NEW Achieve for *Economics*

Engage Every Student

Achieve is a comprehensive set of interconnected teaching and assessment tools. It incorporates the most effective elements from Macmillan's market-leading solutions in a single, easy-to-use platform. Our resources were co-designed with instructors and students, using a foundation of learning research and rigorous testing.

Everything You Need in a Single Learning Path

Achieve is an online learning system that supports students and instructors at every step, from the first point of contact with new content to demonstrating mastery of concepts and skills. Powerful resources including an integrated e-book, robust homework, and a wealth of interactives create an extraordinary learning resource for students.

Learning Objectives Provide Powerful Insights

Every asset you can assign in Achieve is tagged to a learning objective. Insights and reporting help instructors and students understand how they are performing against objectives, enabling more efficient and effective interventions.

PRE-CLASS

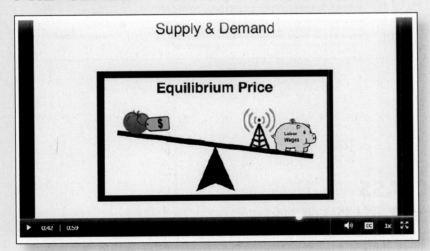

▲ **Pre-Class Tutorials with Bridge Questions** Developed by two pioneers in active-learning methods—Eric Chiang, Florida Atlantic University, and José Vazquez, University of Illinois at Urbana-Champaign—pre-class tutorials foster basic understanding of core economic concepts before students ever set foot in class. Students watch pre-lecture videos and complete bridge questions that prepare them to engage in class. Instructors receive data about student comprehension that can inform the lecture preparation.

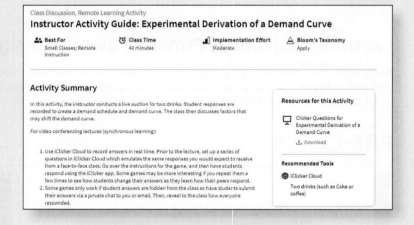

Score: 0/150   Question Value: 35 points

← Back to Study Plan

Lisa has a stand at the local farmer's market where she sells honey from her farm. Every week, Lisa sells out of honey while still having people waiting in line to buy some. What is happening in the market for Lisa's honey?

○ Quantity demanded exceeds quantity supplied, creating a shortage.

○ Quantity demanded exceeds quantity supplied, creating a surplus.

○ Quantity supplied exceeds quantity demanded, creating a surplus.

○ Quantity supplied exceeds quantity demanded, creating a shortage.

Need help on this question?

Read about this topic (no penalty)   Get a hint (fewer points)   Show answer (no points)

◀ **LearningCurve Adaptive Quizzing** With a game-like interface, this popular and effective quizzing engine offers students a low-stakes way to brush up on concepts and help identify knowledge gaps. Questions are linked to relevant e-book sections, providing both the incentive to read and a framework for an efficient reading experience.

IN-CLASS

▶ **Instructor Activity Guides** The guides provide instructors with a structured plan to facilitate an activity that encourages student engagement in both face-to-face and remote learning courses. Each guide is based on a single topic and allows students to participate through questions, group work, presentations, and/or simulations. The guide displays the activity type, estimated prep and class time, implementation instructions, suggestions for remote implementation where applicable, and Learning Objectives and Bloom's level for ease of use. Our Instructor Activity Guides encourage engagement from a Pre-Class Reflection question to prime student interest and offer follow-up iClicker questions to measure comprehension.

Class Discussion, Remote Learning Activity
Instructor Activity Guide: Experimental Derivation of a Demand Curve

Best For Small Classes; Remote Instruction   **Class Time** 40 minutes   **Implementation Effort** Moderate   **Bloom's Taxonomy** Apply

Activity Summary

In this activity, the instructor conducts a live auction for two drinks. Student responses are recorded to create a demand schedule and demand curve. The class then discusses factors that may shift the demand curve.

For video conferencing lectures (synchronous learning):

1. Use iClicker Cloud to record answers in real time. Prior to the lecture, set up a series of questions in iClicker Cloud which emulates the same responses you would expect to receive from a face-to-face class. Go over the instructions for the game, and then have students respond using the iClicker app. Some games may be more interesting if you repeat them a few times to see how students change their answers as they learn how their peers respond.
2. Some games only work if student answers are hidden from the class so have students submit their answers via a private chat to you or email. Then, reveal to the class how everyone responded.

Resources for this Activity

🖥 Clicker Questions for Experimental Derivation of a Demand Curve
⬇ Download

Recommended Tools

◉ iClicker Cloud

Two drinks (such as Coke or coffee)

POST-CLASS

Interactive E-Book The Achieve e-book allows students to highlight and take notes; instructors can choose to assign sections of the e-book as part of their course assignments. The e-book includes step-by-step graphs for complex figures.

Step-by-Step Graphs Available in the e-book, step-by-step graphs mirror how an instructor constructs graphs in the classroom. By breaking down the process into its components, these graphs create more manageable "chunks" for students to understand each step of the process.

▶ **Discovering Data** These exercises require students to use the Federal Reserve Economic Database (FRED) related to the concepts discussed in the chapter. Students will get practical experience manipulating data by being asked, for example, to track the impact of a sales tax on tobacco sales. In working these problems, students will gain a greater understanding of core concepts while also working with an impressive data resource.

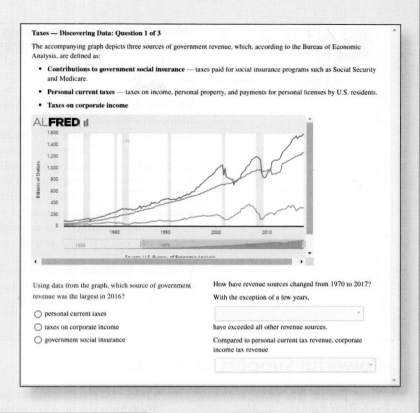

◀ **Work It Out** These skill-building activities pair sample end-of-chapter problems with targeted feedback and video explanations to help students solve problems step by step. This approach allows students to work independently, tests their comprehension of concepts, and prepares them for class and exams.

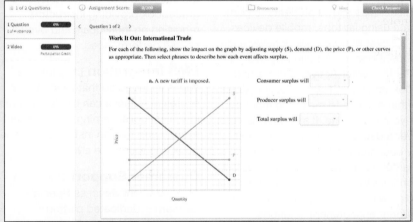

▶ **End-of-Chapter Questions** Developed by economists active in the classroom, these multistep questions are adapted from problems found in the text. Each problem is paired with rich feedback for incorrect and correct responses that guide students through the process of problem solving. These questions also feature our user-friendly graphing tool, designed so students focus entirely on economics and not on how to use the application.

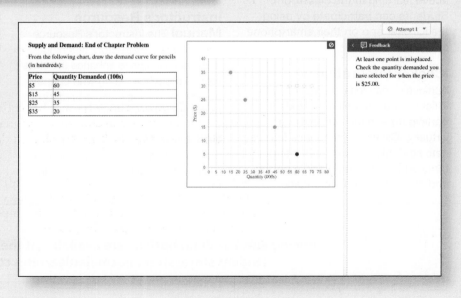

Homework Curated homework problems feature algorithmically generated variables and our user-friendly graphing tool. These problems are multistep with a variety of answer inputs—each with detailed and targeted feedback specific to that answer.

EconoFact Analysis Macmillan Learning has partnered with EconoFact to bring incisive and accessible analysis of current economic and policy trends into the economics classroom. The EconoFact Network provides even-handed and timely analysis of economic issues drawing on relevant data, historical experience, and well-regarded economic frameworks presented in the form of a short memo. In Achieve, instructors can access in-class activity guides to help integrate the memos into their own lectures. Instructors can also access and assign assessment on each memo that starts with basic reading comprehension and builds up to applying the analytical tools students have learned in their course to the economic or policy issue covered in the memo.

Practice Quizzes Designed to be used as a study tool, these quizzes feature questions from the Test Bank and allow for multiple attempts as students familiarize themselves with content.

Powerful Support for Instructors

Test Bank This comprehensive Test Bank contains multiple-choice and short-answer questions to help instructors assess students' comprehension, interpretation, and ability to synthesize.

Lecture Slides These brief, interactive, and visually interesting slides are designed to hold students' attention in class with graphics and animations demonstrating key concepts and real-world examples.

Clicker Slides These slides contain questions to incorporate active learning in the classroom. Students can participate by using the iClicker app on their smartphone or laptop.

iClicker Integration With Achieve's seamless integration with iClicker, you can help any student participate — in the classroom or virtually. iClicker's attendance feature gets students in class, then instructors can choose from flexible polling and quizzing options to engage,

check understanding, and get feedback from students in real time. iClicker also allows students to participate using laptops, mobile devices, or iClicker remotes — whichever each student prefers. Additionally, we offer Instructor Activity Guides and book-specific iClicker question slides within Achieve to make the most out of your class time. It's no surprise that over a decade after being founded by educators, iClicker still leads the market. And thousands of instructors continue to give every student a voice with our simple, award-winning student engagement solutions.

Instructor's Resource Manual The Instructor's Resource Manual offers instructors teaching materials and tips to enhance the classroom experience, along with chapter objectives, outlines, and a breakdown of the large library of MRU videos.

Solutions Manual The Solutions Manual contains detailed solutions to all end-of-chapter problems from the textbook.

Gradebook Assignment scores are collected into a comprehensive gradebook providing instructors reporting on individuals and overall course performance.

LMS Integration LMS Integration is included so that all students' scores in Achieve can easily integrate into a school's learning management system and that an instructor's gradebook and roster are always in sync.

Customer Support Our Achieve Client Success Specialist Team — dedicated platform experts — provides collaboration, software expertise, and consulting to tailor each course to fit your instructional goals and student needs. Start with a demo at a time that works for you to learn more about how to set up your customized course. Talk to your sales representative or visit https://www.macmillanlearning.com /college/us/contact-us/training-and -demos for more information.

Pricing and bundling options are available at the Macmillan student store: store.macmillanlearning.com/

WHAT'S NEW IN THIS EDITION?

There are 60 new opening stories, Business Cases, and Economics in Action applications in this edition — fully one-third of these stories are new, ensuring that the Sixth Edition is truly current and relevant. Many other stories have been updated and refreshed.

11 New Opening Stories

Mastering Textbook Economics
A Bronx Tale
"Shine Bright Like a Diamond"
The Food Court of America
An Affair of the Heart
The Great Mistake of 2011
The Smog of Prosperity
The Malls in Spain Have Mainly Dodged the Pain
Spending to Fight a Recession
That and 900,000 Bolivars Will Get You a Cup of Coffee
Sympathy for the Deficit

13 New Business Cases

Ticket Prices and Music's Reigning Couple
A Market Disruptor Gets Disrupted by the Market
Beyond Impossible: McDonald's and Burger King's Beef-Free Battle
The Rise of the Machine at Amazon
Retail Wars: Big Box Stores in the Age of Amazon
Xcel Energy Goes for a Win-Win
Saving the "Beast": Ecotourism Protects the Jaguars of Brazil
Can America's Entrepreneurial Spirit Survive Threats to the ACA?
Walmart Revolutionizes Its Labor Practices
GM Survives
Paying for a Heads-Up on Inflation
Hyperinflation as a Business Opportunity
German Cars, Made in Spain

36 New Economics in Action Applications

The Cost of Marriage: China's One-Child Policy Creates Millions of Lonely Bachelors
Wait, Then Hurry Up, and Wait Again
When Economists Agree
The Plunging Cost of Solar Panels
Holy Guacamole
Is Facebook Really Free?
The Rise and Fall of the Unpaid Intern
How Price Controls in Venezuela Proved Disastrous
The China Shock
The Steel Tariffs of 2018–2019
Trade War, What Is It Good For?
How the Sharing Economy Reduces Fixed Cost
Pay-for-Delay Runs Out of Time
A Global Pork Shortage Hits Chinese Diners Hard
Are Antitrust Policy Makers Behind the Digital Times?
The Ups and Downs of a Cartel: OPEC Hits the Skids on U.S. Shale Oil
The Price Wars of Christmas: Amazon and Walmart Slug It Out
Over 3,500 Economists Agree: Tax Greenhouse Gas Emissions
American Infrastructure Gets a D+
The Not-So Melancholy Danes
Marginal Productivity and the Minimum Wage Puzzle
The Real Housewives of the United States
Bad Times in Brazil
Argentina's Peso Perplex
Opportunity Knocks
Global Winners and Losers
China's War on Pollution
Three Generations of U.S. Interest Rates
Banks, Successes, and South America
The Rise and Fall of Mortgage Delinquencies
Business Investment in the Great Recession
Who's Afraid of the Death Spiral?
The Spanish Squeeze
Did the Fed Cause the Great Depression?
Debt Fears, Austerity, and the U.S. Recovery Leprechaun Economics

ECONOMICS

Sixth Edition

Paul Krugman
Graduate Center of the City University of New York

Robin Wells

macmillan
international
HIGHER EDUCATION

Senior Vice President, Social Sciences: **Charles Linsmeier**
Program Director, Social Sciences: **Shani Fisher**
Senior Executive Program Manager: **Simon Glick**
Executive Development Editor: **Sharon Balbos**
Senior Development Editor: **Lukia Kliossis**
Development Editor: **Ann Kirby-Payne**
Consultant: **Ryan Herzog**
Director of Media Editorial and Assessment, Social Sciences: **Noel Hohnstine**
Senior Assessment Editor: **Joshua Hill**
Media Editor: **Stephany Harrington**
Assistant Editor: **Amanda Gaglione**
Marketing Manager: **Clay Bolton**
Marketing Assistant: **Steven Huang**
Director, Content Management Enhancement: **Tracey Kuehn**
Senior Managing Editor: **Lisa Kinne**
Senior Content Project Manager: **Martha Emry**
Director of Design, Content Management: **Diana Blume**
Design Services Manager: **Natasha A. S. Wolfe**
Interior Design: **Lumina Datamatics, Inc.**
Cover Design: **Laura de Grasse**
Illustrations: **Network Graphics**
Illustration Coordinator: **Janice Donnola**
Executive Permissions Editor: **Cecilia Varas**
Photo Researcher: **Richard Fox, Lumina Datamatics, Inc.**
Assistant Director, Process Workflow: **Susan Wein**
Senior Workflow Project Manager: **Paul Rohloff**
Production Supervisor: **Lawrence Guerra**
Media Project Manager: **Andrew Vaccaro**
Composition: **Lumina Datamatics, Inc.**
Printing and Binding: **LSC Communications**

ISBN-13: 978-1-319-38352-7
ISBN-10: 1-319-38352-1

Printed in the United States of America
1 2 3 4 5 6   25 24 23 22 21 20

Worth Publishers
One New York Plaza
Suite 4600
New York, NY 10004-1562
www.macmillanlearning.com

About the Authors

PAUL KRUGMAN, recipient of the 2008 Nobel Memorial Prize in Economic Sciences, is a faculty member of the Graduate Center of the City University of New York, associated with the Luxembourg Income Study, which tracks and analyzes income inequality around the world. Prior to that, he taught at Princeton University for 14 years. He received his BA from Yale and his PhD from MIT. Before Princeton, he taught at Yale, Stanford, and MIT. He also spent a year on the staff of the Council of Economic Advisers in 1982–1983. His research has included pathbreaking work on international trade, economic geography, and currency crises. In 1991, Krugman received the American Economic Association's John Bates Clark medal. In addition to his teaching and academic research, Krugman writes extensively for nontechnical audiences. He is a regular op-ed columnist for the *New York Times*. His best-selling trade books include *End This Depression Now!*, *The Return of Depression Economics and the Crisis of 2008*, a history of recent economic troubles and their implications for economic policy, and *The Conscience of a Liberal*, a study of the political economy of economic inequality and its relationship with political polarization from the Gilded Age to the present. His earlier books, *Peddling Prosperity* and *The Age of Diminished Expectations*, have become modern classics.

Ligaya Franklin

ROBIN WELLS was a Lecturer and Researcher in Economics at Princeton University. She received her BA from the University of Chicago and her PhD from the University of California at Berkeley; she then did postdoctoral work at MIT. She has taught at the University of Michigan, the University of Southampton (United Kingdom), Stanford, and MIT.

Vision and Story of *Economics*

This is a book about economics as the study of what people do and how they interact, a study very much informed by real-world experience. These words, this spirit, have served as a guiding principle for us in every edition.

While we were driven to write this book by many small ideas about particular aspects of economics, we also had one big idea: an economics textbook should be built around narratives, many of them pulled from real life, and it should never lose sight of the fact that economics is, in the end, a set of stories about what people do.

Many of the stories economists tell take the form of models—for whatever else they are, economic models are stories about how the world works. But we believe that student understanding of and appreciation for models are greatly enhanced if they are presented, as much as possible, in the context of stories about the real world that both illustrate economic concepts and touch on the concerns we all face living in a world shaped by economic forces. In 2020, the interplay between economics and our everyday lives became clearer than ever as the coronavirus pandemic affected us all, worldwide.

You'll find a rich array of stories in every chapter, in the chapter openers, Economics in Actions, For Inquiring Minds, Global Comparisons, and Business Cases. As always, we include many new stories and update others. We also integrate an international perspective throughout, more extensively than ever before. We have a new focus on how increases in the economy's potential leads to long-run growth, highlighted as a principle in Chapter 1 then throughout the text. An overview of the types of narrative-based features in the text is on p. xii.

We also include pedagogical features that reinforce learning. For example, each major section ends with three related elements devised with the student in mind: (1) the Economics in Actions: a real-world application to help students achieve a fuller understanding of concepts they just read about; (2) a Quick Review of key ideas in list form; and (3) Check Your Understanding self-test questions with answers at the back of the book. Our thought-provoking end-of-chapter problems are another strong feature. The Work It Out feature appears in all end-of-chapter problem sets, offering students online tutorials that guide them step-by-step through solving key problems. Discovering Data exercises offer students the opportunity to use interactive graphs to analyze interesting economic questions. An overview of the text's tools for learning is on p. xiii.

Students also benefit from Achieve, where all of our impressive digital resources are found in one platform. These include several exciting new digital features, such as step-by-step graphs and EconoFact Analysis, as well as adaptive quizzing, tutorials, Bloomberg videos, graphing questions, and data-analysis questions. All have been devised with the goal of supporting instructor teaching and student learning in principles of economics courses.

We hope your experience with this text is a good one. Thank you for introducing it into your classroom.

Paul Krugman   Robin Wells

Engaging Students in the Study of *Economics*

We are committed to the belief that students learn best from a complete textbook program built around narratives, steeped in real life and current events, with a strong emphasis on global matters and with proven technology that supports student success.

Narrative Approach

This is a textbook built around narratives and stories, many pulled from real life. In every chapter, stories are used to teach core concepts and motivate learning. We believe that the best way to introduce concepts and reinforce them is through memorable, real-world stories; students simply relate more easily to them.

Global Focus

This book is unrivaled in the attention paid to global matters. We have thoroughly integrated an international perspective into the text, in the numerous applications, cases, and stories and, of course, in the data-based Global Comparison feature.

Technology That Builds Success

Economics is not just a textbook. With Achieve, it has evolved to become a complete program with interactive features designed and built to extend the goals of the text. This program encourages even stronger student engagement, mastery of the material, and success in the course.

What's New in the Sixth Edition?

Technology that offers the best value and price. Because students' needs are changing, our most powerful learning option is now our most affordable. Achieve is a new digital solution that brings all of the best aspects of Krugman/Wells and Macmillan's digital resources together in one place. Built on best practices in learning science, Achieve provides students with robust tools to succeed in economics while giving instructors insights into their students' understanding and performance.

Current events framed by the world's best communicators of economics. No other text stays as fresh as this one. This edition includes essential coverage of the global effects of COVID-19. For this edition, we've also added cutting-edge online features, including EconoFact Analysis with memos and Bloomberg Analysis with videos. These activities pair journalistic takes on pressing issues with questions based on Bloom's taxonomy. This complements the text's unparalleled coverage of current topics: sustainability, the economic impact of technology, pressing policy debates, and much more.

A richer commitment to broadening students' understanding of the global economy. With unparalleled insight and clarity, the authors use their hallmark narrative approach to take students outside of the classroom and into our global world, starting in Chapter 1 with a new principle on how increases in the economy's potential lead to economic growth over time. To reflect our rapidly changing world, there is an expanded section on market power and the digital economy and an incisive new look at externalities and long-run growth. In addition, there is extensive coverage of the economic impacts and policy responses to the pandemic.

Engaging Students with a Narrative Approach

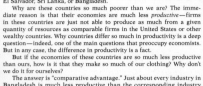
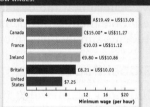

- To engage students, every chapter begins with a compelling story. **What You Will Learn** questions help students focus on key concepts in the chapter.

- So students can immediately see economic concepts applied in the real world, **Economics in Action** applications appear throughout chapters.

- To provide students with an international perspective, the **Global Comparison** feature uses data and graphs to illustrate why countries reach different economic outcomes.

- So students can see key economic principles applied to real-life business situations, each chapter concludes with a **Business Case.**

Engaging Students with Effective Tools for Learning

ECONOMICS >> *in Action*
Trade War, What Is It Good For?

There are, as we've seen, a number of reasons countries sometimes impose tariffs and other restrictions on imports, and these measures often hurt other countries as well as domestic consumers. However, we generally only use the term *trade war* when hurting foreigners isn't a side effect of tariffs, but their purpose—that is, when tariffs are imposed to inflict damage on another country in an attempt to force it to make concessions of some kind.

A classic example is the "chicken war" that broke out between the United States and Europe more than half a century ago. In 1964 the U.S. imposed a 25% tariff on imports of light trucks—a category that today includes most pickups and SUVs. The purpose of the tariff was to put pressure on the European community to eliminate a tariff it had placed on U.S. exports of frozen chicken, which surged with the rise of factory farming. Incredibly, this dispute was never resolved: that 25% tariff remains in place.

Historically, however, trade wars in which countries try to inflict pain have been fairly rare. Before the 1930s, the United States and other countries generally ignored the effects of their trade policies on other countries; since World War II trade wars have mostly been prevented by international trade agreements.

That may, however, be changing. Since 2017 the U.S. government has imposed tariffs on a wide variety of goods and trading partners, with the explicit aim of forcing other countries to change their policies, and some of the countries have responded with tariffs of their own that are explicitly meant to cause pain here.

We have already discussed the steel tariffs recently imposed on Canada and Mexico, at least partly intended to force our neighbors into agreeing to revise the North American Free Trade Agreement. Those tariffs, however, pale in significance compared with the 25% tariff the U.S. government imposed on $250 billion worth of Chinese exports in 2019—almost half of what China sells to the United States—with a threat to expand the tariffs to the rest of China's exports unless China meets policy demands that include protecting U.S. intellectual property and reducing China's trade surplus with the United States.

China has, in turn, retaliated by imposing tariffs on U.S. products, especially agricultural goods, in a clear attempt to raise the political costs of current U.S. policy, for example by hurting U.S. farmers.

What we're experiencing now, in other words, really is a trade war in the classic sense. At the time of writing it was unclear when or how this trade war might be resolved. And the case of the "chicken war" of 1964 suggests that the effects of the current trade conflict might last for a very long time.

In 2019, the United States and China engaged in a classic trade war by levying tariffs on each other's exports.

James Ferguson/Financial Times

>> Quick Review

• The three major justifications for trade protection are national security, job creation, and the infant industry argument.

• Despite the deadweight losses, import protections are often imposed because groups representing import-competing industries are more influential than groups of consumers.

• To further trade liberalization, countries engage in **international trade agreements.** An important purpose of these agreements is to head off the possibility of **trade wars.** Some agreements are among a small number of countries, such as the **North American Free Trade Agreement (NAFTA)** and

---

• To reinforce learning, sections within chapters conclude with three tools: an application of key concepts in the **Economics in Action;** a **Quick Review** of key concepts; and a comprehension check with **Check Your Understanding** questions. Solutions for these questions appear at the back of the text.

• **Pitfalls** teach students to identify and avoid common misconceptions about economic concepts.

• **Discovering Data** exercises offer students the opportunity to use interactive graphs to analyze interesting economic questions.

• End-of-chapter **Work It Out** skill-building problems provide interactive step-by-step help with solving select problems from the text.

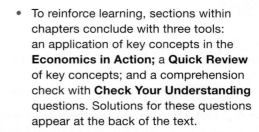

13. Access the Discovering Data exercise for Chapter 8 Problem 13 online to answer the following questions.

a. Rank the states in order of exports to China. Rank in order of most to fewest exports.

b. Calculate the growth in exports from 2002 to 2015 for each state.

c. As a percent of total exports, rank the states in order of most to fewest exports to China.

d. Explain the pattern of trade with China.

PITFALLS

DEMAND VERSUS QUANTITY DEMANDED

When economists say "an increase in demand," they mean a rightward shift of the demand curve, and when they say "a decrease in demand," they mean a leftward shift of the demand curve—that is, when they're being careful.

In ordinary speech most of us, professional economists included, use the word *demand* casually. For example, an economist might say "the demand for air travel has doubled over the past 20 years, partly because of falling airfares" when he or she really means that the *quantity demanded* has doubled.

It's OK to be a bit sloppy in ordinary conversation. But when you're doing economic analysis, it's important to make the distinction between changes in the quantity demanded, which involve movements along a demand curve, and shifts of the demand curve (see Figure 3-3). Sometimes students end up writing something like this: "If demand increases, the price will go up, but that will lead to a fall in demand, which pushes the price down . . ." and then go around in circles.

By making a clear distinction between changes in *demand*, which mean shifts of the demand curve, and changes in *quantity demanded*, which means movement along the demand curve, you can avoid a lot of confusion.

WORK IT OUT

20. The accompanying table gives the annual U.S. demand and supply schedules for pickup trucks.

Price of truck	Quantity of trucks demanded (millions)	Quantity of trucks supplied (millions)
$20,000	20	14
25,000	18	15
30,000	16	16
35,000	14	17
40,000	12	18

a. Plot the demand and supply curves using these schedules. Indicate the equilibrium price and quantity on your diagram.

b. Suppose the tires used on pickup trucks are found to be defective. What would you expect to happen in the market for pickup trucks? Show this on your diagram.

c. Suppose that the U.S. Department of Transportation imposes costly regulations on manufacturers that cause them to reduce supply by one-third at any given price. Calculate and plot the new supply schedule and indicate the new equilibrium price and quantity on your diagram. ∎

Acknowledgments

Our deep appreciation and heartfelt thanks go out to **Ryan Herzog,** Gonzaga University, for his hard work and extensive contributions during every stage of this revision. Ryan's creativity and insights helped us make this Sixth Edition possible. And special thanks to our accuracy checker of page proofs, Thomas Dunn, for his careful attention to detail.

We must also thank the many people at Worth Publishers for their work on this edition: Chuck Linsmeier, Shani Fisher, Simon Glick, Sharon Balbos, Lukia Kliossis, Ann Kirby-Payne, Stephany Harrington, Amanda Gaglione, and Joshua Hill in editorial. We thank Clay Bolton and Travis Long for their enthusiastic and tireless advocacy of this book. Many thanks to the incredible production, design, photo, and media production teams: Tracey Kuehn, Lisa Kinne, Susan Wein, Paul Rohloff, Martha Emry, Diana Blume, Natasha Wolfe, Deb Heimann, Cecilia Varas, Richard Fox, and Andrew Vaccaro.

Our deep appreciation and heartfelt thanks to the following reviewers, whose input helped us shape this Sixth Edition.

Brandon Addison, *Providence Christian College*
Gabriel Azarlian, *California State University, Northridge*
Nestor Azcona, *Providence College*
Christopher Blake, *Oxford College of Emory University*
Bruce Brown, *Santa Monica College*
Terry Brownschidle, *Rider University, Lawrenceville*
Don Carlson, *Williams College*
Humza Chohan, *Coastline Community College*
Brandyn Churchill, *Vanderbilt University*
Charlie Cowell, *Western Iowa Tech Community College*
Meredith Crane, *Cincinnati State Technical & Community College*
Finley Edwards, *Baylor University*
Wayne Edwards, *University of Vermont*

Cynthia Foreman, *Clark College*
Julie Gonzalez, *University of California, Santa Cruz*
Robert Gordon, *Northwestern University, Evanston*
Timothy Haase, *Ramapo College of New Jersey*
Niree Kodaverdian, *Pomona College*
Janet Koscianski, *Shippensburg University of Pennsylvania*
Zhen Li, *Albion College*
Lok Man Lo, *San Francisco State University*
Mark Miller, *Ramapo College of New Jersey*
Margaret Morgan-Davie, *Hamilton College, Clinton*
Michael Nichols, *Baker College of Jackson*
Sanjay Paul, *Elizabethtown College*
Michael Polcen, *Northern Virginia Community College, Loudon*

Collin Rabe, *University of Richmond*
Edward Raupp, *Great Bay Community College*
Jack Reardon, *University of Wisconsin, Eau Claire*
Jeff Sarbaum, *University of North Carolina, Greensboro*
Angela Seidel, *St. Francis College, Loretto*
Ali Shahnawaz, *California State University, Chico*
Jeffrey Stewart, *University of Dayton*
John Tarchick, *Wayne State University*
John Vahaly, *University of Louisville*
Yongqing Wang, *University of Wisconsin, Milwaukee at Waukesha*
Anne M. Wenzel, *San Francisco State University*
Deborah Wright, *Southeastern Community College*
Luo Yilan, *Cerritos College*

We are indebted to the following reviewers, class testers, focus group participants, and other consultants for their suggestions and advice on previous editions.

Carlos Aguilar, *El Paso Community College*
Seemi Ahmad, *Dutchess Community College*
Barbara Alexander, *Babson College*

Terence Alexander, *Iowa State University*
Innocentus Alhamis, *Southern New Hampshire University*
Osbourne Allen, *Miami Dade College*
Morris Altman, *University of Saskatchewan*

Farhad Ameen, *State University of New York, Westchester Community College*
Giuliana Campanelli Andreopoulos, *William Patterson University*
Becca Arnold, *San Diego Mesa College*

Dean Baim, *Pepperdine University*

Jeremy Baker, *Owens Community College*

Christopher P. Ball, *Quinnipiac University*

David Barber, *Quinnipiac University*

Jim Barbour, *Elon University*

Sandra Barone, *Gonzaga University*

Janis Barry-Figuero, *Fordham University at Lincoln Center*

Sue Bartlett, *University of South Florida*

Hamid Bastin, *Shippensburg University*

Scott Beaulier, *Mercer University*

Klaus Becker, *Texas Tech University*

Richard Beil, *Auburn University*

Doris Bennett, *Jacksonville State University*

David Bernotas, *University of Georgia*

Syon Bhanot, *Swarthmore College*

Joydeep Bhattacharya, *Iowa State University*

Marc Bilodeau, *Indiana University and Purdue University, Indianapolis*

Kelly Blanchard, *Purdue University*

Joanne Blankenship, *State Fair Community College*

Emma Bojinova, *Canisius College*

Michael Bonnal, *University of Tennessee, Chattanooga*

Milicia Bookman, *Saint Joseph's University*

Ralph Bradburd, *Williams College*

Mark Brandly, *Ferris State University*

Anne Bresnock, *California State Polytechnic University, Pomona*

Stacey Brook, *University of Iowa*

Kevin Brown, *Asbury University*

Douglas M. Brown, *Georgetown University*

Joseph Calhoun, *Florida State University*

Colleen Callahan, *American University*

Charles Campbell, *Mississippi State University*

Douglas Campbell, *University of Memphis*

Randall Campbell, *Mississippi State University*

Kevin Carlson, *University of Massachusetts, Boston*

Joel Carton, *Florida International University*

Andrew Cassey, *Washington State University*

Shirley Cassing, *University of Pittsburgh*

Semih Cekin, *Texas Tech University*

Sewin Chan, *New York University*

Mitchell M. Charkiewicz, *Central Connecticut State University*

Joni S. Charles, *Texas State University, San Marcos*

Adhip Chaudhuri, *Georgetown University*

Basanta Chaudhuri, *Rutgers University*

Sanjukta Chaudhuri, *University of Wisconsin, Eau Claire*

Eric Chiang, *Florida Atlantic University*

Hayley H. Chouinard, *Washington State University*

Abdur Chowdhury, *Marquette University*

Kenny Christianson, *Binghamton University*

Lisa Citron, *Cascadia Community College*

Timothy Classen, *Loyola University Chicago*

Maryanne Clifford, *Eastern Connecticut State University*

Steven L. Cobb, *University of North Texas*

Greg Colson, *University of Georgia*

Barbara Z. Connolly, *Westchester Community College*

Stephen Conroy, *University of San Diego*

Thomas E. Cooper, *Georgetown University*

Cesar Corredor, *Texas A&M University and University of Texas, Tyler*

Chad Cotti, *University of Wisconsin, Oshkosh*

Jim F. Couch, *University of Northern Alabama*

Patrick Crowley, *Texas A&M University, Corpus Christi*

Attila Cseh, *Valdosta State University*

Maria DaCosta, *University of Wisconsin, Eau Claire*

Daniel Daly, *Regis University*

Dixie Dalton, *Southside Virginia Community College*

H. Evren Damar, *Pacific Lutheran University*

James P. D'Angelo, *University of Cincinnati*

Antony Davies, *Duquesne University*

Greg Delemeester, *Marietta College*

Sean D'Evelyn, *Loyola Marymount University*

Ronald Dieter, *Iowa State University*

Joseph Dipoli, *Salem State University*

Patrick Dolenc, *Keene State College*

Christine Doyle-Burke, *Framingham State College*

Ding Du, *South Dakota State University*

Jerry Dunn, *Southwestern Oklahoma State University*

Thomas Dunn

Robert R. Dunn, *Washington and Jefferson College*

Christina Edmundson, *North Idaho College*

Hossein Eftekari, *University of Wisconsin, River Falls*

Ann Eike, *University of Kentucky*

Harold Elder, *University of Alabama*

Tisha L. N. Emerson, *Baylor University*

Hadi Salehi Esfahani, *University of Illinois*

Mark Evans, *California State University, Bakersfield*

Mohammadmahdi Farsiabi, *Wayne State University*

William Feipel, *Illinois Central College*

Rudy Fichtenbaum, *Wright State University*

David W. Findlay, *Colby College*

Mary Flannery, *University of California, Santa Cruz*

Sherman Folland, *Oakland University*

Cynthia Foreman, *Clark College*

Irene Foster, *George Washington University*

Robert Francis, *Shoreline Community College*

Amanda Freeman, *Kansas State University*

Shelby Frost, *Georgia State University*

John Gahagan, *Shoreline Community College*

Frank Gallant, *George Fox University*

Robert Gazzale, *Williams College*

Bruce Gervais, *California State University, Sacramento*

Satyajit Ghosh, *University of Scranton*

Stuart Glosser, *University of Wisconsin, Whitewater*

Robert Godby, *University of Wyoming*

Fidel Gonzalez, *Sam Houston State University*

Julie Gonzalez, *University of California, Santa Cruz*

Michael G. Goode, *Central Piedmont Community College*

Douglas E. Goodman, *University of Puget Sound*

Marvin Gordon, *University of Illinois at Chicago*

Kathryn Graddy, *Brandeis University*

Alan Gummerson, *Florida International University*
Jason Gurtovoy, *Cerritos College*
Eran Guse, *West Virginia University*
Ian Haberman, *Hunter College*
Alan Day Haight, *State University of New York, Cortland*
Mehdi Haririan, *Bloomsburg University*
Robert Harris, *Indiana University and Purdue University, Indianapolis*
Hadley Hartman, *Santa Fe College*
Clyde A. Haulman, *College of William and Mary*
Richard R. Hawkins, *University of West Florida*
Mickey A. Hepner, *University of Central Oklahoma*
Ryan Herzog, *Gonzaga University*
Michael Hilmer, *San Diego State University*
Tia Hilmer, *San Diego State University*
Jane Himarios, *University of Texas, Arlington*
Jim Holcomb, *University of Texas, El Paso*
Don Holley, *Boise State University*
Alexander Holmes, *University of Oklahoma*
Julie Holzner, *Los Angeles City College*
Robert N. Horn, *James Madison University*
Scott Houser, *Colorado School of Mines*
Grover Howard, *Shoreline Community College*
Steven Husted, *University of Pittsburgh*
Hiro Ito, *Portland State University*
Ali Jalili, *New England College*
Mike Javanmard, *Rio Hondo Community College*
Mervin Jebaraj, *University of Arkansas*
Jonatan Jelen, *The City College of New York*
Carl Jensen, *Seton Hall University*
Robert T. Jerome, *James Madison University*
Donn Johnson, *Quinnipiac University*
Shirley Johnson-Lans, *Vassar College*
David Kalist, *Shippensburg University*
Lillian Kamal, *Northwestern University*
Roger T. Kaufman, *Smith College*
Dennis Kaufman, *University of Wisconsin, Parkside*
Elizabeth Sawyer Kelly, *University of Wisconsin, Madison*
Herb Kessel, *St. Michael's College*

Farida Khan, *University of Wisconsin, Parkside*
Ara Khanjian, *Ventura College*
Rehim Kilic, *Georgia Institute of Technology*
Grace Kim, *University of Michigan, Dearborn*
Miles Kimball, *University of Michigan*
Michael Kimmitt, *University of Hawaii, Manoa*
Robert Kling, *Colorado State University*
Colin Knapp, *University of Florida*
Janet Koscianski, *Shippensburg University*
Sherrie Kossoudji, *University of Michigan*
Stephan Kroll, *Colorado State University*
Charles Kroncke, *College of Mount Saint Joseph*
Reuben Kyle, *Middle Tennessee State University (retired)*
Katherine Lande-Schmeiser, *University of Minnesota, Twin Cities*
Vicky Langston, *Columbus State University*
Richard B. Le, *Cosumnes River College*
Yu-Feng Lee, *New Mexico State University*
David Lehr, *Longwood College*
Mary Jane Lenon, *Providence College*
Noreen Lephardt, *Marquette University*
Mary H. Lesser, *Iona College*
An Li, *Keene State College*
Liaoliao Li, *Kutztown University*
Solina Lindahl, *California Polytechnic Institute, San Luis Obispo*
Haiyong Liu, *East Carolina University*
Jane S. Lopus, *California State University, East Bay*
Fernando Lozano, *Claremont McKenna College*
María José Luengo-Prado, *Northeastern University*
Volodymyr Lugovskyy, *Indiana University*
Rotua Lumbantobing, *North Carolina State University*
Ed Lyell, *Adams State College*
Martin Ma, *Washington State University*
John Marangos, *Colorado State University*
Stephen Marks, *Claremont McKenna College*
Ralph D. May, *Southwestern Oklahoma State University*
Mark E. McBride, *Miami University (Ohio)*

Wayne McCaffery, *University of Wisconsin, Madison*
Larry McRae, *Appalachian State University*
Mary Ruth J. McRae, *Appalachian State University*
Ellen E. Meade, *American University*
Meghan Millea, *Mississippi State University*
Ashley Miller, *Mount Holyoke College*
Norman C. Miller, *Miami University (Ohio)*
Michael Mogavero, *University of Notre Dame*
Khan A. Mohabbat, *Northern Illinois University*
Ross Mohr, *Chapman University*
Myra L. Moore, *University of Georgia*
Jay Morris, *Champlain College in Burlington*
Akira Motomura, *Stonehill College*
Gary Murphy, *Case Western Reserve University*
Kevin J. Murphy, *Oakland University*
Robert Murphy, *Boston College*
Ranganath Murthy, *Bucknell University*
Anna Musatti, *Columbia University*
Christopher Mushrush, *Illinois State University*
Anthony Myatt, *University of New Brunswick, Canada*
Steven Nafziger, *Williams College*
Soloman Namala, *Cerritos College*
Kathryn Nantz, *Fairfield University*
ABM Nasir, *North Carolina Central University*
Gerardo Nebbia, *El Camino College*
Pattabiraman Neelakantan, *East Stroudsburg University*
Randy A. Nelson, *Colby College*
Charles Newton, *Houston Community College*
Daniel X. Nguyen, *Purdue University*
Pamela Nickless, *University of North Carolina, Asheville*
Dmitri Nizovtsev, *Washburn University*
Nick Noble, *Miami University (Ohio)*
Gerald Nyambane, *Davenport University*
Fola Odebunmi, *Cypress College*
Thomas A. Odegaard, *Baylor University*
Constantin Oglobin, *Georgia Southern University*
Charles C. Okeke, *College of Southern Nevada*

Alexandre Olbrecht, *Ramapo College of New Jersey*

Terry Olson, *Truman State University*

Una Okonkwo Osili, *Indiana University and Purdue University, Indianapolis*

Ram Orzach, *Oakland University*

Maxwell Oteng, *University of California, Davis*

Tomi Ovaska, *Youngstown State University*

P. Marcelo Oviedo, *Iowa State University*

Jeff Owen, *Gustavus Adolphus College*

Orgul Demet Ozturk, *University of South Carolina*

Jennifer Pakula, *Cerritos College*

James Palmieri, *Simpson College*

Walter G. Park, *American University*

Elliott Parker, *University of Nevada, Reno*

Tim Payne, *Shoreline College*

Sonia Pereira, *Barnard College, Columbia University*

Michael Perelman, *California State University, Chico*

Nathan Perry, *Utah State University*

Brian Peterson, *Central College*

Dean Peterson, *Seattle University*

Ken Peterson, *Furman University*

David Pieper, *City College of San Francisco*

Paul Pieper, *University of Illinois at Chicago*

Dennis L. Placone, *Clemson University*

Michael Polcen, *Northern Virginia Community College*

Linnea Polgreen, *University of Iowa*

Raymond A. Polchow, *Zane State College*

Eileen Rabach, *Santa Monica College*

Matthew Rafferty, *Quinnipiac University*

Jaishankar Raman, *Valparaiso University*

Tove Rasmussen, *Southern Maine Community College*

Margaret Ray, *Mary Washington College*

Arthur Raymond, *Muhlenberg College*

Jason Reed, *Wayne State University*

Jack Reynolds, *Navarro College*

Tim Reynolds, *Alvin Community College*

Helen Roberts, *University of Illinois at Chicago*

Greg Rose, *Sacramento City College*

Luis Rosero, *Framingham State*

Jeffrey Rubin, *Rutgers University, New Brunswick*

Rose M. Rubin, *University of Memphis*

Lynda Rush, *California State Polytechnic University, Pomona*

Matt Rutledge, *Boston College*

Michael Ryan, *Western Michigan University*

Martin Sabo, *Community College of Denver*

Sara Saderion, *Houston Community College*

Djavad Salehi-Isfahani, *Virginia Tech*

Mikael Sandberg, *University of Florida*

Michael Sattinger, *University at Albany*

Duncan Sattler, *Wilbur Wright College*

Elizabeth Sawyer-Kelly, *University of Wisconsin, Madison*

Jake Schild, *Indiana University*

Lucie Schmidt, *Williams College*

Jesse A. Schwartz, *Kennesaw State University*

Chad Settle, *University of Tulsa*

Steve Shapiro, *University of North Florida*

Robert L. Shoffner III, *Central Piedmont Community College*

Joseph Sicilian, *University of Kansas*

Zamira Simkins, *University of Wisconsin, Superior*

Aschale Siyoum, *Catholic University of America*

Judy Smrha, *Baker University*

Mark Sniderman, *Case Western Reserve University*

John Solow, *University of Iowa*

John Somers, *Portland Community College*

Ralph Sonenshine, *American University*

Stephen Stageberg, *University of Mary Washington*

Monty Stanford, *DeVry University*

Rebecca Stein, *University of Pennsylvania*

James Sterns, *Oregon State University*

William K. Tabb, *Queens College, City University of New York (retired)*

Sarinda Taengnoi, *University of Wisconsin, Oshkosh*

Daniel Talley, *Dakota State University*

Kerry Tan, *Loyola University, Maryland*

Henry Terrell, *George Washington University*

Henry Terrell, *University of Maryland*

Rebecca Achée Thornton, *University of Houston*

Michael Toma, *Armstrong Atlantic State University*

Jill Trask, *Tarrant County College—Southeast*

Julianne Treme, *University of North Carolina at Wilmington*

Brian Trinque, *University of Texas, Austin*

Magda Tsaneva, *Clark University*

Boone A. Turchi, *University of North Carolina, Chapel Hill*

Phillip Tussing, *Alvin Community College*

Nathaniel Udall, *Alvin Community College*

Nora Underwood, *University of Central Florida*

J. S. Uppal, *State University of New York, Albany*

John Vahaly, *University of Louisville*

Lee Van Scyoc, *University of Wisconsin, Oshkosh*

Jose J. Vazquez-Cognet, *University of Illinois, Urbana–Champaign*

Daniel Vazzana, *Georgetown College*

Sujata Verma, *Notre Dame de Namur University*

Aimee Vlachos-Bullard, *Southern Maine Community College*

Roger H. von Haefen, *North Carolina State University*

Andreas Waldkirch, *Colby College*

Christopher Waller, *University of Notre Dame*

Xiao Wang, *University of North Dakota*

Gregory Wassall, *Northeastern University*

Robert Whaples, *Wake Forest University*

Thomas White, *Assumption College*

Michael Williams, *Prairie View A&M University*

Jennifer P. Wissink, *Cornell University*

Mark Witte, *Northwestern University*

Kristen M. Wolfe, *St. Johns River Community College*

Larry Wolfenbarger, *Macon State College*

Louise B. Wolitz, *University of Texas, Austin*

Kelvin Wont, *University of Minnesota*

Hyun Woong Park, *Allegheny College*

Jadrian Wooten, *Pennsylvania State University*

Gavin Wright, *Stanford University*

Bill Yang, *Georgia Southern University*

Kristen Zaborski, *The State College of Florida*

Jason Zimmerman, *South Dakota State University*

Organization of This Book

To help plan your course, we've listed what we consider to be core and optional chapters, with descriptions about the coverage in each.

Optional

Introduction: An Engine for Growth and Discovery
Initiates students into the study of economics using China's Pearl River Delta as the motivating story. Includes basic terms and explains the difference between microeconomics and macroeconomics.

Core

1. **First Principles**
Outlines 12 principles underlying the study of economics: principles of individual choice, interaction between individuals, and economy-wide interaction.

2. **Economic Models: Trade-offs and Trade**
Employs two economic models — the production possibilities frontier and comparative advantage — as an introduction to gains from trade and international comparisons. Also introduces the circular-flow diagram.

Optional

2 Appendix: Graphs in Economics
A comprehensive review of graphing and math skills for students who would find this background helpful.

Core

3. **Supply and Demand**
Covers the essentials of supply, demand, market equilibrium, surplus, and shortage.

4. **Consumer and Producer Surplus**
Introduces market efficiency, the ways markets fail, the role of prices as signals, and property rights.

5. **Price Controls and Quotas: Meddling with Markets**
Covers market interventions and their consequences: price and quantity controls, inefficiency, and deadweight loss.

6. **Elasticity**
Introduces the various elasticity measures and explains how to calculate and interpret them, including price, cross-price and income elasticity of demand, and price elasticity of supply.

7. **Taxes**
Covers basic tax analysis along with a review of the burden of taxation and considerations of equity versus efficiency. The structure of taxation, tax policy, and public spending are also discussed.

Optional

8. **International Trade**
An examination of comparative advantage, tariffs and quotas, the politics of trade protection and international trade agreements, and the controversy over imports from low-wage countries. With new coverage of hyperglobalization, the EU and Brexit, outsourcing, and reshoring.

Core

9. **Decision Making by Individuals and Firms**
Focuses on marginal analysis ("either–or" and "how much" decisions) and the concept of sunk cost, with detailed coverage of behavioral economics, showing the limitations of rational thought.

Optional

9 Appendix: How to Make Decisions Involving Time: Understanding Present Value
Expands on the coverage in the chapter by examining why decisions involving time are different and how to make them.

Core

10. **The Rational Consumer**
Provides a complete treatment of consumer behavior for those who don't cover indifference curves. Includes the budget line, optimal consumption choice, diminishing marginal utility, and substitution effects.

Optional

10 Appendix: Consumer Preferences and Consumer Choice
Offers detailed treatment for those who wish to cover indifference curves.

Core

11. **Behind the Supply Curve: Inputs and Costs**
Develops the production function and the various cost measures of the firm, including discussion of the difference between average cost and marginal cost.

12. **Perfect Competition and the Supply Curve**
Explains the output decision of the perfectly competitive firm, its entry/exit decision, the industry supply curve, and the equilibrium of a perfectly competitive market.

13. **Monopoly**
A complete treatment of monopoly, including topics such as price discrimination, the welfare effects of monopoly, and policy responses.

14. **Oligopoly**
Defines the concept of oligopoly using current, real-world examples, including the demise of OPEC. Offers detailed coverage of basic game theory in both a one-shot and repeated game context.

15. **Monopolistic Competition and Product Differentiation**
Comprehensive coverage of monopolistic competition, the entry/exit decision, efficiency considerations, and advertising, with vivid, current examples.

16. **Externalities**
Revised for clarity and updated to include new content on the economics of climate change. Covers negative externalities and solutions to them, such as Coasian private trades, emissions taxes, and a system of tradable permits. Also explains positive externalities, technological spillovers, and network externalities.

Core

17. Public Goods and Common Resources
Explains how to classify goods into four categories (private goods, common resources, public goods, and artificially scarce goods) based on excludability and rivalry in consumption, to clarify why some goods but not others can be efficiently managed by markets.

Optional

18. The Economics of the Welfare State
Significantly revised and updated, this chapter provides a comprehensive overview of the welfare state and its philosophical foundations. Examines the problem of poverty, the issue of income inequality, and the economics of health care, including the Affordable Care Act.

19. Factor Markets and the Distribution of Income *and* 19 Appendix: Indifference Curve Analysis of Labor Supply
Covers the efficiency-wage model of the labor market as well as the influence of education, discrimination, and market power. The appendix examines the labor-leisure trade-off and the backward bending labor supply curve.

20. Uncertainty, Risk, and Private Information
This unique, applied chapter explains attitudes toward risk, the benefits and limits of diversification, as well as private information, adverse selection, and moral hazard.

Core

21. Macroeconomics: The Big Picture
Introduces the big ideas of macroeconomics with an overview of recessions and expansions, employment and unemployment, long-run growth, inflation versus deflation, and international economics.

22. GDP and the CPI: Tracking the Macroeconomy
Explains how the numbers macroeconomists use are calculated and why, including the basics of national income accounting and price indexes. Sets the stage for upcoming chapters with a newly simplified presentation of the expanded circular-flow diagram.

23. Unemployment and Inflation
Covers the measurement of unemployment, emphasizing that continual job creation and destruction are features of modern economies. Examines the problems inflation poses for policy makers and the economy.

24. Long-Run Economic Growth
Emphasizes an international perspective — economic growth is about the world as a whole — and explains why some countries have been more successful than others, with an updated section on sustainability.

25. Savings, Investment Spending, and the Financial System
An introduction to financial markets and institutions, loanable funds and the determination of interest rates. Includes coverage of present value.

Core

26 Income and Expenditure
Addresses the determinants of consumer and investment spending, introduces the 45-degree diagram, and explains the logic of the multiplier.

Optional

26. Appendix: Deriving the Multiplier Algebraically
A rigorous, mathematical approach to deriving the multiplier.

Core

27. Aggregate Demand and Aggregate Supply
Provides the traditional focus on aggregate price level using the traditional approach to *AD–AS*. In addition, covers the ability of the economy to recover in the long run.

28. Fiscal Policy
Provides an analysis of the role of discretionary fiscal policy, automatic stabilizers, long-run issues of debt and solvency, and the distinction between deficit and debt — with examples of U.S. fiscal stimulus in response to the coronavirus pandemic, Great Recession, and fiscal austerity in Greece.

Optional

28. Appendix: Taxes and the Multiplier
A rigorous derivation of the roles of taxes in reducing the size of the multiplier and acting as an automatic stabilizer.

Core

29. Money, Banking, and the Federal Reserve System
Covers the roles of money, the ways in which banks create money, and the structure and the role of the Federal Reserve and other central banks. Examines the evolution of American banking with detailed coverage of banking crises. The chapter has also been enhanced with the integration of content from our once separate chapter on crises and consequences.

30. Monetary Policy
Covers the role of Federal Reserve policy in driving interest rates and aggregate demand. Bridges the short and long run by showing how interest rates set in the short run reflect the supply and demand of savings in the long run.

Optional

30. Appendix: Reconciling the Two Models of the Interest Rate
Explains why the loanable funds model (long-run discussions) and the liquidity preference approach (short-run discussions) are both valuable.

Core

31. Inflation, Disinflation, and Deflation
Covers the causes and consequences of inflation, the large cost deflation imposes on the economy, and the danger that disinflation leads the economy into a liquidity trap.

Optional

32. Macroeconomics: Events and Ideas
A unique overview of the history of macroeconomic thought, set in the context of changing policy concerns, and the current state of macroeconomic debates.

33. International Macroeconomics
Covers basic topics in international macroeconomics such as balance of payment accounts, foreign exchange markets, and exchange rates.

Contents

Preface x

PART 1 What Is Economics?

INTRODUCTION
An Engine for Growth and Discovery / 1

A Day in the Megacity 1
The Invisible Hand 2
My Benefit, Your Cost 3
Good Times, Bad Times 3
Onward and Upward 4
An Engine for Discovery 4

CHAPTER 1
First Principles / 7

Common Ground 7
Principles That Underlie Individual Choice: The Core of Economics 8
Principle #1: Choices Are Necessary Because Resources Are Scarce 8
Principle #2: The True Cost of Something Is Its Opportunity Cost 9
Principle #3: "How Much" Is a Decision at the Margin 10
Principle #4: People Respond to Incentives, Exploiting Opportunities to Make Themselves Better Off 10
ECONOMICS >> *in Action* The Cost of Marriage: China's One-Child Policy Creates Millions of Lonely Bachelors 11

Interaction: How Economies Work 12
Principle #5: There Are Gains from Trade 13
Principle #6: Markets Move Toward Equilibrium 14
Principle #7: Resources Should Be Used Efficiently to Achieve Society's Goals 15
Principle #8: Markets Usually Lead to Efficiency, But When They Don't, Government Intervention Can Improve Society's Welfare 16
ECONOMICS >> *in Action* Wait, Then Hurry Up, and Wait Again 17

Economy-Wide Interactions 18
Principle #9: One Person's Spending Is Another Person's Income 19
Principle #10: Overall Spending Sometimes Gets Out of Line with the Economy's Productive Capacity; When It Does, Government Policy Can Change Spending 19
Principle #11: Increases in the Economy's Potential Lead to Economic Growth Over Time 20
BUSINESS CASE How Priceline Revolutionized the Travel Industry 22

CHAPTER 2
Economic Models: Trade-offs and Trade / 27

From Kitty Hawk to Dreamliner 27
Models in Economics: Some Important Examples 28
Trade-offs: The Production Possibility Frontier 29
Comparative Advantage and Gains from Trade 34

Comparative Advantage and International Trade, in Reality 37
GLOBAL COMPARISON Pajama Republics 38
Transactions: The Circular-Flow Diagram 38
ECONOMICS >> *in Action* Rich Nation, Poor Nation 40

Using Models 41
Positive versus Normative Economics 41
When and Why Economists Disagree 42
ECONOMICS >> *in Action* When Economists Agree 43
BUSINESS CASE Efficiency, Opportunity Cost, and the Logic of Lean Production 45

CHAPTER 2
Appendix: Graphs in Economics / 51

Getting the Picture 51
Graphs, Variables, and Economic Models 51
How Graphs Work 51
Two-Variable Graphs 51
Curves on a Graph 53

A Key Concept: The Slope of a Curve 54
The Slope of a Linear Curve 54
Horizontal and Vertical Curves and Their Slopes 55
The Slope of a Nonlinear Curve 56
Calculating the Slope Along a Nonlinear Curve 56
Maximum and Minimum Points 58

Calculating the Area Below or Above a Curve 59

Graphs That Depict Numerical Information 59
Types of Numerical Graphs 60
Challenges with Interpreting Numerical Graphs 62

PART 2 Supply and Demand

CHAPTER 3
Supply and Demand / 67

A Natural Gas Boom and Bust 67

Supply and Demand: A Model of a Competitive Market 68

The Demand Curve 68
The Demand Schedule and the Demand Curve 69
Shifts of the Demand Curve 70
GLOBAL COMPARISON Pay More, Pump Less 70
Understanding Shifts of the Demand Curve 72
ECONOMICS >> in Action Beating the Traffic 77

The Supply Curve 78
The Supply Schedule and the Supply Curve 78
Shifts of the Supply Curve 79
Understanding Shifts of the Supply Curve 80
ECONOMICS >> in Action The Plunging Cost of Solar Panels 84

Supply, Demand, and Equilibrium 85
Finding the Equilibrium Price and Quantity 86
Using Equilibrium to Describe Markets 89
ECONOMICS >> in Action The Price of Admission 89

Changes in Supply and Demand 90
What Happens When the Demand Curve Shifts 90
What Happens When the Supply Curve Shifts 91
Simultaneous Shifts of Supply and Demand Curves 92
ECONOMICS >> in Action Holy Guacamole! 94

Competitive Markets—and Others 95
BUSINESS CASE Uber Gives Riders a Lesson in Supply and Demand 96

CHAPTER 4
Consumer and Producer Surplus / 103

Mastering Textbook Economics 103

Consumer Surplus and the Demand Curve 104
Willingness to Pay and the Demand Curve 104
Willingness to Pay and Consumer Surplus 104
How Changing Prices Affect Consumer Surplus 107
FOR INQUIRING MINDS A Matter of Life and Death 109
ECONOMICS >> in Action Is Facebook Really Free? 110

Producer Surplus and the Supply Curve 110
Cost and Producer Surplus 111
How Changing Prices Affect Producer Surplus 113
ECONOMICS >> in Action Highs and Lows on Iowa's Farms 114

Consumer Surplus, Producer Surplus, and the Gains from Trade 115
The Gains from Trade 115
The Efficiency of Markets 116
Equity and Efficiency 120
ECONOMICS >> in Action Take the Keys, Please 120

A Market Economy 121
Why Markets Typically Work So Well 122
A Few Words of Caution 123
ECONOMICS >> in Action A Great Leap—Backward 123
BUSINESS CASE Ticket Prices and Music's Reigning Couple, Beyoncé and Jay-Z 125

CHAPTER 5
Price Controls and Quotas: Meddling with Markets / 131

A Bronx Tale 131

Why Governments Control Prices 132

Price Ceilings 132
Modeling a Price Ceiling 133
How a Price Ceiling Causes Inefficiency 134
FOR INQUIRING MINDS Mumbai's Rent-Control Millionaires 137
Winners, Losers, and Rent Control 138
So Why Are There Price Ceilings? 139
ECONOMICS >> in Action How Price Controls in Venezuela Proved Disastrous 139

Price Floors 141
GLOBAL COMPARISON Check Out Our Low, Low Wages! 141
How a Price Floor Causes Inefficiency 143
So Why Are There Price Floors? 146

ECONOMICS >> *in Action* The Rise and Fall of the Unpaid Intern 146

Controlling Quantities 147

The Anatomy of Quantity Controls 148

The Costs of Quantity Controls 151

ECONOMICS >> *in Action* Crabbing, Quotas, and Saving Lives in Alaska 151

BUSINESS CASE A Market Disruptor Gets Disrupted by the Market 153

CHAPTER 6
Elasticity / 159

Taken for a Ride 159

Defining and Measuring Elasticity 160

Calculating the Price Elasticity of Demand 160

An Alternative Way to Calculate Elasticities: The Midpoint Method 161

ECONOMICS >> *in Action* Estimating Elasticities 163

Interpreting the Price Elasticity of Demand 163

How Elastic Is Elastic? 164

Price Elasticity Along the Demand Curve 168

What Factors Determine the Price Elasticity of Demand? 168

ECONOMICS >> *in Action* Responding to Your Tuition Bill 171

Other Demand Elasticities 172

The Cross-Price Elasticity of Demand 172

The Income Elasticity of Demand 173

GLOBAL COMPARISON Food's Bite in World Budgets 173

ECONOMICS >> *in Action* Spending It 174

The Price Elasticity of Supply 175

Measuring the Price Elasticity of Supply 175

What Factors Determine the Price Elasticity of Supply? 176

ECONOMICS >> *in Action* A Global Commodities Glut 177

An Elasticity Menagerie 178

BUSINESS CASE The American Airline Industry: Fly Less and Charge More 179

PART 3 Individuals and Markets

CHAPTER 7
Taxes / 185

The Founding Taxers 185

The Economics of Taxes: A Preliminary View 186

The Effect of an Excise Tax on Quantities and Prices 186

Price Elasticities and Tax Incidence 189

ECONOMICS >> *in Action* Who Pays the FICA? 191

The Benefits and Costs of Taxation 192

The Revenue from an Excise Tax 192

Tax Rates and Revenue 193

FOR INQUIRING MINDS French Tax Rates and *L'Arc Laffer* 195

The Costs of Taxation 196

Elasticities and the Deadweight Loss of a Tax 199

ECONOMICS >> *in Action* Taxing Tobacco 200

Tax Fairness and Tax Efficiency 202

Two Principles of Tax Fairness 202

Equity versus Efficiency 202

ECONOMICS >> *in Action* Federal Tax Philosophy 203

Understanding the Tax System 204

Tax Bases and Tax Structure 204

Equity, Efficiency, and Progressive Taxation 205

Taxes in the United States 206

Different Taxes, Different Principles 207

GLOBAL COMPARISON You Think Your Taxes Are High? 207

FOR INQUIRING MINDS Taxing Income versus Taxing Consumption 208

ECONOMICS >> *in Action* State Tax Choices 208

BUSINESS CASE A Welcome Tax Hike: Microsoft Raises Its Internal Carbon Tax 210

CHAPTER 8
International Trade / 215

The Everywhere Phone 215

Comparative Advantage and International Trade 216

Production Possibilities and Comparative Advantage, Revisited 217

The Gains from International Trade 219

Comparative Advantage versus Absolute Advantage 220

Popular Misconceptions Arising from Misunderstanding Comparative Advantage 221

GLOBAL COMPARISON Productivity and Wages Around the World 222

Sources of Comparative Advantage 222

FOR INQUIRING MINDS How Scale Effects Drive International Trade 224

ECONOMICS >> *in Action* How Hong Kong Lost Its Shirts 224

Supply, Demand, and International Trade 225

The Effects of Imports 226

The Effects of Exports 228

International Trade and Wages 229

ECONOMICS >> *in Action* The China Shock 231

The Effects of Trade Protection 232

The Effects of a Tariff 232

The Effects of an Import Quota 234

ECONOMICS >> *in Action* The Steel Tariffs of 2018–2019 235

The Political Economy of Trade Protection 236

Arguments for Trade Protection 236

The Politics of Trade Protection 237

International Trade Agreements and the World Trade Organization 237

Challenges to Globalization 238

ECONOMICS >> *in Action* Trade War, What Is It Good For? 239

BUSINESS CASE Li & Fung: From Guangzhou to You 241

PART 4 Economics and Decision Making

CHAPTER 9
Decision Making by Individuals and Firms / 247

Making Decisions in Good Times and Bad 247

Costs, Benefits, and Profits 248

Explicit versus Implicit Costs 248

Accounting Profit versus Economic Profit 249

Making "Either–Or" Decisions 251

ECONOMICS >> *in Action* Airbnb and the Rising Cost of Privacy 252

Making "How Much" Decisions: The Role of Marginal Analysis 252

Marginal Cost 253

Marginal Benefit 255

Marginal Analysis 256

GLOBAL COMPARISON House Sizes Around the World 259

A Principle with Many Uses 259

A Preview: How Consumption Decisions Are Different 259

ECONOMICS >> *in Action* The Cost of a Life 260

Sunk Costs 261

ECONOMICS >> *in Action* Biotech: The World's Biggest Loser 262

Behavioral Economics 262

Rational, but Human, Too 263

Irrationality: An Economist's View 264

FOR INQUIRING MINDS "The Jingle Mail Blues" 265

Rational Models for Irrational People? 267

ECONOMICS >> *in Action* In Praise of Hard Deadlines 268

BUSINESS CASE J.C. Penney's One-Price Strategy Upsets Its Customers 270

CHAPTER 9
Appendix: How to Make Decisions Involving Time: Understanding Present Value / 275

How to Calculate the Present Value of a One-Year Project 275

How to Calculate the Present Value of Multiyear Projects 276

How to Calculate the Present Value of Projects with Revenues and Costs 277

PART 5 The Consumer

CHAPTER 10
The Rational Consumer / 279

The Absolute Last Bite 279

Utility: Getting Satisfaction 280

Utility and Consumption 280

The Principle of Diminishing Marginal Utility 281

ECONOMICS >> *in Action* Is Salmon a Luxury? It Depends 282

Budgets and Optimal Consumption 283

Budget Constraints and Budget Lines 283

Optimal Consumption Choice 285

FOR INQUIRING MINDS Food for Thought on Budget Constraints 287

ECONOMICS >> *in Action* The Great Condiment Craze 287

Spending the Marginal Dollar 288

Marginal Utility per Dollar 288

Optimal Consumption 290

ECONOMICS >> *in Action* Buying Your Way Out of Temptation 291

From Utility to the Demand Curve 292

Marginal Utility, the Substitution Effect, and the Law of Demand 292

The Income Effect 293

ECONOMICS >> *in Action* Lower Gasoline Prices and the Urge to Splurge 294

BUSINESS CASE Beyond Impossible: McDonald's and Burger King's Beef-Free Battle 295

CHAPTER 10
Appendix: Consumer Preferences and Consumer Choice / 301

Mapping the Utility Function 301
Indifference Curves 301
Properties of Indifference Curves 304

Indifference Curves and Consumer Choice 305
The Marginal Rate of Substitution 306
The Tangency Condition 309
The Slope of the Budget Line 310
Prices and the Marginal Rate of Substitution 311
Preferences and Choices 312

Using Indifference Curves: Substitutes and Complements 314
Perfect Substitutes 314
Perfect Complements 316
Less Extreme Cases 316

Prices, Income, and Demand 317
The Effects of a Price Increase 317
Income and Consumption 318
Income and Substitution Effects 321

PART 6 The Production Decision

CHAPTER 11
Behind the Supply Curve: Inputs and Costs / 327

The Farmer's Margin 327

The Production Function 328
Inputs and Output 328
GLOBAL COMPARISON Wheat Yields Around the World 330
From the Production Function to Cost Curves 332
ECONOMICS >> in Action Finding the Optimal Team Size 334

Two Key Concepts: Marginal Cost and Average Cost 335
Marginal Cost 335
Average Total Cost 337
Minimum Average Total Cost 340
Does the Marginal Cost Curve Always Slope Upward? 341
ECONOMICS >> in Action Smart Grid Economics 342

Short-Run versus Long-Run Costs 343
Returns to Scale 346
Summing Up Costs: The Short and Long of It 347

ECONOMICS >> in Action How the Sharing Economy Reduces Fixed Cost 347
BUSINESS CASE The Rise of the Machine at Amazon 349

CHAPTER 12
Perfect Competition and the Supply Curve / 355

Deck the Halls 355

Perfect Competition 356
Defining Perfect Competition 356
Two Necessary Conditions for Perfect Competition 356
FOR INQUIRING MINDS What's a Standardized Product? 357
Free Entry and Exit 358
ECONOMICS >> in Action Pay-for-Delay Runs Out of Time 358

Production and Profits 359
Using Marginal Analysis to Choose the Profit-Maximizing Quantity of Output 360
When Is Production Profitable? 362
The Short-Run Production Decision 365
Changing Fixed Cost 368
Summing Up: The Perfectly Competitive Firm's Profitability and Production Conditions 368
ECONOMICS >> in Action Farmers Know How 369

The Industry Supply Curve 370
The Short-Run Industry Supply Curve 370
The Long-Run Industry Supply Curve 371
The Cost of Production and Efficiency in Long-Run Equilibrium 375
ECONOMICS >> in Action A Global Pork Shortage Hits Chinese Diners Hard 376
BUSINESS CASE Retail Wars: Big Box Stores in the Age of Amazon 377

CHAPTER 13
Monopoly / 383

"Shine Bright Like a Diamond" 383

Types of Market Structure 384

The Meaning of Monopoly 385
Monopoly: Our First Departure from Perfect Competition 385
What Monopolists Do 385
Why Monopolies Exist 386
GLOBAL COMPARISON What Accounts for America's High Drug Prices? 389

ECONOMICS >> *in Action* The Monopoly That Wasn't: China and the Market for Rare Earths 390

How a Monopolist Maximizes Profit 391

The Monopolist's Demand Curve and Marginal Revenue 391

The Monopolist's Profit-Maximizing Output and Price 395

Monopoly versus Perfect Competition 396

Monopoly: The General Picture 396

ECONOMICS >> *in Action* Shocked by the High Price of Electricity 397

Monopoly and Public Policy 399

Welfare Effects of Monopoly 399

Policy Remedies to Monopoly 400

Dealing with Natural Monopoly 401

A New Generation of Market Power 403

A New Generation of Market Power and Monopoly 404

A New Generation of Market Power and Monopsony 404

Policies to Address the New Generation of Market Power 405

ECONOMICS >> *in Action* Are American Antitrust Policy Makers Behind the Digital Times? 406

Price Discrimination 408

The Logic of Price Discrimination 408

Price Discrimination and Elasticity 409

Perfect Price Discrimination 410

BUSINESS CASE Amazon and Hachette Go to War 414

PART 7 Market Structure: Beyond Perfect Competition

CHAPTER 14
Oligopoly / 421

Regulators Give Bridgestone a Flat Tire 421

The Prevalence of Oligopoly 422

ECONOMICS >> *in Action* Is It a Beer-opoly or Not? 423

Understanding Oligopoly 424

A Duopoly Example 424

Collusion and Competition 425

ECONOMICS >> *in Action* The Case Against Chocolate Producers Melts 426

Games Oligopolists Play 427

The Prisoners' Dilemma 428

FOR INQUIRING MINDS Prisoners of the Arms Race and the Resurgent Cold War 430

Overcoming the Prisoners' Dilemma: Repeated Interaction and Tacit Collusion 431

ECONOMICS >> *in Action* The Ups and Downs of a Cartel: OPEC Hits the Skids on U.S. Shale Oil 433

Oligopoly in Practice 434

The Legal Framework 434

GLOBAL COMPARISON The European Union and the United States: Differing Approaches to Antitrust Regulation 435

Tacit Collusion and Price Wars 436

Product Differentiation and Price Leadership 437

How Important Is Oligopoly? 438

ECONOMICS >> *in Action* The Price Wars of Christmas: Amazon and Walmart Slug It Out 439

BUSINESS CASE Virgin Atlantic Blows the Whistle . . . or Blows It? 441

CHAPTER 15
Monopolistic Competition and Product Differentiation / 447

The Food Court of America 447

The Meaning of Monopolistic Competition 448

Large Numbers 448

Differentiated Products 448

Free Entry and Exit in the Long Run 449

Monopolistic Competition: In Sum 449

Product Differentiation 449

Differentiation by Style or Type 449

Differentiation by Location 450

Differentiation by Quality 450

Product Differentiation: In Sum 450

ECONOMICS >> *in Action* Abbondanza! 451

Understanding Monopolistic Competition 452

Monopolistic Competition in the Short Run 452

Monopolistic Competition in the Long Run 453

ECONOMICS >> *in Action* Hits and Flops in the App Store 455

Monopolistic Competition versus Perfect Competition 456

Price, Marginal Cost, and Average Total Cost 456

Is Monopolistic Competition Inefficient? 458

Controversies About Product Differentiation 459

The Role of Advertising 459

Brand Names 460

ECONOMICS >> *in Action* The Perfume Industry: Leading Consumers by the Nose 461

BUSINESS CASE Harry's and the Dollar Shave Club Nick the Profits of Schick and Gillette 463

PART 8 Microeconomics and Public Policy

CHAPTER 16
Externalities / 467

Trouble Underfoot 467

Understanding Externalities 468

FOR INQUIRING MINDS **Driving While Distracted** 468

The Economics of a Negative Externality: Pollution 469

The Costs and Benefits of Pollution 469

Why a Market Economy Produces Too Much Pollution 470

Private Solutions to Externalities 472

ECONOMICS >> *in Action* How Much Does Your Electricity Really Cost? 472

Government Policy and Pollution 473

Environmental Standards 474

Emissions Taxes 474

GLOBAL COMPARISON Economic Growth and Greenhouse Gases in Six Countries 475

Tradable Emissions Permits 476

Comparing Environmental Policies with an Example 477

ECONOMICS >> *in Action* Cap and Trade 478

The Economics of Climate Change 479

The Causes of Climate Change 480

Policies to Address Climate Change 480

Climate Change Mitigation: Costs and Benefits 481

ECONOMICS >> *in Action* Over 3,500 Economists Agree: Tax Greenhouse Gas Emissions 482

The Economics of Positive Externalities 482

Preserved Farmland: A Positive Externality 483

Positive Externalities in Today's Economy 484

ECONOMICS >> *in Action* The Impeccable Economic Logic of Early-Childhood Intervention Programs 485

Network Externalities 485

The External Benefits of a Network Externality 486

ECONOMICS >> *in Action* The Microsoft Case 487

BUSINESS CASE Xcel Energy Goes for a Win-Win 489

CHAPTER 17
Public Goods and Common Resources / 493

The Great Stink 493

Private Goods—and Others 494

Characteristics of Goods 494

Why Markets Can Supply Only Private Goods Efficiently 495

ECONOMICS >> *in Action* From Mayhem to Renaissance 496

Public Goods 496

Providing Public Goods 497

How Much of a Public Good Should Be Provided? 497

FOR INQUIRING MINDS **Voting as a Public Good** 498

GLOBAL COMPARISON Voting as a Public Good: The Global Perspective 500

Cost-Benefit Analysis 501

ECONOMICS >> *in Action* American Infrastructure Gets a D+ 501

Common Resources 503

The Problem of Overuse 503

The Efficient Use and Maintenance of a Common Resource 504

FOR INQUIRING MINDS **When Fertile Farmland Turned to Dust** 505

ECONOMICS >> *in Action* Saving the Oceans with ITQs 506

Artificially Scarce Goods 507

ECONOMICS >> *in Action* Twenty-First Century Piracy 508

BUSINESS CASE Saving the "Beast": Ecotourism Protects the Jaguars of Brazil 509

CHAPTER 18
The Economics of the Welfare State / 515

An Affair of the Heart 515

Poverty, Inequality, and Public Policy 516

The Logic of the Welfare State 516

The Problem of Poverty 517

Trends in Poverty 517

Who Are the Poor? 518

What Causes Poverty? 519

Consequences of Poverty 519

Economic Inequality 520

Mean versus Median Household Income 520

International Comparisons of Inequality 521

When Is Inequality a Problem? 521

Economic Insecurity 522

GLOBAL COMPARISON Income, Redistribution, and Inequality in Rich Countries 523

ECONOMICS >> *in Action* Long-Term Trends in Income Inequality in the United States 523

The U.S. Welfare State 525

Means-Tested Programs 526

Social Security and Unemployment Insurance 526

The Effects of the Welfare State on Poverty and Inequality 527

ECONOMICS >> *in Action* Welfare State Programs and Poverty Rates in the Great Recession, 2007–2010 528

The Economics of Health Care 529

The Need for Health Insurance 529

Health Care in Other Countries 531

The Affordable Care Act 532

Effects of the ACA 533

ECONOMICS >> *in Action* What Medicaid Does 534

The Debate over the Welfare State 535

Problems with the Welfare State 535

The Politics of the Welfare State 536

ECONOMICS >> *in Action* The Not-So Melancholy Danes? 537

BUSINESS CASE Can the Entrepreneurial Spirit of the United States Survive Threats to the ACA? 538

PART 9 Factor Markets and Risk

CHAPTER 19
Factor Markets and the Distribution of Income / 543

The Value of a Degree 543

The Economy's Factors of Production 544

The Factors of Production 544

Why Factor Prices Matter: The Allocation of Resources 544

Factor Incomes and the Distribution of Income 544

FOR INQUIRING MINDS The Factor Distribution of Income and Social Change in the Industrial Revolution 545

ECONOMICS >> *in Action* The Factor Distribution of Income in the United States 545

Marginal Productivity and Factor Demand 546

Value of the Marginal Product 546

Value of the Marginal Product and Factor Demand 548

Shifts of the Factor Demand Curve 550

Market Equilibrium in the Factor Market 551

The Markets for Land and Capital 553

The Marginal Productivity Theory of Income Distribution 554

ECONOMICS >> *in Action* Help Wanted at Flex! 555

Is the Marginal Productivity Theory of Income Distribution Really True? 556

Wage Disparities in Practice 557

Wage Disparities and Marginal Productivity 557

Market Power 559

Efficiency Wages 560

Discrimination 560

FOR INQUIRING MINDS How Labor Works the German Way 561

So Does Marginal Productivity Theory Work? 562

ECONOMICS >> *in Action* Marginal Productivity and the Minimum Wage Puzzle 562

The Supply of Labor 563

Work versus Leisure 563

Wages and Labor Supply 564

Shifts of the Labor Supply Curve 565

GLOBAL COMPARISON The Overworked American? 566

ECONOMICS >> *in Action* The Real Housewives of the United States 567

BUSINESS CASE Walmart Revolutionizes Its Labor Practices 568

CHAPTER 19
Appendix: Indifference Curve Analysis of Labor Supply / 573

The Time Allocation Budget Line 573

The Effect of a Higher Wage Rate 574

Indifference Curve Analysis 576

CHAPTER 20
Uncertainty, Risk, and Private Information / 579

Extreme Weather 579

The Economics of Risk Aversion 580

Expectations and Uncertainty 580

The Logic of Risk Aversion 581

FOR INQUIRING MINDS The Paradox of Gambling 585

Paying to Avoid Risk 585

ECONOMICS >> *in Action* Warranties 586

Buying, Selling, and Reducing Risk 586

Trading Risk 587

Making Risk Disappear: The Power of Diversification 590

FOR INQUIRING MINDS Those Pesky Emotions 592

The Limits of Diversification 592

ECONOMICS >> *in Action* When Lloyd's Almost Lost It 593

Private Information: What You Don't Know Can Hurt You 594

Adverse Selection: The Economics of Lemons 595

Moral Hazard 596

ECONOMICS >> *in Action* Franchise Owners Try Harder 598

BUSINESS CASE PURE — An Insurance Company That Withstands Hurricanes 600

PART 10 Introduction to Macroeconomics

CHAPTER 21
Macroeconomics: The Big Picture / 607

Greek Tragedies 607

The Nature of Macroeconomics 608
Macroeconomic Questions 608
Macroeconomics: The Whole Is Greater Than the Sum of Its Parts 608
Macroeconomics: Theory and Policy 609

ECONOMICS >> *in Action* Fending Off Depression 609

The Business Cycle 611
Charting the Business Cycle 612
The Pain of Recession 612
Taming the Business Cycle 613

FOR INQUIRING MINDS Defining Recessions and Expansions 614
GLOBAL COMPARISON Recessions, Here and There 614
ECONOMICS >> *in Action* Bad Times in Brazil 615

Long-Run Economic Growth 615

ECONOMICS >> *in Action* A Tale of Two Countries 616

Inflation and Deflation 617
The Causes of Inflation and Deflation 618
The Pain of Inflation and Deflation 618

ECONOMICS >> *in Action* A Fast (Food) Measure of Inflation 619

International Imbalances 619

ECONOMICS >> *in Action* Greece's Costly Surplus 620

BUSINESS CASE GM Survives 622

CHAPTER 22
GDP and the CPI: Tracking the Macroeconomy / 627

China Hits the Big Time 627

The National Accounts 628
Following the Money: The Expanded Circular-Flow Diagram 628
Gross Domestic Product 629
Calculating GDP 630

FOR INQUIRING MINDS Our Imputed Lives 632
What GDP Tells Us 635

Real GDP: A Measure of Aggregate Output 635
Calculating Real GDP 636
What Real GDP Doesn't Measure 637

GLOBAL COMPARISON GDP and the Meaning of Life 638
ECONOMICS >> *in Action* Argentina's Peso Perplex 638

Price Indexes and the Aggregate Price Level 639
Market Baskets and Price Indexes 639
The Consumer Price Index 640
Other Price Measures 641

ECONOMICS >> *in Action* Indexing to the CPI 642
BUSINESS CASE Paying for a Heads-Up on Inflation 644

CHAPTER 23
Unemployment and Inflation / 651

The Great Mistake of 2011 651

The Unemployment Rate 652
Defining and Measuring Unemployment 652
The Significance of the Unemployment Rate 653
Growth and Unemployment 655

ECONOMICS >> *in Action* Opportunity Knocks 657

The Natural Rate of Unemployment 658
Job Creation and Job Destruction 658
Frictional Unemployment 659
Structural Unemployment 660
The Natural Rate of Unemployment 663
Changes in the Natural Rate of Unemployment 664

ECONOMICS >> *in Action* Men Not Working 665

Inflation and Deflation 666
The Level of Prices Doesn't Matter . . . 666
. . . But the Rate of Change of Prices Does 667
Winners and Losers from Inflation 670
Inflation Is Easy. Disinflation Is Hard. 671

ECONOMICS >> *in Action* Israel's Experience with Inflation 672
BUSINESS CASE TaskRabbit 673

PART 11 Long-Run Economic Growth

CHAPTER 24
Long-Run Economic Growth / 679

The Smog of Prosperity 679

Comparing Economies Across Time and Space 680
Real GDP per Capita 680
Growth Rates 681

ECONOMICS >> in Action An Economic Breakthrough in Bangladesh 683

The Sources of Long-Run Growth 684
The Crucial Importance of Productivity 684
Explaining Growth in Productivity 684
Accounting for Growth: The Aggregate Production Function 685
What About Natural Resources? 689

ECONOMICS >> in Action The Rise, Fall, and Return of the Productivity Paradox 690

Why Growth Rates Differ 691
Explaining Differences in Growth Rates 692
The Role of Government in Promoting Economic Growth 693

ECONOMICS >> in Action What's the Matter with Italy? 695

Success, Disappointment, and Failure 696
East Asia's Miracle 696
Latin America's Disappointment 698
Africa's Troubles and Promise 698
Left Behind by Growth? 699

GLOBAL COMPARISON Lagging Regions in Rich Countries 699

ECONOMICS >> in Action Global Winners and Losers 701

Is World Growth Sustainable? 702
Natural Resources and Growth, Revisited 702
Economic Growth and the Environment 703

ECONOMICS >> in Action China's War on Pollution 705

BUSINESS CASE Raising the Bar(code) 706

CHAPTER 25
Savings, Investment Spending, and the Financial System / 713

Paying for a Hidden Empire 713

Matching Up Savings and Investment Spending 714
The Savings–Investment Spending Identity 714
The Market for Loanable Funds 718

FOR INQUIRING MINDS Using Present Value 719

ECONOMICS >> in Action Three Generations of U.S. Interest Rates 727

The Financial System 729
Three Tasks of a Financial System 730
Types of Financial Assets 731
Financial Intermediaries 733

GLOBAL COMPARISON Corporate Bonds in the United States and the Euro Area 735

ECONOMICS >> in Action Banks, Success, and South America 736

Financial Fluctuations 736
The Demand for Stocks 737

FOR INQUIRING MINDS How Now, Dow Jones? 737
The Demand for Other Assets 738
Asset Price Expectations 739

FOR INQUIRING MINDS Behavioral Finance 740
Asset Prices and Macroeconomics 741

ECONOMICS >> in Action The Rise and Fall of Mortgage Delinquencies 741

BUSINESS CASE Grameen Bank: Banking Against Poverty 743

PART 12 Short-Run Economic Fluctuations

CHAPTER 26
Income and Expenditure / 749

The Malls in Spain Have Mainly Dodged the Pain 749

The Multiplier: An Informal Introduction 750

ECONOMICS >> in Action To Shale and Back 752

Consumer Spending 753
Current Disposable Income and Consumer Spending 753
Shifts of the Aggregate Consumption Function 756

ECONOMICS >> in Action Famous First Forecasting Failures 758

Investment Spending 759
1. The Interest Rate and Investment Spending 760
2. Expected Future Real GDP, Production Capacity, and Investment Spending 761
3. Inventories and Unplanned Investment Spending 761

ECONOMICS >> in Action Business Investment in the Great Recession 763

The Income-Expenditure Model 763
Planned Aggregate Spending and Real GDP 764
Income–Expenditure Equilibrium 766
The Multiplier Process and Inventory Adjustment 768
What About Exports and Imports? 771

ECONOMICS >> in Action Inventories and the End of a Recession 771

BUSINESS CASE What's Good for America Is Good for GM 773

CHAPTER 26
Appendix: Deriving the Multiplier Algebraically / 779

CHAPTER 27
Aggregate Demand and Aggregate Supply / 781

Different Generations, Different Policies 781

Aggregate Demand 782

Why Is the Aggregate Demand Curve Downward Sloping? 783

The Aggregate Demand Curve and the Income–Expenditure Model 784

Shifts of the Aggregate Demand Curve 786

Government Policies and Aggregate Demand 788

ECONOMICS >> *in Action* Moving Along the Aggregate Demand Curve, 1979–1980 789

Aggregate Supply 790

The Short-Run Aggregate Supply Curve 791

FOR INQUIRING MINDS What's Truly Flexible, What's Truly Sticky 793

Shifts of the Short-Run Aggregate Supply Curve 793

The Long-Run Aggregate Supply Curve 796

From the Short Run to the Long Run 798

ECONOMICS >> *in Action* Sticky Wages in the Great Recession 799

The *AD–AS* Model 800

Short-Run Macroeconomic Equilibrium 800

Shifts of Aggregate Demand: Short-Run Effects 801

Shifts of the *SRAS* Curve 802

Long-Run Macroeconomic Equilibrium 804

FOR INQUIRING MINDS Where's the Deflation? 805

ECONOMICS >> *in Action* Supply Shocks versus Demand Shocks in Practice 807

Macroeconomic Policy 808

Policy in the Face of Demand Shocks 808

FOR INQUIRING MINDS Keynes and the Long Run 808

Responding to Supply Shocks 809

ECONOMICS >> *in Action* Is Stabilization Policy Stabilizing? 810

BUSINESS CASE Toyota Makes Its Move 811

PART 13 Stabilization Policy

CHAPTER 28
Fiscal Policy / 817

Spending to Fight a Recession 817

Fiscal Policy: The Basics 818

Taxes, Purchases of Goods and Services, Government Transfers, and Borrowing 818

The Government Budget and Total Spending 819

Expansionary and Contractionary Fiscal Policy 820

Can Expansionary Fiscal Policy Actually Work? 822

A Cautionary Note: Lags in Fiscal Policy 823

ECONOMICS >> *in Action* A Tale of Two Stimuli 824

Fiscal Policy and the Multiplier 825

Multiplier Effects of an Increase in Government Purchases of Goods and Services 825

Multiplier Effects of Changes in Government Transfers and Taxes 826

How Taxes Affect the Multiplier 827

ECONOMICS >> *in Action* Austerity and the Multiplier 828

The Budget Balance 829

The Budget Balance as a Measure of Fiscal Policy 830

The Business Cycle and the Cyclically Adjusted Budget Balance 830

Should the Budget Be Balanced? 832

ECONOMICS >> *in Action* Trying to Balance Budgets in a Recession 833

Long-Run Implications of Fiscal Policy 834

Deficits, Surpluses, and Debt 835

Potential Dangers Posed by Rising Government Debt 835

GLOBAL COMPARISON The American Way of Debt 836

Deficits and Debt in Practice 837

FOR INQUIRING MINDS What Happened to the Debt from World War II? 838

Implicit Liabilities 838

ECONOMICS >> *in Action* Who's Afraid of a Debt Spiral? 840

BUSINESS CASE Here Comes the Sun 841

CHAPTER 28
Appendix: Taxes and the Multiplier / 847

CHAPTER 29
Money, Banking, and the Federal Reserve System / 849

Not So Funny Money 849

The Meaning of Money 850

What Is Money? 850

Roles of Money 851

GLOBAL COMPARISON The Cash of Nations 851

Types of Money 852

Measuring the Money Supply 853

FOR INQUIRING MINDS All About the Benjamins 854

ECONOMICS >> *in Action* The History of the Dollar 854

The Monetary Role of Banks 855
What Banks Do 856
The Problem of Bank Runs 857
Bank Regulation 858

ECONOMICS >> *in Action* It's a Wonderful Banking System 859

Determining the Money Supply 860
How Banks Create Money 860
Reserves, Bank Deposits, and the Money Multiplier 862
The Money Multiplier in Reality 863

ECONOMICS >> *in Action* Multiplying Money Down 864

The Federal Reserve System 865
The Structure of the Fed 865
What the Fed Does: Reserve Requirements and the Discount Rate 866
Open-Market Operations 867

FOR INQUIRING MINDS Who Gets the Interest on the Fed's Assets? 868
The European Central Bank 869

ECONOMICS >> *in Action* The Fed's Balance Sheet, Normal and Abnormal 870

The Evolution of the U.S. Banking System 871
The Crisis in U.S. Banking in the Early Twentieth Century 871
Responding to Banking Crises: The Creation of the Federal Reserve 872
The Savings and Loan Crisis of the 1980s 873
Back to the Future: The Financial Crisis of 2008 and Its Aftermath 874
Shadow Banking and Its Vulnerabilities 874

ECONOMICS >> *in Action* Financial Regulation After the 2008 Crisis 876

BUSINESS CASE The Perfect Gift: Cash or a Gift Card? 878

CHAPTER 30
Monetary Policy / 885

The Most Powerful Person in Government 885

The Demand for Money 886
The Opportunity Cost of Holding Money 886
The Money Demand Curve 888
Shifts of the Money Demand Curve 889

ECONOMICS >> *in Action* A Yen for Cash 890

Money and Interest Rates 891
The Equilibrium Interest Rate 891
Two Models of Interest Rates? 893
Monetary Policy and the Interest Rate 893
Long-Term Interest Rates 895

ECONOMICS >> *in Action* Up the Down Staircase 896

Monetary Policy and Aggregate Demand 897
Expansionary and Contractionary Monetary Policy 897
Monetary Policy in Practice 898
The Taylor Rule Method of Setting Monetary Policy 899
Inflation Targeting 900

GLOBAL COMPARISON Inflation Targets 900
The Zero Lower Bound Problem 901

ECONOMICS >> *in Action* What the Fed Wants, the Fed Gets 902

Money, Output, and Prices in the Long Run 902
Short-Run and Long-Run Effects of an Increase in the Money Supply 903
Monetary Neutrality 904
Changes in the Money Supply and the Interest Rate in the Long Run 904

ECONOMICS >> *in Action* International Evidence of Monetary Neutrality 905

BUSINESS CASE Parking Your Money at PayPal 907

CHAPTER 30
Appendix: Reconciling the Two Models of the Interest Rate / 911

The Interest Rate in the Short Run 911
The Interest Rate in the Long Run 912

CHAPTER 31
Inflation, Disinflation, and Deflation / 915

That and 900,000 Bolivars Will Get You a Cup of Coffee 915

Money and Inflation 916
The Classical Model of Money and Prices 916
The Inflation Tax 918
The Logic of Hyperinflation 919

ECONOMICS >> *in Action* Behind Venezuela's Inflation 921

Moderate Inflation and Disinflation 921
The Output Gap and the Unemployment Rate 922

FOR INQUIRING MINDS Okun's Law 924
The Short-Run Phillips Curve 924

FOR INQUIRING MINDS The Aggregate Supply Curve and the Short-Run Phillips Curve 926
Inflation Expectations and the Short-Run Phillips Curve 927

ECONOMICS >> *in Action* The Spanish Squeeze 929

Inflation and Unemployment in the Long Run 930
The Long-Run Phillips Curve 930

The Natural Rate of Unemployment, Revisited 931

The Costs of Disinflation 932

GLOBAL COMPARISON Disinflation Around the World 932

ECONOMICS >> in Action The Great Disinflation of the 1980s 933

Deflation 934

Debt Deflation 934

Effects of Expected Deflation 934

ECONOMICS >> in Action Is Europe Turning Japanese? 936

BUSINESS CASE Hyperinflation as a Business Opportunity 938

PART 14 Events and Ideas

CHAPTER 32

Macroeconomics: Events and Ideas / 943

Sympathy for the Deficit 943

Classical Macroeconomics 944

Money and the Price Level 944

The Business Cycle 944

The Great Depression and the Keynesian Revolution 945

Keynes's Theory 945

FOR INQUIRING MINDS The Politics of Keynes 947

Policy to Fight Recessions 947

ECONOMICS >> in Action The End of the Great Depression 948

Challenges to Keynesian Economics 949

The Revival of Monetary Policy 949

Monetarism 949

Limits to Macroeconomic Policy: Inflation and the Natural Rate of Unemployment 950

Rational Expectations and New Classical Economics 951

FOR INQUIRING MINDS Supply-Side Economics 952

The Political Business Cycle 953

ECONOMICS >> in Action Did the Fed Cause the Great Depression? 953

From Great Moderation to Secular Stagnation 955

The Limits of Monetary Policy 955

The Revival of Fiscal Policy 956

Policy in a Low-Interest-Rate World 957

ECONOMICS >> in Action Debt Fears, Austerity, and the U.S. Recovery 958

PART 15 The International Economy

CHAPTER 33

International Macroeconomics / 963

Switzerland Doesn't Want Your Money 963

Capital Flows and the Balance of Payments 964

Balance of Payments Accounts 964

FOR INQUIRING MINDS GDP, GNP, and the Current Account 966

Modeling the Financial Account 968

GLOBAL COMPARISON Big Surpluses 968

Underlying Determinants of International Capital Flows 969

Two-Way Capital Flows 969

ECONOMICS >> in Action Leprechaun Economics 970

The Role of the Exchange Rate 971

Understanding Exchange Rates 971

The Equilibrium Exchange Rate 972

Inflation and Real Exchange Rates 975

Purchasing Power Parity 977

FOR INQUIRING MINDS Burgernomics 977

ECONOMICS >> in Action Strong Dollar Woes 978

Exchange Rate Policy 979

Exchange Rate Regimes 979

How Can an Exchange Rate Be Held Fixed? 980

The Exchange Rate Regime Dilemma 982

FOR INQUIRING MINDS From Bretton Woods to the Euro 983

ECONOMICS >> in Action China Pegs the Yuan 983

Exchange Rates and Macroeconomic Policy 984

Devaluation and Revaluation of Fixed Exchange Rates 985

Monetary Policy Under Floating Exchange Rates 985

International Business Cycles 986

ECONOMICS >> in Action The Little Currency That Could 987

BUSINESS CASE German Cars, Made in Spain 989

Solutions to *Check Your Understanding* Questions S-1

Glossary G-1

Index I-1

Introduction: An Engine for Growth and Discovery

A DAY IN THE MEGACITY

LONDON, NEW YORK, AND TOKYO have something in common: they are megacities — huge metropolitan complexes that contain tens of millions of people and are spread over immense tracts of land. While most people are familiar with these megacities, not everyone knows about the biggest of them all: the vast urban complex known as China's Pearl River Delta (the PRD). Roughly the same size as the state of Delaware, the

Thirty years ago China was very poor with a backward economy. Now it produces sophisticated goods for the world, allowing it to deliver relatively comfortable incomes to many of its people.

PRD is home to more than 65 million people. Driving across the PRD (as one of the authors has done), with its endless succession of factories, office buildings, and apartment towers, is an unforgettable — and very long — experience.

What are all those people doing? A significant percentage of them are engaged in producing goods for world markets, especially, but by no means only, electronic components: just about every smartphone, tablet, and computer contains components produced in the PRD. But the megacity's residents are consumers as well as producers. While the wage of an average worker in the PRD is relatively low by U.S. standards, overall wages and income are high enough to support a vast retail sector, ranging from mom-and-pop local stores to shops selling expensive luxury goods.

But not so long ago, neither the PRD nor the economic dynamism it embodies was visible. As recently as 1980, 800 million people in China subsisted on less than $1.50 a day. The average Chinese citizen more or less had enough to eat and a roof over his or her head, but not much more than that. In fact, the standard of living wasn't much higher than it had been centuries earlier. And from 1959 to 1961, in what is now known as "The Great Leap Backward," the Chinese government got the economy so wrong that millions of Chinese died from man-made famine.

However, in the years since 1980, Chinese incomes have soared more than twentyfold in real terms as the poverty rate (percentage of the population subsisting on less than $1.90 a day) has fallen from 88% in 1981 to 0.2% in 2015. The rise of the PRD is one chapter of an incredible success story in which hundreds of millions of Chinese have been lifted out of abject poverty over the past few decades. Never in human history have so many seen so much progress.

Although this is a remarkable story, it is not entirely unprecedented. From 1840

to 1910, British workers also experienced a marked rise in their standard of living. And this success was repeated soon afterward in the United States, setting the stage for the high levels of prosperity we now enjoy. Commenting on how English workers were lifted out of poverty, the great economist Alfred Marshall made an observation that is equally relevant for Chinese workers today: "The hope that poverty and ignorance may gradually be extinguished, derives indeed much support from the steady progress of the working classes during the nineteenth century."

These unprecedented sets of events have touched our lives today in a dizzying number of ways. You are using smartphones, tablets, and laptops that are manufactured in the PRD as you pursue a first-rate education in the United States, one of the richest countries in the world.

What can economics say about all of this? Quite a lot, it turns out. What you will learn from this book is how these momentous changes, which lifted hundreds of millions of people out of poverty, are related to a simple, but very important, set of questions involving economics. Among these questions are:

- How does our economic system work? That is, how does it manage to deliver the goods?

- When and why does our economic system sometimes go astray, leading people into counterproductive behavior?

- Why are there ups and downs in the economy? That is, why does the economy sometimes have a bad year?

- Why is the long run mainly a story of ups rather than downs? That is, why has China, like Great Britain and the United States, become much richer over time?

Let's take a look at these questions and offer a brief preview of what you will learn in this book. ●

1

An **economy** is a system for coordinating society's productive activities.

Economics is the social science that studies the production, distribution, and consumption of goods and services.

A **market economy** is an economy in which decisions about production and consumption are made by individual producers and consumers.

A booming marketplace in today's China.

‖ The Invisible Hand

The massive industrial and consumer complex that is today's Pearl River Delta is quite a new creation. As recently as 1980 much of the region was an economic backwater; the nucleus, Shenzhen, was then a small and very poor fishing village. How did this backwater turn into the electronics workshop of the world, making it a dynamic creator of wealth?

To achieve the level of prosperity we have in America, a level the average resident of the PRD can only now begin to aspire to, you need a well-functioning system for coordinating productive activities—the activities that create the goods and services people want and get them to the people who want them. That kind of system is what we mean when we talk about the **economy.** And **economics** is the social science that studies the production, distribution, and consumption of goods and services.

An economy succeeds to the extent that it, literally, delivers the goods. And as we've discussed, over the past 30 years the Chinese economy has achieved a spectacular increase in the amount of goods it delivers both to its own citizens and to the rest of the world.

So China's economy must be doing something right, and we might want to compliment the people in charge. But guess what? There isn't anyone in charge—not anymore.

In the 1970s, before the PRD began its incredible rise, China was a *command economy* in which decisions about what factories would produce and what goods would be delivered to households were made by government officials. But experience shows that command economies don't work very well. Producers in command economies like China before 1980 or the Soviet Union before 1991 routinely found themselves unable to produce because they did not have crucial raw materials, or if they succeeded in producing, they found nobody wanted their products. Consumers were often unable to find necessities like toilet paper or milk. Command economies are infamous for long lines at shops. And as we mentioned, from 1959 to 1961, the Chinese government got its command economy terribly wrong, inflicting enormous hardship and causing millions of unnecessary deaths.

In 1978 the Chinese government finally admitted that its economic model wasn't working, and began a remarkable transformation into a **market economy,** one in which production and consumption are the result of decentralized decisions by many firms and individuals. The United States has a market economy. And in today's China there is no central authority telling people what to produce or where to ship it. Each individual producer makes what they think will be most profitable; each consumer buys what they choose. It's important to realize, however, that the Chinese government intervenes in markets much more than the U.S. government does; in particular, while China's government rarely tells producers what to produce, it often tells banks how much to lend and to whom.

If you had never seen a market economy in action, you might imagine that it would be chaotic. After all, nobody is in charge. But market economies are able to coordinate even highly complex activities and reliably provide consumers with the goods and services they want. Indeed, people quite casually trust their lives to the market system: residents of any major city would starve in days if the unplanned yet somehow orderly actions of thousands of businesses did not deliver a steady supply of food. Surprisingly, the unplanned "chaos" of a market economy turns out to be far more orderly than the planning of a command economy. And that's why almost every country in the world—North Korea and Cuba are the only exceptions—has become a market economy.

In 1776, in a famous passage in his book *The Wealth of Nations*, the pioneering Scottish economist Adam Smith wrote about how individuals, in pursuing their own interests, often end up serving the interests of society as a whole. Of a businessman whose pursuit of profit makes the nation wealthier, Smith wrote: "[H]e intends only his own gain, and he is in this, as in many other cases, led by an invisible hand to promote an end which was no part of his intention." Ever since, economists have used the term **invisible hand** to refer to the way a market economy manages to harness the power of self-interest for the good of society.

The study of how individuals make decisions and how these decisions interact is called **microeconomics.** One of the key themes in microeconomics is the validity of Adam Smith's insight: individuals pursuing their own interests often do promote the interests of society as a whole.

So the answer to our first question—"How does our economic system manage to deliver the goods?"—is that we rely on the virtues of a market economy and the power of the invisible hand.

But the invisible hand isn't always our friend. It's also important to understand when and why the individual pursuit of self-interest can lead to counterproductive behavior.

According to Adam Smith, a market economy manages to harness the power of self-interest for the common good.

My Benefit, Your Cost

In most ways, life in the PRD is immensely better than it was in 1980. Two things have, however, gotten much worse: traffic congestion and air quality. At rush hour, the average speed on the PRD's roads is only around 12 miles an hour and the air is seriously unhealthy much of the year.

Why do these problems represent failures of the invisible hand? Consider the case of traffic congestion.

When traffic is congested, each driver is imposing a cost on all the other drivers on the road—she is literally getting in their way (and they are getting in her way). This cost can be substantial: one estimate found that someone driving a car into lower Manhattan on a weekday causes more than three hours of delays to other drivers, and around $160 in monetary losses. Yet when deciding whether or not to drive, commuters have no incentive to take the costs they impose on others into account.

Traffic congestion is a familiar example of a much broader problem: **market failure,** which happens when the individual pursuit of one's own interest, instead of promoting the interests of society as a whole, actually makes society worse off. Another important example of market failure is air pollution, which is all too visible, literally, in the PRD. Water pollution and the overexploitation of natural resources such as fish and forests reflect the same problem.

The environmental costs of self-interested behavior can sometimes be huge. And as the world becomes more crowded and the environmental footprint of human activity continues to grow, issues like climate change and ocean acidification will become increasingly important.

The good news, as you will learn if you study microeconomics, is that economic analysis can be used to diagnose cases of market failure. And often, economic analysis can also be used to devise solutions for the problem.

The **invisible hand** refers to the way in which the individual pursuit of self-interest can lead to good results for society as a whole.

Microeconomics is the branch of economics that studies how people make decisions and how these decisions interact.

When the individual pursuit of self-interest leads to bad results for society as a whole, there is **market failure.**

Good Times, Bad Times

China has become an enormous economic powerhouse in the last 30 years. (And, depending upon the data source used, China and the United States vie for top place among the world's economies.) One somewhat ironic consequence of China's rise is that people around the world get nervous at any signs of trouble in Chinese industry, because it's such a big source of demand for raw materials. And in 2019, there was a lot to be nervous about. Many economic indicators pointed to a sharp slowdown in the economy.

ECONOMICS 101

©Dave Carpenter/Cartoonstock

"Remember, an economic boom is usually followed by an economic kaboom."

Such troubled periods are a regular feature of modern economies. The fact is that the economy does not always run smoothly: it experiences fluctuations, a series of ups and downs. By middle age, a typical American will have experienced three or four downs, known as **recessions.** The U.S. economy experienced serious recessions beginning in 1973, 1981, 1990, 2001, and 2007. During a severe recession, millions of workers may be laid off.

Like market failure, recessions are a fact of life; but also like market failure, they are a problem for which economic analysis offers some solutions. Recessions are one of the main concerns of the branch of economics known as **macroeconomics,** which is concerned with the overall ups and downs of the economy. If you study macroeconomics, you will learn how economists explain recessions and how government policies can be used to minimize the damage from economic fluctuations.

Despite the occasional recession, however, over the long run the stories of all major economies contain many more ups than downs. And that long-run ascent is the subject of our final question.

‖ Onward and Upward

The overall standard of living of the average resident of the PRD, while immensely higher than it was in 1980, is still pretty low by American standards. But then, America wasn't always as rich as it is today. Indeed, at the beginning of the twentieth century, most Americans lived under conditions that we would now think of as extreme poverty. Only 10% of homes had flush toilets, only 8% had central heating, only 2% had electricity, and almost nobody had a car, let alone a washing machine or air conditioning. But over the course of the following century America achieved a remarkable rise in living standards that ultimately led to the great wealth that we see around us today.

Such comparisons are a stark reminder of how much lives around the world have been changed by **economic growth,** the increasing ability of the economy to produce goods and services, leading to higher living standards. Why does the economy grow over time? And why does economic growth occur faster in some places and times than in others? These are key questions for economics, because economic growth is a good thing, for many, as residents of the PRD can attest, and most of us want more of it. But economic growth does come with some costs.

Specifically, despite benefiting the vast majority of people, economic growth has always created losers as well as winners as fast-growing, emerging sectors of the economy eclipse those of the past. For example, the gleaming towers built in the PRD, along with newly constructed dams, displaced many Chinese, a number of them farmers who lost their land and livelihoods.

The environment is another potential loser, unless attention is paid to the question of how to achieve *sustainable long-run economic growth,* which is economic growth over the long term that balances protection of the environment with improved living standards for current and future generations. Today, the goal of balancing the production of goods and services with the health of the environment is a hotly debated policy topic. Economic analysis has a key role to play here because environmental degradation is often a result of market failure.

‖ An Engine for Discovery

We hope we have convinced you that what the great economist Alfred Marshall called the "ordinary business of life," the economic actions and transactions that go on every day not just in the PRD but around the world, is really quite

A **recession** is a downturn in the economy.

Macroeconomics is the branch of economics that is concerned with overall ups and downs in the economy.

Economic growth is the growing ability of the economy to produce goods and services, leading to higher living standards.

extraordinary, if you stop to think about it, and that it can lead us to ask some very interesting and important questions.

In this book, we will describe the answers economists have given to these questions. But this book, like economics as a whole, isn't a list of answers: it's an introduction to a discipline, a way to address questions like those we asked earlier. Or as Alfred Marshall put it: "Economics . . . is not a body of concrete truth, but an engine for the discovery of concrete truth."

So let's turn the key and start the ignition.

KEY TERMS

Economy, p. 2

Economics, p. 2

Market economy, p. 2

Invisible hand, p. 3

Microeconomics, p. 3

Market failure, p. 3

Recession, p. 4

Macroeconomics, p. 4

Economic growth, p. 4

1 ❭ First Principles

THERE WAS A TIME when most of the world's college students were located in wealthy Western nations. Today, however, the number of college students in developing countries like China and India is rapidly overtaking the number in the United States and Western Europe. In fact, China already has more students enrolled in college than the United States does.

And what are these students studying? A variety of subjects, of course. But regardless of the region of the world, a lot of students will be studying economics.

Regardless of where in the world you study, the basic principles of economics are the same.

You might wonder, however, whether the economics being taught at, say, Shanghai University or the University of Mumbai bears much resemblance to the economics being taught in U.S. colleges. After all, there are big differences between nations in levels of income, political institutions, and the problems they face. Doesn't this mean that the economics in these countries is different, too?

The answer is, yes and no. "Yes," because different circumstances and history affect what both students and practitioners need to know. That's why there are international editions of this textbook. Canada, for example, is different enough from the United States to warrant its own edition with explanations about Canadian economic issues and institutions.

The answer is also "no" because much of the material covered in basic economics is the same wherever you are around the world. The reason for this is that all economics is based on a set of common principles that apply to many different issues, regardless of the particular setting.

Some of these principles involve *individual choice* — for economics is, first of all, about the choices that individuals make. Do you save your money and take the bus or do you buy a car? Do you keep your old phone or upgrade to a new one? These decisions involve *making a choice* from among a limited number of alternatives — limited because no one can have everything that he or she wants. Every question in economics at its most basic level involves individuals making choices.

But to understand how an economy works, you need to understand more than how individuals make choices. None of us are like Robinson Crusoe, living alone on an island. Every person must make decisions in an environment that is shaped by the decisions of others. So in this chapter we will learn about four principles of economics that guide the choices made by individuals.

Indeed, in a modern economy even the simplest decisions you make — say, what to have for breakfast — are shaped by the decisions of thousands of other people, from the banana grower in Costa Rica who decided to grow the fruit you eat to the farmer in Iowa who provided the corn in your cornflakes.

Because each of us in a market economy depends on so many others — and they, in turn, depend on us — our choices interact. So although all economics at a basic level is about individual choice, in order to understand how market economies behave we must also understand *economic interaction* — how my choices affect your choices, and vice versa. To that end, in this chapter you will study the four principles that govern how individual choices interact in the economy.

Although many important economic interactions can be understood by looking at the markets for individual goods (like the market for corn), when we consider the economy as a whole, we see that it is composed of an enormous number of markets for individual goods, and these many markets interact. As a result, the larger economy experiences ups and downs. In order to understand economy-wide interactions, in this chapter we will study the three principles that underlie their behavior.

These 11 principles are the basis of all economic analysis. They form the common ground of economics. And they apply just as much in Shanghai or Mumbai as they do in Omaha or Atlanta. ●

WHAT YOU WILL LEARN

- What four principles guide the choices made by individuals?
- What four principles govern how individual choices interact?
- What three principles illustrate economy-wide interactions?

Principles That Underlie Individual Choice: The Core of Economics

Every economic issue involves, at its most basic level, **individual choice**—decisions by an individual about what to do and what not to do. In fact, you might say that it isn't economics if it isn't about choice.

Take Walmart or Amazon. There are thousands of different products available, and it is extremely unlikely that you—or anyone else—could afford to buy everything you might want to have. And anyway, there's only so much space in your dorm room or apartment. So will you buy another bookcase or a mini-refrigerator? Given limitations on your budget and your living space, you must choose which products to buy and which to leave on the shelf.

The fact that those products are on the shelf in the first place involves choice—the store manager chose to put them there, and the manufacturers of the products chose to produce them. All economic activities involve individual choice.

Four economic principles underlie the economics of individual choice, as shown in Table 1-1. We'll now examine each of these principles.

Principle #1: Choices Are Necessary Because Resources Are Scarce

You can't always get what you want. Many of us would like to have a big beautiful house or apartment in a great location, a new car or two, and vacations in exotic locations each year. But even in a rich country like the United States, not many families can afford all that. So they must make choices—like whether to go to Disney World this year or buy a better car, or whether to move to the city where housing is expensive, or accept a longer commute in order to live where housing prices are cheaper.

Limited income isn't the only thing that keeps us from having everything we want. Time is also in limited supply: there are only 24 hours in a day. Choosing to spend time on one activity means choosing not to spend time on something else—studying for an exam means forgoing a night spent watching a movie. Indeed, many people faced with the limited number of hours in the day are willing to trade money for time. For example, local convenience stores typically charge higher prices than a regular supermarket. But they fulfill a valuable role by catering to time-pressed customers who would rather pay more than travel farther to the supermarket.

This leads us to our first principle of individual choice:

People must make choices because resources are scarce.

A **resource** is anything that can be used to produce something else. Lists of the economy's resources usually begin with land, labor (the time of workers), capital (machinery, buildings, and other man-made productive assets), and human capital (the educational achievements and skills of workers). A resource is **scarce** when there's not enough of the resource available to satisfy all the ways a society wants to use it.

There are many scarce resources. These include natural resources that come from the physical environment, such as minerals, lumber, and petroleum. There is also a limited quantity of human resources, such as labor, skill, and intelligence. And in a growing world economy with a rapidly increasing human population, even clean air and water have become scarce resources.

Just as individuals must make choices, the scarcity of resources means that society as a whole must make choices. One way a society with a market economy makes choices is by allowing them to emerge from many individual choices. For example, Americans as a group have only so many hours in a week. How many of those hours will be spent traveling to supermarkets to get lower prices, rather than saving time by shopping at local convenience stores? The answer is the sum of individual decisions: each of the millions of individuals in the economy makes

---

TABLE 1-1 Principles of Individual Choice

1. People must make choices because resources are scarce.

2. The opportunity cost of an item — what you must give up in order to get it — is its true cost.

3. "How much" decisions require making trade-offs at the margin: comparing the costs and benefits of doing a little bit more of an activity versus doing a little bit less.

4. People respond to incentives, exploiting opportunities to make themselves better off.

Ben Heys/Shutterstock

Resources are scarce.

Individual choice is the decision by an individual of what to do, which necessarily involves a decision of what not to do.

A **resource** is anything that can be used to produce something else.

Resources are **scarce**—not enough of the resources are available to satisfy all the various ways a society wants to use them.

a choice about where to shop, and the overall choice is simply the sum of those individual decisions.

The real cost of an item is its **opportunity cost:** what you must give up in order to get it.

Principle #2: The True Cost of Something Is Its Opportunity Cost

It is the last term before you graduate, and your class schedule allows you to take only one elective. There are two, however, that you really want to take: Data Visualization Basics and Introduction to Chinese.

Suppose you decide to take the Intro to Chinese course. What's the cost of that decision? It is, primarily, the fact that you can't take the Data Visualization class, your next best alternative choice. Economists call that kind of cost—what you must give up in order to get an item you want—the **opportunity cost** of that item. This leads us to our second principle of individual choice:

> *The opportunity cost of an item—what you must give up in order to get it—is its true cost.*

So the opportunity cost of taking the Intro to Chinese class includes the benefit you would have derived from the Data Visualization class.

The concept of opportunity cost is crucial to understanding individual choice because, in the end, all costs are opportunity costs. That's because every choice you make means forgoing some other alternative.

Sometimes critics claim that economists are concerned only with costs and benefits that can be measured in dollars and cents. But that is not true. Much economic analysis involves cases like our electives example, where it costs no extra tuition to take one elective course instead of another—that is, there is no direct monetary cost. Nonetheless, the elective you choose has an opportunity cost—the other desirable elective course that you must forgo because time limits permit you to take only one. More specifically, the opportunity cost of a choice is what you forgo by not choosing your next best alternative.

You might think that opportunity cost is an add-on—that is, something *additional* to the monetary cost of an item. But it isn't. Suppose that an elective class costs an additional $750. Now there is a monetary cost to taking Intro to Chinese. Is the opportunity cost of taking that course something separate from that monetary cost?

Yes, it is. Consider that you will have to spend that $750 no matter which class you take. So what you give up to take Intro to Chinese is still the Data Visualization class—you have to spend that $750 either way. But what if the Data Visualization class is free? In that case, what you give up to take the Intro to Chinese class is the benefit from the data visualization class *plus* the benefit you could have gained from spending the $750 on other things.

Either way, the real cost of taking your preferred class is what you must give up to get it. As you expand the set of decisions that underlie each choice—whether to take an elective or not, whether to finish this term or not, whether to drop out or not—you'll realize that all costs are ultimately opportunity costs.

Sometimes the money you have to pay for something is a good indication of its opportunity cost. But many times it is not.

One very important example of how poorly monetary cost can indicate opportunity cost is the cost of attending college. Tuition and housing are major monetary expenses for most students; but even if they were free, attending college would still be an expensive proposition because most college students, if they were not in college, would have a job. By going to college, then, students *forgo* the income they could have earned if they had worked instead. This means that the opportunity cost of attending college is what you pay for tuition and housing plus the forgone income you would have earned in a job.

It's easy to see that the opportunity cost of going to college is especially high for people who could be earning a lot during what would otherwise have been

Mark Zuckerberg, founder of Facebook, understood the concept of opportunity cost.

You make a **trade-off** when you compare the costs with the benefits of doing something.

Decisions about whether to do a bit more or a bit less of an activity are **marginal decisions.**

The study of such decisions is known as **marginal analysis.**

their college years. That is why star athletes and successful entrepreneurs often skip or drop out of college.

Principle #3: "How Much" Is a Decision at the Margin

Some of the decisions we make involve an "either–or" choice—for example, you decide either to go to college or to begin working; you decide either to take economics or something else. But other important decisions involve "how much" choices—for example, if you are taking both economics and chemistry this semester, you must decide how much time to spend studying for each. When it comes to understanding "how much" decisions, economics has an important insight to offer: "how much" is a decision made at the margin.

Suppose you are taking both economics and chemistry. And suppose you are a pre-med student, so your grade in chemistry matters more to you than your grade in economics. Should you spend *all* your study time on chemistry and wing it on the economics exam? Probably not; even if you think your chemistry grade is more important, you should put some effort into studying economics.

Spending more time studying chemistry involves a benefit (a higher expected grade in that course) and a cost (you could have spent that time doing something else, such as studying to get a higher grade in economics). That is, your decision involves a **trade-off**—a comparison of costs and benefits.

How do you decide this kind of "how much" question? The typical answer is that you make the decision a bit at a time, by asking how you should spend the next hour. If both exams are the next day, you will spend the night reviewing your notes for both courses. At 6:00 P.M., you decide that it's a good idea to spend at least an hour on each course. At 8:00 P.M., you decide you need to spend another hour on each course. At 10:00 P.M., you are getting tired and figure you have one more hour to study before bed. Do you study chemistry or economics? If you are pre-med, it's likely to be chemistry; if you are a business major, it's likely to be economics.

Note how you've made the decision to allocate your time: at each point the question is whether or not to spend *one more hour* on either course. In deciding whether to spend that hour studying chemistry, you weigh the costs (an hour forgone of studying economics or an hour forgone of sleeping) versus the benefits (a likely increase in your chemistry grade). As long as the benefit of studying chemistry for one more hour outweighs the cost, you should choose to study for that additional hour.

Decisions of this type—whether to do a bit more or a bit less of an activity, like what to do with your next hour, your next dollar, and so on—are **marginal decisions.** This brings us to our third principle of individual choice:

> *"How much" decisions require making trade-offs at the margin: comparing the costs and benefits of doing a little bit more of an activity versus doing a little bit less.*

The study of such decisions is known as **marginal analysis.** Many of the questions that we face in real life involve marginal analysis: How many minutes should I exercise? How many hours should I work? What is an acceptable rate of negative side effects from a new medicine? Marginal analysis plays a central role in economics because it is the key to deciding "how much" of an activity to do.

Principle #4: People Respond to Incentives, Exploiting Opportunities to Make Themselves Better Off

While listening to the news one day, the authors heard a great tip about cheap parking in Manhattan. At the time, garages in the Wall Street area charged as much as $30 per day. But according to this news report, some people had found a better way: instead of parking in a garage, they had their oil changed at the Manhattan Jiffy Lube for $19.95—and they keep your car all day!

It's a great story, but unfortunately it turned out not to be true—in fact, there is no Jiffy Lube in Manhattan. But if there were, you can be sure there would be a lot of oil changes there. Why? Because when people are offered opportunities to make themselves better off, they take them—and if they could find a way to park their car all day for $19.95 rather than $30, they would.

In this example economists say that people are responding to an **incentive**—an opportunity to make themselves better off, which leads to our fourth principle of individual choice:

> *People respond to incentives, exploiting opportunities to make themselves better off.*

When you try to predict how individuals will behave in an economic situation, it is a very good bet that they will respond to incentives—that is, exploit opportunities to make themselves better off. Furthermore, individuals will *continue* to exploit these opportunities until they have been fully exhausted. If there really were a Manhattan Jiffy Lube and an oil change really were a cheap way to park your car, we can safely predict that before long the waiting list for oil changes would be weeks, if not months.

In fact, the principle that people will exploit opportunities to make themselves better off is the basis of *all* predictions by economists about individual behavior.

In fact, economists tend to be skeptical of any attempt to change behavior that *doesn't* change incentives. For example, a plan aimed at reducing traffic in Manhattan that doesn't offer Manhattan-bound drivers an incentive, like a financial reward, for not driving, or that isn't accompanied by a penalty for driving, is unlikely to succeed. Likewise, a plan that calls on manufacturers to reduce pollution voluntarily probably won't be effective. In contrast, a plan that gives them a financial reward to reduce pollution is a lot more likely to succeed because it has changed their incentives.

So are we ready to do economics? Not yet—because most of the interesting things that happen in the economy are the result not merely of individual choices but of the way in which individual choices interact.

An **incentive** is anything that offers rewards to people to change their behavior.

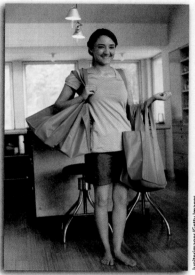

An incentive that cuts waste: Shoppers switch to reusable shopping bags when charged a fee for disposable bags at checkout.

ECONOMICS >> *in Action*
The Cost of Marriage: China's One-Child Policy Creates Millions of Lonely Bachelors

China is the most populous country on Earth, with over 1,420,000,000 people, as of 2019. That's over *one billion four hundred twenty million* people. And trends in Chinese demographics have shifted the cost of marriage over time—specifically, the cost of finding a bride for Chinese bachelors.

In the 1970s, China was very poor and had an already large and growing population. Concerned that it would be unable to adequately provide care for so many people, the Chinese government introduced a one-child policy that restricted most couples to only one child and imposed penalties on those who defied the mandate. By 2016, the average number of children per Chinese woman had fallen to 1.6, from more than 5 before the policy was introduced in 1978.

But the one-child policy has led to an unfortunate unintended consequence on the balance between the sexes in the population. Until recently China was overwhelmingly rural. Because of the physical demands of farming, sons were strongly preferred over daughters. In addition, tradition dictated that sons, not daughters, took care of elderly parents. The effect of the one-child policy was to greatly increase the perceived cost to a Chinese family of a female child. As a result, while some female infants were given up for adoption abroad, many simply "disappeared" during the first year of life, victims of neglect and mistreatment as Chinese families were determined that

The cost of finding a bride is quite high for millions of men in China.

their only child be a son. The Nobel-prize winning economist Amartya Sen calculated that there were milions of "missing women" in Asia due to the perceived higher cost of female children, with estimates running from 45 million to 100 million missing women.

The number of boys in China has outpaced the number of girls for 20 years. Today, there are nearly 34 million *excess* males in the population compared to females. That's the equivalent of the entire population of California—men who will never find wives from among their fellow Chinese.

As of 2018, within the age group of 15- to 29-year-olds, there are 112 men for every 100 women, with projections that there will be as many as 190 young men per 100 young women by 2050. So, although the Chinese government officially ended the one-child policy in 2015, the consequences will endure for decades.

Not surprisingly, some Chinese bachelors are eager to meet eligible women from abroad—particularly from nearby countries such as Vietnam, Laos, and Cambodia that don't have a problem with gender imbalance. And enterprising eligible women from those countries are coming to China to find husbands. Marriage brokers have sprung up in these countries to address the situation in China. For example, one Chinese bachelor, Liu Hua, found happiness with Lili, a Cambodian woman who came to China to find a husband. Before meeting Lili, Liu lived in a village with 60 bachelors and only 2 single women. He ended up paying deposits ranging from $5,000 to $40,000 to three families in nearby villages for the opportunity to date their daughters (not all of which was refunded when the matches didn't work out). He eventually paid a $15,000 broker's fee to marry Lili. Happily married, they now have two children—a boy *and* a girl.

>> Quick Review

• All economic activities involve **individual choice.**

• People must make choices because **resources** are **scarce.**

• The real cost of something is its **opportunity cost**—what you must give up to get it. All costs are opportunity costs. Monetary costs are sometimes a good indicator of opportunity costs, but not always.

• Many choices involve not *whether* to do something but *how much* of it to do. "How much" choices call for making a **trade-off** at the margin. The study of **marginal decisions** is known as **marginal analysis.**

• Because people exploit opportunities to make themselves better off, **incentives** can change people's behavior.

>> Check Your Understanding 1-1
Solutions appear at back of book.

1. Explain how each of the following illustrates one of the four principles of individual choice.
   a. You are on your third trip to a restaurant's all-you-can-eat dessert buffet and are feeling very full. Although it would cost you no additional money, you forgo a slice of coconut cream pie but have a slice of chocolate cake.
   b. Even if there were more resources in the world, there would still be scarcity.
   c. Different teaching assistants teach several Economics 101 tutorials. Those taught by the teaching assistants with the best reputations fill up quickly, with spaces left unfilled in the ones taught by assistants with poor reputations.
   d. To decide how many hours per week to exercise, you compare the health benefits of one more hour of exercise to the effect on your grades of one less hour spent studying.

2. You make $45,000 per year at your current job with Whiz Kids Consultants. You are considering a job offer from Brainiacs, Inc., that will pay you $50,000 per year. Which of the following are elements of the opportunity cost of accepting the new job at Brainiacs, Inc.?
   a. The increased time spent commuting to your new job
   b. The $45,000 salary from your old job
   c. The more spacious office at your new job

‖ Interaction: How Economies Work

An economy is a system for coordinating the productive activities of many people. In a market economy like we live in, coordination takes place without any coordinator: each individual makes his or her own choices.

Yet those choices are by no means independent of one another: each individual's opportunities, and hence choices, depend to a large extent on the choices made by other people. So to understand how a market economy behaves, we have to examine this **interaction** in which my choices affect your choices, and vice versa.

When studying economic interaction, we quickly learn that the end result of individual choices may be quite different from what any one individual intends. Consider the case of American farmers, who, over the past century have adopted new farming techniques and crop strains that have reduced their costs and increased their yields. The end result of each farmer trying to increase his or her own income has actually been to drive many farmers out of business. Because American farmers have been so successful at producing larger yields, agricultural prices have steadily fallen, reducing the incomes of many farmers, and as a result fewer people find farming worth doing. That is, an individual farmer who plants a better variety of corn is better off, but when many farmers plant a better variety of corn, the result may be to make farmers as a group worse off.

There are four principles underlying the economics of interaction. These principles are summarized in Table 1-2 and we will now examine each one.

TABLE 1-2 **Principles of Interaction of Individual Choices**
5. There are gains from trade.
6. Markets move toward equilibrium.
7. Resources should be used efficiently to achieve society's goals.
8. Markets usually lead to efficiency, but when they don't, government intervention can improve society's welfare.

Principle #5: There Are Gains from Trade

Why do the choices I make interact with the choices you make? A family could try to take care of all its own needs—growing its own food, sewing its own clothing, providing itself with entertainment. But trying to live that way would be very hard.

The key to a much better standard of living for everyone is **trade,** in which people divide tasks among themselves and each person provides a good or service that other people want in return for different goods and services that he or she wants.

The reason we have an economy, not many self-sufficient individuals, is that there are **gains from trade:** by dividing tasks and trading, two people (or 6 billion people) can each get more of what they want than they could get by being self-sufficient. This leads us to our fifth principle:

"I hunt and she gathers—otherwise, we couldn't make ends meet."

There are gains from trade.

Gains from trade arise from this division of tasks, which economists call **specialization**—a situation in which different people each engage in a different task, specializing in those tasks that they are good at performing. The advantages of specialization, and the resulting gains from trade, were the starting point for Adam Smith's 1776 book *The Wealth of Nations*, which many regard as the beginning of economics as a discipline.

Smith's book begins with a description of an eighteenth-century pin factory where, rather than each of the 10 workers making a pin from start to finish, each worker specialized in one of the many steps in pin-making:

> One man draws out the wire, another straights it, a third cuts it, a fourth points it, a fifth grinds it at the top for receiving the head; to make the head requires two or three distinct operations; to put it on, is a particular business, to whiten the pins is another; it is even a trade by itself to put them into the paper; and the important business of making a pin is, in this manner, divided into about eighteen distinct operations. . . . Those ten persons, therefore, could make among them upwards of forty-eight thousand

Interaction of choices—my choices affect your choices, and vice versa—is a feature of most economic situations. The results of this interaction are often quite different from what the individuals intend.

In a market economy, individuals engage in **trade:** they provide goods and services to others and receive goods and services in return.

There are **gains from trade:** people can get more of what they want through trade than they could if they tried to be self-sufficient.

An increase in output is due to **specialization:** each person specializes in the task that they are good at performing.

pins in a day. But if they had all wrought separately and independently, and without any of them having been educated to this particular business, they certainly could not each of them have made twenty, perhaps not one pin a day. . . .

The same principle applies when we look at how people divide tasks among themselves and trade in an economy. *The economy, as a whole, can produce more when each person specializes in a task and trades with others.*

The benefits of specialization are the reason a person typically chooses only one career. It takes many years of study and experience to become a physician or a commercial pilot. Many physicians might well have had the potential to become excellent pilots, and vice versa. But it is very unlikely that anyone who decided to pursue both careers would be as good at both as someone who decided at the beginning to specialize in a single field. So it is to everyone's advantage that individuals specialize in their careers.

Markets allow a physician and a pilot to specialize in their own fields. Because markets for commercial flights and for medical care exist, a physician is assured that she can find a flight and a pilot is assured that he can find a physician. As long as individuals know that they can find the goods and services they want in the market, they are willing to forgo self-sufficiency and to specialize. But what assures people that markets will deliver what they want? The answer to that question leads us to our next principle of how individual choices interact.

Principle #6: Markets Move Toward Equilibrium

It's a busy afternoon at the supermarket; there are long lines at the checkout counters. Then one of the previously closed cash registers opens. What happens right away, of course, is a rush to that register. After a couple of minutes, however, things will have settled down. Shoppers will have rearranged themselves so that the line at the newly opened register is about the same length as the lines at all the other registers.

How do we know this? We know from our fourth principle that people will exploit opportunities to make themselves better off. People will rush to the newly opened register to save time standing in line. The rushing around will stop when shoppers can no longer improve their position by switching lines — that is, when the opportunities to make themselves better off have all been exploited.

A story about supermarket checkout lines may seem to have little to do with how individual choices interact, but in fact it illustrates an important principle. A situation in which individuals cannot make themselves better off by doing something different — the situation in which all the checkout lines are the same length — is what economists call an **equilibrium.** An economic situation is in equilibrium when no individual would be better off doing something different.

Recall the story about the mythical Jiffy Lube, where it was supposedly cheaper to leave your car for an oil change than to pay for parking. If the opportunity had really existed and people were still paying $30 to park in garages, the situation would *not* have been an equilibrium. And that should have been a giveaway that the story couldn't be true. In reality, people would have seized an opportunity to park cheaply, just as they seize opportunities to save time at the checkout line. And in so doing they would have eliminated the opportunity! Either it would have become very hard to get an appointment for an oil change or the price of a lube job would have increased to the point that it was no longer an attractive option (unless you really needed an oil change). This brings us to our sixth principle:

> *Because people respond to incentives, markets move toward equilibrium.*

As we will see, markets usually reach equilibrium through changes in prices, which rise or fall until no opportunities for individuals to make themselves better off remain.

Witness equilibrium in action on the checkout line.

An economic situation is in **equilibrium** when no individual would be better off doing something different.

The concept of equilibrium is extremely helpful in understanding economic interactions because it provides a way to cut through the sometimes complex details of those interactions. To understand what happens when a new line opens at a supermarket, you don't need to worry about exactly how shoppers rearrange themselves, which register just opened, and so on. What you need to know is that any time there is a change, the situation will move to an equilibrium.

The fact that markets move toward equilibrium is why we can depend on them to work in a predictable way. In fact, we can trust markets to supply us with the essentials of life. For example, people who live in cities can be sure that the supermarket shelves will always be fully stocked. Why? Because if some merchants who distribute food *didn't* make deliveries, a big profit opportunity would be created for any merchant who did—and there would be a rush to supply food, just like the rush to a newly opened cash register.

So the market ensures that food will always be available for city dwellers. And, returning to our fifth principle, this allows city dwellers to be city dwellers—to specialize in doing city jobs rather than living on farms and growing their own food.

A market economy, as we have seen, allows people to achieve gains from trade. But how do we know how well such an economy is doing? The next principle gives us a standard to use in evaluating an economy's performance.

Principle #7: Resources Should Be Used Efficiently to Achieve Society's Goals

You are attending a lecture in a classroom that is too small for the number of students—many of your fellow classmates are standing or sitting on the floor—despite the fact that large, empty classrooms are available nearby. You would be correct to say that this is no way to run a college. Economists would call this an *inefficient* use of resources. But if an inefficient use of resources is undesirable, just what does it mean to use resources *efficiently?*

You might imagine that the efficient use of resources has something to do with money, maybe that it is measured in dollars-and-cents terms. But in economics, as in life, money is only a means to other ends. The measure that economists really care about is not money but people's happiness or welfare. Economists say that *an economy's resources are used efficiently when they are used in a way that has fully exploited all opportunities to make everyone better off.* Put another way: an economy is **efficient** if it takes all opportunities to make some people better off without making other people worse off.

In our classroom example, there clearly was a way to make everyone better off—move the lecture to a larger room. Students attending the lecture would be made better off without hurting anyone else at the college. This result would be an efficient use of the college's resources. Assigning the course to the smaller classroom was an inefficient use of those resources.

When an economy is efficient, it is producing the maximum gains from trade possible given the resources available. Why? Because there is no way to rearrange how resources are used so that everyone can be made better off. When an economy is efficient, one person can be made better off by rearranging how resources are used *only* by making someone else worse off.

In our example, if all larger classrooms were already occupied, the college would actually have been run efficiently: to make your class better off by moving it to a larger classroom would displace other students already in a larger room. Those students would be made worse off by a move.

We can now state our seventh principle:

> ***Resources should be used as efficiently as possible to achieve society's goals.***

An economy is **efficient** if it takes all opportunities to make some people better off without making other people worse off.

Sometimes equity trumps efficiency.

Should policy makers always strive to achieve economic efficiency? Well, not quite, because efficiency is only a means to achieving society's goals. Sometimes efficiency may conflict with a goal that society has deemed worthwhile to achieve. For example, in most societies, people also care about issues of fairness, or **equity.** And there is typically a trade-off between equity and efficiency: policies that promote equity often come at a cost of decreased efficiency in the economy, and vice versa.

To see this, consider the case of disabled-designated parking spaces in public parking lots. Many people have difficulty walking due to age or disability, so it seems only fair to assign closer parking spaces specifically for their use. You may have noticed, however, that a certain amount of inefficiency is involved. To ensure that a parking space is always available should a disabled person want one, there are typically more such spaces available than there are disabled people who want one. As a result, desirable parking spaces are unused. (And the temptation for nondisabled people to use them is so great that drivers must be dissuaded by fear of getting a ticket.)

So, short of hiring parking valets to allocate spaces, there is a conflict between *equity*, making life "fairer" for disabled people, and *efficiency*, making sure that all opportunities to make people better off have been fully exploited by never letting close-in parking spaces go unused.

Exactly how far policy makers should go in promoting equity over efficiency is a difficult question that goes to the heart of the political process. As such, it is not a question that economists can answer. What is important for economists, however, is always to seek to use the economy's resources as efficiently as possible in the pursuit of society's goals, whatever those goals may be.

Principle #8: Markets Usually Lead to Efficiency, But When They Don't, Government Intervention Can Improve Society's Welfare

There is no branch of the U.S. government entrusted with ensuring the general economic efficiency of our market economy—we don't have agents tasked with checking that brain surgeons aren't plowing fields or that Minnesota farmers aren't trying to grow oranges. The government doesn't need to enforce the efficient use of resources, because in most cases the invisible hand does the job. As explained in the Introduction, the *invisible hand* refers to how a market economy harnesses the power of self-interest for the good of society.

The incentives built into a market economy ensure that resources are usually put to good use and that opportunities to make people better off are not wasted. If a college were known for its habit of crowding students into small classrooms while large classrooms went unused, its enrollment would soon drop, putting the jobs of its administrators at risk. The "market" for college students would respond in a way that induces administrators to run the college efficiently.

A detailed explanation of why markets are usually very good at making sure that resources are used efficiently will have to wait until we have studied how markets actually work. But the most basic reason is that in a market economy, in which individuals are free to choose what to consume and what to produce, people normally take opportunities for mutual gain—that is, gains from trade.

If people encounter an opportunity to make themselves better off, they will take advantage of it. And that is exactly what defines efficiency: all the opportunities to make some people better off without making other people worse off have been exploited. We have now arrived at the first half of our eighth principle:

> *Because people exploit gains from trade, markets usually lead to efficiency.*

However, there are exceptions to this principle that markets are generally efficient. In cases of *market failure*, the individual pursuit of self-interest found in markets makes society worse off—that is, the market outcome is inefficient.

Equity means that everyone gets his or her fair share. Since people can disagree about what's "fair," equity isn't as well defined a concept as efficiency.

Construction Photography/Corbis

Consider the nature of the market failure caused by traffic congestion—commuters driving to work have no incentive to take into account the cost that their actions inflict on other drivers in the form of increased traffic congestion.

Possible remedies to this situation include charging tolls, subsidizing the cost of public transportation, and taxing gasoline sales to individual drivers. These remedies would change the incentives of would-be drivers, motivating them to drive less. But they also share another feature: each relies on government intervention in the market, which leads to the second half of this principle:

> **When markets don't achieve efficiency, government can intervene to improve society's welfare.**

An appropriately designed government policy can sometimes move society closer to an efficient outcome by changing how society's resources are used. And, as we will see next, short of instances of market failure, the general rule is that markets are a remarkably good way of organizing an economy.

ECONOMICS >> *in Action*
Wait, Then Hurry Up, and Wait Again

In a densely populated city like New York, very few people own cars. New Yorkers have typically relied on subways and buses, local taxis, or walking to get where they needed to go. Yet each of these forms of transportation has drawbacks: the subway is often plagued with delays, buses can be slow, taxis are expensive and hard to find during peak travel times, and walking long distances takes time and isn't optimal in bad weather.

Unsurprisingly, the market for transportation changed dramatically with the arrival of ride-hailing services like Uber and Lyft, which have become wildly popular in cities like New York. Hopping into an Uber has been seen as a way to get where you need to go more quickly. In 2018 there were more than 65,000 Uber-affiliated vehicles in New York City, providing an average of 400,000 rides per day. Correspondingly, the number of New Yorkers taking public transportation has declined.

Yet the popularity of ride-hailing services has created one significant drawback. With so many more vehicles on the street, traffic congestion has increased dramatically. A study released in 2018 found that in nine large densely populated metropolitan areas (Boston, Chicago, Los Angeles, Miami, New York, Philadelphia, San Francisco, Seattle, and Washington, DC), there was an overall increase of 160% in driving on city streets. New York City transportation officials describe the city as "crippled" by traffic congestion, and they point to a 40% reduction in travel speeds in Manhattan.

It's an outcome that traffic planners find predictable. Thanks to the new ride-hailing apps that induce more driving and have led to an influx of new cars on city streets, commuters looking for a quick trip in a cab are finding their travel time has increased, making the bus, subway, or walking appealing travel options once again. With commuting times more or less back where they started before ride-hailing services appeared, a new equilibrium has been reached in which travel times across all modes of available transport are unchanged. This predictable outcome resembles what traffic

The fundamental law of traffic congestion is an example of equilibrium in action.

planners call the *fundamental law of traffic congestion:* if a city builds more roads, this induces more driving, and this increase in traffic continues until a new equilibrium is reached, with commuting times more or less back where they started. Whether it's a new ride-hailing app or newly built roads that induces more driving, the ultimate result is that a new equilibrium is reached in which travel times across all modes of transportation are unchanged.

For those who hoped that ride-hailing services would make commuting faster and easier, this result is discouraging. It is, however, a good illustration of the importance of thinking about equilibrium.

>> **Check Your Understanding 1-2**

Solutions appear at back of book.

1. Explain how each of the following illustrates one of the four principles of interaction.
   a. At a college tutoring co-op, students can arrange to provide tutoring in subjects they are good in (like economics) in return for receiving tutoring in subjects they struggle with (like philosophy).
   b. The local municipality imposes a law that requires bars and nightclubs near residential areas to keep their noise levels below a certain threshold.
   c. To provide better care for low-income patients, the local municipality has decided to close some underutilized neighborhood clinics and shift funds to the main hospital.
   d. On Amazon, books of a given title with approximately the same level of wear and tear sell for about the same price.
2. Which of the following describes an equilibrium situation? Which does not? Explain your answer.
   a. The restaurants across the street from the university dining hall serve better-tasting and cheaper meals than those served at the university dining hall. The vast majority of students continue to eat at the dining hall.
   b. You currently take the subway to work. Although taking the bus is cheaper, the ride takes longer. So you are willing to pay the higher subway fare in order to save time.

‖ Economy-Wide Interactions

The economy as a whole—the macroeconomy—has its ups and downs. For example, in 2007 the U.S. economy entered a severe recession in which millions of people lost their jobs, while those who remained employed saw their wages stagnate. It took seven years—until May 2014—for the number of Americans employed to return to its pre-recession level, but wages didn't recover until 2016.

Over time, the behavior of the macroeconomy is a lot like a drive through a mountain range. The trip isn't one continuous upward climb to a destination at high altitude. Instead, you will drive over hills and valleys, with short-term ups and downs during your journey, as you slowly, but inevitably, ascend to your destination.

In the short run, the overall economy experiences ups and downs: good economic times (recoveries) alternate with bad economic times (recessions), with a cycle lasting an average of seven to 10 years. However, over the long run, a period of at least 10 years, the economy grows larger and larger. A graph of the total amount of goods and services the economy produces over time would show a line that looks a lot like our car ride: lots of squiggles up and down, but, over time, the line reaches upward.

To understand why the macroeconomy cycles between recessions and recoveries, but also achieves economic growth over time, we need to look at economy-wide interactions. And understanding the big picture of the economy requires three more economic principles, which are summarized in Table 1-3.

TABLE 1-3 Principles of Economy-Wide Interactions

9. One person's spending is another person's income.

10. Overall spending sometimes gets out of line with the economy's productive capacity; when it does, government policy can change spending.

11. Increases in the economy's potential lead to economic growth over time.

Principle #9: One Person's Spending Is Another Person's Income

Between 2005 and 2011, including a deep recession, U.S. home construction plunged more than 60% because builders found it increasingly hard to make sales. At first the damage was limited to the construction industry. But over time the slump spread throughout the economy, with consumer spending falling across the board.

But why should a fall in home construction mean empty stores in the shopping malls? After all, malls are where families, not builders, do their shopping.

The answer is that lower spending on construction led to lower incomes throughout the economy. People who had been employed either directly in construction, producing goods and services builders need (like roofing shingles), or in producing goods and services new homeowners need (like new furniture), either lost their jobs or were forced to take pay cuts. And as incomes fell, so did spending by consumers. This example illustrates our ninth principle:

> ***One person's spending is another person's income.***

In a market economy, people make a living selling things—including their labor—to other people. If some group in the economy decides, for whatever reason, to spend more, the incomes of other groups will rise. If some group decides to spend less, the incomes of other groups will fall.

And a chain reaction of changes in spending behavior tends to have repercussions that spread economy-wide. For example, a fall in consumer spending at shopping malls leads to reduced family incomes; families respond by reducing their own spending, which leads to another round of income cuts; and so on. These repercussions play an important role in our understanding of recessions and recoveries.

Principle #10: Overall Spending Sometimes Gets Out of Line with the Economy's Productive Capacity; When It Does, Government Policy Can Change Spending

The coronavirus pandemic of 2020 harkened back to a period in the 1930s, known as the Great Depression. Then, as now, a collapse in spending by consumers and businesses led to a plunge in overall spending. In both periods, the plunge in spending led to very high unemployment.

What economists learned from the Great Depression is that overall spending—the amount of goods and services that consumers and businesses want to buy—sometimes doesn't match the amount of goods and services the economy is capable of producing. In the 1930s, as in 2020, spending fell far short of what was needed to keep American workers employed, and the result was a severe economic slump.

It's also possible for overall spending to be too high. In that case, the economy experiences *inflation*, a rise in prices throughout the economy. This rise in prices occurs when the amount that people want to buy outstrips the supply, leading producers to raise their prices and still find willing buyers.

When the economy experiences either shortfalls in spending or excesses in spending, government policies can be used to address the imbalances, which leads to our tenth principle:

> ***Overall spending sometimes gets out of line with the economy's productive capacity; when it does, government policy can change spending.***

The U.S. government spends a lot, on everything from military equipment to health care. Moreover, it can choose to spend more or less, depending upon the state of the economy. Likewise, the government can vary how much it collects in

With advances in technology and greater resources, American farmers today produce far more than they did 100 years ago.

taxes, which in turn affects how much income consumers and businesses have to spend. And the government's control of the quantity of money in circulation gives it another powerful tool with which to affect total spending. Government spending, taxes, and control of money are the tools of *macroeconomic policy*.

Modern governments deploy macroeconomic policy tools in an effort to balance overall spending in the economy, trying to steer it between the perils of recession and inflation. These efforts aren't always successful—recessions still happen, as do periods of inflation. But it's widely believed that aggressive efforts to sustain spending in 2008 and 2009 helped prevent the financial crisis of 2008 from turning into a full-blown depression. And in 2020, Congress passed a $4 trillion relief package for American workers and businesses to cushion the blow from the coronavirus pandemic.

Principle #11: Increases in the Economy's Potential Lead to Economic Growth Over Time

Today's economy is different from the economy of 20 years ago, and drastically different from the economy of a century ago. These changes are due to *economic growth*, the increase in living standards over time. Economic growth has made the United States and other countries far richer over time. Like a car climbing up a mountain range, despite the valleys and hills along the way, the overall path of the economy has been upward in the long run, as Figure 1-1 illustrates.

What accounts for this growth? It is due to the emergence of new technologies and increases in the resources available for production—resources like land, labor, and machinery. As a result, the economy's *potential*, the total amount of goods and services it can produce, rises and leads to higher living standards. For example, in 1820, 80% of American workers were engaged in farming; now, that figure is 2%. Yet there is a far greater quantity and variety of food available now than 200 years ago. The increased mechanization and technological sophistication of agriculture—humongous tractors and satellite imaging—are changes to

---

FIGURE 1-1 Growth in the U.S. Economy Over Time

The overall path of the U.S. economy for the last 200 years, from 1800 to 2000, has been upward, with the inevitable short-term ups and downs along the way.

Data from: Maddison Project Database, version 2018. Jutta Bolt, Robert Inklaar, Herman de Jong, and Jan Luiten van Zanden (2018).

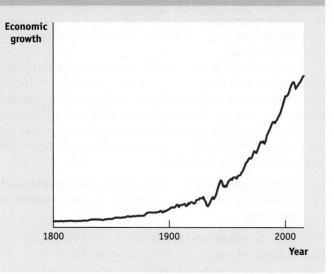

the resources available for production. As a result, the economy's potential has risen: American farmers can now produce vastly more than before and American consumers can now consume vastly more than before.

We have now arrived at our eleventh and final principle:

Increases in the economy's potential lead to economic growth over time.

While economic growth has benefitted a vast number of people, the increase in living standards are usually unequally distributed among a country's residents in the short term. In fact, at any given time, an increase in the economy's potential typically creates *winners and losers.*

For example, over the past 20 years, technological advancements have revolutionized the way we produce energy in the United States. New drilling techniques have made natural gas abundant, and alternative energy sources such as solar and wind power have emerged. These new sources of energy, which pollute less than older sources such as coal, benefit both the economy and the environment—they are the winners in our example. But at the same time, the reduced demand for coal has hurt communities where mining has been a primary source of employment, creating losers.

Yet, in a dynamic market economy, losers won't always stay losers. Remember Principle #4: People usually respond to incentives. It implies that unemployed coal miners will eventually migrate to other sectors of the economy where they can find work. They may, for example, become solar panel installers. However, because it takes time for workers to make such a transition (and it may be impossible for older workers), we can also see why Principle #9 applies: Government intervention can improve society's welfare. Government assistance programs can provide a cushion for dislocated workers.

In the end, just as increases in an economy's potential lead to economic growth over time, economic growth inevitably leads to fundamental economic and social change. With these changes come questions (and debates) that are as relevant today as they were back in the eighteenth century when Adam Smith penned *The Wealth of Nations*—questions about equity, the role of government, and appropriate macroeconomic policy remedies.

>> Check Your Understanding 1-3
Solutions appear at back of book.

1. Explain how each of the following illustrates one of the three principles of economy-wide interactions.
   a. The price of solar panels has fallen by nearly 99% over the past 40 years. Prices are projected to continue falling over the next 30 years.
   b. The financial crisis of 2008 caused unemployment to soar. In response, the White House urged Congress to pass a package of temporary spending increases and tax cuts early in 2009.
   c. With oil prices plummeting, Canadian and U.S. oil companies have been forced to shut down their productive wells. In cities throughout North Dakota, Wyoming, Texas, and Alaska, restaurants and other consumer businesses are failing.

>> Quick Review
- In a market economy, one person's spending is another person's income. As a result, changes in spending behavior have repercussions that spread through the economy.
- Overall spending sometimes gets out of line with the economy's capacity to produce goods and services. When spending is too low, the result is a recession. When spending is too high, it causes inflation.
- When spending is out of line, governments can use macroeconomic policy tools to affect the overall level of spending in an effort to steer the economy between recession and inflation.
- Despite the economy's ups and downs, increases in the economy's potential lead to economic growth in the long term, while creating winners and losers in the short term.

How Priceline Revolutionized the Travel Industry

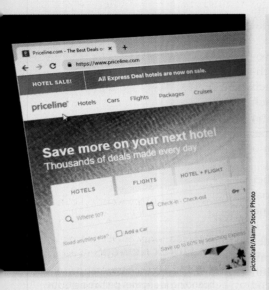

pictoKraft/Alamy Stock Photo

If you bought and held shares of the Priceline Group, the online provider of travel-related reservations and search services, from 2014 to 2019, you would have been one happy camper. During that time, the share price appreciated by 50%, beating the performance of the S&P 500, a widely used overall measure of stock prices, resulting in a company valuation of nearly $80 billion for the company's stock.

Even more remarkable is the fact that in 2002, the company was in such deep trouble that many doubted it would survive. From 1999 to 2002, Priceline lost 95% of its value, going from a company valuation of $9 billion to a paltry $425 million. What went so terribly wrong and then so incredibly right at Priceline?

When the company (originally known as Priceline.com) was formed in 1998, investors were immediately impressed by how it used the internet to revolutionize the travel industry. Before the internet, travelers relied on travel agents and airline staff to book flights and hotels. Information was fragmented and it was difficult to compare prices when shopping for tickets. Because prices were high, far fewer people traveled long distances, for example for the holidays. Priceline's success lay in its ability to spot exploitable opportunities for itself and its customers. The company understood that when a plane departs with empty seats or a hotel has empty beds, there is a cost—the revenue that would have been earned if the seat or bed were filled. Priceline's innovation was to bring airlines and hotels with unsold capacity together with travelers.

It works this way: customers specify the price they are willing to pay for a given trip or hotel, and then Priceline presents them with a list of options from airlines or hotels that are willing to accept that price. Typically, price declines as the trip date nears. Although some travelers like the security of booking their trips well in advance and are willing to pay for that, others are quite happy to wait until the last minute, and risk not getting their first choice flight or hotel in order to benefit from a lower price.

Priceline, then, found a way to make everyone better off—including itself, since it charged a small fee for each trade it facilitated.

Yet, in 2002 the company was at risk of going under. After the terrorist attacks of September 11, 2001, many Americans simply stopped flying. As the economy went into a deep slump, airplanes sat empty on the tarmac and the airlines lost billions of dollars. Several major airlines spiraled toward bankruptcy, and Priceline was losing several million dollars a year.

In order to avert a meltdown of the airline industry, Congress passed a $15 billion aid package that was critical in stabilizing the industry. It was the seed of Priceline's turnaround. The company managed to survive and eventually thrive.

Quick on its feet when it saw its market challenged by newcomers, Expedia and Orbitz, it responded aggressively by moving more of its business toward hotel bookings and into Europe, where the online travel industry was still quite small. Its network was particularly valuable in the European hotel market, composed of many more small hotels compared to the U.S. market, which is dominated by nationwide chains. The efforts paid off, and by 2003 Priceline was turning a profit. Over the years Priceline expanded by acquiring the travel websites Booking.com, KAYAK, agoda.com, rentalcars.com, and OpenTable, transforming itself into the Priceline Group, with revenue of $14.5 billion in 2018.

QUESTION FOR THOUGHT

1. Explain how each of the 11 principles of economics is illustrated in this case.

SUMMARY

1. All economic analysis is based on a set of basic principles that apply to three levels of economic activity. First, we study how individuals make choices; second, we study how these choices interact; and third, we study how the economy functions overall.

2. Everyone has to make choices about what to do and what *not* to do. **Individual choice** is the basis of economics—if it doesn't involve choice, it isn't economics.

3. The reason choices must be made is that **resources**—anything that can be used to produce something else—are **scarce.** Individuals are limited in their choices by money and time; economies are limited by their supplies of human and natural resources.

4. Because you must choose among limited alternatives, the true cost of anything is what you must give up to get it—all costs are **opportunity costs.**

5. Many economic decisions involve questions not of "whether" but of "how much"—how much to spend on some good, how much to produce, and so on. Such decisions must be made by performing a **trade-off** *at the margin*—by comparing the costs and benefits of doing a bit more or a bit less. Decisions of this type are called **marginal decisions,** and the study of them, **marginal analysis,** plays a central role in economics.

6. The study of how people *should* make decisions is also a good way to understand actual behavior. Individuals usually respond to **incentives**—exploiting opportunities to make themselves better off.

7. The next level of economic analysis is the study of **interaction**—how my choices depend on your choices, and vice versa. When individuals interact, the end result may be different from what anyone intends.

8. Individuals interact because there are **gains from trade:** by engaging in the **trade** of goods and services with one another, the members of an economy can all be made better off. **Specialization**—each person specializes in the task they are good at—is the source of gains from trade.

9. Because individuals usually respond to incentives, markets normally move toward **equilibrium**—a situation in which no individual can make himself or herself better off by taking a different action.

10. An economy is **efficient** if all opportunities to make some people better off without making other people worse off are taken. Resources should be used as efficiently as possible to achieve society's goals. But efficiency is not the sole way to evaluate an economy: **equity,** or fairness, is also desirable, and there is often a trade-off between equity and efficiency.

11. Markets usually lead to efficiency, with some well-defined exceptions. But when markets fail and do not achieve efficiency, government intervention can improve society's welfare.

12. Because people in a market economy earn income by selling things, including their own labor, one person's spending is another person's income. As a result, changes in spending behavior can spread throughout the economy.

13. Overall spending in the economy can get out of line with the economy's productive capacity. Spending below the economy's productive capacity leads to a recession; spending in excess of the economy's productive capacity leads to inflation. When overall spending gets out of line, governments can use macroeconomic policy tools to steer the economy between recession and inflation.

14. Increases in the economy's potential lead to economic growth over time. Although economic growth leads to higher living standards for everyone over time, in the short run, increases in the economy's potential lead to both winners and losers.

KEY TERMS

Individual choice, p. 8
Resource, p. 8
Scarce, p. 8
Opportunity cost, p. 9
Trade-off, p. 10

Marginal decisions, p. 10
Marginal analysis, p. 10
Incentive, p. 11
Interaction, p. 13
Trade, p. 13

Gains from trade, p. 13
Specialization, p. 13
Equilibrium, p. 14
Efficient, p. 15
Equity, p. 16

PROBLEMS

1. In each of the following situations, identify which of the 11 principles is at work.

   a. You choose to purchase your textbooks online rather than pay a higher price for the same books through your college bookstore.

   b. On your spring break trip, your budget is limited to $35 a day.

   c. To help reduce traffic congestion, many states have adopted congestion pricing. Under this program, drivers are charged more to use express lanes during peak rush hour.

   d. Congress passes an infrastructure bill to help construction workers who were left jobless after the last recession.

   e. You buy a used textbook from your roommate. Your roommate uses the money to buy songs from iTunes.

   f. You decide how many cups of coffee to have when studying the night before an exam by considering how much more work you can do by having another cup versus how jittery it will make you feel.

   g. There is limited lab space available to do the project required in Chemistry 101. The lab supervisor assigns lab time to each student based on when that student is able to come.

   h. You realize that you can graduate a semester early by forgoing a semester of study abroad.

   i. At the student center, there is a bulletin board on which people advertise used items for sale, such as bicycles. Once you have adjusted for differences in quality, all the bikes sell for about the same price.

   j. You are better at performing lab experiments, and your lab partner is better at writing lab reports. So the two of you agree that you will do all the experiments and she will write up all the reports.

   k. Amazon announces a program to develop a drone delivery system in place of traditional ground shipping.

2. Describe some of the opportunity costs when you decide to do the following:

   a. Attend college instead of taking a job

   b. Watch a movie instead of studying for an exam

   c. Ride the bus instead of driving your car

3. Kim needs to buy a textbook for the next economics class. The price at the college bookstore is $65. One website offers it for $55, and another site, for $57. All prices include sales tax. The accompanying table indicates the typical shipping and handling charges for the textbook ordered online.

Shipping method	Delivery time	Charge
Standard shipping	3–7 days	$3.99
Second-day air	2 business days	8.98
Next-day air	1 business day	13.98

   a. What is the opportunity cost of buying online instead of at the bookstore? Note that if you buy the book online, you must wait to get it.

   b. Show the relevant choices for Kim. What determines which of these options Kim will choose?

4. Use the concept of opportunity cost to explain the following.

   a. More people choose to get graduate degrees when the job market is poor.

   b. More people choose to do their own home repairs when the economy is slow and hourly wages are down.

   c. There are more parks in suburban than in urban areas.

   d. Convenience stores, which have higher prices than supermarkets, cater to busy people.

   e. Fewer students enroll in classes that meet before 10:00 A.M.

5. For the following examples, state how you would use the principle of marginal analysis to make a decision.

   a. Deciding how many days to wait before doing your laundry

   b. Deciding how much time to spend researching before writing your term paper

   c. Deciding how many bags of chips to eat

   d. Deciding how many class lectures to skip

6. This morning you made the following individual choices: you bought a bagel and coffee at the local café, you drove to school in your car during rush hour, and you typed your course notes for your roommate because she was texting in class—in return for which she will do your laundry for a month. For each of these actions, describe how your individual choices interacted with the individual choices made by others. Were other people left better off or worse off by your choices in each case?

7. The Hatfield family lives on the east side of the Hatatoochie River, and the McCoy family lives on the west side. Each family's diet consists of fried chicken and corn-on-the-cob, and each is self-sufficient, raising their own chickens and growing their own corn. Explain the conditions under which each of the following would be true.

   a. The two families are made better off when the Hatfields specialize in raising chickens, the McCoys specialize in growing corn, and the two families trade.

   b. The two families are made better off when the McCoys specialize in raising chickens, the Hatfields specialize in growing corn, and the two families trade.

8. Which of the following situations describes an equilibrium? Which does not? If the situation does not describe an equilibrium, what would an equilibrium look like?

   a. Many people regularly commute from the suburbs to downtown Pleasantville. Due to traffic congestion, the trip takes 30 minutes via highway but only 15 minutes via side streets.

   b. At the intersection of Main and Broadway are two gas stations. One station charges $3.00 per gallon for regular gas and the other charges $2.85 per gallon. Customers can get service immediately at the first station but must wait in a long line at the second.

   c. Every student enrolled in Economics 101 must also attend a weekly tutorial. This year there are two sections offered: section A and section B, which meet at the same time in adjoining classrooms and are taught by equally competent instructors. Section A is overcrowded, with people sitting on the floor and often unable to see what is written on the board at the front of the room. Section B has many empty seats.

9. For each of the following, explain whether you think the situation is efficient or not. If it is not efficient, why not? What actions would make it efficient?

   a. Electricity is included in the rent at your dorm. Some residents in your dorm leave lights, computers, and appliances on when they are not in their rooms.

   b. Although they cost the same amount to prepare, the cafeteria in your dorm consistently provides too many dishes that diners don't like, such as tofu casserole, and too few dishes that diners do like, such as Pad Thai.

   c. The enrollment for a particular course exceeds the spaces available. Some students who need to take this course to complete their major are unable to get a space even though others who are taking it as an elective do get a space.

10. Discuss the efficiency and equity implications of each of the following. How would you go about balancing the concerns of equity and efficiency in these areas?

    a. The government pays the full tuition for every college student to study whatever subject he or she wishes.

    b. When people lose their jobs, the government provides unemployment benefits until they find new ones.

11. Governments often adopt certain policies in order to promote efficiency in society. For each of the following policies, determine what the incentive is and what behavior the government wishes to promote. In each case, why do you think the market is inefficient and why the government might wish to change people's behavior, rather than allow their actions to be solely determined by individual choice?

    a. A tax of $5 per pack is imposed on cigarettes.

    b. The government pays parents $100 when their child is vaccinated for measles.

    c. The government pays college students to tutor children from low-income families.

    d. The government imposes a tax on the amount of air pollution that a company discharges.

12. In each of the following situations, explain how government intervention could improve society's welfare by changing people's incentives. In what sense is the market going wrong?

    a. Pollution from auto emissions has reached unhealthy levels.

    b. Everyone in Woodville would be better off if streetlights were installed in the town. But no individual resident is willing to pay for installation of a streetlight in front of his or her house because it is impossible to recoup the cost by charging other residents for the benefit they receive from it.

13. Tim Geithner, a former U.S. Treasury secretary, has said, "The recession that began in late 2007 was extraordinarily severe. But the actions we took at its height to stimulate the economy helped arrest the free fall, preventing an even deeper collapse and putting the economy on the road to recovery." Which two of the three principles of economy-wide interaction are at work in this statement?

14. A sharp downturn in the U.S. housing market in August 2007 reduced the income of many who worked in the home construction industry. One news source reported that wire-transfer businesses were likely to suffer because many construction workers are foreign nationals who regularly send part of their wages back to relatives in their home countries via wire transfers. With this information, use one of the principles of economy-wide interaction to trace the train of events that explains how reduced spending for U.S. home purchases is likely to affect the performance of the economies in the home countries of these workers.

15. Following the financial crisis of 2008, American consumers cut back on new car purchases. In response to the decline in car sales, Congress passed the program "Cash for Clunkers," which allowed consumers to trade in their old car and receive a cash stipend to purchase a new vehicle. Which principle of economy-wide interactions is at work here?

16. Self-driving cars, also known as autonomous vehicles, will require little or no human input to operate safely. A recent report claims that these vehicles will cost the U.S. economy 4 million jobs but also add nearly $800 billion in annual output. Explain how autonomous vehicles increase potential output and contribute to economic growth. Identify the winners and losers in the development of autonomous vehicles.

Economic Models: Trade-offs and Trade

FROM KITTY HAWK TO DREAMLINER

BOEING'S 787 DREAMLINER was the result of an aerodynamic revolution — a super-efficient airplane designed to cut airline operating costs and the first to use superlight composite materials.

To ensure that the Dreamliner was sufficiently lightweight and aerodynamic, it underwent over 15,000 hours of wind tunnel tests, resulting in subtle design changes that improved its performance, making it more fuel efficient and less pollutant emitting than existing passenger jets. In fact, some budget airlines such as Norwegian Air

The Wright brothers' model made modern airplanes, including the Dreamliner, possible.

(Europe's third-largest budget airline) have been offering transatlantic flights at half the price of their rivals, expecting that the super-fuel-efficient Dreamliner will shrink fuel costs enough to make their discount strategy profitable.

The first flight of the Dreamliner was a spectacular advance from the 1903 maiden voyage of the Wright Flyer, the first successful powered airplane, in Kitty Hawk, North Carolina. Yet the Boeing engineers — and all aeronautical engineers — owe an enormous debt to the Wright Flyer's inventors, Wilbur and Orville Wright.

What made the Wrights truly visionary was their invention of the wind tunnel, an apparatus that let them experiment with many different designs for wings and control surfaces. Doing experiments with a miniature airplane, inside a wind tunnel the size of a shipping crate, gave the Wright Brothers the knowledge that would make heavier-than-air flight possible.

Neither a miniature airplane inside a packing crate nor a miniature model of the Dreamliner inside Boeing's state-of-the-art Transonic Wind Tunnel is the same thing as an actual aircraft in flight. But each is a very useful *model* of a flying plane — a simplified representation of the real thing that can be used to answer crucial questions, such as how much lift a given wing shape will generate at a given airspeed.

Needless to say, testing an airplane design in a wind tunnel is cheaper and safer than building a full-scale version and hoping it will fly. More generally, models play a crucial role in almost all scientific research — economics very much included.

In fact, you could say that economic theory consists mainly of a collection of models, a series of simplified representations of economic reality that allow us to understand a variety of economic issues.

In this chapter, we'll look at three economic models that are crucially important in their own right and illustrate why such models are so useful. We'll conclude with a look at how economists actually use models in their work. ●

WHAT YOU WILL LEARN

- What are economic **models** and why are they so important to economists?

- How do three simple models — the **production possibility frontier, comparative advantage,** and the **circular-flow diagram** — help us understand how modern economies work?

- Why is an understanding of the difference between **positive economics** and **normative economics** important for the real-world application of economic principles?

- Why do economists sometimes disagree?

A **model** is a simplified representation of a real situation that is used to better understand real-life situations.

The **other things equal assumption** means that all other relevant factors remain unchanged.

|| Models in Economics: Some Important Examples

A **model** is any simplified representation of reality that is used to better understand real-life situations. But how do we create a simplified representation of an economic situation?

One possibility—an economist's equivalent of a wind tunnel—is to find or create a real but simplified economy. Take, for example, an economist who wants to know how an increase in the government-mandated minimum wage would affect the U.S. economy. It would be impossible to do an experiment that involved raising the minimum wage across the country and seeing what happens. Instead, the economist will observe the effects of a smaller economy that is raising its minimum wage (like New York City did in 2019) and then extrapolate those results to the larger U.S. economy.

Another possibility is to simulate the workings of the economy on a computer. For example, when changes in tax law are proposed, government officials use *tax models*—large mathematical computer programs—to assess how the proposed changes would affect different types of people.

Models are important because their simplicity allows economists to focus on the effects of only one change at a time. That is, they allow us to hold everything else constant and study how one change affects the overall economic outcome.

So an important assumption when building economic models is the **other things equal assumption,** which means that all other relevant factors remain unchanged.

But you can't always find or create a small-scale version of the whole economy, and a computer program is only as good as the data it uses. (Programmers have a saying: "garbage in, garbage out.") For many purposes, the most effective form of economic modeling is the construction of "thought experiments": simplified, hypothetical versions of real-life situations.

We used the example of how customers checking out at a supermarket rearrange themselves when a new cash register opens to illustrate the concept of equilibrium in Chapter 1. Although we didn't say it, this is an example of a simple model—an imaginary supermarket, in which many details, like what customers were buying, are ignored. This simple model can be used to answer a "what if" question: for example, what if another cash register were to open?

As this checkout story shows, it is possible to describe and analyze a useful economic model in plain English. However, because much of economics involves changes in quantities—in the price of a product, the number of units produced, or the number of workers employed in its production—economists often find that using some mathematics helps clarify an issue. In particular, a numerical example, a simple equation, or—especially—a graph can be key to understanding an economic concept.

Whatever form it takes, a good economic model can be a tremendous aid to understanding. We'll now look at three simple but important economic models and what they tell us.

- First, we will look at the *production possibility frontier,* a model that helps economists think about the trade-offs every economy faces.

- We then turn to *comparative advantage,* a model that clarifies the principle of gains from trade—trade both between individuals and between countries.

- We will also examine the *circular-flow diagram,* a schematic representation that helps us understand how flows of money, goods, and services are channeled through the economy.

Throughout this chapter, and the entire book, we will make considerable use of graphs to represent mathematical relationships. If you are already familiar with how graphs are used, you can skip the appendix to this chapter, which provides a brief introduction to the use of graphs in economics. If not, this would be a good time to read the appendix on graphing.

Trade-offs: The Production Possibility Frontier

The first principle of economics we introduced in Chapter 1 is that resources are scarce and, as a result, any economy faces trade-offs—whether it's an isolated group of a few dozen hunter-gatherers or the nearly 7.8 billion people making up the twenty-first-century global economy. No matter how lightweight the Boeing Dreamliner is, no matter how efficient Boeing's assembly line, producing Dreamliners means using resources that therefore can't be used to produce something else.

To think about the trade-offs that face any economy, economists often use the model known as the **production possibility frontier.** The idea behind this model is to improve our understanding of trade-offs by considering a simplified economy that produces only two goods. This simplification enables us to show the trade-off graphically.

Suppose, for a moment, that the United States was a one-company economy, with Boeing its sole employer and aircraft its only product. But there would still be a choice of what kinds of aircraft to produce—say, Dreamliners versus small commuter jets. Figure 2-1 shows a hypothetical production possibility frontier representing the trade-off this one-company economy would face. The frontier—the line in the diagram—shows the maximum quantity of small jets that Boeing can produce per year *given* the quantity of Dreamliners it produces per year, and vice versa. That is, it answers questions of the form, "What is the maximum quantity of small jets that Boeing can produce in a year if it also produces 9 (or 15, or 30) Dreamliners that year?"

There is a crucial distinction between points *inside* or *on* the production possibility frontier (the shaded area) and *outside* the frontier. If a production point lies inside or on the frontier—like point *C*, at which Boeing produces 20 small jets and 9 Dreamliners in a year—it is feasible. After all, the frontier tells us that if Boeing produces 20 small jets, it could also produce a maximum of 15 Dreamliners that year, so it could certainly make 9 Dreamliners.

However, a production point that lies outside the frontier—such as the hypothetical production point *D*, where Boeing produces 40 small jets and 30 Dreamliners—isn't feasible. Boeing can produce 40 small jets and no Dreamliners, *or* it can produce 30 Dreamliners and no small jets, but it can't do both.

The **production possibility frontier** illustrates the trade-offs facing an economy that produces only two goods. It shows the maximum quantity of one good that can be produced for any given quantity produced of the other.

FIGURE 2-1 The Production Possibility Frontier

The production possibility frontier illustrates the trade-offs Boeing faces in producing Dreamliners and small jets. It shows the maximum quantity of one good that can be produced given the quantity of the other good produced. Here, the maximum quantity of Dreamliners manufactured per year depends on the quantity of small jets manufactured that year, and vice versa. Boeing's feasible production is shown by the area *inside* or *on* the curve. Production at point *C* is feasible but not efficient. Points *A* and *B* are feasible and efficient in production, but point *D* is not feasible.

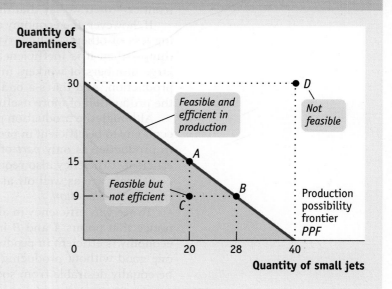

In Figure 2-1 the production possibility frontier intersects the horizontal axis at 40 small jets. This means that if Boeing dedicated all its production capacity to making small jets, it could produce 40 small jets per year but could produce no Dreamliners. The production possibility frontier intersects the vertical axis at 30 Dreamliners. This means that if Boeing dedicated all its production capacity to making Dreamliners, it could produce 30 Dreamliners per year but no small jets.

The figure also shows less extreme trade-offs. For example, if Boeing's managers decide to make 20 small jets this year, they can produce at most 15 Dreamliners; this production choice is illustrated by point *A*. And if Boeing's managers decide to produce 28 small jets, they can make at most 9 Dreamliners, as shown by point *B*.

Thinking in terms of a production possibility frontier simplifies the complexities of reality. The real-world U.S. economy produces millions of different goods. Even Boeing can produce more than two different types of planes. Yet it's important to realize that even in its simplicity, this stripped-down model gives us important insights about the real world.

By simplifying reality, the production possibility frontier helps us understand some aspects of the real economy better than we could without the model: efficiency, opportunity cost, and economic growth.

Efficiency First of all, the production possibility frontier is a good way to illustrate the general economic concept of *efficiency*. Recall from Chapter 1 that an economy is efficient if there are no missed opportunities—there is no way to make some people better off without making other people worse off.

One key element of efficiency is that there are no missed opportunities in production—there is no way to produce more of one good without producing less of other goods. As long as Boeing operates on its production possibility frontier, its production is efficient. At point *A*, 15 Dreamliners are the maximum quantity feasible given that Boeing has also committed to producing 20 small jets; at point *B*, 9 Dreamliners are the maximum number that can be made given the choice to produce 28 small jets; and so on.

But suppose for some reason that Boeing was operating at point *C*, making 20 small jets and 9 Dreamliners. In this case, it would not be operating efficiently and would therefore be *inefficient*: it could be producing more of both planes.

Although we have used an example of the production choices of a one-firm, two-good economy to illustrate efficiency and inefficiency, these concepts also carry over to the real economy, which contains many firms and produces many goods. If the economy as a whole could not produce more of any one good without producing less of something else—that is, if it is on its production possibility frontier—then we say that the economy is *efficient in production*.

If, however, the economy could produce more of some things without producing less of others—which typically means that it could produce more of everything—then it is inefficient in production. For example, an economy in which large numbers of workers are involuntarily unemployed is clearly inefficient in production. And that's a bad thing because these workers could be employed in the production of more useful goods and services.

Although the production possibility frontier helps clarify what it means for an economy to be efficient in production, it's important to understand that efficiency in production is only *part* of what's required for the economy as a whole to be efficient. Efficiency also requires that the economy allocate its resources so that consumers are as well off as possible. If an economy does this, we say that it is *efficient in allocation*.

To see why efficiency in allocation is as important as efficiency in production, notice that points *A* and *B* in Figure 2-1 both represent situations in which the economy is efficient in production, because in each case it can't produce more of one good without producing less of the other. But these two situations may not be equally desirable from society's point of view. Suppose that society prefers to have more small jets and fewer Dreamliners than at point *A;* say, it prefers to have 28 small jets and 9 Dreamliners, corresponding to point *B.* In this case, point *A* is inefficient in allocation from the point of view of the economy as a whole because it would rather have Boeing produce at point *B* instead of point *A.*

This example shows that efficiency for the economy as a whole requires *both* efficiency in production and efficiency in allocation: to be efficient, an economy must produce as much of each good as it can given the production of other goods. It must also produce the mix of goods that people want to consume and deliver those goods to the right people. An economy that gives small jets to international airlines and Dreamliners to commuter airlines serving small rural airports is inefficient, too.

In the real world, command economies, such as the former Soviet Union, are notorious for inefficiency in allocation. For example, it was common for consumers to find stores well stocked with items few people wanted but lacking basics such as soap and toilet paper.

Opportunity Cost   The production possibility frontier is also useful as a reminder of the fundamental point that the true cost of any good isn't the money it costs to buy it, but what must be given up in order to get that good—the *opportunity cost.* If, for example, Boeing decides to change its production from point *A* to point *B*, it will produce 8 more small jets but 6 fewer Dreamliners. So the opportunity cost of 8 small jets is 6 Dreamliners—the 6 Dreamliners that must be forgone in order to produce 8 more small jets. This means that each small jet has an opportunity cost of $6/8 = 3/4$ of a Dreamliner.

Is the opportunity cost of an extra small jet in terms of Dreamliners always the same, no matter how many small jets and Dreamliners are currently produced? In the example illustrated by Figure 2-1, the answer is yes. If Boeing increases its production of small jets from 28 to 40, the number of Dreamliners it produces falls from 9 to zero. So Boeing's opportunity cost per additional small jet is $9/12 = 3/4$ of a Dreamliner, the same as it was when Boeing went from 20 small jets produced to 28.

However, the fact that in this example the opportunity cost of a small jet in terms of a Dreamliner is always the same is a result of an assumption we've made, an assumption that's reflected in how Figure 2-1 is drawn. Specifically, whenever we assume that the opportunity cost of an additional unit of a good doesn't change regardless of the output mix, the production possibility frontier is a straight line.

Moreover, as you might have already guessed, the slope of a straight-line production possibility frontier is equal to the opportunity cost—specifically, the opportunity cost for the good measured on the horizontal axis in terms of the good measured on the vertical axis. In Figure 2-1, the production possibility frontier has a *constant slope* of $-3/4$, implying that Boeing faces a *constant opportunity cost* for 1 small jet equal to $3/4$ of a Dreamliner. (A review of how to calculate the slope of a straight line is found in this chapter's appendix.) This is the simplest case, but the production possibility frontier model can also be used to examine situations in which opportunity costs change as the mix of output changes.

Figure 2-2 illustrates a different assumption, a case in which Boeing faces *increasing opportunity cost.* Here, the more small jets it produces, the more costly it is to produce yet another small jet in terms of forgone production of a Dreamliner. And the same holds true in reverse: the more Dreamliners Boeing produces, the more costly it is to produce yet another Dreamliner in terms of forgone production of small jets. For example, to go from producing zero small jets to producing 20, Boeing has to forgo producing 5 Dreamliners. That is, the opportunity cost of those 20 small jets is 5 Dreamliners. But to increase its production of small jets to 40—that is, to produce an additional 20 small jets—it must forgo producing 25 more Dreamliners, a much higher opportunity cost. As you can see in Figure 2-2, when opportunity costs are increasing rather than constant, the production possibility frontier is a bowed-out curve rather than a straight line.

FIGURE 2-2 Increasing Opportunity Cost

The bowed-out shape of the production possibility frontier reflects increasing opportunity cost. In this example, to produce the first 20 small jets, Boeing must forgo producing 5 Dreamliners. But to produce an additional 20 small jets, Boeing must forgo manufacturing 25 more Dreamliners.

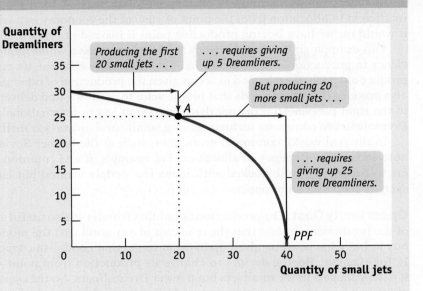

Although it's often useful to work with the simple assumption that the production possibility frontier is a straight line, economists believe that in reality opportunity costs are typically increasing. When only a small amount of a good is produced, the opportunity cost of producing that good is relatively low because the economy needs to use only those resources that are especially well suited for its production.

For example, if an economy grows only a small amount of corn, that corn can be grown in places where the soil and climate are perfect for corn-growing but less suitable for growing anything else, like wheat. So growing that corn involves giving up only a small amount of potential wheat output. Once the economy grows a lot of corn, however, land that is well suited for wheat but isn't so great for corn must be used to produce corn anyway. As a result, the additional corn production involves sacrificing considerably more wheat production. In other words, as more of a good is produced, its opportunity cost typically rises because well-suited inputs are used up and less adaptable inputs must be used instead.

Economic Growth Finally, the production possibility frontier helps us understand what it means to talk about *economic growth*. In the Introduction, we defined the concept of economic growth as *the growing ability of the economy to produce goods and services*. As we saw, economic growth is one of the fundamental features of the real economy. But are we really justified in saying that the economy has grown over time? After all, although the U.S. economy produces more of many things than it did a century ago, it produces less of other things—for example, horse-drawn carriages. Production of many goods, in other words, is actually down. So how can we say for sure that the economy as a whole has grown?

The answer is illustrated in Figure 2-3, where we have drawn two hypothetical production possibility frontiers for the economy. In them we have assumed once again that everyone in the economy works for Boeing and, consequently, the economy produces only two goods, Dreamliners and small jets. Notice how the two curves are nested, with the one labeled "Original *PPF*" lying completely inside the one labeled "New *PPF*." Now we can see graphically what we mean by economic growth of the economy: economic growth means an *expansion of the economy's production possibilities*; that is, the economy *can* produce more of everything.

For example, if the economy initially produces at point *A* (25 Dreamliners and 20 small jets), economic growth means that the economy could move to point *E* (30 Dreamliners and 25 small jets). *E* lies outside the original frontier;

FIGURE 2-3 Economic Growth

Economic growth results in an *outward shift* of the production possibility frontier because production possibilities are expanded. The economy can now produce more of everything. For example, if production is initially at point *A* (25 Dreamliners and 20 small jets), economic growth means that the economy could move to point *E* (30 Dreamliners and 25 small jets).

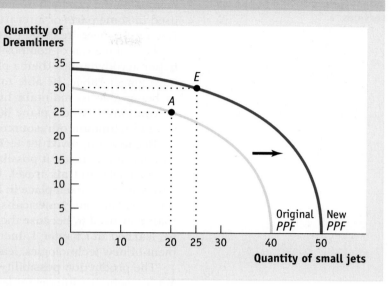

so in the production possibility frontier model, growth is shown as an outward shift of the frontier.

What can lead the production possibility frontier to shift outward? There are basically two sources of economic growth. One is an increase in the economy's **factors of production,** the resources used to produce goods and services. Economists usually use the term *factor of production* to refer to a resource that is not used up in production. For example, in traditional airplane manufacture workers used riveting machines to connect metal sheets when constructing a plane's fuselage; the workers and the riveters are factors of production, but the rivets and the sheet metal are not. Once a fuselage is made, a worker and riveter can be used to make another fuselage, but the sheet metal and rivets used to make one fuselage cannot be used to make another.

Broadly speaking, the main factors of production are the resources: land, labor, physical capital, and human capital. Land is a resource supplied by nature; labor is the economy's pool of workers; physical capital refers to created resources such as machines and buildings; and human capital refers to the educational achievements and skills of the labor force, which enhance its productivity. Of course, each of these is actually a broad category rather than a single factor: land in North Dakota is very different from land in Florida.

To see how adding to an economy's factors of production leads to economic growth, suppose that Boeing builds another construction hangar that allows it to increase the number of planes—small jets or Dreamliners or both—it can produce in a year. The new construction hangar is a factor of production, a resource Boeing can use to increase its yearly output. How many more planes of each type Boeing will produce is a management decision that will depend on, among other things, customer demand. But we can say that Boeing's production possibility frontier has shifted outward because it can now produce more small jets without reducing the number of Dreamliners it makes, or it can make more Dreamliners without reducing the number of small jets produced.

Factors of production are resources used to produce goods and services.

The four factors of production: land, labor, physical capital, and human capital.

Technology is the technical means for producing goods and services.

The other source of economic growth is progress in **technology,** the technical means for the production of goods and services. Composite materials had been used in some parts of aircraft before the Boeing Dreamliner was developed. But Boeing engineers realized that there were large additional advantages to building a whole plane out of composites. The plane would be lighter, stronger, and have better aerodynamics than a plane built in the traditional way. It would therefore have longer range, be able to carry more people, and use less fuel, in addition to being able to maintain higher cabin pressure. So in a real sense Boeing's innovation—a whole plane built out of composites—was a way to do more with any given amount of resources, pushing out the production possibility frontier.

Because improved jet technology has pushed out the production possibility frontier, it has made it possible for the economy to produce more of everything, not just jets and air travel. Over the past 30 years, the biggest technological advances have taken place in information technology, not in construction or food services. Yet some Americans have chosen to buy bigger houses and eat out more than they used to because the economy's growth has made it possible to do so. As we learned in Chapter 1, increases in the economy's potential, like the development of new technologies, lead to economic growth over time.

The production possibility frontier is a very simplified model of an economy. Yet it teaches us important lessons about real-life economies. It gives us our first clear sense of what constitutes economic efficiency, it illustrates the concept of opportunity cost, and it makes clear what economic growth is all about.

Comparative Advantage and Gains from Trade

Another of the eleven principles of economics described in Chapter 1 is the principle of *gains from trade*—the mutual gains that individuals can achieve by specializing in doing different things and trading with one another. Our second illustration of an economic model is a particularly useful model of gains from trade—trade based on *comparative advantage*.

One of the most important insights in all of economics is that there are gains from trade: it makes sense to produce the things you're especially good at producing and to buy from other people the things you aren't as good at producing. This would be true even if you could produce everything for yourself: even if a brilliant brain surgeon *could* repair her own dripping faucet, it's probably a better idea for her to call in a professional plumber.

How can we model the gains from trade? Let's stay with our aircraft example and once again imagine that the United States is a one-company economy where everyone works for Boeing, producing airplanes. Let's now assume, however, that the United States has the ability to trade with Brazil—another one-company economy where everyone works for the Brazilian aircraft company Embraer, which is, in the real world, a successful producer of small commuter jets. (If you fly from one major U.S. city to another, your plane is likely to be a Boeing, but if you fly into a small city, the odds are good that your plane will be an Embraer.)

In our example, the only two goods produced are large jets and small jets. Both countries could produce both kinds of jets. But as we'll see in a moment, they can gain by producing different things and trading with each other. For the purposes of this example, let's return to the simpler case of straight-line production possibility frontiers. America's production possibilities are represented by the production possibility frontier in panel (a) of Figure 2-4, which is similar to the production possibility frontier in Figure 2-1. According to this diagram, the United States can produce 40 small jets if it makes no large jets and can manufacture 30 large jets if it produces no small jets. Recall that this means that the slope of the U.S. production possibility frontier is $-\frac{3}{4}$: its opportunity cost of 1 small jet is $\frac{3}{4}$ of a large jet.

Panel (b) of Figure 2-4 shows Brazil's production possibilities. Like the United States, Brazil's production possibility frontier is a straight line, implying a constant opportunity cost of a small jet in terms of large jets. Brazil's production

FIGURE 2-4 Production Possibilities for Two Countries

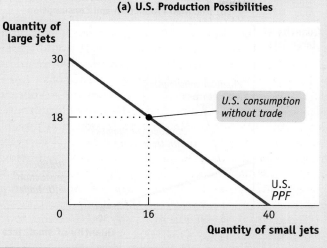

(a) U.S. Production Possibilities

Quantity of large jets

U.S. consumption without trade

U.S. PPF

Quantity of small jets

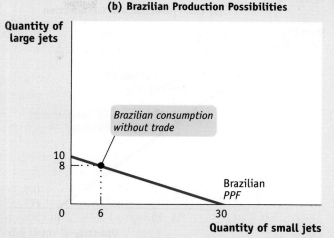

(b) Brazilian Production Possibilities

Quantity of large jets

Brazilian consumption without trade

Brazilian PPF

Quantity of small jets

Here, both the United States and Brazil have a constant opportunity cost of small jets, illustrated by a straight-line production possibility frontier. For the United States,

each small jet has an opportunity cost of ¾ of a large jet. Brazil has an opportunity cost of a small jet equal to ⅓ of a large jet.

possibility frontier has a constant slope of $-\frac{1}{3}$. Brazil can't produce as much of anything as the United States can: at most it can produce 30 small jets or 10 large jets. But it is relatively better at manufacturing small jets than the United States; whereas the United States sacrifices ¾ of a large jet per small jet produced, for Brazil the opportunity cost of a small jet is only ⅓ of a large jet. Table 2-1 summarizes the two countries' opportunity costs of small jets and large jets.

Now, the United States and Brazil could each choose to make their own large and small jets, not trading any of them and consuming only what each produced within its own country. (A country "consumes" an airplane when it is owned by a domestic resident.) Let's suppose that the two countries start out this way and make the consumption choices shown in Figure 2-4: in the absence of trade, the United States produces and consumes 16 small jets and 18 large jets per year, while Brazil produces and consumes 6 small jets and 8 large jets per year.

But is this the best the two countries can do? No, it isn't. Given that the two producers—and therefore the two countries—have different opportunity costs, the United States and Brazil can strike a deal that makes both of them better off.

Table 2-2 shows how such a deal works: the United States specializes in the production of large jets, manufacturing 30 per year, and sells 10 to Brazil. Meanwhile, Brazil specializes in the production of small jets, producing 30 per year, and sells 20 to the United States. The result is shown in Figure 2-5. The United States now

TABLE 2-1 U.S. and Brazilian Opportunity Costs of Small Jets and Large Jets

	U.S. opportunity cost	Brazilian opportunity cost
1 small jet	¾ large jet >	⅓ large jet
1 large jet	4/3 small jets <	3 small jets

TABLE 2-2 How the United States and Brazil Gain from Trade

		Without trade		With trade		Gains from trade
		Production	Consumption	Production	Consumption	
United States	**Large jets**	18	18	30	20	+2
	Small jets	16	16	0	20	+4
Brazil	**Large jets**	8	8	0	10	+2
	Small jets	6	6	30	10	+4

FIGURE 2-5 Comparative Advantage and Gains from Trade

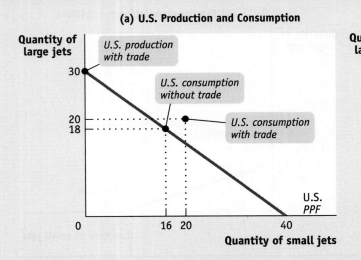

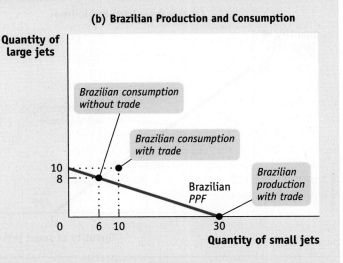

By specializing and trading, the United States and Brazil can produce and consume more of both large jets and small jets. The United States specializes in manufacturing large jets, its comparative advantage, and Brazil — which has an *absolute* disadvantage in both goods but a *comparative* advantage in small jets — specializes in manufacturing small jets. With trade, both countries can consume more of both goods than either could without trade.

---

consumes more of both small jets and large jets than before: instead of 16 small jets and 18 large jets, it now consumes 20 small jets and 20 large jets. Brazil also consumes more, going from 6 small jets and 8 large jets to 10 small jets and 10 large jets. As Table 2-2 also shows, both the United States and Brazil reap gains from trade, consuming more of both types of planes than they would have without trade.

Both countries are better off when they each specialize in what they are good at and trade. It's a good idea for the United States to specialize in the production of large jets because its opportunity cost of a large jet is smaller than Brazil's: $\frac{4}{3} < 3$. Correspondingly, Brazil should specialize in the production of small jets because its opportunity cost of a small jet is smaller than the United States: $\frac{1}{3} < \frac{3}{4}$.

What we would say in this case is that the United States has a comparative advantage in the production of large jets and Brazil has a comparative advantage in the production of small jets. A country has a **comparative advantage** in producing something if the opportunity cost of that production is lower for that country than for other countries. The same concept applies to firms and people: a firm or an individual has a comparative advantage in producing something if its, his, or her opportunity cost of production is lower than for others.

One point of clarification before we proceed further. You may have wondered why the United States traded 10 large jets to Brazil in return for 20 small jets. Why not some other deal, like trading 10 large jets for 12 small jets? The answer to that question has two parts. First, there may indeed be other trades that the United States and Brazil might agree to. Second, there are some deals that we can safely rule out — one like 10 large jets for 10 small jets.

To understand why, reexamine Table 2-1 and consider the United States first. Without trading with Brazil, the U.S. opportunity cost of a small jet is $\frac{3}{4}$ of a large jet. So it's clear that the United States will not accept any trade that requires it to give up more than $\frac{3}{4}$ of a large jet for a small jet. Trading 10 large jets in return for 12 small jets would require the United States to pay an opportunity cost of $\frac{10}{12} = \frac{5}{6}$ of a large jet for a small jet. Because $\frac{5}{6}$ is greater than $\frac{3}{4}$, this is a deal that the United States would reject. Similarly, Brazil won't accept a trade that gives it less than $\frac{1}{3}$ of a large jet for a small jet.

A country has a **comparative advantage** in producing a good or service if its opportunity cost of producing the good or service is lower than other countries' cost. Likewise, an individual has a comparative advantage in producing a good or service if his or her opportunity cost of producing the good or service is lower than it is for other people.

The point to remember is that the United States and Brazil will be willing to trade only if the "price" of the good each country obtains in the trade is less than its own opportunity cost of producing the good domestically. Moreover, this is a general statement that is true whenever two parties—countries, firms, or individuals—trade voluntarily.

While our story clearly simplifies reality, it teaches us some very important lessons that apply to the real economy, too.

First, the model provides a clear illustration of the gains from trade: through specialization and trade, both countries produce more and consume more than if they were self-sufficient.

Second, the model demonstrates a very important point that is often over-looked in real-world arguments: each country has a comparative advantage in producing something. This applies to firms and people as well: *everyone has a comparative advantage in something, and everyone has a comparative disadvantage in something.*

Crucially, in our example it doesn't matter if, as is probably the case in real life, American workers are just as good as or even better than Brazilian workers at producing small jets. Suppose that the United States is actually better than Brazil at all kinds of aircraft production. In that case, we would say that the United States has an **absolute advantage** in both large-jet and small-jet production: in an hour, an American worker can produce more of either a large jet or a small jet than a Brazilian worker. You might be tempted to think that in that case the United States has nothing to gain from trading with the less productive Brazil.

But we've just seen that the United States can indeed benefit from trading with Brazil because *comparative, not absolute, advantage is the basis for mutual gain.* It doesn't matter whether it takes Brazil more resources than the United States to make a small jet; what matters for trade is that for Brazil the opportunity cost of a small jet is lower than the U.S. opportunity cost. So Brazil, despite its absolute disadvantage, even in small jets, has a comparative advantage in the manufacture of small jets. Meanwhile the United States, which can use its resources most productively by manufacturing large jets, has a comparative *dis*advantage in manufacturing small jets.

> A country has an **absolute advantage** in producing a good or service if the country can produce more output per worker than other countries. Likewise, an individual has an absolute advantage in producing a good or service if he or she is better at producing it than other people. Having an absolute advantage is not the same thing as having a comparative advantage.

Comparative Advantage and International Trade, in Reality

Look at the label on a manufactured good sold in the United States, and there's a good chance you will find that it was produced in some other country—in China, or Japan, or even in Canada. On the other side, many U.S. industries sell a large fraction of their output overseas. This is particularly true of agriculture, high technology, and entertainment.

PITFALLS

MISUNDERSTANDING COMPARATIVE ADVANTAGE

Students do it, pundits do it, and politicians do it all the time: they confuse *comparative advantage* with *absolute advantage*. For example, back in the 1980s, when the U.S. economy seemed to be lagging behind that of Japan, news commentators could be heard warning that if we didn't improve our productivity, we would soon have no comparative advantage in anything.

What those commentators meant was that we would have no *absolute advantage* in anything—that there might come a time when the Japanese were better at everything than we were. (It didn't turn out that way, but that's another story.) And they had the idea that in that case we would no longer be able to benefit from trade with Japan.

But just as Brazil, in our example, was able to benefit from trade with the United States (and vice versa) despite the fact that the United States was better at manufacturing both large and small jets, in real life nations can still gain from trade even if they are less productive in all industries than the countries they trade with.

Should all this international exchange of goods and services be celebrated, or is it cause for concern? Politicians and the public often question the desirability of international trade, arguing that the nation should produce goods for itself rather than buying them from foreigners. Industries around the world demand protection from foreign competition: Japanese farmers want to keep out American rice, American steelworkers want to keep out European steel. And these demands are often supported by public opinion.

Economists, however, have a very positive view of international trade. Why? Because they view it in terms of comparative advantage. As we learned from our example of American large jets and Brazilian small jets, international trade benefits both countries. Each country can consume more than if it doesn't trade and remains self-sufficient. Moreover, these mutual gains don't depend on each country being better than other countries at producing one kind of good. Even if one country has, say, higher output per worker in both industries—that is, even if one country has an absolute advantage in both industries—there are still gains from trade. The following Global Comparison illustrates just this point.

GLOBAL COMPARISON **PAJAMA REPUBLICS**

A terrible industrial disaster made headlines when a building that housed five clothing factories collapsed in Bangladesh in 2013, killing more than a thousand garment workers trapped inside. Attention soon focused on the substandard working conditions in those factories, as well as the many violations of building codes and safety procedures—including those required by Bangladeshi law—that set the stage for the tragedy.

While this disaster provoked a justified outcry, it also highlighted the remarkable rise of Bangladesh's clothing industry, which has become a major player in world markets—second only to China in total exports—and a desperately needed source of income and employment in a very poor country.

It's not that Bangladesh has especially high productivity in clothing manufacturing. In fact, estimates by the consulting firm McKinsey and Company suggest that it's about a quarter less productive than China. Rather, it has even lower productivity in other industries, giving it a comparative advantage in clothing manufacturing. This is typical in poor countries, which often rely heavily on clothing exports during the early phases of their economic development. An official from one such country once joked, "We are not a banana republic—we are a pajama republic."

The figure plots the per capita income of several such "pajama republics" (the total income of the country divided by the size of the population) against the share of total exports accounted for by clothing; per capita income is measured as a percentage of the U.S.

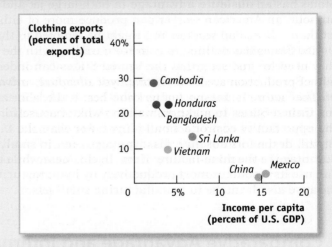

level in order to give you a sense of just how poor these countries are. As you can see, they are very poor indeed—and the poorer they are, the more they depend on clothing exports.

It's worth pointing out, by the way, that relying on clothing exports is not necessarily a bad thing, despite tragedies like the one in Bangladesh. Indeed, Bangladesh, although still desperately poor, is more than four and a half times as rich as it was two decades ago, when it began its dramatic rise as a clothing exporter. (Also see the upcoming Economics in Action on Bangladesh.)

Data from: The World Bank.

Transactions: The Circular-Flow Diagram

Trade takes the form of **barter** when people directly exchange goods or services that they have for goods or services that they want.

The model economies that we've studied so far—each containing only one firm—are huge simplifications. We've also greatly simplified trade between the United States and Brazil, assuming that they engage only in the simplest of economic transactions, **barter,** in which one party directly trades a good or service for another good or service without using money. In a modern economy, simple barter is rare: usually people trade goods or services for money—pieces of colored paper with no inherent value—and then trade those pieces of colored paper for the goods or services they want. That is, they sell goods or services and buy other goods or services.

And they both sell and buy a lot of different things. The U.S. economy is a vastly complex entity, with more than a hundred million workers employed by millions of companies, producing millions of different goods and services. Yet you can learn some very important things about the economy by considering the simple graphic shown in Figure 2-6, the **circular-flow diagram.** This diagram represents the transactions that take place in an economy by two kinds of flows around a circle: flows of physical things such as goods, services, labor, or raw materials in one direction, and flows of money that pay for these physical things in the opposite direction. In this case the physical flows are shown in blue, the money flows in green.

The simplest circular-flow diagram illustrates an economy that contains only two kinds of inhabitants: **households** and **firms.** A household consists of either an individual or a group of people (usually, but not necessarily, a family) that share their income. A firm is an organization that produces goods and services for sale—and that employs members of households.

As you can see in Figure 2-6, there are two kinds of markets in this simple economy. On the left side, there are **markets for goods and services** in which households buy the goods and services they want from firms. This produces a flow of goods and services to households and a return flow of money to firms.

On the right side, there are **factor markets** in which firms buy the resources they need to produce goods and services. Recall from earlier that the main factors of production are land, labor, physical capital, and human capital.

The factor market most of us know best is the labor market, in which workers sell their services. In addition, we can think of households as owning and selling the other factors of production to firms. For example, when a firm buys physical capital in the form of machines, the payment ultimately goes to the households that own the machine-making firm. In this case, the transactions occur in the *capital market,* the market in which capital is bought and sold. As we'll examine in detail later, factor markets ultimately determine an economy's **income distribution,** how the total income created in an economy is allocated between less skilled workers, highly skilled workers, and the owners of capital and land.

The **circular-flow diagram** represents the transactions in an economy by flows around a circle.

A **household** is a person or a group of people that share their income.

A **firm** is an organization that produces goods and services for sale.

Firms sell goods and services that they produce to households in **markets for goods and services.**

Firms buy the resources they need to produce goods and services in **factor markets.**

An economy's **income distribution** is the way in which total income is divided among the owners of the various factors of production.

FIGURE 2-6 The Circular-Flow Diagram

This diagram represents the flows of money and of goods and services in the economy. In the markets for goods and services, households purchase goods and services from firms, generating a flow of money to the firms and a flow of goods and services to the households. The money flows back to households as firms purchase factors of production from the households in factor markets.

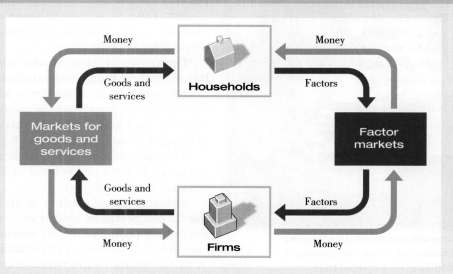

The circular-flow diagram ignores a number of real-world complications in the interests of simplicity. A few examples:

- In the real world, the distinction between firms and households isn't always that clear-cut. Consider a small, family-run business—a farm, a shop, a small hotel. Is this a firm or a household? A more complete picture would include a separate box for family businesses.

- Many of the sales that firms make are not to households but to other firms; for example, steel companies sell mainly to other companies such as auto manufacturers, not to households. A more complete picture would include these flows of goods, services, and money within the business sector.

- The figure doesn't show the government, which in the real world diverts quite a lot of money out of the circular flow in the form of taxes but also injects a lot of money back into the flow in the form of spending.

Figure 2-6, in other words, is by no means a complete picture either of all the types of inhabitants of the real economy or of all the flows of money and physical items that take place among these inhabitants.

Despite its simplicity, however, the circular-flow diagram is a very useful aid to thinking about the economy.

ECONOMICS >> *in Action*
Rich Nation, Poor Nation

Try taking off your clothes—at a suitable time and in a suitable place, of course—and taking a look at the labels inside that say where they were made. It's a very good bet that much, if not most, of your clothes were manufactured overseas, in a country that is much poorer than the United States—say, in El Salvador, Sri Lanka, or Bangladesh.

Why are these countries so much poorer than we are? The immediate reason is that their economies are much less *productive*—firms in these countries are just not able to produce as much from a given quantity of resources as comparable firms in the United States or other wealthy countries. Why countries differ so much in productivity is a deep question—indeed, one of the main questions that preoccupy economists. But in any case, the difference in productivity is a fact.

But if the economies of these countries are so much less productive than ours, how is it that they make so much of our clothing? Why don't we do it for ourselves?

The answer is "comparative advantage." Just about every industry in Bangladesh is much less productive than the corresponding industry in the United States. But the productivity difference between rich and poor countries varies across goods; it is very large in the production of sophisticated goods like aircraft but not that large in the production of simpler goods like clothing. So Bangladesh's position with regard to clothing production is like Embraer's position with respect to producing small jets: it's not as good at it as Boeing, but it's the thing Embraer does comparatively well.

Although less productive than the American economy, Bangladesh's economy has a comparative advantage in clothing production.

Although Bangladesh is at an absolute disadvantage compared with the United States in almost everything, it has a comparative advantage in clothing production. This means that both the United States and Bangladesh are able to consume more because they specialize in producing different things, with Bangladesh supplying our clothes and the United States supplying Bangladesh with more sophisticated goods.

>> *Check Your Understanding* 2-1

Solutions appear at back of book.

1. True or false? Explain your answer.
   a. An increase in the amount of resources available to Boeing for use in producing Dreamliners and small jets does not change its production possibility frontier.
   b. A technological change that allows Boeing to build more small jets for any amount of Dreamliners built results in a change in its production possibility frontier.
   c. The production possibility frontier is useful because it illustrates how much of one good an economy must give up to get more of another good regardless of whether resources are being used efficiently.

2. In Italy, an automobile can be produced by 8 workers in one day and a washing machine by 3 workers in one day. In the United States, an automobile can be produced by 6 workers in one day and a washing machine by 2 workers in one day.
   a. Which country has an absolute advantage in the production of automobiles? In washing machines?
   b. Which country has a comparative advantage in the production of washing machines? In automobiles?
   c. What pattern of specialization results in the greatest gains from trade between the two countries?

3. Using Table 2-1, explain why the United States and Brazil are willing to engage in a trade of 10 large jets for 15 small jets.

4. Use the circular-flow diagram to explain how an increase in the amount of money spent by households results in an increase in the number of jobs in the economy. Describe in words what the circular-flow diagram predicts.

‖ Using Models

We have now seen how economic analysis is mainly a matter of creating models that draw on a set of basic principles but add some more specific assumptions that allow the modeler to apply those principles to a particular situation. But what do economists actually *do* with their models?

Positive versus Normative Economics

Imagine that you are an economic adviser to the governor of your state. What kinds of questions might the governor ask you to answer?

Well, here are three possible questions:

1. How much revenue will the tolls on the state turnpike yield next year?
2. How much would that revenue increase if the toll were raised from $1 to $1.50?
3. Should the toll be raised, bearing in mind that a toll increase will reduce traffic and air pollution near the road but will impose some financial hardship on frequent commuters?

There is a big difference between the first two questions and the third one. The first two are questions about facts. Your forecast of next year's toll collection will be proved right or wrong when the numbers actually come in. Your estimate of the impact of a change in the toll is a little harder to check—revenue depends on other factors besides the toll, and it may be hard to disentangle the causes of any change in revenue. Still, in principle there is only one right answer.

But the question of whether tolls should be raised may not have a "right" answer—two people who agree on the effects of a higher toll could still disagree about whether raising the toll is a good idea. For example, someone who lives near the turnpike but doesn't commute on it will care a lot about noise and air

Positive economics is the branch of economic analysis that describes the way the economy actually works.

Normative economics makes prescriptions about the way the economy should work.

A **forecast** is a simple prediction of the future.

pollution but not so much about commuting costs. A regular commuter who doesn't live near the turnpike will have the opposite priorities.

This example highlights a key distinction between two roles of economic analysis. Analysis that tries to answer questions about the way the world works, which have definite right and wrong answers, is known as **positive economics.** In contrast, analysis that involves saying how the world *should* work is known as **normative economics.** To put it another way, positive economics is about description; normative economics is about prescription.

Positive economics occupies most of the time and effort of the economics profession. And models play a crucial role in almost all positive economics. As we mentioned earlier, the U.S. government uses a computer model to assess proposed changes in national tax policy, and many state governments have similar models to assess the effects of their own tax policy.

It's worth noting that there is a subtle but important difference between the first and second questions we imagined the governor asking. Question 1 asked for a simple prediction about next year's revenue—a **forecast.** Question 2 was a "what if" question, asking how revenue would change if the tax law were changed. Economists are often called upon to answer both types of questions, but models are especially useful for answering "what if" questions.

The answers to such questions often serve as a guide to policy, but they are still predictions, not prescriptions. That is, they tell you what will happen if a policy were changed; they don't tell you whether or not that result is good.

Suppose your economic model tells you that the governor's proposed increase in highway tolls will raise property values in communities near the road but will hurt people who must use the turnpike to get to work. Does that make this proposed toll increase a good idea or a bad one? It depends on whom you ask. As we've just seen, someone who is very concerned with the communities near the road will support the increase, but someone who is very concerned with the welfare of drivers will feel differently. That's a value judgment—it's not a question of economic analysis.

Still, economists often do engage in normative economics and give policy advice. How can they do this when there may be no "right" answer?

One answer is that economists are also citizens, and we all have our opinions. But economic analysis can often be used to show that some policies are clearly better than others, regardless of anyone's opinions.

Suppose that policies A and B achieve the same goal, but policy A makes everyone better off than policy B—or at least makes some people better off without making other people worse off. Then A is clearly more efficient than B. That's not a value judgment: we're talking about how best to achieve a goal, not about the goal itself.

For example, two different policies have been used to help low-income families obtain housing: rent control, which limits the rents landlords are allowed to charge, and rent subsidies, which provide families with additional money to pay rent. Almost all economists agree that subsidies are the more efficient policy. And so the great majority of economists, whatever their personal politics, favor subsidies over rent control.

When policies can be clearly ranked in this way, then economists generally agree. But it is no secret that economists sometimes disagree.

‖ When and Why Economists Disagree

Economists have a reputation for arguing with each other. Where does this reputation come from, and is it justified?

One important answer is that media coverage tends to exaggerate the real differences in views among economists. If nearly all economists agree on an issue—for example, the proposition that rent controls lead to housing shortages—reporters and editors are likely to conclude that it's not a story worth covering, leaving the professional consensus unreported. But an issue on which prominent economists take opposing sides—for example, whether cutting taxes right now would help the economy—makes a news story worth reporting. So you hear much more about the areas of disagreement within economics than you do about the large areas of agreement.

It is also worth remembering that economics is, unavoidably, often tied up in politics. On a number of issues powerful interest groups know what opinions they want to hear; they therefore have an incentive to find and promote economists who profess those opinions, giving these economists a prominence and visibility out of proportion to their support among their colleagues.

While the appearance of disagreement among economists exceeds the reality, it remains true that economists often *do* disagree about important things. For example, some well-respected economists argue vehemently that the U.S. government should replace the income tax with a *value-added tax* (a national sales tax, which is the main source of government revenue in many European countries). Other equally respected economists disagree. Why this difference of opinion?

One important source of differences lies in values: as in any diverse group of individuals, reasonable people can differ. In comparison to an income tax, a value-added tax typically falls more heavily on people of modest means. So an economist who values a society with more social and income equality for its own sake will tend to oppose a value-added tax. An economist with different values will be less likely to oppose it.

A second important source of differences arises from economic modeling. Because economists base their conclusions on models, which are simplified representations of reality, two economists can legitimately disagree about which simplifications are appropriate—and therefore arrive at different conclusions.

Suppose that the U.S. government were considering introducing a value-added tax. Economist A may rely on a model that focuses on the administrative costs of tax systems—that is, the costs of monitoring, processing papers, collecting the tax, and so on. This economist might then point to the well-known high costs of administering a value-added tax and argue against the change. But economist B may think that the right way to approach the question is to ignore the administrative costs and focus on how the proposed law would change savings behavior. This economist might point to studies suggesting that value-added taxes promote higher consumer saving, a desirable result.

Because the economists have used different models—that is, made different simplifying assumptions—they arrive at different conclusions. And so the two economists may find themselves on different sides of the issue.

ECONOMICS >> *in Action*
When Economists Agree

"If all the economists in the world were laid end to end, they still couldn't reach a conclusion," goes an economist joke. But do economists really disagree that much? Not according to an ongoing survey. The Booth School of Business at the University of Chicago has assembled a panel of 51 economists, all with exemplary professional reputations, representing a mix of regions, schools, and political

These four economists are on the panel (clockwise from top left): Cecilia Rouse of Princeton, David Cutler of Harvard, Hilary Hoynes of UC Berkeley, and Raj Chetty of Harvard.

affiliations. They are regularly polled on questions of policy or political interest, often ones on which there are bitter divides among politicians or the general public.

Yet the survey shows much more agreement among economists than rumor would have it, even on supposedly controversial topics. For example, 85% of the panel agreed that trade with China makes most Americans better off and nearly the same percentage agreed that Americans who work in the production of competing goods, like clothing, are made worse off by trade with China. Roughly the same percentage (82%) disagreed with the proposition that rent control increases the supply of quality, affordable housing.

In the first case, the panel overwhelmingly agreed with a position widely considered liberal in American politics, while in the second case they agreed with one widely considered politically conservative.

Disagreements tended to involve untested economic policies. There was, for example, an almost even split over whether new policies adopted by the Federal Reserve aimed at boosting the economy during the deep recession of 2007 to 2009 would work. Ideology played a limited role in these disagreements: Economists known to be liberals did have slightly different positions, on average, from those known to be conservatives, but the differences weren't nearly as large as those among the general public.

So economists do disagree quite a lot on some issues, especially in macroeconomics. But there is a large area of common ground.

>> Quick Review

• **Positive economics** — the focus of most economic research — is the analysis of the way the world works, in which there are definite right and wrong answers. It often involves making **forecasts. Normative economics,** which makes prescriptions about how things *ought to be,* inevitably involves value judgments.

• Economists do disagree — though not as much as legend has it — for two main reasons. One, they may disagree about which simplifications to make in a model. Two, economists may disagree — like everyone else — about values.

>> Check Your Understanding 2-2

Solutions appear at back of book.

1. Which of the following is a positive statement? Which is a normative statement?
   a. Society should take measures to prevent people from engaging in dangerous personal behavior.
   b. People who engage in dangerous personal behavior impose higher costs on society through higher medical costs.

2. True or false? Explain your answer.
   a. Policy choice A and policy choice B attempt to achieve the same social goal. Policy choice A, however, results in a much less efficient use of resources than policy choice B. Therefore, economists are more likely to agree on choosing policy choice B.
   b. When two economists disagree on the desirability of a policy, it's typically because one of them has made a mistake.

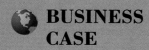
Efficiency, Opportunity Cost, and the Logic of Lean Production

In January 2020, the Boeing 777X, an update to the widely popular 777, took its maiden flight. The 777X was the product of what Boeing calls its *advanced manufacturing* process. With it, Boeing extended its extremely successful process known as *lean production* to newer production methods, such as robotics.

Lean manufacturing, pioneered by Toyota Motors of Japan, is based on the practice of having parts arrive on the factory floor just as they are needed for production. This reduces the amount of parts Boeing holds in inventory as well as the amount of the factory floor needed for production. To help move from lean production to advanced manufacturing Boeing has turned to Toyota, hiring some of their top engineers.

Boeing first adopted lean manufacturing in 1999 in the manufacture of the 737, the most popular commercial airplane. By 2005, after constant refinement, it achieved a 50% reduction in the time it takes to produce a plane and a nearly 60% reduction in parts inventory. An important feature is a continuously moving assembly line, moving products from one assembly team to the next at a steady pace and eliminating the need for workers to wander across the factory floor from task to task or in search of tools and parts.

Toyota's lean production techniques have been the most widely adopted, revolutionizing manufacturing worldwide. In simple terms, lean production is focused on organization and communication. Workers and parts are organized so as to ensure a smooth and consistent workflow that minimizes wasted effort and materials. Lean production is also designed to be highly responsive to changes in the desired mix of output—for example, quickly producing more SUVs and fewer sedans according to changes in customer demand.

Toyota's methods were so successful that they transformed the global auto industry and severely threatened once-dominant American automakers. Until the 1980s, the "Big Three"—Chrysler, Ford, and General Motors—dominated the American auto industry, with virtually no foreign-made cars sold in the United States. In the 1980s, however, Toyotas became increasingly popular due to their high quality and relatively low price—so popular that the Big Three eventually prevailed upon the U.S. government to protect them by restricting the sale of Japanese autos in the United States. Over time, Toyota responded by building assembly plants in the United States, bringing along its lean production techniques, which then spread throughout American manufacturing.

QUESTIONS FOR THOUGHT

1. What is the opportunity cost associated with having a worker wander across the factory floor from task to task or in search of tools and parts?

2. Explain how lean manufacturing improves the economy's efficiency in allocation.

3. Before lean manufacturing innovations, Japan mostly sold consumer electronics to the United States. How did lean manufacturing innovations alter Japan's comparative advantage vis-à-vis the United States?

4. How do you think the shift in the location of Toyota's production from Japan to the United States has altered the pattern of comparative advantage in automaking between the two countries?

SUMMARY

1. Almost all economics is based on **models,** "thought experiments" or simplified versions of reality, many of which use mathematical tools such as graphs. An important assumption in economic models is the **other things equal assumption,** which allows analysis of the effect of a change in one factor by holding all other relevant factors unchanged.

2. One important economic model is the **production possibility frontier.** It illustrates *opportunity cost* (showing how much less of one good can be produced if more of the other good is produced); *efficiency* (an economy is efficient in production if it produces on the production possibility frontier and efficient in allocation if it produces the mix of goods and services that people want to consume); and *economic growth* (an outward shift of the production possibility frontier). There are two basic sources of growth: an increase in **factors of production**—resources such as land, labor, capital, and human capital, inputs that are not used up in production—and improved **technology.**

3. Another important model is **comparative advantage,** which explains the source of gains from trade between individuals and countries. Everyone has a comparative advantage in something—some good or service in which that person has a lower opportunity cost than everyone else. But it is often confused with **absolute advantage,** an ability to produce a particular good or service better than anyone else. This confusion leads some to erroneously conclude that there are no gains from trade between people or countries.

4. In the simplest economies people **barter**—trade goods and services for one another—rather than trade them for money, as in a modern economy. The **circular-flow diagram** represents transactions within the economy as flows of goods, services, and money between **households** and **firms.** These transactions occur in **markets for goods and services** and **factor markets,** markets for factors of production—land, labor, physical capital, and human capital. The circular-flow diagram is useful in understanding how spending, production, employment, income, and growth are related in the economy. Ultimately, factor markets determine the economy's **income distribution,** how an economy's total income is allocated to the owners of the factors of production.

5. Economists use economic models for both **positive economics,** which describes how the economy works, and for **normative economics,** which prescribes how the economy *should* work. Positive economics often involves making **forecasts.** Economists can determine correct answers for positive questions but typically not for normative questions, which involve value judgments. The exceptions are when policies designed to achieve a certain objective can be clearly ranked in terms of efficiency.

6. There are two main reasons economists disagree. One, they may disagree about which simplifications to make in a model. Two, economists may disagree—like everyone else—about values.

KEY TERMS

Model, p. 28
Other things equal assumption, p. 28
Production possibility frontier, p. 29
Factors of production, p. 33
Technology, p. 34
Comparative advantage, p. 36

Absolute advantage, p. 37
Barter, p. 38
Circular-flow diagram, p. 39
Household, p. 39
Firm, p. 39
Markets for goods and services, p. 39

Factor markets, p. 39
Income distribution, p. 39
Positive economics, p. 42
Normative economics, p. 42
Forecast, p. 42

PRACTICE QUESTIONS

1. Penelope Pundit, an economics reporter, states that the European Union (EU) is increasing its productivity very rapidly in all industries. She claims that this productivity advance is so rapid that output from the EU in these industries will soon exceed that of the United States and, as a result, the United States will no longer benefit from trade with the EU.

   a. Do you think Penelope Pundit is correct or not? If not, what do you think is the source of her mistake?

   b. If the EU and the United States continue to trade, what do you think will characterize the goods that the EU sells to the United States and the goods that the United States sells to the EU?

2. The inhabitants of the fictional economy of Atlantis use money in the form of cowry shells. Draw a circular-flow diagram showing households and firms. Firms produce potatoes and fish, and households buy potatoes and fish. Households also provide the land

and labor to firms. Identify where in the flows of cowry shells or physical things (goods and services, or resources) each of the following impacts would occur. Describe how this impact spreads around the circle.

a. A devastating hurricane floods many of the potato fields.

b. A very productive fishing season yields a very large number of fish caught.

c. The inhabitants of Atlantis discover Shakira and spend several days a month at dancing festivals.

3. An economist might say that colleges and universities "produce" education, using faculty members and students as inputs. According to this line of reasoning, education is then "consumed" by households. Construct a circular-flow diagram to represent the sector of the economy devoted to college education: colleges and universities represent firms, and households both consume education and provide faculty and students to universities. What are the relevant markets in this diagram? What is being bought and sold in each direction? What would happen in the diagram if the government decided to subsidize 50% of all college students' tuition?

4. A representative of the American clothing industry made the following statement: "Workers in Asia often work in sweatshop conditions earning only pennies an hour. American workers are more productive and as a result earn higher wages. In order to preserve the dignity of the American workplace, the government should enact legislation banning imports of low-wage Asian clothing."

a. Which parts of this quote are positive statements? Which parts are normative statements?

b. Is the policy that is being advocated consistent with the preceding statements about the wages and productivities of American and Asian workers?

c. Would such a policy make some Americans better off without making any other Americans worse off? That is, would this policy be efficient from the viewpoint of all Americans?

d. Would Asian workers earning low wages benefit from or be hurt by such a policy?

5. Evaluate the following statement: "It is easier to build an economic model that accurately reflects events that have already occurred than to build an economic model to forecast future events." Do you think this is true or not? Why? What does this imply about the difficulties of building good economic models?

6. Economists who work for the government are often called on to make policy recommendations. Why do you think it is important for the public to be able to differentiate normative statements from positive statements in these recommendations?

PROBLEMS

1. Two important industries on the island of Bermuda are fishing and tourism. According to data from the Food and Agriculture Organization of the United Nations and the Bermuda Department of Statistics, in 2014 the 315 registered fishermen in Bermuda caught 497 metric tons of marine fish. And the 2,446 people employed by hotels produced 580,209 hotel stays (measured by the number of visitor arrivals). Suppose that this production point is efficient in production. Assume also that the opportunity cost of 1 additional metric ton of fish is 2,000 hotel stays and that this opportunity cost is constant (the opportunity cost does not change).

a. If all 315 registered fishermen were to be employed by hotels (in addition to the 2,446 people already working in hotels), how many hotel stays could Bermuda produce?

b. If all 2,446 hotel employees were to become fishermen (in addition to the 315 fishermen already working in the fishing industry), how many metric tons of fish could Bermuda produce?

c. Draw a production possibility frontier for Bermuda, with fish on the horizontal axis and hotel stays on the vertical axis, and label Bermuda's actual production point for 2014.

2. According to data from the U.S. Department of Agriculture's National Agricultural Statistics Service, 124 million acres of land in the United States were used for wheat or corn farming in a recent year. Of those 124 million acres, farmers used 50 million acres to grow 2.158 billion bushels of wheat and 74 million acres to grow 11.807 billion bushels of corn. Suppose that U.S. wheat and corn farming is efficient in production. At that production point, the opportunity cost of producing 1 additional bushel of wheat is 1.7 fewer bushels of corn. However, because farmers have increasing opportunity costs, additional bushels of wheat have an opportunity cost greater than 1.7 bushels of corn. For each of the following production points, decide whether that production point is (i) feasible and efficient in production, (ii) feasible but not efficient in production, (iii) not feasible, or (iv) unclear as to whether or not it is feasible.

a. Farmers use 40 million acres of land to produce 1.8 billion bushels of wheat, and they use 60 million acres of land to produce 9 billion bushels of corn. The remaining 24 million acres are left unused.

b. From their original production point, farmers transfer 40 million acres of land from corn to wheat production. They now produce 3.158 billion bushels of wheat and 10.107 bushels of corn.

c. Farmers reduce their production of wheat to 2 billion bushels and increase their production of corn to 12.044 billion bushels. Along the production possibility frontier, the opportunity cost of going from 11.807 billion bushels of corn to 12.044 billion bushels of corn is 0.666 bushel of wheat per bushel of corn.

3. In the ancient country of Roma, only two goods, spaghetti and meatballs, are produced. There are two tribes in Roma, the Tivoli and the Frivoli. By themselves, the Tivoli each month can produce either 30 pounds of spaghetti and no meatballs, or 50 pounds of meatballs and no spaghetti, or any combination in between. The Frivoli, by themselves, each month can produce 40 pounds of spaghetti and no meatballs, or 30 pounds of meatballs and no spaghetti, or any combination in between.

   a. Assume that all production possibility frontiers are straight lines. Draw one diagram showing the monthly production possibility frontier for the Tivoli and another showing the monthly production possibility frontier for the Frivoli. Show how you calculated them.

   b. Which tribe has the comparative advantage in spaghetti production? In meatball production?

   In A.D. 100 the Frivoli discover a new technique for making meatballs that doubles the quantity of meatballs they can produce each month.

   c. Draw the new monthly production possibility frontier for the Frivoli.

   d. After the innovation, which tribe now has an absolute advantage in producing meatballs? In producing spaghetti? Which has the comparative advantage in meatball production? In spaghetti production?

4. One July, the United States sold aircraft worth $1 billion to China and bought aircraft worth only $19,000 from China. During the same month, however, the United States bought $83 million worth of men's pants, shorts, and jeans from China but sold only $8,000 worth of pants, shorts, and jeans to China. Using what you have learned about how trade is determined by comparative advantage, answer the following questions.

   a. Which country has the comparative advantage in aircraft production? In production of pants, shorts, and jeans?

   b. Can you determine which country has the absolute advantage in aircraft production? In production of pants, shorts, and jeans?

5. You are in charge of allocating residents to your dormitory's baseball and basketball teams. You are down to the last four people, two of whom must be allocated to baseball and two to basketball. The accompanying table gives each person's batting average and free-throw average.

Name	Batting average	Free-throw average
Taylor	70%	60%
Nico	50%	50%
Annie	10%	30%
Ryan	80%	70%

   a. Explain how you would use the concept of comparative advantage to allocate the players. Begin by establishing each player's opportunity cost of free throws in terms of batting average.

   b. Why is it likely that the other basketball players will be unhappy about this arrangement but the other baseball players will be satisfied? Nonetheless, why would an economist say that this is an efficient way to allocate players for your dorm's sports teams?

6. Your roommate plays loud music most of the time; you, however, would prefer more peace and quiet. You suggest that she buy some headphones. She responds that although she would be happy to use headphones, she has many other things that she would prefer to spend her money on right now. You discuss this situation with a friend who is an economics major. The following exchange takes place:

   Friend: How much would it cost to buy headphones?
   You: $15.
   Friend: How much do you value having some peace and quiet for the rest of the semester?
   You: $30.
   Friend: It is efficient for you to buy the headphones and give them to your roommate. You gain more than you lose; the benefit exceeds the cost. You should do that.
   You: It just isn't fair that I have to pay for the headphones when I'm not the one making the noise.

   a. Which parts of this conversation contain positive statements and which parts contain normative statements?

   b. Construct an argument supporting your viewpoint that your roommate should be the one to change her behavior. Similarly, construct an argument from the viewpoint of your roommate that you should be the one to buy the headphones. If your dormitory has a policy that gives residents the unlimited right to play music, whose argument is likely to win? If your dormitory has a rule that a person must stop playing music whenever a roommate complains, whose argument is likely to win?

7. Are the following statements true or false? Explain your answers.

   a. "When people must pay higher taxes on their wage earnings, it reduces their incentive to work" is a positive statement.

   b. "We should lower taxes to encourage more work" is a positive statement.

   c. Economics cannot always be used to completely decide what society ought to do.

   d. "The system of public education in this country generates greater benefits to society than the cost of running the system" is a normative statement.

   e. All disagreements among economists are generated by the media.

8. The mayor of Gotham City, worried about a potential epidemic of deadly influenza this winter, asks an economic

adviser the following series of questions. Determine whether a question requires the economic adviser to make a positive assessment or a normative assessment.

a. How much vaccine will be in stock in the city by the end of November?

b. If we offer to pay 10% more per dose to the pharmaceutical companies providing the vaccines, will they provide additional doses?

c. If there is a shortage of vaccine in the city, whom should we vaccinate first—the elderly or the very young? (Assume that a person from one group has an equal likelihood of dying from influenza as a person from the other group.)

d. If the city charges $25 per shot, how many people will pay?

e. If the city charges $25 per shot, it will make a profit of $10 per shot, money that can go to pay for inoculating poor people. Should the city engage in such a scheme?

WORK IT OUT

9. Atlantis is a small, isolated island in the South Atlantic. The inhabitants grow potatoes and catch fish. The accompanying table shows the maximum annual output combinations of potatoes and fish that can be produced. Obviously, given their limited resources and available technology, as they use more of their resources for potato production, there are fewer resources available for catching fish.

Maximum annual output options	Quantity of potatoes (pounds)	Quantity of fish (pounds)
A	1,000	0
B	800	300
C	600	500
D	400	600
E	200	650
F	0	675

a. Draw a production possibility frontier with potatoes on the horizontal axis and fish on the vertical axis illustrating these options, showing points *A–F.*

b. Can Atlantis produce 500 pounds of fish and 800 pounds of potatoes? Explain. Where would this point lie relative to the production possibility frontier?

c. What is the opportunity cost of increasing the annual output of potatoes from 600 to 800 pounds?

d. What is the opportunity cost of increasing the annual output of potatoes from 200 to 400 pounds?

e. Can you explain why the answers to parts c and d are not the same? What does this imply about the slope of the production possibility frontier? ∎

Graphs in Economics

Getting the Picture

When reading about economics in the *Wall Street Journal* or in your economics textbook, you will see many graphs. Visual images can make it much easier to understand verbal descriptions, numerical information, or ideas. In economics, graphs are the type of visual image used to facilitate understanding. So, you need to be familiar with how to interpret and construct these visual aids. This appendix explains how to do this.

Graphs, Variables, and Economic Models

One reason to attend college is that a bachelor's degree provides access to higher paying jobs. Additional degrees, such as MBAs or law degrees, increase earnings even more. If you were to read an article about the relationship between educational attainment and income, you would probably see a graph showing the income levels for workers with different amounts of education. And this graph would depict the idea that, in general, more education increases income.

This graph, like most of those in economics, would depict the relationship between two economic variables. A **variable** is a quantity that can take on more than one value, such as the number of years of education a person has, the price of a can of soda, or a household's income.

As you learned in Chapter 2, economic analysis relies heavily on *models*, simplified descriptions of real situations. Most economic models describe the relationship between two variables, simplified by holding constant other variables that may affect the relationship.

For example, an economic model might describe the relationship between the price of a can of soda and the number of cans of soda that consumers will buy, assuming that everything else affecting consumers' purchases of soda stays constant. This type of model can be described mathematically or verbally, but illustrating the relationship in a graph makes it easier to understand, as you'll see next.

How Graphs Work

Most graphs in economics are based on a grid built around two perpendicular lines that show the values of two variables, helping you visualize the relationship between them. Let's see how this works.

Two-Variable Graphs

Figure 2A-1 shows a typical two-variable graph. It illustrates the data in the accompanying table on outside temperature and the number of sodas a typical vendor can expect to sell at a baseball stadium during one game. The first column shows the values of outside temperature (the first variable) and the second column shows the values of the number of sodas sold (the second variable). Five combinations or pairs of the two variables are shown, each denoted by *A* through *E* in the third column.

Now let's turn to graphing the data in this table. In any two-variable graph, one variable is called the *x*-variable and the other is called the *y*-variable. Here we have

A quantity that can take on more than one value is called a **variable**.

FIGURE 2A-1 Plotting Points on a Two-Variable Graph

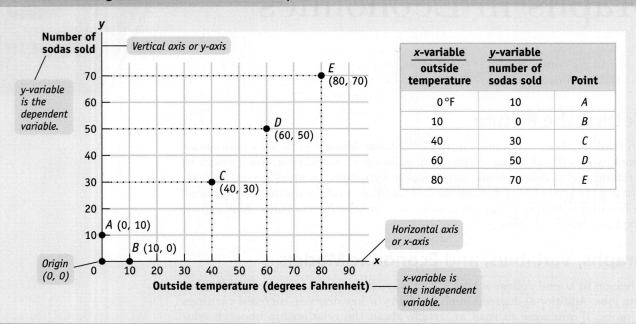

The data from the table are plotted where outside temperature (the independent variable) is measured along the horizontal axis and number of sodas sold (the dependent variable) is measured along the vertical axis. Each of the five combinations of temperature and sodas sold is represented by a point: A, B, C, D, and E. Each point in the graph is identified by a pair of values. For example, point C corresponds to the pair (40, 30)—an outside temperature of 40°F (the value of the x-variable) and 30 sodas sold (the value of the y-variable).

The line along which values of the x-variable are measured is called the **horizontal axis** or **x-axis.** The line along which values of the y-variable are measured is called the **vertical axis** or **y-axis.** The point where the axes of a two-variable graph meet is the **origin.**

A **causal relationship** exists between two variables when the value taken by one variable directly influences or determines the value taken by the other variable. In a causal relationship, the determining variable is called the **independent variable;** the variable it determines is called the **dependent variable.**

made outside temperature the x-variable and number of sodas sold the y-variable. The solid horizontal line in the graph is called the **horizontal axis** or **x-axis,** and values of the x-variable—outside temperature—are measured along it. Similarly, the solid vertical line in the graph is called the **vertical axis** or **y-axis,** and values of the y-variable—number of sodas sold—are measured along it.

At the **origin,** the point where the two axes meet, each variable is equal to zero. As you move rightward from the origin along the x-axis, values of the x-variable are positive and increasing. As you move up from the origin along the y-axis, values of the y-variable are positive and increasing.

You can plot each of the five points A through E on this graph by using a pair of numbers—the values that the x-variable and the y-variable take on for a given point. In Figure 2A-1, at point C, the x-variable takes on the value 40 and the y-variable takes on the value 30. You plot point C by drawing a line straight up from 40 on the x-axis and a horizontal line across from 30 on the y-axis. We write point C as (40, 30). We write the origin as (0, 0).

Looking at point A and point B in Figure 2A-1, you can see that when one of the variables for a point has a value of zero, it will lie on one of the axes. If the value of the x-variable is zero, the point will lie on the vertical axis, like point A. If the value of the y-variable is zero, the point will lie on the horizontal axis, like point B.

Most graphs that depict relationships between two economic variables represent a **causal relationship,** a relationship in which the value taken by one variable directly influences or determines the value taken by the other variable. In a causal relationship, the determining variable is called the **independent variable;** the variable it determines is called the **dependent variable.** In our example of soda sales, the outside temperature is the independent variable.

It directly influences the number of sodas that are sold, the dependent variable in this case.

By convention, we put the independent variable on the horizontal axis and the dependent variable on the vertical axis. Figure 2A-1 is constructed consistent with this convention; the independent variable (outside temperature) is on the horizontal axis and the dependent variable (number of sodas sold) is on the vertical axis.

An important exception to this convention is in graphs showing the economic relationship between the price of a product and quantity of the product: although price is generally the independent variable that determines quantity, it is always measured on the vertical axis.

> A **curve** is a line on a graph that depicts a relationship between two variables. It may be either a straight line or a curved line. If the curve is a straight line, the variables have a **linear relationship.** If the curve is not a straight line, the variables have a **nonlinear relationship.**

Curves on a Graph

Panel (a) of Figure 2A-2 contains some of the same information as Figure 2A-1, with a line drawn through the points *B, C, D,* and *E.* Such a line on a graph is called a **curve,** regardless of whether it is a straight line or a curved line. If the curve that shows the relationship between two variables is a straight line, or linear, the variables have a **linear relationship.** When the curve is not a straight line, or nonlinear, the variables have a **nonlinear relationship.**

A point on a curve indicates the value of the *y*-variable for a specific value of the *x*-variable. For example, point *D* indicates that at a temperature of 60°F, a vendor can expect to sell 50 sodas. The shape and orientation of a curve reveal the general nature of the relationship between the two variables. The upward tilt of the curve in panel (a) of Figure 2A-2 means that vendors can expect to sell more sodas at higher outside temperatures.

FIGURE 2A-2 Drawing Curves

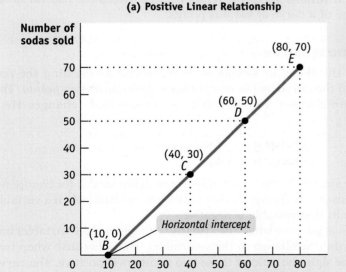

(a) Positive Linear Relationship

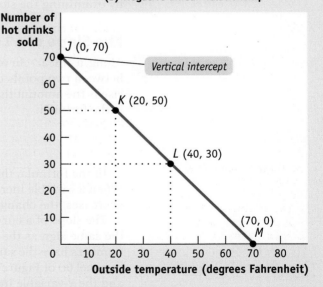

(b) Negative Linear Relationship

The curve in panel (a) illustrates the relationship between the two variables, outside temperature and number of sodas sold. The two variables have a positive linear relationship: positive because the curve has an upward tilt, and linear because it is a straight line. It implies that an increase in the *x*-variable (outside temperature) leads to an increase in the *y*-variable (number of sodas sold). The curve in panel (b) is also a straight line, but it tilts downward. The two variables

here, outside temperature and number of hot drinks sold, have a negative linear relationship: an increase in the *x*-variable (outside temperature) leads to a decrease in the *y*-variable (number of hot drinks sold). The curve in panel (a) has a horizontal intercept at point *B,* where it hits the horizontal axis. The curve in panel (b) has a vertical intercept at point *J,* where it hits the vertical axis, and a horizontal intercept at point *M,* where it hits the horizontal axis.

Two variables have a **positive relationship** when an increase in the value of one variable is associated with an increase in the value of the other variable. It is illustrated by a curve that slopes upward from left to right.

Two variables have a **negative relationship** when an increase in the value of one variable is associated with a decrease in the value of the other variable. It is illustrated by a curve that slopes downward from left to right.

The **horizontal intercept** of a curve is the point at which it hits the horizontal axis; it indicates the value of the *x*-variable when the value of the *y*-variable is zero.

The **vertical intercept** of a curve is the point at which it hits the vertical axis; it shows the value of the *y*-variable when the value of the *x*-variable is zero.

The **slope** of a line or curve is a measure of how steep it is. The slope of a line is measured by "rise over run"—the change in the *y*-variable between two points on the line divided by the change in the *x*-variable between those same two points.

When variables are related this way—that is, when an increase in one variable is associated with an increase in the other variable—the variables are said to have a **positive relationship.** It is illustrated by a curve that slopes upward from left to right. Because this curve is also linear, the relationship between outside temperature and number of sodas sold illustrated by the curve in panel (a) of Figure 2A-2 is a positive linear relationship.

When an increase in one variable is associated with a decrease in the other variable, the two variables are said to have a **negative relationship.** It is illustrated by a curve that slopes downward from left to right, like the curve in panel (b) of Figure 2A-2. Because this curve is also linear, the relationship it depicts is a negative linear relationship. Two variables that might have such a relationship are the outside temperature and the number of hot drinks a vendor can expect to sell at a baseball stadium.

Return for a moment to the curve in panel (a) of Figure 2A-2 and you can see that it hits the horizontal axis at point *B*. This point, known as the **horizontal intercept,** shows the value of the *x*-variable when the value of the *y*-variable is zero. In panel (b) of Figure 2A-2, the curve hits the vertical axis at point *J*. This point, called the **vertical intercept,** indicates the value of the *y*-variable when the value of the *x*-variable is zero.

A Key Concept: The Slope of a Curve

The **slope** of a curve is a measure of how steep it is and indicates how sensitive the *y*-variable is to a change in the *x*-variable. In our example of outside temperature and the number of cans of soda a vendor can expect to sell, the slope of the curve would indicate how many more cans of soda the vendor could expect to sell with each 1 degree increase in temperature. Interpreted this way, the slope gives meaningful information. Even without numbers for *x* and *y,* it is possible to arrive at important conclusions about the relationship between the two variables by examining the slope of a curve at various points.

The Slope of a Linear Curve

Along a linear curve the slope, or steepness, is measured by dividing the *rise* between two points on the curve by the *run* between those same two points. The rise is the amount that *y* changes, and the run is the amount that *x* changes. Here is the formula:

$$\frac{\text{Change in } y}{\text{Change in } x} = \frac{\Delta y}{\Delta x} = \text{Slope}$$

In the formula, the symbol Δ (the Greek uppercase delta) stands for *change in*. When a variable increases, the change in that variable is positive; when a variable decreases, the change in that variable is negative.

The slope of a curve is positive when the rise (the change in the *y*-variable) has the same sign as the run (the change in the *x*-variable). That's because when two numbers have the same sign, the ratio of those two numbers is positive. The curve in panel (a) of Figure 2A-2 has a positive slope: along the curve, both the *y*-variable and the *x*-variable increase.

The slope of a curve is negative when the rise and the run have different signs. That's because when two numbers have different signs, the ratio of those two numbers is negative. The curve in panel (b) of Figure 2A-2 has a negative slope: along the curve, an increase in the *x*-variable is associated with a decrease in the *y*-variable.

Figure 2A-3 illustrates how to calculate the slope of a linear curve. Let's focus first on panel (a). From point *A* to point *B* the value of the *y*-variable changes from

FIGURE 2A-3 Calculating the Slope

(a) Negative Constant Slope

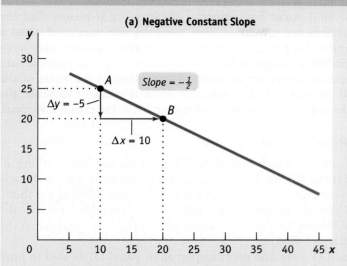

(b) Positive Constant Slope

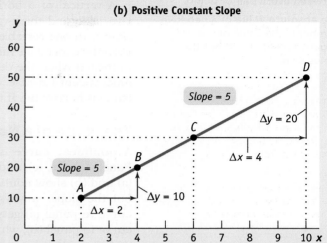

Panels (a) and (b) show two linear curves. Between points A and B on the curve in panel (a), the change in y (the rise) is −5 and the change in x (the run) is 10. So the slope from A to B is $\frac{\Delta y}{\Delta x} = \frac{-5}{10} = -\frac{1}{2} = -0.5$, where the negative sign indicates that the curve is downward sloping. In panel (b), the curve has a slope from A to B of $\frac{\Delta y}{\Delta x} = \frac{10}{2} = 5$. The slope from C to D is $\frac{\Delta y}{\Delta x} = \frac{20}{4} = 5$. The slope is positive, indicating that the curve is upward sloping. Furthermore, the slope between A and B is the same as the slope between C and D, making this a linear curve. The slope of a linear curve is constant: it is the same regardless of where it is measured along the curve.

25 to 20 and the value of the x-variable changes from 10 to 20. So the slope of the line between these two points is:

$$\frac{\text{Change in } y}{\text{Change in } x} = \frac{\Delta y}{\Delta x} = \frac{-5}{10} = -\frac{1}{2} = -0.5$$

Because a straight line is equally steep at all points, the slope of a straight line is the same at all points. In other words, a straight line has a constant slope. You can check this by calculating the slope of the linear curve between points A and B and between points C and D in panel (b) of Figure 2A-3.

Between A and B: $\qquad\qquad \dfrac{\Delta y}{\Delta x} = \dfrac{10}{2} = 5$

Between C and D: $\qquad\qquad \dfrac{\Delta y}{\Delta x} = \dfrac{20}{4} = 5$

Horizontal and Vertical Curves and Their Slopes

When a curve is horizontal, the value of the y-variable along that curve never changes—it is constant. Everywhere along the curve, the change in y is zero. Now, zero divided by any number is zero. So, regardless of the value of the change in x, the slope of a horizontal curve is always zero.

If a curve is vertical, the value of the x-variable along the curve never changes—it is constant. Everywhere along the curve, the change in x is zero. This means that the slope of a vertical curve is a ratio with zero in the denominator.

A **nonlinear curve** is one in which the slope is not the same between every pair of points.

The **absolute value** of a negative number is the value of the negative number without the minus sign.

A ratio with zero in the denominator is equal to infinity—that is, an infinitely large number. So the slope of a vertical curve is equal to infinity.

A vertical or a horizontal curve has a special implication: it means that the *x*-variable and the *y*-variable are unrelated. Two variables are unrelated when a change in one variable (the independent variable) has no effect on the other variable (the dependent variable). Or to put it a slightly different way, two variables are unrelated when the dependent variable is constant regardless of the value of the independent variable. If, as is usual, the *y*-variable is the dependent variable, the curve is horizontal. If the dependent variable is the *x*-variable, the curve is vertical.

The Slope of a Nonlinear Curve

A **nonlinear curve** is one in which the slope changes as you move along it. Panels (a), (b), (c), and (d) of Figure 2A-4 show various nonlinear curves. Panels (a) and (b) show nonlinear curves whose slopes change as you move along them, but the slopes always remain positive. Although both curves tilt upward, the curve in panel (a) gets steeper as you move from left to right in contrast to the curve in panel (b), which gets flatter.

A curve that is upward sloping and gets steeper, as in panel (a), is said to have *positive increasing* slope. A curve that is upward sloping but gets flatter, as in panel (b), is said to have *positive decreasing* slope.

When we calculate the slope along these nonlinear curves, we obtain different values for the slope at different points. How the slope changes along the curve determines the curve's shape. For example, in panel (a) of Figure 2A-4, the slope of the curve is a positive number that steadily increases as you move from left to right, whereas in panel (b), the slope is a positive number that steadily decreases.

The slopes of the curves in panels (c) and (d) are negative numbers. Economists often prefer to express a negative number as its **absolute value,** which is the value of the negative number without the minus sign. In general, we denote the absolute value of a number by two parallel bars around the number; for example, the absolute value of −4 is written as $|-4| = 4$.

In panel (c), the absolute value of the slope steadily increases as you move from left to right. The curve therefore has *negative increasing* slope. And in panel (d), the absolute value of the slope of the curve steadily decreases along the curve. This curve therefore has *negative decreasing* slope.

Calculating the Slope Along a Nonlinear Curve

We've just seen that along a nonlinear curve, the value of the slope depends on where you are on that curve. So how do you calculate the slope of a nonlinear curve? We will focus on two methods: the *arc method* and the *point method*.

The Arc Method of Calculating the Slope   An arc of a curve is some piece or segment of that curve. For example, panel (a) of Figure 2A-4 shows an arc consisting of the segment of the curve between points *A* and *B*. To calculate the slope along a nonlinear curve using the arc method, you draw a straight line between the two endpoints of the arc. The slope of that straight line is a measure of the average slope of the curve between those two endpoints.

You can see from panel (a) of Figure 2A-4 that the straight line drawn between points *A* and *B* increases along the *x*-axis from 6 to 10 (so that $\Delta x = 4$) as it increases along the *y*-axis from 10 to 20 (so that $\Delta y = 10$). Therefore the slope of the straight line connecting points *A* and *B* is:

$$\frac{\Delta y}{\Delta x} = \frac{10}{4} = 2.5$$

This means that the average slope of the curve between points *A* and *B* is 2.5.

FIGURE 2A-4 Nonlinear Curves

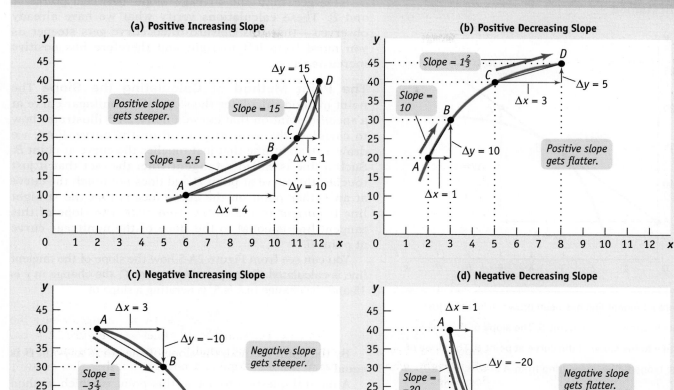

In panel (a) the slope of the curve from A to B is $\frac{y}{x} = \frac{10}{4} = 2.5$, and from C to D it is $\frac{\Delta y}{\Delta x} = \frac{15}{1} = 15$. The slope is positive and increasing; the curve gets steeper as you move to the right. In panel (b) the slope of the curve from A to B is $\frac{\Delta y}{\Delta x} = \frac{10}{1} = 10$, and from C to D it is $\frac{\Delta y}{\Delta x} = \frac{5}{3} = 1\frac{2}{3}$. The slope is positive and decreasing; the curve gets flatter as you move to the right. In panel (c) the slope from A to B is $\frac{\Delta y}{\Delta x} = \frac{-10}{3} = -3\frac{1}{3}$, and from C to D it is $\frac{\Delta y}{\Delta x} = \frac{-15}{1} = -15$. The slope is negative and increasing; the curve gets steeper as you move to the right. And in panel (d) the slope from A to B is $\frac{\Delta y}{\Delta x} = \frac{-20}{1} = -20$, and from C to D it is $\frac{\Delta y}{\Delta x} = \frac{-5}{3} = -1\frac{2}{3}$. The slope is negative and decreasing; the curve gets flatter as you move to the right. The slope in each case has been calculated by using the arc method—that is, by drawing a straight line connecting two points along a curve. The average slope between those two points is equal to the slope of the straight line between those two points.

Now consider the arc on the same curve between points C and D. A straight line drawn through these two points increases along the x-axis from 11 to 12 ($\Delta x = 1$) as it increases along the y-axis from 25 to 40 ($\Delta y = 15$). So the average slope between points C and D is:

$$\frac{\Delta y}{\Delta x} = \frac{15}{1} = 15$$

FIGURE 2A-5 Calculating the Slope Using the Point Method

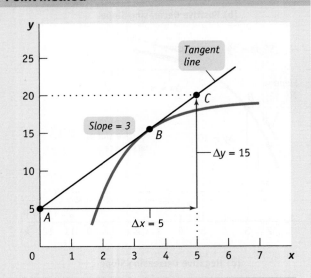

Here a tangent line has been drawn, a line that just touches the curve at point B. The slope of this line is equal to the slope of the curve at point B. The slope of the tangent line, measuring from A to C, is $\frac{\Delta y}{\Delta x} = \frac{15}{5} = 3$.

Therefore the average slope between points C and D is larger than the average slope between points A and B. These calculations verify what we have already observed—that this upward-tilted curve gets steeper as you move from left to right and therefore has positive increasing slope.

The Point Method of Calculating the Slope The point method calculates the slope of a nonlinear curve at a specific point on that curve. Figure 2A-5 illustrates how to calculate the slope at point B on the curve. First, we draw a straight line that just touches the curve at point B. Such a line is called a **tangent line:** the fact that it just touches the curve at point B and does not touch the curve at any other point on the curve means that the straight line is *tangent* to the curve at point B. The slope of this tangent line is equal to the slope of the nonlinear curve at point B.

You can see from Figure 2A-5 how the slope of the tangent line is calculated. From point A to point C, the change in y is 15 and the change in x is 5, generating a slope of

$$\frac{\Delta y}{\Delta x} = \frac{15}{5} = 3$$

By the point method, the slope of the curve at point B is equal to 3.

A natural question to ask at this point is which method should I use—the arc method or the point method—in calculating the slope of a nonlinear curve? The answer depends on the curve itself and the data used to construct it.

Use the arc method when you don't have enough information to be able to draw a smooth curve. For example, suppose that in panel (a) of Figure 2A-4 you have only the data represented by points A, C, and D and don't have the data represented by point B or any of the rest of the curve. Clearly, then, you can't use the point method to calculate the slope at point B; you would have to use the arc method to approximate the slope of the curve in this area by drawing a straight line between points A and C.

But if you have sufficient data to draw the smooth curve shown in panel (a) of Figure 2A-4, then you could use the point method to calculate the slope at point B—and at every other point along the curve as well.

Maximum and Minimum Points

The slope of a nonlinear curve can change from positive to negative or vice versa. When the slope of a curve changes from positive to negative, it creates what is called a *maximum* point of the curve. When the slope of a curve changes from negative to positive, it creates a *minimum* point.

Panel (a) of Figure 2A-6 illustrates a curve in which the slope changes from positive to negative as you move from left to right. When x is between 0 and 50, the slope of the curve is positive. At x equal to 50, the curve attains its highest point—the largest value of y along the curve. This point is called the **maximum** of the curve. When x exceeds 50, the slope becomes negative as the curve turns downward. Many important curves in economics, such as the curve that represents how the profit of a firm changes as it produces more output, are hill-shaped like this.

In contrast, the curve shown in panel (b) of Figure 2A-6 is U-shaped: it has a slope that changes from negative to positive. At x equal to 50, the curve reaches its lowest point—the smallest value of y along the curve. This point is called the

A **tangent line** is a straight line that just touches, or is tangent to, a nonlinear curve at a particular point. The slope of the tangent line is equal to the slope of the nonlinear curve at that point.

A nonlinear curve may have a **maximum** point, the highest point along the curve. At the maximum, the slope of the curve changes from positive to negative.

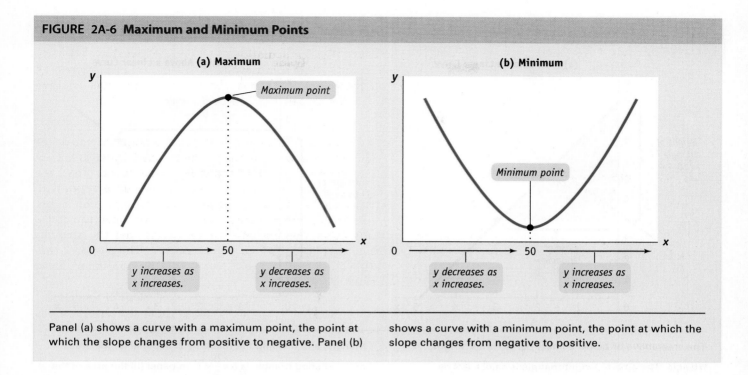

FIGURE 2A-6 Maximum and Minimum Points

(a) Maximum

Maximum point

y increases as x increases.

y decreases as x increases.

(b) Minimum

Minimum point

y decreases as x increases.

y increases as x increases.

Panel (a) shows a curve with a maximum point, the point at which the slope changes from positive to negative. Panel (b) shows a curve with a minimum point, the point at which the slope changes from negative to positive.

minimum of the curve. Various important curves in economics are U-shaped like this.

Calculating the Area Below or Above a Curve

It is useful to know how to measure the size of the area below or above a curve. For the sake of simplicity, we'll only calculate the area below or above a linear curve.

How large is the shaded area below the linear curve in panel (a) of Figure 2A-7? First note that this area has the shape of a right triangle. A right triangle is a triangle that has two sides that make a right angle with each other. We will refer to one of these sides as the *height* of the triangle and the other side as the *base* of the triangle. For our purposes, it doesn't matter which of these two sides we refer to as the base and which as the height.

Calculating the area of a right triangle is straightforward: multiply the height of the triangle by the base of the triangle, and divide the result by 2. The height of the triangle in panel (a) of Figure 2A-7 is $10 - 4 = 6$. And the base of the triangle is $3 - 0 = 3$. So the area of that triangle is:

$$\frac{6 \times 3}{2} = 9$$

How about the shaded area above the linear curve in panel (b) of Figure 2A-7? We can use the same formula to calculate the area of this right triangle. The height of the triangle is $8 - 2 = 6$. And the base of the triangle is $4 - 0 = 4$. So the area of that triangle is:

$$\frac{6 \times 4}{2} = 12$$

Graphs That Depict Numerical Information

Graphs are also a convenient way to summarize and display data without assuming some underlying causal relationship. Graphs that simply display numerical information are called *numerical graphs*.

A nonlinear curve may have a **minimum** point, the lowest point along the curve. At the minimum, the slope of the curve changes from negative to positive.

FIGURE 2A-7 Calculating the Area Below and Above a Linear Curve

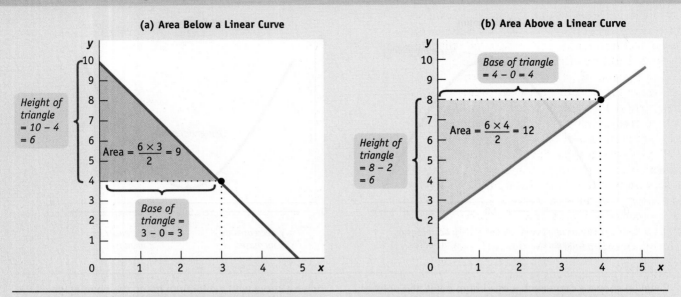

The area above or below a linear curve forms a right triangle. The area of a right triangle is calculated by multiplying the height of the triangle by the base of the triangle, and dividing the result by 2. In panel (a) the area of the shaded triangle is $6 \times \dfrac{3}{2} = 9$. In panel (b) the area of the shaded triangle is $6 \times \dfrac{4}{2} = 12$.

Here we will consider four types of numerical graphs: *time-series graphs, scatter diagrams, pie charts,* and *bar graphs*. These are widely used to display real, empirical data about different economic variables because they often help economists and policy makers identify patterns or trends in the economy. But it's important to be aware of both the usefulness and the limitations of numerical graphs to avoid misinterpreting them or drawing unwarranted conclusions from them.

Types of Numerical Graphs

You have probably seen graphs that show what has happened over time to economic variables such as the unemployment rate or stock prices. A **time-series graph** has successive dates on the horizontal axis and the values of a variable that occurred on those dates on the vertical axis.

For example, Figure 2A-8 shows real gross domestic product (GDP) per capita—a rough measure of a country's standard of living—in the United States from 1950 to 2019. A line connecting the points that correspond to real GDP per capita for each calendar quarter during those years gives a clear idea of the overall trend in the standard of living over these years.

Figure 2A-9 is an example of a different kind of numerical graph. It represents information from a sample of 180 countries on the standard of living, again measured by GDP per capita, and the amount of carbon emissions per capita, a measure of environmental pollution. Each point here indicates an average resident's standard of living and his or her annual carbon emissions for a given country.

The points lying in the upper right of the graph, which show combinations of a high standard of living and high carbon emissions, represent economically advanced countries such as the United States. (The country with the highest

A **time-series graph** has dates on the horizontal axis and values of a variable that occurred on those dates on the vertical axis.

carbon emissions, at the top of the graph, is Qatar.) Points lying in the bottom left of the graph, which show combinations of a low standard of living and low carbon emissions, represent economically less advanced countries such as Afghanistan and Sierra Leone.

The pattern of points indicates that there is a positive relationship between living standard and carbon emissions per capita: on the whole, people create more pollution in countries with a higher standard of living.

This type of graph is called a **scatter diagram,** in which each point corresponds to an actual observation of the x-variable and the y-variable. In scatter diagrams, a curve is typically fitted to the scatter of points; that is, a curve is drawn that approximates as closely as possible the general relationship between the variables. As you can see, the fitted line in Figure 2A-9 is upward sloping, indicating the underlying positive relationship between the two variables. Scatter diagrams are often used to show how a general relationship can be inferred from a set of data.

A **pie chart** shows the share of a total amount that is accounted for by various components, usually expressed in percentages. For example, Figure 2A-10 is a pie chart that depicts the education levels of workers who in 2018 were paid the federal minimum wage or less. As you can see, the majority of workers paid at or below the minimum wage had no college degree. Only 14% of workers who were paid at or below the minimum wage had a bachelor's degree or higher.

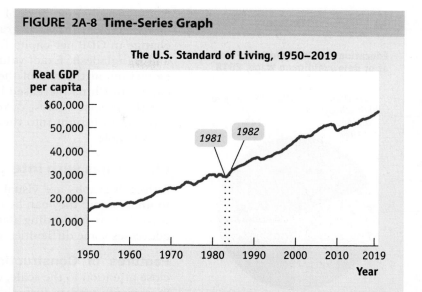

FIGURE 2A-8 Time-Series Graph

The U.S. Standard of Living, 1950–2019

Time-series graphs show successive dates on the x-axis and values for a variable on the y-axis. This time-series graph shows real gross domestic product per capita, a measure of a country's standard of living, in the United States from 1950 to early 2019.
Data from: The Federal Reserve Bank of St. Louis.

A **scatter diagram** shows points that correspond to actual observations of the x- and y-variables. A curve is usually fitted to the scatter of points.

A **pie chart** shows how some total is divided among its components, usually expressed in percentages.

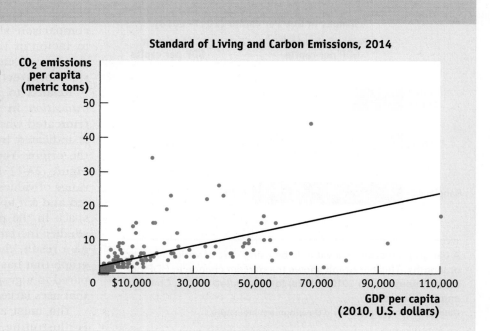

FIGURE 2A-9 Scatter Diagram

In a scatter diagram, each point represents the corresponding values of the x- and y-variables for a given observation. Here, each point indicates the GDP per capita and the amount of carbon dioxide emissions per capita for a given country for a sample of 180 countries. The upward-sloping fitted line here is the best approximation of the general relationship between the two variables.
Data from: World Development Indicators.

Standard of Living and Carbon Emissions, 2014

FIGURE 2A-10 Pie Chart

FIGURE 2A-10 Pie Chart

Education Levels of Workers Paid at or Below Minimum Wage, 2018

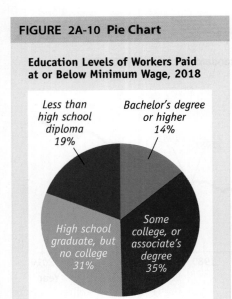

A pie chart shows the percentages of a total amount that can be attributed to various components. This pie chart shows the percentages of workers with given education levels who were paid at or below the federal minimum wage in 2018. (Numbers may not add to 100 due to rounding.)
Data from: Bureau of Labor Statistics.

Bar graphs use bars of various heights or lengths to indicate values of a variable. In the bar graph in Figure 2A-11, the bars show the percent change in GDP per capita from 2017 to 2018 for the United States, China, and Bangladesh. Exact values of the variable that is being measured may be written at the end of the bar, as in this figure. For instance, GDP per capita for China increased by 6.1% between 2017 and 2018. But even without the precise values, comparing the heights or lengths of the bars can give useful insight into the relative magnitudes of the different values of the variable.

Challenges with Interpreting Numerical Graphs

Although graphs are visual images that make ideas or information easier to understand, they can be constructed (intentionally or unintentionally) in ways that are misleading and can lead to inaccurate conclusions. This section addresses some difficulties you may have when you are analyzing graphs.

Features of Construction When evaluating a numerical graph, pay close attention to the scale, or size of increments, shown on the axes. Small increments tend to visually exaggerate changes in the variables, whereas large increments tend to visually diminish them. So the scale used in construction of a graph can influence your interpretation of the significance of the changes it illustrates—perhaps in an unwarranted way.

Take, for example, Figure 2A-12, which shows real GDP per capita in the United States from 1981 to 1982 using increments of $500. You can see that real GDP per capita fell from $30,316 to $29,186. A decrease, sure, but is it as enormous as the scale chosen for the vertical axis makes it seem? It is not.

If you reexamine Figure 2A-8, which shows real GDP per capita in the United States from 1950 to 2019, you will see that it includes the same data shown in Figure 2A-12. But, Figure 2A-8 is constructed with a scale having increments of $10,000 rather than $500. From it you can see that the fall in real GDP per capita from 1981 to 1982 was, in fact, relatively insignificant.

In fact, the story of real GDP per capita—a measure of the standard of living—in the United States is mostly a story of ups, not downs. This comparison shows that if you are not careful to factor in the choice of scale in interpreting graphs, you can arrive at very different, and possibly incorrect, conclusions.

Related to the choice of scale is the use of *truncation* in constructing a graph. An axis is **truncated** when part of the range is omitted. This is indicated by two slashes (//) in the axis near the origin. You can see that the vertical axis of Figure 2A-12 has been truncated—some of the range of values from 0 to $29,000 have been omitted and a // appears in the axis. Truncation saves space in the presentation of a graph and allows smaller increments to be used in constructing it. As a result, changes in the variable depicted on a graph that has been truncated appear larger compared to a graph that has not been truncated and that uses larger increments.

You must also consider exactly what a graph is illustrating. For example, in Figure 2A-11, you

FIGURE 2A-11 Bar Graph

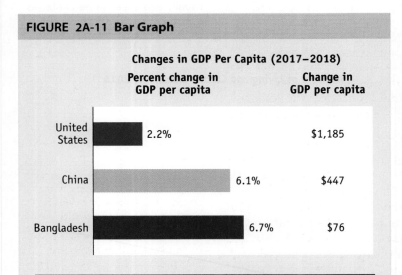

Changes in GDP Per Capita (2017–2018)

	Percent change in GDP per capita	Change in GDP per capita
United States	2.2%	$1,185
China	6.1%	$447
Bangladesh	6.7%	$76

A bar graph measures a variable by using bars of various heights or lengths. This bar graph shows the percent change in GDP per capita (measured in 2010 dollars) for the United States, China, and Bangladesh.
Data from: World Bank, World Development Indicators.

FIGURE 2A-12 Interpreting Graphs: The Effect of Scale

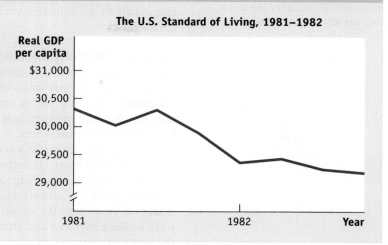

Some of the same data for the years 1981 and 1982 used in Figure 2A-8 are represented here, except that here they are shown using increments of $500 rather than increments of $10,000. As a result of this change in scale, changes in the standard of living look much larger in this figure compared to Figure 2A-8.

Data from: Bureau of Economic Analysis.

should recognize that what is being shown are *percent* changes in GDP per capita, not *numerical* changes. The growth rate for Bangladesh increased by the highest percentage, 6.7% in this example. If you were to confuse numerical changes with percent changes, you would erroneously conclude the country with the greatest change in GDP per capita was Bangladesh.

In fact, a correct interpretation of Figure 2A-11 shows that the greatest dollar change in GDP per capita was for the United States: GDP per capita increased by $1,185 for the United States, which is greater than the increase in GDP per capita for China, which is $447 in this example. Although there was a higher percentage increase in GDP per capita for China, the dollar increase for China from 2017 to 2018 was smaller than the change for the United States, leading to a smaller change in GDP per capita for China than the United States. The same can be said for Bangladesh, where GDP per capita grew by 6.7%, but that only resulted in a $76 increase in actual GDP per capita.

Omitted Variables From a scatter diagram that shows two variables moving either positively or negatively in relation to each other, it is easy to conclude that there is a causal relationship. But relationships between two variables are not always due to direct cause and effect. Quite possibly an observed relationship between two variables is due to the *unobserved* effect of a third variable on each of the other two variables.

An unobserved variable that, through its influence on other variables, creates the erroneous appearance of a direct causal relationship among those variables is called an **omitted variable.** For example, in New England, a greater amount of snowfall during a given week will typically cause people to buy more snow shovels. It will also cause people to buy more de-icer fluid. But if you omitted the influence of the snowfall and simply plotted the number of snow shovels sold versus the number of bottles of de-icer fluid sold, you would produce a scatter diagram that showed an upward tilt in the pattern of points, indicating a positive relationship between snow shovels sold and de-icer fluid sold.

To attribute a causal relationship between these two variables, however, is misguided. More snow shovels sold do not cause more de-icer fluid to be sold, or vice versa. They move together because they are both influenced by a third, determining, variable—the weekly snowfall, which is the omitted variable in this case.

A **bar graph** uses bars of varying heights or lengths to show the comparative sizes of different observations of a variable.

An axis is **truncated** when some of the values on the axis are omitted, usually to save space.

An **omitted variable** is an unobserved variable that, through its influence on other variables, creates the erroneous appearance of a direct causal relationship among those variables.

The error of **reverse causality** is committed when the true direction of causality between two variables is reversed.

So before assuming that a pattern in a scatter diagram implies a cause-and-effect relationship, it is important to consider whether the pattern is instead the result of an omitted variable. Or to put it another way: correlation is not causation.

Reverse Causality   Even when you are confident that there is no omitted variable and that there is a causal relationship between two variables shown in a numerical graph, you must also be sure to avoid making the mistake of **reverse causality**—coming to an erroneous conclusion about which is the dependent and which is the independent variable by reversing the true direction of causality between the two variables.

For example, imagine a scatter diagram that depicts the grade point averages (GPAs) of 20 of your classmates on one axis and the number of hours that each classmate spends studying on the other. A line fitted between the points will probably have a positive slope, showing a positive relationship between GPA and hours of studying. We could reasonably infer that hours spent studying is the independent variable and that GPA is the dependent variable. But you could make the error of reverse causality: you could infer that a high GPA causes a student to study more, whereas a low GPA causes a student to study less.

As you've just seen, it is important to understand how graphs can mislead or be interpreted incorrectly. Policy decisions, business decisions, and political arguments are often based on interpretation of the types of numerical graphs we've just discussed. Problems of misleading features of construction, omitted variables, and reverse causality can lead to important and undesirable consequences.

PROBLEMS

1. Study the four accompanying diagrams. Consider the following statements and indicate which diagram matches each statement. Which variable would appear on the horizontal and which on the vertical axis? In each of these statements, is the slope positive, negative, zero, or infinity?

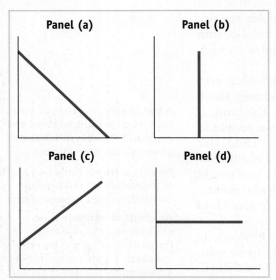

Panel (a)   **Panel (b)**

Panel (c)   **Panel (d)**

a. If the price of movies increases, fewer consumers go to see movies.

b. More experienced workers typically have higher incomes than less experienced workers.

c. Whatever the temperature outside, Americans consume the same number of tacos per day.

d. Consumers buy more frozen yogurt when the price of ice cream goes up.

e. Research finds no relationship between the number of diet books purchased and the number of pounds lost by the average dieter.

f. Regardless of its price, Americans buy the same quantity of salt.

2. During the Reagan administration, economist Arthur Laffer argued in favor of lowering income tax rates in order to increase tax revenues. Like most economists, he believed that at tax rates above a certain level, tax revenue would fall because high taxes would discourage some people from working and that people would refuse to work at all if they received no income after paying taxes. This relationship between tax rates and tax revenue is graphically summarized in what is widely known as the Laffer curve. Plot the Laffer curve relationship assuming that it has the shape of a nonlinear curve. The following questions will help you construct the graph.

a. Which is the independent variable? Which is the dependent variable? On which axis do you therefore measure the income tax rate? On which axis do you measure income tax revenue?

b. What would tax revenue be at a 0% income tax rate?

c. The maximum possible income tax rate is 100%. What would tax revenue be at a 100% income tax rate?

d. Estimates now show that the maximum point on the Laffer curve is (approximately) at a tax rate of 80%. For tax rates less than 80%, how would you describe the relationship between the tax rate and tax revenue, and how is this relationship reflected in the slope? For tax rates higher than 80%, how would you describe the relationship between the tax rate and tax revenue, and how is this relationship reflected in the slope?

3. In the accompanying figures, the numbers on the axes have been lost. All you know is that the units shown on the vertical axis are the same as the units on the horizontal axis.

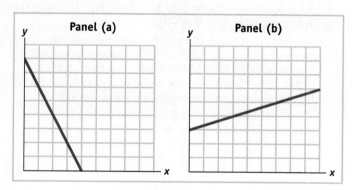

a. In panel (a), what is the slope of the line? Show that the slope is constant along the line.

b. In panel (b), what is the slope of the line? Show that the slope is constant along the line.

4. Answer each of the following questions by drawing a schematic diagram.

a. Taking measurements of the slope of a curve at three points farther and farther to the right along the horizontal axis, the slope of the curve changes from –0.3, to –0.8, to –2.5, measured by the point method. Draw a schematic diagram of this curve. How would you describe the relationship illustrated in your diagram?

b. Taking measurements of the slope of a curve at five points farther and farther to the right along the horizontal axis, the slope of the curve changes from 1.5, to 0.5, to 0, to –0.5, to –1.5, measured by the point method. Draw a schematic diagram of this curve. Does it have a maximum or a minimum?

5. For each of the accompanying diagrams, calculate the area of the shaded right triangle.

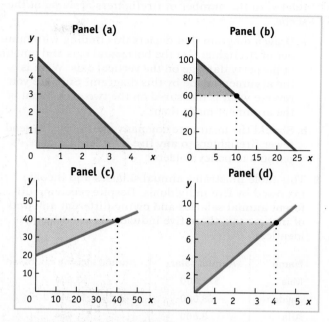

6. The base of a right triangle is 10, and its area is 20. What is the height of this right triangle?

7. The accompanying table shows the relationship between workers' hours of work per week and their hourly wage rate. Apart from the fact that they receive a different hourly wage rate and work different hours, these five workers are otherwise identical.

Name	Quantity of labor (hours per week)	Wage rate (per hour)
Akiko	30	$15
Ben	35	30
Cameron	37	45
Diego	36	60
Emily	32	75

a. Which variable is the independent variable? Which is the dependent variable?

b. Draw a scatter diagram illustrating this relationship. Draw a (nonlinear) curve that connects the points. Put the hourly wage rate on the vertical axis.

c. As the wage rate increases from $15 to $30, how does the number of hours worked respond according to the relationship depicted here? What is the average slope of the curve between Akiko's and Ben's data points using the arc method?

d. As the wage rate increases from $60 to $75, how does the number of hours worked respond according to the relationship depicted here? What is the average slope of the curve between Diego's and Emily's data points using the arc method?

8. An insurance company has found that the severity of property damage in a fire is positively related to the number of firefighters arriving at the scene.

    a. Draw a diagram that depicts this finding with number of firefighters on the horizontal axis and amount of property damage on the vertical axis. What is the argument made by this diagram? Suppose you reverse what is measured on the two axes. What is the argument made then?

    b. Should the insurance company ask the city to send fewer firefighters to any fire in order to reduce its payouts to policy holders?

9. This table illustrates annual salaries and income tax owed by five individuals. Despite receiving different annual salaries and owing different amounts of income tax, these five individuals are otherwise identical.

Name	Annual salary	Annual income tax owed
Mila	$22,000	$3,304
Jayden	63,000	14,317
Aria	3,000	454
Logan	94,000	23,927
Saeed	37,000	7,020

    a. If you were to plot these points on a graph, what would be the average slope of the curve between the points for Jayden's and Logan's salaries and taxes using the arc method? How would you interpret this value for slope?

    b. What is the average slope of the curve between the points for Aria's and Mila's salaries and taxes using the arc method? How would you interpret that value for slope?

    c. What happens to the slope as salary increases? What does this relationship imply about how the level of income taxes affects a person's incentive to earn a higher salary?

WORK IT OUT

10. Studies have found a relationship between a country's yearly rate of economic growth and the yearly rate of increase in airborne pollutants. It is believed that a higher rate of economic growth allows a country's residents to have more cars and travel more, thereby releasing more airborne pollutants.

    a. Which variable is the independent variable? Which is the dependent variable?

    b. Suppose that in the country of Sudland, when the yearly rate of economic growth fell from 3.0% to 1.5%, the yearly rate of increase in airborne pollutants fell from 6% to 5%. What is the average slope of a nonlinear curve between these points using the arc method?

    c. Assume that when the yearly rate of economic growth rose from 3.5% to 4.5%, the yearly rate of increase in airborne pollutants rose from 5.5% to 7.5%. What is the average slope of a nonlinear curve between these two points using the arc method?

    d. How would you describe the relationship between the two variables here? ■

3 > Supply and Demand

A NATURAL GAS BOOM AND BUST

FOR ALMOST A DECADE, Karnes County has been on a wild economic roller-coaster ride. From 2010 to 2018, the Texas county, which sits close to two major geological oil formations, has gone from boom to bust to recovery. What accounted for the swift changes was the advent of hydraulic fracturing, also known as fracking.

From 2010 to 2015, Karnes County went through an extreme cycle of boom and bust as the price of natural gas (per thousand cubic feet) went from nearly $8 to under $2 because of fracking. *Fracking* is a method of extracting natural gas from deposits trapped between layers of shale rock thousands of feet underground using powerful jets of chemical-laden water. For almost a century in the United States vast deposits of natural gas within these shale formations lay untapped because drilling for them was too difficult.

It was only about 80 years ago that new drilling technologies made it possible to reach these deeply embedded deposits. But what finally pushed energy companies to invest in these new extraction technologies was a

The adoption of new drilling technologies has led to cheaper natural gas, but not without controversy and environmental costs.

surge in the price of natural gas — a quadrupling from 2002 to 2006. Two principal factors explain the surge: the demand for natural gas and the supply of natural gas.

First, the demand side. In 2002, the U.S. economy was mired in recession; with economic activity low and job losses high, people and businesses cut their energy consumption. For example, to save money, homeowners turned down their thermostats in winter and turned them up in the summer. But by 2006, the U.S. economy came roaring back, and natural gas consumption rose.

Second, the supply side. In 2005, Hurricane Katrina devastated the American Gulf Coast, site of most of the country's natural gas production at the time. So by 2006 the demand for natural gas surged while supply was severely curtailed. As a result, natural gas prices peaked at around $14 per thousand cubic feet, up from around $2 in 2002.

Fast-forward to 2013: natural gas prices once again fell to $2 per thousand cubic feet. But a slow economy was not the reason this time; instead it was due to advances in fracking technology. From 2010 to 2012, U.S. production of natural gas from shale deposits nearly doubled. By 2018, the United States had become the world's largest producer of natural gas, as well as a net exporter of natural gas to other countries.

Despite the massive increase in supply, prices during 2018 averaged around $3.15, well over the historical lows of under $2. Why? Because although supply surged, demand increased as well. First, electric power plants increased their use of natural gas while shifting away from coal. Second, homeowners increased their consumption of natural gas and shifted away from heating oil. And, third, U.S. natural gas exports to Europe surged given that it was cheaper than comparable energy sources.

Yet the benefits of natural gas — which include the creation of tens of thousands of new jobs, a robust economic boom in Karnes

County starting in 2016, and lower energy costs for those who once used pricier coal and oil — have been accompanied by deep reservations and controversy over the environmental effects of fracking. While there are clear environmental benefits from the switch to natural gas (which burns cleaner than the other, heavily polluting fossil fuels, such as oil and coal), fracking has sparked another set of environmental worries. One is potential for contamination of local groundwater by the chemicals used. Another is that cheap natural gas may discourage the adoption of renewable energy sources like solar and wind power, furthering dependence on fossil fuels (although others have noted that an abundant supply of natural gas could actually increase the adoption of renewables: natural gas-powered "mini-power plants" can be fired up when the sun isn't shining or the wind isn't blowing).

Let's return to the topic at hand: the supply of and demand for natural gas. But what does *supply and demand* mean? Many people use the terms as a sort of catchphrase to mean "the laws of the marketplace at work." To economists, however, the concept of supply and demand has a precise meaning: it is a *model of how a market behaves* that is extremely useful for understanding many — but not all — markets.

In this chapter, we lay out the pieces that make up the *supply and demand model*, put them together, and show you how this model can be used. ●

WHAT YOU WILL LEARN

- What is a **competitive market**?
- What are **supply** and **demand curves**?
- How do supply and demand curves lead to an **equilibrium price** and **equilibrium quantity** in the market?
- What are **shortages** and **surpluses** and why do price movements eliminate them?

A **competitive market** is a market in which there are many buyers and sellers of the same good or service, none of whom can influence the price at which the good or service is sold.

The **supply and demand model** is a model of how a competitive market behaves.

Supply and Demand: A Model of a Competitive Market

Natural gas sellers and natural gas buyers constitute a market—a group of producers and consumers who exchange a good or service for payment. In this chapter, we'll focus on a particular type of market known as a *competitive market*. A **competitive market** is a market in which there are many buyers and sellers of the same good or service. More precisely, the key feature of a competitive market is that no individual's actions have a noticeable effect on the price at which the good or service is sold. It's important to understand, however, that this is not an accurate description of every market.

For example, it's not an accurate description of the market for carbonated soft drinks. That's because in this market, Coca-Cola and Pepsi account for such a large proportion of total sales that they are able to influence the price at which their beverages are bought and sold. But it is an accurate description of the market for natural gas. The global marketplace for natural gas is so huge that even the biggest U.S. driller for natural gas—Exxon Mobil—accounts for such a small share of total global transactions that it is unable to influence the price at which natural gas is bought and sold.

It's a little hard to explain why competitive markets are different from other markets until we've seen how a competitive market works. So let's take a rain check—we'll return to that issue at the end of this chapter. For now, let's just say that it's easier to model competitive markets than other markets. When taking an exam, it's always a good strategy to begin by answering the easier questions. In this book, we're going to do the same thing. So we will start with competitive markets.

When a market is competitive, its behavior is well described by the **supply and demand model.** And because many markets are competitive, the supply and demand model is a very useful one indeed.

There are five key elements in this model:

- The *demand curve*
- The *supply curve*
- The set of factors that cause the demand curve to shift and the set of factors that cause the supply curve to shift
- The *market equilibrium,* which includes the *equilibrium price* and *equilibrium quantity*
- The way the market equilibrium changes when the supply curve or demand curve shifts

To understand the supply and demand model, we will examine each of these elements.

The Demand Curve

How much natural gas will American consumers want to buy in a given year? You might at first think that we can answer this question by simply adding up the amounts each American household and business consumes in that year. But that's not enough to answer the question, because how much natural gas Americans want to buy depends on the price of natural gas.

When the price of natural gas falls, as it did from 2006 to 2015, consumers will generally respond to the lower price by using more natural gas—for example, by turning up their thermostats to keep their houses warmer in the winter or switching to vehicles powered by natural gas. In general, the amount of natural gas, or of any good or service that people want to buy, depends upon the price. The higher the price, the less of the good or service people want to purchase; alternatively, the lower the price, the more they want to purchase.

So the answer to the question "How many units of natural gas do consumers want to buy?" depends on the price of a unit of natural gas. If you don't yet know what the price will be, you can start by making a table of how many units of natural gas people would want to buy at a number of different prices. Such a table is known as a *demand schedule*. This, in turn, can be used to draw a *demand curve*, which is one of the key elements of the supply and demand model.

A **demand schedule** shows how much of a good or service consumers will want to buy at different prices.

The Demand Schedule and the Demand Curve

A **demand schedule** is a table showing how much of a good or service consumers will want to buy at different prices. At the right of Figure 3-1, we show a hypothetical demand schedule for natural gas. It's expressed in BTUs (British thermal units), a commonly used measure of quantity of natural gas. It's a hypothetical demand schedule—it doesn't use actual data on American demand for natural gas.

According to the table, if a BTU of natural gas costs $3, consumers will want to purchase 10 trillion BTUs of natural gas over the course of a year. If the price is $3.25 per BTU, they will want to buy only 8.9 trillion BTUs; if the price is only $2.75 per BTU, they will want to buy 11.5 trillion BTUs. The higher the price, the fewer BTUs of natural gas consumers will want to purchase. So, as the price rises,

FIGURE 3-1 The Demand Schedule and the Demand Curve

Demand Schedule for Natural Gas	
Price of natural gas (per BTU)	Quantity of natural gas demanded (trillions of BTUs)
$4.00	7.1
3.75	7.5
3.50	8.1
3.25	8.9
3.00	10.0
2.75	11.5
2.50	14.2

The demand schedule for natural gas yields the corresponding demand curve, which shows how much of a good or service consumers want to buy at any given price. The demand curve and the demand schedule reflect the law of demand: as price rises, the quantity demanded falls. Similarly, a fall in price raises the quantity demanded. As a result, the demand curve is downward sloping.

The **quantity demanded** is the actual amount of a good or service consumers are willing to buy at some specific price.

A **demand curve** is a graphical representation of the demand schedule. It shows the relationship between quantity demanded and price.

The **law of demand** says that a higher price for a good or service, other things equal, leads people to demand a smaller quantity of that good or service.

the **quantity demanded** of natural gas—the actual amount consumers are willing to buy at some specific price—falls.

The graph in Figure 3-1 is a visual representation of the information in the table. (You might want to review the discussion of graphs in economics in the appendix to Chapter 2.) The vertical axis shows the price of a BTU of natural gas and the horizontal axis shows the quantity of natural gas in trillions of BTUs. Each point on the graph corresponds to one of the entries in the table. The curve that connects these points is a **demand curve.** A demand curve is a graphical representation of the demand schedule, another way of showing the relationship between the quantity demanded and price.

Note that the demand curve shown in Figure 3-1 slopes downward. This reflects the inverse relationship between price and the quantity demanded: a higher price reduces the quantity demanded, and a lower price increases the quantity demanded. We can see this from the demand curve in Figure 3-1. As price falls, we move down the demand curve and quantity demanded increases. And as price increases, we move up the demand curve and quantity demanded falls.

In the real world, demand curves almost always *do* slope downward. (The exceptions are so rare that for practical purposes we can ignore them.) Generally, the proposition that a higher price for a good, *other things equal*, leads people to demand a smaller quantity of that good is so reliable that economists are willing to call it a "law"—the **law of demand.**

Shifts of the Demand Curve

Although natural gas prices in 2006 were higher than they had been in 2002, U.S. consumption of natural gas was higher in 2006. How can we reconcile this fact with the law of demand, which says that a higher price reduces the quantity demanded, other things equal?

The answer lies in the crucial phrase *other things equal*. In this case, other things weren't equal: the U.S. economy had changed between 2002 and 2006 in ways that increased the amount of natural gas demanded at any given price. For one thing, the U.S. economy was much stronger in 2006 than in 2002. Figure 3-2 illustrates this phenomenon using the demand schedule and demand curve for natural gas. (As before, the numbers in Figure 3-2 are hypothetical.)

The table in Figure 3-2 shows two demand schedules. The first is the demand schedule for 2002, the same as shown in Figure 3-1. The second is the demand

---

GLOBAL COMPARISON   **PAY MORE, PUMP LESS**

For a real-world illustration of the law of demand, consider how gasoline consumption varies according to the prices consumers pay at the pump. Because of high taxes, gasoline and diesel fuel are more than twice as expensive in most European countries and in many East Asian countries than in the United States. According to the law of demand, this should lead Europeans to buy less gasoline than Americans—and they do. As you can see from the figure, per person, Europeans consume less than half as much fuel as Americans, mainly because they drive smaller cars with better mileage.

Prices aren't the only factor affecting fuel consumption, but they're probably the main cause of the difference between European and American fuel consumption per person.

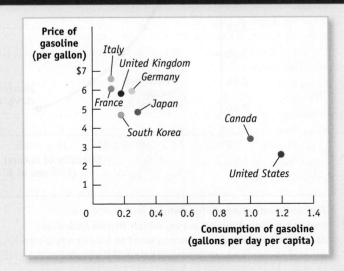

Data from: Bloomberg and U.S. Energy Information Administration, 2018.

FIGURE 3-2 An Increase in Demand

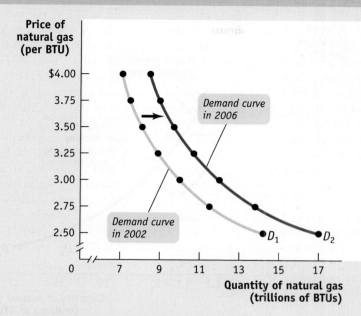

Demand Schedules for Natural Gas		
Price of natural gas (per BTU)	Quantity of natural gas demanded (trillions of BTUs)	
	in 2002	in 2006
$4.00	7.1	8.5
3.75	7.5	9.0
3.50	8.1	9.7
3.25	8.9	10.7
3.00	10.0	12.0
2.75	11.5	13.8
2.50	14.2	17.0

A strong economy is one factor that increases the demand for natural gas — a rise in the quantity demanded at any given price. This is represented by the two demand schedules — one showing the demand in 2002 when the economy was weak, the other showing the demand in 2006, when the economy was strong — and their corresponding demand curves. The increase in demand shifts the demand curve to the right.

schedule for 2006. It differs from the 2002 schedule because of the stronger U.S. economy, leading to an increase in the quantity of natural gas demanded at any given price. So at each price the 2006 schedule shows a larger quantity demanded than the 2002 schedule. For example, the quantity of natural gas consumers wanted to buy at a price of $3 per BTU increased from 10 trillion to 12 trillion BTUs per year; the quantity demanded at $3.25 per BTU went from 8.9 trillion to 10.7 trillion, and so on.

What is clear from this example is that the changes that occurred between 2002 and 2006 generated a *new* demand schedule, one in which the quantity demanded was greater at any given price than in the original demand schedule. The two curves in Figure 3-2 show the same information graphically. As you can see, the demand schedule for 2006 corresponds to a new demand curve, D_2, that is to the right of the demand schedule for 2002, D_1. This **shift of the demand curve** shows the change in the quantity demanded at any given price, represented by the change in position of the original demand curve D_1 to its new location at D_2.

It's crucial to make the distinction between such shifts of the demand curve and **movements along the demand curve,** changes in the quantity demanded of a good arising from a change in that good's price. Figure 3-3 illustrates the difference.

The movement from point A to point B is a movement along the demand curve: the quantity demanded rises due to a fall in price as you move down D_1. Here, a fall in the price of natural gas from $3.50 to $3 per BTU generates a rise in the quantity demanded from 8.1 trillion to 10 trillion BTUs per year. But the quantity demanded can also rise when the price is unchanged if there is an *increase in demand*—a rightward shift of the demand curve. This is illustrated in Figure 3-3 by the shift of the demand curve from D_1 to D_2. Holding the price constant at $3.50 per BTU, the quantity demanded rises from 8.1 trillion BTUs at point A on D_1 to 9.7 trillion BTUs at point C on D_2.

A **shift of the demand curve** is a change in the quantity demanded at any given price, represented by the shift of the original demand curve to a new position, denoted by a new demand curve.

A **movement along the demand curve** is a change in the quantity demanded of a good arising from a change in the good's price.

FIGURE 3-3 Movement Along the Demand Curve versus Shift of the Demand Curve

The rise in quantity demanded when going from point A to point B reflects a movement along the demand curve: it is the result of a fall in the price of the good. The rise in quantity demanded when going from point A to point C reflects a shift of the demand curve: it is the result of a rise in the quantity demanded at any given price.

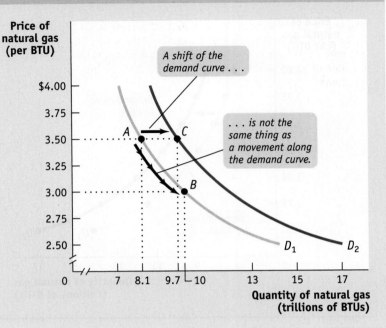

When economists say "the demand for X increased" or "the demand for Y decreased," they mean that the demand curve for X or Y shifted—not that the quantity demanded rose or fell because of a change in the price.

Understanding Shifts of the Demand Curve

Figure 3-4 illustrates the two basic ways in which demand curves can shift.

1. When economists talk about an increase in demand, they mean a *rightward* shift of the demand curve: at any given price, consumers demand a larger quantity of the good or service than before. This is shown by the rightward shift of the original demand curve D_1 to curve D_2.

2. When economists talk about a decrease in demand, they mean a *leftward* shift of the demand curve: at any given price, consumers demand a smaller quantity of the good or service than before. This is shown by the leftward shift of the original demand curve D_1 to curve D_3.

What caused the demand curve for natural gas to shift? As we mentioned earlier, the reason was the stronger U.S. economy in 2006 compared to 2002. If you think

---

PITFALLS

DEMAND VERSUS QUANTITY DEMANDED

When economists say "an increase in demand," they mean a rightward shift of the demand curve, and when they say "a decrease in demand," they mean a leftward shift of the demand curve—that is, when they're being careful.

In ordinary speech most of us, professional economists included, use the word *demand* casually. For example, an economist might say "the demand for air travel has doubled over the past 20 years, partly because of falling airfares" when he or she really means that the *quantity demanded* has doubled.

It's OK to be a bit sloppy in ordinary conversation. But when you're doing economic analysis, it's important to make the distinction between changes in the quantity demanded, which involve movements along a demand curve, and shifts of the demand curve (see Figure 3-3). Sometimes students end up writing something like this: "If demand increases, the price will go up, but that will lead to a fall in demand, which pushes the price down . . ." and then go around in circles.

By making a clear distinction between changes in *demand,* which mean shifts of the demand curve, and changes in *quantity demanded,* which means movement along the demand curve, you can avoid a lot of confusion.

FIGURE 3-4 Shifts of the Demand Curve

Any event that increases demand shifts the demand curve to the right, reflecting a rise in the quantity demanded at any given price. Any event that decreases demand shifts the demand curve to the left, reflecting a fall in the quantity demanded at any given price.

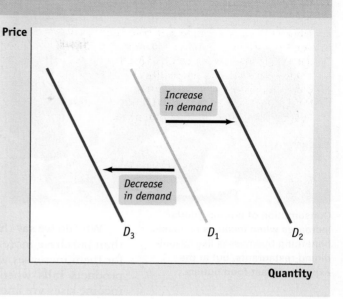

about it, you can come up with other factors that would be likely to shift the demand curve for natural gas. For example, suppose that the price of heating oil rises. This will induce some consumers, who heat their homes and businesses in winter with heating oil, to switch to natural gas instead, increasing the demand for natural gas.

Economists believe that there are five principal factors that shift the demand curve for a good or service:

- Changes in the prices of related goods or services
- Changes in income
- Changes in tastes
- Changes in expectations
- Changes in the number of consumers

Although this list is not exhaustive, it contains the five most important factors that can shift demand curves. When we say that the quantity of a good or service demanded falls as its price rises, *other things equal*, we are in fact stating that the factors that shift demand are remaining unchanged. Let's now explore how those factors shift the demand curve.

Changes in the Prices of Related Goods or Services Heating oil is what economists call a *substitute* for natural gas. A pair of goods are **substitutes** if a rise in the price of one good (heating oil) makes consumers more likely to buy the other good (natural gas). Substitutes are usually goods that in some way serve a similar function: coffee and tea, muffins and doughnuts, train rides and air flights. A rise in the price of the alternative good induces some consumers to purchase the original good *instead* of the substitute, shifting demand for the original good to the right.

But sometimes a rise in the price of one good makes consumers *less* willing to buy another good. Such pairs of goods are known as **complements.** Complements are usually goods that in some sense are consumed together: smartphones and apps, coffee and a breakfast burrito, cars and gasoline. Because consumers like to consume a good and its complement together, a change in the price of one of the goods will affect the demand for its complement. In particular, when the price of one good rises, the demand for its complement decreases, shifting the demand curve for the complement to the left. So, for example, when the price of gasoline began to rise in 2009 from under $3 per gallon to close to $4 per gallon in 2011, the demand for gas-guzzling cars fell.

Two goods are **substitutes** if a rise in the price of one of the goods leads to an increase in the demand for the other good.

Two goods are **complements** if a rise in the price of one good leads to a decrease in the demand for the other good.

Consumption of normal goods increases when incomes increase, benefiting businesses like casual-dining restaurants, but at the expense of fast-food outlets.

Changes in Income Why did the stronger economy in 2006 lead to an increase in the demand for natural gas compared to the demand during the weak economy of 2002? It was because the economy was stronger and Americans had more income, making them more likely to purchase more of *most* goods and services at any given price. For example, with a higher income you are likely to keep your house warmer in the winter than if your income is low.

And, the demand for natural gas, a major source of fuel for electricity-generating power plants, is tied to the demand for other goods and services. For example, businesses must consume power in order to provide goods and services to households. So when the economy is strong and household incomes are high, businesses will consume more electricity and, indirectly, more natural gas.

Why do we say that people are likely to purchase more of "*most* goods," rather than purchase more of "*all* goods"? Most goods are **normal goods**—the demand for them increases when consumer income rises. However, the demand for some products falls when income rises. Goods for which demand decreases when income rises are known as **inferior goods.** Usually an inferior good is considered less desirable than more expensive alternatives—such as a bus ride versus a taxi ride. When they can afford to, people stop buying an inferior good and switch their consumption to the preferred, more expensive alternative. So when a good is inferior, a rise in income shifts the demand curve to the left. And, not surprisingly, a fall in income shifts the demand curve to the right.

One example of the distinction between normal and inferior goods that has drawn attention in the business press is the difference between so-called casual-dining restaurants such as Buffalo Wild Wings or Olive Garden and fast-food chains such as Burger King or McDonald's. When their incomes rise, Americans tend to eat out more at casual-dining restaurants. However, some of that increased dining out comes at the expense of fast-food venues—to some extent, people visit McDonald's less often once they can afford to move upscale. So casual dining is a normal good, whereas fast-food consumption appears to be an inferior good.

Changes in Tastes Why do people want what they want? Fortunately, we don't need to answer that question—we just need to acknowledge that people have certain preferences, or tastes, that determine what they choose to consume and that these tastes can change. Economists usually lump together changes in demand due to trends, beliefs, cultural shifts, and so on under the heading of changes in tastes or preferences.

For example, once upon a time men wore hats. Up until around World War II, a respectable man wasn't fully dressed unless he wore a dignified hat along with his suit. But the returning troops adopted a more informal style. And President Eisenhower, who had been supreme commander of Allied Forces before becoming president, often went hatless. After World War II, it was clear that the demand curve for hats had shifted leftward, reflecting a decrease in the demand for hats.

Economists have relatively little to say about the forces that influence consumers' tastes. (Although marketers and advertisers have plenty to say about them!) However, a change in tastes does have a predictable impact on demand. When tastes change in favor of a good, more people want to buy it at any given price, so the demand curve shifts to the right. When tastes change against a good, fewer people want to buy it at any given price, so the demand curve shifts to the left.

Changes in Expectations When consumers have some choice about when to make a purchase, current demand for a good is often affected by expectations about its future price. For example, savvy shoppers often wait for seasonal sales—say, buying next year's holiday decorations during the post-holiday

When a rise in income increases the demand for a good—the normal case—it is a **normal good.**

When a rise in income decreases the demand for a good, it is an **inferior good.**

markdowns. In this case, expectations of a future drop in price lead to a decrease in demand today. Alternatively, expectations of a future rise in price are likely to cause an increase in demand today.

In addition, the fall in gas prices in recent years to around $2 per BTU has spurred more consumers to switch to natural gas from other fuel types than when natural gas fell to $2 per BTU in 2002. But why are consumers more willing to switch now? Because in 2002, consumers didn't expect the fall in the price of natural gas to last—and they were right.

In 2002, natural gas prices fell because of the weak economy. That situation changed in 2006 when the economy came roaring back and the price of natural gas rose dramatically. In contrast, consumers have come to expect that the more recent fall in the price of natural gas will not be temporary because it is based on a permanent change: the ability to tap much larger deposits of natural gas.

Expected changes in future income can also lead to changes in demand: if you expect your income to rise in the future, you will typically borrow today and increase your demand for certain goods; if you expect your income to fall in the future, you are likely to save today and reduce your demand for some goods.

Changes in the Number of Consumers Another factor that can cause a change in demand is a change in the number of consumers of a good or service. For example, population growth in the United States eventually leads to higher demand for natural gas as more homes and businesses need to be heated in the winter and cooled in the summer.

Let's introduce a new concept: the **individual demand curve,** which shows the relationship between quantity demanded and price for an individual consumer. For example, suppose that the Gonzalez family is a consumer of natural gas for heating and cooling their home. Panel (a) of Figure 3-5 shows how many

> An **individual demand curve** illustrates the relationship between quantity demanded and price for an individual consumer.

FIGURE 3-5 Individual Demand Curves and the Market Demand Curve

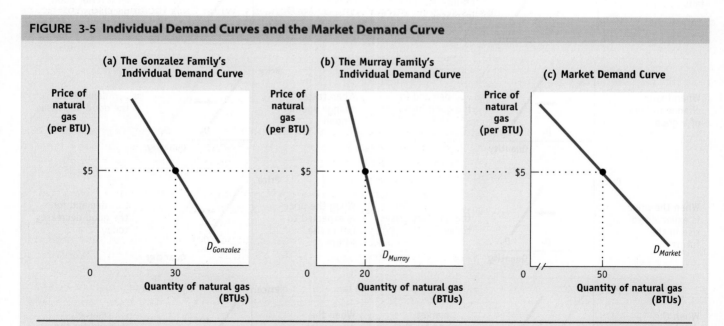

The Gonzalez family and the Murray family are the only two consumers of natural gas in the market. Panel (a) shows the Gonzalez family's individual demand curve: the number of BTUs they will buy per year at any given price. Panel (b) shows the Murray family's individual demand curve. Given that the Gonzalez family and the Murray family are the only two consumers, the *market demand curve,* which shows the quantity of BTUs demanded by all consumers at any given price, is shown in the panel (c). The market demand curve is the *horizontal sum* of the individual demand curves of all consumers. In this case, at any given price, the quantity demanded by the market is the sum of the quantities demanded by the Gonzalez family and the Murray family.

TABLE 3-1 Factors That Shift Demand

When this happens . . .	. . . demand increases	But when this happens . . .	. . . demand decreases
When the price of a substitute rises . . .	. . . demand for the original good increases.	When the price of a substitute falls . . .	. . . demand for the original good decreases.
When the price of a complement falls . . .	. . . demand for the original good increases.	When the price of a complement rises . . .	. . . demand for the original good decreases.
When income rises . . .	. . . demand for a normal good increases.	When income falls . . .	. . . demand for a normal good decreases.
When income falls . . .	. . . demand for an inferior good increases.	When income rises . . .	. . . demand for an inferior good decreases.
When tastes change in favor of a good . . .	. . . demand for the good increases.	When tastes change against a good . . .	. . . demand for the good decreases.
When the price is expected to rise in the future . . .	. . . demand for the good increases today.	When the price is expected to fall in the future . . .	. . . demand for the good decreases today.
When the number of consumers rises . . .	. . . market demand for the good increases.	When the number of consumers falls . . .	. . . market demand for the good decreases.

BTUs of natural gas they will buy per year at any given price. The Gonzalez family's individual demand curve is $D_{Gonzalez}$.

The *market demand curve* shows how the combined quantity demanded by all consumers depends on the market price of the good. (Most of the time when economists refer to the demand curve they mean the market demand curve.) The market demand curve is the *horizontal sum* of the individual demand curves of all consumers in that market.

To see what we mean by the term *horizontal sum*, assume for a moment that there are only two consumers of natural gas, the Gonzalez family and the Murray family. The Murray family consumes natural gas to fuel their natural gas–powered car. The Murray family's individual demand curve, D_{Murray}, is shown in panel (b). Panel (c) shows the market demand curve. At any given price, the quantity demanded by the market is the sum of the quantities demanded by the Gonzalez family and the Murray family. For example, at a price of $5 per BTU, the Gonzalez family demands 30 BTUs of natural gas per year and the Murray family demands 20 BTUs per year. So the quantity demanded by the market is 50 BTUs per year, as seen on the market demand curve, D_{Market}.

Clearly, the quantity demanded by the market at any given price is larger with the Murray family present than it would be if the Gonzalez family were the only consumer. The quantity demanded at any given price would be even larger if we added a third consumer, then a fourth, and so on. So an increase in the number of consumers leads to an increase in demand.

For a review of the factors that shift demand, see Table 3-1.

ECONOMICS >> *in Action*
Beating the Traffic

All big cities have traffic problems, and many local authorities try to discourage driving in the crowded city center. If we think of an auto trip to the city center as a good that people consume, we can use the economics of demand to analyze anti-traffic policies.

One common strategy is to reduce the demand for auto trips by lowering the prices of substitutes. Many metropolitan areas subsidize bus and rail service, hoping to lure commuters out of their cars. An alternative is to raise the price of complements: several major U.S. cities impose high taxes on commercial parking garages and impose short time limits on parking meters, both to raise revenue and to discourage people from driving into the city.

A few major cities—including Singapore, London, Oslo, Stockholm, and Milan—have been willing to adopt a direct and politically controversial approach: reducing congestion by raising the price of driving. Under *congestion pricing*, a charge is imposed on cars entering the city center during business hours. Drivers buy passes, which are then debited electronically as they drive by monitoring stations. Compliance is monitored with cameras that photograph license plates.

The standard cost of driving into London is currently £11.50 (about $15). Drivers who don't pay and are caught pay a fine of £130 (about $171) for each transgression.

Not surprisingly, studies have shown that after the implementation of congestion pricing, traffic does decrease. In the 1990s, London had some of the worst traffic in Europe. The introduction of its congestion charge in 2003 immediately reduced traffic in the city center by about 15%. Fifteen years later, by 2018, the policy was still working, as traffic volumes are still 25% lower than they were in the late 1990s. And there has been increased use of substitutes, such as public

Cities can reduce traffic congestion by raising the price of driving.

transportation, bicycles, and ride-hailing. From 2001 to 2011, bike trips in London increased by 79%, and bus usage was up by 30%.

And less congestion led not just to fewer accidents, but to a lower *rate* of accidents as fewer cars jostled for space. One study found that from 2000 to 2010 the number of accidents per mile driven in London fell by 40%. Stockholm experienced effects similar to those in London: traffic fell by 22% in 2013 compared to pre-congestion charge levels, transit times fell by one-third to one-half, and air quality measurably improved. A 2018 article found that serious childhood asthma attacks declined significantly in Stockholm after the congestion charge was imposed.

Congestion pricing is now getting the attention of city planners in the United States. New York City will become the first American city to implement congestion pricing as of 2020, with Los Angeles, Seattle, and Portland, Oregon, currently considering plans to do the same.

>> Check Your Understanding 3-1
Solutions appear at back of book.

1. Explain whether each of the following events represents (i) a *shift of* the demand curve or (ii) a *movement along* the demand curve.
   a. A store owner finds that customers are willing to pay more for umbrellas on rainy days.
   b. When Circus Cruise Lines offered reduced prices for summer cruises in the Caribbean, their number of bookings increased sharply.
   c. People buy more long-stem roses the week of Valentine's Day, even though the prices are higher than at other times during the year.
   d. A sharp rise in the price of gasoline leads many commuters to join carpools in order to reduce their gasoline purchases.

‖ The Supply Curve

Some deposits of natural gas are easier to tap than others. Before the widespread use of fracking, drillers would limit their natural gas wells to deposits that lay in easily reached pools beneath the earth. How much natural gas they would tap from existing wells, and how extensively they searched for new deposits and drilled new wells, depended on the price they expected to get for the natural gas. The higher the price, the more they would tap existing wells as well as drill and tap new wells.

So just as the quantity of natural gas that consumers want to buy depends upon the price they have to pay, the quantity that producers of natural gas, or of any good or service, are willing to produce and sell—the **quantity supplied**—depends upon the price they are offered.

The Supply Schedule and the Supply Curve

The table in Figure 3-6 shows how the quantity of natural gas made available varies with the price—that is, it shows a hypothetical **supply schedule** for natural gas.

A supply schedule works the same way as the demand schedule shown in Figure 3-1: in this case, the table shows the number of BTUs of natural gas producers are willing to sell at different prices. At a price of $2.50 per BTU, producers are willing to sell only 8 trillion BTUs of natural gas per year. At $2.75 per BTU, they're willing to sell 9.1 trillion BTUs. At $3, they're willing to sell 10 trillion BTUs, and so on.

The **quantity supplied** is the actual amount of a good or service people are willing to sell at some specific price.

A **supply schedule** shows how much of a good or service would be supplied at different prices.

FIGURE 3-6 The Supply Schedule and the Supply Curve

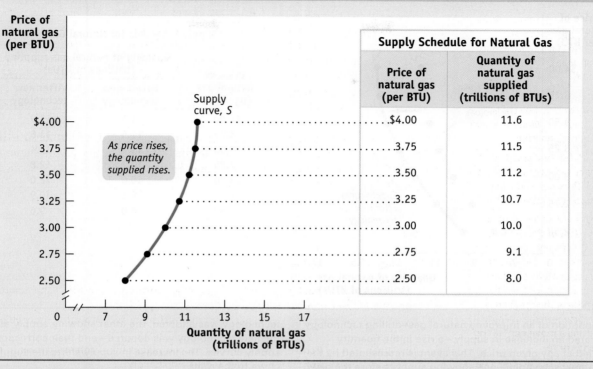

Supply Schedule for Natural Gas	
Price of natural gas (per BTU)	Quantity of natural gas supplied (trillions of BTUs)
$4.00	11.6
3.75	11.5
3.50	11.2
3.25	10.7
3.00	10.0
2.75	9.1
2.50	8.0

The supply schedule for natural gas is plotted to yield the corresponding supply curve, which shows how much of a good producers are willing to sell at any given price. The supply curve and the supply schedule reflect the fact that supply curves are usually upward sloping: the quantity supplied rises when the price rises.

In the same way that a demand schedule can be represented graphically by a demand curve, a supply schedule can be represented by a **supply curve,** as shown in Figure 3-6. Each point on the curve represents an entry from the table.

Suppose that the price of natural gas rises from $3 to $3.25; we can see that the quantity of natural gas that producers are willing to sell rises from 10 trillion to 10.7 trillion BTUs. This is the normal situation for a supply curve, that a higher price leads to a higher quantity supplied. So just as demand curves normally slope downward, supply curves normally slope upward: the higher the price being offered, the more of any good or service producers will be willing to sell.

Shifts of the Supply Curve

As we discussed in the introduction to this chapter, innovations in the technology of drilling natural gas deposits have led to a huge increase in U.S. production of natural gas. Figure 3-7 illustrates these events in terms of the supply schedule and the supply curve for natural gas. The table in Figure 3-7 shows two supply schedules. The schedule before improved natural gas–drilling technology was adopted is the same one as in Figure 3-6. The second schedule shows the supply of natural gas *after* the improved technology was adopted.

Just as a change in demand schedules leads to a shift of the demand curve, a change in supply schedules leads to a **shift of the supply curve**—a change in the quantity supplied at any given price. This is shown in Figure 3-7 by the shift of the supply curve before the adoption of new natural gas–drilling technology, S_1,

A **supply curve** shows the relationship between quantity supplied and price.

A **shift of the supply curve** is a change in the quantity supplied of a good or service at any given price. It is represented by the change of the original supply curve to a new position, denoted by a new supply curve.

FIGURE 3-7 An Increase in Supply

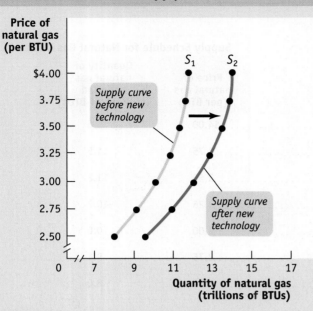

Supply Schedules for Natural Gas		
Price of natural gas (per BTU)	Quantity of natural gas supplied (trillions of BTUs)	
	Before new technology	After new technology
$4.00	11.6	13.9
3.75	11.5	13.8
3.50	11.2	13.4
3.25	10.7	12.8
3.00	10.0	12.0
2.75	9.1	10.9
2.50	8.0	9.6

The adoption of an improved natural gas–drilling technology generated an increase in supply—a rise in the quantity supplied at any given price. This event is represented by the two supply schedules—one showing supply before the new technology was adopted, the other showing supply after the new technology was adopted—and their corresponding supply curves. The increase in supply shifts the supply curve to the right.

to its new position after the adoption of new natural gas–drilling technology, S_2. Notice that S_2 lies to the right of S_1, a reflection of the fact that quantity supplied rises at any given price.

As in the analysis of demand, it's crucial to draw a distinction between such shifts of the supply curve and **movements along the supply curve**—changes in the quantity supplied arising from a change in price. We can see this difference in Figure 3-8. The movement from point *A* to point *B* is a movement along the supply curve: the quantity supplied rises along S_1 due to a rise in price. Here, a rise in price from $3 to $3.50 leads to a rise in the quantity supplied from 10 trillion to 11.2 trillion BTUs of natural gas. But the quantity supplied can also rise when the price is unchanged if there is an increase in supply—a rightward shift of the supply curve. This is shown by the rightward shift of the supply curve from S_1 to S_2. Holding the price constant at $3, the quantity supplied rises from 10 trillion BTUs at point *A* on S_1 to 12 billion BTUs at point *C* on S_2.

Understanding Shifts of the Supply Curve

Figure 3-9 illustrates the two basic ways in which supply curves can shift. When economists talk about an "increase in supply," they mean a *rightward* shift of the supply curve: at any given price, producers supply a larger quantity of the good than before. This is shown in Figure 3-9 by the rightward shift of the original supply curve S_1 to S_2. And when economists talk about a "decrease in supply," they mean a *leftward* shift of the supply curve: at any given price, producers supply a smaller quantity of the good than before. This is represented by the leftward shift of S_1 to S_3.

A **movement along the supply curve** is a change in the quantity supplied of a good arising from a change in the good's price.

FIGURE 3-8 Movement Along the Supply Curve versus Shift of the Supply Curve

The increase in quantity supplied when going from point *A* to point *B* reflects a movement along the supply curve: it is the result of a rise in the price of a good. The increase in quantity supplied when going from point *A* to point *C* reflects a shift of the supply curve: it is the result of an increase in the quantity supplied at any given price.

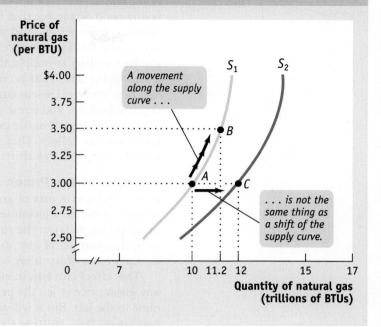

Economists believe that shifts of the supply curve for a good or service are mainly the result of five factors (though, as with demand, there are other possible causes):

- Changes in input prices
- Changes in the prices of related goods or services
- Changes in technology
- Changes in expectations
- Changes in the number of producers

FIGURE 3-9 Shifts of the Supply Curve

Any event that increases supply shifts the supply curve to the right, reflecting a rise in the quantity supplied at any given price. Any event that decreases supply shifts the supply curve to the left, reflecting a fall in the quantity supplied at any given price.

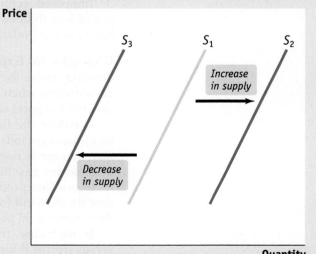

An **input** is a good or service that is used to produce another good or service.

Changes in Input Prices To produce output, you need inputs. For example, to make vanilla ice cream, you need vanilla beans, cream, sugar, and so on. An **input** is any good or service that is used to produce another good or service. Inputs, like outputs, have prices. And an increase in the price of an input makes the production of the final good more costly for those who produce and sell it. So producers are less willing to supply the final good at any given price, and the supply curve shifts to the left. That is, supply decreases. For example, fuel is a major cost for airlines. When oil prices surged in 2007–2008, airlines began cutting back on their flight schedules and some went out of business or merged with larger airlines.

Similarly, a fall in the price of an input makes the production of the final good less costly for sellers. They are more willing to supply the good at any given price, and the supply curve shifts to the right. That is, supply increases.

Changes in the Prices of Related Goods or Services A single producer often produces a mix of goods rather than a single product. For example, an oil refinery produces gasoline from crude oil, but it also produces heating oil and other products from the same raw material. When a producer sells several products, the quantity of any one good it is willing to supply at any given price depends on the prices of its other co-produced goods.

This effect can run in either direction. An oil refiner will supply less gasoline at any given price when the price of heating oil rises, shifting the supply curve for gasoline to the left. But it will supply more gasoline at any given price when the price of heating oil falls, shifting the supply curve for gasoline to the right. This means that gasoline and other co-produced oil products are *substitutes in production* for refiners.

In contrast, due to the nature of the production process, other goods can be *complements in production*. Producers of natural gas often find that natural gas wells also produce oil as a by-product of extraction. The higher the price at which a driller can sell its oil, the more willing it will be to drill natural gas wells and the more natural gas it will supply at any given price. Higher oil prices then lead to more natural gas supplied at any given price because oil and natural gas can be tapped simultaneously. As a result, oil is a complement in the production of natural gas. The reverse is also true: natural gas is a complement in the production of oil.

Changes in Technology As the opening story illustrates, changes in technology affect the supply curve. Technology improvements enable producers to spend less on inputs (in this case, drilling equipment, labor, land purchases, and so on), yet still produce the same amount of output. When a better technology becomes available, reducing the cost of production, supply increases and the supply curve shifts to the right.

Improved technology enabled natural gas producers to more than double output in less than two years. Technology is also the main reason that natural gas has remained relatively cheap, even as demand has grown.

Changes in Expectations Just as changes in expectations can shift the demand curve, they can also shift the supply curve. When suppliers have some choice about when they put their good up for sale, changes in the expected future price of the good can lead a supplier to supply less or more of the good today.

Consider the fact that gasoline and other oil products are often stored for significant periods of time at oil refineries before being sold to consumers. In fact, storage is normally part of producers' business strategy. Knowing that the demand for gasoline peaks in the summer, oil refiners normally store some of their gasoline produced during the spring for summer sale. Similarly, knowing that the demand for heating oil peaks in the winter, they normally store some of their heating oil produced during the fall for winter sale.

In each case, there's a decision to be made between selling the product now versus storing it for later sale. The choice a producer makes depends on a comparison of the current price and the expected future price. This example illustrates how changes in expectations can alter supply: an increase in the anticipated future price of a good or service reduces supply today, a leftward shift of the supply curve. But a fall in the anticipated future price increases supply today, a rightward shift of the supply curve.

Changes in the Number of Producers Just as changes in the number of consumers affect the demand curve, changes in the number of producers affect the supply curve. Let's examine the **individual supply curve,** by looking at panel (a) in Figure 3-10. The individual supply curve shows the relationship between quantity supplied and price for an individual producer. For example, suppose that Louisiana Drillers is a natural gas producer and that panel (a) of Figure 3-10 shows the quantity of BTUs it will supply per year at any given price. Then $S_{Louisiana}$ is its individual supply curve.

The *market supply curve* shows how the combined total quantity supplied by all individual producers in the market depends on the market price of that good. Just as the market demand curve is the horizontal sum of the individual demand curves of all consumers, the market supply curve is the horizontal sum of the individual supply curves of all producers. Assume for a moment that there are only two natural gas producers, Louisiana Drillers and Allegheny Natural Gas. Allegheny's individual supply curve is shown in panel (b). Panel (c) shows the market supply curve. At any given price, the quantity supplied to the market is the sum of the quantities supplied by Louisiana Drillers and Allegheny Natural Gas. For example, at a price of $1 per BTU, Louisiana Drillers supplies 200,000 BTUs and Allegheny Natural Gas supplies 100,000 BTUs per year, making the quantity supplied to the market 300,000 BTUs.

Clearly, the quantity supplied to the market at any given price is larger when Allegheny Natural Gas is also a producer than it would be if Louisiana Drillers were the only supplier. The quantity supplied at a given price would be even larger if we added a third producer, then a fourth, and so on. So an increase in the number of producers leads to an increase in supply and a rightward shift of the supply curve.

For a review of the factors that shift supply, see Table 3-2.

> An **individual supply curve** illustrates the relationship between quantity supplied and price for an individual producer.

FIGURE 3-10 The Individual Supply Curve and the Market Supply Curve

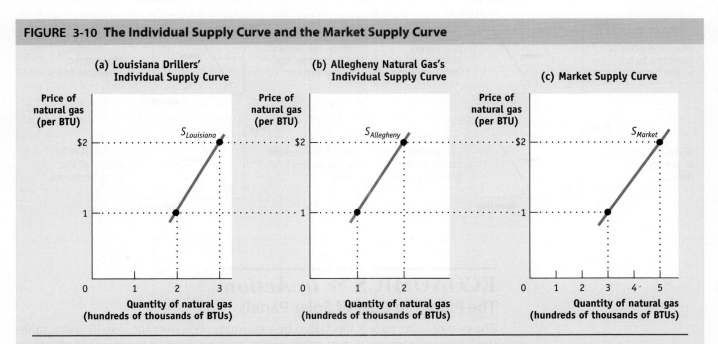

Panel (a) shows the individual supply curve for Louisiana Drillers, $S_{Louisiana}$, the quantity it will sell at any given price. Panel (b) shows the individual supply curve for Allegheny Natural Gas, $S_{Allegheny}$. The market supply curve, which shows the quantity of natural gas supplied by all producers at any given price is shown in panel (c). The market supply curve is the horizontal sum of the individual supply curves of all producers.

TABLE 3-2 Factors That Shift Supply

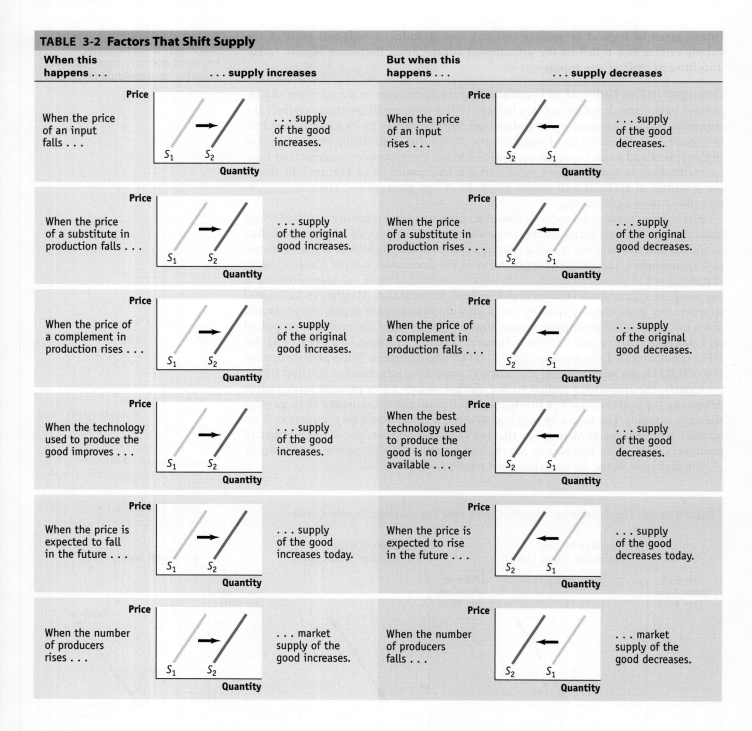

When this happens . . .	. . . supply increases	But when this happens . . .	. . . supply decreases
When the price of an input falls . . .	. . . supply of the good increases.	When the price of an input rises . . .	. . . supply of the good decreases.
When the price of a substitute in production falls . . .	. . . supply of the original good increases.	When the price of a substitute in production rises . . .	. . . supply of the original good decreases.
When the price of a complement in production rises . . .	. . . supply of the original good increases.	When the price of a complement in production falls . . .	. . . supply of the original good decreases.
When the technology used to produce the good improves . . .	. . . supply of the good increases.	When the best technology used to produce the good is no longer available . . .	. . . supply of the good decreases.
When the price is expected to fall in the future . . .	. . . supply of the good increases today.	When the price is expected to rise in the future . . .	. . . supply of the good decreases today.
When the number of producers rises . . .	. . . market supply of the good increases.	When the number of producers falls . . .	. . . market supply of the good decreases.

ECONOMICS >> *in Action*
The Plunging Cost of Solar Panels

The cost of solar panels has fallen by a stunning 99% over the last 40 years, making large-scale generation of solar energy an even more economical choice than more conventional forms of energy, such as coal-generated power. The lower cost of solar panels accounts for the proliferation of skyward-facing blue rectangles visible all across the United States. And, the cost of solar panels is projected to keep falling. Costs are projected to decline by 60% from 2019 to 2050 under the current state of technology, according to the National Renewable Energy Laboratory. Technological breakthroughs could result in an even greater decline.

What accounts for the enormous reductions in the cost of solar energy? There are two explanations. First, advances in technology played a major part. Over time, engineers discovered new, more efficient ways to convert solar rays into usable energy. These new technologies allowed solar panel producers to reduce the cost of production, increasing supply, which shifted the supply curve to the right.

The second driver of the plunge in solar panel prices began with an event that actually caused the price to increase: a change in the cost of a key input—polysilicon—that then led to a change in the number of producers.

Until 2008, solar panels were still relatively expensive and the market for them, while growing, was still small. That same year, polysilicon, the main input in solar panels (as well as semiconductor chips), surged to $475 per kilogram, up from around $30 four years earlier. The reason for this price surge—an increase of 1,500%—was that demand for both solar panels and semiconductor chips was growing. As a result, the demand for polysilicon was growing as well. But at the time, the market supply curve for polysilicon remained unchanged, ultimately contributing to the high price of polysilicon and a leftward shift in the supply curve for solar panels.

Although the high price of polysilicon in 2008 initially contributed to higher solar panel prices, it also prompted new polysilicon producers to enter the market, leading to a massive increase in supply. As a result, by 2014, the price of polysilicon had dropped from $475 to under $16 as the market supply curve shifted outward. Solar panel prices then dropped further and sales increased.

The U.S. Energy Information Administration estimates that in 2019 nearly 20% of new power plant capacity will be powered by solar energy. The amount of solar energy generated increased nearly 100-fold in the 10 years from 2008 to 2018.

Advances in technology and a change in the number of producers of polysilicon, a key input, contributed to the plunging cost of solar panels.

>> *Quick Review*

• The **supply schedule** shows how the **quantity supplied** depends on the price. The **supply curve** illustrates this relationship.

• Supply curves are normally upward sloping: at a higher price, producers are willing to supply more of a good or service.

• A change in price results in a **movement along the supply curve** and a change in the quantity supplied.

• Increases or decreases in supply lead to **shifts of the supply curve.** An increase in supply is a rightward shift: the quantity supplied rises for any given price. A decrease in supply is a leftward shift: the quantity supplied falls for any given price.

• The five main factors that can shift the supply curve are changes in (1) **input** prices, (2) prices of related goods or services, (3) technology, (4) expectations, and (5) number of producers.

• The market supply curve is the horizontal sum of the **individual supply curves** of all producers in the market.

>> *Check Your Understanding* **3-2**

Solutions appear at back of book.

1. Explain whether each of the following events represents (i) a *shift of* the supply curve or (ii) a *movement along* the supply curve.
   a. More homeowners put their houses up for sale during a real estate boom that causes house prices to rise.
   b. Many strawberry farmers open temporary roadside stands during harvest season, even though prices are usually low at that time.
   c. Immediately after the school year begins, fast-food chains must raise wages, which represent the price of labor, to attract workers.
   d. Many construction workers temporarily move to areas that have suffered hurricane damage, lured by higher wages.
   e. Since new technologies have made it possible to build larger cruise ships (which are cheaper to run per passenger), Caribbean cruise lines offer more cabins, at lower prices, than before.

|| Supply, Demand, and Equilibrium

We have now covered the first three key elements in the supply and demand model: the demand curve, the supply curve, and the set of factors that shift each curve. The next step is to put these elements together to show how they can be used to predict the actual price at which the good is bought and sold, as well as the actual quantity transacted.

A competitive market is in equilibrium when price has moved to a level at which the quantity of a good or service demanded equals the quantity of that good or service supplied. The price at which this takes place is the **equilibrium price**, also referred to as the **market-clearing price.** The quantity of the good or service bought and sold at that price is the **equilibrium quantity.**

What determines the price at which a good or service is bought and sold? What determines the quantity transacted of the good or service? In Chapter 1 we learned the general principle that *markets move toward equilibrium*, a situation in which no individual would be better off taking a different action. In the case of a competitive market, we can be more specific: a competitive market is in equilibrium when the price has moved to a level at which the quantity of a good demanded equals the quantity of that good supplied. At that price, no individual seller could make herself better off by offering to sell either more or less of the good and no individual buyer could make himself better off by offering to buy more or less of the good. In other words, at the market equilibrium, price has moved to a level that exactly matches the quantity demanded by consumers to the quantity supplied by sellers.

The price that matches the quantity supplied and the quantity demanded is the **equilibrium price;** the quantity bought and sold at that price is the **equilibrium quantity.** The equilibrium price is also known as the **market-clearing price:** it is the price that "clears the market" by ensuring that every buyer willing to pay that price finds a seller willing to sell at that price, and vice versa. So how do we find the equilibrium price and quantity?

Finding the Equilibrium Price and Quantity

The easiest way to determine the equilibrium price and quantity in a market is by putting the supply curve and the demand curve on the same diagram. Since the supply curve shows the quantity supplied at any given price and the demand curve shows the quantity demanded at any given price, the price at which the two curves cross is the equilibrium price: the price at which quantity supplied equals quantity demanded.

Figure 3-11 combines the demand curve from Figure 3-1 and the supply curve from Figure 3-6. They *intersect* at point *E*, which is the equilibrium of this market; $3 is the equilibrium price and 10 trillion BTUs is the equilibrium quantity.

Let's confirm that point *E* fits our definition of equilibrium. At a price of $3 per BTU, natural gas producers are willing to sell 10 trillion BTUs a year and natural

---

FIGURE 3-11 **Market Equilibrium**

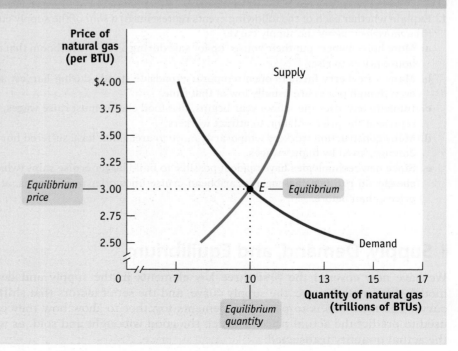

Market equilibrium occurs at point *E*, where the supply curve and the demand curve intersect. In equilibrium, the quantity demanded is equal to the quantity supplied. In this market, the equilibrium price is $3 per BTU and the equilibrium quantity is 10 trillion BTUs per year.

gas consumers want to buy 10 trillion BTUs a year. So at the price of $3 per BTU, the quantity of natural gas supplied equals the quantity demanded. Notice that at any other price the market would not clear: every willing buyer would not be able to find a willing seller, or vice versa. More specifically, if the price were more than $3, the quantity supplied would exceed the quantity demanded; if the price were less than $3, the quantity demanded would exceed the quantity supplied.

The model of supply and demand, then, predicts that given the demand and supply curves shown in Figure 3-11, 10 trillion BTUs would change hands at a price of $3 per BTU. But how can we be sure that the market will arrive at the equilibrium price? We begin by answering three simple questions:

1. Why do all sales and purchases in a market take place at the same price?
2. Why does the market price fall if it is above the equilibrium price?
3. Why does the market price rise if it is below the equilibrium price?

1. Why Do All Sales and Purchases in a Market Take Place at the Same Price?

There are some markets in which the same good can sell for many different prices, depending on who is selling or who is buying. For example, have you ever bought a souvenir in a tourist trap and then seen the same item on sale somewhere else for a lower price? Because tourists don't know which shops offer the best deals and don't have time for comparison shopping, sellers in tourist areas can charge different prices for the same good.

But in any market in which both buyers and sellers have been around for some time, sales and purchases tend to converge at a generally uniform price, so we can safely talk about *the* market price. It's easy to see why. Suppose a seller offered a potential buyer a price noticeably above what the buyer knew other people to be paying. The buyer would clearly be better off shopping elsewhere—unless the seller were prepared to offer a better deal.

Conversely, a seller would not be willing to sell for significantly less than the amount she knew most buyers were paying; she would be better off waiting to get a more reasonable customer. So in any well-established, ongoing market, all sellers receive and all buyers pay approximately the same price. This is what we call the *market price*.

2. Why Does the Market Price Fall If It Is Above the Equilibrium Price?

Suppose the supply and demand curves are as shown in Figure 3-11 but the market price is above the equilibrium level of $3—say, $3.50. This situation is illustrated in Figure 3-12. Why can't the price stay there?

As the figure shows, at a price of $3.50 there would be more BTUs of natural gas available than consumers wanted to buy: 11.2 trillion BTUs versus 8.1 trillion BTUs. The difference of 3.1 trillion BTUs is the **surplus**—also known as the *excess supply*—of natural gas at $3.50.

This surplus means that some natural gas producers are frustrated: at the current price, they cannot find consumers who want to buy their natural gas. The surplus offers an incentive for those frustrated would-be sellers to offer a lower price in order to poach business from other producers and entice more consumers to buy. The result of this price cutting will be to push the prevailing price down until it reaches the equilibrium price. So the price of a good will

There is a **surplus** of a good or service when the quantity supplied exceeds the quantity demanded. Surpluses occur when the price is above its equilibrium level.

FIGURE 3-12 Price Above Its Equilibrium Level Creates a Surplus

The market price of $3.50 is above the equilibrium price of $3. This creates a surplus: at a price of $3.50, producers would like to sell 11.2 trillion BTUs but consumers want to buy only 8.1 trillion BTUs, so there is a surplus of 3.1 trillion BTUs. This surplus will push the price down until it reaches the equilibrium price of $3.

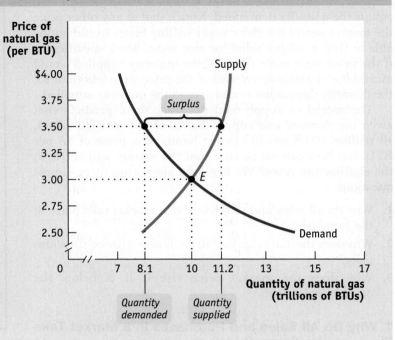

fall whenever there is a surplus—that is, whenever the market price is above its equilibrium level.

3. Why Does the Market Price Rise If It Is Below the Equilibrium Price? Now suppose the price is below its equilibrium level—say, at $2.75 per BTU, as shown in Figure 3-13. In this case, the quantity demanded, 11.5 trillion

FIGURE 3-13 Price Below Its Equilibrium Level Creates a Shortage

The market price of $2.75 is below the equilibrium price of $3. This creates a shortage: consumers want to buy 11.5 trillion BTUs, but only 9.1 trillion BTUs are for sale, so there is a shortage of 2.4 trillion BTUs. This shortage will push the price up until it reaches the equilibrium price of $3.

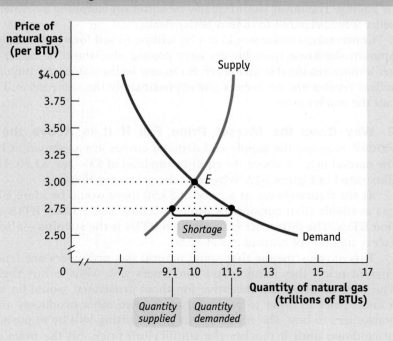

BTUs, exceeds the quantity supplied, 9.1 trillion BTUs, implying that there are would-be buyers who cannot find natural gas: there is a **shortage,** also known as an *excess demand,* of 2.4 trillion BTUs.

When there is a shortage, there are frustrated would-be buyers—people who want to purchase natural gas but cannot find willing sellers at the current price. In this situation, either buyers will offer more than the prevailing price or sellers will realize that they can charge higher prices. Either way, the result is to drive up the prevailing price.

This bidding up of prices happens whenever there are shortages—and there will be shortages whenever the price is below its equilibrium level. So the market price will always rise if it is below the equilibrium level.

> There is a **shortage** of a good or service when the quantity demanded exceeds the quantity supplied. Shortages occur when the price is below its equilibrium level.

Using Equilibrium to Describe Markets

We have now seen that a market tends to have a single price, the equilibrium price. If the market price is above the equilibrium level, the ensuing surplus leads buyers and sellers to take actions that lower the price. And if the market price is below the equilibrium level, the ensuing shortage leads buyers and sellers to take actions that raise the price. So the market price always *moves toward* the equilibrium price, the price at which there is neither surplus nor shortage.

ECONOMICS >> *in Action*
The Price of Admission

The market equilibrium, so the theory goes, is pretty egalitarian because the equilibrium price applies to everyone. That is, all buyers pay the same price—the equilibrium price—and all sellers receive that same price. But is this realistic?

The market for concert tickets is an example that seems to contradict the theory—there's one price at the box office, and there's another price (typically much higher) for the same event online where people who already have tickets resell them. For example, compare the box office price for a Billie Eilish concert in Philadelphia, Pennsylvania, in March 2020 to the StubHub.com price for seats in the same location: $149.50 versus $348.00.

Puzzling as this may seem, there is no contradiction once we take opportunity costs and tastes into account. For major events, buying tickets from the box office can mean waiting in very long "digital" lines. Ticket buyers who use online resellers have decided that the opportunity cost of their time is too high to spend waiting in line. And tickets for major events being sold at face value by online box offices often sell out within minutes. In this case, some people who want to go to the concert badly but have missed out on the opportunity to buy cheaper tickets from the online box office are willing to pay the higher online reseller price.

The competitive market model determines the price you pay for concert tickets.

Not only that, but by comparing prices across sellers for seats close to one another, you can see that markets really do move to equilibrium. For example, for a seat in Section 105, Row 12, StubHub's price was $278.80 while SeatGeek's price for a nearby seat was $278.00. As the competitive market model predicts, units of the same good will end up selling for approximately the same price.

In fact, e-commerce has made markets move to equilibrium more quickly by doing the price comparisons for you. The website SeatGeek compares ticket prices across more than 100 ticket resellers, allowing customers to instantly choose the best deal. Tickets that are priced lower than those of competitors will be snapped up, while higher priced tickets will languish unsold.

And tickets on StubHub can sell for less than the face value for events with little appeal, while they can skyrocket for events in high demand. For example, in 2019, the average ticket price on StubHub for Game 6 of the NBA Finals was over $3,300, with one fan paying nearly $70,000 for a pair of courtside seats to watch the Toronto Raptors win their first NBA championship. Even StubHub's chief executive said the site is "the embodiment of supply-and-demand economics."

So the theory of competitive markets isn't just speculation. If you want to experience it for yourself, try buying tickets to a concert or an NBA championship.

>> Quick Review

• Price in a competitive market moves to the **equilibrium price,** or **market-clearing price,** where the quantity supplied is equal to the quantity demanded. This quantity is the **equilibrium quantity.**

• All sales and purchases in a market take place at the same price. If the price is above its equilibrium level, there is a **surplus** that drives the price down to the equilibrium level. If the price is below its equilibrium level, there is a **shortage** that drives the price up to the equilibrium level.

>> Check Your Understanding 3-3
Solutions appear at back of book.

1. In the following three situations, the market is initially in equilibrium. Explain the changes in either supply or demand that result from each event. After each event described below, does a surplus or shortage exist at the original equilibrium price? What will happen to the equilibrium price as a result?
   a. 2018 was a very good year for California wine-grape growers, who produced a bumper crop.
   b. After a hurricane, Florida hoteliers often find that many people cancel their upcoming vacations, leaving them with empty hotel rooms.
   c. After a heavy snowfall, many people want to buy second-hand snowblowers at the local home improvement store.

‖ Changes in Supply and Demand

The huge fall in the price of natural gas from $14 to $2 per BTU from 2006 to 2013 may have come as a surprise to consumers, but to suppliers it was no surprise at all. Suppliers knew that advances in drilling technology had opened up vast reserves of natural gas that had been too costly to tap in the past. And, predictably, an increase in supply reduces the equilibrium price.

The adoption of improved drilling technology is an example of an event that shifted the supply curve for a good without having an effect on the demand curve. There are many such events. There are also events that shift the demand curve without shifting the supply curve. For example, a medical report that chocolate is good for you increases the demand for chocolate but does not affect the supply. Events often shift either the supply curve or the demand curve, but not both; it is therefore useful to ask what happens in each case.

We have seen that when a curve shifts, the equilibrium price and quantity change. We will now concentrate on exactly how the shift of a curve alters the equilibrium price and quantity.

What Happens When the Demand Curve Shifts

Heating oil and natural gas are substitutes: if the price of heating oil rises, the demand for natural gas will increase, and if the price of heating oil falls, the demand for natural gas will decrease. But how does the price of heating oil affect the *market equilibrium* for natural gas?

Figure 3-14 shows the effect of a rise in the price of heating oil on the market for natural gas. The rise in the price of heating oil increases the demand for natural gas. Point E_1 shows the equilibrium corresponding to the original demand curve, with P_1 the equilibrium price and Q_1 the equilibrium quantity bought and sold.

An increase in demand is indicated by a *rightward* shift of the demand curve from D_1 to D_2. At the original market price P_1, this market is no longer in equilibrium: a shortage occurs because the quantity demanded exceeds the quantity supplied. So the price of natural gas rises and generates an increase in the quantity supplied, an upward *movement along the supply curve*. A new equilibrium is established at point E_2, with a higher equilibrium price, P_2, and higher equilibrium

FIGURE 3-14 Equilibrium and Shifts of the Demand Curve

The original equilibrium in the market for natural gas is at E_1, at the intersection of the supply curve and the original demand curve, D_1. A rise in the price of heating oil, a substitute, shifts the demand curve rightward to D_2. A shortage exists at the original price, P_1, causing both the price and quantity supplied to rise, a movement along the supply curve. A new equilibrium is reached at E_2, with a higher equilibrium price, P_2, and a higher equilibrium quantity, Q_2. When demand for a good or service increases, the equilibrium price and the equilibrium quantity of the good or service both rise.

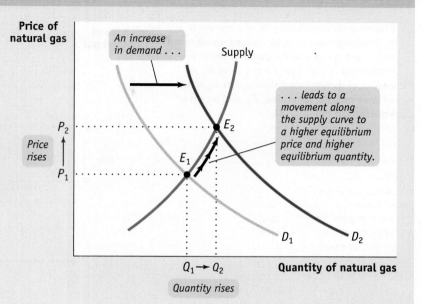

quantity, Q_2. This sequence of events reflects a general principle: *When demand for a good or service increases, the equilibrium price and the equilibrium quantity of the good or service both rise.*

What would happen in the reverse case, a fall in the price of heating oil? A fall in the price of heating oil reduces the demand for natural gas, shifting the demand curve to the *left*. At the original price, a surplus occurs as quantity supplied exceeds quantity demanded. The price falls and leads to a decrease in the quantity supplied, resulting in a lower equilibrium price and a lower equilibrium quantity. This illustrates another general principle: *When demand for a good or service decreases, the equilibrium price and the equilibrium quantity of the good or service both fall.*

To summarize how a market responds to a change in demand: *An increase in demand leads to a rise in both the equilibrium price and the equilibrium quantity. A decrease in demand leads to a fall in both the equilibrium price and the equilibrium quantity.*

What Happens When the Supply Curve Shifts

For most goods and services, it is a bit easier to predict changes in supply than changes in demand. Physical factors that affect supply, like weather or the availability of inputs, are easier to get a handle on than the fickle tastes that affect demand. Still, with supply as with demand, what we can best predict are the *effects* of shifts of the supply curve.

As we mentioned in the opening story, improved drilling technology significantly increased the supply of natural gas from 2006 onward. Figure 3-15 shows how this shift affected the market equilibrium. The original equilibrium is at E_1, the point of intersection of the original supply curve, S_1, with an equilibrium price P_1 and equilibrium quantity Q_1. As a result of the improved technology, supply increases and S_1 shifts *rightward* to S_2. At the original price P_1, a surplus of natural gas now exists and the market is no longer in equilibrium. The surplus causes a fall in price and an increase in the quantity demanded, a *downward movement along the demand curve.* The new equilibrium is at E_2, with an equilibrium price P_2 and an equilibrium quantity Q_2. In the new equilibrium

---

FIGURE 3-15 Equilibrium and Shifts of the Supply Curve

The original equilibrium in the market is at E_1. Improved technology causes an increase in the supply of natural gas and shifts the supply curve rightward from S_1 to S_2. A new equilibrium is established at E_2, with a lower equilibrium price, P_2, and a higher equilibrium quantity, Q_2.

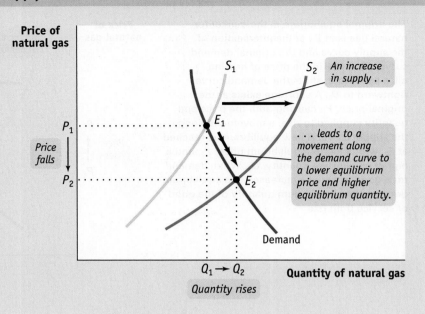

E_2, the price is lower and the equilibrium quantity is higher than before. This can be stated as a general principle: *When supply of a good or service increases, the equilibrium price of the good or service falls and the equilibrium quantity of the good or service rises.*

What happens to the market when supply falls? A fall in supply leads to a *leftward* shift of the supply curve. At the original price a shortage now exists. As a result, the equilibrium price rises and the quantity demanded falls. This describes what happened to the market for natural gas after Hurricane Katrina damaged natural gas production in the Gulf of Mexico in 2005. We can formulate a general principle: *When supply of a good or service decreases, the equilibrium price of the good or service rises and the equilibrium quantity of the good or service falls.*

To summarize how a market responds to a change in supply: *An increase in supply leads to a fall in the equilibrium price and a rise in the equilibrium quantity. A decrease in supply leads to a rise in the equilibrium price and a fall in the equilibrium quantity.*

Simultaneous Shifts of Supply and Demand Curves

Finally, it sometimes happens that events shift *both* the demand and supply curves at the same time. This is not unusual; in real life, supply curves and demand curves for many goods and services shift quite often because the economic environment continually changes.

Figure 3-16 illustrates two examples of simultaneous shifts. In both panels there is an increase in supply—that is, a rightward shift of the supply curve from S_1 to S_2—representing, for example, adoption of an improved drilling technology. Notice that the rightward shift in panel (a) is smaller than the one in panel (b): we can suppose that panel (a) represents a small, incremental change in technology while panel (b) represents a big advance in technology.

Both panels show a decrease in demand—that is, a leftward shift from D_1 to D_2. Also notice that the leftward shift in panel (a) is relatively larger than the one in panel (b): we can suppose that panel (a) reflects the effect on demand of

---

PITFALLS

WHICH CURVE IS IT?

When the price of a good or service changes, in general, we can say that this reflects a change in either supply or demand. But which one is it? A helpful clue is the direction of change in the quantity. If the quantity sold changes in the *same* direction as the price—for example, if both the price and the quantity rise—it is likely that the demand curve has shifted. If the price and the quantity move in *opposite* directions, the likely cause is a shift of the supply curve.

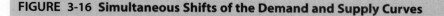

FIGURE 3-16 **Simultaneous Shifts of the Demand and Supply Curves**

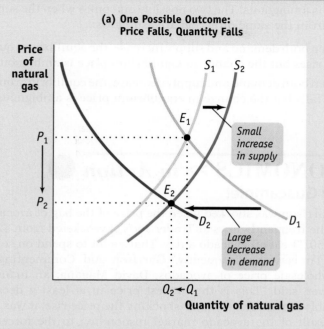

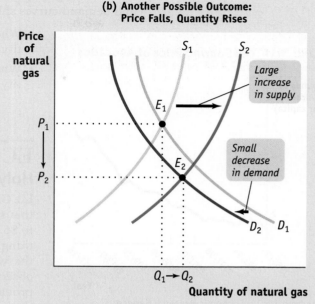

In panel (a) there is a simultaneous leftward shift of the demand curve and a rightward shift of the supply curve. Here the decrease in demand is relatively larger than the increase in supply, so the equilibrium quantity falls as the equilibrium price also falls. In panel (b) there is also a simultaneous leftward shift of the demand curve and rightward shift of the supply curve. Here the increase in supply is large relative to the decrease in demand, so the equilibrium quantity rises as the equilibrium price falls.

a deep recession in the overall economy, while panel (b) reflects the effect of a mild winter.

In both cases the equilibrium price falls from P_1 to P_2 as the equilibrium moves from E_1 to E_2. But what happens to the equilibrium quantity, the quantity of natural gas bought and sold? In panel (a) the decrease in demand is large relative to the increase in supply, and the equilibrium quantity falls as a result. In panel (b) the increase in supply is large relative to the decrease in demand, and the equilibrium quantity rises as a result. That is, when demand decreases and supply increases, the actual quantity bought and sold can go either way depending on *how much* the demand and supply curves have shifted.

In general, when supply and demand shift in opposite directions, we can't predict what the ultimate effect will be on the quantity bought and sold. What we can say is that a curve that shifts a disproportionately greater distance than the other curve will have a disproportionately greater effect on the quantity bought and sold. That said, we can make the following prediction about the outcome when the supply and demand curves shift in opposite directions:

- When demand decreases and supply increases, the equilibrium price falls but the change in the equilibrium quantity is ambiguous.
- When demand increases and supply decreases, the equilibrium price rises but the change in the equilibrium quantity is ambiguous.

But suppose that the demand and supply curves shift in the same direction. This is what has happened in the United States, as the economy made a gradual recovery from the recession in 2008, resulting in an increase in both demand and supply. Can we safely make any predictions about the changes in price and quantity? In this situation, the change in quantity bought and sold can be predicted, but the change in price is ambiguous. The two possible outcomes when the supply and demand curves shift in the same direction are as follows:

- When both demand and supply increase, the equilibrium quantity rises but the change in equilibrium price is ambiguous.
- When both demand and supply decrease, the equilibrium quantity falls but the change in equilibrium price is ambiguous.

FIGURE 3-17 The Soaring Price of Avocados

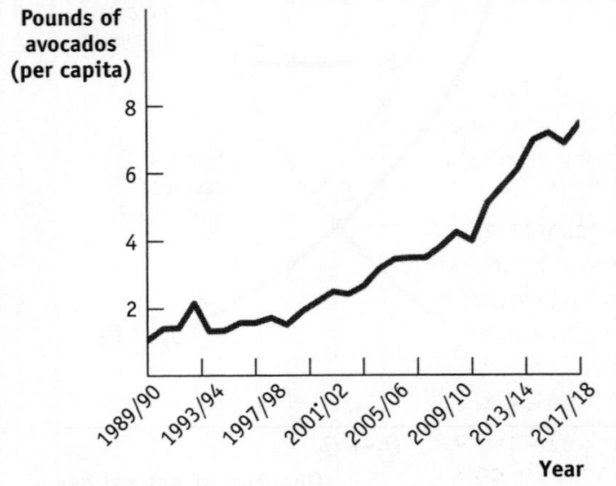

Pounds of avocados (per capita)

Data from: USDA, Economic Research Service.

ECONOMICS >> *in Action*
Holy Guacamole!

Liz Garrison was shocked when the price of the bag of avocados that she frequently buys at Trader Joe's skyrocketed from $2.50 to $6.50. "I eat an avocado a day. That's a lot to spend on something I'm eating so frequently," Garrison said. Commenting on the wholesale price of avocados, David Magaña, an industry observer, said "This is the highest price in at least a decade, probably more." Yet, however shocking the price rise, it was just the result of the avocado market responding to the forces of supply and demand.

First, you can thank Americans' fast-growing appetite (demand) for all things avocado: guacamole, avocado toast, and avocado smoothies. In 2018 the average American ate nearly 7.5 pounds of the fruit per year, compared to 1.1 pounds per year in 1989. In addition, demand for avocados is growing in other places such as Europe and China. Both of these events shifted the demand curve rightward.

Second, there's supply. In 2019 the California avocado harvest was the smallest in a decade following a severe heatwave, coming in nearly 50% lower than in 2018. In addition, two other major avocado growing areas—Peru and South Africa—experienced year-on-year declines in output. These events shifted the supply curve leftward.

Inevitably, an increase in demand coupled with a sharp fall in supply leads to sharply rising prices for avocados. It's economic logic, after all. Until demand falls, or supply rises, or both, the price of satisfying America's avocado cravings will remain high, as shown in Figure 3-17.

However, there's a bright spot on the horizon for avocado lovers. Heavy winter rainfall in California early in 2019 gave growers (and their crops) a boost, according to market analysts. So keep your tortilla chips on hand and ready for dipping.

>> Quick Review

- Changes in the equilibrium price and quantity in a market result from shifts of the supply curve, the demand curve, or both.

- An increase in demand increases both the equilibrium price and the equilibrium quantity. A decrease in demand decreases both the equilibrium price and the equilibrium quantity.

- An increase in supply drives the equilibrium price down but increases the equilibrium quantity. A decrease in supply raises the equilibrium price but reduces the equilibrium quantity.

- Often fluctuations in markets involve shifts of both the supply and demand curves. When they shift in the same direction, the change in equilibrium quantity is predictable but the change in equilibrium price is not. When they shift in opposite directions, the change in equilibrium price is predictable but the change in equilibrium quantity is not. When there are simultaneous shifts of the demand and supply curves, the curve that shifts the greater distance has a greater effect on the change in equilibrium price and quantity.

>> Check Your Understanding 3-4

Solutions appear at back of book.

1. For each of the following, determine (i) the market in question; (ii) whether a shift in demand or supply occurred, the direction of the shift, and what induced the shift; and (iii) the effect of the shift on the equilibrium price and the equilibrium quantity.
   a. As U.S. gasoline prices fall, more people buy large cars.
   b. As technological innovation has lowered the cost of recycling used paper, fresh paper made from recycled stock is used more frequently.
   c. When a local cable company offers cheaper on-demand films, local movie theaters have more unfilled seats.
2. When a new, faster computer chip is introduced, demand for computers using the older, slower chips decreases. Simultaneously, computer makers increase their

production of computers containing the old chips in order to clear out their stocks of old chips.

a. Draw two diagrams of the market for computers containing the old chips: one in which the equilibrium quantity falls in response to these events and one in which the equilibrium quantity rises.

b. What happens to the equilibrium price in each diagram?

|| Competitive Markets — and Others

Earlier in this chapter we defined a competitive market and explained that the supply and demand framework is a model of competitive markets. But why does it matter whether or not a market is competitive? Now that we've seen how the supply and demand model works, we can offer some explanation.

To understand why competitive markets are different from other markets, compare the problems facing two individuals: a wheat farmer who must decide whether to grow more wheat and the president of a giant aluminum company—say, Alcoa—who must decide whether to produce more aluminum.

For the wheat farmer, the question is simply whether the extra wheat can be sold at a price high enough to justify the extra production cost. The farmer need not worry about whether producing more wheat will affect the price of the wheat he or she was already planning to grow. That's because the wheat market is competitive. There are thousands of wheat farmers, and one farmer's decision will not impact the market price.

But for the Alcoa executive, the aluminum market is *not* competitive. There are only a few big producers, including Alcoa, and each of them is well aware that its actions *do* have a noticeable impact on the market price. This adds a whole new level of complexity to the decisions producers have to make. Alcoa can't decide whether or not to produce more aluminum just by asking whether the additional product will sell for more than it costs to make. The company also has to ask whether producing more aluminum will drive down the market price and reduce its *profit*, its net gain from producing and selling its output.

When a market is competitive, individuals can base decisions on less complicated analyses than those used in a noncompetitive market. This in turn means that it's easier for economists to build a model of a competitive market than of a noncompetitive market.

This doesn't mean that economic analysis has nothing to say about noncompetitive markets. On the contrary, economists can offer some very important insights into how other kinds of markets work. But those insights require other models.

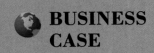
Uber Gives Riders a Lesson in Supply and Demand

JEENAH MOON/The New York Times/Redux

Two young entrepreneurs, Garrett Camp and Travis Kalanick, created Uber in 2009 to alleviate a common frustration: how to find a taxi when you need to get somewhere and there aren't any taxis available. In densely populated cities like New York City, finding a taxi is relatively easy on most days—stand on a corner, stick out your arm, and before long a taxi will stop to pick you up. And you know exactly what taxi fare rates will be before you step into the car, because they are set by city regulators.

But at other times, it can be difficult to find a taxi, and you can wait a very long time for one—for example, on rainy days or during rush hour. As you wait, you will probably notice empty taxis passing you by—drivers who have quit working for the day and are headed home. Moreover, there are times when it is simply impossible to hail a taxi—such as during a snowstorm or on New Year's Eve.

Uber was created to address this problem. Using an app, Uber connects people who want a ride to drivers with cars. It also registers drivers, sets fares, and automatically collects payment from a registered rider's credit card. Uber then keeps 25% of the fare, with the rest going to the driver. As of 2019, Uber was operating in 65 countries and in more than 600 cities, and booked $11.3 billion in rides.

Studies have shown that Uber fares are either roughly equal to or less than regular taxi fares during normal driving hours. The qualification *during normal driving hours* is important because at other times Uber's rates fluctuate. When there are more people looking for a ride than cars available, Uber uses what it calls *surge pricing:* setting the rate higher until everyone who wants a car at the going price can get one. For example, during a snowstorm or on New Year's Eve, Uber rides cost around 9 to 10 times the standard price. Enraged, some Uber customers have accused it of price gouging.

But according to their founders, Uber's surge pricing is simply a method of keeping customers happy because the surge price is calculated to leave as few people as possible without a ride. As Kalanick explains, "We do not own cars nor do we employ drivers. Higher prices are required to get cars on the road and keep them on the road during the busiest times." However, with more drivers joining Uber's fleet, drivers are finding that it takes longer hours to make sufficient income. So in cities like San Diego where passengers have limited access to taxi services, Uber drivers have banded together to take "synchronized breaks" during peak hours, such as Saturday nights. These breaks cause prices to surge, which prompts the drivers to jump into their cars. Clearly these Uber drivers know how supply and demand works.

QUESTIONS FOR THOUGHT

1. What accounts for the fact that before Uber's arrival, there were typically enough taxis available for everyone who wanted one on good weather days, but not enough available on bad weather days?

2. How does Uber's surge pricing solve the problem? Assess Kalanick's claim that the price is set to leave as few people possible without a ride.

3. Use a supply and demand diagram to illustrate how Uber drivers can cause prices to surge by taking coordinated breaks. Why is this strategy unlikely to work in New York, a large city with an established fleet of taxis?

SUMMARY

1. The **supply and demand model** illustrates how a **competitive market,** one with many buyers and sellers, none of whom can influence the market price, works.

2. The **demand schedule** shows the **quantity demanded** at each price and is represented graphically by a **demand curve. The law of demand** says that demand curves slope downward; that is, a higher price for a good or service leads people to demand a smaller quantity, other things equal.

3. A **movement along the demand curve** occurs when a price change leads to a change in the quantity demanded. When economists talk of increasing or decreasing demand, they mean **shifts of the demand curve**—a change in the quantity demanded at any given price. An increase in demand causes a rightward shift of the demand curve. A decrease in demand causes a leftward shift.

4. There are five main factors that shift the demand curve:
   - A change in the prices of related goods or services, such as **substitutes** or **complements**
   - A change in income: when income rises, the demand for **normal goods** increases and the demand for **inferior goods** decreases
   - A change in tastes
   - A change in expectations
   - A change in the number of consumers

5. The market demand curve for a good or service is the horizontal sum of the **individual demand curves** of all consumers in the market.

6. The **supply schedule** shows the **quantity supplied** at each price and is represented graphically by a **supply curve.** Supply curves usually slope upward.

7. A **movement along the supply curve** occurs when a price change leads to a change in the quantity supplied. When economists talk of increasing or decreasing supply, they mean **shifts of the supply curve**—a

change in the quantity supplied at any given price. An increase in supply causes a rightward shift of the supply curve. A decrease in supply causes a leftward shift.

8. There are five main factors that shift the supply curve:
   - A change in **input** prices
   - A change in the prices of related goods and services
   - A change in technology
   - A change in expectations
   - A change in the number of producers

9. The market supply curve for a good or service is the horizontal sum of the **individual supply curves** of all producers in the market.

10. The supply and demand model is based on the principle that the price in a market moves to its **equilibrium price,** or **market-clearing price,** the price at which the quantity demanded is equal to the quantity supplied. This quantity is the **equilibrium quantity.** When the price is above its market-clearing level, there is a **surplus** that pushes the price down. When the price is below its market-clearing level, there is a **shortage** that pushes the price up.

11. An increase in demand increases both the equilibrium price and the equilibrium quantity; a decrease in demand has the opposite effect. An increase in supply reduces the equilibrium price and increases the equilibrium quantity; a decrease in supply has the opposite effect.

12. Shifts of the demand curve and the supply curve can happen simultaneously. When they shift in opposite directions, the change in equilibrium price is predictable but the change in equilibrium quantity is not. When they shift in the same direction, the change in equilibrium quantity is predictable but the change in equilibrium price is not. In general, the curve that shifts the greater distance has a greater effect on the changes in equilibrium price and quantity.

KEY TERMS

Competitive market, p. 68
Supply and demand model, p. 68
Demand schedule, p. 69
Quantity demanded, p. 70
Demand curve, p. 70
Law of demand, p. 70
Shift of the demand curve, p. 71
Movement along the demand curve, p. 71

Substitutes, p. 73
Complements, p. 73
Normal good, p. 74
Inferior good, p. 74
Individual demand curve, p. 75
Quantity supplied, p. 78
Supply schedule, p. 78
Supply curve, p. 79
Shift of the supply curve, p. 79

Movement along the supply curve, p. 80
Input, p. 82
Individual supply curve, p. 83
Equilibrium price, p. 86
Equilibrium quantity, p. 86
Market-clearing price, p. 86
Surplus, p. 87
Shortage, p. 89

PRACTICE QUESTIONS

1. In the market for automobiles explain how demand responds to (i) an increase in the price of automobiles today and (ii) an expected increase in the future price of automobiles.

2. Explain why the following statement is misleading: "Apple increases supply of watches following an unexpected increase in demand."

3. In each of the following, what is the mistake that underlies the statement? Explain the mistake in terms of supply and demand and the factors that influence them.

   a. Consumers are illogical because they are buying more Starbucks beverages in 2019 despite the fact that Starbucks has raised prices 10 to 30 cents per drink.

   b. Consumers are illogical because they buy less at Cost-U-Less Warehouse Superstore when their incomes go up.

   c. Consumers are illogical for buying an iPhone 11 when an iPhone X costs less.

4. Two students are debating the effects of an expected decline in future home prices. One student claims that a decline in home prices will increase the total quantity of homes while the other student claims that the quantity of homes will decline. Which student is correct? Explain. Be sure to discuss how expected price changes shift demand and/or supply.

PROBLEMS

1. A study conducted by Yahoo! revealed that chocolate is the most popular flavor of ice cream in America. For each of the following, indicate the possible effects on demand, supply, or both as well as equilibrium price and quantity of chocolate ice cream.

   a. A severe drought in the Midwest causes dairy farmers to reduce the number of milk-producing cattle in their herds by a third. These dairy farmers supply cream that is used to manufacture chocolate ice cream.

   b. A new report by the American Medical Association reveals that chocolate does, in fact, have significant health benefits.

   c. The discovery of cheaper synthetic vanilla flavoring lowers the price of vanilla ice cream.

   d. New technology for mixing and freezing ice cream lowers manufacturers' costs of producing chocolate ice cream.

2. In a supply and demand diagram, draw the shift of the demand curve for hamburgers in your hometown due to the following events. In each case, show the effect on equilibrium price and quantity.

   a. The price of tacos increases.

   b. All hamburger sellers raise the price of their french fries.

   c. Income falls in town. Assume that hamburgers are a normal good for most people.

   d. Income falls in town. Assume that hamburgers are an inferior good for most people.

   e. Hot dog stands cut the price of hot dogs.

3. The market for many goods changes in predictable ways according to the time of year, in response to events such as holidays, vacation times, seasonal changes in production, and so on. Using supply and demand, explain the change in price in each of the following cases. Note that supply and demand may shift simultaneously.

   a. Lobster prices usually fall during the summer peak lobster harvest season, despite the fact that people like to eat lobster during the summer more than at any other time of year.

   b. The price of a Christmas tree is lower after Christmas than before but fewer trees are sold.

   c. The price of a round-trip ticket to Paris on Air France falls by more than $200 after the end of school vacation in September. This happens despite the fact that generally worsening weather increases the cost of operating flights to Paris, and Air France therefore reduces the number of flights to Paris at any given price.

4. Show in a diagram the effect on the demand curve, the supply curve, the equilibrium price, and the equilibrium quantity of each of the following events.

   a. The market for hotel rooms in your town

      Case 1: The wages of housekeepers go up.

      Case 2: A major political convention will be held in your town, attracting many visitors from across the country.

   b. The market for Kansas City Chiefs cotton T-shirts

      Case 1: The Chiefs win the Super Bowl.

      Case 2: The price of cotton increases.

   c. The market for bagels

      Case 1: People realize that bagels are high in calories and sugar.

      Case 2: People have less time to cook breakfast in the morning.

   d. The market for the Krugman and Wells economics textbook

      Case 1: Your professor makes it required reading for all of his or her students.

      Case 2: Printing costs for textbooks are lowered by the use of synthetic paper.

5. Let's assume that each person in the United States consumes an average of 37 gallons of soft drinks (nondiet) at an average price of $2 per gallon and that the U.S. population is 294 million. At a price of $1.50 per gallon, each individual consumer would demand 50 gallons of soft drinks. From this information about the individual demand schedule, calculate the market demand schedule for soft drinks for the prices of $1.50 and $2 per gallon.

6. Suppose that the supply schedule of Maine lobsters is as follows:

Price of lobster (per pound)	Quantity of lobster supplied (pounds)
$25	800
20	700
15	600
10	500
5	400

Suppose that Maine lobsters can be sold only in the United States. The U.S. demand schedule for Maine lobsters is as follows:

Price of lobster (per pound)	Quantity of lobster demanded (pounds)
$25	200
20	400
15	600
10	800
5	1,000

a. Draw the demand curve and the supply curve for Maine lobsters. What are the equilibrium price and quantity of lobsters?

Now suppose that Maine lobsters can be sold in France. The French demand schedule for Maine lobsters is as follows:

Price of lobster (per pound)	Quantity of lobster demanded (pounds)
$25	100
20	300
15	500
10	700
5	900

b. What is the demand schedule for Maine lobsters now that French consumers can also buy them? Draw a supply and demand diagram that illustrates the new equilibrium price and quantity of lobsters. What will happen to the price at which fishermen can sell lobster? What will happen to the price paid by U.S. consumers? What will happen to the quantity consumed by U.S. consumers?

7. Find the flaws in reasoning in the following statements, paying particular attention to the distinction between shifts of and movements along the supply and demand curves. Draw a diagram to illustrate what actually happens in each situation.

a. "A technological innovation that lowers the cost of producing a good might seem at first to result in a reduction in the price of the good to consumers. But a fall in price will increase demand for the good, and higher demand will send the price up again. It is not certain, therefore, that an innovation will really reduce price in the end."

b. "A study shows that eating a clove of garlic a day can help prevent heart disease, causing many consumers to demand more garlic. This increase in demand results in a rise in the price of garlic. Consumers, seeing that the price of garlic has gone up, reduce their demand for garlic. This causes the demand for garlic to decrease and the price of garlic to fall. Therefore, the ultimate effect of the study on the price of garlic is uncertain."

8. The following table shows a demand schedule for a normal good.

Price	Quantity demanded
$23	70
21	90
19	110
17	130

a. Do you think that the increase in quantity demanded (say, from 90 to 110 in the table) when price decreases (from $21 to $19) is due to a rise in consumers' income? Explain clearly (and briefly) why or why not.

b. Now suppose that the good is an inferior good. Would the demand schedule still be valid for an inferior good?

c. Lastly, assume you do not know whether the good is normal or inferior. Devise an experiment that would allow you to determine which one it was. Explain.

9. In recent years, the number of car producers in China has increased rapidly. In fact, China now has more car brands than the United States. In addition, car sales have climbed every year and automakers have increased their output at even faster rates, causing fierce competition and a decline in prices. At the same time, Chinese consumers' incomes have risen. Assume that cars are a normal good. Draw a diagram of the supply and demand curves for cars in China to explain what has happened in the Chinese car market.

10. Aaron Hank is a star hitter for the Bay City baseball team. He is close to breaking the major league record for home runs hit during one season, and it is widely anticipated that in the next game he will break that record. As a result, tickets for the team's next game have been a hot commodity. But today it is announced that, due to a knee injury, he will not in fact play in the team's next game. Assume that season ticket-holders are able to

resell their tickets if they wish. Use supply and demand diagrams to explain your answers to parts a and b.

a. Show the case in which this announcement results in a lower equilibrium price and a lower equilibrium quantity than before the announcement.

b. Show the case in which this announcement results in a lower equilibrium price and a higher equilibrium quantity than before the announcement.

c. What accounts for whether case a or case b occurs?

d. Suppose that a scalper had secretly learned before the announcement that Aaron Hank would not play in the next game. What actions do you think he would take?

11. Fans of music often bemoan the high price of concert tickets. One superstar has argued that it isn't worth hundreds, even thousands, of dollars to see her perform. Let's assume this star sold out arenas around the country at an average ticket price of $75.

a. How would you evaluate the argument that ticket prices are too high?

b. Suppose that due to this star's protests, ticket prices were lowered to $50. In what sense is this price too low? Draw a diagram using supply and demand curves to support your argument.

c. Suppose the superstar really wanted to bring down ticket prices. Since she controls the supply of her services, what would you recommend she do? Explain using a supply and demand diagram.

d. Suppose this performer's next album was a total dud. Do you think she would still have to worry about ticket prices being too high? Why or why not? Draw a supply and demand diagram to support your argument.

e. Suppose the performer announced that her next tour was going to be her last. What effect would this likely have on the demand for and price of tickets? Illustrate with a supply and demand diagram.

12. After several years of decline, the market for handmade acoustic guitars is making a comeback. These guitars are usually made in small workshops employing relatively few highly skilled luthiers. Assess the impact on the equilibrium price and quantity of handmade acoustic guitars as a result of each of the following events. In your answers indicate which curve(s) shift(s) and in which direction.

a. Environmentalists succeed in having the use of Brazilian rosewood banned in the United States, forcing luthiers to seek out alternative, more costly woods.

b. A foreign producer reengineers the guitar-making process and floods the market with identical guitars.

c. Music featuring handmade acoustic guitars makes a comeback as audiences tire of heavy metal and alternative rock music.

d. The country goes into a deep recession and the income of the average American falls sharply.

13. *Demand twisters:* Sketch and explain the demand relationship in each of the following statements.

a. I would never buy a Taylor Swift album! You couldn't even give me one for nothing.

b. I generally buy a bit more coffee as the price falls. But once the price falls to $2 per pound, I'll buy out the entire stock of the supermarket.

c. I spend more on orange juice even as the price rises. (Does this mean that I must be violating the law of demand?)

d. Due to a tuition rise, most students at a college find themselves with less disposable income. Almost all of them eat more frequently at the school cafeteria and less often at restaurants, even though prices at the cafeteria have risen, too. (This one requires that you draw both the demand and the supply curves for school cafeteria meals.)

14. Will Shakespeare is a struggling playwright in sixteenth-century London. As the price he receives for writing a play increases, he is willing to write more plays. For the following situations, use a diagram to illustrate how each event affects the equilibrium price and quantity in the market for Shakespeare's plays.

a. The playwright Christopher Marlowe, Shakespeare's chief rival, is killed in a bar brawl.

b. The bubonic plague, a deadly infectious disease, breaks out in London.

c. To celebrate the defeat of the Spanish Armada, Queen Elizabeth declares several weeks of festivities, which involves commissioning new plays.

15. This year, the small town of Middling experiences a sudden doubling of the birth rate. After three years, the birth rate returns to normal. Use a diagram to illustrate the effect of these events on the following.

a. The market for an hour of babysitting services in Middling this year

b. The market for an hour of babysitting services 14 years into the future, after the birth rate has returned to normal, by which time children born today are old enough to work as babysitters

c. The market for an hour of babysitting services 30 years into the future, when children born today are likely to be having children of their own

16. Use a diagram to illustrate how each of the following events affects the equilibrium price and quantity of pizza.

a. The price of mozzarella cheese rises.

b. The health hazards of hamburgers are widely publicized.

c. The price of tomato sauce falls.

d. The incomes of consumers rise, and pizza is an inferior good.

e. Consumers expect the price of pizza to fall next week.

17. Although he was a prolific artist, Pablo Picasso painted only 1,000 canvases during his "Blue Period." Picasso is now dead, and all of his Blue Period works are currently on display in museums and private galleries throughout Europe and the United States.

   a. Draw a supply curve for Picasso Blue Period works. Why is this supply curve different from ones you have seen?

   b. Given the supply curve from part a, the price of a Picasso Blue Period work will be entirely dependent on what factor(s)? Draw a diagram showing how the equilibrium price of such a work is determined.

   c. Suppose rich art collectors decide that it is essential to acquire Picasso Blue Period art for their collections. Show the impact of this on the market for these paintings.

18. Draw the appropriate curve in each of the following cases. Is it like or unlike the curves you have seen so far? Explain.

   a. The demand for cardiac bypass surgery, given that the government pays the full cost for any patient

   b. The demand for elective cosmetic plastic surgery, given that the patient pays the full cost

   c. The supply of reprints of Annie Leibovitz photographs

19. In 2018 the price of oil fell to a 14-year low. For drivers, the cost of driving fell significantly as gasoline prices plunged. For the airline industry, the cost of operation also fell significantly because jet fuel is a major expense.

   a. Draw a supply and demand diagram that illustrates the effect of a fall in the price of jet fuel on the supply of air travel.

   b. Draw a supply and demand diagram that illustrates the effect of a fall in the price of oil on the demand for air travel. (*Hint:* think about this in terms of the substitutes for air travel, like driving.)

   c. Put the diagrams from parts a and b together. What happens to the equilibrium price and quantity of air travel?

Despite the fall in the cost of driving, many more Americans chose to fly to their destinations during 2018 as incomes rose and people splurged on vacations that had been postponed during the Great Recession.

   d. Using your results from part c, modify your diagram to illustrate an outcome in which the equilibrium price of air travel rises as people take more vacations by air.

▚ WORK IT OUT

20. The accompanying table gives the annual U.S. demand and supply schedules for pickup trucks.

Price of truck	Quantity of trucks demanded (millions)	Quantity of trucks supplied (millions)
$20,000	20	14
25,000	18	15
30,000	16	16
35,000	14	17
40,000	12	18

   a. Plot the demand and supply curves using these schedules. Indicate the equilibrium price and quantity on your diagram.

   b. Suppose the tires used on pickup trucks are found to be defective. What would you expect to happen in the market for pickup trucks? Show this on your diagram.

   c. Suppose that the U.S. Department of Transportation imposes costly regulations on manufacturers that cause them to reduce supply by one-third at any given price. Calculate and plot the new supply schedule and indicate the new equilibrium price and quantity on your diagram. ∎

4 ❯ Consumer and Producer Surplus

MASTERING TEXTBOOK ECONOMICS

ALTHOUGH YOU ARE JUST BEGINNING your study of economics, chances are that you have already made a number of economic decisions regarding your textbooks — this one included. It is likely you've had several options to choose from. Do you purchase an e-book subscription, a new copy of the actual textbook, or a used copy? Do you rent the book or borrow a copy? According to a survey by Campusbooks.com, a significant number of students are still choosing to purchase physical textbooks. Of those surveyed, 67% had bought a used textbook and 25% purchased a new text.

Rawpixel.com/Shutterstock

How much am I willing to pay for my textbook?

With so many students choosing to use physical textbooks, there is also a very lively market in used textbooks. And whenever a market exists, it means that people are making decisions. Students who own a physical textbook will make a decision at the end of the course whether or not to keep their books: is the money made by selling their used textbook worth more than keeping the book? Likewise, students looking to purchase a textbook will determine whether the price of a somewhat battered used textbook is low enough that they are better

off buying it rather than renting the book, or buying a new book or an e-book subscription.

Both students who sell their books and those who buy them clearly benefit from the existence of the second-hand book market whether it is online, in the college bookstore, or elsewhere. But can we put a number on what used textbook sellers and buyers gain from these transactions? Can we answer the question, "How much do the buyers and sellers of textbooks gain from the existence of the used-book market"?

Yes, we can. In this chapter we will see how to measure benefits, such as those to buyers of used textbooks, from being able to purchase a good — known as *consumer surplus*. And we will see that there is a corresponding measure, *producer surplus,* of the benefits sellers receive from being able to sell a good.

The concepts of consumer surplus and producer surplus are extremely useful for analyzing a wide variety of economic issues. They let us calculate how much benefit producers and consumers receive from the existence of a market. They also allow us to calculate how the welfare of consumers and producers is affected by changes in market prices. Such calculations play a crucial role in evaluating many economic policies.

What information do we need to calculate consumer and producer surplus? Surprisingly, all we need are the demand and supply curves for a good. That is, the supply and demand model isn't just a model of how a competitive market works — it's also a model of how much consumers and producers gain from participating in that market.

So our first step will be to learn how consumer and producer surplus can be derived from the demand and supply curves. We will then see how these concepts can be applied to actual economic issues. ●

‖ Consumer Surplus and the Demand Curve

The market in used textbooks is a big business in terms of dollars and cents—estimated to transact over a billion dollars each year. More importantly for us, it is a convenient starting point for developing the concepts of consumer and producer surplus. We'll use the concepts of consumer and producer surplus to understand exactly how buyers and sellers benefit from a competitive market and how big those benefits are. In addition, these concepts play important roles in analyzing what happens when competitive markets don't work well or there is interference in the market.

So let's begin by looking at the market for used textbooks, starting with the buyers. To keep the discussion simple, we'll assume that all transactions are done through the campus bookstore. The key point, as we'll see in a minute, is that the demand curve is derived from their tastes or preferences—and that those same preferences also determine how much they gain from the opportunity to buy used books.

Willingness to Pay and the Demand Curve

A used book is not as good as a new book—it will be battered and coffee-stained, may include someone else's highlighting, and may not be completely up to date. How much this bothers you depends on your preferences. Some potential buyers would prefer to buy the used book even if it is only slightly cheaper than a new one; others would buy the used book only if it is considerably cheaper.

Let's define a potential buyer's **willingness to pay** as the maximum price at which they would buy a good, in this case a used textbook. An individual won't buy the good if it costs more than this amount but they are eager to do so if it costs less. If the price is just equal to an individual's willingness to pay, they are indifferent between buying and not buying. For the sake of simplicity, we'll assume that the individual buys the good in this case.

The table in Figure 4-1 shows five potential buyers of a used book that costs $100 new, listed in order of their willingness to pay. At one extreme is Aisha, who will buy a second-hand book even if the price is as high as $59. Ben is less willing to have a used book and will buy one only if the price is $45 or less. Chloe is willing to pay only $35, and Darsh, only $25. And Elena, who really doesn't like the idea of a used book, will buy one only if it costs no more than $10.

How many of these five students will actually buy a used book? It depends on the price. If the price of a used book is $55, only Aisha buys one; if the price is $40, Aisha and Ben both buy used books, and so on. So the information in the table can be used to construct the *demand schedule* for used textbooks.

We can use this demand schedule to derive the market demand curve shown in Figure 4-1. Because we are considering only a small number of consumers, this curve doesn't look like the smooth demand curves of Chapter 3, where markets contained hundreds or thousands of consumers. Instead, this demand curve is step-shaped, with alternating horizontal and vertical segments. Each horizontal segment—each step—corresponds to one potential buyer's willingness to pay.

However, we'll see shortly that for the analysis of consumer surplus it doesn't matter whether the demand curve is step-shaped, as in this figure, or whether there are many consumers, making the curve smooth.

Willingness to Pay and Consumer Surplus

Suppose that the campus bookstore makes used textbooks available at a price of $30. In that case Aisha, Ben, and Chloe will buy books. Do they gain from their purchases, and if so, how much?

The answer, shown in Table 4-1, is that each student who purchases a book does achieve a net gain but that the amount of the gain differs among students.

FIGURE 4-1 The Demand Curve for Used Textbooks

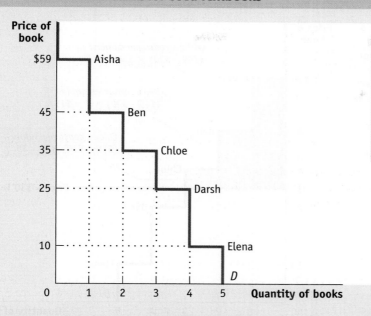

Potential buyers	Willingness to pay
Aisha	$59
Ben	45
Chloe	35
Darsh	25
Elena	10

With only five potential consumers in this market, the demand curve is step-shaped. Each step represents one consumer, and its height indicates that consumer's willingness to pay — the maximum price at which they will buy a used textbook — as indicated in the table. Aisha has the highest willingness to pay at $59, Ben has the next highest at $45, and so on down to Elena with the lowest willingness to pay at $10. At a price of $59, the quantity demanded is one (Aisha); at a price of $45, the quantity demanded is two (Aisha and Ben); and so on until you reach a price of $10, at which all five students are willing to purchase a used textbook.

Aisha would have been willing to pay $59, so her net gain is $59 – $30 = $29. Ben would have been willing to pay $45, so his net gain is $45 – $30 = $15. Chloe would have been willing to pay $35, so her net gain is $35 – $30 = $5. Darsh and Elena, however, won't be willing to buy a used book at a price of $30, so they neither gain nor lose.

The net gain that a buyer achieves from the purchase of a good is called that buyer's **individual consumer surplus.** What we learn from this example is that whenever a buyer pays a price less than their willingness to pay, the buyer achieves some individual consumer surplus.

The sum of the individual consumer surpluses achieved by all the buyers of a good is known as the **total consumer surplus** achieved in the market. In Table 4-1, the total consumer surplus is the sum of the individual consumer surpluses achieved by Aisha, Ben, and Chloe: $29 + $15 + $5 = $49.

Economists often use the term **consumer surplus** to refer to both individual and total consumer surplus. We will follow this practice; it will always be clear in context whether we are referring to the consumer surplus achieved by an individual or by all buyers.

Individual consumer surplus is the net gain to an individual buyer from the purchase of a good. It is equal to the difference between the buyer's willingness to pay and the price paid.

Total consumer surplus is the sum of the individual consumer surpluses of all the buyers of a good in a market.

The term **consumer surplus** is often used to refer both to individual and to total consumer surplus.

TABLE 4-1 Consumer Surplus If the Price of a Used Textbook = $30

Potential buyer	Willingness to pay	Price paid	Individual consumer surplus = Willingness to pay – Price paid
Aisha	$59	$30	$29
Ben	45	30	15
Chloe	35	30	5
Darsh	25	—	—
Elena	10	—	—
All buyers			**Total consumer surplus = $49**

FIGURE 4-2 Consumer Surplus in the Used-Textbook Market

At a price of $30, Aisha, Ben, and Chloe each buy a book but Darsh and Elena do not. Aisha, Ben, and Chloe receive individual consumer surpluses equal to the difference between their willingness to pay and the price, illustrated by the areas of the shaded rectangles. Both Darsh and Elena have a willingness to pay less than $30, so they are unwilling to buy a book in this market; they receive zero consumer surplus. The total consumer surplus is given by the entire shaded area — the sum of the individual consumer surpluses of Aisha, Ben, and Chloe — equal to $29 + $15 + $5 = $49.

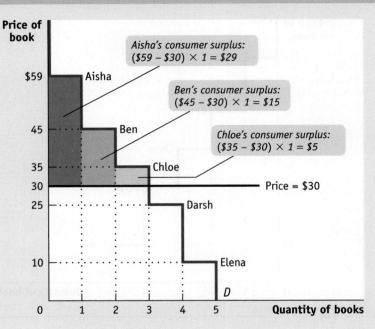

Total consumer surplus can be represented graphically. Figure 4-2 reproduces the demand curve from Figure 4-1. Each step in that demand curve is one book wide and represents one consumer. For example, the height of Aisha's step is $59, her willingness to pay. This step forms the top of a rectangle, with $30 — the price she actually pays for a book — forming the bottom. The area of Aisha's rectangle, ($59 – $30) × 1 = $29, is her consumer surplus from purchasing one book at $30. So the individual consumer surplus Aisha gains is the *area of the dark blue rectangle* shown in Figure 4-2.

In addition to Aisha, Ben and Chloe will also each buy a book when the price is $30. Like Aisha, they benefit from their purchases, though not as much, because they each have a lower willingness to pay. Figure 4-2 also shows the consumer surplus gained by Ben and Chloe; again, this can be measured by the areas of the appropriate rectangles. Darsh and Elena, because they do not buy books at a price of $30, receive no consumer surplus.

The total consumer surplus achieved in this market is just the sum of the individual consumer surpluses received by Aisha, Ben, and Chloe. So total consumer surplus is equal to the combined area of the three rectangles — the entire shaded area in Figure 4-2. Another way to say this is that total consumer surplus is equal to the area below the demand curve but above the price.

Figure 4-2 illustrates the following general principle: *The total consumer surplus generated by purchases of a good at a given price is equal to the area below the demand curve but above that price.* The same principle applies regardless of the number of consumers.

When we consider large markets, this graphical representation of consumer surplus becomes extremely helpful. Consider, for example, the sales of iPhones to millions of potential buyers. Each potential buyer has a maximum price that they are willing to pay. With so many potential buyers, the demand curve will be smooth, like the one shown in Figure 4-3.

Suppose that at a price of $500, a total of 1 million iPhones are purchased. How much do consumers gain from being able to buy those 1 million iPhones? We could answer that question by calculating the individual consumer surplus of

FIGURE 4-3 Consumer Surplus

The demand curve for iPhones is smooth because there are many potential buyers. At a price of $500, 1 million iPhones are demanded. The consumer surplus at this price is equal to the shaded area: the area below the demand curve but above the price. This is the total net gain to consumers generated from buying and consuming iPhones when the price is $500.

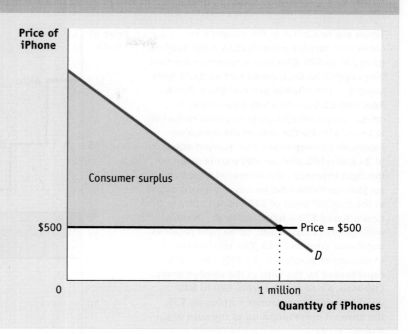

each buyer and then adding these numbers up to arrive at a total. But it is much easier just to look at Figure 4-3 and use the fact that total consumer surplus is equal to the shaded area. As in our original example, consumer surplus is equal to the area below the demand curve but above the price. (To refresh your memory on how to calculate the area of a right triangle, see the appendix to Chapter 2.)

How Changing Prices Affect Consumer Surplus

It is often important to know how much consumer surplus *changes* when the price changes. For example, we may want to know how much consumers are hurt if a flood in cotton-growing areas of Pakistan drives up cotton prices or how much consumers gain if the introduction of fish farming makes salmon steaks less expensive. The same approach we have used to derive consumer surplus can be used to answer questions about how changes in prices affect consumers.

Let's return to the example of the market for used textbooks. Suppose that the bookstore decided to sell used textbooks for $20 instead of $30. How much would this fall in price increase consumer surplus?

The answer is illustrated in Figure 4-4. As shown in the figure, there are two parts to the increase in consumer surplus. The first part, shaded dark blue, is the gain of those who would have bought books even at the higher price of $30. Each of the students who would have bought books at $30—Aisha, Ben, and Chloe—now pays $10 less, and therefore each gains $10 in consumer surplus from the fall in price to $20. So the dark blue area represents the $10 × 3 = $30 increase in consumer surplus to those three buyers.

The second part, shaded light blue, is the gain to those who would not have bought a book at $30 but are willing to pay more than $20. In this case that gain goes to Darsh, who would not have bought a book at $30 but does buy one at $20. He gains $5—the difference between his willingness to pay of $25 and the new price of $20. So the light blue area represents a further $5 gain in consumer surplus.

The total increase in consumer surplus is the sum of the shaded areas, $35. Likewise, a rise in price from $20 to $30 would decrease consumer surplus by an amount equal to the sum of the shaded areas.

FIGURE 4-4 Consumer Surplus and a Fall in the Price of Used Textbooks

There are two parts to the increase in consumer surplus generated by a fall in price from $30 to $20. The first is given by the dark blue rectangle: each person who would have bought at the original price of $30 — Aisha, Ben, and Chloe — receives an increase in consumer surplus equal to the total reduction in price, $10. So the area of the dark blue rectangle corresponds to an amount equal to $3 \times \$10 = \$30$. The second part is given by the light blue area: the increase in consumer surplus for those who would not have bought at the original price of $30 but who buy at the new price of $20 — namely, Darsh. Darsh's willingness to pay is $25, so he now receives consumer surplus of $5. The total increase in consumer surplus is $(3 \times \$10) + \$5 = \$35$, represented by the sum of the shaded areas. Likewise, a rise in price from $20 to $30 would decrease consumer surplus by $35, the amount corresponding to the sum of the shaded areas.

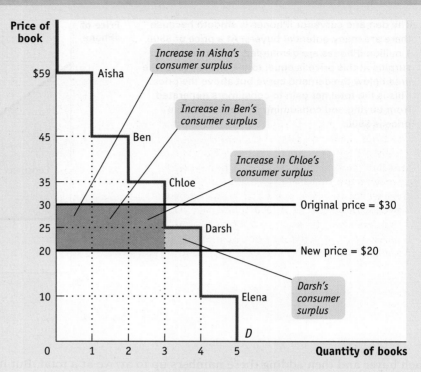

Figure 4-4 illustrates that when the price of a good falls, the area under the demand curve but above the price—which we have seen is equal to total consumer surplus—increases. Figure 4-5 shows the same result for the case of a smooth demand curve, the demand for iPhones. Here we assume that the price of iPhones falls from $2,000 to $500, leading to an increase in the quantity demanded from 200,000 to 1 million units.

As in the used-textbook example, we divide the gain in consumer surplus into two parts.

1. The dark blue rectangle in Figure 4-5 corresponds to the dark blue area in Figure 4-4: it is the gain to the 200,000 people who would have bought iPhones even at the higher price of $2,000. As a result of the price reduction, each receives additional surplus of $1,500.

2. The light blue triangle in Figure 4-5 corresponds to the light blue area in Figure 4-4: it is the gain to people who would not have bought the good at the higher price but are willing to do so at a price of $500. For example, the light blue triangle includes the gain to someone who would have been willing to pay $1,000 for an iPhone and therefore gains $500 in consumer surplus when it is possible to buy an iPhone for only $500.

As before, the total gain in consumer surplus is the sum of the shaded areas: the increase in the area under the demand curve but above the price.

What would happen if the price of a good were to rise instead of fall? We would do the same analysis in reverse. Suppose that the price of iPhones rises from $500 to $2,000. This would lead to a fall in consumer surplus, equal to the sum of the shaded areas in Figure 4-5. This loss consists of two parts.

1. The dark blue rectangle represents the loss to consumers who would still buy an iPhone, even at a price of $2,000.

2. The light blue triangle represents the loss to consumers who decide not to buy an iPhone at the higher price.

FIGURE 4-5 A Fall in the Price Increases Consumer Surplus

A fall in the price of an iPhone from $2,000 to $500 leads to an increase in the quantity demanded and an increase in consumer surplus. The change in total consumer surplus is given by the sum of the shaded areas: the total area below the demand curve and between the old and new prices. Here, the dark blue area represents the increase in consumer surplus for the 200,000 consumers who would have bought an iPhone at the original price of $2,000; they each receive an increase in consumer surplus of $1,500. The light blue area represents the increase in consumer surplus for those willing to buy at a price equal to or greater than $500 but less than $2,000. Similarly, a rise in the price of an iPhone from $500 to $2,000 generates a decrease in consumer surplus equal to the sum of the two shaded areas.

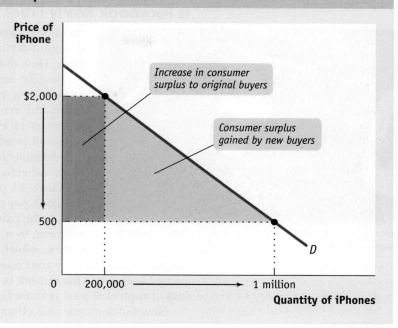

FOR INQUIRING MINDS   A Matter of Life and Death

In 2018, an average of 20 Americans died every day because of a shortage of organs for transplant. In 2019, over 113,000 were wait-listed.

Since the number of people who need organs far exceeds availability, and the demand for organs continues to grow faster than the supply, what is the best way to allocate the available organs? A market isn't feasible. And for understandable reasons, the sale of human body parts is illegal in this country. So the task for establishing a protocol for these situations has fallen to the nonprofit group United Network for Organ Sharing (UNOS).

Kidney transplants, the most common kind of transplant, were the focus of attention when UNOS reformulated its guidelines for allocating organs in 2013. Under the previous guidelines, a donated kidney would go to the person waiting the longest: an available kidney would, for example, go to a 75-year-old who had been waiting for two years rather than to a 25-year-old who had been waiting a year — despite the fact that

the 25-year-old is likely to live longer and therefore benefit from the organ for a longer period of time.

So, UNOS formulated a new set of guidelines based on a concept called *net survival benefit*. Available kidneys are ranked according to how long they are likely to last; recipients are ranked according to how long they are likely to live once receiving a kidney. A kidney is then matched to the recipient expected to achieve the greatest survival time from that kidney. That is, a kidney expected to last many decades will be given to a young person, while a kidney with a shorter expected life span will be given to an older recipient.

So what does kidney transplantation have to do with consumer surplus? The UNOS concept of *net survival benefit* is a lot like individual consumer surplus — the individual consumer surplus generated from getting a new kidney. In essence, UNOS has devised a system that allocates a kidney according to who gets the greatest consumer surplus, thereby

maximizing the total consumer surplus from the available pool of kidneys. In terms of results, the UNOS system operates a lot like a competitive market, but without the purchase and sale of kidneys.

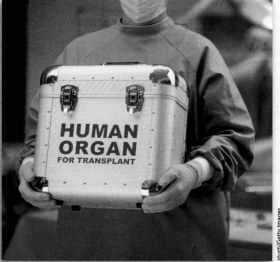

Organ recipients are determined based on who will receive the greatest individual consumer surplus from a transplant.

ECONOMICS >> *in Action*
Is Facebook Really Free?

Would you be willing to pay for a version of Facebook without ads?

Facebook earned nearly $56 billion in revenue in 2018 even though it doesn't charge consumers to use its social media platform. How did the company manage this impressive feat?

Despite being a high-tech company, Facebook earns its money in a rather old-fashioned way: by selling advertising space. Advertisers pay Facebook for the right to place their ads on users' Facebook pages. In addition, Facebook gathers personal information from its users—location, age, gender, and profile characteristics—that allow advertisers to target their ads to those individuals who are more likely to purchase their products.

Facebook offers its platform to users at a zero-price—that is, you don't pay money to access it. Yet there still is still an *effective price* to be paid for its use. Although you don't incur a monetary payment, by using Facebook you release control of personal information, which can cause annoyance and distraction as targeted ads are created to sway your purchasing decisions or views. So the effective price of using Facebook is the burden in terms of annoyance and distraction caused by the loss of control of your personal information.

How burdensome this effective price is varies from person to person. We can get a sense of the effective price a person incurs when using Facebook by asking how much they are willing to pay for an ad-free version of Facebook. In fact, a recent survey of American Facebook users did just that. This survey revealed that 63% of Facebook users were unwilling to pay for an ad-free version of the site, while 22% of users were willing to pay, and 15% of users were unsure. Thus, for the majority 63% who were unwilling to pay for an ad-free Facebook, the effective price of Facebook's data collection and advertisements was close to zero. These users gained the most consumer surplus from the current zero-price arrangement. In contrast, the 22% who were willing to pay for an ad-free version incurred a higher effective price and therefore gained less consumer surplus.

So is Facebook really free? For the majority of users it is, but for a significant minority of users, it is not.

>> Quick Review

• The demand curve for a good is determined by each potential consumer's **willingness to pay.**

• **Individual consumer surplus** is the net gain an individual consumer gets from buying a good.

• The **total consumer surplus** in a given market is equal to the area below the market demand curve but above the price.

• A fall in the price of a good increases **consumer surplus** through two channels: a gain to consumers who would have bought at the original price and a gain to consumers who are persuaded to buy by the lower price. A rise in the price of a good reduces consumer surplus in a similar fashion.

>> Check Your Understanding 4-1
Solutions appear at back of book.

1. Consider the market for cheese-stuffed jalapeno peppers. There are two consumers, Teresa and Azar, and their willingness to pay for each pepper is given in the accompanying table. (Neither is willing to consume more than 4 peppers at any price.) Use the table (i) to construct the demand schedule for peppers for prices of $0.00, $0.10, and so on, up to $0.90, and (ii) to calculate the total consumer surplus when the price of a pepper is $0.40.

Quantity of peppers	Teresa's willingness to pay	Azar's willingness to pay
1st pepper	$0.90	$0.80
2nd pepper	0.70	0.60
3rd pepper	0.50	0.40
4th pepper	0.30	0.30

|| Producer Surplus and the Supply Curve

Just as some buyers of a good would have been willing to pay more for their purchase than the price they actually pay, some sellers of a good would have been willing to sell it for less than the price they actually receive. So just as there are consumers who receive consumer surplus from buying in a market, there are producers who receive producer surplus from selling in a market.

Cost and Producer Surplus

Consider a group of students who are potential sellers of used textbooks. Because they have different preferences, the various potential sellers differ in the price at which they are willing to sell their books. The table in Figure 4-6 shows the prices at which several different students would be willing to sell. Andrew is willing to sell the book as long as he can get at least $5; Brianna won't sell unless she can get at least $15; Carlos, unless he can get $25; Desiree, unless she can get $35; Eli, unless he can get $45.

The lowest price at which a potential seller is willing to sell has a special name in economics: it is called the seller's **cost**. So Andrew's cost is $5, Brianna's is $15, and so on.

Using the term *cost*, which people normally associate with the monetary cost of producing a good, may sound a little strange when applied to sellers of used textbooks. The students don't have to manufacture the books, so it doesn't cost the student who sells a used textbook anything to make that book available for sale, does it?

Yes, it does. A student who sells a book won't have it later, as part of their personal collection. So there is an *opportunity* cost to selling a textbook, even if the owner has completed the course for which it was required. And remember that one of the basic principles of economics is that the true measure of the cost of doing something is always its opportunity cost. That is, the real cost of something is what you must give up to get it.

So it is good economics to talk of the minimum price at which someone will sell a good as the "cost" of selling that good, even if they don't spend any money to make the good available for sale. Of course, in most real-world markets the sellers are also those who produce the good and therefore *do* spend money to make it available for sale. In this case, the cost of making the good available for sale includes monetary costs, but it may also include other opportunity costs.

> A seller's **cost** is the lowest price at which they are willing to sell a good.

FIGURE 4-6 The Supply Curve for Used Textbooks

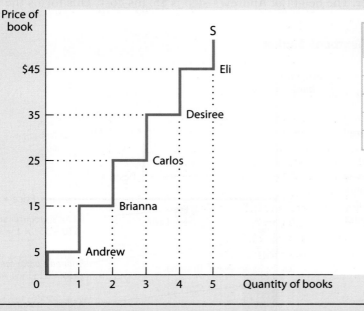

Potential sellers	Cost
Andrew	$5
Brianna	15
Carlos	25
Desiree	35
Eli	45

The supply curve illustrates seller's cost, the lowest price at which a potential seller is willing to sell the good, and the quantity supplied at that price. Each of the five students has one book to sell and each has a different cost, as indicated in the accompanying table. At a price of $5 the quantity supplied is one (Andrew), at $15 it is two (Andrew and Brianna), and so on until you reach $45, the price at which all five students are willing to sell.

Individual producer surplus is the net gain to an individual seller from selling a good. It is equal to the difference between the price received and the seller's cost.

Total producer surplus is the sum of the individual producer surpluses of all the sellers of a good in a market.

Economists use the term **producer surplus** to refer both to individual and to total producer surplus.

Getting back to the example, suppose that Andrew sells his book for $30. Clearly he has gained from the transaction: he would have been willing to sell for only $5, so he has gained $25. This net gain, the difference between the price he actually gets and his cost—the minimum price at which he would have been willing to sell—is known as his **individual producer surplus.**

Just as we derived the demand curve from the willingness to pay of different consumers, we can derive the supply curve from the cost of different producers. The step-shaped curve in Figure 4-6 shows the supply curve implied by the costs shown in the accompanying table. At a price less than $5, none of the students are willing to sell; at a price between $5 and $15, only Andrew is willing to sell, and so on.

As in the case of consumer surplus, we can add the individual producer surpluses of sellers to calculate the **total producer surplus,** the total net gain to all sellers in the market. Economists use the term **producer surplus** to refer to either individual or total producer surplus. Table 4-2 shows the net gain to each of the students who would sell a used book at a price of $30: $25 for Andrew, $15 for Brianna, and $5 for Carlos. The total producer surplus is $25 + $15 + $5 = $45.

TABLE 4-2 Producer Surplus When the Price of a Used Textbook = $30

Potential seller	Cost	Price received	Individual producer surplus = Price received – Cost
Andrew	$5	$30	$25
Brianna	15	30	15
Carlos	25	30	5
Desiree	35	—	—
Eli	45	—	—
All sellers			**Total producer surplus = $45**

As with consumer surplus, the producer surplus gained by those who sell books can be represented graphically. Figure 4-7 reproduces the supply curve from Figure 4-6. Each step in that supply curve is one book wide and represents one seller. The height of Andrew's step is $5, his cost. This forms the bottom of a

FIGURE 4-7 Producer Surplus in the Used-Textbook Market

At a price of $30, Andrew, Brianna, and Carlos each sell a book but Desiree and Eli do not. Andrew, Brianna, and Carlos get individual producer surpluses equal to the difference between the price and their cost, illustrated here by the shaded rectangles. Desiree and Eli each have a cost that is greater than the price of $30, so they are unwilling to sell a book and so receive zero producer surplus. The total producer surplus is given by the entire shaded area, the sum of the individual producer surpluses of Andrew, Brianna, and Carlos, equal to $25 + $15 + $5 = $45.

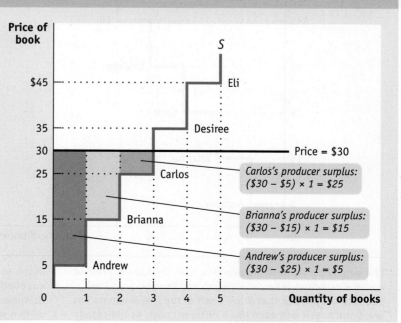

FIGURE 4-8 Producer Surplus

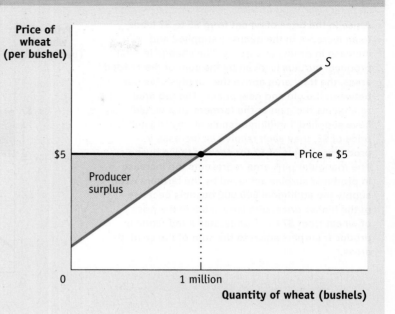

Here is the supply curve for wheat. At a price of $5 per bushel, farmers supply 1 million bushels. The producer surplus at this price is equal to the shaded area: the area above the supply curve but below the price. This is the total gain to producers—farmers in this case—from supplying their product when the price is $5.

rectangle, with $30, the price he actually receives for his book, forming the top. The area of this rectangle, ($30 – $5) × 1 = $25, is his producer surplus. So the producer surplus Andrew gains from selling his book is the *area of the red rectangle* shown in the figure.

Let's assume that the campus bookstore is willing to buy all the used copies of this book that students are willing to sell at a price of $30. Then, in addition to Andrew, Brianna and Carlos will also sell their books. They will also benefit from their sales, though not as much as Andrew, because they have higher costs. Andrew, as we have seen, gains $25. Brianna gains a smaller amount: since her cost is $15, she gains only $15. Carlos gains even less, only $5.

Again, as with consumer surplus, we have a general rule for determining the total producer surplus from sales of a good: *The total producer surplus from sales of a good at a given price is the area above the supply curve but below that price.*

This rule applies both to examples like the one shown in Figure 4-7, where there are a small number of producers and a step-shaped supply curve, and to more realistic examples, where there are many producers and the supply curve is smooth.

Consider, for example, the supply of wheat. Figure 4-8 shows how producer surplus depends on the price per bushel. Suppose that, as shown in the figure, the price is $5 per bushel and farmers supply 1 million bushels. What is the benefit to the farmers from selling their wheat at a price of $5? Their producer surplus is equal to the shaded area in the figure—the area above the supply curve but below the price of $5 per bushel.

How Changing Prices Affect Producer Surplus

As with the case of consumer surplus, a change in price alters producer surplus. But the effects are opposite. While a fall in price increases consumer surplus, it reduces producer surplus. And a rise in price reduces consumer surplus but increases producer surplus.

To see this, let's first consider a rise in the price of the good. Producers of the good will experience an increase in producer surplus, though not all producers gain the same amount. Some producers would have produced the good even at

FIGURE 4-9 A Rise in the Price Increases Producer Surplus

A rise in the price of wheat from $5 to $7 leads to an increase in the quantity supplied and an increase in producer surplus. The change in total producer surplus is given by the sum of the shaded areas: the total area above the supply curve but between the old and new prices. The red area represents the gain to the farmers who would have supplied 1 million bushels at the original price of $5; they each receive an increase in producer surplus of $2 for each of these bushels. The triangular pink area represents the increase in producer surplus achieved by the farmers who supply the additional 500,000 bushels because of the higher price. Similarly, a fall in the price of wheat from $7 to $5 generates a reduction in producer surplus equal to the sum of the shaded areas.

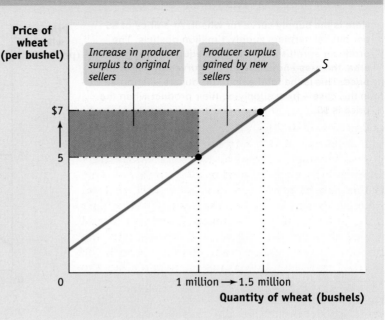

the original price; they will gain the entire price increase on every unit they produce. Other producers will enter the market because of the higher price; they will gain only the difference between the new price and their cost.

Figure 4-9 is the supply counterpart of Figure 4-5. It shows the effect on producer surplus of a rise in the price of wheat from $5 to $7 per bushel. The increase in producer surplus is the sum of the shaded areas, which consists of two parts. First, there is a red rectangle corresponding to the gains to those farmers who would have supplied wheat even at the original $5 price. Second, there is an additional pink triangle that corresponds to the gains to those farmers who would not have supplied wheat at the original price but are drawn into the market by the higher price.

If the price were to fall from $7 to $5 per bushel, the story would run in reverse. The sum of the shaded areas would now be the decline in producer surplus, the decrease in the area above the supply curve but below the price. The loss would consist of two parts, the loss to farmers who would still grow wheat at a price of $5 (the red rectangle) and the loss to farmers who cease to grow wheat because of the lower price (the pink triangle).

ECONOMICS >> *in Action*
Highs and Lows on Iowa's Farms

The price of Iowa farmland is very sensitive to changes in the world economy—specifically, changes in world supply and demand for food commodities. In fact, from 2000 to 2013, the price of Iowa farmland had a spectacular upward run, with the average price of farmland hitting an all-time record high of $8,716 per acre in 2013. That year, the price was more than 1.5 times the 2010 price and more than 4 times the 2000 price.

Figure 4-10 shows the explosive increase in the price of Iowa farmland during these years. And there was no mystery as to why farmland prices rose so dramatically: it was all about the high prices being paid for corn, wheat, and soybeans.

From 2009 to 2013, the price of corn jumped by 75%, soybeans by 45%, and wheat by 40%.

The escalating Iowa farmland prices also reflect shifts in the world economy. Higher demand for food in rising-income economies like China and India have lifted the prices of Iowa food products to higher levels compared to a decade earlier. In addition, poor weather in competing food-producing countries like Australia contributed to the surge in food prices in 2012 and 2013.

But, as you can see in the diagram, the price of Iowa farmland started to drop in 2014. By early 2019, the price had dropped by 22%, to $6,794. This decline can be attributed to lower prices for food products, caused by an increase in supply as farmers in the United States and competing farmers abroad produced more corn, wheat, and soybeans during this time. An escalating trade dispute between the United States and China also contributed to the price drop. The dispute put a damper on food product prices, as U.S. growers became wary that China would restrict imports of U.S. farm products.

So a person who buys farmland in Iowa buys the producer surplus generated by that acre of land. As we've just seen, higher long-term prices for corn, wheat, and soybeans, which raise the producer surplus of Iowa farmers, will make Iowa farmland more valuable. Correspondingly, lower prices for Iowa's food products will make Iowa farmland less valuable.

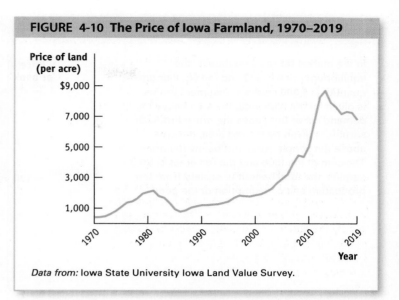

FIGURE 4-10 The Price of Iowa Farmland, 1970–2019

Data from: Iowa State University Iowa Land Value Survey.

>> Check Your Understanding 4-2

Solutions appear at back of book.

1. Consider again the market for cheese-stuffed jalapeno peppers. There are two producers, Cara and Jamie, and their costs of producing each pepper are given in the accompanying table. (Neither is willing to produce more than 4 peppers at any price.)

Quantity of peppers	Cara's cost	Jamie's cost
1st pepper	$0.10	$0.30
2nd pepper	0.10	0.50
3rd pepper	0.40	0.70
4th pepper	0.60	0.90

   a. Use the accompanying table to construct the supply schedule for peppers for prices of $0.00, $0.10, and so on, up to $0.90.
   b. Calculate the total producer surplus when the price of a pepper is $0.70.

Consumer Surplus, Producer Surplus, and the Gains from Trade

One of the 11 core principles of economics is that markets are a remarkably effective way to organize economic activity: they generally make society as well off as possible given the available resources. The concepts of consumer surplus and producer surplus can help us deepen our understanding of why this is so.

The Gains from Trade

Let's return to the market in used textbooks but now consider a much bigger market—say, one at a large state university. There are many potential buyers and sellers, so the market is competitive. Let's line up incoming students who are

FIGURE 4-11 Total Surplus

In the market for used textbooks, the equilibrium price is $30 and the equilibrium quantity is 1,000 books. Consumer surplus is given by the blue area, the area below the demand curve but above the price. Producer surplus is given by the red area, the area above the supply curve but below the price. The sum of the blue and the red areas is total surplus, the total benefit to society from the production and consumption of the good.

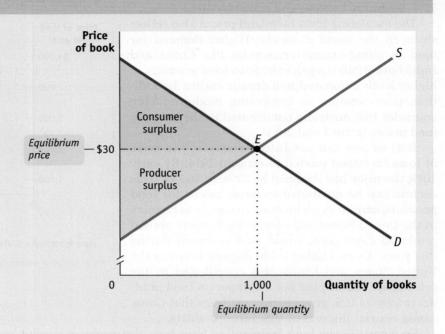

potential buyers of a book in order of their willingness to pay, so that the entering student with the highest willingness to pay is potential buyer number 1, the student with the next highest willingness to pay is number 2, and so on. Then we can use their willingness to pay to derive a demand curve like the one in Figure 4-11.

Similarly, we can line up outgoing students, who are potential sellers of the book, in order of their cost—starting with the student with the lowest cost, then the student with the next lowest cost, and so on—to derive a supply curve like the one shown in the same figure.

As we have drawn the curves, the market reaches equilibrium at a price of $30 per book, and 1,000 books are bought and sold at that price. The two shaded triangles show the consumer surplus (blue) and the producer surplus (red) generated by this market. The sum of consumer and producer surplus is known as the **total surplus** generated in a market.

The striking thing about this picture is that both consumers and producers gain. Both are made better off because there is a market in this good. This should come as no surprise—it illustrates another core principle of economics: *There are gains from trade.* Gains from trade are the reason everyone is better off participating in a market economy than they would be if each individual tried to be self-sufficient.

But are we as well off as we could be? This brings us to the question of the efficiency of markets.

The Efficiency of Markets

Markets produce gains from trade, but in Chapter 1 we made an even bigger claim: that markets are usually *efficient.* That is, once the market has produced its gains from trade, there is no way to make some people better off without making other people worse off, except under some well-defined conditions.

The analysis of consumer and producer surplus helps us understand why markets are usually efficient. To gain more intuition into why this is so, consider the fact that market equilibrium is just *one* way of deciding who consumes the good and who sells the good. There are other possible ways of making that decision.

The **total surplus** generated in a market is the total net gain to consumers and producers from trading in the market. It is the sum of the producer and the consumer surplus.

Consider, again, the case of kidney transplants, in which a decision must be made about who receives one. It is not possible to use a market to decide because in this situation, human organs are involved. Instead, in the past, kidneys were allocated according to a recipient's wait time—a very inefficient method. It has since been replaced with a new system created by the United Network for Organ Sharing, or UNOS, based on *net survival benefit*, a concept an awful lot like consumer surplus that, although not a market system, succeeds in reproducing the efficiency of one.

To further our understanding of why markets usually work so well, imagine a committee charged with improving on the market equilibrium by deciding who gets and who gives up a used textbook. The committee's ultimate goal is to bypass the market outcome and devise another arrangement, one that would produce higher total surplus.

Let's consider the three ways in which the committee might try to increase the total surplus:

1. Reallocate consumption among consumers
2. Reallocate sales among sellers
3. Change the quantity traded

Reallocate Consumption Among Consumers The committee might try to increase total surplus by selling books to different consumers. Figure 4-12 shows why this will result in lower surplus compared to the market equilibrium outcome. Here we have smooth demand and supply curves because there are many buyers and sellers. Points *A* and *B* show the positions on the demand curve of two potential buyers of used books, Ana and Braxton. As we can see from the figure, Ana is willing to pay $35 for a book, but Braxton is willing to pay only $25. Since the market equilibrium price is $30, under the market outcome Ana buys a book and Braxton does not.

Now suppose the committee reallocates consumption. This would mean taking the book away from Ana and giving it to Braxton. Since the book is worth $35 to Ana but only $25 to Braxton, this change *reduces total consumer surplus* by

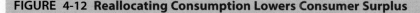

FIGURE 4-12 Reallocating Consumption Lowers Consumer Surplus

Ana (point *A*) has a willingness to pay of $35. Braxton (point *B*) has a willingness to pay of only $25. At the market equilibrium price of $30, Ana purchases a book but Braxton does not. If we rearrange consumption by taking a book from Ana and giving it to Braxton, consumer surplus declines by $10, and, as a result, total surplus declines by $10.

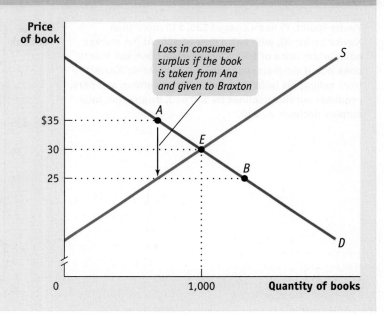

$35 – $25 = $10. Moreover, this result doesn't depend on which two students we pick. Every student who buys a book at the market equilibrium has a willingness to pay of $30 or more, and every student who doesn't buy a book has a willingness to pay of less than $30.

So reallocating the good among consumers always means taking a book away from a student who values it more and giving it to one who values it less. This necessarily reduces total consumer surplus.

Reallocate Sales Among Sellers The committee might try to increase total surplus by altering who sells their books, taking sales away from sellers who would have sold their books at the market equilibrium and instead compelling those who would not have sold their books at the market equilibrium to sell them.

Figure 4-13 shows why this will result in lower surplus. Here points *X* and *Y* show the positions on the supply curve of Xavier, who has a cost of $25, and Yvette, who has a cost of $35. At the equilibrium market price of $30, Xavier would sell his book but Yvette would not sell hers. If the committee reallocated sales, forcing Xavier to keep his book and Yvette to sell hers, total producer surplus would be reduced by $35 – $25 = $10.

Again, it doesn't matter which two students we choose. Any student who sells a book at the market equilibrium has a lower cost than any student who keeps a book. So reallocating sales among sellers necessarily increases total cost and reduces total producer surplus.

Change the Quantity Traded The committee might try to increase total surplus by compelling students to trade either more books or fewer books than the market equilibrium quantity.

Figure 4-14 shows why this will result in lower surplus. It shows all four students: potential buyers Ana and Braxton, and potential sellers Xavier and Yvette. To reduce sales, the committee will have to prevent a transaction that would have occurred in the market equilibrium—that is, prevent Xavier from selling to Ana. Since Ana is willing to pay $35 and Xavier's cost is $25, preventing this transaction reduces total surplus by $35 – $25 = $10.

FIGURE 4-13 Reallocating Sales Lowers Producer Surplus

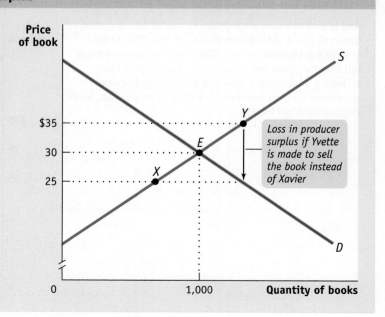

Yvette (point *Y*) has a cost of $35, $10 more than Xavier (point *X*), who has a cost of $25. At the market equilibrium price of $30, Xavier sells a book but Yvette does not. If we rearrange sales by preventing Xavier from selling his book and compelling Yvette to sell hers, producer surplus declines by $10 and, as a result, total surplus declines by $10.

FIGURE 4-14 Changing the Quantity Lowers Total Surplus

If Xavier (point *X*) were prevented from selling his book to someone like Ana (point *A*), total surplus would fall by $10, the difference between Ana's willingness to pay ($35) and Xavier's ($25). This means that total surplus falls whenever fewer than 1,000 books—the equilibrium quantity—are transacted. Likewise, if Yvette (point *Y*) were compelled to sell her book to someone like Braxton (point *B*), total surplus would also fall by $10, the difference between Yvette's cost ($35) and Braxton's willingness to pay ($25). This means that total surplus falls whenever more than 1,000 books are transacted. These two examples show that at market equilibrium, all mutually beneficial transactions—and only mutually beneficial transactions—occur.

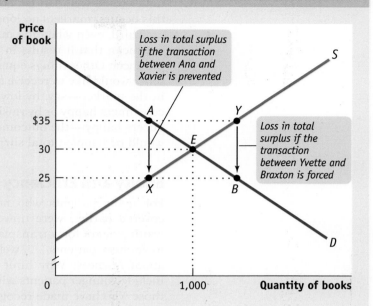

Once again, this result doesn't depend on which two students we pick: any student who would have sold the book at the market equilibrium has a cost of $30 or less, and any student who would have purchased the book at the market equilibrium has a willingness to pay of $30 or more. So preventing any sale that would have occurred in the market equilibrium necessarily reduces total surplus.

Finally, the committee might try to increase sales by forcing Yvette, who would not have sold her book at the market equilibrium, to sell it to someone like Braxton, who would not have bought a book at the market equilibrium. Because Yvette's cost is $35, but Braxton is only willing to pay $25, this transaction reduces total surplus by $10. And once again it doesn't matter which two students we pick—anyone who wouldn't have bought the book has a willingness to pay of less than $30, and anyone who wouldn't have sold has a cost of more than $30.

The key point to remember is that once this market is in equilibrium, there is no way to increase the gains from trade. Any other outcome reduces total surplus. We can summarize our results by stating that an efficient market performs four important functions:

1. It allocates consumption of the good to the potential buyers who most value it, as indicated by the fact that they have the highest willingness to pay.

2. It allocates sales to the potential sellers who most value the right to sell the good, as indicated by the fact that they have the lowest cost.

3. It ensures that every consumer who makes a purchase values the good more than every seller who makes a sale, so that all transactions are mutually beneficial.

4. It ensures that every potential buyer who doesn't make a purchase values the good less than every potential seller who doesn't make a sale, so that no mutually beneficial transactions are missed.

As a result of these four functions, *any way of allocating the good other than the market equilibrium outcome lowers total surplus.*

There are three caveats, however. First, although a market may be efficient, it isn't necessarily *fair*. In fact, fairness, or *equity*, is often in conflict with efficiency. We'll discuss this in the next section.

The second caveat is that markets sometimes *fail*. As mentioned in Chapter 1, under some well-defined conditions, markets can fail to deliver efficiency. When this occurs, markets no longer maximize total surplus.

Third, even when the market equilibrium maximizes total surplus, this does not mean that it results in the best outcome for every *individual* consumer and producer. Other things equal, each buyer would like to pay a lower price and each seller would like to receive a higher price. So if the government were to intervene in the market—say, by lowering the price below the equilibrium price to make consumers happy or by raising the price above the equilibrium price to make producers happy—the outcome would no longer be efficient. Although some people would be happier, total surplus would be lower.

Equity and Efficiency

For many patients who need kidney transplants, the new UNOS guidelines, covered earlier, were unwelcome news. Unsurprisingly, those who have been waiting years for a transplant have found the guidelines, which give precedence to younger patients, . . . well . . . unfair. And the guidelines raise other questions about fairness: Why limit potential transplant recipients to Americans? Why include younger patients with other chronic diseases? Why not give precedence to those who have made recognized contributions to society? And so on.

The point is that efficiency is about *how to achieve goals, not what those goals should be*. For example, UNOS decided that its goal is to maximize the life span of kidney recipients. Some might have argued for a different goal, and efficiency does not address which goal is the best. *What efficiency does address is the best way to achieve a goal once it has been determined*—in this case, using the UNOS concept of net survival benefit.

It's easy to get carried away with the idea that markets are always right and that economic policies that interfere with efficiency are bad. But that would be misguided because there is another factor to consider: society cares about equity, or what's "fair."

There is often a trade-off between equity and efficiency: policies that promote equity often come at the cost of decreased efficiency, and policies that promote efficiency often result in decreased equity. So it's important to realize that a society's choice to sacrifice some efficiency for the sake of equity, however it defines equity, is a valid one. And it's important to understand that fairness, unlike efficiency, can be very hard to define. Fairness is a concept about which well-intentioned people often disagree.

Owners use marketplaces like Airbnb to turn unused resources into cash.

ECONOMICS >> *in Action*
Take the Keys, Please

"Airbnb was really born from a math problem," said its co-founder, Joe Gebbia. "We quit our jobs to be entrepreneurs, and the landlord raised our rent beyond our means. And so we had a math problem to solve. It just so happened that that coming weekend, a design conference came to San Francisco that just wiped out the hotels in the city. We connected the dots. We had extra space in our apartment. So thus was born the air bed-and-breakfast."

From that bout of desperation-induced ingenuity sprang a company that is now the largest single source of lodging in the world. As of 2019, 500 million people searching for a bed have availed themselves of Airbnb's marketplace and, on average, more than 2 million people stay at an Airbnb rental each night. The website now lists 6 million dwellings worldwide, including 4,000 castles and 2,400 tree houses.

Airbnb is the most famous and successful purveyor in what is called "the sharing economy": companies that provide a marketplace in which people can share the use of goods. And there is a dizzying array of others: Turo and Getaround let you rent cars from their owners; Boatbound facilitates boat rentals, Desktime offers office space for rent, JustPark provides parking spaces, and Rent the Runway offers designer clothing.

What's motivating all this sharing? Well, it isn't an outbreak of altruism—it's plain dollars and cents. If there are unused resources sitting around, why not make money by renting them to someone else? As Judith Chevalier, a Yale School of Management economist, says, "These companies let you wring a little bit of value out of . . . goods that are just sitting there." And generating a bit more surplus from your possessions leads to a more efficient use of those resources. As a result, says Arun Sundararajan, a professor at the NYU Stern School of Business, "That makes it possible for people to rethink the way they consume."

>> Check Your Understanding 4-3

Solutions appear at back of book.

1. Using the tables in Check Your Understanding 4-1 and 4-2, find the equilibrium price and quantity in the market for cheese-stuffed jalapeno peppers. What is total surplus in the equilibrium in this market, and who receives it?

2. Show how each of the following three actions reduces total surplus:
   a. Having Azar consume one fewer pepper, and Teresa one more pepper, than in the market equilibrium
   b. Having Cara produce one fewer pepper, and Jamie one more pepper, than in the market equilibrium
   c. Having Azar consume one fewer pepper, and Cara produce one fewer pepper, than in the market equilibrium

3. Suppose UNOS decides to further alter its guidelines for the allocation of donated kidneys, no longer relying solely on the concept of net survival benefit but also giving preference to patients with small children. If "total surplus" in this case is defined to be the total life span of kidney recipients, is this new guideline likely to reduce, increase, or leave total surplus unchanged? How might you justify this new guideline?

|| A Market Economy

As we learned earlier, in a market economy decisions about production and consumption are made via markets. In fact, the economy as a whole is made up of many *interrelated markets*. Up until now, to learn how markets work, we've been examining a single market—the market for used textbooks. But in reality, consumers and producers do not make decisions in isolated markets. For example, a student's decision in the market for used textbooks might be affected by how much interest must be paid on a student loan; thus, the decision in the used textbook market would be influenced by what is going on in the market for money.

We know that an efficient market equilibrium maximizes total surplus—the gains to buyers and sellers in that market. Is there a comparable result for an economy as a whole, an economy composed of a vast number of individual markets? The answer is yes, but with qualifications.

When each and every market in the economy maximizes total surplus, the economy as a whole is efficient. This is a very important result: just as it is impossible to make someone better off without making other people worse off in a single market when it is efficient, the same is true when each and every market in that economy is efficient. However, it is important to realize that this

Property rights are the rights of owners of valuable items, whether resources or goods, to dispose of those items as they choose.

An **economic signal** is any piece of information that helps people make better economic decisions.

is a *theoretical* result: it is virtually impossible to find an economy in which every market is efficient.

For now, let's examine why markets and market economies typically work so well. Once we understand why, we can then briefly address why markets sometimes get it wrong.

Why Markets Typically Work So Well

Economists have written volumes about why markets are an effective way to organize an economy. In the end, well-functioning markets owe their effectiveness to two powerful features: *property rights* and the role of prices as *economic signals*.

Property Rights By **property rights** we mean a system in which valuable items in the economy have specific owners who can dispose of them as they choose. In a system of property rights, by purchasing a good you receive *ownership rights:* the right to use and dispose of the good as you see fit. Property rights are what make the mutually beneficial transactions in the used-textbook market, or any market, possible.

To see why property rights are crucial, imagine that students do not have full property rights in their textbooks and are prohibited from reselling them when the semester ends. This restriction on property rights would prevent many mutually beneficial transactions. Some students would be stuck with textbooks they will never reread when they would be much happier receiving some cash instead. Other students would be forced to pay full price for brand-new books when they would be happier getting slightly battered copies at a lower price.

Price is the most important economic signal in a market economy.

Economic Signals Once a system of well-defined property rights is in place, the second necessary feature of well-functioning markets—prices as economic signals—can operate. An **economic signal** is any piece of information that helps people and businesses make better economic decisions. For example, business forecasters say that sales of cardboard boxes are a good early indicator of changes in industrial production: if businesses are buying lots of cardboard boxes, you can be sure that they will soon increase their production.

But prices are far and away the most important signals in a market economy, because they convey essential information about other people's costs and their willingness to pay. If the equilibrium price of used books is $30, this in effect tells everyone both that there are consumers willing to pay $30 and up and that there are potential sellers with a cost of $30 or less. The signal given by the market price ensures that total surplus is maximized by telling people whether to buy books, sell books, or do nothing at all.

Each potential seller with a cost of $30 or less learns from the market price that it's a good idea to sell their book; if they have a higher cost, it's a good idea to keep it. Likewise, each consumer willing to pay $30 or more learns from the market price that it's a good idea to buy a book; if they are unwilling to pay $30, then it's a good idea not to buy a book.

This example shows that the market price "signals" to consumers with a willingness to pay equal to or more than the market price that they should buy the good, just as it signals to producers with a cost equal to or less than the market price that they should sell the good. And since, in equilibrium, the quantity demanded equals the quantity supplied, all willing consumers will find willing sellers.

Prices can sometimes fail as economic signals. Sometimes a price is not an accurate indicator of how desirable a good is. When there is uncertainty about the quality of a good, price alone may not be an accurate indicator of the value of the good. For example, you can't infer from the price alone whether a used car is good or a "lemon." In fact, a well-known problem in economics is "the market for lemons," a market in which prices don't work well as economic signals.

A Few Words of Caution

Markets are an amazingly effective way to organize economic activity. But as we've seen, markets can sometimes get it wrong. We first learned about this in Chapter 1 in our eighth principle: *When markets don't achieve efficiency, government intervention can improve society's welfare.*

When markets are **inefficient,** there are missed opportunities—ways in which production or consumption can be rearranged that would make some people better off without making other people worse off. In other words, there are gains from trade that go unrealized: total surplus could be increased. And when a market or markets are inefficient, the economy in which they are embedded is also inefficient.

Markets can be rendered inefficient for a number of reasons. Two of the most important are a lack of property rights and inaccuracy of prices as economic signals. When a market is inefficient, we have a **market failure.** We will examine various types of market failure in later chapters. For now, let's review the three main ways in which markets sometimes fall short of efficiency.

> A market or an economy is **inefficient** if there are missed opportunities: some people could be made better off without making other people worse off.
>
> **Market failure** occurs when a market fails to be efficient.

1. *Market Power:* Markets can fail due to *market power,* which occurs when a firm has the ability to raise the market price. In this case the assumption that underlies supply and demand analysis—that no one can have a noticeable effect on the market price—is no longer valid. As we'll see in Chapter 13, the presence of market power leads to inefficiency as the firm manipulates the market price in order to increase profits and thereby prevents mutually beneficial trades from occurring.

2. *Externalities:* Markets can fail due to *externalities,* which arise when actions have side effects on the welfare of others. The most common example of an externality is pollution. Because the market price doesn't capture the negative effect pollution has on others, the market outcome is inefficient. In Chapter 16 we'll learn more about externalities and how societies try to cope with them.

3. *Public Goods, Common Resources, and Private Information:* Markets can fail when the nature of the good makes it unsuitable for efficient allocation by a market. This is true for *public goods* like national defense. Because it cannot be bought and sold by people, national defense cannot be allocated efficiently by a market. It is also true for *common resources,* like the fish in our oceans. Markets generally fail in these cases due to incomplete property rights. Markets will also fail when some people possess information about goods that others don't have, as in the market for used cars that we just discussed. In Chapters 17 and 20 we will learn about how society copes in these situations.

But even with these limitations, it's remarkable how well markets work at maximizing gains from trade.

ECONOMICS >> *in Action*
A Great Leap—Backward

Of any country in the world, China is perhaps the one most associated with free-wheeling markets. From the endless street markets for food in Shanghai, to the bustling export-goods markets in Guangzhou that specialize in everything from eyeglasses to electronics, to the massive mall in Shenzhen where you can

Although some aspects of central planning remain, China's economy has moved closer to a free-market system.

find finely tailored custom suits and fake designer bags, the shopping possibilities in China are endless.

Yet, not so long ago, China was a country almost completely lacking in markets. That's because until the 1980s, China was largely a *planned economy* in which a central planner, rather than markets, made consumption and production decisions. Russia, many Eastern European countries, and several Southeast Asian countries once had planned economies. In addition, India and Brazil once had significant parts of their economies under central planning.

Planned economies are notorious for their inefficiency, and probably the most compelling example of that is the so-called Great Leap Forward, an ambitious economic plan instituted in China during the late 1950s by its leader Mao Zedong. Its intention was to speed up the country's industrialization. Key to this plan was a shift from urban to rural manufacturing: farming villages were supposed to start producing heavy industrial goods such as steel. Unfortunately, the plan backfired.

Diverting farmers from their usual work led to a sharp fall in food production. Meanwhile, because raw materials for steel, such as coal and iron ore, were sent to ill-equipped and inexperienced rural producers rather than to urban factories, industrial output declined as well. The plan, in short, led to a fall in the production of everything in China.

Because China was a very poor country to start with, the results were catastrophic. The famine that followed is estimated to have reduced China's population by as much as 30 million.

China's transition to a free-market system has put it on the path to greater economic growth, increased wealth, and led to the emergence of a middle class. But some aspects of central planning still remain, largely in the allocation of financial capital and in state-owned enterprises. As a result, significant central planning inefficiencies persist. In addition, as it transitions to a free-market system, China is now experiencing excessive pollution, an inefficiency arising from market failure. Many economists have observed that these inefficiencies must be addressed if China is to sustain its rapid growth and satisfy the aspirations of billions of Chinese in a sustainable way.

>> Quick Review

• In a market economy, markets are interrelated. When each and every market in an economy is efficient, the economy as a whole is efficient. But in the real world, some markets in a market economy will almost certainly fail to be efficient.

• A system of **property rights** and the operation of prices as **economic signals** are two key factors that enable a market to be efficient. But under conditions in which property rights are incomplete or prices give inaccurate economic signals, markets can fail.

• Under certain conditions, **market failure** occurs and the market is **inefficient:** gains from trade are unrealized. The three principal causes of market failure are market power, externalities, and a good that, by its nature, makes it unsuitable for a market to allocate efficiently.

>> Check Your Understanding 4-4
Solutions appear at back of book.

1. In some states that are rich in natural resources, such as oil, the law separates the right to above-ground use of the land from the right to drill below ground (called "mineral rights"). Someone who owns both the above-ground rights and the mineral rights can sell the two rights separately. Explain how this division of the property rights enhances efficiency compared to a situation in which the two rights must always be sold together.

2. Suppose that in the market for used textbooks the equilibrium price is $30, but it is mistakenly announced that the equilibrium price is $300. How does this affect the efficiency of the market? Be specific.

3. What is wrong with the following statement? "Markets are always the best way to organize economic activity. Any policies that interfere with markets reduce society's welfare."

Ticket Prices and Music's Reigning Couple, Beyoncé and Jay-Z

Larry Busacca/PW18/Getty Images

Beyoncé and Jay-Z are the reigning couple of music, estimated to be worth $1.4 billion. And a good chunk of that money was earned by touring. In 2018, their "On the Run II Tour" grossed a staggering $253 million with nearly 2.2 million tickets sold. The couple also had a very profitable year in 2014 when their initial "On the Run Tour" grossed over $100 million. One music industry expert noted that no one should be surprised by this. "With nearly 200 million records sold between them

and 36 total Grammys, Beyoncé and Jay-Z are a creative force to be reckoned with. When their talents are combined, the sky is the limit—at least as far as ticket prices are concerned." And, the market seems to agree. TicketIQ estimated that the average online reseller ticket price for the 2018 tour was $403.

Yet, despite the high demand for tickets to their performances, Beyoncé and Jay-Z receive significantly less than this amount for an average ticket. Why? Omar Al-Joulani, the producer of the tour explained that tickets are priced to be *inclusive*. At the MetLife Stadium event in New Jersey in 2018, prices for direct-sale tickets on Live Nation ranged from $25 to $380. Al-Joulani continued: "Our strategy was to price tickets so that wherever you were on that ticket chain you had an opportunity to attend the show."

So if you were able to obtain a ticket from a direct seller, you could have made a pretty penny by reselling your ticket at the market price. Perhaps this was Beyoncé and Jay-Z's way of sharing the wealth as well as their music.

QUESTIONS FOR THOUGHT

1. Use the concepts of consumer surplus and producer surplus to analyze the exchange between Beyoncé and Jay-Z and their fans in the absence of ticket resellers. (That is, assume that everyone buys a ticket directly and goes to the concert.) Draw a diagram to illustrate.

2. Referring to the diagram drawn in response to question 1, explain the effect of resellers on the allocation of consumer surplus and producer surplus among Beyoncé and Jay-Z and their fans.

SUMMARY

1. The **willingness to pay** of each individual consumer determines the demand curve. When price is less than or equal to the willingness to pay, the potential consumer purchases the good. The difference between willingness to pay and price is the net gain to the consumer, the **individual consumer surplus.**

2. **Total consumer surplus** in a market, the sum of all individual consumer surpluses in a market, is equal to the area below the market demand curve but above the price. A rise in the price of a good reduces consumer surplus; a fall in the price increases consumer surplus. The term **consumer surplus** is often used to refer to both individual and total consumer surplus.

3. The **cost** of each potential producer, the lowest price at which they are willing to supply a unit of a particular good, determines the supply curve. If the price of a good is above a producer's cost, a sale generates a net gain to the producer, known as the **individual producer surplus.**

4. **Total producer surplus** in a market, the sum of the individual producer surpluses in a market, is equal to the area above the market supply curve but below the price. A rise in the price of a good increases producer surplus; a fall in the price reduces producer surplus. The term **producer surplus** is often used to refer to both individual and total producer surplus.

5. **Total surplus,** the total gain to society from the production and consumption of a good, is the sum of consumer and producer surplus.

6. Usually markets are efficient and achieve the maximum total surplus. Any possible reallocation of consumption or sales, or a change in the quantity bought and sold, reduces total surplus. However, society also cares about equity. So government intervention in a market that reduces efficiency but increases equity can be a valid choice by society.

7. An economy composed of efficient markets is also efficient, although this is virtually impossible to achieve in reality. The keys to the efficiency of a market economy are **property rights** and the operation of prices as **economic signals.** Under certain conditions, **market failure** occurs, making a market **inefficient.** The three principal causes of market failure are market power, externalities, and a good which, by its nature, makes it unsuitable for a market to allocate efficiently.

KEY TERMS

Willingness to pay, p. 104
Individual consumer surplus, p. 105
Total consumer surplus, p. 105
Consumer surplus, p. 105
Cost, p. 111

Individual producer surplus, p. 112
Total producer surplus, p. 112
Producer surplus, p. 112
Total surplus, p. 116
Property rights, p. 122

Economic signal, p. 122
Inefficient, p. 123
Market failure, p. 123

PRACTICE QUESTIONS

1. Assume that due to a decrease in demand, the average domestic airline fare decreased from $375 in the third quarter of 2019 to $360 in the fourth quarter of the same year, a decrease of $15. The number of passenger tickets sold in the third quarter was 185 million, and it was 175 million in the fourth quarter. Over the same period, the airlines' costs remained roughly the same: the price of jet fuel averaged around $2 per gallon in both quarters, and airline pilots' salaries remained roughly the same, averaging $117,000 per year in 2019.

   Using this information, determine precisely how much producer surplus has decreased as a result of the $15 decrease in the average fare. If you cannot be precise, determine whether it will be less than, or more than, a specific amount?

2. During the summer of 2019 Hurricane Dorian, considered to be the most intense hurricane in history,

languished off the coast of Florida before weakening and making landfall in North Carolina. While it threatened Florida, the local residents scrambled to stock up on basic necessities, including bread, gas, and water. Given the limited supplies, residents quickly noticed some places had increased prices by more than 300%, an act known as price gouging. Explain how price gouging can result in an increase in consumer surplus.

3. In the early 1990s, the Chrysler Corporation released the best-selling SUV, the Jeep Grand Cherokee. At the time of release, the Grand Cherokee came in three different models, each model offering unique features. Today, the Grand Cherokee is sold in ten unique models. Why do firms provide unique models and how does increasing the number of models affect producer surplus?

PROBLEMS

1. Determine the amount of consumer surplus generated in each of the following situations.

  a. Bo goes to the clothing store to buy a new T-shirt, for which he is willing to pay up to $10. He picks out one he likes with a price tag of exactly $10. When he is paying for it, he learns that the T-shirt has been discounted by 50%.

  b. Alberto goes to the music store hoping to find a used copy of Nirvana's *Nevermind* for up to $30. The store has one copy of the record selling for $30, which he purchases.

  c. After soccer practice, Stephany is willing to pay $2 for a bottle of mineral water. The 7-Eleven sells mineral water for $2.25 per bottle, so she declines to purchase it.

2. Determine the amount of producer surplus generated in each of the following situations.

  a. Conner lists his old Lionel electric trains on eBay. He sets a minimum acceptable price, known as his reserve price, of $75. After five days of bidding, the final high bid is exactly $75. He accepts the bid.

  b. So-Hee advertises her car for sale in the used-car section of the student newspaper for $2,000, but she is willing to sell the car for any price higher than $1,500. The best offer she gets is $1,200, which she declines.

  c. Sanjay likes his job so much that he would be willing to do it for free. However, his annual salary is $80,000.

3. There are six potential consumers of computer games, each willing to buy only one game. Consumer 1 is willing to pay $40 for a computer game, consumer 2 is willing to pay $35, consumer 3 is willing to pay $30, consumer 4 is willing to pay $25, consumer 5 is willing to pay $20, and consumer 6 is willing to pay $15.

  a. Suppose the market price is $29. What is the total consumer surplus?

  b. The market price decreases to $19. What is the total consumer surplus now?

  c. When the price falls from $29 to $19, how much does each consumer's individual consumer surplus change? How does total consumer surplus change?

4. a. In an auction, potential buyers compete for a good by submitting bids. Adam Galinsky, a social psychologist at Northwestern University, compared eBay auctions in which the same good was sold. He found that, on average, the larger the number of bidders, the higher the sales price. For example, in two auctions of identical iPads, the one with the larger number of bidders brought a higher selling price. According to Galinsky, this explains why smart sellers on eBay set absurdly low opening prices (the lowest price that the seller will accept), such as 1 cent for a new iPad. Use the concepts of consumer and producer surplus to explain Galinsky's reasoning.

  b. You are considering selling your first car. If the car is in good condition, it is worth a lot; if it is in poor condition, it is useful only as scrap. Assume that your car is in excellent condition but that it costs a potential buyer $40 for a CARFAX report to determine the car's condition. Use what you learned in part a to explain whether or not you should pay for the CARFAX report and share the results with all interested buyers.

5. The accompanying table shows the supply and demand schedules for used copies of the fifth edition of this textbook. The supply schedule is derived from offers at Amazon. The demand schedule is hypothetical.

Price of book	Quantity of books demanded	Quantity of books supplied
$55	50	0
60	35	1
65	25	3
70	17	3
75	14	6
80	12	9
85	10	10
90	8	18
95	6	22
100	4	31
105	2	37
110	0	42

  a. Calculate consumer and producer surplus at the equilibrium in this market.

  b. Now the sixth edition of this textbook becomes available. As a result, the willingness to pay of each potential buyer for a second-hand copy of the fifth edition falls by $20. In a table, show the new demand schedule and again calculate consumer and producer surplus at the new equilibrium.

6. On Thursday nights, a local restaurant has a pasta special. Ari likes the restaurant's pasta, and his willingness to pay for each serving is shown in the accompanying table.

Quantity of pasta (servings)	Willingness to pay for pasta (per serving)
1	$10
2	8
3	6
4	4
5	2
6	0

  a. If the price of a serving of pasta is $4, how many servings will Ari buy? How much consumer surplus does he receive?

b. The following week, Ari is back at the restaurant again, but now the price of a serving of pasta is $6. By how much does his consumer surplus decrease compared to the previous week?

c. One week later, he goes to the restaurant again. He discovers that the restaurant is offering an "all-you-can-eat" special for $25. How much pasta will Ari eat, and how much consumer surplus does he receive now?

d. Suppose you own the restaurant and Ari is a typical customer. What is the highest price you can charge for the "all-you-can-eat" special and still attract customers?

7. You are the manager of Fun World, a small amusement park. The accompanying diagram shows the demand curve of a typical customer at Fun World.

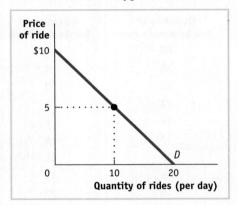

a. Suppose that the price of each ride is $5. At that price, how much consumer surplus does an individual consumer get? (Recall that the area of a right triangle is $\frac{1}{2}$ × the height of the triangle × the base of the triangle.)

b. Suppose that Fun World considers charging an admission fee, even though it maintains the price of each ride at $5. What is the maximum admission fee it could charge? (Assume that all potential customers have enough money to pay the fee.)

c. Suppose that Fun World lowered the price of each ride to zero. How much consumer surplus does an individual consumer get? What is the maximum admission fee Fun World could charge?

8. The accompanying diagram illustrates a taxi driver's individual supply curve (assume that each taxi ride is the same distance).

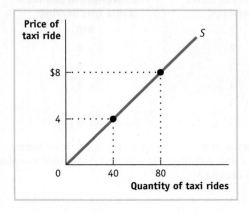

a. Suppose the city sets the price of taxi rides at $4 per ride, and at $4 the taxi driver is able to sell as many taxi rides as he desires. What is this taxi driver's producer surplus? (Recall that the area of a right triangle is $\frac{1}{2}$ × the height of the triangle × the base of the triangle.)

b. Suppose that the city keeps the price of a taxi ride set at $4, but it decides to charge taxi drivers a "licensing fee." What is the maximum licensing fee the city could extract from this taxi driver?

c. Suppose that the city allowed the price of taxi rides to increase to $8 per ride. Again assume that, at this price, the taxi driver sells as many rides as he is willing to offer. How much producer surplus does an individual taxi driver now get? What is the maximum licensing fee the city could charge this taxi driver?

9. Spotify, Pandora, and Google Play are some of the more popular music streaming services. These companies offer free access to music. For a small monthly fee users can purchase premium access and listen to millions of songs on demand and ad free. But not all artists are fans of free streaming music. Taylor Swift's move to prevent Spotify from playing her 2014 release, *1989*, for free, made national headlines. When Spotify refused to restrict access to only paying customers, Swift would not allow the company to play her music for free. She is not alone. Adele, Dr. Dre, Garth Brooks, and Coldplay have all had run-ins with free streaming services.

a. If music lovers obtain music and video content via free music streaming services, instead of buying it directly or paying for premium access, what would the record companies' producer surplus be from music sales? What are the implications for record companies' incentive to produce music content in the future?

b. If Taylor Swift and other artists were not allowed to pull their music from the free streaming services, what would happen to mutually beneficial transactions (the producing and buying of music) in the future?

10. On December 17, 2015, tickets for Adele's highly anticipated U.S. concert tour went on sale at Ticketmaster on a first come, first served basis. Throughout the day, a record 10 million people tried to purchase the 750,000 tickets available. In an attempt to prevent ticket scalping, Adele and Ticketmaster limited buyers to four tickets per concert and required that premium seat holders present the credit card used to purchase tickets to get into the concert. Despite these attempts to restrict resale, tickets on secondary sites like StubHub were selling for 10 times their face value.

a. Draw a supply and demand diagram that depicts the market for Adele concert tickets. Assume all tickets cost $150. Label the equilibrium price, quantity, and resulting shortage.

b. In your diagram, highlight or label the areas that correspond to consumer surplus, producer surplus, and total surplus.

c. Use your diagram to explain how reselling tickets on secondary sites can increase consumer surplus.

11. Uber has long been criticized for its use of surge pricing, setting prices based on current supply and demand factors, which, at times, results in a sudden and drastic increase in prices. In a *Wall Street Journal* article, the CEO of Uber was asked if we are seeing the end of surge pricing. His response: ". . . at the end of the day, Friday night is three or five times bigger than a Sunday night in any city around the world. And if you've got enough supply on the system so that we were perfectly supplied on a Friday night for as much demand as a city could ever throw at us, then the rest of the week you have drivers not making a living."

a. Draw a demand and supply graph for Uber rides in Miami on a Sunday night. How does demand change on a Friday night? How does the supply of Uber rides change? Label the shortage of Uber cars that results on a Friday night without surge pricing.

b. In your diagram, show what happens to consumer and producer surplus on a Friday night without surge pricing.

c. Using your diagram explain how surge pricing changes consumer and producer surplus.

12. Hollywood screenwriters negotiate a new agreement with movie producers stipulating that they will receive 10% of the revenue from every rental of a movie they wrote. They have no such agreement for movies shown on on-demand television.

a. When the new writers' agreement comes into effect, what will happen in the market for movie rentals—that is, will supply or demand shift, and how? And, as a result, how will consumer surplus in the market for movie rentals change? Illustrate with a diagram. Will the writers' agreement be popular with consumers who rent movies?

b. Consumers consider movie rentals and on-demand movies substitutable to some extent. When the new writers' agreement comes into effect, what will happen in the market for on-demand movies—that is, will supply or demand shift, and how? And, as a result, how will producer surplus in the market for on-demand movies change? Illustrate with a diagram. Will the writers' agreement be popular with the cable television companies that show on-demand movies?

c. More consumers are shifting their movie-watching preferences from Redbox rentals to streaming services like Netflix and Amazon Prime. What will happen in the market for movie rentals after the shift in movie preferences? How will producer surplus in the market for movie rentals change? Illustrate with a diagram. Use your diagram to explain how the shift to streaming movies will affect movie rental companies and Hollywood screenwriters.

▦ WORK IT OUT

13. The accompanying diagram shows the demand and supply curves for taxi rides in New York City.

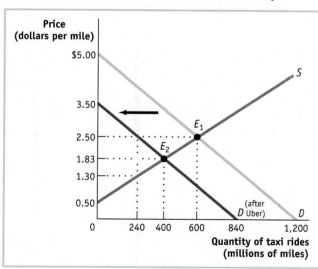

a. At E_1 the market is at equilibrium with 600 million miles of rides transacted at an equilibrium price of $2.50. Calculate consumer surplus, producer surplus, and total surplus at E_1.

b. Uber's entry into the market reduces the quantity of rides demanded from taxis by 30% at every price, shifting the demand curve leftward. Assume that New York City lawmakers respond by imposing a regulated price of $2.50 per mile. Calculate consumer surplus, producer surplus, and total surplus for the taxi market after Uber has entered the market.

c. After complaints from riders, New York removes the regulated price of $2.50 per mile. What happens to the equilibrium price and quantity? How will taxi drivers and riders be affected? ▪

5 ▷ Price Controls and Quotas: Meddling with Markets

A BRONX TALE

STEPHANIE KIRNON WAS WORRIED. How would she, a landlord, afford the $29,000 needed to repair the leaky roof of the 26-unit apartment building she owns in the Bronx, a borough of New York City? In contrast, Gloribel Castillo, a tenant in a nearby apartment building, was relieved, knowing that she would no longer have to worry about affording her monthly rent.

The source of this contrast was a tightening of rent-control regulations. These laws prevent landlords from raising rents or evicting tenants in rent-controlled apartments without permission from a city agency. In 2019, New York State made it much more difficult for landlords to obtain that permission. The revised regulations also prohibit landlords from switching apartments from rent-controlled to unregulated status. Once apartments are unregulated, landlords can charge much higher market rents.

Tenant groups, who had lobbied hard for these regulatory changes, cheered. Many of their members were working class, like

While tenant Gloribel Castillo (left) cheered the tightening of New York rent-control laws, landlord Stephanie Kirnon (right) worried she would now be unable to afford necessary building repairs.

Gloribel Castillo, a hotel cleaner who worked two shifts in order to pay the rent on her rent-controlled apartment. For decades, the Bronx has been home to working-class and lower-income New Yorkers. But by 2019, the Bronx was undergoing a *gentrification* process—less desirable locations became more desirable as people with higher incomes moved in, and lower income residents were forced out. As a result, rents were beginning to increase. Until the tighter restrictions were adopted, tenants in rent-controlled apartments faced the very real possibility that landlords would find a loophole in the law to raise their rents or evict them.

Another group also benefited from the new tighter regulations: owners of unregulated apartments. Now that it was illegal to shift rent-controlled apartments to unregulated status, there would be fewer unregulated apartments available. As a result, the rents for unregulated apartments would rise. But landlords of rent-controlled buildings, like Stephanie Kirnon, were facing a real bind. The tightened regulations made it harder to afford the necessary renovations and maintenance. Stephanie also knew that less rental income made it harder for her to afford her mortgage payments.

What will the future hold for Bronx residents? In the 1970s, when rent-control laws had been applied very strictly, many buildings were abandoned as landlords were unable to charge rents high enough to cover their costs. The Bronx declined dramatically during these years: there was a shortage of inhabitable apartments and crime soared as empty buildings were used for nefarious purposes. Only time will tell whether the Bronx will become a tenant's paradise or revert to being a tenant's nightmare.

Rent control is a type of *market intervention,* a policy imposed by government to prevail over the market forces of supply and demand—in this case, over the market

forces of the supply and demand for rental apartments in the Bronx. Although rent-control laws were introduced during World War II in many major American cities to protect the interests of tenants, the problems they created led most cities to discard them. New York City and San Francisco are notable exceptions, although rent control covers only a small and diminishing proportion of rental apartments in both cities.

As we will learn in this chapter, when a government tries to dictate either a market price or a market quantity that's different from the equilibrium price or quantity, the market will strike back in predictable ways. A shortage of apartments is one example of what happens when the logic of the market is defied: a market intervention like rent control keeps the price of apartment rentals below market equilibrium level, creating the shortage and other serious problems. And, as we'll see, those problems inevitably create winners and losers.

Although there are specific winners and losers from market intervention, we will learn how and why society as a whole loses—a result that has led economists to be generally skeptical of market interventions except in certain well-defined situations. ●

WHAT YOU WILL LEARN

- What is a market intervention and why are **price controls** and **quantity controls** the two main forms it takes?

- Why do price and quantity controls create **deadweight losses?**

- Who benefits and who loses from market interventions?

- Why are economists often skeptical of market interventions? And why do governments undertake market interventions even though they create losses to society?

Price controls are legal restrictions on how high or low a market price may go. They can take two forms: a **price ceiling,** a maximum price sellers are allowed to charge for a good or service, or a **price floor,** a minimum price buyers are required to pay for a good or service.

Why Governments Control Prices

As we know from Chapter 3, a market moves to equilibrium—the market price moves to the level at which the quantity supplied equals the quantity demanded. But this equilibrium price does not necessarily please either buyers or sellers.

After all, buyers would always like to pay less if they could. Sometimes they can make a strong moral or political case for this, such as when the equilibrium rental rates are not affordable for an average working person. In that case, a government might well be under pressure to impose limits on the rents landlords can charge.

Similarly, sellers would always like to get higher prices. Sometimes they can make a strong moral or political case for this, such as when the equilibrium wage rate for a worker who sells their labor in the labor market results in an income below the poverty level. In that case, a government might well be pressured to require employers to pay a rate no lower than some specified minimum wage.

So there are often strong political demands for governments to intervene in markets with powerful interests often making a compelling case that market intervention in their favor is "fair." When a government intervenes to regulate prices, we say that it imposes **price controls.** These controls typically take the form either of an upper limit, a **price ceiling,** or a lower limit, a **price floor.**

However, it's not that easy to tell a market what to do. When a government tries to legislate prices—whether it legislates them down by imposing a price ceiling or up by imposing a price floor—there are certain predictable and unpleasant side effects.

Yet, there are two important caveats to consider. First, we assume in this chapter that the markets in question are efficient before price controls are imposed. But markets can sometimes be inefficient—for example, a market dominated by a monopolist, a single seller that has the power to influence the market price. When markets are inefficient, price controls don't necessarily cause problems and can potentially move markets closer to efficiency. Second, short-term price controls in response to shortages caused by natural disasters can be justified on the basis of equity and social welfare. For example, during the coronavirus pandemic of 2020, a shortage of ventilators necessary to keep people alive would have led to skyrocketing prices in a free market, thereby making them only available to the well-off. So the government on state and federal levels acted to allocate ventilators according to need, making for a far more equitable allocation of life and death.

Price Ceilings

Aside from rent control, there are not many price ceilings in the United States today. But at times they have been widespread. Price ceilings are typically imposed during crises—wars, harvest failures, natural disasters—because these events often lead to sudden price increases that hurt many people but produce big gains for a lucky few.

The U.S. government imposed ceilings on many prices during World War II: the war sharply increased demand for raw materials, such as aluminum and steel, and price controls prevented those with access to these raw materials from earning huge profits. Price controls on oil were imposed in 1973, when an embargo by Arab oil-exporting countries seemed likely to generate huge profits for U.S. oil companies. Price controls were instituted again in 2012 by New York and New Jersey authorities in the aftermath of Hurricane Sandy, as gas shortages led to rampant price-gouging.

Rent control in New York is, as we mention in the opening story, a legacy of World War II: it was imposed because wartime production led to an economic boom that increased demand for apartments at a time when the labor and raw materials that might have been used to build them were being used to win the war instead. Although most price controls were removed soon after the war ended, New York's rent limits were retained and gradually extended to buildings not previously covered, leading to some very strange situations.

You can rent a one-bedroom apartment in Manhattan on fairly short notice—if you are able and willing to pay several thousand dollars a month and live in a less desirable area. Yet some people pay only a small fraction of this for comparable apartments, and others pay hardly more for bigger apartments in the most desirable locations.

Aside from producing great deals for some renters, however, what are the broader consequences of New York's rent-control system? To answer this question, we turn to the model we developed in Chapter 3: the supply and demand model.

Modeling a Price Ceiling

To see what can go wrong when a government imposes a price ceiling on an efficient market, consider Figure 5-1, which shows a simplified model of the market for apartments in New York. For the sake of simplicity, we imagine that all apartments are exactly the same and would rent for the same price in an unregulated market.

The table in Figure 5-1 shows the demand and supply schedules; the demand and supply curves are shown on the left. We show the quantity of apartments on the horizontal axis and the monthly rent per apartment on the vertical axis. You can see that in an unregulated market the equilibrium would be at point *E*: 2 million apartments would be rented for $1,000 each per month.

Now suppose that the government imposes a price ceiling, limiting rents to a price below the equilibrium price—say, no more than $800.

FIGURE 5-1 The Market for Apartments in the Absence of Price Controls

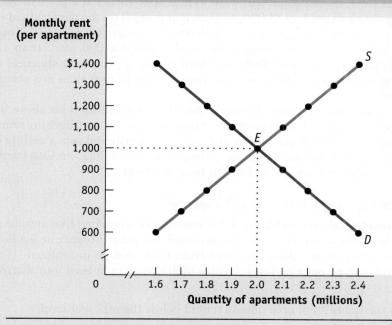

Monthly rent (per apartment)	Quantity of apartments (millions)	
	Quantity demanded	Quantity supplied
$1,400	1.6	2.4
1,300	1.7	2.3
1,200	1.8	2.2
1,100	1.9	2.1
1,000	2.0	2.0
900	2.1	1.9
800	2.2	1.8
700	2.3	1.7
600	2.4	1.6

Without government intervention, the market for apartments reaches equilibrium at point *E* with a market rent of $1,000 per month and 2 million apartments rented.

FIGURE 5-2 The Effects of a Price Ceiling

The black horizontal line represents the government-imposed price ceiling on rents of $800 per month. This price ceiling reduces the quantity of apartments supplied to 1.8 million, point *A*, and increases the quantity demanded to 2.2 million, point *B*. This creates a persistent shortage of 400,000 units: 400,000 people who want apartments at the legal rent of $800 but cannot get them.

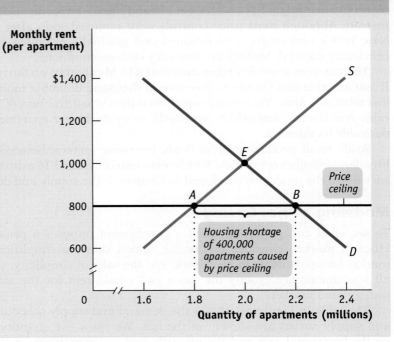

Figure 5-2 shows the effect of the price ceiling, represented by the line at $800. At the enforced rental rate of $800, landlords have less incentive to offer apartments, so they won't be willing to supply as many as they would at the equilibrium rate of $1,000. They will choose point *A* on the supply curve, offering only 1.8 million apartments for rent, 200,000 fewer than in the unregulated market.

At the same time, more people will want to rent apartments at a price of $800 than at the equilibrium price of $1,000; as shown at point *B* on the demand curve, at a monthly rent of $800 the quantity of apartments demanded rises to 2.2 million, 200,000 more than in the unregulated market and 400,000 more than are actually available at the price of $800. So there is now a persistent shortage of rental housing: at that price, 400,000 more people want to rent than are able to find apartments.

Do price ceilings always cause shortages? No. If a price ceiling is set above the equilibrium price, it won't have any effect. Suppose that the equilibrium rental rate on apartments is $1,000 per month and the city government sets a ceiling of $1,200. Who cares? In this case, the price ceiling won't be *binding*—it won't actually constrain market behavior—and it will have no effect.

How a Price Ceiling Causes Inefficiency

The housing shortage shown in Figure 5-2 is not merely annoying: like any shortage induced by price controls, it can be seriously harmful because it leads to inefficiency. In other words, there are gains from trade that go unrealized.

Rent control, like all price ceilings, creates inefficiency in at least four distinct ways.

1. It reduces the quantity of apartments rented below the efficient level.
2. It typically leads to inefficient allocation of apartments among would-be renters.
3. It leads to wasted time and effort as people search for apartments.
4. It leads landlords to maintain apartments in inefficiently low quality or condition.

In addition to inefficiency, price ceilings give rise to illegal behavior as people try to circumvent them. We'll now look at each of these inefficiencies caused by price ceilings.

Inefficiently Low Quantity In Chapter 4 we learned that the market equilibrium of an efficient market leads to the "right" quantity of a good or service being bought and sold—that is, the quantity that maximizes the sum of producer and consumer surplus. Because rent controls reduce the number of apartments supplied, they reduce the number of apartments rented, too.

Figure 5-3 shows the implications for total surplus. Recall that total surplus is the sum of the area above the supply curve and below the demand curve. If the only effect of rent control was to reduce the number of apartments available, it would cause a loss of surplus equal to the area of the shaded triangle in the figure.

The area represented by that triangle has a special name in economics, **deadweight loss:** the lost surplus associated with the transactions that no longer occur due to the market intervention. In this example, the deadweight loss is the lost surplus associated with the apartment rentals that no longer occur due to the price ceiling, a loss that is experienced by both disappointed renters and frustrated landlords. Economists often call triangles like the one in Figure 5-3 a *deadweight-loss triangle.*

Deadweight loss is a key concept in economics, one that we will encounter whenever an action or a policy leads to a reduction in the quantity transacted below the efficient market equilibrium quantity. It is important to realize that deadweight loss is a *loss to society*—it is a reduction in total surplus, a loss in surplus that accrues to no one as a gain. It is not the same as a loss in surplus to one person that then accrues as a gain to someone else, what an economist would call a *transfer* of surplus from one person to another. In the next section we look at how a price ceiling can create deadweight loss as well as a transfer of surplus between renters and landlords.

> **Deadweight loss** is the loss in total surplus that occurs whenever an action or a policy reduces the quantity transacted below the efficient market equilibrium quantity.

FIGURE 5-3 A Price Ceiling Causes Inefficiently Low Quantity

A price ceiling reduces the quantity supplied below the market equilibrium quantity, leading to a deadweight loss. The area of the shaded triangle corresponds to the amount of total surplus lost due to the inefficiently low quantity transacted.

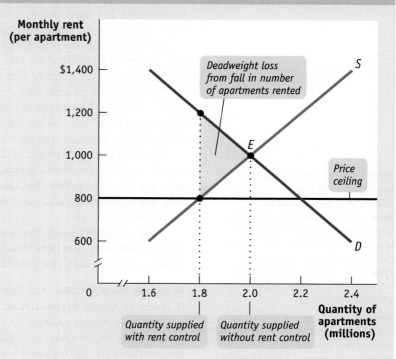

A price ceiling like rent control leads to inefficiency in the market for rental apartments.

Deadweight loss is not the only type of inefficiency that arises from a price ceiling. The types of inefficiency created by rent control go beyond reducing the quantity of apartments available. These additional inefficiencies—inefficient allocation to consumers, wasted resources, and inefficiently low quality—lead to a loss of surplus over and above the deadweight loss.

Inefficient Allocation to Consumers Rent control doesn't just lead to too few apartments being available. It can also lead to misallocation of the apartments that are available: people who badly need a place to live may not be able to find an apartment, but some apartments may be occupied by people with much less urgent needs.

In the case shown in Figure 5-2, 2.2 million people would like to rent an apartment at $800 per month, but only 1.8 million apartments are available. Of those 2.2 million who are seeking an apartment, some want one badly and are willing to pay a high price to get it. Others have a less urgent need and are only willing to pay a low price, perhaps because they have alternative housing.

An efficient allocation of apartments would reflect these differences: people who really want an apartment will get one and people who aren't all that eager to find an apartment won't. In an inefficient distribution of apartments, the opposite will happen: some people who are not especially interested in finding an apartment will get one and others who are very eager to find an apartment won't.

Because people usually get apartments through luck or personal connections under rent control, it generally results in an **inefficient allocation to consumers** of the few apartments available.

To see the inefficiency involved, consider the plight of the Lees, a family with young children who have no alternative housing and would be willing to pay up to $1,500 for an apartment—but are unable to find one. Also consider George, a retiree who lives most of the year in Florida but still has a lease on the New York apartment he moved into 40 years ago. George pays $800 per month for this apartment, but if the rent were even slightly more—say, $850—he would give it up and stay with his children when he visits New York.

This allocation of apartments—George has one and the Lees do not—is a missed opportunity: there is a way to make the Lees and George both better off at no additional cost. The Lees would be happy to pay George, say, $1,200 a month to sublease his apartment, which he would happily accept since the apartment is worth no more than $849 a month to him. George would prefer the money he gets from the Lees to keeping his apartment; the Lees would prefer to have the apartment rather than the money. So both would be made better off by this transaction—and nobody else would be made worse off.

Generally, if people who really want apartments could sublease them from people who are less eager to live there, both those who gain apartments and those who trade their occupancy for money would be better off. However, subletting is illegal under rent control because it would occur at prices above the price ceiling.

The fact that subletting is illegal doesn't mean it never happens. In fact, chasing down illegal subletting is a major business for New York private investigators who are hired to prove that the legal tenants in rent-controlled apartments actually live somewhere else, and have sublet their apartments at two or three times the controlled rent.

This subletting leads to the emergence of a black market, which we will discuss shortly. For now, just note that landlords and legal agencies actively discourage the practice. As a result, the problem of inefficient allocation of apartments remains.

Wasted Resources Another reason a price ceiling causes inefficiency is that it leads to **wasted resources**: people expend money, effort, and time to cope with the shortages caused by the price ceiling. Back in 1979, U.S. price controls on gasoline led to shortages that forced millions of Americans to wait in lines at gas stations for hours each week. The opportunity cost of the time spent in gas lines—the wages not earned, the leisure time not enjoyed—constituted wasted resources from the point of view of consumers and of the economy as a whole.

Price ceilings often lead to inefficiency in the form of **inefficient allocation to consumers**: some people who want the good badly and are willing to pay a high price don't get it, and some who care relatively little about the good and are only willing to pay a low price do get it.

Price ceilings typically lead to inefficiency in the form of **wasted resources**: people expend money, effort, and time to cope with the shortages caused by the price ceiling.

FOR INQUIRING MINDS   Mumbai's Rent-Control Millionaires

Mumbai, India, like New York City, has rent-controlled apartments. Currently, about 60% of apartments in Mumbai's city center are rent-controlled. Although Mumbai is half a world away from New York City, the economics of rent control works just the same: rent control leads to shortages, low quality, inefficient allocation to consumers, wasted resources, and black markets.

Mumbai landlords, who often pay more in taxes and maintenance than what they receive in rent, sometimes simply abandon their properties to decay. And a black market in rent-controlled apartments thrives in Mumbai as old tenants sell the right to occupy apartments to new tenants.

And, like many major cities, New York included, Mumbai has its "rent-control millionaires." One renter lived in a 2,600 square foot apartment paying just $20 per month in an area where apartments not under rent control often go for $2,000 a month. He refused to leave when his roof collapsed, and after three years of negotiations was paid $2.5 million by a developer to vacate the apartment so that a luxury building could be constructed. Similarly, in recent years, three New York City tenants were paid $25 *million* by a property developer to move from their rent-controlled apartments.

With its shortage of land for development, and its desirability as a place to live for the rapidly expanding number of high-income Indians, Mumbai has thousands of rent-controlled tenants who have become millionaires upon vacating their apartments.

Because of rent control, the Lees will spend all their spare time for several months searching for an apartment, time they would rather have spent working or in family activities. That is, there is an opportunity cost to the Lees' prolonged search for an apartment—the leisure or income they had to forgo.

If the market for apartments worked freely, the Lees would quickly find an apartment at the equilibrium rent of $1,000, leaving them time to earn more or to enjoy themselves—an outcome that would make them better off without making anyone else worse off. Again, rent control creates missed opportunities.

Inefficiently Low Quality   Yet another way a price ceiling creates inefficiency is by causing goods to be of inefficiently low quality. **Inefficiently low quality** means that sellers offer low-quality goods at a low price even though buyers would rather have higher quality and would be willing to pay a higher price for it.

Again, consider rent control. Landlords have no incentive to provide better conditions because they cannot raise rents to cover their repair costs but are able to find tenants easily. In many cases, tenants would be willing to pay much more for improved conditions than it would cost for the landlord to provide them—for example, upgrading an outdated electrical system that cannot safely run air conditioners or computers. But any additional payment for such improvements would be legally considered a rent increase, which is prohibited.

Indeed, rent-controlled apartments are notoriously badly maintained, rarely painted, subject to frequent electrical and plumbing problems, sometimes even hazardous to inhabit. As one manager of a Manhattan building described: "At unregulated apartments we'd do most things that the tenants requested. But on the rent-regulated units, we did absolutely only what the law required. . . . We had a perverse incentive to make those tenants unhappy." This whole situation is a missed opportunity—some tenants would be happy to pay for better conditions, and landlords would be happy to provide them for payment. But such an exchange would occur only if the market were allowed to operate freely.

Black Markets   In addition to these four inefficiencies there is a final aspect of price ceilings: the incentive they provide for illegal activities, specifically the emergence of **black markets.** We have already described one kind of black market activity—illegal subletting by tenants. But it does not stop there. Clearly, there is a temptation for a landlord to say to a potential tenant, "Look, you can have the place if you slip me an extra few hundred in cash each month"—and for the tenant to agree if they are one of those people who would be willing to pay much more than the maximum legal rent.

So, what's wrong with black markets? In general, it's a bad thing if people break any law, because it encourages disrespect for the law in general. Worse yet, in this case illegal activity worsens the position of those who are honest. If the

Price ceilings often lead to inefficiency in that the goods being offered are of **inefficiently low quality:** sellers offer low-quality goods at a low price even though buyers would prefer a higher quality at a higher price.

A **black market** is a market in which goods or services are bought and sold illegally—either because it is illegal to sell them at all or because the prices charged are legally prohibited by a price ceiling.

Lees are scrupulous about upholding the rent-control law but other people—who may need an apartment less than the Lees—are willing to bribe landlords or grab illegal sublets, the Lees may never find an apartment.

Yet black markets can diminish *some* of the inefficiency of rent control. For example, if George allows the Lees to sublet his rent-controlled apartment (a black market deal since it is illegal), society is better off (as are the Lees) than if there were no deal. But in the end, society as a whole is made worse off by the presence of a black market relative to a market that is completely free of rent control.

Winners, Losers, and Rent Control

We've just seen how price controls can lead to inefficiencies. These inefficiencies, in turn, create winners and losers as some people benefit from policies like rent control while others are made worse off.

Using consumer and producer surplus, we can graphically evaluate the winners and the losers from rent control. Panel (a) of Figure 5-4 shows the consumer surplus and producer surplus in the equilibrium of the unregulated market for apartments before rent control. Recall that the *consumer surplus*, represented by the area below the demand curve and above the price, is the total net gain to consumers in the market equilibrium. Likewise, *producer surplus*, represented by the area above the supply curve and below the price, is the total net gain to producers in the market equilibrium.

Panel (b) of this figure shows the consumer and producer surplus in the market after the price ceiling of $800 has been imposed. As you can see, for consumers who can still obtain apartments under rent control, consumer surplus has increased. These renters are clearly winners: they obtain an apartment at $800, paying $200 less than the unregulated market price. These people receive a direct transfer of surplus from landlords in the form of lower rent.

FIGURE 5-4 Winners and Losers from Rent Control

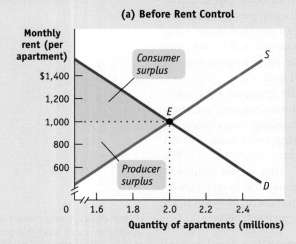
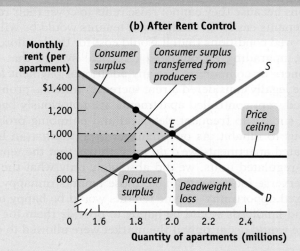

Price ceilings like rent control reduce total surplus. Panel (a) shows the producer and consumer surplus created in the unregulated market for apartments. Total surplus is greatest at the market equilibrium: a monthly rent of $1,000 and a quantity of 2.0 million apartments transacted. Panel (b) shows the producer and consumer surplus in the market after a price ceiling of $800 is imposed, resulting in a fall in total surplus. At the mandated rent of $800, landlords reduce the quantity of apartments supplied from 2.0 million to 1.8 million.

For renters who can find an apartment, their consumer surplus has increased. This increase in consumer surplus is a direct transfer from landlords, represented by the purple-shaded rectangle. However, consumer surplus declines for those who are now unable to rent an apartment. Their loss, as well as the loss to landlords from renting fewer apartments, is represented by the deadweight loss triangle shaded in yellow. The deadweight loss represents the total loss to society from the imposition of rent control.

But not all renters win: there are fewer apartments to rent now than if the market had remained unregulated, making it hard, if not impossible, for some to find a place to call home.

Without direct calculation of the surpluses gained and lost, it is generally unclear whether renters as a whole are made better or worse off by rent control. What we can say is that the greater the deadweight loss—the larger the reduction in the quantity of apartments rented—the more likely it is that renters as a whole lose. We saw this in the opening story: the deadweight loss incurred in the Bronx during the 1970s was very large. Renters as a whole lost as the neighborhood declined and as they were faced with a shortage of inhabitable apartments.

However, we can say unambiguously that landlords are worse off: producer surplus has clearly decreased. Landlords who continue to rent out their apartments get $200 a month less in rent, and others withdraw their apartments from the market altogether. The deadweight-loss triangle, shaded yellow in panel (b), represents the value lost to both renters and landlords from rentals that essentially vanish thanks to rent control.

So Why Are There Price Ceilings?

We have seen three common results of price ceilings:

- A persistent shortage of the good
- Inefficiency arising from this persistent shortage in the form of inefficiently low quantity (deadweight loss), inefficient allocation of the good to consumers, resources wasted in searching for the good, and the inefficiently low quality of the good offered for sale
- The emergence of illegal, black market activity

Given these unpleasant consequences of price ceilings, why do governments still sometimes impose them? Why does rent control, in particular, persist in New York?

One answer is that although price ceilings may have adverse effects, they do benefit some people. In practice, New York's rent-control rules—which are more complex than our simple model—hurt most residents but give a small minority of renters much cheaper housing than they would get in an unregulated market. And those who benefit from the controls are typically better organized and more vocal than those who are harmed by them.

Also, when price ceilings have been in effect for a long time, buyers may not have a realistic idea of what would happen without them. In our earlier example, the rental rate in an unregulated market (Figure 5-1) would be only 25% higher than in the regulated market (Figure 5-2): $1,000 instead of $800. But how would renters know that? Indeed, they might have heard about black market transactions at much higher prices—the Lees or some other family paying George $1,200 or more—and would not realize that these black market prices are much higher than the price that would prevail in a fully unregulated market.

A last answer is that government officials often do not understand supply and demand analysis! It is a great mistake to suppose that economic policies in the real world are always sensible or well informed.

ECONOMICS >> *in Action*
How Price Controls in Venezuela Proved Disastrous

By all accounts, Venezuela is a rich country as one of the world's top producers of oil. But despite its wealth, price controls have so distorted its economy that the country is struggling to feed its citizens and provide health care. Necessities like toilet paper, rice, coffee, corn, flour, milk, and meat are chronically lacking. Hospitals operate without basic supplies and with broken equipment.

Venezuela's food shortages show how price controls disproportionately hurt the people they were designed to benefit.

Today, Venezuelans line up for hours to purchase price-controlled goods at state-run stores, but often came away empty handed. "Empty shelves and no one to explain why a rich country has no food. It's unacceptable," said Jesús López, a 90-year-old farmer.

The origins of the shortages can be traced to policies espoused by Venezuela's former president, Hugo Chávez. First elected in 1998 on a platform that promised to favor the poor and working classes over the country's economic elite, Chávez implemented price controls on basic foodstuffs. Prices were set so low that farmers reduced production, so that by 2006 shortages were severe. As a result, Venezuela went from being self-sufficient in food in 1998 to importing more than 70% of its food. By 2019, researchers had documented widespread weight loss and increasing malnutrition among the Venezuelan population.

At the same time, generous government programs for the poor and working class created higher demand. The reduced supply of goods due to price controls combined with higher demand led to sharply rising prices for black market goods that, in turn, generated even greater demand for goods sold at the controlled prices. Smuggling became rampant, as a bottle of milk sold across the border in Colombia for seven or eight times the controlled price in Venezuela. Not surprisingly, fresh milk was rarely seen in Venezuelan markets.

The irony of the situation is that the policies put in place to help the poor and working classes have disproportionately hurt them. In 2019, the minimum monthly wage allowed Venezuelan's to afford only 24 eggs, three-quarters of a pizza, or half a burger on the black market. People were spending up to 12 hours at a time in line to purchase basic foodstuffs. As one shopper in a low-income area said, "It fills me with rage to have to spend the one free day I have wasting my time for a bag of rice. I end up paying more at the resellers [the black market]. In the end, all these price controls proved useless."

The lack of basic necessities—food and medicine—coupled with soaring crime led to a mass exodus of more than 3 million people from Venezuela to neighboring countries in 2019. As one woman said, "I'm leaving with nothing. But I have to do this. Otherwise, we will just die hungry here."

>> Quick Review

• **Price controls** take the form of either legal maximum prices—**price ceilings**—or legal minimum prices—**price floors.**

• A price ceiling below the equilibrium price benefits successful buyers but causes predictable adverse effects such as persistent shortages, which lead to four types of inefficiencies: **deadweight loss, inefficient allocation to consumers, wasted resources,** and **inefficiently low quality.**

• A deadweight loss is a loss of total surplus that occurs whenever a policy or action reduces the quantity transacted below the efficient market equilibrium level.

• Price ceilings also lead to **black markets,** as buyers and sellers attempt to evade the price controls.

• Price ceilings can be justified when the market is inefficient or when a natural disaster leads to shortages that, if left to a free market, would greatly diminish equity and social welfare.

>> Check Your Understanding 5-1

Solutions appear at back of book.

1. On game days, homeowners near Middletown University's stadium used to rent parking spaces in their driveways to fans at a going rate of $11. A new town ordinance now sets a maximum parking fee of $7. Use the accompanying supply and demand diagram to explain how each of the following corresponds to a price-ceiling concept.
   a. Some homeowners now think it's not worth the hassle to rent out spaces.
   b. Some fans who used to carpool to the game now drive alone.
   c. Some fans can't find parking and leave without seeing the game.
   Explain how each of the following adverse effects arises from the price ceiling.
   d. Some fans now arrive several hours early to find parking.

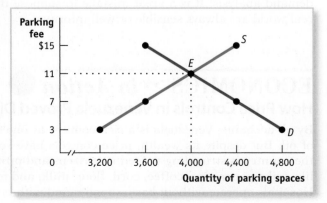

    e. Friends of homeowners near the stadium regularly attend games, even if they aren't big fans. But some serious fans have given up because of the parking situation.

    f. Some homeowners rent spaces for more than $7 but pretend that the buyers are nonpaying friends or family.

2. True or false? Explain your answer. A price ceiling below the equilibrium price of an otherwise efficient market does the following:

    a. Increases quantity supplied

    b. Makes some people who want to consume the good worse off

    c. Makes all producers worse off

3. Which of the following create deadweight loss? Which do not and are simply a transfer of surplus from one person to another? Explain your answer.

    a. You have been evicted from your rent-controlled apartment after the landlord discovered your pet boa constrictor. The apartment is quickly rented to someone else at the same price. You and the new renter do not necessarily have the same willingness to pay for the apartment.

    b. In a contest, you won a ticket to a concert. But you can't go because you have an exam the next day, and the terms of the contest do not allow you to sell the ticket or give it to someone else. Would your answer to this question change if you could not sell the ticket but could give it to someone else?

    c. Your school's dean of students, who is a proponent of a low-fat diet, decrees that ice cream can no longer be served on campus.

    d. Your ice-cream cone falls on the ground and your dog eats it. (Take the liberty of counting your dog as a member of society, and assume that, if he could, your dog would be willing to pay the same amount for the ice-cream cone as you.)

‖ Price Floors

Sometimes governments intervene to push market prices up instead of down. *Price floors* have been widely legislated for agricultural products, such as wheat and milk, as a way to support the incomes of farmers. Historically, there were also price floors—legally mandated minimum prices—on such services as trucking and air travel, although these were phased out by the U.S. government in the 1970s.

    If you have ever worked in a fast-food restaurant, you are likely to have encountered a price floor: governments in the United States and many other countries maintain a lower limit on the hourly wage rate of a worker's labor; that is, a floor on the price of labor called the **minimum wage.**

The **minimum wage** is a legal floor on the wage rate, which is the market price of labor.

GLOBAL COMPARISON   **CHECK OUT OUR LOW, LOW WAGES!**

The minimum wage rate in the United States, as you can see in this graph, is actually quite low compared with that in other rich countries. Since minimum wages are set in national currency—the British minimum wage is set in British pounds, the French minimum wage is set in euros, and so on—the comparison depends on the exchange rate on any given day. As of 2019, Australia had a minimum wage nearly twice as high as the U.S. rate, with France, Canada, and Ireland not far behind.

    You can see one effect of this difference in the supermarket checkout line. In the United States there is usually someone to bag your groceries—someone typically paid the minimum wage or at best slightly more. In Europe, where hiring a bagger is a lot more expensive, you're almost always expected to do the bagging yourself.

Australia   A$19.49 = US$13.09
Canada   C$15.00* = US$11.27
France   €10.03 = US$11.12
Ireland   €9.80 = US$10.86
Britain   £8.21 = US$10.03
United States $7.25

Minimum wage (per hour)

Data from: Organization for Economic Cooperation and Development (OECD).
*The Canadian minimum wage varies by province from C$11.05 to C$15.00.

FIGURE 5-5 The Market for Butter in the Absence of Government Controls

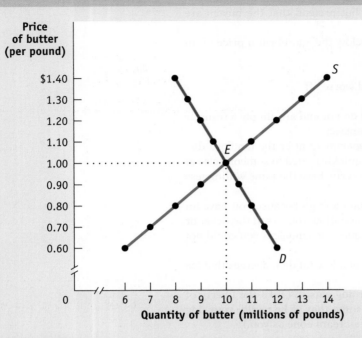

Price of butter (per pound)	Quantity of butter (millions of pounds)	
	Quantity demanded	Quantity supplied
$1.40	8.0	14.0
1.30	8.5	13.0
1.20	9.0	12.0
1.10	9.5	11.0
1.00	10.0	10.0
0.90	10.5	9.0
0.80	11.0	8.0
0.70	11.5	7.0
0.60	12.0	6.0

Without government intervention, the market for butter reaches equilibrium at a price of $1 per pound with 10 million pounds of butter bought and sold.

Just like price ceilings, price floors are intended to help some people but generate predictable and undesirable side effects. Figure 5-5 shows hypothetical supply and demand curves for butter. Left to itself, the market would move to equilibrium at point *E*, with 10 million pounds of butter bought and sold at a price of $1 per pound.

Now suppose that the government, in order to help dairy farmers, imposes a price floor on butter of $1.20 per pound. Its effects are shown in Figure 5-6, where the line at $1.20 represents the price floor. At a price of $1.20 per pound, producers would want to supply 12 million pounds (point *B* on the supply curve) but consumers would want to buy only 9 million pounds (point *A* on the demand curve). So the price floor leads to a persistent surplus of 3 million pounds of butter.

Does a price floor always lead to an unwanted surplus? No. Just as in the case of a price ceiling, the floor may not be binding—that is, it may be irrelevant. If the equilibrium price of butter is $1 per pound but the floor is set at only $0.80, the floor has no effect.

But suppose that a price floor is binding: what happens to the unwanted surplus? The answer depends on government policy. In the case of agricultural price floors, governments buy up unwanted surplus. As a result, the U.S. government, for example, has at times found itself warehousing thousands of tons of butter, cheese, and other farm products. The government then has to find a way to dispose of these unwanted goods.

Some countries pay exporters to sell products at a loss overseas; this is standard procedure for the European Union. The United States gives surplus food away to citizens in need as well as to schools, which use the products in school lunches. In some cases, governments have actually destroyed the surplus production.

When the government is not prepared to purchase the unwanted surplus, a price floor means that would-be sellers cannot find buyers. This is what happens

FIGURE 5-6 The Effects of a Price Floor

The black horizontal line represents the government-imposed price floor of $1.20 per pound of butter. The quantity of butter demanded falls to 9 million pounds, and the quantity supplied rises to 12 million pounds, generating a persistent surplus of 3 million pounds of butter.

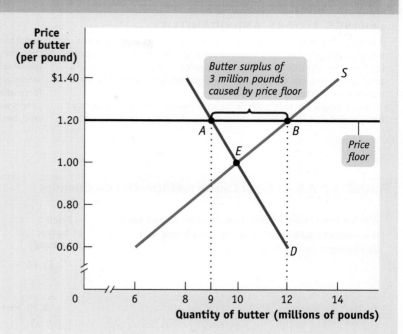

when there is a price floor on the wage rate paid for an hour of labor, the minimum wage: when the minimum wage is above the equilibrium wage rate, some people who are willing to work—that is, sell labor—cannot find buyers—that is, employers—willing to give them jobs.

How a Price Floor Causes Inefficiency

The persistent surplus that results from a price floor creates missed opportunities—inefficiencies—that resemble those created by the shortage that results from a price ceiling. Like a price ceiling, a price floor creates inefficiency in at least four ways:

1. It creates deadweight loss by reducing the quantity transacted to below the efficient level.
2. It leads to an inefficient allocation of sales among sellers.
3. It leads to a waste of resources.
4. It leads to sellers providing an inefficiently high-quality level.

In addition to inefficiency, like a price ceiling, a price floor leads to illegal behavior as people break the law to sell below the legal price.

Inefficiently Low Quantity Because a price floor raises the price of a good to consumers, it reduces the quantity of that good demanded; because sellers can't sell more units of a good than buyers are willing to buy, a price floor reduces the quantity of a good bought and sold below the market equilibrium quantity and leads to a deadweight loss. Notice that this is the *same* effect as a price ceiling. You might be tempted to think that a price floor and a price ceiling have opposite effects, but both have the effect of reducing the quantity of a good bought and sold (see the accompanying Pitfalls).

Since the equilibrium of an efficient market maximizes the sum of consumer and producer surplus, a price floor that reduces the quantity below the equilibrium quantity reduces total surplus. Figure 5-7 shows the implications for total

CEILINGS, FLOORS, AND QUANTITIES

A price ceiling pushes the price of a good *down*. A price floor pushes the price of a good *up*. So it's easy to assume that the effects of a price floor are the opposite of the effects of a price ceiling. In particular, if a price ceiling reduces the quantity of a good bought and sold, doesn't a price floor increase the quantity?

No, it doesn't. In fact, both floors and ceilings reduce the quantity bought and sold. Why? When the quantity of a good supplied isn't equal to the quantity demanded, the actual quantity sold is determined by the "short side" of the market—whichever quantity is less. If sellers don't want to sell as much as buyers want to buy, it's the sellers who determine the actual quantity sold, because buyers can't force unwilling sellers to sell. If buyers don't want to buy as much as sellers want to sell, it's the buyers who determine the actual quantity sold, because sellers can't force unwilling buyers to buy.

FIGURE 5-7 A Price Floor Causes Inefficiently Low Quantity

A price floor reduces the quantity demanded below the market equilibrium quantity and leads to a deadweight loss.

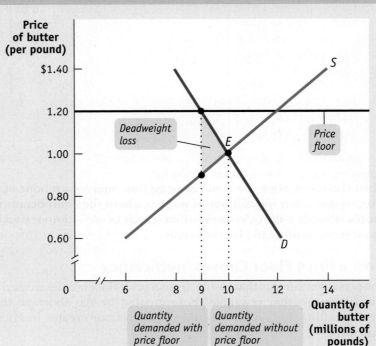

surplus of a price floor on the price of butter. Total surplus is the sum of the area above the supply curve and below the demand curve.

By reducing the quantity of butter sold, a price floor causes a deadweight loss equal to the area of the shaded triangle in the figure. As in the case of a price ceiling, however, deadweight loss is only one of the forms of inefficiency that the price control creates.

Inefficient Allocation of Sales Among Sellers Like a price ceiling, a price floor can lead to *inefficient allocation*—in this case, an **inefficient allocation of sales among sellers:** sellers who are willing to sell at the lowest price are unable to make sales, while sales go to sellers who are only willing to sell at a higher price.

One example of the inefficient allocation of selling opportunities caused by a price floor is the "two-tier" labor market found in many European countries that emerged in the 1980s and persists to this day. A high minimum wage led to a two-tier labor system, composed of the fortunate who had good jobs in the formal labor market, and the rest who were locked out without any prospect of ever finding a good job.

Price floors can lead to **inefficient allocation of sales among sellers:** sellers who are willing to sell at the lowest price are unable to make sales while sales go to sellers who are only willing to sell at a higher price.

Either unemployed or underemployed in dead-end jobs in the black market for labor, the unlucky ones are disproportionately young, from the ages of 18 to early 30s. Although eager for good jobs in the formal sector and willing to accept less than the minimum wage—that is, willing to sell their labor for a lower price—it is illegal for employers to pay them less than the minimum wage. For example, in 2019, unemployment for young Italian workers stood at nearly 20%.

The inefficiency of unemployment and underemployment is compounded as generations of young people are unable to get adequate job training, develop careers, and save for their future. These young people are also more likely to engage in crime. The worst hit countries—such as Greece, Spain, Italy, and France—have seen many of their best and brightest young people emigrate, leading to a permanent reduction in the future performance of their economies.

Wasted Resources Also like a price ceiling, a price floor generates inefficiency by *wasting resources*. The most graphic examples involve government purchases of the unwanted surpluses of agricultural products caused by price floors. The surplus production is sometimes destroyed, which is pure waste; in other cases, the stored produce goes, as officials euphemistically put it, "out of condition" and must be thrown away.

Price floors also lead to wasted time and effort. Consider the minimum wage. Would-be workers who spend many hours searching for jobs, or waiting in line in the hope of getting jobs, play the same role in the case of price floors as hapless families searching for apartments in the case of price ceilings.

Inefficiently High Quality Again like price ceilings, price floors lead to inefficiency in the quality of goods produced.

We saw that when there is a price ceiling, suppliers produce products that are of inefficiently low quality: buyers prefer higher-quality products and are willing to pay for them, but sellers refuse to improve the quality of their products because the price ceiling prevents their being compensated for doing so. This same logic applies to price floors, but in reverse: suppliers offer goods of **inefficiently high quality.**

How can this be? Isn't high quality a good thing? Yes, but only if it is worth the cost. Suppose that suppliers spend a lot to make goods of very high quality but that this quality isn't worth much to consumers, who would rather receive the money spent on that quality in the form of a lower price. This represents a missed opportunity: suppliers and buyers could make a mutually beneficial deal in which buyers got goods of lower quality for a much lower price.

A good example of the inefficiency of excessive quality comes from the days when transatlantic airfares were set artificially high by international treaty. Forbidden to compete for customers by offering lower ticket prices, airlines instead offered expensive services, like lavish in-flight meals that went largely uneaten—an especially wasteful practice, considering that what passengers really wanted was less food and lower airfares.

Since the deregulation of U.S. airlines in the 1970s, American passengers have experienced a large decrease in ticket prices accompanied by a decrease in the quality of in-flight service—smaller seats, lower-quality food, and so on. Everyone complains about the service—but thanks to lower fares, the number of people flying on U.S. carriers has grown from 130 billion passenger miles when deregulation began to approximately 1,016 billion in 2019.

Illegal Activity In addition to the four inefficiencies we analyzed, like price ceilings, price floors provide incentives for illegal activity. For example, in countries where the minimum wage is far above the equilibrium wage rate, workers desperate for jobs sometimes agree to work off the books for employers who conceal their employment from the government—or bribe the government inspectors. This practice, known in Europe as *black labor,* is especially common in Southern European countries such as Italy and Spain.

Price floors often lead to inefficiency in that goods of **inefficiently high quality** are offered: sellers offer high-quality goods at a high price, even though buyers would prefer a lower quality at a lower price.

So Why Are There Price Floors?

To sum up, a price floor creates various negative side effects:

- A persistent surplus of the good
- Inefficiency arising from the persistent surplus in the form of inefficiently low quantity (deadweight loss), inefficient allocation of sales among sellers, wasted resources, and an inefficiently high level of quality offered by suppliers
- The temptation to engage in illegal activity, particularly bribery and corruption of government officials

So why do governments impose price floors when they have so many negative side effects? The reasons are similar to those for imposing price ceilings. Government officials often disregard warnings about the consequences of price floors either because they believe that the relevant market is poorly described by the supply and demand model or, more often, because they do not understand the model. Above all, just as price ceilings are often imposed because they benefit some influential buyers of a good, price floors are often imposed because they benefit some influential sellers.

ECONOMICS >> *in Action*
The Rise and Fall of the Unpaid Intern

"We have an opening for a part-time unpaid intern, which could lead to a full-time unpaid internship."

The best-known example of a price floor is the minimum wage. Most economists believe, however, that the minimum wage has relatively little effect on the overall job market in the United States, mainly because the floor is set so low. In 1964, the U.S. minimum wage was 53% of the average wage of blue-collar production workers; by 2019, it had fallen to about 30%. However, there is one sector of the U.S. job market where it appears that the minimum wage can indeed be binding: the market for interns.

Starting in 2011, a spate of lawsuits brought by former unpaid interns claiming they were cheated out of wages brought the matter to public attention. A common thread in these complaints was that interns were assigned grunt work with no educational value, such as tracking lost cell phones. In other cases, unpaid interns complained that they were given the work of full-salaried employees. And by 2015, many of those lawsuits proved successful: Condé Nast Publications settled for $5.8 million, Sirius SatelliteXM Radio settled for $1.3 million, and Viacom Media settled for $7.2 million. Even the Olsen twins had to cough up $140,000 in payments to unpaid interns for their fashion company, Dualstar Entertainment, in 2017.

In 2018, the U.S. Department of Labor, the agency that formulates federal labor laws, issued a directive stating that unless their programs can clearly demonstrate an educational component such as course credit, companies have to pay their interns minimum wage or shut down their programs altogether.

Some observers worry that the end of the unpaid internship means that programs that once offered valuable training will be lost. But as one lawyer commented, "The law says that when you work, you have to get paid [at least the minimum wage]."

>> Check Your Understanding 5-2

Solutions appear at back of book.

1. The state legislature mandates a price floor for gasoline of P_F per gallon. Assess the following statements and illustrate your answer using the figure provided.

   a. Proponents of the law claim it will increase the income of gas station owners. Opponents claim it will hurt gas station owners because they will lose customers.

   b. Proponents claim consumers will be better off because gas stations will provide better service. Opponents claim consumers will be generally worse off because they prefer to buy gas at cheaper prices.

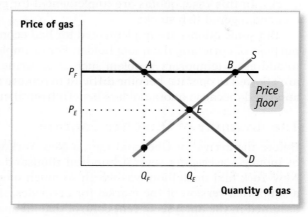

   c. Proponents claim that they are helping gas station owners without hurting anyone else. Opponents claim that consumers are hurt and will end up doing things like buying gas in a nearby state or on the black market.

>> Quick Review

• The most familiar price floor is the **minimum wage.** Price floors are also commonly imposed on agricultural goods.

• A price floor above the equilibrium price benefits successful sellers but causes predictable adverse effects such as a persistent surplus, which leads to four kinds of inefficiencies: deadweight loss from inefficiently low quantity, **inefficient allocation of sales among sellers,** wasted resources, and **inefficiently high quality.**

• Price floors encourage illegal activity, such as workers who work off the books, often leading to official corruption.

Controlling Quantities

In the 1930s, New York City instituted a system of licensing for taxicabs: only taxis with a "medallion" were allowed to pick up passengers, hailing them from the street. Because this system was intended to assure quality, medallion owners were supposed to maintain certain standards, including safety and cleanliness. A total of 11,787 medallions were issued, with taxi owners paying $10 for each medallion.

In 1995, there were still only 11,787 licensed taxicabs in New York, even though the city had meanwhile become the financial capital of the world, a place where hundreds of thousands of people in a hurry tried to hail a cab every day. By 2019, the number of licensed cabs had risen to only 13,587. And up until a few years ago, this restriction on the number of New York City taxi medallions made them a very valuable item: if you wanted to operate a taxi in the city, you had to lease a medallion from someone or buy one.

Yet restrictions on the number of taxis induced people to try to circumvent them, eventually leading to the emergence of mobile-app-based car services like Uber and Lyft. Their cars aren't hailed from the street like taxis—in fact, their drivers are forbidden from picking up riders from the street. Instead, riders arrange trips on their smartphones, directing available drivers to their location. Of course, the ubiquity of smartphones also contributed to the emergence of these car services.

Since 2013, Uber and Lyft have fundamentally altered the market for car rides in New York City and most other major cities. But let's postpone the discussion of those effects until we learn more about how the market worked when only licensed taxicabs could operate.

A taxi medallion is a form of **quantity control,** or **quota,** by which the government regulates the quantity of a good that can be bought and sold rather than the price at which it is transacted. It is another way that government intervenes in markets along with price ceilings and price floors. The total amount of the good that can be transacted under the quantity control is called the **quota limit.** Typically, the government limits quantity in a market by issuing **licenses;** only people with a license can legally supply the good.

A **quantity control,** or **quota,** is an upper limit on the quantity of some good that can be bought or sold. The total amount of the good that can be legally transacted is the **quota limit.**

A **license** gives its owner the right to supply a good.

A taxi medallion is just such a license. The government of New York City limited the number of taxi rides that can be sold by limiting the number of taxis to only those who hold medallions. More generally, quantity controls, or quotas, set an upper limit on the quantity of a good that can be transacted. For example, quotas have been used frequently to limit the size of the catch of endangered fish stocks. In this case, quotas are implemented for good economic reasons: to protect endangered fish stocks.

But some quotas are implemented for bad economic reasons, typically for the purpose of enriching the quota holder. For example, quantity controls introduced to address a temporary problem such as assuring that only safe and clean taxis are allowed to operate, become difficult to remove later, once the problem has disappeared, because quota holders benefit from them and exert political pressure.

The Anatomy of Quantity Controls

Before the arrival of Uber and Lyft, a New York taxi medallion was worth a lot of money—averaging several hundred thousand dollars. To understand why a New York taxi medallion was worth so much money in those days, we consider a simplified version of the market for taxi rides, shown in Figure 5-8. Just as we assumed in the analysis of rent control that all apartments are the same, we now suppose that all taxi rides are the same—ignoring the real-world complication that some taxi rides are longer, and so more expensive, than others.

The table in the figure shows supply and demand schedules. The equilibrium—indicated by point E in the figure and by the shaded entries in the table—is a fare of $5 per ride, with 10 million rides taken per year. (You'll see in a minute why we present the equilibrium this way.)

In this example, the New York medallion system limits the number of taxis, but each taxi driver can offer as many rides as they can manage. To simplify our analysis, however, we will assume that a medallion system limits the number of taxi rides that can legally be given to 8 million per year.

Until now, we have derived the demand curve by answering questions of the form: "How many taxi rides will passengers want to take if the price is $5 per

FIGURE 5-8 The Market for Taxi Rides in the Absence of Government Controls

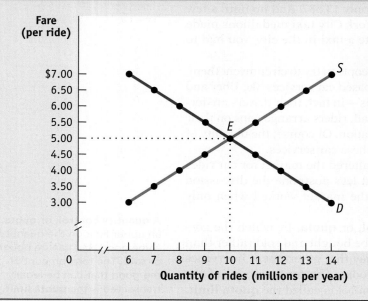

Fare (per ride)	Quantity of rides (millions per year)	
	Quantity demanded	Quantity supplied
$7.00	6	14
6.50	7	13
6.00	8	12
5.50	9	11
5.00	10	10
4.50	11	9
4.00	12	8
3.50	13	7
3.00	14	6

Without government intervention, the market reaches equilibrium with 10 million rides taken per year at a fare of $5 per ride.

ride?" But it is possible to reverse the question and ask instead: "At what price will consumers want to buy 10 million rides per year?" The price at which consumers want to buy a given quantity—in this case, 10 million rides at $5 per ride—is the **demand price** of that quantity. You can see from the demand schedule in Figure 5-8 that the demand price of 6 million rides is $7 per ride, the demand price of 7 million rides is $6.50 per ride, and so on.

Similarly, the supply curve represents the answer to questions of the form: "How many taxi rides would taxi drivers supply at a price of $5 each?" But we can also reverse this question to ask: "At what price will suppliers be willing to supply 10 million rides per year?" The price at which suppliers will supply a given quantity—in this case, 10 million rides at $5 per ride—is the **supply price** of that quantity. We can see from the supply schedule in Figure 5-8 that the supply price of 6 million rides is $3 per ride, the supply price of 7 million rides is $3.50 per ride, and so on.

Now we are ready to analyze a quota. We have assumed that the city government limits the quantity of taxi rides to 8 million per year. Medallions, each of which carries the right to provide a certain number of taxi rides per year, are made available to selected people in such a way that a total of 8 million rides will be provided. Medallion-holders may then either drive their own taxis or rent their medallions to others for a fee.

Figure 5-9 shows the resulting market for taxi rides, with the black vertical line at 8 million rides per year representing the quota limit. Because the quantity of rides is limited to 8 million, consumers must be at point A on the demand curve, corresponding to the shaded entry in the demand schedule: the demand price of 8 million rides is $6 per ride. Meanwhile, taxi drivers must be at point B on the supply curve, corresponding to the shaded entry in the supply schedule: the supply price of 8 million rides is $4 per ride.

> The **demand price** of a given quantity is the price at which consumers will demand that quantity.
>
> The **supply price** of a given quantity is the price at which producers will supply that quantity.

FIGURE 5-9 Effect of a Quota on the Market for Taxi Rides

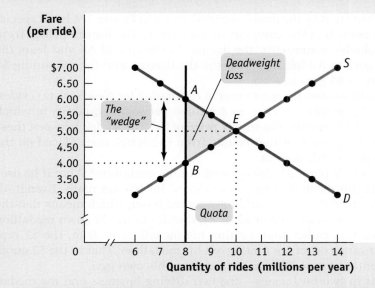

Fare (per ride)	Quantity of rides (millions per year)	
	Quantity demanded	Quantity supplied
$7.00	6	14
6.50	7	13
6.00	8	12
5.50	9	11
5.00	10	10
4.50	11	9
4.00	12	8
3.50	13	7
3.00	14	6

The table shows the demand price and the supply price corresponding to each quantity: the price at which that quantity would be demanded and supplied, respectively. The city government imposes a quota of 8 million rides by selling licenses for only 8 million rides, represented by the black vertical line. The price paid by consumers rises to $6 per ride, the demand price of 8 million rides, shown by point A.

The supply price of 8 million rides is only $4 per ride, shown by point B. The difference between these two prices is the quota rent per ride, the earnings that accrue to the owner of a license. The quota rent drives a wedge between the demand price and the supply price. And since the quota discourages mutually beneficial transactions, it creates a deadweight loss equal to the shaded triangle.

But how can the price received by taxi drivers be $4 when the price paid by taxi riders is $6? The answer is that in addition to the market in taxi rides, there is also a market in medallions. Medallion-holders may not always want to drive their taxis: they may be ill or on vacation. Those who do not want to drive their own taxis will sell the right to use the medallion to someone else.

So we need to consider two sets of transactions here, and so two prices: (1) the transactions in taxi rides and the price at which these will occur, and (2) the transactions in medallions and the price at which these will occur. It turns out that since we are looking at two markets, the $4 and $6 prices will both be right.

To see how this all works, consider two imaginary New York taxi drivers, Ali and Jean. Ali has a medallion but can't use it because he's recovering from a severely sprained wrist. So he's looking to rent his medallion out to someone else. Jean doesn't have a medallion but would like to rent one. Furthermore, at any point in time there are many other people like Jean who would like to rent a medallion. Suppose Ali agrees to rent his medallion to Jean. To make things simple, assume that any driver can give only one ride per day and that Ali is renting his medallion to Jean for one day. What rental price will they agree on?

To answer this question, we need to look at the transactions from the viewpoints of both drivers. Once she has the medallion, Jean knows she can make $6 per day—the demand price of a ride under the quota. And she is willing to rent the medallion only if she makes at least $4 per day—the supply price of a ride under the quota. So Ali cannot demand a rent of more than $2—the difference between $6 and $4. And if Jean offered Ali less than $2—say, $1.50—there would be other eager drivers willing to offer him more, up to $2. So, in order to get the medallion, Jean must offer Ali at least $2. Since the rent can be no more than $2 and no less than $2, it must be exactly $2.

It is no coincidence that $2 is exactly the difference between $6, the demand price of 8 million rides, and $4, the supply price of 8 million rides. In every case in which the supply of a good is legally restricted, there is a **wedge** between the demand price of the quantity transacted and the supply price of the quantity transacted.

This wedge, illustrated by the double-headed arrow in Figure 5-9, has a special name: the **quota rent.** It is the earnings that accrue to the license-holder from ownership of a valuable commodity, the license. In the case of Ali and Jean, the quota rent of $2 goes to Ali because he owns the license, and the remaining $4 from the total fare of $6 goes to Jean.

Figure 5-9 also illustrates the quota rent in the market for New York taxi rides. The quota limits the quantity of rides to 8 million per year, a quantity at which the demand price of $6 exceeds the supply price of $4. The wedge between these two prices, $2, is the quota rent that results from the restrictions placed on the quantity of taxi rides in this market.

But wait a second. What if Ali doesn't rent out his medallion? What if he uses it himself? Doesn't this mean that he gets a price of $6? No, not really. Even if Ali doesn't rent out his medallion, he could have rented it out, which means that the medallion has an *opportunity cost* of $2: if Ali decides to use his own medallion and drive his own taxi rather than renting his medallion to Jean, the $2 represents his opportunity cost of not renting out his medallion. That is, the $2 quota rent is now the rental income he forgoes by driving his own taxi.

In effect, Ali is in two businesses—the taxi-driving business and the medallion-renting business. He makes $4 per ride from driving his taxi and $2 per ride from renting out his medallion. It doesn't make any difference that in this particular case he has rented his medallion to himself! So under quantity controls, the medallion is a valuable asset regardless of whether the medallion owner uses it or rents it out to others. In 2010, before the rise of Uber and Lyft effectively eliminated the quantity controls, New York taxi medallions were trading for around $500,000. Notice, by the way, that quotas—like price ceilings and price floors—don't always have a real effect. If the quota were set at 12 million rides—that is,

A quantity control, or quota, drives a **wedge** between the demand price and the supply price of a good; that is, the price paid by buyers ends up being higher than that received by sellers.

The difference between the demand and supply price at the quota limit is the **quota rent,** the earnings that accrue to the license-holder from ownership of the right to sell the good. It is equal to the market price of the license when the licenses are traded.

above the equilibrium quantity in an unregulated market—it would have no effect because it would not be binding.

The Costs of Quantity Controls

Like price controls, quantity controls can have some predictable and undesirable side effects. The first is the by-now-familiar problem of inefficiency due to missed opportunities: quantity controls create deadweight loss by preventing mutually beneficial transactions from occurring, transactions that would benefit both buyers and sellers.

Looking back at Figure 5-9, you can see that starting at the quota limit of 8 million rides, New Yorkers would be willing to pay at least $5.50 per ride when 9 million rides are offered, 1 million more than the quota, and that taxi drivers would be willing to provide those rides as long as they got at least $4.50 per ride. These are rides that would have taken place if there were no quota limit.

The same is true for the next 1 million rides: New Yorkers would be willing to pay at least $5 per ride when the quantity of rides is increased from 9 to 10 million, and taxi drivers would be willing to provide those rides as long as they got at least $5 per ride. Again, these rides would have occurred without the quota limit.

Only when the market has reached the unregulated market equilibrium quantity of 10 million rides are there no "missed-opportunity rides." The quota limit of 8 million rides has caused 2 million "missed-opportunity rides."

Generally, *as long as the demand price of a given quantity exceeds the supply price, there is a deadweight loss*. A buyer would be willing to buy the good at a price that the seller would be willing to accept, but such a transaction does not occur because it is forbidden by the quota. The deadweight loss arising from the 2 million in missed-opportunity rides is represented by the shaded triangle in Figure 5-9.

And because there are transactions that people would like to make but are not allowed to, quantity controls generate an incentive to circumvent them. In the days before Uber and Lyft, a substantial number of unlicensed taxis simply defied the law and picked up passengers without a medallion. These unregulated, unlicensed taxis contributed to a disproportionately large share of accidents.

However, Uber and Lyft cars legally circumvent the restriction that a car without a medallion can't be hailed from the street. By 2018, Uber had over 78,000 cars in New York City, significantly more than the 13,587 licensed taxicabs.

Clearly, the quantity restriction on New York City taxicabs has been substantially undermined. In effect, the quota line in Figure 5-9 has shifted rightward, closer to the equilibrium quantity, with the entry of Uber and Lyft.

In the past few years, as quota rents to owners of a taxi medallion have fallen, the prices of taxi medallions have fallen significantly as well. In 2018 and 2019, prices for New York City taxi medallions ranged from $185,000 to $130,000, a steep fall from the $500,000 pricetag in 2010. In sum, quantity controls typically create the following undesirable side effects:

- Deadweight loss because some mutually beneficial transactions don't occur
- Incentives for illegal activities

ECONOMICS >> *in Action*
Crabbing, Quotas, and Saving Lives in Alaska

Alaskan king and snow crabs are considered delicacies worldwide. And crab fishing is one of the most important industries in the Alaskan economy. So many were justifiably concerned when, in 1983, the annual crab catch fell by

The quota-share system protects Alaska's crab population and saves the lives of crabbers.

90% due to overfishing. In response, marine biologists set a *total allowable catch quota system,* which limited the amount of crab that could be harvested annually in order to allow the crab population to return to a healthy, sustainable level.

Notice, by the way, that the Alaskan crab quota is an example of a quota that was justified by broader economic and environmental considerations—unlike the New York City taxicab quota, which has long since lost any economic rationale. Another important difference is that, unlike New York City taxicab medallions, owners of Alaskan crab boats did not have the ability to buy or sell individual quotas. So although depleted crab stocks eventually recovered with the total catch quota system in place, there was another, unintended and deadly consequence.

The Alaskan crabbing season is fairly short, running roughly from October to January, and it can be further shortened by bad weather. By the 1990s, Alaskan crab fishermen were engaging in "fishing derbies." To stay within the quota limit when the crabbing season began, boat crews rushed to fish for crab in dangerous, icy, rough water, straining to harvest in a few days a haul that could be worth several hundred thousand dollars. As a result, boats often became overloaded and capsized, making Alaskan crab fishing one of the most dangerous jobs, with an average of 7.3 deaths a year, about 80 times the fatality rate for an average worker. And after the brief harvest, the market for crab was flooded with supply, lowering the prices fishermen received.

In 2006 fishery regulators instituted another quota system called *quota share*—aimed at protecting Alaska's crabbers and crabs. Under individual quota share, each boat received a quota to fill during the three-month season. Moreover, the individual quotas could be sold or leased. These changes transformed the industry as owners of bigger boats bought the individual quotas of smaller boats, shrinking the number of crabbing boats dramatically. Bigger boats are much less likely to capsize, improving crew safety.

In addition, by extending the fishing season, the quota-share system boosted the crab population and crab prices. With more time to fish, fishermen could make sure that juvenile and female crabs were returned to the sea rather than harvested. And with a longer fishing season, the catch comes to market more gradually, eliminating the downward plunge in prices when supply hits the market. Predictably, an Alaskan crab fisherman earns more money under the quota-share system than under the total catch quota system.

>> Quick Review

• **Quantity controls,** or **quotas,** are government-imposed limits on how much of a good may be bought or sold. The quantity allowed for sale is the **quota limit.** The government then issues a **license** — the right to sell a given quantity of a good under the quota.

• When the quota limit is smaller than the equilibrium quantity in an unregulated market, the **demand price** is higher than the **supply price** — there is a **wedge** between them at the quota limit.

• This wedge is the **quota rent,** the earnings that accrue to the license-holder from ownership of the right to sell the good — whether by actually supplying the good or by renting the license to someone else. The market price of a license equals the quota rent.

• Like price controls, quantity controls create deadweight loss and encourage illegal activity.

>> Check Your Understanding 5-3

Solutions appear at back of book.

1. Suppose that the supply and demand for taxi rides is given by Figure 5-8 but the quota is set at 6 million rides instead of 8 million. Find the following and indicate them on Figure 5-8.
   a. The price of a ride
   b. The quota rent
   c. The deadweight loss
   d. Suppose the quota limit on taxi rides is increased to 9 million. What happens to the quota rent? To the deadweight loss?
2. Assume that the quota limit is 8 million rides. Suppose demand decreases due to a decline in tourism. What is the smallest parallel leftward shift in demand that would result in the quota no longer having an effect on the market? Illustrate your answer using Figure 5-8.

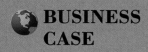

BUSINESS CASE

A Market Disruptor Gets Disrupted by the Market

Michael Nagle/Bloomberg/Getty Images

August 8, 2019, was a grim day at the San Francisco headquarters of Uber, the global leader in ride-hailing companies. That day it announced a staggering loss of $5.2 *billion* in just the previous 3 months. This was in addition to the loss of more than $1 billion in the first quarter of the year. Equally ominous was news of a significant drop in the annual growth rate in the number of rides provided. These results led some observers to question the company's long-term viability.

For a company that had been the darling of the high-tech business world, this day was a spectacular humbling. Investors had believed that only one company—namely Uber—would come to dominate the ride-hailing industry, ultimately making it very profitable. What had gone so wrong?

Uber was the brainchild of two friends, Travis Kalanick and Garret Camp, conceived after a difficult search for a taxi in Paris. When it launched in 2010 in San Francisco, Uber was the first company to enable ride hailing via a smartphone app. It provided easy access to lower-priced cab rides. Uber expanded rapidly, eventually extending its reach to over 600 cities worldwide. The company focused, in particular, on expansion in cities where the existing taxi market was highly regulated and restricted. Ridership grew explosively, so that by 2019 Uber was completing nearly 14 million rides each day.

But Uber's success did not go unnoticed. Seeing the opportunity to make money, some people wanted to become Uber drivers while others wanted to start up rival companies. In 2012, for example, Lyft launched a competing service. In Latin America, China, and India, home-grown challengers emerged. Uber responded by rolling out costly initiatives. For example, to keep its ridership high, Uber began subsidizing rides—that is, it provided discount codes and coupons that lowered the price of rides below the actual cost of providing them.

Whether Uber can get back on track—turning its losses around, recapturing its high growth rates of the past, and fulfilling its early promise—remains to be seen.

QUESTIONS FOR THOUGHT

1. How did quantity controls for taxi rides contribute to Uber's high rates of growth in its early years?

2. Based on what you've learned in the chapter, explain whether Uber's recent difficulties were predictable or the result of bad luck.

3. How likely is it that Uber can regain its past high rates of growth?

4. How has the allocation of surplus changed in this market over time? Who benefitted when Uber began competing with existing taxi companies? Who benefited when rival ride-hailing companies began competing with Uber?

SUMMARY

1. Even when a market is efficient, governments often intervene to pursue greater fairness or to please a powerful interest group. Interventions can take the form of **price controls** or quantity controls, both of which generate predictable and undesirable side effects consisting of various forms of inefficiency and illegal activity.

2. A **price ceiling,** a maximum market price below the equilibrium price, benefits successful buyers but creates persistent shortages. Because the price is maintained below the equilibrium price, the quantity demanded is increased and the quantity supplied is decreased compared to the equilibrium quantity. This leads to predictable problems: inefficiencies in the form of **deadweight loss** from inefficiently low quantity, **inefficient allocation to consumers, wasted resources,** and **inefficiently low quality.** It also encourages illegal activity as people turn to **black markets** to get the good. Because of these problems, price ceilings have generally lost favor as an economic policy tool. However, price ceilings can be justified when the market is inefficient or when a natural disaster leads to shortages that, if left to a free market, would greatly diminish equity and social welfare.

3. A **price floor,** a minimum market price above the equilibrium price, benefits successful sellers but creates persistent surplus. Because the price is maintained above the equilibrium price, the quantity demanded is decreased and the quantity supplied is increased compared to the equilibrium quantity. This leads to predictable problems: inefficiencies in the form of deadweight loss from inefficiently low quantity, **inefficient allocation of sales among sellers,** wasted resources, and **inefficiently high quality.** It also encourages illegal activity and black markets. The most well-known kind of price floor is the **minimum wage,** but price floors are also commonly applied to agricultural products.

4. **Quantity controls,** or **quotas,** limit the quantity of a good that can be bought or sold. The quantity allowed for sale is the **quota limit.** The government issues **licenses** to individuals, the right to sell a given quantity of the good. The owner of a license earns a **quota rent,** earnings that accrue from ownership of the right to sell the good. It is equal to the difference between the **demand price** at the quota limit, what consumers are willing to pay for that quantity, and the **supply price** at the quota limit, what suppliers are willing to accept for that quantity. Economists say that a quota drives a **wedge** between the demand price and the supply price; this wedge is equal to the quota rent. Quantity controls lead to deadweight loss in addition to encouraging illegal activity.

KEY TERMS

Price controls, p. 132
Price ceiling, p. 132
Price floor, p. 132
Deadweight loss, p. 135
Inefficient allocation to consumers, p. 136
Wasted resources, p. 136

Inefficiently low quality, p. 137
Black market, p. 137
Minimum wage, p. 141
Inefficient allocation of sales among sellers, p. 144
Inefficiently high quality, p. 145
Quantity control, p. 147

Quota, p. 147
Quota limit, p. 147
License, p. 147
Demand price, p. 149
Supply price, p. 149
Wedge, p. 150
Quota rent, p. 150

PRACTICE QUESTIONS

1. Oregon recently became the first state to adopt legislation capping housing rents statewide. Explain how Oregon's policy will affect landlords, renters, and the quality of rental units available.

2. In your state the minimum wage is $12 per hour. Yet, you notice that many fast-food restaurants have posted help wanted signs for jobs paying $15 per hour. What does this tell you about the minimum wage and the availability of restaurant work in your town?

3. Many Washington State residents and politicians are concerned about the declining salmon population, a primary food source for local wildlife, including the endangered orca whale. To protect the salmon population from overfishing, politicians are considering two policies. The first is a binding price ceiling in the market for salmon. The second policy is a quota: permits would be sold to those who fish commercially in order to restrict their salmon catch. As events have unfolded, it's become clear that politicians tend to favor the quota system while those who catch fish for a living prefer a price ceiling. Why do you think this is the case?

PROBLEMS

1. In order to appeal to voters, the mayor of Gotham City decides to lower the price of taxi rides. Assume, for simplicity, that all taxi rides are the same distance and therefore cost the same. The accompanying table shows the demand and supply schedules for taxi rides.

Fare (per ride)	Quantity of rides (millions per year)	
	Quantity demanded	Quantity supplied
$7.00	10	12
6.50	11	11
6.00	12	10
5.50	13	9
5.00	14	8
4.50	15	7

a. Assume that there are no restrictions on the number of taxi rides that can be supplied (there is no medallion system). Find the equilibrium price and quantity.

b. Suppose that the mayor sets a price ceiling at $5.50. How large is the shortage of rides? Illustrate with a diagram. Who loses and who benefits from this policy?

c. Suppose that the stock market crashes and, as a result, people in Gotham City are poorer. This reduces the quantity of taxi rides demanded by 6 million rides per year at any given price. What effect will the mayor's new policy have now? Illustrate with a diagram.

d. Suppose that the stock market rises and the demand for taxi rides returns to normal (that is, returns to the demand schedule given in the table). The mayor now decides to ingratiate himself with taxi drivers. He announces a policy in which operating licenses are given to existing taxi drivers; the number of licenses is restricted such that only 10 million rides per year can be given. Illustrate the effect of this policy on the market, and indicate the resulting price and quantity transacted. What is the quota rent per ride?

2. In the late eighteenth century, the price of bread in New York City was controlled, set at a predetermined price above the market price.

a. Draw a diagram showing the effect of the policy. Did the policy act as a price ceiling or a price floor?

b. What kinds of inefficiencies were likely to have arisen when the controlled price of bread was above the market price? Explain in detail.

One year during this period, a poor wheat harvest caused a leftward shift in the supply of bread and therefore an increase in its market price. New York bakers found that the controlled price of bread in New York was below the market price.

c. Draw a diagram showing the effect of the price control on the market for bread during this one-year period. Did the policy act as a price ceiling or a price floor?

d. What kinds of inefficiencies do you think occurred during this period? Explain in detail.

3. In 2019, the U.S. House of Representatives approved a new farm bill modifying the price supports for dairy farmers. The new program, the Dairy Margin Coverage, supports dairy farmers when the margin between feed costs and milk prices falls below $0.08 per pound. Suppose that current feed costs are $0.10 per pound, which means the program creates a price floor for milk at $0.18 per pound. At that price, in 2019, the quantity of milk supplied is 240 billion pounds, and the quantity demanded is 140 billion pounds. To support the price of milk at the price floor, the U.S. Department of Agriculture (USDA) has to buy up 100 billion pounds of surplus milk. The supply and demand curves in the following diagram illustrate the market for milk.

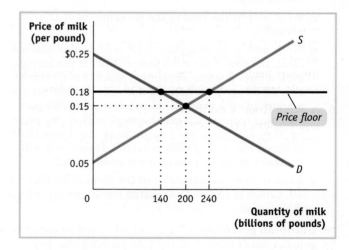

a. In the absence of a price floor, how much consumer surplus is created? How much producer surplus? What is the total surplus (producer surplus plus consumer surplus)?

b. With the price floor at $0.18 per pound of milk, consumers buy 140 billion pounds of milk. How much consumer surplus is created now?

c. With the price floor at $0.18 per pound of milk, producers sell 240 billion pounds of milk (some to consumers and some to the USDA). How much producer surplus is created now?

d. How much money does the USDA spend to buy surplus milk?

e. Taxes must be collected to pay for the purchases of surplus milk by the USDA. As a result, total surplus is reduced by the amount the USDA spent buying surplus milk. Using your answers from parts b, c, and d, what is the total surplus when there is a price floor? How does this total surplus compare to the total surplus without a price floor from part a?

4. The accompanying table shows hypothetical demand and supply schedules for milk per year. The U.S. government decides that the incomes of dairy farmers should be maintained at a level that allows the traditional family dairy farm to survive. So it implements a price floor of $1 per pint by buying surplus milk until the market price is $1 per pint.

Price of milk (per pint)	Quantity of milk (millions of pints per year)	
	Quantity demanded	Quantity supplied
$1.20	550	850
1.10	600	800
1.00	650	750
0.90	700	700
0.80	750	650

a. In a diagram, show the deadweight loss from the inefficiently low quantity bought and sold.

b. How much surplus milk will be produced as a result of this policy?

c. What will be the cost to the government of this policy?

d. Since milk is an important source of protein and calcium, the government decides to provide the surplus milk it purchases to elementary schools at a price of only $0.60 per pint. Assume that schools will buy any amount of milk available at this low price. But parents now reduce their purchases of milk at any price by 50 million pints per year because they know their children are getting milk at school. How much will the dairy program now cost the government?

e. Explain how inefficiencies in the form of inefficient allocation to sellers and wasted resources arise from this policy.

5. European governments tend to make greater use of price controls than does the U.S. government. For example, the French government sets minimum starting yearly wages for new hires who have completed *le bac*, a certification roughly equivalent to a high school diploma. The demand schedule for new hires with *le bac* and the supply schedule for similarly credentialed new job seekers are given in the accompanying table. The price here—given in euros, the currency used in France—is the same as the yearly wage.

Wage (per year)	Quantity demanded (new job offers per year)	Quantity supplied (new job seekers per year)
€45,000	200,000	325,000
40,000	220,000	320,000
35,000	250,000	310,000
30,000	290,000	290,000
25,000	370,000	200,000

a. In the absence of government interference, what are the equilibrium wage and number of graduates hired per year? Illustrate with a diagram. Will there

be anyone seeking a job at the equilibrium wage who is unable to find one—that is, will there be anyone who is involuntarily unemployed?

b. Suppose the French government sets a minimum yearly wage of €35,000. Is there any involuntary unemployment at this wage? If so, how much? Illustrate with a diagram. What if the minimum wage is set at €40,000? Also illustrate with a diagram.

c. Given your answer to part b and the information in the table, what do you think is the relationship between the level of involuntary unemployment and the level of the minimum wage? Who benefits from such a policy? Who loses? What is the missed opportunity here?

6. In many European countries high minimum wages have led to high levels of unemployment and under-employment, and a two-tier labor system. In the formal labor market, workers have good jobs that pay at least the minimum wage. In the informal or black market for labor, workers have poor jobs and receive less than the minimum wage.

a. Draw a demand and supply diagram showing the effect of the imposition of a minimum wage on the overall market for labor, with wage on the vertical axis and hours of labor on the horizontal axis. Your supply curve should represent the hours of labor offered by workers according to the wage, and the demand curve should represent the hours of labor demanded by employers according to the wage. On your diagram show the deadweight loss from the imposition of a minimum wage. What type of shortage is created? Illustrate on your diagram the size of the shortage.

b. Assume that the imposition of the high minimum wage causes a contraction in the economy so that employers in the formal sector cut their production and their demand for workers. Illustrate the effect of this on the overall market for labor. What happens to the size of the deadweight loss? The shortage? Illustrate with a diagram.

c. Assume that the workers who cannot get a job paying at least the minimum wage move into the informal labor market where there is no minimum wage. What happens to the size of the informal market for labor as a result of the economic contraction? What happens to the equilibrium wage in the informal labor market? Illustrate with a supply and demand diagram for the informal market.

7. For the last 85 years the U.S. government has used price supports to provide income assistance to American farmers. To implement these price supports, at times the government has used price floors, which it maintains by buying up the surplus farm products. At other times, it has used target prices, a policy by which the government gives the farmer an amount equal to the difference between the market price and the target price for each unit sold. Consider the market for corn depicted in the accompanying diagram.

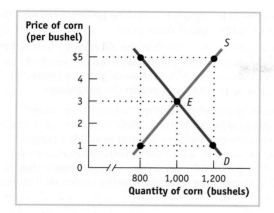

a. If the government sets a price floor of $5 per bushel, how many bushels of corn are produced? How many are purchased by consumers? By the government? How much does the program cost the government? How much revenue do corn farmers receive?

b. Suppose the government sets a target price of $5 per bushel for any quantity supplied up to 1,000 bushels. How many bushels of corn are purchased by consumers and at what price? By the government? How much does the program cost the government? How much revenue do corn farmers receive?

c. Which of these programs (in parts a and b) costs corn consumers more? Which program costs the government more? Explain.

d. Is one of these policies less inefficient than the other? Explain.

8. The waters off the North Atlantic coast were once teeming with fish. But because of overfishing by the commercial fishing industry, the stocks of fish became seriously depleted. In 1991, the National Marine Fisheries Service of the U.S. government implemented a quota to allow fish stocks to recover. In 2016 the quota limited the amount of swordfish caught per year by all U.S.-licensed fishing boats to 7 million pounds. As soon as the U.S. fishing fleet had met the quota limit, the swordfish catch was closed down for the rest of the year. The accompanying table gives the hypothetical demand and supply schedules for swordfish caught in the United States per year.

Price of swordfish (per pound)	Quantity of swordfish (millions of pounds per year)	
	Quantity demanded	Quantity supplied
$20	6	15
18	7	13
16	8	11
14	9	9
12	10	7

a. Use a diagram to show the effect of the quota on the market for swordfish in 1991. In your diagram, illustrate the deadweight loss from inefficiently low quantity.

b. How do you think fishermen will change how they fish in response to this policy?

9. In Maine, you must have a license to harvest lobster commercially; these licenses are issued yearly. The state of Maine is concerned about the dwindling supplies of lobsters found off its coast. The state fishery department has decided to place a yearly quota of 80,000 pounds of lobsters harvested in all Maine waters. It has also decided to give licenses this year only to those fishermen who had licenses last year. The accompanying diagram shows the demand and supply curves for Maine lobsters.

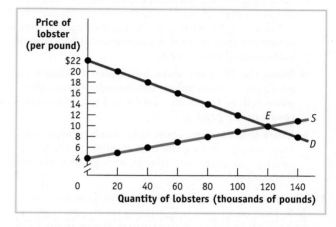

a. In the absence of government restrictions, what are the equilibrium price and quantity?

b. What is the *demand price* at which consumers wish to purchase 80,000 pounds of lobsters?

c. What is the *supply price* at which suppliers are willing to supply 80,000 pounds of lobsters?

d. What is the *quota rent* per pound of lobster when 80,000 pounds are sold? Illustrate the quota rent and the deadweight loss on the diagram.

e. Explain a transaction that benefits both buyer and seller but is prevented by the quota restriction.

10. The Venezuelan government has imposed a price ceiling on the retail price of roasted coffee beans. The accompanying diagram shows the market for coffee beans. In the absence of price controls, the equilibrium is at point E, with an equilibrium price of P_E and an equilibrium quantity bought and sold of Q_E.

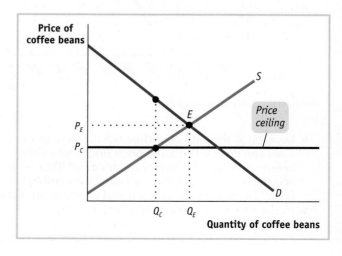

a. Show the consumer and producer surplus before the introduction of the price ceiling.

After the introduction of the price ceiling, the price falls to P_C and the quantity bought and sold falls to Q_C.

b. Show the consumer surplus after the introduction of the price ceiling (assuming that the consumers with the highest willingness to pay get to buy the available coffee beans; that is, assuming that there is no inefficient allocation to consumers).

c. Show the producer surplus after the introduction of the price ceiling (assuming that the producers with the lowest cost get to sell their coffee beans; that is, assuming that there is no inefficient allocation of sales among producers).

d. Using the diagram, show how much of what was producer surplus before the introduction of the price ceiling has been transferred to consumers as a result of the price ceiling.

e. Using the diagram, show how much of what was total surplus before the introduction of the price ceiling has been lost. That is, how great is the dead-weight loss?

11. The accompanying diagram shows data from the U.S. Bureau of Labor Statistics on the average price of an airline ticket in the United States from 1975 until 1985, adjusted to eliminate the effect of *inflation* (the general increase in the prices of all goods over time). In 1978, the U.S. Airline Deregulation Act removed the price floor on airline fares, and it also allowed the airlines greater flexibility to offer new routes.

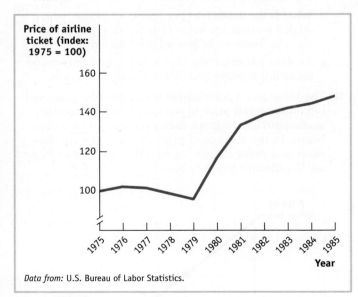

Price of airline ticket (index: 1975 = 100)

Data from: U.S. Bureau of Labor Statistics.

a. Looking at the data on airline ticket prices in the diagram, do you think the price floor that existed before 1978 was binding or nonbinding? That is, do you think it was set above or below the equilibrium price? Draw a supply and demand diagram, showing

where the price floor that existed before 1978 was in relation to the equilibrium price.

b. Most economists agree that the average airline ticket price per mile traveled actually *fell* as a result of the Airline Deregulation Act. How might you reconcile that view with what you see in the diagram?

12. Many college students attempt to land internships before graduation to burnish their resumes, gain experience in a chosen field, or try out possible careers. The hope shared by all of these prospective interns is that they will find internships that pay more than typical summer jobs, such as waiting tables or flipping burgers.

a. With wage measured on the vertical axis and number of hours of work on the horizontal axis, draw a supply and demand diagram for the market for interns in which the minimum wage is nonbinding at the market equilibrium.

b. Assume that a market downturn reduces the demand for interns by employers. However, many students are willing and eager to work in unpaid internships. As a result, the new market equilibrium wage is equal to zero. Draw another supply and demand diagram to illustrate this new market equilibrium. As in Figure 5-7, include a shaded triangle that represents the deadweight loss from the minimum wage. Using the diagram, explain your findings.

WORK IT OUT

13. Suppose it is decided that rent control in New York City will be abolished and that market rents will now prevail. Assume that all rental units are identical and so are offered at the same rent. To address the plight of residents who may be unable to pay the market rent, an income supplement will be paid to all low-income households equal to the difference between the old controlled rent and the new market rent.

a. Use a diagram to show the effect on the rental market of the elimination of rent control. What will happen to the quality and quantity of rental housing supplied?

b. Use a second diagram to show the additional effect of the income-supplement policy on the market. What effect does it have on the market rent and quantity of rental housing supplied in comparison to your answers to part a?

c. Are tenants better or worse off as a result of these policies? Are landlords better or worse off? Is society as a whole better or worse off?

d. From a political standpoint, why do you think cities have been more likely to resort to rent control rather than a policy of income supplements to help low-income people pay for housing? ■

6 Elasticity

TAKEN FOR A RIDE

IF YOU ARE EXPERIENCING a true emergency, you aren't likely to quibble about the price of an ambulance ride to the nearest emergency room. But what if it isn't an emergency? Take the case of Kira Milas, who doesn't even know who called an ambulance after she swam into the side of a swimming pool, breaking three teeth. Shaken, she accepted the ambulance ride to a local hospital, 15 minutes away. A week later, she received the bill: $1,772.42. Stunned, she said: "We only drove nine miles and it was a non-life-threatening injury. I needed absolutely no emergency treatment."

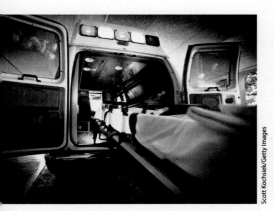

Scott Kochsiek/Getty Images

The demand for ambulance rides to the hospital is relatively unresponsive to the price.

Kira's experience is by no means exceptional. Although ambulances are often requested by a bystander or by 911 dispatchers, it is the patient who receives the bill. Undoubtedly, in a true medical emergency, a patient feels fortunate when an ambulance pulls up. But in nonemergency cases, like Kira's, many patients feel obliged to get into the ambulance once it arrives. And just like Kira, they are uninformed about the cost of the ride to the hospital. And while many

people have health insurance that will cover some or all of the cost of the ambulance service, the patient is ultimately responsible for paying the rest.

Each year an estimated 40 million ambulance trips, at a cost of $14 billion, are provided by nonprofit entities such as local fire departments and by for-profit companies in the United States. Sensing profit-making opportunities, in recent years for-profit companies have significantly expanded their operations, often taking over from nonprofit operators. And big investors are betting that ambulance services will generate significant profits: two private ambulance providers were recently bought by investors, one for $3 billion and another for $438 million. A similar dynamic has occurred in the air ambulance market, where high profits have led to explosive growth and patients have been handed bills for tens of thousands of dollars for trips that would have been shorter and more safely taken by land.

Charges for an ambulance ride vary wildly across the country, from several hundred dollars to tens of thousands of dollars. The price may depend on many things other than the patient's medical needs, from the level of skill of the ambulance team to the distance traveled, or in some cases whether a friend or relative rides along (which can add hundreds of dollars to the cost).

What accounts for the extreme variation in the cost of ambulance services? How are these services able to charge thousands of dollars, regardless of whether an ambulance is actually needed? Or to charge for an

ambulance equipped with heart resuscitation capabilities when the patient only has a broken leg? The answer to these questions is *price unresponsiveness:* in the heat of the moment, many consumers — particularly those with true emergencies — are *unresponsive* to the price of an ambulance. Ambulance operators judge correctly that a significant number of patients won't ask "How much is this ride to the emergency room going to cost?" before getting onboard. In other words, a large increase in the price of an ambulance ride leaves the quantity demanded by a significant number of consumers relatively unchanged.

Let's consider a very different scenario. Suppose that the maker of a particular brand of breakfast cereal decided to charge 10 times the original price. It would be extremely difficult, if not impossible, to find consumers willing to pay the much higher price. In other words, consumers of breakfast cereal are much more responsive to price than consumers of ambulance rides.

But how do we define *responsiveness?* Economists measure responsiveness of consumers to price with a particular number, called the *price elasticity of demand.* In this chapter we will show how the price elasticity of demand is calculated and why it is the best measure of how the quantity demanded responds to changes in price. We will then see that the price elasticity of demand is only one of a family of related concepts, including the *income elasticity of demand, cross-price elasticity of demand,* and *price elasticity of supply.* ●

WHAT YOU WILL LEARN

- Why is **elasticity** used to measure the response to changes in prices or income?
- What are the different elasticity measures and what do they mean?

- What factors influence the size of these various elasticities?
- Why is it vitally important to determine the size of the relevant elasticity before setting prices or government fees?

The **price elasticity of demand** is the ratio of the percent change in the quantity demanded to the percent change in the price as we move along the demand curve.

‖ Defining and Measuring Elasticity

In order for investors to know whether they can earn significant profits in the ambulance business, they need to know the *price elasticity of demand* for ambulance rides. With this information, investors can accurately predict whether or not a significant rise in the price of an ambulance ride results in an increase in revenue.

Calculating the Price Elasticity of Demand

Figure 6-1 shows a hypothetical demand curve for an ambulance ride. At a price of $200 per ride, consumers would demand 10 million rides per year (point *A*); at a price of $210 per ride, consumers would demand 9.9 million rides per year (point *B*).

Figure 6-1, then, tells us the change in the quantity demanded for a particular change in the price. But how can we turn this into a measure of price responsiveness? The answer is to calculate the *price elasticity of demand*.

The **price elasticity of demand** is the ratio of the *percent change in quantity demanded* to the *percent change in price* as we move along the demand curve. As we'll see later in this chapter, the reason economists use percent changes is to obtain a measure that doesn't depend on the units in which a good is measured (say, a 1-mile ambulance trip versus a 10-mile ambulance trip). But before we get to that, let's look at how elasticity is calculated.

To calculate the price elasticity of demand, we first calculate the *percent change in the quantity demanded* and the corresponding *percent change in the price* as we move along the demand curve. These are defined as follows:

$$\text{(6-1)} \quad \% \text{ change in quantity demanded} = \frac{\text{Change in quantity demanded}}{\text{Initial quantity demanded}} \times 100$$

and

$$\text{(6-2)} \quad \% \text{ change in price} = \frac{\text{Change in price}}{\text{Initial price}} \times 100$$

In Figure 6-1, we see that when the price rises from $200 to $210, the quantity demanded falls from 10 million to 9.9 million rides, yielding a change in the

---

FIGURE 6-1 The Demand for Ambulance Rides

At a price of $200 per ambulance ride, the quantity of ambulance rides demanded is 10 million per year (point *A*). When price rises to $210 per ambulance ride, the quantity demanded falls to 9.9 million ambulance rides per year (point *B*).

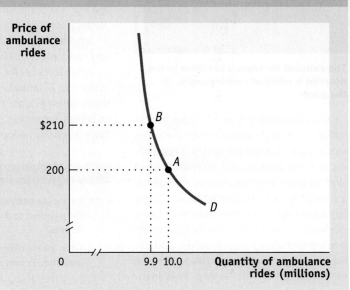

quantity demanded of 0.1 million rides. So the percent change in the quantity demanded is:

$$\% \text{ change in quantity demanded} = \frac{-0.1 \text{ million rides}}{10 \text{ million rides}} \times 100 = -1\%$$

The initial price is \$200 and the change in the price is \$10, so the percent change in price is:

$$\% \text{ change in price} = \frac{\$10}{\$200} \times 100 = 5\%$$

To calculate the price elasticity of demand, we find the ratio of the percent change in the quantity demanded to the percent change in the price:

(6-3) $\text{Price elasticity of demand} = \dfrac{\% \text{ change in quantity demanded}}{\% \text{ change in price}}$

In Figure 6-1, the price elasticity of demand is therefore:

$$\text{Price elasticity of demand} = \frac{1\%}{5\%} = 0.2$$

Notice that the minus sign that appeared in the calculation of the percent change in the quantity demanded has been dropped when we calculate this last equation, the price elasticity of demand. Why have we done this? The *law of demand* says that demand curves are downward sloping, so price and quantity demanded always move in opposite directions. In other words, a positive percent change in price (a rise in price) leads to a negative percent change in the quantity demanded; a negative percent change in price (a fall in price) leads to a positive percent change in the quantity demanded. This means that the price elasticity of demand is, in strictly mathematical terms, a negative number.

However, it is inconvenient to repeatedly write a minus sign. So when economists talk about the price elasticity of demand, they usually drop the minus sign and report the *absolute value* of the price elasticity of demand. In this case, for example, economists would usually say "the price elasticity of demand is 0.2," taking it for granted that you understand they mean *minus* 0.2. We follow this convention here.

The larger the price elasticity of demand, the more responsive the quantity demanded is to the price. When the price elasticity of demand is large—when consumers change their quantity demanded by a large percentage compared to the percent change in the price—economists say that demand is highly elastic.

As we'll see shortly, a price elasticity of 0.2 indicates a small response of quantity demanded to price. That is, the quantity demanded will fall by a relatively small amount when price rises. This is what economists call *inelastic* demand. And inelastic demand is exactly what enables an ambulance operator to increase the total amount earned by raising the price of an ambulance ride.

An Alternative Way to Calculate Elasticities: The Midpoint Method

Price elasticity of demand compares the *percent change in quantity demanded* with the *percent change in price*. When we look at some other elasticities, which we will do shortly, we'll learn why it is important to focus on percent changes. But at this point we need to discuss a technical issue that arises when you calculate percent changes in variables.

The best way to understand the issue is with a real example. Suppose you were trying to estimate the price elasticity of demand for gasoline by comparing gasoline prices and consumption in different countries. Because of high taxes, gasoline usually costs about three times as much per gallon in Europe as it does

The **midpoint method** is a technique for calculating the percent change. In this approach, we calculate changes in a variable compared with the average, or midpoint, of the starting and final values.

in the United States. So what is the percent difference between American and European gas prices?

Well, it depends on which way you measure it. Because the price of gasoline in Europe is approximately three times higher than in the United States, it is 200% higher. Because the price of gasoline in the United States is one-third as high as in Europe, it is 66.7% lower.

This is a nuisance: we'd like to have a percent measure of the difference in prices that doesn't depend on which way you measure it. To avoid computing different elasticities for rising and falling prices we use the *midpoint method*.

The **midpoint method** replaces the usual definition of the percent change in a variable, X, with a slightly different definition:

$$(6\text{-}4) \quad \% \text{ change in } X = \frac{\text{Change in } X}{\text{Average value of } X} \times 100$$

where the average value of X is defined as:

$$\text{Average value of } X = \frac{\text{Starting value of } X + \text{Final value of } X}{2}$$

When calculating the price elasticity of demand using the midpoint method, both the percent change in the price and the percent change in the quantity demanded are found using this method. To see how this method works, suppose you have the following data for some good:

Situation	Price	Quantity demanded
A	$0.90	1,100
B	$1.10	900

To calculate the percent change in quantity going from situation A to situation B, we compare the change in the quantity demanded—a fall of 200 units—with the *average* of the quantity demanded in the two situations. So we calculate:

$$\% \text{ change in quantity demanded} = \frac{-200}{(1{,}100 + 900)/2} \times 100 = \frac{-200}{1{,}000} \times 100 = -20\%$$

In the same way, we calculate:

$$\% \text{ change in price} = \frac{\$0.20}{(\$0.90 + \$1.10)/2} \times 100 = \frac{\$0.20}{\$1.00} \times 100 = 20\%$$

So in this case we would calculate the price elasticity of demand to be:

$$\text{Price elasticity of demand} = \frac{\% \text{ change in quantity demanded}}{\% \text{ change in price}} = \frac{20\%}{20\%} = 1$$

again dropping the minus sign.

The important point is that we would get the same result, a price elasticity of demand of 1, whether we go up the demand curve from situation A to situation B or down the demand curve from situation B to situation A.

To arrive at a more general formula for price elasticity of demand, suppose that we have data for two points on a demand curve. At point 1 the quantity demanded and price are (Q_1, P_1); at point 2 they are (Q_2, P_2). Then the formula for calculating the price elasticity of demand is:

$$(6\text{-}5) \quad \text{Price elasticity of demand} = \frac{\dfrac{Q_2 - Q_1}{(Q_1 + Q_2)/2}}{\dfrac{P_2 - P_1}{(P_1 + P_2)/2}}$$

As before, when finding a price elasticity of demand calculated by the midpoint method, we drop the minus sign and use the absolute value.

ECONOMICS >> *in Action*

Estimating Elasticities

You might think it's easy to estimate price elasticities of demand from real-world data: just compare percent changes in prices with percent changes in quantities demanded. Unfortunately, it's rarely that simple because changes in price aren't the only thing affecting changes in the quantity demanded: other factors—such as changes in income, changes in tastes, and changes in the prices of other goods—shift the demand curve, thereby changing the quantity demanded at any given price.

To estimate price elasticities of demand, economists must use careful statistical analysis to separate the influence of the change in price, holding other things equal.

Economists have estimated price elasticities of demand for a number of goods and services. Table 6-1 summarizes some of these and shows a wide range of price elasticities. There are some goods, like gasoline, for which demand hardly responds at all to changes in the price. There are other goods, such as airline travel for leisure, or Coke and Pepsi, for which the quantity demanded is very sensitive to the price.

Notice that Table 6-1 is divided into two parts: inelastic and elastic demand. We'll explain the significance of that division in the next section.

TABLE 6-1 Some Estimated Price Elasticities of Demand

Good	Price elasticity of demand
Inelastic demand	
Gasoline (short-run)	0.09
Gasoline (long-run)	0.24
College (in-state tuition)	0.60–0.75
Airline travel (business)	0.80
Soda	0.80
Elastic demand	
Housing	1.2
College (out-of-state tuition)	1.2
Airline travel (leisure)	1.5
Coke/Pepsi	3.3

>> Check Your Understanding 6-1

Solutions appear at back of book.

1. The price of strawberries falls from $1.50 to $1.00 per carton and the quantity demanded goes from 100,000 to 200,000 cartons. Use the midpoint method to find the price elasticity of demand.
2. At the present level of consumption, 4,000 movie tickets, and at the current price, $10 per ticket, the price elasticity of demand for movie tickets is 1. Using the midpoint method, calculate the percentage by which the owners of movie theaters must reduce price in order to sell 5,000 tickets.
3. The price elasticity of demand for ice-cream sandwiches is 1.2 at the current price of $0.50 per sandwich and the current consumption level of 100,000 sandwiches. Calculate the change in the quantity demanded when price rises by $0.05. Use Equations 6-1 and 6-2 to calculate percent changes and Equation 6-3 to relate price elasticity of demand to the percent changes.

>> Quick Review

• The **price elasticity of demand** is equal to the percent change in the quantity demanded divided by the percent change in the price as you move along the demand curve, and dropping any minus sign.

• In practice, percent changes are best measured using the **midpoint method,** in which the percent changes are calculated using the average of starting and final values.

|| Interpreting the Price Elasticity of Demand

In a true emergency, a patient is unlikely to question the price of the ambulance ride to the hospital. But even in a nonemergency, like Kira's broken teeth, patients are often unlikely to respond to an increase in the price of an ambulance by reducing their quantity demanded, because they are not aware of the cost. As a result, investors in private ambulance companies see profit-making opportunities in delivering ambulance services, because the price elasticity of demand is small. But what does that mean? How low does a price elasticity have to be for us to classify it as low? How high does it have to be for us to consider it high? And what determines whether the price elasticity of demand is high or low anyway?

To answer these questions, we need to look more deeply at the price elasticity of demand.

Demand is **perfectly inelastic** when the quantity demanded does not respond at all to changes in the price. When demand is perfectly inelastic, the demand curve is a vertical line.

Demand is **perfectly elastic** when any price increase will cause the quantity demanded to drop to zero. When demand is perfectly elastic, the demand curve is a horizontal line.

How Elastic Is Elastic?

As a first step toward classifying price elasticities of demand, let's look at the extreme cases.

First, consider the demand for a good when people pay no attention to the price—say, snake anti-venom. Suppose that consumers will buy 1,000 doses of anti-venom per year regardless of the price. In this case, the demand curve for anti-venom would look like the curve shown in panel (a) of Figure 6-2: it would be a vertical line at 1,000 doses of anti-venom. Since the percent change in the quantity demanded is zero for *any* change in the price, the price elasticity of demand in this case is zero. The case of a zero price elasticity of demand is known as **perfectly inelastic demand.**

The opposite extreme occurs when even a tiny rise in the price will cause the quantity demanded to drop to zero or even a tiny fall in the price will cause the quantity demanded to get extremely large.

Panel (b) of Figure 6-2 shows the case of pink tennis balls; we suppose that tennis players really don't care what color their balls are and that other colors, such as neon green and vivid yellow, are available at $5 per dozen balls. In this case, consumers will buy no pink balls if they cost more than $5 per dozen but will buy only pink balls if they cost less than $5. The demand curve will therefore be a horizontal line at a price of $5 per dozen balls. As you move back and forth along this line, there is a change in the quantity demanded but no change in the price. Roughly speaking, when you divide a number by zero, you get infinity, denoted by the symbol ∞. So a horizontal demand curve implies an infinite price elasticity of demand. When the price elasticity of demand is infinite, economists say that demand is **perfectly elastic.**

The price elasticity of demand for the vast majority of goods is somewhere between these two extreme cases. Economists use one main criterion for classifying these intermediate cases: they ask whether the price elasticity of demand is

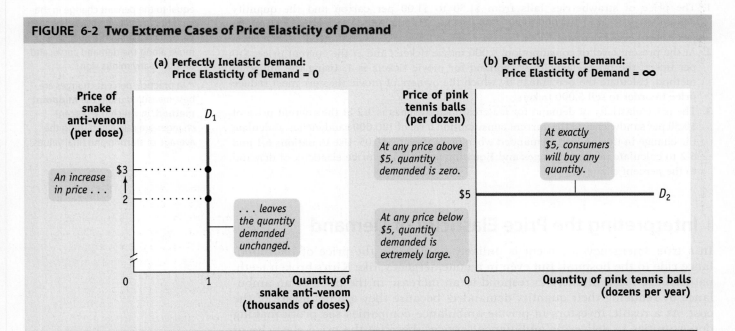

FIGURE 6-2 Two Extreme Cases of Price Elasticity of Demand

Panel (a) shows a perfectly inelastic demand curve, which is a vertical line. The quantity of snake anti-venom demanded is always 1,000 doses, regardless of price. As a result, the price elasticity of demand is zero—the quantity demanded is unaffected by the price. Panel (b) shows a perfectly elastic demand curve, which is a horizontal line. At a price of $5, consumers will buy any quantity of pink tennis balls, but they will buy none at a price above $5. If the price falls below $5, they will buy an extremely large number of pink tennis balls and none of any other color.

greater than or less than 1. When the price elasticity of demand is greater than 1, economists say that demand is **elastic.** When the price elasticity of demand is less than 1, they say that demand is **inelastic.** The borderline case is **unit-elastic demand,** where the price elasticity of demand is—surprise—exactly 1.

To see why a price elasticity of demand equal to 1 is a useful dividing line, let's consider a hypothetical example: a toll bridge operated by the state highway department. Other things equal, the number of drivers who use the bridge depends on the toll, the price the highway department charges vehicles to cross the bridge: the higher the toll, the fewer the drivers who use the bridge.

Figure 6-3 shows three hypothetical demand curves—one in which demand is unit-elastic, one in which it is inelastic, and one in which it is elastic. In each case, point A shows the quantity demanded if the toll is $0.90 and point B shows the quantity demanded if the toll is $1.10. An increase in the toll from $0.90 to $1.10 is an increase of 20% if we use the midpoint method to calculate percent changes.

Panel (a) shows what happens when the toll is raised from $0.90 to $1.10 and the demand curve is unit-elastic. Here the 20% price rise leads to a fall in the quantity of cars using the bridge each day from 1,100 to 900, which is a 20%

> Demand is **elastic** if the price elasticity of demand is greater than 1, **inelastic** if the price elasticity of demand is less than 1, and **unit-elastic** if the price elasticity of demand is exactly 1.

FIGURE 6-3 Unit-Elastic Demand, Inelastic Demand, and Elastic Demand

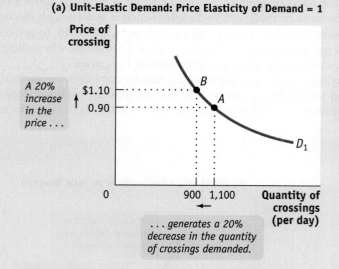

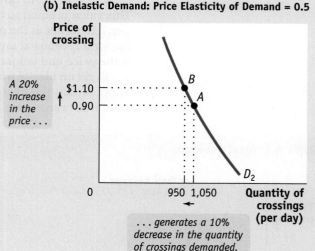

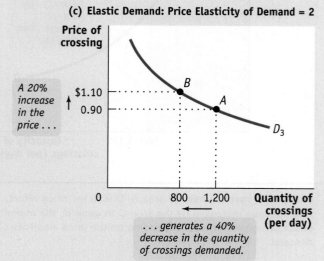

Panel (a) shows a case of unit-elastic demand: a 20% increase in price generates a 20% decline in quantity demanded, implying a price elasticity of demand of 1. Panel (b) shows a case of inelastic demand: a 20% increase in price generates a 10% decline in quantity demanded, implying a price elasticity of demand of 0.5. A case of elastic demand is shown in panel (c): a 20% increase in price causes a 40% decline in quantity demanded, implying a price elasticity of demand of 2. All percentages are calculated using the midpoint method.

The **total revenue** is the total value of sales of a good or service. It is equal to the price multiplied by the quantity sold.

decline (again using the midpoint method). So the price elasticity of demand is 20%/20% = 1.

Panel (b) shows a case of inelastic demand when the toll is raised from $0.90 to $1.10. The same 20% price rise reduces the quantity demanded from 1,050 to 950. That's only a 10% decline, so in this case the price elasticity of demand is 10%/20% = 0.5.

Panel (c) shows a case of elastic demand when the toll is raised from $0.90 to $1.10. The 20% price increase causes the quantity demanded to fall from 1,200 to 800—a 40% decline, so the price elasticity of demand is 40%/20% = 2.

Why does it matter whether demand is unit-elastic, inelastic, or elastic? Because this classification predicts how changes in the price of a good will affect the *total revenue* earned by producers from the sale of that good. In many real-life situations, it is crucial to know how price changes affect total revenue. **Total revenue** is defined as the total value of sales of a good or service, equal to the price multiplied by the quantity sold.

(6-6) Total revenue = Price × Quantity sold

Total revenue has a useful graphical representation that can help us understand why knowing the price elasticity of demand is crucial when we ask whether a price rise will increase or reduce total revenue. Panel (a) of Figure 6-4 shows the same demand curve as panel (a) of Figure 6-3. We see that 1,100 drivers will use the bridge if the toll is $0.90. So the total revenue at a price of $0.90 is $0.90 × 1,100 = $990. This value is equal to the area of the green rectangle, which is drawn with the bottom left corner at the point (0, 0) and the top right corner at (1,100, 0.90). In general, the total revenue at any given price is equal to the area of a rectangle whose height is the price and whose width is the quantity demanded at that price.

To get an idea of why total revenue is important, consider the following scenario. Suppose that the toll on the bridge is currently $0.90 but that the highway department must raise extra money for road repairs. One way to do this is to raise the toll

FIGURE 6-4 Total Revenue

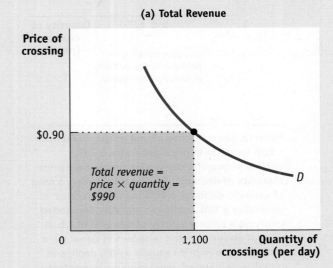

(a) Total Revenue

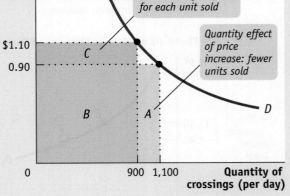

(b) Effect of a Price Increase on Total Revenue

The green rectangle in panel (a) shows the total revenue generated from 1,100 drivers who each pay a toll of $0.90. Panel (b) shows how total revenue is affected when the price increases from $0.90 to $1.10. Due to the quantity effect, total revenue falls by area *A*. Due to the price effect, total revenue increases by the area *C*. In general, the overall effect can go either way, depending on the price elasticity of demand.

on the bridge. But this plan might backfire, since a higher toll will reduce the number of drivers who use the bridge. And if traffic on the bridge dropped a lot, a higher toll would actually reduce total revenue instead of increasing it. So it's important for the highway department to know how drivers will respond to a toll increase.

We can see graphically how the toll increase affects total bridge revenue by examining panel (b) of Figure 6-4. At a toll of $0.90, total revenue is given by the sum of the areas *A* and *B*. After the toll is raised to $1.10, total revenue is given by the sum of areas *B* and *C*. So when the toll is raised, revenue represented by area *A* is lost but revenue represented by area *C* is gained.

These two areas have important interpretations. Area *C* represents the revenue gain that comes from the additional $0.20 paid by drivers who continue to use the bridge. That is, the 900 drivers who continue to use the bridge contribute an additional $0.20 × 900 = $180 per day to total revenue, represented by area *C*. But 200 drivers who would have used the bridge at a price of $0.90 no longer do so, generating a loss to total revenue of $0.90 × 200 = $180 per day, represented by area *A*. (In this particular example, because demand is unit-elastic—the same as in panel (a) of Figure 6-3—the rise in the toll has no effect on total revenue; areas *A* and *C* are the same size.)

Except in the rare case of a good with perfectly elastic or perfectly inelastic demand, when a seller raises the price of a good, two countervailing effects are present:

- *A price effect:* After a price increase, each unit sold sells at a higher price, which tends to raise revenue.

- *A quantity effect:* After a price increase, fewer units are sold, which tends to lower revenue.

But then, you may ask, what is the ultimate net effect on total revenue: does it go up or down? The answer is that, in general, the effect on total revenue can go either way—a price rise may either increase total revenue or lower it. If the price effect, which tends to raise total revenue, is the stronger of the two effects, then total revenue goes up. If the quantity effect, which tends to reduce total revenue, is the stronger, then total revenue goes down. And if the strengths of the two effects are exactly equal—as in our toll bridge example, where a $180 gain offsets a $180 loss—total revenue is unchanged by the price increase.

The price elasticity of demand tells us what happens to total revenue when price changes: its size determines which effect—the price effect or the quantity effect—is stronger. Specifically:

- If demand for a good is *unit-elastic* (the price elasticity of demand is 1), an increase in price does not change total revenue. In this case, the quantity effect and the price effect exactly offset each other.

- If demand for a good is *inelastic* (the price elasticity of demand is less than 1), a higher price increases total revenue. In this case, the quantity effect is weaker than the price effect.

- If demand for a good is *elastic* (the price elasticity of demand is greater than 1), an increase in price reduces total revenue. In this case, the quantity effect is stronger than the price effect.

Table 6-2 shows how the effect of a price increase on total revenue depends on the price elasticity of demand, using the same data as in

The highway department uses the price elasticity of demand to calculate the change in revenue from higher tolls.

TABLE 6-2 **Price Elasticity of Demand and Total Revenue**		
	Price of toll = $0.90	Price of toll = $1.10
Unit-elastic demand (price elasticity of demand = 1)		
Quantity demanded	1,100	900
Total revenue	$990	$990
Inelastic demand (price elasticity of demand = 0.5)		
Quantity demanded	1,050	950
Total revenue	$945	$1,045
Elastic demand (price elasticity of demand = 2)		
Quantity demanded	1,200	800
Total revenue	$1,080	$880

Figure 6-3. An increase in the price from $0.90 to $1.10 leaves total revenue unchanged at $990 when demand is unit-elastic. When demand is inelastic, the quantity effect is dominated by the price effect; the same price increase leads to an increase in total revenue from $945 to $1,045. And when demand is elastic, the quantity effect dominates the price effect; the price increase leads to a decline in total revenue from $1,080 to $880.

The price elasticity of demand also predicts the effect of a *fall* in price on total revenue. When the price falls, the same two countervailing effects are present, but they work in the opposite direction as compared to the case of a price rise. There is the price effect of a lower price per unit sold, which tends to lower revenue. This is countered by the quantity effect of more units sold, which tends to raise revenue. Which effect dominates depends on the price elasticity. Here is a quick summary:

- When demand is *unit-elastic*, the two effects exactly balance; so a fall in price has no effect on total revenue.
- When demand is *inelastic*, the quantity effect is dominated by the price effect; so a fall in price reduces total revenue.
- When demand is *elastic*, the quantity effect dominates the price effect; so a fall in price increases total revenue.

Price Elasticity Along the Demand Curve

Suppose an economist says that "the price elasticity of demand for coffee is 0.25." What they mean is that *at the current price* the elasticity is 0.25. In the previous discussion of the toll bridge, what we were really describing was the elasticity *at the toll price* of $0.90. Why this qualification? Because for the vast majority of demand curves, the price elasticity of demand at one point along the curve is different from the price elasticity of demand at other points along the same curve.

To see this, consider the table in Figure 6-5, which shows a hypothetical demand schedule. It also shows in the last column the total revenue generated at each price and quantity combination in the demand schedule. The upper panel of the graph in Figure 6-5 shows the corresponding demand curve. The lower panel illustrates the same data on total revenue: the height of the bar at each quantity demanded—which corresponds to a particular price—measures the total revenue generated at that price.

In Figure 6-5, you can see that when the price is low, raising the price increases total revenue: starting at a price of $1, raising the price to $2 increases total revenue from $9 to $16. This means that when the price is low, demand is inelastic. Moreover, you can see that demand is inelastic on the entire section of the demand curve from a price of $0 to a price of $5.

When the price is high, however, raising it further reduces total revenue: starting at a price of $8, raising the price to $9 reduces total revenue, from $16 to $9. This means that when the price is high, demand is elastic. Furthermore, you can see that demand is elastic over the section of the demand curve from a price of $5 to $10.

For the vast majority of goods, the price elasticity of demand changes along the demand curve. So whenever you measure a good's elasticity, you are really measuring it at a particular point or section of the good's demand curve.

What Factors Determine the Price Elasticity of Demand?

Investors in private ambulance companies believe that the price elasticity of demand for an ambulance ride is low for two important reasons. First, in many if not most cases, an ambulance ride is a medical necessity. Second, in an emergency there really is no substitute for the standard of care that an ambulance

FIGURE 6-5 The Price Elasticity of Demand Changes Along the Demand Curve

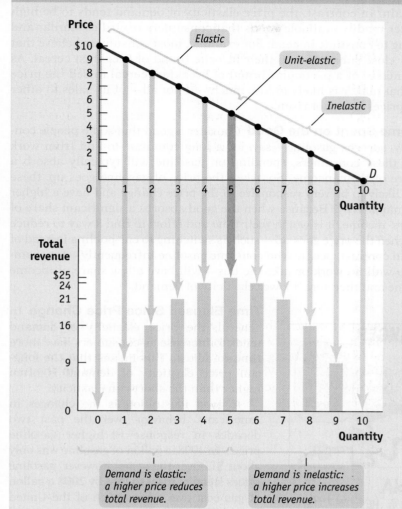

Demand Schedule and Total Revenue for a Linear Demand Curve		
Price	Quantity demanded	Total revenue
$0	10	$0
1	9	9
2	8	16
3	7	21
4	6	24
5	5	25
6	4	24
7	3	21
8	2	16
9	1	9
10	0	0

The upper panel of the graph shows a demand curve corresponding to the demand schedule in the table. The lower panel shows how total revenue changes along that demand curve: at each price and quantity combination, the height of the bar represents the total revenue generated. You can see that at a low price, raising the price increases total revenue. So demand is inelastic at low prices. At a high price, however, a rise in price reduces total revenue. So demand is elastic at high prices.

provides. And even among ambulances there are typically no substitutes because in any given geographical area there is usually only one ambulance provider. The exceptions are very densely populated areas, but even in those locations an ambulance dispatcher is unlikely to give you a choice of ambulance providers with an accompanying price list.

In general there are four main factors that determine elasticity: whether a good is a necessity or luxury, the availability of close substitutes, the share of income a consumer spends on the good, and how much time has elapsed since a change in price. We'll briefly examine each of these factors.

Whether the Good Is a Necessity or a Luxury As our opening story illustrates, the price elasticity of demand tends to be low if a good is something you must have, like a life-saving ambulance ride to the hospital. The price elasticity of demand tends to be high if the good is a luxury—something you can easily live without. For example, most people would consider a 98-inch ultra-high-definition TV a luxury—nice to have, but something they can live without. Therefore, the price elasticity of demand for it will be much higher than for a life-saving ambulance ride to the hospital.

The Availability of Close Substitutes As we just noted, the price elasticity of demand tends to be low if there are no close substitutes or if they are very difficult to obtain. In contrast, the price elasticity of demand tends to be high if there are other readily available goods that consumers regard as similar and would be willing to consume instead. For example, most consumers believe that there are fairly close substitutes to their favorite brand of breakfast cereal. As a result, if the maker of a particular brand of breakfast cereal raised the price significantly, that maker is likely to lose much—if not all—of its sales to other brands whose prices have not risen.

Share of Income Spent on the Good Consider a good that some people consume frequently, such as gasoline—say, for a long commute to and from work every day. For these consumers, spending on gasoline will typically absorb a significant share of their income. So, when the price of gasoline goes up, these consumers are likely to be very responsive to the price change and have a higher elasticity of demand. Why? Because when the good absorbs a significant share of these consumers' income, it is worth their time and effort to find a way to reduce their demand when the price goes up—such as switching to car-pooling instead of driving alone. In contrast, people who consume gasoline infrequently—for example, people who walk to work or take the bus—will have a low share of income spent on gasoline and therefore a lower elasticity of demand.

Time Elapsed Since Price Change In general, the price elasticity of demand tends to increase as consumers have more time to adjust. This means that the long-run price elasticity of demand is often higher than the short-run elasticity.

A good illustration is the changes in Americans' behavior over the past two decades in response to higher gasoline prices. In 1998, a gallon of gasoline was only about $1. Over the years, however, gasoline prices steadily rose, so that by 2008 a gallon of gas cost over $4 in much of the United States. Over time, however, people changed their habits and choices in ways that enabled them to gradually reduce their gasoline consumption. These changes are reflected in the data on American gasoline consumption: the trend line of consumption fluctuated until about 2003, then took a nosedive. By 2013, Americans were purchasing less than 350 million gallons of gas daily, less than the nearly 380 million gallons purchased daily in 2007, and far less than 450 million gallons a day, the amount Americans would have purchased if they had followed previous trends of ever-increasing gasoline consumption. This confirms that the long-run price elasticity of demand for gasoline is much larger than the short-run elasticity.

Gas prices dropped dramatically from 2014 to 2019, with the average price over that period down to around $2.50 per gallon. Not surprisingly, gasoline consumption rose when prices fell. In 2016, when prices fell as low as $1.75, American consumption jumped to nearly 400 million gallons of gasoline per day, as consumers switched back to their gas-guzzlers. As the economy recovered in 2017 and 2018, gasoline prices inched up. Higher gasoline prices and improved fuel efficiency of new cars combined to render U.S. gasoline consumption virtually flat in during 2017 and 2018, a situation that persisted until the sharp fall in demand caused by the coronavirus pandemic in 2020.

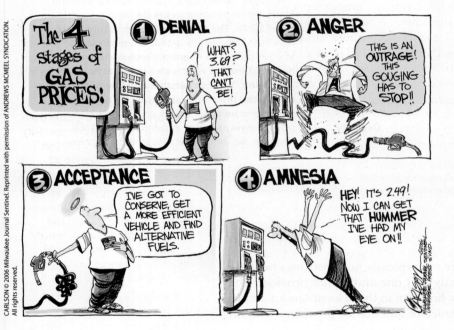

ECONOMICS >> *in Action*
Responding to Your Tuition Bill

If it seems like the cost of college keeps going up—it's because it has. It is estimated that over the past 15 years the average annual increase in tuition has exceeded the inflation rate by approximately 5% to 6% every year. An important question for educators and policy makers is whether the rise in tuition deters people from going to college. And if so, by how much?

Several studies have shown that tuition increases lead to consistently negative effects on enrollment numbers, with estimates of the price elasticity of demand ranging from 0.67 to 0.76 for four-year institutions. So a 3% rise in tuition at a four-year institution leads to a fall in enrollment of approximately 2% (3 × 0.67) to 2.3% (3 × 0.76). Two-year institutions were found to have a significantly higher response: a 3% increase in tuition leads to a 2.7% fall in enrollment, implying a price elasticity of demand of 0.9.

For students receiving financial aid, the price elasticity of demand rises to 1.18, implying that a 3% rise in tuition leads to a 3.54% fall in enrollment. While grant and loan disbursements lead to increases in enrollment, their effects are modest: with a price elasticity of demand of 0.33, a 3% increase in grant monies leads to a 1% increase in enrollment, and with an elasticity of 0.12, a 3% increase in loan monies leads to a 0.36% increase in enrollment.

These results indicate that an increase in tuition accompanied by an equal increase in financial aid leads to lower enrollment. That is, students care not just about *net tuition*, defined as the full price of tuition minus financial aid, but they also care about the composition of how their tuition bill is paid, preferring a lower full-price tuition to one with higher tuition and more financial aid.

So the increase in tuition *is* a barrier to college, and it is more of a barrier for students at two-year institutions than four-year institutions. This makes sense in light of evidence suggesting that students at two-year schools are more likely to be paying their own way, so they are spending a higher share of income on tuition compared to students at four-year institutions (who are more likely to be counting on their parents' income).

Students at two-year schools are also more responsive to changes in the unemployment rate. Higher unemployment leads to higher enrollments, indicating that these students are making a trade-off by going to school instead of working and they consider school a substitute for their time. Both of these factors—the high share of income spent on tuition and viewing school as a substitute for their time—will lead students at two-year colleges to be more responsive to changes in tuition than students at four-year colleges.

An increase in tuition is also more of a barrier for students receiving financial aid than for students paying full tuition. Financial aid recipients may be more responsive to the full cost of tuition for fear of losing their grant money or out of concern about the cost of paying back their student loans.

Students at two-year schools are more responsive to the price of tuition than students at four-year schools.

> *Blend Images/Andersen Ross/Getty Images*

>> *Quick Review*

• Demand is **perfectly inelastic** if it is completely unresponsive to price. It is **perfectly elastic** if it is infinitely responsive to price.

• Demand is **elastic** if the price elasticity of demand is greater than 1. It is **inelastic** if the price elasticity of demand is less than 1. It is **unit-elastic** if the price elasticity of demand is exactly 1.

• When demand is elastic, the quantity effect of a price increase dominates the price effect and **total revenue** falls. When demand is inelastic, the quantity effect is dominated by the price effect and total revenue rises.

• Because the price elasticity of demand can change along the demand curve, economists refer to a particular point on the demand curve when speaking of the price elasticity of demand.

• Ready availability of close substitutes makes demand for a good more elastic, as does a longer length of time elapsed since the price change. Demand for a necessity is less elastic, and demand for a luxury good is more elastic. Demand tends to be inelastic for goods that absorb a small share of a consumer's income and elastic for goods that absorb a large share of income.

>> *Check Your Understanding* 6-2

Solutions appear at back of book.

1. For each case, choose the condition that characterizes demand: elastic demand, inelastic demand, or unit-elastic demand.
   a. Total revenue decreases when price increases.
   b. The additional revenue generated by an increase in quantity sold is exactly offset by revenue lost from the fall in price received per unit.
   c. Total revenue falls when output increases.
   d. Producers in an industry find they can increase their total revenues by coordinating a reduction in industry output.

The **cross-price elasticity of demand** between two goods measures the effect of the change in one good's price on the quantity demanded of the other good. It is equal to the percent change in the quantity demanded of one good divided by the percent change in the other good's price.

2. What is the elasticity of demand for the following goods? Explain. What is the shape of the demand curve?
   a. Demand for a blood transfusion by an accident victim
   b. Demand by students for green erasers

Other Demand Elasticities

The quantity of a good demanded depends not only on the price of that good but also on other variables. In particular, demand curves shift because of changes in the prices of related goods and changes in consumers' incomes. It is often important to have a measure of these other effects, and the best measures are—you guessed it—elasticities. Specifically, we can best measure how the demand for a good is affected by prices of other goods using a measure called the *cross-price elasticity of demand*, and we can best measure how demand is affected by changes in income using the *income elasticity of demand*.

The Cross-Price Elasticity of Demand

In Chapter 3 you learned that the demand for a good is often affected by the prices of other, related goods—goods that are substitutes or complements. There you saw that a change in the price of a related good shifts the demand curve of the original good, reflecting a change in the quantity demanded at any given price. The strength of such a "cross" effect on demand can be measured by the **cross-price elasticity of demand,** defined as the ratio of the percent change in the quantity demanded of one good to the percent change in the price of the other. Like the price elasticity of demand, the cross-price elasticity is calculated using the midpoint method.

(6-7) Cross-price elasticity of demand between goods A and B

$$= \frac{\% \text{ change in quantity of A demanded}}{\% \text{ change in price of B}}$$

When two goods are substitutes, like hot dogs and hamburgers, the cross-price elasticity of demand is positive: a rise in the price of hot dogs increases the demand for hamburgers—that is, it causes a rightward shift of the demand curve for hamburgers. If the goods are close substitutes, the cross-price elasticity will be positive and large. If they are not close substitutes, the cross-price elasticity will be positive and small. So when the cross-price elasticity of demand is positive, its size is a measure of how closely substitutable the two goods are.

When two goods are complements, like hot dogs and hot dog buns, the cross-price elasticity is negative: a rise in the price of hot dogs decreases the demand for hot dog buns—that is, it causes a leftward shift of the demand curve for hot dog buns. As with substitutes, the size of the cross-price elasticity of demand between two complements tells us how strongly complementary they are: if the cross-price elasticity is only slightly below zero, they are weak complements; if it is very negative, they are strong complements.

Note that in the case of the cross-price elasticity of demand, the sign (plus or minus) is very important: it tells us whether the two goods are complements or substitutes. So we cannot drop the minus sign as we did for the price elasticity of demand.

Our discussion of the cross-price elasticity of demand is a useful place to return to a point we made earlier: elasticity is a *unit-free* measure—that is, it doesn't depend on the units in which goods are measured.

To see how this could be a potential problem, suppose someone told you that "if the price of hot dog buns rises by $0.30, Americans will buy 10 million fewer hot dogs this year." If you've ever bought hot dog buns, you'll immediately wonder: is that a $0.30 increase in the price *per bun*, or is it a $0.30 increase in the price *per package*? Buns are usually sold in packages of eight. It makes a big difference what units we are talking about! However, if someone says that the cross-price elasticity of demand between buns and hot dogs is −0.3, it doesn't matter whether buns are sold individually or by the package. Thus, elasticity is defined as a ratio of percent changes, as a way of making sure that confusion over units doesn't arise.

> The **income elasticity of demand** is the percent change in the quantity of a good demanded when a consumer's income changes divided by the percent change in the consumer's income.

The Income Elasticity of Demand

The **income elasticity of demand** is a measure of how much the demand for a good is affected by changes in consumers' incomes. It allows us to determine whether a good is a normal or inferior good as well as to measure how intensely the demand for the good responds to changes in income.

(6-8) Income elasticity of demand = $\dfrac{\%\ \text{change in quantity demanded}}{\%\ \text{change in income}}$

Just as the cross-price elasticity of demand between two goods can be either positive or negative, depending on whether the goods are substitutes or complements, the income elasticity of demand for a good can also be either positive or negative. Recall from Chapter 3 that goods can be either *normal goods*, for which demand increases when income rises, or *inferior goods*, for which demand decreases when income rises. These definitions relate directly to the sign of the income elasticity of demand:

- When the income elasticity of demand is positive, the good is a normal good. In this case, the quantity demanded at any given price increases as income increases. Correspondingly, the quantity demanded at any given price decreases as income falls.

- When the income elasticity of demand is negative, the good is an inferior good. In this case, the quantity demanded at any given price decreases as income increases. Likewise, the quantity demanded at any given price increases as income falls.

🌐 GLOBAL COMPARISON   FOOD'S BITE IN WORLD BUDGETS

The income elasticity of demand for food is less than 1—it is income-inelastic. As consumers grow richer, other things equal, spending on food rises less than income.

Given these facts, we would expect to find that people in poor countries spend a larger share of their income on food than people in rich countries. And that's exactly what the data show. In this graph, we compare per capita income—a country's total income, divided by the population—with the share of income that is spent on food. (To make the graph a manageable size, per capita income is measured as a percentage of U.S. per capita income.)

In very poor countries like Pakistan, people spend a large percent of their income on food. In middle-income countries, like Israel and Mexico, the share of spending that goes to food is much lower. And it's lower still in rich countries like the United States.

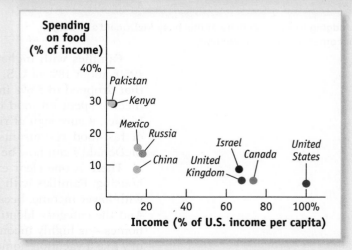

Data from: USDA and IMF, World Economic Outlook.

The demand for a good is **income-elastic** if the income elasticity of demand for that good is greater than 1.

The demand for a good is **income-inelastic** if the income elasticity of demand for that good is positive but less than 1.

Economists often use estimates of the income elasticity of demand to predict which industries will grow most rapidly as the incomes of consumers grow over time. In doing this, they often find it useful to make an additional distinction among normal goods, identifying which normal goods are *income-elastic* and which are *income-inelastic*.

- The demand for a good is **income-elastic** if the income elasticity of demand for that good is greater than 1. When income rises, the demand for income-elastic goods rises *faster* than income. Luxury goods such as second homes and international travel tend to be income-elastic.

- The demand for a good is **income-inelastic** if the income elasticity of demand for that good is positive but less than 1. When income rises, the demand for income-inelastic goods rises, but more slowly than income. Necessities such as food and clothing tend to be income-inelastic.

ECONOMICS >> *in Action*
Spending It

The U.S. Bureau of Labor Statistics carries out extensive surveys of how families spend their incomes. This is not just a matter of intellectual curiosity. Quite a few government benefit programs involve some adjustment for changes in the cost of living. To estimate those changes, the government must know how people spend their money. But an additional payoff to these surveys is data on the income elasticity of demand for various goods.

What stands out from these studies? The classic result is that the income elasticity of demand for "food eaten at home" is considerably less than 1: as a family's income rises, the share of its income spent on food prepared at home falls. Correspondingly, the lower a family's income, the higher the share of income spent on food consumed at home.

In poor countries, many families spend more than half their income on food consumed at home. Although the income elasticity of demand for "food eaten at home" is estimated at less than 0.5 in the United States, the income elasticity of demand for "food eaten away from home" (restaurant meals) is estimated to be much higher—close to 1.

Judging from the activity at this busy McDonald's in Saigon, incomes are rising in Vietnam.

Families with higher incomes eat out more often and at fancier places. In 1950, about 18% of U.S. income was spent on food consumed at home, a number that dropped to 5.6% in 2018. But over the same time period, the share of U.S. income spent on food consumed away from home has stayed constant at 5%. In fact, a sure sign of rising income levels in developing countries is the arrival of fast-food restaurants that cater to newly affluent customers. For example, McDonald's can now be found in Hanoi, Jakarta, and Mumbai.

There is one clear example of an inferior good found in the surveys: rental housing. Families with higher income actually spend less on rent than families with lower income, because they are much more likely to own their own homes. And the category identified as "other housing"—which basically means second homes—is highly income-elastic. Only higher-income families can afford a luxury like a vacation home, so "other housing" has an income elasticity of demand greater than 1.

>> *Check Your Understanding* **6-3**
Solutions appear at back of book.

1. After Charlotte's income increased from $12,000 to $18,000 a year, her purchases of movie downloads increased from 10 to 40 downloads a year. Calculate Charlotte's income elasticity of demand for movies using the midpoint method.

2. Expensive restaurant meals are income-elastic goods for most people, including Sanjay. Suppose his income falls by 10% this year. What can you predict about the change in Sanjay's consumption of expensive restaurant meals?

3. As the price of margarine rises by 20%, a manufacturer of baked goods increases its quantity of butter demanded by 5%. Calculate the cross-price elasticity of demand between butter and margarine. Are butter and margarine substitutes or complements for this manufacturer?

‖ The Price Elasticity of Supply

A fundamental characteristic of any market for ambulance services, no matter where it is located, is limited supply. For example, it would have been much harder to charge Kira Milas $1,772.42 for a 15-minute ride to the hospital if there had been many ambulance providers cruising nearby and offering a lower price. But there are good economic reasons why there are not: who among those experiencing a true health emergency would trust their health and safety to a low-price ambulance? And who would want to be a supplier, paying the expense of providing quality ambulance services, without being able to charge high prices to recoup costs? Not surprisingly, then, in most locations there is only one ambulance provider available.

In sum, a critical element in the ability of ambulance providers to charge high prices is limited supply: a low responsiveness in the quantity of output supplied to the higher prices charged for an ambulance ride. To measure the response of ambulance providers to price changes, we need a measure parallel to the price elasticity of demand—the *price elasticity of supply*, as we'll see next.

Measuring the Price Elasticity of Supply

The **price elasticity of supply** is defined the same way as the price elasticity of demand, although since it is always positive there is no minus sign to be eliminated:

(6-9) Price elasticity of supply = $\dfrac{\%\text{ change in quantity supplied}}{\%\text{ change in price}}$

It is also calculated using the midpoint method. The only difference is that now we consider movements along the supply curve rather than movements along the demand curve.

Suppose that the price of tomatoes rises by 10%. If the quantity of tomatoes supplied also increases by 10% in response, the price elasticity of supply of tomatoes is 1 (10%/10%) and supply is unit-elastic. If the quantity supplied increases by 5%, the price elasticity of supply is 0.5 and supply is inelastic; if the quantity increases by 20%, the price elasticity of supply is 2 and supply is elastic.

As in the case of demand, the extreme values of the price elasticity of supply have a simple graphical representation. Panel (a) of Figure 6-6 shows the supply of cell phone frequencies, the portion of the radio spectrum that is suitable for sending and receiving cell phone signals. Governments own the right to sell the use of this part of the radio spectrum to cell phone operators inside their borders. But governments can't increase or decrease the number of cell phone frequencies that they have to offer—for technical reasons, the quantity of frequencies suitable for cell phone operation is a fixed quantity.

The **price elasticity of supply** is a measure of the responsiveness of the quantity of a good supplied to the price of that good. It is the ratio of the percent change in the quantity supplied to the percent change in the price as we move along the supply curve.

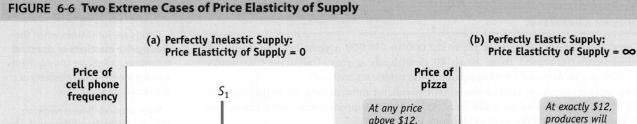

FIGURE 6-6 Two Extreme Cases of Price Elasticity of Supply

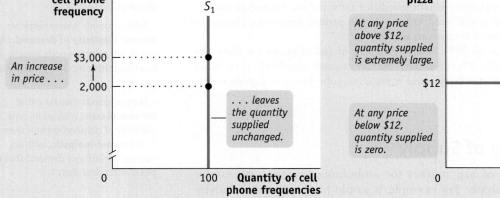

Panel (a) shows a perfectly inelastic supply curve, which is a vertical line. The price elasticity of supply is zero: the quantity supplied is always the same, regardless of price. Panel (b) shows a perfectly elastic supply curve, which is a horizontal line. At a price of $12, producers will supply any quantity, but they will supply none at a price below $12. If price rises above $12, they will supply an extremely large quantity.

There is **perfectly inelastic supply** when the price elasticity of supply is zero, so that changes in the price of the good have no effect on the quantity supplied. A perfectly inelastic supply curve is a vertical line.

There is **perfectly elastic supply** when even a tiny increase or reduction in the price will lead to very large changes in the quantity supplied, so that the price elasticity of supply is infinite. A perfectly elastic supply curve is a horizontal line.

So the supply curve for cell phone frequencies is a vertical line, which we have assumed is set at the quantity of 100 frequencies. As you move up and down that curve, the change in the quantity supplied by the government is zero, whatever the change in price. So panel (a) illustrates a case in which the price elasticity of supply is zero. This is a case of **perfectly inelastic supply.**

Panel (b) shows the supply curve for pizza. We suppose that it costs $12 to produce a pizza, including all opportunity costs. At any price below $12, it would be unprofitable to produce pizza and all the pizza parlors in America would go out of business. Alternatively, there are many producers who could operate pizza parlors if they were profitable. The ingredients—flour, tomatoes, and cheese—are plentiful. And if necessary, more tomatoes could be grown, more milk could be produced to make mozzarella, and so on. So any price above $12 would elicit an extremely large quantity of pizzas supplied. The implied supply curve is therefore a horizontal line at $12.

Since even a tiny increase in the price would lead to a huge increase in the quantity supplied, the price elasticity of supply would be more or less infinite. This is a case of **perfectly elastic supply.**

As our cell phone frequencies and pizza examples suggest, real-world instances of both perfectly inelastic and perfectly elastic supply are easy to find—much easier than their counterparts in demand.

What Factors Determine the Price Elasticity of Supply?

Our examples tell us the main determinant of the price elasticity of supply: the availability of inputs. In addition, as with the price elasticity of demand, time may also play a role in the price elasticity of supply. Here we briefly summarize the two factors.

The Availability of Inputs The price elasticity of supply tends to be large when inputs are readily available and can be shifted into and out of production at a relatively low cost. It tends to be small when inputs are difficult to obtain—and can be shifted into and out of production only at a relatively high cost. In the case of ambulance services, the high cost of providing quality ambulance services is the crucial element in keeping the elasticity of supply very low.

Time The price elasticity of supply tends to grow larger as producers have more time to respond to a price change. This means that the long-run price elasticity of supply is often higher than the short-run elasticity.

The price elasticity of the supply of pizza is very high because the inputs needed to expand the industry are readily available. The price elasticity of cell phone frequencies is zero because an essential input—the radio spectrum—cannot be increased at all.

Many industries are like pizza production and have large price elasticities of supply: they can be readily expanded because they don't require any special or unique resources. In contrast, the price elasticity of supply is usually substantially less than perfectly elastic for goods that involve limited natural resources: minerals like gold or copper, agricultural products like coffee that flourish only on certain types of land, and renewable resources like ocean fish that can only be exploited up to a point without destroying the resource.

But given enough time, producers are often able to significantly change the amount they produce in response to a price change, even when production involves a limited natural resource or a very costly input. Agricultural markets provide a good example. When American farmers receive much higher prices for a given commodity, like wheat (because of a drought in a big wheat-producing country like Australia), in the next planting season they are likely to switch their acreage planted from other crops to wheat.

For this reason, economists often make a distinction between the short-run elasticity of supply, usually referring to a few weeks or months, and the long-run elasticity of supply, usually referring to several years. In most industries, the long-run elasticity of supply is larger than the short-run elasticity.

ECONOMICS >> *in Action*
A Global Commodities Glut

The rapidly growing Chinese economy has been a voracious consumer of commodities—metals, foodstuffs, and fuel—as its economy rapidly expanded to become a global manufacturing powerhouse. As China's demand for commodities to support its transformation soared, the countries providing those commodities also saw their incomes soar.

However, when the Chinese economy faltered in 2016, the commodities boom came to an abrupt end. Global commodity producers saw the demand for their goods fall dramatically, just as many of them were investing in costly projects to increase supplies. For example, Chile, the world's major copper producer, had undertaken a massive expansion of its copper mines, digging up 1.7 billion tons of material as copper prices plummeted around the world. India was building railroad lines to connect its underused coal mines to the export market just as a worldwide glut of coal opened up. And Australia was planning to increase its natural gas production by 150% just as natural gas companies around the world went bankrupt due to shrinking fuel demand and plunging prices.

Because these countries had invested many billions of dollars into increasing their supply capacity over several years, they could not simply shut down production. So production continued, worsening the existing glut of commodities.

What the commodity producers appear to have forgotten is the logic of the price elasticity of supply: combine persistently high prices with the easy availability of inputs to increase supply capacity (in this case, the chief input was financial capital), and the predictable result is a big increase in the supply of commodities—a rightward shift of the supply curve.

Commodity producers, who had greatly expanded capacity to supply a booming Chinese economy, faltered badly when the Chinese economy slumped in 2016.

Also predictable is that once the growth in demand for the commodities slowed down, a steep drop in prices would follow. As one commodities expert at the Council of Foreign Relations said, "Producers ended up being their own worst enemies. No one ever worried they would produce too much, but that is exactly what has happened and gotten them into this mess."

>> Check Your Understanding 6-4

Solutions appear at back of book.

1. Using the midpoint method, calculate the price elasticity of supply for web-design services when the price per hour rises from $100 to $150 and the number of hours transacted increases from 300,000 to 500,000. Is supply elastic, inelastic, or unit-elastic?
2. Are each of the following statements true or false? Explain.
   a. If the demand for milk rose, then, in the long run, milk drinkers would be better off if supply were elastic rather than inelastic.
   b. Long-run price elasticities of supply are generally larger than short-run price elasticities of supply. As a result, the short-run supply curves are generally flatter than the long-run supply curves.
   c. When supply is perfectly elastic, changes in demand have no effect on price.

‖ An Elasticity Menagerie

We've just run through quite a few different elasticities. Table 6-3 summarizes all of them and their implications.

TABLE 6-3 An Elasticity Menagerie

Price elasticity of demand = $\dfrac{\text{\% change in quantity demanded}}{\text{\% change in price}}$ (dropping the minus sign)	
0	**Perfectly inelastic:** price has no effect on quantity demanded (vertical demand curve).
Between 0 and 1	**Inelastic:** a rise in price increases total revenue.
Exactly 1	**Unit-elastic:** changes in price have no effect on total revenue.
Greater than 1, less than ∞	**Elastic:** a rise in price reduces total revenue.
∞	**Perfectly elastic:** any rise in price causes quantity demanded to fall to 0. Any fall in price leads to an infinite quantity demanded (horizontal demand curve).
Cross-price elasticity of demand = $\dfrac{\text{\% change in quantity demanded of \emph{one good}}}{\text{\% change in price of \emph{another good}}}$	
Negative	**Complements:** quantity demanded of one good falls when the price of another rises.
Positive	**Substitutes:** quantity demanded of one good rises when the price of another rises.
Income elasticity of demand = $\dfrac{\text{\% change in quantity demanded}}{\text{\% change in income}}$	
Negative	**Inferior good:** quantity demanded falls when income rises.
Positive, less than 1	**Normal good, income-inelastic:** quantity demanded rises when income rises, but not as rapidly as income.
Greater than 1	**Normal good, income-elastic:** quantity demanded rises when income rises, and more rapidly than income.
Price elasticity of supply = $\dfrac{\text{\% change in quantity supplied}}{\text{\% change in price}}$	
0	**Perfectly inelastic:** price has no effect on quantity supplied (vertical supply curve).
Greater than 0, less than ∞	ordinary upward-sloping supply curve.
∞	**Perfectly elastic:** any fall in price causes quantity supplied to fall to 0. Any rise in price elicits an infinite quantity supplied (horizontal supply curve).

The American Airline Industry: Fly Less and Charge More

AP Photo/Ted S. Warren

In 2019, the top four intra-North American airlines accounted for 67% of all passenger air-miles traveled in the United States. In contrast, the top five intra-European airlines accounted for around 50% of all European air-miles traveled. Moreover, U.S. airlines are the most profitable in the world, earning more than twice as much profit per passenger as the global average. Since 2010, the U.S. airline industry has been profitable every year.

However, it wasn't always like this. The U.S. airline industry suffered heavy losses for many decades, accumulating an industry-wide loss of $52 billion between 1977 to 2009. Those years were also a time of greater fragmentation across the industry: then, the top four airlines accounted for only 49% of air-miles traveled, instead of the 67% share of today. As the accompanying table shows, from 2005 onward, consolidation among the 10 major American carriers led to the 4 major carriers left today: American, Delta, United, and Southwest.

Acquiring airline	Acquired airline	Date
American Airlines	TWA	2001
U.S. Airways	America West	2005
American Airlines	U.S. Airways	2013
Delta	Northwest	2008
United	Continental	2010
Southwest	AirTran	2010

How did the U.S. airline industry achieve such a dramatic turnaround? Simple: fly less and charge more. The catalyst was a particularly nasty recession in 2008, which pushed the U.S. airline industry to the edge of disaster. When the economy cratered, people stopped flying, and the industry lost a staggering $11 billion that year. The largest carriers were forced to significantly slash their capacity—flying fewer planes—to match the lower demand for seats. Smaller carriers, saddled with years of losses, were no longer viable. They merged with their larger rivals and redundant flights were cut. As a result, starting in 2010 flights became a lot more crowded, with only about 1 in 7 seats empty.

Airlines also began charging more: beginning in 2010, the industry enjoyed several years of significant fare increases. One way the airlines accomplished this was by varying ticket prices according to the day and time of departure, as well as the day the ticket was purchased. For example, Wednesday became the cheapest day to fly, with Friday and Saturday the most expensive. The least expensive flight of the day is the first flight of the morning (the one that requires you to get up at 4 A.M.). And buying tickets on Tuesdays at 3 P.M. Eastern Standard time results in the cheapest fares, while tickets purchased on the weekend cost the most.

And it didn't stop there, as every beleaguered traveler knows. In 2010 airlines began imposing new fees and increased old ones—fees for food, blankets, baggage, the right to board first or choose your seat in advance, and so on. These fees are now a major source of airlines' revenue, all while providing a seemingly ever-shrinking amount of leg room.

However, recent events may be turning in consumers' favor. Since 2015 fare increases have been small as low-cost carriers like Spirit Air and Alaska Airlines have expanded as the economy gathered steam. One airline industry researcher, commenting on the long-term profitability of airlines, had this to say: "The wild card is always capacity discipline. All it takes is one carrier to begin to add capacity aggressively, and then we follow and we undo all the good work that's been done."

QUESTIONS FOR THOUGHT

1. How would you describe the price elasticity of demand for airline flights given the information in this case? Explain.

2. Using the concept of elasticity, explain why airlines would create such great variations in the price of a ticket depending on when it is purchased and the day and time the flight departs. Assume that some people are willing to spend time shopping for deals as well as fly at inconvenient times, but others are not.

3. Using the concept of elasticity, explain why airlines have imposed fees on things such as checked bags. Why might they try to hide or disguise fees?

4. Use an elasticity concept to explain under what conditions the airline industry will be able to maintain its high profitability in the future. Explain.

SUMMARY

1. Many economic questions depend on the size of consumer or producer responses to changes in prices or other variables. *Elasticity* is a general measure of responsiveness that can be used to answer such questions.

2. The **price elasticity of demand**—the percent change in the quantity demanded divided by the percent change in the price (dropping the minus sign)—is a measure of the responsiveness of the quantity demanded to changes in the price. In practical calculations, it is usually best to use the **midpoint method,** which calculates percent changes in prices and quantities based on the average of starting and final values.

3. The responsiveness of the quantity demanded to price can range from **perfectly inelastic demand,** where the quantity demanded is unaffected by the price, to **perfectly elastic demand,** where there is a unique price at which consumers will buy as much or as little as they are offered. When demand is perfectly inelastic, the demand curve is a vertical line; when it is perfectly elastic, the demand curve is a horizontal line.

4. The price elasticity of demand is classified according to whether it is more or less than 1. If it is greater than 1, demand is **elastic;** if it is less than 1, demand is **inelastic;** if it is exactly 1, demand is **unit-elastic.** This classification determines how **total revenue,** the total value of sales, changes when the price changes. If demand is elastic, total revenue falls when the price increases and rises when the price decreases. If demand is inelastic, total revenue rises when the price increases and falls when the price decreases. If demand is unit-elastic, total revenue is unchanged by a change in price.

5. The price elasticity of demand depends on whether there are close substitutes for the good in question (it is higher), whether the good is a necessity (it is lower) or a luxury (it is higher), the share of income spent on the good (it is higher), and the length of time that has elapsed since the price change (it is higher).

6. The **cross-price elasticity of demand** measures the effect of a change in one good's price on the quantity demanded of another good. The cross-price elasticity of demand can be positive, in which case the goods are substitutes, or negative, in which case they are complements.

7. The **income elasticity of demand** is the percent change in the quantity of a good demanded when a consumer's income changes divided by the percent change in income. The income elasticity of demand indicates how intensely the demand for a good responds to changes in income. It can be negative; in that case the good is an inferior good. Goods with positive income elasticities of demand are normal goods. If the income elasticity is greater than 1, a good is **income-elastic;** if it is positive and less than 1, the good is **income-inelastic.**

8. The **price elasticity of supply** is the percent change in the quantity of a good supplied divided by the percent change in the price. If the quantity supplied does not change at all, we have an instance of **perfectly inelastic supply;** the supply curve is a vertical line. If the quantity supplied is zero below some price but infinite above that price, we have an instance of **perfectly elastic supply;** the supply curve is a horizontal line.

9. The price elasticity of supply depends on the availability of resources to expand production and on time. It is higher when inputs are available at relatively low cost and the longer the time elapsed since the price change.

KEY TERMS

Price elasticity of demand, p. 160
Midpoint method, p. 162
Perfectly inelastic demand, p. 164
Perfectly elastic demand, p. 164
Elastic demand, p. 165

Inelastic demand, p. 165
Unit-elastic demand, p. 165
Total revenue, p. 166
Cross-price elasticity of demand, p. 172
Income elasticity of demand, p. 173

Income-elastic demand, p. 174
Income-inelastic demand, p. 174
Price elasticity of supply, p. 175
Perfectly inelastic supply, p. 176
Perfectly elastic supply, p. 176

PRACTICE QUESTIONS

1. You recently came across the following headlines:

   i. "Private schools cut tuition and fail to reach enrollment goals"

   ii. "University of California raises tuition on out-of-state students, still at capacity"

   What does each statement say about the elasticity of demand for university tuition? Is each statement consistent with what you learned about the factors that determine elasticity?

2. You and your classmate were discussing some recent observations on your college campus. Using the concepts of elasticity, how would you explain each of these situations:

   i. Textbook prices at the campus bookstore are 20% to 30% more expensive than online retailers.

ii. You notice that at the restaurant where you wait tables, the bar gives away free salty snacks like popcorn and peanuts.

iii. The athletics department charges lower prices for football tickets to students than those to the general public.

iv. Parking prices increased 25% for the school year and you still have difficulty finding an open spot.

3. There is a debate about whether sterile hypodermic needles should be passed out free of charge in cities with high drug use. Proponents argue that doing so will reduce the incidence of diseases, such as HIV/AIDS, that are often spread by needle sharing among drug users. Opponents believe that doing so will

encourage more drug use by reducing the risks of this behavior. As an economist asked to assess the policy, you must know the following: (i) how responsive the spread of diseases like HIV/AIDS is to the price of sterile needles and (ii) how responsive drug use is to the price of sterile needles. Assuming that you know these two things, use the concepts of price elasticity of demand for sterile needles and the cross-price elasticity between drugs and sterile needles to answer the following questions.

a. In what circumstances do you believe this is a beneficial policy?

b. In what circumstances do you believe this is a bad policy?

PROBLEMS

1. Do you think the price elasticity of demand for Ford sport-utility vehicles (SUVs) will increase, decrease, or remain the same when each of the following events occurs? Explain your answer.

a. Other car manufacturers, such as General Motors, decide to make and sell SUVs.

b. SUVs produced in foreign countries are banned from the U.S. market.

c. Due to ad campaigns, Americans believe that SUVs are much safer than ordinary passenger cars.

d. The time period over which you measure the elasticity lengthens. During that longer time, new models such as four-wheel-drive cargo vans appear.

2. In the United States, 2018 was a bad year for growing wheat. And as wheat supply decreased, the price of wheat rose dramatically, leading to a lower quantity demanded (a movement along the demand curve). The accompanying table describes what happened to prices and the quantity of wheat demanded.

	2017	2018
Quantity demanded (bushels)	2.3 billion	1.7 billion
Average price (per bushel)	$4.02	$4.98

a. Using the midpoint method, calculate the price elasticity of demand for winter wheat.

b. What is the total revenue for U.S. wheat farmers in 2017 and 2018?

c. Did the bad harvest increase or decrease the total revenue of U.S. wheat farmers? How could you have predicted this from your answer to part a?

3. The accompanying table gives part of the supply schedule for personal computers in the United States.

Price of computer	Quantity of computers supplied
$1,100	12,000
900	8,000

a. Calculate the price elasticity of supply when the price increases from $900 to $1,100 using the midpoint method. Is it elastic, inelastic, or unit-elastic?

b. Suppose firms produce 1,000 more computers at any given price due to improved technology. As price increases from $900 to $1,100, is the price elasticity of supply now greater than, less than, or the same as it was in part a?

c. Suppose a longer time period under consideration means that the quantity supplied at any given price is 20% higher than the figures given in the table. As price increases from $900 to $1,100, is the price elasticity of supply now greater than, less than, or the same as it was in part a?

4. The accompanying table lists the cross-price elasticities of demand for several goods, where the percent quantity change is measured for the first good of the pair, and the percent price change is measured for the second good.

Good	Cross-price elasticities of demand
Air-conditioning units and kilowatts of electricity	−0.34
Coke and Pepsi	+0.63
High-fuel-consuming sport-utility vehicles (SUVs) and gasoline	−0.28
McDonald's burgers and Burger King burgers	+0.82
Butter and margarine	+1.54

a. Explain the sign of each of the cross-price elasticities. What does it imply about the relationship between the two goods in question?

b. Compare the absolute values of the cross-price elasticities and explain their magnitudes. For example, why is the cross-price elasticity of McDonald's burgers and Burger King burgers less than the cross-price elasticity of butter and margarine?

c. Use the information in the table to calculate how a 5% increase in the price of Pepsi affects the quantity of Coke demanded.

d. Use the information in the table to calculate how a 10% decrease in the price of gasoline affects the quantity of SUVs demanded.

5. What can you conclude about the price elasticity of demand in each of the following statements?

a. "The pizza delivery business in this town is very competitive. I'd lose half my customers if I raised the price by as little as 10%."

b. "I owned both of the two John Lennon autographed lithographs in existence. I sold one on eBay for a high price. But when I sold the second one, the price dropped by 80%."

c. "My economics professor has chosen to use the Krugman/Wells textbook for this class. I have no choice but to buy this book."

d. "I always spend a total of exactly $10 per week on coffee."

6. Take a linear demand curve like that shown in Figure 6-5, where the range of prices for which demand is elastic and inelastic is labeled. In each of the following scenarios, the supply curve shifts. Show along which portion of the demand curve (that is, the elastic or the inelastic portion) the supply curve must have shifted in order to generate the event described. In each case, show on the diagram the quantity effect and the price effect.

a. Recent attempts by the Colombian army to stop the flow of illegal drugs into the United States have actually benefited drug dealers.

b. New construction increased the number of seats in the football stadium and resulted in greater total revenue from box-office ticket sales.

c. A fall in input prices has led to higher output of Porsches. But total revenue for the Porsche Company has declined as a result.

7. The accompanying table shows the price and yearly quantity of souvenir T-shirts demanded in the town of Crystal Lake according to the average income of the tourists visiting.

Price of T-shirt	Quantity of T-shirts demanded when average tourist income is $20,000	Quantity of T-shirts demanded when average tourist income is $30,000
$4	3,000	5,000
5	2,400	4,200
6	1,600	3,000
7	800	1,800

a. Using the midpoint method, calculate the price elasticity of demand when the price of a T-shirt rises from $5 to $6 and the average tourist income is $20,000. Also calculate it when the average tourist income is $30,000.

b. Using the midpoint method, calculate the income elasticity of demand when the price of a T-shirt is $4 and the average tourist income increases from $20,000 to $30,000. Also calculate it when the price is $7.

8. A recent study determined the following elasticities for Honda Civics:

Price elasticity of demand = 2

Income elasticity of demand = 1.5

The supply of Civics is elastic. Based on this information, are the following statements true or false? Explain your reasoning.

a. A 10% increase in the price of a Civic will reduce the quantity demanded by 20%.

b. An increase in consumer income will increase the price and quantity of Civics sold.

9. In each of the following cases, do you think the price elasticity of supply is (i) perfectly elastic; (ii) perfectly inelastic; (iii) elastic, but not perfectly elastic; or (iv) inelastic, but not perfectly inelastic? Explain using a diagram.

a. An increase in demand this summer for luxury cruises leads to a huge jump in the sales price of a cabin on the *Queen Mary 2*.

b. The price of a kilowatt of electricity is the same during periods of high electricity demand as during periods of low electricity demand.

c. Fewer people want to fly during February than during any other month. The airlines cancel about 10% of their flights as ticket prices fall about 20% during this month.

d. Owners of vacation homes in Maine rent them out during the summer. Due to the soft economy this year, a 30% decline in the price of a vacation rental leads more than half of homeowners to occupy their vacation homes themselves during the summer.

10. Use an elasticity concept to explain each of the following observations.

a. During economic booms, the number of new personal care businesses, such as gyms and tanning salons, is proportionately greater than the number of other new businesses, such as grocery stores.

b. Cement is the primary building material in Mexico. After new technology makes cement cheaper to produce, the supply curve for the Mexican cement industry becomes relatively flatter.

c. Some goods that were once considered luxuries, like a telephone, are now considered virtual necessities. As a result, the demand curve for telephone services has become steeper over time.

d. Consumers in a less developed country like Guatemala spend proportionately more of their income on equipment for producing things at home, like sewing machines, than consumers in a more developed country like Canada.

11. Taiwan is a major world supplier of semiconductor chips. A recent earthquake severely damaged the production facilities of Taiwanese chip-producing companies, sharply reducing the amount of chips they could produce.

a. Assume that the total revenue of a typical non-Taiwanese chip manufacturer rises due to these events. In terms of an elasticity, what must be true for this to happen? Illustrate the change in total revenue with a diagram, indicating the price effect and the quantity effect of the Taiwan earthquake on this company's total revenue.

b. Now assume that the total revenue of a typical non-Taiwanese chip manufacturer falls due to these events. In terms of an elasticity, what must be true for this to happen? Illustrate the change in total revenue with a diagram, indicating the price effect and the quantity effect of the Taiwan earthquake on this company's total revenue.

12. Worldwide, the average coffee grower has increased the amount of acreage under cultivation over the past few years. The result has been that the average coffee plantation produces significantly more coffee than it did 10 to 20 years ago. Unfortunately for the growers, however, this has also been a period in which their total revenues have plunged. In terms of an elasticity, what must be true for these events to have occurred? Illustrate these events with a diagram, indicating the quantity effect and the price effect that gave rise to these events.

13. A 2015 article published by the *American Journal of Preventive Medicine* studied the effects of an increase in alcohol prices on the incidence of new cases of sexually transmitted diseases. In particular, the researchers studied the effects that a Maryland policy increasing alcohol taxes had on the decline in gonorrhea cases. The report concluded that an increase in the alcohol tax rate by 3% resulted in 1,600 fewer cases of gonorrhea. Assume that prior to the tax increase, the number of gonorrhea cases was 7,450. Use the midpoint method to determine the percent decrease in gonorrhea cases, and then calculate the cross-price elasticity of demand between alcohol and the incidence of gonorrhea. According to your estimate of this cross-price elasticity of demand, are alcohol and gonorrhea complements or substitutes?

14. The U.S. government is considering reducing the amount of carbon dioxide that firms are allowed to produce by issuing a limited number of tradable allowances for carbon dioxide (CO_2) emissions. In a recent report, the U.S. Congressional Budget Office (CBO) argues that "most of the cost of meeting a cap on CO_2 emissions would be borne by consumers, who would face persistently higher prices for products such as electricity and gasoline . . . poorer households would bear a larger burden relative to their income than wealthier households would." What assumption about one of the elasticities you learned about in this chapter has to be true for poorer households to be disproportionately affected?

15. According to data from the U.S. Department of Energy, sales of the fuel-efficient Toyota Prius hybrid fell from 194,108 vehicles sold in 2014 to 180,603 in 2015. Over the same period, according to data from the U.S. Energy Information Administration, the average price of regular gasoline fell from $3.36 to $2.43 per gallon. Using the midpoint method, calculate the cross-price elasticity of demand between Toyota Prii (the official plural of "Prius" is "Prii") and regular gasoline. According to your estimate of the cross-price elasticity, are the two goods complements or substitutes? Does your answer make sense?

▓▓ WORK IT OUT

16. Nile.com, the online bookseller, wants to increase its total revenue. One strategy is to offer a 10% discount on every book it sells. Nile.com knows that its customers can be divided into two distinct groups according to their likely responses to the discount. The accompanying table shows how the two groups respond to the discount.

	Group A (sales per week)	Group B (sales per week)
Volume of sales before the 10% discount	1.55 million	1.50 million
Volume of sales after the 10% discount	1.65 million	1.70 million

a. Using the midpoint method, calculate the price elasticities of demand for group A and group B.

b. Explain how the discount will affect total revenue from each group.

c. Suppose Nile.com knows which group each customer belongs to when they log on and can choose whether or not to offer the 10% discount. If Nile.com wants to increase its total revenue, should discounts be offered to group A or to group B, to neither group, or to both groups? ■

7 Taxes

THE FOUNDING TAXERS

LONG-STANDING GRIEVANCES boiled over in 1794, and outraged farmers banded together in widespread revolt. Officials responded with deadly force: shots were fired, and several people killed, before government forces finally prevailed.

George Washington's 1791 tax on distillers, imposed to raise much needed government revenue, was widely viewed as unfair and sparked a rebellion.

It wouldn't be surprising if you mistook this as an episode from the French Revolution. But, in fact, it occurred in western Pennsylvania — an event that severely shook the early American nation, and its first president, George Washington. Although the Whiskey Rebellion was eventually suppressed, it permanently reshaped American politics.

So what was the fighting about? Taxes. Facing a large debt after the War of Independence and unable to raise taxes any higher on imported goods, the Washington administration, at the suggestion of Treasury Secretary Alexander Hamilton, enacted a tax on whiskey distillers in 1791. Whiskey was a popular drink at the time, so such a tax could raise a lot of revenue. Meanwhile, a tax would encourage more "upstanding behavior" on the part of the young country's hard-drinking citizenry.

Yet the way the tax was applied was perceived as deeply unfair. Distillers could either pay a flat amount or pay by the gallon. Large distillers could afford the flat amount, but small distillers could not and paid by the gallon. As a result, the small distillers — farmers who distilled whiskey to supplement their income — paid a higher proportion of their earnings in tax than large distillers.

Moreover, in the frontier of western Pennsylvania, cash was commonly hard to acquire and whiskey was often used as payment in transactions. By discouraging small distillers from producing whiskey, the tax left the local economy with less income and fewer means to buy and sell other goods.

Although the rebellion against the whiskey tax was eventually put down, the political party that supported the tax — the Federalist Party of Alexander Hamilton — never fully recovered its popularity. The Whiskey Rebellion paved the way for the emergence of a new political party: Thomas Jefferson's Republican Party, which repealed the tax in 1800.

There are two main morals to this story. One, taxes are necessary: all governments need money to function. Without taxes, governments could not provide the services we want, from national defense to public parks. But taxes have a cost that normally exceeds the money actually paid to the government. That's because taxes distort incentives to engage in mutually beneficial transactions.

And that leads us to the second moral: making tax policy isn't easy — in fact, if you are a politician, it can be dangerous to your professional health. But the story also illustrates some crucial issues in tax policy — issues that economic models help clarify.

One principle used for guiding tax policy is efficiency: the idea that taxes should be designed to distort incentives as little as possible. But efficiency is not the only concern when designing tax rates. As the Washington administration learned from the Whiskey Rebellion, it's also important that a tax be seen as fair. Tax policy always involves striking a balance between the pursuit of efficiency and the pursuit of perceived fairness.

In this chapter, we will look at how taxes affect efficiency and fairness as well as raise revenue for the government. ●

WHAT YOU WILL LEARN

- How do taxes affect supply and demand?
- What factors determine who bears the burden of a tax?
- What are the costs and benefits of a tax, and why is the cost greater than the tax revenue generated?
- What is the difference between **progressive** and **regressive taxes**?
- Why is there a **trade-off between equity and efficiency** in the design of a tax system?
- How is the U.S. tax system structured?

An **excise tax** is a tax on sales of a good or service.

|| The Economics of Taxes: A Preliminary View

To understand the economics of taxes, it's helpful to look at a simple type of tax known as an **excise tax**—a tax charged on each unit of a good or service that is sold. Most tax revenue in the United States comes from other kinds of taxes, which we'll describe later in the chapter. But excise taxes are common. For example, there are excise taxes on gasoline, cigarettes, and foreign-made trucks, and many local governments impose excise taxes on services such as hotel room rentals. The lessons we'll learn from studying excise taxes apply to other, more complex taxes as well.

The Effect of an Excise Tax on Quantities and Prices

Suppose that the supply and demand for hotel rooms in the city of Potterville are as shown in Figure 7-1. We'll make the simplifying assumption that all hotel rooms are the same. In the absence of taxes, the equilibrium price of a room is $80 per night and the equilibrium quantity of hotel rooms rented is 10,000 per night.

Now suppose that Potterville's government imposes an excise tax of $40 per night on hotel rooms—that is, every time a room is rented for the night, the owner of the hotel must pay the city $40. For example, if a customer pays $80, $40 is collected as a tax, leaving the hotel owner with only $40. As a result, hotel owners are less willing to supply rooms at any given price.

What does this imply about the supply curve for hotel rooms in Potterville? To answer this question, we must compare the incentives of hotel owners *pre*-tax (before the tax is levied) to their incentives *post*-tax (after the tax is levied).

From Figure 7-1 we know that pre-tax, hotel owners are willing to supply 5,000 rooms per night at a price of $60 per room. But after the $40 tax per room is levied, they are willing to supply the same amount, 5,000 rooms, only if they receive $100 per room—$60 for themselves plus $40 paid to the city as tax. This

---

FIGURE 7-1 **The Supply and Demand for Hotel Rooms in Potterville**

In the absence of taxes, the equilibrium price of hotel rooms is $80 a night, and the equilibrium number of rooms rented is 10,000 per night, as shown by point *E*. The supply curve, *S,* shows the quantity supplied at any given price pre-tax. At a price of $60 a night, hotel owners are willing to supply 5,000 rooms, shown by point *B.* But post-tax, hotel owners are willing to supply the same quantity only at a price of $100: $60 for themselves plus $40 paid to the city as a tax. This is shown by point *A.*

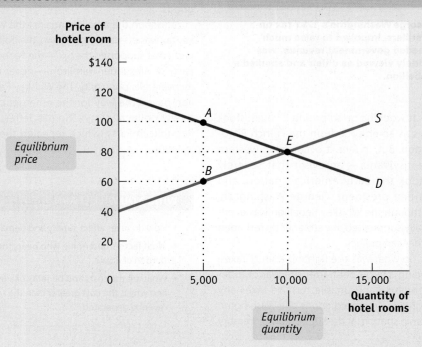

is shown by point *A*. In other words, for hotel owners to be willing to supply the same quantity post-tax as they would have pre-tax, they must receive an additional $40 per room, the amount of the tax.

This implies that the post-tax supply curve shifts up, decreasing by the amount of the tax compared to the pre-tax supply curve. At every quantity supplied, the supply price—the price that producers must receive to produce a given quantity—has increased by $40.

The upward shift of the supply curve caused by the tax is shown in Figure 7-2, where S_1 is the pre-tax supply curve and S_2 is the post-tax supply curve. As you can see, as a result of the tax the market equilibrium moves from *E*, at the equilibrium price of $80 per room and 10,000 rooms rented each night, to *A*, at a market price of $100 per room and only 5,000 rooms rented each night. *A* is, of course, on both the demand curve *D* and the new supply curve S_2.

Although $100 is the demand price of 5,000 rooms, hotel owners receive only $60 of that price because they must pay $40 of it in tax. From the point of view of hotel owners, it is as if they were on their original supply curve at point *B*.

Let's check this again. How do we know that 5,000 rooms will be supplied at a price of $100? Because the price net of tax is $60, and according to the original supply curve, 5,000 rooms will be supplied at a price of $60, as shown by point *B* in Figure 7-2.

Does this look familiar? It should. In Chapter 5 we described the effects of a quota on sales: a quota *drives a wedge* between the price paid by consumers and the price received by producers. An excise tax does the same thing. As a result of this wedge, consumers pay more and producers receive less.

In our example, consumers—people who rent hotel rooms—end up paying $100 a night, $20 more than the pre-tax price of $80. At the same time, producers—the hotel owners—receive a price net of tax of $60 per room, $20 less than the pre-tax price. In addition, the tax creates missed opportunities: 5,000 potential consumers who would have rented hotel rooms—those willing to pay $80 but not $100 per night—are discouraged from doing so. Correspondingly, 5,000 rooms that would have been made available by hotel owners if they received $80 are not

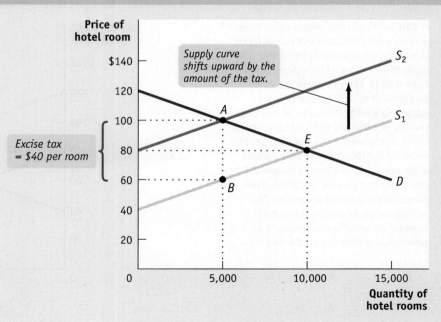

FIGURE 7-2 An Excise Tax Imposed on Hotel Owners

A $40 per room tax imposed on hotel owners shifts the supply curve from S_1 to S_2, an upward shift of $40. The equilibrium price of hotel rooms rises from $80 to $100 per night, and the equilibrium quantity of rooms rented falls from 10,000 to 5,000. Although hotel owners pay the tax, they actually bear only half the burden: the price they receive net of tax falls only $20, from $80 to $60. Guests who rent rooms bear the other half of the burden, because the price they pay rises $20, from $80 to $100.

The **incidence** of a tax is a measure of who really pays it.

offered when they receive only $60. Like a quota, this tax leads to inefficiency by distorting incentives and creating missed opportunities for mutually beneficial transactions.

It's important to recognize that as we've described it, Potterville's hotel tax is a tax on the hotel owners, not their guests—it's a tax on the producers, not the consumers. Yet the price received by producers, net of tax, falls by only $20, half the amount of the tax, and the price paid by consumers rises by $20. In effect, half the tax is being paid by consumers.

What would happen if the city levied a tax on consumers instead of producers? That is, suppose that instead of requiring hotel owners to pay $40 a night for each room they rent, the city required hotel *guests* to pay $40 for each night they stayed in a hotel. The answer is shown in Figure 7-3. If a hotel guest must pay a tax of $40 per night, then the price for a room paid by that guest must be reduced by $40 for the quantity of hotel rooms demanded post-tax to be the same as that demanded pre-tax. Thus, the demand curve shifts *downward*, from D_1 to D_2, by the amount of the tax.

At every quantity demanded, the demand price—the price that consumers must be offered to demand a given quantity—has fallen by $40. This shifts the equilibrium from E to B, where the market price of hotel rooms is $60 and 5,000 hotel rooms are rented. In effect, hotel guests pay $100 when the tax is included. So from the point of view of guests, it is as if they were on their original demand curve at point A.

If you compare Figures 7-2 and 7-3, you will immediately notice that they show equivalent outcomes. In both cases consumers pay $100, producers receive $60, and 5,000 hotel rooms are bought and sold. *In fact, it doesn't matter who officially pays the tax—the outcome is the same.*

This insight illustrates a general principle of the economics of taxation: the **incidence** of a tax—who really bears the burden of the tax—is typically not a question you can answer by asking who writes the check to the government. In this particular case, a $40 tax on hotel rooms is reflected in a $20 increase in the price paid by consumers and a $20 decrease in the price received by producers. Here, regardless of whether the tax is levied on consumers or producers, the incidence of the tax is evenly split between them.

FIGURE 7-3 An Excise Tax Imposed on Hotel Guests

A $40 per room tax imposed on hotel guests shifts the demand curve from D_1 to D_2, a downward shift of $40. The equilibrium price of hotel rooms falls from $80 to $60 per night, and the quantity of rooms rented falls from 10,000 to 5,000. Although in this case the tax is officially paid by consumers, while in Figure 7-2 the tax was paid by producers, the outcome is the same: after taxes, hotel owners receive $60 per room but guests pay $100. This illustrates a general principle: *The incidence of an excise tax doesn't depend on whether consumers or producers officially pay the tax.*

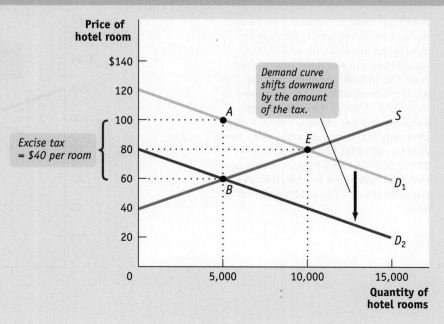

Price Elasticities and Tax Incidence

We've just learned that the incidence of an excise tax doesn't depend on who officially pays it. In the example shown in Figures 7-1 through 7-3, a tax on hotel rooms falls equally on consumers and producers, no matter who the tax is levied on.

But it's important to note that this 50–50 split between consumers and producers is a result of our assumptions in this example. In the real world, the incidence of an excise tax usually falls unevenly between consumers and producers, as one group bears more of the burden than the other.

What determines how the burden of an excise tax is allocated between consumers and producers? The answer is that it depends on the shapes of the supply and the demand curves. *More specifically, the incidence of an excise tax depends on the price elasticity of supply and the price elasticity of demand.* We first look at a case in which consumers pay most of an excise tax, then at a case in which producers pay most of the tax.

When an Excise Tax Is Paid Mainly by Consumers Figure 7-4 shows an excise tax that falls mainly on consumers: an excise tax on gasoline, which we set at $1 per gallon. (There really is a federal excise tax on gasoline, though it is actually only about $0.18 per gallon in the United States. In addition, states impose excise taxes between $0.12 and $0.50 per gallon.) According to Figure 7-4, in the absence of the tax, gasoline would sell for $2 per gallon.

Two key assumptions are reflected in the shapes of the supply and demand curves in Figure 7-4.

1. The price elasticity of demand for gasoline is assumed to be very low, so the demand curve is relatively steep. Recall that a low price elasticity of demand means that the quantity demanded changes little in response to a change in price—a feature of a steep demand curve.
2. The price elasticity of supply of gasoline is assumed to be very high, so the supply curve is relatively flat. A high price elasticity of supply means that the quantity supplied changes a lot in response to a change in price—a feature of a relatively flat supply curve.

We have learned that an excise tax drives a wedge, equal to the size of the tax, between the price paid by consumers and the price received by producers. This

FIGURE 7-4 An Excise Tax Paid Mainly by Consumers

The relatively steep demand curve here reflects a low price elasticity of demand for gasoline. The relatively flat supply curve reflects a high price of elasticity of supply. The pre-tax price per gallon of gasoline is $2.00. When a tax of $1.00 per gallon is imposed, the price paid by consumers rises by $0.95 to $2.95. This reflects the fact that most of the burden of the tax falls on consumers. Only a small portion of the tax is borne by producers: the price they receive falls by only $0.05 to $1.95.

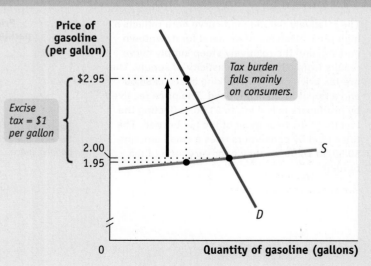

wedge drives the price paid by consumers up and the price received by producers down. But as we can see from Figure 7-4, in this case those two effects are very unequal in size. The price received by producers falls only slightly, from $2.00 to $1.95, but the price paid by consumers rises by a lot, from $2.00 to $2.95. In this case consumers bear the greater share of the tax burden.

This example illustrates another general principle of taxation: *When the price elasticity of demand is low and the price elasticity of supply is high, the burden of an excise tax falls mainly on consumers.* Why? A low price elasticity of demand means that consumers have few substitutes, and therefore little alternative to buying higher-priced gasoline. In contrast, a high price elasticity of supply results from the fact that producers have many production substitutes for their gasoline (that is, other uses for the crude oil from which gasoline is refined).

This gives producers much greater flexibility in refusing to accept lower prices for their gasoline. And, not surprisingly, the party with the least flexibility—in this case, consumers—gets stuck paying most of the tax. This is a good description of how the burden of the most significant excise taxes actually collected in the United States today, such as those on cigarettes and alcoholic beverages, is allocated between consumers and producers.

When an Excise Tax Is Paid Mainly by Producers Figure 7-5 shows an example of an excise tax paid mainly by producers, a $5.00 per day tax on downtown parking in a small city. In the absence of the tax, the market equilibrium price of parking is $6.00 per day.

We've assumed in this case that the price elasticity of supply is very low because the lots used for parking have very few alternative uses. This makes the supply curve for parking spaces relatively steep. The price elasticity of demand, however, is assumed to be high: substitutes are readily available as consumers can easily switch from the downtown spaces to other parking spaces a few minutes' walk from downtown, spaces that are not subject to the tax. This makes the demand curve relatively flat.

The tax drives a wedge between the price paid by consumers and the price received by producers. In this example, however, the tax causes the price paid by consumers to rise only slightly, from $6.00 to $6.50, but causes the price received by producers to fall a lot, from $6.00 to $1.50. In the end, consumers bear only $0.50 of the $5.00 tax burden, with producers bearing the remaining $4.50.

FIGURE 7-5 An Excise Tax Paid Mainly by Producers

The relatively flat demand curve here reflects a high price elasticity of demand for downtown parking, and the relatively steep supply curve results from a low price elasticity of supply. The pre-tax price of a daily parking space is $6.00 and a tax of $5.00 is imposed. The price received by producers falls a lot, to $1.50, reflecting the fact that they bear most of the tax burden. The price paid by consumers rises a small amount, $0.50, to $6.50, so they bear very little of the burden.

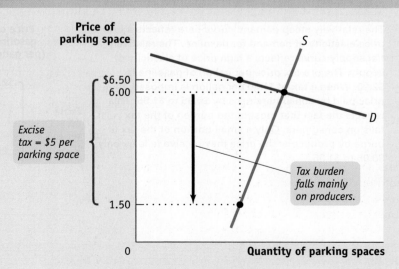

Again, this example illustrates a general principle: *When the price elasticity of demand is high and the price elasticity of supply is low, the burden of an excise tax falls mainly on producers.* A real-world example is a tax on purchases of existing houses. Before the collapse of the housing market that began in 2007, house prices in many American cities and towns rose significantly, as well-off outsiders moved into desirable locations and purchased homes from the less-well-off original occupants.

Some of these towns have imposed taxes on house sales intended to extract money from the new arrivals. But this ignores the fact that the price elasticity of demand for houses in a particular town is often high, because potential buyers can choose to move to other towns. Furthermore, the price elasticity of supply is often low because most sellers must sell their houses due to job transfers or to provide funds for their retirement. So taxes on home purchases are actually paid mainly by the less well-off sellers—not, as town officials imagine, by wealthy buyers.

Putting It All Together   We've just seen that when the price elasticity of supply is high and the price elasticity of demand is low, an excise tax falls mainly on consumers. And when the price elasticity of supply is low and the price elasticity of demand is high, an excise tax falls mainly on producers. This leads us to the general rule: *When the price elasticity of demand is higher than the price elasticity of supply, an excise tax falls mainly on producers. When the price elasticity of supply is higher than the price elasticity of demand, an excise tax falls mainly on consumers.*

So elasticity—not who officially pays the tax—determines the incidence of an excise tax.

ECONOMICS >> *in Action*
Who Pays the FICA?

Anyone who works for an employer receives a paycheck that itemizes not only the wages paid but also the money deducted from the paycheck for various taxes. For most people, one of the big deductions is *FICA*, also known as the payroll tax. FICA, which stands for the Federal Insurance Contributions Act, pays for the Social Security and Medicare systems, federal social insurance programs that provide income and medical care to retired and disabled Americans.

In 2019, most American workers paid 7.65% of their earnings in FICA. But this is literally only the half of it: each employer is required to pay an amount equal to the contributions of its employees.

How should we think about FICA? Is it really shared equally by workers and employers? We can use our previous analysis to answer that question because FICA is like an excise tax—a tax on the sale and purchase of labor. Half of it is a tax levied on the sellers—that is, workers. The other half is a tax levied on the buyers—that is, employers.

Contrary to widely held beliefs, for 70% of Americans it's the FICA, not the income tax, that takes the biggest bite from their paychecks.

But we already know that the incidence of a tax does not really depend on who actually makes out the check. Almost all economists agree that FICA is a tax actually paid by workers, not by their employers. The reason for this conclusion lies in a comparison of the price elasticities of the supply of labor by households and the demand for labor by firms.

Evidence indicates that the price elasticity of demand for labor is quite high, at least 3. That is, an increase in average wages of 1% would lead to at least a 3% decline in the number of hours of work demanded by employers. Labor economists believe, however, that the price elasticity of supply of labor is very low. The reason is that although a fall in the wage rate reduces the incentive to work more hours, it also makes people poorer and less able to afford leisure time.

The strength of this second effect is shown in the data: the number of hours people are willing to work falls very little—if at all—when the wage per hour goes down.

Our general rule of tax incidence says that when the price elasticity of demand is much higher than the price elasticity of supply, the burden of an excise tax falls mainly on the suppliers. So the FICA falls mainly on the suppliers of labor, that is, workers—even though on paper half the tax is paid by employers. In other words, the FICA is largely borne by workers in the form of lower wages, rather than by employers in the form of lower profits.

This conclusion tells us something important about the American tax system: the FICA, rather than the much-maligned income tax, is the main tax burden on most families. For most workers, FICA is 15.3% of all wages and salaries up to $132,900 per year (note that 7.65% + 7.65% = 15.3%). That is, the great majority of workers in the United States pay 15.3% of their wages in FICA. Only a minority of American families pay more than 15% of their income in income tax. In fact, according to estimates by the Congressional Budget Office, for nearly 70% of families FICA is Uncle Sam's main bite out of their income.

>> Quick Review

- An **excise tax** drives a wedge between the price paid by consumers and that received by producers, leading to a fall in the quantity transacted. It creates inefficiency by distorting incentives and creating missed opportunities.

- The **incidence** of an excise tax doesn't depend on who the tax is officially levied on. Rather, it depends on the price elasticities of demand and of supply.

- The higher the price elasticity of supply and the lower the price elasticity of demand, the heavier the burden of an excise tax on consumers. The lower the price elasticity of supply and the higher the price elasticity of demand, the heavier the burden on producers.

>> Check Your Understanding 7-1

Solutions appear at back of book.

1. Consider the market for butter, shown in the accompanying figure. The government imposes an excise tax of $0.30 per pound of butter. What is the price paid by consumers post-tax? What is the price received by producers post-tax? What is the quantity of butter transacted? How is the incidence of the tax allocated between consumers and producers? Show this on the figure.

2. The demand for economics textbooks is very inelastic, but the supply is somewhat elastic. What does this imply about the incidence of an excise tax? Illustrate with a diagram.

3. True or false? When a substitute for a good is readily available to consumers, but it is difficult for producers to adjust the quantity of the good produced, then the burden of a tax on the good falls more heavily on producers. Explain your answer.

4. The supply of bottled spring water is very inelastic, but the demand for it is somewhat elastic. What does this imply about the incidence of a tax? Illustrate with a diagram.

5. True or false? Other things equal, consumers would prefer to face a less elastic supply curve for a good or service when an excise tax is imposed. Explain your answer.

"What taxes would you like to see imposed on other people?"

‖ The Benefits and Costs of Taxation

When a government is considering whether to impose a tax or how to design a tax system, it has to weigh the benefits of a tax against its costs. We don't usually think of a tax as something that provides benefits, but governments need money to provide things people want, such as national defense and health care for those unable to afford it. The benefit of a tax is the revenue it raises for the government to pay for these services. Unfortunately, this benefit comes at a cost—a cost that is normally greater than the amount consumers and producers pay. Let's look first at what determines how much money a tax raises, then at the costs a tax imposes.

The Revenue from an Excise Tax

How much revenue does the government collect from an excise tax? In our hotel tax example, the revenue is equal to the area of the shaded rectangle in Figure 7-6.

FIGURE 7-6 The Revenue from an Excise Tax

The revenue from a $40 excise tax on hotel rooms is $200,000, equal to the tax rate, $40 — the size of the wedge that the tax drives between the supply price and the demand price — multiplied by the number of rooms rented, 5,000. This is equal to the area of the shaded rectangle.

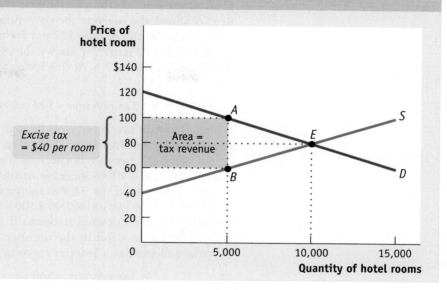

To see why this area represents the revenue collected by a $40 tax on hotel rooms, notice that the height of the rectangle is $40, equal to the tax per room. It is also, as we've seen, the size of the wedge that the tax drives between the supply price (the price received by producers) and the demand price (the price paid by consumers). Meanwhile, the width of the rectangle is 5,000 rooms, equal to the equilibrium quantity of rooms given the $40 tax. With that information, we can make the following calculations.

The tax revenue collected is:

$$\text{Tax revenue} = \$40 \text{ per room} \times 5{,}000 \text{ rooms} = \$200{,}000$$

The area of the shaded rectangle is:

$$\text{Area} = \text{Height} \times \text{Width} = \$40 \text{ per room} \times 5{,}000 \text{ rooms} = \$200{,}000$$

or

$$\text{Tax revenue} = \text{Area of shaded rectangle}$$

This is a general principle: *The revenue collected by an excise tax is equal to the area of the rectangle whose height is the tax wedge between the supply and demand curves and whose width is the quantity transacted under the tax.*

Tax Rates and Revenue

In Figure 7-6, $40 per room is the *tax rate* on hotel rooms. A **tax rate** is the amount of tax levied per unit of the taxed item. Sometimes tax rates are defined in terms of dollar amounts per unit of a good or service; for example, $2.46 per pack of cigarettes sold. In other cases, they are defined as a percentage of the price; for example, the payroll tax is 15.3% of a worker's earnings up to $128,400 in 2018.

There's obviously a relationship between tax rates and revenue. That relationship is not, however, one-for-one. In general, doubling the excise tax rate on a good or service won't double the amount of revenue collected, because the tax increase will reduce the quantity of the good or service transacted. And the relationship between the level of the tax and the amount of revenue collected may not even be positive: in some cases raising the tax rate actually *reduces* the amount of revenue the government collects.

A **tax rate** is the amount of tax people are required to pay per unit of whatever is being taxed.

We can illustrate these points using our hotel room example. Figure 7-6 showed the revenue the government collects from a \$40 tax on hotel rooms. Figure 7-7 shows the revenue the government would collect from two alternative tax rates—a lower tax of only \$20 per room and a higher tax of \$60 per room.

Panel (a) of Figure 7-7 shows the case of a \$20 tax, equal to half the tax rate illustrated in Figure 7-6. At this lower tax rate, 7,500 rooms are rented, generating tax revenue of:

$$\text{Tax revenue} = \$20 \text{ per room} \times 7,500 \text{ rooms} = \$150,000$$

Recall that the tax revenue collected from a \$40 tax rate is \$200,000. So the revenue collected from a \$20 tax rate, \$150,000, is only 75% of the amount collected when the tax rate is twice as high (\$150,000/\$200,000 × 100 = 75%). To put it another way, a 100% increase in the tax rate from \$20 to \$40 per room leads to only a one-third, or 33.3%, increase in revenue, from \$150,000 to \$200,000 ((\$200,000 − \$150,000)/\$150,000 × 100 = 33.3%).

Panel (b) depicts what happens if the tax rate is raised from \$40 to \$60 per room, leading to a fall in the number of rooms rented from 5,000 to 2,500. The revenue collected at a \$60 per room tax rate is:

$$\text{Tax revenue} = \$60 \text{ per room} \times 2,500 \text{ rooms} = \$150,000$$

This is also *less* than the revenue collected by a \$40 per room tax. So raising the tax rate from \$40 to \$60 actually reduces revenue. More precisely, in this case raising the tax rate by 50% ((\$60 − \$40)/\$40 × 100 = 50%) lowers the tax revenue by 25% ((\$150,000 − \$200,000)/\$200,000 × 100 = −25%). Why did this happen? Because the fall in tax revenue caused by the reduction in the number of rooms rented more than offset the increase in the tax revenue caused by the rise in the

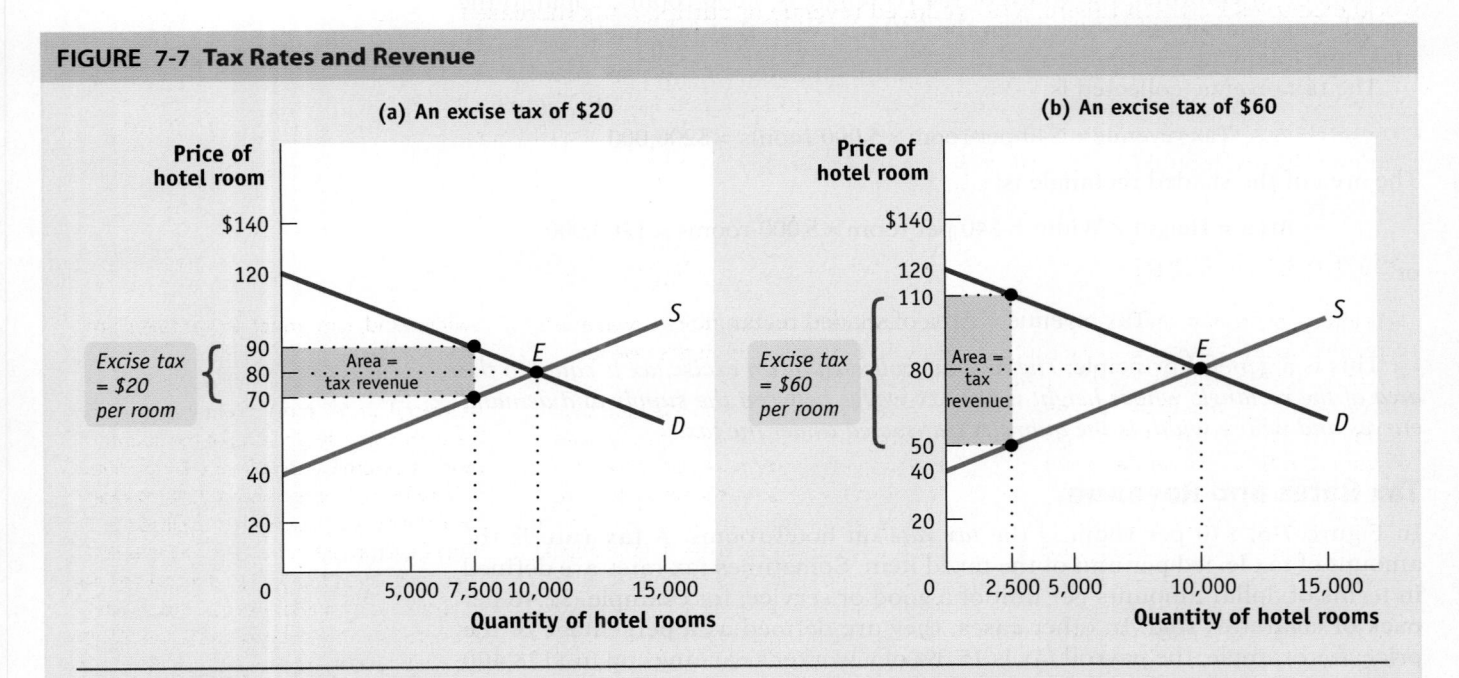

FIGURE 7-7 Tax Rates and Revenue

In general, doubling the excise tax rate on a good or service won't double the amount of revenue collected, because the tax increase will reduce the quantity of the good or service bought and sold. And the relationship between the level of the tax and the amount of revenue collected may not even be positive. Panel (a) shows the revenue raised by a tax of \$20 per room, only half the tax rate in Figure 7-6. The tax revenue raised, equal to the area of the shaded rectangle, is \$150,000. That is 75% of \$200,000, the revenue raised by a \$40 tax rate. Panel (b) shows that the revenue raised by a \$60 tax is also \$150,000. So raising the tax rate from \$40 to \$60 actually reduces tax revenue.

tax rate. In other words, setting a tax rate so high that it deters a significant number of transactions will likely lead to a fall in tax revenue.

One way to think about the revenue effect of increasing an excise tax is that the tax increase affects tax revenue in two ways. On one side, the tax increase means that the government raises more revenue for each unit of the good sold, which other things equal would lead to a rise in tax revenue. On the other side, the tax increase reduces the quantity of sales, which other things equal would lead to a fall in tax revenue. The end result depends both on the price elasticities of supply and demand and on the initial level of the tax.

If the price elasticities of both supply and demand are low, the tax increase won't reduce the quantity of the good sold very much, so tax revenue will definitely rise. If the price elasticities are high, the result is less certain; if they are high enough, the tax reduces the quantity sold so much that tax revenue falls. Also, if the initial tax rate is low, the government doesn't lose much revenue from the decline in the quantity of the good sold, so the tax increase will definitely increase tax revenue. If the initial tax rate is high, the result is again less certain. Tax revenue is likely to fall or rise very little from a tax increase only in cases in which the price elasticities are high and there is already a high tax rate.

The possibility that a higher tax rate can reduce tax revenue, and the corresponding possibility that cutting taxes can increase tax revenue, is a basic principle of taxation that policy makers take into account when setting tax rates. That is, when considering a tax created for the purpose of raising revenue (in contrast to taxes created to discourage undesirable behavior, known as *sin taxes*), a well-informed policy maker won't impose a tax rate so high that cutting the tax would increase revenue.

In the real world, however, policy makers aren't always well informed, but they usually aren't complete fools either. That's why it's very hard to find real-world examples in which raising a tax reduced revenue or cutting a tax increased revenue. Nonetheless, the theoretical possibility that a tax reduction increases tax revenue has played an important role in the folklore of American politics. As explained in For Inquiring Minds, an economist who sketched out the figure of a revenue-increasing income tax reduction had a significant impact on the economic policies adopted in the United States in the 1980s.

FOR INQUIRING MINDS French Tax Rates and *L'Arc Laffer*

One afternoon in 1974, the American economist Arthur Laffer drew on a napkin a diagram that came to be known as the *Laffer curve*. According to this diagram, raising tax rates initially increases tax revenue, but beyond a certain level a continued rise in tax rates causes tax revenues to fall as people forgo economic activity. Correspondingly, a reduction in tax rates from that threshold results in an increase in economic activity as more people are willing to undertake economic transactions.

Although not a new idea, Laffer's diagram captured the American political debate at the time. In 1981, newly elected President Ronald Reagan enacted tax cuts with the promise that they would pay for themselves—that is, that the tax cuts

would increase economic activity so much that the federal government's revenue would not fall.

Very few economists now believe that Reagan's tax cuts actually increased government revenue because, on the whole, American tax rates were simply not high enough to provide a significant deterrent to economic activity. Yet there is a theoretical case that the Laffer curve does exist at high tax rate levels. And the case of the French tax hike appears to present a real-world illustration.

A 1997 change to the French tax law significantly raised taxes on wealthy French citizens. Moreover, unlike in the United States, it is relatively easy for a French person to move to a neighboring country, such as Belgium or

Switzerland, with much lower taxes on the wealthy.

The matter exploded in a public fracas between France's most celebrated president, Francois Hollande, and one of the country's most celebrated actors, Gerard Depardieu, when Hollande announced a 75% tax rate on incomes over $1.2 million to close a huge government deficit. It is estimated that several hundred billion dollars in assets left France, along with French citizens who chose to leave the country to escape higher tax rates. Among them was Depardieu, who renounced his French citizenship and decamped for Belgium. In addition, bankruptcies of businesses accelerated and firms slashed investment. Then, in 2015, the policy was abandoned and the tax rate on high incomes returned to its previous level.

The Costs of Taxation

What is the cost of a tax? Is it the money taxpayers pay to the government? In other words, is the cost of a tax the tax revenue collected? The answer to this question is actually more complex. Suppose the government uses the tax revenue to provide services that taxpayers want. Or that it just hands the tax revenue right back to taxpayers. Could we say in those cases that the tax didn't actually cost anything?

No, we could not—because a tax, like a quota, prevents mutually beneficial transactions from occurring. Consider Figure 7-6 once more. Here, with a $40 tax on hotel rooms, guests pay $100 per room but hotel owners receive only $60 per room. Because of the wedge created by the tax, we know that some transactions don't occur that would have occurred without the tax.

For example, we know from the supply and demand curves that there are some potential guests who would be willing to pay up to $90 per night and some hotel owners who would be willing to supply rooms if they received at least $70 per night. If these two sets of people were allowed to trade with each other without the tax, they would engage in mutually beneficial transactions—hotel rooms would be rented.

But such deals would be illegal, because the $40 tax would not be paid. In our example, 5,000 potential hotel room rentals that would have occurred in the absence of the tax, to the mutual benefit of guests and hotel owners, do not take place because of the tax. Specifically, 5,000 (the number of lost rentals) is equal to 10,000 (the equilibrium quantity at an untaxed rate of $80) minus 5,000 (the rooms that are rented with the tax).

So an excise tax imposes costs over and above the tax revenue collected in the form of inefficiency, which occurs because the tax discourages mutually beneficial transactions. As we learned in Chapter 5, the cost to society of this kind of inefficiency—the value of the forgone mutually beneficial transactions—is called the *deadweight loss*. While all real-world taxes impose some deadweight loss, a badly designed tax imposes a larger deadweight loss than a well-designed one.

To measure the deadweight loss from a tax, we turn to the concepts of producer and consumer surplus. Figure 7-8 shows the effects of an excise tax

FIGURE 7-8 A Tax Reduces Consumer and Producer Surplus

Before the tax, the equilibrium price and quantity are P_E and Q_E, respectively. After an excise tax of T per unit is imposed, the price to consumers rises to P_C and consumer surplus falls by the sum of the dark blue rectangle, labeled A, and the light blue triangle, labeled B. The tax also causes the price to producers to fall to P_P; producer surplus falls by the sum of the red rectangle, labeled C, and the pink triangle, labeled F. The government receives revenue from the tax equal to $Q_T \times T$, which is given by the sum of the areas A and C. Areas B and F represent the losses to consumer and producer surplus that are not collected by the government as revenue. They are the deadweight loss to society of the tax.

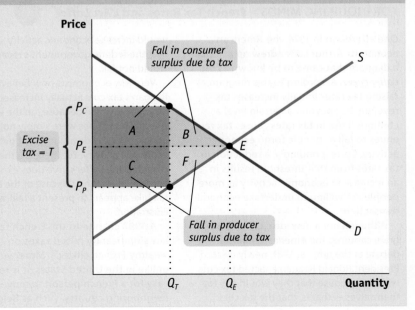

on consumer and producer surplus. In the absence of the tax, the equilibrium is at E and the equilibrium price and quantity are P_E and Q_E, respectively. An excise tax drives a wedge equal to the amount of the tax between the price received by producers and the price paid by consumers, reducing the quantity sold. In this case, where the tax is T dollars per unit, the quantity sold falls to Q_T. The price paid by consumers rises to P_C, the demand price of the reduced quantity, Q_T, and the price received by producers falls to P_P, the supply price of that quantity. The difference between these prices, $P_C - P_P$, is equal to the excise tax, T.

Using the concepts of producer and consumer surplus, we can show exactly how much surplus producers and consumers lose as a result of the tax. From Figure 5-4 we learned that a fall in the price of a good generates a gain in consumer surplus that is equal to the sum of the areas of a rectangle and a triangle. Similarly, a price increase causes a loss to consumers that is represented by the sum of the areas of a rectangle and a triangle. So it's not surprising that in the case of an excise tax, the rise in the price paid by consumers causes a loss equal to the sum of the areas of a rectangle and a triangle: the dark blue rectangle labeled A and the area of the light blue triangle labeled B in Figure 7-8.

Meanwhile, the fall in the price received by producers leads to a fall in producer surplus. This, too, is equal to the sum of the areas of a rectangle and a triangle. The loss in producer surplus is the sum of the areas of the red rectangle labeled C and the pink triangle labeled F in Figure 7-8.

Of course, although consumers and producers are hurt by the tax, the government gains revenue. The revenue the government collects is equal to the tax per unit sold, T, multiplied by the quantity sold, Q_T. This revenue is equal to the area of a rectangle Q_T wide and T high. And we already have that rectangle in the figure: it is the sum of rectangles A and C. So the government gains part of what consumers and producers lose from an excise tax.

But it is important to note that a portion of the loss to producers and consumers from the tax is not offset by a gain to the government—specifically, the two triangles B and F. The deadweight loss caused by the tax is equal to the combined area of these two triangles. It represents the total surplus lost to society because of the tax—that is, the amount of surplus that would have been generated by transactions that now do not take place because of the tax.

Figure 7-9 replicates Figure 7-8, but without the rectangles A (the surplus shifted from consumers to the government) and C (the surplus shifted from producers to the government) and shows only the deadweight loss, here drawn as a triangle shaded yellow. The base of that triangle is equal to the tax wedge, T; the height of the triangle is equal to the reduction in the quantity transacted due to the tax, $Q_E - Q_T$. Clearly, the larger the tax wedge and the larger the reduction in the quantity transacted, the greater the inefficiency from the tax.

But also note an important, contrasting point: if the excise tax somehow *didn't* reduce the quantity bought and sold in this market—if Q_T remained equal to Q_E after the tax was levied—the yellow triangle would disappear and the deadweight loss from the tax would be zero. This observation is simply the flip-side of the principle found earlier in the chapter: a tax causes inefficiency because it discourages mutually beneficial transactions between buyers and sellers. So if a tax does not discourage transactions, which would be true if either supply or demand were perfectly inelastic, it causes no deadweight loss. In this case, the tax simply shifts surplus straight from consumers and producers to the government.

Using a triangle to measure deadweight loss is a technique used in many economic applications. For example, triangles are used to measure the deadweight

FIGURE 7-9 The Deadweight Loss of a Tax

A tax leads to a deadweight loss because it creates inefficiency: some mutually beneficial transactions never take place because of the tax — namely, the transactions $Q_E - Q_T$. The yellow area here represents the value of the deadweight loss: it is the total surplus that would have been gained from the $Q_E - Q_T$s transactions. If the tax had not discouraged transactions — had the number of transactions remained at Q_E because of either perfectly inelastic supply or perfectly inelastic demand — no deadweight loss would have been incurred.

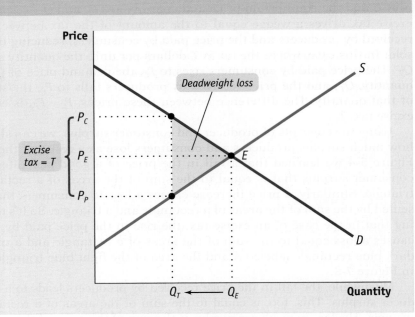

loss produced by types of taxes other than excise taxes. They are also used to measure the deadweight loss produced by monopoly, another kind of market distortion. And deadweight-loss triangles are often used to evaluate the benefits and costs of public policies besides taxation — such as whether to impose stricter safety standards on a product.

In considering the total amount of inefficiency caused by a tax, we must also take into account something not shown in Figure 7-9: the resources actually used by the government to collect the tax, and by taxpayers to pay it, over and above the amount of the tax. These lost resources are called the **administrative costs** of the tax. The most familiar administrative cost of the U.S. tax system is the time individuals spend filling out their income tax forms or the money they pay for tax return preparation services like those provided by companies like H&R Block. (The latter is considered an inefficiency from the point of view of society because resources spent on return preparation could be used for other, non-tax-related purposes.)

Society ultimately pays the administrative costs of taxes.

Included in the administrative costs that taxpayers incur are resources used to evade the tax, both legally and illegally. The costs of operating the Internal Revenue Service, the arm of the federal government tasked with collecting the federal income tax, are actually quite small in comparison to the administrative costs paid by taxpayers.

So we get:

The **administrative costs** of a tax are the resources used for its collection, for the method of payment, and for any attempts to evade the tax.

Total inefficiency of tax = Deadweight loss + Administrative costs

The general rule for economic policy is that, other things equal, a tax system should be designed to minimize the total inefficiency it imposes on society. In practice, other considerations also apply, but this principle nonetheless gives valuable guidance. Administrative costs are usually well known, more or less determined by the current technology of collecting taxes (for example, filing paper returns versus filing electronically).

But how can we predict the size of the deadweight loss associated with a given tax? Not surprisingly, as in our analysis of the incidence of a tax, the price elasticities of supply and demand play crucial roles in making such a prediction.

Elasticities and the Deadweight Loss of a Tax

We know that the deadweight loss from an excise tax arises because it prevents some mutually beneficial transactions from occurring. In particular, the producer and consumer surplus that is forgone because of these missing transactions is equal to the size of the deadweight loss itself. This means that the larger the number of transactions that are prevented by the tax, the larger the deadweight loss.

This fact gives us an important clue in understanding the relationship between elasticity and the size of the deadweight loss from a tax. Recall that when demand or supply is elastic, the quantity demanded or the quantity supplied is relatively responsive to changes in the price. So a tax imposed on a good for which either demand or supply, or both, is elastic will cause a relatively large decrease in the quantity transacted and a relatively large deadweight loss. In addition, the greater the elasticity of either demand or supply, the greater the deadweight loss from a tax. Correspondingly, a tax imposed when demand or supply, or both, is inelastic will cause a relatively small decrease in the quantity transacted and a relatively small deadweight loss.

The four panels of Figure 7-10 illustrate the positive relationship between a good's price elasticity of either demand or supply and the deadweight loss from taxing that good. Each panel represents the same amount of tax imposed but on a different good; the size of the deadweight loss is given by the area of the shaded triangle. In panel (a), the deadweight-loss triangle is large because demand for this good is relatively elastic—a large number of transactions fail to occur because of the tax. In panel (b), the same supply curve is drawn as in panel (a), but demand for this good is relatively inelastic; as a result, the triangle is small because only a small number of transactions are forgone. Likewise, panels (c) and (d) contain the same demand curve but different supply curves. In panel (c), an elastic supply curve gives rise to a large deadweight-loss triangle, but in panel (d) an inelastic supply curve gives rise to a small deadweight-loss triangle.

The implication of this result is clear: if you want to minimize the efficiency costs of taxation, you should choose to tax only those goods for which demand or supply, or both, is relatively inelastic. For such goods, a tax has little effect on behavior because behavior is relatively unresponsive to changes in the price. In the extreme case in which demand is perfectly inelastic (a vertical demand curve), the quantity demanded is unchanged by the imposition of the tax. As a result, the tax imposes no deadweight loss. Similarly, if supply is perfectly inelastic (a vertical supply curve), the quantity supplied is unchanged by the tax and there is also no deadweight loss.

So if the goal in choosing whom to tax is to minimize deadweight loss, then taxes should be imposed on goods and services that have the most inelastic response—that is, goods and services for which consumers or producers will change their behavior the least in response to the tax. (Unless they have a tendency to revolt, of course.) And this lesson carries a flip-side: using a tax to purposely decrease the amount of a harmful activity, such as underage drinking, will have the most impact when that activity is elastically demanded or supplied.

FIGURE 7-10 Deadweight Loss and Elasticities

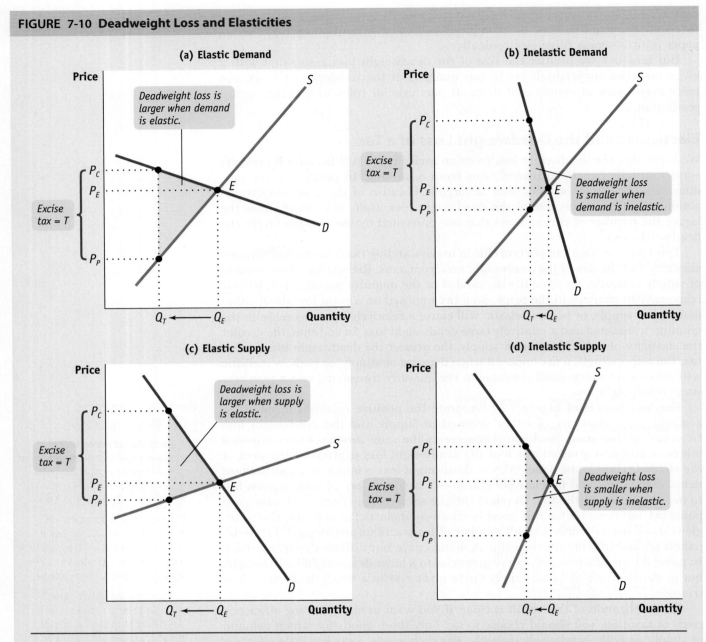

Demand is elastic in panel (a) and inelastic in panel (b), but the supply curves are the same. Supply is elastic in panel (c) and inelastic in panel (d), but the demand curves are the same. The deadweight losses are larger in panels (a) and (c) than in panels (b) and (d) because the greater the price elasticity of demand or supply, the greater the tax-induced fall in the quantity transacted. In contrast, the lower the price elasticity of demand or supply, the smaller the tax-induced fall in the quantity transacted and the smaller the deadweight loss.

ECONOMICS >> *in Action*
Taxing Tobacco

One of the most prominent excise taxes in the United States is the tax on cigarettes. The federal government imposes a tax of $1.01 a pack; state governments impose taxes that range from $0.17 cents per pack in Missouri to $4.50 per pack in Washington D.C., and many cities impose further taxes.

In general, tax rates on cigarettes have increased over time, because more governments have seen them not just as a source of revenue but as a way to discourage smoking. But the rise in cigarette taxes has not been gradual. Usually, once a state government decides to raise cigarette taxes, it raises them a lot—which provides economists with useful data on what happens when there is a big tax increase.

Table 7-1 shows the results of big increases in cigarette taxes. In each case, sales fell, just as our analysis predicts. Although it's theoretically possible for tax revenue to fall after such a large tax increase, in reality tax revenue rose in each case. That's because cigarettes have a low price elasticity of demand.

TABLE 7-1 Results of Increases in Cigarette Taxes

State	Increase in tax (per pack)	New state tax (per pack)	Change in quantity transacted	Change in tax revenue
Louisiana	$0.50	$0.86	−23.9%	81.0%
Kansas	0.50	1.29	−6.4	56.3
Nevada	1.00	1.80	−33.1	51.6
Pennsylvania	1.00	2.60	−18.1	31.3
West Virginia	0.65	1.20	−15.8	83.7

Data from: Orzechowski & Walker, Tax Burden on Tobacco. U.S. Alcohol and Tobacco Tax and Trade Bureau.

>> Check Your Understanding 7-2

Solutions appear at back of book.

1. The accompanying table shows five consumers' willingness to pay for one can of diet soda each, as well as five producers' costs of selling one can of diet soda each. Each consumer buys at most one can of soda; each producer sells at most one can of soda. The government asks your advice about the effects of an excise tax of $0.40 per can of diet soda. Assume that there are no administrative costs from the tax.

Consumer	Willingness to pay	Producer	Cost
Ana	$0.70	Zachary	$0.10
Brianna	0.60	Yves	0.20
Chizuko	0.50	Xavier	0.30
Dylan	0.40	William	0.40
Ella	0.30	Vern	0.50

   a. Without the excise tax, what is the equilibrium price and the equilibrium quantity of soda transacted?
   b. The excise tax raises the price paid by consumers post-tax to $0.60 and lowers the price received by producers post-tax to $0.20. With the excise tax, what is the quantity of soda transacted?
   c. Without the excise tax, how much individual consumer surplus does each of the consumers gain? How much with the tax? How much total consumer surplus is lost as a result of the tax?
   d. Without the excise tax, how much individual producer surplus does each of the producers gain? How much with the tax? How much total producer surplus is lost as a result of the tax?
   e. How much government revenue does the excise tax create?
   f. What is the deadweight loss from the imposition of this excise tax?
2. In each of the following cases, focus on the price elasticity of demand and use a diagram to illustrate the likely size—small or large—of the deadweight loss resulting from a tax. Explain your reasoning.
   a. Gasoline
   b. Milk chocolate bars

>> Quick Review

• An excise tax generates tax revenue equal to the **tax rate** times the number of units of the good or service transacted but reduces consumer and producer surplus.

• The government tax revenue collected is less than the loss in total surplus because the tax creates inefficiency by discouraging some mutually beneficial transactions.

• The difference between the tax revenue from an excise tax and the reduction in total surplus is the deadweight loss from the tax. The total amount of inefficiency resulting from a tax is equal to the deadweight loss plus the **administrative costs** of the tax.

• The larger the number of transactions prevented by a tax, the larger the deadweight loss. As a result, taxes on goods with a greater price elasticity of supply or demand, or both, generate higher deadweight losses. There is no deadweight loss when the number of transactions is unchanged by the tax. (That is, when supply or demand is perfectly inelastic.)

According to the **benefits principle** of tax fairness, those who benefit from public spending should bear the burden of the tax that pays for that spending.

According to the **ability-to-pay principle** of tax fairness, those with greater ability to pay a tax should pay more tax.

A **lump-sum tax** is the same for everyone, regardless of any actions people take.

‖ Tax Fairness and Tax Efficiency

We've just seen how economic analysis can be used to determine the inefficiency caused by a tax. It's clear that, other things equal, policy makers should choose a tax that creates less inefficiency over a tax that creates more. But that guideline still leaves policy makers with wide discretion in choosing what to tax and, consequently, who bears the burden of the tax. How should they exercise this discretion?

One answer is that policy makers should make the tax system fair. But what exactly does fairness mean? Moreover, however you define fairness, how should policy makers balance considerations of fairness versus considerations of efficiency?

Two Principles of Tax Fairness

Fairness, like beauty, is often in the eyes of the beholder. When it comes to taxes, however, most debates about fairness rely on one of two principles of tax fairness: the *benefits principle* and the *ability-to-pay principle*.

The Benefits Principle According to the **benefits principle** of tax fairness, those who benefit from public spending should bear the burden of the tax that pays for that spending. For example, those who benefit from a road should pay for that road's upkeep, those who fly on airplanes should pay for air traffic control, and so on. The benefits principle is the basis for some parts of the U.S. tax system. For example, revenue from the federal tax on gasoline is specifically reserved for the maintenance and improvement of federal roads, including the Interstate Highway System. In this way motorists who benefit from the highway system also pay for it.

The benefits principle is attractive from an economic point of view because it matches well with one of the major justifications for public spending—the theory of *public goods,* which explains why government action is sometimes needed to provide people with goods that markets alone would not provide, goods like national defense or a sewer system. If that's the role of government, it seems natural to charge each person in proportion to the benefits they get from those goods.

Practical considerations, however, make it impossible to base the entire tax system on the benefits principle. It would be too cumbersome to have a specific tax for each of the many distinct programs that the government offers. Also, attempts to base taxes on the benefits principle often conflict with the other major principle of tax fairness: the *ability-to-pay principle.*

The Ability-to-Pay Principle According to the **ability-to-pay principle,** those with greater ability to pay a tax should pay more. This principle is usually interpreted to mean that high-income individuals should pay more in taxes than low-income individuals. Often the ability-to-pay principle is used to argue not only that high-income individuals should pay more taxes but also that they should pay a higher *percentage* of their income in taxes. We'll consider the issue of how taxes vary as a percentage of income later.

The Whiskey Rebellion described in the opening story was basically a protest against the failure of the whiskey tax to take the ability-to-pay principle into account. In fact, the tax made small distillers—farmers of modest means—pay a higher proportion of their income than large, relatively well-off distillers. It's not surprising that farmers were upset that the new tax completely disregarded the ability-to-pay principle.

Equity versus Efficiency

Under the whiskey tax, the flat amount of tax paid by large distillers (in contrast to the per-gallon tax paid by small distillers) was an example of a **lump-sum tax,** a tax that is the same regardless of any actions people take. In this case, the large distillers paid the same amount of tax regardless of how many gallons they produced.

Lump-sum taxes are widely perceived to be much less fair than a tax that is proportional to the amount of the transaction. And this was true in the Whiskey Rebellion: although the small farmers were unhappy to pay a proportional tax, it was still less than they would have owed with the lump-sum tax, which would have imposed an even more unfair burden on them.

But the per-gallon whiskey tax definitely distorted incentives to engage in mutually beneficial transactions and created deadweight loss. Because of the tax, some farmers would have reduced how much whiskey they distilled, with some forgoing distilling altogether. The result, surely, was a lower production of whiskey and less income earned by farmers because of the tax.

In contrast, a lump-sum tax does not distort incentives. Because under a lump-sum tax people have to pay the same amount of tax regardless of their actions, it does not lead them to change their actions and therefore causes no deadweight loss. So lump-sum taxes, although unfair, are better than other taxes at promoting economic efficiency.

A tax system can be made fairer by moving it in the direction of the benefits principle or the ability-to-pay principle. But this will come at a cost because the tax system will now tax people more heavily based on their actions, increasing the amount of deadweight loss. This observation reflects a general principle that we learned in Chapter 1: there is often a trade-off between equity and efficiency.

Here, unless a tax system is badly designed, it can be made fairer only by sacrificing efficiency. Conversely, it can be made more efficient only by making it less fair. This means that there is normally a **trade-off between equity and efficiency** in the design of a tax system.

It's important to understand that economic analysis cannot say how much weight a tax system should give to equity and how much to efficiency. That choice is a value judgment, one we make through the political process.

> In a well-designed tax system, there is a **trade-off between equity and efficiency:** the system can be made more efficient only by making it less fair, and vice versa.

ECONOMICS >> *in Action*
Federal Tax Philosophy

What is the principle underlying the federal tax system? (By federal, we mean taxes collected by the federal government, as opposed to the taxes collected by state and local governments.) The answer is that it depends on the tax.

The best-known federal tax, accounting for about half of all federal revenue, is the income tax. The structure of the income tax reflects the ability-to-pay principle: families with low incomes pay little or no income tax. In fact, some families pay negative income tax: a program known as the Earned Income Tax Credit "tops up," or adds to, the earnings of low-wage workers. Meanwhile, those with high incomes not only pay a lot of income tax but also must pay a larger share of their income in income taxes than the average family.

Some types of federal taxes that you pay are based on the benefits principle, while other types are based on the ability to pay principle.

The second most important federal tax, FICA, also known as the payroll tax, is set up very differently. It was originally introduced in 1935 to pay for Social Security, a program that guarantees retirement income to qualifying older Americans and also provides benefits to workers who become disabled and to family members of workers who die. (Part of the payroll tax is now also used to pay for Medicare, a program that pays most medical bills of older Americans.)

The Social Security system was set up to resemble a private insurance program: people pay into the system during their working years, then receive benefits based on their payments. And the tax more or less reflects the benefits principle: because the benefits of Social Security are mainly intended to assist lower- and middle-income people, and don't increase substantially for the rich, the Social Security tax is levied only on incomes up to a maximum level—$137,700 in 2020. (The Medicare portion of the payroll tax has no upper limit.) As a result, a high-income family doesn't pay much more in payroll taxes than a middle-income family.

Table 7-2 illustrates the difference in the two taxes, using data from a Congressional Budget Office study. The study divided American families into quintiles: the bottom quintile is the poorest 20% of families, the second quintile is the next poorest 20%, and so on. The second column shows the share of total U.S. pre-tax income received by each quintile. The third column shows the share of total federal income tax collected that is paid by each quintile.

As you can see, low-income families actually paid negative income tax through the Earned Income Tax Credit program. Even middle-income families paid a substantially smaller share of total income tax collected than their share of total income. In contrast, the fifth or top quintile, the richest 20% of families, paid a much higher share of total federal income tax collected compared with their share of total income. The fourth column shows the share of total payroll tax collected that is paid by each quintile, and the results are very different: the share of total payroll tax paid by the top quintile is substantially less than their share of total income.

TABLE 7-2 Share of Pre-Tax Income, Federal Income Tax, and Payroll Tax, by Quintile in 2016

Income group	Percent of total pre-tax income received	Percent of total federal income tax paid	Percent of total payroll tax paid
Bottom quintile	3.8%	−4.2%	4.7%
Second quintile	8.9	−1.0	9.7
Third quintile	13.6	4.2	15.5
Fourth quintile	20.5	13.7	24.3
Top quintile	54.4	87.3	45.7

Data from: Congressional Budget Office.

>> Quick Review

• Other things equal, government tax policy aims for tax efficiency. But it also tries to achieve tax fairness.

• There are two important principles of tax fairness: the **benefits principle** and the **ability-to-pay principle.**

• A lump-sum tax is efficient because it does not distort incentives, but it is generally considered unfair. In any well-designed tax system, there is a **trade-off between equity and efficiency.** How the tax system should weight equity and efficiency is a value judgment to be decided by the political process.

>> Check Your Understanding 7-3

Solutions appear at back of book.

1. Assess each of the following taxes in terms of the benefits principle versus the ability-to-pay principle. What, if any, actions are distorted by the tax? Assume for simplicity in each case that the purchaser of the good bears 100% of the burden of the tax.
   a. A federal tax of $500 for each new car purchased that finances highway safety programs
   b. A local tax of 20% on hotel rooms that finances local government expenditures
   c. A local tax of 1% on the assessed value of homes that finances local schools
   d. A 1% sales tax on food that pays for government food safety regulation and inspection programs

‖ Understanding the Tax System

An excise tax is the easiest tax to analyze, making it a good vehicle for understanding the general principles of tax analysis. However, in the United States today, excise taxes are actually a relatively minor source of government revenue. In this section, we develop a framework for understanding more general forms of taxation and look at some of the major taxes used in the United States.

Tax Bases and Tax Structure

The **tax base** is the measure or value, such as income or property value, that determines how much tax an individual or firm pays.

The **tax structure** specifies how the tax depends on the tax base.

Every tax consists of two pieces: a *base* and a *structure*. The **tax base** is the measure or value that determines how much tax an individual or firm pays. It is usually a monetary measure, like income or property value. The **tax structure** specifies how the tax depends on the tax base. It is usually expressed in percentage terms; for example, homeowners in some areas might pay yearly property taxes equal to 2% of the value of their homes.

Some important taxes and their tax bases are as follows:

- **Income tax:** a tax that depends on the income of an individual or family from wages and investments
- **Payroll tax:** a tax that depends on the earnings an employer pays to an employee
- **Sales tax:** a tax that depends on the value of goods sold (also known as an excise tax)
- **Profits tax:** a tax that depends on a firm's profits
- **Property tax:** a tax that depends on the value of property, such as the value of a home
- **Wealth tax:** a tax that depends on an individual's wealth

Once the tax base has been defined, the next question is how the tax depends on the base. The simplest tax structure is a **proportional tax,** also sometimes called a *flat tax*, which is the same percentage of the base regardless of the tax-payer's income or wealth. For example, a property tax that is set at 2% of the value of the property, whether the property is worth $10,000 or $10,000,000, is a proportional tax.

Many taxes, however, are not proportional. Instead, different people pay different percentages, usually because the tax law tries to incorporate either the benefits principle or the ability-to-pay principle.

Because taxes are ultimately paid out of income, economists classify taxes according to how they vary with the income of individuals. A tax that rises *more* than in proportion to income, so that high-income taxpayers pay a larger per-centage of their income than low-income taxpayers, is a **progressive tax.** A tax that rises *less* than in proportion to income, so that higher-income taxpayers pay a smaller percentage of their income than low-income taxpayers, is a **regressive tax.** A proportional tax on income would be neither progressive nor regressive.

The U.S. tax system contains a mixture of progressive and regressive taxes, though it is somewhat progressive overall.

Equity, Efficiency, and Progressive Taxation

Most, though not all, people view a progressive tax system as fairer than a regres-sive system. The reason is the ability-to-pay principle: a high-income family that pays 35% of its income in taxes is still left with a lot more money than a low-income family that pays only 15% in taxes. But attempts to make taxes strongly progressive run up against the trade-off between equity and efficiency.

To see why, consider a hypothetical example, illustrated in Table 7-3. We assume that there are two kinds of people in the nation of Taxmania: half of the population earns $40,000 a year and half earns $80,000, so the aver-age income is $60,000 a year. We also assume that the Taxmanian government needs to collect 25% of that income—$15,000 a year per person—in taxes.

One way to raise this revenue would be through a proportional tax that takes 25% of everyone's income. The results of this propor-tional tax are shown in the second column of Table 7-3: after taxes, lower-income Taxmanians would be left with an income of $30,000 a year and higher-income Taxmanians, $60,000.

Even this system might have some negative effects on incentives. Suppose, for example, that finishing college improves a Taxmanian's chance of getting a higher-paying job. Some people who would invest time and effort in going to college in hopes of raising their income from $40,000 to $80,000, a $40,000 gain, might not bother if the potential gain is only $30,000, the after-tax difference in pay between a lower-paying and higher-paying job.

An **income tax** is a tax on an individual's or family's income.

A **payroll tax** is a tax on the earnings an employer pays to an employee.

A **sales tax** is a tax on the value of goods sold.

A **profits tax** is a tax on a firm's profits.

A **property tax** is a tax on the value of property, such as the value of a home.

A **wealth tax** is a tax on an individual's wealth.

A **proportional tax** is the same percentage of the tax base regardless of the taxpayer's income or wealth.

A **progressive tax** takes a larger share of the income of high-income taxpayers than of low-income taxpayers.

A **regressive tax** takes a smaller share of the income of high-income taxpayers than of low-income taxpayers.

TABLE 7-3 Proportional versus Progressive Taxes in Taxmania

Pre-tax income	After-tax income with proportional taxation	After-tax income with progressive taxation
$40,000	$30,000	$40,000
$80,000	$60,000	$50,000

The **marginal tax rate** is the percentage of an increase in income that is taxed away.

But a strongly progressive tax system could create a much bigger incentive problem. Suppose that the Taxmanian government decided to exempt the poorer half of the population from all taxes but still wanted to raise the same amount of revenue. To do this, it would have to collect $30,000 from each individual earning $80,000 a year. As the third column of Table 7-3 shows, people earning $80,000 would then be left with income after taxes of $50,000—only $10,000 more than the after-tax income of people earning half as much. In effect, 75% of their income over $40,000 has been taxed away. This would greatly reduce the incentive for people to invest time and effort to raise their earnings.

The point here is that any income tax system will tax away part of the gain an individual gets by moving up the income scale, reducing the incentive to earn more. But a progressive tax takes away a larger share of the gain than a proportional tax, creating a more adverse effect on incentives. In comparing the incentive effects of tax systems, economists often focus on the **marginal tax rate:** the percentage of an increase in income that is taxed away. In this example, the marginal tax rate on income above $40,000 is 25% with proportional taxation but 75% with progressive taxation.

Our hypothetical example is much more extreme than the reality of progressive taxation in the modern United States—although in previous decades the marginal tax rates paid by high earners were very high indeed. In the 1950s, the top marginal tax rate for American taxpayers was over 90%. However, these have moderated over time as concerns arose about the severe incentive effects of extremely progressive taxes. In short, the ability-to-pay principle pushes governments toward a highly progressive tax system, but efficiency considerations push them the other way.

Taxes in the United States

Table 7-4 shows the revenue raised by major taxes in the United States in 2018. Some of the taxes are collected by the federal government and the others by state and local governments.

There is a major tax corresponding to five of the six tax bases we identified earlier. There are income taxes, payroll taxes, sales taxes, profits taxes, and property taxes, all of which play an important role in the overall tax system. The only item missing is a wealth tax. In fact, the United States does have a wealth tax, the *estate tax*, which depends on the value of someone's estate after they die. But it raises much less money than the taxes shown in the table.

In addition to the taxes shown, state and local governments collect substantial revenue from other sources as varied as driver's license fees and sewer charges. These fees and charges are an important part of the tax burden, but they are very difficult to summarize or analyze.

Are the taxes in Table 7-4 progressive or regressive? It depends on the tax. The personal income tax is strongly progressive. The payroll tax, which, except for the Medicare portion, is paid only on earnings up to $137,700 is somewhat regressive. Sales taxes are generally regressive, because higher-income families save more of their income and thus spend a smaller share of it on taxable goods than do lower-income families. In addition, there are other taxes principally levied at the state and local level that are typically quite regressive: it costs the same amount to renew a driver's license no matter what your income is.

Overall, the taxes collected by the federal government are quite progressive. The second column of Table 7-5 shows estimates of the average federal tax rate paid by families at different levels of income earned in 2016. These estimates don't count just the money families pay directly. They also attempt to estimate the incidence of

TABLE 7-4 Major Taxes in the United States, 2018

Federal taxes ($ billion)		State and local taxes ($ billion)	
Income	$1,620.2	Income	$420.9
Payroll	1,334.4	Sales	411.9
Profits	147.4	Profits	58.4
		Property	562.0

Data from: Bureau of Economic Analysis.

TABLE 7-5 Federal, State, and Local Taxes as a Percentage of Income, by Income Category, 2016

Income group	Federal	State and local	Total
Bottom quintile	1.7%	11.4%	13.1%
Second quintile	9.4	10.1	19.5
Third quintile	13.9	9.9	23.8
Fourth quintile	17.9	9.5	27.4
Next 15%	22.0	8.9	30.9
Next 4%	26.8	8.0	34.8
Top 1%	33.3	7.4	40.7
Average	13.3	9.4	22.7

Data from: Congressional Budget Office; Institute on Taxation and Economic Policy; and author's calculation.

taxes directly paid by businesses, like the tax on corporate profits, which ultimately falls on individual shareholders. The table shows that the federal tax system is indeed progressive, with low-income families paying a relatively small share of their income in federal taxes and high-income families paying a greater share of their income.

Starting in 2000, the federal government cut income taxes for most families. The largest cuts, both as a share of income and as a share of federal taxes collected, went to families with high incomes. As a result, the federal system became less progressive because the share of income paid by high-income families fell relative to the share paid by middle- and low-income families. More recently, there have been two major changes in income tax rates. In 2013 some of those tax cuts were allowed to expire for Americans with high incomes, and additional taxes were imposed on top incomes to help pay for health reform. But tax rates for high income earners were again lowered with the passage of the Tax Cuts and Job Act of 2017. While the average federal tax rate for the richest Americans was about the same in 2016 as it was in 2000, it has probably fallen significantly at the time of writing.

As the third column of Table 7-5 shows, however, taxes at the state and local levels are generally regressive. That's because the sales tax, the largest source of revenue for most states, is somewhat regressive, and other items, such as vehicle licensing fees, are strongly regressive. As we explain in the upcoming Economics in Action, there is wide variation in tax systems across states.

In sum, the U.S. tax system is somewhat progressive, with the richest fifth of the population paying a somewhat higher share of income in taxes than families in the middle, and the poorest fifth paying considerably less.

Yet there are important differences within the American tax system: the federal income tax is more progressive than the payroll tax. And as can be seen from Table 7-5, federal taxation is more progressive than state and local taxation.

Different Taxes, Different Principles

Why are some taxes progressive but others regressive? Can't the government make up its mind?

There are two main reasons for the mixture of regressive and progressive taxes in the U.S. system: the difference between levels of government and the fact that different taxes are based on different principles.

State and especially local governments generally do not make much effort to apply the ability-to-pay principle. This is largely because they are subject to *tax competition:* a state or local government that imposes high taxes on people

GLOBAL COMPARISON   YOU THINK YOUR TAXES ARE HIGH?

Everyone, everywhere complains about taxes. But citizens of the United States actually have less to complain about than citizens of most other wealthy countries.

To assess the overall level of taxes, economists usually calculate taxes as a share of *gross domestic product* or *GDP*—the total value of goods and services produced in a country. By this measure, as you can see in the accompanying figure, in 2017, U.S. taxes were near the bottom of the scale. Even our neighbor Canada has significantly higher taxes. Tax rates in Europe, where governments need a lot of revenue to pay for extensive benefits such as guaranteed health care and generous unemployment benefits, are 40% to 70% higher than in the United States.

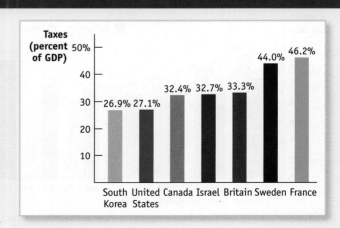

Data from: OECD.

The U.S. government taxes people mainly on the money they *make,* not on the money they spend on consumption. Yet most tax experts argue that this policy badly distorts incentives. Someone who earns income and then invests that income for the future gets taxed twice: once on the original sum and again on any earnings made from the investment.

So a system that taxes income rather than consumption discourages people from saving and investing, instead providing an incentive to spend their income today. And encouraging savings and investing is an important policy goal for two reasons. First, empirical evidence shows that Americans tend to save too little for retirement and health care expenses in their later years. Second, savings and investment both contribute to economic growth.

Moving from a system that taxes income to one that taxes consumption would solve this problem. In fact, the governments of many countries get much of their revenue from a value-added tax, or VAT, which acts like a national sales tax. In some countries VAT rates are very high; in Sweden, for example, the rate is 25%.

The United States does not have a value-added tax mainly because it is difficult, though not impossible, to make a consumption tax progressive.

with high incomes faces the prospect that those people may move to other locations where taxes are lower. This is much less of a concern at the national level, although a handful of very rich people have given up their U.S. citizenship to avoid paying U.S. taxes.

Although the federal government is in a better position than state or local governments to apply principles of fairness, it applies different principles to different taxes. We saw an example of this in the preceding Economics in Action. The most important tax, the federal income tax, is strongly progressive, reflecting the ability-to-pay principle. But the second most important tax, the federal payroll tax, or FICA, is somewhat regressive, because most of it is linked to specific programs—Social Security and Medicare—and, reflecting the benefits principle, is levied more or less in proportion to the benefits received from these programs.

ECONOMICS >> *in Action*
State Tax Choices

While federal taxes are strongly progressive, and state and local taxes are generally regressive, there is wide variation in tax systems across states.

You can see how big these differences can get by comparing taxation in the two most populous states, California and Texas, shown in Figure 7-11. California taxes are represented by the burgundy bars and Texas taxes are represented by the orange bars.

Texas has a relatively small government compared to California, so that average taxes as a percentage of income are lower. But the two states also make very different choices about how to collect revenue. California imposes an income tax that can reach 13.3% of income, whereas Texas has no income tax. In addition, California offers a number of tax breaks to lower- and middle-income residents that Texas does not. The result is that average tax rates are actually slightly lower in California for the lower half of the income distribution, but much higher for higher-income residents.

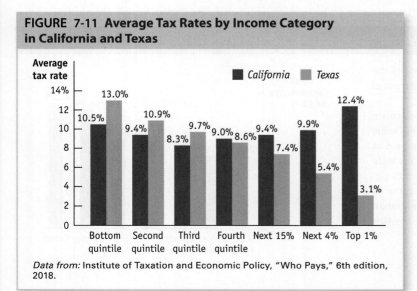

FIGURE 7-11 Average Tax Rates by Income Category in California and Texas

Data from: Institute of Taxation and Economic Policy, "Who Pays," 6th edition, 2018.

So although some states like Texas may advertise themselves as low-tax states, and politicians almost everywhere boast about keeping taxes low, an important question to always ask is "low rates for whom?" That is, which residents are benefitting from the low tax rates?

This comparison teaches us that tax policy isn't one-dimensional. There are many choices involved in setting up a tax system, and keeping taxes low for some people may involve making them higher for others.

>> Check Your Understanding 7-4
Solutions appear at back of book.

1. An income tax taxes 1% of the first $10,000 of income and 2% on all income above $10,000.
   a. What is the marginal tax rate for someone with income of $5,000? How much total tax does this person pay? How much is this as a percentage of their income?
   b. What is the marginal tax rate for someone with income of $20,000? How much total tax does this person pay? How much is this as a percentage of their income?
   c. Is this income tax proportional, progressive, or regressive?

2. When comparing households at different income levels, economists find that consumption spending grows more slowly than income. Assume that when income grows by 50%, from $10,000 to $15,000, consumption grows by 25%, from $8,000 to $10,000. Compare the percent of income paid in taxes by a family with $15,000 in income to that paid by a family with $10,000 in income under a 1% tax on consumption purchases. Is this a proportional, progressive, or regressive tax?

3. True or false? Explain your answers.
   a. Payroll taxes do not affect a person's incentive to take a job because they are paid by employers.
   b. A lump-sum tax is a proportional tax because it is the same amount for each person.

>> Quick Review
- Every tax consists of a **tax base** and a **tax structure**.
- Among the types of taxes are **income taxes, payroll taxes, sales taxes, profits taxes, property taxes,** and **wealth taxes.**
- Tax systems are classified as being **proportional, progressive,** or **regressive.**
- Progressive taxes are often justified by the ability-to-pay principle. But strongly progressive taxes lead to high **marginal tax rates,** which create major incentive problems.
- The United States has a mixture of progressive and regressive taxes. However, the overall structure of taxes is progressive.

A Welcome Tax Hike: Microsoft Raises Its Internal Carbon Tax

Chona Kasinge/Bloomberg/Getty Images

Microsoft just hiked a tax—on itself. In April of 2019, the company announced that it would nearly double its internal carbon tax, from $8 to $15 per metric ton of carbon dioxide. While the company has made steady progress toward its corporate goal of cutting carbon emissions by 75% by 2030, "the magnitude and speed of the world's environmental changes have made it increasingly clear that we must do more," in the words of Microsoft's president, Brad Smith. The company now vows to reach its goal seven years earlier, in 2023.

Microsoft's various business units—such as its Intelligent Cloud Division—are assessed on their performance by senior management each quarter (every three months). One of the major factors in the performance review is quarterly profit—that is, how much did the business unit earn over and above its costs. So it might be surprising to learn that one type of cost that Microsoft's business units must pay is a tax: a carbon tax that is levied internally by Microsoft on its own units. Microsoft began implementing an internal carbon tax in 2012, and since then the policy has quickly grown in popularity. Today, well over 1,400 firms and organizations—from Google, Disney, and ExxonMobil to Yale University—levy an internal carbon tax on their operations.

A *carbon tax* is a tax on a good or service assessed according to the amount of carbon dioxide created by the production of that good or service. Carbon dioxide is one of the main pollutants behind global climate change.

A Microsoft business unit determines its carbon tax levy by calculating the total amount of energy that it consumes for its operations—such as the energy consumed for its office space, data centers, or business travel. Next, the amount of energy consumed is converted into metric tons of carbon—the amount of carbon emissions generated by the unit's consumption of energy. Microsoft's Environmental Sustainability Team then calculates each unit's carbon tax. It is a substantial sum: even before the 2019 tax hike, Microsoft collected approximately $30 million in carbon tax revenue from its business units.

The carbon tax revenue is placed in a fund that pays for a range of clean energy projects within Microsoft. For example, at its corporate headquarters in Redmond, Washington, carbon tax revenue paid for a data collection and software system that optimized energy use across 125 buildings, leading to huge cost and carbon-emissions savings. In just its first three years, the carbon tax system led to a $10 million savings for Microsoft through reduced energy consumption and a 7.5 million metric ton reduction in carbon emissions.

Although the internal carbon tax scheme reduces the company's profit in the short run, Microsoft's shareholders support the scheme. They believe that reducing energy consumption in the long run will lead to higher future profits. For example, through research and development generated by their own internal carbon tax program, Microsoft has developed important skills and technology, particularly in the area of artificial intelligence. That new capability is now being used to create similar programs for its customers who also want to reduce their carbon emissions and save energy. In the words of Smith, "Already we're helping empower our customers and partners with new technology to help them drive efficiencies, transform their businesses, and create their own solutions to create a more sustainable planet."

QUESTIONS FOR THOUGHT

1. To save energy and reduce carbon emissions, why do you think that Microsoft instituted a tax rather than issuing a company-wide directive?

2. How is Microsoft behaving like a government? Why is this preferable to business units acting independently?

3. What trade-offs should Microsoft consider in determining the size of the carbon tax? What happens if the tax is too high? Too low?

4. What does this case tell you about the relationship between an objective and the size of the tax created to achieve that objective? Should they be determined independently or jointly?

SUMMARY

1. **Excise taxes**—taxes on the purchase or sale of a good—raise the price paid by consumers and reduce the price received by producers, driving a wedge between the two. The **incidence** of the tax—how the burden of the tax is divided between consumers and producers—does not depend on who officially pays the tax.

2. The incidence of an excise tax depends on the price elasticities of supply and demand. If the price elasticity of demand is higher than the price elasticity of supply, the tax falls mainly on producers; if the price elasticity of supply is higher than the price elasticity of demand, the tax falls mainly on consumers.

3. The tax revenue generated by a tax depends on the **tax rate** and on the number of taxed units transacted. Excise taxes cause inefficiency in the form of deadweight loss because they discourage some mutually beneficial transactions. Taxes also impose **administrative costs:** resources used to collect the tax, to pay it (over and above the amount of the tax), and to evade it.

4. An excise tax generates revenue for the government but lowers total surplus. The loss in total surplus exceeds the tax revenue, resulting in a deadweight loss to society. This deadweight loss is represented by a triangle, the area of which equals the value of the transactions discouraged by the tax. The greater the elasticity of demand or supply, or both, the larger the deadweight loss from a tax. If either demand or supply is perfectly inelastic, there is no deadweight loss from a tax.

5. An efficient tax minimizes both the sum of the deadweight loss due to distorted incentives and the administrative costs of the tax. However, tax fairness is also a goal of tax policy.

6. There are two major principles of tax fairness, the **benefits principle** and the **ability-to-pay principle.** The most efficient tax, a **lump-sum tax,** does not distort incentives but performs badly in terms of fairness. The fairest taxes in terms of the ability-to-pay principle, however, distort incentives the most and perform badly on efficiency grounds. So in a well-designed tax system, there is a **trade-off between equity and efficiency.**

7. Every tax consists of a **tax base,** which defines what is taxed, and a **tax structure,** which specifies how the tax depends on the tax base. Different tax bases give rise to different taxes—the **income tax, payroll tax, sales tax, profits tax, property tax,** and **wealth tax.** A **proportional tax** is the same percentage of the tax base for all taxpayers.

8. A tax is **progressive** if higher-income people pay a higher percentage of their income in taxes than lower-income people and **regressive** if they pay a lower percentage. Progressive taxes are often justified by the ability-to-pay principle. However, a highly progressive tax system significantly distorts incentives because it leads to a high **marginal tax rate,** the percentage of an increase in income that is taxed away, on high earners. The U.S. tax system is progressive overall, although it contains a mixture of progressive and regressive taxes.

KEY TERMS

Excise tax, p. 186
Incidence, p. 188
Tax rate, p. 193
Administrative costs, p. 198
Benefits principle, p. 202
Ability-to-pay principle, p. 202
Lump-sum tax, p. 202

Trade-off between equity and efficiency, p. 203
Tax base, p. 204
Tax structure, p. 204
Income tax, p. 205
Payroll tax, p. 205
Sales tax, p. 205

Profits tax, p. 205
Property tax, p. 205
Wealth tax, p. 205
Proportional tax, p. 205
Progressive tax, p. 205
Regressive tax, p. 205
Marginal tax rate, p. 206

PRACTICE QUESTIONS

1. The state needs to raise money, and the governor has a choice of imposing an excise tax of the same amount on one of two previously untaxed goods: restaurant meals or gasoline. Both the demand for and the supply of restaurant meals are more elastic than the demand for and the supply of gasoline. If the governor wants to minimize the deadweight loss caused by the tax, which good should be taxed? For each good, draw a diagram that illustrates the deadweight loss from taxation.

2. Assume that demand for gasoline is inelastic and supply is relatively elastic. The government imposes a sales tax on gasoline. The tax revenue is used to fund research into clean fuel alternatives to gasoline, which will improve the air we all breathe.

   a. Who bears more of the burden of this tax, consumers or producers? Show in a diagram who bears how much of the burden.

   b. Is this tax based on the benefits principle or the ability-to-pay principle? Explain.

3. You are advising the government on how to pay for national defense. There are two proposals for a tax system to fund national defense. Under both proposals, the tax base is an individual's income. Under proposal A, all citizens pay exactly the same lump-sum tax, regardless of income. Under proposal B, individuals with higher incomes pay a greater proportion of their income in taxes.

   a. Is the tax in proposal A progressive, proportional, or regressive? What about the tax in proposal B?

   b. Is the tax in proposal A based on the ability-to-pay principle or on the benefits principle? What about the tax in proposal B?

   c. In terms of efficiency, which tax is better? Explain.

4. You work for the Council of Economic Advisers, providing economic advice to the White House. The president wants to overhaul the income tax system and asks your advice. Suppose that the current income tax system consists of a proportional tax of 10% on all income and that there is one person in the country who earns $110 million; everyone else earns less than $100 million. The president proposes a tax cut targeted at the very rich so that the new tax system would consist of a proportional tax of 10% on all income up to $100 million and a marginal tax rate of 0% (no tax) on income above $100 million. You are asked to evaluate this tax proposal.

   a. For incomes of $100 million or less, is this proposed tax system progressive, regressive, or proportional? For incomes of more than $100 million? Explain.

   b. Would this tax system create more or less tax revenue, other things equal? Is this tax system more or less efficient than the current tax system? Explain.

PROBLEMS

1. The United States imposes an excise tax on the sale of domestic airline tickets. Let's assume that in 2015 the total excise tax was $6.10 per airline ticket (consisting of a $3.60 flight segment tax plus a $2.50 September 11 fee). According to data from the Bureau of Transportation Statistics, in 2015, 643 million passengers traveled on domestic airline trips at an average price of $380.00 per trip. The accompanying table shows the supply and demand schedules for airline trips. The quantity demanded at the average price of $380.00 is actual data; the rest is hypothetical.

Price of trip	Quantity of trips demanded (millions)	Quantity of trips supplied (millions)
$380.02	642	699
380.00	643	698
378.00	693	693
373.90	793	643
373.82	913	642

   a. What is the government tax revenue in 2015 from the excise tax?

   b. On January 1, 2016, the total excise tax increased to $6.20 per ticket. What is the quantity of tickets transacted now? What is the average ticket price now? What is the 2016 government tax revenue?

   c. Does this increase in the excise tax increase or decrease government tax revenue?

2. In 1990, the United States began to levy a tax on sales of luxury cars. For simplicity, assume that the tax was an excise tax of $6,000 per car. The accompanying figure shows hypothetical demand and supply curves for luxury cars.

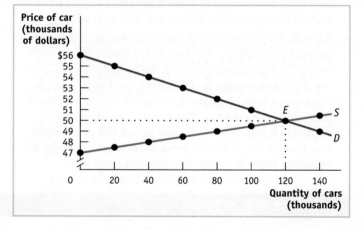

   a. Under the tax, what is the price paid by consumers? What is the price received by producers? What is the government tax revenue from the excise tax?

   Over time, the tax on luxury automobiles was slowly phased out (and completely eliminated in 2002). Suppose that the excise tax falls from $6,000 per car to $4,500 per car.

   b. After the reduction in the excise tax from $6,000 to $4,500 per car, what is the price paid by consumers? What is the price received by producers? What is tax revenue now?

   c. Compare the tax revenue created by the taxes in parts a and b. What accounts for the change in tax revenue from the reduction in the excise tax?

3. All states impose excise taxes on gasoline. According to data from the Federal Highway Administration, the state of California imposes an excise tax of $0.40 per gallon of gasoline. In 2015, gasoline sales in California totaled 14.6 billion gallons. What was California's tax revenue from the gasoline excise tax? If California doubled the excise tax, would tax revenue double? Why or why not?

4. In the United States, each state government can impose its own excise tax on the sale of cigarettes. Suppose that in the state of North Texarkana, the state government imposes a tax of $2.00 per pack sold within the state. In contrast, the neighboring state of South Texarkana imposes no excise tax on cigarettes. Assume that in both states the pre-tax price of a pack of cigarettes is $1.00. Assume that the total cost to a resident of North Texarkana to smuggle a pack of cigarettes from South Texarkana is $1.85 per pack. (This includes the cost of time, gasoline, and so on.) Assume that the supply curve for cigarettes is neither perfectly elastic nor perfectly inelastic.

   a. Draw a diagram of the supply and demand curves for cigarettes in North Texarkana showing a situation in which it makes economic sense for a North Texarkanan to smuggle a pack of cigarettes from South Texarkana to North Texarkana. Explain your diagram.

   b. Draw a corresponding diagram showing a situation in which it does not make economic sense for a North Texarkanan to smuggle a pack of cigarettes from South Texarkana to North Texarkana. Explain your diagram.

   c. Suppose the demand for cigarettes in North Texarkana is perfectly inelastic. Draw a corresponding diagram to illustrate how high the cost of smuggling a pack of cigarettes could go until a North Texarkanan no longer found it profitable to smuggle. Explain your diagram.

   d. Still assume that demand for cigarettes in North Texarkana is perfectly inelastic and that all smokers in North Texarkana are smuggling their cigarettes at a cost of $1.85 per pack, so no tax is paid. Is there any inefficiency in this situation? If so, how much per pack? Suppose chip-embedded cigarette packaging makes it impossible to smuggle cigarettes across the state border. Is there any inefficiency in this situation? If so, how much per pack?

5. In each of the following cases involving taxes, explain: (i) whether the incidence of the tax falls more heavily on consumers or producers, (ii) why government revenue raised from the tax is not a good indicator of the true cost of the tax, and (iii) how deadweight loss arises as a result of the tax.

   a. The government imposes an excise tax on the sale of all college textbooks. Before the tax was imposed, 1 million textbooks were sold every year at a price of $50. After the tax is imposed, 600,000 books are sold yearly; students pay $55 per book, $30 of which publishers receive.

   b. The government imposes an excise tax on the sale of all airline tickets. Before the tax was imposed, 3 million airline tickets were sold every year at a price of $500. After the tax is imposed, 1.5 million tickets are sold yearly; travelers pay $550 per ticket, $450 of which the airlines receive.

   c. The government imposes an excise tax on the sale of all toothbrushes. Before the tax, 2 million toothbrushes were sold every year at a price of $1.50. After the tax is imposed, 800,000 toothbrushes are sold every year; consumers pay $2 per toothbrush, $1.25 of which producers receive.

6. The accompanying diagram shows the market for cigarettes. The current equilibrium price per pack is $4, and every day 40 million packs of cigarettes are sold. In order to recover some of the health care costs associated with smoking, the government imposes a tax of $2 per pack. This will raise the equilibrium price to $5 per pack and reduce the equilibrium quantity to 30 million packs.

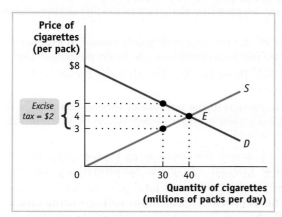

The economist working for the tobacco lobby claims that this tax will reduce consumer surplus for smokers by $40 million per day, since 40 million packs now cost $1 more per pack. The economist working for the lobby for sufferers of second-hand smoke argues that this is an enormous overestimate and that the reduction in consumer surplus will be only $30 million per day, since after the imposition of the tax only 30 million packs of cigarettes will be bought and each of these packs will now cost $1 more. They are both wrong. Why? Include a calculation of consumer surplus before and after the tax in your answer.

7. Consider the original market for pizza in Collegetown, illustrated in the accompanying table. Collegetown officials decide to impose an excise tax on pizza of $4 per pizza.

Price of pizza	Quantity of pizza demanded	Quantity of pizza supplied
$10	0	6
9	1	5
8	2	4
7	3	3
6	4	2
5	5	1
4	6	0
3	7	0
2	8	0
1	9	0

a. What is the quantity of pizza bought and sold after the imposition of the tax? What is the price paid by consumers? What is the price received by producers?

b. Calculate the consumer surplus and the producer surplus after the imposition of the tax. By how much has the imposition of the tax reduced consumer surplus? By how much has it reduced producer surplus?

c. How much tax revenue does Collegetown earn from this tax?

d. Calculate the deadweight loss from this tax.

8. Assess the following four tax policies in terms of the benefits principle versus the ability-to-pay principle.

a. A tax on gasoline that finances maintenance of state roads

b. An 8% tax on imported goods valued in excess of $800 per household brought in on passenger flights

c. Airline-flight landing fees that pay for air traffic control

d. A reduction in the amount of income tax paid based on the number of dependent children in the household.

9. ⬜ Access the Discovering Data exercise for Chapter 7 Problem 9 online to answer the following questions.

a. Which source of government revenue is the largest? How have revenue sources changed over time?

b. Calculate the growth rate of each source of government revenue since December 2007. Which has grown the fastest?

c. Explain how the three sources of government revenue have changed over time and what happened to each source of revenue during the Great Recession.

10. Each of the following tax proposals has income as the tax base. In each case, calculate the marginal tax rate for each level of income. Then calculate the percentage of income paid in taxes for an individual with a pre-tax income of $5,000 and for an individual with a pre-tax income of $40,000. Classify the tax as being proportional, progressive, or regressive. (*Hint:* You can calculate the marginal tax rate as the percentage of an additional $1 in income that is taxed away.)

a. All income is taxed at 20%.

b. All income up to $10,000 is tax-free. All income above $10,000 is taxed at a constant rate of 20%.

c. All income between $0 and $10,000 is taxed at 10%. All income between $10,000 and $20,000 is taxed at 20%. All income higher than $20,000 is taxed at 30%.

d. Each individual who earns more than $10,000 pays a lump-sum tax of $10,000. If the individual's income is less than $10,000, that individual pays in taxes exactly what their income is.

e. Of the four tax policies, which is likely to cause the worst incentive problems? Explain.

11. In Transylvania the basic income tax system is fairly simple. The first 40,000 sylvers (the official currency of Transylvania) earned each year are free of income tax. Any additional income is taxed at a rate of 25%. In addition, every individual pays a social security tax, which is calculated as follows: all income up to 80,000 sylvers is taxed at an additional 20%, but there is no additional social security tax on income above 80,000 sylvers.

a. Calculate the marginal tax rates (including income tax and social security tax) for Transylvanians with the following levels of income: 20,000 sylvers, 40,000 sylvers, and 80,000 sylvers. (*Hint:* You can calculate the marginal tax rate as the percentage of an additional 1 sylver in income that is taxed away.)

b. Is the income tax in Transylvania progressive, regressive, or proportional? Is the social security tax progressive, regressive, or proportional?

c. Which income group's incentives are most adversely affected by the combined income and social security tax systems?

WORK IT OUT

12. The U.S. government wants to help the American auto industry compete against foreign automakers that sell trucks in the United States. It can do this by imposing an excise tax on each foreign truck sold in the United States. The hypothetical pre-tax demand and supply schedules for imported trucks are given in this table.

Price of imported truck	Quantity of imported trucks (thousands)	
	Quantity demanded	Quantity supplied
$32,000	100	400
31,000	200	350
30,000	300	300
29,000	400	250
28,000	500	200
27,000	600	150

a. In the absence of government interference, what is the equilibrium price of an imported truck? The equilibrium quantity? Illustrate with a diagram.

b. Assume that the government imposes an excise tax of $3,000 per imported truck. Illustrate the effect of this excise tax in your diagram from part a. How many imported trucks are now purchased and at what price? How much does the foreign automaker receive per truck?

c. Calculate the government revenue raised by the excise tax in part b. Illustrate it on your diagram.

d. How does the excise tax on imported trucks benefit American automakers? Whom does it hurt? How does inefficiency arise from this government policy? ∎

8 ▷ International Trade

THE EVERYWHERE PHONE

WHAT DO AMERICANS DO with their time? The answer is that they largely spend it staring at small screens. In 2018, the average American spent three hours and 43 minutes a day looking at a smartphone (especially an iPhone) or a tablet, slightly more time than they spent watching TV.

The production and consumption of smartphones are examples of today's hyperglobal world with its soaring levels of international trade.

Where do these small screens come from? Specifically, where does an iPhone come from?

Apple, which sells the iPhone, is an American company. But if you said that iPhones come from America, you're mostly wrong: Apple develops products, but contracts almost all of the manufacturing of those products to other companies that are mainly located overseas. But it's not really right to answer "China," either, even though that's where iPhones are assembled. Assembly is the last phase of iPhone production, in which the pieces are put together in the familiar metal-and-glass case.

In fact, a study of the iPhone X estimated that of the average wholesale price of about $800 per phone, less than $25 stayed in the Chinese economy. A substantially larger amount went to South Korean manufacturers, who supplied the display and memory chips. There were also substantial outlays for raw materials, which are sourced all over the world. And the biggest share of the price — more than half — consisted of Apple's profit margin, which was largely a reward for research, development, and design.

So where do iPhones come from? Lots of places. And the case of the iPhone isn't unusual: the car you drive, the clothing you wear, even the food you eat are generally the end products of complex supply chains that span the globe. Large-scale international trade like this isn't new. It was fairly common by the early twentieth century. In recent decades, however, new technologies for transportation and communication have interacted with pro-trade policies to produce an era of *hyperglobalization* in which international trade has soared thanks to complex chains of production like the one that puts an iPhone in front of your nose.

These global supply chains make the world economy much more productive and, as a result, richer than it would be if each country tried to be self-sufficient. And it isn't just the world as a whole that benefits from international trade: it's almost certain that every country benefits, too. But international trade is nonetheless controversial, because it sometimes hurts particular groups *within* countries. For these reasons, we must have a full picture of international trade to understand how national economies work.

This chapter examines the economics of international trade. We start from the model of comparative advantage, which, as we saw in Chapter 2, explains why there are gains from international trade. We will briefly recap that model here, then turn to a more detailed examination of the causes and consequences of globalization. •

WHAT YOU WILL LEARN

- What is comparative advantage and why does it lead to international trade?
- What are the sources of comparative advantage?
- Who gains and who loses from international trade?

- Why do **trade protections** like **tariffs** and **import quotas** create inefficiency?
- Why do governments engage in trade protection and how do **international trade agreements** counteract this?

Goods and services purchased from other countries are **imports;** goods and services sold to other countries are **exports.**

Globalization is the phenomenon of growing economic linkages among countries.

‖ Comparative Advantage and International Trade

The United States buys smartphones—and many other goods and services—from other countries. At the same time, it sells many goods and services to other countries. Goods and services purchased from abroad are **imports;** goods and services sold abroad are **exports.**

As illustrated by the opening story, international trade plays an increasingly important role in the world economy. Panel (a) of Figure 8-1 shows the ratio of goods crossing national borders to *world GDP*—the total value of goods and services produced in the world as a whole—since 1870. As you can see, the long-term trend has been upward, although there have been some periods of declining trade—for example, the sharp but brief dip in trade during the global financial crisis of 2008 and its aftermath.

Panel (b) illustrates imports and exports as a percentage of GDP for a number of countries. It shows that foreign trade is significantly more important for many other countries than it is for the United States.

Foreign trade isn't the only way countries interact economically. In the modern world, investors from one country often invest funds in another nation; many companies are multinational, with subsidiaries operating in several countries; and a growing number of people work in a country different from the one in which they were born. The growth of all these forms of economic linkages among countries is often called **globalization.**

Globalization isn't a new phenomenon. As you can see from panel (a) of Figure 8-1, there was rapid growth in trade between 1870 and the beginning of World War I, as railroads and steamships effectively made shipping goods long

---

FIGURE 8-1 The Growing Importance of International Trade

(a) World Trade, 1870–2017

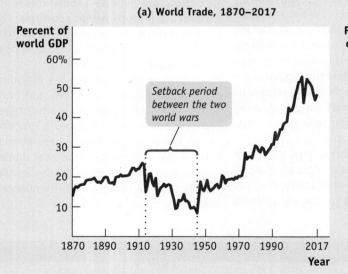

(b) Imports and Exports for Different Countries, 2017

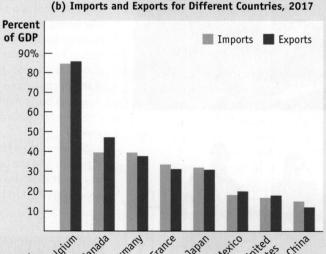

Panel (a) shows the long-term history of the ratio of world trade to world production. The trend has been generally upward, thanks to technological progress in transportation and communication, although there was a long setback during the period between the two world wars. Panel (b) demonstrates that international trade is significantly more important to many other countries than it is to the United States.

Data from: [panel (a)] Klasing, M. J., and P. Milionis, "Quantifying the Evolution of World Trade, 1870–1949," *Journal of International Economics* (2013); and Feenstra, Robert C., Robert Inklaar, and Marcel P. Timmer, "The Next Generation of the Penn World Table" *American Economic Review* 105, no. 10 (2015): 3150–3182, available for download at www.ggdc.net/pwt; [panel (b)] World Development Indicators.

distances faster and cheaper, effectively shrinking the world. This growth of trade was accompanied by large-scale international investment and migration. However, globalization went into reverse for almost 40 years after World War I, as governments imposed limits on trade. And by several measures, globalization didn't return to 1913 levels until the 1980s.

Since then, however, there has been a further dramatic increase in international linkages, sometimes referred to as **hyperglobalization.** The manufacture of iPhones and other high-tech goods, which often involve supply chains of production that span the globe, are an example of hyperglobalization. Each stage of a good's production takes place in a different country—all made possible by advances in communication and transportation technology. (For a real-life example, see this chapter's business case.)

One big question in international economics is whether hyperglobalization will continue in the decades ahead. As you can see from looking closely at Figure 8-1, the big rise in the ratio of exports to world GDP leveled off around 2005. Since then, many reports have appeared about companies deciding that the money they saved by buying goods from suppliers thousands of miles away is more than offset by the disadvantages of long shipping times and other inconveniences. (Even now, it takes around two weeks for a container ship from China to arrive in California, and a month to reach the East Coast.) As a result, there has been some move toward *reshoring*, bringing production closer to markets.

More recently, international disputes over trade have heated up, and governments may once again impose the kind of restrictions on trade that caused globalization to decline after World War I. Although international trade is likely to remain important to world economies, it is possible that hyperglobalization may become less prevalent than it is today.

To understand why international trade occurs and why economists believe it is beneficial to the economy, we will first review the concept of comparative advantage.

Hyperglobalization is the phenomenon of extremely high levels of international trade.

Thanks to cheap and fast ways of transporting goods, extremely high levels of international trade are a feature of today's economy.

Production Possibilities and Comparative Advantage, Revisited

To produce phones, any country must use resources—land, labor, and capital—that could have been used to produce other things. The opportunity cost of that phone is the potential production of other goods a country must forgo to produce it.

In some cases, it's easy to see why the opportunity cost of producing a good is especially low in a given country. Consider, for example, shrimp—much of which now comes from seafood farms in Vietnam and Thailand. It's a lot easier to produce shrimp in Vietnam, where the climate is nearly ideal and there's plenty of coastal land suitable for shellfish farming, than it is in the United States.

Conversely, other goods are not produced as easily in Vietnam as in the United States. For example, Vietnam doesn't have the base of skilled workers and technological know-how that makes the United States so good at producing high-technology goods. So the opportunity cost of a ton of shrimp, in terms of other goods such as aircraft, is much less in Vietnam than it is in the United States.

In other cases, the trade-off is less obvious. For example, it is as easy to assemble smartphones in the United States as in China. And Chinese electronics workers are, if anything, less productive than their U.S. counterparts. But Chinese workers are even less productive than U.S. workers in other areas, such as automobile and chemical production. So we say that China has a comparative advantage in producing smartphones. Let's repeat the definition of comparative advantage from Chapter 2: *A country has a comparative advantage in producing a good or service if the opportunity cost of producing the good or service is lower for that country than for other countries.*

The **Ricardian model of international trade** analyzes international trade under the assumption that opportunity costs are constant.

Employing a Chinese worker to assemble phones is more productive than employing a U.S. worker to assemble phones because the U.S. worker can be even more productively employed elsewhere. That is, the opportunity cost of smartphone assembly in China is less than it is in the United States.

Notice that we said the opportunity cost of phone *assembly*. As we've seen, most of the value of a "Chinese made" phone actually comes from other countries. For the sake of exposition, however, let's ignore that complication and consider a hypothetical case in which China makes phones from scratch.

Figure 8-2 provides a hypothetical numerical example of comparative advantage in international trade. We assume that only two goods are produced and consumed, phones and Caterpillar heavy trucks. (The United States doesn't export many ordinary trucks, but Caterpillar, which makes earth-moving equipment, is a major exporter.) And we assume that there are only two countries in the world, the United States and China. The figure shows hypothetical production possibility frontiers for the United States and China.

As in Chapter 2, we simplify the model by assuming that the production possibility frontiers are straight lines, as shown in Figure 2-1, rather than the more realistic bowed-out shape in Figure 2-2. The straight-line shape implies that the opportunity cost of a phone in terms of trucks in each country is constant—it does not depend on how many units of each good the country produces. The analysis of international trade under the assumption that opportunity costs are constant, which makes production possibility frontiers straight lines, is known as the **Ricardian model of international trade,** named after the English economist David Ricardo, who introduced this analysis in the early nineteenth century.

In Figure 8-2 we show a situation in which the United States can produce 100,000 trucks if it produces no phones, or 100 million phones if it produces no trucks. Thus, the slope of the U.S. production possibility frontier, or *PPF*, is −100,000/100 = −1,000. That is, to produce an additional million phones, the United States must forgo the production of 1,000 trucks. Likewise, to produce one more truck, the United States must forgo 1,000 phones (equal to 1 million phones divided by 1,000 trucks).

FIGURE 8-2 Comparative Advantage and the Production Possibility Frontier

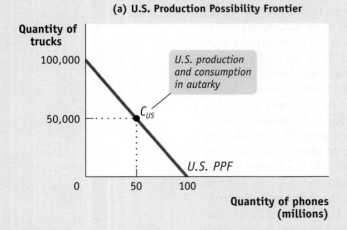

(a) U.S. Production Possibility Frontier

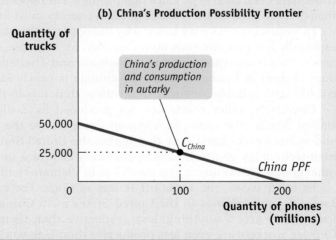

(b) China's Production Possibility Frontier

The U.S. opportunity cost of 1 million phones in terms of trucks is 1,000: for every 1 million phones, 1,000 trucks must be forgone. The Chinese opportunity cost of 1 million phones in terms of trucks is 250: for every additional 1 million phones, only 250 trucks must be forgone. As a result, the United States has a comparative advantage in truck production, and China has a comparative advantage in phone production. In autarky, each country is forced to consume only what it produces: 50,000 trucks and 50 million phones for the United States; 25,000 trucks and 100 million phones for China.

Similarly, China can produce 50,000 trucks if it produces no phones or 200 million phones if it produces no trucks. Thus, the slope of China's *PPF* is −50,000/200 = −250. That is, to produce an additional million phones, China must forgo the production of 250 trucks. Likewise, to produce one more truck, China must forgo 4,000 phones (1 million phones divided by 250 trucks).

> **Autarky** is a situation in which a country does not trade with other countries.

Historically, countries have almost always traded with each other. Yet economists find it helpful as a first step to illustrate the choices a country would make if it were unable to engage in international trade. Economists use the term **autarky** to refer to a situation in which a country does not trade with other countries. In our example, we assume that in autarky the United States chooses to produce and consume 50 million phones and 50,000 trucks. We also assume that in autarky China produces 100 million phones and 25,000 trucks.

The trade-offs facing the two countries when they don't trade are summarized in Table 8-1. As you can see, the United States has a comparative advantage in the production of trucks because it has a lower opportunity cost in terms of phones than China has: producing a truck costs the United States only 1,000 phones, while it costs China 4,000 phones. Correspondingly, China has a comparative advantage in phone production: 1 million phones costs only 250 trucks, while it costs the United States 1,000 trucks.

TABLE 8-1 U.S. and Chinese Opportunity Costs of Phones and Trucks

	U.S. Opportunity Cost		Chinese Opportunity Cost
1 million phones	1,000 trucks	>	250 trucks
1 truck	1,000 phones	<	4,000 phones

As we learned in Chapter 2, each country can do better by engaging in trade than it could by not trading. A country can accomplish this by specializing in the production of the good in which it has a comparative advantage and exporting that good, while importing the good in which it has a comparative disadvantage.

Let's see how this works.

The Gains from International Trade

Figure 8-3 illustrates how both countries can gain from specialization and trade, by showing a hypothetical rearrangement of production and consumption that allows *each* country to consume more of *both* goods. Again, panel (a) represents the United States and panel (b) represents China. In each panel we indicate again the autarky production and consumption assumed in Figure 8-2.

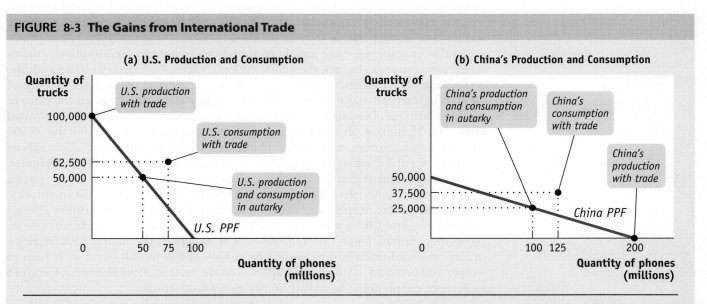

FIGURE 8-3 The Gains from International Trade

(a) U.S. Production and Consumption

U.S. production with trade
U.S. consumption with trade
U.S. production and consumption in autarky
U.S. PPF

(b) China's Production and Consumption

China's production and consumption in autarky
China's consumption with trade
China's production with trade
China PPF

Trade increases world production of both goods, allowing both countries to consume more. Here, each country specializes its production as a result of trade: the United States concentrates on producing trucks, and China concentrates on producing phones. Total world production of both goods rises, which means that it is possible for both countries to consume more of both goods.

TABLE 8-2 How the United States and China Gain from Trade

		In Autarky		With Trade		
		Production	Consumption	Production	Consumption	Gains from trade
United States	Million phones	50	50	0	75	+25
	Trucks	50,000	50,000	100,000	62,500	+12,500
China	Million phones	100	100	200	125	+25
	Trucks	25,000	25,000	0	37,500	+12,500

Once trade becomes possible, however, everything changes. With trade, each country can move to producing only the good in which it has a comparative advantage—trucks for the United States and phones for China. Because the world production of both goods is now higher than in autarky, trade makes it possible for each country to consume more of both goods.

Table 8-2 sums up the changes as a result of trade and shows why both countries can gain. The left part of the table shows the autarky situation, before trade, in which each country must produce the goods it consumes. The right part of the table shows what happens as a result of trade. After trade, the United States specializes in the production of trucks, producing 100,000 trucks and no phones; China specializes in the production of phones, producing 200 million phones and no trucks.

The result is a rise in total world production of both goods. As you can see in the table, there are gains from trade to both countries:

- The United States can consume both more trucks (12,500 more) and phones (25 million more) than before, even though it no longer produces phones, because it can import phones from China.

- China can also consume more of both goods (12,500 more trucks and 25 million more phones), even though it no longer produces trucks, because it can import trucks from the United States.

The key to this mutual gain is the fact that trade liberates both countries from self-sufficiency—from the need to produce the same mixes of goods they consume. Because each country can concentrate on producing the good in which it has a comparative advantage, total world production rises, making a higher standard of living possible in both nations.

In this example we have simply assumed the post-trade consumption bundles of the two countries. In fact, the consumption choices of a country reflect both the preferences of its residents and the *relative prices*—the prices of one good in terms of another in international markets. Although we have not explicitly given the price of trucks in terms of phones, that price is implicit in our example: China sells the United States the 75 million phones the United States consumes in return for the 37,500 trucks China consumes, so 1 million phones are traded for 500 trucks. This tells us that the price of a truck on world markets must be equal to the price of 2,000 phones.

One requirement that the relative price must satisfy is that no country pays a relative price greater than its opportunity cost of obtaining the good in autarky. That is, the United States won't pay more than 1,000 trucks for 1 million phones from China, and China won't pay more than 4,000 phones for each truck from the United States. Once this requirement is satisfied, the actual relative price in international trade is determined by supply and demand—and we'll turn to supply and demand in international trade in the next section. However, first let's look more deeply into the nature of the gains from trade.

Comparative Advantage versus Absolute Advantage

It's easy to accept the idea that Vietnam and Thailand have a comparative advantage in shrimp production: they have a tropical climate that's better suited to shrimp farming than the climate of the United States, and they have a lot of usable coastal area. So the United States imports shrimp from Vietnam and Thailand. But as we have seen in the case of cell phone assembly, the gains from trade often depend on *comparative advantage*, rather than on absolute advantage. It would take less labor to assemble a phone in the United States than in China. That is, the productivity of Chinese electronics workers is less than that of their U.S. counterparts. But what determines comparative advantage is not the amount of resources used to produce a good but the opportunity cost of that good—in this case, the quantity of other goods forgone in order to produce a phone. And the opportunity cost of phones is lower in China than in the United States.

The tropical climates of Vietnam and Thailand give them a comparative advantage in shrimp production.

Here's how it works: Chinese workers have low productivity compared with U.S. workers in the electronics industry. But Chinese workers have even lower productivity compared with U.S. workers in other industries. Because Chinese labor productivity in industries other than electronics is relatively very low, producing a phone in China, even though it takes a lot of labor, does not require forgoing the production of large quantities of other goods.

In the United States, the opposite is true: very high productivity in other industries (such as automobiles) means that assembling electronic products in the United States, even though it doesn't require much labor, requires sacrificing lots of other goods. So the opportunity cost of producing electronics is less in China than in the United States. Despite its lower labor productivity, China has a comparative advantage in the production of many consumer electronics, although the United States has an absolute advantage.

The source of China's comparative advantage in consumer electronics is reflected in global markets by the wages Chinese workers are paid. That's because a country's wage rates, in general, reflect its labor productivity. In countries where labor is highly productive in many industries, employers are willing to pay high wages to attract workers, so competition among employers leads to an overall high wage rate. In countries where labor is less productive, competition for workers is less intense and wage rates are correspondingly lower.

As the Global Comparison shows, there is indeed a strong relationship between overall levels of productivity and wage rates around the world. Because China has generally low productivity, it has a relatively low wage rate. Low wages, in turn, give China a cost advantage in producing goods where its productivity is only moderately low, like consumer electronics. As a result, it's cheaper to produce these goods in China than in the United States.

Popular Misconceptions Arising from Misunderstanding Comparative Advantage

The kind of trade that takes place between low-wage, low-productivity economies like China and high-wage, high-productivity economies like the United States gives rise to two common misperceptions:

- The *pauper labor fallacy* is the belief that when a country with high wages imports goods produced by workers who are paid low wages, it must hurt the standard of living of workers in the importing country.

- The *sweatshop labor fallacy* is the belief that trade must be bad for workers in poor exporting countries because those workers are paid very low wages by our standards.

Both fallacies miss the nature of gains from trade: it's to the advantage of both countries if the poorer, lower-wage country exports goods in which it has a comparative advantage, even if its cost advantage in these goods depends on low wages. That is, both countries are able to achieve a higher standard of living through trade.

It's particularly important to understand that buying a good made by someone who is paid much lower wages than most U.S. workers doesn't necessarily

---

GLOBAL COMPARISON PRODUCTIVITY AND WAGES AROUND THE WORLD

Is it true that both the pauper labor argument and the sweatshop labor argument are fallacies? Yes, it is. The real explanation for low wages in poor countries is low overall productivity.

The graph shows estimates of labor productivity, measured by the value of output (GDP) per worker, and wages, measured by the hourly compensation of the average worker, for several countries in 2018. Both productivity and wages are expressed as percentages of U.S. productivity and wages; for example, productivity and wages in Japan were 66% and 68%, respectively, of their U.S. levels. You can see the strong positive relationship between productivity and wages. The relationship isn't perfect. For example, Iceland has higher wages than its productivity might lead you to expect. But simple comparisons of wages give a misleading sense of labor costs in poor countries: their low wage advantage is mostly offset by low productivity.

Data from: The OECD and the World Bank, World Development Indicators.

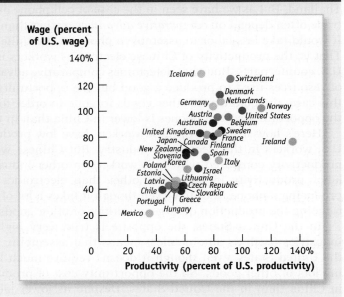

imply that you're taking advantage of that person. It depends on the alternatives. Because workers in poor countries have low productivity across the board, they are offered low wages whether they produce goods exported to the United States or goods sold in local markets. A job that looks terrible by rich-country standards can be a step up for someone in a poor country.

International trade that depends on low-wage exports can nonetheless raise the exporting country's standard of living. This is especially true of very-low-wage nations. For example, Bangladesh and similar countries would be much poorer than they are—their citizens might even be starving—if they weren't able to export goods such as clothing based on their low wage rates.

Sources of Comparative Advantage

International trade is driven by comparative advantage, but where does comparative advantage come from? Economists who study international trade have found three main sources of comparative advantage: international differences in *climate*, international differences in *factor endowments*, and international differences in *technology*.

Differences in Climate One key reason the opportunity cost of producing shrimp in Vietnam and Thailand is less than in the United States is that shrimp need warm water—Vietnam has plenty of that, but the United States doesn't. In general, differences in climate play a significant role in international trade. Tropical countries export tropical products like coffee, sugar, bananas, and shrimp. Countries in the temperate zones export crops like wheat and corn. Some trade is even driven by the difference in seasons between the northern and southern hemispheres: winter deliveries of Chilean grapes have become commonplace in U.S. and European supermarkets.

Differences in Factor Endowments The United States does more trade with Canada than with any other country (China comes in second). Among other things, Canada sells us a lot of forest products—lumber and products derived from lumber, like pulp and paper. These exports don't reflect the special skill of

A greater endowment of forestland gives Canada a comparative advantage in forest products.

Johner Images/Alamy

Canadian lumberjacks. Canada has a comparative advantage in forest products because its forested area is much greater compared to the size of its labor force than the ratio of forestland to the labor force in the United States.

Forestland, like labor and capital, is a *factor of production:* an input used to produce goods and services. (Recall from Chapter 2 that the factors of production are land, labor, physical capital, and human capital.) Due to history and geography, the mix of available factors of production differs among countries, providing an important source of comparative advantage. The relationship between comparative advantage and factor availability is described in an influential model of international trade, the *Heckscher–Ohlin model,* developed by two Swedish economists in the first half of the twentieth century.

Two key concepts in the model are *factor abundance* and *factor intensity.* Factor abundance refers to how large a country's supply of a factor is relative to its supply of other factors. **Factor intensity** refers to the ranking of goods according to which factor is used in relatively greater quantities in production compared to other factors. So oil refining is a capital-intensive good because it tends to use a high ratio of capital to labor, but phone production is a labor-intensive good because it tends to use a high ratio of labor to capital.

According to the **Heckscher–Ohlin model,** *a country that has an abundant supply of a factor of production will have a comparative advantage in goods whose production is intensive in that factor.* So a country that has a relative abundance of capital will have a comparative advantage in capital-intensive industries such as oil refining, but a country that has a relative abundance of labor will have a comparative advantage in labor-intensive industries such as phone production.

The basic intuition behind this result is simple and based on opportunity cost.

- The opportunity cost of a given factor—the value that the factor would generate in alternative uses—is low for a country when it is relatively abundant in that factor.
- Relative to the United States, China has an abundance of low-skilled labor.
- As a result, the opportunity cost of the production of low-skilled, labor-intensive goods is lower in China than in the United States.

World trade in clothing is the most dramatic example of the validity of the Heckscher–Ohlin model in practice. Clothing production is a labor-intensive activity: it doesn't take much physical capital, nor does it require a lot of human capital in the form of highly educated workers. So you would expect labor-abundant countries such as China and Bangladesh to have a comparative advantage in clothing production. And they do.

The fact that international trade is the result of differences in factor endowments helps explain another fact: international specialization of production is often *incomplete.* That is, a country often maintains some domestic production of a good that it imports. A good example is British trade in oil. Britain imports most of the petroleum it consumes, mainly from Norway, which has huge offshore reserves. But Britain has some offshore reserves of its own, mostly off the coast of Scotland, so it's a significant oil producer itself.

In our supply and demand analysis in the next section, we'll consider incomplete specialization by a country to be the norm. We should emphasize, however, that the fact that countries often incompletely specialize does not in any way change the conclusion that there are gains from trade.

Differences in Technology In the 1970s and 1980s, Japan became by far the world's largest exporter of automobiles, selling large numbers to the United States and the rest of the world. Japan's comparative advantage in automobiles wasn't

The **factor intensity** of a good is a measure of which factor is used in relatively greater quantities than other factors in production.

According to the **Heckscher–Ohlin model,** a country has a comparative advantage in a good whose production is intensive in the factors that are abundantly available in that country.

Most analyses of international trade focus on how differences between countries—differences in climate, factor endowments, and technology—create national comparative advantage. While comparative advantage is the single most significant cause of international trade, economists have also pointed out another reason for international trade: the role of *increasing returns to scale.*

Production of a good is characterized by increasing returns to scale if the productivity of labor and other resources used in production rise with the quantity of output. For example, in an industry characterized by increasing returns to scale, increasing output by 10% might require only 8% more labor and 9% more raw materials.

One example of how increasing returns drive international trade is the large passenger aircraft sector. Producing large passenger airplanes efficiently requires

enormous factories—for example, Boeing's wide-bodied passenger jets are assembled in a factory in Everett, Washington, that covers almost 100 acres. Developing a new aircraft also requires huge, one-time investments in research and development. As a result, a small number of companies with large-scale factories dominate world aircraft production. In fact, wide-bodied passenger aircraft are mainly produced in only two places in the world—near Seattle, Washington, and in Toulouse, France. As a result of increasing returns in large passenger aircraft manufacture, there is a great deal of international trade in those aircraft.

The financial services industry is another example of international trade generated by increasing returns. The industry is dominated by a relatively small number of very large banks. These banks also find it advantageous to cluster in the same location in order

to facilitate face-to-face interaction on deals, as well as to have access to a large pool of skilled workers. As a result, the world financial industry is dominated by banks located in two cities—New York and London.

Increasing returns also explain the large amount of trade that takes place between countries that have similar natural endowments of resources. Forestland aside, the United States and Canada don't look very different in terms of technology or resources. Yet they export huge quantities of manufactured goods to each other. The reason is that increasing returns lead each country to specialize in producing a limited range of products and to import the goods it doesn't produce. Increasing returns to scale probably play an especially large role in the trade in manufactured goods between advanced countries, which is about 25% of the total value of world trade.

---

the result of climate. Nor can it easily be attributed to differences in factor endowments: aside from a scarcity of land, Japan's mix of available factors is quite similar to that in other advanced countries. Instead, Japan's comparative advantage in automobiles was based on the superior production techniques developed by its manufacturers, which allowed them to produce more cars with a given amount of labor and capital than their American or European counterparts.

Japan's comparative advantage in automobiles was a case of comparative advantage caused by differences in technology—the techniques used in production.

The causes of differences in technology are somewhat mysterious. Sometimes they seem to be based on knowledge accumulated through experience—for example, Switzerland's comparative advantage in watches reflects a long tradition of watchmaking. Sometimes they are the result of a set of innovations that for some reason occur in one country but not in others.

Technological advantage, however, is often transitory. By adopting *lean production* (techniques designed to improve manufacturing productivity through increased efficiency), American auto manufacturers closed much of the gap in productivity with their Japanese competitors. Similarly, Europe's aircraft industry eventually closed a comparable gap with the U.S. aircraft industry. At any given point in time, however, differences in technology are a major source of comparative advantage.

ECONOMICS >> *in Action*
How Hong Kong Lost Its Shirts

The rise of Hong Kong was one of the most improbable-sounding economic success stories of the twentieth century. When a communist regime took over China in 1949, Hong Kong—which was at that time still a British colony—became in effect a city without a hinterland, largely cut off from economic relations with the territory just over the border. Until that point the people of Hong Kong had made a living largely by serving as a point of entry into China. However, after the city became cut off from China, it did not languish. Instead, Hong Kong prospered to such an extent that today the city—now returned to China, but governed as a special autonomous region—has a GDP per capita comparable to that of the United States.

Much of Hong Kong's ascent was the result of its clothing industry. In 1980 Hong Kong's garment and textile sectors employed almost 450,000 workers, close to 20% of total employment on the island. These workers overwhelmingly made apparel — shirts, trousers, dresses, and more—for export, especially to the United States.

More recently, the Hong Kong clothing industry has fallen sharply—in fact, it has almost disappeared and along with it, Hong Kong's apparel exports. Figure 8-4 shows Hong Kong's share of U.S. apparel imports since 1989, along with the share of a relative newcomer to the industry, Bangladesh. As you can see, Hong Kong has more or less dropped off the chart, while Bangladesh's share has risen significantly.

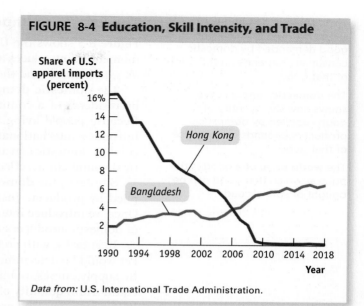

FIGURE 8-4 Education, Skill Intensity, and Trade

Data from: U.S. International Trade Administration.

Why did Hong Kong lose its comparative advantage in making clothing? It wasn't because the city's garment workers became less productive. Instead, it was because the city got better at other things. Apparel production is a labor-intensive, relatively low-tech industry; comparative advantage in that industry has historically always rested with poor, labor-abundant economies. Hong Kong no longer fits that description; Bangladesh does. Hong Kong's garment industry was a victim of the city's success.

>> Check Your Understanding 8-1

Solutions appear at back of book.

1. In the United States, the opportunity cost of 1 ton of corn is 50 bicycles. In China, the opportunity cost of 1 bicycle is 0.01 ton of corn.
   a. Determine the pattern of comparative advantage.
   b. In autarky, the United States can produce 200,000 bicycles if no corn is produced, and China can produce 3,000 tons of corn if no bicycles are produced. Draw each country's production possibility frontier assuming constant opportunity cost, with tons of corn on the vertical axis and bicycles on the horizontal axis.
   c. With trade, each country specializes its production. The United States consumes 1,000 tons of corn and 200,000 bicycles; China consumes 3,000 tons of corn and 100,000 bicycles. Indicate the production and consumption points on your diagrams, and use them to explain the gains from trade.
2. Explain the following patterns of trade using the Heckscher–Ohlin model.
   a. France exports wine to the United States, and the United States exports movies to France.
   b. Brazil exports shoes to the United States, and the United States exports shoe-making machinery to Brazil.

Supply, Demand, and International Trade

Simple models of comparative advantage are helpful for understanding the fundamental causes of international trade. However, to analyze the effects of international trade at a more detailed level and to understand trade policy, it helps to return to the supply and demand model. We'll start by looking at the effects of imports on domestic producers and consumers, then turn to the effects of exports.

>> Quick Review

• **Imports** and **exports** account for a growing share of the U.S. economy and the economies of many other countries.

• The growth of international trade and other international linkages is known as **globalization.** Extremely high levels of international trade are known as **hyperglobalization.**

• International trade is driven by comparative advantage. **The Ricardian model of international trade** shows that trade between two countries makes both countries better off than they would be in **autarky**— that is, there are gains from international trade.

• The main sources of comparative advantage are international differences in climate, factor endowments, and technology.

• The **Heckscher–Ohlin model** shows how comparative advantage can arise from differences in factor endowments: goods differ in their **factor intensity,** and countries tend to export goods that are intensive in the factors they have in abundance.

The **domestic demand curve** shows how the quantity of a good demanded by domestic consumers depends on the price of that good.

The **domestic supply curve** shows how the quantity of a good supplied by domestic producers depends on the price of that good.

The **world price** of a good is the price at which that good can be bought or sold abroad.

The Effects of Imports

Figure 8-5 shows the U.S. market for phones, ignoring international trade for a moment. It introduces a few new concepts: the *domestic demand curve*, the *domestic supply curve*, and the domestic or autarky price.

The **domestic demand curve** shows how the quantity of a good demanded by residents of a country depends on the price of that good. Why "domestic"? Because people living in other countries may demand the good, too. Once we introduce international trade, we need to distinguish between purchases of a good by domestic consumers and purchases by foreign consumers. So the domestic demand curve reflects only the demand of residents of our own country.

Similarly, the **domestic supply curve** shows how the quantity of a good supplied by producers inside our own country depends on the price of that good. Once we introduce international trade, we need to distinguish between the supply of domestic producers and foreign supply—supply brought in from abroad.

In autarky, with no international trade in phones, the equilibrium in this market would be determined by the intersection of the domestic demand and domestic supply curves, point A. The equilibrium price of phones would be P_A, and the equilibrium quantity of phones produced and consumed would be Q_A. As always, both consumers and producers gain from the existence of the domestic market. In autarky, consumer surplus would be equal to the area of the blue-shaded triangle in Figure 8-5. Producer surplus would be equal to the area of the red-shaded triangle. And total surplus would be equal to the sum of these two shaded triangles.

Now let's imagine opening up this market to imports. To do this, we must make an assumption about the supply of imports. The simplest assumption, which we will adopt here, is that unlimited quantities of phones can be purchased from abroad at a fixed price. The price at which a good can be bought or sold abroad is known as the **world price.** Figure 8-6 shows a situation in which the world price of a phone, P_W, is lower than the price of a phone that would prevail in the domestic market in autarky, P_A.

Given that the world price is below the domestic price of a phone, it is profitable for importers to buy phones abroad and resell them domestically. The imported phones increase the supply of phones in the domestic market, driving

FIGURE 8-5 Consumer and Producer Surplus in Autarky

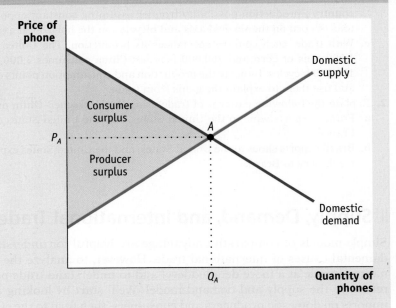

In the absence of trade, the domestic price is P_A, the autarky price at which the domestic supply curve and the domestic demand curve intersect. The quantity produced and consumed domestically is Q_A. Consumer surplus is represented by the blue-shaded area, and producer surplus is represented by the red-shaded area.

down the domestic market price. Phones will continue to be imported until the domestic price falls to a level equal to the world price.

The result is shown in Figure 8-6. Because of imports, the domestic price of a phone falls from P_A to P_W. The quantity of phones demanded by domestic consumers rises from Q_A to Q_D, and the quantity supplied by domestic producers falls from Q_A to Q_S. The difference between the domestic quantity demanded and the domestic quantity supplied, $Q_D - Q_S$, is filled by imports.

Now let's turn to the effects of imports on consumer surplus and producer surplus. Because imports of phones lead to a fall in their domestic price, consumer surplus rises and producer surplus falls. Figure 8-7 shows how this works. We label four areas: W, X, Y, and Z. The autarky consumer surplus we identified in Figure 8-5 corresponds to W, and the autarky producer surplus corresponds to the sum of X and Y. The fall in the domestic price to the world price leads to an increase in consumer surplus; it increases by X and Z, so consumer surplus now equals the sum of W, X, and Z. At the same time, producers lose X in surplus, so producer surplus now equals only Y.

The table in Figure 8-7 summarizes the changes in consumer and producer surplus when the phone market is opened to imports. Consumers gain surplus equal to the areas $X + Z$. Producers lose surplus equal to X. So the sum of producer and consumer surplus—the total surplus generated in the phone market—increases by Z. As a result of trade, consumers gain and producers lose, but the gain to consumers exceeds the loss to producers.

This is an important result. We have just shown that opening up a market to imports leads to a net gain in total surplus, which is what we should have expected given the proposition that there are gains from international trade.

However, we have also learned that although the country as a whole gains, some groups—in this case, domestic producers of phones—lose as a result of international trade. As we'll see shortly, the fact that international trade creates losers as well as winners is crucial for understanding the politics of trade policy.

We turn next to the case in which a country exports a good.

FIGURE 8-6 The Domestic Market with Imports

Here the world price of phones, P_W, is below the autarky price, P_A. When the economy is opened to international trade, imports enter the domestic market, and the domestic price falls from the autarky price, P_A, to the world price, P_W. As the price falls, the domestic quantity demanded rises from Q_A to Q_D and the domestic quantity supplied falls from Q_A to Q_S. The difference between domestic quantity demanded and domestic quantity supplied at P_W, the quantity $Q_D - Q_S$, is filled by imports.

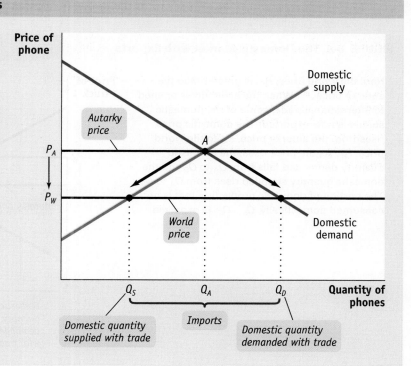

FIGURE 8-7 The Effects of Imports on Surplus

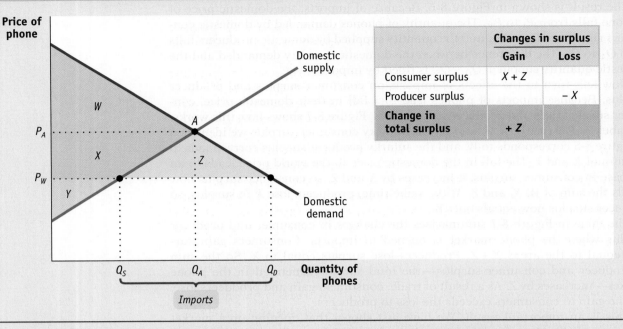

	Changes in surplus	
	Gain	**Loss**
Consumer surplus	$X + Z$	
Producer surplus		$-X$
Change in total surplus	**$+Z$**	

When the domestic price falls to P_W as a result of international trade, consumers gain additional surplus (areas $X + Z$) and producers lose surplus (area X). Because the gains to consumers outweigh the losses to producers, there is an increase in the total surplus in the economy as a whole (area Z).

The Effects of Exports

Figure 8-8 shows the effects on a country when it exports a good, in this case trucks. For this example, we assume that unlimited quantities of trucks can be sold abroad at a given world price, P_W, which is higher than the price that would prevail in the domestic market in autarky, P_A.

FIGURE 8-8 The Domestic Market with Exports

Here the world price, P_W, is greater than the autarky price, P_A. When the economy is opened to international trade, some of the domestic supply is now exported. The domestic price rises from the autarky price, P_A, to the world price, P_W. As the price rises, the domestic quantity demanded falls from Q_A to Q_D and the domestic quantity supplied rises from Q_A to Q_S. The portion of domestic production that is not consumed domestically, $Q_S - Q_D$, is exported.

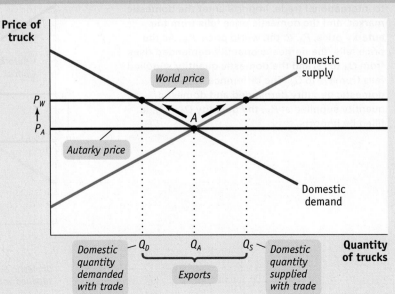

The higher world price makes it profitable for exporters to buy trucks domestically and sell them overseas. The purchases of domestic trucks drive the domestic price up until it is equal to the world price. As a result, the quantity demanded by domestic consumers falls from Q_A to Q_D and the quantity supplied by domestic producers rises from Q_A to Q_S. This difference between domestic production and domestic consumption, $Q_S - Q_D$, is exported.

Like imports, exports lead to an overall gain in total surplus for the exporting country but also create losers as well as winners. Figure 8-9 shows the effects of truck exports on producer and consumer surplus. In the absence of trade, the price of each truck would be P_A. Consumer surplus in the absence of trade is the sum of areas W and X, and producer surplus is area Y. As a result of trade, price rises from P_A to P_W, consumer surplus falls to W, and producer surplus rises to $Y + X + Z$. So producers gain $X + Z$, consumers lose X, and, as shown in the table accompanying the figure, the economy as a whole gains total surplus in the amount of Z.

We have learned, then, that imports of a particular good hurt domestic producers of that good but help domestic consumers, whereas exports of a particular good hurt domestic consumers of that good but help domestic producers. In each case, the gains are larger than the losses.

International Trade and Wages

So far we have focused on the effects of international trade on producers and consumers in a particular industry. For many purposes this is a very helpful approach. However, producers and consumers are not the only parts of society affected by trade; the owners of factors of production are also affected. In particular, the owners of labor, land, and capital employed in producing goods that are exported, or goods that compete with imported goods, can be deeply affected by trade.

Moreover, the effects of trade aren't limited to just those industries that export or compete with imports because *factors of production can often move between*

FIGURE 8-9 The Effects of Exports on Surplus

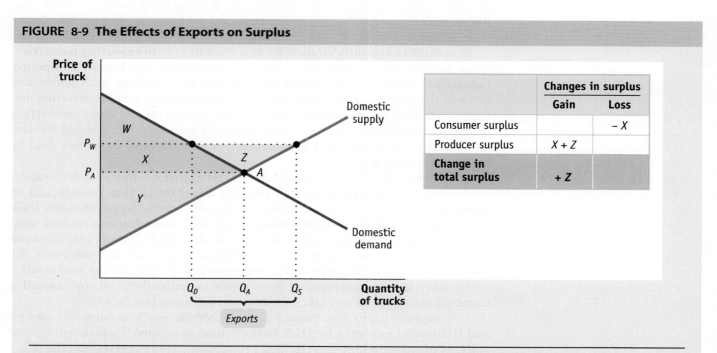

	Changes in surplus	
	Gain	**Loss**
Consumer surplus		– X
Producer surplus	X + Z	
Change in total surplus	**+ Z**	

When the domestic price rises to P_W as a result of trade, producers gain additional surplus (area $X + Z$) but consumers lose surplus (area X). Because the gains to producers outweigh the losses to consumers, there is an increase in the total surplus in the economy as a whole (area Z).

Exporting industries produce goods and services that are sold abroad.

Import-competing industries produce goods and services that are also imported.

industries. So now we turn our attention to the long-run effects of international trade on income distribution—how a country's total income is allocated among its various factors of production.

To begin our analysis, consider the position of Mia, who is initially employed as an accountant in an industry that is shrinking as a result of growing international trade. Suppose, for example, that she works in the U.S. apparel (clothing) industry, which formerly employed millions of people but has largely been displaced by imports from low-wage countries. Mia is likely to find a new job in another industry, such as health care, which has been expanding rapidly over time. How will the move affect her earnings?

The answer is, there probably won't be much effect. According to the U.S. Bureau of Labor Statistics, accountants earn roughly the same amount in health care that they do in what's left of the apparel industry—about $65,000 a year. So we shouldn't think of Mia as a producer of apparel who is hurt by competition from imports. Instead, we should think of her as a worker with particular skills who is affected by imports—mainly by the extent to which those imports change the wages of accountants in the economy as a whole.

The wage rate of accountants is a *factor price*—the price employers have to pay for the services of a factor of production. One key question about international trade is how it affects factor prices—not just narrowly defined factors of production like accountants, but broadly defined factors such as capital, unskilled labor, and college-educated labor.

Earlier in this chapter we described the Heckscher–Ohlin model of trade, which states that comparative advantage is determined by a country's factor endowment. This model also suggests how international trade affects factor prices in a country: compared to autarky, international trade tends to raise the prices of factors that are abundantly available and reduce the prices of factors that are scarce.

We won't work this out in detail, but the idea is simple. The prices of factors of production, like the prices of goods and services, are determined by supply and demand. If international trade increases the demand for a factor of production, that factor's price will rise; if international trade reduces the demand for a factor of production, that factor's price will fall.

Now think of a country's industries as consisting of both **exporting industries,** which produce goods and services that are sold abroad, and **import-competing industries,** which produce goods and services that compete with goods and services that are imported from abroad. Compared with autarky, international trade leads to higher production in exporting industries and lower production in import-competing industries. This indirectly increases the demand for factors used by exporting industries and decreases the demand for factors used by import-competing industries.

In addition, the Heckscher–Ohlin model shows that a country tends to export goods that are intensive in factors that are abundant in that country and to import goods that are intensive in factors that are scarce. *So international trade tends to increase the demand for factors that are more abundant in a country compared with other countries, and to decrease the demand for factors that are more scarce in a country compared with other countries. As international trade grows, the prices of abundant factors tend to rise, and the prices of scarce factors tend to fall.*

In other words, international trade tends to redistribute income toward a country's abundant factors and away from its less abundant factors.

U.S. exports tend to be human-capital-intensive (such as high-tech design and Hollywood movies) while U.S. imports tend to be unskilled-labor-intensive (such as phone assembly and clothing production). This suggests that the effect of international trade on the U.S. factor markets is to raise the wage rate of highly educated American workers and reduce the wage rate of unskilled American workers.

This effect has been a source of much concern in recent years. Wage inequality—the gap between the wages of high-paid and low-paid workers—has increased substantially over the last 40 years. Some economists believe that growing international trade is an important factor in that trend. If international trade has the effects predicted by the Heckscher–Ohlin model, its growth raises the wages of highly educated American workers, who already have relatively high wages, and lowers the wages of less educated American workers, who already have relatively low wages.

But keep in mind another phenomenon: trade reduces the income inequality between countries as poor countries improve their standard of living by exporting to rich countries.

The effects of trade on wages in the United States have generated considerable controversy in recent years. Most economists who have studied the issue agree that growing imports of labor-intensive products from newly industrializing economies, and the export of high-technology goods in return, have helped cause a widening wage gap between highly educated and less educated workers in the United States. However, most economists believe that it is only one of several forces explaining the growth in American wage inequality.

ECONOMICS >> *in Action*
The China Shock

If you go into a Walmart or other large store and look at the labels on the products, it can seem as if everything is made in China these days. That's not really true, but we do buy a lot from China, which supplies almost a quarter of U.S. imported goods.

This is a fairly recent phenomenon. Imports from China, though growing, were small until the late 1990s when they took a great leap upward. In 2000, imports from China were less than 1% of U.S. national income and by 2007 they were more than 2%, after which they began to level off. The surge in Chinese imports corresponded to a change in the structure of the global economy—in particular, a transfer of production and transportation technology from advanced countries to China. China's admittance to the World Trade Organization, a global institution for regulating international trade, also contributed to the surge, known as the *China Shock.*

We have seen that international trade often creates losers as well as winners. In this case, the surge in imports from China was good for U.S. consumers, who paid less for many goods. The price of clothing, in particular, fell about 10% during the China Shock, even as overall consumer prices rose about 25%. It was, however, hard on some U.S. industries. Producers of clothing, furniture, and some electronic goods, suddenly faced greatly increased competition. The losers were American companies that produced those goods, many of which were forced to close plants and their laid-off workers.

Several estimates of the effects of the China Shock indicate that as many as a million manufacturing jobs may have been lost to imports from China from 2000 to 2007. These job losses were offset by job gains elsewhere: overall U.S. employment rose by 5 million over the period. But the communities experiencing job gains weren't the same as those experiencing job losses, and some communities were hard hit as shown in Figure 8-10.

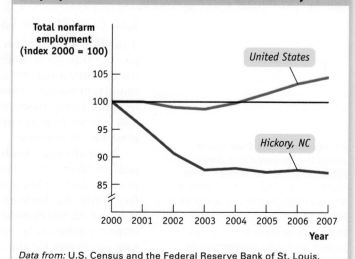

FIGURE 8-10 **The Effect of Chinese Imports on Employment in the American Furniture Industry**

Data from: U.S. Census and the Federal Reserve Bank of St. Louis.

An economy has **free trade** when the government does not attempt either to reduce or to increase the levels of exports and imports that occur naturally as a result of supply and demand.

Policies that limit imports are known as **trade protection** or simply as **protection.**

A **tariff** is a tax levied on imports.

For example, increased imports from China were probably the main reason the U.S. furniture industry lost around 150,000 jobs between 2000 and 2007, even as overall U.S. employment rose. For the overall U.S. economy, this wasn't that big a deal: almost 2 million U.S. workers are laid off every month, even in good times. But for communities like Hickory, North Carolina, where 1 in 6 workers were employed in the furniture industry, the consequences were devastating. Not only were furniture workers laid off, but additional jobs were lost as these workers stopped spending in the local economy. As Figure 8-10 shows, overall employment fell sharply and stagnated in the Hickory area even as it rose in the nation as a whole.

>> **Check Your Understanding 8-2**
Solutions appear at back of book.

1. Due to a strike by truckers, trade in food between the United States and Mexico is halted. In autarky, the price of Mexican grapes is lower than that of U.S. grapes. Using a diagram of the U.S. domestic demand curve and the U.S. domestic supply curve for grapes, explain the effect of the strike on the following.
   a. U.S. grape consumers' surplus
   b. U.S. grape producers' surplus
   c. U.S. total surplus
2. What effect do you think the strike will have on Mexican grape producers? Mexican grape pickers? Mexican grape consumers? U.S. grape pickers?

The Effects of Trade Protection

Ever since David Ricardo laid out the principle of comparative advantage in the early nineteenth century, most economists have advocated **free trade.** That is, they have argued that government policy should not attempt either to reduce or to increase the levels of exports and imports that occur naturally as a result of supply and demand.

Despite the free-trade arguments of economists, however, many governments use taxes and other restrictions to limit imports. Less frequently, governments offer subsidies to encourage exports. Policies that limit imports, usually with the goal of protecting domestic producers in import-competing industries from foreign competition, are known as **trade protection** or simply as **protection.**

Let's look at the two most common protectionist policies, *tariffs* and *import quotas*, then turn to the reasons governments follow these policies.

The Effects of a Tariff

A **tariff** is a form of excise tax, levied only on sales of imported goods. For example, the U.S. government could declare that anyone bringing phones for sale into the country must pay a tariff of $100 per unit. In the distant past, tariffs were an important source of government revenue because they were relatively easy to collect. But in the modern world, tariffs are usually intended to discourage imports and protect import-competing domestic producers, and not levied as a source of government revenue.

A tariff raises both the price received by domestic producers and the price paid by domestic consumers. Suppose, for example, that our country imports phones, and a phone costs $200 on the world market. As we saw earlier, under free trade the domestic price would also be $200. But if a tariff of $100 per unit is imposed, the domestic price will rise to $300, because it won't be profitable to import phones unless the price in the domestic market is high enough to compensate importers for the cost of paying the tariff.

Figure 8-11 illustrates the effects of a tariff on imports of phones. As before, we assume that P_W is the world price of a phone. Before the tariff is imposed, imports

FIGURE 8-11 The Effect of a Tariff

A tariff raises the domestic price of the good from P_W to P_T. The domestic quantity demanded shrinks from Q_D to Q_{DT}, and the domestic quantity supplied increases from Q_S to Q_{ST}. As a result, imports — which had been $Q_D - Q_S$ before the tariff was imposed — shrink to $Q_{DT} - Q_{ST}$ after the tariff is imposed.

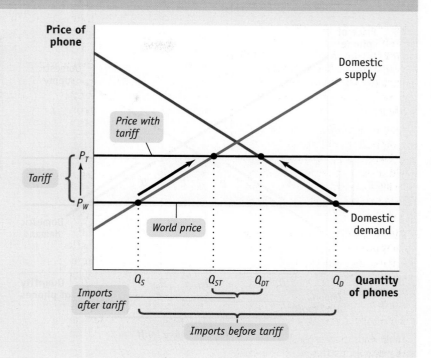

have driven the domestic price down to P_W, so that pre-tariff domestic production is Q_S, pre-tariff domestic consumption is Q_D, and pre-tariff imports are $Q_D - Q_S$.

Now suppose that the government imposes a tariff on each phone imported. As a consequence, it is no longer profitable to import phones unless the domestic price received by the importer is greater than or equal to the world price plus the tariff. So the domestic price rises to P_T, which is equal to the world price, P_W, plus the tariff. Domestic production rises to Q_{ST}, domestic consumption falls to Q_{DT}, and imports fall to $Q_{DT} - Q_{ST}$.

A tariff, then, raises domestic prices, leading to increased domestic production and reduced domestic consumption compared to the situation under free trade. Figure 8-12 shows three effects:

1. The higher domestic price increases producer surplus, a gain equal to area *A*.
2. The higher domestic price reduces consumer surplus, a reduction equal to the sum of areas *A*, *B*, *C*, and *D*.
3. The tariff yields revenue to the government. How much revenue? The government collects the tariff—which, remember, is equal to the difference between P_T and P_W on each of the $Q_{DT} - Q_{ST}$ units imported. So total revenue is $(P_T - P_W) \times (Q_{DT} - Q_{ST})$. This is equal to area *C*.

The welfare effects of a tariff are summarized in the table in Figure 8-12. Producers gain, consumers lose, and the government gains. But consumer losses are greater than the sum of producer and government gains, leading to a net reduction in total surplus equal to areas *B* + *D*.

An excise tax creates inefficiency, or deadweight loss, because it prevents mutually beneficial trades from occurring. In the case of a tariff, the deadweight loss imposed on society is equal to the loss in total surplus represented by areas *B* + *D*.

Tariffs generate deadweight losses because they create inefficiencies in two ways:

1. Some mutually beneficial trades go unexploited: some consumers who are willing to pay more than the world price, P_W, do not purchase the good, even

FIGURE 8-12 A Tariff Reduces Total Surplus

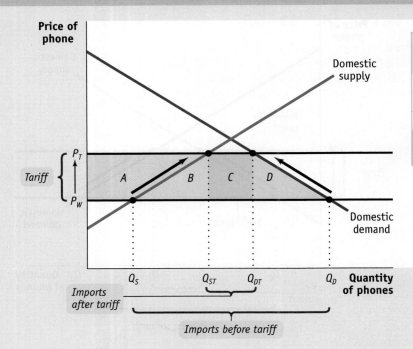

	Changes in surplus	
	Gain	**Loss**
Consumer surplus		$-(A + B + C + D)$
Producer surplus	A	
Government revenue	C	
Change in total surplus		$-(B + D)$

When the domestic price rises as a result of a tariff, producers gain additional surplus (area A), the government gains revenue (area C), and consumers lose surplus (areas $A + B + C + D$). Because the losses to consumers outweigh the gains to producers and the government, the economy as a whole loses surplus (areas B and D).

though P_W is the true cost of a unit of the good to the economy. The cost of this inefficiency is represented in Figure 8-12 by area D.

2. The economy's resources are wasted on inefficient production: some producers whose cost exceeds P_W produce the good, even though an additional unit of the good can be purchased abroad for P_W. The cost of this inefficiency is represented in Figure 8-12 by area B.

The Effects of an Import Quota

An **import quota,** another form of trade protection, is a legal limit on the quantity of a good that can be imported. For example, a U.S. import quota on Chinese phones might limit the quantity imported each year to 50 million units. Import quotas are usually administered through licenses: a number of licenses are issued, each giving the license-holder the right to import a limited quantity of the good each year.

A quota on sales has the same effect as an excise tax, with one difference: the money that would otherwise have accrued to the government as tax revenue under an excise tax becomes license-holders' revenue under a quota—also known as quota rents. (*Quota rent* is defined in Chapter 5.) Similarly, an import quota has the same effect as a tariff, with one difference: the money that would otherwise have been government revenue becomes quota rents to license-holders.

Look again at Figure 8-12. An import quota that limits imports to $Q_{DT} - Q_{ST}$ will raise the domestic price of phones by the same amount as the tariff we considered previously. That is, it will raise the domestic price from P_W to P_T. However, area C will now represent quota rents rather than government revenue.

An **import quota** is a legal limit on the quantity of a good that can be imported.

Who receives import licenses and so collects the quota rents? In the case of U.S. import protection, the answer may surprise you: the most important import licenses—mainly for clothing, and to a lesser extent for sugar—are granted to foreign governments.

Because the quota rents for most U.S. import quotas go to foreigners, the cost to the nation of such quotas is larger than that of a comparable tariff (a tariff that leads to the same level of imports). In Figure 8-12 the net loss to the United States from such an import quota would be equal to areas $B + C + D$, the difference between consumer losses and producer gains.

ECONOMICS >> *in Action*
The Steel Tariffs of 2018–2019

U.S. law grants the president authority to impose tariffs unilaterally, without going to Congress, under certain circumstances. This authority was intended to allow prompt responses to trade challenges without opening up a political process that, history shows, tends to be rife with special-interest politics. In general, presidents have used this authority sparingly. However, in 2018 President Donald Trump moved to impose high tariffs on multiple countries and multiple products, with the most dramatic move being a 25% tariff on steel imports from all major suppliers, of which Canada was the most important.

Some of the president's statements seemed to imply that he believed foreign exporters, not American consumers, would be paying these tariffs. Market data, however, showed a sharp rise in U.S. steel prices as the tariffs went into effect, while world prices were mostly flat. Figure 8-13 shows one example, the price of hot rolled band—a form of steel that is sold to manufacturers of products that use steel. The figure includes data from late 2017 until July 2019. The tariffs were phased in over the course of 2018, then removed in 2019 after the United States, Canada, and Mexico reached a new trade agreement.

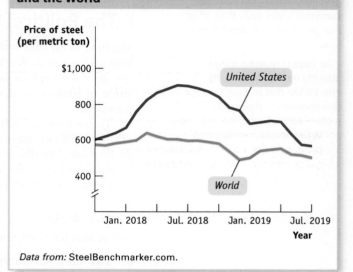

FIGURE 8-13 **Tariffs and Steel Prices, United States and the World**

Data from: SteelBenchmarker.com.

As you can see, after the tariffs took effect, the U.S. price soared above the world price; then U.S. prices fell sharply when the tariffs were removed.

Who gained and who lost from the steel tariffs? U.S. steel companies clearly benefited, as higher prices raised their profits. They also responded to the higher prices by reopening some closed production facilities and planning some expansion of their capacity.

At least initially, however, steel workers didn't seem to be sharing much of the benefit: their wages weren't rising much more than those of workers in other industries.

On the other side, higher steel prices hurt steel users. Ordinary Americans, of course, don't buy steel directly. The metal is used, instead, to make a variety of manufactured goods, such as cars—and U.S. companies that buy steel complained bitterly about higher costs, assigning the tariff partial responsibility for some plant closings and layoffs. They also passed at least some of the tariff on to their customers in the form of higher prices.

The steel tariffs of 2018, then, played out pretty much the way standard analysis would have predicted. Producers of import-competing goods—U.S. steel companies—gained. Consumers—manufacturers who use steel, and, ultimately, the buyers of these manufacturers' goods—were hurt.

>> *Check Your Understanding* 8-3
Solutions appear at back of book.

1. Suppose the world price of butter is $0.50 per pound and the domestic price in autarky is $1.00 per pound. Use a diagram similar to Figure 8-10 to show the following.
   a. If there is free trade, domestic butter producers want the government to impose a tariff of no less than $0.50 per pound. Compare the outcome with a tariff of $0.25 per pound.
   b. What happens if a tariff greater than $0.50 per pound is imposed?
2. Suppose the government imposes an import quota rather than a tariff on butter. What quota limit would generate the same quantity of imports as a tariff of $0.50 per pound?

|| The Political Economy of Trade Protection

We have seen that international trade produces mutual benefits to the countries that engage in it. We have also seen that tariffs and import quotas, although they produce winners as well as losers, reduce total surplus. Yet many countries continue to impose tariffs and import quotas as well as to enact other protectionist measures.

To understand why trade protection takes place, we will first look at some common justifications for protection. Then we will look at the politics of trade protection. Finally, we will look at an important feature of trade protection in today's world: tariffs and import quotas are the subject of international negotiation and are policed by international organizations.

Arguments for Trade Protection

Advocates for tariffs and import quotas offer three common arguments:

1. The *national security* argument is based on the proposition that overseas sources of goods are vulnerable to disruption in times of international conflict. A country should protect domestic suppliers of crucial goods with the aim to be self-sufficient in the production of those goods. For example, during the coronavirus pandemic of 2020, 90% of medical masks used in the United States were produced overseas. As a result, masks were in extremely short supply and rose sharply in price as countries scrambled for supplies of this critical good.

2. The *job creation* argument points to the additional jobs created in import-competing industries as a result of trade protection. Economists argue that these jobs are offset by the jobs lost elsewhere, such as industries that use imported inputs and now face higher input costs. But noneconomists don't always find this argument persuasive.

3. The *infant industry* argument, often raised in newly industrializing countries, holds that new industries require a temporary period of trade protection to get established. For example, in the 1950s many countries in Latin America imposed tariffs and import quotas on manufactured goods, in an effort to switch from their traditional role as exporters of raw materials to a new status as industrial countries.

   In theory, the argument for infant industry protection can be compelling, particularly in high-tech industries that increase a country's overall skill level. Reality, however, is more complicated: it is most often industries that are politically influential that gain protection. In addition, governments tend to be poor predictors of the best emerging technologies. Finally, it is often very difficult to wean an industry from protection when it should be mature enough to stand on its own.

The Politics of Trade Protection

In reality, much trade protection has little to do with the arguments just described. Instead, it reflects the political influence of import-competing producers.

We've seen that a tariff or import quota leads to gains for import-competing producers and losses for consumers. Producers, however, usually have much more influence over trade policy decisions. The producers who compete with imports of a particular good are usually a smaller, more cohesive group than the consumers of that good.

For example, in 2018, the U.S. government imposed a 30% tariff on imports of solar panels, many of which come from China. While it helped U.S. producers, who employed about 2,000 workers, it hurt a much larger group, including tens of thousands of solar panel installers, whose business was hurt when panels became more expensive, leading to a decline in new installations. However, the voices of panel producers were heard much more clearly in Washington than the voices of concern from those who buy panels or install them.

It would be nice to say that the main reason trade protection isn't more extensive is that economists have convinced governments of the virtues of free trade. A more important reason, however, is the role of *international trade agreements*.

International Trade Agreements and the World Trade Organization

When a country engages in trade protection, it hurts two groups. We've already addressed the adverse effect on domestic consumers, but protection also hurts foreign export industries. This means that countries care about one anothers' trade policies: the Canadian lumber industry, for example, has a strong interest in keeping U.S. tariffs on forest products low.

Because countries care about one anothers' trade policies, they enter into **international trade agreements:** treaties in which a country promises to engage in less trade protection against the exports of another country in return for a promise by the other country to do the same for its own exports. International trade agreements are especially important as a way to head off potential **trade wars,** in which countries impose tariffs and other protectionist measures against other countries' products in an attempt to force them to make policy concessions. Most world trade is now governed by such agreements.

Some international trade agreements involve just two countries or a small group of countries. For example, in 1993 the United States, Canada, and Mexico joined together in the **North American Free Trade Agreement,** or **NAFTA.** By 2008 NAFTA had removed most barriers to trade among the three nations. In 2018 the countries negotiated a revised agreement, the United States-Mexico-Canada Agreement or USMCA, which made some changes but kept the main structure of NAFTA intact. For accuracy's sake, we will refer to the current trade agreement as **NAFTA-USMCA.**

Most European countries are part of an even more comprehensive agreement, the **European Union,** or **EU.** Unlike members of NAFTA-USMCA, the 27 members of the EU agree to charge the same tariffs on goods imported from non-EU countries. The EU also sets rules on policies other than trade, most notably requiring that each member nation freely accept migrants from any other member, while collecting fees from member nations to pay for things like agricultural subsidies. These rules and fees are often unpopular and controversial. In June 2016, Britain held a referendum on whether to leave the EU—a proposal popularly known

International trade agreements are treaties in which a country promises to engage in less trade protection against the exports of other countries in return for a promise by other countries to do the same for its own exports.

In a **trade war,** countries deliberately try to impose pain on their trading partners, as a way to extract policy concessions.

The **North American Free Trade Agreement,** or **NAFTA,** is a trade agreement among the United States, Canada, and Mexico. The current version of the agreement is **NAFTA-USMCA.**

The **European Union,** or **EU,** is a customs union among 27 European nations.

The **World Trade Organization,** or **WTO,** oversees international trade agreements and rules on disputes between countries over those agreements.

as *Brexit* (short for "British exit"), which was approved by a narrow majority of voters. Negotiations over the details of Britain's exit from the EU, and its future relationship with it, were still in progress as this book went to press.

There are also global trade agreements covering most of the world. Such global agreements are overseen by the **World Trade Organization,** or **WTO,** an international organization composed of member countries—164 of them currently, accounting for the bulk of world trade. The WTO plays two roles:

1. It provides the framework for the massively complex negotiations involved in a major international trade agreement (the full text of the last major agreement, approved in 1994, was 24,000 pages long).

2. The WTO resolves disputes between its members that typically arise when one country claims that another country's policies violate its previous agreements.

An example of the WTO at work is the dispute between the United States and Brazil over American subsidies to its cotton farmers. These subsidies, in the amount of $3 billion to $4 billion a year, are illegal under WTO rules. Brazil argued that they artificially reduced the price of American cotton on world markets and hurt Brazilian cotton farmers. In 2005 the WTO ruled against the United States and in favor of Brazil, and the United States responded by cutting some export subsidies on cotton. However, in 2007 the WTO ruled that the United States had not done enough to fully comply, such as eliminating government loans to cotton farmers. In 2010, after Brazil threatened, in turn, to impose import tariffs on U.S.-manufactured goods, the two sides agreed to a framework for the solution to the cotton dispute.

The WTO rules do allow trade protection under certain circumstances. One such circumstance occurs when the foreign competition is "unfair" under certain technical criteria. Trade protection is also allowed as a temporary measure when a sudden surge of imports threatens to disrupt a domestic industry. For example, although both Vietnam and Thailand are members of the WTO, the United States has, on and off, imposed tariffs on shrimp imports from these countries.

The WTO is sometimes, with great exaggeration, described as a world government. In fact, it has no army, no police, and no direct enforcement power. The grain of truth in that description is that when a country joins the WTO, it agrees to accept the organization's judgments—and these judgments apply not only to tariffs and import quotas but also to domestic policies that the organization considers trade protection disguised under another name. So in joining the WTO a country does give up some of its sovereignty.

Challenges to Globalization

The forward march of globalization over the past century is generally considered a major political and economic success because it has brought rising living standards to hundreds of millions of people. But it is also true that many people, including some economists and policy makers, are having second thoughts about globalization. These second thoughts arise largely from the decline of manufacturing in richer countries and *offshore outsourcing* that jeopardizes the jobs of non-manufacturing workers, once considered immune from foreign competition.

The Decline of Manufacturing We have seen that international trade has an effect on factor prices, particularly wages. Forty years ago, U.S. imports from poorer countries consisted mostly of raw materials and goods that depended upon the climate, like bananas and coffee beans. So U.S. wages were relatively unaffected by international trade. But that is no longer the case. Today many of the manufactured goods consumed in the United States are imported from poorer countries. As a result, international trade now has a much larger effect on income inequality in the United States.

Trade with Asia has raised the greatest concerns among those who study the effect of international trade on wage levels in rich countries. China, despite its rapid economic growth and rising wages in recent years, is still a very low-wage country compared with the United States. Its hourly compensation in manufacturing is approximately 10% of the U.S. level. Other manufacturing exporters, such as India, Bangladesh, and Vietnam, have wage levels less than half of China's. As we discussed earlier in the chapter, it's clear that imports from these countries have placed downward pressure on the wages of less skilled U.S. workers and possibly contributed to income inequality.

Offshore outsourcing takes place when businesses hire people in another country to perform various tasks.

Outsourcing Chinese exports to the United States overwhelmingly consist of labor-intensive manufactured goods. However, some U.S. workers have also found themselves facing a new form of international competition. *Outsourcing,* in which a company hires another company to perform a task, such as running the corporate computer system, is a long-standing business practice. Until recently, however, outsourcing was normally done locally, with a company hiring another company in the same city or country.

Now, modern telecommunications increasingly make it possible to engage in **offshore outsourcing,** in which businesses hire people in another country to perform various tasks. The classic example is call centers: the person answering the phone when you call a company's help line may well be in India, which has taken the lead in attracting offshore outsourcing. Offshore outsourcing has also spread to fields such as software design and even health care: the radiologist examining your X-rays, like the person giving you computer help, may be on another continent.

Offshore outsourcing has the potential to disrupt the job prospects of millions of U.S. workers.

The threat of offshore outsourcing differs from the threat posed by large-scale imports of manufactured goods from poorer countries. By and large, offshore outsourcing hits higher-skilled U.S. workers who imagined their jobs were safe from foreign competition. An example is U.S. computer programmers, many of whom have their jobs outsourced to India or Eastern Europe. Although offshore outsourcing still accounts for a relatively small portion of international trade, some economists have warned that millions or even tens of millions of workers in rich countries may face unpleasant surprises in the not-too-distant future—workers such as bookkeepers, claims adjusters, and mortgage processors.

Do these challenges of globalization undermine the argument that international trade is a good thing? The great majority of economists would argue that the gains from trade protection still exceed the losses. However, as international trade has grown and job losses in vulnerable sectors have mounted, the politics of international trade has become increasingly difficult and has led to calls for protectionist trade policies. In this debate it's important to understand that government programs, such as unemployment benefits, easily accessible health care, and retraining projects, can reduce the opposition to free trade by helping cushion the losses of those hurt by trade.

ECONOMICS >> *in Action*
Trade War, What Is It Good For?

There are, as we've seen, a number of reasons countries sometimes impose tariffs and other restrictions on imports, and these measures often hurt other countries as well as domestic consumers. However, we generally only use the term *trade*

In 2019, the United States and China engaged in a classic trade war by levying tariffs on each other's exports.

>> Quick Review

• The three major justifications for trade protection are national security, job creation, and the infant industry argument.

• Despite the deadweight losses, import protections are often imposed because groups representing import-competing industries are more influential than groups of consumers.

• To further trade liberalization, countries engage in **international trade agreements.** An important purpose of these agreements is to head off the possibility of **trade wars.** Some agreements are among a small number of countries, such as the **North American Free Trade Agreement (NAFTA)** and the **European Union (EU).** The current version of NAFTA is known as **NAFTA-USMCA.** The **World Trade Organization (WTO)** oversees global trade agreements and referees trade disputes between members.

• Resistance to globalization has emerged in response to a surge in imports of manufacturing goods from poorer countries and the threat of **offshore outsourcing** many jobs that were once considered safe from foreign competition.

war when hurting foreigners isn't a side effect of tariffs, but their purpose—that is, when tariffs are imposed to inflict damage on another country in an attempt to force it to make concessions of some kind.

A classic example is the "chicken war" that broke out between the United States and Europe more than half a century ago. In 1964 the U.S. imposed a 25% tariff on imports of light trucks—a category that today includes most pickups and SUVs. The purpose of the tariff was to put pressure on the European community to eliminate a tariff it had placed on U.S. exports of frozen chicken, which surged with the rise of factory farming. Incredibly, this dispute was never resolved: that 25% tariff remains in place.

Historically, however, trade wars in which countries try to inflict pain have been fairly rare. Before the 1930s, the United States and other countries generally ignored the effects of their trade policies on other countries; since World War II trade wars have mostly been prevented by international trade agreements.

That may, however, be changing. Since 2017 the U.S. government has imposed tariffs on a wide variety of goods and trading partners, with the explicit aim of forcing other countries to change their policies, and some of the countries have responded with tariffs of their own that are explicitly meant to cause pain here.

We have already discussed the steel tariffs recently imposed on Canada and Mexico, at least partly intended to force our neighbors into agreeing to revise the North American Free Trade Agreement. Those tariffs, however, pale in significance compared with the 25% tariff the U.S. government imposed on $250 billion worth of Chinese exports in 2019—almost half of what China sells to the United States—with a threat to expand the tariffs to the rest of China's exports unless China meets policy demands that include protecting U.S. intellectual property and reducing China's trade surplus with the United States.

China has, in turn, retaliated by imposing tariffs on U.S. products, especially agricultural goods, in a clear attempt to raise the political costs of current U.S. policy, for example by hurting U.S. farmers.

What we're experiencing now, in other words, really is a trade war in the classic sense. At the time of writing it was unclear when or how this trade war might be resolved. And the case of the "chicken war" of 1964 suggests that the effects of the current trade conflict might last for a very long time.

>> Check Your Understanding 8-4

Solutions appear at back of book.

1. In 2017, the United States imposed a tariff on steel imports from a number of countries. Steel is an input in a large number and variety of U.S. industries. Explain why political lobbying to eliminate these tariffs is more likely to be effective than political lobbying to eliminate tariffs on consumer goods such as sugar or clothing.

2. Over the years, the WTO has increasingly found itself adjudicating trade disputes that involve not just tariffs or quota restrictions but also restrictions based on quality, health, and environmental considerations. Why do you think this has occurred? What method would you, as a WTO official, use to decide whether a quality, health, or environmental restriction is in violation of a free-trade agreement?

Li & Fung: From Guangzhou to You

It's a very good bet that as you read this, you're wearing something manufactured in Asia. And if you are, it's also a good bet that the Hong Kong company Li & Fung was involved in getting your garment designed, produced, and shipped to your local store. From Levi's to Walmart, Li & Fung is a critical conduit from factories around the world to the shopping mall nearest you.

The company was founded in 1906 in Guangzhou, China. According to Victor Fung, the company's chairman, his grandfather's "value added" was that he spoke English, which allowed him to serve as an interpreter in business deals between Chinese and foreigners. When Mao's Communist Party seized control in mainland China, the company moved to Hong Kong. As Hong Kong's market economy took off during the 1960s and 1970s, Li & Fung grew as an export broker, bringing together Hong Kong manufacturers and foreign buyers.

However, the real transformation of the company came as Asian economies grew and changed. Hong Kong's rapid growth led to rising wages, making Li & Fung increasingly uncompetitive in garments, its main business. So the company reinvented itself: rather than being a simple broker, it became a "supply chain manager." It would not only allocate production of a good to a manufacturer, it would break the allocations of inputs down according to steps in the production process and then allocate final assembly of the good among its 12,000+ suppliers around the globe. Sometimes production would be done in sophisticated economies like those of Hong Kong or even Japan, where high wages reflect high quality and productivity. Sometimes production would be done in less advanced economies such as that of mainland China or Thailand, where labor is less productive but also cheaper.

For example, suppose you own a U.S. retail chain and want to sell garment-washed blue jeans. Rather than simply arrange for production of the jeans, Li & Fung will work with you on design, providing you with the latest production and style information such as what materials and colors are trendy. After the design has been finalized, Li & Fung will arrange for the creation of a prototype, find the most cost-effective way to manufacture it, and then place an order on your behalf. Li & Fung might secure fabric made in Korea and dyed in Taiwan, and then have the jeans assembled in Thailand or mainland China. And because production takes place in so many locations, Li & Fung provides transport logistics as well as quality control.

Li & Fung has been enormously successful. In 2019, the company had a market value of $13.2 billion, with offices and distribution centers in more than 50 countries.

You might ask, by the way, how Li & Fung has been affected by the U.S.-China trade war. The answer is that U.S. tariffs on Chinese exports hurt one important aspect of the company's business, but also opened other opportunities. Li & Fung has been helping U.S. customers shift to alternative sources, such as Vietnam and Bangladesh; it has also been helping customers in Europe and other locations take advantage of the low prices offered by Chinese suppliers shut out of U.S. markets.

QUESTIONS FOR THOUGHT

1. Why do you think it was profitable for Li & Fung to go beyond brokering exports to becoming a supply chain manager, breaking down the production process and sourcing the inputs from various suppliers across many countries?

2. What principle do you think underlies Li & Fung's decisions on how to allocate production of a good's inputs and its final assembly among various countries?

3. Why do you think a retailer prefers to have Li & Fung arrange international production of its jeans rather than purchase them directly from a jeans manufacturer in mainland China?

4. What is the source of Li & Fung's success? Is it based on human capital, on ownership of a natural resource, or on ownership of capital?

SUMMARY

1. International trade is of growing importance to the United States and of even greater importance to most other countries. International trade, like trade among individuals, arises from comparative advantage: the opportunity cost of producing an additional unit of a good is lower in some countries than in others. Goods and services purchased from abroad are **imports;** those sold abroad are **exports.** Foreign trade, like other economic linkages between countries, has been growing rapidly, a phenomenon called **globalization. Hyperglobalization,** the phenomenon of extremely high levels of international trade, has occurred as advances in communication and transportation technology have allowed supply chains of production to span the globe.

2. The **Ricardian model of international trade** assumes that opportunity costs are constant. It shows that there are gains from trade: two countries are better off with trade than in **autarky.**

3. In practice, comparative advantage reflects differences between countries in climate, factor endowments, and technology. The **Heckscher–Ohlin model** shows how differences in factor endowments determine comparative advantage: goods differ in **factor intensity,** and countries tend to export goods that are intensive in the factors they have in abundance.

4. The **domestic demand curve** and the **domestic supply curve** determine the price of a good in autarky. When international trade occurs, the domestic price is driven to equality with the **world price,** the price at which the good is bought and sold abroad.

5. If the world price is below the autarky price, a good is imported. This leads to an increase in consumer surplus, a fall in producer surplus, and a gain in total surplus. If the world price is above the autarky price, a good is exported. This leads to an increase in producer surplus, a fall in consumer surplus, and a gain in total surplus.

6. International trade leads to expansion in **exporting industries** and contraction in **import-competing industries.** This raises the domestic demand for abundant factors of production, reduces the demand for scarce factors, and so affects factor prices, such as wages.

7. Most economists advocate **free trade,** but in practice many governments engage in **trade protection.** The two most common forms of **protection** are tariffs and quotas. In rare occasions, export industries are subsidized.

8. A **tariff** is a tax levied on imports. It raises the domestic price above the world price, hurting consumers, benefiting domestic producers, and generating government revenue. As a result, total surplus falls. An **import quota** is a legal limit on the quantity of a good that can be imported. It has the same effects as a tariff, except that the revenue goes not to the government but to those who receive import licenses.

9. Although several popular arguments have been made in favor of trade protection, in practice the main reason for protection is probably political: import-competing industries are well organized and well informed about how they gain from trade protection, while consumers are unaware of the costs they pay. Still, U.S. trade is fairly free, mainly because of the role of **international trade agreements,** in which countries agree to reduce trade protection against one another's exports. Trade agreements also help prevent **trade wars.** The **North American Free Trade Agreement (NAFTA), NAFTA-USMCA,** and the **European Union (EU)** cover a small number of countries. In contrast, the **World Trade Organization (WTO)** covers a much larger number of countries, accounting for the bulk of world trade. It oversees trade negotiations and adjudicates disputes among its members.

10. In the past few years, many concerns have been raised about the effects of globalization. One issue is the increase in income inequality due to the surge in manufacturing imports from poorer countries over the past 20 years particularly countries in Asia. Another concern is the increase in **offshore outsourcing,** as many jobs that were once considered safe from foreign competition have been moved abroad.

KEY TERMS

Imports, p. 216
Exports, p. 216
Globalization, p. 216
Hyperglobalization, p. 217
Ricardian model of international trade, p. 218
Autarky, p. 219
Factor intensity, p. 223
Heckscher–Ohlin model, p. 223

Domestic demand curve, p. 226
Domestic supply curve, p. 226
World price, p. 226
Exporting industries, p. 230
Import-competing industries, p. 230
Free trade, p. 232
Trade protection, p. 232
Protection, p. 232
Tariff, p. 232

Import quota, p. 234
International trade agreements, p. 237
Trade wars, p. 237
North American Free Trade Agreement (NAFTA), p. 237
NAFTA-USMCA, p. 237
European Union (EU), p. 237
World Trade Organization (WTO), p. 238
Offshore outsourcing, p. 239

PRACTICE QUESTIONS

1. Evaluate the following statement: is it true, false, or uncertain? "The United States can produce more tomatoes and avocados compared to Mexico, therefore there is no need for the United States to trade with Mexico for these goods."

2. In the context of supply and demand under international trade, when will a country decide to export a particular good? Import a good? Who gains and loses under each decision?

3. In 2018 the United States announced 25% tariffs on avocados imported from Mexico and that the higher price of avocados would be paid entirely by Mexico. Supporters of the tariff claimed that the increased price would be paid Mexico. Evaluate the validity of this claim. (*Hint:* Use a figure in the chapter to support your conclusion.)

PROBLEMS

1. Both Canada and the United States produce lumber and footballs with constant opportunity costs. The United States can produce either 10 tons of lumber and no footballs, or 1,000 footballs and no lumber, or any combination in between. Canada can produce either 8 tons of lumber and no footballs, or 400 footballs and no lumber, or any combination in between.

   a. Draw the U.S. and Canadian production possibility frontiers in two separate diagrams, with footballs on the horizontal axis and lumber on the vertical axis.

   b. In autarky, if the United States wants to consume 500 footballs, how much lumber can it consume? Label this point *A* in your diagram. Similarly, if Canada wants to consume 1 ton of lumber, how many footballs can it consume in autarky? Label this point *C* in your diagram.

   c. Which country has the absolute advantage in lumber production?

   d. Which country has the comparative advantage in lumber production?

   Suppose each country specializes in the good in which it has the comparative advantage, and there is trade.

   e. How many footballs does the United States produce? How much lumber does Canada produce?

   f. Is it possible for the United States to consume 500 footballs and 7 tons of lumber? Label this point *B* in your diagram. Is it possible for Canada at the same time to consume 500 footballs and 1 ton of lumber? Label this point *D* in your diagram.

2. For each of the following trade relationships, explain the likely source of the comparative advantage of each of the exporting countries.

   a. The United States exports software to Venezuela, and Venezuela exports oil to the United States.

   b. The United States exports airplanes to China, and China exports clothing to the United States.

   c. The United States exports wheat to Colombia, and Colombia exports coffee to the United States.

3. According to data from the U.S. Census Bureau, since 2000, the value of U.S. imports of men's and boy's shirts from China has more than tripled from a relatively small $244 million in 2000 to $753 million in 2017. What prediction does the Heckscher–Ohlin model make about the wages received by labor in China?

4. Shoes are labor-intensive and satellites are capital-intensive to produce. The United States has abundant capital. China has abundant labor. According to the Heckscher–Ohlin model, which good will China export? Which good will the United States export? In the United States, what will happen to the price of labor (the wage) and to the price of capital?

5. Before the North American Free Trade Agreement (NAFTA) gradually eliminated import tariffs on goods, the autarky price of tomatoes in Mexico was below the world price and in the United States was above the world price. Similarly, the autarky price of poultry in Mexico was above the world price and in the United States was below the world price. Draw diagrams with domestic supply and demand curves for each country and each of the two goods. (You will need to draw four diagrams, total.) As a result of NAFTA, the United States now imports tomatoes from Mexico and the United States now exports poultry to Mexico. How would you expect the following groups to be affected?

   a. Mexican and U.S. consumers of tomatoes. Illustrate the effect on consumer surplus in your diagram.

   b. Mexican and U.S. producers of tomatoes. Illustrate the effect on producer surplus in your diagram.

   c. Mexican and U.S. tomato workers.

   d. Mexican and U.S. consumers of poultry. Illustrate the effect on consumer surplus in your diagram.

   e. Mexican and U.S. producers of poultry. Illustrate the effect on producer surplus in your diagram.

   f. Mexican and U.S. poultry workers.

6. The accompanying table indicates the U.S. domestic demand schedule and domestic supply schedule for commercial jet airplanes. Suppose that the world price of a commercial jet airplane is $100 million.

Price of jet (millions)	Quantity of jets demanded	Quantity of jets supplied
$120	100	1,000
110	150	900
100	200	800
90	250	700
80	300	600
70	350	500
60	400	400
50	450	300
40	500	200

a. In autarky, how many commercial jet airplanes does the United States produce, and at what price are they bought and sold?

b. With trade, what will the price for commercial jet airplanes be? Will the United States import or export airplanes? How many?

7. The accompanying table shows the U.S. domestic demand schedule and domestic supply schedule for oranges. Suppose that the world price of oranges is $0.30 per orange.

Price of orange	Quantity of oranges demanded (thousands)	Quantity of oranges supplied (thousands)
$1.00	2	11
0.90	4	10
0.80	6	9
0.70	8	8
0.60	10	7
0.50	12	6
0.40	14	5
0.30	16	4
0.20	18	3

a. Draw the U.S. domestic supply curve and domestic demand curve.

b. With free trade, how many oranges will the United States import or export?

Suppose that the U.S. government imposes a tariff on oranges of $0.20 per orange.

c. How many oranges will the United States import or export after introduction of the tariff?

d. In your diagram, shade the gain or loss to the economy as a whole from the introduction of this tariff.

8. The U.S. domestic demand schedule and domestic supply schedule for oranges was given in Problem 7. Suppose that the world price of oranges is $0.30. The United States introduces an import quota of 3,000 oranges and assigns the quota rents to foreign orange exporters.

a. Draw the domestic demand and supply curves.

b. What will the domestic price of oranges be after introduction of the quota?

c. Illustrate the area representing the quota rent on your graph. What is the value of the quota rents that foreign exporters of oranges receive?

9. The Observatory of Economic Complexity (OEC) is a data visualization that models international trade data among countries. Go to the website at atlas.media.mit.edu to answer the following questions.

a. Start by selecting "Countries" and enter "United States" in the search bar. In 2017, what was the largest exported good (in dollars) for the United States? What was the value of exports for "Planes, Helicopters, and/or Spacecraft"? What was the largest imported good for the United States?

b. Repeat the steps above for Brazil. In 2017, what was the largest exported good for Brazil? What was the value of exports for, "Planes, Helicopters, and/or Spacecraft"? What was the largest imported good for the Brazil?

c. On the left sidebar click on the link "Explore on Visualization Page." On the new page, in the left sidebar select "Exports," under "Country" select "Brazil," under "Partner" select "United States," and then "Build Visualization." What is the total value of Brazilian exports to the United States? What is Brazil's largest exported good (in dollars) compared to the United States? What type of goods does Brazil generally export to the United States? What is the value of exports related to "Planes, Helicopters, and/or Spacecraft"?

d. Now repeat the steps from part c for exports from the United States to Brazil. Change "Country" to "United States," change "Partner" to "Brazil," and select "Build Visualization." What is the total value of exports from the United States to Brazil? What is the United States' largest export (in dollars) to Brazil? What types of goods does the United States export to Brazil? What is the value of exports related to "Planes, Helicopters, and/or Spacecraft"?

10. Comparative advantage creates an opportunity for less productive economies like Bangladesh to trade with more productive economies like the United States. Using the OEC website from Problem 9, how much did Bangladesh export to the United States? What was its largest export to the United States? In general, what type of goods did Bangladesh export to the United States?

11. Once again, using the OEC website from Problems 9 and 10, identify which country has a comparative advantage for each of the following goods. For each good, include the country's share of global exports and the total dollar value of that share.

a. Computers

b. Maple syrup

c. Soybeans

d. Cocoa beans

e. Beer

12. Over the past five years the United States has become the world's largest producer of natural gas. But gas producers have struggled to find methods to liquefy natural gas so that it can be exported across the Atlantic. Enter Cheniere Energy, a Houston-based natural gas company that has developed a natural gas export terminal located on the Sabine Pass leading into the Gulf of Mexico. The terminal will give U.S. companies access to markets all over the world.

a. Explain how the development of a natural gas export terminal will affect the market for natural gas in the United States.

b. Assuming natural gas prices are $3.00 per BTU, illustrate the effect of an export terminal on the demand for natural gas in the United States. Explain your findings.

c. Assuming natural gas prices in Europe are $6.00 per BTU, draw a diagram to illustrate how the development of a natural gas terminal in the United States will affect supply and demand in the natural gas market for Europe. Explain your findings.

d. How will the exporting of natural gas from the United States to Europe affect consumers and producers in both places?

13. [icon] Access the Discovering Data exercise for Chapter 8 Problem 13 online to answer the following questions.

a. Rank the states in order of exports to China. Rank in order of most to fewest exports.

b. Calculate the growth in exports from 2002 to 2015 for each state.

c. As a percent of total exports, rank the states in order of most to fewest exports to China.

d. Explain the pattern of trade with China.

14. The accompanying diagram illustrates the U.S. domestic demand curve and domestic supply curve for beef.

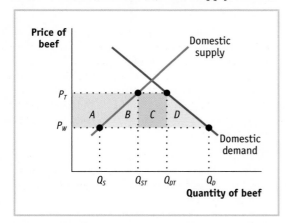

The world price of beef is P_W. The United States currently imposes an import tariff on beef, so the price of beef is P_T. Congress decides to eliminate the tariff. In terms of the areas marked in the diagram, answer the following questions.

a. With the elimination of the tariff what is the gain/loss in consumer surplus?

b. With the elimination of the tariff what is the gain/loss in producer surplus?

c. With the elimination of the tariff what is the gain/loss to the government?

d. With the elimination of the tariff what is the gain/loss to the economy as a whole?

15. As the United States has opened up to trade, it has lost many of its low-skill manufacturing jobs, but it has gained jobs in high-skill industries, such as the software industry. Explain whether the United States as a whole has been made better off by trade.

16. The United States is highly protective of its agricultural (food) industry, imposing import tariffs, and sometimes quotas, on imports of agricultural goods. This chapter presented three arguments for trade protection. For each argument, discuss whether it is a valid justification for trade protection of U.S. agricultural products.

17. In World Trade Organization (WTO) negotiations, if a country agrees to reduce trade barriers (tariffs or quotas), it usually refers to this as a *concession* to other countries. Do you think that this terminology is appropriate?

18. Producers in import-competing industries often make the following argument: "Other countries have an advantage in production of certain goods purely because workers abroad are paid lower wages. In fact, American workers are much more productive than foreign workers. So import-competing industries need to be protected." Is this a valid argument? Explain your answer.

▪▪▪ WORK IT OUT

19. Assume Saudi Arabia and the United States face the production possibilities for oil and cars shown in the accompanying table.

Saudi Arabia		United States	
Quantity of oil (millions of barrels)	Quantity of cars (millions)	Quantity of oil (millions of barrels)	Quantity of cars (millions)
0	4	0	10.0
200	3	100	7.5
400	2	200	5.0
600	1	300	2.5
800	0	400	0

a. What is the opportunity cost of producing a car in Saudi Arabia? In the United States? What is the opportunity cost of producing a barrel of oil in Saudi Arabia? In the United States?

b. Which country has the comparative advantage in producing oil? In producing cars?

c. Suppose that in autarky, Saudi Arabia produces 200 million barrels of oil and 3 million cars; and suppose that the United States produces 300 million barrels of oil and 2.5 million cars. Without trade, can Saudi Arabia produce more oil *and* more cars? Without trade, can the United States produce more oil *and* more cars?

Suppose now that each country specializes in the good in which it has the comparative advantage, and the two countries trade. Also assume that for each country the value of imports must equal the value of exports.

d. What is the total quantity of oil produced? What is the total quantity of cars produced?

e. Is it possible for Saudi Arabia to consume 400 million barrels of oil and 5 million cars and for the United States to consume 400 million barrels of oil and 5 million cars?

f. Suppose that, in fact, Saudi Arabia consumes 300 million barrels of oil and 4 million cars and the United States consumes 500 million barrels of oil and 6 million cars. How many barrels of oil does the United States import? How many cars does the United States export? Suppose a car costs $10,000 on the world market. How much, then, does a barrel of oil cost on the world market? ■

9

Decision Making by Individuals and Firms

MAKING DECISIONS IN GOOD TIMES AND BAD

WHEN MACKENZIE MCQUADE graduated from college with a degree in biology, she found a job right away. This experience was a surprise to her because just four years earlier, her older brother, Adam, had endured a very different experience. Graduating in 2010, Adam had earned a similar degree, but he had a very hard time finding a job. By the time he left school, he had been rejected by more than a dozen companies. Stressed out and nervous, he finally landed a position that forced him to move to another state. Many in the dismal 2010 job market chose yet another option: they went back to school. That year, colleges and universities across the country reported a surge in applications for all sorts of degree programs.

The differing fortunes of Mackenzie and Adam weren't due to Mackenzie being any more able than Adam. Rather, they were the result of economic fluctuations. Unfortunately for Adam, he graduated during a very tough job market, when the unemployment rate was nearly 10%, the worst it had been in several decades. By the time Mackenzie graduated in 2014, the job market had improved considerably; the unemployment rate was down to about 6.1%. But despite the improved job market, the picture was less than rosy: in 2014, the same year that Mackenzie found her job, 44% of college graduates aged 24 to 27 were stuck in low-paying jobs that didn't require a college degree.

Regardless of the circumstances, millions of people every year make decisions about their careers. Mackenzie, with several job offers, had to decide which job to take. Adam had to decide whether to take a not-so-great job that forced him to move, or to take a gamble and continue looking. And millions have made the decision to go back to school rather than endure a low-paying, dead-end job or a prolonged job search.

This chapter is about the economics of making decisions: how to make a decision that results in the best possible — often called *optimal* — economic outcome. Economists have formulated principles or methods of decision making that lead to optimal outcomes, regardless of whether the decision maker is an individual or a firm.

We'll start by examining the decision problem of an individual and learn about the three different types of economic decisions, each with a corresponding principle of decision making that leads to the best possible economic outcome. With this chapter we'll come to understand why economists consider decision making to be the very essence of microeconomics.

Despite the fact that people should use the principles of economic decision making to achieve optimal economic outcomes, they sometimes fail to do so. In other words, people are not always rational decision makers. For example, a shopper may knowingly spend more on gasoline in pursuit of a bargain than they save. Yet economists have discovered that people are *irrational in predictable ways*. A discussion of *behavioral economics*, the branch of economics that studies predictably irrational behavior, concludes this chapter. ●

Ackerman + Gruber

Due to economic fluctuations, siblings Mackenzie and Adam McQuade had very different experiences landing their first jobs after graduating from college.

WHAT YOU WILL LEARN

- Why does good decision making depend on accurately defining costs and benefits?

- What is the difference between **explicit** and **implicit** costs?

- What is the difference between **accounting profit** and **economic profit,** and why is economic profit the correct basis for decisions?

- What are the three types of economic decisions?

- Why do people behave in irrational yet predictable ways sometimes?

- Why are decisions involving time different, and how they should be made? (In this chapter's appendix.)

An **explicit cost** is a cost that requires an outlay of money.

An **implicit cost** does not require an outlay of money. It is measured by the value, in dollar terms, of benefits that are forgone.

‖ Costs, Benefits, and Profits

In making any type of decision, it's critical to define the costs and benefits of that decision accurately. If you don't know the costs and benefits, it is nearly impossible to make a good decision. So that is where we begin.

An important first step is to recognize the role of *opportunity cost,* a concept we first encountered in Chapter 1, where we learned that opportunity costs arise because *resources are scarce.* Because resources are scarce, the true cost of anything is what you must give up to get it—its opportunity cost.

Whether you decide to continue in school for another year or leave to find a job, each choice has costs and benefits. Because your time—a resource—is scarce, you cannot be both a full-time student and a full-time worker. If you choose to be a full-time student, the opportunity cost of that choice is the income you would have earned at a full-time job. And there may be additional opportunity costs, such as the value of the experience you would have gained by working.

When making decisions, it is crucial to think in terms of opportunity cost, because the opportunity cost of an action is often considerably more than the cost of any outlays of money.

Economists use the concepts of *explicit costs* and *implicit costs* to compare the relationship between opportunity costs and monetary outlays. We'll discuss these two concepts first. Then we'll define the concepts of *accounting profit* and *economic profit,* which are *ways of measuring whether the benefit of an action is greater than the cost.* Armed with these concepts for assessing costs and benefits, we will be in a position to consider our first principle of economic decision making: how to make "either–or" decisions.

Explicit versus Implicit Costs

Suppose that, like Adam McQuade, you face two choices upon graduation: take a less-than-ideal job, or return to school for another year to get a graduate degree.

In order to make that decision correctly, you need to know the cost of an additional year of school.

Here is where it is important to remember the concept of opportunity cost: the cost of the year spent getting an advanced degree includes what you forgo by not taking a job for that year. The opportunity cost of an additional year of school, like any cost, can be broken into two parts: the *explicit* cost of the year's schooling and the *implicit* cost.

An **explicit cost** is a cost that requires an outlay of money. For example, the explicit cost of the additional year of schooling includes tuition. An **implicit cost,** though, does not involve an outlay of money. Instead, it is measured by the value, in dollar terms, of the benefits that are forgone. For example, the implicit cost of the year spent in school includes the income you would have earned if you had taken a job instead.

A common mistake, both in economic analysis and in life—whether individual or business—is to ignore implicit costs and focus exclusively on explicit costs. But often the implicit cost of an activity is quite substantial—indeed, sometimes it is much larger than the explicit cost.

Table 9-1 gives a breakdown of hypothetical explicit and implicit costs associated with spending an additional year in school instead of taking a job. The explicit cost consists of tuition, books, supplies, and a computer for doing assignments—all of which require you to spend money. The implicit cost is the salary you would have earned if you had taken a job instead. As you can see, the total opportunity cost of attending an additional year of schooling is $44,500, the sum of

TABLE 9-1 Opportunity Cost of an Additional Year of School

Explicit cost		Implicit cost	
Tuition	$7,000	Forgone salary	$35,000
Books and supplies	1,000		
Computer	1,500		
Total explicit cost	**9,500**	**Total implicit cost**	**35,000**
Total opportunity cost = Total explicit cost + Total implicit cost = $44,500			

the total implicit cost—$35,000 in forgone salary, and the total explicit cost—$9,500 in outlays on tuition, supplies, and a computer. Because the implicit cost is more than three times as much as the explicit cost, ignoring the implicit cost could lead to a seriously misguided decision. This example illustrates a general principle: *the opportunity cost of any activity is equal to its explicit cost plus its implicit cost.*

A slightly different way of looking at the implicit cost in this example can deepen our understanding of opportunity cost:

- The forgone salary is the cost of using your own resources—your time—in going to school rather than working.

- The use of your time for more schooling, despite the fact that you don't have to spend any money on it, is still costly to you.

This explanation illustrates an important aspect of opportunity cost:

- In considering the cost of an activity, you should include the cost of using any of your own resources for that activity. You can calculate the cost of using your own resources by determining what they would have earned in their next best use.

Understanding the role of opportunity costs makes clear the reason for the surge in school applications in 2010: a rotten job market. Starting in 2009, the U.S. job market deteriorated sharply as the economy entered a severe recession. By 2010, the job market was still quite weak; although job openings had begun to reappear, a relatively high proportion of those openings were for jobs with low wages and no benefits. As a result, the opportunity cost of another year of schooling had declined significantly, making spending another year at school a much more attractive choice than when the job market was strong.

> **Accounting profit** is equal to revenue minus explicit cost.

‖ Accounting Profit versus Economic Profit

Let's return to Adam McQuade and imagine that he faces the choice of either completing a two-year full-time graduate program to become a pharmacist, or spending two years working. We'll assume that in order to be certified as a pharmacist, he must complete the entire two-year graduate program. Which choice should he make?

To get started, let's consider what Adam gains by getting the degree—what we might call his revenue from the pharmacology degree. Once he has completed the degree two years from now, he will receive earnings from the degree valued today at $600,000 over the rest of his lifetime. In contrast, if he doesn't get the degree and instead takes the job currently offered to him, two years from now his future lifetime earnings will be valued today at $500,000. The cost of the tuition for his pharmacology degree is $40,000, which he pays for with a student loan that costs him $4,000 in interest.

At this point, what he should do might seem obvious: if he chooses the pharmacology degree, he gets a lifetime increase in the value of earnings of $600,000 − $500,000 = $100,000, and he pays $40,000 in tuition plus $4,000 in interest. That means he makes a profit of $100,000 − $40,000 − $4,000 = $56,000 by getting his pharmacology degree. This $56,000 is Adam's **accounting profit** from obtaining the degree: his revenue minus his explicit cost. In this example his explicit cost of getting the pharmacology degree is $44,000, the amount of his tuition plus student loan interest.

"I've done the numbers, and I will marry you."

Although accounting profit is a useful measure, it would be misleading for Adam to use it alone in making his decision. To make the right decision, the one that leads to the best possible economic outcome for him, he needs to calculate his **economic profit**—the revenue he receives from the pharmacology degree minus his opportunity cost of staying in school (which is equal to his explicit cost *plus* his implicit cost of staying in school). In general, the economic profit of a given project will be less than the accounting profit because there are almost always implicit costs in addition to explicit costs.

When economists use the term *profit*, they are referring to *economic* profit, not *accounting* profit. This will be our convention in the rest of the book: when we use the term *profit*, we mean economic profit.

How does Adam's economic profit from staying in school differ from his accounting profit? We've already encountered one source of the difference: his two years of forgone job earnings. This is an implicit cost of going to school full time for two years. We assume that the value today of Adam's forgone earnings for the two years is $57,000.

Once we factor in Adam's implicit costs and calculate his economic profit, we see that he is better off not getting a degree in pharmacology. You can see this in Table 9-2: his economic profit from getting the pharmacology degree is –$1,000. In other words, he incurs an *economic loss* of $1,000 if he gets the degree. Clearly, he is better off going to work now.

TABLE 9-2 Adam's Economic Profit from Acquiring a Pharmacology Degree	
Value of increase in lifetime earnings	$100,000
Explicit cost:	
Tuition	–40,000
Interest paid on student loan	–4,000
Accounting Profit	**56,000**
Implicit cost:	
Value of income forgone during 2 years spent in school	–57,000
Economic Profit	**–1,000**

Let's consider a slightly different scenario to make sure that the concepts of opportunity costs and economic profit are well understood. Let's suppose that Adam does not have to take out $40,000 in student loans to pay his tuition. Instead, he can pay for it with an inheritance from his grandmother. As a result, he doesn't have to pay $4,000 in interest. In this case, his accounting profit is $60,000 rather than $56,000. Would the right decision now be for him to get the pharmacology degree? Wouldn't the economic profit of the degree now be $60,000 – $57,000 = $3,000?

The answer is no, because in this scenario Adam is using his own *capital* to finance his education, and the use of that capital has an opportunity cost even when he owns it.

Capital is the total value of the assets of an individual or a firm. An individual's capital usually consists of cash in the bank, stocks, bonds, and the ownership value of real estate such as a house. In the case of a business, capital also includes its equipment, its tools, and its inventory of unsold goods and used parts. (Economists like to distinguish between *financial assets*, such as cash, stocks, and bonds, and *physical assets*, such as buildings, equipment, tools, and inventory.)

The point is that even if Adam owns the $40,000, using it to pay tuition incurs an opportunity cost—what he forgoes in the next best use of that $40,000. If he hadn't used the money to pay his tuition, his next best use of the money would have been to deposit it in a bank to earn interest.

To keep things simple, let's assume that he earns $4,000 on that $40,000 once it is deposited in a bank. Now, rather than pay $4,000 in explicit costs in the form of student loan interest, Adam pays $4,000 in implicit costs from the forgone interest he could have earned.

This $4,000 in forgone interest earnings is what economists call the **implicit cost of capital**—the income the owner of the capital could have earned if the capital had been employed in its next best alternative use. The net effect is that it makes no difference whether Adam finances his tuition with a student loan or by using his own funds. This comparison reinforces how carefully you must keep track of opportunity costs when making a decision.

Economic profit is equal to revenue minus the opportunity cost of resources used. It is usually less than the accounting profit.

Capital is the total value of assets owned by an individual or firm—physical assets plus financial assets.

The **implicit cost of capital** is the opportunity cost of the use of one's own capital—the income earned if the capital had been employed in its next best alternative use.

Making "Either–Or" Decisions

An "either–or" decision is one in which you must choose between two activities. That's in contrast to a "how much" decision, which requires you to choose how much of a given activity to undertake. For example, Adam faced an "either–or" decision: to spend two years in graduate school to obtain a degree in pharmacology, or to work. In contrast, a "how much" decision would be deciding how many hours to study or how many hours to work at a job. Table 9-3 contrasts a variety of "either–or" and "how much" decisions.

In making economic decisions, as we have already emphasized, it is vitally important to calculate opportunity costs correctly. The best way to make an "either–or" decision, the method that leads to the best possible economic outcome, is the straightforward **principle of "either–or" decision making.** According to this principle, *when making an "either–or" choice between two activities, choose the one with the positive economic profit.*

Let's examine Adam's dilemma from a different angle in order to understand how this principle works. If he takes the job he is currently offered, the value of his total lifetime earnings is $57,000 (the value today of his earnings over the next two years) + $500,000 (the value today of his total lifetime earnings thereafter) = $557,000. If he gets his pharmacology degree instead and works as a pharmacist, the value today of his total lifetime earnings is $600,000 (value today of his lifetime earnings after two years in school) –$40,000 (tuition) – $4,000 (interest payments) = $556,000. The economic profit from taking the job versus becoming a pharmacist is $557,000 – $556,000 = $1,000.

So the right choice for Adam is to begin work immediately, which gives him an economic profit of $1,000, rather than become a pharmacist, which would give him an economic profit of –$1,000. In other words, by becoming a pharmacist he loses the $1,000 economic profit he would have gained by starting work immediately.

In making "either–or" decisions, mistakes most commonly arise when people or businesses use their own assets in projects rather than rent or borrow assets. That's because they fail to account for the implicit cost of using self-owned capital. This would have been true of Adam, if he were to use his own savings to pay the tuition for pharmacology school. In contrast, when they rent or borrow assets, these rental or borrowing costs show up as explicit costs. If, for example, a restaurant owns its equipment and tools, it would have to compute its implicit cost of capital by calculating how much the equipment could be sold for and how much could be earned by using those funds in the next best alternative project.

In addition, businesses run by the owner (an *entrepreneur*) often fail to calculate the opportunity cost of the owner's time in running the business. In that way, small businesses often underestimate their opportunity costs and overestimate their economic profit of staying in business.

Are we implying that the hundreds of thousands who chose to go back to school rather than find work in 2010 were misguided? Not necessarily. As we mentioned before, the poor job market of 2010

> According to the **principle of "either–or" decision making,** when faced with an "either–or" choice between two activities, choose the one with the positive economic profit.

TABLE 9-3 "Either–Or" versus "How Much" Decisions

"Either–or" decisions	"How much" decisions
Tide or Cheer?	How many days before you do your laundry?
Buy a car or not?	How many miles do you go before an oil change in your car?
An order of nachos or a sandwich?	How many jalapenos on your nachos?
Run your own business or work for someone else?	How many workers should you hire in your company?
Prescribe drug A or drug B for your patients?	How much should a patient take of a drug that generates side effects?
Graduate school or not?	How many hours to study?

PITFALLS

WHY ARE THERE ONLY TWO CHOICES?

In "either–or" decision making, we have assumed that there are only two activities to choose from. But, what if, instead of just two alternatives, there are three or more? Does the principle of "either–or" decision making still apply?

Yes, it does. That's because any choice between three (or more) alternatives can always be boiled down to a series of choices between two alternatives. Here's an illustration using three alternative activities: A, B, or C. (Remember that this is an "either–or" decision: you can choose only one of the three alternatives.)

Let's say you begin by considering A versus B: in this comparison, A has a positive economic profit but B yields an economic loss. At this point, you should discard B as a viable choice because A will always be superior to B. The next step is to compare A to C: in this comparison, C has a positive economic profit but A yields an economic loss. You can now discard A because C will always be superior to A. You are now done: since A is better than B, and C is better than A, C is the correct choice.

greatly diminished the opportunity cost of forgone wages for many students, making continuing their education the optimal choice for them.

ECONOMICS >> *in Action*
Airbnb and the Rising Cost of Privacy

One of the benefits of getting older is having the higher income to acquire a place of one's own and the privacy that comes with it. No longer will you be forced to endure a messy roommate or wait to use the bathroom. But in many places across the country, that's changing as more people share their homes and apartments with strangers. You can thank websites like Airbnb and VRBO for the change and for the loss of privacy.

It's simply a matter of opportunity cost. The rise of space-sharing websites makes it easy to rent out your extra living space for cash. If you live in an area where there is high demand for short-term stays—like San Francisco or Austin—renting out your spare room can be very lucrative. In Austin a private room (shared bathroom) rents for more than $50 per night, while in San Francisco a loft bedroom (shared bathroom) rents for nearly $170 per night. So in many places the opportunity cost of an empty spare room—that is, the opportunity cost of your privacy—has risen substantially.

Not surprisingly, builders have taken notice of the trend and are constructing homes with rentable spaces. In one survey, 35% of young adults said that they wanted to be able to rent out space in their homes at least part time. "A lot of their motivation for doing that is to make the financial step of buying their home more doable," said Linda Mamet, an executive at a home-building company.

Deciding to rent out a spare room is the right choice when the rent exceeds the opportunity cost of your privacy.

>> Quick Review

• All costs are opportunity costs. They can be divided into **explicit costs** and **implicit costs.**

• An activity's **accounting profit** is not necessarily equal to its **economic profit.**

• Due to the **implicit cost of capital**—the opportunity cost of using self-owned **capital**—and the opportunity cost of one's own time, economic profit is often substantially less than accounting profit.

• The **principle of "either–or" decision making** says that when making an "either–or" choice between two activities, choose the one with the positive economic profit.

>> Check Your Understanding 9-1

Solutions appear at back of book.

1. Marisol and Logan run a furniture-refinishing business from their home. Which of the following represent an explicit cost of the business and which represent an implicit cost?
   a. Supplies such as paint stripper, varnish, polish, sandpaper, and so on
   b. Basement space that has been converted into a workroom
   c. Wages paid to a part-time helper
   d. A van that they inherited and use only for transporting furniture
   e. The job at a larger furniture restorer that Marisol gave up in order to run the business
2. Assume that Adam has a third alternative to consider: entering a two-year apprenticeship program for skilled machinists that would, upon completion, make him a licensed machinist. During the apprenticeship, he earns a reduced salary of $15,000 per year. At the end of the apprenticeship, the value of his lifetime earnings is $725,000. What is Adam's best career choice?
3. Suppose you have three alternatives—A, B, and C—and you can undertake only one of them. In comparing A versus B, you find that B has an economic profit and A yields an economic loss. But in comparing A versus C, you find that C has an economic profit and A yields an economic loss. How do you decide what to do?

Making "How Much" Decisions: The Role of Marginal Analysis

Although many decisions in economics are "either–or," many others are "how much." Not many people will give up their cars if the price of gasoline goes up, but many people will drive less. How much less? A rise in corn prices won't necessarily persuade a lot of people to take up farming for the first time, but it will persuade farmers who were already growing corn to plant more. How much more?

Recall from our principles of microeconomics that "how much" is a decision at the margin. So to understand "how much" decisions, we will use an approach known as *marginal analysis*. Marginal analysis involves comparing the benefit of doing a little bit more of some activity with the cost of doing a little bit more of that activity. The benefit of doing a little bit more of something is what economists call its *marginal benefit*, and the cost of doing a little bit more of something is what they call its *marginal cost*.

Why is this called "marginal" analysis? A margin is an edge; what you do in marginal analysis is push out the edge a bit and see whether that is a good move. We will study marginal analysis by considering a hypothetical decision of how many years of school to complete. We'll consider the case of Alexa, who studies computer science in the hopes of becoming an app designer. Since there are a wide variety of topics that can be learned one year at a time (programming, hardware, applications, user interface), at the end of each year Alexa can decide whether to continue her studies or not.

Unlike Adam, who faced an "either–or" decision of whether to get a pharmacology degree or not, Alexa faces a "how much" decision of how many years to study computer science. For example, she could study one more year, or five more years, or any number of years in between. We'll begin our analysis of Alexa's decision problem by defining Alexa's *marginal cost* of another year of study.

> The **marginal cost** of producing a good or service is the additional cost incurred by producing one more unit of that good or service.

Marginal Cost

We'll assume that each additional year of schooling costs Alexa $10,000 in explicit costs—tuition, interest on a student loan, and so on. In addition to the explicit costs, she also has an implicit cost—the income forgone by spending one more year in school.

Unlike Alexa's explicit costs, which are constant (that is, the same each year), Alexa's implicit cost changes each year. That's because each year she spends in school leaves her better trained than the year before; and the better trained she is, the higher the salary she can command. Consequently, the income she forgoes by not working rises each additional year she stays in school. In other words, the greater the number of years Alexa has already spent in school, the higher her implicit cost of another year of school.

Table 9-4 contains the data on how Alexa's cost of an additional year of schooling changes as she completes more years. The second column shows how her total cost of schooling changes as the number of years she has completed increases. For example, Alexa's first year has a total cost of $30,000: $10,000 in explicit costs of tuition and the like as well as $20,000 in forgone salary.

The second column also shows that the total cost of attending two years is $70,000: $30,000 for her first year plus $40,000 for her second year. During her second year in school, her explicit costs have stayed the same ($10,000) but her implicit cost of forgone salary has gone up to $30,000. That's because she's a more valuable worker with one year of schooling under her belt than with no schooling.

Likewise, the total cost of three years of schooling is $130,000: $30,000 in explicit cost for three years of tuition plus $100,000 in implicit cost of three years of forgone salary. The total cost of attending four years is $220,000, and $350,000 for five years.

The change in Alexa's total cost of schooling when she goes to school an additional year is her *marginal cost* of the one-year increase in years of schooling. In general, the **marginal cost** of producing a good or service (in this case, producing one's own education) is the additional cost incurred by producing one more unit of that good or

TABLE 9-4 Alexa's Marginal Cost of Additional Years in School

Quantity of schooling (years)	Total cost	Marginal cost
0	$0	
		$30,000
1	30,000	
		40,000
2	70,000	
		60,000
3	130,000	
		90,000
4	220,000	
		130,000
5	350,000	

Production of a good or service has **increasing marginal cost** when each additional unit costs more to produce than the previous one.

The **marginal cost curve** shows how the cost of producing one more unit depends on the quantity that has already been produced.

Production of a good or service has **constant marginal cost** when each additional unit costs the same to produce as the previous one.

Production of a good or service has **decreasing marginal cost** when each additional unit costs less to produce than the previous one.

service. The arrows, which zigzag between the total costs in the second column and the marginal costs in the third column, are there to help you to see how marginal cost is calculated from total cost.

Similarly, total cost can be calculated from marginal cost: the total cost of a given quantity is the sum of the marginal costs of that quantity and of all of the previous ones. So the total cost of three years of schooling is $30,000 + $40,000 + $60,000 = $130,000; that is, the marginal cost of year 1 plus the marginal cost of year 2 plus the marginal cost of year 3.

As already mentioned, the third column of Table 9-4 shows Alexa's marginal costs of more years of schooling, which have a clear pattern: they are increasing. They go from $30,000 to $40,000, to $60,000, to $90,000, and finally to $130,000 for the fifth year of schooling. That's because each year of schooling would make Alexa a more valuable and highly paid employee if she were to work. As a result, forgoing a job becomes much more costly as she becomes more educated. This is an example of what economists call **increasing marginal cost,** which occurs when each unit of a good costs more to produce than the previous unit.

Figure 9-1 shows the **marginal cost curve,** a graphical representation of Alexa's marginal costs. The height of each shaded bar corresponds to the marginal cost of a given year of schooling. The red line connecting the dots at the midpoint of the top of each bar is Alexa's marginal cost curve. Alexa has an upward-sloping marginal cost curve because she has increasing marginal cost of additional years of schooling.

Although increasing marginal cost is a frequent phenomenon in real life, it's not the only possibility. **Constant marginal cost** occurs when the cost of producing an additional unit is the same as the cost of producing the previous unit. Plant nurseries, for example, typically have constant marginal cost—the cost of growing one more plant is the same, regardless of how many plants have already been produced. With constant marginal cost, the marginal cost curve is a horizontal line.

There can also be **decreasing marginal cost,** which occurs when marginal cost falls as the number of units produced increases. With decreasing marginal cost, the marginal cost line is downward sloping. Decreasing marginal cost is often due to *learning effects* in production: for complicated tasks, such as assembling a new model of a car, workers are often slow and mistake-prone when

FIGURE 9-1 Marginal Cost

The height of each shaded bar corresponds to Alexa's marginal cost of an additional year of schooling. The height of each bar is higher than the preceding one because each year of schooling costs more than the previous years. As a result, Alexa has increasing marginal cost and the marginal cost curve, the line connecting the midpoints at the top of each bar, is upward sloping.

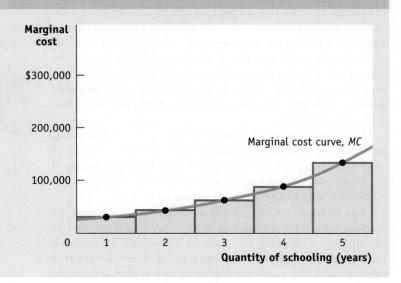

PITFALLS

TOTAL COST VERSUS MARGINAL COST

It can be easy to conclude that marginal cost and total cost must always move in the same direction. That is, if total cost is rising, then marginal cost must also be rising. Or if marginal cost is falling, then total cost must be falling as well. But the following example shows that this conclusion is wrong.

Let's consider the example of auto production, which is likely to involve learning effects. Suppose that for the first batch of cars of a new model, each car costs $10,000 to assemble. As workers gain experience with the new model, they become better at production. As a result, the per-car cost of assembly falls to $8,000 for the second batch. For the third batch, the per-car assembly cost falls again to $6,500 as workers continue to gain expertise. For the fourth batch, the per-car cost of assembly falls to $5,000 and remains constant for the rest of the production run.

In this example, marginal cost is *decreasing* over batches one through four, falling from $10,000 to $5,000. However, it's important

to note that total cost is still *increasing* over the entire production run because marginal cost is greater than zero.

To see this point, assume that each batch consists of 100 cars. Then the total cost of producing the first batch is 100 × $10,000 = $1,000,000. The total cost of producing the first and second batches of cars is $1,000,000 + (100 × $8,000) = $1,800,000. Likewise, the total cost of producing the first, second, and third batches is $1,800,000 + (100 × $6,500) = $2,450,000, and so on. As you can see, although marginal cost is decreasing over the first few batches of cars, total cost is increasing over the same batches.

This shows us that total cost and marginal cost can sometimes move in opposite directions. So it is wrong to assert that they always move in the same direction. What we can assert is that *total cost increases whenever marginal cost is positive,* regardless of whether marginal cost is increasing or decreasing.

---

assembling the earliest units, making for higher marginal cost on those units. But as workers gain experience, assembly time and the rate of mistakes fall, generating lower marginal cost for later units. As a result, overall production has decreasing marginal cost.

Finally, for the production of some goods and services the shape of the marginal cost curve changes as the number of units produced increases. For example, auto production is likely to have decreasing marginal costs for the first batch of cars produced as workers iron out kinks and mistakes in production. Then production has constant marginal costs for the next batch of cars as workers settle into a predictable pace.

But at some point, as workers produce more cars, marginal cost begins to increase as they run out of factory floor space and the auto company incurs costly overtime wages. This gives rise to what we call a "swoosh"-shaped marginal cost curve—a topic we discuss in Chapter 11. For now, we'll stick to the simpler example of an increasing marginal cost curve.

> The **marginal benefit** of a good or service is the additional benefit derived from producing one more unit of that good or service.

Marginal Benefit

Alexa benefits from higher lifetime earnings as she completes more years of school. Exactly how much she benefits is shown in Table 9-5. Column 2 shows Alexa's total benefit according to the number of years of school completed, expressed as the value of her lifetime earnings. The third column shows Alexa's *marginal benefit* from an additional year of schooling. In general, the **marginal benefit** of producing a good or service is the additional benefit earned from producing one more unit.

As in Table 9-4, the data in the third column of Table 9-5 show a clear pattern. However, this time the numbers are decreasing rather than increasing. The first year of schooling gives Alexa a $300,000 increase in the value of her lifetime earnings. The second year also gives her a positive return, but the size of that return has fallen to $150,000; the third year's return is also positive, but its size has fallen yet again to $90,000; and so on. In other words, the more years of school that Alexa has already completed, the smaller the increase in the value of her lifetime earnings from attending one more year.

TABLE 9-5 Alexa's Marginal Benefit of Additional Years in School

Quantity of schooling (years)	Total benefit	Marginal benefit
0	$0	
		$300,000
1	300,000	
		150,000
2	450,000	
		90,000
3	540,000	
		60,000
4	600,000	
		50,000
5	650,000	

FIGURE 9-2 Marginal Benefit

The height of each shaded bar corresponds to Alexa's marginal benefit of an additional year of schooling. The height of each bar is lower than the one preceding it because an additional year of schooling has decreasing marginal benefit. As a result, Alexa's marginal benefit curve, the curve connecting the midpoints at the top of each bar, is downward sloping.

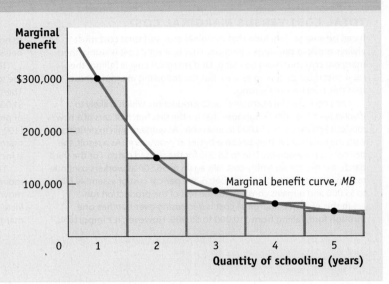

There is **decreasing marginal benefit** from an activity when each additional unit of the activity yields less benefit than the previous unit.

The **marginal benefit curve** shows how the benefit from producing one more unit depends on the quantity that has already been produced.

Alexa's schooling decision has what economists call **decreasing marginal benefit:** each additional year of school yields a smaller benefit than the previous year. Or, to put it slightly differently, with decreasing marginal benefit, the benefit from producing one more unit of the good or service falls as the quantity already produced rises.

Just as marginal cost can be represented by a marginal cost curve, marginal benefit can be represented by a **marginal benefit curve,** shown in blue in Figure 9-2. Alexa's marginal benefit curve slopes downward because she faces decreasing marginal benefit from additional years of schooling.

Not all goods or activities exhibit decreasing marginal benefit. In fact, there are many goods for which the marginal benefit of production is constant—that is, the additional benefit from producing one more unit is the same regardless of the number of units already produced. In later chapters, we will see that the shape of a firm's marginal benefit curve from producing output has important implications for how that firm behaves within its industry. We'll also see why constant marginal benefit is considered the norm for many important industries.

Now we are ready to see how the concepts of marginal benefit and marginal cost are brought together to answer the question of how many years of additional schooling Alexa should undertake.

Marginal Analysis

Table 9-6 shows the marginal cost and marginal benefit numbers from Tables 9-4 and 9-5. It also adds an additional column: the additional profit to Alexa from staying in school one more year, equal to the difference between the marginal benefit and the marginal cost of that additional year in school. (Remember that it is Alexa's economic profit that we care about, not her accounting profit.) We can now use Table 9-6 to determine how many additional years of schooling Alexa should undertake in order to maximize her total profit.

TABLE 9-6 Alexa's Profit from Additional Years of Schooling

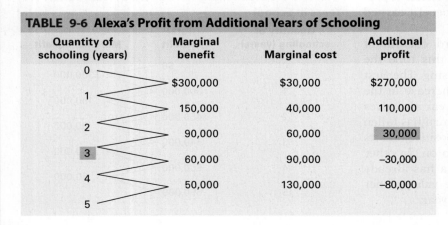

Quantity of schooling (years)	Marginal benefit	Marginal cost	Additional profit
0			
1	$300,000	$30,000	$270,000
2	150,000	40,000	110,000
3	90,000	60,000	30,000
4	60,000	90,000	–30,000
5	50,000	130,000	–80,000

First, imagine that Alexa chooses not to attend any additional years of school. We can see from column 4 that this is a mistake if Alexa wants to achieve the highest total profit from her schooling—the sum of the additional profits generated by another year of schooling. If she attends one additional year of school, she increases the value of her lifetime earnings by $270,000, the profit from the first additional year attended.

Now, let's consider whether Alexa should attend the second year of school. The additional profit from the second year is $110,000, so Alexa should attend the second year as well. What about the third year? The additional profit from that year is $30,000; so, yes, Alexa should attend the third year as well.

What about a fourth year? In this case, the additional profit is negative: it is −$30,000. Alexa loses $30,000 of the value of her lifetime earnings if she attends the fourth year. Clearly, Alexa is worse off by attending the fourth additional year rather than taking a job. And the same is true for the fifth year as well: it has a negative additional profit of −$80,000.

What have we learned? That Alexa should attend three additional years of school and stop at that point. Although the first, second, and third years of additional schooling increase the value of her lifetime earnings, the fourth and fifth years diminish it. So three years of additional schooling lead to the quantity that generates the maximum possible total profit. It is what economists call the **optimal quantity**—the quantity that generates the maximum possible total profit.

Figure 9-3 shows how the optimal quantity can be determined graphically. Alexa's marginal benefit and marginal cost curves are shown together. If Alexa chooses fewer than three additional years (that is, years 0, 1, or 2), she will choose a level of schooling at which her marginal benefit curve lies *above* her marginal cost curve. She can make herself better off by staying in school.

If instead she chooses more than three additional years (years 4 or 5), she will choose a level of schooling at which her marginal benefit curve lies *below* her

> The **optimal quantity** is the quantity that generates the highest possible total profit.

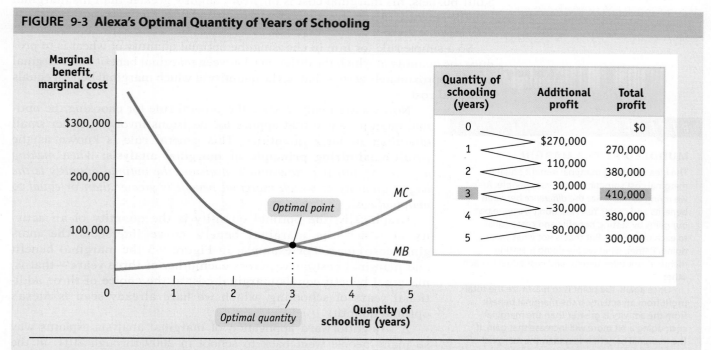

FIGURE 9-3 Alexa's Optimal Quantity of Years of Schooling

Quantity of schooling (years)	Additional profit	Total profit
0		$0
1	$270,000	270,000
2	110,000	380,000
3	30,000	410,000
4	−30,000	380,000
5	−80,000	300,000

The optimal quantity is the quantity that generates the highest possible total profit. It is the quantity at which marginal benefit is greater than or equal to marginal cost. Equivalently, it is the quantity at which the marginal benefit and marginal cost curves intersect. Here, they intersect at 3 additional years of schooling. The table confirms that 3 is indeed the optimal quantity: it leads to the maximum total profit of $410,000.

According to the **profit-maximizing principle of marginal analysis,** when faced with a profit-maximizing "how much" decision, the optimal quantity is the largest quantity at which the marginal benefit is greater than or equal to marginal cost.

marginal cost curve. She can make herself better off by choosing not to attend the additional year of school and taking a job instead.

The table in Figure 9-3 confirms our result. The second column repeats information from Table 9-6, showing Alexa's marginal benefit minus marginal cost—the additional profit per additional year of schooling. The third column shows Alexa's total profit for different years of schooling. The total profit, for each possible year of schooling, is simply the sum of numbers in the second column up to and including that year.

For example, Alexa's profit from additional years of schooling is $270,000 for the first year and $110,000 for the second year. So the total profit for two additional years of schooling is $270,000 + $110,000 = $380,000. Similarly, the total profit for three additional years is $270,000 + $110,000 + $30,000 = $410,000. Our claim that three years is the optimal quantity for Alexa is confirmed by the data in the table in Figure 9-3: at three years of additional schooling, Alexa reaps the greatest total profit, $410,000.

Alexa's decision problem illustrates how you go about finding the optimal quantity when the choice involves a small number of quantities. (In this example, one through five years.) With small quantities, the rule for choosing the optimal quantity is: *increase the quantity as long as the marginal benefit from one more unit is greater than the marginal cost, but stop before the marginal benefit becomes less than the marginal cost.*

In contrast, when a "how much" decision involves relatively large quantities, the rule for choosing the optimal quantity simplifies to this: *The optimal quantity is the quantity at which marginal benefit is equal to marginal cost.*

To see why this is so, consider the example of a farmer who finds that his optimal quantity of wheat produced is 5,000 bushels. Typically, he will find that in going from 4,999 to 5,000 bushels, his marginal benefit is only very slightly greater than his marginal cost—that is, the difference between marginal benefit and marginal cost is close to zero. Similarly, in going from 5,000 to 5,001 bushels, his marginal cost is only very slightly greater than his marginal benefit—again, the difference between marginal cost and marginal benefit is very close to zero.

So a simple rule for him in choosing the optimal quantity of wheat is to produce the quantity at which the difference between marginal benefit and marginal cost is approximately zero—that is, the quantity at which marginal benefit equals marginal cost.

Now we are ready to state the general rule for choosing the optimal quantity—one that applies for decisions involving either small quantities or large quantities. This general rule is known as the **profit-maximizing principle of marginal analysis:** *When making a profit-maximizing "how much" decision, the optimal quantity is the largest quantity at which marginal benefit is greater than or equal to marginal cost.*

Graphically, the optimal quantity is the quantity of an activity at which the marginal benefit curve intersects the marginal cost curve. For example, in Figure 9-3 the marginal benefit and marginal cost curves cross each other at three years—that is, marginal benefit equals marginal cost at the choice of three additional years of schooling, which we have already seen is Alexa's optimal quantity.

A straightforward application of marginal analysis explains why so many people went back to school in 2009 through 2011: in the depressed job market, the marginal cost of another year of school fell because the opportunity cost of forgone wages had fallen.

A straightforward application of marginal analysis can also explain many facts, such as why average new house sizes are typically larger

PITFALLS

MUDDLED AT THE MARGIN

The idea of setting marginal benefit equal to marginal cost sometimes confuses people. Aren't we trying to maximize the *difference* between benefits and costs? Yes. And don't we wipe out our gains by setting benefits and costs equal to each other? Yes. But that is not what we are doing. Rather, what we are doing is setting *marginal,* not *total,* benefit and cost equal to each other.

Once again, the point is to maximize the total profit from an activity. If the marginal benefit from the activity is greater than the marginal cost, doing a bit more will increase that gain. If the marginal benefit is less than the marginal cost, doing a bit less will increase the total profit. *So only when the marginal benefit and marginal cost are equal is the difference between total benefit and total cost at a maximum.*

GLOBAL COMPARISON   HOUSE SIZES AROUND THE WORLD

Although Americans usually think they have the biggest of everything, when it comes to house size, Australia takes first place. In 2015, the average new house size in Australia was 2,303 square feet, compared to 2,164 square feet in the United States. Close behind was Canada, with an average new house size of 1,948 square feet, followed by the other countries listed in the figure.

The larger homes can be explained by the lower average prices for land in those countries. Compared to countries like Germany or Japan, Australia, the United States, and Canada have much more land relative to the size of their populations. This greater supply of land leads to lower average prices, and hence lower costs for building bigger houses.

The figure also shows how the forces of supply and demand determine opportunity cost, which then drives consumer choice. The blue bars measure the average new house size per country, while the green bars measure the country land size. As you can see, there is a strong positive relationship between house size and country land size.

But you can also see that there is not a perfect one-to-one relationship between house size and land size. The most notable anomaly is China, with the largest land mass and the

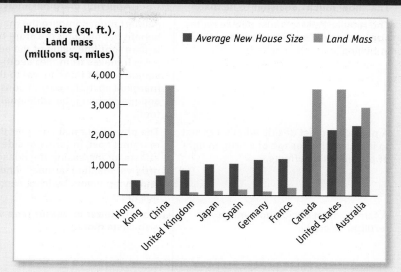

second-to-smallest average new house size, a result that is also consistent with opportunity cost. Compared to the residents of the other countries in the sample, and despite rapidly rising incomes, Chinese residents are still significantly poorer. Although, given how poor China was 20 years ago, it's an extraordinary achievement that the average new Chinese house is only 20% smaller than one in the United Kingdom.

Data from: Shrink That Footprint, www.shrinkthatfootprint.com.

in Australia, Canada, and the United States than those in countries with smaller land mass (as we explain in the Global Comparison).

A Principle with Many Uses

The profit-maximizing principle of marginal analysis can be applied to just about any "how much" decision in which you want to maximize the total profit for an activity. It is equally applicable to production decisions, consumption decisions, and policy decisions. Furthermore, decisions where the benefits and costs are not expressed in dollars and cents can also be made using marginal analysis (as long as benefits and costs can be measured in some type of common units). Table 9-7 includes three examples of decisions that are suitable for marginal analysis.

A Preview: How Consumption Decisions Are Different

We've established that marginal analysis is an extraordinarily useful tool. It is used in "how much" decisions that are applied to both consumption choices and to profit maximization. Producers use it to make optimal production decisions at the margin and individuals use it to make optimal consumption decisions at the margin. But consumption decisions differ from production decisions. Why the difference? Because when individuals make choices, they face a limited amount of income. As a result, when they choose more of one good to consume (say, new clothes), they must choose less of another good (say, restaurant dinners).

TABLE 9-7 Making Decisions Using Marginal Analysis

The "how much" decision to be made	Applying marginal analysis	Arriving at the optimal quantity
The retailer PalMart must decide on the size of the new store it is constructing in Beijing.	PalMart must compare the marginal benefit of enlarging the store by 1 square foot (the value of the additional sales it makes from that additional square foot of floor space) to the marginal cost (the cost of constructing and maintaining the additional square foot).	The optimal store size for PalMart is the largest size at which marginal benefit is greater than or equal to marginal cost.
A physician must decide whether or not to increase the dosage of a drug in light of possible side effects.	The physician must consider the marginal cost, in terms of side effects, of increasing the dosage of a drug versus the marginal benefit of improving health by increasing the dosage.	The optimal dosage level is the largest level at which the marginal benefit of disease amelioration is greater than or equal to the marginal cost of side effects.
A farmer must decide how much fertilizer to apply.	More fertilizer increases crop yield but also costs more.	The optimal amount of fertilizer is the largest quantity at which the marginal benefit of higher crop yield is greater than or equal to the marginal cost of purchasing and applying more fertilizer.

In contrast, decisions that involve maximizing profit by producing a good or service—such as years of education or tons of wheat—are not affected by income limitations. For example, in Alexa's case, she is not limited by income because she can always borrow to pay for another year of school. In the next chapter we will see how consumption decisions differ from—yet are similar to—production decisions.

ECONOMICS >> *in Action* 🌐
The Cost of a Life

What's the marginal benefit to society of saving a human life? You might be tempted to answer that human life is infinitely precious. But in the real world, resources are scarce, so we must decide how much to spend on saving lives since we cannot spend infinite amounts. After all, we could surely reduce highway deaths by dropping the speed limit on interstates to 40 miles per hour, but the cost of a lower speed limit—in time and money—is more than most people are willing to pay.

Generally, people are reluctant to talk in a straightforward way about comparing the marginal cost of a life saved with the marginal benefit—it sounds too callous. Sometimes, however, the question becomes unavoidable.

For example, the cost of saving a life became an object of intense discussion in the United Kingdom after a horrible train crash near London's Paddington Station killed 31 people. There were accusations that the British government was spending too little on rail safety. However, the government estimated that improving rail safety would cost an additional $4.5 million per life saved. But if that amount was worth spending—that is, if the estimated marginal benefit of saving a life exceeded $4.5 million—then the implication was that the British government was spending far too little on rail safety.

In contrast, the estimated marginal cost per life saved through highway improvements was only $1.5 million, making it a much better deal than saving lives through greater rail safety.

1. For each of the "how much" decisions listed in Table 9-3, describe the nature of the marginal cost and of the marginal benefit.

2. Suppose that Alexa's school charges a fixed fee of $70,000 for four years of schooling. If Alexa drops out before she finishes those four years, she still has to pay the $70,000. Alexa's total cost for different years of schooling is now given by the data in the accompanying table. Assume that Alexa's total benefit and marginal benefit remain as reported in Table 9-5.

Use this information to calculate (i) Alexa's new marginal cost, (ii) her new profit, and (iii) her new optimal years of schooling. What kind of marginal cost does Alexa now have—constant, increasing, or decreasing?

Quantity of schooling (years)	Total cost
0	$0
1	90,000
2	120,000
3	170,000
4	250,000
5	370,000

Sunk Costs

When making decisions, knowing what to ignore can be as important as what to include. Although we have devoted much attention in this chapter to costs that are important to take into account when making a decision, some costs should be ignored when doing so. We will now focus on the kinds of costs that people should ignore when making decisions—what economists call *sunk costs*—and why they should be ignored.

To gain some intuition, consider the following scenario. You own a car that is a few years old, and you have just replaced the brake pads at a cost of $250. But then you find out that the entire brake system is defective and also must be replaced. This will cost you an additional $1,500. Alternatively, you could sell the car and buy another of comparable quality, but with no brake defects, by spending an additional $1,600. What should you do: fix your old car, or sell it and buy another?

Some might say that you should take the latter option. After all, this line of reasoning goes, if you repair your car, you will end up having spent $1,750: $1,500 for the brake system and $250 for the brake pads. If instead you sell your old car and buy another, you would spend only $1,600.

But this reasoning, although it sounds plausible, is wrong. It is wrong because the $250 for the brake pads has already been spent. That $250 cannot be recovered; therefore, it should be ignored and should have no effect on your decision whether or not to repair your car and keep it.

From a rational viewpoint, the real cost at this time of repairing and keeping your car is $1,500, not $1,750. So the correct decision is to repair your car and keep it rather than spend $1,600 on a new car.

In this example, the $250 that has already been spent and cannot be recovered is what economists call a **sunk cost.** Sunk costs should be ignored in making decisions about future actions because they have no influence on their actual costs and benefits. Once something can't be recovered, it is irrelevant in making decisions about what to do in the future.

It is often psychologically hard to ignore sunk costs. And if, in fact, you haven't yet incurred the costs, then you should take them into consideration. That is, if you had known at the beginning that it would cost $1,750 to repair your car, then the right choice at that time would have been to buy a new car for $1,600. But once you have already paid the $250 for brake pads, you should no longer include it in your decision making about your next actions. It may be hard to accept that "bygones are bygones," but it is the right way to make a decision.

The $250 already spent on brake pads is irrelevant because it is a sunk cost.

A **sunk cost** is a cost that has already been incurred and is nonrecoverable. A sunk cost should be ignored in decisions about future actions.

ECONOMICS >> *in Action*
Biotech: The World's Biggest Loser

The biotech industry has been built on the premise that sunk costs don't matter.

Biotech firms use cutting-edge bioengineering techniques to discover new therapies to combat disease. But the vast majority of projects that they undertake end in failure. Medscape Medical News estimated that only one out of 5,000 to 10,000 drugs examined in early trials ever makes it to the consumer. And in 2016 it was estimated that over 90% of publicly traded biotech companies would lose money in the upcoming year.

So if there is any industry that exemplifies the principle that sunk costs don't matter, it is the biotech industry. According to Arthur Levinson, chairman of Genentech, one of the largest and most successful of these firms, biotechnology has been "one of the biggest money-losing industries in the history of mankind." It is estimated that the industry has lost well over $100 billion since 1976. (Yes, that's *billion*.)

How, then, do biotech companies survive? It is thanks to savvy investors who know that although thousands of experimental drugs will fail, a tiny minority will succeed. And when they do, the returns will be enormous. These investors ignore past losses—which are sunk costs—and focus, instead, on a company's technical ability and the breadth of the drugs in their development pipeline.

The drug company Xoma is a case in point. Since its founding in 1981, Xoma has accumulated losses of more than $1 billion. Yet investors have been willing to provide it with more money year after year because Xoma possesses a very promising antibody technology and, of course, because shrewd investors understand the principle of sunk costs.

>> Quick Review

• **Sunk costs** should be ignored in decisions regarding future actions. Because they have already been incurred and are nonrecoverable, they have no effect on future costs and benefits.

>> Check Your Understanding 9-3
Solutions appear at back of book.

1. You have decided to go into the ice-cream business and have bought a used ice-cream truck for $8,000. Now you are reconsidering. What is your sunk cost in the following scenarios?
   a. The truck cannot be resold.
   b. The truck can be resold, but only at a 50% discount.
2. You have gone through two years of medical school but are suddenly wondering whether you would be happier as a musician. Which of the following statements are potentially valid arguments and which are not?
   a. "I can't give up now, after all the time and money I've put in."
   b. "If I had thought about it from the beginning, I never would have gone to med school, so I should give it up now."
   c. "I wasted two years, but never mind—let's start from here."
   d. "My parents would kill me if I stopped now." (*Hint:* We're discussing your decision-making ability, not your parents'.)

‖ Behavioral Economics

Most economic models assume that people make choices based on achieving the best possible economic outcome for themselves. Human behavior, however, is often not so simple. Rather than acting like economic computing machines, people often make choices that fall short—sometimes far short—of the greatest possible economic outcome, or payoff. **Behavioral economics** is a branch of economics that combines economic modeling with insights from human psychology in order to understand how people actually—instead of theoretically—make economic choices. Behavioral economics has become very influential over the past 20 years by delivering insights that allow economists to more accurately model decision making in certain circumstances.

First, we should note that, despite the assumptions of most economic models, sometimes it is *rational* for people to make choices that do not lead to the highest possible monetary payoff. These choices are rational when people value something other than a monetary payoff. For example, Alexa may decide to study computer science for two years rather than three years, the optimal number that maximizes her earnings, because she wants to spend some time traveling. This is a rational choice if Alexa values travel more than she values the additional income that another year of school would provide. As we'll discuss shortly, there are many examples of rational choices that don't maximize monetary payoffs.

Yet it's well documented that people also engage in *irrational* behavior, choosing an option that leaves them worse off than other available options. The study of irrational economic behavior was largely pioneered by Daniel Kahneman and Amos Tversky. Kahneman won the 2002 Nobel Prize in economics for his work integrating insights from the psychology of human judgment and decision making into economics. Their work and the insights of others into why people often behave irrationally are having a significant influence on how economists analyze financial markets, labor markets, and other economic concerns.

Rational, but Human, Too

If you are **rational,** you will choose the available option that leads to the outcome you most prefer. But is the outcome you most prefer always the same as the one that gives you the highest possible monetary payoff? No. It can be entirely rational to choose an option that gives you a lower monetary payoff because you care about something other than the size of the monetary payoff. There are four principal reasons why people might prefer a lower monetary payoff: concerns about fairness, nonmonetary rewards, bounded rationality, and risk aversion.

Concerns About Fairness In social situations, people often care about fairness as well as about the size of the economic payoff to themselves. For example, no law requires you to tip your server when you go to a restaurant. But concern for fairness leads most people to leave a tip (unless they've had outrageously bad service) because a tip is seen as fair compensation for good service according to society's norms. Tippers are reducing their own monetary payoff in order to be fair to restaurant servers. A related behavior is gift-giving: if you care about another person's welfare, it's rational for you to reduce your monetary payoff in order to give that person a gift.

Nonmonetary Rewards More than older generations, young people today seem to understand the meaning of an old saying, "There's more to life than dollars and cents." And despite the fact that economists spend their careers tracking dollars and cents, they would all agree. **Nonmonetary rewards** typically take the form of "feel-good" experiences, such as vacation travel, quality time spent with family and friends, playing a sport, or volunteering at a local soup kitchen. A recent report showed that 9 out of 10 millennials (those born between 1981 and 1996) would take a pay cut to work at a company with similar values to their own, whereas only 9% of baby boomers would do the same. In contrast to activities that lead to higher monetary payoffs that are used for consuming more goods and services, nonmonetary rewards directly generate feelings of satisfaction.

Behavioral economics is a branch of economics that combines economic modeling with insights from human psychology to understand how people actually make decisions.

A **rational** decision maker chooses the available option that leads to the outcome they most prefer.

Nonmonetary rewards are benefits or payoffs that are not financial in nature; examples include increased leisure time and "feel-good" experiences.

A decision maker operating with **bounded rationality** makes a choice that is close to but not exactly the one that leads to the best possible economic outcome.

Risk aversion is the willingness to sacrifice some economic payoff in order to avoid a potential loss.

An **irrational** decision maker chooses an option that leaves her worse off than choosing another available option.

The desire for nonmonetary rewards can, in fact, be explained by economics. It is an outcome of the *principle of diminishing marginal utility*, a concept covered in Chapter 10. Simply stated, according to the principle of diminishing marginal utility, the satisfaction gained by consuming one more unit of a good falls as the amount of the good already consumed rises. For example, your first pair of Converse sneakers may have felt very special. However, by the time you purchase your ninth pair, another pair doesn't feel so special. So instead of working to earn money in order to buy the tenth pair, you choose a feel-good experience instead: for example, you quit your regular job and take a position leading backpacking tours in return for room and board.

Surveys show that once people acquire enough goods to live comfortably, they increasingly prefer noneconomic rewards over higher monetary payoffs. According to a recent survey by the travel website Expedia, this is particularly true for millennials: "Millennials are leading the charge in placing a newfound value on experiences, more than things."

Bounded Rationality Being an economic computing machine—choosing the option that gives you the best economic payoff—can require a fair amount of work: sizing up the options, computing the opportunity costs, calculating the marginal amounts, and so on. The mental effort required has its own opportunity cost. This realization led economists to the concept of **bounded rationality**—making a choice that is close to but not exactly the one that leads to the highest possible payoff because the effort of finding the best payoff is too costly. In other words, bounded rationality is the "good enough" method of decision making.

For example, you may have many criteria, and many options, to consider when making a choice about what to eat during your lunch break. What's convenient? What's fastest? What's affordable? What's healthy? What will be most satisfying? Selecting the optimal outcome—the one that will meet all of these criteria—would probably cost more economic computing power than you are willing to devote to the task. And so, you'll opt for a "good enough" option—one that will satisfy one or two of these criteria, and get on with your day. Behavioral economists have studied the concept of bounded rationality and found that we often make choices in this way. And businesses and policy makers can appeal to this tendency to influence our choices, as we'll learn later in the chapter.

Risk Aversion Because life is uncertain and the future unknown, sometimes a choice comes with significant risk. Although you may receive a high payoff if things turn out well, the possibility also exists that things may turn out badly and leave you worse off.

So even if you think a choice will give you the best payoff of all your available options, you may forgo it because you find the possibility that things could turn out badly too, well, risky. This is called **risk aversion**—the willingness to sacrifice some potential economic payoff in order to avoid a potential loss. (We'll discuss risk in detail in Chapter 20.) Because risk makes most people uncomfortable, it's rational for them to give up some potential economic gain in order to avoid it. In fact, if it weren't for risk aversion, there would be no such thing as insurance.

Irrationality: An Economist's View

Sometimes, though, instead of being rational, people are **irrational**—they make choices that leave them worse off than if they had chosen another available option. Is there anything systematic that economists and psychologists can say about economically irrational behavior? Yes, because most people are irrational in predictable ways. People's irrational behavior *typically* stems from seven

FOR INQUIRING MINDS   "The Jingle Mail Blues"

As of 2019, U.S. house prices had grown steadily for the past six years. Yet, just a few years ago, the U.S. housing market was rocked by a cataclysm. In 2008, the great American housing bust hit and house prices began a multiyear slide. Four years later, at the bottom of the bust, American house prices had fallen by nearly 30% from their pre-bust levels. Despite the fact that U.S. house prices have now recovered all the losses incurred during the housing bust, many observers know that the U.S. housing market was forever changed by it. One game-changer has been the rise of *strategic default*: a situation in which a homeowner is financially capable of paying the mortgage, but chooses not to pay it. (A *mortgage* is a loan taken out to buy a house.) Strategic default then precipitates *foreclosure*, when a mortgage lender repossesses the house.

Strategic defaults became so prevalent during the housing bust that a new term was created: *jingle mail*, when a homeowner

seals the keys to their house in an envelope and leaves them with the bank that holds the mortgage on the house.

"Officer, that couple is just walking away from their mortgage!"

Mortgage lenders were stunned by strategic defaults. In the past, homeowners did everything they could to avoid losing their homes. But all of that changed with the housing bust of 2008. A significant portion of homeowners (those who had

bought when housing prices were high) found themselves *underwater*, meaning that they owed more on their homes than they could sell them for. Some houses were worth significantly less than the mortgage amount. These homeowners also discovered that they could rent comparable houses for less than their monthly mortgage payments.

However, those who strategically defaulted did not walk away unscathed: they lost down payments, money spent on repairs and renovation, moving expenses, and so on. But in the words of a Florida resident, who had paid $215,000 for an apartment in Miami where similar units were selling for $90,000, "There is no financial sense in staying." Realizing their losses were sunk costs, underwater homeowners walked away. Perhaps they hadn't made the best economic decision when purchasing their houses, but in leaving they showed impeccable economic logic.

mistakes they make when thinking about economic decisions. The mistakes are listed in Table 9-8, and we will discuss each in turn.

Misperceptions of Opportunity Cost As we discussed at the beginning of this chapter, people tend to ignore opportunity costs when they are nonmonetary—that is, opportunity costs that don't involve an outlay of cash. Another common misperception of opportunity cost leads to the **sunk cost fallacy:** making a decision based on the belief that a sunk cost is an opportunity cost. But as we know from the previous section, a sunk cost is not an opportunity cost. Once an outlay is unrecoverable (sunk), it is no longer an opportunity cost and should be ignored in future decision making. For example, many college students refuse to withdraw from a course even when they are unlikely to complete it with a passing grade. Often, this is because they are falling prey to the sunk cost fallacy by including the cost of tuition—which has already been spent and cannot be refunded—in their analysis. A better analysis would ignore this sunk cost, and focus on the opportunity cost of remaining in the course, which includes time and effort that might be better spent studying for other courses.

Overconfidence It's a function of ego: we tend to think we know more than we actually do. And even if alerted to how widespread overconfidence is, people tend to think that it's someone else's problem, not theirs. (Certainly not yours or mine!)

For example, one study asked students to estimate how long it would take them to complete their thesis "if everything went as well as it possibly could" and "if everything went as poorly as it possibly could." The results: the typical student thought it would take them 33.9 days to finish, with an average estimate of 27.4 days if everything went well and 48.6 days if everything went poorly. In fact,

TABLE 9-8 The Seven Common Mistakes in Economic Decision Making

1. Misperceptions of opportunity cost
2. Overconfidence
3. Unrealistic expectations about future behavior
4. Counting dollars unequally
5. Loss aversion
6. Framing bias
7. Status quo bias

The **sunk cost fallacy** is the mistaken belief that a sunk cost represents an opportunity cost.

Mental accounting is the habit of mentally assigning dollars to different accounts so that some dollars are worth more than others.

Loss aversion is an oversensitivity to loss, leading to unwillingness to recognize a loss and move on.

the average time it took to complete a thesis was much longer, 55.5 days. Students were, on average, from 14% to 102% more confident than they should have been about the time it would take to complete their theses.

Overconfidence can cause problems with meeting deadlines. But it can cause far more trouble by having a strong adverse effect on people's financial health. Overconfidence often persuades people that they are in better financial shape than they actually are. It can also lead to bad investment and spending decisions. For example, nonprofessional investors who engage in a lot of speculative investing—such as quickly buying and selling stocks—on average have significantly worse results than professional brokers because of their misguided faith in their ability to spot a winner. Similarly, overconfidence can lead people to make a large spending decision, such as buying a car, without doing research on the pros and cons, relying instead on anecdotal evidence. Even worse, people tend to remain overconfident because they remember their successes, and explain away or forget their failures.

Unrealistic Expectations About Future Behavior Another form of overconfidence is being overly optimistic about your future behavior: tomorrow you'll study, tomorrow you'll give up ice cream, tomorrow you'll spend less and save more, and so on. Of course, as we all know, when tomorrow arrives, it's still just as hard to study or give up something that you like as it is right now.

Strategies that keep a person on the straight-and-narrow over time are often, at their root, ways to deal with the problem of unrealistic expectations about one's future behavior. Examples are automatic payroll deduction savings plans, diet plans with prepackaged foods, and mandatory attendance at study groups. By providing a way for someone to commit today to an action tomorrow, such plans counteract the habit of pushing difficult actions off into the future.

Counting Dollars Unequally Have you ever spent more on something when paying with a credit card than you would have if you had to pay with cash? Or noticed that students who get an allowance from their parents are less careful with their money than those who live on their own earnings? Both of these scenarios are examples of **mental accounting,** which is the habit of mentally assigning dollars to different accounts, making some dollars worth more than others.

By spending more with a credit card, you are in effect treating dollars in your wallet as more valuable than dollars on your credit card balance, although in reality they count equally in your budget. Likewise, if you spend more from an allowance than you would from your own earnings, you are treating dollars you earned as more valuable than dollars your parents give you. Both of these examples stem from the failure to understand that, regardless of the form it comes in, a dollar is a dollar.

A dollar is a dollar, whether you pay it in cash or with your credit card.

Loss Aversion **Loss aversion** is an oversensitivity to loss, leading to an unwillingness to recognize a loss and move on. In fact, in the lingo of financial markets, "selling discipline"—being able and willing to quickly acknowledge when a stock you've bought is a loser and sell it—is a highly desirable trait to have.

Many investors, though, are reluctant to acknowledge that they've lost money on a stock and won't make it back. Although it's rational to sell the stock at that point and redeploy the remaining funds, most people find it so painful to admit a loss that they avoid selling for much longer than they should. According to Daniel Kahneman and Amos Tversky, most people feel the misery of losing $100 about twice as keenly as they feel the pleasure of gaining $100.

Loss aversion can help explain why sunk costs are so hard to ignore: ignoring a sunk cost means recognizing that the money you spent is unrecoverable and therefore lost.

Framing Bias Have you ever wondered why, in a discount store like Walmart, prices are rarely in whole numbers like $1.00 or $2.00? Instead, prices almost always end in the number "99"—such as $0.99 or $1.99? The reason why is due to what economists call **framing bias:** the tendency to make a decision based upon how the choices are presented, or framed, rather than upon a comparison of their true values. By offering prices that end in the number 99 rather than the next whole number, Walmart is exploiting shoppers' framing bias. The company knows that it will make many more sales of an item if it is priced at $0.99 rather than $1.00 because shoppers irrationally perceive $0.99 to be a much more attractive deal than $1.00. Essentially, this is a mental shortcut that people often take when faced with a lot of data, as noted in the bounded rationality discussion earlier in this chapter.

Limited-time sales like Labor Day sales and Black Friday sales are another example of how retailers take advantage of shoppers' framing bias. Retailers know that, overall, shoppers will buy more when prices are perceived to be low for a limited amount of time compared to a policy of keeping prices at a constant, low level. Retailers are exploiting shoppers' irrational perception that "I had better buy a lot now, because prices will never be this low again."

Framing isn't only about prices. Advertisers know that you are much more likely to buy a medicine if the advertisement says "effective in 75% of cases" than if it says "ineffective in 25% of cases," although both statements are equally true.

Retailers also make use of shoppers' tendency to engage in what social scientists call *anchoring*, making decisions according to some perceived benchmark or reference point. For example, retailers attempt to influence shoppers' belief about whether they are getting a good deal by showing both the full price (the anchor) and the discounted price.

Status Quo Bias Another irrational behavior is **status quo bias,** the tendency to avoid making a decision altogether. A well-known example is the way that employees make decisions about investing in their employer-directed retirement accounts, known as 401(k)s. With a 401(k), employees can, through payroll deductions, set aside part of their salary tax-free, a practice that saves a significant amount of money every year in taxes. Some companies operate on an opt-in basis: employees have to actively choose to participate in a 401(k). Other companies operate on an opt-out basis: employees are automatically enrolled in a 401(k) unless they choose to opt out.

If everyone behaved rationally, then the proportion of employees enrolled in 401(k) accounts at opt-in companies would be roughly equal to the proportion enrolled at opt-out companies. In other words, your decision about whether to participate in a 401(k) should be independent of the default choice at your company. But, in reality, when companies switch to automatic enrollment and an opt-out system, employee enrollment rises dramatically. Clearly, people tend to just go with the status quo. Yet, rational people know that, in the end, the act of not making a choice is still a choice.

Why do people exhibit status quo bias? Some claim it's a form of "decision paralysis": when given more options, people find it harder to make a decision. Others claim it's due to loss aversion and the fear of regret, to thinking that "if I do nothing, then I won't have to regret my choice." Irrational, yes. But not altogether surprising. The recognition of status quo bias has led to the practice of incorporating **nudges** into the status quo choices in order to "nudge" people to make more rational choices. Automatic enrollment into a 401(K) is a classic example of a nudge.

However, rational people know that, in the end, the act of not making a choice is still a choice.

Rational Models for Irrational People?

So why do economists still use models based on rational behavior when people are at times manifestly irrational? For one thing, models based on rational behavior still provide robust predictions about how people behave in most markets.

Framing bias is the tendency to make decisions based upon how choices are presented rather than on a comparison of their true values.

The **status quo bias** is the tendency to avoid making a decision and sticking with the status quo.

A **nudge** is a formulation of the status quo choice intended to shift people to more rational choices when they are prone to status quo bias.

For example, the great majority of farmers will use less fertilizer when it becomes more expensive—a result consistent with rational behavior.

Another explanation is that sometimes market forces can compel people to behave more rationally over time. For example, if you are a small-business owner who persistently exaggerates your abilities or refuses to acknowledge that your favorite line of items is a loser, then sooner or later you will be out of business unless you learn to correct your mistakes. As a result, it is reasonable to assume that when people are disciplined for their mistakes, as happens in most markets, rationality will win out over time.

Finally, economists depend on the assumption of rationality for the simple but fundamental reason that it makes modeling so much simpler. Remember that models are built on generalizations, and it's much harder to extrapolate from messy, irrational behavior. Even behavioral economists, in their research, search for *predictably* irrational behavior in an attempt to build better models of how people behave. Clearly, there is an ongoing dialogue between behavioral economists and the rest of the economics profession, and economics itself has been irrevocably changed by it.

ECONOMICS >> *in Action*
In Praise of Hard Deadlines

Dan Ariely, a professor of psychology and behavioral economics, likes to do experiments with his students that help him explore the nature of irrationality. In his book *Predictably Irrational*, Ariely describes an experiment that gets to the heart of procrastination and ways to address it.

At the time, Ariely was teaching the same subject matter to three different classes, but he gave each class different assignment schedules. The grade in all three classes was based on three equally weighted papers.

Students in the first class were required to choose their own personal deadlines for submitting each paper. Once set, the deadlines could not be changed. Late papers would be penalized at the rate of 1% of the grade for each day late. Papers could be turned in early without penalty but also without any advantage, since Ariely would not grade papers until the end of the semester.

Students in the second class could turn in the three papers whenever they wanted, with no preset deadlines, as long as it was before the end of the term. Again, there would be no benefit for early submission.

Students in the third class faced what Ariely called the "dictatorial treatment." He established three hard deadlines at the fourth, eighth, and twelfth weeks.

So which classes do you think achieved the best and the worst grades? As it turned out, the class with the least flexible deadlines—the one that received the dictatorial treatment—got the best grades. The class with complete flexibility got the worst grades. And the class that got to choose its deadlines performed in the middle.

Ariely learned two simple things about overconfidence from these results. First—no surprise—students tend to procrastinate. Second, hard, equally spaced deadlines are the best cure for procrastination.

But the biggest revelation came from the class that set its own deadlines. The majority of those students spaced their deadlines far apart and got grades as good as those of the students under the dictatorial treatment. Some, however, did not space their deadlines far enough apart, and a few did not space them out at all. These last two groups did less well, putting the average of the entire class below the average of the class with the least flexibility. As Ariely notes, without well-spaced deadlines, students procrastinate and the quality of their work suffers.

This experiment provides two important insights:

1. People who acknowledge their tendency to procrastinate are more likely to use tools for committing to a path of action.
2. Providing those tools allows people to make themselves better off.

If you procrastinate, hard deadlines, as irksome as they may be, are truly for your own good.

>> Check Your Understanding 9-4

Solutions appear at back of book.

1. Which of the types of irrational behavior are suggested by the following events?
    a. Although the housing market has fallen and Jenny wants to move, she refuses to sell her house for any amount less than what she paid for it.
    b. When Leo shops, he likes to take advantage of the "two-for-one" or "three-for-two" offers that stores frequently display. As a result, he often buys more than he needs and ends up giving much of it away.
    c. Danilo has just started his first job and deliberately decided to opt out of the company's savings plan. His reasoning is that he is very young and there is plenty of time in the future to start saving. Why not enjoy life now?
    d. Emma's company requires employees to download and fill out a form if they want to participate in the company-sponsored savings plan. One year after starting the job, Emma had still not submitted the form needed to participate in the plan.
2. How would you determine whether a decision you made was rational or irrational?

J.C. Penney's One-Price Strategy Upsets Its Customers

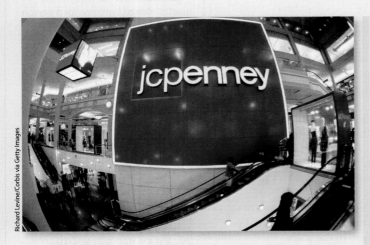

Richard Levine/Corbis via Getty Images

Before Walmart and Target, there was J.C. Penney. At its peak, it had over 2,000 stores across America, selling everything from jewelry to appliances. But in 2019, the 117-year old retailer was in a race for its survival—beset by shrinking sales, dowdy stores, and haphazard merchandise selection. Having borrowed heavily in recent years to keep itself going as sales declined, it faced a do-or-die moment: could it perform a turnaround quickly enough to both repay its massive debt and upgrade its merchandise and stores?

Analysts estimate that the company's sharp decline began in 2011, when Ron Johnson was hired as CEO to reinvigorate the company. Before Johnson arrived, J.C. Penney's way of attracting shoppers was to hold sales. In 2010, it held 590 sales, and almost three-quarters of its goods were marked down 50% or more. Yet, under the old strategy, customers weren't actually paying less. The company would just raise the prices of the merchandise on the racks and then discount prices during the promotions. But, as Johnson argued, why play a game that is costly to the company when it is simply an illusion for customers? So in 2012 he instituted a new retailing strategy of "everyday low prices." That is, instead of offering periodic sales, J.C. Penney now marketed itself to customers as offering low prices every day. In addition, prices were no longer set as numbers ending in 9 or 7, but were changed to whole numbers.

The new strategy seemed like a no-brainer. Rather than continue to promote sales and offer coupons, customers were now assured a low price at all times, regardless of the season and without clipping coupons. Moreover, the company reaped benefits from the new strategy in the form of cost savings from more accurate inventory and profit projections, from more consistent revenues, and by eliminating the cost of paying sales staff to continually change prices. As John T. Gourville, a marketing professor at Harvard Business School, noted, a one-price pricing strategy "makes the operations side of things much easier to predict. You don't have the whiplash effects of selling, say, a ton of Diet Coke one week and virtually none the next week."

But there were problems with this pricing strategy as well. Just how low J.C. Penney's "everyday low prices" were wasn't clear. In effect, "Trust us" was the message J.C. Penney communicated to its shoppers. Unlike Walmart, the company did not offer to match competitors' prices nor could it depend upon a high volume of regular customers to compensate for tiny per-item profits. It could not depend upon membership fees the way Costco did. Moreover, a one-price strategy didn't draw customers in during seasonal high-intensity shopping times, like Labor Day or Christmas.

In the end, J.C. Penney lost the allegiance of shoppers like Tracie Fobes, who runs the *Penny Pinchin' Mom* blog, and who commented, ". . . seeing that something is marked down 20%, then being able to hand over the coupon to save, it just entices me." The loss of these shoppers was devastating: in two short years J.C. Penney's revenues dropped by 30% and its sales dropped 25%. By early 2013, Johnson was unceremoniously fired.

With Johnson's departure, J.C. Penney quickly backtracked and began offering coupons and weekly sales again. The store assistants went back to work, marking items up in order to then immediately mark them back down again. Yet the damage had been done. Starved of revenue, its stores and merchandise declined, nimbler rivals stole its customers, and debt accumulated. As one industry analyst observed about the company's chances for survival, "It's a race to the finish line right now."

QUESTIONS FOR THOUGHT

1. Give an example of a type of rational decision making illustrated by this case and explain your choice.

2. Give an example of a type of irrational decision making illustrated by this case and explain your choice.

3. What purpose does Walmart's price-match guarantee serve? What do you predict would happen if it dropped this policy? Would you predict its competitors—say, the local supermarket or Target—would adopt the same policy?

SUMMARY

1. All economic decisions involve the allocation of scarce resources. Some decisions are "either–or" decisions, in which the question is whether or not to do something. Other decisions are "how much" decisions, in which the question is how much of a resource to put into a given activity.

2. The cost of using a resource for a particular activity is the opportunity cost of that resource. Some opportunity costs are **explicit costs;** they involve a direct outlay of money. Other opportunity costs, however, are **implicit costs;** they involve no outlay of money but are measured by the dollar value of the benefits that are forgone. Both explicit and implicit costs should be taken into account in making decisions. Many decisions involve the use of **capital** and time, for both individuals and firms. So they should base decisions on **economic profit,** which takes into account implicit costs such as the opportunity cost of time and the **implicit cost of capital.** Making decisions based on **accounting profit** can be misleading. It is often considerably larger than economic profit because it includes only explicit costs and not implicit costs.

3. According to the **principle of "either–or" decision making,** when faced with an "either–or" choice between two activities, one should choose the activity with the positive economic profit.

4. A "how much" decision is made using marginal analysis, which involves comparing the benefit to the cost of doing an additional unit of an activity. The **marginal cost** of producing a good or service is the additional cost incurred by producing one more unit of that good or service. The **marginal benefit** of producing a good or service is the additional benefit earned by producing one more unit. The **marginal cost curve** is the graphical illustration of marginal cost, and the **marginal benefit curve** is the graphical illustration of marginal benefit.

5. In the case of **constant marginal cost,** each additional unit costs the same amount to produce as the previous unit. However, marginal cost and marginal benefit typically depend on how much of the activity has already been done. With **increasing marginal cost,** each unit costs more to produce than the previous unit and is represented by an upward-sloping marginal cost curve. With **decreasing marginal cost,** each unit costs

less to produce than the previous unit, leading to a downward-sloping marginal cost curve. In the case of **decreasing marginal benefit,** each additional unit produces a smaller benefit than the unit before.

6. The **optimal quantity** is the quantity that generates the highest possible total profit. According to the **profit-maximizing principle of marginal analysis,** the optimal quantity is the quantity at which marginal benefit is greater than or equal to marginal cost. It is the quantity at which the marginal cost curve and the marginal benefit curve intersect.

7. A cost that has already been incurred and that is nonrecoverable is a **sunk cost.** Sunk costs should be ignored in decisions about future actions because they have no effect on future benefits and costs. The **sunk cost fallacy** is the mistaken belief that sunk costs should be counted in making a decision.

8. **Behavioral economics,** a branch of economics that has become very influential in the past 20 years, combines economic modeling with insights from psychology to understand how people actually make decisions.

9. With **rational** behavior, individuals will choose the available option that leads to the outcome they most prefer. However, it may be rational to choose an outcome with a lower economic payoff. The four principal reasons why are concerns over fairness, **nonmonetary rewards,** bounded rationality, and risk aversion. **Bounded rationality** occurs because the effort needed to find the best economic payoff is costly. **Risk aversion** causes individuals to sacrifice some economic payoff in order to avoid a potential loss.

10. An **irrational** choice leaves a person worse off than if they had chosen another available option. There are seven common forms that irrational behavior takes: misperceptions of opportunity cost; overconfidence; unrealistic expectations about future behavior; **mental accounting,** in which dollars are valued unequally; **loss aversion,** an oversensitivity to loss; **framing bias,** in which decisions are made based upon how choices are presented rather than on their true value; and **status quo bias,** avoiding a decision by sticking with the status quo. **Nudges,** changes to the status quo in order to induce more rational choices, are frequently used.

KEY TERMS

Explicit cost, p. 248
Implicit cost, p. 248
Accounting profit, p. 249
Economic profit, p. 250
Capital, p. 250
Implicit cost of capital, p. 250
Principle of "either–or" decision making, p. 251
Marginal cost, p. 253
Increasing marginal cost, p. 254
Marginal cost curve, p. 254
Constant marginal cost, p. 254
Decreasing marginal cost, p. 254
Marginal benefit, p. 255
Decreasing marginal benefit, p. 256
Marginal benefit curve, p. 256
Optimal quantity, p. 257

Profit-maximizing principle of marginal analysis, p. 258

Sunk cost, p. 261

Behavioral economics, p. 263

Rational, p. 263

Nonmonetary rewards, p. 263

Bounded rationality, p. 264

Risk aversion, p. 264

Irrational, p. 264

Sunk cost fallacy, p. 265

Mental accounting, p. 266

Loss aversion, p. 266

Framing bias, p. 267

Status quo bias, p. 267

Nudges, p. 267

PRACTICE QUESTIONS

1. A study on student loan default rates by the Brookings Institute found an interesting correlation. Generally students that needed to borrow more money to attend a four-year institution were less likely to default than students with a lower level of debt. Students that started college in 2003 borrowed an average of $15,000 and had a default rate of 17.1%. Breaking down the data, students that completed a four-year bachelor's degree borrowed an average of $25,000 but had a significantly lower default rate of only 5.6%. Whereas, students that dropped out of college only borrowed $7,500 but had a default rate that was more than four times greater, 23.9%. Use the concept of marginal analysis to explain the student loan default rate data above.

2. Discuss how each of the following statements represent framing bias:

   i. Financial advisors will provide guidance on retirement and savings options for a small fee. They often promote their investing abilities over other advisors. The stock market has fallen 5% for the year but you see an ad for a financial advisor, "our investments have outperformed our competitors by 2%." Why doesn't the advisor want to advertise their actual return?

   ii. A recent study found that high school seniors and community college students were less likely to attend a four-year institution when offered a financial aid package that included the word "loan" when compared with a financially equivalent package that omitted the word "loan." In fact, when using the term "loan," students were 10% less likely to attending that particular university.

3. You and your roommate are in a dilemma. You are both taking economics and accounting and have an economics exam tomorrow afternoon. You're worried that you won't have enough study time and are debating skipping accounting to use the time to study for the exam. You're not worried about your accounting grade, but your roommate is still trying to convince you to not skip accounting because you've already paid your tuition. Explain how your roommate is guilty of committing a sunk cost fallacy.

PROBLEMS

1. Jackie owns and operates a website design business. To keep up with new technology, she spends $5,000 per year upgrading her computer equipment. She runs the business out of a room in her home. If she didn't use the room as her business office, she could rent it out for $2,000 per year. Jackie knows that if she didn't run her own business, she could return to her previous job at a large software company that would pay her a salary of $60,000 per year. Jackie has no other expenses.

   a. How much total revenue does Jackie need to make in order to break even in the eyes of her accountant? That is, how much total revenue would give Jackie an accounting profit of just zero?

   b. How much total revenue does Jackie need to make in order for her to want to remain self-employed? That is, how much total revenue would give Jackie an economic profit of just zero?

2. You own and operate a bike store. Each year, you receive revenue of $200,000 from your bike sales, and it costs you $100,000 to obtain the bikes. In addition, you pay $20,000 for electricity, taxes, and other expenses per year. Instead of running the bike store, you could become an accountant and receive a yearly salary of $40,000. A large clothing retail chain wants to expand and offers to rent the store from you for $50,000 per year. How do you explain to your friends that despite making a profit, it is too costly for you to continue running your store?

3. Suppose you have just paid a nonrefundable fee of $1,000 for your meal plan for this academic term. This allows you to eat dinner in the cafeteria every evening.

   a. You are offered a part-time job in a restaurant where you can eat for free each evening. Your parents say that you should eat dinner in the cafeteria anyway, since you have already paid for those meals. Are your parents right? Explain why or why not.

   b. You are offered a part-time job in a different restaurant where, rather than being able to eat for free, you receive only a large discount on your meals. Each meal there will cost you $2; if you eat there each evening this semester, it will add up to $200. Your roommate says that you should eat in the restaurant since it costs less than the $1,000 that you paid for the meal plan. Is your roommate right? Explain why or why not.

4. You have bought a $10 ticket in advance for the college soccer game, a ticket that cannot be resold. You know that going to the soccer game will give you a benefit equal to $20. After you have bought the ticket, you hear that there will be a professional baseball post-season game at the same time. Tickets to the baseball game

cost $20, and you know that going to the baseball game will give you a benefit equal to $35. You tell your friends the following: "If I had known about the baseball game before buying the ticket to the soccer game, I would have gone to the baseball game instead. But now that I already have the ticket to the soccer game, it's better for me to just go to the soccer game." Are you making the correct decision? Justify your answer by calculating the benefits and costs of your decision.

5. Amy, Bill, and Carla all mow lawns for money. Each of them operates a different lawn mower. The accompanying table shows the total cost to Amy, Bill, and Carla of mowing lawns.

Quantity of lawns mowed	Amy's total cost	Bill's total cost	Carla's total cost
0	$0	$0	$0
1	20	10	2
2	35	20	7
3	45	30	17
4	50	40	32
5	52	50	52
6	53	60	82

a. Calculate Amy's, Bill's, and Carla's marginal costs, and draw each of their marginal cost curves.

b. Who has increasing marginal cost, who has decreasing marginal cost, and who has constant marginal cost?

6. You are the manager of a gym, and you have to decide how many customers to admit each hour. Assume that each customer stays exactly one hour. Customers are costly to admit because they inflict wear and tear on the exercise equipment. Moreover, each additional customer generates more wear and tear than the customer before. As a result, the gym faces increasing marginal cost. The accompanying table shows the marginal costs associated with each number of customers per hour.

Quantity of customers per hour	Marginal cost of customer
0	
	$14.00
1	
	14.50
2	
	15.00
3	
	15.50
4	
	16.00
5	
	16.50
6	
	17.00
7	

a. Suppose that each customer pays $15.25 for a one-hour workout. Use the profit-maximizing principle of marginal analysis to find the optimal number of customers that you should admit per hour.

b. You increase the price of a one-hour workout to $16.25. What is the optimal number of customers per hour that you should admit now?

7. Georgia and Lauren are economics students who go to a karate class together. Both have to choose how many classes to go to per week. Each class costs $20. The accompanying table shows Georgia's and Lauren's estimates of the marginal benefit that each of them gets from each class per week.

Quantity of classes	Lauren's marginal benefit of each class	Georgia's marginal benefit of each class
0		
	$23	$28
1		
	19	22
2		
	14	15
3		
	8	7
4		

a. Use marginal analysis to find Lauren's optimal number of karate classes per week. Explain your answer.

b. Use marginal analysis to find Georgia's optimal number of karate classes per week. Explain your answer.

8. The Centers for Disease Control and Prevention (CDC) recommended against vaccinating the whole population against the smallpox virus because the vaccination has undesirable, and sometimes fatal, side effects. Suppose the accompanying table gives the data that are available about the effects of a smallpox vaccination program.

Percent of population vaccinated	Deaths due to smallpox	Deaths due to vaccination side effects
0%	200	0
10	180	4
20	160	10
30	140	18
40	120	33
50	100	50
60	80	74

a. Calculate the marginal benefit (in terms of lives saved) and the marginal cost (in terms of lives lost) of each 10% increment of smallpox vaccination. Calculate the net increase in human lives for each 10% increment in population vaccinated.

b. Using marginal analysis, determine the optimal percentage of the population that should be vaccinated.

9. Paige delivers pizza using her own car, and she is paid according to the number of pizzas she delivers. The accompanying table shows Paige's total benefit and total cost when she works a specific number of hours.

Quantity of hours worked	Total benefit	Total cost
0	$0	$0
1	30	10
2	55	21
3	75	34
4	90	50
5	100	70

a. Use marginal analysis to determine Paige's optimal number of hours worked.

b. Calculate the total profit to Paige from working 0 hours, 1 hour, 2 hours, and so on. Now suppose Paige chooses to work for 1 hour. Compare her total profit from working for 1 hour with her total profit from working the optimal number of hours. How much would she lose by working for only 1 hour?

10. Assume De Beers is the sole producer of diamonds. When it wants to sell more diamonds, it must lower its price in order to induce shoppers to buy more. Furthermore, each additional diamond that is produced costs more than the previous one due to the difficulty of mining for diamonds. De Beers's total benefit schedule is given in the accompanying table, along with its total cost schedule.

Quantity of diamonds	Total benefit	Total cost
0	$0	$0
1	1,000	50
2	1,900	100
3	2,700	200
4	3,400	400
5	4,000	800
6	4,500	1,500
7	4,900	2,500
8	5,200	3,800

a. Draw the marginal cost curve and the marginal benefit curve and, from your diagram, graphically derive the optimal quantity of diamonds to produce.

b. Calculate the total profit to De Beers from producing each quantity of diamonds. Which quantity gives De Beers the highest total profit?

11. In each of the following examples, explain whether the decision is rational or irrational. Describe the type of behavior exhibited.

a. Madison likes to give her best friend Mikayla gift cards that Mikayla can use at her favorite stores. Mikayla often forgets to use the cards before their expiration date or loses them, but she is careful with her own cash.

b. Panera Bread Company opened a store in Clayton, Missouri, that allowed customers to pay any amount they like for their orders; instead of prices, the store listed suggested donations based on the cost of the goods. All profits went to a charitable foundation set up by Panera. A year later, the store was pleased with the success of the program.

c. Dominic has just gotten his teaching degree and has two job offers. One job, replacing a teacher who has gone on leave, will last only two years. It is at a prestigious high school, and he will be paid $35,000 per year. He thinks he will probably be able to find another good job in the area after the two years are up but isn't sure. The other job, also at a high school, pays $25,000 per year and is virtually guaranteed for five years; after those five years, he will be evaluated for a permanent teaching position at the school. About 75% of the teachers who start at the school are hired for permanent positions. Dominic takes the five-year position at $25,000 per year.

d. Kimora has planned a trip to Florida during spring break in March. She has several school projects due after her return. Rather than do them in February, she figures she can take her books with her to Florida and complete her projects there.

e. Sahir overpaid when buying a used car that has turned out to be a lemon. He could sell it for parts, but instead he lets it sit in his garage and deteriorate.

f. Barry considers himself an excellent investor in stocks. He selects new stocks by finding ones with characteristics similar to those of his previous winning stocks. He chalks up losing trades to ups and downs in the macroeconomy.

12. You have been hired as a consultant by a company to develop the company's retirement plan, taking into account different types of predictably irrational behavior commonly displayed by employees. State at least two types of irrational behavior employees might display with regard to the retirement plan and the steps you would take to forestall such behavior.

WORK IT OUT

13. Hiro owns and operates a small business that provides economic consulting services. During the year he spends $57,000 on travel to clients and other expenses. In addition, he owns a computer that he uses for business. If he didn't use the computer, he could sell it and earn yearly interest of $100 on the money created through this sale. Hiro's total revenue for the year is $100,000. Instead of working as a consultant for the year, he could teach economics at a small local college and make a salary of $50,000.

a. What is Hiro's accounting profit?

b. What is Hiro's economic profit?

c. Should Hiro continue working as a consultant, or should he teach economics instead? ∎

How to Make Decisions Involving Time: Understanding Present Value

As we learned in Chapter 9, the basic rule to follow when deciding whether or not to undertake a project is to compare the benefits of the project with its costs—explicit as well as implicit—and choose the course of action with the higher economic profit.

But many economic decisions involve choices in which the benefits and the costs arrive at different times, making comparisons between those choices more difficult. For example, the decision about whether to go back to school and get an advanced degree or to get a job, is one of those types of comparisons. If you, Alexa, or Adam choose to get an advanced degree, the costs—forgone wages, tuition, and books—are incurred immediately, while the benefits—higher earnings—are reaped in the future. In other cases, the benefits of a project come earlier than the costs, such as taking out a loan to pay for a vacation that must be repaid in the future. So how should we make decisions when time is a factor?

The economically correct way is to use a concept called *present value*. Using present value calculations allows you to convert costs and/or benefits that arrive in the future into a value today. This way, we can always compare projects that occur over time by comparing their values today. You might wonder why you didn't see present value calculations when we analyzed the decisions in Chapter 9. The fact is that present value was used, but implicitly. For example, statements like "he will receive earnings from the degree valued today at $600,000 over the rest of his lifetime" mean that the future benefits had already been converted into a value today—that value being $600,000.

Now let's see exactly how present value works.

How to Calculate the Present Value of a One-Year Project

Suppose that you will graduate exactly one year from today and you will need $1,000 to rent your first apartment. In order to have $1,000 one year from now, how much do you need today? It's not $1,000, and the reason why has to do with the *interest rate*. The **interest rate,** which we will denote by r, is the price charged a borrower for borrowing money expressed as a percentage of the amount borrowed. And let's use X to denote the amount you need today in order to have $1,000 one year from now. If you put X in the bank today and earn an interest rate r on it, then after one year the bank will pay you $X \times (1 + r)$. If the amount paid to you by the bank one year from now is $1,000, then the amount you need to deposit with the bank today is given by the following equation:

(9A-1) $X \times (1 + r) = \$1,000$

You can apply some basic algebra to find that:

(9A-2) $X = \$1,000/(1 + r)$

When someone borrows money for a year, the **interest rate** is the price, calculated as a percentage of the amount borrowed, charged by the lender.

The **present value** of X is the amount of money needed today in order to receive X at a future date given the interest rate.

So the amount you need today to be assured of having $1,000 one year from now, X, is equal to $1,000 divided by $(1+r)$. Notice that the value of X depends on the interest rate, r, which is always greater than zero. This fact implies that X is always less than $1,000. For example, if $r = 5\%$ (that is, $r = 0.05$), then $X = \$1,000/1.05 = \$952.38$. In other words, $952.38 is the value today of receiving $1,000 one year from now given an interest rate of 5%.

Now we can define the **present value** of X: it is the amount of money needed today in order to receive X in the future given the interest rate. In this example, $952.38 is the present value of $1,000 today given an interest rate of 5%.

The concept of present value is very useful when making decisions that require paying upfront costs now for benefits that arrive in the future. Say you had two options, A and B: the choice of taking a one-year job that pays $10,000 immediately (option A) or taking a one-year course that costs $1,000 now but allows you to earn a one-time payment of $12,000 one year from now (option B). Which one should you take?

On the one hand, the present value of option A is simply $10,000 because you receive its payoff immediately. On the other hand, the present value of option B, with an interest rate of 5%, is:

(9A-3) $\$12,000/1.05 - \$1,000 = \$11,429 - \$1,000 = \$10,429$

Since the present value of option B ($10,429) is greater than the present value of option A ($10,000), you should choose option B.

This example illustrates a general principle: when evaluating choices where the costs and/or benefits arrive over time, make your choice by converting the payoffs into their present values and choose the one with the highest present value. Next we will see how to use present value when projects have a time span of more than one year.

How to Calculate the Present Value of Multiyear Projects

Let's represent the value of $1 to be received two years from now as $X_{2\text{yrs}}$. If you lend out $X_{2\text{yrs}}$ today for two years, you will receive:

(9A-4) $X_{2\text{yrs}} \times (1+r)$ at the end of one year

which you then reinvest to receive:

(9A-5) $X_{2\text{yrs}} \times (1+r) \times (1+r) = X_{2\text{yrs}} \times (1+r)^2$ at the end of two years

From Equation 9A-5 we can calculate how much you would have to lend today in order to receive $1 two years from now:

(9A-6) $X_{2\text{yrs}}(1+r)^2 = \$1$

To solve for $X_{2\text{yrs}}$, divide both sides of Equation 9A-6 by $(1+r)^2$ to arrive at:

(9A-7) $X_{2\text{yrs}} = \$1/(1+r)^2$

For example, if $r = 0.10$, then $X_{2\text{yrs}} = \$1/(1.10)^2 = \$1/1.21 = \$0.83$.

Equation 9A-7 points the way toward the general expression for present value, where $1 is paid after N years. It is:

(9A-8) $X_{N\text{yrs}} = \$1/(1+r)^N$

In other words, the present value of $1 to be received N years from now is equal to $\$1/(1+r)^N$.

How to Calculate the Present Value of Projects with Revenues and Costs

Now let's suppose you have to choose which one of three projects to undertake. Project A gives you an immediate payoff of $100. Project B costs you $10 now and pays $115 a year from now. Project C gives you an immediate payoff of $119 but requires you to pay $20 a year from now. We will assume that $r = 0.10$.

In order to compare these three projects, you must evaluate costs and revenues that are expended or realized at different times. It is here, of course, that the concept of present value is extremely handy: by using present value to convert any dollars realized in the future into today's value, you can factor out differences in time. Once differences in time are factored out, you can compare the three projects by calculating each one's *net present value*, the present value of current and future revenues minus the present value of current and future costs. The best project to undertake is the one with the highest net present value.

Table 9A-1 shows how to calculate the net present value of each of the three projects. The second and third columns show how many dollars are realized and when they are realized; costs are indicated by a minus sign. The fourth column shows the equations used to convert the flows of dollars into their present value, and the fifth column shows the actual amounts of the total net present value for each of the three projects.

For instance, to calculate the net present value of project B, you need to calculate the present value of $115 received one year from now. The present value of $1 received one year from now is $1/(1 + r)$. So the present value of $115 received one year from now is $\$115 \times 1/(1 + r) = \$115/(1 + r)$. The net present value of project B is the present value of current and future revenues minus the present value of current and future costs: $-\$10 + \$115/(1 + r)$.

From the fifth column, we can immediately see that, at an interest rate of 10%, project C is the best project. It has the highest net present value, $100.82, which is higher than the net present value of project A ($100) and much higher than the net present value of project B ($94.55).

This example shows how important the concept of present value is. If we had failed to use the present value calculations and had instead simply added up the revenues and costs, we would have been misled into believing that project B was the best project and C was the worst one.

TABLE 9A-1 The Net Present Value of Three Hypothetical Projects

Project	Dollars realized today	Dollars realized one year from today	Present value formula	Net present value given $r = 0.10$
A	$100	—	$100	$100.00
B	−$10	$115	$-\$10 + \$115/(1 + r)$	$94.55
C	$119	−$20	$\$119 - \$20/(1 + r)$	$100.82

PROBLEMS

1. Suppose that a major city's main thoroughfare, which is also an interstate highway, will be completely closed to traffic for two years, from January 2018 to December 2019, for reconstruction at a cost of $535 million. If the construction company were to keep the highway open for traffic during construction, the highway reconstruction project would take much longer and be more expensive. Suppose that construction would take four years if the highway were kept open, at a total cost of $800 million. The state department of transportation had to make its decision in 2017, one year before the start of construction (so that the first payment was one year away). So the department of transportation had the following choices:

   (i) Close the highway during construction, at an annual cost of $267.5 million per year for two years.

   (ii) Keep the highway open during construction, at an annual cost of $200 million per year for four years.

   a. Suppose the interest rate is 10%. Calculate the present value of the costs incurred under each plan. Which reconstruction plan is less expensive?

   b. Now suppose the interest rate is 80%. Calculate the present value of the costs incurred under each plan. Which reconstruction plan is now less expensive?

2. You have won the state lottery. There are two ways in which you can receive your prize. You can either have $1 million in cash now, or you can have $1.2 million that is paid out as follows: $300,000 now, $300,000 in one year's time, $300,000 in two years' time, and $300,000 in three years' time. The interest rate is 20%. How would you prefer to receive your prize?

3. The drug company Pfizer is considering whether to invest in the development of a new cancer drug. Development will require an initial investment of $10 million now; beginning one year from now, the drug will generate annual profits of $4 million for three years.

   a. If the interest rate is 12%, should Pfizer invest in the development of the new drug? Why or why not?

   b. If the interest rate is 8%, should Pfizer invest in the development of the new drug? Why or why not?

10 > The Rational Consumer

THE ABSOLUTE LAST BITE

A POPULAR STYLE OF RESTAURANT, found in many towns across America, is the all-you-can-eat buffet. For example, at the Happy Family Chinese Buffet in Humble, Texas, for $11.99 you can choose from a wide variety of items, such as egg rolls, crab legs, and sushi, all in unlimited quantities.

When is more of a good thing too much?

But why hasn't the owner of Happy Family Chinese Buffet been eaten out of business by his customers? In other words, what prevents his average customer from wolfing down an amount of food costing far more than $11.99 — say 10 servings of crab legs?

The answer is that even though every once in a while some customers will take advantage of the offer and pile their plates high with 10 servings of crab legs, it's a rare occurrence in real life. That's because the average person knows that, while 1 or 2 servings of crab legs is a treat, 10 servings is likely to lead to an upset stomach. In fact, any sensible person who pays for an all-you-can-eat meal wants to make the

most of it, but making the most of it means knowing when one more bite would be one bite too many.

Notice that last sentence. We said that customers in a restaurant want to "make the most" of their meal; that sounds as if they are trying to maximize something. And we also said that they will stop when consuming one more bite would be a mistake; they are making a marginal decision.

But it is a marginal decision that also involves a person's tastes. While economists can't say much about where tastes come from, they can say a lot about how a rational individual uses marginal analysis to satisfy their tastes. And that is in fact the way that economists think about consumer choice. They work with a model of a *rational consumer* — a consumer who knows what they want and makes the most of the available opportunities.

In this chapter, we will show how to analyze the decisions of a rational consumer. We will begin by showing how the concept of *utility* — a measure of consumer satisfaction — allows us to think about rational consumer choice.

We will then look at how *budget constraints* determine what a consumer can afford to buy and how marginal analysis can be used to determine the consumption choice that maximizes utility.

Finally, we will see how this analysis can be used to understand the law of demand and why the demand curve slopes downward.

For those interested in a more detailed treatment of consumer behavior and coverage of indifference curves, see the appendix that follows this chapter. ●

WHAT YOU WILL LEARN

- What factors determine how consumers spend their income?
- Why do economists use the concept of **utility** to describe people's tastes?
- Why does the **principle of diminishing marginal utility** accurately describe consumer behavior?
- What is the **optimal consumption bundle** and why do we use marginal analysis to determine it?
- How do **income** and **substitution effects** show the effects of changes in income and prices on consumers' choices?

The **utility** of a consumer is a measure of the satisfaction the consumer derives from consumption of goods and services.

An individual's **consumption bundle** is the collection of all the goods and services consumed by that individual.

An individual's **utility function** gives the total utility generated by their consumption bundle.

A **util** is a unit of utility.

‖ Utility: Getting Satisfaction

When analyzing consumer behavior, we're talking about people trying to get satisfaction—that is, about subjective feelings. Yet there is no simple way to measure subjective feelings. How much satisfaction do I get from my third egg roll? Is it less or more than yours? Does it even make sense to ask the question?

Luckily, we don't need to make comparisons between your feelings and mine. All that is required to analyze consumer behavior is to suppose that each individual is trying to maximize some personal measure of the satisfaction gained from consumption of goods and services. That measure is known as the consumer's **utility,** a concept we use to understand behavior but don't expect to measure in practice. Nonetheless, we'll see that the assumption that consumers maximize utility helps us think clearly about consumer choice.

Utility and Consumption

An individual's utility depends on everything that individual consumes, from apples to Ziploc bags. The set of all the goods and services an individual consumes is known as the individual's **consumption bundle.** The relationship between an individual's consumption bundle and the total amount of utility it generates for that individual is known as the **utility function.** The utility function is a personal matter; two people with different tastes will have different utility functions. Someone who actually likes to consume 20 egg rolls in a sitting must have a utility function that looks different from that of someone who would rather stop at 3 egg rolls.

So we can think of consumers as using consumption to "produce" utility, much in the same way as in later chapters we will think of producers as using inputs to produce output. However, it's obvious that people do not have a little computer in their heads that calculates the utility generated by their consumption choices. Nonetheless, people must make choices, and they usually base them on at least a rough attempt to decide which choice will give them greater satisfaction. I can have either a Coke or lemonade with my dinner. Which will I enjoy more? I can go backpacking through Europe this summer or save the money toward buying a new car. Which will make me happier?

The concept of a utility function is just a way of representing the fact that when people consume, they take into account their preferences and tastes in a more or less rational way.

How do we measure utility? For the sake of simplicity, it is useful to suppose that we can measure utility in hypothetical units called—what else?—**utils.**

Figure 10-1 illustrates a utility function. It shows the total utility that Cassie, who likes egg rolls, gets from an all-you-can-eat buffet. We suppose that her consumption bundle consists of a Coke plus a number of egg rolls to be determined. The table that accompanies the figure shows how Cassie's total utility depends on the number of egg rolls; the curve in panel (a) of the figure shows that same information graphically.

Cassie's utility function slopes upward over most of the range shown, but it gets flatter as the number of egg rolls consumed increases. And in this example it eventually turns downward. According to the information in the table in Figure 10-1, 9 egg rolls is an egg roll too many. Adding that additional egg roll actually makes Cassie worse off: it would lower her total utility. If she's rational, of course, Cassie will realize that and not consume the 9th egg roll.

So when Cassie chooses how many egg rolls to consume, she will make this decision by considering the *change* in her total utility from consuming one more egg roll. This illustrates the general point: to maximize *total* utility, consumers must focus on *marginal* utility.

FIGURE 10-1 Cassie's Total Utility and Marginal Utility

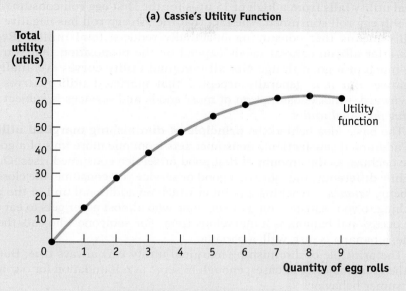

(a) Cassie's Utility Function

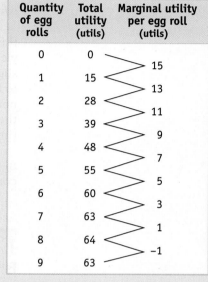

Quantity of egg rolls	Total utility (utils)	Marginal utility per egg roll (utils)
0	0	
		15
1	15	
		13
2	28	
		11
3	39	
		9
4	48	
		7
5	55	
		5
6	60	
		3
7	63	
		1
8	64	
		−1
9	63	

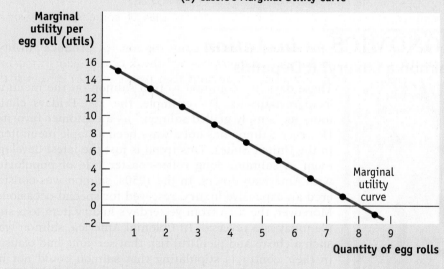

(b) Cassie's Marginal Utility Curve

Panel (a) shows how Cassie's total utility depends on her consumption of egg rolls. It increases until it reaches its maximum utility level of 64 utils at 8 egg rolls consumed and decreases after that. Marginal utility is calculated in the table. Panel (b) shows the marginal utility curve, which slopes downward due to diminishing marginal utility. That is, each additional egg roll gives Cassie less additional utility than the previous egg roll.

The Principle of Diminishing Marginal Utility

In addition to showing how Cassie's total utility depends on the number of egg rolls she consumes, the table in Figure 10-1 also shows the **marginal utility** generated by consuming each additional egg roll—that is, the *change* in total utility from consuming one additional egg roll. Panel (b) shows the implied **marginal utility curve.** Following our practice in Chapter 9 with the marginal benefit curve, the marginal utility curve is constructed by plotting points at the midpoint of the unit intervals.

The **marginal utility** of a good or service is the change in total utility generated by consuming one additional unit of that good or service. The **marginal utility curve** shows how marginal utility depends on the quantity of a good or service consumed.

According to the **principle of diminishing marginal utility,** each successive unit of a good or service consumed adds less to total utility than the previous unit.

The marginal utility curve slopes downward: each successive egg roll adds less to total utility than the previous egg roll. This is reflected in the table: marginal utility falls from a high of 15 utils for the first egg roll consumed to –1 for the 9th egg roll consumed. The fact that the 9th egg roll has negative marginal utility means that consuming it actually reduces total utility. (Restaurants that offer all-you-can-eat meals depend on the proposition that you can have too much of a good thing.) Not all marginal utility curves eventually become negative. But it is generally accepted that marginal utility curves do slope downward—that consumption of most goods and services is subject to *diminishing marginal utility.*

The basic idea behind the **principle of diminishing marginal utility** is that the additional satisfaction a consumer gets from one more unit of a good or service declines as the amount of that good or service consumed rises. Or, to put it slightly differently, the more of a good or service you consume, the closer you are to being *satiated*—reaching a point at which an additional unit of the good adds nothing to your satisfaction. For someone who almost never gets to eat a banana, the occasional banana is a marvelous treat. For someone who eats them all the time, a banana is just, well, a banana.

The principle of diminishing marginal utility isn't always true. But it is true in the great majority of cases, enough to serve as a foundation for our analysis of consumer behavior.

ECONOMICS >> *in Action*
Is Salmon a Luxury? It Depends

Diminishing marginal utility and changes in supply have put salmon on a culinary roller-coaster.

These days, it's common to find salmon on the menu at local restaurants. For example, the TGI Fridays chain touts its "simply grilled salmon," as a customer favorite. However, salmon has not always been a staple menu item in the United States. This trend is just the latest development in salmon's long roller-coaster ride of popularity with American diners. In the 1950s, salmon was considered an expensive luxury, reserved for special occasions. Moreover, the turn from yesterday's luxury item to a staple today is a reversal. In Colonial America, salmon was such a cheap and plentiful fish that servants had clauses in their contracts stipulating that salmon could not be served to them more than a certain number of times a week.

What's behind the extreme changes in salmon's status? The answer is diminishing marginal utility coupled with changes in supply. In the unspoiled nature of Colonial America, salmon was so plentiful that the fish glutted rivers, lakes, and streams. But by the 1980s, pollution and overfishing threatened salmon with extinction. As a *New York Times* article from 1981 stated, "Only in the last 25 years, because of dwindling numbers, has salmon climbed the culinary scale to become a luxury."

Since then, salmon supply has made a massive comeback, thanks to the advances made by aquaculture, commonly known as fish farming. In 1982, 13,265 tons of fish-farmed salmon was produced worldwide. By 2015, that number had increased 1500% to well over 2 million tons.

So in Colonial times, when salmon was extraordinarily plentiful and eaten all the time, diminishing marginal utility made one more serving of salmon a low marginal utility event. And, in the 1980s, when salmon was near extinction, its rarity made one more serving a high marginal utility event. Now that supplies are somewhat plentiful again, salmon is neither a luxury nor a food to be avoided. Instead, it falls somewhere in between—an appealing option to be found on the menu at restaurants near you.

>> Check Your Understanding 10-1

Solutions appear at back of book.

1. Explain why a rational consumer who has diminishing marginal utility for a good would not consume an additional unit when it generates negative marginal utility, even when that unit is free.

2. Marta drinks three cups of coffee a day, for which she has diminishing marginal utility. Which of her three cups generates the greatest increase in total utility? Which generates the least?

3. In each of the following cases, determine if the consumer experiences diminishing marginal utility. Explain your answer.
   a. The more Mabel exercises, the more she enjoys each additional visit to the gym.
   b. Although Mei's collection of vinyl records is huge, her enjoyment from buying another album has not changed as her collection has grown.
   c. When Dexter was a struggling student, his enjoyment from a good restaurant meal was greater than it is now that he can afford to have them more frequently.

‖ Budgets and Optimal Consumption

The principle of diminishing marginal utility explains why most people eventually reach a limit, even at an all-you-can-eat buffet where the cost of another egg roll is measured only in future indigestion. Under ordinary circumstances, however, it costs some additional resources to consume more of a good, and consumers must take that cost into account when making choices.

What do we mean by cost? As always, the fundamental measure of cost is *opportunity cost.* Because the amount of money a consumer can spend is limited, a decision to consume more of one good is also a decision to consume less of some other good.

Budget Constraints and Budget Lines

Consider Sammy, whose appetite is exclusively for egg rolls and Coke. He has a weekly income of $20 and since, given his appetite, more of either good is better than less, he spends all of it on egg rolls and Coke. We will assume that egg rolls cost $4 per roll and Coke costs $2 per bottle. What are his possible choices?

Whatever Sammy chooses, we know that the cost of his consumption bundle cannot exceed his income, the amount of money he has to spend. That is:

(10-1) Expenditure on egg rolls + Expenditure on Coke ≤ Total income

Consumers always have limited income, which constrains how much they can consume. So the requirement illustrated by Equation 10-1—that a consumer must choose a consumption bundle that costs no more than their income—is known as the consumer's **budget constraint.** It's a simple way of saying that a consumer can't spend more than the total amount of income available to them. In other words, consumption bundles are affordable when they obey the budget constraint. We call the set of all of Sammy's affordable consumption bundles his **consumption possibilities.** In general, whether or not a particular consumption bundle is included in a consumer's consumption possibilities depends on the consumer's income and the prices of goods and services.

Figure 10-2 shows Sammy's consumption possibilities. The quantity of egg rolls in his consumption bundle is measured on the horizontal axis and the

A **budget constraint** requires that the cost of a consumer's consumption bundle be no more than the consumer's income.

A consumer's **consumption possibilities** is the set of all consumption bundles that can be consumed given the consumer's income and prevailing prices.

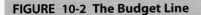

FIGURE 10-2 The Budget Line

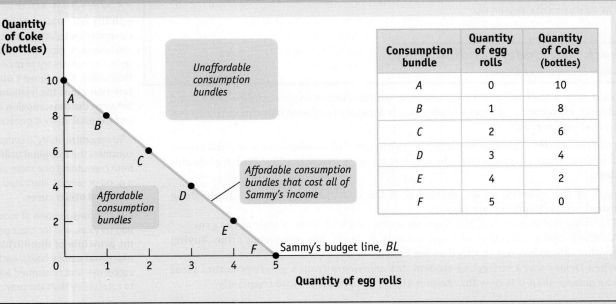

Consumption bundle	Quantity of egg rolls	Quantity of Coke (bottles)
A	0	10
B	1	8
C	2	6
D	3	4
E	4	2
F	5	0

The *budget line* represents the consumption bundles available to Sammy when he spends all of his income. Also, it is the boundary between the set of affordable consumption bundles (the *consumption possibilities*) and unaffordable ones. Given that egg rolls cost $4 per roll and Cokes cost $2 per bottle, if Sammy spends all of his income on egg rolls (bundle *F*), he can purchase 5 egg rolls. If he spends all of his income on Cokes (bundle *A*), he can purchase 10 bottles of Coke.

quantity of Cokes on the vertical axis. The downward-sloping line connecting points *A* through *F* shows which consumption bundles are affordable and which are not. Every bundle on or inside this line (the shaded area) is affordable; every bundle outside this line is unaffordable.

As an example of one of the points, let's look at point *C*, representing 2 egg rolls and 6 Cokes, and check whether it satisfies Sammy's budget constraint. The cost of bundle *C* is 6 bottles of Coke × $2 per bottle + 2 egg rolls × $4 per roll = $12 + $8 = $20. So bundle *C* does indeed satisfy Sammy's budget constraint: it costs no more than his weekly income of $20. In fact, bundle *C* costs exactly as much as Sammy's income. By doing the arithmetic, you can check that all the other points lying on the downward-sloping line are also bundles at which Sammy spends all of his income.

The downward-sloping line has a special name, the **budget line.** It shows all the consumption bundles available to Sammy when he spends all of his income. It's downward sloping because when Sammy is consuming all of his income, say consuming at point *A* on the budget line, then in order to consume more egg rolls he must consume fewer Cokes—that is, he must move to a point like *B*. In other words, when Sammy chooses a consumption bundle that is on his budget line, the opportunity cost of consuming more egg rolls is consuming fewer Cokes, and vice versa. As Figure 10-2 indicates, any consumption bundle that lies above the budget line is unaffordable.

Do we need to consider the other bundles in Sammy's consumption possibilities, the ones that lie *within* the shaded region in Figure 10-2 bounded by the budget line? The answer is, for all practical situations, no: as long as Sammy continues to get positive marginal utility from consuming either good (in other words, Sammy doesn't get *satiated*)—and he doesn't get any utility from saving income rather than spending it—then he will always choose to consume a bundle that lies on his budget line and not within the shaded area.

Given his $20 per week budget, which point on his budget line will Sammy choose?

A consumer's **budget line** shows the consumption bundles available to a consumer who spends all of their income.

Optimal Consumption Choice

Sammy will choose a consumption bundle that lies on his budget line. That's the best he can do given his budget constraint. We want to find the consumption bundle—the point on the budget line—that maximizes Sammy's total utility. This bundle is Sammy's **optimal consumption bundle,** the consumption bundle that maximizes his total utility given the budget constraint.

Table 10-1 shows how much utility Sammy gets from consuming different amounts of egg rolls and Cokes. As you can see, Sammy has a healthy appetite; the more of either good he consumes, the higher his utility. (Although the quantities are not so large that an additional egg roll or Coke would give him *negative utility,* meaning they wouldn't be rational to consume.)

A consumer's **optimal consumption bundle** is the consumption bundle that maximizes the consumer's total utility given their budget constraint.

TABLE 10-1 Sammy's Utility from Egg Roll and Coke Consumption

Utility from egg roll consumption		Utility from Coke consumption	
Quantity of egg rolls	Utility from egg rolls (utils)	Quantity of Coke (bottles)	Utility from Cokes (utils)
0	0	0	0
1	15	1	11.5
2	25	2	21.4
3	31	3	29.8
4	34	4	36.8
5	36	5	42.5
		6	47.0
		7	50.5
		8	53.2
		9	55.2
		10	56.7

But because he has a limited budget, he must make a trade-off: the more egg rolls he consumes, the fewer bottles of Coke, and vice versa. That is, he must choose a point on his budget line.

Table 10-2 shows how Sammy's total utility varies for the different consumption bundles along his budget line. Each of the six possible consumption bundles, *A* through *F* from Figure 10-2, is listed in the first column. The second column shows the number of egg rolls consumed corresponding to each bundle. The third column shows the utility Sammy gets from consuming those egg rolls. The fourth column shows the quantity of Cokes Sammy can afford *given* the level of egg roll consumption. This quantity goes down as the number of egg rolls consumed goes up, because he is sliding down the budget line. The fifth column shows the utility he gets from consuming those Cokes. And the final column shows his *total utility.* In this example, Sammy's total utility is the sum of the utility he gets from egg rolls and the utility he gets from Cokes.

TABLE 10-2 Sammy's Budget and Total Utility

Consumption bundle	Quantity of egg rolls	Utility from egg rolls (utils)	Quantity of Coke (bottles)	Utility from Cokes (utils)	Total utility (utils)
A	0	0	10	56.7	56.7
B	1	15	8	53.2	68.2
C	2	25	6	47.0	72.0
D	3	31	4	36.8	67.8
E	4	34	2	21.4	55.4
F	5	36	0	0	36.0

Figure 10-3 gives a visual representation of the data in Table 10-2. Panel (a) shows Sammy's budget line, to remind us that when he decides to consume more egg rolls he is also deciding to consume fewer Cokes. Panel (b) then shows how his total utility depends on that choice. The horizontal axis in panel (b) has two sets of labels: it shows both the quantity of egg rolls, increasing from left to right, and the quantity of Cokes, increasing from right to left.

The reason we can use the same axis to represent consumption of both goods is, of course, the budget line: the more egg rolls Sammy consumes, the fewer bottles of Coke he can afford, and vice versa.

Clearly, the consumption bundle that makes the best of the trade-off between egg roll consumption and Coke consumption, the optimal consumption bundle, is the one that maximizes Sammy's total utility. That is, Sammy's optimal consumption bundle puts him at the highest point of the total utility curve.

FIGURE 10-3 Optimal Consumption Bundle

Panel (a) shows Sammy's budget line and his six possible consumption bundles. Panel (b) shows how his total utility is affected by his consumption bundle, which must lie on his budget line. The quantity of egg rolls is measured from left to right on the horizontal axis, and the quantity of Cokes is measured from right to left. His total utility is maximized at bundle *C*, the highest point on his utility function, where he consumes 2 egg rolls and 6 bottles of Coke. This is Sammy's *optimal consumption bundle*.

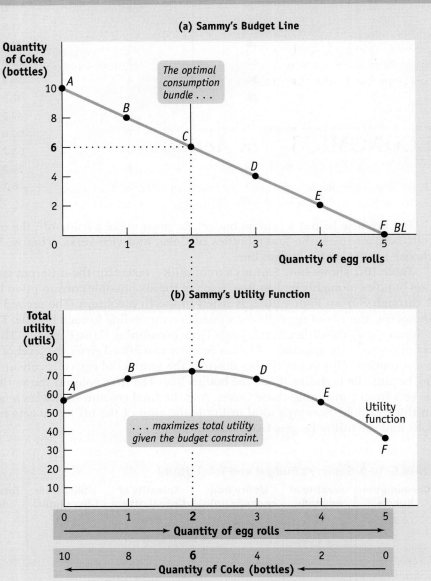

Budget constraints aren't just about money. In fact, there are many other budget constraints affecting our lives. You face a budget constraint if you have a limited amount of closet space for your clothes. All of us face a budget constraint on time: there are only so many hours in the day. And people trying to lose weight or improve their health often face a budget constraint on the foods they eat.

The Weight Watchers diet program is designed to formalize people's food budgets, in order to help them achieve or maintain a healthy weight. The Weight Watchers plan assigns each food a specific number of points based on calories, saturated fat, sugar, and protein content. For example, a 4-ounce scoop of premium ice cream might be 8 points, a slice of cheese pizza with a medium crust 7 points; most fruits are zero

points per serving. Members are allowed a maximum number of points (their points budget) each day but are free to choose which foods they eat.

In other words, someone on the Weight Watchers plan is just like a consumer choosing a consumption bundle: points are the equivalent of prices, and the overall point limit is the equivalent of total income.

As always, we can find the highest point of the curve by direct observation. We can see from Figure 10-3 that Sammy's total utility is maximized at point *C*, his optimal consumption bundle, which contains 2 egg rolls and 6 bottles of Coke. Here we've solved Sammy's optimal consumption choice problem by calculating and comparing the utility generated by each bundle. But since it is a "how much" problem, marginal analysis will give us greater insight than direct calculation. So in the next section we turn to representing and solving the optimal consumption choice problem with marginal analysis.

ECONOMICS >> *in Action*
The Great Condiment Craze

Have you ever found yourself overwhelmed in the grocery store, trying to decide which mustard to choose? Your grandparents probably never had that problem. In their day, the only kind of mustard available in American grocery stores was a runny, fluorescent yellow concoction packaged in plastic squeeze bottles. Ditto for ketchup and mayonnaise—what little selection there was, tasted the same.

No longer. Americans have developed an intense liking for condiments—in a dizzying array of varieties. Who wants plain mustard when you can get mustard flavored with roasted garlic, apricot, or even bourbon/molasses? Likewise, would you like saffron and garlic mayonnaise or sriracha mayonnaise on your sandwich? And sales of salsa in the United States have long since overtaken ketchup sales. In 2019, U.S. condiment and sauce sales reached $42.7 billion. Over the next five years, sales are projected to grow faster than the previous five years.

So what happened? Tastes changed and budgets changed. Mass media, immigration, and global trade mean that Americans are continuously exposed to different cultures and cuisines, making them more willing to try—or even seek out—new flavors. Not only are people wanting to try more flavors, with growing incomes, many Americans also have the financial ability to spend more on higher quality condiments that aren't runny and florescent yellow. The explosion of varieties also stems from the fact that it's fairly easy to make bottled condiments. This enables smaller companies to experiment with exotic flavors, finding the ones that appeal to consumers' increasingly sophisticated tastes. Eventually, the flavors that attract a significant following are picked up by the larger companies such as Kraft. As one industry analyst put it, "People want cheaper, more specialized gourmet products. It's like fashion."

Changing tastes and budgets drove the American condiment craze.

>> *Check Your Understanding* **10-2**
Solutions appear at back of book.

1. In the following two examples, find all the consumption bundles that lie on the consumer's budget line. Illustrate these consumption possibilities in a diagram and draw the budget line through them.
   a. The consumption bundle consists of movie tickets and buckets of popcorn. The price of each ticket is $10.00, the price of each bucket of popcorn is $5.00, and the consumer's income is $20.00. In your diagram, put movie tickets on the vertical axis and buckets of popcorn on the horizontal axis.
   b. The consumption bundle consists of underwear and socks. The price of each pair of underwear is $4.00, the price of each pair of socks is $2.00, and the consumer's income is $12.00. In your diagram, put pairs of socks on the vertical axis and pairs of underwear on the horizontal axis.

‖ Spending the Marginal Dollar

As we've just seen, we can find Sammy's optimal consumption choice by finding the total utility he receives from each consumption bundle on his budget line and then choosing the bundle at which total utility is maximized. But we can use marginal analysis instead, turning Sammy's problem of finding his optimal consumption choice into a "how much" problem.

To do this, think about choosing an optimal consumption bundle as a problem of *how much to spend on each good.* That is, to find the optimal consumption bundle with marginal analysis, ask whether Sammy can make himself better off by spending a little bit more of his income on egg rolls and less on Cokes, or by doing the opposite—spending a little bit more on Cokes and less on egg rolls. In other words, the marginal decision is a question of how to *spend the marginal dollar*—how to allocate an additional dollar between egg rolls and bottles of Coke in a way that maximizes utility.

Our first step in applying marginal analysis is to ask if Sammy is made better off by spending an additional dollar on either good; and if so, by how much is he better off. To answer this question we must calculate the **marginal utility per dollar** spent on either egg rolls or Cokes—how much additional utility Sammy gets from spending an additional dollar on either good.

Marginal Utility per Dollar

We've already introduced the concept of *marginal utility,* the additional utility a consumer gets from consuming one more unit of a good or service; now let's see how this concept can be used to derive the related measure of marginal utility per dollar.

Table 10-3 shows how to calculate the marginal utility per dollar spent on egg rolls and Cokes, respectively.

In panel (a) of the table, the first column shows different possible amounts of egg roll consumption. The second column shows the utility Sammy derives from each amount of egg roll consumption; the third column then shows the marginal utility, the increase in utility Sammy gets from consuming an additional egg roll. Panel (b) provides the same information for Cokes. The next step is to derive marginal utility *per dollar* for each good. To do this, we must divide the marginal utility of the good by its price in dollars.

To see why we must divide by the price, compare the third and fourth columns of panel (a). Consider what happens if Sammy increases his egg roll consumption from 2 rolls to 3 rolls. As we can see, this increase in egg roll consumption raises his total utility by 6 utils. But he must spend $4 for that additional roll, so the increase in his utility per additional dollar spent on egg rolls is 6 utils/$4 = 1.5 utils per dollar.

The **marginal utility per dollar** spent on a good or service is the additional utility from spending one more dollar on that good or service.

TABLE 10-3 Sammy's Marginal Utility per Dollar

(a) Egg rolls (price = $4 per roll)				(b) Cokes (price = $2 per bottle)			
Quantity of egg rolls	Utility from egg rolls (utils)	Marginal utility per roll (utils)	Marginal utility per dollar (utils/$)	Quantity of Coke (bottles)	Utility from Cokes (utils)	Marginal utility per bottle of Coke (utils)	Marginal utility per dollar (utils/$)
0	0			0	0		
		15	3.75			11.5	5.75
1	15			1	11.5		
		10	2.50			9.9	4.95
2	25			2	21.4		
		6	1.50			8.4	4.20
3	31			3	29.8		
		3	0.75			7.0	3.50
4	34			4	36.8		
		2	0.50			5.7	2.85
5	36			5	42.5		
						4.5	2.25
				6	47.0		
						3.5	1.75
				7	50.5		
						2.7	1.35
				8	53.2		
						2.0	1.00
				9	55.2		
						1.5	0.75
				10	56.7		

Similarly, if he increases his egg roll consumption from 3 rolls to 4 rolls, his marginal utility is 3 utils but his marginal utility per dollar is 3 utils/$4 = 0.75 util per dollar. Notice that because of diminishing marginal utility, Sammy's marginal utility per egg roll falls as the quantity of rolls he consumes rises. As a result, his marginal utility per dollar spent on egg rolls also falls as the quantity of rolls he consumes rises.

So the last column of panel (a) shows how Sammy's marginal utility per dollar spent on egg rolls depends on the quantity of rolls he consumes. Similarly, the last column of panel (b) shows how his marginal utility per dollar spent on Coke depends on the quantity of bottles of Coke he consumes. Again, marginal utility per dollar spent on each good declines as the quantity of that good consumed rises, due to diminishing marginal utility.

We will use the symbols MU_r and MU_c to represent the marginal utility per egg roll and bottle of Coke, respectively. And we will use the symbols P_r and P_c to represent the price of egg rolls (per roll) and the price of Coke (per bottle). Then the marginal utility per dollar spent on egg rolls is MU_r/P_r and the marginal utility per dollar spent on Cokes is MU_c/P_c. In general, the additional utility generated from an additional dollar spent on a good is equal to:

(10-2) Marginal utility per dollar spent on a good
= Marginal utility of one unit of the good/Price of one unit of the good
= MU_{Good}/P_{Good}

Now let's see how this concept helps us find the consumer's optimal consumption bundle using marginal analysis.

Optimal Consumption

Let's consider Figure 10-4. As in Figure 10-3, we can measure both the quantity of egg rolls and the quantity of bottles of Coke on the horizontal axis due to the budget constraint. Along the horizontal axis of Figure 10-4—also as in Figure 10-3—the quantity of egg rolls increases as you move from left to right, and the quantity of Cokes increases as you move from right to left. The curve labeled MU_r/P_r in Figure 10-4 shows Sammy's marginal utility per dollar spent on egg rolls as derived in Table 10-3. Likewise, the curve labeled MU_c/P_c shows his marginal utility per dollar spent on Cokes. Notice that the two curves, MU_r/P_r and MU_c/P_c, cross at the optimal consumption bundle, point *C*, consisting of 2 egg rolls and 6 bottles of Coke.

Moreover, Figure 10-4 illustrates an important feature of Sammy's optimal consumption bundle: when Sammy consumes 2 egg rolls and 6 bottles of Coke, his marginal utility per dollar spent is the same, 2, for both goods. That is, at the optimal consumption bundle $MU_r/P_r = MU_c/P_c = 2$.

This isn't an accident. Consider another one of Sammy's possible consumption bundles—say, *B* in Figure 10-3, at which he consumes 1 egg roll and 8 bottles of Coke. The marginal utility per dollar spent on each good is shown by points B_r and B_c in Figure 10-4. At that consumption bundle, Sammy's marginal utility per dollar spent on egg rolls would be approximately 3, but his marginal utility per dollar spent on Cokes would be only approximately 1. This shows that he has made a mistake: he is consuming too many Cokes and not enough egg rolls.

How do we know this? If Sammy's marginal utility per dollar spent on egg rolls is higher than his marginal utility per dollar spent on Cokes, he has a simple way to make himself better off while staying within his budget: spend $1 less on Cokes and $1 more on egg rolls. We can illustrate this with points B_r and B_c in Figure 10-4. By spending an additional dollar on egg rolls, he gains the amount of utility given by B_r, about 3 utils. By spending $1 less on Cokes, he loses the amount of utility given by B_c, only about 1 util.

Because his marginal utility per dollar spent is higher for egg rolls than for Cokes, reallocating his spending toward egg rolls and away from Cokes would

---

FIGURE 10-4 Marginal Utility per Dollar

Sammy's optimal consumption bundle is at point *C*, where his marginal utility per dollar spent on egg rolls, MU_r/P_r, is equal to his marginal utility per dollar spent on Cokes, MU_c/P_c. This illustrates the *utility-maximizing principle of marginal analysis*: at the optimal consumption bundle, the marginal utility per dollar spent on each good and service is the same. At any other consumption bundle on Sammy's budget line, such as bundle *B* in Figure 10-3, represented here by points B_r and B_c, consumption is not optimal: Sammy can increase his utility at no additional cost by reallocating his spending.

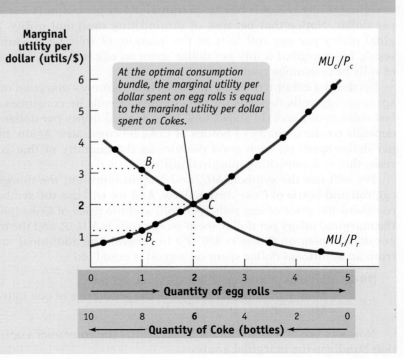

At the optimal consumption bundle, the marginal utility per dollar spent on egg rolls is equal to the marginal utility per dollar spent on Cokes.

THE RIGHT MARGINAL COMPARISON

Marginal analysis solves "how much" decisions by weighing costs and benefits at the margin: the *benefit* of doing a little bit more versus the *cost* of doing a little bit more. However, the form of the marginal analysis can differ, depending upon whether you are making a production decision that maximizes profits or a consumption decision that maximizes utility. Let's review that difference by returning to an example from Chapter 9.

In Chapter 9, Alexa's decision was a production decision because the problem she faced was maximizing the profit from years of schooling. The optimal quantity of years that maximized her profit was found using marginal analysis: at the optimal quantity, the marginal benefit of another year of schooling was equal to its marginal cost. Alexa did not face a budget constraint because she could always borrow to finance another year of school.

But if you were to extend the way we solved Alexa's production problem to Sammy's consumption problem without any change in form, you might be tempted to say that Sammy's optimal consumption bundle is the one at which the marginal utility of egg rolls is equal to the marginal utility of Cokes, or that the marginal utility of egg rolls is equal to the price of egg rolls. But both those statements would be wrong because they don't properly account for Sammy's budget constraint.

In general, unlike producers, consumers face budget constraints. Consuming more of one good requires consuming less of another. So the consumer's objective is to maximize the utility his limited budget can deliver. The right way to find the optimal consumption bundle is to set the *marginal utility per dollar* equal for each good in the consumption bundle.

When this condition is satisfied, the "bang per buck" is the same across all the goods and services consumed. Only then is there no way to rearrange consumption and get more utility from one's budget.

---

increase his total utility. But if his marginal utility per dollar spent on Cokes is higher, he can increase his utility by spending less on egg rolls and more on Cokes. So if Sammy has in fact chosen his optimal consumption bundle, his marginal utility per dollar spent on egg rolls and Cokes must be equal.

This is a general principle, which we call the **utility-maximizing principle of marginal analysis:** when a consumer maximizes utility in the face of a budget constraint, the marginal utility per dollar spent on each good or service in the consumption bundle is the same. That is, for any two goods r and c the optimal consumption rule says that at the optimal consumption bundle:

$$(10\text{-}3) \quad \frac{MU_r}{P_r} = \frac{MU_c}{P_c}$$

It's easiest to understand this rule using examples in which the consumption bundle contains only two goods, but it applies no matter how many goods or services a consumer buys: in the optimal consumption bundle, the marginal utilities per dollar spent for each and every good or service in that bundle are equal.

ECONOMICS >> *in Action*
Buying Your Way Out of Temptation

It might seem odd to pay more to get less. But snack food companies have discovered that consumers are indeed willing to pay more for smaller portions, and that exploiting this trend is a recipe for success. A company executive explained why small packages are popular—they help consumers control portions without having to spend time packaging individual servings themselves. "The irony," said David Adelman, a food industry analyst, "is if you take Wheat Thins or Goldfish, buy a large-size box, count out the items and put them in a Ziploc bag, you'd have essentially the same product." He estimates that snack packs are about 20% more profitable for snack makers than larger packages.

In this case consumers are making a calculation: the extra utility gained from not having to count out individual portions themselves is worth the extra cost. As one shopper said, "They're pretty expensive, but they're worth it. It's individually packaged for the amount I need, so I don't go overboard." So it's clear that consumers aren't being irrational here. Rather, they're being entirely rational: in addition to their snack, they're buying a little hand-to-mouth restraint.

According to the **utility-maximizing principle of marginal analysis,** the marginal utility per dollar spent must be the same for all goods and services in the optimal consumption bundle.

>> Check Your Understanding 10-3

Solutions appear at back of book.

1. In Table 10-3 you can see that marginal utility per dollar spent on egg rolls and marginal utility per dollar spent on Cokes are equal when Sammy increases his consumption of egg rolls from 3 to 4 rolls and his consumption of Cokes from 9 to 10 bottles. Explain why this is not Sammy's optimal consumption bundle. Illustrate your answer using the budget line in Figure 10-3.

2. Explain what is faulty about the following statement, using data from Table 10-3: "In order to maximize utility, Sammy should consume the bundle that gives him the maximum marginal utility per dollar for each good."

‖ From Utility to the Demand Curve

We have now analyzed the optimal consumption choice of a consumer with a given amount of income who faces one particular set of prices—in our Sammy example, $20 of income per week, $4 per egg roll, and $2 per bottle of Coke.

But the main reason for studying consumer behavior is to go behind the market demand curve—to explain how the utility-maximizing behavior of individual consumers leads to the downward slope of the market demand curve.

Marginal Utility, the Substitution Effect, and the Law of Demand

Suppose that the price of egg rolls, P_r, rises. The price increase doesn't change the marginal utility a consumer gets from an additional egg roll, MU_r, at any given level of egg roll consumption. However, it does reduce the marginal utility *per dollar spent* on egg rolls, MU_r/P_r. And the decrease in marginal utility per dollar spent on egg rolls gives the consumer an incentive to consume fewer egg rolls when the price of egg rolls rises.

To see why, recall the utility-maximizing principle of marginal analysis: a utility-maximizing consumer chooses a consumption bundle for which the marginal utility per dollar spent on all goods is the same. If the marginal utility per dollar spent on egg rolls falls because the price of egg rolls rises, the consumer can increase their utility by purchasing fewer egg rolls and more of other goods.

The opposite happens if the price of egg rolls falls. In that case the marginal utility per dollar spent on egg rolls, MU_r/P_r, increases at any given level of egg roll consumption. As a result, a consumer can increase their utility by purchasing more egg rolls and less of other goods when the price of egg rolls falls.

So when the price of a good increases, an individual will normally consume less of that good and more of other goods. Correspondingly, when the price of a good decreases, an individual will normally consume more of that good and less of other goods. This explains why the individual demand curve, which relates an individual's consumption of a good to the price of that good, normally slopes downward—that is, it obeys the law of demand. And since—as we learned in Chapter 3—the market demand curve is the horizontal sum of all the individual demand curves of consumers, it, too, will slope downward.

An alternative way to think about why demand curves slope downward is to focus on opportunity costs. When the price of egg rolls decreases, an individual doesn't have to give up as many units of other goods in order to buy one more egg roll. So consuming egg rolls becomes more attractive. Conversely, when the price of a good increases, consuming that good becomes a less attractive use of resources, and the consumer buys less.

This effect of a price change on the quantity consumed is always present. It is known as the **substitution effect**—the change in the quantity consumed as the consumer substitutes other goods that are now relatively cheaper in place of the good that has become relatively more expensive. When a good absorbs only a small share of the consumer's spending, the substitution effect provides

The **substitution effect** of a change in the price of a good is the change in the quantity of that good consumed as the consumer substitutes other goods that are now relatively cheaper in place of the good that has become relatively more expensive.

the complete explanation of why the consumer's individual demand curve slopes downward. Therefore, when a good absorbs only a small share of the average consumer's spending, the substitution effect provides the sole explanation of why the market demand curve slopes downward.

However, some goods, such as housing, absorb a large share of a typical consumer's spending. For such goods, the story behind the individual demand curve and the market demand curve becomes slightly more complicated.

The Income Effect

For the vast majority of goods, the slopes of the individual and market demand curves are completely determined by the substitution effect. There are, however, some goods, like food or housing, that account for a substantial share of many consumers' spending. In such cases another effect, called the *income effect*, also comes into play.

Consider the case of a family that spends half its income on rental housing. Now suppose that the price of housing increases everywhere. This will have a substitution effect on the family's demand: other things equal, the family will have an incentive to consume less housing—say, by moving to a smaller apartment—and more of other goods. But the family will also, in a real sense, be made poorer by that higher housing price—its income will buy less housing than before.

The amount of income adjusted to reflect its true purchasing power is often termed "real income," in contrast to "money income" or "nominal income," which has not been adjusted. And this reduction in a consumer's real income will have an additional effect, beyond the substitution effect, on the family's consumption bundle, including its consumption of housing.

The change in the quantity of a good consumed that results from a change in the overall purchasing power of the consumer due to a change in the price of that good is known as the **income effect** of the price change. In this case, a change in the price of a good effectively changes a consumer's income because it alters the consumer's purchasing power. Along with the substitution effect, the income effect is another means by which changes in prices alter consumption choices.

It's possible to give more precise definitions of the substitution effect and the income effect of a price change, and we do this in the appendix to this chapter. For most purposes, however, there are only two things you need to know about the distinction between these two effects.

1. For the great majority of goods and services, the income effect is not important and has no significant effect on individual consumption. So most market demand curves slope downward solely because of the substitution effect.

2. When it matters at all, the income effect usually reinforces the substitution effect. That is, when the price of a good that absorbs a substantial share of income rises, consumers of that good become a bit poorer because their purchasing power falls.

As we learned in Chapter 3, the vast majority of goods are *normal goods*, goods for which demand decreases when income falls. So this effective reduction in income leads to a reduction in the quantity demanded and reinforces the substitution effect.

However, in the case of an *inferior good*, a good for which demand increases when income falls, the income and substitution effects work in opposite directions. Although the substitution effect tends to produce a decrease in the quantity of any good demanded as its price increases, in the case of an inferior good the income effect of a price increase tends to produce an *increase* in the quantity demanded.

As a result, it is possible that preferences and income effects can combine to generate a kind of inferior good in which the distinction between income and substitution effects is important. The most extreme example of this is a **Giffen good,** a good that has an upward-sloping demand curve.

Until recently, Giffen goods were treated as a hypothetical case—theoretically possible, but not observed in reality. However, a recent examination of the consumption patterns of Chinese peasants documents a real-world example of a

The **income effect** of a change in the price of a good is the change in the quantity of that good consumed that results from a change in the consumer's purchasing power due to the change in the price of the good.

A **Giffen good** is a hypothetical inferior good for which the income effect outweighs the substitution effect and the demand curve slopes upward.

Giffen good: consumption of rice and noodles, staples in the diet of Chinese peasants, goes up as the price of rice and noodles goes up. Because cheap food like rice and noodles helps these peasants reach a certain required minimum amount of daily calories, it is a necessary part of the diet. But when the price of rice or noodles goes up, more expensive foods like meat or fish have to be forgone. As a result, peasants eat more rice and noodles when the prices go up.

Admittedly, this is a rare case; it's likely to arise only when consumers are very poor and one good, a necessity, accounts for a large part of their budget. So as a practical matter, Giffen goods aren't a subject we need to worry about when discussing the demand for most goods. Typically, income effects are important only for a very limited number of goods.

ECONOMICS >> *in Action*
Lower Gasoline Prices and the Urge to Splurge

For American consumers, 2015 was a year to indulge the urge to splurge, made possible by plunging gasoline prices. From early 2014 to late 2015, gas prices fell nearly 45%, according to a study by the JP Morgan Institute based upon data from millions of credit card and debit card users. This translated into a windfall of approximately $700 for the average American family.

Consumers spent about 80% of their windfall, saving the remaining 20%. Fast-food chains like McDonald's, Wendy's, or Taco Bell, often located near gas stations and which cater to lower-income consumers, were the biggest beneficiaries of this spending as people chose to eat out more frequently or added extras like bacon to their burgers.

This should come as no surprise as low-income households experienced the largest *income effect* from the fall in gas prices—gasoline purchases accounted for a significant share of household spending, especially for those earning less than $29,999 per year. Those households experienced a 1.6% increase in their average income from the fall in gas prices, while households earning $79,700 or more saw their average income increase by only 0.5%.

And data indicate that the *substitution effect*—lower gas prices leading to purchases of more gas and less of other goods—also affected consumers' choices. Not only did people buy more gasoline, they bought higher grades of gasoline. Predictably, sales of electric vehicles, which use much less gas per mile, dropped sharply in 2015 (about 15%) after rising sharply from 2011 to 2013, a period of high gas prices. Simultaneously, gas-guzzling SUVs saw an uptick in sales.

>> Check Your Understanding 10-4
Solutions appear at back of book.

1. In each of the following cases, state whether the income effect, the substitution effect, or both are significant. In which cases do they move in the same direction? In opposite directions? Why?
   a. Orange juice represents a small share of Clare's spending. She buys more lemonade and less orange juice when the price of orange juice goes up. She does not change her spending on other goods.
   b. Apartment rents have risen dramatically this year. Since rent absorbs a major part of her income, Delia moves to a smaller apartment. Assume that rental housing is a normal good.
   c. The cost of a semester-long meal ticket at the student cafeteria rises, representing a significant increase in living costs. Assume that cafeteria meals are an inferior good.
2. In the example described in Question 1c, how would you determine whether or not cafeteria meals are a Giffen good?

>> Quick Review

• Most goods absorb only a small fraction of a consumer's spending. For such goods, the **substitution effect** of a price change is the only important effect of the price change on consumption. It causes individual demand curves and the market demand curve to slope downward.

• When a good absorbs a large fraction of a consumer's spending, the **income effect** of a price change is present in addition to the substitution effect.

• For normal goods, demand rises when a consumer is richer and falls when a consumer is poorer, so that the income effect reinforces the substitution effect. For inferior goods, demand rises when a consumer is poorer and falls when a consumer is richer, so that the income and substitution effects move in opposite directions.

• In the rare case of a **Giffen good,** a type of inferior good, the income effect is so strong that the demand curve slopes upward.

Beyond Impossible: McDonald's and Burger King's Beef-Free Battle

Geoff Robins/Getty Images

After decades of dependable growth, the fortunes of McDonald's have been on a roller coaster for the past several years. During the Great Recession, McDonald's had outperformed other fast-food restaurants and chain restaurants, such as TGI Friday's, as price-conscious customers were drawn to McDonald's "Dollar Menu." However, by 2013 the Dollar Menu was no longer profitable. When it was replaced with the "Dollar Menu and More," which included items costing up to $5, customer reaction was definitely not positive: from 2014 to 2015 revenue fell by 7.4% and, for the first time ever, McDonald's closed more restaurants than it opened in the United States. As Steve Easterbrook, CEO of McDonald's said at the time, "As we moved away from the Dollar Menu, we didn't replace it with offers of an equivalent form of value. And customers have voted with their feet."

McDonald's tried to lure back customers with its 2016 "McPick 2 Menu," which allowed customers to pick two items for $2. But as the economy slowly recovered, McDonald's found itself struggling to keep its price-conscious customers, while at the same time losing ground to the quickest growing segment of the restaurant industry: fast-casual restaurants that cater to customers with higher incomes. Fast-casual chains such as Chipotle and Panera offer a healthier menu using fresh ingredients, customizable, build-your-own selections, and a more comfortable dining environment. While the average McDonald's meal costs from $5 to $7, the typical Chipotle customer spends $12 for a meal. Despite their lower cost, McDonald's healthier menu options haven't sold particularly well because health-conscious customers tend to view McDonald's as the place to go for a quick burger and fries.

McDonald's also was caught flat-footed by the success of Burger King's plant-based Impossible Whopper burger in 2019. Costing $1 more than a regular beef burger, Impossible Burgers are completely meat-free, yet re-create the taste and feel of a beef burger. As the CEO of Restaurant Brands International, the parent company of Burger King, said, sales of the Impossible Whopper have been "highly incremental and have attracted new types of guests into our restaurant. We see a lot of millennial and Gen Z customers who tend to really connect with the message around sustainability." The strong demand for the Impossible Whopper lifted Burger's King sales by nearly 11% in late 2019 while McDonald's comparable sales grew by less than 5% over the same period.

McDonald's is now playing catch-up, rolling out its own plant-based Beyond Burger, called PLT, in selected markets. So the question in the minds of industry analysts is this: having succeeded in dominating the price-conscious but low-profitability segment of the food market, can McDonald's now transform itself in the minds of health-conscious and environmentally conscious customers who are willing to pay more for healthier and more sustainable food? Can it go beyond its identity as a place to buy a cheap beef burger and fries?

QUESTIONS FOR THOUGHT

1. How does the McPick 2 promotion resemble a consumer's optimal choice problem?

2. Give an example of a normal good and an inferior good mentioned in this case. Cite examples of income and substitution effects from the case.

3. Give an example of differences in consumer preferences illustrated by the case.

SUMMARY

1. Consumers maximize a measure of satisfaction called **utility.** Each consumer has a **utility function** that determines the level of total utility generated by their **consumption bundle,** the goods and services that are consumed. We measure utility in hypothetical units called **utils.**

2. A good's or service's **marginal utility** is the additional utility generated by consuming one more unit of the good or service. We usually assume that the **principle of diminishing marginal utility** holds: consumption of another unit of a good or service yields less additional utility than the previous unit. As a result, the **marginal utility curve** slopes downward.

3. A **budget constraint** limits a consumer's spending to no more than their income. It defines the consumer's **consumption possibilities,** the set of all affordable consumption bundles. A consumer who spends all of their income will choose a consumption bundle on the **budget line.** An individual chooses the consumption bundle that maximizes total utility, the **optimal consumption bundle.**

4. We use marginal analysis to find the optimal consumption bundle by analyzing how to allocate the marginal dollar. According to the **utility-maximizing principle of marginal analysis,** at the optimal consumption bundle the **marginal utility per dollar** spent on each good

and service—the marginal utility of a good divided by its price—is the same.

5. Changes in the price of a good affect the quantity consumed in two possible ways: the **substitution effect** and the **income effect.** Most goods absorb only a small share of a consumer's spending; for these goods, only the substitution effect—buying less of the good that has become relatively more expensive and more of goods that are now relatively cheaper—is significant. It causes the individual and the market demand curves to slope downward. When a good absorbs a large fraction of spending, the income effect is also significant: an increase in a good's price makes a consumer poorer, but a decrease in price makes a consumer richer. This change in purchasing power makes consumers demand less or more of a good, depending on whether the good is normal or inferior. For normal goods, the substitution and income effects reinforce each other. For inferior goods, however, they work in opposite directions. The demand curve of a **Giffen good** slopes upward because it is an inferior good in which the income effect outweighs the substitution effect. However, Giffen goods are exceedingly rare: they are likely to arise only when consumers are very poor and one good, a necessity, absorbs a large share of their budget.

KEY TERMS

Utility, p. 280
Consumption bundle, p. 280
Utility function, p. 280
Util, p. 280
Marginal utility, p. 281
Marginal utility curve, p. 281

Principle of diminishing marginal utility, p. 282
Budget constraint, p. 283
Consumption possibilities, p. 283
Budget line, p. 284
Optimal consumption bundle, p. 285

Marginal utility per dollar, p. 288
Utility-maximizing principle of marginal analysis, p. 291
Substitution effect, p. 292
Income effect, p. 293
Giffen good, p. 293

PRACTICE QUESTIONS

1. For each of the following situations, decide whether Al has diminishing marginal utility. Explain.

   a. The more economics classes Al takes, the more he enjoys the subject. And the more classes he takes, the easier each one gets, making him enjoy each additional class even more than the one before.

   b. Al likes loud music. In fact, according to him, "the louder, the better." Each time he turns the volume up a notch, he adds 5 utils to his total utility.

   c. Al enjoys watching reruns of the *X Files*. He claims that these episodes are always exciting, but he does admit that the more times he sees an episode, the less exciting it gets.

   d. Al loves toasted marshmallows. The more he eats, however, the fuller he gets and the less he enjoys each additional marshmallow. And there is a point at which he becomes satiated: beyond that point, more marshmallows actually make him feel worse rather than better.

2. Use the concept of marginal utility to explain the following. Newspaper vending machines are designed so that once you have paid for one paper, you could take more than one paper at a time. But soda vending machines, once you have paid for one soda, dispense only one soda at a time.

3. You and your roommate both enjoy Blue Bunny cookie dough ice cream. At the campus store you can buy a pint of ice cream for $3. In your last visit to the store, you noticed Blue Bunny ice cream was on sale for 50% off. You are excited for the sale and stock up on pints of ice cream but to your surprise, your roommate purchases fewer pints of Blue Bunny, opting instead to purchase more of Ben and Jerry's ice cream. Explain how each decision relates to concepts of income and substitution effects.

4. Many colleges offer on-campus meal plans that allow students to purchase a set number of meals per week; the meals are nonrefundable. Most students purchase a meal plan that allows students to eat 20 meals per week at on-campus dining locations. Toward the end of the week you notice most students eating off campus despite not using all of their on-campus meals. Use the concept of marginal utility to explain student's behavior for spending money to eat off campus instead of consuming "free" on-campus meals.

PROBLEMS

1. Bruno can spend his income on two different goods: smoothies and energy bars. For each of the following three situations, decide if the given consumption bundle is within Bruno's consumption possibilities. Then decide if it lies *on* the budget line or not.

   a. Smoothies cost $2 each, and energy bars cost $3 each. Bruno has income of $60. He is considering a consumption bundle containing 15 smoothies and 10 energy bars.

   b. Smoothies cost $2 each, and energy bars cost $5 each. Bruno has income of $110. He is considering a consumption bundle containing 20 smoothies and 10 energy bars.

   c. Smoothies cost $3 each, and energy bars cost $10 each. Bruno has income of $50. He is considering a consumption bundle containing 10 smoothies and 3 energy bars.

2. Bruno, the consumer in Problem 1, is best friends with Ruby who shares Bruno's love for energy bars and smoothies. The accompanying table shows Ruby's utilities from smoothies and energy bars.

Quantity of smoothies	Utility from smoothies (utils)	Quantity of energy bars	Utility from energy bars (utils)
0	0	0	0
1	32	2	28
2	60	4	52
3	84	6	72
4	104	8	88
5	120	10	100

The price of an energy bar is $2, the price of a smoothie is $4, and Ruby has $20 of income to spend.

   a. Which consumption bundles of energy bars and smoothies can Ruby consume if she spends all her income? Illustrate Ruby's budget line with a diagram, putting smoothies on the horizontal axis and energy bars on the vertical axis.

   b. Calculate the marginal utility of each energy bar and the marginal utility of each smoothie. Then calculate the marginal utility per dollar spent on energy bars and the marginal utility per dollar spent on smoothies.

   c. Draw a diagram like Figure 10-4 in which both the marginal utility per dollar spent on energy bars and the marginal utility per dollar spent on smoothies are illustrated. Draw the quantity of energy bars increasing from left to right, and the quantity of smoothies increasing from right to left. Using this diagram and the utility-maximizing principle of marginal analysis, predict which bundle—from all the bundles on her budget line—Ruby will choose.

3. For each of the following situations, decide whether the bundle Lakshani is considering is optimal or not. If it is not optimal, how could Lakshani improve her overall level of utility? That is, determine which good she should spend more on and which good she should spend less on.

   a. Lakshani has $200 to spend on sneakers and sweaters. Sneakers cost $50 per pair, and sweaters cost $20 each. She is thinking about buying 2 pairs of sneakers and 5 sweaters. She tells her friend that the additional utility she would get from the second pair of sneakers is the same as the additional utility she would get from the fifth sweater.

   b. Lakshani has $5 to spend on pens and pencils. Each pen costs $0.50 and each pencil costs $0.10. She is thinking about buying 6 pens and 20 pencils. The last pen would add five times as much to her total utility as the last pencil.

   c. Lakshani has $50 per season to spend on tickets to football games and tickets to soccer games. Each football ticket costs $10 and each soccer ticket costs $5. She is thinking about buying 3 football tickets and 2 soccer tickets. Her marginal utility from the third football ticket is twice as much as her marginal utility from the second soccer ticket.

4. Cal "Cool" Cooper has $200 to spend on Nikes and sunglasses.

   a. Each pair of Nikes costs $100 and each pair of sunglasses costs $50. Which bundles lie on Cal's budget line? Draw a diagram like Figure 10-4 in which both the marginal utility per dollar spent on Nikes and the marginal utility per dollar spent on sunglasses are illustrated. Draw the quantity of Nikes increasing from left to right, and the quantity of sunglasses increasing from right to left. Use this diagram and the optimal consumption rule to decide how Cal should allocate his money. That is, from all the bundles on his budget line, which bundle will Cal choose? The accompanying table gives his utility of Nikes and sunglasses.

Quantity of Nikes (pairs)	Utility from Nikes (utils)	Quantity of sunglasses (pairs)	Utility from sunglasses (utils)
0	0	0	0
1	400	2	600
2	700	4	700

b. The price of a pair of Nikes falls to $50 each, but the price of sunglasses remains at $50 per pair. Which bundles lie on Cal's budget line? Draw a diagram like Figure 10-4 in which both the marginal utility per dollar spent on Nikes and the marginal utility per dollar spent on sunglasses are illustrated. Use this diagram and the utility-maximizing principle of marginal analysis to decide how Cal should allocate his money. That is, from all the bundles on his budget line, which bundle will Cal choose? The accompanying table gives his utility of Nikes and sunglasses.

Quantity of Nikes (pairs)	Utility from Nikes (utils)	Quantity of sunglasses (pairs)	Utility from sunglasses (utils)
0	0	0	0
1	400	1	325
2	700	2	600
3	900	3	825
4	1,000	4	700

c. How does Cal's consumption of Nikes change as the price of Nikes falls? In words, describe the income effect and the substitution effect of this fall in the price of Nikes, assuming that Nikes are a normal good.

5. Damien Matthews is a busy actor. He allocates his free time to watching movies and working out at the gym. The accompanying table shows his utility from the number of times per week he watches a movie or goes to the gym.

Quantity of gym visits per week	Utility from gym visits (utils)	Quantity of movies per week	Utility from movies (utils)
1	100	1	60
2	180	2	110
3	240	3	150
4	280	4	180
5	310	5	190
6	330	6	195
7	340	7	197

Damien has 14 hours per week to spend on watching movies and going to the gym. Each movie takes 2 hours and each gym visit takes 2 hours. (*Hint:* Damien's free time is analogous to income he can spend. The hours needed for each activity are analogous to the price of that activity.)

a. Which bundles of gym visits and movies can Damien consume per week if he spends all his time either going to the gym or watching movies? Draw Damien's budget line in a diagram with gym visits on the horizontal axis and movies on the vertical axis.

b. Calculate the marginal utility of each gym visit and the marginal utility of each movie. Then calculate the marginal utility per hour spent at the gym and the marginal utility per hour spent watching movies.

c. Draw a diagram like Figure 10-4 in which both the marginal utility per hour spent at the gym and the marginal utility per hour spent watching movies are illustrated. Draw the quantity of gym visits increasing from left to right, and the quantity of movies increasing from right to left. Use this diagram and the utility-maximizing principle of marginal analysis to decide how Damien should allocate his time.

6. Anna Jenniferson is an actress who currently spends several hours each week watching movies and going to the gym. She likes watching movies much more than going to the gym. In fact, she says that if she had to give up seeing 1 movie, she would need to go to the gym twice to make up for the loss in utility from not seeing the movie. A movie takes 2 hours, and a gym visit also lasts 2 hours. Should Anna watch more movies or spend more time at the gym?

7. Sven is a low-income student who covers most of his dietary needs by eating cheap breakfast cereal, since it contains most of the important vitamins. As the price of cereal increases, he decides to buy even less of other foods and even more breakfast cereal to maintain his intake of important nutrients. This makes breakfast cereal a Giffen good for Sven. Describe in words the substitution effect and the income effect from this increase in the price of cereal. In which direction does each effect move, and why? What does this imply for the slope of Sven's demand curve for cereal?

8. In each of the following situations, describe the substitution effect and, if it is significant, the income effect. In which direction does each of these effects move? Why?

a. Ed spends a large portion of his income on his children's education. Because tuition fees rise, one of his children has to withdraw from college.

b. Homer spends much of his monthly income on home mortgage payments. The interest on his adjustable-rate mortgage falls, lowering his mortgage payments, and Homer decides to move to a larger house.

c. Pam thinks that Spam is an inferior good. Yet as the price of Spam rises, she decides to buy less of it.

9. Restaurant meals and housing (measured in the number of rooms) are the only two goods that Neha buys. She has income of $1,000. Initially, she buys a consumption bundle such that she spends exactly half her income on restaurant meals and the other half of her income on housing. Then her income increases by 50%, but the price of restaurant meals increases by 100% (it doubles). The price of housing remains the same. After these changes, if she wanted to, could Neha still buy the same consumption bundle as before?

10. Scott finds that the higher the price of orange juice, the more money he spends on orange juice. Does that mean that Scott has discovered a Giffen good?

11. Margo's marginal utility of one dance lesson is 100 utils per lesson. Her marginal utility of a new pair of dance shoes is 300 utils per pair. The price of a dance lesson is $50 per lesson. She currently spends all her income, and she buys her optimal consumption bundle. What is the price of a pair of dance shoes?

12. According to data from the U.S. Department of Energy, the average retail price of regular gasoline rose from $1.16 in 1990 to $2.52 in 2015, a 117% increase.

a. Other things equal, describe the effect of this price increase on the quantity of gasoline demanded. In your explanation, make use of the utility-maximizing principle of marginal analysis and describe income and substitution effects.

In fact, however, other things were not equal. Over the same time period, the prices of other goods and services rose as well. According to data from the Bureau of Labor Statistics, the overall price of a bundle of goods and services consumed by an average consumer rose by 81%.

b. Taking into account the rise in the price of gasoline and in overall prices, other things equal, describe the effect on the quantity of gasoline demanded.

However, this is not the end of the story. Between 1990 and 2015, the typical consumer's nominal income increased, too: the U.S. Census Bureau reports that U.S. median household nominal income rose from $29,943 in 1990 to $56,516 in 2015, an increase of 89%.

c. Taking into account the rise in the price of gasoline, in overall prices, and in consumers' incomes, describe the effect on the quantity of gasoline demanded.

▊▙ WORK IT OUT

13. Brenda likes to have bagels and coffee for breakfast. The accompanying table shows Brenda's total utility from various consumption bundles of bagels and coffee.

Consumption bundle		Total utility (utils)
Quantity of bagels	Quantity of coffee (cups)	
0	0	0
0	2	28
0	4	40
1	2	48
1	3	54
2	0	28
2	2	56
3	1	54
3	2	62
4	0	40
4	2	66

Suppose Brenda knows she will consume 2 cups of coffee for sure. However, she can choose to consume different quantities of bagels: she can choose either 0, 1, 2, 3, or 4 bagels.

a. Calculate Brenda's marginal utility from bagels as she goes from consuming 0 bagels to 1 bagel, from 1 bagel to 2 bagels, from 2 bagels to 3 bagels, and from 3 bagels to 4 bagels.

b. Draw Brenda's marginal utility curve of bagels. Does Brenda have diminishing marginal utility of bagels? Explain.

c. Brenda has $8 of income to spend on bagels and coffee. Bagels cost $2 each, and coffee costs $2 per cup. Which bundles are on Brenda's budget line? For each of these bundles, calculate the level of utility (in utils) that Brenda enjoys. Which bundle is her optimal bundle?

d. The price of bagels increases to $4, but the price of coffee remains at $2 per cup. Which bundles are now on Brenda's budget line? For each bundle, calculate Brenda's level of utility (in utils). Which bundle is her optimal bundle? ■

Consumer Preferences and Consumer Choice

Different people have different preferences. And for any given person, there will be different consumption bundles that yield the same total utility. This insight leads to the concept of *indifference curves*, a useful way to represent individual preferences. In this appendix, we will look closely at indifference curves.

Using indifference curves to analyze consumer behavior will serve us in three ways.

1. Indifference curves show how diminishing marginal utility determines the trade-off a consumer makes between consuming more of one good and less of another.
2. They provide a framework for a more in-depth analysis of income and substitution effects—how changes in price and income alter the optimal consumption bundle.
3. Indifference curves allow us to illustrate differences in tastes between two people, and how those differences in tastes lead to different optimal consumption bundles.

Indifference curves, then, allow us to get a deeper understanding of what it means to be a rational consumer.

‖ Mapping the Utility Function

In Chapter 10 we introduced the concept of a utility function, which determines a consumer's total utility given his or her consumption bundle. In Figure 10-1 we saw how Cassie's total utility changed as we changed the quantity of egg rolls consumed, holding fixed the quantities of other items in her bundle. That is, in Figure 10-1 we showed how total utility changed as consumption of only *one* good changed. But we also learned in Chapter 10, from our example of Sammy, that finding the optimal consumption bundle involves the problem of how to allocate the last dollar spent between *two* goods, egg rolls and bottles of Coke.

In this appendix we will extend the analysis by learning how to express total utility as a function of consumption of two goods. In this way we will deepen our understanding of the trade-off involved when choosing the optimal consumption bundle and of how the optimal consumption bundle itself changes in response to changes in the prices of goods. In order to do that, we now turn to a different way of representing a consumer's utility function, based on the concept of *indifference curves*.

Indifference Curves

Ingrid is a consumer who buys only two goods: housing, measured in the number of rooms, and restaurant meals. How can we represent her utility function in a way that takes account of her consumption of both goods?

One way is to draw a three-dimensional picture. Figure 10A-1 shows a three-dimensional *utility hill*. The distance along the horizontal axis measures the quantity of housing Ingrid consumes in terms of numbers of rooms; the distance along the vertical axis measures the number of restaurant meals she consumes. The altitude or height of the hill at each point is indicated by a contour line, along which the height of the hill is constant. For example, point *A*, which corresponds

FIGURE 10A-1 Ingrid's Utility Function

The three-dimensional hill shows how Ingrid's total utility depends on her consumption of housing and restaurant meals. Point *A* corresponds to consumption of 3 rooms and 30 restaurant meals. The consumption bundle yields Ingrid 450 utils, corresponding to the height of the hill at point *A*. The lines running around the hill are contour lines, along which the height is constant. Every point on a given contour line generates the same level of utility. So point *B*, corresponding to 6 rooms and 15 restaurants, generates the same level of utility as point *A*, 450 utils, since they lie on the same contour line.

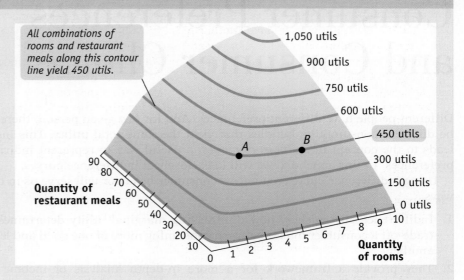

to a consumption bundle of 3 rooms and 30 restaurant meals, lies on the contour line labeled 450. So the total utility Ingrid receives from consuming 3 rooms and 30 restaurant meals is 450 utils.

A three-dimensional picture like Figure 10A-1 helps us think about the relationship between consumption bundles and total utility. But anyone who has ever used a topographical map to plan a hiking trip knows that it is possible to represent a three-dimensional surface in only two dimensions. A topographical map doesn't offer a three-dimensional view of the terrain; instead, it conveys information about altitude solely through the use of contour lines.

The same principle can be applied to representing the utility function. In Figure 10A-2, Ingrid's consumption of rooms is measured on the horizontal axis and her consumption of restaurant meals on the vertical axis. The curve here

FIGURE 10A-2 An Indifference Curve

An indifference curve is a contour line along which total utility is constant. In this case, we show all the consumption bundles that yield Ingrid 450 utils. Consumption bundle *A*, consisting of 3 rooms and 30 restaurant meals, yields the same total utility as bundle *B*, consisting of 6 rooms and 15 restaurant meals. That is, Ingrid is indifferent between bundle *A* and bundle *B*.

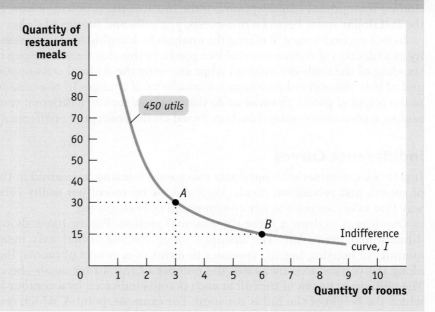

corresponds to the contour line in Figure 10A-1, drawn at a total utility of 450 utils. This curve shows all the consumption bundles that yield a total utility of 450 utils. One point on that contour line is A, a consumption bundle consisting of 3 rooms and 30 restaurant meals. Another point on that contour line is B, a consumption bundle consisting of 6 rooms but only 15 restaurant meals. Because B lies on the same contour line, it yields Ingrid the same total utility—450 utils—as A. We say that Ingrid is *indifferent* between A and B: because bundles A and B yield the same total utility level, Ingrid is equally well off with either bundle.

A contour line that maps consumption bundles yielding the same amount of total utility is known as an **indifference curve.** An individual is always indifferent between any two bundles that lie on the same indifference curve. For a given consumer, there is an indifference curve corresponding to each possible level of total utility. For example, the indifference curve in Figure 10A-2 shows consumption bundles that yield Ingrid 450 utils; different indifference curves would show consumption bundles that yield Ingrid 400 utils, 500 utils, and so on.

A collection of indifference curves that represents a given consumer's entire utility function, with each indifference curve corresponding to a different level of total utility, is known as an **indifference curve map.** Figure 10A-3 shows three indifference curves—I_1, I_2, and I_3—from Ingrid's indifference curve map, as well as several consumption bundles, A, B, C, and D. The accompanying table lists each bundle, its composition of rooms and restaurant meals, and the total utility it yields.

Because bundles A and B generate the same number of utils, 450, they lie on the same indifference curve, I_2. Although Ingrid is indifferent between A and B, she is certainly not indifferent between A and C: as you can see from the table, C generates only 391 utils, a lower total utility than A or B. So Ingrid prefers consumption bundles A and B to bundle C. This is represented by the fact that

An **indifference curve** is a line that shows all the consumption bundles that yield the same amount of total utility for an individual.

The entire utility function of an individual can be represented by an **indifference curve map,** a collection of indifference curves in which each curve corresponds to a different total utility level.

FIGURE 10A-3 An Indifference Curve Map

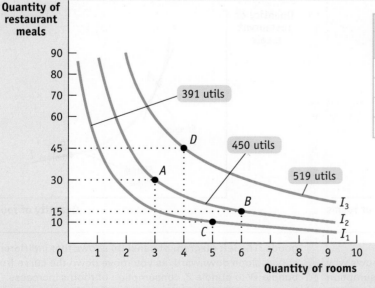

Consumption bundle	Quantity of rooms	Quantity of meals	Total utility (utils)
A	3	30	450
B	6	15	450
C	5	10	391
D	4	45	519

The utility function can be represented in greater detail by increasing the number of indifference curves drawn, each corresponding to a different level of total utility. In this figure bundle C lies on an indifference curve corresponding to a total utility of 391 utils. As in Figure 10A-2, bundles A and B lie on an indifference curve corresponding to a total utility of 450 utils. Bundle D lies on an indifference curve corresponding to a total utility of 519 utils. Ingrid prefers any bundle on I_2 to any bundle on I_1, and she prefers any bundle on I_3 to any bundle on I_2.

C is on indifference curve I_1, and I_1 lies below I_2. Bundle D, though, generates 519 utils, a higher total utility than A and B. It is on I_3, an indifference curve that lies above I_2. Clearly, Ingrid prefers D to either A or B. And, even more strongly, she prefers D to C.

Properties of Indifference Curves

No two individuals have the same indifference curve map because no two individuals have the same preferences. But economists believe that, regardless of the person, every indifference curve map has two general properties. These are illustrated in panel (a) of Figure 10A-4:

FIGURE 10A-4 Properties of Indifference Curves

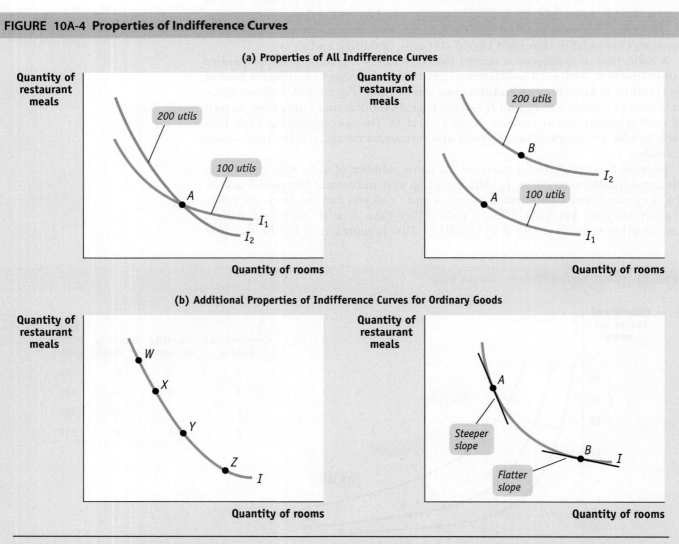

(a) Properties of All Indifference Curves

(b) Additional Properties of Indifference Curves for Ordinary Goods

Panel (a) represents two general properties that all indifference curve maps share. The left diagram shows why indifference curves cannot cross: if they did, a consumption bundle such as A would yield both 100 and 200 utils, a contradiction. The right diagram of panel (a) shows that indifference curves that are farther out yield higher total utility: bundle B, which contains more of both goods than bundle A, yields higher total utility. Panel (b) depicts two additional properties of indifference curves for ordinary goods. The left diagram of panel (b) shows that indifference curves slope downward: as you move down the curve from bundle W to bundle Z, consumption of rooms increases. To keep total utility constant, this must be offset by a reduction in quantity of restaurant meals. The right diagram of panel (b) shows a convex-shaped indifference curve. The slope of the indifference curve gets flatter as you move down the curve to the right, a feature arising from diminishing marginal utility.

- *Indifference curves never cross.* Suppose that we tried to draw an indifference curve map like the one depicted in the left diagram in panel (a), in which two indifference curves cross at *A*. What is the total utility at *A*? Is it 100 utils or 200 utils? Indifference curves cannot cross because each consumption bundle must correspond to a unique total utility level—not, as shown at *A*, two different total utility levels.

- *The farther out an indifference curve lies—the farther it is from the origin—the higher the level of total utility it indicates.* The reason, illustrated in the right diagram in panel (a), is that we assume that more is better—we consider only the consumption bundles for which the consumer is not satiated. Bundle *B*, on the outer indifference curve, contains more of both goods than bundle *A* on the inner indifference curve. So *B*, because it generates a higher total utility level (200 utils), lies on a higher indifference curve than *A*.

Furthermore, economists believe that, for most goods, consumers' indifference curve maps also have two additional properties. They are illustrated in panel (b) of Figure 10A-4:

- *Indifference curves slope downward.* Here, too, the reason is that more is better. The left diagram in panel (b) shows four consumption bundles on the same indifference curve: *W*, *X*, *Y*, and *Z*. By definition, these consumption bundles yield the same level of total utility. But as you move along the curve to the right, from *W* to *Z*, the quantity of rooms consumed increases. The only way a person can consume more rooms without gaining utility is by giving up some restaurant meals. So the indifference curve must slope downward.

- *Indifference curves have a convex shape.* The right diagram in panel (b) shows that the slope of each indifference curve changes as you move down the curve to the right: the curve gets flatter. If you move up an indifference curve to the left, the curve gets steeper. So the indifference curve is steeper at *A* than it is at *B*. When this occurs, we say that an indifference curve has a *convex* shape—it is bowed-in toward the origin. This feature arises from diminishing marginal utility, a principle we discussed in Chapter 10. Recall that when a consumer has diminishing marginal utility, consumption of another unit of a good generates a smaller increase in total utility than the previous unit consumed. In the next section, we will examine in detail how diminishing marginal utility gives rise to convex-shaped indifference curves.

Goods that satisfy all four properties of indifference curve maps are called *ordinary goods*. The vast majority of goods in any consumer's utility function fall into this category. In the next section, we will define ordinary goods and see the key role that diminishing marginal utility plays for them.

Indifference Curves and Consumer Choice

At the beginning of the last section, we used indifference curves to represent the preferences of Ingrid, whose consumption bundles consist of rooms and restaurant meals. Our next step is to show how to use Ingrid's indifference curve map to find her utility-maximizing consumption bundle given her budget constraint, the fact that she must choose a consumption bundle that costs no more than her total income.

It's important to understand how our analysis here relates to what we did in Chapter 10. We are not offering a new theory of consumer behavior in this appendix—just as in Chapter 10, consumers are assumed to maximize total utility. In particular, we know that consumers will follow the *optimal consumption rule* from Chapter 10: the optimal consumption bundle lies on the budget line, and the marginal utility per dollar is the same for every good in the bundle.

But as we'll see shortly, we can derive this optimal consumer behavior in a somewhat different way—a way that yields deeper insights into consumer choice.

The Marginal Rate of Substitution

The first element of our approach is a new concept, the *marginal rate of substitution*. The essence of this concept is illustrated in Figure 10A-5.

Recall from the last section that for most goods, consumers' indifference curves are downward sloping and convex. Figure 10A-5 shows such an indifference curve. The points labeled *V, W, X, Y,* and *Z* all lie on this indifference curve—that is, they represent consumption bundles that yield Ingrid the same level of total utility. The table accompanying the figure shows the components of each of the bundles.

As we move along the indifference curve from *V* to *Z*, Ingrid's consumption of housing steadily increases from 2 rooms to 6 rooms, her consumption of restaurant meals steadily decreases from 30 meals to 10 meals, and her total utility is kept constant. As we move down the indifference curve, then, Ingrid is trading more of one good in place of less of the other, with the *terms* of that trade-off—the ratio of additional rooms consumed to restaurant meals sacrificed—chosen to keep her total utility constant.

Notice that the quantity of restaurant meals that Ingrid is willing to give up in return for an additional room changes along the indifference curve. As we move from *V* to *W*, housing consumption rises from 2 to 3 rooms and restaurant meal consumption falls from 30 to 20—a trade-off of 10 restaurant meals for 1 additional room. But as we move from *Y* to *Z*, housing consumption rises from 5 to 6 rooms and restaurant meal consumption falls from 12 to 10, a trade-off of only 2 restaurant meals for an additional room.

To put it in terms of slopes, the slope of the indifference curve between *V* and *W* is –10: the change in restaurant meal consumption, –10, divided by the change in housing consumption, 1. Similarly, the slope of the indifference curve between *Y* and *Z* is –2. So the slope decreases and the indifference curve gets flatter as we

FIGURE 10A-5 The Changing Slope of an Indifference Curve

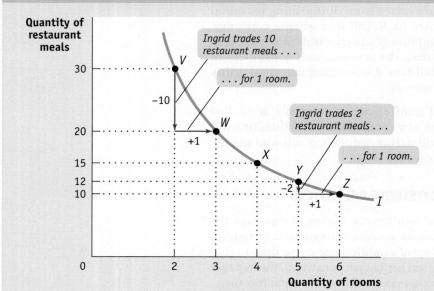

Consumption bundle	Quantity of rooms	Quantity of restaurant meals
V	2	30
W	3	20
X	4	15
Y	5	12
Z	6	10

This indifference curve is downward sloping and convex, implying that restaurant meals and rooms are ordinary goods for Ingrid. As Ingrid moves down her indifference curve from *V* to *Z*, she trades reduced consumption of restaurant meals for increased consumption of housing. However, the terms of that trade-off change. As she moves from *V* to *W*, she is willing to give up 10 restaurant meals in return for 1 more room. As her consumption of rooms rises and her consumption of restaurant meals falls, she is willing to give up fewer restaurant meals in return for each additional room. The flattening of the slope as you move from left to right arises from diminishing marginal utility.

move down it to the right—that is, it has a convex shape, one of the four proper-ties of an indifference curve for ordinary goods.

Why does the trade-off change in this way? Let's think about it intuitively, then work through it more carefully. When Ingrid moves down her indifference curve, whether from *V* to *W* or from *Y* to *Z*, she gains utility from her additional con-sumption of housing but loses an equal amount of utility from her reduced con-sumption of restaurant meals. But at each step, the initial position from which Ingrid begins is different. At *V*, Ingrid consumes only a small quantity of rooms; because of diminishing marginal utility, her marginal utility per room at that point is high. At *V*, then, an additional room adds a lot to Ingrid's total utility. But at *V* she already consumes a large quantity of restaurant meals, so her marginal utility of restaurant meals is low at that point. This means that it takes a large reduction in her quantity of restaurant meals consumed to offset the increased utility she gets from the extra room of housing.

At *Y*, in contrast, Ingrid consumes a much larger quantity of rooms and a much smaller quantity of restaurant meals than at *V*. This means that an additional room adds fewer utils, and a restaurant meal forgone costs more utils, than at *V*. So Ingrid is willing to give up fewer restaurant meals in return for another room of housing at *Y* (where she gives up 2 meals for 1 room) than she is at *V* (where she gives up 10 meals for 1 room).

Now let's express the same idea—that the trade-off Ingrid is willing to make depends on where she is starting from—by using a little math. We do this by examining how the slope of the indifference curve changes as we move down it.

Moving down the indifference curve—reducing restaurant meal consump-tion and increasing housing consumption—will produce two opposing effects on Ingrid's total utility: lower restaurant meal consumption will reduce her total utility, but higher housing consumption will raise her total utility. And since we are moving down the indifference curve, these two effects must exactly cancel out:

Along the indifference curve:
(10A-1) (Change in total utility due to lower restaurant meal consumption) +
(Change in total utility due to higher housing consumption) = 0

or, rearranging terms,

Along the indifference curve:
(10A-2) –(Change in total utility due to lower restaurant meal consumption) =
(Change in total utility due to higher housing consumption)

Let's now focus on what happens as we move only a short distance down the indifference curve, trading off a small increase in housing consumption in place of a small decrease in restaurant meal consumption. Following our notation from Chapter 10, let's use MU_R and MU_M to represent the marginal utility of rooms and restaurant meals, respectively, and ΔQ_R and ΔQ_M to represent the changes in room and meal consumption, respectively.

In general, the change in total utility caused by a small change in consump-tion of a good is equal to the change in consumption multiplied by the *marginal utility* of that good. This means that we can calculate the change in Ingrid's total utility generated by a change in her consumption bundle using the follow-ing equations:

(10A-3) Change in total utility due to a change in restaurant meal
consumption = $MU_M \times \Delta Q_M$

and

(10A-4) Change in total utility due to a change in housing consumption
= $MU_R \times \Delta Q_R$

So we can write Equation 10A-2 in symbols as:

(10A-5) *Along the indifference curve:* $-MU_M \times \Delta Q_M = MU_R \times \Delta Q_R$

Note that the left-hand side of Equation 10A-5 has a minus sign; it represents the loss in total utility from decreased restaurant meal consumption. This must equal the gain in total utility from increased room consumption, represented by the right-hand side of the equation.

What we want to know is how this translates into the slope of the indifference curve. To find the slope, we divide both sides of Equation 10A-5 by ΔQ_R, and again by $-MU_M$, in order to get the ΔQ_M, ΔQ_R terms on one side and the MU_R, MU_M terms on the other. This results in:

(10A-6) *Along the indifference curve:* $\dfrac{\Delta Q_M}{\Delta Q_R} = -\dfrac{MU_R}{MU_M}$

The left-hand side of Equation 10A-6 is the slope of the indifference curve; it is the rate at which Ingrid is willing to trade rooms (the good on the horizontal axis) in place of restaurant meals (the good on the vertical axis) without changing her total utility level. The right-hand side of Equation 10A-6 is minus the ratio of the marginal utility of rooms to the marginal utility of restaurant meals—that is, the ratio of what she gains from one more room to what she gains from one more meal.

Putting all this together, we see that Equation 10A-6 shows that, along the indifference curve, the quantity of restaurant meals Ingrid is willing to give up in return for a room, $\Delta Q_M / \Delta Q_R$, is exactly equal to minus the ratio of the marginal utility of a room to that of a meal, $-MU_R / MU_M$. Only when this condition is met will her total utility level remain constant as she consumes more rooms and fewer restaurant meals.

Economists have a special name for the ratio of the marginal utilities found in the right-hand side of Equation 10A-6: it is called the **marginal rate of substitution,** or **MRS,** of rooms (the good on the horizontal axis) in place of restaurant meals (the good on the vertical axis). That's because as we slide down Ingrid's indifference curve, we are substituting more rooms in place of fewer restaurant meals in her consumption bundle. As we'll see shortly, the marginal rate of substitution plays an important role in finding the optimal consumption bundle.

Recall that indifference curves get flatter as you move down them to the right. The reason, as we've just discussed, is diminishing marginal utility: as Ingrid consumes more housing and fewer restaurant meals, her marginal utility from housing falls and her marginal utility from restaurant meals rises. So her marginal rate of substitution, which is equal to minus the slope of her indifference curve, falls as she moves down the indifference curve.

The flattening of indifference curves as you slide down them to the right—which reflects the same logic as the principle of diminishing marginal utility—is known as the principle of **diminishing marginal rate of substitution.** It says that an individual who consumes only a little bit of good A and a lot of good B will be willing to trade a lot of B in return for one more unit of A; an individual who already consumes a lot of A and not much B will be less willing to make that trade-off.

We can illustrate this point by referring back to Figure 10A-5. At point V, a bundle with a high proportion of restaurant meals to rooms, Ingrid is willing to forgo 10 restaurant meals in return for 1 room. But at point Y, a bundle with a low proportion of restaurant meals to rooms, she is willing to forgo only 2 restaurant meals in return for 1 room.

From this example we can see that, in Ingrid's utility function, rooms and restaurant meals possess the two additional properties that characterize ordinary goods. Ingrid requires additional rooms to compensate her for the loss of a meal, and vice versa; so her indifference curves for these two goods slope

The **marginal rate of substitution,** or **MRS,** of good R in place of good M is equal to MU_R / MU_M, the ratio of the marginal utility of R to the marginal utility of M.

The principle of **diminishing marginal rate of substitution** states that the more of good R a person consumes in proportion to good M, the less M he or she is willing to substitute for another unit of R.

downward. And her indifference curves are convex: the slope of her indifference curve—*minus* the marginal rate of substitution—becomes flatter as we move down it. In fact, an indifference curve is convex only when it has diminishing marginal rate of substitution—these two conditions are equivalent.

With this information, we can define **ordinary goods,** which account for the great majority of goods in any consumer's utility function. A pair of goods are ordinary goods in a consumer's utility function if they possess two properties: the consumer requires more of one good to compensate for less of the other, and the consumer experiences a diminishing marginal rate of substitution when substituting one good in place of the other.

Next we will see how to determine Ingrid's optimal consumption bundle using indifference curves.

> Two goods, *R* and *M*, are **ordinary goods** in a consumer's utility function when (1) the consumer requires additional units of *R* to compensate for less *M*, and vice versa; and (2) the consumer experiences a diminishing marginal rate of substitution when substituting one good in place of another.

The Tangency Condition

Now let's put some of Ingrid's indifference curves on the same diagram as her budget line, to illustrate an alternative way of representing her optimal consumption choice. Figure 10A-6 shows Ingrid's budget line, *BL*, when her income is $2,400 per month, housing costs $150 per room each month, and restaurant meals cost $30 each. What is her optimal consumption bundle?

To answer this question, we show several of Ingrid's indifference curves: I_1, I_2, and I_3. Ingrid would like to achieve the total utility level represented by I_3, the highest of the three curves, but she cannot afford to because she is constrained by her income: no consumption bundle on her budget line yields that much total utility. But she shouldn't settle for the level of total utility generated by *B*, which lies on I_1: there are other bundles on her budget line, such as *A*, that clearly yield higher total utility than *B*.

In fact, *A*—a consumption bundle consisting of 8 rooms and 40 restaurant meals per month—is Ingrid's optimal consumption choice. The reason is that *A* lies on the highest indifference curve Ingrid can reach given her income.

At the optimal consumption bundle *A*, Ingrid's budget line *just touches* the relevant indifference curve—the budget line is *tangent* to the indifference curve.

FIGURE 10A-6 The Optimal Consumption Bundle

The budget line, *BL,* shows Ingrid's possible consumption bundles given an income of $2,400 per month, when rooms cost $150 per month and restaurant meals cost $30 each. I_1, I_2, and I_3 are indifference curves. Consumption bundles such as *B* and *C* are not optimal because Ingrid can move to a higher indifference curve. The optimal consumption bundle is *A*, where the budget line is just tangent to the highest possible indifference curve.

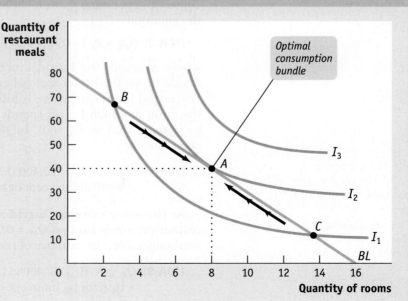

The **tangency condition** between the indifference curve and the budget line holds when the indifference curve and the budget line just touch. This condition determines the optimal consumption bundle when the indifference curves have the typical convex shape.

This **tangency condition** between the indifference curve and the budget line applies to the optimal consumption bundle when the indifference curves have the typical convex shape: *at the optimal consumption bundle, the budget line just touches—is tangent to—the indifference curve.*

To see why, let's look more closely at how we know that a consumption bundle that *doesn't* satisfy the tangency condition can't be optimal. Reexamining Figure 10A-6, we can see that the consumption bundles B and C are both affordable because they lie on the budget line. However, neither is optimal. Both of them lie on the indifference curve I_1, which cuts through the budget line at both points. But because I_1 cuts through the budget line, Ingrid can do better: she can move down the budget line from B or up the budget line from C, as indicated by the arrows. In each case, this allows her to get onto a higher indifference curve, I_2, which increases her total utility.

Ingrid cannot, however, do any better than I_2: any other indifference curve either cuts through her budget line or doesn't touch it at all. And the bundle that allows her to achieve I_2 is, of course, her optimal consumption bundle.

The Slope of the Budget Line

Figure 10A-6 shows us how to use a graph of the budget line and the indifference curves to find the optimal consumption bundle, the bundle at which the budget line and the indifference curve are tangent. But rather than rely on drawing graphs, we can determine the optimal consumption bundle by using a bit of math.

As you can see from Figure 10A-6, at A, the optimal consumption bundle, the budget line and the indifference curve have the same slope. Why? Because two curves can only touch each other if they have the same slope at their point of tangency. Otherwise, they would cross each other somewhere. And we know that if we are on an indifference curve that crosses the budget line (like I_1 in Figure 10A-6), we can't be on the indifference curve that contains the optimal consumption bundle (like I_2).

So we can use information about the slopes of the budget line and the indifference curve to find the optimal consumption bundle. To do that, we must first analyze the slope of the budget line, a fairly straightforward task. We know that Ingrid will get the highest possible utility by spending all of her income and consuming a bundle on her budget line. So we can represent Ingrid's budget line, the consumption bundles available to her when she spends all of her income, with the equation:

(10A-7) $(Q_R \times P_R) + (Q_M \times P_M) = N$

where N stands for Ingrid's income. To find the slope of the budget line, we divide its vertical intercept (where the budget line hits the vertical axis) by its horizontal intercept (where it hits the horizontal axis). The vertical intercept is the point at which Ingrid spends all her income on restaurant meals and none on rooms (that is, $Q_R = 0$). In that case the number of restaurant meals she consumes is:

(10A-8) $Q_M = N/P_M = \$2,400/(\$30 \text{ per meal}) = 80 \text{ meals}$
= Vertical intercept of budget line

At the other extreme, Ingrid spends all her income on rooms and none on restaurant meals (so that $Q_M = 0$). This means that at the horizontal intercept of the budget line, the number of rooms she consumes is:

(10A-9) $Q_R = N/P_R = \$2,400/(\$150 \text{ per room}) = 16 \text{ rooms}$
= Horizontal intercept of budget line

Now we have the information needed to find the slope of the budget line. It is:

(10A-10) Slope of budget line = –(Vertical intercept)/(Horizontal intercept)

$$= -\frac{\frac{N}{P_M}}{\frac{N}{P_R}} = -\frac{P_R}{P_M}$$

Notice the minus sign in Equation 10A-10; it's there because the budget line slopes downward. The quantity P_R/P_M is known as the **relative price** of rooms in terms of restaurant meals, to distinguish it from an ordinary price in terms of dollars. In this example it is equal to $150/$30 = 5. Because buying one more room requires Ingrid to give up P_R/P_M quantity of restaurant meals, or 5 meals, we can interpret the relative price P_R/P_M as the rate at which a room trades for restaurant meals in the market; it is the price—in terms of restaurant meals—Ingrid has to "pay" to get one more room.

Looking at this another way, the slope of the budget line—minus the relative price—tells us the opportunity cost of each good in terms of the other. The relative price illustrates the opportunity cost to an individual of consuming one more unit of one good in terms of how much of the other good in his or her consumption bundle must be forgone. This opportunity cost arises from the consumer's limited resources—his or her limited budget.

It's useful to note that Equations 10A-8, 10A-9, and 10A-10 give us all the information we need about what happens to the budget line when relative price or income changes. From Equations 10A-8 and 10A-9 we can see that a change in income, N, leads to a parallel shift of the budget line: both the vertical and horizontal intercepts will shift. That is, how far out the budget line is from the origin depends on the consumer's income. If a consumer's income rises, the budget line moves outward. If the consumer's income shrinks, the budget line shifts inward. In each case, the slope of the budget line stays the same because the relative price of one good in terms of the other does not change.

In contrast, a change in the relative price P_R/P_M will lead to a change in the slope of the budget line. We'll analyze these changes in the budget line and how the optimal consumption bundle changes when the relative price changes or when income changes in greater detail later in the appendix.

Prices and the Marginal Rate of Substitution

Now we're ready to bring together the slope of the budget line and the slope of the indifference curve to find the optimal consumption bundle. From Equation 10A-6, we know that the slope of the indifference curve at any point is equal to minus the marginal rate of substitution:

(10A-11) Slope of indifference curve = $-\frac{MU_R}{MU_M}$

As we've already noted, at the optimal consumption bundle the slope of the budget line and the slope of the indifference curve are equal. We can write this formally by putting Equations 10A-10 and 10A-11 together, which gives us the **relative price rule** for finding the optimal consumption bundle:

(10A-12) *At the optimal consumption bundle:* $-\frac{MU_R}{MU_M} = -\frac{P_R}{P_M}$

or $\frac{MU_R}{MU_M} = \frac{P_R}{P_M}$

The **relative price** of good R in terms of good M is equal to P_R/P_M, the rate at which R trades for M in the market.

The **relative price rule** says that at the optimal consumption bundle, the marginal rate of substitution between two goods is equal to their relative price.

FIGURE 10A-7 Understanding the Relative Price Rule

The *relative price* of rooms in terms of restaurant meals is equal to minus the slope of the budget line. The *marginal rate of substitution* of rooms in place of restaurant meals is equal to minus the slope of the indifference curve. The *relative price rule* says that at the optimal consumption bundle, the marginal rate of substitution must equal the relative price. This point can be demonstrated by considering what happens when the marginal rate of substitution is not equal to the relative price. At consumption bundle B, the marginal rate of substitution is larger than the relative price; Ingrid can increase her total utility by moving down her budget line, *BL*. At C, the marginal rate of substitution is smaller than the relative price, and Ingrid can increase her total utility by moving up the budget line. Only at A, where the relative price rule holds, is her total utility maximized given her budget constraint.

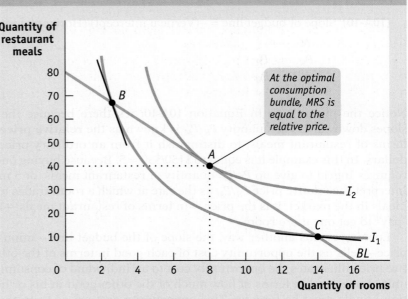

At the optimal consumption bundle, MRS is equal to the relative price.

That is, at the optimal consumption bundle, the marginal rate of substitution between any two goods is equal to the ratio of their prices. Or to put it in a more intuitive way, at Ingrid's optimal consumption bundle, the rate at which she would trade a room in exchange for having fewer restaurant meals along her indifference curve, MU_R/MU_M, is equal to the rate at which rooms are traded for restaurant meals in the market, P_R/P_M.

What would happen if this equality did not hold? We can see by examining Figure 10A-7. There, at point B, the slope of the indifference curve, $-MU_R/MU_M$, is greater in absolute value than the slope of the budget line, $-P_R/P_M$. This means that, at B, Ingrid values an additional room in place of meals *more* than it costs her to buy an additional room and forgo some meals. As a result, Ingrid would be better off moving down her budget line toward A, consuming more rooms and fewer restaurant meals—and because of that, B could not have been her optimal bundle!

Likewise, at C, the slope of Ingrid's indifference curve is less than the slope of the budget line. The implication is that, at C, Ingrid values additional meals in place of a room *more* than it costs her to buy additional meals and forgo a room. Again, Ingrid would be better off moving along her budget line—consuming more restaurant meals and fewer rooms—until she reaches A, her optimal consumption bundle.

But suppose that we do the following transformation to the last term of Equation 10A-12: divide both sides by P_R and multiply both by MU_M. Then the relative price rule becomes (from Chapter 10, Equation 10-3):

(10A-13) *Optimal consumption rule:* $\dfrac{MU_R}{P_R} = \dfrac{MU_M}{P_M}$

So using either the optimal consumption rule (from Chapter 10) or the relative price rule (from this appendix), we find the same optimal consumption bundle.

Preferences and Choices

Now that we have seen how to represent the optimal consumption choice in an indifference curve diagram, we can turn briefly to the relationship between consumer preferences and consumer choices.

When we say that two consumers have different preferences, we mean that they have different utility functions. This in turn means that they will have indifference curve maps with different shapes. And those different maps will translate into different consumption choices, even among consumers with the same income and who face the same prices.

To see this, suppose that Ingrid's friend Lars also consumes only housing and restaurant meals. However, Lars has a stronger preference for restaurant meals and a weaker preference for housing. This difference in preferences is shown in Figure 10A-8, which shows *two* sets of indifference curves: panel (a) shows Ingrid's preferences and panel (b) shows Lars's preferences. Note the difference in their shapes.

Suppose, as before, that rooms cost $150 per month and restaurant meals cost $30. Let's also assume that both Ingrid and Lars have incomes of $2,400 per month, giving them identical budget lines. Nonetheless, because they have different preferences, they will make different consumption choices, as shown in Figure 10A-8. Ingrid will choose 8 rooms and 40 restaurant meals; Lars will choose 4 rooms and 60 restaurant meals.

FIGURE 10A-8 Difference in Preferences

Ingrid and Lars have difference preferences, reflected in the different shapes of their indifference curve maps. So they will choose different consumption bundles even when they have the same possible choices. Both of them have an income of $2,400 per month and face prices of $30 per meal and $150 per room. Panel (a) shows Ingrid's consumption choice: 8 rooms and 40 restaurant meals. Panel (b) shows Lars's choice: even though he has the same budget line, he consumes fewer rooms (4) and more restaurant meals (60).

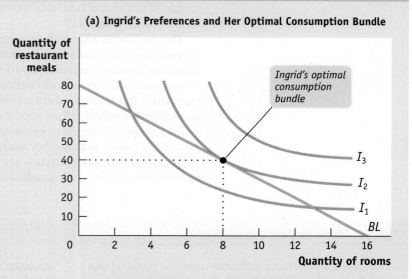

(a) Ingrid's Preferences and Her Optimal Consumption Bundle

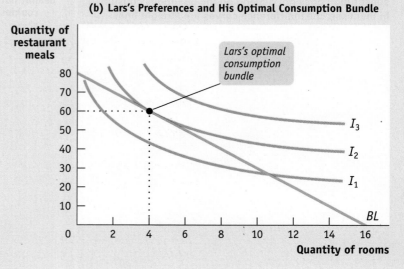

(b) Lars's Preferences and His Optimal Consumption Bundle

Two goods are **perfect substitutes** if the marginal rate of substitution of one good in place of the other good is constant, regardless of how much of each an individual consumes.

Using Indifference Curves: Substitutes and Complements

Now let's apply indifference curve analysis to deepen our understanding of how a consumer classifies different goods based upon his or her preferences. First, we'll consider the distinction between *substitutes* and *complements*.

Back in Chapter 3, we pointed out that the price of one good often affects the demand for another but that the direction of this effect can go either way: a rise in the price of tea increases the demand for coffee, but a rise in the price of cream reduces the demand for coffee. Tea and coffee are substitutes; cream and coffee are complements.

But what determines whether two goods are substitutes or complements? It depends on the shape of a consumer's indifference curves. This relationship can be illustrated with two extreme cases: the cases of *perfect substitutes* and *perfect complements*.

Perfect Substitutes

Consider Cokie, who likes cookies. She isn't particular: it doesn't matter to her whether she has 3 peanut butter cookies and 7 chocolate chip cookies, or vice versa. What would her indifference curves between peanut butter and chocolate chip cookies look like?

The answer is that they would be straight lines like I_1 and I_2 in Figure 10A-9. For example, I_1 shows that any combination of peanut butter cookies and chocolate chip cookies that adds up to 10 cookies yields Cokie the same utility.

A consumer whose indifference curves are straight lines is always willing to substitute the same amount of one good in place of one unit of the other, regardless of how much of either good he or she consumes. Cokie, for example, is always willing to accept one less peanut butter cookie in exchange for one more chocolate chip cookie, making her marginal rate of substitution *constant*.

When indifference curves are straight lines, we say that goods are **perfect substitutes.** When two goods are perfect substitutes, there is only one relative

---

FIGURE 10A-9 Perfect Substitutes

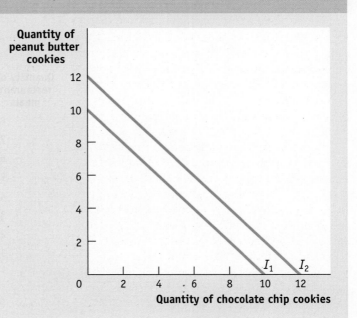

Two goods are perfect substitutes when the marginal rate of substitution does not depend on the quantities consumed. In that case, the indifference curves are straight lines.

FIGURE 10A-10 Consumer Choice Between Perfect Substitutes

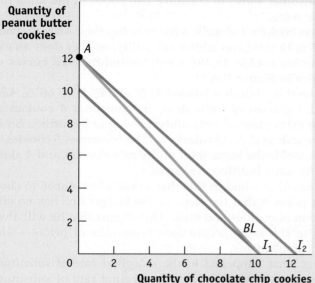

(a) Cokie Buys Only Peanut Butter Cookies

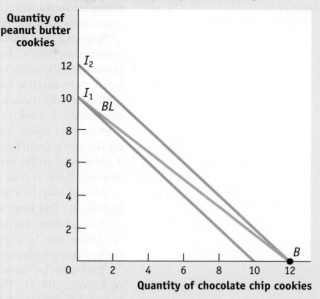

(b) Cokie Buys Only Chocolate Chip Cookies

When two goods are perfect substitutes, small price changes lead to large changes in the consumption bundle. In panel (a), the relative price of chocolate chip cookies is slightly higher than the marginal rate of substitution of chocolate chip cookies in place of peanut butter cookies; this is enough to induce Cokie to choose consumption bundle *A*, which consists entirely of peanut butter cookies. In panel (b), the relative price of chocolate chip cookies is slightly lower than the marginal rate of substitution of chocolate chip cookies in place of peanut butter cookies; this induces Cokie to choose bundle *B*, consisting entirely of chocolate chip cookies.

price at which consumers will be willing to purchase both goods; a slightly higher or lower relative price will cause consumers to buy only one of the two goods.

Figure 10A-10 illustrates this point. The indifference curves are the same as those in Figure 10A-9, but now we include Cokie's budget line, *BL*. In each panel we assume that Cokie has $12 to spend. In panel (a) we assume that chocolate chip cookies cost $1.20 and peanut butter cookies cost $1.00. Cokie's optimal consumption bundle is then at point *A*: she buys 12 peanut butter cookies and no chocolate chip cookies. In panel (b) the situation is reversed: chocolate chip cookies cost $1.00 and peanut butter cookies cost $1.20. In this case, her optimal consumption is at point *B*, where she consumes only chocolate chip cookies.

Why does such a small change in the price cause Cokie to switch all her consumption from one good to the other? Because her marginal rate of substitution is constant and therefore doesn't depend on the composition of her consumption bundle. If the relative price of chocolate chip cookies is more than the marginal rate of substitution of chocolate chip cookies in place of peanut butter cookies, she buys only peanut butter cookies; if it is less, she buys only chocolate chip. And if the relative price of chocolate chip cookies is equal to the marginal rate of substitution, Cokie can maximize her utility by buying any bundle on her budget line. That is, she will be equally happy with any combination of chocolate chip cookies and peanut butter cookies that she can afford. As a result, in this case we cannot predict which particular bundle she will choose among all the bundles that lie on her budget line.

Two goods are **perfect complements** when a consumer wants to consume the goods in the same ratio regardless of their relative price.

Perfect Complements

The case of perfect substitutes represents one extreme form of consumer preferences; the case of perfect complements represents the other. Goods are **perfect complements** when a consumer wants to consume two goods in the same ratio, regardless of their relative price.

Suppose that Aaron likes cookies and milk—but only together. An extra cookie without an extra glass of milk yields no additional utility; neither does an extra glass of milk without another cookie. In this case, his indifference curves will form right angles, as shown in Figure 10A-11.

To see why, consider the three bundles labeled A, B, and C. At B, on I_4, Aaron consumes 4 cookies and 4 glasses of milk. At A, he consumes 4 cookies and 5 glasses of milk; but the extra glass of milk adds nothing to his utility. So A is on the same indifference curve as B, I_4. Similarly, at C he consumes 5 cookies and 4 glasses of milk, but this yields the same total utility as 4 cookies and 4 glasses of milk. So C is also on the same indifference curve, I_4.

Also shown in Figure 10A-11 is a budget line that would allow Aaron to choose bundle B. The important point is that the slope of the budget line has no effect on his relative consumption of cookies and milk. This means that he will always consume the two goods in the same proportions regardless of prices—which makes the goods perfect complements.

You may be wondering what happened to the marginal rate of substitution in Figure 10A-11. That is, exactly what is Aaron's marginal rate of substitution between cookies and milk, given that he is unwilling to make any substitutions between them? The answer is that in the case of perfect complements, the marginal rate of substitution is *undefined* because an individual's preferences don't allow *any* substitution between goods.

Less Extreme Cases

There are real-world examples of pairs of goods that are very close to being perfect substitutes. For example, the list of ingredients on a package of Bisquick pancake mix says that it contains "soybean and/or cottonseed oil": the producer uses whichever is cheaper, since consumers can't tell the difference. There are other pairs of goods that are very close to being perfect complements—for example, cars and tires.

FIGURE 10A-11 Perfect Complements

When two goods are perfect complements, a consumer wants to consume the goods in the same ratio regardless of their relative price. Indifference curves take the form of right angles. In this case, Aaron will choose to consume 4 glasses of milk and 4 cookies (bundle B) regardless of the slope of the budget line passing through B. The reason is that neither an additional glass of milk without an additional cookie (bundle A) nor an additional cookie without an additional glass of milk (bundle C) adds to his total utility.

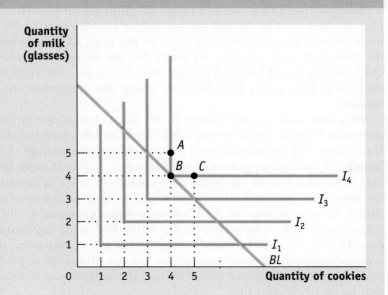

In most cases, however, the possibilities for substitution lie somewhere between these extremes. In some cases it isn't easy to be sure whether goods are substitutes or complements.

Prices, Income, and Demand

Let's return now to Ingrid's consumption choices. In the situation we've considered, her income was $2,400 per month, housing cost $150 per room, and restaurant meals cost $30 each. Her optimal consumption bundle, as seen in Figure 10A-7, contained 8 rooms and 40 restaurant meals.

Let's now ask how her consumption choice would change if either the rent per room or her income changed. As we'll see, we can put these pieces together to deepen our understanding of consumer demand.

The Effects of a Price Increase

Suppose that for some reason there is a sharp increase in housing prices. Ingrid must now pay $600 per room instead of $150. Meanwhile, the price of restaurant meals and her income remain unchanged. How does this change affect her consumption choices?

When the price of rooms rises, the relative price of rooms in terms of restaurant meals rises; as a result, Ingrid's budget line changes (for the worse—but we'll get to that). She responds to that change by choosing a new consumption bundle.

Figure 10A-12 shows Ingrid's original (BL_1) and new (BL_2) budget lines—again, under the assumption that her income remains constant at $2,400 per month. With housing costing $150 per room and a restaurant meal costing $30, her budget line, BL_1, intersected the horizontal axis at 16 rooms and the vertical axis at 80 restaurant meals. After the price of a room rises to $600 per room, the budget line, BL_2, still hits the vertical axis at 80 restaurant meals, but it hits the horizontal axis at only 4 rooms. That's because we know from Equation (10A-9) that the new horizontal intercept of the budget line is now $2,400/$600 = 4. Her budget line has rotated inward and become steeper, reflecting the new, higher relative price of a room in terms of restaurant meals.

FIGURE 10A-12 Effects of a Price Increase on the Budget Line

An increase in the price of rooms, holding the price of restaurant meals constant, increases the relative price of rooms in terms of restaurant meals. As a result, Ingrid's original budget line, BL_1, rotates inward to BL_2. Her maximum possible purchase of restaurant meals is unchanged, but her maximum possible purchase of rooms is reduced.

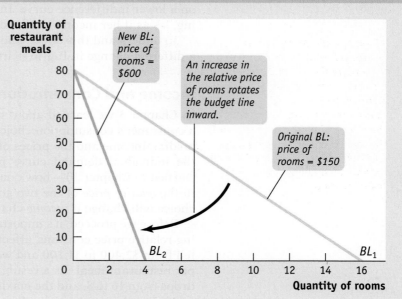

FIGURE 10A-13 Responding to a Price Increase

Ingrid responds to the higher relative price of rooms by choosing a new consumption bundle with fewer rooms and more restaurant meals. Her new optimal consumption bundle, *C,* contains 1 room instead of 8 and 60 restaurant meals instead of 40.

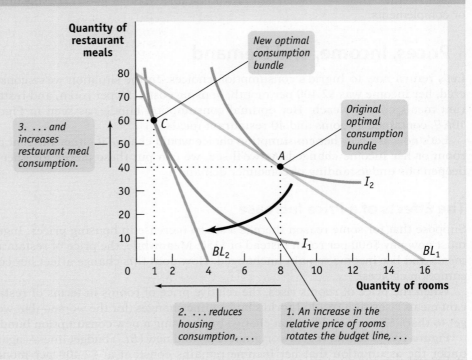

Figure 10A-13 shows how Ingrid responds to her new circumstances. Her original optimal consumption bundle consists of 8 rooms and 40 meals. After her budget line rotates in response to the change in relative price, she finds her new optimal consumption bundle by choosing the point on BL_2 that brings her to as high an indifference curve as possible. At the new optimal consumption bundle, she consumes fewer rooms and more restaurant meals than before: 1 room and 60 restaurant meals.

Why does Ingrid's consumption of rooms fall? Part—but only part—of the reason is that the rise in the price of rooms reduces her purchasing power, making her poorer. That is, the higher relative price of rooms rotates her budget line inward toward the origin, reducing her consumption possibilities and putting her on a lower indifference curve. In a sense, when she faces a higher price of housing, it's as if her income declined.

To understand this effect, and to see why it isn't the whole story, let's consider a different change in Ingrid's circumstances: a change in her income.

Income and Consumption

In Chapter 3 we learned about the individual demand curve, which shows how a consumer's consumption choice will change as the price of one good changes, holding income and the prices of other goods constant. That is, movement along the individual demand curve primarily shows the substitution effect, as we learned in Chapter 10—how quantity consumed changes in response to changes in the *relative price* of the two goods. But we can also ask how the consumption choice will change if *income* changes, holding relative price constant.

Before we proceed, it's important to understand how a change in income, holding relative price constant, affects the budget line. Suppose that Ingrid's income fell from $2,400 to $1,200 and we hold prices constant at $150 per room and $30 per restaurant meal. As a result, the maximum number of rooms she can afford drops from 16 to 8, and the maximum number of restaurant meals drops from 80 to 40. In other words, Ingrid's consumption possibilities have shrunk, as shown

FIGURE 10A-14 **Effect of a Change in Income on the Budget Line**

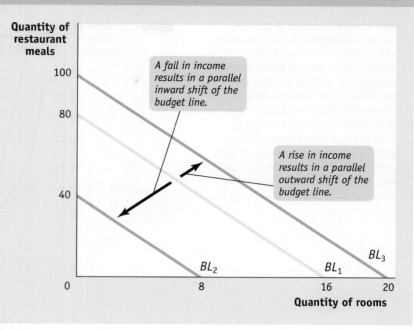

When relative prices are held constant, the budget line shifts parallel in response to changes in income. For example, if Ingrid's income falls from $2,400 to $1,200, she is clearly worse off: her budget line shifts inward from BL_1 to its new position at BL_2. In contrast, if Ingrid's income rises from $2,400 to $3,000, she is clearly better of: her budget line shifts outward from BL_1 to its new position at BL_3.

A fall in income results in a parallel inward shift of the budget line.

A rise in income results in a parallel outward shift of the budget line.

by the parallel inward shift of the budget line in Figure 10A-14 from BL_1 to BL_2. It's a parallel shift because the slope of the budget line—the relative price—remains unchanged when income changes.

Alternatively, suppose Ingrid's income rises from $2,400 to $3,000. She can now afford a maximum of 20 rooms or 100 meals, leading to a *parallel outward shift* of the budget line—the shift from BL_1 to BL_3 in Figure 10A-14. In this case, Ingrid's consumption possibilities have expanded.

Now we are ready to consider how Ingrid responds to a direct change in income—that is, a change in her income level holding relative price constant. Figure 10A-15 compares Ingrid's budget line and optimal consumption choice at an income of $2,400 per month ($BL_1$) with her budget line and optimal consumption choice at an income of $1,200 per month ($BL_2$), keeping prices constant at $150 per room and $30 per restaurant meal. Point *A* is Ingrid's optimal consumption bundle at an income of $2,400, and point *B* is her optimal consumption bundle at an income of $1,200. In each case, her optimal consumption bundle is given by the point at which the budget line is tangent to the indifference curve. As you can see, at the lower income her budget line shifts inward compared to her budget line at the higher income but maintains the same slope because relative price has not changed.

This means that she must reduce her consumption of either housing or restaurant meals, or both. As a result, she is at a lower level of total utility, represented by a lower indifference curve.

As it turns out, Ingrid chooses to consume less of both goods when her income falls: as her income goes from $2,400 to $1,200, her consumption of housing falls from 8 to 4 rooms and her consumption of restaurant meals falls from 40 to 20. This is because in her utility function both goods are *normal goods,* as defined in Chapter 3: goods for which demand increases when income rises and for which demand decreases when income falls.

Although most goods are normal goods, we also pointed out in Chapter 3 that some goods are *inferior goods,* goods for which demand moves in the opposite direction to the change in income: demand decreases when income rises, and demand increases when income falls. An example might be second-hand furniture. Whether a good is an inferior good depends on the consumer's indifference

FIGURE 10A-15 Income and Consumption: Normal Goods

At a monthly income of $2,400, Ingrid chooses bundle A, consisting of 8 rooms and 40 restaurant meals. When relative price remains unchanged, a fall in income shifts her budget line inward to BL_2. At a monthly income of $1,200, she chooses bundle B, consisting of 4 rooms and 20 restaurant meals. Since Ingrid's consumption of both restaurant meals and rooms falls when her income falls, both goods are normal goods.

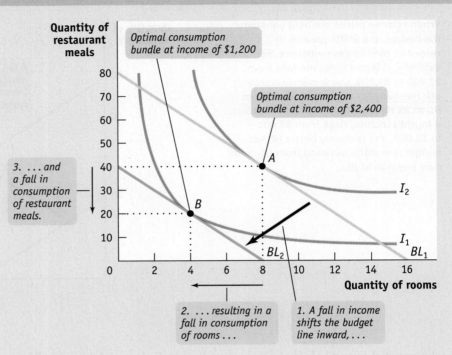

curve map. Figure 10A-16 illustrates such a case, where second-hand furniture is measured on the horizontal axis and restaurant meals are measured on the vertical axis. Note that when Ingrid's income falls from $2,400 ($BL_1$) to $1,200 ($BL_2$), and her optimal consumption bundle goes from D to E, her consumption of second-hand furniture increases—implying that second-hand furniture is an inferior good. Simultaneously, her consumption of restaurant meals decreases—implying that restaurant meals are a normal good.

FIGURE 10A-16 Income and Consumption: An Inferior Good

When Ingrid's income falls from $2,400 to $1,200, her optimal consumption bundle changes from D to E. Her consumption of second-hand furniture increases, implying that second-hand furniture is an inferior good. In contrast, her consumption of restaurant meals falls, implying that restaurant meals are a normal good.

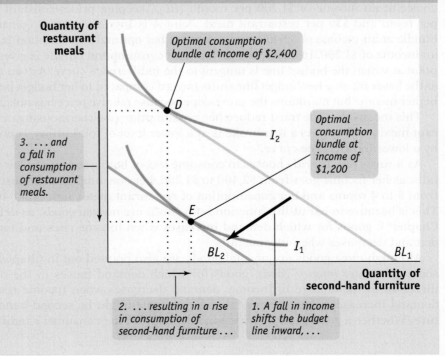

Income and Substitution Effects

Now that we have examined the effects of a change in income, we can return to the issue of a change in price—and show in a more specific way that the effect of a higher price on demand has an income component.

Figure 10A-17 shows, once again, Ingrid's original (BL_1) and new (BL_2) budget lines and consumption choices with a monthly income of $2,400. At a housing price of $150 per room, Ingrid chooses the consumption bundle at *A;* at a housing price of $600 per room, she chooses the consumption bundle at *C.*

Let's notice again what happens to Ingrid's budget line after the increase in the price of housing. It continues to hit the vertical axis at 80 restaurant meals; that is, if Ingrid were to spend all her income on restaurant meals, the increase in the price of housing would not affect her. But the new budget line hits the horizontal axis at only 4 rooms. So the budget line has rotated, *shifting inward* and *becoming steeper,* as a consequence of the rise in the relative price of rooms.

We already know what happens: Ingrid's consumption of housing falls from 8 rooms to 1 room. But the figure suggests that there are *two* reasons for the fall in Ingrid's housing consumption. One reason she consumes fewer rooms is that, because of the higher relative price of rooms, the opportunity cost of a room measured in restaurant meals—the quantity of restaurant meals she must give up to consume an additional room—has increased. This change in opportunity cost, which is reflected in the steeper slope of the budget line, gives her an incentive to substitute restaurant meals in place of rooms in her consumption. She now consumes more restaurant meals: 60 instead of 40.

But the other reason Ingrid consumes fewer rooms after their price increases is that the rise in the price of rooms makes her *poorer.* True, her money income hasn't changed. But she must pay more for rooms, and as a result her budget line has rotated inward. So she cannot reach the same level of total utility as before, meaning that her real income has fallen. That is why she ends up on a lower indifference curve.

In the real world, these effects—an increase in the price of a good raises its opportunity cost and also makes consumers poorer—usually go together. But in our imagination we can separate them. In Chapter 10 we introduced

FIGURE 10A-17 Income and Substitution Effects

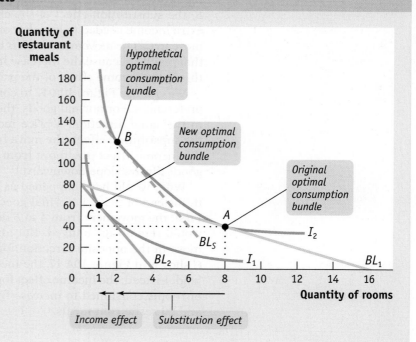

The movement from Ingrid's original optimal consumption bundle when the price of rooms is $150, *A,* to her new optimal consumption bundle when the price of rooms is $600, *C,* can be decomposed into two parts. The movement from *A* to *B*—the movement along the original indifference curve, I_2, as relative price changes— is the pure substitution effect. It captures how her consumption would change if she were given a hypothetical increase in income that just compensates her for the increase in the price of rooms, leaving her total utility unchanged. The movement from *B* to *C,* the change in consumption when we remove that hypothetical income compensation, is the income effect of the price increase—how her consumption changes as a result of the fall in her purchasing power.

the distinction between the *substitution effect* of a price change (the change in consumption that arises from the substitution of the good that is now relatively cheaper in place of the good that is now relatively more expensive) and the *income effect* (the change in consumption caused by the change in purchasing power arising from a price change). Now we can show these two effects more clearly.

To isolate the substitution effect, let's temporarily change the story about why Ingrid faces an increase in rent: it's not that housing has become more expensive, it's the fact that she has moved from Cincinnati to San Jose, where rents are higher. But let's consider a hypothetical scenario—let's suppose momentarily that she earns more in San Jose and that the higher income is just enough to *compensate* her for the higher price of housing, so that her total utility is exactly the same as before.

Figure 10A-17 shows her situation before and after the move. The bundle labeled *A* represents Ingrid's original consumption choice: 8 rooms and 40 restaurant meals. When she moves to San Jose, she faces a higher price of housing, so her budget line becomes steeper. But we have just assumed that her move increases her income by just enough to compensate for the higher price of housing—that is, just enough to let her reach the original indifference curve. So her new *hypothetical* optimal consumption bundle is at *B*, where the steeper dashed hypothetical budget line (BL_S) is just tangent to the original indifference curve (I_2). By assuming that we have compensated Ingrid for the loss in purchasing power due to the increase in the price of housing, we isolate the *pure substitution effect* of the change in relative price on her consumption.

At *B*, Ingrid's consumption bundle contains 2 rooms and 120 restaurant meals. This costs $4,800 (2 rooms at $600 each, and 120 meals at $30 each). So if Ingrid faces an increase in the price of housing from $150 to $600 per room, but also experiences a rise in her income from $2,400 to $4,800 per month, she ends up with the same level of total utility.

The movement from *A* to *B* is the pure substitution effect of the price change. It is the effect on Ingrid's consumption choice when we change the relative price of housing while keeping her total utility constant.

Now that we have isolated the substitution effect, we can bring back the income effect of the price change. That's easy: we just go back to the original story, in which Ingrid faces an increase in the price of housing *without* any rise in income. We already know that this leads her to *C* in Figure 10A-17. But we can think of the move from *A* to *C* as taking place in two steps. First, Ingrid moves from *A* to *B*, the substitution effect of the change in relative price. Then we take away the extra income needed to keep her on the original indifference curve, causing her to move to *C*. The movement from *B* to *C* is the additional change in Ingrid's demand that results because the increase in housing prices actually reduces her utility. So this is the income effect of the price change.

We can use Figure 10A-17 to confirm that rooms are a normal good in Ingrid's preferences. For normal goods, the income effect and the substitution effect work in the same direction: a price increase induces a fall in quantity consumed by the substitution effect (the move from *A* to *B*) and a fall in quantity consumed by the income effect (the move from *B* to *C*). That's why demand curves for normal goods always slope downward.

What would have happened as a result of the increase in the price of housing if, instead of being a normal good, rooms had been an inferior good for Ingrid? First, the movement from *A* to *B* depicted in Figure 10A-17, the substitution effect, would remain unchanged. But an income change causes quantity consumed to move in the opposite direction for an inferior good. So the movement from *B* to *C* shown in Figure 10A-17, the income effect for a normal good, would no longer hold. Instead, the income effect for an inferior good would cause Ingrid's quantity of rooms consumed to *increase* from *B*—say, to a bundle consisting of 3 rooms and 20 restaurant meals.

In the end, the demand curves for inferior goods normally slope downward: if Ingrid consumes 3 rooms after the increase in the price of housing, it is still 5 fewer rooms than she consumed before. So although the income effect moves in the opposite direction of the substitution effect in the case of an inferior good, in this example the substitution effect is stronger than the income effect.

But what if there existed a type of inferior good in which the income effect is so strong that it dominates the substitution effect? Would a demand curve for that good then slope upward—that is, would quantity demanded increase when price increases? The answer is yes: you have encountered such a good already—it is called a *Giffen good*, and it was described in Chapter 10. As we noted there, Giffen goods are rare creatures, but they cannot be ruled out.

Is the distinction between income and substitution effects important in practice? For analyzing the demand for goods, the answer is that it usually isn't that important. However, in Chapter 19 we'll discuss how individuals make decisions about how much of their labor to supply to employers. In that case income and substitution effects work in opposite directions, and the distinction between them becomes crucial.

PRACTICE QUESTIONS

1. The four properties of indifference curves for ordinary goods illustrated in Figure 10A-4 rule out certain indifference curves. Determine whether those general properties allow each of the following indifference curves. If not, state which of the general principles rules out the curves.

a.
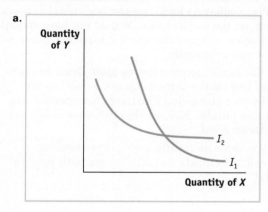

b.
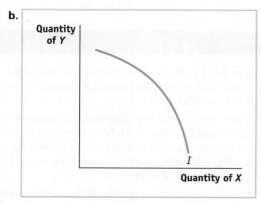

c.
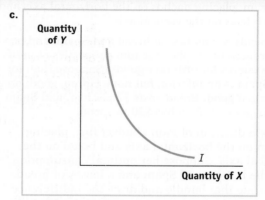

d.
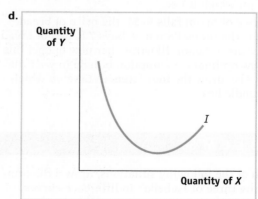

2. Ralph and Lauren are talking about how much they like going to the gym and how much they like eating out at their favorite restaurant and they regularly do some of each. A session at the gym costs the same as a meal at the restaurant. Ralph says that, for his current consumption of gym sessions and restaurant meals,

he values 1 more meal twice as much as he values 1 more session at the gym. Lauren is studying economics, and she tells him that his current consumption bundle cannot be optimal.

a. Is Lauren right? Why or why not? Draw a diagram of Ralph's budget line and the indifference curve that he is on by making his current consumption choice. Place restaurant meals on the horizontal axis and gym sessions on the vertical axis.

b. How should Ralph adjust his consumption so that it is optimal? Illustrate an optimal choice in your diagram.

3. For Norma, both nachos and french fries are normal goods. They are also ordinary goods for Norma. The price of nachos rises, but the price of french fries remains unchanged.

a. Can you determine definitively whether she consumes more or fewer nachos? Explain with a diagram, placing nachos on the horizontal axis and french fries on the vertical axis.

b. Can you determine definitively whether she consumes more or less french fries? Explain with a diagram, placing nachos on the horizontal axis and french fries on the vertical axis.

4. Pam spends her money on bread and Spam, and her indifference curves obey the four properties of indifference curves for ordinary goods. Suppose that, for Pam, Spam is an inferior, but not a Giffen, good; bread is a normal good. Bread costs $2 per loaf, and Spam costs $2 per can. Pam has $20 to spend.

a. Draw a diagram of Pam's budget line, placing Spam on the horizontal axis and bread on the vertical axis. Suppose her optimal consumption bundle is 4 cans of Spam and 6 loaves of bread. Illustrate that bundle and draw the indifference curve on which it lies.

b. The price of Spam falls to $1; the price of bread remains the same. Pam now buys 7 loaves of bread and 6 cans of Spam. Illustrate her new budget line and new optimal consumption bundle in your diagram. Also draw the indifference curve on which this bundle lies.

c. In your diagram, show the income and substitution effects from this fall in the price of Spam. Remember that Spam is an inferior good for Pam.

5. Katya commutes to work. She can either use public transport or her own car. Her indifference curves obey the four properties of indifference curves for ordinary goods.

a. Draw Katya's budget line with car travel on the vertical axis and public transport on the horizontal axis. Suppose that Katya consumes some of both goods. Draw an indifference curve that helps you illustrate her optimal consumption bundle.

b. Now the price of public transport falls. Draw Katya's new budget line.

c. For Katya, public transport is an inferior, but not a Giffen, good. Draw an indifference curve that illustrates her optimal consumption bundle after the price of public transport has fallen. Is Katya consuming more or less public transport?

d. Show the income and substitution effects from this fall in the price of public transport.

6. Carmen consumes nothing but cafeteria meals and music albums. Her indifference curves exhibit the four general properties of indifference curves. Cafeteria meals cost $5 each, and albums cost $10. Carmen has $50 to spend.

a. Draw Carmen's budget line and an indifference curve that illustrates her optimal consumption bundle. Place cafeteria meals on the horizontal axis and albums on the vertical axis. You do not have enough information to know the specific tangency point, so choose one arbitrarily.

b. Now Carmen's income rises to $100. Draw her new budget line on the same diagram, as well as an indifference curve that illustrates her optimal consumption bundle. Assume that cafeteria meals are an inferior good.

c. Can you draw an indifference curve showing that cafeteria meals and albums are both inferior goods?

PROBLEMS

1. For each of the following situations, draw a diagram containing three of Isabella's indifference curves.

a. For Isabella, cars and tires are perfect complements, but in a ratio of 1:4; that is, for each car, Isabella wants exactly four tires. Be sure to label and number the axes of your diagram. Place tires on the horizontal axis and cars on the vertical axis.

b. Isabella gets utility only from her caffeine intake. She can consume Valley Dew or cola, and Valley Dew contains twice as much caffeine as cola.

Be sure to label and number the axes of your diagram. Place cola on the horizontal axis and Valley Dew on the vertical axis.

c. Isabella gets utility from consuming two goods: leisure time and income. Both have diminishing marginal utility. Be sure to label the axes of your diagram. Place leisure on the horizontal axis and income on the vertical axis.

d. Isabella can consume two goods: skis and bindings. For each ski she wants exactly one binding. Be sure to label and number the axes of your diagram. Place bindings on the horizontal axis and skis on the vertical axis.

e. Isabella gets utility from consuming soda. But she gets no utility from consuming water: any more, or any less, water leaves her total utility level unchanged. Be sure to label the axes of your diagram. Place water on the horizontal axis and soda on the vertical axis.

2. Use the four properties of indifference curves for ordinary goods illustrated in Figure 10A-4 to answer the following questions.

a. Can you rank the following two bundles? If so, which property of indifference curves helps you rank them?

Bundle *A:* 2 movie tickets and 3 cafeteria meals

Bundle *B:* 4 movie tickets and 8 cafeteria meals

b. Can you rank the following two bundles? If so, which property of indifference curves helps you rank them?

Bundle *A:* 2 movie tickets and 3 cafeteria meals

Bundle *B:* 4 movie tickets and 3 cafeteria meals

c. Can you rank the following two bundles? If so, which property of indifference curves helps you rank them?

Bundle *A:* 12 videos and 4 bags of chips

Bundle *B:* 5 videos and 10 bags of chips

d. Suppose you are indifferent between the following two bundles:

Bundle *A:* 10 breakfasts and 4 dinners

Bundle *B:* 4 breakfasts and 10 dinners

Now compare bundle *A* and the following bundle:

Bundle *C:* 7 breakfasts and 7 dinners

Can you rank bundle *A* and bundle *C*? If so, which property of indifference curves helps you rank them? (*Hint:* It may help if you draw this, placing dinners on the horizontal axis and breakfasts on the vertical axis. And remember that breakfasts and dinners are ordinary goods.)

3. Restaurant meals and housing (measured by the number of rooms) are the only two goods that Neha can buy. She has income of $1,000, and the price of each room is $100. The relative price of 1 room in terms of restaurant meals is 5. How many restaurant meals can she buy if she spends all her money on them?

4. Answer the following questions based on two assumptions: (1) Inflation increases the prices of all goods by 20%. (2) Ina's income increases from $50,000 to $55,000.

a. Has Ina's budget line become steeper, less steep, or equally as steep?

b. Has Ina's budget line shifted outward, inward, or not at all?

5. Kory has an income of $50, which she can spend on two goods: music albums and cups of hot chocolate. Both are normal goods for her. Each album costs $10, and each cup of hot chocolate costs $2. For each of the following situations, decide whether this is Kory's optimal consumption bundle. If not, what should Kory do to achieve her optimal consumption bundle?

a. Kory is considering buying 4 albums and 5 cups of hot chocolate. At that bundle, her marginal rate of substitution of albums in place of hot chocolate is 1; that is, she would be willing to forgo only 1 cup of hot chocolate to acquire 1 album.

b. Kory is considering buying 2 albums and 15 cups of hot chocolate. Kory's marginal utility of the second album is 25, and her marginal utility of the fifteenth cup of hot chocolate is 5.

c. Kory is considering buying 1 album and 10 cups of hot chocolate. At that bundle, her marginal rate of substitution of albums in place of hot chocolate is 5; that is, she would be just willing to exchange 5 cups of hot chocolate for 1 album.

6. Raul has 4 Cal Ripken and 2 Nolan Ryan baseball cards. The prices of these baseball cards are $24 for Cal and $12 for Nolan. Raul, however, would be willing to exchange 1 Cal card for 1 Nolan card.

a. What is Raul's marginal rate of substitution of Cal Ripken in place of Nolan Ryan baseball cards?

b. Can Raul buy and sell baseball cards to make himself better off? How?

c. Suppose Raul has traded baseball cards and after trading still has some of each kind of card. Also, he now no longer wants to make any more trades. What is his marginal rate of substitution of Cal Ripken in place of Nolan Ryan cards now?

7. Sabine can't tell the difference between Coke and Pepsi—the two taste exactly the same to her.

a. What is Sabine's marginal rate of substitution of Coke in place of Pepsi?

b. Draw a few of Sabine's indifference curves for Coke and Pepsi. Place Coke on the horizontal axis and Pepsi on the vertical axis.

c. Sabine has $6 to spend on cola this week. Coke costs $1.50 per bottle and Pepsi costs $1.00. Draw Sabine's budget line for Coke and Pepsi on the same diagram.

d. What is Sabine's optimal consumption bundle? Show this on your diagram.

e. If the price of Coke and Pepsi is the same, what combination of Coke and Pepsi will Sabine buy?

8. Gus spends his income on gas for his car and food. The government raises the tax on gas, thereby raising the price of gas. But the government also lowers the income tax, thereby increasing Gus's income. And this rise in income is just enough to place Gus on the same indifference curve as the one he was on before the price of gas rose. Will Gus buy more, less, or the same amount of gas as before these changes? Illustrate your answer with a diagram, placing gas on the horizontal axis and food on the vertical axis.

9. For Crandall, cheese cubes and crackers are perfect complements: he wants to consume exactly 1 cheese cube with each cracker. He has $2.40 to spend on cheese and crackers. One cheese cube costs 20 cents, and 1 cracker costs 10 cents. Draw a diagram, with crackers on the horizontal axis and cheese cubes on the vertical axis, to answer the following questions.

a. Which bundle will Crandall consume?

b. The price of crackers rises to 20 cents. How many cheese cubes and how many crackers will Crandall consume?

c. Show the income and substitution effects from this price rise.

10. The Japanese Ministry of Internal Affairs and Communications collects data on the prices of goods and services in the Ku-area of Tokyo, as well as data on the average Japanese household's monthly income. The accompanying table shows some of this data. (¥ denotes the Japanese currency the yen.)

Year	Price of eggs (per pack of 10)	Price of tuna (per 100-gram portion)	Average monthly income
2013	¥187	¥392	¥524,810
2015	231	390	524,585

a. For each of the two years for which you have data, what is the maximum number of packs of eggs that an average Japanese household could have consumed each month? The maximum number of 100-gram portions of tuna? In one diagram, draw the average Japanese household's budget line in 2013 and in 2015. Place the quantity of eggs on the y-axis and the quantity of tuna on the x-axis.

b. Calculate the relative price of eggs in terms of tuna for each year. Use the relative price rule to determine how the average household's consumption of eggs and tuna would have changed between 2013 and 2015.

WORK IT OUT

11. Tyrone is a utility maximizer. His income is $100, which he can spend on cafeteria meals and on notepads. Each meal costs $5, and each notepad costs $2. At these prices Tyrone chooses to buy 16 cafeteria meals and 10 notepads.

a. Draw a diagram that shows Tyrone's choice using an indifference curve and his budget line, placing notepads on the vertical axis and cafeteria meals on the horizontal axis. Label the indifference curve I_1 and the budget line BL_1.

b. The price of notepads falls to $1; the price of cafeteria meals remains the same. On the same diagram, draw Tyrone's budget line with the new prices and label it BL_H.

c. Lastly, Tyrone's income falls to $90. On the same diagram, draw his budget line with this income and the new prices and label it BL_2. Is he worse off, better off, or equally as well off with these new prices and lower income than compared to the original prices and higher income? (*Hint:* Determine whether Tyrone can afford to buy his original consumption bundle of 16 meals and 10 notepads with the lower income and new prices.) Illustrate your answer using an indifference curve and label it I_2.

d. Give an intuitive explanation of your answer to part c. ∎

11 › Behind the Supply Curve: Inputs and Costs

THE FARMER'S MARGIN

"O BEAUTIFUL FOR SPACIOUS SKIES, for amber waves of grain." So begins the song "America the Beautiful." And those amber waves of grain are for real: though farmers are now only a small minority of America's population, our agricultural industry is immensely productive and feeds much of the world.

How intensively an acre of land is worked — a decision at the margin — depends on the price of wheat a farmer faces.

If you look at agricultural statistics, however, something may seem rather surprising: when it comes to yield per acre, U.S. farmers are often nowhere near the top. Farmers in Western European countries grow much more: about three times as much wheat per acre as their U.S. counterparts. Are the Europeans better at growing wheat than we are?

No: European farmers are very skillful, but no more so than Americans. They produce more wheat per acre because they employ more inputs — more fertilizer and, especially, more labor — per acre. Of course, this means that European farmers have higher costs than their American counterparts. But because of government policies,

European farmers receive a much higher price for their wheat than American farmers. This gives them an incentive to use more inputs and to expend more effort at the margin to increase the crop yield per acre.

Notice our use of the phrase "at the margin." Like most decisions that involve a comparison of benefits and costs, decisions about inputs and production involve a comparison of marginal quantities — the marginal cost versus the marginal benefit of producing a bit more from each acre.

In Chapter 9 we considered the case of Alexa, who had to choose the number of years of schooling that maximized her profit from an education. There we used the profit-maximizing principle of marginal analysis to find the optimal quantity of years of schooling. In this chapter, we will encounter producers who have to make similar "how much" decisions: choosing the quantity of output produced to maximize profit.

Here and in Chapter 12, we will show how marginal analysis can be used to understand these output decisions — decisions that lie behind the supply curve. The first step in this analysis is to show how the relationship between a firm's inputs and its output — its *production function* — determines its *cost curves,* the relationship between cost and quantity of output produced. That is what we will examine in this chapter. In Chapter 12, we will use our understanding of the firm's cost curves to derive the individual and the market supply curves. •

Terrance Klassen/AGE Fotostock

A **production function** is the relationship between the quantity of inputs a firm uses and the quantity of output it produces.

A **fixed input** is an input whose quantity is fixed for a period of time and cannot be varied.

A **variable input** is an input whose quantity the firm can vary at any time.

The **long run** is the time period in which all inputs can be varied.

The **short run** is the time period in which at least one input is fixed.

The **total product curve** shows how the quantity of output depends on the quantity of the variable input, for a given quantity of the fixed input.

|| The Production Function

A *firm* is an organization that produces goods or services for sale. To do this, it must transform inputs into output. The quantity of output a firm produces depends on the quantity of inputs; this relationship is known as the firm's **production function.** As we'll see, a firm's production function underlies its *cost curves.* As a first step, let's look at the characteristics of a hypothetical production function.

Inputs and Output

To understand the concept of a production function, let's consider a farm that we assume, for the sake of simplicity, produces only one output, wheat, and uses only two inputs, land and labor. This particular farm is owned by a couple named Riley and Tyler. They hire workers to do the physical labor on the farm. Moreover, we will assume that all potential workers are of the same quality—they are all equally knowledgeable and capable of performing farmwork.

Riley and Tyler's farm sits on 10 acres of land. No more acres are available to them, and they are currently unable to either increase or decrease the size of their farm by selling, buying, or leasing acreage. Land here is what economists call a **fixed input**—an input whose quantity is fixed for a period of time and cannot be varied. Riley and Tyler are, however, free to decide how many workers to hire. The labor provided by these workers is called a **variable input**—an input whose quantity the firm can vary at any time.

In reality, whether or not the quantity of an input is really fixed depends on the time horizon. In the **long run**—that is, given that a long enough period of time has elapsed—firms can adjust the quantity of any input. For example, in the long run, Riley and Tyler can vary the amount of land they farm by buying or selling land. So there are no fixed inputs in the long run.

In contrast, the **short run** is defined as the time period during which at least one input is fixed. Later in this chapter, we'll look more carefully at the distinction between the short run and the long run. But for now, we will restrict our attention to the short run and assume that at least one input is fixed.

Riley and Tyler know that the quantity of wheat they produce depends on the number of workers they hire. Using modern farming techniques, one worker can cultivate the 10-acre farm, albeit not very intensively. When an additional worker is added, the land is divided equally among all the workers: each worker has 5 acres to cultivate when 2 workers are employed, each cultivates $3\frac{1}{3}$ acres when 3 are employed, and so on. So as additional workers are employed, the 10 acres of land are cultivated more intensively and more bushels of wheat are produced.

The relationship between the quantity of labor and the quantity of output, for a given amount of the fixed input, constitutes the farm's production function. The production function for Riley and Tyler's farm, where land is the fixed input and labor is a variable input, is shown in the first two columns of the table in Figure 11-1; the diagram there shows the same information graphically. The curve in Figure 11-1 shows how the quantity of output depends on the quantity of the variable input, for a given quantity of the fixed input. It is called the farm's **total product curve.**

The physical quantity of output, bushels of wheat, is measured on the vertical axis; the quantity of the variable input, labor (that is, the number of workers employed), is measured on the horizontal axis. The total product curve here slopes upward, reflecting the fact that more bushels of wheat are produced as more workers are employed.

Although the total product curve in Figure 11-1 slopes upward along its entire length, the slope isn't constant: as you move up the curve to the right, it flattens out. To understand why the slope changes, look at the third column of

FIGURE 11-1 Production Function and Total Product Curve for Riley and Tyler's Farm

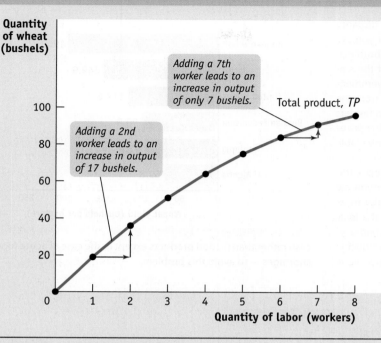

Quantity of labor L (workers)	Quantity of wheat Q (bushels)	Marginal product of labor $MPL = \Delta Q / \Delta L$ (bushels per worker)
0	0	
		19
1	19	
		17
2	36	
		15
3	51	
		13
4	64	
		11
5	75	
		9
6	84	
		7
7	91	
		5
8	96	

The table shows the production function, the relationship between the quantity of the variable input (labor, measured in number of workers) and the quantity of output (wheat, measured in bushels) for a given quantity of the fixed input. It also calculates the marginal product of labor on Riley and Tyler's farm. The total product curve shows the production function graphically. It slopes upward because more wheat is produced as more workers are employed. It also becomes flatter because the marginal product of labor declines as more and more workers are employed.

the table in Figure 11-1, which shows the *change in the quantity of output* that is generated by adding one more worker. This is called the *marginal product of labor,* or *MPL:* the additional quantity of output from using one more unit of labor (where one unit of labor is equal to one worker). In general, the **marginal product** of an input is the additional quantity of output that is produced by using one more unit of that input.

In this example, we have data on changes in output at intervals of 1 worker. Sometimes data aren't available in increments of 1 unit—for example, you might have information only on the quantity of output when there are 40 workers and when there are 50 workers. In this case, we use the following equation to calculate the marginal product of labor:

(11-1) $\quad \begin{array}{l} \text{Marginal} \\ \text{product} \\ \text{of labor} \end{array} = \begin{array}{l} \text{Change in quantity of} \\ \text{output produced by one} \\ \text{additional unit of labor} \end{array} = \dfrac{\text{Change in quantity of output}}{\text{Change in quantity of labor}}$

Or

$$MPL = \frac{\Delta Q}{\Delta L}$$

In this equation, Δ, the Greek uppercase delta, represents the change in a variable.

Now we can explain the significance of the slope of the total product curve: it is equal to the marginal product of labor. The slope of a line is equal to "rise" over "run" (explained in the Chapter 2 graph appendix). This implies that the slope of the total product curve is the change in the quantity of output (the "rise", ΔQ) divided by the change in the quantity of labor (the "run", ΔL). And this, as we can see from Equation 11-1, is simply the marginal product of labor. So in Figure 11-1,

The **marginal product** of an input is the additional quantity of output that is produced by using one more unit of that input.

GLOBAL COMPARISON WHEAT YIELDS AROUND THE WORLD

Wheat yields differ substantially around the world. The disparity between the European Union and the United States that you see in this graph is particularly striking, given that they are both rich economies with comparable agricultural technology. Yet the reason for that disparity is straightforward: differing government policies. In the United States, farmers receive payments from the government to supplement their incomes, but European farmers benefit from price floors. Since European farmers get higher prices for their output than American farmers, they employ more variable inputs and produce significantly higher yields.

Interestingly, in poor countries like Algeria and Ethiopia, foreign aid can lead to significantly depressed yields. Foreign aid from wealthy countries has often taken the form of surplus food, which depresses local market prices, severely hurting the local agriculture that poor countries normally depend on. Charitable organizations like OXFAM have asked wealthy food-producing countries to modify their aid policies — principally, to give aid in cash rather than in food products except in the case of acute food shortages — to avoid this problem.

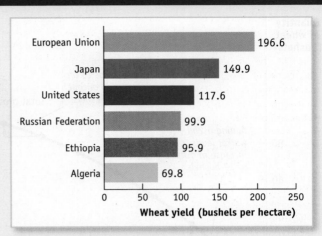

Data from: USDA, 2019.

---

the fact that the marginal product of the first worker is 19 also means that the slope of the total product curve in going from 0 to 1 worker is 19. Similarly, the slope of the total product curve in going from 1 to 2 workers is the same as the marginal product of the second worker, 17, and so on.

In this example, the marginal product of labor steadily declines as more workers are hired—that is, each successive worker adds less to output than the previous worker. So as employment increases, the total product curve gets flatter.

Figure 11-2 shows how the marginal product of labor depends on the number of workers employed on the farm. The marginal product of labor, *MPL,* is measured on the vertical axis in units of physical output—bushels of wheat—produced per additional worker, and the number of workers employed is measured on the horizontal axis. You can see from the table in Figure 11-1 that if 5 workers are employed instead of 4, output rises from 64 to 75 bushels; in this case the marginal product of labor is 11 bushels—the same number found in Figure 11-2. To indicate that 11 bushels is the marginal product when employment rises from 4 to 5, we place the point corresponding to that information halfway between 4 and 5 workers.

In this example the marginal product of labor falls as the number of workers increases. That is, there are *diminishing returns to labor* on Riley and Tyler's farm. In general, there are **diminishing returns to an input** when an increase in the quantity of that input, holding the quantity of all other inputs fixed, reduces that input's marginal product. Due to diminishing returns to labor, the *MPL* curve is negatively sloped.

To grasp why diminishing returns can occur, think about what happens as Riley and Tyler add more and more workers without increasing the number of acres of land. As the number of workers increases, the land is farmed more intensively and the number of bushels produced increases. But each additional worker is working with a smaller share of the 10 acres—the fixed input—than the previous worker. As a result, the additional worker cannot produce as much output as the previous worker. So it's not surprising that the marginal product of the additional worker falls.

The crucial point to emphasize about diminishing returns is that, like many propositions in economics, it is an "other things equal" proposition: each

There are **diminishing returns to an input** when an increase in the quantity of that input, holding the levels of all other inputs fixed, leads to a decline in the marginal product of that input.

FIGURE 11-2 Marginal Product of Labor Curve for Riley and Tyler's Farm

The marginal product of labor curve plots each worker's marginal product, the increase in the quantity of output generated by each additional worker. The change in the quantity of output is measured on the vertical axis and the number of workers employed is measured on the horizontal axis. On Riley and Tyler's 10-acre farm, the first worker employed generates an increase in output of 19 bushels, the second worker generates an increase of 17 bushels, and so on. The curve slopes downward due to diminishing returns to labor.

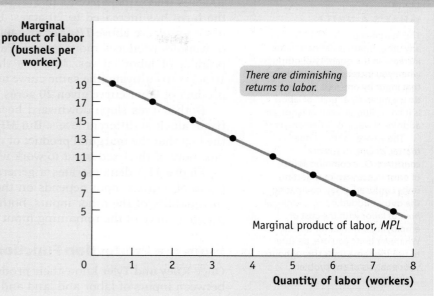

successive unit of an input will raise production by less than the last *if the quantity of all other inputs is held fixed.*

What would happen if the levels of other inputs were allowed to change? You can see the answer illustrated in Figure 11-3. Panel (a) shows two total product

FIGURE 11-3 Total Product, Marginal Product, and the Fixed Input

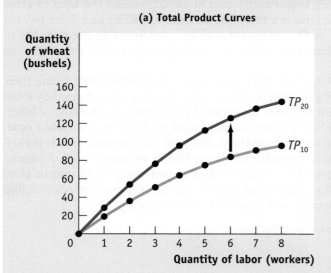

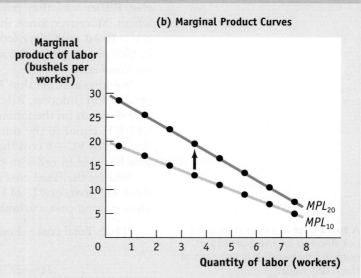

This figure shows how the quantity of output and the marginal product of labor depend on the level of the fixed input. Panel (a) shows two total product curves for Riley and Tyler's farm, TP_{10} when their farm is 10 acres and TP_{20} when it is 20 acres. With more land, each worker can produce more wheat. So an increase in the fixed input shifts the total product curve up from TP_{10} to TP_{20}. This implies that the

marginal product of each worker is higher when the farm is 20 acres than when it is 10 acres. Panel (b) shows the marginal product of labor curves. The increase in acreage also shifts the marginal product of labor curve up from MPL_{10} to MPL_{20}. Note that both marginal product of labor curves still slope downward due to diminishing returns to labor.

curves, TP_{10} and TP_{20}. TP_{10} is the farm's total product curve when its total area is 10 acres (the same curve as in Figure 11-1). TP_{20} is the total product curve when the farm has increased to 20 acres. Except when 0 workers are employed, TP_{20} lies everywhere above TP_{10} because with more acres available, any given number of workers produces more output. Panel (b) shows the corresponding marginal product of labor curves. MPL_{10} is the marginal product of labor curve given 10 acres to cultivate (the same curve as in Figure 11-2), and MPL_{20} is the marginal product of labor curve given 20 acres.

Both curves slope downward because, in each case, the amount of land is fixed, albeit at different levels. But MPL_{20} lies everywhere above MPL_{10}, reflecting the fact that the marginal product of the same worker is higher when that worker has more of the fixed input to work with.

Figure 11-3 demonstrates a general result: the position of the total product curve of a given input depends on the quantities of other inputs. If you change the quantity of the other inputs, both the total product curve and the marginal product curve of the remaining input will shift.

From the Production Function to Cost Curves

Once Riley and Tyler know their production function, they know the relationship between inputs of labor and land and output of wheat. But if they want to maximize their profits, they need to translate this knowledge into information about the relationship between the quantity of output and cost. Let's see how they can do this.

To translate information about a firm's production function into information about its costs, we need to know how much the firm must pay for its inputs. We will assume that Riley and Tyler face either an explicit or an implicit cost of $400 for the use of the land. As we learned in Chapter 9, it is irrelevant whether Riley and Tyler must rent the 10 acres of land for $400 from someone else or whether they own the land themselves and forgo earning $400 from renting it to someone else. Either way, they pay an opportunity cost of $400 by using the land to grow wheat. Moreover, since the land is a fixed input, the $400 Riley and Tyler pay for it is a **fixed cost,** denoted by FC—a cost that does not depend on the quantity of output produced (in the short run). In business, fixed cost is often referred to as *overhead cost*.

We also assume that Riley and Tyler must pay each worker $200. Using their production function, Riley and Tyler know that the number of workers they must hire depends on the amount of wheat they intend to produce. So the cost of labor, which is equal to the number of workers multiplied by $200, is a **variable cost,** denoted by VC—a cost that depends on the quantity of output produced. It is variable because in order to produce more they have to employ more units of input.

Adding the fixed cost and the variable cost of a given quantity of output gives the **total cost,** or TC, of that quantity of output. We can express the relationship among fixed cost, variable cost, and total cost as an equation:

(11-2) Total cost = Fixed cost + Variable cost

Or

$$TC = FC + VC$$

The table in Figure 11-4 shows how total cost is calculated for Riley and Tyler's farm. The second column shows the number of workers employed, L. The third column shows the corresponding level of output, Q, taken from the table in Figure 11-1. The fourth column shows the variable cost, VC, equal to the number of workers multiplied by $200, the cost per worker. The fifth column shows the fixed cost, FC, which is $400 regardless of how many workers are employed. The sixth column shows the total cost of output, TC, which is the variable cost plus the fixed cost.

A **fixed cost** is a cost that does not depend on the quantity of output produced. It is the cost of the fixed input.

A **variable cost** is a cost that depends on the quantity of output produced. It is the cost of the variable input.

The **total cost** of producing a given quantity of output is the sum of the fixed cost and the variable cost of producing that quantity of output.

FIGURE 11-4 Total Cost Curve for Riley and Tyler's Farm

The table shows the variable cost, fixed cost, and total cost for various output quantities on Riley and Tyler's 10-acre farm. The total cost curve shows how total cost (measured on the vertical axis) depends on the quantity of output (measured on the horizontal axis). The labeled points on the curve correspond to the rows of the table. The total cost curve slopes upward because the number of workers employed, and hence total cost, increases as the quantity of output increases. The curve gets steeper as output increases due to diminishing returns to labor.

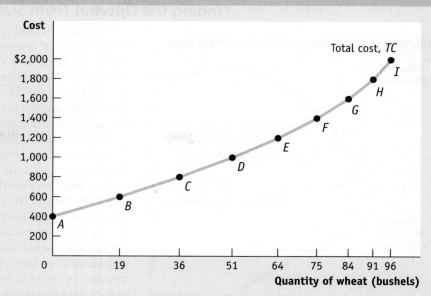

Point on graph	Quantity of labor *L* (workers)	Quantity of wheat *Q* (bushels)	Variable cost *VC*	Fixed cost *FC*	Total cost *TC = FC + VC*
A	0	0	$ 0	$400	$400
B	1	19	200	400	600
C	2	36	400	400	800
D	3	51	600	400	1,000
E	4	64	800	400	1,200
F	5	75	1,000	400	1,400
G	6	84	1,200	400	1,600
H	7	91	1,400	400	1,800
I	8	96	1,600	400	2,000

The first column labels each row of the table with a letter, from *A* to *I*. These labels will be helpful in understanding our next step: drawing the **total cost curve,** a curve that shows how total cost depends on the quantity of output.

Riley and Tyler's total cost curve is shown in the diagram in Figure 11-4, where the horizontal axis measures the quantity of output in bushels of wheat and the vertical axis measures total cost in dollars. Each point on the curve corresponds to one row of the table in Figure 11-4. For example, point *A* shows the situation when 0 workers are employed: output is 0, and total cost is equal to fixed cost, $400. Similarly, point *B* shows the situation when 1 worker is employed: output is 19 bushels, and total cost is $600, equal to the sum of $400 in fixed cost and $200 in variable cost.

Like the total product curve, the total cost curve slopes upward: due to the variable cost, the more output produced, the higher the farm's total cost. But unlike the total product curve, which gets flatter as employment rises, the total cost curve gets *steeper.* That is, the slope of the total cost curve is greater as the amount of output produced increases. As we will soon see, the steepening of the total cost curve is also due to diminishing returns to the variable input. Before we can understand this, we must first look at the relationships among several useful measures of cost.

The **total cost curve** shows how total cost depends on the quantity of output.

ECONOMICS >> *in Action*
Finding the Optimal Team Size

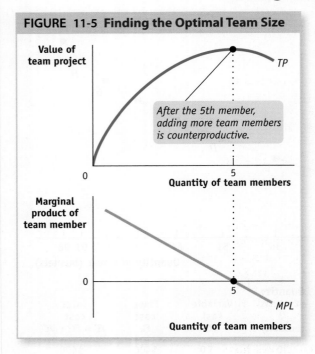

FIGURE 11-5 Finding the Optimal Team Size

After the 5th member, adding more team members is counterproductive.

In both offices and learning environments, team projects are a favorite way of organizing work. They have also been a topic of research. According to one study, the most efficient team size is between 4 and 5 people (4.6 team members, to be exact). Yet researchers have found that project designers routinely create teams that are too large to be efficient. What are project designers failing to understand?

It's true that a larger team has access to more resources, specifically more labor and more human capital. But keep in mind that how large a team should be is a decision at the margin. And studies have shown that adding another person to a team of 5 generally *reduces* the marginal product of existing members. This result is due to a phenomenon called *social loafing:* as the size of the team increases, it's easier to hide individual lack of effort, and the connection between individual effort and reward weakens. So team members loaf. As a result, the marginal product of the 6th member is equal to his personal contribution *minus* the loss due to social loafing that his presence inflicts on other team members.

A larger team must also spend more time coordinating its activities, which reduces the marginal product of each team member. With the addition of each member, team losses get larger. So at some point, team losses from social loafing and coordination costs outweigh the individual contribution made by the 6th team member. This result is well documented among teams of software programmers: at some point, adding another team member reduces the output of the entire team.

This situation is illustrated in Figure 11-5. The top part of the figure shows how the value of the team project varies with the number of team members. Each additional member accomplishes less than the previous one, and beyond a certain point an additional member is actually counterproductive. The bottom part of the figure shows the marginal product of each successive team member, which falls as more team members are employed and eventually becomes negative. In other words, the 6th team member has a negative marginal product.

It appears that project designers are creating teams that are too large by mistakenly focusing on the individual contribution of an additional team member, rather than on the marginal product generated by the *entire* team when another person is added. So, instead of having one large project performed by a team of 10 people, it would be more efficient and productive to split the large project into two smaller projects performed by teams of 5 people. By thinking at the margin, we can understand why, in teamwork, 5 + 5 doesn't equal 10: two teams of 5 people will produce more than one team of 10 people.

>> Quick Review

• The firm's **production function** is the relationship between quantity of inputs and quantity of output. The **total product curve** shows how the quantity of output depends on the quantity of the **variable input** for a given quantity of the **fixed input,** and its slope is equal to the **marginal product** of the variable input. In the **short run,** the fixed input cannot be varied; in the **long run** all inputs are variable.

• When the levels of all other inputs are fixed, **diminishing returns to an input** may arise, yielding a downward-sloping marginal product curve and a total product curve that becomes flatter as more output is produced.

• The **total cost** of a given quantity of output equals the **fixed cost** plus the **variable cost** of that output. The **total cost curve** becomes steeper as more output is produced due to diminishing returns to the variable input.

>> Check Your Understanding 11-1

Solutions appear at back of book.

1. Bernie's ice-making company produces ice cubes using a 10-ton machine and electricity. The quantity of output, measured in terms of pounds of ice, is given in the accompanying table.
   a. What is the fixed input? What is the variable input?
   b. Construct a table showing the marginal product of the variable input. Does it show diminishing returns?

Quantity of electricity (kilowatts)	Quantity of ice (pounds)
0	0
1	1,000
2	1,800
3	2,400
4	2,800

c. Suppose a 50% increase in the size of the fixed input increases output by 100% for any given amount of the variable input. What is the fixed input now? Construct a table showing the quantity of output and marginal product in this case.

Two Key Concepts: Marginal Cost and Average Cost

Now that we've learned how to derive a firm's total cost curve from its production function, let's take a deeper look at total cost by deriving two extremely useful measures: *marginal cost* and *average cost*. As we'll see, these two measures of the cost of production have a somewhat surprising relationship to each other. Moreover, they will prove to be vitally important in Chapter 12, where we will use them to analyze the firm's output decision and the market supply curve.

Marginal Cost

We defined *marginal cost* in Chapter 9: it is the change in total cost generated by producing one more unit of output. We've already seen that the marginal product of an input is easiest to calculate if data on output are available in increments of one unit of that input. Similarly, marginal cost is easiest to calculate if data on total cost are available in increments of one unit of output. When the data come in less convenient increments, it's still possible to calculate marginal cost. But for the sake of simplicity, let's work with an example in which the data come in convenient one-unit increments.

Selena's Gourmet Salsas produces bottled salsa and Table 11-1 shows how its costs per day depend on the number of cases of salsa it produces per day. The firm has fixed cost of $108 per day, shown in the second column, which

TABLE 11-1 Costs at Selena's Gourmet Salsas

Quantity of salsa Q (cases)	Fixed cost FC	Variable cost VC	Total cost TC = FC + VC	Marginal cost of case MC = $\Delta TC/\Delta Q$
0	$108	$0	$108	
				$12
1	108	12	120	
				36
2	108	48	156	
				60
3	108	108	216	
				84
4	108	192	300	
				108
5	108	300	408	
				132
6	108	432	540	
				156
7	108	588	696	
				180
8	108	768	876	
				204
9	108	972	1,080	
				228
10	108	1,200	1,308	

represents the daily cost of its food-preparation equipment. The third column shows the variable cost, and the fourth column shows the total cost. Panel (a) of Figure 11-6 plots the total cost curve. Like the total cost curve for Riley and Tyler's farm in Figure 11-4, this curve slopes upward, getting steeper as you move up it to the right.

The significance of the slope of the total cost curve is shown by the fifth column of Table 11-1, which calculates *marginal cost:* the additional cost of each additional unit. The general formula for marginal cost is:

(11-3) Marginal cost = $\dfrac{\text{Change in total cost generated by one additional unit of output}}{} = \dfrac{\text{Change in total cost}}{\text{Change in quantity of output}}$

Or

$$MC = \frac{\Delta TC}{\Delta Q}$$

As in the case of marginal product, marginal cost is equal to "rise" (the increase in total cost) divided by "run" (the increase in the quantity of output). So just as marginal product is equal to the slope of the total product curve, marginal cost is equal to the slope of the total cost curve.

Now we can understand why the total cost curve gets steeper as we move up it to the right: as you can see in Table 11-1, marginal cost at Selena's Gourmet Salsas rises as output increases. Panel (b) of Figure 11-6 shows the marginal cost curve corresponding to the data in Table 11-1. Notice that, as in Figure 11-2, we plot the marginal cost for increasing output from 0 to 1 case of salsa halfway between 0 and 1, the marginal cost for increasing output from 1 to 2 cases of salsa halfway between 1 and 2, and so on.

Why does the marginal cost curve slope upward? Because there are diminishing returns to inputs in this example. As output increases, the marginal product of the variable input declines. This implies that more and more of the variable

FIGURE 11-6 Total Cost and Marginal Cost Curves for Selena's Gourmet Salsas

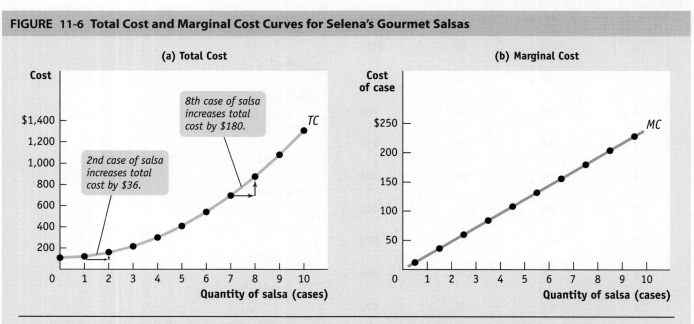

Panel (a) shows the total cost curve from Table 11-1. Like the total cost curve in Figure 11-4, it slopes upward and gets steeper as we move up it to the right. Panel (b) shows the marginal cost curve. It also slopes upward, reflecting diminishing returns to the variable input.

input must be used to produce each additional unit of output as the amount of output already produced rises. And since each unit of the variable input must be paid for, the additional cost per additional unit of output also rises.

In addition, recall that the flattening of the total product curve is also due to diminishing returns: the marginal product of an input falls as more of that input is used if the quantities of other inputs are fixed. The flattening of the total product curve as output increases and the steepening of the total cost curve as output increases are just flip-sides of the same phenomenon. That is, as output increases, the marginal cost of output also increases because the marginal product of the variable input decreases.

We will return to marginal cost in Chapter 12, when we consider the firm's profit-maximizing output decision. Our next step is to introduce another measure of cost: *average cost.*

Average Total Cost

In addition to total cost and marginal cost, it's useful to calculate another measure, **average total cost,** often simply called **average cost.** The average total cost is total cost divided by the quantity of output produced; that is, it is equal to total cost per unit of output. If we let *ATC* denote average total cost, the equation looks like this:

(11-4) $ATC = \dfrac{\text{Total cost}}{\text{Quantity of output}} = \dfrac{TC}{Q}$

Average total cost is important because it tells the producer how much the *average* or *typical* unit of output costs to produce. Marginal cost, meanwhile, tells the producer how much *one more* unit of output costs to produce. Although they may look very similar, these two measures of cost typically differ.

Table 11-2 uses data from Selena's Gourmet Salsas to calculate average total cost. For example, the total cost of producing 4 cases of salsa is $300, consisting of $108 in fixed cost and $192 in variable cost (from Table 11-1). So the average total cost of producing 4 cases of salsa is $300/4 = $75. You can see from Table 11-2 that as quantity of output increases, average total cost first falls, then rises.

Figure 11-7 plots that data to yield the *average total cost curve,* which shows how average total cost depends on output. As before, cost in dollars is measured on the vertical axis and quantity of output is measured on the horizontal axis. The average total cost curve has a distinctive U shape that corresponds to how average total cost first falls and then rises as output increases. Economists believe that such **U-shaped average total cost curves** are the norm for producers in many industries.

Average total cost, often referred to simply as **average cost,** is total cost divided by quantity of output produced.

A **U-shaped average total cost curve** falls at low levels of output, then rises at higher levels.

Average fixed cost is the fixed cost per unit of output.

Average variable cost is the variable cost per unit of output.

TABLE 11-2 Average Costs for Selena's Gourmet Salsas

Quantity of salsa Q (cases)	Total cost TC	Average total cost of case ATC = TC/Q	Average fixed cost of case AFC = FC/Q	Average variable cost of case AVC = VC/Q
1	$120	$120.00	$108.00	$12.00
2	156	78.00	54.00	24.00
3	216	72.00	36.00	36.00
4	300	75.00	27.00	48.00
5	408	81.60	21.60	60.00
6	540	90.00	18.00	72.00
7	696	99.43	15.43	84.00
8	876	109.50	13.50	96.00
9	1,080	120.00	12.00	108.00
10	1,308	130.80	10.80	120.00

To help our understanding of why the average total cost curve is U-shaped, Table 11-2 breaks average total cost into its two underlying components, *average fixed cost* and *average variable cost.* **Average fixed cost,** or *AFC,* is fixed cost divided by the quantity of output, also known as the fixed cost per unit of output. For example, if Selena's Gourmet Salsas produces 4 cases of salsa, average fixed cost is $108/4 = $27 per case. **Average variable cost,** or *AVC,* is variable cost divided by the quantity of output, also known as variable cost per unit of output. At an output of 4 cases, average variable cost is $192/4 = $48 per case.

FIGURE 11-7 Average Total Cost Curve for Selena's Gourmet Salsas

The average total cost curve at Selena's Gourmet Salsas is U-shaped. At low levels of output, average total cost falls because the *spreading effect* of falling average fixed cost dominates the *diminishing returns effect* of rising average variable cost. At higher levels of output, the opposite is true and average total cost rises. At point *M*, corresponding to an output of 3 cases of salsa per day, average total cost is at its minimum level, the minimum average total cost.

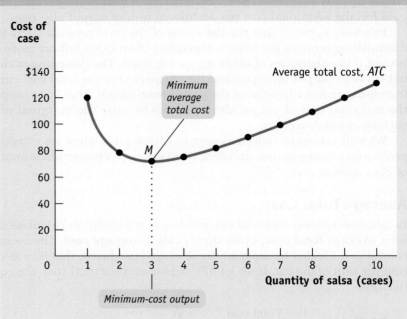

Writing these in the form of equations:

(11-5) $AFC = \dfrac{\text{Fixed cost}}{\text{Quantity of output}} = \dfrac{FC}{Q}$

$AVC = \dfrac{\text{Variable cost}}{\text{Quantity of output}} = \dfrac{VC}{Q}$

Average total cost is the sum of average fixed cost and average variable cost. It has a U shape because these components move in opposite directions as output rises.

Average fixed cost falls as more output is produced because the numerator (the fixed cost) is a fixed number but the denominator (the quantity of output) increases as more is produced. Another way to think about this relationship is that, as more output is produced, the fixed cost is spread over more units of output; the end result is that the fixed cost *per unit of output*—the average fixed cost—falls. You can see this effect in the fourth column of Table 11-2: average fixed cost drops continuously as output increases.

Average variable cost, however, rises as output increases. As we've seen, this reflects diminishing returns to the variable input: each additional unit of output incurs more variable cost to produce than the previous unit. So variable cost rises at a faster rate than the quantity of output increases.

So increasing output has two opposing effects on average total cost:

1. *The spreading effect.* The larger the output, the greater the quantity of output over which fixed cost is spread, leading to lower average fixed cost.

2. *The diminishing returns effect.* The larger the output, the greater the amount of variable input required to produce additional units, leading to higher average variable cost.

At low levels of output, the spreading effect is very powerful because even small increases in output cause large reductions in average fixed cost. So at low levels of output, the spreading effect dominates the diminishing returns effect and causes the average total cost curve to slope downward. But when output is large, average fixed cost is already quite small, so increasing output further has only a very small spreading effect.

Diminishing returns, however, usually grow increasingly important as output rises. As a result, when output is large, the diminishing returns effect dominates the spreading effect, causing the average total cost curve to slope upward. At the bottom of the U-shaped average total cost curve, point *M* in Figure 11-7, the two effects exactly balance each other. At this point average total cost is at its minimum level, the minimum average total cost.

Figure 11-8 brings together in a single picture four members of the family of cost curves that we have derived from the total cost curve for Selena's Gourmet Salsas: the marginal cost curve (*MC*), the average total cost curve (*ATC*), the average variable cost curve (*AVC*), and the average fixed cost curve (*AFC*). All are based on the information in Tables 11-1 and 11-2. As before, cost is measured on the vertical axis and the quantity of output is measured on the horizontal axis.

Let's take a moment to note some features of the various cost curves.

- Marginal cost slopes upward—the result of diminishing returns that make an additional unit of output more costly to produce than the one before.

- Average variable cost also slopes upward—again, due to diminishing returns—but is flatter than the marginal cost curve. This is because the higher cost of an additional unit of output is averaged across all units, not just the additional units, in the average variable cost measure.

- Average fixed cost slopes downward because of the spreading effect.

- The marginal cost curve intersects the average total cost curve from below, crossing it at its lowest point, point *M* in Figure 11-8. This last feature is our next subject of study.

FIGURE 11-8 Marginal Cost and Average Cost Curves for Selena's Gourmet Salsas

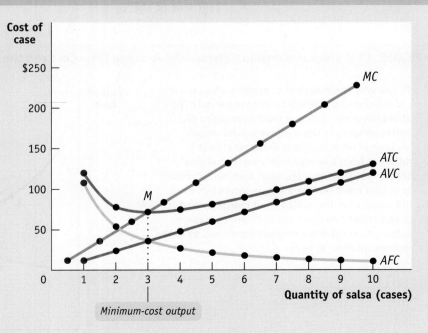

Here we have the family of cost curves for Selena's Gourmet Salsas: the marginal cost curve (*MC*), the average total cost curve (*ATC*), the average variable cost curve (*AVC*), and the average fixed cost curve (*AFC*). Note that the average total cost curve is U-shaped and the marginal cost curve crosses the average total cost curve at the bottom of the U, point *M*, corresponding to the minimum average total cost from Table 11-2 and Figure 11-7.

The **minimum-cost output** is the quantity of output at which average total cost is lowest—the bottom of the U-shaped average total cost curve.

Minimum Average Total Cost

For a U-shaped average total cost curve, average total cost is at its minimum level at the bottom of the U. Economists call the quantity of output that corresponds to the minimum average total cost the **minimum-cost output.** In the case of Selena's Gourmet Salsas, the minimum-cost output is 3 cases of salsa per day.

In Figure 11-8, the bottom of the U is at the level of output at which the marginal cost curve crosses the average total cost curve from below. Is this an accident? No—it reflects three general principles that are always true about a firm's marginal cost and average total cost curves:

1. At the minimum-cost output, average total cost *is equal to* marginal cost.
2. At output less than the minimum-cost output, marginal cost *is less than* average total cost and average total cost is falling.
3. At output greater than the minimum-cost output, marginal cost *is greater than* average total cost and average total cost is rising.

To understand these principles, think about how your grade in one course—say, a 3.0 in sociology—affects your overall grade point average. If your GPA before receiving that grade was more than 3.0, the new grade lowers your average.

Similarly, if marginal cost—the cost of producing one more unit—is less than average total cost, producing that extra unit lowers average total cost. This is shown in Figure 11-9 by the movement from A_1 to A_2. In this case, the marginal cost of producing an additional unit of output is low, as indicated by the point MC_L on the marginal cost curve. When the cost of producing the next unit of output is less than average total cost, increasing production reduces average total cost. So any quantity of output at which marginal cost is less than average total cost must be on the downward-sloping segment of the U.

But if your grade in sociology is more than the average of your previous grades, this new grade raises your GPA. Similarly, if marginal cost is greater than average total cost, producing that extra unit raises average total cost. This is illustrated by the movement from B_1 to B_2 in Figure 11-9, where the marginal cost, MC_H, is higher than average total cost. So any quantity of output at which marginal cost is greater than average total cost must be on the upward-sloping segment of the U.

FIGURE 11-9 The Relationship Between the Average Total Cost and the Marginal Cost Curves

To see why the marginal cost curve (*MC*) must cut through the average total cost curve (*ATC*) at the minimum average total cost (point *M*), corresponding to the minimum-cost output, we look at what happens if marginal cost is different from average total cost. If marginal cost is *less* than average total cost, an increase in output must reduce average total cost, as in the movement from A_1 to A_2. If marginal cost is *greater* than average total cost, an increase in output must increase average total cost, as in the movement from B_1 to B_2.

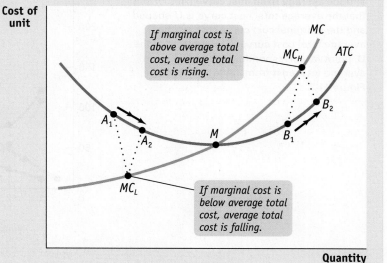

Finally, if a new grade is exactly equal to your previous GPA, the additional grade neither raises nor lowers that average—it stays the same. This corresponds to point *M* in Figure 11-9: when marginal cost equals average total cost, we must be at the bottom of the U, because only at that point is average total cost neither falling nor rising.

Does the Marginal Cost Curve Always Slope Upward?

Up to this point, we have emphasized the importance of diminishing returns, which lead to a marginal product curve that always slopes downward and a marginal cost curve that always slopes upward. In practice, however, economists believe that marginal cost curves often slope *downward* as a firm increases its production from zero up to some low level, sloping upward only at higher levels of production: they look like the curve *MC* in Figure 11-10.

This initial downward slope occurs because a firm often finds that, when it starts with only a very small number of workers, employing more workers and expanding output allows its workers to specialize in various tasks. This, in turn, lowers the firm's marginal cost as it expands output. For example, one individual producing salsa would have to perform all the tasks involved: selecting and preparing the ingredients, mixing the salsa, bottling and labeling it, packing it into cases, and so on. As more workers are employed, they can divide the tasks, with each worker specializing in one or a few aspects of salsa-making.

This specialization leads to *increasing returns* to the hiring of additional workers and results in a marginal cost curve that initially slopes downward. But once there are enough workers to have completely exhausted the benefits of further specialization, diminishing returns to labor set in and the marginal cost curve changes direction and slopes upward. So typical marginal cost curves actually have the "swoosh" shape shown by *MC* in Figure 11-10. For the same reason, average variable cost curves typically look like *AVC* in Figure 11-10: they are U-shaped rather than strictly upward sloping.

However, as Figure 11-10 also shows, the key features we saw from the example of Selena's Gourmet Salsas remain true: the average total cost curve is U-shaped, and the marginal cost curve passes through the point of minimum average total cost.

FIGURE 11-10 More Realistic Cost Curves

A realistic marginal cost curve has a "swoosh" shape. Starting from a very low output level, marginal cost often falls as the firm increases output. That's because hiring additional workers allows greater specialization of their tasks and leads to increasing returns. Once specialization is achieved, however, diminishing returns to additional workers set in and marginal cost rises. The corresponding average variable cost curve is now U-shaped, like the average total cost curve.

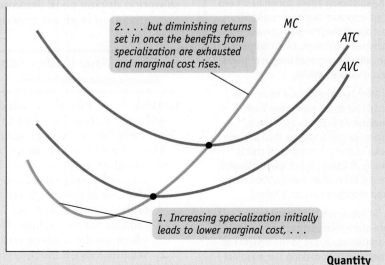

Cost of unit

2. . . . but diminishing returns set in once the benefits from specialization are exhausted and marginal cost rises.

MC

ATC

AVC

1. Increasing specialization initially leads to lower marginal cost, . . .

Quantity

ECONOMICS >> *in Action*
Smart Grid Economics

With SMART Grid technology, consumers save money by basing their demand for electricity on marginal cost rather than average cost.

Astro-0/Getty Images

If you like to listen to music, write term papers, or do laundry in the middle of the night, your local electricity grid would like to thank you. Why? Because you are using electricity when it is least costly to generate.

The problem is that energy cannot be stored efficiently on a large scale. So power plant operators maintain both the main power stations that are designed to run continuously, as well as smaller power plants that operate only during periods of peak demand—such as during daytime working hours or periods of extreme outside temperatures.

These smaller power plants are more expensive to operate, incurring higher marginal cost per kilowatt generated than the average cost of generating a kilowatt (that is, cost averaged over kilowatts generated by the large and small plants). According to the U.S. Government Accountability Office, it can cost up to 10 times more to generate electricity during a summer afternoon (when air conditioners are running at maximum capacity) compared to during the night.

But consumers typically aren't aware that the marginal cost of electricity varies over the course of a day or according to the weather. Instead, consumers see prices on their electricity bills based on the average cost of electricity generation. As a result, electricity demand is inefficient—too high during high marginal cost periods and too low during low marginal cost periods. In the end, consumers end up paying more than they should for their electricity, as utility companies must eventually raise their prices to cover production costs.

To solve this inefficiency, utility companies, appliance manufacturers, and the federal government are working together to develop SMART Grid technologies that help consumers adjust their usage according to the true marginal cost of a kilowatt in real time. "Smart" meters installed in homes allow the price to the consumer to vary according to the true marginal cost, which the consumer can see. And appliances such as dishwashers, refrigerators, dryers, and hot water heaters have been developed to run when electricity rates are lowest.

Studies have consistently shown that when consumers see the real marginal cost fluctuations and are asked to pay accordingly, they scale back their consumption during peak demand times. Clearly, SMART Grid technologies are just an application of smart economics.

>> Quick Review

- Marginal cost is equal to the slope of the total cost curve. Diminishing returns cause the marginal cost curve to slope upward.

- **Average total cost** (or **average cost**) is equal to the sum of **average fixed cost** and **average variable cost**. When the **U-shaped average total cost curve** slopes downward, the spreading effect dominates: fixed cost is spread over more units of output. When it slopes upward, the diminishing returns effect dominates: an additional unit of output requires more variable inputs.

- Marginal cost is equal to average total cost at the **minimum-cost output**. At higher output levels, marginal cost is greater than average total cost and average total cost is rising. At lower output levels, marginal cost is lower than average total cost and average total cost is falling.

- At low levels of output there are often increasing returns to the variable input due to the benefits of specialization, making the marginal cost curve "swoosh"-shaped: initially sloping downward before sloping upward.

>> *Check Your Understanding* 11-2
Solutions appear at back of book.

1. Aidy's Apple Pies is a roadside business. Aidy must pay $9.00 in rent each day. In addition, it costs her $1.00 to produce the first pie of the day, and each subsequent pie costs 50% more to produce than the one before. For example, the second pie costs $1.00 \times 1.5 = $1.50 to produce, and so on.
   a. Calculate Aidy's marginal cost, variable cost, average total cost, average variable cost, and average fixed cost as her daily pie output rises from 0 to 6. (*Hint:* The variable cost of two pies is just the marginal cost of the first pie, plus the marginal cost of the second, and so on.)
   b. Indicate the range of pies for which the spreading effect dominates and the range for which the diminishing returns effect dominates.
   c. What is Aidy's minimum-cost output? Explain why making one more pie lowers her average total cost when output is lower than the minimum-cost output. Similarly, explain why making one more pie raises Aidy's average total cost when output is greater than the minimum-cost output.

‖ Short-Run versus Long-Run Costs

Up to this point, we have treated fixed cost as completely outside the control of a firm because we have focused on the short run. But as we noted earlier, all inputs are variable in the long run: this means that in the long run fixed cost may also be varied. *In the long run,* in other words, *a firm's fixed cost becomes a variable it can choose.* For example, given time, Selena's Gourmet Salsas can acquire additional food-preparation equipment or dispose of some of its existing equipment.

In this section, we will examine how a firm's costs behave in the short run and in the long run. We will also see that the firm will choose its fixed cost in the long run based on the level of output it expects to produce.

Let's begin by supposing that Selena's Gourmet Salsas is considering whether to acquire additional food-preparation equipment. Acquiring additional machinery will affect its total cost in two ways. First, the firm will have to either rent or buy the additional equipment; either way, that will mean higher fixed cost in the short run. Second, if the workers have more equipment, they will be more productive: fewer workers will be needed to produce any given output, so variable cost for any given output level will be reduced.

The table in Figure 11-11 shows how acquiring an additional machine affects costs. In our original example, we assumed that Selena's Gourmet Salsas had a fixed cost of $108. The left half of the table shows variable cost as well as total cost and average total cost assuming a fixed cost of $108. The average total cost curve for this level of fixed cost is given by ATC_1 in Figure 11-11. Let's compare that to a situation in which the firm buys additional food-preparation equipment, doubling its fixed cost to $216 but reducing its variable cost at any given level of output. The right half of the table shows the firm's variable cost, total cost, and average total cost with this higher level of fixed cost. The average total cost curve corresponding to $216 in fixed cost is given by ATC_2 in Figure 11-11.

From the figure you can see that when output is small, 4 cases of salsa per day or fewer, average total cost is smaller when Selena's Gourmet Salsas forgoes the additional equipment and maintains the lower fixed cost of $108: ATC_1 lies below ATC_2. For example, at 3 cases per day, average total cost is $72 without the additional machinery and $90 with the additional machinery. But as output increases beyond 4 cases per day, the firm's average total cost is lower if it acquires the additional equipment, raising its fixed cost to $216. So, at 9 cases of salsa per day, average total cost is $120 when fixed cost is $108 but only $78 when fixed cost is $216.

Why does average total cost change like this when fixed cost increases? When output is low, the increase in fixed cost from the additional equipment outweighs the reduction in variable cost from higher worker productivity—that is, there are too few units of output over which to spread the additional fixed cost. So if Selena's Gourmet Salsas plans to produce 4 or fewer cases per day, it would be better off choosing the lower level of fixed cost, $108, to achieve a lower average total cost of production. When planned output is high, however, it should acquire the additional machinery.

In general, for each output level there is some choice of fixed cost that minimizes the firm's average total cost for that output level. So when the firm has a desired output level that it expects to maintain over time, it should choose the level of fixed cost optimal for that level—that is, the level of fixed cost that minimizes its average total cost.

Now that we are studying a situation in which fixed cost can change, we need to take time into account when discussing average total cost. All of the average total cost curves we have considered until now are defined for a given level of fixed cost—that is, they are defined for the short run, the period of time over which fixed cost doesn't vary. To reinforce that distinction, for the rest of this chapter we will refer to these average total cost curves as *short-run average total cost curves.*

FIGURE 11-11 Choosing the Level of Fixed Cost for Selena's Gourmet Salsas

For any given level of output, there is a trade-off: a choice between lower fixed cost and higher variable cost, or higher fixed cost and lower variable cost. ATC_1 is the average total cost curve corresponding to a fixed cost of $108; it leads to lower fixed cost and higher variable cost. ATC_2 is the average total cost curve corresponding to a higher fixed cost of $216 but lower variable cost. At low output levels, at 4 or fewer cases of salsa per day, ATC_1 lies below ATC_2: average total cost is lower with only $108 in fixed cost. But as output goes up, average total cost is lower with the higher amount of fixed cost, $216: at more than 4 cases of salsa per day, ATC_2 lies below ATC_1.

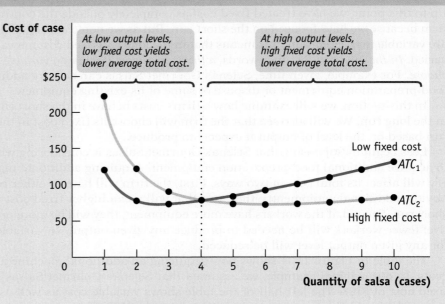

	Low fixed cost (FC = $108)			High fixed cost (FC = $216)		
Quantity of salsa (cases)	High variable cost	Total cost	Average total cost of case ATC_1	Low variable cost	Total cost	Average total cost of case ATC_2
1	$12	$120	$120.00	$6	$222	$222.00
2	48	156	78.00	24	240	120.00
3	108	216	72.00	54	270	90.00
4	192	300	75.00	96	312	78.00
5	300	408	81.60	150	366	73.20
6	432	540	90.00	216	432	72.00
7	588	696	99.43	294	510	72.86
8	768	876	109.50	384	600	75.00
9	972	1,080	120.00	486	702	78.00
10	1,200	1,308	130.80	600	816	81.60

For most firms, it is realistic to assume that there are many possible choices of fixed cost, not just two. The implication: for such a firm, many possible short-run average total cost curves will exist, each corresponding to a different choice of fixed cost and so giving rise to what is called a firm's "family" of short-run average total cost curves.

At any given point in time, a firm will find itself on one of its short-run cost curves, the one corresponding to its current level of fixed cost; a change in output will cause it to move along that curve. If the firm expects that change in output level to be long-standing, then it is likely that the firm's current level of fixed cost is no longer optimal. Given sufficient time, it will want to adjust its fixed cost to a new level that minimizes average total cost for its new output level.

For example, if Selena's Gourmet Salsas had been producing 2 cases of salsa per day with a fixed cost of $108 but found itself increasing its output to 8 cases per day for the foreseeable future, then in the long run it should purchase more equipment and increase its fixed cost to a level that minimizes average total cost at the 8-cases-per-day output level.

Suppose we do a thought experiment and calculate the lowest possible average total cost that can be achieved for each output level if the firm were to choose its fixed cost for each output level. Economists have given this thought experiment a name: the *long-run average total cost curve*. Specifically, the **long-run average total cost curve,** or *LRATC*, is the relationship between output and average total cost when fixed cost has been chosen to minimize average total cost *for each level of output*. If there are many possible choices of fixed cost, the long-run average total cost curve will have the familiar, smooth U shape, as shown by *LRATC* in Figure 11-12.

We can now draw the distinction between the short run and the long run more fully. In the long run, when a producer has had time to choose the fixed cost appropriate for its desired level of output, that producer will be at some point on the long-run average total cost curve. But if the output level is altered, the firm will no longer be on its long-run average total cost curve and will instead be moving along its current short-run average total cost curve. It will not be on its long-run average total cost curve again until it readjusts its fixed cost for its new output level.

Figure 11-12 illustrates this point. The curve ATC_3 shows short-run average total cost if Selena's Gourmet Salsas has chosen the level of fixed cost that minimizes average total cost at an output of 3 cases of salsa per day. This is confirmed by the fact that at 3 cases per day, ATC_3 touches *LRATC*, the long-run average total cost curve. Similarly, ATC_6 shows short-run average total cost if Selena's Gourmet Salsas has chosen the level of fixed cost that minimizes average total cost if its output is 6 cases per day. It touches *LRATC* at 6 cases per day. And ATC_9 shows short-run average total cost if Selena's Gourmet Salsas has chosen the level of fixed cost that minimizes average total cost if its output is 9 cases per day. It touches *LRATC* at 9 cases per day.

Suppose that Selena's Gourmet Salsas initially chose to be on ATC_6. If the firm actually produces 6 cases of salsa per day, it will be at point *C* on both its short-run and long-run average total cost curves. Suppose, however, that Selena's Gourmet Salsas ends up producing only 3 cases of salsa per day. In the short run, the firm's average total cost is indicated by point *B* on ATC_6; it is no longer on *LRATC*. If managers at Selena's had known that it would be producing only 3 cases per

To understand how firms operate over time, be sure to distinguish between short-run and long-run average costs.

The **long-run average total cost curve** shows the relationship between output and average total cost when fixed cost has been chosen to minimize average total cost for each level of output.

FIGURE 11-12 Short-Run and Long-Run Average Total Cost Curves

Short-run and long-run average total cost curves differ because a firm can choose its fixed cost in the long run. If Selena's Gourmet Salsas has chosen the level of fixed cost that minimizes short-run average total cost at an output of 6 cases, and actually produces 6 cases, then it will be at point *C* on *LRATC* and ATC_6. But if the firm produces only 3 cases, it will move to point *B*. If the firm expects to produce only 3 cases for a long time, in the long run it will reduce its fixed cost and move to point *A* on ATC_3. Likewise, if it produces 9 cases (putting it at point *Y*) and expects to continue this for a long time, it will increase its fixed cost in the long run and move to point *X* on ATC_9.

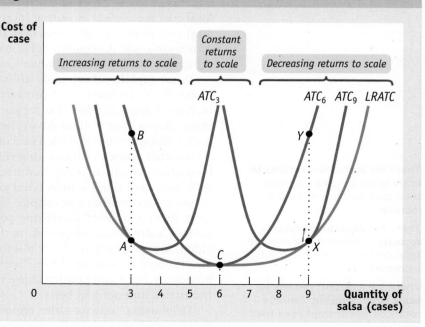

day, they would have been better off choosing a lower level of fixed cost, the one corresponding to ATC_3, thereby achieving a lower average total cost. They could do this, for example, by selling their production plant and purchasing a smaller one. Then the firm would have found itself at point A on the long-run average total cost curve, which lies below point B.

Suppose, conversely, that Selena's Gourmet Salsas ends up producing 9 cases per day even though it initially chose to be on ATC_6. In the short run its average total cost is indicated by point Y on ATC_6. But the firm would be better off purchasing more equipment and incurring a higher fixed cost in order to reduce its variable cost and move to ATC_9. This would allow Selena's Gourmet Salsas to reach point X on the long-run average total cost curve, which lies below Y.

The distinction between short-run and long-run average total costs is extremely important in making sense of how real firms operate over time. A company that has to increase output suddenly to meet a surge in demand will typically find that in the short run its average total cost rises sharply because it is hard to get extra production out of existing facilities. But given time to build new factories or add machinery, short-run average total cost falls.

Returns to Scale

What determines the shape of the long-run average total cost curve? The answer is that *scale,* the size of a firm's operations, is often an important determinant of its long-run average total cost of production. Firms that experience scale effects in production find that their long-run average total cost changes substantially depending on the quantity of output they produce. There are **increasing returns to scale** (also known as *economies of scale*) when long-run average total cost declines as output increases.

As you can see in Figure 11-12, Selena's Gourmet Salsas experiences increasing returns to scale over output levels ranging from 0 to 5 cases of salsa per day—the output levels over which the long-run average total cost curve is declining. In contrast, there are **decreasing returns to scale** (also known as *dis-economies of scale*) when long-run average total cost increases as output increases. For Selena's Gourmet Salsas, decreasing returns to scale occur at output levels greater than 7 cases, the output levels over which its long-run average total cost curve is rising.

There is also a third possible relationship between long-run average total cost and scale: firms experience **constant returns to scale** when long-run average total cost is constant as output increases. In this case, the firm's long-run average total cost curve is horizontal over the output levels for which there are constant returns to scale. As you see in Figure 11-12, Selena's Gourmet Salsas has constant returns to scale when it produces anywhere from 5 to 7 cases of salsa per day.

What explains these scale effects in production? The answer ultimately lies in the firm's technology of production. Increasing returns often arise from the increased *specialization* that larger output levels allow—a larger scale of operation means that individual workers can limit themselves to more specialized tasks, becoming more skilled and efficient at doing them.

Another source of increasing returns is very large initial setup cost; in some industries—such as auto manufacturing, electricity generating, or petroleum refining—incurring a high fixed cost in the form of a plant and equipment is necessary to produce any output.

A third source of increasing returns, found in certain high-tech industries such as software development, is that the value of a good or service to an individual increases when a large number of others own or use the same good or service (known as *network externalities*). As we'll see in Chapter 13, where we study monopoly, increasing returns have very important implications for how firms and industries interact and behave.

Decreasing returns—the opposite scenario—typically arise in large firms due to problems of coordination and communication: as the firm grows in size, it

There are **increasing returns to scale** when long-run average total cost declines as output increases.

There are **decreasing returns to scale** when long-run average total cost increases as output increases.

There are **constant returns to scale** when long-run average total cost is constant as output increases.

becomes ever more difficult and so more costly to communicate and to organize its activities. Although increasing returns induce firms to get larger, decreasing returns tend to limit their size. And when there are constant returns to scale, scale has no effect on a firm's long-run average total cost: it is the same regardless of whether the firm produces 1 unit or 100,000 units.

Summing Up Costs: The Short and Long of It

If a firm is to make the best decisions about how much to produce, it has to understand how its costs relate to the quantity of output it chooses to produce. Table 11-3 provides a quick summary of the concepts and measures of cost you have learned about.

TABLE 11-3 Concepts and Measures of Cost

	Measurement	Definition	Mathematical term
Short run	Fixed cost	Cost that does not depend on the quantity of output produced	FC
	Average fixed cost	Fixed cost per unit of output	$AFC = FC/Q$
Short run and long run	Variable cost	Cost that depends on the quantity of output produced	VC
	Average variable cost	Variable cost per unit of output	$AVC = VC/Q$
	Total cost	The sum of fixed cost (short run) and variable cost	$TC = FC$ (short run) $+ VC$
	Average total cost (Average cost)	Total cost per unit of output	$ATC = TC/Q$
	Marginal cost	The change in total cost generated by producing one more unit of output	$MC = \Delta TC/\Delta Q$
Long run	Long-run average total cost	Average total cost when fixed cost has been chosen to minimize average total cost for each level of output	$LRATC$

ECONOMICS >> *in Action*
How the Sharing Economy Reduces Fixed Cost

Turo is a peer-to-peer car-sharing company: it enables people who own cars to rent them to people who want to use a car but prefer not to buy one. Much like Airbnb, the hugely successful peer-to-peer home-sharing company, Turo is an example of a significant and growing phenomenon: the sharing economy. In the sharing economy, technology allows unrelated parties (firms and individuals) to share assets like office space, houses, computing capacity, cars, small jets, financial capital, books, and designer clothes through market transactions. Even the cloud itself, the vast digital network into which you store your photos and your term papers, is a feature of the sharing economy because it allows firms and individuals to rent computing capacity, storage, and software. But what does this have to do with fixed costs? A lot. If the use of an asset can be obtained only when needed, then it goes from incurring a fixed cost to incurring a variable cost.

Let's explain using the example of a car-sharing market, like Turo. Karenna needs to use a car occasionally. Purchasing a car would mean spending a lot of money: even an older used car will cost Karenna a few thousand dollars. That is,

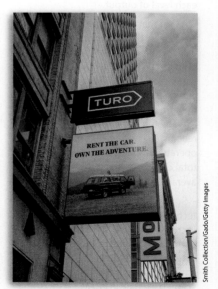

Firms in the sharing economy, like Turo, help convert fixed costs to variable costs and allow for a more efficient use of resources.

Karenna has to incur a sizeable fixed cost if she buys a car. And since she needs the car only occasionally, any car she purchased would sit in her driveway for a significant amount of time.

Suppose that instead of purchasing a car, Karenna uses Turo to rent a car when she needs one. Then she incurs a variable cost—the rental rate for the car—instead of a large fixed cost from ownership. By sharing instead of buying a car, Karenna has transformed what would have been a fixed cost into a variable cost.

Now consider Brianna, who owns a car that she rents out to other drivers through the Turo app. Brianna incurred a fixed cost when she bought the car, some of which she can defray by renting out the car when she doesn't need it. However, since people like Brianna regularly rent out their cars, the total number of cars purchased in the economy falls because people like Karenna no longer needs to buy a car in order to consume car rides. As a result, over the entire economy, for a given quantity demanded of car rides, the number of cars falls. Hence the total outlay of fixed costs in the economy falls for a given quantity demanded of car rides.

In effect, by turning the fixed cost of ownership into the variable cost of sharing, the sharing economy allows people to afford more goods and services (such as car rides) than they would have been able to afford otherwise. Likewise, sharing allows people like Brianna to afford assets like a car—assets that may have been previously unaffordable—because she can now use the car to earn income. The sharing economy marketplace makes for a more efficient use of society's resources because it reduces the total amount of fixed costs incurred in order to generate the desired amounts of goods and services.

>> Check Your Understanding 11-3

Solutions appear at back of book.

1. The accompanying table shows three possible combinations of fixed cost and average variable cost for a single firm. Average variable cost is constant in this example (it does not vary with the quantity of output produced).

Choice	Fixed cost	Average variable cost
1	$8,000	$1.00
2	12,000	0.75
3	24,000	0.25

   a. For each of the three choices, calculate the average total cost of producing 12,000, 22,000, and 30,000 units. For each of these quantities, which choice results in the lowest average total cost?
   b. Suppose that the firm, which has historically produced 12,000 units, experiences a sharp, permanent increase in demand that leads it to produce 22,000 units. Explain how its average total cost will change in the short run and in the long run.
   c. Explain what the firm should do instead if it believes the change in demand indicated in part b is temporary.

2. In each of the following cases, explain what kind of scale effects you think the firm will experience and why.
   a. A telemarketing firm in which employees make sales calls using computers and telephones
   b. An interior design firm in which design projects are based on the expertise of the firm's owner
   c. A diamond-mining company

3. Draw a graph like Figure 11-12 and insert a short-run average total cost curve corresponding to a long-run output choice of 5 cases of salsa per day. Use the graph to show why Selena's Gourmet Salsas should change its fixed cost if it expects to produce only 4 cases per day for a long period of time.

The Rise of the Machine at Amazon

Justin Sullivan/Getty Images

One of the main pillars of Amazon's success is its promise of speedy delivery. For the majority of Prime eligible items, customers receive their orders within two business days. Even better, in select zip codes Amazon can now deliver within 24 hours. And if you happen to live in a major city, odds are that you can receive your delivery in one to two hours. None of its competitors comes close to matching the Amazon's speed. What accounts for Amazon's prodigious delivery abilities?

The answer: robots. Visit an Amazon fulfillment center and you will see hundreds of them swarming an 125,000 square-foot area, engaged in a finely coordinated dance. They haul shelves of merchandise, weighing up to 700 pounds, and deliver them to human "pickers" who assemble orders, and to human "stockers" who sort incoming inventory.

As of 2019 Amazon has more than 100,000 robots working in its 175 fulfillment centers, which shipped out more than 5 billion orders. Before the arrival of robots, human employees did this tedious work, often walking 10 to 15 miles daily, carrying heavy loads. By eliminating the need for humans to walk miles carting merchandise, warehouse operations have become much more efficient. In addition, because robots don't need aisles between shelves like people do, there's more room for merchandise storage in Amazon's fulfillment centers.

Over the past 20 years, Amazon has invested an enormous amount of money perfecting its warehouse management and order fulfillment operations to satisfy customers' desire to receive their items quickly. The company's spokesperson, Phil Hardin, explains the widespread use of robots this way: "It's an investment that has implications for a lot of elements of our cost structure. It has been a great innovation for us, . . . and we think it makes our warehouses more productive." Indeed, some estimates show that, by embracing automation, Amazon has cut the cost of order fulfillment nearly in half.

Amazon's competitors have taken notice. Walmart, for example, also uses robotic systems to speed up delivery times. Robotics companies like 6 River Systems have been working with warehouse management companies such as Flowspace to provide order fulfillment services for non-Amazon sellers. However, with Amazon's huge scale advantage, it remains to be seen whether other retailers can ever catch up.

QUESTIONS FOR THOUGHT

1. Describe the shift in Amazon's cost structure based on the concepts from this chapter. Is Amazon on a short-run or long-run cost curve? What are the relevant returns to scale in Amazon's operations?

2. What are the pros and cons of Amazon's strategy?

3. What advantage does a robotic system give Amazon over its rivals? How likely is it that they will catch up with Amazon? What market factors does it depend upon?

SUMMARY

1. The relationship between inputs and output is a producer's **production function.** In the **short run,** the quantity of a **fixed input** cannot be varied but the quantity of a **variable input** can. In the **long run,** the quantities of all inputs can be varied. For a given amount of the fixed input, the **total product curve** shows how the quantity of output changes as the quantity of the variable input changes. We may also calculate the **marginal product** of an input, the increase in output from using one more unit of that input.

2. There are **diminishing returns to an input** when its marginal product declines as more of the input is used, holding the quantity of all other inputs fixed.

3. **Total cost,** represented by the **total cost curve,** is equal to the sum of **fixed cost,** which does not depend on output, and **variable cost,** which does depend on output. Due to diminishing returns, marginal cost, the increase in total cost generated by producing one more unit of output, normally increases as output increases.

4. **Average total cost** (also known as **average cost**), total cost divided by quantity of output, is the cost of the average unit of output, and marginal cost is the cost of one more unit produced. Economists believe that **U-shaped average total cost curves** are typical, because average total cost consists of two parts: **average fixed cost,** which falls when output increases

(the spreading effect), and **average variable cost,** which rises with output (the diminishing returns effect).

5. When average total cost is U-shaped, the bottom of the U is the level of output at which average total cost is minimized, the point of **minimum-cost output.** This is also the point at which the marginal cost curve crosses the average total cost curve from below. Due to gains from specialization, the marginal cost curve may slope downward initially before sloping upward, giving it a "swoosh" shape.

6. In the long run, a producer can change its fixed input and its level of fixed cost. By accepting higher fixed cost, a firm can lower its variable cost for any given output level, and vice versa. The **long-run average total cost curve** shows the relationship between output and average total cost when fixed cost has been chosen to minimize average total cost at each level of output. A firm moves along its short-run average total cost curve as it changes the quantity of output, and it returns to a point on both its short-run and long-run average total cost curves once it has adjusted fixed cost to its new output level.

7. As output increases, there are **increasing returns to scale** if long-run average total cost declines; **decreasing returns to scale** if it increases; and **constant returns to scale** if it remains constant. Scale effects depend on the technology of production.

KEY TERMS

Production function, p. 328
Fixed input, p. 328
Variable input, p. 328
Long run, p. 328
Short run, p. 328
Total product curve, p. 328
Marginal product, p. 329
Diminishing returns to an input, p. 330

Fixed cost, p. 332
Variable cost, p. 332
Total cost, p. 332
Total cost curve, p. 333
Average total cost, p. 337
Average cost, p. 337
U-shaped average total cost curve,
  p. 337

Average fixed cost, p. 337
Average variable cost, p. 337
Minimum-cost output, p. 340
Long-run average total cost curve,
  p. 345
Increasing returns to scale, p. 346
Decreasing returns to scale, p. 346
Constant returns to scale, p. 346

PRACTICE QUESTIONS

1. Explain the difference between diminishing marginal returns to labor and decreasing returns to scale. Provide an example for each case.

2. Many colleges and universities are witnessing a shift in demographics due to women having fewer children today. The birth rate fell from an average of 2.1 births per woman in 2007 to 1.7 births in 2018. The declining birth rate will reduce the college age population by as much as 15% between 2025 and 2029. How will the declining birth rate affect university operations? Answer the questions below.

a. Do higher-education institutions have large or small fixed costs? What are the variable costs for colleges and universities?

b. Given you answer in part a, how would you describe short-run average total cost?

c. If universities are operating where short-run average total costs are minimized, what will happen to the average cost per student of higher education if universities experience a decline in enrollments?

3. In your economics class, each homework problem set is graded on the basis of a maximum score of 100. You have completed 9 out of 10 of the problem sets for the term, and your current average grade is 88. What range of grades for your 10th problem set will raise your overall average? What range will lower your overall average? Explain your answer.

PROBLEMS

1. Changes in the prices of key commodities have a significant impact on a company's bottom line. For virtually all companies, the price of energy is a substantial portion of their costs. In addition, many industries—such as those that produce beef, chicken, high-fructose corn syrup, and ethanol—are highly dependent on the price of corn. In particular, corn has seen a significant increase in price.

   a. Explain how the cost of energy can be both a fixed cost and a variable cost for a company.

   b. Suppose energy is a fixed cost and energy prices rise. What happens to the company's average total cost curve? What happens to its marginal cost curve? Illustrate your answer with a diagram.

   c. Explain why the cost of corn is a variable cost but not a fixed cost for an ethanol producer.

   d. When the cost of corn goes up, what happens to the average total cost curve of an ethanol producer? What happens to its marginal cost curve? Illustrate your answer with a diagram.

2. Marty's Frozen Yogurt is a small shop that sells cups of frozen yogurt in a university town. Marty owns three frozen-yogurt machines. His other inputs are refrigerators, frozen-yogurt mix, cups, sprinkle toppings, and, of course, workers. He estimates that his daily production function when he varies the number of workers employed (and at the same time, of course, yogurt mix, cups, and so on) is as shown in the accompanying table.

Quantity of labor (workers)	Quantity of frozen yogurt (cups)
0	0
1	110
2	200
3	270
4	300
5	320
6	330

   a. What are the fixed inputs and variable inputs in the production of cups of frozen yogurt?

   b. Draw the total product curve. Put the quantity of labor on the horizontal axis and the quantity of frozen yogurt on the vertical axis.

   c. What is the marginal product of the first worker? The second worker? The third worker? Why does marginal product decline as the number of workers increases?

3. The production function for Marty's Frozen Yogurt is given in Problem 2. Marty pays each of his workers $80 per day. The cost of his other variable inputs is $0.50 per cup of yogurt. His fixed cost is $100 per day.

   a. What is Marty's variable cost and total cost when he produces 110 cups of yogurt? 200 cups? Calculate variable and total cost for every level of output given in Problem 2.

   b. Draw Marty's variable cost curve. On the same diagram, draw his total cost curve.

   c. What is the marginal cost per cup for the first 110 cups of yogurt? For the next 90 cups? Calculate the marginal cost for all remaining levels of output.

4. The production function for Marty's Frozen Yogurt is given in Problem 2. The costs are given in Problem 3.

   a. For each of the given levels of output, calculate the average fixed cost (*AFC*), average variable cost (*AVC*), and average total cost (*ATC*) per cup of frozen yogurt.

   b. On one diagram, draw the *AFC*, *AVC*, and *ATC* curves.

   c. What principle explains why the *AFC* declines as output increases? What principle explains why the *AVC* increases as output increases? Explain your answers.

   d. How many cups of frozen yogurt are produced when average total cost is minimized?

5. Labor costs represent a large percentage of total costs for many firms. According to data from the Bureau of Labor Statistics, U.S. labor costs were up 2.0% in 2019, compared to 2018.

   a. When labor costs increase, what happens to average total cost and marginal cost? Consider a case in which labor costs are only variable costs and a case in which they are both variable and fixed costs.

An increase in labor productivity means each worker can produce more output. Recent data on productivity show that labor productivity in the U.S. nonfarm business sector grew by 1.7% between 1970 and 1999, by 2.6% between 2000 and 2009, and by 1.0% between 2010 and 2019.

   b. When productivity growth is positive, what happens to the total product curve and the marginal product of labor curve? Illustrate your answer with a diagram.

   c. When productivity growth is positive, what happens to the marginal cost curve and the average total cost curve? Illustrate your answer with a diagram.

d. If labor costs are rising over time on average, why would a company want to adopt equipment and methods that increase labor productivity?

6. Magnificent Blooms is a florist specializing in floral arrangements for weddings, graduations, and other events. Magnificent Blooms has a fixed cost associated with space and equipment of $100 per day. Each worker is paid $50 per day. The daily production function for Magnificent Blooms is shown in the accompanying table.

Quantity of labor (workers)	Quantity of floral arrangements
0	0
1	5
2	9
3	12
4	14
5	15

a. Calculate the marginal product of each worker. What principle explains why the marginal product per worker declines as the number of workers employed increases?

b. Calculate the marginal cost of each level of output. What principle explains why the marginal cost per floral arrangement increases as the number of arrangements increases?

7. You have the information shown in the accompanying table about a firm's costs. Complete the missing data.

Quantity of output	TC	MC	ATC	AVC
0	$20		—	—
		$20		
1	?		?	?
		10		
2	?		?	?
		16		
3	?		?	?
		20		
4	?		?	?
		24		
5	?		?	?

8. Evaluate each of the following statements. If a statement is true, explain why; if it is false, identify the mistake and try to correct it.

a. A decreasing marginal product tells us that marginal cost must be rising.

b. An increase in fixed cost increases the minimum-cost output.

c. An increase in fixed cost increases marginal cost.

d. When marginal cost is above average total cost, average total cost must be falling.

9. Sandra and Trey operate a small company that produces souvenir footballs. Their fixed cost is $2,000 per

month. They can hire workers for $1,000 per worker per month. Their monthly production function for footballs is as given in the accompanying table.

Quantity of labor (workers)	Quantity of footballs
0	0
1	300
2	800
3	1,200
4	1,400
5	1,500

a. For each quantity of labor, calculate average variable cost (*AVC*), average fixed cost (*AFC*), average total cost (*ATC*), and marginal cost (*MC*).

b. On one diagram, draw the *AVC*, *ATC*, and *MC* curves.

c. At what level of output is Sandra and Trey's average total cost minimized?

10. You produce widgets. Currently you produce four widgets at a total cost of $40.

a. What is your average total cost?

b. Suppose you could produce one more (the fifth) widget at a marginal cost of $5. If you do produce that fifth widget, what will your average total cost be? Has your average total cost increased or decreased? Why?

c. Suppose instead that you could produce one more (the fifth) widget at a marginal cost of $20. If you do produce that fifth widget, what will your average total cost be? Has your average total cost increased or decreased? Why?

11. In 2017, Tesla Motors released the Model 3. The Model 3 is an all-wheel-drive, luxury sedan. It uses no gasoline and has a range of 220 to 310 miles per charge. Pre-orders for the Model 3 exceeded 450,000 units. To meet demand for the Model 3, Tesla announced it will increase production at its production facility to 6,000 cars per week, or about 300,000 cars per year. Currently, the plant is equipped to produce about 100,000 cars per year. Using the table:

a. Find Tesla's average total cost of production across the various plants for each level of production.

b. Explain why the production costs with size A plant are higher than they would be if Tesla could build a new plant that was equipped to produce 300,000 vehicles.

	Total cost (billions of U.S. dollars)		
Plant size	100,000 cars sold	200,000 cars sold	300,000 cars sold
A	$1.75	$3.25	$5.50
B	2.00	3.00	5.00
C	2.50	4.00	4.50

12. Daniella owns a small concrete-mixing company. Her fixed cost is the cost of the concrete-batching machinery and her mixer trucks. Her variable cost is the cost of the sand, gravel, and other inputs for producing concrete; the gas and maintenance for the machinery and trucks; and her workers. She is trying to decide how many mixer trucks to purchase. She has estimated the costs shown in the accompanying table based on estimates of the number of orders her company will receive per week.

Quantity of trucks	FC	VC		
		20 orders	40 orders	60 orders
2	$6,000	$2,000	$5,000	$12,000
3	7,000	1,800	3,800	10,800
4	8,000	1,200	3,600	8,400

 a. For each level of fixed cost, calculate Daniella's total cost for producing 20, 40, and 60 orders per week.

 b. If Daniella is producing 20 orders per week, how many trucks should she purchase and what will her average total cost be? Answer the same questions for 40 and 60 orders per week.

13. Consider Daniella's concrete-mixing business described in Problem 12. Assume that Daniella purchased 3 trucks, expecting to produce 40 orders per week.

 a. Suppose that, in the short run, business declines to 20 orders per week. What is Daniella's average total cost per order in the short run? What will her average total cost per order in the short run be if her business booms to 60 orders per week?

 b. What is Daniella's long-run average total cost for 20 orders per week? Explain why her short-run average total cost of producing 20 orders per week when the number of trucks is fixed at 3 is greater than her long-run average total cost of producing 20 orders per week.

 c. Draw Daniella's long-run average total cost curve. Draw her short-run average total cost curve if she owns 3 trucks.

14. True or false? Explain your reasoning.

 a. The short-run average total cost can never be less than the long-run average total cost.

 b. The short-run average variable cost can never be less than the long-run average total cost.

 c. In the long run, choosing a higher level of fixed cost shifts the long-run average total cost curve upward.

15. Wolfsburg Wagon (WW) is a small automaker. The accompanying table shows WW's long-run average total cost.

Quantity of cars	LRATC of car
1	$30,000
2	20,000
3	15,000
4	12,000
5	12,000
6	12,000
7	14,000
8	18,000

 a. For which levels of output does WW experience increasing returns to scale?

 b. For which levels of output does WW experience decreasing returns to scale?

 c. For which levels of output does WW experience constant returns to scale?

WORK IT OUT

16. The accompanying table shows a car manufacturer's total cost of producing cars.

Quantity of cars	TC
0	$500,000
1	540,000
2	560,000
3	570,000
4	590,000
5	620,000
6	660,000
7	720,000
8	800,000
9	920,000
10	1,100,000

 a. What is this manufacturer's fixed cost?

 b. For each level of output, calculate the variable cost (VC). For each level of output except zero output, calculate the average variable cost (AVC), average total cost (ATC), and average fixed cost (AFC). What is the minimum-cost output?

 c. For each level of output, calculate this manufacturer's marginal cost (MC).

 d. On one diagram, draw the manufacturer's AVC, ATC, and MC curves. ■

12 Perfect Competition and the Supply Curve

DECK THE HALLS

ONE SURE SIGN it's the holiday season is the sudden appearance of Christmas tree sellers, who set up shop in vacant lots, parking lots, and garden centers all across the country. Until the 1950s, virtually all Christmas trees were obtained by individuals going to local forests to cut down their own. However, by the 1950s increased demand from population growth and diminished supply from the loss of forests created a market opportunity. Seeing an ability to profit by growing and selling Christmas trees, farmers responded.

Joe Raedle/Getty Images

Whether it's Christmas trees or smartphones, how a good is produced determines its cost of production.

So rather than venturing into the forest to cut your own tree, you now have a wide range of tree sizes and varieties to choose from — and they are available close to home. In 2018, nearly 33 million farmed trees were sold in the United States for a total of over $2 billion.

Note that the supply of Christmas trees is relatively price inelastic for two reasons: it takes time to acquire land for planting, and it takes time for the trees to grow. However, these limits apply only in the short run. Over time, farms that are already in operation can increase

their capacity and new tree farmers can enter the business. And, over time, the trees will mature and be ready to harvest. Additionally, if prices of live trees continue to increase while artificial trees become cheaper, many consumers will buy artificial trees. So the increase in the quantity supplied in response to an increase in price will be much larger in the long run than in the short run.

Where does the supply curve come from? Why is there a difference between the short-run and the long-run supply curve? In this chapter we will use our understanding of costs, developed in Chapter 11, as the basis for an analysis of the supply curve. As we'll see, this will require that we understand the behavior both of individual firms and of an entire industry, composed of these many individual firms.

Our analysis in this chapter assumes that the industry in question is characterized by *perfect competition*. We begin by explaining the concept of perfect competition, providing a brief introduction to the conditions that give rise to a perfectly competitive industry. We then show how a producer under perfect competition decides how much to produce. Finally, we use the cost curves of the individual producers to derive the *industry supply curve* under perfect competition.

By analyzing the way a competitive industry evolves over time, we will come to understand the distinction between the short-run and long-run effects of changes in demand on a competitive industry — such as, for example, the effect of America's preference for readily available trees for the holidays on the Christmas tree farming industry. We will conclude with a deeper discussion of the conditions necessary for an industry to be perfectly competitive. ●

WHAT YOU WILL LEARN

- What is perfect competition and why do economists consider it an important benchmark?
- What factors make a firm or an industry perfectly competitive?
- How does a **perfectly competitive industry** determine the profit-maximizing output level?
- What determines if a firm is profitable or unprofitable?
- Why does it make sense for a firm to behave differently in the short run versus the long run?
- How does the **short-run industry supply curve** differ from the **long-run industry supply curve**?

A **price-taking producer** is a producer whose actions have no effect on the market price of the good or service it sells.

A **price-taking consumer** is a consumer whose actions have no effect on the market price of the good or service that consumer buys.

A **perfectly competitive market** is a market in which all market participants are price-takers.

A **perfectly competitive industry** is an industry in which producers are price-takers.

‖ Perfect Competition

Suppose that Yves and Zoe are neighboring farmers, both of whom grow Christmas trees. Both sell their output to the same set of Christmas tree consumers so, in a real sense, Yves and Zoe compete with each other.

Does this mean that Yves should try to stop Zoe from growing Christmas trees or that Yves and Zoe should form an agreement to grow less? Almost certainly not: there are thousands of Christmas tree farmers, and Yves and Zoe are competing with all those other growers as well as with each other. Because so many farmers sell Christmas trees, if any one of them produced more or less, there would be no measurable effect on market prices.

When people talk about business competition, the image they often have in mind is a situation in which two or three rival firms are intensely struggling for advantage. But economists know that when an industry consists of a few main competitors, it's actually a sign that competition is fairly limited. As the example of Christmas trees suggests, when there is enough competition, it doesn't even make sense to identify your rivals: there are so many competitors that you cannot single out any one of them as a rival.

We can put it another way: Yves and Zoe are **price-taking producers.** A producer is a price-taker when its actions cannot affect the market price of the good or service it sells. As a result, a price-taking producer considers the market price as given. When there is enough competition—when competition is what economists call "perfect"—then every producer is a price-taker.

And there is a similar definition for consumers: a **price-taking consumer** is a consumer who cannot influence the market price of the good or service by their actions. That is, the market price is unaffected by how much or how little of the good the consumer buys.

Defining Perfect Competition

In a **perfectly competitive market,** all market participants, both consumers and producers, are price-takers. That is, neither consumption decisions by individual consumers nor production decisions by individual producers affect the market price of the good.

The supply and demand model, which we introduced in Chapter 3 and have used repeatedly since then, is a model of a perfectly competitive market. It depends fundamentally on the assumption that no individual buyer or seller of a good, such as coffee beans or Christmas trees, believes that it is possible to affect the price at which they can buy or sell the good.

As a general rule, consumers are indeed price-takers. Instances in which consumers are able to affect the prices they pay are rare. It is, however, quite common for producers to have a significant ability to affect the prices they receive, a phenomenon we'll address in the next chapter. So the model of perfect competition is appropriate for some but not all markets. An industry in which producers are price-takers is called a **perfectly competitive industry.** Clearly, some industries aren't perfectly competitive; in later chapters we'll learn how to analyze industries that don't fit the perfectly competitive model.

Under what circumstances will all producers be price-takers? In the next section we will find that there are two necessary conditions for a perfectly competitive industry and that a third condition is often present as well.

Two Necessary Conditions for Perfect Competition

The markets for major grains, like wheat and corn, are perfectly competitive: individual wheat and corn farmers, as well as individual buyers of wheat and corn, take market prices as given. In contrast, the markets for some of the food items made from these grains—in particular, breakfast cereals—are by no means perfectly competitive. There is intense competition among cereal brands, but not *perfect* competition. To understand the difference between the market for wheat and the market for shredded wheat cereal is to understand the importance of the two necessary conditions for perfect competition.

First, for an industry to be perfectly competitive, it must contain many producers, none of whom have a large **market share.** A producer's market share is the fraction of the total industry output accounted for by that producer's output. The distribution of market share constitutes a major difference between the grain industry and the breakfast cereal industry. There are thousands of wheat farmers, none of whom account for more than a tiny fraction of total wheat sales.

The breakfast cereal industry, however, is dominated by four producers: Kellogg's, General Mills, Post Foods, and Quaker. Kellogg's and General Mills alone account for 85% of all cereal sales in the United States. Kellogg's executives know that if they try to sell more cornflakes, they are likely to drive down the market price of cornflakes. That is, they know that their actions influence market prices, simply because they are such a large part of the market that changes in their production will significantly affect the overall quantity supplied. It makes sense to assume that producers are price-takers only when an industry does *not* contain any large producers like Kellogg's.

Second, an industry can be perfectly competitive only if consumers regard the products of all producers as equivalent. This clearly isn't true in the breakfast cereal market: consumers don't consider Cap'n Crunch to be a good substitute for Wheaties. As a result, the maker of Wheaties has some ability to increase its price without fear that it will lose all its customers to the maker of Cap'n Crunch.

Contrast this with the case of a **standardized product,** which is a product that consumers regard as the same good even when it comes from different producers, sometimes known as a **commodity.** Because wheat is a standardized product, consumers regard the output of one wheat producer as a perfect substitute for that of another producer. Consequently, one farmer cannot increase the price for their wheat without losing all sales to other wheat farmers. *So the second necessary condition for a competitive industry is that the industry output is a standardized product* (see the accompanying For Inquiring Minds).

> A producer's **market share** is the fraction of the total industry output accounted for by that producer's output.
>
> A good is a **standardized product,** also known as a **commodity,** when consumers regard the products of different producers as the same good.

FOR INQUIRING MINDS **What's a Standardized Product?**

A perfectly competitive industry must produce a standardized product. But is it enough for the products of different firms actually to be the same? No: people must also *think* that they are the same. And producers often go to great lengths to convince consumers that they have a distinctive, or *differentiated*, product, even when they don't.

Consider, for example, champagne — not the superexpensive premium champagnes but the more ordinary stuff. Most people cannot tell the difference between champagne actually produced in the Champagne region of France, where the product originated, and similar products from Spain or California. But the French government has sought and obtained legal protection for the winemakers of Champagne, ensuring that around the

world only bubbly wine from that region can be called champagne. If it's from someplace else, all the seller can do is say that it was produced using the *méthode Champenoise*. This creates a differentiation in the minds of consumers and lets the champagne producers of Champagne charge higher prices.

Similarly, Korean producers of kimchi, the spicy fermented cabbage that is the Korean national side dish, are doing their best to convince consumers that the same product packaged by Japanese firms is just not the real thing. The purpose is, of course, to ensure higher prices for Korean kimchi.

So is an industry perfectly competitive if it sells products that are indistinguishable except in name but that consumers, for whatever reason, don't think

If you can't be persuaded to pay more for Korean kimchi than for Japanese kimchi, then kimchi is a standardized product.

are standardized? No. When it comes to defining the nature of competition, the consumer is always right.

An industry has **free entry and exit** when new producers can easily enter into an industry and existing producers can easily leave that industry.

Free Entry and Exit

All perfectly competitive industries have many producers with small market shares, producing a standardized product. Most perfectly competitive industries are also characterized by one more feature: it is easy for new firms to enter the industry or for firms that are currently in the industry to leave. That is, no obstacles in the form of government regulations or limited access to key resources prevent new producers from entering the market. And no additional costs are associated with shutting down a company and leaving the industry.

Economists refer to the arrival of new firms into an industry as *entry;* they refer to the departure of firms from an industry as *exit.* When there are no obstacles to entry into or exit from an industry, we say that the industry has **free entry and exit.**

Free entry and exit is not strictly necessary for perfect competition. In Chapter 5 we described the case of Alaskan crab fishing, where regulations place a quota on the amount of Alaskan crab that can be caught during a season, so entry is limited to established boat owners that have been given quotas. Despite this, there are enough boats operating that the crab fisherman are price-takers. But free entry and exit is a key factor in most competitive industries. It ensures that the number of producers in an industry can adjust to changing market conditions. And, in particular, it ensures that producers in an industry cannot act to keep new firms out.

To sum up, then, perfect competition depends on two necessary conditions.

1. The industry must contain many producers, each having a small market share.
2. The industry must produce a standardized product.

In addition, perfectly competitive industries are normally characterized by free entry and exit.

How does an industry that meets these three criteria behave? As a first step toward answering that question, let's look at how an individual producer in a perfectly competitive industry maximizes profit.

ECONOMICS >> *in Action*
Pay-for-Delay Runs Out of Time

Sometimes it is possible to watch as a market becomes perfectly competitive. This is the case in the pharmaceutical industry, when the patent on a popular drug expires and a *generic* rival drug enters the market served by that drug.

Let's start with some background on why the market was originally uncompetitive. A company that develops a new drug is given a *patent*, which gives it a *legal monopoly*—the exclusive right to sell the drug—for 20 years. Legally, no one else can sell the drug without the patent-holder's permission. This allows the developer to recoup the costs of development.

When the patent expires after 20 years, the market is open for entry by other companies to produce and sell *generics*, alternative but medically equivalent versions of the drug. As a result, the price drops dramatically. On average, a generic drug costs about 15% of the price of the equivalent patent-protected drug, which will lose up to 90% of its market share. In the case of Lipitor, Pfizer's blockbuster drug for cholesterol, the generic version was only 8% of the price of Lipitor.

That sequence of events is what is *supposed* to happen. However, makers of the original patent-protected drugs have

Patents allow drug makers to have a legal monopoly on new medications for 20 years.

employed a variety of strategies to block or forestall the entry of generic competitors. One very successful tactic has been *pay-for-delay,* an agreement in which the patent holder pays the generic drug maker to delay the entry of the generic drug in return for compensation. As a result, the patent holder continues to charge high prices, the generic drug maker gets a lucrative payment, and the consumer suffers.

In 2012 and 2013, at the height of the use of pay-for-delay agreements, the Federal Trade Commission (FTC) estimated that as many as 142 generic versions of patented drugs had been delayed an average of five years, and as long as nine years in some cases. The agency estimated that pay-for-delay agreements cost consumers an estimated $3.5 billion dollars annually from 2005 to 2013. But the situation changed drastically in 2014, when U.S. Supreme Court ruled that federal regulators had the authority to prosecute pay-for-delay deals as anti-competitive. Subsequently, the number of such deals dropped dramatically. With its new authority, the Federal Trade Commission scored a $1.2 billion settlement from drug maker Teva over allegations it engaged in pay for delay over their sleep-disorder drug Provigil. In addition, in 2019 Teva had to pay consumers nearly $66 million for its anti-competitive behavior. For the pharmaceutical industry, pay-for-delay has clearly run out of time.

>> Check Your Understanding 12-1

Solutions appear at back of book.

1. In each of the following situations, do you think the industry described will be perfectly competitive or not? Explain your answer.
   a. There are two producers of aluminum in the world, a good sold in many places.
   b. The price of natural gas is determined by global supply and demand. A small share of that global supply is produced by a handful of companies located in the North Sea.
   c. Dozens of designers sell high-fashion clothes. Each designer has a distinctive style and a loyal clientele.
   d. There are many baseball teams in the United States, one or two in each major city and each selling tickets to its hometown events.

>> Quick Review

- Neither the actions of a **price-taking producer** nor those of a **price-taking consumer** can influence the market price of a good.

- In a **perfectly competitive market** all producers and consumers are price-takers. Consumers are almost always price-takers, but this is often not true of producers. An industry in which producers are price-takers is a **perfectly competitive industry.**

- A perfectly competitive industry contains many producers, each of which produces a standardized **product** (also known as a **commodity**) but none of which has a large **market share.**

- Most perfectly competitive industries are also characterized by **free entry and exit.**

‖ Production and Profits

Consider Noelle, who runs a Christmas tree farm. Suppose that the market price of Christmas trees is $72 per tree and that Noelle is a price-taker—she can sell as many as she likes at that price. Then we can use the data in Table 12-1 to find her profit-maximizing level of output by direct calculation.

The first column shows the quantity of output in number of trees, and the second column shows Noelle's total revenue from her output: the market value of trees she produced. Total revenue, *TR,* is equal to the market price multiplied by the quantity of output:

(12-1) $TR = P \times Q$

In this example, total revenue is equal to $72 per tree times the quantity of output in trees.

The third column of Table 12-1 shows Noelle's total cost. The fourth column shows her profit, equal to total revenue minus total cost:

(12-2) Profit = $TR - TC$

As indicated by the numbers in the table, profit is maximized at an output of 50 trees, where profit is equal to $720. But we can gain more insight into the profit-maximizing choice of output by viewing it as a problem of marginal analysis, a task we'll do next.

TABLE 12-1 Profit for Noelle's Farm When Market Price Is $72

Quantity of trees *Q*	Total revenue *TR*	Total cost *TC*	Profit *TR – TC*
0	$0	$560	–$560
10	720	1,200	–480
20	1,440	1,440	0
30	2,160	1,760	400
40	2,880	2,240	640
50	3,600	2,880	720
60	4,320	3,680	640
70	5,040	4,640	400

Marginal revenue is the change in total revenue generated by an additional unit of output.

According to the **optimal output rule,** profit is maximized by producing the quantity of output at which the marginal revenue of the last unit produced is equal to its marginal cost.

Using Marginal Analysis to Choose the Profit-Maximizing Quantity of Output

Recall from Chapter 9 the *profit-maximizing principle of marginal analysis:* the optimal amount of an activity is the level at which marginal benefit is equal to marginal cost. To apply this principle, consider the effect on a producer's profit of increasing output by one unit. The marginal benefit of that unit is the additional revenue generated by selling it; this measure has a name—it is called the **marginal revenue** of that unit of output. The general formula for marginal revenue is:

(12-3) Marginal revenue = $\dfrac{\text{Change in total revenue generated by one additional unit of output}}{} = \dfrac{\text{Change in total revenue}}{\text{Change in quantity of output}}$

or

$$MR = \frac{\Delta TR}{\Delta Q}$$

So Noelle maximizes her profit by producing trees up to the point at which the marginal revenue is equal to marginal cost. We can summarize this as the producer's **optimal output rule:** profit is maximized by producing the quantity at which the marginal revenue of the last unit produced is equal to its marginal cost. That is, $MR = MC$ at the optimal quantity of output.

We can learn how to apply the optimal output rule with the help of Table 12-2, which provides various short-run cost measures for Noelle's farm. The second column contains the farm's variable cost, and the third column shows its total cost of output based on the assumption that the farm incurs a fixed cost of $560. The fourth column shows marginal cost. Notice that, in this example, the marginal cost initially falls but then rises as output increases. This gives the marginal cost curve the "swoosh" shape described in Chapter 11. Shortly it will become clear that this shape has important implications for short-run production decisions.

The fifth column contains the farm's marginal revenue, which has an important feature: Noelle's marginal revenue equal to price is constant at $72 for every output level.

TABLE 12-2 Short-Run Costs for Noelle's Farm

Quantity of trees Q	Variable cost VC	Total cost TC	Marginal cost of tree $MC = \Delta TC / \Delta Q$	Marginal revenue of tree MR	Net gain of tree = MR − MC
0	$0	$560			
			$64	$72	$8
10	640	1,200			
			24	72	48
20	880	1,440			
			32	72	40
30	1,200	1,760			
			48	72	24
40	1,680	2,240			
			64	72	8
50	2,320	2,880			
			80	72	−8
60	3,120	3,680			
			96	72	−24
70	4,080	4,640			

The sixth and final column shows the calculation of the net gain per tree, which is equal to marginal revenue minus marginal cost—or, equivalently in this case, market price minus marginal cost. As you can see, it is positive for the 1st through 50th trees; producing each of these trees raises Noelle's profit. For the 51st through 70th trees, however, net gain is negative: producing them would decrease, not increase, profit. So to maximize profits, Noelle will produce up to the point at which the marginal revenue of the last unit produced is greater than or equal to the marginal cost of the last unit produced; any more reduces her profit. Hence, 50 trees is Noelle's profit-maximizing output.

Because Noelle receives $72 for every tree produced, we know that her farm is a price-taking firm. A price-taking firm cannot influence the market price by its actions. It always takes the market price as given because it cannot lower the market price by selling more or raise the market price by selling less. So, for a price-taking firm, the additional revenue generated by producing one more unit is always the market price. Be sure to keep this fact in mind in future chapters, where

FIGURE 12-1 The Price-Taking Firm's Profit-Maximizing Quantity of Output

At the profit-maximizing quantity of output, the market price is equal to marginal cost. It is located at the point where the marginal cost curve crosses the marginal revenue curve, which is a horizontal line at the market price. Here, the profit-maximizing point is at an output of 50 trees, the output quantity at point E.

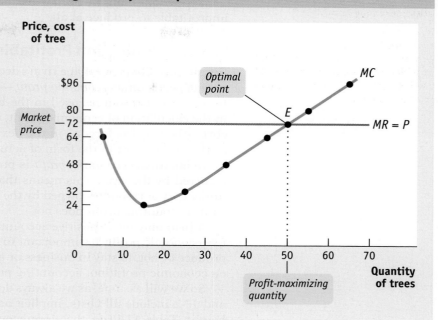

we will learn that marginal revenue is not equal to the market price if the industry is not perfectly competitive. As a result, firms are not price-takers when an industry is not perfectly competitive. For the remainder of this chapter, we will assume that the industry in question is like Christmas tree farming, perfectly competitive.

Figure 12-1 shows that Noelle's profit-maximizing quantity of output is, indeed, 50 trees. The figure shows the marginal cost curve, *MC*, drawn from the data in the fourth column of Table 12-2. As in Chapter 9, we plot the marginal cost of increasing output from 10 to 20 trees halfway between 10 and 20, and so on. The *MC* curve is smooth, allowing us to see how *MC* changes as one more tree is produced. The horizontal line at $72 is Noelle's **marginal revenue curve**.

Note that whenever a firm is a price-taker, its marginal revenue curve is a horizontal line at the market price: it can sell as much as it likes at the market price. Regardless of whether it sells more or less, the market price is unaffected. *In effect, the individual firm faces a horizontal,* perfectly elastic demand curve for its output—an individual demand curve for its output that is equivalent to its marginal revenue curve. The marginal cost curve crosses the marginal revenue curve at point *E* where *MC* = *MR*. Sure enough, the quantity of output at *E* is 50 trees.

This example illustrates another general rule derived from marginal analysis— the **price-taking firm's optimal output rule,** which says that a price-taking firm's profit is maximized by producing the quantity of output up to the point at which the market price is equal to the marginal cost of the last unit produced. That is, *P* = *MC* at the price-taking firm's optimal quantity of output. In fact, the price-taking firm's optimal output rule is just an application of the optimal output rule to the particular case of a price-taking firm. Why? Because *in the case of a price-taking firm, marginal revenue is equal to the market price.*

Does this mean that the price-taking firm's production decision can be entirely summed up as "produce up to the point where the marginal cost of production is equal to the price"? No, not quite. Before applying the profit-maximizing principle of marginal analysis to determine how much to produce, a potential producer must as a first step answer an "either–or" question: should it produce at all? If the answer to that question is yes, it then proceeds to the second step—a "how much" decision: maximizing profit by choosing the quantity of output at which marginal cost is equal to price.

PITFALLS

WHAT IF MARGINAL REVENUE AND MARGINAL COST AREN'T EXACTLY EQUAL?

The optimal output rule says that to maximize profit, you should produce the quantity at which marginal revenue is equal to marginal cost. But what do you do if there is no output level at which marginal revenue exactly equals marginal cost? In that case, you produce the largest quantity for which marginal revenue exceeds marginal cost. The simpler version of the optimal output rule applies when production involves large numbers, such as hundreds or thousands of units. In such cases marginal cost comes in small increments, and there is always a level of output at which marginal cost almost exactly equals marginal revenue.

The **marginal revenue curve** shows how marginal revenue varies as output varies.

According to the **price-taking firm's optimal output rule,** a price-taking firm's profit is maximized by producing the quantity of output at which the market price is equal to the marginal cost of the last unit produced.

To understand why the first step in the production decision involves an "either–or" question, we need to ask how we determine whether it is profitable or unprofitable to produce at all.

When Is Production Profitable?

Recall from Chapter 9 that a firm's decision whether or not to stay in a given business depends on its *economic profit*—the measure of profit based on the opportunity cost of resources used in the business. To put it a slightly different way: in the calculation of economic profit, a firm's total cost incorporates the implicit cost—the benefits forgone in the next best use of the firm's resources—as well as the explicit cost in the form of actual cash outlays.

In contrast, *accounting profit* is profit calculated using only the explicit costs incurred by the firm. This means that economic profit incorporates the opportunity cost of resources owned by the firm and used in the production of output, while accounting profit does not.

A firm may make positive accounting profit while making zero or even negative economic profit. It's important to understand clearly that a firm's decision to produce or not, to stay in business or to close down permanently, should be based on economic profit, not accounting profit.

So we will assume, as we always do, that the cost numbers given in Tables 12-1 and 12-2 include all costs, implicit as well as explicit, and that the profit numbers in Table 12-1 are therefore economic profit. So what determines whether Noelle's farm earns a profit or generates a loss? The answer is that, *given the farm's cost curves, whether or not it is profitable depends on the market price of trees— specifically, whether the market price is more or less than the farm's minimum average total cost.*

In Table 12-3 we calculate short-run average variable cost and short-run average total cost for Noelle's farm. These are short-run values because we take fixed cost as given. (We'll turn to the effects of changing fixed cost shortly.) The short-run average total cost curve, *ATC*, is shown in Figure 12-2, along with the marginal cost curve, *MC*, from Figure 12-1. As you can see, average total cost is minimized at point *C*, corresponding to an output of 40 trees—the *minimum-cost output*—and an average total cost of $56 per tree.

TABLE 12-3 Short-Run Average Costs for Noelle's Farm

Quantity of trees Q	Variable cost VC	Total cost TC	Short-run average variable cost of tree $AVC = VC/Q$	Short-run average total cost of tree $ATC = TC/Q$
10	$640.00	$1,200.00	$64.00	$120.00
20	880.00	1,440.00	44.00	72.00
30	1,200.00	1,760.00	40.00	58.67
40	1,680.00	2,240.00	42.00	56.00
50	2,320.00	2,880.00	46.40	57.60
60	3,120.00	3,680.00	52.00	61.33
70	4,080.00	4,640.00	58.29	66.29

To see how these curves can be used to decide whether production is profitable or unprofitable, recall that profit is equal to total revenue minus total cost, $TR - TC$. This means:

- If the firm produces a quantity at which $TR > TC$, the firm is profitable.
- If the firm produces a quantity at which $TR = TC$, the firm breaks even.
- If the firm produces a quantity at which $TR < TC$, the firm incurs a loss.

We can also express this idea in terms of revenue and cost per unit of output. If we divide profit by the number of units of output, Q, we obtain the following expression for profit per unit of output:

(12-4) $\text{Profit}/Q = TR/Q - TC/Q$

TR/Q is average revenue, which is the market price. TC/Q is average total cost. So a firm is profitable if the market price for its product is more than the average total cost of the quantity the firm produces; a firm loses money if the

FIGURE 12-2 Costs and Production in the Short Run

This figure shows the marginal cost curve, *MC,* and the short-run average total cost curve, *ATC.* When the market price is $56, output will be 40 trees (the minimum-cost output), represented by point *C.* The price of $56, equal to the firm's minimum average total cost, is the firm's *break-even price.*

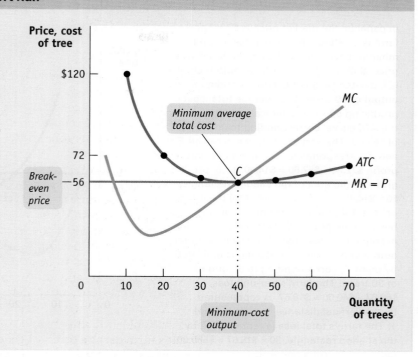

market price is less than average total cost of the quantity the firm produces. This means:

- If the firm produces a quantity at which $P > ATC,$ the firm is profitable.
- If the firm produces a quantity at which $P = ATC,$ the firm breaks even.
- If the firm produces a quantity at which $P < ATC,$ the firm incurs a loss.

Figure 12-3 illustrates this result, showing how the market price determines whether a firm is profitable. It also shows how profits are depicted graphically. Each panel shows the marginal cost curve, *MC,* and the short-run average total cost curve, *ATC.* Average total cost is minimized at point *C.* Panel (a) shows the case we have already analyzed, in which the market price of trees is $72 per tree. Panel (b) shows the case in which the market price of trees is lower, $40 per tree.

In panel (a), we see that at a price of $72 per tree the profit-maximizing quantity of output is 50 trees, indicated by point *E,* where the marginal cost curve, *MC,* intersects the marginal revenue curve—which for a price-taking firm is a horizontal line at the market price. At that quantity of output, average total cost is $57.60 per tree, indicated by point *Z.* Since the price per tree exceeds average total cost per tree, Noelle's farm is profitable.

Noelle's total profit when the market price is $72 is represented by the area of the shaded rectangle in panel (a). To see why, notice that total profit can be expressed in terms of profit per unit:

(12-5) $\text{Profit} = TR - TC = (TR/Q - TC/Q) \times Q$

or, equivalently,

$$\text{Profit} = (P - ATC) \times Q$$

since *P* is equal to *TR/Q* and *ATC* is equal to *TC/Q.* The height of the shaded rectangle in panel (a) corresponds to the vertical distance between points *E* and *Z.* It is equal to $P - ATC = \$72.00 - \$57.60 = \$14.40$ per tree. The shaded rectangle has a width equal to the output: $Q = 50$ trees. So the area of that rectangle is equal

FIGURE 12-3 Profitability and the Market Price

In panel (a) the market price is $72. The farm is profitable because price exceeds minimum average total cost, the break-even price, $56. The farm's optimal output choice is indicated by point E, corresponding to an output of 50 trees. The average total cost of producing 50 trees is indicated by point Z on the ATC curve, corresponding to an amount of $57.60. The vertical distance between E and Z corresponds to the farm's per-unit profit, $72.00 − $57.60 = $14.40. Total profit is given by the area of the shaded rectangle, $50 \times $14.40 = 720.00. In panel (b) the market price is $40; the farm is unprofitable because the price falls below the minimum average total cost, $56. The farm's optimal output choice when producing is indicated by point A, corresponding to an output of 30 trees. The farm's per-unit loss, $58.67 − $40.00 = $18.67, is represented by the vertical distance between A and Y. The farm's total loss is represented by the shaded rectangle, $30 \times $18.67 = 560.00 (adjusted for rounding error).

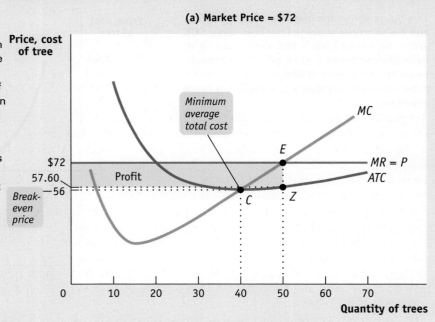

(a) Market Price = $72

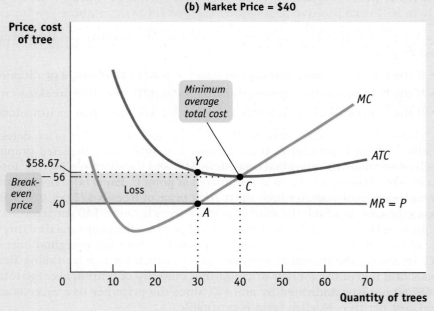

(b) Market Price = $40

to Noelle's profit: 50 trees × $14.40 profit per tree = $720.00 — the same number we calculated in Table 12-1.

What about the situation illustrated in panel (b)? Here the market price of trees is $40 per tree. Setting price equal to marginal cost leads to a profit-maximizing output of 30 trees, indicated by point A. At this output, Noelle has an average total cost of $58.67 per tree, indicated by point Y. At the profit-maximizing output quantity—30 trees—average total cost exceeds the market price. This means that Noelle's farm generates a loss, not a profit.

How much does she lose by producing when the market price is $40? On each tree she loses $ATC − P = $58.67 − $40.00 = 18.67, an amount corresponding to the vertical distance between points *A* and *Y*. And she would produce 30 trees, which corresponds to the width of the shaded rectangle. So the total value of the losses is $18.67 × 30 = $560.00 (adjusted for rounding error), an amount that corresponds to the area of the shaded rectangle in panel (b).

But how does a producer know, in general, whether or not its business will be profitable? It turns out that the crucial test lies in a comparison of the market price to the producer's *minimum average total cost*. On Noelle's farm, minimum average total cost, which is equal to $56, occurs at an output quantity of 40 trees, indicated by point *C*.

Whenever the market price exceeds minimum average total cost, the producer can find some output level for which the average total cost is less than the market price. In other words, the producer can find a level of output at which the firm makes a profit. So Noelle's farm will be profitable whenever the market price exceeds $56. And she will achieve the highest possible profit by producing the quantity at which marginal cost equals the market price.

Conversely, if the market price is less than minimum average total cost, there is no output level at which price exceeds average total cost. As a result, the firm will be unprofitable at any quantity of output. As we saw, at a price of $40—an amount less than minimum average total cost—Noelle did indeed lose money. By producing the quantity at which marginal cost equals the market price, Noelle did the best she could, but the best that she could do was a loss of $560. Any other quantity would have increased the size of her loss.

The minimum average total cost of a price-taking firm is called its **break-even price,** the price at which it earns zero profit. (Recall that's *economic profit*.) A firm will earn positive profit when the market price is above the break-even price, and it will suffer losses when the market price is below the break-even price. Noelle's break-even price of $56 is the price at point *C* in Figures 12-2 and 12-3.

So the rule for determining whether a producer of a good is profitable depends on a comparison of the market price of the good to the producer's break-even price—its minimum average total cost:

* Whenever the market price exceeds minimum average total cost, the producer is profitable.

* Whenever the market price equals minimum average total cost, the producer breaks even.

* Whenever the market price is less than minimum average total cost, the producer is unprofitable.

The Short-Run Production Decision

You might be tempted to say that if a firm is unprofitable because the market price is below its minimum average total cost, it shouldn't produce any output. In the short run, however, this conclusion isn't right.

In the short run, sometimes the firm should produce even if price falls below minimum average total cost. The reason is that total cost includes *fixed cost*—cost that does not depend on the amount of output produced and can only be altered in the long run.

In the short run, fixed cost must still be paid, regardless of whether or not a firm produces. For example, if Noelle rents a refrigerated truck for the year, she has to pay the rent on the truck regardless of whether she produces any trees. *Since it cannot be changed in the short run, her fixed cost is irrelevant to her decision about whether to produce or shut down in the short run.*

Although fixed cost should play no role in the decision about whether to produce in the short run, other costs—variable costs—do matter. An example of variable costs is the wages of workers who must be hired to help with planting

The **break-even price** of a price-taking firm is the market price at which it earns zero profit.

A firm will cease production in the short run if the market price falls below the **shut-down price,** which is equal to minimum average variable cost.

and harvesting. Variable costs can be saved by *not* producing; so they should play a role in determining whether or not to produce in the short run.

Let's turn to Figure 12-4: it shows both the short-run average total cost curve, *ATC,* and the short-run average variable cost curve, *AVC,* drawn from the information in Table 12-3. Recall that the difference between the two curves—the vertical distance between them—represents average fixed cost, the fixed cost per unit of output, *FC/Q.*

Because the marginal cost curve has a "swoosh" shape—falling at first before rising—the short-run average variable cost curve is U-shaped: the initial fall in marginal cost causes average variable cost to fall as well, before rising marginal cost eventually pulls it up again. The short-run average variable cost curve reaches its minimum value of $40 at point *A,* at an output of 30 trees.

We are now prepared to fully analyze the optimal production decision in the short run. We need to consider two cases:

1. When the market price is below minimum average *variable* cost
2. When the market price is greater than or equal to minimum average *variable* cost

When the market price is below minimum average variable cost, the price the firm receives per unit is not covering its variable cost per unit. A firm in this situation should cease production immediately. Why? Because there is no level of output at which the firm's total revenue covers its variable costs—the costs it can avoid by not operating.

In this case the firm maximizes its profits by not producing at all—by, in effect, minimizing its losses. It will still incur a fixed cost in the short run, but it will no longer incur any variable cost. This means that the minimum average variable cost is equal to the **shut-down price,** the price at which the firm ceases production in the short run. In the example of Noelle's tree farm, she will cease production in the short run by laying off workers and halting all planting and harvesting of trees.

When price is greater than minimum average variable cost, however, the firm should produce in the short run. In this case, the firm maximizes profit—or minimizes loss—by choosing the output quantity at which its marginal cost is equal

FIGURE 12-4 The Short-Run Individual Supply Curve

When the market price equals or exceeds Noelle's *shut-down price* of $40, the minimum average variable cost indicated by point *A,* she will produce the output quantity at which marginal cost is equal to price. So at any price equal to or above the minimum average *variable* cost, the short-run individual supply curve is the firm's marginal cost curve; this corresponds to the upward-sloping segment of the individual supply curve. When market price falls below minimum average variable cost, the firm ceases operation in the short run. This corresponds to the vertical segment of the individual supply curve along the vertical axis.

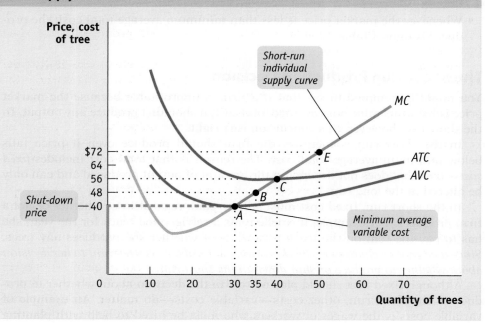

to the market price. For example, if the market price of each tree is $72, Noelle should produce at point *E* in Figure 12-4, corresponding to an output of 50 trees. Note that point *C* in Figure 12-4 corresponds to the farm's break-even price of $56 per tree. Since *E* lies above *C*, Noelle's farm will be profitable; she will generate a per-tree profit of $72.00 – $56.00 = $16.00 when the market price is $72.

But what if the market price lies between the shut-down price and the break-even price—that is, between minimum average *variable* cost and minimum average *total* cost? In the case of Noelle's farm, this corresponds to prices anywhere between $40 and $56—say, a market price of $48. At $48, Noelle's farm is not profitable; since the market price is below minimum average total cost, the farm is losing the difference between price and average total cost per unit produced.

Yet even if it isn't covering its total cost per unit, it is covering its variable cost per unit and some—but not all—of the fixed cost per unit. If a firm in this situation shuts down, it would incur no variable cost but would incur the *full* fixed cost. As a result, shutting down generates an even greater loss than continuing to operate.

This means that whenever price lies between minimum average total cost and minimum average variable cost, the firm is better off producing some output in the short run. The reason is that by producing, it can cover its variable cost per unit and at least some of its fixed cost, even though it is incurring a loss. In this case, the firm maximizes profit—that is, minimizes loss—by choosing the quantity of output at which its marginal cost is equal to the market price. So if Noelle faces a market price of $48 per tree, her profit-maximizing output is given by point *B* in Figure 12-4, corresponding to an output of 35 trees.

It's worth noting that the decision to produce when the firm is covering its variable costs but not all of its fixed cost is similar to the decision to ignore *sunk costs*. You may recall from Chapter 9 that a sunk cost is a cost that has already been incurred and cannot be recouped; and because it cannot be changed, it should have no effect on any current decision.

In the short-run production decision, fixed cost is, in effect, like a sunk cost—it has been spent, and it can't be recovered in the short run. This comparison also illustrates why variable cost does indeed matter in the short run: it can be avoided by not producing.

And what happens if market price is exactly equal to the shut-down price, minimum average variable cost? In this instance, the firm is indifferent between producing 30 units or 0 units. As we'll see shortly, this is an important point when looking at the behavior of an industry as a whole. For the sake of clarity, we'll assume that the firm, although indifferent, does indeed produce output when price is equal to the shut-down price.

Putting everything together, we can now draw the **short-run individual supply curve** of Noelle's farm, the red line in Figure 12-4; it shows how the profit-maximizing quantity of output in the short run depends on the price. As you can see, the curve is in two segments. The upward-sloping red segment starting at point *A* shows the short-run profit-maximizing output when market price is equal to or above the shut-down price of $40 per tree.

As long as the market price is equal to or above the shut-down price, Noelle produces the quantity of output at which marginal cost is equal to the market price. That is, at market prices equal to or above the shut-down price, the firm's short-run supply curve corresponds to its marginal cost curve. But at any market price below minimum average variable cost—in this case, $40 per tree—the firm shuts down and output drops to zero in the short run. This corresponds to the vertical segment of the curve that lies on top of the vertical axis.

Do firms really shut down temporarily without going out of business? Yes. In fact, in some businesses temporary shut-downs are routine. The most common examples are industries in which demand is highly seasonal, like outdoor amusement parks in climates with cold winters. Such parks would have to offer very

The **short-run individual supply curve** shows how an individual producer's profit-maximizing output quantity depends on the market price, taking fixed cost as given.

low prices to entice customers during the colder months—prices so low that the owners would not cover their variable costs (principally wages and electricity). The wiser choice economically is to shut down until warm weather brings enough customers who are willing to pay a higher price.

Changing Fixed Cost

Buying or selling equipment allows a firm to change its fixed cost.

Although fixed cost cannot be altered in the short run, in the long run firms can acquire or get rid of machines, buildings, and so on. In the long run the level of fixed cost is a matter of choice. We saw in Chapter 11 that a firm will choose the level of fixed cost that minimizes the average total cost for its desired output quantity. Now we will focus on an even bigger question facing a firm when choosing its fixed cost: whether to incur *any* fixed cost at all by remaining in its current business.

In the long run, a producer can always eliminate fixed cost by selling off its plant and equipment. If it does so, of course, it can't ever produce—it has exited the industry. In contrast, a potential producer can take on some fixed cost by acquiring machines and other resources, which puts it in a position to produce—it can enter the industry. In most perfectly competitive industries the set of producers, although fixed in the short run, changes in the long run as firms enter or exit the industry.

Consider Noelle's farm once again. In order to simplify our analysis, we will sidestep the problem of choosing among several possible levels of fixed cost. Instead, we will assume from now on that Noelle has only one possible choice of fixed cost if she operates, the amount of $560, Noelle's minimum average total cost, that was the basis for the calculations in Tables 12-1, 12-2, and 12-3. (With this assumption, Noelle's short-run average total cost curve and long-run average total cost curve are one and the same.) Alternatively, she can choose a fixed cost of zero if she exits the industry.

Suppose that the market price of trees is consistently less than $56 over an extended period of time. In that case, Noelle never fully covers her fixed cost: her business runs at a persistent loss. In the long run, then, she can do better by closing her business and leaving the industry. In other words, *in the long run* firms will exit an industry if the market price is consistently less than their break-even price—their minimum average total cost.

Conversely, suppose that the price of Christmas trees is consistently above the break-even price, $56, for an extended period of time. Because her farm is profitable, Noelle will remain in the industry and continue producing.

But things won't stop there. The Christmas tree industry meets the criterion of *free entry:* there are many potential tree producers because the necessary inputs are easy to obtain. And the cost curves of those potential producers are likely to be similar to those of Noelle, since the technology used by other producers is likely to be very similar to that used by Noelle. If the price is high enough to generate profits for existing producers, it will also attract some of these potential producers into the industry. So *in the long run* a price in excess of $56 should lead to entry: new producers will come into the Christmas tree industry.

As we will see next, exit and entry lead to an important distinction between the *short-run industry supply curve* and the *long-run industry supply curve.*

Summing Up: The Perfectly Competitive Firm's Profitability and Production Conditions

In this chapter, we've studied where the supply curve for a perfectly competitive, price-taking firm comes from. Every perfectly competitive firm makes its production decisions by maximizing profit, and these decisions determine the supply curve. Table 12-4 summarizes the perfectly competitive firm's profitability and production conditions. It also relates them to entry into and exit from the industry.

TABLE 12-4 Summary of the Perfectly Competitive Firm's Profitability and Production Conditions

Profitability condition (minimum *ATC* = break-even price)	Result
P > minimum *ATC*	Firm profitable. Entry into industry in the long run.
P = minimum *ATC*	Firm breaks even. No entry into or exit from industry in the long run.
P < minimum *ATC*	Firm unprofitable. Exit from industry in the long run.
Profitability condition (minimum AVC = shut-down price)	**Result**
P > minimum *AVC*	Firm produces in the short run. If *P* < minimum *ATC*, firm covers variable cost and some but not all of fixed cost. If *P* > minimum *ATC*, firm covers all variable cost and fixed cost.
P = minimum *AVC*	Firm indifferent between producing in the short run or not. Just covers variable cost.
P < minimum *AVC*	Firm shuts down in the short run. Does not cover variable cost.

ECONOMICS >> *in Action*
Farmers Know How

If there is one profession that requires a clear understanding of profit-maximization, it's farming. Farmers must respond to constantly fluctuating prices for their output, as well as constantly changing input prices. Furthermore, the farming industry satisfies the condition of a competitive market because it is composed of thousands of individual, price-taking farmers.

For a good illustration of farmers' economic acumen we can examine American crop prices over the past two decades, a period marked by boom and then retrenchment. From 2003 to 2013, prices for corn and soybeans rose to all-time highs, increasing by 300% and 250%, respectively.

The impressive rise in prices from 2003 to 2013 was mainly due to two demand-based factors. First, corn prices benefited from a congressional mandate to increase the use of corn-based ethanol, a biofuel that is blended into gasoline, as a means of reducing American dependency on imported oil. Second, crop prices were pushed upward by rapidly rising exports to China and other developing countries. Being smart profit-maximizers, farmers responded by farming their land more intensively—using more fertilizer, for example—and by increasing their acreage. By 2013, fertilizer prices had doubled compared to 2005. And over the decade from 2003 to 2013, the average price of farmland tripled, with some farmland selling for 10 times its 2003 price.

Each of these strategies made complete economic sense, as each farmer moved up their individual supply curve. And because the individual supply curve is the marginal cost curve, each farmer's costs also went up as more inputs were employed to produce more output.

However, things changed dramatically in 2014, when farmland prices plunged nearly 9% and by 2019 prices were down 23% on an inflation-adjusted basis from their 2013 peak. Various factors related to both the supply and the demand of farmers' output contributed to this fall. On the demand side, the boom in shale oil production, a substitute for ethanol, pushed down the price of ethanol while

Farmers show their economic acumen by moving up and down their supply curves as crop prices change.

R. Hamilton Smith/Getty Images

a strong U.S. dollar reduced the demand by foreign buyers for American crops. More recently, retaliation by the Chinese government against U.S. tariffs imposed in 2018 and 2019 significantly reduced demand for American agricultural products. On the supply side, bumper harvests also sharply depressed crop prices.

Thinking like economists, farmers responded by moving back down their supply curve, withdrawing from production the most expensive land to cultivate and reducing their demand for additional acreage. As a result, the average price of farmland has trended downward. And, unsurprisingly, from 2012 to 2019 the price of fertilizer has fallen significantly, nearly 50%, from its highs. So if you want to see profit-maximization in action, watch a farmer.

>> **Quick Review**

• A producer chooses output according to the **optimal output rule.** For a price-taking firm, **marginal revenue** is equal to price and it chooses output according to the **price-taking firm's optimal output rule,** $P = MC$.

• A firm is profitable whenever price exceeds its **break-even price,** equal to its minimum average total cost. Below that price it is unprofitable. It breaks even when price is equal to its break-even price.

• Fixed cost is irrelevant to the firm's optimal short-run production decision. When price exceeds its **shut-down price,** minimum average variable cost, the price-taking firm produces the quantity of output at which marginal cost equals price. When price is lower than its shut-down price, it ceases production in the short run. This defines the firm's **short-run individual supply curve.**

• Over time, fixed cost matters. If price consistently falls below minimum average total cost, a firm will exit the industry. If price exceeds minimum average total cost, the firm is profitable and will remain in the industry; other firms will enter the industry in the long run.

>> **Check Your Understanding 12-2**

Solutions appear at back of book.

1. Draw a short-run diagram showing a U-shaped average total cost curve, a U-shaped average variable cost curve, and a "swoosh"-shaped marginal cost curve. On it, indicate the range of output and the range of price for which the following actions are optimal.
   a. The firm shuts down immediately.
   b. The firm operates in the short run despite sustaining a loss.
   c. The firm operates while making a profit.
2. Maine has a very active lobster industry, which harvests lobsters during the summer months. The rest of the year lobsters can be obtained from other parts of the world, but at a much higher price. Maine is also full of "lobster shacks," roadside restaurants serving lobster dishes that are open only during the summer. Explain why it is optimal for lobster shacks to operate only in the summer.

‖ The Industry Supply Curve

Why will an increase in the demand for Christmas trees lead to a large price increase at first but a much smaller increase in the long run? The answer lies in the behavior of the **industry supply curve**—the relationship between the price and the total output of an industry as a whole. The industry supply curve is what we referred to in earlier chapters as *the* supply curve or the market supply curve. But here we take some extra care to distinguish between the *individual supply curve* of a single firm and the supply curve of the industry as a whole.

As you might guess from the previous section, the industry supply curve must be analyzed in somewhat different ways for the short run and the long run. Let's start with the short run.

The Short-Run Industry Supply Curve

Recall that in the short run the number of producers in an industry is fixed—there is no entry or exit. And you may also remember from Chapter 3 that the market supply curve is the horizontal sum of the individual supply curves of all producers—you find it by summing the total output across all suppliers at every given price. We will do that exercise here under the assumption that all the producers are alike—an assumption that makes the derivation particularly simple. So let's assume there are 100 Christmas tree farms, each with the same costs as Noelle's farm.

Each of these 100 farms will have an individual short-run supply curve like the one in Figure 12-4. At a price below $40, no farms will produce. At a price of $40 or more, each farm will produce the quantity of output at which its marginal cost is equal to the market price. As you can see from Figure 12-4, this will lead each farm to produce 40 trees if the price is $56 per tree, 50 trees if the price is $72, and so on. So if there are 100 tree farms and the price of Christmas trees is $72 per tree, the industry as a whole will produce 5,000 trees, corresponding to 100 farms × 50 trees per farm, and so on. The result is the **short-run industry supply curve,** shown as *S* in Figure 12-5. This curve shows the quantity that producers will supply at each price, *taking the number of producers as given.*

The **industry supply curve** shows the relationship between the price of a good and the total output of the industry as a whole.

The **short-run industry supply curve** shows how the quantity supplied by an industry depends on the market price given a fixed number of producers.

FIGURE 12-5 The Short-Run Market Equilibrium

The short-run industry supply curve, *S*, is the industry supply curve taking the number of producers—here, 100—as given. It is generated by adding together the individual supply curves of the 100 producers. Below the shut-down price of $40, no producer wants to produce in the short run. Above $40, the short-run industry supply curve slopes upward, as each producer increases output as price increases. It intersects the demand curve, *D*, at point E_{MKT}, the point of short-run market equilibrium, corresponding to a market price of $72 and a quantity of 5,000 trees.

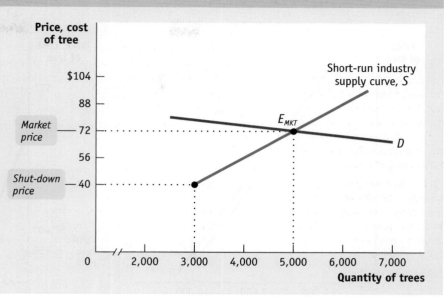

The demand curve *D* in Figure 12-5 crosses the short-run industry supply curve at E_{MKT}, corresponding to a price of $72 and a quantity of 5,000 trees. Point E_{MKT} is a **short-run market equilibrium:** the quantity supplied equals the quantity demanded, taking the number of producers as given. But the long run may look quite different, because in the long run farms may enter or exit the industry.

There is a **short-run market equilibrium** when the quantity supplied equals the quantity demanded, taking the number of producers as given.

The Long-Run Industry Supply Curve

Suppose that in addition to the 100 farms currently in the Christmas tree business, there are many other potential producers. Suppose also that each of these potential producers would have the same cost curves as existing producers like Noelle if they entered the industry.

When will additional producers enter the industry? Whenever existing producers are making a profit—that is, whenever the market price is above the break-even price of $56 per tree, the minimum average total cost of production. For example, at a price of $72 per tree, new firms will enter the industry.

What will happen as additional producers enter the industry? Clearly, the quantity supplied at any given price will increase. The short-run industry supply curve will shift to the right. This will, in turn, alter the market equilibrium and result in a lower market price. Existing firms will respond to the lower market price by reducing their output, but the total industry output will increase because of the larger number of firms in the industry.

Figure 12-6 illustrates the effects of this chain of events on an existing firm and on the market; panel (a) shows how the market responds to entry, and panel (b) shows how an individual existing firm responds to entry. (Note that these two graphs have been rescaled in comparison to Figures 12-4 and 12-5 to better illustrate how profit changes in response to price.) In panel (a), S_1 is the initial short-run industry supply curve, based on the existence of 100 producers. The initial short-run market equilibrium is at E_{MKT}, with an equilibrium market price of $72 and a quantity of 5,000 trees. At this price existing producers are profitable, which is reflected in panel (b): an existing firm makes a total profit represented by the green-shaded rectangle labeled *A* when market price is $72.

These profits will induce new producers to enter the industry, shifting the short-run industry supply curve to the right. For example, the short-run industry supply curve when the number of producers has increased to 167 is S_2. Corresponding to this supply curve is a new short-run market equilibrium labeled

FIGURE 12-6 The Long-Run Market Equilibrium

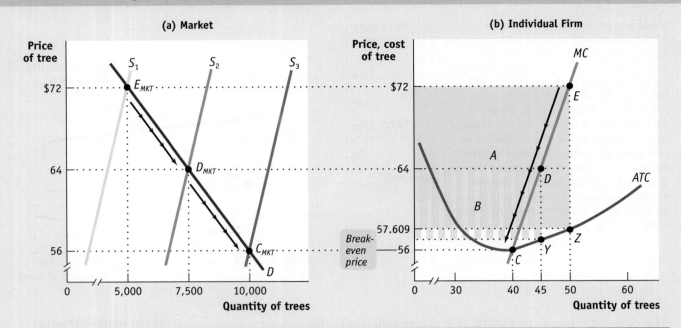

Point E_{MKT} of panel (a) shows the initial short-run market equilibrium. Each of the 100 existing producers makes an economic profit, illustrated in panel (b) by the green rectangle labeled A, the profit of an existing firm. Profits induce entry by additional producers, shifting the short-run industry supply curve outward from S_1 to S_2 in panel (a), resulting in a new short-run equilibrium at point D_{MKT}, at a lower market price of $64 and higher industry output. Existing firms

reduce output and profit falls to the area given by the striped rectangle labeled B in panel (b). Entry continues to shift out the short-run industry supply curve, as price falls and industry output increases yet again. Entry of new firms ceases at point C_{MKT} on supply curve S_3 in panel (a). Here market price is equal to the break-even price; existing producers make zero economic profits, and there is no incentive for entry or exit. So C_{MKT} is also a long-run market equilibrium.

D_{MKT}, with a market price of $64 and a quantity of 7,500 trees. At $64, each firm produces 45 trees, so that industry output is $167 \times 45 = 7{,}500$ trees (rounded).

From panel (b) you can see the effect of the entry of 67 new producers on an existing firm: the fall in price causes it to reduce its output, and its profit falls to the area represented by the striped rectangle labeled B.

Although diminished, the profit of existing firms at D_{MKT} means that entry will continue and the number of firms will continue to rise. If the number of producers rises to 250, the short-run industry supply curve shifts out again to S_3, and the market equilibrium is at C_{MKT}, with a quantity supplied and demanded of 10,000 trees and a market price of $56 per tree.

Like E_{MKT} and D_{MKT}, C_{MKT} is a short-run equilibrium. But it is also something more. Because the price of $56 is each firm's break-even price, an existing producer makes zero economic profit—neither a profit nor a loss, earning only the opportunity cost of the resources used in production—when producing its profit-maximizing output of 40 trees.

At this price there is no incentive either for potential producers to enter or for existing producers to exit the industry. So C_{MKT} corresponds to a **long-run market equilibrium**—a situation in which the quantity supplied equals the quantity demanded given that sufficient time has elapsed for producers to either enter or exit the industry. In a long-run market equilibrium, all existing and potential producers have fully adjusted to their optimal long-run choices; as a result, no producer has an incentive to either enter or exit the industry.

To explore further the significance of the difference between short-run and long-run equilibrium, consider the effect of an increase in demand on an industry

A market is in **long-run market equilibrium** when the quantity supplied equals the quantity demanded, given that sufficient time has elapsed for entry into and exit from the industry to occur.

with free entry that is initially in long-run equilibrium. Panel (b) in Figure 12-7 shows the market adjustment; panels (a) and (c) show how an existing individual firm behaves during the process.

In panel (b) of Figure 12-7, D_1 is the initial demand curve and S_1 is the initial short-run industry supply curve. Their intersection at point X_{MKT} is both a short-run and a long-run market equilibrium because the equilibrium price of $56 leads to zero economic profit—and therefore neither entry nor exit. It corresponds to point X in panel (a), where an individual existing firm is operating at the minimum of its average total cost curve.

Now suppose that the demand curve shifts out for some reason to D_2. As shown in panel (b), in the short run, industry output moves along the short-run industry supply curve S_1 to the new short-run market equilibrium at Y_{MKT}, the intersection of S_1 and D_2. The market price rises to $72 per tree, and industry output increases from Q_X to Q_Y. This corresponds to an existing firm's movement from X to Y in panel (a) as the firm increases its output in response to the rise in the market price.

But we know that Y_{MKT} is not a long-run equilibrium, because $72 is higher than minimum average total cost, so existing producers are making economic profits. This will lead additional firms to enter the industry.

Over time entry will cause the short-run industry supply curve to shift to the right. In the long run, the short-run industry supply curve will have shifted out

FIGURE 12-7 The Effect of an Increase in Demand in the Short Run and the Long Run

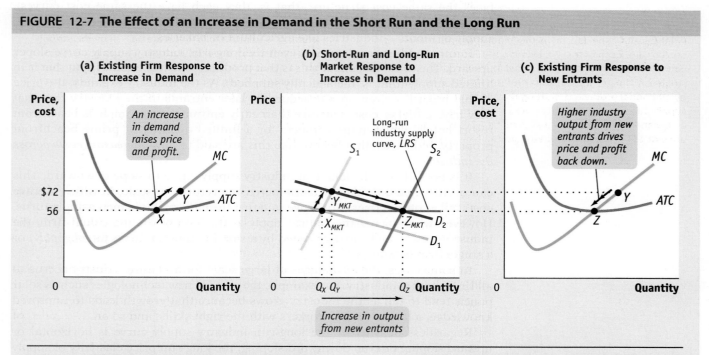

Panel (b) shows how an industry adjusts in the short run and long run to an increase in demand; panels (a) and (c) show the corresponding adjustments by an existing firm. Initially the market is at point X_{MKT} in panel (b), a short-run and long-run equilibrium at a price of $56 and industry output of Q_X. An existing firm makes zero economic profit, operating at point X in panel (a) at minimum average total cost. Demand increases as D_1 shifts rightward to D_2 in panel (b), raising the market price to $72. Existing firms increase their output, and industry output moves along the short-run industry supply curve S_1 to a short-run equilibrium at Y_{MKT}. Correspondingly, the existing firm in panel (a) moves from point X to point Y. But at a price of $72 existing firms are profitable. As shown in panel (b), in the long run new entrants arrive and the short-run industry supply curve shifts rightward, from S_1 to S_2. There is a new equilibrium at point Z_{MKT}, at a lower price of $56 and higher industry output of Q_Z. An existing firm responds by moving from Y to Z in panel (c), returning to its initial output level and zero economic profit. Production by new entrants accounts for the total increase in industry output, $Q_Z - Q_X$. Like X_{MKT}, Z_{MKT} is also a short-run and long-run equilibrium: with existing firms earning zero economic profit, there is no incentive for any firms to enter or exit the industry. The horizontal line passing through X_{MKT} and Z_{MKT}, LRS, is the long-run industry supply curve: at the break-even price of $56, producers will produce any amount that consumers demand in the long run.

The **long-run industry supply curve** shows how the quantity supplied responds to the price once producers have had time to enter or exit the industry.

to S_2, and the equilibrium will be at Z_{MKT}—with the price falling back to \$56 per tree and industry output increasing yet again, from Q_Y to Q_Z. Like X_{MKT} before the increase in demand, Z_{MKT} is both a short-run and a long-run market equilibrium.

The effect of entry on an existing firm is illustrated in panel (c), in the movement from Y to Z along the firm's individual supply curve. The firm reduces its output in response to the fall in the market price, ultimately arriving back at its original output quantity, corresponding to the minimum of its average total cost curve. In fact, every firm that is now in the industry—the initial set of firms and the new entrants—will operate at the minimum of its average total cost curve, at point Z. This means that the entire increase in industry output, from Q_X to Q_Z, comes from production by new entrants.

The line LRS that passes through X_{MKT} and Z_{MKT} in panel (b) is the **long-run industry supply curve.** It shows how the quantity supplied by an industry responds to the price given that producers have had time to enter or exit the industry.

In this particular case, the long-run industry supply curve is horizontal at \$56. In other words, in this industry supply is *perfectly elastic* in the long run: given time to enter or exit, producers will supply any quantity that consumers demand at a price of \$56. Perfectly elastic long-run supply is actually a good assumption for many industries. In this case we speak of there being *constant costs across the industry:* each firm, regardless of whether it is an incumbent or a new entrant, faces the same cost structure (that is, they each have the same cost curves). Industries that satisfy this condition are those in which there is a perfectly elastic supply of inputs—industries like agriculture or bakeries.

In other industries, however, even the long-run industry supply curve slopes upward. The usual reason for this is that producers must use some input that is in limited supply (that is, inelastically supplied). As the industry expands, the price of that input is driven up. Consequently, later entrants in the industry find that they have a higher cost structure than early entrants. An example is beachfront resort hotels, which must compete for a limited quantity of prime beachfront property. Industries that behave like this are said to have *increasing costs across the industry.*

It is possible for the long-run industry supply curve to slope downward. This can occur when an industry faces increasing returns to scale, in which average costs fall as output rises. Notice we said that the *industry* faces increasing returns. However, when increasing returns apply at the level of the individual firm, the industry usually ends up dominated by a small number of firms (an *oligopoly*) or a single firm (a *monopoly*).

In some cases, the advantages of large scale for an entire industry accrue to all firms in that industry. For example, the costs of new technologies such as solar panels tend to fall as the industry grows because that growth leads to improved knowledge, a larger pool of workers with the right skills, and so on.

Regardless of whether the long-run industry supply curve is horizontal or upward sloping or even downward sloping, the long-run price elasticity of supply is *higher* than the short-run price elasticity whenever there is free entry and exit. As shown in Figure 12-8, the long-run industry supply curve is always flatter than the short-run industry supply curve. The reason is entry and exit: a high price caused by an increase in demand attracts entry by new producers, resulting in a rise in industry output and an eventual fall in price; a low price caused by a decrease in demand induces existing firms to exit, leading to a fall in industry output and an eventual increase in price.

The distinction between the short-run industry supply curve and the long-run industry supply curve is very important in practice. We often see a sequence of events like that shown in Figure 12-7: an increase in demand initially leads to a large price increase, but prices return to their initial level once new firms have entered the industry. Or we see the sequence in reverse: a fall in demand reduces prices in the short run, but they return to their initial level as producers exit the industry.

FIGURE 12-8 Comparing the Short-Run and Long-Run Industry Supply Curves

The long-run industry supply curve may slope upward, but it is always flatter—more elastic—than the short-run industry supply curve. This is because of entry and exit: a higher price attracts new entrants in the long run, resulting in a rise in industry output and a fall in price; a lower price induces existing producers to exit in the long run, generating a fall in industry output and an eventual rise in price.

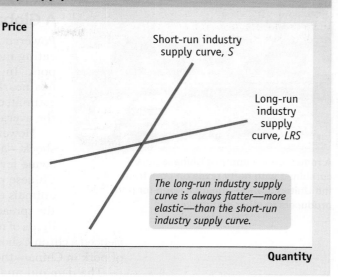

The long-run industry supply curve is always flatter—more elastic—than the short-run industry supply curve.

The Cost of Production and Efficiency in Long-Run Equilibrium

Our analysis leads us to three conclusions about the cost of production and efficiency in the long-run equilibrium of a perfectly competitive industry. These results will be important in our discussion in Chapter 13 of how monopoly gives rise to inefficiency.

1. *In a perfectly competitive industry in equilibrium, the value of marginal cost is the same for all firms.* That's because all firms produce the quantity of output at which marginal cost equals the market price, and as price-takers they all face the same market price.

2. *In a perfectly competitive industry with free entry and exit, each firm will have zero economic profit in long-run equilibrium.* Each firm produces the quantity of output that minimizes its average total cost—corresponding to point *Z* in panel (c) of Figure 12-7. So the total cost of production of the industry's output is minimized in a perfectly competitive industry.

The exception is an industry with increasing costs across the industry. Given a sufficiently high market price, early entrants make positive economic profits, but the last entrants do not as the market price falls. Costs are minimized for later entrants, as the industry reaches long-run equilibrium, but not necessarily for the early ones.

3. *The long-run market equilibrium of a perfectly competitive industry is efficient: no mutually beneficial transactions go unexploited.* To understand this, recall a fundamental requirement for efficiency: all consumers who have a willingness to pay greater than or equal to sellers' costs actually get the good. In addition, when a market is efficient (except under certain, well-defined conditions), the market price matches all consumers with a willingness to pay greater than or equal to the market price to all sellers who have a cost of producing the good less than or equal to the market price.

So in the long-run equilibrium of a perfectly competitive industry, production is efficient: costs are minimized and no resources are wasted. In addition, the allocation of goods to consumers is efficient: every consumer willing to pay the cost of producing a unit of the good gets it. Indeed, no mutually beneficial transaction is left unexploited. Moreover, this condition tends to persist over time as the environment changes: the force of competition makes producers responsive to changes in consumers' desires and to changes in technology.

PITFALLS

ECONOMIC PROFIT, AGAIN

Some readers may wonder why a firm would want to enter an industry if the market price is only slightly greater than the break-even price. Wouldn't a firm prefer to go into another business that yields a higher profit?

The answer is that here, as always, when we calculate cost, we mean *opportunity cost*—that is, cost that includes the return a firm could get by using its resources elsewhere. And so the profit that we calculate is *economic profit;* if the market price is above the break-even level, no matter how slightly, the firm can earn more in this industry than they could elsewhere.

A reduction in supply of Chinese pork —
combined with hefty taxes on pork from
the United States — meant a boon for pork
producers in other countries.

ECONOMICS >> *in Action*
A Global Pork Shortage Hits Chinese Diners Hard

Powered by rapidly rising incomes, Chinese consumers have been eating more meat, and their meat of preference has definitely been pork. In the past 20 years, pork consumption per capita in China has nearly doubled. In 2020, the average Chinese consumer ate an estimated 66 pounds of pork per year, compared to 53 pounds for the average American.

However, the market for pork in China hit a devastating supply shock—a leftward shift of the supply curve—in 2018, when African swine fever, a deadly and rapidly spreading disease, first appeared in Chinese pig stocks. Because there was no vaccine against the disease, animals exposed to the disease had to be destroyed immediately to stop the spread. By late 2019, some 40% of Chinese pigs—equivalent to hundreds of millions of animals—had been lost. As a result, China has experienced a chronic shortage of pork and sky-rocketing pork prices. The producer price of pork in China—the price at the farm—has more than doubled, rising by 125%.

The demand and supply reverberations have spread globally. As the world's largest consumer of pork, China "has a major influence on the price and availability of pork worldwide," according to a study commission by the U.S. National Pork Board. In 2019, there was a global surge in pork and bacon prices, registering the steepest rise seen in 15 years. As one market observer commented, "It doesn't matter where you are in the world at the moment, pork prices are up."

Reduction in the supply of Chinese-produced pork has been a boon to pork producers in other countries. Pork producers in Brazil, Australia, and the European Union have entered the Chinese market on a large scale. (Due to the Trump administration tariffs against China, U.S. pork producers have benefited less.) By late 2019, imports of foreign pork into China had surged by 150%. The import surge increased the supply curve for Chinese consumers relative to the right, dampening the rise in pork prices.

Yet, the gain to non-Chinese pork producers may be short-lived; 50% of China's domestically produced pork comes from small-scale farms—farms which are typically too small to effectively fight against a disease like African swine fever. Decimated by the epidemic, small-scale pork farms are being forced to exit the market, and modern, large-scale pork farms are expanding their share of total output. By modernizing its methods of pork production, China hopes never to be hit with a devastating pork shortage like this again.

>> Quick Review

• The **industry supply curve** corresponds to the supply curve of earlier chapters. In the short run, the time period over which the number of producers is fixed, the **short-run market equilibrium** is given by the intersection of the **short-run industry supply curve** and the demand curve. In the long run, the time period over which producers can enter or exit the industry, the **long-run market equilibrium** is given by the intersection of the **long-run industry supply curve** and the demand curve. In the long-run market equilibrium, no producer has an incentive to enter or exit the industry.

• The long-run industry supply curve is often horizontal, although it may slope upward when a necessary input is in limited supply. It is always more elastic than the short-run industry supply curve.

• In the long-run market equilibrium of a perfectly competitive industry, each firm produces at the same marginal cost, which is equal to the market price, and the total cost of production of the industry's output is minimized. It is also efficient.

>> Check Your Understanding 12-3
Solutions appear at back of book.

1. Which of the following events will induce firms to enter an industry? Which will induce firms to exit? When will entry or exit cease? Explain your answers.
   a. A technological advance lowers the fixed cost of production of every firm in the industry.
   b. The wages paid to workers in the industry go up for an extended period of time.
   c. A permanent change in consumer tastes increases demand for the good.
   d. The price of a key input rises due to a long-term shortage of that input.
2. Assume that the egg industry is perfectly competitive and is in long-run equilibrium with a perfectly elastic long-run industry supply curve. Health concerns about cholesterol then lead to a decrease in demand. Construct a figure similar to Figure 12-7, showing the short-run behavior of the industry and how long-run equilibrium is reestablished.

Retail Wars: Big Box Stores in the Age of Amazon

AP Images/Gerry Broome

The large number of defunct or dying shopping malls littered across the United States confirms that the brick-and-mortar retail industry has undergone what Robin Lewis, author of *The New Rules of Retail*, describes as "a period that would only be paralleled by the Industrial Revolution." Online shopping has decimated many long-established retailers such as Sears and J.C. Penney, and even newer ones such as Circuit City and Toys "R" Us.

But in the last few years, several brick-and-mortar retailers such as Walmart and Target have put up a vigorous fight. To combat consumers' penchant for *showrooming*—visiting a brick-and-mortar store to inspect the merchandise, and then buying it with a mobile shopping app on their smartphone at a cheaper price—Target stocks products that manufacturers have slightly modified as Target exclusives, making it harder to find an online comparison. Both Target and Walmart have beefed up their online retail presence, and they send discount alerts and coupons directly to customers' phones. Both stores leveraged their existing infrastructure by pairing digital commerce with brick-and-mortar convenience, allowing customers to order online and pick up (and return) merchandise in stores, a challenge to Amazon's warehouse and delivery model. Walmart also

instituted a price-match guarantee, in which customers receive Walmart gift cards for the value of any price difference.

Yet the most innovative counter-assault is the brainchild of Hubert Joly, the CEO of Best Buy. In 2012, by all appearances Best Buy was soon to follow its rival, electronics superstore Circuit City, into bankruptcy. However, by 2019, Best Buy was consistently beating its Wall Street earnings forecasts. How did Joly deliver? The first and perhaps most necessary strategy was price-matching: "Until I match Amazon's prices, the customers are ours to lose," Mr. Joly said. Second, Best Buy distinguished itself in an area that couldn't be captured by using robots or fast delivery: customer service. To keep its sales associates well-informed and happy, Joly reinstated a much-loved employee discount and instituted an ambitious training program to ensure that employees could answer questions about entirely new categories such as virtual reality headsets. Third, Joly transformed Best Buy's delivery infrastructure, so that it could ship its items nearly as fast as Amazon could. In the end, Joly has found a way to change showroomers into customers.

For brick-and-mortar retailers, today's retail environment is a race for survival. As one analyst said, "Only a couple of retailers can play the lowest-price game. This is going to accelerate the demise of retailers who do not have either competitive pricing or standout store experience."

QUESTIONS FOR THOUGHT

1. From the evidence in the case, what can you infer about whether or not the retail market for electronics satisfied the conditions for perfect competition before the advent of comparison price shopping via mobile app? What was the most important impediment to competition?

2. What effect is the introduction of shopping apps having on competition in the retail market for electronics? On the profitability of brick-and-mortar retailers like Best Buy? What, on average, will be the effect on the consumer surplus of purchasers of these items?

3. Why are some retailers responding by having manufacturers make slightly modified or exclusive versions of products for them? Is this trend likely to increase or diminish?

SUMMARY

1. In a **perfectly competitive market** all producers are **price-taking producers** and all consumers are **price-taking consumers**—no one's actions can influence the market price. Consumers are normally price-takers, but producers often are not. In a **perfectly competitive industry,** all producers are price-takers.

2. There are two necessary conditions for a perfectly competitive industry: there are many producers, none of whom have a large **market share,** and the industry produces a **standardized product** or **commodity**—goods that consumers regard as equivalent. A third condition is often satisfied as well: **free entry and exit** into and from the industry.

3. A producer chooses output according to the **optimal output rule:** produce the quantity at which **marginal revenue** equals marginal cost. For a price-taking firm, marginal revenue is equal to price and its **marginal revenue curve** is a horizontal line at the market price. It chooses output according to the **price-taking firm's optimal output rule:** produce the quantity at which price equals marginal cost. However, a firm that produces the optimal quantity may not be profitable.

4. A firm is profitable if total revenue exceeds total cost or, equivalently, if the market price exceeds its **break-even price**—minimum average total cost. If market price exceeds the break-even price, the firm is profitable; if it is less, the firm is unprofitable; if it is equal, the firm breaks even. When profitable, the firm's per-unit profit is $P - ATC$; when unprofitable, its per-unit loss is $ATC - P$.

5. Fixed cost is irrelevant to the firm's optimal short-run production decision, which depends on its **shut-down price**—its minimum average variable cost—and the market price. When the market price is equal to or exceeds the shut-down price, the firm produces the output quantity where marginal cost equals the market price. When the market price falls below the shut-down

price, the firm ceases production in the short run. This generates the firm's **short-run individual supply curve.**

6. Fixed cost matters over time. If the market price is below minimum average total cost for an extended period of time, firms will exit the industry in the long run. If above, existing firms are profitable and new firms will enter the industry in the long run.

7. The **industry supply curve** depends on the time period. The **short-run industry supply curve** is the industry supply curve given that the number of firms is fixed. The **short-run market equilibrium** is given by the intersection of the short-run industry supply curve and the demand curve.

8. The **long-run industry supply curve** is the industry supply curve given sufficient time for entry into and exit from the industry. In the **long-run market equilibrium**—given by the intersection of the long-run industry supply curve and the demand curve—no producer has an incentive to enter or exit. The long-run industry supply curve is often horizontal. It may slope upward if there is limited supply of an input, resulting in increasing costs across the industry. It may even slope downward, the case of decreasing costs across the industry. But it is always more elastic than the short-run industry supply curve.

9. In the long-run market equilibrium of a competitive industry, profit maximization leads each firm to produce at the same marginal cost, which is equal to market price. Free entry and exit means that each firm earns zero economic profit—producing the output corresponding to its minimum average total cost. So the total cost of production of an industry's output is minimized. The outcome is efficient because every consumer with a willingness to pay greater than or equal to marginal cost gets the good.

KEY TERMS

Price-taking producer, p. 356
Price-taking consumer, p. 356
Perfectly competitive market, p. 356
Perfectly competitive industry, p. 356
Market share, p. 357
Standardized product, p. 357
Commodity, p. 357

Free entry and exit, p. 358
Marginal revenue, p. 360
Optimal output rule, p. 360
Marginal revenue curve, p. 361
Price-taking firm's optimal output rule, p. 361
Break-even price, p. 365

Shut-down price, p. 366
Short-run individual supply curve, p. 367
Industry supply curve, p. 370
Short-run industry supply curve, p. 370
Short-run market equilibrium, p. 371
Long-run market equilibrium, p. 372
Long-run industry supply curve, p. 374

PRACTICE QUESTIONS

1. A recent report found that Christmas trees have doubled in price over the last three years. The price surge is partly due to a glut of trees 10 years prior. During the Great Recession of 2008 many consumers reduced their purchases leading to a surplus of trees and lower prices. Explain how a glut in trees 10 years prior could lead to higher prices today. Focus on how farms changed operations in response to the price decrease.

2. Given the assumptions of a perfectly competitive industry, explain why firms operating in that industry are reluctant to invest in new technological development.

3. Washington state is the largest producer of apples in the United States. In 2018, farms in Washington produced 171 million bushels of apples, nearly five times more than the next highest producing state, New York. Many apple farms in Washington depend on migrant labor from Mexico and Central America. These countries were once reliable sources of labor, but farmers are now experiencing a large shortage of labor. Most migrant workers are choosing year-round positions in the construction industry instead of the seasonal work offered in agriculture, leaving apple farms relying on undocumented migrant labor. With fewer undocumented workers, labor costs have soared, forcing many farmers to invest in expensive mechanical harvesting devices. Explain how both the labor shortage and investing in mechanical harvesting devices will change the farms' cost structure and industry dynamics.

4. Your roommate is having difficulty understanding how a firm can keep operating despite losing money, earning a negative profit. How will firms respond to losing money?

PROBLEMS

1. For each of the following, is the business a price-taking producer? Explain your answers.

   a. A cappuccino café in a university town where there are dozens of very similar cappuccino cafés

   b. The makers of Pepsi

   c. One of many sellers of zucchini at a local farmers' market

2. For each of the following, is the industry perfectly competitive? Referring to market share, standardization of the product, and/or free entry and exit, explain your answers.

   a. Aspirin

   b. Alicia Keys concerts

   c. SUVs

3. Bob produces flower pots for sale, which he designs and manufactures using 3-D printing technology. Bob rents a building for $30,000 per month and rents machinery for $20,000 a month. Those are his fixed costs. His variable cost per month is given in the accompanying table.

Quantity of flower pots	VC
0	$0
1,000	5,000
2,000	8,000
3,000	9,000
4,000	14,000
5,000	20,000
6,000	33,000
7,000	49,000
8,000	72,000
9,000	99,000
10,000	150,000

   a. Calculate Bob's average variable cost, average total cost, and marginal cost for each quantity of output.

   b. There is free entry into the industry, and anyone who enters will face the same costs as Bob.

Suppose that currently the price of a flower pot is $25. What will Bob's profit be? Is this a long-run equilibrium? If not, what will the price of a flower pot be in the long run?

4. Consider Bob's company described in Problem 3. Assume that flower pot production is a perfectly competitive industry. For each of the following questions, explain your answers.

   a. What is Bob's break-even price? What is his shut-down price?

   b. Suppose the price of a flower pot is $2. What should Bob do in the short run?

   c. Suppose the price of a flower pot is $7. What is the profit-maximizing quantity of flower pots that Bob should produce? What will his total profit be? Will he produce or shut down in the short run? Will he stay in the industry or exit in the long run?

   d. Suppose instead that the price of a flower pot is $20. Now what is the profit-maximizing quantity of flower pots that Bob should produce? What will his total profit be now? Will he produce or shut down in the short run? Will he stay in the industry or exit in the long run?

5. Consider again Bob's company described in Problem 3.

   a. Draw Bob's marginal cost curve.

   b. Over what range of prices will Bob produce no flower pots in the short run?

   c. Draw Bob's individual supply curve. In your graph, plot the price range from $0 to $60 in increments of $10.

6. a. A profit-maximizing business incurs an economic loss of $10,000 per year. Its fixed cost is $15,000 per year. Should it produce or shut down in the short run? Should it stay in the industry or exit in the long run?

   b. Suppose instead that this business has a fixed cost of $6,000 per year. Should it produce or shut down in the short run? Should it stay in the industry or exit in the long run?

7. The first sushi restaurant opens in town. Initially people are very cautious about eating tiny portions of raw fish, as this is a town where large portions of grilled meat have always been popular. Soon, however, an influential health report warns consumers against grilled meat and suggests that they increase their consumption of fish, especially raw fish. The sushi restaurant becomes very popular and its profit increases.

a. What will happen to the short-run profit of the sushi restaurant? What will happen to the number of sushi restaurants in town in the long run? Will the first sushi restaurant be able to sustain its short-run profit over the long run? Explain your answers.

b. Local steakhouses suffer from the popularity of sushi and start incurring losses. What will happen to the number of steakhouses in town in the long run? Explain your answer.

8. A perfectly competitive firm has the following short-run total cost:

Quantity	TC
0	$5
1	10
2	13
3	18
4	25
5	34
6	45

Market demand for the firm's product is given by the following market demand schedule:

Price	Quantity demanded
$12	300
10	500
8	800
6	1,200
4	1,800

a. Calculate this firm's marginal cost and, for all output levels except zero, the firm's average variable cost and average total cost.

b. There are 100 firms in this industry that all have costs identical to those of this firm. Draw the short-run industry supply curve. In the same diagram, draw the market demand curve.

c. What is the market price, and how much profit will each firm make?

9. A new vaccine against a deadly disease has just been discovered. Presently, 55 people die from the disease each year. The new vaccine will save lives, but it is not completely safe. Some recipients of the shots will die from adverse reactions. The projected effects of the inoculation are given in the accompanying table:

Percent of population inoculated	Total deaths due to disease	Total deaths due to inoculation	Marginal benefit of inoculation	Marginal cost of inoculation	"Profit" of inoculation
0	55	0			
10	45	0	—	—	—
20	36	1	—	—	—
30	28	3	—	—	—
40	21	6	—	—	—
50	15	10	—	—	—
60	10	15	—	—	—
70	6	20	—	—	—
80	3	25	—	—	—
90	1	30	—	—	—
100	0	35	—	—	—

a. What are the interpretations of "marginal benefit" and "marginal cost" here? Calculate marginal benefit and marginal cost per each 10% increase in the rate of inoculation. Write your answers in the table.

b. What proportion of the population should optimally be inoculated?

c. What is the interpretation of "profit" here? Calculate the profit for all levels of inoculation.

10. Evaluate each of the following statements. If a statement is true, explain why; if it is false, identify the mistake and try to correct it.

a. A profit-maximizing firm in a perfectly competitive industry should select the output level at which the difference between the market price and marginal cost is greatest.

b. An increase in fixed cost lowers the profit-maximizing quantity of output produced in the short run.

11. The production of agricultural products like wheat is one of the few examples of a perfectly competitive industry. In this question, we analyze results from a recent study released by the U.S. Department of Agriculture about wheat production in the United States.

a. The average variable cost per acre planted with wheat was $115 per acre. Assuming a yield of 44 bushels per acre, calculate the average variable cost per bushel of wheat.

b. The average price of wheat received by a farmer in 2016 was $4.89 per bushel. Do you think the average farm would have exited the industry in the short run? Explain.

c. With a yield of 44 bushels of wheat per acre, the average total cost per farm was $7.71 per bushel. The harvested acreage for wheat in the United States decreased from 48.8 million acres in 2013 to 43.9 million acres in 2016. Using the information on prices and costs here and in parts a and b, explain why this might have happened.

d. Using the information in parts a, b, and c, what do you think will happen to wheat production and prices after 2016?

12. The accompanying table presents prices for washing and ironing a man's shirt taken from a survey of California dry cleaners.

Dry cleaner	City	Price
A-1 Cleaners	Santa Barbara	$1.50
Regal Cleaners	Santa Barbara	1.95
St. Paul Cleaners	Santa Barbara	1.95
Zip Kleen Dry Cleaners	Santa Barbara	1.95
Effie the Tailor	Santa Barbara	2.00
Magnolia Too	Goleta	2.00
Master Cleaners	Santa Barbara	2.00
Santa Barbara Cleaners	Goleta	2.00
Sunny Cleaners	Santa Barbara	2.00
Casitas Cleaners	Carpinteria	2.10
Rockwell Cleaners	Carpinteria	2.10
Norvelle Bass Cleaners	Santa Barbara	2.15
Ablitt's Fine Cleaners	Santa Barbara	2.25
California Cleaners	Goleta	2.25
Justo the Tailor	Santa Barbara	2.25
Pressed 4 Time	Goleta	2.50
King's Cleaners	Goleta	2.50

a. What is the average price per shirt washed and ironed in Goleta? In Santa Barbara?

b. Draw typical marginal cost and average total cost curves for California Cleaners in Goleta, assuming it is a perfectly competitive firm but is making a profit on each shirt in the short run. Mark the short-run equilibrium point and shade the area that corresponds to the profit made by the dry cleaner.

c. Assume $2.25 is the short-run equilibrium price in Goleta. Draw a typical short-run demand and supply curve for the market. Label the equilibrium point.

d. Observing profits in the Goleta area, another dry-cleaning service, Diamond Cleaners, enters the market. It charges $1.95 per shirt. What is the new average price of washing and ironing a shirt in Goleta? Illustrate the effect of entry on the average Goleta price by a shift of the short-run supply curve, the demand curve, or both.

e. Assume that California Cleaners now charges the new average price and just breaks even (that is, makes zero economic profit) at this price. Show the likely effect of the entry on your diagram in part b.

f. If the dry-cleaning industry is perfectly competitive, what does the average difference in price between Goleta and Santa Barbara imply about costs in the two areas?

13. Over the last three years, Christmas tree prices have increased from an average of $35 per tree to over $75 per tree. How would a Christmas tree farm and the overall industry respond to the price change under the following circumstances? Be sure to explain how your answer depends on the elasticity of supply:

a. The price increase is a result of an increase in demand from younger generations, mainly millennials, increasing their desire to purchase real Christmas trees.

b. The price increase is a result of fewer Christmas tree farms harvesting trees in response to consumers purchasing more artificial trees.

WORK IT OUT

14. Kate's Katering provides catered meals, and the catered meals industry is perfectly competitive. Kate's machinery costs $100 per day and is the only fixed input. Her variable cost consists of the wages paid to the cooks and the food ingredients. The variable cost per day associated with each level of output is given in the accompanying table.

Quantity of meals	VC
0	0
10	200
20	300
30	480
40	700
50	1,000

a. Calculate the total cost, the average variable cost, the average total cost, and the marginal cost for each quantity of output.

b. What is the break-even price and quantity? What is the shut-down price and quantity?

c. Suppose that the price at which Kate can sell catered meals is $21 per meal. In the short run, will Kate earn a profit? In the short run, should she produce or shut down?

d. Suppose that the price at which Kate can sell catered meals is $17 per meal. In the short run, will Kate earn a profit? In the short run, should she produce or shut down?

e. Suppose that the price at which Kate can sell catered meals is $13 per meal. In the short run, will Kate earn a profit? In the short run, should she produce or shut down? ■

13 ▷ Monopoly

"SHINE BRIGHT LIKE A DIAMOND"

RIHANNA, THE SUPERSTAR song-stylist, fashion icon, and makeup mogul, is well known for her association with diamond gemstones. Her 2012 hit song "Diamonds" topped the charts in over 20 countries. In 2018 she became the brand ambassador for one of the oldest and most exclusive purveyors of diamond jewelry, Chopard of Paris. Her annual Diamond Ball raises millions of dollars for charity.

ANGELA WEISS/Getty Images

Got stones?

But why does Rihanna focus on diamonds? Diamonds are a symbol of luxury, valued not only for their appearance but for their perceived rarity.

Yet, as geologists will tell you, diamonds aren't actually all that rare. In fact, according to the *Dow Jones-Irwin Guide to Fine Gems and Jewelry*, diamonds are "more common than any other gem-quality colored stone. They only seem rarer."

Why do diamonds seem more precious and rare than rubies, emeralds, and other stones? Part of the answer is a brilliant marketing campaign. But the main reason diamonds seem to be rare is the legacy of a company named De Beers which *made* them rare. For 100 years, De Beers controlled most of the world's diamond mines, allowing it to limit the quantity of diamonds supplied to the market.

In previous chapters we have concentrated exclusively on perfectly competitive markets — markets in which the producers are perfect competitors. But the diamond market has historically been very different. At the height of its power, De Beers controlled the global diamond market and was unlike the producers we've studied so far. It was a *monopolist,* the sole (or almost sole) producer of a good. Monopolists behave differently from producers in perfectly competitive industries: whereas perfect competitors take the price at which they can sell their output as given, monopolists know that their actions affect market prices and take that into account when deciding how much to produce.

Before we begin our analysis, let's step back and look at *monopoly* and perfect competition as parts of a broader system for classifying markets. Perfect competition and monopoly are particular types of *market structure.* They are specific categories in a system economists use to classify markets and industries according to two main dimensions. This chapter begins with a brief overview of types of market structure. It will help us here and in subsequent chapters to understand on a deeper level why markets differ and why producers in those markets behave quite differently. ●

WHAT YOU WILL LEARN

- What is the significance of **monopoly,** a type of industry in which only one producer, a **monopolist,** operates?

- How does being a monopolist affect a firm's price and output decisions?

- Why does the presence of monopoly typically reduce social welfare?

- What tools do policy makers use to address the problem of monopoly?

- How do digital giants like Amazon, Google, and Facebook fit into our model of monopoly and what special challenges do they present?

- What is **price discrimination** and why is it so prevalent in certain industries?

‖ Types of Market Structure

In the real world, there is a mind-boggling array of different markets. We observe widely different behavior patterns by producers across markets. In some markets, firms are extremely competitive. In others, firms seem somehow to coordinate their actions to avoid competing with one another. And, as we have just described, some markets are monopolies in which there is no competition at all.

To develop principles and make predictions about markets and how producers will behave in them, economists have developed four primary models of market structure: *monopoly, oligopoly, perfect competition,* and *monopolistic competition.* This system of market structures is based on two dimensions:

1. The number of firms in the market (one, few, or many)
2. Whether the goods offered are identical or *differentiated*

Differentiated goods are goods that are different from each other in some ways but considered at least somewhat substitutable by consumers (think Coke versus Pepsi). Whether a market has differentiated products or identical products depends on the nature of the good and consumer preferences. Some goods—soft drinks, economics textbooks, breakfast cereals—can readily be made into different varieties in the eyes and tastes of consumers. Other goods—Christmas trees or pencils, for example—are much less easy to differentiate.

Figure 13-1 provides a simple visual summary of the four types of market structure classified according to the two dimensions. In *monopoly,* a single producer sells a single, undifferentiated product. In *oligopoly,* a few producers—more than one but not a large number—sell products that may be either identical or differentiated. In *perfect competition,* as we know, many firms each sell an identical product. And finally, in *monopolistic competition,* many firms each sell a differentiated product (think of producers of economics textbooks).

Over the course of this chapter and the next two we will see what determines the number of firms in a market: whether there is one (monopoly), a few (oligopoly), or many (perfect competition and monopolistic competition). We will just briefly note that in the long run it depends on whether there are conditions that make it difficult for new firms to enter the market. When these conditions are present, industries tend to be monopolies or oligopolies; when they are not present, industries tend to be perfectly competitive or monopolistically competitive.

FIGURE 13-1 Types of Market Structure

The behavior of any given firm and the market it occupies are analyzed using one of four models of market structure—monopoly, oligopoly, perfect competition, or monopolistic competition. This system for categorizing market structure is based on two dimensions: (1) whether products are differentiated or identical, and (2) the number of producers in the industry—one, a few, or many.

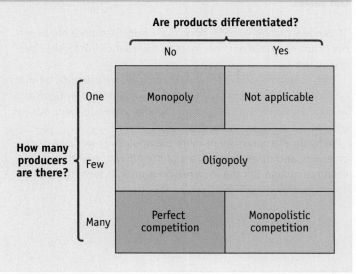

Although this chapter is devoted to monopoly, important aspects of monopoly carry over to oligopoly and monopolistic competition. In the next section, we will define monopoly and review the conditions that make it possible. These same conditions, in less extreme form, also give rise to oligopoly. We then show how a monopolist can increase profit by limiting the quantity supplied to a market—behavior that also occurs in oligopoly and monopolistic competition.

As we'll see, this kind of behavior is good for the producer but bad for consumers; it also causes inefficiency. An important topic of study will be the ways in which public policy tries to limit the damage. Finally, we turn to one of the surprising effects of monopoly—one that is very often present in oligopoly and monopolistic competition as well: the fact that different consumers often pay different prices for the same good.

‖ The Meaning of Monopoly

The De Beers monopoly was created in South Africa in the 1880s by Cecil Rhodes, a British imperialist and businessman. At that time, South Africa was the largest single source of diamonds, and South African mines dominated the world's supply of diamonds. There were, however, many mining companies, all competing with each other. Rhodes bought the great majority of those mines and consolidated them into a single company, De Beers. By 1889 De Beers controlled almost all of the world's diamond production.

De Beers, in other words, became a **monopolist.** A producer is a monopolist if it is the sole supplier of a good that has no close substitutes. When a firm is a monopolist, the industry is a **monopoly.**

Monopoly: Our First Departure from Perfect Competition

As we saw in Chapter 12, the supply and demand model of a market is not universally valid. Instead, it's a model of perfect competition, which is only one of several different types of market structure. A market will be perfectly competitive only if there are many producers, all of whom produce the same good. Monopoly is the most extreme departure from perfect competition.

In practice, true monopolies are hard to find in the modern American economy, partly because of legal obstacles. If a contemporary entrepreneur tried to consolidate all the firms in an industry the way that Rhodes did with diamond mining, that person would soon land in court, accused of breaking *antitrust* laws, which are intended to prevent monopolies from emerging. Oligopoly, a market structure in which there is a small number of large producers, is much more common. In fact, most of the goods you buy, from cars to airline tickets, are supplied by oligopolies.

Monopolies do, however, play an important role in some sectors of the economy, such as pharmaceuticals. Furthermore, an analysis of monopoly provides a foundation for other departures from perfect competition that we have mentioned, such as oligopoly and monopolistic competition.

What Monopolists Do

Why did Rhodes want to consolidate South African diamond producers into a single company, and what difference did it make to the world diamond market? Figure 13-2 offers a preliminary view of the effects of monopoly. It shows an industry in which the supply curve under perfect competition intersects the demand curve at C, leading to the price P_C and the output Q_C.

Suppose that this industry is consolidated into a monopoly. The monopolist *moves up the demand curve* by reducing quantity supplied to a point like M, at which the quantity produced, Q_M, is lower, and the price, P_M, is higher than under perfect competition.

A **monopolist** is a firm that is the only producer of a good that has no close substitutes. An industry controlled by a monopolist is known as a **monopoly.**

FIGURE 13-2 What a Monopolist Does

Under perfect competition, the price and quantity are determined by supply and demand. Here, the competitive equilibrium is at *C*, where the price is P_C and the quantity is Q_C. A monopolist reduces the quantity supplied to Q_M and moves up the demand curve from *C* to *M*, raising the price to P_M.

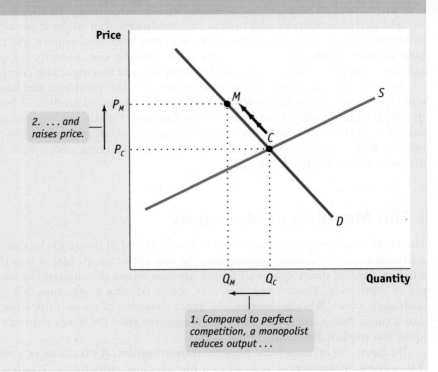

2. . . . and raises price.

1. Compared to perfect competition, a monopolist reduces output . . .

The ability of a monopolist to raise the price of its product above the competitive level by reducing output is known as **market power.** And market power is what monopoly is all about. A wheat farmer who is 1 of 100,000 wheat farmers has no market power: the farmer must sell wheat at the going market price. However, your local water utility does have market power: it can raise prices and still keep many (though not all) of its customers, because they have no other way to get water. In short, it's a monopolist.

The reason a monopolist reduces output and raises price compared to the perfectly competitive industry levels is to increase profit. Cecil Rhodes consolidated the diamond producers into De Beers because he realized that the whole would be worth more than the sum of its parts—the monopoly would generate more profit than the sum of the profits of the individual competitive firms. Under perfect competition economic profits (revenue over and above the opportunity costs of the firm's resources) normally vanish in the long run as competitors enter the market. Under monopoly the profits don't go away—a monopolist is able to continue earning economic profits in the long run.

In fact, monopolists are not the only types of firms that possess market power. In the next chapter we will study *oligopolists*, firms that can have market power as well. Under certain conditions, oligopolists can earn positive economic profits in the long run by restricting output like monopolists do.

But why don't profits get competed away? What allows monopolists to be monopolists?

Why Monopolies Exist

A monopolist making profits will not go unnoticed by others. Why don't other firms crash the party, grab a piece of the action, and drive down prices and profits in the long run?

Market power is the ability of a firm to raise prices.

For a monopoly to persist, something must keep others from going into the same business; that "something" is known as a **barrier to entry.** There are five principal types of barriers to entry: control of a scarce resource or input, increasing returns to scale, technological superiority, network externalities, and a government-created barrier to entry.

1. Control of a Scarce Resource or Input
A monopolist that controls a resource or input crucial to an industry can prevent other firms from entering its market. For example, Cecil Rhodes created the De Beers monopoly by establishing control over the mines that produced the great bulk of the world's diamonds. The market for diamonds also offers an example of what happens when a monopolist loses control of its scarce resource or input. De Beers's hold on the market was seriously weakened by the opening of rival diamond mines in Russia, Canada, and Australia in the 1990s. More recently, the advent of high-quality manufactured diamonds has effectively ended De Beers's monopoly position.

2. Increasing Returns to Scale
Many Americans have natural gas piped into their homes for cooking and heating. Invariably, the local gas company is a monopolist. Why don't rival companies compete to provide gas?

In the early nineteenth century, when the gas industry was starting up, companies did compete for local customers. However, the cost of laying gas lines did not depend on the amount of gas sold and the large fixed costs it required to provide gas lines gave an advantage to companies with a larger volume of sales. Firms with a larger volume of sales had a cost advantage because they were able to spread the fixed costs over a larger volume, and so had lower average total costs than smaller firms. Soon local gas supply became a monopoly in every town.

Local gas supply is an industry in which average cost falls as output increases. As we learned in Chapter 11, this phenomenon is called *increasing returns to scale:* when average total cost falls as output increases, firms tend to grow larger. In an industry characterized by increasing returns to scale, larger companies are more profitable and drive out smaller ones. For the same reason, established companies have a cost advantage over any potential entrant—a potent barrier to entry. So increasing returns to scale—also known as *economies of scale*—can both give rise to and sustain monopoly.

A monopoly created and sustained by increasing returns to scale is called a **natural monopoly.** The defining characteristic of a natural monopoly is that it possesses increasing returns to scale over the range of output that is relevant for the industry. This is illustrated in Figure 13-3, showing the firm's average total cost curve and the market demand curve, *D*. Here we can see that the natural monopolist's *ATC* curve declines over the output levels at which price is greater than or equal to average total cost.

So the natural monopolist has increasing returns to scale over the entire range of output for which any firm would want to remain in the industry—the range of output at which the firm would at least break even in the long run. The source of this condition is large fixed costs: when large fixed costs are required to operate, a given quantity of output is produced at lower average total cost by one large firm than by two or more smaller firms.

The most visible natural monopolies in the modern economy are local utilities—water, natural gas, power generation, and fiber optic cable. As we'll see later, natural monopolies pose a special challenge to public policy.

3. Technological Superiority
A firm that maintains a consistent technological advantage over potential competitors can establish itself as a monopolist. For example, from the 1970s through the 1990s, the semiconductor chip manufacturer Intel was able to maintain a consistent advantage over potential competitors in both the design and the production of microprocessors, the chips that run

To earn economic profits, a monopolist must be protected by a **barrier to entry**—something that prevents other firms from entering the industry.

A **natural monopoly** exists when increasing returns to scale provide a large cost advantage to a single firm that produces all of an industry's output.

FIGURE 13-3 Increasing Returns to Scale Lead to Natural Monopoly

A natural monopoly can arise when fixed costs required to operate are very high. When this occurs, the firm's *ATC* curve declines over the range of output at which price is greater than or equal to average total cost. This gives the firm increasing returns to scale over the entire range of output at which the firm would at least break even in the long run. As a result, a given quantity of output is produced more cheaply by one large firm than by two or more smaller firms.

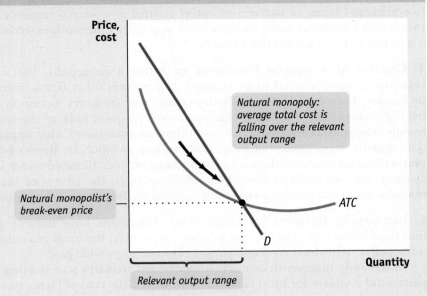

Natural monopoly: average total cost is falling over the relevant output range

Natural monopolist's break-even price

ATC

D

Relevant output range

computers. But technological superiority is typically not a barrier to entry over the longer term: over time competitors will invest in upgrading their technology to match that of the technology leader. In fact, Intel's technological superiority was eventually eroded by a competitor, AMD, which developed chips that are as fast and as powerful as Intel chips.

The fact that technological change can erode monopoly power is also illustrated by the diamond market. As noted earlier, the quality of manufactured diamonds has improved to the point that they rival the real thing, which contributed to the erosion of DeBeers's monopoly position.

4. Network Externalities If you were the only person in the world with an internet connection, what would that connection be worth to you? The answer, of course, is nothing. Your internet connection is valuable only because other people are also connected. And, in general, the more people who are connected, the more valuable your connection is. A **network externality** exists when the value of a good or service to an individual is greater if many others use the same good or service. The value of a network externality derives from enabling its users to participate in a network of other users.

The earliest form of network externalities arose in transportation, when the value of a road or airport increased as the number of people who had access to it rose. Network externalities are especially prevalent in the digital technology and communications sectors of the economy.

Network externalities are a pervasive feature of the digital economy. The classic case is computer operating systems. Worldwide, most personal computers run on Microsoft Windows. Although many believe that Apple has a superior operating system, the wider use of Windows in the early days of personal computers attracted more software development and technical support, giving it a lasting dominance. More recent examples of firms that have come to dominate their industries through network externalities are eBay, Facebook, Amazon, Netflix, Google, PayPal, and Snapchat.

A **network externality** exists when the value of a good or service to an individual is greater when many other people use the good or service as well.

When a network externality exists, the firm with the largest network of customers using its product has an advantage in attracting new customers, one that may allow it to become a monopolist. At a minimum, the dominant firm can charge a higher price and so earn higher profits than competitors. Moreover, a network externality gives an advantage to the firm with the deepest pockets, not necessarily the firm with the best technology. Companies with the most money on hand can sell the most goods at a loss with the expectation that doing so will give them the largest customer base and, eventually, a monopoly.

In practice, a network externality behaves a lot like a case of increasing returns to scale: for the larger firm, the cost of accessing a new customer is less than for a smaller firm. Like natural monopoly, network externalities present a difficult problem for public policy makers. We will examine these issues in more detail later in this chapter.

5. Government-Created Barriers The pharmaceutical company Merck introduced Propecia, a drug effective against hair loss, in 1998. Although Propecia was very profitable and other drug companies had the know-how to produce it, no other firms challenged Merck's monopoly. That's because the U.S. government had given Merck the sole legal right to produce the drug in the United States. Propecia is an example of a monopoly protected by government-created barriers.

GLOBAL COMPARISON WHAT ACCOUNTS FOR AMERICA'S HIGH DRUG PRICES?

Although providing cheap patent-protected drugs to patients in poor countries is a new phenomenon, charging different prices to consumers in different countries is not: it's an example of *price discrimination*.

A monopolist will maximize profits by charging a higher price in the country with a lower price elasticity (the rich country) and a lower price in the country with a higher price elasticity (the poor country). Interestingly, however, drug prices can differ substantially even among countries with comparable income levels. How do we explain this?

The answer is differences in regulation.

This graph shows a price comparison of Advair, an asthma medication, across the United States and four other high-income countries. As you can see, Americans pay much more than residents of other wealthy nations, like Canada and the United Kingdom. The retail price for a monthly supply of Advair in the United States is $309.60, with Canadians paying about one-fourth and Australians paying about one-tenth of the U.S. price. While some Americans receive the discounted price of $154.80 through their health insurance, that is still 50% higher than the Canadian price and 81% higher than the Australian price.

The example of Advair is not unusual. Americans consistently pay more for top-selling drugs than residents of other countries do. According to a recent study, annual U.S. spending on pharmaceuticals exceeded $1,000 per person, 30% to 190% higher than in nine other advanced countries.

The reason? Governments in these other countries regulate drug prices more actively than the U.S. government does, helping to keep drug prices affordable for their citizens. So it's not surprising that some Americans travel to Canada and Mexico to purchase their drugs, or buy them from abroad over the internet to save money.

American drug makers contend that higher drug prices are necessary to cover the high cost of research and development,

The Price Consumers of Various Countries Pay for the Drug Advair

which can run into the tens of millions of dollars over several years for successful drugs. Critics of the drug companies counter that American drug prices are in excess of what is needed for a socially desirable level of drug innovation. Instead, they say that drug companies are too often focused on developing drugs that generate high profits rather than those that improve health or save lives.

What's indisputable is that some level of profit is necessary to fund innovation.

It is also clear that through the high prices that they pay, Americans effectively subsidize research and development for new drugs that benefit patients worldwide. However, with rising drug prices drawing the attention of policy makers, insurers, and consumers, how long this will continue has become a question.

Data from: Bloomberg News, https://www.bloomberg.com/graphics/2015-drug-prices/.

A **patent** gives an inventor a temporary monopoly in the use or sale of an invention.

A **copyright** gives the creator of a literary or artistic work sole rights to profit from that work.

Most legally created monopolies today arise from *patents* and *copyrights*. A **patent** gives an inventor the sole right to make, use, or sell that invention for a period that in most countries lasts between 14 and 20 years. Patents are given to the creators of new products, such as drugs or mechanical devices. Similarly, a **copyright** gives the creator of a literary or artistic work the sole right to profit from that work, usually for a period equal to the creator's lifetime plus 70 years.

The justification for patents and copyrights is a matter of incentives. If inventors were not protected by patents, they would gain little reward from their efforts: as soon as a valuable invention was made public, others would copy it and sell products based on it. And if inventors could not expect to profit from their inventions, then there would be no incentive to incur the costs of invention in the first place. Likewise for the creators of literary or artistic works. The law allows a monopoly to exist temporarily by granting property rights that encourage invention and creation.

Patents and copyrights are temporary because the law strikes a compromise between the interests of producers and the interests of consumers. The higher price for the good that holds while the legal protection is in effect compensates inventors for the cost of invention; conversely, the lower price that results once the legal protection lapses benefits consumers.

Because the lifetime of the temporary monopoly cannot be tailored to specific cases, this system is imperfect and leads to some missed opportunities. In some cases there can even be significant welfare issues. For example, the violation of U.S. drug patents by pharmaceutical companies in poor countries has been a major source of controversy, pitting the needs of poor patients who cannot afford to pay retail drug prices against the interests of the drug manufacturers that have incurred high research costs to discover and test these drugs.

To solve this problem, some U.S. drug companies and poor countries have negotiated deals in which the patents are honored but the U.S. companies sell their drugs at deeply discounted prices. (This is an example of *price discrimination*, which we'll learn about shortly.)

ECONOMICS >> *in Action*
The Monopoly That Wasn't: China and the Market for Rare Earths

A quiver of panic shot through the U.S. technology and military sectors in 2010. Rare earths, a group of 17 elements that are a critical input in the manufacture of high-tech products like smartphones and military jet components, had suddenly become much harder to obtain.

China controlled 85% to 95% of the global supply of rare earths and, until 2009, made them relatively abundant and cheap on world markets. However, in 2010 China adopted an *export quota*—a limit on the amount of rare earths that could be exported, severely restricting supply on the world market and leading to sharply higher prices. For example, the rare earth dysprosium went from $166 per kilo in 2010 to nearly $1,000 per kilo in 2011, a nearly fivefold increase.

But the panic proved to be temporary. China's dominance in rare earths was due to its low cost of production, and not to a monopoly position. In fact, only about a third of the world's rare earth reserves are found in China. Rare earths mines in Australia and the United States, which had been mothballed during the period of low prices, were reopened in response to the sharply higher prices. In addition, other sources emerged, such as recovering rare earths from discarded computer equipment.

The episode revealed to government and business leaders outside of China how vulnerable they were to disruptions in the supply of Chinese rare earths. As a result, they committed to keeping the alternative sources operating, even if prices should fall. And China's leaders learned that without control over the global sources of rare earths, what looked like a monopoly position, in fact, wasn't.

>> Check Your Understanding 13-1
Solutions appear at back of book.

1. Currently, Texas Tea Oil Co. is the only local supplier of home heating oil in Frigid, Alaska. This winter residents were shocked that the price of a gallon of heating oil had doubled and believed that they were the victims of market power. Explain which of the following pieces of evidence support or contradict that conclusion.
   a. There is a national shortage of heating oil, and Texas Tea could procure only a limited amount.
   b. Last year, Texas Tea and several other competing local oil-supply firms merged into a single firm.
   c. The cost to Texas Tea of purchasing heating oil from refineries has gone up significantly.
   d. Recently, some nonlocal firms have begun to offer heating oil to Texas Tea's regular customers at a price much lower than Texas Tea's.
   e. Texas Tea has acquired an exclusive government license to draw oil from the only heating oil pipeline in the state.
2. Suppose the government is considering extending the length of a patent from 20 years to 30 years. How would this change each of the following?
   a. The incentive to invent new products
   b. The length of time during which consumers have to pay higher prices
3. Explain the nature of the network externality in each of the following cases.
   a. A new type of web-based payment system called PayMo
   b. A new type of car engine, which runs on solar cells
   c. A website for trading locally provided goods and services

How a Monopolist Maximizes Profit

Once Cecil Rhodes consolidated the competing diamond producers of South Africa into a single company, the industry's behavior changed: the quantity supplied fell and the market price rose. We will now learn how a monopolist increases its profit by reducing output. And we will see the crucial role that market demand plays in leading a monopolist to behave differently from a perfectly competitive industry.

The Monopolist's Demand Curve and Marginal Revenue

Recall the firm's optimal output rule: a profit-maximizing firm produces the quantity of output at which the marginal cost of producing the last unit of output equals marginal revenue—the change in total revenue generated by that last unit of output. That is, $MR = MC$ at the profit-maximizing quantity of output.

Although the optimal output rule holds for all firms, we will see shortly that its application leads to different profit-maximizing output levels for a monopolist compared to a firm in a perfectly competitive industry—that is, a price-taking firm. We can see the difference by comparing the demand curve faced by a monopolist to the demand curve faced by an individual perfectly competitive firm.

>> Quick Review
- In a **monopoly,** a single firm uses its **market power** to charge higher prices and produce less output than a competitive industry, generating profits in the short run and long run. For a monopoly to succeed, there must be no close substitutes to the good.

- Monopoly profits will not persist in the long run unless there is a **barrier to entry** such as control of a scarce resource, increasing returns to scale, technological superiority, network externalities, or legal restrictions imposed by governments.

- A **natural monopoly** arises when average total cost declines over the output range relevant for the industry. This creates a barrier to entry because an established **monopolist** has a lower average total cost than an entrant.

- In the digital economy, **network externalities** are prevalent. Because the value of using a good or service is greater as the number of other people using it rises, a network externality can lead to monopoly because rival firms shrink and fail as customers move to the firm with the largest number of customers. Both natural monopolies and network externalities present special challenges to policy makers.

- **Patents** and **copyrights,** government-created barriers, are a source of temporary monopoly that attempt to balance the need for higher prices as compensation to an inventor for the cost of invention against the increase in consumer surplus from lower prices and greater efficiency. Patents and copyrights expire after a certain amount of time. So, like technological superiority, which typically erodes over time, they are not long-term barriers to entry.

FIGURE 13-4 Comparing the Demand Curves of a Perfectly Competitive Producer and a Monopolist

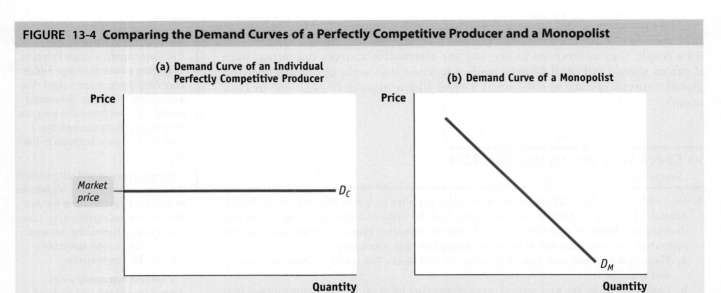

Because an individual perfectly competitive producer cannot affect the market price of a good, it faces the horizontal demand curve D_C, as shown in panel (a), allowing it to sell as much as it wants at the market price.

A monopolist, though, can affect the price. Because it is the sole supplier in the industry, it faces the market demand curve D_M, as shown in panel (b). To sell more output, it must lower the price; by reducing output, it raises the price.

Comparing Demand Curves Recall that each of the firms in a perfectly competitive industry faces a *perfectly elastic* demand curve that is horizontal at the market price, like D_C in panel (a) of Figure 13-4. A perfectly competitive firm can sell as much as it likes at the market price, yet will lose all of its sales if it attempts to charge more. Therefore the marginal revenue of a perfectly competitive producer is simply the market price. As a result, the price-taking firm's optimal output rule is to produce the output level at which the marginal cost of the last unit produced is equal to the market price.

In contrast, a monopolist is the sole supplier of its good. So its demand curve is simply the market demand curve. Like virtually all market demand curves, it slopes downward, like D_M in panel (b) of Figure 13-4. As a result, a monopolist must cut its price to sell more. *This downward slope creates a difference—a "wedge"—between the price of the good and the marginal revenue received by the monopolist for that good.*

Table 13-1 shows this wedge between price and marginal revenue for a monopolist, by calculating the monopolist's total revenue and marginal revenue schedules from its demand schedule.

Comparing Marginal Revenue and Price Now let's examine how the wedge between the monopolist's marginal revenue and price changes according to the quantity of output. The first two columns of Table 13-1 show a hypothetical demand schedule for De Beers diamonds. For the sake of simplicity, we assume that all diamonds are exactly alike. And to make the arithmetic easy, we suppose that the number of diamonds sold is far smaller than is actually the case. For instance, at a price of $500 per diamond, we assume that only 10 diamonds are sold. The demand curve implied by this schedule is shown in panel (a) of Figure 13-5.

The third column of Table 13-1 shows De Beers's total revenue from selling each quantity of diamonds—the price per diamond multiplied by the number of diamonds sold. The last column calculates marginal revenue, the change in total revenue from producing and selling another diamond.

After the first diamond, the marginal revenue a monopolist receives from selling one more unit is less than the price at which that unit is sold. For example, if De Beers sells 10 diamonds, the price at which the 10th diamond is sold is $500. But the marginal revenue—the change in total revenue in going from 9 to 10 diamonds—is only $50.

The marginal revenue from that 10th diamond is less than the price because an increase in production by a monopolist has two opposing effects on revenue:

1. *A quantity effect.* One more unit is sold, increasing total revenue by the price at which the unit is sold (in this case +$500).
2. *A price effect.* To sell the last unit, the monopolist must cut the market price on *all* units sold. This decreases total revenue (in this case, by $9 \times -\$50 = -\$450$).

The quantity effect and the price effect when the monopolist goes from selling 9 diamonds to 10 diamonds are illustrated by the two shaded areas in panel (a) of Figure 13-5. Increasing diamond sales from 9 to 10 means moving down the demand curve from *A* to *B*, reducing the price per diamond from $550 to $500. The green-shaded area represents the quantity effect: De Beers sells the 10th diamond at a price of $500. This is offset, however, by the price effect, represented by the yellow-shaded area. To sell that 10th diamond, De Beers must reduce the price on all its diamonds from $550 to $500. So it loses $9 \times \$50 = \$450$ in revenue, the yellow-shaded area. As point *C* indicates, the total effect on revenue of selling one more diamond—the marginal revenue—derived from an increase in diamond sales from 9 to 10 is only $50.

Point *C* lies on the monopolist's marginal revenue curve, labeled *MR* in panel (a) of Figure 13-5 and taken from the last column of Table 13-1. The crucial point about the monopolist's marginal revenue curve is that it is always *below* the demand curve. That's because of the price effect: a monopolist's marginal revenue from selling an additional unit is always less than the price the monopolist receives for the previous unit. It is the price effect that creates the wedge between the monopolist's marginal revenue curve and the demand curve: to sell an additional diamond, De Beers must cut the market price on all units sold.

In fact, this wedge exists for any firm that possesses market power, such as an oligopolist as well as a monopolist. Having market power means that the firm faces a downward-sloping demand curve. As a result, there will always be a price effect from an increase in its output. So for a firm with market power, the marginal revenue curve always lies below its demand curve.

Take a moment to compare the monopolist's marginal revenue curve with the marginal revenue curve for a perfectly competitive firm, one without market power. For such a firm there is no price effect from an increase

TABLE 13-1 Demand, Total Revenue, and Marginal Revenue for the De Beers Monopoly

Price of diamond *P*	Quantity of diamonds *Q*	Total revenue $TR = P \times Q$	Marginal revenue $MR = \Delta TR / \Delta Q$
$1,000	0	$0	
			$950
950	1	950	
			850
900	2	1,800	
			750
850	3	2,550	
			650
800	4	3,200	
			550
750	5	3,750	
			450
700	6	4,200	
			350
650	7	4,550	
			250
600	8	4,800	
			150
550	9	4,950	
			50
500	10	5,000	
			−50
450	11	4,950	
			−150
400	12	4,800	
			−250
350	13	4,550	
			−350
300	14	4,200	
			−450
250	15	3,750	
			−550
200	16	3,200	
			−650
150	17	2,550	
			−750
100	18	1,800	
			−850
50	19	950	
			−950
0	20	0	

FIGURE 13-5 A Monopolist's Demand, Total Revenue, and Marginal Revenue Curves

Panel (a) shows the monopolist's demand and marginal revenue curves for diamonds from Table 13-1. The marginal revenue curve lies below the demand curve. To see why, consider point A on the demand curve, where 9 diamonds are sold at $550 each, generating total revenue of $4,950. To sell a 10th diamond, the price on all 10 diamonds must be cut to $500, as shown by point B. As a result, total revenue increases by the green area (the quantity effect: +$500) but decreases by the yellow area (the price effect: –$450). So the marginal revenue from the 10th diamond is $50 (the difference between the green and yellow areas), which is much lower than its price, $500. Panel (b) shows the monopolist's total revenue curve for diamonds. As output goes from 0 to 10 diamonds, total revenue increases. It reaches its maximum at 10 diamonds—the level at which marginal revenue is equal to 0—and declines thereafter. The quantity effect dominates the price effect when total revenue is rising; the price effect dominates the quantity effect when total revenue is falling.

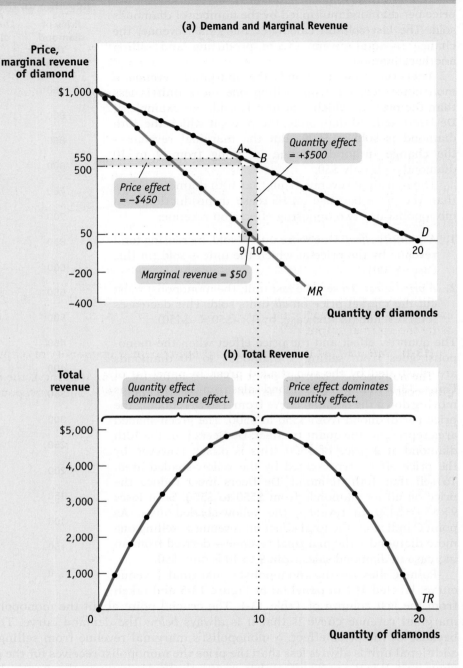

in output: its marginal revenue curve is simply its horizontal demand curve. For a perfectly competitive firm, then, market price and marginal revenue are always equal.

To emphasize how the quantity and price effects offset each other for a firm with market power, De Beers's total revenue curve is shown in panel (b) of Figure 13-5. Notice that it is hill-shaped: as output rises from 0 to 10 diamonds, total revenue increases. This reflects the fact that at *low levels of output, the quantity effect is stronger than the price effect:* as the monopolist sells more, it has to lower the price on only very few units, so the price effect is small. As output rises beyond 10 diamonds, total revenue actually falls. This reflects the fact that *at high levels of output, the price effect is stronger than the quantity effect:* as the monopolist sells more, it now has to lower the price on many units of output, making the price effect very large.

Correspondingly, the marginal revenue curve lies below 0 at output levels above 10 diamonds. For example, an increase in diamond production from 11 to 12 yields only $400 for the 12th diamond, simultaneously reducing the revenue from diamonds 1 through 11 by $550. As a result, the marginal revenue of the 12th diamond is –$150.

The Monopolist's Profit-Maximizing Output and Price

To complete the story of how a monopolist maximizes profit, we now bring in the monopolist's marginal cost. Let's assume that there is no fixed cost of production; we'll also assume that the marginal cost of producing an additional diamond is constant at $200, no matter how many diamonds De Beers produces. Then marginal cost will always equal average total cost, and the marginal cost curve (and the average total cost curve) is a horizontal line at $200, as shown in Figure 13-6.

To maximize profit, the monopolist compares marginal cost with marginal revenue. If marginal revenue exceeds marginal cost, De Beers increases profit by producing more; if marginal revenue is less than marginal cost, De Beers increases profit by producing less. So the monopolist maximizes its profit by using the optimal output rule:

(13-1) $MR = MC$ at the monopolist's profit-maximizing quantity of output

The monopolist's optimal point is shown in Figure 13-6. At point A, the marginal cost curve, MC, crosses the marginal revenue curve, MR. The corresponding

FIGURE 13-6 The Monopolist's Profit-Maximizing Output and Price

This figure shows demand, marginal revenue, and marginal cost curves. Marginal cost per diamond is constant at $200, so the marginal cost curve is horizontal at $200. According to the optimal output rule, the profit-maximizing quantity of output for the monopolist is at $MR = MC$, shown by point A, where the marginal cost and marginal revenue curves cross at an output of 8 diamonds. The price De Beers can charge per diamond is found by going to the point on the demand curve directly above point A, which is point B here — a price of $600 per diamond. It makes a profit of $400 × 8 = $3,200. A perfectly competitive industry produces the output level at which $P = MC$, given by point C, where the demand curve and marginal cost curves cross. So a competitive industry produces 16 diamonds, sells at a price of $200, and makes zero profit.

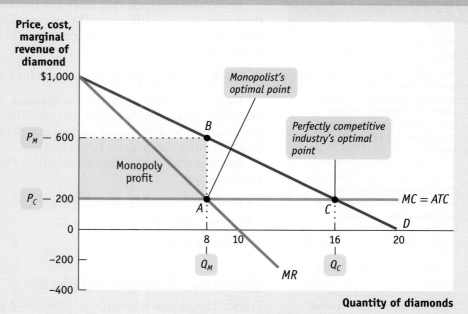

output level, 8 diamonds, is the monopolist's profit-maximizing quantity of output, Q_M. The price at which consumers demand 8 diamonds is $600, so the monopolist's price, P_M, is $600—corresponding to point *B*. The average total cost of producing each diamond is $200, so the monopolist earns a profit of $600 – $200 = $400 per diamond, and total profit is $8 \times $400 = $3,200, as indicated by the shaded area.

Monopoly versus Perfect Competition

When Cecil Rhodes consolidated many independent diamond producers into De Beers, he converted a perfectly competitive industry into a monopoly. We can now use our analysis to see the effects of such a consolidation.

Let's look again at Figure 13-6 and ask how this same market would work if, instead of being a monopoly, the industry were perfectly competitive. We will continue to assume that there is no fixed cost and that marginal cost is constant, so average total cost and marginal cost are equal.

If the diamond industry consists of many perfectly competitive firms, each of those producers takes the market price as given. For each firm, marginal revenue is equal to the market price. So each firm within the industry uses the price-taking firm's optimal output rule:

(13-2) $P = MC$ at the perfectly competitive firm's profit-maximizing
quantity of output

In Figure 13-6, this corresponds to producing at point *C*, where the price per diamond, P_C, is $200, equal to the marginal cost of production. So the profit-maximizing output of an industry under perfect competition, Q_C, is 16 diamonds.

But does the perfectly competitive industry earn any profits at point *C*? No: the price of $200 is equal to the average total cost per diamond. So there are no economic profits for this industry when it produces at the perfectly competitive output level.

We've already seen that once the industry is consolidated into a monopoly, the result is very different. The monopolist's calculation of marginal revenue takes the price effect into account, so that marginal revenue is less than the price. That is:

(13-3) $P > MR = MC$ at the monopolist's profit-maximizing quantity of output

We've also seen that the monopolist produces less than the competitive industry—8 diamonds rather than 16. The price under monopoly is $600, compared with only $200 under perfect competition. The monopolist earns a positive profit, but the competitive firm does not.

As suggested earlier, compared with a competitive industry, a monopolist does the following:

• Produces a smaller quantity: $Q_M < Q_C$
• Charges a higher price: $P_M > P_C$
• Earns a profit

Monopoly: The General Picture

Figure 13-6 involved specific numbers and assumed that marginal cost was constant, that there was no fixed cost, and, therefore, that the average total cost curve was a horizontal line. Figure 13-7 shows a more general picture of monopoly in action: *D* is the market demand curve; *MR*, the marginal revenue curve; *MC*, the marginal cost curve; and *ATC*, the average total cost curve. Here we return to the usual assumption that the marginal cost curve has a "swoosh" shape and the average total cost curve is U-shaped.

PITFALLS

FINDING THE MONOPOLY PRICE

To find the *profit-maximizing quantity of output* for a monopolist, look for the point where the marginal revenue curve crosses the marginal cost curve. Point *A* in Figure 13-6 is an example.

However, it's important not to make the mistake of imagining that point *A* also shows the *price* at which the monopolist sells its output. It doesn't. Instead, it shows the *marginal revenue* received by the monopolist, which is less than the price.

To find the monopoly price, you have to go up vertically from point *A* to the demand curve. There you find the price at which consumers demand the profit-maximizing quantity. So the profit-maximizing price–quantity combination is always a point on the demand curve, like point *B* in Figure 13-6.

FIGURE 13-7 The Monopolist's Profit

In this case, the marginal cost curve has a "swoosh" shape and the average total cost curve is U-shaped. The monopolist maximizes profit by producing the level of output at which $MR = MC$, given by point A, generating quantity Q_M. It finds its monopoly price, P_M, from the point on the demand curve directly above point A, point B here. The average total cost of Q_M is shown by point C. Profit is given by the area of the shaded rectangle.

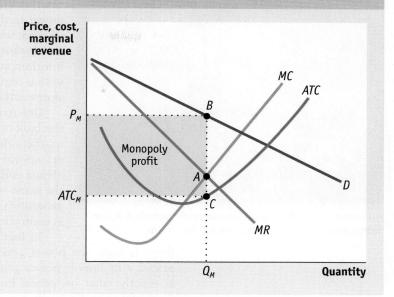

Applying the optimal output rule, we see that the profit-maximizing level of output is the output at which marginal revenue equals marginal cost, indicated by point A. The profit-maximizing quantity of output is Q_M, and the price charged by the monopolist is P_M. At the profit-maximizing level of output, the monopolist's average total cost is ATC_M, shown by point C.

Recalling how we calculated profit in Equation 12-5, profit is equal to the difference between total revenue and total cost. So we have:

$$(13\text{-}4) \quad \text{Profit} = TR - TC$$
$$= (P_M \times Q_M) - (ATC_M \times Q_M)$$
$$= (P_M - ATC_M) \times Q_M$$

Profit is equal to the area of the shaded rectangle in Figure 13-7, with a height of $P_M - ATC_M$ and a width of Q_M.

From Chapter 12 we know that a perfectly competitive industry can have profits in the *short run but not in the long run*. In the short run, price can exceed average total cost, allowing a perfectly competitive firm to make a profit. But we also know that this cannot persist.

In the long run, any profit in a perfectly competitive industry will be competed away as new firms enter the market. In contrast, barriers to entry allow a monopolist to make profits in *both the short run and the long run*.

ECONOMICS >> *in Action*
Shocked by the High Price of Electricity

Historically, electric utilities in the United States were recognized as natural monopolies. A utility serviced a defined geographical area and owned both the plants that generated electricity and the transmission lines that delivered it to retail customers. The rates charged to customers were regulated by the government and were set at a level to cover the utility's cost of operation plus a modest return on capital to its shareholders.

Beginning in the late 1990s, however, there was a move toward deregulation, based on the belief that competition would deliver lower retail electricity prices. Competition occurs at two junctures in the channel from power generation to

Although some electric utilities were deregulated in the 1990s, the current trend is to reregulate them.

retail customers: (1) distributors compete to sell electricity to retail customers, and (2) power generators compete to supply power to distributors.

That was the theory, at least. By 2018, only 16 states had instituted some form of electricity deregulation, while 7 had started but then suspended deregulation, leaving 27 states to continue with a regulated monopoly electricity provider. Why did so few states actually follow through on electricity deregulation?

One major obstacle is the lack of choice in power generators, the bulk of which still entail large up-front fixed costs. In many markets there is only one power generator. Although consumers appear to have a choice in their electricity distributor, the choice is illusory, since everyone must get their electricity from the same source in the end. Even when there is choice in power generators, there is frequently no choice in transmission, which is controlled by monopoly power line companies.

In fact, deregulation can make consumers worse off when there is only one power generator. Unfettered by regulations that set consumer prices, a monopoly power generator can engage in market manipulation. And that is exactly what happened in California during 2000 and 2001. After California deregulated its electricity market, an "energy crisis" suddenly occurred that brought blackouts and billions of dollars in electricity surcharges to homes and businesses. It turned out that a monopoly power generator intentionally reduced the amount of power supplied to consumers in order to drive up prices. After an investigation, regulators discovered audiotapes on which executives could be heard discussing plans to shut down power plants during times of peak energy demand, joking about how they were "stealing" more than $1 million a day from California's electricity consumers.

Another problem associated with deregulation of energy markets is it tends to lead to insufficient investment in new power plants. Without regulation, power generators are no longer guaranteed a market price that gives them a profitable rate of return on new power plants. As a result, in many states power generators have refused to invest in new plants. This has led to a shortfall in capacity as electricity demand has grown. For example, Texas, a deregulated state, has experienced massive blackouts due to insufficient capacity, and in New Jersey and Maryland, regulators have intervened to compel producers to build more power plants.

Lastly, consumers in deregulated states have been subject to big spikes in their electricity bills, often paying much more than consumers in regulated states. Angry customers and exasperated regulators have prompted many states to shift into reverse, with Illinois, Montana, and Virginia moving to regulate their industries. California and Montana have gone so far as to mandate that their electricity distributors reacquire power plants that were sold off during deregulation. In addition, regulators have been on the prowl, fining utilities in Texas, New York, and Illinois for market manipulation.

>> Check Your Understanding 13-2

Solutions appear at back of book.

1. Use the accompanying total revenue schedule of Emerald, Inc., a monopoly producer of 10-carat emeralds, to calculate the answers to parts a–d. Then answer part e.
   a. The demand schedule
   b. The marginal revenue schedule
   c. The quantity effect component of marginal revenue per output level
   d. The price effect component of marginal revenue per output level
   e. What additional information is needed to determine Emerald, Inc.'s profit-maximizing output?

Quantity of emeralds demanded	Total revenue
1	$100
2	186
3	252
4	280
5	250

2. Use Figure 13-6 to show what happens to the following when the marginal cost of diamond production rises from $200 to $400.
   - Marginal cost curve
   - Profit-maximizing price and quantity
   - Profit of the monopolist
   - Perfectly competitive industry profits

‖ Monopoly and Public Policy

It's profitable to be a monopolist, but it's not so beneficial to be a monopolist's customer. A monopolist, by reducing output and raising prices, benefits at the expense of consumers. But buyers and sellers always have conflicting interests: buyers want lower prices while sellers want higher prices. Is the conflict under monopoly any different than it is under perfect competition?

The answer is yes, because monopoly is a source of inefficiency: the losses to consumers from monopoly behavior are larger than the gains to the monopolist. Because monopoly leads to net losses to society's welfare, governments often try either to prevent the emergence of monopolies or to limit their effects. In this section, we will see why monopoly leads to inefficiency and examine the policies governments adopt in an attempt to prevent this inefficiency.

Welfare Effects of Monopoly

By restricting output below the level at which marginal cost is equal to the market price, a monopolist increases its profit but hurts consumers. When comparing the monopolist's gain in profit to the loss in consumer surplus, we learn that the loss in consumer surplus is larger than the monopolist's gain. As a result, monopoly causes a net loss for society.

To see why, let's return to the case where the marginal cost curve is horizontal, as shown in the two panels of Figure 13-8. Here the marginal cost curve is MC, the demand curve is D, and, in panel (b), the marginal revenue curve is MR.

FIGURE 13-8 Monopoly Causes Inefficiency

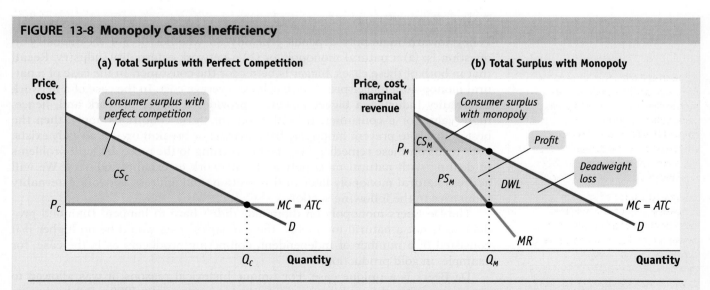

Panel (a) depicts a perfectly competitive industry: output is Q_C, and market price, P_C, is equal to MC. Since price is exactly equal to each producer's average total cost of production per unit, there is no profit and no producer surplus. So total surplus is equal to consumer surplus, the entire shaded area. Panel (b) depicts the industry under monopoly: the monopolist decreases output to Q_M and charges P_M. Consumer surplus (blue area) has shrunk: a portion of it has been captured as profit (green area), and a portion of it has been lost to deadweight loss (yellow area), the value of mutually beneficial transactions that do not occur because of monopoly behavior. As a result, total surplus falls.

Panel (a) shows what happens if this industry is perfectly competitive. Equilibrium output is Q_C; the price of the good, P_C, is equal to marginal cost, and marginal cost is also equal to average total cost because there is no fixed cost and marginal cost is constant. Each firm is earning exactly its average total cost per unit of output, so there is no profit and no producer surplus in this equilibrium.

The consumer surplus generated by the market is equal to the area of the blue shaded triangle CS_C shown in panel (a). Since there is no producer surplus when the industry is perfectly competitive, CS_C also represents the total surplus.

Panel (b) shows the results for the same market, but this time assuming that the industry is a monopoly. The monopolist produces the level of output Q_M, at which marginal cost is equal to marginal revenue, and it charges the price P_M. The industry now earns profit—which is also the producer surplus—equal to the area of the green rectangle, PS_M. Note that this profit is surplus captured from consumers as consumer surplus shrinks to the area of the blue triangle, CS_M.

By comparing panels (a) and (b), we see that in addition to the redistribution of surplus from consumers to the monopolist, another important change has occurred: the sum of profit and consumer surplus—total surplus—is *smaller* under monopoly than under perfect competition. That is, the sum of CS_M and PS_M in panel (b) is less than the area CS_C in panel (a). In Chapter 7, we analyzed how taxes generated *deadweight loss* to society. Here we show that monopoly creates a deadweight loss to society equal to the area of the yellow triangle, DWL. So monopoly produces a net loss for society.

This net loss arises because some mutually beneficial transactions do not occur. There are people for whom an additional unit of the good is worth more than the marginal cost of producing it but who don't consume it because they are not willing to pay P_M.

If you recall our discussion of the deadweight loss from the chapter on taxes, you will notice that the deadweight loss from monopoly looks quite similar. Indeed, by driving a wedge between price and marginal cost, monopoly acts much like a tax on consumers and produces the same kind of inefficiency.

So monopoly hurts the welfare of society as a whole and is a source of market failure. Is there anything government policy can do about it?

Policy Remedies to Monopoly

Policy toward monopoly depends crucially on whether or not the industry in question is: (a) a natural monopoly or (b) a network externality industry. Recall that in both of these cases, bigger is better for the consumer. In the case of a natural monopoly, a bigger producer has lower average cost. In the case of a network externality industry, a bigger producer provides a bigger network and, hence, more value for a consumer. If neither one of those conditions apply, then the best policy is to prevent monopoly from arising or break it up if it already exists. Let's focus on these remedies first, before turning to the more difficult problems of dealing with natural monopoly and a network externality industry. We will address natural monopoly later in this section, and address network externality industries in the following section.

The De Beers monopoly on diamonds didn't have to happen. Diamond production is not a natural monopoly: the industry's costs would be no higher if it consisted of a number of independent, competing producers as is the case, for example, in gold production.

De Beers is a unique case. For unique historical reasons, it was allowed to remain a monopoly until it was overtaken by events in the 1990s. But beginning in the late nineteenth century, most similar monopolies have been broken up. Regulators focused on monopolies that had arisen, like De Beers, from the consolidation of rival firms in an industry into common ownership. The most celebrated example in the United States is Standard Oil, founded by John D. Rockefeller in 1870. By 1878 Standard Oil controlled almost all U.S. oil refining; but in 1911 a court order broke the company into a number of smaller units, including the companies that later became Exxon and Mobil (and merged in 1999 to become ExxonMobil).

The government policies used to prevent or eliminate monopolies are known as *antitrust policies*, which we will discuss in the next chapter.

Dealing with Natural Monopoly

Breaking up a monopoly that isn't natural is clearly a good idea: the gains to consumers outweigh the loss to the producer. But it's not so clear whether a natural monopoly, one in which a large producer has lower average total costs than small producers, should be broken up, because this would raise average total cost. For example, a town government that tried to prevent a single company from dominating local gas supply—which, as we've discussed, is almost surely a natural monopoly—would raise the cost of providing gas to its residents.

Yet even in the case of a natural monopoly, a profit-maximizing monopolist acts in a way that causes inefficiency—it charges consumers a price that is higher than marginal cost and, by doing so, prevents some potentially beneficial transactions. Also, it can seem unfair that a firm that has managed to establish a monopoly position earns a large profit at the expense of consumers.

Two policy options can be adopted to deal with the inefficiencies of monopoly: public ownership and regulation.

1. Public Ownership In many countries, the preferred answer to the problem of natural monopoly has been **public ownership.** Instead of allowing a private monopolist to control an industry, the government establishes a public agency to provide the good and protect consumers' interests. Well-known examples of public ownership in the United States are Amtrak, the passenger rail service, and the U.S. Postal Service. In general, critical transportation channels such as major airports, major bridges, subways, and major ports are owned by a state government authority. And some cities, including Los Angeles, have publicly owned electrical power companies.

> In **public ownership** of a monopoly, the good is supplied by the government or by a firm owned by the government.
>
> **Price regulation** limits the price that a monopolist is allowed to charge.

Amtrak, a public company, has provided train service, at a loss, to destinations that attract few passengers.

The advantage of public ownership, in principle, is that a publicly owned natural monopoly can set prices based on the criterion of efficiency rather than profit maximization. In a perfectly competitive industry, profit-maximizing behavior is efficient because producers produce the quantity at which price is equal to marginal cost; that is why there is no economic argument for public ownership of, say, Christmas tree farms.

Experience suggests, however, that public ownership as a solution to the problem of natural monopoly often works badly in practice. One reason is that publicly owned firms are often less eager than private companies to keep costs down or offer high-quality products. Another is that publicly owned companies all too often end up serving political interests—providing contracts or jobs to people with the right connections. For example, Amtrak has notoriously provided train service at a loss to destinations that attract few passengers—but that are located in the districts of influential members of Congress.

2. Regulation In the United States, the more common policy tool used to address natural monopoly has been to leave the industry in private hands but subject it to regulation. For example, most local utilities are covered by **price regulation** that limits the prices they can charge.

As we've learned, imposing a *price ceiling* on a competitive industry is a recipe for shortages, black markets, and other nasty side effects. Doesn't imposing a limit on the price that, say, a local gas company can charge have the same effects?

Not necessarily: a price ceiling on a monopolist need not create a shortage—in the absence of a price ceiling, a monopolist would charge a price that is higher than its marginal cost of production. So even if forced to charge a lower price—as long as that price is above *MC* and the monopolist at least breaks even on total output—the monopolist still has an incentive to produce the quantity demanded at that price.

Figure 13-9 shows an example of price regulation of a natural monopoly—a highly simplified version of a local gas company. The company faces a demand curve *D*, with an associated marginal revenue curve *MR*. For simplicity, we assume that the firm's total costs consist of two parts: a fixed cost and variable costs that are incurred at a constant proportion to output. In this case, marginal cost is constant, and the marginal cost curve (which here is also the average variable cost curve) is the horizontal line *MC*.

The average total cost curve is the downward-sloping curve *ATC*; it slopes downward because the higher the output, the lower the average fixed cost (the fixed cost per unit of output). Because average total cost slopes downward over the range of output relevant for market demand, this is a natural monopoly.

Panel (a) illustrates a case of natural monopoly without regulation. The unregulated natural monopolist chooses the monopoly output Q_M and charges the price P_M. Since the monopolist receives a price greater than its average total cost, it earns a profit. This profit is exactly equal to the producer surplus in this market, represented by the green-shaded rectangle. Consumer surplus is given by the blue-shaded triangle.

Now suppose that regulators impose a price ceiling on local gas deliveries—one that falls below the monopoly price P_M but above *ATC*, say, at P_R in panel (a). At that price the quantity demanded is Q_R.

FIGURE 13-9 Unregulated and Regulated Natural Monopoly

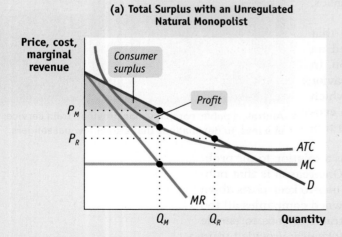

(a) Total Surplus with an Unregulated Natural Monopolist

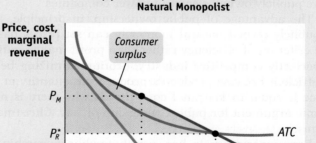

(b) Total Surplus with a Regulated Natural Monopolist

This figure shows the case of a natural monopolist. In panel (a), if the monopolist is allowed to charge P_M, it makes a profit, shown by the green area; consumer surplus is shown by the blue area. If it is regulated and must charge the lower price P_R, output increases from Q_M to Q_R and consumer surplus increases. Panel (b) shows what happens when the monopolist must charge a price equal to average total cost, the price P_R^*. Output expands to Q_R^*, and consumer surplus is now the entire blue area. The monopolist makes zero profit. This is the greatest total surplus possible when the monopolist is allowed to at least break even, making P_R^* the best regulated price.

Does the company have an incentive to produce that quantity? Yes. If the price at which the monopolist can sell its product is fixed by regulators, the firm's output no longer affects the market price. The monopolist ignores the *MR* curve and is willing to expand output to meet the quantity demanded as long as the price it receives for the next unit is greater than marginal cost and the monopolist at least breaks even on total output. So with price regulation, the monopolist produces more, at a lower price.

Of course, the monopolist will not be willing to produce at all if the imposed price means producing at a loss. That is, the price ceiling has to be set high enough to allow the firm to cover its average total cost. Panel (b) shows a situation in which regulators have pushed the price down as far as possible, at the level where the average total cost curve crosses the demand curve.

At any lower price the firm loses money. The price here, P_R^*, is the best regulated price: the monopolist is just willing to operate and produces Q_R^*, the quantity demanded at that price. Consumers and society gain as a result.

The welfare effects of this regulation can be seen by comparing the shaded areas in the two panels of Figure 13-9. Consumer surplus is increased by the regulation, with the gains coming from two sources. First, profits are eliminated and added instead to consumer surplus. Second, the larger output and lower price lead to an overall welfare gain—an increase in total surplus. In fact, panel (b) illustrates the largest total surplus possible.

This all looks terrific: consumers are better off, profits are eliminated, and overall welfare increases. Unfortunately, things are rarely that easy in practice. There two main problems. First is the problem of inadequate information: regulators don't have the information required to set the price exactly at the level at which the demand curve crosses the average total cost curve. Sometimes they set it too low, creating shortages; at other times they set it too high. Also, regulated monopolies, like publicly owned firms, tend to exaggerate their costs to regulators and to provide inferior quality to consumers. Second is the problem of *regulatory capture:* because vast sums of money are at stake, regulators can be unduly influenced by the companies they are supposed to oversee.

However, as the Economics in Action of the last section, "Shocked by the High Price of Electricity," shows, some level of regulation and oversight of a natural monopoly is generally much better than none at all.

A New Generation of Market Power

These days, an old-fashioned monopolist like DeBeers is hard to find. Except in the cases of monopolies that arise from natural monopoly, government protection, or technological advantage (usually short-lived), examples of industries in which there is truly only one seller that has sole control of a good are found almost exclusively in history books.

There's a reason for that. As we explained earlier, a U.S. company that tried to become a monopolist by acquiring control of a scarce natural resource by buying up rival firms (as Cecil Rhodes did) would soon be accused of breaking U.S. antitrust laws.

Yet the topic of monopoly and antitrust regulation has recently become one of the hottest topics of economic discussion in recent years. Why? It's due to the rise of the digital economy and the network externalities that it creates. Companies such as Facebook, Microsoft, Apple, Google, eBay, Uber, and PayPal have transformed the economy. They represent the fastest growing and among the most profitable firms in the economy. However, they represent a unique set of problems in policy making. While the old-fashioned way of becoming a monopolist is no longer viable, network externalities provide a number of ways of gaining market power and, potentially, of becoming a monopolist (or very close to one). In this section we'll explore the special nature of market power that arises from network externalities. We will also learn about an important variation of market power called monopsony—an industry in which there is only one buyer—which has been on the rise due to the growth of network externalities.

In the past few years, the digital economy and its network externalities have generated significant urgency in answering the questions of how to manage market power, both in the case of monopoly and of monopsony. In this section we'll learn why and about the special challenges that policy makers now face.

A New Generation of Market Power and Monopoly

As we learned earlier, increasing returns to scale and network externalities share the critical feature that "bigger is better." Recall that when network externalities are present in an industry, the firm with the largest network is preferred by consumers to firms with smaller networks. Hence the biggest firm in the industry gets bigger while smaller firms shrink. Eventually, the biggest firm—the *dominant* firm—will become large enough relative to any rivals to exert market power and behave like a monopolist.

As in standard monopoly, the dominant firm in a network externalities industry creates a deadweight loss to society if it raises price and reduces output in order to capture surplus from consumers. And in fast-moving digital industries, there's another potential inefficiency caused by market power: *stifling innovation*. The dominant firm, by using its size advantage to deter rivals from entering the market or using their network, stifles the innovation that they can bring.

Microsoft is the best example of a network externalities firm that used its size to vanquish rivals and stifle innovation. A federal court found Microsoft guilty of engaging in "monopolization": using its market dominance in the PC operating systems market to harm Netscape, a rival to Microsoft's Internet Explorer in the internet browser market. The federal court also found that Microsoft had undertaken steps against a number of rival software companies to crush any challenge to its near-monopoly position in the operating-system market, the source of the network externality—companies that possessed superior technology to Microsoft's. Rather than breaking Microsoft up into smaller companies, the court mandated that Microsoft open up its operating-system software to allow rival software companies to work with it. However, Microsoft's position was by then so dominant that rival software companies were never able to establish a significant market share. A case in point: after having an initial market share of 90% share of the internet browser market, Netscape eventually disappeared. Not surprisingly, Microsoft's software division remains highly profitable, reporting profits of nearly $13 billion in 2019.

More recently, in 2018 and in 2019, the EU's antitrust authorities accused Google of engaging in anti-competitive behavior and stifling innovation by blocking rivals across a number of different platforms, such as online shopping searches and the market for Android phone operating systems, hitting it with over $9 billion in fines. However, the final verdicts in these cases will probably take years to decide; if history is any judge, by that time Google's dominance will be sealed.

A New Generation of Market Power and Monopsony

Is it possible for the buyer and not the seller to have market power? Put another way, is it possible to have a market in which there is only one buyer but many sellers, so that the buyer can use its power to capture surplus from the sellers? The answer is yes, and that market is called a **monopsony.**

A **monopsony** exists when there is only one buyer of a good. A **monopsonist** is a firm that is the sole buyer in a market.

Like a monopolist, a **monopsonist** will distort the competitive market outcome in order to capture more of the surplus, except that the monopsonist will do this through quantity purchased and price paid for goods rather than through quantity sold and price charged for goods.

The classic example is a single employer in a small town—say, the local factory—that is purchasing labor services from workers. Recall that a monopolist, realizing that it can affect the price at which its goods are sold, reduces output in order to get a higher price and increase its profits. A monopsonist does much the same thing, but with a twist: realizing that it can affect the wage it pays by moving down the labor supply curve, it reduces the number of employees hired and pays a lower wage in order to increase its profits.

Just as a monopolist creates a deadweight loss by producing too little output, a monopsonist creates a deadweight loss by hiring too few workers and paying wages that are too low. As a result it also produces too little output.

In the past, monopsony was a relatively rare phenomenon as sellers would find a way to offer their goods and services to a rival. For example, workers subject to a local monopsonist employer could in most cases simply move away and find employment elsewhere. However, with the advent of the digital economy, monopsony behavior appears to be on the rise. Giant e-commerce platforms like Amazon or the Apple App Store can now use their power to win concessions from sellers who use their platforms to sell their merchandise. They can capture surplus from sellers by forcing them to accept lower prices for their merchandise in various ways—such as by charging them high fees, by developing competing in-house brands (i.e., the Amazon Basics brand), and the like. Eventually, sellers will reduce their sales on the platform. Output falls and deadweight loss is incurred.

The recent and ongoing legal case of *Apple v. Pepper* is an example of monopsony behavior arising from a network externality. In the legal proceedings, consumers and app designers charged that Apple's requirement that all iOS apps be purchased through its Apple App Store allowed Apple to exert monopsony power over app designers. By charging app designers 30% of their sales price, the plaintiffs claimed that Apple was using the dominance of its e-commerce platform to capture surplus from app suppliers. App suppliers, as a result, had to either accept lower surplus or try to pass the 30% "Apple tax" onto consumers. Either way, output falls in comparison to the competitive outcome, in which app suppliers and consumers can freely trade with one another. However, because app designers want to sell on the e-commerce platform visited by the largest number of customers, while customers want to visit the platform with the largest number of apps supplied—dealing with monopsony behavior based on network externalities presents the same policy difficulty as dealing with monopoly behavior based on network externalities.

Policies to Address the New Generation of Market Power

The examples discussed here illustrate the thorny challenge that market power arising from network externalities poses to policy makers. Like natural monopoly, the firm with the largest network is likely to become dominant enough to exert market power. And it could, eventually, become a monopolist or a monopsonist as smaller firms disappear. Yet, policy makers have also recognized that, like natural monopoly, welfare will be reduced if the dominant firm was split into smaller firms with smaller networks. In time, the problem of market power would reappear as consumers migrate to the firm with the larger network, repeating the dynamic in which the largest firm grows larger while smaller firms shrink and disappear. And when it comes to fostering innovation, there also lies a conundrum. While with monopoly or monopsony behavior the digital giants can stifle innovation created by rivals, it's clear that the digital giants themselves are also huge sources of innovation. Thus poorly implemented regulation of the giants can stifle innovation as well. To regulate them on account of their size, these companies argue, is simply to penalize them for their success in delivering to consumers what they want.

Given the explosive growth of the digital economy, it's arguable that the problem of how to manage the new generation of market power is one of the most difficult challenges facing economists and policy makers. As the following Economics in Action shows, as of the time of writing there are few clear answers.

ECONOMICS >> *in Action*
Are American Antitrust Policy Makers Behind the Digital Times?

imageBROKER/Alamy Stock Photo

The digital giants—Google, Facebook, and Amazon—have presented difficult regulatory challenges for antitrust policy makers.

The digital giants, Amazon, Facebook, and Google, are the quintessential firms of the digital economy. Amazon, which began as an online retailer of books, has grown into a corporate behemoth: a general retailer, a marketing platform, a provider of delivery and logistical services, a payment service, a credit lender, an auction house, a major book publisher, a producer of television and films, a hardware manufacturer, a fashion creator, and a leading provider of cloud services and computing power.

Facebook is the world's dominant social platform, with nearly 2.3 billion active users as of 2018. Google accounts for 92% of global search engine activity. Together, Facebook and Google account for 73% of digital advertising in the United States. In 2018, Amazon reported annual revenue of over $142 billion; Facebook reported nearly $56 billion; and Google reported over $136 billion. (This data was found using Google, written on a computer purchased on Amazon, while not looking at any open Facebook pages.)

But economists and historians have noted a striking feature of these three companies: each one has relied on practices that, in previous eras, were found to be either anti-competitive, or had created critical large-scale infrastructure that warranted regulation as a natural monopoly.

For example, all three firms have taken actions to eliminate rivals. Amazon has purchased a myriad of e-retailing companies—such as Audible, Diapers. com, and Zappos—to maintain its dominance as the one-stop shopping website. Likewise, Facebook has bought rival social-networking platforms Friendster, Instagram, and WhatsApp. According to EU antitrust authorities, Google has harmed competitors by requiring equipment manufacturers to install its search engine on their products.

Amazon's massive warehouse system of over 100 warehouses across the country, manned by fleets of robots, enables it to provide super-fast delivery. And the volume discounts it receives from delivery companies like UPS aren't available to smaller rivals. So goods suppliers, like Eveready Batteries, find it necessary to list their products on Amazon Marketplace. Yet, this enables Amazon to gather finely detailed data on customers' shopping habits, which they then can use to create their own "Amazon Basics" brand, which directly competes against the goods suppliers at lower prices. Finally, recent revelations about Facebook's use of its users' private data has led to calls for intervention.

So what explains U.S. policy makers' lack of action?

One explanation for this inaction is that, like in the case of natural monopoly, policy makers understand that there is no easy fix to the problem of market dominance when there are network externalities. A second explanation is that policy makers don't think the firms are exploiting their dominant positions because there is no clear evidence that consumers are being charged monopoly prices and that output is being restricted. And it is certainly true that consumers have gained vast benefits from the three firms. A third explanation is that U.S. policy makers fear that regulation could stifle innovation and thereby reduce society's welfare in the long run.

Yet, others are not so sanguine. According to some economists and historians, policy makers have a view of social welfare that is too restrictive. In the case of Amazon, they assert that the welfare of goods suppliers should also be taken into account along with that of consumers. They argue that Amazon's actions will eventually force some goods suppliers out of their markets, reducing innovation as well as the quality and diversity of products available, and allowing Amazon to eventually raise prices. For example, the parent company of Diapers.com rebuffed an offer from Amazon to buy the company in 2009. Amazon responded by creating its own brand of diapers and baby products, undercutting the prices on Diapers.com. So in 2010, the company gave in and allowed itself to be purchased by Amazon.

Also, economists and historians argue that the antitrust framework of the past doesn't take into account the enormous advantages that Amazon, Facebook, and Google have in acquiring and using their users' data in a way that reinforces their market dominance. They argue that in Amazon's case, its constantly fluctuating and personalized pricing system simply doesn't allow regulators the ability to monitor if Amazon is indeed inflating its prices. Finally, they raise the concern that the enormous economic weight of the digital giants will translate into outsized political power, making it harder to check their dominance and their exercise of market power. This echoes one of the primary concerns that led to the creation of U.S. antitrust law in the 1890s (which we will discuss in the next chapter).

So far, EU regulators have acted far more aggressively than U.S. regulators. As of 2019, the EU had fined Google over $9 billion, claiming that it had abused its market dominance in several sectors, such as advertising and the Android operating system. In 2020, the EU announced that it planned to formally charge Amazon with abusing its power by gathering data from its small sellers and using that information to launch competing products. It has moved against Facebook's lax handling of users' private data and, in 2020, announced a formal investigation into abuse of market power by Apple's App store.

Are U.S. policy makers moving too slowly? Or are EU policy makers moving to aggressively? At this point, the answer is unclear. Moreover, some observers say that despite the more active stance by EU policy makers, it's not clear that their actions will ultimately alter the firms' market dominance.

Whatever the ultimate policy stance, it's clear that antitrust policy will be a topic of intense debate for the foreseeable future.

>> Check Your Understanding 13-3
Solutions appear at back of book.

1. What policy should the government adopt in the following cases? Explain.
   a. Internet service in Anytown, Ohio, is provided by cable. Customers feel they are being overcharged, but the cable company claims it must charge prices that allow it to recover the costs of laying cable.
   b. The only two airlines that currently fly to Alaska need government approval to merge. Other airlines wish to fly to Alaska but need government-allocated landing slots to do so.
2. True or false? Explain your answer.
   a. Society's welfare is lower under monopoly because some consumer surplus is transformed into profit for the monopolist.
   b. A monopolist causes inefficiency because there are consumers who are willing to pay a price greater than or equal to marginal cost but less than the monopoly price.
3. Suppose a monopolist mistakenly believes that its marginal revenue is always equal to the market price. Assuming constant marginal cost and no fixed cost, draw a diagram comparing the level of profit, consumer surplus, total surplus, and deadweight loss for this misguided monopolist compared to a smart monopolist.
4. Some social media industry observers claim that Facebook is so dominant in the social media market that it is now like a utility, such as a water utility. What have you learned about monopoly that might validate this claim? What evidence might invalidate this claim?

>> **Quick Review**

• By reducing output and raising price above marginal cost, a monopolist captures some of the consumer surplus as profit and causes deadweight loss. To avoid deadweight loss, government policy attempts to curtail monopoly behavior.

• When monopolies are "created" rather than natural, governments should act to prevent them from forming and break up existing ones.

• One method of managing natural monopoly is by **public ownership.** However, publicly owned companies are often poorly run. Another method is **price regulation.** A price ceiling imposed on a monopolist does not create shortages as long as it is not set too low.

• Owing to the rise of the digital economy, market power arising from network externalities has become a topic of intense debate as digital giants engage in monopoly and **monopsony** behavior. A **monopsonist** can affect the price of the good it buys: it captures surplus from sellers by reducing how much it purchases and thereby lowers the price paid to the seller. Like a monopoly, it creates deadweight loss as too little output is produced.

• Because consumers benefit from bigger networks, market power arising from network externalities is a difficult challenge for policy makers. The digital giants can exercise market power, creating deadweight loss and stifling innovation by deterring rivals. Yet, the digital giants are also sources of innovation and are successful because consumers prefer them. Moreover, if they are broken up, dominant firms with market power are likely to reemerge.

‖ Price Discrimination

Up to this point, we have considered only the case of a **single-price monopolist,** one that charges all consumers the same price. As the term suggests, not all monopolists do this. In fact, many if not most monopolists find that they can increase their profits by charging different customers different prices for the same good: they engage in **price discrimination.**

One of the most striking examples of price discrimination involves airline tickets. Although there are a number of airlines, most air routes in the United States are serviced by only one or two carriers. As a result, these carriers have market power and can set prices. So any regular airline passenger quickly becomes aware that the question "How much will it cost me to fly there?" rarely has a simple answer.

If you are willing to buy a nonrefundable ticket a month in advance and happen to purchase the ticket on Tuesday or Wednesday evening, the round trip may cost only $150—or less if you are a senior citizen or a student. But if you have to go on a business trip tomorrow, which happens to be Tuesday, and come back on Wednesday, the same round trip might cost $550. Yet the business traveler and the visiting grandparent receive the same product—the same cramped seat, the same awful food (if indeed any food is served).

You might argue that airlines are not usually monopolists—that in most flight markets the airline industry is an oligopoly because there is more than one firm offering flights to most destinations. In fact, price discrimination takes place under oligopoly and monopolistic competition as well as monopoly because these firms have some market power and can therefore influence prices. But it doesn't happen under perfect competition, where firms have no ability to influence prices. And once we've seen why monopolists sometimes price-discriminate, we'll be in a good position to understand why it happens in oligopoly and monopolistic competition, too.

The Logic of Price Discrimination

Let's begin by looking at why price discrimination might be more profitable than charging all consumers the same price. Imagine that Air Sunshine offers the only nonstop flights between Bismarck, North Dakota, and Fort Lauderdale, Florida. Assume that there are no capacity problems—the airline can fly as many planes as the number of passengers warrants. Also assume that there is no fixed cost. The marginal cost to the airline of providing a seat is $125, however many passengers it carries. Further assume that the airline knows there are two kinds of potential passengers: 2,000 business travelers who want to travel between these destinations each week, and 2,000 students who want to do the same.

Will potential passengers take the flight? It depends on the price. The business travelers, it turns out, really need to fly; they will take the plane as long as the price is no more than $550. Since they are flying purely for business, we assume that cutting the price below $550 will not lead to any increase in business travel. The students, however, have less money and more time; if the price goes above $150, they will take the bus. The implied demand curve is shown in Figure 13-10.

So what should the airline do? If it has to charge everyone the same price, its options are limited. It could charge $550; that way it would get as much as possible out of the business travelers but lose the student market. Or it could charge only $150; that way it would get both types of travelers but would make significantly less money from sales to business travelers.

We can quickly calculate the profits from each of these alternatives. If the airline charged $550, it would sell 2,000 tickets to the business travelers, earning total revenue of 2,000 × $550 = $1.1 million and incurring costs of 2,000 × $125 = $250,000; so its profit would be $850,000, illustrated by the shaded area *B* in Figure 13-10.

FIGURE 13-10 Two Types of Airline Customers

Air Sunshine has two types of customers, business travelers willing to pay at most $550 per ticket and students willing to pay at most $150 per ticket. There are 2,000 of each kind of customer. Air Sunshine has a constant marginal cost of $125 per seat. If Air Sunshine could charge these two types of customers different prices, it would maximize its profit by charging business travelers $550 and students $150 per ticket. It would capture all of the consumer surplus as profit.

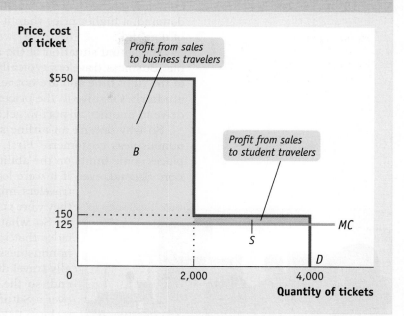

If the airline charged only $150, it would sell 4,000 tickets, receiving revenue of $4,000 \times \$150 = \$600,000$ and incurring costs of $4,000 \times \$125 = \$500,000$; in this case, its profit would be $100,000. If the airline must charge everyone the same price, charging the higher price and forgoing sales to students is clearly more profitable.

What the airline would really like to do, however, is charge the business travelers the full $550 but offer $150 tickets to the students. That's a lot less than the price paid by business travelers, but it's still above marginal cost; so if the airline could sell those extra 2,000 tickets to students, it would make an additional $50,000 in profit. That is, it would make a profit equal to the areas *B* plus *S* in Figure 13-10.

It would be more realistic to suppose that there is some "give" in each group's demand: at a price below $550, there would be some increase in business travel; and at a price above $150, some students would still purchase tickets. But this, it turns out, does not do away with the argument for price discrimination.

The important point is that the two groups of consumers differ in their *sensitivity to price*—that a high price has a larger effect in discouraging purchases by students than purchases by business travelers. As long as different groups of customers respond differently to the price, a monopolist will find that it can capture more consumer surplus and increase its profit by charging them different prices.

Price Discrimination and Elasticity

A more realistic description of the demand that airlines face would not specify particular prices at which different types of travelers would choose to fly. Instead, it would distinguish between the groups on the basis of their sensitivity to the price—their price elasticity of demand.

Suppose that a company sells its product to two easily identifiable groups of people—business travelers and students. It just so happens that business travelers are very insensitive to the price: there is a certain amount of the product they just have to have whatever the price, but they cannot be persuaded to buy much more than that no matter how cheap it is. Students, though, are more flexible: offer a good enough price and they will buy quite a lot, but raise the price too high and they will switch to something else. What should the company do?

The answer is the one already suggested by our simplified example: the company should charge business travelers, who have a low price elasticity of demand, a higher price than it charges students, who have a high price elasticity of demand.

The actual situation of the airlines is very much like this hypothetical example. Business travelers typically place a high priority on being at the right place at the right time and are not very sensitive to the price. But nonbusiness travelers are fairly sensitive to the price: faced with a high price, they might take the bus, drive to another airport to get a lower fare, or skip the trip altogether.

So why doesn't an airline simply announce different prices for business and nonbusiness customers? First, this would probably be illegal because U.S. law places some limits on the ability of companies to practice open price discrimination. Second, even if it were legal, it would be a hard policy to enforce: business travelers might be willing to wear casual clothing and claim they were visiting family in Ft. Lauderdale in order to save $400.

So what the airlines do—quite successfully—is impose rules that indirectly have the effect of charging business and nonbusiness travelers different fares. Business travelers usually travel during the week and want to be home on the weekend; so the round-trip fare is much higher if you don't stay over a Saturday night. The requirement of a weekend stay for a cheap ticket effectively separates business from nonbusiness travelers.

Similarly, business travelers often visit several cities in succession rather than make a simple round trip; so round-trip fares are much lower than twice the one-way fare. Many business trips are scheduled on short notice; so fares are much lower if you book far in advance. Fares are also lower if you purchase a last-minute ticket, taking your chances on whether you actually get a seat—business travelers have to make it to that meeting; people visiting their relatives don't.

On many airline routes, the fare you pay depends on the type of traveler you are.

Because customers must show their ID at check-in, airlines make sure there are no resales of tickets between the two groups that would undermine their ability to price-discriminate—students can't buy cheap tickets and resell them to business travelers. Look at the rules that govern ticket-pricing, and you will see an ingenious implementation of profit-maximizing price discrimination.

Perfect Price Discrimination

Let's return to the example of business travelers and students traveling between Bismarck and Fort Lauderdale, illustrated in Figure 13-10, and ask what would happen if the airline could distinguish between the two groups of customers to charge each a different price.

Clearly, the airline would charge each group its willingness to pay—that is, the maximum that each group is willing to pay. For business travelers, the willingness to pay is $550; for students, it is $150. As we have assumed, the marginal cost is $125 and does not depend on output, making the marginal cost curve a horizontal line. As we noted earlier, we can easily determine the airline's profit: it is the sum of the areas of the rectangle *B* and the rectangle *S*.

In this case, the consumers do not get any consumer surplus! The entire surplus is captured by the monopolist in the form of profit. When a monopolist is able to capture the entire surplus in this way, we say that it achieves **perfect price discrimination.**

Perfect price discrimination takes place when a monopolist charges each consumer their willingness to pay—the maximum that the consumer is willing to pay.

In general, the greater the number of different prices a monopolist is able to charge, the closer it can get to perfect price discrimination. Figure 13-11 shows a monopolist facing a downward-sloping demand curve, a monopolist who we

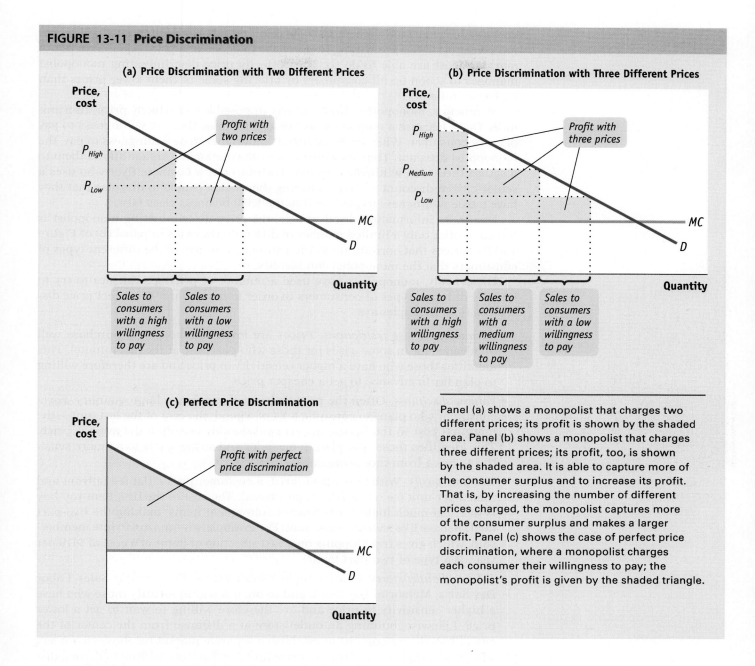

FIGURE 13-11 Price Discrimination

(a) Price Discrimination with Two Different Prices

(b) Price Discrimination with Three Different Prices

(c) Perfect Price Discrimination

Panel (a) shows a monopolist that charges two different prices; its profit is shown by the shaded area. Panel (b) shows a monopolist that charges three different prices; its profit, too, is shown by the shaded area. It is able to capture more of the consumer surplus and to increase its profit. That is, by increasing the number of different prices charged, the monopolist captures more of the consumer surplus and makes a larger profit. Panel (c) shows the case of perfect price discrimination, where a monopolist charges each consumer their willingness to pay; the monopolist's profit is given by the shaded triangle.

assume is able to charge different prices to different groups of consumers, with the consumers who are willing to pay the most being charged the most.

In panel (a) the monopolist charges two different prices; in panel (b) the monopolist charges three different prices. Two things are apparent:

1. The greater the number of prices the monopolist charges, the lower the lowest price—that is, some consumers will pay prices that approach marginal cost.
2. The greater the number of prices the monopolist charges, the more money it extracts from consumers.

With a very large number of different prices, the picture would look like panel (c), a case of perfect price discrimination. Here, consumers least willing to buy the good pay marginal cost, and the entire consumer surplus is extracted as profit.

Both our airline example and the example in Figure 13-11 can be used to make another point: a monopolist that can engage in perfect price discrimination doesn't cause any inefficiency! The source of inefficiency is eliminated: all potential consumers who are willing to purchase the good at a price equal to or above marginal cost are able to do so. The perfectly price-discriminating monopolist manages to scoop up all consumers by offering some of them lower prices than it charges others.

In practice, monopolists find it nearly impossible to perfectly price discriminate. That's because a monopolist is not able to know the true willingness to pay of every consumer. While each consumer knows their true willingness to pay, the monopolist does not. Thus the consumer's information advantage allows them to disguise their true willingness to pay. For example, a business flyer who uses a senior citizen discount when purchasing their ticket is able to disguise that they have a true willingness to pay equal to the $550 business class fare.

Due to its information disadvantage, the price-discriminating monopolist is forced to offer only a limited number of different prices (as in panel (b) of Figure 13-11)—prices that correspond to the willingness to pay of the different types of consumers that the monopolist can identify.

Historically, monopolists have used a number of pricing strategies to try to identify different types of consumers in order to move closer to perfect price discrimination. Examples are:

- *Advance purchase restrictions.* Prices are lower for those who purchase well in advance (or in some cases for those who purchase at the last minute). This identifies those who have a higher sensitivity to price and are therefore willing to plan far in advance to get a cheaper price.

- *Volume discounts.* Often the price is lower if you buy a large quantity. For a consumer who plans to consume a lot of a good, the cost of the last unit—the marginal cost to the consumer—is considerably less than the average price. This identifies those who plan to buy a lot and so are likely to be more sensitive to price from those who don't.

- *Two-part tariffs.* With a two-part tariff, a customer pays a flat fee upfront and then a per-unit fee on each item purchased. The cost of the first item you buy is in effect much higher than that of subsequent items, making the two-part tariff behave like a volume discount. For example, an Amazon Prime membership, which gives free shipping on a vast selection of items at a cost of $119 per year, is a type of two-part tariff.

- *Sales and outlet stores.* Holding regular sales such as Black Friday Sales, Labor Day Sales, Memorial Day Sales, and so on, is a way to identify those who have a higher sensitivity to price and are therefore willing to wait to get a lower price. Likewise, building an outlet store at a distance from the center of the city allows the monopolist to establish a separate market for those customers who have a higher sensitivity to price and are therefore willing to drive a distance to get a lower price.

- *Digital personalized pricing.* The fastest-growing method of price discrimination is digital personalized pricing. By gathering personal data on shoppers' online choices and characteristics, online retailers can greatly reduce the information advantages that shoppers have about their true willingness to pay. For example, the online travel agency Orbitz discovered that Mac computer users spend as much as 30% more a night on hotels. So it shows them a fancier and costlier menu of hotels than it shows to PC users. Digital personalized pricing has the potential to achieve a closer approximation to perfect price discrimination than any other method because of its ability to collect and analyze very precise information about shoppers.

Compared to a single-price monopolist, price discrimination—even when it is not perfect—can increase the efficiency of the market. For example, with price discrimination, firms can sell to consumers who were formerly priced out of the market. Those who are now able to purchase the good at a lower price generate enough surplus to offset the loss in surplus to those now facing a higher price and no longer buying the good. In this way total surplus increases when price discrimination is introduced. This explanation of price discrimination also helps explain why government policies on monopoly typically focus on preventing deadweight losses, not preventing price discrimination—unless it causes serious issues of equity.

For example, consider a drug that is disproportionately prescribed to senior citizens, who are often on fixed incomes and so are very sensitive to price. A policy that allows a drug company to charge senior citizens a low price and everyone else a high price may indeed increase total surplus. But price discrimination that creates serious concerns about equity is likely to be prohibited—for example, an ambulance service that charges patients based on the severity of their emergency.

>> Check Your Understanding 13-4

Solutions appear at back of book.

1. True or false? Explain your answer.
   a. A single-price monopolist sells to some customers that a price-discriminating monopolist refuses to.
   b. A price-discriminating monopolist creates more inefficiency than a single-price monopolist because it captures more of the consumer surplus.
   c. Under price discrimination, a customer with highly elastic demand will pay a lower price than a customer with inelastic demand.
2. Which of these are cases of price discrimination and which are not? In the cases of price discrimination, identify the consumers with high and those with low price elasticity of demand.
   a. Damaged merchandise is marked down.
   b. Restaurants have senior citizen discounts.
   c. Food manufacturers place discount coupons for their merchandise in newspapers.
   d. Airline tickets cost more during the summer peak flying season.

Amazon and Hachette Go to War

Horacio Villalobos/Getty Images

In May 2014, all-out war broke out between Amazon, the third largest U.S. book retailer, and Hachette, the fourth largest book publisher. Suddenly Amazon took weeks to deliver Hachette publications (paper and e-books), including best sellers from authors like Stephen Colbert, Dan Brown, and J. D. Salinger, meanwhile offering shoppers suggestions for non-Hachette books as alternatives. In addition, preorder options for forthcoming Hachette books—including one by J. K. Rowling of Harry Potter fame—disappeared from Amazon's website along with many other Hachette books. These same books were readily available, often at lower prices, at rival book retailers, such as Barnes and Noble.

All publishers pay retailers a share of sales prices. In this case, hostilities were set off by Amazon's demand that Hachette raise that share from 30% to 50%. This was a familiar story: Amazon demanded ever-larger percentages during yearly contract negotiations. Since it won't carry a publisher's books without an agreement, protracted disagreement and the resulting loss of sales are disastrous for publishers. This time, however, Hachette refused to give in and went public with Amazon's demands.

Amazon claimed that the publisher could pay more out of its profit margin—around 75% on e-books, 60% on paperbacks, and 40% on hardcovers. Indeed, Amazon openly admitted that its long-term objective was to displace publishers altogether, and deal directly with authors itself. This model has been popularized by companies like Netflix that are now producing their own media content. Amazon has already received support from some famous authors, including Dean Koontz and Michael Lewis. Ironically, publishers countered that Amazon's calculations ignored the costs of editing, marketing, advertising, and at times supporting struggling writers until they became successful; yet recently, Amazon has found success in publishing as many large publishers have cut their marketing and editing budgets. Amazon, they claimed, would eventually destroy the book industry, and now the publishing industry.

In the conflict, Amazon faced some very angry authors. Douglas Preston, a best-selling Hachette author of thrillers, saw his sales drop by at least 60%. Speaking of the comfortable lifestyle that his writing supported, Preston observed that if Amazon decided not to sell his books at all, "All this goes away." In the end, the conflict became a public relations disaster for Amazon as writers and even some readers turned against them. So, Amazon eventually capitulated and agreed to allow Hachette to set the price of its e-books. However, given Amazon's size and influence, authors remain wary about the future.

In fact, a few years later, Amazon became the largest U.S. book retailer. This is largely due to Amazon's costly investments in its website and its vast warehouse and speedy delivery system, despite sometimes charging higher prices than rival websites. These upgrades have been funded by Amazon investors, who waited patiently for 20 years, incurring billions of dollars in losses. But 2015 was a turning point for Amazon. That year, the company made a small profit, and each year since, it has experienced increased profitability. In 2018, Amazon made over $10 billion. The wait for its investors finally paid off. Over the same time period, Amazon's share price increased by nearly 500%.

QUESTIONS FOR THOUGHT

1. What is the source of surplus in this industry? Who generates it? How is it divided among the various agents (authors, publishers, and retailers)?

2. What are the various sources of market power here? What is at risk for the various parties?

SUMMARY

1. There are four main types of market structure based on the number of firms in the industry and product differentiation: perfect competition, monopoly, oligopoly, and monopolistic competition.

2. A **monopolist** is a producer who is the sole supplier of a good without close substitutes. An industry controlled by a monopolist is a **monopoly.**

3. The key difference between a monopoly and a perfectly competitive industry is that a single perfectly competitive firm faces a horizontal demand curve but a monopolist faces a downward-sloping demand curve. This gives the monopolist **market power,** the ability to raise the market price by reducing output compared to a perfectly competitive firm.

4. To persist, a monopoly must be protected by a **barrier to entry.** This can take the form of control of a natural resource or input, increasing returns to scale that give rise to **natural monopoly,** technological superiority, a **network externality,** or government rules that prevent entry by other firms, such as **patents** or **copyrights.** Neither technological superiority nor patents and copyrights provide long-term barriers to entry.

5. The marginal revenue of a monopolist is composed of a quantity effect (the price received from the additional unit) and a price effect (the reduction in the price at which all units are sold). Because of the price effect, a monopolist's marginal revenue is always less than the market price, and the marginal revenue curve lies below the demand curve.

6. At the monopolist's profit-maximizing output level, marginal cost equals marginal revenue, which is less than market price. At the perfectly competitive firm's profit-maximizing output level, marginal cost equals the market price. So in comparison to perfectly competitive industries, monopolies produce less, charge higher prices, and earn profits in both the short run and the long run.

7. A monopoly creates deadweight losses by charging a price above marginal cost: the loss in consumer surplus exceeds the monopolist's profit. The government should intervene to prevent the formation of monopolies that are created to exploit monopoly power and earn monopoly profits. If they already exist, the government should break them up. Monopolies based on government-created barriers and technological superiority will disappear over time. However, breaking up a natural monopoly will raise costs and reduce welfare.

8. Natural monopolies can still cause deadweight losses. To limit these losses, governments sometimes impose **public ownership** and at other times impose **price regulation.** A price ceiling on a monopolist, as opposed to a perfectly competitive industry, need not cause shortages and can increase total surplus.

9. How to manage market power arising from network externalities is a much-debated topic as digital giants engage in monopoly and **monopsony** behavior. A **monopsonist**—the single buyer of a good in an industry—captures surplus from sellers by reducing its purchases and lowering the price paid to sellers. Too little output is produced and a deadweight loss is incurred.

10. Market power arising from network externalities poses a difficult policy problem because consumers benefit from bigger networks. On the one hand, market power imposes deadweight loss, and stifles innovation in fast-moving digital industries. On the other hand, the digital giants innovate as well, and are successful because consumers have preferred them. Moreover, given the dynamics of network externalities, if the digital giant is broken up, dominant firms with market power are likely to reemerge.

11. Not all monopolists are **single-price monopolists.** Monopolists, as well as oligopolists and monopolistic competitors, often engage in **price discrimination** to make higher profits, using various techniques to differentiate consumers based on their sensitivity to price, charging those with less elastic demand higher prices. Compared to a single-price monopoly, price discrimination reduces deadweight loss. The most widely used techniques are advance purchase restrictions; volume discounts; two-part tariffs; sales and outlet stores; and digital personalized pricing.

12. Digital personalized pricing comes the closest to achieving **perfect price discrimination,** in which each consumer pays a price equal to their willingness to pay. While the monopolist captures the total surplus in the market, no deadweight loss is incurred because all mutually beneficial transactions occur. Unless it causes serious equity issues, governments tend to focus on preventing deadweight loss and not preventing price discrimination.

KEY TERMS

Monopolist, p. 385

Monopoly, p. 385

Market power, p. 386

Barrier to entry, p. 387

Natural monopoly, p. 387

Network externality, p. 388

Patent, p. 390

Copyright, p. 390

Public ownership, p. 401

Price regulation, p. 401

Monopsony, p. 404

Monopsonist, p. 404

Single-price monopolist, p. 408

Price discrimination, p. 408

Perfect price discrimination, p. 410

PRACTICE QUESTIONS

1. Skyscraper City has a subway system, for which a one-way fare is $1.50. There is pressure on the mayor to reduce the fare by one-third, to $1.00. The mayor is dismayed, thinking that this will mean Skyscraper City is losing one-third of its revenue from sales of subway tickets. The mayor's economic adviser reminds her that she is focusing only on the price effect and ignoring the quantity effect. Explain why the mayor's estimate of a one-third loss of revenue is likely to be an overestimate. Illustrate with a diagram.

2. This diagram illustrates your local electric company's natural monopoly. It shows the demand curve for kilowatt-hours (kWh) of electricity, the company's marginal revenue (*MR*) curve, its marginal cost (*MC*) curve, and its average total cost (*ATC*) curve. The government wants to regulate the monopolist by imposing a price ceiling.

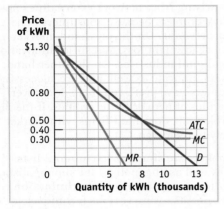

   a. If the government does not regulate this monopolist, which price will it charge? Illustrate the inefficiency this creates by shading the deadweight loss from monopoly.

   b. If the government imposes a price ceiling equal to the marginal cost, $0.30, will the monopolist make profits or lose money? Shade the area of profit (or loss) for the monopolist. If the government does impose this price ceiling, do you think the firm will continue to produce in the long run?

   c. If the government imposes a price ceiling of $0.50, will the monopolist make a profit, lose money, or break even?

3. A monopolist knows that in order to expand the quantity of output it produces from 8 to 9 units it must lower the price of its output from $2 to $1. Calculate the quantity effect and the price effect. Use these results to calculate the monopolist's marginal revenue of producing the 9th unit. The marginal cost of producing the 9th unit is positive. Is it a good idea for the monopolist to produce the 9th unit?

4. Explain the following situations.

   a. In Europe, when a service contract is purchased, many cell phone service providers give away for free what would otherwise be very expensive cell service. Why might a company want to do that?

   b. In England, the country's antitrust authority prohibited the cell phone service provider Vodafone from offering a plan that gave customers free calls to other Vodafone customers. Why might Vodafone have wanted to offer these calls for free? Why might a government want to step in and ban this practice? Why might it not be a good idea for a government to interfere in this way?

5. For people with life-threatening allergies, carrying a device that can automatically inject epinephrine (called an *autoinjector*) is a necessity. In the summer of 2016, Mylan, the maker of the widely used autoinjector EpiPen, found itself with a virtual monopoly. A year earlier its primary competitor, Auvi-Q, was recalled amid fears that it would malfunction and deliver the wrong dose. In addition, the FDA denied a third drug producer, Teva, from releasing a generic autoinjector. Prior to these events, a two-pack EpiPen sold for approximately $100. But during that summer, Mylan raised the price to over $600 per pack, leading to extensive news coverage, popular online petitions, and outrage on the part of consumers. Mylan countered that many consumers received their EpiPens through their medical insurance, hence they were protected from the price increase. For those who didn't have insurance coverage and had to pay the full price, Mylan offered a $300 savings card.

   a. Draw a graph that shows consumer and producer surplus in a competitive market for epinephrine autoinjectors. Assume firms have a constant marginal cost of $100 per pack.

   b. Next, using that graph, show how much consumer surplus, producer surplus, and deadweight loss change after the Auvi-Q recall and the denied entry of Teva by the FDA.

   c. How is the savings card offered to those without insurance an example of price discrimination? (*Hint:* Patients who are covered by medical insurance are like consumers who have high incomes and can therefore afford to pay full price.) Draw a graph showing how consumer and producer surplus will change under the savings card program.

PROBLEMS

1. Each of the following firms possesses market power. Explain its source.

   a. Merck, the producer of the patented cholesterol-lowering drug Zetia

   b. Waterworks, a provider of piped water

   c. Chiquita, a supplier of bananas and owner of most banana plantations

   d. The Walt Disney Company, the creators of Mickey Mouse

2. Bob, Bill, Ben, and Brad Baxter have just made a documentary movie about their basketball team. They are thinking about making the movie available for download on the internet, and they can act as a single-price monopolist if they choose to. Each time the movie is downloaded, their internet service provider charges them a fee of $4. The Baxter brothers are arguing about which price to charge customers per download. The accompanying table shows the demand schedule for their film.

Price of download	Quantity of downloads demanded
$10	0
8	1
6	3
4	6
2	10
0	15

   a. Calculate the total revenue and the marginal revenue per download.

   b. Bob is proud of the film and wants as many people as possible to download it. Which price would he choose? How many downloads would be sold?

   c. Bill wants as much total revenue as possible. Which price would he choose? How many downloads would be sold?

   d. Ben wants to maximize profit. Which price would he choose? How many downloads would be sold?

   e. Brad wants to charge the efficient price. Which price would he choose? How many downloads would be sold?

3. Mateo's room overlooks a major league baseball stadium. He decides to rent a telescope for $50.00 a week and charge his friends to use it to peep at the games for 30 seconds. He can act as a single-price monopolist for renting out "peeps." For each person who takes a 30-second peep, it costs Mateo $0.20 to clean the eyepiece. The accompanying table shows the information Mateo has gathered about the weekly demand for the service.

Price of peep	Quantity of peeps demanded
$1.20	0
1.00	100
0.90	150
0.80	200
0.70	250
0.60	300
0.50	350
0.40	400
0.30	450
0.20	500
0.10	550

   a. For each price in the table, calculate the total revenue from selling peeps and the marginal revenue per peep.

   b. At what quantity will Mateo's profit be maximized? What price will he charge? What will his total profit be?

   c. Mateo's landlady complains about all the visitors and tells him to stop selling peeps. But, if he pays her $0.20 for every peep he sells, she won't complain. What effect does the $0.20-per-peep bribe have on Mateo's marginal cost per peep? What is the new profit-maximizing quantity of peeps? What effect does the $0.20-per-peep bribe have on Mateo's total profit?

4. Suppose that De Beers is a single-price monopolist in the diamond market. De Beers has five potential customers: Raquel, Jackie, Jake, Elijah, and Jordan. Each of these customers will buy at most one diamond—and only if the price is just equal to, or lower than, their willingness to pay. Raquel's willingness to pay is $400; Jackie's, $300; Jake's, $200; Elijah's, $100; and Jordan's, $0. De Beers's marginal cost per diamond is $100. The result is a demand schedule for diamonds as follows:

Price of diamond	Quantity of diamonds demanded
$500	0
400	1
300	2
200	3
100	4
0	5

   a. Calculate De Beers's total revenue and its marginal revenue. From your calculation, draw the demand curve and the marginal revenue curve.

   b. Explain why De Beers faces a downward-sloping demand curve and why the marginal revenue from an additional diamond sale is less than the price of the diamond.

c. Suppose De Beers currently charges $200 for its diamonds. If it lowers the price to $100, how large is the price effect? How large is the quantity effect?

d. Add the marginal cost curve to your diagram from part a and determine which quantity maximizes De Beers's profit and which price De Beers will charge.

5. Use the demand schedule for diamonds given in Problem 4. The marginal cost of producing diamonds is constant at $100. There is no fixed cost.

a. If De Beers charges the monopoly price, how large is the individual consumer surplus that each buyer experiences? Calculate total consumer surplus by summing the individual consumer surpluses. How large is producer surplus?

Suppose that upstart Russian and Asian producers enter the market and it becomes perfectly competitive.

b. What is the perfectly competitive price? What quantity will be sold in this perfectly competitive market?

c. At the competitive price and quantity, how large is the consumer surplus that each buyer experiences? How large is total consumer surplus? How large is producer surplus?

d. Compare your answer to part c to your answer to part a. How large is the deadweight loss associated with monopoly in this case?

6. Use the demand schedule for diamonds given in Problem 4. De Beers is a monopolist, but it can now price-discriminate perfectly among all five of its potential customers. De Beers's marginal cost is constant at $100. There is no fixed cost.

a. If De Beers can price-discriminate perfectly, to which customers will it sell diamonds and at what prices?

b. How large is each individual consumer surplus? How large is total consumer surplus? Calculate producer surplus by summing the producer surplus generated by each sale.

7. Download Records decides to release an album by the group Mary and the Little Lamb. It produces the album with no fixed cost, but the total cost of creating a digital album and paying Mary her royalty is $6 per album. Download Records can act as a single-price monopolist. Its marketing division finds that the demand schedule for the album is as shown in the accompanying table.

Price of album	Quantity of albums demanded
$22	0
20	1,000
18	2,000
16	3,000
14	4,000
12	5,000
10	6,000
8	7,000

a. Calculate the total revenue and the marginal revenue per album.

b. The marginal cost of producing each album is constant at $6. To maximize profit, what level of output should Download Records choose, and which price should it charge for each album?

c. Mary renegotiates her contract and will be paid a higher royalty per album. So the marginal cost rises to be constant at $14. To maximize profit, what level of output should Download Records now choose, and which price should it charge for each album?

8. The Collegetown movie theater serves 900 students and 100 professors in town. Each student's willingness to pay for a movie ticket is $5. Each professor's willingness to pay is $10. Each will buy only one ticket. The movie theater's marginal cost per ticket is constant at $3, and there is no fixed cost.

a. Suppose the movie theater cannot price-discriminate and charges both students and professors the same price per ticket. If the movie theater charges $5, who will buy tickets and what will the movie theater's profit be? How large is consumer surplus?

b. If the movie theater charges $10, who will buy movie tickets and what will the movie theater's profit be? How large is consumer surplus?

c. Assume the movie theater can price-discriminate between students and professors by requiring students to show their student ID. If the movie theater charges students $5 and professors $10, how much profit will the movie theater make? How large is consumer surplus?

9. In the United States, the Federal Trade Commission (FTC) is charged with promoting competition and challenging mergers that would likely lead to higher prices. Several years ago, Staples and Office Depot, two of the largest office supply superstores, announced their agreement to merge.

a. Some critics of the merger argued that, in many parts of the country, a merger between the two companies would create a monopoly in the office supply superstore market. Based on the FTC's argument and its mission to challenge mergers that would likely lead to higher prices, do you think it allowed the merger?

b. Staples and Office Depot argued that, while in some parts of the country they might create a monopoly in the office supply superstore market, the FTC should consider the larger market for all office supplies, which includes many smaller stores that sell office supplies (such as grocery stores and other retailers). In that market, Staples and Office Depot would face competition from many other, smaller stores. If the market for all office supplies is the relevant market that the FTC should consider, would it make the FTC more or less likely to allow the merger?

10. Prior to the late 1990s, the same company that generated your electricity also distributed it to you over high-voltage lines. Since then, 16 states and

the District of Columbia have begun separating the generation from the distribution of electricity, allowing competition between electricity generators and between electricity distributors.

a. Assume that the market for electricity distribution was and remains a natural monopoly. Use a graph to illustrate the market for electricity distribution if the government sets price equal to average total cost.

b. Assume that deregulation of electricity generation creates a perfectly competitive market. Also assume that electricity generation does not exhibit the characteristics of a natural monopoly. Use a graph to illustrate the cost curves in the long-run equilibrium for an individual firm in this industry.

11. In 2014, Time Warner and Comcast announced their intention to merge. This prompted questions of monopoly because the combined company would supply cable access to an overwhelming majority of Americans. It also raised questions of monopsony since the combined company would be virtually the only purchaser of programming for broadcast shows. Although the merger was ultimately disallowed, assume that it had occurred. In each of the following, determine whether it is evidence of monopoly, monopsony, or neither.

a. The monthly cable fee for consumers increases significantly more than the increase in the cost of producing and delivering programs over cable.

b. Companies that advertise on cable TV find that they must pay higher rates for advertising.

c. Companies that produce broadcast shows find they must produce more shows for the same amount they were paid before.

d. Consumers find that there are more shows available for the same monthly cable fee.

12. Walmart is the world's largest retailer. As a consequence, it has sufficient bargaining power to push its suppliers to lower their prices so it can honor its slogan of "Save Money. Live Better" for its customers.

a. Is Walmart acting like a monopolist or monopsonist when purchasing goods from suppliers? Explain.

b. How does Walmart affect the consumer surplus of its customers? The producer surplus of its suppliers?

c. Over time, what is likely to happen to the quality of products produced by Walmart suppliers?

 WORK IT OUT

13. Consider an industry with the demand curve (*D*) and marginal cost curve (*MC*) shown in the accompanying diagram. There is no fixed cost. If the industry is a single-price monopoly, the monopolist's marginal revenue curve would be *MR*. Answer the following questions by naming the appropriate points or areas.

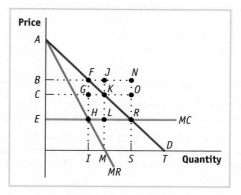

a. If the industry is perfectly competitive, what will be the total quantity produced? At what price?

b. Which area reflects consumer surplus under perfect competition?

c. If the industry is a single-price monopoly, what quantity will the monopolist produce? Which price will it charge?

d. Which area reflects the single-price monopolist's profit?

e. Which area reflects consumer surplus under single-price monopoly?

f. Which area reflects the deadweight loss to society from single-price monopoly?

g. If the monopolist can price-discriminate perfectly, what quantity will the perfectly price-discriminating monopolist produce? ◼

14 > Oligopoly

REGULATORS GIVE BRIDGESTONE A FLAT TIRE

WITH SALES OF OVER $33 BILLION IN 2019, Bridgestone is the largest tire company by sales in the United States. But only 5 years ago it suffered a particularly humiliating turn of events, courtesy of U.S. regulators. In 2014 Bridgestone admitted that for several years it had participated in meetings with competitors Hitachi Automotive and Mitsubishi Electric. At those meetings, the companies set prices and split up the market for rubber automotive parts, behavior called *price-fixing*. In all, 26 companies pled guilty to price-fixing for rubber automotive parts, 32 people were indicted, and a total of more than $2 billion in fines were assessed by the U.S. government.

In 2019, the giant tire manufacturer Bridgestone admitted to engaging in price-fixing with its competitors.

What Bridgestone and their co-conspirators were doing was illegal. According to the indictment issued by the Justice Department, their actions were undertaken to "suppress and eliminate competition." The effect of these actions was to raise the price of auto parts to auto manufacturers throughout the country — from General Motors to Toyota to Chrysler. In this chapter we will come to understand how regulators made that determination, and how Bridgestone's actions hurt consumers.

The case brought against Bridgestone and its co-conspirators illustrates the issues posed by *oligopoly* — an industry that is neither perfectly competitive nor purely monopolistic. Oligopoly is a type of market structure in which there are only a few producers. In the real world, oligopoly occurs much more frequently than monopoly. And it is arguably more typical of modern economies than perfect competition.

The problems posed by oligopoly keep regulators at the U.S. Justice Department very busy investigating dozens of cases of allegedly anti-competitive behavior. For example, in 2020, the Justice Department announced it would bring criminal charges against several generic drug manufacturers for colluding to keep drug prices high and costing patients billions of dollars. In 2019, Starkist, the market leader for packaged tuna in the United States, paid a $100 million fine after the Justice Department charged it with working with rivals Bumble Bee and Chicken of the Sea to fix the price of canned tuna. Other recent cases have involved price-fixing in the credit card industry by Visa and MasterCard, in the sea transport industry, and by one-way truck rental companies U-Haul and Avis.

When there are only a few producers in an industry, as is the case with oligopoly, the issue of *strategic behavior* arises: how one firm behaves affects the behavior of other firms. Because firms can affect each other's behavior, they are tempted to coordinate their actions, or *collude,* in order to stifle competition and raise profits, as Bridgestone and its co-conspirators did. As a result of this behavior, regulators often intervene in oligopolistic industries to protect consumers.

In this chapter, we'll begin by examining what oligopoly is and why it is so important. Then we'll turn to the behavior of oligopolistic industries. Finally, we'll look at *antitrust policy,* which is adopted by regulators to maintain competition in oligopolistic industries, thereby keeping oligopolies "well behaved." ●

WHAT YOU WILL LEARN

- What is **oligopoly** and why does it occur?
- Why do **oligopolists** benefit from **collusion** and how are consumers hurt by it?
- How do the insights gained from **game theory** help us to understand the strategic behavior of oligopolists?
- Why is **antitrust policy,** policy which is aimed at preventing collusion among oligopolists, a critical function of government?

An **oligopoly** is an industry with only a small number of producers. A producer in such an industry is known as an **oligopolist.**

When no one firm has a monopoly, but producers nonetheless realize that they can affect market prices, an industry is characterized by **imperfect competition.**

|| The Prevalence of Oligopoly

During the period of price-fixing by Bridgestone and its co-conspirators, no one company controlled the world market for rubber auto parts, but there were only a few major producers. An industry with only a few sellers is known as an **oligopoly;** a firm in such an industry is known as an **oligopolist.**

Oligopolists obviously compete with one another for sales. But neither Bridgestone nor Mitsubishi was like a firm in a perfectly competitive industry, which takes the price at which it can sell its product as given. Each of these firms knew that its decision about how much to produce would affect the market price. That is, like monopolists, each of the firms had some *market power.* So the competition in this industry wasn't "perfect."

Economists refer to a situation in which firms compete but also possess market power—which enables them to affect market prices—as **imperfect competition.** As we saw in Chapter 13, there are actually two important forms of imperfect competition: oligopoly and *monopolistic competition.* Of these, oligopoly is probably the more important in practice.

Although rubber automotive parts is a multibillion-dollar business, it is not exactly a product familiar to most consumers. However, many familiar goods and services are supplied by only a few competing sellers, which means the industries in question are oligopolies. For example, Google has a market share of 62.5% in the American search engine market, while Bing/Microsoft and Yahoo/Verizon Media have a combined share of 36.6%. In the U.S. smartphone market, Apple and Samsung have market shares of 56% and 27% respectively. In the American toothpaste market, Colgate-Palmolive accounts for 48% of the market, while Crest and Sensodyne account for 29% and 22% respectively. Verizon, AT&T, and T-Mobile collectively account for about 88% of the American wireless telephone subscriptions, and most domestic airline routes are covered by only two to three carriers. This list could go on for several more pages.

It's important to realize that an oligopoly isn't necessarily made up of large firms. What matters isn't size per se; the question is how many competitors there are. When a small town has only two grocery stores, grocery service there is just as much an oligopoly as air shuttle service between New York and Washington.

Why are oligopolies so prevalent? Essentially, oligopoly is the result of some of the same factors that sometimes produce monopoly, but in weaker form. The most important source of oligopoly is the existence of *increasing returns to scale,* which give bigger producers a cost advantage over smaller ones. When these effects are very strong, they lead to monopoly; when they are moderately strong, they lead to an industry with a small number of firms.

For example, larger grocery stores typically have lower costs than smaller ones. But the advantages of large scale taper off once grocery stores are reasonably large, which is why two or three stores often survive in small towns.

If oligopoly is so common, why has most of this book focused on competition in industries where the number of sellers is very large? And why did we study monopoly, which is relatively uncommon, first? The answer has two parts.

First, much of what we learn from the study of perfectly competitive markets—about costs, entry and exit, and efficiency—remains valid despite the fact that many industries are not perfectly competitive. Second, the analysis of oligopoly rests on the notion of *interdependence* between firms—in oligopoly, the actions of one firm directly affect other firms within the industry. When firms are interdependent, there are a multitude of different possible outcomes depending upon how the firms behave. This is unlike either perfect competition and monopoly, where there will be one rational choice for a firm and one market equilibrium. So by studying perfect competition and monopoly before oligopoly, we are following a rule that is generally good to follow: first, deal with the questions you can easily answer (perfect competition and monopoly), and then address the harder ones (oligopoly).

ECONOMICS >> *in Action*
Is It a Beer-opoly or Not?

In practice, it's not always easy to determine an industry's market structure by looking solely at the number of producers. The market for beer is one example: although there are dozens of beer brewers, many of them are small niche producers (makers of craft beer), leaving the overall market dominated by two very large brewers. Anheuser-Busch InBev and MillerCoors account for 40.8% and 23.5%, respectively, of American beer sales. You can see the distribution of brewers in Figure 14-1.

So, economists often use a measure called the *Herfindahl–Hirschman Index*, or HHI, to gauge the nature of competition in a given industry. The HHI for an industry is calculated as the square of each firm's market share summed over the firms in the industry. (We defined *market share* in Chapter 12.) For example, if an industry contains three firms with market shares of 60%, 25%, and 15%, the HHI for the industry is:

$$HHI = 60^2 + 25^2 + 15^2 = 4{,}450$$

By squaring each market share, the HHI is much larger when the industry is dominated by a small number of firms, making it a better measure of how concentrated an industry is.

It's not just an academic matter. The HHI is used by the Justice Department and the Federal Trade Commission to formulate *antitrust policy*. Their mission is to support adequate competition in an industry by prosecuting price-fixing, breaking up economically inefficient monopolies, and disallowing mergers between firms that will reduce competition.

FIGURE 14-1 Market Share for the U.S. Beer Industry in 2018, HHI = 2,332

Pabst Brewing 2.1%
Heineken USA 3.5%
Constellation/Crown Imports 9.9%
All others* 20%
Anheuser-Busch InBev 40.8%
Miller Coors, LLC 23.5%

Data from: America's Beer Distributors.

According to Justice Department guidelines, an HHI below 1,500 indicates an unconcentrated industry—one that is not dominated by a small number of firms and therefore operates competitively. An HHI between 1,500 and 2,500 indicates moderate concentration, and an HHI over 2,500 indicates a highly concentrated industry—in other words, an oligopoly or a monopoly. In moderately or highly concentrated industries, mergers between firms that raise the HHI will receive scrutiny from Justice Department economists and will, potentially, be prohibited.

The 2016 merger of beer makers Anheuser-Busch InBev and SABMiller, the owner of the MillerCoors brand, is a good example of how the HHI is used in making regulatory policy. Anheuser-Busch InBev wanted the merger in order to access the rapidly growing foreign markets in which SABMiller already operated. But before the merger, the U.S. beer industry was highly concentrated, with an HHI of 2,598. Therefore, the two companies knew they would have to obtain Justice Department approval to proceed.

The Justice Department did eventually allow the merger, but only after stringent conditions were met. SABMiller was required to sell its MillerCoors brand, so that Anheuser-Busch InBev and MillerCoors remained competitors. And beer distributors, the local companies that deliver beer to restaurants and bars in a geographical area, were part of the deal. These distributors are often owned by the big brewers, and craft beer makers complain that this discourages sales of their craft beers. So as part of the deal, the newly merged company was forbidden to take actions with distributors that discouraged competition. But even with the agreement, regulators, lawmakers, and competitors have made clear that they are keeping an eye on future developments in the beer industry and will take any anti-competitive actions by the new company very seriously. By 2019, the HHI for the beer industry has fallen to 2,332, moving it from a highly concentrated to a moderately concentrated industry.

>> Quick Review

• In addition to perfect competition and monopoly, **oligopoly** and monopolistic competition are also important types of market structure. They are forms of **imperfect competition.**

• Oligopoly is a common market structure, one in which there are only a few firms, called **oligopolists,** in the industry. It arises from the same forces that lead to monopoly, except in weaker form.

• The Herfindahl–Hirschman Index, the sum of the squares of the market shares of each firm in the industry, is a widely used measure of industry concentration.

When a firm's decision significantly affects the profits of other firms in the industry, the firms are in a situation of **interdependence.**

An oligopoly consisting of only two firms is a **duopoly.** Each firm is known as a **duopolist.**

Sellers engage in **collusion** when they cooperate to raise their joint profits. A **cartel** is an agreement among several producers to obey output restrictions in order to increase their joint profits.

>> Check Your Understanding 14-1

Solutions appear at back of book.

1. Explain why each of the following industries is an oligopoly, not a perfectly competitive industry.
   a. The world oil industry, where a few countries near the Persian Gulf control much of the world's oil reserves
   b. The microprocessor industry, where two firms, Intel and its bitter rival AMD, dominate the technology
   c. The wide-body passenger jet industry, composed of the American firm Boeing and the European firm Airbus, where production is characterized by extremely large fixed cost
2. The accompanying table shows the market shares for search engines in 2019.
   a. Calculate the HHI in this industry.
   b. If Yahoo! and Bing were to merge, what would the HHI be?

Search engine	Market share
Google	62.5%
Bing/Microsoft	24.9
Yahoo!/Verizon Media	11.7
Ask	0.9

‖ Understanding Oligopoly

Oligopolists can behave very differently than firms in other types of market structure because they operate in a state of **interdependence.** This means that the pricing and production decisions of one firm significantly affect the profits of its rivals. To begin to understand how oligopolies think and behave, we will start with an example.

A Duopoly Example

We'll now examine the simplest version of oligopoly, an industry in which there are only two producing firms—a **duopoly**—and each is known as a **duopolist.**

Going back to our opening story, imagine that there are only two producers of auto tires, Bridgestone and Hitachi. To make things simpler, suppose that once a company has incurred the fixed cost needed to produce tires, the marginal cost of producing another tire is zero. So the companies are concerned only with the revenue they receive from sales, and not with their costs.

Table 14-1 shows a hypothetical demand schedule for tires and the total revenue of the industry at each price–quantity combination.

If this were a perfectly competitive industry, each firm would have an incentive to produce more as long as the market price was above marginal cost. Since the marginal cost is assumed to be zero, this would mean that at equilibrium tires would be provided free. Firms would produce until price equals zero, yielding a total output of 120 million tires and zero revenue for both firms.

Yet, surely the firms would not be that stupid. With only two firms in the industry, each would realize that by producing more, it drives down the market price. So each firm would, like a monopolist, realize that profits would be higher if it and its rival limited their production.

So how much will the two firms produce?

One possibility is that the two companies will engage in **collusion**—they will cooperate to raise their joint profits. The strongest form of collusion is a **cartel,** an arrangement between producers that determines how much each is allowed

TABLE 14-1 Demand Schedule for Tires

Price of tire	Quantity of tires demanded (millions)	Total revenue (millions)
$12	0	$0
11	10	110
10	20	200
9	30	270
8	40	320
7	50	350
6	60	360
5	70	350
4	80	320
3	90	270
2	100	200
1	110	110
0	120	0

to produce. The world's most famous cartel is the Organization of the Petroleum Exporting Countries (OPEC), described in an Economics in Action later in the chapter.

As its name indicates, OPEC is actually an agreement among governments rather than firms. There's a reason this cartel is an agreement among governments: cartels among firms are illegal in the United States and many other jurisdictions. But let's ignore the law for a moment (which is, of course, what Bridgestone did in real life—to its detriment).

Let's illustrate with an example of a cartel formed by only two firms, Bridgestone and Hitachi. We'll assume that this cartel decided to act as if it were a monopolist, maximizing total industry profits. It's obvious from Table 14-1 that in order to maximize the combined profits of the two firms, the cartel should set total industry output at 60 million tires, which would sell at a price of $6 per tire, leading to revenue of $360 million, the maximum possible.

Then the only question would be how much of that 60 million tires each firm gets to produce. A fair solution might be for each firm to produce 30 million tires with revenues for each firm of $180 million.

But even if the two firms agreed on such a deal, they might have a problem: each of the firms would have an incentive to break its word and produce more than the agreed-upon quantity.

Collusion and Competition

Suppose that the presidents of Bridgestone and Hitachi were to agree that each would produce 30 million tires over the next year. Both would understand that this plan maximizes their combined profits. And both would have an incentive to cheat.

To see why, consider what would happen if Hitachi honored its agreement, producing only 30 million tires, but Bridgestone ignored its promise and produced 40 million tires. This increase in total output would drive the price down from $6 to $5 per tire, the price at which 70 million tires are demanded. The industry's total revenue would fall from $360 million ($6 × 60 million tires) to $350 million ($5 × 70 million tires). However, Bridgestone's revenue would *rise*, from $180 million ($6 × 30 million tires) to $200 million ($5 × 40 million tires). Since we are assuming a marginal cost of zero, this would mean a $20 million increase in Bridgestone's profits.

But Hitachi's president might make exactly the same calculation. And if both firms were to produce 40 million tires, the price would drop to $4 per tire. So each firm's profits would fall, from $180 million to $160 million.

Why do individual firms have an incentive to produce more than the quantity that maximizes their joint profits? Because neither firm has as strong an incentive to limit its output as a true monopolist would.

Let's go back for a minute to the theory of monopoly. We know that a profit-maximizing monopolist sets marginal cost (which in this case is zero) equal to marginal revenue. But what is marginal revenue? Recall that producing an additional unit of a good has two effects:

1. A positive *quantity* effect: one more unit is sold, increasing total revenue by the price at which that unit is sold.

2. A negative *price* effect: in order to sell one more unit, the monopolist must cut the market price on *all* units sold.

The negative price effect is the reason marginal revenue for a monopolist is less than the market price. In the case of oligopoly, when considering the effect of increasing production, a firm is concerned only with the price effect on its *own* units of output, not those of its fellow oligopolists. Both Bridgestone and Hitachi suffer a negative price effect if Bridgestone decides to produce extra tires and so

When firms ignore the effects of their actions on each others' profits, they engage in **noncooperative behavior.**

drives down the price. But Bridgestone cares only about the negative price effect on the units it produces, not about the loss to Hitachi.

This tells us that an individual firm in an oligopolistic industry faces a smaller price effect from an additional unit of output than does a monopolist; therefore, the marginal revenue that such a firm calculates is higher. So it will seem to be profitable for any one company in an oligopoly to increase production, even if that increase reduces the profits of the industry as a whole. But if everyone thinks that way, the result is that everyone earns a lower profit!

Until now, we have been able to analyze producer behavior by asking what a producer should do to maximize profits. But even if Bridgestone and Hitachi are both trying to maximize profits, what does this predict about their behavior? Will they engage in collusion, reaching and holding to an agreement that maximizes their combined profits? Or will they engage in **noncooperative behavior,** with each firm acting in its own self-interest, even though this has the effect of driving down everyone's profits? Both strategies sound like profit maximization. Which will actually describe their behavior?

Now you see why oligopoly, with only a small number of players, makes collusion a real possibility. If there were dozens or hundreds of firms, it would be safe to assume they would behave noncooperatively. Yet when there are only a handful of firms in an industry, collusion isn't inevitable. For reasons we explain in the next section, oligopolists are often unable to collude.

Since collusion is ultimately more profitable than noncooperative behavior, firms do have an incentive to collude if they can. One way to do so is to formalize it—sign an agreement (maybe even draw up a legal contract) or establish some financial incentives for the companies to set their prices high. But in the United States and many other nations, you can't do that—at least not legally. Companies cannot make a legal contract to keep prices high: not only is the contract unenforceable, but writing it is a one-way ticket to jail. Neither can they sign an informal agreement that lacks the force of law but perhaps rests on threats of retaliation—that's illegal, too.

In fact, executives from rival companies rarely meet without lawyers present, who make sure that the conversation does not stray into inappropriate territory. Even hinting at how nice it would be if prices were higher can bring you an unwelcome interview with the Justice Department or the Federal Trade Commission.

For example, in an emblematic 2013 case, the Justice Department launched a price-fixing case against Monsanto and other large producers of genetically modified seeds. The Justice Department was alerted by a series of meetings held between Monsanto and Pioneer Hi-Bred International, two companies that accounted for 60% of the U.S. market in corn and soybean seeds. The two companies, parties to a licensing agreement involving genetically modified seeds, claimed that no illegal discussions of price-fixing occurred in those meetings. But the fact that the two firms discussed prices as part of the licensing agreement was enough to trigger action by the Justice Department.

Sometimes, as we've seen, oligopolistic firms just ignore the rules. But more often they find ways to achieve collusion without a formal agreement, as we'll soon see.

ECONOMICS >> *in Action* 🌐
The Case Against Chocolate Producers Melts

In the Bridgestone case, company executives admitted to price-fixing, giving investigators indisputable evidence of collusion that was used to prosecute the company. However, without solid evidence, the prosecution of price-fixing can be a tricky business. The differing outcomes of price-fixing allegations in the U.S. and Canadian chocolate industry make that point abundantly clear.

In late 2015, an eight-year-long probe into collusion by the major Canadian chocolate makers finally ended. It started when Cadbury Canada disclosed that it had colluded with Hershey Canada, Nestlé Canada, and Mars Canada. In the ensuing court case, 13 Cadbury Canada executives revealed their contacts with the other companies, including one episode in which a Nestlé Canada executive handed over details about a forthcoming price hike to Cadbury Canada. According to court documents, top executives of Hershey Canada, Nestlé Canada, and Mars Canada secretly met to set prices. After protracted litigation, all four producers settled the case and paid fines totaling more than $23 million that were then distributed among consumers.

Are chocolate makers engaging in price-fixing?

South of the border, several of the largest U.S. grocery chains and snack retailers were convinced that they, too, had been victims of collusion by chocolate makers. In 2010, one of these stores, SuperValu, filed a lawsuit against the U.S. divisions of the four chocolate makers. In contrast to Canada, where the big four controlled a little less than 50% of the market, in the U.S. market they controlled over 75%. SuperValu claimed that the U.S. companies had been fixing prices since 2002, regularly increasing prices by mid-single-digit to double-digit amounts within a few days of one another.

Indeed, over that period the price of chocolate candy in the United States had soared, climbing by 17% from 2008 to 2010, far in excess of the rate of inflation. U.S. chocolate makers, however, defended their actions, contending that they were simply passing on the higher costs of cocoa beans, dairy products, and sugar. And as antitrust experts pointed out, without solid evidence such as conversations or written agreements between companies, price-fixing can be very difficult to prove because it is not illegal for producers to raise prices at the same time.

In 2014, a U.S. judge threw out the collusion case against the U.S. chocolate producers, stating that closely timed price increases were not sufficient proof of collusion and that there was no evidence that U.S. producers knew of the collusion between their Canadian counterparts. Federal Judge Christopher Conner concluded that the companies engaged in "rational, competitive behavior" when they increased prices to counter anticipated cost increases. In 2015, Canadian regulators finally closed their books on the case, deciding against bringing further criminal charges against the four companies.

>> Check Your Understanding 14-2

Solutions appear at back of book.

1. Which of the following factors increase the likelihood that an oligopolist will collude with other firms in the industry? Which increase the likelihood that an oligopolist will act noncooperatively and raise output? Explain your answers.
   a. The firm's initial market share is small. (*Hint:* Think about the price effect.)
   b. The firm has a cost advantage over its rivals.
   c. The firm's customers face additional costs when they switch from the use of one firm's product to another firm's product.
   d. The oligopolist has a lot of unused production capacity but knows that its rivals are operating at their maximum production capacity and cannot increase the amount they produce.

>> Quick Review

• Oligopolies operate in a state of **interdependence,** in which a firm's pricing and production decisions directly affect the other firm(s) in the industry.

• Some of the key issues in oligopoly can be understood by looking at the simplest case, a **duopoly**—an industry containing only two firms, called **duopolists.**

• By acting as if they were a single monopolist, oligopolists can maximize their combined profits. So there is an incentive to form a **cartel.**

• However, each firm has an incentive to cheat—to produce more than it is supposed to under the cartel agreement. So there are two principal outcomes: successful **collusion** or behaving **noncooperatively** by cheating.

‖ Games Oligopolists Play

In our duopoly example and in real life, each oligopolistic firm realizes that it is interdependent: its profit depends on what its competitor does and its competitor's profit depends on what it does. Each firm's decisions, then, will

The study of behavior in situations of interdependence is known as **game theory.**

The reward received by a player in a game, such as the profit earned by an oligopolist, is that player's **payoff.**

A **payoff matrix** shows how the payoff to each of the participants in a two-player game depends on the actions of both. Such a matrix helps us analyze situations of interdependence.

significantly affect the profit of the other firm (or firms, in the case of more than two).

In effect, the two firms are playing a game in which the profit of each player depends not only on its own actions but on those of the other player (or players). In order to understand more fully how oligopolists behave, economists, along with mathematicians, developed the area of study of such games, known as **game theory.** It has many applications, not just to economics but also to military strategy, politics, and other social sciences.

Let's see how game theory helps us understand oligopoly.

The Prisoners' Dilemma

Game theory deals with any situation in which the reward to any one player—the **payoff**—depends not only on their own actions but also on those of other players in the game. In the case of oligopolistic firms, the payoff is simply the firm's profit.

When there are only two players, as in a duopoly, the interdependence between the players can be represented with a **payoff matrix** like that shown in Figure 14-2. Each row corresponds to an action by one player (in this case, Bridgestone); each column corresponds to an action by the other (in this case, Hitachi). For simplicity, let's assume that Bridgestone can pick only one of two alternatives: produce 30 million tires or produce 40 million tires. Hitachi has the same pair of choices.

The matrix contains four boxes, each divided by a diagonal line. Each box shows the payoff to the two firms that results from a pair of choices: the number below the diagonal shows Bridgestone's profits; the number above the diagonal shows Hitachi's profits.

These payoffs show what we concluded from our earlier analysis: the combined profit of the two firms is maximized if they each produce 30 million tires. Either firm, however, can increase its own profit by producing 40 million tires while the other produces only 30 million tires. But if both produce the larger quantity, both will have lower profits than if they had both held their output down.

FIGURE 14-2 A Payoff Matrix

Two firms, Bridgestone and Hitachi, must decide how many tires to produce. The profits of the two firms are *interdependent:* each firm's profit depends not only on its own decision but also on the other's decision. Each row represents an action by Bridgestone; each column an action by Hitachi. Both firms will be better off if they both choose the lower output, but it is in each firm's individual interest to choose the higher output.

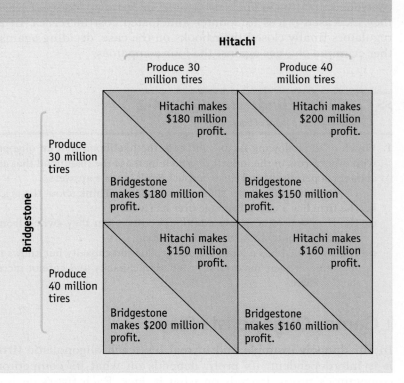

The particular situation shown here is a version of a famous—and seemingly paradoxical—case of interdependence that appears in many contexts. Known as the **prisoners' dilemma,** it is a type of game in which the payoff matrix implies the following:

- Each player has an incentive, regardless of what the other player does, to cheat—to take an action that benefits it at the other's expense.

- When both players cheat, both are worse off than they would have been if neither had cheated.

The original illustration of the prisoners' dilemma occurred in a fictional story about two accomplices in crime—let's call them Thelma and Louise—who have been caught by the police. The police have enough evidence to put them behind bars for 5 years. They also know that the pair have committed a more serious crime, one that carries a 20-year sentence; unfortunately, they don't have enough evidence to convict the women on that charge. To do so, they would need each of the prisoners to implicate the other in the second crime.

So the police put the miscreants in separate cells and say the following to each: "Here's the deal: if neither of you confesses, you know that we'll send you to jail for 5 years. If you confess and implicate your partner, and she doesn't do the same, we'll reduce your sentence from 5 years to 2. But if your partner confesses and you don't, you'll get the maximum 20 years. And if both of you confess, we'll give you both 15 years."

Figure 14-3 shows the payoffs that face the prisoners, depending on the decision of each to remain silent or to confess. (Usually the payoff matrix reflects the players' payoffs, and higher payoffs are better than lower payoffs. This case is an exception: a higher number of years in prison is bad, not good!) Let's assume that the prisoners have no way to communicate and that they have not sworn an oath not to harm each other or anything of that sort. So each acts in her own self-interest. What will they do?

The answer is clear: both will confess. Look at it first from Thelma's point of view: she is better off confessing, regardless of what Louise does. If Louise doesn't confess,

Prisoners' dilemma is a game based on two premises: (1) Each player has an incentive to choose an action that benefits itself at the other player's expense; (2) When both players act in this way, both are worse off than if they had acted cooperatively.

FIGURE 14-3 The Prisoners' Dilemma

Each of two prisoners, held in separate cells, is offered a deal by the police — a light sentence if she confesses and implicates her accomplice but her accomplice does not do the same, a heavy sentence if she does not confess but her accomplice does, and so on. It is in the joint interest of both prisoners not to confess; it is in each one's individual interest to confess.

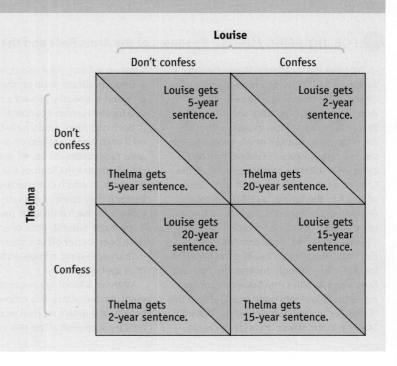

An action is a **dominant strategy** when it is a player's best action regardless of the action taken by the other player.

A **Nash equilibrium,** also known as a **noncooperative equilibrium,** results when each player in a game chooses the action that maximizes their payoff given the actions of other players, ignoring the effects of their action on the payoffs received by those other players.

Thelma's confession reduces her own sentence from 5 years to 2. If Louise *does* confess, Thelma's confession reduces her sentence from 20 to 15 years. Either way, it's clearly in Thelma's interest to confess. And because she faces the same incentives, it's clearly in Louise's interest to confess, too. To confess in this situation is a type of action that economists call a *dominant strategy*. An action is a **dominant strategy** when it is the player's best action regardless of the action taken by the other player.

It's important to note that not all games have a dominant strategy—it depends on the structure of payoffs in the game. But in the case of Thelma and Louise, it is clearly in the interest of the police to structure the payoffs so that confessing is a dominant strategy for each person. So as long as the two prisoners have no way to make an enforceable agreement that neither will confess (something they can't do if they can't communicate, and the police certainly won't allow them to do so because the police want to compel each one to confess), Thelma and Louise will each act in a way that hurts the other.

So if each prisoner acts rationally in her own interest, both will confess. Yet if neither of them had confessed, both would have received a much lighter sentence! In a prisoners' dilemma, each player has a clear incentive to act in a way that hurts the other player—but when both make that choice, it leaves both of them worse off.

When Thelma and Louise both confess, they reach an *equilibrium* of the game. We have used the concept of equilibrium many times; it is an outcome in which no individual or firm has any incentive to change their own action.

In game theory, this kind of equilibrium, in which each player takes the action that is best for her given the actions taken by other players, and vice versa, is known as a **Nash equilibrium,** after the mathematician and Nobel laureate John Nash. (Nash's life was chronicled in the best-selling biography *A Beautiful Mind*, which was made into a movie.) Because the players in a Nash equilibrium do not take into account the effect of their actions on others, this is also known as a **noncooperative equilibrium.**

Now look back at Figure 14-2: Bridgestone and Hitachi are in the same situation as Thelma and Louise. Each firm is better off producing the higher output, regardless of what the other firm does. Yet if both produce 40 million tires, both are worse off than if they had followed their agreement and produced only 30 million tires. In both cases, then, the pursuit of individual self-interest—the effort to maximize profits or to minimize jail time—has the perverse effect of hurting both players.

FOR INQUIRING MINDS   Prisoners of the Arms Race and the Resurgent Cold War

In 2016 the North Atlantic Treaty Organization, or NATO, the defensive alliance of 28 countries spanning Europe and North America, raised its military spending for the first time in years. Most experts attribute the increase to Russia's newly more aggressive military posture in Europe, evidenced by its 2014 invasion and annexation of the Crimea, a region of Ukraine. It was a case of "back to the future," as NATO members (including the United States) found themselves drawn into an arms race with Russia.

Between World War II and the 1980s, the United States and its allies (NATO) were locked in a seemingly endless struggle with Russia and its allies (the Soviet Union) that never broke out into open war. Dubbed the "Cold War," during this period the United States and the Soviet Union spent huge sums on military equipment, sums that were a significant drain on the U.S. economy and eventually proved a crippling burden for the Russian economy.

Both countries would have been better off if each had spent less on arms. Yet the arms race continued for 40 years. The arms race illustrates the logic of the prisoner's dilemma, in which both parties would be better if they could cooperate, but it is rational for each individual party to act in its own self-interest. Both countries would have been better off in a stalemate with low military spending, compared to one with high spending.

Without a binding cooperative agreement, each country was rational to spend heavily: if it didn't, its rival would gain military superiority. The two countries tried to escape this trap by repeatedly negotiating limits on weapons. However, these agreements were hard to negotiate and very difficult to verify. Ultimately, the issue was resolved as heavy military spending hastened the collapse of the Soviet Union in 1991. For the next 20 years, the arms race between the United States and Russia largely faded away.

That is until 2016, when the Russian annexation of the Crimea provided a clear sign that the arms race had returned as Russia had regained its economic footing. Russian military spending climbed 60% from 2008 to 2015, before settling back to earlier levels in 2017 and 2018. The increased NATO spending in response has made it abundantly clear that the logic of the arms race is still very much alive.

Prisoners' dilemmas appear in many situations. Clearly, the players in any prisoners' dilemma would be better off if they had some way of enforcing cooperative behavior—if Thelma and Louise had both sworn to a code of silence or if Bridgestone and Hitachi had signed an enforceable agreement not to produce more than 30 million tires.

But in the United States an agreement setting the output levels of two oligopolists isn't just unenforceable, it's illegal. So it seems that a noncooperative equilibrium is the only possible outcome. Or is it?

Overcoming the Prisoners' Dilemma: Repeated Interaction and Tacit Collusion

Thelma and Louise in their cells are playing what is known as a *one-shot* game—that is, they play the game with each other only once. They get to choose once and for all whether to confess or hang tough, and that's it. However, most of the games that oligopolists play aren't one-shot; instead, they expect to play the game repeatedly with the same rivals.

An oligopolist usually expects to be in business for many years, and it knows that its decision today about whether to cheat is likely to affect the way other firms treat it in the future. So a smart oligopolist doesn't just decide what to do based on the effect on profit in the short run. Instead, it engages in **strategic behavior,** taking account of the effects of the action it chooses today on the future actions of other players in the game. And under some conditions oligopolists that behave strategically can manage to behave as if they had a formal agreement to collude.

Suppose that Bridgestone and Hitachi expect to be in the tire business for many years and therefore expect to play the game of cheat versus collude shown in Figure 14-2 many times. Would they really betray each other time and again?

Probably not. Suppose that Bridgestone considers two strategies. In one strategy it always cheats, producing 40 million tires each year, regardless of what Hitachi does. In the other strategy, it starts with good behavior, producing only 30 million tires in the first year, and watches to see what its rival does. If Hitachi also keeps its production down, Bridgestone will stay cooperative, producing 30 million tires again for the next year. But if Hitachi produces 40 million tires, Bridgestone will take the gloves off and also produce 40 million tires the next year. This latter strategy—start by behaving cooperatively, but thereafter do whatever the other player did in the previous period—is generally known as **tit for tat.**

Tit for tat is a form of strategic behavior, which we have just defined as behavior intended to influence the future actions of other players. Tit for tat offers a reward to the other player for cooperative behavior—if you behave cooperatively, so will I. It also provides a punishment for cheating—if you cheat, don't expect me to be nice in the future.

The payoff to Bridgestone of each of these strategies would depend on which strategy Hitachi chooses. Consider the four possibilities, shown in Figure 14-4:

1. If Bridgestone plays tit for tat and so does Hitachi, both firms will make a profit of $180 million each year.

2. If Bridgestone plays always cheat but Hitachi plays tit for tat, Bridgestone makes a profit of $200 million the first year but only $160 million per year thereafter.

3. If Bridgestone plays tit for tat but Hitachi plays always cheat, Bridgestone makes a profit of only $150 million in the first year but $160 million per year thereafter.

4. If Bridgestone plays always cheat and Hitachi does the same, both firms will make a profit of $160 million each year.

Which strategy is better? In the first year, Bridgestone does better playing always cheat, whatever its rival's strategy: it assures itself that it will get either $200 million

PLAYING FAIR IN THE PRISONERS' DILEMMA

One common reaction to the prisoners' dilemma is to assert that it isn't rational for either prisoner to confess. Thelma wouldn't confess because she'd be afraid Louise would beat her up, or Thelma would feel guilty because Louise wouldn't do that to her.

But this kind of answer is, well, cheating—it amounts to changing the payoffs in the payoff matrix. To understand the dilemma, you have to play fair and imagine prisoners who care *only* about the length of their sentences.

Luckily, when it comes to oligopoly, it's a lot easier to believe that the firms care only about their profits. There is no indication that anyone at Bridgestone felt either fear of or affection for Hitachi, or vice versa; it was strictly about business.

A firm engages in **strategic behavior** when it attempts to influence the future behavior of other firms.

A strategy of **tit for tat** involves playing cooperatively at first, then doing whatever the other player did in the previous period.

FIGURE 14-4 How Repeated Interaction Can Support Collusion

A strategy of tit for tat involves playing cooperatively at first, then following the other player's move. This rewards good behavior and punishes bad behavior. If the other player cheats, playing tit for tat will lead to only a short-term loss in comparison to playing always cheat. But if the other player plays tit for tat, also playing tit for tat leads to a long-term gain. So a firm that expects other firms to play tit for tat may well choose to do the same, leading to successful tacit collusion.

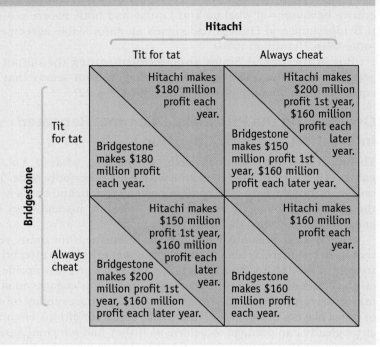

or $160 million (which of the two payoffs it actually receives depends on whether Hitachi plays tit for tat or always cheat). This is better than what it would get in the first year if it played tit for tat: either $180 million or $150 million. But by the second year, a strategy of always cheat gains Bridgestone only $160 million per year for the second and all subsequent years, regardless of Hitachi's actions.

Over time, the total amount gained by Bridgestone by playing always cheat is less than the amount it would gain by playing tit for tat: for the second and all subsequent years, it would never get any less than $160 million and would get as much as $180 million if Hitachi played tit for tat as well. Which strategy, always cheat or tit for tat, is more profitable depends on two things: how many years Bridgestone expects to play the game and what strategy its rival follows.

If Bridgestone expects the tire business to end in the near future, it is in effect playing a one-shot game. So it might as well cheat and grab what it can. Even if Bridgestone expects to remain in the tire business for many years (therefore to find itself repeatedly playing this game with Hitachi) and, for some reason, expects Hitachi always to cheat, it should also always cheat. That is, Bridgestone should follow the old rule "Do unto others before they do unto you."

But if Bridgestone expects to be in the business for a long time and thinks Hitachi is likely to play tit for tat, it will make more profits over the long run by playing tit for tat, too. It could have made some extra short-term profits by cheating at the beginning, but this would provoke Hitachi into cheating, too, and would, in the end, mean lower profits.

The lesson of this story is that when oligopolists expect to compete with one another over an extended period of time, each individual firm will often conclude that it is in its own best interest to be helpful to the other firms in the industry. So it will restrict its output in a way that raises the profits of the other firms, expecting them to return the favor. Despite the fact that firms have no way of making an enforceable agreement to limit output and raise prices (and are in legal jeopardy if they even discuss prices), they manage to act "as if" they had such an agreement. When this happens, we say that firms engage in **tacit collusion.**

When firms limit production and raise prices in a way that raises one anothers' profits, even though they have not made any formal agreement, they are engaged in **tacit collusion.**

ECONOMICS >> *in Action*
The Ups and Downs of a Cartel: OPEC Hits the Skids on U.S. Shale Oil

The Organization of the Petroleum Exporting Countries (OPEC), composed of the 17 countries of Algeria, Angola, Austria, Cameroon, Ecuador, Gabon, Iran, Iraq, Kuwait, Libya, Nigeria, Qatar, Saudi Arabia, Republic of Congo, Syria, the United Arab Emirates, and Venezuela, is a cartel that controlled 44% of global crude oil output in 2019. The cartel accounts for 72% of proven crude oil reserves and generates 60% of global crude oil exports. Unlike corporations that are legally prohibited from forming cartels, national governments can do whatever they like in setting prices.

For many years OPEC was the largest, most successful, and most economically important cartel in the world. Its members met regularly to set price and production quotas for oil.

Figure 14-5 shows the price of oil (in constant dollars) since 1947. OPEC first demonstrated its muscle in 1973: during the Yom Kippur War in the Middle East, OPEC producers limited their output—and they liked the resulting price increase so much that they decided to continue the practice. Following a second wave of turmoil from the Iran-Iraq War in 1979, output quotas fell further and prices shot even higher.

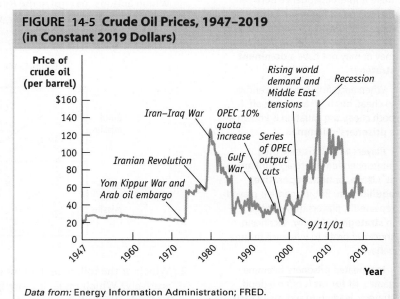

FIGURE 14-5 Crude Oil Prices, 1947–2019 (in Constant 2019 Dollars)

Data from: Energy Information Administration; FRED.

Higher oil prices spurred more exploration and production, so by the mid-1980s a growing glut of oil on world markets and cheating by cash-strapped OPEC members led to a price collapse. But in the late 1990s OPEC emerged successful once again, as Saudi Arabia, the largest producer by far, began acting as the "swing producer": allowing other members to produce as much as they wanted, then adjusting its own output to meet the overall production limit. By 2008, the price of oil had soared to $145 per barrel.

Yet, by late 2015, OPEC was nearly dead as a successful cartel as the price of oil had dropped to under $30 a barrel, a victim of surging oil exports from Russia, which accounts for the third largest share of reserves and output in the world. After having suffered a huge fall in production in the late 1990s during a period of political instability, Russia ramped up its production enough to precipitate a plunge in prices by 2015. So by late 2016, Russia and OPEC agreed to jointly limit their oil production, sending oil prices surging to above $55 per barrel.

In fact, few industry observers believe that OPEC (or OPEC plus Russia) will ever regain its glory days, with a consensus of $60 per barrel as the most likely maximum price for the near future. One important factor is the rising popularity of renewables as more and more countries shift their economies toward green technology and away from fossil fuels like oil. But the most important near-term factor dampening the rise in oil prices is the vast expansion of oil supply from the United States arising from new fracking technologies. Within five years, the United States is expected to overtake Saudi Arabia as the world's largest oil producer. As one analyst said, "U.S. shale is a huge game changer for OPEC. If prices rise to $60 and a large volume of oil can come back quickly, that's a very significant constraint on the ability of OPEC to manage the oil market." And, unlike Russia, it is virtually impossible that U.S. producers (of whom there are thousands) will ever agree to a voluntary output limitation.

>> Check Your Understanding 14-3

Solutions appear at back of book.

1. Find the Nash (noncooperative) equilibrium actions for the following payoff matrix. Which actions maximize the total payoff of Nikita and Margaret? Why is it unlikely that they will choose those actions without some communication?

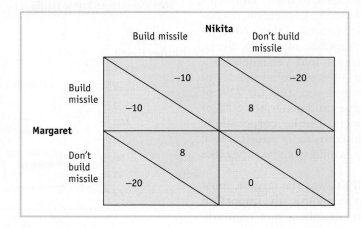

2. Which of the following factors make it more likely that oligopolists will play noncooperatively? Which make it more likely that they will engage in tacit collusion? Explain.
   a. Each oligopolist expects several new firms to enter the market in the future.
   b. It is very difficult for a firm to detect whether another firm has raised output.
   c. The firms have coexisted while maintaining high prices for a long time.

Oligopoly in Practice

In an earlier Economics in Action, we described how the four leading chocolate companies in Canada were colluding to raise prices for many years. Collusion is not, fortunately, the norm. But how do oligopolies usually work in practice? The answer depends both on the legal framework that limits what firms can do and on the underlying ability of firms in a given industry to cooperate without formal agreements.

The Legal Framework

To understand oligopoly pricing in practice, we must be familiar with the legal constraints under which oligopolistic firms operate. In the United States, oligopoly first became an issue during the second half of the nineteenth century, when the growth of railroads—themselves an oligopolistic industry—created a national market for many goods.

Large firms producing oil, steel, and many other products soon emerged. The industrialists quickly realized that profits would be higher if they could limit price competition. So, many industries formed cartels—that is, they signed formal agreements to limit production and raise prices. Until 1890, when the first federal legislation against such cartels was passed, this was perfectly legal.

However, although these cartels were legal, they weren't legally *enforceable*—members of a cartel couldn't ask the courts to force a firm that was violating its agreement to reduce its production. And firms often did violate their agreements, for the reason already suggested by our duopoly example: there is always a temptation for each firm in a cartel to produce more than it is supposed to.

In 1881, clever lawyers at John D. Rockefeller's Standard Oil Company came up with a solution—the so-called trust. In a trust, shareholders of all the major companies in an industry placed their shares in the hands of a board of trustees who controlled the companies. This, in effect, merged the companies into a single firm that could then engage in monopoly pricing. In this way, the Standard Oil Trust established what was essentially a monopoly of the oil industry, and it was soon followed by trusts in sugar, whiskey, lead, cottonseed oil, and linseed oil.

Eventually there was a public backlash, driven partly by concern about the economic effects of the trust movement, partly by fear that the owners of the trusts were simply becoming too powerful. The result was the Sherman Antitrust Act of 1890, which was intended both to prevent the creation of more monopolies and to break up existing ones. At first this law went largely unenforced. But over the decades that followed, the federal government became increasingly committed to making it difficult for oligopolistic industries either to become monopolies or to behave like them. Such efforts are known to this day as **antitrust policy.**

One of the most striking early actions of antitrust policy was the breakup of Standard Oil in 1911. (Its components formed the nuclei of many of today's large oil companies—Standard Oil of New Jersey became Exxon, Standard Oil of New York became Mobil, and so on.) In the 1980s a long-running case led to the breakup of Bell Telephone, which once had a monopoly over phone service in the United States. As we mentioned earlier, the Justice Department reviews proposed mergers between companies in the same industry and will bar mergers that it believes will reduce competition.

Among advanced countries, the United States is unique in its long tradition of antitrust policy. Until recently, other advanced countries did

Antitrust policy consists of efforts undertaken by the government to prevent oligopolistic industries from becoming or behaving like monopolies.

"*Frankly, I'm dubious about amalgamated smelting and refining pleading innocent to their anti-trust violation due to insanity.*"

GLOBAL COMPARISON   THE EUROPEAN UNION AND THE UNITED STATES: DIFFERING APPROACHES TO ANTITRUST REGULATION

Like the Federal Trade Commission (FTC) in the United States, the European Union's Competition Commission (CC) enforces competition and antitrust regulation for the 28 member nations. It wields the authority to block mergers, force companies to sell subsidiaries, and impose heavy fines if it determines that companies have acted unfairly to inhibit competition.

Although companies are able to dispute charges at a hearing once a complaint has been issued, if the Competition Commission feels that its own case is convincing, it rules against the firm and levies a penalty. Companies that believe they have been unfairly treated have only limited recourse. Critics complain that the commission acts as prosecutor, judge, and jury.

In contrast, charges of unfair competition in the United States must be made in court, where lawyers for the Federal Trade Commission have to present their evidence to independent judges. Companies employ legions of highly trained and highly paid lawyers to counter the government's case. For U.S. regulators, there is no guarantee of success. In fact, judges in many cases have found in favor of companies and against the regulators. Moreover, companies can appeal unfavorable decisions, so reaching a final verdict can take several years.

Companies, not surprisingly, prefer the American system. The accompanying figure further shows why. In recent years, on average, fines for unfair competition have been higher in the European Union than in the United States.

Observers, however, criticize both systems for their inadequacies. In the slow-moving, litigious, and expensive U.S. system, consumers and rival companies may wait a very long time to secure protection. And companies often prevail, raising questions about how well consumers are protected. But some charge that the EU system gives inadequate protection to companies that are accused.

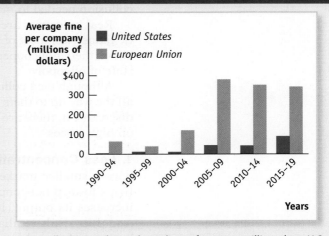

Overall, EU regulators have been far more willing than U.S. regulators to take aim at tech giants, having opened multiple investigations of Apple, Google, and Facebook. In 2017 the European Union fined Google $2.7 billion for anticompetitive behavior in the internet search market, arguing that it unfairly favored its own search engine over those of rivals. This was more than double the previous largest penalty in this type of antitrust case. And in 2018 the European Union fined Google a record $5.8 billion for anticompetitive behavior in the Android software market. While some claim that the European Union is unfairly targeting U.S. firms, seeking to give them an advantage over EU firms, others dispute that characterization, saying that consumers need more protection from antitrust behavior and privacy invasions by tech giants. And the FTC is taking notice: Joseph Simons, the chairman of the FTC, said in 2018, "Let me just say we're going to read what the EU put out very closely. We're very interested in what they are doing."

not have policies against price-fixing, and some had even supported the creation of cartels, believing that it would help their own firms against foreign rivals. But the situation has changed radically over the past 30 years, as the European Union (EU)—a supranational body tasked with enforcing antitrust policy for its member countries—has moved toward U.S. practices. Today, EU and U.S. regulators often target the same firms because price-fixing has "gone global" as international trade has expanded.

During the early 1990s, the United States instituted an amnesty program in which a price-fixer receives a much-reduced penalty if it informs on its co-conspirators. In addition, Congress increased the maximum fines levied upon conviction. These two new policies clearly made informing on your cartel partners a dominant strategy, and it has paid off as executives from Belgium, the United Kingdom, Canada, France, Germany, Italy, Mexico, the Netherlands, South Korea, and Switzerland, as well as from the United States, have been convicted in U.S. courts of cartel crimes. As one lawyer commented, "You get a race to the courthouse" as each conspirator seeks to be the first to come clean.

Life has gotten much tougher over the past few years if you want to operate a cartel. So what's an oligopolist to do?

Tacit Collusion and Price Wars

If a real industry were as simple as our tire example, it probably wouldn't be necessary for the company presidents to meet or do anything that could land them in jail. Both firms would realize that it was in their mutual interest to restrict output to 30 million tires each and that any short-term gains to either firm from producing more would be much less than the later losses as the other firm retaliated. So even without any explicit agreement, the firms would probably achieve the tacit collusion needed to maximize their combined profits.

Real industries are nowhere near that simple. Nonetheless, in most oligopolistic industries, most of the time, the sellers do appear to succeed in keeping prices above their noncooperative level. Tacit collusion, in other words, is the normal state of oligopoly.

Although tacit collusion is common, it rarely allows an industry to push prices all the way up to their monopoly level; collusion is usually far from perfect. As we discuss next, there are four factors that make it hard for an industry to coordinate on high prices.

1. Less Concentration In a less concentrated industry, the typical firm will have a smaller market share than in a more concentrated industry. This tilts firms toward noncooperative behavior because when a smaller firm cheats and increases its output, it gains for itself all of the profit from the higher output. And if its rivals retaliate by increasing their output, the firm's losses are limited because of its relatively modest market share. A less concentrated industry is often an indication that there are low barriers to entry.

2. Complex Products and Pricing Schemes In our tire example the two firms produce only one product. In reality, however, oligopolists often sell thousands or even tens of thousands of different products. Under these circumstances, keeping track of what other firms are producing and the prices they are charging is difficult. This makes it hard to determine whether a firm is cheating on the tacit agreement.

3. Differences in Interests In the tire example, a tacit agreement for the firms to split the market equally is a natural outcome, probably acceptable to both firms. In real industries, however, firms often differ both in their perceptions about what is fair and in their real interests.

For example, suppose that Hitachi was a long-established tire producer and Bridgestone a more recent entrant to the industry. Hitachi might feel that it deserved to continue producing more than Bridgestone, but Bridgestone might feel that it was entitled to 50% of the business.

Alternatively, suppose that Bridgestone's marginal costs were lower than Hitachi's. Even if they could agree on market shares, they would then disagree about the profit-maximizing level of output.

4. Bargaining Power of Buyers Often oligopolists sell not to individual consumers but to large buyers—other industrial enterprises, nationwide chains of stores, and so on. These large buyers are in a position to bargain for lower prices from the oligopolists: they can ask for a discount from an oligopolist and warn that they will go to a competitor if they don't get it. An important reason why large retailers like Walmart are able to offer lower prices to customers than small retailers is precisely their ability to use their size to extract lower prices from their suppliers.

These difficulties in enforcing tacit collusion have sometimes led companies to defy the law and create illegal cartels. We've already examined the cases of the tire industry and the chocolate industry. Recent examples include the generic drug industry, canned tuna, and the two major credit card companies. An older, classic example is the U.S. electrical equipment conspiracy of the 1950s, which led to the prosecution of and jail sentences for some executives. It provides a classic illustration of the factors that make tacit collusion especially difficult to achieve.

- There were many firms—40 companies were indicted.
- They produced a very complex array of products, often more or less custombuilt for particular clients.
- They differed greatly in size, from giants like General Electric to family firms with only a few dozen employees.
- The customers in many cases were large buyers like electrical utilities, which would normally try to force suppliers to compete for their business.

Tacit collusion just didn't seem practical—so executives met secretly and illegally to decide who would bid what price for which contract.

Because tacit collusion is often hard to achieve, most oligopolies charge prices that are well below what the same industry would charge if it were controlled by a monopolist—or what they would charge if they were able to collude explicitly. In addition, sometimes collusion breaks down and there is a **price war.** A price war sometimes involves simply a collapse of prices to their noncooperative level. Sometimes they even go *below* that level, as sellers try to put each other out of business or at least punish what they regard as cheating.

Product Differentiation and Price Leadership

In our hypothetical example of Bridgestone and Hitachi tire companies, we have assumed that their tires are perfect substitutes. That is, consumers regard them as identical. In many oligopolies, however, firms produce products that consumers regard as similar but not identical. A $10 difference in price won't make many customers switch from a Samsung smartphone to an iPhone, or vice versa.

Sometimes the differences between products are real, like differences between Froot Loops and Wheaties; sometimes, like differences between brands of vodka (which is supposed to be tasteless), they exist mainly in the minds of consumers. Either way, the effect is to reduce the intensity of competition among the firms: consumers will not all rush to buy whichever product is cheapest.

As you might imagine, oligopolists welcome the extra market power that comes when consumers think that their product is different from that of competitors. So in many oligopolistic industries, firms make considerable efforts to create the perception that their product is different—that is, they engage in **product differentiation.**

A **price war** occurs when tacit collusion breaks down and prices collapse.

Product differentiation is an attempt by a firm to convince buyers that its product is different from the products of other firms in the industry.

In **price leadership,** one firm sets its price first, and other firms then follow.

Firms that have a tacit understanding not to compete on price often engage in intense **nonprice competition,** using advertising and other means to try to increase their sales.

A firm that tries to differentiate its product may do so by altering what it actually produces, adding "extras," or choosing a different design. It may also use advertising and marketing campaigns to create a differentiation in the minds of consumers, even though its product is more or less identical to the products of rivals.

A classic case of how products may be perceived as different even when they are really pretty much the same is over-the-counter medication. For many years there have been just a few pain relievers available without a prescription—aspirin, ibuprofen, acetaminophen, and naproxen. These pain relievers are widely available as generic brands yet many consumers choose to spend more for the name brands of Bayer, Advil, Tylenol, and Aleve. Each brand uses a marketing campaign that implies some special superiority over their generic competitors (store brands), which are essentially the same thing (one classic slogan was "contains the pain reliever doctors recommend most"—that is, aspirin).

Whatever the nature of product differentiation, oligopolists producing differentiated products often reach a tacit understanding not to compete on price. For example, during the years when the great majority of cars sold in the United States were produced by the Big Three auto companies (General Motors, Ford, and Chrysler), there was an unwritten rule that none of the three companies would try to gain market share by making its cars noticeably cheaper than those of the other two.

But then who would decide on the overall price of cars? The answer was normally General Motors: as the biggest of the three, it would announce its prices for the year first, and the other companies would match it. This pattern of behavior, in which one company tacitly sets prices for the industry as a whole, is known as **price leadership.**

Interestingly, firms that have a tacit agreement not to compete on price often engage in vigorous **nonprice competition**—adding new features to their products, spending large sums on ads that proclaim the inferiority of their rivals' offerings, and so on.

Perhaps the best way to understand the mix of cooperation and competition in such industries is with a political analogy. During the long Cold War between the United States and the Soviet Union, the two countries engaged in intense rivalry for global influence. They not only provided financial and military aid to their allies; they sometimes supported forces trying to overthrow governments allied with their rival (as the Soviet Union did in Vietnam in the 1960s and early 1970s, and as the United States did in Afghanistan from 1979 until the collapse of the Soviet Union in 1991). They even sent their own soldiers to support allied governments against rebels (as the United States did in Vietnam and the Soviet Union did in Afghanistan). But they did not get into direct military confrontations with each other; open warfare between the two superpowers was regarded by both as too dangerous—and was tacitly avoided.

Price wars aren't as serious as shooting wars, but the principle is the same.

How Important Is Oligopoly?

We have seen that, across industries, oligopoly is far more common than either perfect competition or monopoly. When we try to analyze oligopoly, the economist's usual way of thinking—asking how self-interested individuals would behave, then analyzing their interaction—does not work as well as we might hope because we do not know whether rival firms will engage in noncooperative behavior or manage to engage in some kind of collusion.

Given the prevalence of oligopoly, then, is the analysis we developed in earlier chapters, which was based on perfect competition, still useful?

The conclusion of the great majority of economists is yes. For one thing, important parts of the economy are fairly well described by perfect competition.

And even though many industries are oligopolistic, in many cases the limits to collusion keep prices relatively close to marginal costs—in other words, the industry behaves "almost" as if it were perfectly competitive.

It is also true that predictions from supply and demand analysis are often valid for oligopolies. For example, in Chapter 5 we saw that price controls will produce shortages. Strictly speaking, this conclusion is certain only for perfectly competitive industries. But in the 1970s, when the U.S. government imposed price controls on the definitely oligopolistic oil industry, the result was indeed to produce shortages and lines at the gas pumps.

So how important is it to take account of oligopoly? Most economists adopt a pragmatic approach. As we have seen in this chapter, the analysis of oligopoly is far more difficult and messy than that of perfect competition; so in situations where they do not expect the complications associated with oligopoly to be crucial, economists prefer to adopt the working assumption of perfectly competitive markets. They always keep in mind the possibility that oligopoly might be important; they recognize that there are important issues, from antitrust policies to price wars, where trying to understand oligopolistic behavior is crucial.

We will follow the same approach in the chapters that follow.

ECONOMICS >> *in Action*
The Price Wars of Christmas: Amazon and Walmart Slug It Out

It's the Christmas season—and in the aisles and websites of American retail, there's a slugfest going on. Market observers are carefully watching which retailer will come to dominate the biggest selling season of the year. Online sales, which accounted for nearly one-half of total Christmas sales in 2019, have weaponized head-to-head price competition. Such direct competition creates the potential for a race to the bottom, with big and small retailers, as well as suppliers, suffering the consequences.

If Amazon is the King Kong of retail, then Walmart is the up-and-coming Godzilla, a fight that experts say has the potential to go beyond a conventional price war. On price alone, several studies have shown Amazon to be the low-price leader. Over time, Walmart fell behind Amazon in terms of price-competitiveness as Walmart continued to focus on sales in its physical stores.

There's a price war going on in the toy aisle.

Yet by Christmas of 2019, Walmart was clearly closing the gap. Research from Boomerang Commerce found that "Amazon and Walmart are nearly neck-and-neck on pricing" for popular gifts. Their review of featured Thanksgiving weekend deals on both sites in 2019, for example, showed Walmart featuring 40 items on its home page, compared to 26 items for Amazon, and discounts at Walmart averaged of 33.9%, compared to Amazon's 36.9%. In addition, Walmart began offering lower prices to customers who picked up their online purchases in the store, betting that they would make additional purchases while there.

In order to soften direct price competition, retailers are also using strategies like bundling products with services (such as offering in-home assembly), time-sensitive discounting, and customized products. Yet the competitive pressures are definitely present: the holiday sale season has lengthened over time, as each retailer tries to capture more sales from its rivals by starting its discounting earlier. Not so long ago, Black Friday, the day after Thanksgiving, marked the start of the selling season. Now, it starts at Halloween, the fourth busiest day of the year for online sales.

As one market commented on the state of the retail industry during the Christmas season, "I don't think it's just a price war. I think it's a strategic price war, or a smart price war. In the end, no retailer wants to lose money."

>> **Check Your Understanding 14-4**
Solutions appear at back of book.

1. Which of the following factors are likely to support the conclusion that there is tacit collusion in this industry? Which are not? Explain.
   a. For many years the price in the industry has changed infrequently, and all the firms in the industry charge the same price. The largest firm publishes a catalog containing a "suggested" retail price. Changes in price coincide with changes in the catalog.
   b. There has been considerable variation in the market shares of the firms in the industry over time.
   c. Firms in the industry build into their products unnecessary features that make it hard for consumers to switch from one company's products to another company's products.
   d. Firms meet yearly to discuss their annual sales forecasts.
   e. Firms tend to adjust their prices upward at the same times.

Virgin Atlantic Blows the Whistle . . . or Blows It?

Ian Waldie/Getty Images

The United Kingdom is home to two long-haul airline carriers (carriers that fly between continents): British Airways and its rival, Virgin Atlantic. Although British Airways is the dominant company, with a market share generally between 50% and 100% on routes between London and various American cities, Virgin has been a tenacious competitor.

The rivalry between the two has ranged from relatively peaceable to openly hostile over the years. In the 1990s, British Airways lost a court case alleging it had engaged in "dirty tricks" to drive Virgin out of business. In April 2010, however, British Airways may well have wondered if the tables had been turned.

It all began in mid-July 2004, when oil prices were rising. British prosecutors alleged that the two airlines had plotted to levy fuel surcharges on passengers. For the next two years, according to the prosecutors, the rivals had established a cartel through

which they coordinated increases in surcharges. British Airways first introduced a £5 ($8.25) surcharge on long-haul flights when a barrel of oil traded at about $38. It increased the surcharge six times, so that by 2006, when oil was trading at about $69 a barrel, the surcharge was £70 ($115). At the same time, Virgin Atlantic also levied a £70 fee. These surcharges increased within days of each other.

Eventually, three Virgin executives decided to blow the whistle in exchange for immunity from prosecution. British Airways immediately suspended its executives under suspicion and paid fines of nearly $500 million to U.S. and U.K. authorities. And in 2010 four British Airways executives were prosecuted by British authorities for their alleged role in the conspiracy.

The lawyers for the executives argued that although the two airlines had swapped information, this was not proof of a criminal conspiracy. In fact, they argued, Virgin was so fearful of American regulators that it had admitted to criminal behavior before confirming that it had indeed committed an offense.

One of the defense lawyers, Clare Montgomery, argued that because U.S. laws against anti-competitive behavior are much tougher than those in the United Kingdom, companies may be compelled to

blow the whistle to avoid investigation. "It's a race," she said. "If you don't get to them and confess first, you can't get immunity. The only way to protect yourself is to go to the authorities, even if you haven't [done anything]." The result was that the Virgin executives were given immunity in both the United States and the United Kingdom, but the British Airways executives were subject to prosecution (and possible multiyear jail terms) in both countries.

In late 2011 the case came to a shocking end for Virgin Atlantic and U.K. authorities. Citing e-mails that Virgin was forced to turn over by the court, the judge found insufficient evidence that there was ever a conspiracy between the two airlines. The court was incensed enough to threaten to rescind the immunity granted to the three Virgin executives.

QUESTIONS FOR THOUGHT

1. Explain why Virgin Atlantic and British Airways might collude in response to increased oil prices. Was the market conducive to collusion or not?

2. How would you determine whether illegal behavior actually occurred? What might explain these events other than illegal behavior?

3. Explain the dilemma facing the two airlines as well as their individual executives.

SUMMARY

1. Many industries are **oligopolies:** there are only a few sellers. In particular, a **duopoly** has only two sellers. Oligopolies exist for more or less the same reasons that monopolies exist, but in weaker form. They are characterized by **imperfect competition:** firms compete but possess market power.

2. Oligopolists operate in a state of **interdependence** in which the actions of one firm have a significant effect on the profits of its rivals. The firms in an oligopoly could maximize their combined profits by acting as a **cartel,** setting output levels for each firm as if they were a single monopolist; to the extent that firms manage to do this, they engage in **collusion.** But each individual firm has an incentive to produce more than it would in such an arrangement—to engage in **noncooperative behavior.**

3. The situation of interdependence, in which each firm's profit depends noticeably on what other firms do, is the subject of **game theory.** In the case of a game with two players, the **payoff** of each player depends both on its own actions and on the actions of the other; this interdependence can be represented as a **payoff matrix.** Depending on the structure of payoffs in the payoff matrix, a player may have a **dominant** strategy—an action that is always the best regardless of the other player's actions.

4. **Duopolists** face a particular type of game known as a **prisoners' dilemma;** if each acts independently in its own interest, the resulting **Nash equilibrium** or **noncooperative equilibrium** will be bad for both. However, firms that expect to play a game repeatedly tend to engage in **strategic behavior,** trying to influence each other's future actions. A particular strategy that seems to work well in maintaining **tactic collusion** is **tit for tat.**

5. In order to limit the ability of oligopolists to collude and act like monopolists, most governments pursue an **antitrust policy** designed to make collusion more difficult. In practice, however, tacit collusion is widespread.

6. A variety of factors make tacit collusion difficult: large numbers of firms, complex products and pricing, differences in interests, and bargaining power of buyers. When tacit collusion breaks down, there is a **price war.** Oligopolists try to avoid price wars in various ways, such as through **product differentiation** and through **price leadership,** in which one firm sets prices for the industry. Another is through **nonprice competition,** such as advertising.

KEY TERMS

Oligopoly, p. 422
Oligopolist, p. 422
Imperfect competition, p. 422
Interdependence, p. 424
Duopoly, p. 424
Duopolist, p. 424
Collusion, p. 424
Cartel, p. 424
Noncooperative behavior, p. 426
Game theory, p. 428
Payoff, p. 428
Payoff matrix, p. 428
Prisoners' dilemma, p. 429
Dominant strategy, p. 430
Nash equilibrium, p. 430
Noncooperative equilibrium, p. 430
Strategic behavior, p. 431
Tit for tat, p. 431
Tacit collusion, p. 432
Antitrust policy, p. 435
Price war, p. 437
Product differentiation, p. 437
Price leadership, p. 438
Nonprice competition, p. 438

PRACTICE QUESTIONS

1. Epic Games's massively popular online game *Fortnite* starts with 100 players who are dropped onto an island to face off in a game that resembles the one in Suzanne Collins's book series *The Hunger Games.* Each player must scavenge or barter for weapons and eliminate the other players in their path; the last player standing wins. Launched in 2017, today the game boasts more than 300 million users. Players can play for free but often spend money on special skins (costumes) and pay for access to specific battles. However, developers at Epic Games recently noticed a worrying trend: more advanced players were colluding in the game. In response to the collusion, Epic Games is now banning any player that colludes.

   a. What is the incentive for players to collude in *Fortnite*?

   b. Why would Epic Games want to eliminate collusion in *Fortnite*?

2. In George R.R. Martin's novel *A Storm of Swords* (one of the books that inspired HBO's *Game of Thrones*), the young and sadistic King Joffrey has the largest army in the realm at his command. Joffrey is offered the following advice by his grandfather, Lord Tywin, who is also the army commander: "Joffrey, when your enemies defy you, you must serve them steel and fire. When they go to their knees, however, you must help them back to their feet. Elsewise no man will ever bend the knee to you."

a. Assume that King Joffrey has one enemy and can make two choices: serve them steel and fire (violence) or offer them a hand (forgiveness). King Joffrey's enemy must also make a decision to fight or surrender. In a single game, what is the likely outcome between King Joffrey and his enemy?

b. Now suppose King Joffrey faces potential threats from multiple enemies. What is the likely outcome for King Joffrey if he ignores Lord Tywin's advice?

c. What type of strategy does Lord Tywin propose? Explain how it will likely lead to a different outcome?

PROBLEMS

1. The accompanying table presents market share data for the U.S. breakfast cereal market.

Company	Market share
Kellogg's	30.0%
General Mills	29.9
Post	18.9
Private Label	7.5
Quaker Oats	6.5
Other	7.2

Data from: Advertising Age.

a. Use the data provided to calculate the Herfindahl–Hirschman Index (HHI) for the market.

b. Based on this HHI, how would you describe the market structure in the U.S. breakfast cereal market?

2. The accompanying table shows the demand schedule for vitamin D. Suppose that the marginal cost of producing vitamin D is zero.

Price of vitamin D (per ton)	Quantity of vitamin D demanded (tons)
$8	0
7	10
6	20
5	30
4	40
3	50
2	60
1	70

a. Assume that BASF is the only producer of vitamin D and acts as a monopolist. It currently produces 40 tons of vitamin D at $4 per ton. If BASF were to produce 10 more tons, what would be the price effect for BASF? What would be the quantity effect? Would BASF have an incentive to produce those 10 additional tons?

b. Now assume that Roche enters the market by also producing vitamin D and the market is now a duopoly. BASF and Roche agree to produce 40 tons of vitamin D in total, 20 tons each. BASF cannot be punished for deviating from the agreement with Roche. If BASF, on its own, were to deviate from that agreement and produce 10 more tons, what

would be the price effect for BASF? What would be the quantity effect for BASF? Would BASF have an incentive to produce those 10 additional tons?

3. The market for olive oil in New York City is controlled by two families, the Sopranos and the Contraltos. Both families will ruthlessly eliminate any other family that attempts to enter the New York City olive oil market. The marginal cost of producing olive oil is constant and equal to $40 per gallon. There is no fixed cost. The accompanying table gives the market demand schedule for olive oil.

Price of olive oil (per gallon)	Quantity of olive oil demanded (gallons)
$100	1,000
90	1,500
80	2,000
70	2,500
60	3,000
50	3,500
40	4,000
30	4,500
20	5,000
10	5,500

a. Suppose the Sopranos and the Contraltos form a cartel. For each of the quantities given in the table, calculate the total revenue for their cartel and the marginal revenue for each additional gallon. How many gallons of olive oil would the cartel sell in total and at what price? The two families share the market equally (each produces half of the total output of the cartel). How much profit does each family make?

b. Uncle Junior, the head of the Soprano family, breaks the agreement and sells 500 more gallons of olive oil than under the cartel agreement. Assuming the Contraltos maintain the agreement, how does this affect the price for olive oil and the profit earned by each family?

c. Anthony Contralto, the head of the Contralto family, decides to punish Uncle Junior by increasing his sales by 500 gallons as well. How much profit does each family earn now?

4. In France, the market for bottled water is controlled by two large firms, Perrier and Evian. Each firm has a fixed cost of €1 million and a constant marginal cost of €2 per liter of bottled water (€1 = 1 euro). The following table gives the market demand schedule for bottled water in France.

Price of bottled water (per liter)	Quantity of bottled water demanded (millions of liters)
€10	0
9	1
8	2
7	3
6	4
5	5
4	6
3	7
2	8
1	9

a. Suppose the two firms form a cartel and act as a monopolist. Calculate marginal revenue for the cartel. What will the monopoly price and output be? Assuming the firms divide the output evenly, how much will each produce and what will each firm's profit be?

b. Now suppose Perrier decides to increase production by 1 million liters. Evian doesn't change its production. What will the new market price and output be? What is Perrier's profit? What is Evian's profit?

c. What if Perrier increases production by 3 million liters? Evian doesn't change its production. What would Perrier's output and profit be relative to those in part b?

d. What do your results tell you about the likelihood of cheating on such agreements?

5. To preserve the North Atlantic fish stocks, it is decided that only two fishing fleets, one from the United States and the other from the European Union, can fish in those waters. Suppose that this fisheries agreement breaks down, so that the fleets behave noncooperatively. Assume that the United States and the European Union each can send out either one or two fleets. The more fleets in the area, the more fish they catch in total but the lower the catch of each fleet. The accompanying matrix shows the profit (in dollars) per week earned by each side.

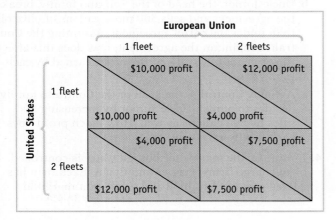

a. What is the noncooperative Nash equilibrium? Will each side choose to send out one or two fleets?

b. Suppose that the fish stocks are being depleted. Each region considers the future and comes to a tit-for-tat agreement whereby each side will send only one fleet out as long as the other does the same. If either of them breaks the agreement and sends out a second fleet, the other will also send out two and will continue to do so until its competitor sends out only one fleet. If both play this tit-for-tat strategy, how much profit will each make every week?

6. Untied and Air "R" Us are the only two airlines operating flights between Collegeville and Bigtown. That is, they operate in a duopoly. Each airline can charge either a high price or a low price for a ticket. The accompanying matrix shows their payoffs, in profits per seat (in dollars), for any choice that the two airlines can make.

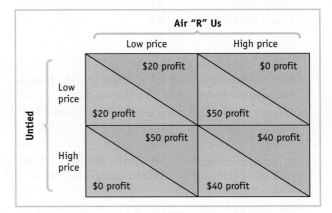

a. Suppose the two airlines play a one-shot game—that is, they interact only once and never again. What will be the Nash (noncooperative) equilibrium in this one-shot game?

b. Now suppose the two airlines play this game twice. And suppose each airline can play one of two strategies: it can play either always charge the low price or tit for tat—that is, it starts off charging the high price in the first period, and then in the second period it does whatever the other airline did in the previous period. Write down the payoffs to Untied from the following four possibilities:

   i. Untied plays always charge the low price when Air "R" Us also plays always charge the low price.

   ii. Untied plays always charge the low price when Air "R" Us plays tit for tat.

   iii. Untied plays tit for tat when Air "R" Us plays always charge the low price.

   iv. Untied plays tit for tat when Air "R" Us also plays tit for tat.

7. Suppose that Coke and Pepsi are the only two producers of cola drinks, making them duopolists. Both companies have zero marginal cost and a fixed cost of $100,000.

a. Assume first that consumers regard Coke and Pepsi as perfect substitutes. Currently both are sold for

$0.20 per can, and at that price each company sells 4 million cans per day.

i. How large is Pepsi's profit?

ii. If Pepsi were to raise its price to $0.30 per can, and Coke did not respond, keeping its price at $0.20 per can, what would happen to Pepsi's profit?

b. Now suppose that each company advertises to differentiate its product from the other company's. As a result of advertising, Pepsi realizes that if it raises or lowers its price, it will sell less or more of its product, as shown by the demand schedule in the accompanying table.

Price of Pepsi (per can)	Quantity of Pepsi demanded (millions of cans)
$0.10	5
0.20	4
0.30	3
0.40	2
0.50	1

If Pepsi now were to raise its price to $0.30 per can, what would happen to its profit?

c. Comparing your answer to part a(i) and to part b, what is the maximum amount Pepsi would be willing to spend on advertising?

8. Schick and Gillette spend huge sums of money each year to advertise their razors in an attempt to steal customers from each other. Suppose each year Schick and Gillette have to decide whether or not they want to spend money on advertising. If neither firm advertises, each will earn a profit of $2 million. If they both advertise, each will earn a profit of $1.5 million. If one firm advertises and the other does not, the firm that advertises will earn a profit of $2.8 million and the other firm will earn $1 million.

a. Use a payoff matrix to depict this problem.

b. Suppose Schick and Gillette can write an enforceable contract about what they will do. What is the cooperative solution to this game?

c. What is the Nash equilibrium without an enforceable contract? Explain why this is the likely outcome.

9. Over the last 40 years the Organization of Petroleum Exporting Countries (OPEC) has had varied success in forming and maintaining its cartel agreements. Explain how the following factors may contribute to the difficulty of forming and/or maintaining its price and output agreements.

a. New oil fields are discovered and increased drilling is undertaken in the Gulf of Mexico and the North Sea by nonmembers of OPEC.

b. Crude oil is a product that is differentiated by sulfur content: it costs less to refine low-sulfur crude oil into gasoline. Different OPEC countries possess oil reserves of different sulfur content.

c. Cars powered by hydrogen are developed.

10. Suppose you are an economist working for the Antitrust Division of the Justice Department. In each of the following cases you are given the task of determining whether the behavior warrants an antitrust investigation for possible illegal acts or is just an example of undesirable, but not illegal, tacit collusion. Explain your reasoning.

a. Two companies dominate the industry for industrial lasers. Several people sit on the boards of directors of both companies.

b. Three banks dominate the market for banking in a given state. Their profits have been going up recently as they add new fees for customer transactions. Advertising among the banks is fierce, and new branches are springing up in many locations.

c. The two oil companies that produce most of the petroleum for the western half of the United States have decided to forgo building their own pipelines and to share a common pipeline, the only means of transporting petroleum products to that market.

d. The two major companies that dominate the market for herbal supplements have each created a subsidiary that sells the same product as the parent company in large quantities but with a generic name.

e. The two largest credit card companies, Passport and OmniCard, have required all retailers who accept their cards to agree to limit their use of rival credit cards.

11. In 2015, Anheuser-Busch InBev offered $104.2 billion to acquire SABMiller. The U.S. Justice Department approved the merger, but only after the two beer giants agreed to sell off a number of brands, including Miller Lite, Peroni, and Snow (the world's top selling beer produced in China). Anheuser-Busch InBev sought the merger to increase its global market share. The accompanying table presents the global market share before and after the merger for the world's ten largest brewers.

Brewers	Market share Before merger	Market share After merger
AB InBev	21%	29%
SABMiller	10	–
Heineken	9	11
Carlsberg	6	6
China Resource Brewery Ltd.	6	6
Tsingtao Brewery Group	4	4
Molson-Coors	3	4
Yanjing	3	3
Kirin	2	2
BGI/Groupe Castel	2	2

a. Using the table, calculate the HHI for the global beer market both before and after the merger.

b. Based on the HHI calculated in part a, how has the market structure for the global beer industry changed?

12. In 2011, the Justice Department rejected AT&T's proposal to purchase T-Mobile for $39 billion due to anti-competitive concerns. A few years later, Sprint launched its own attempt to purchase T-Mobile. In 2019, Sprint's discussions with T-Mobile about a potential takeover were still ongoing, with a proposed merger close to complete.

a. Use the accompanying table to calculate the HHI before and after the proposed 2011 merger of AT&T and T-Mobile.

b. Use the table to calculate the HHI before and after the proposed merger of Sprint and T-Mobile in 2019.

c. Based on your calculations in parts a and b, do you think the Justice Department is likely to approve a merger between Sprint and T-Mobile?

Carrier	2011	2019
Verizon	34%	29%
AT&T	32	40
Sprint	17	13
T-Mobile	10	16

13. Use these steps to find the antitrust claim made by the Justice Department to prevent the merger of Anheuser-Busch InBev and Grupo Modelo. Refer to the antitrust claim to answer the questions that follow.

i. Go to U.S. Department of Justice, Antitrust Division (www.justice.gov/atr).

ii. Click on "Antitrust Case Filings" in the bar at the left and then click "Filter and Sort."

iii. Set Date to "2013," Case Type to "Civil Merger."

iv. Find the case *U.S. v. Anheuser-Busch InBev SA/NV and Grupo Modelo S.A.B. de C.V.* Click on the title to go to the website for the case.

v. Scroll to the bottom of the web page and click on "Complaint." Then click on "Attachment" to review the case.

a. Prior to the merger, what is the U.S. market share for Anheuser-Busch InBev and Grupo Modelo? (See the pie chart on page 2.)

b. In part IV, section C (Relevant Geographic Market), how does the Justice Department define a beer market? Why?

c. Based on the information in part V, in how many markets would the proposed merger exceed the HHI threshold of 2,500 points and be considered highly concentrated?

d. In Appendix A, find the postmerger HHI calculations. Note that "Delta HHI" means the change in HHI. Which market experiences the greatest increase in the HHI ratio and is the most concentrated? Which market is the least concentrated? After the merger, what happens to the HHI for the United States as a whole?

WORK IT OUT

14. Let's revisit the fisheries agreement introduced in Problem 5 stating that to preserve the North Atlantic fish stocks, only two fishing fleets, one from the United States (U.S.) and the other from the European Union (EU), can fish in those waters. The accompanying table shows the market demand schedule per week for fish from these waters. The only costs are fixed costs, so fishing fleets maximize profit by maximizing revenue.

Price of fish (per pound)	Quantity of fish demanded (pounds)
$17	1,800
16	2,000
15	2,100
14	2,200
12	2,300

a. If both fishing fleets collude, what is the revenue-maximizing output for the North Atlantic fishery? What price will a pound of fish sell for?

b. If both fishing fleets collude and share the output equally, what is the revenue to the EU fleet? To the U.S. fleet?

c. Suppose the EU fleet cheats by expanding its own catch by 100 pounds per week. The U.S. fleet doesn't change its catch. What is the revenue to the U.S. fleet? To the EU fleet?

d. In retaliation for the cheating by the EU fleet, the U.S. fleet also expands its catch by 100 pounds per week. What is the revenue to the U.S. fleet? To the EU fleet? ■

15 > Monopolistic Competition and Product Differentiation

THE FOOD COURT OF AMERICA

WITH OVER 500 STORES covering over 5 million square feet catering to over 40 million visitors annually, the Mall of America, located in Bloomington, Minnesota, is the largest mall in the United States. To make sure that the thousands who visit it daily have plenty of energy to shop, it also contains the largest and most extensive food court in the country, with over 70 restaurants. There you can find Panda Express, Sbarro, Qdoba Mexican Eats, Chick-fil-A, A&W Restaurant, Burger King, Long John Silvers, Kabob's Indian Grill, and many, many more. With its enormous variety, the "Food Court of America" is a microcosm of the American fast-food industry.

So how would you describe the fast-food industry? On the one side, it clearly isn't a monopoly. When you go to a fast-food court, you have a choice among vendors, and there is real competition between them. For example, there is competition between A&W and Burger King for the burger diners, as well as competition between the burger vendors and the pizza vendors. On the other side, in a way each vendor *does* possess some aspects of a monopoly because each vendor offers a different menu and a different eating experience. For example, Burger King is the "home of the Whopper," a flame-grilled hamburger, but if you prefer a Big Mac, you can only find one at McDonalds. The point is that each fast-food provider offers a product that is *differentiated* from its rivals' products.

In the fast-food industry, many firms compete to satisfy more or less the same demand — the desire of consumers for something tasty and quick. But each firm offers to satisfy that demand with a distinctive, differentiated product — products that

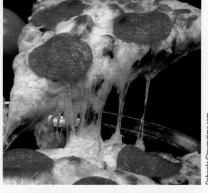

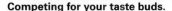

Competing for your taste buds.

consumers typically view as close but not perfect substitutes.

When there are many firms offering competing, differentiated products, as there are in the fast-food industry, economists say that the industry is characterized by *monopolistic competition*. This is the fourth and final market structure that we will discuss (having covered perfect competition, monopoly, and oligopoly in earlier chapters).

We'll start by defining monopolistic competition more carefully and explaining its characteristic features. Then we'll explore how firms differentiate their products; this will allow us to analyze how monopolistic competition works. The chapter concludes with a discussion of some ongoing controversies about product differentiation — in particular, the question of why advertising is effective. ●

WHAT YOU WILL LEARN

- What is **monopolistic competition?**
- Why do oligopolists and monopolistically competitive firms differentiate their products?
- How are prices and profits determined in monopolistic competition in the short run and the long run?
- How does monopolistic competition pose a trade-off between lower prices and greater product diversity?
- What is the economic significance of advertising and **brand names?**

447

Monopolistic competition is a market structure in which there are many competing producers in an industry, each producer sells a differentiated product, and there is free entry into and exit from the industry in the long run.

‖ The Meaning of Monopolistic Competition

Leo owns the Wonderful Wok stand in the food court of a big shopping mall. He offers the only dim sum and fried rice there, but there are more than a dozen other vendors from Bodacious Burgers to Pizza Paradise. When deciding what to charge for a meal, Leo knows that he must take those alternatives into account: even people who normally prefer fried rice won't order a $20 lunch from Leo when they can get a burger, fries, and drink for $6.

But Leo also knows that he won't lose all his business even if his lunches cost a bit more than the alternatives. Fried rice and dim sum aren't the same things as burgers or pizza. Some people will really be in the mood for fried rice that day, and they will buy from Leo even if they could dine more cheaply on burgers. Of course, the reverse is also true: even if a meal at Wonderful Wok is a bit cheaper, some people will choose burgers instead. In other words, Leo does have some market power: he has *some* ability to set his own price.

So how would you describe Leo's situation? He definitely isn't a price-taker, so he isn't in a situation of perfect competition. But you wouldn't exactly call him a monopolist, either. Although he's the only seller of Chinese food in that food court, he does face competition from other food vendors.

Yet it would also be wrong to call him an oligopolist. Oligopoly, remember, involves competition among a small number of interdependent firms in an industry protected by some—albeit limited—barriers to entry and whose profits are highly interdependent. Because their profits are highly interdependent, oligopolists have an incentive to collude, tacitly or explicitly. But in Leo's case there are *lots* of vendors in the shopping mall, too many to make tacit collusion feasible.

Economists describe Leo's situation as one of **monopolistic competition.** Monopolistic competition is particularly common in service industries like restaurants and gas stations, but it also exists in some manufacturing industries. It involves three conditions: large numbers of competing producers, differentiated products, and free entry into and exit from the industry in the long run.

In a monopolistically competitive industry, each producer has some ability to set the price of their differentiated product. But exactly how high they can set it is limited by the competition they face from other existing and potential producers that produce close, but not identical, products.

Large Numbers

In a monopolistically competitive industry, there are many producers. Such an industry does not look either like a monopoly, where the firm faces no competition, or an oligopoly, where each firm has only a few rivals. Instead, each seller has many competitors. For example, there are many vendors in a big food court, many gas stations along a major highway, and many hotels at a popular beach resort.

Differentiated Products

In a monopolistically competitive industry, each producer has a product that consumers view as somewhat distinct from the products of competing firms; at the same time, though, consumers see these competing products as close substitutes. If Leo's food court contained 15 vendors selling exactly the same kind and quality of food, there would be perfect competition: any seller who tried to charge a higher price would have no customers. But suppose that Wonderful Wok is the only Chinese food vendor, Bodacious Burgers is the only hamburger stand, and so on. The result of this differentiation is that each seller has some ability to set their own price: each producer has some—albeit limited—market power.

Free Entry and Exit in the Long Run

In monopolistically competitive industries, new producers, with their own distinct products, can enter the industry freely in the long run. For example, other food vendors would open outlets in the food court if they thought it would be profitable to do so. In addition, firms will exit the industry if they find they are not covering their costs in the long run.

Monopolistic Competition: In Sum

Monopolistic competition, then, differs from the three market structures we have examined so far. It's not the same as perfect competition: firms have some power to set prices. It's not pure monopoly: firms face some competition. And it's not the same as oligopoly: because there are many firms and free entry, the potential for collusion so important in oligopoly no longer exists.

We'll see in a moment how prices, output, and the number of products available are determined in monopolistically competitive industries. But first, let's look a little more closely at what it means to have differentiated products.

‖ Product Differentiation

Product differentiation often plays an important role in oligopolistic industries because it reduces the intensity of competition between firms when tacit collusion cannot be achieved. Product differentiation plays an even more crucial role in monopolistically competitive industries. Because tacit collusion is virtually impossible when there are many producers, product differentiation is the only way monopolistically competitive firms can acquire some market power.

How do firms in the same industry—such as fast-food vendors, gas stations, or chocolate makers—differentiate their products? Sometimes the difference is mainly in the minds of consumers rather than in the products. We'll discuss the role of advertising and the importance of brand names in achieving this kind of product differentiation later in the chapter. But, in general, firms differentiate their products by—surprise!—actually making them different.

The key to product differentiation is that consumers have different preferences and are willing to pay somewhat more to satisfy those preferences. Each producer can carve out a market niche by producing something that caters to the particular preferences of some group of consumers better than the products of other firms.

There are three important forms of product differentiation:

1. By style or type
2. By location
3. By quality

Differentiation by Style or Type

The other sellers in Leo's food court offer different types of fast food: hamburgers, pizza, tacos, and so on. Each consumer arrives at the food court with some preference for one or another of these offerings. This preference may depend on the consumer's mood, their diet, or what they have already eaten that day. These preferences will not make consumers indifferent to price: if Wonderful Wok were to charge $15 for an egg roll, everybody would go to Bodacious Burgers or Pizza Paradise instead. But some people will choose a more expensive meal if that type of food is closer to their preference. So the products of the different vendors are substitutes, but they aren't *perfect* substitutes—they are *imperfect substitutes*.

Vendors in a food court aren't the only sellers that differentiate their offerings by type. Clothing stores concentrate on women's or men's clothes, on business or casual clothes, on trendy or classic styles, and so on. Auto manufacturers offer sedans, minivans, sport-utility vehicles, and sports cars, each type aimed at drivers with different needs and tastes.

Books offer yet another example of differentiation by type and style. Mysteries are differentiated from romances; among mysteries, we can differentiate among hard-boiled detective stories, whodunits, and police procedurals. And no two writers of fantasy and science fiction are exactly alike: J. K. Rowling and George R. R. Martin each have their devoted fans.

In fact, product differentiation is characteristic of most consumer goods. As long as people differ in their tastes, producers find it possible and profitable to produce a wide variety of goods.

Differentiation by Location

Gas stations along a road offer differentiated products. True, the gas may be exactly the same. But the location of the stations is different, and location matters to consumers: it's more convenient to stop for gas near your home, near your workplace, or near wherever you are when the gas gauge gets low.

In fact, many monopolistically competitive industries supply goods differentiated by location. This is especially true in service industries, from car mechanics to drugstores, where customers often choose the seller who is closest rather than cheapest.

Differentiation by Quality

Do you have a craving for chocolate? How much are you willing to spend on it? You see, there's chocolate and then there's chocolate: although ordinary chocolate may not be very expensive, gourmet chocolate can cost several dollars per bite.

With chocolate, as with many goods, there is a range of possible qualities. You can get a usable bicycle for less than $100; you can get a much fancier bicycle for 10 times as much. It all depends on how much the additional quality matters to you and how much you will miss the other things you could have purchased with that money.

Because consumers vary in what they are willing to pay for higher quality, producers can differentiate their products by quality—some offering lower-quality, inexpensive products and others offering higher-quality products at a higher price.

Product Differentiation: In Sum

Product differentiation, then, can take several forms. Whatever form it takes, however, there are two important features of industries with differentiated products:

1. *There is competition among sellers:* even though sellers of differentiated products are not offering identical goods, they are to some extent competing for a limited market. If more businesses enter the market, each will find that it sells less quantity at any given price. For example, if a new gas station opens along a particular road, each of the existing gas stations will sell a bit less.
2. *There is value in variety:* consumers benefit from the proliferation of differentiated products. A food court with eight vendors makes consumers happier than one with only six vendors, even if the prices are the same, because some customers will get a meal that is closer to what they had in mind. A road on which there is a gas station every two miles is more convenient for motorists than a road where gas stations are five miles apart. Likewise, when a product is available with a range of quality standards, fewer people are forced to pay for higher quality than they need or to settle for lower quality than they want.

Buddy Mays/Alamy

For industries that differentiate by location, proximity is everything.

As we'll see next, competition among the sellers of differentiated products is the key to understanding how monopolistic competition works.

ECONOMICS >> *in Action*
Abbondanza!

Has the experience of trying to choose a pasta sauce among the dozens of varieties on the shelves in the grocery store ever left you feeling overwhelmed? If so, you have one person to thank and to blame: Howard Moskowitz. Thirty years ago, making your selection was much simpler: there was no Newman's Sockarooni, no Barilla's Spicy Marinara with Roasted Garlic, no Emeril's Homestyle, no Classico's Tomato Basil. In fact, there were only two brands available, Prego and Ragú. And they offered only one variety each—plain spaghetti sauce.

In the late 1980s, Prego was in a slump compared to its rival, Ragú. While searching for a way to turn their business around, the company concluded that Prego and Ragú pasta sauces were relatively indistinguishable. But rather than engage in a price war with its rival, Prego hired market researcher Howard Moskowitz, who realized that the answer to Prego's dilemma was to find out what appealed to consumers' taste buds and then use this to distinguish Prego from Ragú. Moskowitz proceeded to create 45 varieties of pasta sauces, varied on every conceivable measure: sweetness, spiciness, tartness, saltiness, thickness, and so on. He then taste-tested them around the country. What stood out was consumers' preference for extra chunky sauce—an unavailable option at the time, when both Prego and Ragú offered highly blended, watery sauces.

A dizzying variety of pasta sauces is available—thanks to monopolistic competition.

In 1989 Prego launched its Extra Chunky variety, and it was extraordinarily successful. It's a measure of Moskowitz's success that today it is hard to appreciate the radicalness of his approach. Thirty years ago, the food industry believed it should strive to create a "platonic dish"—some ideal version that would completely satisfy consumers' tastes. Prego and Ragú offered thin pasta sauces because their ideal reflected how sauce was made in Italy. But Prego came to understand the importance of setting itself apart while avoiding head-to-head price competition with Ragú, which would ultimately be self-defeating. Along came Moskowitz, who freed the food industry to indulge American consumers' iconoclastic desire for variety and distinctive flavors. So the next time you are puzzling over which pasta sauce to buy, think of Howard Moskowitz and his radical ideas.

>> *Check Your Understanding* 15-1

Solutions appear at back of book.

1. Each of the following goods and services is a differentiated product. Which are differentiated as a result of monopolistic competition and which are not? Explain your answers.
   a. Ladders
   b. Soft drinks
   c. Clothing stores
   d. Steel

2. You must determine which of two types of market structure better describes an industry, but you are allowed to ask only one question about the industry. What question should you ask to determine if an industry is:
   a. Perfectly competitive or monopolistically competitive?
   b. A monopoly or monopolistically competitive?

> ## >> *Quick Review*
>
> • In **monopolistic competition** there are many competing producers, each with a differentiated product, and free entry and exit in the long run.
>
> • Product differentiation can occur in oligopolies that fail to achieve tacit collusion as well as in monopolistic competition. It takes three main forms: by style or type, by location, or by quality. The products of competing sellers are considered imperfect substitutes.
>
> • Producers compete for the same market, so entry by more producers reduces the quantity each existing producer sells at any given price. In addition, consumers gain from the increased diversity of products.

‖ Understanding Monopolistic Competition

Suppose an industry is monopolistically competitive: it consists of many producers, all competing for the same consumers but offering differentiated products. How does such an industry behave?

As the term *monopolistic competition* suggests, this market structure combines some features typical of monopoly with others typical of perfect competition. Because each firm is offering a distinct product, it is in a way like a monopolist: it faces a downward-sloping demand curve and has some market power—the ability within limits to determine the price of its product. However, unlike a pure monopolist, a monopolistically competitive firm does face competition: the amount of its product it can sell depends on the prices and products offered by other firms in the industry.

The same, of course, is true of an oligopoly. In a monopolistically competitive industry, however, there are *many* producers, as opposed to the small number that defines an oligopoly. This means that the puzzle of oligopoly—will firms collude or will they behave noncooperatively?—does not arise in the case of monopolistically competitive industries. True, if all the gas stations or all the restaurants in a town could agree—explicitly or tacitly—to raise prices, it would be in their mutual interest to do so.

But such collusion is virtually impossible when the number of firms is large and, by implication, there are no barriers to entry. So in situations of monopolistic competition, we can safely assume that firms behave noncooperatively and ignore the potential for collusion.

Monopolistic Competition in the Short Run

Recall the distinction between short-run and long-run equilibrium. The short-run equilibrium of an industry takes the number of firms as given. The long-run equilibrium, by contrast, is reached only after enough time has elapsed for firms to enter or exit the industry. To analyze monopolistic competition, we focus first on the short run and then on how an industry moves from the short run to the long run.

Panels (a) and (b) of Figure 15-1 show two possible situations that a typical firm in a monopolistically competitive industry might face in the short run. In each case, the firm looks like any monopolist: it faces a downward-sloping demand curve, which implies a downward-sloping marginal revenue curve.

We assume that every firm has an upward-sloping marginal cost curve but that it also faces some fixed costs, so that its average total cost curve is U-shaped. This assumption doesn't matter in the short run, but, as we'll see shortly, it is crucial to understanding the long-run equilibrium.

In each case the firm, in order to maximize profit, sets marginal revenue equal to marginal cost. So how do these two figures differ? In panel (a) the firm is profitable; in panel (b) it is unprofitable. (Recall that we are referring always to economic profit, not accounting profit—that is, a profit given that all factors of production are earning their opportunity costs.)

In panel (a) the firm faces the demand curve D_P and the marginal revenue curve MR_P. It produces the profit-maximizing output Q_P, the quantity at which marginal revenue is equal to marginal cost, and sells it at the price P_P. This price is above the average total cost at this output, ATC_P. The firm's profit is indicated by the area of the shaded rectangle.

In panel (b) the firm faces the demand curve D_U and the marginal revenue curve MR_U. It chooses the quantity Q_U at which marginal revenue is equal to marginal cost. However, in this case the price P_U is *below* the average total cost ATC_U; so at this quantity the firm loses money. Its loss is equal to the area of the shaded rectangle. Since Q_U is the profit-maximizing quantity—which means, in this case, the loss-minimizing quantity—there is no way for a firm in this situation to make a profit.

FIGURE 15-1 The Monopolistically Competitive Firm in the Short Run

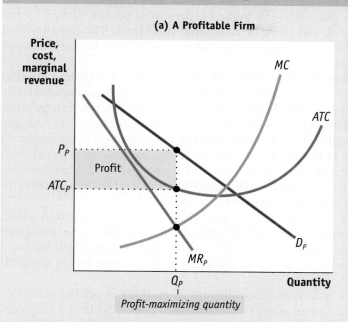

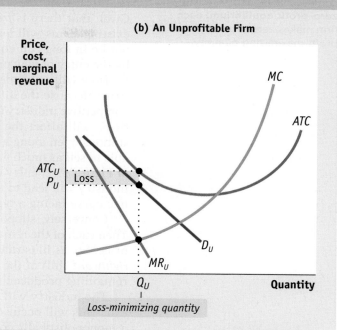

The firm in panel (a) can be profitable for some output quantities: the quantities for which its average total cost curve, ATC, lies below its demand curve, D_P. The profit-maximizing output quantity is Q_P, the output at which marginal revenue, MR_P, is equal to marginal cost, MC. The firm charges price P_P and earns a profit, represented by the area of the green-shaded rectangle. The firm in panel (b), however, can never be profitable because its average total cost curve lies above its demand curve, D_U, for every output quantity. The best that it can do if it produces at all is to produce quantity Q_U and charge price P_U. This generates a loss, indicated by the area of the yellow-shaded rectangle. Any other output quantity results in a greater loss.

We can confirm this by noting that at *any* quantity of output, the average total cost curve in panel (b) lies above the demand curve D_U. Because $ATC > P$ at all quantities of output, this firm always suffers a loss.

As this comparison suggests, the key to whether a firm with market power is profitable or unprofitable in the short run lies in the relationship between its demand curve and its average total cost curve. In panel (a) the demand curve D_P crosses the average total cost curve, meaning that some of the demand curve lies above the average total cost curve. So there are some price–quantity combinations available at which price is higher than average total cost, indicating that the firm can choose a quantity at which it makes positive profit.

In panel (b), by contrast, the demand curve D_U does not cross the average total cost curve—it always lies below it. So the price corresponding to each quantity demanded is always less than the average total cost of producing that quantity. There is no quantity at which the firm can avoid losing money.

These figures, showing firms facing downward-sloping demand curves and their associated marginal revenue curves, look just like ordinary monopoly analysis. The "competition" aspect of monopolistic competition comes into play, however, when we move from the short run to the long run.

Monopolistic Competition in the Long Run

Obviously, an industry in which existing firms are losing money, like the one in panel (b) of Figure 15-1, is not in long-run equilibrium. When existing firms are losing money, some firms will *exit* the industry. The industry will not be in long-run equilibrium until the persistent losses have been eliminated by the exit of some firms.

In the long run, a monopolistically competitive industry ends up in **zero-profit equilibrium:** each firm makes zero profit at its profit-maximizing quantity.

It may be less obvious that an industry in which existing firms are earning profits, like the one in panel (a) of Figure 15-1, is also not in long-run equilibrium. Given that there is *free entry* into the industry, persistent profits earned by the existing firms will lead to the entry of additional producers. The industry will not be in long-run equilibrium until the persistent profits have been eliminated by the entry of new producers.

How will entry or exit by other firms affect the profits of a typical existing firm? Because the differentiated products offered by firms in a monopolistically competitive industry compete for the same set of customers, entry or exit by other firms will affect the demand curve facing every existing producer. If new gas stations open along a highway, each of the existing gas stations will no longer be able to sell as much gas as before at any given price. So, as illustrated in panel (a) of Figure 15-2, entry of additional producers into a monopolistically competitive industry will lead to a *leftward* shift of the demand curve and the marginal revenue curve facing a typical existing producer.

Conversely, suppose that some of the gas stations along the highway close. Then each of the remaining stations will be able to sell more gasoline at any given price. So, as illustrated in panel (b), exit of firms from an industry will lead to a *rightward* shift of the demand curve and marginal revenue curve facing a typical remaining producer.

The industry will be in long-run equilibrium when there is neither entry nor exit. This will occur only when every firm earns zero profit. So in the long run, a monopolistically competitive industry will end up in **zero-profit equilibrium,** in which firms just manage to cover their costs at their profit-maximizing output quantities. (The app industry offers an example of this principle, as you will see in the upcoming Economics in Action.)

We have seen that a firm facing a downward-sloping demand curve will earn positive profits if any part of that demand curve lies above its average total cost

FIGURE 15-2 Entry and Exit Shift Existing Firm's Demand Curve and Marginal Revenue Curve

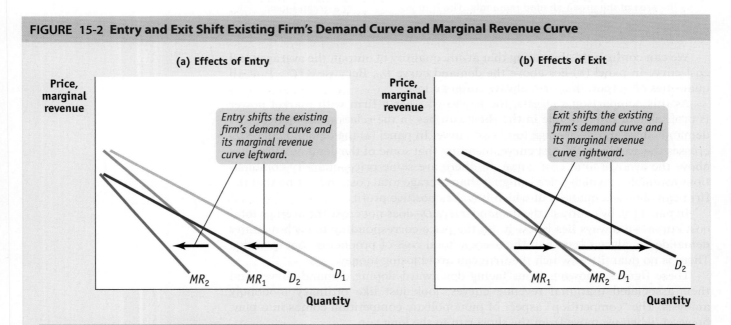

Entry will occur in the long run when existing firms are profitable. In panel (a), entry causes each existing firm's demand curve and marginal revenue curve to shift to the left. The firm receives a lower price for every unit it sells, and its profit falls. Entry will cease when firms make zero profit. Exit will occur in the long run when existing firms are unprofitable. In panel (b), exit from the industry shifts each remaining firm's demand curve and marginal revenue curve to the right. The firm receives a higher price for each unit it sells, and profit rises. Exit will cease when the remaining firms make zero profit.

FIGURE 15-3 The Long-Run Zero-Profit Equilibrium

If existing firms are profitable, entry will occur and shift each existing firm's demand curve leftward. If existing firms are unprofitable, each remaining firm's demand curve shifts rightward as some firms exit the industry. Entry and exit will cease when every existing firm makes zero profit at its profit-maximizing quantity. So, in long-run zero-profit equilibrium, the demand curve of each firm is tangent to its average total cost curve at its profit-maximizing quantity: at the profit-maximizing, Q_{MC}, price, P_{MC}, equals average total cost, ATC_{MC}. A monopolistically competitive firm is like a monopolist without monopoly profits.

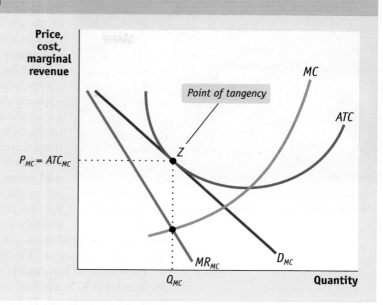

curve; it will incur a loss if its demand curve lies everywhere below its average total cost curve. So in zero-profit equilibrium, the firm must be in a borderline position between these two cases; its demand curve must just touch its average total cost curve. That is, it must be just *tangent* to it at the firm's profit-maximizing output quantity—the output quantity at which marginal revenue equals marginal cost.

If this is not the case, the firm operating at its profit-maximizing quantity will find itself making either a profit or loss, as illustrated in the panels of Figure 15-1. But we also know that free entry and exit means that this cannot be a long-run equilibrium. Why? In the case of a profit, new firms will enter the industry, shifting the demand curve of every existing firm leftward until all profits are extinguished. In the case of a loss, some existing firms will exit and so shift the demand curve of every remaining firm to the right until all losses are extinguished. All entry and exit ceases only when every existing firm makes zero profit at its profit-maximizing quantity of output.

Figure 15-3 shows a typical monopolistically competitive firm in such a zero-profit equilibrium. The firm produces Q_{MC}, the output at which $MR_{MC} = MC$, and charges price P_{MC}. At this price and quantity, represented by point Z, the demand curve is just tangent to its average total cost curve. The firm earns zero profit because price, P_{MC}, is equal to average total cost, ATC_{MC}.

The normal long-run condition of a monopolistically competitive industry, then, is that each producer is in the situation shown in Figure 15-3. Each producer acts like a monopolist, facing a downward-sloping demand curve and setting marginal cost equal to marginal revenue so as to maximize profits. But this is just enough to achieve zero economic profit. The producers in the industry are like monopolists without monopoly profits.

ECONOMICS >> *in Action*
Hits and Flops in the App Store

There's no denying that some apps have been extremely lucrative creations. King Digital Entertainment, the company that created the wildly popular game app Candy Crush, was purchased by Activision, owners of Call of Duty, Guitar Hero, and Skylanders, for nearly $6 billion in 2016. That same year, Uber, the

Although a few apps have been extraordinarily profitable, the app industry can't escape the zero-profit equilibrium.

ride-hailing app, was valued at an astounding $66 billion. Spurred by these success stories, an unprecedented number of people have rushed to develop mobile apps. But lost in the rush is the fact that the vast majority of apps have flopped or are barely alive.

The app industry looks a lot like an example of monopolistic competition. First, there is free entry in app design. And second, apps are differentiated products. They are differentiated by platform: the iOS (Apple) platform, the Android (Google) platform, or the Microsoft platform. They are also differentiated by function: sharing photos, digital coloring books, a virtual koi pond, travel pricing and reservations, personal finance management, and so on. And within each functional subgroup of apps there are variations, each trying to capture a larger share of the market. In 2019, the iOS platform had 2.2 million available apps, slightly less than the 2.6 million apps available from Google Play. The two platforms generated close to 105 billion downloads in 2019. But as one industry observer, Frank Bi, commented, ". . . the easy money is gone."

Hundreds of thousands of apps now languish in obscurity for every breakout hit like TikTok, Snapchat, or Clash of Clans. The original App Store model of selling apps is outdated. Today most apps are downloaded for free or at a minimum expense. In 2011, 63% of apps were paid downloads at an average price of $3.64; by 2019 that figure dropped to less than 7% with an average price of $1.01. It's estimated that in 75% of downloads, the app is used once and never again.

At this point, many app developers are struggling to survive, unable to generate enough download revenue to continue operations. In other words, the app creation industry has reached the zero-profit equilibrium state that characterizes monopolistic competition. So, in the end, this cutting edge, high-tech industry cannot escape the consequences of the economics of monopolistic competition.

>> **Quick Review**

• Like a monopolist, each firm in a monopolistically competitive industry faces a downward-sloping demand curve and marginal revenue curve. In the short run, it may earn a profit or incur a loss at its profit-maximizing quantity.

• If the typical firm earns positive profit, new firms will enter the industry in the long run, shifting each existing firm's demand curve to the left. If the typical firm incurs a loss, some existing firms will exit the industry in the long run, shifting the demand curve of each remaining firm to the right.

• The long-run equilibrium of a monopolistically competitive industry is a **zero-profit equilibrium** in which firms just break even. The typical firm's demand curve is tangent to its average total cost curve at its profit-maximizing quantity.

>> *Check Your Understanding* **15-2**
Solutions appear at back of book.

1. Currently a monopolistically competitive industry, composed of firms with U-shaped average total cost curves, is in long-run equilibrium. Describe how the industry adjusts, in both the short and long run, in each of the following situations.
   a. A technological change that increases fixed cost for every firm in the industry
   b. A technological change that decreases marginal cost for every firm in the industry
2. Why, in the long run, is it impossible for firms in a monopolistically competitive industry to create a monopoly by joining together to form a single firm?

Monopolistic Competition versus Perfect Competition

In a way, long-run equilibrium in a monopolistically competitive industry looks a lot like long-run equilibrium in a perfectly competitive industry. In both cases, there are many firms; in both cases, profits have been competed away; in both cases, the price received by every firm is equal to the average total cost of production.

However, the two versions of long-run equilibrium are different—in ways that are economically significant.

Price, Marginal Cost, and Average Total Cost

Figure 15-4 compares the long-run equilibrium of a typical firm in a perfectly competitive industry with that of a typical firm in a monopolistically competitive

FIGURE 15-4 Comparing Long-Run Equilibrium in Perfect Competition and Monopolistic Competition

(a) Long-Run Equilibrium in Perfect Competition

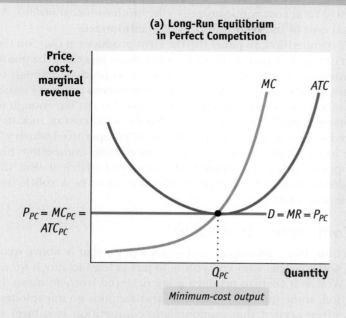

(b) Long-Run Equilibrium in Monopolistic Competition

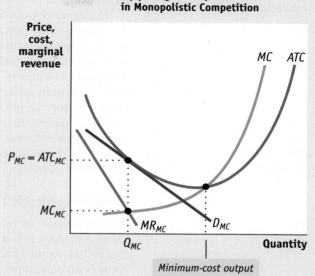

Panel (a) shows the situation of the typical firm in long-run equilibrium in a perfectly competitive industry. The firm operates at the minimum-cost output Q_{PC}, sells at the competitive market price P_{PC}, and makes zero profit. It is indifferent to selling another unit of output because P_{PC} is equal to its marginal cost, MC_{PC}. Panel (b) shows the situation of the typical firm in long-run equilibrium in

a monopolistically competitive industry. At Q_{MC} it makes zero profit because its price, P_{MC}, just equals average total cost, ATC_{MC}. At Q_{MC} the firm would like to sell another unit at price P_{MC} since P_{MC} exceeds marginal cost, MC_{MC}. But it is unwilling to lower price to make more sales. It therefore operates to the left of the minimum-cost output level and has excess capacity.

industry. Panel (a) shows a perfectly competitive firm facing a market price equal to its minimum average total cost; panel (b) reproduces Figure 15-3. Comparing the panels, we see two important differences.

First, in the case of the perfectly competitive firm shown in panel (a), the price, P_{PC}, received by the firm at the profit-maximizing quantity, Q_{PC}, is equal to the firm's marginal cost of production, MC_{PC}, at that quantity of output. By contrast, at the profit-maximizing quantity chosen by the monopolistically competitive firm in panel (b), Q_{MC}, the price, P_{MC}, is *higher* than the marginal cost of production, MC_{MC}.

This difference translates into a difference in the attitude of firms toward consumers. A wheat farmer, who can sell as much wheat as they like at the going market price, would not get particularly excited if you offered to buy some more wheat at the market price. Since that farmer has no desire to produce more at that price and can sell the wheat to someone else, you are not doing them a favor.

But if you decide to fill up your tank at Jamil's gas station rather than at Katy's, you are doing Jamil a favor. He is not willing to cut his price to get more customers—he's already made the best of that trade-off. But if he gets a few more customers than he expected at the *posted* price, that's good news: an additional sale at the posted price increases his revenue more than it increases his costs because the posted price exceeds marginal cost.

The fact that monopolistic competitors, unlike perfect competitors, want to sell more at the going price is crucial to understanding why they engage in activities like advertising that help increase sales.

The other difference between monopolistic competition and perfect competition that is visible in Figure 15-4 involves the position of each firm on its average

Firms in a monopolistically competitive industry have **excess capacity:** they produce less than the output at which average total cost is minimized.

total cost curve. In panel (a), the perfectly competitive firm produces at point Q_{PC}, at the bottom of the U-shaped *ATC* curve. That is, each firm produces the quantity at which average total cost is minimized—the *minimum-cost output*. As a consequence, the total cost of industry output is also minimized.

Under monopolistic competition, in panel (b), the firm produces at Q_{MC}, on the *downward-sloping* part of the U-shaped *ATC* curve: it produces less than the quantity that would minimize average total cost. This failure to produce enough to minimize average total cost is sometimes described as the **excess capacity** issue. The typical vendor in a food court or gas station along a road is not big enough to take maximum advantage of available cost savings. So the total cost of industry output is not minimized in the case of a monopolistically competitive industry.

Some people have argued that, because every monopolistic competitor has excess capacity, monopolistically competitive industries are inefficient. But the issue of efficiency under monopolistic competition turns out to be a subtle one that does not have a clear answer.

Is Monopolistic Competition Inefficient?

A monopolistic competitor, like a monopolist, charges a price that is above marginal cost. As a result, some people who are willing to pay at least as much for an egg roll at Wonderful Wok as it costs to produce it are deterred from doing so. In monopolistic competition, some mutually beneficial transactions go unexploited.

Furthermore, it is often argued that monopolistic competition is subject to another kind of inefficiency: that the excess capacity of every monopolistic competitor implies *wasteful duplication* because monopolistically competitive industries offer too many varieties. According to this argument, it would be better if there were only two or three vendors in the food court, not six or seven. If there were fewer vendors, they would each have lower average total costs and so could offer food more cheaply.

Is this argument against monopolistic competition right—that it lowers total surplus by causing inefficiency? Not necessarily. It's true that if there were fewer gas stations along a highway, each gas station would sell more gasoline and so would have lower costs per gallon. But there is a drawback: motorists would be inconvenienced because gas stations would be farther apart. The point is that the diversity of products offered in a monopolistically competitive industry is beneficial to consumers. So the higher price consumers pay because of excess capacity is offset to some extent by the value they receive from greater diversity.

There is, in other words, a trade-off: more producers means higher average total costs but also greater product diversity. Does a monopolistically competitive industry arrive at the socially optimal point on this trade-off? Probably not—but it is hard to say whether there are too many firms or too few! Most economists now believe that duplication of effort and excess capacity in monopolistically competitive industries are not important issues in practice.

>> Check Your Understanding 15-3

Solutions appear at back of book.

1. True or false? Explain your answers.
   a. Like a firm in a perfectly competitive industry, a firm in a monopolistically competitive industry is willing to sell a good at any price that equals or exceeds marginal cost.
   b. Suppose there is a monopolistically competitive industry in long-run equilibrium that possesses excess capacity. All the firms in the industry would be better off if they merged into a single firm and produced a single product, but whether consumers are made better off by this is ambiguous.
   c. Fads and fashions are more likely to arise in monopolistic competition or oligopoly than in monopoly or perfect competition.

‖ Controversies About Product Differentiation

Up to this point, we have assumed that products are differentiated in a way that corresponds to some real desire of consumers. For example, there is real convenience in having a gas station nearby. Likewise, your taste buds know that Chinese and Mexican cuisines are different from one another.

In the real world, however, some instances of product differentiation can seem puzzling if you think about them. What is the real difference between Crest and Colgate toothpaste? Between Energizer and Duracell batteries? Or a Marriott and a Hilton hotel room? Most people would be hard-pressed to answer any of these questions. Yet the producers of these goods make considerable efforts to convince consumers that their products are different from and better than those of their competitors.

No discussion of product differentiation is complete without spending at least a bit of time on the two related issues—and puzzles—of *advertising* and *brand names*.

The Role of Advertising

Wheat farmers don't advertise their wares online and on billboards, but car dealers do. That's not because farmers are shy and car dealers are outgoing; it's because advertising is worthwhile only in industries in which firms have at least some market power.

The purpose of advertisements is to convince people to buy more of a seller's product at the going price. A perfectly competitive firm, which can sell as much as it likes at the going market price, has no incentive to spend money convincing consumers to buy more. Only a firm that has some market power, and that therefore charges a price above marginal cost, can gain from advertising. Industries that are more or less perfectly competitive, like the milk industry, do advertise—but these ads are sponsored by an association on behalf of the industry as a whole, not on behalf of the milk that comes from the cows on a particular farm.

Given that advertising works, it's not hard to see why firms with market power would spend money on it. But the big question about advertising is *why* it works. A related question is whether advertising is, from society's point of view, a waste of resources.

Not all advertising poses a puzzle. Much of it is straightforward: it's a way for sellers to inform potential buyers about what they have to offer (or, occasionally, for buyers to inform potential sellers about what they want). Nor is there much controversy about the economic usefulness of ads that provide information: the real estate ad that declares "sunny, charming, 2 br, 1 ba, a/c" tells you things you need to know (even if a few euphemisms are involved—"charming," of course, means "small").

But what information is being conveyed when Jay-Z touts Samsung cell phones, or when Gigi Hadid promotes BMW? Surely nobody believes that Jay-Z is personally vouching for the superior operating system of a Samsung phone, or that Gigi Hadid's engineering know-how led her to choose a BMW over a rival car. Yet companies believe, with good reason, that money spent on such promotions increases their sales—and that they would be in big trouble if they stopped advertising but their competitors continued to do so.

Why are consumers influenced by ads and endorsements by media influencers that do not really provide any information about the product? One answer is that consumers are not as rational as economists typically

"The active ingredient is marketing."

Barbara Smaller/CartoonStock

assume. Perhaps consumers' judgments, or even their tastes, can be influenced by things that economists think ought to be irrelevant, such as which company has hired the most attractive and charismatic celebrity to endorse its product. And there is surely some truth to this. As we learned in Chapter 9, consumer rationality is a useful working assumption; it is not an absolute truth.

However, another answer is that consumer response to advertising is not entirely irrational because ads can serve as indirect signals in a world where consumers don't have good information about products. Suppose, to take a common example, that you need to avail yourself of some service that you don't use regularly—finding a dentist or a mover. When searching online, you will see firms with sponsored listings pop up at the top or with larger displays. You know that these listings appear as they do because the firms paid extra for them; still, it may be quite rational to call one of the firms with a big display ad. After all, the big ad probably means that it's a relatively large, successful company—otherwise, the company wouldn't have found it worth spending the money for the larger ad.

The same principle may partly explain why ads feature celebrities. You don't really believe that Justin Bieber prefers one brand of underwear over another. But the fact that Calvin Klein is willing and able to pay the Biebs nearly $70 million to put his name on its product tells you that it is a major company that is likely to stand behind its product. According to this reasoning, an expensive advertisement serves to establish the quality of a firm's products in the eyes of consumers.

The possibility that it is rational for consumers to respond to advertising also has some bearing on the question of whether advertising is a waste of resources. If ads only work by manipulating the weak-minded, the hundreds of billions of dollars that U.S. businesses spend annually will have been an economic waste—except to the extent that ads sometimes provide entertainment. To the extent that advertising conveys important information, however, it is an economically productive activity after all.

Brand Names

You've been driving all day, and you decide that it's time to find a place to sleep. On your right, you see a sign for the Bates Motel; on your left, you see a sign for a Motel 6, or a Best Western, or some other national chain. Which one do you choose?

Unless they are familiar with the area, most people would head for the chain. In fact, most motels in the United States are members of major chains; the same is true of most fast-food restaurants and many, if not most, stores in shopping malls.

Motel chains and fast-food restaurants are only one aspect of a broader phenomenon: the role of **brand names,** names owned by particular companies that differentiate their products in the minds of consumers. In many cases, a company's brand name is the most important asset it possesses: clearly, McDonald's is worth far more than the sum of the deep-fat fryers and hamburger grills the company owns.

In fact, companies often go to considerable lengths to defend their brand names, suing anyone else who uses them without permission. You may talk about blowing your nose on a kleenex or using scotch tape to wrap gifts, but unless the product in question comes from Kleenex or Scotch, legally the seller must describe it as a facial tissue or adhesive tape.

As with advertising, with which they are closely linked, the social usefulness of brand names is a source of dispute. Does the preference of consumers for known brands reflect consumer irrationality? Or do brand names convey real information? That is, do brand names create unnecessary market power, or do they serve a real purpose?

As in the case of advertising, the answer is probably some of both. On one side, brand names often do create unjustified market power. Many consumers

A **brand name** is a name owned by a particular firm that distinguishes its products from those of other firms.

will pay more for brand-name goods in the supermarket even though consumer experts assure us that the cheaper store brands are equally good. Similarly, many common medicines, like aspirin, are cheaper—with no loss of quality—in their generic form.

On the other side, for many products the brand name does convey information. A traveler arriving in a strange town can be sure of what awaits in a Holiday Inn or a McDonald's; a tired and hungry traveler may find this preferable to trying an independent hotel or restaurant that might be better—but might be worse.

In addition, brand names offer some assurance that the seller is engaged in repeated interaction with its customers and so has a reputation to protect. If a traveler eats a bad meal at a restaurant in a tourist trap and vows never to eat there again, the restaurant owner may not care, since the chance is small that the traveler will be in the same area again in the future. But if that traveler eats a bad meal at McDonald's and vows never to eat there again, that matters to the company. This gives McDonald's an incentive to provide consistent quality, thereby assuring travelers that quality controls are in place. Not surprisingly, branding has become a feature of peer-to-peer e-commerce as companies recognize that many customers will pay extra for assurances of quality and safety in anonymous, online transactions. Hence Uber created its Premium class of ride, that uses luxury cars driven by drivers with high ratings. Likewise Airbnb created the category of Plus properties, accommodations that are vetted by Airbnb staff and have a record of great reviews.

ECONOMICS >> *in Action*
The Perfume Industry: Leading Consumers by the Nose

The perfume industry has remarkably few barriers to entry: to make a fragrance, it is easy to purchase ingredients, mix them, and bottle the result. Even if you don't think you have a very good "nose," consultants are readily available to help you create something special (or even copy someone else's fragrance). So how is it possible that a successful perfume can generate a profit rate of almost 100%? Why don't rivals enter and compete away those profits?

A clue to the answer is that the most successful perfumes these days are heavily promoted by celebrities. Rihanna, Beyoncé, Taylor Swift, and Zendaya all have perfumes that are marketed by them. Britney Spears has 28! In fact, the cost of producing what is in the bottle is minuscule compared to the total cost of selling a successful perfume—only about 3% of the production cost and less than 1% of the retail price. The remaining 97% of the production cost goes into packaging, marketing, and advertising.

The extravagant bottles that modern perfumes come in—some shaped like spaceships or encrusted with rhinestones—incur a cost of four to six times that of the perfume inside. Top bottle designers earn well over $100,000 for a single design. Add onto that the cost of advertising, in-store employees who spritz and hawk, and commissions to salespeople.

Finally, include the cost of celebrity endorsements that run into the millions of dollars. For example, Beyoncé reportedly has earned more than $40 million on her fragrance, Heat. Moreover, in comparison to older fragrances that have been around for decades, like Chanel or Dior, modern fragrances are made with much cheaper synthetic ingredients. So while a scent like Chanel would last 24 hours, modern fragrances last only a few hours at best.

In the perfume industry, it's packaging and advertising that generate profits.

As one celebrated "nose," Roja Dova, commented, "Studies show that people will say that a particular perfume is one of their favorites, but in a blind test they hate it. The trouble is that most people buy scent for their ego, after seeing an image in an advert and wanting to identify themselves in a certain way."

So here's a metaphysical question: even if perfume buyers really hate a fragrance in a blind test, but advertising convinces them that it smells wonderful, who are we to say that they are wrong to buy it? Isn't the attractiveness of a scent in the mind of the beholder?

>> Check Your Understanding 15-4

Solutions appear at back of book.

1. In which of the following cases is advertising likely to be economically useful? Economically wasteful? Explain your answer.
   a. Advertisements on the benefits of aspirin
   b. Advertisements for Bayer aspirin
   c. Advertisements on the benefits of drinking orange juice
   d. Advertisements for Tropicana orange juice
   e. Advertisements that state how long a plumber or an electrician has been in business

2. Some industry analysts have stated that a successful brand name is like a barrier to entry. Explain the reasoning behind this statement.

Harry's and the Dollar Shave Club Nick the Profits of Schick and Gillette

Mary Altaffer/ASSOCIATED PRESS

For 95 years, the historical market leaders of the American razor industry, Schick and Gillette, had enjoyed a comfortable if competitive long-term relationship. King Gillette invented the safety razor in 1901, and in 1921 Colonel Jacob Schick introduced another version of the safety razor. Now owned by large companies (Procter & Gamble and Energizer, respectively), the razor business has been incredibly profitable. Razor cartridges are the most profitable category of packaged goods. So much so that Gillette and Schick shared a $20 billion dollar global industry in 2019.

To keep these profits rolling in, Schick and Gillette introduced new feature after new feature, such as hydrating gel reservoirs, multiblade heads, and swiveling ball-hinges. For example, Gillette boasted that its Pro-Glide Shield (which sells for $22) with FlexBall technology "responds to contours and gets virtually every hair." In addition, both companies spent hundreds of millions of dollars on advertising and celebrity endorsements.

It was the culmination of a long-standing strategy undertaken by both companies: sell cheap razor handles, and make money on expensive cartridge refills. The two rivals created an arms-race dynamic in the market—going from two blades to three, then four and five to six—which forced customers to upgrade their razors every few years.

Then, in 2011 and 2012, came Dollar Shave Club and Harry's, two direct-to-consumer razor brands. For both companies, simplicity was the point: both offer a very limited range of razors, priced around $2 per cartridge. "The average guy does not like shopping and comparing 27 different things," said Katz-Mayfield, Harry's CEO.

Greg Lesko, a 56-year-old from the Pittsburgh area, said he became "fed up" with Gillette's high prices. "I figured there was nothing to lose so I gave Harry's a try. I wouldn't go back [to Gillette razors] if you paid me."

By 2018, the two startups had captured 14% of U.S. razor blade sales and were growing furiously. Both companies based themselves on a simple premise: a subscriber sets up a regular monthly order online, to be shipped to their home, at a fraction of the $10 to $20 retail cost of razors from Schick or Gillette. By the time Dollar Shave Club was purchased by Unilever in 2016, its annual sales were close to $200 million. It was purchased for $1 billion, a remarkable price for a five-year-old startup. In 2019, Schick followed, announcing a planned acquisition of Harry's for an even greater sum of $1.37 billion. However, in early 2020, the FTC sued to block the merger, with the complaint alleging that Harry's has shaken up a "comfortable duopoly." Harry's "has forced its rivals to offer lower prices, and more options, to consumers across the country," according to Daniel Francis, deputy director of the FTC's Bureau of Competition. Not surprisingly, Gillette and Schick have started their own inexpensive, subscription-based lines of razors.

QUESTIONS FOR THOUGHT

1. What explains the complexity of and high rate of innovation in razors by Gillette and Schick?

2. Why is the razor business so profitable? What explains the size of the advertising budgets of Schick and Gillette?

3. What explains the popularity of Harry's and the Dollar Shave Club? What dilemma do Schick and Gillette face in deciding to create their own lines of inexpensive subscription-based razors? What does this indicate about the welfare value to customers of the innovation in razors?

SUMMARY

1. **Monopolistic competition** is a market structure in which there are many competing producers, each producing a differentiated product, and there is free entry and exit in the long run. Product differentiation takes three main forms: by style or type, by location, or by quality. Products of competing sellers are considered imperfect substitutes, and each firm has its own downward-sloping demand curve and marginal revenue curve.

2. Short-run profits will attract entry of new firms in the long run. This reduces the quantity each existing producer sells at any given price and shifts its demand curve to the left. Short-run losses will induce exit by some firms in the long run. This shifts the demand curve of each remaining firm to the right.

3. In the long run, a monopolistically competitive industry is in **zero-profit equilibrium:** at its profit-maximizing quantity, the demand curve for each existing firm is tangent to its average total cost curve. There are zero profits in the industry and no entry or exit.

4. In long-run equilibrium, firms in a monopolistically competitive industry sell at a price greater than marginal cost. They also have **excess capacity** because they produce less than the minimum-cost output; as a result, they have higher costs than firms in a perfectly competitive industry. Whether or not monopolistic competition is inefficient is ambiguous because consumers value the diversity of products that it creates.

5. A monopolistically competitive firm will always prefer to make an additional sale at the going price, so it will engage in advertising to increase demand for its product and enhance its market power. Advertising and **brand names** that provide useful information to consumers are economically valuable. But they are economically wasteful when their only purpose is to create market power. In reality, advertising and brand names are likely to be some of both: economically valuable and economically wasteful.

KEY TERMS

Monopolistic competition, p. 448
Zero-profit equilibrium, p. 454

Excess capacity, p. 458

Brand name, p. 460

PRACTICE QUESTIONS

1. The market structure of the local gas station industry is monopolistic competition. Suppose that currently each gas station incurs a loss. Draw a diagram for a typical gas station to show this short-run situation. Then, in a separate diagram, show what will happen to the typical gas station in the long run. Explain your reasoning.

2. The local hairdresser industry has the market structure of monopolistic competition. Your hairdresser boasts that they are making a profit and that if they continue to do so, they will be able to retire in five years. Use a diagram to illustrate your hairdresser's current situation. Do you expect this to last? In a separate diagram, draw what you expect to happen in the long run. Explain your reasoning.

3. Magnificent Blooms is a florist in a monopolistically competitive industry. It is a successful operation, producing the quantity that minimizes its average total cost and making a profit. The owner also says that at its current level of output, its marginal cost is above marginal revenue. Illustrate the current situation of Magnificent Blooms in a diagram. Answer the following questions by illustrating with a diagram.

   a. In the short run, could Magnificent Blooms increase its profit?

   b. In the long run, could Magnificent Blooms increase its profit?

PROBLEMS

1. Use the three conditions for monopolistic competition discussed in the chapter to decide which of the following firms are likely to be operating as monopolistic competitors. If they are not monopolistically competitive firms, are they monopolists, oligopolists, or perfectly competitive firms?

   a. A local band that plays for weddings, parties, and so on

   b. Minute Maid, a producer of individual-serving juice boxes

   c. Your local dry cleaner

   d. A farmer who produces soybeans

2. You are thinking of setting up a coffee shop. The market structure for coffee shops is monopolistic competition. There are three Starbucks shops and two other coffee shops very much like Starbucks in your town already. In order for you to have some degree of market power, you may want to differentiate your coffee shop. Thinking about the three different ways in which

products can be differentiated, explain how you would decide whether you should copy Starbucks or whether you should sell coffee in a completely different way.

3. "In the long run, there is no difference between monopolistic competition and perfect competition." Discuss whether this statement is true, false, or ambiguous with respect to the following criteria.

   a. The price charged to consumers

   b. The average total cost of production

   c. The efficiency of the market outcome

   d. The typical firm's profit in the long run

4. "In both the short run and in the long run, the typical firm in monopolistic competition and a monopolist each make a profit." Do you agree with this statement? Explain your reasoning.

5. The market for clothes has the structure of monopolistic competition. What impact will fewer firms in this industry have on you as a consumer? Address the following issues.

   a. Variety of clothes

   b. Differences in quality of service

   c. Price

6. For each of the following situations, decide whether advertising is directly informative about the product or simply an indirect signal of its quality. Explain your reasoning.

   a. Football great Peyton Manning drives a Buick in a TV commercial and claims that he prefers it to any other car.

   b. A Craigslist ad states, "For sale: 1999 Honda Civic, 160,000 miles, new transmission."

   c. McDonald's spends millions of dollars on an advertising campaign that proclaims: "I'm lovin' it."

   d. Subway advertises one of its sandwiches by claiming that it contains 6 grams of fat and fewer than 300 calories.

7. In each of the following cases, explain how the advertisement functions as a signal to a potential buyer. Explain what information the buyer lacks that is being supplied by the advertisement and how the information supplied by the advertisement is likely to affect the buyer's willingness to buy the good.

   a. "Looking for work. Excellent references from previous employers available."

   b. "Electronic equipment for sale. All merchandise carries a one-year, no-questions-asked warranty."

   c. "Car for sale by original owner. All repair and maintenance records available."

8. The accompanying table shows the Herfindahl–Hirschman Index (HHI) for the restaurant, cereal, movie studio, and laundry detergent industries as well as the advertising expenditures of the top 10 firms in each industry. Use the information in the table to answer the following questions.

Industry	HHI	Advertising expenditures (millions)
Restaurants	179	$1,784
Cereal	2,598	732
Movie studios	918	3,324
Laundry detergent	2,750	132

   a. Which market structure—oligopoly or monopolistic competition—best characterizes each of the industries?

   b. Based on your answer to part a, which type of market structure has higher advertising expenditures? Use the characteristics of each market structure to explain why this relationship might exist.

9. McDonald's spends millions of dollars each year on legal protection of its brand name, thereby preventing any unauthorized use of it. Explain what information this conveys to you as a consumer about the quality of McDonald's products.

10. Before the existence of food-delivery companies UberEats, Grubhub, DoorDash, and Postmates, many students who attended college in small towns faced a pizza dilemma. While up late studying, hungry students had limited food options: in most locations there was only one late night food delivery option, usually pizza. Analyze the short-run and long-run effect of entrance of food-delivery companies in the market for late night delivery in small college towns.

11. Have you ever wondered why there are so many mattress stores? There is no question that we value a good night's rest and are willing to spend countless dollars on finding the perfect mattress. Despite an overwhelmingly large number of mattress stores, there seems to be an increasing number of new mattress companies selling online. Companies like Purple, Casper, Puffy, and even Amazon have started selling mattresses online. Assuming the brick-and-mortar mattress stores operated in a monopolistically competitive industry, how would you model the cost curves for these mattress companies in the short run? How have online mattress stores disrupted the industry?

WORK IT OUT

12. The restaurant business in town is a monopolistically competitive industry in long-run equilibrium. One restaurant owner asks for your advice. This owner tells you that, each night, not all tables in the restaurant are full. The owner also tells you that the restaurant would attract more customers if it lowered the prices on the menu and that doing so would lower the average total cost. Should the restaurant lower prices? Draw a diagram showing the demand curve, marginal revenue curve, marginal cost curve, and average total cost curve for this restaurant to explain your advice. Show in your diagram what would happen to the restaurant owner's profit if the restaurant were to lower the price so that it sells at the minimum-cost output. ∎

16 ⟩ Externalities

TROUBLE UNDERFOOT

WHEN RESEARCHERS AT DUKE University published a paper with an unassuming title, "Increased stray gas abundance in a subset of drinking water wells near Marcellus shale gas extraction," the effects of that publication were anything but restrained. While its results are not definitive, the paper presented evidence that fracking — the

Does pollution from fracking for natural gas endanger underground sources of drinking water? If so, how should society make the trade-off?

extraction of natural gas by fracturing underground shale deposits with chemical-laden pressurized jets of water — at the Marcellus gas field in Pennsylvania had contaminated underground drinking water supplies with ethane and propane.

The Duke paper provided support to some critics of fracking who claim that it poses an intolerable pollution threat to drinking water supplies. It also helped fuel an increasingly polarized debate over the costs and benefits of fracking.

You may recall from our discussion in Chapter 3 that fracking has dramatically reduced the cost of energy in the United States, leading to lower heating bills for homeowners and lower production costs for suppliers. And fracking has the potential to significantly reduce air pollution as consumers and industries move from dirtier-burning gasoline and coal to cleaner-burning natural gas.

However, as anticipated in Chapter 3, the environmental benefits of cleaner air from cheaper natural gas have been challenged by the specter of polluted drinking water from fracking. A key question in assessing the trade-off is the role of government: should regulators do more to protect groundwater supplies? Would more regulatory oversight of how fracking wells are drilled reduce groundwater contamination? What amount of contamination would regulators find acceptable? And how would they enforce it?

The dilemma posed by fracking is just one example of the dilemmas that are caused by *externalities*. An externality occurs when individuals impose costs or deliver benefits to others, but don't have an economic incentive to take those costs or benefits into account when making decisions. We briefly noted the concept of externalities

in Chapters 1 and 4. There we stated that one of the principal sources of market failure is actions that create *side effects* that are not properly taken into account — that is, actions that create externalities.

In this chapter we'll examine the economics of externalities, seeing how they can get in the way of market efficiency and lead to market failure, why they provide a reason for government intervention in markets, and how economic analysis can be used to guide government policy.

Externalities arise from the side effects of actions. First, we'll study the case of pollution, which generates a *negative externality* — a side effect that imposes costs on others. Whenever a side effect can be directly observed and quantified, it can be regulated: by imposing direct controls on it, taxing it, or subsidizing it. As we will see, government intervention in this case should be aimed directly at moving the market to the right quantity of the side effect. ●

WHAT YOU WILL LEARN

- What are **externalities** and why do they lead to inefficiency and government intervention in the market?

- How do **negative externalities, positive externalities,** and *network externalities* differ?

- What is the **Coase theorem** and how does it explain that private individuals can sometimes remedy externalities?

- Why are some government policies to deal with externalities efficient while others are not?

- Why are network externalities an important feature of high-tech industries?

An **external cost** is an uncompensated cost that an individual or firm imposes on others.

An **external benefit** is a benefit that an individual or firm confers on others without receiving compensation.

External costs and benefits are known as **externalities.** External costs are **negative externalities,** and external benefits are **positive externalities.**

‖ Understanding Externalities

The environmental costs of pollution are the best known and most important example of an **external cost**—an uncompensated cost that an individual or firm imposes on others. In a modern economy there are many examples of an external cost that an individual or firm imposes on others. A very familiar one is the external cost of traffic congestion: an individual who chooses to drive during rush hour increases congestion and has no incentive to take into account the inconvenience inflicted on other drivers. Another familiar example is the cost created by people who text while driving, increasing the risk of accidents that will harm others as well as themselves (see the upcoming For Inquiring Minds).

Pollution leads to an external cost because, in the absence of government intervention, those who decide how much pollution to create have no incentive to take into account the costs of pollution that they impose on others. In the case of air pollution from a coal-fired power plant, the power company has no incentive to take into account the health costs imposed upon people who breathe dirty air. Instead, the company's incentives are determined by the private monetary costs and benefits of generating power, such as the price of coal, the price earned for a kilowatt of energy, and so on.

We'll see later in this chapter that there are also important examples of **external benefits,** benefits that individuals or firms confer on others without receiving compensation. For example, when you get a flu shot, you are less likely to pass on the flu virus to your roommates. Yet you alone incur the monetary cost of the vaccination and the painful jab. Businesses that develop new technologies also generate external benefits, because their ideas often contribute to innovation by other firms.

External costs and benefits are jointly known as **externalities,** with external costs called **negative externalities** and external benefits called **positive externalities.** Externalities can lead to private decisions—that is, decisions by individuals or firms—that are not optimal for society as a whole. Let's take a closer look at why by focusing on the case of pollution.

FOR INQUIRING MINDS Driving While Distracted

Why is that person in the car in front of us driving so erratically? Is the driver drunk? No, the driver is texting or using their cell phone to check social media or make calls.

According to a recent survey, 69% of drivers between the ages of 18 and 64 admitted to using their phones while driving. Traffic safety experts take the risks posed by driving while using a cell phone very seriously: a driver is 23 times more likely to have an accident while texting.

The National Safety Council estimated that approximately 1 in 4 traffic accidents was attributable to the use of cell phones while driving and nearly 10% of fatal car crashes were tied to distracted drivers. Car crashes are the leading cause of teen deaths, and texting and driving is a large, contributing factor. In 2017, there were nearly 275 teenager deaths attributed to distracted driving.

And using hands-free, voice-activated devices to make a call doesn't seem to help much because the main danger is distraction. As one traffic consultant put it, "It's not where your eyes are; it's where your head is."

The National Safety Council urges people not to use cell phones while driving. Most states have some restrictions on cell phone use while driving. But in response to a growing number of accidents, several states have banned cell phone use behind the wheel altogether. In 48 states the District of Columbia, Puerto Rico, Guam, and the U.S. Virgin Islands it is illegal to text and drive. Cell phone use while driving is illegal in many countries as well, including Japan and Israel.

Why not leave the decision up to the driver? Because the risk posed by driving while using a cell phone isn't just a risk to the driver; it's also a safety risk to

Using a cell phone while driving makes you a danger to others as well as yourself.

others—to a driver's passengers, to pedestrians, and to people in other cars. Even if a driver decides that the benefit of using their cell phone while driving is worth the cost, they aren't taking into account the cost to other people. Driving while using a cell phone, in other words, generates a serious—and sometimes fatal—negative externality.

The Economics of a Negative Externality: Pollution

Pollution is a bad thing. Yet most pollution is a side effect of activities that provide us with good things: our air is polluted by power plants generating the electricity that lights our cities, and our rivers are damaged by fertilizer runoff from farms that grow our food. And groundwater contamination may occur from fracking, which also produces cleaner-burning fuel. Why shouldn't we accept a certain amount of pollution as the cost of a good life?

Actually, we do. Even highly committed environmentalists don't think that we can or should completely eliminate pollution—even an environmentally conscious society would accept *some* pollution as the cost of producing useful goods and services. What environmentalists argue is that unless there is a strong and effective environmental policy, our society will generate *too much* pollution—too much of a bad thing. And the great majority of economists agree.

To see why, we need a framework that lets us think about how much pollution a society *should* have. We'll then be able to see why a market economy, left to itself, will produce more pollution than it should. We'll start by adopting the simplest framework to study the problem—assuming that the amount of pollution emitted by a polluter is directly observable and controllable.

The Costs and Benefits of Pollution

How much pollution should society allow? The answer to this question involves comparing the marginal benefit from an additional unit of pollution with the marginal cost of an additional unit of pollution.

The **marginal social cost of pollution** is the additional cost imposed on society as a whole by an additional unit of pollution.

For example, sulfur dioxide from coal-fired power plants mixes with rainwater to form acid rain, which damages fisheries, crops, and forests, while groundwater contamination, which may be a side effect of fracking, damages health. Typically, the marginal social cost of pollution is increasing—each additional unit of pollution emitted causes a greater level of damage than the unit before. That's because nature can often safely handle low levels of pollution but is increasingly harmed as pollution reaches higher levels.

The **marginal social benefit of pollution** is the benefit to society from an additional unit of pollution. This may seem like a confusing concept—how can there be any benefit to society from pollution? The answer lies in the understanding that pollution can be reduced—but at a cost. For example, air pollution from coal-fired power plants can be reduced by using more-expensive coal and expensive scrubbing technology; contamination of drinking water due to fracking can be limited with more-expensive drilling techniques; wastewater contamination of rivers and oceans can be reduced by building water treatment facilities.

All these methods of reducing pollution have an opportunity cost. That is, avoiding pollution requires using scarce resources that could have been employed to produce other goods and services. So the marginal social benefit of pollution is the goods and services that could be had by society if it tolerated another unit of pollution.

Comparisons between the pollution levels tolerated in rich and poor countries illustrate the importance of the level of the marginal social benefit of pollution in deciding how much pollution a society wishes to tolerate. Because poor countries have a higher opportunity cost of resources spent on reducing pollution than richer countries, they tolerate higher levels of pollution. For example, the World Health Organization has estimated that 3.8 million people in poor countries die prematurely from breathing polluted indoor air caused by burning dirty fuels like wood, dung, and coal to heat and cook—a situation that residents of rich countries can afford to avoid.

Using hypothetical numbers, Figure 16-1 shows how we can determine the **socially optimal quantity of pollution**—the quantity of pollution that society

The **marginal social cost of pollution** is the additional cost imposed on society as a whole by an additional unit of pollution.

The **marginal social benefit of pollution** is the additional gain to society as a whole from an additional unit of pollution.

The **socially optimal quantity of pollution** is the quantity of pollution that society would choose if all the costs and benefits of pollution were fully accounted for.

would choose if all the social costs and benefits were fully accounted for. The upward-sloping marginal social cost curve, *MSC*, shows how the marginal cost to society of an additional unit of pollution varies with the quantity of pollution. It is typically upward sloping because the harm inflicted by a unit of pollution typically increases since more pollution has already been emitted. In contrast, the marginal social benefit curve, *MSB*, is downward sloping. At high levels of pollution, the cost of achieving a reduction in pollution is fairly small. However, as pollution levels drop, it becomes progressively more costly to engineer a further fall in pollution as more expensive techniques must be used, so the *MSB* is higher at lower levels of pollution.

As we can see from Figure 16-1, the socially optimal quantity of pollution in this example isn't zero. It's Q_{OPT}, the quantity corresponding to point *O*, where *MSB* crosses *MSC*. At Q_{OPT}, the marginal social benefit from an additional unit of pollution and its marginal social cost are equalized at $200.

But will a market economy, left to itself, arrive at the socially optimal quantity of pollution? No, it won't.

Why a Market Economy Produces Too Much Pollution

While pollution yields both benefits and costs to society, in a market economy without government intervention too much pollution will be produced. In that case it is polluters alone—owners of power plants or gas-drilling companies, for example—who decide how much pollution is created. And they have no incentive to take into account the cost that pollution inflicts on others. Instead, the company's incentives are determined by the private monetary costs and benefits of generating power, such as the price of coal, the price earned for a kilowatt of energy, and so on.

Figure 16-2 shows the result of this asymmetry between who reaps the benefits and who pays the costs. In a market economy without government intervention, since polluters are the only ones making the decisions, only the private

---

FIGURE 16-1 The Socially Optimal Quantity of Pollution

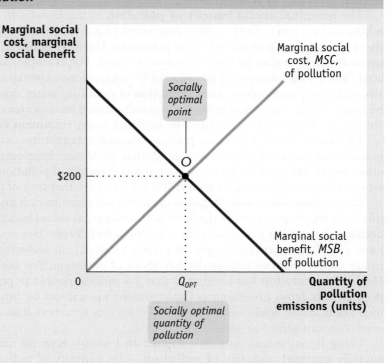

Pollution yields both costs and benefits. Here the *MSC* curve shows how the marginal cost to society as a whole from emitting one more unit of pollution emissions depends on the quantity of emissions. The *MSC* curve is upward sloping, so the marginal social cost increases as pollution increases. The *MSB* curve shows how the marginal benefit to society as a whole of emitting an additional unit of pollution emissions depends on the quantity of pollution emissions. The *MSB* curve is downward sloping, so the marginal social benefit falls as pollution increases. The socially optimal quantity of pollution is Q_{OPT}; at that quantity, the marginal social benefit of pollution is equal to the marginal social cost, corresponding to $200.

FIGURE 16-2 Why a Market Economy Produces Too Much Pollution

In the absence of government intervention, the quantity of pollution will be Q_{MKT}, the level at which the marginal social benefit of pollution is zero. This is an inefficiently high quantity of pollution: the marginal social cost, $400, greatly exceeds the marginal social benefit, $0. An optimal Pigouvian tax* of $200, the value of the marginal social cost of pollution when it equals the marginal social benefit of pollution, can move the market to the socially optimal quantity of pollution, Q_{OPT}.

*Pigouvian taxes will be covered in the next section on pollution policy.

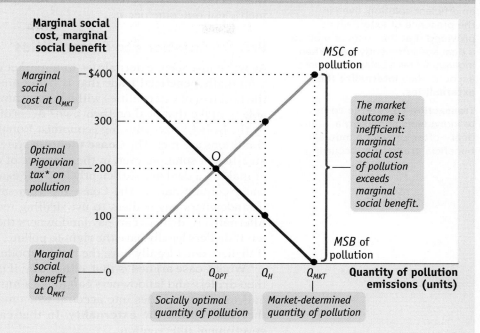

Marginal social cost, marginal social benefit

Marginal social cost at Q_{MKT} — $400

300

Optimal Pigouvian tax* on pollution — 200

100

Marginal social benefit at Q_{MKT} — 0

MSC of pollution

O

The market outcome is inefficient: marginal social cost of pollution exceeds marginal social benefit.

MSB of pollution

Q_{OPT} Q_H Q_{MKT} Quantity of pollution emissions (units)

Socially optimal quantity of pollution

Market-determined quantity of pollution

benefits of pollution are taken into account when choosing how much pollution to produce, rather than the costs to society. So instead of producing the socially optimal quantity, Q_{OPT}, the market economy will generate the amount Q_{MKT}. At Q_{MKT}, the marginal social benefit of an additional unit of pollution is zero, while the marginal social cost of an additional unit is much higher—$400.

Why? Well, take a moment to consider what the polluter would do if they were emitting Q_{OPT} of pollution. Remember that the *MSB* curve represents the resources made available by tolerating one more unit of pollution. The polluter would notice that if they increase their emission of pollution by moving down the *MSB* curve from Q_{OPT} to Q_H, they would gain $200 – $100 = $100. That gain of $100 comes from using less-expensive but higher-emission production techniques. Remember, they suffer none of the costs of doing this—only others do. However, it won't stop there. At Q_H, they notice that if emissions are increased from Q_H to Q_{MKT}, they would gain another $100 as they move down the *MSB* curve yet again. This would be achieved by using even cheaper and higher-emission production techniques. They will stop at Q_{MKT} because at this emission level the marginal social benefit of a unit of pollution is zero. That is, at Q_{MKT} they gain nothing by using yet cheaper and dirtier production techniques and emitting more pollution.

The market outcome, Q_{MKT}, is inefficient. Recall that an outcome is inefficient if someone could be made better off without someone else being made worse off. At an inefficient outcome, a mutually beneficial trade is being missed. At Q_{MKT}, the benefit accruing to the polluter of the last unit of pollution is very low—virtually zero. But the cost imposed on society of that last unit of pollution is quite high—$400. So by reducing the quantity of pollution at Q_{MKT} by one unit, the total social cost of pollution falls by $400 but the total social benefit falls by virtually zero.

So total surplus rises by approximately $400 if the quantity of pollution at Q_{MKT} is reduced by one unit. At Q_{MKT}, society would be willing to pay the polluter up to $400 not to emit the last unit of pollution, and the polluter would be willing

According to the **Coase theorem,** the economy can always reach an efficient solution, even in the presence of externalities, provided that the costs of making a deal are sufficiently low. When individuals take externalities into account, they **internalize the externalities.**

Transaction costs—the costs to individuals of making a deal—often prevent a mutually beneficial trade from occurring.

to accept their offer since that last unit gains them virtually nothing. But because there is no means in this market economy for this transaction to take place, an inefficient outcome occurs.

Private Solutions to Externalities

As we've just seen, externalities in a market economy cause inefficiency: there is a mutually beneficial trade that is being missed. So can the private sector solve the problem of externalities without government intervention? Will individuals be able to make that deal on their own? According to the *Coase theorem*, formulated by the Nobel Prize–winning economist Ronald Coase, the answer is yes if certain conditions are met. The **Coase theorem** states that the economy can always reach an efficient solution, even in the presence of externalities, provided that the costs of making a deal are sufficiently low. For example, if fracking is causing groundwater contamination, the Coase theorem says that the problem can be avoided if landowners pay drillers to use drilling technology that creates less pollution. Alternatively, drillers can pay landowners the cost of damage to their groundwater. If drillers legally have the right to pollute, then the first outcome is more likely. If drillers don't legally have the right to pollute, then the second is more likely.

What Coase argued is that, either way, if transaction costs are sufficiently low, then drillers and landowners can make a mutually beneficial deal. When individuals take externalities into account when making decisions, economists say that they **internalize the externality.** In that case the outcome is efficient without government intervention.

So why don't private parties always internalize externalities? The problem is **transaction costs**—the costs of making a deal—often prevent a mutually beneficial trade from occurring. Transaction costs are a barrier particularly when those who are hurt by the externality are widely dispersed, such as in the case of air pollution or *greenhouse gases*. When this happens, the cost of communication and negotiation is simply too high to achieve an efficient outcome.

When transaction costs prevent the private sector from dealing with externalities, it is time to look for government solutions. We turn to public policy in the next section.

ECONOMICS >> *in Action*
How Much Does Your Electricity Really Cost?

Three leading economists, Nicholas Z. Muller, Robert Mendelsohn, and Nobel Prize-winner William Nordhaus, estimated the external cost of pollution by various U.S. industries. The costs took a variety of forms, from harmful effects on health to reduced agricultural yields. In the case of the electricity-generation sector they estimated the costs of carbon dioxide emissions—one of the many greenhouse gases that cause *climate change*.

The authors used a relatively low estimate of the external costs because their valuation is a contentious issue—in part because the external costs will fall on future generations. They compared the total external costs of pollution (TEC) for the coal-fired and natural gas–fired power sector, and compared this to each sectors' value added (VA)—the market value of its output.

The accompanying table shows the TEC to VA ratios and the TEC to kilowatt-hour ratios for the two sectors. As you can see, both modes of electricity generation impose large external costs, exceeding their value added.

What is the social cost of carbon?

Denis Pepin/Shutterstock

But the TEC per kilowatt-hour generated with natural gas is much lower than that of one generated with coal, because burning natural gas releases both less carbon dioxide and fewer other pollutants. A conservative estimate is that the external cost of a kilowatt hour is one-third of the retail price of electricity when generated by coal, and one-twentieth when generated by natural gas.

	TEC/VA	TEC/Kilowatt-hour
Coal	$2.83	$0.039
Natural gas	1.30	0.005

In 2014, the Obama administration issued rules that limited carbon emissions from newly constructed power plants, with the intent of compelling new coal-fired plants to adopt carbon-capture technology. In 2018, the Trump administration significantly relaxed those rules in a bid to revive the coal industry. Yet industry analysts observed that this relaxation of the limits on carbon emissions was unlikely to reverse the coal industry's long-term decline. By 2016, fracking had rendered natural gas–fired plants cheaper to operate than coal-fired plants. In that year, for the first time in history, more U.S. energy was generated by natural gas than by coal. And by 2018, some clean energy plants were even cheaper than natural gas–fired plants.

>> Check Your Understanding 16-1

Solutions appear at back of book.

1. Wastewater runoff from large poultry farms adversely affects their neighbors. Explain the following:
   a. The nature of the external cost imposed
   b. The outcome in the absence of government intervention or a private deal
   c. The socially optimal outcome
2. According to Yasmin, any student who borrows a book from the university library and fails to return it on time imposes a negative externality on other students. She claims that rather than charging a modest fine for late returns, the library should charge a huge fine so that borrowers will never return a book late. Is Yasmin's economic reasoning correct?

|| Government Policy and Pollution

By the 1960s, vast tracts of ghostly, withered trees in the northeastern United States and southeastern Canada revealed an ominous truth: these great forests were dying. Moreover, the lakes and streams within them were dying too, as the stock of fish and other aquatic life plummeted.

The culprit was acid rain, a phenomenon that occurs when rain mixes with airborne sulfur dioxide pollutants from coal-burning power plants. The result is highly acidic rain that poisons trees and aquatic life. Before 1970, there were no rules governing the amount of sulfur dioxide that coal-burning power plants in the United States could emit.

In 1970, Congress adopted the Clean Air Act, which set rules forcing power plants to reduce their emissions. And it worked—the acidity of rainfall declined significantly. Economists, however, argued that a more flexible system of rules that exploits the effectiveness of markets could reduce pollution at a lower cost. In 1990 this theory was put into effect with a modified version of the Clean Air Act. And guess what? The economists were right!

In this section we'll look at the three types of policies governments typically use to deal with pollution: environmental standards, emissions taxes, and tradable emissions permits.

We will also see how economic analysis has been used to improve those policies. And we will look at the issue of climate change and how government policy can be used to address it.

Environmental Standards

Among the most serious negative externalities we face today are those associated with actions that damage the environment—air pollution, water pollution, habitat destruction, and so on. Protection of the environment has become a major role of government in all developed nations. In the United States, the Environmental Protection Agency is the principal enforcer of environmental policies at the national level, supported by the actions of state and local governments.

How does a country protect its environment? At present the main policy tools are **environmental standards,** rules that protect the environment by specifying actions by producers and consumers. A familiar example is the law that requires almost all vehicles to have catalytic converters, which reduce the emission of toxic gases and other pollutants that cause smog and lead to health problems. Other rules require communities to treat their sewage or factories to avoid or limit certain kinds of pollution. And as we just saw in the Economics in Action, environmental standards were put in place in 2014, compelling new coal- and gas-fired power plants to adopt cleaner-burning technologies.

"They have very strict antipollution laws in this state."

Environmental standards came into widespread use in the 1960s and 1970s, and they have had considerable success in reducing pollution. For example, since the United States passed the Clean Air Act in 1970, overall emission of pollutants into the air has fallen by more than a third, even though the population has grown by a third and the size of the economy has more than doubled.

Emissions Taxes

Another policy tool to address pollution is to charge polluters an **emissions tax.** Emissions taxes depend on the amount of pollution a firm emits. As we learned in Chapter 7, a tax imposed on an activity will reduce the level of that activity.

Recall that without government intervention, polluters have an incentive to increase pollution beyond the socially optimal quantity of pollution. In fact, polluters will push pollution up to the quantity Q_{MKT}, shown in Figure 16-2, the point at which marginal social benefit equals zero.

As shown in that figure, if the marginal social benefit and marginal social cost of an additional unit of pollution are equal at $200, a tax on polluters of $200 per unit of pollution will induce them to reduce their emissions to Q_{OPT}, the socially optimal quantity. This illustrates a general result: an emissions tax equal to the marginal social cost at the socially optimal quantity of pollution induces polluters to internalize the externality—to take into account the true cost to society of their actions.

An emissions tax is also a more efficient way to reduce pollution than environmental standards because the tax ensures that the marginal benefit of pollution is equal for all sources of pollution. Environmental standards, by contrast, treat all polluters the same, when they actually differ according to their costs of pollution reduction.

The term *emissions tax* may convey the misleading impression that taxes are a solution to only one kind of negative externality, pollution. In fact, taxes can be used to discourage any activity that generates negative externalities, such as driving (which inflicts environmental damage greater than the cost of producing gasoline) or smoking (which inflicts health costs on society far greater than the cost of making a cigarette).

In general, taxes designed to reduce the costs imposed on society from a negative externality are known as **Pigouvian taxes,** after the economist A. C. Pigou, who emphasized their usefulness in his classic 1920 book, *The Economics of Welfare.*

Environmental standards are rules that protect the environment by specifying actions by producers and consumers.

An **emissions tax** is a tax that depends on the amount of pollution a firm produces.

Taxes designed to reduce the costs imposed on society from a negative externality are known as **Pigouvian taxes.**

GLOBAL COMPARISON ECONOMIC GROWTH AND GREENHOUSE GASES IN SIX COUNTRIES

At first glance, a comparison of the per capita greenhouse gas emissions of various countries, shown in panel (a) of this graph, suggests that Canada, the United States, and Australia are the worst offenders. In 2018, the average American is responsible for 16.6 tonnes of greenhouse gas emissions (measured in carbon dioxide, CO_2, equivalents)—the pollution that causes climate change—compared to only 2.8 tonnes for the average Uzbek, 7.1 tonnes for the average Chinese, and 2.0 tonnes for the average Indian. (A tonne, also called a metric ton, equals 1.10 ton.)

Such a conclusion, however, ignores an important factor in determining the level of a country's greenhouse gas emissions: its gross domestic product, or GDP—the total value of a country's domestic output. Output typically cannot be produced without more energy, and more energy usage typically results in more pollution. In fact, some have argued that criticizing a country's level of greenhouse gases without taking account of its level of economic development is misguided. It would be equivalent to faulting a country for being at a more advanced stage of economic development.

A more meaningful way to compare pollution across countries is to measure emissions per $1 million of a country's GDP, as shown in panel (b). On this basis, the United States, Canada, and Australia are now "green" countries, but China, India, and Uzbekistan are

not. What explains the reversal once GDP is accounted for? The answer is scarce resources.

Countries that are poor, such as Uzbekistan, China (historically), and India have viewed resources spent on pollution reduction as better spent on other things. They have argued that they are too poor to afford the same environmental priorities as wealthy developed countries. To impose a wealthy country's environmental standards on them would, they claimed, jeopardize their economic growth.

However, the scientific evidence pointing to *greenhouse gases* as the cause of *climate change* and the falling price of nonpolluting energy sources has changed attitudes in poorer countries. Realizing that their citizens are likely to suffer disproportionately more from climate change, poor countries joined forces with rich countries to sign the *Paris Agreement* in 2015, an agreement between 196 countries to limit their greenhouse gas emissions, to keep global temperatures from increasing less than 2 degrees Celsius, the temperature at which the effects of climate change are considered to be catastrophic and irreversible. At the time of writing, the United States has announced its intent to withdraw from the agreement in November 2020, the only country in the world to reject the agreement.

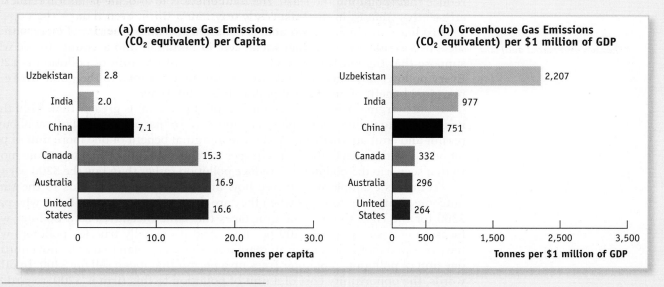

Data from: Global Carbon Atlas; IMF—World Economic Outlook.

In our example, the optimal Pigouvian tax is $200. As you can see from Figure 16-2, this corresponds to the marginal social cost of pollution at the optimal output quantity, Q_{OPT}.

The main shortcoming of emissions taxes compared to environmental standards is that, government officials usually aren't sure how high the tax should be set. If they set it too low, pollution reduction would be insufficient. If they set it too high, emissions will be reduced by more than is efficient. This uncertainty around the optimal level of the emissions tax can't be eliminated, but the nature of the risks can be changed by using an alternative policy, issuing tradable emissions permits. However, emissions taxes can have political advantages: voters may be more willing to approve of them when the tax revenue is rebated back to consumers.

Tradable emissions permits are licenses to emit limited quantities of pollutants that can be bought and sold by polluters.

Tradable Emissions Permits

Tradable emissions permits are licenses to emit limited quantities of pollutants that can be bought and sold by polluters. Tradable emissions permits work in practice much like the tradable quotas (discussed in Chapter 5) in which regulators created a system of tradable licenses to fish for crabs. The tradable licenses resulted in an efficient way to allocate the right to fish—boat owners with the safest and lowest cost of operation purchase the rights of owners with less safe, higher cost boats. Although tradable emissions permits involve trading a "bad" like pollution instead of a "good" like crab, both systems work to allocate an activity efficiently because the permits, like licenses, are *tradable*.

Here's why this system works in the case of pollution. Firms that pollute typically have different costs of reducing pollution—for example, it will be more costly for plants using older technology to reduce pollution than plants using newer technology. Regulators begin the system by issuing polluters with permits to pollute based on some formula—say, for example, equal to 50% of a given firm's historical level of emissions. Firms then have the right to trade permits among themselves.

Under this system, a market in permits to pollute will emerge. Polluters who place a higher value on the right to pollute—those with older technology—will purchase permits from polluters who place a lower value on the right to pollute—those with newer technology. As a result, a polluter with a higher value for a unit of emissions will pollute more than a polluter with a lower value.

In the end, those with the lowest cost of reducing pollution will reduce their pollution the most, while those with the highest cost of reducing pollution will reduce their pollution the least. The total effect is to allocate pollution reduction efficiently—that is, in the least costly way.

Just like emissions taxes, tradable emissions permits provide polluters with an incentive to take the marginal social cost of pollution into account. To see why, suppose that the market price of a permit to emit one unit of pollution is $200. Every polluter now has an incentive to limit its emissions to the point where its marginal benefit of one unit of pollution is $200. Why?

If the marginal benefit of one more unit of pollution is greater than $200 then it is cheaper to pollute more than to pollute less. In that case the polluter will buy a permit and emit another unit. And if the marginal benefit of one more unit of pollution is less than $200, then it is cheaper to reduce pollution than to pollute more. In that scenario the polluter will reduce pollution rather than buy the $200 permit.

From this example we can see how an emissions permit leads to the same outcome as an emissions tax when they are the same amount: a polluter who pays $200 for the right to emit one unit faces the same incentives as a polluter who faces an emissions tax of $200 per unit. And it's equally true for polluters who have received more permits from regulators than they plan to use: by not emitting one unit of pollution, a polluter frees up a permit that it can sell for $200. In other words, the opportunity cost of a unit of pollution to this firm is $200, regardless of whether it is used.

Recall that when using emissions taxes to arrive at the optimal level of pollution, the problem arises of finding the right amount of the tax: if the tax is too low, too much pollution is emitted; if the tax is too high, too little pollution is emitted (in other words, too many resources are spent reducing pollution). A similar problem with tradable emissions permits is getting the quantity of permits right, which is much like the flip-side of getting the level of the tax right.

Because it is difficult to determine the optimal quantity of pollution, regulators can find themselves either issuing too many permits, so that there is insufficient pollution reduction, or issuing too few, so that there is too much pollution reduction.

In the case of sulfur dioxide pollution, the U.S. government first relied on environmental standards, but then turned to a system of tradable emissions permits. Currently the largest emissions permit trading system is the European Union system for controlling emissions of carbon dioxide.

Comparing Environmental Policies with an Example

Figure 16-3 shows a hypothetical industry consisting of only two plants, plant A and plant B. We'll assume that plant A uses newer technology, giving it a lower cost of pollution reduction, while plant B uses older technology and has a higher cost of pollution reduction. Reflecting this difference, plant A's marginal benefit of pollution curve, MB_A, lies below plant B's marginal benefit of pollution curve, MB_B. Because it is more costly for plant B to reduce its pollution at any output quantity, an additional unit of pollution is worth more to plant B than to plant A.

In the absence of government action, we know that polluters will pollute until the marginal social benefit of a unit of pollution is equal to zero. As a result, without government intervention each plant will pollute until its own marginal benefit of pollution is equal to zero. This corresponds to an emissions quantity of 600 units for each plant—the quantities of pollution at which MB_A and MB_B are equal to zero. So although plant A and plant B have different costs of pollution reduction, they will each choose to emit the same amount of pollution.

Now suppose that regulators decide that the overall pollution from this industry should be cut in half, from 1,200 units to 600 units. Panel (a) of Figure 16-3 shows this might be achieved with an environmental standard that requires each plant to cut its emissions in half, from 600 to 300 units. The standard has the

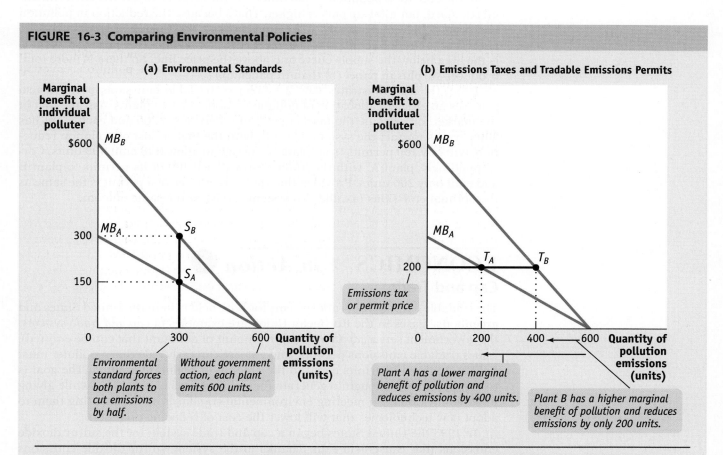

FIGURE 16-3 Comparing Environmental Policies

In both panels, MB_A shows the marginal benefit of pollution to plant A and MB_B shows the marginal benefit of pollution to plant B. In the absence of government intervention, each plant would emit 600 units. However, the cost of reducing emissions is lower for plant A, as shown by the fact that MB_A lies below MB_B Panel (a) shows the result of an environmental standard that requires both plants to cut emissions in half; this is inefficient, because it leaves the marginal benefit of pollution higher for plant B than for plant A. Panel (b) shows that an emissions tax as well as a system of tradable permits achieves the same quantity of overall pollution efficiently. Faced with either an emissions tax of $200 per unit, or a market price of a permit of $200 per unit, each plant reduces pollution to the point where its marginal benefit is $200.

desired effect of reducing overall emissions from 1,200 to 600 units but accomplishes it inefficiently.

As you can see from panel (a), the environmental standard leads plant A to produce at point S_A, where its marginal benefit of pollution is $150, but plant B produces at point S_B, where its marginal benefit of pollution is twice as high, $300.

This difference in marginal benefits between the two plants tells us that the same quantity of pollution can be achieved at lower total cost by allowing plant B to pollute more than 300 units but inducing plant A to pollute less. In fact, the efficient way to reduce pollution is to ensure that at the industry-wide outcome, the marginal benefit of pollution is the same for all plants. When each plant values a unit of pollution equally, there is no way to rearrange pollution reduction among the various plants that achieves the optimal quantity of pollution at a lower total cost.

We can see from panel (b) how an emissions tax achieves exactly that result. Suppose both plant A and plant B pay an emissions tax of $200 per unit, so that the marginal cost of an additional unit of emissions to each plant is now $200 rather than zero. As a result, plant A produces at T_A and plant B produces at T_B. So plant A reduces its pollution more than it would under an inflexible environmental standard, cutting its emissions from 600 to 200 units. Meanwhile, plant B reduces its pollution less, going from 600 to 400 units.

In the end, total pollution—600 units—is the same as under the environmental standard, but total surplus is higher. That's because the reduction in pollution has been achieved efficiently, allocating most of the reduction to plant A, the plant that can reduce emissions at a lower cost. (Remember that producer surplus is the area below the supply curve and above the price line. So there is more total producer surplus in panel (b) than in panel (a).)

Panel (b) also illustrates why a system of tradable emissions permits also achieves an efficient allocation of pollution among the two plants. Assume that in the market for permits, the market price of a permit is $200 and each plant has 300 permits to start the system. Plant B, with the higher cost of pollution reduction, will buy 100 permits from plant A, enough to allow it to emit 400 units. Correspondingly, plant A, with the lower cost, will sell 100 of its permits to plant B and emit only 200 units. Provided that the market price of a permit is the same as the optimal emissions tax, the two systems arrive at the same outcome.

ECONOMICS >> *in Action*
Cap and Trade

The tradable emissions permit systems for both acid rain in the United States and greenhouse gases in the European Union are examples of *cap and trade systems:* the government sets a *cap* (a maximum amount of pollutant that can be emitted), issues tradable emissions permits, and enforces a yearly rule that a polluter must hold a number of permits equal to the amount of pollutant emitted. The goal is to set the cap low enough to generate the efficient level of pollution, while giving polluters flexibility in meeting environmental standards and motivating them to adopt new technologies that will lower the cost of reducing pollution.

In 1995 the United States began a cap and trade system for the sulfur dioxide emissions that cause acid rain. Thanks to the system, sulfur dioxide emissions have fallen by 91% from 1994 to 2018. Economists have estimated that it would have been 80% more expensive to reduce emissions by the same amount using a non-market-based regulatory policy.

In 2005 the first cap and trade system for trading greenhouse gases—called *carbon trading*—was launched in the European Union. Nearly two decades later, carbon trading has grown rapidly around the world and now covers 20% of all man-made greenhouse gas emissions. In the past few years, several new greenhouse gas markets have been launched covering California, South Korea, Quebec, and three major industrial centers in China. In 2019, approximately $214 billion in permits were traded globally. This number is expected to grow rapidly as China plans to start a national trading scheme.

Yet cap and trade systems are not silver bullets for the world's pollution problems. While they are appropriate for pollution that's geographically dispersed, like sulfur dioxide and greenhouse gases, they don't work for pollution that's localized, like groundwater contamination. Second, there must be vigilant monitoring of compliance for the system to deliver its goals. Finally, the system attracts political interference which has, in practice, led to caps that are too high to achieve the efficient level of emissions.

Like emissions taxes, cap and trade systems are susceptible to political interference from companies that lobby to get more generous terms. As of 2018, only five countries with cap and trade systems (Finland, France, Sweden, Norway, and Switzerland) had permit prices that met or exceeded $44 per metric ton, the carbon price that the International Emissions Trading Association estimates is required to avert catastrophic climate change. As one energy economist stated, "It is politically difficult to get carbon prices to levels that have an effect." As a result, policy makers are sometimes returning to the use of environmental standards. Two examples are Obama administration era regulations: rules that limit the emissions from newly built coal-fired and natural gas–fired plants; and mandates that required the doubling of the fuel efficiency of cars by 2025.

>> Check Your Understanding 16-2
Solutions appear at back of book.

1. Some opponents of tradable emissions permits object to them on the grounds that polluters that sell their permits benefit monetarily from their contribution to polluting the environment. Assess this argument.
2. Explain the following.
   a. Why an emissions tax smaller than or greater than the marginal social cost at Q_{OPT} leads to a smaller total surplus compared to the total surplus generated if the emissions tax had been set optimally
   b. Why a system of tradable emissions permits that sets the total quantity of allowable pollution higher or lower than Q_{OPT} leads to a smaller total surplus compared to the total surplus generated if the number of permits had been set optimally
   c. How a carbon tax, which is a tax on carbon emissions, would encourage consumers to use more renewable energy sources

‖ The Economics of Climate Change

It is safe to say that one of the most challenging problems that the world will face during your lifetime is **climate change.** Science has conclusively shown that emissions of *greenhouse gases* are changing Earth's climate. On a global scale, **greenhouse gases** trap heat in Earth's atmosphere, leading to extreme weather patterns around the world—drought, flooding, extreme temperatures, destructive storm activity, and rising sea levels. Climate change inflicts huge costs and suffering, as crops fail, homes are washed away, tropical diseases spread, animal species are lost, and areas become uninhabitable. Moreover, the burden of this cost will fall more heavily on poorer countries, which have fewer resources to cope with the change.

In 2018, a scientific report by 13 federal agencies warned that unmitigated climate change could lower U.S. GDP by 10% by 2100. One study estimated that 20% of world GDP would be lost under the same conditions. Economists and scientists widely recognize that the direct cost of fossil-fuel consumption greatly underestimates the social cost. In a World Bank study, Nobel prize–winning economists Joseph Stiglitz and Nicholas Stern estimated that the true environmental cost of carbon emissions ranges from $50 to $100 per ton as of 2017, and may climb as high as $400 by 2050.

An accumulation of greenhouse gases caused by the use of fossil fuels has led to changes in Earth's climate, known as **climate change.**

Greenhouse gases are gas emissions that trap heat in Earth's atmosphere.

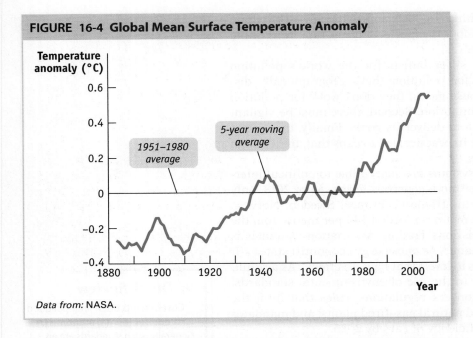

FIGURE 16-4 Global Mean Surface Temperature Anomaly

Data from: NASA.

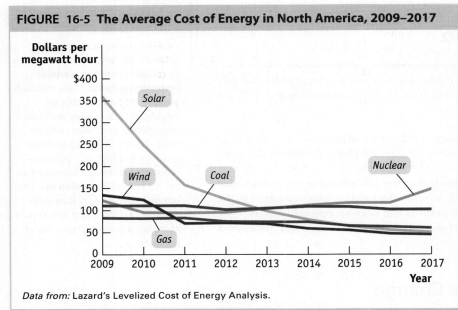

FIGURE 16-5 The Average Cost of Energy in North America, 2009–2017

Data from: Lazard's Levelized Cost of Energy Analysis.

According to industry observers, the plunge in national electricity demand caused by the pandemic of 2020 is likely to hasten the permanent closure of many coal plants.

The Causes of Climate Change

The rise in Earth's temperature began in the first half of the nineteenth century and has accelerated since the 1980s as Figure 16-4 shows. The source of the vast majority of greenhouse gases is human activity—specifically, the burning of **fossil fuels** such as coal, oil, and natural gas, which are derived from fossil sources and are used to generate electricity or power vehicles. Burning fossil fuels releases carbon into the atmosphere, which turns into greenhouse gases. While fossil fuels are in limited supply, **renewable energy sources** are inexhaustible. Examples are solar and wind-generated power. Unlike fossil fuels, renewables are **clean energy sources** because they do not emit greenhouse gases.

Over the past decade, government subsidies, environmental regulation, and the threat of emissions taxes have spurred huge investments in clean energy sources, leading to dramatic cost reductions for renewables. While coal (the most polluting fossil fuel) was once the energy source of choice in the United States, accounting for nearly 60% of power generation, environmental restrictions and technological innovations have rendered it more costly than natural gas or renewables. By 2019, the use of coal as a power source had fallen to 20%, which is even lower than the 23% share accounted for by renewables. In fact, in many instances, prices for industrial-scale solar power and wind power have become even cheaper than cleaner-burning natural gas power as Figure 16-5 shows.

Despite these advances, world energy consumption remains overwhelmingly dependent upon fossil fuels. In 2018 they accounted for approximately 85% of total consumption, while renewables accounted for only 10.8%. (Nuclear energy accounts for the difference of approximately 4%.) Why? It's dollars and cents. Historically, fossil fuels have been a cheaper source of energy than renewables. In much of the world, energy is generated by aging power plants that run on coal. This is true of both China and India where 70% or more of the electricity is generated by coal.

Fossil fuels such as coal and oil are fuels derived from fossil sources.

Renewable energy sources such as solar and wind power are inexhaustible sources of energy (unlike fossil-fuel sources, which are exhaustible).

Clean energy sources are those that do not emit greenhouse gases. Renewable energy sources are also clean energy sources.

Policies to Address Climate Change

Earlier in this chapter, we learned about government policies aimed at achieving an efficient level of greenhouse gas emissions. These included regulations or mandates, emissions taxes, and cap-and-trade systems.

However, history has shown that to solve a complex and global negative externality problem like greenhouse gas emissions, other policies are needed. These include both government subsidies to research and development (R&D) and multilateral agreements.

Government Subsidies to R&D Since the 1980s, the U.S. government has provided billions of dollars in subsidies for R&D dedicated to lowering the cost of clean energy sources. These subsidies were critical in kick-starting innovation in the clean energy sector that has become increasingly cost competitive with the fossil-fuel industry. According to the Energy Information Administration, since 2016 the federal government has spent almost $7 billion on subsidies for renewable energy. These subsidies have the advantage of allowing the government to encourage energy innovation while avoiding imposing taxes on fossil fuels or regulating them—both less popular policies that have the potential to provoke a political backlash.

Multilateral Agreements Most countries would be disinclined to undertake costly policies to reduce greenhouse gas emissions if other countries refuse to do the same. To encourage cooperation, *multilateral agreements* set common objectives and allocate burden-sharing across countries, significantly increasing the chances of success in tackling climate change. In 2015, 196 countries came together under the **Paris Agreement,** committing to reduce emissions of greenhouse gases, with a common goal of limiting the increase in Earth's temperature to 2° centigrade, the level beyond which the effects of climate change are considered to be catastrophic and irreversible. Another example of a successful multilateral agreement was the *Montreal Protocol* of 1987. By setting limits on the production of ozone-depleting chemicals around the world, this agreement is credited with saving the Earth's ozone layer, a part of the upper atmosphere that protects Earth from the harmful effects of ultraviolet radiation coming from the sun.

Incentives for Individual Choices Incentives aimed at individual choices have an important role to play in addressing climate change. For example, through smart-metering, individuals are motivated to conserve energy, a fast and cost-effective way to reduce greenhouse gases. Higher gasoline taxes and wider availability of charging stations can motivate drivers to switch to electrically-powered cars. Individuals can also privately alter their choices, such as using less air conditioning, taking public transportation, or eating less meat (an emissions-heavy source of nutrition).

Climate Change Mitigation: Costs and Benefits

Reducing greenhouse gas emissions to sustainable levels requires a major structural shift in the economy that will inevitably affect growth rates and consumption. Consequently, some have claimed that attempts to mitigate climate change should be abandoned because the costs to consumers are too high.

However, that argument fails under a cost-benefit analysis. In a review of the latest scientific evidence, the Intergovernmental Panel on Climate Change concluded that meeting the Paris Agreement goals would mean that global consumption would shrink by 3–11% by 2100 compared to the status quo. But this number is quite a modest loss given that the world economy will continue growing, with an average growth rate of around 3% over the last several years.

The **Paris Agreement** is an international agreement by 196 countries to reduce their greenhouse gas emissions.

And as mentioned earlier, global losses by 2100 from runaway climate change are estimated at 20% of GDP.

Moreover, when the direct health costs from fossil-fuel air pollution are taken into account, the losses from runaway climate change climb significantly. The World Health Organization estimates that 4.6 million people die annually from air pollution caused by burning fossil fuels.

Nearly 1.25 million "excess" deaths are estimated to occur each year in China, alone, from fossil-fuel fouled air. The health benefits of switching to clean energy is estimated to be as much as 5% of global GDP. In addition, the estimates of the costs of mitigating climate change don't incorporate the rapidly dropping price of clean energy sources as technology advances.

So claims that the costs of addressing climate change are too high don't withstand scrutiny. That's why, as the next Economics in Action describes, over 3,500 economists have advocated for a carbon tax to combat climate change.

ECONOMICS >> *in Action*
Over 3,500 Economists Agree: Tax Greenhouse Gas Emissions

In 2019, 3,558 economists from across the ideological spectrum—4 former chairs of the Federal Reserve System, 27 Nobel laureates, 15 former chairs of the Council of Economic Advisers, and 2 former Secretaries of the Department of Treasury—signed a joint statement calling for a tax on greenhouse gas emissions to fight climate change, with the proceeds of the tax to be distributed to American consumers. In their words, "Global climate change is a serious problem calling for immediate national action." Published in the *Wall Street Journal*, it was the largest public statement by economists in history.

According to the statement, an emissions tax is needed to quickly reduce emissions, and it should be raised every year until emissions reductions goals are set. A tax, they argue, is more efficient that regulations. By distributing the tax revenues to American consumers in the form of a "carbon dividend," they also believe that this system is politically more viable and more equitable than a cap and trade system. Finally, they argue that imports from abroad should also be taxed according to their true environmental cost, so that U.S. firms aren't put at a cost-disadvantage relative to foreign firms. For the economics profession, it was an indisputable show of support for the validity of the economics of climate change.

>> *Check Your Understanding* **16-3**
Solutions appear at back of book.

1. What are the types of fossil fuels? What are the main clean energy sources? What are their relationships to climate change?
2. What market failure led to climate change? What are the estimated losses to GDP from unmitigated climate change?
3. Why are government subsidies an important policy tool in addressing climate change? Multilateral agreements? Incentives to individual choice?
4. How would you respond to the argument that the structural change to the economy required to address climate change is too costly?

|| The Economics of Positive Externalities

New Jersey is the most densely populated state in the United States, lying along the northeastern corridor, an area of almost continuous development stretching from Washington, D.C., to Boston. Yet a drive through New Jersey reveals a surprising feature: acre upon acre of farmland, growing everything from corn to pumpkins to the famous Jersey tomatoes. This is no accident: starting in 1961, New Jerseyans have voted in a series of measures that subsidize farmers to permanently preserve their farmland rather than sell it to developers. By 2016, the Green Acres Program, administered by the state, had preserved over 680,000 acres of open space.

Why have New Jersey citizens voted to raise their own taxes to subsidize the preservation of farmland? Because they believe that preserved farmland in an already heavily developed state provides benefits, such as natural beauty, access to fresh food, and the conservation of wild bird populations. In addition, preservation alleviates the negative externalities that come with more development, such as pressure on roads, water supplies, and municipal services—and, inevitably, more pollution. The Trust for Public Land estimated that every $1 invested in state land preservation programs returns $10 in economic value by diminishing local pollution, enhancing the natural environment, and reducing flood risk. Not surprisingly, the average value of nearby homes increased by 16%.

In this section we'll explore the topic of positive externalities. They are, in many ways, the mirror images of negative externalities. Left to its own, the market will produce too little of a good (in this case, preserved New Jersey farmland) that generates benefits on others. But society as a whole is better off when policies are adopted that increase the supply of such a good.

New Jerseyans understand that preserving local farmland makes them better off.

Preserved Farmland: A Positive Externality

Preserved farmland yields both benefits and costs to society. In the absence of government intervention, the farmer who wants to sell his land incurs all the costs of preservation—namely, the forgone profit to be made from selling the farmland to a developer. But the benefits of preserved farmland accrue not to the farmer but to neighboring residents, who have no right to influence how the farmland is disposed of.

Figure 16-6 illustrates society's problem. The marginal social cost of preserved farmland, shown by the *MSC* curve, is the additional cost imposed on society

FIGURE 16-6 Why a Market Economy Preserves Too Little Farmland

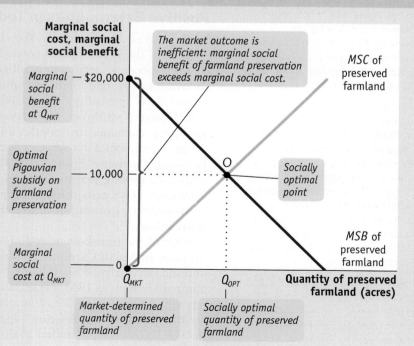

Without government intervention, the quantity of preserved farmland will be zero, the level at which the marginal social cost of preservation is zero. This is an inefficiently low quantity of preserved farmland: the marginal social benefit is $20,000, but the marginal social cost is zero. An optimal Pigouvian subsidy of $10,000, the value of the marginal social benefit of preservation when it equals the marginal social cost, can move the market to the socially optimal level of preservation, Q_{OPT}.

The market outcome is inefficient: marginal social benefit of farmland preservation exceeds marginal social cost.

A **Pigouvian subsidy** is a payment designed to encourage activities that generate positive externalities.

A **technology spillover** is a positive externality that results when knowledge spreads among individuals and firms.

by an additional acre of such farmland. This represents the forgone profits that would have accrued to farmers if they had sold their land to developers. The line is upward sloping because when very few acres are preserved and there is plenty of land available for development, the profit that could be made from selling an acre to a developer is small. But as the number of preserved acres increases and few are left for development, the amount a developer is willing to pay for them, and therefore the forgone profit, increases as well.

The *MSB* curve represents the marginal social benefit of preserved farmland. It is the additional benefit that accrues to society—in this case, the farmer's neighbors—when an additional acre of farmland is preserved. The curve is downward sloping because as more farmland is preserved, the benefit to society of preserving another acre falls.

As Figure 16-6 shows, the socially optimal point, *O*, occurs when the marginal social cost and the marginal social benefit are equalized—here, at a price of $10,000 per acre. At the socially optimal point, Q_{OPT} acres of farmland are preserved.

The market alone will not provide Q_{OPT} acres of preserved farmland. Instead, in the market outcome no acres will be preserved; the level of preserved farmland, Q_{MKT}, is equal to zero. That's because farmers will set the marginal social cost of preservation—their forgone profits—at zero and sell all their acres to developers. Because farmers bear the entire cost of preservation but gain none of the benefits, an inefficiently low quantity of acres will be preserved in the market outcome.

This is clearly inefficient because at zero acres preserved, the marginal social benefit of preserving an acre of farmland is $20,000. So how can the economy be induced to produce Q_{OPT} acres of preserved farmland, the socially optimal level? The answer is a **Pigouvian subsidy:** a payment designed to encourage activities that generate positive externalities. The optimal Pigouvian subsidy, as shown in Figure 16-6, is equal to the marginal social benefit of preserved farmland at the socially optimal level, Q_{OPT}—that is, $10,000 per acre.

So New Jersey voters are indeed implementing the right policy to raise their social welfare—taxing themselves in order to provide subsidies for farmland preservation.

Positive Externalities in Today's Economy

In the overall U.S. economy, the single most important source of positive externalities is the creation of knowledge. In industries such as programming, app design, robotics, artificial intelligence, green technology, and bioengineering, innovations by one firm are quickly emulated and improved upon by rival firms. Such spreading of knowledge across individuals and firms is known as a **technology spillover.** In today's economy, the greatest sources of technology spillovers are major universities and research institutes.

In technologically advanced countries such as the United States, Japan, England, Germany, France, and Israel, there is an ongoing exchange of people and ideas among private industries, major universities, and research institutes located in close proximity. The dynamic interplay that occurs in these *research clusters* spurs innovation and competition, theoretical advances, and practical applications.

One of the best-known and most successful research clusters is the Research Triangle in North Carolina, anchored by Duke University, North Carolina State, and the University of North Carolina, several other universities and hospitals, and companies such as IBM, Pfizer, and Qualcomm. Ultimately, the areas of technology spillover increase the economy's productivity and raise living standards.

But research clusters don't appear out of thin air. Except in a few instances in which firms have funded basic research on a long-term basis, research clusters have grown up around major universities. And like farmland preservation in New Jersey, major universities and their research activities are subsidized by government. In fact, government policy makers have long understood that the positive externalities generated by knowledge, stemming from basic education to high-tech research, are key to the economy's growth over time.

ECONOMICS >> *in Action*
The Impeccable Economic Logic of Early-Childhood Intervention Programs

One of the most vexing problems facing any society is how to break what research-ers call the *cycle of poverty:* children who grow up in disadvantaged socioeconomic circumstances are far more likely to remain trapped in poverty as adults, even after we account for differences in ability. They are more likely to be unemployed or underemployed, to engage in crime, and to suffer chronic health problems.

Early-childhood intervention programs offer hope for breaking the cycle. A study by the RAND Corporation found that high-quality early-childhood programs that focus on education and health care lead to significant social, intellectual, and financial advantages for kids who would otherwise be at risk of dropping out of high school and of engaging in criminal behavior. Children in programs like Head Start were less likely to engage in such destructive behaviors and more likely to end up with a job and to earn a high salary later in life.

Another study by researchers at the University of Pittsburgh measured the benefits of early-childhood intervention programs in monetary terms, finding from $4 to $7 in benefits for every $1 spent, while a RAND study put the figure as high as $17 per $1 spent. The Pittsburgh study also pointed to one program whose participants, by age 20, were 26% more likely to have finished high school, 35% less likely to have been charged in juvenile court, and 40% less likely to have repeated a grade compared to individuals of similar socioeconomic background who did not attend preschool.

The observed benefits to society of these programs are so large that the Brookings Institution predicts that providing high-quality preschool education to every American child would result in an increase in the total value of a country's domestic output (its GDP) by almost 2%, representing over 3 million more jobs.

Early-childhood intervention programs focusing on education and health offer many benefits to society.

>> Check Your Understanding 16-4
Solutions appear at back of book.

1. In 2019, the U.S. Department of Education spent almost $120 billion on college student aid. Explain why this can be an optimal policy to encourage the creation of knowledge.
2. In each of the following cases, determine whether a negative or positive externality is imposed and what an appropriate policy response would be.
   a. Trees planted in urban areas improve air quality and lower summer temperatures.
   b. Water-saving toilets reduce the need to pump water from rivers and aquifers. The cost of a gallon of water to homeowners is virtually zero.
   c. Bottled drinks are packaged in plastic that does not decompose when discarded. As a result, they take up vast amounts of landfill space or must be burned, releasing pollutants.

>> Quick Review

• When there are positive externalities, a market economy, left to itself, will typically produce too little of the good or activity. The socially optimal quantity of the good or activity can be achieved by an optimal **Pigouvian subsidy.**

• The most important example of a positive externalities in the economy is the creation of knowledge through **technology spillover.**

‖ Network Externalities

As explained in Chapter 13, a *network externality* exists when the value of a good or service increases as the number of other people who also use the good or service increases. Although network externalities are common in technology-driven and communication-driven sectors of the economy, the phenomenon is considerably more widespread than that.

Consider the case of a car. You might not think that the value of having a car depends on how many others also have cars, but in the early days of car consumerism it certainly did. That's because when very few cars existed, service stations and repair shops were few and far between, and local governments had little or no incentive to upgrade roads to make them car-worthy. However, as more people purchased cars, service stations and repair shops sprang up, and roads were improved. As a result, owning a car became even more valuable.

What a network externality shares with positive and negative externalities is an external effect: one person's actions affect the payoff to another person's actions. Network externalities play a key role both in the economy and in a number of regulatory policy controversies.

The External Benefits of a Network Externality

We can now deepen our understanding of network externalities by noting that a network externality involves an external benefit: one person's adoption of a good or service extends an external benefit to another person who also adopts that good or service. As a result, the marginal benefit of the good or service to any one person depends on the number of other people who also use it.

Although the most common network externalities involve methods of communication—the internet, cell phones, social media, and so on—they are also frequently present in transportation. For example, the value to a traveler of a given airport increases as more travelers use that airport as well, making more airlines and more destinations available from it. A marketplace website like eBay is more valuable to use, either to buy or to sell, the greater the number of other people also using that site. Similarly, many of us value banking with a particular bank because of the number of ATMs it has, and it will have more ATMs if it has a larger customer base.

The classic case of network externalities in the tech industry arises from computer operating systems. Most personal computers around the world run on Windows by Microsoft rather than on Apple's competing system. In 2019 nearly 6 new PCs that run Windows were sold for every Apple Mac sold. Why does Windows dominate personal computers? There are two answers to the question, both involving network externalities. First, there is a direct effect: it is easier for a Windows user to get help and advice from other Windows users. Second, is an indirect effect: Windows' early dominance attracted more software developers, so more programs were developed to run on Windows than on a competing system. (This second effect has largely vanished now, but it was important in the early days of making PCs dominant.)

When a network externality arises from the use of a good or service, it leads to **positive feedback,** also known as a *bandwagon effect:* if large numbers of people use it, other people become more likely to use it, too. And if fewer people use the good or service, others become less likely to use it as well. This leads to a chicken-versus-egg problem: if one person's value of the good depends on whether another person also uses the good, how do you get anyone to buy the good in the first place?

Not surprisingly, producers of goods and services with network externalities are aware of this problem. They understand that of two competing products, the one with the largest network—not necessarily the one that's the better product—will win in the end. The product with the larger network will continue to grow and dominate the market, while its rival will shrink and eventually disappear.

An important way to gain an advantage at the early stages of a market with network externalities is to sell the product cheaply, perhaps at a loss, in order to

A good is subject to **positive feedback** when success breeds greater success and failure breeds further failure.

increase the size of the network of users. For example, Skype, the first widely successful internet calling company, allows free calls only between members. This builds Skype's network of users, who will then pay for using Skype to call a non-Skype contact or to place a call to a landline phone. Today, Skype is used heavily for international calling. Newer companies such as WhatsApp and Snapchat likewise increase the size of their network by allowing free interaction between members, allowing them to generate more revenue from selling ads and user data. And as we explain in the following Economics in Action, the fact that all web browsers—including Internet Explorer, Chrome, and Firefox—are free to download is a legacy of Microsoft's early strategy of providing Internet Explorer free on its computers in order to buttress its Windows operating-system dominance.

Network externalities present special challenges for antitrust regulators because the antitrust laws do not, strictly speaking, forbid monopoly. Rather, they only prohibit *monopolization*—efforts to create a monopoly. If you just happen to end up ruling an industry, that's okay, but if you take actions designed to drive out competition, that's not okay. So we could argue that monopolies in goods with network externalities, because they occur naturally, should not pose legal problems.

Unfortunately, it isn't that simple. Firms investing in new technologies are clearly trying to establish monopoly positions. Furthermore, in the face of positive feedback, firms have an incentive to engage in aggressive strategies to push their goods in order to increase their network size and tip the market in their favor. So what is the dividing line between legal and illegal actions? In the Microsoft antitrust case, described in the next Economics in Action, reasonable economists and legal experts disagreed sharply about whether the company had broken the law.

ECONOMICS >> *in Action*
The Microsoft Case

A consent decree between Microsoft and a federal court prohibiting certain business practices expired in 2011, marking the end of an era for the company. Beginning in 1998, the federal Justice Department as well as 20 states and the District of Columbia sued Microsoft, alleging predatory practices against competitors to protect the monopoly position held by its Windows operating system.

At the time, Microsoft was by any reasonable definition a monopoly, as just about all personal computers in the late 1990s ran Windows. And the key feature supporting this dominance was a network externality: people used Windows because other people used Windows.

Despite urging by some economists, the Justice Department did not challenge the Windows monopoly itself, as most experts agreed that monopoly was the natural outcome of an industry with network externalities. What Justice Department lawyers did claim, however, was that Microsoft had used the monopoly position of its Windows operating system to give its other products an unfair advantage over competitors.

The Microsoft case was a good example of the pros and cons raised by goods with network externalities.

For example, by bundling Internet Explorer free as part of Windows, it was alleged that Microsoft had given itself an unfair advantage over rival web browser Netscape, because it prevented Netscape from charging customers for its use.

The Justice Department argued that this was harmful because it discouraged innovation: potential software innovators were unwilling to invest large sums out of fear that Microsoft would bundle equivalent software with Windows for free. Microsoft, in contrast, argued that by setting the precedent that companies would be punished for success, the government was the real opponent of innovation.

After many years of legal wrangling, the consent decree was signed in 2002, which barred Microsoft from excluding rivals from its computers and forced the company to make Windows seamlessly interoperable with non-Microsoft software. This eliminated any advantage Microsoft had through free bundling of its own programs into the Windows package.

Although the case against Microsoft consumed many tens of millions of dollars in legal costs and is considered one of the most significant antitrust cases of its generation, its long-term effects are hotly debated. Some say that the case essentially had no effect, as the cutting edge of technology moved into mobile devices like smartphones and tablets, leaving Microsoft and its PC-centered business behind. Others argue that, although the case may not have dampened overall innovation as Microsoft claimed, it changed the culture of Microsoft itself, making it more cautious and therefore unable to explore and capitalize on new technological trends.

Two effects, however, are beyond dispute. Because of Microsoft's example, products with network externalities are often priced at a loss or even at zero—as in the case of today's web browsers, Chrome and Firefox, which are available for free. Second, rival tech companies now routinely charge one another with predatory behavior that exploits a network externality advantage—as in Microsoft's charges against Google for its advantage in the search engine market.

>> Check Your Understanding 16-5

Solutions appear at back of book.

1. For each of the following goods, explain the nature of the network externality present.
   a. Appliances using a particular voltage, such as 110 volts versus 220 volts
   b. 8½-by-11-inch paper versus 8-by-12½-inch paper
2. Suppose there are two competing companies in an industry that has a network externality. Explain why it is likely that the company able to sustain the largest initial losses will eventually dominate the market.

iurii/Shutterstock

Historically, renewables have been more expensive than fossil fuels, and federal subsidies to the renewable energy industry have been critical in bringing costs to consumers down as well as in funding innovation. However, over the years, those subsidies have frequently been at risk. For example, from 2012 to 2013, newly installed wind capacity plunged by 93% from when federal subsidies ended. In 2014 and 2015, wind capacity revived when those subsidies were restored. But in 2017 a new pattern appeared: when federal subsidies for renewable energy were again at risk as Congress debated whether to cut them, the percentage of newly installed power capacity that was accounted for by renewables fell only modestly—from nearly 50% in 2017 to 48% in 2018. In 2020, the future of the subsidies are again unclear: without congressional action, they will largely expire at the end of 2021. However, by 2020 renewables are projected to account for 78% of newly installed power capacity. Will the threat to end subsidies stall their meteoric rise?

Benjamin Fowke, the CEO of Xcel Energy of Colorado, thinks not and is undeterred. HE is trained in finance and accounting, so it's safe to say that he is no starry-eyed dreamer. Xcel Energy has announced that across is eight-state system, 60% of its energy will be generated by renewables and its carbon emissions will be reduced by 80% by 2030.

Fowke is positioning Xcel Energy to take advantage of the *learning curve* associated with the cost of renewable energy. The term is used to describe the dramatic fall in costs that is often achieved after a new technology is introduced. Adoption of the new technology spreads because scientists, innovators, and manufacturers get better at exploiting it. A virtuous cycle is generated as costs fall and adoption of the new technology increases, spurring further investment and additional reductions in costs.

An example is solar energy: the price to consumers of a watt of solar energy has dropped by more than 75% since 1998. The learning curve has been steepest in the last decade, with solar prices dropping by 60%. In the case of wind energy, prices have dropped by more than 90% since 1980.

According to Fowke, it is now cheaper to build new wind turbines than to operate its lowest-cost existing coal plants. For example, in 2017 Xcel purchased wind energy at a cost of $15 to $20 per megawatt-hour, compared to $25 to $35 for natural gas–generated power, the main energy source competing with renewables.

Unsurprisingly, competition with conventional fossil-fuel producers encourages the solar and wind industries, along with producers of other renewables, to keep improving their product and prices to stay ahead of the competition.

QUESTIONS FOR THOUGHT

1. Explain how subsidies affect the future adoption of a new technology that is subject to steep learning curve effects. Relate this to the role of government intervention when externalities are present.

2. Is Fowke right or wrong to persist in the adoption of renewables when federal subsidies are under threat? Analyze the investment decision that a CEO like Fowke must make in deciding whether and when to invest more capacity in renewables instead of in fossil-fuel sources.

3. How does this case illustrate the way in which business and government can work together in a market economy?

SUMMARY

1. When pollution can be directly observed and controlled, government policies should be geared directly to producing the **socially optimal quantity of pollution,** the quantity at which the **marginal social cost of pollution** is equal to the **marginal social benefit of pollution.** In the absence of government intervention, a market produces too much pollution because polluters take only their benefit from polluting into account, not the costs imposed on others.

2. The costs to society of pollution are an example of an **external cost;** in some cases, however, economic activities yield **external benefits.** External costs and benefits are jointly known as **externalities,** with external costs called **negative externalities** and external benefits called **positive externalities.**

3. According to the **Coase theorem,** individuals can find a way to **internalize the externality,** making government intervention unnecessary, as long as **transaction costs**—the costs of making a deal—are sufficiently low. However, in many cases transaction costs are too high to permit such deals.

4. Governments often deal with pollution by imposing **environmental standards,** a method, economists argue, that is usually an inefficient way to reduce pollution. Two efficient (cost-minimizing) methods for reducing pollution are **emissions taxes,** a form of **Pigouvian tax,** and **tradable emissions permits.** The optimal Pigouvian tax on pollution is equal to its marginal social cost at the socially optimal quantity of pollution. These methods also provide incentives for the creation and adoption of production technologies that cause less pollution.

5. A history of heavy reliance on **fossil fuels** that emit **greenhouse gases** has led to problems created by **climate change.** Unlike fossil fuels, **renewable energy sources** are inexhaustible. Policies such as taxes, tax credits, subsidies, and mandates, as well as consumer use of smart metering and industrial commitments, can help ensure a wide-scale shift toward renewable **clean energy sources.** Multilateral agreements such as the **Paris Agreement** commit many countries to common objectives and allocate burden-sharing across countries in order to tackle climate change.

6. When a good or activity yields positive externalities, such as **technology spillovers,** then an optimal **Pigouvian subsidy** to producers moves the market to the socially optimal quantity of production.

7. Communications, transportation, and high-technology goods are frequently subject to *network externalities,* which arise when the value of a good or service increases as the number of other people who use the good or service increases. Such goods are likely to be subject to **positive feedback:** if large numbers of people buy the good, other people are more likely to buy it, too. So success breeds greater success and failure breeds further failure: the good with the larger network will eventually dominate, and rival goods will disappear. As a result, producers have an incentive to take aggressive action in the early stages of the market to increase the size of their network. Markets with network externalities tend to be monopolies. They are especially challenging for antitrust regulators because differentiating between the natural progression of the network externality and illegal monopolization efforts by producers can be hard to do.

KEY TERMS

External cost, p. 468
External benefit, p. 468
Externalities, p. 468
Negative externalities, p. 468
Positive externalities, p. 468
Marginal social cost of pollution, p. 469
Marginal social benefit of pollution, p. 469

Socially optimal quantity of pollution, p. 469
Coase theorem, p. 472
Internalize the externality, p. 472
Transaction costs, p. 472
Environmental standards, p. 474
Emissions tax, p. 474
Pigouvian taxes, p. 474
Tradable emissions permits, p. 476

Climate change, p. 479
Greenhouse gases, p. 479
Fossil fuels, p. 480
Renewable energy sources, p. 480
Clean energy sources, p. 480
Paris Agreement, p. 481
Pigouvian subsidy, p. 484
Technology spillover, p. 484
Positive feedback, p. 486

PRACTICE QUESTIONS

1. To recline or not to recline? In early 2020, a passenger on an American Airlines flight was caught on video continuously punching the back of the seat in front of him, in which another passenger sat in the reclined position. The video went viral and sparked a national debate on whether passengers should recline their seats. Who is entitled to the 2 inches of space directly behind the airplane seat? Using the Coase theorem, recommend one remedy that can provide an efficient solution to this problem.

2. The Global Carbon Project brings together the international science community to "establish a common and mutually agreed knowledge base to support policy debate and action to slow down and ultimately stop the increase of greenhouse gases in the atmosphere." Go to their website, Global Carbon Atlas, www.globalcarbonatlas.org and find the data map by selecting the tab "CO2 Emissions" on the top of the page.

The default map will present $MtCO_2$ (metric tons of CO_2) by country. What countries produced the most carbon emissions? What do you notice about the high-carbon-emitting countries? Next, in the left-hand tool bar, change the units to tCO_2 (total CO_2) per person. What do you notice about the disparity across countries? What happened with the high-emitting countries you identified previously?

PROBLEMS

1. What type of externality (positive or negative) is present in each of the following examples? Is the marginal social benefit of the activity greater than or equal to the marginal benefit to the individual? Is the marginal social cost of the activity greater than or equal to the marginal cost to the individual? Without intervention, will there be too little or too much (relative to what would be socially optimal) of this activity?

    a. Mr. Chau plants lots of colorful flowers in his front yard.

    b. Your next-door neighbor likes to build bonfires in his backyard, and sparks often drift onto your house.

    c. Maija, who lives next to an apple orchard, decides to keep bees to produce honey.

    d. Justine buys a large SUV that consumes a lot of gasoline.

2. Many dairy farmers in California are adopting a new technology that allows them to produce their own electricity from methane gas captured from animal waste. (One cow can produce up to 2 kilowatts a day.) This practice reduces the amount of methane gas released into the atmosphere. In addition to reducing their own utility bills, the farmers are allowed to sell any electricity they produce at favorable rates.

    a. Explain how the ability to earn money from capturing and transforming methane gas behaves like a Pigouvian tax on methane gas pollution and can lead dairy farmers to emit the efficient amount of methane gas pollution.

    b. Suppose some dairy farmers have lower costs of transforming methane into electricity than others. Explain how this system of capturing and selling methane gas leads to an efficient allocation of emissions reduction among farmers.

3. Voluntary environmental programs were extremely popular in the United States, Europe, and Japan in the 1990s. Part of their popularity stems from the fact that these programs do not require legislative authority, which is often hard to obtain. The 33/50 program started by the Environmental Protection Agency (EPA) is an example of such a program. With this program, the EPA attempted to reduce industrial emissions of 17 toxic chemicals by providing information on relatively inexpensive methods of pollution control. Companies were asked to voluntarily commit to reducing emissions from their 1988 levels by 33% by 1992 and by 50% by 1995. The program actually met its second target by 1994.

    a. As in Figure 16-3, draw marginal benefit curves for pollution generated by two plants, A and B, in 1988. Assume that without government intervention, each plant emits the same amount of pollution, but that at all levels of pollution less than this amount, plant A's marginal benefit of polluting is less than that of plant B. Label the vertical axis "Marginal benefit to individual polluter" and the horizontal axis "Quantity of pollution emissions." Mark the quantity of pollution each plant produces without government action.

    b. Do you expect the total quantity of pollution before the program was put in place to have been less than or more than the optimal quantity of pollution? Why?

    c. Suppose the plants whose marginal benefit curves you depicted in part a were participants in the 33/50 program. In a replica of your graph from part a, mark targeted levels of pollution in 1995 for the two plants. Which plant was required to reduce emissions more? Was this solution necessarily efficient?

    d. What kind of environmental policy does the 33/50 program most closely resemble? What is the main shortcoming of such a policy? Compare it to two other types of environmental policies discussed in this chapter.

4. According to a report from the U.S. Census Bureau, "the average [lifetime] earnings of a full-time, year-round worker with a high school education are about $1.2 million compared with $2.1 million for a college graduate." This indicates that there is a considerable benefit to a graduate from investing in their own education. Tuition at most state universities covers only about two-thirds to three-quarters of the cost, so the state applies a Pigouvian subsidy to college education.

    If a Pigouvian subsidy is appropriate, is the externality created by a college education a positive or a negative externality? What does this imply about the differences between the costs and benefits that accrue privately to students compared to social costs and benefits? What are some reasons for the differences?

5. The city of Falls Church, Virginia, subsidizes the planting of trees in homeowners' front yards when the yards are within 15 feet of the street.

    a. Using concepts in the chapter, explain why a municipality would subsidize planting trees on private property, but near the street.

b. Draw a diagram similar to Figure 16-4 that shows the marginal social benefit, the marginal social cost, and the optimal Pigouvian subsidy on planting trees.

6. Fishing for sablefish had been so intensive that sablefish were threatened with extinction. After several years of banning such fishing, the government is now proposing to introduce tradable vouchers, each of which entitles its holder to a catch of a certain size. Explain how uncontrolled fishing generates a negative externality and how the voucher scheme may overcome the inefficiency created by this externality.

7. The two dry-cleaning companies in Collegetown, College Cleaners and Big Green Cleaners, are a major source of air pollution. Together they currently produce 350 units of air pollution, which the town wants to reduce to 200 units. The accompanying table shows the current pollution level produced by each company and each company's marginal cost of reducing its pollution. The marginal cost is constant.

Companies	Initial pollution level (units)	Marginal cost of reducing pollution (per unit)
College Cleaners	230	$5
Big Green Cleaners	120	$2

a. Suppose that Collegetown passes an environmental standards law that limits each company to 100 units of pollution. What would be the total cost to the two companies of each reducing its pollution emissions to 100 units?

Suppose instead that Collegetown issues 100 pollution vouchers to each company, each entitling the company to one unit of pollution, and that these vouchers can be traded.

b. How much is each pollution voucher worth to College Cleaners? To Big Green Cleaners? (That is, how much would each company, at most, be willing to pay for one more voucher?)

c. Who will sell vouchers and who will buy them? How many vouchers will be traded?

d. What is the total cost to the two companies of the pollution controls under this voucher system?

8. a. EAuction and EMarketplace are two competing internet auction sites, where buyers and sellers transact goods. Each auction site earns money by charging sellers for listing their goods. EAuction has decided to eliminate fees for the first transaction for sellers that are new to its site. Explain why this is likely to be a good strategy for EAuction in its competition with EMarketplace.

b. EMarketplace complained to the Justice Department that EAuction's practice of eliminating fees for new sellers was anti-competitive and would lead to monopolization of the internet auction industry. Is EMarketplace correct? How should the Justice Department respond?

c. EAuction stopped its practice of eliminating fees for new sellers. But since it provided much better

technical service than its rival, EMarketplace, buyers and sellers came to prefer EAuction. Eventually, EMarketplace closed down, leaving EAuction as a monopolist. Should the Justice Department intervene to break EAuction into two companies? Explain.

d. EAuction is now a monopolist in the internet auction industry. It also owns a site that handles payments over the internet, called PayForIt. It is competing with another internet payment site, called PayBuddy. EAuction has now stipulated that any transaction on its auction site must use PayForIt, rather than PayBuddy, for the payment. Should the Justice Department intervene? Explain.

9. Which of the following are characterized by network externalities? Which are not? Explain.

a. The choice between installing 110-volt electrical current in structures rather than 220-volt

b. The choice between purchasing a Toyota versus a Ford

c. The choice of a printer, where each printer requires its own specific type of ink cartridge

d. The choice of whether to purchase an iPad Air or an iPad Mini.

▪ WORK IT OUT

10. The loud music coming from the sorority next to your dorm is a negative externality that can be directly quantified. The accompanying table shows the marginal social benefit and the marginal social cost per decibel (dB, a measure of volume) of music.

Volume of music (dB)	Marginal social benefit of dB	Marginal social cost of dB
90		
	$36	$0
91		
	30	2
92		
	24	4
93		
	18	6
94		
	12	8
95		
	6	10
96		
	0	12
97		

a. Draw the marginal social benefit curve and the marginal social cost curve. Use your diagram to determine the socially optimal volume of music.

b. Only the members of the sorority benefit from the music, and they bear none of the cost. Which volume of music will they choose?

c. The college imposes a Pigouvian tax of $3 per decibel of music played. From your diagram, determine the volume of music the sorority will now choose. ▪

17 Public Goods and Common Resources

THE GREAT STINK

BY THE MIDDLE OF THE NINETEENTH century, London had become the world's largest city, with close to 2.5 million inhabitants. Unfortunately, all those people produced a lot of waste — and there was no place for it to go except into the Thames, the river flowing through the city. Nobody with a working nose could ignore the results. And the river didn't just smell bad — it carried dangerous waterborne diseases like cholera and typhoid. London neighborhoods close to the Thames had death rates from cholera more than six times greater than the neighborhoods farthest

London's River Thames, in the nineteenth century (top) and now. Government intervention turned it from an open sewer to a pristine waterway.

away. And the great majority of Londoners drew their drinking water from the Thames.

What the city needed, said reformers, was a sewage system to carry waste away from the river. Yet no private individual was willing to build such a system, and influential people were opposed to the idea that the government should take responsibility for the problem.

But the hot summer of 1858 brought what came to be known as the Great Stink, which was so bad that one health journal reported "men struck down with the stench." Even the privileged and powerful suffered: Parliament met in a building next to the river. After unsuccessful efforts to stop the smell by covering the windows with chemical-soaked curtains, Parliament finally approved a plan for an immense system of sewers and pumping stations to direct sewage away from the city.

The system, opened in 1865, brought dramatic improvement in the city's quality of life; cholera and typhoid epidemics, which had been regular occurrences, completely disappeared. The Thames was turned from the filthiest to the cleanest metropolitan river in the world, and the sewage system's principal engineer, Sir Joseph Bazalgette, was lauded as having "saved more lives than any single Victorian public official." It was estimated at the time that his sewer system added 20 years to the life span of the average Londoner.

The story of the Great Stink and the policy response that followed illustrate two important reasons for government intervention in the economy. London's new sewage system was a clear example of a *public good* — a good that benefits many people, whether or not they have paid for it, and whose benefits to any one individual do not depend on how many others also benefit. As we will see, public goods differ in important ways from the *private goods* we have studied so far — and these differences mean that public goods cannot be efficiently supplied by the market.

In addition, clean water in the Thames is an example of a *common resource,* a good that many people can consume whether

or not they have paid for it but whose consumption by each person reduces the amount available to others. Such goods tend to be overused by individuals in a market system unless the government takes action.

In earlier chapters, we saw that markets sometimes fail to deliver efficient levels of production and consumption of a good or activity. We saw how inefficiency can arise from market power, which allows monopolists and colluding oligopolists to charge prices that are higher than marginal cost, thereby preventing mutually beneficial transactions from occurring. We also saw how inefficiency can arise from positive and negative externalities, which cause a divergence between the costs and benefits of an individual's or industry's actions and the costs and benefits of those actions borne by society as a whole.

In this chapter, we will take a somewhat different approach to the question of why markets sometimes fail. Here we focus on how *the characteristics of goods often determine whether markets can deliver them efficiently*. When goods have the "wrong" characteristics, the resulting market failures resemble those associated with externalities or market power. This alternative way of looking at sources of inefficiency deepens our understanding of why markets sometimes don't work well and how government can take actions that increase society's welfare. ●

WHAT YOU WILL LEARN

- What is a **public good** and how is it different from a **private good?**

- What is a **common resource** and why is it overused?

- What is an **artificially scarce good** and why is it underconsumed?

- Why do markets typically fail to supply these types of goods efficiently?

- How can government intervention make society better off in the production and consumption of these types of goods?

A good is **excludable** if the supplier of that good can prevent people who do not pay from consuming it.

A good is **rival in consumption** if the same unit of the good cannot be consumed by more than one person at the same time.

A good that is both excludable and rival in consumption is a **private good.**

When a good is **nonexcludable,** the supplier cannot prevent consumption by people who do not pay for it.

A good is **nonrival in consumption** if more than one person can consume the same unit of the good at the same time.

‖ Private Goods — and Others

What's the difference between installing a new bathroom in a house and building a municipal sewage system? What's the difference between growing wheat and fishing in the open ocean?

These aren't trick questions. In each case there is a basic difference in the characteristics of the goods involved. Bathroom fixtures and wheat have the characteristics necessary to allow markets to work efficiently. Public sewage systems and fish in the sea do not.

Let's look at these crucial characteristics and why they matter.

Characteristics of Goods

Goods like bathroom fixtures or wheat have two characteristics that, as we'll soon see, are essential if a good is to be efficiently provided by a market economy.

- They are **excludable:** suppliers of the good can prevent people who don't pay from consuming it.
- They are **rival in consumption:** the same unit of the good cannot be consumed by more than one person at the same time.

When a good is both excludable and rival in consumption, it is called a **private good.** Wheat is an example of a private good. It is *excludable:* the farmer can sell a bushel to one consumer without having to provide wheat to everyone in the county. And it is *rival in consumption:* if I eat bread baked with a farmer's wheat, that wheat cannot be consumed by someone else.

But not all goods possess these two characteristics. Some goods are **nonexcludable**—the supplier cannot prevent consumption of the good by people who do not pay for it. Fire protection is one example: a fire department that puts out fires before they spread protects the whole city, not just people who have made contributions to the Firemen's Benevolent Association. An improved environment is another: the city of London couldn't have ended the Great Stink for some residents while leaving the River Thames foul for others.

Nor are all goods rival in consumption. Goods are **nonrival in consumption** if more than one person can consume the same unit of the good at the same time. TV shows are nonrival in consumption: your decision to watch a show does not prevent other people from watching the same show.

Because goods can be either excludable or nonexcludable, rival or nonrival in consumption, there are four types of goods, illustrated by the matrix in Figure 17-1:

- *Private goods,* which are excludable and rival in consumption, like wheat
- *Public goods,* which are nonexcludable and nonrival in consumption, like a public sewer system
- *Common resources,* which are nonexcludable but rival in consumption, like clean water in a river
- *Artificially scarce goods,* which are excludable but nonrival in consumption, like on-demand movies on Amazon Prime

There are, of course, many other characteristics that distinguish between types of goods—necessities versus luxuries, normal versus inferior, and so on. Why focus on whether goods are excludable and rival in consumption?

FIGURE 17-1 Four Types of Goods

	Rival in consumption	Nonrival in consumption
Excludable	**Private goods** • Wheat • Bathroom fixtures	**Artificially scarce goods** • On-demand movies • Computer software
Non-excludable	**Common resources** • Clean water • Biodiversity	**Public goods** • Public sanitation • National defense

There are four types of goods. The type of a good depends on (1) whether or not it is excludable — whether a producer can prevent someone from consuming it; and (2) whether or not it is rival in consumption — whether it is impossible for the same unit of a good to be consumed by more than one person at the same time.

Why Markets Can Supply Only Private Goods Efficiently

As we learned in earlier chapters, markets are typically the best means for a society to deliver goods and services to its members; that is, markets are efficient except in the case of the well-defined problems of market power, externalities, or other instances of market failure. But there is yet another condition that must be met, one rooted in the nature of the good itself: markets cannot supply goods and services efficiently unless they are private goods—excludable and rival in consumption.

To see why excludability is crucial, suppose that a farmer had only two choices: either produce no wheat or provide a bushel of wheat to every resident of the county who wants it, whether or not that resident pays for it. It seems unlikely that anyone would grow wheat under those conditions.

Yet the operator of a municipal sewage system faces pretty much the same problem as our hypothetical farmer. A sewage system makes the whole city cleaner and healthier—but that benefit accrues to all the city's residents, whether or not they pay the system operator. That's why no private entrepreneur came forward with a plan to end London's Great Stink.

The general point is that if a good is nonexcludable, self-interested consumers won't be willing to pay for it—they will take a "free ride" on anyone who *does* pay. So there is a **free-rider problem.** Examples of the free-rider problem are familiar from daily life. One you may have encountered is when students are required to do a group project. There is often a tendency for some group members to shirk, relying on others in the group to get the work done. The shirkers *free-ride* on someone else's effort.

Because of the free-rider problem, the forces of self-interest alone do not lead to an efficient level of production for a nonexcludable good. Even though consumers would benefit from increased production of the good, no one individual is willing to pay for more, and so no producer is willing to supply it. The result is that nonexcludable goods suffer from *inefficiently low production*. That is, they are undersupplied in a market economy. In fact, in the face of the free-rider problem, self-interest may not ensure that any amount of the good—let alone the efficient quantity—is produced.

Goods that are excludable and nonrival in consumption, like on-demand movies, suffer from a different kind of inefficiency. As long as a good is excludable, it is possible to earn a profit by making it available only to those who pay. Therefore producers are willing to supply an excludable good. But the marginal cost of letting an additional viewer watch an on-demand movie is zero because it is nonrival in consumption. So the efficient price to the consumer is also zero—or, to put it another way, individuals should watch movies up to the point where their marginal benefit is zero.

But if Amazon actually charges viewers $4 for on-demand movies, viewers will consume the good only up to the point where their marginal benefit is $4. When consumers must pay a price greater than zero for a good that is nonrival in consumption, the price they pay is higher than the marginal cost of allowing them to consume that good, which is zero. So in a market economy, goods that are nonrival in consumption suffer from *inefficiently low consumption*—they are underconsumed.

Now we can see why private goods are the only goods that can be efficiently produced and consumed in a competitive market. (That is, a private good will be efficiently produced and consumed in a market free of market power, externalities, or other instances of market failure.) Because private goods are excludable, producers can charge for them and so have an incentive to produce them. And because they are also rival in consumption, it is efficient for consumers to pay a positive price—a price equal to the marginal cost of production. If one or both of these characteristics are lacking, a market economy will not lead to efficient production and consumption of the good.

Fortunately for the market system, most goods are private goods. Food, clothing, shelter, and most other desirable things in life are excludable and rival in consumption, so markets can provide us with most things. Yet there are crucial goods that don't meet these criteria—and in most cases, that means that the government must step in.

Goods that are nonexcludable suffer from the **free-rider problem:** many individuals are unwilling to pay for their own consumption and instead will take a "free ride" on anyone who does pay.

PITFALLS

MARGINAL COST OF WHAT EXACTLY?

In the case of a good that is nonrival in consumption, it's easy to confuse the marginal cost of *producing* a unit of the good with the marginal cost of *allowing* a unit of the good *to be consumed*.

For example, Amazon Prime Video incurs a marginal cost in making an on-demand movie available to its subscribers that is equal to the cost of the resources it uses to produce and broadcast that movie. However, *once that movie is being broadcast,* no marginal cost is incurred by letting an additional family watch it. In other words, no costly resources are used up when one more family consumes a movie that has already been produced and is being broadcast.

This complication does not arise, however, when a good is rival in consumption. In that case, the resources used to produce a unit of the good are used up by a person's consumption of it—they are no longer available to satisfy someone else's consumption. So when a good is rival in consumption, the marginal cost to society of allowing an individual to consume a unit is equal to the resource cost of producing that unit—that is, equal to the marginal cost of producing it.

The emergence of institutions to maintain law and order laid the foundation for the flowering of the Renaissance.

ECONOMICS >> *in Action*
From Mayhem to Renaissance

Life during the European Middle Ages—from approximately 1100 to 1500—was difficult and dangerous, with high rates of violent crime, banditry, and war casualties. According to researchers, murder rates in Europe in 1200 were 30 to 40 per 100,000 people. But by 1500 the rate had been halved to around 20 per 100,000; today, it is less than 1 per 100,000. What accounts for the sharp decrease in mayhem over the last 900 years?

Think public goods, as the history of medieval Italian city-states illustrates.

Starting around the year 900 in Venice and 1100 in other city-states like Milan and Florence, citizens began to organize and create institutions for protection. In Venice, citizens built a defensive fleet to battle the pirates who regularly attacked them. Other city-states built strong defensive walls to encircle their cities and formed defensive militias. Institutions were created to maintain law and order: cadres of guards, watchmen, and magistrates were hired; courthouses and jails were built.

As a result, trade, commerce, and banking flourished, as well as literacy, numeracy, and the arts. By 1300, the leading cities of Venice, Milan, and Florence had each grown to over 100,000 people. As resources and the standard of living increased, the rate of violent deaths diminished.

The Republic of Venice became known as *La Serenissima*—the Most Serene One—because of its enlightened governance, overseen by a council of leading citizens. Owing to its stability, diplomatic prowess, and prodigious fleet of vessels, Venice became enormously wealthy in the fifteenth and sixteenth centuries.

The provision of public goods brought stability, high literacy, and numeracy that made Florence the banking center of Italy. During the fifteenth century it was ruled by the Medici, an immensely wealthy banking family. It was their patronage of artists such as Leonardo da Vinci and Michelangelo that ushered in the Renaissance.

So Western Europe was able to move from mayhem to Renaissance through the creation of public goods, like good governance and defense, that benefited everyone and could not be diminished by any one person's use.

>> *Check Your Understanding* 17-1
Solutions appear at back of book.

1. Classify each of the following goods according to whether they are excludable and whether they are rival in consumption. What kind of good is each?
   a. Use of a public space such as a park
   b. A cheese burrito
   c. Information from a website that is password-protected
   d. Publicly announced information on the path of an incoming hurricane
2. Which of the goods in Question 1 will be provided by a competitive market? Which will not be? Explain your answer.

>> Quick Review

- Goods can be classified according to two attributes: whether they are **excludable** and whether they are **rival in consumption.**

- Goods that are both excludable and rival in consumption are **private goods.** Private goods can be efficiently produced and consumed in a competitive market.

- When goods are **nonexcludable,** there is a **free-rider problem:** consumers will not pay producers, leading to inefficiently low production.

- When goods are **nonrival in consumption,** the efficient price for consumption is zero. But if a positive price is charged to compensate producers for the cost of production, the result is inefficiently low consumption.

A **public good** is both nonexcludable and nonrival in consumption.

‖ Public Goods

A **public good** is the exact opposite of a private good: it is a good that is both nonexcludable and nonrival in consumption. A public sewer system is an example of a public good: you can't keep a river clean without making it clean for everyone who lives near its banks, and my protection from great stinks does not come at my neighbor's expense.

Here are some other examples of public goods:

- *Disease prevention.* When doctors act to stamp out an epidemic before it can spread, they protect people around the world.
- *National defense.* A strong military protects all citizens.
- *Scientific research.* More knowledge benefits everyone.

Because these goods are nonexcludable, they suffer from the free-rider problem, so no private firm would be willing to produce them. And because they are nonrival in consumption, it would be inefficient to charge people for consuming them. As a result, society must find nonmarket methods for providing these goods.

Providing Public Goods

Public goods are provided through a variety of means. The government doesn't always get involved—in many cases a nongovernmental solution has been found for the free-rider problem. But these solutions are usually imperfect in some way.

Some public goods are supplied through voluntary contributions. For example, private donations support a considerable amount of scientific research. But they are insufficient to finance huge, socially important projects like basic medical research.

Some public goods are supplied by self-interested individuals or firms because those producing the goods are able to make money in an indirect way. The classic example is broadcast television, which in the United States is supported entirely by advertising. The downside of such indirect funding is that it skews the nature and quantity of the public goods that are supplied, as well as imposing additional costs on consumers. TV stations show the programs that yield the most advertising revenue (that is, programs best suited for selling prescription drugs, weight-loss remedies, and the like to the segment of the population that buys them), which are not necessarily the programs people most want to see. And viewers must also endure many commercials.

Some potentially public goods are deliberately made excludable and therefore subject to charge, like on-demand movies. In the United Kingdom, where most television programming is paid for by a yearly license fee assessed on every television owner (£154.50, or about $200 in 2019), television viewing is made artificially excludable by the use of television detection vans that roam neighborhoods in an attempt to locate televisions in nonlicensed households and fine the residents. However, as noted earlier, when suppliers charge a price greater than zero for a nonrival good, consumers will consume an inefficiently low quantity of that good.

In small communities, a high level of social encouragement or pressure can be brought to bear on people to contribute money or time to provide the efficient level of a public good. Volunteer fire departments, which depend both on the volunteered services of the firefighters themselves and on contributions from local residents, are a good example. But as communities grow larger and more anonymous, social pressure is increasingly difficult to apply, compelling larger towns and cities to tax residents to provide salaried firefighters for fire protection services.

As this last example suggests, when these other solutions fail, it is up to the government to provide public goods. Indeed, the most important public goods—national defense, the legal system, disease control, fire protection in municipalities, and so on—are provided by government and paid for by taxes. Economic theory tells us that the provision of public goods is one of the crucial roles of government.

How Much of a Public Good Should Be Provided?

In some cases, provision of a public good is an "either–or" decision: London would either have a sewage system—or not. But in most cases, governments must decide not only whether to provide a public good but also *how much* of that public good to provide. For example, street cleaning is a public good—but how often should the streets be cleaned? Once a month? Twice a month? Every other day?

Imagine a city in which there are only two residents, Theo and Abby. Assume that the public good in question is street cleaning and that Theo and Abby truthfully tell the government how much they value a unit of the public good, where a unit is equal to one street cleaning per month. Specifically, each of them tells the government *their willingness to pay for another unit of the public good supplied*—an amount that corresponds to that *individual's marginal benefit* of another unit of the public good.

Using this information plus information on the cost of providing the good, the government can use marginal analysis to find the efficient level of providing the public good: the level at which the *marginal social benefit* of the public good is equal to the marginal cost of producing it. Recall from Chapter 16 that the marginal social benefit of a good is the benefit that accrues to society as a whole from the consumption of one additional unit of the good.

But what is the marginal social benefit of another unit of a public good—a unit that generates utility for *all* consumers, not just one consumer, because it is non-excludable and nonrival in consumption? This question leads us to an important principle: *In the special case of a public good, the marginal social benefit of a unit of the good is equal to the sum of the individual marginal benefits that are enjoyed by all consumers of that unit.*

Or to consider it from a slightly different angle, if a consumer could be compelled to pay for a unit before consuming it (the good is made excludable), then the marginal social benefit of a unit is equal to the *sum* of each consumer's willingness to pay for that unit. Using this principle, the marginal social benefit of an additional street cleaning per month is equal to Theo's individual marginal benefit from that additional cleaning *plus* Abby's individual marginal benefit.

We all benefit when someone does the cleaning up.

Why? Because a public good is nonrival in consumption—Theo's benefit from a cleaner street does not diminish Abby's benefit from that same clean street, and vice versa. Because people can all simultaneously consume the same unit of a public good, the marginal social benefit of an additional unit of that good is the *sum* of the individual marginal benefits of all who enjoy the public good. And the efficient quantity of a public good is the quantity at which the marginal social benefit is equal to the marginal cost of providing it.

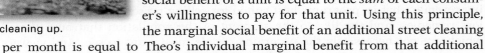

FOR INQUIRING MINDS   Voting as a Public Good

It's a sad fact that many Americans who are eligible to vote don't bother to. As a result, their interests tend to be ignored by politicians. Yet what is self-defeating on a public level is completely rational on an individual level.

As economist Mancur Olson pointed out in a famous book titled *The Logic of Collective Action,* voting is a public good, one that suffers from severe free-rider problems.

Imagine that you are one of a million people who would stand to gain the equivalent of $100 each if some plan is passed in a statewide referendum—say, a plan to improve public schools. And suppose that

the opportunity cost of the time it would take you to vote is $10. Will you be sure to go to the polls and vote for the referendum? If you are rational, the answer is no because it is very unlikely that your vote will decide the issue, either way. If the measure passes, you benefit, even if you didn't bother to vote—the benefits are nonexcludable. If the measure doesn't pass, your vote would not have changed the outcome. By not voting and free-riding on those who do vote you save $10.

Of course, many people do vote out of a sense of civic duty. But because political action is a public good, typically people

devote too little effort to defending their own interests.

The result, Olson pointed out, is that when a large group of people share a common political interest, they are likely to exert too little effort promoting their cause and so will be ignored. Conversely, small, well-organized interest groups that act on issues narrowly targeted in their favor tend to have disproportionate power.

Is this a reason to distrust democracy? Winston Churchill said it best: "Democracy is the worst form of government, except for all the other forms that have been tried."

Figure 17-2 illustrates the efficient provision of a public good, showing three marginal benefit curves. Panel (a) shows Theo's individual marginal benefit curve from street cleaning, MB_T: he would be willing to pay \$25 for the city to clean its streets once a month, an additional \$18 to have it done a second time, and so on. Panel (b) shows Abby's individual marginal benefit curve from street cleaning, MB_A. Panel (c) shows the marginal social benefit curve from street cleaning, MSB: it is the vertical sum of Theo and Abby's individual marginal benefit curves, MB_T and MB_A.

To maximize society's welfare, the government should clean the street up to the level at which the marginal social benefit of an additional cleaning is no

FIGURE 17-2 A Public Good

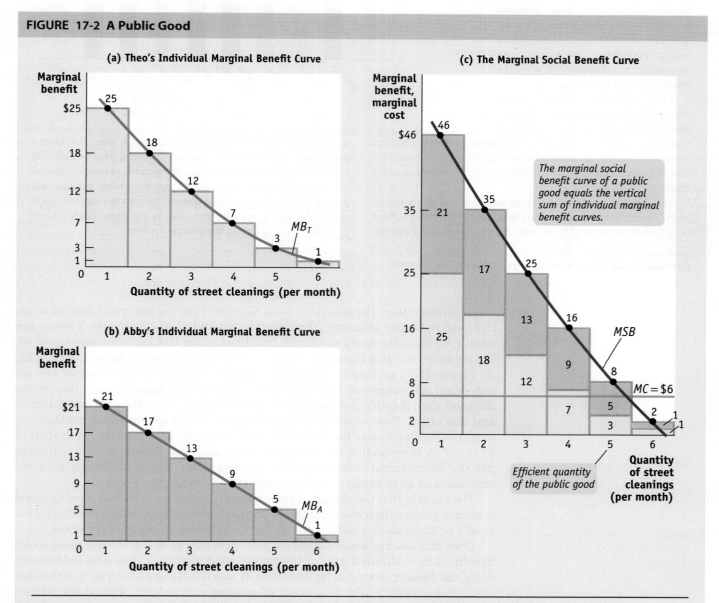

Panel (a) shows Theo's individual marginal benefit curve of street cleanings per month, MB_T, and panel (b) shows Abby's individual marginal benefit curve, MB_A. Panel (c) shows the marginal social benefit of the public good, equal to the sum of the individual marginal benefits to all consumers (in this case, Theo and Abby). The marginal social benefit curve,

MSB, is the vertical sum of the individual marginal benefit curves MB_T and MB_A. At a constant marginal cost of \$6, there should be 5 street cleanings per month, because the marginal social benefit of going from 4 to 5 cleanings is \$8 (\$3 for Theo plus \$5 for Abby), but the marginal social benefit of going from 5 to 6 cleanings is only \$2.

Despite the fact that choosing not to vote can be an entirely rational choice, many countries consistently achieve astonishingly high turnout rates in their elections by adopting policies that encourage voting. In Belgium, Singapore, and Australia, voting is compulsory; eligible voters are penalized if they fail to do their civic duty by casting their ballots. These penalties are effective at getting out the vote. When Venezuela dropped its mandatory voting requirement, the turnout rate dropped 30%; it dropped 20% when the Netherlands did the same.

Other countries have policies that reduce the cost of voting; for example, declaring election day a work holiday (giving citizens ample time to cast their ballots), allowing voter registration on election day (eliminating the need for advance planning), and permitting voting by mail (increasing convenience).

This figure shows turnout rates in several countries, measured as the percentage of eligible voters who cast ballots, over the most recent election up to 2019. As you can see, Singapore, Australia,

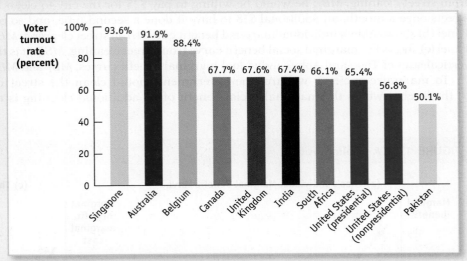

and Belgium have the highest voter turnout rates. The United States has a below-average level of turnout during presidential elections. However, turnout drops significantly in nonpresidential elections, when the United States has the lowest turnout rate among advanced countries. In general, the past four decades have seen a decline in voter turnout rates in the major democracies, most dramatically among the youngest voters.

Data from: International Institute for Democracy and Electoral Assistance.

longer greater than the marginal cost. Suppose that the marginal cost of street cleaning is $6 per cleaning. Then the city should clean its streets 5 times per month, because the marginal social benefit of going from 4 to 5 cleanings is $8, but going from 5 to 6 cleanings would yield a marginal social benefit of only $2.

Figure 17-2 can help reinforce our understanding of why we cannot rely on individual self-interest to yield provision of an efficient quantity of public goods. Suppose that the city did one fewer street cleaning than the efficient quantity and that either Theo or Abby was asked to pay for the last cleaning. Neither one would be willing to pay for it! Theo would personally gain only the equivalent of $3 in utility from adding one more street cleaning—so he wouldn't be willing to pay the $6 marginal cost of another cleaning. Abby would personally gain the equivalent of $5 in utility—so she wouldn't be willing to pay either.

The point is that the marginal social benefit of one more unit of a public good is always greater than the individual marginal benefit to any one individual. That is why no individual is willing to pay for the efficient quantity of the good.

Does this description of the public good problem, in which the marginal social benefit of an additional unit of the public good is greater than any individual's marginal benefit, sound a bit familiar? It should: we encountered a somewhat similar situation in our discussion of *positive externalities*. Remember that in the case of a positive externality, the marginal social benefit accruing to all consumers of another unit of the good is greater than the price that the producer receives for that unit; as a result, the market produces too little of the good.

In the case of a public good, the individual marginal benefit of a consumer plays the same role as the price received by the producer in the case of positive externalities: both cases create insufficient incentive to provide an efficient amount of the good.

The problem of providing public goods is very similar to the problem of dealing with positive externalities; in both cases there is a market failure that calls for government intervention. One basic rationale for the existence of government is that it provides a way for citizens to tax themselves in order to provide public goods—particularly a vital public good like national defense.

Of course, if society really consisted of only two individuals, they would probably manage to strike a deal to provide the good. But imagine a city with a million residents, each of whose individual marginal benefit from provision of the good is only a tiny fraction of the marginal social benefit. It would be impossible for people to reach a voluntary agreement to pay for the efficient level of street cleaning—the potential for free-riding makes it too difficult to make and enforce an agreement among so many people. But they could and would vote to tax themselves to pay for a citywide sanitation department.

> **Cost-benefit analysis** is the estimation and comparison of the social costs and social benefits of providing a public good.

Cost-Benefit Analysis

How do governments decide in practice how much of a public good to provide? Sometimes policy makers just guess—or do whatever they think will get them reelected. However, responsible governments try to estimate and compare both the social benefits and the social costs of providing a public good, a process known as **cost-benefit analysis.**

It's straightforward to estimate the cost of supplying a public good. Estimating the benefit is harder. In fact, it is a very difficult problem.

Now you might wonder why governments can't figure out the marginal social benefit of a public good just by asking people their willingness to pay for it (their individual marginal benefit). But it turns out that it's hard to get an honest answer.

This is not a problem with private goods: we can determine how much an individual is willing to pay for one more unit of a private good by looking at that individual's actual choices. But because people don't actually pay for public goods, the question of willingness to pay is always hypothetical.

Worse yet, it's a question that people have an incentive not to answer truthfully. People naturally want more rather than less. Because they cannot be made to pay for whatever quantity of the public good they use, people are apt to overstate their true feelings when asked how much they desire a public good. For example, if street cleaning were scheduled according to the stated wishes of homeowners alone, the streets would be cleaned every day—an inefficient level of provision.

So governments must be aware that they cannot simply rely on the public's statements when deciding how much of a public good to provide—if they do, they are likely to provide too much. In contrast, as the preceding For Inquiring Minds explains, relying on the public to indicate how much of the public good they want through voting has problems as well—and is likely to lead to too little of the public good being provided.

ECONOMICS >> *in Action*
American Infrastructure Gets a D+

New Jersey is the third richest state in the country, with the third highest median household income; much of its income is derived through its close economic links to New York City's financial industry. On a typical day, several hundred thousand New Jerseyans take a train or a bus into New York City on the second busiest commuter route in the country. Public transportation the lifeblood of New Jersey's economy, with nearly a million people—10% of the state's population—taking a bus or a train each day.

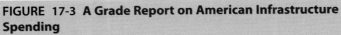

FIGURE 17-3 A Grade Report on American Infrastructure Spending

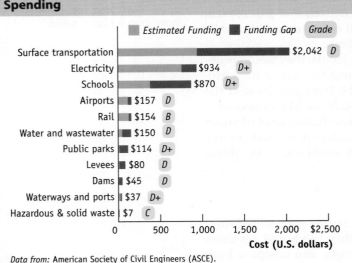

Data from: American Society of Civil Engineers (ASCE).

Yet, despite the critical importance of the public transportation system to New Jersey's economy, it has been chronically underfunded. In recent years the state contribution to the system's operating budget was only 10% of what it had been in 2009. By 2020 the department was running an annual deficit in excess of $135 million. Capital investment has plunged by 20% as ridership has increased by 20%. Predictably, buses are persistently late, overcrowded, and prone to break down. As one commuter said, "It's gotten me in trouble with work quite a bit. They think I'm making it up." And in September 2016 a packed New Jersey Transit commuter train slammed into a train station at full speed, injuring 114 people and killing 1. Tragically, New Jersey Transit Authority had delayed installation of an automatic braking system in its trains the previous year.

New Jersey's infrastructure woes are not unique; in fact, they are the norm across the country. A 2017 study showed that state and local spending on infrastructure—schools, water treatment plants, roads, highways, and bridges—is at a 30-year low. Every four years the American Society of Civil Engineers (ASCE) assesses the state of American infrastructure and issues a report card. In 2017, the United States received a D+ "based on a significant backlog of overdue maintenance across our infrastructure system [and] a pressing need for modernization" arising from decades of underfunding. According to ASCE, an estimated $4.6 trillion in spending is needed by 2027 in order to bring American infrastructure up to a grade B (good). Based on current funding gaps, it is estimated that almost $4 trillion in gross domestic product will be lost by 2025, translating into an annual loss to each household of $3,400.

Figure 17-3 shows the projected funding, the funding gap, and the 2017 grade for types of infrastructure. As you can see, the funding gaps for much of our basic infrastructure are extensive, with surface transportation, schools, and waterways suffering most from funding shortages. Across the board, grades for each of these infrastructure types are consistently bad. They make it clear that infrastructure improvements are needed.

Why has infrastructure in the United States been allowed to deteriorate so badly? It has been a casualty of both the political conflict in Congress and state legislatures, as well as short-sightedness that undervalues infrastructure as a long-term asset.

For years, political gridlock prevented federal and state governments from borrowing money or raising taxes to adequately fund infrastructure. As a result, the country has run down its existing stock to perilous levels. During the past few years Congress has allocated larger sums, as the costs of deteriorating roads, schools, water quality, and more have grown too great to ignore. It's a start, but it will take many years of higher funding for the country to dig out of its infrastructure pothole.

>> Quick Review

• A **public good** is both nonexcludable and nonrival in consumption.

• Because most forms of public-good provision by the private sector have serious defects, they are typically provided by the government and paid for with taxes.

• The marginal social benefit of an additional unit of a public good is equal to the sum of each consumer's individual marginal benefit from that unit. At the efficient quantity, the marginal social benefit equals the marginal cost of providing the good.

• No individual has an incentive to pay for providing the efficient quantity of a public good because each individual's marginal benefit is less than the marginal social benefit. This is a primary justification for the existence of government.

• Although governments should rely on **cost-benefit analysis** to determine how much of a public good to supply, doing so is problematic because individuals tend to overstate the good's value to them.

>> Check Your Understanding 17-2

Solutions appear at back of book.

1. The town of Centreville, population 16, has two types of residents, Homebodies and Revelers. Using the accompanying table, the town must decide how much to spend on its New Year's Eve party. No individual resident expects to directly bear the cost of the party.

a. Suppose there are 10 Homebodies and 6 Revelers. Determine the marginal social benefit schedule of money spent on the party. What is the efficient level of spending?

b. Suppose there are 6 Homebodies and 10 Revelers. How do your answers to part a change? Explain.

c. Suppose that the individual marginal benefit schedules are known but no one knows the true proportion of Homebodies versus Revelers. Individuals are asked their preferences. What is the likely outcome if each person assumes that others will pay for any additional amount of the public good? Why is it likely to result in an inefficiently high level of spending? Explain.

Money spent on party	Individual marginal benefit of additional $1 spent on party	
	Homebody	Reveler
$0		
	$0.05	$0.13
1		
	0.04	0.11
2		
	0.03	0.09
3		
	0.02	0.07
4		

|| Common Resources

A **common resource** is a good that is nonexcludable but is rival in consumption. An example is the stock of fish in a limited fishing area, like the fisheries off the coast of New England. Traditionally, anyone who had a boat could go out to sea and catch fish—fish in the sea were a nonexcludable good. Yet because the total number of fish is limited, the fish that one person catches are no longer available to be caught by someone else. So fish in the sea are rival in consumption.

Other examples of common resources are clean air and water as well as the diversity of animal and plant species on the planet (biodiversity). In each of these cases the fact that the good, though rival in consumption, is nonexcludable poses a serious problem.

The Problem of Overuse

Because common resources are nonexcludable, individuals cannot be charged for their use. Yet because they are rival in consumption, an individual who uses a unit depletes the resource by making that unit unavailable to others. As a result, a common resource is subject to **overuse:** an individual will continue to use it until that individual's marginal benefit of its use is equal to their own individual marginal cost, ignoring the cost that this action inflicts on society as a whole. As we will see shortly, the problem of overuse of a common resource is similar to a problem we studied in Chapter 16: the problem of a good that generates a negative externality, such as groundwater contamination from fracking or climate change from greenhouse gas emissions.

Fishing is a classic example of a common resource. In heavily fished waters, my fishing imposes a cost on others by reducing the fish population and making it harder for others to catch fish. But I have no personal incentive to take this cost into account, since I cannot be charged for fishing. As a result, from society's point of view, I catch too many fish.

Traffic congestion is another example of overuse of a common resource. A major highway during rush hour can accommodate only a certain number of vehicles per hour. If I decide to drive to work alone rather than carpool or work at home, I make the commute of many other people a bit longer; but I have no incentive to take these consequences into account.

In the case of a common resource, the *marginal social cost* of my use of that resource is higher than my *individual marginal cost*, the cost to me of using an additional unit of the good.

Figure 17-4 illustrates this point. It shows the demand curve for fish, which measures the marginal benefit of fish—the benefit to consumers when an

A **common resource** is nonexcludable and rival in consumption: you can't stop me from consuming the good, and more consumption by me means less of the good available for you.

Common resources left to the market suffer from **overuse:** individuals ignore the fact that their use depletes the amount of the resource remaining for others.

FIGURE 17-4 A Common Resource

The supply curve *S*, which shows the marginal cost of production of the fishing industry, is composed of the individual supply curves of the individual fishermen. But each fisherman's individual marginal cost does not include the cost that their actions impose on others: the depletion of the common resource. As a result, the marginal social cost curve, *MSC*, lies above the supply curve; in an unregulated market, the quantity of the common resource used, Q_{MKT}, exceeds the efficient quantity of use, Q_{OPT}.

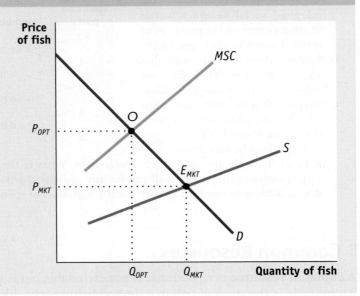

additional unit of fish is caught and consumed. It also shows the supply curve for fish, which measures the marginal cost of production of the fishing industry. We know that the industry supply curve is the horizontal sum of each individual fisherman's supply curve—equivalent to their individual marginal cost curve. The fishing industry supplies the quantity where its marginal cost is equal to the price, the quantity Q_{MKT}.

But the efficient outcome is to catch the quantity Q_{OPT}, the quantity of output that equates the marginal benefit to the marginal social cost, not to the fishing industry's marginal cost of production. The market outcome results in overuse of the common resource.

As we noted, there is a close parallel between the problem of managing a common resource and the problem posed by negative externalities. In the case of an activity that generates a negative externality, the marginal social cost of production is greater than the industry's marginal cost of production, the difference being the marginal external cost imposed on society. Here, the loss to society arising from a fisherman's depletion of the common resource plays the same role as the external cost plays when there is a negative externality. In fact, many negative externalities (such as pollution) can be thought of as involving common resources (such as clean air).

The Efficient Use and Maintenance of a Common Resource

Because common resources pose problems similar to those created by negative externalities, the solutions are also similar. To ensure efficient use of a common resource, society must find a way of getting individual users of the resource to take into account the costs they impose on other users. This is basically the same principle as that of getting individuals to internalize a negative externality that arises from their actions.

There are three fundamental ways to induce people who use common resources to internalize the costs they impose on others.

- Tax or otherwise regulate the use of the common resource
- Create a system of tradable licenses for the right to use the common resource
- Make the common resource excludable and assign property rights to some individuals

FOR INQUIRING MINDS   When Fertile Farmland Turned to Dust

Ashley Yost's grandfather sank a well deep underneath his prime Kansas farmland and struck a source of water so bountiful that he could pump 1,600 gallons to the surface every minute. Now, 50 years later, his grandson is having trouble getting just 300 gallons of water per minute. And that water is so contaminated by sediment that tens of thousands of dollars' worth of pumping equipment has been destroyed. As Mr. Yost ruefully remarked, "That's prime land. I've raised 294 bushels of corn an acre before. . . . Now, it's over." In west-central Kansas, the problem is widespread. Wells in up to a fifth of the irrigated farmland have already gone dry. In the Texas Panhandle, many farms have been abandoned and rural communities hollowed out as once highly productive farmland returns to prairie.

This is the sad consequence of mismanagement of a remarkable common resource, the Ogallala Aquifer, one of the world's largest underground reservoirs of water. It stretches across portions of eight Great Plains states and underlies

approximately 174,000 square miles, supplying drinking water for millions of people. The water in the Ogallala Aquifer was deposited 2 to 6 million years ago when the Great Plains region was geologically active. As you might guess, water that was deposited millions of years ago cannot be replenished quickly. For the many parts of the Ogallala that are now dry, it would take over 6,000 years of rainfall to fill them back up.

How did this happen? The decimation of the Ogallala began in the 1950s with the large scale irrigation of Plains farmland with groundwater. The virtually unrestricted pumping of groundwater turned millions of acres of the semi-arid Great Plains into one of the world's most productive areas for the cultivation of wheat, corn, and other crops. However, as a common resource, farmers had no interest in conserving the Ogallala's water. As a result even the most arid areas, like the Texas Panhandle, were coaxed into growing water-thirsty crops like corn.

While some areas in the northern Plains states still have enough groundwater for

approximately 200 years, farmers and residents of the southern Plains know that the days of endless water supplies have ended, as much of the Ogallala Aquifer has been pumped to dangerously low levels.

Some farmers have given up all together, while others have switched to less thirsty crops or to livestock farming. Everyone in the supply chain, from seed dealers to tractor sellers and railroads, is ending up with less income.

What's needed is a multistate response since the aquifer extends across several state lines. Unfortunately, there has been little coordinated response. "The thing is, we've built some pretty nice schools and some pretty nice hospitals, and we have a nice tax base all based on irrigated ground," says a local authority. "The light switch has been on for a while now, and when it gets switched to dark, people have to be ready." Although what the future holds is unknown, at the time of writing, it's clear that the days of ignoring the Ogallala Aquifer, a common resource, are gone.

Like activities that generate negative externalities, use of a common resource can be reduced to the efficient quantity by imposing a Pigouvian tax. For example, some countries have imposed congestion charges on those who drive during rush hour, in effect charging them for use of the common resource of city streets. Likewise, visitors to national parks must pay a fee, and the number of visitors to any one park is restricted.

A second way to correct the problem of overuse is to create a system of tradable licenses for the use of the common resource much like the systems designed to address negative externalities. The policy maker issues the number of licenses that corresponds to the efficient level of use of the good. Making the licenses tradable ensures that the right to use the good is allocated efficiently—that is, those who end up using the good (those willing to pay the most for a license) are those who gain the most from its use.

But when it comes to common resources, often the most natural solution is simply to assign property rights. At a fundamental level, common resources are subject to overuse because *nobody owns them*. The essence of ownership of a good—the *property right* over the good—is that you can limit who can and cannot use the good as well as how much of it can be used.

When a good is nonexcludable, in a very real sense no one owns it because a property right cannot be enforced—and consequently no one has an incentive to use it efficiently. So one way to correct the problem of overuse is to make the good excludable and assign property rights over it to someone. The good then has an owner who has an incentive to protect the value of the good—to use it efficiently rather than overuse it.

As the following Economics in Action shows, a system of tradable licenses, called individual transferable quotas, or ITQs, has been a successful strategy in some fisheries.

ECONOMICS >> *in Action*

Saving the Oceans with ITQs

The world's oceans are in serious trouble. According to a study by the International Program on the State of the Oceans, there is an imminent risk of widespread extinctions of multiple species of fish. As of 2019, 40% of North Atlantic fish stocks and 87% of Mediterranean fish stocks are in danger of collapse. In the North Sea, 93% of cod are fished before they can breed. And bluefin tuna, a favorite in Japanese sushi, are in danger of imminent extinction, with current stocks at less than 97% of their natural, unfished levels.

Not surprisingly, the principal culprit is overfishing. The decline of fishing stocks has worsened as fishermen trawl in deeper waters with their very large nets to catch the remaining fish, unintentionally killing many other marine animals in the process.

The fishing industry is in crisis, too, as fishermen's incomes decline and they are compelled to fish for longer periods of time and in more dangerous waters in order to make a living.

Will ITQs help save the North Sea cod?

But individual transferable quotas, or ITQs, may provide a solution to both crises. Under an ITQ scheme, a fisherman receives a license entitling him to catch an annual quota within a given fishing ground. The ITQ is given for a long period of time, sometimes indefinitely. Because it is transferable, the owner can sell or lease it.

Researchers who analyzed 121 established ITQ schemes around the world concluded that ITQs can help reverse the collapse of fisheries because each ITQ holder has a financial interest in the long-term maintenance of his particular fishery. This view is endorsed by Arne Fuglvog, a commercial fisherman, who explained that owning part of the resource has led to more careful oversight of it: "We want to keep the resource healthy. We don't want to overfish it. We want to keep making a living at it for as long as we can and keep it for future generations."

ITQ schemes (also called catch-share schemes) are common in New Zealand, Australia, Iceland, and increasingly in the United States and Canada. (The quota share program for Alaska crab fishing analyzed in Chapter 5 is an example of an American ITQ.) The Alaskan halibut fishery is one example of a successful ITQ scheme. When it was implemented, the annual fishing season had shrunk from four months to two or three days, resulting in dangerous races by the boats. Now the season lasts nearly eight months. Steve Gaines, director of the Marine Science Institute at the University of California at Santa Barbara says, "Halibut fishermen were barely squeaking by—but now the fishery is insanely profitable."

>> Quick Review

• A **common resource** is rival in consumption but nonexcludable.

• The problem with common resources is **overuse**: a user depletes the amount of the common resource available to others but does not take this cost into account when deciding how much to use the common resource.

• Like negative externalities, a common resource can be efficiently managed by Pigouvian taxes, by the creation of a system of tradable licenses for its use, or by making it excludable and assigning property rights.

>> Check Your Understanding 17-3

Solutions appear at back of book.

1. Rocky Mountain Forest is a government-owned forest in which private citizens were allowed in the past to harvest as much timber as they wanted free of charge. State in economic terms why this is problematic from society's point of view.

2. You are the new forest service commissioner and have been instructed to come up with ways to preserve the forest for the general public. Name three different methods you could use to maintain the efficient level of tree harvesting and explain how each would work. For each method, what information would you need to know in order to achieve an efficient outcome?

‖ Artificially Scarce Goods

An **artificially scarce good** is a good that is excludable but nonrival in consumption. As we've already seen, on-demand movies are a familiar example. The marginal cost to society of allowing an individual to watch the movie is zero, because one person's viewing doesn't interfere with other people's viewing. Yet Amazon and companies like it prevent individuals from seeing on-demand movies if they haven't paid. Goods like software, video games, or digital books, which are valued for the information they embody (and are sometimes called *information goods*), are also artificially scarce.

As we've already seen, markets will supply artificially scarce goods: because they are excludable, the producers can charge people for consuming them.

But artificially scarce goods are nonrival in consumption, which means that the marginal cost of an individual's consumption is zero. So the price that the supplier of an artificially scarce good charges exceeds marginal cost. Because the efficient price is equal to the marginal cost of zero, the good is "artificially scarce," and consumption of the good is inefficiently low. However, unless the producer can somehow earn revenue for producing and selling the good, the producer will be unwilling to produce at all—an outcome that leaves society even worse off than it would otherwise be with positive but inefficiently low consumption.

Figure 17-5 illustrates the loss in total surplus caused by artificial scarcity. The demand curve shows the quantity of on-demand movies watched at any given price. The marginal cost of allowing an additional person to watch the movie is zero, so the efficient quantity of movies viewed is Q_{OPT}. Amazon charges a positive price, in this case $4 to watch the movie, and as a result only Q_{MKT} on-demand movies will be watched. This leads to a deadweight loss equal to the area of the shaded triangle.

Does this look familiar? Like the problems that arise with public goods and common resources, the problem created by artificially scarce goods is similar to the problem of *natural monopoly*. A natural monopoly, you will recall, is an industry in which average total cost is above marginal cost for the relevant output range. In order to be willing to produce output, the producer must charge a price at least as high as average total cost—that is, a price above marginal cost. But a price above marginal cost leads to inefficiently low consumption.

> An **artificially scarce good** is excludable but nonrival in consumption.

FIGURE 17-5 An Artificially Scarce Good

An artificially scarce good is excludable and nonrival in consumption. It is made artificially scarce because producers charge a positive price, but the marginal cost of allowing one more person to consume the good is zero. In this example, the market price of an on-demand movie is $4 and the quantity demanded at that price is Q_{MKT}. But the efficient level of consumption is Q_{OPT}, the quantity demanded when the price is zero. The efficient quantity, Q_{OPT}, exceeds the quantity demanded in an unregulated market, Q_{MKT}. The shaded area represents the loss in total surplus from charging a price of $4.

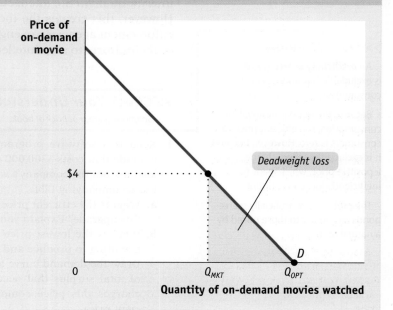

ECONOMICS >> *in Action*
Twenty-First Century Piracy

Intellectual property piracy, or IPP, is the illegal copying, distribution, or use of intellectual property. Intellectual property has accounted for a larger and larger share of the U.S. economy: as of 2019, patented intellectual property account for 74% of U.S. exports. Hence the extent of IPP is carefully monitored, with the FBI devoting substantial resources to fighting it.

The most common forms include the piracy of software, sophisticated digital hardware, counterfeit goods, movies, music, and games. It is a global industry that has cost the owners of intellectual property rights—musicians, actors, movie studios, software companies, and creators of software and games—over $1 trillion in 2019. For example, Torrentfreak.com, a website that tracks illegal downloads, found that the final episode of *Game of Thrones* was illegally downloaded 1.5 million times within eight hours of its airing. And the Business Software Alliance estimates that 36% of all software in use is pirated.

Authorities have stepped up their efforts to combat IPP. In Canada, ISPs (internet service providers) now keep track of illegal downloads, with fines up to $5,000 per illegal download. The FBI has now teamed up with Interpol, the international crime-fighting agency, to find, charge, and extradite to the United States individuals who run large-scale pirating operations abroad.

Intellectual property goods, like video games, must be made artificially scarce, which creates an incentive to pirate them.

What is the connection to artificially scarce goods? It stems from the fact that, once an intellectual property good is created, the marginal cost to deliver another unit to a consumer is virtually zero—it involves only a few seconds-long internet download. And because intellectual property goods are nonrival in consumption, my consumption of a bootleg version of the movie *Avengers* or a computer game doesn't impede or reduce your consumption of them.

However, if movie and game creators are unable to charge for the right to use their products, they won't produce them in the first place. (This explains why free versions of software or games are knock-offs of commercial versions and are of inferior quality.) So, intellectual property goods must be made artificially scarce. However, this creates the incentive to pirate them. So you can be sure that law enforcement agencies are engaged in their own version of the game whack-a-mole in their efforts to stop intellectual property piracy.

>> Quick Review

• An **artificially scarce good** is excludable but nonrival in consumption.

• Because the good is nonrival in consumption, the efficient price to consumers is zero. However, because it is excludable, sellers charge a positive price, which leads to inefficiently low consumption.

• The problems of artificially scarce goods are similar to those posed by a natural monopoly.

>> Check Your Understanding 17-4
Solutions appear at back of book.

1. Xena is a software program produced by Xenoid. Each year Xenoid produces an upgrade that costs $300,000 to produce. It costs nothing to allow customers to download it from the company's website. The demand schedule for the upgrade is shown in the accompanying table.

   a. What is the efficient price to a consumer of this upgrade? Explain your answer.

   b. What is the lowest price at which Xenoid is willing to produce and sell the upgrade? Draw the demand curve and show the loss of total surplus that occurs when Xenoid charges this price compared to the efficient price.

Price of upgrade	Quantity of upgrades demanded
$180	1,700
150	2,000
120	2,300
90	2,600
0	3,500

Saving the "Beast": Ecotourism Protects the Jaguars of Brazil

Hal Beral/VW Pics/Universal Images Group via Getty Images

"It's *Fera*—that's 'Beast' in Portuguese. She's almost four now, 145 pounds," whispered Haberfeld to a jeep full of gawking humans, as they stared at a lounging jaguar a mere 20 yards away. Just a few years ago, Fera's life would have been in great danger if she had allowed human beings to come so close to her. Now, thanks to the work of Mario Haberfeld and his Onçafari Project, Fera and her offspring are thriving.

Today, jaguars are the superstars of Caiman Ecological Refuge, a 131,000-acre luxury ecotourism property in Brazil. Jaguars used to range from the Grand Canyon to Argentina. But having lost half of their natural range, Caiman refuge is now a crucial bastion for the big cats. It's the world's largest tropical wetland, a vast savanna larger than England. In the rainy season it brims with wildlife; in the dry season, it's home to a robust free-range cattle industry. At Caiman refuge, more than 100 jaguars—with males weighing as much as 300 pounds—cross paths with 30,000 head of cattle.

And there's the rub. Although it is illegal to hunt jaguars in Brazil, the law was routinely flouted as cowboys and landowners shot the apex predators on sight. As the project biologist commented, "People associate jaguars with losing money. They are seen as the villain." Haberfeld's insight was not to attempt to enforce existing law. Rather, it was to make ranchers start to see jaguars as profit-drivers rather than loss-makers.

To accomplish that, Haberfeld presented a clear cost-benefit proposition to them. Jaguars kill about 1% of ranchers' stock in a year. "So for him [the rancher], it's nothing," in Haberfeld's words. But by adding high-end jaguar-focused ecotourism lodges to their vast ranches, landowners could make money both on cattle and the big cats, he argued. Once he convinced ranchers to spare the animals, he worked with biologists to habituate them to nearby human presence.

And it worked. In 2012, only 7% of Caiman refuge visitors saw jaguars, and often expressed disappointment in not seeing them. By 2016, 72% of guests saw the big cats, rising to 95% in the dry season. And the economic impact is real: surveys show that 85% of Caiman refuge visitors choose a lodge according to its rate of jaguar sightings, with the most successful lodges earning about $7,000 per visitor. The key, according to Haberfeld, was to understand that ranchers are above all businessmen and that the bottom line will ultimately prevail. Haberfeld sees his mission in shifting the attitudes of ranchers. That is, to create the conditions so that, as Haberfeld says of the ranchers: "then the guy will understand, 'Wow, I'm losing money by killing jaguars.'"

QUESTIONS FOR THOUGHT

1. Using the concepts you learned in this chapter, explain the economic incentives behind the loss of jaguars' natural habitat and the killing of the animals.

2. Also using the concepts from this chapter, explain the change in incentives that led to the protection of the jaguars of the Caiman Ecological Refuge.

SUMMARY

1. Goods may be classified according to whether or not they are **excludable** and whether or not they are **rival in consumption.**

2. Free markets can deliver efficient levels of production and consumption for **private goods,** which are both excludable and rival in consumption. When goods are nonexcludable or nonrival in consumption, or both, free markets cannot achieve efficient outcomes.

3. When goods are **nonexcludable,** there is a **free-rider problem:** some consumers will not pay for the good, consuming what others have paid for and leading to inefficiently low production. When goods are **nonrival in consumption,** they should be free, and any positive price leads to inefficiently low consumption.

4. A **public good** is nonexcludable and nonrival in consumption. In most cases a public good must be supplied by the government. The marginal social benefit of a public good is equal to the sum of the individual marginal benefits to each consumer. The efficient quantity of a public good is the quantity at which marginal social benefit equals the marginal cost of providing the good. Like a positive externality, marginal social benefit is greater than any one individual's marginal benefit, so no individual is willing to provide the efficient quantity.

5. One rationale for the presence of government is that it allows citizens to tax themselves in order to provide public goods. Governments use **cost-benefit analysis** to determine the efficient provision of a public good. Such analysis is difficult, however, because individuals have an incentive to overstate the good's value to them.

6. A **common resource** is rival in consumption but non-excludable. It is subject to **overuse,** because an individual does not take into account the fact that their use depletes the amount available for others. This is similar to the problem of a negative externality: the marginal social cost of an individual's use of a common resource is always higher than the individual marginal cost. Pigouvian taxes, the creation of a system of tradable licenses, or the assignment of property rights are possible solutions.

7. **Artificially scarce goods** are excludable but nonrival in consumption. Because no marginal cost arises from allowing another individual to consume the good, the efficient price is zero. A positive price compensates the producer for the cost of production but leads to inefficiently low consumption. The problem of an artificially scarce good is similar to that of a natural monopoly.

KEY TERMS

Excludable, p. 494
Rival in consumption, p. 494
Private good, p. 494
Nonexcludable, p. 494
Nonrival in consumption, p. 494
Free-rider problem, p. 495
Public good, p. 496
Cost-benefit analysis, p. 501
Common resource, p. 503
Overuse, p. 503
Artificially scarce good, p. 507

PRACTICE QUESTIONS

1. Prior to 2003, the city of London was often one big parking lot. Traffic jams were common, and it could take hours to travel a couple of miles. Each additional commuter contributed to the congestion, which can be measured by the total number of cars on London roads. Although each commuter suffered by spending valuable time in traffic, none of them paid for the inconvenience they caused others. The total cost of travel includes the opportunity cost of time spent in traffic and any fees levied by London authorities.

   a. Draw a graph illustrating the overuse of London roads, assuming that there is no fee to enter London in a vehicle and that roads are a common resource. Put the cost of travel on the vertical axis and the quantity of cars on the horizontal axis. Draw typical demand, individual marginal cost (MC), and marginal social cost (MSC) curves and label the equilibrium point. (*Hint:* The marginal cost takes into account the opportunity cost of spending time on

   the road for individual drivers but not the inconvenience they cause to others.)

   b. In February 2003, the city of London began charging a £5 congestion fee on all vehicles traveling in central London. Illustrate the effects of this congestion charge on your graph and label the new equilibrium point. Assume the new equilibrium point is not optimally set (that is, assume that the £5 charge is too low relative to what would be efficient).

   c. The congestion fee was raised to £9 in January 2011. Illustrate the new equilibrium point on your graph, assuming the new charge is now optimally set.

2. Butchart Gardens is a very large garden in Victoria, British Columbia, renowned for its beautiful plants. It is so large that it could hold many times more visitors than currently visit it. The garden charges an admission fee of $30. At this price, 1,000 people visit the garden each day. If admission were free, 2,000 people would visit each day.

a. Are visits to Butchart Gardens excludable or nonexcludable? Are they rival in consumption or nonrival? What type of good is it?

b. In a diagram, illustrate the demand curve for visits to Butchart Gardens. Indicate the situation when Butchart Gardens charges an admission fee of $30. Also indicate the situation when Butchart Gardens charges no admission fee.

c. Illustrate the deadweight loss from charging a $30 admission fee. Explain why charging a $30 admission fee is inefficient.

3. In developing a vaccine for the COVID-19 virus, a pharmaceutical company incurs a very high fixed cost. The marginal cost of delivering the vaccine to patients, however, is negligible (consider it to be equal to zero). The pharmaceutical company holds the exclusive patent to the vaccine. You are a regulator who must decide what price the pharmaceutical company is allowed to charge.

a. Draw a diagram that shows the price for the vaccine that would arise if the company is unregulated, and label it P_M. What is the efficient price for the vaccine? Show the deadweight loss that arises from the price P_M.

b. On another diagram, show the lowest price that the regulator can enforce that would still induce the pharmaceutical company to develop the vaccine. Label it P^*. Show the deadweight loss that arises from this price. How does it compare to the deadweight loss that arises from the price P_M?

c. Suppose you have accurate information about the pharmaceutical company's fixed cost. How could you use price regulation of the pharmaceutical company, combined with a subsidy to the company, to have the efficient quantity of the vaccine provided at the lowest cost to the government?

PROBLEMS

1. The government is involved in providing many goods and services. For each of the goods or services listed, determine whether it is rival or nonrival in consumption and whether it is excludable or nonexcludable. What type of good is it? Without government involvement, would the quantity provided be efficient, inefficiently low, or inefficiently high?

a. Street signs

b. Amtrak rail service

c. Regulations limiting pollution

d. A congested interstate highway without tolls

e. A lighthouse on the coast

2. An economist gives the following advice to a museum director: "You should introduce 'peak pricing.' At times when the museum has few visitors, you should admit visitors for free. And at times when the museum has many visitors, you should charge a higher admission fee."

a. When the museum is quiet, is it rival or nonrival in consumption? Is it excludable or nonexcludable? What type of good is the museum at those times? What would be the efficient price to charge visitors during that time, and why?

b. When the museum is busy, is it rival or nonrival in consumption? Is it excludable or nonexcludable? What type of good is the museum at those times? What would be the efficient price to charge visitors during that time, and why?

3. In many planned communities, various aspects of community living are subject to regulation by a homeowners' association. These rules can regulate house architecture; require snow removal from sidewalks; exclude outdoor equipment, such as backyard swimming pools; require appropriate conduct in shared spaces such as the community clubhouse; and so on.

Suppose there has been some conflict in one such community because some homeowners feel that some of the regulations mentioned above are overly intrusive. You have been called in to mediate. Using what you have learned about public goods and common resources, how would you decide what types of regulations are warranted and what types are not?

4. The accompanying table shows Tanisha's and Ari's individual marginal benefit of different amounts of street cleanings per month. Suppose that the marginal cost of street cleanings is constant at $9 each.

Quantity of street cleanings per month	Tanisha's individual marginal benefit	Ari's individual marginal benefit
0		
	$10	$8
1		
	6	4
2		
	2	1
3		

a. If Tanisha had to pay for street cleaning on her own, how many street cleanings would there be?

b. Calculate the marginal social benefit of street cleaning. What is the optimal number of street cleanings?

c. Consider the optimal number of street cleanings. The last street cleaning of the optimal number of street cleanings costs $9. Is Tanisha willing to pay for that last cleaning on her own? Is Ari willing to pay for that last cleaning on his own?

5. Anyone with a radio receiver can listen to public radio, which is funded largely by donations.

a. Is public radio excludable or nonexcludable? Is it rival in consumption or nonrival? What type of good is it?

b. Should the government support public radio? Explain your reasoning.

c. In order to finance itself, public radio decides to transmit only to satellite radios, for which users have to pay a fee. What type of good is public radio then? Will the quantity of radio listening be efficient? Why or why not?

6. Your economics professor assigns a group project for the course. Describe the free-rider problem that can lead to a suboptimal outcome for your group. To combat this problem, the instructor asks you to evaluate the contribution of your peers in a confidential report. Will this evaluation have the desired effects?

7. The village of Upper Bigglesworth has a village "commons," a piece of land on which each villager, by law, is free to graze cows. Use of the commons is measured in units of the number of cows grazing on it. Assume that the marginal private cost curve of cow-grazing on the commons is upward sloping (say due to more time spent herding). There is also a marginal social cost curve of cow-grazing on the commons: each additional cow grazed means less grass available for others, and the damage done by overgrazing of the commons increases as the number of cows grazing increases. Finally, assume that the private benefit to the villagers of each additional cow grazing on the commons declines as more cows graze, since each additional cow has less grass to eat than the previous one.

a. Is the commons excludable or nonexcludable? Is it rival in consumption or nonrival? What kind of good is the commons?

b. Draw a diagram showing the marginal social cost, marginal private cost, and the marginal private benefit of cow-grazing on the commons, with the quantity of cows that graze on the commons on the horizontal axis. How does the quantity of cows grazing in the absence of government intervention compare to the efficient quantity? Show both in your diagram.

c. The villagers hire you to tell them how to achieve an efficient use of the commons. You tell them that there are three possibilities: a Pigouvian tax, the assignment of property rights over the commons, and a system of tradable licenses for the right to graze a cow. Explain how each one of these options would lead to an efficient use of the commons. In the assignment of property rights, assume that one person is assigned the rights to the commons and the rights to all the cows. Draw a diagram that shows the Pigouvian tax.

8. The accompanying table shows six consumers' willingness to pay (their individual marginal benefit) to download a Jay-Z album. The marginal cost of making the file accessible to one additional consumer is constant, at zero.

Consumer	Individual marginal benefit
Adriana	$2
Bhagesh	15
Chizuko	1
Denzel	10
Emma	5
Frank	4

a. What would be the efficient price to charge for a download of the file?

b. All six consumers are able to download the file for free from a file-sharing service, Pantster. Which consumers will download the file? What will be the total consumer surplus to those consumers?

c. Pantster is shut down for copyright law infringement. In order to download the file, consumers now have to pay $4.99 at a commercial music site. Which consumers will download the file? What will be the total consumer surplus to those consumers? How much producer surplus accrues to the commercial music site? What is the total surplus? What is the deadweight loss from the new pricing policy?

9. Software has historically been an artificially scarce good—it is nonrival because the cost of replication is negligible once the investment to write the code is made, but software companies make it excludable by charging for user licenses. But then open-source software emerged, most of which is free to download and can be modified and maintained by anyone.

a. Discuss the free-rider problem that might exist in the development of open-source software. What effect might this have on quality? Why does this problem not exist for proprietary software, such as the products of a company like Microsoft or Adobe?

b. Some argue that open-source software serves an unsatisfied market demand that proprietary software ignores. Draw a typical diagram that illustrates how proprietary software may be underproduced. Put the price and marginal cost of software on the vertical axis and the quantity of software on the horizontal axis. Draw a typical demand curve and a marginal cost curve (*MC*) that is always equal to zero. Assume that the software company charges a positive price, *P*, for the software. Label the equilibrium point and the efficient point.

10. Americans have become passionate consumers of the Asian hot sauce Sriracha. Sriracha is produced by Huy Fong Foods in Irwindale, California. Each year the company processes over 100 million pounds of chili peppers to make their delectable sauce. But roasting all of those chili peppers has had an unintended consequence: pollution. Recently, local residents began complaining about a pungent odor from the plant that they believed led to heartburn, nosebleeds, and coughing.

The hypothetical table shows the estimated marginal social benefit (*MSB*) and marginal social cost (*MSC*) of pollution that arises from odor emissions.

Quantity of odor emissions (thousands of odor units)	Marginal social benefit ($ per odor unit)	Marginal social cost ($ per odor unit)
0	$80	$0
1	72	8
2	64	16
3	56	24
4	48	32
5	40	40
6	32	48
7	24	56
8	16	64
9	8	72
10	0	80

a. How can the pollution that results from Sriracha production have a marginal social benefit?

b. Graph the marginal social cost and marginal social benefit of odor.

c. What is the market-determined quantity of odor?

d. What is the social gain from reducing the market-determined quantity of odor by one odor unit?

WORK IT OUT

11. A residential community has 100 residents who are concerned about security. The accompanying table gives the total cost of hiring a 24-hour security service as well as each individual resident's total benefit.

Quantity of security guards	Total cost	Total individual benefit to each resident
0	$0	$0
1	150	10
2	300	16
3	450	18
4	600	19

a. Explain why the security service is a public good for the residents of the community.

b. Calculate the marginal cost, the individual marginal benefit for each resident, and the marginal social benefit.

c. If an individual resident were to decide about hiring and paying for security guards on their own, how many guards would that resident hire?

d. If the residents act together, how many security guards will they hire? ■

18

The Economics of the Welfare State

AN AFFAIR OF THE HEART

IN 2018 Kenneth Young, a 53-year-old Virginia plumber with heart problems, wasn't taking his medicine. He didn't have insurance, and he couldn't afford to pay for the drug out of pocket.

But he was able to resume treatment in 2019: on January 1 of that year Virginia expanded Medicaid, a government program that covers health expenses for lower-income Americans, and Young was among the first wave of new enrollees. Medicaid would pay for his treatment.

More than 110 million Americans — around a third of the population — receive health coverage from the government, mainly via Medicaid and Medicare, a program that covers all legal U.S. residents age 65 and older. Millions more receive government subsidies to help them purchase private insurance. Nor is health care the only area where government aid is a big factor in people's lives. More than 60 million Americans receive benefits from Social Security, which supports retirees and those with disabilities. More than 35 million receive aid in purchasing food under the Supplemental Nutrition Assistance Program, often referred to as "food stamps." And more than 25 million receive subsidies that add to their wage income via the Earned Income Tax Credit.

In each case, the government provides some form of aid to individuals in an attempt to limit economic insecurity and reduce economic inequality. The collection of programs that serve this purpose is known as the *welfare state*. As the numbers we've just given show, the U.S. welfare state is quite extensive. But the welfare state plays an even bigger role in the economies of most other wealthy countries.

There is intense political dispute about the appropriate size and role of the welfare state. Indeed, you can argue that this dispute is what politics is mainly about, with liberals seeking to expand the welfare state's reach and conservatives seeking to scale it back.

Yet there is a broad political consensus that troubled families should receive some help. And they do: even conservatives generally accept a fairly extensive welfare state as a fact of life. Governments of all wealthy nations play a large role in everything from health care, to retirement, to aid to the poor and jobless.

We start this chapter by discussing the rationale for welfare state programs. Then we look at the two main programs operating in the United States: *income support programs,* of which Social Security is by far the largest, and *health care programs,* dominated by Medicare and Medicaid, but with the Affordable Care Act playing a growing role. •

Kristen Prahl/Getty Images

Implementation of the Affordable Care Act (ACA) was a major expansion of the U.S. welfare state.

WHAT YOU WILL LEARN

- What is the **welfare state** and how does it benefit society?
- What are the causes and consequences of poverty?
- How has income inequality in the United States changed over time?
- How do **social insurance programs** like Social Security affect poverty and income inequality?
- Why is there debate over the size of the welfare state?
- What are the special concerns about **private health insurance** and how have governments acted to address them?

The **welfare state** is the collection of government programs designed to alleviate economic hardship.

A **government transfer** is a government payment to an individual or a family.

A **poverty program** is a government program designed to aid the poor.

A **social insurance program** is a government program designed to provide protection against unpredictable financial distress.

‖ Poverty, Inequality, and Public Policy

The term **welfare state** has come to refer to the collection of government programs that are designed to alleviate economic hardship. A large share of the government spending of all wealthy countries consists of **government transfers**—payments by the government to individuals and families—that provide financial aid to the poor, assistance to unemployed workers, guaranteed income for the elderly, and assistance in paying medical bills for those with large health care expenses.

The Logic of the Welfare State

There are three major economic rationales for the creation of the welfare state. We'll turn now to a discussion of each.

1. Alleviating Income Inequality Suppose that the Taylor family, which has an income of only $15,000 a year, receives a government check for $1,500, which might help them afford things that significantly improve their quality of life, such as a better place to live or a more nutritious diet. Also suppose that the Fisher family, which has an income of $300,000 a year, faces an extra tax of $1,500. This probably wouldn't make much difference to their quality of life: at worst, they might have to give up a few minor luxuries.

This hypothetical exchange illustrates the first major rationale for the welfare state: *alleviating income inequality*. Because a marginal dollar is worth more to a poor person than to a rich one, modest transfers from the rich to the poor will do the rich little harm but benefit the poor a lot. So, according to this argument, a government that plays Robin Hood, taking modest amounts from the rich to give to the poor, does more good than harm. As long as the amounts are relatively modest, the inefficiencies created by the transfers will be outweighed by the benefits to society. Programs that are designed to aid the poor are known as **poverty programs.**

2. Alleviating Economic Insecurity The second major rationale for the welfare state is *alleviating economic insecurity*. When bad things happen, such as a flood, or an illness, they almost always happen to a limited number of people. For example, during the devastating floods that hit Texas in 2017 millions of Texans were rendered homeless. But the floods left the rest of the United States unscathed.

Imagine 10 families, each of which can expect an income next year of $50,000 if nothing goes wrong. But suppose the odds are that something *will* go wrong for one of the families, although nobody knows which one. For example, suppose each of the families has a 1 in 10 chance of experiencing a sharp drop in income because one family member incurs large medical bills or their home is badly flooded. And assume that this event will produce severe hardship for the family—a family member will have to drop out of school or the family will lose its home.

Now suppose there's a government program that provides aid to families in distress, paying for that aid by taxing families that are having a good year. Arguably, this program will make all the families better off, because even families that don't currently receive aid from the program might need it at some point in the future. Each family will therefore feel safer knowing that the government stands ready to help when disaster strikes. Programs designed to provide protection against unpredictable financial distress are known as **social insurance programs.**

These two rationales for the welfare state, alleviating income inequality and alleviating economic insecurity, are closely related to the *ability-to-pay principle* we learned about in Chapter 7. Recall how the ability-to-pay principle is used to justify progressive taxation: it says that people with low incomes, for whom an additional dollar makes a big difference to economic well-being, should pay a smaller fraction of their income in taxes than people with higher incomes, for whom an additional dollar makes much less difference. The same principle suggests that those with very low incomes should actually get money back from the tax system.

3. Reducing Poverty and Providing Access to Health Care The third and final major rationale for the welfare state involves the *social benefits of poverty reduction and access to health care,* especially when applied to children of poor households. Researchers have documented that such children, on average, suffer lifelong disadvantage. Even after adjusting for ability, children from economically disadvantaged backgrounds are more likely to be underemployed or unemployed, engage in crime, and suffer chronic health problems—all of which impose significant social costs. So, according to the evidence, programs that help to alleviate poverty and provide access to health care generate external benefits to society.

More broadly, some political philosophers argue that principles of social justice demand that society take care of the poor and unlucky. Others disagree, arguing that welfare state programs go beyond the proper role of government. To an important extent, the difference between those two philosophical positions defines what we mean in politics by *liberalism* and *conservatism.*

But before we get carried away, it's important to realize that things aren't quite that cut and dried. Even conservatives who believe in limited government typically support some welfare state programs. And even economists who support the goals of the welfare state are concerned about the effects of large-scale aid to the poor and the unlucky on their incentives to work and save. Like taxes, welfare state programs can create substantial deadweight losses, so their true economic costs can be considerably larger than the direct monetary cost.

We'll turn to the costs and benefits of the welfare state later in this chapter. First, however, let's examine the problems the welfare state is supposed to address.

The Problem of Poverty

What, exactly, do we mean by poverty? Any definition is somewhat arbitrary. Since 1965, however, the U.S. government has maintained an official definition of the **poverty threshold,** a minimum annual income that is considered adequate to purchase the necessities of life. Families whose incomes fall below the poverty threshold are considered poor.

The official poverty threshold depends on the size and composition of a family and is adjusted every year to reflect changes in the cost of living. In 2018 the poverty threshold for an adult living alone was $12,140; for a household consisting of two adults and two children, it was $25,100.

Trends in Poverty

Although the United States as a whole has grown much richer over the past several decades, the orange line in Figure 18-1 shows the official U.S. **poverty rate**—the percentage of the U.S. population living below the poverty threshold—has not declined. The orange line in Figure 18-1 shows the poverty rate from 1967 to 2018. As you can see, since 1967 poverty has fluctuated up and down, with no clear trend over the long run. In 2018, the poverty rate was approximately the same as it had been during the 1960s, even though the United States as a whole was far richer.

In response to this surprising result, researchers have identified a number of limitations to the official poverty measure, of which the most important is that the definition of income doesn't actually include many forms of government aid. For example, it excludes the monetary value of food stamps. So the U.S. Census Bureau now releases a *Supplemental Poverty Measure* that includes income from

The **poverty threshold** is the annual income below which a family is officially considered poor.

The **poverty rate** is the percentage of the population living below the poverty threshold.

FIGURE 18-1 Trends in the U.S. Poverty Rate, 1967–2018

The official poverty rate has shown no clear trend since the late 1960s. However, an alternative measure, known as the supplemental poverty measure, or SPM, which most experts consider to be more accurate, has declined modestly.

Data from: U.S. Census Bureau; Fox, Liana, et al., NBER Report No. w19789.

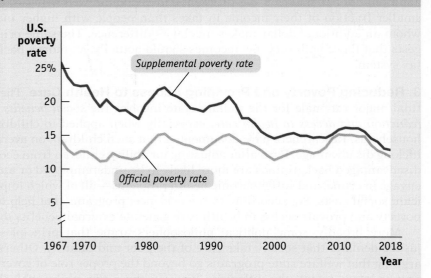

government aid, a measure that experts consider to be more accurate. The burgundy line in Figure 18-1 shows how the rate of poverty according to this measure has changed over time. While it shows more progress than the standard measure, the change is still surprisingly little considering that total real income in the United States has risen by more than 250%.

Who Are the Poor?

There's a widely held image of poverty in the United States: an African-American or Hispanic family with no husband present and the female head of the household unemployed at least part of the time. This picture isn't completely off base: poverty is disproportionately high among African-Americans and Hispanics as well as among female-headed households. But a majority of the poor don't fit the stereotype.

In 2018, 38.1 million Americans were in poverty—11.8% of the population, or slightly more than one in seven persons. Of those in poverty, the single largest group is non-Hispanic Whites, making up 41% of the total. Hispanics follow, representing 28% of those in poverty; then African-Americans at 23%, and Asians at 5%. However, African-Americans, Hispanics, and Asians are more likely to be poor than non-Hispanic Whites. And one-third of all people in poverty are children: about one of six children in the United States live in poverty.

There is also a correlation between family makeup and poverty. Female-headed families with no spouse present had a very high poverty rate: 24.9%. Married couples were much less likely to be poor, with a poverty rate of only 4.7%; still, about 39% of the families in poverty were in married households with both spouses present.

What really stands out in the data, however, is the association between poverty and inadequate employment. Adults who work full time are very unlikely to be poor: only 2.3% of full-time workers were poor in 2018. Many industries, particularly in the retail and service sectors, now rely primarily on part-time workers who typically lack benefits such as health plans, paid vacation days, and retirement benefits. These jobs also usually pay a lower hourly wage than comparable full-time work. As a result, many of the poor are members of what analysts call the *working poor:* workers whose incomes fall at or below the poverty threshold. The coronavirus pandemic illustrated many of the challenges that the working poor face: for financial reasons, choosing to work while sick or choosing to forgo medical care.

What Causes Poverty?

Poverty is often blamed on lack of education, and educational attainment clearly has a strong positive effect on income level—those with more education earn, on average, higher incomes than those with less education. For example, in 1979 the median weekly wage of men with a bachelor's degree was 29% higher than that of men with only a high school diploma; by 2019, the "college premium" had increased to 92%.

Lack of proficiency in English is also a barrier to higher income. For example, Mexican-born male workers in the United States—two-thirds of whom have not graduated from high school and many of whom have poor English skills—earn less than half of what native-born men earn.

And it's important not to overlook the role of racial and gender discrimination; although less pervasive today than 60 years ago, discrimination still erects formidable barriers to advancement for many Americans. Non-Whites earn less and are less likely to be employed than Whites with comparable levels of education. Studies find that African-American males suffer persistent discrimination by employers in favor of Whites, African-American women, and Hispanic immigrants. Women earn lower incomes than men with similar qualifications.

The United States has a high poverty rate compared to other rich countries.

Another important source of poverty that should not be overlooked is bad luck. Many families find themselves impoverished when a wage-earner loses a job, a family business fails, or a family member falls seriously ill.

Some of the bad luck that leads to poverty afflicts groups of people rather than individuals. In particular, there are high concentrations of poor Americans in geographic regions that have been left behind by economic change. Consider, for example, Harlan County, Kentucky, a former coal-mining center that has been left behind by changes in markets and technology. More than 40% of the county's residents—who are 96% White—are below the poverty line.

Consequences of Poverty

The consequences of poverty are often severe and long-lasting, particularly for children. Poverty is often associated with lack of access to health care, which can lead to health problems that erode the ability to attend school and work later in life. Affordable housing is also frequently a problem, leading poor families to move often, disrupting school and work schedules.

Recent medical studies have shown that children raised in severe poverty tend to suffer from lifelong learning disabilities. As a result, American children growing up in or near poverty tend to be at a disadvantage throughout their lives. Even talented children who come from poor families are unlikely to finish college.

A long-term survey conducted by the U.S. Department of Education tracked students, starting in eighth grade, according to ability and parental income and employment. Among students who scored in the top 25% on aptitude tests but who came from economically disadvantaged backgrounds, only 29% finished college. Equally talented students from families with higher incomes had a 74% chance of finishing. The results show that because children from less advantaged backgrounds are much less likely to complete the education they need to overcome poverty, to an important degree, poverty is self-perpetuating.

Economists Raj Chetty, John Friedman, and Nathaniel Hendren, of the Opportunity Insights Project of Harvard University, found that the geographic concentration of poverty is especially deleterious. Children who grow up in poor neighborhoods that have higher rates of unstable family structures have a much more difficult time escaping poverty. Neighborhoods with more stable family structures (lower divorce rates and higher marriage rates) tend to have higher levels of upward mobility regardless of whether a child is from a single-parent or two-parent family. In other words, the average family structure of the neighborhood counts more than the child's own family structure. In addition, neighborhoods with stronger support structures and role models of upward mobility also have higher rates of escape from poverty. As a result, according to the researchers, when poor children move to neighborhoods with more stable family structures, stronger support networks, and more role models, they are more likely to graduate from school and earn higher incomes. As Chetty comments, "One of the strongest patterns that emerges is that what you are exposed to as a child—in terms of career pathways, crime, marriage, etc.— impacts how you grow up."

Economic Inequality

The United States is a rich country. The average household income in 2018 was $90,021. How is it possible, then, that so many Americans still live in poverty? The answer is that income is unequally distributed, with many households earning much less than the average and others earning much more.

Table 18-1 shows the distribution of pre-tax income—income before federal income taxes are paid—among U.S. families in 2018, as estimated by the Census Bureau. Households are grouped into *quintiles*, each containing 20%, or one-fifth, of the population. The first, or bottom, quintile contains households whose income put them below the 20th percentile in income, the second quintile contains households whose income put them between the 20th and 40th percentiles, and so on.

For each group, Table 18-1 shows three numbers. The second column shows the income ranges that define the group. For example, in 2018, the bottom quintile consisted of households with annual incomes of less than $25,600, the next quintile of households had incomes between $25,601 and $50,000, and so on. The third column shows the average income in each group, ranging from $13,775 for the bottom fifth to $416,520 for the top 5%. The fourth column shows the percentage of total U.S. income received by each group.

TABLE 18-1 U.S. Income Distribution in 2018

Income group	Income ranges	Average income	Percent of total income
Bottom quintile	$25,600 and under	$13,775	3.1%
Second quintile	$25,601 to $50,000	37,293	8.3
Third quintile	$50,001 to $79,542	63,572	14.1
Fourth quintile	$79,543 to $130,000	101,570	22.6
Top quintile	$130,001 and over	233,895	52.0
Top 5%	$248,728 and over	416,520	23.1
Mean income = $90,021		Median income = $63,179	

Data from: U.S. Census Bureau.

Mean versus Median Household Income

At the bottom of Table 18-1 are two useful numbers for thinking about the incomes of American households. **Mean household income,** also called average household income, is the total income of all U.S. households divided by the number of households. **Median household income** is the income of a household in the exact middle of the income distribution—the level of income at which half of all households have lower income and half have higher income. It's very important to realize that these two numbers do not measure the same thing.

Economists often illustrate the difference by asking people first to imagine a room containing several dozen more or less ordinary wage-earners, then to think about what happens to the mean and median incomes of the people in the room if a Silicon Valley billionaire walks in. The mean income soars because the billionaire's income pulls up the average, but the median income hardly rises at all.

This example explains why economists regard median income as a better guide to the economic status of typical American families than mean income: mean income is strongly affected by the incomes of a relatively small number of very-high-income Americans, who are not representative of the population as a whole; median income is not.

Mean household income is the average income across all households.

Median household income is the income of the household lying at the exact middle of the income distribution.

What we learn from Table 18-1 is that income in the United States is quite unequally distributed. The average income of the poorest fifth, those in the bottom quintile, of families is less than a quarter of the average income of families in the middle, and the richest fifth, those in the top quintile, have an average income more than three times that of families in the middle. The incomes of the richest fifth of the population are, on average, about 17 times as high as those of the poorest fifth. In fact, the distribution of income in the United States has become more unequal since 1980, rising to a level that has made it a significant political issue. The upcoming Economics in Action discusses long-term trends in U.S. income inequality, which declined in the 1930s and 1940s, was stable for more than 30 years after World War II, but began rising again in the late 1970s.

It's important to note that the data in Table 18-1 overstate the true degree of inequality in the United States to some degree, for two reasons:

- Household incomes vary from year to year. In any given year, many households at the bottom of the income distribution are having a particularly bad year, just as many at the top are having a particularly good year. Their average incomes over a number of years aren't as unequal as those in a single year.

- Household incomes vary over the lifetime. Young people, and retired people, on average have lower income than people in their prime working years. So data that mixes people of different ages will show more income inequality than data that makes comparisons among people of similar ages.

Despite those qualifications, there is a considerable amount of genuine income inequality in the United States, and income has become considerably more unequal since 1980.

> The **Gini coefficient** is a number that summarizes a country's level of income inequality based on how unequally income is distributed across quintiles.

International Comparisons of Inequality

A good way to gain some perspective on the level of income inequality in the United States is to compare it to levels in other countries. To do that economists created the **Gini coefficient,** a measure of income inequality based on the type of data found in Table 18-1. Mathematically, a country's Gini coefficient can range from 0, indicating a perfectly equal distribution of income, to 1, indicating the most unequal distribution of income possible—one in which all the income goes to a single person.

Figure 18-2 shows recent estimates of the Gini coefficient for many of the world's countries. Countries with a high degree of income inequality have a Gini coefficient close to 0.5. Aside from a few countries in Africa, the highest levels of income inequality are found in Latin America, especially Brazil. Countries with a very equal income distribution have Gini coefficients around 0.25. The most equal distributions of income are in Europe, especially in Scandinavia. According to the most recent data, the United States has a Gini coefficient of 0.41. So, compared to other wealthy countries, the United States has unusually high inequality, though it isn't as unequal as Latin America. In 2016, the top 1% income bracket in the United States ($390,000 and up) garnered 20% of national income, compared to 6% in Denmark and 14% in Canada.

When Is Inequality a Problem?

Some level of income inequality in an economy is desirable. In a market-based economy, a significant share of the observed inequality will represent the economic reward to skill, effort, innovation, and education. Without such a reward, incentives would suffer and the economy would stagnate.

Yet high income inequality is a problem because it means that a significant share of a country's population is not sharing in the country's overall prosperity. In the United States, inequality has been rising for 40 years; it is the reason the poverty rate has not fallen even though the United States has become considerably richer. A further concern is how inequality is perpetuated across generations.

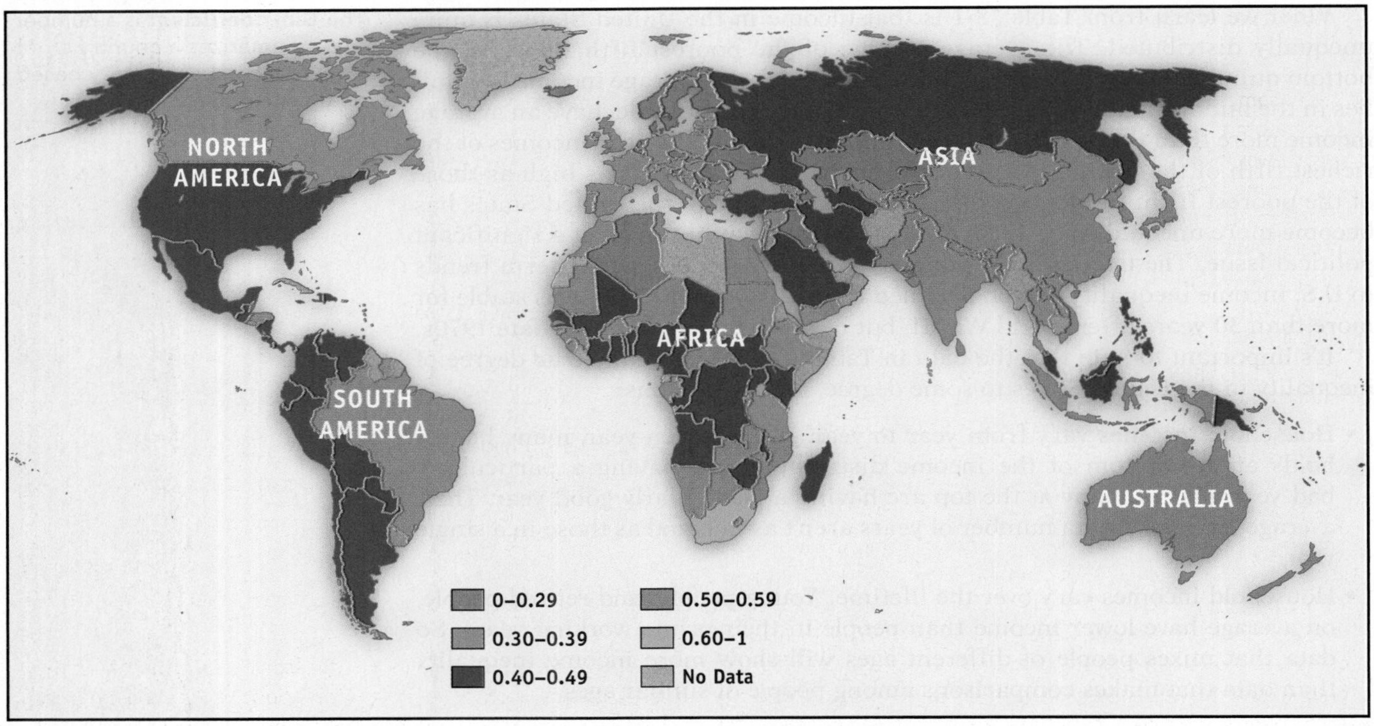

■ 0–0.29		■ 0.50–0.59	
■ 0.30–0.39		■ 0.60–1	
■ 0.40–0.49		■ No Data	

FIGURE 18-2 Income Inequality Around the World

The highest levels of income inequality are found in Africa and Latin America. The most equal distributions of income are in Europe, especially in Scandinavia. Compared to other wealthy countries, the States, with a Gini coefficient of 0.41, has unusually high inequality. (Gini coefficients are from 2008 to 2017.)

Data from: World Bank, *World Development Indicators,* 2019.

The children of poor parents are much more likely to be poor than the children of affluent parents—a correlation that is stronger in the United States than in other rich countries.

Extreme inequality can hurt a nation's long-term economic prospects if, as is often the case, it limits opportunities. Those born into low-income families may fail to receive adequate nutrition and health care, limiting their productivity as adults; they may also lack access to education and job opportunities, limiting their ability to make contributions to economic growth. In some cases, high inequality also contributes to social and political instability, which further damages a nation's economic performance.

Economic Insecurity

As we stated earlier, although the rationale for the welfare state rests in part on the social benefits of reducing poverty and inequality, it also rests in part on the benefits of reducing economic insecurity, which afflicts even relatively well-off families.

One form economic insecurity takes is the risk of a sudden loss of income, which usually happens when a family member loses a job and either spends an extended period without work or is forced to take a new job that pays considerably less. For example, in the wake of the COVID-19 pandemic in the spring of 2020, the unemployment rate jumped from less than 5% to nearly 15%. And economic inequality sharply increased as 40% of low-income Americans (those with incomes below $40,000) reported losing their jobs, while only 13% of households with incomes over $100,000 reported a job loss. Moreover, a third of those who lost their jobs or had their wages cut said they couldn't cover their monthly expenses.

Even if a family doesn't face a loss in income, it can face a surge in expenses. Until implementation of the Affordable Care Act in 2014, the most common reason for such a surge was a medical problem that required expensive treatment, such as heart disease or cancer. Estimates show that 60% of personal bankruptcies in the United States in 2009 were due to medical expenses.

GLOBAL COMPARISON   INCOME, REDISTRIBUTION, AND INEQUALITY IN RICH COUNTRIES

Spend some time traveling around the United States, then spend some more time traveling around Denmark. You'll almost surely come away with the impression that Denmark has substantially less income inequality than the United States, that the rich aren't as rich and the poor aren't as poor. And the numbers confirm this impression: the Gini coefficient for Denmark, and indeed for most of Western Europe, is substantially lower than in the United States. But why?

The answer, to an important extent, is the role of government. Even in the United States, government plays a significant role in redistributing income away from those with the highest incomes to those who earn the least. But European nations have substantially bigger welfare states than we do, and do a lot more income redistribution.

The accompanying figure shows two measures of the Gini coefficient for a number of rich countries. (The figure focuses on households in which everyone is under 60, because differences in retirement ages skew results among older families.) A country with a perfectly equal income distribution—one in which every household had the same income—would have a Gini coefficient of zero. At the other extreme, a country in which all of the income goes to one household would have a Gini coefficient of 1. For each country, the purple bars show the actual Gini, a measure of the observed inequality in income before taxes and transfers are made. The orange bars show what each country's Gini would be after taxes and transfers are made. It turns out that the inequality of market incomes in Denmark is somewhat lower than that in the United States, but much of the difference in observed inequality is the result of Denmark's bigger welfare state.

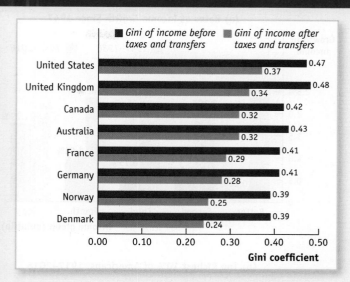

There are some caveats to this conclusion. On one side, the data are unlikely to do a very good job of tracking very high incomes, which are probably a bigger factor in the United States than elsewhere. On the other side, European welfare states may indirectly increase measured income inequality through their effects on incentives. Still, the data strongly suggest that differences in inequality among rich countries reflect different policies as well as differences in the underlying economic situation.

Data from: Janet C. Gornick and Branko Milanovic, "Income Inequality in the United States in Cross-National Perspective: Redistribution Revisited," Luxembourg Income Study Center, May 4, 2015.

ECONOMICS >> *in Action*
Long-Term Trends in Income Inequality in the United States

Does inequality tend to rise, fall, or stay the same over time? The answer is yes—all three. Over the course of the past century, the United States has gone through periods characterized by all three trends: an era of falling inequality during the 1930s and 1940s, an era of stable inequality for about 35 years after World War II, and an era of rising inequality over the past 40 years.

Detailed U.S. data on income by quintiles, as shown in Table 18-1, are available starting in 1947. Panel (a) of Figure 18-3 shows the annual rate of growth of income, adjusted for inflation, for each quintile over two periods: from 1947 to 1980, and from 1980 to 2018. There's a clear difference between the two periods. In the first period, income within each group grew at about the same rate—that is, there wasn't much change in the inequality of income, just growing incomes across the board.

After 1980, however, incomes grew much more quickly at the top than in the middle, and more quickly in the middle than at the bottom. So inequality has increased substantially since 1980. Overall, inflation-adjusted income for families in the top quintile rose 83% between 1980 and 2018, significantly more than the 10% increase experienced by families in the bottom quintile.

FIGURE 18-3 Trends in U.S. Income Inequality

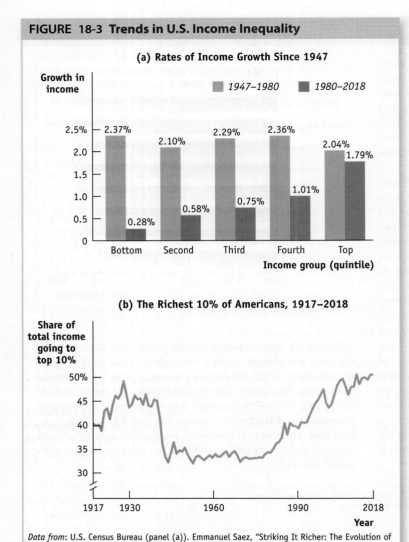

(a) Rates of Income Growth Since 1947

Growth in income

1947–1980   1980–2018

Income group (quintile)	1947–1980	1980–2018
Bottom	2.37%	0.28%
Second	2.10%	0.58%
Third	2.29%	0.75%
Fourth	2.36%	1.01%
Top	2.04%	1.79%

(b) The Richest 10% of Americans, 1917–2018

Share of total income going to top 10%

50%
45
40
35
30

1917 1930 1960 1990 2018

Year

Data from: U.S. Census Bureau (panel (a)). Emmanuel Saez, "Striking It Richer: The Evolution of Top Incomes in the United States." University of California, Berkeley, discussion paper, 2008 (updated 2019)(panel (b)).

Although detailed data on income distribution aren't available before 1947, economists have used other information, such as income tax data, to estimate the share of income going to the top 10% of the population all the way back to 1917. Panel (b) of Figure 18-3 shows this measure from 1917 to 2018. These data, like the more detailed data available since 1947, show that American inequality was more or less stable between 1947 and the late 1970s but has risen substantially since.

The longer-term data also show, however, that the relatively equal distribution of 1947 was something new. In the late nineteenth century, often referred to as the Gilded Age, American income was very unequally distributed. This high level of inequality persisted into the 1930s. But inequality declined sharply between the late 1930s and the end of World War II. In a famous paper, Claudia Goldin and Robert Margo, two economic historians, dubbed this narrowing of income inequality *the Great Compression*.

The Great Compression roughly coincided with World War II, a period during which the U.S. government imposed special controls on wages and prices. Evidence indicates that these controls were applied in ways that reduced inequality—for example, it was much easier for employers to get approval to increase the wages of their lowest-paid employees than to increase executive salaries. What remains puzzling is that the equality imposed by wartime controls lasted for decades after those controls were lifted in 1946.

As we've already seen, inequality has increased substantially since the 1970s. In fact, pre-tax income appears to be as unequally distributed in the United States today as it was in the 1920s, prompting many commentators to describe the current state of the nation as a new Gilded Age—albeit one in which the effects of inequality are moderated by taxes and the existence of the welfare state.

There is intense debate among economists about the causes of this widening inequality. The most popular explanation is rapid technological change, which has increased the demand for highly skilled or talented workers more rapidly than the demand for other workers, leading to a rise in the wage gap between the highly skilled and other workers. Growing international trade may also have contributed by allowing the United States to import labor-intensive products from low-wage countries rather than making them domestically, reducing the demand for less skilled American workers and depressing their wages. Rising immigration may be yet another source. On average, immigrants have lower education levels than native-born workers and increase the supply of low-skilled labor while depressing low-skilled wages.

However, these explanations fail to account for one key feature: much of the rise in inequality doesn't reflect a rising gap between highly educated workers and those with less education but rather growing differences among highly educated workers themselves. For example, schoolteachers and top business executives have similarly high levels of education, but executive paychecks have risen dramatically and teachers' salaries have not. For some reason, a few super-stars—a group that includes literal superstars in the entertainment world but also such groups as Wall Street traders and top corporate executives—now earn much higher incomes than was the case a generation ago. It's still unclear what caused the change.

>> Check Your Understanding 18-1

Solutions appear at back of book.

1. Indicate whether each of the following programs is a poverty program or a social insurance program.
   a. A pension guarantee program, which provides pensions for retirees if they have lost their employment-based pension due to their employer's bankruptcy
   b. The federal program known as SCHIP, which provides health care for children in families that are above the poverty threshold but still have relatively low income
   c. The Section 8 housing program, which provides housing subsidies for low-income households
   d. The federal flood program, which provides financial help to communities hit by major floods

2. Recall that the poverty threshold is not adjusted to reflect changes in the standard of living. As a result, is the poverty threshold a relative or an absolute measure of poverty? That is, does it define poverty according to how poor someone is relative to others or according to some fixed measure that doesn't change over time? Explain.

3. The accompanying table gives the distribution of income for a very small economy.
   a. What is the mean income? What is the median income? Which measure is more representative of the income of the average person in the economy? Why?
   b. What income range defines the first quintile? The third quintile?

	Income
Sephora	$39,000
Kelly	17,500
Raul	900,000
Vijay	15,000
Oskar	28,000

4. Which of the following statements more accurately reflects the principal source of rising inequality in the United States today?
   a. The salary of the manager of the local branch of Sunrise Bank has risen relative to the salary of the neighborhood gas station attendant.
   b. The salary of the CEO of Sunrise Bank has risen relative to the salary of the local branch bank manager, although the two have similar education levels.

|| The U.S. Welfare State

In 2019 the U.S. welfare state consisted of three huge programs (Social Security, Medicare, and Medicaid); several other fairly big programs, including the Affordable Care Act, Temporary Assistance for Needy Families, food stamps, and the Earned Income Tax Credit; and a number of smaller programs. Table 18-2 shows one useful way to categorize the programs existing in 2019, along with spending on each listed program.

First, the table distinguishes between programs that are **means-tested** and those that are not. In means-tested programs, benefits are available only to families or individuals whose income or wealth falls below some minimum. Basically, means-tested programs are poverty programs designed to help only those with low incomes. By contrast, non-means-tested programs provide their benefits to everyone, although, as we'll see, they tend in practice to reduce income inequality.

Second, the table distinguishes between programs that provide monetary transfers that beneficiaries can spend as they choose and those that provide

>> Quick Review

• **Welfare state** programs, which include **government transfers,** absorb a large share of government spending in wealthy countries.

• The ability-to-pay principle explains one rationale for the welfare state: alleviating income inequality. **Poverty programs** do this by aiding the poor. **Social insurance programs** address a second rationale: alleviating economic insecurity. The external benefits to society of poverty reduction and access to health care, especially for children, is a third rationale for the welfare state.

• The official U.S. **poverty threshold** is adjusted yearly to reflect changes in the cost of living but not in the average standard of living. But even though average income has risen significantly, the U.S. **poverty rate** is no lower than it was 50 years ago.

• The causes of poverty can include lack of education, the legacy of racial and gender discrimination, and bad luck. The consequences of poverty are dire for children.

• **Median household income** is a better indicator of typical household income than **mean household income.** A comparison of **Gini coefficients** across countries shows that the United States has less income inequality than poor countries but more than all other rich countries.

• The United States has seen both declining and increasing income inequality. Since 1980, income inequality has increased substantially, largely due to increased inequality among highly educated workers.

A **means-tested** program is a program available only to individuals or families whose incomes fall below a certain level.

TABLE 18-2 Major U.S. Welfare State Programs, 2019

	Monetary transfers	In-kind
Means-tested	Temporary Assistance for Needy Families: $20.7 billion	Food stamps: $71.2 billion
	Supplemental Security Income: $53.0 billion	Medicaid: $418.7 billion
	Earned Income Tax Credit: $60.6 billion	Affordable Care Act: $48.9 billion
Not means-tested	Social Security: $1,041.2 billion	Medicare: $644.9 billion
	Unemployment insurance: $26.8 billion	

Data from: Office of Management and Budget and Congressional Budget Office; all data is the projected amount for 2019.

One of every seven Americans receives food stamps, officially known as SNAP.

An **in-kind benefit** is a benefit given in the form of goods or services.

A **negative income tax** is a program that supplements the income of low-income working families.

in-kind benefits, which are given in the form of goods or services rather than money. As the numbers suggest, in-kind benefits are dominated by Medicare and Medicaid, which pay for health care. We'll discuss health care in the next section of this chapter. For now, let's examine the other major programs.

Means-Tested Programs

When people use the term *welfare*, they're often referring to monetary aid to poor families. The main source of such monetary aid in the United States is Temporary Assistance for Needy Families, or TANF. This program does not aid everyone who is poor; it is available only to poor families with children and only for a limited period of time.

TANF was introduced in the 1990s to replace a highly controversial program known as Aid to Families with Dependent Children, or AFDC. The older program was widely accused of creating perverse incentives for the poor, including encouraging family breakup. Partly as a result of the change in programs, the benefits of modern "welfare" are considerably less generous than those available a generation ago, once the data are adjusted for inflation. Also, TANF contains time limits, so welfare recipients—even single parents—must eventually seek work. As you can see from Table 18-2, TANF is a relatively small part of the modern U.S. welfare state.

Other means-tested programs, though more expensive, are less controversial. The Supplemental Security Income program aids disabled Americans who are unable to work and have no other source of income. The food stamp program, or SNAP—officially the Supplemental Nutrition Assistance Program, since it now provides debit cards rather than stamps—helps low-income families and individuals, who can use those debit cards to buy food staples but not other items.

Finally, economists use the term **negative income tax** for a program that supplements the earnings of low-income working families. The United States has a program known as the Earned Income Tax Credit (EITC), which provides additional income to millions of workers. It has become more generous as traditional welfare has become less generous. Only workers who earn income are eligible for the EITC. Over a certain range of incomes, the more a worker earns, the higher the amount of EITC received. In 2019, married couples with two children would receive a tax credit equal to 40% of their income up to $14,550. For 2019, the EITC is capped at $5,828. (Payments were slightly lower for single-parent families or workers without children.) The EITC starts to phase out at incomes over $24,800. As of 2019, the payment ceased at an income of $52,493 for married couples with two children.

Social Security and Unemployment Insurance

Social Security, the largest program in the U.S. welfare state, is a non-means-tested program that guarantees retirement income to qualifying older Americans. It also provides benefits to workers who become disabled and "survivor benefits" to family members of workers who die.

Social Security is supported by a dedicated tax on wages: the Social Security portion of the payroll tax pays for Social Security benefits. The benefits workers receive on retirement depend on their taxable earnings during their working years: the more you earn up to the maximum amount subject to Social Security taxes ($132,900 in 2019), the more you receive in retirement. Benefits are not, however, strictly proportional to earnings. Instead, they're determined by a formula that gives high earners more than low earners, but with a sliding scale that makes the program relatively more generous for low earners.

Because most seniors don't receive pensions from their former employers and most don't own enough assets to provide them with a living, Social Security benefits are an enormously important source of income for them. At least 50% of married couples and 70% of unmarried persons 65 and older rely on Social Security for more than half their income. Social Security accounts for at least 90% of income for 21% of married couples and 45% of unmarried persons over 65. In most cases, these people have no income at all except for Social Security.

Unemployment insurance, although normally a much smaller amount of government transfers than Social Security, is another key social insurance program. It provides workers who lose their jobs with about 35% of their previous salary until they find a new job or until 26 weeks have passed. Like Social Security, unemployment insurance is not means-tested.

President Franklin D. Roosevelt signed the Social Security Act in 1935, creating the modern welfare state.

The Effects of the Welfare State on Poverty and Inequality

The U.S. welfare state redistributes income from those with higher incomes and wealth to those with less. Government statistics show that this redistribution significantly reduces the U.S. poverty rate. However, statistics show only the *direct* effect of taxes and transfers, not the *indirect* effect, such as changes in behavior. For example, we know that many older Americans who are now retired would instead be working if they didn't receive Social Security checks. Yet, the statistics can't capture this effect. As a result, statistics reveal only a partial indicator of the effects of the welfare state. Nonetheless, the results are striking.

Table 18-3 shows how a number of government programs affected the poverty rate, as measured by the Supplemental Poverty Measure, for the population as a whole and for different age groups in 2012 (the most current data available). For each program it shows the amount, in percentage points,

TABLE 18-3 Effects of Government Programs on Reducing the Rate of Poverty, 2012

	All people	Children	Nonelderly adults	65 years and older
Social Security	8.56%	1.97%	4.08%	39.86%
Refundable Tax Credits	3.02	6.66	2.25	0.20
SNAP (food stamps)	1.62	3.01	1.27	0.76
Unemployment insurance	0.79	0.82	0.88	0.31
Supplemental Security Income	1.07	0.84	1.12	1.21
Housing subsidies	0.91	1.39	0.66	1.12
School lunch	0.38	0.91	0.25	0.03
Temporary Assistance for Needy Families	0.21	0.46	0.14	0.05
WIC (Women, Infants, and Children)	0.13	0.29	0.09	0.00

Data from: Council of Economic Advisers.

TABLE 18-4 Effects of Taxes and Transfers on Income Distribution, 2016

Quintiles	Share of aggregate income without taxes and transfers	Share of aggregate income with taxes and transfers
Bottom quintile	3.8%	7.7%
Second quintile	8.9	11.1
Third quintile	13.6	14.7
Fourth quintile	20.5	20.3
81st–99th percentiles	38.5	35.1
Top 1%	15.8	12.5

Data from: Congressional Budget Office.

FIGURE 18-4 Poverty Rates in the Great Recession

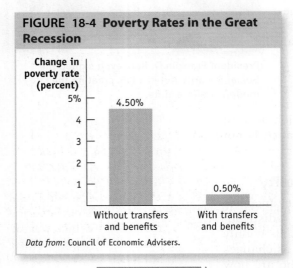

Data from: Council of Economic Advisers.

> **Quick Review**

• **Means-tested** programs are designed to reduce poverty, but non-means-tested programs do so as well. Programs are classified according to whether they provide monetary or **in-kind benefits.**

• "Welfare," or TANF, is far less generous today than a generation ago due to concerns about its effect on incentives to work and family breakup. The **negative income tax** addresses these concerns: it supplements the incomes of only low-income working families.

• Social Security, the largest program in the U.S. welfare state, is a non-means-tested program that provides retirement income for the elderly. Unemployment insurance is also a key social insurance program that is not means-tested.

• Overall, the American welfare state is redistributive. It increases the share of income going to the poorest 80% while reducing the share going to the richest 20%.

by which that group's poverty rate was reduced by the program. For example, it shows that without Social Security, the poverty rate among older Americans would have been almost 40 percentage points higher than it was.

Table 18-4 shows a Congressional Budget Office estimate of the effect of taxes and transfers on the share of aggregate income going to each quintile of the income distribution in 2016 (the latest available date). The effect of government programs was to increase the share of income going to the poorest 80% of the population, especially the share going to the poorest 20%, while reducing the share of income going to the richest 20%.

ECONOMICS >> *in Action*
Welfare State Programs and Poverty Rates in the Great Recession, 2007–2010

In 2007 the U.S. economy entered a deep downturn, the worst since the 1930s. Recovery officially began in 2009, but it was slow and disappointing. It took over six years for both average and median family income, adjusted for inflation, to return to pre-recession levels.

Given this poor economic performance, you might have expected to see a sharp rise in poverty, and the official poverty rate did in fact move up, as you can see in Figure 18-4. But while the Great Recession and its aftermath certainly hurt many American families, the country never seemed as desperate as it did during the Great Depression, or even during the last big slump, in 1981–1982. And sure enough, the Supplemental Poverty Measure, which most experts consider a better measure of economic hardship, rose only slightly. Why?

The main answer, it turns out, was antipoverty programs, which automatically expanded during the slump and were further reinforced by legislation that temporarily expanded food stamps and other forms of aid. Figure 18-4 shows an estimate of how much the poverty rate would have risen between 2007 and 2010 in the absence of welfare state programs, compared with how much it actually rose. Without transfers and benefits the poverty rate would have risen by 4.50%; but with transfers and benefits it rose only 0.50%. The U.S. welfare state didn't prevent the slump or stop people from losing their jobs or homes. But it did strikingly limit the rise in poverty.

> **Check Your Understanding 18-2**
Solutions appear at back of book.

1. Explain how the negative income tax avoids the disincentive to work that characterizes poverty programs that simply give benefits based on low income.

2. According to Table 18-3, what effect does the U.S. welfare state have on the overall poverty rate? On the poverty rate for those aged 65 and over?

The Economics of Health Care

A large part of the welfare state, in both the United States and other wealthy countries, is devoted to paying for health care. In most wealthy countries, the government pays between 70% and 80% of all medical costs. The private sector plays a larger role in the U.S. health care system. Yet even in the United States the government pays roughly half of all health care costs; furthermore, it indirectly subsidizes private health insurance through the federal tax code.

Figure 18-5 shows who paid for U.S. health care in 2018. Only 12% of health care consumption spending (all spending on health care except investment in health care buildings and facilities) was expenses "out of pocket"—that is, paid directly by individuals. Most health care spending, 88%, was paid for by some kind of insurance. Of this 88%, considerably less than half was private insurance; the rest was some kind of government insurance, mainly Medicare and Medicaid. To understand why, we need to examine the special economics of health insurance.

The Need for Health Insurance

In 2018, U.S. personal health care expenses were $11,121 per person—17.8% of gross domestic product. This did not, however, mean that the typical American spent nearly $10,000 on medical treatment. In fact, in any given year half the population incurs only minor medical expenses. But a small percentage of the population faces huge medical bills, with 10% of the population typically accounting for almost two-thirds of medical costs.

Is it possible to predict who will have high medical costs? To a limited extent, yes: there are broad patterns to illness. For example, the elderly are more likely to need expensive surgery or drugs than the young. But the fact is that anyone can suddenly need very expensive medical treatment, costing many thousands of dollars in a very short time—far beyond what most families can easily afford. Yet nobody wants to be unable to afford such treatment if it becomes necessary. As a result, most people would like to be covered by *health insurance*—insurance that covers the costs of medical bills.

The Problem with Private Health Insurance Under **private health insurance,** each member of a large pool of individuals agrees to pay a fixed amount annually (called a *premium*) into a common fund that is managed by a private company, which then pays most of the medical expenses of the pool's members. The problem with private health insurance is that it is subject to market failure. Let's examine why.

People typically don't want to purchase health insurance until they are already sick, to avoid paying premiums when they are healthy. But, as a result, the average person who purchases a private health insurance policy is sicker and has higher medical expenses than the average person who does not. Premiums have to be raised to account for the higher medical expenses, which in turn leads more of the relatively healthy insured people to stop buying insurance and leave the pool. Without some type of intervention, this dynamic continues for more rounds until only extremely sick people are left in the pool. In some cases this means that the private insurance company collapses, unable to charge high enough premiums to cover its medical cost outlays. Economists call this phenomenon the *private health insurance market death spiral.*

Private health insurers employ several methods to counteract the death spiral: refusing insurance to anyone who had any sign of a preexisting medical

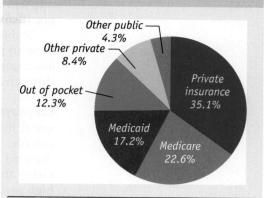

FIGURE 18-5 Who Paid for U.S. Health Care in 2018?

- Other public 4.3%
- Other private 8.4%
- Out of pocket 12.3%
- Private insurance 35.1%
- Medicaid 17.2%
- Medicare 22.6%

In the United States in 2018, insurance paid for 88% of health care consumption costs: the sum of 35.1% (private insurance), 22.6% (Medicare), 17.2% (Medicaid), 8.4% (other private), and 4.3% (other public). The percentage paid for by private insurance, 35.1%, was a uniquely high number among advanced countries. Even so, substantially more U.S. health care was paid for by Medicare, Medicaid, and other government programs than by other means. (Total may not add up to 100 due to rounding.)

Data from: Department of Health and Human Services Centers for Medicare and Medicaid Services.

Under **private health insurance,** each member of a large pool of individuals pays a fixed amount annually to a private company that agrees to pay most of the medical expenses of the pool's members.

condition; dropping coverage of those who did develop an illness while insured; and refusing to cover some procedures such as delivering a baby. But these methods leave a significant number of people uninsured—particularly those with preexisting conditions, who need it most.

So how do people get health insurance when private insurance markets perform so poorly? There are three principal ways: employment-based health insurance; government health insurance; and government intervention in the market through the Affordable Care Act.

Employment-Based Health Insurance Private insurers can avoid the death spiral by selling insurance indirectly, to peoples' employers rather than to individuals. The advantage of *employment-based health insurance* is that employees enrolled are likely to be a representative mix of healthy and less healthy people, rather than a group of people who want insurance because they expect to incur high medical bills. This is especially true if the employer is a large company with thousands of workers. Employers require their employees to participate in the company health insurance plan because allowing employees to opt out (which healthier ones will be tempted to do) raises the cost of providing insurance for everyone else.

There's another reason employment-based health insurance is widespread in the United States: it gets special, favorable tax treatment. Workers pay taxes on their paychecks, but workers who receive health insurance from their employers don't pay taxes on the value of the benefit. So employment-based health insurance is, in effect, subsidized by the U.S. tax system. Economists estimate the value of this subsidy at about $150 billion each year.

However, many working Americans don't receive employment-based health insurance. Those who aren't covered include most older Americans, because relatively few employers offer workers insurance that continues after they retire; the many workers whose employers don't offer coverage (especially part-time workers); and the unemployed.

Government Health Insurance Table 18-5 shows the breakdown of health insurance coverage across the U.S. population in 2018. A majority of Americans, 178 million people, received health insurance through their employers. The majority of those who didn't have private insurance were covered by two government programs, Medicare and Medicaid. (The numbers don't add up because some people have more than one form of coverage. For example, many recipients of Medicare also have supplemental coverage either through Medicaid or private policies.)

Medicare, financed by payroll taxes, is available to all Americans 65 and older, regardless of their income and wealth. You can get an idea of how much difference Medicare makes to the finances of elderly Americans by comparing the median income per person of Americans 65 and older—$43,696—with average annual Medicare payments per recipient, which were more than $13,000 in 2018. As with health care spending in general, however, the average can be misleading: in a given year, about 7% of Medicare recipients account for 50% of the costs.

TABLE 18-5 Number of Americans Covered by Health Insurance, 2018 (millions)	
Covered by private health insurance	**217.8**
Employment-based	178.4
Direct purchase	34.9
Covered by government	**111.3**
Medicaid	57.7
Medicare	57.8
Military health care	11.4
Uninsured/not covered	**27.5**

Data from: U.S. Census Bureau.

Unlike Medicare, Medicaid is a means-tested program, paid for with federal and state government revenues. There's no simple way to summarize the criteria for eligibility because it is partly paid for by state governments and each state sets its own rules. Of the nearly 57.7 million Americans covered by Medicaid in 2018, 35 million were children under 18 and many of the rest were parents of children under 19. Most of the cost of Medicaid, however, is accounted for by a small number of older Americans, especially those needing long-term care.

More than 11.4 million Americans receive health insurance as a consequence of military service. Unlike Medicare and Medicaid, which pay medical bills but don't deliver health care directly, the Veterans Health Administration, which has more than 9 million clients, runs hospitals and clinics around the country.

The U.S. health care system, then, offers a mix of private insurance, mainly from employers, and public insurance of various forms. Most Americans have health insurance either from private insurance companies or through various forms of government insurance. Yet in 2012, before the implementation of the Affordable Care Act—which extended health insurance to many previously uninsured Americans—almost 48 million, or 15.4% of the population, had no health insurance at all.

"For me, crime pays for what Medicare doesn't cover."

Health Care in Other Countries

Health care is one area in which the United States is very different from other wealthy countries. In fact, we're distinctive in three ways. First, we rely much more on private health insurance than any other wealthy country does. Second, we spend much more on health care per person. Third, even after passage of the Affordable Care Act, we remain the only wealthy country in which substantial numbers of people lack health insurance.

Table 18-6 compares the United States with three other wealthy countries: Britain, Canada, and Switzerland. Each of these countries takes a very different approach to providing health care.

In Britain, most health care is provided directly by a government agency, the National Health Service (NHS). The NHS operates hospitals and pays most doctors' salaries. Medical care is provided free of charge. In the United States the Veterans Health Administration operates similarly—though on a smaller scale—providing care to veterans through a network of hospitals and clinics.

Canada has a **single-payer system:** a health care system in which the government acts as the principal payer of medical bills funded through taxes. For comparison, Medicare is essentially a single-payer system for older Americans—and the Canadian system is, in fact, called Medicare.

Finally, Switzerland has a somewhat complex system in which all citizens are required to purchase insurance from nonprofit insurance organizations, with lower-income individuals receiving government subsidies to help them afford the premiums.

Britain, Canada, and Switzerland provide health insurance to all their citizens; the United States does not. Yet all three spend much less on health care per person than we do. Many Americans assume this must mean that foreign health

TABLE 18-6 Health Care Systems in Advanced Countries, 2018				
	Government share of health care spending	Health care spending per capita (US$, purchasing power parity)	Life expectancy (total population at birth, years)	Infant mortality (deaths per 1,000 live births)
United States	40.4%	$10,586	78.5	5.60
Britain	77.1	4,069	81.4	3.64
Canada	69.7	4.974	82.8	4.30
Switzerland	63.7	7,317	83.3	3.70

Data from: OECD, World Bank, and CMS.gov.

A **single-payer system** is a health care system in which the government is the principal payer of medical bills funded through taxes.

care is inferior in quality. But many health care experts disagree with the claim that the health care systems of other wealthy countries deliver poor-quality care. As they point out, other wealthy countries generally match or exceed the United States in many measures of health care provision, such as the number of doctors, nurses, and hospital beds per 100,000 people. It's true that U.S. medical care includes more advanced technology in some areas and many more expensive surgical procedures. U.S. patients also have shorter waiting times for elective surgery than patients in Canada or Britain. But some countries with low health spending have very short waiting times.

Surveys of patients seem to suggest that there are no significant differences in the quality of care received by patients in Canada, Europe, and the United States. And as Table 18-6 shows, the United States does considerably worse than other advanced countries in terms of basic measures such as life expectancy and infant mortality, although our poor performance on these measures may have causes other than the quality of medical care—notably our relatively high levels of poverty and income inequality.

So why does the United States spend so much more on health care than other wealthy countries? Some of the disparity is the result of higher doctors' salaries, but most studies suggest that this is a secondary factor. One possibility is that Americans are getting better care than their counterparts abroad, but in ways that don't show up in either surveys of patient experiences or statistics on health performance.

However, the most likely explanation is that the U.S. system has suffered from serious inefficiencies that other countries manage to avoid. Critics of the U.S. system emphasize the fact that its reliance on private insurance companies made it highly fragmented, as individual insurance companies each expended resources on overhead and on activities such as marketing and trying to identify and weed out high-risk patients, leading to high operating costs. On average, the operating costs of private health insurers consume 14% of the premiums clients pay, leaving only 86% to spend on providing health care.

By contrast, Medicare spends only 3% of its funds on operating costs, leaving 97% to spend on health care. A study by the McKinsey Global Institute found that the United States spends almost six times as much per person on health care administration as other wealthy countries. Americans also pay higher prices for prescription drugs because, in other countries, government agencies bargain with pharmaceutical companies to receive lower drug prices.

Recognition of the serious inefficiencies in the U.S. system, along with a steep rise in the number of uninsured, led to the passage of the Affordable Care Act by Congress.

The Affordable Care Act

In 2010 Congress passed the Affordable Care Act (ACA), which went fully into effect in 2014. At the time, the U.S. health care system was clearly in trouble. One source of the trouble was the rapid growth in the uninsured. The percentage of working-age Americans without health insurance grew from 1997 to 2010, peaking with almost a quarter of working-age Americans uninsured. Most of the uninsured were low-wage workers, employed at jobs that lacked health insurance benefits, and unable to afford private insurance on their own.

Meanwhile, health care spending was rising rapidly, leading to sharply higher insurance premiums. In fact, health care spending has tripled as a share of U.S. income since 1965. The ACA was the largest expansion of the American welfare state since the creation of Medicare and Medicaid in 1965. It had two major objectives: covering the uninsured and controlling costs. Let's look at each in turn.

Covering the Uninsured The ACA moved to cover the uninsured in two ways. First, it expanded eligibility for Medicaid, covering most of the expense for states that were willing to expand Medicaid to cover everyone up to 133% of the poverty line. (As of 2019, 37 states including the District of Columbia had expanded Medicaid; Virginia, which we featured in the opening story, voted for expansion in 2018.)

Second, the ACA moved to make private insurance available to more Americans. On one side, insurance companies were prohibited from denying insurance or charging higher premiums to people with preexisting medical conditions. On the other, many lower- and middle-income households were given subsidies to make insurance more affordable.

Cost Control Before the ACA, private insurers had high operating costs due to the amounts they spent on marketing and weeding out high-cost applicants. But because the ACA eliminated insurers' ability to spend resources on weeding out applicants, it has the potential to increase efficiency.

The ACA also contained a number of additional measures, many of them involving Medicare, intended to help control health care costs. Health care providers were encouraged to band together to form "accountable care organizations," coordinating care in ways that save money; organizations that did so would receive a share of the savings. Hospitals were encouraged to provide effective care by rules that reduced payments to hospitals whose patients tend to be readmitted at high rates. Special taxes on "Cadillac" health insurance—extremely generous plans—aimed to discourage excessive treatment. And the ACA eliminated copayments for preventive care, in the hope that patients would be encouraged to take care of medical issues before they required expensive treatment.

As it turns out, the rate at which health costs were rising slowed sharply around 2010, just as the ACA was passed. It's unclear how much of this cost slowdown was caused by the law's provisions.

Effects of the ACA

Although the Affordable Care Act was passed in 2010, its most important provisions didn't take effect until the beginning of 2014. By 2017, however, its main effects were clear.

The first effect can be seen in Figure 18-6, which shows the percentage of the working-age population that is uninsured. This percentage began dropping after 2010, partly because of a recovering economy, but also because some provisions of the ACA went into effect, notably a rule allowing Americans under the age of 26 to remain on their parents' policies. And after 2013, with the law in full effect, the number of uninsured fell sharply. By 2017 the percent of working-age adults without health insurance had been cut almost in half.

Yet a sizable number of people remain uninsured. The law does not cover undocumented immigrants, and a significant number of states have chosen not to accept the federally funded expansion of Medicaid, leaving several million people in a *gap* where they receive neither Medicaid nor subsidies to buy private insurance. So progress toward covering the uninsured has been substantial but incomplete.

Furthermore, in 2017 Republicans in Congress succeeded in repealing one important

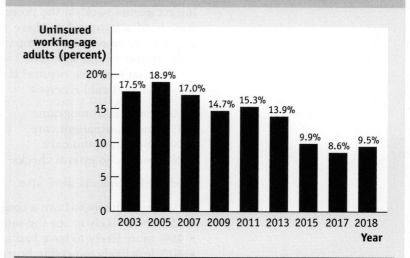

FIGURE 18-6 Uninsured Working-Age Americans, 2003–2018

Before the ACA was implemented, the share of uninsured working-age adults, those that were employed full-time, was rising dramatically. Since the ACA's implementation, the share has fallen sharply.
Data from: U.S. Census.

provision of the ACA, the requirement that all legal residents have insurance, although the rest of the law remained intact. This change is generally believed to have driven up premiums, because fewer healthy people signed up, although many beneficiaries were insulated from this premium increase thanks to the subsidies mandated by the law. Some states, like New Jersey, imposed their own requirements that residents have coverage, and saw premiums drop noticeably. But in states that didn't do this, the move probably led to a significant fall in the number of insured Americans, seen in the slight uptick for uninsured rates in 2018.

ECONOMICS >> *in Action*
What Medicaid Does

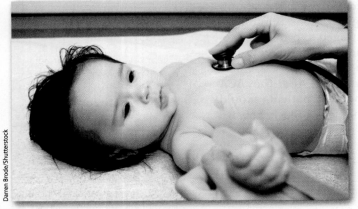

Medicaid has been shown to make a big difference in the well-being of recipients.

Do social insurance programs actually help their beneficiaries? The answer isn't always as obvious as you might think. Take the example of Medicaid, which provides health insurance to low-income Americans. Some skeptics about the program's effectiveness have argued that in the absence of Medicaid, the poor would still find ways to get essential health care, and that there is no clear evidence that receiving Medicaid actually leads to better health.

Testing such assertions is tricky. You can't just compare people who are on Medicaid with people who aren't, since the program's beneficiaries differ in many ways from those who aren't on the program. And we don't normally get to do controlled experiments in which otherwise comparable groups receive different government benefits.

Once in a while, however, events provide the equivalent of a controlled experiment—and that's what happened with Medicaid. In 2008, the state of Oregon—which had sharply curtailed its Medicaid program because it lacked sufficient funds—found itself with enough money to put some but not all deserving recipients back on the program. To allocate the limited number of slots, the state used a lottery. And there you had it: in effect, a controlled experiment, in which researchers could compare a random sample of people receiving Medicaid with similar people who didn't win the lottery.

So what were the results? It turned out that Medicaid made a big difference. Those on Medicaid received:

- 60% more mammograms
- 35% more outpatient care
- 30% more hospital care
- 20% more cholesterol checks

Medicaid recipients were also:

- 70% more likely to have a consistent source of care
- 55% more likely to see the same doctor over time
- 45% more likely to have had a Pap test within the last year (for women)
- 40% less likely to need to borrow money or skip payment on other bills because of medical expenses
- 25% more likely to report themselves in "good" or "excellent" health
- 15% more likely to use prescription drugs
- 15% more likely to have had a blood test for high blood sugar or diabetes
- 10% less likely to screen positive for depression

In short, Medicaid led to major improvements in access to medical care and in the well-being of those receiving it. So although there is a valid debate over the size of a state's Medicaid program because it costs taxpayers a significant amount of money, the Oregon results show that one criticism of Medicaid—the claim that it doesn't work at all—isn't valid.

>> Check Your Understanding 18-3

Solutions appear at back of book.

1. If you are enrolled in a four-year degree program, it is likely that you are required to enroll in a health insurance program run by your school unless you can show proof of existing insurance coverage.
    a. Explain how you and your parents benefit from this health insurance program even though, given your age, it is unlikely that you will need expensive medical treatment.
    b. Explain how your school's health insurance program avoids the problem of the adverse selection death spiral faced by private insurance.

2. According to its critics, what accounts for the higher costs of the U.S. health care system compared to those of other wealthy countries?

‖ The Debate over the Welfare State

The goals of the welfare state seem laudable: to help the poor, protect against severe economic hardship, and ensure access to essential health care. But good intentions don't always make for good policy. There is an intense debate about how large the welfare state should be, partly reflecting differences in philosophy but also reflecting concern about the possibly counterproductive effects on incentives of welfare state programs. Disputes about the size of the welfare state are one of the defining issues of modern American politics.

Problems with the Welfare State

There are two different arguments against the welfare state. One is based on philosophical concerns about the proper role of government. Some political theorists believe that redistributing income is not a legitimate role of government. Rather, they believe that government's role should be limited to maintaining the rule of law, providing public goods, and managing externalities.

The more conventional argument against the welfare state involves the trade-off between efficiency and equity. As we've learned, the *ability-to-pay-principle*—the argument that an extra dollar of income matters more to a less well-off individual than to a more well-off individual—implies that the government can help the poor at relatively little cost to the well-off. But this redistribution of income from well-off to poor requires that the well-off be taxed more heavily, paying a higher percentage of their income in taxes than those with lower incomes. This is the principle behind progressive taxation.

As a result, the goals of the welfare state must be balanced against the efficiency costs of higher tax rates on the well-off that can reduce their incentive to work hard or make risky investments. A progressive tax system, then, tends to make society as a whole somewhat poorer, and could hurt even those the system was intended to help. A larger welfare state requires higher tax revenue and higher tax rates than a smaller welfare state, which restricts itself to mainly providing public goods such as national defense. So in making policy that affects the size of the welfare state, government must make a trade-off between efficiency versus equity.

>> Quick Review

• Health insurance satisfies an important need because expensive medical treatment is unaffordable for most families. **Private health insurance** has an inherent problem: those who buy insurance are disproportionately sicker than the average person, which drives up costs and premiums, leading more healthy people to forgo insurance, further driving up costs and premiums and ultimately leading private insurance companies to fail. Employment-based health insurance, the way most Americans are covered, avoids this problem altogether.

• The majority of Americans not covered by private insurance are covered by Medicare, which is a non-means-tested **single-payer system** for those over 65, and Medicaid, which is means-tested.

• Compared to other wealthy countries, the United States depends more heavily on private health insurance, has higher health care spending per person, higher administrative costs, and higher drug prices, but without clear evidence of better health outcomes.

• Health care costs everywhere are increasing rapidly due to medical progress. The 2010 ACA legislation was designed to address the large and growing share of American uninsured and to reduce the rate of growth of health care spending.

One way to reduce the cost of the welfare state is to means-test benefits: make them available only to those who need them. But means-testing creates a different kind of trade-off between equity and efficiency. Consider the following example: Suppose there is some means-tested benefit, worth $2,000 per year, that is available only to families with incomes of less than $20,000 per year. Now suppose that a family currently has an income of $19,500 but that one family member is deciding whether to take a new job that will raise the family's income to $20,500. Well, taking that job will actually make the family worse off because it will gain $1,000 in earnings but lose the $2,000 in government benefits. This effect is known as a *benefits notch*.

Unless means-testing is carefully designed, poor families can face a large fall in their effective income when their income rises to the level at which they are no longer eligible for benefits, reducing their incentive to work. One 2005 study found that a family of two adults and two children that raised its income from $20,000 a year — just above the poverty threshold in 2005 — to $35,000 would find almost all its increase in after-tax income offset by loss of benefits such as food stamps, the Earned Income Tax Credit, and Medicaid.

The Politics of the Welfare State

During the French Revolution of the eighteenth century, France was governed by the Legislative Assembly, a congress of representatives seated according to social class: the upper classes, who pretty much liked the way things were, sat on the right; commoners, who wanted big changes, sat on the left. Ever since, political commentators refer to politicians as being on the "right" (more conservative) or on the "left" (more liberal).

Today, U.S. politicians also fall on a "right-left" divide, and they mainly disagree about the appropriate size of the welfare state. The debate over the ACA was an example, with the vote on the bill breaking down entirely according to party lines — Democrats (on the left) in favor of the ACA and Republicans (on the right) opposed.

You might think that it's a huge oversimplification to say political debate is really about just one thing — how big to make the welfare state. But political scientists have found that once you carefully rank members of Congress from right to left on past legislation, a congressperson's position in that ranking is a very good predictor of that person's votes on future legislation.

The same studies also show that American politics has become more polarized. Forty years ago, there was a substantial overlap between the parties: some Democrats were to the right of some Republicans, or, if you prefer, some Republicans were to the left of some Democrats. Today, however, the rightmost Democrats appear to be to the left of the leftmost Republicans.

Can economic analysis help resolve this political conflict? Only up to a point. Some of the political controversy involves differences in opinion about the trade-offs we have just discussed: if you believe that the disincentive effects of more generous benefits and higher taxes are very large, you will look less favorably on welfare state programs than if you believe they're fairly small. Economic analysis, by improving our knowledge of the facts, can help resolve some of these differences. Yet some of the disagreements over the welfare state are the result of a misunderstanding of economics — for example, how health insurance markets work. And some of the conflict is based on a misunderstanding of how economic policy is made. For example, it is important to realize that a promise to maintain social programs cannot be met if, at the same time, cuts will be made to the tax revenue those programs depend upon.

To an important extent, however, differences of opinion on the size of the welfare state reflect differences in values and philosophy. And those are differences economics can't resolve.

ECONOMICS >> *in Action*

The Not-So Melancholy Danes?

The United States has the smallest welfare state of any major advanced economy. Denmark has one of the largest. As a result, Denmark has much higher social spending than the United States as a percentage of total national income, and Danish citizens face much higher tax rates than Americans. One argument against a large welfare state is that it has negative effects on efficiency. Does Danish experience support this argument?

On the face of it, the answer would seem to be a clear yes. Table 18-7 shows that Danish GDP per capita—the total value of the economy's output, divided by the total population—is about 16% lower than GDP per capita in the United States. But is the size of the Danish welfare state responsible for that difference, and is lower Danish GDP per capita a sign of trouble?

Not necessarily. Once one looks at the sources of relatively low Danish GDP, a more nuanced picture emerges.

As a matter of basic arithmetic, GDP per capita reflects three factors:

- The fraction of the population that is employed
- How much the average worker produces in an hour
- The number of hours each worker works

With one of the largest welfare states in the world, Denmark guarantees health care for all its citizens.

TABLE 18-7 Difference Between Denmark and the United States, in Percent (2017)

GDP per capita	−16%
Employed share of population	+7%
Productivity	−1%
Hours worked	−20%

Data from: Total Economy Database.

So Danes are actually slightly more likely to be employed than Americans (7% more likely) and they basically have the same productivity (1% more productive). The reason Denmark has lower GDP per capita than we do (16% lower) is that employed Danes work fewer hours over the course of a year (20% fewer). This in turn largely reflects deliberate policy: where Americans take fewer vacations than citizens of any other wealthy country, Danish employers are legally required to give employees 5 weeks of paid leave each year, and the country's strong union movement has in many cases negotiated additional time off.

This deliberate choice puts a different spin on Denmark's lower GDP per capita, since it's not at all clear that trading off somewhat less income for more time with one's family or other pursuits is a bad deal. For what it's worth, surveys that ask how satisfied people are with their lives rank Denmark consistently high—and consistently above the United States.

To be fair, it's not clear that every country would do as well with a huge welfare state as Denmark appears to. But in Denmark, the welfare state seems to work.

>> Check Your Understanding 18-4

Solutions appear at back of book.

1. Explain how each of the following policies creates a disincentive to work or undertake a risky investment.
   a. A high sales tax on consumer items
   b. The complete loss of a housing subsidy when yearly income rises above $25,000

2. Over the past 40 years, has the polarization in Congress increased, decreased, or stayed the same?

>> Quick Review

- Intense debate on the size of the welfare state centers on philosophy and on equity-versus-efficiency concerns. The high marginal tax rates needed to finance an extensive welfare state can reduce the incentive to work. Holding down the cost of the welfare state by means-testing can also cause inefficiency by creating high effective marginal tax rates for benefit recipients.

- Politics is often depicted as an opposition between left and right; in the modern United States, that division mainly arises from three sources: differences in views on the size of the equity-versus-efficiency trade-off, a misunderstanding of economics, and philosophical differences.

- Studies show that American politics has become more polarized between left and right. Economics can help resolve some but not all of the political conflict. Economic analysis can help determine the facts when there are disagreements about the size of the terms of a trade-off. However, economics cannot help when differences are based on a basic misunderstanding of economics.

Can the Entrepreneurial Spirit of the United States Survive Threats to the ACA?

Fedor Selivanov/Shutterstock

In 2016, Stinson Dean faced a critical decision. A savvy trader employed by a firm that traded lumber as a commodity, Dean could see that the lumber market was ripe for a dramatic upswing as the home construction industry recovered from the housing bust. Yet to personally profit from that upswing, he would have to quit his job and open his own firm.

But becoming an entrepreneur carried significant risk. By going out on his own, he would have to sacrifice the employer-provided health insurance that covered him, his wife, and their three young children. In making his decision, Dean declared: "One of the things I wasn't willing to risk was the health of my family." In fact, the tendency of workers to stay in a job that they would rather leave for fear of losing their health care benefits is so pervasive that economists have a term for it: *job lock*.

In the end, Dean made the jump because he was able to purchase affordable health insurance for himself and his family through the ACA. And the move paid off as the surge in home construction boosted Dean's business far beyond his expectations.

In fact, business was so good that, by 2017, Dean wanted to expand and hire three or four new people. However, by that time congressional threats to repeal the ACA generated a stumbling block not only to his expansion plans, but to his future as an entrepreneur in the long run.

"What that's doing for me is preventing me to convince folks who are in a similar situation to where I was—a nice corporate job, making good money, with great benefits, with kids—convincing them to leave that to come to work for me with no benefits," he says. As a result, in 2017, Dean was having trouble convincing others to take a chance and come work for him. Moreover, he wondered whether he would eventually be forced to close his firm and resume his corporate job in order to assure health insurance for his family.

QUESTIONS FOR THOUGHT

1. A recent study of employees with chronic health conditions who have employer-provided health care coverage found that these workers were 40% less likely to leave their jobs than similar employees without chronic health conditions. A RAND Corporation study found that making health insurance more accessible to individuals could increase self-employment and entrepreneurship in the United States by a third. What pattern would you expect to see in the size and number of newly created companies after the implementation of the ACA compared to before?

2. Historically, small businesses and entrepreneurs have been more innovative than larger companies. What does this imply for the rate of innovation in the United States before implementation of the ACA? After? And what would you expect now that the ACA has come under threat?

SUMMARY

1. The **welfare state** absorbs a large share of government spending in all wealthy countries. **Government transfers** are the payments made by the government to individuals and families. **Poverty programs** alleviate income inequality by helping the poor; **social insurance programs** alleviate economic insecurity. Welfare state programs also deliver external benefits to society through poverty reduction and improved access to health care, particularly for children.

2. Despite the fact that the **poverty threshold** is adjusted according to the cost of living but not according to the standard of living, and that the average American income has risen substantially over the last 30 years, the **poverty rate,** the percentage of the population with an income below the poverty threshold, is no lower than it was 30 years ago. There are various causes of poverty: lack of education, the legacy of discrimination, and bad luck. The consequences of poverty are particularly harmful for children, resulting in more chronic disease, lower lifetime earnings, and higher rates of criminality.

3. **Median household income,** the income of a family at the center of the income distribution, is a better indicator of the income of the typical household than **mean household income** because it is not distorted by the inclusion of a small number of very wealthy households. The **Gini coefficient,** a number that summarizes a country's level of income inequality based on how unequally income is distributed across quintiles, is used to compare income inequality across countries.

4. Both **means-tested** and non-means-tested programs reduce poverty. The major **in-kind benefits** programs are Medicare and Medicaid, which pay for medical care. Due to concerns about the effects on incentives to work and on family cohesion, aid to poor families has become significantly less generous even as the **negative income tax** has become more generous. Social Security, the largest U.S. welfare state program, has significantly reduced poverty among the elderly. Unemployment insurance is also a key social insurance program.

5. Health insurance satisfies an important need because most families cannot afford expensive medical treatment. **Private health insurance,** unless it is employment-based or carefully screens applicants, has the potential to fall into an adverse selection death spiral. Most Americans are covered by employment-based private health insurance; the majority of the remaining are covered by Medicare (a **single-payer system** for those 65 and over in which the government pays for most medical bills from tax revenue) or Medicaid (for those with low incomes).

6. Compared to other countries, the United States relies more heavily on private health insurance and has substantially higher health care costs per person without clearly providing better care. Health care costs are rising as medicine has become more advanced. The rising number of uninsured and the financial distress caused by lack of insurance prompted the passage in 2010 of the Affordable Care Act, or ACA. Its objective is to reduce the number of uninsured and reduce the rate of growth of health care costs.

7. Debates over the size of the welfare state are based on philosophical and equity-versus-efficiency considerations. The equity-versus-efficiency debate arises from the fact that an extensive welfare state requires high taxes on the well-off, which can diminish society's wealth by reducing their incentive to work and make risky investments. Means-testing of benefits can reduce the cost of the welfare state but must be carefully designed to avoid reducing the incentive to work by the poor.

8. Politicians on the left tend to favor a bigger welfare state and those on the right to oppose it. American politics has become more polarized in recent decades. Differences arise from views on the size of the equity-versus-efficiency trade-off, misunderstandings about how markets work, and philosophical differences.

KEY TERMS

Welfare state, p. 516
Government transfer, p. 516
Poverty program, p. 516
Social insurance program, p. 516
Poverty threshold, p. 517
Poverty rate, p. 517
Mean household income, p. 520
Median household income, p. 520
Gini coefficient, p. 521
Means-tested, p. 525
In-kind benefit, p. 526
Negative income tax, p. 526
Private health insurance, p. 529
Single-payer system, p. 531

PRACTICE QUESTIONS

1. In this question you are going to explore the trends in income inequality across countries. Go to the World Inequality Database, wid.world and select "Country Graphs." Open up the data for Finland and the Netherlands.

   a. Compare the income shares in each country for the most recent year of data. What do you notice?

   b. How has inequality changed over time?

   c. How does the after-tax income distribution differ from the pre-tax distribution?

   d. How does the trend compare with that of the United States?

   e. Explore other countries in the database.

2. Using the World Inequality Database, wid.world, from the previous question select the data for the United States. In the upper left corner of the page is an option to "select a subregion" or state. Select the data for California, Indiana, Michigan, and New York.

   a. What are the current values of the income share for the top 10% and 1% of earners for each state?

   b. How has share of income going to the top income earners changed over time for each state?

   c. What are the likely factors that explain the increase in income going to the top of the distribution across these three states? What factors explain the difference across states today?

3. A recent feature in the *New York Times*, "How Working-Class Life Is Killing Americans, in Charts," shows a substantial increase in the *Deaths of Despair*, deaths from drugs, alcohol, and suicide. In 2000, the death rate from these causes for Whites, under 50, without a college degree was less than 50 deaths per 100,000 people. By 2017, the death rate has increased by nearly 300%. Meanwhile, the death rate for those with a college degree was significantly lower in 2000, less than 20 deaths per 100,000 people. The death rate for those with a college degree has increased but by only 40%. How have changes to the welfare state contributed to the rise in the deaths by despair? What policies would you advocate to help reduce the deaths of despair?

PROBLEMS

1. The accompanying table contains data on the U.S. economy for the years 1983 and 2019. The second column shows the poverty threshold. The third column shows the consumer price index (CPI), a measure of the overall level of prices. And the fourth column shows U.S. gross domestic product (GDP) per capita, a measure of the standard of living.

Year	Poverty threshold	CPI (1982–1984 = 100)	GDP per capita
1983	$5,180	99.6	$15,525
2019	13,064	255.7	65,212

Data from: U.S. Census Bureau; Bureau of Labor Statistics; Bureau of Economic Analysis.

   a. By what factor has the poverty threshold increased from 1983 to 2019? That is, has it doubled, tripled, and so on?

   b. By what factor has the CPI increased from 1983 to 2019? That is, has it doubled, tripled, and so on?

   c. By what factor has GDP per capita increased from 1983 to 2019? That is, has it doubled, tripled, and so on?

   d. What do your results tell you about how people officially classified as "poor" have done economically relative to other U.S. citizens?

2. In the city of Metropolis, there are 100 residents, each of whom lives until age 75. Residents of Metropolis have the following incomes over their lifetime: Through age 14, they earn nothing. From age 15 until age 29, they earn 200 metros (the currency of Metropolis) per year. From age 30 to age 49, they earn 400 metros. From age 50 to age 64, they earn 300 metros. Finally, at age 65 they retire and are paid a pension of 100 metros per year until they die at age 75. Each year, everyone consumes whatever their income is that year (that is, there is no saving and no borrowing). Currently, 20 residents are 10 years old, 20 residents are 20 years old, 20 residents are 40 years old, 20 residents are 60 years old, and 20 residents are 70 years old.

   a. Study the income distribution among all residents of Metropolis. Split the population into quintiles according to their income. How much income does a resident in the lowest quintile have? In the second, third, fourth, and top quintiles? What share of total income of all residents goes to the residents in each quintile? Construct a table showing the share of total income that goes to each quintile. Does this income distribution show inequality?

   b. Now look only at the 20 residents of Metropolis who are currently 40 years old, and study the income distribution among only those residents. Split those 20 residents into quintiles according to their income. How much income does a resident in the lowest quintile have? In the second, third, fourth, and top quintiles? What share of total income of all 40-year-olds goes to the residents in each quintile? Does this income distribution show inequality?

   c. What is the relevance of these examples for assessing data on the distribution of income in any country?

3. The accompanying table presents data from the U.S. Census Bureau on median and mean income of male workers for the years 1972 and 2018. The income figures are adjusted to eliminate the effect of inflation.

Year	Median income	Mean income
	(in 2018 dollars)	
1972	$40,102	$46,481
2018	41,615	61,180

Data from: U.S. Census Bureau.

a. By what percentage has median income changed over this period? By what percentage has mean income changed over this period?

b. Between 1972 and 2018, has the income distribution become less or more unequal? Explain.

4. There are 100 households in the economy of Equalor. Initially, 99 of them have an income of $10,000 each, and one household has an income of $1,010,000.

a. What is the median income in this economy? What is the mean income?

Through its poverty programs, the government of Equalor now redistributes income: it takes $990,000 away from the richest household and distributes it equally among the remaining 99 households.

b. What is the median income in this economy now? What is the mean income? Has the median income changed? Has the mean income changed? Which indicator (mean or median household income) is a better indicator of the typical Equalorian household's income? Explain.

5. The country of Marxland has the following income tax and social insurance system. Each citizen's income is taxed at an average tax rate of 100%. A social insurance system then provides transfers to each citizen such that each citizen's after-tax income is exactly equal. That is, each citizen gets (through a government transfer payment) an equal share of the income tax revenue. What is the incentive for one individual citizen to work and earn income? What will the total tax revenue in Marxland be? What will be the after-tax income (including the transfer payment) for each citizen? Do you think such a tax system that creates perfect equality will work?

6. The tax system in Taxilvania includes a negative income tax. For all incomes below $10,000, individuals pay an income tax of –40% (that is, they receive a payment of 40% of their income). For any income above the $10,000 threshold, the tax rate on that additional income is 10%.

Scenarios	
1	Lowani earns income of $8,000
2	Midram earns income of $40,000
3	Hi-Wan earns income of $100,000

a. For each scenario in the table, calculate the amount of income tax to be paid and after-tax income.

b. Can you find a situation in this tax system where earning more pre-tax income actually results in less after-tax income? Explain.

7. In the city of Notchingham, each worker is paid a wage rate of $10 per hour. Notchingham administers its own unemployment benefit, which is structured as follows: If you are unemployed (that is, if you do not work at all), you get unemployment benefits (a transfer from the government) of $50 per day. As soon as you work for only one hour, the unemployment benefit is completely withdrawn. That is, there is a notch in the benefit system.

a. How much income does an unemployed person have per day? How much daily income does an individual who works four hours per day have? How many hours do you need to work to earn just the same as if you were unemployed?

b. Will anyone ever accept a part-time job that requires working four hours per day, rather than being unemployed?

c. Suppose that Notchingham now changes the way in which the unemployment benefit is withdrawn. For each additional dollar an individual earns, $0.50 of the unemployment benefit is withdrawn. How much daily income does an individual who works four hours per day now have? Is there an incentive now to work four hours per day rather than being unemployed?

8. The accompanying table shows data on the total number of people in the United States and the number of all people who were uninsured, for selected years from 2005 to 2017. It also shows data on the total number of poor children in the United States—those under 18 and below the poverty threshold—and the number of poor children who were uninsured.

Year	Total people	Uninsured people	Total poor children	Uninsured poor children
	(millions)			
2005	293.8	44.8	12.9	8.0
2007	299.1	45.7	13.3	8.1
2009	304.3	50.7	15.5	7.5
2011	308.8	48.6	16.1	7.0
2013	313.1	41.8	15.8	5.4
2015	318.4	29.0	14.5	4.5
2017	322.5	28.5	12.8	3.8

Data from: U.S. Census Bureau.

For each year, calculate the percentage of all people who were uninsured and the percentage of poor children who were uninsured. How have these percentages changed over time? What is a possible explanation for the change in the percentage of uninsured poor children?

9. The American National Election Studies conducts periodic research on the opinions of U.S. voters. The accompanying table shows the percentage of people, in selected years from 1952 to 2016, who agreed with the statement "There are important differences in what the Republicans and Democrats stand for." What do these data say about the degree of partisanship in U.S. politics over time?

Year	Agree with statement
1952	50%
1972	46
1992	60
2004	76
2008	78
2012	81
2016	85

Data from: American National Election Studies.

10. For this Discovering Data exercise, go to FRED (fred.stlouisfed.org) to create a line graph that compares poverty rates for different counties across the United States. In the search bar enter "Estimated Percent of People of All Ages in Poverty for United States" and select the subsequent series. Follow the steps below to add the series for additional counties. Then answer the questions that follow.

   I. Select "Edit Graph" and under "Add Line" enter "Estimated Percent of People in Poverty for Wayne County, MI," which includes Detroit, Michigan.

   II. Repeat step I to add the following counties:

   i. King County, WA (for Seattle, Washington)

   ii. Miami-Dade County, FL (for Miami, Florida)

   iii. San Francisco County/City, CA (for San Francisco, California)

   iv. Cuyahoga County, OH (for Cleveland, OH)

III. In the graph frame change the start date to 1997-01-01 and the end date to 2014-01-01.

   a. Which counties have the lowest poverty rates? Highest? How do poverty rates compare to the national average?

   b. How has the difference in poverty rates changed from 2004 (prior to the Great Recession) to 2012 (after the Great Recession)?

   c. Create a second line graph including "Estimated Percent of People of All Ages in Poverty for United States" and a second line with your home county. How does the poverty rate in your home county compare with that of the national average?

11. In a private insurance market, there are two different kinds of people: some who are more likely to require expensive medical treatment and some who are less likely to require medical treatment and who, if they do, require less expensive treatment. One health insurance policy is offered, tailored to the average person's health care needs: the premium is equal to the average person's medical expenses (plus the insurer's expenses and normal profit).

   a. Explain why such an insurance policy is unlikely to be feasible.

   In an effort to avoid the adverse selection death spiral, a private health insurer offers two health insurance policies: one that is intended for those who are more likely to require expensive treatment (and therefore charges a higher premium) and one that is intended for those who are less likely to require treatment (and therefore charges a lower premium).

   b. Could this system overcome the problem created by adverse selection?

   c. How does the British National Health Service avoid these problems?

19 Factor Markets and the Distribution of Income

THE VALUE OF A DEGREE

DOES HIGHER EDUCATION PAY? Yes, it does: in the modern economy, employers are willing to pay a premium for workers with more education. And the size of that premium has increased a lot over the last few decades. In 2019, Americans with four-year college degrees made 85% more per week on average than those without a degree. That percentage is up from 72% in 2004, and 45% in the early 1980s. In fact, according to David Autor, a professor of economics at MIT, the true cost of a college degree is approximately *negative* $500,000. That is, a college degree is cheaper than free.

In other words, not getting a college degree will cost you about half a million dollars over your lifetime. That's roughly double what the negative cost was 35 years ago. And because having a bachelor's degree is so valuable, more Americans than ever are getting one: in 2019, 39% of those aged 25 to 29 had at least a bachelor's degree, compared to 24.7% in 1995.

Who decided that the wages of workers with a four-year college degree would be so much more than for workers without one? The answer, of course, is that nobody decided it. Wage rates are prices, the prices of different kinds of labor; and they are decided, like other prices, by supply and demand.

Still, there is a qualitative difference between the wage rate of high school grads and the price of used textbooks: the wage rate isn't the price of a *good,* it's the price of a *factor of production.* And although markets for factors of production are in many ways similar to those for goods, there are also some important differences.

In this chapter, we examine *factor markets,* the markets in which the factors of production such as labor, land, and capital are traded. Factor markets, like markets for goods and services, play a crucial role in the economy: they allocate productive resources to producers and help ensure that those resources are used efficiently.

We begin by describing the major factors of production and the demand for factors of production, which leads to a crucial insight: the *marginal productivity theory of income distribution.* We then consider some challenges to the marginal productivity theory and examine the markets for capital and for land. The chapter concludes with a discussion of the supply of the most important factor, labor. ●

If you have doubts about completing college, consider this: not getting a college degree will cost you about half a million dollars over your lifetime.

WHAT YOU WILL LEARN

- How are resources like land, labor, **physical capital,** and **human capital** traded in factor markets, and how does this determine the **factor distribution of income?**

- What is the **marginal productivity theory of income distribution?**

- What are the sources of wage disparities, and what is the role of discrimination?

- How does market power affect labor markets?

- How do decisions about **time allocation** determine labor supply?

Physical capital—often referred to simply as *capital*—consists of manufactured productive resources such as equipment, buildings, tools, and machines.

Human capital is the improvement in labor created by education and knowledge that is embodied in the workforce.

|| The Economy's Factors of Production

You may recall that we have already defined a factor of production in Chapter 2 in the context of the circular-flow diagram of the economy: it is any resource that is used by firms to produce goods and services for consumption by households. Factors of production are bought and sold in *factor markets*, and the prices in factor markets are known as *factor prices*.

What are these factors of production, and why do factor prices matter?

The Factors of Production

Economists divide factors of production into four principal classes: land, labor, physical capital, and human capital. Land is a resource provided by nature; labor is the work done by human beings.

In Chapter 9 we defined *capital*: it is the value of the assets that are used by a firm in producing its output. There are two broad types of capital. **Physical capital**—often referred to simply as *capital*—consists of manufactured resources such as equipment, buildings, tools, and machines.

In the modern economy, **human capital,** the improvement in labor created by education and knowledge, and embodied in the workforce, is at least equally significant. The importance of human capital has increased greatly because of the progress of technology, which has made a high level of technical knowledge essential to many jobs—one cause of the increased premium paid for workers with advanced degrees.

Why Factor Prices Matter: The Allocation of Resources

Factor markets and factor prices play a key role in one of the most important processes that must take place in any economy: the allocation of resources among producers. As we will see, it is through the allocation of resources that an economy decides what and how much to produce.

To see how factor markets operate in the allocation of an economy's resources, consider Midland, Texas, which is at the heart of the new Texas oil boom. During the oil boom of 2016 to 2019, employment in Midland rose 24%, six times the growth in America as a whole, led by surging employment in the oil fields.

What ensured that workers came to Midland? The factor market: the high demand for workers drove up wages, not just for those directly employed in the oil fields, but for those providing services to those workers, like barbers. In fact, by 2019 barbers willing to move to Midland could earn as much as $180,000 a year. In other words, the markets for factors of production—oil field workers and barbers in this example—allocate the factors of production to where they are needed. In this sense factor markets are similar to goods markets, which allocate goods among consumers. But there are two features that make factor markets special. The first is that demand in a factor market is called *derived demand;* that is, demand for the factor is derived from a firm's output choice. This is different from demand in a market for goods. The second feature is that factor markets are where most of us get the largest shares of our income (government transfers being the next largest source of income in the economy).

Factor Incomes and the Distribution of Income

Most American families get most of their income in the form of wages and salaries—that is, they get their income by selling their own labor. Some people, however, get most of their income from physical capital: when you own stock in a company, what you really own is a share of that company's physical capital. And some people get much of their income from rents earned on land they own.

As a consequence, then, the prices of factors of production have a major impact on how the economic pie is sliced among different groups. For example, a higher wage rate, other things equal, means that a larger proportion of the

PITFALLS

WHAT IS A FACTOR? WHAT ISN'T?

Imagine a business that produces shirts. It will make use of workers and machines—that is, of labor and capital. But it will also use other inputs, such as electricity and cloth. Are all of these inputs factors of production? No: labor and capital are factors of production, but cloth and electricity are not.

The key distinction to remember: a factor of production earns income from the selling of its services over and over again but an input cannot.

A worker earns income over time from repeatedly selling their efforts; the owner of a machine earns income over time from repeatedly selling the use of that machine. So a factor of production, such as labor and capital, represents an enduring source of income.

An input like electricity or cloth, however, is used up in the production process. Once exhausted, it cannot be a source of future income for its owner.

economy's total income goes to people who derive their income from labor, and less goes to those who derive their income from capital or land. Economists refer to how the economic pie is sliced as the *distribution of income*. Specifically, factor prices determine the **factor distribution of income**—how the total income of the economy is divided among labor, land, and capital.

As the following Economics in Action explains, the factor distribution of income in the United States has been relatively stable over the past few decades. In other times and places, however, large changes have taken place in the factor distribution. One notable example: during the Industrial Revolution, the share of total income earned by English landowners fell sharply, while the share earned by English capital owners rose. As explained in the For Inquiring Minds, this shift had a profound effect on society.

> The **factor distribution of income** is the division of total income among labor, land, and capital.

ECONOMICS >> *in Action*
The Factor Distribution of Income in the United States

When we talk about the factor distribution of income, what are we talking about in practice?

In the United States, as in all advanced economies, payments to labor account for most of the economy's total income. Figure 19-1 shows the factor distribution of income in the United States in 2019: in that year, 68.9% of total income in the economy took the form of *compensation of employees*—a number that includes both wages and benefits such as health insurance. This number is somewhat low by historical standards (it was 72.1% in 1972 and 70.2% in 2007). It reflects the slow recovery after the Great Recession where unemployment and wage rates took more than five years to return to pre-recession levels.

However, measured wages and benefits don't capture the full income of "labor" because a significant fraction of total income in the United States (usually 7% to 10%) is *proprietors' income*—the earnings of people who own their own businesses. Part of that income should be considered wages these business owners pay themselves. So the true share of labor in the economy is probably a few percentage points higher than the reported "compensation of employees" share.

But much of what we call compensation of employees is really a return on human capital. A surgeon isn't just supplying the services of a pair of ordinary hands (at least the patient hopes not!): that individual is also supplying the result of many years and hundreds of thousands of dollars invested in training and experience. We can't directly measure what fraction of wages is really a payment for education and training, but many economists believe that human capital has become *the* most important factor of production in modern economies.

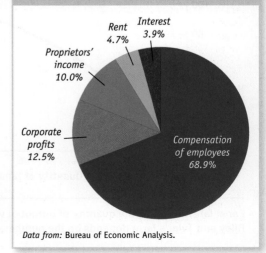

FIGURE 19-1 Factor Distribution of Income in the United States in 2019

Rent 4.7%
Interest 3.9%
Proprietors' income 10.0%
Corporate profits 12.5%
Compensation of employees 68.9%

Data from: Bureau of Economic Analysis.

>> *Check Your Understanding* **19-1**
Solutions appear at back of book.

1. Suppose that the government places price controls on the market for college professors, imposing a wage that is lower than the market wage. Describe the effect of this policy on the production of college degrees. What sectors of the economy do you think will be adversely affected by this policy? What sectors of the economy might benefit?

Marginal Productivity and Factor Demand

All economic decisions are based on comparing costs to benefits—and usually about comparing marginal costs to marginal benefits. This goes both for a consumer, deciding whether to undertake another year of schooling, and for a producer, deciding whether to hire an additional worker.

Although there are some important exceptions, most factor markets in the modern American economy are perfectly competitive, meaning that buyers and sellers of a given factor are price-takers. And in a competitive labor market, it's clear how to define an employer's marginal cost of a worker: it is simply the worker's wage rate. But what is the benefit of that worker? To answer that question, we return to a concept first introduced in Chapter 11: the *production function*, which relates inputs to output. And as in Chapter 12, we will assume throughout this chapter that all producers are price-takers in their output markets—that is, they operate in a perfectly competitive industry.

Value of the Marginal Product

Figure 19-2 reproduces Figures 11-1 and 11-2, which showed the production function for wheat on Riley and Tyler's farm. Panel (a) uses the total product curve to show how total wheat production depends on the number of workers employed on the farm; panel (b) shows how the *marginal product* of labor, the increase in output from employing one more worker, depends on the number of

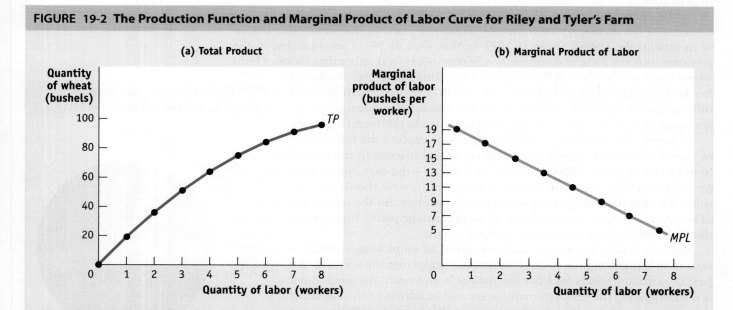

FIGURE 19-2 The Production Function and Marginal Product of Labor Curve for Riley and Tyler's Farm

Panel (a) shows how the quantity of output of wheat on Riley and Tyler's farm depends on the number of workers

employed. Panel (b) shows how the marginal product of labor depends on the number of workers employed.

workers employed. Table 19-1, which reproduces the table in Figure 11-1, shows the numbers behind the figure.

Assume that Riley and Tyler want to maximize their profit, that workers must be paid $200 each, and that wheat sells for $20 per bushel. What is their optimal number of workers? That is, how many workers should they employ to maximize profit?

Riley and Tyler use marginal analysis to answer this question in several steps (which we showed in Chapters 11 and 12).

- In Chapter 11 we used information from the producer's production function to derive the firm's total cost and its marginal cost.

- In Chapter 12 we derived the *price-taking firm's optimal output rule:* a price-taking firm's profit is maximized by producing the quantity of output at which the marginal cost of the last unit produced is equal to the market price.

- Having determined the optimal quantity of output, we can go back to the production function and find the optimal number of workers—it is simply the number of workers needed to produce the optimal quantity of output.

TABLE 19-1 Employment and Output for Riley and Tyler's Farm

Quantity of labor L (workers)	Quantity of wheat Q (bushels)	Marginal product of labor $MPL = \dfrac{\Delta Q}{\Delta L}$ (bushels per worker)
0	0	
		19
1	19	
		17
2	36	
		15
3	51	
		13
4	64	
		11
5	75	
		9
6	84	
		7
7	91	
		5
8	96	

There is, however, another way to use marginal analysis to find the number of workers that maximizes a producer's profit. We can go directly to the question of what level of employment maximizes profit. This alternative approach is equivalent to the approach we outlined in the preceding list—it's just a different way of looking at the same thing. But it gives us more insight into the demand for factors as opposed to the supply of goods.

To see how this alternative approach works, let's suppose that Riley and Tyler are considering whether or not to employ an additional worker. At each level of employment, they would compare the cost to the benefit of hiring. The increase in *cost* from employing that additional worker is the wage rate, W. The *benefit* to Riley and Tyler from employing that extra worker is the value of the extra output that worker can produce. What is this value? It is the marginal product of labor, *MPL*, multiplied by the price per unit of output, *P*. This amount—the extra value of output that is generated by employing one more unit of labor—is known as the **value of the marginal product** of labor, or *VMPL:*

(19-1) Value of the marginal product of labor = $VMPL = P \times MPL$

So should Riley and Tyler hire that extra worker? The answer is yes if the value of the extra output is more than the cost of the worker—that is, if $VMPL > W$. Otherwise they shouldn't hire that worker.

So the decision to hire labor is a marginal decision, in which the marginal benefit to the producer from hiring an additional worker (*VMPL*) should be compared with the marginal cost to the producer (*W*). And as with any marginal decision, the optimal choice is where marginal benefit is just equal to marginal cost. That is, to maximize profit Riley and Tyler will employ workers up to the point at which, for the last worker employed:

(19-2) $VMPL = W$ at the profit-maximizing level of employment

This rule doesn't apply only to labor; it applies to any factor of production. The value of the marginal product of any factor is its marginal product times the price of the good it produces. Applying this rule to all factors of production gives

The **value of the marginal product** of a factor is the value of the additional output generated by employing one more unit of that factor.

The **price-taking producer's optimal employment rule** says that a price-taking producer's profit is maximized by employing each factor of production up to the level at which the value of the marginal product is equal to the factor's price.

The **value of the marginal product curve** of a factor shows how the value of the marginal product of that factor depends on the quantity of the factor employed.

us the **price-taking producer's optimal employment rule:** *a profit-maximizing price-taking producer employs each factor of production up to the level at which the value of the marginal product is equal to that factor's price.*

It's important to realize that this rule doesn't conflict with our analysis in Chapters 11 and 12. There we saw that a profit-maximizing producer of a good chooses the level of output at which the price of that good is equal to the marginal cost of production. It's just a different way of looking at the same rule. If the level of output is chosen so that price equals marginal cost, then it is also true that at that output level the value of the marginal product of labor will equal the wage rate.

Now let's look more closely at why choosing the level of employment at which the value of the marginal product of the last worker employed is equal to the wage rate is the right method, and how it helps us understand factor demand.

Value of the Marginal Product and Factor Demand

Table 19-2 calculates the value of the marginal product of labor on Riley and Tyler's farm, on the assumption that the price of wheat is $20 per bushel. In Figure 19-3 the horizontal axis shows the number of workers employed; the vertical axis measures the value of the marginal product of labor *and* the wage rate. The curve shown is the **value of the marginal product curve** of labor. This curve, like the marginal product of labor curve, slopes downward because of diminishing returns to labor in production. That is, the value of the marginal product of each worker is less than that of the preceding worker, because the marginal product of each worker is less than that of the preceding worker.

We have just seen that to maximize profit, Riley and Tyler must hire workers up to the point at which the wage rate is equal to the value of the marginal product of the last worker employed. Let's use the example to see how this principle really works.

Assume that Riley and Tyler currently employ 3 workers and that workers must be paid the market wage rate of $200. Should they employ an additional worker?

Looking at Table 19-2, we see that if Riley and Tyler currently employ 3 workers, the value of the marginal product of an additional worker is $260. So if they employ an additional worker, they will increase the value of their production by $260 but increase their cost by only $200, yielding an increased profit of $60. In fact, a producer can always increase total profit by employing one more unit of a factor of production as long as the value of the marginal product produced by that unit exceeds its factor price.

Alternatively, suppose that Riley and Tyler employ 8 workers. By reducing the number of workers to 7, they can save $200 in wages. In addition, the value of the marginal product of the last one, the 8th worker, was only $100. So, by reducing employment by one worker, they can increase profit by $200 − $100 = $100. In other words, a producer can always increase total profit by employing one less unit of a factor of production as long as the value of the marginal product produced by that unit is less than the factor price.

Using this method, we can see from Table 19-2 that the profit-maximizing employment level is 5 workers given a wage rate of $200. The value of the marginal product of the 5th worker is $220, so adding the 5th worker results in $20 of additional profit. But Riley and Tyler should not hire more than 5 workers: the value of the marginal product of the 6th worker is only $180, $20 less than the cost

TABLE 19-2 Value of the Marginal Product of Labor for Riley and Tyler's Farm

Quantity of labor *L* (workers)	Marginal product of labor *MPL* (bushels per worker)	Value of the marginal product of labor $VMPL = P \times MPL$
0		
	19	$380
1		
	17	340
2		
	15	300
3		
	13	260
4		
	11	220
5		
	9	180
6		
	7	140
7		
	5	100
8		

FIGURE 19-3 The Value of the Marginal Product Curve

This curve shows how the value of the marginal product of labor depends on the number of workers employed. It slopes downward because of diminishing returns to labor in production. To maximize profit, Riley and Tyler choose the level of employment at which the value of the marginal product of labor is equal to the market wage rate. For example, at a wage rate of $200 the profit-maximizing level of employment is 5 workers, shown by point *A*. The value of the marginal product curve of a factor is the producer's individual demand curve for that factor.

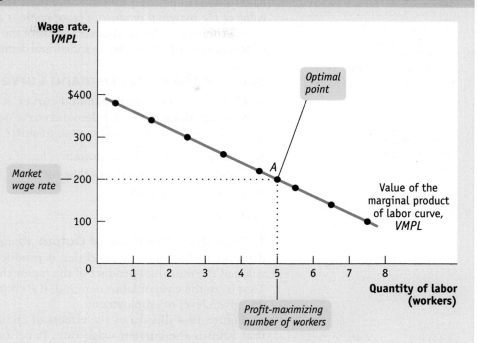

of that worker. So, to maximize total profit, Riley and Tyler should employ workers up to, but not beyond the point at which the value of the marginal product of the last worker employed is equal to the wage rate.

Now look again at the value of the marginal product curve in Figure 19-3. To determine the profit-maximizing level of employment, we set the value of the marginal product of labor equal to the price of labor—a wage rate of $200 per worker. This means that the profit-maximizing level of employment is at point *A*, corresponding to an employment level of 5 workers. If the wage rate were higher than $200, we would simply move up the curve and reduce the number of workers employed; if the wage rate were lower than $200, we would move down the curve and increase the number of workers employed.

In this example, Riley and Tyler have a small farm in which the potential employment level varies from 0 to 8 workers, and they hire workers up to the point at which the value of the marginal product of the last worker is greater than or equal to the wage rate. (To go beyond this point and hire workers for which the wage exceeds the value of the marginal product would reduce Riley and Tyler's profit.)

Suppose, however, that the producer in question is large and has the potential of hiring many workers. When there are many employees, the value of the marginal product of labor falls only slightly when an additional worker is employed. As a result, there will be some worker whose value of the marginal product almost exactly equals the wage rate. (In keeping with the Riley and Tyler example, this means that some worker generates a value of the marginal product of approximately $200.) In this case, the producer maximizes profit by choosing a level of employment at which the value of the marginal product of the last worker hired *equals* (to a very good approximation) the wage rate.

Firms continue to hire workers until the value of the marginal product of the last worker hired equals the wage rate.

In the interest of simplicity, we will assume from now on that producers use this rule to determine the profit-maximizing level of employment. *This means that the value of the marginal product of labor curve is the individual producer's labor demand curve.* And, in general, a producer's value of the marginal product curve for any factor of production is that producer's individual demand curve for that factor of production.

Shifts of the Factor Demand Curve

As in the case of ordinary demand curves, it is important to distinguish between movements along the factor demand curve and shifts of the factor demand curve. What causes factor demand curves to shift? There are three main causes:

1. Changes in the price of output
2. Changes in the supply of other factors
3. Changes in technology

Let's look at each in detail.

1. Changes in the Price of Output Remember that factor demand is derived demand: if the price of a good that is produced with a factor changes, so will the value of the marginal product of the factor that is employed to produce that good. That is, in the case of labor demand, if P changes, $VMPL = P \times MPL$ will change at any given level of employment.

Figure 19-4 illustrates the effects of changes in the price of wheat, assuming that $200 is the current wage rate. Panel (a) shows the effect of an *increase* in the price of wheat. This shifts the value of the marginal product of labor curve upward, because $VMPL$ rises at any given level of employment. If the wage rate remains unchanged at $200, the optimal point moves from point A to point B: the profit-maximizing level of employment rises.

Panel (b) shows the effect of a *decrease* in the price of wheat. This shifts the value of the marginal product of labor curve downward. If the wage rate

FIGURE 19-4 Shifts of the Value of the Marginal Product Curve

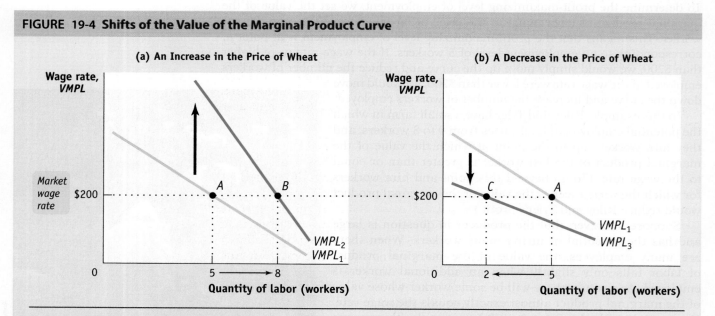

Panel (a) shows the effect of an increase in the price of wheat on Riley and Tyler's demand for labor. The value of the marginal product of labor curve shifts upward, from $VMPL_1$ to $VMPL_2$. If the market wage rate remains at $200, profit-maximizing employment rises from 5 workers to 8 workers, shown by the movement from point A to point B.

Panel (b) shows the effect of a decrease in the price of wheat. The value of the marginal product of labor curve shifts downward, from $VMPL_1$ to $VMPL_3$. At the market wage rate of $200, profit-maximizing employment falls from 5 workers to 2 workers, shown by the movement from point A to point C.

remains unchanged at $200, the optimal point moves from point *A* to point *C:* the profit-maximizing level of employment falls.

2. Changes in the Supply of Other Factors Suppose that Riley and Tyler acquire more land to cultivate—say, by clearing a woodland on their property. Each worker now produces more wheat because each one has more land to work with. As a result, the marginal product of labor on the farm rises at any given level of employment. This has the same effect as an increase in the price of wheat, which is illustrated in panel (a) of Figure 19-4: the value of the marginal product of labor curve shifts upward, and at any given wage rate the profit-maximizing level of employment rises.

In contrast, suppose Riley and Tyler cultivate less land. This leads to a fall in the marginal product of labor at any given employment level. Each worker produces less wheat because each has less land to work with. As a result, the value of the marginal product of labor curve shifts downward—as in panel (b) of Figure 19-4—and the profit-maximizing level of employment falls.

3. Changes in Technology In general, the effect of technological progress on the demand for any given factor can go either way: improved technology can either increase or reduce the demand for a given factor of production. And, frequently, a decrease in one factor leads to an increase in another.

How can technological progress reduce factor demand? Consider horses, which were once an important factor of production. The development of substitutes for horse power, such as cars and tractors, greatly reduced the demand for horses. At the same time, however, demand increased for other factors such as drivers, manufacturers, and skilled auto mechanics.

In today's economy, the expanding use of automation and robots as a substitute for human labor has some analysts predicting that the factor demand for human workers will decrease in certain industries in the coming decades. Robots can collect goods from warehouse shelves and lay bricks at construction sites, eliminating the need for humans to perform these tasks. And, as you might predict, at the same time, the demand for other factors such as software developers and robotics engineers will increase.

The usual effect of technological progress is to increase the demand for a given factor by raising its productivity. So despite persistent fears that machinery and automation would reduce the demand for labor, over the long term the U.S. economy has seen both large wage increases and large increases in employment. That's because technological progress has raised labor productivity, and as a result increased the demand for labor.

Market Equilibrium in the Factor Market

We've now seen that each perfectly competitive producer in a perfectly competitive factor market maximizes profit by hiring labor up to the point at which its value of the marginal product is equal to its price—in the case of labor, to the point where $VMPL = W$. What does this tell us about labor's share in the factor distribution of income? To answer that question, we need to examine equilibrium in the labor market. From that vantage point we will go on to learn about the markets for land and capital and about how they also influence the factor distribution of income.

Let's start by assuming that the labor market is in equilibrium: at the current market wage rate, the number of workers that producers want to employ is equal to the number of workers willing to work. Thus, all employers pay the *same* wage rate, and *each* employer, whatever they are producing, employs labor up to the point at which the value of the marginal product of the last worker hired is equal to the market wage rate.

This situation is illustrated in Figure 19-5, which shows the value of the marginal product curves of two producers—Farmer Garcia, who produces wheat, and Farmer Freeman, who produces corn. Despite the fact that they produce

FIGURE 19-5 All Producers Face the Same Wage Rate

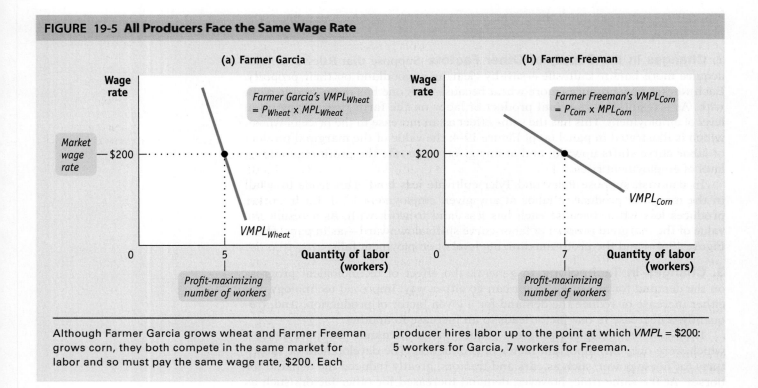

(a) Farmer Garcia

Wage rate

Market wage rate — $200 ⋯⋯⋯⋯⋯⋯⋯⋯⋯⋯⋯●⋯

Farmer Garcia's $VMPL_{Wheat}$ = P_{Wheat} × MPL_{Wheat}

$VMPL_{Wheat}$

0   5   **Quantity of labor (workers)**

Profit-maximizing number of workers

(b) Farmer Freeman

Wage rate

$200 ⋯⋯⋯⋯⋯⋯⋯⋯⋯⋯●⋯

Farmer Freeman's $VMPL_{Corn}$ = P_{Corn} × MPL_{Corn}

$VMPL_{Corn}$

0   7   **Quantity of labor (workers)**

Profit-maximizing number of workers

Although Farmer Garcia grows wheat and Farmer Freeman grows corn, they both compete in the same market for labor and so must pay the same wage rate, $200. Each producer hires labor up to the point at which $VMPL$ = $200: 5 workers for Garcia, 7 workers for Freeman.

different products, they compete for the same workers and so must pay the same wage rate, $200. When both farmers maximize profit, both hire labor up to the point at which its value of the marginal product is equal to the wage rate. In the figure, this corresponds to employment of 5 workers by Garcia and 7 by Freeman.

Figure 19-6 illustrates the labor market as a whole. The *market labor demand curve*, like the market demand curve for a good (shown in Figure 3-5), is the

FIGURE 19-6 Equilibrium in the Labor Market

The market labor demand curve is the horizontal sum of the individual labor demand curves of all producers. Here the equilibrium wage rate is W^*, the equilibrium employment level is L^*, and every producer hires labor up to the point at which $VMPL = W^*$. So labor is paid its equilibrium value of the marginal product, the value of the marginal product of the last worker hired in the labor market as a whole.

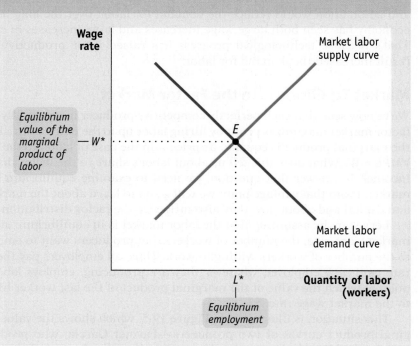

Wage rate

Market labor supply curve

Equilibrium value of the marginal product of labor — W^* ⋯⋯⋯⋯⋯⋯⋯●E⋯

Market labor demand curve

L^* **Quantity of labor (workers)**

Equilibrium employment

horizontal sum of all the individual labor demand curves of all the producers who hire labor. And recall that each producer's individual labor demand curve is the same as their value of the marginal product of labor curve. For now, let's simply assume an upward-sloping labor supply curve; we'll discuss labor supply later in this chapter. Then the equilibrium wage rate is the wage rate at which the quantity of labor supplied is equal to the quantity of labor demanded. In Figure 19-6, this leads to an equilibrium wage rate of W^* and the corresponding equilibrium employment level of L^*. (The equilibrium wage rate is also known as the market wage rate.)

And as we showed in the examples of the farms of Riley and Tyler and of Farmer Garcia and Farmer Freeman (where the equilibrium wage rate is $200), each farm hires labor up to the point at which the value of the marginal product of labor is equal to the equilibrium wage rate. Therefore, in equilibrium, the value of the marginal product of labor is the same for all employers. So the equilibrium (or market) wage rate is equal to the **equilibrium value of the marginal product** of labor—the additional value produced by the last unit of labor employed in the labor market as a whole. It doesn't matter where that additional unit is employed, since equilibrium *VMPL* is the same for all producers.

What we have just learned, then, is that the market wage rate is equal to the equilibrium value of the marginal product of labor. And the same is true of each factor of production: in a perfectly competitive market economy, the market price of each factor is equal to its equilibrium value of the marginal product. Let's examine the markets for land and (physical) capital now. (From this point on, we'll refer to physical capital as simply *capital*.)

The Markets for Land and Capital

If we maintain the assumption that the markets for goods and services are perfectly competitive, the result that we derived for the labor market also applies to other factors of production. Suppose, for example, that a farmer is considering whether to rent an additional acre of land for the next year. The farmer will compare the cost of renting that acre with the value of the additional output generated by employing an additional acre—the value of the marginal product of an acre of land. To maximize profit, the farmer must employ land up to the point at which the value of the marginal product of an acre of land is equal to the rental rate per acre.

What if the farmer already owns the land? We already saw the answer in Chapter 9, which dealt with economic decisions: even if you own land, there is an implicit cost—the opportunity cost—of using it for a given activity, because it could be used for something else, such as renting it out to other farmers at the market *rental rate*. So a profit-maximizing producer employs additional acres of land up to the point at which the cost of the last acre employed, explicit or implicit, is equal to the value of the marginal product of that acre.

The same is true for capital. The explicit or implicit cost of using a unit of land or capital for a set period of time is called its **rental rate.** In general, a unit of land or capital is employed up to the point at which that unit's value of the marginal product is equal to its rental rate over that time period. How are the rental rates for land and capital determined? By the equilibria in the land market and the capital market, of course. Figure 19-7 illustrates those outcomes.

Panel (a) shows the equilibrium in the market for land. Summing over the individual demand curves for land of all producers gives us the market demand curve for land. Due to diminishing returns, the demand curve slopes downward, like the demand curve for labor. As we have drawn it, the supply curve of land is relatively steep and therefore relatively inelastic. This reflects the fact that finding new supplies of land for production is typically difficult and expensive—for example, creating new farmland through expensive irrigation. The equilibrium rental rate for land, R^*_{Land}, and the equilibrium quantity of land employed in production, Q^*_{Land}, are given by the intersection of the two curves.

The **equilibrium value of the marginal product** of a factor is the additional value produced by the last unit of that factor employed in the factor market as a whole.

The **rental rate** of either land or capital is the cost, explicit or implicit, of using a unit of that asset for a given period of time.

FIGURE 19-7 Equilibria in the Land and Capital Markets

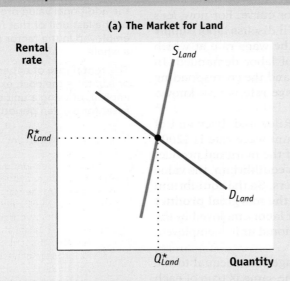

(a) The Market for Land

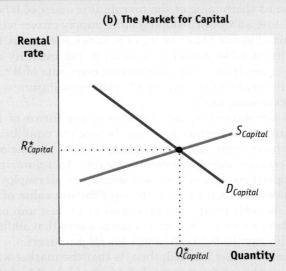

(b) The Market for Capital

Panel (a) illustrates equilibrium in the market for land; panel (b) illustrates equilibrium in the market for capital. The supply curve for land is relatively steep, reflecting the high cost of increasing the quantity of productive land. The supply curve for capital, in contrast, is relatively flat, due to the relatively high responsiveness of savings to changes in the rental rate for capital. The equilibrium rental rates for land and capital, as well as the equilibrium quantities transacted, are given by the intersections of the demand and supply curves. In a competitive land market, each unit of land will be paid the equilibrium value of the marginal product of land, R^*_{Land}. Likewise, in a competitive capital market, each unit of capital will be paid the equilibrium value of the marginal product of capital, $R^*_{Capital}$.

Panel (b) shows the equilibrium in the market for capital. In contrast to the supply curve for land, the supply curve for capital is relatively elastic. That's because the supply of capital is relatively responsive to price: capital is paid for with funds that come from the savings of investors, and the amount of savings that investors make available is relatively responsive to the rental rate for capital. The equilibrium rental rate for capital, $R^*_{Capital}$, and the equilibrium quantity of capital employed in production, $Q^*_{Capital}$, are given by the intersection of the two curves.

The Marginal Productivity Theory of Income Distribution

So we have learned that when the markets for goods and services and the factor markets are perfectly competitive, a factor of production will be employed up to the point at which its value of the marginal product is equal to its market equilibrium price. That is, it will be paid its equilibrium value of the marginal product.

What does this say about the factor distribution of income? It leads us to the **marginal productivity theory of income distribution,** which says that each factor is paid the value of the output generated by the last unit of that factor employed in the factor market as a whole—its equilibrium value of the marginal product.

To understand why the marginal productivity theory of income distribution is important, look back at Figure 19-1, which shows the factor distribution of income in the United States, and ask yourself this question: who or what decided that labor would get 69% of total U.S. income? Why not 90% or 50%?

The answer, according to the marginal productivity theory of income distribution, is that the division of income among the economy's factors of production isn't arbitrary: it is determined by each factor's marginal productivity at the economy's equilibrium. The wage rate earned by *all* workers in the economy is equal to

According to the **marginal productivity theory of income distribution,** every factor of production is paid its equilibrium value of the marginal product.

the increase in the value of output generated by the last worker employed in the economy-wide labor market.

So far we have treated factor markets as if every unit of each factor were identical. That is, as if all land were identical, all labor were identical, and all capital were identical. But in reality factors differ considerably with respect to productivity. For example, workers have different skills and abilities.

Rather than thinking of one land market for all land resources in an economy, and similarly one capital market and one labor market, think, instead, of different markets for different types of land, physical capital, human capital, and labor. For example, the market for computer programmers is different from the market for pastry chefs.

When we consider that there are separate factor markets for different types of factors, we can still apply the marginal productivity of income distribution. That is, when the labor market for software programmers is in equilibrium, the theory says that the wage rate earned by all software programmers is equal to the market's equilibrium value of the marginal product—the value of the marginal product of the last computer programmer hired in that market.

The marginal productivity theory of income distribution rests on the assumption that factor markets as well as goods and services markets are perfectly competitive. Yet, as we discuss in the next section, many markets don't satisfy that criterion. So it is useful as a benchmark, but not as an exact representation of the real world.

And it's important to note that to the extent the marginal productivity theory of income distribution works, it's an explanation of what markets do, not a statement about what is fair or right. That is, it doesn't tell us what the income distribution "ought" to be. Rather, the marginal productivity theory of income distribution can serve as a benchmark to help society decide what is the right trade-off between equity and efficiency.

> ### PITFALLS
>
> #### GETTING MARGINAL PRODUCTIVITY THEORY RIGHT
>
> Carefully consider what the marginal productivity theory of income distribution says: *all* units of a factor get paid the factor's equilibrium value of the marginal product—the additional value produced by the *last* unit of the factor employed.
>
> The most common source of error is to forget that the relevant value of the marginal product is the equilibrium value, not the value of the marginal products you calculate on the way to equilibrium. In looking at Table 19-2, it is tempting to think that because the first worker has a value of the marginal product of $380, that worker is paid $380 in equilibrium. Not so: if the equilibrium value of the marginal product in the labor market is equal to $200, then *all* workers receive $200.

ECONOMICS >> *in Action*
Help Wanted at Flex!

Flextronics International (Flex) is the second largest electronics manufacturing services and design company in the world. An American company headquartered in Singapore, it produces everything from Fitbits to electric motorcycles and components for electric cars. And as a manufacturing company, it employs thousands of skilled machinists.

As of March 2019, according to Payscale.com, the average American skilled machinist earned $73,157 at Flex, excluding benefits. Like most skilled machinists in the United States, Flex's machinists are very productive: according to the U.S. Census Annual Survey of Manufacturers, in 2017, the average production worker in computer and electronic product manufacturing generated approximately $270,548 in value added.

But there is a nearly $200,000 gap between the salary paid to an average American skilled machinist at Flex, and what is a reasonable estimate of the value added they create. Does this mean that the marginal productivity theory of income distribution doesn't hold? Doesn't the theory imply that machinists should be paid $270,548, the average value added that each one generates? The answer to both questions is no, for two reasons:

The marginal productivity theory of income distribution holds for skilled machinists.

1. The $270,548 figure is averaged over *all machinists currently employed*. The theory says that machinists will be paid the value of the marginal product of the *last machinist hired*, and due to diminishing returns to labor, that value will be lower than the average over all machinists currently employed.

2. A worker's equilibrium wage rate includes other costs, such as employee benefits, that have to be added to the $73,157 salary. The marginal productivity theory of income distribution says that workers are paid a wage rate, *including all benefits,* equal to the value of the marginal product.

You can see all these costs are present at Flex. There the machinists have good benefits and job security, which add to their salary. Including these benefits, machinists' total compensation will be equal to the value of the marginal product of the last machinist employed.

In Flex's case, there is yet another factor that explains the nearly $200,000 gap: there are not enough machinists at the current wage rate. As of early 2019, Flex was trying to hire more. Why doesn't Flex raise its wages in order to attract more skilled machinists? The problem is that the work they do is so specialized that it is hard to hire from the outside, even when the company raises wages as an inducement.

To address this problem, companies like Flex spend significant amounts of money training each new hire, costs that can run well over $100,000 per trainee. In the end, it does appear that the marginal productivity theory of income distribution holds.

>> Check Your Understanding 19-2

Solutions appear at back of book.

1. In the following cases, state the direction of the shift of the demand curve for labor and what will happen, other things equal, to the market equilibrium wage rate and quantity of labor employed as a result.
   a. Service industries, such as retailing and banking, experience an increase in demand. These industries use relatively more labor than nonservice industries.
   b. Due to overfishing, there is a fall in the amount of fish caught per day by commercial fishers; this decrease affects their demand for workers.

2. Explain the following statement: "When producers in different industries all compete for the same workers, then the value of the marginal product of the last worker hired will be equal across all producers regardless of whether they are in different industries."

Is the Marginal Productivity Theory of Income Distribution Really True?

Although the marginal productivity theory of income distribution is a well-established part of economic theory, closely linked to the analysis of markets in general, it is a source of some controversy. There are two main objections to it.

First, in the real world we see large disparities in income between factors of production that, in the eyes of some observers, should receive the same payment. Perhaps the most conspicuous examples in the United States are the large differences in the average wages between women and men and among various racial and ethnic groups. Do these wage differences really reflect differences in marginal productivity, or is something else going on?

Second, many people wrongly believe that the marginal productivity theory of income distribution gives a *moral* justification for the distribution of income, implying that the existing distribution is fair and appropriate. This misconception sometimes leads other people, who believe that the current distribution of income is unfair, to reject marginal productivity theory.

To address these controversies, we'll start by looking at income disparities across gender and ethnic groups. Then we'll ask what factors might account for these disparities and whether these explanations are consistent with the marginal productivity theory of income distribution.

Wage Disparities in Practice

Wage rates in the United States cover a very wide range. In 2018, nearly two million workers received the legal federal minimum of $7.25 per hour. At the other extreme, the chief executives of several companies were paid more than $100 million, which works out to $20,000 per hour even if they worked 100-hour weeks. Even leaving out these extremes, there is a huge range of wage rates. Are people really that different in their marginal productivities?

A particular source of concern is the existence of systematic wage differences across gender and ethnicity. Figure 19-8 compares annual median earnings in 2018 of full-time workers age 25 or older classified by gender and race. As a group, White males had the highest earnings. Other data show that women (averaging across all races) earned only about 72% as much; African-American workers (male and female combined), only 70% as much; Hispanic workers (again, male and female combined), only 62% as much. Do marginal productivity differences really explain these persistent differences across gender and race?

We are a nation founded on the belief that all men are created equal—and if the Constitution were rewritten today, we would say that *all people* are created equal. So why do they receive such unequal pay? Let's start with the marginal productivity explanations, then look at other influences.

Wage Disparities and Marginal Productivity

A large part of the observed disparity in wages can be explained by differences that are consistent with the marginal productivity theory of income distribution. In particular, there are three well-understood sources of differences in wages across workers and occupations.

First is the existence of **compensating differentials.** Across different jobs, wages that are often higher or lower depend on how attractive or unattractive the job is. These wage differences are known as compensating differentials. Workers with unpleasant or dangerous jobs demand a higher wage than workers with jobs that require the same skill and effort but lack the unpleasant or dangerous qualities. For example, truckers who haul hazardous loads are paid more than truckers who haul nonhazardous loads. During the height of the 2020 pandemic, retailers like Amazon

Compensating differentials are wage differences across jobs that reflect the fact that some jobs are less pleasant than others.

FIGURE 19-8 Median Earnings by Gender and Ethnicity, 2018

The U.S. labor market continues to show large differences across workers according to gender and ethnicity. Women are paid substantially less than men; African-American and Hispanic workers are paid substantially less than White male workers.

Data from: U.S. Census Bureau.

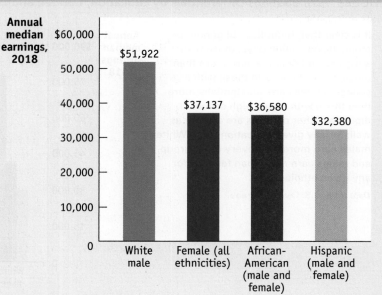

and Kroger gave their in-store and warehouse workers extra pay to compensate for the hazard of catching the virus. But for any *given* job, the marginal productivity theory of income distribution generally holds true. For example, hazardous-load truckers are paid a wage equal to the equilibrium value of the marginal product of the last person employed in the labor market for hazardous-load truckers.

A second reason for wage disparities that is consistent with marginal productivity theory is differences in *ability*. A higher-ability person, by producing a better product, commands a higher price than a person with lower abilities. The person with higher abilities also generates a higher value of the marginal product, and this difference in the value of the marginal product translates into differences in earning potential. Professional sports is a good example: practice is important, but most of the population doesn't have what it takes to throw passes like Tom Brady or hit tennis balls like Serena Williams. The same is true in other fields of endeavor.

A third reason for wage differences is differences in the quantity of human capital. Recall that *human capital*—education and training—is at least as important in the modern economy as physical capital in the form of buildings and machines. Different people embody quite different quantities of human capital, and a person with a higher quantity of human capital typically generates a higher value of the marginal product by producing a product that commands a higher price. So differences in human capital account for substantial differences in wages. People with high levels of human capital, such as skilled surgeons or engineers, who undergo many years of education and training, generally receive high wages.

The most direct way to see the effect of human capital on wages is to look at the relationship between educational levels and earnings. Figure 19-9 shows earnings differentials by gender, ethnicity, and three educational levels for people aged 25 or older in 2018. As you can see, regardless of gender or ethnicity, higher education is associated with higher median earnings. For example, in 2018 White females with 9 to 12 years of schooling but without a high school diploma had median earnings 32% less than those with a high school diploma and 63% less than those with a college degree—and similar patterns exist for the other five groups. Because even now men typically have had more years of education than women, and Whites more years than non-Whites, differences in level of education are part of the explanation for the earnings differences shown in Figure 19-8.

FIGURE 19-9 Earnings Differentials by Education, Gender, and Ethnicity, 2018

It is clear that, regardless of gender or ethnicity, education pays: those with a high school diploma earn more than those without one, and those with a college degree earn substantially more than those with only a high school diploma. Other patterns are evident as well: for any given education level, White males earn more than every other group, and males earn more than females for any given ethnic group.

Data from: U.S. Census Bureau.

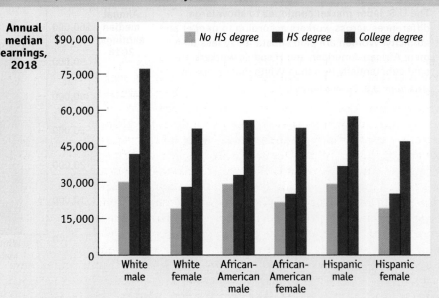

But formal education is not the only source of human capital; on-the-job training and work experience also generate human capital and lead to wage differences that are consistent with marginal productivity theory. Workers with longer job tenure tend to have more work experience, and therefore higher wages.

There are other factors that influence differences in wages. A good illustration is found in research on the *gender-wage gap*, the persistent difference in the earnings of men compared to women. In the U.S. labor market, researchers have found that the gender gap is largely explained by differences in:

- human capital (women tend to have lower levels of it than men)
- choice of occupation (women have tended to choose occupations such as nursing and teaching, in which they earn less)
- career interruptions (women move in and out of the labor force more frequently)
- part-time status (women are more likely to work part-time rather than full-time)
- overtime status (women are less likely to work overtime)

For example, a recent U.S. Department of Labor study indicates that the gender-wage gap fell from 20.4% to 5.0% once the preceding factors were accounted for. Moreover, over the past 37 years even the unadjusted gender-wage gap has fallen significantly, from 37.7% in 1979 to 18.9% in 2018, as women have begun to close in on men in terms of these five factors.

But it's also important to emphasize that earnings differences arising from these factors are not necessarily fair. The U.S. lags behind other advanced countries in providing government or legal support for child care. As a result, American women face more career interruptions than men, and are also less able to work full time than men. Similarly, a society in which non-White children receive a poor education because they live in underfunded school districts, then go on to earn low wages because they are poorly educated, may have labor markets that are well described by marginal productivity theory (and would be consistent with the earnings differences across racial and ethnic groups and between the genders shown in Figure 19-8). Yet many people would still consider the resulting distribution of income unfair.

Still, many observers think that actual wage differentials cannot be entirely explained by compensating differentials, differences in ability or talent, and differences in human capital. They believe that market power, *efficiency wages*, and discrimination also play an important role. We examine these forces next.

Market Power

The marginal productivity theory of income distribution is based on the assumption that factor markets are perfectly competitive. In such markets we can expect workers to be paid the equilibrium value of their marginal product, regardless of who they are. But how valid is this assumption?

We studied markets that are *not* perfectly competitive in preceding chapters. Now let's touch briefly on the ways in which labor markets may deviate from the competitive assumption. One undoubted source of differences in wages between otherwise similar workers is the role of **unions**—organizations that try to raise wages and improve working conditions for their members. Unions are a source of power in factor markets. When they are successful, unions replace one-on-one wage deals between workers and employers with *collective bargaining*, in which the employer must negotiate wages with union representatives. Without question, this leads to higher wages for those workers who are represented by unions. In 2019, the median weekly earnings of union members in the United States were $1,082, compared to $892 for workers not represented by unions—more than a 20% difference. Studies have shown that unionization helps reduce the wage differences between White men and women, as well as between White and non-White workers.

Unions are organizations of workers that try to raise wages and improve working conditions for their members by bargaining collectively with employers.

According to the **efficiency-wage model,** some employers pay an above-equilibrium wage as an incentive for better performance.

How much does collective action, either by workers or by employers, affect wages in the modern United States? Several decades ago, when around 30% of American workers were union members, unions probably had a significant upward effect on wages. Today, however, most economists think unions exert a fairly minor influence.

In 2019, less than 8% of the employees of private businesses were represented by unions. Just as unionized workers can extract higher wages than they would otherwise receive, if an employer is large enough, it can exercise market power and *lower* wages below the competitive level. As you may recall from Chapter 13, this type of market power is called *monopsony*. When firms exercise monopsony power in labor markets, workers are paid less than their value of marginal product. Let's consider the market for nurses. The median annual salary for nurses is around $72,000. Data suggest that in a perfectly competitive market, nurses' salary would be much higher: in the range of $90,000 to $200,000. But, because many areas in the United States have few hospitals, medical institutions can pay nurses lower wages knowing there are limited opportunities for their nurses to leave for higher-paying jobs at rival hospitals. Recent research has found evidence of considerable monopsony power in many U.S. labor markets, with this issue growing in importance because of industry consolidation.

Efficiency Wages

Another source of wage differentials is the phenomenon of *efficiency wages*—a type of incentive scheme used by employers to motivate workers to work hard and to reduce worker turnover. Suppose a worker performs a job that is extremely important but that the employer can observe how well the job is being performed only at infrequent intervals—say, serving as a caregiver for the employer's child. Then it makes sense for the employer to pay more than the worker could earn in an alternative job—that is, more than the equilibrium wage. Why? Because earning a premium makes losing this job quite costly for the worker.

The **efficiency-wage model** states that when it is difficult to observe a worker's performance, it may be economically rational for an employer to pay a wage greater than the market equilibrium level as an incentive for better performance. The threat of losing a job that pays a premium motivates the worker to do the job well and avoid being fired. Likewise, paying a premium also reduces worker turnover—the frequency with which an employee leaves a job voluntarily. Despite the fact that it may take no more effort and skill to be a child's caregiver than to be a hospital care aide, efficiency wages show why it often makes economic sense for a parent to pay a caregiver more than the equilibrium wage of hospital care aides.

Like price floors and, in particular, much like the minimum wage—efficiency wages lead to a surplus of labor in labor markets where they are used. This surplus of labor translates into unemployment—some workers are actively searching for a high-paying efficiency-wage job but are unable to get one, and other more fortunate but no more deserving workers are able to acquire one.

As a result, two workers with exactly the same profile—the same skills and same job history—may earn unequal wages: the worker who is lucky enough to get an efficiency-wage job earns more than the worker who gets a standard job (or who remains unemployed while searching for a higher-paying job).

Efficiency wages are a response to a type of market failure that arises when some employees are able to hide the fact that they don't always perform as well as they should. As a result, employers use nonequilibrium wages to motivate their employees, leading to an inefficient outcome.

Discrimination

Workplace discrimination has been a long-standing feature of the U.S. economy. Although formal discrimination on the basis of gender or race was made illegal nearly 60 years ago, researchers find that informal discrimination still exists.

For example, researchers found that when they submit fictitious job applications using identical resumes but with ethnically identifiable names, White-identified applicants receive 36% more call-backs than African-American–identified applicants, and 24% more than Hispanic-identified applicants.

It is a real and ugly fact that throughout history there has been discrimination against workers who are considered to be of the wrong race, ethnicity, gender, or other characteristics. How does this fit into our economic models?

Discrimination is *not* a natural consequence of market competition. On the contrary, market forces tend to work against discrimination. To see why, consider the incentives that would exist if social convention dictated that women be paid 30% less than men with equivalent qualifications and experience. Companies would be able to reduce their costs by hiring women rather than men. The result would be to create an excess demand for female workers, which would eventually drive up their wages.

But if market competition works against discrimination, how is it that so much discrimination has taken place? The answer is twofold.

First, when labor markets don't work well, employers may have the ability to discriminate without hurting their profits. For example, market interferences (such as unions or minimum-wage laws) or market failures (such as efficiency wages) can lead to wages that are above their equilibrium levels. In these cases, there are more job applicants than there are jobs, leaving employers free to discriminate among applicants. In 2011, with unemployment over 9%, the Equal Employment Opportunity Commission, the federal agency tasked with investigating employment discrimination charges, reported that the complaints from workers and job-seekers had hit an all-time high, the most logged in the agency's 46-year history.

Second, discrimination has sometimes been institutionalized in government policy. This institutionalization of discrimination has made it easier to maintain it against market pressure, and historically it is the form that discrimination has typically taken. For example, at one time in the United States, African-Americans were barred from attending "Whites-only" public schools and universities in many parts of the country and forced to attend inferior schools.

Although market competition tends to work against *current* discrimination, it is not a remedy for past discrimination, which typically has had an impact on the education and experience of its victims and thereby reduces their income.

FOR INQUIRING MINDS   How Labor Works the German Way

Germany is home to some of the finest manufacturing firms in the world. From the automotive sector to beer brewing, and from home appliances to chemical engineering and pharmaceuticals, German products are considered among the highest quality available. And unlike in the United States, blue-collar jobs — those that don't require college degrees — pay high enough wages that they are still prized. If you ask Germans what accounts for their ability to combine a highly successful manufacturing sector with well-paying blue-collar jobs, two overlapping institutions will top their lists: Germany's works councils system and their apprenticeship system.

Enshrined in the German constitution, works councils exist in every factory to encourage management and employees to work together on issues like work conditions, productivity, and wages, with the goal of discouraging costly conflict. Workers are given seats in management organizations such as a company's board of directors. This collaborative environment, in turn, supports higher levels of unionization within German manufacturing. As a result, German unions are more successful at raising the wages of their members.

But what allows German manufacturing to compete successfully while paying higher wages? One explanation is the German apprentice system, which is promoted and accredited by the German government. These programs provide hands-on training to young workers in specific skills from automotive electronics to hairdressing. About 60% of German high school students train in an apprenticeship program, graduating with a formal certificate, and often landing a permanent job at the company where they were trained. As a result, the typical German manufacturing worker starts a job with higher levels of job-specific human capital than their American counterpart.

So integral is the apprenticeship system to the success of German manufacturing that German companies have been replicating it at their plants in the United States. In South Carolina, where BMW and Tognum, a German engine maker, are located, apprenticeship programs have been created in partnership with local and state governments to assure that young workers are trained in the skills that the companies need. And, needless to say, the apprentices welcome such training and the well-paying jobs that it will bring.

So Does Marginal Productivity Theory Work?

The main conclusion you should draw from this discussion is that the marginal productivity theory of income distribution is not a perfect description of how factor incomes are determined, but that it is still a very useful tool for economic analysis. The deviations are important. But, by and large, in a modern economy with well-functioning labor markets, factors of production are paid the equilibrium value of the marginal product—the value of the marginal product of the last unit employed in the market as a whole.

It's important to emphasize, once again, that this does not mean that the factor distribution of income is morally justified.

ECONOMICS >> *in Action*
Marginal Productivity and the Minimum Wage Puzzle

The U.S. government, like many other governments, puts a floor under wages: nationally, employers aren't allowed to pay workers less than $7.25 an hour. However, many states and some cities impose their own minimum wages, in some cases well above the national standard. For example, Arizona requires that employers pay at least $12.00 an hour. Seattle requires payment of $16.39 an hour.

Labor economists have devoted a lot of attention to state and local minimum wages, both because they affect millions of workers and because they serve as "natural experiments": by looking at what happens when a state increases its minimum wage, and especially by comparing the results with developments in neighboring states, economists can gather important information about how labor markets actually work in the real world.

The results of such an experiment may seem readily apparent: a state that increases its minimum wage, say from $7.25 to $16.39, raises the cost of labor. Minimum-wage workers, like employees at fast-food restaurants, are now more expensive to hire. Wouldn't these higher costs lead employers to reduce employment and workers to lose their jobs? But that's not what seems to happen, according to many labor economists (although there are some dissenters). Instead, even significant minimum-wage hikes, while they do raise wages for many workers, appear to have no effect on employment. How is this possible?

The answer, suggest some of the economists who have pioneered this line of research, is *monopsony:* because large employers use their market power to hold down wages, paying workers less than their marginal product, moderate increases in the minimum wage do not discourage hiring because even the new higher wage is still below labor's marginal product, so employing workers is still profitable.

If correct, this analysis has implications well beyond minimum wage policy, because it casts doubt on how well the marginal productivity theory of income distribution works for the economy as a whole.

>> *Check Your Understanding* 19-3
Solutions appear at back of book.

1. Assess each of the following statements. Do you think they are true, false, or ambiguous? Explain.
   a. The marginal productivity theory of income distribution is inconsistent with the presence of income disparities associated with gender, race, or ethnicity.
   b. Companies that engage in workplace discrimination but whose competitors do not are likely to have lower profits as a result of their actions.
   c. Workers who are paid less because they have less experience are not the victims of discrimination.
   d. Walmart moves into a small, rural town forcing many small businesses to close. Workers are the victims of discrimination as they take lower paying jobs at Walmart.

>> Quick Review

• Existing large disparities in wages both among individuals and across groups lead some to question the marginal productivity theory of income distribution.

• **Compensating differentials,** as well as differences in the values of the marginal products of workers that arise from differences in talent, job experience, job status, and human capital, account for some wage disparities.

• Market power, in the form of **unions** or monopsony behavior by employers, as well as the **efficiency-wage model,** in which employers pay an above-equilibrium wage to induce better performance, also explain how some wage disparities arise.

• Discrimination has historically been a major factor in wage disparities. Market competition tends to work against discrimination. But discrimination can leave a long-lasting legacy of diminished human capital acquisition.

The Supply of Labor

Up to this point we have focused on the demand for factors, which determines the quantities demanded of labor, capital, or land by producers as a function of their factor prices. What about the supply of factors?

In this section we focus exclusively on the supply of labor. We do this for two reasons. First, in the modern U.S. economy, labor is the most important factor of production, accounting for most of factor income. Second, as we'll see, labor supply is the area in which factor markets look most different from markets for goods and services.

> Decisions about labor supply result from decisions about **time allocation:** how many hours to spend on different activities.
>
> **Leisure** is time available for purposes other than earning money to buy marketed goods.

Work versus Leisure

In the labor market, the roles of firms and households are the reverse of what they are in markets for goods and services. A good such as wheat or smartphones is supplied by firms and demanded by households; labor, though, is demanded by firms and supplied by households. How do people decide how much labor to supply?

As a practical matter, most people have limited control over their work hours: either you take a job that involves working a set number of hours per week, or you don't get the job at all. To understand the logic of labor supply, however, it helps to put realism to one side for a bit and imagine an individual who can choose to work as many or as few hours as that individual likes.

Why wouldn't such an individual work as many hours as possible? Because workers are human beings, too, and have other uses for their time. An hour spent on the job is an hour not spent on other, presumably more pleasant, activities. So the decision about how much labor to supply involves making a decision about **time allocation**—how many hours to spend on different activities.

By working, people earn income that they can use to buy goods. The more hours an individual works, the more goods that individual can afford to buy. But this increased purchasing power comes at the expense of a reduction in **leisure,** the time spent not working. (Leisure doesn't necessarily mean time spent goofing off. It could mean time spent with one's family, pursuing hobbies, exercising, and so on.) And though purchased goods yield utility, so does leisure. Indeed, we can think of leisure itself as a normal good, which most people would like to consume more of as their incomes increase.

How does a rational individual decide how much leisure to consume? By making a marginal comparison, of course. In analyzing consumer choice, we asked how a utility-maximizing consumer uses a marginal *dollar.* In analyzing labor supply, we ask how an individual uses a marginal *hour.*

Consider Jaden, an individual who likes both leisure and the goods money can buy. Suppose that his wage rate is $10 per hour. In deciding how many hours he wants to work, he must compare the marginal utility of an additional hour of leisure with the additional utility he gets from $10 worth of goods. If $10 worth of goods adds more to his total utility than an additional hour of leisure, he can increase his total utility by giving up an hour of leisure to work an additional hour. If an extra hour of leisure adds more to his total utility than $10 worth of goods, he can increase his total utility by working one fewer hour in order to gain an hour of leisure.

At Jaden's optimal labor supply choice, then, his marginal utility of one hour of leisure is equal to the marginal utility he gets from the goods that his hourly wage can purchase. This is very similar to the *optimal consumption rule* we encountered in Chapter 10, except that it is a rule about time rather than money.

Every worker faces a trade-off between leisure and work.

The **individual labor supply curve** shows how the quantity of labor supplied by an individual depends on that individual's wage rate.

Our next step is to ask how Jaden's decision about time allocation is affected when his wage rate changes.

Wages and Labor Supply

Suppose that Jaden's wage rate doubles, from $10 to $20 per hour. How will he change his time allocation?

You could argue that Jaden will work longer hours, because his incentive to work has increased: by giving up an hour of leisure, he can now gain twice as much money as before. But you could equally well argue that he will work less, because he doesn't need to work as many hours to generate the income to pay for the goods he wants.

As these opposing arguments suggest, the quantity of labor Jaden supplies can either rise or fall when his wage rate rises. To understand why, let's recall the distinction between *substitution effects* and *income effects* that we learned in Chapter 10 and its appendix. We saw there that a price change affects consumer choice in two ways: by changing the opportunity cost of a good in terms of other goods (the substitution effect) and by making the consumer richer or poorer (the income effect).

Now think about how a rise in Jaden's wage rate affects his demand for leisure. The opportunity cost of leisure—the amount of money he gives up by taking an hour off instead of working—rises. That substitution effect gives him an incentive, other things equal, to consume *less* leisure and work *longer* hours. Conversely, a higher wage rate makes Jaden richer—and this income effect leads him, other things equal, to want to consume *more* leisure and work *fewer* hours, because leisure is a normal good.

So in the case of labor supply, the substitution effect and the income effect work in opposite directions. If the substitution effect is so powerful that it dominates the income effect, an increase in Jaden's wage rate leads him to supply *more* hours of labor. If the income effect is so powerful that it dominates the substitution effect, an increase in the wage rate leads him to supply *fewer* hours of labor.

We see, then, that the **individual labor supply curve**—the relationship between the wage rate and the number of hours of labor supplied by an individual worker—does not necessarily slope upward. If the income effect dominates, a higher wage rate will reduce the quantity of labor supplied.

Figure 19-10 illustrates the two possibilities for labor supply. If the substitution effect dominates the income effect, the individual labor supply curve slopes upward; panel (a) shows an increase in the wage rate from $10 to $20 per hour leading to a *rise* in the number of hours worked from 40 to 50. However, if the income effect dominates, the quantity of labor supplied goes down when the wage rate increases. Panel (b) shows the same rise in the wage rate leading to a *fall* in the number of hours worked from 40 to 30. (Economists refer to an individual labor supply curve that contains both upward-sloping and downward-sloping segments as a "backward-bending labor supply curve"—a concept that we analyze in detail in this chapter's appendix.)

Is a negative response of the quantity of labor supplied to the wage rate a real possibility? Yes: many labor economists believe that income effects on the supply of labor may be somewhat stronger than substitution effects. The most compelling piece of evidence for this belief comes from Americans' increasing consumption of leisure over the past century. At the end of the nineteenth century, wages adjusted for inflation were only about one-eighth what they are today; the typical workweek was 70 hours, and very few workers retired at age 65. Today the typical workweek is less than 40 hours, and most people retire at age 65 or earlier. So it seems that Americans have chosen to take advantage of higher wages in part by consuming more leisure.

FIGURE 19-10 The Individual Labor Supply Curve

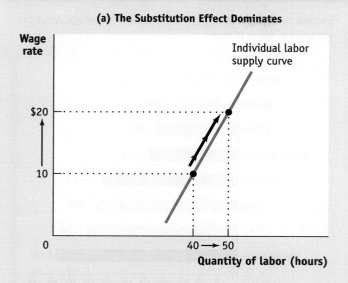

(a) The Substitution Effect Dominates

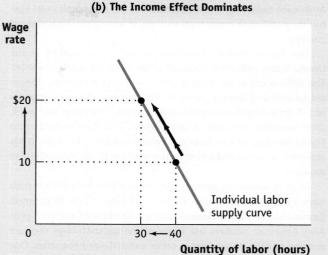

(b) The Income Effect Dominates

When the substitution effect of a wage increase dominates the income effect, the individual labor supply curve slopes upward, as in panel (a). Here a rise in the wage rate from $10 to $20 per hour increases the number of hours worked from 40 to 50. But when the income effect of a wage increase dominates the substitution effect, the individual labor supply curve slopes downward, as in panel (b). Here the same rise in the wage rate reduces the number of hours worked from 40 to 30. The individual labor supply curve shows how the quantity of labor supplied by an individual depends on that individual's wage rate.

Shifts of the Labor Supply Curve

Now that we have examined how income and substitution effects shape the individual labor supply curve, we can turn to the market labor supply curve. In any labor market, the market supply curve is the horizontal sum of the individual labor supply curves of all workers in that market. A change in any factor *other than the wage* that alters workers' willingness to supply labor causes a shift of the labor supply curve. A variety of factors can lead to such shifts, including changes in preferences and social norms, changes in population, changes in opportunities, and changes in wealth.

Changes in Preferences and Social Norms Changes in preferences and social norms can lead workers to increase or decrease their willingness to work at any given wage. A striking example of this phenomenon is the large increase in the number of employed women—particularly married employed women—that has occurred in the United States since the 1960s. Until that time, women who could afford to largely avoided working outside the home. Changes in preferences and norms in post–World War II America (helped along by the invention of labor-saving home appliances such as washing machines, increasing urbanization of the population, and higher female education levels) have induced large numbers of American women to join the workforce—a phenomenon often repeated in other countries that experience similar social and technological forces.

Changes in Population Changes in the population size generally lead to shifts of the labor supply curve. A larger population tends to shift the labor supply curve rightward as more workers are available at any given wage; a smaller population tends to shift the labor supply curve leftward. From 1990 to 2019,

GLOBAL COMPARISON THE OVERWORKED AMERICAN?

Americans today may work less than they did a hundred years ago, but they still work more than workers in any other industrialized country.

This figure compares average annual hours worked in the United States with those worked in other industrialized countries. The differences result from a combination of Americans' longer workweeks and shorter vacations. For example, the great majority of full-time American workers put in at least 40 hours per week. Until recently, however, a government mandate limited most French workers to a 35-hour workweek; collective bargaining has achieved a similar reduction in the workweek for many German workers.

In 2019, American workers got, on average, ten paid vacation days, but 24% of American workers got none at all. In contrast, German workers are guaranteed six weeks of paid vacation a year. Also, American workers use fewer of the vacation days they are entitled to than do workers in other industrialized countries. One survey found that American workers used only 51% of the vacation days they are entitled to, compared to 90% in France. Why do Americans work so much more than others? Unlike their counterparts in other industrialized countries, Americans are not legally

entitled to paid vacation days; as a result, the average American worker gets fewer of them.

Data from: OECD.

the U.S. labor force has grown approximately 1% per year, generated by immigration and a relatively high birth rate. As a result, from 1990 to 2019 the U.S. labor market had a rightward-shifting labor supply curve. However, while the population continued to grow after 2008, from 2008 through 2011 the size of the labor force temporarily shrunk as workers disillusioned by bad job prospects left the labor force. As a result, the U.S. labor supply curve shifted leftward during this period.

Changes in Opportunities At one time, teaching was the only occupation considered suitable for well-educated women. However, as opportunities in other professions opened up to women starting in the 1960s, many women left teaching and potential female teachers chose other careers. This generated a leftward shift of the supply curve for teachers, reflecting a fall in the willingness to work at any given wage and forcing school districts to pay more to maintain an adequate teaching staff. These events illustrate a general result: when superior alternatives arise for workers in another labor market, the supply curve in the original labor market shifts leftward as workers move to the new opportunities. Similarly, when opportunities diminish in one labor market—say, layoffs in the manufacturing industry due to increased foreign competition—the supply in alternative labor markets increases as workers move to these other markets.

Changes in Wealth A person whose wealth increases will buy more normal goods, including leisure. So when a class of workers experiences a general rise in their wealth levels—say, due to a stock market boom—the income effect from the wealth increase will shift the labor supply curve associated with those workers leftward as workers consume more leisure and work less. Note that *the income effect caused by a change in wealth shifts the labor supply curve,* but *the income effect from a wage rate increase*—as we discussed in the case of the individual labor supply curve—*is a movement along the labor supply curve.*

ECONOMICS >> *in Action*

The Real Housewives of the United States

If you watch old TV shows, you might think that the United States in the 1950s was a land of traditional families, with a male breadwinner and a stay-at-home housewife. The reality wasn't that stark: even in 1960, more than 40% of women in their prime working years (ages 25–54) were in the paid labor force. But that compared with 97% labor force participation for men in the same age group.

Over the 35 years that followed, women moved in large numbers into jobs outside the home: by the mid-1990s, more than 75% of prime-working-age women were in the paid workforce. But over the next few decades women's employment stagnated, or even declined a bit.

The high cost of child care in the United States depresses American women's labor supply in comparison to other wealthy countries.

The funny thing is that this didn't happen in other wealthy countries, where women's employment continued to rise. By 2019, around 85% of prime-working-age women in northern European countries and Canada were in the workforce, while the United States was still at 75%. Even Japan, which used to be famous for blatant gender discrimination, had higher female employment than the United States.

Why did the United States diverge? The most likely explanation is public policy that affects labor supply decisions. Most other wealthy countries either directly provide day care for children of working mothers, or subsidize and regulate private day care. The United States doesn't have a comparable policy, so the costs of going to work are much higher for U.S. women with children than for their counterparts abroad.

One implication of this explanation is that changing policy could have large implications for labor supply. Some U.S. politicians are now advocating creation of a national program that subsidizes child care. They argue that such a program would partly (not completely) pay for itself, because more women would take paying jobs, and would as a result pay higher taxes. The logic of labor supply says that these claims are probably right.

>> Check Your Understanding 19-4

Solutions appear at back of book.

1. Formerly, Jaden was free to work as many or as few hours per week as he wanted. But a new law limits the maximum number of hours he can work per week to 35. Explain under what circumstances, if at all, he is made:
   a. Worse off
   b. Equally as well off
   c. Better off

2. Explain in terms of the income and substitution effects how a fall in Jaden's wage rate can induce him to work more hours than before.

>> Quick Review

• The choice of how much labor to supply is a problem of **time allocation:** a choice between work and **leisure.**

• A rise in the wage rate causes both an income and a substitution effect on an individual's labor supply. The substitution effect of a higher wage rate induces more hours of work supplied, other things equal. This is countered by the income effect: higher income leads to a higher demand for leisure, a normal good. If the income effect dominates, a rise in the wage rate can actually cause the individual labor supply curve to slope the "wrong" way: downward.

• The market labor supply curve is the horizontal sum of the **individual labor supply curves** of all workers in that market. It shifts for four main reasons: changes in preferences and social norms, changes in population, changes in opportunities, and changes in wealth.

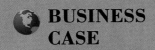

Walmart Revolutionizes
Its Labor Practices

With 2.2 million employees in 2019—roughly 1.5% of the country's working population—Walmart is America's largest private employer. The big-box retail chain is so large that Walmart's employee policies are considered a barometer of the current state of the labor market for retail workers.

Yet in the 1990s and early-to-mid 2000s, Walmart was considered a notoriously bad place to work. It was known for failing to provide workers with consistent schedules, for offering few benefits, and for paying wages so low that some employees qualified for food stamps and other antipoverty programs. During this period, Walmart was hit with several lawsuits alleging overtime violations, sexual harassment by managers, and gender discrimination.

Not only were Walmart employees unsatisfied—customers were too. They complained of dirty bathrooms, empty shelves, endless checkout lines, and impossible-to-find sales help. "Walmart's relentless focus on costs does seem to have taken some toll on in-store conditions and stock levels," an analyst explained, adding "If an item is not on the shelf, then you cannot sell it." As of 2015, only 16% of Walmart stores were meeting the company's own customer service goals.

But in 2015, Walmart suddenly began to overhaul its labor practices. At first the changes were fairly modest: higher wages and more consistent work scheduling. By 2016, Walmart's average pay for a nonmanagerial full-time worker was $13.69 per hour, up 16% from 2014 (but still below Costco's hourly rate of nearly $20 per hour).

The changes produced clear results. Customer feedback improved markedly: by 2016, 75% of Walmart stores were hitting their customer service targets. Walmart sales, which had been sliding relative to those of competitors, rose.

The changes didn't stop there. In 2018, in the midst of a strong economy, the company raised starting pay, introduced a year-end bonus to employees, and added 10 weeks of fully paid maternity leave for full-time employees. As one market observer said, "Those are 'sticky benefits'—the kind that might keep you from leaving Walmart just to earn 50 cents or $1 an hour more, or might woo you to Walmart in the first place."

At the same time, in order to counter the threat from rival retailer Amazon, Walmart has been investing more in worker training while investing heavily in its own e-commerce capabilities. Now customers can "click and collect" in their local Walmart store. When an item isn't on the shelf, customers can order it online. If necessary, a Walmart sales associate will walk a customer through that process. The company has created "Walmart Academies," located in the back of stores, where associates can expand their skills by learning about management responsibilities and mobile shopping apps.

Yes, indeed, a revolution is underway in Aisle 6.

QUESTIONS FOR THOUGHT

1. Use the marginal productivity theory of income distribution to explain how companies like Walmart can pay workers so little that they fall below the poverty line.

2. Use the case to explain how similar workers in the same labor market can end up being paid different wages in equilibrium. Also explain why Walmart believed it could improve its profitability by raising its labor costs.

3. Some politicians want to encourage more companies to adopt a high-wage strategy. What are the possible positive and negative effects of such a policy?

4. When an employer introduces "sticky benefits," like generous child-care benefits, what does that imply about the costs of worker turnover to employer?

5. What factors do you think compelled Walmart to change its labor practices? Be specific.

SUMMARY

1. Just as there are markets for goods and services, there are markets for factors of production, including labor, land, and both **physical capital** and **human capital.** These markets determine the **factor distribution of income.**

2. According to the **price-taking producer's optimal employment rule,** a price-taking producer's profit is maximized by employing each factor of production up to the level at which its **value of the marginal product** is equal to the factor's price. The value of the marginal product of a factor is equal to its marginal product multiplied by the price of the output it produces. The **value of the marginal product curve** is therefore the individual price-taking producer's demand curve for a factor.

3. The market demand curve for labor is the horizontal sum of the individual demand curves of producers in that market. It shifts for three main reasons: changes in output price, changes in the supply of other factors, and technological changes.

4. When a competitive labor market is in equilibrium, the market wage is equal to the **equilibrium value of the marginal product** of labor, the additional value produced by the last worker hired in the labor market as a whole. The same principle applies to other factors of production: the **rental rate** of land or capital is equal to the equilibrium value of the marginal products. This insight leads to the **marginal productivity theory of income distribution,** according to which each factor is paid the value of the marginal product of the last unit of that factor employed in the factor market as a whole.

5. Large disparities in wages raise questions about the validity of the marginal productivity theory of income distribution. Many disparities can be explained by **compensating differentials** and by differences in talent, job experience, job status, and human capital across workers. Market interference in the forms of **unions** and collective action by employers also creates wage disparities. The **efficiency-wage model,** which arises from a type of market failure, shows how wage disparities can result from employers' attempts to increase worker performance. Free markets tend to diminish discrimination, but discrimination remains a real source of wage disparity, especially through its effects on human capital acquisition. Discrimination is typically maintained either through problems in labor markets or (historically) through institutionalization in government policies.

6. Labor supply is the result of decisions about **time allocation,** where each worker faces a trade-off between **leisure** and work. An increase in the hourly wage rate tends to increase work hours via the substitution effect but to reduce work hours via the income effect. If the net result is that a worker increases the quantity of labor supplied in response to a higher wage, the **individual labor supply curve** slopes upward. If the net result is that a worker reduces work hours, the individual labor supply curve—unlike supply curves for goods and services—slopes downward.

7. The market labor supply curve is the horizontal sum of the individual labor supply curves of all workers in that market. It shifts for four main reasons: changes in preferences and social norms, changes in population, changes in opportunities, and changes in wealth.

KEY TERMS

Physical capital, p. 544
Human capital, p. 544
Factor distribution of income, p. 545
Value of the marginal product, p. 547
Price-taking producer's optimal employment rule, p. 548

Value of the marginal product curve, p. 548
Equilibrium value of the marginal product, p. 553
Rental rate, p. 553
Marginal productivity theory of income distribution, p. 554

Compensating differentials, p. 557
Unions, p. 559
Efficiency-wage model, p. 560
Time allocation, p. 563
Leisure, p. 563
Individual labor supply curve, p. 564

PRACTICE QUESTIONS

1. The market for school teachers appears to be very competitive, but similar to nursing, many cities have only a few employers. Most regions have one or two school districts that employ the majority of teachers. How can monopsony power within school districts contribute to lower wages and gender wage discrimination?

2. The OECD (Organization for Economic Cooperation and Development) presents average wage data across developed countries. The database also includes data on the gender wage gap and share of low- and high-wage workers. For this problem go to the website: data.oecd.org/earnwage/average-wages.htm. In the left sidebar, select the tab for gender wage gap.

a. What is the definition of the gender wage gap?

b. What is the gender wage gap for the United States? Provide an interpretation of the value.

c. What are the primary factors that explain the gender wage gap? Do these factors rule out discrimination?

3. A recent study by economists at Northwestern University and UCLA researched the wage and employment effects of economic consolidation in the hospital industry across the United States. The authors looked at three distinct groups of workers:

i. Unskilled workers whose occupations are not constricted to the health care industry, such as custodial and cafeteria workers

ii. Skilled workers whose skills are not specific to the industry, such as human resources personnel and Equal Employment Opportunity Commission compliance officers

iii. Skilled health care professionals such as nurses or pharmacy workers

Which group of workers do you think was most affected by the consolidations? Why?

PROBLEMS

1. In 2019, national income in the United States was $18,155.2 billion. In the same year, 152 million workers were employed, at an average wage, including benefits, of $75,138 per worker per year.

a. How much compensation of employees was paid in the United States in 2019?

b. Analyze the factor distribution of income. What percentage of national income was received in the form of compensation to employees in 2019?

c. Suppose that a huge wave of corporate downsizing leads many terminated employees to open their own businesses. What is the effect on the factor distribution of income?

d. Suppose the supply of labor rises due to an increase in the retirement age. What happens to the percentage of national income received in the form of compensation of employees?

2. Marty's Frozen Yogurt has the production function per day shown in the accompanying table. The equilibrium wage rate for a worker is $80 per day. Each cup of frozen yogurt sells for $2.

Quantity of labor (workers)	Quantity of frozen yogurt (cups)
0	0
1	110
2	200
3	270
4	300
5	320
6	330

a. Calculate the marginal product of labor for each worker and the value of the marginal product of labor per worker.

b. How many workers should Marty employ?

3. The production function for Patty's Pizza Parlor is given in the table in Problem 12. The price of pizza is $2, but the hourly wage rate rises from $10 to $15. Use a diagram to determine how Patty's demand for workers responds as a result of this wage rate increase.

4. Jameel runs a driver education school. The more driving instructors he hires, the more driving lessons he can sell. But because he owns a limited number of training automobiles, each additional driving instructor adds less to Jameel's output of driving lessons. The accompanying table shows Jameel's production function per day. Each driving lesson can be sold at $35 per hour.

Quantity of labor (driving instructors)	Quantity of driving lessons (hours)
0	0
1	8
2	15
3	21
4	26
5	30
6	33

Determine Jameel's labor demand schedule (his demand schedule for driving instructors) for each of the following daily wage rates for driving instructors: $160, $180, $200, $220, $240, and $260.

5. Dale and Dana work at a self-service gas station and convenience store. Dale opens up every day, and Dana arrives later to help stock the store. They are both paid the current market wage of $9.50 per hour. But Dale feels he should be paid much more because the revenue generated from the gas pumps he turns on every morning is much higher than the revenue generated by the items that Dana stocks. Assess this argument.

6. A *New York Times* article observed that the wage of farmworkers in Mexico was $11 an hour but the wage of immigrant Mexican farmworkers in California was $9 an hour.

a. Assume that the output sells for the same price in the two countries. Does this imply that the marginal product of labor of farmworkers is higher in Mexico or in California? Explain your answer, and illustrate with a diagram that shows the demand and supply curves for labor in the respective markets. In your diagram, assume that the quantity supplied of labor for any given wage rate is the same for Mexican farmworkers as it is for immigrant Mexican farm-workers in California.

b. Now suppose that farmwork in Mexico is more arduous and more dangerous than farmwork in California. As a result, the quantity supplied of labor for any given wage rate is not the same for Mexican farmworkers as it is for immigrant Mexican farmworkers in California. How does this change your answer to part a? What concept best accounts for the difference between wage rates for Mexican farmworkers and immigrant Mexican farmworkers in California?

c. Illustrate your answer to part b with a diagram. In this diagram, assume that the quantity of labor demanded for any given wage rate is the same for Mexican employers as it is for Californian employers.

7. Kendra is the owner of Wholesome Farms, a commercial dairy. Kendra employs labor, land, and capital. In her operations, Kendra can substitute between the amount of labor she employs and the amount of capital she employs. That is, to produce the same quantity of output she can use more labor and less capital; similarly, to produce the same quantity of output she can use less labor and more capital. Let w^* represent the annual cost of labor in the market, let r_L^* represent the annual cost of a unit of land in the market, and let r_k^* represent the annual cost of a unit of capital in the market.

a. Suppose that Kendra can maximize her profits by employing less labor and more capital than she is currently using but the same amount of land. What three conditions must now hold for Kendra's operations (involving her value of the marginal product of labor, land, and capital) for this to be true?

b. Kendra believes that she can increase her profits by renting and using more land. However, if she uses more land, she must use more of both labor and capital; if she uses less land, she can use less of both labor and capital. What three conditions must hold (involving her value of the marginal product of labor, land, and capital) for this to be true?

8. For each of the following situations in which similar workers are paid different wages, give the most likely explanation for these wage differences.

a. Test pilots for new jet aircraft earn higher wages than airline pilots.

b. College graduates usually have higher earnings in their first year on the job than workers without college degrees have in their first year on the job.

c. Full professors command higher salaries than assistant professors for teaching the same class.

d. Unionized workers are generally better paid than non-unionized workers.

9. Research consistently finds that despite nondiscrimination policies, African-American workers on average receive lower wages than White workers do. What are the possible reasons for this? Are these reasons consistent with marginal productivity theory?

10. Greta is an enthusiastic amateur gardener and spends a lot of her free time working in her yard. She also has

a demanding and well-paid job as a freelance advertising consultant. Because the advertising business is going through a difficult time, the hourly consulting fee Greta can charge falls. Greta decides to spend more time gardening and less time consulting. Explain her decision in terms of income and substitution effects.

11. You are the governor's economic policy adviser. The governor wants to put in place policies that encourage employed people to work more hours at their jobs and that encourage unemployed people to find and take jobs. Assess each of the following policies in terms of reaching that goal. Explain your reasoning in terms of income and substitution effects, and indicate when the impact of the policy may be ambiguous.

a. The state income tax rate is lowered, which has the effect of increasing workers' after-tax wage rate.

b. The state income tax rate is increased, which has the effect of decreasing workers' after-tax wage rate.

c. The state property tax rate is increased, which reduces workers' after-tax income.

WORK IT OUT

12. Patty's Pizza Parlor has the production function per hour shown in the accompanying table. The hourly wage rate for each worker is $10. Each pizza sells for $2.

Quantity of labor (workers)	Quantity of pizza
0	0
1	9
2	15
3	19
4	22
5	24

a. Calculate the marginal product of labor for each worker and the value of the marginal product of labor per worker.

b. Draw the value of the marginal product of labor curve. Use your diagram to determine how many workers Patty should employ.

c. The price of pizza increases to $4. Calculate the value of the marginal product of labor per worker, and draw the new value of the marginal product of labor curve in your diagram. Use your diagram to determine how many workers Patty should employ now.

Now let's assume that Patty buys a new high-tech pizza oven that allows her workers to become twice as productive as before. That is, the first worker now produces 18 pizzas per hour instead of 9, and so on.

d. Calculate the new marginal product of labor and the new value of the marginal product of labor at the original price of $2 per pizza.

e. Use a diagram to determine how Patty's hiring decision responds to this increase in the productivity of her workforce. ■

Indifference Curve Analysis of Labor Supply

In the chapter, you learned why the labor supply curve can slope downward instead of upward: the substitution effect of a higher wage rate, which provides an incentive to work longer hours, can be outweighed by the income effect of a higher wage rate, which may lead individuals to consume more leisure. In this appendix we will see how this analysis can be carried out using the *indifference curves* introduced in the Chapter 10 appendix.

The Time Allocation Budget Line

Let's return to the example of Jaden, who likes leisure but also likes having money to spend. We now assume that Jaden has a total of 80 hours per week that he could spend either working or enjoying as leisure time. (The remaining hours in his week, we assume, are taken up with necessary activities, mainly sleeping.) Let's also assume, initially, that his hourly wage rate is $10.

His consumption possibilities are defined by the **time allocation budget line** in Figure 19A-1, a budget line that shows Jaden's trade-offs between consumption of leisure and income. Hours of leisure per week are measured on the horizontal axis, and the money he earns from working is measured on the vertical axis.

The horizontal intercept, point *X*, is at 80 hours: if Jaden didn't work at all, he would have 80 hours of leisure per week but would not earn any money. The vertical intercept, point *Y*, is at $800: if Jaden worked all the time, he would earn $800 per week.

Why can we use a budget line to describe Jaden's time allocation choice? The budget lines found in Chapter 10 and its appendix represent the trade-offs facing consumers deciding how to allocate their income among different goods. Here, instead of asking how Jaden allocates his income, we ask how he allocates his

A **time allocation budget line** shows an individual's trade-off between consumption of leisure and the income that allows consumption of marketed goods.

FIGURE 19A-1 The Time Allocation Budget Line

Jaden's time allocation budget line shows his trade-off between work, which pays a wage rate of $10 per hour, and leisure. At point *X* he allocates all his time, 80 hours, to leisure but has no income. At point *Y* he allocates all his time to work, earning $800, but consumes no leisure. His hourly wage rate of $10, the opportunity cost of an hour of leisure, is equal to minus the slope of the time allocation budget line. We have assumed that point *A*, at 40 hours of leisure and $400 in income, is Jaden's optimal time allocation choice. It obeys the optimal time allocation rule: the additional utility Jaden gets from one more hour of leisure must equal the additional utility he gets from the goods he can purchase with one hour's wages.

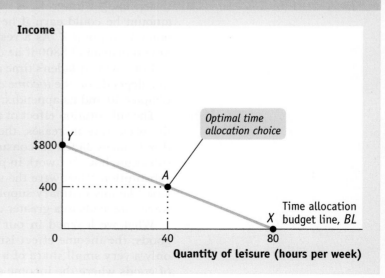

The **optimal time allocation rule** says that an individual should allocate time so that the marginal utility gained from the income earned from an additional hour worked is equal to the marginal utility of an additional hour of leisure.

time. But the principles underlying the allocation of income and the allocation of time are the same: each involves allocating a fixed amount of a resource (80 hours of time in this case) with a constant trade-off (Jaden must forgo $10 for each additional hour of leisure). So using a budget line is just as appropriate for time allocation as it is for income allocation.

As in the case of ordinary budget lines, opportunity cost plays a key role. The opportunity cost of an hour of leisure is what Jaden must forgo by working one less hour—$10 in income. This opportunity cost is, of course, Jaden's hourly wage rate and is equal to minus the slope of his time allocation budget line. You can verify this by noting that the slope is equal to minus the vertical intercept, point *Y*, divided by the horizontal intercept, point *X*—that is, –$800/(80 hours) = –$10 per hour.

To maximize his utility, Jaden must choose the optimal point on the time allocation budget line in Figure 19A-1. In Chapter 10 we saw that a consumer who allocates spending to maximize utility finds the point on the budget line that satisfies the *utility-maximizing principle of marginal analysis:* the marginal utility per dollar spent on two goods must be equal. Although Jaden's choice involves allocating time rather than money, the same principles apply.

Since Jaden "spends" time rather than money, the counterpart of the utility-maximizing principle of marginal analysis is the **optimal time allocation rule:** the marginal utility Jaden gets from the extra money earned from an additional hour spent working must equal the marginal utility of an additional hour of leisure.

The Effect of a Higher Wage Rate

Depending on his tastes, Jaden's utility-maximizing choice of hours of leisure and income could lie anywhere on the time allocation budget line in Figure 19A-1. Let's assume that his optimal choice is point *A*, at which he consumes 40 hours of leisure and earns $400. Now we are ready to link the analysis of time allocation to labor supply.

When Jaden chooses a point like *A* on his time allocation budget line, he is also choosing the quantity of labor he supplies to the labor market. By choosing to consume 40 of his 80 available hours as leisure, he has also chosen to supply the other 40 hours as labor.

Now suppose that Jaden's wage rate doubles, from $10 to $20 per hour. The effect of this increase in his wage rate is shown in Figure 19A-2. His time allocation budget line rotates outward: the vertical intercept, which represents the amount he could earn if he devoted all 80 hours to work, shifts upward from point *Y* to point *Z*. As a result of the doubling of his wage, Jaden would earn $1,600 instead of $800 if he devoted all 80 hours to working.

But how will Jaden's time allocation actually change? As we saw in the chapter, this depends on the *income effect* and *substitution effect* that we learned about in Chapter 10 and its appendix.

The substitution effect of an increase in the wage rate works as follows. When the wage rate increases, the opportunity cost of an hour of leisure increases; this induces Jaden to consume less leisure and work more hours—that is, to substitute hours of work in place of hours of leisure as the wage rate rises. If the substitution effect were the whole story, the individual labor supply curve would look like any ordinary supply curve and would always slope upward—a higher wage rate leads to a greater quantity of labor supplied.

What we learned in our analysis of demand was that for most consumer goods, the income effect isn't very important because most goods account for only a very small share of a consumer's spending. In addition, in the few cases of goods where the income effect is significant—for example, major purchases like housing—it usually reinforces the substitution effect: most goods are

FIGURE 19A-2 An Increase in the Wage Rate

The two panels show Jaden's initial optimal choice, point A or BL_1, the time allocation budget line corresponding to a wage rate of $10. After his wage rate rises to $20, his budget line rotates out to the new budget line, BL_2: if he spends all his time working, the amount of money he earns rises from $800 to $1,600, reflected in the movement from point Y to point Z. This generates two opposing effects: the substitution effect pushes him to consume less leisure and to work more hours; the income effect pushes him to consume more leisure and to work fewer hours. Panel (a) shows the change in time allocation when the substitution effect is stronger: Jaden's new optimal choice is point B, representing a decrease in hours of leisure to 30 hours and an increase in hours of labor to 50 hours. In this case the individual labor supply curve slopes upward. Panel (b) shows the change in time allocation when the income effect is stronger: point C is the new optimal choice, representing an increase in hours of leisure to 50 hours and a decrease in hours of labor to 30 hours. Now the individual labor supply curve slopes downward.

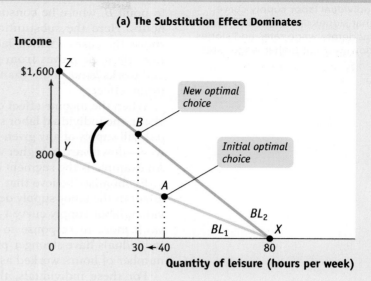

(a) The Substitution Effect Dominates

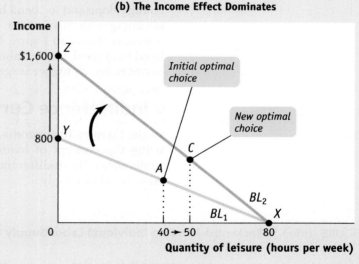

(b) The Income Effect Dominates

normal goods, so when a price increase makes a consumer poorer, that consumer buys less of that good.

In the labor/leisure choice, however, the income effect takes on a new significance, for two reasons. First, most people get the great majority of their income from wages. This means that the income effect of a change in the wage rate is *not* small: an increase in the wage rate will generate a significant increase in income. Second, leisure is a normal good: when income rises, other things equal, people tend to consume more leisure and work fewer hours.

So the income effect of a higher wage rate tends to *reduce* the quantity of labor supplied, working in opposition to the substitution effect, which tends to *increase* the quantity of labor supplied. So the net effect of a higher wage rate on the quantity of labor Jaden supplies could go either way—depending on his preferences, he might choose to supply more labor, or he might choose to supply less labor. The two panels of Figure 19A-2 illustrate these two outcomes. In each panel, point A represents Jaden's initial consumption choice.

A backward-bending individual labor supply curve is an individual labor supply curve that slopes upward at low to moderate wage rates and slopes downward at higher wage rates.

Panel (a) shows the case in which Jaden works more hours in response to a higher wage rate. An increase in the wage rate induces him to move from point *A* to point *B*, where he consumes less leisure than at *A* and therefore works more hours. Here the substitution effect prevails over the income effect. Panel (b) shows the case in which Jaden works fewer hours in response to a higher wage rate. Here, he moves from point *A* to point *C*, where he consumes more leisure and works *fewer* hours than at *A*. Here the income effect prevails over the substitution effect.

When the income effect of a higher wage rate is stronger than the substitution effect, the individual labor supply curve, which shows how much labor an individual will supply at any given wage rate will have a segment that slopes the "wrong" way—downward: a higher wage rate leads to a smaller quantity of labor supplied. An example is the segment connecting points *B* and *C* in Figure 19A-3.

Economists believe that the substitution effect usually dominates the income effect in the labor supply decision when an individual's wage rate is low. An individual labor supply curve typically slopes upward for lower wage rates as people work more in response to rising wage rates. But they also believe that many individuals have stronger preferences for leisure and will choose to cut back the number of hours worked as their wage rate continues to rise.

For these individuals, the income effect eventually dominates the substitution effect as the wage rate rises, leading their individual labor supply curves to change slope and to "bend backward" at high wage rates. An individual labor supply curve with this feature, called a **backward-bending individual labor supply curve,** is shown in Figure 19A-3. Although an *individual* labor supply curve may bend backward, *market* labor supply curves almost always slope upward over their entire range as higher wage rates draw more new workers into the labor market.

Indifference Curve Analysis

In the Chapter 10 appendix, we learned that consumer choice can be represented using the concept of *indifference curves*, which provide a "map" of consumer preferences. But indifference curves are also especially useful for addressing the issue of labor supply.

FIGURE 19A-3 A Backward-Bending Individual Labor Supply Curve

At lower wage rates, the substitution effect dominates the income effect for Jaden. This is illustrated by the movement along the individual labor supply curve from point *A* to point *B*: a rise in the wage rate from W_1 to W_2 leads the quantity of labor supplied to increase from L_1 to L_2. But at higher wage rates, the income effect dominates the substitution effect, shown by the movement from point *B* to point *C*: here, a rise in the wage rate from W_2 to W_3 leads the quantity of labor supplied to decrease from L_2 to L_3.

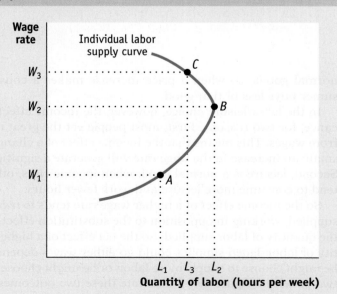

FIGURE 19A-4 Labor Supply Choice: The Indifference Curve Approach

Point *A*, on *BL₁*, is Jaden's initial optimal choice. After a wage rate increase, his income and utility level increase: his new time allocation budget line is *BL₂* and his new optimal choice is point *C*. This change can be decomposed into the substitution effect, the fall in the hours of leisure from point *A* to point *S*, and the income effect, the increase in the number of hours of leisure from point *S* to point *C*. As shown here, the income effect dominates the substitution effect: the net result of an increase in the wage rate is an increase in the hours of leisure consumed and a decrease in the hours of labor supplied.

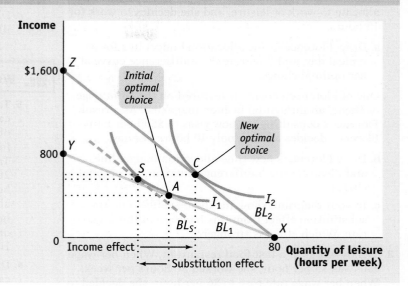

Using indifference curves, Figure 19A-4 shows how an increase in the wage rate can lead to a fall in the quantity of labor supplied. Point *A* is Jaden's initial optimal choice, given an hourly wage rate of $10. It is the same as point *A* in Figure 19A-1; this time, however, we include an indifference curve to show that it is a point at which the budget line is tangent to the highest possible indifference curve.

Now consider the effect of a rise in the wage rate to $20. Imagine, for a moment, that at the same time Jaden was offered a higher wage, he was told that he had to start repaying his student loan and that the combination of good and bad news left his utility unchanged. Then he would find himself at point *S:* on the same indifference curve as at *A*, but tangent to a steeper budget line, the dashed line *BLₛ* in Figure 19A-4, which is parallel to *BL₂*. The move from point *A* to point *S* is the substitution effect of his wage increase: it leads him to consume less leisure and therefore supply more labor.

But now cancel the repayment on the student loan, and Jaden is able to move to a higher indifference curve. His new optimum is at point *C*, which corresponds to *C* in panel (b) of Figure 19A-2. The move from point *S* to point *C* is the income effect of his wage increase. And we see that this income effect can outweigh the substitution effect: at *C* he consumes more leisure, and therefore supplies less labor, than he did at *A*.

PROBLEMS

1. Leandro has 16 hours per day that he can allocate to work or leisure. His job pays a wage rate of $20. Leandro decides to consume 8 hours of leisure. His indifference curves have the usual shape: they slope downward, they do not cross, and they have the characteristic convex shape.

   a. Draw Leandro's time allocation budget line for a typical day. Then illustrate the indifference curve at his optimal choice.

   Now Leandro's wage rate falls to $10.

   b. Draw Leandro's new budget line.

   c. Suppose that Leandro now works only 4 hours as a result of his reduced wage rate. Illustrate the indifference curve at his new optimal choice.

   d. Leandro's decision to work less as the wage rate falls is the result of a substitution effect and an income effect. In your diagram, show the income effect and the substitution effect from this reduced wage rate. Which effect is stronger?

2. Florence is a highly paid fashion consultant who earns $100 per hour. She has 16 hours per day that she can allocate to work or leisure, and she decides to work for 12 hours.

   a. Draw Florence's time allocation budget line for a typical day, and illustrate the indifference curve at her optimal choice.

   One of Florence's clients is featured on the front page of *Vague*, an influential fashion magazine. As a result, Florence's consulting fee now rises to $500 per hour. Florence decides to work only 10 hours per day.

   b. Draw Florence's new time allocation budget line, and illustrate the indifference curve at her optimal choice.

   c. In your diagram, show the income effect and the substitution effect from this increase in the wage rate. Which effect is stronger?

3. Wendy works at a fast-food restaurant. When her wage rate was $5 per hour, she worked 30 hours per week. When her wage rate rose to $6 per hour, she decided to work 40 hours. But when her wage rate rose further to $7, she decided to work only 35 hours.

   a. Draw Wendy's individual labor supply curve.

   b. Is Wendy's behavior irrational, or can you find a rational explanation? Explain your answer.

4. Over the past 50 years the average American's leisure time has increased by between 4 and 8 hours a week. Some economists think that this increase is primarily driven by a rise in wage rates.

   a. Use the income and substitution effects to describe the labor supply for the average American. Which effect dominates?

   b. In addition to increasing wages, a study by the Bureau of Labor Statistics finds labor force participation for women is projected to steadily increase through 2024. For the average woman who has entered the labor force, which effect dominates?

   c. Draw typical individual labor supply curves that illustrate your answers to part a and part b above.

WORK IT OUT

5. Tamara has 80 hours per week that she can allocate to work or leisure. Her job pays a wage rate of $20 per hour, but Tamara is being taxed on her income in the following way. On the first $400 that Tamara makes, she pays no tax. That is, for the first 20 hours she works, her net wage—what she takes home after taxes—is $20 per hour. On all income above $400, Tamara pays a 75% tax. That is, for all hours above the first 20 hours, her net wage rate is only $5 per hour. Tamara decides to work 30 hours. Her indifference curves have the usual shape.

   a. Draw Tamara's time allocation budget line for a typical week. Also illustrate the indifference curve at her optimal choice.

   The government changes the tax scheme. Now only the first $100 of income is tax-exempt. That is, for the first 5 hours she works, Tamara's net wage rate is $20 per hour. But the government reduces the tax rate on all other income to 50%. That is, for all hours above the first 5 hours, Tamara's net wage rate is now $10. After these changes, Tamara finds herself exactly equally as well off as before. That is, her new optimal choice is on the same indifference curve as her initial optimal choice.

   b. Draw Tamara's new time allocation budget line on the same diagram. Also illustrate her optimal choice. Bear in mind that she is equally as well off (on the same indifference curve) as before the tax changes occurred.

   c. Will Tamara work more or less than before the changes to the tax scheme? Why? ■

20 Uncertainty, Risk, and Private Information

EXTREME WEATHER

IN DECEMBER 2019, as heavy rains blanketed the state, a collective sigh of relief could be heard across California: nearly eight years of severe drought had finally come to an end. The drought years had exacted a heavy toll on California and neighboring western states. During 2017, 2018, and 2019, a series of catastrophic wildfires across the west, as well as Alaska, burning several million acres, claiming 163 lives, and destroying tens of thousands of building. The cumulative loss was estimated at over $53 billion.

While drought and wildfires ravaged the western United States, other parts of the country were repeatedly hit by other types of extreme weather. In 2019 alone, Tropical Storm Imelda, Hurricane Dorian, and a number of tornadoes caused a cumulative loss of $18 billion to the U.S. economy. In the Midwest, a series of floods caused losses totaling $20 billion. From the Dakotas to the Carolinas, torrential rain, wind, hailstorms, and flooding destroyed homes, buildings, crops, livestock, and infrastructure. Moreover, observers believe that the estimated damage significantly understates the true cost because many people fail to report their losses.

As these extreme weather events illustrate, uncertainty is a feature of the real world. Up to this point we have assumed that people make decisions with knowledge of exactly how the future will unfold. (The exception is our coverage of health insurance decisions.) Yet, as anyone who lives on the Atlantic Seaboard, or in the tornado-prone Great Plains, or in the drought-stricken Western states, now realizes, making decisions when the future is uncertain carries with it the *risk of loss*. In fact, both climatologists and the property insurance industry largely agree that extreme weather events have become more frequent as a result of climate change.

It is often possible for individuals to use markets to reduce their risk. For example, hurricane victims who had insurance were able to receive some, if not complete, compensation for their losses. In fact, through insurance and other devices, the modern economy offers many ways for individuals to reduce their exposure to risk.

However, a market economy cannot always solve the problems created by uncertainty. Markets do very well at coping with risk when two conditions hold: (1) when risk can be reasonably well *diversified* and (2) when the probability of loss is equally well known by everyone. However, the increase in extreme weather events over the past several years has led many insurers to stop relying on *diversification* for weather-related losses and instead to sharply reduce their coverage of such losses.

In practice, the second condition is often the more limiting one. Markets run into trouble when some people know things that others do not — a situation that involves what is called *private information*. We'll see that private information can cause inefficiency by preventing mutually beneficial transactions from occurring — especially in insurance markets.

In this chapter we'll examine why most people dislike risk. Then we'll explore how a market economy allows people to reduce risk at a price. Finally, we'll turn to the special problems created for markets by private information. ●

The wildfires that tore through California in 2019 illustrate that uncertainty is an important feature of the real world.

JOSH EDELSON/AFP/Getty Images

WHAT YOU WILL LEARN

- Why is **risk** a key feature of the economy?
- Why does diminishing marginal utility make people **risk-averse** and how does it determine what they are willing to pay to reduce risk?
- How do insurance markets lead to mutually beneficial trades of risk?
- What is **private information** and what special problems does it pose for markets?

A **random variable** is a variable with an uncertain future value.

The **expected value** of a random variable is the weighted average of all possible values, where the weights on each possible value correspond to the probability of that value occurring.

A **state of the world** is a possible future event.

Risk is uncertainty about future outcomes. When the uncertainty is about monetary outcomes, it becomes **financial risk.**

‖ The Economics of Risk Aversion

In general, people don't like risk and are willing to pay a price to avoid it. Just ask the U.S. insurance industry, which collects more than $1 trillion in premiums every year. But what exactly is *risk?* And why don't most people like it? To answer these questions, we need to look briefly at the concept of *expected value* and the meaning of *uncertainty.* Then we can turn to why people dislike risk.

Expectations and Uncertainty

The Lee family doesn't know how big its medical bills will be next year. If all goes well, they won't have any medical expenses at all. Let's assume that there's a 50% chance of that happening. But if a family member requires hospitalization or expensive drugs, they will face medical expenses of $10,000. Let's assume that there's also a 50% chance that these high medical expenses will materialize.

In this example—which is designed to illustrate a point, rather than to be realistic—the Lees' medical expenses for the coming year are a **random variable,** a variable that has an uncertain future value. No one can predict which of its possible values, or outcomes, a random variable will take. But that doesn't mean we can say nothing about the Lees' future medical expenses. On the contrary, an actuary (a person trained in evaluating uncertain future events) could calculate the **expected value** of expenses next year—the weighted average of all possible values, where the weights on each possible value correspond to the probability of that value occurring. In this example, the expected value of the Lees' medical expenses is $(0.5 \times \$0) + (0.5 \times \$10,000) = \$5,000$.

To derive the general formula for the expected value of a random variable, we imagine that there are a number of different **states of the world,** possible future events. Each state is associated with a different realized value—the value that actually occurs—of the random variable. You don't know which state of the world will actually occur, but you can assign probabilities, one for each state of the world.

Let's assume that P_1 is the probability of state 1, P_2 the probability of state 2, and so on. And you know the realized value of the random value in each state of the world: S_1 in state 1, S_2 in state 2, and so on. Let's also assume that there are N possible states. Then the expected value of a random variable is:

(20-1) *Expected value of a random variable*
$$EV = (P_1 \times S_1) + (P_2 \times S_2) + \ldots + (P_N \times S_N)$$

In the case of the Lee family, there are only two possible states of the world, each with a probability of 0.5.

Notice, however, that the Lee family doesn't actually expect to pay $5,000 in medical bills next year. That's because in this example there is no state of the world in which the family pays exactly $5,000. Either the family pays nothing, or it pays $10,000. So the Lees face considerable uncertainty about their future medical expenses.

But what if the Lee family can buy health insurance that will cover its medical expenses, whatever they turn out to be? Suppose, in particular, that the family can pay $5,000 up front in return for full coverage of whatever medical expenses actually arise during the coming year. Then the Lees' future medical expenses are no longer uncertain *for them:* in return for $5,000—an amount equal to the expected value of the medical expenses—the insurance company assumes all responsibility for paying those medical expenses. Would this be a good deal from the Lees' point of view?

Yes, it would—or at least most families would think so. Most people prefer, other things equal, to reduce **risk**—uncertainty about future outcomes. (We'll focus here on **financial risk,** in which the uncertainty is about monetary outcomes, as opposed to uncertainty about outcomes that can't be assigned a monetary value.) In fact, most people are willing to pay a substantial price to reduce their risk; that's why we have an insurance industry.

But before we study the market for insurance, we need to understand why people feel that risk is a bad thing, an attitude that economists call *risk aversion*. The source of risk aversion lies in a concept we first encountered in our analysis of consumer demand, back in Chapter 10: *diminishing marginal utility*.

The Logic of Risk Aversion

To understand how diminishing marginal utility gives rise to risk aversion, we need to look not only at the Lees' medical costs but also at how those costs affect the income the family has left after medical expenses. Let's assume the family knows that it will have an income of $30,000 next year. If the family has no medical expenses, it will be left with all of that income. If its medical expenses are $10,000, its income after medical expenses will be only $20,000. Since we have assumed that there is an equal chance of these two outcomes, the expected value of the Lees' income after medical expenses is $(0.5 \times \$30,000) + (0.5 \times \$20,000) = \$25,000$. At times we will simply refer to this as expected income.

But as we'll now see, if the family's utility function has the shape typical of most families', its **expected utility**—the expected value of its total utility given uncertainty about future outcomes—is less than it would be if the family didn't face any risk and knew with certainty that its income after medical expenses would be $25,000.

To see why, we need to look at how total utility depends on income. Panel (a) of Figure 20-1 shows a hypothetical utility function for the Lee family, where total utility depends on income—the amount of money the Lees have available for consumption of goods and services (after they have paid any medical bills). The table within the figure shows how the family's total utility varies over the income range of $20,000 to $30,000. As usual, the utility function slopes upward, because more income leads to higher total utility. Notice as well that the curve gets flatter as we move up and to the right, which reflects diminishing marginal utility.

In Chapter 10 we applied the principle of diminishing marginal utility to individual goods and services: each successive unit of a good or service that a consumer purchases adds less to their total utility. The same principle applies to income used for consumption: each successive dollar of income adds less to total utility than the previous dollar.

Panel (b) shows how marginal utility varies with income, confirming that marginal utility of income falls as income rises. As we'll see in a moment, diminishing marginal utility is the key to understanding the desire of individuals to reduce risk.

To analyze how a person's utility is affected by risk, economists start from the assumption that individuals facing uncertainty maximize their *expected* utility. We can use the data in Figure 20-1 to calculate the Lee family's expected utility. We'll first do the calculation assuming that the Lees have no insurance, and then we'll recalculate it assuming that they have purchased insurance.

Without insurance, if the Lees are lucky and don't incur any medical expenses, they will have an income of $30,000, generating total utility of 1,080 utils. But if they have no insurance and are unlucky, incurring $10,000 in medical expenses, they will have just $20,000 of their income to spend on consumption and total utility of only 920 utils. So *without insurance,* the family's expected utility is $(0.5 \times 1,080) + (0.5 \times 920) = 1,000$ utils.

Now let's suppose that an insurance company offers to pay whatever medical expenses the family incurs during the next year in return for a **premium**—a payment to the insurance company—of $5,000. Note that the amount of the premium in this case is equal to the expected value of the Lees' medical expenses—the

Expected utility is the expected value of an individual's total utility given uncertainty about future outcomes.

A **premium** is a payment to an insurance company in return for the insurance company's promise to pay a claim in certain states of the world.

FIGURE 20-1 The Utility Function and Marginal Utility Curve of a Risk-Averse Family

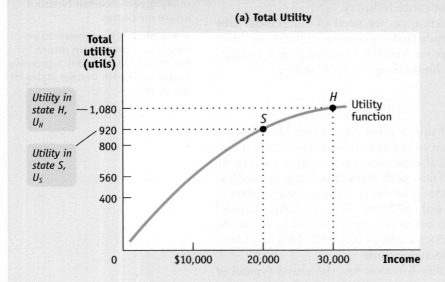

Income	Total utility (utils)
$20,000	920
21,000	945
22,000	968
23,000	989
24,000	1,008
25,000	1,025
26,000	1,040
27,000	1,053
28,000	1,064
29,000	1,073
30,000	1,080

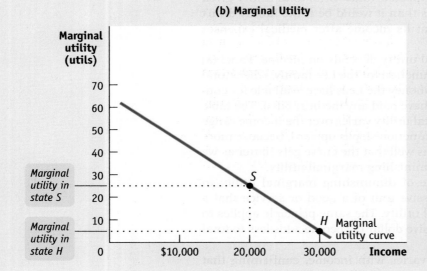

Panel (a) shows how the total utility of the Lee family depends on its income available for consumption (that is, its income after medical expenses). The curve slopes upward: more income leads to higher total utility. But it gets flatter as we move up it and to the right, reflecting diminishing marginal utility. Panel (b) reflects the negative relationship between income and marginal utility when there is risk aversion: the marginal utility from each additional $1,000 of income is lower the higher your income. So the marginal utility of income is higher when the family has high medical expenses and therefore low income (point S) than when it has low medical expenses and therefore high income (point H).

expected value of their future claim against the policy. An insurance policy with this feature, for which the premium is equal to the expected value of the claim, has a special name—a **fair insurance policy.**

If the family purchases this fair insurance policy, the expected value of its income available for consumption is the *same* as it would be without insurance: $25,000—that is, $30,000 minus the $5,000 premium. But the family's risk has been eliminated: the family has an income available for consumption of $25,000 *for sure*, which means that it receives the utility level associated with an income of $25,000.

Reading from the table in Figure 20-1, we see that this utility level is 1,025 utils. Or to put it a slightly different way, their expected utility with insurance is $1 \times 1,025 = 1,025$ utils, because with insurance they will receive a utility of 1,025 utils with a probability of 1. And this is higher than the level of expected utility without insurance—only 1,000 utils. So by eliminating risk through the purchase of a fair insurance policy, the family increases its expected utility even though its expected income hasn't changed.

A **fair insurance policy** is an insurance policy for which the premium is equal to the expected value of the claim.

TABLE 20-1 The Effect of Fair Insurance on the Lee Family's Income Available for Consumption and Expected Utility

| | Income in different states of the world | | Expected value of income available for consumption | Expected utility |
	$0 in medical expenses (0.5 probability)	$10,000 in medical expenses (0.5 probability)		
Without insurance	$30,000	$20,000	(0.5 × $30,000) + (0.5 × $20,000) = $25,000	(0.5 × 1,080 utils) + (0.5 × 920 utils) = 1,000 utils
With fair insurance	$25,000	$25,000	(0.5 × $25,000) + (0.5 × $25,000) = $25,000	(0.5 × 1,025 utils) + (0.5 × 1,025 utils) = 1,025 utils

The calculations for this example are summarized in Table 20-1. This example shows that the Lees, like most people in real life, are **risk-averse:** they will choose to reduce the risk they face when the cost of that reduction leaves the expected value of their income or wealth unchanged. So the Lees, like most people, will be willing to buy fair insurance.

You might think that this result depends on the specific numbers we have chosen. In fact, however, the proposition that purchase of a fair insurance policy increases expected utility depends on only one assumption: diminishing marginal utility. The reason is that *with diminishing marginal utility, a dollar gained when income is low adds more to utility than a dollar gained when income is high.*

That is, having an additional dollar matters more when you are facing hard times than when you are facing good times. And as we will shortly see, a fair insurance policy is desirable because it transfers a dollar from high-income states (where it is valued less) to low-income states (where it is valued more).

But first, let's see how diminishing marginal utility leads to risk aversion by examining expected utility more closely. In the case of the Lee family, there are two states of the world; let's call them H and S, for healthy and sick. In state H the family has no medical expenses; in state S it has $10,000 in medical expenses. We'll use the symbols U_H and U_S to represent the Lee family's total utility in each state. Then the family's expected utility is:

(20-2) Expected utility = (Probability of state H × Total utility in state H) + (Probability of state S × Total utility in state S)

= $(0.5 \times U_H) + (0.5 \times U_S)$

The fair insurance policy *reduces* the family's income available for consumption in state H by $5,000, but it *increases* it in state S by the same amount. As we've just seen, we can use the utility function to directly calculate the effects of these changes on expected utility. But as we have also seen in many other contexts, we gain more insight into individual choice by focusing on *marginal* utility.

To use marginal utility to analyze the effects of fair insurance, let's imagine introducing the insurance a bit at a time, say in 5,000 small steps. At each of these steps, we reduce income in state H by $1 and simultaneously increase income in state S by $1. At each of these steps, total utility in state H falls by the marginal utility of income in that state but total utility in state S rises by the marginal utility of income in that state.

Now look again at panel (b) of Figure 20-1, which shows how marginal utility varies with income. Point S shows marginal utility when the Lee family's income is $20,000; point H shows marginal utility when income is $30,000. Clearly, marginal utility is higher when income after medical expenses is low. Because of diminishing marginal utility, an additional dollar of income adds more to total utility when the family has low income (point S) than when it has high income (point H).

This tells us that the gain in expected utility from increasing income in state S is larger than the loss in expected utility from reducing income in state H by the same

Risk-averse individuals will choose to reduce the risk they face when that reduction leaves the expected value of their income or wealth unchanged.

amount. So at each step of the process of reducing risk, by transferring $1 of income from state *H* to state *S*, expected utility increases. This is the same as saying that the family is risk-averse. That is, risk aversion is a result of diminishing marginal utility.

Almost everyone is risk-averse, because almost everyone has diminishing marginal utility. But the degree of risk aversion varies among individuals—some people are more risk-averse than others. To illustrate this point, Figure 20-2 compares two individuals, Danny and Mel. We suppose that each of them earns the same income now but is confronted with the possibility of earning either $1,000 more or $1,000 less.

Panel (a) of Figure 20-2 shows how each individual's total utility would be affected by the change in income. Danny would gain very few utils from a rise in income, which moves him from *N* to H_D, but lose a large number of utils from a fall in income, which moves him from *N* to L_D. That is, he is highly risk-averse. This is reflected in panel (b) by his steeply declining marginal utility curve.

FIGURE 20-2 Differences in Risk Aversion

As shown in panel (a), Danny and Mel have different utility functions. Danny is highly risk-averse: a gain of $1,000 in income, which moves him from *N* to H_D, adds only a few utils to his total utility, but a $1,000 fall in income, which moves him from *N* to L_D, reduces his total utility by a large number of utils. By contrast, Mel gains almost as many utils from a $1,000 rise in income (the movement from *N* to H_M) as he loses from a $1,000 fall in income (the movement from *N* to L_M). Panel (b) illustrates this difference using the two men's marginal utility curves. The slope of Danny's marginal utility curve is steeper than Mel's, which means that Danny would be willing to pay much more for insurance than Mel.

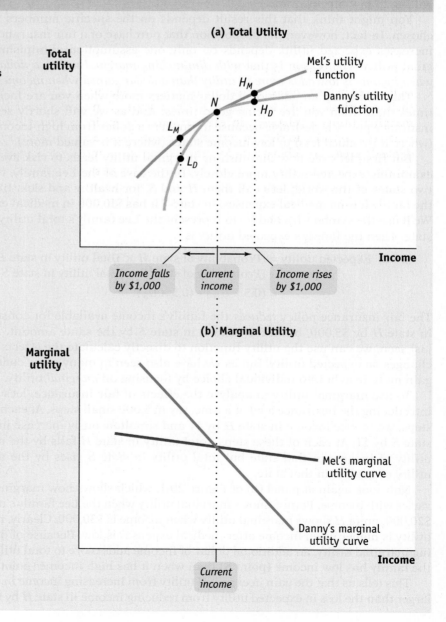

FOR INQUIRING MINDS **The Paradox of Gambling**

If most people are risk-averse and risk-averse individuals won't take a fair gamble, how come Las Vegas and other places where gambling is legal do so much business?

After all, a casino doesn't even offer gamblers a fair gamble: all the games in any gambling facility are designed so that, on average, the casino makes money. So why would anyone play their games?

You might argue that the gambling industry caters to the minority of people who are actually the opposite of risk-averse: risk-loving. But a glance at the customers of Las Vegas hotels quickly refutes that hypothesis: most of them aren't daredevils who also skydive and go bungee-jumping. Instead, most of them are ordinary people who have health and life insurance and who wear seat belts. In other words, they are risk-averse like the rest of us.

So why do people gamble? Presumably because they enjoy the experience.

Also, gambling may be one of those areas where the assumption of rational behavior goes awry. Psychologists have concluded that gambling can be addictive in ways that are not that different from the addictive effects of drugs. Taking dangerous drugs is irrational; so is excessive gambling. Alas, both happen all the same.

Mel, though, as shown in panel (a), would gain almost as many utils from higher income, which moves him from N to H_M, as he would lose from lower income, which moves him from N to L_M. He is barely risk-averse at all. This is reflected in his marginal utility curve in panel (b), which is almost horizontal. So, other things equal, Danny will gain a lot more utility from insurance than Mel will. Someone who is completely insensitive to risk is called **risk-neutral.**

Individuals differ in risk aversion for two main reasons: differences in preferences and differences in initial income or wealth.

1. *Differences in preferences.* Other things equal, people simply differ in how much their marginal utility is affected by their level of income. Someone whose marginal utility is relatively unresponsive to changes in income will be much less sensitive to risk. In contrast, someone whose marginal utility depends greatly on changes in income will be much more risk-averse.

2. *Differences in initial income or wealth.* The possible loss of $1,000 makes a big difference to a family living below the poverty threshold; it makes very little difference to someone who earns $1 million a year. In general, people with high incomes or high wealth will be less risk-averse.

Differences in risk aversion have an important consequence: they affect how much an individual is willing to pay to avoid risk.

Paying to Avoid Risk

The risk-averse Lee family is clearly better off taking out a fair insurance policy—a policy that leaves their expected income unchanged but eliminates their risk. Unfortunately, real insurance policies are rarely fair: because insurance companies have to cover other costs, such as salaries for salespeople and actuaries, they charge more than they expect to pay in claims.

Will the Lee family still want to purchase an "unfair" insurance policy—one for which the premium is larger than the expected claim?

It depends on the size of the premium. Look again at Table 20-1. We know that without insurance expected utility is 1,000 utils and that insurance costing $5,000 raises expected utility to 1,025 utils. If the premium were $6,000, the Lees would be left with an income of $24,000, which, as you can see from Figure 20-1, would give them a total utility of 1,008 utils—which is still higher than their expected utility if they had no insurance at all. So the Lees would be willing to buy insurance with a $6,000 premium. But they wouldn't be willing to pay $7,000, which would reduce their income to $23,000 and their total utility to 989 utils.

This example shows that risk-averse individuals are willing to make deals that reduce their expected income but also reduce their risk: they are willing to pay a premium that exceeds their expected claim.

A **risk-neutral** person is completely insensitive to risk.

PITFALLS

BEFORE OR AFTER THE FACT?
Why is an insurance policy different from a doughnut?

No, it's not a riddle. Although the supply and demand for insurance behave like the supply and demand for any good or service, the payoff is very different. When you buy a doughnut, you know what you're going to get. When you buy insurance, by definition you *don't* know what you're going to get. If you bought car insurance and then didn't have an accident, you got nothing from the policy, except peace of mind, and might wish that you hadn't bothered. But if you did have an accident, you probably would be glad that you bought insurance that covered the cost.

This means we have to be careful in assessing the rationality of insurance purchases (or, for that matter, any decision made in the face of uncertainty). *After the fact*—after the uncertainty has been resolved—such decisions are almost always subject to second-guessing. But that doesn't mean that the decision was wrong *before the fact,* given the information available at the time.

One highly successful Wall Street investor told the authors that he never looks back—as long as he believes he made the right decision given what he knew when he made it, he never reproaches himself if things turn out badly. That's the right attitude, and it almost surely contributes to his success.

The more risk-averse they are, the higher the premium they are willing to pay. That willingness to pay is what makes the insurance industry possible. In contrast, a risk-neutral person is unwilling to pay at all to reduce their risk.

"Call me when you invent the warranty."

ECONOMICS >> *in Action*
Warranties

Many expensive consumer goods—electronics, major appliances, cars—come with some form of *warranty*. Typically, the manufacturer guarantees to repair or replace the item if something goes wrong with it during some specified period after purchase—usually six months or one year.

Why do manufacturers offer warranties? Part of the answer is that warranties *signal* to consumers that the goods are of high quality. But mainly warranties are a form of consumer insurance. For many people, the cost of repairing or replacing an expensive item like a smartphone or a car would be a serious burden. If they were obliged to come up with the cash, their consumption of other goods would be restricted; as a result, their marginal utility of income would be higher than if they didn't have to pay for repairs.

So a warranty that covers the cost of repair or replacement increases the consumer's expected utility, even if the cost of the warranty is greater than the expected future claim paid by the manufacturer.

>> Quick Review

• The **expected value** of a **random variable** is the weighted average of all possible values, where the weight corresponds to the probability of a given value occurring.

• Uncertainty about **states of the world** entails **risk**, or **financial risk** when there is an uncertain monetary outcome. When faced with uncertainty, consumers choose the option yielding the highest level of **expected utility**.

• Most people are **risk-averse:** they would be willing to purchase a **fair insurance policy** in which the premium is equal to the expected value of the claim.

• Risk aversion arises from diminishing marginal utility. Differences in preferences and in income or wealth lead to differences in risk aversion.

• Depending on the size of the **premium,** a risk-averse person may be willing to purchase an "unfair" insurance policy with a premium larger than the expected claim. The greater your risk aversion, the greater the premium you are willing to pay. A **risk-neutral** person is unwilling to pay any premium to avoid risk.

>> Check Your Understanding 20-1
Solutions appear at back of book.

1. Compare two families who own homes near the coast in Florida. Which family is likely to be more risk-averse—(i) a family with income of $2 million per year or (ii) a family with income of $60,000 per year? Would either family be willing to buy an "unfair" insurance policy to cover losses to their Florida home?

2. Karma's income next year is uncertain: there is a 60% probability she will make $22,000 and a 40% probability she will make $35,000. The accompanying table shows some income and utility levels for Karma.

Income	Total utility (utils)
$22,000	850
25,000	1,014
26,000	1,056
35,000	1,260

   a. What is Karma's expected income? Her expected utility?
   b. What certain income level leaves her as well off as her uncertain income? What does this imply about Karma's attitudes toward risk? Explain.
   c. Would Karma be willing to pay some amount of money greater than zero for an insurance policy that guarantees her an income of $26,000? Explain.

‖ Buying, Selling, and Reducing Risk

Lloyd's of London is the oldest existing commercial insurance company, and it is an institution with an illustrious past. Originally formed in the eighteenth century to help merchants cope with the risks of commerce, it grew in the heyday of the British Empire into a mainstay of imperial trade.

The basic idea of Lloyd's was simple. In the eighteenth century, shipping goods on sailing vessels was risky: the chance that a ship would sink in a storm or be captured by pirates was fairly high. The merchant who owned the ship and its cargo could easily be ruined financially by such an event. Lloyd's matched shipowners seeking insurance with wealthy investors who promised to compensate a merchant if his ship were lost. In return, the merchant paid the investor a fee in advance. If his ship *didn't* sink, the investor still kept the fee.

In effect, the merchant paid a price to relieve himself of risk. By matching people who wanted to purchase insurance with people who wanted to provide it, Lloyd's performed the functions of a market. The fact that British merchants could use Lloyd's to reduce their risk made many more Brits willing to undertake merchant trade.

Insurance companies have changed quite a lot from the early days of Lloyd's. But asking why Lloyd's worked to the mutual benefit of merchants and investors is a good way to understand how the market economy as a whole "trades" and thereby transforms risk.

The insurance industry rests on these two principles, which we will consider in turn.

1. Trade in risk, like trade in any good or service, can produce mutual gains. In this case, the gains come when those less willing to bear risk transfer it to people who are more willing to bear it.
2. Some risk can be made to disappear through *diversification*.

Trading Risk

It may seem a bit strange to talk about "trading" risk. After all, risk is a bad thing—and aren't we supposed to be trading goods and services?

But people often trade away things they don't like to other people who dislike them less. Suppose you have just bought a house for $300,000, the average price for a house in your community. But you have now learned, to your horror, that the building next door is being turned into a nightclub. You want to sell the house immediately and are willing to accept $285,000 for it. But who will now be willing to buy it? The answer: a person who doesn't really mind late-night noise. Such a person might be willing to pay up to $300,000. So there is an opportunity here for a mutually beneficial deal—you are willing to sell for as little as $285,000, and the other person is willing to pay as much as $300,000, so any price in between will benefit both of you.

The key point is that the two parties have different sensitivities to noise, which enables those who most dislike noise, in effect, to pay other people to make their lives quieter. Trading risk works exactly the same way: people who want to reduce the risk they face can pay other people who are less sensitive to risk to take some of their risk away.

As we saw in the previous section, individual preferences account for some of the variations in people's attitudes toward risk, but differences in income and wealth are probably the principal reason behind different risk sensitivities. Lloyd's made money by matching wealthy investors who were more risk-tolerant with less wealthy and therefore more risk-averse shipowners.

Suppose, staying with our Lloyd's of London story, that a merchant whose ship went down would lose £1,000 and that there was a 10% chance of such a disaster. The expected loss in this case would be $0.10 \times £1,000 = £100$. But the merchant, whose whole livelihood was at stake, might have been willing to pay £150 to be compensated in the amount of £1,000 if the ship sank. Meanwhile, a wealthy investor for whom the loss of £1,000 was no big deal would have been willing to take this risk for a return only slightly better than the expected loss—say, £110.

Clearly, there is room for a mutually beneficial deal here: the merchant pays something less than £150 and more than £110—say, £130—in return for compensation if the ship goes down. In effect, they have paid a less risk-averse individual to bear the burden of their risk. Everyone has been made better off by this transaction.

The funds that an insurer places at risk when providing insurance are called the insurer's **capital at risk.**

An **efficient allocation of risk** is an allocation of risk in which those who are most willing to bear risk are those who end up bearing it.

The funds that an insurer places at risk when providing insurance are called the insurer's **capital at risk.** In our example, the wealthy Lloyd's investor places capital of £1,000 at risk in return for a premium of £130. In general, the amount of capital that potential insurers are willing to place at risk depends, other things equal, on the premium offered. If every ship is worth £1,000 and has a 10% chance of going down, nobody would offer insurance for less than a £100 premium, equal to the expected claim. In fact, only an investor who isn't risk-averse at all—that is, who is risk-neutral—would be willing to offer a policy at that price, because accepting a £100 premium would leave the insurer's expected income unchanged while increasing that insurer's risk.

Suppose there is one investor who is risk-neutral. But the next most willing investor is slightly risk-averse and insists on a £105 premium. The next investor, being somewhat more risk-averse, demands a premium of £110, and so on. By varying the premium and asking how many insurers would be willing to provide insurance at that premium, we can trace out a supply curve for insurance, as shown in Figure 20-3. As the premium increases as we move up the supply curve, more risk-averse investors are induced to provide coverage.

Meanwhile, potential buyers will consider their willingness to pay a given premium, defining the demand curve for insurance. In Figure 20-4, the highest premium that any shipowner is willing to pay is £200. Who's willing to pay this? The most risk-averse shipowner, of course. A slightly less risk-averse shipowner might be willing to pay £190, an even slightly less risk-averse shipowner is willing to pay £180, and so on.

Now imagine a market in which there are thousands of shipowners and potential insurers, so that the supply and demand curves for insurance are smooth lines. In this market, as in markets for ordinary goods and services, there will be an equilibrium price and quantity. Figure 20-5 illustrates such a market equilibrium at a premium of £130, with a total quantity of 5,000 policies bought and sold, representing a total capital at risk of £5,000,000.

Notice that in this market risk is transferred from the people who most want to get rid of it (the most risk-averse shipowners) to the people least bothered by risk (the least risk-averse investors). So just as markets for goods and services typically produce an efficient allocation of resources, markets for risk also typically lead to an **efficient allocation of risk**—an allocation of risk in which those who

---

FIGURE 20-3 The Supply of Insurance

This is the supply of insurance policies to provide £1,000 in coverage to a merchant ship that has a 10% chance of being lost. Each investor has £1,000 of capital at risk. The lowest possible premium at which a policy is offered is £100, equal to the expected claim, and only a risk-neutral investor is willing to supply this policy. As the premium increases, investors who are more risk-averse are induced to supply policies to the market, increasing the quantity of policies supplied.

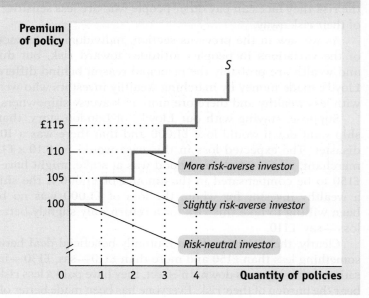

FIGURE 20-4 The Demand for Insurance

This is the demand for insurance policies for £1,000 in coverage of a merchant ship that has a 10% chance of being lost. In this example, the highest premium at which anyone demands a policy is £200, which only the most risk-averse shipowners will desire. As the premium falls, shipowners who are less risk-averse are induced to demand policies, increasing the quantity of policies demanded.

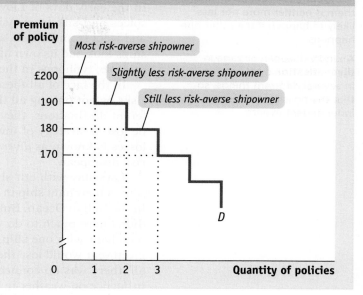

are most willing to bear risk are those who end up bearing it. But as in the case of the markets for goods and services, there is an important qualification to this result: there are well-defined cases in which the market for risk fails to achieve efficiency. These arise from the presence of *private information*, which we will discuss in the next section.

The trading of risk between individuals who differ in their degree of risk aversion plays an extremely important role in the economy, but it is not the only way that markets can help people cope with risk. Under some circumstances, markets can perform a sort of magic trick: they can make some (though rarely all) of the risk that individuals face simply disappear.

FIGURE 20-5 Insurance Market

Here we represent the hypothetical market for insuring a merchant ship, where each ship requires £1,000 in coverage. The demand curve is made up of shipowners who wish to buy insurance, and the supply curve is made up of wealthy investors who wish to supply insurance. In this example, at a premium of £200, only the most risk-averse shipowners will purchase insurance; at a premium of £100, only risk-neutral investors are willing to supply insurance. The equilibrium is at a premium of £130 with 5,000 policies bought and sold. In the absence of *private information* (explained in the next section), the insurance market leads to an efficient allocation of risk.

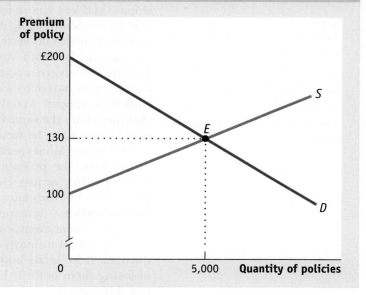

Two possible events are **independent events** if each of them is neither more nor less likely to happen if the other one happens.

An individual can engage in **diversification** by investing in several different things, so that the possible losses are independent events.

Making Risk Disappear: The Power of Diversification

In the early days of Lloyd's, British merchant ships traversed the world, trading spices and silk from Asia, tobacco and rum from the New World, and textiles and wool from Britain, among other goods. Each of the many routes that British ships took had its own unique risks—pirates in the Caribbean, gales in the North Atlantic, typhoons in the Indian Ocean.

In the face of all these risks, merchants were able to survive by reducing their risks by not putting all their eggs in one basket: by sending different ships to different destinations, they could reduce the probability that all their ships would be lost. A strategy of investing in such a way to reduce the probability of severe losses is known as *diversification*, which can often make some of the economy's risk disappear.

Let's stay with our shipping example. It was all too likely that a pirate might seize a merchant ship in the Caribbean or that a typhoon might sink another ship in the Indian Ocean. But the key point here is that the various threats to shipping didn't have much to do with each other. So it was considerably less likely that a merchant with one ship in the Caribbean and another in the Indian Ocean in a given year would lose them both, one to a pirate and the other to a typhoon. After all, there was no connection: the actions of cutthroats in the Caribbean had no influence on weather in the Indian Ocean, or vice versa.

Statisticians refer to such unconnected events as **independent events**—one is no more likely to happen if the other does than if it does not. Many unpredictable events are independent of each other. If you toss a coin twice, the probability that it will come up heads on the second toss is the same whether it came up heads or tails on the first toss. If your house burns down today, it does not affect the probability that my house will burn down the same day (unless we live next door to each other or employ the services of the same incompetent electrician).

There is a simple rule for calculating the probability that two independent events will both happen: multiply the probability that one event would happen on its own by the probability that the other event would happen on its own. If you toss a coin once, the probability that it will come up heads is 0.5. If you toss the coin twice, the probability that it will come up heads *both* times is $0.5 \times 0.5 = 0.25$.

But what did it matter to shipowners or Lloyd's investors that ship losses in the Caribbean and ship losses in the Indian Ocean were independent events? The answer is that by spreading their investments across different parts of the world, they could make some of the riskiness of the shipping business simply disappear.

Let's suppose that Joseph Moneypenny, Esq., is wealthy enough to outfit two ships—and let's ignore for a moment the possibility of insuring his ships. Should Mr. Moneypenny equip two ships for the Caribbean trade and send them off together? Or should he send one ship to Barbados and one to Calcutta?

Assume that both voyages will be equally profitable if successful, yielding £1,000 if the voyage is completed. Also assume that there is a 10% chance both that a ship sent to Barbados will run into a pirate and that a ship sent to Calcutta will be sunk by a typhoon. And if two ships travel to the same destination, we will assume that they share the same fate. So if Mr. Moneypenny were to send both his ships to either destination, he would face a probability of 10% of losing all his investment.

But if Mr. Moneypenny were instead to send one ship to Barbados and one to Calcutta, the probability that he would lose both of them would be only $0.1 \times 0.1 = 0.01$, or just 1%. As we will see shortly, his expected payoff would be the same—but the chance of losing it all would be much less. So by engaging in **diversification**—investing in several different things, where the possible losses are independent events—he could make some of his risk disappear.

Table 20-2 summarizes Mr. Moneypenny's options and their possible consequences. If he sends both ships to the same destination, he runs a 10% chance of losing them both. If he sends them to different destinations, there are three possible outcomes.

TABLE 20-2 How Diversification Reduces Risk

If both ships are sent to the same destination			
State	**Probability**	**Payoff**	**Expected payoff**
Both ships arrive	0.9 = 90%	£2,000	$(0.9 \times £2,000) + (0.1 \times £0) = £1,800$
Both ships lost	0.1 = 10%	0	
If one ship is sent east, the other west			
State	**Probability**	**Payoff**	**Expected payoff**
Both ships arrive	$0.9 \times 0.9 = 81\%$	£2,000	$(0.81 \times £2,000) + (0.01 \times £0) +$
Both ships lost	$0.1 \times 0.1 = 1\%$	0	$(0.18 \times £1,000) = £1,800$
One ship arrives	$(0.9 \times 0.1 + (0.1 \times 0.9) = 18\%$	1,000	

1. Both ships could arrive safely: because there is a 0.9 probability of either one making it, the probability that both will make it is $0.9 \times 0.9 = 81\%$.
2. Both could be lost—but the probability of that happening is only $0.1 \times 0.1 = 1\%$.
3. Only one ship can arrive. The probability that the first ship arrives and the second ship is lost is $0.9 \times 0.1 = 9\%$. The probability that the first ship is lost but the second ship arrives is $0.1 \times 0.9 = 9\%$. So the probability that only one ship makes it is $9\% + 9\% = 18\%$.

You might think that diversification is a strategy available only to the wealthy. But there are ways for even small investors to diversify. Even if Mr. Moneypenny can only afford to equip one ship, he can enter a partnership with another merchant. They can jointly outfit two ships, agreeing to share the profits equally, and then send those ships to different destinations. That way each investor faces less risk than if he equips one ship alone.

In the modern economy, diversification is made much easier for investors by the fact that they can easily buy shares in many companies by using the *stock market*. The owner of a **share** in a company is the owner of part of that company—typically a very small part, one-millionth or less. An individual who put all of their wealth in shares of a single company would lose all of that wealth if the company went bankrupt. But most investors hold shares in many companies, which makes the chance of losing all their investment very small.

In fact, Lloyd's of London wasn't just a way to trade risks; it was also a way for investors to diversify. To see how this worked, let's introduce Lady Penelope, a wealthy aristocrat, who decides to increase her income by placing £1,000 of her capital at risk via Lloyd's. She could use that capital to insure just one ship. But more typically she would enter a *syndicate*, a group of investors, who would jointly insure a number of ships going to different destinations, agreeing to share the cost if any one of those ships went down. Because it would be much less likely for all the ships insured by the syndicate to sink than for any one of them to go down, Lady Penelope would be at much less risk of losing her entire capital.

In some cases, an investor can make risk almost entirely disappear by taking a small share of the risk in many independent events. This strategy is known as **pooling.**

Consider the case of a health insurance company, which has millions of policyholders, with thousands of them requiring expensive treatment each year. The insurance company can't know whether any given individual will, say, require a heart bypass operation. But heart problems for two different individuals are pretty much independent events. And when there are many possible independent events, it is possible, using statistical analysis, to predict with great accuracy *how many* events of a given type will happen. For example, if you toss a coin 1,000 times, it will come up heads about 500 times—and it is very unlikely to be more than a percent or two off that figure.

A **share** in a company is a partial ownership of that company.

Pooling is a strong form of diversification in which an investor takes a small share of the risk in many independent events. This produces a payoff with very little total overall risk.

Mike Twohy The New Yorker Collection/The Cartoon Bank

FOR INQUIRING MINDS Those Pesky Emotions

For a small investor (someone investing less than several hundred thousand dollars), financial economists agree that the best strategy for investing in stocks is to buy an index fund.

Why index funds? Because they contain a wide range of stocks that reflect the overall market, they achieve diversification, and they have low management fees. In addition, financial economists agree that it's a losing strategy to try to "time" the market: to buy when the stock market is low and sell when it's high. Instead, small investors should buy a fixed dollar amount of stocks and other financial assets every year, regardless of the state of the market.

Yet many, if not most, small investors don't follow this advice. Instead, they buy individual stocks or funds that charge high fees. They spend endless hours online chasing the latest hot tip or sifting through data trying to discern patterns in stocks' behavior. They try to time the market but invariably buy when stocks are high and refuse to

"Your mother called to remind you to diversify."

sell losers. And they fail to diversify, instead concentrating too much money in a few stocks they think are winners.

So why are humans so dense when it comes to investing? According to experts, the culprit is emotion. In his book *Your Money and Your Brain*, Jason Zweig states, "the brain is not an optimal tool for making financial decisions." As he explains it, the

problem is that the human brain evolved to detect and interpret simple patterns. (Is there a lion lurking in that bush?) As a consequence, "when it comes to investing, our incorrigible search for patterns leads us to assume that order exists where it often doesn't." In other words, investors fool themselves into believing that they've discovered a lucrative stock market pattern when, in fact, stock market behavior is largely random.

Not surprisingly, financial decision making is a major topic of study in the area of behavioral economics, a branch of economics that studies why human beings often fail to behave rationally.

So, what's the typical twenty-first-century investor to do? According to Mr. Zweig, there's hope: if you recognize the influence of your emotions, then you can tame them.

So a company offering fire insurance can predict very accurately how many of its clients' homes will burn down in a given year; a company offering health insurance can predict very accurately how many of its clients will need heart surgery in a given year; a life insurance company can predict how many of its clients will . . . Well, you get the idea.

When an insurance company is able to take advantage of the predictability that comes from aggregating a large number of independent events, it is said to engage in *pooling of risks*. And this pooling often means that even though insurance companies protect people from risk, the owners of the insurance companies may not themselves face much risk.

Lloyd's of London wasn't just a way for wealthy individuals to get paid for taking on some of the risks of less wealthy merchants. It was also a vehicle for pooling some of those risks. The effect of that pooling was to shift the supply curve in Figure 20-5 rightward: to make investors willing to accept more risk, at a lower price, than would otherwise have been possible.

The Limits of Diversification

Diversification can reduce risk. In some cases it can eliminate it. But these cases are not typical, because there are important limits to diversification. We can see the most important reason for these limits by returning to Lloyd's one more time.

In Lloyd's early days, there was one important hazard facing British shipping other than pirates or storms: war. Between 1690 and 1815, Britain fought a series of wars, mainly with France (which, among other things, went to war with Britain in support of the American Revolution). Each time, France would sponsor privateers—basically pirates with official backing—to raid British shipping and thus indirectly damage Britain's war effort.

Whenever war broke out between Britain and France, losses of British merchant ships would increase. Unfortunately, merchants could not protect themselves against this eventuality by sending ships to different ports: the privateers would prey on British ships anywhere in the world. So the loss of a ship to French privateers in the Caribbean and the loss of another ship to French privateers in the Indian Ocean would *not* be independent events. It would be quite likely that they would happen in the same year.

When an event is more likely to occur if some other event occurs, these two events are said to be **positively correlated.** And like the risk of having a ship seized by French privateers, many financial risks are, alas, positively correlated.

Here are some of the positively correlated financial risks that investors in the modern world face:

- *Severe weather.* Within any given region, losses due to weather are definitely not independent events. When a hurricane hits Florida, a lot of Florida homes will suffer hurricane damage. To some extent, insurance companies can diversify away this risk by insuring homes in many states. But events like El Niño (a recurrent temperature anomaly in the Pacific Ocean that disrupts weather around the world) can cause simultaneous flooding across the United States and elsewhere. And as we have seen, over the past several years, there has been a significant increase in extreme weather.

- *Political events.* Modern governments do not, thankfully, license privateers. Even today, however, some kinds of political events such as a war or revolution in a key raw-material-producing area—can damage business around the globe.

- *Business cycles.* The causes of *business cycles,* fluctuations in the output of the economy as a whole, are a subject for macroeconomics. What we can say here is that if one company suffers a decline in business because of a nationwide economic slump, many other companies will also suffer such declines. So these events will be positively correlated.

When events are positively correlated, the risks they pose cannot be diversified away. An investor can protect herself from the risk that any one company will do badly by investing in many companies; this investor cannot use the same technique to protect against an economic slump in which *all* companies do badly.

An insurance company can protect itself against the risk of losses from local flooding by insuring houses in many different places. But a global weather pattern that produces floods in many places will defeat this strategy. Not surprisingly, insurers pulled back from writing policies when it became clear that extreme weather patterns had become worse. They could no longer be confident that profits from policies written in good weather areas would be sufficient to compensate for losses incurred on policies in hurricane and drought prone areas.

So institutions like insurance companies and stock markets cannot make risk go away completely. There is always an irreducible core of risk that cannot be diversified. Markets for risk, however, do accomplish two things: First, they enable the economy to eliminate the risk that can be diversified. Second, they allocate the risk that remains to the people most willing to bear it.

> Two events are **positively correlated** if each event is more likely to occur if the other event also occurs.

ECONOMICS >> *in Action*
When Lloyd's Almost Lost It

At the end of the 1980s, Lloyd's found itself in severe trouble. Investors who had placed their capital at risk, believing that the risks were small and the return on their investments more or less assured, found themselves required to make large payments to satisfy enormous claims. A number of investors, including members of some very old aristocratic families, found themselves pushed into bankruptcy.

Insurance companies cannot completely eliminate risk, as the overwhelming number of asbestos claims faced by Lloyd's made clear.

What happened? Part of the answer is that ambitious managers at Lloyd's had persuaded investors to take on risks that were much larger than the investors realized. (Or to put it a different way, the premiums the investors accepted were too small for the true level of risk contained in the policies.)

But the biggest single problem was that many of the events against which Lloyd's had become a major insurer were *not* independent. In the 1970s and 1980s, Lloyd's had become a major provider of corporate liability insurance in the United States: it protected American corporations against the possibility that they might be sued for selling defective or harmful products. Everyone expected such suits to be more or less independent events. Why should one company's legal problems have much to do with another's?

The answer turned out to lie in one word: asbestos. For decades, this fireproofing material had been used in many products, which meant that many companies were responsible for its use. Then it turned out that asbestos can cause severe damage to the lungs, especially in children. The result was a torrent of lawsuits by people who believed they were injured by asbestos and billions of dollars in damage awards—many of them ultimately paid by Lloyd's investors.

>> Quick Review

• Insurance markets exist because there are gains from trade in risk. Except in the case of private information, they lead to an **efficient allocation of risk:** those who are most willing to bear risk place their **capital at risk** to cover the financial losses of those least willing to bear risk.

• When **independent events** are involved, a strategy of **diversification** can substantially reduce risk. Diversification is made easier by the existence of institutions like the stock market, in which people trade **shares** of companies. A form of diversification, relevant especially to insurance companies, is **pooling.**

• When events are **positively correlated,** there is a core of risk that cannot be eliminated, no matter how much individuals diversify.

>> Check Your Understanding 20-2

Solutions appear at the back of book.

1. Explain how each of the following events would change the equilibrium premium and quantity of insurance in the market, indicating any shifts in the supply and demand curves.
   a. An increase in the number of ships traveling the same trade routes and so facing the same kinds of risks
   b. An increase in the number of trading routes, with the same number of ships traveling a greater variety of routes and so facing different kinds of risk
   c. An increase in the degree of risk aversion among the shipowners in the market
   d. An increase in the degree of risk aversion among the investors in the market
   e. An increase in the risk affecting the economy as a whole
   f. A fall in the wealth levels of investors in the market

Private Information: What You Don't Know Can Hurt You

Markets do very well at dealing with diversifiable risk and with risk due to uncertainty: situations in which nobody knows what is going to happen, whose house will be flooded, or who will get sick. However, markets have much more trouble with situations in which *some people know things that other people don't know*—situations of **private information.**

As we will see, private information can distort economic decisions and sometimes prevent mutually beneficial economic transactions from taking place. (Sometimes economists use the term *asymmetric information* rather than *private information,* but they are equivalent.)

Why is some information private? The main reason is that people generally know more about themselves than other people do. For example, you know whether or not you are a careful driver. But unless you have already been in several accidents, your auto insurance company does not. You are more likely to have a better estimate than your insurance company of whether or not you will need an expensive medical procedure. And if you are selling me your used car, you are more likely to be aware of any problems with it than I am.

But why are such differences in who knows what a problem? It turns out that there are two distinct sources of trouble: *adverse selection,* which arises from having private information about the way things are, and *moral hazard,* which arises from having private information about what people do.

Private information is information that some people have but others do not.

Adverse Selection: The Economics of Lemons

Suppose that someone offers to sell you an almost brand-new car—purchased just three months ago, with only 2,000 miles on the odometer and no dents or scratches. Will you be willing to pay almost the same for it as for a car direct from the dealer?

Probably not, for one main reason: you cannot help but wonder why this car is being sold. Is it because the owner has discovered something wrong with it—that it is a "lemon"? Having driven the car for a while, the owner knows more about it than you do—and people are more likely to sell cars that give them trouble.

You might think that sellers of used cars are at an advantage because they know more about them than buyers do. But potential buyers know that potential sellers are likely to offer them lemons—they just don't know which car is a lemon. For this reason, buyers will offer a lower price than they would if they had a guarantee of the car's quality. And this poor opinion of used cars tends to be self-reinforcing, precisely because it depresses the prices that buyers offer. Used cars sell at a significant discount because buyers expect a disproportionate share of those cars to be lemons.

Even a used car that is not a lemon would sell only at a large discount because buyers don't know whether it's a lemon or not. But potential sellers who have good cars ("plums") are unwilling to sell them at a deep discount, except under exceptional circumstances. So good used cars are rarely offered for sale, and used cars that are offered for sale have a strong tendency to be lemons. (This is why people who have a compelling reason to sell a car, such as moving overseas, make a point of revealing that information to potential buyers—as if to say "This car is not a lemon!").

The end result, then, is not only that used cars sell for low prices and that there are a large number of them with hidden problems. Equally important, many potentially beneficial transactions—sales of good cars by people who would like to get rid of them to people who would like to buy them—end up being frustrated by the inability of potential sellers to convince potential buyers that their cars are actually worth the higher price being asked. So some mutually beneficial trades between those who want to sell used cars and those who want to buy them go unexploited.

Although economists sometimes refer to situations like this as the *lemons problem*, the more formal name of the problem is **adverse selection.** The reason for the name is obvious: because the potential sellers know more about the quality of what they are selling than the potential buyers, they have an incentive to select the worst things to sell.

Adverse selection does not apply only to used cars. It is a problem for many parts of the economy—notably for insurance companies, and most notably for health insurance companies.

Suppose that a health insurance company were to offer a standard policy to everyone with the same premium. The premium would reflect the *average* risk of incurring a medical expense. But that would make the policy look very expensive to healthy people, who know that they are less likely than the average person to incur medical expenses. So healthy people would be less likely than less healthy people to buy the policy, leaving the health insurance company with exactly the customers it doesn't want: people with a higher-than-average risk of needing medical care, who would find the premium to be a good deal.

In order to cover its expected losses from this sicker customer pool, the health insurance company is compelled to raise premiums, driving away more of the remaining healthier customers, and so on. Because the insurance company can't determine who is healthy and who is not, it must charge everyone the same premium, thereby discouraging healthy people from purchasing policies and encouraging unhealthy people to buy policies.

Before the passage of the Affordable Care Act, adverse selection could lead to a phenomenon called an *adverse selection death spiral* as the market for health

How do I know whether or not this used car is a lemon?

Adverse selection occurs when an individual knows more about the way things are than other people do. Private information leads buyers to expect hidden problems in items offered for sale, leading to low prices and the best items being kept off the market.

Adverse selection can be reduced through **screening:** using observable information about people to make inferences about their private information.

Adverse selection can be diminished by people **signaling** their private information through actions that credibly reveal what they know.

A long-term **reputation** allows an individual to reassure others that they are not concealing adverse private information.

insurance collapsed: insurance companies refused to offer policies because there was no premium at which the company could cover its losses. Because of the severe adverse selection problems, governments in many advanced countries have assumed the role of providing health insurance to their citizens. In the United States, adverse selection in health insurance is avoided in two ways:

1. U.S. government insurance programs, which provided almost half of the total payments for medical care in the United States in 2019, are financed by dedicated taxes that people cannot opt out of.
2. The ACA requires that everyone have health insurance, so healthy people cannot opt out of paying premiums.

However, adverse selection still exists in other insurance markets such as auto insurance. In general, people or firms faced with the problem of adverse selection follow one of several well-established strategies for dealing with it. One strategy is **screening:** using observable information to make inferences about private information. If you apply to purchase auto insurance, you'll find that the insurance company will ask about your driving record in an attempt to "screen out" unsafe drivers—people they will refuse to insure or will insure only at very high premiums.

Auto insurance companies provide a very good example of the use of statistics in screening to reduce adverse selection. They may not know whether you are a careful driver, but they have statistical data on the accident rates of people who resemble your profile—and use those data in setting premiums. A 19-year-old male who drives a sports car and has already had a fender-bender is likely to pay a much higher premium than a 40-year-old female who drives an SUV and has never had an accident.

In some cases, this may be unfair: some adolescent males are very careful drivers, and some women drive SUVs as if they were F-16's. But nobody can deny that the insurance companies are right on average.

Another strategy to counter the problems caused by adverse selection is for good prospects to do some **signaling** of their private information—taking some action that wouldn't be worth taking unless they were indeed good prospects. For example, reputable used-car dealers often offer warranties—promises to repair any problems with the cars they sell that arise within a given amount of time. This isn't just a way of insuring their customers against possible expenses; it's a way of credibly showing that they are not selling lemons. As a result, more sales occur and dealers can command higher prices for their used cars.

Finally, in the face of adverse selection, it can be very valuable to establish a good **reputation:** a used-car dealership will often advertise how long it has been in business to show that it has continued to satisfy its customers. As a result, new customers will be willing to purchase cars and pay more for that dealer's cars.

Moral Hazard

In the late 1970s, New York and other major cities experienced an epidemic of suspicious fires that appeared to be deliberately set. Investigators eventually became aware of patterns in a number of the fires. Particular landlords who owned several buildings seemed to have an unusually large number of their buildings burn down. Although it was difficult to prove, police suspected that most of these fireprone landlords were hiring professional arsonists to torch their own properties.

Why burn your own building? These buildings were typically in neighborhoods where rising crime and middle-class flight had led to a decline in property values. But the insurance policies on the buildings were written to compensate owners based on historical property values, and so would pay the owner of a destroyed building more than the building was worth in the current market. For an unscrupulous landlord who knew the right people, this presented a profitable opportunity.

The arson epidemic became less severe during the 1980s, partly because insurance companies began making it difficult to overinsure properties, and partly because a boom in real estate values made many previously arson-threatened buildings worth more unburned.

The arson episodes make it clear that it is a bad idea for insurance companies to let customers insure buildings for more than their value—it gives the customers some destructive incentives. You might think, however, that the incentive problem would go away as long as the insurance is no more than 100% of the value of what is being insured.

But, unfortunately, anything close to 100% insurance still distorts incentives by inducing policyholders to behave differently than they would in the absence of insurance. The reason is that preventing fires requires effort and cost on the part of a building's owner. Fire alarms and sprinkler systems have to be kept in good repair, and fire safety rules have to be strictly enforced. All of this takes time and money that the owner may not find worth spending if the insurance policy will provide close to full compensation for any losses.

Of course, the insurance company could specify in the policy that it won't pay if basic safety precautions were unmet. But it isn't always easy to tell how careful a building's owner has been—the owner knows, but the insurance company does not.

The point is that the building's owner has private information about their own actions: whether they have really taken all appropriate precautions. As a result, the insurance company is likely to face more claims than if it were able to determine exactly how much effort a building owner exerts to prevent a loss. The problem of distorted incentives that arises when an individual has private information about their own actions but someone else bears the costs of a lack of care or effort is known as **moral hazard.**

To deal with moral hazard, individuals with private information need to be given some personal stake in what happens so they have a reason to exert effort even if others cannot verify that they have done so. Moral hazard is the reason salespeople in many stores receive a commission on sales: it's hard for managers to be sure how hard salespeople are really working, and if they were paid only a straight salary, they would not have an incentive to exert effort to make those sales.

Insurance companies deal with moral hazard by requiring a **deductible:** they compensate for losses only above a certain amount, so that coverage is always less than 100%. The insurance on your car, for example, may pay for repairs only after the first $500 in loss. This means that a careless driver who gets into a fender-bender will end up paying $500 for repairs even if they are insured, which provides at least some incentive to be careful and reduces moral hazard.

In addition to reducing moral hazard, deductibles provide a partial solution to the problem of adverse selection. Your insurance premium often drops substantially if you are willing to accept a large deductible. This is an attractive option to people who know they are low-risk customers; it is less attractive to people who know they are high-risk—and are likely to have an accident and end up paying the deductible. By offering a menu of policies with different premiums and deductibles, insurance companies can screen their customers, inducing them to sort themselves out on the basis of their private information.

As the example of deductibles suggests, moral hazard limits the ability of the economy to allocate risks efficiently. You generally can't get full (100%) insurance on your home or car, even though you would like to buy it, and you bear the risk of large deductibles, even though you would prefer not to. The following Economics in Action illustrates how in some cases moral hazard limits the ability of investors to diversify their investments.

Moral hazard occurs when an individual knows more about their own actions than other people do. This leads to a distortion of incentives to take care or to exert effort when someone else bears the costs of the lack of care or effort.

A **deductible** in an insurance policy is a sum that the insured individual must pay before being compensated for a claim.

ECONOMICS >> *in Action*
Franchise Owners Try Harder

Franchise owners face risk, which motivates them to work harder than salaried managers.

When Americans want a quick meal, they often end up at one of the fast-food chains—Subway, Taco Bell, Pizza Hut, McDonald's, and so on. Because these are large corporations, customers may assume that the people who serve them are employees of large corporations. But usually they aren't. Most fast-food restaurants—for example, 85% of McDonald's outlets—are franchises. That is, some individual has paid the parent company for the right to operate a restaurant selling its product. This person may look like an arm of a giant company but is in fact a small-business owner.

Becoming a franchisee is not a guarantee of success. You must put up a large amount of money, both to buy the license and to set up the restaurant itself. For example, in 2019 it cost between $1 and $2.2 million to open a McDonald's franchise. And although McDonald's takes care that its franchises are not too close to each other, they often face stiff competition from rival chains and even from a few truly independent restaurants. Becoming a franchise owner, in other words, involves taking on a lot of risk.

But why should people be willing to take these risks? Didn't we just learn that it is better to diversify, to spread your wealth among many investments?

The logic of diversification would seem to say that it's better for someone with $1.7 million to invest in a wide range of stocks rather than put it all into one Taco Bell. This implies that Taco Bell would find it hard to attract franchisees: nobody would be willing to be a franchisee unless they expected to earn considerably more than they would as a hired manager with their wealth invested in a diversified portfolio of stocks. So wouldn't it be more profitable for Pizza Hut or Taco Bell simply to hire managers to run their restaurants?

It turns out that it isn't, because the success of a restaurant depends a lot on how hard the manager works, on the effort they put into choosing the right employees, on keeping the place clean and attractive to customers, and so on. The problem is moral hazard: the manager knows how effectively they are running their restaurant, but company headquarters—which bears the costs of a poorly run restaurant—does not. So a salaried manager, who gets paid even without doing everything possible to make the restaurant a success, does not have the incentive to do that extra bit—an incentive the owner does have because they have a substantial personal stake in the restaurant's success.

In other words, there is a moral hazard problem when a salaried manager runs a Pizza Hut, where the private information is how hard the manager works. Franchising solves this problem. A franchisee, whose wealth is tied up in the business and who stands to profit personally from its success, has every incentive to work extremely hard.

The result is that fast-food chains rely mainly on franchisees to operate their restaurants, even though the contracts with these owner-managers allow the franchisees on average to make much more than it would have cost the companies to employ store managers. The higher earnings of franchisees compensate them for the risk they accept, and the companies are compensated by higher sales that lead to higher license fees.

In addition, licensing agreements forbid franchisees from taking actions that reduce their risk exposure to their business, such as selling shares of the franchise to others. It's an illustration of the fact that given a manager's action is subject to moral hazard, the parent company won't allow them to eliminate their risk through diversification.

>> Check Your Understanding 20-3

Solutions appear at the back of book.

1. Your car insurance premiums are lower if you have had no moving violations for several years. Explain how this feature tends to decrease the potential inefficiency caused by adverse selection.

2. A common feature of home construction contracts is that when it costs more to construct a building than was originally estimated, the contractor must absorb the additional cost. Explain how this feature reduces the problem of moral hazard but also forces the contractor to bear more risk than the contractor would like.

3. True or false? Explain your answer, stating what concept analyzed in this chapter accounts for the feature.

   People with higher deductibles on their auto insurance:
   a. Generally drive more carefully
   b. Pay lower premiums
   c. Generally are wealthier

PURE—An Insurance Company That Withstands Hurricanes

ntzolov/Getty Images

Ross Buchmueller went where few others dared to go: he went to Florida to underwrite homeowner insurance policies soon after Hurricane Katrina and Hurricane Rita hit the American Gulf Coast in 2005 (An *underwriter* "produces" insurance by measuring the risk, calculating the premium, and writing the insurance contract.) Katrina alone was the most expensive natural disaster in U.S. history: 1,800 people were killed and $41 billion in insured losses were incurred, enough to wipe out 25 years' worth of insurance industry premiums. And with more bad weather to come, by the end of 2005, insurers had incurred $71 billion in losses, the worst year on record.

In the years after Katrina, major national insurers significantly reduced their policy writing in hurricane-prone coastal areas. And for homeowners in those areas who could still obtain insurance, both premiums and deductibles sky-rocketed. Millions of Americans who built or purchased homes in hurricane-prone coastal areas with the expectation of being able to buy affordable insurance faced a costly and risky dilemma.

So in 2007, some industry professionals were skeptical when Privilege Underwriters Reciprocal Exchange (PURE), the company created by Ross Buchmueller, began underwriting policies in Florida. Michael Koziol, an insurance industry analyst, observed "Like any new company, there's a certain risk. More new companies go under than old companies." The common industry view was that although Florida insurance premiums were at record highs, they were still too low to offset the potential costs from extreme weather events.

However, Buchmueller had a two-pronged strategy for making a profit. First, after studying industry statistics on past hurricane-related claims, he limited his sales to homes worth more than $1 million that were fairly new, solidly built, and equipped with strong shutters and high-grade windows that repelled flying debris. Second, Buchmueller purchased policies from big, global insurance companies that covered 75% of his potential losses. The size and global reach of their portfolios allowed these companies to treat the exposure to Florida hurricane losses as a relatively small risk.

Buchmueller was confident in his approach: for his select group of customers, not only did he offer policies at lower premiums than competitors, he often offered policies to homeowners that no one else would cover. One of PURE's first customers, Ellis Kern, who had previously been insured by Lloyd's of London, saw his premium fall by nearly 55%.

So how has PURE fared over time? As of 2019, not only has PURE survived, it has thrived, growing by 30% to 40% in *each* of the past 10 years. PURE's successes in Florida allowed it to expand nationwide, so that it now offers coverage in 49 states plus the District of Columbia. In early 2020, the international insurance company, Tokio Marine, purchased PURE for $3.1 *billion*.

QUESTIONS FOR THOUGHT

1. What is one example of moral hazard by homeowners in hurricane-prone areas? Explain.

2. How does the case illustrate market failure due to adverse selection?

3. What were the sources of Buchmueller's innovation that allowed him to succeed in the presence of moral hazard and adverse selection?

4. Why did Buchmueller purchase insurance policies from big, global insurance companies to cover up to 75% of his own losses? What principle does this illustrate?

SUMMARY

1. The **expected value** of a **random variable** is the weighted average of all possible values, where the weight corresponds to the probability of a given value occurring.

2. **Risk** is uncertainty about future events or **states of the world.** It is **financial risk** when the uncertainty is about monetary outcomes.

3. Under uncertainty, people maximize **expected utility.** A **risk-averse** person will choose to reduce risk when that reduction leaves the expected value of their income or wealth unchanged. A **fair insurance policy** has that feature: the **premium** is equal to the expected value of the claim. A **risk-neutral** person is completely insensitive to risk and therefore unwilling to pay any premium to avoid it.

4. Risk aversion arises from diminishing marginal utility: an additional dollar of income generates higher marginal utility in low-income states than in high-income states. A fair insurance policy increases a risk-averse person's utility because it transfers a dollar from a high-income state (a state when no loss occurs) to a low-income state (a state when a loss occurs).

5. Differences in preferences and income or wealth lead to differences in risk aversion. Depending on the size of the premium, a risk-averse person is willing to purchase "unfair" insurance, a policy for which the premium exceeds the expected value of the claim. The greater your risk aversion, the higher the premium you are willing to pay.

6. There are gains from trade in risk, leading to an **efficient allocation of risk:** those who are most willing to bear risk put their **capital at risk** to cover the losses of those least willing to bear risk.

7. Risk can also be reduced through **diversification,** investing in several different things that correspond to **independent events.** The stock market, where **shares** in companies are traded, offers one way to diversify. Insurance companies can engage in **pooling,** insuring many independent events so as to eliminate almost all risk. But when the underlying events are **positively correlated,** all risk cannot be diversified away.

8. **Private information** can cause inefficiency in the allocation of risk. One problem is **adverse selection,** private information about the way things are. It creates the "lemons problem" in used-car markets, where sellers of high-quality cars drop out of the market. Adverse selection can be limited in several ways—through **screening** of individuals, through the **signaling** that people use to reveal their private information, and through the building of a **reputation.**

9. A related problem is **moral hazard:** individuals have private information about their actions, which distorts their incentives to exert effort or care when someone else bears the costs of that lack of effort or care. It limits the ability of markets to allocate risk efficiently. Insurance companies try to limit moral hazard by imposing **deductibles,** placing more risk on the insured.

KEY TERMS

Random variable, p. 580
Expected value, p. 580
State of the world, p. 580
Risk, p. 580
Financial risk, p. 580
Expected utility, p. 581
Premium, p. 581
Fair insurance policy, p. 582

Risk-averse, p. 583
Risk-neutral, p. 585
Capital at risk, p. 588
Efficient allocation of risk, p. 588
Independent events, p. 590
Diversification, p. 590
Share, p. 591
Pooling, p. 591

Positively correlated, p. 593
Private information, p. 594
Adverse selection, p. 595
Screening, p. 596
Signaling, p. 596
Reputation, p. 596
Moral hazard, p. 597
Deductible, p. 597

PRACTICE QUESTIONS

1. Insurance companies are using technology to learn more about their customer's behavior. Explain how each of the following devices reduces the adverse selection problem. Which customers are most likely to use the devices?

   a. GPS car trackers that monitor speed, time of day, and erratic driving

   b. Fitness and diet health trackers

2. Many star college athletes are faced with the difficult decision of going pro and earning millions or choosing to stay in school to complete their degree. What are the financial risks faced by the college athlete? How can insurance be used to mitigate these risks?

PROBLEMS

1. For each of the following situations, calculate the expected value.

   a. Tanisha owns one share of IBM stock, which is currently trading at $80. There is a 50% chance that the share price will rise to $100 and a 50% chance that it will fall to $70. What is the expected value of the future share price?

   b. Sharon buys a ticket in a small lottery. There is a probability of 0.7 that she will win nothing, of 0.2 that she will win $10, and of 0.1 that she will win $50. What is the expected value of Sharon's winnings?

   c. Aaron is a farmer whose rice crop depends on the weather. If the weather is favorable, he will make a profit of $100. If the weather is unfavorable, he will make a profit of –$20 (that is, he will lose money). The weather forecast reports that the probability of weather being favorable is 0.9 and the probability of weather being unfavorable is 0.1. What is the expected value of Aaron's profit?

2. Vicky is considering investing some of her money in a startup company. She currently has income of $4,000, and she is considering investing $2,000 of that in the company. There is a 0.5 probability that the company will succeed and will pay out $8,000 to Vicky (her original investment of $2,000 plus $6,000 of the company's profits). And there is a 0.5 probability that the company will fail and Vicky will get nothing (and lose her investment). The accompanying table illustrates Vicky's utility function.

Income	Total utility (utils)
$0	0
1,000	50
2,000	85
3,000	115
4,000	140
5,000	163
6,000	183
7,000	200
8,000	215
9,000	229
10,000	241

   a. Calculate Vicky's marginal utility of income for each income level. Is Vicky risk-averse?

   b. Calculate the expected value of Vicky's income if she makes this investment.

   c. Calculate Vicky's expected utility from making the investment.

   d. What is Vicky's utility from not making the investment? Will Vicky therefore invest in the company?

Income	Total utility(utils)	Marginal utility (utils)
$0	0	
		50
1,000	50	
		35
2,000	85	
		30
3,000	115	
		25
4,000	140	
		23
5,000	163	
		20
6,000	183	
		17
7,000	200	
		15
8,000	215	
		14
9,000	229	
		12
10,000	241	

3. Vicky's utility function was given in Problem 2. As in Problem 2, Vicky currently has income of $4,000. She is considering investing in a startup company, but the investment now costs $4,000 to make. If the company fails, Vicky will get nothing from the company. But if the company succeeds, she will get $10,000 from the company (her original investment of $4,000 plus $6,000 of the company's profits). Each event has a 0.5 probability of occurring. Will Vicky invest in the company?

4. You have $1,000 that you can invest. If you buy Ford stock, you face the following returns and probabilities from holding the stock for one year: with a probability of 0.2 you will get $1,500; with a probability of 0.4 you will get $1,100; and with a probability of 0.4 you will get $900. If you put the money into the bank, in one year's time you will get $1,100 for certain.

   a. What is the expected value of your earnings from investing in Ford stock?

   b. Suppose you are risk-averse. Can we say for sure whether you will invest in Ford stock or put your money into the bank?

5. Wilbur is an airline pilot who currently has income of $60,000. If he gets sick and loses his flight medical certificate, he loses his job and has only $10,000 income. His probability of staying healthy is 0.6, and his probability of getting sick is 0.4. Wilbur's utility function is given in the accompanying table.

Income	Total utility (utils)
$0	0
10,000	60
20,000	110
30,000	150
40,000	180
50,000	200
60,000	210

a. What is the expected value of Wilbur's income?

b. What is Wilbur's expected utility?

Wilbur thinks about buying "loss-of-license" insurance that will compensate him if he loses his flight medical certificate.

c. One insurance company offers Wilbur full compensation for his income loss (that is, the insurance company pays Wilbur $50,000 if he loses his flight medical certificate), and it charges a premium of $40,000. That is, regardless of whether he loses his flight medical certificate, Wilbur's income after insurance will be $20,000. What is Wilbur's utility? Will he buy the insurance?

d. What is the highest premium Wilbur would be willing to pay for full insurance (insurance that completely compensates him for the income loss)?

6. According to the FBI's Uniform Crime Reports, approximately 1 in 365 cars was stolen in the United States in 2018. Beth owns a car worth $20,000 and is considering purchasing an insurance policy to protect herself from car theft. For the following questions, assume that the chance of car theft is the same in all regions and across all car models.

a. What should the premium for a fair insurance policy have been in 2018 for a policy that replaces Beth's car if it is stolen? (*Hint:* In your calculation, round up to three decimal places.)

b. Suppose an insurance company charges 0.6% of the car's value for a policy that pays for replacing a stolen car. How much will the policy cost Beth?

c. Will Beth purchase the insurance in part b if she is risk-neutral?

d. Discuss a possible moral hazard problem facing Beth's insurance company if she purchases the insurance.

7. Hugh's income is currently $5,000. His utility function is shown in the accompanying table.

Income	Total utility (utils)
$0	0
1,000	100
2,000	140
3,000	166
4,000	185
5,000	200
6,000	212
7,000	222
8,000	230
9,000	236
10,000	240

a. Calculate Hugh's marginal utility of income. What is his attitude toward risk?

b. Hugh is thinking about gambling in a casino. With a probability of 0.5 he will lose $3,000, and with a probability of 0.5 he will win $5,000. What is the expected value of Hugh's income? What is Hugh's expected utility? Will he decide to gamble? (Suppose that he gets no extra utility from going to the casino.)

c. Suppose that the "spread" (how much he can win versus how much he can lose) of the gamble narrows, so that with a probability of 0.5 Hugh will lose $1,000, and with a probability of 0.5 he will win $3,000. What is the expected value of Hugh's income? What is his expected utility? Is this gamble better for him than the gamble in part b? Will he decide to gamble?

8. Eva is risk-averse. Currently she has $50,000 to invest. She faces the following choice: she can invest in the stock of a startup company, or she can invest in IBM stock. If she invests in the startup company, then with a probability of 0.5 she will lose $30,000, but with a probability of 0.5 she will gain $50,000. If she invests in IBM stock, then with a probability of 0.5 she will lose $10,000, but with a probability of 0.5 she will gain $30,000. Can you tell which investment she will prefer to make?

9. Suppose you have $1,000 that you can invest in Ted and Larry's Ice Cream Parlor and/or Ethel's House of Cocoa. The price of a share of stock in either company is $100. The fortunes of each company are closely linked to the weather. When it is warm, the value of Ted and Larry's stock rises to $150 but the value of Ethel's stock falls to $60. When it is cold, the value of Ethel's stock rises to $150 but the value of Ted and Larry's stock falls to $60. There is an equal chance of the weather being warm or cold.

a. If you invest all your money in Ted and Larry's, what is your expected stock value? What if you invest all your money in Ethel's?

b. Suppose you diversify and invest half of your $1,000 in each company. How much will your total stock be worth if the weather is warm? What if it is cold?

c. Suppose you are risk-averse. Would you prefer to put all your money in Ted and Larry's, as in part a? Or would you prefer to diversify, as in part b? Explain your reasoning.

10. LifeStrategy Conservative Growth and Small Cap Growth are two portfolios constructed and managed by the Vanguard Group of mutual funds, comprised of stocks of conservatively managed U.S. companies and stocks of small U.S. firms, mostly in healthcare or technology. The accompanying table shows historical annualized return from the period 2010 to 2020, which suggests the expected value of the annual percentage returns associated with these portfolios.

Portfolio	Expected value of return (percent)
LifeStrategy Conservative Growth	5.88%
Small Cap Growth	11.01

a. Which portfolio would a risk-neutral investor prefer?

b. Juan, a risk-averse investor, chooses to invest in the LifeStrategy Conservative Growth portfolio. What can be inferred about the risk of the two portfolios from Juan's choice of investment? Based on historical performance, would a risk-neutral investor ever choose LifeStrategy Conservative Growth?

c. Juan is aware that diversification can reduce risk. He considers a portfolio in which half his investment is in conservatively managed companies and the other half in small high tech or healthcare companies. What is the expected value of the return for this combined portfolio? Would you expect this combined portfolio to be more risky or less risky than the LifeStrategy Conservative Growth portfolio? Why or why not?

11. You are considering buying a second-hand Volkswagen. From reading car magazines, you know that half of all Volkswagens have problems of some kind (they are "lemons") and the other half run just fine (they are "plums"). If you knew that you were getting a plum, you would be willing to pay $10,000 for it: this is how much a plum is worth to you. You would also be willing to buy a lemon, but only if its price was no more than $4,000: this is how much a lemon is worth to you. And someone who owns a plum would be willing to sell it at any price above $8,000. Someone who owns a lemon would be willing to sell it for any price above $2,000.

a. For now, suppose that you can immediately tell whether the car that you are being offered is a lemon or a plum. Suppose someone offers you a plum. Will there be trade?

Now suppose that the seller has private information about the car they are selling: the seller knows whether they have a lemon or a plum. But when the seller offers you a Volkswagen, you do not know whether it is a lemon or a plum. So this is a situation of adverse selection.

b. Since you do not know whether you are being offered a plum or a lemon, you base your decision on the expected value to you of a Volkswagen, assuming you are just as likely to buy a lemon as a plum. Calculate this expected value.

c. Suppose, from driving the car, the seller knows they have a plum. However, you don't know whether this particular car is a lemon or a plum, so the most you are willing to pay is your expected value. Will there be trade?

12. You own a company that produces chairs, and you are thinking about hiring one more employee. Each chair produced gives you revenue of $10. There are two potential employees, Fred and Sylvia. Fred is a fast worker who produces 10 chairs per day, creating revenue for you of $100. Fred knows that he is fast and so will work for you only if you pay him more than $80 per day. Sylvia is a slow worker who produces only five chairs per day, creating revenue for you of $50. Sylvia knows that she is slow and so will work for you if you pay her more than $40 per day. Although Sylvia

knows she is slow and Fred knows he is fast, you do not know who is fast and who is slow. So this is a situation of adverse selection.

a. Since you do not know which type of worker you will get, you think about what the expected value of your revenue will be if you hire one of the two. What is that expected value?

b. Suppose you offered to pay a daily wage equal to the expected revenue you calculated in part a. Whom would you be able to hire: Fred, or Sylvia, or both, or neither?

c. If you know whether a worker is fast or slow, which one would you prefer to hire and why? Can you devise a compensation scheme to guarantee that you employ only the type of worker you prefer?

13. For each of the following situations, do the following: first describe whether it is a situation of moral hazard or of adverse selection. Then explain what inefficiency can arise from this situation and explain how the proposed solution reduces the inefficiency.

a. When you buy a second-hand car, you do not know whether it is a lemon (low quality) or a plum (high quality), but the seller knows. A solution is for sellers to offer a warranty with the car that pays for repair costs.

b. Some people are prone to see doctors unnecessarily for minor complaints like headaches, and health maintenance organizations do not know how urgently you need a doctor. A solution is for insurees to have to make a co-payment of a certain dollar amount (for example, $10) each time they visit a health care provider. All insurees are risk-averse.

c. When airlines sell tickets, they do not know whether a buyer is a business traveler (who is willing to pay a lot for a seat) or a leisure traveler (who has a low willingness to pay). A solution for a profit-maximizing airline is to offer an expensive ticket that is very flexible (it allows date and route changes) and a cheap ticket that is very inflexible (it has to be booked in advance and cannot be changed).

d. A company does not know whether workers on an assembly line work hard or whether they slack off. A solution is to pay the workers "piece rates," that is, pay them according to how much they have produced each day. All workers are risk-averse, but the company is not risk-neutral.

e. When making a decision about hiring you, prospective employers do not know whether you are a productive or unproductive worker. A solution is for productive workers to provide potential employers with references from previous employers.

14. Kory owns a house that is worth $300,000. If the house burns down, she loses all $300,000. If the house

does not burn down, she loses nothing. Her house burns down with a probability of 0.02. Kory is risk-averse.

a. What would a fair insurance policy cost?

b. Suppose an insurance company offers to insure her fully against the loss from the house burning down, at a premium of $1,500. Can you say for sure whether Kory will or will not take the insurance?

c. Suppose an insurance company offers to insure her fully against the loss from the house burning down, at a premium of $6,000. Can you say for sure whether Kory will or will not take the insurance?

d. Suppose that an insurance company offers to insure her fully against the loss from the house burning down, at a premium of $9,000. Can you say

for sure whether Kory will or will not take the insurance?

WORK IT OUT

15. You have $1,000 that you can invest. If you buy General Motors stock, then, in one year's time: with a probability of 0.4 you will get $1,600; with a probability of 0.4 you will get $1,100; and with a probability of 0.2 you will get $800. If you put the money into the bank, in one year's time you will get $1,100 for certain.

a. What is the expected value of your earnings from investing in General Motors stock?

b. Suppose you prefer putting your money into the bank to investing it in General Motors stock. What does that tell us about your attitude toward risk? ■

21 ▷ Macroeconomics: The Big Picture

GREEK TRAGEDIES

CONSTANTINE KAKOYIANNIS, an engineer, grew up in Greece. But these days he lives in Dusseldorf, Germany. He's one of many Greeks who have settled there since 2010, so many that Dusseldorf has become known as a "mini-Athens."

Why did he and so many others leave home? Because there were no jobs. In 2016, when Kakoyiannis left, Greece's *unemployment rate*—the percentage of those looking for work who couldn't find it—was 24%. As of December 2019, unemployment in Greece had fallen but was still 16.5%. For the sake of comparison, in the United States the unemployment rate was only 3.5% although it shot up to 14.7% a few months later when the economy was locked down in an attempt to limit the spread of COVID-19.

Yet Greece hasn't always had sky-high unemployment. In 2007 the unemployment rate was only about 8%. Greece was still poorer than northern European countries like Germany, but it had been doing

Greeks in Germany, where the jobs are.

Felix Brüggemann/The New York Times/Redux Pictures

relatively well, and Greeks were feeling optimistic about their prospects.

Then Greece plunged into a severe economic downturn—a *recession*—which led to a collapse in employment. Many businesses went bust and people suffered economic hardship. And Greece wasn't alone. After 2007, much of the world, including the United States, plunged into a deep recession, which came to be known as the *Great Recession*. By 2019 the United States had mostly recovered, but some parts of Europe, Greece in particular, had not.

Yet, as bad as things were during the Great Recession, the global economy had seen much worse. Beginning in 1929, a severe global economic slump known as the *Great Depression* hit and lasted over a decade, until the start of World War II in 1940. The Great Recession was less severe than the Great Depression for many reasons. But one significant factor was that economists had learned something about what to do from the earlier catastrophe. As the Great Depression began in 1929, political leaders and their economic advisers had no idea what policies might help or hinder recovery.

Microeconomics, which is concerned with the consumption and production decisions of individual consumers and producers and with the allocation of scarce resources among industries, was already a well-developed branch of economics. But *macroeconomics,* which focuses on the behavior of the economy as a whole, was still in its infancy. In contrast, by 2007 macroeconomics had advanced enough that economists knew what needed to be done when the Great Recession hit.

In normal economic times, when there is no recession or depression, workers who lose their jobs are able to find

employment somewhere else. However, the Great Depression was no normal time: in the United States the unemployment rate hit 23% and the value of the economy's output (GDP) fell by 26%. Economists realized that they needed to understand the nature of the catastrophe that had overtaken the United States and much of the rest of the world in order to extricate themselves, as well as to learn how to avoid such economic disasters in the future. To this day, the effort to understand economic slumps and find ways to prevent them is at the core of macroeconomics. Over time, however, macroeconomics has broadened its reach to encompass a number of other subjects, such as long-run economic growth, inflation, and international macroeconomics.

This chapter offers an overview of macroeconomics. We start with a general description of the difference between macroeconomics and microeconomics, then briefly describe some of the field's major concerns. ●

WHAT YOU WILL LEARN

- What is the difference between macroeconomics and microeconomics?
- What are **business cycles** and why do policy makers try to diminish their severity?
- How does **long-run economic growth** determine a country's standard of living?
- What are **inflation** and **deflation,** and why is **price stability** preferred?
- Why does **international macroeconomics** matter, and how do economies interact through **trade deficits** and **trade surpluses?**

‖ The Nature of Macroeconomics

Macroeconomics differs from microeconomics by focusing on the behavior of the economy as a whole.

Macroeconomic Questions

Table 21-1 lists some typical economic questions from the perspectives of microeconomists in the left column, and macroeconomists in the right column. By comparing the questions, you can begin to get a sense of the difference between microeconomics and macroeconomics.

As these questions illustrate, microeconomics focuses on how decisions are made by individuals and firms and the consequences of those decisions. For example, we use microeconomics to determine how much it would cost a university or college to offer a new course, including the instructor's salary, the cost of class materials, and so on. The school can then decide whether to offer the course by weighing the costs and benefits.

TABLE 21-1 Microeconomic versus Macroeconomic Questions	
Microeconomic Questions	**Macroeconomic Questions**
Should I go to business school or take a job right now?	How many people are employed in the economy as a whole this year?
What determines the salary Google offers to Cherie Camajo, a new MBA?	What determines the overall salary levels paid to workers in a given year?
What determines the cost to a university or college of offering a new course?	What determines the overall level of prices in the economy as a whole?
What government policies should be adopted to make it easier for low-income students to attend college?	What government policies should be adopted to promote employment and growth in the economy as a whole?
What determines whether Citibank opens a new office in Shanghai?	What determines the overall trade in goods, services, and financial assets between the United States and the rest of the world?
Why was there a shortage of toilet paper during the coronavirus pandemic?	How did a fall in consumer spending during the pandemic affect overall employment?

Macroeconomics, in contrast, examines the *overall* behavior of the economy—how the actions of all the individuals and firms in the economy interact to produce a particular economy-wide level of economic performance. For example, macroeconomics is concerned with the general level of prices in the economy and how high or how low that level is relative to the general level of prices last year, rather than with the price of one particular good or service.

You might imagine that macroeconomic questions can be answered simply by adding up microeconomic answers. For example, the model of supply and demand introduced in Chapter 3 tells us how the equilibrium price of an individual good or service is determined in a competitive market. So you might think that applying supply and demand analysis to every good and service in the economy, then summing the results, is the way to understand the overall level of prices in the economy as a whole.

But that is incorrect: although basic concepts such as supply and demand are essential to macroeconomics, answering macroeconomic questions requires an additional set of tools and an expanded frame of reference.

Macroeconomics: The Whole Is Greater Than the Sum of Its Parts

If you drive on a highway, you probably know what a rubbernecking traffic jam is and why it is so annoying. Someone pulls over to the side of the road, perhaps to fix a flat tire, and, pretty soon, a long traffic jam occurs as drivers slow down to take a look.

What makes it so annoying is that the length of the traffic jam is greatly out of proportion to the minor event that precipitated it. Because some drivers hit their brakes to rubberneck, the drivers behind them must also hit their brakes, those behind them must do the same, and so on. The accumulation of all the individual hitting of brakes eventually leads to a long, wasteful traffic jam as each driver slows down a little bit more than the driver ahead. In other words, each person's response leads to an amplified response by the next person.

Understanding rubbernecking gives us some insight into one very important way in which macroeconomics differs from microeconomics: many thousands

Just as individual actions on the road can unintentionally lead to a traffic jam, individual actions in the economy can produce an unintended macroeconomic effect.

or millions of individual actions compound upon one another to produce an outcome that isn't simply the sum of those individual actions.

Consider, for example, what macroeconomists call the *paradox of thrift:* when families and businesses are worried about the possibility of economic hard times, they prepare by cutting their spending. This reduction in spending depresses the economy as consumers spend less and businesses react by laying off workers. As a result, families and businesses may end up worse off than if they hadn't tried to act responsibly by cutting their spending.

This is a paradox because seemingly virtuous behavior—preparing for hard times by saving more—ends up harming everyone. The flip-side to this story is that when families and businesses are feeling optimistic about the future, they spend more today. This stimulates the economy, leading businesses to hire more workers, which further expands the economy. Seemingly profligate behavior leads to good times for all.

A key insight of macroeconomics, then, is that the combined effect of individual decisions can have results that are very different from what any one individual intended, results that are sometimes perverse. The behavior of the macroeconomy is, indeed, greater than the sum of individual actions and market outcomes.

Macroeconomics: Theory and Policy

To a much greater extent than microeconomists, macroeconomists are concerned with questions about *policy*, about what the government can do to make macroeconomic performance better. This policy focus was strongly shaped by history, in particular by the Great Depression of the 1930s.

Before the 1930s, economists tended to regard the economy as **self-regulating:** they believed that problems such as unemployment would be corrected through the working of the "invisible hand" and that government attempts to improve the economy's performance would be ineffective at best—and would probably make things worse.

The Great Depression changed all that. The sheer scale of the catastrophe, which left a quarter of the U.S. workforce without jobs and threatened the political stability of many countries, created a demand for action. It also led to a major effort on the part of economists to understand economic slumps and find ways to prevent them.

In 1936 the British economist John Maynard Keynes (pronounced "canes") published *The General Theory of Employment, Interest, and Money*, a book that transformed macroeconomics. According to **Keynesian economics,** a depressed economy is the result of inadequate spending. In addition, Keynes argued that government intervention can help a depressed economy through *monetary policy* and *fiscal policy*. **Monetary policy** uses changes in the quantity of money to alter interest rates, which in turn affect the level of overall spending. **Fiscal policy** uses changes in taxes and government spending to affect overall spending.

In general, Keynes established the idea that managing the economy is a government responsibility. Keynesian ideas continue to have a strong influence on both economic theory and public policy: in 2008 and 2009, Congress, the White House, and the Federal Reserve (a quasi-governmental agency that manages U.S. monetary policy) took steps to fend off an economic slump that were clearly Keynesian in spirit, as described in the following Economics in Action.

In a **self-regulating economy,** problems such as unemployment are resolved without government intervention, through the working of the invisible hand.

According to **Keynesian economics,** economic slumps are caused by inadequate spending, and they can be mitigated by government intervention.

Monetary policy uses changes in the quantity of money to alter interest rates and affect overall spending.

Fiscal policy uses changes in government spending and taxes to affect overall spending.

"If you wear it like this you can't see any economic forecasts."

Matt Pritchett/The Daily Telegraph

ECONOMICS >> *in Action*
Fending Off Depression

In 2008 the world economy experienced a severe financial crisis reminiscent of the early days of the Great Depression. Major banks teetered on the edge of collapse and world trade slumped. In reviewing the 2009 data, economic historians Barry Eichengreen and Kevin O'Rourke pointed out that "globally we are tracking or even doing worse than the Great Depression."

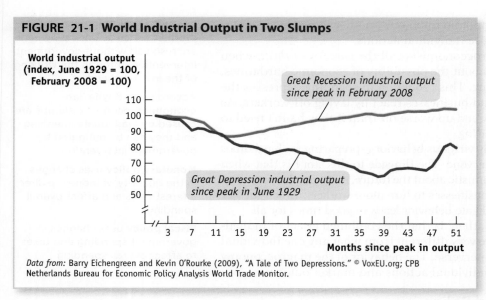

FIGURE 21-1 World Industrial Output in Two Slumps

World industrial output
(index, June 1929 = 100,
February 2008 = 100)

Great Recession industrial output since peak in February 2008

Great Depression industrial output since peak in June 1929

Months since peak in output

Data from: Barry Eichengreen and Kevin O'Rourke (2009), "A Tale of Two Depressions." © VoxEU.org; CPB Netherlands Bureau for Economic Policy Analysis World Trade Monitor.

But the worst did not, in the end, come to pass. Figure 21-1 shows one of Eichengreen and O'Rourke's measures of economic activity, world industrial production, during the Great Depression (the bottom line) and during the Great Recession (the top line). During the first year the two crises were indeed comparable. But fortunately, 11 months into the Great Recession, world production leveled off and turned around. In contrast, three years into the Great Depression world production continued to fall. Why the difference?

At least part of the answer is that policy makers responded very differently. During the Great Depression, it was widely argued that the slump should be allowed to run its course. Any attempt to mitigate the ongoing catastrophe, declared Joseph Schumpeter—the Austrian-born Harvard economist now famed for his work on innovation—would "leave the work of depression undone." In the early 1930s, some countries' monetary authorities actually raised interest rates in the face of the slump, while governments cut spending and raised taxes—actions that deepened the recession.

In the aftermath of the 2008 crisis, by contrast, interest rates were slashed, and a number of countries, the United States included, used temporary increases in spending and reductions in taxes in an attempt to sustain spending. Governments also moved to shore up their banks with loans, aid, and guarantees.

Many of these measures were controversial, to say the least. But most economists believe that by responding actively to the Great Recession—and doing so using the knowledge gained from the study of macroeconomics—governments helped avoid a global economic catastrophe.

>> Quick Review

• Microeconomics focuses on decision making by individuals and firms and the consequences of the decisions made. Macroeconomics focuses on the overall behavior of the economy.

• The combined effect of individual actions can have unintended consequences and lead to worse or better macroeconomic outcomes for everyone.

• Before the 1930s, economists tended to regard the economy as **self-regulating.** After the Great Depression, **Keynesian economics** provided the rationale for government intervention through **monetary policy** and **fiscal policy** to help a depressed economy.

>> Check Your Understanding 21-1

Solutions appear at back of book.

1. Which of the following questions involve microeconomics, and which involve macroeconomics? In each case, explain your answer.
   a. Why did consumers switch to smaller cars in 2008?
   b. Why did overall consumer spending slow down in 2008?
   c. Why did the standard of living rise more rapidly in the first generation after World War II than in the second?
   d. Why have starting salaries for students with economics degrees risen sharply as of late?
   e. What determines the choice between rail and road transportation?
   f. Why did laptops get much cheaper between 2000 and 2017?
   g. Why did inflation fall in the 2010s?

2. In 2008, problems in the financial sector led to a drying up of credit around the country: home-buyers were unable to get mortgages, students were unable to get student loans, car-buyers were unable to get car loans, and so on.
   a. Explain how the drying up of credit can lead to compounding effects throughout the economy and result in an economic slump.
   b. If you believe the economy is self-regulating, what would you advocate that policy makers do?
   c. If you believe in Keynesian economics, what would you advocate that policy makers do?

‖ The Business Cycle

The Great Depression was by far the worst economic crisis in U.S. history. Although the economy managed to avoid catastrophe in the decades that followed, it has experienced many ups and downs.

It's true that the ups have consistently been bigger than the downs: a chart of any of the major numbers used to track the U.S. economy shows a strong upward trend over time. For example, panel (a) of Figure 21-2 shows total U.S. private-sector employment (the total number of jobs offered by private businesses) measured along the left vertical axis, with the data from 1985 to 2020 given by the purple line. The graph also shows the index of industrial production (a measure of the total output of U.S. factories) measured along the right vertical axis, with the data from 1985 to 2020 given by the red line. Both private-sector employment and industrial production were much higher at the end of this period than at the beginning, and in most years both measures rose.

But they didn't rise steadily. As you can see from the figure, there were four periods—in the early 1990s, in the early 2000s, beginning in late 2007, and again in 2020—when both employment and industrial output stumbled. Panel (b) emphasizes these stumbles by showing the *rate of change* of employment and industrial production over the previous year. For example, the percent change in employment for October 2009 was –0.6 because employment in October 2009 was 0.6% lower than it had been in October 2008. The big downturns stand out clearly. What's more, a detailed look at the data makes it clear that in each period the stumble wasn't confined to only a few industries: in each downturn, just about every sector of the U.S. economy cut back on production and on the number of people employed.

FIGURE 21-2 U.S. Growth, Interrupted, 1985–2020

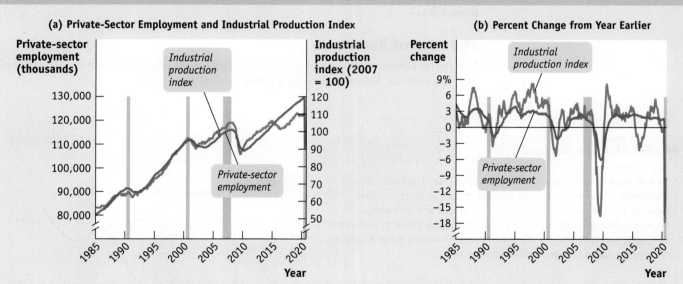

Panel (a) shows two important economic numbers, the industrial production index and total private-sector employment. Both numbers grew substantially from 1985 to 2020, but they didn't grow steadily. Instead, both suffered from downturns associated with recessions, which are indicated by the shaded areas in the figure.

Panel (b) emphasizes those downturns by showing the annual rate of change of industrial production and employment, that is, the percentage increase over the past year. The simultaneous downturns in both numbers during the recessions are clear.

Data from: Federal Reserve Bank of St. Louis.

Recessions, or contractions, are periods of economic downturn when output and employment are falling.

Expansions, or recoveries, are periods of economic upturn when output and employment are rising.

The **business cycle** is the short-run alternation between recessions and expansions.

The point at which the economy turns from expansion to recession is a **business-cycle peak.**

The point at which the economy turns from recession to expansion is a **business-cycle trough.**

The economy's forward march, in other words, isn't smooth. And the uneven pace of the economy's progress, its ups and downs, is one of the main preoccupations of macroeconomics.

Charting the Business Cycle

Figure 21-3 shows a stylized representation of the way the economy evolves over time. The vertical axis shows either employment or an indicator of how much the economy is producing, such as industrial production or *real gross domestic product (real GDP)*, a measure of the economy's overall output that we'll learn about in Chapter 22. As the data in Figure 21-2 suggest, these two measures tend to move together. Their common movement is the starting point for a major theme of macroeconomics: the economy's alternation between short-run downturns and upturns.

A widespread downturn, in which output and employment in many industries fall, is called a **recession** (sometimes referred to as a *contraction*). Recessions are officially declared by the National Bureau of Economic Research, or NBER (discussed in the upcoming For Inquiring Minds), and are indicated by the shaded areas in Figure 21-2. When the economy isn't in a recession, when most economic numbers are following their normal upward trend, the economy is said to be in an **expansion** (sometimes referred to as a *recovery*).

The alternation between recessions and expansions is known as the **business cycle.** The point in time at which the economy shifts from expansion to recession is known as a **business-cycle peak;** the point at which the economy shifts from recession to expansion is known as a **business-cycle trough.**

The business cycle is an enduring feature of the economy. Table 21-2 shows the official list of business-cycle peaks and troughs. As you can see, there have been recessions and expansions for at least the past 160 years. Whenever there is a prolonged expansion, as there was in the 1960s and again in the 1990s, books and articles come out proclaiming the end of the business cycle. Such proclamations have always been proved wrong: the cycle always comes back.

The Pain of Recession

Not many people complain about the business cycle when the economy is expanding. Recessions, however, create a great deal of pain.

FIGURE 21-3 The Business Cycle

This is a stylized picture of the business cycle. The vertical axis measures either employment or total output in the economy. Periods when these two variables turn down are *recessions;* periods when they turn up are *expansions.* The point at which the economy turns down is a *business-cycle peak;* the point at which it turns up again is a *business-cycle trough.*

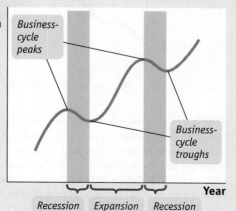

The most important effect of a recession is its effect on the ability of workers to find and hold jobs. The most widely used indicator of conditions in the labor market is the *unemployment rate*. We'll explain how that rate is calculated in Chapter 23, but for now it's enough to say that a high unemployment rate tells us that jobs are scarce and a low unemployment rate tells us that jobs are easy to find.

Figure 21-4 shows the unemployment rate from 1988 to 2020. As you can see, the U.S. unemployment rate surged during and after each recession but eventually fell during periods of expansion. The rising unemployment rate in April 2020 due to the COVID-19 economic shutdown was a sign that a new recession might be under way, which was later confirmed by the NBER to have begun in February 2020.

Because recessions cause many people to lose their jobs and make it hard to find new ones, they reduce the standard of living of households across the country. Recessions are usually associated with a rise in the number of people living below the poverty line, an increase in the number of people who lose their homes because they can't afford the mortgage payments, and a fall in the percentage of Americans with health insurance coverage. But workers are not the only group that suffers during a recession. Recessions are also bad for firms: profits fall during recessions, and many small businesses fail.

All in all, then, recessions are bad for almost everyone. Can anything be done to reduce their frequency and severity?

Taming the Business Cycle

Modern macroeconomics largely came into being as a response to the worst recession in history—the 43-month downturn that began in 1929 and continued into 1933, ushering in the Great Depression. The havoc wreaked by the 1929–1933 recession spurred economists to search both for understanding and for solutions: they wanted to know how such things could happen and how to prevent them.

TABLE 21-2 The History of the Business Cycle

Business-cycle peak	Business-cycle trough
no prior data available	December 1854
June 1857	December 1858
October 1860	June 1861
April 1865	December 1867
June 1869	December 1870
October 1873	March 1879
March 1882	May 1885
March 1887	April 1888
July 1890	May 1891
January 1893	June 1894
December 1895	June 1897
June 1899	December 1900
September 1902	August 1904
May 1907	June 1908
January 1910	January 1912
January 1913	December 1914
August 1918	March 1919
January 1920	July 1921
May 1923	July 1924
October 1926	November 1927
August 1929	March 1933
May 1937	June 1938
February 1945	October 1945
November 1948	October 1949
July 1953	May 1954
August 1957	April 1958
April 1960	February 1961
December 1969	November 1970
November 1973	March 1975
January 1980	July 1980
July 1981	November 1982
July 1990	March 1991
March 2001	November 2001
December 2007	June 2009
February 2020	

Data from: National Bureau of Economic Research.
Economy is currently in a recession at time of publication.

FIGURE 21-4 The U.S. Unemployment Rate, 1988–2020

The unemployment rate, a measure of joblessness, rises sharply during recessions and usually falls during expansions.
Data from: Bureau of Labor Statistics.

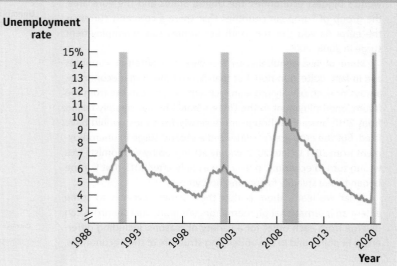

FOR INQUIRING MINDS   Defining Recessions and Expansions

You may be wondering exactly how recessions and expansions are defined. The truth is that there are no exact definitions!

In many countries, economists adopt the rule that a recession is a period of at least two consecutive quarters (a quarter is three months) during which the total output of the economy shrinks. The two-consecutive-quarters requirement is designed to avoid classifying brief hiccups in the economy's performance, with no lasting significance, as recessions.

Sometimes, however, this seems too strict. For example, three months of sharply declining output, then three months of slightly positive growth, then another three months of rapid decline, should surely be considered a recession.

In the United States, the task of determining when a recession begins and ends is assigned to an independent panel of experts at the National Bureau of Economic Research (NBER). This panel looks at a variety of economic indicators, then makes a judgment call.

Sometimes this judgment is controversial. In fact, there is lingering controversy over the 2001 recession. According to the NBER, that recession began in March 2001 and ended in November 2001 when output began rising. Some critics argued that the recession began several months earlier, when industrial production began falling. Other critics argue that the recession didn't end in 2001 because employment continued to fall and the job market remained weak for another year and a half.

"I can't move in with my parents. They moved in with my grandparents."

As explained earlier, the work of John Maynard Keynes suggested that monetary and fiscal policies could be used to mitigate the effects of recessions, and to this day governments turn to Keynesian policies when recession strikes. Later work, notably that of another great macroeconomist, Milton Friedman, led to a consensus that it's important to rein in booms as well as to fight slumps. So modern policy makers try to "smooth out" the business cycle. They haven't been completely successful, as a look back at Figure 21-2 makes clear. It's widely believed, however, that policy guided by macroeconomic analysis has helped make the economy more stable.

Although the business cycle has historically played a crucial role in fostering development of the field, macroeconomists are also concerned with other issues such as long-run growth, inflation and deflation, and international imbalances, which we examine next.

GLOBAL COMPARISON   RECESSIONS, HERE AND THERE

This figure shows unemployment from 2007 to 2020 in two of the world's biggest economies: the United States and the euro area, the group of European countries that share a common currency, the euro. As you can see, both economies saw unemployment surge in 2008–2009.

More or less simultaneous recessions in different countries are, in fact, quite common. But that doesn't mean that economies always or even usually move in lockstep. As you can see from the figure, unemployment in the United States began steadily falling from 2010 onward, although more slowly than most would have liked. But the euro area experienced a second surge in unemployment from 2011 to late 2012, widely attributed by economists to a wrong turn in economic policy. It was only after 2013 that Europe began to see steadily falling unemployment.

What we learn, then, is that the business cycle is to some extent an international phenomenon. But individual countries can diverge from each other for a variety of reasons, including differences in policy and in the underlying structure of their economies.

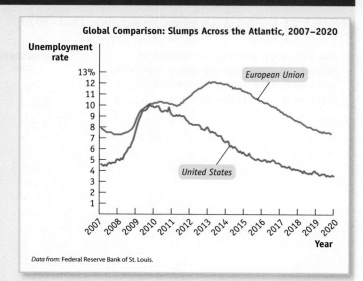

Global Comparison: Slumps Across the Atlantic, 2007–2020

Data from: Federal Reserve Bank of St. Louis.

ECONOMICS >> *in Action*
Bad Times in Brazil

The Great Recession afflicted almost all the world's economies, although some suffered more than others. Sometimes, however, individual countries have their own macroeconomic troubles. Five years after the U.S. recession ended, Brazil—the economic powerhouse of Latin America, often hailed as a country on the rise—entered a recession far worse than anything the United States had experienced in the last half century.

Figure 21-5 compares real GDP, a measure of the economy's total output, in the U.S. Great Recession and Brazil's later slump. In each case we measure output as a percentage of the maximum output just before recession struck. As you can see, Brazil's slump was much deeper and lasted much longer.

What caused Brazil's slump? It seems to have been a combination of a fall in the prices of some goods, like soybeans, that Brazil sells on world markets, and a pullback by Brazilian consumers, who had run up too much debt.

But why was the slump so severe? A large part of the answer is that Brazil, unlike the United States in 2007 and after, didn't take policy steps to minimize the downturn. Instead of cutting interest rates and increasing government spending, Brazil did the opposite. Brazil had reasons for these policies, largely political ones, but nonetheless the policies still had the effect of causing a much deeper downturn than experienced in the United States.

FIGURE 21-5 The Tale of Two Recoveries

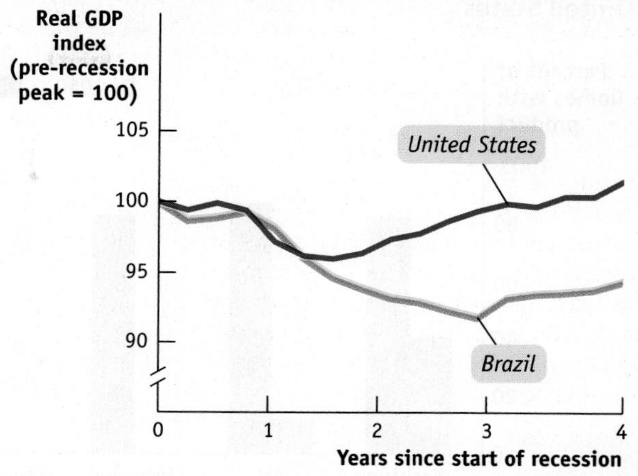

Real GDP index (pre-recession peak = 100) vs. *Years since start of recession*, comparing United States and Brazil.

Data from: Federal Reserve Bank of St. Louis and OECD, "Main Economic Indicators—complete database."

>> **Quick Review**

• The **business cycle,** the short-run alternation between **recessions** and **expansions,** is a major concern of modern macroeconomics.

• The point at which expansion shifts to recession is a **business-cycle peak.** The point at which recession shifts to expansion is a **business-cycle trough.**

>> *Check Your Understanding* **21-2**
Solutions appear at back of book.

---

1. Why do we talk about business cycles for the economy as a whole, rather than just talking about the ups and downs of particular industries?

2. Describe who gets hurt in a recession, and how.

‖ Long-Run Economic Growth

In 1960, most Americans believed, rightly, that they were better off than the citizens of any other nation, past or present. Yet they were quite poor by today's standards. Figure 21-6 shows the percentage of U.S. homes equipped with selected appliances in 1960 and 2015. In 1960, only a minority of households had a washing machine, very few had air conditioning, and of course nobody had smartphones or computers. And if we turn the clock back to, say, 1900, we find that life for many Americans was startlingly primitive by today's standards.

Why are the vast majority of Americans today able to afford conveniences that many Americans lacked in 1960? The answer is **long-run economic growth,** the sustained rise in the quantity of goods and services the economy produces. This sustained rise, in turn, reflects one of our basic principles of economics: Increases in the economy's potential lead to economic growth over time. Figure 21-7 shows estimates of real GDP per capita, a measure of total output per person, for two countries—the United States and Britain—for selected years going back to the Middle Ages. Both countries have experienced an enormous long-run rise in production per person, dwarfing the ups and downs of the business cycle.

Long-run economic growth is the sustained upward trend in the economy's output over time.

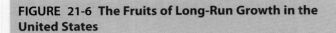

FIGURE 21-6 The Fruits of Long-Run Growth in the United States

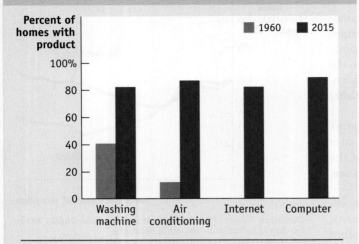

Americans have become able to afford many more material goods over time thanks to long-run economic growth.
Data from: U.S. Census.

FIGURE 21-7 Economic Growth, the Long View

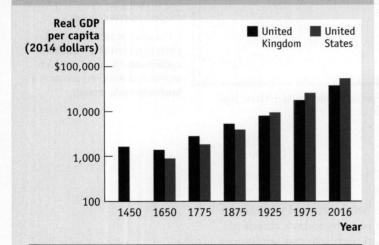

Over the long run, real GDP per capita has increased in both Britain and the United States. For about 300 years, real GDP per capita was greater in Britain. But early in the twentieth century, the United States surpassed Britain, becoming the richer country.
Data from: Maddison Data Project, revision 2018.

Two points are, however, worth noting:

1. Long-run economic growth is a modern invention: Britain wasn't any richer in 1650 than it was two centuries earlier, and overall world incomes didn't start rising until around 1890.

2. Countries don't necessarily grow at the same rate. Britain was once substantially richer than the United States, but it was overtaken by the rapidly growing new nation after 1875.

Long-run economic growth is fundamental to many of the most pressing economic questions today. Responses to key policy questions, such as the country's ability to bear the future costs of government programs such as Social Security and Medicare, depend in part on how fast the U.S. economy grows over the next few decades.

More broadly, the public's sense that the country is making progress depends crucially on success in achieving long-run growth. When growth slows, as it did in the 1970s, it can generate a national mood of pessimism. In particular, *long-run growth per capita*—a sustained upward trend in output per person—is the key to higher wages and a rising standard of living. A major concern of macroeconomics—and the theme of Chapter 24—is trying to understand the forces behind long-run growth.

Long-run growth is an even more urgent concern in poorer, less developed countries. In these countries, which would like to achieve a higher standard of living, the question of how to accelerate long-run growth is the central concern of economic policy.

As we'll see, macroeconomists don't use the same models to think about long-run growth that they use to think about the business cycle. It's important to keep both sets of models in mind, because what is good in the long run can be bad in the short run, and vice versa. For example, we've already mentioned the paradox of thrift: an attempt by households to increase their savings can cause a recession. But a higher level of savings, as we'll see in Chapter 25, plays a crucial role in encouraging long-run economic growth.

ECONOMICS >> *in Action*
A Tale of Two Countries

Many countries have experienced long-run growth, but not all have done equally well. One of the most informative contrasts is between Canada and Argentina, two countries that, at the beginning of the twentieth century, seemed to be in a good economic position.

From today's vantage point, it's surprising to realize that Canada and Argentina looked rather similar before World War I. Both were major exporters of agricultural products; both attracted large numbers of European immigrants; both also attracted large amounts of European investment, especially in the railroads that opened up their agricultural hinterlands. Economic historians believe that the average level of per capita income was comparable in the two countries as late as the 1930s.

After World War II, however, Argentina's economy performed poorly, largely due to political instability and bad macroeconomic policies. Argentina experienced several periods of extremely high inflation, during which the cost of living soared. Meanwhile, Canada made steady progress. Thanks to the fact that Canada has achieved sustained long-run growth since 1930, but Argentina has not, Canada's standard of living today is almost as high as that of the United States—and is about two and a half times as high as Argentina's.

>> Check Your Understanding 21-3

Solutions appear at back of book.

1. Many poor countries have high rates of population growth. What does this imply about the long-run growth rates of overall output that they must achieve in order to generate a higher standard of living per person?

2. Argentina used to be as rich as Canada; now it's much poorer. Does this mean that Argentina is poorer than it was in the past? Explain.

‖ Inflation and Deflation

In January 1980, the average production worker in the United States was paid $6.57 an hour. By January 2020, the average hourly earnings for such a worker had risen to $23.88 an hour. Three cheers for economic progress!

But wait. U.S. workers were paid much more in 2020 than they had been in 1980, but they also faced a much higher cost of living. Figure 21-8 compares the percentage increase in hourly earnings between 1980 and 2020 with the increases in the cost of some major types of consumer spending. As you can see, the average worker's paycheck went farther in terms of some goods,

>> Quick Review

• Because the U.S. economy has achieved **long-run economic growth,** Americans live much better than they did a half-century or more ago.

• Long-run economic growth is crucial for many economic concerns, such as a higher standard of living or financing government programs. It's especially crucial for poorer countries.

FIGURE 21-8 Rising Prices

Between 1980 and 2020, American workers' hourly earnings rose by 263%. But the cost of some major types of consumer spending also rose, some by more. Overall, the rising cost of living offset most of the rise in the average U.S. worker's wage.

Data from: Bureau of Labor Statistics.

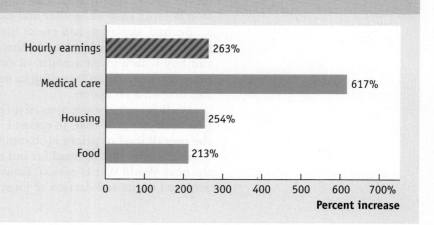

A rising overall level of prices is **inflation.**

A falling overall level of prices is **deflation.**

The economy has **price stability** when the overall level of prices changes slowly or not at all.

but less far in terms of others. Overall, the cost of living from 1980 to 2020 rose by 232%, which wiped out almost all of the wage gains of the typical U.S. worker during that period. In other words, once inflation is taken into account, the living standard of the typical U.S. worker barely rose from 1980 to the present.

The point is that between 1980 and 2020 the economy experienced substantial **inflation:** a rise in the overall level of prices. Understanding the causes of inflation and its opposite, **deflation**—a fall in the overall level of prices—is another main concern of macroeconomics.

The Causes of Inflation and Deflation

You might think that changes in the overall level of prices are just a matter of supply and demand. For example, higher gasoline prices reflect the higher price of crude oil, and higher crude oil prices reflect such factors as the exhaustion of major oil fields, growing demand from China and other emerging economies as more people grow rich enough to buy cars, and so on. Can't we just add up what happens in each of these markets to find out what happens to the overall level of prices?

No, because supply and demand can only explain why a particular good or service becomes more expensive *relative to other goods and services.* It can't explain why, for example, the price of chicken has risen over time in spite of the fact that chicken production has become more efficient and chicken has become substantially cheaper compared to other goods.

What causes the overall level of prices to rise or fall? As we'll learn in Chapter 23, in the short run, movements in inflation are closely related to the business cycle. When the economy is depressed and jobs are hard to find, inflation tends to fall; when the economy is booming, inflation tends to rise. For example, prices of most goods and services fell sharply during the Great Depression.

In the long run, by contrast, the overall level of prices is mainly determined by changes in the money supply, the total quantity of assets that can be readily used to make purchases. As we'll see in Chapter 31, hyperinflation, in which prices rise by thousands or hundreds of thousands of percent, invariably occurs when governments print money to pay a large part of their bills.

The Pain of Inflation and Deflation

Both inflation and deflation can pose problems for the economy. Let's look at two examples.

First, inflation discourages people from holding onto cash, because cash loses value over time if the overall price level is rising. That is, the amount of goods and services you can buy with a given amount of cash falls. In extreme cases, people stop holding cash altogether and turn to barter.

Second, deflation can cause the reverse problem. If the price level is falling, cash gains value over time. In other words, the amount of goods and services you can buy with a given amount of cash increases. So holding on to cash becomes more attractive than investing in new factories and other productive assets. This can deepen a recession.

We'll describe other costs of inflation and deflation in Chapters 23 and 31. For now, let's just note that, in general, economists regard **price stability**—in which the overall level of prices is changing only slowly—as a desirable goal. Price stability is a goal that seemed far out of reach for much of the U.S. economy during the post–World War II period. However, from the 1990s to the present, it has been achieved to the satisfaction of most macroeconomists.

ECONOMICS >> *in Action*
A Fast (Food) Measure of Inflation

The original McDonald's opened in 1948. It offered fast service—it was, indeed, the original fast-food restaurant. And it was also very inexpensive: hamburgers cost $0.15, $0.25 with fries. By 2020, a hamburger at a typical McDonald's cost more than six times as much, about $1.00. Has McDonald's lost touch with its fast-food roots? Have burgers become luxury cuisine?

No—in fact, compared with other consumer goods, a burger is a better bargain today than it was in 1948. Burger prices were about 6.5 times as high in 2020 as they were in 1948. But the consumer price index, the most widely used measure of the cost of living, was about 11 times as high in 2020 as it was in 1948.

Even though a burger costs six times more than it did when McDonald's first opened, it's still a good bargain compared to other consumer goods.

>> Check Your Understanding 21-4
Solutions appear at back of book.

1. Which of these sound like inflation, which sound like deflation, and which are ambiguous?
   a. Gasoline prices are up 10%, food prices are down 20%, and the prices of most services are up 1–2%.
   b. Gas prices have doubled, food prices are up 50%, and most services seem to be up 5% or 10%.
   c. Gas prices haven't changed, food prices are way down, and services have gotten cheaper, too.

‖ International Imbalances

The United States is an **open economy:** an economy that trades goods and services with other countries. There have been times when that trade was more or less balanced—when the United States sold about as much to the rest of the world as it bought. But this isn't one of those times.

In 2018, the United States ran a big **trade deficit**—that is, the value of the goods and services U.S. residents bought from the rest of the world was a lot larger than the value of the goods and services U.S. producers sold to customers abroad. Meanwhile, some other countries were in the opposite position, selling much more to foreigners than they bought.

Figure 21-9 shows the exports and imports of goods for three important economies in 2018. As you can see, the United States imported much more than it exported, but Germany and China did the reverse: they each ran a **trade surplus.** A country runs a trade surplus when the value of the goods and services it buys from the rest of the world is smaller than the value of the goods and services it sells abroad.

Was the U.S. trade deficit a sign that something was wrong with our economy—that we weren't able to make things that people in other countries wanted to buy? No, not really. Trade deficits and their opposite, trade surpluses, are macroeconomic phenomena. They're the result of situations in which the whole is very different from the sum of its parts. You might think that countries with highly productive workers or widely desired products and services to sell run trade surpluses and countries with unproductive workers or poor-quality

>> Quick Review

• A dollar today doesn't buy what it did in 1980, because the prices of most goods have risen. This rise in the overall price level has wiped out most if not all of the wage increases received by the typical American worker over the past 40 years.

• One area of macroeconomic study is in the overall level of prices. Because either **inflation** or **deflation** can cause problems for the economy, economists typically advocate maintaining **price stability.**

An **open economy** is an economy that trades goods and services with other countries.

A country runs a **trade deficit** when the value of goods and services bought from foreigners is more than the value of goods and services it sells to them. It runs a **trade surplus** when the value of goods and services bought from foreigners is less than the value of the goods and services it sells to them.

FIGURE 21-9 Unbalanced Trade

In 2018, the goods and services the United States bought from other countries were worth considerably more than the goods and services we sold abroad. Germany and China were in the reverse position. Trade deficits and trade surpluses reflect macroeconomic forces, especially differences in savings and investment spending.

Data from: International Monetary Fund, International Financial Statistics.

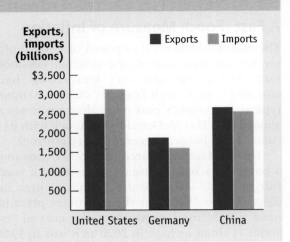

products and services to sell run trade deficits. But the reality is that there's no simple relationship between the success of an economy and whether it runs trade surpluses or trade deficits.

In Chapter 2 we learned that international trade is the result of comparative advantage: countries export goods they're relatively good at producing and import goods they're not as good at producing. That's why the United States exports wheat and imports coffee. What the concept of comparative advantage doesn't explain, however, is why the value of a country's imports is sometimes much larger than the value of its exports, or vice versa.

So what does determine whether a country runs a trade surplus or a trade deficit? Later on we'll learn the surprising answer: the determinants of the overall balance between exports and imports lie in decisions about savings and investment spending—spending on goods like machinery and factories that are in turn used to produce goods and services for consumers. Countries with high investment spending relative to savings run trade deficits; countries with low investment spending relative to savings run trade surpluses.

FIGURE 21-10 Greece's Current Account Balance, 1999–2018

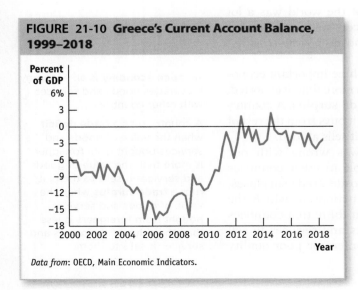

Data from: OECD, Main Economic Indicators.

ECONOMICS >> *in Action*
Greece's Costly Surplus

In 1999, Greece took a momentous step: it gave up its national currency, the drachma, in order to adopt the euro, a shared currency intended to promote closer economic and political union among the nations of Europe. How did this affect Greece's international trade?

Figure 21-10 shows Greece's current account balance—a broad definition of its trade balance—from 2000 to 2018. A negative current account balance, as shown here, means the country is running a trade deficit. As you can see, after Greece switched to the euro it began running large trade deficits, which at their peak equaled almost 16% of the total value of goods and services Greece produced. After 2008, however, the trade deficit began shrinking rapidly, and by 2013 Greece was nearly running a surplus.

Did this mean that Greece's economy was doing badly in the mid-2000s, and better thereafter? Just the opposite. When Greece adopted the euro, foreign investors became highly optimistic about its prospects, and money poured into the country, fueling rapid economic expansion. Unfortunately, this optimism eventually evaporated, and the inflows of foreign capital dried up. One consequence was that Greece could no longer run large trade deficits, and by 2013 was forced into nearly running a surplus. Another consequence was a severe recession, leading to a scarcity of jobs—the scarcity that led Constantine Kakoyiannis, the engineer we mentioned at the start of this chapter, to give up and move to Germany.

>> Check Your Understanding 21-5
Solutions appear at back of book.

1. Which of the following reflect comparative advantage, and which reflect macroeconomic forces?
   a. Thanks to the development of huge oil sands in the province of Alberta, Canada has become an exporter of oil and an importer of manufactured goods.
   b. Like many consumer goods, the Apple iPad is assembled in China, although many of the components are made in other countries.
   c. Since 2002, Germany has been running huge trade surpluses, exporting much more than it imports.
   d. The United States, which had roughly balanced trade in the early 1990s, began running large trade deficits later in the decade, as the technology boom took off.

>> Quick Review

• Comparative advantage can explain why an **open economy** exports some goods and services and imports others, but it can't explain why a country imports more than it exports, or vice versa.

• **Trade deficits** and **trade surpluses** are macroeconomic phenomena, determined by decisions about investment spending and savings.

GM Survives

G.J. McCARTHY/Tribune News Service/ARLINGTON/TX/USA/ Newscom

Once upon a time, General Motors (GM) was widely regarded as the world's greatest corporation. It was the largest employer in the United States; its success was so bound up with that of the nation as a whole that in 1953 its CEO declared that "what was good for our country was good for General Motors, and vice versa. The difference did not exist."

By 2008, however, GM was not the company it had been. It no longer dominated the U.S. car market, thanks in part to rising competition from foreign automakers. It had high "legacy" costs resulting from contracts to pay pensions and health benefits to retired workers. And the company was bleeding cash, losing more than $30 billion in 2008. It seemed possible that GM would not just declare formal bankruptcy, failing to pay its debts, but that it would go into actual liquidation, shutting down as a business.

GM executives appealed to the government for help and got it: the federal government provided almost $50 billion in cash, receiving in return majority ownership of the company.

There was intense negative reaction to this bailout, with many critics predicting that the company would be unable to come back, and that the aid provided to GM would be money down the drain. In the end, however, GM did stage a comeback, returning to profitability. By 2010, it repaid its federal loans, and eventually the U.S. government sold all the stock it had acquired, although the price it got for that stock left taxpayers with a $10 billion overall loss.

Why was GM able to survive and become profitable again? The company did undertake a number of cost-cutting measures. But the main secret of its turnaround was that 2008 was an exceptionally bad year for the auto industry, and that things improved dramatically in the years that followed.

The key point is that car sales are very sensitive to the state of the economy. When the economy as a whole stumbles, and workers have either lost their jobs or are worried about future job loss, they tend to postpone buying a new car. Figure 21-11 shows total U.S. sales of light vehicles (which includes both passenger cars and SUVs) over the past several decades. As you can see, sales plunged dramatically—around 40%—during the Great Recession, far more than the economy as a whole. It was predictable, however, that sales would surge again if and when the economy recovered.

The prospect of rapid growth in sales if the economy recovered is

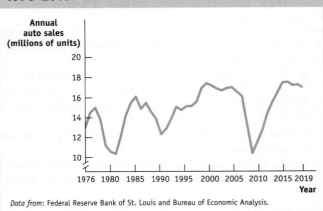

FIGURE 21-11 Automobile and Light Truck Sales, 1976–2019

Data from: Federal Reserve Bank of St. Louis and Bureau of Economic Analysis.

what made bailing out GM in 2009 a better bet than looking at the company's losses might have suggested. Despite its comeback, the company is nothing like the colossus it once was. But it has survived.

QUESTIONS FOR THOUGHT

1. While sales of many goods fell during the Great Recession, cars took a much bigger hit than groceries. Why?

2. Looking at Figure 21-11, you can see that car sales fell much less during the previous two recessions than they did during the Great Recession. What might explain the difference?

3. General Motors, somewhat unusually for U.S. firms outside the banking industry, has consistently employed a highly regarded economist, who among other things helps the economy make forecasts. (As of 2019 the position was held by Elaine Buckberg, a former student of one of the authors.) Why do you think GM might place a higher priority on economic analysis than, say, Walmart would?

SUMMARY

1. Macroeconomics is the study of the behavior of the economy as a whole, which can be different from the sum of its parts. Macroeconomics differs from microeconomics in the type of questions it tries to answer. Macroeconomics also has a strong policy focus: **Keynesian economics,** which emerged during the Great Depression, advocates the use of **monetary policy** and **fiscal policy** to fight economic slumps. Prior to the Great Depression, the economy was thought to be **self-regulating.**

2. One key concern of macroeconomics is the **business cycle,** the short-run alternation between **recessions,** periods of falling employment and output, and **expansions,** periods of rising employment and output. The point at which expansion turns to recession is a **business-cycle peak.** The point at which recession turns to expansion is a **business-cycle trough.**

3. Another key area of macroeconomic study is **long-run economic growth,** the sustained upward trend in the economy's output over time. Long-run economic growth is the force behind long-term increases in living standards and is important for financing some economic programs. It is especially important for poorer countries.

4. When the prices of most goods and services are rising, so that the overall level of prices is going up, the economy experiences **inflation.** When the overall level of prices is going down, the economy is experiencing **deflation.** In the short run, inflation and deflation are closely related to the business cycle. In the long run, prices tend to reflect changes in the overall quantity of money. Because both inflation and deflation can cause problems, economists and policy makers generally aim for **price stability.**

5. Although comparative advantage explains why **open economies** export some things and import others, macroeconomic analysis is needed to explain why countries run **trade surpluses** or **trade deficits.** The determinants of the overall balance between exports and imports lie in decisions about savings and investment spending.

KEY TERMS

Self-regulating economy, p. 609
Keynesian economics, p. 609
Monetary policy, p. 609
Fiscal policy, p. 609
Recession, p. 612
Expansion, p. 612

Business cycle, p. 612
Business-cycle peak, p. 612
Business-cycle trough, p. 612
Long-run economic growth, p. 615
Inflation, p. 618
Deflation, p. 618

Price stability, p. 618
Open economy, p. 619
Trade deficit, p. 619
Trade surplus, p. 619

PRACTICE QUESTIONS

1. The U.S. Department of Labor reports statistics on employment and earnings that are used as key indicators by many economists to gauge the health of the economy. Figure 21-4 plots historical data on the unemployment rate each month. Noticeably, the numbers were high during the recessions in the early 1990s, in 2001, and in the aftermath of the Great Recession, 2007–2009.

   a. Locate the latest data on the national unemployment rate. (*Hint:* Go to the Bureau of Labor Statistics at www.bls.gov, in the search bar enter "Employment Situation Summary," and select the subsequent page.)

   b. Compare the current numbers with those during the early 1990s, 2001, and following the Great Recession, as well as with the periods of relatively high economic growth just before the recessions. Are the current numbers indicative of a recessionary trend?

2. In the 1990s, there were some dramatic economic events that came to be known as the *Asian financial crisis.* A decade later similar events came to be known as the *global financial crisis.* The accompanying figure shows the growth rate of real GDP in the United States and Japan from 1996 to 2018. Using the graph, explain why the two sets of events are referred to this way.

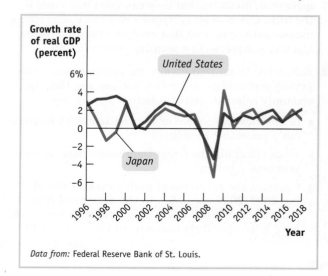

Data from: Federal Reserve Bank of St. Louis.

3. The accompanying figure illustrates the trade deficit of the United States since 1987. The United States has been consistently and, on the whole, increasingly importing more goods than it has been exporting. One of the countries it runs a trade deficit with is China. Which of the following statements are valid possible explanations of this fact? Explain.

a. Many products, such as televisions, that were formerly manufactured in the United States are now manufactured in China.

b. The wages of the average Chinese worker are far lower than the wages of the average American worker.

c. Investment spending in the United States is high relative to its level of savings.

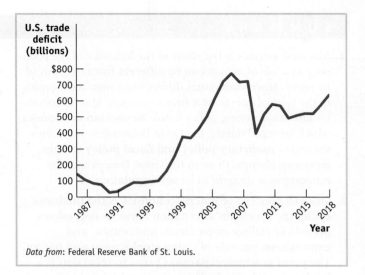

Data from: Federal Reserve Bank of St. Louis.

1. Which of the following questions are relevant for the study of macroeconomics and which for microeconomics?

a. How will Ms. Martin's tips change when a large manufacturing plant near the restaurant where she works closes?

b. What will happen to spending by consumers when the economy enters a downturn?

c. How will the price of oranges change when a late frost damages Florida's orange groves?

d. How will wages at a manufacturing plant change when its workforce is unionized?

e. What will happen to U.S. exports as the dollar becomes less expensive in terms of other currencies?

f. What is the relationship between a nation's unemployment rate and its inflation rate?

2. When one person saves more, that person's wealth is increased, meaning that they can consume more in the future. But when everyone saves more, everyone's income falls, meaning that everyone must consume less today. Explain this seeming contradiction.

3. Before the Great Depression, the conventional wisdom among economists and policy makers was that the economy is largely self-regulating.

a. Is this view consistent or inconsistent with Keynesian economics? Explain.

b. What effect did the Great Depression have on conventional wisdom?

c. Contrast the response of policy makers during the 2007–2009 recession to the actions of policy makers during the Great Depression. What would have been the likely outcome of the 2007–2009

recession if policy makers had responded in the same fashion as policy makers during the Great Depression?

4. How do economists in the United States determine when a recession begins and when it ends? How do other countries determine whether or not a recession is occurring?

5. Access the Discovering Data exercise for Chapter 21, Problem 5 online to answer the following questions.

a. What was real GDP per capita for Canada and Argentina in 1950?

b. How much did real GDP per capita increase for Canada and Argentina from 1950 through 2017?

c. Calculate the relative income difference between Canada and Argentina in 1950.

d. Calculate the relative income difference between Canada and Argentina in 2017.

6. Access the Discovering Data exercise for Chapter 21, Problem 6 online to answer the following questions.

a. What was the percentage decline in industrial production for Greece from 2007 to 2009? What was it from 2007 to 2016?

b. What country had the largest decline in industrial production from 2007 to 2009? Rank the countries, in order, from the largest decline in industrial production to the smallest.

c. Find the decline in industrial production from 2007 to 2009 for each of the countries.

d. What country experienced the fastest recovery from the financial crisis? The slowest recovery?

e. How long did it take Germany to fully recover from the financial crisis? How long did it take the United States?

7. a. What three measures of the economy tend to move together during the business cycle? Which way do they move during an upturn? During a downturn?

b. Who in the economy is hurt during a recession? How?

c. How did Milton Friedman alter the consensus that had developed in the aftermath of the Great Depression on how the economy should be managed? What is the current goal of policy makers in managing the economy?

8. Why do we consider a business-cycle expansion different from long-run economic growth? Why do we care about the size of the long-run growth rate of real GDP relative to the size of the growth rate of the population?

9. In 1798, Thomas Malthus's *Essay on the Principle of Population* was published. In it, he wrote: "Population, when unchecked, increases in a geometrical ratio. Subsistence increases only in an arithmetical ratio. . . . This implies a strong and constantly operating check on population from the difficulty of subsistence." Malthus was saying that the growth of the population is limited by the amount of food available to eat; people will live at the subsistence level forever. Why didn't Malthus's description apply to the world after 1800?

10. Each year, *The Economist* publishes data on the price of the Big Mac in different countries and exchange rates. The accompanying table shows some data from 2007 and 2019. Use this information to answer the following questions.

Country	2007 Price of Big Mac (in local currency)	2007 Price of Big Mac (in U.S. dollars)	2019 Price of Big Mac (in local currency)	2019 Price of Big Mac (in U.S. dollars)
Argentina	peso8.25	$2.65	peso120.0	$2.87
Canada	C$3.63	$3.08	C$6.77	$5.16
Euro area	€2.94	$3.82	€4.08	$4.58
Japan	¥280	$2.31	¥390	$3.59
United States	$3.22	$3.22	$5.74	$5.74

a. Where was it cheapest to buy a Big Mac in U.S. dollars in 2007?

b. Where was it cheapest to buy a Big Mac in U.S. dollars in 2019?

c. Using the increase in the local currency price of the Big Mac in each country to measure the percent change in the overall price level from 2007 to 2019, which nation experienced the most inflation? Did any of the nations experience deflation?

11. College tuition has risen significantly in the last few decades. For the sake of this problem, let's assume that over the last 20 years the cost of college, including total tuition, room, and board paid by full-time undergraduate students went from $2,871 to $16,789 at public institutions, a 485% price increase, and from $6,330 to $33,716 at private institutions, a 433% increase. Over the same time, average personal income after taxes rose from $9,785 to $39,409 per year, an increase of 302%. Have these tuition increases made it more difficult for the average student to afford college tuition?

22 > GDP and the CPI: Tracking the Macroeconomy

 ## CHINA HITS THE BIG TIME

WE OPENED THIS BOOK with a portrait of the Pearl River Delta, the huge urban complex in southeastern China that, taken as a whole, is now the world's biggest city. The world's biggest city also has a very big economy, larger than that of many nations. And China as a whole, by some measures, now has the world's largest economy. Other measures show that the U.S. economy is still larger.

But what does it mean to have the largest economy in the world? If you compare China with the United States, you find that they do quite different things. China, for example, produces much of the world's clothing, while the U.S. clothing industry has largely disappeared. On the other hand, America produces around half of the world's passenger jets, while China is just getting into the aircraft industry. So you might think that trying to compare the sizes of the two economies would be a matter of comparing apples and oranges — well, pajamas and Boeings, but you get the idea.

China has become an economic superpower, surpassing Japan.

In fact, however, economists routinely do compare the sizes of economies across both space and time — for example, they compare the size of the U.S. economy with that of China, and they also compare the size of the U.S. economy today with its size in the past. They do this using a measure known as *gross domestic product,* or *GDP,* the total value of goods and services produced in a country, and a closely related measure, *real GDP,* which corrects GDP for price changes. When number-crunchers say that one country's economy has overtaken the other's, they mean that China's real GDP has surpassed that of the United States (or that the United States' real GDP has surpassed that of China).

GDP and real GDP are two of the most important measures used to track the macroeconomy — that is, to quantify movements in the overall level of output and prices. Measures like GDP and *price indexes* play an important role in formulating economic policy, since policy makers need to know what's going on, and anecdotes are no substitute for hard data. Measures are also important for business decisions — to such an extent that, as the Business Case at the end of the chapter illustrates, corporations and other players seek independent estimates when they don't trust official numbers.

In this chapter, we explain how macroeconomists measure key aspects of the economy. We first explore ways to measure the economy's total output and total income. We then turn to the problem of how to measure the level of prices and the change in prices in the economy. ●

WHAT YOU WILL LEARN

- How do economists use aggregate measures to track the performance of the economy?

- What is **gross domestic product,** or **GDP,** and how is it calculated?

- What is the difference between **real GDP** and **nominal GDP,** and why is real GDP the appropriate measure of real economic activity?

- What is a **price index,** and how is it used to calculate the **inflation rate?**

The **national income and product accounts,** or **national accounts,** keep track of the flows of money between different sectors of the economy.

Government purchases of goods and services are total expenditures on goods and services by federal, state, and local governments.

Consumer spending is household spending on goods and services.

Investment spending is spending on productive physical capital—such as machinery and construction of buildings—and on changes to inventories.

Goods and services sold to other countries are **exports.** Goods and services purchased from other countries are **imports.**

‖ The National Accounts

Almost all countries calculate a set of numbers known as the *national income and product accounts.* In fact, the accuracy of a country's accounts is a remarkably reliable indicator of its state of economic development—in general, the more reliable the accounts, the more economically advanced the country. When international economic agencies seek to help a less developed country, typically the first order of business is to send a team of experts to audit and improve the country's accounts.

In the United States, these numbers are calculated by the Bureau of Economic Analysis, a division of the U.S. government's Department of Commerce. The **national income and product accounts,** often referred to simply as the **national accounts,** keep track of the spending of consumers, the sales of producers, business investment spending, government purchases, and a variety of other flows of money between different sectors of the economy. Let's see how they work.

Following the Money: The Expanded Circular-Flow Diagram

To understand the principles behind the national accounts, it helps to look at Figure 22-1, which is an expanded version of the circular-flow diagram we introduced in Chapter 2 (see Figure 2-6). Figure 22-1 shows the flows of money through the economy. For the purposes of this chapter, however, we will focus only on the left side of the diagram, where green arrows represent the "real" economy—flows of money associated with the production and sales of goods and services. We'll turn to the "financial" economy, represented by the blue arrows, in Chapter 25—borrowing, lending, and other money flows—that are crucial but have only an indirect effect on production.

As Figure 22-1 shows, spending on goods and services—flows of money *into* the markets for goods and services—comes from four distinct kinds of buyers:

1. Governments at the local, state, and federal level spend tax revenue in two broad areas: **government purchases of goods and services** like education or defense, where the government buys things for its own use, and *transfer payments* like Social Security, where the government gives money to households. For now, in this chapter, we will focus only on government purchases.
2. Households—that's your family, ours, and tens of millions of others. Households engage in **consumer spending** by purchasing goods and services through the markets for goods and services from firms or imports from the rest of the world.
3. Firms—firms buy goods and services from each other when they engage in **investment spending,** spending on productive capital, such as machinery and construction of buildings.
4. Rest of the world—a fourth source of spending comes from **exports,** goods and services sold to residents of other countries.

All four of these money flows involve spending on goods and services. However, some of the goods and services purchased by a country's residents are produced abroad. For example, many consumer goods sold in the United States are made in China. Goods and services that are purchased by households, governments, or firms, but produced by residents of another country, are known as **imports.** The purchase of imports leads to a flow of money *out* of the market for goods and services and *out* of the economy.

Suppose we add up consumer spending on goods and services, investment spending, government purchases of goods and services, and the value of exports, then subtract the value of imports. This gives us a measure of the overall market value of the goods and services the economy produces. That measure has a name: it's a country's *gross domestic product.* But before we can formally define gross domestic product, or GDP, we have to examine an important distinction between classes of goods and services: the difference between *final goods and services,* on one side, and *intermediate goods and services* on the other.

FIGURE 22-1 An Expanded Circular-Flow Diagram: The Flows of Money Through the Economy

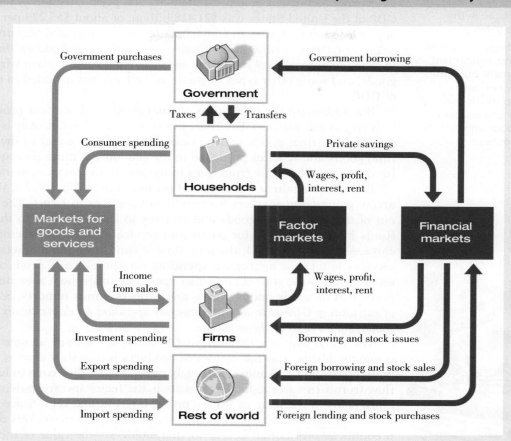

A circular flow of money connects the four sectors of the economy: government, households, firms, and the rest of the world, via three types of markets: markets for goods and services, factor markets, and financial markets. Money flows from firms to households in the form of wages, profit, interest, and rent through the factor markets. Households use that money to pay taxes to the government, to save it in the form of private savings that flows to the financial markets, or to pay for consumer spending on goods and services from firms or imports from the rest of the world. The government uses tax revenue to purchase goods and services from firms or the rest of the world. It can also use tax revenue to transfer money to households in the form of subsidies or the social safety net (Social Security or unemployment insurance payments, for example). Firms use the money they receive from the financial markets via borrowing or issuing stocks or bonds to pay for investment spending, which involves spending on goods and services such as machinery and building construction, which will increase their production in the future. Finally, the rest of the world purchases the economy's exports. To understand national income accounting, we focus on the flows to and from the markets for goods and services, which represent the "real" economy, shown on the left side of the diagram, in green. The right side of the diagram, in blue, represents the "financial" economy, which we will examine in Chapter 25.

Gross Domestic Product

A consumer's purchase of a new car from a dealer is one example of a sale of **final goods and services:** goods and services sold to the final, or end, user. But an automobile manufacturer's purchase of steel from a steel foundry or glass from a glassmaker is an example of purchasing **intermediate goods and services:** goods and services that are inputs for production of final goods and services. In the case of intermediate goods and services, the purchaser—another firm—is *not* the final user.

Final goods and services are goods and services sold to the final, or end, user.

Intermediate goods and services are goods and services—bought from one firm by another firm—that are inputs for production of final goods and services.

Gross domestic product, or **GDP,** is the total value of all final goods and services produced in the economy during a given year.

Aggregate spending, the sum of consumer spending, investment spending, government purchases of goods and services, and exports minus imports, is the total spending on domestically produced final goods and services in the economy.

Gross domestic product, or **GDP,** is the total value of all *final goods and services* produced in an economy during a given period, usually a year. In 2019 the GDP of the United States was $21,428 billion, or about $65,223 per person. If you are an economist trying to construct a country's national accounts, *one way to calculate GDP is to calculate it directly: survey firms and add up the total value of their production of final goods and services.* We'll soon explain why intermediate goods, and some other types of goods as well, are not included in the calculation of GDP.

But adding up the total value of final goods and services produced isn't the only way of calculating GDP. There are two other ways. One way is based on total spending on final goods and services. Since GDP is equal to the total value of final goods and services produced in the economy, it must also equal the flow of funds received by firms from sales in the goods and services market.

If you look again at the circular-flow diagram in Figure 22-1, you will see the arrow going from markets for goods and services to firms. The flow of funds out of the markets for goods and services to firms is equal to the total flow of funds into the markets for goods and services from other sectors. And as you can see from Figure 22-1, the total flow of funds into the markets for goods and services is total or **aggregate spending** on domestically produced final goods and services—the sum of consumer spending, investment spending, government purchases of goods and services, and exports minus imports. *So a second way of calculating GDP is to add up aggregate spending on domestically produced final goods and services in the economy.*

The third way of calculating GDP is based on total income earned in the economy. Firms, and the factors of production that they employ, are owned by households. So firms must ultimately pay out what they earn to households. The flow from firms to the factor markets is the factor income paid out by firms to households in the form of wages, profit, interest, and rent. Since all the income earned by firms belongs to someone—if it doesn't go to workers or bondholders, it counts as profits that accrue to shareholders—the value of the flow of factor income from firms to households must be equal to the flow of money into firms from the markets for goods and services. And this last value, we know, is the total value of production in the economy—GDP.

Why is GDP equal to the total value of factor income paid by firms in the economy to households? Because each sale in the economy must accrue to someone as income—either as wages, profit, interest, or rent. *So a third way of calculating GDP is to sum the total factor income earned by households from firms in the economy.*

"You wouldn't think there'd be much money in potatoes, chickens, and woodchopping, but it all adds up."

Calculating GDP

We've just explained the three methods for calculating GDP:

1. Survey and add up total value of all final goods and services produced.
2. Add up aggregate spending on all domestically produced goods and services in the economy.
3. Add up the total factor income earned by households from firms in the economy.

Government statisticians use all three methods. To illustrate how these three methods work, we will consider a simplified hypothetical economy, shown in Figure 22-2. This economy consists of three firms—National Motors, Inc., which produces one car per year; National Steel, Inc., which produces the steel that goes into the car; and National Ore, Inc., which mines the iron ore that goes into the steel. So GDP is $21,500, the value of the one car per year the economy produces. Let's look at how the three different methods of calculating GDP yield the same result.

FIGURE 22-2 Calculating GDP

In this simplified hypothetical economy consisting of three firms, GDP can be calculated in three different ways: (1) measuring GDP as the value of production of final goods and services, by summing each firm's value added; (2) measuring GDP as aggregate spending on domestically produced final goods and services; and (3) measuring GDP as factor income earned by households from firms in the economy.

2. Aggregate spending on domestically produced final goods and services = $21,500

	National Ore, Inc.	National Steel, Inc.	National Motors, Inc.	Total factor income
Value of sales	$4,200 (iron ore)	$9,000 (steel)	$21,500 (car)	
Intermediate goods	0	4,200 (iron ore)	9,000 (steel)	
Wages	2,000	3,700	10,000	$15,700
Interest payments	1,000	600	1,000	2,600
Rent	200	300	500	1,000
Profit	1,000	200	1,000	2,200
Total expenditure by firm	4,200	9,000	21,500	
Value added per firm = Value of sales − Cost of intermediate goods	4,200	4,800	12,500	

3. Total payments to factors = $21,500

1. Value of production of final goods and services, sum of value added = $21,500

Measuring GDP as the Value of Production of Final Goods and Services

The first method for calculating GDP is to add up the value of all the final goods and services produced in the economy—a calculation that excludes the value of intermediate goods and services. Why are intermediate goods and services excluded? After all, don't they represent a very large and valuable portion of the economy?

To understand why only final goods and services are included in GDP, look at the simplified economy described in Figure 22-2. Should we measure the GDP of this economy by adding up the total sales of the iron ore producer, the steel producer, and the auto producer? If we did, we would in effect be counting the value of the steel twice—once when it is sold by the steel plant to the auto plant, and again when the steel auto body is sold to a consumer as a finished car. And we would be counting the value of the iron ore *three* times—once when it is mined and sold to the steel company, a second time when it is made into steel and sold to the auto producer, and a third time when the steel is made into a car and sold to the consumer.

So counting the full value of each producer's sales would cause us to count the same items several times and artificially inflate the calculation of GDP. For example, in Figure 22-2, the total value of all sales, intermediate and final, is $34,700: $21,500 from the sale of the car, plus $9,000 from the sale of the steel, plus $4,200 from the sale of the iron ore. Yet we know that GDP is only $21,500. The way we avoid double-counting is to count only each producer's **value added** in the calculation of GDP: the difference between the value of its sales and the value of the intermediate goods and services it purchases from other businesses.

That is, we subtract the cost of inputs—the intermediate goods—at each stage of the production process. In this case, the value added of the auto producer is the dollar value of the cars it manufactures *minus* the cost of the steel it buys, or $12,500. The value added of the steel producer is the dollar value of

The **value added** of a producer is the value of its sales minus the value of its purchases of intermediate goods and services.

Steel is an intermediate good because it is sold to other product manufacturers, such as automakers, and rarely to final buyers, such as consumers.

aaltair/Shutterstock

the steel it produces *minus* the cost of the ore it buys, or $4,800. Only the ore producer, which we have assumed doesn't buy any inputs, has value added equal to its total sales, $4,200. The sum of the three producers' value added is $21,500, equal to GDP.

Measuring GDP as Spending on Domestically Produced Final Goods and Services

Another way to calculate GDP is by adding up aggregate spending on domestically produced final goods and services. That is, GDP can be measured by the flow of funds into firms. Like the method that estimates GDP as the value of domestic production of final goods and services, this measurement must be carried out in a way that avoids double-counting.

In terms of our steel and auto example, we don't want to count both consumer spending on a car (represented in Figure 22-2 by $21,500, the sales price of the car) and the auto producer's spending on steel (represented in Figure 22-2 by $9,000, the price of a car's worth of steel). If we counted both, we would be counting the steel embodied in the car twice.

We solve this problem by counting only the value of sales to *final buyers*, such as consumers, firms that purchase investment goods, the government, or foreign buyers. In other words, to avoid double-counting of spending, we omit sales of inputs from one business to another when estimating GDP using spending data. You can see from Figure 22-2 that aggregate spending on final goods and services—the finished car—is $21,500.

As we've already pointed out, the national accounts *do* include investment spending by firms as a part of final spending. That is, an auto company's purchase of steel to make a car isn't considered a part of final spending, but the company's purchase of new machinery for its factory *is* considered a part of final spending. What's the difference? Steel is an input that is used up in production; machinery will last for a number of years. Since purchases of capital goods that will last for a considerable time aren't closely tied to current production, the national accounts consider such purchases a form of final sales.

In later chapters, we will make use of the proposition that GDP is equal to aggregate spending on domestically produced goods and services by final buyers. We will also develop models of how final buyers decide how much to spend. With that in mind, we'll now examine the types of spending that make up GDP.

FOR INQUIRING MINDS   Our Imputed Lives

An old line says that when a person marries the household cook, GDP falls. And it's true: when someone provides services for pay, those services are counted as a part of GDP. But the services family members provide to each other are not. Some economists have produced alternative measures that try to "impute" the value of household work—that is, assign an estimate of what the market value of that work would have been if it had been paid for. But the standard measure of GDP doesn't contain that imputation.

GDP estimates do, however, include an imputation for the value of owner-occupied housing. That is, if you buy the home you were formerly renting, GDP does not go down. It's true that because you no longer pay rent to your landlord, the landlord no longer sells a service to you—namely, use of the house or apartment. But the statisticians make an estimate of what you would have paid if you rented your dwelling, whether it's an apartment or a house. For the purposes of the statistics, it's as if you were renting from yourself.

If you think about it, this makes a lot of sense. In a country like the United States, the pleasure we derive from owning a home is an important part of the standard of living. So to be accurate, estimates of GDP must take into account the value of housing that is occupied by owners as well as the value of rental housing.

The value of the services that family members provide to each other is not counted as part of GDP.

Look again at the markets for goods and services in the circular-flow diagram in Figure 22-1, and you will see that one component of sales by firms is consumer spending. Let's denote consumer spending with the symbol C. Figure 22-1 also shows three other components of sales: sales of investment goods to other businesses, or investment spending, which we will denote by I; government purchases of goods and services, which we will denote by G; and sales to foreigners—that is, exports—which we will denote by X.

In reality, not all of this final spending goes toward domestically produced goods and services. We must take account of spending on imports, which we will denote by IM. Income spent on imports is income not spent on domestic goods and services—it is income that has "leaked" across national borders. So to accurately value domestic production using spending data, we must subtract out spending on imports to arrive at spending on domestically produced goods and services. Putting this all together gives us the following equation, which breaks GDP down by the four sources of aggregate spending:

(22-1) $GDP = C + I + G + X - IM$

We'll be seeing a lot of Equation 22-1 in later chapters.

Measuring GDP as Factor Income Earned from Firms in the Economy

A final way to calculate GDP is to add up all the income earned by factors of production from firms in the economy—the wages earned by labor; the interest paid to those who lend their savings to firms and the government; the rent earned by those who lease their land or structures to firms; and dividends, the profits paid to the shareholders, the owners of the firms' physical capital.

Figure 22-2 shows how this calculation works for our simplified economy. The numbers shaded in the column at far right show the total wages, interest, and rent paid by all these firms as well as their total profit. Summing up all of these items yields total factor income of $21,500—again, equal to GDP.

PITFALLS

GDP: WHAT'S IN AND WHAT'S OUT

It's easy to confuse what is included in and excluded from GDP. For example, investment spending—spending on productive physical capital (including construction of residential and commercial structures), and changes to inventories (goods and raw materials held to facilitate business operations)—is included in GDP. But spending on intermediate goods and services, like the steel used to make cars, is not. Why?

The answer is that we only include items that are newly produced (unlike, say, used cars), and aren't used up in production (like the steel in new cars). Here's a table summarizing what's in or out.

IN	OUT
Investment spending	**Spending on intermediate goods and services**
Spending on productive physical capital (including construction of residential and commercial structures) and changes to inventories	Inputs for production of final goods and services
Capital spending	**Used goods**
Considered part of investment spending	To include them would be to double-count: counting them once when sold as new and again when sold as used
Domestically produced final goods and services	**Financial assets like stocks and bonds**
Includes capital goods and new construction of structures produced by firms (also includes owner-occupied home-based businesses like child care provided by households, and educational and other such services provided by the government)	They don't represent either the production or the sale of final goods and services: a *bond* represents a promise to repay with interest; a *stock* represents a proof of ownership
	Import Spending
	Spending on goods and services produced outside the country are not part of domestic production and are excluded

We won't emphasize factor income as much as the other two methods of calculating GDP. It's important to keep in mind, however, that all the money spent on domestically produced goods and services generates factor income to households.

The Components of GDP Now that we know how GDP is calculated in principle, let's see what it looks like in practice.

Figure 22-3 shows the first two methods of calculating GDP side by side. The height of each bar above the horizontal axis represents the GDP of the U.S. economy in 2019: $21,428 billion. Each bar is divided to show the breakdown of that total in terms of where the value was added and how the money was spent.

In the left bar in Figure 22-3, we see the breakdown of GDP by value added according to sector, the first method of calculating GDP. Of the $21,428 billion, $16,328 billion consisted of value added by businesses. Another $2,687 billion of value added was added by households and institutions; a large part of that was the imputed services of owner-occupied housing, described in the For Inquiring Minds "Our Imputed Lives." Finally, $2,412 billion consisted of value added by government, in the form of military, education, and other government services.

The right bar in Figure 22-3 corresponds to the second method of calculating GDP, showing the breakdown by the four types of aggregate spending. The total length of the right bar is longer than the total length of the left bar, a difference of $632 billion (which, as you can see, is the amount by which the right bar extends below the horizontal axis). That's because the total length of the right bar represents total spending in the economy, spending on both domestically produced and foreign-produced final goods and services. Within the bar, consumer spending (*C*), which is 68.0% of GDP, dominates overall spending.

FIGURE 22-3 U.S. GDP in 2019: Two Methods of Calculating GDP

The two bars show two equivalent ways of calculating GDP. The height of each bar above the horizontal axis represents $22,060 billion, U.S. GDP in 2019. The left bar shows the breakdown of GDP according to the value added of each sector of the economy: government, households, and firms. The right bar shows the breakdown of GDP according to the four types of aggregate spending: $C + I + G + X - IM$. The right bar has a total length of $22,060 billion + $632 billion = $21,428 billion. The $632 billion, shown as the area extending below the horizontal axis, is the amount of total spending absorbed by net exports, which were negative in 2019. (Numbers may not add due to rounding.)

Data from: Bureau of Economic Analysis.

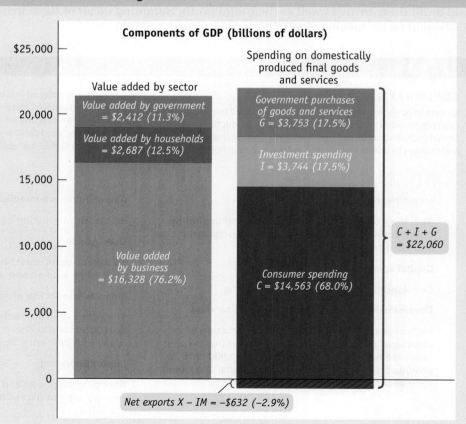

Components of GDP (billions of dollars)

Value added by sector
- Value added by government = $2,412 (11.3%)
- Value added by households = $2,687 (12.5%)
- Value added by business = $16,328 (76.2%)

Spending on domestically produced final goods and services
- Government purchases of goods and services G = $3,753 (17.5%)
- Investment spending I = $3,744 (17.5%)
- Consumer spending C = $14,563 (68.0%)

$C + I + G = $22,060

Net exports X – IM = –$632 (–2.9%)

But some of that spending was absorbed by foreign-produced goods and services. In 2019, **net exports,** the difference between the value of exports and the value of imports ($X - IM$ in Equation 22-1) was negative—the United States was a net importer of foreign goods and services. The 2019 value of $X - IM$ was −$632 billion, or −2.9% of GDP. Thus, a portion of the right bar extends below the horizontal axis by $632 billion to represent the amount of total spending that was absorbed by net imports and so did not lead to higher U.S. GDP. Investment spending (I) constituted 17.5% of GDP; government purchases of goods and services (G) constituted 17.5% of GDP.

Net exports are the difference between the value of exports and the value of imports.

What GDP Tells Us

We've now seen the various ways that gross domestic product is calculated. But what does the measurement of GDP tell us?

The most important use of GDP is as a measure of the size of the economy. For example, suppose you want to compare the economies of different nations. A natural approach is to compare their GDPs. In 2019, as we've seen, U.S. GDP was $21,428 billion, China's GDP was $14,140 billion, and the combined GDP of the 28 countries that make up the European Union was $18,292 billion.

But wait—didn't we open this chapter by stating that by some measures, China has the world's largest economy, while other measures show that the U.S. economy is still larger? Well, it turns out that one must be careful when using GDP numbers in comparing countries, and especially when making comparisons over time. That's because part of the increase in the value of GDP over time represents increases in the *prices* of goods and services rather than an increase in output. For example, U.S. GDP was $8,578 billion in 1997 and had more than doubled to $21,428 billion by 2019. But the U.S. economy didn't actually double in size over that period. To measure actual changes in aggregate output, we need a modified version of GDP that is adjusted for price changes, known as *real GDP.*

A similar issue arises when comparing the United States and China, because many goods and services sold inside China are much cheaper than they are in the United States, and estimates that take this into account find that China's real GDP is bigger than the unadjusted number suggests. We'll see next how real GDP is calculated.

>> Check Your Understanding 22-1

Solutions appear at back of book.

1. Explain why the three methods of calculating GDP produce the same estimate of GDP.

2. What are the various sectors to which firms make sales? What are the various ways in which households are linked with other sectors of the economy?

3. Consider the first row of Figure 22-2 and suppose you mistakenly believed that total value added was $30,500, the sum of the sales price of a car and a car's worth of steel. What items would you be counting twice?

>> Quick Review

• A country's **national income and product accounts,** or **national accounts,** track flows of money among economic sectors.

• There are four flows of money into the markets for goods and services: **consumer spending, government purchases of goods and services, exports,** and **investment spending.**

• Part of spending on goods and services flows out of the country via **imports.** The rest becomes sales by domestic producers.

• **Gross domestic product,** or **GDP,** can be calculated in three different ways: add up the **value added** by all firms; add up all spending on domestically produced **final goods and services,** an amount equal to **aggregate spending;** or add up all factor income paid by firms. **Intermediate goods and services** are not included in the calculation of GDP.

|| Real GDP: A Measure of Aggregate Output

The U.S. economy had a pretty good year in 2019: the nation gained 2.1 million jobs, while the unemployment rate fell from 4.0% to 3.5%. It was certainly a better year than 1982, when a severe recession reduced employment by 2 million and sent unemployment soaring. Strange to say, however, gross domestic product rose slightly faster in 1982 (4.2%) than it did in 2019 (4.1%). How is that possible?

Aggregate output is the economy's total quantity of output of final goods and services.

Real GDP is the total value of all final goods and services produced in the economy during a given year, calculated using the prices of a selected base year.

Nominal GDP is the value of all final goods and services produced in the economy during a given year, calculated using the prices current in the year in which the output is produced.

The answer is that back in 1982 GDP was rising for a bad reason—inflation, which raised the prices of the goods and services America produced—not because the economy was actually growing. Inflation was much lower in 2019 so the rise in GDP really did correspond to economic progress.

In order to accurately measure the economy's growth, we need a measure of **aggregate output:** the total quantity of final goods and services the economy produces. The measure that is used for this purpose is known as *real GDP.* By tracking real GDP over time, we avoid the problem of changes in prices distorting the value of changes in production of goods and services over time. Let's look first at how real GDP is calculated, then at what it means.

Calculating Real GDP

To understand how real GDP is calculated, imagine an economy in which only two goods, apples and oranges, are produced and in which both goods are sold only to final consumers. The outputs and prices of the two fruits for two consecutive years are shown in Table 22-1.

The first thing we can say about these data is that the value of sales increased from year 1 to year 2. In the first year, the total value of sales was (2,000 billion × $0.25) + (1,000 billion × $0.50) = $1,000 billion; in the second it was (2,200 billion × $0.30) + (1,200 billion × $0.70) = $1,500 billion, which is 50% larger. But it is also clear from the table that this increase in the dollar value of GDP overstates the real growth in the economy. Although the quantities of both apples and oranges increased, the prices of both apples and oranges also rose. So part of the 50% increase in the dollar value of GDP from year 1 to year 2 simply reflects higher prices, not higher production of output.

TABLE 22-1 Calculating GDP and Real GDP in a Simple Economy

	Year 1	Year 2
Quantity of apples (billions)	2,000	2,200
Price of apple	$0.25	$0.30
Quantity of oranges (billions)	1,000	1,200
Price of orange	$0.50	$0.70
GDP (billions of dollars)	$1,000	$1,500
Real GDP (billions of year 1 dollars)	$1,000	$1,150

To estimate the true increase in aggregate output produced, we have to ask: how much would GDP have gone up if prices had *not* changed? To answer this question, we need to find the value of output in year 2 expressed in year 1 prices. In year 1 the price of apples was $0.25 each and the price of oranges $0.50 each. So year 2 output *at year 1 prices* is (2,200 billion × $0.25) + (1,200 billion × $0.50) = $1,150 billion. And output in year 1 at year 1 prices was $1,000 billion. So in this example GDP measured in year 1 prices rose 15%—from $1,000 billion to $1,150 billion.

Now we can define **real GDP:** it is the total value of final goods and services produced in the economy during a year, calculated as if prices had stayed constant at the level of some given base year. A real GDP number always comes with information about what the base year is.

A GDP number that has not been adjusted for changes in prices is calculated using the prices in the year in which the output is produced. Economists call this measure **nominal GDP,** GDP at current prices. If we had used nominal GDP to measure the true change in output from year 1 to year 2 in our apples and oranges example, we would have overstated the true growth in output: we would have claimed it to be 50%, when in fact it was only 15%. By comparing output in the two years using a common set of prices—the year 1 prices in this example—we are able to focus solely on changes in the quantity of output by eliminating the influence of changes in prices.

Table 22-2 shows a real-life version of our apples and oranges example. The second column shows nominal GDP in

TABLE 22-2 Nominal versus Real GDP in 2005, 2012, and 2019

	Nominal GDP (billions of current dollars)	Real GDP (billions of 2012 dollars)
2005	$13,037	$14,913
2012	16,197	16,197
2019	$21,428	$19.073

2005, 2012, and 2019. The third column shows real GDP for each year in 2012 dollars. For 2012 the two numbers are the same. But real GDP in 2005 expressed in 2012 dollars was higher than nominal GDP in 2005, reflecting the fact that prices were in general higher in 2012 than in 2005. Real GDP in 2019 expressed in 2012 dollars, however, was less than nominal GDP in 2019 because prices in 2012 were lower than in 2019.

You might have noticed that there is an alternative way to calculate real GDP using the data in Table 22-1. Why not measure it using the prices of year 2 rather than year 1 as the base-year prices? This procedure seems equally valid. According to that calculation, real GDP in year 1 at year 2 prices is $(2,000 \text{ billion} \times \$0.30) + (1,000 \text{ billion} \times \$0.70) = \$1,300$ billion; real GDP in year 2 at year 2 prices is \$1,500 billion, the same as nominal GDP in year 2. So using year 2 prices as the base year, the growth rate of real GDP is equal to $(\$1,500 \text{ billion} - \$1,300 \text{ billion})/\$1,300 \text{ billion} = 0.154$, or 15.4%. This is slightly higher than the figure we got from the previous calculation, in which year 1 prices were the base-year prices. In that calculation, we found that real GDP increased by 15%. Neither answer, 15.4% versus 15%, is more "correct" than the other.

In reality, the government economists who put together the U.S. national accounts have adopted a method known as chain-linking to measure the change in real GDP; they use the average between the GDP growth rate calculated using an early base year and the GDP growth rate calculated using a late base year. As a result, U.S. statistics on real GDP are always expressed in **chained dollars**.

What Real GDP Doesn't Measure

GDP, nominal or real, is a measure of a country's aggregate output. Other things equal, a country with a larger population will have higher GDP simply because there are more people working. So if we want to compare GDP across countries but want to eliminate the effect of differences in population size, we use the measure **GDP per capita**—GDP divided by the size of the population, equivalent to the average GDP per person.

Real GDP per capita can be a useful measure in some circumstances, such as in a comparison of labor productivity between countries. However, despite the fact that it is a rough measure of the average real output per person, real GDP per capita has well-known limitations as a measure of a country's living standards. Every once in a while economists are accused of believing that growth in real GDP per capita is the only thing that matters—that is, thinking that increasing real GDP per capita is a goal in itself. In fact, economists rarely make that mistake; the idea that economists care only about real GDP per capita is a sort of urban legend.

Let's take a moment to be clear about why a country's real GDP per capita is not a sufficient measure of human welfare in that country and why growth in real GDP per capita is not an appropriate policy goal in itself.

One way to think about this is to say that an increase in real GDP means an expansion in the economy's production possibility frontier. Because the economy has increased its productive capacity, society can achieve more things. But whether society actually makes good use of that increased potential to improve living standards is another matter. To put it in a slightly different way, your income may be higher this year than last year, but whether you use that higher income to improve your quality of life is your choice.

Real GDP per capita, then, is a measure of an economy's average aggregate output per person. A country with a high GDP can afford for its citizens to be healthy, to be well educated, and in general, to have a good quality of life. But there is not a one-to-one match between GDP and the quality of life.

Chained dollars is the method of calculating changes in real GDP using the average between the growth rate calculated using an early base year and the growth rate calculated using a late base year.

GDP per capita is GDP divided by the size of the population; it is equivalent to the average GDP per person.

GLOBAL COMPARISON **GDP AND THE MEANING OF LIFE**

"I've been rich and I've been poor," the actress Mae West famously declared. "Believe me, rich is better." But is the same true for countries?

This figure shows two pieces of information for a number of countries: how rich they are, as measured by GDP per capita, and how people assess their well-being. Well-being was measured by a Gallup world survey that asked people to rate how satisfied they were with their lives on a scale of 0 to 10. The figure seems to tell us three things:

1. *Rich is better.* Richer countries on average have a higher well-being than poor countries.

2. *Money matters less as you grow richer.* As GDP rises, the average gain in life satisfaction per extra dollar gets smaller and smaller. Going from per capita GDP of $20,000 to $40,000 seems to produce no more gain than going from $10,000 to $20,000.

3. *Money isn't everything.* Costa Ricans, whose nation is only middle-income, seem more satisfied with their lives than citizens of much richer countries, like Japan.

These results are consistent with the observation that high GDP per capita makes it easier to achieve a good life but that countries aren't equally successful in taking advantage of that possibility.

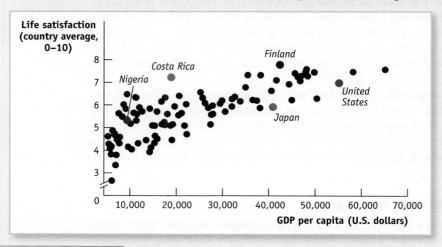

Data from: World Happiness Report (2019); World Bank.

ECONOMICS >> *in Action*
Argentina's Peso Perplex

The South American nation of Argentina has had a troubled economic history, to the point where it has almost become a byword for economic crisis. In 2018 Argentina was in trouble again, suffering from a sudden loss of investor confidence. The country's unemployment rate shot up from 7.2% in late 2017 to 9.1% in late 2018.

But how could this be? After all, Argentina's GDP was rising rapidly, growing 43% from the last quarter of 2017 to the last quarter of 2018.

The answer was that this was the growth in *nominal* GDP, and one of Argentina's problems was high inflation. *Real* GDP fell by more than 6% in 2018.

Argentina's woes therefore offer a good example of why it's important to distinguish between nominal and real GDP. They also demonstrate the importance of measuring inflation carefully—something that, as we explain in this chapter's Business Case, Argentina's government hasn't always done.

>> Check Your Understanding 22-2
Solutions appear at back of book.

1. Assume there are only two goods in the economy, french fries and onion rings. In 2019, 1,000,000 servings of french fries were sold at $0.40 each and 800,000 servings of onion rings at $0.60 each. From 2019 to 2020 the price of french fries rose by 25%

and the servings sold fell by 10%; the price of onion rings fell by 15% and the servings sold rose by 5%.

    a. Calculate nominal GDP in 2019 and 2020. Calculate real GDP in 2020 using 2019 prices.

    b. Why would an assessment of growth using nominal GDP be misguided?

2. From 2016 to 2020, the price of electronic equipment fell dramatically and the price of housing rose dramatically. What are the implications of this in deciding whether to use 2016 or 2020 as the base year in calculating 2018 real GDP?

The **aggregate price level** is a measure of the overall level of prices in the economy.

A **market basket** is a hypothetical set of consumer purchases of goods and services.

‖ Price Indexes and the Aggregate Price Level

In early 2020, drivers had something to celebrate: gasoline prices had tumbled to an average of $1.77 per gallon, down 40% from their peak, a year earlier. But while driving was getting cheaper, having someplace to live when you arrived was getting more expensive: by the end of 2019, average rents were 3.7% higher than they had been when gas was its most expensive. So was the cost of living going up or down?

    Clearly, there was a need for a single number summarizing what was happening to consumer prices. Just as macroeconomists find it useful to have a single number representing the overall level of output, they also find it useful to have a single number representing the overall level of prices: the **aggregate price level.** Yet a huge variety of goods and services are produced and consumed in the economy. How can we summarize the prices of all these goods and services with a single number? The answer lies in the concept of a *price index*—a concept best introduced with an example.

Market Baskets and Price Indexes

Suppose that a frost in Florida destroys most of the citrus harvest. As a result, the price of an orange rises from $0.20 to $0.40, the price of a grapefruit rises from $0.60 to $1.00, and the price of a lemon rises from $0.25 to $0.45. How much has the price of citrus fruit increased?

    One way to answer that question is to state three numbers—the changes in prices for oranges, grapefruit, and lemons. But this is a very cumbersome method. Rather than having to recite three numbers in an effort to track changes in the prices of citrus fruit, we would prefer to have some kind of overall measure of the *average* price change.

    To measure average price changes for consumer goods and services, economists track changes in the cost of a typical consumer's *consumption bundle*—the typical basket of goods and services purchased before the price changes. A hypothetical consumption bundle, used to measure changes in the overall price level, is known as a **market basket.** Suppose that before the frost a typical consumer bought 200 oranges, 50 grapefruit, and 100 lemons over the course of a year, our market basket for this example.

    Table 22-3 shows the pre-frost and post-frost cost of this market basket. Before the frost, it cost $95; after the frost, the same bundle of goods cost $175. Since $175/$95 = 1.842, the post-frost basket costs 1.842 times the cost of the pre-frost

TABLE 22-3 Calculating the Cost of a Market Basket		
	Pre-frost	**Post-frost**
Price of orange	$0.20	$0.40
Price of grapefruit	0.60	1.00
Price of lemon	0.25	0.45
Cost of market basket (200 oranges, 50 grapefruit, 100 lemons)	(200 × $0.20) + (50 × $0.60) + (100 × $0.25) = $95.00	(200 × $0.40) + (50 × $1.00) + (100 × $0.45) = $175.00

A **price index** measures the cost of purchasing a given market basket in a given year, where that cost is normalized so that it is equal to 100 in the selected base year.

The **inflation rate** is the percent change per year in a price index—typically the consumer price index.

The **consumer price index,** or **CPI,** measures the cost of the market basket of a typical urban American family.

basket, a cost increase of 84.2%. In this example, the average price of citrus fruit has increased 84.2% since the base year as a result of the frost, where the base year is the initial year used in the measurement of the price change.

Economists use the same method to measure changes in the overall price level over time. For example, to measure the change in the overall price level from 2010 (the base year) to 2020, they compare the cost of purchasing the market basket in 2010 to the cost in 2020. So they *normalize* the measure of the aggregate price level, meaning that they set the cost of the market basket equal to 100 in the chosen base year. Working with a market basket and a base year, and after normalizing, we arrive at a **price index,** a normalized measure of the overall price level. It is always cited along with the year for which the aggregate price level is being measured and the base year. A price index can be calculated using the following formula:

(22-2) $\text{Price index in a given year} = \dfrac{\text{Cost of market basket in a given year}}{\text{Cost of market basket in base year}} \times 100$

In our example, the citrus fruit market basket cost $95 in the base year, the year before the frost. So by Equation 22-2 we define the price index for citrus fruit as (cost of market basket in a given year/$95) × 100, yielding an index of 100 for the period before the frost and 184.2 after the frost. You should note that the price index for the base year always results in a price index equal to 100. This is because the price index in the base year is equal to: (cost of market basket in base year/cost of market basket in base year) × 100 = 100.

Thus, the price index makes it clear that the average price of citrus has risen 84.2% as a consequence of the frost. Because of its simplicity and intuitive appeal, the method we've just described is used to calculate a variety of price indexes to track average price changes among a variety of different groups of goods and services. For example, the *consumer price index*, which we'll discuss shortly, is the most widely used measure of the aggregate price level, the overall price level of final consumer goods and services across the economy.

Price indexes are also the basis for measuring inflation. The **inflation rate** is the annual percent change in an official price index. The inflation rate from year 1 to year 2 is calculated using the following formula, where we assume that year 1 and year 2 are consecutive years:

(22-3) $\text{Inflation rate} = \dfrac{\text{Price index in year 2} - \text{Price index in year 1}}{\text{Price index in year 1}} \times 100$

Typically, a news report that cites "the inflation rate" is referring to the annual percent change in the consumer price index.

The Consumer Price Index

The most widely used measure of prices in the United States is the **consumer price index** (often referred to simply as the **CPI**), which is intended to show how the cost of all purchases by a typical urban family has changed over time. It is calculated by surveying market prices for a market basket that is constructed to represent the consumption of a typical family of four living in a typical American city. The base period for the index is currently 1982–1984; that is, the index is calculated so that the average of consumer prices in 1982–1984 is 100.

The market basket used to calculate the CPI is far more complex than the three-fruit market basket we just described. In fact, to calculate the CPI, the Bureau of Labor Statistics sends its employees out to survey supermarkets, gas stations, hardware stores, and so on—some 23,000 retail outlets in 87 cities. Every month it tabulates about 80,000 prices, on everything from romaine lettuce to a medical check-up.

Figure 22-4 shows the weight of major categories in the consumer price index as of December 2018. For example, motor fuel, mainly gasoline, accounted for 3.8% of the CPI. On the other hand, housing accounted for more than 42% of the CPI. So that 30% plunge in gasoline prices would have reduced the CPI by roughly 1.1% (0.30 × 3.8%), while the much smaller percentage rise in housing costs of 3.5% actually had a bigger positive effect on the overall price index of 1.5% (0.035 × 42.2%).

Figure 22-5 shows how the CPI has changed since measurement began in 1913. Since 1940, the CPI has risen steadily, although its annual percent increases in recent years have been much smaller than those of the 1970s and early 1980s. (A logarithmic scale is used so that equal percent changes in the CPI have the same slope.)

The United States is not the only country that calculates a consumer price index. In fact, nearly every country has one. As you might expect, the market baskets that make up these indexes differ quite a lot from country to country. In poor countries, where people must spend a high proportion of their income just to feed themselves, food makes up a large share of the price index. Among high-income countries, differences in consumption patterns lead to differences in the price indexes: the Japanese price index puts a larger weight on raw fish and a smaller weight on beef than ours does, and the French price index puts a larger weight on wine.

FIGURE 22-4 The Makeup of the Consumer Price Index in 2018

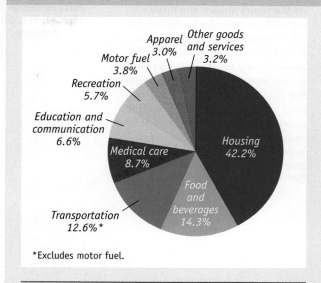

*Excludes motor fuel.

This chart shows the percentage shares of major types of spending in the CPI as of December 2018. Housing, food, transportation, and motor fuel made up about 73% of the CPI market basket. (Numbers don't add to 100% due to rounding.)
Data from: Bureau of Labor Statistics.

Other Price Measures

There are two other price measures that are also widely used to track economy-wide price changes. One is the **producer price index** (or **PPI**, which used to be known as the *wholesale price index*). As its name suggests, the PPI measures the cost of a typical basket of goods and services—containing raw commodities such as steel, electricity, coal, and so on—purchased by producers.

The **producer price index,** or **PPI,** measures changes in the prices of goods purchased by producers.

FIGURE 22-5 The CPI, 1913–2020

Since 1940, the CPI has risen steadily. But the annual percentage increases in recent years have been much smaller than those of the 1970s and early 1980s. (The vertical axis is measured on a logarithmic scale so that equal percent changes in the CPI have the same slope.)
Data from: Bureau of Labor Statistics.

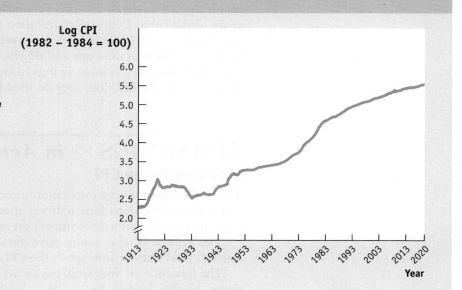

FIGURE 22-6 The CPI, the PPI, and the GDP Deflator

As the figure shows, the three different measures of inflation, the PPI (orange), the CPI (green), and the GDP deflator (purple), usually move closely together. Each reveals a drastic acceleration of inflation during the 1970s and a return to relative price stability in the 1990s. With the exception of a brief period of deflation in 2009, prices have remained stable from 2000 to 2019.

Data from: Bureau of Labor Statistics; Bureau of Economic Analysis.

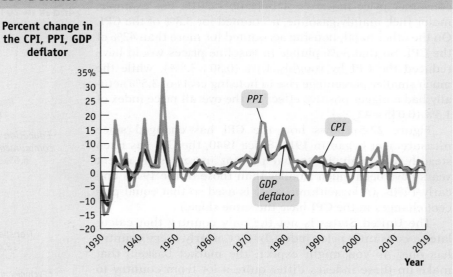

The **GDP deflator** for a given year is 100 times the ratio of nominal GDP to real GDP in that year.

Because commodity producers are relatively quick to change prices when they perceive a change in overall demand for their goods, the PPI often responds to inflationary or deflationary pressures more quickly than the CPI. As a result, a change in the PPI is often regarded as an early warning signal of changes in the inflation rate.

The other widely used price measure is the *GDP deflator;* it isn't exactly a price index, although it serves the same purpose. Recall in our discussion of Table 22-2 we distinguished between *nominal GDP* (GDP in current prices) and *real GDP* (GDP calculated using the prices of a base year). The **GDP deflator** for a given year is equal to 100 times the ratio of nominal GDP for that year to real GDP for that year. Since real GDP is currently expressed in 2012 dollars, the GDP deflator for 2012 is equal to 100. If nominal GDP doubles but real GDP does not change, the GDP deflator indicates that the aggregate price level doubled.

Perhaps the most important point about the different inflation rates generated by these three measures of prices is that they usually move closely together (although the PPI tends to fluctuate more than either of the other two measures). Figure 22-6 shows the annual percent changes in the three indexes since 1930. By all three measures, the U.S. economy experienced deflation during the early years of the Great Depression, inflation during World War II, accelerating inflation during the 1970s, and a return to relative price stability in the 1990s. Notice, by the way, the dramatic ups and downs in producer prices from 2000 to 2019 on the graph; this reflects large swings in energy and food prices, which play a much bigger role in the PPI than they do in either the CPI or the GDP deflator.

ECONOMICS >> *in Action*
Indexing to the CPI

Although GDP is a very important number for shaping economic policy, official statistics on GDP don't have a direct effect on people's lives. The CPI, by contrast, has a direct and immediate impact on millions of Americans.

The reason is that many payments are tied, or *indexed*, to the CPI—the amount paid rises or falls when the CPI rises or falls.

The practice of indexing payments to consumer prices goes back to the dawn of the United States as a nation. In 1780 the Massachusetts State

Legislature recognized that the pay of its soldiers fighting the British needed to be increased because of inflation that occurred during the Revolutionary War. The legislature adopted a formula that made a soldier's pay proportional to the cost of a market basket that consisted of 5 bushels of corn, 68 $\frac{4}{7}$ pounds of beef, 10 pounds of sheep's wool, and 16 pounds of shoe leather.

Today, 63 million people receive payments from Social Security, a national retirement program that accounts for almost a quarter of current total federal spending—more than the defense budget. The amount of an individual's Social Security payment is determined by a formula that reflects each person's previous payments into the system and other factors. In addition, all Social Security payments are adjusted each year to offset any increase in consumer prices over the previous year. The CPI is used to calculate the official estimate of the inflation rate used to adjust these payments yearly. So every percentage point added to the official estimate of the rate of inflation adds 1% to the checks received by tens of millions of individuals.

Other government payments, such as disability benefits, are also indexed to the CPI. In addition, income tax brackets, the bands of income levels that determine a taxpayer's income tax rate, are indexed to the CPI. (Individuals in a higher income bracket pay a higher income tax rate in a progressive tax system like ours.) Indexing also extends to the private sector, where some private contracts, including some wage settlements, contain cost-of-living allowances (called COLAs) that adjust payments in proportion to changes in the CPI.

Because the CPI plays such an important and direct role in people's lives, it's a politically sensitive number. The Bureau of Labor Statistics, which calculates the CPI, takes great care in collecting and interpreting price and consumption data. It uses a complex method in which households are surveyed to determine what they buy and where they shop, and a carefully selected sample of stores are surveyed to get representative prices.

A small change in the CPI has large consequences for those dependent on Social Security payments.

>> Check Your Understanding 22-3

Solutions appear at back of book.

1. Consider Table 22-3 but suppose that the market basket is composed of 100 oranges, 50 grapefruit, and 200 lemons. How does this change the pre-frost and post-frost price indexes? Explain. Generalize your explanation to how the construction of the market basket affects the price index.

2. For each of the following events, how would an economist using a 10-year-old market basket create a bias in measuring the change in the cost of living today?
   a. A typical family owns more cars than it would have a decade ago. Over that time, the average price of a car has increased more than the average prices of other goods.
   b. Virtually no households had broadband internet access 20 years ago. Now many households have it, and the price has regularly fallen each year.

3. The consumer price index in the United States (base period 1982–1984) was 254.943 in 2019 and 255.902 in 2020. Calculate the inflation rate from 2019 to 2020.

>> Quick Review

• Changes in the **aggregate price level** are measured by the cost of buying a particular **market basket** during different years. A **price index** for a given year is the cost of the market basket in that year normalized so that the price index equals 100 in a selected base year.

• The **inflation rate** is calculated as the percent change in a price index. The most commonly used price index is the **consumer price index,** or **CPI,** which tracks the cost of a basket of consumer goods and services. The **producer price index,** or **PPI,** does the same for goods and services used as inputs by firms. The **GDP deflator** measures the aggregate price level as the ratio of nominal to real GDP times 100. These three measures normally behave quite similarly.

Paying for a Heads-Up on Inflation

Javier Ghersi/Getty Images

Normally we rely on governments to produce key economic statistics. But what if you can't trust the government's numbers? That's what happened in Argentina from 2007 to 2016, where it was common knowledge that the government was manipulating the data to make inflation look lower than it really was. In response, researchers at MIT and Harvard created what they called The Billion Prices Project, using online prices to create their own measures of inflation, first for Argentina, then for a number of other countries, including the United States. The researchers found that by the middle of 2015 inflation in Argentina had risen to nearly 27.18%, but official measures showed an annual inflation rate of 14.85%. The story was a bit different for the United States. While official inflation measures reported an inflation rate of 0.17%, the project reported an annual inflation rate of −0.60%.

The Billion Prices Project played a surprisingly important role in the U.S. economic debate around 2011–2012. At the time a number of prominent commentators were claiming that official U.S. measures of consumer prices were understating the true rate of inflation. One way to see whether this was really happening was to compare the official inflation rate with the independently calculated Billion Prices measure. As it happened, there was very little difference between the two measures; the U.S. government was, in fact, reporting the numbers honestly.

But if the government numbers are okay, who needs an independent private inflation measure? The answer is that the Billion Prices measure, which is based on online data, can track inflation more or less in real time, unlike the CPI, which is only released once a month.

And there is, it turns out, a market for early reads on the inflation rate. PriceStats, a company owned by State Street Bank, uses Billion Prices data to produce real-time inflation estimates, which are made available to customers—mainly businesses—who pay a subscription fee. PriceStats data give you a heads-up on inflation trends, a few weeks before everyone else has the official data. And people are willing to pay for that heads-up.

QUESTIONS FOR THOUGHT

1. Why do you think the government of Argentina might have wanted to pretend that inflation was lower than it really was?

2. If researchers can produce a pretty good inflation measure just using online data, why do we need the elaborate process used to create the CPI?

3. Elaborating on Question 2, what things might the Billion Prices index miss? Think about what we said about the weights of various goods in the CPI.

SUMMARY

1. Economists keep track of the flows of money between sectors with the **national income and product accounts,** or **national accounts.** Demand for goods and services comes from **consumer spending, investment spending,** and **government purchases of goods and services. Exports** generate an inflow of funds into the country from the rest of the world, but **imports** lead to an outflow of funds to the rest of the world.

2. **Gross domestic product,** or **GDP,** measures the value of all **final goods and services** produced in the economy. It does not include the value of **intermediate goods and services,** but it does include **net exports** $(X - IM)$. It can be calculated in three ways: add up the **value added** by all producers; add up all spending on domestically produced final goods and services, leading to the equation GDP $= C + I + G + X - IM$, also known as **aggregate spending;** or add up all the income paid by domestic firms to factors of production. These three methods are equivalent because in the economy as a whole, total income paid by domestic firms to factors of production must equal total spending on domestically produced final goods and services.

3. **Real GDP** is the value of the final goods and services produced calculated using the prices of a selected base year. Except in the base year, real GDP is not the same as **nominal GDP,** the value of **aggregate output** calculated using current prices. Analysis of the growth rate of aggregate output must use real GDP because doing so eliminates any change in the value of aggregate output due solely to price changes. Real **GDP per capita** is a measure of average aggregate output per person but is not in itself an appropriate policy goal. U.S. statistics on real GDP are always expressed in **chained dollars.**

4. To measure the **aggregate price level,** economists calculate the cost of purchasing a **market basket.** A **price index** is the ratio of the current cost of that market basket to the cost in a selected base year, multiplied by 100.

5. The **inflation rate** is the yearly percent change in a price index, typically based on the **consumer price index,** or **CPI,** the most common measure of the aggregate price level. A similar index for goods and services purchased by firms is the **producer price index,** or **PPI.** Finally, economists also use the **GDP deflator,** which measures the price level by calculating the ratio of nominal GDP to real GDP times 100.

KEY TERMS

National income and product accounts (national accounts), p. 628
Government purchases of goods and services, p. 628
Consumer spending, p. 628
Investment spending, p. 628
Exports, p. 628
Imports, p. 628
Final goods and services, p. 629

Intermediate goods and services, p. 629
Gross domestic product (GDP), p. 630
Aggregate spending, p. 630
Value added, p. 631
Net exports, p. 635
Aggregate output, p. 636
Real GDP, p. 636
Nominal GDP, p. 636
Chained dollars, p. 637

GDP per capita, p. 637
Aggregate price level, p. 639
Market basket, p. 639
Price index, p. 640
Inflation rate, p. 640
Consumer price index (CPI), p. 640
Producer price index (PPI), p. 641
GDP deflator, p. 642

PRACTICE QUESTIONS

1. Go to the Bureau of Labor Statistics home page at www.bls.gov. Click on the "Economic Releases" tab and then click on "Major Economic Indicators" in the drop-down menu that appears. Once on the "Major Economic Indicators" page, click on "Consumer Price Index." On that page, under "Table of Contents," click on "Table 1: Consumer Price Index for All Urban Consumers." Using the "unadjusted" figures, determine what the CPI was for the previous month. How did it change from the previous month? How does the CPI compare to the same month one year ago?

2. Explain the difference between intermediate and investment goods. Are intermediate and investment goods included in GDP? Explain.

3. Analyze the following statement: "GDP has increased by 2% from last year. This is a good indicator of economic well-being as it represents an average increase in incomes."

4. Using Figure 22-4, explain how the current weighting of the CPI index could lead to either over or understating the actual inflation rate for your household.

PROBLEMS

1. At right is a simplified circular-flow diagram for the economy of Micronia. (Note that there is no investment spending and no transfers in Micronia.)

a. What is the value of GDP in Micronia?

b. What is the value of net exports?

c. What is the value of disposable income?

d. Does the total flow of money out of households—the sum of taxes paid and consumer spending—equal the total flow of money into households?

e. How does the government of Micronia finance its purchases of goods and services?

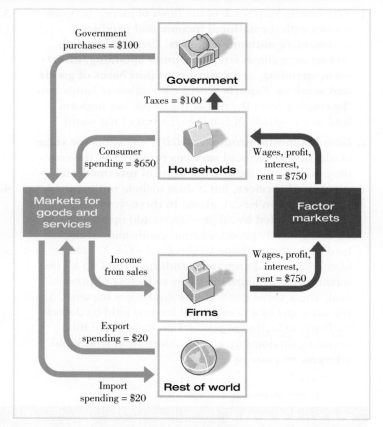

2. A more complex circular-flow diagram for the economy of Macronia is shown at right.

a. What is the value of GDP in Macronia?

b. What is the value of net exports?

c. What is the value of disposable income?

d. Does the total flow of money out of households—the sum of taxes paid, consumer spending, and private savings—equal the total flow of money into households?

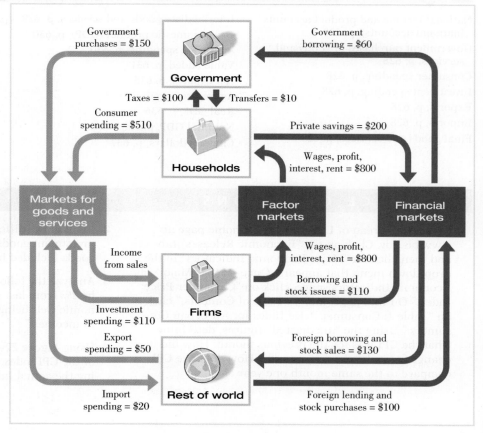

3. The components of GDP in the accompanying table were produced by the Bureau of Economic Analysis.

Category	Components of GDP in 2018 (billions of dollars)
Consumer spending	
Durable goods	$1,475.1
Nondurable goods	2,889.2
Services	9,633.9
Private investment spending	
Fixed investment spending	3,573.6
Nonresidential	2,786.9
Structures	633.2
Equipment and intellectual property products	931.1
Residential	786.7
Change in private inventories	54.7
Net exports	
Exports	2,510.3
Imports	3,148.5
Government purchases of goods and services and investment spending	
Federal	1,347.3
National defense	793.6
Nondefense	553.7
State and local	2,244.2

a. Calculate 2018 consumer spending.

b. Calculate 2018 private investment spending.

c. Calculate 2018 net exports.

d. Calculate 2018 government purchases of goods and services and government investment spending.

e. Calculate 2018 gross domestic product.

f. Calculate 2018 consumer spending on services as a percentage of total consumer spending.

g. Calculate 2018 exports as a percentage of imports.

h. Calculate 2018 government purchases on national defense as a percentage of federal government purchases of goods and services.

4. The small economy of Pizzania produces three goods (bread, cheese, and pizza), each produced by a separate company. The bread and cheese companies produce all the inputs they need to make bread and cheese, respectively. The pizza company uses the bread and cheese from the other companies to make its pizzas. All three companies employ labor to help produce their goods, and the difference between the value of goods sold and the sum of labor and input costs is the firm's profit. The accompanying table summarizes the activities of the three companies when all the bread and cheese produced are sold to the pizza company as inputs in the production of pizzas.

	Bread company	Cheese company	Pizza company
Cost of inputs	$0	$0	$50 (bread) 35 (cheese)
Wages	15	20	75
Value of output	50	35	200

a. Calculate GDP as the value added in production.

b. Calculate GDP as spending on final goods and services.

c. Calculate GDP as factor income.

5. In the economy of Pizzania (from Problem 4), bread and cheese produced are sold both to the pizza company for inputs in the production of pizzas and to consumers as final goods. The accompanying table summarizes the activities of the three companies.

	Bread company	Cheese company	Pizza company
Cost of inputs	$0	$0	$50 (bread) 35 (cheese)
Wages	25	30	75
Value of output	100	60	200

a. Calculate GDP as the value added in production.

b. Calculate GDP as spending on final goods and services.

c. Calculate GDP as factor income.

6. Which of the following transactions will be included in GDP for the United States?

a. Coca-Cola builds a new bottling plant in the United States.

b. Delta sells one of its existing airplanes to Korean Air.

c. Ms. Moneybags buys an existing share of Disney stock.

d. A California winery produces a bottle of Chardonnay and sells it to a customer in Montreal, Canada.

e. An American buys a bottle of French perfume in Tulsa.

f. A book publisher produces too many copies of a new book; the books don't sell this year, so the publisher adds the surplus books to inventories.

7. Access the Discovering Data exercise for Chapter 22, Problem 7 online to answer the following questions.

a. What was GDP for the United States last year?

b. Calculate the absolute change in U.S. GDP between last year and the year before.

c. Which component of GDP was the largest last year? Which was the smallest? What is the most recent year in which net exports were positive?

d. What happened to the size of government spending during the 1940s? What factors likely caused the shift?

e. How has each of the four components, as a percent of GDP, changed since the 1940s?

8. The accompanying table shows data on nominal GDP (in billions of dollars), real GDP (in billions of 2012 dollars), and population (in thousands) of the United States in 1968, 1978, 1988, 1998, 2008, and 2018. The U.S. price level rose consistently over the period 1965–2018.

Year	Nominal GDP (billions of dollars)	Real GDP (billions of 2012 dollars)	Population (thousands)
1968	$941	$4,792	200,745
1978	2,352	6,569	222,629
1988	5,236	8,866	245,061
1998	9,063	12,038	276,154
2008	14,713	15,605	304,543
2018	20,580	18,638	327,436

a. Why is real GDP greater than nominal GDP for all years until 2008 and lower for 2018?

b. Calculate the percent change in real GDP from 1968 to 1978, 1978 to 1988, 1988 to 1998, 1998 to 2008, and 2008 to 2018. Which period had the highest growth rate?

c. Calculate real GDP per capita for each of the years in the table.

d. Calculate the percent change in real GDP per capita from 1968 to 1978, 1978 to 1988, 1988 to 1998, 1998 to 2008, and 2008 to 2018. Which period had the highest growth rate?

e. How do the percent change in real GDP and the percent change in real GDP per capita compare? Which is larger? Do we expect them to have this relationship?

9. Eastland College is concerned about the rising price of textbooks that students must purchase. To better identify the increase in the price of textbooks, the dean asks you, the Economics Department's star student, to create an index of textbook prices. The average student purchases three English, two math, and four economics textbooks per year. The prices of these books are given in the accompanying table.

	2018	2019	2020
English textbook	$100	$110	$114
Math textbook	140	144	148
Economics textbook	160	180	200

a. What is the percent change in the price of an English textbook from 2018 to 2020?

b. What is the percent change in the price of a math textbook from 2018 to 2020?

c. What is the percent change in the price of an economics textbook from 2018 to 2020?

d. Using 2019 as a base year, create a price index for these books for all years.

e. What is the percent change in the price index from 2018 to 2020?

10. The consumer price index, or CPI, measures the cost of living for a typical urban household by multiplying the price for each category of expenditure (housing, food, and so on) times a measure of the importance of that expenditure in the average consumer's market basket and summing over all categories. However, using data from the CPI, we can see that changes in the cost of living for different types of consumers can vary a great deal. Let's compare the cost of living for a hypothetical retired person and a hypothetical college student. Let's assume that the market basket of a retired person is allocated in the following way: 10% on housing, 15% on food, 5% on transportation, 60% on medical care, 0% on education, and 10% on recreation. The college student's market basket is allocated as follows: 5% on housing, 15% on food, 20% on transportation, 0% on medical care, 40% on education, and 20% on recreation. The accompanying table shows the August 2019 CPI for each of the relevant categories.

	CPI August 2019
Housing	169.5
Food	162.2
Transportation	146.4
Medical care	210.8
Education	266.8
Recreation	120.4

Calculate the overall CPI for the retired person and for the college student by multiplying the CPI for each of the categories by the relative importance of that category to the individual and then summing each of the categories. The CPI for all items in August 2019 was 158.4. How do your calculations for a CPI for the retired person and the college student compare to the overall CPI?

11. The accompanying table provides the annual real GDP (in billions of 2012 dollars) and nominal GDP (in billions of dollars) for the United States.

a. Calculate the GDP deflator for each year.

b. Use the GDP deflator to calculate the inflation rate for all years except 2012.

	2012	2013	2014	2015	2016	2017	2018
Real GDP (billions of 2012 dollars)	16,197	16,495	16,912	17,404	17,689	18,108	18,638
Nominal GDP (billions of dollars)	16,197	16,785	17,527	18,225	18,715	19,519	20,580

12. The accompanying table contains two price indexes for the years 2016, 2017, and 2018: the GDP deflator and the CPI. For each price index, calculate the inflation rate from 2016 to 2017 and from 2017 to 2018.

Year	GDP deflator	CPI
2016	106.551	241.432
2017	108.713	246.524
2018	111.256	251.233

13. Access the Discovering Data exercise for Chapter 22, Problem 13 online to answer the following questions.

a. What was the CPI for the United States last year?

b. What was the inflation rate, the percent change in the CPI, from 2018 to 2019? From 1989 to 1990?

c. Which component of CPI grew the fastest from 1983 through 2019? The slowest?

d. CPI measured by the BLS is most likely to be overstated for which group of people? Understated?

e. Calculate your personal CPI index.

WORK IT OUT

14. The economy of Britannica produces three goods: computers, pens, and pizza. The accompanying table shows the prices and output of the three goods for the years 2018, 2019, and 2020.

a. What is the percent change in production of each of the goods from 2018 to 2019 and from 2019 to 2020?

b. What is the percent change in prices of each of the goods from 2018 to 2019 and from 2019 to 2020?

c. Calculate nominal GDP in Britannica for each of the three years. What is the percent change in nominal GDP from 2018 to 2019 and from 2019 to 2020?

d. Calculate real GDP in Britannica using 2018 prices for each of the three years. What is the percent change in real GDP from 2018 to 2019 and from 2019 to 2020?

Year	Computers Price	Quantity	Pens Price	Quantity	Pizza Price	Quantity
2018	$900	10	$10	100	$15	2
2019	1,000	10.5	12	105	16	2
2020	1,050	12	14	110	17	3

23 ▶ Unemployment and Inflation

THE GREAT MISTAKE OF 2011

THE EURO, A CURRENCY SHARED BY 19 EUROPEAN COUNTRIES, was introduced in 1999. Like all modern currencies, the euro is managed by a *central bank* — an institution that has the power to create or destroy money. Along with this power comes the ability to determine certain crucial interest rates, like the rates at which private banks lend to each other, and the rate they are paid on money they deposit with the central bank. Decisions about the quantity of money and key interest rates are called *monetary policy,* and are a central part of overall macroeconomic policy. In the United States, monetary policy is set by the Federal Reserve, commonly referred to as the Fed. In Europe, monetary policy is run by the rather boringly named European Central Bank or ECB.

In 2011 the ECB made a big mistake. Like the Fed, it had cut interest rates sharply in the face of the 2008 financial crisis. But in 2011 it raised rates again, even though Europe had barely begun to recover from the aftereffects of that crisis.

The chair of the Federal Reserve balances the goals of low unemployment and price stability when deciding whether to give the economy more gas or hit the brakes. Bernanke chose wisely in 2011; Trichet did not.

Why did the ECB raise rates? Macroeconomic policy usually focuses mainly on trying to mitigate the two great evils of macroeconomics, high unemployment and high inflation. High unemployment incurs human and economic waste because willing workers can't find jobs. High inflation undermines the monetary system through rapidly rising prices. So the two principal goals of macroeconomic policy are low unemployment and price stability, usually defined as a low but positive rate of inflation.

Sometimes, unfortunately, these twin goals can be in conflict. At those times, macroeconomic policy makers must make a trade-off based on judgment and guesswork. And the goals did indeed seem to be in conflict in Europe in 2011: unemployment was still high in the aftermath of the 2008 financial crisis, but inflation had also accelerated sharply. The ECB, led at the time by France's Jean-Claude Trichet, decided that inflation was the greater threat, and raised rates despite high unemployment.

As it turned out, this was the wrong call. (By contrast, Ben Bernanke, the leader of the Fed, and his colleagues, facing a similar situation, got it right.) The rise in inflation reflected temporary factors, like a surge in world oil prices, that soon went away, while unemployment continued to rise. By the end of 2011 the ECB had reversed its rate hikes.

In this chapter, we'll explore the dynamics of unemployment and inflation in the economy. We'll learn how they are measured and why accurate measurement is a critical function of government. From there we will go on to understand why low unemployment and price stability are the main goals of macroeconomic policy. Yet, as we just noted, sometimes those goals are in conflict. ●

WHAT YOU WILL LEARN

- How is **unemployment** measured and how is the **unemployment rate** calculated?
- What is the significance of the unemployment rate for the economy?
- What is the relationship between the unemployment rate and economic growth?
- What factors determine the **natural rate of unemployment**?
- What are the economic costs of inflation?
- How do inflation and deflation create winners and losers?
- Why do policy makers try to maintain a stable rate of inflation?

Employment is the number of people currently employed in the economy, either full time or part time.

Unemployment is the number of people who are actively looking for work but aren't currently employed.

The **labor force** is equal to the sum of employment and unemployment.

The **labor force participation rate** is the percentage of the population aged 16 or older that is in the labor force.

‖ The Unemployment Rate

Figure 23-1 shows the U.S. unemployment rate from 1948 to 2020; as you can see, unemployment soared during the Great Recession of 2007–2009 and fell only gradually in the years that followed, and spiked again in spring 2020 as a result of the COVID-19 crisis. What did the elevated unemployment rate mean, and why was it such a big factor in people's lives? To understand why policy makers pay so much attention to employment and unemployment, we need to understand how they are both defined and measured.

Defining and Measuring Unemployment

It's easy to define employment: you're employed if and only if you have a job. **Employment** is the total number of people currently employed, either full time or part time.

Unemployment, however, is a more subtle concept. Just because a person isn't working doesn't mean that we consider that person unemployed. For example, as of February 2020, there were 49.8 million retired workers in the United States receiving Social Security checks. Most of them were probably happy that they were no longer working, so we wouldn't consider someone who has settled into a comfortable, well-earned retirement to be unemployed. There were also 13.4 million disabled, under the age of 65, U.S. workers receiving benefits because they were unable to work. Again, although they weren't working, we don't consider them to be unemployed.

The U.S. Census Bureau, the federal agency tasked with collecting data on unemployment, considers the unemployed only to be those who are "jobless, looking for jobs, and available for work." Retired people don't count because they aren't looking for jobs; the disabled don't count because they aren't available for work. More specifically, an individual is considered unemployed if they don't currently have a job and have been actively seeking a job during the past four weeks. So **unemployment** is defined as the total number of people who are actively looking for work but aren't currently employed.

A country's **labor force** is the sum of employment and unemployment—that is, of people who are currently working and people who are currently looking for work, respectively. The **labor force participation rate,** defined as the

---

FIGURE 23-1 The U.S. Unemployment Rate, 1948–2020

The unemployment rate has fluctuated widely over time. It always rises during recessions, which are shown by the shaded bars. It usually, but not always, falls during periods of economic expansion.

Data from: Bureau of Labor Statistics; National Bureau of Economic Research.

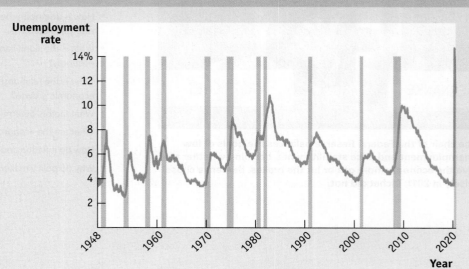

percentage of the working-age population that is in the labor force, is calculated as follows:

(23-1) $\text{Labor force participation rate} = \dfrac{\text{Labor force}}{\text{Population age 16 and older}} \times 100$

The **unemployment rate,** defined as the percentage of the total number of people in the labor force who are unemployed, is calculated as follows:

(23-2) $\text{Unemployment rate} = \dfrac{\text{Number of unemployed workers}}{\text{Labor force}} \times 100$

To estimate the numbers that go into calculating the unemployment rate, the U.S. Census Bureau carries out a monthly survey called the Current Population Survey, which involves interviewing a random sample of approximately 60,000 American households. People are asked whether they are currently employed. If they are not employed, they are asked whether they have been looking for a job during the past four weeks. The results are then scaled up, using estimates of the total population, to estimate the total number of employed and unemployed Americans.

The Significance of the Unemployment Rate

In general, the unemployment rate is a good although imperfect indicator of how easy or difficult it is to find a job given the current state of the economy. You can see this by the strong correlation between the unemployment rate and other indicators of job market conditions, like the *quit rate*—the fraction of workers voluntarily leaving their jobs in any given month. In 2009, with the unemployment rate close to 10%, very few workers were quitting, because someone who left a job had little assurance of finding another. By early 2020, with unemployment below 4%, the quit rate had doubled. In the spring of 2020, as unemployment soared in the face of COVID-19, quits plunged.

Although the unemployment rate is a good indicator of current labor market conditions, it's not a literal measure of the percentage of people who want a job but can't find one. That's because in some ways the unemployment rate exaggerates the difficulty people have in finding jobs. But in other ways, the opposite is true—a low unemployment rate can conceal deep frustration over the lack of job opportunities.

How the Unemployment Rate Can Overstate the True Level of Unemployment If you are searching for work, it's normal to take at least a few weeks to find a suitable job. Yet a worker who is quite confident of finding a job, but has not yet accepted a position, is counted as unemployed. As a consequence, the unemployment rate never falls to zero, even in boom times when jobs are plentiful. Even in the buoyant labor market of February 2020, when it was easy to find work, the unemployment rate was still 3.4%. Later in this chapter, we'll discuss in greater depth the reasons that measured unemployment persists even when jobs are abundant.

How the Unemployment Rate Can Understate the True Level of Unemployment Frequently, people who would like to work but aren't working still don't get counted as unemployed. In particular, an individual who has given up looking for a job for the time being because there are no jobs available—say, a laid-off steelworker in a deeply depressed steel town—isn't counted as unemployed because he or she has not been searching for a job during the previous four weeks. Individuals who want to work but have told government researchers that they aren't currently searching because they see little prospect of finding a job given the state of the job market are called **discouraged workers.** Because it does not count discouraged workers, the measured unemployment rate may understate the percentage of people who want to work but are unable to find jobs.

The **unemployment rate** is the percentage of the total number of people in the labor force who are unemployed.

Discouraged workers are nonworking people who are capable of working but have given up looking for a job given the state of the job market.

FIGURE 23-2 Alternative Measures of Unemployment, 1996–2020

The unemployment number usually quoted in the news media counts someone as unemployed only if that person has been looking for work during the past four weeks. Broader measures also count discouraged workers, marginally attached workers, and the underemployed. These broader measures show a higher unemployment rate, but they move closely in parallel with the standard rate.

Data from: Bureau of Labor Statistics.

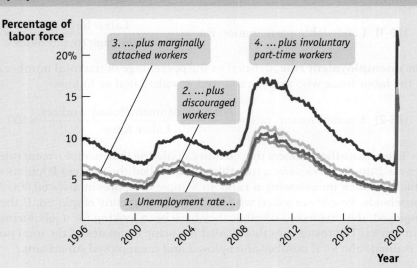

Discouraged workers are part of a larger group—**marginally attached workers.** These are people who say they would like to have a job and have looked for work in the recent past but are not currently looking for work. They are also not included when calculating the unemployment rate. Finally, another category of workers who are frustrated in their ability to find work but aren't counted as unemployed are the **underemployed:** workers who would like to find full-time jobs but are currently working part time "for economic reasons"—that is, they can't find a full-time job. Again, they aren't counted in the unemployment rate.

The *Bureau of Labor Statistics* is the federal agency that calculates the official unemployment rate. It also calculates broader "measures of labor underutilization" that include the three categories of frustrated workers. Figure 23-2 shows what happens to the measured unemployment rate once discouraged workers, other marginally attached workers, and the underemployed are counted. The broadest measure of unemployment and underemployment, known as *U-6,* is the sum of these three measures plus the unemployed. It is substantially higher than the rate usually quoted by the news media. But U-6 and the unemployment rate move very much in parallel, so changes in the unemployment rate remain a good guide to what's happening in the overall labor market, including frustrated workers.

Finally, it's important to realize that the unemployment rate varies greatly among demographic groups. Other things equal, jobs are generally easier to find for more experienced workers and for workers during their prime working years, that is, from ages 25 to 54. For younger workers, as well as workers nearing retirement age, jobs are typically harder to find, other things equal.

Figure 23-3 shows unemployment rates for different groups in 2000, when the overall unemployment rate was low by historical standards, in 2010, when the rate was high in the aftermath of the Great Recession, and in 2020, when it had come down to pre-crisis levels before the pandemic. As you can see, the unemployment rate for African-American workers is consistently much higher than the national average; the unemployment rate for White teenagers (ages 16–19) is normally even higher; and the unemployment rate for African-American teenagers is higher still. (Bear in mind that a teenager isn't considered unemployed, even if they aren't working, unless that teenager is looking for work but can't find it.) So even at times when the overall unemployment rate is relatively low, jobs are hard to find for some groups.

Marginally attached workers would like to be employed and have looked for a job in the recent past but are not currently looking for work.

Underemployment is the number of people who work part time because they cannot find full-time jobs.

FIGURE 23-3 Unemployment Rates of Different Groups in 2000, 2010, and 2020

Unemployment rates vary greatly among different demographic groups. For example, although the overall unemployment rate in February 2020 was 3.5%, the unemployment rate among African-American teenagers was 20.4%. As a result, even during periods of low overall unemployment, unemployment remains a serious problem for some groups.

Data from: Bureau of Labor Statistics.

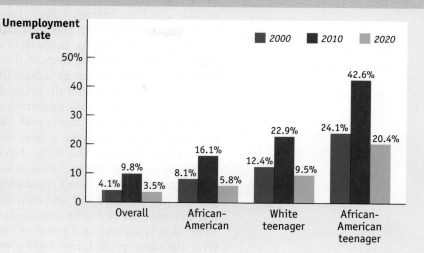

So you should interpret the unemployment rate as an indicator of overall labor market conditions, not as an exact measure of the percentage of people unable to find jobs. The unemployment rate is, however, a very good indicator: its ups and downs closely reflect economic changes that have a significant impact on people's lives. Let's turn now to the causes of these fluctuations.

Growth and Unemployment

Compared to Figure 23-1, Figure 23-4 shows the U.S. unemployment rate over a somewhat shorter period, from 1979 through 2020. The shaded bars represent periods of recession. As you can see, during every recession, without exception, the unemployment rate rose. The severe recession of 2007–2009, like the earlier one of 1981–1982, led to a large rise in unemployment. The 2020 pandemic led to both a recession and an even larger spike in unemployment.

Correspondingly, during periods of economic expansion the unemployment rate usually falls. The long economic expansion of the 1990s and the recovery

FIGURE 23-4 Unemployment and Recessions, 1979–2020

This figure shows a close-up of the unemployment rate for the past three decades, with the shaded bars indicating recessions. It's clear that unemployment always rises during recessions and *usually* falls during expansions. But in both the early 1990s and the early 2000s, unemployment continued to rise for some time after the recession was officially declared over.

Data from: Bureau of Labor Statistics; National Bureau of Economic Research.

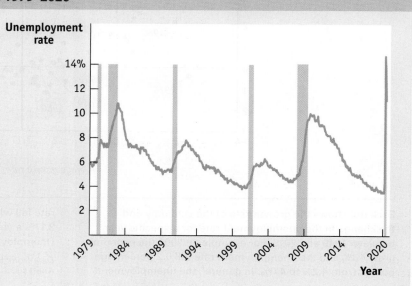

from the Great Recession eventually brought the unemployment rate down below 4.0%. However, it's important to recognize that *economic expansions aren't always periods of falling unemployment*. Look at the periods immediately following the recessions of 1990–1991 and 2001 in Figure 23-4. In each case the unemployment rate continued to rise for more than a year after the recession was officially over. The explanation in both cases is that although the economy was growing, it was not growing fast enough to reduce the unemployment rate.

Figure 23-5 is a scatter diagram showing U.S. data for the period from 1949 to 2019. The horizontal axis measures the annual rate of growth in real GDP—the percent by which each year's real GDP changed compared to the previous year's real GDP. (Notice that there were 10 years in which growth was negative—that is, real GDP shrank.) The vertical axis measures the *change* in the average unemployment rate over the previous year in percentage points—last year's unemployment rate minus this year's unemployment rate. Each dot represents the observed growth rate of real GDP and change in the unemployment rate for a given year. For example, in 2000 the average unemployment rate fell to 4.0% from 4.2% in 1999; this is shown as a value of –0.2 along the vertical axis for the year 2000. Over the same period, real GDP grew by 4.1%; this is the value shown along the horizontal axis for the year 2000.

The downward trend of the scatter diagram in Figure 23-5 shows that there is a generally strong negative relationship between growth in the economy and the rate of unemployment. Years of high growth in real GDP were also years in which the unemployment rate fell, and years of low or negative growth in real GDP were years in which the unemployment rate rose.

The green vertical line in Figure 23-5 at the value of 3.17% indicates the average growth rate of real GDP over the period from 1949 to 2019. Points lying to the right of the vertical line are years of above-average growth. In these years, the value on the vertical axis is usually negative, meaning that the unemployment

FIGURE 23-5 Growth and Changes in Unemployment, 1949–2019

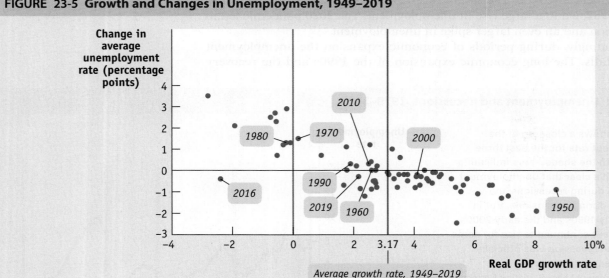

Each dot shows the growth rate of the economy and the change in the unemployment rate for a specific year between 1949 and 2019. For example, in 2000 the economy grew 4.1% and the unemployment rate fell 0.2 percentage points, from 4.2% to 4.0%. In general, the unemployment rate fell when growth was above its average rate of 3.17% a year and rose when growth was below average. Unemployment always rose when real GDP fell.

Data from: Bureau of Labor Statistics; Bureau of Economic Analysis.

rate fell. That is, years of above-average growth were usually years in which the unemployment rate was falling. Conversely, points lying to the left of the green vertical line were years of below-average growth. In these years, the value on the vertical axis is usually positive, meaning that the unemployment rate rose. That is, years of below-average growth were usually years in which the unemployment rate was rising.

A period in which real GDP is growing at a below-average rate and unemployment is rising is called a **jobless recovery** or a *growth recession*. Since 1990, there have been three recessions, each of which was followed by a period of jobless recovery. But true recessions, periods when real GDP falls, are especially painful for workers. As illustrated by the points to the left of the purple vertical line in Figure 23-5 (representing years in which the real GDP growth rate is negative), falling real GDP is always associated with a rising rate of unemployment, causing a great deal of hardship for families.

> A **jobless recovery** is a period in which the real GDP growth rate is positive but the unemployment rate is still rising.

ECONOMICS >> *in Action*
Opportunity Knocks

Do you need a college degree to get a well-paying job? It definitely helps. But sometimes opportunity knocks even for those without a BA. A 2019 article in the *Wall Street Journal* highlighted the good fortune of Cassandra Eaton, a 23-year-old high school graduate in Biloxi, Mississippi. After leaving school, Ms. Eaton was employed by a day-care center that paid $8.25 an hour. But by early 2019 she was making $18.90 an hour as an apprentice welder at a nearby shipyard.

No doubt Ms. Eaton did much to earn her new position, but there were a lot of stories like hers in 2019: many employers were willing to hire and train workers they might not have been interested in a few years earlier. Why? Because the job market was very good, and employers couldn't afford to be choosy. That *Wall Street Journal* article was titled "Inside the hottest job market of the past half century."

Figure 23-6 illustrates the point, showing unemployment rates for adults over age 25 with high school and college degrees respectively over the period from 2007 to 2020. Adults without a college degree always have somewhat higher unemployment than their more credentialed peers, but the gap depends a lot on the overall state of employment. In the terrible job market of 2010, with overall unemployment near 10%, the gap was huge. In fact, some commentators warned that America was suffering from a "skills gap," with many workers lacking the qualifications the modern economy requires.

By 2019, however, overall unemployment was below 4%, and unemployment among workers who only had a high school degree was only modestly higher than for the college-educated. To the extent that there was still a skills gap, employers themselves were trying to close it by giving workers the training they needed.

The moral of the story is that the state of the labor market, which the unemployment rate helps us track, makes a huge difference in peoples' lives, even those who stay employed.

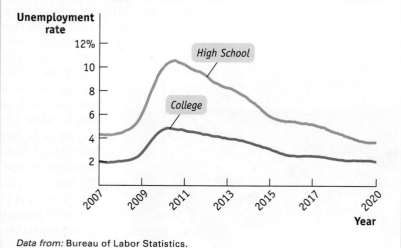

FIGURE 23-6 Unemployment Rate for College and High School Graduates, 2007–2020

Data from: Bureau of Labor Statistics.

>> Quick Review

• The **labor force,** equal to **employment** plus **unemployment,** does not include discouraged workers. Nor do labor statistics contain data on **underemployment.** The **labor force participation rate** is the percentage of the population age 16 and over in the labor force.

• The **unemployment rate** is an indicator of the state of the labor market, not an exact measure of the percentage of workers who can't find jobs. It can overstate the true level of unemployment because workers often spend time searching for a job even when jobs are plentiful. But it can also understate the true level of unemployment because it excludes **discouraged workers, marginally attached workers,** and **underemployed** workers.

• There is a strong negative relationship between growth in real GDP and changes in the unemployment rate. When growth is above average, the unemployment rate generally falls. When growth is below average, the unemployment rate generally rises — a period called a **jobless recovery** that typically follows a deep recession.

>> Check Your Understanding 23-1

Solutions appear at back of book.

1. Suppose employment websites develop new software that enables job-seekers to find suitable jobs more quickly and employers to better screen potential employees. What effect will this have on the unemployment rate over time? Also suppose that these websites encourage job-seekers who had given up their searches to begin looking again. What effect will this have on the unemployment rate?

2. In which of the following cases is a worker counted as unemployed? Explain.
   a. Rosa, an older worker who has been laid off and who gave up looking for work months ago
   b. Anthony, a schoolteacher who is not working during his three-month summer break
   c. Kanako, an investment banker who has been laid off and is currently searching for another position
   d. Sergio, a classically trained musician who can only find work playing for local parties
   e. Natasha, a graduate student who went back to school because jobs were scarce

3. Which of the following are consistent with the observed relationship between growth in real GDP and changes in the unemployment rate as shown in Figure 23-5? Which are not?
   a. A rise in the unemployment rate accompanies a fall in real GDP.
   b. An exceptionally strong business recovery is associated with a greater percentage of the labor force being employed.
   c. Negative real GDP growth is associated with a fall in the unemployment rate.

‖ The Natural Rate of Unemployment

Fast economic growth tends to reduce the unemployment rate. So how low can the unemployment rate go? You might be tempted to say zero, but that isn't feasible. Over the past half-century, the national unemployment rate has never dropped below 2.9%.

During boom times, how can there be so much unemployment even when many employees are actively searching for work? To answer this question, we need to examine the nature of labor markets and why they normally lead to substantial measured unemployment even when jobs are plentiful. Our starting point is the observation that even in the best of times, jobs are constantly being created and destroyed.

Job Creation and Job Destruction

Even during good times, most Americans know someone who has lost a job. In December 2019, the U.S. unemployment rate was only 3.5%, very low by historical standards. Yet in that month there were 5.7 million *job separations* — terminations of employment that occur because a worker is either fired or quits voluntarily.

There are many reasons for such job loss. One is structural change in the economy: industries rise and fall as new technologies emerge and consumers' tastes change. For example, employment in coal mining has declined to a small fraction of its one-time high due to both automation and a switch to other sources of energy. However, structural change also brings the creation of new jobs: employment in solar power surged after 2010 as a combination of rapidly improving technology and tax incentives led to a rapid growth in the use of solar panels.

Poor management performance or bad luck at individual companies also leads to job loss for employees. For example, in early 2018, J.C. Penney announced the closure of 140 stores and offered early retirement to 6,000 workers. In the same year, Toys

"At this point, I'm just happy to still have a job."

"R" Us closed 735 stores, causing 31,000 layoffs. Meanwhile, online retailers like Amazon continued to expand, building distribution centers all over the country.

Continual job creation and destruction are features of modern economies, making a naturally occurring amount of unemployment inevitable. Within this naturally occurring amount, there are two types of unemployment—*frictional* and *structural*.

Workers who spend time looking for employment are engaged in **job search.**

Frictional unemployment is unemployment due to the time workers spend in job search.

Frictional Unemployment

When a worker loses a job involuntarily due to job destruction, that worker often doesn't take the first new job offered. For example, suppose a skilled programmer, laid off because their software company's product line was unsuccessful, sees an online job posting for a receptionist. The programmer might apply and get the receptionist job—but that would be foolish. Instead, they should take the time to look for a job that takes advantage of their skills and pays accordingly. In addition, individual workers are constantly leaving jobs voluntarily, typically for personal reasons—family moves, dissatisfaction, and better job prospects elsewhere.

Economists say that workers who spend time looking for employment are engaged in **job search.** If all workers and all jobs were alike, job search wouldn't be necessary; if information about jobs and workers was perfect, job search would be very quick. In practice, however, it's normal for a worker who loses a job, or a young worker seeking a first job, to spend at least a few weeks searching.

Frictional unemployment is unemployment due to the time workers spend in job search. A certain amount of frictional unemployment is inevitable due to the constant process of economic change. As we just mentioned, during the low-unemployment month of December 2019 there were nonetheless more than 5 million job separations, in which workers left or lost their jobs. Total employment grew because these separations were more than offset by an even larger number of hires. Inevitably, some of the workers who left or lost their jobs spent at least some time unemployed, as did some of the workers newly entering the labor force.

Figure 23-7 shows the average monthly flows of workers among three states: employed, unemployed, and not in the labor force during December 2019. What the figure suggests is how much churning is constantly taking place in the labor market. An inevitable consequence of that churning is a significant number of workers who haven't yet found their next job—that is, frictional unemployment.

A limited amount of frictional unemployment is relatively harmless and may even be a good thing. The economy is more productive if workers take the time to find jobs that are well matched to their skills, and workers who are unemployed

FIGURE 23-7 Labor Market Flows in December 2019

Even in December 2019, a low-unemployment month, large numbers of workers moved into and out of both employment and unemployment.
Data from: Bureau of Labor Statistics.

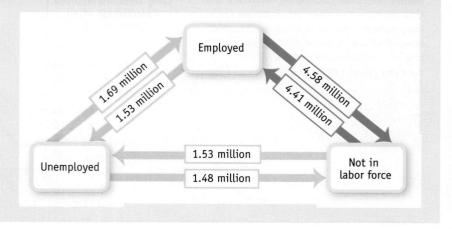

FIGURE 23-8 Distribution of the Unemployed by Duration of Unemployment, February 2020

When the unemployment rate is low, most unemployed workers are unemployed for only a short period. In February 2020, 35.1% of the unemployed had been unemployed for less than 5 weeks and 66% for less than 15 weeks. The short duration of unemployment for most workers suggests that much of the unemployment was frictional. (Total may not add up to 100 due to rounding.)

Data from: Bureau of Labor Statistics.

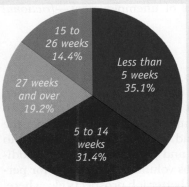

for a brief period while searching for the right job don't experience great hardship. In fact, when there is a low unemployment rate, periods of unemployment tend to be quite short, suggesting that much of the unemployment is frictional.

Figure 23-8 shows the composition of unemployment in February 2020. Approximately 35% of the unemployed had been unemployed for less than 5 weeks, and only 34% had been unemployed for 15 or more weeks. Only about one in five unemployed workers were considered to be *long-term unemployed*—those unemployed for 27 or more weeks.

In periods of higher unemployment, however, workers tend to be jobless for longer periods of time, suggesting that the amount of frictional unemployment is small relative to the amount of unemployment arising from the downturn in the business cycle. Figure 23-9 shows the fraction of the unemployed who had been out of work for 6 months or more from 2007 to 2020. It jumped to 45% after the Great Recession, but came gradually down as the economy recovered.

Structural Unemployment

Frictional unemployment exists even when the number of people seeking jobs is equal to the number of jobs being offered—that is, the existence of frictional unemployment doesn't mean that there is a surplus of labor. Sometimes, however, there is a *persistent surplus* of job-seekers in a particular labor market, even when the economy is at the peak of the business cycle. There may be more workers with a particular skill than there are jobs available using that skill, or there may be more workers in a particular geographic region than there are jobs available in that region. **Structural unemployment** is unemployment that results when there are more people seeking jobs in a particular labor market than there are jobs available at the current wage rate. Economists try to gauge the level of structural unemployment in an economy by looking at the level of unemployment at the peak of the business cycle.

In **structural unemployment,** more people are seeking jobs in a particular labor market than there are jobs available at the current wage rate, even when the economy is at the peak of the business cycle.

FIGURE 23-9 Percentage of Unemployed U.S. Workers Who Had Been Unemployed for Six Months or Longer, 2007–2019

Before the Great Recession, relatively few U.S. workers had been unemployed for long periods. However, the percentage of long-term unemployed shot up after 2007, and came down only gradually.

Data from: Bureau of Labor Statistics.

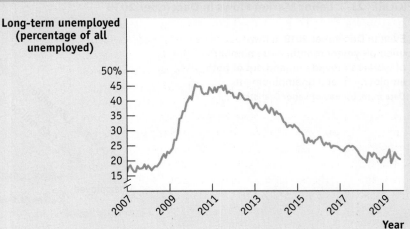

FIGURE 23-10 The Effect of a Minimum Wage on a Labor Market

When the government sets a minimum wage, W_F, that exceeds the market equilibrium wage rate in that market, W_E, the number of workers who would like to work at that minimum wage, Q_S, is greater than the number of workers demanded at that wage rate, Q_D. This surplus of labor is structural unemployment.

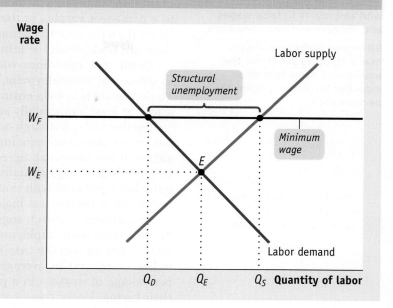

The supply and demand model tells us that the price of a good, service, or factor of production tends to move toward an equilibrium level that matches the quantity supplied with the quantity demanded. This is equally true, in general, of labor markets. Figure 23-10 shows a typical market for labor. The downward-sloping labor demand curve indicates that when the price of labor—the wage rate—increases, employers demand less labor. The upward-sloping labor supply curve indicates that when the price of labor increases, more workers are willing to supply labor at the prevailing wage rate. These two forces coincide to lead to an equilibrium wage rate for any given type of labor in a particular location. That equilibrium wage rate is shown as W_E.

Even at the equilibrium wage rate W_E, there will still be some frictional unemployment. That's because there will always be some workers engaged in job search even when the number of jobs available is equal to the number of workers seeking jobs. But there wouldn't be any structural unemployment in this labor market. *Structural unemployment occurs when the wage rate is, for some reason, persistently above W_E.* Several factors can lead to a wage rate in excess of W_E, the most important being *minimum wages, unions, efficiency wages,* the side effects of government policies, and mismatches between employees and employers.

Minimum Wages A **minimum wage** is a government-mandated floor on the wage rate. In the United States, the federally mandated minimum wage in early 2020 was $7.25 an hour. A number of state and local governments also determine the minimum wage within their jurisdictions, typically for the purpose of setting it higher than the federal level. For example, the city of Seattle has set a minimum wage at $15 an hour. For many American workers, the minimum wage is irrelevant; the market equilibrium wage for these workers is well above the national price floor. But for less-skilled workers, the minimum wage can be binding—that is, it raises their wage above the equilibrium level. As a result, it can lead to structural unemployment.

A **minimum wage** is a government-mandated floor on the wage rate.

California's minimum wage will be raised incrementally to $15 by 2022.

A **union** is an organization of workers that bargains collectively with employers to raise wages and improve working conditions.

Efficiency wages are wages that employers set above the equilibrium wage rate as an incentive for better employee performance.

Figure 23-10 shows the effect of a binding minimum wage. In this market, the minimum wage is W_F, which is above the equilibrium wage rate, W_E. This leads to a persistent surplus in the labor market: the quantity of labor supplied, Q_S, is larger than the quantity demanded, Q_D. In other words, more people want to work than can find jobs at the minimum wage, leading to structural unemployment.

Given that minimum wages—that is, binding minimum wages—can lead to structural unemployment, you might wonder why governments impose them. The rationale is to help ensure that people who work can earn enough income to afford at least a minimally adequate standard of living.

Furthermore, although economists broadly agree that a high minimum wage has the employment-reducing effects shown in Figure 23-10, there is widespread, although not universal, agreement that this isn't a good description of how the U.S. minimum wage actually works. The minimum wage in the United States is quite low compared with that in other wealthy countries, and as already noted, it isn't binding for the vast majority of workers.

In addition, research suggests that minimum wage increases do not seem to be associated with employment declines and may actually lead to higher employment when, as was the case in the United States at one time, the minimum wage is low compared to average wages. They argue that firms employing a large percentage of workers in a particular market can keep wages low by restricting their hiring. Under these conditions, a moderate rise in the minimum wage will not lead to a loss of jobs. Most economists, however, agree that a sufficiently high minimum wage *does* lead to structural unemployment.

Unions The actions of **unions,** organizations of workers that bargain collectively with employers to raise wages and improve living standards of their members, can have effects similar to those of minimum wages, leading to structural unemployment. By bargaining collectively for all of a firm's workers, unions can often win higher wages from employers than workers would have obtained by bargaining individually. This process, known as *collective bargaining*, is intended to tip the scales of bargaining power more toward workers and away from employers. Labor unions exercise bargaining power by threatening firms with a *labor strike*, a collective refusal to work. The threat of a strike can have serious consequences for firms. In such cases, workers acting collectively can exercise more power than they could if acting individually.

Employers have acted to counter the bargaining power of unions by threatening and enforcing *lockouts*—periods in which union workers are locked out and rendered unemployed—while hiring replacement workers.

When workers have increased bargaining power, they tend to demand and receive higher wages. Unions also bargain over benefits, such as health care and pensions, which we can think of as additional wages. Indeed, economists who study the effects of unions on wages find that unionized workers earn higher wages and more generous benefits than non-union workers with similar skills. The result of these increased wages can be the same as the result of a minimum wage: labor unions push the wage that workers receive above the equilibrium wage. Like a binding minimum wage, this leads to structural unemployment. In the United States, however, due to a low level of unionization, the amount of unemployment generated by union demands is likely to be very small. And in countries such as Germany and Japan, unions and management collaborate on devising more efficient work practices that support higher equilibrium wages.

Efficiency Wages Actions by firms can contribute to structural unemployment. Firms may choose to pay **efficiency wages**—wages that employers set above the equilibrium wage rate as an incentive for their workers to perform better.

Employers may feel the need for such incentives for several reasons. For example, employers often have difficulty observing directly how hard an employee works. They can, however, elicit more work effort by paying above-market wages:

employees receiving these higher wages are more likely to work harder to ensure that they aren't fired, which would cause them to lose their higher wages.

For example, in 2018, the average hourly worker at Costco made over $22 per hour, while the average worker at Walmart made only $14 per hour. As a result, Costco's employees were reported to be more satisfied with their jobs, more productive, and less likely to search for better opportunities elsewhere.

When many firms pay efficiency wages, the result is a pool of workers who want jobs but can't find them. With Costco paying efficiency wages, a lot of workers are willing to work at Costco but not Walmart. So the use of efficiency wages by firms may lead to structural unemployment.

Side Effects of Government Policies In addition, government policies designed to help workers who lose their jobs can lead to structural unemployment as an unintended side effect. Most economically advanced countries provide benefits to laid-off workers as a way to tide them over until they find a new job. In the United States, these benefits typically replace only about 45% of a worker's income and expire after 26 weeks. (Benefits were extended in some cases to 99 weeks during the period of high unemployment in 2009–2011). In other countries, particularly in Europe, benefits are more generous and last longer. The drawback to this generosity is that it reduces a worker's incentive to quickly find a new job. During the 1980s, it was often argued that unemployment benefits in some European countries were one of the causes of *Eurosclerosis*, persistently high unemployment that afflicted a number of European economies.

Mismatches Between Employees and Employers It takes time for workers and firms to adjust to shifts in the economy. The result can be a mismatch between what employees have to offer and what employers are looking for. A skills mismatch is one form; for example, in the aftermath of the housing bust of 2009, there were more construction workers looking for jobs than there were jobs available. Another form is geographic, as is the case in the "eastern heartland" regions that, as described in Economics in Action, have been left behind by economic change. Until the mismatch is resolved through a big enough fall in wages of the surplus workers to induce retraining or relocation, there will be structural unemployment.

The Natural Rate of Unemployment

Because some frictional unemployment is inevitable and because many economies also suffer from structural unemployment, a certain amount of unemployment is normal, or "natural." Actual unemployment fluctuates around this normal level. The **natural rate of unemployment** is the normal unemployment rate around which the actual unemployment rate fluctuates. It is the rate of unemployment that arises from the effects of frictional plus structural unemployment.

Cyclical unemployment is the deviation of the actual rate of unemployment from the natural rate; that is, it is the difference between the actual and natural rates of unemployment. As the name suggests, cyclical unemployment is the share of unemployment that arises from the downturns of the business cycle.

We'll see in Chapter 31 that an economy's natural rate of unemployment is a critical policy variable because a government cannot keep the unemployment rate persistently below the natural rate without leading to accelerating inflation.

We can summarize the relationships between the various types of unemployment as follows:

(23-3) Natural unemployment =
Frictional unemployment + Structural unemployment

(23-4) Actual unemployment =
Natural unemployment + Cyclical unemployment

The **natural rate of unemployment** is the unemployment rate that arises from the effects of frictional plus structural unemployment.

Cyclical unemployment is the deviation of the actual rate of unemployment from the natural rate due to downturns in the business cycle.

Perhaps because of its name, people often imagine that the natural rate of unemployment is a constant that doesn't change over time and can't be affected by government policy. Neither proposition is true. Let's take a moment to stress two facts:

1. The natural rate of unemployment changes over time.
2. It can be affected by government policies.

Changes in the Natural Rate of Unemployment

Private-sector economists and government agencies need estimates of the natural rate of unemployment both to make forecasts and to conduct policy analyses. Almost all these estimates show that the U.S. natural rate rises and falls over time. For example, the Congressional Budget Office, the independent agency that conducts budget and economic analyses for Congress, believes that the U.S. natural rate of unemployment was 5.3% in 1950, rose to 6.3% by the end of the 1970s, but fell to 4.4% by 2020. In June 2020, the Federal Reserve, which makes projections about the future natural rate, left its projection unchanged at between 4.0% and 4.3% despite the COVID-19 crisis. European countries have experienced even larger swings in their natural rates of unemployment.

What causes the natural rate of unemployment to change? The most important factors are changes in labor force characteristics, changes in labor market institutions, and changes in government policies. Let's look briefly at each factor.

Changes in Labor Force Characteristics In February 2020, before COVID-19, the rate of unemployment in the United States was 3.5%. Young workers, however, had much higher unemployment rates: 11.0% for teenagers and 6.4% for workers aged 20 to 24. Workers aged 25 to 54 had an unemployment rate of only 3.0%.

In general, unemployment rates tend to be lower for experienced than for inexperienced workers. Because experienced workers tend to stay in a given job longer than do inexperienced ones, they have lower frictional unemployment. Also, because older workers are more likely than young workers to be family breadwinners, they have a stronger incentive to find and keep jobs. One reason the natural rate of unemployment rose during the 1970s was a large rise in the number of new workers—children of the post–World War II baby boom, as well as a rising percentage of women, entered the labor force. As Figure 23-11 shows, both the percentage of the labor force less than 25 years old and the percentage

FIGURE 23-11 The Changing Makeup of the U.S. Labor Force, 1950–2020

In the 1970s the percentage of women in the labor force rose rapidly, as did the percentage of those under age 25. These changes reflected the entry of large numbers of women into the paid labor force for the first time and the fact that baby boomers were reaching working age. The natural rate of unemployment may have risen because many of these workers were relatively inexperienced. Today, the labor force is much more experienced, which is one possible reason the natural rate has fallen since the 1970s.

Data from: Bureau of Labor Statistics.

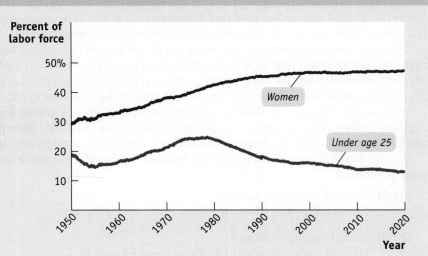

of women in the labor force grew rapidly in the 1970s. By the end of the 1990s, however, the share of women in the labor force had leveled off, and the percentage of workers under 25 had fallen sharply. As a result, the labor force as a whole is more experienced today than it was in the 1970s, one likely reason that the natural rate of unemployment is lower today than in the 1970s.

Changes in Labor Market Institutions As we pointed out earlier, unions that negotiate wages above the equilibrium level can be a source of structural unemployment. Some economists believe that the high natural rate of unemployment in Europe is caused, in part, by strong labor unions. In the United States, a sharp fall in union membership after 1980 may have been one reason the natural rate of unemployment fell between the 1970s and the 1990s.

Other institutional changes may also be at work. For example, some labor economists believe that temporary employment agencies have reduced frictional unemployment by helping match workers to jobs. Likewise, the proliferation of gig economy companies like Uber and TaskRabbit has reduced frictional and structural unemployment by making it easier for workers to earn money quickly and accept wages below a minimum wage, if it is binding.

Technological change, coupled with labor market institutions, can also affect the natural rate of unemployment. Technological change tends to increase the demand for skilled workers who are familiar with the relevant technology and reduce the demand for unskilled workers. Economic theory predicts that wages should increase for skilled workers and decrease for unskilled workers as technology advances. But if wages for unskilled workers cannot go down—say, due to a binding minimum wage—increased structural unemployment, and therefore a higher natural rate of unemployment, will result during periods of faster technological change.

Changes in Government Policies A high minimum wage can cause structural unemployment. Generous unemployment benefits can increase both structural and frictional unemployment as workers feel less pressured financially to immediately accept a job. So government policies intended to help workers can have the undesirable side effect of raising the natural rate of unemployment.

Some government policies, however, may reduce the natural rate. Two examples are job training and employment subsidies. *Job-training programs* are supposed to provide unemployed workers with skills that widen the range of jobs they can perform. *Employment subsidies* are payments either to workers or to employers that provide a financial incentive to accept or offer jobs.

ECONOMICS >> *in Action*
Men Not Working

The United States is a vast country: California is as far from Maine as France is from Siberia. Yet we often talk as if the whole country constituted a single labor market. And to be fair, American workers often move to wherever the jobs are.

But not all workers are able or willing to move. This creates problems for workers who find themselves stuck in a region in which the demand for labor has declined, for whatever reason. Such "stranded" workers are especially likely to suffer from structural unemployment.

Economists who study this issue generally prefer *not* to look at the standard unemployment rate, because people are only counted as unemployed if they're actively seeking work, which may not happen in places that persistently lack employment opportunities. Instead, recent research tends to focus on

The decline in employment in traditionally male-dominated sectors hit some regions harder than others, and has contributed to a surge in social problems.

a different indicator: the percentage of men in what are usually the prime working years, ages 25 to 54, who aren't working.

Why men specifically, rather than adults in general? Despite changing cultural norms, U.S. men remain less likely than women to choose voluntarily to be stay-at-home parents, caregivers, or homemakers. So when you see large numbers of prime-aged men not working, it suggests a troubled labor market.

So where do we see large numbers of men not working? Mainly in a region the economists Benjamin Austin, Edward Glaeser, and Lawrence Summers call the "eastern heartland"—an arc that runs from western Pennsylvania down to Alabama and Mississippi.

A few decades ago, many of this region's residents were still employed in traditional sectors like farming, coal mining, and industries like steel that were closely linked to coal. Since the 1970s, however, those traditional sources of employment have declined, while employers in rising "knowledge-based" industries tend to prefer large metropolitan areas with highly educated workforces.

The result appears to be persistent high structural unemployment in the troubled region. In West Virginia, for example, only 75 percent of prime-aged men are working, compared with almost 90 percent in growing states like New Jersey and Texas.

Sadly, the lack of job opportunities in the eastern heartland appears to be contributing to a variety of social problems, including opioid addiction. Most grimly, the region has seen a surge in mortality, via what the economists Anne Case and Angus Deaton call "deaths of despair"—deaths from suicide, alcohol, and drugs. This demonstrates another reason the state of the job market matters: job opportunities aren't just about money, they're about dignity.

>> *Check Your Understanding* **23-2**
Solutions appear at back of book.

1. Explain the following statements.
   a. Frictional unemployment is higher when the pace of technological advance quickens.
   b. Structural unemployment is higher when the pace of technological advance quickens.
   c. Frictional unemployment accounts for a larger share of total unemployment when the unemployment rate is low.
2. Why does collective bargaining have the same general effect on unemployment as a minimum wage? Illustrate your answer with a diagram.
3. Suppose that at the peak of the business cycle the United States dramatically increases benefits for unemployed workers. Explain what will happen to the natural rate of unemployment.

‖ Inflation and Deflation

As we mentioned in the opening story, macroeconomic policy makers are usually focused on two big evils, unemployment and inflation. It's easy to see why high unemployment is a problem. But why is inflation something to worry about? The answer is that inflation can impose costs on the economy—but not in the way most people think.

The Level of Prices Doesn't Matter . . .

The most common complaint about *inflation*, which is an increase in the price level, is that it makes everyone poorer—after all, a given amount of money buys less. But inflation does not make everyone poorer. To see why, it's helpful to imagine what would happen if the United States did something other countries have done from time to time—replacing the dollar with a new currency.

An example of this kind of currency conversion happened in 2002, when France, like a number of other European countries, replaced its national currency, the franc, with the new pan-European currency, the euro. People turned in their franc coins and notes, and received euro coins and notes in exchange, at a rate of precisely 6.55957 francs per euro. At the same time, all contracts were restated in euros at the same rate of exchange. For example, if a French citizen had a home mortgage debt of 500,000 francs, this became a debt of 500,000/6.55957 = 76,224.51 euros. If a worker's contract specified that they should be paid 100 francs per hour, it became a contract specifying a wage of 100/6.55957 = 15.2449 euros per hour, and so on.

You could imagine doing the same thing in the case of the dollar, replacing the dollar with a "new dollar" at a rate of exchange of, say, 7 to 1. If you owed $140,000 on your home, that would become a debt of 20,000 new dollars. If you had a wage rate of $14 an hour, it would become 2 new dollars an hour, and so on. This would bring the overall U.S. price level back to about what it was in 1962, when John F. Kennedy was president.

So would everyone be richer as a result because prices would be only one-seventh as high? Of course not. Prices would be lower, but so would wages and incomes in general. If you cut a worker's wage to one-seventh of its previous value, but also cut all prices to one-seventh of their previous level, the worker's **real wage**—the wage rate divided by the price level—hasn't changed. In fact, bringing the overall price level back to what it was during the Kennedy administration would have no effect on overall purchasing power because doing so would reduce income exactly as much as it reduced prices.

Conversely, the rise in prices that has actually taken place since the early 1960s hasn't made the United States poorer because it has also raised incomes by the same amount: **real incomes**—incomes divided by the price level—haven't been affected by the rise in overall prices.

The moral of this story is that the *level* of prices doesn't matter: the rise in prices in the U.S. economy over the past 50 years hasn't made us any poorer.

> The **real wage** is the wage rate divided by the price level.
>
> **Real income** is income divided by the price level.

. . . But the Rate of Change of Prices Does

The conclusion that the level of prices doesn't matter might seem to imply that the inflation rate doesn't matter either. But that's not true.

To see why, it's crucial to distinguish between the *level of prices* and the *inflation rate:* the percent increase in the overall level of prices per year. Recall from Chapter 22 that the inflation rate is defined as follows:

$$\text{Inflation rate} = \frac{\text{Price index in year 2} - \text{Price index in year 1}}{\text{Price index in year 1}} \times 100$$

Figure 23-12 highlights the difference between the price level and the inflation rate in the United States over the last half-century, with the price level measured along the left vertical axis and the inflation rate measured along the right vertical axis. In the 2000s, the overall level of prices in the United States was much higher than it had been in 1960—but that, as we've learned, didn't matter. The inflation rate in the 2000s, however, was much lower than in the 1970s—and that almost certainly made the economy richer than it would have been if high inflation had continued.

Economists believe that high rates of inflation impose significant economic costs as resources are wasted. The most important of these costs are *shoe-leather costs, menu costs,* and *unit-of-account costs.* We'll discuss each in turn.

Shoe-Leather Costs People hold money—cash in their wallets and bank deposits—for convenience in making transactions. A high inflation rate, however, discourages people from holding money because the purchasing power of the cash

FIGURE 23-12 The Price Level versus the Inflation Rate, 1960–2020

With the exception of 2009, over the past half-century the price level has continuously increased. But the *inflation rate* — the rate at which prices are rising — has had both ups and downs. And in 2009, the inflation rate briefly turned negative, a phenomenon called *deflation*.

Data from: Bureau of Labor Statistics.

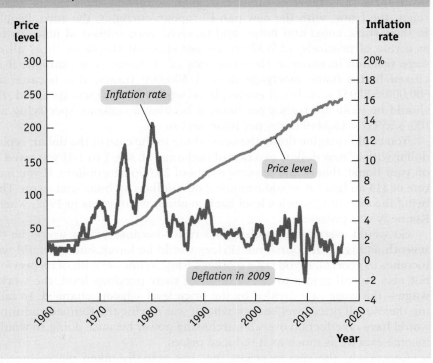

in your wallet and the funds in your bank account steadily erode as the overall level of prices rises. This leads people to move funds into assets they believe will hold value and to reduce the amount of money they hold, often at considerable economic cost. For example, when Venezuelan inflation hit around 1 million percent in 2018, meaning that prices more than doubled every month, people began holding cigarettes and electronic currency (like Bitcoin) instead of Venezuelan currency.

During the most famous of all inflations, the German *hyperinflation* of 1921–1923, merchants employed runners to take their cash to the bank many times a day to convert it into something that would hold its value, such as a stable foreign currency. Hyperinflation occurs when prices rise by 50% or more per month, making an annual inflation rate of around 13,000%. In such cases, to avoid having the purchasing power of their money eroded, people use up valuable resources, such as the labor of the German runners, that could be used productively elsewhere. During the German hyperinflation, so many banking transactions were taking place that the number of employees at German banks nearly quadrupled—from around 100,000 in 1913 to 375,000 in 1923.

More recently, Brazil experienced hyperinflation during the early 1990s; during that episode, the Brazilian banking sector grew so large that it accounted for 15% of GDP, more than twice the size of the financial sector in the United States measured as a share of GDP. The large increase in the Brazilian banking sector needed to cope with the consequences of inflation, which represented a loss of real resources to its society.

Increased costs of transactions caused by inflation are known as **shoe-leather costs,** an allusion to the wear and tear caused by the extra running around that takes place when people are trying to avoid holding money. Shoe-leather costs are substantial in economies with very high inflation, as anyone who has lived in such an economy—say, one suffering inflation of 100% or more per year—can attest. Most estimates suggest, however, that the shoe-leather costs of inflation at the rates seen in the United States—which in peacetime has never had inflation above 15%—are quite small.

Shoe-leather costs are the increased costs of transactions caused by inflation.

Menu Costs In a modern economy, most of the things we buy have a listed price. There's a price listed under each item on a supermarket shelf, a price listed for goods sold on any online retailer's website, such as Amazon or Zappos, and a price listed for each dish on a restaurant's menu. Changing a listed price has a real cost, called a **menu cost.** Although the potential burden imposed by menu costs have diminished in advanced economies as more sales have shifted online and prices can be changed electronically, they still exist. For example, to change prices in a supermarket or a clothing store requires sending clerks to change the listed price with each item. In the face of inflation, of course, firms are forced to change prices more often than they would if the aggregate price level was more or less stable. This means higher costs for the economy as a whole.

In times of very high inflation, menu costs can be substantial. During the Brazilian inflation of the early 1990s, for instance, supermarket workers reportedly spent half of their time replacing old price stickers with new ones. When inflation is high, merchants may decide to stop listing prices in terms of the local currency and use either an artificial unit—in effect, measuring prices relative to one another—or a more stable currency, such as the U.S. dollar. This is exactly what the Israeli real estate market began doing in the mid-1980s: prices were quoted in U.S. dollars, even though payment was made in Israeli shekels. And this is also what happened in Zimbabwe when, in May 2008, official estimates of the inflation rate reached 1,694,000%. By 2009, the government had suspended the Zimbabwean dollar, allowing Zimbabweans to buy and sell goods using foreign currencies.

Menu costs are also present in low-inflation economies, but they are not severe. In low-inflation economies, businesses might update their prices only sporadically—not daily or even more frequently, as is the case in high-inflation or hyperinflation economies.

> The **menu cost** is the real cost of changing a listed price.
>
> The **unit-of-account costs** of inflation are the costs arising from the way inflation makes money a less reliable unit of measurement.

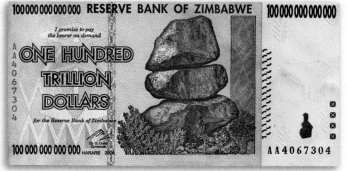

When one hundred trillion dollar bills are in circulation as they were in Zimbabwe, menu costs are substantial.

Unit-of-Account Costs In the Middle Ages, contracts were often specified "in kind": tenants might, for example, be obliged to provide their landlord with a certain number of cattle each year (the phrase *in kind* actually comes from an ancient word for *cattle*). This may have made sense at the time, but it would be an awkward way to conduct modern business. Instead, we state contracts in monetary terms: renters owe a certain number of dollars per month, a company that issues a bond promises to pay the bondholder the dollar value of the bond when it comes due, and so on. We also tend to make our economic calculations in dollars: a family planning its budget, or a small business owner trying to figure out how well the business is doing, makes estimates of the amount of money coming in and going out.

This role of the dollar as a basis for contracts and calculation is called the *unit-of-account* role of money. It's an important aspect of the modern economy. Yet it's a role that can be degraded by inflation, which causes the purchasing power of a dollar to change over time—a dollar next year is worth less than a dollar this year. The effect, many economists argue, is to reduce the quality of economic decisions: the economy as a whole makes less efficient use of its resources because of the uncertainty caused by changes in the unit of account, the dollar. The **unit-of-account costs** of inflation are the costs arising from the way inflation makes money a less reliable unit of measurement.

Unit-of-account costs may be particularly important in the tax system because inflation can distort the measures of income on which taxes are collected. Here's an example: assume that the inflation rate is 10%, so the overall level of prices rises 10% each year. Suppose that a business buys an asset, such as a piece of land, for $100,000, then resells it a year later for $110,000. In a fundamental

The **interest rate** on a loan is the price, calculated as a percentage of the amount borrowed, that lenders charge borrowers the use of their savings for one year.

The **nominal interest rate** is the interest rate expressed in dollar terms.

The **real interest rate** is the nominal interest rate minus the rate of inflation.

sense, the business didn't make a profit on the deal: in real terms, it got no more for the land than it paid for it. But U.S. tax law would say that the business made a capital gain of $10,000, and it would have to pay taxes on that phantom gain.

During the 1970s, when the United States had relatively high inflation, the distorting effects of inflation on the tax system were a serious problem. Some businesses were discouraged from productive investment spending because they found themselves paying taxes on phantom gains. Meanwhile, some unproductive investments became attractive because they led to phantom losses that reduced tax bills. When inflation fell in the 1980s—and tax rates were reduced—these problems became much less important.

Winners and Losers from Inflation

As we've just learned, a high inflation rate imposes costs on the economy through a waste of resources. In addition, inflation can produce winners and losers within the economy. The main reason inflation sometimes helps some people while hurting others is that economic transactions often involve contracts that extend over a period of time, such as loans, and these contracts are normally specified in nominal—that is, in dollar—terms.

In the case of a loan, the borrower receives a certain amount of funds at the beginning, and the loan contract specifies the *interest rate* on the loan and when it must be paid off. The **interest rate** is the return a lender receives for allowing borrowers the use of their savings for one year, calculated as a percentage of the amount borrowed.

But what that dollar is worth in real terms—that is, in terms of purchasing power—depends greatly on the rate of inflation over the intervening years of the loan. Economists summarize the effect of inflation on borrowers and lenders by distinguishing between the *nominal* interest rate and the *real* interest rate. The **nominal interest rate** is the interest rate in dollar terms—for example, the interest rate on a student loan. The **real interest rate** is the nominal interest rate minus the rate of inflation. For example, if a loan carries an interest rate of 8%, but there is 5% inflation, the real interest rate is 8% − 5% = 3%.

When a borrower and a lender enter into a loan contract, the contract is normally written in dollar terms—that is, the interest rate it specifies is a nominal interest rate. But each party to a loan contract has an expectation about the future rate of inflation and therefore an expectation about the real interest rate on the loan. If the actual inflation rate is *higher* than expected, borrowers gain at the expense of lenders: borrowers will repay their loans with funds that have a lower real value than had been expected. Conversely, if the inflation rate is *lower* than expected, lenders will gain at the expense of borrowers: borrowers must repay their loans with funds that have a higher real value than had been expected.

In the modern United States, home mortgages are the most important source of gains and losses from inflation. While some mortgage interest rates are linked to the inflation rate, the vast majority are not, creating big winners and losers when inflation rates have changed unexpectedly. Americans who took out mortgages in the early 1970s quickly found the real cost of their payments reduced by higher-than-expected inflation. In contrast, those who took out mortgages in the early 1990s lost. The inflation rate fell to lower-than-expected levels in the following years and raised the cost of their payments.

Because gains for some and losses for others result from inflation that is either higher or lower than expected, yet another problem arises: uncertainty about the future inflation rate discourages people from entering into any form of long-term contract. This is an additional cost of high inflation, because high rates of inflation are usually unpredictable. In countries with high and uncertain inflation, long-term loans are rare, which makes it difficult in many cases to make long-term investments.

One last point: unexpected *deflation*—a surprise fall in the price level—creates winners and losers, too. Between 1929 and 1933, as the U.S. economy plunged into the Great Depression, the consumer price index fell by 35%. This meant that debtors, including many farmers and homeowners, saw a sharp rise in the real value of their debts, which led to widespread bankruptcy and helped create a banking crisis, as lenders found their customers unable to pay back their loans. And as you can see in Figure 23-12, deflation occurred again in 2009, when the inflation rate fell to −2% at the trough of a deep recession. Like the Great Depression (but to a much lesser extent), the unexpected deflation of 2009 imposed heavy costs on debtors. We will discuss the effects of deflation in more detail in Chapter 31.

> **Disinflation** is the process of bringing the inflation rate down.

Inflation Is Easy. Disinflation Is Hard.

There is not much evidence that a rise in the inflation rate from 2% to 5% would do a great deal of harm to the economy. Still, policy makers generally move forcefully to bring inflation back down when it creeps above 2% or 3%. Why? Because experience shows that bringing the inflation rate down—a process called **disinflation**—is very difficult and costly once a higher rate of inflation has become well established in the economy.

Figure 23-13 shows what happened during two major episodes of disinflation in the United States, in the mid-1970s and in the early 1980s. The horizontal axis shows the unemployment rate. The vertical axis shows *core inflation* over the previous year, a measure that excludes volatile food and energy prices and is widely considered a better measure of underlying inflation than overall consumer prices. Each marker represents the inflation rate and the unemployment rate for one month. In each episode, unemployment and inflation followed a sort of clockwise spiral, with high inflation gradually falling in the face of an extended period of very high unemployment.

According to many economists, these periods of high unemployment that temporarily depressed the economy were necessary to reduce inflation that had become deeply embedded in the economy. The best way to avoid having to put the economy through a wringer to reduce inflation, however, is to avoid having a serious inflation problem in the first place. So, as a form of preventive medicine for the economy, policy makers respond forcefully to signs that inflation may be accelerating.

FIGURE 23-13 The Cost of Disinflation

There were two major periods of disinflation in modern U.S. history, in the mid-1970s and the early 1980s. This figure shows the track of the unemployment rate and the core inflation rate, which excludes food and energy, during these two episodes. In each case bringing inflation down required a temporary but very large increase in the unemployment rate, demonstrating the high cost of disinflation.
Data from: Bureau of Labor Statistics.

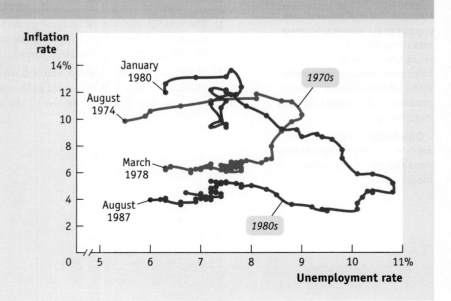

ECONOMICS >> *in Action*
Israel's Experience with Inflation

During a period of high inflation in the mid-1980s, Israelis held very little cash, forcing them to make repeated trips to banks.

It's frequently hard to see the costs of inflation clearly because serious inflation problems are often associated with other problems that disrupt economic life, notably war or political instability (or both). In the mid-1980s, however, Israel experienced a "clean" inflation: there was no war, the government was stable, and there was order in the streets. Yet a series of policy errors led to very high inflation, with prices often rising more than 10% a month.

As it happens, one of the authors spent a month visiting at Tel Aviv University at the height of the inflation, so we can give a first-hand account of the effects.

First, the shoe-leather costs of inflation were substantial. At the time, debit cards had not yet been introduced. So Israelis spent a lot of time in lines at the bank, moving money in and out of accounts that provided high enough interest rates to offset inflation. People walked around with very little cash in their wallets; they had to go to the bank whenever they needed to make even a moderately large cash payment. Banks responded by opening a lot of branches, a costly business expense.

Second, although menu costs weren't that visible to a visitor, what you could see were the efforts businesses made to minimize them. For example, restaurant menus often didn't list prices. Instead, they listed numbers that you had to multiply by another number, written on a chalkboard and changed every day, to figure out the price of a dish.

Finally, it was hard to make decisions because prices changed so much and so often. It was a common experience to walk out of a store because prices were 25% higher than at one's usual shopping destination, only to discover that prices had just been increased 25% there, too.

>> Quick Review

• The **real wage** and **real income** are unaffected by the level of prices.

• Inflation, like unemployment, is a major concern of policy makers — so much so that in the past they have accepted high unemployment as the price of reducing inflation.

• While the overall level of prices is irrelevant, high rates of inflation impose real costs on the economy: **shoe-leather costs, menu costs,** and **unit-of-account costs.**

• The **interest rate** is the return a lender receives for use of their funds for a year. The **real interest rate** is equal to the **nominal interest rate** minus the inflation rate. As a result, unexpectedly high inflation helps borrowers and hurts lenders. With high and uncertain inflation, people will often avoid long-term investments.

• **Disinflation** is very costly, so policy makers try to avoid getting into situations of high inflation in the first place.

>> Check Your Understanding 23-3

Solutions appear at back of book.

1. The widespread use of technology has revolutionized the banking industry, making it much easier for customers to access and manage their assets. Does this mean that the shoe-leather costs of inflation are higher or lower than they used to be?

2. Most people in the United States have grown accustomed to a modest inflation rate of around 2% to 3%. Who would gain and who would lose if inflation unexpectedly came to a complete stop over the next 15 or 20 years?

ABIR SULTAN/Newscom/European Pressphoto Agency/Jerusalem/Israel

TaskRabbit

STEPHEN LAM/REUTERS/Newscom

"Moving is the worst. Yard work is the worst. Building IKEA furniture is the worst." So began a 2015 report on TaskRabbit, a company founded in 2008 (under the name RunMyErrand), that helps people hire others to do their chores. As of 2019 there were about 140,000 of these freelancers, whom the company calls Taskers, and TaskRabbit operated in 53 U.S. cities, Great Britain, and Canada.

Why would becoming a Tasker seem appealing to some workers? The great majority of Taskers are part-time workers, who want flexibility in their employment; the company's pitch to potential Taskers contains the slogan "Earn money your way," and features testimonials from workers who combined employment with parenting, careers in the arts, and so on.

Working part time for a variety of clients isn't a new phenomenon. On urban street corners across the United States, workers still line up early each morning in the hope of getting day jobs in industries like construction, where the need for workers fluctuates, sometimes unpredictably. For more skilled workers, there are numerous online resources as well as temporary staffing agencies, like Allegis Group, that provide workers on a subcontracting basis, from a few days to months at a time. And some people still find temporary jobs by calling numbers listed in classified ads, or even going door to door.

But TaskRabbit—founded the year after Apple introduced its first iPhone—tries to use the ubiquity of smartphones to simplify the process. Originally it was set up as a kind of auction market, in which potential employers and workers placed bids, but since 2014 it has relied on a streamlined system that is very similar to the way car services like Uber or Lyft match riders with willing drivers. TaskRabbit's app let those seeking help make their needs known simply by tapping on one of a few common chores; potential workers can then offer to do jobs that match the locations and skills they have put in their profiles, again simply by tapping on jobs that appear on their smartphones. (They have already specified their hourly rate.) The process takes a lot less time and effort than standing on street corners, pounding the pavement, or performing online job searches.

How big a deal are enterprises like TaskRabbit? Some observers suggest that we're seeing the rise of a *gig economy*, in which large numbers of people freelance, moving from job to job rather than being formal employees of a large firm. There's probably some hype in these pronouncements, but real change does seem to be happening. So far, however, there isn't a lot of evidence for a major shift in the nature of employment.

QUESTIONS FOR THOUGHT

1. How is the matching of job-seekers and employers through services like TaskRabbit likely to affect frictional unemployment?

2. What is the likely effect of such services on the number of people considered to be in the labor force?

3. Some analysts suggest that most freelancers have other jobs, and only do gig economy work on the side. How does that statement help explain the lack of clear evidence for a growing gig economy?

SUMMARY

1. The two principal objectives of macroeconomic policy are price stability (a low, but positive, level of inflation) and low unemployment.

2. **Employment** is the number of people employed; **unemployment** is the number of people unemployed and actively looking for work. Their sum is equal to the **labor force,** and the **labor force participation rate** is the percentage of the population age 16 or older that is in the labor force.

3. The **unemployment rate,** the percentage of the labor force that is unemployed and actively looking for work, can both overstate and understate the true level of unemployment. It can overstate because it counts as unemployed those who are continuing to search for a job despite having been offered one. It can understate because it ignores frustrated workers, such as **discouraged workers, marginally attached workers,** and the **underemployed.** In addition, the unemployment rate varies greatly among different groups in the population; it is typically higher for younger workers and for workers near retirement age than for workers in their prime working years.

4. There is a negative relationship between the growth rate of GDP and the change in unemployment. During a recession, when the GDP growth rate is less than zero, unemployment rises; the deeper the recession, the greater the rise in unemployment. During a strong expansion, when the GDP growth rate is above average, unemployment falls; the stronger the expansion, the greater the fall in unemployment. A **jobless recovery** occurs when the GDP growth rate is positive but below average, resulting in rising unemployment.

5. Job creation and destruction, as well as voluntary job separations, lead to natural unemployment, composed of **frictional unemployment** and **structural unemployment. Job search** leads to frictional unemployment. Structural unemployment arises when the prevailing wage rate is above the equilibrium wage rate, resulting in persistent unemployment. It is due to a number of factors, such as **minimum wages, unions, efficiency wages,** government policies, and mismatch between employers and employees. As a result, the **natural rate of unemployment,** the sum of frictional and structural unemployment, is well above zero, even when jobs are plentiful.

6. The actual unemployment rate is equal to the natural rate of unemployment, the share of unemployment that is independent of the business cycle, plus **cyclical unemployment,** the share of unemployment that depends on fluctuations in the business cycle.

7. The natural rate of unemployment changes over time, largely in response to changes in labor force characteristics, labor market institutions, and government policies.

8. Inflation does not, as many assume, make everyone poorer by raising the level of prices. That's because wages and incomes are adjusted to take into account a rising price level, leaving **real wages** and **real income** unaffected. However, a high inflation rate imposes overall costs on the economy: **shoe-leather costs, menu costs,** and **unit-of-account costs.**

9. Inflation can produce winners and losers within the economy, because long-term contracts are generally written in dollar terms. The **interest rate** specified in a loan is typically a **nominal interest rate,** which differs from the **real interest rate** due to inflation. A higher-than-expected inflation rate is good for borrowers and bad for lenders. A lower-than-expected inflation rate is good for lenders and bad for borrowers.

10. Many believe policies that depress the economy and produce high unemployment are necessary to reduce embedded inflation. Because **disinflation** is very costly, policy makers try to prevent inflation from becoming excessive in the first place.

KEY TERMS

Employment, p. 652
Unemployment, p. 652
Labor force, p. 652
Labor force participation rate, p. 652
Unemployment rate, p. 653
Discouraged workers, p. 653
Marginally attached workers, p. 654
Underemployment, p. 654
Jobless recovery, p. 657

Job search, p. 659
Frictional unemployment, p. 659
Structural unemployment, p. 660
Minimum wage, p. 661
Union, p. 662
Efficiency wages, p. 662
Natural rate of unemployment, p. 663
Cyclical unemployment, p. 663
Real wage, p. 667

Real income, p. 667
Shoe-leather costs, p. 668
Menu costs, p. 669
Unit-of-account costs, p. 669
Interest rate, p. 670
Nominal interest rate, p. 670
Real interest rate, p. 670
Disinflation, p. 671

1. Each month, usually on the first Friday of the month, the Bureau of Labor Statistics releases the Employment Situation Summary for the previous month. Go to www.bls.gov and find the latest report. On the Bureau of Labor Statistics home page, at the top of the page, select the "Economic Releases" tab, find "Latest Releases," and select "Employment Situation." You will find the Employment Situation Summary listed at the top. How does the current unemployment rate compare to the rate one month earlier? How does the current unemployment rate compare to the rate one year earlier?

2. In 2018, the Bureau of Labor Statistics released the report "Contingent and Alternative Employment Arrangements," which included independent contractors, those in the gig economy. The report found 16.5 million people working in contingent or independent jobs. Surprisingly, the share of all workers classified as either contingent or independent contractors had declined from 11.5% in 2005 to 10.7% in 2017. The BLS report stated, "The government figures only count workers whose gig arrangements are their main job, and only includes those who've worked in that job in the last week." In what ways did the BLS understate the reported numbers? Who was likely being omitted from these calculations?

1. In general, how do changes in the unemployment rate vary with changes in real GDP? After several quarters of a severe recession, explain why we might observe a decrease in the official unemployment rate. Explain why we could see an increase in the official unemployment rate after several quarters of a strong expansion.

2. In each of the following situations, what type of unemployment is Melanie facing?

   a. After completing a complex programming project, Melanie is laid off. Her prospects for a new job requiring similar skills are good, and she has signed up with a programmer placement service. She has passed up offers for low-paying jobs.

   b. When Melanie and her co-workers refused to accept pay cuts, her employer outsourced their programming tasks to workers in another country. This phenomenon is occurring throughout the programming industry.

   c. Due to the current slump, Melanie has been laid off from her programming job. Her employer promises to rehire her when business picks up.

3. Part of the information released in the Employment Situation Summary concerns how long individuals have been unemployed. Go to www.bls.gov to find the latest report. Use the same technique as in Practice Questions Problem 1 to find the Employment Situation Summary. Near the end of the Employment Situation, click on Table A-12, titled "Unemployed persons by duration of unemployment." Use the seasonally adjusted numbers to answer the following questions.

   a. How many workers were unemployed less than 5 weeks? What percentage of all unemployed workers do these workers represent? How do these numbers compare to the previous month's data?

   b. How many workers were unemployed for 27 or more weeks? What percentage of all unemployed workers do these workers represent? How do these numbers compare to the previous month's data?

   c. How long has the average worker been unemployed (average duration, in weeks)? How does this compare to the average for the previous month's data?

   d. Comparing the latest month for which there are data with the previous month, has the problem of long-term unemployment improved or deteriorated?

4. A country's labor force is the sum of the number of employed and unemployed workers. The accompanying table provides data on the size of the labor force and the number of unemployed workers for different regions of the United States.

Region	Labor force (thousands)		Unemployed (thousands)	
	December 2018	December 2019	December 2018	December 2019
Northeast	28,536	28,729	1,083	1,080
South	60,112	60,909	2,183	2,074
Midwest	34,971	35,063	1,275	1,244
West	38,704	39,166	1,608	1,489

Data from: Bureau of Labor Statistics.

   a. Calculate the number of workers employed in each of the regions in December 2018 and December 2019. Use your answers to calculate the change in the total number of workers employed between December 2018 and December 2019.

   b. For each region, calculate the growth in the labor force from December 2018 to December 2019.

   c. Compute unemployment rates in the different regions of the country in December 2018 and December 2019.

   d. What can you infer about the fall in unemployment rates over this period? Was it caused by a net gain in the number of jobs or by a large fall in the number of people seeking jobs?

5. Access the Discovering Data exercise for Chapter 23 Problem 5 online to answer the following questions.

   a. What is the current federal minimum wage?

   b. In what year was the federal minimum wage last increased?

   c. What is the current value for the real minimum wage?

   d. In what year was the real minimum wage the highest? The lowest?

   e. In general, since 1970, how has the purchasing power of the minimum wage changed over time?

6. In which of the following cases is it more likely for efficiency wages to exist? Why?

   a. Jane and her boss work as a team selling ice cream.

   b. Jane sells ice cream without any direct supervision by her boss.

   c. Jane speaks Korean and sells ice cream in a neighborhood in which Korean is the primary language. It is difficult to find another worker who speaks Korean.

7. How will the following changes affect the natural rate of unemployment?

   a. The government reduces the time during which an unemployed worker can receive unemployment benefits.

   b. More teenagers focus on their studies and do not look for jobs until after college.

   c. Greater access to the internet leads both potential employers and potential employees to use the internet to list and find jobs.

   d. Union membership declines.

8. With its tradition of a job for life for most citizens, Japan once had a much lower unemployment rate than that of the United States; from 1960 to 1995, the unemployment rate in Japan exceeded 3% only once. However, since the crash of its stock market in 1989 and slow economic growth in the 1990s, the job-for-life system has broken down and unemployment rose to more than 5% in 2003.

   a. Explain the likely effect of the breakdown of the job-for-life system in Japan on the Japanese natural rate of unemployment.

   b. As the accompanying diagram shows, the rate of growth of real GDP picked up in Japan after 2001 and before the global economic crisis of 2007–2009. Explain the likely effect of this increase in real GDP growth on the unemployment rate. Was the likely cause of the change in the unemployment rate during this period a change in the natural rate of unemployment or a change in the cyclical unemployment rate?

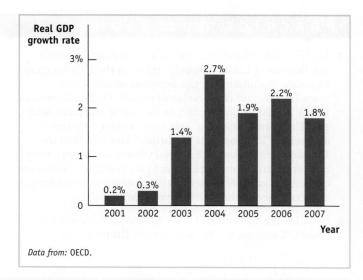

Data from: OECD.

9. In the following examples, is inflation creating winners and losers at no net cost to the economy or is inflation imposing a net cost on the economy? If a net cost is being imposed, which type of cost is involved?

   a. When inflation is expected to be high, workers get paid more frequently and make more trips to the bank.

   b. Lanwei is reimbursed by her company for her work-related travel expenses. Sometimes, however, the company takes a long time to reimburse her. So when inflation is high, she is less willing to travel for her job.

   c. Hector has a mortgage with a fixed nominal interest rate of 6% that he took out five years ago. Over the years, the inflation rate has crept up unexpectedly to its present level of 7%.

   d. In response to unexpectedly high inflation, the manager of Cozy Cottages of Cape Cod must reprint and resend expensive color brochures correcting the price of rentals this season.

10. The accompanying diagram shows the interest rate on one-year loans and inflation from 2005 to 2020 in the economy of Albernia. When would one-year loans have been especially attractive and why?

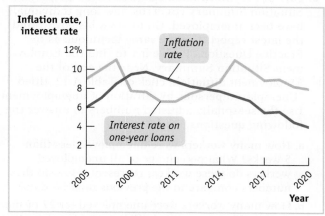

11. The accompanying table provides the inflation rate in the year 2005 and the average inflation rate over the period 2006–2019 for seven different countries.

Country	Inflation rate in 2005	Average inflation rate in 2006–2019
Brazil	6.87%	5.47%
China	1.77	2.68
France	1.74	1.23
Indonesia	10.45	5.83
Japan	-0.28	0.35
Turkey	8.18	9.53
United States	3.39	1.95

Data from: IMF.

a. Given the expected relationship between average inflation and menu costs, rank the countries in descending order of menu costs using average inflation over the period 2006–2019.

b. Rank the countries in order of inflation rates that most favored borrowers with ten-year loans that were taken out in 2005. Assume that the loans were agreed upon with the expectation that the inflation rate for 2006 to 2019 would be the same as the inflation rate in 2005.

c. Did borrowers who took out ten-year loans in Japan gain or lose overall versus lenders? Explain.

12. Access the Discovering Data exercise for Chapter 23 Problem 12 online to answer the following questions.

a. What is the current level of employment for individuals without a high school diploma?

b. How much has employment changed for high school graduates from 2007 through 2016?

c. Since 2007, which education group has experienced the largest increase in employment?

d. Since the end of the Great Recession in 2009, how has employment changed for the different education levels? Calculate the net gain (or loss) of jobs for each category to answer.

e. What percent of the employed had a bachelor's degree in January 1992? What percent has a bachelor's degree today?

f. Calculate the change in the share of employment by education level since 1992.

13. The accompanying diagram shows the inflation rate in the United Kingdom from 1980 to 2019.

a. Between 1980 and 1985, policy makers in the United Kingdom worked to lower the inflation rate. What would you predict happened to unemployment between 1980 and 1985?

b. Policy makers in the United Kingdom react forcefully when the inflation rate rises above a target rate of 2%. Why would it be harmful if inflation rose from 0.7% (the level in 2019) to, say, a level of 5%?

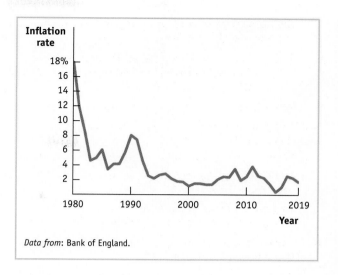

Data from: Bank of England.

WORK IT OUT

14. There is only one labor market in Profunctia. All workers have the same skills, and all firms hire workers with these skills. Use the accompanying diagram, which shows the supply of and demand for labor, to answer the following questions. Illustrate each answer with a diagram.

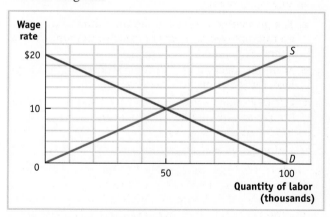

a. What is the equilibrium wage rate in Profunctia? At this wage rate, what are the level of employment, the size of the labor force, and the unemployment rate?

b. If the government of Profunctia sets a minimum wage equal to $12, what will be the level of employment, the size of the labor force, and the unemployment rate?

c. If unions bargain with the firms in Profunctia and set a wage rate equal to $14, what will be the level of employment, the size of the labor force, and the unemployment rate?

d. If the concern for retaining workers and encouraging high-quality work leads firms to set a wage rate equal to $16, what will be the level of employment, the size of the labor force, and the unemployment rate? ■

24 Long-Run Economic Growth

 THE SMOG OF PROSPERITY

DELHI, THE CAPITAL OF INDIA, has terrible air quality — which is a bad thing. But it's a by-product of a very good thing: the remarkable growth of India's economy over the past few decades.

Until around 1980, India's economic story was one of disappointment: living standards weren't much higher than they had been when the nation won independence in 1947. But after 1980 the economy took off. India is still very poor by U.S. or European standards, but it has a rapidly growing middle class, which can finally afford the things middle-class families tend to want everywhere: bigger houses, household appliances like washing machines and, of course, cars.

As recently as 2001 India had only 53 motor vehicles per 1,000 inhabitants, around a tenth as many as in advanced countries. By 2015, however, that number had more than tripled.

Hence the air quality problem. The streets of Delhi, which has 18 million residents, are now clogged with cars and trucks; the city is also surrounded with factories producing consumer goods and power plants supplying the electricity to run them.

And all these cars, factories, and power plants emit spectacular amounts of pollution. In November 2017, visibility in much of Delhi dropped to a few feet, and health experts said that just being outdoors during the Great Smog of Delhi was the equivalent of smoking 50 cigarettes a day. Nor was this a one-time event. In November 2019 another extended period of severe pollution forced the city to close all its schools.

As we said, however, Delhi's air quality crisis is a by-product of a very good thing, economic success. And if the experience of other countries is any guide, India will eventually bring its air pollution under control. Beijing, the capital of China, is even bigger than Delhi, with considerably more cars, and it used to have a severe air quality problem, too. But China, which has had even more economic success than India, has begun to put effective pollution controls in place, and this has helped literally clear the air. Meanwhile, China's living standards have continued to rise.

And despite the pollution, India's recent history is a hugely impressive example of *long-run economic growth* — a sustained increase in output per capita. True, India is still a relatively poor country; but that's only because other nations began the process of long-run economic growth many decades ago. In the case of the United States and European countries, long-run economic growth began more than a century and a half ago.

Many economists have argued that long-run economic growth — why it happens and how to achieve it — is the single most important issue in macroeconomics because of its direct effect on living standards.

In this chapter, we present some facts about long-run growth, look at the factors that economists believe determine the pace at which long-run growth takes place, and examine how government policies can help or hinder growth. We will also address questions about the environmental sustainability of long-run growth. ●

Rapid, uncontrolled economic growth has resulted in much higher living standards in places like Delhi, but at the cost of very high levels of pollution.

DOMINIQUE FAGET/Getty Images

WHAT YOU WILL LEARN

- Why is long-run economic growth measured as the increase in real GDP per capita? How has real GDP per capita changed over time in different countries?
- Why is **productivity** the key to long-run economic growth? How is productivity driven by **physical capital, human capital,** and **technological progress?**
- Why do long-run growth rates differ so much among countries?
- How does growth vary among several important regions of the world? Why does the **convergence hypothesis** apply to economically advanced countries?
- How do scarcity of natural resources and environmental degradation pose a challenge to **sustainable long-run economic growth?**

‖ Comparing Economies Across Time and Space

Before we analyze the sources of long-run economic growth, it's useful to have a sense of just how much the U.S. economy has grown over time and how large the gaps are between wealthy countries like the United States and countries that have yet to achieve comparable growth. So let's take a look at the numbers.

Real GDP per Capita

The key statistic used to track economic growth is *real GDP per capita*—real GDP divided by the population size. We focus on GDP because, as we learned in Chapter 22, GDP measures the total value of an economy's production of final goods and services as well as the income earned in that economy in a given year. We use *real* GDP because we want to separate changes in the quantity of goods and services from the effects of a rising price level. We focus on real GDP *per capita* because we want to isolate the effect of changes in the population. For example, other things equal, an increase in the population lowers the standard of living for the average person—there are now more people to share a given amount of real GDP. An increase in real GDP that only matches an increase in population leaves the average standard of living unchanged.

Although we also learned that growth in real GDP per capita should not be a policy goal in and of itself, it does serve as a very useful summary measure of a country's economic progress over time. Figure 24-1 shows real GDP per capita for the United States, India, and China, measured in 2011 dollars, from 1900 to 2016. The vertical axis is drawn on a logarithmic scale so that equal percent changes in real GDP per capita across countries are the same size in the graph.

To give a sense of how much the U.S. economy grew during the last century, Table 24-1 shows real GDP per capita at selected years, expressed two ways: as a percentage of the 1900 level and as a percentage of the 2016 level. In 1920, the U.S. economy already produced 136% as much per person as it did in 1900. In 2016, it produced 848% as much per person as it did in 1900, more than an eightfold increase. Alternatively, in 1900 the U.S. economy produced only 12% as much per person as it did in 2016.

FIGURE 24-1 Economic Growth in the United States, India, and China over the Past Century

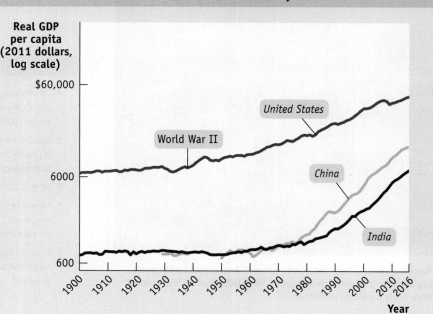

Real GDP per capita from 1900 to 2016, measured in 2011 dollars, is shown for the United States, India, and China. Equal percent changes in real GDP per capita are drawn the same size. As the steeper slopes of the lines representing China and India show, since 1980 India and China had a much higher growth rate than the United States. The standard of living achieved in the United States in 1900 was attained by China in 2000 and by India in 2016 (approximately for both). Note that the break in China data from 1940 to 1950 is due to war.

Data from: Maddison Project Database, version 2018. Jutta Bolt, Robert Inklaar, Herman de Jong, and Jan Luiten van Zanden (2018), "Rebasing 'Maddison': New income comparisons and the shape of long-run economic development," Maddison Project Working Paper 10.

The income of the typical family normally grows more or less in proportion to per capita income. For example, a 1% increase in real GDP per capita corresponds, roughly, to a 1% increase in the income of the median or typical family—a family at the center of the income distribution. In 2016, the median American household had an income of about $57,500. Since Table 24-1 tells us that real GDP per capita in 1900 was only 12% of its 2016 level, a typical family in 1900 probably had a purchasing power only 12% as large as the purchasing power of a typical family in 2016. That's around $6,250 in 2016 dollars, representing a standard of living that we would now consider severe poverty. Today's typical American family, if transported back to the United States of 1900, would feel quite a lot of deprivation.

Many people in the world have a standard of living equal to or lower than that of the average American of many generations ago. That's the message about China and India in Figure 24-1: despite dramatic economic growth in China over the last four decades and the more recent acceleration of economic growth in India, China's per capita GDP is only about as high as America's was in 1930, while India is roughly at our level in 1900.

You can get a sense of how poor much of the world remains by looking at Figure 24-2, a map of the world in which countries are classified according to their 2018 levels of GDP per capita, in U.S. dollars. As you can see, in large parts of the world, people have very low incomes. Generally speaking, the countries of Europe and North America, as well as a few in the Pacific, have high incomes. Many Asian countries, including China and India, have experienced rapid economic growth, moving them into the middle-income categories. Africa, however, is dominated by countries with GDP less than $5,000 per capita. In fact, about 25% of the world's people live in countries with a lower standard of living than the United States had a century ago.

Growth Rates

How did the United States manage to produce over eight times as much real GDP per person in 2016 than in 1900? A little bit at a time. Long-run economic growth

TABLE 24-1 U.S. Real GDP per Capita

Year	Percentage of 1900 real GDP per capita	Percentage of 2016 real GDP per capita
1900	100%	12%
1920	136	16
1940	181	21
1980	474	56
2000	734	87
2016	848	100

Data from: Maddison Project Database, version 2018. Jutta Bolt, Robert Inklaar, Herman de Jong, and Jan Luiten van Zanden (2018), "Rebasing 'Maddison': New income comparisons and the shape of long-run economic development," Maddison Project Working Paper 10.

FIGURE 24-2 Incomes Around the World, 2018

Although the countries of Europe and North America — along with a few in the Pacific — have high incomes, much of the world is still very poor. Today, about a quarter of the world's population lives in countries with a lower standard of living than the United States had a century ago.

Data from: World Development Indicators, World Bank.

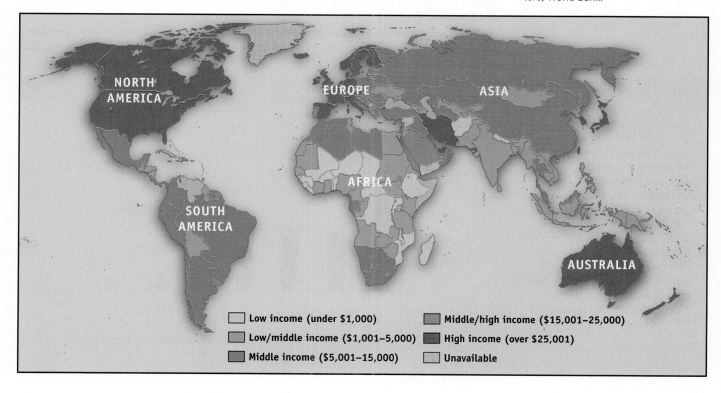

- ☐ Low income (under $1,000)
- ☐ Low/middle income ($1,001–5,000)
- ■ Middle income ($5,001–15,000)
- ▨ Middle/high income ($15,001–25,000)
- ■ High income (over $25,001)
- ☐ Unavailable

According to the **Rule of 70,** the time it takes a variable that grows gradually over time to double is approximately 70 divided by that variable's annual growth rate.

is normally a gradual process in which real GDP per capita grows at most a few percent per year. From 1900 to 2016, real GDP per capita in the United States increased an average of 1.9% each year.

To have a sense of the relationship between the annual growth rate of real GDP per capita and the long-run change in real GDP per capita, it's helpful to keep in mind the **Rule of 70,** a mathematical formula that tells us how long it takes real GDP per capita, or any other variable that grows gradually over time, to double. The approximate answer is:

(24-1) $\text{Number of years for variable to double} = \dfrac{70}{\text{Annual growth rate of variable}}$

(Note that the Rule of 70 can only be applied to a positive growth rate.) So, if real GDP per capita grows at 1% per year, it will take 70 years to double. If it grows at 2% per year, it will take only 35 years to double. In fact, U.S. real GDP per capita rose, on average, 1.9% per year over the last century.

Applying the Rule of 70 to this information implies that it should have taken 37 years for real GDP per capita to double; it would have taken 111 years—three periods of 37 years each—for U.S. real GDP per capita to double three times. That is, the Rule of 70 implies that over the course of 111 years, U.S. real GDP per capita should have increased by a factor of $2 \times 2 \times 2 = 8$. And this does turn out to be a pretty good approximation of reality. Between 1900 and 2016—a period of 116 years—real GDP per capita rose just over eightfold.

Figure 24-3 shows the average annual rate of growth of real GDP per capita for selected countries from 1980 to 2018. Some countries were notable success stories: for example, China, though still quite poor, has made spectacular progress. India, although not matching China's performance, has also achieved impressive growth. The same is true for Bangladesh, as discussed in the following Economics in Action.

Some countries, though, have had very disappointing growth. Argentina was once considered a wealthy nation. In the early years of the twentieth century, it was in the same league as the United States and Canada. But since then it has lagged far behind more dynamic economies. And still others, like Venezuela, have slid backward.

What explains these differences in growth rates? To answer that question, we need to examine the sources of long-run economic growth, which we turn to next.

FIGURE 24-3 Comparing Recent Growth Rates

The average annual rate of growth of real GDP per capita from 1980 to 2018 is shown here for selected countries. China and, to a lesser extent, India and Ireland achieved impressive growth. The United States and France had moderate growth. Once considered an economically advanced country, Argentina had more sluggish growth. Still others, such as Venezuela, slid backward.

Data from: World Development Indicators.

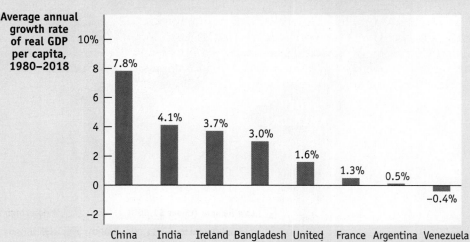

PITFALLS

CHANGE IN LEVEL VERSUS RATE OF CHANGE

When studying economic growth, it's important to understand the difference between a *change in level* and a *rate of change*. When we say that real GDP "grew," economists mean that the *level* of real GDP increased at a certain point in time. For example, we might say that U.S. real GDP grew during 2019 by $435 billion.

But statements about economic growth over a period of years almost always refer to changes in the growth rate. For example, if we knew the level of U.S. real GDP in 2018, we could also represent the amount of 2019 growth in terms of a

rate of change. For example, if U.S. real GDP in 2018 had been $18,638 billion, then U.S. real GDP in 2019 would have been $18,638 billion + $435 billion = $19,073 billion. We could calculate the rate of change, or the growth rate, of U.S. real GDP during 2019 as: (($19,073 billion − $18,638 billion) / $18,638 billion) × 100 = ($435 billion / $18,638 billion) × 100 = 2.3%. So when we say that "U.S. growth fell during the 1970s," we mean that the U.S. growth rate of real GDP was lower in the 1970s compared to the 1960s. When we say that "growth accelerated during the early 1990s," we mean that the growth rate increased year after year in the early 1990s—for example, going from 3% to 3.5% to 4%.

ECONOMICS >> *in Action* 🌐
An Economic Breakthrough in Bangladesh

Western news media rarely mention Bangladesh: it's not a political hot spot, it doesn't have oil, and it's overshadowed by its immense neighbor, India. Yet it is home to more than 160 million people—and although it is still very poor, it is nonetheless one of the greatest economic success stories of the past generation.

As recently as the 1980s, real GDP per capita in Bangladesh—which achieved independence from Pakistan in 1971, after a brutal war—was barely higher than it had been in 1950, when the country was so poor that it literally lived on the edge of starvation. In the early 1990s, however, the nation began a process of political and economic reform, making the transition from military rule to democracy, freeing up markets, and achieving monetary and fiscal stability. And growth took off, most notably with the rise of Bangladesh as a major exporter of clothing to Western markets. Real GDP per capita tripled over the period from 1990 to 2019. Other measures also showed dramatic improvements in the quality of life: life expectancy rose by a dozen years, child mortality fell by 70%, and school enrollment rose sharply, especially for girls.

Make no mistake, Bangladesh is still incredibly poor by American standards. Wages are very low although rising, while working conditions are often terrible and dangerous—a point highlighted in 2013, when a factory complex collapsed, killing more than a thousand workers. But compared with its own past, Bangladesh has achieved a lot of progress—and demonstrated that economic growth brings real human benefits, too.

Although Bangladesh remains a very poor country, a high growth rate has improved living standards over the last 25 years.

Michael Runkel/AGE Fotostock

>> Check Your Understanding 24-1
Solutions appear at back of book.

1. Why do economists use real GDP per capita to measure economic progress rather than some other measure, such as nominal GDP per capita or real GDP?

2. Apply the Rule of 70 to the data in Figure 24-3 to determine how many years it will take each of the countries listed there (except Venezuela) to double its real GDP per capita. Would India's real GDP per capita exceed that of the United States in the future if growth rates remain as shown in Figure 24-3? Why or why not?

>> Quick Review

• Economic growth is measured using real GDP per capita.

• In the United States, real GDP per capita increased eightfold since 1900, resulting in a large increase in living standards.

• Many countries have real GDP per capita much lower than that of the United States. About 25% of the world's population has living standards worse than those existing in the United States in the early 1900s.

• The long-term rise in real GDP per capita is the result of gradual growth. The **Rule of 70** tells us how many years at a given annual rate of growth it takes to double real GDP per capita.

• Growth rates of real GDP per capita differ substantially among nations.

Labor productivity, often referred to simply as **productivity,** is output per worker.

Physical capital consists of human-made resources such as buildings and machines.

3. Although China and India currently have growth rates much higher than the U.S. growth rate, the typical Chinese or Indian household is far poorer than the typical American household. Explain why.

‖ The Sources of Long-Run Growth

One of our fundamental principles of economics is that *increases in economic potential lead to economic growth over time.* More specifically, long-run economic growth depends almost entirely on one ingredient: rising *productivity.* However, a number of factors affect the growth of productivity. Let's look first at why productivity is the key ingredient and then examine what affects it.

The Crucial Importance of Productivity

Sustained economic growth occurs only when the amount of output produced by the average worker increases steadily. The term **labor productivity,** or **productivity** for short, is used to refer either to output per worker or, in some cases, to output per hour. (The number of hours worked by an average worker differs to some extent across countries, although this isn't an important factor in the difference between living standards in, say, India and the United States.) For the economy as a whole, productivity—output per worker—is simply real GDP divided by the number of people working.

You might wonder why we say that higher productivity is the only source of long-run growth. Can't an economy also increase its real GDP per capita by putting more of the population to work? The answer is, yes, but . . .

For short periods of time, an economy can experience a burst of growth in output per capita by putting a higher percentage of the population to work. That happened in the United States during World War II, when millions of women who previously worked only in the home entered the paid workforce. The percentage of adult civilians employed outside the home rose from 50% in 1941 to 58% in 1944, and you can see the resulting bump in real GDP per capita during those years in Figure 24-1.

Over the longer run, however, the rate of employment growth is never very different from the rate of population growth. Over the course of the twentieth century, for example, the population of the United States rose at an average rate of 1.3% per year and employment rose 1.5% per year. Real GDP per capita rose 1.9% per year; of that, 1.7%—that is, almost 90% of the total—was the result of rising productivity. In general, overall real GDP can grow because of population growth, but any large increase in real GDP *per capita* must be the result of increased output *per worker.* That is, it must be due to higher productivity.

So increased productivity is the key to long-run economic growth. But what leads to higher productivity?

Explaining Growth in Productivity

There are three main reasons why the average U.S. worker today produces far more than their counterpart a century ago. First, the modern worker has far more *physical capital,* such as machinery and office space, to work with. Second, the modern worker is much better educated and so possesses much more *human capital.* Finally, modern firms have the advantage of a century's *technological progress.*

Let's look at each of these three sources of productivity growth.

Increases in Physical Capital Economists define **physical capital** as manufactured resources such as buildings and machines. Physical capital makes workers more productive. For example, a worker operating a backhoe can dig a lot more feet of trench per day than one equipped only with a shovel.

The average U.S. private-sector worker today is backed up by nearly $400,000 worth of physical capital—far more than a U.S. worker had 100 years ago and far more than the average worker in most other countries has today.

Increase in Human Capital It's not enough for a worker to have good equipment—they must also know what to do with it. **Human capital** refers to the improvement in labor created by the education and knowledge embodied in the workforce.

The human capital of the United States has increased dramatically over the past century. A century ago, although most Americans were able to read and write, very few had an extensive education. In 1910, only 13.5% of Americans over 25 had graduated from high school and only 3% had four-year college degrees. By 2018, the percentages were 90% and 35%, respectively. It would be impossible to run today's economy with a population as poorly educated as the American populace a century ago.

Analyses based on *growth accounting*, described later in this chapter, suggest that education—and its effect on productivity—is an even more important determinant of growth than increases in physical capital.

Technological Progress Probably the most important driver of productivity growth is **technological progress,** which is broadly defined as an advance in the technical means of the production of goods and services. We'll see shortly how economists measure the impact of technology on growth. Workers today are able to produce more than those in the past, even with the same amount of physical and human capital, because technology has advanced over time. It's important to realize that economically important technological progress need not be flashy or rely on cutting-edge science.

Historians have noted that past economic growth has been driven not only by major inventions, such as the railroad or the semiconductor chip, but also by thousands of modest innovations, such as the precut cardboard boxes used to deliver practically everything we order online, which were invented in 1890, and the Post-it® note, introduced in 1980, which has had surprisingly large benefits for office productivity.

Experts attribute much of a productivity surge that took place in the United States from about 1995 to 2005 to new technology adopted by service-producing companies like Walmart rather than to high-technology companies.

Accounting for Growth: The Aggregate Production Function

Productivity is higher, other things equal, when workers are equipped with more physical capital, more human capital, better technology, or any combination of the three. But can we put numbers to these effects? To do this, economists make use of estimates of the **aggregate production function,** which shows how productivity depends on the quantities of physical capital per worker and human capital per worker as well as the state of technology.

In general, all three factors tend to rise over time, as workers are equipped with more machinery, receive more education, and benefit from technological advances. What the aggregate production function does is allow economists to disentangle the effects of these three factors on overall productivity.

An example of an aggregate production function applied to real data comes from a 2015 study by Keting Shen, Jing Wang, and John Whalley comparing growth in the United States, India, and China from 1979 (when China began a major shift toward becoming a market economy) to 2008. One of their production functions took the form:

GDP per worker = $T \times$ (Physical capital per worker)$^{1/3} \times$ (Human capital per worker)$^{2/3}$

Human capital is the improvement in labor created by the education and knowledge embodied in the workforce.

Technological progress is an advance in the technical means of the production of goods and services.

The **aggregate production function** is a hypothetical function that shows how productivity (real GDP per worker) depends on the quantities of physical capital per worker and human capital per worker as well as the state of technology.

An aggregate production function exhibits **diminishing returns to physical capital** when, holding the amount of human capital per worker and the state of technology fixed, each successive increase in the amount of physical capital per worker leads to a smaller increase in productivity.

where T represented an estimate of the level of technology, and they related human capital to years of education. Over this period, China moved well up the scale, from GDP per capita only 5% that of the United States to 17% that of the United States (a number that had risen to around 25% by 2018). Most of this relative growth, they found, was due to an increase in China's relative T, from around 10% that of the United States to 25% that of the United States.

In analyzing historical economic growth, economists have discovered a crucial fact about the estimated aggregate production function: it exhibits **diminishing returns to physical capital.** That is, when the amount of human capital per worker and the state of technology are held fixed, each successive increase in the amount of physical capital per worker leads to a smaller increase in productivity.

Figure 24-4 and the table to its right give a hypothetical example of how the level of physical capital per worker might affect the level of real GDP per worker, holding human capital per worker and the state of technology fixed. In this example, we measure the quantity of physical capital in dollars.

To see why the relationship between physical capital per worker and productivity exhibits diminishing returns, think about how the availability of farm equipment affects the productivity of farmworkers. A little bit of equipment makes a big difference: a worker equipped with a tractor can do much more than a worker without one. And a worker using more expensive equipment will, other things equal, be more productive: a worker with a $40,000 tractor will normally be able to cultivate more farmland in a given amount of time than a worker with

FIGURE 24-4 Physical Capital and Productivity

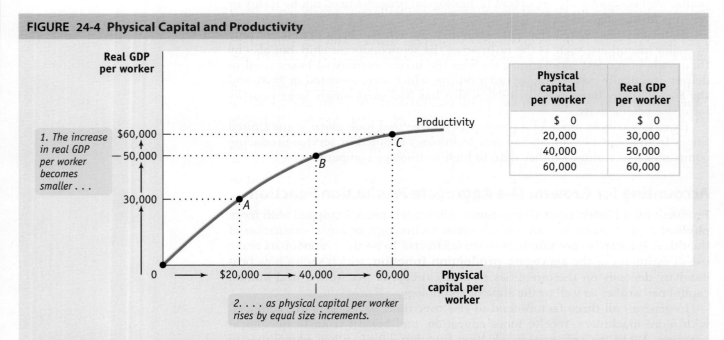

Physical capital per worker	Real GDP per worker
$ 0	$ 0
20,000	30,000
40,000	50,000
60,000	60,000

1. The increase in real GDP per worker becomes smaller . . .

2. . . . as physical capital per worker rises by equal size increments.

The aggregate production function shows how, in this case, holding human capital per worker and technology fixed, productivity increases as physical capital per worker rises. Other things equal, a greater quantity of physical capital per worker leads to higher real GDP per worker but is subject to diminishing returns: each successive addition to physical capital per worker produces a smaller increase in productivity. Starting at the origin, 0, a $20,000 increase in physical capital per worker leads to an increase in real GDP per worker of $30,000, indicated by point A. Starting from point A, another $20,000 increase in physical capital per worker leads to an increase in real GDP per worker but only of $20,000, indicated by point B. Finally, a third $20,000 increase in physical capital per worker leads to only a $10,000 increase in real GDP per worker, indicated by point C.

a $20,000 tractor because the more expensive machine will be more powerful, perform more tasks, or both.

But will a worker with a $40,000 tractor, holding human capital and technology constant, be twice as productive as a worker with a $20,000 tractor? Probably not: there's a huge difference between not having a tractor at all and having even an inexpensive tractor; there's much less difference between having an inexpensive tractor and having a better tractor. And we can be sure that a worker with a $200,000 tractor won't be 10 times as productive: a tractor can be improved only so much. Because the same is true of other kinds of equipment, the aggregate production function shows diminishing returns to physical capital.

Diminishing returns to physical capital imply a relationship between physical capital per worker and output per worker like the one shown in Figure 24-4. As the productivity curve for physical capital and the accompanying table illustrate, more physical capital per worker leads to more output per worker. But each $20,000 increment in physical capital per worker adds less to productivity.

As you can see from the table, there is a big payoff for the first $20,000 of physical capital: real GDP per worker rises by $30,000. The second $20,000 of physical capital also raises productivity, but not by as much: real GDP per worker goes up by only $20,000. The third $20,000 of physical capital raises real GDP per worker by only $10,000. By comparing points along the curve you can also see that as physical capital per worker rises, output per worker also rises—but at a diminishing rate.

Going from the origin at 0 to point A, a $20,000 increase in physical capital per worker, leads to an increase of $30,000 in real GDP per worker. Going from point A to point B, a second $20,000 increase in physical capital per worker, leads to an increase of only $20,000 in real GDP per worker. And from point B to point C, a $20,000 increase in physical capital per worker, increased real GDP per worker by only $10,000.

It's important to realize that diminishing returns to physical capital is an "other things equal" phenomenon: additional amounts of physical capital are less productive *when the amount of human capital per worker and the technology are held fixed.* Diminishing returns may disappear if we increase the amount of human capital per worker, or improve the technology, or both at the same time the amount of physical capital per worker is increased.

For example, a worker with a $40,000 tractor who has also been trained in the most advanced cultivation techniques may in fact be more than twice as productive as a worker with only a $20,000 tractor and no additional human capital.

But diminishing returns to any one input—regardless of whether it is physical capital, human capital, or number of workers—is a pervasive characteristic of production. Typical estimates suggest that in practice a 1% increase in the quantity of physical capital per worker increases output per worker by only one-third of 1%, or 0.33%.

In practice, all the factors contributing to higher productivity rise during the course of economic growth: both physical capital and human capital per worker increase, and technology advances as well. To disentangle the effects of these factors, economists use **growth accounting,** which estimates the contribution of each major factor in the aggregate production function to economic growth. For example, suppose the following are true:

- The amount of physical capital per worker grows 3% per year.

- According to estimates of the aggregate production function, each 1% rise in physical capital per worker, holding human capital and technology constant, raises output per worker by one-third of 1%, or 0.33%.

Growth accounting estimates the contribution of each major factor in the aggregate production function to economic growth.

IT MAY BE DIMINISHED . . . BUT IT'S STILL POSITIVE!

As we've seen, the term *diminishing returns to physical capital* means that when holding the amount of human capital per worker and the technology fixed, each successive increase in the amount of physical capital per worker results in a smaller increase in real GDP per worker.

But avoid falling into a common trap. The term does not mean that real GDP per worker will eventually fall as more and more physical

capital is added. What happens instead is that the increase in real GDP per worker will get smaller and smaller, while remaining at or above zero. So an increase in physical capital per worker never reduces productivity.

But due to diminishing returns, at some point, increasing the amount of physical capital per worker will no longer produce an economic payoff. At this point, the increase in output will be so small that it's not worth the cost of the additional physical capital.

In that case, we would estimate that growing physical capital per worker is responsible for $3\% \times 0.33 = 1$ percentage point of productivity growth per year. A similar but more complex procedure is used to estimate the effects of growing human capital. The procedure is more complex because there aren't simple dollar measures of the quantity of human capital.

Growth accounting allows us to calculate the effects of greater physical and human capital on economic growth. But how can we estimate the effects of technological progress? We do so by estimating what is left over after the effects of physical and human capital have been taken into account. For example, let's imagine that there was no increase in human capital per worker so that we can focus on changes in physical capital and in technology.

In Figure 24-5, the lower curve shows the same hypothetical relationship between physical capital per worker and output per worker shown in Figure 24-4. Let's assume that this was the relationship given the technology available in 1950. The upper curve also shows a relationship between physical capital per worker and productivity, but this time given the technology available in 2020.

FIGURE 24-5 Technological Progress and Productivity Growth

Technological progress raises productivity at any given level of physical capital per worker, and therefore shifts the aggregate production function upward. Here we hold human capital per worker fixed. We assume that the lower curve (the same curve as in Figure 24-4) reflects technology in 1950 and the upper curve reflects technology in 2020. Holding technology and human capital fixed, tripling physical capital per worker from $20,000 to $60,000 leads to a doubling of real GDP per worker, from $30,000 to $60,000. This is shown by the movement from point *A* to point *C*, reflecting an approximately 1% per year rise in real GDP per worker. In reality, technological progress raised productivity at any given level of physical capital — shown here by the upward shift of the curve — and the actual rise in real GDP per worker is shown by the movement from point *A* to point *D*. Real GDP per worker grew 2% per year, leading to a quadrupling during the period. The extra 1% in growth of real GDP per worker is due to higher total factor productivity.

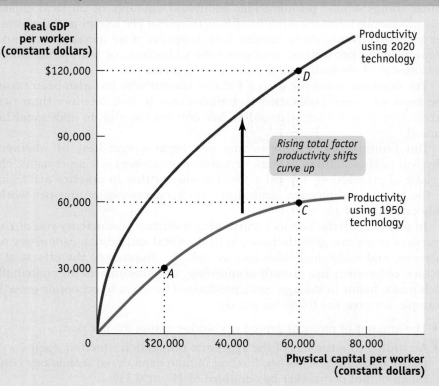

(We've chosen a 70-year stretch to allow us to use the Rule of 70.) The 2020 curve is shifted up compared to the 1950 curve because technologies developed over the previous 70 years make it possible to produce more output for a given amount of physical capital per worker than was possible with the technology available in 1950. (Note that the two curves are measured in constant dollars.)

Let's assume that between 1950 and 2020 the amount of physical capital per worker tripled from $20,000 to $60,000. If this increase in physical capital per worker had taken place without any technological progress, the economy would have moved from *A* to *C:* output per worker would have risen, but only from $30,000 to $60,000, or 1% per year (using the Rule of 70 tells us that a 1% growth rate over 70 years doubles output). In fact, however, the economy moved from *A* to *D:* output rose from $30,000 to $120,000, or 2% per year. There was an increase in both physical capital per worker and technological progress, which shifted the aggregate production function.

In this case, 50% of the annual 2% increase in productivity—that is, 1% in annual productivity growth—is due to higher **total factor productivity,** the amount of output that can be produced with a given amount of factor inputs. So when total factor productivity increases, the economy can produce more output with the same quantity of physical capital, human capital, and labor.

Increases in total factor productivity are central to a country's economic growth. And economists believe that technological progress drives increases in total factor productivity. By reducing the limitations imposed on growth by a given amount of physical capital, technological progress is crucial to economic growth. The Bureau of Labor Statistics estimates the growth rate of both labor productivity and total factor productivity for nonfarm businesses in the United States. According to the Bureau's estimates, over the period from 1948 to 2019 American labor productivity rose 2.1% per year. Less than half of that rise, approximately 49%, is explained by increases in physical and human capital per worker; the rest is explained by rising total factor productivity—that is, by technological progress.

In the United States, labor productivity and total factor productivity have risen continuously for at least two centuries, although the rate of increase has varied a lot over time. For example, productivity growth was very high for a generation after World War II, doubling living standards in a single generation. Since then, productivity growth has been much slower, despite impressive innovations like computers, smartphones, and social media.

What About Natural Resources?

In our discussion so far, we haven't mentioned natural resources, which certainly have an effect on productivity. Other things equal, countries that are abundant in valuable natural resources, such as highly fertile land or rich mineral deposits, have higher real GDP per capita than less fortunate countries.

The most obvious modern example is the Middle East, where enormous oil deposits have made a few sparsely populated countries very rich. For example, the United Arab Emirates (UAE) has about the same level of real GDP per capita as Germany, but the UAE's wealth is based on oil, not manufacturing, the source of Germany's high output per worker.

But other things are often not equal. In the modern world, natural resources are a much less important determinant of productivity than human or physical capital for the great majority of countries. For example, some nations with very high real GDP per capita, such as Japan, have very few natural resources, while some resource-rich nations, such as Nigeria (which has sizable oil deposits), are very poor.

Historically, natural resources played a much more prominent role in determining productivity. In the nineteenth century, the countries with the highest real GDP per capita were those abundant in rich farmland and mineral deposits: the United States, Canada, Argentina, and Australia. As a consequence, natural resources figured prominently in the development of economic thought.

Total factor productivity is the amount of output that can be achieved with a given amount of factor inputs.

In a famous book published in 1798, *An Essay on the Principle of Population*, the English economist Thomas Malthus made the fixed quantity of land in the world the basis of a pessimistic prediction about future productivity. As population grew, he pointed out, the amount of land per worker would decline. And this, other things equal, would cause productivity to fall.

His view, in fact, was that improvements in technology or increases in physical capital would lead only to temporary improvements in productivity because they would always be offset by the pressure of rising population and more workers on the supply of land. In the long run, he concluded, the great majority of people were condemned to living on the edge of starvation. Only then would death rates be high enough and birth rates low enough to prevent rapid population growth from outstripping productivity growth.

It hasn't turned out that way, although many historians believe that Malthus's prediction of stagnant productivity was valid for much of human history. Population pressure probably did prevent large productivity increases until the eighteenth century. But in the time since Malthus wrote his book, any negative effects on productivity from population growth have been far outweighed by other, positive factors—advances in technology, increases in human and physical capital, and the opening up of enormous amounts of cultivable land in the New World.

It remains true, however, that we live on a finite planet, with limited supplies of resources such as oil and limited ability to absorb environmental damage. We address the concerns these limitations pose for economic growth in the final section of this chapter.

ECONOMICS >> *in Action*
The Rise, Fall, and Return of the Productivity Paradox

We live in an era of revolutionary technological change—or that's what everyone says. And to be fair, there are good reasons for the excitement. After all, your smartphone is thousands of times faster and can store millions of times more data than the computers available to the astronauts who landed on the moon. But is the dramatic increase in computing power translating into equally dramatic economic growth? Economists have been asking that question for decades—and the answer still isn't clear.

Modern information technology began in the 1970s, with the introduction of the first microprocessor—in effect, a whole computer taking the form of tiny transistors and circuits etched on a piece of silicon. Spectacular increases in computing power have transformed how we use and disseminate information. The 1980s brought personal computers, replacing hulking machines that had to be programmed with punch cards, and the first cell phones. The 1990s brought the internet. With the twenty-first century came broadband, smartphones (the first iPhone was introduced in 2007), video streaming, and more.

You might have expected these developments to produce an explosion in total factor productivity. In fact, however, as Figure 24-6 shows, total factor productivity grew much more rapidly in the generation that followed World War II than it has since. Economists sometimes refer to

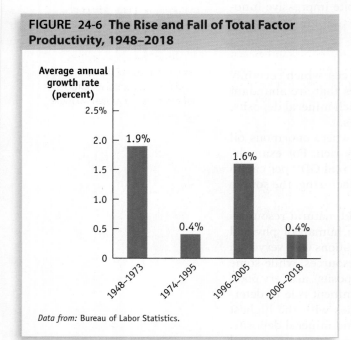

FIGURE 24-6 The Rise and Fall of Total Factor Productivity, 1948–2018

Data from: Bureau of Labor Statistics.

this disconnect between what looks like rapid technological progress and actual productivity as the "productivity paradox."

True, there was a decade, from 1996 to 2005, when information technology finally seemed to be paying off, and the paradox seemed to be disappearing. Much of this rise came in the service sector, especially retailing, where stores like Walmart achieved major gains in efficiency by using real-time information from cash registers to manage inventory, ordering, and other seemingly mundane aspects of their business. But progress slowed again and remains sluggish even now.

The truth is that nobody knows why modern technology doesn't seem to be doing more for the economy. As we noted in the text, however, a lot of real-world progress comes from technologies that aren't at all flashy, like precut cardboard boxes. Maybe the flip side of this observation is that an era of flashy new technologies isn't necessarily one of rapid progress across the economy as a whole.

>> Check Your Understanding 24-2

Solutions appear at back of book.

1. Predict the effect of each of the following events on the growth rate of productivity.
   a. The amounts of physical and human capital per worker are unchanged, but there is significant technological progress.
   b. The amount of physical capital per worker grows at a steady pace, but the level of human capital per worker and technology are unchanged.

2. Output in the economy of Erewhon has grown 3% per year over the past 30 years. The labor force has grown at 1% per year, and the quantity of physical capital has grown at 4% per year. The average education level hasn't changed. Estimates by economists say that each 1% increase in physical capital per worker, other things equal, raises productivity by 0.3%. (*Hint:* % change in (X/Y) = % change in X – % change in Y.)
   a. How fast has productivity in Erewhon grown?
   b. How fast has physical capital per worker grown?
   c. How much has growing physical capital per worker contributed to productivity growth? What percentage of productivity growth is that?
   d. How much has technological progress contributed to productivity growth? What percentage of productivity growth is that?

3. Multinomics, Inc. is a large company with many offices around the country. It has just adopted a new computer system that will affect virtually every function performed within the company. Why might a period of time pass before employees' productivity is improved by the new computer system? Why might there be a temporary decrease in employees' productivity?

>> Quick Review

- Long-run increases in living standards arise almost entirely from growing **labor productivity,** often simply referred to as **productivity.**

- An increase in **physical capital** is one source of higher productivity, but it is subject to **diminishing returns to physical capital.**

- **Human capital** and **technological progress** are also sources of increases in productivity.

- The **aggregate production function** is used to estimate the sources of increases in productivity. **Growth accounting** has shown that rising **total factor productivity,** interpreted as the effect of technological progress, is central to long-run economic growth.

- Natural resources are less important today than physical and human capital as sources of productivity growth in most economies.

‖ Why Growth Rates Differ

In 1800, according to estimates by the economic historian Angus Maddison, Mexico's real GDP per capita was 1.5 times greater than Japan. Today, Japan has higher real GDP per capita than most European nations and Mexico is a relatively poor country, though by no means among the poorest. The difference? Over the long run—since 1800—real GDP per capita grew at 1.7% per year in Japan but at only 1.1% per year in Mexico. Today Japan's real GDP per capita is 2.5 times greater than Mexico.

As this example illustrates, even small differences in growth rates have large consequences over the long run. So why do growth rates differ across countries and across periods of time?

Explaining Differences in Growth Rates

As we've seen, economies with rapid growth tend to add physical capital, increase their human capital, or experience rapid technological progress. Striking economic success stories, like Japan in the 1950s and 1960s or China more recently, tend to be countries that do all three:

1. Rapidly add to their physical capital through high savings and investment spending.
2. Increase their human capital by improving their educational institutions.
3. Make fast technological progress through research and development.

Evidence also points to the importance of government policies and practices in fostering the sources of growth. We'll look at the role of government as well.

Savings and Investment Spending One reason for differences in growth rates between countries is that some countries are increasing their stock of physical capital much more rapidly than others, through high rates of investment spending. In the 1960s, Japan was the fastest-growing major economy. It also spent a much higher share of its GDP on investment goods than did other major economies. In recent years, China has been the fastest-growing major economy, and it similarly spends a very large share of its GDP on investment goods. In 2019, investment spending was 43% of China's GDP, compared with only 21% in the United States.

Where does the money for high investment spending come from? It comes from savings. In the next chapter we'll analyze how financial markets channel savings into investment spending. For now, however, the key point is that investment spending must be paid for either out of savings from domestic households or by savings from foreign households—that is, an inflow of foreign capital.

Foreign capital has played an important role in the long-run economic growth of some countries, including the United States, which relied heavily on foreign funds during its early industrialization. For the most part, however, countries that invest a large share of their GDP are able to do so because they have high domestic savings. In fact, China in 2019 saved an even higher percentage of its GDP than it invested at home. The extra savings were invested abroad, largely in the United States.

Education Just as countries differ substantially in the rate at which they add to their physical capital, there have been large differences in the rate at which countries add to their human capital through education.

A case in point is the comparison between Argentina and China. In both countries the adult literacy rate has risen steadily over time, but it has risen much faster in China.

Figure 24-7 shows the percentage of people over the age of 15 who can both read and write in China, which we have highlighted as an example of spectacular long-run growth, and in Argentina, a country whose growth has been disappointing. Thirty-five years ago, Argentina had a much more educated population, while many Chinese were still illiterate. Today, the average educational level and adult literacy rate in China is still slightly below that in Argentina—but that's mainly because there

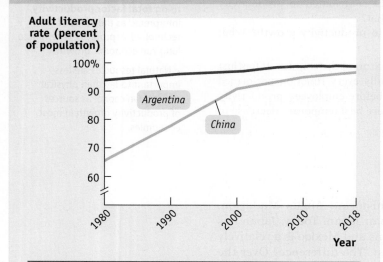

FIGURE 24-7 China's Students Are Catching Up, 1980–2018

Although China still lags behind Argentina in adult literacy, it is rapidly catching up. China's success at adding human capital is one key to the spectacular rise in its long-run growth rate in recent decades.

Data from: World Development Indicators, World Bank.

are still many elderly adults in China who never received basic education. In terms of secondary and tertiary education, China has outstripped once-rich Argentina.

Research and Development The advance of technology is a key force behind economic growth. What drives technological progress?

Scientific advances make new technologies possible. To take the most spectacular example in today's world, the semiconductor chip—which is the basis for all modern information technology—could not have been developed without the theory of quantum mechanics in physics.

But science alone is not enough: scientific knowledge must be translated into useful products and processes. And that often requires devoting a lot of resources to **research and development,** or **R&D,** spending to create new technologies and apply them to practical use.

Although some research and development is conducted by governments, much R&D is paid for by the private sector. The United States became the world's leading economy in large part because U.S. businesses were among the first to make systematic research and development a part of their operations. In fact, back in 1875 Thomas Edison created the first modern industrial research laboratory.

Developing new technology is one thing; applying it is another. There have often been notable differences in the pace at which different countries take advantage of new technologies. For example, since 2000, Italy has suffered a significant decline in its total factor productivity, while the United States has moved ahead (see the Economics in Action on Italy at the end of this section). The sources of these national differences are the subject of a great deal of economic research.

The Role of Government in Promoting Economic Growth

Governments can play an important role in promoting—or blocking—all three sources of long-term economic growth: physical capital, human capital, and technological progress. They can either affect growth directly through subsidies to factors that enhance growth or by creating an environment that either fosters or hinders growth.

Government policies can increase the economy's growth rate through the following six channels.

1. Government Subsidies to Infrastructure Governments play an important direct role in building **infrastructure:** roads, power lines, ports, information networks, and other large-scale physical capital projects that provide a foundation for economic activity. Although some infrastructure is provided by private companies, much of it is either provided by the government or requires a great deal of government regulation and support.

China offers a spectacular example of a country that uses public spending on infrastructure to promote economic growth. Infrastructure spending on everything from roads to high-speed rail amounts to about 8% of China's GDP, four times the percentage in the United States. In fact, China spends more on infrastructure than Western Europe and North America combined.

Poor infrastructure, such as a power grid that frequently fails and cuts off electricity, is a major obstacle to economic growth in many countries. To provide good infrastructure, an economy must not only be able to afford it, but it must also have the political discipline to maintain it.

Perhaps the most crucial infrastructure is something we, in an advanced country, rarely think about: basic public health measures in the form of a clean water supply and disease control. Poor health infrastructure is a major obstacle to economic growth in poor countries, especially those in Africa.

Research and development, or **R&D,** is spending to create and implement new technologies.

Roads, power lines, ports, information networks, and other underpinnings for economic activity are known as **infrastructure.**

2. Government Subsidies to Education In contrast to physical capital, which is mainly created by private investment spending, much of an economy's human capital is the result of government spending on education. In the United States, various levels of government fund the bulk of primary and secondary education. Government funding subsidizes a significant share of higher education as well: over 70% of students attend public colleges and universities. In addition, the federal government significantly subsidizes research performed at private colleges and universities.

Differences in the rate at which countries add to their human capital largely reflect government policy. As we saw in Figure 24-7, the adult literacy rate in China has been increasing more rapidly than in Argentina. This isn't because China is richer than Argentina; until recently, China was, on average, poorer than Argentina. Instead, it reflects the fact that the Chinese government has made education and raising the literacy rate high priorities.

3. Government Subsidies to R&D Technological progress is largely the result of private initiative. But in the more advanced countries, important R&D is done by government agencies as well. For example, the internet grew out of a system, the Advanced Research Projects Agency Network (ARPANET), created by the U.S. Department of Defense, then extended to educational institutions by the National Science Foundation.

4. Maintaining a Well-Functioning Financial System Governments play an important indirect role in making high rates of private investment spending possible. Both the amount of savings and the ability of an economy to direct savings into productive investment spending depend on the economy's institutions, especially its financial system. A well-regulated and well-functioning financial system is very important for economic growth because in most countries it is the principal way in which savings are channeled into investment spending.

If a country's citizens trust their banks, they will place their savings in bank deposits, which the banks will then lend to their business customers. But if people distrust their banks, they will hoard gold or foreign currency, keeping their savings in safe deposit boxes or under the mattress, where it cannot be turned into productive investment spending. A well-functioning financial system requires appropriate government regulation to assure depositors that their funds are protected from loss.

5. Protection of Property Rights *Property rights* are the legal rights held by owners of valuable items to dispose of those items as they choose. A subset, *intellectual property rights*, are the rights of innovators to accrue the rewards of their innovations. The state of property rights generally, and intellectual property rights in particular, are important factors in explaining differences in growth rates across economies. Why? Because no one would bother to spend the effort and resources required to innovate if someone else could appropriate that innovation and capture the rewards. So, for innovation to flourish, intellectual property rights must receive protection.

Sometimes protecting property rights is accomplished by the nature of the innovation: it may be too difficult or expensive to copy. But, generally, the government has to protect intellectual property rights. A *patent* is a government-created temporary monopoly given to innovators for the use or sale of their innovations. It's a temporary rather than permanent monopoly because while it's in society's interests to give innovators an incentive to invent, it's also in society's interest to eventually encourage competition.

6. Political Stability and Good Governance There's not much point in investing in a business if rioting mobs are likely to destroy it, or in saving your money if someone with political connections can steal it. Political stability and

"I'm thinking of giving this up to campaign for orderly, competent government."

good governance (including the protection of property rights) are essential ingredients in fostering economic growth in the long run.

Long-run economic growth in successful economies, like that of the United States, has been possible because there are good laws, institutions that enforce those laws, and a stable political system that maintains those institutions. The law must say that your property is really yours so that someone else can't take it away. The courts and the police must be honest so that they can't be bribed to ignore the law. And the political system must be stable so that laws don't change capriciously.

Americans take these preconditions for granted, but they are by no means guaranteed. Aside from the disruption caused by war or revolution, many countries find that their economic growth suffers due to corruption among the government officials who should be enforcing the law. For example, until 1991 the Indian government imposed many bureaucratic restrictions on businesses, which often had to bribe government officials to get approval for even routine activities—a tax on business, in effect. Economists have argued that a reduction in this burden of corruption was one reason India experienced a surge of economic growth after 1990 that continues to this day.

Even when the government isn't corrupt, excessive government intervention can be a brake on economic growth. If large parts of the economy are supported by wasteful government subsidies, protected from imports, subject to unnecessary monopolization, or otherwise insulated from competition, productivity tends to suffer because of a lack of incentives. As we'll see in the next section, excessive government intervention is one often-cited explanation for slow growth in Latin America.

ECONOMICS >> *in Action*
What's the Matter with Italy?

Italy was once considered a remarkable economic success story. A century ago it was still a poor country—so poor that in the late nineteenth and early twentieth century millions of Italians emigrated to the United States and other destinations in search of a better life. After World War II, however, Italy experienced decades of rapid growth, with real GDP per capita quadrupling between 1950 and 1990. By the end of that growth spurt, as you can see from Figure 24-8, Italy was significantly richer than the United Kingdom, the nation that had led the Industrial Revolution.

But at that point Italian growth stalled. Real GDP per capita was stagnant after the late 1990s, and began falling after 2008, as Italy's economy suffered a severe downturn as a result of the European debt crisis. What went wrong?

Part of the answer involves slow growth of the factors of production. Italy's low birth rate has meant a rapidly aging population, with a declining percentage of working-age adults. Italy has also lagged in education, with the lowest college-educated share of the population in the European Union. Italy also seems to be having trouble taking advantage of technological progress. In fact, measured total factor productivity in Italy has declined since 2000. Why?

FIGURE 24-8 Real GDP per Capita for Italy and the United Kingdom, 1960–2018

Real GDP per capita (2010 dollars)

Data from: The World Bank.

>> **Quick Review**

• Countries differ greatly in their growth rates of real GDP per capita due to differences in the rates at which they accumulate physical capital and human capital as well as differences in technological progress. A prime cause of differences in growth rates is differences in rates of domestic savings and investment spending as well as differences in education levels, and **research and development,** or **R&D,** levels. R&D largely drives technological progress.

• Government actions can promote or hinder the sources of long-term growth.

• Government policies that directly promote growth are subsidies to **infrastructure,** particularly public health infrastructure, subsidies to education, subsidies to R&D, and the maintenance of a well-functioning financial system.

• Governments improve the environment for growth by protecting property rights (particularly intellectual property rights through patents), by providing political stability, and through good governance. Poor governance includes corruption and excessive government intervention.

Some economists suggest that the explanation may lie in its business culture. In particular, Italian management practices have been widely criticized because promotion and financial rewards all too often reflect seniority rather than performance, giving few incentives to adopt new technology and best business practices.

Underlying this low-performance culture may be a lack of effective competition in many markets, which means that even badly run companies can stay in business indefinitely. The absence of competition within the Italian economy points to a government policy failure, perhaps arising from the relationship between established firms and government being too cozy. In an economy dominated by established firms, there's little incentive to invest or innovate. Italy's troubles show that even countries with a history of economic success can stumble. Achieving sustained economic growth, it turns out, isn't easy.

>> **Check Your Understanding 24-3**
Solutions appear at back of book.

1. Explain the link between a country's growth rate, its investment spending as a percent of GDP, and its domestic savings.

2. U.S. centers of academic biotechnology research have closer connections with private biotechnology companies than do their European counterparts. What effect might this have on the pace of innovation and development of new drugs in the United States versus Europe?

3. During the 1990s in the former Soviet Union a lot of property was seized and controlled by those in power. How might this have affected the country's growth rate at that time? Explain.

Success, Disappointment, and Failure

As Figure 24-2 illustrates, rates of long-run economic growth differ quite a lot around the world. We'll now look at three regions of the world that have had quite different experiences with economic growth over the last several decades. We've chosen these three regions—East Asia, Latin America, and Africa—because they illustrate the challenges of sustained productivity growth.

Figure 24-9 shows trends since 1960 in real GDP per capita in 2010 dollars for three countries: Argentina, Nigeria, and South Korea. (As in Figure 24-1, the vertical axis is drawn in logarithmic scale.) We have chosen these countries because each is a particularly striking example of what has happened in its region. South Korea's amazing rise is part of a broad "economic miracle" in East Asia. Argentina's slow progress, interrupted by repeated setbacks, is more or less typical of the disappointing growth that has characterized Latin America. Like Argentina, Nigeria also had a little growth in real GDP until 2000. Since then both countries have fared better.

East Asia's Miracle

In 1960 South Korea was a very poor country. In fact, in 1960 its real GDP per capita was lower than that of India today. But, as you can see from Figure 24-9, beginning in the early 1960s South Korea began an extremely rapid economic ascent: real GDP per capita grew about 7% per year for more than 30 years. Today South Korea, though still somewhat poorer than Europe or the United States, looks very much like an economically advanced country.

South Korea's economic growth is unprecedented in history: it took the country only 35 years to achieve growth that required centuries elsewhere. Yet South

FIGURE 24-9 Success and Disappointment

Real GDP per capita from 1960 to 2018, measured in 2010 dollars, is shown for Argentina, South Korea, and Nigeria, using a logarithmic scale. South Korea and some other East Asian countries have been highly successful at achieving economic growth. Argentina, like much of Latin America, has had several setbacks, slowing its growth. Nigeria's standard of living in 2018 was only barely higher than it had been in 1960, an experience shared by many African countries. Neither Argentina nor Nigeria exhibited much growth over the 58-year period, although both have had significantly higher growth in recent years.
Data from: World Development Indicators.

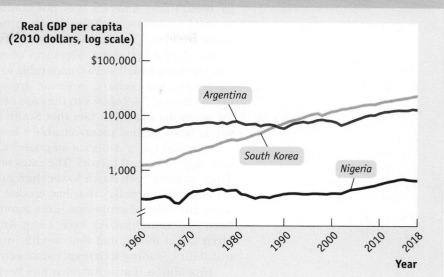

Korea is only part of a broader phenomenon, often referred to as the East Asian economic miracle. High growth rates first appeared in South Korea, Taiwan, Hong Kong, and Singapore but then spread across the region, most notably to China. Since 1975, the whole region has increased real GDP per capita by 6% per year, more than three times America's historical rate of growth.

How have the Asian countries achieved such high growth rates? The answer is that all of the sources of productivity growth have been firing on all cylinders. Very high savings rates, the percentage of GDP that is saved nationally in any given year, have allowed the countries to significantly increase the amount of physical capital per worker. Very good basic education has permitted a rapid improvement in human capital. And these countries have experienced substantial technological progress.

Why were such high rates of growth unheard of in the past? Most economic analysts think that East Asia's growth spurt was possible because of its *relative* backwardness. That is, by the time that East Asian economies began to move into the modern world, they could benefit from adopting the technological advances that had been generated in technologically advanced countries such as the United States.

In 1900, the United States could not have moved quickly to a modern level of productivity because much of the technology that powers the modern economy, from jet planes to computers, hadn't been invented yet. In 1970, South Korea probably still had lower labor productivity than the United States had in 1900, but it could rapidly upgrade its productivity by adopting technology that had been developed in the United States, Europe, and Japan over the previous century. This was aided by a huge investment in human capital through widespread schooling.

The East Asian experience demonstrates that economic growth can be especially fast in countries that are playing catch-up to other countries with higher GDP per capita. On this basis, many economists have suggested a general principle known as the **convergence hypothesis.** It says that differences in real GDP per capita among countries tend to narrow over time because countries that start with lower real GDP per capita tend to have higher growth rates.

However, starting with a relatively low level of real GDP per capita is no guarantee of rapid growth, as the examples of Latin America and Africa both demonstrate.

According to the **convergence hypothesis,** international differences in real GDP per capita tend to narrow over time.

Latin America's Disappointment

In 1900, Latin America was not considered an economically backward region. Natural resources, including both minerals and cultivable land, were abundant. Some countries, notably Argentina, attracted millions of immigrants from Europe in search of a better life. Measures of real GDP per capita in Argentina, Uruguay, and southern Brazil were comparable to those in economically advanced countries.

For the last century, however, growth in Latin America has been disappointing. As Figure 24-9 shows in the case of Argentina, growth has been disappointing for many decades. The fact that South Korea is now much richer than Argentina would have seemed inconceivable a few generations ago.

Why did Latin America stagnate? Comparisons with East Asian success stories suggest several factors. The rates of savings and investment spending in Latin America have been much lower than in East Asia, partly as a result of irresponsible government policy that has eroded savings through high inflation, bank failures, and other disruptions. Education—especially broad basic education—has been underemphasized: even Latin American nations rich in natural resources often failed to channel that wealth into their educational systems. And political instability, leading to irresponsible economic policies, has taken a toll.

In addition, Latin America has been unable to grow through the adoption of technology developed elsewhere. This has led to chronic disappointment among Latin Americans in their standard of living, which has further fueled political instability.

In the 1980s, many economists came to believe that Latin America was suffering from excessive government intervention in markets. They recommended opening the economies to imports, selling off government-owned companies, and, in general, freeing up individual initiative. The hope was that this would produce an East Asian–type economic surge. So far, however, only one Latin American nation, Chile, has achieved sustained rapid growth.

Africa's Troubles and Promise

Africa south of the Sahara is home to more than 1 billion people, more than three times the population of the United States. On average, they are very poor, nowhere close to U.S. living standards 100 or even 200 years ago. In fact, real GDP per capita in sub-Saharan Africa actually fell 13% from 1980 to 1994, although it has recovered since then. However, since 1995, growth rates across most of Africa have been much higher, averaging about 5% a year if the big economies of Nigeria, Angola, and South Africa are excluded. What explains the dramatic turnaround?

First and foremost, many African countries have tackled the problem of political instability. In the years after 1975, large parts of Africa experienced devastating civil wars (often with outside powers backing rival sides) that killed millions of people and made productive investment spending impossible. The threat of war and general anarchy also inhibited other important preconditions for growth, such as education and provision of basic infrastructure.

Slow and uneven economic growth in sub-Saharan Africa has led to extreme and ongoing poverty for many of its people.

Property rights are also a major problem. The lack of legal safeguards means that property owners are often subject to extortion because of government corruption, making them averse to owning property or improving it. This is especially damaging in a country that is very poor.

While many economists see political instability and government corruption as the leading causes of underdevelopment in Africa, some—most notably Jeffrey Sachs of Columbia University and the United Nations—believe the opposite.

They argue that Africa is politically unstable because it is poor. And Africa's poverty, they go on to claim, stems from its extremely unfavorable geographic conditions—much of the continent is landlocked, hot, infested with tropical diseases, and cursed with poor soil.

Sachs, along with economists from the World Health Organization, has highlighted the importance of health problems in Africa. In poor countries, worker productivity is often severely hampered by malnutrition and disease. In particular, tropical diseases such as malaria can only be controlled with an effective public health infrastructure, something that is lacking in much of Africa. Economists are studying certain regions of Africa to determine whether modest amounts of aid given directly to residents for the purposes of increasing crop yields, reducing malaria, and increasing school attendance can produce self-sustaining gains in living standards.

Although the example of African countries represents a warning that long-run economic growth cannot be taken for granted, there are some signs of hope. As we saw in Figure 24-9, Nigeria's per capita GDP, after decades of stagnation, turned upward after 2000, and it achieved an average annual growth rate of 3.0% from 2008 through 2018.

Left Behind by Growth?

Historically, rising real GDP per capita has translated into rising real income for the great majority of a nation's residents. However, there's no guarantee that this will happen. One of the principles we laid out in Chapter 1 is that economic change often produces losers as well as winners, and this is true of the changes that come with long-run economic growth. Gains from long-run economic growth may be very unequally distributed, and in some cases significant shares of the population may see their incomes fall even while the overall income of the nation is rising.

This isn't just a theoretical possibility. In the United States, and to a lesser extent in other wealthy countries, the share of income going to families near the top of the income distribution, and especially to the 1% of families with the

---

GLOBAL COMPARISON   **LAGGING REGIONS IN RICH COUNTRIES**

Growing regional disparities aren't a uniquely U.S. problem. On the contrary, similar forces—economic trends that appear to favor large, highly educated metropolitan areas over rural and older industrial areas—are clearly at work in virtually all wealthy nations. In Britain, London's economy has surged while the old coal-mining and industrial towns of England's northeast have struggled. France presents a similar contrast between greater Paris and the coal-and-steel belt of the country's north. Italy has long been divided between a wealthy north and a poor south, especially in Sicily. More than 30 years after the fall of the Berlin Wall, the former East Germany remains poorer than the rest of the country.

Comparing regional disparities across countries is tricky, because we don't define regions the same way: the United States collects data for states and metropolitan areas, while European data are based on the "Nomenclature des Unités territoriales statistiques"—yes, NUTS. For what it's worth, however, the figure, which shows real GDP of several countries' poorest region as a percent of the national average, suggests that regional disparities are similar across the Western world, and if anything slightly bigger in the United States.

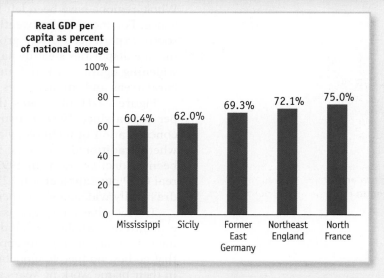

Data from: Nomenclature des Unités territoriales statistiques and Bureau of Economic Analysis.

FIGURE 24-10 The Growing Income Divide, 1953–2018

In the United States, from 1953 through 1980, both real per capita GDP and the real income of the median family grew at nearly identical rates because the distribution of income was quite stable. After 1980, however, the share of national income going to the richest Americans rose significantly. And while real GDP per capita continued to grow, real median income — the income earned by families in the middle of the income distribution — lagged behind. This means that since 1980 many of those families in the middle have been left behind by economic growth.

Data from: U.S. Census; FRED.

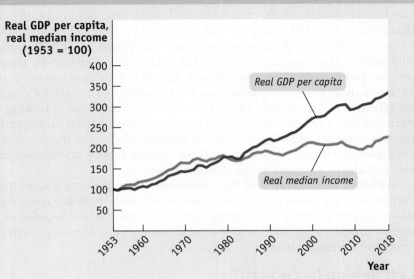

highest incomes, has grown substantially since 1980. Figure 24-10 shows one consequence of this rise in inequality. The figure compares the growth since 1953 of real per capita GDP in the United States and the real income of the *median family* — the family at the exact middle of the income scale, with half of all families richer and half poorer. Both numbers are shown as indexes, with 1953 = 100.

Until 1980 the two numbers grew at nearly the same rate because the distribution of income was quite stable. After 1980, however, a growing share of income went to a relatively small number of people at the top. As a result, the income of the median family — which arguably reflects the experience of the typical American — rose much more slowly than real GDP per capita. Many U.S. families, in other words, were to some extent left behind by economic growth.

Nor was it simply individual families that were left behind by recent growth. Whole regions have been left behind, reversing a historical trend toward convergence. For most of the twentieth century, the poorest U.S. states, mainly in the south, experienced faster growth than the nation as a whole, so that regional income disparities steadily narrowed. In recent decades, however, gaps have been widening again, with high-income metropolitan areas pulling away both from rural areas and smaller cities that used to be hubs of manufacturing.

Figure 24-11 illustrates this point by comparing the growth in real GDP per capita since 1997 in two states: Massachusetts, a rich state thanks to the concentration of technology and finance in and around Boston, and Kentucky, where traditional economic mainstays like coal mining and agriculture have been in decline. Even in 1997 Kentucky was poorer than Massachusetts, with real GDP per capita around 25 percent lower. But the gap between the states has drastically widened since then.

The fact that some regions of the United States are lagging even as the national economy as a whole grows is disturbing in itself. What makes it even more disturbing is that lagging regions appear to be suffering from significant social problems that go beyond merely monetary losses. In these regions, a high fraction of adults in their prime working years are without jobs, although they aren't all counted as unemployed, because some have given up even searching for work. And perhaps as a consequence of the lack of employment opportunities, these regions also suffer disproportionately from what the economists Anne Case and Angus Deaton have called "deaths of despair": mortality caused by drug overdoses, suicide, and alcohol.

FIGURE 24-11 **The Income Gap Between Rich and Poor States, 1997–2018**

In recent decades high-income states have widened the gap with poorer states. From 1997 through 2018 gross domestic product in Massachusetts has grown by nearly 50% compared with only 10% growth for Kentucky. In 1997, per capita income in Massachusetts was 31% greater than Kentucky, by 2018 the gap had widened to 75%.

Data from: U.S. Census; FRED.

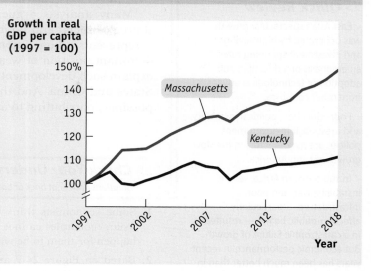

It is important, however, to acknowledge two qualifications to this somewhat downbeat note about growth in the United States. First, in the broad sweep of history it is still true that economic growth raises the standard of living of the great majority of the population. Second, it would be wrong to imagine that global economic growth, even in recent decades, has mainly benefited a well-off minority. On the contrary, as explained in the Economics in Action below, from a worldwide perspective the most conspicuous aspect of recent growth has been the rise of a *global middle class*—rapidly rising incomes among hundreds of millions of previously poor people in China and other emerging economies.

ECONOMICS >> *in Action*
Global Winners and Losers

Within the United States, the gains from economic growth since around 1980 have been unevenly distributed. Incomes at the top have soared, but incomes of most families have grown much more slowly. As a result, inequality has risen.

But is the same true for the world as a whole? No, the global picture is more complicated. In fact, even the question "Is global inequality rising or falling?" turns out to not be very meaningful. Inequality *within* many countries, especially in richer nations, has gone up. But inequality *between* nations has gone down, thanks to rapid growth in China, India, and other countries that used to be very poor.

One helpful way to think about who benefits from global growth is to divide the world's population into four groups: the untouched, the developing-country middle class, the advanced-country working class, and the global elite.

At the bottom there are still a large number of people, perhaps as many as 2 billion, who have yet to be touched by long-run economic growth. Most of sub-Saharan Africa, and even some parts of both China and India, still have per capita incomes not much higher than they had a century ago.

Above this group, however, is another large group, more than 1 billion strong, of people in China, India, and other rapidly growing economies who were very poor in living memory but now constitute a rapidly rising global middle class.

The story is less happy for the next group, the working class in advanced countries—for example, blue-collar workers in the United States. This group still has above-average incomes compared with the world as a whole, but as we've seen, these incomes have grown slowly since around 1980.

Finally, a small group of very well-off people, mostly but not entirely in wealthy nations, has seen big income gains.

Many analysts argue that this uneven pattern of gains is an important source of social and political friction. The rise of the global middle class, while it represents a huge improvement in human welfare, has also eroded the once-dominant position of wealthy nations in the world economic system, helping to explain such developments as the emergence of trade conflict between the United States and China. And the working class in wealthy countries feels left behind, possibly contributing to a populist backlash.

>> Check Your Understanding 24-4
Solutions appear at back of book.

1. Some economists think the high rates of growth of productivity achieved by many Asian economies cannot be sustained. Why might they be right? What would have to happen for them to be wrong?

2. Based on Figure 24-9 and the discussion in this section, which regions would you predict to follow the convergence hypothesis? Why?

3. Some economists think the best way to help African countries is for wealthier countries to provide more funds for basic infrastructure. Others think this policy will have no long-run effect unless African countries have the financial and political means to maintain this infrastructure. What policies would you suggest?

‖ Is World Growth Sustainable?

Earlier in the chapter we described the views of Thomas Malthus, the late-eighteenth-century economist who warned that the pressure of population growth would tend to limit the standard of living. Malthus was right about the past: for around 58 centuries, from the origins of civilization until his own time, limited land supplies effectively prevented any large rise in real incomes per capita. Since then, however, technological progress and rapid accumulation of physical and human capital have allowed the world to defy Malthusian pessimism.

But will this always be the case? Some skeptics have expressed doubt about whether **sustainable long-run economic growth** is possible—that is, growth that can continue in the face of the limited supply of natural resources and, perhaps even more important, given the negative effects of past economic growth on the environment.

Natural Resources and Growth, Revisited

"Neo-Malthusian" theories—claims that economic growth will be severely limited by lack of resources—have emerged at intervals ever since modern long-run economic growth began. In 1865 the British economist William Stanley Jevons wrote an influential book warning that reserves of coal, which fueled the Industrial Revolution, might soon be exhausted. In 1972 a famous report by a group called the Club of Rome warned that shortages of natural resources in general would lead to collapsing growth. In the early 2000s there were widespread concerns about "peak oil," a crisis that would supposedly be brought on by the exhaustion of world oil supplies.

So far, however, none of these warnings have proved accurate, largely because technological advances have circumvented previous limits. For example, since 2005 there have been dramatic developments in energy production, with large amounts of previously unreachable oil and gas extracted through fracking and with a huge decline in the cost of electricity generated by wind and solar power.

Most, though not all, economists believe that modern economies can almost always find ways to work around limits on the supply of natural resources. One reason for this optimism is the fact that resource scarcity leads to high resource prices. These high prices, in turn, provide strong incentives to conserve the scarce resource and find alternatives. For example, after the sharp oil price increases of the 1970s, U.S. consumers turned to smaller, more fuel-efficient cars as U.S. industry greatly intensified its efforts to reduce energy bills.

Given such responses to prices, economists generally tend to see resource scarcity as a problem that modern economies handle fairly well and not as a fundamental limit to long-run economic growth. Environmental issues, however, pose a more difficult problem for economies because dealing with them requires effective political action.

Economic Growth and the Environment

Economic growth, other things equal, tends to increase the adverse impact of human activity on the environment, including an increase in pollution, the loss of wildlife habitats, the extinction of species, and reduced biodiversity. As we saw in this chapter's opening story, India's economic growth has also brought a spectacular increase in air pollution in its cities.

In analyzing economic growth and its environmental impact, it is useful to distinguish between *local* environmental degradation, which affects a geographically limited area, and *global* environmental degradation, which is far-reaching, with worldwide impact. As we'll see, it has proven to be far more difficult to address global environmental degradation and, in particular, the problem of *climate change*.

In fact, the improved air quality in the cities of today's advanced economies indicates that local environmental harm can be greatly reduced when there is sufficient political will and resources are devoted to finding a solution. As described in the Economics in Action below, in recent years China has dramatically improved air quality in its major cities while continuing to achieve rapid economic growth.

However, *climate change*—changes in Earth's climate brought about by human activity, including pollution—has been a much harder problem to solve because policies must be implemented on a global scale, requiring the cooperation of many countries.

There is broad scientific consensus that burning fossil fuels—coal, oil, and natural gas—leads to increasing levels of carbon dioxide in the atmosphere. Carbon dioxide is a type of *greenhouse gas*. Such gases trap the sun's energy, raising the planet's temperature, and lead to shifts in weather patterns, which, in turn, impose high human, economic, and environmental costs. These costs include extreme weather, rising sea levels that increase the risk of flooding, the disruption of agriculture, including crop failures, and more. A recent estimate put the cost of unmitigated climate change at 20% of world gross domestic product by 2100. Moreover, these costs tend to fall more heavily on poor countries.

The problem of climate change is linked to economic growth: the larger the economy, the more homes, factories, and vehicles, will have to be powered, typically by burning fossil fuels. At present, world energy consumption is overwhelmingly dependent upon fossil fuels, which account for 85% of total consumption, while clean, renewable sources account for only 11%. Why? Because historically, fossil fuels have been cheaper to use. Most of today's wealthy countries grew their economies through industrialization and the burning of fossil fuels over the last century. To reduce the global emission of greenhouse gases, developed countries and large rapidly developing countries, such as China and India, will have to undertake a transition from a heavy reliance on fossil fuels to greater use of clean, renewable energy sources such as wind and solar power.

FIGURE 24-12 Climate Change and Growth

Greenhouse gas emissions are positively related to growth. As shown here by the United States and Europe, wealthy countries have historically been responsible for the great bulk of carbon dioxide emissions — which make up more than three-quarters of all greenhouse gas emissions — because of their richer and faster-growing economies. As China and other emerging economies have grown, they began to emit much more carbon dioxide. China has since overtaken the United States and Europe in emissions. *Data from:* Energy Information Administration.

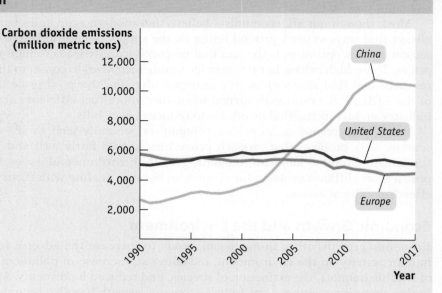

Until recently, effective action against climate change had been stymied by disagreement among countries on how to pay the cost of shifting from fossil fuel to clean energy sources. As Figure 24-12 shows, today's wealthy economies have historically been responsible for most of the carbon dioxide emissions—and carbon dioxide alone accounts for approximately three-quarters of all global greenhouse gas emissions. But newly emerging economies like China and India are responsible for the recent growth. Inevitably, rich countries are reluctant to pay the price of reducing emissions only to have their efforts frustrated by rapidly growing emissions from new players. But relatively poor countries like China and India consider it unfair that they should be expected to bear the burden of protecting an environment threatened by the past actions of rich nations.

In acknowledgment of the seriousness of the problem, in 2015, 196 countries came together under the **Paris Agreement,** committing to reduce their emissions of greenhouse gases in an effort to limit the rise in Earth's temperature to no more than 2 degrees Celsius. The linchpin of the agreement was cooperation between China, India, and the United States. China and India agreed to limit their emissions, and the United States, along with other rich countries, committed to develop various forms of public and private financing to help poorer countries pay the cost. Despite originally committing to the Paris Agreement, at the time of writing the Trump administration had announced plans for the United States to withdraw from it in November 2020.

Is it possible to maintain long-run growth while averting the effects of climate change? The answer, according to most economists who have studied the issue, is yes. While there will be economic costs, those costs have been falling as technological innovation in clean energy sources advances. The best available estimates show that even a large reduction in greenhouse gas emissions over the next few decades would cause only a modest reduction in the long-term rise in real GDP per capita.

To achieve long-run economic growth with environmental protection, governments will need to use regulations and environmental standards, and institute policies that create market incentives to encourage individuals and firms to make the transition to clean energy sources. Finally, governments—both rich and poor—will need to continue to cooperate with one another. Getting political consensus around the necessary policies will be key.

Under the **Paris Agreement** of 2015, 196 countries agreed to reduce their greenhouse gas emissions in an effort to limit the rise in Earth's temperature to no more than 2 degrees Celsius.

ECONOMICS >> *in Action*
China's War on Pollution

Beijing, the capital of China, is even bigger than New Delhi: the metropolitan area is home to 24 million people. And not long ago it was synonymous with air pollution. In 2014, when the city was host to Asia-Pacific Economic Cooperation, a high-profile international forum, the authorities imposed temporary pollution controls that literally cleared the air for a while; this was such a rare occurrence at the time that residents coined the term "APEC blue" for the unusual appearance of natural-colored skies.

In that same year, however, the Chinese government declared a longer-term "war on pollution." This involved a number of measures, including restrictions on coal burning and the closing of some of the oldest, most polluting plants; restrictions on highly polluting vehicles in major cities; and the introduction of highly subsidized electric buses.

As Beijing pivots to electric vehicles, the air is beginning to clear.

These measures worked: the air got a lot cleaner. Beijing's air is still much worse than air in, say, greater New York, which has a similar population; pollution hovers between "moderate" and "unhealthy." But it's far better than it was.

The striking thing is that China achieved this significant reduction in air pollution while remaining one of the world's fastest-growing economies. Chinese real GDP grew 38% between 2014 and 2019, or 6.4% a year, even as the air got steadily clearer. In other words, long-term economic growth can go along with an improving environment.

>> Check Your Understanding 24-5
Solutions appear at back of book.

1. Are economists typically more concerned about the limits to growth imposed by environmental degradation or those imposed by resource scarcity? Explain, noting the role of negative externalities (costs imposed by individuals or firms on others without the requirement to pay compensation), in your answer.

2. What is the link between greenhouse gas emissions and growth? What is the expected effect on growth from emissions reduction? Why is international burden sharing of greenhouse gas emissions reduction a contentious problem?

>> Quick Review

• Economists generally believe that environmental degradation poses a major challenge to **sustainable long-run economic growth.** They also generally believe that modern economies can find ways to alleviate limits to growth from natural resource scarcity through the price response that promotes conservation and the creation of alternatives.

• Economic growth tends to harm the environment unless actions are taken to protect it. Local environmental degradation can be addressed through political will and resources. Global environmental degradation is harder to address because it requires cooperation across many countries.

• The accumulation of greenhouse gases, a by-product of burning fossil fuels, has led to climate change, the raising of Earth's temperature. In order to avert the impact of climate change, effective government intervention is required.

• Developed countries and large countries that are rapidly growing need to shift from a heavy reliance on fossil fuels to using clean, energy sources like solar and wind power. This will come at a modest cost to the rise in real GDP per capita, a cost that is falling as technological innovation in clean energy sources advances.

• In the **Paris Agreement** of 2015, 196 countries agreed to reduce their greenhouse gas emissions in an effort to limit the rise in Earth's temperature.

Raising the Bar(code)

Bloomberg/Getty Images

When we think about innovation and technological progress, we tend to focus on the dramatic changes: cars replacing horses and buggies, electric light bulbs replacing gaslights, computers replacing adding machines and typewriters. However, much more progress is incremental and almost invisible to most people, yet has huge effects over time. Consider, for example, the simple bar-code scanner.

Bar codes were first used commercially in 1974, when a 10-pack of Wrigley's chewing gum was rung up with a scanner produced by the National Cash Register Corporation (now NCR Corp). Since then bar codes and their two-dimensional descendants—visual patterns that are meaningless to human eyes but are instantly recognizable by scanners and smartphones—have become ubiquitous, used to identify and route everything from shipping containers to airline passengers.

The benefits from machine-readable labels are enormous, extending well beyond what consumers in the checkout line can see. For example, retailers use them to continuously track sales, telling them when to reorder merchandise and restock shelves, what to keep in their warehouses, how productive individual workers

are, and more. Grocery retailing is a labor-intensive industry, and economists estimate that the adoption of bar-code technology reduced labor costs by as much as 40%. Ultimately, bar-code technology helped drive the computerization of the entire retail industry.

And this story isn't over. A growing number of retailers offer self-checkout, where customers scan items themselves and pay electronically. Some stores offer smartphone apps that offer even more convenience by letting customers scan items as they put them into the shopping cart.

You might think, then, that NCR, which remains a major player in point-of-service technologies like scanners, ATMs, and so forth, made a fortune from its leading role in this technology revolution. But while the company has done well, scanner sales in the early years weren't enormous: the adoption of bar-code scanners was relatively slow compared with the spread of smartphones a couple of decades later. Only about a third of supermarkets adopted them in the first decade after that historic pack of gum.

Why? To realize the full potential of bar-code technology, both retailers and firms had to spend substantial money up front to buy the scanners and the information-processing systems they served. Equally important, manufacturers had to install the equipment to put bar codes on their products. This created a chicken-and-egg problem, with retailers waiting to have more scanner-readable products available and manufacturers waiting for more scanner-ready stores.

Over time this problem was resolved as retailers and manufacturers made the necessary investments, setting the stage for widespread use of information technology. In fact, during the productivity surge from 1995 to 2005, retailing was one of the leading sources of overall productivity growth in the U.S. economy.

Adoption was slower in Europe. In the United States, big stores were the first to install scanners, and the technology fostered greater concentration of retailing at the expense of small, mom-and-pop stores that couldn't afford to implement scanner technology. In Europe, however, government policies—especially land-use policy—protected these stores.

Eventually, however, Europe began to follow the trend, too. Bar-code technology has spread from the United States to become almost universal, at least in advanced economies.

QUESTIONS FOR THOUGHT

1. Bar-code technology spurred a lot of investment in retailing. How did it alter the retailing production function? What would a similar amount of investment have accomplished without the new technology?

2. The spread of bar codes was delayed in the United States because everyone was waiting for someone else to move. What policy could have been adopted to address the delays? Would it have been a good idea?

3. Use the case to explain why international growth rates vary.

4. Despite initial barriers, bar codes have spread globally. What does this imply about differences in economic growth across countries?

SUMMARY

1. Growth is measured as changes in real GDP per capita in order to eliminate the effects of changes in the price level and changes in population size. Levels of real GDP per capita vary greatly around the world: about a quarter of the world's population lives in countries that are still poorer than the United States was in 1900. GDP per capita in the United States is about eight times as high as it was in 1900.

2. Growth rates of real GDP per capita also vary widely. According to the **Rule of 70,** the number of years it takes for real GDP per capita to double is equal to 70 divided by the annual growth rate of real GDP per capita.

3. The key to long-run economic growth is rising **labor productivity,** or just **productivity,** which is output per worker. Increases in productivity arise from increases in **physical capital** per worker and **human capital** per worker as well as **technological progress.** The **aggregate production function** shows how real GDP per worker depends on these three factors. Other things equal, there are **diminishing returns to physical capital:** holding human capital per worker and technology fixed, each successive addition to physical capital per worker yields a smaller increase in productivity than the one before. Equivalently, more physical capital per worker results in a lower, but still positive, increase in productivity. **Growth accounting,** which estimates the contribution of each factor to a country's economic growth, has shown that rising **total factor productivity,** the amount of output produced from a given amount of factor inputs, is key to long-run growth. It is usually interpreted as the effect of technological progress. In contrast to earlier times, natural resources are a less significant source of productivity growth in most countries today.

4. The large differences in countries' growth rates are largely due to differences in their rates of accumulation of physical and human capital as well as differences in technological progress. Although inflows of foreign savings from abroad help, a prime factor is differences in domestic savings and investment spending rates, since most countries that have high investment spending on physical capital finance it by high domestic savings. Technological progress is largely a result of **research and development,** or **R&D.**

5. Governments can help or hinder growth. Government policies that directly foster growth are subsidies to **infrastructure,** particularly public health infrastructure, subsidies to education and R&D, and maintenance of a well-functioning financial system that channels savings into investment spending, education, and R&D. Governments can enhance the environment for growth by protecting property rights (particularly intellectual property rights through patents), by being politically stable and by providing good governance. Poor governance includes corruption and excessive government intervention.

6. The world economy contains examples of success and failure in the effort to achieve long-run economic growth. East Asian economies have done many things right and achieved very high growth rates. The low growth rates of Latin American and African economies over many years led economists to believe that the **convergence hypothesis,** the claim that differences in real GDP per capita across countries narrow over time, fits the data only when factors that affect growth, such as education, infrastructure, and favorable government policies and institutions, are held equal across countries. In recent years, there has been an uptick in growth among some Latin American and sub-Saharan African countries, largely due to a boom in commodity exports.

7. Not only is economic growth uneven across countries, there are many cases where economic growth is uneven within countries. In the United States this is shown by a divergence in mean and median per capita income, highlighted by the growing income divide between rich and poor states.

8. Economists generally believe that environmental degradation pose a major challenge to **sustainable long-run economic growth.** Addressing the problem will require effective governmental intervention.

9. Climate change is linked to growth and there is broad consensus that government action is needed to address it. To avert the impact of climate change, countries will need to shift from a heavy reliance on fossil fuel to using clean, renewable energy sources. This will come at a modest cost to the rise in real GDP per capita, a cost that is falling as technological innovation in clean energy sources advances. Countries also need to cooperate with each other to realize the terms of the 2015 **Paris Agreement,** in which 196 signatory countries agreed to reduce their greenhouse gas emissions in an effort to limit the rise in Earth's temperature.

Rule of 70, p. 682
Labor productivity, p. 684
Productivity, p. 684
Physical capital, p. 684
Human capital, p. 685
Technological progress, p. 685

Aggregate production function, p. 685
Diminishing returns to physical
 capital, p. 686
Growth accounting, p. 687
Total factor productivity, p. 689
Research and development (R&D), p. 693

Infrastructure, p. 693
Convergence hypothesis, p. 697
Sustainable long-run economic growth,
 p. 702
Paris Agreement, p. 704

PRACTICE QUESTIONS

1. The accompanying table shows data from the World
Bank, World Development Indicators, for real GDP
per capita in 2010 U.S. dollars for Argentina, Ghana,
South Korea, and the United States for 1960, 1980,
2000, and 2018.

  a. Complete the table by expressing each year's real GDP
  per capita as a percentage of its 1960 and 2018 levels.

  b. How does the growth in living standards from 1960
  to 2018 compare across these four nations? What
  might account for these differences?

| | **Argentina** | | | **Ghana** | | | **South Korea** | | | **United States** | | |
| | Real GDP per capita (2010 dollars) | Percentage of | | Real GDP per capita (2010 dollars) | Percentage of | | Real GDP per capita (2010 dollars) | Percentage of | | Real GDP per capita (2010 dollars) | Percentage of | |
Year		1960 real GDP per capita	2018 real GDP per capita		1960 real GDP per capita	2018 real GDP per capita		1960 real GDP per capita	2018 real GDP per capita		1960 real GDP per capita	2018 real GDP per capita
1960	$5,643	?	?	$1,056	?	?	$944	?	?	$17,551	?	?
1980	7,908	?	?	881	?	?	3,700	?	?	28,590	?	?
2000	8,224	?	?	952	?	?	15,105	?	?	44,727	?	?
2018	10,044	?	?	1,807	?	?	26,762	?	?	54,579	?	?

2. The country of Androde is currently using Method 1
for its production function. By chance, scientists
stumble onto a technological breakthrough that will
enhance Androde's productivity. This technological breakthrough is reflected in another production
function, Method 2. The accompanying table shows
combinations of physical capital per worker and
output per worker for both methods, assuming that
human capital per worker is fixed.

Method 1		**Method 2**	
Physical capital per worker	Real GDP per worker	Physical capital per worker	Real GDP per worker
0	0.00	0	0.00
50	35.36	50	70.71
100	50.00	100	100.00
150	61.24	150	122.47
200	70.71	200	141.42
250	79.06	250	158.11
300	86.60	300	173.21
350	93.54	350	187.08
400	100.00	400	200.00
450	106.07	450	212.13
500	111.80	500	223.61

  a. Using the data in the accompanying table, draw the
  two production functions in one diagram. Androde's
  current amount of physical capital per worker is
  100. In your figure, label that point A.

  b. Starting from point A, over a period of 70 years,
  the amount of physical capital per worker in
  Androde rises to 400. Assuming Androde still uses
  Method 1, in your diagram, label the resulting
  point of production B. Using the Rule of 70, calculate by how many percent per year output per
  worker has grown.

  c. Now assume that, starting from point A, over the
  same period of 70 years, the amount of physical
  capital per worker in Androde rises to 400, but
  that during that time period, Androde switches
  to Method 2. In your diagram, label the resulting
  point of production C. Using the Rule of 70, calculate by how many percent per year output per
  worker has grown now.

  d. As the economy of Androde moves from point A
  to point C, what share of the annual productivity
  growth is due to higher total factor productivity?

3. The Bureau of Labor Statistics regularly releases
the "Productivity and Costs" report for the previous
month. Go to www.bls.gov and find the latest report.

(On the Bureau of Labor Statistics home page, from the tab "Subjects," select the link to "Productivity: Labor Productivity & Costs"; then, from the heading "LPC News Releases," find the most recent "Productivity and Costs" report.) What were the percent changes in business and nonfarm business productivity for the previous quarter? How does the percent change in that quarter's productivity compare to the percent change from the same quarter a year ago?

4. Why would you expect real GDP per capita in California and Pennsylvania to exhibit convergence but not in California and Baja California, a state of Mexico that borders the United States? What changes would allow California and Baja California to converge?

5. According to the U.S. Energy Information Administration, the proven oil reserves existing in the world in 2018 consisted of 1,663 billion barrels. In that year, the U.S. Energy Information Administration reported that the world daily oil production was 82.92 million barrels a day.

a. At this rate, for how many years will the proven oil reserves last? Discuss the Malthusian view in the context of the number you just calculated.

b. In order to do the calculation in part a, what did you assume about the total quantity of oil reserves over time? About oil prices over time? Are these assumptions consistent with the Malthusian view on resource limits?

c. Discuss how market forces may affect the amount of time the proven oil reserves will last, assuming that no new oil reserves are discovered and that the demand curve for oil remains unchanged.

PROBLEMS

1. The following table shows the average annual growth rate in real GDP per capita for Argentina, Ghana, and South Korea using data from the World Bank, World Development Indicators, for the past few decades.

Years	Average annual growth rate of real GDP per capita		
	Argentina	Ghana	South Korea
1968–1978	1.21%	−0.34%	9.02%
1978–1988	−0.25	−1.64	7.47
1988–1998	2.13	1.50	5.59
1998–2008	1.52	2.71	5.10
2008–2018	−0.16	4.12	2.55

a. For each 10-year period and for each country, use the Rule of 70 where possible to calculate how long it would take for that country's real GDP per capita to double.

b. Suppose that the average annual growth rate that each country achieved over the period 2008–2018 continues indefinitely into the future. Starting from 2018, use the Rule of 70 to calculate, where possible, the year in which a country will have doubled its real GDP per capita.

2. The following table provides approximate statistics on per capita income levels and growth rates for regions defined by income levels. According to the Rule of 70, starting in 2018 the high-income countries are projected to double their per capita GDP in approximately 70 years, in 2088. Throughout this question, assume constant growth rates for each of the regions are equal to their average value between 2000 and 2018.

Region	Real GDP per capita (2018)	Average annual growth rate of real GDP per capita (2000–2018)
High-income countries	$43,559	1.0%
Middle-income countries	5,149	3.6
Low-income countries	740	2.1

Data from: World Bank.

a. Calculate the ratio of per capita GDP in 2018 of the following:

   i. Middle-income to high-income countries

   ii. Low-income to high-income countries

   iii. Low-income to middle-income countries

b. Calculate the number of years it will take the low-income and middle-income countries to double their per capita GDP.

c. Calculate the per capita GDP of each of the regions in 2088. (*Hint:* How many times does their per capita GDP double in 70 years, the number of years from 2018 to 2088?)

d. Repeat part a with the projected per capita GDP in 2088.

e. Compare your answers to parts a and d. Comment on the change in economic inequality between the regions.

3. What roles do physical capital, human capital, technology, and natural resources play in influencing long-run economic growth of aggregate output per capita?

4. How have U.S. policies and institutions influenced the country's long-run economic growth?

5. Over the next 100 years, real GDP per capita in Groland is expected to grow at an average annual rate of 2.0%. In Sloland, however, growth is expected to be somewhat slower, at an average annual growth rate of 1.5%. If both countries have a real GDP per capita today of $20,000, how will their real GDP per capita differ in 100 years? [*Hint:* A country that has a real GDP today of x and grows at y% per year will achieve a real GDP of $\$x \times (1 + (y/100))^z$ in z years. We assume that $0 \le y \le 100$.]

6. The accompanying table shows data from the World Bank, World Development Indicators, for real GDP per capita (2010 U.S. dollars) in France, Japan, the United Kingdom, and the United States in 1960 and 2018. Complete the table. Have these countries reduced the income gap with the United States?

	1960		2018	
	Real GDP per capita (2010 dollars)	Percentage of U.S. real GDP per capita	Real GDP per capita (2010 dollars)	Percentage of U.S. real GDP per capita
France	$12,744	?	$43,664	?
Japan	8,608	?	48,920	?
United Kingdom	13,934	?	43,325	?
United States	17,551	?	54,579	?

7. The accompanying table shows data from the World Bank, World Development Indicators for real GDP per capita (2010 U.S. dollars) for Argentina, Ghana, South Korea, and the United States in 1960 and 2018. Complete the table. Have these countries caught up economically?

	1960		2018	
	Real GDP per capita (2010 dollars)	Percentage of U.S. real GDP per capita	Real GDP per capita (2010 dollars)	Percentage of U.S. real GDP per capita
Argentina	$5,643	?	$10,404	?
Ghana	1,056	?	1,807	?
South Korea	944	?	26,762	?
United States	17,551	?	54,579	?

8. Access the Discovering Data exercise for Chapter 24 online to answer the following questions.

   a. What was the ratio of Japanese GDP per capita relative to the United States in 1950 and 1991?

   b. Why has Japan's GDP caught up to that of the United States?

c. Rank the countries in order of richest to poorest (with 1 being the richest) in 1960 and 2010?

d. What was the ratio of GDP per capita for Spain relative to the United States in 1960 and 2010?

e. Which two countries experienced the fastest rate of convergence from 1960 through 2010?

f. Why are lower income countries, like Korea in 1960, able to grow faster than rich countries?

g. If countries continue along a similar path, will Japan, Korea, Chile, or Spain be the first country to reach the level of real GDP per capita in the United States?

9. The accompanying table shows the annual growth rate for the years 2000–2014 in per capita emissions of carbon dioxide (CO_2) and the annual growth rate in real GDP per capita for selected countries.

Country	2000–2014 Average annual growth rate	
	Real GDP per capita	CO_2 emissions per capita
Argentina	1.69%	1.17%
Bangladesh	4.33	4.47
Canada	0.96	0.01
China	9.24	7.48
Germany	1.20	−0.41
Ireland	1.30	−2.56
Japan	0.70	0.11
South Korea	3.51	2.32
Mexico	0.67	0.42
Nigeria	5.03	−1.30
Russia	4.16	1.35
South Africa	1.64	−0.02
United Kingdom	1.02	−2.20
United States	0.85	−1.27

Data from: Energy Information Administration; World Bank.

a. Rank the countries in terms of their growth in CO_2 emissions, from highest to lowest. What five countries have the highest growth rate in emissions? What five countries have the lowest growth rate in emissions?

b. Now rank the countries in terms of their growth in real GDP per capita, from highest to lowest. What five countries have the highest growth rate? What five countries have the lowest growth rate?

c. Would you infer from your results that CO_2 emissions are linked to growth in output per capita?

d. Do high growth rates necessarily lead to high CO_2 emissions?

▦ WORK IT OUT

10. You are hired as an economic consultant to the countries of Albernia and Brittania. Each country's current relationship between physical capital per worker and output per worker is given by the curve labeled "Productivity$_1$" in the accompanying diagram. Albernia is at point A and Brittania is at point B.

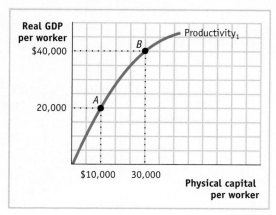

a. In the relationship depicted by the curve Productivity$_1$, what factors are held fixed? Do these countries experience diminishing returns to physical capital per worker?

b. Assuming that the amount of human capital per worker and the technology are held fixed in each country, can you recommend a policy to generate a doubling of real GDP per capita in Albernia?

c. How would your policy recommendation change if the amount of human capital per worker could be changed? Assume that an increase in human capital doubles the output per worker when physical capital per worker equals $10,000. Draw a curve on the diagram that represents this policy for Albernia. ▪

25

Savings, Investment Spending, and the Financial System

PAYING FOR A HIDDEN EMPIRE

AMAZON.COM IS THE WORLD'S LARGEST and most famous online retailer. Millions of people routinely visit its website to buy everything from books to electronics to pet supplies. You click a mouse or tap your smartphone, and a few days later the item you want shows up at your door, seemingly untouched by human hands.

Bloomberg/Getty Images

Through the financial system Amazon obtained billions of dollars to finance its expansion, making it the world's largest online retailer.

But the impression one sometimes has of a disembodied organization that summons consumer goods out of thin air is misleading: Amazon is by no means a virtual company. Behind those convenient online interactions and deliveries lies a vast, if mostly hidden, physical empire of server farms handling data and warehouses. In fact, that network of physical facilities is widely regarded as a key factor in Amazon's success. According to one recent analysis, Amazon has more than 175 warehouses ("fulfillment centers," in Amazon-speak) that employ 250,000 workers; half the U.S. population lives within 20 miles of one of these centers.

The existence of these warehouses, so close to major markets and containing a huge inventory of popular products, is what allows the firm to offer one- or two-day delivery on many items. And this superiority in distribution — some of you may have bought your textbook from Amazon! — gives the company a big competitive advantage.

We don't know exactly how much Amazon has spent to build this hidden physical empire, but the cost has surely run to many billions of dollars. Where did that money come from?

Not from reinvestment of the company's profits: Amazon, founded in 1994, basically earned no profits until 2016. But the company was able to convince outside investors that it would eventually become highly profitable. And the prospect of future profits was enough to bring in large amounts of money from outside investors.

Some of these investors bought equity — essentially shares in those expected future profits. In a move that was unusual for tech companies but was standard practice for many traditional companies, Amazon also, early in its history, sold debt: promises to pay investors a fixed amount each year, whatever happens. Those debt sales were controversial at the time, but are now widely viewed as having given Amazon a crucial advantage over competitors, who weren't able to make the same kind of investment in physical plant, especially those in warehouses.

Amazon, then, was able to get the money it needed for massive investment spending long before that spending could yield financial results. It was, in a way, a kind of financial miracle. But while Amazon is an exceptional case, the same kind of financial miracle happens all the time in modern economies.

The long-run growth we analyzed in the previous chapter depends crucially on a set of markets and institutions, collectively known as the *financial system,* that channels the funds of savers into productive investment spending. Without this system, businesses like Amazon would not be able to purchase much of the physical capital that is an important source of productivity growth. And savers would be forced to accept a lower return on their funds.

Historically, financial systems channeled funds into investment spending projects such as railroads and factories. Today, financial systems channel funds into new sources of growth such as green technology, social media, and investments in human capital. Without a well-functioning financial system, a country will suffer stunted economic growth.

In this chapter, we begin by focusing on the economy as a whole. We will examine the relationship between savings and investment spending. Next, we go behind this relationship and analyze the financial system, the means by which savings is transformed into investment spending.

We'll see how the financial system works by creating assets, markets, and institutions that increase the welfare of both savers (those with funds to invest) and borrowers (those with investment spending projects to finance). Finally, we examine the behavior of financial markets and why they often resist economists' attempts at explanation. ●

WHAT YOU WILL LEARN

- **What is the relationship between savings and investment spending?**

- **How does the loanable funds market match savers with borrowers?**

- **What are the purposes of the four principal types of financial assets: loans, bonds, stocks, and bank deposits?**

- **How do financial intermediaries help investors achieve diversification?**

- **What are the competing views about how asset prices are determined and why asset market fluctuations can be a source of macroeconomic instability?**

According to the **savings–investment spending identity,** savings and investment spending are always equal for the economy as a whole.

Matching Up Savings and Investment Spending

We learned in the previous chapter that two of the essential ingredients in economic growth are increases in the economy's levels of *human capital* and *physical capital.* Human capital is largely provided by governments through public education. (In countries with a large private education sector, like the United States, private post-secondary education is also an important source of human capital.) But physical capital, with the exception of infrastructure, is mainly created through private investment spending—that is, spending by firms rather than by the government.

Who pays for private investment spending? In some cases it's the people or corporations that actually do the spending—for example, a family that owns a business might use its own savings to buy new equipment or a new building, or a corporation might reinvest some of its own profits to build a new factory. In the modern economy, however, individuals and firms that create physical capital often do it with other people's money—money that they borrow or raise by selling stock.

You may recall Figure 22-1, which showed an extended version of the circular flow of funds through the economy. In Chapter 22 we focused on the left side of that diagram, the green arrows showing flows of money into and out of the markets for goods and services. In this chapter we focus on the blue arrows on the right side of the diagram, specifically those flowing into and out of the *financial markets,* markets in which the government, firms, and individuals trade not goods but promises to pay in the future.

To understand financial markets and how investment spending is financed, we need to look first at how savings and investment spending are related for the economy as a whole. Then we will examine how savings are allocated among investment spending projects.

The Savings–Investment Spending Identity

The most basic point to understand about savings and investment spending is that they are always equal. This is not a theory; it's a fact of accounting called the **savings–investment spending identity.**

To see why the savings–investment spending identity must be true, let's look again at the national income accounting that we learned in Chapter 22. Recall that GDP is equal to total spending on domestically produced final goods and services, and that we can write the following equation (which is the same as Equation 22-1):

(25-1) $GDP = C + I + G + X - IM$

where C is spending by consumers, I is investment spending, G is government purchases of goods and services, X is the value of exports to other countries, and IM is spending on imports from other countries.

The Savings–Investment Spending Identity in a Closed Economy   In a closed economy, there are no exports or imports. So $X = 0$ and $IM = 0$, which makes Equation 25-1 simpler. As we learned in Chapter 22, the overall income of this simplified economy would, by definition, equal total spending. Why? Recall one of the basic principles of economics from Chapter 1, that one person's spending is another person's income: the only way people can earn income is by selling something to someone else, and every dollar spent in the economy creates income for somebody. This is represented by Equation 25-2: on the left, GDP represents total income earned in the economy, and on the right, $C + I + G$ represents total spending in the economy:

(25-2) $GDP = C + I + G$
                Total income = Total spending

Now, what can be done with income? It can either be spent on consumption—consumer spending (*C*) plus government purchases of goods and services (*G*)—or saved (*S*). So it must be true that:

(25-3) $GDP = C + G + S$
                Total income = Consumption spending + Savings

where *S* is savings. Meanwhile, as Equation 25-2 tells us, total spending consists of either consumption spending (*C* + *G*) or investment spending (*I*):

(25-4) $GDP = C + G + I$
                Total income = Consumption spending + Investment spending

Putting Equations 25-3 and 25-4 together, we get:

(25-5) $C + G + S = C + G + I$
                Consumption spending + Savings = Consumption spending +
                                Investment spending

Subtract consumption spending (*C* + *G*) from both sides, and we get:

(25-6) $S = I$
                Savings = Investment spending

As we said, then, it's a basic accounting fact that savings equals investment spending for the economy as a whole.

Now, let's take a closer look at savings. Households are not the only parties that can save in an economy. In any given year, the government can save, too, if it collects more tax revenue than it spends. When this occurs, the difference is called a **budget surplus** and is equivalent to savings by government.

If, alternatively, government spending exceeds tax revenue, there is a **budget deficit**—a negative budget surplus. In this case, we often say that the government is *dissaving:* by spending more than its tax revenues, the government is engaged in the opposite of savings. One way to finance a budget deficit is by borrowing. **Government borrowing** is the total amount of funds borrowed by federal, state, and local governments in the financial markets.

We'll define the term **budget balance** to refer to both cases, with the understanding that the budget balance can be positive (a budget surplus) or negative (a budget deficit). The budget balance is defined as:

(25-7) $S_{Government} = T - G - TR$

where *T* is the value of tax revenues and *TR* is the value of government transfers. The budget balance is equivalent to savings by government—if it's positive, the government is saving; if it's negative, the government is dissaving. **National savings,** which we just called savings, for short, is equal to the sum of the budget balance and private savings, where private savings is disposable income (income plus government transfers minus taxes) minus consumption. It is given by:

(25-8) $S_{National} = S_{Government} + S_{Private}$

So Equations 25-6 and 25-8 tell us that, in a closed economy, the savings–investment spending identity has the following form:

(25-9) $S_{National} = I$
                National savings = Investment spending

The Savings–Investment Spending Identity in an Open Economy
In an open or international economy, goods and money can flow into and out of the country. This changes the savings–investment spending identity because savings

The **budget surplus** is the difference between tax revenue and government spending when tax revenue exceeds government spending.

The **budget deficit** is the difference between tax revenue and government spending when government spending exceeds tax revenue.

Government borrowing is the total amount of funds borrowed by federal, state, and local governments in the financial markets.

The **budget balance** is the difference between tax revenue and government spending.

National savings, the sum of private savings and the budget balance, is the total amount of savings generated within the economy.

THE DIFFERENT KINDS OF CAPITAL

It's important to understand clearly the three different kinds of capital: physical capital, human capital, and financial capital (as explained in the previous chapter):

1. *Physical capital* consists of manufactured resources such as buildings and machines.

2. *Human capital* is the improvement in the labor force generated by education and knowledge.

3. *Financial capital* is funds from savings that are available for investment spending. A country that has a positive net capital inflow is experiencing a flow of funds into the country from abroad that can be used for investment spending.

need not be spent on investment spending projects in the same country in which the savings are generated. That's because the savings of people who live in any one country can be used to finance investment spending that takes place in other countries. So any given country can receive *inflows* of funds—foreign savings that finance investment spending in that country. Any given country can also generate *outflows* of funds—domestic savings that finance investment spending in another country.

The net effect of international inflows and outflows of funds on the total savings available for investment spending in any given country is known as the **net capital inflow** into that country, equal to the total inflow of foreign funds minus the total outflow of domestic funds to other countries. Like the budget balance, a net capital inflow can be negative—that is, more capital can flow out of a country than flows into it. In recent years, the United States has experienced a consistent positive net capital inflow from foreigners, who view our economy as an attractive place to put their savings. In 2018, for example, net capital inflows into the United States were $509.5 billion.

It's important to note that, from a national perspective, a dollar generated by national savings and a dollar generated by capital inflow are not equivalent. Yes, they can both finance the same dollar's worth of investment spending. But any dollar borrowed from a saver must eventually be repaid with interest. A dollar that comes from national savings is repaid with interest to someone domestically—either a private party or the government.

But a dollar that comes as capital inflow must be repaid with interest to a foreigner. So a dollar of investment spending financed by a capital inflow comes at a higher *national* cost—the interest that must eventually be paid to a foreigner—than a dollar of investment spending financed by national savings.

The fact that a net capital inflow represents funds borrowed from foreigners is an important aspect of the savings–investment spending identity in an international economy. Consider an individual who spends more than their income; that person must borrow the difference from others. Similarly, a country that spends more on imports than it earns from exports must borrow the difference from foreigners. And that difference, the amount of funds borrowed from foreigners, is the country's net capital inflow. As we explain more fully in Chapter 33, this means the net capital inflow into a country is equal to the difference between imports and exports:

(25-10) $$NCI = IM - X$$
Net capital inflow = Imports – Exports

Rearranging Equation 25-1 we get:

(25-11) $I = (GDP - C - G) + (IM - X)$

Using Equation 25-3 we know that $GDP - C - G$ is equal to national savings, so that:

(25-12) $I = S_{National} + (IM - X) = S_{National} + NCI$
Investment spending = National savings + Net capital inflow

So the application of the savings–investment spending identity to an economy that is open to inflows or outflows of capital means that investment spending is equal to savings, where savings is equal to national savings *plus* net capital inflow. That is, in an economy with a positive net capital inflow, some investment spending is funded by the savings of foreigners. And in an economy with a negative net capital inflow (that is, more capital is flowing out than flowing in), some portion of national savings is funding investment spending in other countries.

Net capital inflow is the total inflow of funds into a country minus the total outflow of funds out of a country.

U.S. investment spending in 2018 totaled $4,315.5 billion. Private savings totaled $4,478.4 billion, and government savings equaled –$683.2 billion, leading to national savings of $3,795.2 billion. Net capital inflow was $509.5 billion. Notice that these numbers don't quite add up. Because data collection isn't perfect, there is a statistical discrepancy of $10.8 billion, the amount that national savings plus net capital inflow exceeded investment spending. We know this is a data error because the savings–investment spending identity must hold.

Figure 25-1 shows what the savings–investment spending identity looked like in 2018 for two of the world's major economies, those of the United States and Germany. To make the two economies easier to compare, we've measured savings and investment spending as percentages of GDP. In each panel the orange bars on the left show total investment spending and the multicolored bars on the right show the components of savings. U.S. investment spending was 21.0% of GDP, financed by a combination of private savings (24.1% of GDP) and positive net capital inflow (2.4% of GDP) and partly offset by a government budget deficit (–5.7% of GDP). German investment spending was higher as a percentage of GDP, at 21.8%. It was financed by a higher level of private savings as a percentage of GDP (27.2%), and a government budget surplus (1.9% of GDP), but was offset by a negative capital inflow or capital outflow (–7.3% of GDP).

The economy's savings finance its investment spending. But how are these funds that are available for investment spending allocated among various projects? That is, what determines which projects get financed (such as Amazon's fulfillment centers) and which don't? We'll see shortly that funds get allocated to investment spending projects using a familiar method: by the market, via supply and demand.

FIGURE 25-1 The Savings–Investment Spending Identity in Open Economies: The United States and Germany, 2018

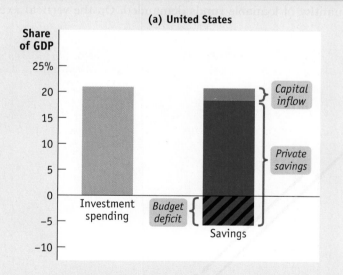

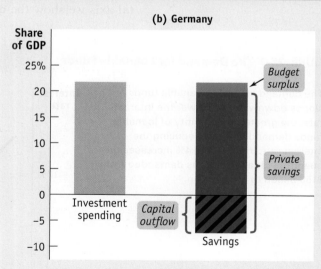

U.S. investment spending in 2018 (equal to 21.0% of GDP) was financed by a combination of private savings (24.1% of GDP) and a capital inflow (2.4% of GDP), which were partially offset by a government budget deficit (–5.7% of GDP). German investment spending in 2018 was slightly higher as a percentage of GDP (21.8%). It was financed by a higher level of private savings as a percentage of GDP (27.2%), and a small government budget surplus (1.9% of GDP), but was offset by a capital outflow (–7.3% of GDP). Bars may not equal due to statistical discrepancy.

Data from: International Monetary Fund.

The **loanable funds market** is a hypothetical market that illustrates the market outcome of the demand for funds generated by borrowers and the supply of funds provided by lenders.

The Market for Loanable Funds

For the economy as a whole, savings always equals investment spending. In a closed economy, savings is equal to national savings. In an international or open economy, savings is equal to national savings plus capital inflow. At any given time, however, savers, the people with funds to lend, are usually not the same as borrowers, the people who want to borrow to finance their investment spending. How are savers and borrowers brought together?

Savers and borrowers are matched up with one another in much the same way producers and consumers are matched up: through markets governed by supply and demand.

To understand this, it helps to consider a somewhat simplified version of reality. In the actual economy, there are a large number of different financial markets. These include markets for *bonds* and *loans,* which are both promises to pay a fixed amount whatever happens, and for *stocks,* which give investors a share of future profits. However, economists often work with a simplified model in which they assume that there is just one market that brings together those who want to lend money (savers) and those who want to borrow (firms with investment spending projects).

This hypothetical market is known as the **loanable funds market.** The price that is determined in the loanable funds market is the interest rate, denoted by *r.* As we noted in Chapter 23, loans typically specify a nominal interest rate. So although we call *r* "the interest rate," it is with the understanding that *r* is a nominal interest rate—an interest rate that is unadjusted for inflation.

We're not quite done simplifying things. There are, in reality, many different kinds of interest rates, because there are many different kinds of loans—short-term loans, long-term loans, loans made to corporate borrowers, loans made to governments, and so on. In the interest of simplicity, we'll ignore those differences and assume that there is only one type of loan.

OK, now we're ready to analyze how savings and investment get matched up.

The Demand for Loanable Funds Figure 25-2 illustrates a hypothetical demand curve for loanable funds, *D,* which slopes downward. On the horizontal axis we show the quantity of loanable funds demanded. On the vertical axis

---

FIGURE 25-2 The Demand for Loanable Funds

The demand curve for loanable funds slopes downward: the lower the interest rate, the greater the quantity of loanable funds demanded. Here, reducing the interest rate from 12% to 4% increases the quantity of loanable funds demanded from $150 billion to $450 billion.

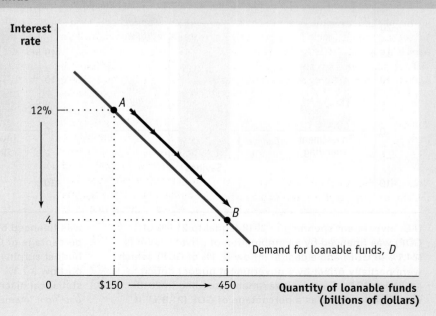

we show the interest rate, which is the "price" of borrowing. But why does the demand curve for loanable funds slope downward?

To answer this question, consider what a firm is doing when it engages in investment spending—say, by buying new equipment. Investment spending means laying out money right now, expecting that this outlay will lead to higher profits at some point in the future. In fact, however, the promise of a dollar five or ten years from now is worth less than an actual dollar right now. So an investment is worth making only if it generates a future return that is *greater* than the monetary cost of making the investment today. How much greater?

To answer that, we need to take into account the present value of the future return the firm expects to get. We examine the concept of *present value* in the accompanying For Inquiring Minds. As you'll recall, we learned in the Chapter 9 appendix how the concept of present value can be applied to dollars earned multiple years in the future. The appendix also addressed how present value is used to calculate the prices of shares of stock and bonds.

FOR INQUIRING MINDS   Using Present Value

An understanding of the concept of present value shows why the demand curve for loanable funds slopes downward. A simple way to grasp the essence of present value is to consider an example that illustrates the difference in value between having a sum of money today and having the same sum of money a year from now.

Suppose that exactly one year from today you will graduate, and you want to reward yourself by taking a trip that will cost $1,000. In order to have $1,000 a year from now, how much do you need today? It's not $1,000, and the reason why has to do with the interest rate.

Let's call the amount you need today X. We'll use r to represent the interest rate you receive on funds deposited in the bank. If you put X into the bank today and earn interest rate r on it, then after one year, the bank will pay you $X \times (1+r)$. If what the bank will pay you a year from now is equal to $1,000, then the amount you need today is:

$$X \times (1+r) = \$1,000$$

You can apply some basic algebra to find that:

$$X = \$1,000/(1+r)$$

Notice that the value of X depends on the interest rate r, which is always greater than 0. This fact implies that X is always less than $1,000. For example, if r = 5% (that is, r = 0.05), then X = $952.38. In other words, having $952.38 today is equivalent to having $1,000 a year from now when the interest rate is 5%. That is, $952.38 is the value of $1,000 today given an interest rate of 5%.

Now we can define the *present value* of X: it is the amount of money needed today in order to receive X in the future given the interest rate. In this numerical example, $952.38 is the present value of $1,000 received one year from now given an interest rate of 5%.

The concept of present value also applies to decisions made by firms. Think about a firm that has two potential investment projects in mind, each of which will yield $1,000 a year from now. However, each project has different initial costs—say, one requires that the firm borrow $900 right now and the other requires that the firm borrow $950. Which, if any, of these projects is worth borrowing money to finance and undertake?

The answer depends on the interest rate, which determines the present value of $1,000 a year from now. If the interest rate is 10%, the present value of $1,000 delivered a year from now is $909. In other words, at an interest rate of 10%, a $909 loan requires a repayment of $1,000 in a year's time. A loan less than $909 requires a repayment less than $1,000, while a loan of more than $909 requires a repayment of more than $1,000. So only the first project, which has an initial cost of less than $909, is profitable, because its return in a year's time is more than the amount of the loan repayment.

With an interest rate of 10%, the return on any project costing more than $909 is less than the amount the firm has to repay on its loan and is therefore unprofitable. If the interest rate is only 5%, however, the present value of $1,000 rises to $952. At this interest rate, both projects are profitable,

because $952 exceeds both projects' initial cost. So a firm will borrow more and engage in more investment spending when the interest rate is lower.

Meanwhile, similar calculations will be taking place at other firms. So a lower interest rate will lead to higher investment spending in the economy as a whole: the demand curve for loanable funds slopes downward.

When making financial decisions, individuals and firms must always keep in mind that having $1,000 today is worth more than having $1,000 a year from now.

In present value calculations, we use the interest rate to determine how the value of a dollar in the future compares to the value of a dollar today. But the fact is that future dollars are worth less than a dollar today, and they are worth even less when the interest rate is higher.

The intuition behind present value calculations is simple. The interest rate measures the opportunity cost of investment spending that results in a future return: instead of spending money on an investment spending project, a company could simply put the money into the bank and earn interest on it. And the higher the interest rate, the more attractive it is to simply put money into the bank and let it earn interest instead of investing it in an investment spending project.

In other words, the higher the interest rate, the higher the opportunity cost of investment spending. And, the higher the opportunity cost of investment spending, the lower the number of investment spending projects firms want to carry out, and therefore the lower the quantity of loanable funds demanded. It is this insight that explains why the demand curve for loanable funds is downward sloping.

When businesses engage in investment spending, they spend money right now in return for an expected payoff in the future. To evaluate whether a particular investment spending project is worth undertaking, a business must compare the present value of the future payoff with the current cost of that project. If the present value of the future payoff is greater than the current cost, a project is profitable and worth investing in. If the interest rate falls, then the present value of any given project rises, so more projects pass that test. If the interest rate rises, then the present value of any given project falls, and fewer projects pass that test.

So total investment spending, and hence the demand for loanable funds to finance that spending, is negatively related to the interest rate. Thus, the demand curve for loanable funds slopes downward. You can see this in Figure 25-2. When the interest rate falls from 12% to 4%, the quantity of loanable funds demanded rises from $150 billion (point *A*) to $450 billion (point *B*).

The Supply of Loanable Funds Figure 25-3 shows a hypothetical supply curve for loanable funds, *S*. Again, the interest rate plays the same role that the price plays in ordinary supply and demand analysis. But why is this curve upward sloping?

FIGURE 25-3 The Supply of Loanable Funds

The supply curve for loanable funds slopes upward: the higher the interest rate, the greater the quantity of loanable funds supplied. Here, increasing the interest rate from 4% to 12% increases the quantity of loanable funds supplied from $150 billion to $450 billion.

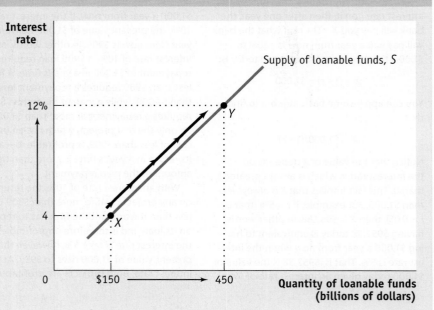

The answer is that loanable funds are supplied by savers, and savers incur an opportunity cost when they lend to a business: the funds could instead be spent on consumption—say, a nice vacation. Whether a given saver becomes a lender by making funds available to borrowers depends on the interest rate received in return. By saving your money today and earning interest on it, you are rewarded with higher consumption in the future when the loan you made is repaid with interest. So it is a good assumption that more people are willing to forgo current consumption and make a loan to a borrower when the interest rate is higher.

As a result, our hypothetical supply curve of loanable funds slopes upward. In Figure 25-3, lenders will supply $150 billion to the loanable funds market at an interest rate of 4% (point X); if the interest rate rises to 12%, the quantity of loanable funds supplied will rise to $450 billion (point Y).

The Equilibrium Interest Rate The interest rate at which the quantity of loanable funds supplied equals the quantity of loanable funds demanded is called the **equilibrium interest rate.** As you can see in Figure 25-4, the equilibrium interest rate, r^*, and the total quantity of lending, Q^*, are determined by the intersection of the supply and demand curves, at point E.

Here, the equilibrium interest rate is 8%, at which $300 billion is lent and borrowed. In this equilibrium, only investment spending projects that are profitable if the interest rate is 8% or higher are funded. Projects that are profitable only when the interest rate falls below 8% are not funded. Correspondingly, only lenders who are willing to accept an interest rate of 8% or less will have their offers to lend funds accepted; lenders who demand an interest rate higher than 8% do not have their offers to lend accepted.

Figure 25-4 shows how the market for loanable funds matches up desired savings with desired investment spending: in equilibrium, the quantity of funds that savers want to lend is equal to the quantity of funds that firms want to borrow. The figure also shows that this match-up is efficient, in two senses. First, the right investments get made: the investment spending projects that are actually financed have higher payoffs (in terms of present value) than those that do not get financed. Second, the right people do the saving and lending: the savers who actually lend funds are willing to lend for lower interest rates than those who do not.

The interest rate at which the quantity of loanable funds supplied equals the quantity of loanable funds demanded is the **equilibrium interest rate.**

FIGURE 25-4 Equilibrium in the Loanable Funds Market

At the equilibrium interest rate, the quantity of loanable funds supplied equals the quantity of loanable funds demanded. Here, the equilibrium interest rate is 8%, with $300 billion of funds lent and borrowed. Lenders who demand an interest rate of 8% or lower have their offers of loans accepted; those who demand a higher interest rate do not. Projects that are profitable at an interest rate of 8% or higher are funded; those that are profitable only when the interest rate falls below 8% are not.

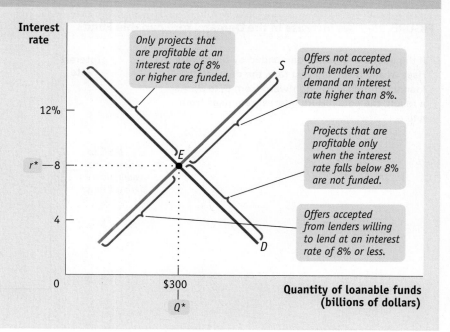

The insight that the loanable funds market leads to an efficient use of savings, although drawn from a highly simplified model, has important implications for real life. As we'll see shortly, it is the reason that a well-functioning financial system increases an economy's long-run economic growth rate.

Before we get to that, let's look at how the market for loanable funds responds to shifts of demand and supply. As in the standard model of supply and demand, where the equilibrium price changes in response to shifts of the demand or supply curves, here, the equilibrium interest rate changes when there are shifts of the demand curve for loanable funds, the supply curve for loanable funds, or both.

Shifts of the Demand for Loanable Funds Let's start by looking at the causes and effects of changes in demand.

The factors that can cause the demand curve for loanable funds to shift include the following:

1. *Changes in perceived business opportunities.* A change in beliefs about the payoff of investment spending can increase or decrease the amount of desired spending at any given interest rate. For example, during the 1990s there was great excitement over the business possibilities created by the internet, which had just begun to be widely used. As a result, businesses rushed to buy computer equipment, put fiber-optic cables in the ground, launch websites, and so on. This shifted the demand for loanable funds to the right. By 2001, the failure of many dot-com businesses had led to disillusionment with technology-related investment; this shifted the demand for loanable funds back to the left.

2. *Changes in government borrowing.* A government runs a budget deficit when, in a given year, it spends more than it receives. A government that runs budget deficits can be a major source of demand for loanable funds. For example, in 2009 the U.S. federal government was running a budget deficit in excess of $1.413 trillion, but by 2016 the federal deficit had been cut by $1 trillion to a little more than $330 billion. The federal government greatly reduced its borrowing needs. This change in the federal budget position had the effect, other things equal, of shifting the demand curve for loanable funds to the left.

Figure 25-5 shows the effects of an increase in the demand for loanable funds. S is the supply of loanable funds, and D_1 is the initial demand curve. The initial equilibrium interest rate is r_1. An increase in the demand for loanable funds means

---

FIGURE 25-5 An Increase in the Demand for Loanable Funds

If the quantity of funds demanded by borrowers rises at any given interest rate, the demand for loanable funds shifts rightward from D_1 to D_2. As a result, the equilibrium interest rate rises from r_1 to r_2.

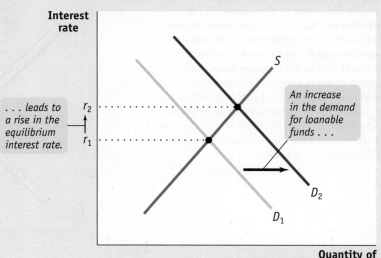

that the quantity of funds demanded rises at any given interest rate, so the demand curve shifts rightward to D_2. As a result, the equilibrium interest rate rises to r_2.

The fact that an increase in the demand for loanable funds leads, other things equal, to a rise in the interest rate has one especially important implication: it tells us that increasing or persistent government budget deficits are cause for concern because an increase in the government's deficit shifts the demand curve for loanable funds to the right, which leads to a higher interest rate. If the interest rate rises, businesses will cut back on their investment spending.

So, other things equal, a rise in the government budget deficit tends to reduce overall investment spending. Economists call the negative effect of government budget deficits on investment spending **crowding out.** Concerns about crowding out are one key reason to worry about increasing or persistent budget deficits.

However, it's important to add a qualification here: crowding out may not occur if the economy is depressed. When the economy is operating far below full employment, government spending can lead to higher incomes, and these higher incomes lead to increased savings at any given interest rate. Higher savings allows the government to borrow without raising interest rates. Many economists believe, for example, that the large budget deficits that the U.S. government ran from 2008 to 2013 in the face of a depressed economy caused little if any crowding out.

Crowding out occurs when a government budget deficit drives up the interest rate and leads to reduced investment spending.

Shifts of the Supply of Loanable Funds Like the demand for loanable funds, the supply of loanable funds can shift. Among the factors that can cause the supply of loanable funds to shift are the following:

1. *Changes in private savings behavior.* A number of factors can cause the level of private savings to change at any given interest rate. For example, following the coronavirus pandemic and concerns of a growing recession, households cut back on spending. In April 2020, the personal saving rate, savings as a percent of disposable income, increased to 33% from about 8% earlier in the year. This had the effect of shifting the supply curve of loanable funds to the right.

2. *Changes in net capital inflows.* Capital flows into and out of a country can change as investors' perceptions of that country change. For example, Greece experienced large net capital inflows after the creation of the euro, Europe's common currency, in 1999, because investors believed that Greece's adoption of the euro as its currency had made it a safe place to put their funds. By 2009, however, worries about the Greek government's solvency (and the discovery that it had been understating its debt) led to a collapse in investor confidence, and the net inflow of funds dried up. The effect of shrinking capital inflows was to shift the supply curve in the Greek loanable funds market to the left.

    In the mid-2000s, the United States received large net capital inflows, with much of the money coming from China and the Middle East. Those inflows helped fuel a big increase in residential investment spending—newly constructed homes—from 2003 to 2006. As a result of the bursting of the U.S. housing bubble in 2006–2007 and the subsequent deep recession, those inflows declined, and as of 2019 were still much smaller, as a percentage of GDP, than they had been at their peak.

Figure 25-6 shows the effects of an increase in the supply of loanable funds. D is the demand for loanable funds, and S_1 is the initial supply curve. The initial equilibrium interest rate is r_1. An increase in the supply of loanable funds means that the quantity of funds supplied rises at any given interest rate, so the supply curve shifts rightward to S_2. As a result, the equilibrium interest rate falls to r_2.

A Global Market for Loanable Funds? As we've noted, international capital flows can be an important influence on interest rates. What determines these capital flows? Most of the time, capital flows from countries where interest rates are relatively low to countries where interest rates are relatively high. And the result of these flows is to raise interest rates where they were low, and reduce rates where they were high.

FIGURE 25-6 An Increase in the Supply of Loanable Funds

If the quantity of funds supplied by lenders rises at any given interest rate, the supply of loanable funds shifts rightward from S_1 to S_2. As a result, the equilibrium interest rate falls from r_1 to r_2.

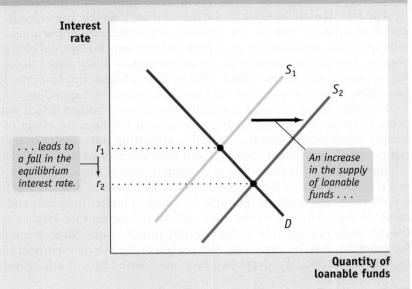

... leads to a fall in the equilibrium interest rate.

An increase in the supply of loanable funds ...

A **global loanable funds market** arises when international capital flows are so large that they equalize interest rates across countries.

For some purposes, it is useful to think about what would happen if this process went all the way—if international capital flows were so large that they had the effect of completely equalizing interest rates across countries. In that case we could talk about a **global loanable funds market.**

Figure 25-7 shows how such a market would work. We imagine a world consisting of only two countries, the United States and Britain. Panel (a) shows the loanable funds market in the United States, where the equilibrium in the absence of international capital flows is at point E_{US}, with an interest rate of 6%. Panel (b) shows the loanable funds market in Britain, where the equilibrium in the absence of international capital flows is at point E_B, with an interest rate of 2%.

FIGURE 25-7 Loanable Funds Markets in a Two-Country World

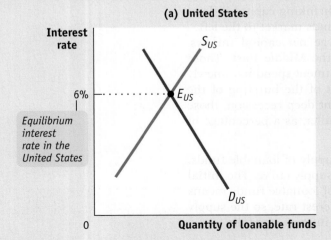

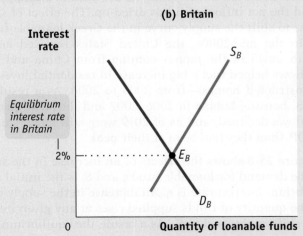

Here we show two countries, the United States and Britain, each with its own loanable funds market. The equilibrium interest rate is 6% in the U.S. market

but only 2% in the British market. This creates an incentive for capital to flow from Britain to the United States.

Will the actual interest rate in the United States remain at 6% and that in Britain at 2%? Not if it is easy for British residents to make loans to Americans. In that case, British lenders, attracted by high U.S. interest rates, will send some of their loanable funds to the United States. This capital inflow will increase the quantity of loanable funds supplied to American borrowers, pushing the U.S. interest rate down. It will also reduce the quantity of loanable funds supplied to British borrowers, pushing the British interest rate up. So international capital flows will narrow the gap between U.S. and British interest rates.

Let's further suppose that British lenders consider a loan to an American to be just as good as a loan to one of their own compatriots, and that U.S. borrowers regard a debt to a British lender as no more costly than a debt to a U.S. lender. In that case, the flow of funds from Britain to the United States will continue until the gap between their interest rates is eliminated. In other words, when residents of the two countries believe that foreign assets and foreign liabilities are as good as domestic ones, then international capital flows will equalize the interest rates in the two countries.

Figure 25-8 shows how an international equilibrium in the loanable funds market arises. In this case, the equilibrium interest rate is 4% in both the United States and Britain. At this interest rate, the quantity of loanable funds demanded by U.S. borrowers exceeds the quantity of loanable funds supplied by U.S. lenders. This gap is filled by "imported" funds—a capital inflow from Britain. At the same time, the quantity of loanable funds supplied by British lenders is greater than the quantity of loanable funds demanded by British borrowers. This excess is "exported" in the form of a capital outflow to the United States. A global loanable funds market arises as the two markets are in equilibrium at a common interest rate of 4%. At that rate, the total quantity of loans demanded by borrowers across the two markets is equal to the total quantity of loans supplied by lenders across the two markets.

In short, international flows of capital are like international flows of goods and services. Capital moves from places where it would be cheap in the absence of international capital flows to places where it would be expensive in the absence of such flows.

FIGURE 25-8 International Capital Flows in a Two-Country World

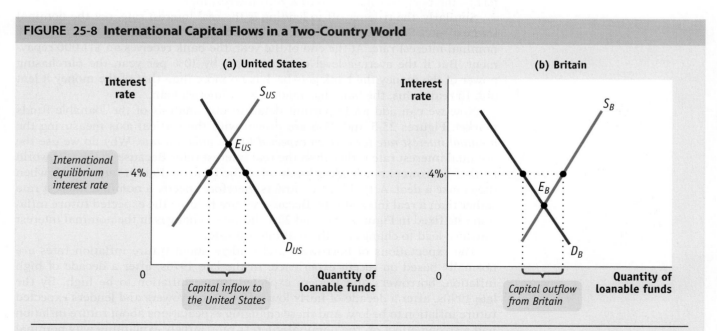

British lenders lend to borrowers in the United States, leading to equalization of interest rates at 4% in both countries. At that rate, U.S. borrowing exceeds U.S. lending; the difference is made up by capital inflows to the United States. Meanwhile, British lending exceeds British borrowing; the excess is a capital outflow from Britain.

In practice, this picture is complicated by various factors. In particular, countries use different currencies—the United States uses dollars, Britain uses pounds—and when you compare the interest rate on loans in dollars with the rate on loans in pounds, you need to take into account the possibility that the value of a pound in dollars can change over time. Still, the concept of a global market for loanable funds is very useful for some purposes, and we will return to this concept in later chapters.

Inflation and Interest Rates Anything that shifts either the supply of loanable funds curve or the demand for loanable funds curve changes the interest rate. Historically, major changes in interest rates have been driven by many factors, including changes in government policy and technological innovations that created new investment opportunities.

However, arguably the most important factor affecting interest rates over time—the main reason, for example, that interest rates today are much lower than they were in the late 1970s and early 1980s—is changing expectations about future inflation, which shift both the supply and the demand for loanable funds.

To understand the effect of expected future inflation on interest rates, recall our discussion in Chapter 23 of the way inflation creates winners and losers—for example, the way that higher than expected U.S. inflation in the 1970s and 1980s reduced the real value of homeowners' mortgages, which was good for the homeowners but bad for the banks. We also learned that economists summarize the effect of inflation on borrowers and lenders by distinguishing between the *nominal interest rate* and the *real interest rate,* where the difference is:

Real interest rate = Nominal interest rate − Inflation rate

The true cost of borrowing is the real interest rate, not the nominal interest rate. To see why, suppose a firm borrows $10,000 for one year at a 10% nominal interest rate. At the end of the year, it must repay $11,000—the amount borrowed plus the interest. But suppose that over the course of the year the average level of prices increases by 10%, so that the real interest rate is zero. Then the $11,000 repayment has the same purchasing power as the original $10,000 loan. In real terms, the borrower has received a zero-interest loan.

Similarly, the true payoff to lending is the real interest rate, not the nominal interest rate. Suppose that a bank makes a $10,000 loan for one year at a 10% nominal interest rate. At the end of the year, the bank receives an $11,000 repayment. But if the average level of prices rises by 10% per year, the purchasing power of the money the bank gets back is no more than that of the money it lent out. In real terms, the bank has made a zero-interest loan.

Now we can add an important detail to our analysis of the loanable funds market. Figures 25-5 and 25-6 are drawn with the vertical axis measuring the *nominal interest rate for a given expected future inflation rate.* Why do we use the nominal interest rate rather than the real interest rate? Because in the real world neither borrowers nor lenders know what the future inflation rate will be when they make a deal. Actual loan contracts therefore specify a nominal interest rate rather than a real interest rate. Because we are holding the expected future inflation rate fixed in Figures 25-5 and 25-6, however, changes in the nominal interest rate also lead to changes in the real interest rate.

The expectations of borrowers and lenders about future inflation rates are normally based on recent experience. In the late 1970s, after a decade of high inflation, borrowers and lenders expected future inflation to be high. By the late 1990s, after a decade of fairly low inflation, borrowers and lenders expected future inflation to be low. And these changing expectations about future inflation had a strong effect on the nominal interest rate, largely explaining why nominal interest rates were much lower in the early years of the twenty-first century than they were in the early 1980s.

Let's look at how changes in the expected future rate of inflation are reflected in the loanable funds model.

FIGURE 25-9 The Fisher Effect

D_0 and S_0 are the demand and supply curves for loanable funds when the expected future inflation rate is 0%. At an expected inflation rate of 0%, the equilibrium nominal interest rate is 4%. An increase in expected future inflation pushes both the demand and supply curves upward by 1 percentage point for every percentage point increase in expected future inflation. D_{10} and S_{10} are the demand and supply curves for loanable funds when the expected future inflation rate is 10%. The 10 percentage point increase in expected future inflation raises the equilibrium nominal interest rate to 14%. The expected real interest rate remains at 4%, and the equilibrium quantity of loanable funds also remains unchanged.

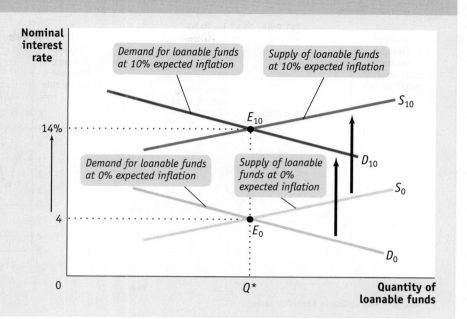

In Figure 25-9, the curves S_0 and D_0 show the supply and demand for loanable funds given that the expected future rate of inflation is 0%. In that case, equilibrium is at E_0, and the equilibrium nominal interest rate is 4%. Because expected future inflation is 0%, the equilibrium expected real interest rate over the life of the loan is also 4%.

Now suppose that the expected future inflation rate rises to 10%. The demand curve for loanable funds shifts upward to D_{10}: borrowers are now willing to borrow as much at a nominal interest rate of 14% as they were previously willing to borrow at 4%. That's because with a 10% inflation rate, a 14% nominal interest rate corresponds to a 4% real interest rate.

Similarly, the supply curve of loanable funds shifts upward to S_{10}: lenders require a nominal interest rate of 14% to persuade them to lend as much as they would previously have lent at 4%. The new equilibrium is at E_{10}: the result of an expected future inflation rate of 10% is that the equilibrium nominal interest rate rises from 4% to 14%.

This situation can be summarized as a general principle, known as the **Fisher effect** (after the U.S. economist Irving Fisher, who proposed it in 1930): *the expected real interest rate is unaffected by changes in expected future inflation.*

According to the Fisher effect, an increase in expected future inflation drives up the nominal interest rate, where each additional percentage point of expected future inflation drives up the nominal interest rate by 1 percentage point. The central point is that both lenders and borrowers base their decisions on the expected real interest rate. As a result, a change in the expected rate of inflation does not affect the equilibrium quantity of loanable funds or the expected real interest rate; all it affects is the equilibrium nominal interest rate.

According to the **Fisher effect,** an increase in expected future inflation drives up the nominal interest rate, leaving the expected real interest rate unchanged.

ECONOMICS >> *in Action*
Three Generations of U.S. Interest Rates

There have been some large movements in U.S. interest rates dating back to the 1950s. These movements clearly show how both changes in expected future inflation and changes in the expected return on investment spending move interest rates.

FIGURE 25-10 Changes in U.S. Expected Inflation and Interest Rates

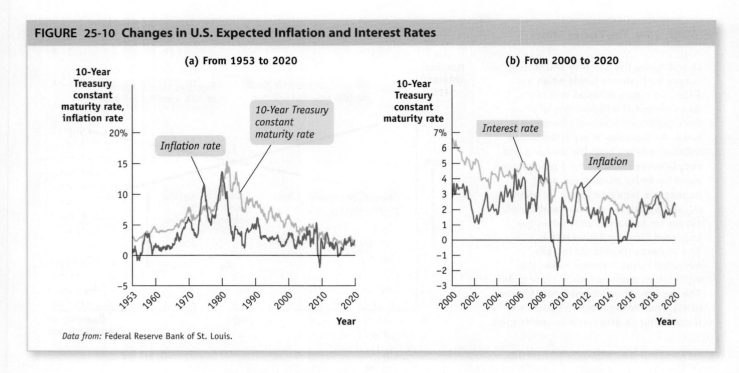

Data from: Federal Reserve Bank of St. Louis.

Panel (a) of Figure 25-10 illustrates the first effect. It shows the average interest rate on bonds issued by the U.S. government—specifically, bonds for which the government promises to repay the full amount after 10 years—from 1953 to 2020, along with the rate of consumer price inflation over the same period. As you can see, the big story about interest rates is the way they soared in the 1970s, before coming back down in the 1980s.

It's not hard to see why that happened: inflation shot up during the 1970s, leading to widespread expectations that high inflation would continue. And as we've seen, a higher expected inflation rate raises the equilibrium interest rate. As the inflation rate came down in the 1980s, so did expectations of future inflation, and this brought interest rates down as well.

Panel (b) illustrates the second effect: changes in the expected return on investment spending and interest rates, with a "close-up" of interest rates and inflation from 2000 to 2020. Interest rates have been much lower in recent years—usually below 2%—than they were at the beginning of the twenty-first century, when they typically exceeded 5%. Yet inflation didn't fall very much. In fact, surveys and other evidence suggest that expected inflation has been stable, at around 2%, for the past couple of decades. What happened instead seems to have been a decline in perceived investment returns. Economists are still debating the causes of this decline, although many point to slowing population growth, which has reduced the need for new housing, office buildings, and other forms of capital.

Throughout this whole process, total savings was equal to total investment spending, and the rise and fall of the interest rate played a key role in matching lenders with borrowers.

>> Check Your Understanding 25-1

Solutions appear at back of book.

1. Use a diagram of the loanable funds market to illustrate the effect of the following events on the equilibrium interest rate and investment spending.
   a. An economy is opened to international movements of capital, and a net capital inflow occurs.
   b. Retired people generally save less than working people at any interest rate. The proportion of retired people in the population goes up.

2. Explain what is wrong with the following statement: "Savings and investment spending may not be equal in the economy as a whole because when the interest rate rises, households will want to save more money than businesses will want to invest."

3. Suppose that expected inflation rises from 3% to 6%.
   a. How will the real interest rate be affected by this change?
   b. How will the nominal interest rate be affected by this change?
   c. What will happen to the equilibrium quantity of loanable funds?

• Because government borrowing competes with private borrowers in the loanable funds market, a government deficit can cause **crowding out,** which is less likely if the economy is in a slump.

• Capital flows allow countries to export their savings to borrowers in other countries. Capital flows from a country with a lower interest rate to a country with a higher interest rate, reducing the difference in those rates. If capital flows are large, a **global loanable funds market** arises, equalizing interest rates across countries.

• Higher expected future inflation raises the nominal interest rate through the **Fisher effect,** leaving the real interest rate unchanged.

‖ The Financial System

A well-functioning financial system that brings together the funds of investors and the vision of entrepreneurs has made the rise of Amazon possible. But to think that this is an exclusively modern phenomenon would be misguided. Financial markets raised the funds that were used to develop colonial markets in India, to build canals across Europe, and to finance the Napoleonic wars in the eighteenth and early nineteenth centuries. Capital inflows financed the early economic development of the United States, funding investment spending in mining, railroads, and canals. In fact, many of the principal features of financial markets and assets have been well understood in Europe and the United States since the eighteenth century. These features are no less relevant today. So let's begin by understanding exactly what is traded in financial markets.

Financial markets are where households invest their current savings and their accumulated savings, or **wealth,** by purchasing *financial assets*. A **financial asset** is a paper claim that entitles the buyer to future income from the seller. For example, when a saver lends funds to a company, the loan is a financial asset sold by the company that entitles the lender (the buyer of the financial asset) to future income from the company.

A household can also invest its current savings or wealth by purchasing a **physical asset,** a tangible object that can be used to generate future income such as a preexisting house or preexisting piece of equipment. Purchasing a physical asset gives the owner the right to dispose of the object as they wish (for example, rent it or sell it).

Recall that the purchase of a financial or physical asset is typically called investing. So if you purchase a preexisting piece of equipment—say, a used airliner—you are investing in a physical asset. In contrast, if you spend funds that *add* to the stock of physical capital in the economy—say, purchasing a newly manufactured airplane—you are engaging in investment spending.

If you get a loan from your local bank—say, to buy a new car—you and the bank are creating a financial asset: your loan. A *loan* is one important kind of financial asset in the real world, one that is owned by the lender—in this case, your local bank. In creating that loan, you and the bank are also creating a **liability,** a requirement to pay income in the future.

So although your loan is a financial asset from the bank's point of view, it is a liability from your point of view. In addition to loans, there are three other important kinds of financial assets: *stocks, bonds,* and *bank deposits*. Because a financial asset is a claim to future income that someone has to pay, it is also someone else's liability. We'll explain in detail shortly who bears the liability for each type of financial asset.

These four types of financial assets—loans, stocks, bonds, and bank deposits—exist because the economy has developed a set of specialized markets, like the stock market and the bond market, and specialized institutions, like banks, that facilitate the flow of funds from lenders to borrowers. Taken together, these institutions and markets are known as the financial system.

A well-functioning financial system is a critical ingredient in achieving long-run growth because it encourages greater savings and investment spending. It also ensures that savings and investment spending are undertaken efficiently.

Financial markets are where households invest their current and accumulated savings. A household's **wealth** is the value of its accumulated savings.

A **financial asset** is a paper claim that entitles the buyer to future income from the seller.

A **physical asset** is a tangible object that can be used to generate future income.

A **liability** is a requirement to pay income in the future.

Transaction costs are the expenses of negotiating and executing a deal.

Financial risk is uncertainty about future outcomes that involve financial losses or gains.

To understand how this occurs, we first need to know what tasks the financial system needs to accomplish. Then we can see how the job gets done.

Three Tasks of a Financial System

Our earlier analysis of the loanable funds market ignored three important problems facing borrowers and lenders: *transaction costs, risk,* and the desire for *liquidity.* The three tasks of a financial system are to reduce these problems in a cost-effective way that enhances the efficiency of financial markets and makes it more likely that lenders and borrowers will make mutually beneficial trades—trades that make society as a whole richer. We'll turn now to examining how financial assets are designed and how institutions are developed to cope with these problems.

Task 1: Reducing Transaction Costs The expenses of actually putting together and executing a deal are known as **transaction costs.** For example, arranging a loan requires spending time and money negotiating the terms of the deal, verifying the borrower's ability to pay, drawing up and executing legal documents, and so on.

Suppose a large business decided that it wanted to raise $1 billion for investment spending. No individual would be willing to lend that much. And negotiating individual loans from thousands of different people, each willing to lend a modest amount, would impose very large total costs because each individual transaction would incur a cost. Total costs would be so large that the entire deal would probably be unprofitable for the business.

Fortunately, that's not necessary: when large businesses want to borrow money, they either go to a bank or sell bonds in the bond market. Obtaining a loan from a bank avoids large transaction costs by involving only a single borrower and a single lender. We'll explain more about how bonds work in the next section. For now, it is enough to know that the principal reason a bond market exists is to allow companies to borrow large sums of money without incurring large transaction costs.

Task 2: Reducing Risk Another problem that real-world borrowers and lenders face is **financial risk,** uncertainty about future outcomes that involve financial losses or gains. Financial risk, or simply risk, is a problem because the future is uncertain, containing the potential for losses as well as gains. For example, owning and driving a car entails the financial risk of a costly accident. Most people view potential losses and gains in an *asymmetrical* way: most people experience the loss in welfare from losing a given amount of money more intensely than they experience the increase in welfare from gaining the same amount of money.

A person who is more sensitive to a loss than to a gain of an equal dollar amount is called *risk-averse.* Most people are risk-averse, although to differing degrees. For example, people who are wealthy are typically less risk-averse than those who are not so well-off.

A well-functioning financial system helps people reduce their exposure to risk, which risk-averse people would like to do. Suppose the owner of a business expects to make a greater profit if they buy additional capital equipment, but they aren't completely sure that this greater profit will happen. The business owner could pay for the equipment by using their savings or selling their house. But if the profit is significantly less than expected, the business owner will have lost savings, a house, or both. That is, the owner would be exposed to a lot of risk due to uncertainty about how well or poorly the business performs. (This is why business owners, who typically have a significant portion of their own personal wealth tied up in their businesses, are usually more tolerant of risk than the average person.)

So, being risk-averse, this business owner wants to share the risk of purchasing new capital equipment with someone, even if that requires sharing some of the profit if all goes well. A business owner can do this by selling shares of the company to other people and using the money received from selling shares, rather than money from the sale of other assets, to finance the equipment purchase. By selling shares in the company, the business owner reduces personal losses if the profit is less than expected: the owner won't have lost any other assets. But if things go well, the shareholders earn a share of the profit as a return on their investment.

By selling a share of the business, the owner has achieved *diversification:* the owner has been able to invest in several things in a way that lowers total risk. The owner has maintained their investment in their bank account, a financial asset; in ownership of their house, a physical asset; and in ownership of the unsold portion of their business, a financial asset. These investments are likely to carry some risk of their own; for example, the bank may fail or the house may burn down (though in the modern United States it is likely that the business owner is partly protected against these risks by insurance).

But even in the absence of insurance, the business owner is better off having maintained investments in these different assets because their different risks are *unrelated,* or *independent, events*. This means, for example, that the house is no more likely to burn down if the business does poorly and that the bank is no more likely to fail if the house burns down.

To put it another way, if one asset performs poorly, it is very likely that the other assets will be unaffected and, as a result, the total risk of loss has been reduced. But if the business owner had invested all their wealth in their business, the owner would have faced the prospect of losing everything if the business had performed poorly. By engaging in **diversification**—investing in several assets with unrelated, or independent, risks—our business owner has lowered the total risk of loss.

The desire of individuals to manage and reduce their total risk by engaging in diversification is why we have stocks and a stock market, as we'll explain in detail in the next section.

Task 3: Providing Liquidity The financial system also exists to provide investors with *liquidity*, a concern that—like risk—arises because the future is uncertain. Suppose that, having made a loan, a lender suddenly finds themself in need of cash—say, to meet a medical emergency. Unfortunately, if that loan was made to a business that used it to buy new equipment, the business cannot repay the loan on short notice to satisfy the lender's need to recover the money. Knowing in advance that there is a danger of needing to get the money back before the term of the loan is up, our lender might be reluctant to lock up the money by lending it to a business.

An asset is **liquid** if it can be quickly converted into cash with relatively little loss of value, **illiquid** if it cannot. As we'll see, stocks and bonds are a partial answer to the problem of liquidity. Banks provide an additional way for individuals to hold liquid assets and still finance illiquid investment spending projects, such as buying capital equipment for a business.

To help lenders and borrowers make mutually beneficial deals, then, the economy needs ways to reduce transaction costs, to reduce and manage risk through diversification, and to provide liquidity. How does it achieve these tasks?

Types of Financial Assets

Recall that in the modern economy there are four main types of financial assets: *loans, bonds, stocks,* and *bank deposits*. In addition, financial innovation has allowed the creation of a wide range of *loan-backed securities*. Each asset serves a somewhat different purpose. We'll examine loans, bonds, stocks, and loan-backed securities now, reserving our discussion of bank deposits until the following section.

Loans A lending agreement made between an individual lender and an individual borrower is a **loan.** Most people encounter loans in the form of a student loan

---

An individual can engage in **diversification** by investing in several different assets so that the possible losses are independent events.

An asset is **liquid** if it can be quickly converted into cash with relatively little loss of value.

An asset is **illiquid** if it cannot be quickly converted into cash with relatively little loss of value.

A **loan** is a lending agreement between an individual lender and an individual borrower.

A **default** occurs when a borrower fails to make payments as specified by the loan or bond contract.

A **loan-backed security** is an asset created by pooling individual loans and selling shares in that pool.

or a bank loan to finance the purchase of a car or a house. And small businesses usually use bank loans to buy new equipment.

The good aspect of loans is that a given loan is usually tailored to the needs of the borrower. Before a small business can get a loan, it usually has to discuss its business plans, its profits, and so on with the lender. This results in a loan that meets the borrower's needs and ability to pay.

The bad aspect of loans is that making a loan to an individual person or a business typically involves a lot of transaction costs, such as the cost of negotiating the terms of the loan, investigating the borrower's credit history and ability to repay, and so on. To minimize these costs, large borrowers such as major corporations and governments often take a more streamlined approach: they sell (or issue) bonds.

Bonds An IOU issued by a borrower is known as a bond. Normally, the seller of the bond promises to pay a fixed sum of interest each year and to repay the principal—the value stated on the face of the bond—to the owner of the bond on a particular date. So a bond is a financial asset from its owner's point of view and a liability from its issuer's point of view.

A bond issuer sells a number of bonds with a given interest rate and maturity date to whoever is willing to buy them, a process that avoids costly negotiation of the terms of a loan with many individual lenders.

Bond purchasers can acquire information free of charge on the quality of the bond issuer, such as the bond issuer's credit history, from bond-rating agencies rather than incurring the expense of investigating it themselves. A particular concern for investors is the possibility of **default,** the risk that the bond issuer will fail to make payments as specified by the bond contract. Once a bond's risk of default has been rated, it can be sold on the bond market as a more or less standardized product, one with clearly defined terms and quality. In general, bonds with a higher default risk must pay a higher interest rate to attract investors.

Another important advantage of bonds is that they are easy to resell. This provides liquidity to bond purchasers. Indeed, a bond will often pass through many hands before it finally comes due. Loans, in contrast, are much more difficult to resell because, unlike bonds, they are not standardized: they differ in size, quality, terms, and so on. This makes them a lot less liquid than bonds.

Loan-Backed Securities Assets created by pooling individual loans and selling shares in that pool (a process called *securitization*) are called **loan-backed securities.** This type of asset has become extremely popular over the past two decades. While mortgage-backed securities—in which thousands of individual home mortgages are pooled and shares are sold to investors—are the best-known example, securitization has also been widely applied to student loans, credit card loans, and auto loans.

These loan-backed securities are traded on financial markets like bonds; they are preferred by investors because they provide more diversification and liquidity than individual loans. However, with so many loans packaged together, it can be difficult to assess the true quality of the asset. That difficulty came to haunt investors during the financial crisis of 2008, when the bursting of the housing bubble led to widespread defaults on mortgages and large losses for holders of supposedly "safe" mortgage-backed securities, pain that spread throughout the entire financial system.

Stocks A share in the ownership of a company is a stock. A share of stock is a financial asset from its owner's point of view and a liability from the company's point of view. Not all companies sell shares of their stock; privately held companies are owned by an individual or a few partners, who get to keep all of the company's profit. Most large companies, however, do sell stock. For example, Microsoft has nearly 8 billion shares outstanding; if you buy one of those shares, you are entitled to one eight billionth of the company's profit, as well as 1 of 8 billion votes on company decisions.

Why does Microsoft, historically a very profitable company, allow you to buy a share in its ownership? Why didn't Bill Gates and Paul Allen, the two founders of Microsoft, keep complete ownership for themselves and just sell bonds for their investment spending needs? The reason, as we have just learned, is risk: few individuals are risk-tolerant enough to face the risk involved in being the sole owner of a large company.

Reducing the risk that business owners face, however, is not the only way in which the existence of stocks improves society's welfare: it also improves the welfare of investors who buy stocks. Shareowners are able to enjoy the higher returns over time that stocks generally offer in comparison to bonds. Over the past century, stocks have typically yielded about 7% after adjusting for inflation; bonds have yielded only about 2%. But as investment companies warn you, "past performance is no guarantee of future results."

And there is a downside: owning the stock of a given company is riskier than owning a bond issued by the same company. Why? Loosely speaking, a bond is a promise while a stock is a hope: by law, a company must pay what it owes its lenders before it distributes any profit to its shareholders. And if the company should fail (that is, be unable to pay its interest obligations and declare bankruptcy), its physical and financial assets go to its bondholders—its lenders—while its shareholders generally receive nothing. So although a stock generally provides a higher return to an investor than a bond, it also carries higher risk.

But the financial system has devised ways to help investors as well as business owners simultaneously manage risk and enjoy somewhat higher returns. It does that through the services of institutions known as *financial intermediaries*.

Financial Intermediaries

A **financial intermediary** is an institution that transforms funds gathered from many individuals into financial assets. The most important types of financial intermediaries are *mutual funds, pension funds, life insurance companies,* and *banks*. About three-quarters of the financial assets Americans own are held through these intermediaries rather than directly.

Mutual Funds As we've seen, owning shares of a company entails accepting risk in return for a higher potential reward. But it should come as no surprise that stock investors can lower their total risk by engaging in diversification. By owning a *diversified portfolio* of stocks—a group of stocks in which risks are unrelated to, or offset by, one another—rather than concentrating investment in the shares of a single company or a group of related companies, investors can reduce their risk.

In addition, financial advisers, aware that most people are risk-averse, almost always advise their clients to diversify not only their stock portfolio but also their entire wealth by holding other assets in addition to stock—assets such as bonds and cash. (And, for good measure, to have plenty of insurance in case of accidental losses.)

However, for individuals who don't have a large amount of money to invest— say, $1 million or more—building a diversified stock portfolio can incur high transaction costs (particularly fees paid to stockbrokers) because they are buying a few shares of a lot of companies. Fortunately for such investors, *mutual funds* help solve the problem of achieving diversification without high transaction costs.

A **mutual fund** is a financial intermediary that creates a stock portfolio by buying and holding shares in companies and then selling shares of the stock portfolio to individual investors. By buying these shares, investors with a relatively small amount of money to invest can indirectly hold a diversified portfolio,

A **financial intermediary** is an institution that transforms the funds it gathers from many individuals into financial assets.

A **mutual fund** is a financial intermediary that creates a stock portfolio and then resells shares of this portfolio to individual investors.

TABLE 25-1 Vanguard 500 Index Fund, Top Holdings (as of January 2020)

Company	Percent of mutual fund assets invested in a company
Microsoft Corp.	5.03%
Apple Inc.	4.64
Amazon.com Inc.	3.19
Facebook Inc. A	1.88
Alphabet Inc. A	1.63
Alphabet Inc. C	1.63
Berkshire Hathaway Inc. B	1.60
Johnson & Johnson	1.44
JPMorgan Chase & Co.	1.43
Visa Inc. A	1.27

Data from: Morningstar.

achieving a better return for any given level of risk than they could otherwise achieve. Table 25-1 shows an example of a diversified mutual fund, the Vanguard 500 Index Fund. It shows the percentage of investors' money invested in the stocks of the largest companies in the mutual fund's portfolio.

Many mutual funds also perform market research on the companies they invest in. This is important because there are thousands of stock-issuing U.S. companies (not to mention foreign companies), each differing in terms of its likely profitability, dividend payments, and so on. It would be extremely time-consuming and costly for an individual investor to do adequate research on even a small number of companies. Mutual funds save transaction costs by doing this research for their customers.

The mutual fund industry represents a huge portion of the modern U.S. economy, not just of the U.S. financial system. In total, U.S. mutual funds had assets of $17.7 trillion at the end of 2019. In 2019, the largest mutual fund company was Vanguard, with $3.4 trillion in assets in mutual funds.

We should mention, by the way, that mutual funds charge fees for their services. These fees are quite small for mutual funds that simply hold a diversified portfolio of stocks without trying to pick winners. But the fees charged by mutual funds that claim to have special expertise in investing your money can be quite high.

Pension Funds and Life Insurance Companies In addition to mutual funds, many Americans have holdings in **pension funds,** nonprofit institutions that collect the savings of their members and invest those funds in a wide variety of assets, providing their members with income when they retire. Although pension funds are subject to some special rules and receive special treatment for tax purposes, they function much like mutual funds. They invest in a diverse array of financial assets, allowing their members to achieve more cost-effective diversification and market research than they would be able to achieve individually. At the end of 2019, pension funds in the United States held more than $24.4 trillion in assets.

Americans also have substantial holdings in the policies of **life insurance companies,** which guarantee a payment to the policyholder's beneficiaries (typically, the family) when the policyholder dies. By enabling policyholders to cushion their beneficiaries from financial hardship arising from their death, life insurance companies also improve welfare by reducing risk.

Banks Recall the problem of liquidity: other things equal, people want assets that can be readily converted into cash. Bonds and stocks are much more liquid than physical assets or loans, yet the transaction cost of selling bonds or stocks to meet a sudden expense can be large. Furthermore, for many small and moderate-size companies, the cost of issuing bonds and stocks is too large given the modest amount of money they seek to raise. A *bank* is an institution that helps resolve the conflict between lenders' needs for liquidity and the financing needs of borrowers who don't want to use the stock or bond markets.

A bank works by first accepting funds from *depositors:* when you put your money in a bank, you are essentially becoming a lender by lending the bank your money. In return, you receive credit for a **bank deposit**—a claim on the bank, which is obliged to give you your cash if and when you demand it. So a bank deposit is a financial asset owned by the depositor and a liability of the bank that holds it.

A **pension fund** is a type of mutual fund that holds assets in order to provide retirement income to its members.

A **life insurance company** sells policies that guarantee a payment to a policyholder's beneficiaries when the policyholder dies.

A **bank deposit** is a claim on a bank that obliges the bank to give the depositor their cash when demanded.

GLOBAL COMPARISON CORPORATE BONDS IN THE UNITED STATES AND THE EURO AREA

A business that wants to borrow funds could do this two ways: by selling bonds to investors or by getting loans from banks. There are advantages and disadvantages to each strategy.

On the one hand, issuing bonds tends to be cheaper than borrowing from a bank, because it eliminates the middleman. Also, banks often place conditions on loans, restricting the borrower's freedom to conduct its business as it chooses. On the other hand, bank loans can be less risky than issuing bonds. If a borrower gets into difficulty, its bank will typically be supportive, offering more time to repay if a good plan is in place to fix their problems. Bond holders are much less flexible.

It's a tough choice — and interestingly, companies in the United States and their counterparts in Europe generally make different choices. The figure shows the value of bonds issued by nonfinancial corporations in the United States and in the euro area, the group of European countries using the euro as a common currency, both expressed as a percentage of GDP in 2019. U.S. companies issue more bonds than their European counterparts, who rely much more on bank borrowing.

Why the difference? Generally, U.S. companies are more inclined to take risks. Also, European households are more inclined than U.S. households to leave large sums in bank accounts. As a result, European banks have more money to lend than their U.S. counterparts.

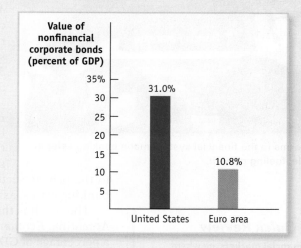

Data from: BIS Statistics Explorer.

A bank, however, keeps only a fraction of its customers' deposits in the form of ready cash. Most of its deposits are lent out to businesses, buyers of new homes, and other borrowers. These loans come with a long-term commitment by the bank to the borrower: as long as the borrower makes their payments on time, the loan cannot be recalled by the bank and converted into cash. So a bank enables those who wish to borrow for long lengths of time to use the funds of those who wish to lend but simultaneously want to maintain the ability to get their cash back on demand.

More formally, a **bank** is a financial intermediary that provides liquid financial assets in the form of deposits to lenders and uses their funds to finance the illiquid investment spending needs of borrowers. In essence, a bank is engaging in a kind of mismatch: lending for long periods of time while subject to the condition that its depositors could demand their funds back at any time. How can it manage that?

The bank counts on the fact that, on average, only a small fraction of its depositors will want their cash at the same time. On any given day, some people will make withdrawals and others will make new deposits; these will roughly cancel each other out. So the bank needs to keep only a limited amount of cash on hand to satisfy its depositors.

In addition, if a bank becomes financially incapable of paying its depositors, individual bank deposits are guaranteed to depositors up to $250,000 by the Federal Deposit Insurance Corporation, or FDIC, a federal agency. This reduces the risk to a depositor of holding a bank deposit, in turn reducing the incentive to withdraw funds if concerns about the financial state of the bank should arise. So, under normal conditions, banks need to hold only a fraction of their depositors' cash.

By reconciling the needs of savers for liquid assets with the needs of borrowers for long-term financing, banks play a key economic role. As the following Economics in Action explains, the creation of a well-functioning banking system seems to be an important condition for economic success.

A **bank** is a financial intermediary that provides liquid assets in the form of bank deposits to lenders and uses those funds to finance the illiquid investment spending needs of borrowers.

ECONOMICS >> *in Action*
Banks, Success, and South America

Reforms to the financial system made banking safer in Chile, fueling growth.

Argentina, as we noted in Chapter 24, is a notable example of disappointing long-run economic growth. In the early twentieth century it was considered a rich country, but GDP per capita has grown only slowly since then. And in the past few decades Argentina has fallen well behind some of its neighbors, especially Chile, Latin America's biggest economic success story. As recently as 1990 Argentina was slightly richer than Chile, but since then Chile's GDP per capita has risen at an annual rate of 3.3%, versus only 1.7% in Argentina, so that Chile is now about 50% richer than its neighbor.

What explains this difference in fortunes? There are surely multiple reasons, but financial development is probably an important factor. After a banking crisis in the early 1980s, Chile implemented reforms that made banks safer, encouraging savers to increase deposits and allowing rapid growth in loans to the private sector. Argentina, by contrast, continued to experience a series of banking crises, as well as bouts of inflation that eroded the real value of deposits.

The result is that there is vastly more financial intermediation in Chile than in Argentina. Economists often use domestic credit to the private sector, measured as a percentage of GDP, as a rough measure of the amount of financial intermediation in an economy. In advanced countries with well-developed financial institutions this number typically ranges between 100% and 200%. In 2018 Chile's domestic credit was 116% of GDP, similar to that of advanced countries. In Argentina the number was only 16%, indicating an economy with very limited financial intermediation. This probably means that Chile is doing a much better job than its once-richer neighbor of channeling its savings into productive investments.

>> Quick Review

• **Financial markets** are where households can invest their current savings or their **wealth** by purchasing either **financial assets** or **physical assets.** A financial asset is a seller's **liability.**

• A well-functioning financial system reduces **transaction costs,** reduces **financial risk** by enabling **diversification,** and provides **liquid** assets, which investors prefer to **illiquid** assets.

• The four main types of financial assets are **loans,** bonds, stocks, and **bank deposits.** A recent innovation is **loan-backed securities,** which are more liquid and more diversified than individual loans. Bonds with a higher **default** risk typically must pay a higher interest rate.

• The most important types of **financial intermediaries** are **mutual funds, pension funds, life insurance companies,** and **banks.**

• A bank accepts bank deposits, which obliges it to return depositors' cash on demand, and lends those funds to borrowers for long lengths of time.

>> Check Your Understanding 25-2
Solutions appear at back of book.

1. Rank the following assets in terms of (i) level of transaction costs, (ii) level of risk, (iii) level of liquidity.
   a. A bank deposit with a guaranteed interest rate
   b. A share of a highly diversified mutual fund, which can be quickly sold
   c. A share of the family business, which can be sold only if you find a buyer and all other family members agree to the sale

2. What relationship would you expect to find between the level of development of a country's financial system and its level of economic development? Explain in terms of the country's level of savings and level of investment spending.

‖ Financial Fluctuations

We've learned that the financial system is an essential part of the economy; without stock markets, bond markets, and banks, long-run economic growth would be hard to achieve. Yet the news isn't entirely good: the financial system sometimes doesn't function well and instead is a source of instability in the short run.

In fact, the financial consequences of a sharp fall in housing prices became a major problem for economic policy makers starting in the summer of 2007. By the fall of 2008, it was clear that the U.S. economy faced a severe slump as it adjusted to the consequences of greatly reduced home values, and unemployment stayed elevated for years. We could easily write a whole book on asset market fluctuations. In fact, many people have. Here, we briefly discuss the causes of asset price fluctuations.

The Demand for Stocks

Once a company issues shares of stock to investors, those shares can then be resold to other investors in the stock market. And thanks to cable TV and the internet, you can easily spend all day watching stock market fluctuations—the movement up and down of the prices of individual stocks—as well as summary measures of stock prices like the Dow Jones Industrial Average. These fluctuations reflect changes in supply and demand by investors. But what causes the supply and demand for stocks to shift?

Remember that stocks are financial assets: they are shares in the ownership of a company. Unlike a good or service, whose value to its owner comes from its consumption, the value of an asset comes from its ability to generate higher future consumption of goods or services.

A financial asset allows higher future consumption in two ways. First, many financial assets provide regular income to their owners in the form of interest payments or dividends. But many companies don't pay dividends; instead, they retain their earnings to finance future investment spending. Investors purchase non-dividend-paying stocks in the belief that they will earn income from selling the stock in the future at a profit, the second way of generating higher future income. Even in the cases of a bond or a dividend-paying stock, investors will not want to purchase an asset that they believe will sell for less in the future than today, because such an asset will reduce their wealth when they sell it.

So the value of a financial asset today depends on investors' beliefs about the future value or price of the asset. If investors believe that it will be worth more in the future, they will demand more of the asset today at any given price; consequently, today's equilibrium price of the asset will rise. Conversely, if investors believe the asset will be worth less in the future, they will demand less today at any given price; consequently, today's equilibrium price of the asset will fall. Today's stock prices will change according to changes in investors' expectations about future stock prices.

Suppose an event occurs that leads to a rise in the expected future price of a company's shares—say, for example, Apple announces that it forecasts higher

---

FOR INQUIRING MINDS   How Now, Dow Jones?

Financial news reports often lead with the day's stock market action, as measured by changes in the Dow Jones Industrial Average, the S&P 500, and the NASDAQ.

All three are stock market indices. Like the consumer price index, they are numbers constructed as a summary of average prices—in this case, prices of stocks.

- The Dow, created by the financial analysis company Dow Jones, is an index of the prices of stock in 30 leading companies.

- The S&P 500 is an index of 500 companies, created by Standard and Poor's, another financial company.

- The NASDAQ is compiled by the National Association of Securities Dealers, which trades the stocks of smaller new companies.

Because these indices contain different groups of stocks, they track somewhat different things. The Dow, because it contains only 30 of the largest companies, tends to reflect traditional business powerhouses. The NASDAQ is heavily influenced by technology stocks. The S&P 500, a broad measure, is in between.

These indexes give investors a quick, snapshot view of how stocks from certain sectors of the economy are doing. And the price of a stock embodies investors' expectations about the future prospects of the underlying company. By implication, an index composed of stocks drawn from companies in a particular sector embodies investors' expectations of the future prospects of that sector of the economy.

The numbers tell the tale.

than expected profitability due to torrential sales of the latest version of the iPhone. Demand for Apple shares will increase. At the same time, existing shareholders will be less willing to supply their shares to the market at any given price, leading to a decrease in the supply of Apple shares. And as we know, an increase in demand or a decrease in supply (or both) leads to a rise in price.

Alternatively, suppose that an event occurs that leads to a fall in the expected future price of a company's shares—say, Home Depot announces that it expects lower profitability because a slump in home sales has depressed the demand for home improvements. Demand for Home Depot shares will decrease. At the same time, supply will increase because existing shareholders will be more willing to supply their Home Depot shares to the market. Both changes lead to a fall in the stock price.

So stock prices are determined by the supply and demand for shares—which, in turn, depend on investors' expectations about the future stock price.

Stock prices are also affected by changes in the attractiveness of substitute assets, like bonds. As we learned early on, the demand for a particular good decreases when purchasing a substitute good becomes more attractive—say, due to a fall in its price. The same lesson holds true for stocks: when purchasing bonds becomes more attractive due to a rise in interest rates, stock prices will fall. And when purchasing bonds becomes less attractive due to a fall in interest rates, stock prices will rise.

The Demand for Other Assets

Everything we've just said about stocks applies to other assets as well, including physical assets. Consider the demand for commercial real estate—office buildings, shopping malls, and other structures that provide space for business activities. An investor who buys an office building does so for two reasons. First, because space in the building can be rented out, the owner of the building receives income in the form of rent. Second, the investor may expect the building to rise in value, meaning that it can be sold at a higher price at some future date.

As in the case of stocks, the demand for commercial real estate also depends on the attractiveness of substitute assets, especially bonds. When interest rates rise, the demand for commercial real estate decreases; when interest rates fall, the demand for commercial real estate increases.

Most Americans don't own commercial real estate. Only half of the population owns any stock, even indirectly through mutual funds, and for most of those people, stock ownership is well under $50,000. However, at the end of 2019 about 65% of American households owned another kind of asset: their own homes. What determines housing prices?

You might wonder whether home prices can be analyzed the same way we analyze stock prices or the price of commercial real estate. After all, stocks pay dividends, commercial real estate yields rents, but when a family lives in its own home, no money changes hands.

In economic terms, however, that doesn't matter very much. To a large extent, the benefit of owning your own home is the fact that you don't have to pay rent to someone else—or, to put it differently, it's as if you were paying rent to yourself. In fact, the U.S. government includes *implicit rent*—an estimate of the amount that homeowners, in effect, pay to themselves—in its estimates of GDP. The amount people are willing to pay for a house depends in part on the implicit rent they expect to receive from that house.

The demand for housing, like the demand for other assets, also depends on what people expect to happen to future prices: they're willing to pay more for a house if they believe they can sell it at a higher price sometime in the future.

Last but not least, the demand for houses depends on interest rates: a rise in the interest rate increases the cost of a mortgage and leads to a decrease in housing demand; a fall in the interest rate reduces the cost of a mortgage and causes an increase in housing demand.

All asset prices, then, are determined by a similar set of factors. But we haven't yet fully answered the question of what determines asset prices because we haven't explained what determines investors' *expectations* about future asset prices.

Asset Price Expectations

There are two principal competing views about how asset price expectations are determined. One view, which comes from traditional economic analysis, emphasizes the rational reasons why expectations *should* change. The other, widely held by market participants and also supported by some economists, emphasizes the irrationality of market participants.

The Efficient Markets Hypothesis Suppose you were trying to assess what Home Depot's stock is really worth. To do this, you would look at the *fundamentals,* the underlying determinants of the company's future profits. These would include factors like the changing shopping habits of the U.S. public and the prospects for home remodeling. You would also want to compare the earnings you could expect to receive from Home Depot with the likely returns on other financial assets, such as bonds.

According to one view of asset prices, the value you would come up with after a careful study of this kind would, in fact, turn out to be the price at which Home Depot stock is already selling in the market. Why? Because all publicly available information about Home Depot's fundamentals is already embodied in its stock price. Any difference between the market price and the value suggested by a careful analysis of the underlying fundamentals indicates a profit opportunity to smart investors, who then sell Home Depot stock if it looks overpriced and buy it if it looks underpriced.

The **efficient markets hypothesis** is the general form of this view; it means that asset prices always embody all publicly available information. One implication of the efficient markets hypothesis is that at any point in time, stock prices are fairly valued: they reflect all currently available information about fundamentals. So they are neither overpriced nor underpriced.

Another implication of the efficient markets hypothesis is that the prices of stocks and other assets should change only in response to new information about the underlying fundamentals. Since new information is by definition unpredictable—if it were predictable, it wouldn't be new information—movements in asset prices are also unpredictable. As a result, the movement of, say, stock prices will follow a **random walk**—the general term for the movement over time of an unpredictable variable.

The efficient markets hypothesis plays an important role in understanding how financial markets work. Most investment professionals and many economists, however, regard it as an oversimplification. Investors, they claim, aren't that rational.

Irrational Markets? Many people who actually trade in the markets, such as individual investors and professional money managers, are skeptical of the efficient markets hypothesis. They believe that markets often behave irrationally and that a smart investor can engage in successful *market timing*—buying stocks when they are underpriced and selling them when they are overpriced.

Although economists are generally skeptical about claims that there are sure-fire ways to outsmart the market, many have also challenged the efficient markets hypothesis. It's important to understand, however, that finding particular examples where the market got it wrong does not disprove the efficient markets hypothesis. If the price of Home Depot stock plunges from $40 to $10 because of

According to the **efficient markets hypothesis,** asset prices embody all publicly available information.

A **random walk** is the movement over time of an unpredictable variable.

FOR INQUIRING MINDS   Behavioral Finance

Individuals often make irrational— sometimes predictably irrational—choices that leave them worse off economically than would other, feasible alternatives. People also have a habit of repeating the same decision-making mistakes. This kind of behavior is the subject of *behavioral economics,* which includes the rapidly growing subfield of *behavioral finance,* the study of how investors in financial markets often make predictably irrational choices. In fact, the 2013 Nobel Prize in Economics was awarded to Yale professor Robert Shiller (along with two others), for his work showing how financial markets exhibit clear signs of irrationality.

Like most people, investors depart from rationality in systematic ways. In particular, they are prone to

- *Overconfidence:* having a misguided faith that they are able to spot a winning stock
- *Loss aversion:* being unwilling to sell an unprofitable asset and accept the loss
- A *herd mentality:* buying an asset when its price has already been driven high and selling it when its price has already been driven low

This irrational behavior raises an important question: can investors who *are* rational make a lot of money at the expense of those investors who aren't—for example, by buying a company's stock if irrational fears make it cheap?

The answer to this question is sometimes yes and sometimes no. Some professional investors have made huge profits by betting against irrational moves in the market—buying when there is irrational selling and selling when there is irrational buying. For example, the billionaire hedge fund manager John Paulson made $4 billion by betting against subprime mortgages during the U.S. housing bubble of 2007–2008 because he understood that these financial assets were being sold at inflated prices.

But sometimes even a rational investor cannot profit from market irrationality. For example, a money manager has to obey customers' orders to buy or sell even when those actions are irrational. Likewise, it can be much safer for professional money managers to follow the herd: if they do that and their investments go badly, they have the career-saving excuse that no one foresaw a problem.

But if they've gone against the herd and their investments go south, they are likely to be fired for making poor choices. So rational investors can even exacerbate the irrational moves in financial markets.

Some observers of historical trends hypothesize that financial markets alternate between periods of complacency and forgetfulness, which breed bubbles as investors irrationally believe that prices can only go up, followed by a crash, which in turn leads investors to avoid financial markets altogether and renders asset prices irrationally cheap.

Clearly, the events of the past 20 years, with a huge housing bubble followed by extreme turmoil in financial markets, have given researchers in the area of behavioral finance a lot of material to work with.

a sudden change in buying patterns, this doesn't mean that the market was inefficient in originally pricing the stock at $40. The fact that buying patterns were about to change wasn't publicly available information, so it wasn't embodied in the earlier stock price.

Serious challenges to the efficient markets hypothesis focus instead either on evidence of systematic misbehavior of market prices or on evidence that individual investors don't behave in the way the theory suggests. For example, some economists believe they have found strong evidence that stock prices fluctuate more than can be explained by news about fundamentals.

Others believe they have strong evidence that individual investors behave in systematically irrational ways. For example, people seem to expect that a stock that has risen in the past will keep on rising, even though the efficient markets hypothesis tells us there is no reason to expect this. The same appears to be true of other assets, especially housing: the great housing bubble, discussed in the Economics in Action that follows this section, arose in large part because homebuyers assumed that home prices would continue rising in the future.

Asset Prices and Macroeconomics

How should macroeconomists and policy makers deal with the fact that asset prices fluctuate a lot and that these fluctuations can have important economic effects? This question has become one of the major problems facing macroeconomic policy.

On one side, policy makers are reluctant to assume that the market is wrong—that asset prices are either too high or too low. In part, this reflects the efficient markets hypothesis, which says that any information that is publicly available is already accounted for in asset prices. More generally, it's hard to make the case that government officials are better judges of appropriate prices than private investors who are putting their own money on the line.

On the other side, the past 25 years were marked by not one but two huge asset bubbles, each of which created major macroeconomic problems when it burst. In the late 1990s the prices of technology stocks, including but not limited to dot-com internet firms, soared to hard-to-justify heights. When the bubble burst, these stocks lost, on average, two-thirds of their value in a short time, helping to cause the 2001 recession and a period of high unemployment. A few years later there was a major bubble in housing prices. The collapse of this bubble in 2008 triggered a severe financial crisis followed by a deep recession, and the lingering effects of the crisis afflicted the U.S. economy years later.

These events have prompted much debate over whether and how to limit financial instability. We discuss financial regulation and the efforts to make it more effective in Chapter 29.

ECONOMICS >> *in Action*
The Rise and Fall of Mortgage Delinquencies

For the past 40 years about a quarter of U.S. investment spending, on average, has been "residential fixed investment": building places for people to live. Because these are mainly single-family homes or condos rather than apartment buildings, families must come up with large sums to purchase their dwellings, and relatively few people can afford to pay cash.

Instead, home purchases are typically paid for by taking out a mortgage—a loan from a bank or other financial intermediary that gives the lender the right to seize your house if you fail to make scheduled payments. That might sound like a risky proposition for the borrower; what if one or more members of the family lose their jobs or face unexpected medical expenses, and can't keep up the payments? In practice, however, "delinquencies"—missed payments—are normally rare, affecting only about 1 mortgage in 40. One reason the rate is so low is that families in financial difficulties can often sell their houses and pay off their loans.

As panel (a) of Figure 25-11 shows, however, there was a huge surge in mortgage delinquencies from 2007 to 2010, at which point almost 1 in 8 families was missing payments. This period of widespread mortgage delinquencies lasted several years, before beginning a gradual decline. As of 2019 delinquencies were back down to normal historical levels.

What happened? As panel (b) of Figure 25-11 shows, there was a dramatic increase in mortgage debt between 2000 and 2007, which was closely associated with a period of rapidly rising home prices. Both borrowers and lenders believed that it was safe for homebuyers to borrow more than in the past, because rising prices would make it easy to sell houses and repay loans even if borrowers experienced financial difficulties.

As it turned out, however, the big rise in home prices was a bubble—and the bursting of the bubble provoked a severe recession, which led to high unemployment and greater financial distress. So delinquencies surged.

FIGURE 25-11 Debt and Delinquencies

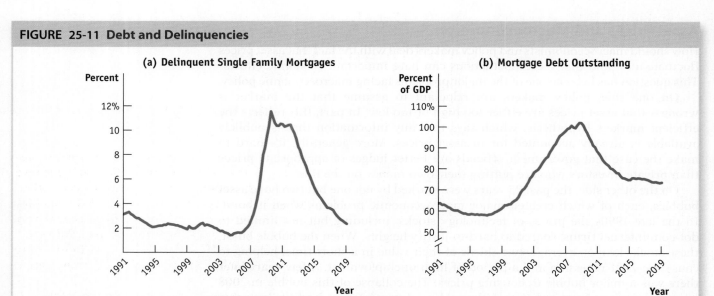

Data from: Panel (a): Board of Governors of the Federal Reserve System. Panel (b): Bureau of Economic Analysis and Board of Governors of the Federal Reserve System.

Eventually, as you can see in the figure, reduced borrowing and economic recovery reduced the level of mortgage debt relative to income, and delinquencies returned to more or less normal levels.

>> **Check Your Understanding 25-3**

Solutions appear at back of book.

1. What is the likely effect of each of the following events on the stock price of a company? Explain your answers.
   a. The company announces that although profits are low this year, it has discovered a new line of business that will generate high profits next year.
   b. The company announces that although it had high profits this year, those profits will be less than had been previously announced.
   c. Other companies in the same industry announce that sales are unexpectedly slow this year.
   d. The company announces that it is on track to meet its previously forecast profit target.

2. Assess the following statement: "Although many investors may be irrational, it is unlikely that over time they will behave irrationally in exactly the same way—such as always buying stocks the day after the Dow has risen by 1%."

>> **Quick Review**

• Financial market fluctuations can be a source of short-run macroeconomic instability.

• Asset prices are driven by supply and demand as well as by the desirability of competing assets like bonds. Supply and demand also reflect expectations about future asset prices. One view of expectations is the **efficient markets hypothesis,** which leads to the view that stock prices follow a **random walk.**

• Market participants and some economists question the efficient markets hypothesis. In practice, policy makers don't assume that they can outsmart the market, but they also don't assume that markets will always behave rationally.

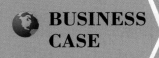

Grameen Bank:
Banking Against Poverty

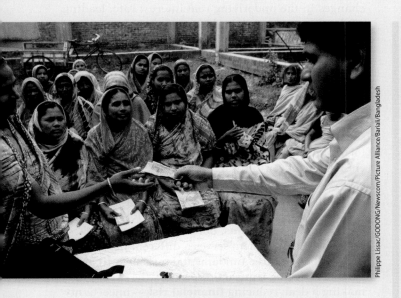

Philippe Lissac/GODONG/Newscom/Picture Alliance/Bariali/Bangladesh

An old joke says that a banker will only lend you money if you don't need it. So when Guadalupe Perez found it hard to pay the rent for her party decoration store in Queens, New York, as the Great Recession hurt her business, she normally would have been forced to close her doors. Instead she was able to turn for help to Grameen America, obtaining a loan to tide her over. "It opened up a way for me to keep my business," she said. "It was a loan that I could pay little by little; I felt it was a good choice for me." And she returned to Grameen, borrowing several more times to expand her store and invest in more inventory.

Grameen America is a subsidiary of Grameen Bank in Bangladesh, which pioneered the business of *microcredit*, providing small loans to poor individuals. It was created in the mid-1970s by Muhammad Yunus, a Bangladeshi economist with a PhD from Vanderbilt University. Regular banks require a borrower to have an established credit history and/or assets that are put up as collateral for the loan (and will be seized if the loan isn't repaid on time)—requirements that a poor person can rarely meet.

Instead, Grameen Bank relies on collective responsibility to ensure that its loans are repaid: each borrower is part of a five-member group that approves each other's loan and provides oversight. The group doesn't have any legal obligation to repay the loan, but in practice the group usually does take financial responsibility if a borrower gets into difficulties. If everyone in the group repays on time, each member is able to borrow a larger amount the next time.

Grameen operates in over 100 countries, from the United States to Uganda. The great majority of its customers are rural women seeking to escape poverty by starting small businesses. Since its inception it has lent over $30 billion to well over nine million women.

Even in a rich country like the United States, *microlending*—defined as a loan of less than $50,000—has become a booming business. Since 2008, when it was founded, through 2019 Grameen America has made over 530,000 microloans to women and dispensed nearly $1.4 billion. The company estimates that borrowers have increased their income by an average of $1,800 annually.

However, microcredit isn't a panacea. Multiple studies have found that while microcredit does increase small-business investment, its impacts in reducing poverty and improving family well-being are limited. And in some cases it leads to excessive debt. Still, the overall impact of microcredit is positive, especially when combined with other efforts to expand access to the financial system.

Fittingly, in 2006 Yunus and Grameen received the Nobel Peace Prize for their contributions to development and poverty reduction.

QUESTIONS FOR THOUGHT

1. What market inefficiency is being exploited by Grameen Bank? What is the source of this inefficiency?

2. What tasks of a financial system does microlending perform?

3. What do you predict is the effect of Grameen Bank's lending on a community?

SUMMARY

1. Investment in physical capital is necessary for long-run economic growth. So in order for an economy to grow, it must channel savings into investment spending.

2. According to the **savings–investment spending identity,** savings and investment spending are always equal for the economy as a whole. The government is a source of savings when it runs a positive **budget balance,** also known as a **budget surplus;** it is a source of dissavings when it runs a negative budget balance, also known as a **budget deficit.** One way a government can finance a budget deficit is by borrowing. **Government borrowing** is the total amount of funds borrowed by federal, state, and local governments in the financial markets. In a closed economy, savings is equal to **national savings,** the sum of private savings plus the budget balance. In an open or international economy, savings is equal to national savings plus **net capital inflow** of foreign savings. When a negative net capital inflow occurs, some portion of national savings is funding investment spending in other countries.

3. The hypothetical **loanable funds market** shows how loans from savers are allocated among borrowers with investment spending projects. At the **equilibrium interest rate** the quantity of loans demanded equals the quantity of loans offered. Only those investment projects with an expected return greater or equal to the equilibrium interest rate are funded. By showing how gains from trade between lenders and borrowers are maximized, the loanable funds market shows why a well-functioning financial system leads to greater long-run economic growth. Increasing or persistent government budget deficits can lead to **crowding out:** higher interest rates and reduced investment spending. Changes in perceived business opportunities and in government borrowing shift the demand curve for loanable funds; changes in private savings and capital inflows shift the supply curve.

4. In order to evaluate a project in which the return, X, is realized in the future, you must transform X into its present value using the interest rate, r. The present value of $1 received one year from now is $1/(1 + r)$, the amount of money you must lend out today to have $1 one year from now. The present value of a given project rises as the interest rate falls and falls as the interest rate rises. This tells us that the demand curve for loanable funds is downward sloping.

5. Capital flows narrow differences in interest rates across countries by flowing from low interest rate countries to high interest rate countries. When flows are large, a **global loanable funds market** arises in which interest rates are equalized across countries.

6. Because neither borrowers nor lenders can know the future inflation rate, loans specify a nominal interest rate rather than a real interest rate. For a given expected future inflation rate, shifts of the demand and supply curves of loanable funds result in changes in the underlying real interest rate, leading to changes in the nominal interest rate. According to the **Fisher effect,** an increase in expected future inflation raises the nominal interest rate one-to-one so that the expected real interest rate remains unchanged.

7. **Financial markets** are where households invest their current savings or **wealth**—their accumulated savings—by purchasing assets. Assets come in the form of either a **financial asset,** a paper claim that entitles the buyer to future income from the seller, or a **physical asset,** a tangible object that can generate future income. A financial asset is also a **liability** from the point of view of its seller. There are four main types of financial assets: **loans,** bonds, stocks, and **bank deposits.** Each of them serves a different purpose in addressing the three fundamental tasks of a financial system: reducing **transaction costs**—the cost of making a deal; reducing **financial risk**—uncertainty about future outcomes that involves financial gains and losses; and providing **liquid** assets—assets that can be quickly converted into cash without much loss of value (in contrast to **illiquid** assets, which are not easily converted).

8. Although many small and moderate borrowers use bank loans to fund investment spending, larger companies typically issue bonds. Bonds with a higher risk of **default** must typically pay a higher interest rate. Business owners reduce their risk by selling stock. Although stocks usually generate a higher return than bonds, investors typically wish to reduce their risk by engaging in **diversification,** owning a wide range of assets whose returns are based on unrelated, or independent, events. Most people are risk-averse, more sensitive to a loss than to an equal-size gain. **Loan-backed securities,** a recent innovation, are assets created by pooling individual loans and selling shares of that pool to investors. Because they are more diversified and more liquid than individual loans, bonds are preferred by investors. It can be difficult, however, to assess a bond's quality.

9. **Financial intermediaries**—institutions such as **mutual funds, pension funds, life insurance companies,** and **banks**—are critical components of the financial system. Mutual funds and pension funds allow small investors to diversify, and life insurance companies reduce risk.

10. A bank allows individuals to hold liquid bank deposits that are then used to finance illiquid loans. Banks can perform this mismatch because on average only a small fraction of depositors withdraw their funds at any one time. A well-functioning banking sector is a key ingredient of long-run economic growth.

11. Asset market fluctuations can be a source of short-run macroeconomic instability. Asset prices are determined by supply and demand as well as by the desirability of competing assets, like bonds: when the interest rate rises, prices of stocks and physical assets such as real estate generally fall, and vice versa. Expectations drive the supply of and demand for assets: expectations of higher future prices push today's asset prices higher, and expectations of lower future prices drive them lower. One view of how expectations are formed is the **efficient markets hypothesis,** which holds that the prices of assets embody all publicly available information. It implies that fluctuations are inherently unpredictable—they follow a **random walk.**

12. Many market participants and economists believe that, based on actual evidence, financial markets are not as rational as the efficient markets hypothesis claims. Such evidence includes the fact that stock price fluctuations are too great to be driven by fundamentals alone. Likewise, policy makers do not believe that markets always behave rationally or that they can outsmart them.

KEY TERMS

Savings–investment spending identity, p. 714
Budget surplus, p. 715
Budget deficit, p. 715
Government borrowing, p. 715
Budget balance, p. 715
National savings, p. 715
Net capital inflow, p. 716
Loanable funds market, p. 718
Equilibrium interest rate, p. 721
Crowding out, p. 723
Global loanable funds market, p. 724

Fisher effect, p. 727
Financial markets, p. 729
Wealth, p. 729
Financial asset, p. 729
Physical asset, p. 729
Liability, p. 729
Transaction costs, p. 730
Financial risk, p. 730
Diversification, p. 731
Liquid, p. 731
Illiquid, p. 731

Loan, p. 731
Default, p. 732
Loan-backed securities, p. 732
Financial intermediary, p. 733
Mutual fund, p. 733
Pension fund, p. 734
Life insurance company, p. 734
Bank deposit, p. 734
Bank, p. 735
Efficient markets hypothesis, p. 739
Random walk, p. 739

PRACTICE QUESTIONS

1. Explain why equilibrium in the loanable funds market maximizes efficiency.

2. How would you respond to a friend who claims that the government should eliminate all purchases that are financed by borrowing because such borrowing crowds out private investment spending?

3. What are the important types of financial intermediaries in the U.S. economy? What are the primary assets of these intermediaries, and how do they facilitate investment spending and saving?

PROBLEMS

1. Given the following information about the closed economy of Brittania, what is the level of investment spending and private savings, and what is the budget balance? What is the relationship among the three? Is national savings equal to investment spending? There are no government transfers.

   GDP = $1,000 million   T = $50 million
   C = $850 million   G = $100 million

2. Given the following information about the international economy of Regalia, what is the level of investment spending and private savings, and what are the budget balance and net capital inflow? What is the relationship among the four? There are no government transfers. [*Hint:* Net capital inflow equals the value of imports (*IM*) minus the value of exports (*X*).]

   GDP = $1,000 million   G = $100 million
   C = $850 million   X = $100 million
   T = $50 million   IM = $125 million

3. The accompanying table shows the percentage of GDP accounted for by private savings, investment spending, and net capital inflow in the economies of Capsland and Marsalia. Capsland is currently experiencing a positive net capital inflow and Marsalia, a negative net capital inflow. What is the budget balance (as a percentage of GDP) in both countries? Are Capsland and Marsalia running a budget deficit or surplus?

	Capsland	Marsalia
Investment spending as a percentage of GDP	20%	20%
Private savings as a percentage of GDP	10	25
Net capital inflow as a percentage of GDP	5	–2

4. Assume the economy is open to capital inflows and outflows and therefore net capital inflow equals imports (*IM*) minus exports (*X*). Calculate each of the following.

a. X = $125 million
 IM = $80 million
 Budget balance = –$200 million
 I = $350 million

 Calculate private savings.

b. X = $85 million
 IM = $135 million
 Budget balance = $100 million
 Private savings = $250 million

 Calculate I.

c. X = $60 million
 IM = $95 million
 Private savings = $325 million
 I = $300 million

 Calculate the budget balance.

d. Private savings = $325 million
 I = $400 million
 Budget balance = $10 million
 Calculate $IM - X$.

5. The government is running a budget balance of zero when it decides to increase education spending by $200 billion and finance the spending by selling bonds. The accompanying diagram shows the market for loanable funds before the government sells the bonds. Assume that there are no capital inflows or outflows. How will the equilibrium interest rate and the equilibrium quantity of loanable funds change? Is there any crowding out in the market?

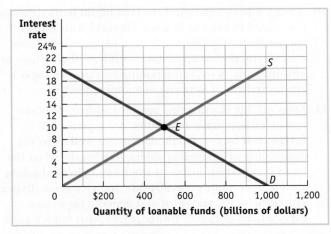

6. Congress estimated that the cost of increasing support and expanding pre-kindergarten education and infant and toddler child care would cost $28 billion in 2014. Since the U.S. government was running a budget deficit at the time, assume that the new pre-K funding was financed by government borrowing, which increases the demand for loanable funds without affecting supply. This question considers the likely effect of this government expenditure on the interest rate.

a. Draw typical demand (D_1) and supply (S_1) curves for loanable funds without the cost of the expanded pre-K programs accounted for. Label the vertical axis "Interest rate" and the horizontal axis "Quantity of loanable funds." Label the equilibrium point (E_1) and the equilibrium interest rate (r_1).

b. Now draw a new diagram with the cost of the expanded pre-K programs included in the analysis. Shift the demand curve in the appropriate direction. Label the new equilibrium point (E_2) and the new equilibrium interest rate (r_2).

c. How does the equilibrium interest rate change in response to government expenditure on the expanded pre-K programs? Explain.

7. Lynn agrees to lend Boris $10,000, which Boris will repay with interest in one year. They agree to a nominal interest rate of 8%, reflecting a real interest rate of 3% on the loan and a commonly shared expected inflation rate of 5% over the next year.

a. If the inflation rate is actually 4% over the next year, how does that lower-than-expected inflation rate affect Boris and Lynn? Who is better off?

b. If the actual inflation rate is 7% over the next year, how does that affect Boris and Lynn? Who is better off?

8. Using the accompanying diagram, explain what will happen to the market for loanable funds when there is a fall of 2 percentage points in the expected future inflation rate. How will the change in the expected future inflation rate affect the equilibrium quantity of loanable funds?

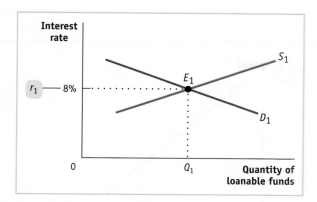

9. The accompanying diagram shows data for the interest rate on 10-year euro area government bonds and inflation rate for the euro area from 1996 through early 2020, as reported by the European Central Bank. How would you describe the relationship between the two? How does the pattern compare to that of the United States in Figure 25-10?

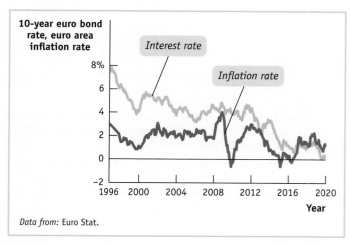

Data from: Euro Stat.

10. For each of the following, is it an example of investment spending, investing in financial assets, or investing in physical assets?

   a. Rupert, a wealthy investor, buys 100 shares of existing Coca-Cola stock.

   b. Rhonda, the star of a blockbuster film franchise, spends $10 million to buy a mansion built in the 1970s.

   c. Rhonda's costar, Ronald, spends $10 million to build a new mansion with a view of the Pacific Ocean.

   d. Rawlings builds a new plant to make catcher's mitts.

   e. Russia buys $100 million in U.S. government bonds.

11. Explain how a well-functioning financial system increases savings and investment spending, holding the budget balance and any capital flows fixed.

12. Explain the effect on a company's stock price today of each of the following events, other things held constant.

   a. The interest rate on bonds falls.

   b. Several companies in the same sector announce surprisingly higher sales.

   c. A change in the tax law passed last year reduces this year's profit.

   d. The company unexpectedly announces that due to an accounting error, it must amend last year's accounting statement and reduce last year's reported profit by $5 million. It also announces that this change has no implications for future profits.

13. Sallie Mae is a quasi-governmental agency that packages individual student loans into pools of loans and sells shares of these pools to investors as Sallie Mae bonds.

   a. What is this process called? What effect will it have on investors compared to situations in which they could only buy and sell individual student loans?

   b. What effect do you think Sallie Mae's actions will have on the ability of students to get loans?

   c. Suppose that a very severe recession hits and, as a consequence, many graduating students cannot get jobs and default on their student loans. What effect will this have on Sallie Mae bonds? Why is it likely that investors now believe Sallie Mae bonds to be riskier than expected? What will be the effect on the availability of student loans?

14. Access the Discovering Data activity for Chapter 25, Problem 14 online.

   a. What is the relationship between domestic investment and national saving? How has the relationship changed over time?

   b. Calculate the difference between investment and national saving in 2008, 2014, and 2019. What does the value represent?

   c. Using the loanable funds framework, predict what would happen to interest rates in 2008, 2014, and 2019.

15. Access the Discovering Data activity for Chapter 25, Problem 15 online.

   a. In what year did the United States last run a government surplus?

   b. Calculate the deficit as a percent of GDP in 1971, 1983, 1992, 2003, and 2010. What year had the largest deficit as a percent of GDP?

   c. How would you describe the relationship between government debt and long-term interest rates?

   d. Have larger deficits increased the crowding out of private investment?

⋮⋮ WORK IT OUT

16. Use the market for loanable funds shown in the accompanying diagram to explain what happens to private savings, private investment spending, and the interest rate if each of the following events occur. Assume that there are no capital inflows or outflows.

    a. The government reduces the size of its deficit to zero.

    b. At any given interest rate, consumers decide to save more. Assume the budget balance is zero.

    c. At any given interest rate, businesses become very optimistic about the future profitability of investment spending. Assume the budget balance is zero.

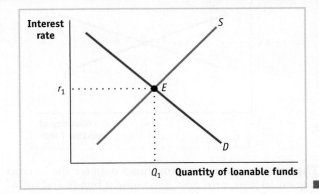

26 | Income and Expenditure

THE MALLS IN SPAIN HAVE MAINLY DODGED THE PAIN

WHEN PUERTO VENECIA, IN THE CITY OF ZARAGOZA, SPAIN, opened in October 2012, it was one of Europe's biggest shopping malls. Like some U.S. mega-malls, it offers more than just shopping: it's meant to be a destination experience, with cinemas, a skating rink, an artificial surfing wave, and a lake with rowboats.

The timing of its opening, however, appeared to be terrible: Spain's economy was at a low point. Two back-to-back crises — the global financial crisis of 2008, and the crisis of the euro, Europe's shared currency, which began in 2010 — had pushed Spain into a deep recession. The Spanish unemployment rate when the mall opened was almost 26%. It was not, you might have thought, a great time to open a high-end shopping complex.

Fortunately for Puerto Venecia's investors, however, late 2012 marked Spain's low point. Over the next few years the economy rebounded, largely thanks to a surge in exports, especially cars: by

A mall that was saved by Spain's recovery.

2018 Spain was producing more than 2 million cars a year, more than any other European nation other than Germany. And with the economy's recovery came a surge in consumer spending, especially, as it happens, in large shopping centers.

But wait: why should good news for Spain's auto industry also be good news for its shopping malls?

The answer is that the increased sales of cars and other exports meant higher incomes for Spanish households, who spent much of this higher income on other goods and services. This meant another round of income increases among Spaniards producing or selling these goods and services. And the process didn't stop there: rising income led to even more consumer spending, leading to even more income gains, and so on.

Spain's recovery illustrates the way booms and busts happen for the economy as a whole. The business cycle is often driven by ups or downs in one particular kind of spending — either exports, as was the case in Spain, or investment spending. These first-round changes in spending then lead to changes in consumer spending, which magnify — or, as economists usually say, *multiply* — the effect of the initial changes on the economy as a whole.

In this chapter we'll study how this process works, showing how *multiplier* analysis helps us understand the business cycle. As a first step, we introduce the concept of the multiplier informally. ●

WHAT YOU WILL LEARN

- What is the importance of the **multiplier,** which summarizes how initial changes in spending lead to further changes?
- What is the **aggregate consumption function?**
- How do expected future income and aggregate wealth affect consumer spending?
- What determines investment spending and why do we need to distinguish between **planned investment spending** and **unplanned inventory investment?**
- How does the inventory adjustment process move the economy to a new equilibrium after a change in demand?
- Why is investment spending considered a leading indicator of the future state of the economy?

|| The Multiplier: An Informal Introduction

The story of Spain's recovery involves a sort of chain reaction in which an initial rise or fall in aggregate spending leads to changes in income, which lead to further changes in aggregate spending, and so on. Let's examine that chain reaction more closely, this time thinking through the effects of changes in aggregate spending in the economy as a whole.

For the sake of this analysis, we'll initially make four simplifying assumptions that will have to be reconsidered later.

1. We assume that *producers are willing to supply additional output at a fixed price.* That is, if consumers or businesses buying investment goods decide to spend an additional $1 billion, that will translate into the production of $1 billion worth of additional goods and services without driving up the overall level of prices. As a result, *changes in aggregate spending translate into changes in aggregate output,* as measured by real GDP. As we'll learn in the next chapter, this assumption isn't too unrealistic in the short run, but it needs to be changed when we think about the long-run effects of changes in demand.

2. We take the interest rate as given.

3. We assume that there is no government spending and no taxes.

4. We assume that exports and imports are zero (which is obviously a departure from our Spanish example, but in a later section we'll see how to bring trade back).

Given these simplifying assumptions, consider what happens if there is a change in investment spending. For example, imagine that for some reason home builders decide to spend an extra $100 billion on home construction over the next year.

The direct effect of this increase in investment spending will be to increase income and the value of aggregate output by the same amount. That's because each dollar spent on home construction translates into a dollar's worth of income for construction workers, suppliers of building materials, electricians, and so on. If the process stopped there, the increase in housing investment spending would raise overall income by exactly $100 billion.

But the process doesn't stop there. The increase in aggregate output leads to an increase in disposable income that flows to households in the form of profits and wages. The increase in households' disposable income leads to a rise in consumer spending, which, in turn, induces firms to increase output yet again. This generates another rise in disposable income, which leads to another round of consumer spending increases, and so on. So there are multiple rounds of increases in aggregate output.

How large is the total effect on aggregate output if we sum the effect from all these rounds of spending increases? To answer this question, we need to introduce the concept of the **marginal propensity to consume,** or **MPC:** the increase in consumer spending when disposable income rises by $1. When consumer spending changes because of a rise or fall in disposable income, *MPC* is the change in consumer spending divided by the change in disposable income:

$$(26\text{-}1) \quad MPC = \frac{\Delta \text{ Consumer spending}}{\Delta \text{ Disposable income}}$$

where the symbol Δ (delta) means "change in." For example, if consumer spending goes up by $6 billion when disposable income goes up by $10 billion, *MPC* is $6 billion/$10 billion = 0.6.

Because consumers normally spend part but not all of an additional dollar of disposable income, *MPC* is a number between 0 and 1. The additional disposable income that consumers don't spend is saved; the **marginal propensity to save,** or **MPS,** is the fraction of an additional dollar of disposable income that is saved. *MPS* is equal to $1 - MPC$.

The **marginal propensity to consume,** or **MPC,** is the increase in consumer spending when disposable income rises by $1.

The **marginal propensity to save,** or **MPS,** is the increase in household savings when disposable income rises by $1.

Because we assumed that there are no taxes and no international trade, each $1 increase in aggregate spending raises both real GDP and disposable income by $1. So the $100 billion increase in investment spending initially raises real GDP by $100 billion. This leads to a second-round increase in consumer spending, which raises real GDP by a further $MPC \times \$100$ billion. It is followed by a third-round increase in consumer spending of $MPC \times MPC \times \$100$ billion, and so on. After an infinite number of rounds, the total effect on real GDP is:

$$
\begin{aligned}
\text{Increase in investment spending} &= & \$100 \text{ billion} \\
+ \text{ Second-round increase in consumer spending} &= MPC & \times \$100 \text{ billion} \\
+ \text{ Third-round increase in consumer spending} &= MPC^2 & \times \$100 \text{ billion} \\
+ \text{ Fourth-round increase in consumer spending} &= MPC^3 & \times \$100 \text{ billion}
\end{aligned}
$$

$$
\vdots \qquad\qquad \vdots
$$

$$
\text{Total increase in real GDP} = (1 + MPC + MPC^2 + MPC^3 + \ldots) \times \$100 \text{ billion}
$$

So the $100 billion increase in investment spending sets off a chain reaction in the economy. The net result of this chain reaction is that a $100 billion increase in investment spending leads to a change in real GDP that is a *multiple* of the size of that initial change in spending.

How large is this multiple? It's a mathematical fact that an infinite series of the form $1 + x + x^2 + x^3 + \ldots$, where x is between 0 and 1, is equal to $1/(1 - x)$. So the total effect of a $100 billion increase in investment spending, I, taking into account all the subsequent increases in consumer spending (and assuming no taxes and no international trade), is given by:

(26-2) Total increase in real GDP from a $100 billion rise in I

$$
= \frac{1}{1 - MPC} \times \$100 \text{ billion}
$$

Let's consider a numerical example in which $MPC = 0.6$: each $1 in additional disposable income causes a $0.60 rise in consumer spending. In that case, a $100 billion increase in investment spending raises real GDP by $100 billion in the first round. The second-round increase in consumer spending raises real GDP by another $0.6 \times \$100$ billion, or $60 billion. The third-round increase in consumer spending raises real GDP by another $0.6 \times \$60$ billion, or $36 billion. Table 26-1 shows the successive stages of increases, where "..." means the process goes on an infinite number of times. In the end, real GDP rises by $250 billion as a consequence of the initial $100 billion rise in investment spending:

TABLE 26-1 Rounds of Increases in Real GDP When $MPC = 0.6$

Rounds	Increase in real GDP (billions)	Total increase in real GDP (billions)
First	$100	$100
Second	60	160
Third	36	196
Fourth	21.6	217.6
...	...	...
Final	0	250

$$
\frac{1}{0.6} \times \$100 \text{ billion} = 2.5 \times \$100 \text{ billion} = \$250 \text{ billion}
$$

Notice that even though there are an infinite number of rounds of expansion of real GDP, the total rise in real GDP is limited to $250 billion. The reason is that at each stage some of the rise in disposable income "leaks out" because it is saved. How much of an additional dollar of disposable income is saved depends on MPS, the marginal propensity to save.

We've described the effects of a change in investment spending, but the same analysis can be applied to any other change in aggregate spending. The important thing is to distinguish between the initial change in aggregate spending, before real GDP rises, and the additional change in aggregate spending caused by the change in real GDP as the chain reaction unfolds. For example, suppose that a boom in housing prices makes consumers feel richer and that, as a result, they become willing to spend more at any given level of disposable income. This will lead to an initial rise in consumer spending, before real GDP rises. But it will also lead to second and later rounds of higher consumer spending as real GDP rises.

An **autonomous change in aggregate spending** is an initial change in the desired level of spending by firms, households, or government at a given level of real GDP.

The **multiplier** is the ratio of the total change in real GDP caused by an autonomous change in aggregate spending to the size of that autonomous change.

An initial rise or fall in aggregate spending at a given level of real GDP is called an **autonomous change in aggregate spending.** It's autonomous—which means self-governing—because it's the cause, not the result, of the chain reaction we've just described. Formally, the **multiplier** is the ratio of the total change in real GDP caused by an autonomous change in aggregate spending to the size of that autonomous change.

If we let ΔAAS stand for autonomous change in aggregate spending and ΔY stand for the change in real GDP, then the multiplier is equal to $\Delta Y / \Delta AAS$. And we've already seen how to find the value of the multiplier. Assuming no taxes and no trade, the change in real GDP caused by an autonomous change in spending is:

(26-3) $\Delta Y = \dfrac{1}{1 - MPC} \times \Delta AAS$

So the multiplier is:

(26-4) $\text{Multiplier} = \dfrac{\Delta Y}{\Delta AAS} = \dfrac{1}{1 - MPC}$

Notice that the size of the multiplier depends on MPC. If the marginal propensity to consume is high, so is the multiplier. This is true because the size of MPC determines how large each round of expansion is compared with the previous round. To put it another way, the higher MPC is, the less disposable income leaks out into savings at each round of expansion.

In later chapters we'll use the concept of the multiplier to analyze the effects of fiscal and monetary policies. We'll also see that the formula for the multiplier changes when we introduce various complications, including taxes and foreign trade. First, however, we need to look more deeply at what determines consumer spending.

ECONOMICS >> *in Action*
To Shale and Back

For most of America, recovery from the severe recession of 2007–2009 was disappointingly slow. But a few parts of the country experienced rapid growth—and none more rapid than North Dakota, whose economy grew 60% between 2009 and 2012. That's an annual growth rate of 15%, more than five times the growth of the U.S. economy as a whole.

There's no mystery about the North Dakota boom: it was all about shale oil. Fracking made it possible to extract oil from the Bakken shale, which underlies the state. Oil companies and other investors rushed in, along with thousands of oil-field workers, more than doubling the output of the mining sector in just two years.

But as Figure 26-1 shows, mining and related industries weren't the only sectors growing fast. North Dakota also saw much faster growth than other states in a number of areas, notably retail and wholesale trade, banking, and utilities. Why?

The answer was the multiplier. As high-paying shale-related jobs surged, so did consumer spending—much of which ended up in the hands of local shops, bank branches, companies supplying electricity and heating oil, and so on. These local suppliers, in turn, hired more workers, whose incomes added to consumer spending and fed additional rounds of expansion.

Obviously this extraordinary growth couldn't last. In fact, the shale boom came to an abrupt end in late 2014, as falling oil prices led to a drastic slowdown: mining

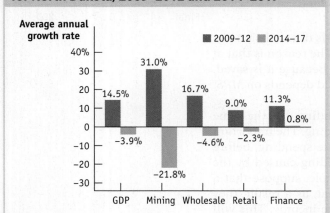

FIGURE 26-1 Comparing Industry Growth Rates for North Dakota, 2009–2012 and 2014–2017

Data from: Bureau of Economic Analysis.

employment in North Dakota fell more than 50% between October 2014 and July 2016, which had a ripple effect throughout the state's economy. But the boom was fun while it lasted, and it also gave an excellent example of the multiplier at work.

>> Check Your Understanding 26-1

Solutions appear at back of book.

1. Explain why a decline in investment spending caused by a change in business expectations leads to a fall in consumer spending.

2. What is the multiplier if the marginal propensity to consume is 0.5? What is it if *MPC* is 0.8?

3. As a percentage of GDP, savings accounts for a larger share of the economy in the country of Scania compared to the country of Amerigo. Which country is likely to have the larger multiplier? Explain.

|| Consumer Spending

Should you splurge on a restaurant meal or save money by eating at home? Should you buy a new car and, if so, how expensive a model? Should you redo that bathroom or live with it for another year? In the real world, households are constantly confronted with such choices—not just about the consumption mix but also about how much to spend in total.

These choices, in turn, have a powerful effect on the economy: consumer spending normally accounts for two-thirds of total spending on final goods and services. In particular, as we've just seen, the decision about how much of an additional dollar in income to spend—the marginal propensity to consume—determines the size of the multiplier, which determines the ultimate effect on the economy of autonomous changes in spending.

But what determines how much consumers spend?

Current Disposable Income and Consumer Spending

The most important factor affecting a family's consumer spending is its current disposable income—income after taxes are paid and government transfers are received. It's obvious from daily life that people with high disposable incomes on average drive more expensive cars, live in more expensive houses, and spend more on meals and clothing than people with lower disposable incomes. And the relationship between current disposable income and spending is clear in the data.

The Bureau of Labor Statistics (BLS) collects annual data on family income and spending. Families are grouped by levels of before-tax income, and after-tax income for each group is also reported. Since the income figures include transfers from the government, what the BLS calls a household's after-tax income is equivalent to its current disposable income.

Figure 26-2 is a scatter diagram illustrating the relationship between household current disposable income and household consumer spending for American households by income group in 2018. For example, point *A* shows that in 2018 the middle fifth of the population had an average current disposable income of $51,211 and average spending of $51,729. The pattern of the dots slopes upward from left to right, making it clear that households with higher current disposable income had higher consumer spending.

It's very useful to represent the relationship between an individual household's current disposable income and its consumer spending with an equation. The **consumption function** is an equation showing how an individual household's consumer spending

>> **Quick Review**

• A change in investment spending arising from a change in expectations starts a chain reaction in which the initial change in real GDP leads to changes in consumer spending, leading to further changes in real GDP, and so on. The total change in aggregate output is a multiple of the initial change in investment spending.

• Any **autonomous change in aggregate spending,** a change in spending that is not caused by a change in real GDP, generates the same chain reaction. The total size of the change in real GDP depends on the size of the **multiplier.** Assuming that there are no taxes and no trade, the multiplier is equal to $1/(1- MPC)$, where **MPC** is the **marginal propensity to consume.** The total change in real GDP, ΔY, is equal to $1/(1- MPC) \times \Delta AAS$.

The **consumption function** is an equation showing how an individual household's consumer spending varies with the household's current disposable income.

People with lower disposable incomes may avoid higher-priced brand-name goods in favor of generics that cost less.

Richard Levine/Alamy Stock Photo

FIGURE 26-2 Current Disposable Income and Consumer Spending for U.S. Households in 2018

For each income group of households, average current disposable income in 2018 is plotted versus average consumer spending in 2018. For example, the middle income group, with current disposable income of $41,490 to $70,367, is represented by point A, indicating a household average current disposable income of $51,211 and average household consumer spending of $51,729. The data clearly show a positive relationship between current disposable income and consumer spending: families with higher current disposable income have higher consumer spending.

Data from: Bureau of Labor Statistics.

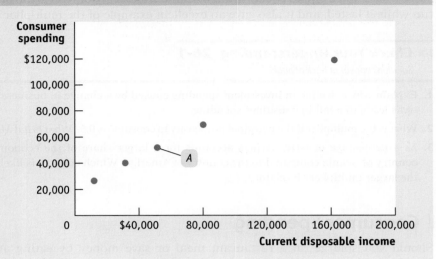

varies with the household's current disposable income. The simplest version of a consumption function is a linear equation:

(26-5) $c = a + MPC \times yd$

where lowercase letters indicate variables measured for an individual household.

In this equation, c is individual household consumer spending and yd is individual household current disposable income. Recall that MPC, the marginal propensity to consume, is the amount by which consumer spending rises if current disposable income rises by $1. Finally, a is a constant term—individual household *autonomous consumer spending*, the amount of spending a household would have if it had zero disposable income. We assume that a is greater than zero because a household with zero disposable income is able to fund some consumption by borrowing or using its savings.

Notice, by the way, that we're using y for income. That's standard practice in macroeconomics, even though *income* isn't actually spelled "yncome." The reason is that I is reserved for investment spending.

Recall that we expressed MPC as the ratio of a change in consumer spending to the change in current disposable income. We've rewritten it for an individual household as Equation 26-6:

(26-6) $MPC = \Delta c / \Delta yd$

Multiplying both sides of Equation 26-6 by Δyd, we get:

(26-7) $MPC \times \Delta yd = \Delta c$

Equation 26-7 tells us that when yd goes up by $1, c goes up by $MPC \times 1.

Figure 26-3 shows what Equation 26-5 looks like graphically, plotting yd on the horizontal axis and c on the vertical axis. Individual household autonomous consumer spending, a, is the value of c when yd is zero—it is the vertical *intercept* of the consumption function, cf. MPC is the *slope* of the line, measured by rise over run. If current disposable income rises by Δyd, household consumer spending, c, rises by Δc. Since MPC is defined as $\Delta c / \Delta yd$, the slope of the consumption function is:

(26-8) Slope of consumption function
= Rise over run
= $\Delta c / \Delta yd$
= MPC

In reality, actual data has never fit Equation 26-5 perfectly, but the fit can be pretty good. Figure 26-4 shows the data from Figure 26-2 again, together with a

FIGURE 26-3 The Consumption Function

The consumption function relates a household's current disposable income to its consumer spending. The vertical intercept, *a*, is individual household autonomous consumer spending: the amount of a household's consumer spending if its current disposable income is zero. The slope of the consumption function line, *cf*, is the marginal propensity to consume, or *MPC:* of every additional $1 of current disposable income, *MPC* × $1 is spent.

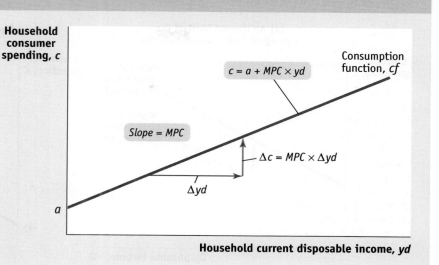

line drawn to fit the data as closely as possible. According to the data on households' consumer spending and current disposable income, the best estimate of *a* is $20,195 and of *MPC* is 0.60. So the consumption function fitted to the data is:

$$c = \$20{,}195 + 0.60 \times yd$$

That is, the data suggest a marginal propensity to consume of approximately 0.60. This implies that the marginal propensity to save (*MPS*)—the amount of an additional $1 of disposable income that is saved—is approximately 0.40, and the multiplier is approximately 1/0.40 = 2.50.

It's important to realize that Figure 26-4 shows a *microeconomic* relationship between the current disposable income of individual households and their spending on goods and services. However, macroeconomists assume that a similar relationship holds *for the economy as a whole:* that there is a relationship, called the **aggregate consumption function,** between aggregate current disposable income and aggregate consumer spending. We'll assume that it has the same form as the household-level consumption function:

(26-9) $C = A + MPC \times YD$

The **aggregate consumption function** is the relationship for the economy as a whole between aggregate current disposable income and aggregate consumer spending.

FIGURE 26-4 A Consumption Function Fitted to Data

The data from Figure 26-2 are reproduced here, along with a line drawn to fit the data as closely as possible. For U.S. households in 2018 the best estimate of the average household's autonomous consumer spending, *a*, is $20,195 and the best estimate of *MPC* is 0.60.

Data from: Bureau of Labor Statistics.

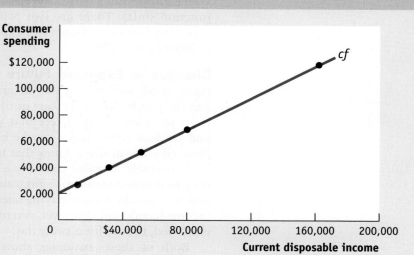

FIGURE 26-5 Shifts of the Aggregate Consumption Function

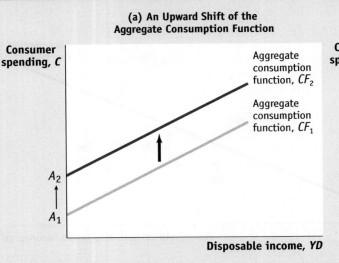

(a) An Upward Shift of the Aggregate Consumption Function

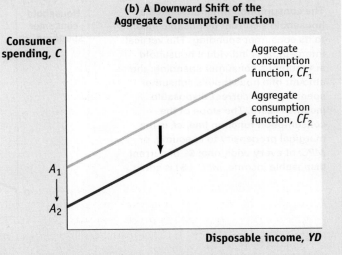

(b) A Downward Shift of the Aggregate Consumption Function

Panel (a) illustrates the effect of an increase in expected aggregate future disposable income. Consumers will spend more at every given level of aggregate current disposable income, *YD*. As a result, the initial aggregate consumption function CF_1, with aggregate autonomous consumer spending A_1, shifts up to a new position at CF_2 and aggregate autonomous consumer spending A_2. An increase in aggregate wealth will also shift the aggregate consumption function up.

Panel (b), in contrast, illustrates the effect of a reduction in expected aggregate future disposable income. Consumers will spend less at every given level of aggregate current disposable income, *YD*. Consequently, the initial aggregate consumption function CF_1, with aggregate autonomous consumer spending A_1, shifts down to a new position at CF_2 and aggregate autonomous consumer spending A_2. A reduction in aggregate wealth will have the same effect.

Here, C is aggregate consumer spending (called just "consumer spending"); YD is aggregate current disposable income (called, for simplicity, just "disposable income"); and A is aggregate autonomous consumer spending, the amount of consumer spending when YD equals zero. This is the relationship represented in Figure 26-5 by CF, analogous to cf in Figure 26-3.

Shifts of the Aggregate Consumption Function

The aggregate consumption function shows the relationship between disposable income and consumer spending for the economy as a whole, other things equal. When things other than disposable income change, the aggregate consumption function shifts. There are two principal causes of shifts of the aggregate consumption function: changes in expected future disposable income and changes in aggregate wealth.

Changes in Expected Future Disposable Income Suppose you land a really good, well-paying job on graduating from college in May—but the job, and the paychecks, won't start until September. So your disposable income hasn't risen yet. Even so, it's likely that you will start spending more on final goods and services right away—maybe buying nicer work clothes than you originally planned—because you know that higher income is coming.

Conversely, suppose you have a good job but learn that the company is planning to downsize your division, raising the possibility that you may lose your job and have to take a lower-paying one somewhere else. Even though your disposable income hasn't gone down yet, you might well cut back on spending even while still employed, to save for a rainy day.

Both of these examples show how expectations about future disposable income can affect consumer spending. The two panels of Figure 26-5, which plot disposable income against consumer spending, show how changes in expected future disposable income affect the aggregate consumption function. In both panels, CF_1 is the initial aggregate consumption function. Panel (a) shows the effect of good news: information that leads consumers to expect higher disposable income in the future than they did before.

Consumers will now spend more at any given level of current disposable income, YD, corresponding to an increase in A, aggregate autonomous consumer spending, from A_1 to A_2. The effect is to shift the aggregate consumption function up, from CF_1 to CF_2. Panel (b) shows the effect of bad news: information that leads consumers to expect lower disposable income in the future than they did before. Consumers will now spend less at any given level of current disposable income, YD, corresponding to a fall in A from A_1 to A_2. The effect is to shift the aggregate consumption function down, from CF_1 to CF_2.

In a famous 1957 book, *A Theory of the Consumption Function*, Milton Friedman showed that taking the effects of expected future income into account explains an otherwise puzzling fact about consumer behavior. If we look at consumer spending during any given year, we find that people with high current income save a larger fraction of their income than those with low current income. (This is obvious from the data in Figure 26-4: people with higher incomes spend considerably less than their income; those with lower incomes spend more than their income.) You might think this implies that the overall savings rate will rise as the economy grows and average current incomes rise; in fact, however, this hasn't happened.

Friedman pointed out that when we look at individual incomes in a given year, there are systematic differences between current and expected future income that create a positive relationship between current income and the savings rate. On one side, people with low current incomes are often having an unusually bad year. For example, they may be workers who have been laid off but will probably find new jobs eventually. They are people whose expected future income is higher than their current income, so it makes sense for them to have low or even negative savings. On the other side, people with high current incomes in a given year are often having an unusually good year. For example, they may have investments that happened to do extremely well. They are people whose expected future income is lower than their current income, so it makes sense for them to save most of their windfall.

When the economy grows, by contrast, current and expected future incomes rise together. Higher current income tends to lead to higher savings today, but higher expected future income tends to lead to less savings today. As a result, there's a weaker relationship between current income and the savings rate.

Friedman argued that consumer spending ultimately depends mainly on the income people expect to have over the long term rather than on their current income. This argument is known as the *permanent income hypothesis*.

Changes in Aggregate Wealth Imagine two individuals, Maria and Mark, both of whom expect to earn $30,000 this year. Suppose, however, that they have different histories. Maria has been working steadily for the past 10 years, owns her own home, and has $200,000 in the bank. Mark is the same age as Maria, but he has been in and out of work, hasn't managed to buy a house, and has very little in savings. In this case, Maria has something that Mark doesn't have: *wealth*. Even though they have the same disposable income, other things equal, you'd expect Maria to spend more on consumption than Mark. That is, wealth has an effect on consumer spending.

The effect of wealth on spending is emphasized by an influential economic model of how consumers make choices about spending versus saving called the *life-cycle hypothesis.* According to this hypothesis, consumers plan their spending over a lifetime, not just in response to their current disposable income. As a result, people try to smooth their consumption over their lifetimes—they save some of their current disposable income during their years of peak earnings (typically occurring during a worker's 40s and 50s) and during their retirement live off the wealth they accumulated while working.

We won't go into the details of this hypothesis but will simply point out that it implies an important role for wealth in determining consumer spending. For example, a middle-aged couple who have accumulated a lot of wealth—who have paid off the mortgage on their house and already own plenty of stocks and bonds—will, other things equal, spend more on goods and services than a couple who have the same current disposable income but still need to save for their retirement.

Because wealth affects household consumer spending, changes in wealth across the economy can shift the aggregate consumption function. A rise in aggregate wealth—say, because of a booming stock market—increases the vertical intercept *A*, aggregate autonomous consumer spending. This, in turn, shifts the aggregate consumption function up in the same way as does an expected increase in future disposable income. A decline in aggregate wealth—say, because of a fall in housing prices as occurred in 2008—reduces *A* and shifts the aggregate consumption function down.

ECONOMICS >> *in Action*
Famous First Forecasting Failures

The Great Depression created modern macroeconomics. It also gave birth to the modern field of *econometrics*—the use of statistical techniques to fit economic models to empirical data. The aggregate consumption function was one of the first things econometricians studied. And, sure enough, they quickly experienced one of the first major failures of economic forecasting: consumer spending after World War II was much higher than estimates of the aggregate consumption function based on prewar data would have predicted.

Figure 26-6 tells the story. Panel (a) shows aggregate data on disposable income and consumer spending from 1929 to 1941, measured in billions of 2005

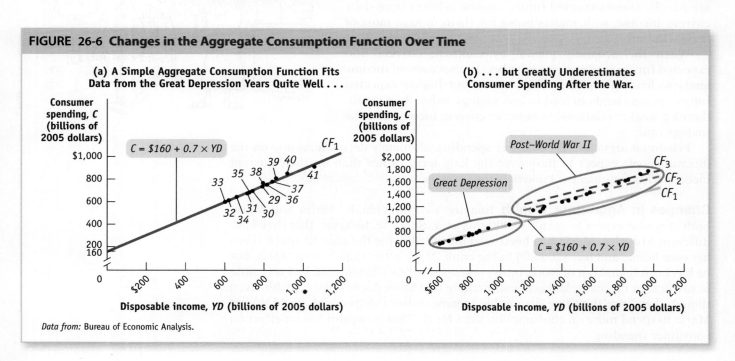

FIGURE 26-6 Changes in the Aggregate Consumption Function Over Time

(a) A Simple Aggregate Consumption Function Fits Data from the Great Depression Years Quite Well . . .

$C = \$160 + 0.7 \times YD$

(b) . . . but Greatly Underestimates Consumer Spending After the War.

$C = \$160 + 0.7 \times YD$

Data from: Bureau of Economic Analysis.

dollars. A simple linear consumption function, CF_1, seems to fit the data very well. And many economists thought this relationship would continue to hold in the future. But panel (b) shows what actually happened in later years. The points in the circle at the left are the data from the Great Depression shown in panel (a). The points in the circle at the right are data from 1946 to 1960. (Data from 1942 to 1945 aren't included because rationing during World War II prevented consumers from spending normally.)

The solid line in the figure, CF_1, is the consumption function fitted to 1929–1941 data. As you can see, post–World War II consumer spending was much higher than the relationship from the Depression years would have predicted. For example, in 1960 consumer spending was 13.5% higher than the level predicted by CF_1.

Why was extrapolating from the earlier relationship so misleading? The answer is that from 1946 onward, both expected future disposable income and aggregate wealth were steadily rising. Consumers grew increasingly confident that the Great Depression wouldn't reemerge and that the post–World War II economic boom would continue. At the same time, wealth was steadily increasing. As indicated by the dashed lines in panel (b), CF_2 and CF_3, the increases in expected future disposable income and in aggregate wealth shifted the aggregate consumption function up a number of times.

In macroeconomics, failure—whether of economic policy or of economic prediction—often leads to intellectual progress. The embarrassing failure of early estimates of the aggregate consumption function to predict post–World War II consumer spending led to important progress in our understanding of consumer behavior.

>> Check Your Understanding 26-2

Solutions appear at back of book.

1. Suppose the economy consists of three people: Angelina, Felicia, and Marina. The table shows how their consumer spending varies as their current disposable income rises by $10,000.

   a. Derive each individual's consumption function, where *MPC* is calculated for a $10,000 change in current disposable income.

   b. Derive the aggregate consumption function.

Current disposable income	Consumer spending		
	Angelina	Felicia	Marina
$0	$8,000	$6,500	$7,250
10,000	12,000	14,500	14,250

2. Suppose that problems in the capital markets make consumers unable either to borrow or to put money aside for future use. What implication does this have for the effects of expected future disposable income on consumer spending?

|| Investment Spending

Although consumer spending is much larger than investment spending, booms and busts in investment spending tend to drive the business cycle. In fact, most recessions originate as a fall in investment spending. Figure 26-7 illustrates this point; it shows the annual percent change of investment spending and consumer spending in the United States, measured in real terms, during six recessions from 1973 to 2009. As you can see, swings in investment spending are much more dramatic than those in consumer spending. In addition, due to the multiplier process, economists believe that declines in consumer spending are usually the result of a process that begins with a slump in investment spending. Soon we'll examine in more detail how a slump in investment spending generates a fall in consumer spending through the multiplier process.

Before we do that, however, let's analyze the factors that determine investment spending, which are somewhat different from those that determine consumer

FIGURE 26-7 Fluctuations in Investment Spending and Consumer Spending

The bars illustrate the annual percent change in investment spending and consumer spending during six recent recessions. As the lengths of the bars show, swings in investment spending were much larger in percentage terms than those in consumer spending. This pattern has led economists to believe that recessions typically originate as a slump in investment spending.

Data from: Bureau of Economic Analysis.

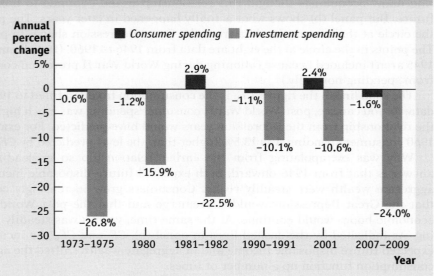

spending. The most important ones are the interest rate and expected future real GDP. We'll also revisit a fact that we noted in Chapter 25: the level of investment spending businesses *actually* carry out is sometimes not the same level as **planned investment spending,** the investment spending that firms *intend* to undertake during a given period.

Planned investment spending depends on three principal factors that we'll analyze next.

1. The interest rate
2. The expected future level of real GDP
3. The current level of production capacity

First, we'll analyze the effect of the interest rate.

1. The Interest Rate and Investment Spending

Interest rates have their clearest effect on one particular form of investment spending: spending on residential construction—that is, on the construction of homes. The reason is straightforward: home builders only build houses they think they can sell, and houses are more affordable—and so more likely to sell—when the interest rate is low.

Consider a family that needs to borrow $350,000 to buy a new house. At an interest rate of 6.5%, a 30-year home mortgage will mean payments of $2,212 per month. At an interest rate of 4.0%, those payments would be only $1,722 per month, making houses significantly more affordable.

Interest rates also affect other forms of investment spending. Firms with investment spending projects will only go ahead with a project if they expect a rate of return higher than the cost of the funds they would have to borrow to finance that project. As we saw in Chapter 25, if the interest rate rises, fewer projects will pass that test, and as a result investment spending will be lower.

You might think that the trade-off a firm faces is different if it can fund its investment project with its past profits rather than through borrowing. Past profits used to finance investment spending are called *retained earnings*. But even if a firm pays for investment spending out of retained earnings, the trade-off it must make in deciding whether or not to fund a project remains the same because it

Planned investment spending is the investment spending that businesses intend to undertake during a given period.

must take into account the opportunity cost of its funds. For example, instead of purchasing new equipment, the firm could lend out the funds and earn interest. The forgone interest earned is the opportunity cost of using retained earnings to fund an investment project.

So the trade-off the firm faces when comparing a project's rate of return to the market interest rate has not changed when it uses retained earnings rather than borrowed funds, which means that regardless of whether a firm funds investment spending through borrowing or retained earnings, a rise in the market interest rate makes any given investment project less profitable.

Conversely, a fall in the interest rate makes some investment projects that were unprofitable before profitable at the now lower interest rate. So some projects that had been unfunded before will be funded now.

So planned investment spending—spending on investment projects that firms voluntarily decide whether or not to undertake—is negatively related to the interest rate. Other things equal, a higher interest rate leads to a lower level of planned investment spending.

2. Expected Future Real GDP, Production Capacity, and Investment Spending

Suppose a firm has enough capacity to continue to produce the amount it is currently selling but doesn't expect its sales to grow in the future. Then it will engage in investment spending only to replace existing equipment and structures that wear out or are rendered obsolete by new technologies. But if, instead, the firm expects its sales to grow rapidly in the future, it will find its existing production capacity insufficient for its future production needs. So the firm will undertake investment spending to meet those needs. This implies that, other things equal, firms will undertake more investment spending when they expect their sales to grow.

Now suppose that the firm currently has considerably more capacity than necessary to meet current production needs. Even if it expects sales to grow, it won't have to undertake investment spending for a while—not until the growth in sales catches up with its excess capacity. This illustrates the fact that, other things equal, the current level of productive capacity has a negative effect on investment spending: other things equal, the higher the current capacity, the lower the investment spending.

If we combine the effects on investment spending of both growth in expected future sales and the size of current production capacity, we can see one situation in which we can be reasonably sure that firms will undertake high levels of investment spending: when they expect sales to grow rapidly. In that case, even excess production capacity will soon be used up, leading firms to resume investment spending.

What is an indicator of high expected growth of future sales? It's a high expected future growth rate of real GDP. A higher expected future growth rate of real GDP results in a higher level of planned investment spending, but a lower expected future growth rate of real GDP leads to lower planned investment spending. This relationship is summarized in a proposition known as the **accelerator principle.** Generally, the effects of the accelerator principle play an important role in *investment spending slumps*, periods of low investment spending.

3. Inventories and Unplanned Investment Spending

Most firms maintain **inventories,** stocks of goods held to satisfy future sales. Firms hold inventories so they can quickly satisfy buyers—a consumer can purchase an item off the shelf rather than waiting for it to be manufactured. In addition, businesses often hold inventories of their inputs to be sure they have a steady supply of necessary materials and spare parts. At the end of December 2019, the

According to the **accelerator principle,** a higher growth rate of real GDP leads to higher planned investment spending, but a lower growth rate of real GDP leads to lower planned investment spending.

Inventories are stocks of goods held to satisfy future sales.

Inventory investment is the value of the change in total inventories held in the economy during a given period.

Unplanned inventory investment is an unintended swing in inventory that occurs when actual sales are higher or lower than expected sales.

Actual investment spending is the sum of planned investment spending and unplanned inventory investment.

overall value of inventories in the U.S. economy was estimated at $2.04 trillion, just under 10% of GDP.

A firm that increases its inventories is engaging in a form of investment spending. Suppose, for example, that the U.S. auto industry produces 800,000 cars per month but sells only 700,000. The remaining 100,000 cars are added to the inventory at auto company warehouses or car dealerships, ready to be sold in the future. **Inventory investment** is the value of the change in total inventories held in the economy during a given period. Unlike other forms of investment spending, inventory investment can actually be negative. If, for example, the auto industry reduces its inventory over the course of a month, we say that it has engaged in negative inventory investment.

To understand inventory investment, think about a manager stocking the canned goods section of a supermarket. The manager tries to keep the store fully stocked so that shoppers can almost always find what they're looking for. But the manager does not want the shelves too heavily stocked because shelf space is limited and products can spoil. Similar considerations apply to many firms and typically lead them to manage their inventories carefully.

However, sales fluctuate. And because firms cannot always accurately predict sales, they often find themselves holding more or less inventories than they had intended. These unintended swings in inventories due to unforeseen changes in sales are called **unplanned inventory investment.** They represent investment spending, positive or negative, that occurred but was unplanned.

So in any given period, **actual investment spending** is equal to planned investment spending plus unplanned inventory investment. If we let $I_{Unplanned}$ represent unplanned inventory investment, $I_{Planned}$ represent planned investment spending, and I represent actual investment spending, then the relationship among all three can be represented as:

(26-10) $I = I_{Unplanned} + I_{Planned}$

Alexander Chaikin/Shutterstock

When the economy slumps, as it did in 2009, consumer spending plunges and inventory—such as cars at auto dealers—goes unsold, leading to a rise in unplanned inventory investment.

To see how unplanned inventory investment can occur, let's continue to focus on the auto industry and make the following assumptions. First, let's assume that the industry must determine each month's production volume in advance, before it knows the volume of actual sales. Second, let's assume that it anticipates selling 800,000 cars next month and that it plans neither to add to nor subtract from existing inventories. In that case, it will produce 800,000 cars to match anticipated sales.

Now imagine that next month's actual sales are less than expected, only 700,000 cars. As a result, the value of 100,000 cars will be added to investment spending as unplanned inventory investment.

The auto industry will, of course, eventually adjust to this slowdown in sales and the resulting unplanned inventory investment. The industry will probably cut next month's production volume in order to reduce inventories.

In fact, economists who study macroeconomic variables in an attempt to determine the future path of the economy pay careful attention to changes in inventory levels. Rising inventories typically indicate positive unplanned inventory investment and a slowing economy, as sales are less than had been forecast. Falling inventories typically indicate negative unplanned inventory investment and a growing economy, as sales are greater than forecast.

In the next section, we will see how production adjustments in response to fluctuations in sales and inventories ensure that the value of final goods and services actually produced is equal to desired purchases of those final goods and services.

ECONOMICS >> *in Action*
Business Investment in the Great Recession

Between December 2007 and June 2009 the U.S. economy experienced its worst economic downturn since the 1930s. Almost all economists agree that the principal driver of the Great Recession was the housing market: as a huge housing bubble deflated, residential investment—construction of new housing—plunged, and falling home values also reduced consumer wealth and therefore consumption spending.

But the Great Recession wasn't just about residential investment. As Figure 26-8 shows, nonresidential investment—which basically consists of business spending on new factories, office parks, warehouses, and so on—also plunged. Why?

The answer is that the sharp fall in residential investment and consumer spending left U.S. businesses with a great deal of *excess capacity*, as shown by the orange line in Figure 26-8. That is, because people weren't buying as much as before, there were many idle assembly lines, empty offices, unused space in warehouses, and so on. And since businesses weren't using the capacity they had, they saw little reason to build more.

As a result, a sharp drop in housing construction led to a further drop in non-housing investment, deepening the recession.

The good news is that once the economy stabilized and began growing again, excess business capacity was put back in use, and soon businesses began investing again.

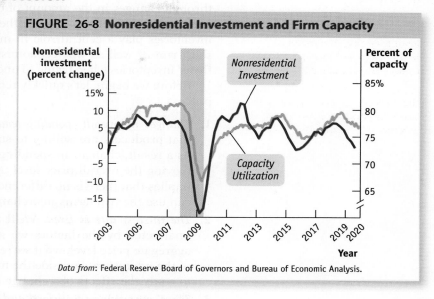

FIGURE 26-8 Nonresidential Investment and Firm Capacity

Data from: Federal Reserve Board of Governors and Bureau of Economic Analysis.

>> Check Your Understanding 26-3

Solutions appear at back of book.

1. For each event, explain whether planned investment spending or unplanned inventory investment will change and in what direction.
   a. An unexpected increase in consumer spending
   b. A sharp rise in the cost of business borrowing
   c. A sharp increase in the economy's growth rate of real GDP
   d. An unanticipated fall in sales

2. Historically, investment spending has experienced more extreme upward and downward swings than consumer spending. Why do you think this is so? (*Hint:* Consider the marginal propensity to consume and the accelerator principle.)

3. Consumer spending was sluggish in late 2007, and economists worried that an *inventory overhang*—a high level of unplanned inventory investment throughout the economy—would make it difficult for the economy to recover anytime soon. Explain why an inventory overhang might, like the existence of too much production capacity, depress current economic activity.

> ## >> Quick Review
>
> • **Planned investment spending** is negatively related to the interest rate and positively related to expected future real GDP. According to the **accelerator principle,** there is a positive relationship between planned investment spending and the expected future growth rate of real GDP.
>
> • Firms hold **inventories** to sell in the future. **Inventory investment,** a form of investment spending, can be positive or negative.
>
> • When actual sales are more or less than expected, **unplanned inventory investment** occurs. **Actual investment spending** is equal to planned investment spending plus unplanned inventory investment.

‖ The Income–Expenditure Model

Earlier in this chapter, we described how autonomous changes in spending—such as a fall in investment spending when a housing bubble bursts—lead to a multistage process through the actions of the multiplier that magnifies the effect of these changes on real GDP. We will now examine this multistage process more closely.

We'll see that the multiple rounds of changes in real GDP are accomplished through changes in the amount of output produced by firms—changes that they make in response to changes in their inventories. We'll come to understand why inventories play a central role in macroeconomic models of the economy in the short run as well as why economists pay particular attention to the behavior of firms' inventories when trying to understand the likely future state of the economy.

Before we begin, let's quickly recap the assumptions underlying the multiplier process.

1. *Changes in overall spending lead to changes in aggregate output.* We assume that producers are willing to supply additional output at a fixed price level. As a result, changes in spending translate into changes in output rather than moving the overall price level up or down. A fixed aggregate price level also implies that there is no difference between nominal GDP and real GDP. So we can use the two terms interchangeably in this chapter.

2. *The interest rate is fixed.* We'll take the interest rate as predetermined and unaffected by the factors we analyze in the model. As in the case of the aggregate price level, what we're really doing here is leaving the determinants of the interest rate outside the model. As we'll see, the model can still be used to study the effects of a change in the interest rate.

3. *Taxes, government transfers, and government purchases are all zero.*

4. *Exports and imports are both zero.*

In all subsequent chapters, we will drop the assumption that the aggregate price level is fixed. The Chapter 28 appendix addresses how taxes affect the multiplier process. We'll discuss how foreign trade enters the picture briefly later in this chapter, and bring it fully into the model in Chapter 33.

Planned Aggregate Spending and Real GDP

In an economy with no government and no foreign trade, there are only two sources of aggregate spending: consumer spending, C, and investment spending, I. And since we assume that there are no taxes or transfers, aggregate disposable income is equal to GDP (which, since the aggregate price level is fixed, is the same as real GDP): the total value of final sales of goods and services ultimately accrues to households as income. So in this highly simplified economy, there are two basic equations of national income accounting:

(26-11) $GDP = C + I$

(26-12) $YD = GDP$

As we learned earlier, the aggregate consumption function shows the relationship between disposable income and consumer spending. Let's continue to assume that the aggregate consumption function is of the same form as in Equation 26-9:

(26-13) $C = A + MPC \times YD$

In our simplified model, we will also assume planned investment spending, $I_{Planned}$, is fixed.

We need one more concept before putting the model together: **planned aggregate spending,** the total amount of planned spending in the economy. Unlike firms, households don't take unintended actions like unplanned inventory investment. So planned aggregate spending is equal to the sum of consumer spending and planned investment spending. We denote planned aggregate spending by $AE_{Planned}$, so:

(26-14) $AE_{Planned} = C + I_{Planned}$

Planned aggregate spending is the total amount of planned spending in the economy.

The level of planned aggregate spending in a given year depends on the level of real GDP in that year. To see why, let's look at a specific example, shown in Table 26-2. We assume that the aggregate consumption function is:

(26-15) $C = 300 + 0.6 \times YD$

Real GDP, YD, C, $I_{Planned}$, and $AE_{Planned}$ are all measured in billions of dollars, and we assume that the level of planned investment, $I_{Planned}$, is fixed at $500 billion per year. The first column shows possible levels of real GDP. The second column shows disposable income, YD, which in our simplified model is equal to real GDP. The third column shows consumer spending, C, equal to $300 billion plus 0.6 times disposable income, YD. The fourth column shows planned investment spending, $I_{Planned}$, which we have assumed is $500 billion regardless of the level of real GDP. Finally, the last column shows planned aggregate spending, $AE_{Planned}$, the sum of aggregate consumer spending, C, and planned investment spending, $I_{Planned}$. (To economize on notation, we'll assume that it is understood from now on that all the variables in Table 26-2 are measured in billions of dollars per year.)

As you can see, a higher level of real GDP leads to a higher level of disposable income: every 500 increase in real GDP raises YD by 500, which in turn raises C by $500 \times 0.6 = 300$ and $AE_{Planned}$ by 300.

Figure 26-9 illustrates the information in Table 26-2 graphically. Real GDP is measured on the horizontal axis. CF is the aggregate consumption function; it shows how consumer spending depends on real GDP. $AE_{Planned}$, the planned aggregate spending line, corresponds to the aggregate consumption function shifted up by 500 (the amount of $I_{Planned}$). It shows how planned aggregate spending depends on real GDP. Both lines have a slope of 0.6, equal to MPC, the marginal propensity to consume.

But this isn't the end of the story. Table 26-2 reveals that real GDP equals planned aggregate spending, $AE_{Planned}$, only when the level of real GDP is at 2,000.

TABLE 26-2 Equilibrium When Real $GDP = YD = AE_{Planned}$

Real GDP	YD	C	$I_{Planned}$	$AE_{Planned}$
(billions of dollars)				
$0	$0	$300	$500	$800
500	500	600	500	1,100
1,000	1,000	900	500	1,400
1,500	1,500	1,200	500	1,700
2,000	2,000	1,500	500	2,000
2,500	2,500	1,800	500	2,300
3,000	3,000	2,100	500	2,600
3,500	3,500	2,400	500	2,900

FIGURE 26-9 The Aggregate Consumption Function and Planned Aggregate Spending

The lower line, *CF*, is the aggregate consumption function constructed from the data in Table 26-2. The upper line, $AE_{Planned}$, is the planned aggregate spending line, also constructed from the data in Table 26-2. It is equivalent to the aggregate consumption function shifted up by $500 billion, the amount of planned investment spending, $I_{Planned}$.

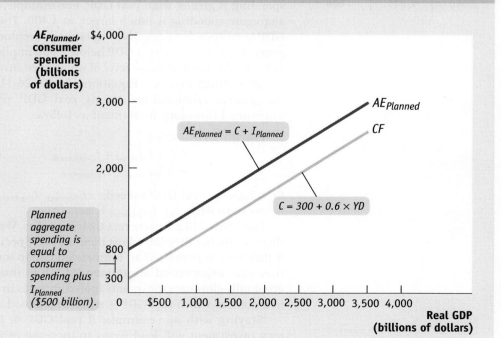

Real GDP does not equal $AE_{Planned}$ at any other level. Is that possible? Didn't we learn in Chapter 22, with the circular-flow diagram, that total spending on final goods and services in the economy is equal to the total value of output of final goods and services? The answer is that for *brief* periods of time, planned aggregate spending can differ from real GDP because of the role of *unplanned* aggregate spending—$I_{Unplanned}$, unplanned inventory investment.

But as we'll see next, the economy moves over time to a situation in which there is no unplanned inventory investment, a situation called *income–expenditure equilibrium*. And when the economy is in income–expenditure equilibrium, planned aggregate spending on final goods and services equals aggregate output.

Income–Expenditure Equilibrium

For all but one value of real GDP shown in Table 26-2, real GDP is either more or less than $AE_{Planned}$, the sum of consumer spending and *planned* investment spending. For example, when real GDP is 1,000, consumer spending, C, is 900 and planned investment spending is 500, making planned aggregate spending 1,400. This is 400 *more* than the corresponding level of real GDP. Now consider what happens when real GDP is 2,500; consumer spending, C, is 1,800 and planned investment spending is 500, making planned aggregate spending only 2,300, which is 200 *less* than real GDP.

As we've just explained, planned aggregate spending can be different from real GDP only if there is unplanned inventory investment, $I_{Unplanned}$, in the economy. Let's examine Table 26-3, which includes the numbers for real GDP and for planned aggregate spending from Table 26-2. It also includes the levels of unplanned inventory investment, $I_{Unplanned}$, that each combination of real GDP and planned aggregate spending implies. For example, if real GDP is 2,500, planned aggregate spending is only 2,300. This 200 excess of real GDP over $AE_{Planned}$ must consist of positive unplanned inventory investment. This can happen only if firms have overestimated sales and produced too much, leading to unintended additions to inventories.

More generally, any level of real GDP in excess of 2,000 corresponds to a situation in which firms are producing more than consumers and other firms want to purchase, creating an unintended increase in inventories.

Conversely, a level of real GDP below 2,000 implies that planned aggregate spending is *greater* than real GDP. For example, when real GDP is 1,000, planned aggregate spending is much larger, at 1,400. The 400 excess of $AE_{Planned}$ over real GDP corresponds to negative unplanned inventory investment equal to –400. More generally, any level of real GDP below 2,000 implies that firms have underestimated sales, leading to a negative level of unplanned inventory investment in the economy.

By putting together Equations 26-10, 26-11, and 26-14, we can summarize the general relationships among real GDP, planned aggregate spending, and unplanned inventory investment as follows:

(26-16) $GDP = C + I$
$$= C + I_{Planned} + I_{Unplanned}$$
$$= AE_{Planned} + I_{Unplanned}$$

So whenever real GDP exceeds $AE_{Planned}$, $I_{Unplanned}$ is positive; whenever real GDP is less than $AE_{Planned}$, $I_{Unplanned}$ is negative.

But firms will act to correct their mistakes. We've assumed that they don't change their prices, but they *can* adjust their output. Specifically, they will reduce production if they have experienced an unintended rise in inventories or increase production if they have experienced an unintended fall in inventories. And these responses will eventually eliminate the unanticipated changes in inventories and move the economy to a point at which real GDP is equal to planned aggregate spending.

Staying with our example, if real GDP is 1,000, negative unplanned inventory investment will lead firms to increase production, leading to a rise in real

TABLE 26-3 Equilibrium When $I_{Unplanned} = 0$

Real GDP	$AE_{Planned}$	$I_{Unplanned}$
(billions of dollars)		
$0	$800	–$800
500	1,100	–600
1,000	1,400	–400
1,500	1,700	–200
2,000	2,000	0
2,500	2,300	200
3,000	2,600	400
3,500	2,900	600

GDP. In fact, this will happen whenever real GDP is less than 2,000—that is, whenever real GDP is less than planned aggregate spending. Conversely, if real GDP is 2,500, positive unplanned inventory investment will lead firms to reduce production, leading to a fall in real GDP. This will happen whenever real GDP is greater than planned aggregate spending.

The only situation in which firms won't have an incentive to change output in the next period is when aggregate output, measured by real GDP, is equal to planned aggregate spending in the current period, an outcome known as **income–expenditure equilibrium.** In Table 26-3, income–expenditure equilibrium is achieved when real GDP is 2,000, the only level of real GDP at which unplanned inventory investment is zero. From now on, we'll denote the real GDP level at which income–expenditure equilibrium occurs as Y^* and call it the **income–expenditure equilibrium GDP.**

Figure 26-10 illustrates the concept of income–expenditure equilibrium graphically. Real GDP is on the horizontal axis and planned aggregate spending, $AE_{Planned}$, is on the vertical axis. There are two lines in the figure. The solid line is the planned aggregate spending line. It shows how $AE_{Planned}$, equal to $C + I_{Planned}$, depends on real GDP; it has a slope of 0.6, equal to the marginal propensity to consume, MPC, and a vertical intercept equal to $A + I_{Planned}$ (300 + 500 = 800). The dashed line, which goes through the origin with a slope of 1 (often called a 45-degree line), shows all the possible points at which planned aggregate spending is equal to real GDP.

This line allows us to easily spot the point of income–expenditure equilibrium, which must lie on both the 45-degree line and the planned aggregate spending line. So the point of income–expenditure equilibrium is at E, where the two lines cross. And the income–expenditure equilibrium GDP, Y^*, is 2,000—the same outcome we derived in Table 26-3.

Now consider what happens if the economy isn't in income–expenditure equilibrium. We can see from Figure 26-10 that whenever real GDP is less than Y^*,

> The economy is in **income-expenditure equilibrium** when aggregate output, measured by real GDP, is equal to planned aggregate spending.
>
> **Income–expenditure equilibrium GDP** is the level of real GDP at which real GDP equals planned aggregate spending.

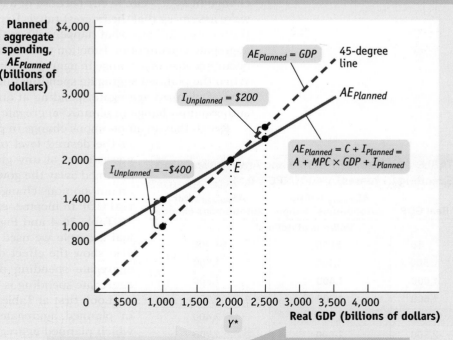

FIGURE 26-10 Income–Expenditure Equilibrium

Income–expenditure equilibrium occurs at E, the point where the planned aggregate spending line, $AE_{Planned}$, crosses the 45-degree line. At E, the economy produces real GDP of $2,000 billion per year, the only point at which real GDP equals planned aggregate spending, $AE_{Planned}$, and unplanned inventory investment, $I_{Unplanned}$, is zero. This is the level of income–expenditure equilibrium GDP, Y^*. At any level of real GDP less than Y^*, $AE_{Planned}$ exceeds real GDP. As a result, unplanned inventory investment, $I_{Unplanned}$, is negative and firms respond by increasing production. At any level of real GDP greater than Y^*, real GDP exceeds $AE_{Planned}$. Unplanned inventory investment, $I_{Unplanned}$, is positive and firms respond by reducing production.

The **Keynesian cross** diagram identifies income–expenditure equilibrium as the point where the planned aggregate spending line crosses the 45-degree line.

the planned aggregate spending line lies above the 45-degree line and $AE_{Planned}$ exceeds real GDP. In this situation, $I_{Unplanned}$ is negative: as shown in the figure, at a real GDP of 1,000, $I_{Unplanned}$ is –400. As a consequence, real GDP will rise. In contrast, whenever real GDP is greater than Y^*, the planned aggregate expenditure line lies below the 45-degree line. Here, $I_{Unplanned}$ is positive: as shown, at a real GDP of 2,500, $I_{Unplanned}$ is 200. The unanticipated accumulation of inventory leads to a fall in real GDP.

The type of diagram shown in Figure 26-10, which identifies income–expenditure equilibrium as the point at which the planned aggregate spending line crosses the 45-degree line, has a special place in the history of economic thought. Known as the **Keynesian cross,** it was developed by Paul Samuelson, one of the greatest economists of the twentieth century (as well as a Nobel Prize winner), to explain the ideas of John Maynard Keynes, the founder of macroeconomics as we know it.

The Multiplier Process and Inventory Adjustment

We've just learned about a very important feature of the macroeconomy: when planned spending by households and firms does not equal the current aggregate output by firms, this difference shows up in changes in inventories. The response of firms to those inventory changes moves real GDP over time to the point at which real GDP and planned aggregate spending are equal. That's why, as we mentioned earlier, changes in inventories are considered a leading indicator of future economic activity.

Now that we understand how real GDP moves to achieve income–expenditure equilibrium for a given level of planned aggregate spending, let's turn to understanding what happens when there is *a shift of the planned aggregate spending line.* How does the economy move from the initial point of income–expenditure equilibrium to a new point of income–expenditure equilibrium? And what are the possible sources of changes in planned aggregate spending?

In our simple model there are only two possible sources of a shift of the planned aggregate spending line: a change in planned investment spending, $I_{Planned}$, or a shift of the aggregate consumption function, CF. For example, a change in $I_{Planned}$ can occur because of a change in the interest rate. (Remember, we're assuming that the interest rate is fixed by factors that are outside the model. But we can still ask what happens when the interest rate changes.) A shift of the aggregate consumption function (that is, a change in its vertical intercept, A) can occur because of a change in aggregate wealth—say, due to a rise in house prices. When the planned aggregate spending line shifts—when there is a change in the level of planned aggregate spending at any given level of real GDP—there is an autonomous change in planned aggregate spending.

Recall that an autonomous change in planned aggregate spending is a change in the desired level of spending by firms, households, and government at any given level of real GDP (although we've assumed away the government for the time being). How does an autonomous change in planned aggregate spending affect real GDP in income–expenditure equilibrium?

Table 26-4 and Figure 26-11 start from the same numerical example we used in Table 26-3 and Figure 26-10. They also show the effect of an autonomous increase in planned aggregate spending of 400—what happens when planned aggregate spending is 400 higher at each level of real GDP.

Look first at Table 26-4. Before the autonomous increase in planned aggregate spending, the level of real GDP at which planned aggregate spending is equal to real GDP, Y^*, is 2,000. After the autonomous change, Y^* has risen to 3,000. The same result is visible in Figure 26-11. The initial income–expenditure equilibrium is at E_1, where Y_1^* is 2,000. The autonomous rise in planned aggregate spending shifts

TABLE 26-4 Real GDP Before and After Autonomous Spending Increases by 400 ($MPC = 0.6$)

Real GDP	$AE_{Planned}$ before autonomous change	$AE_{Planned}$ after autonomous change
	(billions of dollars)	
$0	$800	$1,200
500	1,100	1,500
1,000	1,400	1,800
1,500	1,700	2,100
2,000	2,000	2,400
2,500	2,300	2,700
3,000	2,600	3,000
3,500	2,900	3,300
4,000	3,200	3,600

FIGURE 26-11 The Multiplier

This figure illustrates the change in Y^* caused by an autonomous increase in planned aggregate spending. The economy is initially at equilibrium point E_1 with an income–expenditure equilibrium GDP, Y_1^*, equal to 2,000. An autonomous increase in $AE_{Planned}$ of 400 shifts the planned aggregate spending line upward by 400. The economy is no longer in income–expenditure equilibrium: real GDP is equal to 2,000 but $AE_{Planned}$ is now 2,400, represented by point X. The vertical distance between the two planned aggregate spending lines, equal to 400, represents $I_{Unplanned} = -400$—the negative inventory investment that the economy now experiences. Firms respond by increasing production, and the economy eventually reaches a new income–expenditure equilibrium at E_2 with a higher level of income–expenditure equilibrium GDP, Y_2^*, equal to 3,000.

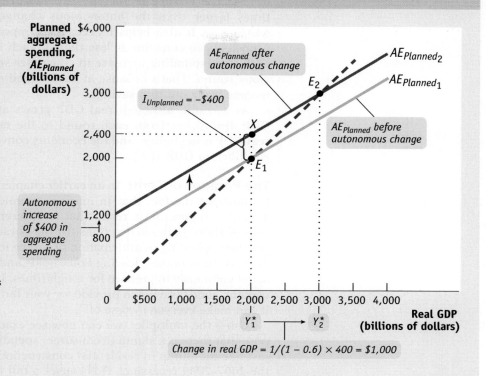

the planned aggregate spending line up, leading to a new income–expenditure equilibrium at E_2, where Y_2^* is 3,000.

The fact that the rise in income–expenditure equilibrium GDP, from 2,000 to 3,000, is much larger than the autonomous increase in aggregate spending, which is only 400, has a familiar explanation: the multiplier process. In the specific example we have just described, an autonomous increase in planned aggregate spending of 400 leads to an increase in Y^* from 2,000 to 3,000, a rise of 1,000. So the multiplier in this example is $1,000/400 = 2.5$.

We can examine in detail what underlies the multistage multiplier process by looking more closely at Figure 26-11. First, starting from E_1, the autonomous increase in planned aggregate spending leads to a gap between planned aggregate spending and real GDP. This is represented by the vertical distance between X, at 2,400, and E_1, at 2,000. This gap illustrates an unplanned fall in inventory investment: $I_{Unplanned} = -400$. Firms respond by increasing production, leading to a rise in real GDP from Y_1^*. The rise in real GDP translates into an increase in disposable income, YD.

That's the first stage in the chain reaction. But it doesn't stop there—the increase in YD leads to a rise in consumer spending, C, which sets off a second-round rise in real GDP. This in turn leads to a further rise in disposable income and consumer spending, and so on. And we could play this process in reverse: an autonomous fall in aggregate spending will lead to a chain reaction of reductions in real GDP and consumer spending.

We can summarize these results in an equation, where $\Delta AAE_{Planned}$ represents the autonomous change in $AE_{Planned}$, and $\Delta Y^* = Y_2^* - Y_1^*$, the subsequent change in income–expenditure equilibrium GDP:

(26-17) $\Delta Y^* = \text{Multiplier} \times \Delta AAE_{Planned} = \dfrac{1}{1 - MPC} \times \Delta AAE_{Planned}$

Recalling that the multiplier, $1/(1 - MPC)$, is greater than 1, Equation 26-17 tells us that the change in income–expenditure equilibrium GDP, ΔY^*, is several times larger than the autonomous change in planned aggregate spending, $\Delta AAE_{Planned}$. It also helps us recall an important point: because the marginal propensity to consume is less than 1, each increase in disposable income and each corresponding increase in consumer spending is smaller than in the previous round. That's because at each round some of the increase in disposable income leaks out into savings.

As a result, although real GDP grows at each round, the increase in real GDP diminishes from each round to the next. At some point the increase in real GDP is negligible, and the economy converges to a new income–expenditure equilibrium GDP at Y_2^*.

The Paradox of Thrift In an earlier chapter we mentioned the paradox of thrift to illustrate the fact that in macroeconomics the outcome of many individual actions can generate a result that is different from and worse than the simple sum of those individual actions. In the paradox of thrift, households and firms cut their spending in anticipation of future tough economic times. These actions depress the economy, leaving households and firms worse off than if they hadn't acted virtuously to prepare for tough times. It is called a paradox because what's usually "good" (saving to provide for your family in hard times) is "bad" (because it can make everyone worse off).

Using the multiplier, we can now see exactly how this scenario unfolds. Suppose that there is a slump in consumer spending or investment spending, or both, just like the slump in residential construction investment spending leading up to the 2007–2009 recession. This causes a fall in income–expenditure equilibrium GDP that is several times larger than the original fall in spending. The fall in real GDP leaves consumers and producers worse off than they would have been if they hadn't cut their spending.

Conversely, prodigal behavior is rewarded: if consumers or producers increase their spending, the resulting multiplier process makes the increase in income–expenditure equilibrium GDP several times larger than the original increase in spending. So lavish spending makes consumers and producers better off than if they had been cautious spenders.

It's important to realize that our result that the multiplier is equal to $1/(1 - MPC)$ depends on the simplifying assumption that there are no taxes or transfers, so that disposable income is equal to real GDP. In the Chapter 28 appendix, we'll bring taxes into the picture, which makes the expression for the multiplier more complicated and the multiplier itself smaller.

But the general principle we just learned remains valid: an autonomous change in planned aggregate spending leads to a change in income–expenditure equilibrium GDP, both directly and through an induced change in consumer spending.

As we've seen, declines in planned investment spending are usually the major factor causing recessions, because historically they have been the most common source of autonomous reductions in aggregate spending. The tendency of the consumption function to shift upward over time, which as noted earlier in the Economics in Action, "Famous First Forecasting Failures," means that autonomous changes in both planned investment spending and consumer spending play important roles in expansions. But regardless of the source, there are multiplier effects in the economy that magnify the size of the initial change in aggregate spending.

Lavish spending after a slump makes everyone better off thanks to the multiplier effect.

Rawpixel.com/Shutterstock

What About Exports and Imports?

The simple version of the income–expenditure model that we have just laid out assumes that there is no international trade. But, as you may have noticed, the opening story for this chapter deviates in an important way from this simple version of the model. Spain's economic rebound was largely the result of a strong boost in exports of automobiles. And in a basic sense the boom in North Dakota, described in an earlier Economics in Action, also involved trade—North Dakota's shale oil is sold to other states and countries, not to local consumers.

So how does bringing exports and imports back in change the story? The answer is that the basic multiplier story continues to work, with two modifications.

First, income earned from exports is a source of spending on domestically produced goods and services, just like consumption and investment. Changes in exports act just like autonomous changes in spending, like an investment boom or slump. In Spain's case, the boost in automobile exports led to a direct increase in Spanish incomes. This then led to an increase in the demand for consumer goods, which led to a further increase in income, and so on, exactly the way an increase in investment spending leads via the multiplier process to an economic expansion.

Second, the multiplier process itself is made somewhat weaker thanks to foreign trade: when consumer spending rises or falls, part of that change is reflected in changes in spending on imports, which don't affect a nation's own income. Suppose, for example, that U.S. consumer spending rises by $1 billion. If the United States didn't engage in foreign trade, all of that rise in spending would translate directly into a rise in U.S. GDP. In reality, however, a significant part of the total—say $200 million—will be a rise in spending on goods produced in Canada, Mexico, China, or elsewhere. And this spending *isn't* part of U.S. GDP. As economists sometimes put it, part of any spending change "leaks" abroad.

The effect of this leakage is to reduce the size of the multiplier. The extent to which the multiplier falls depends on how much of an additional dollar of spending falls on imports rather than domestic goods—the *marginal propensity to import*. In the case of the United States, which is a very large economy with only limited international trade, leaks from imports have only a modest effect on the size of the multiplier. In small countries that engage in a lot of trade, trade may greatly reduce the multiplier.

One final point about the effect of trade: it creates interdependence among national economies, because each country's exports are some other country's imports. Suppose that the U.S. economy enters a recession. This will lead, other things equal, to a decline in the amount we spend on goods produced in Canada, which means a decline in Canadian exports. And this spillover will tend to drag Canada's economy down, too. More broadly, the trade links between economies are one reason business cycles are often international, even global, in scope: many countries tend to have recessions and recoveries at the same time.

One thing is important to realize, however, about exports and imports: while they can change the size of the multiplier, they don't change the fundamental story about how aggregate spending rises and falls.

ECONOMICS >> *in Action*
Inventories and the End of a Recession

A very clear example of the role of inventories in the multiplier process took place in late 2001, as that year's recession came to an end. The driving force behind the recession was a slump in business investment spending. It took several years before investment spending bounced back in the form of a housing boom. By late 2001 the economy had begun to recover, largely due to an increase in consumer spending—especially on durable goods such as automobiles.

FIGURE 26-12 Inventories and the End of a Recession

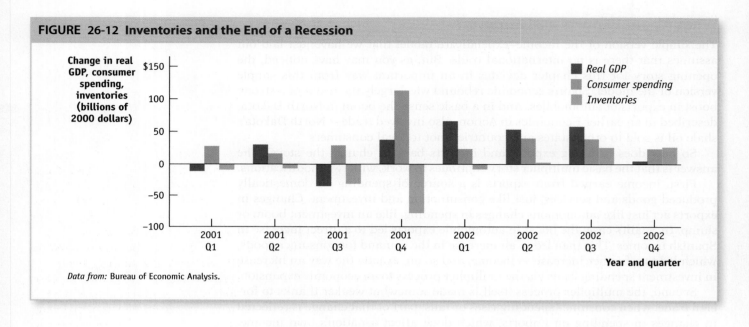

Data from: Bureau of Economic Analysis.

Initially, this increase in consumer spending caught manufacturers by surprise. Figure 26-12 shows changes in real GDP, real consumer spending, and real inventories in each quarter of 2001 and 2002. Notice the surge in consumer spending in the fourth quarter of 2001. Initially, it didn't lead to significant GDP growth because it was offset by a plunge in inventories. But in the first quarter of 2002, producers greatly increased their production, leading to a jump in real GDP.

>> Check Your Understanding 26-4

Solutions appear at back of book.

1. Although economists believe that recessions typically begin as slumps in investment spending, they also believe that consumer spending eventually slumps during a recession. Explain why.

2. **a.** Use a diagram like Figure 26-11 to show what happens when there is an autonomous fall in planned aggregate spending. Describe how the economy adjusts to a new income–expenditure equilibrium.

   b. Suppose Y^* is originally $500 billion, the autonomous reduction in planned aggregate spending is $300 million ($0.3 billion), and $MPC = 0.5$. Calculate Y^* after such a change.

>> Quick Review

- The economy is in **income–expenditure equilibrium** when **planned aggregate spending** is equal to real GDP.

- At any output level greater than **income–expenditure equilibrium GDP,** real GDP exceeds planned aggregate spending and inventories are rising. At any lower output level, real GDP falls short of planned aggregate spending and inventories are falling.

- After an autonomous change in planned aggregate spending, the economy moves to a new income–expenditure equilibrium through the inventory adjustment process, as illustrated by the **Keynesian cross.** Because of the multiplier effect, the change in income–expenditure equilibrium GDP is a multiple of the autonomous change in aggregate spending.

- The multiplier effect is modified but not fundamentally changed by international trade. Changes in imports operate in the same way as changes in consumption and investment spending. Imports create leakages of spending, which make the size of the multiplier smaller than it is in an economy with no imports.

What's Good for America Is Good for GM

Bill Pugliano/Getty Images

With the economy in a steep nose-dive in 2009, the U.S. government took many stabilization measures, some of which were highly controversial. The decision to use taxpayer's funds to bail out General Motors, which was teetering on the edge of bankruptcy, was among the most controversial. To keep the company afloat, the U.S. government gave it $49.5 billion in loans that were then converted into stock, giving the government temporary ownership of 61% of the company.

General Motors—or GM, as it was often called in its heyday—was once a U.S. icon, so dominant that in the 1950s the company's president, who had been nominated as Secretary of Defense, famously claimed that any conflict of interest was inconceivable: "I thought what was good for our country was good for General Motors, and vice versa."

By 2009 the fate of GM and the fate of the United States seemed less intertwined. Still, the case for the bailout rested crucially on the belief that GM's problems weren't entirely self-made, that the company was in trouble because the U.S. economy was in trouble, and that national recovery would make a big difference to the automaker's fortune, too.

On the face of it, this interdependence wasn't entirely obvious: the 2007–2009 recession was driven by a housing bust and troubles in the banking sector, not by developments in the auto industry. But multiplier effects had indeed led to a plunge in auto sales, as shown in Figure 26-13. And sure enough, as the economy began to recover, auto sales made up most of their lost ground, with GM sharing in the industry's resurgence.

Did saving GM justify the bailout? The company's recovery meant that taxpayers got most of their money back—

but not all of it. Recall that the government loan of almost $50 billion was converted into GM stock. Over time, the government sold off its stake for roughly $40 billion—leaving taxpayers with a $10 billion loss.

Defenders of the bailout nonetheless declared it a success, because it resuscitated the U.S. auto industry and saved many jobs, not just in the auto companies and their suppliers, but in the many businesses whose sales depend on the incomes of workers employed in the auto industry. In the summer of 2009 the unemployment rate in Michigan, still the U.S. automotive heartland, rose above 14%—but it then began a rapid decline, falling below the national average to 4.5% by the summer of 2016. Few would argue that the speedy recovery in employment in Michigan would have happened without the auto bailout.

In the end, GM bounced back because the U.S. economy recovered; what was good for America was indeed still good for General Motors. And what was good for General Motors was clearly good for Michigan—and maybe, arguably, for the United States as a whole.

QUESTIONS FOR THOUGHT

1. Why did a national slump that began with housing affect companies like General Motors?

2. Why was it reasonable in June 2009 to predict that auto sales would improve in the near future?

3. How does this story about General Motors help explain how a slump in housing—a relatively small part of the U.S. economy—could produce such a deep national recession?

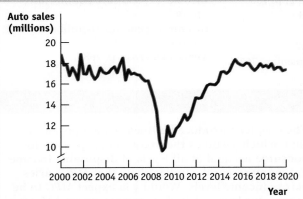

FIGURE 26-13 U.S. Auto Sales 2000–2020

Data from: Federal Reserve Bank of St. Louis.

SUMMARY

1. An **autonomous change in aggregate spending** leads to a chain reaction in which the total change in real GDP is equal to the **multiplier** times the initial change in aggregate spending. The size of the multiplier, $1/(1 - MPC)$, depends on the **marginal propensity to consume, MPC,** the fraction of an additional dollar of disposable income spent on consumption. The larger the MPC, the larger the multiplier and the larger the change in real GDP for any given autonomous change in aggregate spending. The **marginal propensity to save, MPS,** is equal to $1 - MPC$.

2. The **consumption function** shows how an individual household's consumer spending is determined by its current disposable income. The **aggregate consumption function** shows the relationship for the entire economy. According to the life-cycle hypothesis, households try to smooth their consumption over their lifetimes. As a result, the aggregate consumption function shifts in response to changes in expected future disposable income and changes in aggregate wealth.

3. **Planned investment spending** depends negatively on the interest rate and on existing production capacity; it depends positively on expected future real GDP. The **accelerator principle** says that investment spending is greatly influenced by the expected growth rate of real GDP.

4. Firms hold **inventories** of goods so that they can satisfy consumer demand quickly. **Inventory investment** is positive when firms add to their inventories, negative when they reduce them. Often, however, changes in inventories are unintended. They arise when expected sales and actual sales don't match. The result is unplanned inventory investment. **Actual investment spending** is the sum of planned investment spending and unplanned inventory investment.

5. In **income–expenditure equilibrium, planned aggregate spending,** which in a simplified model with no government and no trade is the sum of consumer spending and planned investment spending, is equal to real GDP. At the **income–expenditure equilibrium GDP,** or Y^*, unplanned inventory investment is zero. When planned aggregate spending is larger than Y^*, unplanned inventory investment is negative; there is an unanticipated reduction in inventories and firms increase production. When planned aggregate spending is less than Y^*, unplanned inventory investment is positive; there is an unanticipated increase in inventories and firms reduce production. The **Keynesian cross** shows how the economy self-adjusts to income–expenditure equilibrium through inventory adjustments.

6. After an autonomous change in planned aggregate spending, the inventory adjustment process moves the economy to a new income–expenditure equilibrium. The change in income–expenditure equilibrium GDP arising from an autonomous change in spending is equal to $(1/(1 - MPC)) \times \Delta AAE_{Planned}$.

7. When trade is introduced, the basic multiplier story continues to work but it is modified in two ways: first, income earned from exports is a source of spending on domestically produced goods and services, just like consumption and investment; and second, imports reduce the size of the multiplier.

KEY TERMS

Marginal propensity to consume (MPC), p. 750

Marginal propensity to save (MPS), p. 750

Autonomous change in aggregate spending, p. 752

Multiplier, p. 752

Consumption function, p. 753

Aggregate consumption function, p. 755

Planned investment spending, p. 760

Accelerator principle, p. 761

Inventories, p. 761

Inventory investment, p. 762

Unplanned inventory investment, p. 762

Actual investment spending, p. 762

Planned aggregate spending, p. 764

Income–expenditure equilibrium, p. 767

Income–expenditure equilibrium GDP, p. 767

Keynesian cross, p. 768

PRACTICE QUESTIONS

1. Explain how each of the following actions will affect the level of planned investment spending and unplanned inventory investment. Assume the economy is initially in income–expenditure equilibrium.

   a. The Federal Reserve raises the interest rate.

   b. There is a rise in the expected growth rate of real GDP.

   c. A sizable inflow of foreign funds into the country lowers the interest rate.

   d. A large economic shutdown of nonessential businesses causes a significant reduction in consumer spending.

2. The chapter introduced a linear consumption function, which assumes the marginal propensity to consume is equal at all levels of disposable income. Yet many research studies show that MPC varies across income levels. Would you expect MPC to be greater for lower or higher income groups? How would relaxing the assumption of a constant MPC, allowing it to vary across income groups, change the multiplier?

PROBLEMS

1. Due to an increase in consumer wealth, there is a $40 billion autonomous increase in consumer spending in the economies of Westlandia and Eastlandia. Assuming that the aggregate price level is constant, the interest rate is fixed in both countries, and there are no taxes and no foreign trade, complete the accompanying tables to show the various rounds of increased spending that will occur in both economies if the marginal propensity to consume is 0.5 in Westlandia and 0.75 in Eastlandia. What do your results indicate about the relationship between the size of *MPC* and the multiplier?

	Westlandia	
Rounds	**Incremental change in GDP**	**Total change in GDP**
1	$\Delta C = \$40$ billion	?
2	$MPC \times \Delta C =$?	?
3	$MPC \times MPC \times \Delta C =$?	?
4	$MPC \times MPC \times MPC \times \Delta C =$?	?
...	...	...
Total change in GDP	$(1/(1 - MPC)) \times \Delta C = ?$	

	Eastlandia	
Rounds	**Incremental change in GDP**	**Total change in GDP**
1	$\Delta C = \$40$ billion	?
2	$MPC \times \Delta C =$?	?
3	$MPC \times MPC \times \Delta C =$?	?
4	$MPC \times MPC \times MPC \times \Delta C =$?	?
...	...	...
Total change in GDP	$(1/(1 - MPC)) \times \Delta C = ?$	

2. Assuming that the aggregate price level is constant, the interest rate is fixed, and there are no taxes and no foreign trade, what will be the change in GDP if the following events occur?

   a. There is an autonomous increase in consumer spending of $25 billion; the marginal propensity to consume is 2/3.

   b. Firms reduce investment spending by $40 billion; the marginal propensity to consume is 0.8.

   c. The government increases its purchases of military equipment by $60 billion; the marginal propensity to consume is 0.6.

3. Economists observed the only five residents of a very small economy and estimated each one's consumer spending at various levels of current disposable income. The accompanying table shows each resident's consumer spending at three income levels.

Individual consumer spending by	Individual current disposable income		
	$0	**$20,000**	**$40,000**
Andre	$1,000	$15,000	$29,000
Barbara	2,500	12,500	22,500
Casey	2,000	20,000	38,000
Declan	5,000	17,000	29,000
Elena	4,000	19,000	34,000

   a. What is each resident's consumption function? What is *MPC* for each resident?

   b. What is the economy's aggregate consumption function? What is *MPC* for the economy?

4. From 2014 to 2019, Eastlandia experienced large fluctuations in both aggregate consumer spending and disposable income, but wealth, the interest rate, and expected future disposable income did not change. The accompanying table shows the level of aggregate consumer spending and disposable income in millions of dollars for each of these years. Use this information to answer the following questions.

Year	Disposable income (millions of dollars)	Consumer spending (millions of dollars)
2014	$100	$180
2015	350	380
2016	300	340
2017	400	420
2018	375	400
2019	500	500

   a. Plot the aggregate consumption function for Eastlandia.

   b. What is *MPC*? What is *MPS*?

   c. What is the aggregate consumption function?

5. The Bureau of Economic Analysis reported that, in real terms, overall consumer spending increased by $335.5 billion in 2019.

   a. If *MPC* is 0.50, by how much will real GDP change in response?

   b. If there are no other changes to autonomous spending other than the increase in consumer spending in part a, and unplanned inventory investment, $I_{Unplanned}$, decreased by $100 billion, what is the change in real GDP?

   c. GDP at the end of 2019 was $18,638.2 billion. If GDP were to increase by the amount calculated in part b, what would be the percent increase in GDP?

6. During the early 2000s, the Case–Shiller U.S. Home Price Index, a measure of average home prices, rose continuously until it peaked in March 2006. From March 2006 to May 2009, the index lost 32% of its value. Meanwhile, the stock market experienced similar ups and downs. From March 2003 to October 2007, the Standard and Poor's 500 (S&P 500) stock index, a broad measure of stock market prices, almost doubled, from 800.73 to a high of 1,565.15. From that time until March 2009, the index fell by almost 60%, to a low of 676.53. How do you think the movements in home prices both influenced the growth in real GDP during the first half of the decade and added to the concern about maintaining consumer spending after the collapse in the housing market that began in 2006? To what extent did the movements in the stock market hurt or help consumer spending?

7. How will planned investment spending change as the following events occur?

a. The interest rate falls as a result of Federal Reserve policy.

b. The U.S. Environmental Protection Agency decrees that corporations must upgrade or replace their machinery in order to reduce their emissions of sulfur dioxide.

c. Baby boomers begin to retire in large numbers and reduce their savings, resulting in higher interest rates.

8. In an economy with no government and no foreign sectors, autonomous consumer spending is $250 billion, planned investment spending is $350 billion, and the marginal propensity to consume is 2/3.

a. Plot the aggregate consumption function and planned aggregate spending.

b. What is unplanned inventory investment when real GDP equals $600 billion?

c. What is Y^*, income–expenditure equilibrium GDP?

d. What is the value of the multiplier?

e. If planned investment spending rises to $450 billion, what will be the new Y^*?

9. An economy has a marginal propensity to consume of 0.5, and Y^*, income–expenditure equilibrium GDP, equals $500 billion. Given an autonomous increase in planned investment of $10 billion, show the rounds of increased spending that take place by completing the accompanying table. The first and second rows are filled in for you. In the first row, the increase of planned investment spending of $10 billion raises real GDP and YD by $10 billion, leading to an increase in consumer spending of $5 billion ($MPC \times$ change in disposable income) in row 2, raising real GDP and YD by a further $5 billion.

Rounds	Change in $I_{Planned}$ or C	Change in real GDP	Change in YD
	(billions of dollars)		
1	$\Delta I_{Planned}$ = $10.00	$10.00	$10.00
2	ΔC = $5.00	$5.00	$5.00
3	ΔC = ?	?	?
4	ΔC = ?	?	?
5	ΔC = ?	?	?
6	ΔC = ?	?	?
7	ΔC = ?	?	?
8	ΔC = ?	?	?
9	ΔC = ?	?	?
10	ΔC = ?	?	?

a. What is the total change in real GDP after the 10 rounds? What is the value of the multiplier? What would you expect the total change in Y^* to be based on the multiplier formula? How do your answers to the first and third questions compare?

b. Redo the table starting from round 2, assuming MPC is 0.75. What is the total change in real GDP after 10 rounds? What is the value of the multiplier? As the marginal propensity to consume increases, what happens to the value of the multiplier?

10. Although the United States is one of the richest nations in the world, it is also the world's largest debtor nation. We often hear that the problem is the nation's low savings rate. Suppose policy makers attempt to rectify this by encouraging greater savings in the economy. What effect will their successful attempts have on real GDP?

11. The U.S. economy slowed significantly in early 2008, and policy makers were extremely concerned about growth. To boost the economy, Congress passed several relief packages (the Economic Stimulus Act of 2008 and the American Recovery and Reinvestment Act of 2009) that combined would deliver about $700 billion in government spending. Assume, for the sake of argument, that this spending was in the form of payments made directly to consumers. The objective was to boost the economy by increasing the disposable income of American consumers.

a. Calculate the initial change in aggregate consumer spending as a consequence of this policy measure if MPC in the United States is 0.5. Then calculate the resulting change in real GDP arising from the $700 billion in payments.

b. Illustrate the effect on real GDP with the use of a graph depicting the income–expenditure equilibrium. Label the vertical axis "Planned aggregate spending, $AE_{Planned}$" and the horizontal axis "Real GDP." Draw two planned aggregate expenditure curves ($AE_{Planned1}$ and $AE_{Planned2}$) and a 45-degree line to show the effect of the autonomous policy change on the equilibrium.

12. Access the Discovery Data exercise for Chapter 26, Problem 12 online.

  a. Calculate the marginal propensity to consume for the United States from 2002 through 2019.

  b. Find the change in real exports of goods and services from 2008 to 2009 and 2017 to 2018.

  c. Using *MPC* from part a, calculate the multiplier and the effect of a change in real exports from part b on real GDP.

13. Access the Discovering Data exercise for Chapter 26, Problem 13 online.

  a. The United Kingdom and most of Europe suffered from the Long Depression from 1873 to 1896. Calculate *MPC* in the United Kingdom using data from 1830 through 1900.

  b. Find the change in real investment expenditures from 1877 to 1880 and 1883 to 1886.

  c. Using the multiplier from part a, calculate multiplier and the effect of a change in real exports from part b on real GDP. How does your calculation compare with the actual change in real GDP?

WORK IT OUT

14. a. The accompanying table shows gross domestic product (GDP), disposable income (*YD*), consumer spending (*C*), and planned investment spending ($I_{Planned}$) in an economy. Assume there is no government or foreign sector in this economy. Complete the table by calculating planned aggregate spending ($AE_{Planned}$) and unplanned inventory investment ($I_{Unplanned}$).

  b. What is the aggregate consumption function?

  c. What is Y^*, income–expenditure equilibrium GDP?

  d. What is the value of the multiplier?

  e. If planned investment spending falls to $200 billion, what will be the new Y^*?

  f. If autonomous consumer spending rises to $200 billion, what will be the new Y^*?

GDP	YD	C	$I_{Planned}$	$AE_{Planned}$	$I_{Unplanned}$
(billions of dollars)					
$0	$0	$100	$300	?	?
400	400	400	300	?	?
800	800	700	300	?	?
1,200	1,200	1,000	300	?	?
1,600	1,600	1,300	300	?	?
2,000	2,000	1,600	300	?	?
2,400	2,400	1,900	300	?	?
2,800	2,800	2,200	300	?	?
3,200	3,200	2,500	300	?	?

Deriving the Multiplier Algebraically

This appendix shows how to derive the multiplier algebraically. First, recall that in this chapter planned aggregate spending, $AE_{Planned}$, is the sum of consumer spending, C, which is determined by the consumption function, and planned investment spending, $I_{Planned}$. That is, $AE_{Planned} = C + I_{Planned}$. Rewriting this equation to express all its terms fully, we have:

(26A-1) $AE_{Planned} = A + MPC \times YD + I_{Planned}$

Because there are no taxes or government transfers in this model, disposable income is equal to GDP, so Equation 26A-1 becomes:

(26A-2) $AE_{Planned} = A + MPC \times GDP + I_{Planned}$

The income–expenditure equilibrium GDP, Y^*, is equal to planned aggregate spending:

(26A-3) $Y^* = AE_{Planned}$
$= A + MPC \times Y^* + I_{Planned}$
in income–expenditure equilibrium

Just two more steps. Subtract $MPC \times Y^*$ from both sides of Equation 26A-3:

(26A-4) $Y^* - MPC \times Y^* = Y^* \times (1 - MPC) = A + I_{Planned}$

Finally, divide both sides by $(1 - MPC)$:

(26A-5) $Y^* = \dfrac{A + I_{Planned}}{1 - MPC}$

Equation 26A-5 tells us that a \$1 autonomous change in planned aggregate spending—a change in either A or $I_{Planned}$—causes a $\$1/(1 - MPC)$ change in income–expenditure equilibrium GDP, Y^*. The multiplier in our simple model is therefore:

(26A-6) Multiplier $= 1/(1 - MPC)$

PROBLEMS

1. Complete the following table by calculating the value of the multiplier and identifying the change in Y^* due to the change in autonomous spending. How does the value of the multiplier change with the marginal propensity to consume?

MPC	Value of multiplier	Change in spending	Change in Y^*
0.5	?	$\Delta C = +\$50$ million	?
0.6	?	$\Delta I = -\$10$ million	?
0.75	?	$\Delta C = -\$25$ million	?
0.8	?	$\Delta I = +\$20$ million	?
0.9	?	$\Delta C = -\$2.5$ million	?

2. In an economy without government purchases, transfers, or taxes, and without imports or exports, aggregate autonomous consumer spending is \$500 billion, planned investment spending is \$250 billion, and the marginal propensity to consume is 0.5.

   a. Write the expression for planned aggregate spending as in Equation 26A-1.

   b. Solve for Y^* algebraically.

   c. What is the value of the multiplier?

   d. How will Y^* change if autonomous consumer spending falls to \$450 billion?

27 〉 Aggregate Demand and Aggregate Supply

DIFFERENT GENERATIONS, DIFFERENT POLICIES

UNEMPLOYMENT AND INFLATION are the two great evils of macroeconomics, and policy makers do their best to keep both under control. Sometimes, however, this task isn't straightforward, as we learned in Chapter 23: policies to control inflation can worsen unemployment and policies aimed at reducing unemployment can cause inflation. So at times it's hard to know whether inflation or unemployment poses the bigger risk to the economy.

Policy makers at the Federal Reserve, also known as the Fed, found themselves facing such a quandary in 2011, when the unemployment rate, at around 9%, was very high by historical standards, but inflation had spiked to almost 4%, twice the widely accepted policy target of 2%. So should policy remain expansionary, to fight unemployment, or should it be contractionary, to reduce inflation?

In the end, the Fed decided to keep its foot on the gas and continue with a strong expansionary monetary policy — it reduced interest rates with the goal of boosting the economy. Fed officials believed that the inflation surge was a blip caused by a temporary rise in oil prices, and that it would soon dissipate. Time proved them right: once the oil price rise ran its course, inflation quickly fell back below 2%. The Fed's counterpart in Europe, the European Central Bank, or ECB, faced a similar situation: a 10% unemployment rate and 3% inflation.

Officials who came of age in the 1970s probably worry about inflation.

Yet it made the opposite policy choice: contractionary monetary policy — raising interest rates with the goal of slowing the economy.

Why did these two central banks, facing similar circumstances, move in opposite directions? Differences in the ages of the two bank leaders may provide a clue: Jean-Claude Trichet, President of the ECB, was 68, while Ben Bernanke, the chairman of the Fed, was 57. The 11-year age difference may seem inconsequential, but it was in fact significant because it corresponded to differences in the kinds of economic problems that dominated when each man was coming of age.

In fact, Neil Irwin of the *New York Times* has found a strong correlation between the ages of policy makers and their policy stances. Those like Mr. Trichet, who spent their young adulthood during the high-inflation 1970s, were more likely to call for interest-rate hikes and tightening monetary policy to head off inflation than were younger policy makers, like Mr. Bernanke, who, in contrast, were more concerned about unemployment and growth.

Bernanke understood that an economic slump can arise from different types of shocks. This understanding requires a model of the economy that can distinguish between different types of short-run economic fluctuations, a model that extends beyond the income–expenditure framework we studied in the previous chapter.

So why was Bernanke right in this case? Because the recessions of the 1970s were very different from the severe slump that began in 2007 and was still afflicting the economy in 2011. The recessions of the 1970s were largely caused by *supply shocks,* while the Great Recession of 2007–2009 was the result of a *demand shock.* (We discuss supply and demand shocks at length in the chapter.) Unlike Trichet, Bernanke seemed to have grasped the fact that times had changed.

In this chapter, we will develop the *AD–AS model* to help you understand how these shocks affect the economy. We'll proceed in three steps. First, we'll develop the concept of *aggregate demand.* Then we'll turn to the parallel concept of *aggregate supply.* Finally, we'll put the two concepts together. ●

WHAT YOU WILL LEARN

- How does the **aggregate demand curve** illustrate the relationship between the aggregate price level and the quantity of aggregate output demanded?

- How does the **aggregate supply curve** illustrate the relationship between the aggregate price level and the quantity of aggregate output supplied?

- Why is the aggregate supply curve different in the short run compared to the long run?

- How is the *AD–AS* **model** used to analyze economic fluctuations?

- How can monetary policy and fiscal policy stabilize the economy?

H. Armstrong Roberts/ClassicStock/Getty Images

The **aggregate demand curve** shows the relationship between the aggregate price level and the quantity of aggregate output demanded by households, businesses, the government, and the rest of the world.

|| Aggregate Demand

The Great Depression, the great majority of economists agree, was the result of a massive negative demand shock. What does that mean? In Chapter 3 we explained that when economists talk about a fall in the demand for a particular good or service, they're referring to a leftward shift of the demand curve. Similarly, when economists talk about a negative demand shock to the economy as a whole, they're referring to a leftward shift of the **aggregate demand curve,** a curve that shows the relationship between the aggregate price level and the quantity of aggregate output demanded by households, firms, the government, and the rest of the world.

Figure 27-1 shows what the aggregate demand curve may have looked like in 1933, at the end of the 1929–1933 recession. The horizontal axis shows the total quantity of domestic goods and services demanded, measured in 2012 dollars. We use real GDP to measure aggregate output and will often use the two terms interchangeably.

The vertical axis shows the aggregate price level, measured by the GDP deflator. With these variables on the axes, we can draw a curve, *AD*, showing how much aggregate output would have been demanded at any given aggregate price level. Since *AD* is meant to illustrate aggregate demand, the point labeled 1933 on the curve corresponds to actual data from that year, when the aggregate price level was 9.4 and the total quantity of domestic final goods and services purchased was $817 billion in 2012 dollars.

The aggregate demand curve in Figure 27-1 is downward sloping, indicating a negative relationship between the aggregate price level and the quantity of aggregate output demanded. A higher aggregate price level, other things equal, reduces the quantity of aggregate output demanded; a lower aggregate price level, other things equal, increases the quantity of aggregate output demanded. According to Figure 27-1, if the price level in 1933 had been 5 instead of 9.4, the total quantity of domestic final goods and services demanded would have been $1,109 billion in 2012 dollars instead of $817 billion.

The first key question about the aggregate demand curve is: why should the curve be downward sloping?

FIGURE 27-1 The Aggregate Demand Curve

The aggregate demand curve shows the relationship between the aggregate price level and the quantity of aggregate output demanded. The curve is downward sloping due to the wealth effect of a change in the aggregate price level and the interest rate effect of a change in the aggregate price level. Corresponding to actual 1933 data, here the total quantity of goods and services demanded at an aggregate price level of 9.4 is $817 billion in 2012 dollars. According to our hypothetical curve, however, if the aggregate price level had been only 5.0, the quantity of aggregate output demanded would have risen to $1,109 billion.

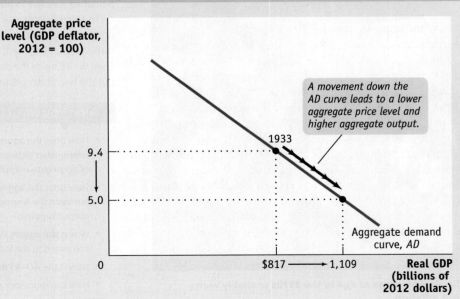

Why Is the Aggregate Demand Curve Downward Sloping?

In Figure 27-1, the curve *AD* is downward sloping. Why? Recall the basic equation of national income accounting:

(27-1) $GDP = C + I + G + X - IM$

where *C* is consumer spending, *I* is investment spending, *G* is government purchases of goods and services, *X* is exports to other countries, and *IM* is imports. If we measure these variables in constant dollars—that is, in prices of a base year—then $C + I + G + X - IM$ is the quantity of domestically produced final goods and services demanded during a given period. *G* is decided by the government, but the other variables are private-sector decisions. To understand why the aggregate demand curve slopes downward, we need to understand why a rise in the aggregate price level reduces *C*, *I*, and $X - IM$.

You might think that the downward slope of the aggregate demand curve is a natural consequence of the *law of demand* defined back in Chapter 3. That is, since the demand curve for any one good is downward sloping, isn't it natural that the demand curve for aggregate output is also downward sloping? This turns out, however, to be a misleading parallel. The demand curve for any individual good shows how the quantity demanded depends on the price of that good, *holding the prices of other goods and services constant*. The main reason the quantity of a good demanded falls when the price of that good rises—that is, the quantity of a good demanded falls as we move up the demand curve—is that people switch their consumption to other goods and services.

But when we consider movements up or down the aggregate demand curve, we're considering *a simultaneous change in the prices of all final goods and services*. Furthermore, changes in the composition of goods and services in consumer spending aren't relevant to the aggregate demand curve: if consumers decide to buy fewer clothes but more cars, this doesn't necessarily change the total quantity of final goods and services they demand.

Why, then, does a rise in the aggregate price level lead to a fall in the quantity of all domestically produced final goods and services demanded? There are two main reasons: the *wealth effect* and the *interest rate effect* of a change in the aggregate price level.

The Wealth Effect An increase in the aggregate price level, other things equal, reduces the purchasing power of many assets. Consider, for example, someone who has $5,000 in a bank account. If the aggregate price level were to rise by 25%, what used to cost $5,000 would now cost $6,250, and would no longer be affordable. And what used to cost $4,000 would now cost $5,000, so that the $5,000 in the bank account would now buy only as much as $4,000 would have bought previously. With the loss in purchasing power, the owner of that bank account would probably scale back their consumption plans. Millions of other people would respond the same way, leading to a fall in spending on final goods and services, because a rise in the aggregate price level reduces the purchasing power of everyone's bank account.

Correspondingly, a fall in the aggregate price level increases the purchasing power of consumers' assets and leads to more consumer demand. The **wealth effect of a change in the aggregate price level** is the effect on consumer spending caused by the effect of a change in the aggregate price level on the purchasing power of consumers' assets. Because of the wealth effect, consumer spending, *C*, falls when the aggregate price level rises, leading to a downward-sloping aggregate demand curve.

The Interest Rate Effect Economists use the term *money* in its narrowest sense to refer to cash and bank accounts on which people can use a debit card and write checks. People and firms hold money because it reduces the cost and

The **wealth effect of a change in the aggregate price level** is the effect on consumer spending caused by the effect of a change in the aggregate price level on the purchasing power of consumers' assets.

The **interest rate effect of a change in the aggregate price level** is the effect on consumer spending and investment spending caused by the effect of a change in the aggregate price level on the purchasing power of consumers' and firms' money holdings.

inconvenience of making transactions. An increase in the aggregate price level, other things equal, reduces the purchasing power of a given amount of money holdings. To purchase the same basket of goods and services as before, people and firms now need to hold more money. So, in response to an increase in the aggregate price level, the public tries to increase its money holdings, either by borrowing more or by selling assets such as bonds. This reduces the funds available for lending to other borrowers and drives interest rates up.

In Chapter 25 we learned that a rise in the interest rate reduces investment spending because it makes the cost of borrowing higher. It also reduces consumer spending because households save more of their disposable income. So a rise in the aggregate price level depresses investment spending, *I*, and consumer spending, *C*, through its effect on the purchasing power of money holdings, an effect known as the **interest rate effect of a change in the aggregate price level.** This also leads to a downward-sloping aggregate demand curve.

We'll have a lot more to say about money and interest rates in Chapter 30 on monetary policy. We'll also see, in Chapter 33, which covers international macroeconomics, that a higher interest rate indirectly tends to reduce exports (*X*) and increase imports (*IM*). For now, the important point is that the aggregate demand curve is downward sloping due to both the wealth effect and the interest rate effect of a change in the aggregate price level.

The Aggregate Demand Curve and the Income–Expenditure Model

In the preceding chapter we introduced the *income–expenditure model*, which shows how the economy arrives at *income–expenditure equilibrium.* Now we've introduced the aggregate demand curve, which relates the overall demand for goods and services to the overall price level. How do these concepts fit together?

Recall that one of the assumptions of the income–expenditure model is that the aggregate price level is fixed. We now drop that assumption. We can still use the income–expenditure model, however, to ask what aggregate spending would be *at any given aggregate price level,* which is precisely what the aggregate demand curve shows. So the *AD* curve is actually derived from the income–expenditure model. Economists sometimes say that the income–expenditure model is "embedded" in the *AD–AS* model.

Figure 27-2 shows, once again, how income–expenditure equilibrium is determined. Real GDP is on the horizontal axis; real planned aggregate spending is on the vertical axis. Other things equal, planned aggregate spending, equal to consumer spending plus planned investment spending, rises with real GDP. This is illustrated by the upward-sloping lines $AE_{Planned_1}$ and $AE_{Planned_2}$. Income–expenditure equilibrium, as we learned in Chapter 26, is at the point where the line representing planned aggregate spending crosses the 45-degree line. For example, if $AE_{Planned_1}$ is the relationship between real GDP and planned aggregate spending, then income–expenditure equilibrium is at point E_1, corresponding to a level of real GDP equal to Y_1.

We've just seen, however, that changes in the aggregate price level change the level of planned aggregate spending *at any given level of real GDP.* This means that when the aggregate price level changes, the $AE_{Planned}$ curve shifts. For example, suppose that the aggregate price level falls. As a result of both the wealth effect and the interest rate effect, the fall in the aggregate price level will lead to higher planned aggregate spending at any given level of real GDP. So the $AE_{Planned}$ curve will shift up, as illustrated in Figure 27-2 by the shift from $AE_{Planned_1}$ to $AE_{Planned_2}$. The increase in planned aggregate spending leads to a multiplier process that moves the income–expenditure equilibrium from point E_1 to point E_2, raising real GDP from Y_1 to Y_2.

Figure 27-3 shows how this result can be used to derive the aggregate demand curve. In Figure 27-3, we show a fall in the aggregate price level from P_1 to P_2.

FIGURE 27-2 How Changes in the Aggregate Price Level Affect Income–Expenditure Equilibrium

Income–expenditure equilibrium occurs at the point where the curve $AE_{Planned}$, which shows real aggregate planned spending, crosses the 45-degree line. A fall in the aggregate price level causes the $AE_{Planned}$ curve to shift from $AE_{Planned_1}$ to $AE_{Planned_2}$, leading to a rise in income–expenditure equilibrium GDP from Y_1 to Y_2.

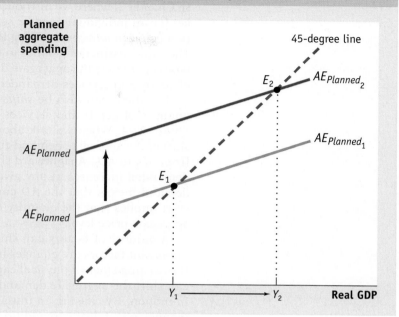

We see in Figure 27-2 that a fall in the aggregate price level would lead to an upward shift of the $AE_{Planned}$ curve and hence a rise in real GDP. We can see this same result in Figure 27-3 as a movement along the AD curve: as the aggregate price level falls, real GDP rises from Y_1 to Y_2.

So the aggregate demand curve doesn't replace the income–expenditure model. Instead, it's a way to summarize what the income–expenditure model says about the effects of changes in the aggregate price level.

In practice, economists often use the income–expenditure model to analyze short-run economic fluctuations, even though strictly speaking it should be seen as a component of a more complete model. In the short run, in particular, this is usually a reasonable shortcut.

FIGURE 27-3 The Income–Expenditure Model and the Aggregate Demand Curve

Figure 27-2 shows how a fall in the aggregate price level shifts the planned aggregate spending curve up, leading to a rise in real GDP. Here we see that same result as a movement along the aggregate demand curve. If the aggregate price level falls from P_1 to P_2, real GDP rises from Y_1 to Y_2. The AD curve is therefore downward sloping.

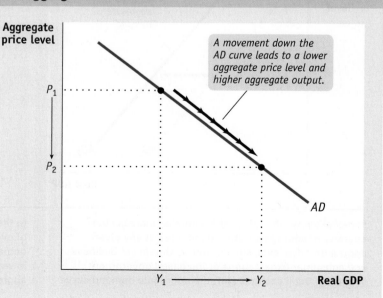

Shifts of the Aggregate Demand Curve

In Chapter 3, where we introduced the analysis of supply and demand in the market for an individual good or service, we stressed the importance of the distinction between *movements along* the demand curve and *shifts of* the demand curve. The same distinction applies to the aggregate demand curve. Figure 27-1 shows a *movement along* the aggregate demand curve, a change in the aggregate quantity of goods and services demanded as the aggregate price level changes.

But there can also be *shifts of* the aggregate demand curve, changes in the quantity of goods and services demanded at any given price level, as shown in Figure 27-4. When we talk about an increase in aggregate demand, we mean a shift of the aggregate demand curve to the right, as shown in panel (a) by the shift from AD_1 to AD_2. A rightward shift occurs when the quantity of aggregate output demanded increases at any given aggregate price level. A decrease in aggregate demand means that the AD curve shifts to the left, as in panel (b). A leftward shift implies that the quantity of aggregate output demanded falls at any given aggregate price level.

A number of factors can shift the aggregate demand curve. Among the most important factors are changes in expectations, changes in wealth, and the size of the existing stock of physical capital. In addition, both fiscal and monetary policy can shift the aggregate demand curve. All five factors set the multiplier process in motion. By causing an initial rise or fall in real GDP, they change disposable income, which leads to additional changes in aggregate spending, which lead to further changes in real GDP, and so on. For an overview of factors that shift the aggregate demand curve, see Table 27-1.

Changes in Expectations Both consumer spending and planned investment spending depend in part on people's expectations about the future. Consumers base their spending not only on the income they have now but also on the income they expect to have in the future. Firms base their planned investment spending not only on current conditions but also on the sales they expect to make in the future.

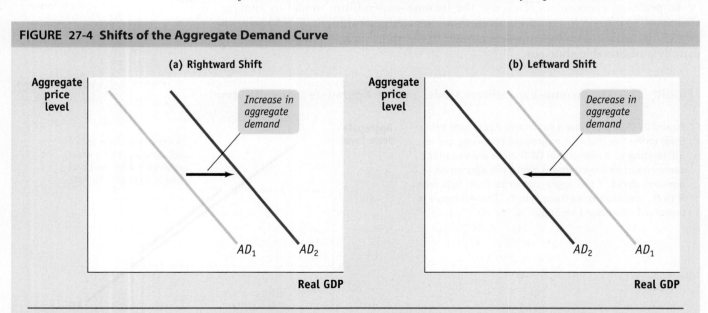

FIGURE 27-4 Shifts of the Aggregate Demand Curve

Panel (a) shows the effect of events that increase the quantity of aggregate output demanded at any given aggregate price level, such as improvements in business and consumer expectations or increased government spending. Such changes shift the aggregate demand curve to the right, from AD_1 to AD_2. Panel (b) shows the effect of events that decrease the quantity of aggregate output demanded at any given aggregate price level, such as a fall in wealth caused by a stock market decline. This shifts the aggregate demand curve leftward from AD_1 to AD_2.

TABLE 27-1 Factors That Shift Aggregate Demand

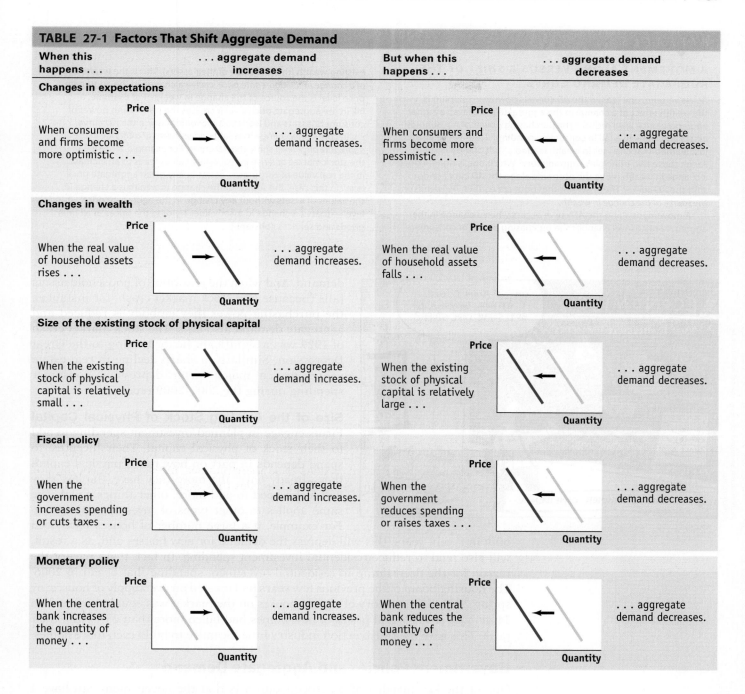

When this happens . . .	. . . aggregate demand increases	But when this happens . . .	. . . aggregate demand decreases
Changes in expectations			
When consumers and firms become more optimistic . . .	. . . aggregate demand increases.	When consumers and firms become more pessimistic . . .	. . . aggregate demand decreases.
Changes in wealth			
When the real value of household assets rises . . .	. . . aggregate demand increases.	When the real value of household assets falls . . .	. . . aggregate demand decreases.
Size of the existing stock of physical capital			
When the existing stock of physical capital is relatively small . . .	. . . aggregate demand increases.	When the existing stock of physical capital is relatively large . . .	. . . aggregate demand decreases.
Fiscal policy			
When the government increases spending or cuts taxes . . .	. . . aggregate demand increases.	When the government reduces spending or raises taxes . . .	. . . aggregate demand decreases.
Monetary policy			
When the central bank increases the quantity of money . . .	. . . aggregate demand increases.	When the central bank reduces the quantity of money . . .	. . . aggregate demand decreases.

As a result, changes in expectations can push consumer spending and planned investment spending up or down. If consumers and firms become more optimistic, aggregate spending rises; if they become more pessimistic, aggregate spending falls.

In fact, short-run economic forecasters pay careful attention to surveys of consumer and business sentiment. In particular, forecasters watch the Consumer Confidence Index, a monthly measure calculated by The Conference Board, and the Michigan Consumer Sentiment Index, a similar measure calculated by the University of Michigan.

Changes in Wealth Consumer spending depends in part on the value of household assets. When the real value of these assets rises, the purchasing power they embody also rises, leading to an increase in aggregate spending. For example, in the 1990s there was a significant rise in the stock market that increased aggregate

A MOVEMENT ALONG VERSUS A SHIFT OF THE AGGREGATE DEMAND CURVE

As we've seen, one reason the *AD* curve is downward sloping is the wealth effect of a change in the aggregate price level: a higher aggregate price level reduces the purchasing power of households' assets and leads to a fall in consumer spending, *C*. But we've also just learned that changes in wealth lead to a shift of the *AD* curve. Aren't those two principles contradictory? Which one is right—does a change in wealth move the economy along the *AD* curve or does it shift the *AD* curve? The answer is that both are correct: *it depends on the source of the change in wealth.*

A movement along the *AD* curve occurs when a change in the aggregate price level changes the purchasing power of consumers'

existing wealth (the real value of their assets). This is the *wealth effect of a change in the aggregate price level*—a change in the aggregate price level is the source of the change in wealth. For example, a fall in the aggregate price level increases the purchasing power of consumers' assets and leads to a movement down the *AD* curve.

In contrast, a change in wealth *independent of a change in the aggregate price level* shifts the *AD* curve. For example, a rise in the stock market or a rise in real estate values leads to an increase in the real value of consumers' assets at any given aggregate price level. In this case, the source of the change in wealth is a change in the values of assets without any change in the aggregate price level—that is, a change in asset values holding the prices of all final goods and services constant.

Joel Pett Editorial Cartoon used with the permission of Joel Pett and the Cartoonist Group

demand. And when the real value of household assets falls (because of a stock market crash, for instance), the purchasing power they embody is reduced and aggregate demand also falls. The stock market crash of 1929 was a significant factor leading to the Great Depression. Similarly, a sharp decline in real estate values was a major factor depressing consumer spending during the 2007–2009 recession.

Size of the Existing Stock of Physical Capital

Firms engage in planned investment spending to add to their stock of physical capital. Their incentive to spend depends in part on how much physical capital they already have: the more they have, the less they will feel a need to add more, other things equal. The same applies to other types of investment spending. For example, if a large number of houses have been built in recent years, this will depress the demand for new houses and, as a result, will also tend to reduce residential investment spending. In fact, that's part of the reason for the deep slump in residential investment spending that began in 2006. The housing boom of the previous few years had created an oversupply of houses: by spring 2009, the inventory of unsold houses on the market was equal to more than 14 months of sales, and prices of new homes had fallen more than 25% from their peak. This gave the construction industry little incentive to build even more homes.

Government Policies and Aggregate Demand

One of the key insights of macroeconomics is that the government can have a powerful influence on aggregate demand and that, in some circumstances, this influence can be used to improve economic performance.

The two main ways the government can influence the aggregate demand curve are through fiscal policy and monetary policy. We'll briefly discuss their influence on aggregate demand, leaving a full-length discussion for upcoming chapters.

Fiscal Policy The use of either government spending—government purchases of final goods and services and government transfers—or tax policy to stabilize the economy is known as fiscal policy. In practice, governments often respond to recessions by increasing spending, cutting taxes, or both. They often respond to inflation by reducing spending or increasing taxes.

The effect of government purchases of final goods and services, *G*, on the aggregate demand curve is *direct* because government purchases are themselves a component of aggregate demand. So an increase in government purchases shifts the aggregate demand curve to the right and a decrease shifts it to the left. History's most dramatic example of how increased government purchases affect aggregate demand was the effect of wartime government spending during World War II.

Because of the war, U.S. federal purchases surged 400%. This increase in purchases is usually credited with ending the Great Depression. In the 1990s Japan used large public works projects—such as government-financed construction of roads, bridges, and dams—in an effort to increase aggregate demand in the face of a slumping economy. Similarly, in 2009, in the wake of the Great Recession, the United States began spending more than $100 billion on infrastructure projects such as improving highways, bridges, public transportation, and more, to stimulate overall spending.

In contrast, changes in either tax rates or government transfers influence the economy *indirectly* through their effect on disposable income. A lower tax rate means that consumers get to keep more of what they earn, increasing their disposable income. An increase in government transfers also increases consumers' disposable income. In either case, this increases consumer spending and shifts the aggregate demand curve to the right. A higher tax rate or a reduction in transfers reduces the amount of disposable income received by consumers. This reduces consumer spending and shifts the aggregate demand curve to the left.

During the onset of the coronavirus pandemic in 2020, many businesses closed, requiring the federal government to implement an unprecedented economic relief package. It included transfer payments through unemployment insurance for those laid off and a one-time tax rebate of $1,200 to individuals earning less than $75,000 with an extra $500 per child dependent. These measures were designed to stabilize consumer spending, preventing a further decline in aggregate demand, minimizing the economic shock from the virus.

"No player may move, collect money, or buy anything."

Matt Pritchett/The Daily Telegraph

Monetary Policy We opened this chapter by talking about the problems faced by the Federal Reserve in 2011. The Fed controls monetary policy—the use of changes in the quantity of money or the interest rate to stabilize the economy. We've just discussed how a rise in the aggregate price level, by reducing the purchasing power of money holdings, causes a rise in the interest rate. That, in turn, reduces both investment spending and consumer spending.

But what happens if the quantity of money in the hands of households and firms changes? In modern economies, the quantity of money in circulation is largely determined by the decisions of a *central bank* created by the government. As we'll learn in Chapter 29, the Federal Reserve, the U.S. central bank, is a special institution that is neither exactly part of the government nor exactly a private institution. When the central bank increases the quantity of money in circulation, households and firms have more money, which they are willing to lend out. The effect is to drive the interest rate down at any given aggregate price level, leading to higher investment spending and higher consumer spending.

That is, increasing the quantity of money shifts the aggregate demand curve to the right. Reducing the quantity of money has the opposite effect: households and firms have fewer money holdings than before, leading them to borrow more and lend less. This raises the interest rate, reduces investment spending and consumer spending, and shifts the aggregate demand curve to the left.

ECONOMICS >> *in Action*
Moving Along the Aggregate Demand Curve, 1979–1980

When looking at data, it's often hard to distinguish between changes in spending that represent *movements along* the aggregate demand curve and those that represent *shifts of* the aggregate demand curve. One telling exception, however, is what happened right after the oil crisis of 1979. Faced with a sharp increase

During the 1979 oil crisis, the interest rate effect from a rise in the aggregate price level pushed the economy up the AD curve, leading to a fall in aggregate output.

in the aggregate price level—the rate of consumer price inflation reached 14.8% in March of 1980—the Fed stuck to a policy of increasing the quantity of money slowly. The aggregate price level was rising steeply, but the quantity of money circulating in the economy was growing slowly. The net result was that the purchasing power of the quantity of money in circulation fell.

This led to an increase in the demand for borrowing and a surge in interest rates. The *prime rate*, which is the interest rate banks charge their best customers, climbed above 20%. High interest rates, in turn, caused both consumer spending and investment spending to fall: in 1980 purchases of durable consumer goods like cars fell by 5.3% and real investment spending fell by 8.9%.

In other words, in 1979–1980 the economy responded just as we'd expect if it were moving upward along the aggregate demand curve from right to left: due to the wealth effect and the interest rate effect of a change in the aggregate price level, the quantity of aggregate output demanded fell as the aggregate price level rose. This does not explain, of course, why the aggregate price level rose. But as we'll see in the upcoming section on the *AD–AS* model, the answer to that question lies in the behavior of the *short-run aggregate supply curve*.

>> **Quick Review**

• The **aggregate demand curve** is downward sloping because of the **wealth effect of a change in the aggregate price level** and the **interest rate effect of a change in the aggregate price level.**

• The aggregate demand curve shows how income–expenditure equilibrium GDP changes when the aggregate price level changes.

• Changes in consumer spending caused by changes in wealth and expectations about the future shift the aggregate demand curve. Changes in investment spending caused by changes in expectations and by the size of the existing stock of physical capital also shift the aggregate demand curve.

• Fiscal policy affects aggregate demand directly through government purchases and indirectly through changes in taxes or government transfers. Monetary policy affects aggregate demand indirectly through changes in the interest rate.

>> **Check Your Understanding 27-1**

Solutions appear at back of book.

1. Determine the effect on aggregate demand of each of the following events. Explain whether it represents a movement along the aggregate demand curve (up or down) or a shift of the curve (leftward or rightward).
   a. A rise in the interest rate caused by a change in monetary policy
   b. A fall in the real value of money in the economy due to a higher aggregate price level
   c. News of a worse-than-expected job market next year
   d. A fall in tax rates
   e. A rise in the real value of assets in the economy due to a lower aggregate price level
   f. A rise in the real value of assets in the economy due to a surge in real estate values

‖ Aggregate Supply

Between 1929 and 1933, there was a sharp fall in aggregate demand—a reduction in the quantity of goods and services demanded at any given price level. One consequence of the economy-wide decline in demand was a fall in the prices of most goods and services. By 1933, the GDP deflator (one of the price indexes we defined in Chapter 22) was 26% below its 1929 level, and other indexes were down by similar amounts. A second consequence was a decline in the output of most goods and services: by 1933, real GDP was 27% below its 1929 level. A third consequence, closely tied to the fall in real GDP, was a surge in the unemployment rate from 3% to 25%.

The association between the plunge in real GDP and the plunge in prices wasn't an accident. Between 1929 and 1933, the U.S. economy was moving down its **aggregate supply curve,** which shows the relationship between the economy's aggregate price level (the overall price level of final goods and services in the economy) and the total quantity of final goods and services, or aggregate output, producers are willing to supply. (As you will recall, we use real GDP to measure aggregate output. So we'll often use the two terms interchangeably.) More specifically, between 1929 and 1933 the U.S. economy moved down its *short-run aggregate supply curve.*

The **aggregate supply curve** shows the relationship between the aggregate price level and the quantity of aggregate output supplied in the economy.

The Short-Run Aggregate Supply Curve

The period from 1929 to 1933 demonstrated that there is a positive relationship in the short run between the aggregate price level and the quantity of aggregate output supplied. That is, a rise in the aggregate price level is associated with a rise in the quantity of aggregate output supplied, other things equal; a fall in the aggregate price level is associated with a fall in the quantity of aggregate output supplied, other things equal. To understand why this positive relationship exists, consider the most basic question facing a producer: is producing a unit of output profitable or not? Let's define profit per unit:

(27-2) Profit per unit of output =
           Price per unit of output – Production cost per unit of output

Thus, the answer to the question depends on whether the price the producer receives for a unit of output is greater than or less than the cost of producing that unit of output. At any given point in time, many of the costs producers face are fixed per unit of output and can't be changed for an extended period of time. Typically, the largest source of inflexible production cost is the wages paid to workers. *Wages* here refers to all forms of worker compensation, such as employer-paid health care and retirement benefits in addition to earnings.

Wages are typically an inflexible production cost because the dollar amount of any given wage paid, called the **nominal wage,** is often determined by contracts that were signed some time ago. And even when there are no formal contracts, there are often informal agreements between management and workers, making companies reluctant to change wages in response to economic conditions. For example, companies usually will not reduce wages during poor economic times—unless the downturn has been particularly long and severe—for fear of generating worker resentment. Correspondingly, they typically won't raise wages during better economic times—until they are at risk of losing workers to competitors—because they don't want to encourage workers to routinely demand higher wages.

As a result of both formal and informal agreements, then, the economy is characterized by **sticky wages:** nominal wages that are slow to fall even in the face of high unemployment and slow to rise even in the face of labor shortages. It's important to note, however, that nominal wages cannot be sticky forever: ultimately, formal contracts and informal agreements will be renegotiated to take into account changed economic circumstances. As the upcoming For Inquiring Minds explains, how long it takes for nominal wages to become flexible is an integral component of what distinguishes the short run from the long run.

To understand how the fact that many costs are fixed in nominal terms gives rise to an upward-sloping short-run aggregate supply curve, it's helpful to know that prices are set somewhat differently in different kinds of markets. In *perfectly competitive markets*, producers take prices as given; in *imperfectly competitive markets*, producers have some ability to choose the prices they charge. In both kinds of markets, there is a short-run positive relationship between prices and output, but for slightly different reasons.

Let's start with the behavior of producers in perfectly competitive markets; remember, they take the price as given. Imagine that, for some reason, the aggregate price level falls, which means that the price received by the typical producer of a final good or service falls. Because many production costs are fixed in the short run, production cost per unit of output doesn't fall by the same proportion as the fall in the price of output. So the profit per unit of output declines, leading perfectly competitive producers to reduce the quantity supplied in the short run.

On the other hand, suppose that for some reason the aggregate price level rises. As a result, the typical producer receives a higher price for its final

The **nominal wage** is the dollar amount of the wage paid.

Sticky wages are nominal wages that are slow to fall even in the face of high unemployment and slow to rise even in the face of labor shortages.

The **short-run aggregate supply curve** shows the relationship between the aggregate price level and the quantity of aggregate output supplied that exists in the short run, the time period when many production costs can be taken as fixed.

good or service. Again, many production costs are fixed in the short run, so production cost per unit of output doesn't rise by the same proportion as the rise in the price of a unit. And since the typical perfectly competitive producer takes the price as given, profit per unit of output rises and output increases.

Now consider an imperfectly competitive producer that is able to set its own price. If there is a rise in the demand for this producer's product, it will be able to sell more at any given price. Given stronger demand for its products, it will probably choose to increase its prices as well as its output, as a way of increasing profit per unit of output. In fact, industry analysts often talk about variations in an industry's *pricing power:* when demand is strong, firms with pricing power are able to raise prices—and they do.

Conversely, if there is a fall in demand, firms will normally try to limit the fall in their sales by cutting prices.

Both the responses of firms in perfectly competitive industries and those of firms in imperfectly competitive industries lead to an upward-sloping relationship between aggregate output and the aggregate price level. The positive relationship between the aggregate price level and aggregate output in the short run is illustrated by an upward-sloping **short-run aggregate supply curve.** Along this curve, producers are willing to supply final goods and services during the time period when many production costs, particularly nominal wages, can be taken as fixed. Figure 27-5 shows a hypothetical short-run aggregate supply curve, *SRAS*, that matches actual U.S. data for 1929 and 1933. On the horizontal axis is aggregate output (or, equivalently, real GDP)—the total quantity of final goods and services supplied in the economy—measured in 2012 dollars. On the vertical axis is the aggregate price level as measured by the GDP deflator, with the value for the year 2012 equal to 100. In 1929, the aggregate price level was 9.4 and real GDP was $1,109 billion. In 1933, the aggregate price level was 7.0 and real GDP was only $817 billion. The movement down the *SRAS* curve corresponds to the deflation and fall in aggregate output experienced over those years.

FIGURE 27-5 The Short-Run Aggregate Supply Curve

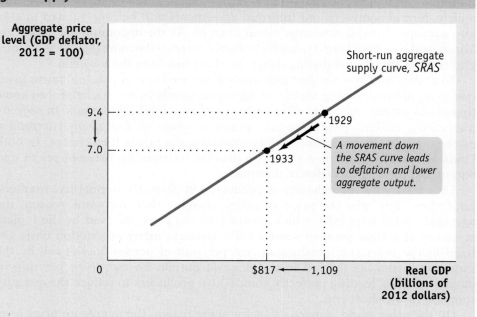

The short-run aggregate supply curve shows the relationship between the aggregate price level and the quantity of aggregate output supplied in the short run, the period in which many production costs such as nominal wages are fixed. It is upward sloping because a higher aggregate price level leads to higher profit per unit of output and higher aggregate output given fixed nominal wages. Here we show numbers corresponding to early in the Great Depression, from 1929 to 1933. When deflation occurred and the aggregate price level fell from 9.4 (in 1929) to 7.0 (in 1933), firms responded by reducing the quantity of aggregate output supplied from $1,109 billion to $817 billion measured in 2012 dollars.

FOR INQUIRING MINDS   *What's Truly Flexible, What's Truly Sticky*

Most macroeconomists agree that the picture shown in Figure 27-5 is correct: there is, other things equal, a positive short-run relationship between the aggregate price level and aggregate output. But many would argue that the details are a bit more complicated.

So far we've stressed a difference in the behavior of the aggregate price level and the behavior of nominal wages. That is, we've said that the aggregate price level is flexible but nominal wages are sticky in the short run. Although this assumption is a good way to explain why the short-run aggregate supply curve is upward sloping, empirical data on wages and prices don't wholly support a sharp distinction between

flexible prices of final goods and services and sticky nominal wages.

On one side, some nominal wages are in fact flexible even in the short run because some workers are not covered by a contract or informal agreement with their employers. Since some nominal wages are sticky but others are flexible, we observe that the *average nominal wage*—the nominal wage averaged over all workers in the economy—falls when there is a steep rise in unemployment. For example, nominal wages fell substantially in the early years of the Great Depression.

On the other side, some prices of final goods and services are sticky rather than flexible. For example, some firms,

particularly the makers of luxury or name-brand goods, are reluctant to cut prices even when demand falls. Instead they prefer to cut output even if their profit per unit hasn't declined.

These complications, as we've said, don't change the basic picture. When the aggregate price level falls, some producers cut output because the nominal wages they pay are sticky. And some producers don't cut their prices in the face of a falling aggregate price level, preferring instead to reduce their output. In both cases, the positive relationship between the aggregate price level and aggregate output is maintained. So, in the end, the short-run aggregate supply curve is still upward sloping.

Shifts of the Short-Run Aggregate Supply Curve

Figure 27-5 shows a *movement along* the short-run aggregate supply curve, as the aggregate price level and aggregate output fell from 1929 to 1933. But there can also be *shifts of* the short-run aggregate supply curve, as shown in Figure 27-6. Panel (a) shows a *decrease in short-run aggregate supply*—a leftward shift of the short-run aggregate supply curve. Aggregate supply decreases when producers reduce the quantity of aggregate output they are willing to supply at any given aggregate price level. Panel (b) shows an *increase in short-run aggregate supply*—a rightward shift of the short-run aggregate supply curve. Aggregate supply increases when producers increase the quantity of aggregate output they are willing to supply at any given aggregate price level.

FIGURE 27-6 Shifts of the Short-Run Aggregate Supply Curve

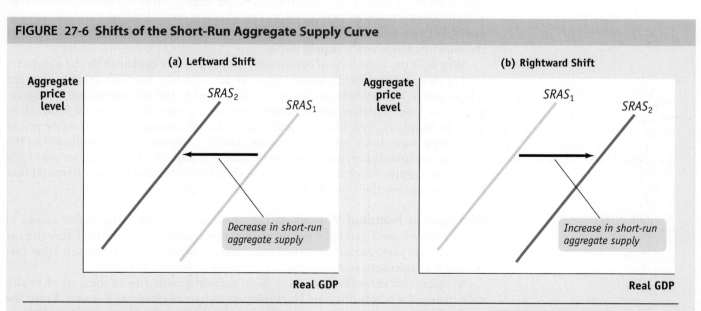

Panel (a) shows a decrease in short-run aggregate supply: the short-run aggregate supply curve shifts leftward from $SRAS_1$ to $SRAS_2$, and the quantity of aggregate output supplied at any given aggregate price level falls. Panel (b)

shows an increase in short-run aggregate supply: the short-run aggregate supply curve shifts rightward from $SRAS_1$ to $SRAS_2$, and the quantity of aggregate output supplied at any given aggregate price level rises.

To understand why the short-run aggregate supply curve can shift, it's important to recall that producers make output decisions based on their profit per unit of output. The short-run aggregate supply curve illustrates the relationship between the aggregate price level and aggregate output: because some production costs are fixed in the short run, a change in the aggregate price level leads to a change in producers' profit per unit of output and, in turn, leads to a change in aggregate output.

But other factors besides the aggregate price level can affect profit per unit and, in turn, aggregate output. It is changes in these other factors that will shift the short-run aggregate supply curve.

To develop some intuition, suppose that something happens that raises production costs—say, an increase in the price of oil. At any given price of output, a producer now earns a smaller profit per unit of output. As a result, producers reduce the quantity supplied at any given aggregate price level, and the short-run aggregate supply curve shifts to the left. If, in contrast, something happens that lowers production costs—say, a fall in the nominal wage—a producer now earns a higher profit per unit of output at any given price of output. This leads producers to increase the quantity of aggregate output supplied at any given aggregate price level, and the short-run aggregate supply curve shifts to the right.

Now we'll discuss some of the important factors that affect producers' profit per unit and so can lead to shifts of the short-run aggregate supply curve. These factors include changes in commodity prices, changes in nominal wages, and changes in productivity.

Changes in Commodity Prices In the opening story, we saw how the views of Jean-Claude Trichet, the president of the ECB, were shaped by the high inflation of the 1970s. The origins of that inflationary period lay in a sharp and sustained increase in the price of a very important commodity—oil. The high price of oil sharply raised costs for producers around the world.

A *commodity* is a standardized input bought and sold in bulk quantities. An increase in the price of a commodity, such as oil, raises production costs across the economy and reduces the quantity of aggregate output supplied at any given aggregate price level. This shifts the aggregate supply curve to the left. Conversely, a decline in commodity prices reduces production costs, leading to an increase in the quantity supplied at any given aggregate price level and a rightward shift of the short-run aggregate supply curve.

Why isn't the influence of commodity prices already captured by the short-run aggregate supply curve? Because commodities—unlike, say, soft drinks—are not a final good. Hence their prices are not included in the calculation of the aggregate price level. Further, commodities represent a significant cost of production to most suppliers, just like nominal wages do. So changes in commodity prices have large impacts on production costs. And in contrast to noncommodities, the prices of commodities can sometimes change drastically due to industry-specific shocks to supply—such as wars in the Middle East or rising Chinese demand that leaves less oil for the United States.

Changes in Nominal Wages At any given point in time, the dollar wages of many workers are fixed because they are set by contracts or informal agreements made in the past. Nominal wages can change, however, once enough time has passed for contracts and informal agreements to be renegotiated.

Suppose, for example, that there is an economy-wide rise in the cost of health care insurance premiums paid by employers as part of employees' wages. From the employers' perspective, this is equivalent to a rise in nominal wages because it is an increase in employer-paid compensation. So this rise in nominal wages increases production costs and shifts the short-run aggregate supply curve to the left.

Conversely, suppose there is an economy-wide fall in the cost of such premiums. This is equivalent to a fall in nominal wages from the point of view of employers; it reduces production costs and shifts the short-run aggregate supply curve to the right.

An important historical fact is that during the 1970s the surge in the price of oil had the indirect effect of also raising nominal wages. This "knock-on" effect occurred because many wage contracts included *cost-of-living allowances* that automatically raised the nominal wage when consumer prices increased. Through this channel, the surge in the price of oil—which led to an increase in overall consumer prices—ultimately caused a rise in nominal wages.

So the economy, in the end, experienced two leftward shifts of the aggregate supply curve: the first generated by the initial surge in the price of oil, the second generated by the induced increase in nominal wages. The negative effect on the economy of rising oil prices was greatly magnified through the cost-of-living allowances in wage contracts. Today, cost-of-living allowances in wage contracts are rare.

Changes in Productivity An increase in productivity means that a worker can produce more units of output with the same quantity of inputs. For example, the introduction of bar-code scanners in retail stores greatly increased the ability of a single worker to stock, inventory, and resupply store shelves. As a result, the cost to a store of "producing" a dollar of sales fell, profit rose, and the quantity supplied increased. (Think of Walmart and the increase in the number of its stores as an increase in aggregate supply.) So a rise in productivity, whatever the source, increases producers' profits per unit produced and shifts the short-run aggregate supply curve to the right.

Conversely, a fall in productivity—say, due to new regulations that require workers to spend more time filling out forms—reduces the number of units of output a worker can produce with the same quantity of inputs. Consequently, the cost per unit of output rises, leading to a fall in profit per unit produced, and a fall in quantity supplied, shifting the short-run aggregate supply curve to the left.

For a summary of the factors that shift the short-run aggregate supply curve, see Table 27-2.

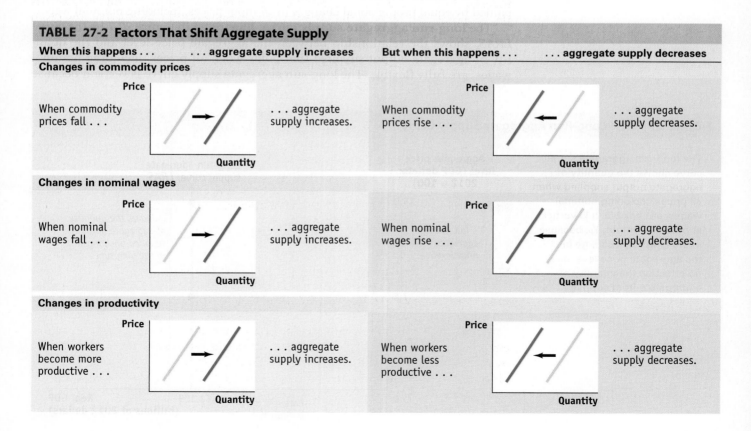

TABLE 27-2 Factors That Shift Aggregate Supply

When this happens . . .	. . . aggregate supply increases	But when this happens . . .	. . . aggregate supply decreases
Changes in commodity prices			
When commodity prices fall . . .	. . . aggregate supply increases.	When commodity prices rise . . .	. . . aggregate supply decreases.
Changes in nominal wages			
When nominal wages fall . . .	. . . aggregate supply increases.	When nominal wages rise . . .	. . . aggregate supply decreases.
Changes in productivity			
When workers become more productive . . .	. . . aggregate supply increases.	When workers become less productive . . .	. . . aggregate supply decreases.

The **long-run aggregate supply curve** shows the relationship between the aggregate price level and the quantity of aggregate output supplied that would exist if all prices, including nominal wages, were fully flexible.

The Long-Run Aggregate Supply Curve

We've just seen that in the short run a fall in the aggregate price level leads to a decline in the quantity of aggregate output supplied because nominal wages are sticky in the short run. But, as mentioned earlier, contracts and informal agreements are renegotiated in the long run. So in the long run, nominal wages will fully adjust to changes in the aggregate price level (they are flexible, not sticky). This fact greatly alters the long-run relationship between the aggregate price level and aggregate supply. In fact, in the long run, the aggregate price level has *no* effect on the quantity of aggregate output supplied.

To see why, let's conduct a thought experiment. Imagine that you could wave a magic wand—or maybe a magic bar-code scanner—and cut *all prices* in the economy in half at the same time. By "all prices" we mean the prices of all inputs, including nominal wages, as well as the prices of final goods and services. What would happen to aggregate output, given that the aggregate price level has been halved and all input prices, including nominal wages, have been halved?

The answer is: nothing. Consider Equation 27-2 again: each producer would receive a lower price for its product, but costs would fall by the same proportion. As a result, every unit of output profitable to produce before the change in prices would still be profitable to produce after the change in prices. So a halving of *all* prices in the economy has no effect on the economy's aggregate output. In other words, changes in the aggregate price level now have no effect on the quantity of aggregate output supplied.

In reality, of course, no one can change all prices by the same proportion at the same time. But now, we'll consider the *long run, the period of time in which all prices, including production costs such as nominal wages, are fully flexible.* In the long run, inflation or deflation has the same effect as someone changing all prices by the same proportion. *As a result, changes in the aggregate price level do not change the quantity of aggregate output supplied in the long run.* That's because changes in the aggregate price level, which is composed of prices of final goods and services, will be accompanied by equal proportional changes in *all* input prices, including nominal wages.

The **long-run aggregate supply curve,** illustrated in Figure 27-7 by the curve *LRAS*, shows the relationship between the aggregate price level and the quantity of aggregate output supplied that holds when all prices, including nominal wages, are fully flexible. The long-run aggregate supply curve is vertical because

FIGURE 27-7 The Long-Run Aggregate Supply Curve

The long-run aggregate supply curve shows the quantity of aggregate output supplied when all prices, including nominal wages, are flexible. It is vertical at potential output, Y_P, because in the long run a change in the aggregate price level has no effect on the quantity of aggregate output supplied.

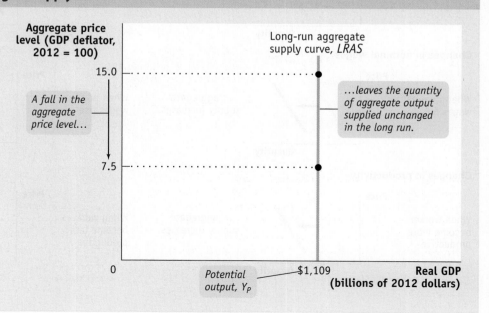

changes in the aggregate price level have *no* effect on aggregate output in the long run. At an aggregate price level of 15.0, the quantity of aggregate output supplied is $1,109 billion in 2012 dollars. If the aggregate price level falls by 50% to 7.5, the quantity of aggregate output supplied is unchanged in the long run at $1,109 billion in 2012 dollars.

It's important to understand not only that the *LRAS* curve is vertical but also that its position along the horizontal axis represents a significant measure. The horizontal intercept in Figure 27-7, where *LRAS* touches the horizontal axis ($1,109 billion in 2009 dollars), is the economy's **potential output,** Y_P: the level of real GDP the economy would produce if all prices, including nominal wages, were fully flexible.

In reality, the actual level of real GDP is almost always either above or below potential output. We'll see why later in this chapter, when we discuss the *AD–AS* model. Still, an economy's potential output is an important number because it defines the trend around which actual aggregate output fluctuates from year to year.

In the United States, the Congressional Budget Office, or CBO, estimates annual potential output for the purpose of federal budget analysis. In Figure 27-8, the CBO's estimates of U.S. potential output from 1990 to 2020 are represented by the orange line and the actual values of U.S. real GDP over the same period are represented by the blue line. Years shaded purple on the horizontal axis correspond to periods in which actual aggregate output fell short of potential output; years shaded green correspond to periods in which actual aggregate output exceeded potential output.

As you can see, U.S. potential output has risen steadily over time—implying a series of rightward shifts of the *LRAS* curve. What has caused these rightward shifts? The answer lies in the factors related to long-run growth that we discussed in Chapter 24, such as increases in physical capital and human capital as well as

> **Potential output** is the level of real GDP the economy would produce if all prices, including nominal wages, were fully flexible.

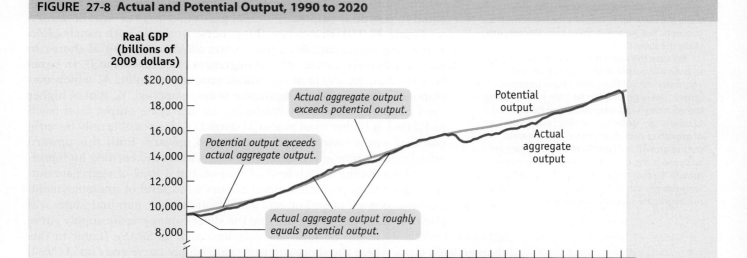

FIGURE 27-8 Actual and Potential Output, 1990 to 2020

This figure shows the performance of actual and potential output in the United States from 1990 to 2020. The orange line shows estimates of U.S. potential output, produced by the Congressional Budget Office, and the blue line shows actual aggregate output. The purple-shaded years are periods in which actual aggregate output fell below potential output, and the years shaded green are periods in which actual aggregate output exceeded potential output. As shown, significant shortfalls occurred in the recessions of the early 1990s and after 2000. Actual aggregate output was significantly above potential output in the boom of the late 1990s, and a huge shortfall occurred after the recession of 2007–2009. Another shortfall occurred in the second quarter of 2020, when the coronavirus pandemic caused economic activity to decline at an annualized rate in excess of 30%.

Data from: Congressional Budget Office; Bureau of Economic Analysis; Federal Reserve Bank of St. Louis.

technological progress. Over the long run, as the size of the labor force and the productivity of labor both rise, the level of real GDP that the economy is capable of producing also rises. Indeed, one way to think about long-run economic growth is that it is the growth in the economy's potential output. We generally think of the long-run aggregate supply curve as shifting to the right over time as an economy experiences long-run growth.

From the Short Run to the Long Run

As you can see in Figure 27-8, the economy normally produces more or less than potential output: actual aggregate output was below potential output in the early 1990s, above potential output in the late 1990s, below potential output for most of the 2000s, and significantly below potential output after the recession of 2007–2009 and during the coronavirus pandemic. So the economy is normally on its short-run aggregate supply curve—but not on its long-run aggregate supply curve. So why is the long-run curve relevant? Does the economy ever move from the short run to the long run? And if so, how?

The first step to answering these questions is to understand that the economy is always in one of only two states with respect to the short-run and long-run aggregate supply curves. It can be on both curves simultaneously by being at a point where the curves cross (as in the few years in Figure 27-8 in which actual aggregate output and potential output roughly coincided). Or it can be on the short-run aggregate supply curve but not the long-run aggregate supply curve (as in the years in which actual aggregate output and potential output *did not* coincide).

But that is not the end of the story. If the economy is on the short-run but not the long-run aggregate supply curve, the short-run aggregate supply curve will shift over time until the economy is at a point where both curves cross—a point where actual aggregate output is equal to potential output.

Figure 27-9 illustrates how this process works. In both panels *LRAS* is the long-run aggregate supply curve, $SRAS_1$ is the initial short-run aggregate supply curve, and the aggregate price level is at P_1. In panel (a) the economy starts at the initial production point, A_1, which corresponds to a quantity of aggregate output supplied, Y_1, that is higher than potential output, Y_P. Producing an aggregate output level (such as Y_1) that is higher than potential output (Y_P) is possible only because nominal wages haven't yet fully adjusted upward. Until this upward adjustment in nominal wages occurs, producers are earning high profits and producing a high level of output. But a level of aggregate output higher than potential output means a low level of unemployment. Because jobs are abundant and workers are scarce, nominal wages will rise over time, gradually shifting the short-run aggregate supply curve leftward. Eventually it will be in a new position, such as $SRAS_2$. (Later in this chapter, we'll show where the short-run aggregate supply curve ends up. As we'll see, that depends on the aggregate demand curve as well.)

In panel (b), the initial production point, A_1, corresponds to an aggregate output level, Y_1, that is lower than potential output, Y_P. Producing an aggregate output level (such as Y_1) that is lower than potential output (Y_P) is possible only because nominal wages haven't yet fully adjusted downward. Until this downward adjustment occurs, producers are earning low (or negative) profits and producing a low level of output. An aggregate output level lower than potential output means high unemployment. Because workers are abundant and jobs are scarce, nominal wages will fall over time, shifting the short-run aggregate supply curve gradually to the right. Eventually it will be in a new position, such as $SRAS_2$.

We'll see shortly that these shifts of the short-run aggregate supply curve will return the economy to potential output in the long run.

PITFALLS

WHAT THE LONG RUN REALLY MEANS

We've used the term *long run* in two different contexts. In an earlier chapter we focused on *long-run economic growth:* growth that takes place over decades. In this chapter we introduced the *long-run aggregate supply curve,* which depicts the economy's potential output: the level of aggregate output that the economy would produce if all prices, including nominal wages, were fully flexible. It might seem that we're using the same term, *long run,* for two different concepts. But we aren't: these two concepts are really the same thing.

Because the economy always tends to return to potential output in the long run, actual aggregate output *fluctuates around* potential output, rarely getting too far from it. As a result, the economy's rate of growth over long periods of time — say, decades — is very close to the rate of growth of potential output. And potential output growth is determined by the factors we analyzed in the chapter on long-run economic growth. So that means that the "long run" of long-run growth and the "long run" of the long-run aggregate supply curve coincide.

FIGURE 27-9 From the Short Run to the Long Run

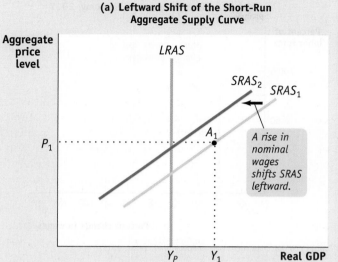

(a) Leftward Shift of the Short-Run Aggregate Supply Curve

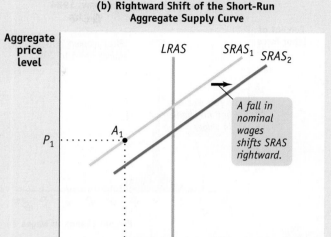

(b) Rightward Shift of the Short-Run Aggregate Supply Curve

In panel (a), the initial short-run aggregate supply curve is $SRAS_1$. At the aggregate price level, P_1, the quantity of aggregate output supplied, Y_1, exceeds potential output, Y_P. Eventually, low unemployment will cause nominal wages to rise, leading to a leftward shift of the short-run aggregate supply curve

from $SRAS_1$ to $SRAS_2$. In panel (b), the reverse happens: at the aggregate price level, P_1, the quantity of aggregate output supplied is less than potential output. High unemployment eventually leads to a fall in nominal wages over time and a rightward shift of the short-run aggregate supply curve.

ECONOMICS >> *in Action*
Sticky Wages in the Great Recession

We've asserted that the aggregate supply curve is upward sloping in the short run mainly because of *sticky wages*—in particular, because employers are reluctant to cut nominal wages (and workers are unwilling to accept wage cuts) even when labor is in excess supply. But what is the evidence for wage stickiness?

The answer is that we can look at what happens to wages at times when we might have expected to see many workers facing wage cuts because similar workers are unemployed and would be willing to work for less. If wages are sticky, what we would expect to find at such times is that many workers' wages don't change at all: there's no reason for employers to give them a raise, but because wages are sticky, they don't face cuts either.

And that is exactly what you find during and after the Great Recession of 2007–2009. Figure 27-10 shows an especially striking illustration: the case of Portugal, which suffered a severe, prolonged slump starting in 2008, with the unemployment rate peaking at more than 17% in early 2013.

Panel (a) shows the distribution of Portuguese wage changes—the percentage of all workers whose wages went up by a given amount—in prosperous times, namely 1984, when the economy was doing fairly well and there was also significant inflation. As you can see, most workers were getting raises of between 15% and 20%, but they were spread over a significant range. Panel (b), by contrast, shows the distribution of wage changes in 2012, when the Portuguese economy was deeply depressed and inflation was near zero. Under those circumstances you might have expected to see widespread wage cuts. But employers are reluctant to cut wages. So what we saw instead was that most workers' wages, nearly 80%, were completely flat, as shown by the spike you see at zero. That is, because wages were sticky, most wages were neither rising nor falling.

FIGURE 27-10 Distribution Wage Changes in Portugal

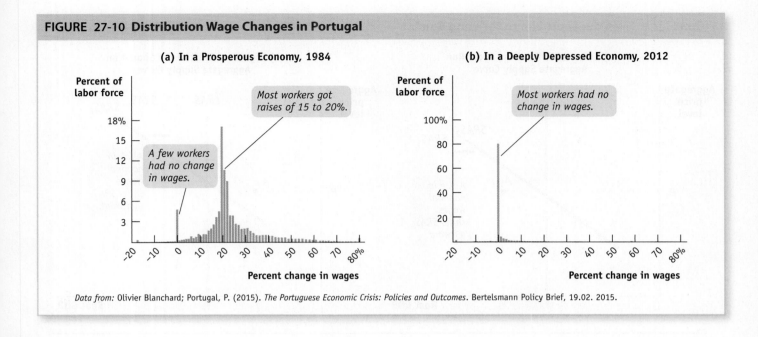

Data from: Olivier Blanchard; Portugal, P. (2015). *The Portuguese Economic Crisis: Policies and Outcomes.* Bertelsmann Policy Brief, 19.02. 2015.

>> Check Your Understanding 27-2
Solutions appear at back of book.

1. Determine the effect on short-run aggregate supply for each of the following events. Explain whether it represents a movement along the *SRAS* curve or a shift of the *SRAS* curve.
   a. A rise in the consumer price index (CPI) leads producers to increase output.
   b. A fall in the price of oil leads producers to increase output.
   c. A rise in legally mandated retirement benefits paid to workers leads producers to reduce output.

2. Suppose the economy is initially at potential output and the quantity of aggregate output supplied increases. What information would you need to determine whether this was due to a movement along the *SRAS* curve or a shift of the *LRAS* curve?

‖ The *AD–AS* Model

From 1929 to 1933, the U.S. economy moved down the short-run aggregate supply curve as the aggregate price level fell. In contrast, from 1979 to 1980 the U.S. economy moved up the aggregate demand curve as the aggregate price level rose. In each case, the cause of the movement along the curve was a shift of the other curve. In 1929–1933, it was a leftward shift of the aggregate demand curve—a major fall in consumer spending. In 1979–1980, it was a leftward shift of the short-run aggregate supply curve—a dramatic fall in short-run aggregate supply caused by the surging price of oil. Although the aggregate price level did not fall during the Great Recession, economists agree that it was caused by a leftward shift of the aggregate demand curve, similar to the 1929–1933 episode.

So to understand the behavior of the economy, we must put the aggregate supply curve and the aggregate demand curve together. The result is the ***AD–AS*** **model,** the basic model we use to understand economic fluctuations.

Short-Run Macroeconomic Equilibrium

We'll begin our analysis by focusing on the short run. Figure 27-11 shows the aggregate demand curve and the short-run aggregate supply curve on the same diagram. The point at which the *AD* and *SRAS* curves intersect, E_{SR}, is the

FIGURE 27-11 The *AD–AS* Model

The *AD–AS* model combines the aggregate demand curve and the short-run aggregate supply curve. Their point of intersection, E_{SR}, is the point of short-run macroeconomic equilibrium where the quantity of aggregate output demanded is equal to the quantity of aggregate output supplied. P_E is the short-run equilibrium aggregate price level, and Y_E is the short-run equilibrium level of aggregate output.

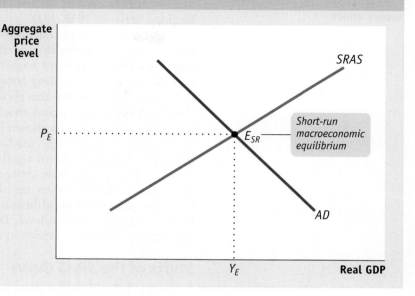

short-run macroeconomic equilibrium: the point at which the quantity of aggregate output supplied is equal to the quantity demanded by domestic households, businesses, the government, and the rest of the world. The aggregate price level at E_{SR}, P_E, is the **short-run equilibrium aggregate price level.** The level of aggregate output at E_{SR}, Y_E, is the **short-run equilibrium aggregate output.**

We saw in the supply and demand model that a shortage of any individual good causes its market price to rise but a surplus of the good causes its market price to fall. These forces ensure that the market reaches equilibrium. The same logic applies to short-run macroeconomic equilibrium. If the aggregate price level is above its equilibrium level, the quantity of aggregate output supplied exceeds the quantity of aggregate output demanded. This leads to a fall in the aggregate price level and pushes it toward its equilibrium level.

If the aggregate price level is below its equilibrium level, the quantity of aggregate output supplied is less than the quantity of aggregate output demanded. This leads to a rise in the aggregate price level, again pushing it toward its equilibrium level. In the discussion that follows, we'll assume that the economy is always in short-run macroeconomic equilibrium.

We'll also make another important simplification based on the observation that in reality there is a long-term upward trend in both aggregate output and the aggregate price level. We'll assume that a fall in either variable really means a fall compared to the long-run trend. For example, if the aggregate price level normally rises 4% per year, a year in which the aggregate price level rises only 3% would count, for our purposes, as a 1% decline. In fact, since the Great Depression there have been very few years in which the aggregate price level of any major nation actually declined—Japan's period of deflation since 1995 is one of the few exceptions. There have, however, been many cases in which the aggregate price level fell relative to the long-run trend.

Short-run equilibrium aggregate output and the short-run equilibrium aggregate price level can change either because of shifts of the *AD* curve or because of shifts of the *SRAS* curve. Let's look at each case in turn.

Shifts of Aggregate Demand: Short-Run Effects

An event that shifts the aggregate demand curve, such as a change in expectations or wealth, the effect of the size of the existing stock of physical capital, or the use of fiscal or monetary policy, is known as a **demand shock.** The Great Depression

The economy is in **short-run macroeconomic equilibrium** when the quantity of aggregate output supplied is equal to the quantity demanded.

The **short-run equilibrium aggregate price level** is the aggregate price level in the short-run macroeconomic equilibrium.

Short-run equilibrium aggregate output is the quantity of aggregate output produced in the short-run macroeconomic equilibrium.

An event that shifts the aggregate demand curve is a **demand shock.**

An event that shifts the short-run aggregate supply curve is a **supply shock.**

was caused by a negative demand shock, the collapse of wealth and of business and consumer confidence that followed the stock market crash of 1929 and the banking crisis of 1930–1931.

The Depression was ended by a positive demand shock—the huge increase in government purchases during World War II. In 2008 the U.S. economy experienced another significant negative demand shock as the housing market turned from boom to bust, leading consumers and firms to scale back their spending.

Figure 27-12 shows the short-run effects of negative and positive demand shocks. A negative demand shock shifts the aggregate demand curve, *AD*, to the left, from AD_1 to AD_2, as shown in panel (a). The economy moves down along the *SRAS* curve from E_1 to E_2, leading to lower short-run equilibrium aggregate output and a lower short-run equilibrium aggregate price level. A positive demand shock shifts the aggregate demand curve, *AD*, to the right, as shown in panel (b). Here, the economy moves up along the *SRAS* curve, from E_1 to E_2. This leads to higher short-run equilibrium aggregate output and a higher short-run equilibrium aggregate price level. Demand shocks cause aggregate output and the aggregate price level to move in the same direction.

Shifts of the *SRAS* Curve

An event that shifts the short-run aggregate supply curve, such as a change in commodity prices, nominal wages, or productivity, is known as a **supply shock.** A *negative* supply shock raises production costs and reduces the quantity producers are willing to supply at any given aggregate price level, leading to a leftward shift of the short-run aggregate supply curve. The U.S. economy experienced severe negative supply shocks following disruptions to world oil supplies in 1973 and 1979.

In contrast, a *positive* supply shock reduces production costs and increases the quantity supplied at any given aggregate price level, leading to a rightward shift of the short-run aggregate supply curve. The United States experienced a positive supply shock between 1995 and 2000, when the increasing use of the internet and other information technologies caused productivity growth to surge.

FIGURE 27-12 Demand Shocks

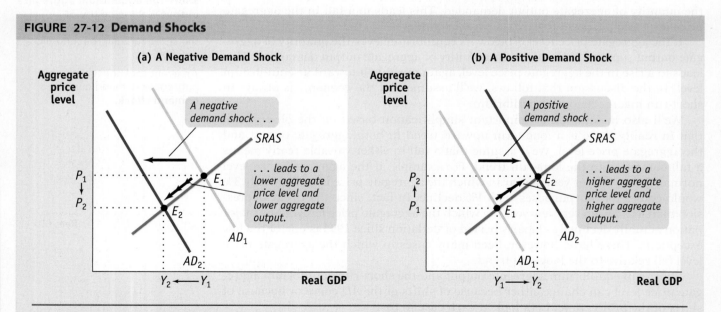

A demand shock shifts the aggregate demand curve, moving the aggregate price level and aggregate output in the same direction. In panel (a), a negative demand shock shifts the aggregate demand curve leftward from AD_1 to AD_2, reducing the aggregate price level from P_1 to P_2 and aggregate output from Y_1 to Y_2. In panel (b), a positive demand shock shifts the aggregate demand curve rightward, increasing the aggregate price level from P_1 to P_2 and aggregate output from Y_1 to Y_2.

The effects of a negative supply shock are shown in panel (a) of Figure 27-13. The initial equilibrium is at E_1, with aggregate price level P_1 and aggregate output Y_1. The disruption in the oil supply causes the short-run aggregate supply curve to shift to the left, from $SRAS_1$ to $SRAS_2$. As a consequence, aggregate output falls and the aggregate price level rises, an upward movement along the AD curve. At the new equilibrium, E_2, the short-run equilibrium aggregate price level, P_2, is higher, and the short-run equilibrium aggregate output level, Y_2, is lower than before.

Stagflation is the combination of inflation and falling aggregate output.

The combination of inflation and falling aggregate output shown in panel (a) has a special name: **stagflation,** for "stagnation plus inflation." Stagflation is unpleasant: falling aggregate output leads to rising unemployment, while the purchasing power of consumers is squeezed by rising prices. Stagflation in the 1970s created a mood of economic pessimism and deeply affected those who lived through it, like Jean-Claude Trichet. It also, as we'll see, poses a dilemma for policy makers.

A positive supply shock, shown in panel (b), has exactly the opposite effects. A rightward shift of the $SRAS$ curve from $SRAS_1$ to $SRAS_2$ results in a rise in aggregate output and a fall in the aggregate price level, a downward movement along the AD curve. The favorable supply shocks of the late 1990s led to a combination of full employment and declining inflation. That is, the aggregate price level fell compared with the long-run trend. This combination produced, for a time, a great wave of national optimism.

The distinctive feature of supply shocks, both negative and positive, is that, unlike demand shocks, they cause the aggregate price level and aggregate output to move in *opposite* directions.

There's another important contrast between supply shocks and demand shocks. As we've seen, monetary policy and fiscal policy enable the government to shift the AD curve, meaning that governments are in a position to create the kinds of shocks shown in Figure 27-12. It's much harder for governments to shift

FIGURE 27-13 Supply Shocks

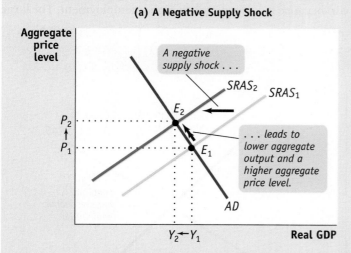

(a) A Negative Supply Shock

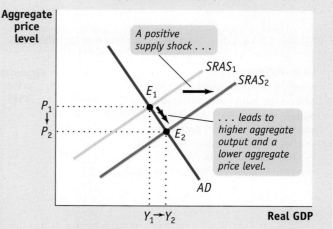

(b) A Positive Supply Shock

A supply shock shifts the short-run aggregate supply curve, moving the aggregate price level and aggregate output in opposite directions. Panel (a) shows a negative supply shock, which shifts the short-run aggregate supply curve leftward and causes *stagflation* — lower output and a higher aggregate price level. Here the short-run aggregate supply curve shifts from $SRAS_1$ to $SRAS_2$, and the economy moves from E_1 to E_2. The aggregate price level rises from P_1 to P_2, and aggregate output falls from Y_1 to Y_2. Panel (b) shows a positive supply shock, which shifts the short-run aggregate supply curve rightward, generating higher aggregate output and a lower aggregate price level. The short-run aggregate supply curve shifts from $SRAS_1$ to $SRAS_2$, and the economy moves from E_1 to E_2. The aggregate price level falls from P_1 to P_2, and aggregate output rises from Y_1 to Y_2.

The economy is in **long-run macroeconomic equilibrium** when the point of short-run macroeconomic equilibrium is on the long-run aggregate supply curve.

There is a **recessionary gap** when aggregate output is below potential output.

the *AS* curve. Are there good policy reasons to shift the *AD* curve? We'll turn to that question soon. First, however, let's look at the difference between short-run macroeconomic equilibrium and *long-run macroeconomic equilibrium*.

Long-Run Macroeconomic Equilibrium

Figure 27-14 combines the aggregate demand curve with both the short-run and long-run aggregate supply curves. The aggregate demand curve, *AD*, crosses the short-run aggregate supply curve, *SRAS*, at E_{LR}. Here we assume that enough time has elapsed that the economy is also on the long-run aggregate supply curve, *LRAS*. As a result, E_{LR} is at the intersection of all three curves—*SRAS*, *LRAS*, and *AD*. So short-run equilibrium aggregate output is equal to potential output, Y_P. Such a situation, in which the point of short-run macroeconomic equilibrium is on the long-run aggregate supply curve, is known as **long-run macroeconomic equilibrium.**

To see the significance of long-run macroeconomic equilibrium, let's consider what happens if a demand shock moves the economy away from long-run macroeconomic equilibrium. In Figure 27-15, we assume that the initial aggregate demand curve is AD_1 and the initial short-run aggregate supply curve is $SRAS_1$. So the initial macroeconomic equilibrium is at E_1, which lies on the long-run aggregate supply curve, *LRAS*. The economy, then, starts from a point of short-run and long-run macroeconomic equilibrium, and short-run equilibrium aggregate output equals potential output at Y_1.

Now suppose that for some reason—such as a sudden worsening of business and consumer expectations—aggregate demand falls and the aggregate demand curve shifts leftward to AD_2. This results in a lower equilibrium aggregate price level at P_2 and a lower equilibrium aggregate output level at Y_2 as the economy settles in the short run at E_2. The short-run effect of such a fall in aggregate demand is what the U.S. economy experienced in 1929–1933: a falling aggregate price level and falling aggregate output.

Aggregate output in this new short-run equilibrium, E_2, is below potential output. When this happens, the economy faces a **recessionary gap.** A recessionary gap inflicts a great deal of pain because it corresponds to high unemployment. The large

FIGURE 27-14 Long-Run Macroeconomic Equilibrium

Here the point of short-run macroeconomic equilibrium also lies on the long-run aggregate supply curve, *LRAS*. As a result, short-run equilibrium aggregate output is equal to potential output, Y_P. The economy is in long-run macroeconomic equilibrium at E_{LR}.

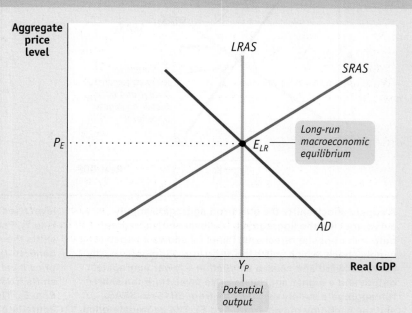

FIGURE 27-15 Short-Run versus Long-Run Effects of a Negative Demand Shock

In the long run the economy is self-correcting: demand shocks have only a short-run effect on aggregate output. Starting at E_1, a negative demand shock shifts AD_1 leftward to AD_2. In the short run the economy moves to E_2 and a recessionary gap arises: the aggregate price level declines from P_1 to P_2, aggregate output declines from Y_1 to Y_2, and unemployment rises. But in the long run nominal wages fall in response to high unemployment at Y_2, and $SRAS_1$ shifts rightward to $SRAS_2$. Aggregate output rises from Y_2 to Y_1, and the aggregate price level declines again, from P_2 to P_3. Long-run macroeconomic equilibrium is eventually restored at E_3.

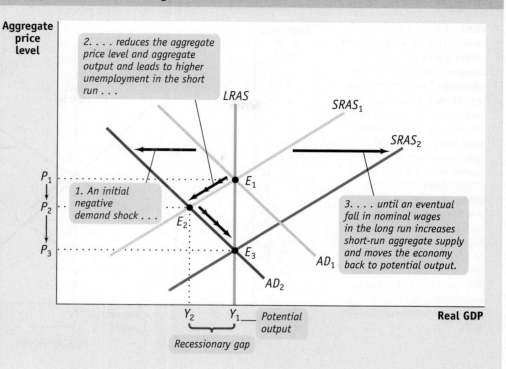

2. . . . reduces the aggregate price level and aggregate output and leads to higher unemployment in the short run . . .

1. An initial negative demand shock . . .

3. . . . until an eventual fall in nominal wages in the long run increases short-run aggregate supply and moves the economy back to potential output.

recessionary gap that had opened up in the United States by 1933 caused intense social and political turmoil. And the devastating recessionary gap that opened up in Germany at the same time played an important role in Hitler's rise to power.

But this isn't the end of the story. In the face of high unemployment, nominal wages eventually fall, as do any other sticky prices, ultimately leading producers to increase output. As a result, a recessionary gap causes the short-run aggregate supply curve to gradually shift to the right over time. This process continues until $SRAS_1$ reaches its new position at $SRAS_2$, bringing the economy to equilibrium at E_3, where AD_2, $SRAS_2$, and $LRAS$ all intersect. At E_3, the economy is back in long-run macroeconomic equilibrium; it is back at potential output Y_1 but at a lower aggregate price level, P_3, reflecting a long-run fall in the aggregate price level. In the end, the economy is *self-correcting* in the long run.

What if, instead, there was an increase in aggregate demand? The results are shown in Figure 27-16, where we again assume that the initial aggregate demand

FOR INQUIRING MINDS   Where's the Deflation?

The *AD–AS* model says that either a negative demand shock or a positive supply shock should lead to a fall in the aggregate price level—that is, deflation. However, since 1949, an actual fall in the aggregate price level has been a rare occurrence in the United States. Similarly, most other countries have had little or no experience with deflation. Japan, which experienced sustained mild deflation in the late 1990s and the early part of the next decade, is the

big (and much discussed) exception. What happened to deflation?

The answer is that since World War II economic fluctuations have largely taken place around a long-run inflationary trend. Before the war, it was common for prices to fall during recessions, but since then negative demand shocks have largely been reflected in a *decline in the rate of inflation* rather than an actual fall in prices. For example, the rate of consumer price inflation fell from more

than 3% at the beginning of the 2001 recession to 1.1% a year later, but it never went below zero.

All of this changed during the recession of 2007–2009. The negative demand shock that followed the 2008 financial crisis was so severe that, for most of 2009, consumer prices in the United States indeed fell. But the deflationary period didn't last long: beginning in 2010, prices again rose, at a rate of between 1% and 4% per year.

FIGURE 27-16 *Short-Run versus Long-Run Effects of a Positive Demand Shock*

Starting at E_1, a positive demand shock shifts AD_1 rightward to AD_2, and the economy moves to E_2 in the short run. This results in an inflationary gap as aggregate output rises from Y_1 to Y_2, the aggregate price level rises from P_1 to P_2, and unemployment falls to a low level. In the long run, $SRAS_1$ shifts leftward to $SRAS_2$ as nominal wages rise in response to low unemployment at Y_2. Aggregate output falls back to Y_1, the aggregate price level rises again to P_3, and the economy self-corrects as it returns to long-run macroeconomic equilibrium at E_3.

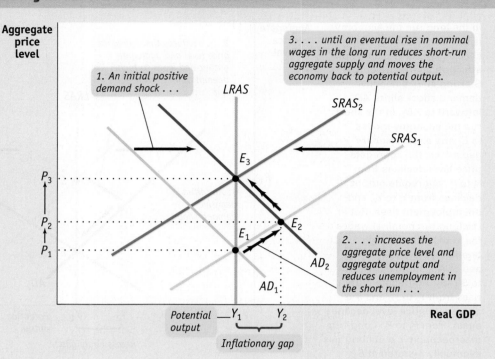

There is an **inflationary gap** when aggregate output is above potential output.

The **output gap** is the percentage difference between actual aggregate output and potential output.

curve is AD_1 and the initial short-run aggregate supply curve is $SRAS_1$, so that the initial macroeconomic equilibrium, at E_1, lies on the long-run aggregate supply curve, $LRAS$. Initially, then, the economy is in long-run macroeconomic equilibrium.

Now suppose that aggregate demand rises, and the AD curve shifts rightward to AD_2. This results in a higher aggregate price level, at P_2, and a higher aggregate output level, at Y_2, as the economy settles in the short run at E_2. Aggregate output in this new short-run equilibrium is above potential output, and unemployment is low in order to produce this higher level of aggregate output. When this happens, the economy experiences an **inflationary gap.**

As in the case of a recessionary gap, the story doesn't end here. In the face of low unemployment, nominal wages will rise, as will other sticky prices. An inflationary gap causes the short-run aggregate supply curve to shift gradually to the left as producers reduce output in the face of rising nominal wages. This process continues until $SRAS_1$ reaches its new position at $SRAS_2$, bringing the economy to equilibrium at E_3, where AD_2, $SRAS_2$, and $LRAS$ all intersect. At E_3, the economy is back in long-run macroeconomic equilibrium. It is back at potential output, but at a higher price level, P_3, reflecting a long-run rise in the aggregate price level. Again, the economy is self-correcting in the long run.

To summarize the analysis of how the economy responds to recessionary and inflationary gaps, we can focus on the **output gap,** the percentage difference between actual aggregate output and potential output. The output gap is calculated as follows:

(27-3) $\text{Output gap} = \dfrac{\text{Actual aggregate output} - \text{Potential output}}{\text{Potential output}} \times 100$

Our analysis says that the output gap always tends toward zero.

If there is a recessionary gap, so that the output gap is negative, nominal wages eventually fall, moving the economy back to potential output and bringing the output gap back to zero. If there is an inflationary gap, so that the output gap is positive, nominal wages eventually rise, also moving the economy back to potential output and again bringing the output gap back to zero. So in the long run the economy is **self-correcting:** shocks to aggregate demand affect aggregate output in the short run but not in the long run.

> The economy is **self-correcting** when shocks to aggregate demand affect aggregate output in the short run, but not the long run.

ECONOMICS >> *in Action* 🌐
Supply Shocks versus Demand Shocks in Practice

How often do supply shocks and demand shocks, respectively, cause recessions? The verdict of most, though not all, macroeconomists is that recessions are mainly caused by demand shocks. But when a negative supply shock does happen, the resulting recession tends to be particularly severe.

Let's get specific. Between World War II and the coronavirus recession of 2020, which was really in a class of its own, there were twelve recessions in the United States. However, two of these, in 1980 and 1981–1982, are often treated as a single *double-dip recession* (that is, a recession followed by a temporary recovery, then followed by another recession), bringing the total number down to eleven. Of these eleven recessions, only two—the recession of 1973–1975 and the double-dip recession of 1980–1982—showed the distinctive combination of falling aggregate output and a surge in the price level that we call stagflation. In each case, the cause of the supply shock was political turmoil in the Middle East—the Arab–Israeli war of 1973 and the Iranian revolution of 1979—that disrupted world oil supplies and sent oil prices skyrocketing. In fact, economists sometimes refer to the two slumps as "OPEC I" and "OPEC II," after the Organization of the Petroleum Exporting Countries, the world oil cartel. The Great Recession that began in 2007 and lasted until 2009 was at least partially exacerbated, if not partially caused, by a spike in oil prices.

So eight of eleven postwar recessions were purely the result of demand shocks, not supply shocks. The few supply-shock recessions, however, were the worst as measured by the unemployment rate. Figure 27-17 shows the U.S. unemployment rate since 1948, with the dates of the 1973 Arab–Israeli war and the 1979 Iranian revolution marked on the figure. Some of the highest unemployment rates since World War II came after these big negative supply shocks.

There's a reason the aftermath of a supply shock tends to be particularly severe for the economy: macroeconomic policy has a much harder time dealing with supply shocks than with demand shocks. We'll see in a moment why supply shocks present such a problem.

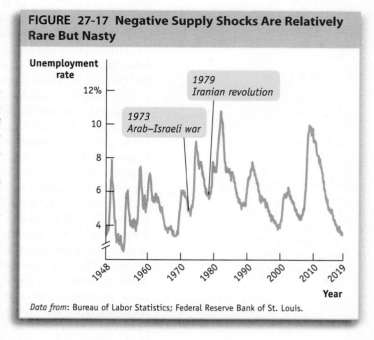

FIGURE 27-17 Negative Supply Shocks Are Relatively Rare But Nasty

Data from: Bureau of Labor Statistics; Federal Reserve Bank of St. Louis.

>> *Check Your Understanding* 27-3

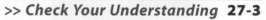

Solutions appear at back of book.

1. Describe the short-run effects of each of the following shocks on the aggregate price level and on aggregate output.
   a. The government sharply increases the minimum wage, raising the wages of many workers.
   b. Solar energy firms launch a major program of investment spending.
   c. Congress raises taxes and cuts spending.
   d. Severe weather destroys crops around the world.

2. A rise in productivity increases potential output, but some worry that demand for the additional output will be insufficient even in the long run. How would you respond?

> ## >> *Quick Review*
>
> • The **AD–AS model** is used to study economic fluctuations.
>
> • **Short-run macroeconomic equilibrium** occurs at the intersection of the short-run aggregate supply and aggregate demand curves. This determines the **short-run equilibrium aggregate price level** and the level of **short-run equilibrium aggregate output.**
>
> • A **demand shock,** a shift of the *AD* curve, causes the aggregate price level and aggregate output to move in the same direction. A **supply shock,** a shift of the *SRAS* curve, causes them to move in opposite directions. **Stagflation** is the consequence of a negative supply shock.
>
> • A fall in nominal wages occurs in response to a **recessionary gap,** and a rise in nominal wages occurs in response to an **inflationary gap.** Both move the economy to **long-run macroeconomic equilibrium,** where the *AD, SRAS,* and *LRAS* curves intersect.
>
> • The **output gap** always tends toward zero because the economy is **self-correcting** in the long run.

Stabilization policy is the use of government policy to reduce the severity of recessions and rein in excessively strong expansions.

‖ Macroeconomic Policy

We've just seen that the economy is self-correcting in the long run: it will eventually trend back to potential output. Most macroeconomists believe, however, that the process of self-correction typically takes a decade or more. In particular, if aggregate output is below potential output, the economy can suffer an extended period of depressed aggregate output and high unemployment before it returns to normal.

This belief is the background to one of the most famous quotations in economics: John Maynard Keynes's declaration, "In the long run we are all dead." We explain the context in which he made this remark in the upcoming For Inquiring Minds.

Economists usually interpret Keynes as having recommended that governments not wait for the economy to correct itself. Instead, it is argued by many economists, but not all, that the government should use monetary and fiscal policy to get the economy back to potential output in the aftermath of a shift of the aggregate demand curve. This is the rationale for an active **stabilization policy,** which is the use of government policy to reduce the severity of recessions and rein in excessively strong expansions.

Can stabilization policy improve the economy's performance? If we reexamine Figure 27-8, the answer certainly appears to be yes. Under active stabilization policy, the U.S. economy returned to potential output in 1996 after an approximately five-year recessionary gap. Likewise, in 2001 it also returned to potential output after an approximately four-year inflationary gap. These periods are much shorter than the decade or more that economists believe it would take for the economy to self-correct in the absence of active stabilization policy. In fact, recovery from the Great Recession took longer—seven years—partly because of political constraints on fiscal policy. And recovery would have taken even longer if Ben Bernanke had not undertaken strongly expansionary monetary policy, as recounted in the opening story. However, as we'll see shortly, the ability to improve the economy's performance is not always guaranteed. It depends on the kinds of shocks the economy faces.

Policy in the Face of Demand Shocks

Imagine that the economy experiences a negative demand shock, like the one shown in Figure 27-15. As we've discussed in this chapter, monetary and fiscal policy shift the aggregate demand curve. If policy makers react quickly to the fall in aggregate demand, they can use monetary or fiscal policy to shift the aggregate demand curve back to the right. And if policy were able to perfectly anticipate shifts

---

FOR INQUIRING MINDS   **Keynes and the Long Run**

The British economist Sir John Maynard Keynes (1883–1946), probably more than any other single economist, created the modern field of macroeconomics. We'll look at his role, and the controversies that still swirl around some aspects of his thought, in a later chapter on macroeconomic events and ideas. But for now let's just look at his most famous quote.

In 1923 Keynes published *A Tract on Monetary Reform*, a small book on the economic problems of Europe after World War I. In it he decried the tendency of many of his colleagues to focus on how things work

out in the long run—as in the long-run macroeconomic equilibrium we have just analyzed—while ignoring the often very painful and possibly disastrous things that can happen along the way. Here's a fuller version of the quote:

This long run is a misleading guide to current affairs. In the long run we are all dead. Economists set themselves too easy, too useless a task if in tempestuous seasons they can only tell us that when the storm is long past the sea is flat again.

Keynes focused the attention of economists of his day on the short run.

of the aggregate demand curve, it could short-circuit the whole process shown in Figure 27-15. Instead of going through a period of low aggregate output and falling prices, the government could manage the economy so that it would stay at E_1.

Why might a policy that short-circuits the adjustment shown in Figure 27-15 and maintains the economy at its original equilibrium be desirable? For two reasons.

1. The temporary fall in aggregate output that would happen without policy intervention is a bad thing, particularly because such a decline is associated with high unemployment.

2. As explained in Chapter 23, price stability is generally regarded as a desirable goal. So preventing deflation—a fall in the aggregate price level—is a good thing.

Does this mean that policy makers should always act to offset declines in aggregate demand? Not necessarily. As we'll see in later chapters, some policy measures to increase aggregate demand, especially those that increase budget deficits, may have long-term costs in terms of lower long-run growth. Furthermore, in the real world policy makers aren't perfectly informed, and the effects of their policies aren't perfectly predictable. This creates the danger that stabilization policy will do more harm than good; that is, attempts to stabilize the economy may end up creating more instability. We'll describe the long-running debate over macroeconomic policy in Chapter 32. Despite these qualifications, most economists believe that a good case can be made for using macroeconomic policy to offset major negative shocks to the *AD* curve.

Should policy makers also try to offset positive shocks to aggregate demand? It may not seem obvious that they should. After all, even though inflation may be a bad thing, isn't more output and lower unemployment a good thing? Not necessarily.

Most economists now believe that any short-run gains from an inflationary gap must be paid back later. So policy makers today usually try to offset positive as well as negative demand shocks. For reasons we'll explain in Chapter 30, attempts to eliminate recessionary gaps and inflationary gaps usually rely on monetary rather than fiscal policy. In 2007 and 2008 the Fed sharply cut interest rates in an attempt to head off a rising recessionary gap; earlier in the decade, when the U.S. economy seemed headed for an inflationary gap, it raised interest rates to generate the opposite effect.

But how should macroeconomic policy respond to supply shocks?

Responding to Supply Shocks

Back in panel (a) of Figure 27-13 we showed the effects of a negative supply shock: in the short run such a shock leads to lower aggregate output but a higher aggregate price level. As we've noted, policy makers can respond to a negative *demand* shock by using monetary and fiscal policy to return aggregate demand to its original level. But what can or should they do about a negative *supply* shock?

In contrast to the aggregate demand curve, there are no easy policies that shift the short-run aggregate supply curve. That is, there is no government policy that can easily affect producers' profitability and so compensate for shifts of the short-run aggregate supply curve. So the policy response to a negative supply shock cannot aim to simply push the curve that shifted back to its original position.

And if you consider using monetary or fiscal policy to shift the aggregate demand curve in response to a supply shock, the right response isn't obvious. Two bad things are happening simultaneously: a fall in aggregate output, leading to a rise in unemployment, *and* a rise in the aggregate price level. Any policy that shifts the aggregate demand curve helps one problem only by making the other worse. If the government acts to increase aggregate demand and limit the rise in unemployment, it reduces the decline in output but causes even more inflation. If it acts to reduce aggregate demand, it curbs inflation but causes a further rise in unemployment.

It's a trade-off with no good answer. In the end, the United States and other economically advanced nations suffering from the supply shocks of the 1970s eventually chose to stabilize prices even at the cost of higher unemployment. This was the same policy that Jean-Claude Trichet adopted in 2011, when he chose to forgo expansionary monetary policy after he mistook a temporary blip in oil prices as a supply shock.

ECONOMICS >> *in Action*
Is Stabilization Policy Stabilizing?

We've described the theoretical rationale for stabilization policy as a way of responding to demand shocks. But does stabilization policy actually stabilize the economy? We can try to answer this question by looking at the long-term historical record.

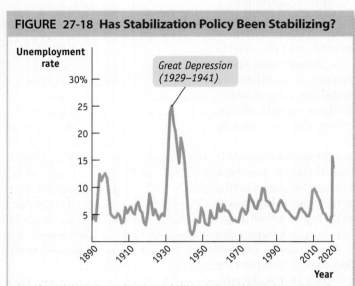

FIGURE 27-18 Has Stabilization Policy Been Stabilizing?

Unemployment rate

Great Depression (1929–1941)

Year

Data from: Christina Romer, "Spurious Volatility in Historical Unemployment Data." *Journal of Political Economy* 94, no. 1 (1986): 1–37 (years 1890–1928); Bureau of Labor Statistics (years 1929–2020).

Before World War II, the U.S. government didn't really have a stabilization policy, largely because macroeconomics as we know it didn't exist, and there was no consensus about what to do. Since World War II, and especially since 1960, active stabilization policy has become standard practice.

So, has the economy actually become more stable since the government began trying to stabilize it? The answer is a qualified yes. It's qualified for two reasons. One is that data from the pre–World War II era are less reliable than modern data. The other is that the severe and protracted slump that began in 2007 has shaken confidence in the effectiveness of government policy. Still, there seems to have been a reduction in the size of fluctuations.

Figure 27-18 shows the number of unemployed as a percentage of the nonfarm labor force since 1890. (We focus on nonfarm workers because farmers, though they often suffer economic hardship, are rarely reported as unemployed.) Even ignoring the huge spike in unemployment during the Great Depression, unemployment seems to have varied a lot more before World War II than after. It's also worth noticing that the peaks in postwar unemployment, in 1975, 1982, and to some extent in 2010, corresponded to major supply shocks—the kind of shock for which stabilization policy has no good answer.

It's possible that the greater stability of the economy reflects good luck rather than policy. But on the face of it, the evidence suggests that stabilization policy is indeed stabilizing.

>> Quick Review

• **Stabilization policy** is the use of fiscal or monetary policy to offset demand shocks. There can be drawbacks, however. Such policies may lead to a long-term rise in the budget deficit and lower long-run growth because of crowding out. And, due to incorrect predictions, a misguided policy can increase economic instability.

• Negative supply shocks pose a policy dilemma because fighting the slump in aggregate output worsens inflation and fighting inflation worsens the slump.

>> Check Your Understanding 27-4
Solutions appear at back of book.

1. Suppose someone says, "Using monetary or fiscal policy to pump up the economy is counterproductive—you get a brief high, but then you have the pain of inflation."
   a. Explain what this means in terms of the *AD–AS* model.
   b. Is this a valid argument against stabilization policy? Why or why not?

2. In 2008, in the aftermath of the collapse of the housing bubble and a sharp rise in the price of commodities, particularly oil, there was much internal disagreement within the Fed about how to respond, with some advocating lowering interest rates and others contending that this would set off a rise in inflation. Explain the reasoning behind each one of these views in terms of the *AD–AS* model.

Toyota Makes Its Move

If you or someone you know bought a new car recently, the odds are pretty good that it was manufactured by one of two Japanese companies, Toyota or Honda. Together, these companies account for about a quarter of total passenger car sales. But this was not always the case. In 1973, the two companies accounted for a mere 2.6% of U.S. auto sales. Over the course of the 1970s and early 1980s, the Japanese share quadrupled. Why?

Toyota did a lot of things right: during the 1960s it had perfected the technique of so-called *just-in-time production* or *lean manufacturing*, a production system that yielded lower costs, higher productivity, and higher quality compared to American production techniques. (You may recall our discussion of lean production in the Chapter 2 Business Case.)

But Toyota was lucky as well. During the 1970s, Americans began to switch from enormous sedans to smaller cars, a market that U.S. car companies had neglected. The few choices they did offer were of poor quality, and included the AMC Gremlin and Ford Pinto, among others. In contrast, Toyota, having long produced small, reliable, fuel-efficient cars for Japan, its home market, was ready to fill the gap.

But why the shift to smaller, fuel-efficient cars? One answer is that the United States experienced a series of severe recessions, which could have induced consumers to seek cheaper alternatives to traditional big cars. As it turns out, however, other recessions have not led to major downsizing in car purchases. Figure 27-19 shows the average number of miles per gallon for new passenger cars since 1975, which has generally trended upward, but increased at a much faster rate in the mid to late 1970s and early 1980s, before stabilizing in the early 1990s—this despite the fact that many consumers were buying more fuel-efficient cars at that time. And, as you can see, there was only a slight increase in average mileage after 2007, even though the Great Recession that began that year was deeper and more prolonged than any slump since the 1930s.

So what was different in the 1970s? At that time, two bad things were happening: unemployment was rising sharply, but so was the price of gasoline. After 2007, as unemployment soared, gas prices fluctuated but eventually came down to levels well below those before the recession. So people bought fewer cars, but not, by and large, smaller cars.

The point is that Toyota got its big break not just by producing good cars, but also by producing the particular kind of good car that suited consumers during the economic troubles of the 1970s.

QUESTIONS FOR THOUGHT

1. Why do you think gas prices rose in the recessions of the 1970s but fell after the Great Recession?

2. What does this say about the causes of the recessions in each case?

3. In the 1970s, Toyota was able to increase its U.S. sales despite interest rates on auto loans surging as high as 17.5%. In contrast, after 2007, U.S. auto loan rates fell to their lowest levels in history; car sales also declined. Explain why. (*Hint:* Examine the connection between inflation and interest rates on loans.)

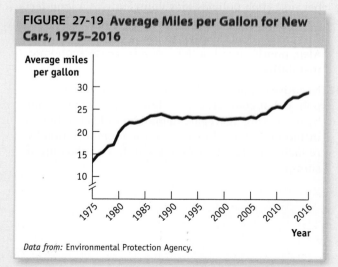

FIGURE 27-19 Average Miles per Gallon for New Cars, 1975–2016

Data from: Environmental Protection Agency.

SUMMARY

1. The **aggregate demand curve** shows the relationship between the aggregate price level and the quantity of aggregate output demanded.

2. The aggregate demand curve is downward sloping for two reasons. The first is the **wealth effect of a change in the aggregate price level**—a higher aggregate price level reduces the purchasing power of households' wealth and reduces consumer spending. The second is the **interest rate effect of a change in the aggregate price level**—a higher aggregate price level reduces the purchasing power of households' and firms' money holdings, leading to a rise in interest rates and a fall in investment spending and consumer spending.

3. The aggregate demand curve shifts because of changes in expectations, changes in wealth not due to changes in the aggregate price level, and the effect of the size of the existing stock of physical capital. Policy makers can use fiscal policy and monetary policy to shift the aggregate demand curve.

4. The **aggregate supply curve** shows the relationship between the aggregate price level and the quantity of aggregate output supplied.

5. The **short-run aggregate supply curve** is upward sloping because **nominal wages** are **sticky** in the short run: a higher aggregate price level leads to higher profit per unit of output and increased aggregate output in the short run.

6. Changes in commodity prices, nominal wages, and productivity lead to changes in producers' profits and shift the short-run aggregate supply curve.

7. In the long run, all prices, including nominal wages, are flexible and the economy produces at its **potential output.** If actual aggregate output exceeds potential output, nominal wages will eventually rise in response to low unemployment and aggregate output will fall. If potential output exceeds actual aggregate output, nominal wages will eventually fall in response to high unemployment and aggregate output will rise. So the **long-run aggregate supply curve** is vertical at potential output.

8. In the *AD–AS model*, the intersection of the short-run aggregate supply curve and the aggregate demand curve is the point of **short-run macroeconomic**

equilibrium. It determines the **short-run equilibrium aggregate price level** and the level of **short-run equilibrium aggregate output.**

9. Economic fluctuations occur because of a shift of the aggregate demand curve (a *demand shock*) or the short-run aggregate supply curve (a *supply shock*). A **demand shock** causes the aggregate price level and aggregate output to move in the same direction as the economy moves along the short-run aggregate supply curve. A **supply shock** causes them to move in opposite directions as the economy moves along the aggregate demand curve. A particularly nasty occurrence is **stagflation**—inflation and falling aggregate output—which is caused by a negative supply shock.

10. Demand shocks have only short-run effects on aggregate output because the economy is **self-correcting** in the long run. In a **recessionary gap,** an eventual fall in nominal wages moves the economy to **long-run macroeconomic equilibrium,** where aggregate output is equal to potential output. In an **inflationary gap,** an eventual rise in nominal wages moves the economy to long-run macroeconomic equilibrium. We can use the **output gap,** the percent difference between actual aggregate output and potential output, to summarize how the economy responds to recessionary and inflationary gaps. Because the economy tends to be self-correcting in the long run, the output gap always tends toward zero.

11. The high cost—in terms of unemployment—of a recessionary gap and the future adverse consequences of an inflationary gap lead many economists to advocate active **stabilization policy:** using fiscal or monetary policy to offset demand shocks. There can be drawbacks, however, because such policies may contribute to a long-term rise in the budget deficit and crowding out of private investment, leading to lower long-run growth. Also, poorly timed policies can increase economic instability.

12. Negative supply shocks pose a policy dilemma: a policy that counteracts the fall in aggregate output by increasing aggregate demand will lead to higher inflation, but a policy that counteracts inflation by reducing aggregate demand will deepen the output slump.

KEY TERMS

Aggregate demand curve, p. 782
Wealth effect of a change in the
  aggregate price level, p. 783
Interest rate effect of a change in the
  aggregate price level, p. 784
Aggregate supply curve, p. 790
Nominal wage, p. 791
Sticky wages, p. 791
Short-run aggregate supply curve,
  p. 792

Long-run aggregate supply curve, p. 796
Potential output, p. 797
AD–AS model, p. 800
Short-run macroeconomic equilibrium,
  p. 801
Short-run equilibrium aggregate price
  level, p. 801
Short-run equilibrium aggregate
  output, p. 801
Demand shock, p. 801

Supply shock, p. 802
Stagflation, p. 803
Long-run macroeconomic equilibrium,
  p. 804
Recessionary gap, p. 804
Inflationary gap, p. 806
Output gap, p. 806
Self-correcting, p. 807
Stabilization policy, p. 808

PRACTICE QUESTIONS

1. Your study partner is confused by the upward-sloping short-run aggregate supply curve and the vertical long-run aggregate supply curve. How would you explain the differences?

2. Suppose that in Wageland all workers sign annual wage contracts each year on January 1. No matter what happens to prices of final goods and services during the year, all workers earn the wage specified in their annual contract. This year, prices of final goods and services fall unexpectedly after the contracts are signed. Answer the following questions using a diagram and assume that the economy starts at potential output.

   a. In the short run, how will the quantity of aggregate output supplied respond to the fall in prices?

   b. What will happen when firms and workers renegotiate their wages?

3. The Conference Board publishes the Consumer Confidence Index (CCI) every month based on a

survey of 5,000 representative U.S. households. It is used by many economists to track the state of the economy. A press release by the Board on March 31, 2020, stated: "The Conference Board Consumer Confidence Index declined sharply in March, following an increase in February. The Index now stands at 120.0 (1985 = 100), down from 132.6 in February."

   a. As an economist, is this news encouraging for economic growth?

   b. Explain your answer to part a with the help of the *AD–AS* model. Draw a typical diagram showing two equilibrium points (E_1) and (E_2). Label the vertical axis "Aggregate price level" and the horizontal axis "Real GDP." Assume that all other major macroeconomic factors remain unchanged.

   c. How should the government respond to this news if the economy is below potential output? If it is above potential output?

PROBLEMS

1. A fall in the value of the dollar against other currencies makes U.S. final goods and services cheaper to foreigners even though the U.S. aggregate price level stays the same. As a result, foreigners demand more U.S. aggregate output. Your study partner says that this represents a movement down the aggregate demand curve because foreigners are demanding more in response to a lower price. You, however, insist that this represents a rightward shift of the aggregate demand curve. Who is right? Explain.

2. The economy is at point *A* in the accompanying diagram. Suppose that the aggregate price level rises from P_1 to P_2. How will aggregate supply adjust in the short run and in the long run to the increase in the aggregate price level? Illustrate with a diagram.

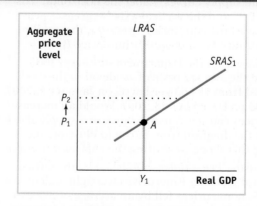

3. Suppose that all households hold all their wealth in assets that automatically rise in value when the aggregate price level rises (an example of this is what is called an "inflation-indexed bond"—a bond whose

interest rate, among other things, changes one-for-one with the inflation rate). What happens to the wealth effect of a change in the aggregate price level as a result of this allocation of assets? What happens to the slope of the aggregate demand curve? Will it still slope downward? Explain.

4. Suppose that the economy is currently at potential output. Also suppose that you are an economic policy maker and that a college economics student asks you to rank, if possible, your most preferred to least preferred type of shock: positive demand shock, negative demand shock, positive supply shock, negative supply shock. How would you rank them and why?

5. Explain whether the following government policies affect the aggregate demand curve or the short-run aggregate supply curve and how.

   a. The government reduces the minimum nominal wage.

   b. The government increases Temporary Assistance for Needy Families (TANF) payments, government transfers to families with dependent children.

   c. To reduce the budget deficit, the government announces that households will pay much higher taxes beginning next year.

   d. The government reduces military spending.

6. In Wageland, all workers sign annual wage contracts each year on January 1. In late January, a new computer operating system is introduced that increases labor productivity dramatically. Explain how Wageland will move from one short-run macroeconomic equilibrium to another. Illustrate with a diagram.

7. There were two major shocks to the U.S. economy in 2007, leading to the severe recession of 2007–2009. One shock was related to oil prices; the other was the slump in the housing market. This question analyzes the effect of these two shocks on GDP using the *AD–AS* framework.

   a. Draw typical aggregate demand and short-run aggregate supply curves. Label the horizontal axis "Real GDP" and the vertical axis "Aggregate price level." Label the equilibrium point E_1, the equilibrium quantity Y_1, and equilibrium price P_1.

   b. Data taken from the Department of Energy indicate that the average price of crude oil in the world increased from $54.63 per barrel on January 5, 2007, to $92.93 on December 28, 2007. Would an increase in oil prices cause a demand shock or a supply shock? Redraw the diagram from part a to illustrate the effect of this shock by shifting the appropriate curve.

   c. The Housing Price Index, published by the Office of Federal Housing Enterprise Oversight, calculates that U.S. home prices fell by an average of 3.0% in the 12 months between January 2007 and January 2008. Would the fall in home prices cause a supply shock or demand shock? Redraw the diagram from part b to illustrate the effect of this shock

by shifting the appropriate curve. Label the new equilibrium point E_3, the equilibrium quantity Y_3, and equilibrium price P_3.

   d. Compare the equilibrium points E_1 and E_3 in your diagram for part c. What was the effect of the two shocks on real GDP and the aggregate price level (increase, decrease, or indeterminate)?

8. Using aggregate demand, short-run aggregate supply, and long-run aggregate supply curves, explain the process by which each of the following economic events will move the economy from one long-run macroeconomic equilibrium to another. Illustrate with diagrams. In each case, what are the short-run and long-run effects on the aggregate price level and aggregate output?

   a. There is a decrease in households' wealth due to a decline in the stock market.

   b. The government lowers taxes, leaving households with more disposable income, with no corresponding reduction in government purchases.

9. Using aggregate demand, short-run aggregate supply, and long-run aggregate supply curves, explain the process by which each of the following government policies will move the economy from one long-run macroeconomic equilibrium to another. Illustrate with diagrams. In each case, what are the short-run and long-run effects on the aggregate price level and aggregate output?

   a. There is an increase in taxes on households.

   b. There is an increase in the quantity of money.

   c. There is an increase in government spending.

10. The economy is in short-run macroeconomic equilibrium at point E_1 in the accompanying diagram. Based on the diagram, answer the following questions.

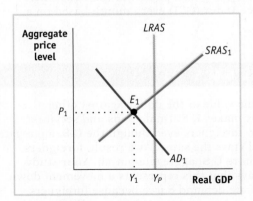

   a. Is the economy facing an inflationary or a recessionary gap?

   b. What policies can the government implement that might bring the economy back to long-run macroeconomic equilibrium? Illustrate with a diagram.

   c. If the government did not intervene to close this gap, would the economy return to long-run macroeconomic equilibrium? Explain and illustrate with a diagram.

d. What are the advantages and disadvantages of the government implementing policies to close the gap?

11. In the accompanying diagram, the economy is in long-run macroeconomic equilibrium at point E_1 when an oil shock shifts the short-run aggregate supply curve to $SRAS_2$. Based on the diagram, answer the following questions.

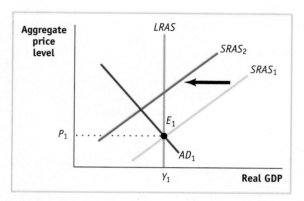

a. How do the aggregate price level and aggregate output change in the short run as a result of the oil shock? What is this phenomenon known as?

b. What fiscal or monetary policies can the government use to address the effects of the supply shock? Use a diagram that shows the effect of policies chosen to address the change in real GDP. Use another diagram to show the effect of policies chosen to address the change in the aggregate price level.

c. Why do supply shocks present a dilemma for government policy makers?

12. The late 1990s in the United States were characterized by substantial economic growth with low inflation; that is, real GDP increased with little, if any, increase in the aggregate price level. Explain this experience using aggregate demand and aggregate supply curves. Illustrate with a diagram.

WORK IT OUT

13. In each of the following cases, in the short run, determine whether the events cause a shift of a curve or a movement along a curve. Determine which curve is involved and the direction of the change.

a. As a result of an increase in the value of the dollar in relation to other currencies, U.S. producers now pay less in dollar terms for foreign steel, a major commodity used in production.

b. An increase in the quantity of money by the Fed increases the quantity of money that people wish to lend, lowering interest rates.

c. Greater union activity leads to higher nominal wages.

d. A fall in the aggregate price level increases the purchasing power of households' and firms' money holdings. As a result, they borrow less and lend more. ∎

28 Fiscal Policy

SPENDING TO FIGHT A RECESSION

2020 was the year of the coronavirus — a rapidly spreading virus that quickly infected millions around the world, in many cases requiring weeks of intensive care and in all too many cases proving fatal. The pandemic also had devastating effects on the economy, leading to the steepest decline in employment and output ever recorded.

In response, in late March Congress enacted the CARES (Coronavirus Aid, Relief, and Economic Security) Act, a $2 trillion package giving cash and loans to individuals, businesses, hospitals, and more. One main purpose of the act was to provide temporary relief to Americans who were laid off as new rules enforcing "social distancing" effectively shut down countless businesses. Across the country, restaurants were closed to limit the spread of the virus, leaving millions of food service workers unemployed.

The restaurant closure caused unemployment claims to spike. By late June 2020, almost 33 million unemployed workers were receiving unemployment compensation.

But the act had a secondary purpose: to sustain those parts of the economy that continued to function. There was good reason to fear that laid-off workers would cut spending on a wide variety of goods and services, leading to unnecessary unemployment in the nation as a whole. So the act gave adults making up to $75,000 per year a $1,200 check and an additional $500 per child. Additionally, the act also greatly increased payments to unemployed workers. Both measures were designed to aid households harmed by stay at-home orders and the closure of nonessential businesses.

While the CARES Act was in part about disaster relief, it was also an example of *fiscal policy:* changes in taxes and government spending to stabilize the economy by shifting the aggregate demand curve. In this case the fiscal policy was *expansionary*, designed to shift the aggregate demand curve *out;* fiscal policies that shift the aggregate demand curve *in* are *contractionary.*

Fiscal policy is often controversial. When in 2009 the government engaged in expansionary fiscal policy — the so-called Obama stimulus — to fight the recession that followed the 2008 financial crisis, some believed it was a mistake to increase government spending at a time of widespread distress. One member of Congress spoke for many when he declared that the government should spend *less* in hard times: "American families are tightening their belts, but they don't see government tightening its belt." There were also concerns that the new spending would widen the budget deficit. But most economists believe that expansionary fiscal policy is appropriate when the economy is depressed.

The qualification — "when the economy is depressed" — is important. In 2017, eight years after the Obama stimulus, the newly elected Trump administration passed new tax cuts. In some respects these measures looked similar to the Obama stimulus, but while some economists supported the Trump stimulus, most did not — including many who had supported the Obama stimulus. Were they being inconsistent? In reality, no: in early 2009 the U.S. economy was deeply depressed and was heading further downward. By contrast, in early 2017 the economy was growing and was close to full employment. The economists who declined to support the Trump stimulus knew that stimulus, delivered at the wrong time, was likely to be counterproductive to the economy. They understood that, in making fiscal policy, timing is crucial.

In this chapter we'll see how fiscal policy fits into the models of economic fluctuation we studied in Chapters 26 and 27. We will also see why budget deficits and government debt can be problems, and why short-run and long-run considerations can pull fiscal policy in opposite directions. ●

WHAT YOU WILL LEARN

- What is fiscal policy and why is it an essential tool in managing economic fluctuations?

- Which policies constitute **expansionary fiscal policy** and which constitute **contractionary fiscal policy?**

- Why does fiscal policy have a multiplier effect and how is this effect influenced by **automatic stabilizers?**

- Why do governments calculate the **cyclically adjusted budget balance?**

- Why can a large **public debt** and **implicit liabilities** of the government be a cause for concern?

‖ Fiscal Policy: The Basics

Modern governments in economically advanced countries spend a great deal of money and collect a lot in taxes. Figure 28-1 shows government spending and tax revenue as percentages of GDP for a selection of high-income countries in 2019. As you can see, the French government sector is relatively large, accounting for more than half of the French economy. The government of the United States plays a smaller role in the economy than those of Canada, Japan, and most European countries. But that role is still sizable, with the government playing a major role in the U.S. economy. As a result, changes in the federal budget—changes in government spending or in taxation—can have large effects on the American economy.

To analyze these effects, we begin by showing how taxes and government spending affect the economy's flow of income. Then we can see how changes in spending and tax policy affect aggregate demand.

Taxes, Purchases of Goods and Services, Government Transfers, and Borrowing

In Figure 22-1 we showed the circular flow of income and spending in the economy as a whole. One of the sectors represented in that figure was the government. Funds flow *into* the government in the form of taxes and government borrowing; funds flow *out* in the form of government purchases of goods and services and government transfers to households.

What kinds of taxes do Americans pay, and where does the money go? Figure 28-2 shows the composition of U.S. tax revenue in 2019. Taxes, of course, are required payments to the government. In the United States, taxes are collected at the national level by the federal government; at the state level by each state government; and at local levels by counties, cities, and towns. At the federal level, the taxes that generate the greatest revenue are income taxes on both personal income and corporate profits as well as *social insurance* taxes, which we'll explain shortly. At the state and local levels, the picture is more complex: these governments rely on a mix of sales taxes, property taxes, income taxes, and fees of various kinds.

Overall, taxes on personal income and corporate profits accounted for 41.2% of total government revenue in 2019; social insurance taxes accounted for 24.6%; and a variety of other taxes, collected mainly at the state and local levels, accounted for the rest.

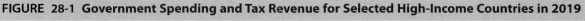

FIGURE 28-1 Government Spending and Tax Revenue for Selected High-Income Countries in 2019

Government spending and tax revenue are represented as a percentage of GDP. France has a particularly large government sector, representing more than half of its GDP. The U.S. government sector, although sizable, is smaller than those of Canada, Japan, and most European countries.

Data from: IMF World Economic Outlook.

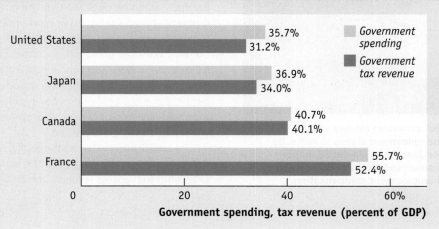

Figure 28-3 shows the composition of total U.S. government spending in 2018, which takes two broad forms. One form is purchases of goods and services. This includes everything from ammunition for the military to the salaries of public school teachers (who are treated in the national accounts as providers of a service—education). The big items here are national defense and education. The category "Other goods and services" consists mainly of state and local spending on a variety of services, from police and firefighters to highway construction and maintenance.

The other form of government spending is government transfers, which are payments by the government to households for which no good or service is provided in return. In the United States, as well as in Canada and Europe, government transfers represent a very large proportion of the budget. Most U.S. government spending on transfer payments is accounted for by the following four programs:

- Social Security, which provides guaranteed income to older Americans, disabled Americans, and the surviving spouses and dependent children of deceased or retired beneficiaries

- Medicare, which covers much of the cost of health care for Americans aged 65 or older

- Medicaid, which covers much of the cost of health care for Americans with low incomes

- The Affordable Care Act (ACA), which seeks to make health insurance available and affordable to all Americans

The term **social insurance** is used to describe government programs that are intended to protect families against economic hardship. These include Social Security, Medicare, Medicaid, and the ACA, as well as smaller programs such as unemployment insurance and food stamps. The ACA works through a system of regulated private insurance markets, subsidies, and an expansion of Medicaid eligibility and is much smaller than the other three large programs. Social insurance programs in the United States are largely paid for with special, dedicated taxes on wages—the social insurance taxes mentioned earlier. The ACA is an exception: it is funded mainly by special taxes on high incomes.

How do tax policy and government spending affect the economy? The answer is that taxation and government spending have a strong effect on total aggregate spending in the economy.

The Government Budget and Total Spending

Let's revisit the basic equation of national income accounting:

(28-1) $GDP = C + I + G + X - IM$

The left-hand side of this equation is GDP, the value of all final goods and services produced in the economy. The right-hand side is aggregate spending, total spending on final goods and services produced in the economy. It is the sum of consumer spending (C), investment spending (I), government purchases of goods and services (G), and the value of exports (X) minus the value of imports (IM). It includes all the sources of aggregate demand.

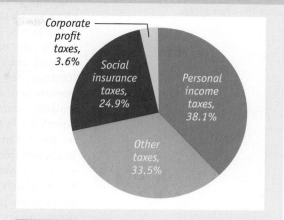

FIGURE 28-2 Sources of Tax Revenue in the United States, 2019

Personal income taxes, taxes on corporate profits, and social insurance taxes account for most government tax revenue. The rest is a mix of property taxes, sales taxes, and other sources of revenue. (Percentages may not add to 100 due to rounding.)
Data from: Bureau of Economic Analysis.

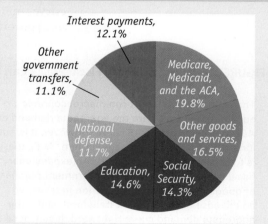

FIGURE 28-3 Government Spending in the United States, 2018

The two types of government spending are purchases of goods and services and government transfers. The biggest items in government purchases are national defense and education. The biggest items in government transfers are Social Security, Medicare, Medicaid, and the Affordable Care Act. (Percentages do not add to 100 due to rounding.)
Data from: Bureau of Economic Analysis.

Social insurance programs are government programs intended to protect families against economic hardship.

The government directly controls one of the variables on the right-hand side of Equation 28-1: government purchases of goods and services (G). But that's not the only effect fiscal policy has on aggregate spending in the economy. Through changes in taxes and transfers, it also influences consumer spending (C) and, in some cases, investment spending (I).

To see why the budget affects consumer spending, recall that *disposable income,* the total income households have available to spend, is equal to the total income they receive from wages, dividends, interest, and rent, *minus* taxes, *plus* government transfers. So either an increase in taxes or a reduction in government transfers *reduces* disposable income. And a fall in disposable income, other things equal, leads to a fall in consumer spending. Conversely, either a decrease in taxes or an increase in government transfers *increases* disposable income. And a rise in disposable income, other things equal, leads to a rise in consumer spending.

The government's ability to affect investment spending is a more complex story, which we won't discuss in detail. The important point is that the government taxes profits, and changes in the rules that determine how much a business owes can increase or reduce the incentive to spend on investment goods.

Because the government itself is one source of spending in the economy, and because taxes and transfers can affect spending by consumers and firms, the government can use changes in taxes or government spending to *shift the aggregate demand curve.* And as we saw in Chapter 27, there are sometimes good reasons to shift the aggregate demand curve.

Expansionary and Contractionary Fiscal Policy

Why would the government want to shift the aggregate demand curve? Because it wants to close either a recessionary gap, created when aggregate output falls below potential output, or an inflationary gap, created when aggregate output exceeds potential output.

Figure 28-4 shows the case of an economy facing a recessionary gap. *SRAS* is the short-run aggregate supply curve, *LRAS* is the long-run aggregate supply curve, and AD_1 is the initial aggregate demand curve. At the initial short-run macroeconomic equilibrium, E_1, aggregate output is Y_1, below potential output,

---

FIGURE 28-4 Expansionary Fiscal Policy Can Close a Recessionary Gap

The economy is in short-run macroeconomic equilibrium at E_1, where the aggregate demand curve, AD_1, intersects the *SRAS* curve. However, it is not in long-run macroeconomic equilibrium. At E_1, there is a recessionary gap of $Y_P - Y_1$. An expansionary fiscal policy—an increase in government purchases of goods and services, a reduction in taxes, or an increase in government transfers—shifts the aggregate demand curve rightward. It can close the recessionary gap by shifting AD_1 to AD_2, moving the economy to a new short-run macroeconomic equilibrium, E_2, which is also a long-run macroeconomic equilibrium.

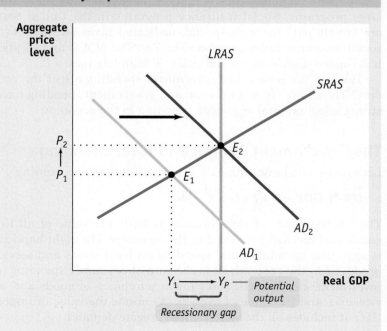

Y_P. What the government would like to do is increase aggregate demand, shifting the aggregate demand curve rightward to AD_2. This would increase aggregate output, making it equal to potential output. Fiscal policy that increases aggregate demand, called **expansionary fiscal policy,** normally takes one of three forms:

1. An increase in government purchases of goods and services
2. A cut in taxes
3. An increase in government transfers

The 2009 stimulus (or the Recovery Act) was a combination of all three: a direct increase in federal spending and aid to state governments to help them maintain spending, tax cuts for most families, and increased aid to the unemployed. The CARES Act consisted mainly of transfers: a one-time check for $1,200 for every American, expanded unemployment benefits, and subsidized loans to businesses. It also included some increase in spending on health care and aid to state governments.

Figure 28-5 shows the opposite case—an economy facing an inflationary gap. Again, *SRAS* is the short-run aggregate supply curve, *LRAS* is the long-run aggregate supply curve, and AD_1 is the initial aggregate demand curve. At the initial equilibrium, E_1, aggregate output is Y_1, above potential output, Y_P. As we'll explain in later chapters, policy makers often try to head off inflation by eliminating inflationary gaps. To eliminate the inflationary gap shown in Figure 28-5, fiscal policy must reduce aggregate demand and shift the aggregate demand curve leftward to AD_2. This reduces aggregate output and makes it equal to potential output. Fiscal policy that reduces aggregate demand, called **contractionary fiscal policy,** is the opposite of expansionary fiscal policy. It is implemented in three possible ways:

1. A reduction in government purchases of goods and services
2. An increase in taxes
3. A reduction in government transfers

A classic example of contractionary fiscal policy occurred in 1968, when U.S. policy makers grew worried about rising inflation. President Lyndon Johnson imposed a temporary 10% surcharge on taxable income—everyone's income taxes were increased by 10%. He also tried to scale back government purchases

Expansionary fiscal policy is fiscal policy that increases aggregate demand.

Contractionary fiscal policy is fiscal policy that reduces aggregate demand.

FIGURE 28-5 Contractionary Fiscal Policy Can Close an Inflationary Gap

The economy is in short-run macroeconomic equilibrium at E_1, where the aggregate demand curve, AD_1, intersects the *SRAS* curve. But it is not in long-run macroeconomic equilibrium. At E_1, there is an inflationary gap of $Y_1 - Y_P$. A contractionary fiscal policy—such as reduced government purchases of goods and services, an increase in taxes, or a reduction in government transfers—shifts the aggregate demand curve leftward. It closes the inflationary gap by shifting AD_1 to AD_2, moving the economy to a new short-run macroeconomic equilibrium, E_2, which is also a long-run macroeconomic equilibrium.

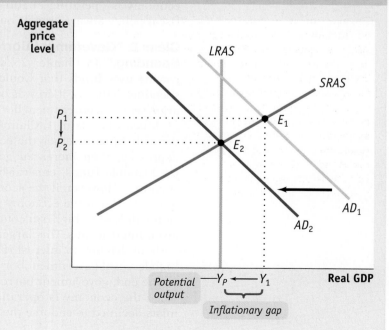

of goods and services, which had risen dramatically because of the cost of the Vietnam War.

Can Expansionary Fiscal Policy Actually Work?

In practice, the use of fiscal policy—in particular, the use of expansionary fiscal policy in the face of a recessionary gap—is often controversial. We'll examine the origins of these controversies in detail in Chapter 32. But for now, let's quickly summarize the major points of the debate over expansionary fiscal policy, so we can understand when the critiques are justified and when they are not.

There are three main arguments against the use of expansionary fiscal policy.

1. Government spending always crowds out private spending.
2. Government borrowing always crowds out private investment spending.
3. Government budget deficits lead to reduced private spending.

The first of these claims is wrong in principle, but it has nonetheless played a prominent role in public debates. The second is valid under some, but not all, circumstances. The third argument, although it raises some important issues, isn't a good reason to believe that expansionary fiscal policy doesn't work.

Claim 1: "Government Spending Always Crowds Out Private Spending."
Some claim that expansionary fiscal policy can never raise aggregate spending and therefore can never raise aggregate income, with reasons that go something like this: "Every dollar that the government spends is a dollar taken away from the private sector. So any rise in government spending must be offset by an equal fall in private spending." In other words, every dollar spent by the government *crowds out*, or displaces, a dollar of private spending.

But the statement is wrong because it assumes that resources in the economy are always fully employed and, as a result, the aggregate income earned in the economy is always a fixed sum—which isn't true. In reality, whether or not government spending crowds out private spending depends upon the state of the economy. In particular, when the economy is suffering from a recessionary gap, there are unemployed resources in the economy, and output (and therefore income) is below its potential level. Expansionary fiscal policy during these periods puts unemployed resources to work and generates higher spending and higher income. Government spending crowds out private spending only when the economy is operating at full employment. So the argument that expansionary fiscal policy always crowds out private spending is wrong in principle.

Claim 2: "Government Borrowing Always Crowds Out Private Investment Spending."
In Chapter 25, we discussed the possibility that government borrowing uses funds that would have otherwise been used for private investment spending—that is, it crowds out private investment spending. So how valid is the argument that government borrowing always reduces private investment spending?

Much like Claim 1, Claim 2 is wrong because whether crowding out occurs depends upon whether the economy is depressed or not. If the economy is not depressed, then increased government borrowing, by increasing the demand for loanable funds, can raise interest rates and crowd out private investment spending. However, if the economy is depressed, crowding out is much less likely to occur. When the economy is at far less than full employment, a fiscal expansion will lead to higher incomes, which in turn leads to increased savings at any given interest rate. This larger pool of savings allows the government to borrow without driving up interest rates. The 2009 stimulus was a case in point: despite high levels of government borrowing, U.S. interest rates stayed near historic lows. In the end, government borrowing crowds out private investment spending only when the economy is operating at full employment (which is why most economists declined to endorse the Trump administration's 2017 tax cuts).

Claim 3: "Government Budget Deficits Lead to Reduced Private Spending." Other things equal, expansionary fiscal policy leads to a larger budget deficit and greater government debt. And higher debt will eventually require the government to raise taxes to pay it off. So, according to the third argument against expansionary fiscal policy, consumers, anticipating that they must pay higher taxes in the future to pay off today's government debt, will cut their spending today in order to save money. This argument, first made by nineteenth-century economist David Ricardo, is known as *Ricardian equivalence*. It is an argument often taken to imply that expansionary fiscal policy will have no effect on the economy because far-sighted consumers will undo any attempts at expansion by the government. (And will also undo any contractionary fiscal policy, for that matter.)

In reality, however, it's doubtful that consumers behave with such foresight and budgeting discipline. Most people, when provided with extra cash (generated by fiscal expansion), will spend at least some of it. So even fiscal policy that takes the form of temporary tax cuts or transfers of cash to consumers probably does have an expansionary effect.

Moreover, it's possible to show that even with Ricardian equivalence, a temporary rise in government spending that involves direct purchases of goods and services—such as a program of road construction—would still lead to a boost in total spending in the near term. That's because even if consumers cut back their current spending in anticipation of higher future taxes, their reduced spending will take place over an extended period as consumers save over time to pay the future tax bill. Meanwhile, the additional government spending will be concentrated in the near future, when the economy needs it.

So although the effects emphasized by Ricardian equivalence may reduce the impact of fiscal expansion, the claim that it makes fiscal expansion completely ineffective is neither consistent with how consumers actually behave nor a reason to believe that increases in government spending have no effect. So, in the end, it's not a valid argument against expansionary fiscal policy.

In Sum The extent to which we should expect expansionary fiscal policy to work depends upon the circumstances. When the economy has a recessionary gap—as it did when the 2009 stimulus was passed—economics tells us that this is just the kind of situation in which expansionary fiscal policy helps the economy. However, when the economy is already at full employment, as it seemed to be in 2017, when the Trump tax cuts went into effect, expansionary fiscal policy is the wrong policy and will lead to crowding out, an overheated economy, and higher inflation. (As it turned out, the economy was probably further from full employment in 2017 than most economists believed, so that the adverse effects of the stimulus weren't obvious.)

A Cautionary Note: Lags in Fiscal Policy

Looking back at Figures 28-4 and 28-5, it may seem obvious that the government should actively use fiscal policy—always adopting an expansionary fiscal policy when the economy faces a recessionary gap and always adopting a contractionary fiscal policy when the economy faces an inflationary gap. But many economists caution against an extremely active stabilization policy, arguing that a government that tries too hard to stabilize the economy—through either fiscal policy or monetary policy—can end up making the economy less stable.

We'll leave discussion of the warnings associated with monetary policy to Chapter 30. In the case of fiscal policy, one key reason for caution is that there are important *time lags* between when the policy is decided upon and when it is implemented. To understand the nature of these lags, consider the three things that have to happen before the government increases spending to fight a recessionary gap.

1. The government has to realize that the recessionary gap exists: economic data take time to collect and analyze, and recessions are often recognized

only months after they have begun. Although the Great Recession is generally considered to have begun in December 2007, as late as September 2008 some economists were still questioning whether the recession was real.

2. The government has to develop a spending plan, which can itself take months, particularly if politicians take time debating how the money should be spent and passing legislation.

3. It takes time to spend money. For example, a road construction project begins with activities such as surveying that don't involve spending large sums. It may be quite some time before the big spending begins. The Recovery Act was passed in the first quarter of 2009, but much of its effect on federal spending, especially purchases of goods and services, didn't come until 2011.

Because of these lags, an attempt to increase spending to fight a recessionary gap may take so long to get going that the economy has already recovered on its own. In fact, the recessionary gap may have turned into an inflationary gap by the time expansionary fiscal policy takes effect. In that case, expansionary fiscal policy will make things worse instead of better.

In making fiscal policy, timing is crucial.

This doesn't mean that fiscal policy should never be actively used. In early 2009 there was good reason to believe that the slump facing the U.S. economy would be both deep and long and that a fiscal stimulus designed to arrive over the next year or two would almost surely push aggregate demand in the right direction. In fact, as we'll see later in this chapter, the 2009 stimulus arguably faded out too soon, leaving the economy still deeply depressed when it ended. But the problem of lags makes the actual use of both fiscal and monetary policy harder than you might think from a simple analysis like the one we have just given.

ECONOMICS >> *in Action*
A Tale of Two Stimuli

There were some broad similarities between the Obama stimulus of 2009 and proposals that were floated by the Trump administration soon after it took office in early 2017, including the passage of new tax cuts that started in 2018 and proposed new infrastructure spending. Yet many economists who supported the Obama stimulus were dubious about the Trump plan, because the state of the economy had changed.

Figure 28-6 shows two indicators that played an important role in policy discussions at both times. One is the unemployment rate. The other is the *quits rate*, the fraction of workers voluntarily leaving their jobs each month. This rate is widely viewed as an indication of how good the labor market is: workers are reluctant to quit if they believe new jobs are very hard to find. For this reason, the quits rate is a useful backup to the unemployment rate: if you're unsure whether the unemployment rate is giving an accurate read on the situation, you can check whether the quits rate is telling the same story.

FIGURE 28-6 Comparing the State of the U.S. Economy in 2009 and 2017

Unemployment rate (percent)

Quits rate (percent of total employment)

Unemployment rate

Quits rate

11%
10
9
8
7
6
5
4

2.25%
2.00
1.75
1.50
1.25
1.00

2007 2009 2011 2013 2015 2017 2019

Year

Data from: Federal Reserve Bank of St. Louis.

What you can see from Figure 28-6 is that in early 2009 the United States showed all the signs of a deeply depressed economy, in the grip of an accelerating plunge, with unemployment high and rising and the quits rate low and falling. By late 2017, when the tax cuts took effect, however, the data were telling the opposite story: a low unemployment rate and a high quits rate indicated that jobs were relatively plentiful.

This difference meant that the case for expansionary fiscal policy was much weaker in 2017 than it had been in 2009: under 2017 conditions it seemed likely that increased government spending would crowd out private spending and that increased government borrowing would crowd out private investment. It was possible to favor the Trump administration's proposals for a variety of reasons. But the macroeconomics of fiscal policy made the potential downside much higher than it had been in 2009.

>> Check Your Understanding 28-1

Solutions appear at back of book.

1. In each of the following cases, determine whether the policy is expansionary or contractionary fiscal policy.
   a. Several military bases around the country, which together employ tens of thousands of people, are closed.
   b. The number of weeks an unemployed person is eligible for unemployment benefits is increased.
   c. The federal tax on gasoline is increased.
2. Explain why federal disaster relief, which quickly disburses funds to victims of natural disasters such as hurricanes, floods, and large-scale crop failures, will stabilize the economy more effectively after a disaster than relief that must be legislated.
3. Is the following statement true or false? Explain. "When the government expands, the private sector shrinks; when the government shrinks, the private sector expands."

‖ Fiscal Policy and the Multiplier

An expansionary fiscal policy, like the 2009 stimulus, pushes the aggregate demand curve to the right. A contractionary fiscal policy pushes the aggregate demand curve to the left. For policy makers, however, knowing the direction of the shift isn't enough: they need estimates of *how much* a given policy will shift the aggregate demand curve. To get these estimates, they use the concept of the multiplier, which we learned about in Chapter 26.

Multiplier Effects of an Increase in Government Purchases of Goods and Services

Suppose that a government decides to spend $50 billion building bridges and roads. The government's purchases of goods and services will directly increase total spending on final goods and services by $50 billion. But as we learned in Chapter 26, there will also be an indirect effect: the government's purchases will start a chain reaction throughout the economy. The firms that produce the goods and services purchased by the government earn revenues that flow to households in the form of wages, profits, interest, and rent. This increase in disposable income leads to a rise in consumer spending. The rise in consumer spending, in turn, induces firms to increase output, leading to a further rise in disposable income, which leads to another round of consumer spending increases, and so on.

As we know, the *multiplier* is the ratio of the change in real GDP caused by an autonomous change in aggregate spending to the size of that autonomous change. An increase in government purchases of goods and services is a prime example of such an autonomous increase in aggregate spending.

Expansionary or contractionary fiscal policy will start a chain reaction throughout the economy.

Grafissimo/Getty Images

In Chapter 26 we considered a simple case in which there are no taxes or international trade, so that any change in GDP accrues entirely to households. We also assumed that the aggregate price level is fixed, so that any increase in nominal GDP is also a rise in real GDP, and that the interest rate is fixed. In that case the multiplier is $1/(1 - MPC)$. Recall that MPC is the *marginal propensity to consume*, the fraction of an additional dollar in disposable income that is spent. For example, if the marginal propensity to consume is 0.5, the multiplier is $1/(1 - 0.5) = 1/0.5 = 2$. Given a multiplier of 2, a $50 billion increase in government purchases of goods and services would increase real GDP by $100 billion. Of that $100 billion, $50 billion is the initial effect from the increase in G, and the remaining $50 billion is the subsequent effect arising from the increase in consumer spending.

What happens if government purchases of goods and services are instead reduced? The math is exactly the same, except that there's a minus sign in front: if government purchases of goods and services fall by $50 billion and the marginal propensity to consume is 0.5, real GDP falls by $100 billion.

Multiplier Effects of Changes in Government Transfers and Taxes

Expansionary or contractionary fiscal policy need not take the form of changes in government purchases of goods and services. Governments can also change transfer payments or taxes. In general, however, a change in government transfers or taxes shifts the aggregate demand curve by *less* than an equal-sized change in government purchases, resulting in a smaller effect on real GDP.

To see why, imagine that instead of spending $50 billion on building bridges, the government simply hands out $50 billion in the form of government transfers. In this case, there is no direct effect on aggregate demand, as there was with government purchases of goods and services. Real GDP goes up because households spend some of that $50 billion—but they won't spend it all.

Table 28-1 shows a hypothetical comparison of two expansionary fiscal policies assuming an MPC equal to 0.5: one in which the government directly purchases $50 billion in goods and services and one in which the government makes transfer payments instead, sending out $50 billion in checks to consumers. In each case there is a first-round effect on real GDP, either from purchases by the government or from purchases by the consumers who received the checks, followed by a series of additional rounds as rising real GDP raises disposable income.

However, the first-round effect of the transfer program is smaller. Because we have assumed that the MPC is 0.5, only $25 billion of the $50 billion is spent, with the other $25 billion saved. And as a result, all the further rounds are smaller, too. In the end, the transfer payment increases real GDP by only $50 billion, equal to $MPC \times 1/(1 - MPC)$. In comparison, a $50 billion increase in government purchases produces a $100 billion increase in real GDP, equal to $1/(1 - MPC)$.

Overall, when expansionary fiscal policy takes the form of a rise in transfer payments, real GDP may rise by either more or less than the initial government outlay—that is, the multiplier may be either more or less than 1 depending upon the size of the MPC. In Table 28-1, with an MPC equal to 0.5, the multiplier is exactly 1: a $50 billion rise in transfer payments increases real GDP by $50 billion. If the MPC is less than 0.5, so that a smaller share of the initial transfer is spent, the multiplier

TABLE 28-1 Hypothetical Effects of a Fiscal Policy When $MPC = 0.5$		
Effect on real GDP	$50 billion rise in government purchases of goods and services	$50 billion rise in government transfer payments
First round	$50 billion	$25 billion
Second round	$25 billion	$12.5 billion
Third round	$12.5 billion	$6.25 billion
·	·	·
·	·	·
·	·	·
Total effect	$100 billion	$50 billion
Total effect in terms of multiplier	$\Delta Y = \Delta G \times 1/(1 - MPC)$	$\Delta Y = \Delta TR \times MPC \times 1/(1 - MPC)$

on that transfer is *less* than 1. If a larger share of the initial transfer is spent, the multiplier is *more* than 1.

A tax cut has an effect similar to the effect of a transfer. It increases disposable income, leading to a series of increases in consumer spending. But the overall effect is smaller than that of an equal-sized increase in government purchases of goods and services: the autonomous increase in aggregate spending is smaller because households save part of the amount of the tax cut.

We should also note that taxes introduce a further complication—they typically change the size of the multiplier. That's because in the real world governments rarely impose **lump-sum taxes,** in which the amount of tax a household owes is independent of its income. With lump-sum taxes there is no change in the multiplier. Instead, the great majority of tax revenue is raised via taxes that are not lump-sum, and so tax revenue depends upon the level of real GDP. As we'll discuss shortly, and analyze in detail in this chapter's appendix, non-lump-sum taxes reduce the size of the multiplier.

In practice, economists often argue that the size of the multiplier determines *who* among the population should get tax cuts or increases in government transfers. For example, compare the effects of an increase in unemployment benefits to a cut in taxes on profits distributed to shareholders as dividends. Consumer surveys suggest that the average unemployed worker will spend a higher share of any increase in their disposable income than would the average recipient of dividend income. That is, people who are unemployed tend to have a higher *MPC* than people who own a lot of stocks because the latter tend to be wealthier and tend to save more of any increase in disposable income. If that's true, a dollar spent on unemployment benefits increases aggregate demand more than a dollar's worth of dividend tax cuts.

How Taxes Affect the Multiplier

When we introduced the analysis of the multiplier in Chapter 26, we simplified matters by assuming that a $1 increase in real GDP raises disposable income by $1. In fact, however, government taxes capture some part of the increase in real GDP that occurs in each round of the multiplier process, since most government taxes depend positively on real GDP. As a result, disposable income increases by considerably less than $1 once we include taxes in the model.

The increase in government tax revenue when real GDP rises isn't the result of a deliberate decision or action by the government. It's a consequence of the way the tax laws are written, which causes most sources of government revenue to increase *automatically* when real GDP goes up. For example, income tax receipts increase when real GDP rises because the amount each individual owes in taxes depends positively on their income, and households' taxable incomes rise when real GDP rises. Sales tax receipts increase when real GDP rises because people with more income spend more on goods and services. And corporate profit tax receipts increase when real GDP rises because profits increase when the economy expands.

The effect of these automatic increases in tax revenue is to reduce the size of the multiplier. Remember, the multiplier is the result of a chain reaction in which higher real GDP leads to higher disposable income, which leads to higher consumer spending, which leads to further increases in real GDP. The fact that the government siphons off some of any increase in real GDP means that at each stage of this process, the increase in consumer spending is smaller than it would be if taxes weren't part of the picture. The result is to reduce the multiplier.

In fact, the effect of taxes on the multiplier is very similar to the effect of international trade, which also reduces the multiplier. In one case the multiplier process is weakened because at each stage some spending "leaks" into imports; in the other case, income "leaks" into taxes. The appendix to this chapter shows how to derive the multiplier when taxes that depend positively on real GDP are taken into account.

Lump-sum taxes are taxes that don't depend on the taxpayer's income.

Automatic stabilizers are government spending and taxation rules that cause fiscal policy to be automatically expansionary when the economy contracts and automatically contractionary when the economy expands.

Discretionary fiscal policy is fiscal policy that is the result of deliberate actions by policy makers rather than rules.

Many macroeconomists believe it's a good thing that taxes reduce the multiplier. In the previous chapter we argued that most, though not all, recessions are the result of negative demand shocks. The same mechanism that makes tax revenue increase when the economy expands makes tax revenue decrease when the economy contracts. Since tax receipts decrease when real GDP falls, the effects of these negative demand shocks are smaller than they would be in a world in which there were no taxes. The decrease in tax revenue reduces the adverse effect of the initial fall in aggregate demand.

The automatic decrease in government tax revenue generated by a fall in real GDP—caused by a decrease in the amount of taxes households pay—acts like an automatic expansionary fiscal policy implemented in the face of a recession. Similarly, when the economy expands, the government finds itself automatically pursuing contractionary fiscal policy—a tax increase. Government spending and taxation rules that cause fiscal policy to be automatically expansionary when the economy contracts and automatically contractionary when the economy expands, without requiring any deliberate action by policy makers, are called **automatic stabilizers.**

The rules that govern tax collection aren't the only automatic stabilizers, although they are the most important ones. Some types of government transfers also play a stabilizing role. For example, more people receive unemployment insurance when the economy is depressed than when it is booming. The same is true of

Medicaid and food stamps. So transfer payments tend to rise when the economy is contracting and fall when the economy is expanding. Like changes in tax revenue, these automatic changes in transfers tend to reduce the size of the multiplier because the total change in disposable income that results from a given rise or fall in real GDP is smaller.

As in the case of government tax revenue, many macroeconomists believe that it's a good thing that government transfers reduce the multiplier. Expansionary and contractionary fiscal policies that are the result of automatic stabilizers are widely considered helpful to macroeconomic stabilization because they blunt the extremes of the business cycle.

But what about fiscal policy that *isn't* the result of automatic stabilizers? **Discretionary fiscal policy** is the direct result of deliberate actions by policy makers rather than automatic adjustment. For example, during a recession, the government may pass legislation that cuts taxes and increases government spending in order to stimulate the economy. In general, economists tend to support the use of discretionary fiscal policy only in the case of a severe recession or sustained economic weakness.

During the Great Depression, the Works Progress Administration (WPA), an example of discretionary fiscal policy, put millions of unemployed Americans to work constructing bridges, roads, buildings, dams, and parks.

ECONOMICS >> *in Action*
Austerity and the Multiplier

We've explained the logic of the fiscal multiplier, but what empirical evidence do economists have about multiplier effects in practice? Until a few years ago, the answer would have been that we didn't have nearly as much evidence as we'd like.

The problem was that large changes in fiscal policy are fairly rare, and usually happen at the same time other things are taking place, making it hard to separate the effects of spending and taxes from those of other factors. For example, the U.S. government drastically increased spending during World War II. But it also instituted rationing of many consumer goods and restricted construction of new homes in order to conserve resources for the war effort. So it is hard to distinguish the effects of the increase in government spending from the transformation of a peacetime economy to a war economy.

However, more recent events offer considerable new evidence. In the wake of the Global Financial Crisis of 2009, several European governments found themselves facing debt crises. As loans they had taken out came due, these governments were either unable to raise new funds or were forced to pay extremely high interest rates. As a result, they had to turn to the rest of Europe for aid. In an attempt to reduce budget deficits, a condition of this aid was *austerity*—sharp cuts in spending plus tax increases. Austerity is a form of contractionary fiscal policy. So by comparing the economic performance of countries forced into austerity with the performance of countries that weren't, we get a relatively clear view of the effects of changes in spending and taxes.

Figure 28-7 compares the amount of austerity imposed in a number of countries between 2009 and 2013 to the growth in their GDP over the same period. (We end the analysis in 2013 because European debt markets calmed down in late 2012, and the pressure for harsh austerity was greatly reduced.) Austerity is measured on the horizontal axis by the change in the *cyclically adjusted budget balance*, defined later in this chapter. As you can see, Greece stands out. It was forced to impose severe spending cuts and suffered a huge fall in output. But even without Greece there is a clear negative relationship. A line fitted through the scatterplot has a slope of –1.5. That is, the figure suggests that spending cuts and tax increases had an average multiplier of 1.5. Put another way, a contractionary fiscal policy that took $1 out of the economy resulted in a $1.50 fall in GDP.

Economists have offered a number of qualifications and caveats to this result, given that this wasn't truly a controlled experiment. Yet recent experience strongly supports the proposition that fiscal policy does indeed move GDP in the predicted direction, with a multiplier of more than 1.

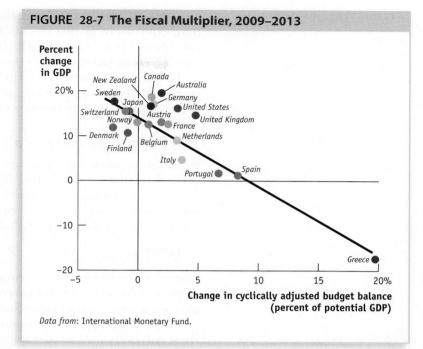

FIGURE 28-7 The Fiscal Multiplier, 2009–2013

Data from: International Monetary Fund.

>> Check Your Understanding 28-2

Solutions appear at back of book.

1. Explain why a $500 million increase in government purchases of goods and services will generate a larger rise in real GDP than a $500 million increase in government transfers.

2. Explain why a $500 million reduction in government purchases of goods and services will generate a larger fall in real GDP than a $500 million reduction in government transfers.

3. The country of Boldovia has no unemployment insurance benefits and a tax system using only lump-sum taxes. The neighboring country of Moldovia has generous unemployment benefits and a tax system in which residents must pay a percentage of their income. Which country will experience greater variation in real GDP in response to positive and negative demand shocks? Explain.

The Budget Balance

Headlines about the government's budget tend to focus on just one point: whether the government is running a surplus or a deficit and, in either case, how big. People usually think of surpluses as good: when the federal government ran a record surplus in 2000, many people regarded it as a cause for celebration. Conversely, people usually think of deficits as bad: when the U.S. federal government ran record deficits from 2009 to 2011, many people regarded it as a cause for concern.

How do surpluses and deficits fit into the analysis of fiscal policy? Are deficits ever a good thing and surpluses a bad thing? To answer those questions, let's look at the causes and consequences of surpluses and deficits.

The Budget Balance as a Measure of Fiscal Policy

What do we mean by surpluses and deficits? The budget balance, which was defined in Chapter 25, is the difference between the government's revenue, in the form of tax revenue, and its spending, both on goods and services and on government transfers, in a given year. That is, the budget balance—savings by government—is defined by Equation 28-2 (which is the same as Equation 25-7):

(28-2) $S_{Government} = T - G - TR$

where T is the value of tax revenues, G is government purchases of goods and services, and TR is the value of government transfers. As we've learned, a budget surplus is a positive budget balance and a budget deficit is a negative budget balance.

Other things equal, expansionary fiscal policies—increased government purchases of goods and services, higher government transfers, or lower taxes—reduce the budget balance for that year. That is, expansionary fiscal policies make a budget surplus smaller or a budget deficit bigger. Conversely, contractionary fiscal policies—reduced government purchases of goods and services, lower government transfers, or higher taxes—increase the budget balance for that year, making a budget surplus bigger or a budget deficit smaller.

You might think this means that changes in the budget balance can be used to measure fiscal policy. In fact, economists often do just that: they use changes in the budget balance as a "quick-and-dirty" way to assess whether current fiscal policy is expansionary or contractionary. But they always keep in mind two reasons this quick-and-dirty approach is sometimes misleading:

1. Two different changes in fiscal policy that have equal-sized effects on the budget balance may have quite unequal effects on the economy. As we have already seen, changes in government purchases of goods and services have a larger effect on real GDP than equal-sized changes in taxes and government transfers.

2. Often, changes in the budget balance are themselves the result, not the cause, of fluctuations in the economy.

To understand the second point, we need to examine the effects of the business cycle on the budget.

The Business Cycle and the Cyclically Adjusted Budget Balance

Historically there has been a strong relationship between the federal government's budget balance and the business cycle. The budget tends to move into deficit when the economy experiences a recession, but deficits tend to get smaller or even turn into surpluses when the economy is expanding. Figure 28-8 shows the federal budget deficit as a percentage of GDP from 1964 to 2019. Shaded areas indicate recessions; unshaded areas indicate expansions. As you can see, the federal budget deficit increased around the time of each recession and usually declined during expansions. In fact, in the late stages of the long expansion from 1991 to through early 2001, the deficit actually became negative—the budget deficit became a budget surplus.

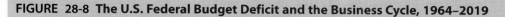

FIGURE 28-8 The U.S. Federal Budget Deficit and the Business Cycle, 1964–2019

The budget deficit as a percentage of GDP tends to rise during recessions (indicated by shaded areas) and fall during expansions.

Data from: Federal Reserve Bank of St. Louis.

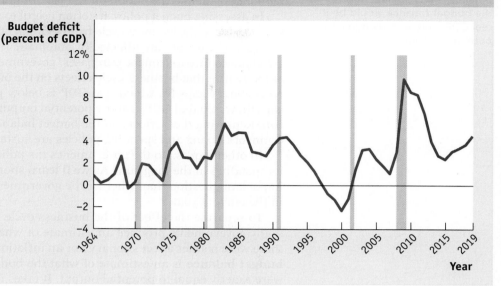

The relationship between the business cycle and the budget balance is even clearer if we compare the budget deficit as a percentage of GDP with the unemployment rate, as we do in Figure 28-9. The budget deficit almost always rises when the unemployment rate rises and falls when the unemployment rate falls.

Is this relationship between the business cycle and the budget balance evidence that policy makers engage in discretionary fiscal policy, using expansionary fiscal policy during recessions and contractionary fiscal policy during expansions? Not necessarily. To a large extent the relationship in Figure 28-9 reflects automatic stabilizers at work. As we saw earlier in the discussion of automatic stabilizers, government tax revenue tends to rise and some government transfers, like unemployment benefit payments, tend to fall when the economy expands. Conversely, government tax revenue tends to fall and some government transfers tend to rise when the economy contracts. So the budget tends to move

FIGURE 28-9 The U.S. Federal Budget Deficit and the Unemployment Rate, 1964–2019

There is a close relationship between the budget balance and the business cycle: a recession moves the budget balance toward deficit, but an expansion moves it toward surplus. Here, the unemployment rate serves as an indicator of the business cycle, and we should expect to see a higher unemployment rate associated with a higher budget deficit. This is confirmed by the figure: the budget deficit as a percentage of GDP moves closely in tandem with the unemployment rate.

Data from: Federal Reserve Bank of St. Louis.

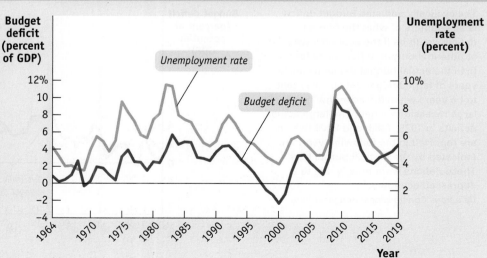

The **cyclically adjusted budget balance** is an estimate of what the budget balance would be if real GDP were exactly equal to potential output.

toward surplus during expansions and toward deficit during recessions even without any deliberate action on the part of policy makers.

In assessing budget policy, it's often useful to separate movements in the budget balance due to the business cycle from movements due to discretionary fiscal policy changes. The former are affected by automatic stabilizers and the latter by deliberate changes in government purchases, government transfers, or taxes. It's important to realize that business-cycle effects on the budget balance are temporary: both recessionary gaps (in which real GDP is below potential output) and inflationary gaps (in which real GDP is above potential output) tend to be eliminated in the long run. Removing their effects on the budget balance sheds light on whether the government's taxing and spending policies are sustainable in the long run.

In other words, do the government's tax policies yield enough revenue to fund its spending in the long run? As we'll learn shortly, this is a fundamentally more important question than whether the government runs a budget surplus or deficit in the current year.

To separate the effect of the business cycle from the effects of other factors, many governments produce an estimate of what the budget balance would be if there were neither a recessionary nor an inflationary gap. The **cyclically adjusted budget balance** is an estimate of what the budget balance would be if real GDP were exactly equal to potential output. It takes into account the extra tax revenue the government would collect and the transfers it would save if a recessionary gap were eliminated—or the revenue the government would lose and the extra transfers it would make if an inflationary gap were eliminated.

Figure 28-10 shows the actual budget deficit and the Congressional Budget Office estimate of the cyclically adjusted budget deficit, both as a percentage of potential GDP, from 1965 to 2019. As you can see, the cyclically adjusted budget deficit doesn't fluctuate as much as the actual budget deficit. In particular, large actual deficits, such as those of 1975, 1983, and 2009 (indicated by the purple bars), are mostly due to a depressed economy.

Should the Budget Be Balanced?

Persistent budget deficits can cause problems for both the government and the economy. Yet politicians are often tempted to run deficits because this allows them to cater to voters by cutting taxes without cutting spending or by increasing

---

FIGURE 28-10 The Actual Budget Deficit versus the Cyclically Adjusted Budget Deficit, 1965–2019

The cyclically adjusted budget deficit is an estimate of what the budget deficit would be if the economy was at potential output. It fluctuates less than the actual budget deficit because years of large budget deficits also tend to be years when the economy has a large recessionary gap. The large actual deficits in 1975, 1983, and 2009 (which are reported in the following year) are indicated by the vertical purple bars. These deficits were mostly due to a depressed economy.

Data from: Congressional Budget Office.

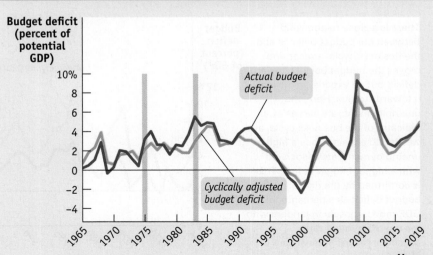

spending without increasing taxes. As a result, there are occasional attempts by policy makers to force fiscal discipline by introducing legislation—even a constitutional amendment—forbidding the government from running budget deficits. This is usually stated as a requirement that the budget be balanced—that revenues at least equal spending each fiscal year. Would it be a good idea to require a balanced budget annually?

Most economists don't think so. They believe that the government should only balance its budget on average—that it should be allowed to run deficits in bad years, offset by surpluses in good years. They don't believe the government should be forced to run a balanced budget *every year* because this would undermine the role of taxes and transfers as automatic stabilizers.

As we've learned, the tendency of tax revenue to fall and transfers to rise when the economy contracts helps to limit the size of recessions. But falling tax revenue and rising transfer payments generated by a downturn in the economy push the budget toward deficit. If constrained by a balanced-budget rule, the government would have to respond to this deficit with contractionary fiscal policies that would tend to deepen a recession.

Yet policy makers concerned about excessive deficits sometimes feel that rigid rules prohibiting—or at least setting an upper limit on—deficits are necessary. In fact, as the following Economics in Action explains, state and local governments do have such rules, which had a major impact on fiscal policy during the Great Recession and in its aftermath.

ECONOMICS >> *in Action*
Trying to Balance Budgets in a Recession

When the Great Recession struck, the U.S. federal government's budget deficit increased from just $160 billion to $1.4 trillion, partly because of stimulus measures but mainly because of automatic stabilizers: revenue fell sharply, while some expenditures, especially unemployment benefits, rose. Many observers worried about this deficit, but most economists thought that trying to balance the budget in the face of a recession would actually make that recession worse.

When it comes to government spending in America, however, the federal government isn't the only player. State and local governments account for about 40% of total government spending, and most government employment. (Most government employees are in positions that deliver essential services, such as schoolteachers, police officers, and firefighters.) And almost all of these state and local governments have rules requiring that they balance their budgets all the time.

There are a number of reasons for these rules, which make sense for each individual state or city. Taken together, however, the rules mean that for a large part of government in the United States, automatic stabilizers don't work. In fact, state and local governments cut back sharply in the face of a depressed economy, especially after 2010, when federal aid from the 2009 stimulus ended. Figure 28-11 shows the number of state and local employees from 2000 to 2020; as you can see, from 2009 until 2013 (the period shaded in purple), there were large cuts, mainly layoffs of teachers, in the face of falling revenues.

FIGURE 28-11 State and Local Government Employment, 2000–2020

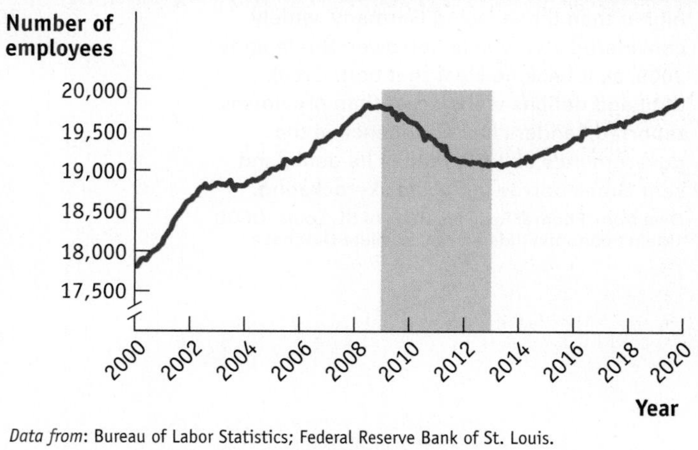

Data from: Bureau of Labor Statistics; Federal Reserve Bank of St. Louis.

These actions at the state and local levels didn't fully offset the effects of automatic stabilizers at the federal level, but they still probably caused the recession to be deeper and the recovery slower than it would have been if we didn't have multiple levels of government, with the lower levels required to run balanced budgets.

>> **Check Your Understanding 28-3**
Solutions appear at back of book.

1. Why is the cyclically adjusted budget balance a better measure of whether government policies are sustainable in the long run than the actual budget balance is?

2. Explain why states required by their constitutions to balance their budgets are likely to experience more severe economic fluctuations than states not held to that requirement.

‖ Long-Run Implications of Fiscal Policy

At the end of 2009, the government of Greece ran into a financial wall. Like most other governments in Europe (and the U.S. government, too), the Greek government was running a large budget deficit, which meant that it needed to keep borrowing more funds, both to cover its expenses and to pay off existing loans as they came due. But governments, like countries or individuals, can only borrow if lenders believe it's likely that they will eventually be willing or able to repay their debts. By 2009 many lenders had lost faith in Greece's financial future, and they were no longer willing to lend to the Greek government. Those few who were willing to lend demanded very high interest rates to compensate them for the risk of loss.

Figure 28-12 compares interest rates on 10-year bonds issued by the governments of Greece and Germany. At the beginning of 2007, Greece could borrow at almost the same rate as Germany, widely considered a very safe borrower. In 2009 its borrowing costs started to climb, and by the end of 2011 Greece had to pay an interest rate around 10 times the rate Germany paid.

What precipitated the crisis? In 2009 it became clear that the Greek government had used creative accounting to hide just how much debt it had already taken on. Government debt is, after all, a promise to make future payments to lenders. By 2010 it seemed likely that the Greek government had already promised more than it could possibly deliver.

FIGURE 28-12 Greek and German Long-Term Interest Rates

As late as 2008, the government of Greece could borrow at interest rates only slightly higher than those facing Germany, widely considered a very safe borrower. But in early 2009, as it became clear that both Greek debt and deficits were larger than previously reported, lenders lost confidence in the government's ability to repay its debts and sent Greek borrowing costs skyrocketing.
Data from: Federal Reserve Bank of St. Louis; OECD "Main Economic Indicators Complete Database."

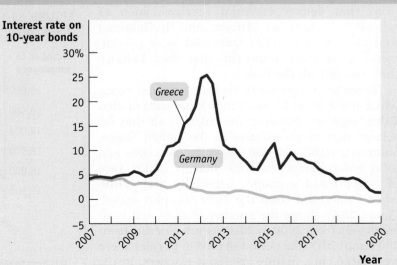

Lenders became deeply worried that the level of Greek government debt was unsustainable—that is, it was unlikely to repay what was owed. As a result, Greece found itself largely shut out of private debt markets. In order to prevent a government collapse, it received emergency loans from other European nations and the International Monetary Fund. But these loans came with the requirement that the Greek government undertake austerity, by making severe spending cuts and sharply raising taxes. Austerity in Greece wreaked havoc with the economy, imposed severe economic hardship on citizens, and led to massive social unrest.

The 2009 crisis in Greece shows why no discussion of fiscal policy is complete without taking into account the long-run implications of government budget surpluses and deficits, especially the implications for government debt. We now turn to those long-run implications.

Deficits, Surpluses, and Debt

When a family spends more than it earns over the course of a year, it has to raise the extra funds either by selling assets or by borrowing. And if a family borrows year after year, it will eventually end up with a lot of debt.

The same is true for governments. With a few exceptions, governments don't raise large sums by selling assets such as national parkland. Instead, when a government spends more than the tax revenue it receives—when it runs a budget deficit—it almost always borrows the extra funds. And governments that run persistent budget deficits end up with substantial debts.

To interpret the numbers that follow, you need to know a slightly peculiar feature of federal government accounting. For historical reasons, the U.S. government does not keep books by calendar years. Instead, budget totals are kept by **fiscal years,** which run from October 1 to September 30 and are labeled by the calendar year in which they end. For example, fiscal 2019 began on October 1, 2018, and ended on September 30, 2019.

At the end of fiscal 2019, the U.S. federal government had total debt equal to $21.2 trillion. However, part of that debt represented special accounting rules specifying that the federal government as a whole owes funds to certain government programs, especially Social Security. We'll explain those rules shortly. For now, however, let's focus on **public debt:** federal government debt held by individuals and institutions outside the government. At the end of fiscal 2019, the federal government's public debt was "only" $16.8 trillion, or 79% of GDP. Federal public debt at the end of 2019 was larger than at the end of 2018 because the government ran a deficit in 2019: a government that runs persistent budget deficits will experience a rising level of public debt. Why is this a problem?

Potential Dangers Posed by Rising Government Debt

There are two reasons to be concerned when a government runs persistent budget deficits that result in government debt that rises over time.

1. Crowding Out When the economy is at full employment and the government borrows funds in the financial markets, it is competing with firms that plan to borrow funds for investment spending. As a result, the government's borrowing may crowd out private investment spending, increasing interest rates and reducing the economy's long-run rate of growth.

2. Financial Pressure and Default Today's deficits, by increasing the government's debt, place financial pressure on future budgets. The impact of current deficits on future budgets is straightforward. Like individuals, governments must

A **fiscal year** runs from October 1 to September 30 and is labeled according to the calendar year in which it ends.

Public debt is government debt held by individuals and institutions outside the government.

PITFALLS

DEFICITS VERSUS DEBT

Deficits and *debt* aren't the same thing.

A *deficit* is the difference between the amount of money a government spends and the amount it receives in taxes over a given period—usually, though not always, a year. Deficit numbers always come with a statement about the time period to which they apply, as in "the U.S. budget deficit *in fiscal 2019* was $984 billion."

A *debt* is the sum of money a government owes at a particular point in time. Debt numbers usually come with a specific date, as in "U.S. public debt *at the end of fiscal 2019* was $16.8 trillion."

Deficits and debt are linked, because government debt grows when governments run deficits. But they are different concepts that can even tell different stories. For example, Italy had a fairly small deficit by historical standards in 2019, but had a very high debt, a legacy of past policies.

A **debt spiral** takes place when the interest on government debt drives that debt even higher.

pay their bills, including interest payments on their accumulated debt. When a government is deeply in debt, those interest payments can be substantial. In fiscal 2019, the U.S. federal government paid 1.8% of GDP, or $347 billion, in interest on its debt. The more heavily indebted government of Italy paid interest of 3.7% of its GDP in 2019, according to estimates.

Other things equal, a government paying large sums in interest must raise more revenue from taxes or spend less than it would otherwise be able to afford—or it must borrow even more to cover the gap. And a government that borrows to pay interest on its outstanding debt may push itself even deeper into debt—a process known as a **debt spiral.** This process can eventually push a government to the point where lenders question its ability to repay. Like a consumer who has maxed out their credit cards, it will find that lenders are unwilling to lend any more funds. The result can be that the government defaults on its debt—it stops paying what it owes. Default is often followed by deep financial and economic turmoil.

Americans aren't used to the idea of government default, but it does happen. In the 1990s Argentina, a relatively high-income developing country, was widely praised for its economic policies—and it was able to borrow large sums from foreign lenders. By 2001, however, Argentina's interest payments were spiraling out of control, and the country defaulted. It eventually reached a settlement with most of its lenders under which it paid less than a third of the amount originally due.

Default creates havoc in a country's financial markets and badly shakes public confidence in both the government and the economy. Argentina's debt default was accompanied by a crisis in the country's banking system and a very severe recession. And even if a highly indebted government avoids default, a heavy debt

GLOBAL COMPARISON   THE AMERICAN WAY OF DEBT

How does the public debt of the United States stack up internationally? In dollar terms, we're number one—but this isn't very informative, since the U.S. economy and so the government's tax base are much larger than those of all but a few other nations. A more informative comparison is the ratio of public debt to GDP.

The figure shows the *net public debt* of a number of rich countries as a percentage of GDP at the end of 2019. Net public debt is government debt minus any assets governments may have—an adjustment that can make a big difference. What you see here is that the United States is more or less in the middle of the pack.

It may not surprise you that Greece heads the list, and most of the other high net debt countries are European nations that made headlines for their debt problems. Interestingly, however, Japan is also high on the list because it has used massive public spending to prop up its economy ever since the 1990s. Investors, however, still consider Japan a reliable government, so its borrowing costs remain low despite high net debt.

In contrast to the other countries, Norway has a large *negative* net public debt

thanks to oil. Norway is one of the world's largest oil exporters. Instead of spending its oil revenues immediately, the government of Norway has used them to build up an investment fund for future needs following the lead of traditional oil producers like Saudi Arabia. As a result, Norway has a huge stock of government assets rather than a large government debt.

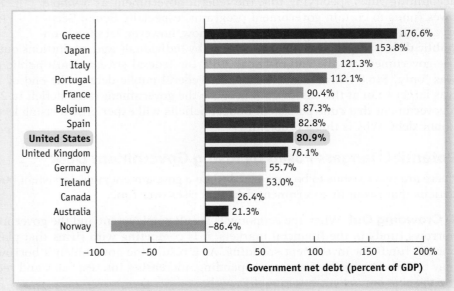

Data from: International Monetary Fund; World Economic Outlook, January 2020.

burden typically forces it to slash spending or raise taxes, politically unpopular measures that can also damage the economy. In some cases, austerity measures intended to reassure lenders that the government can indeed pay end up depressing the economy so much that lender confidence continues to fall.

> The **debt–GDP ratio** is the government's debt as a percentage of GDP.

If it has its own currency, a government that has trouble borrowing can print money to pay its bills. But doing so can lead to another problem: inflation. In fact, budget problems are the main cause of very severe inflation. Governments do not want to find themselves in a position where the choice is between defaulting on their debts and inflating those debts away by printing money.

Concerns about the long-run effects of deficits need not rule out the use of expansionary fiscal policy to stimulate the economy when it is depressed. However, these concerns do mean that governments should try to offset budget deficits in bad years with budget surpluses in good years. In other words, governments should run a budget that is approximately balanced over time. Have they actually done so?

Deficits and Debt in Practice

Figure 28-13 shows the U.S. federal government's budget deficit and how its debt changed from 1940 to 2019. Panel (a) shows the federal deficit as a percentage of GDP. As you can see, the federal government ran huge deficits during World War II. It briefly ran surpluses after the war, but it has normally run deficits ever since, especially after 1980. This seems inconsistent with the advice that governments should offset deficits in bad times with surpluses in good times.

However, panel (b) of Figure 28-13 shows that for most of the period these persistent deficits didn't lead to runaway debt. To assess the ability of governments to pay their debt, we use the **debt–GDP ratio,** the government's debt as a percentage of GDP. We use this measure, rather than simply looking at the size of the debt, because GDP, which measures the size of the economy as a whole, is a good indicator of the potential taxes the government can collect. If the government's debt grows more slowly than GDP, the burden of paying that debt is actually falling

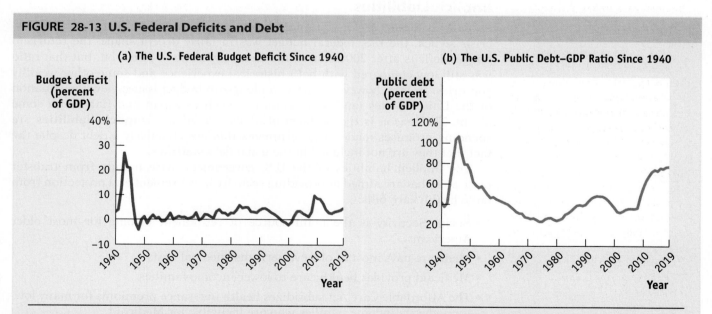

FIGURE 28-13 U.S. Federal Deficits and Debt

(a) The U.S. Federal Budget Deficit Since 1940

(b) The U.S. Public Debt–GDP Ratio Since 1940

Panel (a) shows the U.S. federal budget deficit as a percentage of GDP from 1940 to 2019. The U.S. government ran huge deficits during World War II and has run smaller deficits ever since. Panel (b) shows the U.S. debt–GDP ratio. Comparing panels (a) and (b), you can see that in many years the debt–GDP ratio has declined in spite of government deficits. This seeming paradox reflects the fact that the debt–GDP ratio can fall, even when debt is rising, as long as GDP grows faster than debt.

Data from: Office of Management and Budget; Federal Reserve Bank of St. Louis.

FOR INQUIRING MINDS **What Happened to the Debt from World War II?**

As you can see from Figure 28-13, the U.S. government paid for World War II by borrowing on a huge scale. By the war's end, the public debt was more than 100% of GDP, and many people worried about how it could ever be paid off.

The truth is that it never was paid off. In 1946 public debt was $242 billion; that number dipped slightly in the next few years, as the United States ran postwar budget surpluses, but the government budget went back into deficit in 1950 with the start of the Korean War. By 1962 the public debt was back up to $248 billion.

But by that time nobody was worried about the fiscal health of the U.S. government because the debt–GDP ratio had fallen by more than half. The reason? Vigorous economic growth, plus mild inflation, led to a rapid rise in GDP. The experience was a clear lesson in the peculiar fact that modern governments can run deficits forever, as long as they aren't too large.

compared with the government's potential tax revenue. Under these conditions the underlying economy is strong enough to generate future surpluses, allowing the government to pay off its debt, at a time of its own choosing, and avoid the potential dangers of financial pressure and default.

What we see from panel (b) is that although the federal debt grew in almost every year, the debt–GDP ratio fell for 30 years after the end of World War II. This shows that the debt–GDP ratio can fall, even when debt is rising, as long as GDP grows faster than debt. The accompanying For Inquiring Minds explains how sufficiently high levels of growth and/or inflation can allow a government that runs persistent budget deficits to nevertheless have a declining debt–GDP ratio.

Still, a government that runs persistent *large* deficits will have a rising debt–GDP ratio when debt grows faster than GDP. In the aftermath of the financial crisis of 2008, the U.S. government began running deficits much larger than anything seen since World War II, and the debt–GDP ratio began rising sharply. Similar surges in the debt–GDP ratio could be seen in a number of other countries after 2008. Economists and policy makers agreed that this was not a sustainable trend, and that governments would need to get their spending and revenues back in line.

Implicit Liabilities

Looking at Figure 28-13, you might be tempted to conclude that until the 2008 crisis struck, the U.S. federal budget was in fairly decent shape: the return to budget deficits after 2001 caused the debt–GDP ratio to rise a bit, but that ratio was still low compared with both historical experience and some other wealthy countries. In fact, however, experts on long-run budget issues view the situation of the United States (and other countries such as Japan and Italy) with some alarm. The reason is the problem of *implicit liabilities*. **Implicit liabilities** are spending promises made by governments that are effectively a debt despite the fact that they are not included in the usual debt statistics.

The implicit liabilities of the U.S. government arise mainly from transfer programs that are aimed at providing security in retirement and protection from large health care bills:

- Social Security is the main source of retirement income for most older Americans.

- Medicare pays most of older Americans' medical costs.

- Medicaid provides health care to lower-income families.

- The Affordable Care Act subsidizes health insurance premiums for many low- to moderate-income families who are ineligible for Medicaid.

Implicit liabilities are spending promises made by governments that are effectively a debt despite the fact that they are not included in the usual debt statistics.

In each of these cases, the government has promised to provide transfer payments to future as well as current beneficiaries. So these programs represent a future debt that must be honored, even though the debt does not currently show up in the usual statistics. Together, these programs currently account for approximately half of federal spending.

The implicit liabilities created by these transfer programs worry fiscal experts. Figure 28-14 shows why. It shows actual 2019 spending on Social Security and major health care programs, measured as a percentage of GDP, together with Congressional Budget Office projections for average spending in the 2040s. According to these projections, spending on Social Security will rise substantially over the next few decades and spending on the major health care programs will soar. Why?

In the case of Social Security, the answer is demography. Social Security is a pay-as-you-go system: current workers pay payroll taxes that fund the benefits of current retirees. So the ratio of the number of retirees drawing benefits to the number of workers paying into Social Security has a major impact on the system's finances.

There was a huge surge in the U.S. birth rate between 1946 and 1964, the years of what is commonly called the *baby boom.* Many baby boomers are still of working age—which means they are paying taxes, not collecting benefits. But many are starting to retire, and as more and more of them do so, they will stop earning taxable income and start collecting benefits.

As a result, the ratio of retirees receiving benefits to workers paying into the Social Security system will rise. In 2018 there were 36 retirees receiving benefits for every 100 workers paying into the system. But, by 2050, according to the Social Security Administration, that number will rise to 45. So as baby boomers move into retirement, benefit payments will continue to rise relative to the size of the economy.

The aging of the baby boomers, by itself, poses only a moderately sized long-run fiscal problem. The projected rise in health care spending is a much more serious concern. These projections also reflect the aging of the population, both because more people will be eligible for Medicare and because older people tend to have higher medical costs. But the main story behind projections of higher health care spending is the long-run tendency of such spending to rise faster than overall spending, for both government-funded and privately funded health care.

To some extent, the implicit liabilities of the U.S. government are already reflected in debt statistics. We mentioned earlier that the government had a total debt of $21.2 trillion at the end of fiscal 2019 but that only $16.8 trillion of that total was owed to the public. The main explanation for that discrepancy is that both Social Security and part of Medicare (the hospital insurance program) are supported by *dedicated taxes:* their expenses are paid out of special taxes on wages. At times, these dedicated taxes yield more revenue than is needed to pay current benefits.

In particular, since the mid-1980s the Social Security system has been taking in more revenue than it currently needs in order to prepare for the retirement of the baby boomers. This surplus in the Social Security system has been used to accumulate a *Social Security trust fund,* which was $2.8 trillion at the end of fiscal 2019.

The money in the trust fund is held in the form of U.S. government bonds, which are included in the $21.2 trillion in total debt. You could say that there's something funny about counting bonds in the Social Security trust fund as part of government debt. After all, these bonds are owed by one part of the government (the government outside the Social Security system) to another part of the government (the Social Security system itself). But the debt corresponds to a real, if implicit, liability: promises by the government to pay future retirement benefits. So many economists argue that the gross debt of $21.2 trillion, the sum of public debt and government debt held by Social Security and other trust funds, is a more accurate indication of the government's fiscal health than the smaller amount owed to the public alone.

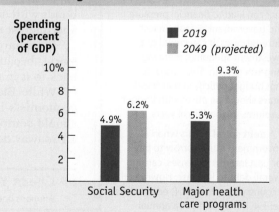

FIGURE 28-14 Future Demands on the Federal Budget

This figure shows actual spending on social insurance programs as a percentage of GDP in 2019 and Congressional Budget Office projections for these same programs in the 2040s. Partly as a result of an aging population, these programs will become much more expensive over time. But, it is the significant increases in health care spending that will pose the most serious problem for the federal budget in the future.

Data from: Congressional Budget Office.

ECONOMICS >> *in Action*
Who's Afraid of a Debt Spiral?

As we explained in the text, one concern about the long-run effects of budget deficits is that they may start to feed on themselves, via a debt spiral. Deficits lead to higher debt; higher debt leads to higher interest payments, which increases the deficit, which leads to even higher debt, and so on. So debt can snowball.

TABLE 28-2 Interest Rates versus Growth		
	Average 10-year interest rate	Nominal GDP growth rate
1990–2019	4.41	4.51
2010–2019	2.40	3.97

But how worried should we be about debt spirals? In January 2019 Olivier Blanchard, the former chief economist of the International Monetary Fund and one of the world's most respected macroeconomists, startled his colleagues at the annual meeting of the American Economic Association, where he gave the presidential address. Blanchard argued that fears of a debt spiral, and concerns about government debt in general, are greatly exaggerated.

Blanchard's argument emphasized a point we also made in the text, about the effects of growth and inflation on the debt–GDP ratio, which is a much better indicator of a government's fiscal health than the simple dollar value of debt. As we noted, rising nominal GDP, which reflects both inflation and real growth, causes the debt–GDP ratio to "melt" away unless the budget deficit is large.

What Blanchard pointed out was that while a rise in debt increases the government's interest payments, it also accelerates the rate of melting, basically because there is more debt to melt. You only get a debt spiral if the higher interest payments caused by higher debt exceed this melting effect. The key question is whether the interest rate the government has to pay is more or less than the rate of growth in nominal GDP.

And as Blanchard noted, the experience of the United States and other advanced economies over the past 30 years, and especially over the past decade, is that interest rates are generally less than nominal growth rates. This point is illustrated in Table 28-2, which compares the average 10-year interest rate on U.S. government bonds with nominal GDP growth over time. Furthermore, the gap between growth and interest rates is even larger in many other advanced countries.

Blanchard also argued that even this comparison overstates the risk of a debt spiral, because some of the money the government pays out in interest comes back to it in tax payments from bondholders.

While Blanchard's speech came as something of a bombshell, many other economists have recently made similar arguments. Nobody is arguing that we should completely ignore debt. But there doesn't seem to be much reason to fear a runaway debt spiral.

>> Quick Review

• Large and persistent budget deficits lead to increases in **public debt.**

• Public debt that rises year after year can lead to financial pressure and government default. In less extreme cases, it can crowd out investment spending, reducing long-run growth. This suggests that budget deficits in bad **fiscal years** should be offset with budget surpluses in good fiscal years.

• A **debt spiral** occurs when a government must borrow to pay for past interest expenses, causing overall debt to increase. However, if a country has rising GDP, economists believe it may safely run annual deficits as long as the **debt–GDP ratio** is stable or falling because GDP is growing faster than the debt.

• In addition to their official public debt, modern governments have implicit liabilities. The U.S. government has large **implicit liabilities** in the form of Social Security, Medicare, Medicaid, and the Affordable Care Act (ACA). With large implicit liabilities, a stable debt–GDP ratio may give a misleading sense of security.

>> Check Your Understanding 28-4
Solutions appear at back of book.

1. Explain how each of the following events would affect the public debt or implicit liabilities of the U.S. government, other things equal. Would the public debt or implicit liabilities be greater or smaller?
   a. A higher growth rate of real GDP
   b. Retirees living longer
   c. A decrease in tax revenue
   d. Government borrowing to pay interest on its current public debt

2. Suppose the economy is in a slump and the current public debt is quite large. Explain the trade-off of short-run versus long-run objectives that policy makers face when deciding whether or not to engage in deficit spending.

3. Explain how a contractionary fiscal policy like austerity can make it more likely that a government is unable to pay its debts.

Here Comes the Sun

Ethan Miller/Getty Images

The Solana power plant covers three square miles of the Sonoran Desert in Gila Bend, Arizona, about 70 miles from Phoenix. Whereas most solar installations rely on photovoltaic panels that convert light directly into electricity, Solana uses a system of mirrors to concentrate the sun's heat on black pipes, which convey that heat to tanks of molten salt. The heat in the salt is, in turn, used to generate electricity. The advantage of this arrangement is that the plant can keep generating power long after the sun has gone down, greatly enhancing its efficiency.

Solana is one of only a small number of concentrated thermal solar plants operating or under construction, and as Figure 28-15 shows, solar power has been rapidly rising in importance, with the amount of solar-generated electricity increasing over 10,000% between 2008 and 2018. There are a number of reasons for this sudden rise, but the 2009 stimulus—which put substantial sums into the promotion of green energy—was a major factor. Solana, in particular, was built by the Spanish company Abengoa with the aid of a $1.45 billion federal loan guarantee. Abengoa also received $1.2 billion for a similar plant in the Mojave Desert.

While Solana is a good example of stimulus spending at work, it is also a good example of why such spending tends to be politically difficult. There were many protests over federal loans to a non-U.S. firm, although Abengoa had the necessary technology, and the construction jobs created by the project were, of course, in the United States. Also, the long-term financial viability of solar power projects depends in part on whether government subsidies and other policies favoring renewable energy will continue, which isn't certain.

In terms of the goals of the stimulus, however, Solana seems to have done what it was supposed to: it generated jobs at a time when borrowing was cheap and many construction workers were unemployed.

FIGURE 28-15 The Solar Sunrise, 2008–2018

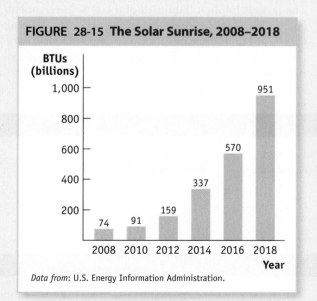

Data from: U.S. Energy Information Administration.

QUESTIONS FOR THOUGHT

1. How did the political reaction to government funding for the Solana project differ from the reaction to more conventional government spending projects such as roads and schools? What does the case tell us about how to assess the value of a fiscal stimulus project?

2. In the chapter we talked about the problem of lags in discretionary fiscal policy. What does the Solana case tell us about this issue?

3. Is the depth of a recession a good or a bad time to undertake an energy project? Why or why not?

SUMMARY

1. The government plays a large role in the economy, collecting a large share of GDP in taxes and spending a large share both to purchase goods and services and to make transfer payments, largely for **social insurance.** *Fiscal policy* is the use of taxes, government transfers, or government purchases of goods and services to shift the aggregate demand curve.

2. Government purchases of goods and services directly affect aggregate demand, and changes in taxes and government transfers affect aggregate demand indirectly by changing households' disposable incomes. **Expansionary fiscal policy** shifts the aggregate demand curve rightward; **contractionary fiscal policy** shifts the aggregate demand curve leftward.

3. Only when the economy is at full employment is there potential for crowding out of private spending and private investment spending by expansionary fiscal policy. The argument that expansionary fiscal policy won't work because of Ricardian equivalence—that consumers will cut back spending today to offset expected future tax increases—appears to be untrue in practice. What is clearly true is that very active fiscal policy may make the economy less stable due to time lags in policy formulation and implementation.

4. Fiscal policy has a multiplier effect on the economy, the size of which depends on the fiscal policy. Except in the case of lump-sum taxes, taxes reduce the size of the multiplier. Expansionary fiscal policy leads to an increase in real GDP, and contractionary fiscal policy leads to a reduction in real GDP. Because part of any change in taxes or transfers is absorbed by savings in the first round of spending, changes in government purchases of goods and services have a more powerful effect on the economy than equal-sized changes in taxes or transfers.

5. Rules governing taxes—with the exception of **lump-sum taxes**—and some transfers act as **automatic stabilizers,** reducing the size of the multiplier and automatically reducing the size of fluctuations in the business cycle. In contrast, **discretionary fiscal policy** arises from deliberate actions by policy makers rather than from the business cycle.

6. Some of the fluctuations in the budget balance are due to the effects of the business cycle. In order to separate the effects of the business cycle from the effects of discretionary fiscal policy, governments determine the **cyclically adjusted budget balance,** an estimate of the budget balance if the economy were at potential output.

7. U.S. government budget accounting is calculated on the basis of **fiscal years.** Persistently large budget deficits have long-run consequences because they lead to an increase in **public debt.** As a result, two potential dangers may arise: crowding out, which reduces long-run economic growth, and financial pressure leading to default, which brings economic and financial turmoil. A **debt spiral** will increase public debt if countries need to take on additional debt to pay past interest expenses.

8. A widely used measure of fiscal health is the **debt–GDP ratio.** This number can remain stable or fall even in the face of persistent budget deficits if GDP rises over time. With large **implicit liabilities,** a stable debt–GDP ratio may give a misleading sense of security. The largest implicit liabilities of the U.S. government come from Social Security, Medicare, Medicaid, and the Affordable Care Act (ACA), the costs of which are increasing due to the aging of the population and rising medical costs.

KEY TERMS

Social insurance, p. 820
Expansionary fiscal policy, p. 821
Contractionary fiscal policy, p. 821
Lump-sum taxes, p. 827
Automatic stabilizers, p. 828

Discretionary fiscal policy, p. 828
Cyclically adjusted budget balance, p. 832
Fiscal year, p. 835
Public debt, p. 835

Debt spiral, p. 836
Debt–GDP ratio, p. 837
Implicit liabilities, p. 838

PRACTICE QUESTIONS

1. The CARES Act was the largest in both nominal and real measures of fiscal relief/stimulus passed in U.S. history. The package will cost more than $2 trillion as it stabilizes consumer spending during a period of unprecedented unemployment. Simultaneously, the global pandemic caused a supply side shock as supply chains experienced delays as households stocked up on basic necessities. In terms of aggregate demand and aggregate supply, explain if the CARES Act would cause a significant rise in the price level?

2. With the CARES Act costing over $2 trillion and the federal government facing a significant decline in tax revenue, explain the effectiveness of fiscal policy using the three claims outlined in the chapter.

3. The government's budget surplus in Macroland has risen consistently over the past five years. Two government policy makers disagree as to why this has happened. One argues that a rising budget surplus indicates a growing economy; the other argues that it shows that the government is using contractionary fiscal policy. Can you determine which policy maker is correct? If not, why not?

PROBLEMS

1. The accompanying diagram shows the current macroeconomic situation for the economy of Albernia. You have been hired as an economic consultant to help the economy move to potential output, Y_P.

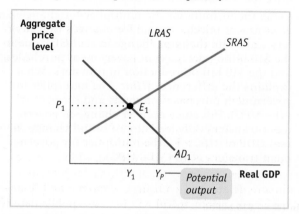

   a. Is Albernia facing a recessionary or inflationary gap?

   b. Which type of fiscal policy—expansionary or contractionary—would move the economy of Albernia to potential output, Y_P? What are some examples of such policies?

   c. Illustrate the macroeconomic situation in Albernia with a diagram after the successful fiscal policy has been implemented.

2. The accompanying diagram shows the current macroeconomic situation for the economy of Brittania; real GDP is Y_1, and the aggregate price level is P_1. You have been hired as an economic consultant to help the economy move to potential output, Y_P.

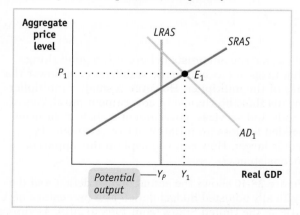

   a. Is Brittania facing a recessionary or inflationary gap?

   b. Which type of fiscal policy—expansionary or contractionary—would move the economy of Brittania to potential output, Y_P? What are some examples of such policies?

   c. Illustrate the macroeconomic situation in Brittania with a diagram after the successful fiscal policy has been implemented.

3. An economy is in long-run macroeconomic equilibrium when each of the following aggregate demand shocks occurs. What kind of gap—inflationary or recessionary—will the economy face after the shock, and what type of fiscal policies would help move the economy back to potential output? How would your recommended fiscal policy shift the aggregate demand curve?

   a. A stock market boom increases the value of stocks held by households.

   b. Firms come to believe that a recession in the near future is likely.

   c. Anticipating the possibility of war, the government increases its purchases of military equipment.

   d. The quantity of money in the economy declines and interest rates increase.

4. During a 2008 interview, then German Finance Minister Peer Steinbruck said, "We have to watch out that in Europe and beyond, nothing like a combination of downward economic [growth] and high inflation rates emerges—something that experts call stagflation." Such a situation can be depicted by the movement of the short-run aggregate supply curve from its original position, $SRAS_1$, to its new position, $SRAS_2$, with the new equilibrium point E_2 in the accompanying figure. In this question, we try to understand why stagflation is particularly hard to fix using fiscal policy.

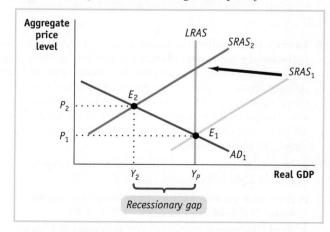

   a. What would be the appropriate fiscal policy response to this situation if the primary concern of the government was to maintain economic growth? Illustrate the effect of the policy on the equilibrium point and the aggregate price level using the diagram.

b. What would be the appropriate fiscal policy response to this situation if the primary concern of the government was to maintain price stability? Illustrate the effect of the policy on the equilibrium point and the aggregate price level using the diagram.

c. Discuss the effectiveness of the policies in parts a and b in fighting stagflation.

5. Show why a $10 billion reduction in government purchases of goods and services will have a larger effect on real GDP than a $10 billion reduction in government transfers by completing the accompanying table for an economy with a marginal propensity to consume (*MPC*) of 0.6. The first and second rows of the table are filled in for you: on the left side of the table, in the first row, the $10 billion reduction in government purchases decreases real GDP and disposable income, *YD*, by $10 billion, leading to a reduction in consumer spending of $6 billion

(*MPC* × change in disposable income) in row 2. However, on the right side of the table, the $10 billion reduction in transfers has no effect on real GDP in round 1 but does lower *YD* by $10 billion, resulting in a decrease in consumer spending of $6 billion in round 2.

a. When government purchases decrease by $10 billion, what is the sum of the changes in real GDP after the 10 rounds?

b. When the government reduces transfers by $10 billion, what is the sum of the changes in real GDP after the 10 rounds?

c. Using the formula for the multiplier for changes in government purchases and for changes in transfers, calculate the total change in real GDP due to the $10 billion decrease in government purchases and the $10 billion reduction in transfers. What explains the difference? [*Hint:* The multiplier for government purchases of goods and services is 1/(1 − *MPC*). But since each $1 change in government transfers only leads to an initial change in real GDP of *MPC* × $1, the multiplier for government transfers is *MPC*/(1 − *MPC*).]

Rounds	Decrease in *G* = −$10 billion (billions of dollars)			Decrease in *TR* = −$10 billion (billions of dollars)		
	Change in *G* or *C*	Change in real GDP	Change in *YD*	Change in *TR* or *C*	Change in real GDP	Change in *YD*
1	$\Delta G = $ −$10.00	−$10.00	−$10.00	$\Delta TR = $ −$10.00	$0.00	−$10.00
2	$\Delta C = $ −6.00	−6.00	−6.00	$\Delta C = $ −6.00	−6.00	−6.00
3	$\Delta C = $?	?	?	$\Delta C = $?	?	?
4	$\Delta C = $?	?	?	$\Delta C = $?	?	?
5	$\Delta C = $?	?	?	$\Delta C = $?	?	?
6	$\Delta C = $?	?	?	$\Delta C = $?	?	?
7	$\Delta C = $?	?	?	$\Delta C = $?	?	?
8	$\Delta C = $?	?	?	$\Delta C = $?	?	?
9	$\Delta C = $?	?	?	$\Delta C = $?	?	?
10	$\Delta C = $?	?	?	$\Delta C = $?	?	?

6. In each of the following cases, either a recessionary or inflationary gap exists. Assume that the aggregate supply curve is horizontal, so that the change in real GDP arising from a shift of the aggregate demand curve equals the size of the shift of the curve. Calculate both the change in government purchases of goods and services and the change in government transfers necessary to close the gap.

a. Real GDP equals $100 billion, potential output equals $160 billion, and the *MPC* is 0.75.

b. Real GDP equals $250 billion, potential output equals $200 billion, and the *MPC* is 0.5.

c. Real GDP equals $180 billion, potential output equals $100 billion, and the *MPC* is 0.8.

7. Most macroeconomists believe it is a good thing that taxes act as automatic stabilizers and lower the size of the multiplier. However, a smaller multiplier means that the change in government purchases of goods and services, government transfers, or taxes needed to close an inflationary or recessionary gap is larger. How can you explain this apparent inconsistency?

8. Figure 28-10 shows the actual budget deficit and the cyclically adjusted budget deficit as a percentage of GDP in the United States from 1965 to 2019. Assuming that potential output was unchanged, use this figure to determine which of the years from 1990 to 2019 the government used expansionary fiscal policy and in which years it used contractionary fiscal policy.

9. You are an economic adviser to a candidate for national office. She asks you for a summary of the economic consequences of a balanced-budget rule for the federal government and for your recommendation on whether she should support such a rule. How do you respond?

10. In 2020, the policy makers of the economy of East-landia projected the debt–GDP ratio and the ratio of the budget deficit to GDP for the economy for the next 10 years under different scenarios for growth in the government's deficit. Real GDP is currently $1,000 billion per year and is expected to grow by 3% per year, the public debt is $300 billion at the beginning of the year, and the deficit is $30 billion in 2020.

Year	Real GDP (billions of dollars)	Debt (billions of dollars)	Budget deficit (billions of dollars)	Debt (percent of real GDP)	Budget deficit (percent of real GDP)
2020	$1,000	$300	$30	?	?
2021	1,030	?	?	?	?
2022	1,061	?	?	?	?
2023	1,093	?	?	?	?
2024	1,126	?	?	?	?
2025	1,159	?	?	?	?
2026	1,194	?	?	?	?
2027	1,230	?	?	?	?
2028	1,267	?	?	?	?
2029	1,305	?	?	?	?
2030	1,344	?	?	?	?

a. Complete the accompanying table to show the debt–GDP ratio and the ratio of the budget deficit to GDP for the economy if the government's budget deficit remains constant at $30 billion over the next 10 years. (Remember that the government's debt will grow by the previous year's deficit.)

b. Redo the table to show the debt–GDP ratio and the ratio of the budget deficit to GDP for the economy if the government's budget deficit grows by 3% per year over the next 10 years.

c. Redo the table again to show the debt–GDP ratio and the ratio of the budget deficit to GDP for the economy if the government's budget deficit grows by 20% per year over the next 10 years.

d. What happens to the debt–GDP ratio and the ratio of the budget deficit to GDP for the economy over time under the three different scenarios?

11. Your study partner argues that the distinction between the government's budget deficit and debt is similar to the distinction between consumer savings and wealth. Your study partner also argues that if you have large budget deficits, you must have a large debt. In what ways is your study partner correct and in what ways incorrect?

12. Access the Discovering Data exercise for Chapter 28 online to answer these questions.

a. Which of these six countries—United States, France, Italy, Greece, Germany, and the United Kingdom—had the largest amount of government debt as a percent of GDP as of 2015? Which had the smallest?

b. Calculate the percent change in government debt from 2007 through 2015 for the same six countries. Which country experienced the largest percent increase in government debt from 2007 through 2015? Which experienced the smallest?

c. Using the six countries as a reference point, what conclusions can you draw about the relationship between government debt and economic growth?

13. In which of the following cases does the size of the government's debt and the size of the budget deficit indicate potential problems for the economy?

a. The government's debt is relatively low, but the government is running a large budget deficit as it builds a high-speed rail system to connect the major cities of the nation.

b. The government's debt is relatively high due to a recently ended deficit-financed war, but the government is now running only a small budget deficit.

c. The government's debt is relatively low, but the government is running a budget deficit to finance the interest payments on the debt.

d. The government's debt is relatively high and the government is running a budget deficit to finance new infrastructure spending.

14. How did or would the following affect the current public debt and implicit liabilities of the U.S. government?

a. In 2003, Congress passed and President George W. Bush signed the Medicare Modernization Act, which provides seniors and individuals with disabilities with a prescription drug benefit. Some of the benefits under this law took effect immediately, but other benefits will not begin until sometime in the future.

b. The age at which retired persons can receive full Social Security benefits is raised to age 70 for future retirees.

c. Social Security benefits for future retirees are limited to those with low incomes.

d. Because the cost of health care is increasing faster than the overall inflation rate, annual increases in Social Security benefits are increased by the annual increase in health care costs rather than the overall inflation rate.

e. The Affordable Care Act (ACA), which went into effect in 2014, created incentives for hospitals to find ways to save the government money.

15. Unlike households, governments are often able to sustain large debts. For example, in 2019, the U.S. government's total debt reached $21.2 trillion, approximately equal to 105.3% of GDP. At the time, according to the U.S. Treasury, the average interest rate paid by the government on its debt was 1.3%. However, running budget deficits becomes hard when very large debts are outstanding.

a. Calculate the dollar cost of the annual interest on the government's total debt assuming the interest rate and debt figures cited above.

b. If the government operates on a balanced budget before interest payments are taken into account, at what rate must GDP grow in order for the debt–GDP ratio to remain unchanged?

c. Calculate the total increase in national debt if the government incurs a deficit of $600 billion in 2020.

d. At what rate would nominal GDP have to grow in order for the debt–GDP ratio to remain unchanged when the deficit in 2020 is $600 billion?

e. Why is the debt–GDP ratio the preferred measure of a country's debt rather than the dollar value of the debt? Why is it important for a government to keep this number under control?

WORK IT OUT

16. The accompanying table shows how consumers' marginal propensities to consume in a particular economy are related to their level of income.

Income range	Marginal propensity to consume
$0–$20,000	0.9
$20,001–$40,000	0.8
$40,001–$60,000	0.7
$60,001–$80,000	0.6
Above $80,000	0.5

a. Suppose the government engages in increased purchases of goods and services. For each of the income groups in the table, what is the value of the multiplier—that is, what is the "bang for the buck" from each dollar the government spends on government purchases of goods and services in each income group?

b. If the government needed to close a recessionary or inflationary gap, at which group should it primarily aim its fiscal policy of changes in government purchases of goods and services? ∎

Taxes and the Multiplier

In the chapter, we described how taxes that depend positively on real GDP reduce the size of the multiplier and act as an automatic stabilizer for the economy. Let's look a little more closely at the mathematics of how this works.

Specifically, let's assume that the government "captures" a fraction t of any increase in real GDP in the form of taxes, where t, the tax rate, is a fraction between 0 and 1. And let's repeat the exercise we carried out in Chapter 26, where we consider the effects of a $100 billion increase in investment spending. The same analysis holds for *any* autonomous increase in aggregate spending—in particular, it is also true for increases in government purchases of goods and services.

The $100 billion increase in investment spending initially raises real GDP by $100 billion (the first round). In the absence of taxes, disposable income would rise by $100 billion. But because part of the rise in real GDP is collected in the form of taxes, disposable income only rises by $(1-t) \times \$100$ billion. The second-round increase in consumer spending, which is equal to the marginal propensity to consume (MPC) multiplied by the rise in disposable income, is $(MPC \times (1-t)) \times \$100$ billion. This leads to a third-round increase in consumer spending of $(MPC \times (1-t)) \times (MPC \times (1-t)) \times \$100$ billion, and so on. So the total effect on real GDP is

Increase in investment spending	=	$100 billion
+ Second-round increase in consumer spending	$= (MPC \times (1-t))$	$\times \$100$ billion
+ Third-round increase in consumer spending	$= (MPC \times (1-t))^2$	$\times \$100$ billion
+ Fourth-round increase in consumer spending	$= (MPC \times (1-t))^3$	$\times \$100$ billion

$$\text{Total increase in real GDP} = [1 + (MPC \times (1-t)) + (MPC \times (1-t))^2 + (MPC \times (1-t))^3 + \ldots] \times \$100 \text{ billion}$$

As explained in Chapter 26, an infinite series of the form $1 + x + x^2 + \ldots$, with $0 < x < 1$, is equal to $1/(1-x)$. In this example, $x = (MPC \times (1-t))$. So the total effect of a $100 billion increase in investment spending, taking into account all the subsequent increases in consumer spending, is to raise real GDP by:

$$\frac{1}{1 - (MPC \times (1-t))} \times \$100 \text{ billion}$$

When we calculated the multiplier assuming away the effect of taxes, we found that it was $1/(1-MPC)$. But when we assume that a fraction t of any change in real GDP is collected in the form of taxes, the multiplier is:

$$\text{Multiplier} = \frac{1}{1 - (MPC \times (1-t))}$$

This is always a smaller number than $1/(1-MPC)$, and its size diminishes as t grows. Suppose, for example, that $MPC = 0.6$. In the absence of taxes, this implies a multiplier of $1/(1-0.6) = 1/0.4 = 2.5$. But now let's assume that $t = 1/3$, that is, that 1/3 of any increase in real GDP is collected by the government. Then the multiplier is:

$$\frac{1}{1 - (0.6 \times (1 - 1/3))} = \frac{1}{1 - (0.6 \times 2/3)} = \frac{1}{1 - 0.4} = \frac{1}{0.6} = 1.667$$

PROBLEMS

1. An economy has a marginal propensity to consume of 0.6, real GDP equals $500 billion, and the government collects 20% of GDP in taxes. If government purchases increase by $10 billion, show the rounds of increased spending that take place by completing the accompanying table. The first and second rows are filled in for you. In the first row, the increase in government purchases of $10 billion raises real GDP by $10 billion, taxes increase by $2 billion, and *YD* increases by $8 billion; in the second row, the increase in *YD* of $8 billion increases consumer spending by $4.80 billion (*MPC* × change in disposable income).

Rounds	Change in *G* or *C*	Change in real GDP	Change in taxes	Change in *YD*
	(billions of dollars)			
1	$\Delta G = \$10.00$	$10.00	$2.00	$8.00
2	$\Delta C = 4.80$	4.80	0.96	3.84
3	$\Delta C = ?$	?	?	?
4	$\Delta C = ?$	?	?	?
5	$\Delta C = ?$	?	?	?
6	$\Delta C = ?$	?	?	?
7	$\Delta C = ?$	?	?	?
8	$\Delta C = ?$	?	?	?
9	$\Delta C = ?$	?	?	?
10	$\Delta C = ?$	?	?	?

a. What is the total change in real GDP after the 10 rounds? What is the value of the multiplier? What would you expect the total change in real GDP to be, based on the multiplier formula? How do your two answers compare?

b. Redo the accompanying table, assuming the marginal propensity to consume is 0.75 and the government collects 10% of the rise in real GDP in taxes. What is the total change in real GDP after 10 rounds? What is the value of the multiplier? How do your two answers compare?

WORK IT OUT

2. Calculate the change in government purchases of goods and services necessary to close the recessionary or inflationary gaps in the following cases. Assume that the short-run aggregate supply curve is horizontal, so that the change in real GDP arising from a shift of the aggregate demand curve equals the size of the shift of the curve.

a. Real GDP equals $100 billion, potential output equals $160 billion, the government collects 20% of any change in real GDP in the form of taxes, and the marginal propensity to consume is 0.75.

b. Real GDP equals $250 billion, potential output equals $200 billion, the government collects 10% of any change in real GDP in the form of taxes, and the marginal propensity to consume is 0.5.

c. Real GDP equals $180 billion, potential output equals $100 billion, the government collects 25% of any change in real GDP in the form of taxes, and the marginal propensity to consume is 0.8. ∎

29 Money, Banking, and the Federal Reserve System

NOT SO FUNNY MONEY

"THE PRODUCT IS CAREFULLY CREATED in rural facilities throughout the Peruvian countryside using cheap labor, then hoarded in stash houses controlled by violent gangs in Lima. Once there, the goods are packed into parcels, loaded onto planes or hidden inside luggage, pottery, hollowed-out Bibles, sneakers, children's toys or massive shipping containers bound for major U.S. ports of entry, such as Miami." So began a *Washington Post* report on Operation Sunset, a huge raid carried out by Peruvian authorities in cooperation with the U.S. Secret Service in 2016. But what was the target of this raid? It wasn't a drug bust; it was a fake money bust.

In recent years, Peru has become a major source for the production of counterfeit U.S. currency; the so-called "Peruvian note" is considered to be the best counterfeit in the business. Workers employed by criminal syndicates meticulously add decorative details to printed bills by hand, creating high-quality fakes that are very hard to detect.

The funny thing is that elaborately decorated pieces of paper have little or no intrinsic value. Indeed, a $100 bill printed with blue or orange ink wouldn't be worth the paper it was printed on.

But if the ink on that piece of paper is just the right shade of green, people will think that it's *money* and will accept it as payment for very real goods and services, because they believe, correctly, that they can do the same thing: exchange that piece of green paper for real goods and services.

In fact, here's a riddle: If a fake $100 bill from Peru enters the United States and is successfully exchanged for a good or service with nobody ever realizing it's a fake, who gets hurt? Accepting a fake $100 bill isn't like buying a car that turns out to be a lemon or a meal that turns out to be inedible. As long as the bill's counterfeit nature remains undiscovered, it will pass from hand to hand just like a real $100 bill.

The answer to the riddle is that the actual victims of the counterfeiting are U.S. taxpayers, because counterfeit dollars reduce the revenues available to pay for the operations of the U.S. government. The Treasury Department believes that only around 0.01% of the currency in circulation, about $200 million, is fake, but that could still mean that taxpayers have been defrauded of hundreds of millions of dollars. Accordingly, the Secret Service diligently monitors the integrity of U.S. currency, promptly investigating any reports of counterfeit dollars. The efforts of the Secret Service attest to the fact that money isn't like ordinary goods and services, and it certainly is not like pieces of colored paper.

In this chapter we'll look at what money is, the role that it plays, the workings of a modern monetary system, and the institutions that sustain and regulate it, including the *Federal Reserve*. ●

Anna Delaw/Alamy

Money is the essential channel that links the various parts of the modern economy.

WHAT YOU WILL LEARN

- What are the various roles that **money** plays and what forms does it take?
- Why is the level of the **money supply** so important to the state of the economy?
- How do the actions of private banks and the Federal Reserve determine the money supply?
- How does the Federal Reserve use **open-market operations** to change the **monetary base**?

Money is any asset that can easily be used to purchase goods and services.

Currency in circulation is cash held by the public.

Checkable bank deposits are bank accounts that can be accessed using checks, debit cards, and digital payments.

The **money supply** is the total value of financial assets in the economy that are considered money.

|| The Meaning of Money

In everyday conversation, we often use the word *money* to mean wealth. If you ask, "How much money does Jeff Bezos, the founder of Amazon, have?" the answer will be something like, "Oh, $172 billion or so, but who's counting?" That is, the number will include the value of the stocks, bonds, real estate, and other assets he owns.

But the economist's definition of money doesn't include all forms of wealth. The dollar bills in your wallet are money; other forms of wealth—such as stocks, bonds, and real estate—aren't money. What, according to economists, distinguishes money from other forms of wealth?

What Is Money?

Money is defined in terms of what it does: **money** is any asset that can easily be used to purchase goods and services. In Chapter 25 we defined an asset as *liquid* if it can easily be converted into cash. Money consists of cash itself, which is liquid by definition, as well as other assets that are highly liquid.

Without a liquid asset like money, making purchases would be much harder.

You can see the distinction between money and other assets by asking yourself how you pay for your morning jolt of java. The cashier will accept dollar bills in return for a double mocha latte—but they won't accept stock certificates or a collection of vintage baseball cards. If you want to convert stock certificates or vintage baseball cards into a latte, you have to sell them—trade them for money—and then use the money to buy your drink.

Of course, the vast majority of stores allow you to buy goods with a debit card linked to your bank account, and many of us pay larger bills (like tuition) with checks written on our accounts. Does that make your bank account money, even if you haven't converted it into cash? Yes. **Currency in circulation**—actual cash in the hands of the public—is considered money. So are **checkable bank deposits**—bank accounts that can be accessed using debit cards, digital payments, and checks.

Some definitions of money include assets other than currency and checkable bank deposits. There are two widely used definitions of the **money supply,** the total value of financial assets in the economy that are considered money.

1. The narrower definition of money considers only the most liquid assets to be money: currency in circulation and checkable bank deposits.

2. The broader definition includes the three categories just noted plus other assets that are "almost" checkable, such as savings account deposits that can easily be transferred into a checking account with a phone call or a few taps on a smartphone. Both definitions of the money supply, however, make a distinction between those assets that can easily be used to purchase goods and services and those that can't.

Money plays a crucial role in generating *gains from trade* because it makes indirect exchange possible. Think of what happens when a cardiac surgeon buys a new refrigerator. The surgeon has valuable services to offer—namely, heart operations. The owner of the store has valuable goods to offer—refrigerators and other appliances. It would be extremely difficult for both parties if, instead of using money, they had to directly barter the goods and services they sell. In a barter system, a cardiac surgeon and an appliance store owner could trade only if the store owner happened to want a heart operation and the surgeon happened to want a new refrigerator.

This is known as the problem of finding a *double coincidence of wants:* in a barter system, two parties can trade only when each wants what the other has to offer. Money solves this problem: individuals can trade what they have to offer for money and trade money for what they want.

Because the ability to make transactions with money rather than relying on bartering makes it easier to achieve gains from trade, the existence of money increases welfare, even though money does not directly produce anything.

Let's take a closer look at the roles money plays in the economy.

Roles of Money

Money plays three main roles in any modern economy: it is a *medium of exchange*, a *store of value*, and a *unit of account*.

1. Medium of Exchange Our cardiac surgeon/refrigerator example illustrates the role of money as a **medium of exchange**—an asset that individuals use to trade for goods and services rather than for consumption. People can't eat dollar bills; rather, they use dollar bills to trade for goods and services.

In normal times, the official money of a given country—the dollar in the United States, the peso in Mexico, and so on—is also the medium of exchange in virtually all transactions in that country. During troubled economic times, however, other goods or assets often play that role instead. For example, during economic turmoil people often turn to other countries' moneys as the medium of exchange: U.S. dollars have played this role in troubled Latin American countries, as have euros in troubled Eastern European countries. In a famous example, cigarettes functioned as the medium of exchange in World War II prisoner-of-war camps: even nonsmokers traded goods and services for cigarettes because the cigarettes could in turn be easily traded for other items. Inmates at federal penitentiaries, where smoking is now banned, reportedly use packages of ramen noodles for many transactions. During the extreme German inflation of 1923, goods such as eggs and lumps of coal became, briefly, mediums of exchange.

2. Store of Value To act as a medium of exchange, money must also be a **store of value**—a means of holding purchasing power over time. To see why this is

A **medium of exchange** is an asset that individuals acquire for the purpose of trading goods and services rather than for their own consumption.

A **store of value** is a means of holding purchasing power over time.

GLOBAL COMPARISON   **THE CASH OF NATIONS**

When did you last pay for something using cash—that is, literally hand over green pieces of paper bearing portraits of historical figures? For many of us, the answer may be that it was days, weeks, and, for some, months ago. These days, many of our day-to-day purchases are made using some form of digital payment, whether it involves a card or a smartphone.

So is cash on its way out? The answer, somewhat surprisingly, is that it depends on what country you live in. One simple measure of the prevalence of cash transactions is the ratio of the value of currency in circulation to GDP, the value of goods and services produced in a nation. The accompanying figure shows this ratio for three countries, Sweden, the United States, and Japan.

At one extreme, Sweden is very nearly a cashless society: most shops don't accept cash, and half of the country's bank branches don't even handle cash. At the other extreme, Japanese still carry around a lot of cash. The United States is somewhere in the middle.

What's odd about this is that all three countries are technologically sophisticated, to about the same degree. Why are they so different when it comes to cash?

In the case of Japan, the answer seems to be mainly cultural: for a variety of reasons, Japanese citizens are still accustomed to using

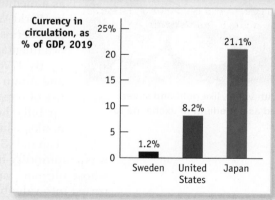

currency and are reluctant to go digital even though their society is every bit as addicted to smartphones as ours.

The U.S. case is different: as For Inquiring Minds on p. 422 explains, a majority of U.S. currency is actually held outside the country, mainly in the form of $100 bills.

Sweden, arguably, is what the monetary future will look like; it is, in fact, considering eliminating cash altogether. And even in the United States a growing number of businesses have stopped accepting cash. But not everyone is happy with that future. Recently, New York City passed a law requiring that stores continue to accept cash as payment, arguing that cashless stores effectively discriminate against people too poor to have a card linked to a bank account.

Data from: Bank for International Settlements, International Monetary Fund.

A **unit of account** is a measure used to set prices and make economic calculations.

Commodity money is a good used as a medium of exchange that has intrinsic value in other uses.

Commodity-backed money is a medium of exchange with no intrinsic value whose ultimate value is guaranteed by a promise that it can be converted into valuable goods.

necessary, imagine trying to operate an economy in which ice cream cones were the medium of exchange. Such an economy would quickly suffer from, well, monetary meltdown: your medium of exchange would likely turn into a sticky puddle before you could use it to buy something else. (As we'll see in Chapter 31, one of the problems caused by high inflation is that, in effect, it causes the value of money to "melt.") Of course, money is by no means the only store of value. Any asset that holds its purchasing power over time is a store of value. So the store-of-value role is a necessary but not distinctive feature of money.

3. Unit of Account Finally, money normally serves as the **unit of account**—the commonly accepted measure individuals use to set prices and make economic calculations. To understand the importance of this role, consider a historical fact: during the Middle Ages, peasants typically were required to provide landowners with goods and labor rather than money. A peasant might, for example, be required to work on the landowner's land one day a week and hand over one-fifth of their harvest.

Today, rents, like other prices, are almost always specified in money terms. That makes things much clearer: imagine how hard it would be to decide which apartment to rent if landlords today followed medieval practice. Suppose, for example, that one landlord says he'll let you have a place if you clean his house twice a week and bring him a pound of steak every day, whereas a second landlord wants you to clean her house just once a week but wants four pounds of chicken every day. Who's offering the better deal? It's hard to say. If, instead, the first landlord wants $600 a month and the other wants $700, the comparison is easy. In other words, without a commonly accepted measure, the terms of a transaction are harder to determine, making it more difficult to make transactions and achieve gains from trade.

Types of Money

In some form or another, money has been in use for thousands of years. For most of that time, people used **commodity money:** the medium of exchange was a good, normally gold or silver, that had intrinsic value in other uses. These alternative uses gave commodity money value independent of its role as a medium of exchange. For example, cigarettes, which served as money in World War II prisoner-of-war camps, were also valuable because many prisoners smoked. Gold was valuable because it was used for jewelry and ornamentation, aside from the fact that it was minted into coins.

By 1776, the year in which the United States declared independence and Adam Smith published *The Wealth of Nations*, there was widespread use of paper money in addition to gold or silver coins. Unlike modern dollar bills, however, this paper money consisted of notes issued by private banks, which promised to exchange their notes for gold or silver coins on demand. So the paper currency that initially replaced commodity money was **commodity-backed money,** a medium of exchange with no intrinsic value whose ultimate value was guaranteed by a promise that it could always be converted into valuable goods on demand.

The big advantage of commodity-backed money over simple commodity money, like gold and silver coins, was that it tied up fewer valuable resources. Although a note-issuing bank still had to keep some gold and silver on hand, it had to keep only enough to satisfy demands for redemption of its notes. And it could rely on the fact that on a normal day only a fraction of its paper notes would be redeemed. So the bank needed to keep only a portion of the total value of its notes in circulation in the form of gold and silver in its vaults. It could then lend out the remaining gold and silver to those who wished to use it. This allowed society to use the remaining gold and silver for other purposes, all with no loss in the ability to achieve gains from trade.

Goods with value, like gold and silver, were used as a medium of exchange for centuries.

By issuing paper notes to function as money instead of gold and silver coins, banks were able to free up valuable resources.

In a famous passage in *The Wealth of Nations,* Adam Smith described paper money as a "waggon-way through the air." Smith was making an analogy between money and an imaginary highway that did not absorb valuable land beneath it. An actual highway provides a useful service but at a cost: land that could be used to grow crops is instead paved over. If the highway could be built through the air, it wouldn't destroy useful land. As Smith understood, when banks replaced gold and silver money with paper notes, they accomplished a similar feat: they reduced the amount of real resources used by society to provide the functions of money.

At this point you may ask: why make any use at all of gold and silver in the monetary system, even to back paper money? In fact, today's monetary system goes even further than the system Smith admired, having eliminated any role for gold and silver. A U.S. dollar bill isn't commodity money, and it isn't even commodity-backed. Rather, its value arises entirely from the fact that it is generally accepted as a means of payment, a role that is ultimately decreed by the U.S. government. Money whose value derives entirely from its official status as a means of exchange is known as **fiat money** because it exists by government fiat, a historical term for a policy declared by a ruler.

Fiat money has two major advantages over commodity-backed money. First, it is even more of a "waggon-way through the air"—creating it doesn't use up any real resources beyond the paper it's printed on. Second, the supply of money can be adjusted based on the needs of the economy, instead of being determined by the amount of gold and silver that prospectors happen to discover.

Fiat money, though, poses some risks. In the opening story, we described one such risk—counterfeiting. Counterfeiters usurp a privilege of the U.S. government, which has the sole legal right to print dollar bills. And the benefit that counterfeiters get by exchanging fake bills for real goods and services comes at the expense of the U.S. federal government, which covers a small but nontrivial part of its own expenses by issuing new currency to meet a growing demand for money.

Another large risk is that governments that can create money whenever they feel like it will be tempted to abuse the privilege. In Chapter 31 we'll learn how governments sometimes rely too heavily on printing money to pay their bills, leading to high inflation. In this chapter, however, we'll stay focused on the question of what money is and how it is managed.

Measuring the Money Supply

The Federal Reserve calculates the size of two **monetary aggregates,** overall measures of the money supply, which differ in how strictly money is defined. The two aggregates are known, rather cryptically, as M1 and M2. (There used to be a third aggregate named—you guessed it—M3, but in 2006 the Federal Reserve stopped measuring it, having determined that it was no longer useful.)

M1, the narrowest definition, contains only currency in circulation (also known as cash) and checkable bank deposits. M2 adds several other kinds of assets, often referred to as **near-moneys**—financial assets that aren't directly usable as a medium of exchange but can be readily converted into cash or checkable bank deposits, such as savings accounts. Examples are time deposits such as small-denomination *certificates of deposit (CDs),* which aren't checkable but can be withdrawn at any time before their maturity date by paying a penalty. Because currency and checkable deposits are directly usable as a medium of exchange, M1 is the most liquid measure of money.

Figure 29-1 shows the actual composition of M1 and M2 as of March 2020, in billions of dollars. M1 was valued at \$4,267.6 billion, with about 41% accounted for by currency in circulation and the rest accounted for by checkable bank deposits. In turn, M1 made up 27% of M2, valued at \$16,103.9 billion. M2 consists of M1 plus other types of assets: two types of bank deposits, known as savings deposits and time deposits, both of which are considered noncheckable, plus money market funds, which are mutual funds that invest only in liquid assets and

Fiat money is a medium of exchange whose value derives entirely from its official status as a means of payment.

A **monetary aggregate** is an overall measure of the money supply.

Near-moneys are financial assets that can't be directly used as a medium of exchange but can be readily converted into cash or checkable bank deposits.

FIGURE 29-1 Monetary Aggregates, March 2020

The Federal Reserve uses two definitions of the money supply, M1 and M2. As panel (a) shows, more than half of M1 consists of checkable bank deposits with currency in circulation making up all of the rest. M2, as panel (b) shows, has a much broader definition: it includes M1 plus a range of other deposits and deposit-like assets, making it almost four times as large. (Numbers may not add to 100% due to rounding.)
Data from: Federal Reserve Bank of St. Louis.

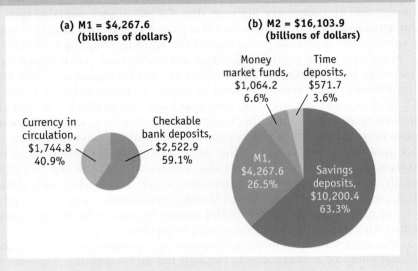

(a) M1 = $4,267.6
(billions of dollars)

Currency in circulation, $1,744.8 40.9%

Checkable bank deposits, $2,522.9 59.1%

(b) M2 = $16,103.9
(billions of dollars)

Money market funds, $1,064.2 6.6%

Time deposits, $571.7 3.6%

M1, $4,267.6 26.5%

Savings deposits, $10,200.4 63.3%

bear a close resemblance to bank deposits. These near-moneys pay interest—cash (currency in circulation) does not—and they typically pay higher interest rates than any offered on checkable bank deposits.

FOR INQUIRING MINDS All About the Benjamins

There is nearly $1.8 trillion of U.S. currency in circulation in the United States, almost $5,500 for every man, woman, and child. Most individuals don't carry this amount in their wallets—the average American holds only about $60 in cash, probably because people increasingly make purchases using debit cards and smartphone apps. So where is all that cash sitting?

Some of it can be found in cash registers. Businesses as well as individuals need to hold cash. However, the largest proportion of these huge currency holdings—approximately 60%—is in the hands of foreign residents who so distrust their own national currencies that the U.S. dollar has

become a widely accepted medium of exchange and store of value.

Cash is also widely used to keep transactions hidden—by criminals such as drug dealers, or businesspeople looking to avoid paying taxes on their income. The prevalence of illegal transactions may explain why around three-quarters of the value of U.S. currency in circulation takes the form of $100 bills—sometimes called "Benjamins," because they bear the portrait of Benjamin Franklin—which many legitimate businesses won't even accept.

The desire to shield transactions from the eyes of authorities helps to explain the growth of Bitcoin, a virtual currency created

in 2009. It is basically a computing algorithm that creates electronic tokens that are accepted by some as currency.

But what leads people to place faith in a virtual currency—to accept it in place of "real" money? As with the dollar, faith in Bitcoin arose from the belief that someone else, at a later date, would accept it in exchange for something real. As long as there are people who want to hide transactions, that's not an unreasonable belief. One drawback to Bitcoin is its susceptibility to hacking. Despite that, the attractions of Bitcoin, and another new virtual currency, Ethereum, are so great that their combined value in April 2020 was approximately $150 billion.

ECONOMICS >> *in Action*
The History of the Dollar

U.S. dollar bills are pure fiat money: they have no intrinsic value, and they are not backed by anything that does. But U.S. money wasn't always like that. In the early days of European settlement, the colonies that would become the United States used commodity money, partly consisting of gold and silver coins minted in Europe. But because such coins were scarce on this side of the Atlantic, the colonists relied on a variety of other forms of commodity money. For example, settlers in Virginia used tobacco as money and settlers in the Northeast used *wampum,* made from a clamshell.

Later in U.S. history, commodity-backed paper money came into widespread use. But this wasn't paper money as we now know it, issued by the U.S. government and bearing the signature of the Secretary of the Treasury. Before the Civil War, the U.S. government didn't issue any paper money. Instead, dollar bills were issued by private banks, which promised that their bills could be redeemed for gold or silver coins on demand. These promises weren't always credible because banks sometimes failed, leaving holders of their bills with worthless pieces of paper. Understandably, people were reluctant to accept currency from any bank rumored to be in financial trouble. In this private money system, some dollars were less valuable than others.

A curious legacy of that time was notes issued by the Citizens' Bank of Louisiana, based in New Orleans, that became among the most widely used bank notes in the southern states. These notes were printed in English on one side and French on the other. (At the time, many people in New Orleans, originally a colony of France, spoke French.) Thus, the $10 bill read *Ten* on one side and *Dix*, the French word for *ten*, on the other. These $10 bills became known as *dixies*, probably the source of the nickname of the U.S. South.

The U.S. government began issuing official paper money, called *greenbacks*, in 1862 as a way to pay for the ongoing Civil War. At first greenbacks had no fixed value in terms of commodities. After 1873, the U.S. government guaranteed the value of a dollar in terms of gold, effectively turning dollars into commodity-backed money.

In 1933, when President Franklin D. Roosevelt broke the link between dollars and gold, his own federal budget director—who feared that the public would lose confidence in the dollar if it wasn't ultimately backed by gold—declared ominously, "This will be the end of Western civilization." It wasn't. The link between the dollar and gold was restored a few years later, then dropped again—seemingly for good—in August 1971. Despite the warnings of doom, the U.S. dollar went on to become the world's most widely used currency.

>> Check Your Understanding 29-1

Solutions appear at back of book.

1. Suppose you have a gift card, good for certain products at participating stores. Is this gift card money? Why or why not?

2. Although most bank accounts pay some interest, depositors can get a higher interest rate by buying a certificate of deposit, or CD. The difference between a CD and a checking account is that the depositor pays a penalty for withdrawing the money before the CD comes due—a period of months or even years. Small CDs are counted in M2 but not in M1. Explain why they are not part of M1.

3. Explain why a system of commodity-backed money uses resources more efficiently than a system of commodity money.

>> Quick Review

• **Money** is any asset that can easily be used to purchase goods and services. **Currency in circulation** and **checkable bank deposits** are both part of the **money supply.**

• Money plays three roles: a **medium of exchange,** a **store of value,** and a **unit of account.**

• Historically, money took the form first of **commodity money,** then of **commodity-backed money.** Today the dollar is pure **fiat money.**

• The money supply is measured by two **monetary aggregates:** M1 and M2. M1 consists of currency in circulation, and checkable deposits. M2 consists of M1 plus various kinds of **near-moneys.**

‖ The Monetary Role of Banks

Roughly 41% of M1, the narrowest definition of the money supply, consists of currency in circulation—$1 bills, $5 bills, and so on. It's obvious where currency comes from: it's printed by the U.S. Treasury. But the rest of M1 consists of checkable bank deposits; savings deposits account for the great bulk of M2, the broader definition of the money supply. By either measure, then, bank deposits are a major component of the money supply. And this fact brings us to our next topic: the monetary role of banks.

Bank reserves are the currency banks hold in their vaults plus their deposits at the Federal Reserve.

A **T-account** is a tool for analyzing a business's financial position by showing, in a single table, the business's assets (on the left) and liabilities (on the right).

What Banks Do

As we learned in Chapter 25, a bank is a *financial intermediary* that uses liquid assets in the form of bank deposits to finance the illiquid investments of borrowers. Banks can create liquidity because it isn't necessary for a bank to keep all of the funds deposited with it in the form of highly liquid assets. Except in the case of a *bank run*—which we'll get to shortly—all of a bank's depositors won't want to withdraw their funds at the same time. So a bank can provide its depositors with liquid assets yet still invest much of the depositors' funds in illiquid assets, such as mortgages and business loans.

Banks can't, however, lend out all the funds placed in their hands by depositors because they have to satisfy any depositor who wants to withdraw their funds. In order to meet these demands, a bank must keep substantial quantities of liquid assets on hand. In the modern U.S. banking system, these assets take the form either of currency in the bank's vault or deposits held in the bank's own account at the Federal Reserve. As we'll see shortly, the latter can be converted into currency more or less instantly. Currency in bank vaults and bank deposits held at the Federal Reserve are called **bank reserves.** Because bank reserves are in bank vaults and at the Federal Reserve, not held by the public, they are not part of currency in circulation.

To understand the role of banks in determining the money supply, we start by introducing a simple tool for analyzing the financial position of a bank or business: a **T-account.** A T-account summarizes the financial position of a bank or business in a single table by showing assets on the left and liabilities on the right.

Figure 29-2 shows the T-account for a hypothetical business that *isn't* a bank—Samantha's Smoothies. According to Figure 29-2, Samantha's Smoothies owns a building worth $30,000 and has $15,000 worth of smoothie-making equipment. These are assets, so they're on the left side of the table. To finance its opening, the business borrowed $20,000 from a local bank. That's a liability, so the loan is on the right side of the table. By looking at the T-account, you can immediately see what Samantha's Smoothies owns and what it owes. Oh, and it's called a T-account because the lines in the table make a T-shape.

Samantha's Smoothies is an ordinary, nonbank business. Now let's look at the T-account for a hypothetical bank, First Street Bank, which is the repository of $1 million in bank deposits.

Figure 29-3 shows First Street Bank's financial position. The loans First Street Bank has made are on the left side because they're assets: they represent funds that those who have borrowed from the bank are expected to repay. The bank's only other assets, in this simplified example, are its reserves, which, as we've learned, can take the form either of cash in the bank's vault or deposits at the Federal Reserve. On the right side are the bank's liabilities, which in this example consist entirely of deposits made by customers at First Street Bank. These are liabilities because they represent funds that must ultimately be repaid to depositors.

Notice that in this example First Street Bank's assets are larger than its liabilities. And that's the way it is supposed to be. Banks are required by law to maintain assets that are larger than their liabilities by a specific percentage.

FIGURE 29-2 A T-Account for Samantha's Smoothies

A T-account summarizes a business's financial position. Its assets, in this case consisting of a building and some smoothie-making machinery, are on the left side. Its liabilities, consisting of the money it owes to a local bank, are on the right side.

Assets		Liabilities	
Building	$30,000	Loan from bank	$20,000
Smoothie-making machines	$15,000		

FIGURE 29-3 Assets and Liabilities of First Street Bank

First Street Bank's assets consist of $1,200,000 in loans and $100,000 in reserves. Its liabilities consist of $1,000,000 in deposits—money owed to people who have placed funds in First Street's hands.

Assets		Liabilities	
Loans	$1,200,000	Deposits	$1,000,000
Reserves	$100,000		

We will assume that First Street Bank holds reserves equal to 10% of its customers' bank deposits. The fraction of bank deposits that a bank holds as reserves is its **reserve ratio.** In the modern U.S. system, the Federal Reserve—which, among other things, regulates banks operating in the United States—sets a minimum required reserve ratio that banks must maintain. To understand why banks are regulated, let's consider a problem banks can face: bank runs.

The **reserve ratio** is the fraction of bank deposits that a bank holds as reserves.

A **bank run** is a phenomenon in which many of a bank's depositors try to withdraw their funds due to fears of a bank failure.

The Problem of Bank Runs

A bank can lend out most of the funds deposited in its care because in normal times only a small fraction of its depositors want to withdraw their funds on any given day. But what would happen if, for some reason, all or at least a large fraction of its depositors tried to withdraw their funds during a short period of time, such as over a couple of days?

If a significant share of its depositors demanded their money back at the same time, the bank wouldn't be able to raise enough cash to meet those demands. The reason for this cash shortfall is that banks convert most of their depositors' funds into loans made to borrowers. That's how banks earn revenue—by charging interest on loans.

Bank loans, however, are illiquid: they can't easily be converted into cash on short notice. To see why, imagine that First Street Bank has lent $100,000 to Drive-a-Peach Used Cars, a local dealership. To raise cash to meet demands for withdrawals, First Street Bank can sell its loan to Drive-a-Peach to someone else—another bank or an individual investor. But if First Street Bank tries to sell the loan quickly, potential buyers will be wary: they will suspect that First Street Bank wants to sell the loan because there is something wrong and the loan might not be repaid. As a result, First Street Bank can sell the loan quickly only by offering it for sale at a deep discount—say, a discount of 40%, for a sale price of $60,000.

The upshot is that if a significant number of First Street Bank's depositors suddenly decided to withdraw their funds, the bank's efforts to raise the necessary cash quickly would force it to sell off its assets very cheaply. Inevitably, this leads to a *bank failure:* the bank would be unable to pay off its depositors in full.

What might start this whole process? That is, what might lead First Street Bank's depositors to rush to pull their money out? A plausible answer is a spreading rumor that the bank is in financial trouble. Even if depositors aren't sure the rumor is true, they are likely to play it safe and get their money out while they still can. And it gets worse: a depositor who simply thinks that *other* depositors are going to panic and try to get their money out will realize that this could "break the bank." So this depositor joins the rush. In other words, fear about a bank's financial condition can be a self-fulfilling prophecy: depositors who believe that other depositors will rush to the exit will rush to the exit themselves.

A **bank run,** then, is a phenomenon in which many of a bank's depositors try to withdraw their funds due to fears of a bank failure. Moreover, bank runs aren't bad only for the bank in question and its depositors. Historically, they have often proved contagious, with a run on one bank leading to a loss of faith in other banks, causing additional bank runs.

Deposit insurance guarantees that a bank's depositors will be paid even if the bank can't come up with the funds, up to a maximum amount per account.

Reserve requirements are rules set by the Federal Reserve that determine the minimum reserve ratio for banks.

The **discount window** is an arrangement in which the Federal Reserve stands ready to lend money to banks in trouble.

The upcoming Economics in Action describes an actual case of just such a contagion, the wave of bank runs that swept across the United States in the early 1930s. In response to that experience and similar experiences in other countries, the United States and most other modern governments established a system of bank regulations that protect depositors and prevent most bank runs.

Bank Regulation

Should you worry about losing money in the United States due to a bank run? As long as it's a conventional bank, the answer is no. After the banking crises of the 1930s, the United States and most other countries put into place a system designed to protect depositors and the economy as a whole against bank runs. This system has four main features: *deposit insurance, capital requirements, reserve requirements,* and, in addition, banks have access to the *discount window,* a source of cash when it's needed.

1. Deposit Insurance Almost all banks in the United States advertise themselves as a "member of the FDIC"—the Federal Deposit Insurance Corporation. The FDIC provides **deposit insurance,** a guarantee that depositors will be paid from FDIC funds, even if the bank is unable to satisfy withdrawals, up to a maximum amount per account. The FDIC currently guarantees the first $250,000 per depositor, per insured bank.

It is worth noting that deposit insurance doesn't just protect depositors if a bank fails. It also greatly reduces the potential for bank failures from bank runs by eliminating the main reason for bank runs: since depositors know their funds are safe even if a bank should fail, they have no incentive to rush to withdraw their accounts because of a rumor that the bank is in trouble.

2. Capital Requirements Although deposit insurance protects the banking system against bank runs, it creates a well-known incentive problem. Because depositors are protected from loss, they have no incentive to monitor their bank's financial health, allowing risky behavior by the bank to go undetected. At the same time, the owners of banks have an incentive to engage in overly risky investment behavior, such as making questionable loans at high interest rates. That's because if all goes well, the owners profit. But if things go badly, the government covers the losses through federal deposit insurance.

To reduce the incentive for excessive risk taking, regulators require that bank owners hold substantially more assets than the value of bank deposits. That way, the bank still has assets larger than its deposits even if some of its loans go bad, and losses will accrue against the bank's assets, not the government. The excess of a bank's assets over its bank deposits and other liabilities is called the *bank's capital.* Bank capital is sometimes referred to as the bank's *net worth* or *owner's equity.* For example, First Street Bank has capital of $300,000, equal to ($1,200,000 + $100,000) − $1,000,000. This is equivalent to $300,000/($1,200,000 + $100,000) = 23% of the total value of its assets. In practice, banks' capital is required to equal at least 7% of the value of their assets.

3. Reserve Requirements Another regulation used to reduce the risk of bank runs is **reserve requirements,** rules set by the Federal Reserve that specify the minimum reserve ratio for banks. For example, in the United States, the minimum reserve ratio for checkable bank deposits is 10%.

4. The Discount Window One final protection against bank runs is the fact that the Federal Reserve, which we discuss more thoroughly later in this chapter, stands ready to lend money to banks in trouble, an arrangement known as the **discount window.** The ability to borrow money means a bank can avoid being forced to sell its assets at fire-sale prices in order to satisfy the demands of a sudden rush of depositors demanding cash. Instead, it can turn to the Fed and borrow the funds it needs to pay off depositors.

Limits to Regulation's Reach: Shadow Banking The modern U.S. banking system is well-protected against old-fashioned bank runs. Unfortunately, as many investors learned to their horror in 2008, although old-fashioned bank runs may be a thing of the past, new-fashioned bank runs—which look very different, but have many of the same effects—can still happen.

How is that possible? The answer lies in a variety of financial arrangements that aren't exactly banking in the traditional sense, but serve more or less the same purposes as conventional banking, and can pose serious risks. These arrangements, referred to as *shadow banking*, are undertaken by nondepository financial firms, including investment banks, insurance companies, hedge fund companies, and money market fund companies. Because they don't accept deposits, firms in the shadow banking sector aren't fully covered by the protections or regulations that have made conventional, depository banking so safe. We'll say more about shadow banking later in the chapter.

ECONOMICS >> *in Action*
It's a Wonderful Banking System

The classic 1946 film *It's a Wonderful Life* is a holiday tradition. It stars Jimmy Stewart as George Bailey, a small-town banker whose life is saved by an angel. One pivotal scene depicts a run on Bailey's bank, as fearful depositors rush to take their funds out.

When the movie was made, such scenes were still fresh memories for Americans who had lived through the Great Depression. There was a wave of bank runs in late 1930, a second wave in the spring of 1931, and a third wave in early 1933. By the end, more than a third of the nation's banks had failed. To bring the panic to an end, on March 6, 1933, the newly inaugurated president, Franklin D. Roosevelt, declared a national *bank holiday,* closing all banks for a week to give bank regulators time to close unhealthy banks and certify healthy ones.

Since then, regulation has protected the United States and other wealthy countries against most bank runs. In fact, the scene in *It's a Wonderful Life* was already out of date when the movie was made. But recent decades have seen several waves of bank runs in developing countries. For example, bank runs played a role in an economic crisis that swept Southeast Asia in 1997–1998 and in the severe economic crisis in Argentina that began in late 2001. And a panic with strong resemblance to a wave of bank runs swept world financial markets in 2008.

Notice that we said *most bank runs*. There are some limits on deposit insurance; in particular, as we've learned, in the United States currently only the first $250,000 of an individual depositor's funds in an insured bank is covered. As a result, there can still be a run on a bank perceived as troubled. In fact, that's exactly what happened in July 2008 to IndyMac Bank, a Pasadena-based lender that had made a large number of questionable home loans. As questions about IndyMac's financial soundness were raised, depositors began pulling out funds, forcing federal regulators to step in and close the bank. In Britain the limits on deposit insurance are much lower, which exposed the bank Northern Rock to a classic bank run in September 2007. Unlike the bank runs of the 1930s, however, most depositors at both IndyMac and Northern Rock got all their funds back—and the panics at these banks didn't spread to other institutions.

Panicky IndyMac depositors lined up to pull their money out of the troubled California bank in July 2008.

>> Check Your Understanding 29-2
Solutions appear at back of book.

1. Suppose you are a depositor at First Street Bank. You hear a rumor that the bank has suffered serious losses on its loans. Every depositor knows that the rumor isn't true, but each thinks that most other depositors believe the rumor. Why, in the absence of deposit insurance, could this lead to a bank run? How does deposit insurance change the situation?

2. A con artist has a great idea: they'll open a bank without investing any capital and lend all the deposits at high interest rates to real estate developers. If the real estate market booms, the loans will be repaid and they'll make high profits. If the real estate market goes bust, the loans won't be repaid and the bank will fail—but they will not lose any of their own wealth. How would modern bank regulation frustrate this scheme?

‖ Determining the Money Supply

Without banks, there would be no checkable deposits, so the quantity of currency in circulation would equal the money supply. In that case, the money supply would be solely determined by whoever controls government minting and printing presses. But banks do exist, and through their creation of checkable bank deposits they affect the money supply in two ways.

1. Banks reduce the money supply by removing some currency from circulation: dollar bills that are sitting in bank vaults, as opposed to sitting in people's wallets, aren't part of the money supply.

2. Much more importantly, banks increase the money supply by making loans, the total value of which is much larger than their reserves. As a result, they make the money supply larger than just the value of currency in circulation.

Our next topic is how banks create money and what determines the amount of money they create.

How Banks Create Money

To see how banks create money, let's examine what happens when someone decides to deposit currency in a bank. Consider the example of Silas, a miser, who keeps a shoebox full of cash under his bed. Suppose Silas realizes that it would be safer, as well as more convenient, to deposit that cash in the bank and to use his debit card when shopping. Assume that he deposits $1,000 into a checkable account at First Street Bank. What effect will Silas's actions have on the money supply?

Panel (a) of Figure 29-4 shows the initial effect of his deposit. First Street Bank credits Silas with $1,000 in his account, so the economy's checkable bank deposits rise by $1,000. Meanwhile, Silas's cash goes into the vault, raising First Street's reserves by $1,000 as well.

This initial transaction has no effect on the money supply. Currency in circulation, part of the money supply, falls by $1,000. Checkable bank deposits, also part of the money supply, rise by the same amount.

But this is not the end of the story, because First Street Bank can now lend out part of Silas's deposit. Assume that it holds 10% of Silas's deposit—$100—in reserves and lends the rest out in cash to Silas's neighbor, Maya. The effect of this second stage is shown in panel (b). First Street's deposits remain unchanged, and so does the value of its assets. But the composition of its assets changes: by making the loan, it reduces its reserves by $900, so that they are only $100 larger than they were before Silas made his deposit. In the place of the $900 reduction in reserves, the bank has acquired an IOU, its $900 cash loan to Maya.

FIGURE 29-4 Effect on the Money Supply of Turning Cash into a Checkable Deposit at First Street Bank

(a) Initial Effect Before Bank Makes a New Loan

Assets		Liabilities	
Loans	No change	Checkable	
Reserves	+$1,000	deposits	+$1,000

(b) Effect When Bank Makes a New Loan

Assets		Liabilities
Loans	+$900	No change
Reserves	−$900	

When Silas deposits $1,000 (which had been stashed under his bed) into a checkable bank account, there is initially no effect on the money supply: currency in circulation falls by $1,000, but checkable bank deposits rise by $1,000. The corresponding entries on the bank's T-account, depicted in panel (a), show deposits initially rising by $1,000 and the bank's reserves initially rising by $1,000. In the second stage, depicted in panel (b), the bank holds 10% of Silas's deposit ($100) as reserves and lends out the rest ($900) to Maya. As a result, its reserves fall by $900 and its loans increase by $900. Its liabilities, including Silas's $1,000 deposit, are unchanged. The money supply, the sum of checkable bank deposits and currency in circulation, has now increased by $900—the $900 now held by Maya.

So by putting $900 of Silas's cash back into circulation by lending it to Maya, First Street Bank has, in fact, increased the money supply. That is, the sum of currency in circulation and checkable bank deposits has risen by $900 compared to what it had been when Silas's cash was still under his bed. Although Silas is still the owner of $1,000, now in the form of a checkable deposit, Maya has the use of $900 in cash from her borrowings.

And this may not be the end of the story. Suppose that Maya uses her cash to buy a television from Acme Merchandise. What does Anne Acme, the store's owner, do with the cash? If she holds on to it, the money supply doesn't increase any further. But suppose she deposits the $900 into a checkable bank deposit—say, at Second Street Bank. Second Street Bank, in turn, will keep only part of that deposit in reserves, lending out the rest, creating still more money.

Assume that Second Street Bank, like First Street Bank, keeps 10% of any bank deposit in reserves and lends out the rest. Then it will keep $90 in reserves and lend out $810 of Anne's deposit to another borrower, further increasing the money supply.

Table 29-1 shows the process of money creation we have described so far. To simplify the table we will assume that, at first, the money supply consists only of Silas's $1,000. After he deposits the cash into a checkable bank deposit and the bank makes a loan, the money supply rises to $1,900. After the second deposit and the second loan, the money supply rises to $2,710. And the process will, of course, continue from there. (Although we have considered the case in which Silas places his cash in a checkable bank deposit, the results would be the same if he put it into any type of near-money.)

This process of money creation may sound familiar. In Chapter 26 we described the *multiplier process:* an initial increase in real GDP leads to a rise in consumer spending, which leads to a further rise in real GDP, which leads to a further rise in consumer spending, and so on. What we have here is another kind of multiplier—the *money multiplier.* We'll now see what determines the size of this multiplier.

TABLE 29-1 How Banks Create Money

	Currency in circulation	Checkable bank deposits	Money supply
First stage Silas keeps his cash under his bed.	$1,000	$0	$1,000
Second stage Silas deposits cash in First Street Bank, which lends out $900 to Maya, who then pays it to Anne Acme.	900	1,000	1,900
Third stage Anne Acme deposits $900 in Second Street Bank, which lends out $810 to another borrower.	810	1,900	2,710

Excess reserves are a bank's reserves over and above its required reserves.

Reserves, Bank Deposits, and the Money Multiplier

In tracing out the effect of Silas's deposit in Table 29-1, we assumed that the funds a bank lends out always end up being deposited either in the same bank or in another bank—so funds disbursed as loans come back to the banking system, even if not to the lending bank itself.

In reality, some of these loaned funds may be held by borrowers in their wallets and not deposited in a bank, meaning that some of the loaned amount "leaks" out of the banking system. Such leaks reduce the size of the money multiplier, just as leaks of real income into savings reduce the size of the real GDP multiplier. (Bear in mind, however, that the leak here comes from the fact that borrowers keep some of their funds in currency, rather than the fact that consumers save some of their income.)

"There's money in there that could be used for other purposes."

But let's set that complication aside for a moment and consider how the money supply is determined in a checkable-deposits-only monetary system, where funds are always deposited in bank accounts and none are held in wallets as currency. That is, in our checkable-deposits-only monetary system, any and all funds borrowed from a bank are immediately deposited into a checkable bank account. We'll assume that banks are required to satisfy a minimum reserve ratio of 10% and that every bank lends out all of its **excess reserves,** reserves over and above the amount needed to satisfy the minimum reserve ratio.

Now suppose that for some reason a bank suddenly finds itself with $1,000 in excess reserves. What happens? The answer is that the bank will lend out that $1,000, which will end up as a checkable bank deposit somewhere in the banking system, launching a money multiplier process very similar to the process shown in Table 29-1.

In the first stage, the bank lends out its excess reserves of $1,000, which becomes a checkable bank deposit somewhere. The bank that receives the $1,000 deposit keeps 10%, or $100, as reserves and lends out the remaining 90%, or $900, which again becomes a checkable bank deposit somewhere. The bank receiving this $900 deposit again keeps 10%, which is $90, as reserves and lends out the remaining $810. The bank receiving this $810 keeps $81 in reserves and lends out the remaining $729, and so on. As a result of this process, the total increase in checkable bank deposits is equal to a sum that looks like:

$$\$1,000 + \$900 + \$810 + \$729 + \dots$$

We'll use the symbol *rr* for the reserve ratio. More generally, the total increase in checkable bank deposits that is generated when a bank lends out $1,000 in excess reserves is:

(29-1) Increase in checkable bank deposits from $1,000 in excess reserves =
$$\$1,000 + (\$1,000 \times (1-rr)) + (\$1,000 \times (1-rr)^2) + (\$1,000 \times (1-rr)^3) + \dots$$

As we saw in Chapter 26, an infinite series of this form can be simplified to:

(29-2) Increase in checkable bank deposits from $1,000 in excess reserves =
$$\$1,000/rr$$

Given a reserve ratio of 10%, or 0.1, a $1,000 increase in excess reserves will increase the total value of checkable bank deposits by $1,000/0.1 = $10,000. In fact, in a checkable-deposits-only monetary system, the total value of checkable bank deposits will be equal to the value of bank reserves divided by the reserve ratio. Or to put it a different way, if the reserve ratio is 10%, each $1 of reserves held by a bank supports $1/*rr* = $1/0.1 = $10 of checkable bank deposits.

The Money Multiplier in Reality

In reality, the determination of the money supply is more complicated than our simple model suggests because it depends not only on the ratio of reserves to bank deposits but also on the fraction of the money supply that individuals choose to hold in the form of currency. In fact, we already saw this in our example of Silas depositing the cash under his bed: when he chose to hold a checkable bank deposit instead of currency, he set in motion an increase in the money supply.

To define the money multiplier in practice, it's important to recognize that the Federal Reserve controls the *sum* of bank reserves and currency in circulation, called the *monetary base*, but it does not control the allocation of that sum between bank reserves and currency in circulation. Consider Silas and his deposit one more time: by taking the cash from under his bed and depositing it in a bank, he reduced the quantity of currency in circulation but increased bank reserves by an equal amount—leaving the *monetary base*, on net, unchanged. The **monetary base,** which is the quantity the monetary authorities control, is the sum of currency in circulation and reserves held by banks.

The monetary base is different from the money supply in two ways.

1. Bank reserves, which are part of the monetary base, aren't considered part of the money supply. A $1 bill in someone's wallet is considered money because it's available for an individual to spend, but a $1 bill held as bank reserves in a bank vault or deposited at the Federal Reserve isn't considered part of the money supply because it's not available for spending.

2. Checkable bank deposits, which are part of the money supply because they are available for spending, aren't part of the monetary base.

Figure 29-5 illustrates the two concepts. The circle on the left represents the monetary base, consisting of bank reserves plus currency in circulation. The circle on the right represents the money supply, consisting mainly of currency in circulation plus checkable or near-checkable bank deposits. As the figure indicates, currency in circulation is part of both the monetary base and the money supply. But bank reserves aren't part of the money supply, and checkable or near-checkable bank deposits aren't part of the monetary base. In practice, most of the monetary base actually consists of currency in circulation, which also makes up about half of the money supply.

Now we can formally define the **money multiplier:** it's the ratio of the money supply to the monetary base. Before the financial crisis of 2008, it was about 1.6, as calculated from official Federal Reserve statistics. After the crisis, it fell

The **monetary base** is the sum of currency in circulation and bank reserves.

The **money multiplier** is the ratio of the money supply to the monetary base.

FIGURE 29-5 The Monetary Base and the Money Supply

The monetary base is equal to bank reserves plus currency in circulation. It is different from the money supply, consisting mainly of checkable or near-checkable bank deposits plus currency in circulation. Each dollar of bank reserves backs several dollars of bank deposits. As a result, in normal economic times, the money supply is larger than the monetary base, making the circle at right larger than the circle on the left. However, in extraordinary economic times, as in the aftermath of the 2008 financial crisis, the monetary base grew, overtaking the money supply, making the circle at right smaller than the circle on the left.

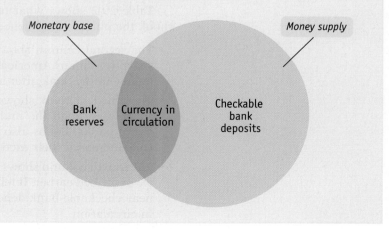

The collapse of Lehman Brothers and the ensuing financial crisis prompted the Federal Reserve to dramatically increase the monetary base in order to stabilize the economy.

to about 0.7. Even before the crisis it was a lot smaller than $1/0.1 = 10$, which would be the money multiplier in a checkable-deposits-only system with a reserve ratio of 10% (the minimum required ratio for most checkable deposits in the United States).

The reason the actual money multiplier has been smaller than 10 is that people hold significant amounts of cash, and a dollar of currency in circulation, unlike a dollar in reserves, doesn't support multiple dollars of the money supply. In fact, before the crisis currency in circulation accounted for more than 90% of the monetary base.

At the beginning of 2009, currency in circulation had dropped to only 40% of the monetary base. Over a decade later, in 2019, the percentage had only increased slightly, to 47%. What happened, basically, is that the Federal Reserve dramatically expanded the monetary base in response to the financial crisis. The Fed undertook this action in an effort to stabilize the economy after Lehman Brothers, a key financial institution, failed in September 2008. However, banks saw few opportunities for safe, profitable lending at the time. So rather than lending out the increase in the monetary base, they parked it at the Federal Reserve in the form of deposits that counted as part of the monetary base. As a result, currency in circulation no longer dominated the monetary base, as the surge in deposits at the Fed made the monetary base larger than M1. As a result, the actual money multiplier fell to less than 1 as banks held much more than the required 10% in reserves at the Fed. It wasn't until 2019 when the money multiplier was finally back above 1: by March 2020 it stood at 1.01.

ECONOMICS >> *in Action*
Multiplying Money Down

TABLE 29-2 The Effects of Bank Runs, 1929–1933			
	Currency in circulation	Checkable bank deposits	M1
	(billions of dollars)		
1929	$3.90	$22.74	$26.64
1933	5.09	14.82	19.91
Percent change	+31%	−35%	−25%

Data from: U.S. Census Bureau (1975), *Historical Statistics of the United States.*

In our hypothetical example illustrating how banks create money, we described Silas the miser taking the currency from under his bed and turning it into a checkable bank deposit. This led to an increase in the money supply as banks engaged in successive waves of lending backed by Silas's funds. It follows that if something happened to make Silas revert to old habits, taking his money out of the bank and putting it back under his bed, the result would be less lending and, ultimately, a decline in the money supply. That's exactly what happened as a result of the bank runs of the 1930s.

Table 29-2 shows what happened between 1929 and 1933, as bank failures shook the public's confidence in the banking system:

- The second column shows the public's holdings of currency. This increased sharply, as many Americans decided that money under the bed was safer than money in the bank after all.

- The third column shows the value of checkable bank deposits. This fell sharply, through the multiplier process, when individuals pulled their cash out of banks. Loans also fell because banks that survived the waves of bank runs increased their excess reserves, just in case another wave began.

- The fourth column shows the value of M1, the first of the monetary aggregates we described earlier. It fell sharply because the total reduction in checkable or near-checkable bank deposits was much larger than the increase in currency in circulation.

1. Assume that total reserves are equal to $200 and total checkable bank deposits are equal to $1,000. Also assume that the public does not hold any currency. Now suppose that the required reserve ratio falls from 20% to 10%. Trace out how this leads to an expansion in bank deposits.

2. Take the example of Silas depositing his $1,000 in cash into First Street Bank and assume that the required reserve ratio is 10%. But now assume that each time someone receives a bank loan, they keep half the loan in cash. Explain the resulting expansion in the money supply.

The Federal Reserve System

Who's in charge of ensuring that banks maintain enough reserves? Who decides how large the monetary base will be? The answer, in the United States, is an institution known as the Federal Reserve, or the Fed. The Federal Reserve is a **central bank**—an institution that oversees and regulates the banking system and controls the monetary base.

Other central banks include the Bank of England, the People's Bank of China, the Bank of Japan, and the European Central Bank, or ECB. The ECB acts as a common central bank for 19 European countries: Austria, Belgium, Cyprus, Estonia, Finland, France, Germany, Greece, Ireland, Italy, Latvia, Lithuania, Luxembourg, Malta, the Netherlands, Portugal, Slovakia, Slovenia, and Spain. The world's oldest central bank is Sweden's Sveriges Riksbank, which awards the Nobel Prize in economics.

The Structure of the Fed

The legal status of the Fed, which was created in 1913, is unusual: it is not exactly part of the U.S. government, but it is not really a private institution either. Strictly speaking, the Federal Reserve system consists of two parts: the Board of Governors and the 12 regional Federal Reserve Banks.

The Board of Governors, which oversees the entire system from its offices in Washington, D.C., is constituted like a government agency: its seven members are appointed by the president and must be approved by the Senate. However, they are appointed for 14-year terms, to insulate them from political pressure in their conduct of monetary policy. (Why this is a potential problem will become clear in the next chapter, when we discuss inflation.)

Although the chair is appointed more frequently—every four years—chairs are often reappointed and serve much longer terms. For example, William McChesney Martin was chair of the Fed from 1951 until 1970. Alan Greenspan, appointed in 1987, served as the Fed's chair until 2006. Ben Bernanke, Greenspan's successor, served until 2014. Janet Yellen, who followed Bernanke, became the first chair to not be reappointed to a second term. Jerome Powell was her successor at the Fed.

The 12 Federal Reserve Banks each serve a region of the country, providing various banking and supervisory services. One of their jobs, for example, is to audit the books of private-sector banks to ensure their financial health. Each regional bank is run by a board of directors chosen from the local banking and business community. The Federal Reserve Bank of New York plays a special role: it carries out *open-market operations*, usually the main tool of monetary policy. Figure 29-6 shows the 12 Federal Reserve districts and the city in which each regional Federal Reserve Bank is located.

Decisions about monetary policy are made by the Federal Open Market Committee, which consists of the Board of Governors plus five of the regional bank presidents. The president of the Federal Reserve Bank of New York is always on the committee, and the other four seats rotate among the 11 other regional bank

A **central bank** is an institution that oversees and regulates the banking system and controls the monetary base.

FIGURE 29-6 The Federal Reserve System

The Federal Reserve System consists of the Board of Governors in Washington, D.C., plus 12 regional Federal Reserve Banks. This map shows each of the 12 Federal Reserve districts.

Data from: Board of Governors of the Federal Reserve System.

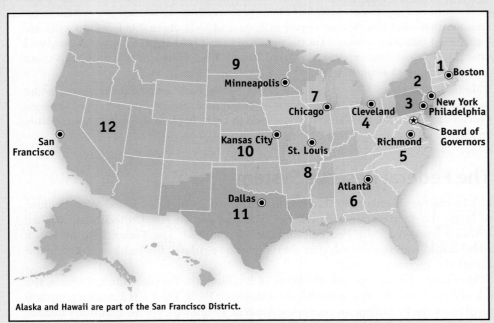

Alaska and Hawaii are part of the San Francisco District.

presidents. The chair of the Board of Governors normally also serves as the chair of the Open Market Committee.

The effect of this complex structure is to create an institution that is ultimately accountable to the voting public because the Board of Governors is chosen by the president and confirmed by the Senate, all of whom are themselves elected officials. But the long terms served by board members, as well as the indirectness of their appointment process, largely insulate them from short-term political pressures.

What the Fed Does: Reserve Requirements and the Discount Rate

The Fed has three main policy tools at its disposal: *reserve requirements,* the *discount rate,* and, most importantly, *open-market operations.*

In our discussion of bank runs, we noted that the Fed sets a minimum reserve ratio requirement, currently equal to 10% for checkable bank deposits. Banks that fail to maintain at least the required reserve ratio on average over a two-week period face penalties.

What does a bank do if it looks as if it has insufficient reserves to meet the Fed's reserve requirement? Normally, it borrows additional reserves from other banks via the **federal funds market,** a financial market that allows banks that fall short of the reserve requirement to borrow reserves (usually just overnight) from banks that are holding excess reserves. The interest rate in this market is determined by supply and demand—but the supply and demand for bank reserves are both strongly affected by Federal Reserve actions. As we'll see in the next chapter, the **federal funds rate,** the interest rate at which funds are borrowed and lent in the federal funds market, plays a key role in modern monetary policy.

Alternatively, banks in need of reserves can borrow from the Fed itself via the *discount window.* The **discount rate** is the rate of interest the Fed charges on those loans. Normally, the discount rate is set 1 percentage point above the federal funds rate in order to discourage banks from turning to the Fed when they are in need of reserves. Beginning in the fall of 2007, however, the Fed reduced the spread between the federal funds rate and the discount rate as part of its response to an ongoing financial crisis, described in the upcoming Economics in Action. As a result, by the

The **federal funds market** allows banks that fall short of the reserve requirement to borrow funds from banks with excess reserves.

The **federal funds rate** is the interest rate at which funds are borrowed and lent in the federal funds market.

The **discount rate** is the rate of interest the Fed charges on loans to banks.

spring of 2008 the discount rate was only 0.25 percentage points above the federal funds rate. And in early 2020, just before the coronavirus crisis struck, the discount rate was still only 0.60 percentage points above the federal funds rate.

In order to alter the money supply, the Fed can change reserve requirements, the discount rate, or both. If the Fed reduces reserve requirements, banks will normally lend a larger percentage of their deposits, leading to more loans and an increase in the money supply via the money multiplier. Alternatively, if the Fed increases reserve requirements, banks are forced to reduce their lending, leading to a fall in the money supply via the money multiplier.

If the Fed reduces the spread between the discount rate and the federal funds rate, the cost to banks of being short of reserves falls. Banks respond by increasing their lending, and the money supply increases via the money multiplier. If the Fed increases the spread between the discount rate and the federal funds rate, bank lending falls—and so will the money supply via the money multiplier.

Under current practice, however, the Fed doesn't use changes in reserve requirements to actively manage the money supply. The last significant change in reserve requirements was in 1992. The Fed normally doesn't use the discount rate either, although, as we mentioned earlier, there was a temporary surge in lending through the discount window beginning in 2007 in response to the financial crisis. Ordinarily, monetary policy is conducted almost exclusively using the Fed's third policy tool: open-market operations.

Open-Market Operations

Like the banks it oversees, the Federal Reserve has assets and liabilities. The Fed's assets normally consist of holdings of debt issued by the U.S. government, mainly short-term U.S. government bonds with a maturity of less than one year, known as U.S. Treasury bills. Remember, the Fed isn't exactly part of the U.S. government, so U.S. Treasury bills held by the Fed are a liability of the government but an asset of the Fed. The Fed's liabilities consist of currency in circulation and bank reserves. Figure 29-7 summarizes the normal assets and liabilities of the Fed in the form of a T-account.

In an **open-market operation** the Federal Reserve buys or sells U.S. Treasury bills, normally through a transaction with *commercial banks* (banks that accept deposits and make loans), and *investment banks* (banks that create and trade assets but don't accept deposits). The Fed never buys U.S. Treasury bills directly from the federal government. There's a good reason for this: when a central bank buys government debt directly from the government, it is lending directly to the government—in effect, the central bank is printing money to finance the government's budget deficit. This has historically been a formula for disastrously high levels of inflation.

The two panels of Figure 29-8 show the changes in the financial position of both the Fed and commercial banks that result from open-market operations. When the Fed buys U.S. Treasury bills from a commercial bank, it pays by crediting the bank's reserve account by an amount equal to the value of the Treasury bills. This is illustrated in panel (a): the Fed buys $100 million of U.S. Treasury bills from commercial banks, which increases the monetary base by $100 million because it increases bank reserves by $100 million. When the Fed sells U.S. Treasury bills to commercial banks, it debits the banks' accounts, reducing their

An **open-market operation** is a purchase or sale of government debt by the Fed.

FIGURE 29-7 The Federal Reserve's Assets and Liabilities

The Federal Reserve holds its assets mostly in short-term government bonds called U.S. Treasury bills. Its liabilities are the monetary base—currency in circulation plus bank reserves.

Assets	Liabilities
Government debt (Treasury bills)	Monetary base (currency in circulation + bank reserves)

FIGURE 29-8 Open-Market Operations by the Federal Reserve

(a) An Open-Market Purchase of $100 Million

	Assets		**Liabilities**	
Federal Reserve	Treasury bills	+$100 million	Monetary base	+$100 million

	Assets		**Liabilities**
Commercial banks	Treasury bills	−$100 million	No change
	Reserves	+$100 million	

(b) An Open-Market Sale of $100 Million

	Assets		**Liabilities**	
Federal Reserve	Treasury bills	−$100 million	Monetary base	−$100 million

	Assets		**Liabilities**
Commercial banks	Treasury bills	+$100 million	No change
	Reserves	−$100 million	

In panel (a), the Federal Reserve increases the monetary base by purchasing U.S. Treasury bills from private commercial banks in an open-market operation. Here, a $100 million purchase of U.S. Treasury bills by the Federal Reserve is paid for by a $100 million addition to private bank reserves, generating a $100 million increase in the monetary base. This will ultimately lead to an increase in the money supply via the money multiplier as banks lend out some of these new reserves. In panel (b), the Federal Reserve reduces the monetary base by selling U.S. Treasury bills to private commercial banks in an open-market operation. Here, a $100 million sale of U.S. Treasury bills leads to a $100 million reduction in private bank reserves, resulting in a $100 million decrease in the monetary base. This will ultimately lead to a fall in the money supply via the money multiplier as banks reduce their loans in response to a fall in their reserves.

reserves. This is shown in panel (b), where the Fed sells $100 million of U.S. Treasury bills. Here, bank reserves and the monetary base decrease.

You might wonder where the Fed gets the funds to purchase U.S. Treasury bills from banks. The answer is that it simply creates them with a mouse click that credits the banks' accounts with extra reserves. (The Fed prints money to pay for Treasury bills only when banks want the additional reserves in the form of currency.) Remember, the modern dollar is fiat money, which isn't backed by anything. So the Fed can create additional monetary base at its own discretion.

FOR INQUIRING MINDS   Who Gets the Interest on the Fed's Assets?

The Fed owns a lot of assets — Treasury bills — that it bought from commercial banks in exchange for additions to the monetary base in the form of credits to banks' reserve accounts. These assets pay interest. Yet the Fed's liabilities consist mainly of the monetary base, liabilities on which the Fed normally *doesn't* pay interest. So the Fed is, in effect, an institution that has the privilege of borrowing funds at a zero interest rate and lending them out at a positive interest rate. That sounds like a pretty profitable business. And the U.S. taxpayers get the profits.

The Fed keeps some of the interest it receives to finance its operations but turns most of it over to the U.S. Treasury. For example, in 2019 the total income of the Federal Reserve system was $55.5 billion, almost all in the form of interest on its assets, of which $54.9 billion was returned to the Treasury. This amount has steadily declined over the last five years; in 2014, the Fed returned over $100 million to the Treasury.

Let's consider our opening story again and the impact of those forged dollars printed in Peru. When, say, a fake $20 bill enters circulation, it has the same economic effect as a real $20 bill printed by the U.S. government. That is, as long as nobody catches the forgery, the fake bill serves, for all practical purposes, as part of the monetary base.

Meanwhile, the Fed decides on the size of the monetary base based on economic considerations — in particular, the Fed normally doesn't let the monetary base get too large because that can cause higher inflation. So every fake $20 bill that enters circulation means that the Fed prints one less real $20 bill. When the Fed prints a $20 bill legally, however, it gets Treasury bills in return — and the interest on those bills helps pay U.S. government expenses. So a counterfeit $20 bill reduces the amount of Treasury bills the Fed can acquire and thereby reduces the interest payments going to the Fed and the U.S. Treasury. Taxpayers, then, bear the real cost of counterfeiting.

The change in bank reserves caused by an open-market operation doesn't directly affect the money supply. Instead, it starts the money multiplier in motion. After the $100 million increase in reserves shown in panel (a) of Figure 29-8, commercial banks will (under normal circumstances) lend out all of their additional reserves, immediately increasing the money supply by $100 million. Some of those loans would be deposited back into the banking system, increasing reserves again and permitting a further round of loans, and so on, leading to a rise in the money supply. An open-market sale has the reverse effect: bank reserves fall, requiring banks to reduce their loans, leading to a fall in the money supply.

Although economists often say, loosely, that the Fed controls the money supply—checkable deposits plus currency in circulation, that statement is not completely accurate. *The Fed literally only controls the monetary base—bank reserves plus currency in circulation. But by increasing or reducing the monetary base, the Fed can exert a powerful influence on both the money supply and interest rates*. This influence is the basis of monetary policy, the subject of the next chapter.

The European Central Bank

We've seen that the Fed is only one of a number of central banks around the world, and it's much younger than Sweden's Sveriges Riksbank and Britain's Bank of England. In general, other central banks operate in much the same way as the Fed. That's especially true of the only other central bank that rivals the Fed in terms of importance to the world economy: the European Central Bank.

The European Central Bank (ECB) was created in January 1999 when 11 European nations abandoned their national currencies, adopted the euro as their common currency, and placed their joint monetary policy in the ECB's hands. More countries have joined since then, with Lithuania becoming the nineteenth European nation to adopt the euro in 2015. The ECB instantly became an extremely important institution: although no single European nation has an economy anywhere near as large as that of the United States, the combined economies of the eurozone, the group of countries that have adopted the euro as their currency, are roughly as big as the U.S. economy. As a result, the ECB and the Fed are the two giants of the monetary world.

Like the Fed, the ECB has a special status: it's not a private institution, but it's not exactly a government agency either. In fact, it can't be a government agency because there is no pan-European government! Luckily for puzzled Americans, there are strong analogies between European central banking and the Federal Reserve system.

First of all, the ECB, which is located in Frankfurt, Germany, isn't really the counterpart of the whole Federal Reserve system: it's the equivalent of the Board of Governors in Washington, D.C. The European counterparts of the regional Federal Reserve Banks are Europe's national central banks: the Bank of France, the Bank of Italy, and so on. Until 1999, each of these national banks was its country's equivalent to the Fed. For example, the Bank of France controlled the French monetary base.

Today these national banks, like regional Feds, provide various financial services to local banks and businesses and conduct open-market operations, but the making of monetary policy has moved upstream to the ECB. Still, the various European national central banks aren't small institutions: in total, they employ more than 50,000 people.

In the eurozone, each country chooses who runs its own national central bank. The ECB's Executive Board is the counterpart of the Fed's Board of Governors; its members are chosen by unanimous consent of the eurozone national governments. The counterpart of the Federal Open Market Committee is the ECB's Governing Council. Just as the Fed's Open Market Committee consists of the Board of Governors plus a rotating group of regional Fed presidents, the ECB's Governing Council consists of the Executive Board plus the heads of the national central banks.

Like the Fed, the ECB is ultimately answerable to voters, and it tries to maintain its independence from short-term political pressures.

ECONOMICS >> *in Action*
The Fed's Balance Sheet, Normal and Abnormal

Figure 29-7 showed a simplified version of the Fed's balance sheet. Here, liabilities consisted entirely of the monetary base and assets consisted entirely of Treasury bills. This is an oversimplification because the Fed's operations are more complicated in reality and its balance sheet contains a number of additional things. But, in normal times, Figure 29-7 is a reasonable approximation: the monetary base typically accounts for 90% of the Fed's liabilities, and 90% of its assets are in the form of claims on the U.S. Treasury (as in Treasury bills).

But in late 2007 it became painfully clear that we were no longer in normal times. The source of the turmoil was the bursting of a huge housing bubble, which led to massive losses for financial institutions that had made mortgage loans or held mortgage-related assets. This led to a widespread loss of confidence in the financial system.

Not only were conventional deposit-taking commercial banks in trouble, but so were nondepository financial institutions like investment banks and insurance companies, which make up the shadow banking sector. Because they carried a lot of debt, faced huge losses from the collapse of the housing bubble, and held illiquid assets, panic hit the shadow banking sector. Within hours the financial system was frozen as financial institutions experienced what were essentially bank runs.

For example, in 2008, many investors became worried about the health of Bear Stearns, a Wall Street investment bank that engaged in complex financial deals, buying and selling financial assets with borrowed funds. When confidence in Bear Stearns dried up, the firm was unable to raise the funds needed to deliver on its end of these deals and it quickly spiraled into collapse. This was followed by the collapse of another investment bank, Lehman Brothers, and set off widespread panic in financial markets.

The Fed sprang into action to contain what was becoming a meltdown across the entire financial sector. It greatly expanded its discount window—making huge loans to deposit-taking banks as well as nondepository financial institutions. This gave financial institutions the liquidity that the financial market had denied them. And as these firms took advantage of the ability to borrow cheaply from the Fed, they pledged their assets on hand as collateral—a motley collection of real estate loans, business loans, and so on.

Examining Figure 29-9, we see that starting in mid-2008, the Fed sharply reduced its holdings of traditional securities like Treasury bills, as its "lending to financial institutions" skyrocketed—referring to discount window lending, but also to loans the Fed made directly to firms like Bear Stearns. "Liquidity to key credit markets" covers purchases by the Fed of assets like corporate bonds, which was necessary to keep interest rates on loans to firms from soaring. Finally, "Federal agency debt" is the debt of Fannie Mae and Freddie Mac, the government-sponsored home mortgage agencies, which the Fed was also compelled to buy in order to prevent collapse in the mortgage market.

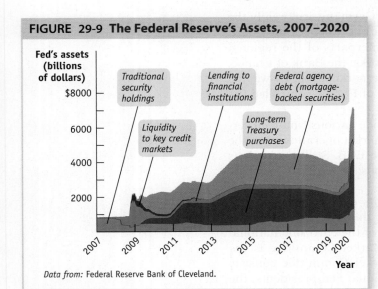

FIGURE 29-9 The Federal Reserve's Assets, 2007–2020

Fed's assets (billions of dollars)

Traditional security holdings

Liquidity to key credit markets

Lending to financial institutions

Long-term Treasury purchases

Federal agency debt (mortgage-backed securities)

Data from: Federal Reserve Bank of Cleveland.

As the crisis subsided in late 2009, the Fed didn't return to its traditional asset holdings. Instead, it shifted into long-term Treasury bills and increased its purchases of Federal agency debt. When the coronavirus pandemic struck in March 2020, threatening to cause another financial meltdown, the Fed moved even further away from tradition, buying trillions more in long-term assets and even pushing some corporate bonds.

>> Check Your Understanding 29-4

Solutions appear at back of book.

1. Assume that any money lent by a bank is always deposited back in the banking system as a checkable deposit, that the reserve ratio is 10%, and that banks don't hold excess reserves. Explain the effects of a $100 million open-market purchase of U.S. Treasury bills by the Fed on the value of checkable bank deposits. What is the size of the money multiplier?

The Evolution of the U.S. Banking System

Up to this point, we have been describing the U.S. banking system and how it works. To fully understand that system, however, it is helpful to understand how and why it was created—a story that is closely intertwined with the story of how and when things went wrong. The key elements of twenty-first century U.S. banking weren't created out of thin air: efforts to change both the regulations that govern banking and the Federal Reserve system that resulted from the 2008 crisis have propelled financial reform to the forefront. This reform promises to continue reshaping the financial system well into future years.

The Crisis in U.S. Banking in the Early Twentieth Century

The creation of the Federal Reserve system in 1913 marked the beginning of the modern era of U.S. banking. From 1864 until 1913, U.S. banking was dominated by a federally regulated system of national banks. They alone were allowed to issue currency, and the currency notes they issued were printed by the federal government with uniform size and design. How much currency a national bank could issue depended on its capital. Although this system was an improvement on the earlier period in which banks issued their own notes with no uniformity and virtually no regulation, the national banking regime still suffered numerous bank failures and major financial crises—at least one and often two per decade.

The main problem afflicting the system was that the money supply was not sufficiently responsive: it was difficult to shift currency around the country to respond quickly to local economic changes. (In particular, there was often a tug-of-war between New York City banks and rural banks for adequate amounts of currency.) Rumors that a bank had insufficient currency to satisfy demands for withdrawals would quickly lead to a bank run. A bank run would then spark a contagion, setting off runs at other nearby banks, sowing widespread panic and devastation in the local economy. In response, bankers in some locations pooled their resources to create local clearinghouses that would jointly guarantee a member's liabilities in the event of a panic, and some state governments began offering deposit insurance on their banks' deposits.

Despite these recurrent crises, calls for monetary reform went unheeded until the Panic of 1907, which led to a four-year national recession, drove home just how vulnerable the system had become.

The Morgan Library & Museum/Art Resource, NY

In both the Panic of 1907 and the financial crisis of 2008, large losses from risky speculation destabilized the banking system.

This crisis originated in institutions in New York known as *trusts*, bank-like institutions that accepted deposits but that were originally intended to manage only inheritances and estates for wealthy clients. Because these trusts were supposed to engage only in low-risk activities, they were less regulated, had lower reserve requirements, and had lower cash reserves than national banks, allowing them to pay their depositors higher returns. As a result, trusts grew rapidly: by 1907, the total assets of trusts in New York City were as large as those of national banks. Meanwhile, the trusts declined to join the New York Clearinghouse, a consortium of New York City national banks that guaranteed one anothers' soundness.

The Panic of 1907 began with the failure of the Knickerbocker Trust, a large New York City trust that failed when it suffered massive losses in unsuccessful stock market speculation. Quickly, other New York trusts came under pressure, and frightened depositors began queuing in long lines to withdraw their funds. The New York Clearinghouse declined to step in and lend to the trusts, and even healthy trusts came under serious assault. Within two days, a dozen major trusts had gone under. Credit markets froze, and the stock market fell dramatically as stock traders were unable to get credit to finance their trades and business confidence evaporated.

Fortunately, New York City's wealthiest man, the banker J. P. Morgan, quickly stepped in to stop the panic. Understanding that the crisis was spreading and would soon engulf healthy institutions, trusts and banks alike, he worked with other bankers, wealthy men such as John D. Rockefeller, and the U.S. Secretary of the Treasury to shore up the reserves of banks and trusts so they could withstand the onslaught of withdrawals. Once people were assured that they could withdraw their money, the panic ceased. Although the panic itself lasted little more than a week, it and the stock market collapse decimated the economy. A four-year recession ensued, with production falling 11% and unemployment rising from 3% to 8%.

Responding to Banking Crises: The Creation of the Federal Reserve

Concerns over the frequency of banking crises and the unprecedented role of J. P. Morgan in saving the financial system prompted the federal government to initiate banking reform. In 1913 the national banking system was eliminated and the Federal Reserve system was created as a way to compel all deposit-taking institutions to hold adequate reserves and to open their accounts to inspection by regulators. The Panic of 1907 convinced many that the time for centralized control of bank reserves had come. In addition, the Federal Reserve was given the sole right to issue currency in order to make the money supply sufficiently responsive to satisfy economic conditions around the country.

Although the new regime standardized and centralized the holding of bank reserves, it did not eliminate the potential for bank runs because banks' reserves were still less than the total value of their deposits. The potential for more bank runs became a reality during the Great Depression. Plunging commodity prices hit U.S. farmers particularly hard, precipitating a series of bank runs in 1930, 1931, and 1933, each of which started at midwestern banks and then spread throughout the country.

After the failure of a particularly large bank in 1930, federal officials realized that the economy-wide effects compelled them to take a less hands-off approach and to intervene more vigorously. In 1932, the Reconstruction Finance

Corporation (RFC) was established and given the authority to make loans to banks in order to stabilize the banking sector. Also, the Glass-Steagall Act of 1933, which created federal deposit insurance and increased the ability of banks to borrow from the Federal Reserve system, was passed. However, the beast had not yet been tamed. Banks became fearful of borrowing from the RFC because doing so signaled weakness to the public.

As noted earlier, the new president, Franklin D. Roosevelt, was inaugurated during the catastrophic bank run of 1933. He immediately declared a "bank holiday," closing all banks until regulators could get a handle on the problem.

In March 1933, emergency measures were adopted that gave the RFC extraordinary powers to stabilize and restructure the banking industry by providing capital to banks through either loans or outright purchases of bank shares. With the new rules, regulators closed nonviable banks and recapitalized viable ones by allowing the RFC to buy preferred shares in banks (shares that gave the U.S. government more rights than regular shareholders) and by greatly expanding banks' ability to borrow from the Federal Reserve. By 1933, the RFC had invested nearly $19 billion (2020 dollars) in bank capital—one-third of the total capital of all banks in the United States at that time—and purchased shares in almost one-half of all banks. The RFC loaned more than $37 billion (2020 dollars) to banks during this period.

Economic historians uniformly agree that the banking crises of the early 1930s greatly exacerbated the severity of the Great Depression, rendering monetary policy ineffective as the banking sector broke down and currency, withdrawn from banks and stashed under beds, reduced the money supply.

Although the powerful actions of the RFC stabilized the banking industry, new legislation was needed to prevent future banking crises. The Glass-Steagall Act of 1933 separated banks into two categories, **commercial banks,** depository banks that are covered by deposit insurance, and nondepository **investment banks,** which engaged in creating and trading financial assets such as stocks and corporate bonds and were not covered by deposit insurance.

Regulation Q prevented commercial banks from paying interest on checking accounts in the belief that this would promote unhealthy competition between banks. In addition, investment banks were much more lightly regulated than commercial banks. The most important measure for the prevention of bank runs, however, was the adoption of federal deposit insurance (with an original limit of $2,500 per deposit).

These measures were clearly successful, and the United States enjoyed a long period of financial and banking stability. As memories of the bad old days dimmed, Depression-era bank regulations were lifted. In 1980, Regulation Q was eliminated; by 1999, the Glass-Steagall Act had been so weakened that offering services like trading financial assets was no longer off-limits to commercial banks.

The Savings and Loan Crisis of the 1980s

Along with banks, the banking industry also included **savings and loans** (also called S&Ls or **thrifts**), institutions designed to accept savings and turn them into long-term mortgages for home-buyers. S&Ls were covered by federal deposit insurance and were tightly regulated for safety. However, trouble hit in the 1970s, as high inflation led savers to withdraw their funds from low-interest-paying S&L accounts and put them into higher-interest-paying money market accounts. In addition, the high inflation rate severely eroded the value of the S&Ls' assets, the long-term mortgages they held on their books.

To improve S&Ls' competitive position vis-à-vis banks, Congress eased regulations to allow S&Ls to undertake much more risky investments in addition to long-term home mortgages. However, the new freedom did not bring with it increased oversight, leaving S&Ls with less oversight than banks. Not surprisingly, during the real estate boom of the 1970s and 1980s, S&Ls engaged in overly

A **commercial bank** accepts deposits and is covered by deposit insurance.

An **investment bank** trades in financial assets and does not accept deposits, so it is not covered by deposit insurance.

A **savings and loan (thrift)** is another type of deposit-taking bank, usually specialized in issuing home loans.

Bank-like activities undertaken by nondepository financial firms such as investment banks and hedge funds, but without regulatory oversight or protection, are known as **shadow banking.**

risky real estate lending. Also, corruption occurred as some S&L executives used their institutions as private piggy banks.

During the late 1970s and early 1980s, political interference from Congress kept insolvent S&Ls open when a bank in a comparable situation would have been quickly shut down by regulators. By the early 1980s, numerous S&Ls had failed. Because accounts were covered by federal deposit insurance, the liabilities of a failed S&L became liabilities of the federal government, and depositors had to be paid from taxpayer funds. From 1986 through 1995, the federal government closed over 1,000 failed S&Ls, costing U.S. taxpayers over $124 billion.

In a classic case of shutting the barn door after the horse has escaped, in 1989 Congress put in place comprehensive oversight of S&L activities. It also empowered Fannie Mae and Freddie Mac to take over much of the home mortgage lending previously done by S&Ls. *Fannie Mae* and *Freddie Mac* are quasi-governmental agencies created during the Great Depression to make homeownership more affordable for low- and moderate-income households. The S&L crisis led to a steep slowdown in the finance and real estate industries, leading to the recession of the early 1990s.

Back to the Future: The Financial Crisis of 2008 and Its Aftermath

The bank regulations introduced in the 1930s led to a long era of relative financial stability. But by the early twenty-first century a new problem had emerged: these regulations didn't cover **shadow banking**—activities, as we explained earlier, that don't look like traditional banking but serve similar purposes while posing significant risks. In 2008 shadow banking was at the center of a crisis that in important ways resembled the crisis of the 1930s.

Shadow Banking and Its Vulnerabilities

The details of shadow banking can be complex. However, much of the shadow banking system involves financial intermediaries—nondepository financial firms like investment banks, insurance companies, hedge funds, and money market funds. These firms borrow short-term—often taking out loans that must be repaid the next day—and use the borrowed funds to buy relatively illiquid assets to put up as collateral. This looks like banking to those lending funds to intermediaries, because their loans are a lot like bank deposits. For example, a corporation with extra cash on hand might lend that extra cash on an overnight basis to a Wall Street investment bank. That way it can get a higher interest rate than if it parked the funds in ordinary bank deposits, and under normal circumstances it can still count on having access to the money with only one day's notice.

Meanwhile, the financial intermediary doesn't have to keep enough cash on hand to repay all of its debts every day. Many of the lenders will simply roll over their loans each day, relending the funds. And when a lender does demand repayment, the borrower will simply raise the cash from another lender. So the shadow banking firm's relationship to its lenders is a lot like a conventional bank's relationship with its depositors, except for two significant differences: there is no deposit insurance and there is much less regulation of the intermediary's actions.

It is a system that can work seamlessly in normal times, but it can also go terribly wrong as it did when the housing bubble it helped to create burst in 2007, leading to the Great Recession.

Subprime Lending and the Housing Bubble The story of the 2008 crisis begins with low interest rates: by 2003, U.S. interest rates were at historically low levels, partly because of Federal Reserve policy and partly because of large inflows of capital from other countries, especially China. These low interest rates helped cause a boom in housing, which in turn pulled the U.S. economy out of recession.

As housing boomed, however, financial institutions took on greater risks that were not well understood.

Traditionally, people were only able to borrow money to buy homes if they could show that they had sufficient income to meet the mortgage payments. Home loans to people who don't meet the usual criteria for borrowing, called **subprime lending,** were only a minor part of overall lending. But in the booming housing market of 2003 to 2006, subprime lending started to seem like a safe bet. According to conventional thinking, since housing prices kept rising, borrowers who were unable to make their mortgage payments could always pay off their mortgages by selling their homes. As a result, subprime lending exploded.

For the most part, these subprime loans were not made by traditional banks that lend out depositors' money. Instead, most of the loans were made by *loan originators,* companies specializing in making subprime loans and quickly selling them off to other investors in the shadow banking market. Large-scale sales of subprime mortgages were made possible by **securitization:** the assembly of pools of loans and sale of shares of the income from these pools. Again, according to conventional thinking at the time, these shares were considered relatively safe investments, based on the belief that large numbers of home-buyers were unlikely to default on their payments at the same time.

But that's exactly what happened. The housing boom turned out to be a bubble, and when home prices started falling in late 2006, significant numbers of subprime borrowers were unable either to meet their mortgage payments or sell their houses for enough to pay off their mortgages. As a result, they defaulted and investors in securities backed by subprime mortgages suffered heavy losses.

These securities were largely held by shadow banking institutions, but also by some traditional, depository banks. Like the trusts that played a key role in the Panic of 1907, these largely unregulated shadow banks offered higher returns to investors but left them extremely vulnerable in a crisis. Without the safety net of deposit insurance, mortgage-related losses led to a collapse of trust in the financial system.

Figure 29-10 shows one measure of the severity of the loss of trust: the quantity of *asset-backed commercial paper,* an important asset class in shadow banking. In the mid-2000s this paper—backed by short-term loans taken out using assets often created by securitization of mortgages and other debts—grew rapidly in volume.

Subprime lending is lending to home-buyers who don't meet the usual criteria for qualifying for a loan.

In **securitization,** a pool of loans is assembled and shares of that pool are sold to investors.

"Honey we're homeless."

Leo Cullum/CartoonStock

FIGURE 29-10 Measuring Lost Trust

In the mid-2000s the use of asset-backed commercial paper, short-term loans created by securitization of mortgages and other debts, and an important component of shadow banking, grew rapidly in volume. But it went into rapid decline after the housing boom went bust, a sign of extreme financial stress as liquidity in the financial system dried up.

Data from: Federal Reserve Bank of St. Louis.

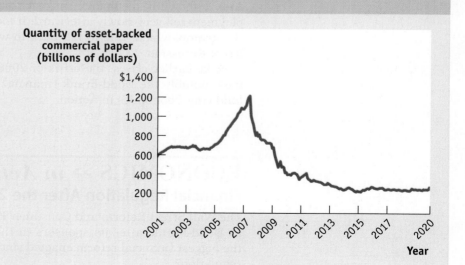

After the housing bust, it went into rapid decline, a sign of extreme financial stress. Although this was not a 1930s-style crash in the money supply in an official sense, it functioned in much the same way because commercial paper was an essential source of liquidity in the financial system.

Crisis and Response Starting in 2007, the bursting of the housing bubble, followed by large losses on the part of financial firms and the collapse in trust in the financial system, led to major disruptions for the economy as a whole. All firms—financial and nonfinancial—found it difficult to borrow, even for short-term operations. Individuals found home loans unavailable and credit card limits reduced. Prices of many assets tumbled, severely reducing household wealth.

Overall, the negative economic effect of the financial crisis bore a strong and extremely troubling resemblance to the banking crisis of the early 1930s, which sparked the Great Depression. Policy makers, noticing the resemblance, tried to prevent a repeat performance. Beginning in August 2007, the Federal Reserve provided liquidity to stop a cascade of defaults, by lending funds to a wide range of institutions and buying commercial paper. The Fed and the Treasury Department also stepped in to rescue individual firms that were deemed too crucial to be allowed to fail, such as the investment bank Bear Stearns and the insurance company AIG.

In September 2008, however, under political pressure to punish "irresponsible bankers," policy makers allowed one major investment bank, Lehman Brothers, to fail. They quickly regretted the decision. Within days of Lehman's failure, widespread panic gripped the financial markets. In response, the U.S. government intervened further to support the financial system. The U.S. Treasury injected capital directly into banks—supplying them with cash in return for shares. The effect was to partly *nationalize* the financial system (take public ownership). The Federal Reserve engaged in novel forms of open-market operations, such as providing massive liquidity through discount window lending and buying a large quantity of other assets—mainly long-term government debt and the debt of Fannie Mae and Freddie Mac (as shown in Figure 29-9 by the huge surge in Fed assets after September 2008).

The Aftermath of the Crisis After many terrifying months, in the fall of 2010 the financial system stabilized, and major institutions had repaid much of the money the federal government had injected during the crisis. However, the recovery of the banks was not matched by a successful turnaround for the overall economy. Although the recession that began in December 2007 officially ended in June 2009, with unemployment reaching a high of 10% in October 2009, unemployment fell very slowly afterward. It took nearly nine years, until May 2016, for the unemployment rate to fall back to where it had been before the start of the Great Recession.

Like earlier crises, the crisis of 2008 led to changes in banking regulation, most notably the Dodd-Frank financial regulatory reform act discussed in the following Economics in Action.

ECONOMICS >> *in Action*
Financial Regulation After the 2008 Crisis

The Wall Street Reform and Consumer Protection Act of 2010—generally known as Dodd-Frank, after its sponsors in the Senate and House, respectively—was the biggest financial reform enacted since the 1930s. How did it change financial regulation?

For traditional depository banks, the main change was the creation of a new agency, the Consumer Financial Protection Bureau. Its mission was to protect borrowers from being exploited through seemingly attractive financial deals they didn't understand.

The main thrust of Dodd-Frank, however, was the regulation of shadow banking institutions. Under the law, a financial institution could be designated as "systematically important"—that is, like Lehman Brothers, it was important enough to the financial system that it could trigger a banking crisis, even though it wasn't a depository bank.

Under Dodd-Frank, these systemically important institutions were subjected to depository bank–style regulation, such as relatively high capital requirements and limits on risk taking. In addition, the federal government asserted *resolution authority*, the right to seize troubled nondepository financial institutions in much the same way that it seized troubled banks.

The Dodd-Frank Act extended old-fashioned bank regulation to today's more complex financial system. More recently, the Trump administration has rolled back some of its provisions.

Dodd-Frank also mandated that most *derivatives*, complex financial instruments that also played a significant role in the 2008 crisis, could be bought and sold on public exchanges in order to make them more transparent and reduce risk.

Overall, the purpose of Dodd-Frank was to extend the spirit of old-fashioned bank regulation to the more complex financial system of the twenty-first century. How well is it working? Relatively well, according to the evidence so far:

- The new rules on systemically important institutions seem to have reduced the incentive to create shadow banks that bypass regulations on conventional banks. An example is the case of GE Capital, an unregulated bank once owned by General Electric. Although it was the main source of profits for its parent company, General Electric sold it off in the wake of Dodd-Frank.

- Resolution authority seems to have led to a reduction in the so-called *too big to fail subsidy:* the lower cost of borrowing enjoyed by big financial institutions compared to smaller ones because it was assumed that only the big ones would be bailed out in a crisis.

- The Consumer Financial Protection Bureau was widely considered to have been quite effective at punishing and deterring financial fraud. Its power and effectiveness were, however, greatly curtailed after 2017, when the newly elected Trump administration moved to reduce the agency's independence and reduce its role.

That said, we won't know how effective Dodd-Frank has been until the next period of financial turbulence.

>> Check Your Understanding 29-5

Solutions appear at back of book.

1. What are the similarities between the Panic of 1907, the S&L crisis, and the crisis of 2008?

2. Why did the creation of the Federal Reserve fail to prevent the bank runs of the Great Depression? What measures stopped the bank runs?

3. Why were extraordinary measures needed to deal with the financial crisis of 2008?

>> Quick Review

- The Federal Reserve system was created in response to the Panic of 1907.

- Widespread bank runs in the early 1930s resulted in greater bank regulation and the creation of federal deposit insurance. Banks were separated into two categories: **commercial** (covered by deposit insurance) and **investment** (not covered).

- In the **savings and loan (thrift)** crisis of the 1970s and 1980s, insufficiently regulated S&Ls incurred huge losses from risky speculation in housing.

- Unregulated **shadow banking** activities created a vulnerability in the financial system. In the mid-2000s, **securitization** spread loans from **subprime lending** throughout the shadow banking sector, and among some traditional banks, leading to a financial crisis when the housing bubble burst. The Federal Reserve and U.S. Treasury undertook extraordinary steps to stabilize financial markets.

- In 2010, Congress passed the Dodd-Frank Act. The law extended both financial regulations — to avoid another financial crisis — and protections against consumer financial fraud.

The Perfect Gift: Cash or a Gift Card?

Richard Levine/Alamy

It's always nice when someone gives you a gift. Over the past few years, more people have been showing their appreciation by giving gift cards, often prepaid plastic cards issued by a retailer that can be redeemed for merchandise in the store or online. The best-selling single item for more than 80% of the top 100 U.S. retailers, according to the website GiftCardUSA, is their gift cards.

What could be more simple and useful than allowing the recipient to choose what they want? And isn't a gift card more personal than cash or a check?

Yet a number of firms are now making a profit from the fact that gift card recipients are often willing to sell their cards at a discount—sometimes at a fairly sizable discount—to turn them into cold, impersonal dollars and cents. Meanwhile, other people are willing to buy those cards, and turn them into goods they want, at a discount.

CardCash is one such site. At the time of writing, it offers to pay cash to a seller of a Walmart gift card equivalent to 88% of the card's face value. For example, the seller of a Walmart card with a value of $100 would receive $88. Cardcash.com profits by reselling the card at a premium over what it paid. So it would sell a Walmart gift card for more than 88% of its face value. The amount of cash offered to sellers of cards will vary by retailer. CardCash offers cash equal to only 75% of a Gap card's face value, for example.

Many consumers will sell at a sizable discount to turn gift cards into cash. But retailers promote the use of gift cards over cash because much of the value of gift cards issued never gets used, a phenomenon known as *breakage*.

How does breakage occur? People lose cards. Or they spend only $47 of a $50 gift card, and never return to spend that last $3. Also, retailers have imposed fees on the use of cards or made them subject to expiration dates, which customers forget about. Sometimes they even forget that they have a gift card. And if a retailer goes out of business, the value of outstanding gift cards disappears with it.

In addition to breakage, retailers benefit when customers intent on using up the value of their gift card find that it is too difficult to spend exactly the amount of the card. Instead, they end up spending even more than the card's face value, sometimes even more than they would have without the gift card.

Gift cards are so beneficial to retailers that instead of rewarding customer loyalty with rebate checks (once a common practice) many have switched loyalty programs to dispensing gift cards. Today retailers are hoping loyal customers reward them with a gift of their own. During the coronavirus shutdown, shuttered restaurants needed cash, quickly, so they turned to selling gift cards. Restaurants were even adding a 20% bonus if you purchased a $50 or $100 gift card. Restaurants were hoping that receiving the cash upfront would help cover their expenses and the cards they dispensed would help retain customer loyalty.

QUESTIONS FOR THOUGHT

1. Why are gift card owners willing to sell their cards for a cash amount less than their face value?

2. Why do gift cards for Walmart sell for a smaller discount than those for the Gap?

3. Use your answer from Question 2 to explain why cash never "sells" at a discount.

4. Explain why retailers prefer to reward loyal customers with gift cards instead of rebate checks.

5. There are now laws restricting retailers' ability to impose fees and expiration dates on their gift cards and mandate greater disclosure of their terms. Why do you think Congress enacted this legislation?

SUMMARY

1. **Money** is any asset that can easily be used to purchase goods and services. **Currency in circulation** and **checkable bank deposits** are both considered part of the **money supply.** Money plays three roles: it is a **medium of exchange** used for transactions, a **store of value** that holds purchasing power over time, and a **unit of account** in which prices are stated.

2. Over time, **commodity money,** which consists of goods possessing value aside from their role as money, such as gold and silver coins, was replaced by **commodity-backed money,** such as paper currency backed by gold. Today the dollar is pure **fiat money,** whose value derives solely from its official role.

3. The Federal Reserve calculates two measures of the money supply. M1 is the narrowest **monetary aggregate,** containing only currency in circulation, and checkable bank deposits. M2 includes a wider range of assets called **near-moneys,** mainly other forms of bank deposits, that can easily be converted into checkable bank deposits.

4. Banks allow depositors immediate access to their funds, but they also lend out most of the funds deposited in their care. To meet demands for cash, they maintain **bank reserves** composed of both currency held in vaults and deposits at the Federal Reserve. The **reserve ratio** is the ratio of bank reserves to bank deposits. A **T-account** summarizes a bank's financial position, with loans and reserves counted as assets and deposits counted as liabilities.

5. Banks have sometimes been subject to **bank runs,** most notably in the early 1930s. To avert this danger, depositors are now protected by **deposit insurance,** bank owners face capital requirements that reduce the incentive to make overly risky loans with depositors' funds, and banks must satisfy **reserve requirements.**

6. When currency is deposited in a bank, it starts a multiplier process in which banks lend out **excess reserves,** leading to an increase in the money supply—so banks create money. If the entire money supply consisted of checkable bank deposits, the money supply would be equal to the value of reserves divided by the reserve ratio. In reality, much of the **monetary base** consists of currency in circulation, and the **money multiplier** is the ratio of the money supply to the monetary base.

7. The monetary base is controlled by the Federal Reserve, the **central bank** of the United States. The Fed regulates banks and sets reserve requirements. To meet those requirements, banks borrow and lend reserves in the **federal funds market** at the **federal funds rate.** Through the **discount window** facility, banks can borrow from the Fed at the **discount rate.**

8. **Open-market operations** by the Fed are the principal tool of monetary policy: the Fed can increase or reduce the monetary base by buying U.S. Treasury bills from banks or selling U.S. Treasury bills to banks.

9. In response to the Panic of 1907, the Fed was created to centralize the holding of reserves, inspect banks' books, and make the money supply sufficiently responsive to varying economic conditions.

10. The Great Depression sparked widespread bank runs in the early 1930s, which greatly worsened and lengthened it. Federal deposit insurance was created, and the government recapitalized banks by lending to them and by buying shares of banks. By 1933, banks had been separated into two categories: **commercial banks** (which accept deposits and are covered by deposit insurance) and **investment banks** (which don't accept deposits and are not covered). Public acceptance of deposit insurance finally stopped the bank runs of the Great Depression.

11. The **savings and loan (thrift)** crisis of the 1980s arose because insufficiently regulated S&Ls engaged in overly risky speculation and incurred huge losses. Depositors in failed S&Ls were compensated with taxpayer funds because they were covered by deposit insurance. The crisis caused steep losses in the financial and real estate sectors, resulting in a recession in the early 1990s.

12. The emergence of **shadow banking,** bank-like activities undertaken by nondepository financial firms not subject to regulatory oversight or protection, made the financial system once again vulnerable to bank-run type panics. In the mid-2000s, **securitization** of mortgage loans from **subprime lending** spread through the shadow banking sector and among some traditional depository banks. When the housing bubble burst in 2007, losses by financial institutions led to panic and a widespread collapse of the financial system in 2008. To prevent another Great Depression, the Federal Reserve and U.S. Treasury undertook extraordinary actions to provide support to the financial system, such as injecting capital into banks through the purchase of bank shares, providing massive liquidity through discount window lending, and buying large amounts of long-term government debt and government-sponsored agency debt. By 2010, the financial system had stabilized but the economy did not fully recover until 2016.

13. In 2010, Congress passed a financial regulation reform act, known as Dodd-Frank, in order to prevent another crisis. Its main purpose was to extend old-fashioned bank regulation to today's more complex financial system. It also extended protection for consumers against financial fraud.

KEY TERMS

Money, p. 850
Currency in circulation, p. 850
Checkable bank deposits, p. 850
Money supply, p. 850
Medium of exchange, p. 851
Store of value, p. 851
Unit of account, p. 852
Commodity money, p. 852
Commodity-backed money, p. 852
Fiat money, p. 853
Monetary aggregate, p. 853

Near-moneys, p. 853
Bank reserves, p. 856
T-account, p. 856
Reserve ratio, p. 857
Bank run, p. 857
Deposit insurance, p. 858
Reserve requirements, p. 858
Discount window, p. 858
Excess reserves, p. 862
Monetary base, p. 863
Money multiplier, p. 863

Central bank, p. 865
Federal funds market, p. 866
Federal funds rate, p. 866
Discount rate, p. 866
Open-market operation, p. 867
Commercial bank, p. 873
Investment bank, p. 873
Savings and loan (thrift), p. 873
Shadow banking, p. 874
Subprime lending, p 875
Securitization, p. 875

PRACTICE QUESTIONS

1. Your roommate is considering purchasing cryptocurrency, as they believe it can be used in place of money. Can cryptocurrency function as money?

2. During the economic collapse of 2020 many people had concerns about the stability of the financial system. As employment fell, many residents were unable to make mortgage, rent, car, or credit card payments. Many wondered: would we see another financial panic, like what occurred following the housing collapse in 2009? Explain how changes in regulations following the Great Recession helped prevent another bank run.

3. How did the Federal Reserve respond to the economic crash of 2020? Using Figure 29-9, explain how the Federal Reserve's response was similar to the response following the bursting of the housing bubble.

PROBLEMS

1. For each of the following transactions, what is the initial effect (increase or decrease) on M1? On M2?

   a. You sell a few shares of stock and put the proceeds into your savings account.

   b. You sell a few shares of stock and put the proceeds into your checking account.

   c. You transfer money from your savings account to your checking account.

   d. You discover $0.25 under the floor mat in your car and deposit it in your checking account.

   e. You discover $0.25 under the floor mat in your car and deposit it in your savings account.

2. There are three types of money: commodity money, commodity-backed money, and fiat money. Which type of money is used in each of the following situations?

   a. Bottles of rum were used to pay for goods in colonial Australia.

   b. Salt was used in many European countries as a medium of exchange.

   c. For a brief time, Germany used paper money (the "Rye Mark") that could be redeemed for a certain amount of rye, a type of grain.

   d. The town of Ithaca, New York, prints its own currency, the Ithaca HOURS, which can be used to purchase local goods and services.

3. The following table shows the components of M1 and M2 in billions of dollars for the month of December in the years 2009 to 2019 reported by the Federal Reserve Bank of St. Louis. Complete the table by calculating M1, M2, currency in circulation as a percentage of M1, and currency in circulation as a percentage of M2. What trends or patterns about M1, M2, currency in circulation as a percentage of M1, and currency in circulation as a percentage of M2 do you see? What might account for these trends?

Year	Currency in circulation	Checkable deposits	Savings deposits	Time deposits	Money market funds	M1	M2	Currency in circulation as a percentage of M1	Currency in circulation as a percentage of M2
2009	$863.7	$829.1	$4,812.0	$1,187.5	$791.1	?	?	?	?
2010	918.8	917.9	5,331.5	934.4	686.7	?	?	?	?
2011	1,001.6	1,162.7	6,033.6	776.9	676.3	?	?	?	?
2012	1,090.7	1,370.4	6,683.3	645.8	655.4	?	?	?	?
2013	1,160.7	1,503.7	7,128.2	570.4	652.0	?	?	?	?
2014	1,253.2	1,687.1	7,573.0	523.4	631.3	?	?	?	?
2015	1,339.5	1,754.4	8,169.7	413.2	653.3	?	?	?	?
2016	1,420.9	1,919.0	8,814.5	353.4	691.3	?	?	?	?
2017	1,525.0	2,082.3	9,110.3	414.2	703.8	?	?	?	?
2018	1,624.8	2,121.7	9,260.9	532.9	811.5	?	?	?	?
2019	1,710.9	2,266.2	9,765.2	580.0	979.9	?	?	?	?

Data from: Federal Reserve Bank of St. Louis.

4. Indicate whether each of the following is part of M1, M2, or neither:

   a. $95 on your campus meal card

   b. $0.55 in the change cup of your car

   c. $1,663 in your savings account

   d. $459 in your checking account

   e. 100 shares of stock worth $4,000

   f. A $1,000 line of credit on your Target credit card

5. Tracy Williams deposits $500 that was in her sock drawer into a checking account at the local bank. The reserve ratio is 10%.

   a. How does the deposit initially change the T-account of the local bank? How does it change the money supply?

   b. If the bank maintains a reserve ratio of 10%, how will it respond to the new deposit?

   c. If every time the bank makes a loan, the loan results in a new checkable bank deposit in a different bank equal to the amount of the loan, by how much could the total money supply in the economy expand in response to Tracy's initial cash deposit of $500?

   d. If every time the bank makes a loan, the loan results in a new checkable bank deposit in a different bank equal to the amount of the loan and the bank maintains a reserve ratio of 5%, by how much could the money supply expand in response to Tracy's initial cash deposit of $500?

6. Ryan Cozzens withdraws $400 from his checking account at the local bank and keeps it in his wallet.

   a. How will the withdrawal change the T-account of the local bank and the money supply?

   b. If the bank maintains a reserve ratio of 10%, how will it respond to the withdrawal? Assume that the bank responds to insufficient reserves by reducing the amount of deposits it holds until its level of reserves satisfies its required reserve ratio. The bank reduces its deposits by calling in some of its loans, forcing borrowers to pay back these loans by taking cash from their checking deposits (at the same bank) to make repayment.

   c. If every time the bank decreases its loans, checkable bank deposits fall by the amount of the loan, by how much will the money supply in the economy contract in response to Ryan's withdrawal of $400?

   d. If every time the bank decreases its loans, checkable bank deposits fall by the amount of the loan and the bank maintains a reserve ratio of 20%, by how much will the money supply contract in response to a withdrawal of $400?

7. The government of Eastlandia uses measures of monetary aggregates similar to those used by the United States, and the central bank of Eastlandia imposes a required reserve ratio of 10%. Given the following information, answer the questions below.

   Bank deposits at the central bank = $200 million
   Currency held by public = $150 million
   Currency in bank vaults = $100 million
   Checkable bank deposits = $500 million

   a. What is M1?

   b. What is the monetary base?

   c. Are the commercial banks holding excess reserves?

   d. Can the commercial banks increase checkable bank deposits? If yes, by how much can checkable bank deposits increase?

8. In Westlandia, the public holds 50% of M1 in the form of currency, and the required reserve ratio is 20%. Estimate how much the money supply will increase in response to a new cash deposit of $500 by completing the accompanying table. (*Hint:* The first row shows that the bank must hold $100 in minimum reserves—20% of the $500 deposit—against this deposit, leaving $400 in excess reserves that can be loaned out. However, since the public wants to hold

50% of the loan in currency, only $400 \times 0.5 = $200 of the loan will be deposited in round 2 from the loan granted in round 1.) How does your answer compare to an economy in which the total amount of the loan is deposited in the banking system and the public doesn't hold any of the loan in currency? What does this imply about the relationship between the public's desire for holding currency and the money multiplier?

Round	Deposits	Required reserves	Excess reserves	Loans	Held as currency
1	$500.00	$100.00	$400.00	$400.00	$200.00
2	200.00	?	?	?	?
3	?	?	?	?	?
4	?	?	?	?	?
5	?	?	?	?	?
6	?	?	?	?	?
7	?	?	?	?	?
8	?	?	?	?	?
9	?	?	?	?	?
Total after 10 rounds	?	?	?	?	?

9. What will happen to the money supply under the following circumstances in a checkable-deposits-only system?

   a. The required reserve ratio is 25%, and a depositor withdraws $700 from their checkable bank deposit and holds it as cash.

   b. The required reserve ratio is 5%, and a depositor withdraws $700 from their checkable bank deposit and holds it as cash.

   c. The required reserve ratio is 20%, and a customer deposits $750 to their checkable bank deposit and holds it as cash.

   d. The required reserve ratio is 10%, and a customer deposits $600 to their checkable bank deposit and holds it as cash.

10. Although the U.S. Federal Reserve doesn't use changes in reserve requirements to manage the money supply, the central bank of Albernia does. The commercial banks of Albernia have $100 million in reserves and $1,000 million in checkable deposits; the initial required reserve ratio is 10%. The commercial banks follow a policy of holding no excess reserves. The public holds no currency, only checkable deposits in the banking system.

   a. How will the money supply change if the required reserve ratio falls to 5%?

   b. How will the money supply change if the required reserve ratio rises to 25%?

11. Using Figure 29-6, find the Federal Reserve district in which you live. Go to www.federalreserve.gov/fomc/ and determine if the president of the regional Federal Reserve bank in your district is currently a voting member of the Federal Open Market Committee (FOMC).

12. Show the changes to the T-accounts for the Federal Reserve and for commercial banks when the Federal Reserve sells $30 million in U.S. Treasury bills. If the public holds a fixed amount of currency (so that all new loans create an equal amount of checkable bank deposits in the banking system) and the minimum reserve ratio is 5%, by how much will checkable bank deposits in the commercial banks change? By how much will the money supply change? Show the final changes to the T-account for the commercial banks when the money supply changes by this amount.

13. The Congressional Research Service estimates that at least $45 million of counterfeit U.S. $100 notes produced by the North Korean government are in circulation.

   a. Why do U.S. taxpayers lose because of North Korea's counterfeiting?

   b. As of December 2016, the interest rate earned on one-year U.S. Treasury bills was 0.87%. At a 0.87% rate of interest, what is the amount of money U.S. taxpayers are losing per year because of these $45 million in counterfeit notes?

14. As shown in Figure 29-9, the portion of the Federal Reserve's assets made up of U.S. Treasury bills has declined since 2007. Go to www.federalreserve.gov. On the top of the page, under "Data" and "Money Stock and Reserve Balances," select the link "Factors Affecting Reserve Balances – H.4.1." Click on the link for the current release.

   a. Under "Condition Statement of Federal Reserve Banks," find the row "Reserve Bank Credit." What is the total amount of reserve bank credit under "Average of Daily Figures" for the most current week ended? What is the amount displayed for "U.S. Treasury securities"? What percentage of the Federal Reserve's total reserve bank credit is currently made up of U.S. Treasury bills?

   b. Do the Federal Reserve's assets consist primarily of U.S. Treasury securities, as they did in January 2007, the beginning of the graph in Figure 29-9, or does the Fed still own a large number of other assets, as it did in early 2020, the end of the graph in Figure 29-9?

15. The accompanying figure shows new U.S. housing starts, in thousands of units per month, between January 1980 and March 2020. The figure shows a large drop in new housing starts from 1984–1991 and 2006–2009. New housing starts are related to the availability of mortgages.

   a. What caused the drop in new housing starts from 1984–1991?

   b. What caused the drop in new housing starts from 2006–2009?

   c. How could better regulation of financial institutions have prevented these two instances?

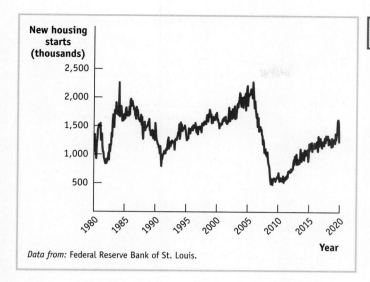

New housing starts (thousands)

Data from: Federal Reserve Bank of St. Louis.

Year

⠿ **WORK IT OUT**

16. Show the changes to the T-accounts for the Federal Reserve and for commercial banks when the Federal Reserve buys $50 million in U.S. Treasury bills. If the public holds a fixed amount of currency (so that all loans create an equal amount of deposits in the banking system), the minimum reserve ratio is 10%, and banks hold no excess reserves, by how much will deposits in the commercial banks change? By how much will the money supply change? Show the final changes to the T-account for commercial banks when the money supply changes by this amount. ∎

30 > Monetary Policy

THE MOST POWERFUL PERSON IN GOVERNMENT

"THE FUNDAMENTALS OF THE U.S. ECONOMY remain strong. However, the coronavirus poses evolving risks to economic activity. In light of these risks and in support of achieving its maximum employment and price stability goals, the Federal Open Market Committee decided today to lower the target range for the federal funds rate by 1/2 percentage point, to 1 to 1-1/4 percent. The Committee is closely monitoring developments and their implications for the economic outlook and will use its tools and act as appropriate to support the economy."

So read a statement issued on March 3, 2020, by the people who set U.S. monetary policy. Just 12 days later they issued another statement, effectively reducing the interest rates they control to zero, while also announcing plans to boost the economy by buying at least $700 billion in bonds.

These two announcements amounted to a major shift in U.S. economic policy. But who was doing the shifting? Neither Congress nor the president has any direct role in setting interest rates. That role falls, instead, to the Board of Governors of the Federal Reserve, an independent agency that was chaired at the time by Jerome Powell. And there is an old saw to the effect that the Fed chair, not the president, is the most powerful person in government.

Yet, at the Federal Reserve, unlike at the nearby White House, there is no pomp and circumstance: no aides dashing around, no splendidly dressed military guards, no ornate paintings on the

walls, and no Secret Service. Instead, workers at the Fed are casually dressed — and often look like graduate students. For example, each day at the New York Federal Reserve Bank, where the Fed's financial operations are performed, billions of dollars' worth of long-term U.S. government bonds are bought and sold in a small room with just five employees. Struck by the ordinariness of it all, one journalist wrote, "Can a spectacle so lacking in the indicia of importance — no pageantry, no emotions, not even speaking — really be the beating heart of capitalism?"

The answer is yes. The source of the power of the Fed chair and the Board of Governors comes from their ability to set *monetary policy*. It's hard to overstate the importance of the Fed's monetary policy to the U.S. economy — for price stability, for job creation, and for the smooth functioning of the financial system. Roughly half the recessions that have occurred since World War II can be attributed, at least partly, to policies undertaken by the Federal Reserve to fight inflation. And during many other periods, Fed policy played a critical role in fighting slumps and promoting recovery. During the financial crisis of 2008 and the ensuing Great Recession, the Fed was at the very center of the fight to keep the economy from plunging into an abyss.

How does the Fed accomplish all this? Through changes in the money supply and interest rates, which are implemented by its unassuming-looking employees trading billions of dollars daily in U.S. government bonds. (And, as we learned in Chapter 29, to a lesser extent, the Fed can influence the money supply by changing the reserve requirements for banks.)

In this chapter we'll learn how monetary policy works — how actions by the Federal Reserve can have a powerful effect on the economy. We'll start by looking at the *demand for money* from households and firms. Then we'll see how the Fed's ability to change the *supply of money* allows it to move interest rates in the short run and thereby affect real GDP. We'll look at U.S. monetary policy in practice and compare it to the monetary policy of other central banks. We'll conclude by examining monetary policy's long-run effects. ●

The chair of the Federal Reserve is arguably the most powerful position in the U.S. government.

REUTERS/Kevin Lamarque

WHAT YOU WILL LEARN

- What is the **money demand curve?**
- Why does the **liquidity preference model** determine the interest rate in the short run?
- How does the Federal Reserve implement monetary policy?
- Why is monetary policy the main tool for stabilizing the economy?
- Why do economists believe in **monetary neutrality?**

A **certificate of deposit (CD)** is a bank-issued asset in which customers deposit funds for a specified amount of time and earn a specified interest rate.

|| The Demand for Money

In the previous chapter we learned about the various types of monetary aggregates: M1, the most commonly used definition of the money supply, consists of currency in circulation (cash) plus checkable bank deposits; and M2, a broader definition of the money supply, consists of M1 plus deposits that can easily be transferred into checkable deposits. We also learned why people hold money—to make it easier to purchase goods and services. Now we'll go deeper, examining what determines how much money individuals and firms want to hold at any given time.

The Opportunity Cost of Holding Money

Most economic decisions involve trade-offs at the margin. That is, individuals decide how much of a good to consume by determining whether the benefit they'd gain from consuming a bit more of any given good is worth the cost. The same decision process is used when deciding how much money to hold.

Michael Trujillo/EyeEm/Getty Images

There is a price to be paid for the convenience of holding money.

Individuals and firms find it useful to hold some of their assets in the form of money because of the convenience that cash provides: money can be used to make purchases directly, but other assets can't. But there is a price to be paid for that convenience: money normally yields no rate of return, or a lower rate of return, than nonmonetary assets.

As an example of how convenience makes it worth incurring some opportunity costs, consider the substantial sums that Americans hold in cash and in zero-interest bank accounts linked to debit cards or money transmitters like PayPal and Venmo. By doing so they forgo the interest that could have been earned by putting those funds into an interest-bearing asset like a certificate of deposit. A **certificate of deposit,** or **CD,** is a bank-issued asset that allows customers to deposit their funds for a specified amount of time, and, in return, the bank pays a specified interest rate. For example, as of April 2020 the bank Capital One was offering a five-year CD paying 1.4% annually and a one-year CD paying 1.5%. But CDs also carry a penalty if funds are withdrawn before the specified amount of time—whether five years or one year—has elapsed.

So making sense of the demand for money is about understanding how individuals and firms trade off the benefit of holding monetary assets that provide convenience but little or no interest (like cash and zero-interest bank accounts) versus the benefit of holding nonmonetary assets—that provide more interest but less convenience (like CDs). And that trade-off is affected by the interest rate. (As before, when we say *the interest rate* it is with the understanding that we mean a nominal interest rate—that is, it's unadjusted for inflation.) Next, we'll examine how that trade-off changed dramatically from March 2019 and March 2020, when there was a big fall in interest rates.

Table 30-1 illustrates the opportunity cost of holding money in a specific month, March 2019. The first row shows the interest rate on one-month Treasury bills—that is, the interest rate individuals could get if they were willing to lend funds to the U.S. government for one month.

In March 2019, one-month Treasury bills yielded 2.45%. The second row shows the interest rate on interest-bearing demand deposits. Funds in these accounts were more accessible than those in Treasury bills, but the price of that convenience was a much lower interest rate, only 0.06%. Finally, the last row shows the interest rate on currency—cash in your wallet—which was, of course, zero.

TABLE 30-1 Selected Interest Rates, March 2019	
One-month Treasury bills	2.45%
Interest-bearing demand deposits	0.06%
Currency	0

Data from: Federal Reserve Bank of St. Louis.

Table 30-1 shows the opportunity cost of holding money at one point in time, but the opportunity cost of holding money changes when the overall level of interest rates changes. Specifically, when the overall level of interest rates falls, the opportunity cost of holding money falls, too.

Table 30-2 illustrates this point by showing how selected interest rates changed between March 2019 and March 2020; as we've already seen, in early 2020 the Fed slashed rates in an effort to fight off a rapidly worsening recession. A comparison between interest rates in those two months illustrates what happens when the opportunity cost of holding money falls sharply. Over the course of a year the federal funds rate, which is the rate the Fed controls most directly, fell by 2.3 percentage points. The interest rate on one-month Treasuries fell by almost the same amount. These interest rates are **short-term interest rates**—rates on financial assets that come due, or mature, within less than a year.

As short-term interest rates fell, the interest rate on money didn't fall by the same amount. The interest rate on currency, of course, remained at zero. The interest rate paid on demand deposits also remained unchanged, at 0.06%. As a comparison of the two columns of Table 30-2 shows, the opportunity cost of holding money fell. The last two rows of Table 30-2 summarize this comparison: they give the differences between the interest rates on Treasuries and demand deposits and between the interest rates on Treasuries and currency.

These differences—the opportunity cost of holding money rather than interest-bearing assets—declined sharply between March 2019 and March 2020. This reflects a general result: *the higher the short-term interest rate, the higher the opportunity cost of holding money; the lower the short-term interest rate, the lower the opportunity cost of holding money.*

The fact that the federal funds rate in Table 30-2 and the interest rate on Treasuries fell by almost the same percentage is not an accident: all short-term interest rates tend to move together, with rare exceptions. The reason short-term interest rates tend to move together is that short-term assets are in effect competing for the same business. Any short-term asset that offers a lower-than-average interest rate will be sold by investors, who will move their wealth into a higher-yielding short-term asset. The selling of the asset, in turn, forces its interest rate up, because investors must be rewarded with a higher rate in order to induce them to buy it.

Conversely, investors will move their wealth into any short-term financial asset that offers an above-average interest rate. The purchase of the asset drives its interest rate down when sellers find they can lower the rate of return on the asset and still find willing buyers. So, interest rates on short-term financial assets tend to be roughly the same because no asset will consistently offer a higher-than-average or a lower-than-average interest rate.

Table 30-2 contains only short-term interest rates. At any given moment, **long-term interest rates**—rates of interest on financial assets that mature, or come due, a number of years into the future—may be different from short-term interest rates. The difference between short-term and long-term interest rates is sometimes important as a practical matter.

Moreover, it's short-term rates rather than long-term rates that affect money demand, because the decision to hold money involves trading off the convenience of holding cash versus the payoff from holding assets that mature in the short term—a year or less. For the moment, however, let's ignore the distinction between short-term and long-term rates and assume that there is only one interest rate.

TABLE 30-2 Interest Rates and the Opportunity Cost of Holding Money

	March 2019	March 2020
Federal funds rate	2.41%	0.08%
One-month Treasury bills	2.45%	0.12%
Interest-bearing demand deposits	0.06%	0.06%
Currency	0	0
Treasury bills minus interest-bearing demand deposits (percentage points)	2.39	0.06
Treasury bills minus currency (percentage points)	2.45	0.12

Data from: Federal Reserve Bank of St. Louis.

Short-term interest rates are the interest rates on financial assets that mature within less than a year.

Long-term interest rates are interest rates on financial assets that mature a number of years in the future.

The **money demand curve** shows the relationship between the interest rate and the quantity of money demanded.

The Money Demand Curve

Because the overall level of interest rates affects the opportunity cost of holding money, the quantity of money individuals and firms want to hold is, other things equal, negatively related to the interest rate. In Figure 30-1, the horizontal axis shows the quantity of money demanded and the vertical axis shows the interest rate, r, which you can think of as a representative short-term interest rate such as the rate on one-month CDs. (As we discussed in Chapter 25, it is the nominal interest rate, not the real interest rate, that influences people's money allocation decisions. Hence, r in Figure 30-1 and all subsequent figures is the nominal interest rate.)

The relationship between the interest rate and the quantity of money demanded by the public is illustrated by the **money demand curve,** *MD*, in Figure 30-1. The money demand curve slopes downward because, other things equal, a higher interest rate increases the opportunity cost of holding money, leading the public to reduce the quantity of money it demands. For example, if the interest rate is very low—say, 1%—the interest forgone by holding money is relatively small. As a result, individuals and firms will tend to hold relatively large amounts of money to avoid the cost and nuisance of converting other assets into money when making purchases.

By contrast, if the interest rate is relatively high—say, 15%, a level it reached in the United States in the early 1980s—the opportunity cost of holding money is high. People will respond by keeping only small amounts in cash and deposits, converting assets into money only when needed.

You might ask why we draw the money demand curve with the interest rate—as opposed to rates of return on other assets, such as stocks or real estate—on the vertical axis. The answer is that for most people the relevant question in deciding how much money to hold is whether to put the funds in the form of other assets that can be turned fairly quickly and easily into money. Many online brokers offer $0 trades. Stocks don't fit that definition because converting stocks to cash can take considerable time, incur substantial fees, or both, and also because stock values fluctuate. Real estate doesn't fit the definition either because selling real estate involves even larger fees and can take a long time as well. So the relevant comparison is with assets that are "close to" money—assets like CDs that are less liquid than money but more liquid than

FIGURE 30-1 The Money Demand Curve

The money demand curve illustrates the relationship between the interest rate and the quantity of money demanded. It slopes downward: a higher interest rate leads to a higher opportunity cost of holding money and reduces the quantity of money demanded. Correspondingly, a lower interest rate reduces the opportunity cost of holding money and increases the quantity of money demanded.

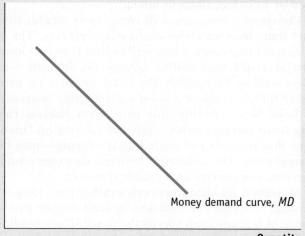

stocks or real estate. And as we've already seen, the interest rates on all these assets normally move closely together.

Shifts of the Money Demand Curve

A number of factors other than the interest rate affect the demand for money. When one of these factors changes, the money demand curve shifts. Figure 30-2 shows shifts of the money demand curve: an increase in the demand for money corresponds to a rightward shift of the *MD* curve, raising the quantity of money demanded at any given interest rate; a decrease in the demand for money corresponds to a leftward shift of the *MD* curve, reducing the quantity of money demanded at any given interest rate.

The most important factors causing the money demand curve to shift are changes in the aggregate price level, changes in real GDP, changes in credit markets and banking technology, and changes in institutions.

Changes in the Aggregate Price Level Americans keep a lot more cash on hand and funds in their checking accounts today than they did in the 1950s. One reason is that they have to if they want to be able to buy anything: almost everything costs more now than it did when you could get a burger, fries, and a drink at McDonald's for 45 cents and a gallon of gasoline for 29 cents. So, other things equal, higher prices increase the demand for money (a rightward shift of the *MD* curve), and lower prices decrease the demand for money (a leftward shift of the *MD* curve).

We can actually be more specific than this: other things equal, the demand for money is *proportional* to the price level. That is, if the aggregate price level rises by 20%, the quantity of money demanded at any given interest rate, such as r_1 in Figure 30-2, also rises by 20%—the movement from M_1 to M_2. Why? Because if the price of everything rises by 20%, it takes 20% more money to buy the same basket of goods and services. And if the aggregate price level falls by 20%, at any given interest rate the quantity of money demanded falls by 20%—shown by the movement from M_1 to M_3 at the interest rate r_1. As we'll see later, the fact that money demand is proportional to the price level has important implications for the long-run effects of monetary policy.

FIGURE 30-2 Increases and Decreases in the Demand for Money

The demand curve for money shifts when non-interest-rate factors that affect the demand for money change. An increase in money demand shifts the money demand curve to the right, from MD_1 to MD_2, and the quantity of money demanded rises at any given interest rate. A decrease in money demand shifts the money demand curve to the left, from MD_1 to MD_3, and the quantity of money demanded falls at any given interest rate.

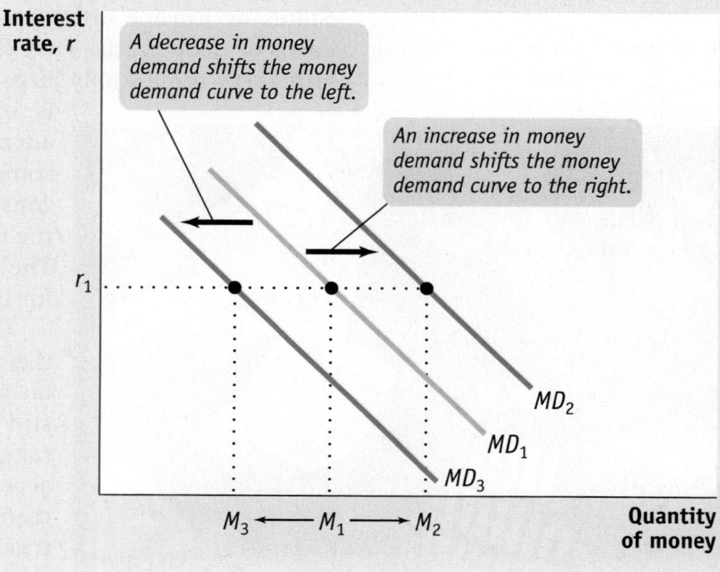

Changes in Real GDP Households and firms hold money as a way to facilitate purchases of goods and services. The larger the quantity of goods and services they buy, the larger the quantity of money they will want to hold at any given interest rate. So, an increase in real GDP—the total quantity of goods and services produced and sold in the economy—shifts the money demand curve rightward. A fall in real GDP shifts the money demand curve leftward.

martin-dm/Getty Images

Since the start of coronavirus pandemic merchants have seen a spike in contactless forms of payment like ApplePay and Google Pay.

Changes in Credit Markets and Banking Technology As late as the 1960s almost all small purchases—lunch, groceries, and more—were made using cash because alternatives were few. Since then, however, the need for cash has been greatly reduced by a series of innovations, from widely available credit cards to debit cards to apps like PayPal that let you pay with your smartphone (see the Business Case at end of chapter to learn more about money transmitters like PayPal and Venmo). ATMs and then online banking also made it much easier to transfer funds between accounts, so it became less necessary to hold a surplus of funds in checking accounts in order to make payments. During the coronavirus pandemic, consumers have preferred contactless payment and have dumped cash in favor of digital platforms like AplePay or Google Pay. All of these developments make it easier for people to make purchases and reduce the demand for money, shifting the demand curve for money to the left.

Changes in Institutions Changes in institutions can increase or decrease the demand for money. For example, until Regulation Q was eliminated in 1980, U.S. banks weren't allowed to offer interest on checking accounts. So the interest you would forgo by holding funds in a checking account instead of an interest-bearing asset made the opportunity cost of holding funds in checking accounts very high. When banking regulations changed, allowing banks to pay interest on checking account funds, the demand for money rose and shifted the money demand curve to the right.

ECONOMICS >> *in Action*
A Yen for Cash

Japan, say financial experts, is still a "cash society." Visitors from the United States or Europe are surprised at how little use the Japanese make of credit cards or debit cards. They do make many purchases with smartphones, yet they still carry remarkably large amounts of cash around in their wallets. Yet Japan is one of the most economically and technologically advanced countries, and superior to the United States in some areas, such as transportation. So why do the citizens of this economic powerhouse often still do business the way Americans and Europeans did a generation ago? The answer highlights the factors affecting the demand for money.

One reason the Japanese use cash so much is that their institutions never made the switch to heavy reliance on plastic. For complex reasons, Japan's retail sector is still dominated by small mom-and-pop stores, which are reluctant to pay the up-front costs that would let them accept credit cards, let alone smartphone apps, as payment. Japan's banks have also been slow about pushing transaction technology; visitors are often surprised to find that ATMs outside of major metropolitan areas close early in the evening rather than staying open all night.

Trevor Mogg/Alamy

No matter what they are shopping for, Japanese consumers tend to pay with cash rather than plastic.

But there's another reason the Japanese hold so much cash: there's little opportunity cost to doing so. Short-term interest rates in Japan have been below 1% since the mid-1990s. It also helps that the Japanese crime rate is quite low, so you are unlikely to have your wallet stolen. So why not hold cash?

>> Check Your Understanding 30-1

Solutions appear at back of book.

1. Explain how each of the following would affect the quantity of money demanded. Does the change cause a movement along the money demand curve or a shift of the money demand curve?
   a. Short-term interest rates rise from 5% to 30%.
   b. All prices fall by 10%.
   c. New "just walk out technology" automatically charges supermarket purchases to credit cards, eliminating the need to stop at the cash register.
   d. In order to avoid paying a sharp increase in taxes, residents of Laguria shift their assets into overseas bank accounts. These accounts are harder for tax authorities to trace but also harder for their owners to tap and convert funds into cash.

2. Which of the following will increase the opportunity cost of holding cash? Which will reduce it? Explain.
   a. In order to attract new customers, the new electronic payment firm, PayBuddy, announces it will pay 0.5% interest on cash balances in a PayBuddy account.
   b. To attract more deposits, banks raise the interest paid on six-month CDs.
   c. In an effort to increase holiday sales, stores offer one-year zero-interest deals on purchases made with store credit cards.

‖ Money and Interest Rates

We started this chapter by quoting from a Federal Reserve press release announcing a change in the target federal funds rate. We learned about the federal funds rate in Chapter 29: it's the rate at which banks lend reserves to each other to meet the required reserve ratio. As the statement implies, at each of its eight-times-a-year meetings, and also sometimes on special occasions between meetings, a group called the Federal Open Market Committee sets a target value for the federal funds rate. It's then up to Fed officials to achieve that target. This is done by the Open Market Desk at the Federal Reserve Bank of New York, which buys and sells short-term U.S. government debt, known as Treasury bills, to achieve that target.

As we've already seen, other short-term interest rates move with the federal funds rate. So when the Fed cut its target for the federal funds rate in March 2020, many other short-term interest rates also fell by about the same amount.

How does the Fed go about achieving a *target federal funds rate?* And more to the point, how is the Fed able to affect interest rates at all?

The Equilibrium Interest Rate

Recall that, for simplicity, we're assuming there is only one interest rate paid on nonmonetary financial assets, both in the short run and in the long run. To understand how the interest rate is determined, consider Figure 30-3, which illustrates the **liquidity preference model of the interest rate;** this model says that the interest rate is determined by the supply and demand for money in the market for money. Figure 30-3 combines the money demand curve, *MD*, with the **money supply curve,** *MS,* which shows how the quantity of money supplied by the Federal Reserve varies with the interest rate.

According to the **liquidity preference model of the interest rate,** the interest rate is determined by the supply and demand for money.

The **money supply curve** shows how the quantity of money supplied varies with the interest rate.

FIGURE 30-3 Equilibrium in the Money Market

The money supply curve, *MS,* is vertical at the money supply chosen by the Federal Reserve, $\overline{M}$. The money market is in equilibrium at the interest rate r_E: the quantity of money demanded by the public is equal to $\overline{M}$, the quantity of money supplied.

At a point such as *L,* the interest rate, r_L, is below r_E and the corresponding quantity of money demanded, M_L, exceeds the money supply, $\overline{M}$. In an attempt to shift their wealth out of nonmoney interest-bearing financial assets and raise their money holdings, investors drive the interest rate up to r_E. At a point such as *H,* the interest rate r_H exceeds r_E and the corresponding quantity of money demanded, M_H, is less than the money supply, $\overline{M}$. In an attempt to shift out of money holdings into nonmoney interest-bearing financial assets, investors drive the interest rate down to r_E.

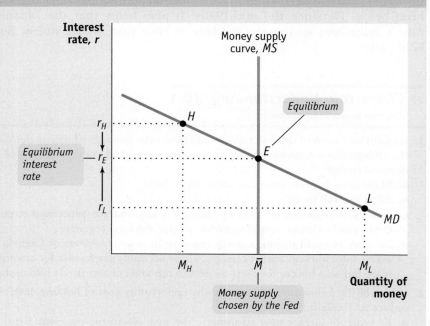

The Federal Reserve can increase or decrease the money supply: it usually does this through *open-market operations,* buying or selling Treasury bills, but it can also lend via the *discount window* or change *reserve requirements.* Let's assume for simplicity that the Fed, using one or more of these methods, simply chooses the level of the money supply that it believes will achieve its interest rate target. Then the money supply curve is a vertical line, *MS* in Figure 30-3, with a horizontal intercept corresponding to the money supply chosen by the Fed, $\overline{M}$. The money market equilibrium is at *E,* where *MS* and *MD* cross. At this point the quantity of money demanded equals the money supply, $\overline{M}$. leading to an equilibrium interest rate of r_E.

To understand why r_E is the equilibrium interest rate, consider what happens if the money market is at a point like *L,* where the interest rate, r_L, is below r_E. At r_L the public wants to hold the quantity of money M_L, an amount larger than the actual money supply, $\overline{M}$. This means that at point *L,* the public wants to shift some of its wealth out of interest-bearing assets such as CDs into money.

This result has two implications.

1. The quantity of money demanded is *more* than the quantity of money supplied.
2. The quantity of interest-bearing nonmoney assets demanded is *less* than the quantity supplied.

So those trying to sell nonmoney assets will find that they have to offer a higher interest rate to attract buyers. As a result, the interest rate will be driven up from r_L until the public wants to hold the quantity of money that is actually available, $\overline{M}$. That is, the interest rate will rise until it is equal to r_E.

Now consider what happens if the money market is at a point such as *H* in Figure 30-3, where the interest rate r_H is above r_E. In that case the quantity of money demanded, M_H, is less than the quantity of money supplied, $\overline{M}$. Correspondingly, the quantity of interest-bearing nonmoney assets demanded is greater than the quantity supplied. Those trying to sell interest-bearing nonmoney assets will find that they can offer a lower interest rate and still find willing buyers. This leads to a fall in the interest rate from r_H. It falls until the public wants to hold the quantity of money that is actually available, $\overline{M}$. Again, the interest rate will end up at r_E.

Two Models of Interest Rates?

You might have noticed that this is the second time we have discussed the determination of the interest rate. In Chapter 25 we studied the *loanable funds model* of the interest rate; according to that model, the interest rate is determined by the equalization of the supply of funds from lenders and the demand for funds by borrowers in the market for loanable funds. But here we have described a seemingly different model in which the interest rate is determined by the equalization of the supply and demand for money in the money market. Which of these models is correct?

The answer is both. We explain how the models are consistent with each other in the appendix to this chapter. For now, let's put the loanable funds model to one side and concentrate on the liquidity preference model of the interest rate. The most important insight from this model is that it shows us how monetary policy—actions by the Federal Reserve and other central banks—works.

Monetary Policy and the Interest Rate

Let's examine how the Federal Reserve can use changes in the money supply to change the interest rate. Figure 30-4 shows what happens when the Fed increases the money supply from $\overline{M}_1$ to $\overline{M}_2$. The economy is originally in equilibrium at E_1, with an equilibrium interest rate of r_1 and money supply, $\overline{M}_1$. An increase in the money supply by the Fed to $\overline{M}_2$ shifts the money supply curve to the right, from MS_1 to MS_2, and leads to a fall in the equilibrium interest rate to r_2. Why? Because r_2 is the only interest rate at which the public is willing to hold the quantity of money actually supplied, $\overline{M}_2$.

So an increase in the money supply drives the interest rate down. Conversely, a reduction in the money supply drives the interest rate up. By adjusting the money supply up or down, the Fed can set the interest rate.

FIGURE 30-4 The Effect of an Increase in the Money Supply on the Interest Rate

The Federal Reserve can lower the interest rate by increasing the money supply. Here, the equilibrium interest rate falls from r_1 to r_2 in response to an increase in the money supply from $\overline{M}_1$ to $\overline{M}_2$. In order to induce people to hold the larger quantity of money, the interest rate must fall from r_1 to r_2.

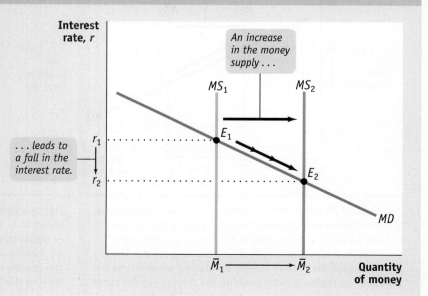

SETTING INTEREST RATES OR THE MONEY SUPPLY: DIFFERENT LOOK, SAME STORY

Over the years, the Federal Reserve has changed the way in which monetary policy is implemented. In the late 1970s and early 1980s, it set a target level for the money supply and altered the monetary base to achieve that target. Under this operating procedure, the federal funds rate fluctuated freely. Today the Fed does the opposite: setting a target for the federal funds rate, allowing the money supply to fluctuate as it pursues that target.

A common mistake is to assume that these changes in the way the Fed operates alter the way the money market works. You may have heard the claim that the interest rate no longer reflects the supply and demand for money because the Fed sets the interest rate.

In fact, the money market works as it always has: the interest rate is determined by the supply and demand for money. The only difference is that now the Fed adjusts the supply of money to achieve its target interest rate. It's important not to confuse a change in the Fed's operating procedure with a change in the way the economy works.

The **target federal funds rate** is the Federal Reserve's desired federal funds rate.

In practice, at each meeting the Federal Open Market Committee decides on the interest rate to prevail for the next six weeks, until its next meeting. The Fed sets a **target federal funds rate,** a desired level for the federal funds rate. This target is then enforced by the Open Market Desk of the Federal Reserve Bank of New York—in those small rooms we mentioned in the opening story—which adjusts the money supply through the purchase and sale of Treasury bills until the actual federal funds rate equals the target rate. The other tools of monetary policy, lending through the discount window and changes in reserve requirements, aren't used on a regular basis (although the Fed used discount window lending in its efforts to address the 2008 financial crisis).

Figure 30-5 shows how this works. In both panels, r_T is the target federal funds rate. In panel (a), the initial money supply curve is MS_1 with money supply $\overline{M}_1$, and the equilibrium interest rate, r_1, is above the target rate. To lower the interest rate to r_T, the Fed makes an open-market purchase of Treasury bills that leads to an increase in the money supply via the money multiplier. This is illustrated in panel (a) by the rightward shift of the money supply curve from MS_1 to MS_2 and an increase in the money supply to $\overline{M}_2$. This drives the equilibrium interest rate down to the target rate, r_T.

Panel (b) shows the opposite case. Again, the initial money supply curve is MS_1 with money supply $\overline{M}_1$. But this time the equilibrium interest rate, r_1, is below the target federal funds rate, r_T. In this case, the Fed will make an open-market sale of Treasury bills, leading to a fall in the money supply to $\overline{M}_2$ via the money multiplier. The money supply curve shifts leftward from MS_1 to MS_2, driving the equilibrium interest rate up to the target federal funds rate, r_T.

FIGURE 30-5 Setting the Federal Funds Rate

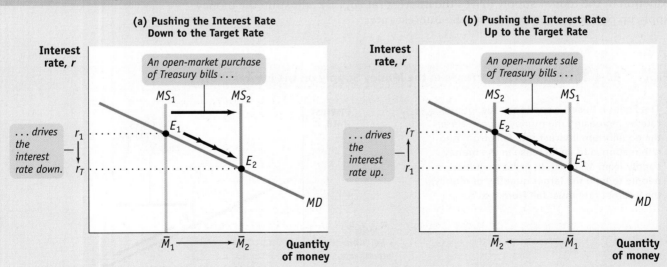

The Federal Reserve sets a target for the federal funds rate and uses open-market operations to achieve that target. In both panels the target rate is r_T. In panel (a) the initial equilibrium interest rate, r_1, is above the target rate. The Fed increases the money supply by making an open-market purchase of Treasury bills, pushing the money supply curve rightward, from MS_1 to MS_2, and driving the interest rate down to r_T. In panel (b) the initial equilibrium interest rate, r_1, is below the target rate. The Fed reduces the money supply by making an open-market sale of Treasury bills, pushing the money supply curve leftward, from MS_1 to MS_2, and driving the interest rate up to r_T.

Long-Term Interest Rates

In early 2015, short-term interest rates were quite similar in the world's wealthy economies, because they were all close to zero. For example, in Germany the short-term interest rate was 0.05%, while in the United States it was 0.15%. But long-term interest rates—rates on bonds or loans that mature in several years—were quite different. The interest rate on 10-year German government bonds was 0.35%, but the corresponding rate for the United States was 1.97%.

Why were these long-term rates so different? Because long-term rates reflect expected future monetary policy, which in turn largely depend on the future economic outlook.

Consider the case of Min, who has already decided to place $10,000 in U.S. government bonds for the next two years. However, she hasn't decided whether to put the money in one-year bonds, at a 4% rate of interest, or two-year bonds, at a 5% rate of interest. If she buys the one-year bond, then in one year, Min will receive the $10,000 she paid for the bond (the *principal*) plus interest earned. If instead she buys the two-year bond, Min will have to wait until the end of the second year to receive her principal and her interest.

You might think that the two-year bonds are a clearly better deal—but they may not be. Suppose that Min expects the rate of interest on one-year bonds to rise sharply next year. If she puts her funds in one-year bonds this year, she will be able to reinvest the money at a much higher rate next year. And this could give her a two-year rate of return that is higher than if she put her funds into the two-year bonds today.

For example, if the rate of interest on one-year bonds rises from 4% this year to 8% next year, putting her funds in a one-year bond today and in another one-year bond a year from now will give her an annual rate of return over the next two years of about 6%, better than the 5% rate on two-year bonds.

The same considerations apply to all investors deciding between short-term and long-term bonds. If they expect short-term interest rates to rise, investors may buy short-term bonds even if long-term bonds bought today offer a higher interest rate today. If they expect short-term interest rates to fall, investors may buy long-term bonds even if short-term bonds bought today offer a higher interest rate today.

As the example suggests, long-term interest rates largely reflect the average expectation in the market about what's going to happen to short-term rates in the future. What happened in 2015 was that investors expected the U.S. economy to continue growing in the near future, which led to the expectation that the Fed would raise short-term interest rates.

Expected monetary policy is not, however, the whole story: risk is also a factor. Let's return to Min's decision: whether to buy one-year or two-year bonds. Suppose that there is some chance she will need to cash in her investment after just one year—say, to meet an emergency medical bill. If she buys two-year bonds, she would have to sell those bonds to meet the unexpected expense. But what price will she get for those bonds? It depends on what has happened to interest rates in the rest of the economy. As we've learned, bond prices and interest rates move in opposite directions: if interest rates rise, bond prices fall, and vice versa.

This means that Min will face extra risk if she buys two-year rather than one-year bonds, because if a year from now bond prices fall and she must sell her bonds in order to raise cash, she will lose money on the bonds. Owing to this risk factor, long-term interest rates are, on average, higher than short-term rates in order to compensate long-term bond purchasers for the higher risk they face (although this relationship is reversed when short-term rates are unusually high).

Advertising during the two world wars increased the demand for government long-term bonds from savers who might have been otherwise reluctant to tie up their funds for several years.

As we will soon see, the fact that long-term rates don't necessarily move with short-term rates is sometimes an important consideration for monetary policy.

ECONOMICS >> *in Action*
Up the Down Staircase

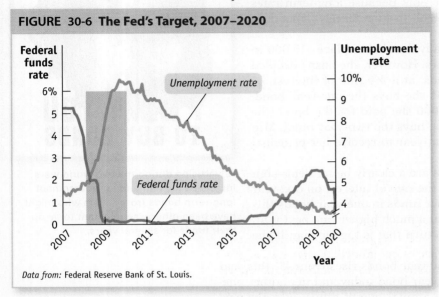

FIGURE 30-6 The Fed's Target, 2007–2020

Data from: Federal Reserve Bank of St. Louis.

We began this chapter with the Fed's March 2020 announcement that it was cutting its target interest rate. By historical standards, however, the target rate was already very low even before that cut. As Figure 30-6 shows, in early 2007, before the financial crisis, the target rate was 5.25%. But when the financial crisis hit in 2008, the Fed drastically cut rates in an effort to fight the Great Recession, and kept them close to zero for seven years.

Why did the Fed keep rates so low? Because a severe recession followed by a slow recovery kept unemployment—also shown in the figure—very high, while inflation stayed low, for a very long time. In effect, the Fed believed that it needed to keep the pedal to the metal.

By late 2015, however, the economy had clearly improved, with unemployment, in particular, down roughly to its pre-crisis level. And in December 2015 the Federal Open Market Committee began inching back toward a more historically normal monetary policy, before reversing course in 2019. But "inching" is the word: even at its 2019 peak, the federal funds rate was still well below what it had been in 2007.

Why was the Fed moving so slowly? For one thing, while the economy had clearly recovered from the worst of the Great Recession, it was hardly experiencing an inflationary boom. In fact, the Fed's preferred measure of inflation was still a bit below its target.

Also, a significant number of economists worried that changes in the economic environment, in particular an aging population and slowing productivity growth, meant that maintaining full employment would require keeping interest rates more or less permanently low by historical standards. Investors seemed to agree: in fact, after rising briefly, by early 2020—that is, before the coronavirus hit—long-term interest rates were only about 1.50%, which implied that, for the foreseeable future, investors didn't expect the Fed to return to the kind of interest rates it used to target.

>> Check Your Understanding 30-2
Solutions appear at back of book.

1. There is an increase in the demand for money at every interest rate. Draw a diagram showing the effect of this on the equilibrium interest rate for a given money supply.

2. Now assume that the Fed is following a policy of targeting the federal funds rate. What will the Fed do in the situation described in Question 1 to keep the federal funds rate unchanged? Illustrate with a diagram.

3. Malia must decide whether to buy a one-year bond today and another one a year from now, or to buy a two-year bond today. In which of the following scenarios is she better off taking the first action? The second action?

   a. This year, the interest on a one-year bond is 4%; next year, it will be 10%. The interest rate on a two-year bond is 5%.

   b. This year, the interest rate on a one-year bond is 4%; next year, it will be 1%. The interest rate on a two-year bond is 3%.

Expansionary monetary policy is monetary policy that increases aggregate demand.

Monetary Policy and Aggregate Demand

We saw how fiscal policy can be used to stabilize the economy in Chapter 28. Now we will see how monetary policy, which we defined earlier as changes in the money supply, and the interest rate, together, can play the same role.

Expansionary and Contractionary Monetary Policy

In Chapter 27 we learned that monetary policy shifts the aggregate demand curve. We can now explain how that works: through the effect of monetary policy on the interest rate.

Figure 30-7 illustrates the process. Suppose, first, that the Federal Reserve wants to reduce interest rates, so it expands the money supply. As you can see in the top portion of the figure, a lower interest rate will lead, other things equal, to more investment spending. This will in turn lead to higher consumer spending, through the multiplier process, and to an increase in aggregate output demanded. In the end, the total quantity of goods and services demanded at any given aggregate price level rises when the quantity of money increases, and the *AD* curve shifts to the right. Monetary policy that increases the demand for goods and services is known as **expansionary monetary policy**. (It is also commonly called *loose monetary policy*.)

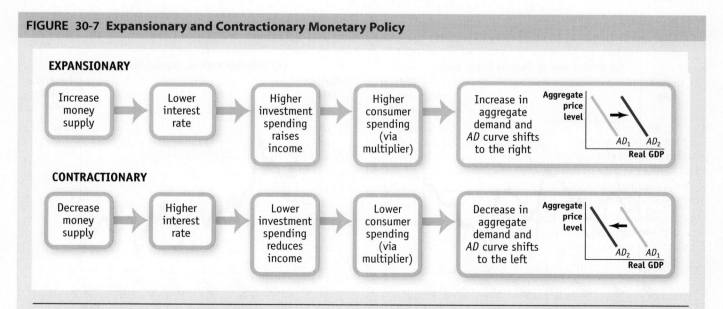

FIGURE 30-7 Expansionary and Contractionary Monetary Policy

The top portion of the diagram shows what happens when the Fed adopts an expansionary monetary policy and increases the money supply. Interest rates fall, leading to higher investment spending, which raises income, which, in turn, raises consumer spending and shifts the *AD* curve to the right. The bottom portion shows what happens when the Fed adopts a contractionary monetary policy and reduces the money supply. Interest rates rise, leading to lower investment spending and a reduction in income. This lowers consumer spending and shifts the *AD* curve to the left.

"I told you the Fed should have tightened."

Contractionary monetary policy
is monetary policy that decreases
aggregate demand.

Suppose, alternatively, that the Federal Reserve wants to increase interest rates, so it contracts the money supply. You can see this process illustrated in the bottom portion of the diagram. Contraction of the money supply leads to a higher interest rate. The higher interest rate leads to lower investment spending, then to lower consumer spending, and then to a decrease in aggregate output demanded. So, the total quantity of goods and services demanded falls when the money supply is reduced, and the *AD* curve shifts to the left. Monetary policy that decreases the demand for goods and services is called **contractionary monetary policy.** (It is also commonly called *tight monetary policy*.)

Monetary Policy in Practice

How does the Fed decide whether to use expansionary or contractionary monetary policy? And how does it decide how much is enough? As we've learned, policy makers try to both fight recessions and ensure *price stability:* low (though usually not zero) inflation. Actual monetary policy reflects a combination of these goals.

In general, the Fed and other central banks tend to engage in expansionary monetary policy when actual real GDP is below potential output. Panel (a) of Figure 30-8 shows the U.S. output gap, defined in Chapter 27 as the percentage difference between actual real GDP and potential output, versus the federal funds rate since 1985. (Recall that the output gap is positive when actual real GDP exceeds potential output.) As you can see, the Fed tends to raise interest rates when the output gap is rising (when the economy is developing an inflationary gap) and cut rates when the output gap is falling. (The exception is the period from 2009 to 2016, and again in 2020, when the federal funds rate was stuck near zero, a phenomenon, called the *zero lower bound on interest rates*.)

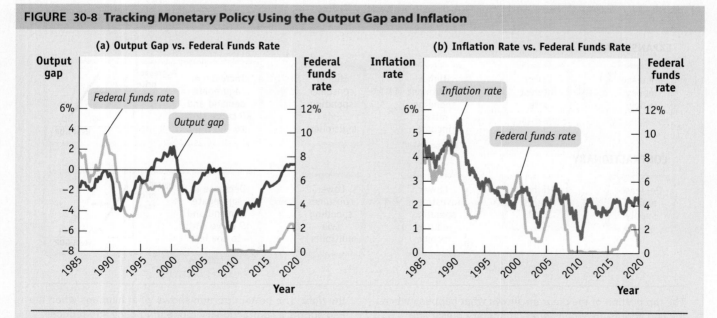

FIGURE 30-8 Tracking Monetary Policy Using the Output Gap and Inflation

Panel (a) shows that the federal funds rate usually rises when the output gap is rising, and falls when the output gap is falling. Panel (b) illustrates that the federal funds rate tends to be high when inflation is high and low when inflation is low.
Data from: Federal Reserve Bank of St. Louis.

The big exception was the late 1990s, when the Fed left rates steady for several years even as the economy developed a positive output gap (which went along with a low unemployment rate). One reason the Fed was willing to keep interest rates low in the late 1990s was that inflation was low.

Panel (b) of Figure 30-8 compares the inflation rate, measured as the rate of change in consumer prices excluding food and energy, with the federal funds rate. You can see how low inflation during the mid-1990s, the early 2000s, and the late 2000s helped encourage loose monetary policy in the late 1990s, in 2002–2003, and again beginning in 2008.

> A **Taylor rule for monetary policy** is a rule that sets the federal funds rate according to the level of the inflation rate and either the output gap or the unemployment rate.

The Taylor Rule Method of Setting Monetary Policy

In 1993 Stanford economist John Taylor suggested that monetary policy should follow a simple rule that takes into account concerns about both the business cycle and inflation. He also suggested that actual monetary policy often looks as if the Federal Reserve was, in fact, more or less following the proposed rule. A **Taylor rule for monetary policy** is a rule for setting interest rates that takes into account the inflation rate and the output gap or, in some cases, the unemployment rate.

A widely cited example of a Taylor rule is a relationship among Fed policy, inflation, and unemployment estimated by economists at the Federal Reserve Bank of San Francisco. These economists found that between 1988 and 2008 the Fed's behavior was well summarized by the following Taylor rule:

$$\text{Federal funds rate} = 2.07 + 1.28 \times \text{inflation rate} - 1.95 \times \text{unemployment gap}$$

where the inflation rate was measured by the change over the previous year in consumer prices excluding food and energy, and the unemployment gap was the difference between the actual unemployment rate and Congressional Budget Office estimates of the natural rate of unemployment.

Figure 30-9 compares the federal funds rate predicted by this rule with the actual federal funds rate from 1985 to 2020. As you can see, the Fed's decisions were quite close to those predicted by this particular Taylor rule from 1985 through the end of 2008. We'll talk about what happened after 2008 shortly.

FIGURE 30-9 The Taylor Rule and the Federal Funds Rate

The purple line shows the federal funds rate predicted by the San Francisco Fed's version of the Taylor rule, which relates the interest rate to the inflation rate and the unemployment rate. The green line shows the actual federal funds rate. The actual rate tracked the predicted rate quite closely through the end of 2008. After that, however, the Taylor rule called for negative interest rates, which is a difficult and problematic goal to achieve.

Data from: Bureau of Labor Statistics; Congressional Budget Office; Federal Reserve Bank of St. Louis; Glenn D. Rudebusch, "The Fed's Monetary Policy Response to the Current Crisis," *FRBSF Economic Letter* #2009–17 (May 22, 2009).

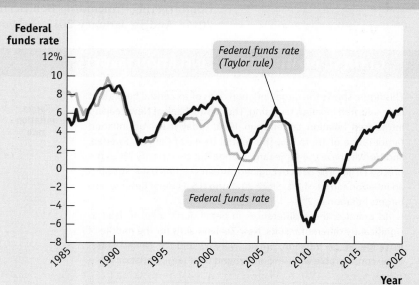

Inflation targeting occurs when the central bank sets an explicit target for the inflation rate and sets monetary policy in order to hit that target.

Inflation Targeting

Until January 2012, the Fed did not explicitly commit itself to achieving a particular inflation rate. However, in January 2012, the Fed announced that it would set its policy to maintain an approximately 2% inflation rate per year. With that statement, the Fed joined a number of other central banks that have explicit inflation targets. So, rather than using a Taylor rule to set monetary policy, they instead announce the inflation rate that they want to achieve—the *inflation target*—and set policy in an attempt to hit that target. This method of setting monetary policy, called **inflation targeting,** involves having the central bank announce the inflation rate it is trying to achieve and set policy in an attempt to hit that target. The central bank of New Zealand, which was the first country to adopt inflation targeting, specified a range for that target of 1% to 3%.

Other central banks commit themselves to achieving a specific number. For example, the Bank of England has committed to keeping inflation at 2%. In practice, there doesn't seem to be much difference between these versions: central banks with a target range for inflation seem to aim for the middle of that range, and central banks with a fixed target tend to give themselves considerable wiggle room.

One major difference between inflation targeting and the Taylor rule method is that inflation targeting is forward-looking rather than backward-looking. That is, the Taylor rule method adjusts monetary policy in response to *past* inflation, but inflation targeting is based on a forecast of future inflation.

Advocates of inflation targeting argue that it has two key advantages over the Taylor rule: *transparency* and *accountability*. First, economic uncertainty is reduced because the central bank's plan is transparent: the public knows the objective of an inflation-targeting central bank. Second, the central bank's success can be judged by seeing how closely actual inflation rates have matched the inflation target, making central bankers accountable.

Critics of inflation targeting argue that it's too restrictive because there are times when other concerns—like the stability of the financial system—should take priority over achieving any particular inflation rate. Indeed, starting in late 2013 the Taylor rule rate and the federal funds rate diverged significantly, as the Fed kept the interest rate close to zero while the Taylor rule rate climbed. The Fed's actions were motivated by the fear that an interest rate rise could push the persistently weak economy back into turmoil and recession.

Many American macroeconomists have had positive things to say about inflation targeting—including Ben Bernanke (the Fed chair from 2006 through early 2014). And in January 2012 the Fed declared that what it means by the "price

GLOBAL COMPARISON   INFLATION TARGETS

This figure shows the target inflation rates of six central banks that have adopted inflation targeting. The central bank of New Zealand introduced inflation targeting in 1990. Today it has an inflation target range of 1% to 3%. The central banks of Canada, Sweden, and Norway have the same target range but also specify 2% as the precise target. The Bank of England, Britain's central bank, specifies an inflation target of 2%. Since 2012, the U.S. Federal Reserve also targets inflation at 2%.

In practice, these differences in detail don't seem to lead to significantly different results. New Zealand aims for the middle of its range, at 2% inflation; Britain, Norway, and the United States allow considerable wiggle room around their target inflation rates.

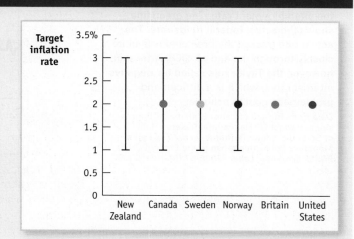

Data from: IMF, Reserve Bank of New Zealand, Bank of Canada, Riksbank, Bank of England, Norges Bank, and Federal Reserve System.

stability" it seeks is 2% inflation, although there was no explicit commitment about when this inflation rate would be achieved.

The Zero Lower Bound Problem

As Figure 30-9 shows, a Taylor rule based on inflation and the unemployment rate does a good job of predicting Federal Reserve policy from 1985 through 2008. After that, however, things go awry, and for a simple reason: with very high unemployment and low inflation, the same Taylor rule called for an interest rate significantly less than zero, which is a difficult and problematic goal to achieve.

Negative interest rates are a problem because people always have the alternative of holding cash, which offers a zero interest rate. Why, then, would they ever buy a bond yielding an interest rate less than zero?

Until 2014 most economists believed that it was basically impossible for interest rates to go below zero. That year, however, the central bank of Switzerland did the previously unthinkable, setting rates slightly below zero. It turns out that even at a slightly negative interest rate, there are limits to how much cash the public is willing to hold, because storing cash is expensive: you need vaults that are secure against loss, both from potential theft and from threats like money-eating mice. (Yes, rodent control turns out to play some role in monetary policy.) By 2016, the Swiss equivalent of the federal funds rate was –0.75%, and both the European Central Bank and the Bank of Japan also had slightly negative rates. (Japan's situation, which economists refer to as being *up against the zero bound*, is addressed in Chapter 31.)

So, the zero lower bound isn't an absolute limit. Still, no central bank has tried to push rates significantly below zero, say down to –3% or –6%, which is what the Taylor rule suggested for the United States in 2009 and 2010. This is explained partly because rates that low would lead to the hoarding of cash. Also, negative interest rates are widely believed to cause big problems for the banking system, with adverse effects on the economy as a whole. This set of circumstances leads to what is called the **zero lower bound for interest rates:** interest rates cannot fall much below zero without causing significant problems.

As a result, the Fed has never been willing to push rates below zero. This in turn means that when inflation is low and the economy is operating far below potential, normal monetary policy—open-market purchases of short-term government debt to expand the money supply—runs out of room to operate because short-term interest rates are already at or near zero. Economists refer to this situation as *running up against the zero lower bound.*

In November 2010 the Fed began an attempt to circumvent the problem caused by its inability to reduce interest rates further despite economic weakness. This attempt went by the somewhat obscure name *quantitative easing.* Instead of purchasing only short-term government debt, it began buying longer-term government debt—five-year or six-year bonds, rather than three-month Treasury bills. And, as we know, long-term interest rates don't exactly follow short-term rates. At the time the Fed began this program, short-term rates were near zero, but rates on longer-term bonds were between 2% and 3%. The Fed hoped that direct purchases of these longer-term bonds would drive down interest rates on long-term debt, exerting an expansionary effect on the economy.

Later the Fed expanded the program further, also purchasing mortgage-backed securities, which normally offer somewhat higher rates than U.S. government debt. Here, too, the hope was that these rates could be driven down, with an expansionary effect on the economy. As with ordinary open-market operations, quantitative easing was undertaken by the Federal Reserve Bank of New York.

Was this policy effective? The Federal Reserve believes that it helped the economy. However, the pace of recovery remained disappointingly slow. Starting in 2016, the Fed began to slowly raise rates by an amount less than a Taylor rule would have predicted, reflecting the sluggish pace of the recovery. And it reversed course in 2019, even before the coronavirus pandemic sent the economy reeling.

The **zero lower bound for interest rates** means that interest rates cannot fall much below zero without causing significant problems.

FIGURE 30-10   When the Fed Wants a Recession

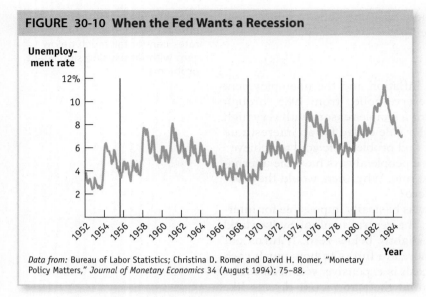

Data from: Bureau of Labor Statistics; Christina D. Romer and David H. Romer, "Monetary Policy Matters," *Journal of Monetary Economics* 34 (August 1994): 75–88.

ECONOMICS >> *in Action*
What the Fed Wants, the Fed Gets

What's the evidence that the Fed can actually cause an economic contraction or expansion? You might think that finding such evidence is just a matter of looking at what happens to the economy when interest rates go up or down. But it turns out that there's a big problem with that approach: the Fed usually changes interest rates in an attempt to tame the business cycle, raising rates if the economy is expanding and reducing rates if the economy is slumping. So in the actual data, it often looks as if low interest rates go along with a weak economy and high rates go along with a strong economy.

In a famous paper titled "Does Monetary Policy Matter?", macroeconomists Christina Romer and David Romer solved this problem by focusing on episodes in which monetary policy wasn't a reaction to the business cycle. Specifically, they used minutes from the Federal Open Market Committee and other sources to identify episodes "in which the Federal Reserve in effect decided to attempt to create a recession to reduce inflation." As we'll learn in Chapter 31, rather than just using monetary policy as a tool of macroeconomic stabilization, sometimes it is used to eliminate *embedded inflation*—inflation that people believe will persist into the future. In such a case, the Fed needs to create a recessionary gap—not just eliminate an inflationary gap—to wring embedded inflation out of the economy.

Figure 30-10 shows the unemployment rate between 1952 and 1984 and also identifies five dates on which, according to Romer and Romer, the Fed decided that it wanted a recession (the vertical lines). In four out of the five cases, the decision to contract the economy was followed, after a modest lag, by a rise in the unemployment rate. On average, Romer and Romer found the unemployment rate rises by 2 percentage points after the Fed decides that unemployment needs to go up.

So yes, the Fed gets what it wants.

>> Quick Review

• The Federal Reserve can use **expansionary monetary policy** to increase aggregate demand and **contractionary monetary policy** to reduce aggregate demand. The Federal Reserve and other central banks generally try to tame the business cycle while keeping the inflation rate low but positive.

• Under a **Taylor rule for monetary policy,** the target federal funds rate rises when there is high inflation and either a positive output gap or very low unemployment; it falls when there is low or negative inflation and either a negative output gap or high unemployment.

• In contrast, some central banks set monetary policy by **inflation targeting,** a forward-looking policy rule, rather than by using the Taylor rule, a backward-looking policy rule. Although inflation targeting has the benefits of transparency and accountability, some think it is too restrictive. Until 2008, the Fed followed a loosely defined Taylor rule. Starting in early 2012, it began inflation targeting with a target of 2% per year.

• There is a **zero lower bound for interest rates**—they cannot fall much below zero without causing significant problems—that limits the effectiveness of monetary policy.

• Because it is subject to fewer lags than fiscal policy, monetary policy is the main tool for macroeconomic stabilization.

>> Check Your Understanding 30-3

Solutions appear at back of book.

1. Suppose the economy is currently suffering from an output gap and the Federal Reserve uses an expansionary monetary policy to close that gap. Describe the short-run effect of this policy on the following.
   a. The money supply curve
   b. The equilibrium interest rate
   c. Investment spending
   d. Consumer spending
   e. Aggregate output

2. In setting monetary policy, which central bank—one that operates according to a Taylor rule or one that operates by inflation targeting—is likely to respond more directly to a financial crisis? Explain.

‖ Money, Output, and Prices in the Long Run

Through its expansionary and contractionary effects, monetary policy is generally the policy tool of choice to help stabilize the economy. However, not all actions by central banks are productive. In particular, central banks sometimes print money, not to fight a recessionary gap but to help the government pay its bills, an action that typically destabilizes the economy.

What happens when a change in the money supply pushes the economy away from, rather than toward, long-run equilibrium? As we've learned, the economy is self-correcting in the long run: a demand shock has only a temporary effect on aggregate output. If the demand shock is the result of a change in the money supply, we can make a stronger statement: in the long run, changes in the quantity of money affect the aggregate price level, but they do not change real aggregate output or the interest rate. To see why, let's look at what happens if the central bank permanently increases the money supply.

Short-Run and Long-Run Effects of an Increase in the Money Supply

To analyze the long-run effects of monetary policy, it's helpful to think of the central bank as choosing a target for the money supply rather than the interest rate. In assessing the effects of an increase in the money supply, we return to the analysis of the long-run effects of an increase in aggregate demand, first introduced in Chapter 27.

Figure 30-11 shows the short-run and long-run effects of an increase in the money supply when the economy begins at potential output, Y_1. The initial short-run aggregate supply curve is $SRAS_1$, the long-run aggregate supply curve is $LRAS$, and the initial aggregate demand curve is AD_1. The economy's initial equilibrium is at E_1, a point of both short-run and long-run macroeconomic equilibrium because it is on both the short-run and the long-run aggregate supply curves. Real GDP is at potential output, Y_1.

Now suppose there is an increase in the money supply. Other things equal, an increase in the money supply reduces the interest rate, which increases investment spending, which leads to a further rise in consumer spending, and so on. So an increase in the money supply increases the quantity of goods and services

---

FIGURE 30-11 The Short-Run and Long-Run Effects of an Increase in the Money Supply

When the economy is already at potential output, an increase in the money supply generates a positive short-run effect, but no long-run effect, on real GDP.

Here, the economy begins at E_1, a point of short-run and long-run macroeconomic equilibrium. An increase in the money supply shifts the AD curve rightward, and the economy moves to a new short-run macroeconomic equilibrium at E_2 and a new real GDP of Y_2. But E_2 is not a long-run equilibrium: Y_2 exceeds potential output, Y_1, leading to an increase in nominal wages over time. In the long run, the increase in nominal wages shifts the short-run aggregate supply curve leftward, to a new position at $SRAS_2$.

The economy reaches a new short-run and long-run macroeconomic equilibrium at E_3 on the $LRAS$ curve, and output falls back to potential output, Y_1. When the economy is already at potential output, the only long-run effect of an increase in the money supply is an increase in the aggregate price level from P_1 to P_3.

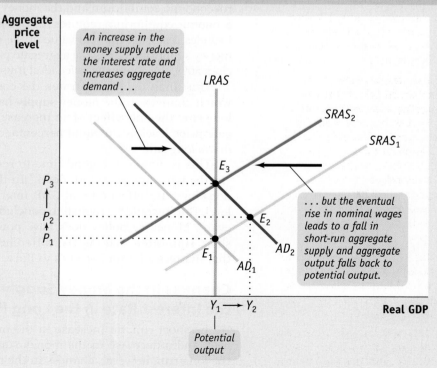

According to the concept of **monetary neutrality,** changes in the money supply have no real effects on the economy.

demanded, shifting the AD curve rightward, to AD_2. In the short run, the economy moves to a new short-run macroeconomic equilibrium at E_2. The price level rises from P_1 to P_2, and real GDP rises from Y_1 to Y_2. That is, both the aggregate price level and aggregate output increase in the short run.

But the aggregate output level, Y_2, is above potential output. As a result, nominal wages will rise over time, causing the short-run aggregate supply curve to shift leftward. This process stops only when the $SRAS$ curve ends up at $SRAS_2$ and the economy ends up at point E_3, a point of both short-run and long-run macroeconomic equilibrium. The long-run effect of an increase in the money supply, then, is that the aggregate price level has increased from P_1 to P_3, but aggregate output is back at potential output, Y_1. In the long run, a monetary expansion raises the aggregate price level but has no effect on real GDP.

We won't describe the effects of a monetary contraction in detail, but the same logic applies. In the short run, a fall in the money supply leads to a fall in aggregate output as the economy moves down the short-run aggregate supply curve. In the long run, however, the monetary contraction reduces only the aggregate price level, and real GDP returns to potential output.

Monetary Neutrality

How much does a change in the money supply change the aggregate price level in the long run? The answer is that a change in the money supply leads to an equal proportional change in the aggregate price level in the long run. For example, if the money supply falls 25%, the aggregate price level falls 25% in the long run; if the money supply rises 50%, the aggregate price level rises 50% in the long run.

How do we know this? Consider the following thought experiment: suppose all prices in the economy—prices of final goods and services and also factor prices, such as nominal wage rates—double. And suppose the money supply doubles at the same time. What difference does this make to the economy in real terms? The answer is none. All real variables in the economy—such as real GDP and the real value of the money supply (the amount of goods and services it can buy)—are unchanged. So there is no reason for anyone to behave any differently.

We can state this argument in reverse: if the economy starts out in long-run macroeconomic equilibrium and the money supply changes, restoring long-run macroeconomic equilibrium requires restoring all real values to their original values. This includes restoring the real value of the money supply to its original level. So if the money supply falls 25%, the aggregate price level must fall 25%; if the money supply rises 50%, the aggregate price level must rise 50%; and so on.

This analysis demonstrates the concept known as **monetary neutrality,** in which changes in the money supply have no real effects on the economy. In the long run, the only effect of an increase in the money supply is to raise the aggregate price level by an equal percentage. Economists argue that *money is neutral in the long run.*

This is, however, a good time to recall the dictum of John Maynard Keynes: "In the long run we are all dead." In the long run, changes in the money supply don't have any effect on real GDP, interest rates, or anything else except the price level. But it would be foolish to conclude from this statement that the Fed is irrelevant. Monetary policy does have powerful real effects on the economy in the short run, often making the difference between recession and expansion. And that matters a lot for society's welfare.

Changes in the Money Supply and the Interest Rate in the Long Run

In the short run, an increase in the money supply leads to a fall in the interest rate, and a decrease in the money supply leads to a rise in the interest rate. In the long run, however, changes in the money supply don't affect the interest rate.

FIGURE 30-12 The Long-Run Determination of the Interest Rate

The economy is initially at E_1, a long-run macroeconomic equilibrium. In the short run, an increase in the money supply, from $\overline{M}_1$ to $\overline{M}_2$ pushes the interest rate down from r_1 to r_2. The economy moves to E_2, a short-run equilibrium. In the long run, however, the aggregate price level rises in proportion to the increase in the money supply, leading to an increase in money demand at any given interest rate in proportion to the increase in the aggregate price level, as shown by the shift from MD_1 to MD_2. The result is that the quantity of money demanded at any given interest rate rises by the same amount as the quantity of money supplied. The economy moves to long-run equilibrium at E_3 and the interest rate returns to r_1.

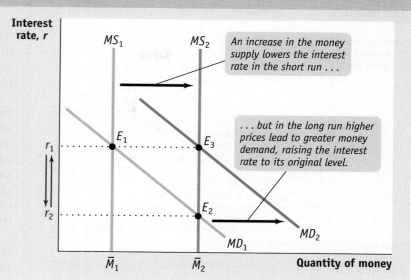

Figure 30-12 shows why. It shows the money supply curve and the money demand curve before and after the Fed increases the money supply. We assume that the economy is initially at E_1, in long-run macroeconomic equilibrium at potential output, and with money supply $\overline{M}_1$. The initial equilibrium interest rate, determined by the intersection of the money demand curve MD_1 and the money supply curve MS_1, is r_1.

Now suppose the money supply increases from $\overline{M}_1$ to $\overline{M}_2$. In the short run, the economy moves from E_1 to E_2 and the interest rate falls from r_1 to r_2. Over time, however, the aggregate price level rises, and this raises money demand, shifting the money demand curve rightward from MD_1 to MD_2. The economy moves to a new long-run equilibrium at E_3, and the interest rate rises to its original level at r_1.

And it turns out that the long-run equilibrium interest rate is the original interest rate, r_1. We know this for two reasons. First, due to monetary neutrality, in the long run the aggregate price level rises by the same proportion as the money supply; so if the money supply rises by, say, 50%, the aggregate price level will also rise by 50%. Second, the demand for money is, other things equal, proportional to the aggregate price level.

So a 50% increase in the money supply raises the aggregate price level by 50%, which increases the quantity of money demanded at any given interest rate by 50%. As a result, the quantity of money demanded at the initial interest rate, r_1, rises exactly as much as the money supply—so that r_1 is still the equilibrium interest rate. In the long run, then, changes in the money supply do not affect the interest rate.

ECONOMICS >> *in Action*
International Evidence of Monetary Neutrality

These days monetary policy is quite similar among developed countries. Each major nation (or, in the case of the euro, the euro area) has a central bank that is insulated from political pressure. All of these central banks try to keep the aggregate price level roughly stable, which usually means inflation of at most 2% to 3% per year.

But if we look at a longer period and a wider group of countries, we see large differences in the growth of the money supply. Between 1983 and 2018, the money supply rose only a few percent per year in some countries, such as

FIGURE 30-13 The Long-Run Relationship Between Money and Inflation

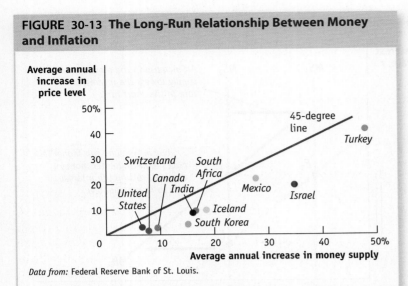

Data from: Federal Reserve Bank of St. Louis.

Switzerland and the United States, but rose much more rapidly in some poorer countries, such as South Africa and Mexico. These differences allow us to see whether it is really true that increases in the money supply lead, in the long run, to equal percent rises in the aggregate price level.

Figure 30-13 shows the annual percentage increases in the money supply and average annual increases in the aggregate price level—that is, the average rate of inflation—for a sample of countries during the period 1983–2018, with each point representing a country. If the relationship between increases in the money supply and changes in the aggregate price level were exact, the points would lie precisely on a 45-degree line.

In fact, the relationship isn't exact, because other factors besides money affect the aggregate price level. But the scatter of points clearly lies close to a 45-degree line, showing a more or less proportional relationship between money and the aggregate price level. That is, the data support the concept of monetary neutrality in the long run.

>> *Check Your Understanding* **30-4**

Solutions appear at back of book.

1. Assume the central bank increases the quantity of money by 25%, even though the economy is initially in both short-run and long-run macroeconomic equilibrium. Describe the effects, in the short run and in the long run (giving numbers where possible), on the following.
   a. Aggregate output
   b. Aggregate price level
   c. Interest rate
2. Why does monetary policy affect the economy in the short run but not in the long run?

Parking Your Money at PayPal

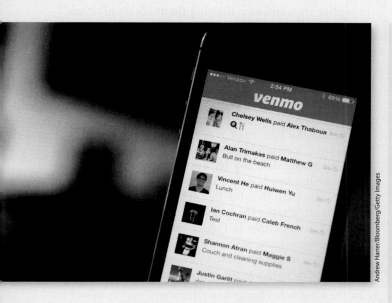

Andrew Harrer/Bloomberg/Getty Images

Officially, PayPal, the electronic funds-transfer firm—which is also the owner of the popular mobile-phone payment service Venmo—isn't considered a bank. Instead, regulators consider it a *money transmitter*, an entity that sends your money someplace rather than holding it and keeping it safe.

However, as users accumulate substantial sums in their PayPal accounts, that distinction has started to look questionable. Venmo users, in particular, often seem willing to let incoming payments sit in their accounts until the funds are spent, the way people once kept cash in their wallets. As a result, PayPal's accounts were estimated to total more than $22.5 billion in 2019. If those billions were considered bank deposits, PayPal would be considered among the 70 largest banks in the United States.

At first glance, leaving significant sums in PayPal accounts seems counterintuitive for two reasons. First, these accounts aren't protected by federal deposit insurance. Second, they pay no interest. But upon closer examination, this behavior makes good economic sense. People will typically hold only a tiny fraction of their wealth in their PayPal account, thereby making the lack of federal deposit insurance an acceptable risk. And interest rates on bank accounts are so low at the time of this writing (around 0.06% in July 2020) that losing that interest is a reasonable price to pay to avoid the hassle of moving funds back and forth between a bank account and a PayPal or Venmo account.

The result is that many people are behaving like one user quoted by the *Wall Street Journal*, who now waits a while before transferring funds out of her Venmo account to her regular bank account: "I'm starting to intentionally keep my money in there a little bit longer."

But will PayPal/Venmo or something like it begin to make major inroads into traditional banking? Some analysts think so. Others suggest, however, that payment systems like Zelle, developed by conventional banks, and eventually rising interest rates will lure customers back to conventional bank deposits. Time will tell.

QUESTIONS FOR THOUGHT

1. PayPal accounts aren't counted as part of the money supply. Should they be? Why or why not?

2. In 2010, only around 25% of mobile phones in the United States were smartphones. By 2020, almost everyone had a smartphone. How does this situation play into the PayPal story, and how does it fit into the broader pattern of monetary history?

3. How might future actions by the Federal Open Market Committee affect the future of PayPal and similar services?

SUMMARY

1. The **money demand curve** arises from a trade-off between the opportunity cost of holding money and the liquidity that money provides. Americans hold substantial sums in cash and in zero-interest bank accounts linked to debit cards or money transmitters like PayPal and Venmo. By doing so they forgo the interest that could have been earned by putting those funds into an interest-bearing asset like a **certificate of deposit (CD).** The opportunity cost of holding money depends on **short-term interest rates,** not **long-term interest rates.** Changes in the aggregate price level, real GDP, technology, and institutions shift the money demand curve.

2. According to the **liquidity preference model of the interest rate,** the interest rate is determined in the money market by the money demand curve and the **money supply curve.** The Federal Reserve can change the interest rate in the short run by shifting the money supply curve. In practice, the Fed uses open-market operations to achieve a **target federal funds rate,** which other short-term interest rates generally track. Although long-term interest rates don't necessarily move with short-term interest rates, they reflect expectations about what's going to happen to short-term rates in the future.

3. **Expansionary monetary policy** reduces the interest rate by increasing the money supply. This increases investment spending and consumer spending, which in turn increases aggregate demand and real GDP in the short run. **Contractionary monetary policy** raises the interest rate by reducing the money supply. This reduces investment spending and consumer spending, which in turn reduces aggregate demand and real GDP in the short run.

4. The Federal Reserve and other central banks try to stabilize the economy, limiting fluctuations of actual output around potential output, while also keeping inflation low but positive. Under a **Taylor rule for monetary policy,** the target federal funds rate rises when there is high inflation and either a positive output gap or very low unemployment; it falls when there is low or negative inflation and either a negative output gap or high unemployment. Some central banks, including the Fed, engage in **inflation targeting,** which is a forward-looking policy rule, whereas the Taylor rule method is a backward-looking policy rule. Because monetary policy is subject to fewer implementation lags than fiscal policy, it is the preferred policy tool for stabilizing the economy. However, because interest rates cannot fall much below zero without causing significant problems, there is a **zero lower bound for interest rates.** As a result, the effectiveness of monetary policy is limited.

5. In the long run, changes in the money supply affect the aggregate price level but not real GDP or the interest rate. Data show that the concept of **monetary neutrality** holds: changes in the money supply have no real effect on the economy in the long run.

KEY TERMS

Certificate of deposit (CD), p. 886
Short-term interest rates, p. 887
Long-term interest rates, p. 887
Money demand curve, p. 888
Liquidity preference model of the interest rate, p. 891

Money supply curve, p. 891
Target federal funds rate, p. 894
Expansionary monetary policy, p. 897
Contractionary monetary policy, p. 898

Taylor rule for monetary policy, p. 899
Inflation targeting, p. 900
Zero lower bound for interest rates, p. 901
Monetary neutrality, p. 904

PRACTICE QUESTIONS

1. The rise of electronic payment systems has encouraged more peer-to-peer lending programs. These programs connect lenders and borrowers outside the traditional banking system. As the Federal Reserve relies on changes to the money supply through open-market operations and ultimately bank lending, how will a rise of peer-to-peer lending networks affect the Federal Reserve's ability to conduct effective monetary policy?

2. John Maynard Keynes said, "In the long run we are all dead." How is this quote consistent with the concept of money neutrality? How is it inconsistent?

3. According to the European Central Bank website, the treaty establishing the European Community "makes clear that ensuring price stability is the most important contribution that monetary policy can make to achieve a favourable economic environment and a high level of employment." If price stability is the only goal of monetary policy, explain how monetary policy would be conducted during recessions. Analyze both the case of a recession that is the result of a demand shock and the case of a recession that is the result of a supply shock.

PROBLEMS

1. Access the Discovering Data exercise for Chapter 30 Problem 1 online to answer the following questions.

   a. What is the target federal funds rate?

   b. Is the target federal funds rate different from the target federal funds rate in the previous FOMC statement? If yes, by how much does it differ?

   c. Does the statement comment on current macroeconomic conditions in the United States? How does it describe the U.S. economy?

2. How will the following events affect the demand for money? In each case, specify whether there is a shift of the demand curve or a movement along the demand curve and its direction.

   a. There is a fall in the interest rate from 12% to 10%.

   b. Thanksgiving arrives and, with it, the beginning of the holiday shopping season.

   c. Increasingly, merchants are adopting electronic payment systems that allow more consumers to use PayPal and Apple Pay to make purchases.

   d. The Fed engages in an open-market purchase of U.S. Treasury bills.

3. **a.** Go to www.treasurydirect.gov. Under "Individuals," go to "Treasury Securities & Programs." Click on "Treasury bills." Under "at a glance," click on "rates in recent auctions." What is the investment rate for the most recently issued 52-week T-bills?

   b. Go to the website of your favorite bank. What is the interest rate for one-year CDs?

   c. Why are the rates for one-year CDs higher than for 52-week Treasury bills?

4. Go to www.treasurydirect.gov. Under "Individuals," go to "Treasury Securities & Programs." Click on "Treasury notes." Under "at a glance," click on "rates in recent auctions." Use the list of Recent Note, Bond, and TIPS Auction Results to answer the following questions.

   a. What are the interest rates on 2-year and 10-year notes?

   b. How do the interest rates on the 2-year and 10-year notes relate to each other? Why is the interest rate on the 10-year note higher (or lower) than the interest rate on the 2-year note?

5. An economy is facing the recessionary gap shown in the accompanying diagram. To eliminate the gap, should the central bank use expansionary or contractionary monetary policy? How will the interest rate, investment spending, consumer spending, real GDP, and the aggregate price level change as monetary policy closes the recessionary gap?

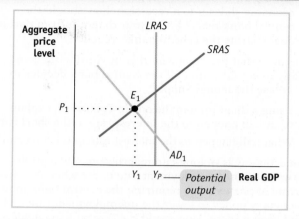

6. An economy is facing the inflationary gap shown in the accompanying diagram. To eliminate the gap, should the central bank use expansionary or contractionary monetary policy? How will the interest rate, investment spending, consumer spending, real GDP, and the aggregate price level change as monetary policy closes the inflationary gap?

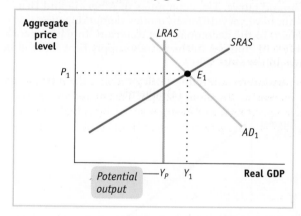

7. In the economy of Eastlandia, the money market is initially in equilibrium when the economy begins to slide into a recession.

   a. Using the accompanying diagram, explain what will happen to the interest rate if the central bank of Eastlandia keeps the money supply constant at $\overline{M}_1$.

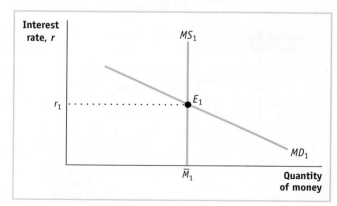

b. If the central bank is instead committed to maintaining an interest rate target of r_1, then as the economy slides into a recession, how should the central bank react? Using your diagram from part a, demonstrate the central bank's reaction.

8. Suppose that the money market in Westlandia is initially in equilibrium and the central bank decides to decrease the money supply.

a. Using a diagram like the one in Problem 7, explain what will happen to the interest rate in the short run.

b. What will happen to the interest rate in the long run?

9. An economy is in long-run macroeconomic equilibrium with an unemployment rate of 5% when the government passes a law requiring the central bank to use monetary policy to lower the unemployment rate to 3% and keep it there. How could the central bank achieve this goal in the short run? What would happen in the long run? Illustrate with a diagram.

10. The effectiveness of monetary policy depends on how easy it is for changes in the money supply to change interest rates. By changing interest rates, monetary policy affects investment spending and the aggregate demand curve. The economies of Albernia and Brittania have very different money demand curves, as shown in the accompanying diagram. In which economy will changes in the money supply be a more effective policy tool? Why?

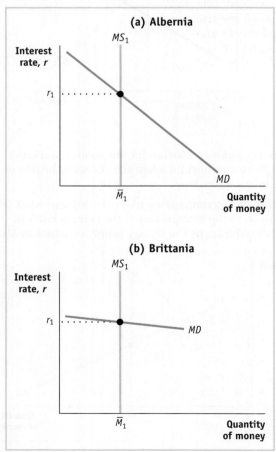

11. During the Great Depression, businesspeople in the United States were very pessimistic about the future of economic growth and reluctant to increase investment spending even when interest rates fell. How did this limit the potential for monetary policy to help alleviate the Depression?

12. Access the Discovering Data exercise for Chapter 30 Problem 12 online to answer the following questions.

a. How does the relationship between the effective federal funds rate and the Taylor rule change throughout the Great Recession?

b. Compare the long-term and short-term interest rate before and after the Great Recession.

▪▪▪ WORK IT OUT

13. Because of the economic slowdown associated with the 2007–2009 recession, the Federal Open Market Committee of the Federal Reserve, between September 18, 2007, and December 16, 2008, lowered the federal funds rate in a series of steps from a high of 5.25% to a rate between zero and 0.25%. The idea was to provide a boost to the economy by increasing aggregate demand.

a. Use the liquidity preference model to explain how the Federal Open Market Committee lowers the interest rate in the short run. Draw a typical graph that illustrates the mechanism. Label the vertical axis "Interest rate" and the horizontal axis "Quantity of money." Your graph should show two interest rates, r_1 and r_2.

b. Explain why the reduction in the interest rate causes aggregate demand to increase in the short run.

c. Suppose that in 2022 the economy is at potential output but that this is somehow overlooked by the Fed, which continues its monetary expansion. Demonstrate the effect of the policy measure on the *AD* curve. Use the *LRAS* curve to show that the effect of this policy measure on the *AD* curve, other things equal, causes the aggregate price level to rise in the long run. Label the vertical axis "Aggregate price level" and the horizontal axis "Real GDP." ▪

Reconciling the Two Models of the Interest Rate

In the liquidity preference model of the interest rate developed in Chapter 30, at the equilibrium interest rate the quantity of money demanded equals the quantity of money supplied. Yet, in the loanable funds model of the interest rate developed in Chapter 25, the equilibrium interest rate matches the quantity of loanable funds supplied by savers with the quantity of loanable funds demanded for investment spending. Can these two models of the interest rate be reconciled? Yes, they can. We will do this in two steps, focusing first on the short run and then on the long run.

The Interest Rate in the Short Run

As explained in the chapter, a fall in the interest rate leads to a rise in investment spending, I, which then leads to a rise in both real GDP and consumer spending, C. The rise in real GDP doesn't lead only to a rise in consumer spending, however. It also leads to a rise in savings: at each stage of the multiplier process, part of the increase in disposable income is saved. How much do savings rise?

In Chapter 25 we introduced the *savings–investment spending identity:* total savings in the economy is always equal to investment spending. *This tells us that when a fall in the interest rate leads to higher investment spending, the resulting increase in real GDP generates exactly enough additional savings to match the rise in investment spending.* To put it another way, after a fall in the interest rate, the quantity of savings supplied rises exactly enough to match the quantity of savings demanded. Understanding this relationship is the key to reconciling the two models of the interest rate.

Figure 30A-1 illustrates how the two models of the interest rate are reconciled in the short run. Panel (a) shows the liquidity preference model of the interest rate where MS_1 and MD_1 are the initial supply and demand curves for money, and r_1, the initial equilibrium interest rate, equalizes the quantity of money supplied to the quantity of money demanded in the money market. Panel (b) shows the loanable funds model of the interest rate where S_1 is the initial supply curve, D is the demand curve for loanable funds, and r_1, the initial equilibrium interest rate, equalizes the quantity of loanable funds supplied to the quantity of loanable funds demanded in the market for loanable funds.

In Figure 30A-1 both the money market and the market for loanable funds are initially in equilibrium at E_1 with the same interest rate, r_1. You might think that this would only happen by accident, but in fact it will always be true. To see why, consider what happens in panel (a), the money market, when the Fed increases the money supply from $\overline{M}_1$ to $\overline{M}_2$, pushing the money supply curve rightward, to MS_2, reducing the equilibrium interest rate in the market to r_2, and moving the economy to a short-run equilibrium at E_2.

What happens in panel (b), the market for loanable funds? In the short run, the fall in the interest rate due to the increase in the money supply leads to a rise in real GDP, which generates a rise in savings through the multiplier process. This rise in savings shifts the supply curve for loanable funds rightward, from S_1 to S_2, moving the equilibrium in the loanable funds market from E_1 to E_2 and reducing the equilibrium interest rate in the loanable funds market. Since the rise

FIGURE 30A-1 The Short-Run Determination of the Interest Rate

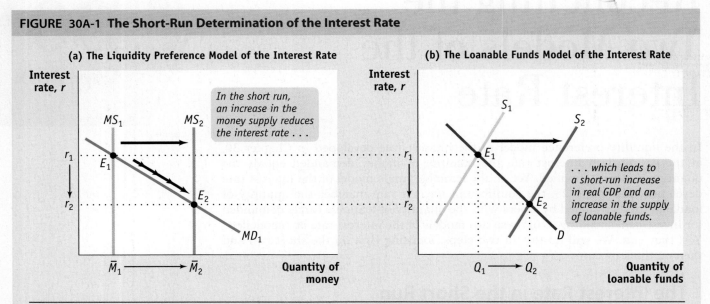

(a) The Liquidity Preference Model of the Interest Rate

(b) The Loanable Funds Model of the Interest Rate

In the short run, an increase in the money supply reduces the interest rate . . .

. . . which leads to a short-run increase in real GDP and an increase in the supply of loanable funds.

Panel (a) shows the liquidity preference model of the interest rate: the equilibrium interest rate matches the money supply to the quantity of money demanded. In the short run, the interest rate is determined in the money market, where an increase in the money supply, from $\overline{M}_1$ to $\overline{M}_2$, pushes the equilibrium interest rates down, from r_1 to r_2. Panel (b) shows the loanable funds model of the interest

rate. The fall in the interest rate in the money market leads, through the multiplier effect, to an increase in real GDP and savings; to a rightward shift of the supply curve of loanable funds, from S_1 to S_2; and to a fall in the interest rate, from r_1 to r_2. As a result, the new equilibrium interest rate in the loanable funds market matches the new equilibrium interest rate in the money market at r_2.

in savings must exactly match the rise in investment spending, the equilibrium rate in the loanable funds market must fall to r_2, the same as the new equilibrium interest rate in the money market.

In the short run, then, the supply and demand for money determine the interest rate, and the loanable funds market follows the lead of the money market until the equilibrium interest rate in the loanable funds market is the same as the equilibrium interest rate in the money market.

Notice our use of the phrase *in the short run*. Changes in aggregate demand affect aggregate output only in the short run. In the long run, aggregate output is equal to potential output. So our story about how a fall in the interest rate leads to a rise in aggregate output, which leads to a rise in savings, applies only to the short run.

In the long run, as we'll see next, the determination of the interest rate is quite different, because the roles of the two markets are reversed. In the long run, the loanable funds market determines the equilibrium interest rate, and it is the market for money that follows the lead of the loanable funds market.

The Interest Rate in the Long Run

In the short run an increase in the money supply leads to a fall in the interest rate, and a decrease in the money supply leads to a rise in the interest rate. In the long run, however, changes in the money supply don't affect the interest rate.

Figure 30A-2 shows why. As in Figure 30A-1, panel (a) shows the liquidity preference model of the interest rate and panel (b) shows the supply and demand for loanable funds. We assume that in both panels the economy is initially at E_1, in long-run macroeconomic equilibrium at potential output with the money supply equal to $\overline{M}_1$. The demand curve for loanable funds is D, and the initial supply curve for loanable funds is S_1. The initial equilibrium interest rate in both markets is r_1.

FIGURE 30A-2 The Long-Run Determination of the Interest Rate

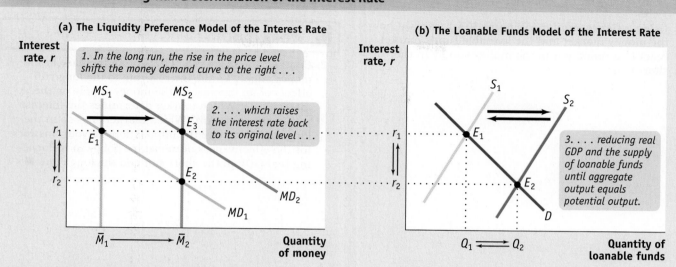

(a) The Liquidity Preference Model of the Interest Rate

1. *In the long run, the rise in the price level shifts the money demand curve to the right . . .*

2. *. . . . which raises the interest rate back to its original level . . .*

MS_1 MS_2

E_3

r_1 E_1

r_2 E_2

MD_2

MD_1

$\overline{M}_1$ ⟶ $\overline{M}_2$

Interest rate, r

Quantity of money

(b) The Loanable Funds Model of the Interest Rate

S_1

S_2

r_1 E_1

3. *. . . . reducing real GDP and the supply of loanable funds until aggregate output equals potential output.*

r_2 E_2

D

$Q_1 \rightleftharpoons Q_2$

Interest rate, r

Quantity of loanable funds

Panel (a) shows the liquidity preference model long-run adjustment to an increase in the money supply from $\overline{M}_1$ to $\overline{M}_2$; panel (b) shows the corresponding long-run adjustment in the loanable funds market. Both panels start from E_1, a long-run macroeconomic equilibrium at potential output and with interest rate r_1. As we discussed in Figure 30A-1, the increase in the money supply reduces the interest rate from r_1 to r_2, increases real GDP, and increases savings in the short run. This is shown in panels (a) and (b) as the movement from E_1 to E_2. In the long run, however, the increase in the money supply raises wages and other nominal prices. This shifts the money demand curve in panel (a) from MD_1 to MD_2, leading to an increase in the interest rate from r_2 to r_1 as the economy moves from E_2 to E_3. The rise in the interest rate causes a fall in real GDP and a fall in savings, shifting the loanable funds supply curve back to S_1 from S_2 and moving the loanable funds market from E_2 back to E_1. In the long run, the equilibrium interest rate is determined by matching the supply of loanable funds to the demand for loanable funds that results when real GDP equals potential output.

Now suppose the money supply rises from $\overline{M}_1$ to $\overline{M}_2$. As in Figure 30A-1, this initially reduces the interest rate to r_2. According to the neutrality of money, in the long run the aggregate price level rises by the same proportion as the increase in the money supply. And we also know that a rise in the aggregate price level increases money demand by the same proportion. So in the long run the money demand curve shifts out to MD_2 as money demand responds to higher prices, and moves the equilibrium interest rate back to its original level, r_1.

Panel (b) of Figure 30A-2 shows what happens in the market for loanable funds. As before, an increase in the money supply leads to a short-run rise in real GDP, and this shifts the supply of loanable funds rightward from S_1 to S_2. In the long run, however, real GDP falls back to its original level as wages and other nominal prices rise. As a result, the supply of loanable funds, S, which initially shifted from S_1 to S_2, shifts back to S_1.

In the long run, then, changes in the money supply do not affect the interest rate. So what determines the interest rate in the long run, r_1, in Figure 30A-2? The answer is the supply and demand for loanable funds. More specifically, in the long run the equilibrium interest rate matches the supply and demand for loanable funds that arise at potential output.

PROBLEMS

1. Using a figure similar to Figure 30A-1, explain how the money market and the loanable funds market react to a reduction in the money supply in the short run.

WORK IT OUT

2. Contrast the short-run effects of an increase in the money supply on the interest rate to the long-run effects of an increase in the money supply on the interest rate. Which market determines the interest rate in the short run? Which market does so in the long run? What are the implications of your answers for the effectiveness of monetary policy in influencing real GDP in the short run and the long run? ∎

31 > Inflation, Disinflation, and Deflation

THAT AND 900,000 BOLIVARS WILL GET YOU A CUP OF COFFEE

IN 2015 THE SOUTH AMERICAN NATION of Venezuela essentially stopped releasing economic statistics, probably in an attempt to hide how badly things were going — and in particular, to avoid admitting the extent of the country's runaway inflation. But it's unlikely that anyone was fooled.

Independent observers came up with their own measures of inflation; for example, Bloomberg News began releasing a "café con leche index" based on the price of Venezuela's favorite drink. And private citizens, well aware that the value of bolivars, the nation's currency, was plunging, made every effort to get rid of the currency as soon as it came into their hands. Shopkeepers wouldn't put money in the cash register, they would run out to spend it on new supplies. Enterprising individuals would buy goods subject to price controls and smuggle them out to sell in neighboring countries. And everyone tried to exchange bolivars for U.S. dollars on the black market.

In 2019 Venezuela's central bank, the equivalent of the Federal Reserve, finally relented and released inflation numbers, which confirmed what everyone already knew. In 2016 the inflation rate was "only" 274%; by 2018 it had reached 130,000%. (Inflation fell slightly in 2019, but few expected the reprieve to last.)

Stacks of currency, worth a lot less than they were even a month earlier.

Guillermo Legaria/Getty Images

Venezuela's experience was shocking, but not unprecedented. In 2008 Zimbabwe briefly reached 500 billion percent inflation before abandoning its currency altogether. In 1994 the inflation rate in Armenia hit 27,000%. In 1991 Nicaraguan inflation exceeded 60,000%. And Zimbabwe's experience was more or less matched by history's most famous example of extreme inflation, which took place in Germany in 1922–1923. Toward the end of the German hyperinflation, prices were rising 16% a *day,* which — through compounding — meant an increase of approximately 500 billion percent over the course of five months.

Germans became so reluctant to hold paper money, which lost value by the hour, that eggs and lumps of coal began to circulate as currency. Firms would pay their workers several times a day so that they could spend their earnings before they lost value (lending new meaning to the term *hourly wage*). Legend has it that customers sitting down at a bar would order two beers at a time, out of fear that the price of a beer would rise before they could order a second round!

The United States has never experienced that kind of inflation. The worst U.S. inflation in modern times took place at the end of the 1970s. From 1978 to 1980 the U.S. inflation rate more than doubled, from 6.4% to 14.5%. Yet inflation at even that rate was profoundly troubling to the American public, and the policies the Federal Reserve pursued in order to get U.S. inflation back down to an acceptable rate led to a severe recession.

What causes inflation to rise and fall? In this chapter, we'll look at the underlying reasons for inflation. We'll see that the underlying causes of very high inflation, the type of inflation suffered by Venezuela, are quite different from the causes of more moderate inflation. We'll also learn why *disinflation,* a reduction in the inflation rate, is often very difficult. Finally, we'll discuss the special problems associated with a falling price level, or deflation. ●

WHAT YOU WILL LEARN

- Why can printing money lead to high rates of inflation and hyperinflation?
- How does the **Phillips curve** describe the short-run trade-off between inflation and unemployment?
- Why does the trade-off between inflation and unemployment cease in the long run?
- Why can even moderate levels of inflation be hard to end?
- Why is deflation a problem for economic policy makers?

Money and Inflation

Moderate levels of inflation such as those experienced in the United States—even the double-digit inflation of the late 1970s—can have complex causes. But very high inflation is always associated with rapid increases in the money supply.

To understand why, we need to revisit the effect of changes in the money supply on the overall price level. Then we'll turn to the reasons governments sometimes increase the money supply very rapidly.

The Classical Model of Money and Prices

In the previous chapter we learned that in the short run, an increase in the money supply increases real GDP by lowering the interest rate and stimulating investment spending and consumer spending. However, in the long run, as nominal wages and other sticky prices rise, real GDP falls back to its original level. So in the long run, an increase in the money supply does not change real GDP. Instead, other things equal, it leads to an equal percent rise in the overall price level. That is, the prices of all goods and services in the economy, including nominal wages and the prices of intermediate goods, rise by the same percentage as the money supply. And when the overall price level rises, the aggregate price level—the prices of all final goods and services—rises as well.

As a result, a change in the *nominal* money supply, *M,* leads in the long run to a change in the aggregate price level that leaves the *real* quantity of money, *M/P,* at its original level, with no long-run effect on aggregate demand or real GDP. For example, when Turkey dropped six zeros from its currency, the Turkish lira, in January 2005, Turkish real GDP did not change. The only thing that changed was the number of zeros in prices: instead of something costing 2,000,000 lira, it cost 2 lira.

This is, to repeat, what happens in the long run. When analyzing large changes in the aggregate price level, however, macroeconomists often find it useful to ignore the distinction between the short run and the long run. Instead, they work with a simplified model in which the effect of a change in the money supply on the aggregate price level takes place instantaneously rather than over a long period of time. You might be concerned about this assumption, given that in previous chapters we've emphasized the difference between the short run and the long run. However, for reasons we'll explain shortly, this is a reasonable assumption to make in the case of high inflation.

A simplified model in which the real quantity of money, *M/P,* is always at its long-run equilibrium level is known as the **classical model of the price level** because it was commonly used by "classical" economists who wrote before the work of John Maynard Keynes. To understand the classical model and why it is useful in the context of high inflation, let's revisit the *AD–AS* model and what it says about the effects of an increase in the money supply. (Unless otherwise noted, we will always be referring to changes in the *nominal* supply of money.)

Figure 31-1 reviews the effects of an increase in the money supply according to the *AD–AS* model. The economy starts at E_1, a point of short-run and long-run macroeconomic equilibrium. It lies at the intersection of the aggregate demand curve, AD_1, and the short-run aggregate supply curve, $SRAS_1$. It also lies on the long-run aggregate supply curve, *LRAS.* At E_1, the equilibrium aggregate price level is P_1.

Now suppose there is an increase in the money supply. This is an expansionary monetary policy, which shifts the aggregate demand curve to the right, to AD_2, and moves the economy to a new short-run macroeconomic equilibrium at E_2. Over time, however, nominal wages adjust upward in response to the rise in the aggregate price level, and the *SRAS* curve shifts to the left, to $SRAS_2$. The new long-run macroeconomic equilibrium is at E_3, and real GDP returns to its initial level. As we learned in Chapter 30, the long-run increase in the aggregate price

According to the **classical model of the price level,** the real quantity of money is always at its long-run equilibrium level.

FIGURE 31-1 The Classical Model of the Price Level

Starting at E_1, an increase in the money supply shifts the aggregate demand curve rightward, as shown by the movement from AD_1 to AD_2. There is a new short-run macroeconomic equilibrium at E_2 and a higher price level at P_2. In the long run, nominal wages adjust upward and push the *SRAS* curve leftward to $SRAS_2$. The total percent increase in the price level from P_1 to P_3 is equal to the percent increase in the money supply. In the *classical model of the price level*, we ignore the transition period and think of the price level as rising to P_3 immediately. This is a good approximation under conditions of high inflation.

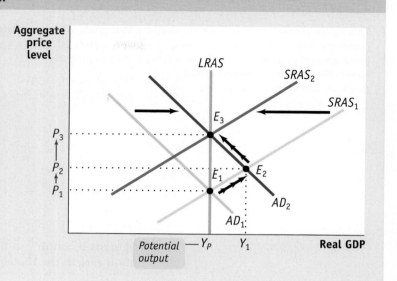

level from P_1 to P_3 is proportional to the increase in the money supply. As a result, in the long run changes in the money supply have no effect on the real quantity of money, M/P, or on real GDP. In the long run, money—as we learned—is *neutral*.

The classical model of the price level ignores the short-run movement from E_1 to E_2, assuming that the economy moves directly from one long-run equilibrium to another long-run equilibrium. In other words, it assumes that the economy moves directly from E_1 to E_3 and that real GDP never changes in response to a change in the money supply. In effect, in the classical model the effects of money supply changes are analyzed as if the short-run as well as the long-run aggregate supply curves were vertical.

This is a poor assumption during periods of low inflation, because it may take a while for workers and firms to react to a monetary expansion by raising wages and prices. As a result, under low inflation there is an upward-sloping *SRAS* curve, and changes in the money supply can indeed change real GDP in the short run.

In the face of high inflation, however, economists have observed that the short-run stickiness of nominal wages and prices tends to vanish. Workers and businesses, sensitized to inflation, are quick to raise their wages and prices in response to changes in the money supply. This implies that under high inflation, there is a quicker adjustment of wages and prices of intermediate goods than occurs in the case of low inflation. So the short-run aggregate supply curve shifts leftward more quickly, and there is a more rapid return to long-run equilibrium under high inflation. As a result, the classical model of the price level is much more likely to be a good approximation of reality for economies experiencing persistently high inflation.

The consequence of this rapid adjustment of all prices in the economy is that in countries with persistently high inflation, changes in the money supply are quickly translated into changes in the inflation rate. Let's look at Venezuela. Figure 31-2 shows the *monthly* rate of growth in the money supply (as measured by the monetary base) and the monthly rate of change of consumer prices from 2016 through 2019. We use monthly rates of change partly because that is how people in very-high-inflation economies tend to think about inflation, partly because otherwise inflation at "only" a few hundred percent per year would be invisible. As you can see, the surge in the growth rate of the money supply coincided with a surge in the inflation rate.

FIGURE 31-2 Money Supply Growth and Inflation in Venezuela

This figure shows *monthly* rates of change in Venezuela's monetary base and consumer prices as the country spiraled into hyperinflation. Surges in the monetary base were quickly reflected in surges in the price level.

Data from: Central Bank of Venezuela.

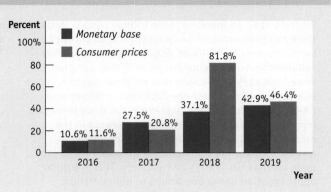

What leads a country to increase its money supply so much that the result is an inflation rate in the thousands of percent per year?

The Inflation Tax

Modern economies use fiat money—pieces of paper that have no intrinsic value but are accepted as a medium of exchange. In the United States and most other wealthy countries, the decision about how many pieces of paper to issue is placed in the hands of a central bank that is somewhat independent of the political process. However, this independence can always be taken away if politicians decide to seize control of monetary policy.

So what is to prevent a government from paying for some of its expenses not by raising taxes or borrowing but simply by printing money? Nothing. In fact, governments, including the U.S. government, do it all the time. How can the U.S. government do this, given that the Federal Reserve issues money, not the U.S. Treasury? The answer is that the Treasury and the Federal Reserve work in concert. The Treasury issues debt to finance the government's purchases of goods and services, and the Fed *monetizes* the debt by creating money and buying the debt back from the public through open-market purchases of Treasury bills. In effect, the U.S. government can and does raise revenue by printing money.

For example, in August 2008, the U.S. monetary base—bank reserves plus currency in circulation—was $18 billion larger than it had been a year earlier. This occurred because, over the course of that year, the Federal Reserve had issued $20 billion in money or its electronic equivalent and put it into circulation through open-market operations. To put it another way, the Fed created money out of thin air and used it to buy valuable government securities from the private sector. It's true that the U.S. government pays interest on debt owned by the Federal Reserve—but the Fed, by law, hands the interest payments it receives on government debt back to the Treasury, keeping only enough to fund its own operations. In effect, then, the Federal Reserve's actions enabled the government to pay off $18 billion in outstanding government debt by printing money.

An alternative way to look at this is to say that the right to print money is itself a source of revenue. Economists refer to the revenue generated by the government's right to print money as *seigniorage,* an archaic term that goes back to the Middle Ages. It refers to the right to stamp gold and silver into coins, and charge a fee for doing so, that medieval lords—*seigniors,* in Medieval France—reserved for themselves.

Seigniorage normally accounts for only a tiny fraction (less than 1%) of the U.S. government's budget. Furthermore, concerns about seigniorage don't have any influence on the Federal Reserve's decisions about how much money to print; the Fed is worried about inflation and unemployment, not revenue. But this hasn't always been true, even in the United States: both the North and the South relied on seigniorage to help cover budget deficits during the Civil War. And there have been many occasions in history when governments turned to their printing presses as a crucial source of revenue.

According to the usual scenario, a government finds itself running a large budget deficit, but lacks either the competence or the political will to eliminate this deficit by raising taxes or cutting spending. Furthermore, the government can't borrow to cover the gap because potential lenders won't extend loans given the fear that the government's weakness will continue and leave it unable to repay its debts.

In such a situation, governments end up printing money to cover the budget deficit. But by printing money to pay its bills, a government increases the quantity of money in circulation. And as we've just seen, increases in the money supply sooner or later translate into equally large increases in the aggregate price level. So printing money to cover a budget deficit leads to inflation.

Who ends up paying for the goods and services the government purchases with newly printed money? The people who currently hold money pay. They pay because inflation erodes the purchasing power of their money holdings. In other words, a government imposes an **inflation tax,** the reduction in the value of the money held by the public, by printing money to cover its budget deficit and creating inflation.

It's helpful to think about what this tax represents. If the inflation rate is 5%, then a year from now $1 will buy goods and services worth only $0.95 today. So a 5% inflation rate in effect imposes a tax rate of 5% on the value of all money held by the public.

But why would any government push the inflation tax to rates of hundreds or thousands of percent? We turn next to the logic of hyperinflation.

The Logic of Hyperinflation

Inflation imposes a tax on individuals who hold money. And, like most taxes, it will lead people to change their behavior. In particular, when inflation is high, people will try to avoid holding money and will instead substitute real goods as well as interest-bearing assets for money. In the opening story we described how, during the German hyperinflation, people began using eggs or lumps of coal as a medium of exchange. They did this because lumps of coal maintained their real value over time, but money didn't. Indeed, during the peak of German hyperinflation, people often burned paper money, which was less valuable than wood.

Moreover, people don't just reduce their nominal money holdings—they reduce their *real* money holdings, cutting the amount of money they hold so much that it actually has less purchasing power than the amount of money they would hold if inflation were low. They do this by using the money to buy goods that last over time or assets that hold

The **inflation tax** is the reduction in the value of money held by the public as a result of inflation.

In the 1920s, hyperinflation made German currency worth so little that children made kites from banknotes.

Keystone/Hulton Archive/Getty Images

their value, like gold. Why? Because the more real money holdings they have, the greater the real amount of resources the government captures from them through the inflation tax.

We are now ready to understand how countries can get themselves into situations of extreme inflation. High inflation arises when the government must print a large quantity of money, imposing a large inflation tax, to cover a large budget deficit.

Now, the seigniorage collected by the government over a short period—say, one month—is equal to the change in the money supply over that period. Let's use M to represent the money supply and use the symbol Δ to mean "monthly change in." Then:

(31-1) Seigniorage $= \Delta M$

The money value of seigniorage, however, isn't very informative by itself. After all, the whole point of inflation is that a given amount of money buys less and less over time. So it's more useful to look at *real* seigniorage, the revenue created by printing money divided by the price level, P:

(31-2) Real seigniorage $= \Delta M/P$

Equation 31-2 can be rewritten by dividing and multiplying by the current level of the money supply, M, giving us:

(31-3) Real seigniorage $= (\Delta M/M) \times (M/P)$

or

Real seigniorage $=$ Rate of growth of the money supply $\times$ Real money supply

But as we've just explained, in the face of high inflation the public reduces the real amount of money it holds, so the far right-hand term in Equation 31-3, M/P, gets smaller. Suppose that the government needs to print enough money to pay for a given quantity of goods and services—that is, it needs to collect a given *real* amount of seigniorage. Then, as the real money supply, M/P, falls as people hold smaller amounts of real money, the government has to respond by accelerating the rate of growth of the money supply, $\Delta M/M$. This will lead to an even higher rate of inflation. And people will respond to this new higher rate of inflation by reducing their real money holdings, M/P, yet again.

As the process becomes self-reinforcing, it can easily spiral out of control. Although the amount of real seigniorage that the government must ultimately collect to pay off its deficit does not change, the inflation rate the government needs to impose to collect that amount rises. So the government is forced to increase the money supply more rapidly, leading to an even higher rate of inflation, and so on.

Here's an analogy: imagine a city government that tries to raise a lot of money with a special fee on parking. The fee will raise the cost of parking in the city, and this will cause people to turn to easily available substitutes, such as walking or taking the bus. As the number of parked cars declines, the government finds that its tax revenue declines, and it must impose a higher fee to raise the same amount of revenue as before. You can imagine the ensuing vicious circle: the government imposes fees on parking, which leads to less parking, which causes the government to raise the fee on parking, which leads to even less parking, and so on.

Substitute the real money supply for parking and the inflation rate for the fee on parking, and you have the story of hyperinflation. A race develops between the government printing presses and the public: the presses churn out money at a faster and faster rate to try to compensate for the fact that the public is reducing its real money holdings. At some point the inflation rate explodes into hyperinflation, and people are unwilling to hold any money at all (and resort to trading in eggs and lumps of coal). The government is then forced to abandon its use of the inflation tax and shut down the printing presses.

ECONOMICS >> *in Action*
Behind Venezuela's Inflation

Venezuela offers the most recent example of a country experiencing very high inflation. Figure 31-2 showed that surges in Venezuela's money supply growth were matched by almost simultaneous surges in its inflation rate. But why did Venezuela's government pursue policies that led to runaway inflation?

Venezuela used to be relatively rich compared with other major Latin American nations. This wealth, however, rested on a very narrow base: the Venezuelan economy was almost completely reliant on oil exports. And many Venezuelans felt that they weren't getting their fair share of the country's income, that it was being siphoned off for the benefit of a small, wealthy minority.

In 1999 Hugo Chavez, a left-wing populist, took power with the promise to use Venezuela's oil wealth to help the poor and working class. For a number of years he delivered at least partly on that promise, increasing spending on social programs and presiding over what appears to have been a substantial reduction in poverty. However, he did nothing to diversify Venezuela away from its dependence on oil.

Chavez died in 2013, and his successor, Nicolas Maduro, soon found himself in trouble, largely because of a collapse in global oil prices. Figure 31-3 shows the real price of oil—that is, the price adjusted for inflation—in the United States since 2010. Prices plunged in 2013, largely because fracking led to a surge in the supply of oil and other hydrocarbons, mainly natural gas. And Venezuela's government, deeply dependent on oil revenue, no longer had the money to pay for Chavez's programs.

Instead of cutting back or seeking new revenue sources, however, the Maduro government tried to close the budget gap by printing money. When this, predictably, led to inflation, the Venezuelan government tried to suppress the inflation with price controls, leading to widespread shortages that probably made the inflation worse.

While there are many unique details to the Venezuela story, overall it fits the classic pattern, in which a government that can't or won't pay for its operations turns to the printing press, and stumbles its way into hyperinflation.

FIGURE 31-3 Real Oil Prices, 2010–2020

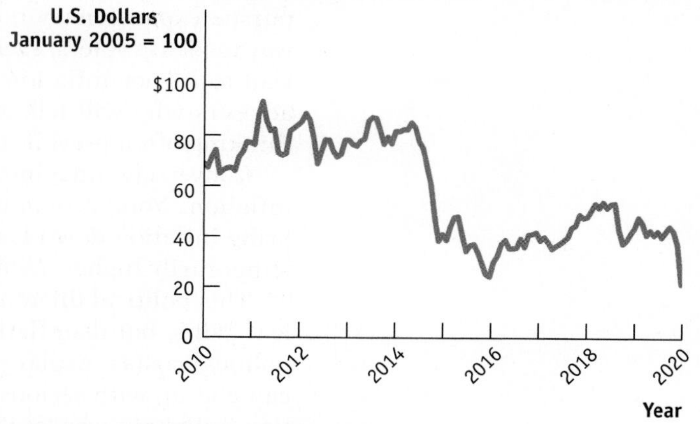

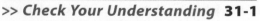

Data from: U.S. Energy Information Administration.

>> *Check Your Understanding* 31-1
Solutions appear at back of book.

1. Suppose there is a large increase in the money supply in an economy that previously had low inflation. As a consequence, aggregate output expands in the short run. What does this say about situations in which the classical model of the price level applies?

2. Suppose that all wages and prices in an economy are indexed to inflation—that is, wages and prices are automatically adjusted to incorporate the latest inflation figures. Can there still be an inflation tax?

>> *Quick Review*

• The **classical model of the price level** does not distinguish between the short and the long run. It explains how increases in the money supply feed directly into inflation. It is a good description of reality only for countries with persistently high inflation or hyperinflation.

• Governments sometimes print money to cover a budget deficit. The resulting loss in the value of money is called the **inflation tax.**

• A high inflation rate causes people to reduce their real money holdings, leading to the printing of more money and higher inflation in order to collect the inflation tax. This can cause a self-reinforcing spiral into hyperinflation.

‖ Moderate Inflation and Disinflation

The governments of wealthy, politically stable countries, like the United States and Britain, don't find themselves forced to print money to pay their bills. Yet over the past 40 years, both countries, along with a number of other nations, have experienced uncomfortable episodes of inflation. In the United States, the inflation rate peaked at 14% at the beginning of the 1980s. In Britain, the inflation rate reached 26% in 1975. Why did policy makers allow this to happen?

The answer, in brief, is that in the short run, policies that produce a booming economy also tend to lead to higher inflation, and policies that reduce inflation tend to depress the economy. This creates both temptations and dilemmas for governments.

First, imagine yourself as a politician facing an election in a year or two, and suppose that inflation is fairly low at the moment. You might well be tempted to pursue expansionary policies that will push the unemployment rate down as a way to please voters, even if your economic advisers warn that this will eventually lead to higher inflation. You might also be tempted to find different economic advisers who will tell you not to worry: in politics, as in ordinary life, wishful thinking often prevails over realistic analysis.

Conversely, imagine yourself as a politician in an economy suffering from inflation. Your economic advisers will probably tell you that the only way to bring inflation down is to push the economy into a recession, which will lead to temporarily higher unemployment. Are you willing to pay that price? Maybe not.

This political dilemma—inflationary policies often produce short-term political gains, but disinflationary policies to bring inflation down carry short-term political costs—explains how countries with no need to impose an inflation tax can end up with serious inflation problems. For example, that 26% rate of inflation in Britain was largely the result of the British government's decision in 1971 to pursue highly expansionary monetary and fiscal policies in order to gain a political advantage. British politicians disregarded warnings that these policies would be inflationary and were extremely reluctant to reverse course when it became clear that the warnings had been accurate.

But why do expansionary policies lead to inflation? To answer that question, we need to look first at the relationship between output and unemployment.

The Output Gap and the Unemployment Rate

In Chapter 27 we introduced the concept of *potential output*, the level of real GDP that the economy would produce once all prices had fully adjusted. Potential output typically grows steadily over time, reflecting long-run growth. However, as we learned from the *AD–AS* model, actual aggregate output fluctuates around potential output in the short run: a recessionary gap arises when actual aggregate output falls short of potential output. An inflationary gap arises when actual aggregate output exceeds potential output.

Recall that the percentage difference between the actual level of real GDP and potential output is called the *output gap*. A positive or negative output gap occurs when an economy is producing more than or less than what would be "expected" because all prices, including wages in the labor market, have not yet adjusted. And wages, as we've learned, are the prices in the labor market.

Meanwhile, we learned in Chapter 23 that the unemployment rate is composed of both cyclical unemployment and natural unemployment (natural unemployment is the portion of the unemployment rate unaffected by the business cycle). So there is a relationship between the unemployment rate and the output gap. This relationship is defined by two rules:

1. When actual aggregate output is equal to potential output, the actual unemployment rate is equal to the natural rate of unemployment.
2. When the output gap is positive (an inflationary gap), the unemployment rate is *below* the natural rate. When the output gap is negative (a recessionary gap), the unemployment rate is *above* the natural rate.

In other words, fluctuations of aggregate output around the long-run trend of potential output correspond to fluctuations of the unemployment rate around the natural rate.

This makes sense. When the economy is producing less than potential output—when the output gap is negative—it is not making full use of its productive resources.

FIGURE 31-4 Cyclical Unemployment and the Output Gap

Panel (a) shows the actual U.S. unemployment rate from 1949 through February 2020, together with the Congressional Budget Office estimate of the natural rate of unemployment. The actual rate fluctuates around the natural rate, often for extended periods. Panel (b) shows cyclical unemployment—the difference between the actual unemployment and the natural rate of unemployment—and the output gap, also estimated by the CBO. The unemployment rate is measured on the left vertical axis, and the output gap is measured with an inverted scale on the right vertical axis. With an inverted scale, it moves in the same direction as the unemployment rate: when the output gap is positive, the actual unemployment rate is below its natural rate. And when the output gap is negative, the actual unemployment rate is above its natural rate. The two series track one another closely, showing the strong relationship between the output gap and cyclical unemployment.

Data from: Federal Reserve Bank of St. Louis.

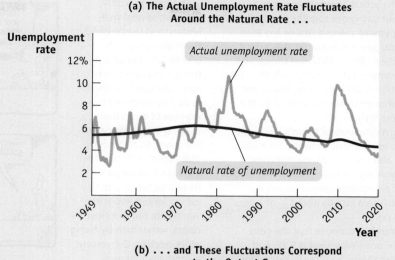

(a) The Actual Unemployment Rate Fluctuates Around the Natural Rate . . .

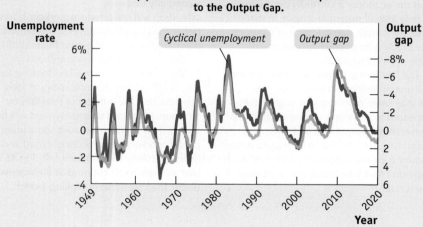

(b) . . . and These Fluctuations Correspond to the Output Gap.

Among the resources that are not fully utilized is labor, the economy's most important resource. So we would expect a negative output gap to be associated with unusually high unemployment. Conversely, when the economy is producing more than potential output, it is temporarily using resources at higher-than-normal rates. With this positive output gap, we would expect to see lower-than-normal unemployment.

Figure 31-4 confirms this rule. Panel (a) shows the actual and natural rates of unemployment, as estimated by the Congressional Budget Office (CBO). Panel (b) shows two series. One is cyclical unemployment: the difference between the actual unemployment rate and the CBO estimate of the natural rate of unemployment, measured on the left. The other is the CBO estimate of the output gap, measured on the right. To make the relationship clearer, the output gap series is inverted—shown upside down—so that the line goes down if actual output rises above potential output and up if actual output falls below potential output.

As you can see, the two series move together quite closely, showing the strong relationship between the output gap and cyclical unemployment. Years of high cyclical unemployment, like 1982, 1992, or 2009, were also years of a strongly negative output gap. Years of low cyclical unemployment, like the late 1960s or late 1990s into the early 2000s, were also years of a strongly positive output gap.

FOR INQUIRING MINDS   Okun's Law

Although cyclical unemployment and the output gap move together, cyclical unemployment seems to move *less* than the output gap. For example, the output gap reached −8% in 1982, but the cyclical unemployment rate reached only 4%. This observation is the basis of an important relationship originally discovered by the economist Arthur Okun.

Modern estimates of **Okun's law**—the negative relationship between the output gap and the cyclical unemployment rate—typically find that a rise in the output gap of 1 percentage point reduces the unemployment rate by about $\frac{1}{2}$ of a percentage point.

For example, suppose that the natural rate of unemployment is 5.2% and that the economy is currently producing at only 98% of potential output. In that case, the output gap is −2%, and Okun's law predicts an unemployment rate of $5.2\% - \frac{1}{2} \times (-2\%) = 6.2\%$.

The fact that a 1% rise in output reduces the unemployment rate by only $\frac{1}{2}$ of 1% may seem puzzling: you might have expected to see a one-to-one relationship between the output gap and unemployment. Doesn't a 1% rise in aggregate output require a 1% increase in employment? And shouldn't that take 1% off the unemployment rate?

The answer is no: there are several well-understood reasons why the relationship isn't one-to-one. For one thing, companies often meet changes in demand in part by changing the number of hours their existing employees work. For example, a company that experiences a sudden increase in demand for its products may cope by asking (or requiring) its workers to put in longer hours, rather than by hiring more workers. Conversely, a company that sees sales drop will often reduce workers' hours rather than lay off employees. This behavior dampens the effect of output fluctuations on the number of workers employed.

Also, the number of workers looking for jobs is affected by the availability of jobs. Suppose that the number of jobs falls by 1 million. Measured unemployment will rise by less than 1 million because some unemployed workers become discouraged and give up actively looking for work. (Recall that workers aren't counted as unemployed unless they are actively seeking work.)

Conversely, if the economy adds 1 million jobs, some people who haven't been actively looking for work will begin doing so. As a result, measured unemployment will fall by less than 1 million.

Finally, the rate of growth of labor productivity generally accelerates during booms and slows down or even turns negative during busts. The reasons for this phenomenon are the subject of some dispute among economists. The consequence, however, is that the effects of booms and busts on the unemployment rate are dampened.

The Short-Run Phillips Curve

We've just seen that expansionary policies lead to a lower unemployment rate. Our next step in understanding the temptations and dilemmas facing governments is to show that there is a short-run trade-off between unemployment and inflation—lower unemployment tends to lead to higher inflation, and vice versa. The key concept is that of the *Phillips curve*.

The origins of this concept lie in a famous 1958 paper by the New Zealand–born economist A. W. H. Phillips. Looking at historical data for Britain, he found that when the unemployment rate was high, the wage rate tended to fall, and when the unemployment rate was low, the wage rate tended to rise. Using data from Britain, the United States, and elsewhere, other economists soon found a similar apparent relationship between the unemployment rate and the rate of inflation—that is, the rate of change in the aggregate price level. For example, Figure 31-5 shows the U.S. unemployment rate and the rate of consumer price inflation over each subsequent year from 1955 to 1968, with each dot representing one year's data.

Looking at evidence like Figure 31-5, many economists concluded that there is a negative short-run relationship between the unemployment rate and the inflation rate, which is called the **short-run Phillips curve,** or *SRPC*. (We'll explain the difference between the short-run and the long-run Phillips curve soon.) Figure 31-6 shows a hypothetical short-run Phillips curve.

Okun's law is the negative relationship between the output gap and cyclical unemployment.

The **short-run Phillips curve** is the negative short-run relationship between the unemployment rate and the inflation rate.

FIGURE 31-5 Unemployment and Inflation, 1955–1968

Each dot shows the average U.S. unemployment rate for one year and the percentage increase in the consumer price index over the subsequent year. Data like this lay behind the initial concept of the Phillips curve.

Data from: Bureau of Labor Statistics.

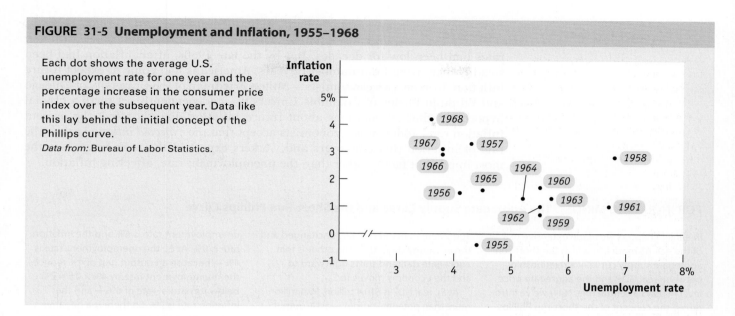

Early estimates of the short-run Phillips curve for the United States were very simple: they showed a negative relationship between the unemployment rate and the inflation rate, without taking account of any other variables. During the 1950s and 1960s, this simple approach seemed, for a while, to be adequate. And this simple relationship is clear in the data in Figure 31-5.

Even at the time, however, some economists argued that a more accurate short-run Phillips curve would include other factors. In Chapter 27 we discussed the effect of *supply shocks,* such as sudden changes in the price of oil, which shift the short-run aggregate supply curve. Such shocks also shift the short-run Phillips curve: surging oil prices were an important factor in the inflation of the 1970s and also played an important role in the acceleration of inflation in 2007–2008. In general, a negative supply shock shifts *SRPC* up as the inflation rate increases for every level of the unemployment rate, and a positive supply shock shifts it down as the inflation rate falls for every level of the unemployment rate. Both outcomes are shown in Figure 31-8.

FIGURE 31-6 The Short-Run Phillips Curve

The short-run Phillips curve, *SRPC,* slopes downward because the relationship between the unemployment rate and the inflation rate is negative.

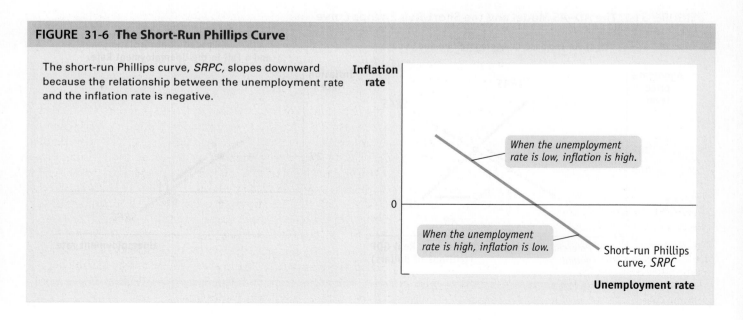

But supply shocks are not the only factors that can change the inflation rate. In the early 1960s, Americans had little experience with inflation because inflation rates had been low for decades. But by the late 1960s, after inflation had been steadily increasing for a number of years, Americans had come to expect future inflation. In 1968, two economists—Milton Friedman of the University of Chicago and Edmund Phelps of Columbia University—independently set forth a crucial hypothesis: that expectations about future inflation directly affect the present inflation rate. Today most economists accept that the *expected inflation rate*—the rate of inflation that employers and workers expect in the near future—is the most important factor, other than the unemployment rate, affecting inflation.

FOR INQUIRING MINDS The Aggregate Supply Curve and the Short-Run Phillips Curve

In earlier chapters we made extensive use of the *AD–AS* model, in which the short-run aggregate supply curve—a relationship between real GDP and the aggregate price level—plays a central role. Now we've introduced the concept of the short-run Phillips curve, a relationship between the unemployment rate and the rate of inflation. How do these two concepts fit together?

We can get a partial answer to this question by looking at panel (a) of Figure 31-7, which shows how changes in the aggregate price level and the output gap depend on changes in aggregate demand. Assume that in year 1 the aggregate demand curve is AD_1, the long-run aggregate supply curve is *LRAS,* and the short-run aggregate supply curve is *SRAS.* The initial macroeconomic equilibrium is at E_1, where the price level is 100 and real GDP is $10 trillion. Notice that at E_1 real GDP is equal to potential output, so the output gap is zero.

Now consider two possible paths for the economy over the next year. One is that

aggregate demand remains unchanged and the economy stays at E_1. The other is that aggregate demand shifts rightward to AD_2 and the economy moves to E_2.

At E_2, real GDP is $10.4 trillion, $0.4 trillion more than potential output—a 4% output gap. Meanwhile, at E_2 the aggregate price level is 102—a 2% increase. So panel (a) tells us that in this example, a zero output gap is associated with zero inflation and a 4% output gap is associated with 2% inflation.

Panel (b) shows what this implies for the relationship between unemployment and inflation. Assume that the natural rate of unemployment is 6% and that a rise of 1 percentage point in the output gap causes a fall of ½ percentage point in the unemployment rate per Okun's law, described in the previous For Inquiring Minds. In that case, the two cases shown in panel (a)—aggregate demand either unchanged or rising—correspond to the two points in panel (b). At E_1, the

unemployment rate is 6% and the inflation rate is 0%. At E_2, the unemployment rate is 4%—because an output gap of 4% reduces the unemployment rate by 4% × 0.5 = 2% below its natural rate of 6%—and the inflation rate is 2%. So there is a negative relationship between unemployment and inflation.

So does the short-run aggregate supply curve say exactly the same thing as the short-run Phillips curve? Not quite. The short-run aggregate supply curve seems to imply a relationship between the *change* in the unemployment rate and the inflation rate, but the short-run Phillips curve shows a relationship between the *level* of the unemployment rate and the inflation rate. Reconciling these views completely would go beyond the scope of this book. The important point is that the short-run Phillips curve is a concept that is closely related, though not identical, to the short-run aggregate supply curve.

FIGURE 31-7 The *AD–AS* Model and the Short-Run Phillips Curve

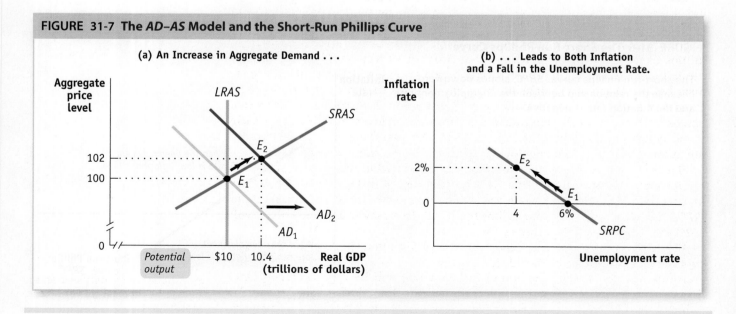

(a) An Increase in Aggregate Demand . . .

(b) . . . Leads to Both Inflation and a Fall in the Unemployment Rate.

FIGURE 31-8 The Short-Run Phillips Curve and Supply Shocks

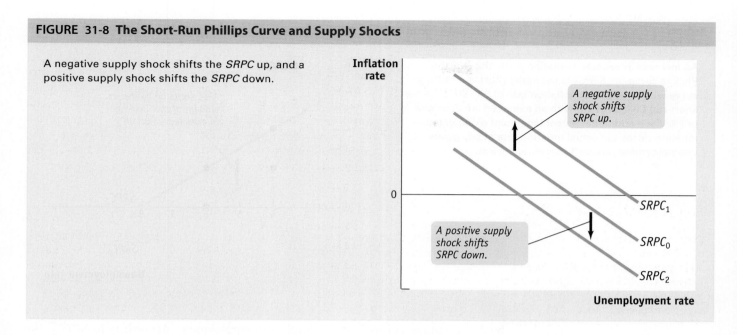

A negative supply shock shifts the *SRPC* up, and a positive supply shock shifts the *SRPC* down.

Inflation Expectations and the Short-Run Phillips Curve

The **expected rate of inflation** is the rate of inflation that employers and workers expect in the near future. One of the crucial discoveries of modern macroeconomics is that changes in the expected rate of inflation affect the short-run trade-off between unemployment and inflation and shift the short-run Phillips curve.

Why do changes in expected inflation affect the short-run Phillips curve? Put yourself in the position of a worker and employer about to sign a contract setting the worker's wages over the next year. For a number of reasons, the wage rate they agree to will be higher if everyone expects high inflation (including rising wages) than if everyone expects prices to be stable. The worker will want a wage rate that takes into account future declines in the purchasing power of earnings. They will also want a wage rate that won't fall behind the wages of other workers. And the employer will be more willing to agree to a wage increase now if hiring workers later will be even more expensive. Also, rising prices will make paying a higher wage rate more affordable for the employer because the employer's output will sell for more.

For these reasons, an increase in expected inflation shifts the short-run Phillips curve upward: the actual rate of inflation at any given unemployment rate is higher when the expected inflation rate is higher. In fact, macroeconomists believe that the relationship between changes in expected inflation and changes in actual inflation is one-to-one. That is, when the expected inflation rate increases, the actual inflation rate at any given unemployment rate will increase by the same amount. When the expected inflation rate falls, the actual inflation rate at any given level of unemployment will fall by the same amount.

Figure 31-9 shows how the expected rate of inflation affects the short-run Phillips curve. First, suppose that the expected rate of inflation is 0%. $SRPC_0$ is the short-run Phillips curve when the public expects 0% inflation. According to $SRPC_0$, the actual inflation rate will be 0% if the unemployment rate is 6%; it will be 2% if the unemployment rate is 4%.

Alternatively, suppose the expected rate of inflation is 2%. In that case, employers and workers will build this expectation into wages and prices: at any given unemployment rate, the actual inflation rate will be 2 percentage points higher than it would be if people expected 0% inflation. $SRPC_2$, which shows the Phillips curve when the expected inflation rate is 2%, is $SRPC_0$ shifted upward

The **expected rate of inflation** is the inflation rate that businesses and workers are expecting in the near future.

FIGURE 31-9 Expected Inflation and the Short-Run Phillips Curve

An increase in expected inflation shifts the short-run Phillips curve up. $SRPC_0$ is the initial short-run Phillips curve with an expected inflation rate of 0%; $SRPC_2$ is the short-run Phillips curve with an expected inflation rate of 2%. Each additional percentage point of expected inflation raises the actual inflation rate at any given unemployment rate by 1 percentage point.

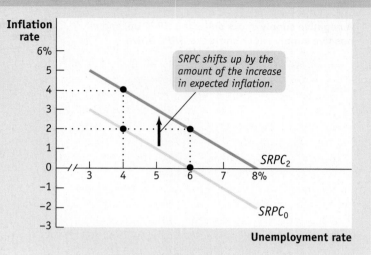

by 2 percentage points at every level of unemployment. According to $SRPC_2$, the actual inflation rate will be 2% if the unemployment rate is 6%; it will be 4% if the unemployment rate is 4%.

What determines the expected rate of inflation? In general, people base their expectations about inflation on experience. If the inflation rate has hovered around 0% in the last few years, people will expect it to be around 0% in the near future. But if the inflation rate has averaged around 5% lately, people will expect inflation to be around 5% in the near future.

Since expected inflation is an important part of the modern discussion about the short-run Phillips curve, you might wonder why it was not in the original formulation of the Phillips curve. The answer lies in history. Think back to what we said about the early 1960s: at that time, people were accustomed to low inflation rates and reasonably expected that future inflation rates would also be low. It was only after 1965 that persistent inflation became a fact of life. So only then did economists begin to argue that expected inflation should play an important role in price setting.

Sure enough, the seemingly clear relationship between inflation and unemployment fell apart after 1969. Figure 31-10 plots the track of U.S. unemployment and inflation rates from 1961 to 1990. As you can see, the track looks more like a tangled piece of yarn than like a smooth curve.

FIGURE 31-10 Unemployment and Inflation, 1961–1990

In the 1970s, the short-run Phillips curve relationship that seemed to hold during the 1950s and 1960s broke down as the U.S. economy experienced a combination of high unemployment and high inflation. Economists believe this was the result of both negative supply shocks and the cumulative effect of several years of higher than expected inflation. Inflation came down during the 1980s, and the 1990s were a time of both low unemployment and low inflation.
Data from: Bureau of Labor Statistics.

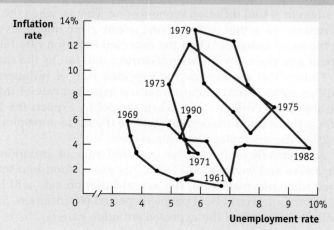

Through much of the 1970s and early 1980s, the economy suffered from a combination of above-average unemployment rates coupled with inflation rates unprecedented in modern American history. This condition came to be known as *stagflation*—for stagnation combined with high inflation. In the late 1990s, by contrast, the economy was experiencing a blissful combination of low unemployment and low inflation. What explains these developments?

Part of the answer can be attributed to a series of negative supply shocks that the U.S. economy suffered during the 1970s. The price of oil, in particular, soared as wars and revolutions in the Middle East led to a reduction in oil supplies and as oil-exporting countries deliberately curbed production to drive up prices. Compounding the oil price shocks, there was also a slowdown in labor productivity growth. Both of these factors shifted the short-run Phillips curve upward. During the 1990s, by contrast, supply shocks were positive. Prices of oil and other raw materials were generally falling, and productivity growth accelerated. As a result, the short-run Phillips curve shifted downward.

Equally important, however, was the role of expected inflation. As mentioned earlier in the chapter, inflation accelerated during the 1960s. During the 1970s, the public came to expect high inflation, and this also shifted the short-run Phillips curve up. It took a sustained and costly effort during the 1980s to get inflation back down. The result, however, was that expected inflation was very low by the late 1990s, allowing actual inflation to be low even with low rates of unemployment.

In fact, most macroeconomists believe that since the 1990s we have recreated conditions somewhat similar to those that prevailed in the 1950s and 1960s: people expect inflation to remain low and stable. As some analysts put it, inflation expectations are now "anchored" at an annual rate of around 2%. As a result, the modern relationship between unemployment and inflation looks a lot like the original Phillips curve.

ECONOMICS >> *in Action*
The Spanish Squeeze

The relationship between unemployment and inflation isn't exact; few relationships in economics are. By February 2020 the U.S. unemployment rate had dropped to just 3.5%, well below its level before the 2008 financial crisis, yet inflation remained low. Economists weren't sure why, although some suggested that the unemployment rate wasn't as good an indicator of labor market tightness as it used to be.

We would still expect, however, to see really big moves in the unemployment rate reflected in the inflation rate. And this is in fact what we see looking at countries that experienced very high unemployment after the crisis.

Spain is an example of a country that has experienced dramatic ups and downs since the start of the twenty-first century. From 2000 to 2007 it experienced a huge boom, driven by an enormous housing bubble, bigger than the one experienced in the United States. When this bubble burst, Spain fell into a deep slump, made worse by large cuts in government spending intended to reassure investors worried about Spain's government debt. As a result, the unemployment rate shot up, reaching an amazing 26% in 2013. Since then Spain has been achieving a gradual recovery.

Did the big swings in Spain's unemployment rate lead to changes in the inflation rate? Yes. Figure 31-11 shows Spanish unemployment versus inflation (as measured by the GDP deflator) from 2000 to 2019.

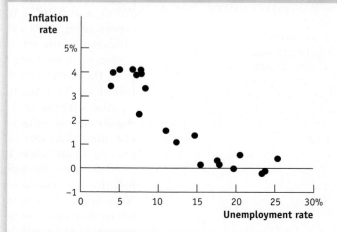

FIGURE 31-11 The Phillips Curve in Spain, 2000–2019

Data from: Organization for Economic Co-operation and Development.

The low-unemployment-rate years were marked by relatively high inflation, the ultra-high-unemployment-rate years by very low inflation.

You may have noticed that for Spain, "low unemployment" still meant unemployment rates of 8% to 10%, high by U.S. standards. Indeed, Spain seems to have high measured unemployment even when the economy appears to be booming. One reason is that quite a few "unemployed" Spaniards actually do have jobs, but are working off the books to avoid taxes and regulations.

>> Check Your Understanding 31-2

Solutions appear at back of book.

1. Explain how the short-run Phillips curve illustrates the negative relationship between cyclical unemployment and the actual inflation rate for a given level of the expected inflation rate.

2. Which way does the short-run Phillips curve move in response to a fall in commodities prices? To a surge in commodities prices? Explain.

Inflation and Unemployment in the Long Run

The short-run Phillips curve says that at any given point in time, there is a trade-off between unemployment and inflation. According to this view, policy makers have a choice: they can choose whether or not to accept the price of high inflation in order to achieve low unemployment. In fact, during the 1960s, many economists believed that this trade-off represented a real choice.

However, this view was greatly altered by the later recognition that expected inflation affects the short-run Phillips curve. In the short run, expectations often diverge from reality. In the long run, however, any consistent rate of inflation will be reflected in expectations. If inflation is consistently high, as it was in the 1970s, people will come to expect more of the same; if inflation is consistently low, as it has been in recent years, that, too, will become part of expectations.

So what does the trade-off between inflation and unemployment look like in the long run, when actual inflation is incorporated into expectations? Most macroeconomists believe that there is, in fact, no long-run trade-off. That is, it is not possible to achieve lower unemployment in the long run by accepting higher inflation. To see why, we need to introduce another concept: the *long-run Phillips curve*.

The Long-Run Phillips Curve

Figure 31-12 reproduces the two short-run Phillips curves from Figure 31-9, $SRPC_0$ and $SRPC_2$. It also adds an additional short-run Phillips curve, $SRPC_4$, representing a 4% expected rate of inflation. In a moment, we'll explain the significance of the vertical long-run Phillips curve, $LRPC$.

Suppose that the economy has, in the past, had a 0% inflation rate. In that case, the current short-run Phillips curve will be $SRPC_0$, reflecting a 0% expected inflation rate. If the unemployment rate is 6%, the actual inflation rate will be 0%.

Also suppose that policy makers decide to trade off lower unemployment for a higher rate of inflation. They use monetary policy, fiscal policy, or both to drive the unemployment rate down to 4%. This puts the economy at point A on $SRPC_0$, leading to an actual inflation rate of 2%.

Over time, the public will come to expect a 2% inflation rate. *This increase in inflationary expectations will shift the short-run Phillips curve upward* to $SRPC_2$. Now, when the unemployment rate is 6%, the actual inflation rate will be 2%. Given this new short-run Phillips curve, policies adopted to keep the unemployment rate at 4% will lead to a 4% actual inflation rate—point B on $SRPC_2$—rather than point A with a 2% actual inflation rate.

FIGURE 31-12 The NAIRU and the Long-Run Phillips Curve

$SRPC_0$ is the short-run Phillips curve when the expected inflation rate is 0%. At a 4% unemployment rate, the economy is at point A with an actual inflation rate of 2%. The higher inflation rate will be incorporated into expectations, and the $SRPC$ will shift upward to $SRPC_2$. If policy makers act to keep the unemployment rate at 4%, the economy will be at point B and the actual inflation rate will rise to 4%. Inflationary expectations will be revised upward again, and $SRPC$ will shift to $SRPC_4$. At a 4% unemployment rate, the economy will be at point C and the actual inflation rate will rise to 6%. Here, an unemployment rate of 6% is the NAIRU, or nonaccelerating inflation rate of unemployment. As long as unemployment is at the NAIRU, the actual inflation rate will match expectations and remain constant. An unemployment rate below 6% requires ever-accelerating inflation. The long-run Phillips curve, $LRPC$, which passes through E_0, E_2, and E_4, is vertical: no long-run trade-off between unemployment and inflation exists.

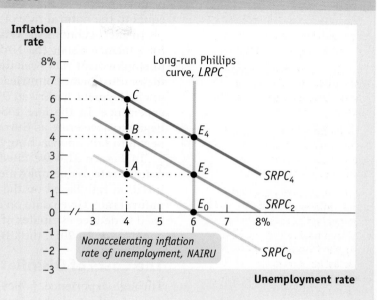

Eventually, the 4% actual inflation rate gets built into expectations about the future inflation rate, and the short-run Phillips curve shifts upward yet again to $SRPC_4$. To keep the unemployment rate at 4% would now require accepting a 6% actual inflation rate, point C on $SRPC_4$, and so on. In short, a persistent attempt to trade off lower unemployment for higher inflation leads to *accelerating* inflation over time.

To avoid accelerating inflation over time, the unemployment rate must be high enough that the actual rate of inflation matches the expected rate of inflation.

This is the situation at E_0 on $SRPC_0$: when the expected inflation rate is 0% and the unemployment rate is 6%, the actual inflation rate is 0%. It is also the situation at E_2 on $SRPC_2$: when the expected inflation rate is 2% and the unemployment rate is 6%, the actual inflation rate is 2%. And it is the situation at E_4 on $SRPC_4$: when the expected inflation rate is 4% and the unemployment rate is 6%, the actual inflation rate is 4%. This relationship between accelerating inflation and the unemployment rate is known as the *natural rate hypothesis*.

The unemployment rate at which inflation does not change over time—6% in Figure 31-12—is known as the **nonaccelerating inflation rate of unemployment,** or **NAIRU** for short. Keeping the unemployment rate below the NAIRU leads to ever-accelerating inflation and cannot be maintained. Most macroeconomists believe that there is a NAIRU and that there is no long-run trade-off between unemployment and inflation.

We can now explain the significance of the vertical line $LRPC$. It is the **long-run Phillips curve,** the relationship between unemployment and inflation in the long run, after expectations of inflation have had time to adjust to experience. It is vertical because any unemployment rate below the NAIRU leads to ever-accelerating inflation. In other words, the long-run Phillips curve shows that there are limits to expansionary policies, because an unemployment rate below the NAIRU cannot be maintained in the long run. Moreover, there is a corresponding point we have not yet emphasized: any unemployment rate above the NAIRU leads to decelerating inflation.

The Natural Rate of Unemployment, Revisited

Recall that the natural rate of unemployment is the portion of the unemployment rate unaffected by the swings of the business cycle. Now we have introduced the concept of the *NAIRU*. How do these two concepts relate to each other?

The **nonaccelerating inflation rate of unemployment,** or **NAIRU,** is the unemployment rate at which inflation does not change over time.

The **long-run Phillips curve** shows the relationship between unemployment and inflation after expectations of inflation have had time to adjust to experience.

The answer is that the NAIRU is another name for the natural rate. The level of unemployment the economy needs in order to avoid accelerating inflation is equal to the natural rate of unemployment.

In fact, economists estimate the natural rate of unemployment by looking for evidence about the NAIRU from the behavior of the inflation rate and the unemployment rate over the course of the business cycle. For example, the way major European countries learned, to their dismay, that their natural rates of unemployment had risen 9% or more by around 1990, was through unpleasant experience. In the late 1980s, and again in the late 1990s, European inflation began to accelerate as European unemployment rates, which had been above 9%, began to fall, approaching 8%.

In Figure 31-4 we cited Congressional Budget Office estimates of the U.S. natural rate of unemployment. The CBO has a model that predicts changes in the inflation rate based on the deviation of the actual unemployment rate from the natural rate. Given data on actual unemployment and inflation, this model can be used to deduce estimates of the natural rate—and that's where the CBO numbers come from. In 2017, the CBO estimate of the U.S. natural rate was 4.7%.

The Costs of Disinflation

Through experience, policy makers have found that bringing inflation down is a much harder task than increasing it. The reason is that once the public has come to expect continuing inflation, bringing inflation down is painful.

A persistent attempt to keep unemployment below the natural rate leads to accelerating inflation that becomes incorporated into expectations. To reduce inflationary expectations, policy makers need to run the process in reverse, adopting contractionary policies that keep the unemployment rate above the natural rate for an extended period of time. The process of bringing down inflation that has become embedded in expectations is known as *disinflation*, a concept discussed in Chapter 23.

Disinflation can be very expensive. As the following Economics in Action documents, the U.S. retreat from high inflation at the beginning of the 1980s appears to have cost the equivalent of about 18% of a year's real GDP, the equivalent of roughly $3.7 trillion today. The justification for paying these costs is that they lead to a permanent gain. Although the economy does not recover the short-term production losses caused by disinflation, it no longer suffers from the costs associated with persistently high inflation. In fact, the United States, Britain, and other wealthy countries that experienced inflation in the 1970s eventually decided that the benefit of bringing inflation down was worth the required suffering—the large reduction in real GDP in the short term.

🌐 GLOBAL COMPARISON DISINFLATION AROUND THE WORLD

The disinflation of the 1980s wasn't unique to the United States. A number of other advanced countries also experienced high inflation during the 1970s, then brought inflation down during the 1980s at the cost of a severe recession. This figure shows the annual rate of inflation in Britain, Italy, and the United States from 1970 to 2019. All three nations experienced high inflation rates following the two oil price shocks of 1973 and 1979, with the U.S. inflation rate the least severe of the three. All three nations then weathered severe recessions in order to bring inflation down. Since the 1980s, inflation has remained low and stable in all wealthy nations.

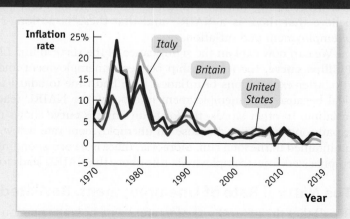

Data from: World Development Indicators, World Bank.

Some economists argue that the costs of disinflation can be reduced if policy makers explicitly state their determination to reduce inflation. A clearly announced, credible policy of disinflation, they contend, can reduce expectations of future inflation and so shift the short-run Phillips curve downward. Some economists believe that the clear determination of the Federal Reserve to combat the inflation of the 1970s was credible enough that the costs of disinflation, huge though they were, were lower than they might otherwise have been.

ECONOMICS >> *in Action*
The Great Disinflation of the 1980s

As we've mentioned, the United States ended the 1970s with a high rate of inflation, at least by its own peacetime historical standards—14% in 1980. Part of this inflation was the result of one-time events, especially a world oil crisis. But expectations of future inflation at 10% or more per year appeared to be firmly embedded in the economy.

By the mid-1980s, however, inflation was running at about 4% per year. Panel (a) of Figure 31-13 shows the annual rate of change in the "core" consumer price index (CPI)—also called the *core inflation rate*. This index, which excludes volatile energy and food prices, is widely regarded as a better indicator of underlying inflation trends than the overall CPI. By this measure, inflation fell from about 12% at the end of the 1970s to about 4% by the mid-1980s.

How was this disinflation achieved? At great cost. Beginning in late 1979, the Federal Reserve imposed strongly contractionary monetary policies, which pushed the economy into a severe recession—at that point the worst since the Great Depression, although it would later be surpassed by the Great Recession of 2007–2009. Panel (b) shows the Congressional Budget Office estimate of the U.S. output gap from 1979 to 1989: by 1982, actual output was 7% below potential output, corresponding to an unemployment rate of more than 9%. Aggregate output didn't get back to potential output until 1987.

Our analysis of the Phillips curve tells us that a temporary rise in unemployment, like that of the 1980s, is needed to break the cycle of inflationary

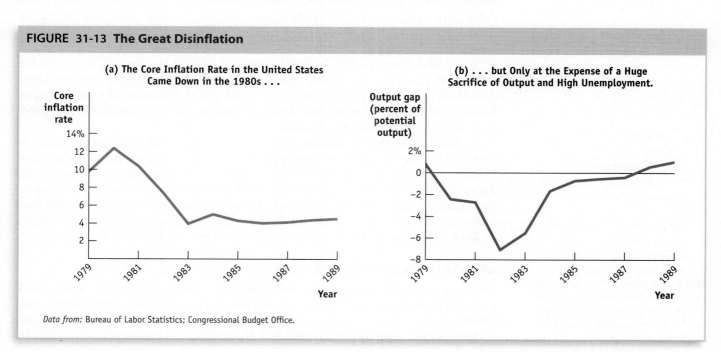

FIGURE 31-13 The Great Disinflation

(a) The Core Inflation Rate in the United States Came Down in the 1980s . . .

(b) . . . but Only at the Expense of a Huge Sacrifice of Output and High Unemployment.

Data from: Bureau of Labor Statistics; Congressional Budget Office.

expectations. Once expectations of inflation are reduced, the economy can return to the natural rate of unemployment at a lower inflation rate. And that's just what happened.

But the cost was huge. If you add up the output gap over 1980–1987, you find that the economy sacrificed approximately 18% of an average year's output over the period. If we had to do the same thing today, that would mean giving up roughly $4 trillion worth of goods and services.

>> *Check Your Understanding* 31-3
Solutions appear at back of book.

1. Why is there no long-run trade-off between unemployment and inflation?

2. British economists believe that the natural rate of unemployment in their country rose sharply during the 1970s, from around 3% to as much as 10%. During that period, Britain experienced a sharp acceleration of inflation, which for a time went above 20%. How might these facts be related?

3. Why is disinflation so costly for an economy? Are there ways to reduce these costs?

‖ Deflation

Before World War II, *deflation*—a falling aggregate price level—was almost as common as inflation. (We introduced deflation in Chapter 21.) In fact, the U.S. consumer price index on the eve of World War II was 30% lower than it had been in 1920. After World War II, inflation became the norm in all countries. But in the 1990s, deflation reappeared in Japan and proved difficult to reverse. Concerns about potential deflation played a crucial role in U.S. monetary policy in the early 2000s and again in the aftermath of the 2008 financial crisis.

Why is deflation a problem? And why is it hard to end?

Debt Deflation

Deflation, like inflation, produces both winners and losers—but in the opposite direction. Due to the falling price level, a dollar in the future has a higher real value than a dollar today. So lenders, who are owed money, gain under deflation because the real value of borrowers' payments increases. Borrowers lose because the real burden of their debt rises.

In a famous analysis at the beginning of the Great Depression, Irving Fisher (who first analyzed the *Fisher effect* of expected inflation on interest rates, described in Chapter 25) claimed that the effects of deflation on borrowers and lenders can worsen an economic slump. Deflation, in effect, takes real resources away from borrowers and redistributes them to lenders.

Fisher argued that borrowers, who lose from deflation, are typically short of cash and will be forced to cut their spending sharply when their debt burden rises. Lenders, however, are unlikely to increase spending sharply when the values of the loans they own rise. The overall effect, said Fisher, is that deflation reduces aggregate demand, deepening an economic slump, which, in a vicious circle, may lead to further deflation. The effect of deflation in reducing aggregate demand, known as **debt deflation,** probably played a significant role in the Great Depression.

Effects of Expected Deflation

Debt deflation is the reduction in aggregate demand arising from the increase in the real burden of outstanding debt caused by deflation.

Like expected inflation, expected deflation affects the nominal interest rate. Look back at Figure 25-9, which demonstrated how expected inflation affects the equilibrium interest rate. In Figure 25-9, the equilibrium nominal interest rate is 4% if the expected inflation rate is 0%. But, if the expected inflation rate is −3%—if the public expects deflation at 3% per year—the equilibrium nominal interest rate would fall to 1%.

But what would happen if the expected rate of inflation is –6%? Would the nominal interest rate fall to –2%, in which lenders are paying borrowers 2% on their debt? Probably not, because they could do better by simply holding cash. As explained in Chapter 30, we now know that there isn't a strict zero lower bound because holding lots of cash is inconvenient. But the nominal rate clearly can't go more than a small amount below zero.

This restriction—called the *zero lower bound problem*—can limit the effectiveness of monetary policy. Suppose the economy is depressed, with output below potential output and the unemployment rate above the natural rate. Normally the central bank can respond by cutting interest rates to increase aggregate demand. If the nominal interest rate is already zero, however, the central bank cannot push it down any further. The central bank is up against the zero lower bound for the nominal interest rate. Banks refuse to lend and consumers and firms refuse to spend because, with a negative inflation rate and a 0% nominal interest rate, holding cash yields a positive real return: with falling prices, a given amount of cash buys more over time. Any further increases in the monetary base will either be held in bank vaults or held as cash by individuals and firms, without being spent.

A situation in which conventional monetary policy to fight a slump—cutting interest rates—can't be used because nominal interest rates can't be cut further is known as a **liquidity trap.** A liquidity trap can occur whenever there is a sharp reduction in demand for loanable funds—which is exactly what happened during the Great Depression. Figure 31-14 shows the interest rate on short-term U.S. government debt from 1920 to 2020. As you can see, during the period from 1933 to the post–World War II recovery, the U.S. economy was either close to or up against the zero lower bound. After World War II, when inflation became the norm around the world, the zero lower bound largely vanished as a problem, as the public came to expect inflation rather than deflation. As a result, economists largely lost interest in the issue.

But, as you can see, the zero lower bound emerged again as a result of the financial crisis of 2008, and again during the coronavirus pandemic. Once more, the interest rate on three-month U.S. Treasury bills was virtually zero. Yet for reasons not entirely clear, the United States did not experience deflation during the Great

> The economy is in a **liquidity trap** when conventional monetary policy is ineffective because the nominal interest rate is up against the zero lower bound.

FIGURE 31-14 The Zero Lower Bound in the U.S. Economy

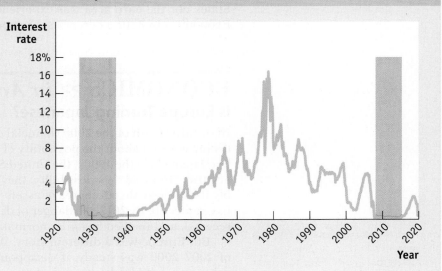

This figure shows U.S. short-term interest rates, specifically the interest rate on three-month Treasury bills, from 1920 to 2020. As shown by the shaded bar at left, for much of the 1930s, interest rates were very close to zero, leaving little room for expansionary monetary policy. After World War II, persistent inflation generally kept interest rates well above zero. However, in late 2008, in the wake of the housing bubble bursting and the financial crisis, the interest rate on three-month Treasury bills was again virtually zero and stayed there for almost eight years — shown by the shaded bar at right.

Data from: National Bureau of Economic Research; Federal Reserve Bank of St. Louis.

FIGURE 31-15 Deflation and the Liquidity Trap in the Japanese Economy

A prolonged economic slump in Japan led to deflation from the late 1990s on. The Bank of Japan responded by cutting interest rates — but eventually ran up against the zero lower bound where it remained in 2020, over 20 years later. *Data from:* Federal Reserve Bank of St. Louis.

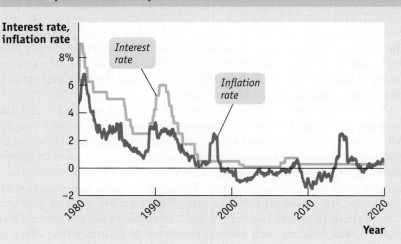

Recession. Sticky wages may have been the cause, since the United States did not experience a significant fall in nominal wages although unemployment shot up.

The recent history of the Japanese economy, shown in Figure 31-15, provides the best modern illustration of the problem of deflation and the liquidity trap. In the 1990s, after the bursting of a huge housing and stock bubble, the Japanese economy entered a period of sustained weakness in which wages and prices fell. In an effort to fight the economic weakness, the Bank of Japan—the equivalent of the Federal Reserve—repeatedly cut interest rates. Eventually, it arrived at the ZIRP: the *zero interest rate policy*. The call money rate, the equivalent of the U.S. federal funds rate, was literally set equal to zero. Because the economy was still depressed, it would have been desirable to cut interest rates even further. But that wasn't possible: Japan was up against the zero lower bound. And it was still there in 2020, nearly 25 years later!

In the aftermath of the 2008 financial crisis, the world's most important central banks—the U.S. Federal Reserve and the European Central Bank—found themselves facing much of the same problems as the Bank of Japan had faced since the 1990s: their economies remained depressed despite policy interest rates close to zero and inflation persistently below target. In 2014, neither the United States nor the euro area was experiencing actual deflation, but as the following Economics in Action describes, Europe did get alarmingly close.

ECONOMICS >> *in Action*
Is Europe Turning Japanese?

In the aftermath of the 2008 financial crisis, officials at the Federal Reserve were deeply worried about the possibility of *Japanification*—that is, they worried that, like Japan since the 1990s, the United States might find itself stuck in a deflationary trap. To avoid this possibility, they took some extraordinary measures, notably the large-scale purchases of assets—so-called *quantitative easing*—described in Chapter 30. By 2017, the danger of deflation in the United States seemed to have receded, and the Fed began to normalize its policy.

But Europe was a different story. Where the U.S. recovery from the recession of 2007–2009 was steady, if disappointingly slow, the euro area, held back by debt crises, slid back into recession in late 2011. Growth resumed in 2013, but as

FIGURE 31-16 Trouble in Europe, 2008–2020

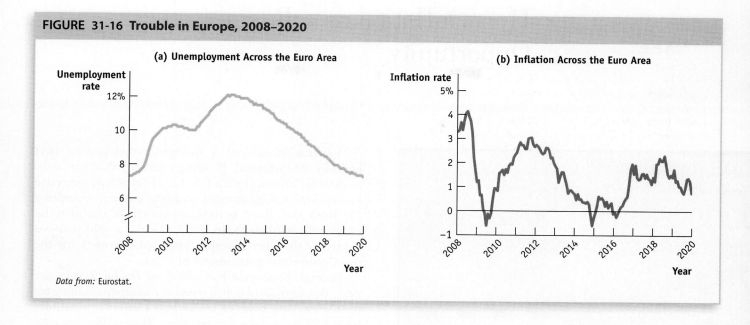

Data from: Eurostat.

you can see from panel (a) of Figure 31-16, it only led to a modest decline in high unemployment. And as panel (b) of Figure 31-16 shows, in 2013–2017 inflation began sliding below 1%, leading to worries that Europe was on track to replicate Japan's economic situation.

While Europe was not yet experiencing sustained deflation as of 2017, it was, as the International Monetary Fund put it, suffering from *lowflation*—inflation persistently below target—and this created many of the same problems. In particular, lower-than-expected inflation was worsening the problems of highly indebted nations, like Portugal, Spain, and Greece.

And like the Bank of Japan a number of years earlier, the European Central Bank was finding it hard to devise an effective answer to the problem. Beginning in June 2014, the ECB took the extraordinary step of reducing one of its key policy rates, the interest rate it pays on deposits of private banks, to *minus* 0.1%—that is, it began actually charging banks a fee for holding their money. But below-target inflation persisted.

>> Check Your Understanding 31-4

Solutions appear at back of book.

1. Why won't anyone lend money at a negative nominal rate of interest? How can this pose problems for monetary policy?

>> **Quick Review**

• Unexpected deflation helps lenders and hurts borrowers. This can lead to **debt deflation,** which has a contractionary effect on aggregate demand.

• Deflation makes it more likely that interest rates will end up against the zero lower bound. When this happens, the economy is in a **liquidity trap,** and monetary policy is ineffective.

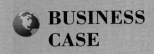

Hyperinflation as a Business Opportunity

Carolina Cabral/Getty Images

We often say that modern governments with fiat currencies simply print their own currencies. But sometimes that's not literally true—what they actually do is hire private companies to print money for them. That's what happened in November 2019, when Venezuela signed a contract with Goznak, a Russian money-printing company, to churn out 300 million bolivar bills, in denominations running from 10,000 to 50,000 bolivars.

Venezuela's use of a foreign money-printer isn't actually that unusual. Printing currency that isn't easy to counterfeit requires a fair bit of technical expertise and specialized equipment, so many countries contract the work out. Even Britain subcontracts the printing of pound banknotes to De La Rue, a 200-year-old company that, for example, supplied currency for the pre-Communist government of China.

Indeed, Venezuela has relied on De La Rue in the past. But as of 2019 it still owed the company money for past work, and none of De La Rue's usual competitors were willing to take the business. Hence the choice of Goznak, which happens to be owned by the Russian government.

There were two unusual things about the Goznak contract. One was the fact that the order was quite small—just $143 million in face value, which isn't much even for a country the size of Venezuela. Yet this amounted to about one-fifth of the value of Venezuelan currency in circulation at the time. The other was the unusually high fee—about 5% of the value of the notes. This high fee partly reflected the low purchasing power of the notes: the cost of printing a 10,000 bolivar note is presumably not very different from the cost of printing, say, a $20 bill, but even at the time the Venezuelan note was worth only around $0.14.

Still, business is business, and Goznak's contract showed that even bad times offer opportunities.

QUESTIONS FOR THOUGHT

1. Why was Venezuela so desperate to hire someone to print more money?

2. Why did such a small order for new currency account for such a large fraction of the existing money supply?

3. How would you classify the fees paid to Goznak under the general category of costs of inflation?

1. In analyzing high inflation, economists use the **classical model of the price level,** which says that changes in the money supply lead to proportional changes in the aggregate price level even in the short run.

2. Governments sometimes print money in order to finance budget deficits. When they do, they impose an **inflation tax,** generating tax revenue equal to the inflation rate times the money supply, on those who hold money. Revenue from the real inflation tax, the inflation rate times the real money supply, is the real value of resources captured by the government. In order to avoid paying the inflation tax, people reduce their real money holdings and force the government to increase inflation to capture the same amount of real inflation tax revenue. In some cases, this leads to a vicious circle of a shrinking real money supply and a rising rate of inflation, leading to hyperinflation and a fiscal crisis.

3. The output gap is the percentage difference between the actual level of real GDP and potential output. A positive output gap is associated with lower-than-normal unemployment; a negative output gap is associated with higher-than-normal unemployment. The relationship between the output gap and cyclical unemployment is described by **Okun's law.**

4. Countries that don't need to print money to cover government deficits can still stumble into moderate inflation, either because of political opportunism or because of wishful thinking.

5. At a given point in time, there is a downward-sloping relationship between unemployment and inflation known as the **short-run Phillips curve.** This curve is shifted by changes in the **expected rate of inflation.** The **long-run Phillips curve,** which shows the relationship between unemployment and inflation once expectations have had time to adjust, is vertical. It defines the **nonaccelerating inflation rate of unemployment,** or **NAIRU,** which is equal to the natural rate of unemployment. *Stagflation,* a combination of high unemployment and high inflation, reflects an upward shift of the short-run Phillips curve.

6. Once inflation has become embedded in expectations, getting inflation back down can be difficult because *disinflation* can be very costly, requiring the sacrifice of large amounts of aggregate output and imposing high levels of unemployment. However, policy makers in the United States and other wealthy countries were willing to pay that price of bringing down the high inflation of the 1970s.

7. Deflation poses several problems. It can lead to **debt deflation,** in which a rising real burden of outstanding debt intensifies an economic downturn. Also, nominal interest rates are more likely to run up against the zero lower bound in an economy experiencing deflation. When this happens, the economy enters a **liquidity trap,** rendering conventional monetary policy ineffective.

Classical model of the price level, p. 916
Inflation tax, p. 919
Okun's law, p. 924

Short-run Phillips curve, p. 924
Expected rate of inflation, p. 927
Nonaccelerating inflation rate of unemployment (NAIRU), p. 931

Long-run Phillips curve, p. 931
Debt deflation, p. 934
Liquidity trap, p. 935

1. Throughout the textbook, we relied on a traditional upward-sloping short-run aggregate supply curve. But across the profession there is a large debate around the actual slope of the short-run aggregate supply curve. Many economists believe the *SRAS* curve is much "flatter" than depicted in the book. Explain how a flatter *SRAS* curve affects the Phillips curve and the short-run trade-off between inflation and unemployment following expansionary monetary and fiscal policy.

2. During the onset of the economic shutdown tied to COVID-19, many economists were debating the effects the economic shutdown and subsequent policy efforts would have on future inflation. Explain how each of the following events will affect the short-run Phillips curve. Treat each part as a unique event.

   a. A decline in consumer spending in expectation of a slowdown in future economic activity.

   b. An increase in expansionary fiscal and monetary policy.

   c. A shutdown of global production has made it difficult for producers to maintain production for essential goods, causing production costs to increase.

3. You recently read two quotes, one from an article in *National Review:* "Then there are the costs of shortening the global supply chains and perhaps re-domesticating

some production. Entirely without economic theory, simply from observing how the world economy." The author came to an inevitable conclusion, "There will be inflation. How much inflation? . . . I'd say low double digits in the United States by the first months of 2022."

And the other from Olivier Blanchard, past chief economist for the International Monetary Fund, "Will falling commodity prices, stumbling oil prices, and a depressed labour market bring low inflation and perhaps even deflation, or will very large increases in fiscal deficits and central bank balance sheets bring inflation?" Blanchard went on to conclude, "The challenge for monetary and fiscal policy is thus likely to be to sustain demand and avoid deflation rather than the reverse."

Given the extreme range of opinions, how would you assess each statement over the next one to two years?

PROBLEMS

1. In the economy of Scottopia, policy makers want to lower the unemployment rate and raise real GDP by using monetary policy. Using the accompanying diagram, show why this policy will ultimately result in a higher aggregate price level but no change in real GDP.

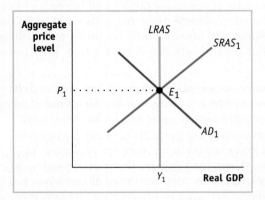

2. In the following examples, would the classical model of the price level be a useful model for analyzing how the economy behaves?

   a. The economy has high unemployment and no history of inflation.

   b. The economy has just experienced five years of hyperinflation.

   c. Although the economy experienced inflation in the 10% to 20% range three years ago, prices have recently been stable and the unemployment rate has approximated the natural rate of unemployment.

3. Access the Discovering Data exercise for Chapter 31 online to answer the following questions.

   a. How much did the monetary base change in the last year?

   b. How did the change in the monetary base help in the government's efforts to finance its deficit?

   c. Why is it important for the central bank to be independent of government policy makers?

4. Answer the following questions about the (real) inflation tax, assuming that the price level starts at 1.

   a. Maria keeps $1,000 in her sock drawer for a year. Over the year, the inflation rate is 10%. What is the real inflation tax paid by Maria for this year?

   b. Maria continues to keep the $1,000 in her drawer for a second year. What is the real value of this $1,000 at the beginning of the second year? Over the year, the inflation rate is again 10%. What is the real inflation tax paid by Maria for the second year?

   c. For a third year, Maria keeps the $1,000 in the drawer. What is the real value of this $1,000 at the beginning of the third year? Over the year, the inflation rate is again 10%. What is the real inflation tax paid by Maria for the third year?

   d. After three years, what is the cumulative real inflation tax paid?

   e. Redo parts a through d with an inflation rate of 25%. Why is hyperinflation such a problem?

5. The inflation tax is often used as a significant source of revenue in developing countries where the tax collection and reporting system is not well developed and tax evasion may be high.

   a. Use the numbers in the accompanying table to calculate the inflation tax in the United States and India (Rp = rupees).

	Inflation in 2019	Money supply in 2019 (billions)	Central government receipts in 2019 (billions)
India	7.66%	Rp36,883	Rp12,828
United States	1.81%	$3,981	$3,331

Data from: Bureau of Economic Analysis; Controller General of Accounts (India); Reserve Bank of India; International Monetary Fund; The World Bank.

   b. How large is the inflation tax for the two countries when calculated as a percentage of government receipts?

6. Concerned about the crowding-out effects of government borrowing on private investment spending, a candidate for president argues that the United States should just print money to cover the government's budget deficit. What are the advantages and disadvantages of such a plan?

7. The accompanying scatter diagram shows the relationship between the unemployment rate and the output gap in the United States from 1996 to 2019. Draw a straight line through the scatter of dots in the figure. Assume that this line represents Okun's law:

$$\text{Unemployment rate} = b - (m \times \text{Output gap})$$

where b is the vertical intercept and $-m$ is the slope.

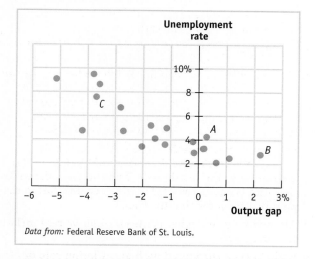

Data from: Federal Reserve Bank of St. Louis.

What is the unemployment rate when aggregate output equals potential output? What would the unemployment rate be if the output gap were 2%? What if the output gap were –3%? What do these results tell us about the coefficient m in Okun's law?

8. After experiencing a recession for the past two years, the residents of Albernia were looking forward to a decrease in the unemployment rate. Yet after six months of strong positive economic growth, the unemployment rate has fallen only slightly below what it was at the end of the recession. How can you explain why the unemployment rate did not fall as much although the economy was experiencing strong economic growth? (*Hint:* Reread the For Inquiring Minds box on Okun's law for help with answering this question.)

9. a. Go to www.bls.gov. Click on link "Subjects"; on the left, under "Inflation & Prices," click on the link "Consumer Price Index," then under the heading "CPI Data," select "Tables" and then "Archived CPI Detailed Report." Download the file for "2009

Detailed Reports" and open file cpid09av.pdf. What is the value of the percent change in the CPI from 2008 to 2009?

b. Now go to www.treasury.gov and under the tab "Data" and "Interest Rates" select "Daily Treasury Bill Rates" and select "2009" under "Select Time Period." Examine the data in "4 Weeks Bank Discount." What is the maximum? The minimum? Then do the same for 2007. How do the data for 2009 and 2007 compare? How would you relate this to your answer in part a? From the data on Treasury bill interest rates, what would you infer about the level of the inflation rate in 2007 compared to 2009? (You can check your answer by going back to the www.bls.gov website to find the percent change in the CPI from 2006 to 2007.)

c. How would you characterize the change in the U.S. economy from 2007 to 2009? What were the implications for the effectiveness of monetary policy?

10. The economy of Brittania has been suffering from high inflation with an unemployment rate equal to its natural rate. Policy makers would like to disinflate the economy with the lowest economic cost possible. Assume that the state of the economy is not the result of a negative supply shock. How can they try to minimize the unemployment cost of disinflation? Is it possible for there to be no cost of disinflation?

11. Who are the winners and losers when a mortgage company lends $100,000 to the Miller family to buy a house worth $105,000 and during the first year prices unexpectedly fall by 10%? What would you expect to happen if the deflation continued over the next few years? How would continuing deflation affect borrowers and lenders throughout the economy as a whole?

WORK IT OUT

12. Due to historical differences, countries often differ in how quickly a change in actual inflation is incorporated into a change in expected inflation. In a country such as Japan, which has had very little inflation in recent memory, it will take longer for a change in the actual inflation rate to be reflected in a corresponding change in the expected inflation rate. In contrast, in a country such as Zimbabwe, which has recently had very high inflation, a change in the actual inflation rate will immediately be reflected in a corresponding change in the expected inflation rate. What does this imply about the short-run and long-run Phillips curves in these two types of countries? What does this imply about the effectiveness of monetary and fiscal policy to reduce the unemployment rate? ■

32 ⟩ Macroeconomics: Events and Ideas

SYMPATHY FOR THE DEFICIT

IN FISCAL 2019, THE U.S. FEDERAL GOVERNMENT ran a budget deficit of almost $1 trillion, 4.7% of GDP. It wasn't the biggest deficit in U.S. history. However, in the past deficits that size occurred only during wars and economic emergencies like the aftermath of the 2008 financial crisis. To run such a big deficit in the face of low unemployment and healthy growth was unprecedented.

You might have expected, then, to see economists warning about fiscal irresponsibility. In fact, however, 2019 also happened to be a year in which several prominent macroeconomists published articles arguing that government debt is a much less pressing problem than many people imagine. In January 2019, Olivier Blanchard, the former chief economist of the International Monetary Fund and about as mainstream and widely respected as any modern macroeconomist, devoted his presidential lecture to the American Economic Association to the issue of public debt, and concluded that it may not do much, if any, damage.

A few weeks later Jason Furman and Lawrence Summers, who had been top economists in the Obama administration, published an article titled "Who's afraid of budget deficits?" that concluded, "It's

Speaking at the American Economic Association's Annual Meeting, President Olivier Blanchard discusses fallacies around issuing public debt.

time for Washington to put away its deficit obsession and focus on bigger things."

Indeed, when budget deficits exploded in 2020 as a result of plunging revenue and emergency spending to cope with the coronavirus, economists surveyed by the University of Chicago supported a program providing income support to unemployed workers, even though this program was adding hundreds of billions to government spending.

Why have influential economists developed a soft spot for budget deficits? The answer, as is often the case in macroeconomics, is that they were strongly influenced by events — in this case both the financial crisis of 2008 and the era of very low interest rates that began during the crisis but continued right through 2020.

Macroeconomic ideas evolve because circumstances change. Solutions that were appropriate when gold and silver were the only monies available are inappropriate in an age of debit cards, Venmo, and digital currency. However, macroeconomic ideas also evolve because there is a steady accumulation of research and evidence that can be applied to the kinds of economic phenomenon that recur over time. The lessons learned in one decade are made available for the benefit of future generations.

To understand the state of macroeconomic thinking today, then, requires a trip through economic history and an understanding of the way economic ideas have evolved in the face of events.

In this chapter we'll trace the development of macroeconomic ideas over the past 90 years: the rise of Keynesian economics in response to the Great Depression, the challenges to policy activism that arose in response to the stagflation of the 1970s, and the revisions to economic thinking induced by changes in the economic environment since the Great Recession. ●

> ### WHAT YOU WILL LEARN
>
> - Why was classical macroeconomics inadequate for the problems posed by the Great Depression?
> - How did John Maynard Keynes and the experience of the Great Depression legitimize **macroeconomic policy activism?**
> - Why did the original focus of **Keynesian economics** on fiscal policy give way to an emphasis on monetary policy?
> - Why did economists come temporarily to have great faith in the power of independent central banks to stabilize the economy?
> - How have events since 2008 undermined that faith, and also changed views on deficits and debt?

‖ Classical Macroeconomics

The term *macroeconomics* appears to have been coined in 1933 by the Norwegian economist Ragnar Frisch. The date, during the worst year of the Great Depression, is no accident. Still, there were economists analyzing what we now consider macroeconomic issues—the behavior of the aggregate price level and aggregate output—before then.

Money and the Price Level

In Chapter 31, we described the *classical model of the price level*. According to the classical model, prices are flexible, making the aggregate supply curve vertical even in the short run. In this model, an increase in the money supply leads, other things equal, to an equal proportional rise in the aggregate price level, with no effect on aggregate output. As a result, increases in the money supply lead to inflation, and that's all. Before the 1930s, the classical model of the price level dominated economic thinking about the effects of monetary policy.

Did classical economists really believe that changes in the money supply affected only aggregate prices, without any effect on aggregate output? Probably not. Historians of economic thought argue that before 1930 most economists were aware that changes in the money supply affect aggregate output as well as aggregate prices in the short run—or, to use modern terms, they were aware that the short-run aggregate supply curve slopes upward. But they regarded such short-run effects as unimportant, stressing that it was the long run that mattered. It was this attitude that led the British economist John Maynard Keynes to scoff at the exclusive focus on the long run: he famously quipped that "in the long run, we are all dead."

The Business Cycle

Despite their lack of interest in the short run, classical economists were aware that the economy did not grow smoothly. Some economic historians argue that the first true recession in the modern sense took place in Britain in 1825–1826, when an overheated boom in canal-building collapsed. As the Industrial Revolution spread beyond Britain, so did the business cycle, which eventually became the object of systematic, quantitative study, pioneered by the American economist Wesley Mitchell. In 1920 Mitchell founded the National Bureau of Economic Research (NBER), an independent, nonprofit organization that to this day has the official role of declaring the beginnings of recessions and expansions. Thanks to Mitchell's work, the *measurement* of business cycles was well advanced by 1930. But there was no widely accepted *theory* of what caused business cycles or what to do about them.

In the absence of any clear theory, conflicts arose among policy makers over how to respond to a recession. Some economists favored expansionary monetary and fiscal policies to fight a recession. Others believed that such policies would worsen the slump or merely postpone the inevitable. For example, in 1934 Harvard's Joseph Schumpeter, now famous for his early recognition of the importance of technological change, warned that any attempt to alleviate the Great Depression with expansionary monetary policy "would, in the end, lead to a collapse worse than the one it was called in to remedy." When the Great Depression hit, policy was paralyzed by this lack of consensus.

Necessity was, however, the mother of invention. As we'll see next, the Great Depression provided an opportunity for economists to develop theories that could serve as a guide to policy.

The Great Depression and the Keynesian Revolution

The Great Depression demonstrated, once and for all, that economists cannot safely ignore the short run. Not only was the economic pain severe; it threatened to destabilize societies and political systems. In particular, the economic plunge helped Adolf Hitler rise to power in Germany, setting the stage for World War II.

The whole world wanted to know how this economic disaster could be happening and what should be done about it. But because there was no widely accepted theory of the business cycle, economists gave conflicting and often harmful advice. Some believed that only a huge change in the economic system—such as having the government take over much of private industry and replace markets with a command economy—could end the slump. Others argued that slumps were natural—even beneficial, helping to correct past excesses—and that nothing should be done.

Some economists, however, argued that slumps were destructive and should be cured. Moreover, they could be cured without compromising the market economy. The most compelling advocate for this view was John Maynard Keynes, who compared the problems of the U.S. and British economies in 1930 to those of a car with a defective starter. Getting the economy running, he argued, would require only a modest repair, not a complete overhaul.

Nice metaphor. But what did he mean, specifically?

Keynes's Theory

In 1936 Keynes presented his analysis of the Great Depression—his explanation of what was wrong with the economy's starter—in a book titled *The General Theory of Employment, Interest, and Money*. In 1946 the great American economist and Nobel Prize–winner Paul Samuelson wrote that "it is a badly written book, poorly organized. . . . Flashes of insight and intuition intersperse tedious algebra. . . . We find its analysis to be obvious and at the same time new. In short, it is a work of genius." Samuelson was correct on both counts: *The General Theory* isn't easy reading, yet it stands with Adam Smith's *The Wealth of Nations* as one of the most influential books on economics ever written.

As Samuelson's description indicates, Keynes's book offers a vast stew of ideas. *Keynesian economics* is principally based on two innovations. First, Keynes emphasized the importance of short-run effects of changes in aggregate demand on aggregate output, unlike the classicists who focused exclusively on the long-run determination of the aggregate price level.

Until *The General Theory* appeared most economists had treated short-run macroeconomics as a minor issue. Keynes shifted the focus of attention of economists away from the unreachable long run to the world in which people actually live, one in which the short-run aggregate supply curve slopes upward and shifts in the aggregate demand curve affect aggregate output and employment as well as aggregate prices.

Figure 32-1 illustrates the difference between Keynesian and classical macroeconomics. Both panels of the figure show the short-run aggregate supply curve, *SRAS;* in both it is assumed that for some reason demand falls and the aggregate demand curve shifts leftward from AD_1 to AD_2—say, for example, in response to a fall in stock market prices that leads households to reduce consumer spending.

Panel (a) shows the classical view: in it, the short-run aggregate supply curve is vertical. Therefore the fall in aggregate demand leads to a fall in the aggregate price level, from P_1 to P_2, but leaves aggregate output unchanged. Panel (b) shows the Keynesian view: in it, the short-run aggregate supply curve slopes upward.

FIGURE 32-1 Classical versus Keynesian Macroeconomics

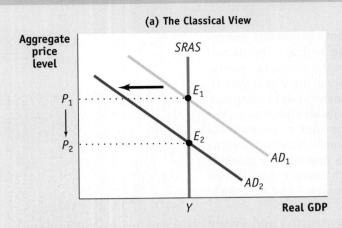

(a) The Classical View

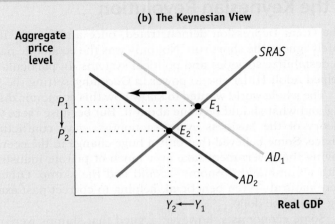

(b) The Keynesian View

One important difference between classical and Keynesian economics involves the short-run aggregate supply curve. Panel (a) shows the classical view: the *SRAS* curve is vertical, so shifts in aggregate demand affect the aggregate price level but not aggregate output. Panel (b) shows the Keynesian view: in the short run the *SRAS* curve slopes upward, so shifts in aggregate demand affect aggregate output as well as aggregate prices.

So a fall in aggregate demand leads to both a fall in the aggregate price level, from P_1 to P_2, and a fall in aggregate output, from Y_1 to Y_2.

As we've already explained, many classical macroeconomists would have agreed that panel (b) portrayed an accurate story in the short run—but they regarded the short run as unimportant. Keynes strongly disagreed, arguing that short-run economic problems caused great social distress and were in fact fixable. (Just to be clear, there isn't any diagram that looks like panel (b) of Figure 32-1 in Keynes's *General Theory*. But Keynes's discussion of aggregate supply, translated into modern terminology, clearly implies an upward-sloping *SRAS* curve.)

Keynes's second innovation concerned the question of what factors shifted the aggregate demand curve and caused business cycles. Classical economists attributed shifts in the demand curve almost exclusively to changes in the money supply. Keynes, by contrast, argued that other factors, especially changes in "animal spirits"—these days usually referred to with the bland term *business confidence*—are mainly responsible for business cycles.

Before Keynes, economists argued that as long as the money supply stayed constant, changes in factors like business confidence would have no effect on either the aggregate price level or aggregate output. Keynes offered a very different picture in which, for example, pessimism about future profits can lead to a fall in investment spending, and this can cause a recession.

Keynesian economics, a view of the business cycle informed by these innovations, has penetrated deeply into the public consciousness, to the extent that many people who have never heard of Keynes, or have heard of him but think they disagree with his theory, use Keynesian ideas all the time. For example, suppose that a business commentator says something like this: "Businesses are holding back on investment spending because they're worried about low consumer demand, and that's why recovery has stalled." Whether the commentator knows it or not, that statement is pure Keynesian economics.

Keynes himself more or less predicted that someday people would make use of his ideas without knowing that they were *Keynesians*. As he famously wrote in *The General Theory*, "Practical men, who believe themselves to be quite

Keynesian economics rests on two main tenets: changes in aggregate demand affect aggregate output, employment, and prices; and changes in business confidence cause the business cycle.

FOR INQUIRING MINDS   The Politics of Keynes

Some political commentators use the term *Keynesian economics* as a synonym for left-wing economics. Because Keynes offered a rationale for some kinds of government activism, these commentators have gone on to claim that he was a leftist of some kind, maybe even a socialist. But the truth is more complicated.

As we explained, Keynesian ideas have actually been accepted among economists and policy makers across a broad range of the political spectrum. In 2004 the American president, George W. Bush, was a conservative, as was his top economist, N. Gregory Mankiw. But Mankiw is also a well-known promoter of Keynesian ideas.

In fact, Keynes was no socialist—and not much of a leftist. At the time *The General Theory* was published, the Depression had convinced many intellectuals that socialism was the only solution to the economy's woes. They believed that the Great Depression was the final crisis of the capitalist economic system and that only

a government takeover of industry could save the economy. Keynes, in contrast, argued that socialism was not the answer. Instead, he said, all the capitalist market system needed was a narrow technical fix. In essence, his ideas were pro-capitalist and politically conservative.

What is true is that the rise of Keynesian economics in the 1940s, 1950s, and 1960s accompanied a general enlargement of the role of government in the economy, and those who favored a larger role for government tended to be enthusiastic Keynesians. Conversely, a swing of the pendulum back toward free-market policies in the 1970s and 1980s was accompanied by a series of challenges to Keynesian ideas, which we will describe in this chapter.

Recent history shows that it is quite easy to find respected economists and policy makers who have conservative political preferences and who simultaneously respect Keynes's fundamental contributions to

macroeconomics. It is equally possible to find those of a liberal bent who question some of Keynes's ideas.

The ideas of John Maynard Keynes have been accepted across the political spectrum.

---

exempt from any intellectual influences, are usually the slaves of some defunct economist."

Policy to Fight Recessions

The greatest consequence of Keynes's work was that it legitimized **macroeconomic policy activism**—the use of monetary and fiscal policy to smooth out the business cycle.

It's true that some economists had called for macroeconomic activism before Keynes, in particular advocating monetary expansion to fight economic downturns. And some economists had even argued, as Keynes did, that temporary budget deficits were a good thing in times of recession. But macroeconomic policy activism at the time was considered deeply controversial and those who advocated it were fiercely attacked.

As a result, when some governments during the 1930s followed policies that we would now call Keynesian, they were carried out in a half-hearted way and were insufficient to turn the Great Depression around. In the United States, the administration of Franklin Roosevelt engaged in modest deficit spending in an effort to create jobs, actions which seemed to gain some traction in improving the economy. But, in 1937 Roosevelt gave in to advice from non-Keynesian economists who urged him to balance the federal budget and raise interest rates, even though the economy was still deeply depressed. The result was a renewed slump.

Over time, however, Keynesian ideas spread, and they were widely accepted among economists after World War II. There were, however, a series of challenges to those ideas, which led to a considerable shift in views even among those economists who continued to believe that Keynes was broadly right about the causes of recessions. Next we'll learn about those challenges and the schools, *new classical economics* and *new Keynesian economics*, that emerged.

Macroeconomic policy activism is the use of monetary and fiscal policy to smooth out the business cycle.

ECONOMICS >> *in Action*
The End of the Great Depression

It would make a good story if Keynes's ideas had led to a change in economic policy that brought the Great Depression to an end. Unfortunately, that's not what happened. Yet the way the Depression finally ended helped convince the economics profession that Keynes was basically right.

What economists learned from Keynes's work was that economic recovery requires aggressive fiscal expansion—deficit spending on a sufficiently large scale to create jobs and push up aggregate demand. And that happened in the United States not because of intentional economic policy, but as the result of a very large war that required an enormous amount of government spending, World War II. The overwhelming evidence that it was government expenditures for World War II that lifted the economy out of the Great Depression finally ended the debate over the validity of Keynes's views.

Figure 32-2 shows the U.S. unemployment rate and the federal budget deficit as a share of GDP from 1930 to 1947. As you can see, deficit spending during the 1930s was on a modest scale. In 1940, as the risk of war grew larger, the United States began a large military buildup, building tanks, planes, military bases, and the like, moving the budget deep into deficit. After the attack on Pearl Harbor on December 7, 1941, the country began deficit spending on an enormous scale: in fiscal 1943, which began in July 1942, the deficit was 30% of GDP. Today that would be equivalent to a deficit of $6 trillion.

What was clear to economists and policy makers was that this enormous surge in government spending led the economy, mired in the Great Depression for well over a decade, to finally recover in a sustainable way. World War II wasn't intended as a Keynesian fiscal policy. And it is hard to believe that any event, short of a world war, would have compelled the U.S. government to spend so much money. Yet unintentional as it was, World War II spending demonstrated that expansionary fiscal policy can lift the economy out of a deep slump.

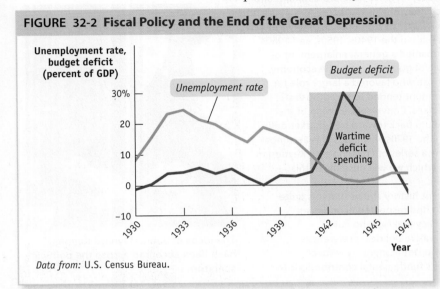

FIGURE 32-2 Fiscal Policy and the End of the Great Depression

Data from: U.S. Census Bureau.

>> Quick Review

• Classical macroeconomists focused on the long-run effects of monetary policy on the aggregate price level, ignoring any short-run effects on aggregate output.

• By the time of the Great Depression, the measurement of business cycles was well advanced, but there was no widely accepted theory about why they happened.

• The key innovations of **Keynesian economics** are an emphasis on the short run, in which the *SRAS* curve slopes upward rather than being vertical, and the belief that changes in business confidence shift the *AD* curve and thereby generate business cycles.

• Keynesian economics legitimized **macroeconomic policy activism.**

• Keynesian ideas are widely used even by people who haven't heard of Keynes or think they disagree with him.

>> Check Your Understanding 32-1
Solutions appear at back of book.

1. In their famous book *A Monetary History of the United States, 1867–1960*, the economists Milton Friedman and Anna Schwartz argued that the Federal Reserve was responsible for the Great Depression, because it failed to pursue a sufficiently expansionary monetary policy. Why would a classical economist have thought that action by the Federal Reserve would not have made a difference in the length or depth of the Great Depression?

2. In a press release during the Great Recession, the National Federation of Independent Business, which calculates the Small Business Optimism Index, stated "The Small Business Optimism Index rose just 0.1 points in January. . . . Historically, optimism remains at recession levels. While small business owners appeared less pessimistic about the outlook for business conditions and real sales growth, that optimism did not materialize in hiring or increased inventories plans." Would this statement seem familiar to a Keynesian economist? Which conclusion would a Keynesian economist draw for the need for public policy?

‖ Challenges to Keynesian Economics

Keynes's ideas fundamentally changed the way economists think about business cycles. They did not, however, go unquestioned. In the wake of the success of government expenditures in ending the Great Depression, Keynesian economics faced a new series of challenges. As a result, by the 1980s the consensus of macroeconomists retreated somewhat from the strong version of Keynesianism that prevailed in the 1950s. In particular, many economists began to suggest limits to the effectiveness of macroeconomic policy activism.

The Revival of Monetary Policy

Many macroeconomists agree with Keynes's view that during a depression monetary policy would be relatively ineffective. We met this phenomenon in Chapter 31 in what we called the *liquidity trap*, a situation in which monetary policy is ineffective because the interest rate cannot be pushed any lower. In the 1930s, when Keynes wrote, interest rates were, in fact, very close to zero.

When the era of near-zero interest rates came to an end after World War II and the economy had recovered, the pendulum had swung so far in favor of Keynesian economics that many economists continued to emphasize fiscal policy and downplay the usefulness of monetary policy. Eventually, however, the pendulum swung partly back as macroeconomists reassessed the importance of monetary policy.

A key milestone in this reassessment was the 1963 publication of *A Monetary History of the United States, 1867–1960*, by Milton Friedman, of the University of Chicago, and Anna Schwartz, of the National Bureau of Economic Research. Friedman and Schwartz showed that business cycles had historically been associated with fluctuations in the money supply. In particular, the money supply fell sharply during the onset of the Great Depression. Friedman and Schwartz persuaded many, though not all, economists that the Great Depression could have been avoided if the Federal Reserve had acted to prevent the monetary contraction by increasing the monetary base. They persuaded most economists that monetary policy should play a key role in economic management.

Milton Friedman and co-author Anna Schwartz played a key role in convincing macroeconomists of the importance of monetary policy.

The revival of interest in monetary policy was significant because it suggested that the burden of managing the economy could be shifted away from fiscal policy—meaning that economic management could largely be taken out of the hands of politicians. This feature was attractive to many because fiscal policy necessarily involves political choices. If the government tries to stimulate the economy by cutting taxes, it must decide whose taxes will be cut. If it tries to stimulate the economy with government spending, it must decide what to spend the money on. As a result, management of the economy would often be bogged down by the political process if fiscal policy were the only tool available.

Monetary policy, in contrast, does not involve such political choices: when the central bank cuts interest rates to fight a recession, it cuts everyone's interest rate at the same time. So a shift from relying on fiscal policy to relying on monetary policy makes macroeconomics a more technical, less political undertaking. In fact, as we've learned, monetary policy in most major economies is set by an independent central bank that is insulated from the political process.

Monetarism

After the publication of *A Monetary History*, Milton Friedman led a movement that sought to eliminate all forms of macroeconomic policy activism—fiscal and

Monetarism asserts that GDP will grow steadily if the money supply grows steadily.

Discretionary monetary policy is the use of changes in the interest rate or the money supply to stabilize the economy.

A **monetary policy rule** is a formula that determines the central bank's actions.

monetary. Instead, he asserted that the best way to manage the economy was with non-activist or *nondiscretionary* monetary policy. **Monetarism** asserts that GDP will grow steadily if the money supply grows steadily. According to the monetarist policy prescription, the central bank should target a constant rate of growth of the money supply, such as 3% per year, and maintain that target regardless of any fluctuations in the economy.

It's important to realize that monetarism retained many Keynesian ideas. Like Keynes, Friedman asserted that the short run is important and that short-run changes in aggregate demand affect aggregate output as well as aggregate prices. Like Keynes, he argued that macroeconomic policy should have been much more expansionary during the Great Depression, even if he believed that only monetary policy was needed.

Monetarists argued, however, that in most cases activist macroeconomic policy to smooth out the business cycle actually makes things worse. In Chapter 28 we described how lags can cause problems for *discretionary fiscal policy*. For example, a government that tries to respond to recessions by increasing spending sometimes finds that by the time it realizes that a recession is underway, takes action, and gets results, the recession is over, and the spending increase feeds a boom instead of fighting a slump. According to monetarists, **discretionary monetary policy,** changes in the interest rate or the money supply by the central bank in order to stabilize the economy, faces similar problems and can easily make the economy less stable.

Friedman also argued that if the central bank followed his advice, adopting a non-activist monetary policy and refusing to change the money supply in response to fluctuations in the economy, fiscal policy would be much less effective than Keynesians believed due to *crowding out*—when government spending crowds out private investment spending. In Chapter 25 we analyzed how this can occur: government spending leads to deficits, which drive up interest rates and reduce investment spending. Friedman and others pointed out that if the money supply is held fixed while the government pursues an expansionary fiscal policy, crowding out will occur as the interest rate rises, limiting the effect of the fiscal expansion on aggregate demand.

As already noted, Friedman didn't favor activist monetary policy either, arguing that the problems of time lags that limit the ability of discretionary fiscal policy to stabilize the economy also apply to discretionary monetary policy. Friedman's solution was to make monetary policy nondiscretionary, to put it on autopilot. The central bank, he argued, should follow a **monetary policy rule,** a formula that determines its actions and leaves it relatively little discretion. During the 1960s and 1970s, most monetarists favored a monetary policy rule of slow, steady growth in the money supply.

Monetarism strongly influenced U.S. monetary policy in the late 1970s and early 1980s as the Fed tried to keep the rate of growth in the money supply constant. It quickly became clear, however, that this didn't ensure steady growth in the economy.

Consequently, traditional monetarists—those who believe that GDP will grow steadily if the money supply grows steadily—are hard to find among today's macroeconomists. However, Friedman's argument that monetary policy can do the job of stabilizing the economy, and that fiscal policy has little role to play, became widespread among economists until it was called into question by the 2008 crisis and its aftermath.

Limits to Macroeconomic Policy: Inflation and the Natural Rate of Unemployment

The problem of time lags in the implementation of activist macroeconomic policy was not the only criticism leveled at Keynesian economics. Another serious concern arose over its effect on inflation. During the 1940s and 1950s, many Keynesian economists believed that expansionary fiscal policy could be used to achieve full employment on a permanent basis. By the 1960s, however, many economists realized that persistently expansionary policies could cause problems with inflation. Yet they still believed that governments could choose to keep unemployment low if they were willing to accept higher inflation.

In 1968, however, Milton Friedman and Edmund Phelps of Columbia University, working independently, argued that there isn't actually a long-run trade-off between unemployment and inflation. (Incidentally, Friedman made his argument in a famous 1969 presidential address to the American Economic Association—the same occasion that Olivier Blanchard used to downplay concerns about public debt 50 years later.) According to Friedman and Phelps's **natural rate hypothesis,** any attempt to keep unemployment below a minimum level would lead not just to inflation but to ever-rising inflation. The important point to recognize here is that, if true, the natural rate hypothesis implies that Keynesian policies can't accomplish as much as macroeconomists previously believed. Because the government can't keep unemployment below the natural rate, its task is not to keep unemployment low but to keep it *stable around the natural rate*—to prevent large fluctuations in unemployment above or below the natural rate.

And the natural rate hypothesis was, in fact, accepted by most economists after the 1970s. The Friedman–Phelps hypothesis made a strong prediction: that the apparent trade-off between unemployment and inflation would not survive an extended period of rising prices. Once inflation was embedded into the public's expectations, it would continue even in the face of high unemployment.

Sure enough, that's exactly what happened in the 1970s. This accurate prediction was one of the triumphs of macroeconomic analysis. It convinced the great majority of economists that the natural rate hypothesis was correct, although some macroeconomists believe that at very low rates of inflation or deflation the hypothesis doesn't work.

Rational Expectations and New Classical Economics

As we have seen, one key difference between classical economics and Keynesian economics is that classical economists believed that the short-run aggregate supply curve is vertical, while Keynesian economics claims that the aggregate supply curve slopes upward in the short run. A consequence of the upward-sloping supply curve is that demand shocks—shifts in the aggregate demand curve—cause fluctuations in aggregate output.

In the 1970s and 1980s, the classical view that shifts in the aggregate demand curve affect only the aggregate price level, not aggregate output, was revived in an approach known as **new classical macroeconomics.** It evolved in two stages. First, some economists challenged traditional arguments about the slope of the short-run aggregate supply curve based on the concept of *rational expectations.* Second, some economists suggested that changes in productivity cause economic fluctuations, a view known as *real business cycle theory.*

In the 1970s a concept known as *rational expectations* had a powerful impact on macroeconomics. **Rational expectations,** originally introduced by John Muth in 1961, claims that individuals and firms make decisions optimally, using all available information.

For example, workers and employers bargaining over long-term wage contracts need to take account of the expected inflation rate over the life of that contract. The concept of rational expectations says that in making estimates of future inflation, they won't just look at past rates of inflation; they will also take into account currently available information about monetary and fiscal policy. Suppose that prices didn't rise last year, but that the monetary and fiscal policies announced by policy makers have made it clear that there will be substantial

According to the **natural rate hypothesis,** because inflation is eventually embedded into expectations, to avoid accelerating inflation over time the unemployment rate should be kept stable around the natural rate.

New classical macroeconomics is an approach to the business cycle that returns to the classical view that shifts in the aggregate demand curve affect only the aggregate price level, not aggregate output.

The concept of **rational expectations** is the view that individuals and firms make decisions optimally, using all available information.

FOR INQUIRING MINDS   Supply-Side Economics

During the 1970s a group of economic writers began propounding what came to be known as *supply-side economics*. Proponents of this view believed that reducing tax rates, and so increasing the incentives to work and invest, would have a powerful positive effect on the growth rate of potential output. The supply-siders urged the government to cut taxes without worrying about matching spending cuts: economic growth, they argued, would offset any negative effects from budget deficits.

Some supply-siders even argued that a cut in tax *rates* would have such a miraculous effect on economic growth that tax *revenues* — the total amount taxpayers pay to the government — would actually rise. That is, some supply-siders argued that the United States was on the wrong side of the *Laffer curve,* a hypothetical relationship between tax rates and total tax revenue

that slopes upward at low tax rates but turns downward when tax rates are very high. Supply-side economics became popular with politicians, and in 1980 Ronald Reagan made supply-side economics the basis of his presidential campaign.

Because supply-side economics emphasizes supply rather than demand, and because the supply-siders are harshly critical of Keynesian economics, it would appear that it belongs in our discussion of new classical macroeconomics. But, in fact, supply-side economics is generally dismissed by economic researchers.

The main reason for this dismissal is lack of supporting evidence. Almost all economists agree that tax cuts increase incentives to work and invest. But attempts to estimate these incentive effects indicate that at current U.S. tax levels, the positive incentive effects aren't nearly strong enough

to support the strong claims made by supply-siders. In particular, the supply-side doctrine implies that large tax cuts, such as the Reagan tax cuts of the early 1980s, should sharply raise potential output, while tax hikes, like the Clinton tax hikes of 1993, should slow potential growth. Yet estimates by the Congressional Budget Office and others showed no sign of either.

Years later, in 2012, the state of Kansas provided the best evidence so far against the usefulness of supply-side economics. That year, Kansas passed large cuts in state taxes. Yet its economy tanked, with economic growth and job creation falling far below the national average, and its state deficit skyrocketed. In 2017, facing a state financial crisis and voters angry over cuts to state services, Kansas ended its experiment in supply-side economics and raised taxes.

---

inflation over the next few years. According to rational expectations, long-term wage contracts will be adjusted today to reflect this future inflation, even though prices haven't yet risen.

Adopting the premise of rational expectations can significantly alter beliefs about the effectiveness of activist macroeconomic policy. According to the original version of the natural rate hypothesis, a government attempt to persistently push the unemployment rate below the natural rate would work in the short run but will eventually fail because higher inflation will get built into expectations. According to rational expectations, we should remove the word *eventually* and replace it with *immediately:* if the government tries to lower unemployment today at the cost of higher inflation in the future, inflation will shoot up immediately without even a temporary fall in unemployment. So, under rational expectations, government intervention fails in the short run and the long run.

In the 1970s Robert Lucas of the University of Chicago used the logic of rational expectations to argue that monetary policy can change the level of output and unemployment only if it comes as a surprise to the public. In 1995 Lucas won the Nobel Prize in economics for this work, which remains widely admired. However, many — perhaps most — macroeconomists, especially those advising policy makers, now believe that his conclusions were overstated. The Federal Reserve certainly thinks that it can play a useful role in economic stabilization.

Why, in the view of many macroeconomists, doesn't Lucas's **rational expectations model** of macroeconomics accurately describe how the economy actually behaves? **New Keynesian economics,** a set of ideas that became influential in the 1990s, provides an explanation. It argues that market imperfections interact to make many prices in the economy temporarily sticky. And with sticky prices, expected inflation can't rise quickly enough to offset activist macroeconomic policy.

Over time, new Keynesian ideas combined with actual experience have reduced the practical influence of the rational expectations concept. However, some macroeconomists went even further than Lucas, arguing that demand shocks play no role in recessions. In the 1980s, a number of economists argued that slowdowns in productivity growth, which they attributed to pauses in technological progress, are the main cause of recessions. **Real business cycle theory**

According to the **rational expectations model** of the economy, expected changes in monetary policy have no effect on unemployment and output and only affect the price level.

According to **new Keynesian economics,** market imperfections can lead to price stickiness for the economy as a whole.

Real business cycle theory claims that fluctuations in the rate of growth of total factor productivity cause the business cycle.

claims that fluctuations in the rate of growth of productivity cause the business cycle.

This theory was strongly influential for some years, reflected by the fact that two of the founders of real business cycle theory, Finn Kydland of Carnegie Mellon University and Edward Prescott of the Federal Reserve Bank of Minneapolis, won the 2004 Nobel Prize in economics. The current status of real business cycle theory, however, is similar to that of rational expectations. It is widely recognized for making a valuable contribution to our understanding of the economy, and for cautioning against an overemphasis on aggregate demand.

But many of the real business cycle theorists themselves now acknowledge that the actual economic data indicate that their models need an upward-sloping aggregate supply curve—and that this gives aggregate demand a potential role in determining aggregate output.

A **political business cycle** results when politicians use macroeconomic policy to serve political ends.

The Political Business Cycle

One final challenge to Keynesian economics focused not on the validity of the economic analysis but on its political consequences. A number of economists and political scientists pointed out that activist macroeconomic policy lends itself to political manipulation.

Statistical evidence suggests that election results are strongly affected by the state of the economy in the months just before the election. In the United States, if the economy is growing rapidly and the unemployment rate is falling in the six months or so before Election Day, the incumbent party tends to be reelected even if the economy performed poorly in the preceding three years. This creates an obvious temptation to abuse activist macroeconomic policy: pump up the economy in an election year, and pay the price in higher inflation and/or higher unemployment later. The consequence will be unnecessary instability in the economy, a **political business cycle** caused by the use of macroeconomic policy to serve political ends.

An often-cited example is the combination of expansionary fiscal and monetary policy that led to rapid growth in the U.S. economy just before the 1972 election and a sharp acceleration in inflation after the election. Kenneth Rogoff, a highly respected macroeconomist who served as chief economist at the International Monetary Fund, has proclaimed Richard Nixon, the president at the time, "the all-time hero of political business cycles."

As we've learned, one way to avoid a political business cycle is to place monetary policy in the hands of an independent central bank, insulated from political pressure. The political business cycle is also a reason to limit the use of discretionary fiscal policy to extreme circumstances like a liquidity trap.

Carsten Reisinger/Shutterstock

AWesleyFloyd/Shutterstock

Political manipulation in order to win votes is a danger of activist macroeconomic policy.

ECONOMICS >> *in Action*
Did the Fed Cause the Great Depression?

The Great Depression gave birth to Keynesian economics and convinced most economists of the need for activist macroeconomic policy. But Friedman and Schwartz's influential *A Monetary History* argued that the Federal Reserve could have prevented the Great Depression if only it had done its job. Some of Milton Friedman's later writings strengthen this view and claim the Fed *caused* the depression.

Did the Fed, in fact, cause the Great Depression or at least allow it to happen through negligence?

The case against the Fed rests largely on the fact that the overall money supply, as measured by M2, fell sharply from 1929 to 1933 as the economy plunged. This monetary contraction is shown in Figure 32-3, where M2 is shown as an index with 1929 = 100. The Friedman–Schwartz view was that the Fed could have prevented the fall in M2 and hence stopped the depression from happening.

FIGURE 32-3 Monetary Policy During the Great Depression

During the Great Depression the Federal Reserve increased the monetary base by over 50% but the overall money supply, measured by M2, declined by 30% before stabilizing in 1933 and slightly increasing in 1934 and 1935. Most economists believe the divergence in M2 and the monetary base stemmed from the widespread bank failures.

Data from: Friedman, Milton, and Anna Jacobson Schwartz. (1970). "Monetary Statistics of the United States: Estimates, Sources, Methods."

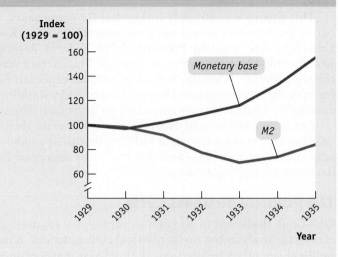

However, the Fed doesn't directly control monetary aggregates like M2, which consist mainly of bank deposits. What the Fed controls directly is the monetary base—currency in circulation plus bank reserves. And as Figure 32-3 also shows, the monetary base actually rose sharply in the early years of the Great Depression.

Why did M2 fall so much even though the monetary base was rising? The main explanation was that a wave of bank runs destroyed confidence in banks' safety: many people chose to convert their deposits into currency, and surviving banks cut back on lending, accumulating reserves instead, so that they would have cash on hand in the event of a run.

Under these conditions, it's not at all clear that the Fed could have prevented the plunge in M2. Interest rates were very low, giving banks little incentive to lend, so even if the Fed had engaged in large open-market operations, adding to bank reserves, the money might well have just sat there.

In fact, that's what happened after the 2008 financial crisis, when the Fed massively increased the monetary base but saw only a small rise in M2.

In short, it's doubtful whether the Fed could have prevented the Great Depression, and it certainly didn't cause it.

>> Check Your Understanding 32-2

Solutions appear at back of book.

1. What are the limits of macroeconomic policy activism?

2. Starting in 2008, as the economy entered the Great Recession, unemployment soared while interest rates and investment spending fell sharply. The Fed accelerated the growth of the monetary base in response.
   a. Do you think Milton Friedman would have agreed with the Fed's policy?
   b. Monetarists, like Friedman, generally believe that discretionary monetary policy and fiscal policy are ineffective. Do you think their objections to fiscal and monetary policy were valid during the Great Recession? Note that unemployment did not return to its pre-recession level until 2016.

3. In late 2008, as it became clear that the United States was experiencing a recession, the Fed reduced its target for the federal funds rate to near zero, as part of a larger aggressively expansionary monetary policy stance (including what the Fed called *quantitative easing*). Most observers agreed that the Fed's aggressive monetary expansion helped reduce the length and severity of the Great Recession.
   a. What would rational expectations theorists say about this conclusion?
   b. What would real business cycle theorists say?

From Great Moderation to Secular Stagnation

The 1970s and the first half of the 1980s were a stormy period for the U.S. economy (and for other major economies, too). There was a severe recession in 1974–1975, then two back-to-back recessions in 1979–1982 that sent the unemployment rate to almost 11%. At the same time, the inflation rate soared into double digits—and then plunged. As we have seen, these events left a strong mark on macroeconomic thought.

After about 1985, however, the economy settled down. The recession of 1990–1991 was much milder than the 1974–1975 recession or the double-dip slump from 1979 to 1982, and the inflation rate generally stayed below 4%. The period of relative calm in the economy from 1985 to 2007 came to be known as the **Great Moderation.** And the calmness of the economy was to a large extent marked by a similar calm in macroeconomic policy discussion. In fact, it seemed that a broad consensus had emerged about several key macroeconomic issues.

To tackle the Great Recession, policy makers were able to use the macroeconomic tools that evolved from the experience of the Great Depression.

However, the global financial crisis of 2008 and its aftermath undermined any sense that policy makers had things under control, and also led to a rethinking of macroeconomic policy—a rethinking that in some ways brought macroeconomists back to a more traditional Keynesian view.

> The **Great Moderation** is the period from 1985 to 2007 when the U.S. economy experienced relatively small fluctuations and low inflation. It led to widespread belief that monetary policy could stabilize the economy.

The Limits of Monetary Policy

In the end, Milton Friedman was unable to convince policy makers that monetarism was a good idea—simply ensuring that the money supply was growing at a steady rate was not enough to stabilize the economy. During the Great Moderation, however, both economists and policy makers generally believed that monetary policy in general was highly effective, and that apolitical technocrats at the Fed and other central banks could do the job of stabilizing the economy.

Events since 2008 have, however, undermined confidence in the ability of central bankers to keep the economy on an even keel. Figure 32-4, which shows the federal funds rate since the beginning of the Great Moderation, illustrates the

---

FIGURE 32-4 Monetary Policy in Recent Recessions

The Federal Reserve responds actively to economic downturns. During each of these four recessions, the Federal Reserve acted quickly to cut interest rates.

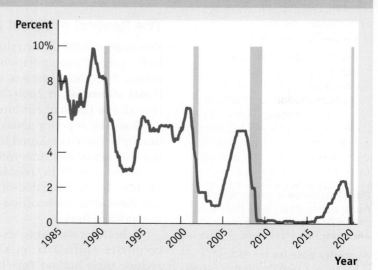

Data from: Federal Reserve Bank of St. Louis.

FIGURE 32-5 Big Money, Small Inflation in the United States, 2007–2020

Quantitative easing led to a huge rise in the U.S. monetary base after the Great Recession, and some economists warned that this would in turn lead to high inflation. The Fed, however, argued that inflation risks were low, and, as you can see from the figure, was vindicated by events: the consumer price index stayed virtually flat, reflecting a very low inflation rate from 2008 onward.

Data from: Federal Reserve Bank of St. Louis.

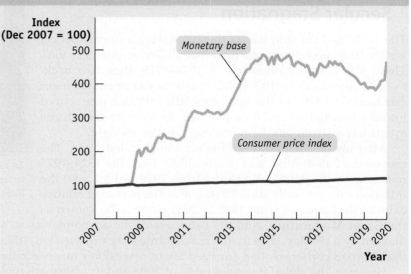

---

problem. Normal monetary policy involves raising or lowering the federal funds rate through open-market operations, and the Fed has in fact cut that rate by about 5 percentage points each time recession has struck.

In 2008, however, cutting the federal funds rate all the way to zero wasn't enough to prevent a severe recession—and recovery from that recession was disappointingly slow. In other words, conventional monetary policy didn't seem up to the job it was supposed to do.

In fact, even unconventional monetary policy seemed to fall short. Normally the Fed only buys short-term government debt. In 2010, however, it tried to boost the economy by buying other assets, including long-term government debt and the debt of government agencies that lend money to home-buyers. As Figure 32-5 shows, this program, generally referred to as *quantitative easing*, led to a huge increase in the monetary base.

Some critics warned that the surge in the monetary base would lead to high inflation. As Figure 32-5 also shows, this didn't happen. On the other hand, it didn't lead to an economic boom either. Fed officials believe that the program had some positive effects, but if so, they weren't dramatic.

The Revival of Fiscal Policy

Events after 2008 showed that monetary policy wasn't as reliable a recession-fighting tool as many economists had believed. This led to a revival of interest in fiscal policy. The United States engaged in significant expansionary fiscal policy, or **fiscal stimulus,** in 2009–2010, because the economy was still contracting even though the Fed had cut interest rates all the way to zero.

Does fiscal policy actually work? Some observers pointed to the fact that U.S. unemployment remained high after the 2009 stimulus as evidence that it doesn't, but this argument runs into the problem that the stimulus was a response to an economy already in trouble. Consider an analogy with visits to the doctor: people tend to see their doctor when they get sick, and many of them are still sick a few days after their office visit. You wouldn't want to cite this as evidence that doctors are useless.

A better test came over the period from 2010–2013, when a number of countries shifted from stimulus to harsh **austerity policies**—attempts to reduce their budget deficits by cutting spending and raising taxes. These policies were largely inspired by events in Greece, which saw interest rates soar

Fiscal stimulus is expansionary fiscal policy that takes the form of temporary spending measures and temporary tax cuts.

Austerity policies try to limit government borrowing by cutting spending and raising taxes.

in 2010 as investors lost confidence in the Greek government's ability to pay its debts.

Fearing a similar fate, many countries, including the United States, engaged in fiscal austerity, but the degree of austerity varied a great deal from country to country. For example, Spain imposed budget cuts equal to around 8% of GDP, while Belgium, which actually had a higher level of debt relative to GDP, imposed almost no cuts.

An influential study from the International Monetary Fund showed a strong correlation between budget cuts and economic growth compared with earlier forecasts: the deeper the budget cuts, the worse the economic performance. Indeed, each dollar of budget cuts seemed to reduce GDP by around $1.50. Together with other evidence, this experience convinced many economists that fiscal policy does indeed have strong effects in a world of low interest rates, with little evidence of crowding out.

As a result, macroeconomists have a much stronger interest in fiscal policy as a tool for stabilizing the economy than they did during the Great Moderation.

Expansionary fiscal policy, however, means higher budget deficits. Shouldn't this be a source of concern? The answer, as we suggested in this chapter's opening story, is that many (though not all) macroeconomists have become less concerned about debt than they once were. This reduced concern has a lot to do with the same phenomenon that has reduced confidence in the effectiveness of monetary policy: persistently low interest rates.

Policy in a Low-Interest-Rate World

We saw in Figure 32-4 that the Fed cut interest rates all the way to zero in the face of the 2008 financial crisis, and found that even this wasn't enough to avoid a severe recession followed by a sluggish recovery. At first, however, most economists—and Federal Reserve officials—believed that the Fed would be able to raise interest rates to historically normal levels once the crisis had passed. But as you can also see in Figure 32-4, the Fed ended up keeping rates close to zero for multiple years, then raised them only slightly, and began cutting again in 2019 amid signs of economic weakness. The coronavirus pandemic forced the Fed to return to their zero interest rate policy.

The persistence of low interest rates wasn't just a U.S. phenomenon. Figure 32-6 shows 10-year interest rates, which are often used as an indicator of long-term

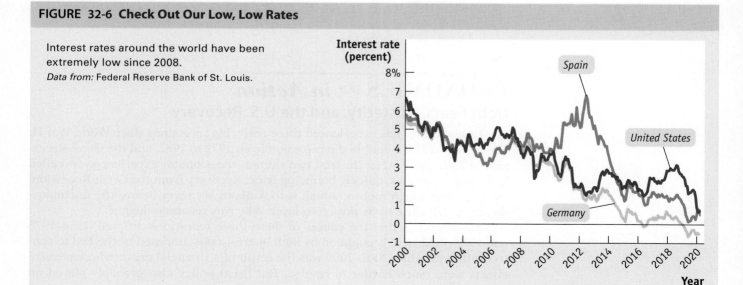

FIGURE 32-6 Check Out Our Low, Low Rates

Interest rates around the world have been extremely low since 2008.

Data from: Federal Reserve Bank of St. Louis.

Secular stagnation occurs when the interest rate that is needed to achieve full employment is consistently below zero.

borrowing costs, for three countries since 2000: the United States, Germany, and Spain. As you can see, interest rates in both the United States and Germany have been on a declining trend—in Germany they're actually negative. Spain saw a temporary rise in rates after the Greek debt crisis caused a panic about other European nations' debt, but the panic soon subsided and by early 2016 Spain's borrowing costs were even lower than those of the United States.

Why have interest rates fallen so much and so persistently? A number of economists, invoking a concept from the 1930s, suggest that underlying factors such as declining population growth and, perhaps, a slowdown in technological progress had put the world's major economies in or on the edge of **secular stagnation,** a state in which the interest rate that is needed to achieve full employment is consistently close to zero.

If very low interest rates are the new normal, as they appear to be, this has two major consequences for economic policy: we shouldn't worry much about debt, and we should worry a lot about fiscal responses to downturns.

We began this chapter by talking about Olivier Blanchard's presidential address to the American Economic Association, in which he argued that fears about debt have been overstated. Low interest rates were central to his argument.

In the past, he noted, people have worried that debt might snowball over time, as interest payments on debt lead to higher deficits, which increase debt, leading to higher interest payments, and so on. As Blanchard noted, however, what matters for the economy is not the absolute size of the debt but the ratio of debt to GDP. And in recent decades interest rates have been well below the economy's growth rate. What this means is that instead of feeding on itself, a high ratio of debt to GDP tends to shrink over time unless the government runs a large non-interest-rate deficit. You might say, we don't need to worry about snowballing debt because the snowball tends to melt.

Indeed, there may be a good case for increasing government debt through further borrowing, if the borrowing is used to pay for things like infrastructure that will strengthen the economy in the future.

At the same time, an economy in which interest rates are persistently low is also an economy in which even medium-size adverse shocks may be too big to offset with monetary policy, simply because the Fed and its counterparts don't have enough room to cut. This suggests that we should strengthen the economy's *automatic stabilizers,* the tax and spending responses that help fight recessions even without new legislation. Some economists also argue that a moderate degree of persistent deficit spending may be a good thing, especially if it involves public investment, because it means that some fiscal stimulus is already in place.

ECONOMICS >> *in Action*
Debt Fears, Austerity, and the U.S. Recovery

The United States has experienced three really big recessions since World War II: one in 1974–1975, a double-dip recession from 1979 to 1982, and the Great Recession of 2007–2009. After the first two slumps, the economy experienced so-called V-shaped recoveries, quickly bouncing back. Recovery from the Great Recession, however, was much more gradual; it took about six years before the unemployment rate fell close to its pre-crisis level. Why was recovery sluggish?

One answer is that the causes of these three recessions differed: 1974–1975 and 1979–1982 were brought on by high interest rates, imposed by the Fed to control inflation, while 2007–2009 was the result of a financial crisis, whose adverse effects were much harder to reverse. But fiscal policy also probably played an important role.

FIGURE 32-7 Austerity, American Style

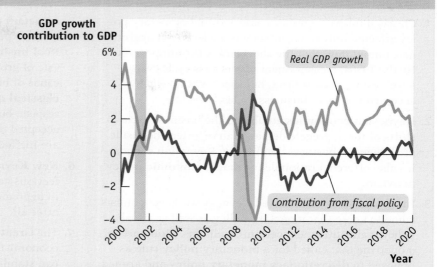

Persistent cuts in government spending after 2011 may have delayed U.S. recovery from the Great Recession.

Data from: Federal Reserve Bank of St. Louis; Hutchins Center on Fiscal and Monetary Policy.

True, the U.S. government enacted a major fiscal stimulus in 2009. But the effects of that stimulus began to fade out in late 2010. And by that time much of Washington's political establishment had decided that public debt was a major danger—that the Greek crisis was a warning to everyone—and began pushing for fiscal austerity in the form of spending cuts.

U.S. fiscal austerity was never as extreme as austerity in, say, Spain, let alone Greece. But it was significant. The Hutchins Center at Washington's Brookings Institution provides regular estimates of what it calls its "fiscal impact measure," which "shows how much local, state, and federal tax and spending policy adds to or subtracts from overall economic growth." Figure 32-7 shows this measure along with real GDP growth over the past 20 years. According to this estimate, austerity imposed a steady, significant drag on economic growth from early 2011 through 2015.

How much difference did this drag make to the pace of recovery? If the Hutchins estimate is correct, without austerity the United States might well have experienced a full recovery, with unemployment falling below 5%, by some time in 2012.

So the United States seems to have paid a large price for austerity imposed in the name of limiting government debt. If economists who now say that debt fears were overblown are right, this was a huge policy mistake.

>> Check Your Understanding 32-3

Solutions appear at back of book.

1. Why did the Great Recession lead to the decline of the Great Moderation consensus? What is the current state of consensus among most economists?

2. Why was there such a fierce debate over both the Fed's unconventional monetary policy and the appropriate level of the Fed's inflation target?

>> Quick Review

• The **Great Moderation,** the period of economic calm from 1985 to 2007, led many economists to believe that monetary policy was sufficient to stabilize the economy. However, the 2008 financial crisis, in which the Fed cut rates to zero and even this wasn't enough to prevent a severe recession, undermined this belief.

• The appearance of limits to monetary policy led to renewed interest in fiscal policy, with a temporary turn to **fiscal stimulus** to fight the Great Recession. However, concerns about government debt led many countries to reverse this policy from 2010 onward, engaging in **austerity policies** instead. The adverse effects of austerity on growth, somewhat ironically, showed that fiscal policy is effective.

• Interest rates have remained very low since the 2008 financial crisis. Some economists believe that we are suffering from **secular stagnation:** declining population growth and slower technological progress led to a state of persistent economic weakness.

• In a low-interest-rate world, former concerns about government debt appear to have been overstated, and there is a much stronger case for fiscal stimulus, especially to fight recessions, but possibly even in normal times.

1. Classical macroeconomics asserted that monetary policy affected only the aggregate price level, not aggregate output, and that the short run was unimportant. By the 1930s, measurement of business cycles was a well-established subject, but there was no widely accepted theory of business cycles.

2. **Keynesian economics** attributed the business cycle to shifts of the aggregate demand curve, often the result of changes in business confidence. Keynesian economics also offered a rationale for **macroeconomic policy activism.**

3. In the decades that followed Keynes's work, economists came to agree that monetary policy as well as fiscal policy is effective under certain conditions. **Monetarism,** a doctrine that called for a **monetary policy rule** as opposed to **discretionary monetary policy** and argued for steady growth in the money supply, was influential for a time but was eventually rejected by many macroeconomists.

4. The **natural rate hypothesis** became almost universally accepted, limiting the role of macroeconomic policy to stabilizing the economy rather than seeking a permanently lower unemployment rate. Fears of a **political business cycle** led to a consensus that monetary policy should be insulated from politics.

5. The concept of **rational expectations** claims that individuals and firms make decisions using all available information. According to the **rational expectations model** of the economy, only unexpected changes in monetary policy affect aggregate output and employment; expected changes merely alter the price level. **Real business cycle theory** claims that changes in the rate of growth of total factor productivity are the main cause of business cycles. Both of these versions of **new classical macroeconomics** received wide attention and respect, but policy makers and many economists haven't accepted the conclusion that monetary and fiscal policy are ineffective in changing aggregate output.

6. **New Keynesian economics** argues that market imperfections can lead to price stickiness, so that changes in aggregate demand have effects on aggregate output after all.

7. The **Great Moderation** from 1985 to 2007 made many economists confident that monetary policy alone can stabilize the economy. But the Great Recession revealed the limits to monetary policy and the potential usefulness of **fiscal stimulus.** On the other hand, after the Greek debt crisis many countries, worried about their levels of government debt, turned to **austerity policies** that appear to have hurt growth and delayed recovery.

8. The persistence of very low interest rates has led to concerns that we face **secular stagnation:** declining population growth and a slowdown in technological progress lead to a state of persistent economic weakness. In any case, low interest rates suggest that governments should focus less on debt, and perhaps engage in more deficit spending.

KEY TERMS

Keynesian economics, p. 946
Macroeconomic policy activism, p. 947
Monetarism, p. 950
Discretionary monetary policy, p. 950
Monetary policy rule, p. 950
Natural rate hypothesis, p. 951

New classical macroeconomics, p. 951
Rational expectations, p. 951
Rational expectations model, p. 952
New Keynesian economics, p. 952
Real business cycle theory, p. 952
Political business cycle, p. 953

Great Moderation, p. 955
Fiscal stimulus, p. 956
Austerity policies, p. 956
Secular stagnation, p. 958

PRACTICE QUESTIONS

1. Figure 32-1 highlights the differences in the *SRAS* for classical and Keynesian economists. What would the different *SRAS* imply about the Phillips curve? Following the Great Recession most research has found a "flattening of the Phillips curve": what does this imply about the two schools of thought?

2. "We are all Keynesians now," is a quote that is often attributed to President Richard Nixon. While the origins of the exact quote remain up for debate, how does this quote, in terms to fiscal stimulus and austerity policies, apply to the lesson we've learned following the Great Recession and the economic shutdown tied to the coronavirus pandemic?

3. At the start of the economic shutdown tied to the coronavirus pandemic, the Congressional Budget Office projected the federal debt to GDP ratio would reach 108% by the end of 2021, an increase of 26 percentage points from their previous projection. Going forward, what lessons can be applied from the record-level debt following World War II? What are the primary factors that will determine if debt snowballs out of control or will slowly melt?

PROBLEMS

1. Since the crash of its stock market in 1989, the Japanese economy has seen little economic growth and some deflation. The accompanying table from the Organization for Economic Cooperation and Development (OECD) shows some key macroeconomic data for Japan for 1991 (a "normal" year) and 1995–2003.

   a. From the data, determine the type of policies Japan's policy makers undertook at that time to promote growth.

   b. We can safely consider a short-term interest rate that is less than 0.1% to effectively be a 0% interest rate. What is this situation called? What does it imply about the effectiveness of monetary policy? Of fiscal policy?

Year	Real GDP annual growth rate	Short-term interest rate	Government debt (percent of GDP)	Government budget deficit (percent of GDP)
1991	3.4%	7.38%	64.8%	−1.81%
1995	1.9	1.23	87.1	4.71
1996	3.4	0.59	93.9	5.07
1997	1.9	0.60	100.3	3.79
1998	−1.1	0.72	112.2	5.51
1999	0.1	0.25	125.7	7.23
2000	2.8	0.25	134.1	7.48
2001	0.4	0.12	142.3	6.13
2002	−0.3	0.06	149.3	7.88
2003	2.5	0.04	157.5	7.67

2. The National Bureau of Economic Research (NBER) maintains the official chronology of past U.S. business cycles. Go to its website at www.nber .org/cycles/cyclesmain.html to answer the following questions.

   a. How many business cycles have occurred since the end of World War II in 1945?

   b. What was the average duration of a business cycle when measured from the end of one expansion (its peak) to the end of the next? That is, what was the average duration of a business cycle in the period from 1945 to 2009?

   c. When was the last announcement by the NBER's Business Cycle Dating Committee, and what was it?

3. The fall of its military rival, the Soviet Union, in 1989 allowed the United States to significantly reduce its defense spending in subsequent years. Using the data in the following table from the Economic Report of the President, replicate Figure 32-2 for the 1990–2000 period. Given the strong economic growth in the United States during the late 1990s, why would a Keynesian see the reduction in defense spending during the 1990s as a good thing?

Year	Budget deficit (percent of GDP)	Unemployment rate
1990	3.9%	5.6%
1991	4.5	6.8
1992	4.7	7.5
1993	3.9	6.9
1994	2.9	6.1
1995	2.2	5.6
1996	1.4	5.4
1997	0.3	4.9
1998	−0.8	4.5
1999	−1.4	4.2
2000	−2.4	4.0

4. In the modern world, central banks are free to increase or reduce the money supply as they see fit. However, some people harken back to the "good old days" of the gold standard. Under the gold standard, the money supply could expand only when the amount of available gold increased.

   a. Under the gold standard, if a growing economy led to a rising demand for money, what would have had to happen to keep prices stable?

   b. Why would modern macroeconomists consider the gold standard a bad idea?

5. The chapter notes that Kenneth Rogoff proclaimed Richard Nixon "the all-time hero of political business cycles." Using the following table of data from the Economic Report of the President, explain why Nixon may have earned that title. (*Note:* Nixon entered office in January 1969 and was reelected in November 1972. He resigned in August 1974.)

Year	Government receipts (billions of dollars)	Government spending (billions of dollars)	Government budget balance (billions of dollars)	M1 growth	M2 growth	3-month Treasury bill rate
1969	$186.9	$183.6	$3.2	3.3%	3.7%	6.68%
1970	192.8	195.6	−2.8	5.1	6.6	6.46
1971	187.1	210.2	−23.0	6.5	13.4	4.35
1972	207.3	230.7	−23.4	9.2	13.0	4.07
1973	230.8	245.7	−14.9	5.5	6.6	7.04

6. The economy of Albernia is facing a recessionary gap, and the leader of that nation calls together its best economists representing the classical, Keynesian, monetarist, real business cycle, Great Moderation consensus, expansionary austerity, and secular stagnationist views of the macroeconomy. Explain what policies each economist would recommend and why.

7. Which of the following policy recommendations are consistent with the classical, Keynesian, monetarist, and/or Great Moderation view, versus secular stagnationist views of the macroeconomy?

   a. Since the long-run growth of GDP is 2%, the money supply should grow at 2%.

   b. Decrease government spending in order to decrease inflationary pressure.

   c. Increase the money supply in order to alleviate a recessionary gap.

   d. Always maintain a balanced budget.

   e. Decrease the budget deficit as a percent of GDP when facing a recessionary gap.

   f. Pursue large, expansionary fiscal policies during a liquidity trap.

8. Using a graph of *AD/AS* and money supply and money demand, show how a monetarist can argue that a contractionary fiscal policy need not lead to a fall in real GDP given a fixed money supply. Explain.

9. In response to the Great Recession, the Federal Reserve took drastic and largely untested measures to stabilize both the financial system and the macroeconomy. These measures caused the monetary base to increase from approximately $850 billion to over $4 trillion. What would an economist from each of the following viewpoints—classical, Keynesian, monetarist, real business cycle, Great Moderation consensus, and secular stagnationists—predict about the effect of these policies, and why? Indicate whether each school would support the Fed's actions.

33 > International Macroeconomics

SWITZERLAND DOESN'T WANT YOUR MONEY

PARKING YOUR MONEY in a Swiss bank is no way to get rich, given the low interest rates Swiss bankers offer. Since 2013, in fact, Swiss banks have paid negative interest on deposits, charging customers for the service of keeping their funds.

But for generations, Swiss bank accounts have been seen as a way to *stay* rich, a safe place to store your wealth. In the troubled years that followed the 2008 financial crisis, the Swiss reputation for safety became especially important. European investors, in particular, poured enormous sums of money into Swiss banks.

And the Swiss hated it. The inflow of foreign funds led to a surge in the value of the Swiss franc that wreaked havoc with Swiss exports.

At the beginning of 2008, one Swiss franc traded for about 0.6 euro. By mid-2011, the franc was trading for around 0.9 euro, a 50% appreciation. That meant that Swiss exporters, other things equal, had seen a 50% rise in their labor costs relative to competitors elsewhere in Europe. Thanks to its reputation for quality, Switzerland has been remarkably successful over the years at selling goods to the world market, despite high labor costs. Nobody expects to get a bargain on Swiss watches or Swiss chocolate. But a 50% appreciation of the Swiss franc pushed Swiss exporters to the breaking point.

So what was to be done? Starting in early 2009, the Swiss National Bank, Switzerland's equivalent of the Federal Reserve, began selling Swiss francs on the foreign exchange market in an attempt to hold down their value. In return, the Swiss National Bank received other currencies, mainly dollars and euros, which it added to its reserves. We're talking about a *lot* of sales: over a period of 2 ½ years, the bank added $180 billion to its foreign exchange reserves, equal to a third of Switzerland's GDP — the equivalent for the United States of selling $5 trillion.

Yet even that wasn't enough to stop the Swiss franc's rise. In September 2011, as the franc seemed headed for a value of 1 euro or more, the Swiss National Bank announced that it would do whatever it took — that is, sell an unlimited amount of francs — to keep the franc below a maximum of 0.833 euro per franc. That announcement finally seemed to halt the franc's rise.

What the extraordinary efforts of the Swiss National Bank illustrated was the importance of a dimension of macroeconomics that we haven't emphasized so far — the fact that modern national economies trade large quantities of goods, services, and assets with the rest of the world. *International macroeconomics* is a branch of macroeconomics that deals with the relationships between national economies (it is sometimes referred to as *open-economy macroeconomics*). As the Swiss story illustrates, economic interactions with the rest of the world can have a profound impact on a domestic economy.

In this chapter we'll learn about some of the key issues in international macroeconomics: the determinants of a country's *balance of payments*, the factors affecting *exchange rates*, the different forms of *exchange rate policy* adopted by various countries, and the relationship between exchange rates and macroeconomic policy. •

The Swiss National Bank undertook extraordinary actions to protect the Swiss economy from massive inflows of foreign money.

Prisma by Dukas Presseagentur GmbH/Alamy

WHAT YOU WILL LEARN

- What are the **balance of payments accounts?**
- What determines international capital flows?
- What roles do the **foreign exchange market** and the **exchange rate** play?
- How do **real exchange rates** affect the **current account?**
- Why do countries choose different **exchange rate regimes,** such as **fixed exchange rates** and **floating exchange rates?**
- How should domestic macroeconomic policy be adjusted as a consequence of international economic considerations?

A country's **balance of payments accounts** are a summary of the country's transactions with other countries for a given year.

‖ Capital Flows and the Balance of Payments

In 2020 people living in the United States sold trillions of dollars' worth of stuff to people living in other countries and bought trillions of dollars' worth of stuff in return. What kind of stuff? All kinds. Residents of the United States (including firms operating in the United States) sold airplanes, bonds, software licenses, wheat, and many other items to residents of other countries. U.S. residents bought cars, stocks, oil, and many other items from residents of other countries.

How can we keep track of these transactions? In Chapter 22 we learned that economists keep track of the domestic economy using the national income and product accounts. Economists keep track of international transactions using a different but related set of numbers, the *balance of payments accounts*.

Balance of Payments Accounts

A country's **balance of payments accounts** are a summary of the country's transactions with other countries for a given year.

To understand the basic idea behind the balance of payments accounts, let's consider a small-scale example: not a country, but a family farm. Let's say that we know the following about how last year went financially for the Costas, who own a small artichoke farm in California:

- They made $100,000 by selling artichokes.
- They spent $70,000 on running the farm, including purchases of new farm machinery, and another $40,000 buying food, paying utility bills, replacing their worn-out car, and so on.
- They received $500 in interest on their bank account but paid $10,000 in interest on their mortgage.
- They took out a new $25,000 loan to help pay for farm improvements but didn't use all the money immediately. So they put the remaining $5,500 in the bank.

TABLE 33-1 The Costas' Financial Year

	Sources of cash	Uses of cash	Net
Sales and purchases of goods and services	Artichoke sales: $100,000	Farm operation and living expenses: $110,000	–$10,000
Interest payments	Interest received on bank account: $500	Interest paid on mortgage: $10,000	–$9,500
Loans and deposits	Funds received from new loan: $25,000	Funds deposited in bank: $5,500	+$19,500
Total	$125,500	$125,500	$0

How could we summarize the Costas' transactions for the year? One way would be with a table like Table 33-1, which shows sources of cash coming in and uses of cash going out, characterized under a few broad headings. The first row of Table 33-1 shows sales and purchases of goods and services: sales of artichokes; purchases of groceries, heating oil, that new car, and so on. The second row shows interest payments: the interest the Costas received from their bank account and the interest they paid on their mortgage. The third row shows loans and deposits: cash coming in from a loan and cash deposited in the bank.

In each row we show the net inflow of cash from that type of transaction. So the net in the first row is –$10,000, because the Costas spent $10,000 more than they earned. The net in the second row is –$9,500, the difference between the interest the Costas received on their bank account and the interest they paid on the mortgage. The net in the third row is $19,500: the Costas brought in $25,000 with their new loan but put only $5,500 of that sum in the bank.

The last row shows the sum of cash coming in from all sources and the sum of all cash used. These sums are equal, by definition: every dollar has a source, and every dollar received gets used somewhere. (What if the Costas hid money under the mattress? Then that would be counted as another "use" of cash.)

A country's balance of payments accounts is a table that summarizes the country's transactions with the rest of the world for a given year in a manner very similar to the way we just summarized the Costas' financial year.

Table 33-2 shows a simplified version of the U.S. balance of payments accounts for 2019. Where the Costas family's accounts show sources and uses of cash, a country's balance of payments accounts show payments from foreigners—sources of cash for the United States as a whole—and payments to foreigners—uses of cash for the United States as a whole.

Row 1 of Table 33-2 shows payments that arise from U.S. sales to foreigners and U.S. purchases from foreigners of goods and services in 2019. For example, the number in the second column of row 1, $2,498 billion, incorporates items such as the value of U.S. wheat exports and the fees foreigners paid to U.S. consulting companies in 2019. The number in the third column of row 1, $3,114 billion, incorporates items such as the value of U.S. oil imports and the fees U.S. companies paid to Indian call centers—the people who often answer your 1-800 calls—in 2019.

Row 2 shows U.S. *factor income* in 2019—the income that foreigners paid to U.S. residents for the use of U.S.-owned factors of production, as well as income paid by Americans to foreigners for the use of foreign-owned factors of production. Factor income mostly consists of investment income, such as interest paid by Americans on loans from overseas, profits of U.S.-owned corporations that operate overseas, and the like. For example, the profits earned by Disneyland Paris, which is owned by the U.S.-based Walt Disney Company, are included in the $1,123 billion figure in the second column of row 2. The profits earned by the U.S. operations of Japanese auto companies are included in the $866 billion figure shown in the third column of row 2. Factor income also includes some labor income. For example, the wages of an American engineer who worked temporarily on a construction site in Dubai are counted in the $1,123 billion figure in the second column.

Row 3 shows *international transfers* for the United States in 2019—funds sent by U.S. residents to residents of other countries and vice versa. The figure in the second column of row 3, $143 billion, includes payments sent home by skilled U.S. workers who work abroad. The third column accounts for the major portion of international transfers. That figure, $282 billion, is composed mainly of remittances that immigrants who reside in the United States, such as the millions of Mexican-born workers employed in the United States, send to their families in their country of origin.

Row 4 of the table shows net payments accruing from sales and purchases of assets between U.S. residents and foreigners in 2019. Such payments involve a wide variety of transactions, from Chinese companies purchasing U.S. firms to U.S. purchases of European stocks and bonds. The details of these transactions are complex, and if you add up all purchases the value is very large, which is why we focus only on the net value. Overall, according to official figures, and as you can see in the table, U.S. residents sold $357 billion more in assets than they purchased.

In laying out Table 33-2, we have separated rows 1, 2, and 3 into one group, to distinguish them from row 4, reflecting a fundamental difference in how these two groups of transactions affect the future. When a U.S. resident sells a good such as wheat to a foreigner, that's the end of the transaction. But a financial asset, such as a bond, is different: it is a promise to pay interest and principal in the future. So when a U.S. resident sells a bond to a foreigner, that sale creates a liability: the U.S. resident will have to pay interest and repay principal in the future. The balance of payments accounts distinguish between transactions that don't create liabilities and those that do.

TABLE 33-2 The U.S. Balance of Payments in 2019 (billions of dollars)

		Payments from foreigners	Payments to foreigners	Net
1	Sales and purchases of goods and services	$2,498	$3,114	−$616
2	Factor income	1,123	866	257
3	Transfers	143	282	−139
	Current account (1 + 2 + 3)			**−498**
4	Asset sales and purchases (financial account)	784	427	357
	Financial account (4)			**357**
	Statistical discrepancy	—	—	**−141**

Data from: Bureau of Economic Analysis.

A country's **balance of payments on current account,** or **current account,** is its balance of payments on goods and services plus net international transfer payments and factor income.

A country's **balance of payments on goods and services** is the difference between its exports and its imports during a given period.

The **merchandise trade balance,** or **trade balance,** is the difference between a country's exports and imports of goods.

A country's **balance of payments on financial account,** or simply its **financial account,** is the difference between its sales of assets to foreigners and its purchases of assets from foreigners for a given period.

Transactions that don't create liabilities are considered part of the **balance of payments on current account,** often referred to simply as the **current account:** the balance of payments on goods and services plus net international transfer payments and factor income. This corresponds to rows 1, 2, and 3 in Table 33-2. In practice, row 4 of the table, amounting to –$616 billion, corresponds to the most important part of the current account: the **balance of payments on goods and services,** the difference between the value of exports and the value of imports during a given period.

In economic news reports, you may see references to another measure, the **merchandise trade balance,** sometimes referred to as the **trade balance,** for short. It is the difference between a country's exports and imports of goods alone—not including services. Economists sometimes focus on the merchandise trade balance, even though it's an incomplete measure, because data on international trade in services aren't as accurate as data on trade in physical goods, and they are also slower to arrive.

Transactions that involve the sale or purchase of assets, and therefore do create future liabilities, are considered part of the **balance of payments on financial account,** or the **financial account** for short, for a given period. This corresponds to row 4 in Table 33-2, which was $357 billion in 2019. (Until a few years ago, economists often referred to the financial account as the *capital account.* We'll use the modern term, but you may run across the older term.)

So how does it all add up? The rows shaded purple in Table 33-2 show the bottom lines: the overall U.S. current account and financial account for 2019. As you can see:

- The United States ran a *current account deficit:* the amount it paid to foreigners for goods, services, factors, and transfers was more than the amount it received.

- Simultaneously, it ran a *financial account surplus:* the value of the assets it sold to foreigners was more than the value of the assets it bought from foreigners.

- In the official data, the U.S. current account deficit and financial account surplus didn't offset each other: the financial account surplus in 2019 was $141 billion smaller than the current account deficit (shown in the final row of the table). But that was just a statistical error, reflecting the imperfection of official data. (The discrepancy may have reflected foreign purchases of U.S. assets that official data somehow missed.)

FOR INQUIRING MINDS   GDP, GNP, and the Current Account

When we discussed national income accounting in Chapter 22, we derived the basic equation relating GDP to the components of spending:

$$Y = C + I + G + X - IM$$

where X and IM are exports and imports, respectively, of goods and services. But as we've learned, the balance of payments on goods and services is only one component of the current account balance. Why doesn't the national income equation use the current account as a whole?

The answer is that gross domestic product, Y, is the value of goods and services produced domestically. So it doesn't include international factor income and international transfers, two sources of income that are included in the calculation of the current account balance. The profits of Ford Motors U.K. aren't included in the

U.S. GDP, and the funds Latin American immigrants send home to their families aren't subtracted from GDP.

Shouldn't we have a broader measure that does include these sources of income? Actually, gross *national* product—GNP—does include international factor income. Estimates of U.S. GNP differ slightly from estimates of GDP because GNP adds in items such as the earnings of U.S. companies abroad and subtracts items such as the interest payments on bonds owned by residents of China and Japan. There isn't, however, any regularly calculated measure that includes transfer payments.

Why do economists usually use GDP rather than a broader measure? Two reasons. First, the original purpose of the national accounts was to track production rather than income. Second, data on international factor income and transfer payments are generally

considered somewhat unreliable. So if you're trying to keep track of movements in the economy, it usually makes sense to focus on GDP, because it doesn't include these unreliable data. (As the Economics in Action on "leprechaun economics" shows, however, sometimes GDP has problems, too.)

The funds Latin American immigrants send abroad are included in GDP because they were earned for services performed in the United States.

In fact, it's a basic rule of balance of payments accounting that the current account and the financial account must sum to zero:

(33-1) Current account (CA) + Financial account $(FA) = 0$

or

$$CA = -FA$$

Why must Equation 33-1 be true? We already saw the fundamental explanation in Table 33-1, which showed the accounts of the Costas family: in total, the sources of cash must equal the uses of cash. The same applies to balance of payments accounts. Figure 33-1, a variant on the circular-flow diagram we have found useful in discussing domestic macroeconomics, may help you visualize how this adding up works. Instead of showing the flow of money *within* a national economy, Figure 33-1 shows the flow of money *between* national economies.

Money flows into the United States from the rest of the world as payment for U.S. exports of goods and services, as payment for the use of U.S.-owned factors of production, and as transfer payments. These flows, indicated by the lower blue arrow, are the positive components of the U.S. current account. Money also flows into the United States from foreigners who purchase U.S. assets. They make up the positive component of the U.S. financial account and are shown by the lower green arrow.

At the same time, money flows from the United States to the rest of the world as payment for U.S. imports of goods and services, as payment for the use of foreign-owned factors of production, and as transfer payments. These flows, indicated by the upper blue arrow, are the negative components of the U.S. current account. Money also flows from the United States to purchase foreign assets. They make up the negative component of the U.S. financial account and are shown by the upper green arrow.

As in all circular-flow diagrams, the flow into a box and the flow out of a box are equal. This means that the sum of the blue and green arrows going into the United States (at the bottom of the diagram) is equal to the sum of the blue and green arrows going out of the United States (at the top of the diagram). That is:

(33-2)

Positive current account entries + Positive financial account entries =
(lower blue arrow)   (lower green arrow)

Negative current account entries + Negative financial account entries
(upper blue arrow)   (upper green arrow)

FIGURE 33-1 The Balance of Payments

The blue arrows represent payments that are counted in the current account. The green arrows represent payments that are counted in the financial account. Because the total flow into the United States must equal the total flow out of the United States, the sum of the current account plus the financial account is zero.

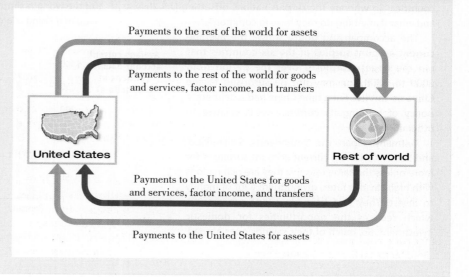

Payments to the rest of the world for assets

Payments to the rest of the world for goods and services, factor income, and transfers

United States

Rest of world

Payments to the United States for goods and services, factor income, and transfers

Payments to the United States for assets

Equation 33-2 can be rearranged as follows:

(33-3)
$$\text{Positive current account entries} - \text{Negative current account entries} +$$
$$\text{Positive financial account entries} - \text{Negative financial account entries} = 0$$

Equation 33-3 is equivalent to Equation 33-1: once we have summed up the positive and negative entries within each account, the current account plus the financial account is equal to zero.

But what determines the current account and the financial account?

Modeling the Financial Account

A country's financial account measures its net sales of assets to foreigners. There is, however, another way to think about the financial account: it's a measure of *capital inflows*, of foreign savings that are available to finance domestic investment spending.

What determines these capital inflows?

Part of the explanation will have to wait until later because some international capital flows are carried out by governments and central banks, which sometimes act very differently from private investors. But we can gain insight into the motivations for capital flows that are the result of private decisions by using the *loanable funds model* developed in Chapter 25 and, in particular, in Figures 25-7 and 25-8. In using this model to analyze the financial account, we make two important simplifications:

1. We assume that all international capital flows are in the form of loans. In reality, capital flows take many forms, including purchases of shares of stock in foreign companies and foreign real estate as well as *direct foreign investment*, in which companies build factories or acquire other productive assets abroad.

GLOBAL COMPARISON   BIG SURPLUSES

As we've seen, the United States generally runs a large deficit in its current account. In fact, the United States leads the world in its current account deficit; other countries run bigger deficits as a share of GDP, but they have much smaller economies, so the U.S. deficit is much bigger in absolute terms.

For the world as a whole, however, deficits on the part of some countries must be matched with surpluses on the part of other countries. So who are the surplus nations offsetting U.S. deficits, and what if anything do they have in common?

The accompanying figure shows the average current account surplus of the six countries that ran the largest surpluses over the period from 2009 to 2018. You may not be surprised to see China on this list. For a time China had a deliberate policy of keeping its currency weak relative to other currencies.

Germany, Japan, the Netherlands, Switzerland, and South Korea run current account surpluses for more or less the same reasons: they are rich nations with high savings rates, giving them a lot of money to invest. They also have slow long-run growth, which reduces the opportunities for domestic investment. So, much of their savings goes abroad,

which means that they run deficits on the financial account and surpluses on the current account.

The current account surpluses of Germany, which tops the list, and the Netherlands have also grown thanks to the declining value of the euro. A lower euro has reduced the cost of their manufacturing goods on world markets, allowing them to export more.

Overall, the surplus countries are a diverse group. If your picture of the world is simply one of U.S. deficits versus Chinese surpluses, you're missing a large part of the story.

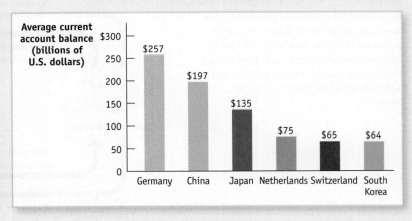

2. We ignore the effects of expected changes in exchange rates, the relative values of different national currencies. We analyze the determination of exchange rates shortly.

Recall Figure 25-7 from our discussion of the global loanable funds market in Chapter 25. It shows a hypothetical world consisting of two countries, the United States and Britain, which would have different equilibrium interest rates—6% in the United States, 2% in Britain—in the absence of international capital flows. But this difference in interest rates will not persist if it is easy for British lenders to make their funds available to U.S. borrowers. In fact, if British lenders consider loans to Americans just as good as domestic loans, interest rates will fall in the United States and rise in Britain until they are the same in both countries, with the United States, in effect, importing loanable funds from Britain. This equalization of interest rates (at 4%) is shown in Figure 25-8.

However, given our two simplifying assumptions, the loanable funds the United States imports from Britain (which are Britain's excess savings or capital outflows), are precisely the U.S. balance of payments on the financial account! So the financial account is determined by the supply and demand for loanable funds: capital moves from places where it would be cheap in the absence of international capital flows to places where it would be expensive in the absence of such flows.

Underlying Determinants of International Capital Flows

While the loanable funds model tells us the direction of capital flows—from countries in which capital is cheap to countries in which capital is expensive—it doesn't explain why. That is, why is capital cheap in one country but expensive in another?

International differences in investment opportunities generate international differences in the demand for capital. A country with a rapidly growing economy, other things equal, will offer more investment opportunities and a higher return to investors than a country with a slowly growing economy. So a country with a rapidly growing economy will typically have a higher demand for capital than the country with a slowly growing economy. As a result, capital tends to flow from slowly growing to rapidly growing economies.

International differences in the supply of funds reflect differences in savings across countries. These may be the result of differences in private savings rates, which vary among countries. They may also reflect differences in savings by governments. In particular, government budget deficits, which reduce overall national savings, can lead to capital inflows.

Now we can put together the demand for capital generated by investment opportunities within a country, with the supply for capital generated by savings within a country, to explain differences in interest rates across countries. Other things equal, countries with a high demand for capital and/or a low supply of capital will have higher interest rates. As a result, they will be the recipients of capital inflows.

Conversely, other things equal, countries with a low demand for funds and/or a high supply of funds will have lower interest rates. As a result, they will be the sources of capital outflows. The classic example of international capital flows is the flow of capital from Britain to the United States and other New World economies from 1870 to 1914. During that era, the United States was rapidly industrializing and had a high demand for capital. But Britain, which already industrialized, had a slowly growing economy with a large amount of accumulated savings.

Two-Way Capital Flows

In fact, it is the direction of *net* capital flows—the excess of inflows into a country over outflows, or vice versa—that is explained by the loanable funds model. The direction of *net* flows, other things equal, is determined by differences in interest rates between countries. However, *gross* flows take place in both directions: for

Many American companies have opened plants in China to access the growing Chinese market and take advantage of low labor costs.

example, the United States both sells assets to foreigners and buys assets from foreigners. Why does capital move in both directions?

The answer to this question is that in the real world, as opposed to the simple model just described, there are other motives for international capital flows besides seeking a higher rate of interest.

Individual investors often seek to diversify against risk by buying stocks in several countries. Stocks in Europe may do well when stocks in the United States do badly, or vice versa, so investors in Europe try to reduce their risk by buying some U.S. stocks, as U.S. investors try to reduce their risk by buying some European stocks. The result is capital flows in both directions.

Meanwhile, corporations often engage in international investment as part of their business strategy—for example, auto companies may find that they can compete better in an overseas market if they assemble some of their cars in that location. Such business investments can also lead to two-way capital flows, as, say, European car makers build plants in the United States even as U.S. computer companies open facilities in Europe.

Finally, some countries, including the United States, are international banking centers: people from all over the world put money in U.S. financial institutions, which then invest many of those funds overseas.

The result of these two-way flows is that modern economies are typically both debtors (countries that owe money to the rest of the world) and creditors (countries to which the rest of the world owes money). Due to years of both capital inflows and outflows, at the end of 2016, the United States had accumulated foreign assets worth $29.3 trillion, and foreigners had accumulated assets in the United States worth $40.3 trillion.

ECONOMICS >> *in Action*
Leprechaun Economics

One factor we didn't mention in our discussion of international capital flows was taxation. Yet tax rates on corporate profits vary considerably between nations. France, for example, has a corporate tax rate of 28%, while Ireland's rate is only 12.5%. These tax differences create an incentive for multinational corporations to report large investments in low-tax countries.

Notice how we worded this: it gives corporations an incentive to *report* large investments in countries like Ireland. Consider the operations of Apple's Irish subsidiary, which buys parts from Apple operations in other countries and sells much of what it makes to other Apple branches; it also pays royalties to the home company for its use of Apple patents. How profitable is that subsidiary? It's hard to say, because both the prices it receives and the prices it pays largely reflect internal Apple decisions rather than some independent market.

So it's easy for Apple to record very large profits on its Irish operations; as long as it doesn't send the profits home, these profits are considered to have been invested in Ireland, even though there isn't any real investment taking place.

Tax avoidance doesn't just distort balance of payments statistics. It can also distort national income accounting, especially for smaller countries. In 2015 Ireland reported that its real GDP rose 26%, which was obviously not the economy's true growth rate. What happened was that several big companies changed their accounting, choosing to attribute more of their value added to Ireland. One of this book's authors immediately dubbed the bizarre reported figure "leprechaun economics," a term quickly picked up by the Irish, who fortunately have a good sense of humor about themselves (and who have developed alternative measures that give a better picture of the economy's true growth.)

Unfortunately, joking aside, this kind of profit shifting has become a major problem for tax collection. The IMF estimates that "phantom" capital flows, done solely to avoid taxes, account for about 40% of international corporate investment. This represents a serious revenue loss for many governments.

>> Check Your Understanding 33-1

Solutions appear at back of book.

1. Which of the balance of payments accounts do the following events affect?
   a. Boeing, a U.S.-based company, sells a newly built airplane to China.
   b. Chinese investors buy stock in Boeing from U.S. residents.
   c. A Chinese company buys a used airplane from American Airlines and ships it to China.
   d. A Chinese investor who owns property in the United States buys a corporate jet, which they will keep in the United States so they can travel around America.

2. What effect do you think the collapse of the U.S. housing bubble in 2008, and the ensuing Great Recession, had on international capital flows into the United States?

‖ The Role of the Exchange Rate

We've just seen how differences in the supply of loanable funds from savings and the demand for loanable funds for investment spending lead to international capital flows. We've also learned that a country's balance of payments on current account plus its balance of payments on financial account add to zero: a country that receives net capital inflows must run a matching current account deficit, and a country that generates net capital outflows must run a matching current account surplus.

The behavior of the financial account—reflecting inflows or outflows of capital—is best described by equilibrium in the global loanable funds market. At the same time, the balance of payments on goods and services, the main component of the current account, is determined by decisions in the international markets for goods and services.

So given that the financial account reflects the movement of capital and the current account reflects the movement of goods and services, what ensures that the balance of payments really does balance? That is, what ensures that the two accounts actually offset each other?

Not surprisingly, a price is what makes these two accounts balance. Specifically, that price is the *exchange rate*, which is determined in the *foreign exchange market*.

Understanding Exchange Rates

In general, goods, services, and assets produced in a country must be paid for in that country's currency. U.S. products must be paid for in dollars; European products must be paid for in euros; Japanese products must be paid for in yen. Occasionally, sellers will accept payment in foreign currency, but they will then exchange that currency for domestic money.

International transactions, then, require a market—the **foreign exchange market**—in which currencies can be exchanged for each other. This market determines **exchange rates,** the prices at which currencies trade. (The foreign exchange market is, in fact, not located in any one geographic spot. Rather, it

Currencies are traded in the **foreign exchange market.**

The prices at which currencies trade are known as **exchange rates.**

When a currency becomes more valuable in terms of other currencies, it **appreciates.**

When a currency becomes less valuable in terms of other currencies, it **depreciates.**

TABLE 33-3 Exchange Rates, May 6, 2020, 11 P.M.

	U.S. dollars	Yen	Euros
One U.S. dollar exchanged for	1	106.27	0.9259
One yen exchanged for	0.0094	1	0.0087
One euro exchanged for	1.0800	114.74	1

is a global electronic market that traders around the world use to buy and sell currencies.)

Table 33-3 shows exchange rates among the world's three most important currencies as of 11 P.M., EDT, on May 6, 2020. Each entry shows the price of the "row" currency in terms of the "column" currency. For example, at that time US$1 exchanged for €0.9259, so it took €0.9259 to buy US$1. Similarly, it took US$1.0800 to buy €1. These two numbers reflect the same rate of exchange between the euro and the U.S. dollar: 1/1.0800 = 0.9259.

There are two ways to write any given exchange rate. In this case, there were €0.9259 to US$1 and US$1.0800 to €1. Which is the correct way to write it? The answer is that there is no fixed rule. In most countries, people tend to express the exchange rate as the price of a dollar in domestic currency. However, this rule isn't universal, and the U.S. dollar–euro rate is commonly quoted both ways. The important thing is to be sure you know which one you are using, as explained in the accompanying Pitfalls.

When discussing movements in exchange rates, economists use specialized terms to avoid confusion. When a currency becomes more valuable in terms of other currencies, economists say that the currency **appreciates.** When a currency becomes less valuable in terms of other currencies, it **depreciates.** Suppose, for example, that the value of €1 went from $1 to $1.25, which means that the value of US$1 went from €1 to €0.80 (because 1/1.25 = 0.80). In this case, we would say that the euro appreciated and the U.S. dollar depreciated.

By the way, although *appreciate* and *depreciate* are the technical, more or less official terms for a rise or fall of a currency against other currencies, you will also often hear it said that an appreciating currency is getting "stronger," or a depreciating currency is getting "weaker." It's important to realize that these terms, while widely used, shouldn't be taken as value judgments: a strong dollar isn't necessarily a good thing and a weak dollar isn't necessarily a bad thing.

Movements in exchange rates, other things equal, affect the relative prices of goods, services, and assets in different countries. Suppose, for example, that the price of a U.S. hotel room is US$100 and the price of a French hotel room is €100. If the exchange rate is €1 = US$1, these hotel rooms have the same price. If the exchange rate is €1.25 = US$1, the French hotel room is 20% cheaper than the U.S. hotel room. If the exchange rate is €0.80 = US$1, the French hotel room is 25% more expensive than the U.S. hotel room.

But what determines exchange rates? Supply and demand in the foreign exchange market.

The Equilibrium Exchange Rate

Imagine, for the sake of simplicity, that there are only two currencies in the world: U.S. dollars and euros. Europeans wanting to purchase U.S. goods, services, and assets come to the foreign exchange market, wanting to exchange euros for U.S. dollars. That is, Europeans demand U.S. dollars from the foreign exchange market and, correspondingly, supply euros to that market. Americans wanting to buy European goods, services, and assets come to the foreign exchange market to exchange U.S. dollars for euros. That is, Americans supply U.S. dollars to the foreign exchange market and, correspondingly, demand euros from that market. (International transfers and payments of factor income also enter into the foreign exchange market, but to make things simple we'll ignore these.)

Figure 33-2 shows how the foreign exchange market works. The quantity of dollars demanded and supplied at any given euro–U.S.

PITFALLS

WHICH WAY IS UP?

Someone says that "The U.S. exchange rate is up." What exactly does that mean?

It isn't clear. Sometimes the exchange rate is measured as the price of a dollar in terms of foreign currency, sometimes as the price of foreign currency in terms of dollars. So the statement could mean either that the dollar appreciated or that it depreciated!

You have to be particularly careful when using published statistics. Most countries other than the United States state their exchange rates in terms of the price of a dollar in their domestic currency—for example, Mexican officials will say that the exchange rate is 10, meaning 10 pesos per dollar. But Britain, for historical reasons, usually states its exchange rate the other way. On May 6, 2020, US$1 was worth £0.8088, and £1 was worth US$1.2364. More often than not, this number is reported as an exchange rate of 1.2364. In fact, on occasion, professional economists and consultants embarrass themselves by getting the direction in which the pound is moving wrong!

By the way, Americans generally follow other countries' lead: we usually say that the exchange rate against Mexico is 10 pesos per dollar but that the exchange rate against Britain is 1.24 dollars per pound. But this rule isn't reliable; exchange rates against the euro are often stated both ways.

So before using exchange rate data, always ask yourself: which way is the exchange rate being measured?

FIGURE 33-2 The Foreign Exchange Market

The foreign exchange market matches up the demand for a currency from foreigners who want to buy domestic goods, services, and assets with the supply of a currency from domestic residents who want to buy foreign goods, services, and assets. Here the equilibrium in the market for dollars is at point *E*, corresponding to an equilibrium exchange rate of €0.80 per US$1.

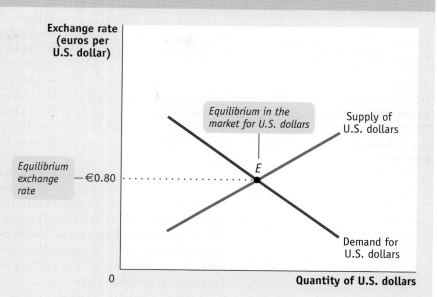

dollar exchange rate is shown on the horizontal axis, and the euro–U.S. dollar exchange rate is shown on the vertical axis. The exchange rate plays the same role as the price of a good or service in an ordinary supply and demand diagram.

The figure shows two curves, the demand curve for U.S. dollars and the supply curve for U.S. dollars. The key to understanding the slopes of these curves is that the level of the exchange rate affects exports and imports. When a country's currency appreciates (becomes more valuable), exports fall and imports rise. When a country's currency depreciates (becomes less valuable), exports rise and imports fall.

To understand why the demand curve for U.S. dollars slopes downward, recall that the exchange rate, other things equal, determines the prices of U.S. goods, services, and assets relative to those of European goods, services, and assets.

If the U.S. dollar rises against the euro (the dollar appreciates), U.S. products will become more expensive to Europeans relative to European products. So Europeans will buy less from the United States and will acquire fewer dollars in the foreign exchange market: the quantity of U.S. dollars demanded falls as the number of euros needed to buy a U.S. dollar rises.

If the U.S. dollar falls against the euro (the dollar depreciates), U.S. products will become relatively cheaper for Europeans. Europeans will respond by buying more from the United States and acquiring more dollars in the foreign exchange market: the quantity of U.S. dollars demanded rises as the number of euros needed to buy a U.S. dollar falls.

A similar argument explains why the supply curve of U.S. dollars in Figure 33-2 slopes upward: the more euros required to buy a U.S. dollar, the more dollars Americans will supply. Again, the reason is the effect of the exchange rate on relative prices. If the U.S. dollar rises against the euro, European products look cheaper to Americans—who will demand more of them. This will require Americans to convert more dollars into euros.

The **equilibrium exchange rate** is the exchange rate at which the quantity of U.S. dollars demanded in the foreign exchange market is equal to the quantity of U.S. dollars supplied. In Figure 33-2, the equilibrium is at point *E*, and the equilibrium exchange rate is €0.80. That is, at an exchange rate of €0.80 per US$1, the quantity of U.S. dollars supplied to the foreign exchange market is equal to the quantity of U.S. dollars demanded.

The **equilibrium exchange rate** is the exchange rate at which the quantity of a currency demanded in the foreign exchange market is equal to the quantity supplied.

TABLE 33-4 A Hypothetical Equilibrium in the Foreign Exchange Market

	Current account	Financial account	Totals
European purchases of U.S. dollars (trillions of dollars)	To buy U.S. goods and services: 1.0	To buy U.S. assets: 1.0	2.0
U.S. sales of U.S. dollars (trillions of dollars)	To buy European goods and services: 1.5	To buy European assets: 0.5	2.0
U.S. balance of payments	−0.5	+0.5	

To understand the significance of the equilibrium exchange rate, it's helpful to consider a numerical example of what equilibrium in the foreign exchange market looks like. A hypothetical example is shown in Table 33-4. The first row shows European purchases of U.S. dollars, either to buy U.S. goods and services or to buy U.S. assets. The second row shows U.S. sales of U.S. dollars, either to buy European goods and services or to buy European assets. At the equilibrium exchange rate, the total quantity of U.S. dollars Europeans want to buy is equal to the total quantity of U.S. dollars Americans want to sell.

Remember that the balance of payments accounts divide international transactions into two types. Purchases and sales of goods and services are counted in the current account. (Again, we're leaving out transfers and factor income to keep things simple.) Purchases and sales of assets are counted in the financial account. At the equilibrium exchange rate, then, we have the situation shown in Table 33-4: the sum of the balance of payments on the current account plus the balance of payments on the financial account is zero.

Now let's briefly consider how a shift in the demand for U.S. dollars affects equilibrium in the foreign exchange market. Suppose that for some reason capital flows from Europe to the United States increase due to a change in the preferences of European investors. The effects are shown in Figure 33-3. The demand for U.S. dollars in the foreign exchange market increases as European investors convert euros into dollars to fund their new investments in the United States. This is shown by the shift of the demand curve from D_1 to D_2. As a result, the U.S. dollar appreciates against the euro: the number of euros per U.S. dollar at the equilibrium exchange rate rises from XR_1 to XR_2.

What are the consequences of this increased capital inflow for the balance of payments? The total quantity of U.S. dollars supplied to the foreign exchange market still must equal the total quantity of U.S. dollars demanded. So the increased capital inflow to the United States—an increase in the balance of payments on the financial account—must be matched by a decline in the balance of

FIGURE 33-3 An Increase in the Demand for U.S. Dollars

An increase in the demand for U.S. dollars might result from a change in the preferences of European investors. The demand curve for U.S. dollars shifts from D_1 to D_2. So the equilibrium number of euros per U.S. dollar rises—the dollar appreciates against the euro. As a result, the balance of payments on current account falls as the balance of payments on financial account rises.

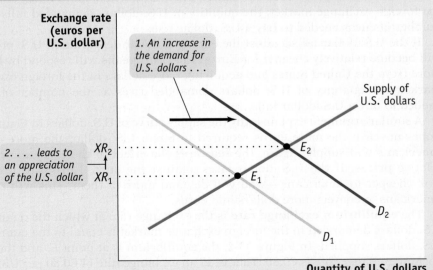

payments on the current account. What causes the balance of payments on the current account to decline? The appreciation of the U.S. dollar. A rise in the number of euros per U.S. dollar leads Americans to buy more European goods and services and Europeans to buy fewer U.S. goods and services.

Table 33-5 shows a hypothetical example of how this might work. Europeans are buying more U.S. assets, increasing the balance of payments on the financial account from 0.5 to 1.0. This is offset by a reduction in European purchases of U.S. goods and services and a rise in U.S. purchases of European goods and services, both the result of the dollar's appreciation.

TABLE 33-5 A Hypothetical Example of Effects of Increased Capital Inflows

	Current account	Financial account	Totals
European purchases of U.S. dollars (trillions of dollars)	To buy U.S. goods and services: 0.75 (down 0.25)	To buy U.S. assets: 1.5 (up 0.5)	2.25
U.S. sales of U.S. dollars (trillions of dollars)	To buy European goods and services: 1.75 (up 0.25)	To buy European assets: 0.5 (no change)	2.25
U.S. balance of payments	−1.0 (down 0.5)	+1.0 (up 0.5)	

So any change in the U.S. balance of payments on financial account generates an equal and opposite reaction in the balance of payments on current account. Movements in the exchange rate ensure that changes in the financial account and in the current account offset each other.

Let's briefly run this process in reverse. Suppose there is a reduction in capital flows from Europe to the United States—again due to a change in the preferences of European investors. The demand for U.S. dollars in the foreign exchange market falls, and the dollar depreciates: the number of euros per U.S. dollar at the equilibrium exchange rate falls. This leads Americans to buy fewer European products and Europeans to buy more U.S. products. Ultimately, this generates an increase in the U.S. balance of payments on current account. So a fall in capital flows into the United States leads to a weaker dollar, which in turn generates an increase in U.S. net exports.

Inflation and Real Exchange Rates

In 1993 one U.S. dollar exchanged, on average, for 3.1 Mexican pesos. By 2020 the peso had fallen against the dollar by nearly 90%, with an average exchange rate of more than 24.3 pesos per dollar. Did Mexican products also become drastically cheaper relative to U.S. products over that 27-year period? Did the price of Mexican products expressed in terms of U.S. dollars also fall by nearly 90%? The answer to both questions is no, because Mexico had much higher inflation than the United States over that period. In fact, the relative price of U.S. and Mexican products fluctuated both up and down between 1993 and 2020, with no clear trend.

To take account of the effects of differences in inflation rates, economists calculate **real exchange rates,** exchange rates adjusted for international differences in aggregate price levels. Suppose that the exchange rate we are looking at is the number of Mexican pesos per U.S. dollar. Let P_{US} and P_{Mex} be indexes of the aggregate price levels in the United States and Mexico, respectively. Then the real exchange rate between the Mexican peso and the U.S. dollar is defined as:

(33-4) Real exchange rate = Mexican pesos per U.S. dollar $\times \dfrac{P_{US}}{P_{Mex}}$

To distinguish it from the real exchange rate, the exchange rate unadjusted for aggregate price levels is sometimes called the *nominal* exchange rate.

To understand the significance of the difference between the real and nominal exchange rates, let's consider the following example. Suppose that the Mexican peso depreciates against the U.S. dollar, with the exchange rate going from 10 pesos per U.S. dollar to 15 pesos per U.S. dollar, a 50% change. But suppose that at the same time the price of everything in Mexico, measured in pesos, increases by 50%, so that the Mexican price index rises from 100 to 150. At the

Real exchange rates are exchange rates adjusted for international differences in aggregate price levels.

same time, suppose that there is no change in U.S. prices, so that the U.S. price index remains at 100. Then the initial real exchange rate is:

$$\text{Pesos per dollar before depreciation} \times \frac{P_{US}}{P_{Mex}} = 10 \times \frac{100}{100} = 10$$

After the peso depreciates and the Mexican price level increases, the real exchange rate is:

$$\text{Pesos per dollar after depreciation} \times \frac{P_{US}}{P_{Mex}} = 15 \times \frac{100}{100} = 10$$

In this example, the peso has depreciated substantially in terms of the U.S. dollar, but the *real* exchange rate between the peso and the U.S. dollar hasn't changed at all. And because the real peso–U.S. dollar exchange rate hasn't changed, the nominal depreciation of the peso against the U.S. dollar will have no effect either on the quantity of goods and services exported by Mexico to the United States or on the quantity of goods and services imported by Mexico from the United States.

Susana Gonzalez/Bloomberg via Getty Images

It's the real exchange rate, not the nominal exchange rate, that counts in decisions about buying and selling abroad.

To see why, consider again the example of a hotel room. Suppose that this room initially costs 1,000 pesos per night, which is $100 at an exchange rate of 10 pesos per dollar. After both Mexican prices and the number of pesos per dollar rise by 50%, the hotel room costs 1,500 pesos per night—but 1,500 pesos divided by 15 pesos per dollar is $100, so the Mexican hotel room still costs $100. As a result, a U.S. tourist considering a trip to Mexico will have no reason to change plans.

The same is true for all goods and services that enter into trade: *the current account responds only to changes in the real exchange rate, not the nominal exchange rate.* A country's products become cheaper to foreigners only when that country's currency depreciates in real terms, and those products become more expensive to foreigners only when the currency appreciates in real terms. As a consequence, economists who analyze movements in exports and imports of goods and services focus on the real exchange rate, not the nominal exchange rate.

Figure 33-4 illustrates just how important it can be to distinguish between nominal and real exchange rates. The line labeled "Nominal exchange rate" shows the number of pesos it took to buy a U.S. dollar from 1993 to 2020. As you

FIGURE 33-4 Real versus Nominal Exchange Rates, 1993–2020

Between November 1993 and February 2020, the price of a dollar in Mexican pesos increased dramatically. But because Mexico had higher inflation than the United States, the real exchange rate, which measures the relative price of Mexican goods and services, ended up roughly where it started.

Data from: Federal Reserve Bank of St. Louis.

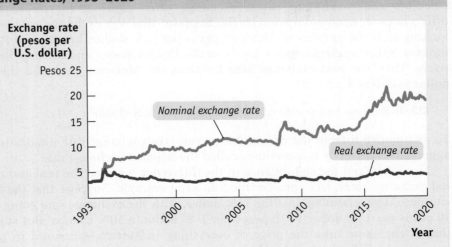

can see, the peso depreciated massively over that period. But the line labeled "Real exchange rate" shows the real exchange rate: it was calculated using Equation 33-4, with price indexes for both Mexico and the United States set so that 1993 = 100. In real terms, the peso depreciated between 1994 and 1995, but not by nearly as much as the nominal depreciation. By 2013, the real peso–U.S. dollar exchange rate was just about back where it started, although it rose again over the next two years.

Purchasing Power Parity

A useful tool for analyzing exchange rates, closely connected to the concept of the real exchange rate, is known as *purchasing power parity*. The **purchasing power parity** between two countries' currencies is the nominal exchange rate at which a given basket of goods and services would cost the same amount in each country. Suppose, for example, that a basket of goods and services that costs $100 in the United States costs 1,000 pesos in Mexico. Then the purchasing power parity is 10 pesos per U.S. dollar: at that exchange rate, 1,000 pesos = $100, so the market basket costs the same amount in both countries.

Calculations of purchasing power parities are usually made by estimating the cost of buying broad market baskets containing many goods and services — everything from cars and groceries to housing and internet service. But as the For Inquiring Minds, "Burgernomics," illustrates, nominal exchange rates almost always differ from purchasing power parities. Some of these differences are systematic: in general, aggregate price levels are lower in poor countries than in rich countries because services tend to be cheaper in poor countries. But even among countries at roughly the same level of economic development, nominal exchange rates vary quite a lot from purchasing power parity.

Figure 33-5 shows the nominal exchange rate between the Canadian dollar and the U.S. dollar, measured as the number of Canadian dollars per U.S. dollar,

> The **purchasing power parity** between two countries' currencies is the nominal exchange rate at which a given basket of goods and services would cost the same amount in each country.

FOR INQUIRING MINDS   Burgernomics

The Economist magazine publishes an annual comparison of the cost in different countries of one particular consumption item that is found around the world — a McDonald's Big Mac. The magazine finds the price of a Big Mac in local currency, then computes two numbers: the price of a Big Mac in U.S. dollars using the prevailing exchange rate and the exchange rate at which the price of a Big Mac would equal the U.S. price.

If purchasing power parity held for Big Macs, the dollar price of a Big Mac would be the same everywhere. If purchasing power parity is a good theory for the long run, the exchange rate at which a Big Mac's price matches the U.S. price should offer some guidance about where the exchange rate will eventually end up.

Table 33-6 shows *The Economist* estimates for selected countries as of January 2020, ranked in increasing order of the dollar price of a Big Mac. The countries with the cheapest Big Macs, and therefore

by this measure with the most undervalued currencies, are Mexico, India, and China, all three developing countries. And topping the list, with a Big Mac some 20% more expensive than in the United States, is Switzerland — the nation that, as we described in the opening story, has taken extraordinary action in an effort to depreciate its currency.

TABLE 33-6 Purchasing Power Parity and the Price of a Big Mac

Country	Big Mac price In local currency	In U.S. dollars	Local currency per dollar Implied PPP	Actual exchange rate
India	Rupee 188	$2.65	33.16	70.98
Mexico	Peso 50	2.66	8.82	18.82
China	Yuan 21.5	3.13	3.79	6.88
Japan	¥ 390	3.54	68.78	110.04
Britain	£ 3.39	4.40	0.60	0.77
Euro area	€ 4.12	4.58	0.73	0.90
Brazil	Real 19.90	4.81	3.51	4.14
United States	$5.67	5.67	1.00	1.00
Switzerland	SFr 6.50	6.70	1.15	0.97

Data from: The Economist.

FIGURE 33-5 Purchasing Power Parity versus the Nominal Exchange Rate, 1990–2019

The purchasing power parity between the United States and Canada — the exchange rate at which a basket of goods and services would have cost the same amount in both countries — changed very little over the period shown, staying near C$1.20 per US$1. But the nominal exchange rate fluctuated widely.

Data from: OECD.

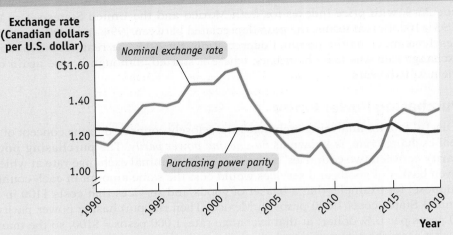

from 1990 to 2019, together with an estimate of the purchasing power parity exchange rate between the United States and Canada over the same period. The purchasing power parity didn't change much over the whole period because the United States and Canada had about the same rate of inflation. For most of the 1990s through 2005, the nominal exchange rate was above the purchasing power parity, so a market basket was much cheaper in Canada than in the United States. But from 2005 to 2015, the Canadian dollar had appreciated, making a market basket more expensive in Canada.

Over the long run, however, purchasing power parities are pretty good at predicting actual changes in nominal exchange rates. In particular, nominal exchange rates between countries at similar levels of economic development tend to fluctuate around levels that lead to similar costs for a given market basket.

ECONOMICS >> *in Action* 🌐
Strong Dollar Woes

Does the exchange rate really matter for business? To answer this question, let's consider what happened to U.S. corporations from 2014 to 2015.

Over the course of these two years, the dollar strengthened sharply against many currencies, especially the euro and the Japanese yen. The dollar's rise largely reflected the weaknesses of other economies: troubles in Europe and Japan kept interest rates and investment demand low, and capital flowed to the United States, which was experiencing steady job growth and overall was doing a much better job recovering from the Great Recession.

While the strong dollar reflected (relatively) good news for the U.S. economy as a whole, it was bad news for U.S. companies that sell a lot to overseas markets—companies like Procter and Gamble, which sells toothpaste and other toiletries around the world, or, Kimberly-Clark, whose

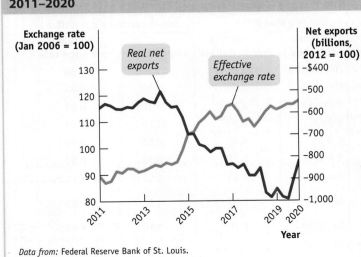

FIGURE 33-6 The Negative Impact of a Strong Dollar, 2011–2020

Data from: Federal Reserve Bank of St. Louis.

Huggies diapers protect many foreign babies' bottoms. Such companies reported large hits to their profits, and began either losing ground to foreign competitors or shifting some of their own production abroad.

Figure 33-6 illustrates the overall picture. It compares the *U.S. effective exchange rate*, a measure of the average value of the dollar against other currencies, with *real net exports*, exports minus imports, measured in 2012 dollars. From early 2014 to early 2016 the dollar rose about 15% on average, then has stayed at this higher level into 2020, while real net exports moved considerably deeper into deficit.

In other words, the exchange rate does matter a lot for businesses that compete with foreign rivals. Earlier we noted that while it's common to describe an appreciating currency as "getting stronger," that doesn't mean it's a good thing. And the stronger dollar of 2014 to 2015 definitely wasn't a good thing for some U.S. companies.

>> **Check Your Understanding** 33-2
Solutions appear at back of book.

1. Mexico discovers huge reserves of oil and starts exporting oil to the United States. Describe how this would affect the following.
   a. The nominal peso–U.S. dollar exchange rate
   b. Mexican exports to the United States of other goods and services
   c. Mexican imports from the United States of goods and services
2. A basket of goods and services that costs $100 in the United States costs 800 pesos in Mexico, and the current nominal exchange rate is 10 pesos per U.S. dollar. Over the next five years, the cost of that market basket rises to $120 in the United States and to 1,200 pesos in Mexico, although the nominal exchange rate remains at 10 pesos per U.S. dollar. Calculate the following.
   a. The real exchange rate now and five years from now, if today's price index in both countries is 100
   b. Purchasing power parity today and five years from now

Exchange Rate Policy

The nominal exchange rate, like other prices, is determined by supply and demand. Unlike the price of wheat or oil, however, the exchange rate is the price of a country's money (in terms of another country's money). Money isn't a good or service produced by the private sector; it's an asset whose quantity is determined by government policy. As a result, governments have much more power to influence nominal exchange rates than they have to influence ordinary prices.

The nominal exchange rate is a very important price for many countries because it determines the price of imports and the price of exports. In economies where exports and imports are large percentages of GDP, movements in the exchange rate can have major effects on aggregate output and the aggregate price level. What do governments do with their power to influence this important price?

The answer is, it depends. At different times and in different places, governments have adopted a variety of *exchange rate regimes*. Let's talk about these regimes, how they are enforced, and how governments choose a regime. (From now on, we'll adopt the convention that we mean the nominal exchange rate when we refer to the exchange rate.)

Exchange Rate Regimes

An **exchange rate regime** is a rule governing policy toward the exchange rate. There are two main kinds of exchange rate regimes. A country has a **fixed exchange rate** when the government keeps the exchange rate against

>> **Quick Review**
• Currencies are traded in the **foreign exchange market,** which determines **exchange rates.**
• Exchange rates can be measured in two ways. To avoid confusion, economists say that a currency **appreciates** or **depreciates.** The **equilibrium exchange rate** matches the supply and demand for currencies on the foreign exchange market.
• To take account of differences in national price levels, economists calculate **real exchange rates.** The current account responds only to changes in the real exchange rate, not the nominal exchange rate.
• **Purchasing power parity** is the nominal exchange rate that equalizes the price of a market basket in two countries. While the nominal exchange rate almost always differs from purchasing power parity, purchasing power parity is a good predictor of actual changes in the nominal exchange rate.

An **exchange rate regime** is a rule governing policy toward the exchange rate.

A country has a **fixed exchange rate** when the government keeps the exchange rate against some other currency at or near a particular target.

		WE BUY AT	WE SELL AT
AUSTRALIA	AUD	.6883	.7964
BRAZIL	BRL	.2861	.3380
CANADA	CAD	.6889	.7768
CHINA	CNY	.1309	.1561
RUSSIA	RR	.0147	.0190
EUROPEAN UNION	EUR	1.0351	1.1830
JAPAN	JPY	.0083	.0095
MEXICO	MXP	.0492	.0561
NORWAY	NOK	.1094	.1254
SWITZERLAND	CHF	.9457	1.0887
UNITED KINGDOM	GBP	1.2117	1.3847

Exchange rates play a very important role in the global economy.

some other currency at or near a particular target. For example, Hong Kong has an official policy of setting an exchange rate of HK$7.80 per US$1. In contrast, a country has a **floating exchange rate** when the government lets market forces determine the exchange rate. This is the policy followed by Britain, Canada, and the United States.

Fixed exchange rates and floating exchange rates aren't the only possibilities. At various times, countries have adopted compromise policies that lie somewhere between fixed and floating exchange rates. These include exchange rates that are fixed at any given time but are adjusted frequently, exchange rates that aren't fixed but are managed by the government to avoid wide swings, and exchange rates that float within a *target zone* but are prevented from leaving that zone. In this chapter, however, we'll focus on the two main exchange rate regimes.

The immediate puzzle posed by a fixed exchange rate is how a government can fix the exchange rate when the exchange rate is determined by supply and demand.

How Can an Exchange Rate Be Held Fixed?

To understand how it is possible for a country to fix its exchange rate, let's consider a hypothetical country, Genovia, which for some reason has decided to fix the value of its currency, the geno, at US$1.50.

The obvious problem is that $1.50 may not be the equilibrium exchange rate in the foreign exchange market: the equilibrium rate may be either higher or lower than the target exchange rate. Figure 33-7 shows the foreign exchange market for genos, with the quantities of genos supplied and demanded on the horizontal axis and the exchange rate of the geno, measured in U.S. dollars per geno, on the vertical axis. Panel (a) shows the case in which the equilibrium value of the geno is *below* the target exchange rate. Panel (b) shows the case in which the equilibrium value of the geno is *above* the target exchange rate.

Consider first the case in which the equilibrium value of the geno is below the target exchange rate. As panel (a) shows, at the target exchange rate of $1.50 per geno, there is a surplus of genos in the foreign exchange market, which would normally push the value of the geno down. How can the Genovian government support the value of the geno to keep the rate where it wants? There are three possible answers, all of which have been used by governments at some point.

One way the Genovian government can support the geno is to soak up the surplus of genos by buying its own currency in the foreign exchange market. A government purchase or sale of currency in the foreign exchange market is called an **exchange market intervention.** To buy genos in the foreign exchange market, of course, the Genovian government must have U.S. dollars to exchange for genos. In fact, most countries maintain **foreign exchange reserves,** stocks of foreign currency (usually U.S. dollars or euros) that they can use to buy their own currency to support its price.

We mentioned earlier in the chapter that an important part of international capital flows is the result of purchases and sales of foreign assets by governments and central banks. Now we can see why governments sell foreign assets: they are supporting their currency through exchange market intervention. As we'll see in a moment, governments that keep the value of their currency *down* through exchange market intervention must *buy* foreign assets. First, however, let's talk about the other ways governments fix exchange rates.

A country has a **floating exchange rate** when the government lets market forces determine the exchange rate.

A government purchase or sale of currency in the foreign exchange market is an **exchange market intervention.**

Foreign exchange reserves are stocks of foreign currency that governments maintain to buy their own currency on the foreign exchange market.

FIGURE 33-7 Exchange Market Intervention

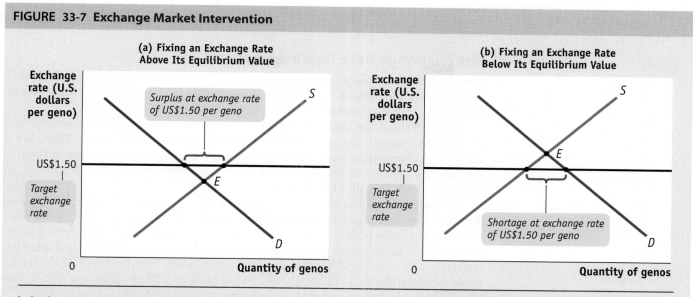

(a) Fixing an Exchange Rate Above Its Equilibrium Value

Exchange rate (U.S. dollars per geno)

Surplus at exchange rate of US$1.50 per geno

S

US$1.50

E

Target exchange rate

D

0

Quantity of genos

(b) Fixing an Exchange Rate Below Its Equilibrium Value

Exchange rate (U.S. dollars per geno)

S

E

US$1.50

Target exchange rate

Shortage at exchange rate of US$1.50 per geno

D

0

Quantity of genos

In both panels, the imaginary country of Genovia is trying to keep the exchange rate of the geno fixed at US$1.50 per geno. In panel (a), the equilibrium exchange rate is below $1.50, leading to a surplus of genos on the foreign exchange market. To keep the geno from falling below $1.50, the

Genovian government can buy genos and sell U.S. dollars. In panel (b), the equilibrium exchange rate is above $1.50, leading to a shortage of genos on the foreign exchange market. To keep the geno from rising above $1.50, the Genovian government can sell genos and buy U.S. dollars.

A second way for the Genovian government to support the geno is to try to shift the supply and demand curves for the geno in the foreign exchange market. Governments usually do this by changing monetary policy. For example, to support the geno the Genovian central bank can raise the Genovian interest rate. This will increase capital flows into Genovia, increasing the demand for genos, at the same time that it reduces capital flows out of Genovia, reducing the supply of genos. So, other things equal, an increase in a country's interest rate will increase the value of its currency.

Third, the Genovian government can support the geno by reducing the supply of genos to the foreign exchange market. It can do this by requiring domestic residents who want to buy foreign currency to get a license and giving these licenses only to people engaging in approved transactions (such as the purchase of imported goods the Genovian government thinks are essential). Licensing systems that limit the right of individuals to buy foreign currency are called **foreign exchange controls.** Other things equal, foreign exchange controls increase the value of a country's currency.

So far we've been discussing a situation in which the government is trying to prevent a depreciation of the geno. Suppose, instead, that the situation is as shown in panel (b) of Figure 33-7, where the equilibrium value of the geno is *above* the target exchange rate of $1.50 per geno and there is a shortage of genos. To maintain the target exchange rate, the Genovian government can apply the same three basic options in the reverse direction. It can intervene in the foreign exchange market, in this case *selling* genos and acquiring U.S. dollars, which it can add to its foreign exchange reserves. It can *reduce* interest rates to increase the supply of genos and reduce the demand. Or it can impose foreign exchange controls that limit the ability of foreigners to buy genos. All of these actions, other things equal, will reduce the value of the geno.

As we said, all three techniques have been used to manage fixed exchange rates. But we haven't said whether fixing the exchange rate is a good idea. In fact,

Foreign exchange controls are licensing systems that limit the right of individuals to buy foreign currency.

the choice of exchange rate regime poses a dilemma for policy makers, because fixed and floating exchange rates each have both advantages and disadvantages.

The Exchange Rate Regime Dilemma

Few questions in macroeconomics produce as many arguments as that of whether a country should adopt a fixed or a floating exchange rate. And there are so many arguments because both sides have a case.

To understand the case for a fixed exchange rate, consider for a moment how easy it is to conduct business across state lines in the United States. There are a number of things that make interstate commerce trouble-free, but one of them is the absence of any uncertainty about the value of money: a dollar is a dollar, in both New York City and Los Angeles.

By contrast, a dollar isn't a dollar in transactions between New York City and Toronto. The exchange rate between the Canadian dollar and the U.S. dollar fluctuates, sometimes widely. If a U.S. firm promises to pay a Canadian firm a given number of U.S. dollars a year from now, the value of that promise in Canadian currency can vary by 10% or more. This uncertainty has the effect of deterring trade between the two countries. So, one benefit of a fixed exchange rate is certainty about the future value of a currency.

There is also, in some cases, an additional benefit to adopting a fixed exchange rate: by committing itself to a fixed rate, a country is also committing itself not to engage in inflationary policies. For example, in 1991 Argentina, which has a long history of irresponsible policies leading to severe inflation, adopted a fixed exchange rate of US$1 per Argentine peso in an attempt to commit itself to non-inflationary policies in the future. (Argentina's fixed exchange rate regime collapsed disastrously in late 2001. But that's another story.)

The point is that there is some economic value in having a stable exchange rate. Indeed, as the accompanying For Inquiring Minds explains, the presumed benefits of stable exchange rates motivated the international system of fixed exchange rates created after World War II. It was also a major reason for the creation of the euro.

However, there are also costs to fixing the exchange rate. To stabilize an exchange rate through intervention, a country must keep large quantities of foreign currency on hand—usually a low-return investment. Furthermore, even large reserves can be quickly exhausted when there are large capital flows out of a country. If a country chooses to stabilize an exchange rate by adjusting monetary policy rather than through intervention, it must divert monetary policy from other goals, notably stabilizing the economy and managing the inflation rate. Finally, foreign exchange controls, like import quotas and tariffs, distort incentives for importing and exporting goods and services. They can also create substantial costs in terms of red tape and corruption.

So there's a dilemma. Should a country let its currency float, which leaves monetary policy available for macroeconomic stabilization but creates uncertainty for business? Or should it fix the exchange rate, which eliminates the uncertainty but means giving up monetary policy, adopting exchange controls, or both?

Different countries reach different conclusions at different times. Most European countries, except for Britain, have long believed that exchange rates among major European economies, which do most of their international trade with each other, should be fixed. But Canada seems happy with a floating exchange rate with the United States, even though the United States accounts for most of Canada's trade.

Fortunately we don't have to resolve this dilemma. For the rest of the chapter, we'll take exchange rate regimes as given and ask how they affect macroeconomic policy.

FOR INQUIRING MINDS From Bretton Woods to the Euro

In 1944, while World War II was still raging, representatives of Allied nations met in Bretton Woods, New Hampshire, to establish a postwar international monetary system of fixed exchange rates among major currencies. The system was highly successful at first, but it broke down in 1971. After a confusing interval during which policy makers tried unsuccessfully to establish a new fixed exchange rate system, by 1973 most economically advanced countries had moved to floating exchange rates.

In Europe, however, many policy makers were unhappy with floating exchange rates, which they believed created too much uncertainty for business. From the late 1970s onward they tried several times to create a system of more or less fixed exchange rates in Europe, culminating in an arrangement known as the Exchange Rate Mechanism. (The Exchange Rate Mechanism was, strictly speaking, a target zone system — European exchange rates were free to move within a narrow band, but not outside it.) And in 1991 they agreed to move to the ultimate in fixed exchange rates: a common European currency, the euro. To the surprise of many analysts, they pulled it off: today most of Europe has abandoned national currencies for the euro.

Figure 33-8 illustrates the history of European exchange rate arrangements. It shows the exchange rate between the French franc and the German mark, measured as francs per mark, from 1971 until their replacement by the euro. The exchange rate fluctuated widely at first. The plateaus you can see in the data — eras

when the exchange rate fluctuated only modestly — are periods when attempts to restore fixed exchange rates were in process. The Exchange Rate Mechanism, after a couple of false starts, became effective in 1987, stabilizing the exchange rate at about 3.4 francs per mark. (The wobbles in the early 1990s reflect two *currency crises* — episodes in which widespread expectations of imminent devaluations led to large but temporary capital flows.)

In 1999 the exchange rate was *locked* — no further fluctuations were allowed as the countries prepared to switch from francs and marks to the euro. At the end of 2001, the franc and the mark ceased to exist.

The transition to the euro has not been without costs. Countries that adopted the euro sacrificed some important policy tools: they could no longer tailor monetary policy to their specific economic circumstances, and they could no longer lower their costs relative to other European nations simply by letting their currencies depreciate.

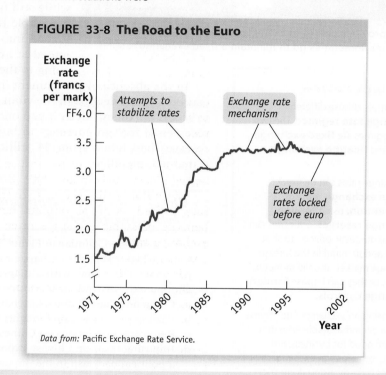

FIGURE 33-8 The Road to the Euro

Data from: Pacific Exchange Rate Service.

ECONOMICS >> *in Action*
China Pegs the Yuan

In the early years of the twenty-first century, China provided a striking example of the lengths to which countries sometimes go to maintain a fixed exchange rate.

In the first act of this story, China acted to keep its currency down. The country's spectacular success as an exporter had produced a rising surplus on current account, and private investors became increasingly eager to shift funds into China, to invest in its growing domestic economy.

These capital flows were somewhat limited by foreign exchange controls — but kept coming in anyway. As a result of the current account surplus and private capital inflows, China found itself in the position described by panel (b) of Figure 33-7: at the target exchange rate, the demand for yuan exceeded the supply. Yet the Chinese government was determined to keep the exchange rate fixed at a value below its equilibrium level.

China provides a striking example of the lengths to which countries sometimes go to maintain a fixed exchange rate.

To keep the rate fixed, China had to engage in large-scale exchange market intervention, selling yuan, buying up other countries' currencies (mainly U.S. dollars) on the foreign exchange market, and adding them to its reserves. Indeed, between early 2009 and early 2014 China added $2 trillion to its foreign exchange reserves, which by mid-2014 had risen to a remarkable $4 trillion, roughly 40% of GDP. Not surprisingly, China's exchange rate policy led to some friction with its trading partners, who felt that it had the effect of subsidizing Chinese exports.

But then came the second act of the story. After 2012 China's current account surplus declined, partly reflecting rising wages and the rise of new competitors like Vietnam and Bangladesh. Also, China's economic growth, while still fast, slowed, and investors grew nervous about a possible financial or political crisis. So capital inflows turned into capital outflows: the 2015 outflow was estimated at an amazing $1 trillion, the great majority of it going to the United States.

In the absence of government intervention, this capital flight might well have caused a sharp decline in the yuan. But the Chinese government was as reluctant to see its currency fall as it had once been to see it rise. So China began using its reserves of foreign currency to buy large quantities of yuan. And by early 2017 reserves had fallen from $4 trillion to approximately $3 trillion, where it has remained into 2020.

>> Check Your Understanding 33-3

Solutions appear at back of book.

1. Draw a diagram, similar to Figure 33-7, representing the foreign exchange situation of China when it kept the exchange rate fixed. Express the exchange rate as U.S. dollars per yuan. Then show with a diagram how each of the following policy changes will eliminate the disequilibrium in the market.
   a. China no longer fixing its exchange rate, allowing it to float freely
   b. Placing restrictions on foreigners who want to invest in China
   c. Removing restrictions on Chinese who want to invest abroad
   d. Imposing taxes on Chinese exports, such as shipments of clothing, that are causing a political backlash in the importing countries

‖ Exchange Rates and Macroeconomic Policy

When the euro was created in 1999, there were celebrations across the nations of Europe where it was seen as a step toward a brighter future. But there were a few notable exceptions. You see, some countries chose not to adopt the new currency. The most important of these was Britain, but other European countries, such as Sweden, also decided that the euro was not for them.

Why did Britain say no? Part of the answer was national pride: if Britain gave up the pound, it would also have to give up currency that bears the portrait of the queen. But there were also serious economic concerns about giving up the pound in favor of the euro. British economists who favored adoption of the euro argued that if Britain used the same currency as its neighbors, the country's international trade would expand and its economy would become more productive. But other economists pointed out that adopting the euro would take away Britain's ability to have an independent monetary policy and might lead to macroeconomic problems.

As this discussion suggests, the fact that modern economies are open to international trade and capital flows adds a new level of complication to our analysis of macroeconomic policy. Let's look at three policy issues raised by international aspects of macroeconomics:

1. Devaluation and revaluation of fixed exchange rates
2. Monetary policy under floating exchange rates
3. International business cycles

> A **devaluation** is a reduction in the value of a currency that is set under a fixed exchange rate regime.
>
> A **revaluation** is an increase in the value of a currency that is set under a fixed exchange rate regime.

Devaluation and Revaluation of Fixed Exchange Rates

Historically, fixed exchange rates haven't been permanent commitments. Sometimes countries with a fixed exchange rate switch to a floating rate. In other cases, they retain a fixed rate but change the target exchange rate. Such adjustments in the target were common during the Bretton Woods era described in the preceding For Inquiring Minds. For example, in 1967 Britain changed the exchange rate of the pound against the U.S. dollar from US$2.80 per £1 to US$2.40 per £1. A modern example is Argentina, which maintained a fixed exchange rate against the dollar from 1991 to 2001 but switched to a floating exchange rate at the end of 2001.

A reduction in the value of a currency that is set under a fixed exchange rate regime is called a **devaluation.** As we've already learned, a *depreciation* is a downward move in a currency. A devaluation is a depreciation that is due to a revision in a fixed exchange rate target. An increase in the value of a currency that is set under a fixed exchange rate regime is called a **revaluation.**

A devaluation, like any depreciation, makes domestic goods cheaper in terms of foreign currency, which leads to higher exports. At the same time, it makes foreign goods more expensive in terms of domestic currency, which reduces imports. The effect is to increase the balance of payments on current account. Similarly, a revaluation makes domestic goods more expensive in terms of foreign currency, which reduces exports, and makes foreign goods cheaper in domestic currency, which increases imports. So a revaluation reduces the balance of payments on current account.

Devaluations and revaluations serve two purposes under fixed exchange rates. First, they can be used to eliminate shortages or surpluses in the foreign exchange market. For example, in 2010 some economists and politicians were urging China to revalue the yuan because they believed that China's exchange rate policy unfairly aided Chinese exports.

Second, devaluation and revaluation can be used as tools of macroeconomic policy. A devaluation, by increasing exports and reducing imports, increases aggregate demand. So a devaluation can be used to reduce or eliminate a recessionary gap. A revaluation has the opposite effect, reducing aggregate demand. So a revaluation can be used to reduce or eliminate an inflationary gap.

Monetary Policy Under Floating Exchange Rates

Under a floating exchange rate regime, a country's central bank retains its ability to pursue independent monetary policy: it can increase aggregate demand by cutting the interest rate or decrease aggregate demand by raising the interest rate. But the exchange rate adds another dimension to the effects of monetary policy. To see why, let's return to the hypothetical country of Genovia and ask what happens if the central bank cuts the interest rate.

Just as in an economy without international linkages, a lower interest rate leads to higher investment spending and higher consumer spending. But the decline in the interest rate also affects the foreign exchange market. Foreigners have less incentive to move funds into Genovia because they will receive a lower interest rate on their loans. As a result, they have less need to exchange U.S. dollars for genos,

FIGURE 33-9 Monetary Policy and the Exchange Rate

Here we show what happens in the foreign exchange market if Genovia cuts its interest rate. Residents of Genovia have a reduced incentive to keep their funds at home, so they invest more abroad. As a result, the supply of genos shifts rightward, from S_1 to S_2. Meanwhile, foreigners have less incentive to put funds into Genovia, so the demand for genos shifts leftward, from D_1 to D_2. The geno depreciates: the equilibrium exchange rate falls from XR_1 to XR_2.

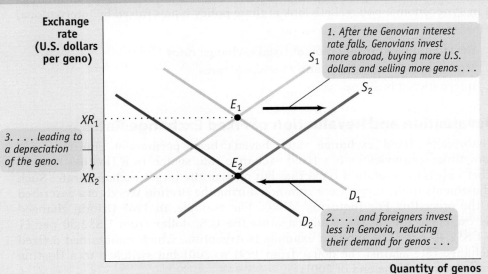

1. After the Genovian interest rate falls, Genovians invest more abroad, buying more U.S. dollars and selling more genos . . .

3. . . . leading to a depreciation of the geno.

2. . . . and foreigners invest less in Genovia, reducing their demand for genos . . .

so the demand for genos falls. At the same time, Genovians have *more* incentive to move funds abroad because the interest rate on loans at home has fallen, making investments outside the country more attractive. As a result, they need to exchange more genos for U.S. dollars, so the supply of genos rises.

Figure 33-9 shows the effect of an interest rate reduction on the foreign exchange market. The demand curve for genos shifts leftward, from D_1 to D_2, and the supply curve shifts rightward, from S_1 to S_2. The equilibrium exchange rate, as measured in U.S. dollars per geno, falls from XR_1 to XR_2. That is, a reduction in the Genovian interest rate causes the geno to *depreciate*.

The depreciation of the geno, in turn, affects aggregate demand. We've already seen that a devaluation—a depreciation that is the result of a change in a fixed exchange rate—increases exports and reduces imports, thereby increasing aggregate demand. A depreciation that results from an interest rate cut has the same effect: it increases exports and reduces imports, increasing aggregate demand.

In other words, monetary policy under floating rates has effects beyond those we've described before. In the absence of international trade and capital flows, a reduction in the interest rate leads to a rise in aggregate demand because it leads to more investment spending and consumer spending. In an economy with a floating exchange rate, the interest rate reduction leads to increased investment spending and consumer spending, but it also increases aggregate demand in another way: it leads to a currency depreciation, which increases exports and reduces imports, and further increases aggregate demand.

International Business Cycles

Up to this point, we have discussed macroeconomics as if all demand shocks originate from the domestic economy. In reality, however, economies sometimes face shocks coming from abroad. For example, recessions in the United States have historically led to recessions in Mexico.

The key point is that changes in aggregate demand affect the demand for goods and services produced abroad as well as at home: other things equal, a recession leads to a fall in imports and an expansion leads to a rise in imports. And one country's imports are another country's exports. This link between aggregate demand in different national economies is one reason business cycles in different countries sometimes—but not always—seem to be synchronized. Prime examples are the Great Depression of the 1930s, the Great Recession of 2008, and the 2020 slump brought on by the coronavirus pandemic, all of which affected countries around the world.

The extent of this link depends, however, on the exchange rate regime. To see why, think about what happens if a recession abroad reduces the demand for Genovia's exports. A reduction in foreign demand for Genovian goods and services is also a reduction in demand for genos in the foreign exchange market. If Genovia has a fixed exchange rate, it responds to this decline with exchange market intervention. But if Genovia has a floating exchange rate, the geno depreciates. Because Genovian goods and services become cheaper to foreigners when the demand for exports falls, the quantity of goods and services exported doesn't fall by as much as it would under a fixed rate. At the same time, the fall in the geno makes imports more expensive to Genovians, leading to a fall in imports. Both effects limit the decline in Genovia's aggregate demand compared to what it would have been under a fixed exchange rate.

One of the virtues of a floating exchange rate, according to advocates of such exchange rates, is that they help insulate countries from recessions originating abroad. This theory looked pretty good in the early 2000s: Britain, with a floating exchange rate, managed to stay out of a recession that affected the rest of Europe, and Canada, which also has a floating rate, suffered a less severe recession than the United States.

In the Great Recession, however, a financial crisis that began in the United States led to a recession in virtually every country. In this case, it appears that "financial contagion"—the spread of market disruption via international linkages among financial markets—was much stronger than any insulation from overseas disturbances provided by floating exchange rates.

Finally, the coronavirus slump was global in large part because of literal contagion: nations around the world put much of their economies on temporary lockdown in an attempt to limit the spread of COVID-19.

ECONOMICS >> *in Action*
The Little Currency That Could

Iceland, with a population around 334,000, is a tiny country. And in 2008, it had a very big economic problem. Between 2003 and 2007 the country's main banks expanded very aggressively, mainly with money borrowed from banks in other countries, and the banking boom led in turn to a booming local economy. But then the boom went bust, as did the banks, and Iceland needed to go back to more mundane ways of making a living, like fishing and tourism. To do this it needed to reduce costs, mainly by cutting wages. It wasn't the only country in this position. Other nations that had borrowed a lot of money, like Greece, also needed to make big adjustments.

But there was one big difference between Iceland and Greece (aside from the weather): Greece no longer had its own currency, because it had adopted the euro, whereas Iceland, tiny though it was, still had its own currency, the krona (plural kronur)—and Icelandic wages are set in kronur, not euros or dollars.

This made the process of cutting wages very different in Iceland than it was in euro-using countries. In Greece, employers actually had to tell workers that they would be paid less—something companies are reluctant to do, because at best it creates bad feelings and at worst it leads to strikes. Iceland, however, could gain competitiveness without wage cuts, simply by letting the krona fall.

Figure 33-10 shows how the different options played out. The red line shows average wages in the euro area as a whole, with 2007 = 100, while the purple line

FIGURE 33-10 Cutting Wages in Iceland and Greece, 2007–2015

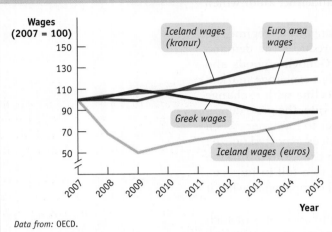

Data from: OECD.

shows Greek wages over the same period. As you can see, Greece did manage to cut wages gradually over time while wages in other European nations rose, so the Greek economy gradually became more competitive. It was, however, a slow and extremely painful process.

The other two lines show Iceland's story. The blue line shows wages in Iceland's own currency, kronur. These continued to rise; there were no nominal wage cuts. The green line shows Icelandic wages in euros, which fell dramatically thanks to the depreciation of the krona.

It would be wrong to say that this process was painless—Icelandic workers saw the prices of imported goods rise, reducing their purchasing power. But it wasn't nearly as painful as Greece's adjustment. In Greece, unemployment rose year after year, peaking at 28% in late 2013 before it began inching down. In Iceland, by contrast, the jobs crisis only lasted about two years, and by late 2014 the unemployment rate was under 5%.

Overall, Iceland's experience was an object lesson in the advantages of having your own currency—even when your country is no bigger than a medium-sized U.S. town.

>> **Quick Review**

• Countries can change fixed exchange rates. A **devaluation,** a reduction in the value of the currency, can help reduce surpluses in the foreign exchange market and can increase aggregate demand. A **revaluation,** an increase in the value of the currency, can help reduce shortages in the foreign exchange market and can reduce aggregate demand.

• In an open economy with a floating exchange rate, interest rates also affect the exchange rate, and so monetary policy affects aggregate demand through the effects of the exchange rate on imports and exports.

• Because one country's imports are another country's exports, business cycles are sometimes synchronized across countries. However, floating exchange rates may reduce this link.

>> **Check Your Understanding 33-4**

Solutions appear at back of book.

1. Look at the data in Figure 33-8. Where do you see devaluations and revaluations of the franc against the mark?

2. In the late 1980s Canadian economists argued that the high interest rate policies of the Bank of Canada weren't just causing high unemployment—they were also making it hard for Canadian manufacturers to compete with the United States. Explain this complaint, using our analysis of how monetary policy works under floating exchange rates.

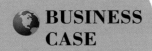
German Cars, Made in Spain

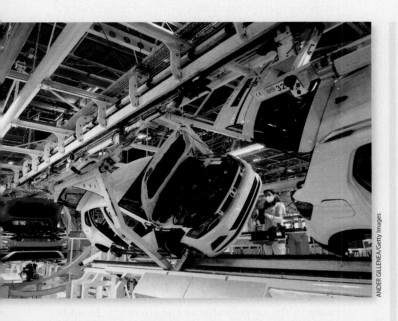

ANDER GILLENEA/Getty Images

The town of Pamplona, Spain, is famous for the "running of the bulls," a summer event in which thrill-seekers attempt to outrun a group of bulls through a cordoned-off section of the town's ancient center. But that is an annual event, and while it does draw in tourists, the town's residents have to make a living all year long. And what many of them actually live off, directly or indirectly, is something you probably don't associate with Spain: automotive manufacturing.

Pamplona is home to a large assembly plant owned by Volkswagen, one of many car producers operating in Spain. Volkswagen, like other automotive firms—especially but not only German corporations—began investing large sums expanding its Spanish operations in the early 2010s. You probably don't think of Spain as an auto-industry powerhouse, since there are no Spanish-owned car companies. But multinational auto companies have flocked to Spain, making it Europe's second-largest producer of cars, behind only Germany.

The Spanish auto industry mainly produces cars for consumers in other countries; 80% of its output is exported. So why are companies like Volkswagen moving production to Spain? In a word, costs.

Spain, like Germany, uses the euro. When it faced a severe recession that drove the unemployment rate to 26%, it couldn't devalue its currency the way Iceland did. However, as we noted in the Economics in Action in Chapter 31, Spanish inflation dropped drastically in the face of high unemployment, while prices in other countries, including Germany, continued to rise. Spanish wages also lagged. From 2010 to 2018, the hourly cost of labor in Spanish manufacturing rose only 0.9% per year, compared with 2.4% in Germany.

Spain's relative wage restraint seems to have mattered a lot for its auto industry. And the booming auto industry has been one of the biggest forces behind Spain's economic recovery.

QUESTIONS FOR THOUGHT

1. How does the story of Spain's auto industry relate to our discussion of the determinants of the current account on p. 542?

2. Spain's adjustment since the early 2010s is sometimes described as "internal devaluation." What do you think that means?

3. Spain's rising auto exports are entirely due to the investments of non-Spanish companies. How might this affect changes in Spain's current account?

SUMMARY

1. A country's **balance of payments accounts** summarize its transactions with the rest of the world. The **balance of payments on current account,** or **current account,** includes the **balance of payments on goods and services** together with balances on factor income and transfers. The **merchandise trade balance,** or **trade balance,** is a frequently cited component of the balance of payments on goods and services. The **balance of payments on financial account,** or **financial account,** measures capital flows. By definition, the balance of payments on current account plus the balance of payments on financial account is zero.

2. The loanable funds model shows that the direction of net capital flows—the excess of inflows over outflows, or vice versa—across countries is determined by differences in interest rates that arise from differences in investment opportunities and savings behavior. Capital flows move to equalize interest rates across countries. In the real world, countries experience two-way capital flows—gross flows of capital in and out—because factors other than interest rate differences affect investors' decisions. Those factors are risk considerations, business strategy, and banking industry expertise.

3. Currencies are traded in the **foreign exchange market;** the prices at which they are traded are **exchange rates.** When a currency rises against another currency, it **appreciates;** when it falls, it **depreciates.** The **equilibrium exchange rate** matches the quantity of that currency supplied to the foreign exchange market to the quantity demanded.

4. To correct for international differences in inflation rates, economists calculate **real exchange rates,** which multiply the exchange rate between two countries' currencies by the ratio of the countries' price levels. The current account responds only to changes in the real exchange rate, not the nominal exchange rate. **Purchasing power parity** is the exchange rate that makes the cost of a basket of goods and services equal in two countries. While purchasing power parity and the nominal exchange rate almost always differ, purchasing power parity is a good predictor of actual changes in the nominal exchange rate.

5. Countries adopt different **exchange rate regimes,** rules governing exchange rate policy. The main types are **fixed exchange rates,** where the government takes action to keep the exchange rate at a target level, and **floating exchange rates,** where the exchange rate is free to fluctuate. Countries can fix exchange rates using **exchange market intervention,** which requires them to hold **foreign exchange reserves** that they use to buy any surplus of their currency. Alternatively, they can change domestic policies, especially monetary policy, to shift the demand and supply curves in the foreign exchange market. Finally, they can use **foreign exchange controls.**

6. Exchange rate policy poses a dilemma: there are economic payoffs to stable exchange rates, but the policies used to fix the exchange rate have costs. Exchange market intervention requires large reserves, and exchange controls distort incentives. If monetary policy is used to help fix the exchange rate, it isn't available to use for domestic policy.

7. Fixed exchange rates aren't always permanent commitments: countries with a fixed exchange rate sometimes engage in **devaluations,** reductions in the target value of the currency, or **revaluations,** increases in the target value of the currency. In addition to helping eliminate a surplus of domestic currency on the foreign exchange market, a devaluation increases aggregate demand. Similarly, a revaluation reduces shortages of domestic currency and reduces aggregate demand.

8. Under floating exchange rates, expansionary monetary policy works in part through the exchange rate: cutting domestic interest rates leads to a depreciation, and through that to higher exports and lower imports, which increases aggregate demand. Contractionary monetary policy has the reverse effect.

9. The fact that one country's imports are another country's exports creates a link between the business cycle in different countries. Floating exchange rates, however, may reduce the strength of that link.

KEY TERMS

Balance of payments accounts, p. 964
Balance of payments on current account (current account), p. 966
Balance of payments on goods and services, p. 966
Merchandise trade balance (trade balance), p. 966
Balance of payments on financial account (financial account), p. 966
Foreign exchange market, p. 971
Exchange rates, p. 971
Appreciates, p. 972
Depreciates, p. 972
Equilibrium exchange rate, p. 973
Real exchange rate, p. 975
Purchasing power parity, p. 977
Exchange rate regime, p. 979
Fixed exchange rate, p. 979
Floating exchange rate, p. 980
Exchange market intervention, p. 980
Foreign exchange reserves, p. 980
Foreign exchange controls, p. 981
Devaluation, p. 985
Revaluation, p. 985

PRACTICE QUESTIONS

1. You recently read a headline that states: "The U.S. loses $500 billion a year to trade with China." This amount would be included as part of the U.S. current account deficit. How is this headline misleading? How do these transactions affect the loanable funds framework?

2. During his presidency, Donald Trump attempted to alleviate the U.S. trade deficit by passing a series of tariffs on Chinese exports. Prior to President Trump taking office, the U.S. had an average tariff rate of 3.1% on Chinese exports but by February of 2020 the average tariff rate had increased to 19.3%. During the same time period, the U.S. dollar appreciated from 6.27 Chinese yuan to 7.10 yuan per U.S. dollar. Using the foreign exchange market, explain how the implementation of the tariffs would change the yuan/dollar exchange rate. Is this consistent with what we observed in the data?

3. With oil priced in U.S. dollars, most Middle Eastern and other oil-producing countries have a fixed exchange rate peg to the U.S. dollar. What are the pros and cons of these countries pegging their currency to the U.S. dollar?

PROBLEMS

1. How would the following transactions be categorized in the U.S. balance of payments accounts? Would they be entered in the current account (as a payment to or from a foreigner) or the financial account (as a sale of assets to or purchase of assets from a foreigner)? How will the balance of payments on the current and financial accounts change?

   a. A French importer buys a case of California wine for $500.

   b. An American who works for a French company deposits her paycheck, drawn on a Paris bank, into her San Francisco bank.

   c. An American buys a bond from a Japanese company for $10,000.

   d. An American charity sends $100,000 to Africa to help local residents buy food after a harvest shortfall.

2. The accompanying diagram shows foreign-owned assets in the United States and U.S.-owned assets abroad, both as a percentage of foreign GDP. As you can see from the diagram, both increased around five-fold from 1980 to 2019.

   a. As U.S.-owned assets abroad increased as a percentage of foreign GDP, does this mean that the United States, over the period, experienced net capital outflows?

   b. Does this diagram indicate that world economies were more tightly linked in 2019 than they were in 1980?

3. In the economy of Scottopia in 2020, exports equaled $400 billion of goods and $300 billion of services, imports equaled $500 billion of goods and $350 billion of services, and the rest of the world purchased $250 billion of Scottopia's assets. What was the merchandise trade balance for Scottopia? What was the balance of payments on current account in Scottopia? What was the balance of payments on financial account? What was the value of Scottopia's purchases of assets from the rest of the world?

4. In the economy of Popania in 2020, total Popanian purchases of assets in the rest of the world equaled $300 billion, purchases of Popanian assets by the rest of the world equaled $400 billion, and Popania exported goods and services equal to $350 billion. What was Popania's balance of payments on financial account in 2020? What was its balance of payments on current account? What was the value of its imports?

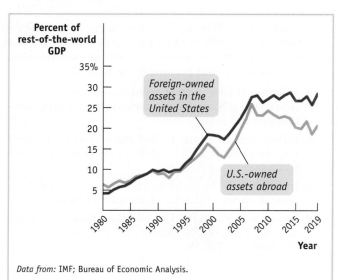

Data from: IMF; Bureau of Economic Analysis.

5. Suppose that Northlandia and Southlandia are the only two trading countries in the world, that each nation runs a balance of payments on both current and financial accounts equal to zero, and that each nation sees the other's assets as identical to its own. Using the accompanying diagrams, explain how the demand and supply of loanable funds, the interest rate, and the balance of payments on current and financial accounts will change in each country if international capital flows are possible.

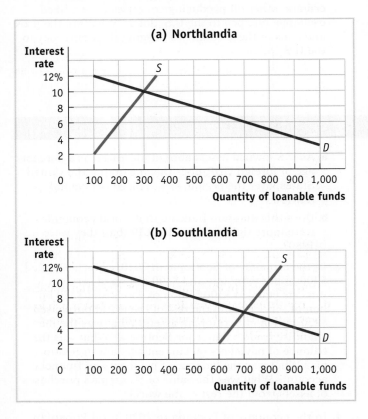

7. Go to http://fx.sauder.ubc.ca. Using the table labeled "The Most Recent Cross-Rates of Major Currencies," determine whether the British pound (GBP), the Canadian dollar (CAD), the Japanese yen (JPY), the euro (EUR), and the Swiss franc (CHF) have appreciated or depreciated against the U.S. dollar (USD) since April 1, 2020. The exchange rates on April 1, 2020 are listed in the table in Problem 6.

8. In January 2001, the U.S. federal funds rate was 6.5%, falling to 2% in November 2004. During the same period, the marginal lending rate at the European Central Bank fell from 5.75% to 3%.

   a. Considering the change in interest rates over the period and using the loanable funds model, would you have expected funds to flow from the United States to Europe or from Europe to the United States over this period?

   b. The accompanying diagram shows the exchange rate between the euro and the U.S. dollar from January 1, 2001, through September 2008. Is the movement of the exchange rate over the period January 2001 to November 2004 consistent with the movement in funds predicted in part a?

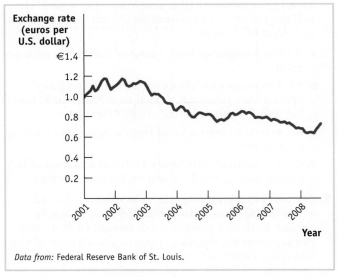

Data from: Federal Reserve Bank of St. Louis.

6. Based on the exchange rates for the trading days of 2019 and 2020 shown in the accompanying table, did the U.S. dollar appreciate or depreciate over the year? Did the movement in the value of the U.S. dollar make American goods and services more or less attractive to foreigners?

April 1, 2019	April 1, 2020
US$1.31 to buy 1 British pound sterling	US$1.24 to buy 1 British pound sterling
30.81 Taiwan dollars to buy US$1	30.29 Taiwan dollars to buy US$1
US$0.75 to buy 1 Canadian dollar	US$0.70 to buy 1 Canadian dollar
111.23 Japanese yen to buy US$1	107.22 Japanese yen to buy US$1
US$1.12 to buy 1 euro	US$1.09 to buy 1 euro
1.00 Swiss franc to buy US$1	0.97 Swiss franc to buy US$1

9. In each of the following scenarios, suppose that the two nations are the only trading nations in the world. Given inflation and the change in the nominal exchange rate, which nation's goods become more attractive?

   a. Inflation is 10% in the United States and 5% in Japan; the U.S. dollar–Japanese yen exchange rate remains the same.

   b. Inflation is 3% in the United States and 8% in Mexico; the price of the U.S. dollar falls from 12.50 to 10.25 Mexican pesos.

   c. Inflation is 5% in the United States and 3% in the euro area; the price of the euro falls from $1.30 to $1.20.

   d. Inflation is 8% in the United States and 4% in Canada; the price of the Canadian dollar rises from US$0.60 to US$0.75.

10. Starting from a position of equilibrium in the foreign exchange market under a fixed exchange rate regime, how must a government react to an increase in the demand for the nation's goods and services by the rest of the world to keep the exchange rate at its fixed value?

11. Suppose that Albernia's central bank has fixed the value of its currency, the bern, to the U.S. dollar (at a rate of US$1.50 to 1 bern) and is committed to that exchange rate. Initially, the foreign exchange market for the bern is also in equilibrium, as shown in the accompanying diagram. However, both Albernians and Americans begin to believe that there are big risks in holding Albernian assets; as a result, they become unwilling to hold Albernian assets unless they receive a higher rate of return on them than they do on U.S. assets. How would this affect the diagram? If the Albernian central bank tries to keep the exchange rate fixed using monetary policy, how will this affect the Albernian economy?

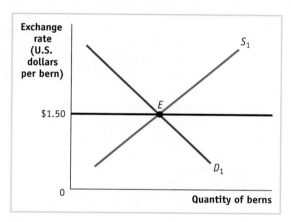

12. Access the Discovering Data exercise for Chapter 33 online to answer the following questions.

a. Using the most current data available, how has the exchange rate changed for Mexico, the United Kingdom, and Switzerland?

b. By how much did each of these three currencies appreciate and depreciate against the U.S. dollar?

c. How will the exchange rate change in each of the three countries affect their exports to the United States?

13. Your study partner asks you, "If central banks lose the ability to use discretionary monetary policy under fixed exchange rates, why would nations agree to a fixed exchange rate system?" How do you respond?

⠿ WORK IT OUT

14. Suppose the United States and Japan are the only two trading countries in the world. What will happen to the value of the U.S. dollar if the following occur, other things equal?

a. Japan relaxes some of its import restrictions.

b. The United States imposes some import tariffs on Japanese goods.

c. Interest rates in the United States rise dramatically.

d. A report indicates that Japanese cars last much longer than previously thought, especially compared with U.S. cars. ■

Solutions to *Check Your Understanding* Questions

This section offers suggested answers to the *Check Your Understanding* questions found within chapters.

‖ CHAPTER ONE

1-1 Check Your Understanding

1. **a.** This illustrates the concept of opportunity cost. Given that a person can only eat so much at one sitting, having a slice of chocolate cake requires that you forgo eating something else, such as a slice of coconut cream pie.

   b. This illustrates the concept that resources are scarce. Even if there were more resources in the world, the total amount of those resources would be limited. As a result, scarcity would still arise. For there to be no scarcity, there would have to be unlimited amounts of everything (including unlimited time in a human life), which is clearly impossible.

   c. This illustrates the concept that people usually exploit opportunities to make themselves better off. Students will seek to make themselves better off by signing up for the tutorials of teaching assistants with good reputations and avoiding those teaching assistants with poor reputations. It also illustrates the concept that resources are scarce. If there were unlimited spaces in tutorials with good teaching assistants, they would not fill up.

   d. This illustrates the concept of marginal analysis. Your decision about allocating your time is a "how much" decision: how much time spent exercising versus how much time spent studying. You make your decision by comparing the benefit of an additional hour of exercising to its cost, the effect on your grades of one less hour spent studying.

2. **a.** Yes. The increased time spent commuting is a cost you will incur if you accept the new job. That additional time spent commuting—or equivalently, the benefit you would get from spending that time doing something else—is an opportunity cost of the new job.

   b. Yes. One of the benefits of the new job is that you will be making $50,000. But if you take the new job, you will have to give up your current job; that is, you have to give up your current salary of $45,000. So $45,000 is one of the opportunity costs of taking the new job.

   c. No. A more spacious office is an additional benefit of your new job and does not involve forgoing something else. So it is not an opportunity cost.

1-2 Check Your Understanding

1. **a.** This illustrates the concept that there are gains from trade. Students trade tutoring services based on their different abilities in academic subjects.

   b. This illustrates the concept that when markets don't achieve efficiency, government intervention can improve society's welfare. In this case the market, left alone, will permit bars and nightclubs to impose costs on their neighbors in the form of loud music, costs that the bars and nightclubs have no incentive to take into account. This is an inefficient outcome because society as a whole can be made better off if bars and nightclubs are induced to reduce their noise.

   c. This illustrates the concept that resources should be used as efficiently as possible to achieve society's goals. By closing neighborhood clinics and shifting funds to the main hospital, better health care can be provided at a lower cost.

   d. This illustrates the concept that markets move toward equilibrium. Here, because books with the same amount of wear and tear sell for about the same price, no buyer or seller can be made better off by engaging in a different trade than he or she undertook. This means that the market for used textbooks has moved to an equilibrium.

2. **a.** This does not describe an equilibrium situation. Many students should want to change their behavior and switch to eating at the restaurants. An equilibrium will be established when students are equally as well off eating at the restaurants as eating at the dining hall—which would happen if, say, prices at the dining hall were higher than at the restaurants.

   b. This does describe an equilibrium situation. By changing your behavior and riding the bus, you would not be made better off. Therefore, you have no incentive to change your behavior.

1-3 Check Your Understanding

1. **a.** This illustrates the principle that increases in the economy's potential lead to economic growth over time. Cheaper solar panels will lower the cost of energy, increasing the economy's potential and economic growth. Solar panel manufacturers will be better off but firms producing competing energy will be worse off.

   b. This illustrates the principle that overall spending sometimes gets out of line with the economy's productive capacity; when it does, government policy can change spending. The tax cut would increase people's after-tax incomes, leading to higher consumer spending.

   c. This illustrates the principle that one person's spending is another person's income. As oil companies decrease their spending on labor by laying off workers and paying remaining workers lower wages, those workers' incomes fall. In turn, those workers decrease their consumer spending, causing restaurants and other consumer businesses to lose income.

CHAPTER TWO

2-1 Check Your Understanding

1. **a.** False. An increase in the resources available to Boeing for use in producing Dreamliners and small jets changes the production possibility frontier by shifting it outward. This is because Boeing can now produce more small jets and Dreamliners than before. In the accompanying figure, the line labeled "Boeing's original PPF" represents Boeing's original production possibility frontier, and the line labeled "Boeing's new PPF" represents the new production possibility frontier that results from an increase in resources available to Boeing.

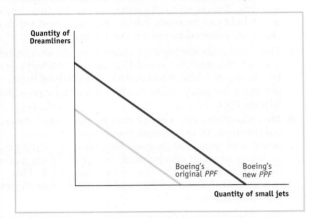

b. True. A technological change that allows Boeing to build more small jets for any amount of Dreamliners built results in a change in its production possibility frontier. This is illustrated in the accompanying figure: the new production possibility frontier is represented by the line labeled "Boeing's new PPF," and the original production frontier is represented by the line labeled "Boeing's original PPF." Since the maximum quantity of Dreamliners that Boeing can build is the same as before, the new production possibility frontier intersects the vertical axis at the same point as the original frontier. But since the maximum possible quantity of small jets is now greater than before, the new frontier intersects the horizontal axis to the right of the original frontier.

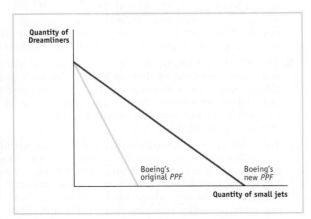

c. False. The production possibility frontier illustrates how much of one good an economy must give up to get more of another good only when resources are used

efficiently in production. If an economy is producing inefficiently—that is, inside the frontier—then it does not have to give up a unit of one good in order to get another unit of the other good. Instead, by becoming more efficient in production, this economy can have more of both goods.

2. **a.** The United States has an absolute advantage in automobile production because it takes fewer Americans (6) to produce a car in one day than Italians (8). The United States also has an absolute advantage in washing machine production because it takes fewer Americans (2) to produce a washing machine in one day than Italians (3).

b. In Italy the opportunity cost of a washing machine in terms of an automobile is $\frac{3}{8}$: $\frac{3}{8}$ of a car can be produced with the same number of workers and in the same time it takes to produce 1 washing machine. In the United States the opportunity cost of a washing machine in terms of an automobile is $\frac{2}{6} = \frac{1}{3}$: $\frac{1}{3}$ of a car can be produced with the same number of workers and in the same time it takes to produce 1 washing machine. Since $\frac{1}{3} < \frac{3}{8}$, the United States has a comparative advantage in the production of washing machines: to produce a washing machine, only $\frac{1}{3}$ of a car must be given up in the United States but $\frac{3}{8}$ of a car must be given up in Italy. This means that Italy has a comparative advantage in automobiles. This can be checked as follows. The opportunity cost of an automobile in terms of a washing machine in Italy is $\frac{8}{3}$, equal to $2\frac{2}{3}$: $2\frac{2}{3}$ washing machines can be produced with the same number of workers and in the time it takes to produce 1 car in Italy. And the opportunity cost of an automobile in terms of a washing machine in the United States is $\frac{6}{2}$, equal to 3:3 washing machines can be produced with the same number of workers and in the time it takes to produce 1 car in the United States. Since $2\frac{2}{3} < 3$, Italy has a comparative advantage in producing automobiles.

c. The greatest gains are realized when each country specializes in producing the good for which it has a comparative advantage. Therefore, the United States should specialize in washing machines and Italy should specialize in automobiles.

3. At a trade of 10 U.S. large jets for 15 Brazilian small jets, Brazil gives up less for a large jet than it would if it were building large jets itself. Without trade, Brazil gives up 3 small jets for each large jet it produces. With trade, Brazil gives up only 1.5 small jets for each large jet from the United States. Likewise, the United States gives up less for a small jet than it would if it were producing small jets itself. Without trade, the United States gives up $\frac{3}{4}$ of a large jet for each small jet. With trade, the United States gives up only $\frac{2}{3}$ of a large jet for each small jet from Brazil.

4. An increase in the amount of money spent by households results in an increase in the flow of goods to households. This, in turn, generates an increase in demand for factors of production by firms. So, there is an increase in the number of jobs in the economy.

2-2 Check Your Understanding

1. **a.** This is a normative statement because it stipulates what should be done. In addition, it may have no "right" answer. That is, should people be prevented from all dangerous personal behavior if they enjoy that

behavior—like skydiving? Your answer will depend on your point of view.

b. This is a positive statement because it is a description of fact.

2. a. True. Economists often have different value judgments about the desirability of a particular social goal. But despite those differences in value judgments, they will tend to agree that society, once it has decided to pursue a given social goal, should adopt the most efficient policy to achieve that goal. Therefore economists are likely to agree on adopting policy choice B.

b. False. Disagreements between economists are more likely to arise because they base their conclusions on different models or because they have different value judgments about the desirability of the policy.

‖ CHAPTER THREE

3-1 Check Your Understanding

1. a. The quantity of umbrellas demanded is higher at any given price on a rainy day than on a dry day. This is a rightward shift of the demand curve, since at any given price the quantity demanded rises. This implies that any specific quantity can now be sold at a higher price.

b. The quantity of summer Caribbean cruises demanded rises in response to a price reduction. This is a movement along the demand curve for summer Caribbean cruises.

c. The demand for roses increases the week of Valentine's Day. This is a rightward shift of the demand curve.

d. The quantity of gasoline demanded falls in response to a rise in price. This is a movement along the demand curve.

3-2 Check Your Understanding

1. a. The quantity of houses supplied rises as a result of an increase in prices. This is a movement along the supply curve.

b. The quantity of strawberries supplied is higher at any given price. This is a rightward shift of the supply curve.

c. The quantity of labor supplied is lower at any given wage. This is a leftward shift of the supply curve compared to the supply curve during school vacation. So, in order to attract workers, fast-food chains have to offer higher wages.

d. The quantity of labor supplied rises in response to a rise in wages. This is a movement along the supply curve.

e. The quantity of cabins supplied is higher at any given price. This is a rightward shift of the supply curve.

3-3 Check Your Understanding

1. a. The supply curve shifts rightward. At the original equilibrium price of the year before, the quantity of grapes supplied exceeds the quantity demanded. This is a case of surplus. The price of grapes will fall.

b. The demand curve shifts leftward. At the original equilibrium price, the quantity of hotel rooms supplied exceeds the quantity demanded. This is a case of surplus. The rates for hotel rooms will fall.

c. The demand curve for second-hand snowblowers shifts rightward. At the original equilibrium price, the quantity of second-hand snowblowers demanded exceeds the quantity supplied. This is a case of shortage. The equilibrium price of second-hand snowblowers will rise.

3-4 Check Your Understanding

1. a. The market for large cars: this is a rightward shift in demand caused by a decrease in the price of a complement, gasoline. As a result of the shift, the equilibrium price of large cars will rise and the equilibrium quantity of large cars bought and sold will also rise.

b. The market for fresh paper made from recycled stock: this is a rightward shift in supply due to a technological innovation. As a result of this shift, the equilibrium price of fresh paper made from recycled stock will fall and the equilibrium quantity bought and sold will rise.

c. The market for movies at a local movie theater: this is a leftward shift in demand caused by a fall in the price of a substitute, on-demand films. As a result of this shift, the equilibrium price of movie tickets will fall and the equilibrium number of people who go to the movies will also fall.

2. Upon the announcement of the new chip, the demand curve for computers using the earlier chip shifts leftward, as demand decreases, and the supply curve for these computers shifts rightward, as supply increases.

a. If demand decreases relatively more than supply increases, then the equilibrium quantity falls, as shown here:

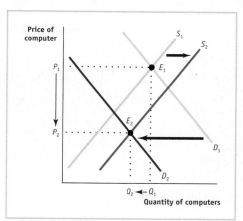

If supply increases relatively more than demand decreases, then the equilibrium quantity rises, as shown here:

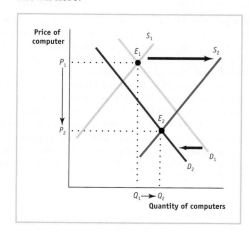

b. In both cases, the equilibrium price falls.

CHAPTER FOUR

4-1 Check Your Understanding

1. A consumer buys each pepper if the price is less than (or just equal to) the consumer's willingness to pay for that pepper. The demand schedule is constructed by asking how many peppers will be demanded at any given price. The accompanying table illustrates the demand schedule.

Price of pepper	Quantity of peppers demanded	Quantity of peppers demanded by Teresa	Quantity of peppers demanded by Azar
$0.90	1	1	0
0.80	2	1	1
0.70	3	2	1
0.60	4	2	2
0.50	5	3	2
0.40	6	3	3
0.30	8	4	4
0.20	8	4	4
0.10	8	4	4
0.00	8	4	4

When the price is $0.40, Teresa's consumer surplus from the first pepper is $0.50, from her second pepper $0.30, from her third pepper $0.10, and she does not buy any more peppers. Teresa's individual consumer surplus is therefore $0.90. Azar's consumer surplus from her first pepper is $0.40, from her second pepper $0.20, from her third pepper $0.00 (since the price is exactly equal to her willingness to pay, she buys the third pepper but receives no consumer surplus from it), and she does not buy any more peppers. Azar's individual consumer surplus is therefore $0.60. Total consumer surplus at a price of $0.40 is therefore $0.90 + $0.60 = $1.50.

4-2 Check Your Understanding

1. a. A producer supplies each pepper if the price is greater than (or just equal to) the producer's cost of producing that pepper. The supply schedule is constructed by asking how many peppers will be supplied at any price. The accompanying table illustrates the supply schedule.

   b. When the price is $0.70, Cara's producer surplus from the first pepper is $0.60, from her second pepper $0.60, from her third pepper $0.30, from her fourth pepper $0.10, and she does not supply any more peppers. Cara's individual producer surplus is therefore $1.60. Jamie's producer surplus from his first pepper is $0.40, from his second pepper $0.20, from his third pepper $0.00 (since the price is exactly equal to his cost, he sells the third pepper but receives no producer surplus from it), and he does not supply any more peppers. Jamie's individual producer surplus is therefore $0.60. Total producer surplus at a price of $0.70 is therefore $1.60 + $0.60 = $2.20.

Price of pepper	Quantity of peppers supplied	Quantity of peppers supplied by Cara	Quantity of peppers supplied by Jamie
$0.90	8	4	4
0.80	7	4	3
0.70	7	4	3
0.60	6	4	2
0.50	5	3	2
0.40	4	3	1
0.30	3	2	1
0.20	2	2	0
0.10	2	2	0
0.00	0	0	0

4-3 Check Your Understanding

1. The quantity demanded equals the quantity supplied at a price of $0.50, the equilibrium price. At that price, a total quantity of five peppers will be bought and sold. Teresa will buy three peppers and receive consumer surplus of $0.40 on her first, $0.20 on her second, and $0.00 on her third pepper. Azar will buy two peppers and receive consumer surplus of $0.30 on her first and $0.10 on her second pepper. Total consumer surplus is therefore $1.00. Cara will supply three peppers and receive producer surplus of $0.40 on her first, $0.40 on her second, and $0.10 on her third pepper. Jamie will supply two peppers and receive producer surplus of $0.20 on his first and $0.00 on his second pepper. Total producer surplus is therefore $1.10. Total surplus in this market is therefore $1.00 + $1.10 = $2.10.

2. a. If Azar consumes one fewer pepper, she loses $0.60 (her willingness to pay for her second pepper); if Teresa consumes one more pepper, she gains $0.30 (her willingness to pay for her fourth pepper). This results in an overall loss of consumer surplus of $0.60 − $0.30 = $0.30.

   b. Cara's cost of the last pepper she supplied (the third pepper) is $0.40, and Jamie's cost of producing one more (his third pepper) is $0.70. Total producer surplus therefore falls by $0.70 − $0.40 = $0.30.

   c. Azar's willingness to pay for her second pepper is $0.60; this is what she would lose if she were to consume one fewer pepper. Cara's cost of producing her third pepper is $0.40; this is what she would save if she were to produce one fewer pepper. If we therefore reduced quantity by one pepper, we would lose $0.60 − $0.40 = $0.20 of total surplus.

3. The new guideline is likely to reduce the total life span of kidney recipients because recipients with small children are more likely to get a kidney compared to the original guideline. As a result, total surplus is likely to fall. However, this new policy can be justified as an acceptable sacrifice of efficiency for fairness because it's a desirable goal to reduce the chance of a small child losing a parent.

4-4 Check Your Understanding

1. When these rights are separated, someone who owns both the above-ground and the mineral rights can sell each of these separately in the market for above-ground rights and the market for mineral rights. And each of these markets will achieve efficiency: if the market price for above-ground rights is higher than the seller's cost, the seller will sell those rights and total surplus increases. If the market price for mineral rights is higher than the seller's cost, the seller will sell those rights and total surplus increases. If the two rights, however, cannot be sold separately, a seller can only sell both rights or none at all. Imagine a situation in which the seller values the mineral rights highly (that is, has a high cost of selling it) but values the above-ground rights much less. If the two rights are separate, the owner may sell the above-ground rights (increasing total surplus) but not the mineral rights. If, however, the two rights cannot be sold separately, and the owner values the mineral rights sufficiently highly, she may not sell either of the two rights. In this case, surplus could have been created through the sale of the above-ground rights but goes unrealized because the two rights could not be sold separately.

2. There will be many sellers willing to sell their books but only a few buyers who want to buy books at that price. As a result, only a few transactions will actually occur, and many transactions that would have been mutually beneficial will not take place. This, of course, is inefficient.

3. Markets, alas, do not always lead to efficiency. When there is market failure, the market outcome may be inefficient. This can occur for three main reasons. Markets can fail when, in an attempt to capture more surplus, one party—a monopolist, for instance—prevents mutually beneficial transactions from occurring. Markets can also fail when one individual's actions have side effects—externalities—on the welfare of others. Finally, markets can fail when the goods themselves—such as goods about which some relevant information is private—are unsuited for efficient management by markets. And when markets don't achieve efficiency, government intervention can improve society's welfare.

‖ CHAPTER FIVE

5-1 Check Your Understanding

1. **a.** Fewer homeowners are willing to rent out their driveways because the price ceiling has reduced the payment they receive. This is an example of a fall in price leading to a fall in the quantity supplied. It is shown in the accompanying diagram by the movement from point E to point A along the supply curve, a reduction in quantity of 400 parking spaces.

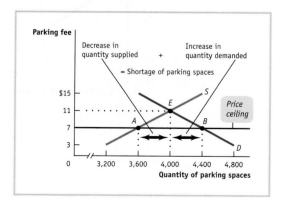

b. The quantity demanded increases by 400 spaces as the price decreases. At a lower price, more fans are willing to drive and rent a parking space. It is shown in the diagram by the movement from point E to point B along the demand curve.

c. Under a price ceiling, the quantity demanded exceeds the quantity supplied; as a result, shortages arise. In this case, there will be a shortage of 800 parking spaces. It is shown by the horizontal distance between points A and B.

d. Price ceilings result in wasted resources. The additional time fans spend to guarantee a parking space is wasted time.

e. Price ceilings lead to inefficient allocation of a good—here, the parking spaces—to consumers.

f. Price ceilings lead to black markets.

2. **a.** False. By lowering the price that producers receive, a price ceiling leads to a decrease in the quantity supplied.

b. True. A price ceiling leads to a lower quantity supplied than in an efficient, unregulated market. As a result, some people who would have been willing to pay the market price, and so would have gotten the good in an unregulated market, are unable to obtain it when a price ceiling is imposed.

c. True. Those producers who still sell the product now receive less for it and are therefore worse off. Other producers will no longer find it worthwhile to sell the product at all and so will also be made worse off.

3. **a.** Since the apartment is rented quickly at the same price, there is no change (either gain or loss) in producer surplus. So any change in total surplus comes from changes in consumer surplus. When you are evicted, the amount of consumer surplus you lose is equal to the difference between your willingness to pay for the apartment and the rent-controlled price. When the apartment is rented to someone else at the same price, the amount of consumer surplus the new renter gains is equal to the difference between their willingness to pay and the rent-controlled price. So this will be a pure transfer of surplus from one person to another only if both your willingness to pay and the new renter's willingness to pay are the same. Since under rent control apartments are not always allocated to those who have the highest willingness to pay, the new renter's willingness to pay may be either equal to, lower than, or higher than your willingness to pay. If the new renter's willingness to pay is lower than yours, this will create additional deadweight loss: there is some additional consumer surplus that is lost. However, if the new renter's willingness to pay is higher than yours, this will create an increase in total surplus, as the new renter gains more consumer surplus than you lost.

b. This creates deadweight loss: if you were able to give the ticket away, someone else would be able to obtain consumer surplus, equal to their willingness to pay for the ticket. You neither gain nor lose any surplus, since you cannot go to the concert whether or not you give the ticket away. If you were able to sell the ticket, the buyer would obtain consumer surplus equal to the difference between their willingness to pay for the ticket and the price at which you sell the ticket. In addition, you would obtain producer surplus equal to the difference between the price at which you sell the ticket and your cost of selling the ticket (which, since you won the ticket, is presumably zero). Since the restriction to neither sell nor give away the ticket means that this surplus cannot be obtained by anybody, it creates deadweight loss. If you could give the ticket away, as just described, there would be consumer surplus that accrues to the recipient of the ticket; and if you give the ticket to the person with the highest willingness to pay, there would be no deadweight loss.

c. This creates deadweight loss. If students buy ice cream on campus, they obtain consumer surplus: their willingness to pay must be higher than the price of the ice cream. Your college obtains producer surplus: the price is higher than your college's cost of selling the ice cream. Prohibiting the sale of ice cream on campus means that these two sources of total surplus are lost: there is deadweight loss.

d. Given that your dog values ice cream equally as much as you do, this is a pure transfer of surplus. As you lose consumer surplus, your dog gains equally as much consumer surplus.

5-2 Check Your Understanding

1. a. Some gas station owners will benefit from getting a higher price. Q_F indicates the sales made by these owners. But some will lose; there are those who make sales at the market equilibrium price of P_E but do not make sales at the regulated price of P_F. These missed sales are indicated on the graph by the fall in the quantity demanded along the demand curve, from point E to point A.

b. Those who buy gas at the higher price of P_F will probably receive better service; this is an example of *inefficiently high quality* caused by a price floor as gas station owners compete on quality rather than price. But opponents are correct to claim that consumers are generally worse off—those who buy at P_F would have been happy to buy at P_E, and many who were willing to buy at a price between P_E and P_F are now unwilling to buy. This is indicated on the graph by the fall in the quantity demanded along the demand curve, from point E to point A.

c. Proponents are wrong because consumers and some gas station owners are hurt by the price floor, which creates "missed opportunities"—desirable transactions between consumers and station owners that never take place. The deadweight loss, the amount of total surplus lost because of missed opportunities, is indicated by the shaded area in the accompanying figure. Moreover, the inefficiency of wasted resources arises as consumers spend time and money driving to other states. The price floor also tempts people to engage in black market activity. With the price floor, only Q_F units are sold. But at prices between P_E and P_F, there are drivers who cumulatively want to buy more than Q_F and owners who are willing to sell to them, a situation likely to lead to illegal activity.

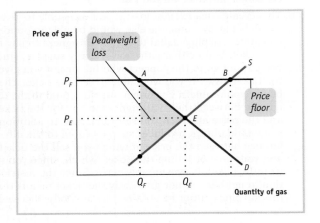

5-3 Check Your Understanding

1. a. The price of a ride is $7 since the quantity demanded at this price is 6 million: $7 is the *demand price* of 6 million rides. This is represented by point A in the accompanying figure.

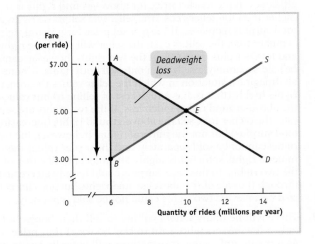

b. At 6 million rides, the supply price is $3 per ride, represented by point B in the figure. The wedge between the demand price of $7 per ride and the supply price of $3 per ride is the quota rent per ride, $4. This is represented in the figure above by the vertical distance between points A and B.

c. The quota discourages 4 million mutually beneficial transactions. The shaded triangle in the figure represents the deadweight loss.

d. At 9 million rides, the demand price is $5.50 per ride, indicated by point C in the accompanying figure, and the supply price is $4.50 per ride, indicated by point D. The quota rent is the difference between the demand price and the supply price: $1. The deadweight loss is represented by the shaded triangle in the figure. As you can see, the deadweight loss is smaller when the quota is set at 9 million rides than when it is set at 6 million rides.

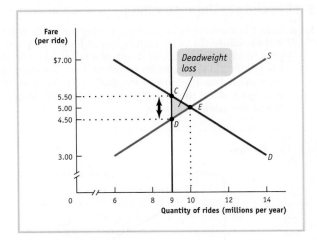

2. The accompanying figure shows a decrease in demand by 4 million rides, represented by a leftward shift of the demand curve from D_1 to D_2: at any given price, the quantity demanded falls by 4 million rides. (For example, at a price of $5, the quantity demanded falls from 10 million to 6 million rides per year.) This eliminates the effect of a quota limit of 8 million rides. At point E_2, the new market equilibrium, the equilibrium quantity is equal to the quota limit; as a result, the quota has no effect on the market.

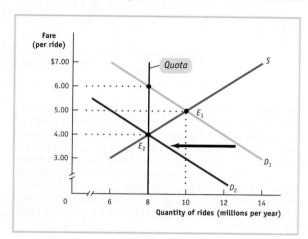

CHAPTER SIX

6-1 Check Your Understanding

1. By the midpoint method, the percent change in the price of strawberries is:

$$\frac{\$1.00 - \$1.50}{(\$1.50 + \$1.00)/2} \times 100 = \frac{-\$0.50}{\$1.25} \times 100 = -40\%$$

Similarly, the percent change in the quantity of strawberries demanded is:

$$\frac{200,000 - 100,000}{(100,000 + 200,000)/2} \times 100 = \frac{100,000}{150,000} \times 100 = 67\%$$

Dropping the minus sign, the price elasticity of demand using the midpoint method is 67%/40% = 1.7.

2. By the midpoint method, the percent change in the quantity of movie tickets demanded in going from 4,000 tickets to 5,000 tickets is:

$$\frac{5,000 - 4,000}{(4,000 + 5,000)/2} \times 100 = \frac{1,000}{4,500} \times 100 = 22\%$$

Since the price elasticity of demand is 1 at the current consumption level, it will take a 22% reduction in the price of movie tickets to generate a 22% increase in quantity demanded.

3. Since price rises, we know that quantity demanded must fall. Given the current price of $0.50, a $0.05 increase in price represents a 10% change, using the method in Equation 6-2. So the price elasticity of demand is:

$$\frac{\text{change in quantity demanded}}{10\%} = 1.2$$

so that the change in quantity demanded (10% × 1.2) equals 12%. A 12% decrease in quantity demanded represents 100,000 × 0.12, or 12,000 sandwiches.

6-2 Check Your Understanding

1. **a.** Elastic demand. Consumers are highly responsive to changes in price. For a rise in price, the quantity effect (which tends to reduce total revenue) outweighs the price effect (which tends to increase total revenue). Overall, this leads to a fall in total revenue.

   b. Unit-elastic demand. Here the revenue lost to the fall in price is exactly equal to the revenue gained from higher sales. The quantity effect exactly offsets the price effect.

   c. Inelastic demand. Consumers are relatively unresponsive to changes in price. For consumers to purchase a given percent increase in output, the price must fall by an even greater percent. The price effect of a fall in price (which tends to reduce total revenue) outweighs the quantity effect (which tends to increase total revenue). As a result, total revenue decreases.

   d. Inelastic demand. Consumers are relatively unresponsive to price, so the percent fall in output is smaller than the percent rise in price. The price effect of a rise in price (which tends to increase total revenue) outweighs the quantity effect (which tends to reduce total revenue). As a result, total revenue increases.

2. **a.** The demand of an accident victim for a blood transfusion is very likely to be perfectly inelastic because there is no substitute and it is necessary for survival. The demand curve will be vertical, at a quantity equal to the needed transfusion quantity.

   b. Students' demand for green erasers is likely to be perfectly elastic because there are easily available substitutes: nongreen erasers. The demand curve will be horizontal, at a price equal to that of nongreen erasers.

6-3 Check Your Understanding

1. By the midpoint method, the percent increase in Charlotte's income is:

$$\frac{\$18,000 - \$12,000}{(\$12,000 + \$18,000)/2} \times 100 = \frac{\$6,000}{\$15,000} \times 100 = 40\%$$

Similarly, the percent increase in her consumption of albums is:

$$\frac{40 - 10}{(10 + 40)/2} \times 100 = \frac{30}{25} \times 100 = 120\%$$

So Charlotte's income elasticity of demand for movies is 120%/40% = 3.

2. Sanjay's consumption of expensive restaurant meals will fall more than 10% because a given percent change in income (a fall of 10% here) induces a larger percent change in consumption of an income-elastic good.

3. The cross-price elasticity of demand is 5%/20% = 0.25. Since the cross-price elasticity of demand is positive, the two goods are substitutes.

6-4 Check Your Understanding

1. By the midpoint method, the percent change in the number of hours of web-design services contracted is:

$$\frac{500,000 - 300,000}{(300,000 + 500,000)/2} \times 100 = \frac{200,000}{400,000} \times 100 = 50\%$$

Similarly, the percent change in the price of web-design services is:

$$\frac{\$150 - \$100}{(\$100 + \$150)/2} \times 100 = \frac{\$50}{\$125} \times 100 = 40\%$$

The price elasticity of supply is 50%/40% = 1.25. So supply is elastic.

2. **a.** True. An increase in demand raises price. If the price elasticity of supply of milk is low, then relatively little additional quantity supplied will be forthcoming as the price rises. As a result, the price of milk will rise substantially to satisfy the increased demand for milk. If the price elasticity of supply is high, then there will be a relatively large increase in quantity supplied when the price rises. As a result, the price of milk will rise only by a little to satisfy the higher demand for milk.

   b. False. It is true that long-run price elasticities of supply are generally larger than short-run elasticities of supply. But this means that the short-run supply curves are generally steeper, not flatter, than the long-run supply curves.

   c. True. When supply is perfectly elastic, the supply curve is a horizontal line. So a change in demand has no effect on price; it affects only the quantity bought and sold.

‖ CHAPTER SEVEN

7-1 Check Your Understanding

1. The following figure shows that, after introduction of the excise tax, the price paid by consumers rises to $1.20; the price received by producers falls to $0.90. Consumers bear $0.20 of the $0.30 tax per pound of butter; producers bear $0.10 of the $0.30 tax per pound of butter. The tax drives a wedge of $0.30 between the price paid by consumers and the price received by producers. As a result, the quantity of butter bought and sold is now 9 million pounds.

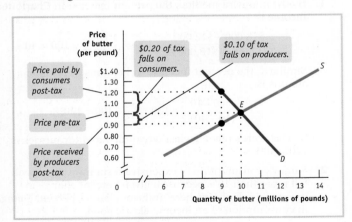

2. The fact that demand is very inelastic means that consumers will reduce their demand for textbooks very little in response to an increase in the price caused by the tax. The fact that supply is somewhat elastic means that suppliers will respond to the fall in the price by reducing supply. As a result, the incidence of the tax will fall heavily on consumers of economics textbooks and very little on publishers, as shown in the accompanying figure.

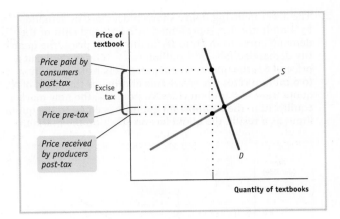

3. True. When a substitute is readily available, demand is elastic. This implies that producers cannot easily pass on the cost of the tax to consumers because consumers will respond to an increased price by switching to the substitute. Furthermore, when producers have difficulty adjusting the amount of the good produced, supply is inelastic. That is, producers cannot easily reduce output in response to a lower price net of tax. So the tax burden will fall more heavily on producers than consumers.

4. The fact that supply is very inelastic means that producers will reduce their supply of bottled water very little in response to the fall in price caused by the tax. Demand, on the other hand, will fall in response to an increase in price because demand is somewhat elastic. As a result, the incidence of the tax will fall heavily on producers of bottled spring water and very little on consumers, as shown in the accompanying figure.

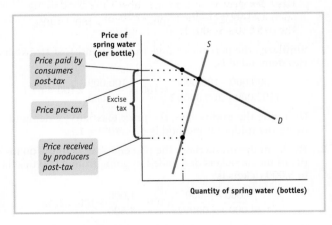

5. True. The lower the elasticity of supply, the more the burden of a tax will fall on producers rather than consumers, other things equal.

7-2 Check Your Understanding

1. **a.** Without the excise tax, Zachary, Yves, Xavier, and William sell, and Ana, Brianna, Chizuko, and Dylan buy one can of soda each, at $0.40 per can. So the quantity bought and sold is 4.

b. At a price to consumers of $0.60, only Ana and Brianna are willing to buy a can of soda. At a price paid to producers of only $0.20, only Zachary and Yves are willing to sell. So the quantity bought and sold is 2.

c. Without the excise tax, Ana's individual consumer surplus is $0.70 − $0.40 = $0.30, Brianna's is $0.60 − $0.40 = $0.20, Chizuko's is $0.50 − $0.40 = $0.10, and Dylan's is $0.40 − $0.40 = $0.00. Total consumer surplus is $0.30 + $0.20 + $0.10 + $0.00 = $0.60. With the tax, Ana's individual consumer surplus is $0.70 − $0.60 = $0.10 and Brianna's is $0.60 − $0.60 = $0.00. Total consumer surplus post-tax is $0.10 + $0.00 = $0.10. So the total consumer surplus lost because of the tax is $0.60 − $0.10 = $0.50.

d. Without the excise tax, Zachary's individual producer surplus is $0.40 − $0.10 = $0.30, Yves's is $0.40 − $0.20 = $0.20, Xavier's is $0.40 − $0.30 = $0.10, and William's is $0.40 − $0.40 = $0.00. Total producer surplus is $0.30 + $0.20 + $0.10 + $0.00 = $0.60. With the tax, Zachary's individual producer surplus is $0.20 − $0.10 = $0.10 and Yves's is $0.20 − $0.20 = $0.00. Total producer surplus post-tax is $0.10 + $0.00 = $0.10. So the total producer surplus lost because of the tax is $0.60 − $0.10 = $0.50.

e. With the tax, two cans of soda are sold, so the government tax revenue from this excise tax is $2 \times \$0.40 = \$0.80$.

f. Total surplus without the tax is $0.60 + $0.60 = $1.20. With the tax, total surplus is $0.10 + $0.10 = $0.20, and government tax revenue is $0.80. So deadweight loss from this excise tax is $1.20 − ($0.20 + $0.80) = $0.20.

2. a. The demand for gasoline is inelastic because there is no close substitute for gasoline itself and it is difficult for drivers to arrange substitutes for driving, such as taking public transportation. As a result, the deadweight loss from a tax on gasoline would be relatively small, as shown in the accompanying diagram.

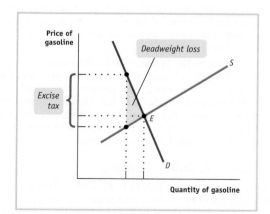

b. The demand for milk chocolate bars is elastic because there are close substitutes: dark chocolate bars, milk chocolate kisses, and so on. As a result, the deadweight loss from a tax on milk chocolate bars would be relatively large, as shown in the accompanying diagram.

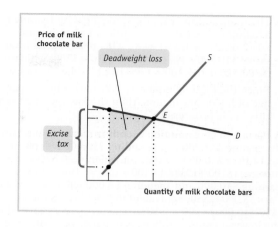

7-3 Check Your Understanding

1. a. Since drivers are the beneficiaries of highway safety programs, this tax performs well according to the benefits principle. But since the level of the tax does not depend on ability to pay the tax, it does not perform well according to the ability-to-pay principle. Since higher-income car purchasers are likely to spend more on a new car, a tax assessed as a percentage of the purchase price of the car would perform better on the ability-to-pay principle. A $500-per-car tax will cause people to buy fewer new cars, but a percentage-based tax will cause people to buy fewer cars and less expensive cars.

b. This tax does not perform well according to the benefits principle because the payers are nonresidents of the local area, but the beneficiaries are local residents who will enjoy greater government services. But to the extent that people who stay in hotels have higher income compared to those who don't, the tax performs well according to the ability-to-pay principle. It will distort the action of staying in a hotel room in this area, resulting in fewer nights of hotel room stays.

c. This tax performs well according to the benefits principle because local homeowners are the users of local schools. It also performs well according to the ability-to-pay principle because it is assessed as a percentage of home value: higher-income residents, who own more expensive homes, will pay higher taxes. It will distort the action of buying a house in this area versus another area with a lower property tax rate. It could also distort the action of making improvements to a house that would increase its assessed value.

d. This tax performs well according to the benefits principle because food consumers are the beneficiaries of government food safety programs. It does not perform well according to the ability-to-pay principle because food is a necessity, and lower-income people will pay approximately as much as higher-income people. This tax will distort the action of buying food, leading people to purchase cheaper varieties of food.

7-4 Check Your Understanding

1. a. The marginal tax rate for someone with income of $5,000 is 1%: for each additional $1 in income, $0.01 or 1%, is taxed away. This person pays total tax of $5,000 × 1% = $50, which is ($50/$5,000) × 100 = 1% of his or her income.

b. The marginal tax rate for someone with income of $20,000 is 2%: for each additional $1 in income, $0.02 or 2%, is taxed away. This person pays total tax of $10,000 × 1% + $10,000 × 2% = $300, which is ($300/$20,000) × 100 = 1.5% of his or her income.

c. Since the high-income taxpayer pays a larger percentage of his or her income than the low-income taxpayer, this tax is progressive.

2. A 1% tax on consumption spending means that a family earning $15,000 and spending $10,000 will pay a tax of 1% × $10,000 = $100, equivalent to 0.67% of its income; ($100/$15,000) × 100 = 0.67%. But a family earning $10,000 and spending $8,000 will pay a tax of 1% × $8,000 = $80, equivalent to 0.80% of its income; ($80/$10,000) × 100 = 0.80%. The tax is regressive, since the lower-income family pays a higher percentage of its income in tax than the higher-income family.

3. a. False. Recall that a seller always bears some burden of a tax as long as his or her supply of the good is not perfectly elastic. Since the supply of labor a worker offers is not perfectly elastic, some of the payroll tax will be borne by the worker, and therefore the tax will affect the person's incentive to take a job.

b. False. Under a proportional tax, the percentage of the tax base is the same for everyone. Under a lump-sum tax, the total tax paid is the same for everyone, regardless of income.

‖ CHAPTER EIGHT

8-1 Check Your Understanding

1. a. To determine comparative advantage, we must compare the two countries' opportunity costs for a given good. Take the opportunity cost of 1 ton of corn in terms of bicycles. In China, the opportunity cost of 1 bicycle is 0.01 ton of corn; so the opportunity cost of 1 ton of corn is 1/0.01 bicycles = 100 bicycles. The United States has the comparative advantage in corn since its opportunity cost in terms of bicycles is 50, a smaller number. Similarly, the opportunity cost in the United States of 1 bicycle in terms of corn is 1/50 ton of corn = 0.02 ton of corn. This is greater than 0.01, the Chinese opportunity cost of 1 bicycle in terms of corn, implying that China has a comparative advantage in bicycles.

b. Given that the United States can produce 200,000 bicycles if no corn is produced, it can produce 200,000 bicycles × 0.02 ton of corn/bicycle = 4,000 tons of corn when no bicycles are produced. Likewise, if China can produce 3,000 tons of corn if no bicycles are produced, it can produce 3,000 tons of corn × 100 bicycles/ton of corn = 300,000 bicycles if no corn is produced. These points determine the vertical and horizontal intercepts of the U.S. and Chinese production possibility frontiers, as shown in the accompanying diagram.

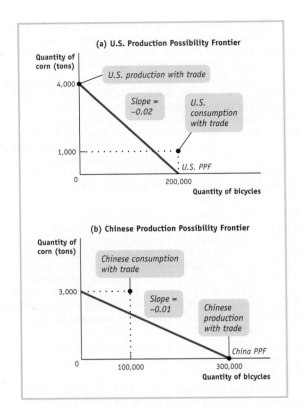

(a) U.S. Production Possibility Frontier

Quantity of corn (tons)

U.S. production with trade

4,000

Slope = −0.02

U.S. consumption with trade

1,000

U.S. PPF

0 · · · · · · · · 200,000

Quantity of bicycles

(b) Chinese Production Possibility Frontier

Quantity of corn (tons)

Chinese consumption with trade

3,000

Slope = −0.01

Chinese production with trade

China PPF

0 · · · · · · · 100,000 · · · · · · · 300,000

Quantity of bicycles

c. The diagram shows the production and consumption points of the two countries. Each country is clearly better off with international trade because each now consumes a bundle of the two goods that lies outside its own production possibility frontier, indicating that these bundles were unattainable in autarky.

2. a. According to the Heckscher–Ohlin model, this pattern of trade occurs because the United States has a relatively larger endowment of factors of production, such as human capital and physical capital, that are suited to the production of movies, but France has a relatively larger endowment of factors of production suited to wine-making, such as vineyards and the human capital of vintners.

b. According to the Heckscher–Ohlin model, this pattern of trade occurs because the United States has a relatively larger endowment of factors of production, such as human and physical capital, that are suited to making machinery, but Brazil has a relatively larger endowment of factors of production suited to shoe-making, such as unskilled labor and leather.

8-2 Check Your Understanding

1. In the accompanying diagram, P_A is the U.S. price of grapes in autarky and P_W is the world price of grapes under international trade. With trade, U.S. consumers pay a price of P_W for grapes and consume quantity Q_D, U.S. grape producers produce quantity Q_S, and the difference, $Q_D - Q_S$, represents imports of Mexican grapes. As a consequence of the strike by truckers, imports are halted, the price paid by American consumers rises to the autarky price, P_A, and U.S. consumption falls to the autarky quantity, Q_A.

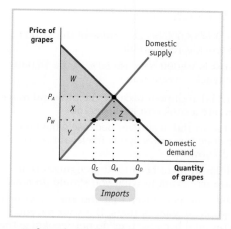

a. Before the strike, U.S. consumers enjoyed consumer surplus equal to areas $W + X + Z$. After the strike, their consumer surplus shrinks to W. So consumers are worse off, losing consumer surplus represented by $X + Z$.

b. Before the strike, U.S. producers had producer surplus equal to the area Y. After the strike, their producer surplus increases to $Y + X$. So U.S. producers are better off, gaining producer surplus represented by X.

c. U.S. total surplus falls as a result of the strike by an amount represented by area Z, the loss in consumer surplus that does not accrue to producers.

2. Mexican grape producers are worse off because they lose sales of exported grapes to the United States, and Mexican grape pickers are worse off because they lose the wages that were associated with the lost sales. The lower demand for Mexican grapes caused by the strike implies that the price Mexican consumers pay for grapes falls, making them better off. U.S. grape pickers are better off because their wages increase as a result of the increase of $Q_A - Q_S$ in U.S. sales.

8-3 Check Your Understanding

1. a. If the tariff is $0.50, the price paid by domestic consumers for a pound of imported butter is $0.50 + $0.50 = $1.00, the same price as a pound of domestic butter. Imported butter will no longer have a price advantage over domestic butter, imports will cease, and domestic producers will capture all the feasible sales to domestic consumers, selling amount Q_A in the accompanying figure. If the tariff is $0.25, the price paid by domestic consumers for a pound of imported butter is $0.50 + $0.25 = $0.75, $0.25 cheaper than a pound of domestic butter. American butter producers will gain sales in the amount of $Q_2 - Q_1$ as a result of the $0.25 tariff. But this is smaller than the amount they would have gained under the $0.50 tariff, the amount $Q_A - Q_1$.

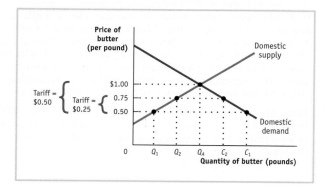

b. As long as the tariff is at least $0.50, increasing it more has no effect. At a tariff of $0.50, all imports are effectively blocked.

2. All imports are effectively blocked at a tariff of $0.50. So such a tariff corresponds to an import quota of 0.

8-4 Check Your Understanding

1. There are many fewer businesses that use steel as an input than there are consumers who buy sugar or clothing. So it will be easier for such businesses to communicate and coordinate among themselves to lobby against tariffs than it will be for consumers. In addition, each business will perceive that the cost of a steel tariff is quite costly to its profits, but an individual consumer is either unaware of or perceives little loss from tariffs on sugar or clothing.

2. Countries are often tempted to protect domestic industries by claiming that an import poses a quality, health, or environmental danger to domestic consumers. A WTO official should examine whether domestic producers are subject to the same stringency in the application of quality, health, or environmental regulations as foreign producers. If they are, then it is more likely that the regulations are for legitimate, non–trade protection purposes; if they are not, then it is more likely that the regulations are intended as trade protection measures.

‖ CHAPTER NINE

9-1 Check Your Understanding

1. a. Supplies are an explicit cost because they require an outlay of money.

   b. If the basement could be used in some other way that generates money, such as renting it to a student, then the implicit cost is that money forgone. Otherwise, the implicit cost is zero.

   c. Wages are an explicit cost.

   d. By using the van for their business, Marisol and Logan forgo the money they could have gained by selling it. So use of the van is an implicit cost.

   e. Marisol's forgone wages from her job are an implicit cost.

2. We need only compare the choice of becoming a machinist to the choice of taking a job in another state in order to make the right choice. We can discard the choice of acquiring a pharmacology degree because we already know that taking a job in another state is always superior to it. Now let's compare the remaining two alternatives: becoming a skilled machinist versus immediately taking a job in another state. As an apprentice machinist, Adam will earn only $30,000 over the first two years, versus $57,000 in the out-of-state job. So he has an implicit cost of $30,000 − $57,000 = −$27,000 by becoming a machinist instead of immediately moving out of state to work. However, two years from now the value of his lifetime earnings as a machinist is $725,000 versus $600,000 in advertising, giving him an accounting profit of $125,000 by choosing to be a machinist. Summing, his economic profit from choosing a career as a machinist over his other career is $125,000 − $27,000 = $98,000. In contrast, his economic profit from choosing the alternative, a career out of state over a career as a machinist, is −$125,000 + $27,000 = −$98,000. By the principle of "either–or" decision making, Adam should choose to be a machinist because that career has a positive economic profit.

3. You can discard alternative A because both B and C are superior to it. But you must now compare B versus C. You should then choose the alternative—B or C—that carries a positive economic profit.

9-2 Check Your Understanding

1. **a.** The marginal cost of doing your laundry is any monetary outlays plus the opportunity cost of your time spent doing laundry today—that is, the value you would place on spending time today on your next best alternative activity, like seeing a movie. The marginal benefit is having more clean clothes today to choose from.

    b. The marginal cost of changing your oil is the opportunity cost of time spent changing your oil now as well as the explicit cost of the oil change. The marginal benefit is the improvement in your car's performance.

    c. The marginal cost is the unpleasant feeling of a burning mouth that you receive from it plus any explicit cost of the jalapeno. The marginal benefit of another jalapeno on your nachos is the pleasant taste that you receive from it.

    d. The marginal cost is the wage you must pay that worker. The marginal benefit of hiring another worker in your company is the value of the output that worker produces.

    e. The marginal cost is the value lost due to the increased side effects from this additional dose. The marginal benefit of another dose of the drug is the value of the reduction in the patient's disease.

    f. The marginal cost is the opportunity cost of your time—what you would have gotten from the next best use of your time. The marginal benefit is the probable increase in your grade.

2. The accompanying table shows Alexa's new marginal cost and her new profit. It also reproduces Alexa's marginal benefit from Table 9-5.

Years of schooling	Total cost	Marginal cost	Marginal benefit	Profit
0	$0			
		$90,000	$300,000	$210,000
1	90,000			
		30,000	150,000	120,000
2	120,000			
		50,000	90,000	40,000
3	170,000			
		80,000	60,000	−20,000
4	250,000			
		120,000	50,000	−70,000
5	370,000			

Alexa's marginal cost is decreasing until she has completed two years of schooling, after which marginal cost increases because of the value of her forgone income. The optimal amount of schooling is still three years. For less than three years of schooling, marginal benefit exceeds marginal cost; for more than three years, marginal cost exceeds marginal benefit.

9-3 Check Your Understanding

1. **a.** Your sunk cost is $8,000 because none of the $8,000 spent on the truck is recoverable.

    b. Your sunk cost is $4,000 because 50% of the $8,000 spent on the truck is recoverable.

2. **a.** This is an invalid argument because the time and money already spent are a sunk cost at this point.

    b. This is also an invalid argument because what you should have done two years ago is irrelevant to what you should do now.

    c. This is a valid argument because it recognizes that sunk costs are irrelevant to what you should do now.

    d. This is a valid argument given that you are concerned about disappointing your parents. But your parents' views are irrational because they do not recognize that the time already spent is a sunk cost.

9-4 Check Your Understanding

1. **a.** Jenny is exhibiting loss aversion. She has an oversensitivity to loss, leading to an unwillingness to ignore sunk costs and move on.

    b. This is an example of framing bias. Retailers are using the multiple-item offers to induce shoppers to buy more under the perception that they are getting a good deal. But it is not a good deal for Leo because he buys more than he needs.

    c. Danilo may have unrealistic expectations of future behavior. Even if he does not want to participate in the plan now, he should find a way to commit to participating at a later date.

    d. Emma is showing signs of status quo bias. She is avoiding making a decision altogether; in other words, she is sticking with the status quo.

2. You would determine whether a decision was rational or irrational by first accurately accounting for all the costs and benefits of the decision. In particular, you must accurately measure all opportunity costs. Then calculate the economic payoff of the decision relative to the next best alternative. If you would still make the same choice after this comparison, then you have made a rational choice. If not, then the choice was irrational.

CHAPTER TEN

10-1 Check Your Understanding

1. Consuming a unit that generates negative marginal utility leaves the consumer with lower total utility than not consuming that unit at all. A rational consumer, a consumer who maximizes utility, would not do that. For example, from Figure 10-1 you can see that Cassie receives 64 utils if she consumes 8 clams; but if she consumes the 9th clam, she loses a util, netting her a total utility of only 63 utils. So whenever consuming a unit generates negative marginal utility, the consumer is made better off by not consuming that unit, even when that unit is free.

2. Since Marta has diminishing marginal utility of coffee, her first cup of coffee of the day generates the greatest increase in total utility. Her third and last cup of the day generates the least.

3. **a.** Mabel does not have diminishing marginal utility of exercising since each additional unit consumed brings more additional enjoyment than the previous unit.

   b. Mei does not have diminishing marginal utility of vinyl records because each additional unit generates the same additional enjoyment as the previous unit.

   c. Dexter has diminishing marginal utility of restaurant meals since the additional utility generated by a good restaurant meal is less when he consumes lots of them than when he consumed few of them.

10-2 Check Your Understanding

1. **a.** The accompanying table shows the consumer's consumption possibilities, A through C. These consumption possibilities are plotted in the accompanying diagram, along with the consumer's budget line, BL.

Consumption bundle	Quantity of popcorn (buckets)	Quantity of movie tickets
A	0	2
B	2	1
C	4	0

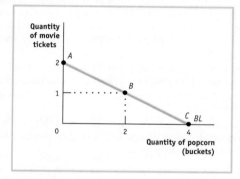

   b. The accompanying table shows the consumer's consumption possibilities, A through D. These consumption possibilities are plotted in the accompanying diagram, along with the consumer's budget line, BL.

Consumption bundle	Quantity of underwear (pairs)	Quantity of socks (pairs)
A	0	6
B	1	4
C	2	2
D	3	0

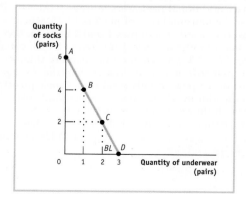

10-3 Check Your Understanding

1. From Table 10-3 you can see that Sammy's marginal utility per dollar from increasing his consumption of egg rolls from 3 rolls to 4, and his marginal utility per dollar from increasing his consumption of Coke from 9 bottles to 10 are the same, 0.75 utils. But a consumption bundle consisting of 4 egg rolls and 10 bottles of Coke is not Sammy's optimal consumption bundle because it is not affordable given his income of $20; 4 egg rolls and 10 bottles of Coke cost $4 × 4 + $2 × 10 = $36, $16 more than Sammy's income. This can be illustrated with Sammy's budget line from panel (a) of Figure 10-3: a bundle of 4 egg rolls and 10 bottles of Coke is represented by point X in the accompanying diagram, a point that lies outside Sammy's budget line. If you look at the horizontal axis of panel (a) of Figure 10-3, it is quite clear that there is no such thing in Sammy's consumption possibilities as a bundle consisting of 4 egg rolls and 10 bottles of Coke.

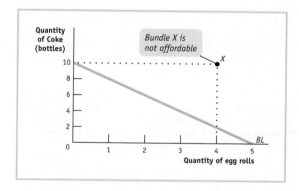

2. Sammy's maximum utility per dollar is generated when he goes from consuming 0 to 1 egg roll (3.75 utils) and as he goes from 0 to 1 bottle of Coke (5.75 utils). But this bundle consisting of 1 egg roll and 1 bottle of Coke generates only 26.5 utils for him. Instead, Sammy should choose the consumption bundle that satisfies his budget constraint and for which the marginal utility per dollar for both goods is equal.

10-4 Check Your Understanding

1. **a.** Since spending on orange juice is a small share of Clare's spending, the income effect from a rise in the price of orange juice is insignificant. Only the substitution effect, represented by the substitution of lemonade in place of orange juice, is significant.

   b. Since rent is a large share of Delia's expenditures, the increase in rent generates a significant income effect, making Delia feel poorer. Since housing is a normal good for Delia, the income and substitution effects move in the same direction, leading her to reduce her consumption of housing by moving to a smaller apartment.

   c. Since a meal ticket is a significant share of the students' living costs, an increase in its price will generate a significant income effect. Because cafeteria meals are an inferior good, the substitution effect (which would induce students to substitute restaurant meals in place of cafeteria meals) and the income effect (which would induce them to eat in the cafeteria more often because they are poorer) move in opposite directions.

2. In order to determine whether any good is a Giffen good, you must first establish whether it is an inferior good. In other words, if students' incomes decrease, other things equal, does the quantity of cafeteria meals demanded increase? Once you have established that the good is an inferior good, you must then establish that the income effect outweighs the substitution effect. That is, as the price of cafeteria meals rises, other things equal, does the quantity of cafeteria meals demanded increase? Be careful that, in fact, all other things remain equal. But if the quantity of cafeteria meals demanded truly increases in response to a price rise, you have found a Giffen good.

|| CHAPTER ELEVEN

11-1 Check Your Understanding

1. **a.** The fixed input is the 10-ton machine, and the variable input is electricity.

   b. As you can see from the declining numbers in the third column of the accompanying table, electricity does indeed exhibit diminishing returns: the marginal product of each additional kilowatt of electricity is less than that of the previous kilowatt.

Quantity of electricity (kilowatts)	Quantity of ice (pounds)	Marginal product of electricity (pounds per kilowatt)
0	0	
		1,000
1	1,000	
		800
2	1,800	
		600
3	2,400	
		400
4	2,800	

   c. A 50% increase in the size of the fixed input means that Bernie now has a 15-ton machine. So the fixed input is now the 15-ton machine. Since it generates a 100% increase in output for any given amount of electricity, the quantity of output and marginal product are now as shown in the accompanying table.

Quantity of electricity (kilowatts)	Quantity of ice (pounds)	Marginal product of electricity (pounds per kilowatt)
0	0	
		2,000
1	2,000	
		1,600
2	3,600	
		1,200
3	4,800	
		800
4	5,600	

11-2 Check Your Understanding

1. **a.** As shown in the accompanying table, the marginal cost for each pie is found by multiplying the marginal cost of the previous pie by 1.5. Variable cost for each output level is found by summing the marginal cost for all the pies produced to reach that output level. So, for example, the variable cost of three pies is $1.00 + $1.50 + $2.25 = $4.75. Average fixed cost for Q pies is calculated as $9.00/$Q$ since fixed cost is $9.00. Average variable cost for Q pies is equal to variable cost for the Q pies divided by Q; for example, the average variable cost of five pies is $13.19/5, or approximately $2.64. Finally, average total cost can be calculated in two equivalent ways: as TC/Q or as $AVC + AFC$.

Quantity of pies	Marginal cost of pie	Variable cost	Average fixed cost of pie	Average variable cost of pie	Average total cost of pie
0		$0.00	—	—	—
	$1.00				
1		1.00	$9.00	$1.00	$10.00
	1.50				
2		2.50	4.50	1.25	5.75
	2.25				
3		4.75	3.00	1.58	4.58
	3.38				
4		8.13	2.25	2.03	4.28
	5.06				
5		13.19	1.80	2.64	4.44
	7.59				
6		20.78	1.50	3.46	4.96

   b. The spreading effect dominates the diminishing returns effect when average total cost is falling: the fall in AFC dominates the rise in AVC for pies 1 to 4. The diminishing returns effect dominates when average total cost is rising: the rise in AVC dominates the fall in AFC for pies 5 and 6.

   c. Aidy's minimum-cost output is 4 pies; this generates the lowest average total cost, $4.28. When output is less than 4, the marginal cost of a pie is less than the average total cost of the pies already produced. So making an additional pie lowers average total cost. For example, the marginal cost of pie 3 is $2.25, whereas the average total cost of pies 1 and 2 is $5.75. So making pie 3 lowers average total cost to $4.58, equal to (2 × $5.75 + $2.25)/3. When output is more than 4, the marginal cost of a pie is greater than the average total cost of the pies already produced. Consequently, making an additional pie raises average total cost. So, although the marginal cost of pie 6 is $7.59, the average total cost of pies 1 through 5 is $4.44. Making pie 6 raises average total cost to $4.96, equal to (5 × $4.44 + $7.59)/6.

11-3 Check Your Understanding

1. **a.** The accompanying table shows the average total cost of producing 12,000, 22,000, and 30,000 units for each of the three choices of fixed cost. For example, if the firm makes choice 1, the total cost of producing 12,000 units of output is $8,000 + 12,000 × $1.00 = $20,000. The average total cost of producing 12,000 units of output is therefore $20,000/12,000 = $1.67. The other average total costs are calculated similarly. So if the firm wanted to produce 12,000 units, it would make choice 1 because this gives it the lowest average total cost. If it wanted to produce 22,000 units, it would make choice 2. If it wanted to produce 30,000 units, it would make choice 3.

	12,000 units	22,000 units	30,000 units
Average total cost from choice 1	$1.67	$1.36	$1.27
Average total cost from choice 2	1.75	1.30	1.15
Average total cost from choice 3	2.25	1.34	1.05

b. Having historically produced 12,000 units, the firm would have adopted choice 1. When producing 12,000 units, the firm would have had an average total cost of $1.67. When output jumps to 22,000 units, the firm cannot alter its choice of fixed cost in the short run, so its average total cost in the short run will be $1.36. In the long run, however, it will adopt choice 2, making its average total cost fall to $1.30.

c. If the firm believes that the increase in demand is temporary, it should not alter its fixed cost from choice 1 because choice 2 generates higher average total cost as soon as output falls back to its original quantity of 12,000 units: $1.75 versus $1.67.

2. **a.** This firm is likely to experience constant returns to scale. To increase output, the firm must hire more workers, purchase more computers, and pay additional telephone charges. Because these inputs are easily available, their long-run average total cost is unlikely to change as output increases.

b. This firm is likely to experience decreasing returns to scale. As the firm takes on more projects, the costs of communication and coordination required to implement the expertise of the firm's owner are likely to increase. As a result, the firm's long-run average total cost will increase as output increases.

c. This firm is likely to experience increasing returns to scale. Because diamond mining requires a large initial set-up cost for excavation equipment, long-run average total cost will fall as output increases.

3. The accompanying diagram shows the long-run average total cost curve (*LRATC*) and the short-run average total cost curve corresponding to a long-run output choice of 5 cases of salsa (*ATC₅*). The curve *ATC₅* shows the short-run average total cost for which the level of fixed cost minimizes average total cost at an output of 5 cases of salsa. This is confirmed by the fact that at 5 cases per day, *ATC₅* touches *LRATC*, the long-run average total cost curve.

If Selena's Gourmet Salsas expects to produce only 4 cases of salsa for a long time, the firm should change its fixed cost. If it does not change its fixed cost and produces 4 cases of salsa, the firm's average total cost in the short run is indicated by point *B* on *ATC₅*; it is no longer on the *LRATC*. If it changes its fixed cost, though, its average total cost could be lower, at point *A*.

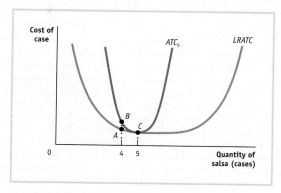

CHAPTER TWELVE

12-1 Check Your Understanding

1. **a.** With only two producers in the world, each producer will represent a sizable share of the market. So the industry will not be perfectly competitive.

b. Because each producer of natural gas from the North Sea has only a small market share of total world supply of natural gas, and since natural gas is a standardized product, the natural gas industry will be perfectly competitive.

c. Because each designer has a distinctive style, high-fashion clothes are not a standardized product. So the industry will not be perfectly competitive.

d. The market described here is the market in each city for tickets to baseball games. Since there are only one or two teams in each major city, each team will represent a sizable share of the market. So the industry will not be perfectly competitive.

12-2 Check Your Understanding

1. **a.** The firm should shut down immediately when price is less than minimum average variable cost, the shutdown price. In the accompanying diagram, this is optimal for prices in the range 0 to *P₁*.

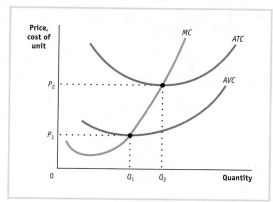

b. When price is greater than minimum average variable cost (the shut-down price) but less than minimum average total cost (the break-even price), the firm should continue to operate in the short run even though it is making a loss. This is optimal for prices in the range P_1 to P_2 and for quantities Q_1 to Q_2.

c. When price exceeds minimum average total cost (the break-even price), the firm makes a profit. This happens for prices in excess of P_2 and results in quantities greater than Q_2.

2. This is an example of a temporary shut-down by a firm when the market price lies below the shut-down price, the minimum average variable cost. In this case, the market price is the price of a lobster meal and variable cost is the variable cost of serving such a meal, such as the cost of the lobster, employee wages, and so on. In this example, however, it is the average variable cost curve rather than the market price that shifts over time, due to seasonal changes in the cost of lobsters. Maine lobster shacks have relatively low average variable cost during the summer, when cheap Maine lobsters are available. During the rest of the year, their average variable cost is relatively high due to the high cost of imported lobsters. So the lobster shacks are open for business during the summer, when their minimum average variable cost lies below price. But they close during the rest of the year, when price lies below their minimum average variable cost.

12-3 Check Your Understanding

1. a. A fall in the fixed cost of production generates a fall in the average total cost of production and, in the short run, an increase in each firm's profit at the current output level. So in the long run new firms will enter the industry. The increase in supply drives down price and profits. Once profits are driven back to zero, entry will cease.

b. An increase in wages generates an increase in the average variable and the average total cost of production at every output level. In the short run, firms incur losses at the current output level, and so in the long run some firms will exit the industry. (If the average variable cost

rises sufficiently, some firms may even shut down in the short run.) As firms exit, supply decreases, price rises, and losses are reduced. Exit will cease once losses return to zero.

c. Price will rise as a result of the increased demand, leading to a short-run increase in profits at the current output level. In the long run, firms will enter the industry, generating an increase in supply, a fall in price, and a fall in profits. Once profits are driven back to zero, entry will cease.

d. The shortage of a key input causes that input's price to increase, resulting in an increase in average variable and average total costs for producers. Firms incur losses in the short run, and some firms will exit the industry in the long run. The fall in supply generates an increase in price and decreased losses. Exit will cease when losses have returned to zero.

2. In the accompanying diagram, point X_{MKT} in panel (b), the intersection of S_1 and D_1, represents the long-run industry equilibrium before the change in consumer tastes. When tastes change, demand falls and the industry moves in the short run to point Y_{MKT} in panel (b), at the intersection of the new demand curve D_2 and S_1, the short-run supply curve representing the same number of egg producers as in the original equilibrium at point X_{MKT}. As the market price falls, an individual firm reacts by producing less—as shown in panel (a)—as long as the market price remains above the minimum average variable cost. If market price falls below minimum average variable cost, the firm would shut down immediately. At point Y_{MKT} the price of eggs is below minimum average total cost, creating losses for producers. This leads some firms to exit, which shifts the short-run industry supply curve leftward to S_2. A new long-run equilibrium is established at point Z_{MKT}. As this occurs, the market price rises again, and, as shown in panel (c), each remaining producer reacts by increasing output (here, from point Y to point Z). All remaining producers again make zero profits. The decrease in the quantity of eggs supplied in the industry comes entirely from the exit of some producers from the industry. The long-run industry supply curve is the curve labeled LRS in panel (b).

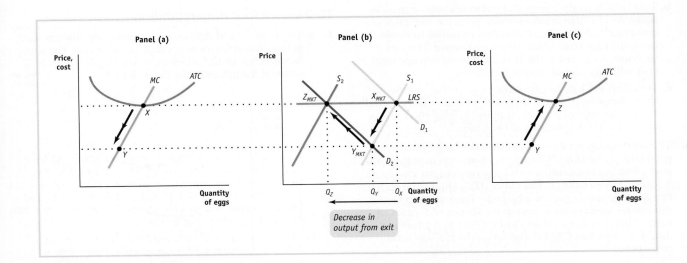

|| CHAPTER THIRTEEN

13-1 Check Your Understanding

1. **a.** This does not support the conclusion. Texas Tea has a limited amount of oil, and the price has risen in order to equalize supply and demand.

   b. This supports the conclusion because the market for home heating oil has become monopolized, and a monopolist will reduce the quantity supplied and raise price to generate profit.

   c. This does not support the conclusion. Texas Tea has raised its price to consumers because the price of its input, home heating oil, has increased.

   d. This supports the conclusion. The fact that other firms have begun to supply heating oil at a lower price implies that Texas Tea must have earned sufficient profits to attract the others to Frigid.

   e. This supports the conclusion. It indicates that Texas Tea enjoys a barrier to entry because it controls access to the only Alaskan heating oil pipeline.

2. **a.** Extending the length of a patent increases the length of time during which the inventor can reduce the quantity supplied and increase the market price. Since this increases the period of time during which the inventor can earn economic profits from the invention, it increases the incentive to invent new products.

   b. Extending the length of a patent also increases the period of time during which consumers have to pay higher prices. So determining the appropriate length of a patent involves making a trade-off between the desirable incentive for invention and the undesirable high price to consumers.

3. **a.** When a large number of other people use PayMo, then any one merchant is more likely to accept it for payment. So the larger the customer base, the more likely PayMo will be accepted for payment.

   b. When a large number of people own a car with a new type of engine, it will be easier to find a knowledgeable mechanic who can repair it.

   c. When a large number of people use such a website, it is more likely that you will be able to find a buyer for something you want to sell or a seller for something you want to buy.

13-2 Check Your Understanding

1. **a.** The price at each output level is found by dividing the total revenue by the number of emeralds produced; for example, the price when 3 emeralds are produced is $252/3 = $84. The price at the various output levels is then used to construct the demand schedule in the accompanying table.

   b. The marginal revenue schedule is found by calculating the change in total revenue as output increases by one unit. For example, the marginal revenue generated by increasing output from 2 to 3 emeralds is ($252 − $186) = $66.

   c. The quantity effect component of marginal revenue is the additional revenue generated by selling one more unit of the good at the market price. For example, as shown in the accompanying table, at 3 emeralds, the

market price is $84; so when going from 2 to 3 emeralds, the quantity effect is equal to $84.

   d. The price effect component of marginal revenue is the decline in total revenue caused by the fall in price when one more unit is sold. For example, as shown in the table, when only 2 emeralds are sold, each emerald sells at a price of $93. However, when Emerald, Inc. sells an additional emerald, the price must fall by $9 to $84. So the price effect component in going from 2 to 3 emeralds is (−$9) × 2 = −$18. That's because 2 emeralds can only be sold at a price of $84 when 3 emeralds in total are sold, although they could have been sold at a price of $93 when only 2 in total were sold.

Quantity of emeralds demanded	Price of emerald	Marginal revenue	Quantity effect component	Price effect component
1	$100			
		$86	$93	−$7
2	93			
		66	84	−18
3	84			
		28	70	−42
4	70			
		−30	50	−80
5	50			

   e. In order to determine Emerald, Inc.'s profit-maximizing output level, you must know its marginal cost at each output level. Its profit-maximizing output level is the one at which marginal revenue is equal to marginal cost.

2. As the accompanying diagram shows, the marginal cost curve shifts upward to $400. The profit-maximizing price rises and quantity falls. Profit falls from $3,200 to $300 × 6 = $1,800. Competitive industry profits, though, are unchanged at zero.

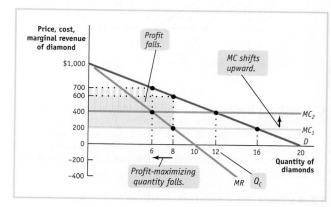

13-3 Check Your Understanding

1. **a.** Cable internet service is a natural monopoly. So the government should intervene only if it believes that price exceeds average total cost, where average total cost is based on the cost of laying the cable. In this case it should impose a price ceiling equal to average total cost. Otherwise, it should do nothing.

   b. The government should approve the merger only if it fosters competition by transferring some of the company's landing slots to another, competing airline.

2. **a.** False. As can be seen from Figure 13-8, panel (b), the inefficiency arises from the fact that some of the consumer surplus is transformed into deadweight loss (the yellow area), not that it is transformed into profit (the green area).

   b. True. If a monopolist sold to all customers who have a valuation greater than or equal to marginal cost, all mutually beneficial transactions would occur and there would be no deadweight loss.

3. As shown in the accompanying diagram, a profit-maximizing monopolist produces Q_M, the output level at which $MR = MC$. A monopolist who mistakenly believes that $P = MR$ produces the output level at which $P = MC$ (when, in fact, $P > MR$, and at the true profit-maximizing level of output, $P > MR = MC$). This misguided monopolist will produce the output level Q_C, where the demand curve crosses the marginal cost curve—the same output level produced if the industry were perfectly competitive. It will charge the price P_C, which is equal to marginal cost, and make zero profit. The entire shaded area is equal to the consumer surplus, which is also equal to total surplus in this case (since the monopolist receives zero producer surplus). There is no deadweight loss since every consumer who is willing to pay as much as or more than marginal cost gets the good. A smart monopolist, however, will produce the output level Q_M and charge the price P_M. Profit equals the green area, consumer surplus corresponds to the blue area, and total surplus is equal to the sum of the green and blue areas. The yellow area is the deadweight loss generated by the monopolist.

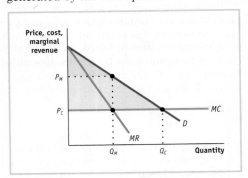

4. Facebook has nearly 2.5 billion users, which has created a network externality. At this point, Facebook is experiencing increasing returns to scale. But at the same time, there are many social media networks, including Twitter, Instagram, and Snapchat, which has reduced Facebook's market share.

13-4 Check Your Understanding

1. **a.** False. A price-discriminating monopolist will sell to some customers that a single-price monopolist will refuse to—namely, customers with a high price elasticity of demand who are willing to pay only a relatively low price for the good.

   b. False. Although a price-discriminating monopolist does indeed capture more of the consumer surplus, inefficiency is lower: more mutually beneficial transactions occur because the monopolist makes more sales to customers with a low willingness to pay for the good.

   c. True. Under price discrimination consumers are charged prices that depend on their price elasticity

of demand. A consumer with highly elastic demand will pay a lower price than a consumer with inelastic demand.

2. **a.** This is not a case of price discrimination because all consumers, regardless of their price elasticities of demand, value the damaged merchandise less than undamaged merchandise. So the price must be lowered to sell the merchandise.

   b. This is a case of price discrimination. Senior citizens have a higher price elasticity of demand for restaurant meals (their demand for restaurant meals is more responsive to price changes) than other patrons. Restaurants lower the price to high-elasticity consumers (senior citizens). Consumers with low price elasticity of demand will pay the full price.

   c. This is a case of price discrimination. Consumers with a high price elasticity of demand will pay a lower price by collecting and using discount coupons. Consumers with a low price elasticity of demand will not use coupons.

   d. This is not a case of price discrimination; it is simply a case of supply and demand.

|| CHAPTER FOURTEEN

14-1 Check Your Understanding

1. **a.** The world oil industry is an oligopoly because a few countries control a necessary resource for production, oil reserves.

   b. The microprocessor industry is an oligopoly because two firms possess superior technology and so dominate industry production.

   c. The wide-body passenger jet industry is an oligopoly because there are increasing returns to scale in production.

2. **a.** The HHI in this industry is $62.5^2 + 24.9^2 + 11.7^2 + 0.9^2 = 4,664$.

   b. If Yahoo! and Bing were to merge, making their combined market $11.7\% + 24.9\% = 36.6\%$, the HHI in this industry would be $62.5^2 + 36.6^2 + 0.9^2 = 5,247$.

14-2 Check Your Understanding

1. **a.** The firm is likely to act noncooperatively and raise output, which will generate a negative price effect. But because the firm's current market share is small, the negative price effect will fall much more heavily on its rivals' revenues than on its own. At the same time, the firm will benefit from a positive quantity effect.

   b. The firm is likely to act noncooperatively and raise output, which will generate a fall in price. Because its rivals have higher costs, they will lose money at the lower price while the firm continues to make profits. So the firm may be able to drive its rivals out of business by increasing its output.

   c. The firm is likely to collude. Because it is costly for consumers to switch products, the firm would have to lower its price quite substantially (by increasing quantity a lot) to induce consumers to switch to its product. So increasing output is likely to be unprofitable given the large negative price effect.

   d. The firm is likely to act noncooperatively because it knows its rivals cannot increase their output in retaliation.

14-3 Check Your Understanding

1. When Margaret builds a missile, Nikita's payoff from building a missile as well is –10; it is –20 if he does not. The same set of payoffs holds for Margaret when Nikita builds a missile: her payoff is –10 if she builds one as well, –20 if she does not. So it is a Nash (or noncooperative) equilibrium for both Margaret and Nikita to build missiles, and their total payoff is (–10) + (–10) = –20. But their total payoff is greatest when neither builds a missile: their total payoff is 0 + 0 = 0. But this outcome—the cooperative outcome—is unlikely. If Margaret builds a missile but Nikita does not, Margaret gets a payoff of +8, rather than the 0 she gets if she doesn't build a missile. So Margaret is better off if she builds a missile but Nikita doesn't. Similarly, Nikita is better off if he builds a missile but Margaret doesn't: he gets a payoff of +8, rather than the 0 he gets if he doesn't build a missile. So both players have an incentive to build a missile. Both will build a missile, and each gets a payoff of –10. So unless Nikita and Margaret are able to communicate in some way to enforce cooperation, they will act in their own individual interests and each will build a missile.

2. **a.** Future entry by several new firms will increase competition and drive down industry profits. As a result, there is less future profit to protect by behaving cooperatively today. So each oligopolist is more likely to behave noncooperatively today.

    b. When it is very difficult for a firm to detect if another firm has raised output, then it is very difficult to enforce cooperation by playing tit for tat. So it is more likely that a firm will behave noncooperatively.

    c. When firms have coexisted while maintaining high prices for a long time, each expects cooperation to continue. So the value of behaving cooperatively today is high, and it is likely that firms will engage in tacit collusion.

14-4 Check Your Understanding

1. **a.** This is likely to be interpreted as evidence of tacit collusion. Firms in the industry are able to tacitly collude by setting their prices according to the published "suggested" price of the largest firm in the industry. This is a form of price leadership.

    b. This is not likely to be interpreted as evidence of tacit collusion. Considerable variation in market shares indicates that firms have been competing to capture one another's business.

    c. This is not likely to be interpreted as evidence of tacit collusion. These features make it more unlikely that consumers will switch products in response to lower prices. So this is a way for firms to avoid any temptation to gain market share by lowering price. This is a form of product differentiation used to avoid direct competition.

    d. This is likely to be interpreted as evidence of tacit collusion. In the guise of discussing sales targets, firms can create a cartel by designating quantities to be produced by each firm.

    e. This is likely to be interpreted as evidence of tacit collusion. By raising prices together, each firm in the industry is refusing to undercut its rivals by leaving its price unchanged or lowering it. Because it could gain market share by doing so, refusing to do it is evidence of tacit collusion.

CHAPTER FIFTEEN

15-1 Check Your Understanding

1. **a.** Ladders are not differentiated as a result of monopolistic competition. A ladder producer makes different ladders (tall ladders versus short ladders) to satisfy different consumer needs, not to avoid competition with rivals. So two tall ladders made by two different producers will be indistinguishable by consumers.

    b. Soft drinks are an example of product differentiation as a result of monopolistic competition. For example, several producers make colas; each is differentiated in terms of taste, which fast-food chains sell it, and so on.

    c. Clothing stores are an example of product differentiation as a result of monopolistic competition. They serve different clienteles that have different price sensitivities and different tastes. They also offer different levels of customer service and are situated in different locations.

    d. Steel is not differentiated as a result of monopolistic competition. Different types of steel (beams versus sheets) are made for different purposes, not to distinguish one steel manufacturer's products from another's.

2. **a.** Perfectly competitive industries and monopolistically competitive industries both have many sellers. So it may be hard to distinguish between them solely in terms of number of firms. And in both market structures, there is free entry into and exit from the industry in the long run. But in a perfectly competitive industry, one standardized product is sold; in a monopolistically competitive industry, products are differentiated. So you should ask whether products are differentiated in the industry.

    b. In a monopoly there is only one firm, but a monopolistically competitive industry contains many firms. So you should ask whether or not there is a single firm in the industry.

15-2 Check Your Understanding

1. **a.** An increase in fixed cost raises average total cost and shifts the average total cost curve upward. In the short run, firms incur losses. In the long run, some will exit the industry, resulting in a rightward shift of the demand curves for those firms that remain in the industry, since each one now serves a larger share of the market. Long-run equilibrium is reestablished when the demand curve for each remaining firm has shifted rightward to the point where it is tangent to the firm's new, higher average total cost curve. At this point each firm's price just equals its average total cost, and each firm makes zero profit.

    b. A decrease in marginal cost lowers average total cost and shifts the average total cost curve and the marginal cost curve downward. Because existing firms now make profits, in the long run new entrants are attracted into the industry. In the long run, this results in a leftward shift of each existing firm's demand curve since each firm now has a smaller share of the market. Long-run equilibrium is reestablished when each firm's demand curve has shifted leftward to the point where it is tangent to the new, lower average total cost curve. At this point each firm's price just equals average total cost, and each firm makes zero profit.

2. If all the existing firms in the industry joined together to create a monopoly, they would achieve monopoly profits. But this would induce new firms to create new, differentiated products and then enter the industry and capture some of the monopoly profits. So in the long run it would be impossible to maintain a monopoly. The problem arises from the fact that because new firms can create new products, there is no barrier to entry that can maintain a monopoly.

15-3 Check Your Understanding

1. **a.** False. As can be seen from panel (b) of Figure 15-4, a monopolistically competitive firm produces at a point where price exceeds marginal cost—unlike a perfectly competitive firm, which produces where price equals marginal cost (at the point of minimum average total cost). A monopolistically competitive firm will refuse to sell at marginal cost. This would be below average total cost and the firm would incur a loss.

   b. True. Firms in a monopolistically competitive industry could achieve higher profits (monopoly profits) if they all joined together and produced a single product. In addition, since the industry possesses excess capacity, producing a larger quantity of output would lower the firm's average total cost. The effect on consumers, however, is ambiguous. They would experience less choice. But if consolidation substantially reduces industry-wide average total cost and therefore substantially increases industry-wide output, consumers may experience lower prices under monopoly.

   c. True. Fads and fashions are created and promulgated by advertising, which is found in oligopolies and monopolistically competitive industries but not in monopolies or perfectly competitive industries.

15-4 Check Your Understanding

1. **a.** This is economically useful because such advertisements are likely to focus on the medical benefits of aspirin.

   b. This is economically wasteful because such advertisements are likely to focus on promoting Bayer aspirin versus a rival's aspirin product. The two products are medically indistinguishable.

   c. This is economically useful because such advertisements are likely to focus on the health and enjoyment benefits of orange juice.

   d. This is economically wasteful because such advertisements are likely to focus on promoting Tropicana orange juice versus a rival's product. The two are likely to be indistinguishable by consumers.

   e. This is economically useful because the longevity of a business gives a potential customer information about its quality.

2. A successful brand name indicates a desirable attribute, such as quality, to a potential buyer. So, other things equal—such as price—a firm with a successful brand name will achieve higher sales than a rival with a comparable product but without a successful brand name. This is likely to deter new firms from entering an industry in which an existing firm has a successful brand name.

CHAPTER SIXTEEN

16-1 Check Your Understanding

1. **a.** The external cost is the pollution caused by the wastewater runoff, an uncompensated cost imposed by the poultry farms on their neighbors.

   b. Since poultry farmers do not take the external cost of their actions into account when making decisions about how much wastewater to generate, they will create more runoff than is socially optimal in the absence of government intervention or a private deal. They will produce runoff up to the point at which the marginal social benefit of an additional unit of runoff is zero; however, their neighbors experience a high, positive level of marginal social cost of runoff from this output level. So the quantity of wastewater runoff is inefficient: reducing runoff by one unit would reduce total social benefit by less than it would reduce total social cost.

   c. At the socially optimal quantity of wastewater runoff, the marginal social benefit is equal to the marginal social cost. This quantity is lower than the quantity of wastewater runoff that would be created in the absence of government intervention or a private deal.

2. Yasmin's reasoning is not correct: allowing some late returns of books is likely to be socially optimal. Although you impose a marginal social cost on others every day that you are late in returning a book, there is some positive marginal social benefit to you of returning a book late—for example, you get a longer period to use it in working on a term paper.

   The socially optimal number of days that a book is returned late is the number at which the marginal social benefit equals the marginal social cost. A fine so stiff that it prevents any late returns is likely to result in a situation in which people return books although the marginal social benefit of keeping them another day is greater than the marginal social cost—an inefficient outcome. In that case, allowing an overdue patron another day would increase total social benefit more than it would increase total social cost. So charging a moderate fine that reduces the number of days that books are returned late to the socially optimal number of days is appropriate.

16-2 Check Your Understanding

1. This is a misguided argument. Allowing polluters to sell emissions permits makes polluters face the cost of polluting in the form of the opportunity cost of the permit. If a polluter chooses not to reduce its emissions, it cannot sell its emissions permits. As a result, it forgoes the opportunity of making money from the sale of the permits. So despite the fact that the polluter receives a monetary benefit from selling the permits, the scheme has the desired effect: to make polluters internalize the externality of their actions.

2. **a.** If the emissions tax is smaller than the marginal social cost at Q_{OPT}, a polluter will face a marginal cost of polluting (equal to the amount of the tax) that is less than the marginal social cost at the socially optimal quantity of pollution. Since a polluter will produce emissions up

to the point where the marginal social benefit is equal to its marginal cost, the resulting amount of pollution will be larger than the socially optimal quantity. As a result, there is inefficiency: if the amount of pollution is larger than the socially optimal quantity, the marginal social cost exceeds the marginal social benefit. A reduction in emissions levels will increase social surplus.

If the emissions tax is greater than the marginal social cost at Q_{OPT}, a polluter will face a marginal cost of polluting (equal to the amount of the tax) that is greater than the marginal social cost at the socially optimal quantity of pollution. This will lead the polluter to reduce emissions below the socially optimal quantity. This also is inefficient: whenever the marginal social benefit is greater than the marginal social cost, an increase in emissions levels will raise social surplus.

b. If the total amount of allowable pollution is set too high, the supply of emissions permits will be high and so the equilibrium price at which permits trade will be low. That is, polluters will face a marginal cost of polluting (the price of a permit) that is "too low"—lower than the marginal social cost at the socially optimal quantity of pollution. As a result, pollution will be greater than the socially optimal quantity. This is inefficient and lowers total surplus.

If the total level of allowable pollution is set too low, the supply of emissions permits will be low and so the equilibrium price at which permits trade will be high. That is, polluters will face a marginal cost of polluting (the price of a permit) that is "too high"—higher than the marginal social cost at the socially optimal quantity of pollution. As a result, pollution will be lower than the socially optimal quantity. This also is inefficient and lowers total surplus.

c. A carbon tax will increase the cost of using fossil fuels, including the prices of gasoline and coal. As the cost of fossil fuels increases, consumers will reduce their use of fossil fuels as energy sources. They will be increasingly likely to purchase more fuel-efficient cars and invest in solar technology for their homes.

16-3 Check Your Understanding

1. Types of fossil fuels are coal, oil, and gas. The main clean energy sources are wind and solar. The burning of fossil fuels creates greenhouse gas emissions, which cause climate change. Clean energy sources do not create greenhouse gas emissions, so do not contribute to climate change.

2. The market failure that led to climate change was the historical underpricing of fossil-fuel consumption. That is, the market price of fossil fuel was too low compared to the true cost of greenhouse gas emissions that they generated. The estimated loss to U.S. GDP from unmitigated climate change is 10%; the estimated loss to world GDP is 20%.

3. Government subsidies to innovations in clean energy are an important policy tool because it is unlikely that the clean energy sector would have become cost competitive with fossil fuels without them. Multilateral agreements between countries are an important policy tool because a country is likely to be unwilling to cut its emissions without a commitment by other countries to do the same. Individual incentives are important because they can lead to fast and effective ways to conserve energy and thus reduce greenhouse gas emissions.

4. Although the structural change required to address climate change will require some loss of GDP, it is small (1) compared to the costs of unmitigated climate change; and (2) compared to the projected growth rate of GDP over time. Also, the direct health costs of unmitigated climate change are significant, resulting in millions of excess deaths and as much as 5% of world GDP.

16-4 Check Your Understanding

1. College education provides external benefits through the creation of knowledge. And student aid acts like a Pigouvian subsidy on higher education. If the marginal social benefit of higher education is indeed $120 billion, then student aid is an optimal policy.

2. **a.** Planting trees generates an external benefit since many people (not just those who plant the trees) benefit from the increased air quality and lower summer temperatures. Without a subsidy, people will plant too few trees, setting the marginal social cost of planting a tree—what they forgo by planting a tree—too low. (Although too low, it may still be more than zero since a homeowner gains some personal benefit from planting a tree.) A Pigouvian subsidy will induce people to plant more trees, bringing the marginal social benefit of planting a tree in line with the marginal social cost.

   b. Water-saving toilets generate an external benefit because they discourage wasting water, thereby reducing the need to pump water from rivers and aquifers. Without a subsidy, homeowners will use water until the marginal social cost of water usage is equal to zero since water is costless to them. A Pigouvian subsidy on water-saving toilets will induce homeowners to reduce their water usage so that the marginal social benefit of water is in line with the marginal social cost.

   c. Discarded plastic drink bottles impose an external cost by degrading the environment. Without a tax, people will discard plastic bottles freely—until the marginal social cost of discarding a bottle (what they must forgo in discarding a bottle) is zero. A Pigouvian tax or subsidy on drink bottles will bring the marginal social benefit of a drink bottle in line with its marginal social cost. This can be done two ways: via a tax or a subsidy. A tax will induce drink manufacturers to shift away from polluting plastic bottles to less polluting containers, like paper cartons. A subsidy for disposing of the containers in an environmentally sound way, such as recycling, will induce drink consumers to dispose of the bottles in a way that reduces the external costs.

16-5 Check Your Understanding

1. **a.** The voltage of an appliance must be consistent with the voltage of the electrical outlet it is plugged into. Consumers will want to have 110-volt appliances when houses are wired for 110-volt outlets, and builders will want to install 110-volt outlets when most prospective

homeowners use 110-volt appliances. So a network externality arises because a consumer will want to use appliances that operate with the same voltage as the appliances used by most other consumers.

b. Printers, copy machines, fax machines, and so on are designed for specific paper sizes. Consumers will want to purchase paper of a size that can be used in these machines, and machine manufacturers will want to manufacture their machines for the size of paper that most consumers use. So a network externality arises because a consumer will want to use the size of paper used by most other consumers—namely, 8½-by-11-inch paper rather than 8-by-12½-inch paper.

2. Of the two competing companies, the company able to achieve the higher number of sales is likely to dominate the market. In a market with a network externality, new consumers will base their buying decisions on the number of existing consumers of a specific product. In other words, the more consumers a company can attract initially, the more consumers will choose to buy that company's product; therefore, the good exhibits *positive feedback*. So it is important for a company to make a large number of sales early on. It can do this by pricing its good cheaply and taking a loss on each unit sold. The company that can best afford to subsidize a large number of sales early on is likely to be the winner of this competition.

CHAPTER SEVENTEEN

17-1 Check Your Understanding

1. a. Use of a public park is nonexcludable, but it may or may not be rival in consumption, depending on the circumstances. For example, if both you and I use the park for jogging, then your use will not prevent my use—use of the park is nonrival in consumption. In this case the public park is a public good. But use of the park is rival in consumption if there are many people trying to use the jogging path at the same time or when my use of the public tennis court prevents your use of the same court. In those cases the public park is a common resource.

b. A cheese burrito is both excludable and rival in consumption. Hence it is a private good.

c. Information from a password-protected website is excludable but nonrival in consumption. So it is an artificially scarce good.

d. Publicly announced information on the path of an incoming hurricane is nonexcludable and nonrival in consumption. So it is a public good.

2. A private producer will supply only a good that is excludable; otherwise, the producer won't be able to charge a price for it that covers the costs of production. So a private producer would be willing to supply a cheese burrito and information from a password-protected website but unwilling to supply a public park or publicly announced information about an incoming hurricane.

17-2 Check Your Understanding

1. a. With 10 Homebodies and 6 Revelers, the marginal social benefit schedule of money spent on the party is as shown in the accompanying table.

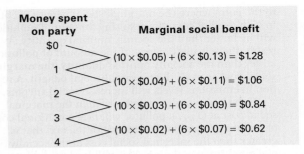

Money spent on party	Marginal social benefit
$0	
	$(10 \times \$0.05) + (6 \times \$0.13) = \$1.28$
1	
	$(10 \times \$0.04) + (6 \times \$0.11) = \$1.06$
2	
	$(10 \times \$0.03) + (6 \times \$0.09) = \$0.84$
3	
	$(10 \times \$0.02) + (6 \times \$0.07) = \$0.62$
4	

The efficient spending level is $2, the highest level for which the marginal social benefit is greater than the marginal cost ($1).

b. With 6 Homebodies and 10 Revelers, the marginal social benefit schedule of money spent on the party is as shown in the accompanying table.

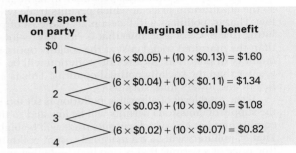

Money spent on party	Marginal social benefit
$0	
	$(6 \times \$0.05) + (10 \times \$0.13) = \$1.60$
1	
	$(6 \times \$0.04) + (10 \times \$0.11) = \$1.34$
2	
	$(6 \times \$0.03) + (10 \times \$0.09) = \$1.08$
3	
	$(6 \times \$0.02) + (10 \times \$0.07) = \$0.82$
4	

The efficient spending level is now $3, the highest level for which the marginal social benefit is greater than the marginal cost ($1). The efficient level of spending has increased from that in part a because with relatively more Revelers than Homebodies, an additional dollar spent on the party generates a higher level of social benefit compared to when there are relatively more Homebodies than Revelers.

c. When the numbers of Homebodies and Revelers are unknown but residents are asked their preferences, Homebodies will pretend to be Revelers to induce a higher level of spending on the public party. That's because a Homebody still receives a positive individual marginal benefit from an additional $1 spent, despite the fact that the individual's marginal benefit is lower than that of a Reveler for every additional $1. In this case the "reported" marginal social benefit schedule of money spent on the party will be as shown in the accompanying table.

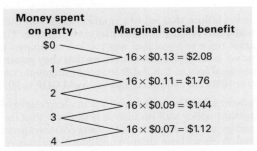

Money spent on party	Marginal social benefit
$0	
	$16 \times \$0.13 = \$2.08$
1	
	$16 \times \$0.11 = \$1.76$
2	
	$16 \times \$0.09 = \$1.44$
3	
	$16 \times \$0.07 = \$1.12$
4	

As a result, $4 will be spent on the party, the highest level for which the "reported" marginal social benefit is greater than the marginal cost ($1). Regardless of whether there are 10 Homebodies and 6 Revelers (part a) or 6 Homebodies and 10 Revelers (part b), spending $4 in total on the party is clearly inefficient because marginal cost exceeds marginal social benefit at this spending level.

As a further exercise, consider how much Homebodies gain by this misrepresentation. In part a, the efficient level of spending is $2. So by misrepresenting their preferences, the 10 Homebodies gain, in total, $10 \times (\$0.03 + \$0.02) = \$0.50$—that is, they gain the marginal individual benefit in going from a spending level of $2 to $4. The 6 Revelers also gain from the misrepresentations of the Homebodies; they gain $6 \times (\$0.09 + \$0.07) = \$0.96$ in total. This outcome is clearly inefficient—when $4 in total is spent, the marginal cost is $1 but the marginal social benefit is only $0.62, indicating that too much money is being spent on the party.

In part b, the efficient level of spending is actually $3. The misrepresentation by the 6 Homebodies gains them, in total, $6 \times \$0.02 = \$0.12$, but the 10 Revelers gain $10 \times \$0.07 = \$0.70$ in total. This outcome is also clearly inefficient—when $4 is spent, marginal social benefit is only $0.12 + \$0.70 = \$0.82$ but marginal cost is $1.

17-3 Check Your Understanding

1. When individuals are allowed to harvest freely, the government-owned forest becomes a common resource, and individuals will overuse it—they will harvest more trees than is efficient. In economic terms, the marginal social cost of harvesting a tree is greater than a private logger's individual marginal cost.

2. The three methods consistent with economic theory are (i) Pigouvian taxes, (ii) a system of tradable licenses, and (iii) allocation of property rights.

   i. *Pigouvian taxes.* You would enforce a tax on loggers that equals the difference between the marginal social cost and the individual marginal cost of logging a tree at the socially efficient harvest amount. In order to do this, you must know the marginal social cost schedule and the individual marginal cost schedule.

   ii. *System of tradable licenses.* You would issue tradable licenses, setting the total number of trees harvested equal to the socially efficient harvest number. The market that arises in these licenses will allocate the right to log efficiently when loggers differ in their costs of logging: licenses will be purchased by those who have a relatively lower cost of logging. The market price of a license will be equal to the difference between the marginal social cost and the individual marginal cost of logging a tree at the socially efficient harvest amount. In order to implement this level, you need to know the socially efficient harvest amount.

   iii. *Allocation of property rights.* Here you would sell or give the forest to a private party. This party will have the right to exclude others from harvesting trees. Harvesting is now a private good—it is excludable and rival in consumption. As a result, there is no longer any divergence between social and private costs, and the private party will harvest the efficient level of trees. You need no additional information to use this method.

17-4 Check Your Understanding

1. **a.** The efficient price to a consumer is $0, since the marginal cost of allowing a consumer to download it is $0.

b. Xenoid will not produce the software unless it can charge a price that allows it at least to make back the $300,000 cost of producing it. So the lowest price at which Xenoid is willing to produce it is $150. At this price, it makes a total revenue of $150 \times 2,000 = \$300,000$; at any lower price, Xenoid will not cover its cost. The shaded area in the accompanying diagram shows the deadweight loss when Xenoid charges a price of $150.

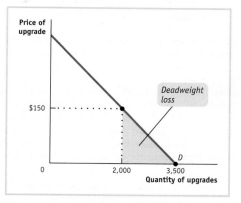

CHAPTER EIGHTEEN

18-1 Check Your Understanding

1. **a.** A pension guarantee program is a social insurance program. The possibility of an employer declaring bankruptcy and defaulting on its obligation to pay employee pensions creates insecurity. By providing pension income to those employees, such a program alleviates this source of economic insecurity.

   b. The SCHIP program is a poverty program. By providing health care to children in low-income households, it targets its spending specifically to the poor.

   c. The Section 8 housing program is a poverty program. By targeting its support to low-income households, it specifically helps the poor.

   d. The federal flood program is a social insurance program. For many people, the majority of their wealth is tied up in the home they own. The potential for a loss of that wealth creates economic insecurity. By providing assistance to those hit by a major flood, the program alleviates this source of insecurity.

2. The poverty threshold is an absolute measure of poverty. It defines individuals as poor if their incomes fall below a level that is considered adequate to purchase the necessities of life, irrespective of how well other people are doing. And that measure is fixed: in 2018, for instance, it took $12,140 for an individual living alone to purchase the necessities of life, regardless of how well-off other Americans were. In particular, the poverty threshold is not adjusted for an increase in living standards: even if other Americans are becoming increasingly well-off over time, in real terms (that is, how many goods an individual at the poverty threshold can buy) the poverty threshold remains the same.

3. **a.** To determine mean (or average) income, we take the total income of all individuals in this economy and divide it by the number of individuals. Mean income is $(\$39,000 + \$17,500 + \$900,000 + \$15,000 + \$28,000)/5 = \$999,500/5 = \$199,900$. To determine median income,

look at the accompanying table, which ranks the five individuals in order of their income.

	Income
Vijay	$15,000
Kelly	17,500
Oskar	28,000
Sephora	39,000
Raul	900,000

The median income is the income of the individual in the exact middle of the income distribution: Oskar, with an income of $28,000. So the median income is $28,000.

Median income is more representative of the income of individuals in this economy: almost everyone earns income between $15,000 and $39,000, close to the median income of $28,000. Only Raul is the exception: it is his income that raises the mean income to $199,900, which is not representative of most incomes in this economy.

b. The first quintile is made up of the 20% (or one-fifth) of individuals with the lowest incomes in the economy. Vijay makes up the 20% of individuals with the lowest incomes. His income is $15,000, so that is the average income of the first quintile. Oskar makes up the 20% of individuals with the third-lowest incomes. His income is $28,000, so that is the average income of the third quintile.

4. As the Economics in Action pointed out, much of the rise in inequality reflects growing differences among highly educated workers. That is, workers with similar levels of education earn very dissimilar incomes. As a result, the principal source of rising inequality in the United States today is reflected by statement b: the rise in the bank CEO's salary relative to that of the branch manager.

18-2 Check Your Understanding

1. The Earned Income Tax Credit (EITC), a negative income tax, applies only to those workers who earn income; over a certain range of incomes, the more a worker earns, the higher the amount of EITC received. A person who earns no income receives no income tax credit. By contrast, poverty programs that pay individuals based solely on low income still make those payments even if the individual does not work at all; once the individual earns a certain amount of income, these programs discontinue payments. As a result, such programs contain an incentive not to work and earn income, since earning more than a certain amount makes individuals ineligible for their benefits. The negative income tax, however, provides an incentive to work and earn income because its payments increase the more an individual works.

2. The second column of Table 18-3 gives the percentage reduction in the overall poverty rate by government programs. So the reduction in the overall poverty rate by the U.S. welfare state is given by adding up the numbers in that second column, which gives a 16.7% reduction in the overall poverty rate. For those aged 65 or over, the welfare state cuts the poverty rate by 43.6%, the amount given by adding up the numbers in the last column of Table 18-3.

18-3 Check Your Understanding

1. a. The program benefits you and your parents because the pool of all college students contains a representative mix of healthy and less healthy people, rather than a selected group of people who want insurance because they expect to pay high medical bills. In that respect, this insurance is like *employment-based health insurance*. Because no student can opt out, the school can offer health insurance based on the health care costs of its average student. If each student had to buy his or her own health insurance, some students would not be able to obtain any insurance and many would pay more than they do to the school's insurance program.

b. Since all students are required to enroll in its health insurance program, even the healthiest students cannot leave the program in an effort to obtain cheaper insurance tailored specifically to healthy people. If this were to happen, the school's insurance program would be left with an adverse selection of less healthy students and so would have to raise premiums, beginning the adverse selection death spiral. But since no student can leave the insurance program, the school's program can continue to base its premiums on the average student's probability of requiring health care, avoiding the adverse selection death spiral.

2. According to critics, part of the reason the U.S. health care system is so much more expensive than those of other countries is its fragmented nature. Since each of the many insurance companies has significant administrative (overhead) costs, the system tends to be more expensive than one in which there is only a single medical insurer. Another part of the explanation is that U.S. medical care includes many more expensive treatments than found in other wealthy countries, pays higher physician salaries, and has higher drug prices.

18-4 Check Your Understanding

1. a. Recall one of the principles from Chapter 1: one person's spending is another person's income. A high sales tax on consumer items is the same as a high marginal tax rate on income. As a result, the incentive to earn income by working or by investing in risky projects is reduced, since the payoff, after taxes, is lower.

b. If you lose a housing subsidy as soon as your income rises above $25,000, your incentive to earn more than $25,000 is reduced. If you earn exactly $25,000, you obtain the housing subsidy; however, as soon as you earn $25,001, you lose the entire subsidy, making you worse off than if you had not earned the additional dollar.

2. Over the past forty years, polarization in Congress has increased. Forty years ago, some Republicans were to the left of some Democrats. Today, the rightmost Democrats appear to be to the left of the leftmost Republicans.

CHAPTER NINETEEN

19-1 Check Your Understanding

1. Many college professors will depart for other lines of work if the government imposes a wage that is lower than the market wage. Fewer professors will result in fewer courses taught and therefore fewer college degrees produced. It will adversely affect sectors of the economy that depend directly on colleges, such as the local shopkeepers who sell goods and services to students and faculty, college textbook publishers, and so on. It will

also adversely affect firms that use the "output" produced by colleges: new college graduates. Firms that need to hire new employees with college degrees will be hurt as a smaller supply results in a higher market wage for college graduates. Ultimately, the reduced supply of college-educated workers will result in a lower level of human capital in the entire economy relative to what it would have been without the policy. And this will hurt all sectors of the economy that depend on human capital. The sectors of the economy that might benefit are firms that compete with colleges in the hiring of would-be college professors. For example, accounting firms will find it easier to hire people who would otherwise have been professors of accounting, and publishers will find it easier to hire people who would otherwise have been professors of English (easier in the sense that the firms can recruit would-be professors with a lower wage than before). In addition, workers who already have college degrees will benefit; they will command higher wages as the supply of college-educated workers falls.

19-2 Check Your Understanding

1. **a.** As the demand for services increases, the price of services will rise. And as the price of the output produced by the industries increases, this shifts the *VMPL* curve upward—that is, the demand for labor rises. This results in an increase in both the equilibrium wage rate and the quantity of labor employed.

    b. The fall in the catch per day means that the marginal product of labor in the industry declines. The *VMPL* curve shifts downward, generating a fall in the equilibrium wage rate and the equilibrium quantity of labor employed.

2. When producers from different industries compete for the same workers, then each worker in the various industries will be paid the same equilibrium wage rate, *W*. And since, by the marginal productivity theory of income distribution, $VMPL = P \times MPL = W$ for the last worker hired in equilibrium, the last worker hired in each of these different industries will have the same value of the marginal product of labor.

19-3 Check Your Understanding

1. **a.** False. Income disparities associated with gender, race, or ethnicity can be explained by the marginal productivity theory of income distribution provided that differences in marginal productivity across people are correlated with gender, race, or ethnicity. One possible source for such correlation is past discrimination. Such discrimination can lower individuals' marginal productivity by, for example, preventing them from acquiring the human capital that would raise their productivity. Another possible source of the correlation is differences in work experience that are associated with gender, race, or ethnicity. For example, in jobs where work experience or length of tenure is important, women may earn lower wages because on average more women than men take child-care-related absences from work.

    b. True. Companies that discriminate when their competitors do not are likely to hire less able workers because they discriminate against more able workers who are considered to be of the wrong gender, race, ethnicity, or other characteristic. And with less able workers, such companies are likely to earn lower profits than their competitors that don't discriminate.

    c. Ambiguous. In general, workers who are paid less because they have less experience may or may not be the victims of discrimination. The answer depends on the reason for the lack of experience. If workers have less experience because they are young or have chosen to do something else rather than gain experience, then they are not victims of discrimination if they are paid less. But if workers lack experience because previous job discrimination prevented them from gaining experience, then they are indeed victims of discrimination when they are paid less.

    d. False. This is not an example of wage discrimination. As long as Walmart doesn't offer differing wages based on gender, age, or race, all workers will be treated the same. This is an example of firms exploiting monopsony power in the labor market. In a small town, Walmart would be the predominant employer for most entry level, lower skill jobs.

19-4 Check Your Understanding

1. **a.** Jaden is made worse off if, before the new law, he had preferred to work more than 35 hours per week. As a result of the law, he can no longer choose his preferred time allocation; he now consumes fewer goods and more leisure than he would like.

    b. Jaden's utility is unaffected by the law if, before the law, he had preferred to work 35 or fewer hours per week. The law has not changed his preferred time allocation.

    c. Jaden can never be made better off by a law that restricts the number of hours he can work. He can only be made worse off (case a) or equally as well off (case b).

2. The substitution effect would induce Jaden to work fewer hours and consume more leisure after his wage rate falls—the fall in the wage rate means the price of an hour of leisure falls, leading Jaden to consume more leisure. But a fall in his wage rate also generates a fall in Jaden's income. The income effect of this is to induce Jaden to consume less leisure and therefore work more hours, since he is now poorer and leisure is a normal good. If the income effect dominates the substitution effect, Jaden will in the end work more hours than before.

CHAPTER TWENTY

20-1 Check Your Understanding

1. The family with the lower income is likely to be more risk-averse. In general, higher income or wealth results in lower degrees of risk aversion, due to diminishing marginal utility. Both families may be willing to buy an "unfair" insurance policy. Most insurance policies are "unfair" in that the expected claim is less than the premium. The degree to which a family is willing to pay more than an expected claim for insurance depends on the family's degree of risk aversion.

2. **a.** Karma's expected income is the weighted average of all possible values of her income, weighted by the probabilities with which she earns each possible value of her income. Since she makes $22,000 with a probability of 0.6 and $35,000 with a probability of 0.4, her expected income is $(0.6 \times \$22,000) + (0.4 \times \$35,000) = \$13,200 + \$14,000 = \$27,200$. Her expected utility is

simply the expected value of the total utilities she will experience. Since with a probability of 0.6 she will experience a total utility of 850 utils (the utility to her from making $22,000), and with a probability of 0.4 she will experience a total utility of 1,260 utils (the utility to her from making $35,000), her expected utility is (0.6 × 850 utils) + (0.4 × 1,260 utils) = 510 utils + 504 utils = 1,014 utils.

b. If Karma makes $25,000 for certain, she experiences a utility level of 1,014 utils. From the answer to part a, we know that this leaves her equally as well off as when she has a risky expected income of $27,200. Since Karma is indifferent between a risky expected income of $27,200 and a certain income of $25,000, you can conclude that she would prefer a certain income of $25,000 to a risky expected income of $27,200. That is, she would definitely be willing to reduce the risk she faces when this reduction in risk leaves her expected income unchanged. In other words, Karma is risk-averse.

c. Yes. Karma experiences a utility level of 1,056 utils when she has a certain income of $26,000. This is higher than the expected utility level of 1,014 utils generated by a risky expected income of $27,200. So Karma is willing to pay a premium to guarantee a certain income of $26,000.

20-2 Check Your Understanding

1. a. An increase in the number of ships implies an increase in the quantity of insurance demanded at any given premium. This is a rightward shift of the demand curve, resulting in a rise in both the equilibrium premium and the equilibrium quantity of insurance bought and sold.

b. An increase in the number of trading routes means that investors can diversify more. In other words, they can reduce risk further. At any given premium, there are now more investors willing to supply insurance. This is a rightward shift of the supply curve for insurance, leading to a fall in the equilibrium premium and a rise in the equilibrium quantity of insurance bought and sold.

c. If shipowners in the market become even more risk-averse, they will be willing to pay even higher premiums for insurance. That is, at any given premium, there are now more people willing to buy insurance. This is a rightward shift of the demand curve for insurance, leading to a rise in both the equilibrium premium and the equilibrium quantity of insurance bought and sold.

d. If investors in the market become more risk-averse, they will be less willing to accept risk at any given premium. This is a leftward shift of the supply curve for insurance, leading to a rise in the equilibrium premium and a fall in the equilibrium quantity of insurance bought and sold.

e. As the overall level of risk increases, those willing to buy insurance will be more willing to buy insurance at any given premium; the demand curve for insurance shifts to the right. But since overall risk cannot be diversified away, those ordinarily willing to take on risk will be less willing to do so, leading to a leftward shift in the supply curve for insurance. As a result, the equilibrium premium will rise; the effect on the equilibrium quantity of insurance is uncertain.

f. If the wealth levels of investors fall, investors will become more risk-averse and so less willing to supply insurance at any given premium. This is a leftward shift of the supply curve for insurance, leading to a rise in the equilibrium premium and a fall in the equilibrium quantity of insurance bought and sold.

20-3 Check Your Understanding

1. The inefficiency caused by adverse selection is that an insurance policy with a premium based on the average risk of all drivers will attract only an adverse selection of bad drivers. Good (that is, safe) drivers will find this insurance premium too expensive and so will remain uninsured. This is inefficient. However, safe drivers are also those drivers who have had fewer moving violations for several years. Lowering premiums for only those drivers allows the insurance company to screen its customers and sell insurance to safe drivers, too. This means that at least some of the good drivers now are also insured, which decreases the inefficiency that arises from adverse selection. In a way, having no moving violations for several years is building a reputation for being a safe driver.

2. The moral hazard problem in home construction arises from private information about what the contractor does: whether the contractor takes care to reduce the cost of construction or allows costs to increase. The homeowner cannot, or can only imperfectly, observe the cost-reduction effort of the contractor. If the contractor were fully reimbursed for all costs incurred during construction, the contractor would have no incentive to reduce costs. Making the contractor responsible for any additional costs above the original estimate means that the contractor now has an incentive to keep costs low. However, this imposes risk on the contractor. For instance, if the weather is bad, home construction will take longer, and will be more costly, than if the weather had been good. Since the contractor pays for any additional costs (such as weather-induced delays) above the original estimate, the contractor now faces risk that they cannot control.

3. a. True. Drivers with higher deductibles have more incentive to be more careful while driving, to avoid paying the deductible. This is a moral hazard phenomenon.

b. True. Suppose you know that you are a safe driver. You have a choice of a policy with a high premium but a low deductible or one with a lower premium but a higher deductible. In this case, you would be more likely to choose the cheap policy with the high deductible because you know that you will be unlikely to have to pay the deductible. When there is adverse selection, insurance companies use screening devices such as this to make inferences about people's private information about how skillful they are as drivers.

c. True. The wealthier you are, the less risk-averse you are. If you are less risk-averse, you are more willing to bear risk yourself. Having an insurance policy with a high deductible means that you are exposed to more risk: you have to pay more of any insurance claim yourself. This is an implication of how risk aversion changes with a person's income or wealth.

CHAPTER TWENTY-ONE

21-1 Check Your Understanding

1. **a.** This is a microeconomic question because it addresses decisions made by consumers about a particular product.

   b. This is a macroeconomic question because it addresses consumer spending in the overall economy.

   c. This is a macroeconomic question because it addresses changes in the overall economy.

   d. This is a microeconomic question because it addresses changes in a particular market, in this case the market for economists.

   e. This is a microeconomic question because it addresses choices made by consumers and producers about which mode of transportation to use.

   f. This is a microeconomic question because it addresses changes in a particular market.

   g. This is a macroeconomic question because it addresses changes in a measure of the economy's overall price level.

2. **a.** When people can't get credit to finance their purchases, they will be unable to spend money. This will weaken the economy, and as others see the economy weaken, they will also cut back on their spending in order to save for future bad times. As a result, the credit shortfall will spark a compounding effect through the economy as people cut back their spending, making the economy worse, leading to more cutbacks in spending, and so on.

   b. If you believe the economy is self-regulating, then you would advocate doing nothing in response to the slump.

   c. If you believe in Keynesian economics, you would advocate that policy makers undertake monetary and fiscal policies to stimulate spending in the economy.

21-2 Check Your Understanding

1. We talk about business cycles for the economy as a whole because recessions and expansions are not confined to a few industries—they reflect downturns and upturns for the economy as a whole. In downturns, almost every sector of the economy reduces output and the number of people employed. Moreover, business cycles are an international phenomenon, sometimes moving in rough synchrony across countries.

2. A recession can hurt people throughout society. They cause large numbers of workers to lose their jobs and make it hard to find new jobs. Recessions hurt the standard of living of many families and are usually associated with a rise in the number of people living below the poverty line, an increase in the number of people who lose their houses because they can't afford their mortgage payments, and a fall in the percentage of Americans with health insurance. Recessions also hurt the profits of firms.

21-3 Check Your Understanding

1. Countries with high rates of population growth will have to maintain higher long-run growth rates of overall output than countries with low rates of population growth in order to achieve an increased standard of living per person, because aggregate output will have to be divided among a larger number of people.

2. No, Argentina is not poorer than it was in the past. Both Argentina and Canada have experienced long-run growth. However, after World War II, Argentina did not make as much progress as Canada, perhaps because of political instability and bad macroeconomic policies. Also, Canada's economy grew much faster than Argentina's. Although Canada is now about three times as rich as Argentina, Argentina still experienced long-run growth.

21-4 Check Your Understanding

1. **a.** As some prices have risen but other prices have fallen, there may be overall inflation or deflation. The answer is ambiguous.

   b. As all prices have risen significantly, this sounds like inflation.

   c. As most prices have fallen and others have not changed, this sounds like deflation.

21-5 Check Your Understanding

1. **a.** This situation reflects comparative advantage. Canada's comparative advantage results from the development of oil—Canada now has an abundance of oil.

   b. This situation reflects comparative advantage. China's comparative advantage results from an abundance of labor; China is good at labor-intensive activities such as assembly.

   c. This situation reflects macroeconomic forces. Germany has been running huge trade surpluses because of underlying decisions regarding savings and investment spending with its savings in excess of its investment spending.

   d. This situation reflects macroeconomic forces. The United States was able to begin running large trade deficits because the technology boom made the United States an attractive place to invest, with investment spending outstripping U.S. savings.

CHAPTER TWENTY-TWO

22-1 Check Your Understanding

1. Let's start by considering the relationship between the total value added of all domestically produced final goods and services and aggregate spending on domestically produced final goods and services. These two quantities are equal because every final good and service produced in the economy is either purchased by someone or added to inventories. And additions to inventories are counted as spending by firms. Next, consider the relationship between aggregate spending on domestically produced final goods and services and total factor income. These two quantities are equal because all spending that is channeled to firms to pay for purchases of domestically produced final goods and services is revenue for firms. Those revenues must be paid out by firms to their factors of production in the form of wages, profit, interest, and rent. Taken together, this means that all three methods of calculating GDP are equivalent.

2. Firms make sales to other firms, households, the government, and the rest of the world. Households are linked to firms through the sale of factors of production to firms, through purchases from firms of final goods and services, and through lending funds to firms in the financial markets.

Households are linked to the government through their payment of taxes, their receipt of transfers, and their lending of funds to the government via the financial markets. Finally, households are linked to the rest of the world through their purchases of imports and transactions with foreigners in financial markets.

3. You would be counting the value of the steel twice—once as it was sold by National Steel to National Motors and once as part of the car sold by National Motors.

22-2 Check Your Understanding

1. **a.** In 2019 nominal GDP was $(1,000,000 \times \$0.40) + (800,000 \times \$0.60) = \$400,000 + \$480,000 = \$880,000$. A 25% rise in the price of french fries from 2019 to 2020 means that the 2020 price of french fries was $1.25 \times \$0.40 = \$0.50$. A 10% fall in servings sold means that $1,000,000 \times 0.9 = 900,000$ servings were sold in 2020. As a result, the total value of sales of french fries in 2020 was $900,000 \times \$0.50 = \$450,000$. A 15% fall in the price of onion rings from 2019 to 2020 means that the 2020 price of onion rings was $0.85 \times \$0.60 = \$0.51$. A 5% rise in servings sold means that $800,000 \times 1.05 = 840,000$ servings were sold in 2020. As a result, the total value of sales of onion rings in 2020 was $840,000 \times \$0.51 = \$428,400$. Nominal GDP in 2020 was $\$450,000 + \$428,400 = \$878,400$. To find real GDP in 2020, we must calculate the value of sales in 2020 using 2019 prices: $(900,000 \text{ french fries} \times \$0.40) + (840,000 \text{ onion rings} \times \$0.60) = \$360,000 + \$504,000 = \$864,000$.

   b. The change in nominal GDP from 2019 to 2020 was $((\$878,400 - \$880,000)/\$880,000) \times 100 = -0.18\%$, a decline. But a comparison using real GDP shows a decline of $((\$864,000 - \$880,000)/\$880,000) \times 100 = -1.8\%$. That is, a calculation based on real GDP shows a drop 10 times larger (1.8%) than a calculation based on nominal GDP (0.18%). In this case, the calculation based on nominal GDP underestimates the true magnitude of the change.

2. A price index based on 2016 prices will contain a relatively high price of electronics and a relatively low price of housing compared to a price index based on 2020 prices. This means that a 2016 price index used to calculate real GDP in 2018 will magnify the value of electronics production in the economy, but a 2020 price index will magnify the value of housing production in the economy.

22-3 Check Your Understanding

1. This market basket costs, pre-frost, $(100 \times \$0.20) + (50 \times \$0.60) + (200 \times \$0.25) = \$20 + \$30 + \$50 = \$100$. The same market basket, post-frost, costs $(100 \times \$0.40) + (50 \times \$1.00) + (200 \times \$0.45) = \$40 + \$50 + \$90 = \$180$. So the price index is $(\$100/\$100) \times 100 = 100$ before the frost and $(\$180/\$100) \times 100 = 180$ after the frost, implying a rise in the price index of 80%. This increase in the price index is less than the 84.2% increase calculated in the text. The reason for this difference is that the new market basket of 100 oranges, 50 grapefruit, and 200 lemons contains proportionately more of the items that have experienced relatively lower price increases (the lemons, whose price has increased by 80%) and proportionately fewer of the items that have experienced relatively large price increases (the oranges, whose price has increased by 100%). This shows that the price index can be very sensitive to the composition of the market basket. If the market basket contains a large proportion of goods whose prices have risen faster than the prices of other goods, it will lead to a higher estimate of the increase in the price level. If it contains a large proportion of goods whose prices have risen more slowly than the prices of other goods, it will lead to a lower estimate of the increase in the price level.

2. **a.** A market basket determined 10 years ago would contain fewer cars than at present. Given that the average price of a car has grown faster than the average prices of other goods, this basket will underestimate the true increase in the cost of living because it contains relatively too few cars.

   b. A market basket determined 20 years ago will not contain broadband internet access. So it cannot track the fall in prices of internet access over the past few years. As a result, it will overestimate the true increase in the cost of living.

3. Using Equation 22-3, the inflation rate from 2017 to 2018 is $((252.723 - 247.901)/247.901) \times 100 = 1.95\%$.

CHAPTER TWENTY-THREE

23-1 Check Your Understanding

1. Software improvements developed by employment websites that enable job-seekers to find jobs more quickly will reduce the unemployment rate over time. However, websites that induce discouraged workers to begin actively looking for work again will lead to an increase in the unemployment rate over time.

2. **a.** Rosa is not counted as unemployed because she is not actively looking for work, but she is counted in broader measures of labor underutilization as a discouraged worker.

   b. Anthony is not counted as unemployed; he is considered employed because he has a job.

   c. Kanako is unemployed; she is not working and is actively looking for work.

   d. Sergio is not unemployed, but underemployed; he is working part time for economic reasons. He is counted in broader measures of labor underutilization.

   e. Natasha is not unemployed, but she is a marginally attached worker. She is counted in broader measures of labor underutilization.

3. Both parts a and b are consistent with the relationship, illustrated in Figure 23-5, between above-average or below-average growth in real GDP and changes in the unemployment rate: during years of above-average growth, the unemployment rate falls, and during years of below-average growth, the unemployment rate rises. However, part c is not consistent: it implies that a recession is associated with a fall in the unemployment rate, which is incorrect.

23-2 Check Your Understanding

1. **a.** When the pace of technological advancement quickens, there will be higher rates of job creation and destruction as old industries disappear and new ones emerge. As a result, frictional unemployment will be higher as workers leave jobs in declining industries in search of jobs in expanding industries.

   b. When the pace of technological advancement quickens, there will be greater mismatch between the skills employees have and the skills employers are looking for, leading to higher structural unemployment.

c. When the unemployment rate is low, frictional unemployment will account for a larger share of total unemployment because other sources of unemployment will be diminished. So the share of total unemployment composed of the frictionally unemployed will rise.

2. A binding minimum wage represents a price floor below which wages cannot fall. As a result, actual wages cannot move toward equilibrium. So a minimum wage causes the quantity of labor supplied to exceed the quantity of labor demanded. Because this surplus of labor reflects unemployed workers, it affects the unemployment rate. Collective bargaining has a similar effect—unions are able to raise the wage above the equilibrium level to a level like W_U in the accompanying diagram. This will act like a minimum wage by causing the number of job-seekers to be larger than the number of workers firms are willing to hire. Collective bargaining causes the unemployment rate to be higher than it otherwise would be, as shown in the accompanying diagram.

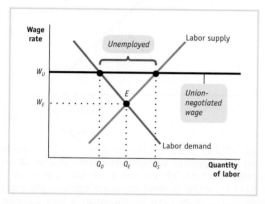

3. An increase in unemployment benefits at the peak of the business cycle reduces the cost to individuals of being unemployed, causing them to spend more time searching for new jobs. So the natural rate of unemployment would increase.

23-3 Check Your Understanding

1. Shoe-leather costs as a result of inflation will be lower because it is now less costly for individuals to manage their assets in order to economize on their money holdings. This reduction in the costs associated with converting other assets into money translates into lower shoe-leather costs.

2. If inflation came to an unexpected and complete stop over the next 15 or 20 years, the inflation rate would be zero, which of course is less than the expected inflation rate of 2% to 3%. Because the real interest rate is the nominal interest rate minus the inflation rate, the real interest rate on a loan would be higher than expected, and lenders would gain at the expense of borrowers. Borrowers would have to repay their loans with funds that have a higher real value than had been expected.

CHAPTER TWENTY-FOUR

24-1 Check Your Understanding

1. Economic progress raises the living standards of the average resident of a country. An increase in overall real GDP does not accurately reflect an increase in an average resident's living standard because it does not account for growth in the number of residents. If, for example, real GDP rises by 10% but population grows by 20%, the living standard of the average resident falls: after the change, the average resident has only $(110/120) \times 100 = 91.6\%$ as much real income as before the change. Similarly, an increase in nominal GDP per capita does not accurately reflect an increase in living standards because it does not account for any change in prices. For example, a 5% increase in nominal GDP per capita generated by a 5% increase in prices implies that there has been no change in living standards. Real GDP per capita is the only measure that accounts for both changes in the population and changes in prices.

2. Using the Rule of 70, the number of years it will take for China to double its real GDP per capita is $(70/7.8) = 8.97$, or approximately 9 years; India, $(70/4.1) = 17.07$, or approximately 17 years; Ireland, $(70/3.7) = 18.92$, or approximately 19 years; Bangladesh, $(70/3) = 23.33$, or approximately 23 years; the United States, $(70/1.6) = 43.75$, or approximately 44 years; France, $(70/1.3) = 53.85$, or approximately 54 years; and Argentina $(70/0.5) = 140$ years. Since the Rule of 70 can only be applied to a positive growth rate, we cannot apply it to the case of Venezuela, which experienced negative growth. If India continues to have a higher growth rate of real GDP per capita than the United States, then India's real GDP per capita will eventually surpass that of the United States.

3. The United States began growing rapidly over a century ago, but China and India have begun growing rapidly only recently. As a result, the living standard of the typical Chinese or Indian household has not yet caught up with that of the typical American household.

24-2 Check Your Understanding

1. **a.** Significant technological progress will result in a positive growth rate of productivity even though physical capital per worker and human capital per worker are unchanged.

   b. The growth rate of productivity will fall but remain positive due to diminishing returns to physical capital.

2. **a.** If output has grown 3% per year and the labor force has grown 1% per year, then productivity—output per person—has grown at approximately $3\% - 1\% = 2\%$ per year.

   b. If physical capital has grown 4% per year and the labor force has grown 1% per year, then physical capital per worker has grown at approximately $4\% - 1\% = 3\%$ per year.

   c. According to estimates, each 1% rise in physical capital, other things equal, increases productivity by 0.3%. So, as physical capital per worker has increased by 3%, productivity growth that can be attributed to an increase in physical capital per worker is $0.3 \times 3\% = 0.9\%$. As a percentage of total productivity growth, this is $0.9\%/2\% \times 100\% = 45\%$.

   d. If the rest of productivity growth is due to technological progress, then technological progress has contributed $2\% - 0.9\% = 1.1\%$ to productivity growth. As a percentage of total productivity growth, this is $1.1\%/2\% \times 100\% = 55\%$.

3. It will take a period of time for workers to learn how to use the new computer system and to adjust their routines. And because there are often setbacks in learning a new system, such as accidentally erasing your computer files, productivity at Multinomics, Inc. may decrease for a period of time.

24-3 Check Your Understanding

1. A country that has high domestic savings is able to achieve a high rate of investment spending as a percent of GDP. This, in turn, allows the country to achieve a high growth rate.

2. It is likely that the United States will experience a greater pace of innovation and development of new drugs because closer links between private companies and academic research centers will lead to research and development more directly focused on producing new drugs rather than on pure research.

3. It is likely that these events resulted in a fall in the country's growth rate because the lack of property rights would have dissuaded people from making investments in a productive capacity.

24-4 Check Your Understanding

1. The conditional version of the convergence hypothesis says that countries grow faster, other things equal, when they start from relatively low GDP per capita. From this we can infer that they grow more slowly, other things equal, when their real GDP per capita is relatively higher. This points to lower future Asian growth. However, other things might not be equal: if Asian economies continue investing in human capital, if savings rates continue to be high, if governments invest in infrastructure, and so on, growth might continue at an accelerated pace.

2. The regions of East Asia, Western Europe, and the United States support the convergence hypothesis because a comparison among them shows that the growth rate of real GDP per capita falls as real GDP per capita rises. Eastern Europe, West Asia, Latin America, and Africa do not support the hypothesis because they all have much lower real GDP per capita than the United States but have either approximately the same growth rate (West Asia and Eastern Europe) or a lower growth rate (Africa and Latin America).

3. The evidence suggests that both sets of factors matter: better infrastructure is important for growth, but so is political and financial stability. Policies should try to address both areas.

24-5 Check Your Understanding

1. Economists are typically more concerned about environmental degradation than resource scarcity. The reason is that in modern economies the price response tends to alleviate the limits imposed by resource scarcity through conservation and the development of alternatives. However, because environmental degradation involves a cost imposed by individuals or firms on others without the requirement to pay compensation (known as a *negative externality*), effective government intervention is required to address it. As a result, economists are more concerned about the limits to growth imposed by environmental degradation because a market response would be inadequate.

2. Growth increases a country's greenhouse gas emissions. The current best estimates are that a large reduction in emissions will result in only a modest reduction in growth. The international burden sharing of greenhouse gas emissions reduction is contentious because rich countries are reluctant to pay the costs of reducing their emissions only to see newly emerging countries like China rapidly increase their emissions. Yet most of the current accumulation of gases is due to the past actions of rich countries. Poorer countries like China are equally reluctant to sacrifice their growth to pay for the past actions of rich countries.

CHAPTER TWENTY-FIVE

25-1 Check Your Understanding

1. **a.** As there is a net capital inflow into the economy, the supply of loanable funds increases. This is illustrated by the shift of the supply curve from S_1 to S_2 in the accompanying diagram. As the equilibrium moves from E_1 to E_2, the equilibrium interest rate falls from r_1 to r_2, and the equilibrium quantity of loanable funds increases from Q_1 to Q_2.

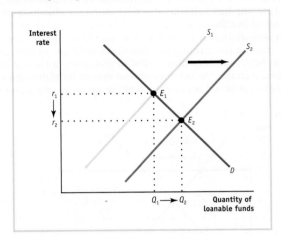

b. Savings fall due to the higher proportion of retired people, and the supply of loanable funds decreases. This is illustrated by the leftward shift of the supply curve from S_1 to S_2 in the accompanying diagram. The equilibrium moves from E_1 to E_2, the equilibrium interest rate rises from r_1 to r_2, and the equilibrium quantity of loanable funds falls from Q_1 to Q_2.

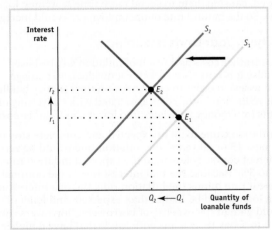

2. We know from the loanable funds market that as the interest rate rises, households want to save more and consume less. But at the same time, an increase in the interest rate lowers the number of investment spending projects with returns at least as high as the interest rate. The statement "households will want to save more money than businesses will want to invest" cannot represent an equilibrium in the loanable funds market because it says that the quantity of loanable funds offered exceeds the quantity of loanable funds demanded. If that were to occur, the interest rate must fall to make the quantity of loanable funds offered equal to the quantity of loanable funds demanded.

3. **a.** The real interest rate will not change. According to the Fisher effect, an increase in expected inflation drives up the nominal interest rate, leaving the real interest rate unchanged.

   b. The nominal interest rate will rise by 3%. Each additional percentage point of expected inflation drives up the nominal interest rate by 1 percentage point.

   c. As we saw in Figure 25-9, as long as inflation is expected, it does not affect the equilibrium quantity of loanable funds. Both the supply and demand curves for loanable funds are pushed upward, leaving the equilibrium quantity of loanable funds unchanged.

25-2 Check Your Understanding

1. The transaction costs for (a) a bank deposit and (b) a share of a mutual fund are approximately equal because each can typically be accomplished by making a phone call, going online, or visiting a branch office. Transaction costs are highest for (c) a share of a family business, since finding a buyer for the share consumes time and resources. The level of risk is lowest for (a) a bank deposit, since these deposits are insured by the Federal Deposit Insurance Corporation (FDIC) up to $250,000; somewhat higher for (b) a share of a mutual fund, since despite diversification, there is still risk associated with holding mutual funds; and highest for (c) a share of a family business, since this investment is not diversified. The level of liquidity is highest for (a) a bank deposit, since withdrawals can usually be made immediately; somewhat lower for (b) a share of a mutual fund, since it may take a few days between selling your shares and the payment being processed; and lowest for (c) a share of a family business, since it can only be sold with the unanimous agreement of other members and it will take some time to find a buyer.

2. Economic development and growth are the result of, among other factors, investment spending on physical capital. Since investment spending is equal to savings, the greater the amount saved, the higher investment spending will be, and so the higher growth and economic development will be. So the existence of institutions that facilitate savings will help a country's growth and economic development. As a result, a country with a financial system that provides low transaction costs, opportunities for diversification of risk, and high liquidity to its savers will experience faster growth and economic development than a country that doesn't.

25-3 Check Your Understanding

1. **a.** Today's stock prices reflect the market's expectation of future stock prices, and according to the efficient markets hypothesis, stock prices always take account of all available information. The fact that this year's profits are low is not new information, so it is already built into the share price. However, when it becomes known that the company's profits will be high next year, the price of a share of its stock will rise today, reflecting this new information.

   b. The expectations of investors about high profits were already built into the stock price. Since profits will be lower than expected, the market's expectations about the company's future stock price will be revised downward. This new information will lower the stock price.

   c. When other companies in the same industry announce that sales are unexpectedly slow this year, investors are likely to conclude that sales will also be unexpectedly slow for this company. As a result, investors will revise their expectations of future profits and of the future stock price downward. This new information will result in a lower stock price today.

   d. This announcement will either have no effect on the company's stock price or will increase it only slightly. It does not add any new information, beyond removing some uncertainty about whether the profit forecast was correct. It should therefore result in either no increase or only a small increase in the stock price.

2. The efficient markets hypothesis states that all available information is immediately taken into account in stock prices. So if investors consistently bought stocks the day after the Dow rose by 1%, a smart investor would *sell* on that day because demand—and so stock prices—would be high. If a profit can be made that way, eventually many investors would be selling, and it would no longer be true that investors always bought stocks the day after the Dow rose by 1%.

CHAPTER TWENTY-SIX

26-1 Check Your Understanding

1. A decline in investment spending, like a rise in investment spending, has a multiplier effect on real GDP—the only difference in this case is that real GDP falls instead of rises. The fall in I leads to an initial fall in real GDP, which leads to a fall in disposable income, which leads to lower consumer spending, which leads to another fall in real GDP, and so on. So consumer spending falls as an indirect result of the fall in investment spending.

2. When MPC is 0.5, the multiplier is equal to $1/(1-0.5) = 1/0.5 = 2$. When MPC is 0.8, the multiplier is equal to $1/(1-0.8) = 1/0.2 = 5$.

3. The greater the share of GDP that is saved rather than spent, the lower the MPC. Disposable income that goes to savings is like a "leak" in the system, reducing the amount of spending that fuels a further expansion. So it is likely that Amerigo will have the larger multiplier.

26-2 Check Your Understanding

1. **a.** Angelina's autonomous consumer spending is $8,000. When her current disposable income rises by $10,000, her consumer spending rises by $12,000 − $8,000 = $4,000. So her MPC is $4,000/$10,000 = 0.4 and her consumption function is $c = \$8,000 + 0.4 \times yd$. Felicia's autonomous consumer spending is $6,500. When her current disposable income rises by $10,000, her consumer spending rises by $14,500 − $6,500 = $8,000. So her MPC is $8,000/$10,000 = 0.8 and her consumption function is $c = \$6,500 + 0.8 \times yd$. Marina's autonomous consumer spending is $7,250. When her current disposable income rises by $10,000, her consumer spending rises by $14,250 − $7,250 = $7,000. So her MPC is $7,000/$10,000 = 0.7 and her consumption function is $c = \$7,250 + 0.7 \times yd$.

   b. The aggregate autonomous consumer spending in this economy is $8,000 + $6,500 + $7,250 = $21,750. A $30,000 increase in disposable income ($3 \times \$10,000$) leads to a $4,000 + $8,000 + $7,000 = $19,000 increase in consumer spending. So the economy-wide MPC is $19,000/$30,000 = 0.63 and the aggregate consumption function is $C = \$21,750 + 0.63 \times YD$.

2. If you expect your future disposable income to fall, you would like to save some of today's disposable income to tide you over in the future. But you cannot do this if you cannot save. If you expect your future disposable income to rise, you would like to spend some of tomorrow's higher income today. But you cannot do this if you cannot borrow. If you cannot save or borrow, your expected future disposable income will have no effect on your consumer spending today. In fact, your *MPC* must always equal 1: you must consume all your current disposable income today, and you will be unable to smooth your consumption over time.

26-3 Check Your Understanding

1. **a.** An unexpected increase in consumer spending will result in a reduction in inventories as producers sell items from their inventories to satisfy this short-term increase in demand. This is negative unplanned inventory investment: it reduces the value of producers' inventories.

   b. A rise in the cost of borrowing is equivalent to a rise in the interest rate: fewer investment spending projects are now profitable to producers, whether they are financed through borrowing or retained earnings. As a result, producers will reduce the amount of planned investment spending.

   c. A sharp increase in the rate of real GDP growth leads to a higher level of planned investment spending by producers, according to the accelerator principle, as they increase production capacity to meet higher demand.

   d. As sales fall, producers sell less, and their inventories grow. This leads to positive unplanned inventory investment.

2. Since the marginal propensity to consume is less than 1—because consumers normally spend part but not all of an additional dollar of disposable income—consumer spending does not fully respond to fluctuations in current disposable income. This behavior diminishes the effect of fluctuations in the economy on consumer spending. In contrast, by the accelerator principle, investment spending is directly related to the expected future growth rate of GDP. As a result, investment spending will magnify fluctuations in the economy: a higher expected future growth rate of real GDP leads to higher planned investment spending; a lower expected future growth rate of real GDP leads to lower planned investment spending.

3. When consumer spending is sluggish, firms with excess production capacity will cut back on planned investment spending because they think their existing capacities are sufficient for expected future sales. Similarly, when consumer spending is sluggish and firms have a large amount of unplanned inventory investment, they are likely to cut back their production of output because they think their existing inventories are sufficient for expected future sales. So an inventory overhang is likely to depress current economic activity as firms cut back on their planned investment spending and on their output.

26-4 Check Your Understanding

1. A slump in planned investment spending will lead to a fall in real GDP in response to an unanticipated increase in inventories. The fall in real GDP will translate into a fall in households' disposable income, and households will respond by reducing consumer spending. The decrease in consumer spending leads producers to further decrease output, further lowering disposable income and leading to further reductions in consumer spending. So although the slump originated in investment spending, it will cause a reduction in consumer spending.

2. **a.** After an autonomous fall in planned aggregate spending, the economy is no longer in equilibrium: real GDP is greater than planned aggregate spending. The accompanying figure shows this autonomous fall in planned aggregate spending by the shift of the aggregate spending curve from AE_1 to AE_2. The difference between the two results in positive unplanned inventory investment: there is an unanticipated increase in inventories. Firms will respond by reducing production. This will eventually move the economy to a new equilibrium. In the accompanying figure, this is illustrated by the movement from the initial income–expenditure equilibrium at E_1 to the new income–expenditure equilibrium at E_2. As the economy moves to its new equilibrium, real GDP falls from its initial income–expenditure equilibrium level at Y_1^* to its new lower level, Y_2^*.

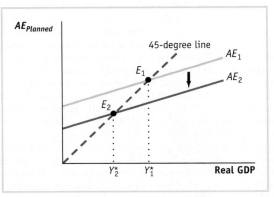

   b. We know that the change in income–expenditure equilibrium GDP is given by Equation 26-17: $\Delta Y^* = \text{Multiplier} \times \Delta AAE_{Planned}$. Here, the multiplier is equal to $1/(1 - 0.5) = 1/0.5 = 2$. So a \$300 million autonomous reduction in planned aggregate spending will lead to a $2 \times \$300$ million = \$600 million (\$0.6 billion) fall in income–expenditure equilibrium GDP. The new Y^* will be \$500 billion – \$0.6 billion = \$499.4 billion.

|| CHAPTER TWENTY-SEVEN

27-1 Check Your Understanding

1. **a.** This is a shift of the aggregate demand curve. A decrease in the quantity of money raises the interest rate, since people now want to borrow more and lend less. A higher interest rate reduces investment and consumer spending at any given aggregate price level. So the aggregate demand curve shifts to the left.

   b. This is a movement up along the aggregate demand curve. As the aggregate price level rises, the real value of money holdings falls. This is the interest rate effect of a change in the aggregate price level: as the value of money falls, people want to hold more money. They do so by borrowing more and lending less. This leads to a rise in the interest rate and a reduction in consumer and investment spending. So it is a movement along the aggregate demand curve.

   c. This is a shift of the aggregate demand curve. Expectations of a poor job market, and so lower average disposable incomes, will reduce people's consumer spending today at any given aggregate price level. So the aggregate demand curve shifts to the left.

d. This is a shift of the aggregate demand curve. A fall in tax rates raises people's disposable income. At any given aggregate price level, consumer spending is now higher. So the aggregate demand curve shifts to the right.

e. This is a movement down along the aggregate demand curve. As the aggregate price level falls, the real value of assets rises. This is the wealth effect of a change in the aggregate price level: as the value of assets rises, people will increase their consumption plans. This leads to higher consumer spending. So it is a movement along the aggregate demand curve.

f. This is a shift of the aggregate demand curve. A rise in the real value of assets in the economy due to a surge in real estate values raises consumer spending at any given aggregate price level. So the aggregate demand curve shifts to the right.

27-2 Check Your Understanding

1. a. This represents a movement along the *SRAS* curve because the CPI—like the GDP deflator—is a measure of the aggregate price level, the overall price level of final goods and services in the economy.

b. This represents a shift of the *SRAS* curve because oil is a commodity. The *SRAS* curve will shift to the right because production costs are now lower, leading to a higher quantity of aggregate output supplied at any given aggregate price level.

c. This represents a shift of the *SRAS* curve because it involves a change in nominal wages. An increase in legally mandated benefits to workers is equivalent to an increase in nominal wages. As a result, the *SRAS* curve will shift leftward because production costs are now higher, leading to a lower quantity of aggregate output supplied at any given aggregate price level.

2. You would need to know what happened to the aggregate price level. If the increase in the quantity of aggregate output supplied was due to a movement along the *SRAS* curve, the aggregate price level would have increased at the same time as the quantity of aggregate output supplied increased. If the increase in the quantity of aggregate output supplied was due to a rightward shift of the *LRAS* curve, the aggregate price level might not rise. Alternatively, you could make the determination by observing what happened to aggregate output in the long run. If it fell back to its initial level in the long run, then the temporary increase in aggregate output was due to a movement along the *SRAS* curve. If it stayed at the higher level in the long run, the increase in aggregate output was due to a rightward shift of the *LRAS* curve.

27-3 Check Your Understanding

1. a. An increase in the minimum wage raises the nominal wage and, as a result, shifts the short-run aggregate supply curve to the left. As a result of this negative supply shock, the aggregate price level rises and aggregate output falls.

b. Increased investment spending shifts the aggregate demand curve to the right. As a result of this positive demand shock, both the aggregate price level and aggregate output rise.

c. An increase in taxes and a reduction in government spending both result in negative demand shocks, shifting the aggregate demand curve to the left. As a result, both the aggregate price level and aggregate output fall.

d. This is a negative supply shock, shifting the short-run aggregate supply curve to the left. As a result, the aggregate price level rises and aggregate output falls.

2. As the rise in productivity increases potential output, the long-run aggregate supply curve shifts to the right. If, in the short run, there is now a recessionary gap (aggregate output is less than potential output), nominal wages will fall, shifting the short-run aggregate supply curve to the right. This results in a fall in the aggregate price level and a rise in aggregate output. As prices fall, we move along the aggregate demand curve due to the wealth and interest rate effects of a change in the aggregate price level. Eventually, as long-run macroeconomic equilibrium is reestablished, aggregate output will rise to be equal to potential output.

27-4 Check Your Understanding

1. a. An economy is overstimulated when an inflationary gap is present. This will arise if an expansionary monetary or fiscal policy is implemented when the economy is currently in long-run macroeconomic equilibrium. This shifts the aggregate demand curve to the right, in the short run raising the aggregate price level and aggregate output and creating an inflationary gap. Eventually nominal wages will rise and shift the short-run aggregate supply curve to the left, and aggregate output will fall back to potential output. This is the scenario envisaged by the speaker.

b. No, this is not a valid argument. When the economy is not currently in long-run macroeconomic equilibrium, an expansionary monetary or fiscal policy does not lead to the outcome described above. Suppose a negative demand shock has shifted the aggregate demand curve to the left, resulting in a recessionary gap. An expansionary monetary or fiscal policy can shift the aggregate demand curve back to its original position in long-run macroeconomic equilibrium. In this way, the short-run fall in aggregate output and deflation caused by the original negative demand shock can be avoided. So, if used in response to demand shocks, fiscal or monetary policy is an effective policy tool.

2. Those within the Fed who advocated lowering interest rates were focused on boosting aggregate demand in order to counteract the negative demand shock caused by the collapse of the housing bubble. Lowering interest rates will result in a rightward shift of the aggregate demand curve, increasing aggregate output but raising the aggregate price level. Those within the Fed who advocated holding interest rates steady were focused on the fact that fighting the slump in aggregate demand in the face of a negative supply shock could result in a rise in inflation. Holding interest rates steady relies on the ability of the economy to self-correct in the long run, with the aggregate price level and aggregate output only gradually returning to their levels before the negative supply shock.

‖ CHAPTER TWENTY-EIGHT

28-1 Check Your Understanding

1. a. This is contractionary fiscal policy because it is a reduction in government purchases of goods and services.

b. This is expansionary fiscal policy because it is an increase in government transfers that will increase disposable income.

c. This is contractionary fiscal policy because it is an increase in taxes that will reduce disposable income.

2. Federal disaster relief that is quickly disbursed is more effective than legislated aid because there is very little time lag between the time of the disaster and the time it is received by victims. So it will stabilize the economy after a disaster. In contrast, legislated aid is likely to entail a time lag in its disbursement, potentially destabilizing the economy.

3. This statement implies that expansionary fiscal policy will result in crowding out of the private sector, and that the opposite, contractionary fiscal policy, will lead the private sector to grow. Whether this statement is true or not depends upon whether the economy is at full employment; it is only then that we should expect expansionary fiscal policy to lead to crowding out. If, instead, the economy has a recessionary gap, then we should expect instead that the private sector grows along with the fiscal expansion, and contracts along with a fiscal contraction.

28-2 Check Your Understanding

1. A $500 million increase in government purchases of goods and services directly increases aggregate spending by $500 million, which then starts the multiplier in motion. It will increase real GDP by $500 million $\times 1/(1 - MPC)$. A $500 million increase in government transfers increases aggregate spending only to the extent that it leads to an increase in consumer spending. Consumer spending rises by $MPC \times \$1$ for every $1 increase in disposable income, where MPC is less than 1. So a $500 million increase in government transfers will cause a rise in real GDP only MPC times as much as a $500 million increase in government purchases of goods and services. It will increase real GDP by $500 million $\times MPC/(1 - MPC)$.

2. This is the same issue as in Problem 1, but in reverse. If government purchases of goods and services fall by $500 million, the initial fall in aggregate spending is $500 million. If there is a $500 million reduction in government transfers, the initial fall in aggregate spending is $MPC \times \$500$ million, which is less than $500 million.

3. Boldovia will experience greater variation in its real GDP than Moldovia because Moldovia has automatic stabilizers while Boldovia does not. In Moldovia the effects of slumps will be lessened by unemployment insurance benefits that will support residents' incomes, while the effects of booms will be diminished because tax revenues will go up. In contrast, incomes will not be supported in Boldovia during slumps because there is no unemployment insurance. In addition, because Boldovia has lump-sum taxes, its booms will not be diminished by increases in tax revenue.

28-3 Check Your Understanding

1. The actual budget balance takes into account the effects of the business cycle on the budget deficit. During recessionary gaps, it incorporates the effect of lower tax revenues and higher transfers on the budget balance; during inflationary gaps, it incorporates the effect of higher tax revenues and reduced transfers. In contrast, the cyclically adjusted budget balance factors out the effects of the business cycle and assumes that real GDP is at potential output. Since, in the long run, real GDP tends to potential output, the cyclically adjusted budget balance is a better measure of the long-run sustainability of government policies.

2. In recessions, real GDP falls. This implies that consumers' incomes, consumer spending, and producers' profits also fall. So in recessions, states' tax revenue (which depends in large part on consumers' incomes, consumer spending, and producers' profits) falls. In order to balance the state budget, states have to cut spending or raise taxes. But that deepens the recession. Without a balanced-budget requirement, states could use expansionary fiscal policy during a recession to lessen the fall in real GDP.

28-4 Check Your Understanding

1. a. A higher growth rate of real GDP implies that tax revenue will increase. If government spending remains constant and the government runs a budget surplus, the size of the public debt will be less than it would otherwise have been.

    b. If retirees live longer, the average age of the population increases. As a result, the implicit liabilities of the government increase because spending on programs for older Americans, such as Social Security and Medicare, will rise.

    c. A decrease in tax revenue without offsetting reductions in government spending will cause the public debt to increase.

    d. Public debt will increase as a result of government borrowing to pay interest on its current public debt.

2. In order to stimulate the economy in the short run, the government can use fiscal policy to increase real GDP. This entails borrowing, increasing the size of the public debt further and leading to undesirable consequences: in extreme cases, governments can be forced to default on their debts. Even in less extreme cases, a large public debt is undesirable because government borrowing crowds out borrowing for private investment spending. This reduces the amount of investment spending, reducing the long-run growth of the economy.

3. A contractionary fiscal policy like austerity reduces government spending, which in turn reduces income and reduces tax revenue. With less tax revenue, the government is less able to pay its debts. Also, a failing economy causes lenders to have less confidence that a government is able to pay its debts and leads them to raise interest rates on the debt. Higher interest rates on the debt make it even less likely the government can repay.

‖ CHAPTER TWENTY-NINE

29-1 Check Your Understanding

1. The defining characteristic of money is its liquidity: how easily it can be used to purchase goods and services. Although a gift card can easily be used to purchase a very defined set of goods or services (the goods or services available at the store issuing the gift card), it cannot be used to purchase any other goods or services. A gift card is therefore not money, since it cannot easily be used to purchase all goods and services.

2. Again, the important characteristic of money is its liquidity: how easily it can be used to purchase goods and services. M1, the narrowest definition of the money supply, contains only currency in circulation and checkable bank deposits. CDs aren't checkable—and they can't be made checkable without incurring a cost because there's a penalty for early withdrawal. This makes them less liquid than the assets counted in M1.

3. Commodity-backed money uses resources more efficiently than simple commodity money, like gold and silver coins,

because commodity-backed money ties up fewer valuable resources. Although a bank must keep some of the commodity—generally gold and silver—on hand, it only has to keep enough to satisfy demand for redemptions. It can then lend out the remaining gold and silver, which allows society to use these resources for other purposes, with no loss in the ability to achieve gains from trade.

29-2 Check Your Understanding

1. Even though you know that the rumor about the bank is not true, you are concerned about other depositors pulling their money out of the bank. And you know that if enough other depositors pull their money out, the bank will fail. In that case, it is rational for you to pull your money out before the bank fails. All depositors will think like this, so even if they all know that the rumor is false, they may still rationally pull their money out, leading to a bank run. Deposit insurance leads depositors to worry less about the possibility of a bank run. Even if a bank fails, the FDIC will currently pay each depositor up to $250,000 per account. This will make you much less likely to pull your money out in response to a rumor. Since other depositors will think the same, there will be no bank run.

2. The aspects of modern bank regulation that would frustrate this scheme are *capital requirements* and *reserve requirements*. Capital requirements mean that a bank has to have a certain amount of capital—the difference between its assets (loans plus reserves) and its liabilities (deposits). So the con artist could not open a bank without putting any of their own wealth in because the bank needs a certain amount of capital—that is, it needs to hold more assets (loans plus reserves) than deposits. So the con artist would be at risk of losing their own wealth if their loans turn out badly.

29-3 Check Your Understanding

1. Since they only have to hold $100 in reserves, instead of $200, banks now lend out $100 of their reserves. Whoever borrows the $100 will deposit it in a bank, which will lend out $100 × (1 − rr) = $100 × 0.9 = $90. Whoever borrows the $90 will put it into a bank, which will lend out $90 × 0.9 = $81, and so on. Overall, deposits will increase by $100/0.1 = $1,000.

2. Silas puts $1,000 in the bank, of which the bank lends out $1,000 × (1 − rr) = $1,000 × 0.9 = $900. Whoever borrows the $900 will keep $450 in cash and deposit $450 in a bank. The bank will lend out $450 × 0.9 = $405. Whoever borrows the $405 will keep $202.50 in cash and deposit $202.50 in a bank. The bank will lend out $202.50 × 0.9 = $182.25, and so on. Overall, this leads to an increase in deposits of $1,000 + $450 + $202.50 + ... But it decreases the amount of currency in circulation: the amount of cash is reduced by the $1,000 Silas puts into the bank. This is offset, but not fully, by the amount of cash held by each borrower. The amount of currency in circulation therefore changes by −$1,000 + $450 + $202.50 + ... The money supply therefore increases by the sum of the increase in deposits and the change in currency in circulation, which is $1,000 − $1,000 + $450 + $450 + $202.50 + $202.50 + . . . and so on.

29-4 Check Your Understanding

1. An open-market purchase of $100 million by the Fed increases banks' reserves by $100 million as the Fed credits their accounts with additional reserves. In other words, this open-market purchase increases the monetary base (currency in circulation plus bank reserves) by $100 million. Banks lend out the additional $100 million. Whoever borrows the money puts it back into the banking system in the form of deposits. Of these deposits, banks lend out $100 million × (1 − rr) = $100 million × 0.9 = $90 million. Whoever borrows the money deposits it back into the banking system. And banks lend out $90 million × 0.9 = $81 million, and so on. As a result, bank deposits increase by $100 million + $90 million + $81 million + . . . = $100 million/$rr$ = $100 million/0.1 = $1,000 million = $1 billion. Since in this simplified example all money lent out is deposited back into the banking system, there is no increase of currency in circulation, so the increase in bank deposits is equal to the increase in the money supply. In other words, the money supply increases by $1 billion. This is greater than the increase in the monetary base by a factor of 10: in this simplified model in which deposits are the only component of the money supply and in which banks hold no excess reserves, the money multiplier is 1/rr = 10.

29-5 Check Your Understanding

1. The Panic of 1907, the S&L crisis, and the crisis of 2008 all involved losses by shadow bank–like financial institutions that were less regulated than traditional depository banks. In the crises of 1907 and 2008, there was a widespread loss of confidence in the financial sector and a collapse of credit markets. Like the crisis of 1907 and the S&L crisis, the crisis of 2008 exerted a powerful negative effect on the economy.

2. The creation of the Federal Reserve failed to prevent bank runs because it did not eradicate the fears of depositors that a bank collapse would cause them to lose their money. The bank runs eventually stopped after federal deposit insurance was instituted and the public came to understand that their deposits were now protected.

3. Extraordinary measures were needed to address the financial crisis of 2008 because the failure of unregulated shadow banks, like Lehman Brothers, led to increased panic in markets as asset prices tumbled and credit markets froze for households and businesses. The failure of shadow banks also put the entire financial system at risk of failure, both the financially sound traditional depository banks and nondepository financial institutions, that were eventually deemed too critical to the economy to fail.

CHAPTER THIRTY

30-1 Check Your Understanding

1. **a.** By increasing the opportunity cost of holding money, a high interest rate reduces the quantity of money demanded. This is a movement up and to the left along the money demand curve.

   b. A 10% fall in prices reduces the quantity of money demanded at any given interest rate, shifting the money demand curve leftward.

   c. This technological change reduces the quantity of money demanded at any given interest rate. So it shifts the money demand curve leftward.

   d. This will increase the demand for money at any given interest rate. With more of the economy's assets in overseas bank accounts that are difficult to access, people will want to hold more cash to finance purchases. The money demand curve shifts to the right.

2. a. The 0.5% interest paid on cash balances will reduce the opportunity cost of holding cash for PayBuddy customers because they now forgo less by holding cash.

   b. An increase in the interest paid on six-month CDs raises the opportunity cost of holding cash because holding cash requires forgoing the higher interest paid.

   c. One year of zero-interest financing on holiday purchases increases the opportunity cost of holding cash. A holiday shopper need not convert interest-paying assets into cash in order to avoid paying interest on credit card purchases. So what a shopper forgoes by paying for holiday purchases with cash instead of charging it on a credit card has increased.

30-2 Check Your Understanding

1. In the accompanying diagram, the increase in the demand for money is shown as a rightward shift of the money demand curve, from MD_1 to MD_2. This raises the equilibrium interest rate from r_1 to r_2.

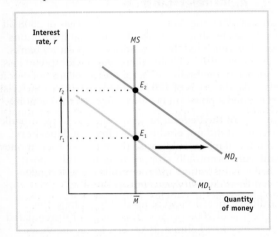

2. In order to prevent the interest rate from rising, the Federal Reserve must make an open-market purchase of Treasury bills, shifting the money supply curve rightward. This is shown in the accompanying diagram as the move from MS_1 to MS_2.

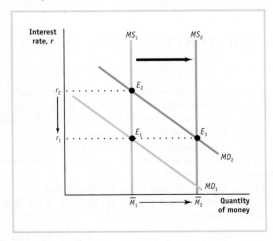

3. a. Malia is better off buying a one-year bond today and a one-year bond next year because this allows her to get the higher interest rate one year from now.

   b. Malia is better off buying a two-year bond today because it gives her a higher interest rate in the second year than if she bought two one-year bonds.

30-3 Check Your Understanding

1. a. The money supply curve shifts to the right.

   b. The equilibrium interest rate falls.

   c. Investment spending rises, due to the fall in the interest rate.

   d. Consumer spending rises, due to the multiplier process.

   e. Aggregate output rises because of the rightward shift of the aggregate demand curve.

2. The central bank that uses a Taylor rule is likely to respond more directly to a financial crisis than one that uses inflation targeting because with a Taylor rule the central bank does not have to set policy to meet a prespecified inflation target. Additionally, under the Taylor rule, central banks will respond directly to a change in the unemployment rate because in a financial crisis unemployment is more likely to increase than inflation is to decrease.

30-4 Check Your Understanding

1. a. Aggregate output rises in the short run, then falls back to equal potential output in the long run.

   b. The aggregate price level rises in the short run, but by less than 25%. It rises further in the long run, for a total increase of 25%.

   c. The interest rate falls in the short run, then rises back to its original level in the long run.

2. In the short run, a change in the interest rate alters the economy because it affects investment spending, which in turn affects aggregate demand and real GDP through the multiplier process. However, in the long run, changes in consumer spending and investment spending will eventually result in changes in nominal wages and the nominal prices of other factors of production. For example, an expansionary monetary policy will eventually cause a rise in factor prices; a contractionary policy will eventually cause a fall in factor prices. In response, the short-run aggregate supply curve will shift to move the economy back to long-run equilibrium. So in the long run, monetary policy has no effect on the economy.

‖ CHAPTER THIRTY-ONE

31-1 Check Your Understanding

1. The inflation rate is more likely to quickly reflect changes in the money supply when the economy has had an extended period of high inflation. That's because an extended period of high inflation sensitizes workers and firms to raise nominal wages and prices of intermediate goods when the aggregate price level rises. As a result, there will be little or no increase in real output in the short run after an increase in the money supply, and the increase in the money supply will simply be reflected in an equal-sized percent increase in prices. In an economy where people are not sensitized to high inflation because of low inflation in the past, an increase in the money supply will lead to an increase in real output in the short run. This illustrates the fact that the classical model of the price level best applies to economies with persistently high inflation, not those with little or no history of high inflation even though they may currently have high inflation.

2. Yes, there can still be an inflation tax because the tax is levied on people who hold money. As long as people hold money, regardless of whether prices are indexed or not, the government is able to use seigniorage to capture real resources from the public.

31-2 Check Your Understanding

1. When real GDP equals potential output, cyclical unemployment is zero and the unemployment rate is equal to the natural rate. This is given by point E_1 in Figure 31-7. Assuming a 0% expected inflation rate, this also corresponds to a 6% unemployment rate on curve $SRPC_0$ in Figure 31-9. Any unemployment in excess of this 6% rate, or less than the 6% rate, represents cyclical unemployment. An increase in aggregate demand leads to a fall in the unemployment rate below the natural rate (negative cyclical unemployment) and an increase in the inflation rate. This is given by the movement from E_1 to E_2 in Figure 31-7 and traces a movement upward along the short-run Phillips curve. A reduction in aggregate demand leads to a rise in the unemployment rate above the natural rate (positive cyclical unemployment) and a fall in the inflation rate. This would be represented by a movement down along the short-run Phillips curve from point E_1. So for a given expected inflation rate, the short-run Phillips curve illustrates the relationship between cyclical unemployment and the actual inflation rate.

2. A fall in commodities prices leads to a positive supply shock, which lowers the aggregate price level and reduces inflation. As a result, any given level of unemployment can be sustained with a lower inflation rate now—meaning that the short-run Phillips curve has shifted downward. In contrast, a surge in commodities prices leads to a negative supply shock, which raises the aggregate price level and increases inflation. Any given level of unemployment can be sustained only with a higher inflation rate—meaning that the short-run Phillips curve has shifted upward.

31-3 Check Your Understanding

1. There is no long-run trade-off between unemployment and inflation because once expectations of inflation adjust, wages will also adjust, returning employment and the unemployment rate to their equilibrium (natural) levels. This implies that once expectations of inflation fully adjust to any change in actual inflation, the unemployment rate will return to the natural rate of unemployment, or NAIRU. This also implies that the long-run Phillips curve is vertical.

2. There are two possible explanations for this. First, negative supply shocks (for example, increases in the price of oil) will cause an increase in unemployment and an increase in inflation. Second, it is possible that British policy makers attempted to lower the unemployment rate below the natural rate of unemployment. Any attempt to lower the unemployment rate below the natural rate will result in an increase in inflation.

3. Disinflation is costly because to reduce the inflation rate, aggregate output in the short run must typically fall below potential output. This, in turn, results in an increase in the unemployment rate above the natural rate. In general, we would observe a reduction in real GDP. The costs of any disinflation will be lower if the central bank is credible and it announces in advance its policy to reduce inflation. In this situation, the adjustment to the disinflationary policy will be more rapid, resulting in a smaller loss of aggregate output.

31-4 Check Your Understanding

1. If the nominal interest rate is negative, an individual is better off simply holding cash, which has a 0% nominal rate of return. If the options facing an individual are to lend and receive a negative nominal interest rate or to hold cash and receive a 0% nominal interest rate, the individual will hold cash. Such a scenario creates the possibility of a liquidity trap, in which monetary policy is ineffective because the nominal interest rate cannot fall more than a small amount below zero. Once the nominal interest rate falls to zero, further increases in the money supply will lead firms and individuals to simply hold the additional cash.

‖ CHAPTER THIRTY-TWO

32-1 Check Your Understanding

1. A classical economist would have said that although expansionary monetary policy would probably have some effect in the short run, the short run was unimportant. Instead, a classical economist would have stressed the long run, claiming expansionary monetary policy would result only in an increase in the aggregate price level without affecting aggregate output.

2. The statement would seem very familiar to a Keynesian economist. According to Keynes, business confidence (which he called "animal spirits") is mainly responsible for recessions. If business confidence is low, a Keynesian economist would think of this as a case for macroeconomic policy activism: that the government should use expansionary monetary and fiscal policy to help the economy recover.

32-2 Check Your Understanding

1. Fiscal policy is limited by time lags in recognizing economic problems, forming a response, passing legislation, and implementing the policies. Monetary policy is also limited by time lags, but these lags are not as severe as those for fiscal policy because the Federal Reserve tends to act more quickly than Congress. Attempts to reduce unemployment below the natural rate via both fiscal and monetary policy are limited by predictions of the natural rate hypothesis: that these attempts will result in accelerating inflation. Also, both fiscal and monetary policy are limited by concerns about the political business cycle: that they will be used to satisfy political ends and will end up destabilizing the economy.

2. **a.** It's likely that Milton Friedman would have agreed with the Fed policy of accelerating the growth of M1, because we know that Friedman believed that the Fed should have undertaken a more expansionary monetary policy in the wake of the Great Depression. Although he may have expressed caution over using discretionary policy.

   b. The monetarist objections to fiscal policy are based on the problems of time lags in its implementation and crowding out. Monetarists also believe time lags undermine the effectiveness of monetary policy, but to a lesser extent than with fiscal policy. However, none of these objections applied during the Great Recession. Because it lasted so long, both fiscal policy and monetary policy were effective despite time lags. And because interest rates and investment spending plunged, crowding out by fiscal policy was not a problem.

3. **a.** Rational expectations theorists would argue that only unexpected changes in the money supply would have any short-run effect on economic activity. They would also argue that expected changes in the money supply

would affect only the aggregate price level, with no short-run effect on aggregate output. So such theorists would give credit to the Fed for limiting the severity of the Great Recession only if the Fed's monetary policy had been more aggressive than individuals expected during this period.

b. Real business cycle theorists would argue that the Fed's policy had no effect on ending the Great Recession because they believe that fluctuations in aggregate output are caused largely by changes in total factor productivity.

32-3 Check Your Understanding

1. The liquidity trap brought on by the Great Recession greatly diminished the Great Moderation consensus, which considered monetary policy to be the main policy tool, and monetary policy was now largely ineffective. The continuing disagreements over fiscal policy were brought to the forefront. The dismal experience of European countries that had adopted fiscal austerity, when compared to the faster recovery of the United States, which had adopted fiscal expansionary policies, has led most economists to more or less agree with the Keynesian view about the effects of fiscal policy.

2. The Fed was criticized by some individuals who thought it was doing too much and by secular stagnationists who thought it was doing too little. Some individuals believed that the huge increase in the monetary base and quantitative easing would lead to high inflation. Secular stagnationists believed the economy was in a liquidity trap and in a state of secular stagnation. Therefore, the stagnationists advocated for a higher inflation target that would allow the Fed to push the real interest rate down while the nominal rate was near zero.

‖ CHAPTER THIRTY-THREE

33-1 Check Your Understanding

1. **a.** The sale of the new airplane to China represents an export of a good to China and so enters the current account.

   b. The sale of Boeing stock to Chinese investors is a sale of a U.S. asset and so enters the financial account.

   c. Even though the plane already exists, when it is shipped to China it is an export of a good from the United States. So the sale of the plane enters the current account.

   d. Because the plane stays in the United States, the Chinese investor is buying a U.S. asset. So this is identical to the answer to part b: the sale of the jet enters the financial account.

2. The collapse of the U.S. housing bubble and the ensuing recession led to a dramatic fall in interest rates in the United States because of the deeply depressed economy. Consequently, capital inflows into the United States dried up.

33-2 Check Your Understanding

1. **a.** The increased purchase of Mexican oil will cause U.S. individuals (and firms) to increase their demand for the peso. To purchase pesos, individuals will increase their supply of U.S. dollars to the foreign exchange market, causing a rightward shift in the supply curve of U.S.

dollars. This will cause the peso price of the dollar to fall (the amount of pesos per dollar will fall). The peso has appreciated and the U.S. dollar has depreciated as a result.

   b. This appreciation of the peso means it will take more U.S. dollars to obtain the same quantity of Mexican pesos. If we assume that the price level (measured in Mexican pesos) of other Mexican goods and services does not change, other Mexican goods and services become more expensive to U.S. households and firms. The dollar cost of other Mexican goods and services will rise as the peso appreciates. So Mexican exports to the United States of goods and services other than oil will fall.

   c. Assuming that the U.S. price level (measured in U.S. dollars) does not change, the appreciation of the peso will make U.S. goods and services cheaper in terms of pesos. So Mexican imports from the United States of goods and services will rise.

2. **a.** The real exchange rate equals

   $$\text{Pesos per U.S. dollar} \times \frac{\text{Aggregate price level in the U.S.}}{\text{Aggregate price level in Mexico}}$$

   Today, the aggregate price levels in both countries are both equal to 100. The real exchange rate today is $10 \times (100/100) = 10$. The aggregate price level in five years in the U.S. will be $100 \times (120/100) = 120$, and in Mexico it will be $100 \times (1,200/800) = 150$. The real exchange rate in five years, assuming the nominal exchange rate does not change, will be $10 \times (120/150) = 8$.

   b. Today, a basket of goods and services that costs $100 costs 800 pesos, so the purchasing power parity is 8 pesos per U.S. dollar. In five years, a basket that costs $120 will cost 1,200 pesos, so the purchasing power parity will be 10 pesos per U.S. dollar.

33-3 Check Your Understanding

1. The accompanying diagram shows the supply of and demand for the yuan, with the U.S. dollar price of the yuan on the vertical axis. In 2005, prior to the revaluation, the exchange rate was pegged at 8.28 yuan per U.S. dollar or, equivalently, 0.121 U.S. dollars per yuan ($0.121). At the target exchange rate of $0.121, the quantity of yuan demanded exceeded the quantity of yuan supplied, creating the shortage depicted in the diagram. Without any intervention by the Chinese government, the U.S. dollar price of the yuan would have been bid up, causing an appreciation of the yuan. The Chinese government, however, intervened to prevent this appreciation.

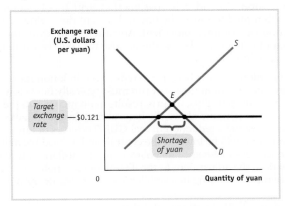

   a. If the exchange rate is allowed to move freely, the U.S. dollar price of the exchange rate will move toward the equilibrium exchange rate (labeled *XR** in the accompanying diagram). This will occur as a result of the shortage, when buyers of the yuan will bid up its U.S. dollar price. As the exchange rate increases, the quantity of yuan demanded will fall and the quantity of yuan supplied will increase. If the exchange rate increases to *XR**, the disequilibrium will be entirely eliminated.

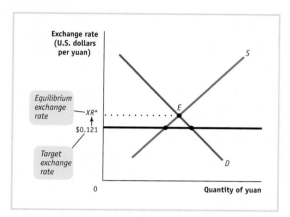

b. Placing restrictions on foreigners who want to invest in China will reduce the demand for the yuan, causing the demand curve to shift in the accompanying diagram from D_1 to a position like D_2. This will cause a reduction in the shortage of the yuan. If demand fell to D_3, the disequilibrium will be completely eliminated.

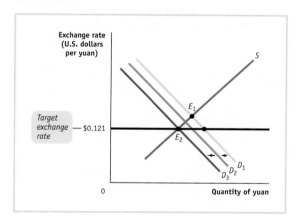

c. Removing restrictions on Chinese who wish to invest abroad will cause an increase in the supply of the yuan and a rightward shift in the supply curve. This increase in supply will also cause a reduction in the size of the shortage. If, for example, supply increased from S_1 to S_2, the disequilibrium will be eliminated completely in the accompanying diagram.

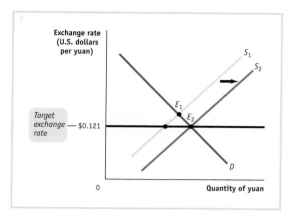

d. Imposing a tax on exports (Chinese goods sold to foreigners) will raise the price of these goods and decrease the amount of Chinese goods purchased. This will also decrease the demand for the yuan. The graphical analysis here is virtually identical to that found in the figure accompanying part b.

33-4 Check Your Understanding

1. The devaluations and revaluations most likely occurred in those periods when there was a sudden change in the franc–mark exchange rate: 1974, 1976, the early 1980s, 1986, and 1993–1994.

2. The high Canadian interest rates would likely have caused an increase in capital inflows to Canada. To obtain these assets (which yielded a relatively higher interest rate) in Canada, investors would first have had to obtain Canadian dollars. The increase in the demand for the Canadian dollar would have caused the Canadian dollar to appreciate. This appreciation of the Canadian currency would have raised the price of Canadian goods to foreigners (measured in terms of the foreign currency). This would have made it more difficult for Canadian firms to compete in other markets.

Glossary

A

ability-to-pay principle the principle of tax fairness by which those with greater ability to pay a tax should pay more tax.

absolute advantage the advantage a country has in producing a good or service if the country can produce more output per worker than other countries. Likewise, an individual has an absolute advantage in producing a good or service if they are better at producing it than other people. Having an absolute advantage is not the same thing as having a comparative advantage.

absolute value the value of a number without regard to a plus or minus sign.

accelerator principle the proposition that a higher growth rate in real GDP results in a higher level of planned investment spending, and a lower growth rate in real GDP leads to lower planned investment spending.

accounting profit revenue minus explicit cost.

actual investment spending the sum of planned investment spending and unplanned inventory investment.

AD–AS model the basic model used to understand fluctuations in aggregate output and the aggregate price level. It uses the aggregate supply curve and the aggregate demand curve together to analyze the behavior of the economy in response to shocks or government policy.

administrative costs (of a tax) the resources used for its collection, for the method of payment, and for any attempts to evade the tax.

adverse selection the case in which an individual knows more about the way things are than other people do. Adverse selection problems can lead to market problems: private information leads buyers to expect hidden problems in items offered for sale, leading to low prices and the best items being kept off the market.

aggregate consumption function the relationship for the economy as a whole between aggregate current disposable income and aggregate consumer spending.

aggregate demand curve a graphical representation that shows the relationship between the aggregate price level and the quantity of aggregate output demanded by households, firms, the government, and the rest of the world. The aggregate demand curve has a negative slope due to the wealth effect of a change in the aggregate price level and the interest rate effect of a change in the aggregate price level.

aggregate output the total quantity of final goods and services the economy produces for a given time period, usually a year. Real GDP is the numerical measure of aggregate output typically used by economists.

aggregate price level a single number that represents the overall price level for final goods and services in the economy.

aggregate production function a hypothetical function that shows how productivity (real GDP per worker) depends on the quantities of physical capital per worker and human capital per worker as well as the state of technology.

aggregate spending the total flow of funds into markets for domestically produced final goods and services; the sum of consumer spending, investment spending, government purchases of goods and services, and exports minus imports.

aggregate supply curve a graphical representation that shows the relationship between the aggregate price level and the total quantity of aggregate output supplied.

antitrust policy legislative and regulatory efforts undertaken by the government to prevent oligopolistic industries from becoming or behaving like monopolies.

appreciation a rise in the value of one currency in terms of other currencies.

artificially scarce good a good that is excludable but nonrival in consumption.

austerity policy a policy that tries to limit government borrowing by cutting spending and raising taxes.

autarky a situation in which a country does not trade with other countries.

automatic stabilizers government spending and taxation rules that cause fiscal policy to be automatically expansionary when the economy contracts and automatically contractionary when the economy expands without requiring any deliberate actions by policy makers. Taxes that depend on disposable income are the most important example of automatic stabilizers.

autonomous change in aggregate spending an initial rise or fall in aggregate spending at a given level of real GDP.

average cost an alternative term for average total cost; the total cost divided by the quantity of output produced.

average fixed cost the fixed cost per unit of output.

average total cost total cost divided by quantity of output produced. Also referred to as average cost.

average variable cost the variable cost per unit of output.

B

backward-bending individual labor supply curve an individual labor supply curve that slopes upward at low to moderate wage rates and slopes downward at higher wage rates.

balance of payments accounts a summary of a country's transactions with other countries for a given year, including two main elements: the balance of payments on current account and the balance of payments on financial account.

balance of payments on current account (current account) transactions that don't create liabilities; a country's balance of payments on goods and services plus net international transfer payments and factor income.

balance of payments on financial account (financial account) international transactions that involve the sale or purchase of assets, and therefore create future liabilities.

balance of payments on goods and services the difference between the value of exports and the value of imports during a given period.

bank a financial intermediary that provides liquid assets in the form of bank deposits to lenders and uses those funds to finance the illiquid investments or investment spending needs of borrowers.

bank deposit a claim on a bank that obliges the bank to give the depositor their cash when demanded.

bank reserves currency held by banks in their vaults plus their deposits at the Federal Reserve.

bank run a phenomenon in which many of a bank's depositors try to withdraw their funds because of fears of a bank failure.

bar graph a graph that uses bars of varying heights or lengths to show the comparative sizes of different observations of a variable.

barrier to entry something that prevents other firms from entering an industry. Crucial in protecting the profits of a monopolist. There are five types of barriers to entry: control over scarce resources or inputs, increasing returns to scale, technological superiority, network externalities, and government-created barriers.

barter trade in the form of the direct exchange of goods or services for other goods or services that people want.

benefits principle the principle of tax fairness by which those who benefit from public spending should bear the burden of the tax that pays for that spending.

black market a market in which goods or services are bought and sold illegally, either because it is illegal to sell them at all or because the prices charged are legally prohibited by a price ceiling.

bounded rationality a basis for decision making that leads to a choice that is close to but not exactly the one that leads to the best possible economic outcome; the "good enough" method of decision making.

brand name a name owned by a particular firm that distinguishes its products from those of other firms.

break-even price the market price at which a price-taking firm earns zero profits.

budget balance the difference between tax revenue and government spending. A positive budget balance is referred to as a budget surplus; a negative budget balance is referred to as a budget deficit.

budget constraint the limitation that the cost of a consumer's consumption bundle be no more than the consumer's income.

budget deficit the difference between tax revenue and government spending when government spending exceeds tax revenue; dissaving by the government in the form of a budget deficit is a negative contribution to national savings.

budget line all the consumption bundles available to a consumer who spends all of their income.

budget surplus the difference between tax revenue and government spending when tax revenue exceeds government spending; saving by the government in the form of a budget surplus is a positive contribution to national savings.

business cycle the short-run alternation between economic downturns, known as recessions, and economic upturns, known as expansions.

business-cycle peak the point in time at which the economy shifts from expansion to recession.

business-cycle trough the point in time at which the economy shifts from recession to expansion.

C

capital the total value of assets owned by an individual or firm—physical assets plus financial assets.

capital at risk funds that an insurer places at risk when providing insurance.

cartel an agreement among several producers to obey output restrictions in order to increase their joint profits.

causal relationship the relationship between two variables in which the value taken by one variable directly influences or determines the value taken by the other variable.

central bank an institution that oversees and regulates the banking system and controls the monetary base.

certificate of deposit (CD) a bank-issued asset in which customers deposit funds for a specified amount of time and earn a specified interest rate.

chained dollars method of calculating real GDP that splits the difference between growth rates calculated using early base years and the growth rate calculated using a late base year.

checkable bank deposits bank accounts that can be accessed by using checks, debit cards, and digital payments.

circular-flow diagram a diagram that represents the transactions in an economy by two kinds of flows around a circle: flows of physical things such as goods or labor in one direction and flows of money to pay for these physical things in the opposite direction.

classical model of the price level a simplified financial model of the price level in which the real quantity of money, M/P, is always at its long-run equilibrium level. This model ignores the distinction between the short run and the long run but is useful for analyzing the case of high inflation.

clean energy sources energy sources that do not emit greenhouse gases. Renewable energy sources are also clean energy sources.

climate change the man-made change in Earth's climate from the accumulation of greenhouse gases caused by the use of fossil fuels.

Coase theorem the proposition that even in the presence of externalities an economy can always reach an efficient solution provided that the costs of making a deal are sufficiently low.

collusion cooperation among producers to limit production and raise prices so as to raise one another's profits.

commercial bank a bank that accepts deposits and is covered by deposit insurance.

commodity output of different producers regarded by consumers as the same good; also referred to as a standardized product.

commodity-backed money a medium of exchange that has no intrinsic value, whose ultimate value is guaranteed by a promise that it can be converted into valuable goods on demand.

commodity money a medium of exchange that is a good, normally gold or silver, that has intrinsic value in other uses.

common resource a resource that is nonexcludable and rival in consumption.

comparative advantage the advantage a country has in producing a good or service if its opportunity cost of producing the good or service is lower than other countries' cost. Likewise, an individual has a comparative advantage in producing a good or service if their opportunity cost of producing the good or service is lower than it is for other people.

compensating differentials wage differences across jobs that reflect the fact that some jobs are less pleasant or more dangerous than others.

competitive market a market in which there are many buyers and sellers of the same good or service, none of whom can influence the price at which the good or service is sold.

complements pairs of goods for which a rise in the price of one good leads to a decrease in the demand for the other good.

constant marginal cost each additional unit costs the same to produce as the previous one.

constant returns to scale long-run average total cost is constant as output increases.

consumer price index (CPI) a measure of prices; calculated by surveying market prices for a market basket intended to represent the consumption of a typical urban American family of four. The CPI is the most commonly used measure of prices in the United States.

consumer spending household spending on goods and services from domestic and foreign firms.

consumer surplus a term often used to refer both to individual consumer surplus and to total consumer surplus.

consumption bundle (of an individual) the collection of all the goods and services consumed by a given individual.

consumption function an equation showing how an individual household's consumer spending varies with the household's current disposable income.

consumption possibilities the set of all consumption bundles that can be consumed given a consumer's income and prevailing prices.

contractionary fiscal policy fiscal policy that reduces aggregate demand by decreasing government purchases, increasing taxes, or decreasing transfers.

contractionary monetary policy monetary policy that, through the raising of the interest rate, reduces aggregate demand and therefore output.

convergence hypothesis a principle of economic growth that holds that international differences in real GDP per capita tend to narrow over time because countries that start with lower real GDP per capita tend to have higher growth rates.

copyright the exclusive legal right of the creator of a literary or artistic work to profit from that work; like a patent, it is a temporary monopoly.

cost (of seller) the lowest price at which a seller is willing to sell a good.

cost-benefit analysis an estimation and comparison of the costs and benefits of providing a good. When governments use cost-benefit analysis, they estimate the social costs and social benefits of providing a public good.

cross-price elasticity of demand a measure of the effect of the change in the price of one good on the quantity demanded of the other; it is equal to the percent change in the quantity demanded of one good divided by the percent change in the price of another good.

crowding out the negative effect of budget deficits on private investment, which occurs because government borrowing drives up interest rates.

currency in circulation actual cash held by the public.

current account (balance of payments on current account) transactions that don't create liabilities; a country's balance of payments on goods and services plus net international transfer payments and factor income.

curve a line on a graph, which may be curved or straight, that depicts a relationship between two variables.

cyclical unemployment the difference between the actual rate of unemployment and the natural rate of unemployment due to downturns in the business cycle.

cyclically adjusted budget balance an estimate of what the budget balance would be if real GDP were exactly equal to potential output.

D

deadweight loss the loss in total surplus that occurs whenever an action or a policy reduces the quantity transacted below the efficient market equilibrium quantity.

debt deflation the reduction in aggregate demand arising from the increase in the real burden of outstanding debt caused by deflation; occurs because borrowers, whose real debt rises as a result of deflation, are likely to cut spending sharply, and lenders, whose real assets are now more valuable, are less likely to increase spending.

debt spiral when the interest on government debt drives that debt even higher.

debt–GDP ratio government debt as a percentage of GDP, frequently used as a measure of a government's ability to pay its debts.

decreasing marginal benefit each additional unit of an activity yields less benefit than the previous unit.

decreasing marginal cost each additional unit costs less to produce than the previous one.

decreasing returns to scale long-run average total cost increases as output increases (also known as diseconomies of scale).

deductible a sum specified in an insurance policy that the insured individual must pay before being compensated for a claim; deductibles reduce moral hazard.

default the failure of a bond issuer to make payments as specified by the bond contract.

deflation a fall in the overall level of prices.

demand curve a graphical representation of the demand schedule. It shows the relationship between quantity demanded and price.

demand price the price of a given quantity at which consumers will demand that quantity.

demand schedule a list or table showing how much of a good or service consumers will want to buy at different prices.

demand shock an event that shifts the aggregate demand curve. A positive demand shock is associated with higher demand for aggregate output at any price level and shifts the curve to the right. A negative demand shock is associated with lower demand for aggregate output at any price level and shifts the curve to the left.

dependent variable the determined variable in a causal relationship.

deposit insurance a guarantee that a bank's depositors will be paid even if the bank can't come up with the funds, up to a maximum amount per account.

depreciation a fall in the value of one currency in terms of other currencies.

devaluation a reduction in the value of a currency that is set under a fixed exchange rate regime.

diminishing marginal rate of substitution the principle that the more of one good that is consumed in proportion to another, the less of the second good the consumer is willing to substitute for another unit of the first good; the more of good R a person consumes in proportion to good M, the less they are willing to substitute for another unit of R.

diminishing returns to an input the effect observed when an increase in the quantity of an input, while holding the levels of all other inputs fixed, leads to a decline in the marginal product of that input.

diminishing returns to physical capital in an aggregate production function when the amount of human capital per worker and the state of technology are held fixed, each successive increase in the amount of physical capital per worker leads to a smaller increase in productivity.

discount rate the rate of interest the Federal Reserve charges on loans to banks that fall short of reserve requirements.

discount window a protection against bank runs in which the Federal Reserve stands ready to lend money to banks in trouble.

discouraged workers individuals who want to work but who have stated to government researchers that they aren't currently searching for a job because they see little prospect of finding one given the state of the job market.

discretionary fiscal policy fiscal policy that is the direct result of deliberate actions by policy makers rather than automatic adjustments or rules.

discretionary monetary policy policy actions, either changes in interest rates or changes in the money supply, undertaken by the central bank based on its assessment of the state of the economy.

disinflation the process of bringing down inflation that has become embedded in expectations.

diversification investment in several different assets with unrelated, or independent, risks, so that the possible losses are independent events.

domestic demand curve a demand curve that shows how the quantity of a good demanded by domestic consumers depends on the price of that good.

domestic supply curve a supply curve that shows how the quantity of a good supplied by domestic producers depends on the price of that good.

dominant strategy in game theory, an action that is a player's best action regardless of the action taken by the other player.

duopolist one of the two firms in a duopoly.

duopoly an oligopoly consisting of only two firms.

E

economic growth the growing ability of the economy to produce goods and services, leading to higher living standards.

economic profit revenue minus the opportunity cost of resources used; usually less than the accounting profit.

economic signal any piece of information that helps people make better economic decisions.

economics the social science that studies the production, distribution, and consumption of goods and services.

economy a system for coordinating society's productive activities.

efficiency wages wages that employers set above the equilibrium wage rate as an incentive for workers to deliver better performance.

efficiency-wage model a model in which some employers pay an above-equilibrium wage as an incentive for better performance.

efficient description of a market or economy that takes all opportunities to make some people better off without making other people worse off.

efficient allocation of risk an allocation of risk in which those most willing to bear risk are those who end up bearing it.

efficient markets hypothesis a principle of asset price determination that holds that asset prices embody all publicly available information. The hypothesis implies that stock prices should be unpredictable, or follow a random walk, since changes should occur only in response to new information about fundamentals.

elastic demand the case in which the price elasticity of demand is greater than 1.

emissions tax a tax that depends on the amount of pollution a firm produces.

employment the total number of people currently employed for pay in the economy, either full time or part time.

environmental standards rules established by a government to protect the environment by specifying actions by producers and consumers.

equilibrium an economic situation in which no individual would be better off doing something different.

equilibrium exchange rate the exchange rate at which the quantity of a currency demanded in the foreign exchange market is equal to the quantity supplied.

equilibrium interest rate a situation where the interest rate at which the quantity of loanable funds supplied equals the quantity of loanable funds demanded.

equilibrium price the price at which the market is in equilibrium, that is, the quantity of a good or service demanded equals the quantity of that good or service supplied; also referred to as the market-clearing price.

equilibrium quantity the quantity of a good or service bought and sold at the equilibrium (or market-clearing) price.

equilibrium value of the marginal product the additional value produced by the last unit of that factor employed in the factor market as a whole.

equity fairness; everyone gets their fair share. Since people can disagree about what is "fair," equity is not as well defined a concept as efficiency.

European Union (EU) a customs union among 27 European nations.

excess capacity the failure to produce enough to minimize average total cost; characteristic of monopolistically competitive firms.

economy a system for coordinating society's productive activities.

excess reserves a bank's reserves over and above the reserves required by law or regulation.

exchange market intervention government purchases or sales of currency in the foreign exchange market.

exchange rate the price at which currencies trade, determined by the foreign exchange market.

exchange rate regime a rule governing policy toward the exchange rate.

excise tax a tax on sales of a good or service.

excludable referring to a good, describes the case in which the supplier can prevent those who do not pay from consuming the good.

expansion a period of economic upturn in which output and employment are rising; most economic numbers are following their normal upward trend; also referred to as a recovery.

expansionary fiscal policy fiscal policy that increases aggregate demand by increasing government purchases, decreasing taxes, or increasing transfers.

expansionary monetary policy monetary policy that, through the lowering of the interest rate, increases aggregate demand and therefore output.

expected rate of inflation the inflation rate that businesses and workers are expecting in the near future.

expected utility the expected value of an individual's total utility given uncertainty about future outcomes.

expected value in reference to a random variable, the weighted average of all possible values, where the weights on each possible value correspond to the probability of that value occurring.

explicit cost a cost that requires an outlay of money.

exporting industries industries that produce goods and services that are sold abroad.

exports goods and services sold to other countries.

external benefit an uncompensated benefit that an individual or firm confers on others; also known as positive externality.

external cost an uncompensated cost that an individual or firm imposes on others; also known as negative externality.

externalities external benefits and external costs.

F

factor distribution of income the division of total income among labor, land, and capital.

factor intensity a measure of which factor is used in relatively greater quantities than other factors in production. For example, oil refining is capital-intensive compared to auto seat production because oil refiners use a higher ratio of capital to labor than do producers of auto seats.

factor markets markets in which firms buy the resources they need to produce goods and services.

factors of production the resources used to produce goods and services.

fair insurance policy an insurance policy for which the premium is equal to the expected value of the claim.

federal funds market a financial market that allows banks that fall short of reserve requirements to borrow funds from banks with excess reserves.

federal funds rate the interest rate at which funds are borrowed and lent in the federal funds market.

fiat money a medium of exchange whose value derives entirely from its official status as a means of payment.

final goods and services goods and services sold to the final, or end, user.

financial account (balance of payments on financial account) international transactions that involve the sale of purchase of assets, and therefore create future liabilities.

financial asset a paper claim that entitles the buyer to future income from the seller. Loans, stocks, bonds, and bank deposits are types of financial assets.

financial intermediary an institution, such as a mutual fund, pension fund, life insurance company, or bank, that transforms the funds it gathers from many individuals into financial assets.

financial markets the banking, stock, and bond markets, which channel private savings and foreign lending into investment spending, government borrowing, and foreign borrowing.

financial risk uncertainty about future outcomes that involve financial losses or gains.

firm an organization that produces goods and services for sale.

fiscal policy changes in government spending and taxes designed to affect overall spending.

fiscal stimulus expansionary fiscal policy that takes the form of temporary spending measures and temporary tax cuts.

fiscal year the time period used for much of government accounting, running from October 1 to September 30 in the United States. Fiscal years are labeled by the calendar year in which they end.

Fisher effect the principle by which an increase in expected future inflation drives up the nominal interest rate, leaving the expected real interest rate unchanged.

fixed cost a cost that does not depend on the quantity of output produced; the cost of a fixed input.

fixed exchange rate an exchange rate regime in which the government keeps the exchange rate against some other currency at or near a particular target.

fixed input an input whose quantity is fixed for a period of time and cannot be varied (for example, land).

floating exchange rate an exchange rate regime in which the government lets market forces determine the exchange rate.

forecast a simple prediction of the future.

foreign exchange controls licensing systems that limit the right of individuals to buy foreign currency.

foreign exchange market the market in which currencies can be exchanged for each other.

foreign exchange reserves stocks of foreign currency that governments can use to buy their own currency on the foreign exchange market.

fossil fuel fuel derived from fossil sources such as coal and oil.

framing bias the tendency to make decisions based on how choices are presented rather than on a comparison of their true values.

free entry and exit describes an industry that potential producers can easily enter or current producers can easily leave.

free trade occurs in an economy when the government does not attempt either to reduce or to increase the levels of exports and imports that occur naturally as a result of supply and demand.

free-rider problem problem that results when individuals who have no incentive to pay for their own consumption of a good take a "free ride" on anyone who does pay; a problem with goods that are nonexcludable.

frictional unemployment unemployment due to time workers spend in job search.

G

gains from trade gains achieved by dividing tasks and trading; in this way people can get more of what they want through trade than they could if they tried to be self-sufficient.

game theory the study of behavior in situations of interdependence. Used to explain the behavior of an oligopoly.

GDP deflator a price measure for a given year that is equal to 100 times the ratio of nominal GDP to real GDP in that year.

GDP per capita GDP divided by the size of the population; equivalent to the average GDP per person.

Giffen good the hypothetical inferior good for which the income effect outweighs the substitution effect and the demand curve slopes upward.

Gini coefficient a number that summarizes a country's level of income inequality based on how unequally income is distributed across quintiles.

global loanable funds market a situation in which international capital flows are so large that they equalize interest rates across countries.

globalization the phenomenon of growing economic linkages among countries.

government borrowing the total amount of funds borrowed by federal, state, and local governments in the financial markets.

government purchases of goods and services total purchases by federal, state, and local governments on goods and services.

government transfers a government payment to an individual or a family for which no good or service is provided in return.

Great Moderation the period from 1985 to 2007 when the U.S. economy experienced small fluctuations and low inflation.

greenhouse gases gas emissions that trap heat in Earth's atmosphere.

gross domestic product (GDP) the total value of all final goods and services produced in the economy during a given period, usually a year.

growth accounting accounting that estimates the contribution of each of the major factors (physical and human capital, labor, and technology) in the aggregate production function.

H

Hecksher–Olin model a model of international trade in which a country has a comparative advantage in a good whose production is intensive in the factors that are abundantly available in that country.

horizontal axis the horizontal number line of a graph along which values of the x-variable are measured; also referred to as the x-axis.

horizontal intercept the point at which a curve hits the horizontal axis; it indicates the value of the x-variable when the value of the y-variable is zero.

household a person or a group of people that share their income.

human capital the improvement in labor created by the education and knowledge embodied in the workforce.

hyperglobalization the phenomenon of extremely high levels of international trade.

I

illiquid describes an asset that cannot be quickly converted into cash with relatively little loss of value.

imperfect competition a market structure in which no firm has a monopoly, but producers nonetheless have market power they can use to affect market prices.

implicit cost a cost that does not require the outlay of money; it is measured by the value, in dollar terms, of benefits that are forgone.

implicit cost of capital the opportunity cost of the use of one's own capital — the income earned if the capital had been employed in its next best alternative use.

implicit liabilities spending promises made by governments that are effectively a debt despite the fact that they are not included in the usual debt statistics. In the United States, the largest implicit liabilities arise from Social Security and Medicare, which promise transfer payments to current and future retirees (Social Security) and to the elderly (Medicare).

import quota a legal limit on the quantity of a good that can be imported.

import-competing industries industries that produce goods and services that are also imported.

imports goods and services purchased from other countries.

incentive anything that offers rewards to people to change their behavior.

incidence (of a tax) a measure of who really pays a tax.

income distribution the way in which total income is divided among the owners of the various factors of production in an economy.

income effect the change in the quantity of a good consumed that results from the change in a consumer's purchasing power due to the change in the price of the good.

income elasticity of demand the percent change in the quantity of a good demanded when a consumer's income changes divided by the percent change in the consumer's income.

income tax a tax on an individual's or family's income.

income-elastic demand the case in which the income elasticity of demand for a good is greater than 1.

income-inelastic demand the case in which the income elasticity of demand for a good is positive but less than 1.

income–expenditure equilibrium a situation in which aggregate output, measured by real GDP, is equal to planned aggregate spending and firms have no incentive to change output.

income–expenditure equilibrium GDP the level of real GDP at which real GDP equals planned aggregate spending.

increasing marginal cost each additional unit costs more to produce than the previous one.

increasing returns to scale long-run average total cost declines as output increases (also referred to as economies of scale).

independent events events for which the occurrence of one does not affect the likelihood of occurrence of any of the others.

independent variable the determining variable in a causal relationship.

indifference curve a contour line that shows all consumption bundles that yield the same amount of total utility for an individual.

indifference curve map a collection of indifference curves for a given individual that represents the individual's entire utility function; each curve corresponds to a different total utility level.

individual choice the decision by an individual of what to do, which necessarily involves a decision of what not to do.

individual consumer surplus the net gain to an individual buyer from the purchase of a good; equal to the difference between the buyer's willingness to pay and the price paid.

individual demand curve a graphical representation of the relationship between quantity demanded and price for an individual consumer.

individual labor supply curve a graphical representation that shows how the quantity of labor supplied by an individual depends on that individual's wage rate.

individual producer surplus the net gain to an individual seller from selling a good; equal to the difference between the price received and the seller's cost.

individual supply curve a graphical representation of the relationship between quantity supplied and price for an individual producer.

industry supply curve a graphical representation that shows the relationship between the price of a good and the total output of the industry for that good.

inefficient describes a market or economy in which there are missed opportunities: some people could be made better off without making other people worse off.

inefficient allocation of sales among sellers a form of inefficiency in which sellers who would be willing to sell a good at the lowest price are unable to make sales while sales go to sellers who are only willing to sell at a higher price; often the result of a price floor.

inefficient allocation to consumers a form of inefficiency in which some people who want the good badly and are willing to pay a high price don't get it, and some who care relatively little about the good and are only willing to pay a low price do get it; often a result of a price ceiling.

inefficiently high quality a form of inefficiency in which sellers offer high-quality goods at a high price even though buyers would prefer a lower quality at a lower price; often the result of a price floor.

inefficiently low quality a form of inefficiency in which sellers offer low-quality goods at a low price even though buyers would prefer a higher quality at a higher price; often a result of a price ceiling.

inelastic demand the case in which the price elasticity of demand is less than 1.

inferior good a good for which a rise in income decreases the demand for the good.

inflation a rise in the overall level of prices.

inflation rate the annual percent change in a price index — typically the consumer price index. The inflation rate is positive when the aggregate price level is rising (inflation) and negative when the aggregate price level is falling (deflation).

inflation targeting an approach to monetary policy that requires that the central bank try to keep the inflation rate near a predetermined target rate.

inflation tax the reduction in the value of money held by the public as a result of inflation.

inflationary gap the gap that exists when aggregate output is above potential output.

infrastructure physical capital, such as roads, power lines, ports, information networks, and other parts of an economy, that provides the underpinnings, or foundation, for economic activity.

in-kind benefit a benefit given in the form of goods or services.

input a good or service used to produce another good or service.

interaction (of choices) my choices affect your choices, and vice versa; a feature of most economic situations. The results of this interaction are often quite different from what the individuals intend.

interdependence a relationship among firms in which their decisions significantly affect one another's profits; characteristic of oligopolies.

interest rate the price, calculated as a percentage of the amount borrowed, charged by the lender.

interest rate effect of a change in the aggregate price level the effect on consumer spending and investment spending caused by a change in the purchasing power of consumers' money holdings when the aggregate price level changes. A rise (fall) in the aggregate price level decreases (increases) the purchasing power of consumers' money holdings. In response, consumers try to increase (decrease) their money holdings, which drives up (down) interest rates, thereby decreasing (increasing) consumption and investment.

intermediate goods and services goods and services—bought from one firm by another firm—that are inputs for production of final goods and services.

internalize the externality when individuals take into account external costs and external benefits.

international trade agreements treaties in which a country promises to engage in less trade protection against the exports of other countries in return for a promise by other countries to do the same for its own exports.

inventories stocks of goods and raw materials held to facilitate business operations.

inventory investment the value of the change in total inventories held in the economy during a given period. Unlike other types of investment spending, inventory investment can be negative if inventories fall.

investment bank a bank that trades in financial assets and does not accept deposits, so it is not covered by deposit insurance.

investment spending spending on productive physical capital—such as machinery and construction of buildings—and on changes to inventories.

invisible hand a phrase used by Adam Smith to refer to the way in which an individual's pursuit of self-interest can lead, without the individual intending it, to good results for society as a whole.

irrational describes a decision maker who chooses an option that leaves them worse off than choosing another available option.

J

job search the time spent by workers in looking for employment.

jobless recovery a period in which real GDP growth rate is positive but the unemployment rate is still rising.

K

Keynesian cross a diagram that identifies income–expenditure equilibrium as the point where the planned aggregate spending line crosses the 45-degree line.

Keynesian economics a school of thought emerging out of the works of John Maynard Keynes; according to Keynesian economics, a depressed economy is the result of a inadequate spending and government intervention can help a depressed economy through monetary policy and fiscal policy.

L

labor force the sum of employment and unemployment; that is, the number of people who are currently working plus the number of people who are currently looking for work.

labor force participation rate the percentage of the population age 16 or older that is in the labor force.

labor productivity output per worker; also referred to as simply productivity. Increases in labor productivity are the only source of long-run economic growth.

law of demand the principle that a higher price for a good or service, other things equal, leads people to demand a smaller quantity of that good or service.

leisure the time available for purposes other than earning money to buy marketed goods.

liability a requirement to pay income in the future.

license the right, conferred by the government or an owner, to supply a good.

life insurance company a financial intermediary that sells policies guaranteeing a payment to a policyholder's beneficiaries when the policyholder dies.

linear relationship the relationship between two variables in which the slope is constant and therefore is depicted on a graph by a curve that is a straight line.

liquid describes an asset that can be quickly converted into cash with relatively little loss of value.

liquidity preference model of the interest rate a model of the market for money in which the interest rate is determined by the supply and demand for money.

liquidity trap the economy is in a liquidity trap when monetary policy is ineffective because nominal interest rates are up against the zero bound.

loan a lending agreement between an individual lender and an individual borrower. Loans are usually tailored to the individual borrower's needs and ability to pay but carry relatively high transaction costs.

loanable funds market a hypothetical market that brings together those who want to lend money (savers) and those who want to borrow (firms with investment spending projects).

loan-backed securities assets created by pooling individual loans and selling shares in that pool.

long run the time period in which all inputs can be varied.

long-run aggregate supply curve a graphical representation that shows the relationship between the aggregate price level and the quantity of aggregate output supplied that would exist if all prices, including nominal wages, were fully flexible. The long-run aggregate supply curve is vertical because the aggregate price level has no effect on aggregate output in the long run; in the long run, aggregate output is determined by the economy's potential output.

long-run average total cost curve a graphical representation showing the relationship between output and average total cost when fixed cost has been chosen to minimize average total cost for each level of output.

long-run economic growth the sustained rise in the quantity of goods and services the economy produces.

long-run industry supply curve a graphical representation that shows how quantity supplied responds to price once producers have had time to enter or exit the industry.

long-run macroeconomic equilibrium the point at which the short-run macroeconomic equilibrium is on the long-run aggregate supply curve; so short-run equilibrium aggregate output is equal to potential output.

long-run market equilibrium an economic balance in which, given that sufficient time has elapsed for entry into and exit from the industry to occur, the quantity supplied equals the quantity demanded.

long-run Phillips curve a graphical representation of the relationship between unemployment and inflation in the long run after expectations of inflation have had time to adjust to experience.

long-term interest rate the interest rate on financial assets that mature a number of years into the future.

loss aversion oversensitivity to loss, leading to unwillingness to recognize a loss and move on.

lump-sum tax a tax that is the same for everyone, regardless of any actions people take.

M

macroeconomic policy activism the use of monetary policy and fiscal policy to smooth out the business cycle.

macroeconomics the branch of economics that is concerned with the overall ups and downs in the economy.

marginal analysis the study of marginal decisions.

marginal benefit the additional benefit derived from producing one more unit of a good or service.

marginal benefit curve a graphical representation showing how the benefit from producing one more unit depends on the quantity that has already been produced.

marginal cost the additional cost incurred by producing one more unit of that good or service.

marginal cost curve a graphical representation showing how the cost of producing one more unit depends on the quantity that has already been produced.

marginal decision a decision made at the "margin" of an activity to do a bit more or a bit less of that activity.

marginal product the additional quantity of output produced by using one more unit of that input.

marginal productivity theory of income distribution the proposition that every factor of production is paid its equilibrium value of the marginal product.

marginal propensity to consume (*MPC*) the increase in consumer spending when disposable income rises by \$1. Because consumers normally spend part but not all of an additional dollar of disposable income, *MPC* is between 0 and 1.

marginal propensity to save (*MPS*) the fraction of an additional dollar of disposable income that is saved; *MPS* is equal to $1 - MPC$.

marginal rate of substitution (*MRS*) the ratio of the marginal utility of one good to the marginal utility of another; if a good R in place of good M is equal to MU_R/MU_M, the ratio of the marginal utility of R to the marginal utility of M.

marginal revenue the change in total revenue generated by an additional unit of output.

marginal revenue curve a graphical representation showing how marginal revenue varies as output varies.

marginal social benefit of pollution the additional gain to society as a whole from an additional unit of pollution.

marginal social cost of pollution the additional cost imposed on society as a whole by an additional unit of pollution.

marginal tax rate the percentage of an increase in income that is taxed away.

marginal utility the change in total utility generated by consuming one additional unit of a good or service.

marginal utility curve a graphical representation showing how marginal utility depends on the quantity of the good or service consumed.

marginal utility per dollar the additional utility gained from spending one more dollar on a good or service.

marginally attached workers nonworking individuals who say they would like a job and have looked for work in the recent past but are not currently looking for work.

market basket a hypothetical consumption bundle of consumer purchases of goods and services, used to measure changes in overall price level.

market economy an economy in which decisions about production and consumption are made by individual producers and consumers.

market failure the point at which the individual pursuit of self-interest found in markets makes society worse off—that is, the market outcome is inefficient.

market power the ability of a firm to raise prices.

market share the fraction of the total industry output accounted for by producer's output.

market-clearing price the price at which the market is in equilibrium, that is, the quantity of a good or service demanded equals the quantity of that good or service supplied; also referred to as the equilibrium price.

markets for goods and services markets in which firms sell goods and services that they produce to households.

maximum the highest point on a nonlinear curve, where the slope of the curve changes from positive to negative.

mean household income the average income across all households.

means-tested describes a program in which benefits are available only to individuals or families whose incomes fall below a certain level.

median household income the income of the household lying at the exact middle of the income distribution.

medium of exchange an asset that individuals acquire for the purpose of trading for goods and services rather than for their own consumption.

mental accounting the habit of mentally assigning dollars to different accounts so that some dollars are worth more than others.

menu cost the real cost of changing a listed price.

merchandise trade balance (trade balance) the difference between a country's exports and imports of goods alone—not including services.

microeconomics the branch of economics that studies how people make decisions and how these decisions interact.

midpoint method a technique for calculating the percent change in which changes in a variable are compared with the average, or midpoint, of the starting and final values.

minimum the lowest point on a nonlinear curve, where the slope of the curve changes from negative to positive.

minimum wage a legal floor on the wage rate, which is the market price of labor.

minimum-cost output the quantity of output at which the average total cost is lowest—the bottom of the U-shaped average total cost curve.

model a simplified representation of a real situation that is used to better understand real-life situations.

monetarism a theory of business cycles, associated primarily with Milton Friedman, that asserts that GDP will grow steadily if the money supply grows steadily.

monetary aggregate an overall measure of the money supply. The most common monetary aggregates in the United States are M1, which includes currency in circulation, traveler's checks, and checkable bank deposits, and M2, which includes M1 as well as near-moneys.

monetary base the sum of currency in circulation and bank reserves.

monetary neutrality the concept that changes in the money supply have no real effects on the economy in the long run and only result in a proportional change in the price level.

monetary policy changes in the quantity of money in circulation designed to alter interest rates and affect the level of overall spending.

monetary policy rule a formula that determines the central bank's actions.

money any asset that can easily be used to purchase goods and services.

money demand curve a graphical representation of the relationship between the interest rate and the quantity of money demanded. The money demand curve slopes downward because, other things equal, a higher interest rate increases the opportunity cost of holding money.

money multiplier the ratio of the money supply to the monetary base.

money supply the total value of financial assets in the economy that are considered money.

money supply curve a graphical representation of the relationship between the quantity of money supplied by the Federal Reserve and the interest rate.

monopolist a firm that is the only producer of a good that has no close substitutes.

monopolistic competition a market structure in which there are many competing producers in an industry, each producer sells a differentiated product, and there is free entry and exit into and from the industry in the long run.

monopoly an industry controlled by a monopolist.

monopsonist a firm that is the sole buyer in a market.

monopsony a market in which there is only one buyer but many sellers of a good.

moral hazard the situation that can exist when an individual knows more about their own actions than other people do. This leads to a distortion of incentives to take care or to expend effort when someone else bears the costs of the lack of care or effort.

movement along the demand curve a change in the quantity demanded of a good that results from a change in the good's price.

movement along the supply curve a change in the quantity supplied of a good that results from a change in the good's price.

multiplier the ratio of total change in real GDP caused by an autonomous change in aggregate spending to the size of that autonomous change.

mutual fund a financial intermediary that creates a stock portfolio by buying and holding shares in companies and then selling shares of this portfolio to individual investors.

N

Nash equilibrium in game theory, the equilibrium that results when all players choose the action that maximizes their payoffs given the actions of other players, ignoring the effect of that action on the payoffs of other players; also known as noncooperative equilibrium.

national income and product accounts (national accounts) a method of calculating and keeping track of consumer spending, sales of producers, business investment spending, government purchases, and a variety of other flows of money between different sectors of the economy.

national savings the sum of private savings and the government's budget balance; the total amount of savings generated within the economy.

natural monopoly a monopoly that exists when increasing returns to scale provide a large cost advantage to a single firm that produces all of an industry's output.

natural rate hypothesis the hypothesis that because inflation is eventually embedded into expectations, to avoid accelerating inflation over time the unemployment rate should be kept stable around the natural rate.

natural rate of unemployment the normal unemployment rate around which the actual unemployment rate fluctuates; the unemployment rate that arises from the effects of frictional and structural unemployment.

near-moneys financial assets that can't be directly used as a medium of exchange but can be readily converted into cash or checkable bank deposits.

negative externalities external costs.

negative income tax a government program that supplements the income of low-income working families.

negative relationship a relationship between two variables in which an increase in the value of one variable is associated with a decrease in the value of the other variable. It is illustrated by a curve that slopes downward from left to right.

net capital inflow the total inflow of funds into a country minus the total outflow of funds out of a country.

net exports the difference between the value of exports and the value of imports. A positive value for net exports indicates that a country is a net exporter of goods and services; a negative value indicates that a country is a net importer of goods and services.

network externality the increase in the value of a good or service to an individual is greater when a large number of others own or use the same good or service.

new classical macroeconomics an approach to the business cycle that returns to the classical view that shifts in the aggregate demand curve affect only the aggregate price level, not aggregate output.

new Keynesian economics a theory that argues that market imperfections can lead to price stickiness for the economy as a whole.

nominal GDP the value of all final goods and services produced in the economy during a given year, calculated using the prices current in the year in which the output is produced.

nominal interest rate the interest rate in dollar terms.

nominal wage the dollar amount of any given wage paid.

nonaccelerating inflation rate of unemployment (NAIRU) the unemployment rate at which, other things equal, inflation does not change over time.

noncooperative behavior actions by firms that ignore the effects of those actions on the profits of other firms.

noncooperative equilibrium in game theory, the equilibrium that results when all players choose the action that maximizes their payoffs given the actions of other players, ignoring the effect of that action on the payoffs of other players; also known as Nash equilibrium.

nonexcludable referring to a good, describes the case in which the supplier cannot prevent consumption by people who do not pay for it.

nonlinear curve a curve in which the slope is not the same between every pair of points.

nonlinear relationship the relationship between two variables in which the slope is not constant and therefore is depicted on a graph by a curve that is not a straight line.

nonmonetary rewards benefits or payoffs that are not financial in nature; examples include increased leisure time and "feel-good" experiences.

nonprice competition competition in areas other than price to increase sales, such as new product features and advertising; especially engaged in by firms that have a tacit understanding not to compete on price.

nonrival in consumption referring to a good, describes the case in which the same unit can be consumed by more than one person at the same time.

normal good a good for which a rise in income increases the demand for that good—the "normal" case.

normative economics the branch of economic analysis that makes prescriptions about the way the economy should work.

North American Free Trade Agreement (NAFTA) a trade agreement among the United States, Canada, and Mexico. Revised in 2018 as USMCA.

nudge a formulation of the status quo choice intended to shift people to more rational choices when they are prone to status quo bias.

O

offshore outsourcing the practice in which businesses hire people in another country to perform various tasks.

offshore outsourcing the practice of businesses hiring people in another country to perform various tasks.

Okun's law the negative relationship between the output gap and the unemployment rate, whereby each additional percentage point of output gap reduces the unemployment rate by about ½ of a percentage point.

oligopolist a firm in an industry with only a small number of producers.

oligopoly an industry with only a small number of producers.

omitted variable an unobserved variable that, through its influence on other variables, creates the erroneous appearance of a direct causal relationship among those variables.

open economy an economy that trades goods and services with other countries.

open-market operation a purchase or sale of U.S. Treasury bills by the Federal Reserve, normally through a transaction with a commercial bank.

opportunity cost the real cost of an item: what you must give up in order to get it.

optimal consumption bundle the consumption bundle that maximizes a consumer's total utility given that consumer's budget constraint.

optimal output rule the principle that profit is maximized by producing the quantity of output at which the marginal revenue of the last unit produced is equal to its marginal cost.

optimal quantity the quantity that generates the highest possible total profit.

optimal time allocation rule the principle that an individual should allocate time so that the marginal utility gained from the income earned from an additional hour worked is equal to the marginal utility of an additional hour of leisure.

ordinary goods in a consumer's utility function, those for which additional units of one good are required to compensate for fewer units of another, and vice versa; and for which the consumer experiences a diminishing marginal rate of substitution when substituting one good in place of another.

other things equal assumption in the development of a model, the assumption that all other relevant factors remain unchanged.

output gap the percentage difference between actual aggregate output and potential output.

overuse the depletion of a common resource that occurs when individuals ignore the fact that their use depletes the amount of the resource remaining for others.

P

Paris Agreement a commitment by 196 countries, signed in 2015, to reduce their greenhouse gas emissions in an effort to limit the rise in the earth's temperature to no more than 2 degrees centigrade.

patent a temporary monopoly given by the government to an inventor for the use or sale of an invention.

payoff in game theory, the reward received by a player (for example, the profit earned by an oligopolist).

payoff matrix in game theory, a diagram that shows how the payoffs to each of the participants in a two-player game depend on the actions of both; a tool in analyzing interdependence.

payroll tax a tax on the earnings an employer pays to an employee.

pension fund a type of mutual fund that holds assets in order to provide retirement income to its members.

perfect complements goods a consumer wants to consume in the same ratio, regardless of their relative price.

perfect price discrimination the price discrimination that results when a monopolist charges each consumer the maximum that the consumer is willing to pay.

perfect substitutes goods for which the indifference curves are straight lines; the marginal rate of substitution of one good in place of another good is constant, regardless of how much of each an individual consumes.

perfectly competitive industry an industry in which all producers are price-takers.

perfectly competitive market a market in which all participants are price-takers.

perfectly elastic demand the case in which any price increase will cause the quantity demanded to drop to zero; the demand curve is a horizontal line.

perfectly elastic supply the case in which even a tiny increase or reduction in the price will lead to very large changes in the quantity supplied, so that the price elasticity of supply is infinite; the perfectly elastic supply curve is a horizontal line.

perfectly inelastic demand the case in which the quantity demanded does not respond at all to changes in the price; the demand curve is a vertical line.

perfectly inelastic supply the case in which the price elasticity of supply is zero, so that changes in the price of the good have no effect on the quantity supplied; the perfectly inelastic supply curve is a vertical line.

physical asset a claim on a tangible object that can be used to generate future income.

physical capital manufactured productive resources, such as equipment, buildings, tools, and machines; often referred to simply as "capital."

pie chart a circular graph that shows how some total is divided among its components, usually expressed in percentages.

Pigouvian subsidy a payment designed to encourage activities that generate external benefits.

Pigouvian taxes taxes designed to reduce the costs imposed on society from a negative externality.

planned aggregate spending the total amount of planned spending in the economy; includes consumer spending and planned investment spending.

planned investment spending the investment spending that firms intend to undertake during a given period. Planned investment spending may differ from actual investment spending due to unplanned inventory investment.

political business cycle a business cycle that results from the use of macroeconomic policy to serve political ends.

pooling a strong form of diversification in which an investor takes a small share of the risk in many independent events, so the payoff has very little total overall risk.

positive economics the branch of economic analysis that describes the way the economy actually works.

positive externalities external benefits.

positive feedback put simply, success breeds success, failure breeds failure; the effect is seen with goods that are subject to network externalities.

positive relationship a relationship between two variables in which an increase in the value of one variable is associated with an increase in the value of the other variable. It is illustrated by a curve that slopes upward from left to right.

positively correlated describes a relationship between events such that each event is more likely to occur if the other event also occurs.

potential output the level of real GDP the economy would produce if all prices, including nominal wages, were fully flexible.

poverty program a government program designed to aid the poor.

poverty rate the percentage of the population with incomes below the poverty threshold.

poverty threshold the annual income below which a family is officially considered poor.

premium a payment to an insurance company in return for the promise to pay a claim in certain states of the world.

present value (of X) the amount of money needed today in order to receive X at a future date given the interest rate.

price ceiling a maximum price sellers are allowed to charge for a good or service; a form of price control.

price controls legal restrictions on how high or low a market price may go.

price discrimination charging different prices to different consumers for the same good.

price elasticity of demand the ratio of the percent change in the quantity demanded to the percent change in the price as we move along the demand curve.

price elasticity of supply a measure of the responsiveness of the quantity of a good supplied to the price of that good; the ratio of the percent change in the quantity supplied to the percent change in the price as we move along the supply curve.

price floor a minimum price buyers are required to pay for a good or service; a form of price control.

price index a measure of the cost of purchasing a given market basket in a given year, where that cost is normalized so that it is equal to 100 in the selected base year; a measure of overall price level.

price leadership a pattern of behavior in which one firm sets its price and other firms in the industry follow.

price regulation limits the price that a monopolist is allowed to charge.

price stability a situation in which the overall cost of living is changing slowly or not at all.

price war a collapse of prices when tacit collusion breaks down.

price-taking consumer a consumer whose actions have no effect on the market price of the good or service that consumer buys.

price-taking firm's optimal output rule the principle that a price-taking firm's profit is maximized by producing the quantity of output at which the market price is equal to the marginal cost of the last unit produced.

price-taking producer a producer whose actions have no effect on the market price of the good or service it sells.

price-taking producer's optimal employment rule a price-taking producer's profit is maximized by employing each factor of production up to the level at which the value of the marginal product is equal to the factor's price.

principle of diminishing marginal utility the proposition that each successive unit of a good or service consumed adds less to total utility than did the previous unit.

principle of "either–or" decision making the principle that, when faced with an "either-or" choice between two activities, choose the one with the positive economic profit.

prisoner's dilemma a game based on two premises: (1) each player has an incentive to choose an action that benefits itself at the other player's expense; and (2) both players are then worse off than if they had acted cooperatively.

private good a good that is both excludable and rival in consumption.

private health insurance a program in which each member of a large pool of individuals pays a fixed amount to a private company that agrees to pay most of the medical expenses of the pool's members.

private information information that some people have, but others do not.

producer price index (PPI) a measure of the cost of a typical basket of goods and services purchased by producers. Because these commodity prices respond quickly to changes in demand, the PPI is often regarded as a leading indicator of changes in the inflation rate.

producer surplus a term often used to refer both to individual producer surplus and to total producer surplus.

product differentiation the attempt by firms to convince buyers that their products are different from those of other firms in the industry. If firms can so convince buyers, they can charge a higher price.

production function the relationship between the quantity of inputs a firm uses and the quantity of output it produces.

production possibility frontier a model that illustrates the trade-offs facing an economy that produces only two goods. It shows the maximum quantity of one good that can be produced for any given quantity produced of the other.

productivity output per worker; a shortened form of the term *labor productivity*.

profit-maximizing principle of marginal analysis the proposition that in a profit-maximizing "how much" decision the optimal quantity is the largest quantity at which marginal benefit is greater than or equal to marginal cost.

profits tax a tax on a firm's profits.

progressive tax a tax that takes a larger share of the income of high-income taxpayers than of low-income taxpayers.

property rights the rights of owners of valuable items, whether resources or goods, to dispose of those items as they choose.

property tax a tax on the value of property, such as the value of a home.

proportional tax a tax that is the same percentage of the tax base regardless of the taxpayer's income or wealth.

protection an alternative term for trade protection; policies that limit imports.

public debt government debt held by individuals and institutions outside the government.

public good a good that is both nonexcludable and nonrival in consumption.

public ownership the case in which goods are supplied by the government or by a firm owned by the government to protect the interests of the consumer in response to natural monopoly.

purchasing power parity (between two countries' currencies) the nominal exchange rate at which a given basket of goods and services would cost the same amount in each country.

Q

quantity control an upper limit, set by the government, on the quantity of some good that can be bought or sold; also referred to as a quota.

quantity demanded the actual amount of a good or service consumers are willing to buy at some specific price.

quantity supplied the actual amount of a good or service producers are willing to sell at some specific price.

quota an upper limit, set by the government, on the quantity of some good that can be bought or sold; also referred to as a quantity control.

quota limit the total amount of a good under a quota or quantity control that can be legally transacted.

quota rent the difference between the demand price and the supply price at the quota limit; this difference, the earnings that accrue to the license-holder from ownership of the right to sell the good, is equal to the market price of the license when the licenses are traded.

R

random variable a variable with an uncertain future value.

random walk the movement over time of an unpredictable variable.

rational describes a decision maker who chooses the available option that leads to the outcome they most prefer.

rational expectations a theory of expectation formation that holds that individuals and firms make decisions optimally, using all available information.

rational expectations model a model of the economy in which expected changes in monetary policy have no effect on unemployment and output and only affect the price level.

real business cycle theory a theory of business cycles that asserts that fluctuations in the growth rate of total factor productivity cause the business cycle.

real exchange rate the exchange rate adjusted for international differences in aggregate price levels.

real GDP the total value of all final goods and services produced in the economy during a given year, calculated using the prices of a selected base year.

real income income divided by the price level.

real interest rate the nominal interest rate minus the inflation rate.

real wage the wage rate divided by the price level.

recession a downturn in the economy when output and employment are falling; also referred to as a contraction.

recessionary gap the gap that exists when aggregate output is below potential output.

regressive tax a tax that takes a smaller share of the income of high-income taxpayers than of low-income taxpayers.

relative price the ratio of the price of one good to the price of another.

relative price rule at the optimal consumption bundle, the marginal rate of substitution of one good in place of another is equal to the relative price.

renewable energy sources energy sources, such as solar and wind power, that are inexhaustible, unlike fossil fuel sources, which are exhaustible.

rental rate the cost, implicit or explicit, of using a unit of land or capital for a given period of time.

reputation a long-term standing in the public regard that serves to reassure others that private information is not being concealed; a valuable asset in the face of adverse selection.

research and development (R&D) spending to create new technologies and prepare them for practical use.

reserve ratio the fraction of bank deposits that a bank holds as reserves. In the United States, the minimum required reserve ratio is set by the Federal Reserve.

reserve requirements rules of the Federal Reserve that set the minimum reserve ratio for banks. For checkable bank deposits in the United States, the minimum reserve ratio is set at 10%.

resource something that can be used to produce something else; includes natural resources (from the physical environment) and human resources (labor, skill, intelligence).

revaluation an increase in the value of a currency that is set under a fixed exchange rate regime.

reverse causality the error committed when the true direction of causality between two variables is reversed, and the independent variable and the dependent variable are incorrectly identified.

Ricardian model of international trade a model that analyzes international trade under the assumption that opportunity costs are constant.

risk uncertainty about future outcomes.

risk-averse describes individuals who choose to reduce risk when that reduction leaves the expected value of their income or wealth unchanged.

risk-aversion the willingness to sacrifice some economic payoff in order to avoid a potential loss.

risk-neutral describes individuals who are completely insensitive to risk.

rival in consumption referring to a good, describes the case in which one unit cannot be consumed by more than one person at the same time.

Rule of 70 a mathematical formula that states that the time it takes real GDP per capita, or any other variable that grows gradually over time, to double is approximately 70 divided by that variable's annual growth rate.

S

sales tax a tax on the value of goods sold.

savings and loans (thrifts) deposit-taking banks, usually specialized in issuing home loans.

savings–investment spending identity an accounting fact that states that savings and investment spending are always equal for the economy as a whole.

scarce in short supply; a resource is scarce when there is not enough of the resource available to satisfy all the various ways a society wants to use it.

scatter diagram a graph that shows points that correspond to actual observations of the x- and y-variables; a curve is usually fitted to the scatter of points to indicate the trend in the data.

screening using observable information about people to make inferences about their private information; a way to reduce adverse selection.

secular stagnation a state in which the interest rate that would be needed to achieve full employment is consistently below zero. Proponents of this view, known as *secular stagnationists*, advocate an active fiscal policy and unconventional monetary policy.

securitization the pooling of loans and mortgages made by a financial institution and the sale of shares in such a pool to other investors.

self-correcting describes an economy in which shocks to aggregate demand affect aggregate output in the short run but not in the long run.

self-regulating economy describes an economy in which problems such as unemployment are resolved without government intervention, through the working of the invisible hand, and in which government attempts to improve the economy's performance would be ineffective at best, and would probably make things worse.

shadow banking bank-like activities undertaken by nondepository financial firms such as investment banks and hedge funds, but without regulatory oversight and protection.

share a partial ownership of a company.

shift of the demand curve a change in the quantity demanded at any given price, represented graphically by the shift of the original demand curve to a new position, denoted by a new demand curve.

shift of the supply curve a change in the quantity supplied of a good or service at any given price. It is represented by the change of the original supply curve to a new position, denoted by a new supply curve.

shoe-leather costs (of inflation) the increased costs of transactions caused by inflation.

short run the time period in which at least one input is fixed.

short-run aggregate supply curve a graphical representation that shows the positive relationship between the aggregate price level and the quantity of aggregate output supplied that exists in the short run, the time period when many production costs, particularly nominal wages, can be taken as fixed. The short-run aggregate supply curve has a positive slope because a rise in the aggregate price level leads to a rise in profits, and therefore output, when production costs are fixed.

short-run equilibrium aggregate output the quantity of aggregate output produced in short-run macroeconomic equilibrium.

short-run equilibrium aggregate price level the aggregate price level in short-run macroeconomic equilibrium.

short-run individual supply curve a graphical representation that shows how an individual producer's profit-maximizing output quantity depends on the market price, taking fixed cost as given.

short-run industry supply curve a graphical representation that shows how the quantity supplied by an industry depends on the market price given a fixed number of producers.

short-run macroeconomic equilibrium the point at which the quantity of aggregate output supplied is equal to the quantity demanded.

short-run market equilibrium an economic balance that results when the quantity supplied equals the quantity demanded, taking the number of producers as given.

short-run Phillips curve a graphical representation of the negative short-run relationship between the unemployment rate and the inflation rate.

short-term interest rate the interest rate on financial assets that mature within less than a year.

shortage the insufficiency of a good or service that occurs when the quantity demanded exceeds the quantity supplied; shortages occur when the price is below the equilibrium price.

shut-down price the price at which a firm will cease production in the short run if the market price falls below the minimum average variable cost.

signaling taking some action to establish credibility despite possessing private information; a way to reduce adverse selection.

single-payer system a health care system in which the government is the principal payer of medical bills funded through taxes.

single-price monopolist a monopolist that offers its product to all consumers at the same price.

slope a measure of how steep a line or curve is. The slope of a line is measured by "rise over run"—the change in the y-variable between two points on the line divided by the change in the x-variable between those same two points.

social insurance government programs—like Social Security, Medicare, unemployment insurance, and food stamps—intended to protect families against economic hardship.

social insurance program a government program designed to provide protection against unpredictable financial distress.

socially optimal quantity of pollution the quantity of pollution that society would choose if all the costs and benefits of pollution were fully accounted for.

specialization the situation in which each person specializes in the task that they are good at performing.

stabilization policy the use of government policy to reduce the severity of recessions and to rein in excessively strong expansions. There are two main tools of stabilization policy: monetary policy and fiscal policy.

stagflation the combination of inflation and falling aggregate output.

standardized product output of different producers regarded by consumers as the same good; also referred to as a commodity.

state of the world a possible future event.

status quo bias the tendency to avoid making a decision and sticking with the status quo.

sticky wages nominal wages that are slow to fall even in the face of high unemployment and slow to rise even in the face of labor shortages.

store of value an asset that is a means of holding purchasing power over time.

strategic behavior actions taken by a firm that attempt to influence the future behavior of other firms.

structural unemployment unemployment that results when there are more people seeking jobs in a particular labor market than there are jobs available at the current wage rate, even when the economy is at the peak of the business cycle.

subprime lending lending to homebuyers who don't meet the usual criteria for qualifying for a loan.

substitutes pairs of goods for which a rise in the price of one of the goods leads to an increase in the demand for the other good.

substitution effect the change in the quantity of a good consumed as the consumer substitutes other goods that are now relatively cheaper in place of the good that has become relatively more expensive.

sunk cost a cost that has already been incurred and is not recoverable. A sunk cost should be ignored in decisions about future actions.

sunk cost fallacy the mistaken belief that a sunk cost represents an opportunity cost.

supply and demand model a model of how a competitive market behaves.

supply curve a graphical representation of the supply schedule, showing the relationship between quantity supplied and price.

supply price the price of a given quantity at which producers will supply that quantity.

supply schedule a list or table showing how much of a good or service producers will supply at different prices.

supply shock an event that shifts the short-run aggregate supply curve. A negative supply shock raises production costs and reduces the quantity supplied at any aggregate price level, shifting the curve leftward. A positive supply shock decreases production costs and increases the quantity supplied at any aggregate price level, shifting the curve rightward.

surplus the excess of a good or service that occurs when the quantity supplied exceeds the quantity demanded; surpluses occur when the price is above the equilibrium price.

sustainable long-run economic growth long-run growth that can continue in the face of the limited supply of natural resources and with less negative impact on the environment.

T

T-account a simple tool that summarizes a business's financial position by showing, in a single table, the business's assets and liabilities, with assets on the left and liabilities on the right.

tacit collusion cooperation among producers, without a formal agreement, to limit production and raise prices so as to raise one another's profits.

tangency condition on a graph of a consumer's budget line and available indifference curves of available consumption bundles, the point at which an indifference curve and the budget line just touch. When the indifference curves have the typical convex shape, this point determines the optimal consumption bundle.

tangent line a straight line that just touches, or is tangent to, a nonlinear curve at a particular point; the slope of the tangent line is equal to the slope of the nonlinear curve at that point.

target federal funds rate the Federal Reserve's desired level for the federal funds rate. The Federal Reserve adjusts the money supply through the purchase and sale of Treasury bills until the actual rate equals the desired rate.

tariff a tax levied on imports.

tax base the measure or value, such as income or property value, that determines how much tax an individual or firm pays.

tax rate the amount of tax people are required to pay per unit of whatever is being taxed.

tax structure specifies how a tax depends on the tax base; usually expressed in percentage terms.

Taylor rule for monetary policy a rule that sets the federal funds rate according to the level of the inflation rate and either the output gap or the unemployment rate.

technological progress an advance in the technical means of production of goods and services.

technology the technical means for producing goods and services.

technology spillover an external benefit, or positive externality, that results when knowledge spreads among individuals and firms.

time allocation the decision about how many hours to spend on different activities, which leads to a decision about how much labor to supply.

time allocation budget line an individual's possible trade-off between consumption of leisure and the income that allows consumption of marketed goods.

time-series graph a two-variable graph that has dates on the horizontal axis and values of a variable that occurred on those dates on the vertical axis.

tit for tat in game theory, a strategy that involves playing cooperatively at first, then doing whatever the other player did in the previous period.

total consumer surplus the sum of the individual consumer surpluses of all the buyers of a good in a market.

total cost the sum of the fixed cost and the variable cost of producing a given quantity of output.

total cost curve a graphical representation of the total cost, showing how total cost depends on the quantity of output.

total factor productivity the amount of output that can be produced with a given amount of factor inputs.

total producer surplus the sum of the individual producer surpluses of all the sellers of a good in a market.

total product curve a graphical representation of the production function, showing how the quantity of output depends on the quantity of the variable input for a given quantity of the fixed input.

total revenue the total value of sales of a good or service (the price of the good or service multiplied by the quantity sold).

total surplus the total net gain to consumers and producers from trading in a market; it is the sum of the producer surplus and the consumer surplus.

tradable emissions permits licenses to emit limited quantities of pollutants that can be bought and sold by polluters.

trade the practice, in a market economy, in which individuals provide goods and services to others and receive goods and services in return.

trade balance (merchandise trade balance) the difference between a country's exports and imports of goods alone—not including services.

trade deficit the deficit that results when the value of the goods and services bought from foreigners is more than the value of the goods and services sold to consumers abroad.

trade protection policies that limit imports.

trade surplus the surplus that results when the value of goods and services bought from foreigners is less than the value of the goods and services sold to them.

trade war occurs when countries deliberately try to impose pain on their trading partners, as a way to extract policy concessions.

trade-off a comparison of costs and benefits of doing something.

trade-off between equity and efficiency the dynamic whereby a well-designed tax system can be made more efficient only by making it less fair, and vice versa.

transaction costs the expenses of negotiating and executing a deal that often prevent a mutually beneficial trade from occurring.

truncated cut; in a truncated axis, some of the range of values are omitted, usually to save space.

U

U-shaped average total cost curve a distinctive graphical representation of the relationship between output and average total cost; the average total cost curve at first falls when output is low and then rises as output increases.

underemployment the number of people who work part time because they cannot find full-time jobs.

unemployment the total number of people who are actively looking for work but aren't currently employed.

unemployment rate the percentage of the total number of people in the labor force who are unemployed, calculated as unemployment/(unemployment + employment).

union an organization of workers that bargains collectively with employers to raise wages and improve working conditions.

unit of account a measure used to set prices and make economic calculations.

unit-elastic demand the case in which the price elasticity of demand is exactly 1.

unit-of-account costs (of inflation) costs arising from the way inflation makes money a less reliable unit of measurement.

United States-Mexico-Canada Agreement or USMCA a revised trade agreement between the United States, Canada, and Mexico to replace NAFTA.

unplanned inventory investment an unintended swing in inventory that occurs when actual sales are higher or lower than expected sales.

util a unit of utility.

utility (of a consumer) a measure of the satisfaction derived from consumption of goods and services.

utility function (of an individual) the total utility generated by an individual's consumption bundle.

utility-maximizing principle of marginal analysis the principle that the marginal utility per dollar spent must be the same for all goods and services in the optimal consumption bundle.

V

value added (of a producer) the value of a producer's sales minus the value of its purchases of intermediate goods and services.

value of the marginal product the value of the additional output generated by employing one more unit of a given factor, such as labor.

value of the marginal product curve a graphical representation showing how the value of the marginal product of a factor depends on the quantity of the factor employed.

variable a quantity that can take on more than one value.

variable cost a cost that depends on the quantity of output produced; the cost of a variable input.

variable input an input whose quantity the firm can vary at any time (for example, labor).

velocity of money the ratio of nominal GDP to the money supply.

vertical axis the vertical number line of a graph along which values of the y-variable are measured; also referred to as the y-axis.

vertical intercept the point at which a curve hits the vertical axis; it shows the value of the y-variable when the value of the x-variable is zero.

W

wasted resources a form of inefficiency in which people expend money, effort, and time to cope with the shortages caused by a price ceiling.

wealth (of a household) the value of accumulated savings.

wealth effect of a change in the aggregate price level the effect on consumer spending caused by the change in the purchasing power of consumers' assets when the aggregate price level changes. A rise in the aggregate price level decreases the purchasing power of consumers' assets, so consumers decrease their consumption; a fall in the aggregate price level increases the purchasing power of consumers' assets, so consumers increase their consumption.

wealth tax a tax on an individual's wealth.

wedge the difference between the demand price of the quantity transacted and the supply price of the quantity transacted for a good when the supply of the good is legally restricted. Often created by a quantity control, or quota. The price paid by buyers ends up being higher than that received by sellers.

welfare state the collection of government programs designed to alleviate economic hardship.

willingness to pay the maximum price at which a consumer is prepared to pay for a good.

world price the price at which that good can be bought or sold abroad.

World Trade Organization (WTO) an international organization of member countries that oversees international trade agreements and rules on disputes between countries over those agreements.

X

x-axis the horizontal number line of a graph along which values of the x-variable are measured; also referred to as the horizontal axis.

Y

y-axis the vertical number line of a graph along which values of the y-variable are measured; also referred to as the vertical axis.

Z

zero lower bound for interest rates statement of the fact that interest rates cannot fall below zero without causing significant problems.

zero-profit equilibrium an economic balance in which each firm makes zero profit at its profit-maximizing quantity; a long-run result of a monopolistically competitive industry.

Index

Note: Key terms appear in
boldface type.

A

Abengoa, 841
ability-to-pay principle
of tax fairness, 202
welfare state and, 516–517, 535
absolute advantage, 37
comparative advantage vs., 37
absolute value, 56
ACA. *See* Affordable Care Act
accelerator principle, 761
account, money as unit of, 852
accountability, inflation targeting
and, 900
accounting, mental, 266
accounting profit, 249, 362
economic profit vs., 249–252
acid rain, 473
Activision, 455
actual inventory investment,
762
AD–AS model, 800–807
increase in money supply and,
916
long-run macroeconomic
equilibrium and, 804–807
shifts of the short-run
aggregate supply curve
and, 802–804
short-run macroeconomic
equilibrium and, 800–801
short-run Phillips curve and,
926
short-run shifts of aggregate
demand curve and,
801–802
supply shocks vs. demand
shocks in practice and,
807
Adelman, David, 291
administrative costs, 198
of a tax, 198–199
advanced manufacturing, 45
Advanced Research Projects
Agency Network
(ARPANET), 694
advance purchase restrictions,
412
adverse selection, 594, 595–596
adverse selection death spiral,
595–596
advertising, monopolistic
competition and, 459–460
AFC. See average fixed cost
AFDC. *See* Aid to Families with
Dependent Children

Affordable Care Act (ACA), 522,
525, 531, 532–534, 819
cost control and, 533
coverage for uninsured under,
532–533
effects of, 533–534
politics and, 533–534, 538
as remedy for job lock, 538
Africa. *See also specific countries*
economic growth of, 698–699
infrastructure spending in, 693
**aggregate consumption
function,** 755–758
shifts of, 756–758
aggregate demand curve,
782–790. *See also* AD–AS
model
downward slope of, 783–784
fiscal policy and, 788–789
government policies and,
788–789
income-expenditure model and,
784–785
Keynesian view of factors
shifting, 946
monetary policy and, 789
movement along during
1979–1980, 789–790
movement along vs. shift of,
788
shifts of, 786–788
short-run effects of changes
in, on aggregate output,
945–946
aggregate output, 636. *See also*
real GDP
aggregate demand and, in
Keynesian vs. classical
macroeconomics, 945–946
fluctuations around long-run
trend of potential output,
unemployment rate and,
922–923
long-run aggregate supply
curve and, 796–798
short-run, equilibrium, 801
short-run changes in aggregate
demand and, 945–946
aggregate price level, 639
changes in, shifts of the money
demand curve and, 889
fall in. *See* deflation
increase in. *See* hyperinflation;
inflation
interest rate effect of a change
in, 783–784
normalizing measure of, 640
short-run, equilibrium, 801

wealth effect of a change in,
783
aggregate production function,
685–689
aggregate spending, 630
autonomous change in, 752
planned, real GDP and,
764–766
aggregate supply curve,
790–800. *See also* AD–AS
model; long-run aggregate
supply curve; short-run
aggregate supply curve
commodity price changes and,
794, 795
nominal wage changes and,
794–795
productivity changes and, 795
short-run Phillips curve and,
926
aggregate wealth, changes in,
aggregate consumption
function and, 757–758
agoda.com, 22
agriculture
farmers' understanding of
profit maximization and,
369–370
farmland preservation and,
483–484
farmland prices and, 114–115
inputs and, 327
wheat yields and, 330
Aid to Families with Dependent
Children (AFDC), 526
AIG, 876
Airbnb, 120–121, 252
aircraft industry
airplane design and, 27
airplane manufacture and, 45
airplane production and, 224
European, 224
international trade and, 224
airline industry
cartel in, 441
deregulation of, 145
oil prices and, 82
Priceline and, 22
ticket prices and, 22, 145, 179,
408–410
air pollution. *See* pollution
Alaskan crab fishing, 151–152
Alcoa, 95
Algeria, wheat yield in, 330
Allegis Group, 673
Allen, Paul, 733
allocation
to consumers, inefficient, 136

of consumption, among
consumers, 117–118
efficiency in, 30–31
of resources, factor prices and,
544
of risk, efficient, 588–589
of sales among sellers,
inefficient, 144–145
of time, 563, 573–574
Amazon, 8, 349, 388, 405,
406–407, 414, 495,
557–558, 659, 669, 713,
729
price war with Walmart,
438–439
ambulance service, price of, 159
AMD, 388
Amtrak, 401
anchoring, 267
Anheuser-Busch InBev, 423
antitrust policy, 435
in EU and United States,
435–436
formulation of, 423
monopoly and, 385, 401,
403–404, 406–407
new generation of market
power and, 403–404,
406–407
oligopoly and, 421
Apple, 215, 388, 403, 405, 422,
456, 486, 970
ApplePay, 890
Apple v. Pepper, 405
appreciation, 972
arc method of calculating slope
along a nonlinear curve,
56–58
area, below or above a curve,
calculating, 59, 60
Argentina
default by, 836
economic crises in, 638
economic growth of, 616–617,
682, 692–693, 698
exchange rate of, 982
financial intermediation
in, 736
inflation in, 644
Ariely, Dan, 268
Armenia, inflation in, 915
arms race, 430
ARPANET. *See* Advanced
Research Projects Agency
Network (ARPANET)
arson, insurance and, 596–597
artificially scarce goods, 494,
507–508

asset(s)
of Fed, 867, 870–871
of Fed, interest on, 868
financial. *See* bank deposits;
bonds; financial assets;
loan(s); loan-backed
securities; stock(s)
illiquid, 731
liquid, 731, 850
physical, 729
asset-backed commercial paper,
875–876
asset prices
expectations and, 739–740
fluctuations of, 736–742
macroeconomics and, 741
asymmetric information, 594. *See
also* private information
ATC. See average total cost
ATMs, 890
in Japan, 890
AT&T, 422
Audible, 406
Austen, Jane, 545
austerity policies, 956–957. *See
also* fiscal austerity
Austin, Benjamin, 666
Australia
drug prices in, 389
economic growth and
greenhouse gases in, 475
Gini coefficient in, 523
government debt of, 836
individual transferable quotas
in, 506
natural gas production in, 177
number of hours worked in,
566
productivity and wages in, 222
voting as a public good in, 500
wages in, 141
Austria, productivity and wages
in, 222
autarky, 219, 226
automatic stabilizers, 828
automation, factor demand and,
551
automobile industry
of Japan, 223–224
lean production techniques
in, 45
product differentiation in, 438
Spanish, 989
U.S., 224, 811
**autonomous change in
aggregate spending,** 752
autonomous consumer spending,
754
AVC. See average variable cost
average cost, 337
average fixed cost (AFC), 337–
338, 339
average total cost, 337–339, 340
minimum, 340–341, 365
monopolistic competition vs.
perfect competition and,
457–458
average total cost curve (ATC)
long-run, 345, 346–347
short-run, 343, 344, 345–346
U-shaped, 337

average variable cost (AVC),
337–338, 339
Avis, 421
avocado prices, demand and
supply and, 94
A&W Restaurant, 447
axes of a graph, 52
truncated, 62

B

baby boom, Social Security and,
839
**backward-bending individual
labor supply curve,** 576
balanced budget. *See* budget
balance
balance of payments accounts,
964–968
exchange rates and, 975
**balance of payments on
current account,**
966, 975
**balance of payments on
financial account,** 966,
975
**balance of payments on goods
and services,** 966
balance sheet, of Fed, 870–871
bandwagon effect, 486
Bangladesh
clothing industry of, 38, 40
economic growth of, 682, 683
bank(s), 734–735
capital of, 858
central. *See* central banks;
European Central Bank
(ECB); Federal Reserve
System (Fed)
commercial, 867, 873
failures of. *See* banking crises;
bank runs
functions of, 856–857
investment. *See* Bear Stearns;
investment banks;
Lehman Brothers
money creation by, 860–861
net worth of, 858
owner's equity of, 858
regulation of, 858–859, 873,
876–877
reserves of. *See* bank reserves
runs on. *See* bank runs
shadow, 874–876
Swiss, 963
bank deposits, 729, 734–735
checkable, 850
bank failures, 857. *See also*
banking crises; bank runs
bank holiday, 859, 873
banking
multiplier process and, 861
shadow, 874–876
technology for, changes in,
shifts of money demand
curve and, 890
banking crises
creation of Federal Reserve
and, 872–873
multiplier and, 864
Panic of 1907 and, 871–872,
875

protection against, 859
savings and loan crisis of 1980s
and, 873–874
banking system. *See* U.S. banking
system
Bank of England, 865, 900
Bank of Japan, 865, 936
bank reserves, 856
excess, 862
money multiplier and, 862
requirements for, 858, 866–867
bank runs, 857–858, 871
in Argentinian economic crisis,
859
during Great Depression, 859,
864, 872–873
on IndyMac Bank, 859
money supply and, 864
on Northern Rock, 859
protection against, 859
in Southeast Asian economic
crisis, 859
bar codes, 706
bar graphs, 62
barriers to entry, 387–390
barter, 38–39
Bazalgette, Joseph, 493
Bear Stearns, 870, 876
A Beautiful Mind, 430
beer market, 423
behavioral economics, 247,
262–269, 740
irrationality and, 264–267
models based on rational
behavior and, 267–268
rationality and, 263–264
behavioral finance, 740
Belgium
fiscal policy in, 957
government debt of, 836
productivity and wages in, 222
voting as a public good in, 500
Bell Telephone, 435
benefits
of climate change mitigation,
481–482
cost-benefit analysis and, 501
external. *See* external benefits;
positive externalities
social. *See* marginal social
benefit *entries;* social
benefit
survival, net, 109, 117
benefits notches, 536
benefits principle, of tax
fairness, 202
Benjamins, 854
Bernanke, Ben, 651, 781, 865
on inflation targeting,
900–901
Best Buy, 377
Best Western, 460
Bezos, Jeff, 850
Big Mac prices, purchasing power
parity and, 977
Billion Prices Project, 644
Bing, 422
biotech firms, 262
Bitcoin, 854
black labor, 145
black markets, 137–138

Blanchard, Olivier, 951
on government debt, 840, 943
on interest rates, 958
BLS. *See* Bureau of Labor
Statistics (BLS)
BMW, 459, 561
Board of Governors, of Fed, 865
Boatbound, 121
Boeing, 27, 45
bonds, 729, 732
corporate, in United States and
Euro area, 735
default on, 732
long-term interest rates and,
895
markets for, 718
Booking.com, 22
book retailers, 414
borrowing. *See* debt; government
borrowing; loan(s);
mortgages; public debt
bounded rationality, 264
brand names, monopolistic
competition and, 460–461
Brazil
dispute with United States
over subsidies to cotton
farmers, 238
ecotourism in, 509
Gini coefficient in, 521
hyperinflation in, 668, 669
purchasing power parity and
Big Mac price in, 977
recession in, 615
breakage, gift cards and, 878
break-even price, 365
breakfast cereal industry, 357
Bretton Woods system, 983
Bridgestone, 421, 424
Britain. *See* United Kingdom
British Airways, 441
Buchmueller, Ross, 599
budget balance, 715, 829–834
business cycle and, 830–832
cyclically adjusted, 829,
830–832
desirability of, 832–833
as measure of fiscal policy, 830
in a recession, 833–834
budget constraints, 279,
283–284, 287
budget deficits, 715
business cycle and, 830–832
crowding out and, 723
debt vs., 835
fiscal policy and, 830–832
government debt and, 835
during Great Recession, 833
in practice, 837–838
private spending and, 823
unemployment rate and, 831
budget line, 284
price increase and, 317–318
slope of, 310–311
time allocation, 573–574
budget surpluses, 277, 715, 830,
836
Buffalo Wild Wings, 74
Bumble Bee, 421
Bureau of Labor Statistics (BLS),
640, 643

consumer price index and, 640
data collection by, 753
unemployment rate calculated by, 654
Burger King, 74, 295, 447
Bush, George W., 947
business confidence, 946
business cycle, 611–615
budget deficits and, 830–832
charting, 612
classical macroeconomics and, 944
cyclically adjusted budget balance and, 830–832
depression and. *See* Great Depression
history of, 613
international, 986–987
Keynesian views on, 946
political, 953
recessions and. *See* Great Recession; recession(s)
risk and, 593
taming, 613–614
business-cycle peaks, 612
business-cycle troughs, 612
business opportunities, perceived, shifts of demand for loanable funds and, 722

C

cabs. *See* taxis
Cadbury Canada, 427
Calvin Klein, 460
Cambodia, clothing industry of, 38
Camp, Garrett, 96, 153
Canada
drug prices in, 389
economic growth and greenhouse gases in, 475
economic growth of, 616–617
gasoline consumption in, 70
Gini coefficient in, 521, 523
government debt of, 836
government spending and tax revenue in, 818
health care in, 531, 532
individual transferable quotas in, 506
inflation and money supply in, 906
inflation targeting in, 900
intellectual property piracy in, 508
NAFTA and, 237, 240
number of hours worked in, 566
productivity and wages in, 222
purchasing power parity exchange rate between United States and, 977–978
spending on food in, 173
taxes in, 207
tradable emissions permits in, 478
trade with United States, 222–223
voting as a public good in, 500
wages in, 141

cap and trade systems, 476, 478–479
capital, 250
of banks, 858
financial, definition of, 716
foreign, economic growth and, 692
human. *See* education; human capital
implicit cost of, 250
physical. *See* physical capital
capital at risk, 588
capital flows
financial account as measure of inflows and, 968
international, two-way, 969–970
international, underlying determinants of, 969
loanable funds model and, 968
net inflow and, 716
capital market, 39
carbon tax, 208
carbon trading, 478–479
CardCash, 878
CARES Act, 821
cartels, 424–425, 434
Case, Anne, 700
cash
Japanese use of, 890–891
uses of, 854
catch-share schemes, 506
causal relationships, 52
CBO. *See* Congressional Budget Office (CBO)
CDs. *See* certificates of deposit (CDs)
cell phones, driving while using, as negative externality, 468
central banks, 651, 865. *See also* European Central Bank (ECB); Federal Reserve System (Fed)
inflation targeting by, 900
monetary policy and. *See* monetary policy
certificates of deposit (CDs), 853, 886
chained dollars, 637
Chanel, 461
Chávez, Hugo, 110, 140, 921
checkable bank deposits, 850
Chetty, Raj, 44, 519
Chevalier, Judith, 121
Chicken of the Sea, 421
Chick-fil-A, 447
Chile
copper production of, 177
financial intermediation in, 736
productivity and wages in, 222
China
air pollution in, 705
clothing industry of, 38
command economy of, 2, 124
currency of, pegging of, 983–984
current account surplus of, 968
demand for commodities of, 177
economic growth and greenhouse gases in, 475
economic growth of, 680–681, 682, 685–686, 692–693, 697

government spending on education in, 694
infrastructure spending in, 693
labor costs in, 970
one-child policy in, 11–12
Pearl River Delta in, 1, 627
pegging of yuan and, 983–984
pork shortage and, 376
purchasing power parity and Big Mac price in, 977
rare earth market and, 390–391
ride-hailing services in, 153
smartphone production of, 217–218, 221
spending on food in, 173
standard of living in, 1, 4
tradable emissions permits in, 479
trade surplus of, 619, 620
trade war with United States, 240
transition to a free-market system, 123–124
U.S. job loss due to imports from, 231–232
China Shock, 231–232
Chipotle, 295
chocolate industry, 426–427
choice. *See* consumer choice; individual choice
Christmas tree market, 355
Chrysler, 45, 421
Churchill, Winston, 498
cigarettes, tax on, 200–201
Circuit City, 377
circular-flow diagram, 38–41
balance of payments and, 967
national accounts and, 628–629
cities. *See also specific cities*
megacities, 1
traffic congestion in. *See* traffic congestion
Citizens' Bank of Louisiana, 855
classical macroeconomics, 944
Keynesian economics vs., 945–946
classical model of the price level, 916–918, 944
Clean Air Act, 473, 474
clean energy sources, 480
climate, comparative advantage and, 222
climate change, 472, 479–482
causes of, 480
costs and benefits of mitigation efforts and, 481–482
economic growth and, 703–704
Paris Agreement and, 704
policies to address, 480–481
closed economies, savings-investment spending identity in, 714–715
clothing industry
comparative advantage in, 38, 40
in Hong Kong, 224–225
Club of Rome, 702
coal industry, decline of, 473
Coase, Ronald, 472
Coase theorem, 472
Coca-Cola, 68, 163

Cold War, 430, 438
collective bargaining, 559, 662
college education
earnings and, 543
opportunity cost of attending college and, 9–10, 265
tuition costs for, 171
unemployment rate for college graduates, 2007–2020 and, 657
collusion, 421, 424–427
tacit, 432
command economies, 2, 124
commercial banks, 873
Fed purchases and sales of Treasury bills and, 867
commercial paper, asset-backed, 875–876
commodities, 357, 794
changes in prices of, short-run aggregate supply curve and, 794, 795
glut of, 177–178
commodity-backed money, 852, 854–855
commodity money, 852
common resources, 123, 493, 494, 503–506
efficient use and maintenance of, 504–505
overuse problem and, 503–504
comparative advantage, 36
absolute advantage vs., 37
in clothing industry, 38, 40
gains from trade and, 34–37
international trade and, 37–38, 217–219
misconceptions about, 221–222
production possibility frontier and, 218–219
in real world, 37–38
sources of, 222–224
compensating differentials, 557–558
compensation of employees, 545. *See also* wages
competition. *See* monopolistic competition; oligopoly; perfect competition
competitive markets, 68, 95
supply and demand model of. *See* demand curve; demand schedule; supply and demand model; supply curve; supply schedule
complements, 73
changes in prices of, shifts of the demand curve and, 73, 76
perfect, 316
in production, 82
computer operating systems, network externalities and, 388
Condé Nast Publications, 146
condiments, demand for, 287
congestion pricing, 77
Congressional Budget Office (CBO), 226, 664, 797, 803
Conner, Christopher, 427

conservatism, 517, 536
constant marginal cost, 254
constant returns to scale, 346
consumer(s)
changes in number of, shifts of the demand curve and, 75–77
excise tax paid mainly by, price elasticities and, 189–190
inefficient allocation to, 136
preferences of. See preferences
price-taking. See Perfect competition
rational. See marginal utility; rational consumer; utility
reallocation of consumption among, total surplus and, 117–118
consumer choice
income and, 318–320
income effect and, 321–323
marginal rate of substitution and, 306–309, 311–312
perfect complements and, 316
perfect substitutes and, 314–315
preferences and, 312–313
price increases and, 317–318
prices and, 311–312
slope of budget line and, 310–311
substitution effect and, 321–323
tangency condition and, 309–310
Consumer Confidence Index, 787
Consumer Financial Protection Bureau, 877
consumer price index (CPI), 619, 640–641
calculation of, 640
indexing to, 642–643
makeup of, 641
consumer spending, 628, 753–759
in aggregate spending, 630
autonomous, 754
budget deficits and, 823
consumption function and, 753–756
crowding out of, 822
current disposable income and, 753–756
shift of aggregate consumption function and, 756–759
consumer surplus, 103
efficiency of markets and, 116–120
gains from trade and, 115–116
imports and, 227
individual, 105
price changes and, 107–109
reduction by taxes, 196–197
rent control and, 138–139
total, 105
willingness to pay and, 104–107
consumption
income and, 318–320
inefficiently low, 495
marginal propensity to consume and, 750–752
nonrivals in, 494

optimal. See optimal consumption entries
reallocation among consumers, total surplus and, 117–118
rivals in, 494, 495
tax on, income tax vs., 208
utility and, 280–281
consumption bundles, 280, 639–640
consumption decisions, marginal analysis and, 259–260
consumption function, 753–756
aggregate, 755–756
consumption possibilities, 283–284
contraction(s). See Great Recession; recession(s)
contractionary fiscal policy, inflationary gaps and, 821–822
contractionary monetary policy, 898
convergence hypothesis, 697
copyrights, 390
core inflation, 671
core inflation rate, 933
coronavirus pandemic
actual and potential output and, 797
CARES Act and, 821
contactless payment and, 890
gasoline consumption and, 170
global effects of, 987
hazard pay and, 558
national security argument, 236
recession associated with, 807, 987
relief package and, 20
risks to economic activity posed by, 885
shortages and, 132
unemployment related to, 652, 653, 654, 664
zero interest rate policy and, 957
cost(s)
administrative, of a tax, 198–199
average. See average entries
of climate change mitigation, 481–482
of college tuition, 171
of disinflation, 932–934
explicit, 248–249
external, 468. See also negative externalities; pollution
of finding a bride in China, 12
fixed. See fixed costs
of fixing the exchange rate, 982
of health care, control under ACA, 533
implicit, 248–249, 250
of a life, 260
marginal. See marginal cost; marginal cost curve
menu, of inflation, 669
opportunity. See opportunity cost
producer surplus and, 111–113

projects with, calculating present value of, 277
of quantity controls, 151–152
shoe-leather, of inflation, 667–668
in short run, 362–363
short- vs. long-run, 343–348
social. See marginal social cost entries
summary of, 347
sunk, 261–262
of taxation, 196–199
total. See total cost
transaction, 472, 730
unit-of-account, of inflation, 669–670
variable, 332
cost-benefit analysis, 501
Costco, 270, 568, 663
cost curves, 327, 328, 332–333
average total, 337, 345–347
marginal, 254, 339, 340, 341
total, 333
counterfeit currency, 849
COVID-19 pandemic. See coronavirus pandemic
CPI. See consumer price index (CPI)
crabs, Alaskan fishing of, 151–152
credit cards, in Japan, 890
credit markets, changes in, shifts of the money demand curve and, 890
cross-price elasticity of demand, 172–173, 178
crowding out, 723
Friedman's views on, 950
by government borrowing, 822
by government spending, 822
rising government debt and, 835
Cuba, economy of, 2
currency(ies). See also dollar (U.S.); euro; exchange rate(s); exchange rate regimes; money
appreciation of, 972
Chinese, pegging of, 983–984
counterfeit, 849
depreciation of, 972
devaluation of, 985
digital (virtual), 854
opportunity cost of holding, 886–887
printing of, 938
quantity in circulation, 850, 851, 854
revaluation of, 985
wages and, 987–988
currency crises, 983
currency in circulation, 850, 854
global comparison of, 851
current account, 966
deficits in, 966, 968
exchange rates and, 976
GDP and GNP and, 966
surpluses in, 968
Current Population Survey, 653
curves, 53–59. See also specific curves

calculating area below or above, 59, 60
horizontal, 55–56
maximum and minimum points on, 58–59
nonlinear, 56–58
slope of, 54–59
vertical, 55–56
Cutler, David, 44
cycle of poverty, 485
cyclically adjusted budget balance, 829
business cycle and, 830–832
cyclical unemployment, 663
output gap and, 923, 924
Czech Republic, productivity and wages in, 222

D

deadlines, 268–269
deadweight loss
from monopoly, 400
price ceilings and, 135
tariffs and, 233–234
of a tax, 196–198, 199–200
deadweight-loss triangle, 135
Deaton, Angus, 700
DeBeers, 383, 385, 386, 387, 391, 400
debit cards, in Japan, 890
debt
budget deficits vs., 835
government. See public debt
monetization of, 918
public. See public debt
debt deflation, 934
debt–GDP ratio, 837–838
debt spiral, 836, 840
decision making, 247–274
accounting profit vs. economic profit and, 239–252
behavioral economics and. See behavioral economics
costs, benefits, and profits and, 248–249
economic, common mistakes in, 265–267
"either-or," 251–252
"how much." See marginal analysis
marginal decisions and, 10. See also marginal analysis
production, short-run, 365–368
sunk costs and, 261–262
decreasing marginal benefit, 256
decreasing marginal cost, 254–255
decreasing returns to scale, 346–347
dedicated taxes, 839
deductibles, 597
default
on bonds, 732
rising government debt and, 835, 836–837
strategic, 265
deficits
budget. See budget deficits
in current account, 966, 968
trade, 619

deflation, 618, 805, 934–937
  causes of, 618
  debt, 934
  expected, effects of, 934–936
  Great Depression and, 671
  in Japan, 936
  pain of, 618
  recessions and, 671
  in United States, 671
De La Rue, 938
demand. *See also* demand curve;
    demand schedule; supply
    and demand model
  aggregate. *See* AD–AS model;
    aggregate demand;
    aggregate demand curve
  for commercial real estate, 738
  cross-price elasticity of, 172–173
  derived, 544
  elastic, 165, 167
  elasticity of. *See* elasticity of
    demand; price elasticity of
    demand
  excess. *See* shortages
  excise taxes and, 186–188
  income-elastic, 174, 178
  income elasticity of, 173–174
  income-inelastic, 174
  inelastic, 161, 165, 167
  law of, 783
  for loanable funds, 718–720
  for money, 886–891
  perfectly elastic, 164–165
  perfectly inelastic, 164
  quantity demanded vs., 72
  for stocks, 737–738
  unit-elastic, 165–166, 167
  for U.S. dollars, foreign
    exchange market and,
    974–975
demand curve, 68–78
  aggregate. *See* aggregate
    demand curve
  consumer surplus and, 104–110
  demand schedule and, 69–70
  domestic, international trade
    and, 226–228
  for factors, shifts of, 550–551
  individual, 75, 77
  for insurance, 588, 589
  market, 77
  of a monopolist, 391–392, 394
  price elasticity along, 168
  shifts of, 70–78
demand price, 149
demand schedule, 69–70, 104
demand shocks, 801–802
  Great Depression caused by,
    782, 801–802
  Great Depression ended by, 802
  Great Recession caused by,
    781, 800
  macroeconomic policy and,
    808–809
  negative, 804
  supply shocks vs., 802–804, 807
Denmark
  Gini coefficient in, 521, 523
  productivity and wages in, 222
  welfare state of, 537

Depardieu, Gerard, 195
dependent variables, 52–53
deposit insurance, 297, 735, 858,
    864
depositors, 734
depreciation, 972
depressions. *See* Great Depression
deregulation
    of airline industry, 145
    of electric utilities, 396–397
derivatives, 877
derived demand, 544
Desktime, 121
devaluation, 985
diamond monopoly, 383, 385, 386,
    387, 391, 400
Diapers.com, 406, 407
Dickens, Charles, 545
digital currency, 854
digital personalized pricing, 412
**diminishing marginal rate of
    substitution,** 308
diminishing marginal utility,
    principle of, 264, 281–282
diminishing returns effect, of
    increasing output on
    average total cost, 338,
    339
diminishing returns to an input,
    330
**diminishing returns to physical
    capital,**
    686–687, 688
Dior, 461
direct foreign investment,
    financial account and, 968
discount(s), volume, 412
discount rate, 866–867
discount window, 858–859, 866,
    892
discouraged workers, 653–654
discretionary fiscal policy, 828,
    950
discretionary monetary policy,
    950
disinflation, 671
  costs of, 932–934
  global comparison of, 932
Disney, 208
Disneyland Paris, 965
disposable income
  current, consumer spending
    and, 753–756
  future, expected, changes in,
    aggregate consumption
    function and, 756–757
  government transfers and, 820
diversification, 579, 590–593, 731
  limits of, 592–593
  mutual funds and, 733
  risk and, 590–592
dixies, 855
Dodd–Frank financial regulatory
    reform act of 2010,
    876–877
"Does Monetary Policy Matter?"
    (Romer and Romer), 902
Dollar Shave Club, 463
dollar (U.S.)
  chained, 637

history of, 854–855
other countries' prices quoted
    in, 669
shift in demand for, foreign
    exchange market and,
    974–975
strong, international trade and,
    978–979
domestic demand curve,
    226–228
domestic supply curve, 226–228
dominant strategy, 430
double coincidence of wants, 850
double-dip recessions, 807
Dow Jones Industrial Average, 737
driving while distracted, as
    negative externality, 468
drugs. *See* pharmaceutical
    industry
Dualstar Entertainment, 146
duopolists, 424
duopoly, 424–425

E

early-childhood intervention
    programs, 485
Earned Income Tax Credit (EITC),
    204, 526, 536
earnings. *See* disposable income;
    income; wages
East Asia. *See also specific
    countries*
  economic growth of, 696–697
  real GDP per capita in, 696, 697
Easterbrook, Steve, 295
eBay, 388, 403
ECB. *See* European Central Bank
    (ECB)
econometrics, 758–759
economic crises. *See also* Great
    Depression; Great
    Recession
  in Argentina, 638
  bank runs during, 859
economic fluctuations. *See*
    business cycle; Great
    Depression; Great
    Recession; recession(s)
economic growth, 4
  change in levels vs. rate of
    change and, 683
  greenhouse gases and, 475
  long-run. *See* long-run
    economic growth;
    sustainable long-run
    economic growth
  over time, 20–21
  production possibility frontier
    and, 32–34
  unemployment and, 655–657
economic inequality, 520–522. *See
    also* poverty
  international comparisons of,
    521
  mean versus median household
    income and, 520–521
  as a problem, 521–522
economic insecurity, 522
  alleviating, as rationale for
    welfare state, 516–517

economic interaction.
    See interaction
economic loss, 250
economic models. *See* models;
    specific models
economic policy. *See also* fiscal
    policy; macroeconomic
    policy; monetary policy;
    stabilization policy
  economists' age and, 781
economic profit, 250, 362, 375
  accounting profit vs., 249–252
economics, 2. *See also*
    macroeconomics;
    microeconomics
  behavioral. *See* behavioral
    economics
  Keynesian. *See* Keynesian
    economics
  positive vs. normative, 41–42
  study of, 7
  supply-side, 952
economic signals, 122–123
The Economics of Welfare (Pigou),
    474–475
economic thought,
    macroeconomic. *See*
    macroeconomics
economies of scale. *See* increasing
    returns to scale
economists
  age of, economic policies and,
    781
  agreement among, 43–44
  disagreement among, 42–43
economy(ies), 2
  closed, savings-investment
    spending identity in,
    714–715
  command (planned), 2, 124
  comparison of sizes of, 627
  convergence of, 697
  gig, 665, 673
  market. *See* market economies
  open, 619
  self-correcting, 805, 807
  self-regulating, 609
  sharing. *See* sharing economy
  trade and interdependence
    among, 771
ecotourism, in Brazil, 509
education. *See also* college
    education; human capital
  accounting profit vs. economic
    profit and, 249–252
  economic growth and, 692–693
  government subsidies to,
    economic growth and, 694
  implicit and explicit costs of,
    248–249
  lack of, poverty and, 519
  marginal cost of a year
    of, 253
effective exchange rate, real net
    exports and, 979
effective price, 110
efficiency, 15–16. *See also*
    inefficiency
  in allocation, 30–31
  of allocation of risk, 588–589

efficiency (*continued*)
conflict between equity and, 16, 120
cost of efficiency in long-run equilibrium and, 375
efficient supply of private goods and, 495
of markets, consumer and producer surplus and, 116–120
in production, 30–31
production possibility frontier and, 30–31
of taxes, equity vs., 202–203, 205–206
trade-off between equity and, 16, 120, 202–203
of use and maintenance of a common resource, 504–505
efficiency-wage model, 560
efficiency wages, 559, 560
structural unemployment and, 662–663
efficient allocation of risk, 588–589
efficient markets hypothesis, 739
Eichengreen, Barry, 609–610
EITC. *See* Earned Income Tax Credit
"either-or" decision making, 251–252
elastic demand, 165, 167
elasticity, 159–184
deadweight loss of a tax and, 199–200
of demand. *See* elasticity of demand; income elasticity of demand; price elasticity of demand
estimating, 163
price. *See* price elasticity of demand
price discrimination and, 409–410
summary of, 178
of supply. *See* elasticity of supply; price elasticity of supply
elasticity of demand
cross-price, 172–173, 178
deadweight loss of a tax and, 196–198, 199–200
income. *See* income elasticity of demand
price. *See* price elasticity of demand
elasticity of supply
deadweight loss of a tax and, 196–198, 199–200
price. *See* price elasticity of supply
electricity
cost of, 489
deregulation of industry, 396–397
SMART Grid technologies and, 342
social cost of, 472–473

El Salvador, clothing industry of, 40
embedded inflation, 902
emissions taxes, 474–475
employers, mismatches between employees and, 663
employment. *See also* labor *entries;* wages
labor supply and. *See* labor supply
number of hours worked and, 566
trade-off between work and leisure and, 563–564, 573–576
workplace discrimination and, 560–561
work vs. labor and, 563–564, 573–576
employment. *See also* labor *entries;* unemployment; unemployment rate; wages
definition of, 652
growth in, 684
productivity and, 684
termination of, 658. *See also* unemployment
employment-based health insurance, 530
employment subsidies, 665
endorsements, monopolistic competition and, 459–460
Energizer, 463
energy. *See also* oil
fossil fuels and climate change and, 703
renewable and clean sources of, 480
solar, 84–85, 841
England. *See* United Kingdom
English language proficiency, lack of, poverty and, 519
entry
barriers to, 387–390
free, 358, 449
in monopolistic competition, 449
environment
pollution and. *See* climate change; pollution
sustainable long-run economic growth and, 703–705
environmental policies, comparison of, 477–478
environmental standards, 474
equilibrium, 14–15, 91–92
income-expenditure. *See* income-expenditure equilibrium; income-expenditure equilibrium GDP
in labor market, 552
in loanable funds market, 721–722
macroeconomic. *See* macroeconomic equilibrium
market. *See* market equilibrium
Nash, 430

noncooperative, 430
shifts of the demand curve and, 90–91
shifts of the supply curve and, 91–92
traffic congestion as example of, 17–18
zero-profit, 454–455
equilibrium exchange rate, 972–975
equilibrium interest rate, 721–722, 891–893
equilibrium price, 86
finding, 86–89
equilibrium quantity, 86
finding, 86–89
equilibrium value of the marginal product, 553
equity, 16
ability-to-pay principle of tax fairness and, 202
behavioral economics and, 263
benefits principle of tax fairness and, 202
trade-off between efficiency and, 16, 120, 202–203
ERM. *See* Exchange Rate Mechanism (ERM)
An Essay on the Principle of Population (Malthus), 690
estate tax, 206
Estonia, productivity and wages in, 222
Ethereum, 854
Ethiopia, wheat yield in, 330
EU. *See* European Union
euro
countries choosing not to adopt, 983–984
transition to, 983
euro area
corporate bonds in, 735
purchasing power parity and Big Mac price in, 977
recovery from recession of 2007–2009 and, 936–937
Europe. *See also* euro area; European Union; *specific countries*
Gini coefficients in, 521
multiplier effects of austerity following Global Financial Crisis of 2009 in, 829
trade war with United States, 240
European Central Bank (ECB), 865, 869–870
interest rates raised by, in 2011, 651, 781
recovery from recession of 2007–2009 and, 936–937
European Union (EU), 237–238
antitrust policy in, 404, 407, 435, 436
recessions in, 614
tradable emissions permits in, 478, 479
wheat yield in, 330
Eurosclerosis, 663
Eveready Batteries, 406

excess capacity, 458
excess demand. *See* shortages
excess reserves, 862
excess supply. *See* surpluses
exchange, money as medium of, 851
exchange market intervention, 980–982
exchange rate(s), 971–988
current account and, 976
devaluation and revaluation and, 985
effective, real net exports and, 979
equilibrium, 972–975
fixed. *See* fixed exchange rates
floating. *See* floating exchange rates
international business cycles and, 986–987
international trade and, 978–979
locked, 983
macroeconomic policy and, 984–988
purchasing power parity and, 977–978
real, inflation and, 975–977
real vs. nominal, 975–977
Exchange Rate Mechanism (ERM), 983
exchange rate regimes, 979–984
Bretton Woods and, 983
dilemma concerning, 982
euro and, 983
fixed, 980–982
pegging of yuan and, 983–984
excise taxes, 186–193
costs of, 196
price elasticities and incidence of, 189–191
quantities and prices and, 186–188
revenue from, 192–193
tariffs as. *See* tariffs
excludability, 494, 495
expansion(s), 612. *See also* business cycle
definition of, 614
Spanish, 749
expansionary fiscal policy, 820–821. *See also* fiscal stimulus
arguments against, 822
budget deficits and, 823
crowding out and, 822
recessionary gaps and, 820–821
expansionary monetary policy, 897
expectations
changes in, shifts of the aggregate demand curve and, 786–787
changes in, shifts of the demand curve and, 74–75, 76
changes in, shifts of the supply curve and, 82–83, 84
for deflation, effects of, 934–936

rational, 951–952
for real GDP, investment spending and, 761
unrealistic, about future behavior, 266
expected rate of inflation, short-run Phillips curve and, 927–929, 930
expected utility, 581
expected value, 580
Expedia, 22
explicit costs, 248–249
export(s), 216, 628. *See also* international trade
net, 635
supply and demand and, 228–229
exporting industries, 230
export quotas, Chinese, on rare earths, 390
external benefits, 468. *See also* positive externalities
of a network externality, 486–487
external costs, 468
externalities, 123, 467–492
internalizing, 472
negative. *See* negative externalities; pollution
network. *See* network externalities
positive. *See* positive externalities
extreme weather, 579, 593
Exxon, 401, 435
ExxonMobil, 68, 208, 401

F

Facebook, 110, 388, 403, 406, 407
factor abundance, 223
factor demand, value of the marginal product and, 548–550
factor demand curve, shifts of, 550–551
factor distribution of income, 545
factor endowments, comparative advantage and, 222–223
factor income
earned from firms in the economy, GDP as, 633–634
income distribution and, 544–545
U.S., 965
factor intensity, 223
factor markets, 39, 543, 544
in circular-flow diagram, 629
factor prices, 230, 544
factors of production, 33, 543, 544–546
change in supply of, shifts of the factor demand curve and, 551
forestland as, 223
movement between industries, 229–230
other inputs vs., 544
production possibility frontier and, 33

fair insurance policies, 582
fairness. *See* equity
Fannie Mae, 870, 873–874
farming. *See* agriculture
farmland
Ogallala Aquifer and, 505
preservation of, 483–484
price of, 114–115
fast-food industry, as monopolistically competitive industry, 447
FC. See fixed costs
FDIC. *See* Federal Deposit Insurance Corporation
Fed. *See* Federal Reserve System
Federal Deposit Insurance Corporation, 858
Federal Deposit Insurance Corporation (FDIC), 735
federal funds market, 866
federal funds rate, 866
lowering target range for, 885
target for, 885, 891, 894, 896
Taylor rule and, 899
Federal Insurance Contributions Act (FICA) tax, 203–204, 205
incidence of, 191–192
Federal Open Market Committee (FOMC), 865–866
Federal Reserve System (Fed), 609, 789, 865–869
ability to cause contractions or expansions, 902
assets of, 867, 868, 870–871
balance sheet of, 870–871
creation of, 871, 872–873
discount rate and, 866–867
Great Depression and, 953–954
Great Recession and, 870–871, 876, 896
interest on assets of, 868
interest rates reduced by, in 2011, 651, 781
liabilities of, 867
monetary base and, 863
monetary policy and. *See* monetary policy
monetization of debt by, 918
money multiplier and, 864
open-market operations of, 867–869
quantitative easing and, 901, 936, 956
reserve requirements and, 866–867
structure of, 865–866
target federal funds rate and, 885, 891, 894, 896
tools for increasing or decreasing the money supply, 892
Federal Trade Commission (FTC), pharmaceutical industry and, 359
fiat money, 853
FICA. *See* Federal Insurance Contributions Act tax

final goods and services, 629
domestically produced, GDP as spending on, 632–633
GDP as value of, 631–632
finance, behavioral, 740
financial account, 966
modeling, 968–969
surplus in, 966
financial assets, 729. *See also* bank deposits; bonds; loan(s); loan-backed securities; stock(s)
asset price expectations and, 739–740
macroeconomics and prices of, 741
price fluctuations of, 736–742
financial capital, definition of, 716
financial crises. *See also* banking crises; bank runs; Great Depression; Great Recession
multiplier effects of austerity following Global Financial Crisis of 2009 and, 829
financial intermediaries, 733–735. *See also* bank(s)
financial markets, 714, 729
in circular-flow diagram, 629
financial pressure, rising government debt and, 835–836
financial risk, 580–581, 730–731
financial services industry, international trade and, 224
financial system, 713, 729–736
financial intermediaries and, 733–735
government regulation of, 694
partial nationalization of, 876
tasks of, 730–731
types of financial assets and, 731–733
well-functioning, economic growth and, 694
Finland
productivity and wages in, 222
tradable emissions permits in, 479
fire protection, 494
as public good, 497
firms, 39, 328. *See also* producer(s)
in circular-flow diagram, 628, 629
factor income earned from, in GDP, 630, 633–634
interdependence between, oligopoly and, 422
spending by, 628, 629
fiscal austerity
in Greece, 829, 956–957
multiplier effects of, 828–829
recovery from Great Recession and, 959
stimulus vs., 956–957
fiscal policy, 609, 817–846
austerity. *See* fiscal austerity
budget and total spending and, 819–820

budget balance as measure of, 830
budget deficits and, 830–832
contractionary, 821–822
dangers posed by rising government debt and, 835–837
debt spiral and, 836, 840
deficits, surpluses, and debt and, 835
deficits and debt in practice and, 837–838
discretionary, 828, 950
expansionary. *See* expansionary fiscal policy; fiscal stimulus
government spending and, 818, 819–820
implicit liabilities and, 838–839
lags in, 823–824
long-run implications of, 834–840
multiplier and, 825–829
shifts of the aggregate demand curve and, 787, 788–789
taxes and, 818, 819
transfer payments and, 819
fiscal stimulus, 956–957. *See also* expansionary fiscal policy
austerity vs., 956–957
under Obama, 821, 824, 959
of Obama vs. Trump, 824–825
Solana power plant and, 841
under Trump, 821
fiscal years, 835
Fisher, Irving, 934
Fisher effect, 727, 934
fishing
as common resource, 503
for crab, Alaskan, 151–152
overfishing and, 503, 506
fixed costs (*FC*), 332
average, 337–338
changing, 368
reduction by sharing economy, 347–348
fixed exchange rates, 979–982
advantages and disadvantages of, 982
devaluation and revaluation of, 985
floating rates vs., 982
fixed inputs, 328, 331
Flextronics International (Flex), 555–556
floating exchange rates, 980
fixed rates vs., 982
monetary policy under, 985–986
Flowspace, 349
FOMC. *See* Federal Open Market Committee
food
fast-food industry as monopolistically competitive industry and, 447
spending on, 173
food stamps, 515, 526, 536
Ford, 45
forecasts, 42

foreclosure, 265
foreign capital, economic growth and, 692
foreign exchange controls, 981
foreign exchange market, 971–972, 973. *See also* exchange rate(s); exchange rate regimes equilibrium in, shift in demand for U.S. dollars and, 974–975
foreign exchange reserves, 980
fossil fuels, 480
climate change and, 703
401(k) accounts, 267
Fowke, Benjamin, 489
fracking, 67, 467, 473, 752
framing bias, 267
France
economic growth of, 682
gasoline consumption in, 70
Gini coefficient in, 523
government debt of, 836
government spending and tax revenue in, 818
number of hours worked in, 566
productivity and wages in, 222
taxes in, 195, 207
tradable emissions permits in, 479
wages in, 141
franchises, 598
Francis, Daniel, 463
Freddie Mac, 870, 873–874
free entry and exit, 358
in monopolistically competitive industries, 449
free-rider problem, 495
free trade, 232
frictional unemployment, 659–660
Friedman, John, 519
Friedman, Milton
on business cycle, 614
on expected future income, 757
on importance of monetary policy, 949, 955
monetarism and, 949–951
A Monetary History of the United States, 1867–1960, 949, 953
natural rate hypothesis and, 951
on prevention of Great Depression, 949
A Theory of the Consumption Function, 757
Frisch, Ragnar, 944
FTC. *See* Federal Trade Commission
fundamentals, 739
Fung, Victor, 241
Furman, Jason, 943

G

gains from trade, 13–14
comparative advantage and, 34–37
consumer surplus and, 115–116
international trade and, 219–220

money and generation of, 850
producer surplus and, 115–116
gambling, 585
game theory, 427–434
arms race and resurgent cold war and, 430
prisoners' dilemma and, 428–431
repeated interaction and tacit collusion and, 431–432
gap, in health insurance coverage, 533
gasoline prices
consumption and, 70, 170
income and substitution effects and, 294
price controls on, 136
price elasticity of demand and, 170
gasoline tax, 202
Gates, Bill, 733
GDP. *See* gross domestic product (GDP)
GDP deflator, 642
GDP per capita, 637. *See also* real GDP per capita
Gebbia, Joe, 120
GE Capital, 877
gender discrimination, poverty and, 519
gender-wage gap, 559
Genentech, 262
General Electric, 877
General Mills, 357
General Motors (GM), 45, 421
bailout of, 622, 773
The General Theory of Employment, Interest and Money (Keynes), 609, 945, 946, 947
generic drugs, 358–359
gentrification, 131
Germany
apprentice system in, 561
current account surplus of, 968
gasoline consumption in, 70
Gini coefficient in, 523
government debt of, 836
inflation in, 668, 915
interest rates in, 957, 958
investment spending in, 717
number of hours worked in, 566
productivity and wages in, 222
savings-investment spending identity in, 717
trade surplus of, 619, 620
Getaround, 121
Giffen goods, 293–294, 323
gift cards, 878
gig economy, 673
reduction of unemployment by, 665
Gilded Age, 524
Gillette, 463
Gillette, King, 463
Gini coefficient, 521
Glaeser, Edward, 666
Glass-Steagall Act of 1933, 873
Global Financial Crisis of 2009, multiplier effects of austerity following, 829

globalization, 216–217. *See also* export(s); export *entries*; import *entries*; international trade; trade challenges to, 238–239
comparative advantage and. *See* comparative advantage
Great Depression and, 987
hyperglobalization and, 215, 217
global loanable funds market, 723–726
global middle class, 701
global supply chains, 215
GM. *See* General Motors
GNP. *See* gross national product
Goldin, Claudia, 524
goods and services
artificially scarce, 494, 507–508
balance of payments on, 966
complements. *See* complements
differentiation of, market structure and, 384
excludable, 494, 495
final. *See* final goods and services
Giffen, 293–294, 323
government purchases of. *See* government purchases of goods and services
inferior, 74, 293, 319–320
information, 507
as inputs. *See* inputs
intermediate, 629
luxury, price elasticity of demand for, 169
markets for, 629, 909
necessities, price elasticity of demand for, 169
nonexcludable, 494
nonrival in consumption, 494
normal, 74, 293, 319, 320
ordinary, 309
private. *See* private goods
public. *See* public goods
related. *See* complements; substitutes
rival in consumption, 494, 495
substitutes. *See* substitutes
Google, 208, 388, 403, 404, 406, 407, 422
Google Pay, 890
Gourville, John T., 270
governance, economic growth and, 694–695
government. *See also* Federal *and* federal *entries*
antitrust policy and. *See* antitrust policy
barriers to entry created by, 389–390
borrowing by, 277, 715, 822, 828
in circular-flow diagram, 628, 629
debt of. *See* public debt
health insurance provided by, 530–531. *See also* Affordable Care Act (ACA); Medicaid; Medicare
implicit liabilities of, 838–839

macroeconomic policy and. *See* fiscal policy; macroeconomic policy; monetary policy; stabilization policy
macroeconomic policy tools of. *See* government spending; tax(es)
market intervention by. *See* price ceilings; price controls; price floors
price controls and, 130. *See also* price ceilings; price floors; rent controls
regulation by. *See* regulation
role in promoting economic growth, 693–695
spending by. *See* government spending
subsidies from, economic growth and, 693–694
taxes and. *See* excise taxes; Federal Insurance Contributions Act tax; tax(es)
government borrowing, 715. *See also* public debt
changes in, shifts in demand for loanable funds and, 722
crowding out by, 822
government budget. *See also* budget *entries*
fiscal policy and, 819–820
government debt. *See* public debt
government policy. *See also* fiscal policy; macroeconomic policy; monetary policy; stabilization policy
to address climate change, 480–481
to address new generation of market power, 405–406
aggregate demand and, 787, 788–789
economic growth and, 693–695
macroeconomic policy tools and, 20
monopoly and, 399–403
natural rate of unemployment and, 665
pollution and, 473–479
spending and, 19
structural unemployment and, 663
government purchases of goods and services, 628
fiscal policy and, 825–826
multiplier effects of, 825–826
during World War II, 948
government spending, 19–20
in aggregate spending, 630
crowding out by, 822
ending of Great Depression and, 948
fiscal austerity and. *See* fiscal austerity
fiscal policy and, 818, 819–820
fiscal stimulus and. *See* fiscal stimulus
time lag and, 824
during World War II, 948

government transfers, 516, 628. *See also* welfare state
  changes in, multiplier effects of, 826–827
  disposable income and, 820
  fiscal policy and, 819
  implicit liability for, 838–839
Goznak, 938
Grameen America, 743
graphs, 51–66. *See also specific curves*
  bar, 62
  calculating area below or above a curve and, 59, 60
  curves on, 53–54
  horizontal and vertical curves on, 55–56
  interpretation of, 62–63
  linear curves on, 53–54
  maximum and minimum points of, 58–59
  models and, 51
  nonlinear curves on, 53, 56–58
  numerical, 60–64
  omitted variables and, 63–64
  pie charts, 61, 62
  reverse causality and, 64
  scale of, 62–63
  scatter diagrams, 60–61
  slope of curves on, 54–59
  time-series, 60, 61
  two-variable, 51–53
  variables and, 51
Great Britain. *See* United Kingdom
Great Compression, 524
Great Depression, 19, 607, 609
  aggregate supply curve during, 800
  bank runs during, 859, 864
  beginning of, 613
  cause of, 782, 801–802, 953–954
  deflation and, 671
  demand shock and, 801–802
  econometrics and, 758–759
  end of, 789, 802, 948
  Friedman and Schwartz's views on, 949
  global effects of, 987
  government spending and end of, 789
  Great Recession compared with, 610
  international impact of, 987
  Keynes' analysis of, 945–947
  liquidity trap in, 935
  nominal wages during, 793
  origin of macroeconomics and, 171, 609, 758, 764
  Roosevelt's efforts to turn around, 947
  Schumpeter's views on, 944
  World War II and, 945
Great Leap Forward, 124
Great Moderation, 955
Great Recession, 607, 609–610
  aftermath of, 876–877, 936–937
  beginning of, 824
  budget deficit during, 830
  business investment in, 763

  demand shock causing, 781, 800
  expansion after, 545
  Fed's response to, 870–871, 876, 896
  fiscal policy revival and, 956–957
  fiscal stimulus and, 821, 824, 959
  Great Depression compared with, 610
  housing bubble and, 870, 874–876
  inability of conventional monetary policy to prevent, 956
  recovery from, 958–959
  shadow banking and, 874–876
  sticky wages in, 799
  welfare state programs and poverty rates in, 528
Great Stink, 493, 494
Greece
  austerity in, 829, 956–957
  budget deficit and debt of, 834
  cutting of wages in, 987–988
  government debt of, 836
  productivity and wages in, 222
  recession in, 607
  trade surplus of, 620–621
  unemployment rate in, 607
Green Acres Program, 483–484
greenbacks, 855
greenhouse gases, 472, 479, 703. *See also* acid rain; pollution
  cap and trade systems and, 476, 478–479
  climate change and, 479–481
  economic growth and, 475
  tax on emissions of, 482
Greenspan, Alan, 865
gross domestic product (GDP), 627, 630
  calculating, 630–635
  components of, 633, 634–635
  current account and, 966
  imputed value in, 632
  income-expenditure equilibrium, 767–768
  information provided by, 635
  life satisfaction and, global comparison of, 638
  marginal propensity to consume and, 750, 751–752
  nominal, 636–637, 638
  per capita, 637
  real. *See* real GDP; real GDP per capita
  uses of, 635
  well-being and, 638
gross national product (GNP), 966
growth accounting, 685, 687–689
growth recessions, 657

H

Hachette, 414
Hamilton, Alexander, 185
Hardin, Phil, 349
Harry's, 463

Head Start program, 485
health care, 529–535
  Affordable Care Act and. *See* Affordable Care Act
  in other countries, 531–532
health insurance
  adverse selection death spiral and, 595–596
  employment-based, 530
  government, 530–531. *See also* Affordable Care Act; Medicaid; Medicare
  need for, 529–530
  private, 529–530
  private health insurance market death spiral and, 529
Heat, 461
Heckscher–Ohlin model, 223, 230, 231
Hendren, Nathaniel, 519
herd mentality, 740
Herfindahl-Hirschman Index (HHI), 423
Hershey Canada, 427
HHI. *See* Herfindahl–Hirschman Index
higher education. *See* college education
Hitachi Automotive, 421, 424
Hitler, Adolf, 805, 945
Holiday Inn, 461
Hollande, Francois, 195
home mortgages. *See* mortgages
homeowner insurance, 599
Honda, 811
Honduras, clothing industry of, 38
Hong Kong
  clothing manufacture in, 224–225
  economic growth of, 697
  Li & Fung and, 241
horizontal axis, 52
horizontal curves, 55–56
horizontal intercept, 54
hourly wage, 915
hours worked, international comparison of, 566
household(s), 39
  in circular-flow diagram, 628, 629
  spending by. *See* consumer spending
  total factor income earned by, GDP as, 630
household income, mean vs. median, 520–521
household work, imputing the value of, 632
housing. *See also* Fannie Mae; Freddie Mac; mortgages
  mortgage delinquencies and, 741–742
  prices of, determination of, 738–739
housing bubble, 870
  subprime lending and, 874–876
"how much" decision making. *See* marginal analysis
Hoynes, Hilary, 44

human capital, 544, 558. *See also* college education; education
  definition of, 716
  increases in, productivity and, 685
  provision of, 714
Hungary, productivity and wages in, 222
hydraulic fracturing, 67
hyperglobalization, 215, 217
hyperinflation
  Armenian, 915
  Brazilian, 668, 669
  German, 668, 915
  logic of, 919–920
  Nicaraguan, 915
  Venezuelan, 915, 938
  Zimbabwean, 669, 915

I

IBM, 484
Iceland
  cutting of wages in, 987–988
  individual transferable quotas in, 506
  inflation and money supply in, 906
  productivity and wages in, 222
illegal activity, price floors and, 145
illiquid assets, 731
IMF. *See* International Monetary Fund (IMF)
imperfect competition, 422. *See also* monopolistic competition; oligopoly
imperfectly competitive markets, price setting in, 791, 792
imperfect substitutes, 449
implicit cost(s), 248–249
implicit cost of capital, 250
implicit liabilities, 838–839
implicit rent, 738
import(s), 216, 628. *See also* international trade
  marginal propensity to import and, 771
  supply and demand and, 226–228
import-competing industries, 230
import quotas, 233
  effects of, 233–234
imputation, of the value of household work, 632
incentives, 10–11
  equilibrium and, 14–15
  for individual choices, to address climate change, 481
incidence, of a tax, 188–191
  price elasticities and, 189–191
income. *See also* wages
  changes in, shifts of the demand curve and, 74, 76
  college education and, 543
  compensation of employees in, 545
  consumption and, 318–320
  disposable. *See* disposable income

income (*continued*)
  factor. *See* factor income
  global comparison of, 523
  household, mean vs. median, 520–521
  poverty threshold and, 517
  real, 667
  risk aversion and, 585
  savings level and, 757
  share spent on a good, price elasticity of demand and, 170
  share spent on food, 173
  spending and, 19
  U.S. regional disparities in, 699–701
income distribution, 39
  factor incomes and, 544–545
  marginal productivity theory of. *See* marginal productivity theory of income distribution
income effect, 293, 294
  consumption and, 321–323
  labor supply and, 564, 574
  market demand curve and, 293–294
income-elastic demand, 174, 178
income elasticity of demand, 173–174
income-expenditure equilibrium, 766–768
  aggregate demand curve and, 784–785
income-expenditure equilibrium GDP, 767–768
income-expenditure model, 763–772
  equilibrium and, 766–768
  international trade and, 771
  multiplier process and inventory adjustment and, 768–770
  planned aggregate spending and real GDP and, 764–766
income-inelastic demand, 174
income inequality. *See also* poverty
  alleviating, as rationale for welfare state, 516
  long-term trends in, in United States, 523–525
  welfare state effects on, 527–528
income support programs. *See* income inequality; poverty; Social Security; welfare state
income tax, 205. *See also* tax(es)
  consumption tax vs., 208
  federal, 203
  negative, 526
  value-added tax vs., 43
increasing marginal cost, 254
increasing returns to scale, 346–347
  international trade and, 224
  monopoly and, 387, 388
  oligopoly and, 422

independent events, 590
independent variable, 52–53
index funds, 592
indexing to the CPI, 642–643
India
  economic growth and greenhouse gases in, 475
  economic growth of, 679, 680–681, 682, 685–686
  inflation and money supply in, 906
  purchasing power parity and Big Mac price in, 977
  railroad lines in, 177
  ride-hailing services in, 153
  voting as a public good in, 500
indifference curve(s), 301–305
  consumer choice and. *See* consumer choice
  labor supply and, 576–578
  marginal rate of substitution and, 306–309, 311–312
  perfect complements and, 316
  perfect substitutes and, 314–315
  preferences and choices and, 312–313
  prices and, 311–312
  properties of, 304–305
  slope of, 305, 306
  slope of budget line and, 310–311
  tangency condition and, 309–310
  utility function and, 301–305
indifference curve maps, 303
individual choice, 7, 8–12
  incentives and, 10–11
  opportunity cost and, 9–10
  resource scarcity and, 8–9
  trade-offs and, 10
individual consumer surplus, 105
individual demand curve, 75, 77
individual labor supply curve, 564–565
  backward-bending, 576
  shifts of, 565–566
individual producer surplus, 112
individual supply curve, 83
  short-run, 366, 367
individual transferable quotas (ITQs), 506
Industrial Revolution, factor distribution of income and social change in, 545
industries. *See also specific industries*
  barriers to entry and, 387–390
  competition in, 423
  concentration of, 423
  exporting, 230
  factor movement between, 229–230
  free entry and exit and, 358, 449
  import-competing, 230
  output of. *See* output; production
  perfectly competitive, 356
  pricing power of, 792

industry supply curve, 370–376
  cost of production and efficiency in long-run equilibrium and, 375
  long-run, 371–375
  short-run, 370–371, 374–375
IndyMac Bank, run on, 859
inefficiency, 123. *See also* efficiency
  of monopolistic competition, 458
  price ceilings causing, 134–138
  price floors causing, 143–145
  taxes causing, 198
  of unemployment, 145
inefficient allocation of sales among sellers, 144–145
inefficient allocation to consumers, 136
inefficiently high quality, 145
inefficiently low consumption, 495
inefficiently low production, 495
inefficiently low quality, 137
inelastic demand, 161, 165, 167
infant industry argument for trade protection, 236–237
inferior goods, 74, 293
  income and consumption of, 319–320
inflation, 19, 617–619, 666–672, 915–942. *See also* hyperinflation
  Argentinian, 644
  Armenian, 915
  Billion Prices Project and, 644
  Brazilian, 668, 669
  causes of, 618
  classical model of the price level and, 916–918
  core, 671
  deflation and. *See* deflation
  disinflation and, 671, 932–934
  embedded, 902
  expected rate of, short-run Phillips curve and, 927–929
  Fisher effect and, 727, 934
  German, 668
  inflation tax and, 918–919
  interest rates and, 934
  Israeli, 669, 672
  long-run Phillips curve and, 930–931
  MacDonald's hamburger prices and, 619
  menu costs of, 669
  Mexican, 975
  monetarist view of, 951
  natural rate of unemployment and, 931–932
  Nicaraguan, 915
  nonaccelerating inflation rate of unemployment and, 931
  Okun's law and, 924
  output gap and unemployment rate and, 922–923
  pain of, 618
  Phillips curve and. *See* long-run Phillips curve; Phillips

curve; short-run Phillips curve
  price levels and, 666–677
  rate of change of prices and, 667–670
  real exchange rates and, 975–977
  shoe-leather costs of, 667–668
  Spanish, unemployment and, 929–930
  unemployment and. *See* long-run Phillips curve; Phillips curve; short-run Phillips curve
  in United Kingdom, 921–922
  in United States, 915, 921–922, 928, 975
  unit-of-account costs of, 669–670
  Venezuelan, 915, 921, 938
  winners and losers from, 670–671
  Zimbabwean, 231, 669, 915, 921
inflationary gaps, 806–807, 922
  contractionary fiscal policy and, 821–822
inflation rate, 640
  core, 933
  expected, short-run Phillips curve and, 927–929
  unemployment rate and. *See* Phillips curve
inflation targeting, 900–901
  global comparison of, 900
inflation tax, 918–919
inflows of funds, 716. *See also* capital flows
information, private. *See* private information
information goods, 507
infrastructure
  government subsidies to, economic growth and, 693
  U.S., deterioration of, 501–502
in kind, 669
in-kind benefits, 526
innovation, stifling, 404
inputs, 82
  agriculture and, 327
  availability of, price elasticity of supply and, 176–177
  changes in prices of, shifts in supply curve and, 82, 84
  diminishing returns to, 330
  factors of production vs., 544
  fixed, 328, 331
  production function and, 328–332
  variable, 328
Instagram, 406
institutions
  changes in, shifts of the money demand curve and, 890
  labor market, changes in, natural rate of unemployment and, 665
insurance, 585, 586–587
  adverse selection and, 595–596
  deductibles and, 597

demand curve for, 588, 589
deposit, 297, 735, 858, 864
fair insurance policies and, 582
health. *See* Affordable Care
Act; health insurance;
Medicaid; Medicare
homeowner, 599
life insurance companies and,
734
limitations of, 593
Lloyd's of London and,
586–587, 590, 593–594
market for, 588–589
moral hazard and, 596–597
premiums for, 529, 581–582
social, 516–517, 820. *See also*
Medicaid; Medicare;
Social Security
supply curve for, 588
underwriters and, 599
Intel, 387–388
intellectual property piracy (IPP),
508
intellectual property rights,
protection of, economic
growth and, 694
interaction, 7, 12–21
economy-wide, 18–21
efficiency and, 15–16
equilibrium and, 14–15
gains from trade and, 13–14
government intervention and,
16–17
interdependence, 424
oligopoly and, 422, 424
interest, on Fed's assets, 868
interest rate(s), 275
discount, 866–867
ECB raises in 2011, 651
equilibrium, 283–284,
721–722, 891–893,
897–899
Fed cut in, to fight Great
Recession, 896
federal funds. *See* federal funds
rate
Fisher effect and, 727
government debt and, 834
inflation and, 670, 934
investment spending and,
760–761
liquidity preference model of,
891
liquidity trap and. *See* liquidity
trap
loanable funds model of, 893
in long run, 914–915
in long run, changes in money
supply and, 904–905
long-term, 887, 895–896
low, monetary policy and,
957–958
models of, 891
nominal, 670
prime, 790
real, 670
in short run, 911–912
short-term, 887
in United States, 727–728
zero lower bound on, 898, 901,
936–936, 957

**interest rate effect of a change
in aggregate price level,**
783–784
**intermediate goods and
services,** 629
internalizing the externality, 472
international business cycles,
986–987
international capital flows
equilibrium exchange rate and,
974–975
financial account as measure of
inflows and, 968
loanable funds model and, 968
savings-investment spending
identity and, 715–717
two-way, 969–970
underlying determinants of, 969
international macroeconomics,
963–994
balance of payments accounts
and, 964–968
exchange rates and. *See*
exchange rate(s);
exchange rate regimes
modeling the financial account
and, 968–969
tax rates and, 970–971
two-way capital flows and,
969–970
underlying determinants of
international capital flows
and, 969
International Monetary Fund
(IMF), 835
international trade, 215–246. *See
also* export(s); import
entries
comparative advantage and. *See*
comparative advantage
export effects and, 228–229
gains from, 219–220
growing importance of,
216–217
import effects and, 226–228
income-expenditure model
and, 771
increasing returns to scale and,
224
lack of, 219
Ricardian model of, 218
trade protection and. *See* trade
protection
wages and, 229–231
international trade agreements,
237–238
inventories
multiplier process and
adjustment of, 768–770
unplanned investment spending
and, 761–762
inventory investment, 762
investing
emotion and, 592
stock market and, 592
investment. *See also* bonds;
stock(s)
inventory, 762
investment spending vs., 714
investment banks, 873
collapse of, 870

Fed purchases and sales of
Treasury bills and, 867
investment spending, 628,
759–763
in aggregate spending, 630
circular-flow diagram and, 629
crowding out of, 723, 822
economic growth and, 692
expected future real GDP and
production capacity and,
761
during Great Recession, 763
interest rate and, 760–761
for inventory, 762
investment vs., 714
opportunity cost of, 720
paradox of thrift and, 770
planned, 760
private, 714
savings-investment spending
identity and, 714–717
slumps in, 761
sources of, 714
trade-off between interest rate
and, 760–761
unplanned, inventories and,
761–762
U.S., 717
invisible hand, 3, 16, 609
IPP. *See* intellectual property
piracy
Ireland
economic growth of, 682
government debt of, 836
productivity and wages
in, 222
tax rate in, 970–971
wages in, 141
irrationality, 264–267
irrational markets, 739–740
Irwin, Neil, 781
Israel
inflation and money supply
in, 906
inflation in, 669, 672
productivity and wages in, 222
spending on food in, 173
taxes in, 207
Italy
disinflation in, 932
economic growth of, 695–696
gasoline consumption in, 70
government debt of, 836
productivity and wages in, 222
ITQs. *See* individual transferable
quotas

J

jaguars, protection by ecotourism,
509
Japan
automobile industry of, 45,
223–224
cash use in, 890–891
currency in circulation of, 851
current account surplus of, 968
deflation and liquidity trap in,
936
economic growth of, 692
gasoline consumption in, 70
government debt of, 836

government spending and tax
revenue in, 818
interest rates in, 891
natural resources and real GDP
per capita of, 689
number of hours worked in,
566
productivity and wages in, 222
purchasing power parity and
Big Mac price in, 977
real GDP per capita of, 691
wheat yield in, 330
Japanification, 936
J.C. Penney, 270, 377, 658
Jevons, William Stanley, 702
jingle mail, 265
job creation argument for trade
protection, 236
jobless recoveries, 657
job lock, 538
job loss, 658–659. *See also*
unemployment
job search, 659
job separations, 658
job-training programs, 665
Johnson, Lyndon, contractionary
fiscal policy under,
821–822
Johnson, Ron, 270
Joly, Hubert, 377
just-in-time production, 811
JustPark, 121

K

Kabob's Indian Grill, 447
Kahneman, Daniel, 263, 266
Kalanick, Travis, 96, 153
KAYAK, 22
Kellogg's, 357
Kenya, spending on food in, 173
Keynes, John Maynard, 609, 614,
808. *See also* Keynesian
economics
analysis of Great Depression,
945–947
*The General Theory of
Employment, Interest and
Money,* 171, 945, 946, 947
on short and long run, 904,
944, 945
A Tract on Monetary Reform,
808
Keynesian cross, 768
Keynesian economics, 609,
945–948
challenges to, 949–954
classical macroeconomics vs.,
945–946
factors shifting aggregate
demand curve and causing
business cycles and, 946
macroeconomic policy activism
and, 947
monetarism vs., 949–950
short-run effects of changes
in aggregate demand on
aggregate output and,
945–946
kidney transplants, 109, 117
Kimberly-Clark, 978–979
King Digital Entertainment, 455

Knickerbocker Trust, 872
Korea. *See* North Korea; South
    Korea
Koziol, Michael, 599
Kydland, Finn, 953

L

labor. *See also* employment;
    unemployment;
    unemployment rate;
    wages
    black, 145
    marginal product of. *See*
        marginal product of labor
    market demand for, 552–553
    pauper labor fallacy and,
        221–222
    sweatshop labor fallacy and,
        221–222
labor force
    changes in characteristics
        of, natural rate of
        unemployment and,
        664–665
    definition of, 652
    women in, during World
        War II, 684
labor force participation rate,
    652–653
labor market
    equilibrium in, 552
    institutions of, changes
        in, natural rate of
        unemployment and, 665
labor productivity, 684. *See also*
    productivity
labor strikes, 662
labor supply, 563–567
    indifference curves and,
        576–578
    shifts of the labor supply curve
        and, 565–566
    wages and, 564–565
    of women in United States, 567
    work vs. leisure and, 563–564
labor supply curve, individual. *See*
    individual labor supply
    curve
labor unions. *See* unions
Laffer, Arthur, 195
Laffer curve, 195
land. *See also* farmland
    market for, 553, 554
Latin America. *See also specific*
    countries
    Gini coefficients in, 521
    ride-hailing services in, 153
Latvia, productivity and wages
    in, 222
law of demand, 70, 783
    price elasticity of demand and,
        161
lean manufacturing (lean
    production), 811
lean production, 45, 224
learning curve, 489
learning disabilities, poverty and,
    519
learning effects, 254–255
Lehman Brothers, 864, 870, 877

leisure, work vs., 563–564, 573–576
lemons problem, 595–596
lending, 731–732. *See also* debt;
    government borrowing;
    mortgages; public debt
    subprime, housing bubble and,
        874–876
Levinson, Arthur, 262
Levi's, 241
Lewis, Robin, 377
liabilities, 729
    of Fed, 867
    implicit, 838–839
liberalism, 517, 536
licenses, 147
life, cost of, 260
life-cycle hypothesis, 758
life insurance companies, 734
life satisfaction, GDP and, global
    comparison of, 638
Li & Fung, 241
linear curves, slope of, 54–55
linear relationships, 53
Lipitor, 358–359
liquid assets, 731, 850
liquidity, 731
**liquidity preference model of
    the interest rate,** 891
liquidity traps, 935, 936
    Great Depression and, 949
Lithuania, productivity and wages
    in, 222
living standard, in China, 1, 4
Lloyd's of London, 586–587, 590,
    593–594
loan(s), 731–732. *See also* debt;
    government borrowing;
    mortgages; public debt
loanable funds market, 718–727
    demand for loanable funds and,
        718–720
    equilibrium interest rate and,
        721–722
    global, 723–726
    inflation and interest rates and,
        726–727
    shifts of demand for loanable
        funds and, 722–723
    shifts of supply for loanable
        funds and, 723
    supply of loanable funds and,
        720–721
loanable funds model, 893
    modeling the financial account
        and, 968–969
loan-backed securities, 731, 732
loan originators, 875
location, product differentiation
    by, 450
locked exchange rates, 983
lockouts, 662
The Logic of Collective Action
    (Olson), 498
London, England
    congestion pricing in, 77
    sewer system in, 493, 494
Long John Silvers, 447
long run, 328
    changes in money supply in,
        interest rate and, 904–905

interest rates in, 904–905,
    914–915
    Keynes on, 904, 944, 945
    meaning of, 798
    money supply increase in,
        effects of, 903–904
    monopolistic competition in,
        453–455
**long-run aggregate supply curve
    (LRAS),** 796–799
    increase in money supply and,
        916, 917
    inflationary gaps and, 821–822
    recessionary gaps and, 820–821
**long-run average total cost
    curve (LRATC),** 345
    returns to scale and, 346–347
long-run economic growth,
    615–617, 679–712
    aggregate production function
        and, 685–689
    change in level vs. rate of
        change and, 683
    differing rates of, 691–702
    global comparison of, 699
    government's role in promoting,
        693–695
    natural resources and,
        689–690, 702–703
    productivity and, 684–689,
        690–691
    rates of, 681–682
    real GDP per capita and,
        680–684
    sources of, 684–691
    sustainable. *See* sustainable
        long-run economic growth
    in United States, India, and
        China, 685–686
long-run growth per capita, 616
long-run industry supply curve,
    371–374
**long-run macroeconomic
    equilibrium,** 804–807
long-run market equilibrium,
    372–373
    cost of production and
        efficiency in, 375
long-run Phillips curve (LRPC),
    930–931
long-term interest rates, 887,
    895–896
long-term unemployed, 660
loose monetary policy, 897
loss aversion, 266, 740
losses
    economic, 250
    risk of, 579
lowflation, 937
LRAS. See long-run aggregate
    supply curve
LRATC. See long-run average total
    cost curve
LRPC. See long-run Phillips curve
Lucas, Robert, 952
luck, bad, poverty and, 519
lump-sum taxes, 202–203, 827
luxury goods, price elasticity of
    demand for, 169
Lyft, 17, 147, 150, 151, 153, 673

M

MacDonald's, 74, 174, 295, 461,
    598, 619
macroeconomic equilibrium
    long-run, 804–807
    short-run, 800–801
macroeconomic ideas, evolution
    of, 943
macroeconomic policy, 609,
    808–810. *See also* fiscal
        policy; monetary policy;
        stabilization policy
    demand shocks and, 808–809
    to fight recessions, 947
    inflation and. *See* inflation
    limits to, 950–951, 955–955
    low interest rates and, 957–958
    policymakers' ages and, 781
    supply shocks and, 809–810
    tools of, 20. *See also*
        government spending;
        tax(es)
    unemployment and. *See*
        unemployment
macroeconomic policy activism,
    947
    monetarism's effort to
        eliminate, 949–950
    rational expectations and, 952
macroeconomic questions, 608
macroeconomics, 4, 607
    business cycle and. *See*
        business cycle
    classical, 944, 945–946
    deflation and. *See* deflation
    evolution of, 943
    Great Depression and,
        Keynesian economics and.
        See Keynesian economics
    Great Moderation and, 955
    inflation and. *See* inflation
    international (open-
        economy). *See* exchange
            rate(s); exchange rate
            regimes; international
            macroeconomics
    Keynesian. *See* Keynesian
        economics
    long-run economic growth and.
        See long-run economic
            growth
    monetarism and, 949–951
    nature of, 608–610
    new classical, 951–953
    new Keynesian, 952
    open-economy. *See* exchange
        rate(s); exchange rate
        regimes; international
        macroeconomics
    origins of, 171, 609, 758, 764
    policy activism and, 947, 949–
        950, 952
    policy and. *See* fiscal policy;
        macroeconomic policy;
        monetary policy;
        stabilization policy
    political business cycle and,
        953
    rational expectations and,
        951–952

real business cycle theory and, 951, 952–953
supply-side economics and, 952
theory and, 609
whole as greater than sum of parts and, 608–609
Maddison, Angus, 691
Maduro, Nicolas, 921
Mall of America, 447
Malthus, Thomas, 690, 702
Mankiw, N. Gregory, 947
manufacturing, decline of, 238–239
Mao Zedong, 124
marginal analysis, 10, 252–261, 327
choosing profit-maximizing quantity of output using, 360–361
consumption decisions and, 259–260
cost of a life and, 260
decisions suitable for, 260
"how much" vs. "either-or" decisions and, 251
marginal benefit and. *See* marginal benefit *entries*
marginal cost and. *See* marginal cost *entries*
profit-maximizing principle of, 257–258
utility-maximizing principle of, 291, 574
marginal benefit, 255–256
of another unit of a public good, 498–500
decreasing, 256
marginal benefit curve (MB), 256
marginal cost, 253–255, 335–337
constant, 254
decreasing, 254–255
of goods nonrival in consumption, 495
increasing, 254
individual, of a common resource, 503–504
monopolistic competition vs. perfect competition and, 457
not equal to marginal revenue, 361
total cost vs., 255
marginal cost curve (MC), 254, 339, 340
slope of, 341
marginal decisions, 10, 279
marginally attached workers, 654
marginal product, 329, 331
equilibrium value of, 553
marginal productivity theory of income distribution, 543, 551–553, 554–562
discrimination and, 560–561
efficiency wages and, 560
market power and, 559–560
minimum wage and, 562
usefulness of, 562
wage disparities and marginal productivity and, 557–559

wage disparities in practice and, 557
marginal product of labor (*MPL*), 329, 331, 546–550
value of, 546–550
marginal propensity to consume (MPC), 750–752
marginal propensity to import, 771
marginal propensity to save (MPS), 750
marginal rate of substitution (MRS), 306–309
diminishing, 308
prices and, 311–312
marginal revenue, 360
of a monopolist, 392–395
not equal to marginal cost, 361
marginal revenue curve, 361
marginal social benefit
of pollution, 469
of a public good, 498–500
marginal social benefit of pollution, 469
marginal social cost
of a common resource, 503–504
of pollution, 469
marginal social cost of pollution, 469
marginal tax rate, 206
marginal utility, 281
diminishing, principle of, 264, 281–282
market demand curve and, 292
marginal utility curve (MU), 281–282
marginal utility per dollar, 288–289, 290, 291
Margo, Robert, 524
market(s)
barriers to entry into, 387–390
beer, 423
black, 137–138
capital, 39
Christmas tree, 355
competitive. *See* competitive markets
credit, changes in, shifts of the money demand curve and, 890
efficiency of. *See* efficiency
efficient supply of private goods, 495
factor, 39, 629, 909
foreign exchange. *See* exchange rate(s); fixed exchange rates; floating exchange rates; foreign exchange market
free entry and exit from, 358, 449
for goods and services, 39, 629, 909
housing. *See* housing *entries*
imperfectly competitive, price setting in, 791, 792
for insurance, 588–589
interrelated, 121
irrational, 739–740
labor. *See* labor market

for land, 553, 554
for loanable funds. *See* loanable funds market
for pasta sauce, product differentiation in, 451
perfectly competitive, 356
for physical capital, 554
rare earth, 390–391
search engine, 422
stock, 591
for tickets, 89–90, 125
toothpaste, 422
used textbook, 103
for used textbooks, 103
wireless telephone, 422
market baskets, 639–640
market-clearing price, 86
market demand, for labor, 552–553
market demand curve, 77, 292–294
income effect and, 293–294
marginal utility and, 292
substitution effect and, 292–293
market economies, 2–3, 121–124
amount of pollution produced by, 470–472
economic signals in, 122–123
inefficiency and, 123
invisible hand and, 16
property rights and, 122
market equilibrium, 86
long-run, 372–373, 375
short-run, 371
market failure, 3, 16–17, 123
market intervention, 131. *See also* price ceilings; price controls; price floors
market power, 123, 386, 403–407
marginal productivity theory of income distribution and, 559–560
new generation of. *See* new generation of market power
market price, 87–89
above equilibrium price, 87–88
below equilibrium price, 88–89
profitability and, 363–365
markets for goods and services, 39
market share, 357
market structure, 383. *See also* monopolistic competition; monopoly; oligopoly; perfect competition
types of, 384–385
market supply curve, 83
market timing, 739
Mars Canada, 427
Marshall, Alfred, 1, 4, 5
Martin, George R. R., 450
Martin, William McChesney, 865
MasterCard, 421
maximum, 58, 59
MB. See marginal benefit curve
MC. See marginal cost curve
McDonald's, Big Mac prices and purchasing power parity and, 977

MD. See money demand curve
mean household income, 520–521
means-tested programs, 525, 526
median household income, 520–521
Medicaid, 515, 525, 530, 536, 819
ACA and, 532–533
effects of, 534–535
medical care. *See* Affordable Care Act; health care; health insurance
Medicare, 515, 525, 530, 532, 819, 839
FICA tax and, 203–204, 205
Medici family, 496
medium of exchange, money as, 851
megacities, 1
Mendelsohn, Robert, 472
mental accounting, 266
menu costs, 669
merchandise trade balance, 966
Merck, 389
Mexico
clothing industry of, 38
inflation and money supply in, 906
inflation in, 975
NAFTA and, 237, 240
productivity and wages in, 222
purchasing power parity and Big Mac price in, 977
real GDP per capita of, 691
spending on food in. 173
U.S. recessions and, 986
Michelangelo, 496
microcredit, 743
microeconomic questions, 608
microeconomics, 3, 607
microlending, 743
microprocessor industry, 387–388
Microsoft, 388, 403, 404, 422, 456, 486, 487, 732–733
Justice Department case against, 487–488
Microsoft 210, 208
middle class, global, 701
midpoint method, 161–162
MillerCoors, 423
minimum, 59
minimum-cost output, 340, 362
monopolistic competition vs. perfect competition and, 457–458
minimum wage, 141, 562
natural rate of unemployment and, 665
structural unemployment and, 661–662
in United States, 661, 662
misfortune, poverty and, 519
Mitchell, Wesley, 944
Mitsubishi Electric, 421
M1 monetary aggregate, 853, 854
M2 monetary aggregate, 853, 854
Great Depression and, 953–954
M3 monetary aggregate, 853
Mobil, 401, 435

models, 27–50
   AD–AS. See AD–AS model
   circular flow diagram as,
      38–41, 190–191, 628–629,
      908–911, 967, 973
   comparative advantage as,
      34–37
   economists' agreement and,
      43–44
   economists' disagreements and,
      42–43
   efficiency-wage, 560
   graphs and, 51. *See also* graphs
   Heckscher–Ohlin, 223, 230, 231
   illustrating with graphs. *See*
      graphs
   income-expenditure. *See*
      income-expenditure
      model
   liquidity preference, of the
      interest rate, 891
   loanable funds, 893, 968–969
   other things equal assumption
      and, 28
   positive vs. negative economics
      and, 41–42
   of price level, classical, 916–918
   production possibility frontier
      as, 29–34
   rational, 267–268
   of rational consumer. *See*
      marginal utility; rational
      consumer; utility
   rational expectations, 951–952
   Ricardian, of international
      trade, 218
   supply and demand. *See*
      demand curve; demand
      schedule; supply and
      demand model; supply
      curve; supply schedule
monetarism, 949–951
   inflation and natural rate
      of unemployment and,
      950–951
   natural rate hypothesis and,
      951
monetary aggregates, 853
monetary base, 863
   quantitative easing and
      increase in, 956
A Monetary History of
      the United States,
      1867–1960 (Friedman and
      Schwartz), 949, 953
monetary neutrality, 904
   international evidence of,
      905–906
monetary policy, 609, 651,
      885–578
   aggregate demand and,
      897–902
   contractionary (tight), 898
   discretionary, 950
   expansionary (loose), 897
   under floating exchange rates,
      985–986
   following oil crisis of 1979,
      789–790
   inflation targeting and, 900–901

influence of, 902
interest rates and, 893–897,
   957–958
limits of, 955–956
monetarist views on, 950
monetary neutrality and, 904,
   905–906
money supply and. *See* money
   supply
in practice, 898–899
revival of interest in, 949
setting interest rates vs. money
   supply and, 894
shifts of the aggregate demand
   curve and, 787, 789
Taylor rule method of setting,
   899
zero lower bound problem and,
   898, 901, 935–936
monetary policy rule, 950
monetization of debt, 918
money, 850–855. *See also*
   currency(ies); dollar (U.S.)
   changes in the aggregate price
      level and, 783–784
   in circulation, 850, 851, 854
   commodity, 852
   commodity-backed, 852,
      854–855
   creation of, by banks, 860–861
   definition of, 850–851
   fiat, 853
   gains from trade and, 850
   opportunity cost of holding,
      886–887, 888
   printing of, 918–919, 938
   roles of, 851–852
   supply of. *See* money supply
   types of, 852–853
   unit-of-account role of, 669
money demand curve (*MD*),
      888–891
   interest rate and, 891–892
   shifts of, 889–890
money multiplier, 863–864
money supply, 850, 860–865
   bank creation of money and,
      860–861
   bank runs and, 864
   changes in, interest rate in the
      long run and, 904–905
   classical macroeconomics and,
      944
   components of, 853
   Fed's tools for increasing or
      decreasing, 892
   Great Depression and, 953–954
   increase in, short- and long-run
      effects of, 903–904
   monetary base and, 863
   monetary neutrality and, 904
   money multiplier in reality and,
      863–864
   reserves, bank deposits, and
      money multiplier and, 862
money supply curve (*MS*),
      interest rate and, 891–892
money transmitters, 886, 907
monopolistic competition, 384,
      422, 447–466

description of, 448–449
inefficiency of, 458
in long run, 453–455
perfect competition vs.,
   456–458
price, marginal cost, and
   average total cost and,
   456–458
product differentiation and. *See*
   product differentiation
in short run, 452–453
monopolists, 383, 385–386
   single-price, 408
monopoly, 374, 385–420
   antitrust policy and, 385
   demand curve and marginal
      revenue of, 391–395
   description of, 385–386
   legal, 358–359
   market power and, 386,
      403–407
   natural, dealing with, 387,
      401–403
   perfect competition vs., 396
   price discrimination and. *See*
      price discrimination
   profit maximization under,
      391–399
   public policy and, 399–403
   reasons for, 386–390
   supply curve for, lack of, 397
   welfare effects of, 399–400
monopsonists, 404
monopsony, 404–405, 560
Monsanto, 426
Montgomery, Clare, 441
Montreal Protocol, 481
moral hazard, 594, 596–597
Morgan, J. P., 872
mortgages
   delinquencies and, 741–742
   strategic default and, 265
   subprime lending and, 874–876
Moskowitz, Howard, 451
Motel 6, 460
movement along the aggregate
   demand curve
   during 1979–1980, 789–790
   shift of the curve vs., 788
**movements along the demand
   curve,** 71
   shifts of the demand curve vs.,
      71, 72
**movements along the supply
   curve,** 80
   shifts along the curve vs., 80, 81
MPC. See marginal propensity to
   consume
MPL. See marginal product of
   labor
MPS. See marginal propensity to
   save
MRS. See marginal rate of
   substitution
MS. See money supply curve
MU. See marginal utility curve
Muller, Nicholas Z., 472
multilateral agreements, to
   address climate change,
   481

multiplier, 749, 750–753
   algebraic derivation of, 779
   austerity and, 828–830
   changes in government
      transfers and taxes and,
      826–827
   increase in government
      purchases of goods
      and services and, 825–826
   international trade and, 771
   inventories at end of recession
      and, 771–772
   inventory adjustment and,
      768–770
   money, 863–864
   paradox of thrift and, 770
   taxes and, 827–828
multiplier process, money
   creation and, 861
Mumbai, India, rent controls in,
   137
Muth, John, 951
mutual funds, 733–734

N

NAFTA. *See* North American Free
   Trade Agreement
NAFTA-USMCA, 237
NAIRU. *See* nonaccelerating
   inflation rate of
   unemployment
NASDAQ, 737
Nash, John, 430
Nash equilibrium, 430
national accounts, 628. *See also*
   national income and
   product accounts
National Bureau of Economic
   Research (NBER), 944
   recessions declared by, 612, 614
National Cash Register
   Corporation, 706
National Health Service (NHS),
   531
**national income and product
   accounts,** 628–635
   circular-flow diagram and,
      628–629
   gross domestic product and,
      629–635
nationalization, partial, of
   financial system, Great
   Recession and, 876
national savings, 715
National Science Foundation, 694
national security argument for
   trade protection, 236
NATO. *See* North Atlantic Treaty
   Organization
natural gas industry
   fracking and, 67, 467, 473
   as natural monopoly, 387
natural monopoly, 387
   artificially scarce goods and,
      507
   dealing with, 401–403
natural rate hypothesis, 951
natural rate of unemployment,
      658–666
   changes in, 664–665

cyclical unemployment and, 663
frictional unemployment and, 659–660
inflation and, 931–932
job creation and job destruction and, 658–659
long-run Phillips curve and, 930–931
NAIRU related to, 931
structural unemployment and, 660–663
natural resources
overexploitation of, as market failure, 3
productivity and, 689–690
sustainable long-run economic growth and, 702–703
NBER. *See* National Bureau of Economic Research
NCR Corp., 706
near-moneys, 853
negative externalities, 467, 468–482. *See also* pollution
private solutions to, 472
negative income tax, 526
negative relationships, 54
Nestlé Canada, 427
net capital inflow, 716
net exports, 635
real, effective exchange rate and, 979
Netflix, 388, 414
Netherlands
current account surplus of, 968
productivity and wages in, 222
net present value, 277
net survival benefit, 109, 117
network externalities, 485–488
external benefits of, 486–487
increasing returns to scale and, 346
monopoly and, 388–389
new generation of market power and, 403–407
new classical macroeconomics, 951–953
new generation of market power, 403–407
monopoly and, 404
monopsony and, 404–405
policies to address, 405–406
New Keynesian economics, 952
The New Rules of Retail (Lewis), 377
New York City
rent controls in, 131, 132–133
taxi medallions in, 147–151
New York Clearinghouse, 872
New Zealand
individual transferable quotas in, 506
inflation targeting in, 900
ITQ schemes in, 506
productivity and wages in, 222
NHS. *See* National Health Service (NHS)
Nicaragua, inflation in, 915
Nigeria
economic growth of, 699

natural resources and real GDP per capita of, 689
Nixon, Richard, 953
nominal exchange rates, real exchange rates vs., 975–977
nominal GDP, 636–637
real GDP vs., 638
nominal interest rate, 670
nominal wage, 791, 793
changes in, short-run aggregate supply curve and, 794–795
nonaccelerating inflation rate of unemployment (NAIRU), 931
noncooperative effect, 426
noncooperative equilibrium, 430
nonexcludability, 494
nonlinear curves, 56
slope of, 56–58
nonlinear relationships, 53
nonmonetary rewards, 263–264
nonprice competition, 438
nonrivals in consumption, 494
Nordhaus, William, 472
normal goods, 74, 293
income and consumption of, 319, 320
normalization, of aggregate price level measure, 640
normative economics, 41–42
North American Free Trade Agreement (NAFTA), 237, 240
North Atlantic Treaty Organization (NATO), 430
Northern Rock, run on, 859
North Korea, economy of, 2
Norway
drug prices in, 389
Gini coefficient in, 523
government debt of, 836
inflation targeting in, 900
productivity and wages in, 222
tradable emissions permits in, 479
Norwegian Air, 27
numerical graphs, 59–64
interpreting, 62–64
types of, 60–62

O

Obama, Barack, fiscal stimulus under, 821, 824–825, 959
Obamacare. *See* Affordable Care Act
Odoba Mexican Eats, 447
offshore outsourcing, 238, 239
Ogallala Aquifer, 505
oil
fracking and, 752
long-run economic growth and, 689
monetary policy following oil crisis of 1979 and, 789–790
OPEC and, 433
price controls and, 132
price shocks and, 929

oil boom, 544
Okun, Arthur, 924
Okun's law, 924
oligopolists, 422
oligopoly, 374, 384, 385, 386, 421–446
collusion and competition and, 425–426
duopoly example of, 424–425
games and. *See* game theory
importance of, 438–439
legal framework of, 434–436
prevalence of, 422–424
price leadership and, 438
price wars and, 436–437
product differentiation and, 437–438
tacit collusion and, 436–437
Olive Garden, 74
Olson, Mancur, 498
omitted variables, 63–64
one-shot games, 431
OPEC. *See* Organization of Petroleum Exporting Countries
open economies, 619
savings-investment spending identity in, 715–717
open-economy macroeconomics. *See* exchange rate(s); exchange rate regimes; international macroeconomics
open-market operations, 865, 867–869, 892
OpenTable, 22
Operation Sunset, 849
opportunities, changes in, shifts of the labor supply curve and, 566
opportunity cost, 9–10, 111, 283
constant, 31
of holding money, 886–887, 888
increasing, 31
of investment spending, 720
production possibility frontier and, 31–32
quantity controls and, 150
of space sharing, 252
Opportunity Insights Project, 519
optimal consumption, 290–291
optimal consumption bundle, 285–287, 309
optimal consumption rule, 305, 312, 563
optimal output rule, 360
optimal quantity, 257
optimal time allocation rule, 574
Orbitz, 22, 412
ordinary goods, 309
Organization of Petroleum Exporting Countries (OPEC), 425, 433
supply shocks caused by, 807
organ transplantation, 109, 117
origin, 52
O'Rourke, Kevin, 609–610
other things equal assumption, 28
outflows of funds, 716

outlet stores, 412
output. *See also* production
aggregate. *See* aggregate output; real GDP
changes in price of, shifts of the factor demand curve and, 550–551
minimum-cost, 340
per worker or per hour. *See* productivity
potential, 797–798, 922
production function and, 328–332
profit-maximizing, of a monopolist, 395–396
profit-maximizing quantity of, choosing, 360–361
output gaps, 806–807
cyclical unemployment and, 923, 924
unemployment rate and, 922–923. *See also* Phillips curve; short-run Phillips curve
outsourcing, 238, 239
overconfidence, 265–266, 740
overfishing, 503
of Alaskan crabs, 151–152
individual transferable quotas and, 506
overuse, 503–504
ownership rights, 122

P

package size, 291
Pakistan
spending on food in, 173
voting as a public good in, 500
Panda Express, 447
Panera, 295
Panic of 1907, 871–872, 875
paradox of thrift, 171, 609, 770, 776
Paris Agreement, 481, 704
pasta sauce market, product differentiation in, 451
patents, 358–359, 390, 694
pauper labor fallacy, 221–222
pay-for-delay tactic, 359
payoff, 428
payoff matrix, 428
PayPal, 388, 403, 886, 890, 907
payroll tax, 205. *See also* Federal Insurance Contributions Act tax
Pearl River Delta (PRD), China, 1, 627
pension funds, 734
People's Bank of China, 865
Pepsi, 68, 163
perfect competition, 355–382, 384
definition of, 356
free entry and exit and, 358
industry supply curve under, 370–376
monopolistic competition vs., 456–458
monopoly vs., 396
necessary conditions for, 356–357
production and profits under, 359–370

perfect complements, 316
perfectly competitive
    industries, 356
perfectly competitive markets,
    356
    price setting in, 791–792
perfectly elastic demand,
    164–165
perfectly elastic supply, 176
perfectly inelastic demand, 164
perfectly inelastic supply, 176
perfect price discrimination,
    410–413
perfect substitutes, 314–315
perfume industry, 461–462
permanent income hypothesis,
    757
petroleum industry. See fracking;
    gasoline; gasoline prices;
    oil; Organization of
    Petroleum Exporting
    Countries
Pfizer, 484
pharmaceutical industry
    drug prices and, 389, 390, 421
    generic drugs and, 358–359
    product differentiation in, 438
Phelps, Edmund, 951
Phillips, A. W. H., 924
Phillips curve
    long-run, 930–931
    short-run, 924–927
    supply shocks and, 925, 927
physical assets, 729
physical capital, 544, 684
    creation of, 714
    definition of, 716
    diminishing returns to,
        686–687, 688
    economic growth and, 684–685
    increases in, productivity and,
        684–685, 687–688, 689
    market for, 554
    size of stock of, shifts of the
        aggregate demand curve
        and, 787, 788
    spending on. See investment
        spending
pie charts, 61, 62
Pigou, A. C., 474–475
Pigouvian subsidies, 484
Pigouvian taxes, 474–475
Pioneer Hi-Bred International,
    426
Pizza Hut, 598
planned aggregate spending,
    real GDP and, 764–766
planned economies, 2, 124
planned investment spending,
    760
point method of calculating
    slope along a nonlinear
    curve, 58
Poland, productivity and wages
    in, 222
political business cycle, 953
political stability, economic
    growth and, 694–695
politics
    ACA and, 533–534, 538

influence on economists'
    opinions, 43
    Keynesian economics and, 947
    risk and, 593
    subsidies for renewable energy
        and, 489
    supply shocks caused by, 807
    of trade protection, 236–240
    of welfare state, 536
    welfare state and, 517
pollution, 469–482, 472, 473. See
    also externalities; negative
    externalities
    amount produced by a market
        economy, 470–472
    in China, 705
    economic growth and, 703–704
    government policy and,
        473–479
    marginal social benefit of, 469
    marginal social cost of, 469
    as market failure, 62–63
    socially optimal quantity of,
        469–470
pooling, 591, 592
population, changes in, shifts of
    the labor supply curve
    and, 565–566
pork shortage, 376
Portugal
    government debt of, 836
    productivity and wages in, 222
    sticky wages during Great
        Recession in, 799–800
positive economics, 41–42
positive externalities, 468,
    482–485
    farmland preservation and,
        483–484
    marginal social benefit and,
        500
    technology spillovers and,
        484–485
positive feedback, 486
positively correlated events, 593
positive relationships, 54
Post Foods, 357
potential output, 797, 922
    long-run aggregate supply
        curve and, 797–798
poverty, 517–520
    causes of, 519
    consequences of, 519–520
    cycle of, 485
    geographic concentration of,
        519–520
    incidence of, 518
    social benefits of reducing, 517
    trends in, 517–518
    welfare state effects on,
        527–528
poverty programs, 516
poverty rate, 517
    in Great Recession, 528
poverty threshold, 517
Powell, Jerome, 865
PPF. See production possibility
    frontier
PPI. See producer price index
PRD. See Pearl River Delta, China

Predictably Irrational (Ariely), 268
preferences
    changes in, shifts of the demand
        curve and, 74, 76
    changes in, shifts of the labor
        supply curve and, 565
    consumer choice and, 312–313
    risk aversion and, 585
premiums, 529, 581–582
Prescott, Edward, 953
present value, 275–278
    of multiyear projects,
        calculating, 276
    net, 277
    of a one-year project,
        calculating, 275–276
    of projects with revenues and
        costs, calculating, 277
Preston, Douglas, 414
price(s)
    of ambulance service, 159
    asset. See asset prices
    of avocados, demand and
        supply and, 94
    Big Mac, purchasing power
        parity and, 977
    break-even, 365
    changes in. See price changes
    of commodities, changes in,
        short-run aggregate
        supply curve and, 794, 795
    deflation and, 618
    demand, 149
    effective, 110
    equilibrium. See equilibrium
        price
    everyday low prices strategy
        and, 270
    factor, 230
    factors inhibiting coordination
        of, 436–437
    of farmland, 114–115
    of financial assets, fluctuations
        of, 736–742
    of fuel, airlines and, 82
    of gasoline. See gasoline prices
    increase in, consumption
        choices and, 317–318
    indexes of. See price indexes
    inflation and. See inflation
    marginal rate of substitution
        and, 311–312
    market, 87–89
    market-clearing, 86
    monopolistic competition vs.
        perfect competition and,
        457
    profit-maximizing, of a
        monopolist, 395–396
    rate of change of, inflation and,
        667–670
    sensitivity to, 409
    setting of, in perfectly and
        imperfectly competitive
        markets, 791–792
    shut-down, 366
    of solar panels, 84–85
    stability of, 180, 618, 898, 904
    supply, 149
    surge pricing and, 96

tariffs and, 232–233
    of tickets, 125
    willingness to pay and. See
        willingness to pay
    world, 226
price ceilings, 132–141, 402
    inefficiency caused by, 134–138
    modeling, 133–134
    quantities and, 144
    reasons for, 139
    winners and losers created by,
        138–139
price changes
    of complements, shifts of the
        demand curve and, 73, 76
    consumer surplus and, 107–109
    of inputs, shifts in supply curve
        and, 82, 84
    of outputs, shifts of the factor
        demand curve and,
        550–551
    producer surplus and, 113–114
    of substitutes, shifts of the
        demand curve and, 73, 76
    of substitutes, shifts of the
        supply curve and, 82, 84
    time elapsed since, price
        elasticity of demand and,
        170
price controls, 131–147. See also
    price ceilings; price floors;
    rent controls
    on oil, 132
    reasons for, 132
    in Venezuela, 139–140
price discrimination, 408–413
    drug prices and, 389, 390
    elasticity and, 409–410
    logic of, 408–409
    perfect, 410–413
price effect
    marginal revenue and, 425
    on marginal revenue of a
        monopolist, 393
    price elasticity of demand and,
        167
price elasticity of demand, 159,
    160–172, 178
    along demand curve, 168
    calculating, 160–162
    elastic demand and, 165, 167
    factors determining, 168–170
    inelastic demand and, 161,
        165, 167
    perfectly elastic demand and,
        164–165
    perfectly inelastic demand and,
        164
    tax incidence and, 189–191
    total revenue and, 166–168
    unit-elastic demand and, 165–
        166, 167
price elasticity of supply,
    175–178
    factors determining, 176–177
    measuring, 175–176
    tax incidence and, 189–191
price-fixing, 421
price floors, 132, 141–147
    inefficiency caused by, 143–145

quantities and, 144
reasons for, 146
price indexes, 639–643
consumer. *See* consumer price index (CPI)
GDP deflator as, 642
market baskets and, 639–640
producer, 641–642
wholesale, 641
price leadership, 438
price levels. *See also* inflation rate
aggregate. *See* aggregate price level
classical model of, 916–918, 944
inflation and, 666–667
inflation and disinflation and. *See* disinflation; inflation
Priceline Group, 22
price-matching, 377
price regulation, 401–403
price setting, in perfectly and imperfectly competitive markets, 791–792
price stability, 618, 898
PriceStats, 644
price-taking consumers, 356. *See also* perfect competition
price-taking firm's optimal output rule, 361, 547
price-taking producers, 356. *See also* perfect competition
price-taking producer's optimal employment rule, 548
price unresponsiveness, 159
price wars, 437, 439–440
pricing power, 792
prime rate, 790
principal, 895
principle of diminishing marginal utility, 264, 281–282
principle of "either-or" decision making, 251
prisoners' dilemma, 428–431
private goods, 494–496
characteristics of, 494
efficient supply by markets, 495
private health insurance, 529–530
under ACA, 533
private health insurance market death spiral, 529
private information, 123, 579, 589, 594–599
adverse selection and, 595–596
moral hazard and, 596–597
private spending
budget deficits and, 823
crowding out of, by expansionary fiscal policy, 822
Privilege Underwriters Reciprocal Exchange (PURE), 599
Procter & Gamble, 463, 978–979
producer(s)
changes in number of, shifts of the supply curve and, 83, 84
excise tax paid mainly by, price elasticities and, 190–191
number of, monopolistic competition and, 448

price-taking, 356. *See also* perfect competition
producer price index (PPI), 641–642
producer surplus, 103
cost and, 111–113
gains from trade and, 115–116
imports and, 227
individual, 112
price changes and, 113–114
reduction by taxes, 196–197
rent control and, 138–139
supply curve and, 110–115
total, 112
product(s). *See* goods and services
product differentiation, 437–438, 448, 449–462
advertising and, 459–460
brand names and, 460–461
competition among sellers and, 450
by location, 450
market structure and, 384
proliferation of differentiated products and, 450
by quality, 450
by style or type, 449–450
production. *See also* output
aggregate production function and, 685–689
complements in, 82
factors of. *See* factors of production; *specific factors*
of final goods and services, GDP as, 631–632
inefficiently low, 495
just-in-time, 811
lean, 45, 138, 811
profitable, 362–365
scale effects in, 346
in short run, 362–363
substitutes in, 82
production capacity, investment spending and, 761
production function, 327, 328–335
aggregate, 685–689
cost curves and, 332–333
inputs and outputs and, 328–332
production possibility frontier (PPF), 29–34
comparative advantage and, 218–219
economic growth and, 32–34
efficiency and, 30–31
opportunity cost and, 31–32
productivity, 684–689
aggregate production function and, 685–689
changes in, short-run aggregate supply curve and, 795
employment and, 684
growth in, 684–685
importance of, 684
long-run economic growth and, 684–689, 690–691
Malthus' predictions regarding, 690

natural resources and, 689–690
total factor, 689, 690–691
profit
accounting vs. economic, 249–252
market price and, 363–365
profit maximization, by a monopolist, 391–399
profit-maximizing price, for a monopolist, 395–396
profit-maximizing principle of marginal analysis, 257–258, 360–361
profit-maximizing quantity of output
choosing using marginal analysis, 360–361
for a monopolist, 395–396
profits tax, 205
progressive taxes, 205
property rights, 122
common resources and, 505
protection of, economic growth and, 694
property tax, 205
proportional taxes, 205
proprietors' income, 545
protection, 232. *See also* trade protection
Provigil, 359
public debt, 835. *See also* government borrowing
budget deficits vs., 835
debt-GDP ratio and, 837–838
default on, 835, 836–837
global comparisons of, 836
in practice, 837–838
rising, potential dangers posed by, 835–837
from World War II, 838–839
public goods, 123, 493, 494, 496–503
amount to be provided, 497–501
benefits principle of tax fairness and, 202
cost-benefit analysis of providing, 501
examples of, 496, 497
provision of, 497
voting as, 498, 500
public ownership, 401
of a natural monopoly, 401
public policy. *See* fiscal policy; government policy; macroeconomic policy; monetary policy; stabilization policy
purchases, government. *See* government purchases of goods and services
purchasing power parity, 977–978
PURE. *See* Privilege Underwriters Reciprocal Exchange

Q

Quaker, 357
Qualcomm, 484
quality

inefficiently high, price floors and, 145
inefficiently low, 137
product differentiation by, 450
quantitative easing, 901, 936, 956
quantity. *See also* shortages; surpluses
equilibrium, 86–89
optimal, 257
price controls and, 144
quantity controls, 147–152
anatomy of, 148–151
costs of, 151
quantity demanded, 70
demand vs., 72
inefficiently low, 135–136, 143–144
quantity effect
marginal revenue and, 425
on marginal revenue of a monopolist, 393
price elasticity of demand and, 167
quantity supplied, 78
quantity traded, change in, total surplus and, 118–120
quintiles, 520
quits rate, 653, 824–825
quota(s), 147. *See also* quantity controls
export, Chinese, on rare earths, 390
import, 233–234
quota limits, 147
quota rents, 150, 233
quota share system, Alaskan crab fishing and, 151–152

R

racial discrimination, poverty and, 519
railroad industry, 434
random variables, 580
random walk, 739
rare earth market, 390–391
rational consumers, 279–300
budgets and optimal consumption and, 283–288
utility and. *See* marginal utility; utility
rational expectations, 951–952
rational expectations model, 952
razor industry, 463
R&D. *See* research and development
Reagan, Ronald, 195
real business cycle theory, 951, 952–953
real estate, commercial, demand for, 738
real exchange rates
inflation and, 975–977
nominal exchange rates vs., 975–977
real GDP, 612, 627, 635–639
actual and potential output and, 797–798, 922
business cycle and, 612

real GDP (*continued*)
calculating, 636–637
changes in, shifts of the money demand curve and, 890
defined, 636–637
future, expected, investment spending and, 761
growth of, unemployment and, 656–657
income-expenditure equilibrium, 767–768
as measure of aggregate output, 636
nominal GDP vs., 638
planned aggregate spending and, 764–766
real GDP per capita, 635–636. *See also* economic growth; GDP per capita; long-run economic growth
global comparison of, 680–681, 682
physical capital and, 686–687
regional disparities in, 699–702
of U. S. and Britain, 615–616
in United States, India, and China, 680–681
real income, 667
real interest rate, 670
real net exports, effective exchange rate and, 979
real wage, 667
recession(s), 4, 612–613. *See also* business cycle; Great Recession
automobile industry and, 811
balancing the budget in, 833–834
Brazilian, 615
coronavirus, 807
definition of, 612, 614
deflation and, 671
demand shocks causing, 781, 800
double-dip, 807
in Europe, 614
first, 944
following Panic of 1907, 871–872
Greek, 607
growth, 657
impact of, 613
inventories at end of, 771–772
investment spending and, 759
of 1970s, supply shocks causing, 781
policy to fight, 947
supply-shock, 781, 807
unemployment and, 613
in United States, 176, 614, 781, 787, 871–872, 955, 958–959, 961
in United States, Mexico and, 986
recessionary gaps, 804–807
expansionary fiscal policy and, 820–821
output gap and, 806
Reconstruction Finance Corporation (RFC), 872–873

recoveries. *See* business cycle; expansion(s)
Recovery Act, 821, 824
regressive taxes, 205
regulation
airline industry deregulation and, 145
antitrust. *See* antitrust policy
of banks, 858–859, 873, 876–877
electricity industry deregulation and, 396–397
of financial system, 694
price, 401–403
of savings and loans, 873–874
Regulation Q, 873, 890
related goods. *See* complements; substitutes
relative price, 311
relative price rule, 311–312
Renaissance, flowering of, 496
renewable energy sources, 480
rent(s)
implicit, 738
quota, 150, 233
rentalcars.com, 22
rental rate, 553
rent controls
consumer and producer surplus and, 138–139
in Mumbai, India, 137
in New York City, 131, 132–133
Rent the Runway, 121
reputation, 596
research and development (R&D)
economic growth and, 693
government subsidies to, economic growth and, 694
government subsidies to, to address climate change, 481
research clusters, 484
Research Triangle (North Carolina), 484
reserve(s)
bank. *See* bank reserves
foreign exchange, 980
reserve ratio, 857
reserve requirements, 858, 892
reshoring, 217
resolution authority, 877
resources, 8
allocation of. *See* allocation
common. *See* common resources
efficient use of. *See* efficiency
natural. *See* natural resources
scarcity of. *See* scarce resources
wasted, 136–137
Restaurant Brands International, 295
retained earnings, 760
returns to scale
constant, 346
decreasing, 346–347
increasing. *See* increasing returns to scale
revaluation, 985
revenue
from an excise tax, 192–193

marginal, 360
projects with, calculating present value of, 277
tax rates and, 193–195
reverse causality, 64
RFC. *See* Reconstruction Finance Corporation (RFC)
Rhodes, Cecil, 385, 386, 387, 391
Ricardian equivalence, 823
Ricardian model of international trade, 218
Ricardo, David, 218, 232, 823
ride-hailing services, 17, 147, 153. *See also* Lyft; Uber
risk
financial, 730–731
stocks and, 733
risk, 580–581
capital at risk and, 588
diversification and, 590–593
efficient allocation of, 588–589
financial, 580–581
of loss, 579
pooling, 591, 592
trading, 587–589
risk-averse people, 583
risk aversion, 264, 580–586
diminishing marginal utility and, 583–584
expectations and uncertainty and, 580–581
logic of, 581–585
paying to avoid risk and, 585–586
risk-neutral people, 585
rivals in consumption, 494, 495
robots, 349
factor demand and, 551
Rockefeller, John D., 400–401, 872
Romer, Christina, 902
Romer, David, 902
Roosevelt, Franklin D., 527, 855
bank holiday declared by, 859, 873
efforts to turn Great Depression around, 947
Rouse, Cecilia, 44
Rowling, J. K., 450
Rule of 70, 682
RunMyErrand, 673
running up against the zero lower bound, 901
Russia
arms race and, 430
oil production of, 433
spending on food in, 173
wheat yield in, 330

S

SABMiller, 423
Sachs, Jeffrey, 698–699
sales, 412
inefficient allocation among sellers, price floors and, 144–145
reallocation among sellers, total surplus and, 118
sales tax, 205
salmon, diminishing marginal utility of, 282–283
Samsung, 422, 459

Samuelson, Paul, 945
Saudi Arabia, oil production of, 433
savings
accumulated. *See* wealth
economic growth and, 692
income level and, 757
marginal propensity to save and, 750
national, 715
paradox of thrift and, 770
savings-investment spending identity and, 714–717
savings and loans, crisis of 1980s and, 873–874
savings-investment spending identity, 714–717
in closed economy, 714–715
in open economy, 715–717
Sbarro, 447
scarce resources, monopoly and, 387
scarcity, 8–9, 248
scatter diagrams, 60–61
Schick, 463
Schick, Jacob, 463
Schumpeter, Joseph, 610, 944
Schwartz, Anna, *A Monetary History of the United States, 1867–1960,* 949, 953
screening, 596
search engine market, 422
Sears, 377
SeatGeek, 89
secular stagnation, 958
securities, loan-backed, 731, 732
securitization, 732, 875–876
seigniorage, 919
self-correcting economies, 805, 807
self-regulating economies, 609
sellers
competition among, in monopolistic competition, 450
inefficient allocation of sales among, price floors and, 144–145
reallocation of sales among, total surplus and, 118
Sen, Amartya, 12
services. *See* final goods and services; goods and services
severe weather, 579, 593
shadow banking, Great Recession and, 874–876
shares, 591
sharing economy, 121
reduction of fixed costs by, 347–348
Shen, Keting, 685
Sherman Antitrust Act of 1890, 435
shifts
of aggregate consumption function, 756–758
of aggregate demand curve, 786–788
of money demand curve, 889–890

shifts of the demand curve, 70–78
  equilibrium and, 90–91
  expectations and, 74–75, 76
  income and, 74, 76
  for labor, 550–551
  movements along the demand curve vs., 71, 72
  number of consumers and, 75–77
  prices of related goods or services and, 73, 76
  simultaneous shifts of the supply curve and, equilibrium and, 92–94
  tastes and, 74, 76
shifts of the supply curve, 79–84
  equilibrium and, 91–92
  expectations and, 82–83, 84
  input prices and, 82, 84
  movements along the curve vs., 80, 81
  number of producers and, 83, 84
  prices of related goods or services and, 82, 84
  simultaneous shifts of the demand curve and, equilibrium and, 92–94
  technological change and, 82, 84
Shiller, Robert, 740
shoe-leather costs, 667–668
shortages, market price and, 88–89
short run, 328
  costs and production in, 362–363
  interest rates in, 911–912
  Keynes on, 904, 944, 945
  monopolistic competition in, 452–453
short-run aggregate supply curve (SRAS), 790, 791–795, 798–799, 926
  commodity price changes and, 794, 795
  increase in money supply and, 916, 917
  inflationary gaps and, 821–822
  nominal wage changes and, 794–795
  productivity changes and, 795
  recessionary gaps and, 820–821
  shifts of, 792, 793–795, 802–803
  sticky wages and, 791, 799
short -run average total cost curve, 343, 344, 345–346
short-run equilibrium aggregate output, 801
short-run equilibrium aggregate price level, 801
short-run individual supply curve, 366, 367
short-run industry supply curve, 370–371
short-run macroeconomic equilibrium, 800–801
short-run market equilibrium, 371
short-run Phillips curve (SRPC), 924–927

expected rate of inflation and, 927–929
short-run production decision, 365–368
short-term interest rates, 887
showrooming, 377
shrimp, Thai and Vietnamese production of, 217, 220–221, 222, 238
shut-down price, 366
signaling, 596
Singapore
  economic growth of, 697
  voting as a public good in, 500
single-payer systems, 531
single-price monopolists, 408
sin taxes, 195
Sirius SatelliteXM Radio, 146
6 River Systems, 349
Skype, 487
slope, 54–59
  along a nonlinear curve, calculating, 56–58
  of budget line, 310–311
  of indifference curves, 305, 306
  of linear curves, 54–55
  of marginal cost curve, 341
Slovakia, productivity and wages in, 222
Slovenia, productivity and wages in, 222
S&Ls. See savings and loans
SMART Grid technologies, 342
smartphone production, 217–218, 221
Smith, Adam, 2–3, 13–14, 852, 853
  The Wealth of Nations, 852, 853, 945
Smith, Brad, 208
SNAP. See Supplemental Nutrition Assistance Program
Snapchat, 388, 487
social benefit. See also marginal social benefit entries
  of poverty reduction, 517
social cost, marginal. See marginal social cost
social insurance, 820. See also Medicaid; Medicare; Social Security
social insurance programs, 516–517
socially optimal quantity of pollution, 469–470
social norms, changes in, shifts of the labor supply curve and, 565
Social Security, 515, 525, 526–527, 628, 643, 652, 819
  dedicated taxes supporting, 839
  FICA tax and, 203–204, 205
  implicit liability for, 839
Social Security trust fund, 839
society, deadweight loss as a loss to, 135
Solana power plant, 841
solar energy, cost of, 489
solar panels, 237
  prices of, 84–85
South Africa

inflation and money supply in, 906
  voting as a public good in, 500
South Korea
  current account surplus of, 968
  economic growth of, 697
  gasoline consumption in, 70
  inflation and money supply in, 906
  productivity and wages in, 222
  real GDP per capita in, 696–697
  taxes in, 207
  tradable emissions permits in, 478
Soviet Union
  Cold War and, 438
  former, Cold War and, 430
S&P 500, 737
Spain
  automobile industry of, 989
  fiscal austerity in, 957
  government debt of, 836
  interest rates in, 957, 958
  productivity and wages in, 222
  recovery of, 749
  unemployment and inflation in, 929–930
specialization, 13–14
  increasing returns to scale and, 346
spending
  aggregate. See aggregate spending
  consumer. See consumer spending
  on domestically produced final goods and services, GDP as, 632–633
  government, 19–20
  government policy and, 19
  income and, 19
  investment. See investment spending
  paradox of thrift and, 171, 609, 770, 776
spreading effect, of increasing output on average total cost, 338–339
SRAS. See short-run aggregate supply curve
Sri Lanka, clothing industry of, 38, 40
SRPC. See short-run Phillips curve
stabilization policy, 808, 810
stagflation, 803, 807, 929
standardized products, 357
standard of living, in China, 1, 4
Standard Oil Company, 434–435
Standard Oil Trust, 435
Standard Pol, 400–401
states of the world, 580
State Street Bank, 644
status quo bias, 267
steel tariffs, 234, 240
Stern, Nicholas, 479
sticky wages, 791, 793
  in Great Recession, 799
  in perfectly vs. imperfectly competitive markets, 791
Stiglitz, Joseph, 479
stimulus. See fiscal stimulus

stock(s), 729, 732–733
  demand for, 737–738
  diversified portfolio of, 733
  market timing and, 739
  mutual funds and, 733
stock market, 591
Stokey, Nancy, 545
store of value, money as, 851–852
strategic behavior, 431–432
strategic default, 265
structural unemployment, 660–663
  efficiency wages and, 662–663
  government policies and, 663
  minimum wage and, 661–662
  mismatches between employees and employers and, 663
  unions and, 662
StubHub.com, 89
style, product differentiation by, 449–450
subprime lending, housing bubble and, 874–876
subsidies
  economic growth and, 693–694
  employment, 665
  Pigouvian, 484
  for renewable energy, 489
  too big to fail, 877
substitutes, 73
  changes in prices of, shifts of the demand curve and, 73, 76
  changes in prices of, shifts of the supply curve and, 82, 84
  perfect, 314–315
  price elasticity of demand and, 170
  in production, 82
substitution, marginal rate of, 306–309
substitution effect, 292, 294
  consumption and, 321–323
  labor supply and, 564, 574
  market demand curve and, 292–293
Subway, 598
Summers, Lawrence, 666, 943
Sundararajan, Arun, 121
sunk cost(s), 261–262
sunk cost fallacy, 265
SuperValu, 427
Supplemental Nutrition Assistance Program (SNAP), 515, 526, 536
Supplemental Poverty Measure, 527–528
supply
  excess. See surpluses
  excise taxes and, 186–188
  of factors of production, change in, shifts of the factor demand curve and, 551
  of labor. See labor supply
  of loanable funds, 720–721
  of money. See money supply
  perfectly elastic, 176
  perfectly inelastic, 176
  price elasticity of. See price elasticity of supply

supply and demand model,
65–99, 67–102, 68. *See
also* AD–AS model;
demand; demand curve;
demand schedule; market
equilibrium; supply;
supply curve; supply
schedule
changes in supply and demand
and, 90–95
competitive markets and, 68, 95
equilibrium and, 85–90
supply chains
global, 215
Li & Fung as manager of, 241
supply curve, 78–85
aggregate. *See* AD–AS model;
aggregate supply curve;
long-run aggregate supply
curve; short-run aggregate
supply curve
domestic, international trade
and, 226–228
individual. *See* individual
supply curve *entries*
industry. *See* industry supply
curve
for insurance, 588
for labor. *See* individual labor
supply curve
market, 83
movements along, 80, 81
shifts of. *See* shifts of the
supply curve
supply schedule and, 78–79
supply price, 149
supply schedule, 78, 79
supply shocks, 802–803
demand shocks vs., 802–804,
807
macroeconomic policy and,
809–810
negative, 802–803, 807
positive, 802–803
recessions of 1970s caused by,
781
short-run Phillips curve and,
925, 927
supply-side economics, 952
surge pricing, 96
surpluses
budget, 715
consumer. *See* consumer
surplus
in current account, 968
in financial account, 966
market price and, 87–88
producer. *See* producer surplus
trade. *See* trade surpluses
**sustainable long-run economic
growth,** 4, 702–705
environment and, 703–705
natural resources and, 702–703
sweatshop labor fallacy, 221–222
Sweden
currency in circulation of, 851
euro and, 984
inflation targeting in, 900
number of hours worked in,
566

productivity and wages in, 222
taxes in, 207
tradable emissions permits in,
479
Swiss franc, rise in value of, 963
Swiss National Bank, 963
Switzerland
bank accounts in, 963
current account surplus of, 968
health care in, 531
inflation and money supply
in, 906
productivity and wages in, 222
purchasing power parity and
Big Mac price in, 977
tradable emissions permits in,
479
syndicates, 591

T

T-accounts, 856
tacit collusion, 432, 436–437
price wars and, 437
Taco Bell, 598
Taiwan, economic growth of, 697
TANF. *See* Temporary Assistance
for Needy Families
tangency condition, 309–310
tangent line, 58
Target, 377
target federal funds rate, 885,
891, 894, 896
tariffs (fees), two-part, 412
tariffs (trade protection), 232
effects of, 232–234
TaskRabbit, 665, 673
tastes. *See* preferences
tax(es), 185–214
carbon, 210
changes in, multiplier effects
of, 826–827
on cigarettes, 200–201
costs of taxation and, 196–199
deadweight loss of, 196–198,
198–200, 199–200
dedicated, 839
emissions, 474–475
equity vs. efficiency of,
202–203, 205–206
estate, 206
excise. *See* excise taxes
fairness of, 202
federal, principles underlying,
203–204, 207–208
fiscal policy and, 818, 819
on gasoline, 202
on greenhouse gas emissions,
482
incidence of, 188, 189–191
income. *See* income tax
on income vs. consumption,
208
inflation, 918–919
Irish, 970–971
Laffer curve and, 195
lump-sum, 202–203, 827
multiplier and, 827–828
payroll, 191–192, 203–204, 205
Pigouvian, 474–475
profits, 205

progressive, 205–206
property, 205
proportional, 205
regressive, 205
sales, 205
sin, 195
social insurance, 839
state and local, 206, 208–209
in United States, 206–207
value-added, 43
wealth, 205
Whiskey Rebellion and, 185,
202
tax bases, 204–205
tax competition, 207–208
taxis
Lyft, 673, 887, 987, 988
medallions for, 147–151
ride-hailing services and, 17,
147, 153. *See also* Lyft;
Uber
Uber, 665, 673, 966, 987, 988
tax rates
marginal, 206
revenue and, 193–195
tax structure, 204
Taylor, John, 899
Taylor rule for monetary policy,
899
team size, optimal, finding, 334
TC. *See* total cost curve
TEC. *See* total external costs of
pollution
technological change
in banking, shifts of the money
demand curve and, 890
natural rate of unemployment
and, 665
technological progress
productivity and, 685, 688–689
R&D and, 693, 694
technology, 34
changes in, shifts of the factor
demand curve and, 551
comparative advantage and,
223–224
monopoly and, 387–388
production possibility frontier
and, 34
robots and, 349, 551
shifts of the supply curve and,
82, 84
SMART Grid, 342
technology spillovers, 484–485
television programming, as public
good, 497
Temporary Assistance for Needy
Families (TANF), 525, 526
Teva, 359
TGI Friday's, 295
Thailand, shrimp production of,
217, 220–221, 222, 238
*A Theory of the Consumption
Function* (Friedman), 757
thrift, paradox of, 171, 609, 770,
776
thrift(s), crisis of 1980s and,
873–874
ticket prices, 125
determination of, 89–90

tight monetary policy, 898
time. *See also* long run; short run
price elasticity of supply and,
177
time allocation, 563
time allocation budget line,
573–574
time lags, in fiscal policy, 823–824
time-series graphs, 60, 61
tire industry, 424
as oligopoly, 421
tit for tat strategy, 431–432
T-Mobile, 422
Tognum, 561
Tokio Marine, 599
too big to fail subsidies, 877
toothpaste market, 422
total consumer surplus, 105
total cost, 332
average. *See* average total cost
marginal cost vs., 255
total cost curve (*TC*), 333
total external costs of pollution
(TEC), 472–473
total factor productivity, 689
in Italy, decline of, 695–696
rise and fall of, 690–691
total producer surplus, 112
total product curve, 328–330, 331
total revenue, price elasticity of
demand and, 166–168
total surplus, 116
exports and, 228
imports and, 227
Toyota, 421, 811
Toyota Motors of Japan, 45
Toys "R" Us, 377, 658–659
A Tract on Monetary Reform
(Keynes), 808
tradable emissions permits, 476,
478–479
trade, 13. *See also* comparative
advantage; export(s);
free trade; gains from
trade; import *entries;*
international trade;
international trade
agreements
comparative advantage and. *See*
comparative advantage
gains from. *See* gains from
trade
trade balance, 966
trade deficits, 619
trade-off(s), 10. *See also*
opportunity cost
autarky and, 219
between equity and efficiency,
16, 120, 202–203,
205–206, 535–536
between interest rate and
investment spending,
760–761
between judgment
and guesswork,
macroeconomic policy
and, 651
production possibility frontier
and. *See* production
possibility frontier

between work and leisure, 563–564, 573–576
trade-off between equity and efficiency, 16, 120, 203, 535–536
progressive taxation and, 205–206
of a tax system, 202–203
trade protection, 232–240
arguments for, 236–237
challenges to globalization and, 238–239
import quotas as, 234–235
international trade agreements and World Trade Organization and, 237–238
politics of, 237
tariffs as, 232–234, 235–236
trade wars and, 237, 239–240
trade surpluses, 619, 620
Greek, 620–621
trade wars, 237, 239–240
traffic congestion
as common resource, 503
congestion pricing and, 77
equilibrium and, 17–18
fundamental law of, 18
as market failure, 3
transaction costs, 472, 730
transfer payments. *See* government transfers
transparency, inflation targeting and, 900
Treasury bills, Fed purchases and sales of, 867–868
Trichet, Jean-Claude, 651, 781, 794, 810
Trump, Donald
fiscal stimulus under, 821, 824–825
steel tariffs under, 234, 240
truncated axes, 62
trusts, 434–435, 872
tuna prices, 421
Turkey
inflation and money supply in, 906
money supply of, 916
Turo, 121
Tversky, Amos, 263, 266
two-part tariffs, 412
type, product differentiation by, 449–450

U

U-6, 655–657
UAE. *See* United Arab Emirates
Uber, 17, 147, 150, 151, 153, 403, 455–456, 665, 673
surge pricing and, 96
U-Haul, 421
underemployment, 654
underwriters, 599
unemployment, 652–666
among men in United States, 665–666
coronavirus pandemic and, 652, 653, 654, 664
cyclical, 663

definition of, 652
duration of, 659–660
economic growth and, 655–657
frictional, 659–660
Greek, 607
growth in the economy and, 655–657
inefficiency of, 145
inflation and. *See* long-run Phillips curve; Phillips curve; short-run Phillips curve
long-term, 660
macroeconomic policy and, 651
measurement of, 652–653, 654
natural rate hypothesis and, 925, 946, 950, 951, 952
recessionary gaps and, 805
recessions and, 613, 655
structural. *See* structural unemployment
U-6 measure of, 652
unemployment benefits, natural rate of unemployment and, 665
unemployment insurance, 527
unemployment rate
budget deficit and, 831
for college graduates, 2007–2020, 657
definition of, 653
of different groups, 654
education and, 657
Greek, 607
inflation rate and. *See* Phillips curve
monetarist view of, 951
natural. *See* natural rate of unemployment
nonaccelerating inflation rate of, 931
output gaps and, 922–923. *See also* Phillips curve; short-run Phillips curve
significance of, 653–655
stimulus plans and, 821
in United States, 214, 652, 928, 934
Unilever, 463
unions, 559–560
natural rate of unemployment and, 665
structural unemployment and, 662
unit(s), 332
United Arab Emirates (UAE), economic growth of, 689
United Kingdom
disinflation in, 932
drug prices in, 389
economic growth of, 615–616
euro and, 984
first recession in, 944
gasoline consumption in, 70
Gini coefficient in, 523
government debt of, 836
health care in, 531, 532
inflation in, 921–922
inflation targeting in, 900
number of hours worked in, 566

printing of currency of, 938
productivity and wages in, 222
purchasing power parity and Big Mac price in, 977
spending on food in, 173
taxes in, 207
television programming in, 497
voting as a public good in, 500
wages in, 141
wars and merchant ships of, 592–593
United Network for Organ Sharing (UNOS), 109, 117
United States. *See also* Federal and federal *entries*
airline industry in, 145, 408
antitrust policy in, 435–436
arms race and, 430
automobile industry of, 45, 224, 811
balance of payments accounts of, 965
banking system of. *See* U.S. banking system
budget deficits of, 943
business cycle in, 611, 612
Cold War and, 430, 438
corporate bonds in, 735
currency in circulation of, 850, 851, 854
current account deficit of, 968
deflation in, 671
disinflation in, 932, 933–934
dispute with Brazil over subsidies to cotton farmers, 238
drug prices in, 389
economic growth of, 20–21, 475, 615–616, 680–681, 682, 685–686, 692
economic inequality in, 520, 521–522
effective exchange rate of, 979
electric utilities in, 396–397
environmental standards in, 474
exports of, 230
factor distribution of income in, 545
gasoline consumption in, 70
GDP per capita and well-being in, 638
Gini coefficient in, 521, 523
government debt of, 836
government spending and tax revenue in, 818
government spending on education in, 694
Great Moderation in, 955
greenhouse gases in, 475
health care in, 531–532
housing bubble in, 870, 874–876
imports of, 230
income inequality in, long-term trends in, 523–525
individual transferable quotas in, 506
inflation and money supply in, 906

inflation in, 915, 921–922, 975
inflation targeting in, 900
infrastructure of, 501–502
interest rates in, 727–728, 957–958
investment spending in, 717
job loss due to imports from China, 231–232
minimum wage in, 661, 662
mutual funds in economy of, 734
NAFTA and, 237, 240
natural gas industry in, 67
number of hours worked in, 566
offshore outsourcing and, 239
as open economy, 619
productivity and wages in, 222
purchasing power parity and Big Mac price in, 977
purchasing power parity exchange rate between Canada and, 977–978
R&D in, 693
recessions in, 614, 807, 811, 955, 958–959. *See also* Great Recession
regional disparities in real GDP per capita in, 699–701
savings-investment spending identity in, 717
spending on food in, 173
taxes in, 206–207
tradable emissions permits in, 478
trade war with China, 240
trade war with Europe, 240
trade with Canada, 222–223
unemployment rate and inflation in, 1961–1990, 928
unemployment rate in, 1948–2020, 652
unions in, 559–560
voting as a public good in, 500
wages in, 141
welfare state in, 525–528
wheat yield in, 330
withdrawal from Paris Agreement, 704
women in labor supply in, 567
zero lower bound in, 898, 901, 935–936, 957
U.S. banking system, 871–877
crisis in early twentieth century, 871–872
Federal Reserve System and. *See* Federal Reserve System (Fed)
regulation of, 876–877
savings and loan crisis of the 1980s and, 873–874
shadow banking and, 874–876
U.S. Census Bureau
Current Population Survey of, 653
unemployment defined by, 652
U.S. Postal Service, 401
United States-Mexico-Canada Agreement (USMCA), 237

unit-elastic demand, 165–166, 167
unit-free measures, 172
unit of account, money as, 669, 852
unit-of-account costs, 669–670
UNOS. *See* United Network for Organ Sharing
unpaid internships, 146
unplanned inventory investment, 762
UPS, 406
used textbook market, 103
U-shaped average total cost curves, 337
USMCA. *See* United States-Mexico-Canada Agreement
util(s), 280
utility, 279, 280–283
   consumption and, 280–281
   expected, 581
   marginal. *See* marginal utility *entries*
utility function, 280, 301–305
   indifference curves and, 301–305
utility hill, 301
utility-maximizing principle of marginal analysis, 291, 574
Uzbekistan, economic growth and greenhouse gases in, 475

V

value
   absolute, 56
   equilibrium, of the marginal product, 553
   expected, 580
   of the marginal product, 546–550
   money as store of, 851–852
   present. *See* present value
value added, 631
value-added tax, 43
value of the marginal product curve, 548–550
value of the marginal product (VMPL), 546–550
   factor demand and, 548–550
Vanguard 500 Index Fund, 734
variable(s), 51, 52–53
   dependent and independent, 52–53
   omitted, 63–64
   random, 580
variable costs, 332
   average, 337–338

variable inputs, 328
VAT. *See* value-added tax
Venezuela
   economic growth of, 682
   growth of money supply of, 917–918
   inflation in, 915, 921, 938
   price controls in, 139–140
   printing of currency of, 938
Venmo, 886, 907, 943
Verizon Media, 422
vertical axis, 52
vertical curves, 55–56
vertical intercept, 54
Veterans Health Administration, 531
Viacom Media, 146
Vietnam
   clothing industry of, 38
   shrimp production of, 217, 220–221, 222, 238
Vinci, Leonardo da, 496
Virgin Atlantic, 441
virtual currency, 854
Visa, 421
VMPL. See value of the marginal product
Volkswagen, 989
volume discounts, 412
voting, as a public good, 498, 500
VRBO, 252

W

wages
   currencies and, 987–988
   disparities in, in practice, 557
   disparities in, marginal productivity and, 557–559
   efficiency, 559, 560, 662–663
   gender-wage gap and, 559
   hourly, 915
   increase in, work vs. leisure and, 573–576
   international trade and, 229–231
   labor supply and, 564–565
   marginal productivity theory of income distribution and. *See* marginal productivity theory of income distribution
   minimum. *See* minimum wage
   nominal. *See* nominal wage
   real, 667
   sticky, 791, 793, 799
   structural unemployment and, 661–662
   unions and, 662

Wall Street Reform and Consumer Protection Act of 2010, 876–877
Walmart, 8, 241, 267, 270, 349, 377, 568, 663
   price war with Amazon, 438–439
Walt Disney Company, 965
wampum, 854
Wang, Jing, 685
warranties, 586
Washington, George, 185
wasted resources, 136–137
   price floors and, 145
water pollution. *See* pollution
wealth, 729
   changes in, shifts of the labor supply curve and, 566
   changes in, shifts of the aggregate demand curve and, 787–788
   risk aversion and, 585
wealth effect of a change in the aggregate price level, 783
The Wealth of Nations (Smith), 2–3, 13–14, 852, 853, 945
wealth tax, 205
weather, extreme, 579, 593
wedges, 150
   driven by excise taxes, 187
   driven by quotas, 150
welfare effects
   of monopoly, 399–400
   of a tariff, 233–234
welfare state, 515–542
   economic inequality and. *See* income inequality
   economic insecurity and, 522
   government transfers and, 516
   in Great Recession, 528
   health care and. *See* health care
   logic of, 516–517
   means-tested programs for, 525, 526
   politics of, 536
   poverty and. *See* poverty
   problems with, 535–536
   Social Security and, 526–527
   unemployment insurance and, 527
   in United States, 525–528
well-being, GDP per capita and, 638
Whalley, John, 685
WhatsApp, 406, 487
wheat yields, 330
Whiskey Rebellion, 185, 202

wholesale price index, 641
willingness to pay, 104
   consumer surplus and, 104–107
wireless telephone market, 422
women, in U.S. work force, 567
work. *See* employment; labor *entries;* unemployment; unemployment rate
working poor, 518
workplace discrimination, 560–561
world price, 226
World Trade Organization (WTO), 238
World War II
   government expenditures for, ending of Great Depression and, 948
   public debt from, 838–839
   women in labor force during, 684
Wright, Wilbur and Orville, 27
Wright Flyer, 27
WTO. *See* World Trade Organization; World Trade Organization (WTO)

X

***x*-axis,** 52
Xcel Energy, 489
Xoma, 262

Y

Yahoo, 422
Yale University, 208
***y*-axis,** 52
Yellen, Janet, 865
Your Money and Your Brain (Zweig), 592
yuan, pegging of, 983–984
Yunus, Mohammad, 743

Z

Zappos, 406, 669
zero interest rate policy (ZIRP), 929–930
zero lower bound for interest rates, 898, 901, 935–936, 957
zero-profit equilibrium, 454–455
Zimbabwe, hyperinflation in, 669, 915
ZIRP (zero interest rate policy), 936
Zuckerberg, Mark, 9
Zweig, Jason, 592